THE
WORLD
ALMANAC®
&BOOK
OF FACTS

Publisher: Edward R. Kennedy, 1972-1975

Editor: George E. Delury

Managing Editor: Vincent P. Bannan

Associate Editors: Kenneth C. Johnston, Hana Umlauf, Barry Youngerman

Assistant Editor: Thomas J. McGuire

Senior Assistant: Florence Byrnes

Assistant to the Editor: Juliana Mace

Senior Editor, Canada: Dr. Paul W. Fox

Assistant Editor: Glenda M. Patrick

e editors acknowledge with thanks the many letters of helpful comment and criticism from
THE WORLD ALMANAC, and invite further suggestions and observations. Because of the
f mail directed to the editorial offices, it is not possible personally to reply to each letter
wever, every communication will be read by the editors and all comments and suggestions
careful attention.

WORLD ALMANAC is published annually in November.

Inquiries regarding contents and purchase orders should be sent to: World Almanac, 230 Park
nue, New York, N.Y.10017.

THE WORLD ALMANAC does not decide wagers.

The first edition of THE WORLD ALMANAC, a 120-page hand-set volume with 12 pages of
rtising, was published by the New York World in 1868, 108 years ago. Annual publication was
nded in 1876. Joseph Pulitzer, publisher of the New York World, revived THE WORLD ALMA-
1886 with the goal of making it a "compendium of universal knowledge." It has been publish-
ually since then. In 1931, it was acquired by the Scripps-Howard Newspapers; until 1951, it
the imprint of the New York World-Telegram and thereafter, until 1967, that of the New York
rld Telegram and Sun. It is now published in paper and clothbound editions by Newspaper Enter-
ise Association, Inc., a Scripps-Howard company.

NEWSPAPER ENTERPRISE ASSOCIATION, INC.,
230 Park Avenue, New York, NY 10017;
1200 West Third Street, Cleveland, OH 44113.
Robert Roy Metz, president; Earl H. Anderson, vice president.

THE AUTHORITY SINCE 1868

THE WORLD ALMANAC

& BOOK OF FACTS

1976

Published Annually by
NEWSPAPER ENTERPRISE ASSO
New York, Cleveland

O31
W92w
1976

General Index

3

Late News, Addenda, Changes

Ford Shakes Up Top Leadership: Schlesinger Out, Kissinger In; Rockefeller Declines

In a sudden, sweeping shake-up of his top administration, Pres. Ford Nov. 3 announced the departure of James R. Schlesinger as secretary of defense and of William E. Colby as director of the Central Intelligence Agency, and the early-1976 resignation of Rogers C.B. Morton as secretary of commerce. Henry A. Kissinger would turn over his job as national security adviser to his assistant, Lt. Gen. Brent Scowcroft. On the same day, Vice Pres. Nelson A. Rockefeller, apparently in anticipation of being "dumped," told Ford he would not be his running-mate in 1976.

Ford named Donald H. Rumsfeld, White House chief of staff, to succeed Schlesinger; George Bush, head of the U.S. mission to Peking, to succeed Colby; Elliot L. Richardson, ambassador to Great Britain, to succeed Morton; and Richard B. Cheney, a deputy White House assistant, to succeed Rumsfeld. (The changes affect information on Pages 317, 334, 335, 342, 678.)

(Continued On Page 40)

Edward R. Kennedy, World Almanac Publisher, Dies

Edward R. Kennedy, publisher of The World Almanac since 1972, died of a heart attack in Cleveland, Ohio, June 16, 1975, at the age of 52.

Mr. Kennedy had been closely associated with The World Almanac since 1966 when it was acquired by Newspaper Enterprise Association. He helped develop a marketing and public service concept that increased the annual reference book's sale from 850,000 to nearly twice that distribution with this edition.

Besides his work as publisher of The World Almanac, Mr. Kennedy was Vice-President — Publications of Newspaper Enterprise Association, chairman of the research and development department of the E.W. Scripps Company and a member of the board of directors of the Scripps-Howard Foundation.

Mr. Kennedy began his newspaper career at the age of 15 and worked briefly as a reporter for the Philadelphia Bulletin before World War II. He joined the Army as a private and rose to the rank of captain, earning Silver and Bronze Stars and three Purple Hearts in Europe.

In 1946, Mr. Kennedy joined Scripps-Howard Newspapers and worked on the Columbus Citizen and Indianapolis Times. Appointed managing editor of the Japan Times in Tokyo in 1952, Mr. Kennedy remained in Asia seven years, including time spent as a special correspondent in Bangkok. He returned to Indianapolis in 1959 and joined Newspaper Enterprise Association in its Cleveland offices in 1960.

Known throughout the fields of book publishing and newspapers as a tough and energetic businessman, Mr. Kennedy was also noted for the warmth, kindness, and charm that affected everyone around him. These qualities, combined with an extraordinary range of knowledge and interests, made him an especially able publisher of The World Almanac and endeared him to its staff.

The World Almanac

and Book of Facts for 1976

Some Major Events and Trends in 1975

The 30-year war in Indochina came to a rapid conclusion in April and May as the pro-American governments of South Vietnam, Cambodia, and Laos succumbed to communist forces and U.S. personnel were evacuated. Almost 150,000 Vietnamese refugees fled to the U.S. Also in May, the U.S. launched an attack in the area to rescue the hijacked container-ship Mayaguez.

Only 17 days separated two bungled assassination attempts against President Ford in September in Northern California. Both attempts were by women apparently more intent on publicity than mayhem. The attempts raised serious questions concerning the safety of the president and the role of the media in perhaps provoking such attempts.

Lower inflation rates accompanied the sharpest economic downturn in a generation as the unemployment rate exceeded nine per cent and the GNP turned steeply negative. By the end of the year, a slow recovery was perceptible along with increased inflation.

Jerusalem and Cairo moved closer to peace in September with the signing of a new interim agreement on Sinai. Both sides made extensive concessions and the U.S. agreed to maintain surveillance of the Sinai buffer zone with some 200 U.S. technicians.

After 28 years as the world's largest democracy, India moved toward dictatorship in late June as Prime Minister Indira Gandhi declared a national emergency, ordered her opponents arrested, and imposed press censorship after a court had found her guilty of corrupt campaign practices and voided her election to Parliament.

Keeping a firm lid on future government spending, President Ford successfully exercised his veto power more than 30 times and reduced the overwhelmingly Democratic 94th Congress to frustrated impotence. In addition, the Democrats were unable to agree on an energy policy, leaving the initiative in that area to the President.

Alternately described as accomplice and victim, Patty Hearst and her SLA companions were objects of intense public interest after her capture by the FBI in September. While her defense attorneys claimed she was brain-washed and half-crazed, the prosecutors indicted her for robbery, kidnapping, and assault amid reports that she may have been involved in still further crimes, including murder during a bank robbery.

Reviled by President Ford as foolish spendthrifts, New York City's politicians and people prepared for the city's almost certain default on over $12 billion of debt. Demanding that city officials not "escape responsibility for their past follies," Ford rejected appeals for federal loan guarantees and promised to veto legislation to help New York City. He called for changes in bankruptcy law to allow a federal judge to take over the city's affairs when default occurred.

Lengthy news stories were also devoted to the intense struggle between Portuguese Communists and moderates for control of their country, the bloody ethnic battles in Lebanon, the disappearance of Teamster leader Jimmy Hoffa, the continuing dispute over school busing, the final verdict of guilty for major figures in the Watergate scandal, and continuing Congressional investigation of the Central Intelligence Agency, the FBI and other federal agencies tarnished by the Watergate brush.

Hats in the Ring
1976 Presidential Contenders

Including all declared major party candidates as of October 1975, and others most often mentioned as possible contenders.

Republicans

President Gerald Ford publicly declared July 8, 1975, that he would run for reelection. (See p. 312 for biography.)

Ronald Reagan was born in Tampico, Ill., Feb. 6, 1911. He graduated from Eureka College in 1932. From then until 1937 he was a sports announcer in Des Moines. In the latter years, Reagan began a 30-year movie and television acting career. He was president of the Screen Actors Guild 1947-52 and 1959-60. While serving as program supervisor for General Electric Theater, he developed a conservative reputation with numerous speaking engagements. He was elected governor of California in 1966 and reelected in 1970. Reagan staked out a leadership role on the right wing of the Republican party, favoring cuts in government programs and conservative approaches to education and social issues. He unsuccessfully sought the Republican presidential nomination in 1968. Reagan is a horse breeder. He is married and has four children.

Democrats

Sen. Birch Evans Bayh was born near Terre Haute, Ind., on Jan. 22, 1928. Bayh, who owns and operates a family farm, received an agricultural degree from Purdue University in 1951, and a law degree from Indiana University in 1960. He served in the Indiana House 1954-62, the last six years as minority leader or speaker. In 1962 he was elected to the U.S. Senate from Indiana as a young liberal in the John F. Kennedy mold. He was reelected in 1968 and 1974. Bayh helped secure passage of the 25th Amendment to the Constitution, on presidential succession; the 26th Amendment, on the 18-year-old vote; and the pending 27th, Equal Rights Amendment. Bayh led the fight against confirmation of Nixon Supreme Court nominees Carswell and Haynsworth. He also sponsored the Juvenile Justice Act. Bayh serves on the Senate Judiciary and Appropriations Committees. An Army veteran, he is married and has one child.

Sen. Lloyd Millard Bentsen was born in Mission, Texas, Feb. 11, 1921. He received an LL.B. degree from the University of Texas in 1942, and served in the Army for the next three years. He was county judge for Hidalgo County, 1946-48, and a member of the U.S. House of Representatives, 1948-55. An insurance millionaire, Bentsen in 1955 became president of Lincoln Consolidated of Houston, a financial holding institution; he has been on the board of directors of numerous major corporations. Bentsen was elected to the U.S. Senate in 1970. His supporters call him a moderate conservative. Bentsen belongs to the Senate Finance, Public Works, and Joint Economic Committees. He is married and has three children.

Jimmy (James Earl) Carter is a former governor of Georgia. He was born Oct. 1, 1924, in rural southwest Georgia. He graduated from the U.S. Naval Academy in 1947 and did graduate work in nuclear physics. Carter served in the Navy from 1947 to 1953, when he returned to Georgia and built up a seed and farm supply business. He became local school board chairman and first president of the Georgia Planning Association. Carter was elected to the Georgia Senate in 1962 and served through 1966. Four years later he won election to a four-year gubernatorial term with a moderate reformist and racial harmony campaign. In office Carter concentrated on education programs and administrative streamlining. He was named national chairman for the 1974 Democratic congressional campaign. Georgia's constitution bars a governor from running for a second consecutive term. Carter is married and has four children.

Fred. R. Harris was born on a farm in Walters, Okla., Nov. 13, 1930. He received a political science degree from the University of Oklahoma in 1952 and a Law Degree from the same university in 1954. Harris was elected to the Oklahoma Senate in 1956 and served until 1964, when he was elected to the U.S. Senate. A proponent of tax reform, anti-trust actions, and minority rights, Harris worked on the 1967 Advisory Commission on Civil Disorders and was co-chairman of the Urban Coalition Commission on the Cities in the 70s. While chairing the Democratic National Committee in 1969-1970, he promoted changes in party rules. Harris did not run for Senate reelection in order to seek the 1972 Democratic presidential nomination; he withdrew from the race for lack of funds. He has since worked with citizens groups on tax, utility, food, and union issues. He has written several books, including *The New Populism.* Harris is married and has three children.

Sen. Hubert Horatio Humphrey was born in Wallace, S.D., May 27, 1911. After several years studying and working as a pharmacist, Humphrey received degrees in political science from the University of Minnesota and Louisiana State University, at both of which he taught 1939-41; he returned to the Univ. of Minn. and Macalester College for teaching stints later in his career. He headed the Minn. division of the Works Progress Administration, and served in several civilian war agencies during World War II. While leading the 1944 Roosevelt-Truman campaign in Minnesota, Humphrey was instrumental in merging the state's Democratic and Farmer-Labor Parties. Humphrey was elected Minneapolis mayor and served 1945-48. At the 1948 Democratic National Convention, Humphrey led the successful fight for a strong civil rights stand. As U.S. Senator, 1948-64, he was one of the nation's leading liberals, and was active in early steps to control nuclear weapons. He was elected majority whip in 1961, and he authored or secured passage of a variety of legislation. Humphrey lost a 1960 bid for the presidential nomination, but was elected vice president in 1964. Four years later, burdened by the Vietnam War issue, he lost the presidential race to Richard Nixon by a razor-thin margin. His try for the 1972 Democratic nomination failed, though he piled up over four million primary votes, more than any other candidate. Humphrey was reelected to the Senate from Minnesota in 1970. He serves on the Senate Agriculture, Foreign Relations, Joint Economic and Select Nutrition Committees. Humphrey is married and has four children.

Sen. Henry Martin Jackson was born in Everett, Wash., May 31, 1912. He received an LL.B. degree from the University of Washington in 1935, and began practicing law. Jackson was Snohomish Co. prosecuting attorney, 1938-40, U.S. Representative from Washington's second district, 1941-53, and has been a U.S. Senator ever since. He was a U.S. delegate to the NATO Parliamentarians Conference from 1956 to 1959, and again in 1966 and 1972. He was chairman of the Democratic National Committee 1960-61. Jackson sought the Democratic presidential nomination in 1972, but withdrew after being overshadowed in the primaries. He was an early environmentalist, though he later stressed a balance between economic growth and conservation. He is an internationalist supporter of a vigorous U.S. role abroad. Jackson chairs the Senate Interior Committee and serves on the Senate Armed Services and Government Operations Committees and the Joint Committee on Atomic Energy. He is married and has two children.

Edward Moore Kennedy, senior senator from Massachusetts, youngest brother of President John F. Kennedy, was born in Boston Feb. 22, 1932. He served in the Army 1951-53. Kennedy obtained a B.A. degree at Harvard in 1954, and an LL.B. at the University of Virginia in 1959. He was Suffolk County, Mass., assistant district attorney 1961-62, and was first elected U.S. Senator from Massachusetts in 1962, during the administration of his brother. Kennedy was Senate Democratic Whip in 1969-70, and currently sits on the Judiciary and Labor and Public Welfare Committees, and on special committees on nutrition and aging. Kennedy is generally regarded as among the most liberal senators. Though he formally renounced interest in the 1976 presidential nomination, he was often reported by polls to be the most popular possible Democratic candidate. But some voters reported lingering doubts about a 1969 Chappaquiddick, Mass. automobile accident in which a female passenger of the Senator was drowned. Kennedy is married and has three children.

Edmund Sixtus Muskie was born in Rumford, Me., March 28, 1914. He graduated from Bates College in 1936, and in 1939 received a law degree at Cornell. He served in the U.S. Naval Reserve 1942-45. In 1948 Muskie was elected to the Maine House of Representatives, and served as Democratic floor leader 1949-51, after which he resumed private law practice. He was elected governor in 1954, and served until his election to the U.S. Senate four years later. He was reelected senator in 1964 and 1970. In 1968 Muskie was the Democratic nominee for vice president. In 1972, he sought the presidential nomination with the support of many party officials and officeholders, but withdrew after uneven results in the primaries. Muskie is a member of the Senate Foreign Relations, Public Works, and Government Operations Committees, and the Special Committee on Aging. Among his areas of concern are the environment and arms control. Muskie is married and has five children.

Terry Sanford was born Aug. 20, 1917, in Laurinberg, N.C. He attended the University of North Carolina, obtaining his B.A. and law degrees in 1939 and 1946 respectively. Sanford was an FBI agent 1941-42, and an Army paratrooper 1942-46. In 1949-50 he was president of the North Carolina Young Democrats. Sanford became secretary-treasurer of the North Carolina Port Authority, 1950-53, and a

member of the North Carolina Senate, 1953-54. He was elected governor in 1960 as an ally of John F. Kennedy, and he carried out school desegregation decisions in his four-year term. He has been president of Duke University since 1969. In 1968, Sanford was an undeclared vice presidential candidate; in 1972 he declared for the presidential nomination, but withdrew when George Wallace defeated him in the North Carolina primary. Sanford has depicted himself as a moderate Southern liberal. He was chairman of the charter commission that wrote the 1974 Democratic Party Constitution. He is married and has two children.

Gov. Milton J. Shapp was born in Cleveland June 25, 1912. He graduated from Case Institute of Technology in 1933 with an electrical engineering degree. He served in the Army during World War II. In 1947 Shapp founded the Jerrold Electronics Corp., one of the first cable television concerns, which he headed until 1966. He was a Peace Corps and Department of

1976 Presidential Primaries

(Scheduled as of Sept. 29, 1975.)
Source: Democratic National Committee

State	Type	Primary Date	Filing Deadline
New Hampshire	A	February 24	December 25, 1975
Massachusetts		March 2	January 2
Florida	P	March 9	February 10
Illinois	A	March 16	December 28, 1975
North Carolina	P	March 23	February 3
New York	DS	April 6	February 19
Wisconsin	P	April 6	March 2
Pennsylvania	A	April 27	February 17
Texas	DS	May 1	February 2
Alabama	DS	May 4	March 1
District of Columbia	P	May 4	March 4
Georgia		May 4	
Indiana	B	May 4	March 24
Tennessee	B	May 6	March 4
Nebraska	A	May 11	March 11
West Virginia	A	May 11	February 7
Maryland	A	May 18	March 25
Michigan	P	May 18	March 19
Idaho	P	May 25	April 24
Kentucky	P	May 25	April 9
Nevada	P	May 25	May 9
Oregon	P	May 25	March 15
Rhode Island	D	June 1	March 20
Mississippi	DS,O	June 1	April 1
Montana	D	June 1	March 22
South Dakota	DS,P	June 1	April 15
Arkansas	P	June 8	April 6
California	P	June 8	March 14
New Jersey	A	June 8	April 28
Ohio	DS	June 8	March 24

(A) Advisory Presidential Preference & Delegate Selection Primary.
(B) Binding. The Rules of the Democratic Party prohibit binding presidential preference primaries unless delegates are allocated to presidential candidates in proportion to the votes such candidate received, provided the candidate received at least 15% of the vote).
(D) Discretionary: State Party Rules determine how the results of the preference primary will be used.
(DS) Delegate Selection only: The names of presidential candidates do not appear separately on the ballot.
(O) Optional.
(P) Proportional: In Arkansas, delegates are allocated proportionally to each presidential candidate who received a sufficient percentage of the vote to entitle him to at least one full delegate; in Michigan and Nevada, National Convention Delegates are allocated proportionallyto each presidential candidate receiving at least 5% of the vote; in Idaho, 80% of the delegates are allocated proportionally to each presidential candidate receiving at least 5 s of the vote; in California, the District of Columbia, and South Dakota, delegates are allocated within each Congressional District to each slate receiving at least 15% of the vote; in Florida and Wisconsin, delegates are allocated proportionally to each presidential candidate receiving at least 15 s of the vote; in North Carolina and Oregon, Party Rules determine the specific proportional allocation of delegates.

Commerce consultant during the Kennedy Administration, and helped organize the Area Redevelopment Administration. He was elected governor of Pennsylvania in 1970 and reelected in 1974. As governor, Shapp stressed management reform and fiscal stability, as well as consumer and other programs. Working as a negotiator, he helped end the 1974 national independent trucker strike. Shapp is the first Jew actively to seek a major party presidential nomination. He is married and has three children.

Robert Sargent Shriver was born Nov. 9, 1915, in Westminster, Md. He received a B.A. degree from Yale in 1938 and an LL.B. in 1941. Shriver served in the Naval Reserve, 1940-45. He was an assistant editor of Newsweek, 1945-46. From 1946 to 1960, Shriver worked on the staff of Joseph P. Kennedy, serving as assistant general manager of Kennedy's Merchandise Mart in Chicago from 1948 on. He was president of Chicago's Board of Education, 1955-60. Shriver joined the administration of his brother-in-law John F. Kennedy in 1961 as first director of the Peace Corps. He was director of the Office of Economic Opportunity, 1964-68, and U.S. Ambassador to France, 1968-70. Shriver served as a special assistant to President Nixon in 1971, but was placed on the Democratic ticket as vice presidential nominee the following year after the withdrawal of the designated candidate Thomas Eagleton. Shriver, a moderate liberal, has the support of many Kennedy family members and political allies. He is married and has five children.

Rep. Mo (Morris King) Udall was born to a political family in a small Mormon settlement in Arizona June 15, 1922. After serving in the Army Air Force 1942-46, he attended the University of Arizona, became student body president, and received an LL.B. in 1949. Udall became chief deputy county attorney for Pima County (Tucson) 1950-52 and county attorney 1953-54. As a private trial lawyer thereafter, he fought for Arizona court reform. Udall helped found the Bank of Tucson. In 1961 he won a special election to succeed his brother Stewart in the U.S. House of Representatives. He has been reelected by large mar-

gins ever since as an activist liberal from a conservative state. He has focused on election and congressional reform and on the environment. Udall is a member of the House Interior and Post Office and Civil Service Committees. He has written three books on law and on congressional reform. He is married and has six children.

George Corley Wallace, governor of Alabama, was born Aug. 25, 1919, the son of Alabama farmers. He was graduated from the University of Alabama Law School in 1942, and served in the Army Air Force in World War II. He was assistant Alabama attorney general, 1946-47, and served in the state's Legislature, 1947-53. Wallace led the fight against the civil rights platform plank at the 1948 Democratic National Convention. As a judge on the 3rd Judicial Circuit of Alabama (1953-58) he defied a federal probe of voting discrimination against blacks. Elected governor in 1962, he tried the next year to block desegregation of the University of Alabama. His wife Lurleen became governor in 1966, but died two years later. As 1968 third-party presidential candidate Wallace garnered nearly 10 million popular votes and 45 electoral votes, campaigning against Vietnam War protesters, liberals, integrationists and Washington "bureaucrats." He was reelected governor in 1970 and 1974. During the 1972 campaign for the Democratic nomination, Wallace piled up strong vote totals in Midwest and Southern primaries, but was shot and partially paralyzed May 15. He then withdrew from the race. In recent years, he moderated his rightist rhetoric, and sought black votes in Alabama by speaking of equal opportunity. Wallace remarried after his wife's death; he has four children.

National Conventions

The Democratic National Convention will be held the week of July 11, 1976, in New York City. The Democrats met twice before in New York, in 1868 and in 192̂

The Repu̶ ̶ans will begin their National Convention Aug. 16, 1̶s̶ ̶in Kansas City, Mo., where they last met in 1928. The ̶̶00 Democratic National Convention was also held in Kansas City.

The Campaign Finance Act

The 1976 presidential and congressional election campaigns will be conducted under a different set of financial rules than have prevailed in the past, because of the Federal Elections Campaign Amendments of 1974. New limits have been set on contributions and spending; partial public financing will be provided for presidential primary and general elections; new, more stringent financial reporting is required; and a new Federal Election Commission has gone into operation to enforce the law.

Contributions

The law sets a maximum contribution per individual donor of $1,000 for each primary, runoff, special, or general election. (All presidential primaries are considered together as one election for this purpose.) No donor may give more than a total of $25,000 to all federal candidates and political committees in any one election year.

A political committee (such as a lobbying or public interest group) may give up to $5,000 for each election, and independent state divisions of these political groups may also each make $5,000 donations. There is no limit on the total amount such committees can donate in one election year, nor on the amount they can give to party organizations backing federal candidates.

A presidential candidate and his or her immediate family can give no more than $50,000 for that candi-

date's own campaign. Senate candidates are limited to $35,000 in personal funds, and House candidates to $25,000.

No individual can spend more than $1,000 on independent, unsolicited actions on behalf of a federal candidate. There is a $100 limit on cash gifts, and all foreign contributions are illegal. No individual can make a contribution in someone else's name.

Unions and corporations, including government contractors, may maintain segregated political funds, but company or union money may not be contributed to the funds. However, such money may be used to finance non-partisan registration or get-out-the-vote drives, and unions or corporations may communicate political views to members or stockholders and their families.

Public Financing

Voluntary public financing is provided for presidential campaigns. Each major party nominee automatically qualifies for a $20 million grant, while minor party candidates can get proportional amounts based on past or current voting strength. If a candidate accepts public money in the general election, he or she may not accept any private contributions.

In the primaries, presidential candidates can qualify for up to $5 million each in matching funds; but only gifts of $250 or less may be matched. In order to qualify, a candidate must amass $100,000, with $5,000 raised in contributions of $250 or less in each of 20 states or the District of Columbia. Only gifts made after Jan. 1, 1975, count for 1976 matching. The funds are to be divided as quickly as possible, with the order of qualification taken into account. If there is not enough money in the fund, each candidate is to receive a pro-rata payment.

In addition, each major party convention will be offered a $2 million subsidy, with smaller amounts going to minor parties.

The federal payments are to come from the Presidential Election Campaign Fund, which is fed by $1 checkoffs from income tax returns. This fund was established by a 1971 law, but its use was postponed until after the 1972 election under threat of a veto by then-President Richard Nixon.

Spending

Presidential candidates may spend up to $10 million for all primaries. Within each state, the candidate may not spend more than twice the amount permitted to Senate candidates in that state. (See below.)

In the general presidential election there is a $20 million spending limit for each candidate, but if a candidate refuses the federal subsidy, the limit is raised to $24 million to cover fund-raising costs. In addition, the national party committees can each donate 2c per eligible voter ($2.9 million in 1976) to their candidates above the $20 million limit. Contributions to a vice presidential candidate are counted as gifts to his presidential running mate.

Senate candidates may spend up to $100,000 or 8c per eligible voter, whichever is greater, in the primary election, and $150,000 or 12c per eligible voter, whichever is greater, in the general election. For House candidates, the limit is $70,000 in the primary and the same amount in the general election, except that a candidate from a one-representative state may spend as much as a Senate candidate from that state is permitted.

In addition, the national and state party committees can each donate up to $20,000 or 2c per eligible voter to Senate candidates in the general election, and $10,000 to House candidates.

As an example, the limit for a Senate general election candidate, counting the national and state party committee allowance and the fund-raising deduction, ranges from $220,000 in Alaska to $2,669,656 in California.

All these spending figures are subject to annual inflation increases, depending on the Labor Department price index. Separate limits on media advertising spending are abolished.

Fund-raising costs of up to 20% of a candidate's total expenses may be excluded from the spending limit. Also excluded are expenses of $500 per donor for food, beverages, invitations, use of personal property, travel costs for volunteers, and other incidental expenses.

Disclosure and Reporting

Each candidate must have a central campaign committee, through which all expenses and gifts of $10 or more must be cleared. Specific bank depositories must be designated.

Full reports, listing all gifts and expenses, must be filed with the Federal Elections Commission ten days before and 30 days after each election, and within ten days of the close of each quarter, unless the committee received or spent less than $1,000 in that quarter. In non-election years, only a year-end report is required. In addition, any gift of $1,000 or more within 15 days of the election must be reported in 48 hours.

Personal loans to a candidate are to be considered as gifts, while bank loans require a cosignor or guarantor for each thousand dollars of outstanding obligation. Any individual who spends or gives over $100 to influence the vote other than to or through a candidate or political committee must also report.

Among other provisions:

The law repealed the prohibition against voluntary political activity by state and local workers in federal campaigns, but similar state laws were allowed to stand.

Federal officials and employees may not accept payment of over $1,000 for a lecture or article, and may not earn over $15,000 per year from such activities.

All interstate campaign literature must be identified by origin.

No campaign funds may be solicited by franked mail (free mail available to congresspersons).

Surplus campaign funds can be used for any lawful purpose, including the expenses of holding public office.

Federal Election Commission

The law is enforced, and the public funds distributed, by the newly created Federal Election Commission, a full-time bi-partisan body. Its members are nominated two each by the President, the Speaker of the House, and the President Pro Tem of the Senate, subject to confirmation by both houses of Congress. The Secretary of the Senate and the Clerk of the House are ex-officio non-voting members; they also serve as custodians of candidates' reports. The commission's first members were confirmed in April 1975.

Commission rulings in interpretation of the la..._ ___ subject to veto by either the House or Senate within 30 days of issue. The commission can give advisory opinions, conduct audits and investigations, subpoena witnesses and information, and seek civil injunctions in court. Criminal cases are turned over to the Department of Justice. Fines for violation of the law run as high as $50,000 in some cases, and a candidate who breaks the law can be banned from running again for that office, until one term plus one year elapses.

The following are some of the major decisions made by the commission in its first 6 months:

National party conventions may accept a wide range of free services from committees funded by private local businesses, when such services would be extended to attract any convention. Certain services, such as free use of automobiles supplied by national automobile companies, cannot be provided free of charge, but their cost would be allowed over and above the $2 million limit for convention spending.

Eligibility for federal matching funds for presidential primary candidates, and the total amount of such funds given to each candidate, will be based on the total amount privately raised, without deducting for fund-raising expenses. Thus, if a candidate spends $50,000 to raise $100,000, the full $100,000 will count toward eligibility and can be matched, not just the $50,000 net income.

When a presidential candidate also runs for the Senate, he may spend in his home state only the amount permitted a Senate candidate in that state, in order to avoid giving him an unfair advantage over his Senate primary opponents.

A political group may spend an unlimited amount on a registration or get-out-the-vote drive, even when the spending is limited to districts where a candidate favored by the group is known to have support. But the potential voters may not be questioned as to their partisan preferences.

The commission also ruled that consititutent service funds ("slush funds"), donated by private sources and used by many Congresspersons, should be subject to the rules of the 1974 law. However, the Senate overturned this ruling Oct. 8 by a 48-47 vote.

The commission has asked Congress to legislate spending and contribution limits on candidates in races for delegate slots at the national conventions. It was feared that without such limits, wealthy donors could get around the $1,000 contribution maximum for presidential candidates by donating large sums to delegates pledged to a candidate supported by the donor.

(Continued From Page 34)

1975 Awards, Prizes (P 542-553)

Nobel Peace Prize: Andrei D. Sakharov, Russian physicist, author, freedom proponent, "father" of the Soviet hydrogren bomb; $140,000.

Nobel Prize in Literature: Eugenio Montale, Italian poet; $143,000.

Nobel Prize in Physiology-Medicine: Drs. David Baltimore and Howard Martin Temin, U.S., and Dr. Renato Dulbecco, Italy-U.S., for tumor virus discoveries; $143,000 shared equally.

Nobel Prize in Physics: Dr. James Rainwater, U.S.; Dr. Hage N. Bohr, Denmark, and Dr. Ben R. Mottelson, U.S.-Denmark, for an atomic nucleus structure theory; $143,000 shared equally.

Nobel Prize in Chemistry: Dr. John Warcup Cornforth, Australia-Great Britain, and Dr. Vladimir Prelog, Yugoslavia-Switzerland, for stereochemistry work; $143,000 shared equally.

Nobel Memorial Prize in Economics: Dr. Tjalling C. Koopmans, Netherlands-U.S., and Dr. Leonid V. Kantorovich, USSR, for contributions to the theory of optimum allocation of resources; $143,000 shared equally.

Loeb Financial Journalism Awards: Vermont Royster, retired editor, Wall Street Journal, $1,500; Allan Sloan, Detroit Free Press; Tom Miller, Huntington (W. Va.) ~~~ ~~ Advertiser; Edwin Darby, Chicago Sun-Ti~~~~, Donald Barlett, James Steel, Philadelph~~~~ quirer, $1,000 each.

~~~iss Black America:** Helen Ford, Miss Mississippi.

Coty Fashion Award: Calvin Klein.

Silver Gavel Award, American Bar Assn.: Charles ~~~ibner's Sons for "The Appearance of Justice" by ~~~. MacKenzie.

~~. ~~ Addams Children's Book Award:** "The Princess a..d the Admiral" by Charlotte Pomerantz.

Louisa Gross Horwitz Prize: Drs. Sune Bergstrom and Bengt Samuelsson, both Sweden, for research on prostaglandins; $25,000 shared.

Japan Foundation Prize; Edwin O. Reischauer, for promotion of U.S.-Japan cultural interchange; $16,600.

Rock Music Awards: Best vocalists, Stevie Wonder, Joni Mitchell; personality, Elton John; album, "Blood on the Tracks," Bob Dylan; single, "You're No Good," Linda Ronstadt; group, Eagles; composer, D. Henley, G. Frey, J.D. Souther, "Best of Love"; rhythm & blues single, "Lady Marmalade," Labelle; r & b album, "That's the Way of the World," Earth, Wind, and Fire; Hall of Fame, Chuck Berry; public service, Joan Baez.

Country Music Assn. Awards: Entertainer and song, John Denver, "Back Home Again"; vocalists, Dolly Parton, Waylon Jennings; single, Freddy Ferner, "Before the Next Teardrop Falls"; duo, Conway Twitty, Loretta Lynn; instrument group, Buck Trent, Roy Clark; instrumentalist Johnny Gimble.

Astronomy (P 754)

Astronomer Charles Kowal, discoverer of Jupiter's 13th moon, reported finding a 14th, 4 mi. in diameter, Oct. 9, 1975.

Holidays (P 262)

Veterans Day will be celebrated Nov. 11, 1976, in at least 46 states. Under a U.S. law signed in 197, Veterans Day will continue to be observed as a federal holiday on the 4th Monday in October (Oct. 26 in 1976) until 1978, when it will revert to Nov. 11.

United Nations (P 671)

There were 142 member states in the United Nations. Papua New Guinea should be added to the list; it became a member Oct. 10, 1975.

Elected nonpermanent members of the Security Council in Oct. 1975 were Pakistan, Dahomey, Libya, Panama, and Romania, replacing Byelorussia, Cameroon, Iraq, Costa Rica, and Mauritania.

Pay of U.S. Officials, Employees, Armed Forces

Pay scales were raised 5% Oct. 1, 1975, by act of Congress. Among those affected, and their new pay, were:

Vice president: raised to $65,625 (P 334).

Chief justice of U.S.; $65,625 (P 337).

Associate justices, Supreme Court; $63,000 (P 337).

Senators, representatives; $44,625 (Pp 343, 345).

Armed Forces; increased 5% (Pp 362, 363).

Salary of the president was not included, (P 334).

U.S. Public Officials

Thomas S. Kleppe was sworn in as Interior secretary, Oct. 17, 1975, succeeding Stanley K. Hathaway who resigned for health reasons (P 335).

Creighton Bolder was confirmed as assistant secretary of Commerce for tourism, Sept. 30 (P 336).

William J. Casey submitted his resignation as president of the Export-Import Bank, Sept. 13 (P 342).

Ray D. Garrett resigned as chairman of the Securities & Exchange Commission, effective Nov. 30, 1975 (P 342).

Frederick L. Webber resigned as assistant secretary of the Treasury, effective Sept. 2 (P 334).

Daniel J. Boorstin was confirmed Sept. 26 as librarian of Congress (P 460).

Sports (P 825-918)

Horse Racing: Honest Pleasure won the $100,000 added Champagne Stakes in 1:36 2/5 for the 1-mi. contest for 2-year-olds Oct. 18, 1975.

Group Plan won the $150,000 added Jockey Club Gold Cup in 3:23 1/5 for the 2-mi. run Oct. 25, 1975.

Snow Knight won the $188,700 Canadian International Championship in 2:43 1/5 over the 1 5/8-mi. course.

Baseball: Fred Lynn, Boston Red Sox outfielder, was named American League Rookie of the Year.

John Montefusco, San Francisco Giants pitcher, was named National League Rookie of the Year.

Springfield, Mass. (P 449)

The editor of the Springfield Union and the Sunday Republican is Arnold S. Friedman.

World Population (P 577)

The UN Statistical Office estimated in Nov. 1975 that world population reached 3.967 billion on July 1, 1975, and will reach 4.044 billion on July 1, 1976.

U.S. Population, ZIP Codes

Oakwood City, Oh., ZIP Code should be 45419 (P 233).

Shiloh, Oh., ZIP Code should be 45415 (P 233).

The name of Lockbourne Air Force Base has been changed to Rickenbacker Air Force Base (P 232).

Census of Counties and States

The New Hampshire county should be spelled Strafford, not Stratford (P 249).

Heads of States (P 677)

Prince Juan Carlos de Borbon became Spain's acting Chief of State, Oct. 30, as Francisco Franco appeared near death (see also Spain, P 652).

Colleges, Universities (P 176)

The new president of Northeastern University, Boston, is Kenneth G. Ryder. He was sworn in Oct. 28.

GOP Finds No Cheering Signs in 1975 Elections

Republican hopes for an off-year turnaround in 1975 elections to set a trend for the 1976 presidential contest were thoroughly dashed by the voters.

The Republicans came close to pulling off a major, stunning upset in Mississippi where Gil Carmichael, a GOP moderate, battled to within only a few votes of Cliff Finch, a "working man's" Democrat. Carmichael would have been the state's first Republican governor in 103 years.

The only other governorship race in the Nov. 4 election was decisively won by Kentucky's Democratic Gov. Julian M. Carroll by almost 2-to-1 over conservative Republican Robert Gable.

If Pres. Ford was looking for good omens, he could find one in the fact that most incumbents were re-

(Continued On Page 41)

Governors of States and Possessions

Reflecting as of Nov. 4, 1975 election

State	Capital	Governor	Party	Term Years	Term Expires	Annual Salary
Alabama	Montgomery	George C. Wallace	Dem.	4	Jan. 1979	$25,000
Alaska	Juneau	Jay Hammond	Rep.	4	Dec. 1978	40,000
Arizona	Phoenix	Raul Castro	Dem.	4	Jan. 1979	35,000
Arkansas	Little Rock	David Pryor	Dem.	2	Jan. 1977	10,000
California	Sacramento	Edmund G. Brown Jr.	Dem.	4	Jan. 1979	49,100
Colorado	Denver	Richard D. Lamm	Dem.	4	Jan. 1979	40,000
Connecticut	Hartford	Ella T. Grasso	Dem.	4	Jan. 1979	35,000
Delaware	Dover	Sherman W. Tribbitt	Dem.	4	Jan. 1977	35,000
Florida	Tallahassee	Reubin Askew	Dem.	4	Jan. 1979	40,000
Georgia	Atlanta	George Busbee	Dem.	4	Jan. 1979	50,000
Hawaii	Honolulu	George R. Ariyoshi	Dem.	4	Dec. 1978	42,000
Idaho	Boise	Cecil D. Andrus	Dem.	4	Jan. 1979	30,000
Illinois	Springfield	Daniel Walker	Dem.	4	Jan. 1977	50,000
Indiana	Indianapolis	Otis R. Bowen	Rep.	4	Jan. 1977	36,000
Iowa	Des Moines	Robert D. Ray	Rep.	4	Jan. 1979	40,000
Kansas	Topeka	Robert F. Bennett	Rep.	4	Jan. 1979	20,000
Kentucky	Frankfort	Julian Carroll	Dem.	4	Dec. 1979	30,000
Louisiana	Baton Rouge	Edwin W. Edwards	Dem.	4	May 1980	28,374
Maine	Augusta	James Longley	Ind.	4	Jan. 1979	35,000
Maryland	Annapolis	Marvin Mandel	Dem.	4	Jan. 1979	25,000
Massachusetts	Boston	Michael S. Dukakis	Dem.	4	Jan. 1979	40,000
Michigan	Lansing	William G. Milliken	Rep.	4	Jan. 1979	45,000
Minnesota	St. Paul	Wendell R. Anderson	Dem.	4	Jan. 1979	41,000
Mississipi	Jackson	Charles C. Finch	Dem.	4	Jan. 1980	35,000
Missouri	Jefferson City	Christopher S. Bond	Rep.	4	Jan. 1977	37,500
Montana	Helena	Thomas L. Judge	Dem.	4	Jan. 1977	25,000
Nebraska	Lincoln	J. James Exon	Dem.	4	Jan. 1979	25,000
Nevada	Carson City	Mike O'Callaghan	Dem.	4	Jan. 1979	30,000
New Hampshire	Concord	Meldrim Thomson Jr.	Rep.	2	Jan. 1977	32,760
New Jersey	Trenton	Brendan T. Byrne	Dem.	4	Jan. 1978	50,000
New Mexico	Santa Fe	Jerry Apodaca	Dem.	4	Jan. 1979	26,000
New York	Albany	Hugh L. Carey	Dem.	4	Jan. 1979	85,000
North Carolina	Raleigh	James E. Holshouser Jr.	Rep.	4	Jan. 1977	35,000
North Dakota	Bismarck	Arthur A. Link	Dem.	4	Jan. 1977	18,000
Ohio	Columbus	James A. Rhodes	Rep.	4	Jan. 1979	50,000
Oklahoma	Oklahoma City	David Boren	Dem.	4	Jan. 1979	35,000
Oregon	Salem	Robert Straub	Dem.	4	Jan. 1979	35,000
Pennsylvania	Harrisburg	Milton J. Shapp	Dem.	4	Jan. 1979	45,000
Rhode Island	Providence	Philip W. Noel	Dem.	2	Jan. 1977	42,500
South Carolina	Columbia	James B. Edwards	Rep.	4	Jan. 1979	35,000
South Dakota	Pierre	Richard F. Kneip	Dem.	4	Jan. 1979	25,000
Tennessee	Nashville	Ray Blanton	Dem.	4	Jan. 1979	50,000
Texas	Austin	Dolph Briscoe	Dem.	4	Jan. 1979	63,000
Utah	Salt Lake City	Calvin L. Rampton	Dem.	4	Jan. 1977	33,000
Vermont	Montpelier	Thomas P. Salmon	Dem.	2	Jan. 1977	35,000
Virginia	Richmond	Mills E. Godwin Jr.	Rep.	4	Jan. 1978	35,000
Washington	Olympia	Daniel J. Evans	Rep.	4	Jan. 1977	34,300
West Virginia	Charleston	Arch A. Moore Jr.	Rep.	4	Jan. 1977	35,000
Wisconsin	Madison	Patrick J. Lucey	Dem.	4	Jan. 1979	25,000
Wyoming	Cheyenne	Ed Herschler	Dem.	4	Jan. 1979	37,500

Possessions

Guam	Agana	Ricardo J. Bordallo	Rep.	4	Jan. 1977	35,000
Puerto Rico	San Juan	Rafael Hernandez Colon	Pop.	4	Jan. 1977	35,000
Virgin Isls.	Charlotte Amalie	Cyril E. King	Rep.	4	Jan. 1977	35,505

(Continued From Page 40)

turned to office in the major mayoralty races.

Results for women were mixed. In New Jersey and New York it turned out to be not the right era yet for ERA as the women's equal rights amendments proposed for the 2 states' constitutions went down to defeat.

But Democrat Evelyn Gandy handily defeated Republican Bill Patrick for lieutenant governor of Mississippi, doing better than her running mate, Finch. And Democrat Thelma Stovall defeated her opponent for lieutenant governor in Kentucky by a margin as large as Gov. Carroll's.

Democrats also kept control of the 4 state legislatures at stake in Kentucky, Mississippi, Virginia and New Jersey.

Voters were bitten by the economy bug, turning down a $4.5-billion bond-and-tax proposal in Ohio and a $922-billion bond package in New Jersey.

Louisiana Gov. Edwin W. Edwards won reelection Nov. 2, taking 62% of the vote over 5 fellow Democrats.

Early in the year, Jan. 7, Henson Moore became the 2d GOP congressman elected from Louisiana in 101 years.

Mayors and City Managers of Larger North American Cities
as of Nov. 4 elections, 1975

Asterisk before name denotes city manager. All others are mayors. For mayors, dates are those of expiration of term, for city managers, they are dates of appointment.

D., Democrat: R., Republican; N-P, Non-Partisan

City	Name	Term
Abilene, Tex.	*Fred Sandlin.	1974, May
Abington, Pa.	*Fred Schaefer	1958, June
Akron, Ohio.	John S. Ballard, R.	1979, Dec.
Alameda, Cal.	*John Goss.	1973, Dec.
Albany, Ga.	*S. A. Roos.	1961, Jan.
Albany, N.Y.	Erastus Corning, 2nd, D.	1977, Dec.
Albuquerque N.M.	Harry Kinney, N-P	1977 Dec.
Alexandria, La.	John K. Snyder, D	1977, June
Alexandria, Va.	*Keith Mulrooney	1974, Nov.
Alhambra, Cal.	*Harry S. Scott.	1968, Sept.
Allen Park, Mich.	Frank J. Lada, N-P	1977, Nov.
Allentown, Pa.	Joseph Daddona, D.	1978, Jan.
Alton, Ill.	Paul A. Lenz, N-P.	1977, Apr.
Altoona, Pa.	William C. Stouffer, R.	1980, Jan.
Amarillo, Tex.	*John S. Stiff.	1963, Sept.
Ames, Iowa.	*J. R. Castner.	1964, Oct.
Anaheim, Cal.	*Keith A. Murdoch.	1958, Nov.
Anchorage, Alas.	*Douglas G. Weiford.	1974, May
Anderson, Inc.	Robert Rock, D.	1980, Jan.
Anderson, S.C.	*Charles B. Martin.	1973, Mar.
Ann Arbor, Mich.	*Sylvester Murray.	1973, July
Appleton, Wis.	James P. Sutherland, N-P	1976, Apr.
Arcadia, Cal.	*Lyman H. Cozad.	1966, Aug.
Arlington, Mass.	*Donald R. Marquis.	1966, Nov.
Arlington, Tex.	*Ross Calhoun.	1973, Feb.
Arlington, Va.	*Bert Johnson.	1962, Dec.
Arlington Hts. Ill.	*L. A. Hanson.	1958, Oct.
Arvada, Col.	*Capp F. Shanks Jr.	1973, Aug.
Asheville, N.C.	*Ernest J. Ward.	1972, Sept.
Athens, Ga.	Upshaw Bentley, D.	1979, Nov.
Atlanta, Ga.	Maynard Jackson, D.	1978, Jan.
Atlantic City, N.J.	Joseph Bradway, Jr., N-P.	1976, May
Auburn, N.Y.	*Bruce L. Clifford.	1966, Aug.
Augusta, Ga.	Lewis A. Newman.	1977, Dec.
Aurora, Col.	*W. Robert Semple.	1972, Feb.
Aurora, Ill.	Albert D. McCoy, N-P.	1977, Apr.
Austin, Tex.	*Dan H. Davidson.	1972, Sept.
Bakersfield, Cal.	*Harold E. Bergen.	1966, July
Baldwin Park, Cal.	*James S. Mocalis.	1971, Dec.
Baltimore, Md.	William Schaefer, D.	1979, Dec.
Bangor, Me.	*Merle F. Goff.	1966, Dec.
Baton Rouge, La.	W. W. Dumas, D.	1976, Dec.
Battle Creek, Mich.	*Aaron Marsh.	1971, Aug.
Bay City, Mich.	*Carlton Laird.	1975, July
Baytown, Tex.	*Fritz Lanham.	1972, May
Beaumont, Tex.	*Howard McDaniel (Act.).	1975, June
Belleville, Ill.	Charles E. Nichols, N-P.	1977, Apr.
Belleville, N.J.	Michael Marotti, N-P.	1979, May
Bellevue, Wash.	*L. Joe Miller.	1961, Jan.
Bellflower, Cal.	*Peter B. Feenstra.	1968, Oct.
Beloit, Wis.	*H. Herbert Holt.	1970, Mar.
Berkeley, Cal.	*John L. Taylor.	1974, Feb.
Berwyn, Ill.	Emil Vacin, D.	1977, Apr.
Bessemer, Ala.	Ed Porter, D.	1978, Oct.
Bethlehem, Pa.	Gordon Mowrer, D.	1977, Dec.
Billings, Mont.	Joseph Leone, D.	1977, May
Biloxi, Miss.	Jerry O'Keefe, D.	1977, July
Binghamton, N.Y.	Alfred J. Libous, R.	1977, Dec.
Birmingham, Ala.	David Vann,.	1979, Nov.
Bismarck, N.D.	Robert Heskin.	1978, Apr.
Bloomfield, N.J.	*H. Joseph North.	1967, Oct.
Bloomington, Ill.	*Dave Anderson.	1975, July
Bloomington, Ind.	Francis X. McCloskey, D.	1979, Dec.
Bloomington, Minn.	*John Pidgeon.	1967, Dec.
Boise, Idaho.	Dick Eardley, R.	1977, Dec.
Bossier City, La.	James Cathey, D.	1977, June
Boston, Mass.	Kevin White, D.	1979, Dec.
Boulder, Col.	*Archie J. Twitchell.	1973, June
Bowie, Md.	*G. C. Moore (Act.).	1975, Sept.
Bowling Green, Ky.	*Paul McCauley.	1973, Jan.
Bridgeport, Conn.	John Mandanici, D.	1977, Nov.
Bristol, Conn.	Henry Wojtusik, D.	1977, Nov.
Brockton, Mass.	David L. Crosby, D.	1977, Dec.
Brookfield, Wis.	Franklin Wirth, R.	1976, Apr.
Brookline, Mass.	Board of Selectmen.	

City	Name	Term
Brooklyn Center, Minn.	*Donald G. Poss.	1966, June
Brownsville, Tex.	*J. W. Sloss.	1975, Jan.
Bryan, Tex.	*J. Louis Odle.	1974, May
Buffalo, N.Y.	Stanley M. Makowsky, D.	1977, Dec.
Burbank, Cal.	*Joseph N. Baker.	1968, Mar.
Burlington, Vt.	Gordon H. Paquette, D.	1977, Apr.
Calumet City, Ill.	Robert C. Stefaniak, D.	1977, Apr.
Cambridge, Mass.	*James L. Sullivan.	1974, Apr.
Camden, N.J.	Angelo Errichetti.	1977, July
Canton, Ohio.	Stanley A. Cmich, R.	1979, Dec.
Cape Girardeau, Mo.	*W. G. Lawley.	1970, July
Carson, Cal.	*E. Frederick Bien.	1968, Apr.
Casper, Wyo.	*Kenneth Erickson.	1969, Oct.
Cedar Rapids, Iowa	Donald J. Canney, N-P.	1977, Dec.
Champaign, Ill.	*Eugene Miller.	1974, Sept.
Charleston, S.C.	J. Palmer Gailliard, D.	1979, Dec.
Charleston, W. Va.	*H. Hugh Bosely.	1973, Apr.
Charlotte, N.C.	*David A. Burkhalter.	1971, May
Charlottesville, Va.	*Cole Hendrix.	1971, Jan.
Chattanooga, Tenn.	Charles A. Rose, N-P.	1979, Apr.
Chesapeake, Va.	*Durwood S. Curling.	1971, Jan.
Chester, Pa.	John Nacrelli, R.	1980, Jan.
Cheyenne, Wyo.	Bill Nation, D.	1976, Dec.
Chicago, Ill.	Richard J. Daley, D.	1979, Apr.
Chicago Hts., Ill.	Charles Panici.	1979, Apr.
Chicopee, Mass.	Howard Redfern.	1977, Dec.
Chula Vista, Cal.	*Lane F. Cole.	1975, Feb.
Cicero, Ill.	John Karner, R.	1976, Apr.
Cincinnati, Ohio	*E. Robert Turner.	1972, June
Clarksville, Tenn.	Charles W. Crow, D.	1979, Jan.
Clearwater, Fla.	*Picot B. Floyd.	1973, Oct.
Cleveland, Ohio.	Ralph J. Perk, R.	1977, Nov.
Cleveland Heights.	*Robert A. Edwards.	1975, June
Clifton, N.J.	*William Holster.	1957, Jan.
Col. Spgs., Col.	*George H. Fellows.	1966, July
Columbia, Mo.	*Terry Novak.	1974, Feb.
Columbia, S.C.	*Graydon V. Olive Jr.	1970, Mar.
Columbus, Ga.	*Franklyn Lambert.	1971, Jan.
Columbus, Ohio.	Tom Moody, R.	1980, Jan.
Commerce, Cal.	*Robert Hinderliter.	1973, Sept.
Compton, Cal.	*James S. Wilson Jr.	1974, Feb.
Concord, Cal.	*F. A. Stewart.	1960, Apr.
Concord, N.H.	*John E. Henchey.	1968, Jan.
Coon Rapids, Minn.	*John K. Cottingham.	1969, July
Coral Gables, Fla.	*J. Martin Gainer.	1975, Jan.
Corpus Christi, Tex.	*R. Marvin Townsend.	1968, Jan.
Corvallis, Ore.	*C. Dean Smith.	1968, Jan.
Costa Mesa, Cal.	*Fred Sorsable.	1970, Nov.
Council Buffs, Ia.	*M. Don Harmon.	1969, Feb.
Covington, Ky.	George Wermeling, D.	1979, Dec.
Cranston, R.I.	James L. Taft Jr., R.	1979, Jan.
Crystal, Minn.	*John Irving.	1964, Jan.
Culver City, Cal.	*Harry D. Jones.	1969, June
Cuyahoga Falls. O.	Robert Quirk, D.	1977, Dec.
Dallas, Tex.	*George R. Schrader.	1972, Dec.
Daly City, Cal.	*David R. Rowe.	1969, Aug.
Danbury, Conn.	Charles A. Ducibella, D.	1977, Dec.
Danville, Ill.	David S. Palmer, N-P.	1979, Apr.
Danville, Va.	*James W. Lord.	1971, Nov.
Davenport, Ia.	Robert Duax, R.	1979, Dec.
Dayton, Ohio.	*James Alloway.	1974, Feb.
Daytona Bch., Fla.	*Russell C. Smith.	1971, Mar.
Dearborn, Mich.	Orville L. Hubbard, N-P.	1978, Jan.
Decatur, Ala.	Russell Bolding, D.	1976, Sept.
Decatur, Ill.	*Leslie T. Allen.	1972, Sept.
Denton, Tex.	*Jim White.	1968, May
Denver, Col.	William H. McNichols, D.	1979, July
Des Moines, Ia.	*Richard A. Wilkey.	1974, Mar.
Des Plaines, Ill.	Herbert Behrel, R.	1977, Apr.
Detroit, Mich.	Coleman A. Young, N-P.	1978, Jan.
Dotham, Ala.	*Christian P. Morris.	1974, Mar.
Downers Grove, Ill.	*James R. Griesemer.	1972, Sept.
Dubuque, Ia.	*Gilbert D. Chavenelle.	1960, July
Duluth, Minn.	Robert Beaudin, R.	1977, Dec.
Durham, N.C.	*I. Harding Hughes Jr.	1963, Jan.

City	Name	Term
E. Chicago, Ind.	Robert A. Pastrick, D.	1979, Dec.
E. Cleveland, Oh.	*Curtis Hall	1973, Jan.
E. Detroit, Mich.	*W. Larry Collins	1975, Mar.
E. Hartford, Conn.	Richard H. Blackstone, D.	1977, Nov.
E. Lansing, Mich.	*John Patriarche	1948, Jan.
E. Orange, N.J.	William S. Hart, D.	1977, Dec.
E. Providence, R.I.	*Paul A. Flynn.	1972, July
E. St. Louis, Ill.	William Mason, D.	1979, May
Eau Claire, Wis.	*Ray E. Wachs	1970, June
Edina, Minn.	*Warren Hyde	1955, May
Edison, N.J.	Thomas Paterniti, D.	1977, Dec.
El Cajon, Cal.	*Robert M. Applegate	1958, Sept.
Elgin, Ill.	*Leo Nelson.	1972, Dec.
Elizabeth, N.J.	Thomas G. Dunn, D.	1976, Dec.
Elkhart, Ind.	Peter Carantos, R.	1979, Dec.
Elmhurst, Ill.	*Robert T. Palmer.	1953, June
Elmira, N.Y.	*Joseph E. Sartori.	1972, June
El Monte, Cal.	*Kenneth Botts	1969, Aug.
El Paso, Tex.	Don Henderson	1977, Apr.
Elyria, Oh.	Marguerite Bowman, R.	1979, Dec.
Enfield, Conn.	*William L. McDivitt.	1975, July
Enid, Okla.	*Tom Sailors Jr.	1969, Oct.
Erie, Pa.	Louis J. Tullio, D.	1977, Dec.
Escondido, Cal.	*George Patterson.	1970, May
Euclid, Oh.	Anthony Sustarsic, R.	1979, Dec.
Eugene, Ore.	*Charles T. Henry.	1975, July
Evanston, Ill.	*Edward A. Martin.	1971, Mar.
Evansville, Ind.	Russell Lloyd, R.	1980, Jan.
Everett, Mass.	Geroge R. McCarthy, D.	1977, Dec.
Everett, Wash.	Robert C. Anderson, N-P.	1978, Jan.
Fairborn, Oh.	*Claude Malone Jr.	1970, July
Fairfield, Cal.	*B. Gale Wilson	1956, Mar.
Fairfield, Conn.	John J. Sullivan, D.	1977, Nov.
Fair Lawn, N.J.	*Frank Vanore	1975, Oct.
Fall River, Mass.	Wilfred C. Driscoll, D.	1979, Dec.
Frmngtn Hills, Mich.	Earl Opperthuser, N-P.	1976, July
Fayetteville, Ark.	*Donald Grimes.	1972, Apr.
Fayetteville, N.C.	*J. Guy Smith.	1971, Jan.
Fitchburg, Mass.	Hedley Bray, D.	1978, Jan.
Flagstaff, Ariz.	*Charles McClain.	1973, Nov.
Flint, Mich.	*Daniel Boggan Jr.	1974, June
Florissant, Mo.	James J. Eagan, D.	1979, Apr.
Fond du Lac, Wis.	*Myron J. Medin Jr.	1967, Nov.
Ft. Collins, Col.	*Robert L. Brunton.	1972, Oct.
Ft. Lauderdale, Fla.	*Robert Anderson.	1975, July
Ft. Lee, N.J.	*James J. Mulcare.	1973, Jan.
Ft. Smith, Ark.	*Ray A. Riley	1972, Dec.
Ft. Wayne, Ind.	Robert Armstrong, R.	1979, Dec.
Ft. Worth, Tex.	*Rodger Line	1971, Apr.
Fremont, Cal.	*Don Driggs.	1967, Jan.
Fresno, Cal.	*Ralph W. Hanley	1973, Sept.
Fullerton, Cal.	*W. F. Cornett.	1966, Oct.
Gadsden, Ala.	Steve Means, D.	1979, Oct.
Gainesville, Fla.	*B. Harold Farmer.	1968, Nov.
Galesburg, Ill.	*Thomas B. Herring.	1960, Nov.
Galveston, Tex.	*Jack Nichols.	1975, June
Gardena, Cal.	*Craig McDowell.	1973, Dec.
Garden Grove, Cal.	*Richard R. Powers.	1972, Apr.
Garfield Hts., Ohio	Raymond Stachewicz, D.	1977, Dec.
Garland, Tex.	*C. E. Duckworth.	1965, Jan.
Gary, Ind.	R. G. Hatcher, D.	1979, Nov.
Gastonia, N.C.	*Gary Hicks	1973, Dec.
Glendale, Ariz.	*S. F. Van de Putte.	1960, Aug.
Glendale, Cal.	*C. E. Perkins.	1952, Apr.
Grand Forks, N.D.	Cyril P. O'Neill, D.	1976, Apr.
Gr. Island, Neb.	*John M. Carpenter	1964, Aug.
Gr. Prairie, Tex.	*Clifford A. Johnson.	1962, Oct.
Gr. Rapids, Mich.	*Joseph R. Grassie.	1970, June
Granite City, Ill.	Paul Schuler, N-P.	1977, Apr.
Great Falls, Mont.	*Richard D. Thomas.	1973, May
Green Bay, Wis.	Michael Monfils	1979, Apr.
Greensboro, N.C.	*Thomas Z. Osborne.	1972, Nov.
Greensville, S.C.	*John J. Dullea	1971, Oct.
Greenwich, Conn.	Ruppert Vernon, R.	1977, Dec.
Groton, Conn.	Donald Sweet, N-P.	1977, May
Gulfport, Miss.	Arthur W. Long Jr., D.	1977, June
Hackensack, N.J.	*Joseph J. Squillace	1964, Oct.
Hagerstown, Md.	Varner L. Paddack, R.	1977, Apr.
Hamden, Conn.	Lucien A. DiMeo, R.	1977, Nov.
Hamilton, Ohio.	*Edward C. Smith	1971, June
Hammond, Ind.	Edward J. Raskowsky, D.	1979, Dec.
Hampton, Va.	*C. E. Johnson.	1958, May
Harlingen, Tex.	*Charles Norwood.	1973, Apr.
Harrisburg, Pa.	Harold Swenson, D.	1978, Jan.

City	Name	Term
Hartford, Conn.	*Edward Curtin.	1971, June
Harvey, Ill.	James A. Haines, R.	1979, Apr.
Hattiesburg, Miss.	A. L. Gerrard Jr., D	1977, July
Haverhill, Mass.	Louis C. Burton.	1977, Dec.
Hawthorne, Cal.	*Donald W. Mansfield.	1972, Jan.
Hayward, Cal.	*William C. Hanley.	1972, Feb.
Hempstead, N.Y.	Dalton R. Miller, R.	1977, Apr.
Hialeah, Fla.	Dale Bennett, D.	1977, Dec.
High Point, N.C.	*Harold R. Cheek.	1960, Mar.
Highland Pk., Ill.	*Larry Rice.	1975, Jan.
Hoboken, N.J.	Steve Cappiello, N-P.	1977, July
Holyoke, Mass.	Ernest Proulx.	1978, Jan.
Hollywood, Fla.	*Tony M. Reasons.	1977, Dec.
Honolulu, Hawaii.	Frank F. Fasi, D.	1977, Jan.
Hot Springs, Ark.	Tom Ellsworth, N-P.	1978, Dec.
Houston, Tex.	(Undecided).	
Huntington, W. Va.	*Barry R. Evans.	1973, Mar.
Huntington Beach,		
Cal.	*David D. Rowlands.	1972, Feb.
Huntsville, Ala.	Joe W. Davis, N-P.	1976, Oct.
Hutchinson, Kan.	*George W. Pyle.	1967, Sept.
Independence, Mo.	*Lyle Alberg.	1968, Sept.
Indianapolis, Ind.	William Hudnut, R.	1979, Dec.
Inglewood, Cal.	*Douglas W. Ayres.	1968, Apr.
Inkster, Mich.	*David S. Williams.	1973, Oct.
Iowa City, Iowa	*Neal Berlin.	1975, Mar.
Irving, Tex.	*Darwin McGill.	1973, June
Irvington, N.J.	Robert Miller, R.	1978, July
Jackson, Mich.	*S. W. McAllister Jr.	197.
Jackson, Miss.	Russell C. Davis, D.	1977, July
Jackson, Tenn.	Bob Conger, D.	1979, July
Jacksonville, Fla.	Hans Tanzler Jr., D.	1979, June
Jamestown, N.Y.	Stanley Lundine, D.	1977, Dec.
Janesville, Wis.	*Robert O. Bailey.	1971, Jan.
Jefferson City, Mo.	Robert Hyder.	1979, Apr.
Jersey City, N.J.	Paul Jordan, D.	1977, July
Johnson City, Tenn.	*William Ricker.	1971, Oct.
Johnstown, Pa.	Herbert Pfuhl, R.	1977, Jan.
Joliet, Ill.	*Lynn Neuhart.	1972, Feb.
Joplin, Mo.	*Robert E. Metzinger.	1968, Mar.
Kalamazoo, Mich.	*Bruce Brown.	1975, Jan.
Kansas City, Kan.	John Reardon, N-P.	1979, Apr.
Kansas City, Mo.	*Robert A. Kipp.	1974, Jan.
Kenosha, Wis.	Wallace E. Burkee, N-P.	1976, Apr.
Kettering, Oh.	*Vacant.	
Key West, Fla.	*Robert J. Stack.	1974, June
Killeen, Tex.	*Robert Brockman.	1972, Jan.
Knoxville, Tenn.	Kyle C. Testerman, R.	1979, Dec.
Kokomo, Ind.	Arthur LaDow, R.	1980, Jan.
LaCrosse, Wis.	Patrick Zielke, N-P.	1977, Apr.
Lafayette, Ind.	James Riehle, D.	1979, Dec.
Lafayette, La.	Kenneth Bowen, D.	1976, June
La Habra, Cal.	*Lee Risner.	1971, Nov.
La Mesa, Cal.	*Gayle T. Martin.	1975, June
La Mirada, Cal.	*Claude J. Klug.	1971, Aug.
Lake Charles, La.	William E. Boyer, D.	1978, June
Lakeland, Fla.	*Robert V. Youkey.	1960, Jan.
Lakewood, Cal.	*Milton R. Farrell.	1971, Dec.
Lakewood, Col.	*Ray Wells.	1974, Sept.
Lakewood, Oh.	Robert M. Lawther, R.	1979, Dec.
Lancaster, Pa.	Richard M. Scott, R	1978, Jan.
Lansing, Mich.	Gerald Graves, N-P.	1977, Dec.
Laredo, Tex.	J. C. Martin Jr., N-P	1978, May
Las Cruces, N.M.	*Harold Yungmeyer.	1975, Jan.
Las Vegas, Nev.	*Arthur R. Trelease.	1965, Jan.
Lawrence, Kan.	*Buford M. Watson Jr.	1970, Jan.
Lawrence, Mass.	John J. Buckley, N-P.	1977, Dec.
Lawton, Okla.	*John R. Thomson.	1975, Feb.
Lewiston, Me.	(Undecided).	
Lexington, Ky.	H. Foster Pettit, D.	1978, Jan.
Lima, Oh.	Harry Moyer, R.	1977, Nov.
Lincoln, Neb.	Helen Boosalis, N-P.	1979, May
Lincoln Pk., Mich.	Melvin L. Gish, N-P.	1977, Dec.
Linden, N.J.	John Gregorio, D.	1978, Dec.
Little Rock, Ark.	*Carleton E. McMullin.	1973, Nov.
Livermore, Cal.	*William H. Parness.	1957, Oct.
Livonia, Mich.	E. H. McNamara, N-P.	1978, Jan.
Lombard, Ill.	*Warren Browning.	1975, Sept.
Long Beach, Cal.	*John R. Mansell.	1961, Mar.
Long Beach, N.Y.	*Richard Bowen.	1974, Apr.
Longview Tex.	*Harry G. Mosley.	1952, July
Los Angeles, Cal.	Thomas Bradley, D.	1977, June

City	Name	Term
Louisville, Ky.	Harvey Sloane, D.	1977, Nov.
Lowell, Mass.	*Vacant.	
L. Merion, Pa.	*Thomas B. Fulweiler.	1968, Jan.
Lubbock, Tex.	*N. B. McCullough	1971, Oct.
Lynchburg, Va.	*David B. Norman.	1970, Nov.
Lynn, Mass.	Anthony J. Marino	1980, Jan.
Lynwood, Cal.	*Stephen Wright	1973, Feb.
Macon, Ga.	Buckner Melton, D.	1979, Nov.
Madison, Wis.	Paul Soglin, N-P.	1977, Apr.
Madison Heights, Mich.	Virginia Solberg.	1977, Apr.
Malden, Mass.	James Conway,	1978, Jan.
Manchester, Conn.	*Robert B. Weiss	1966, Jan.
Manchester, N.H.	Charles Stanton, D.	1977, Dec.
Manitowoc, Wis.	Anthony V. Dufek, N-P	1977, Apr.
Mansfield, Oh.	Richard A. Porter, R.	1976, Dec.
Marion, Ind.	Anthony Maidenberg, D.	1980, Jan.
McKeesport, Pa.	John E. Pribanic, D.	1980, Jan.
Medford, Mass.	*James Nicholson.	1970, Oct.
Melbourne, Fla.	*Ernest E. Watkins.	1969, July
Memphis, Tenn.	Wyeth Chandler, N-P	1979, Dec.
Mentor, Oh.	*Arthur V. Dickard.	1963, Sept.
Meridian, Miss.	*Joel W. Forrester.	1959, May
Mesa, Ariz.	*J. A. Petrie.	1950, Sept.
Mesquite, Tex.	*Billy G. York.	1969, Oct.
Miami, Fla.	*P. W. Andrews.	1973, Aug.
Miami Beach, Fla.	*Frack Spence.	1973, Feb.
Middletown, Oh.	*Dale F. Helsel.	1970, Oct.
Midland, Tex.	*James W. Brown.	1964, Nov.
Midwest City, Okla.	*Jerry Wadw (act.)	1975, Sept.
Milford, Conn.	Joel Baldwin, D.	1977, Nov.
Milwaukee, Wis.	Henry W. Maier, D.	1976, Apr.
Minneapolis.	Charles Stenvig, N-P	1977, Nov.
Minnetonka, Minn.	*Carsten D. Leikvold.	1973, Dec.
Minot, N.D.	*John Arnold.	1972, Oct.
Mobile, Ala.	Robert Doyle.	1976, May
Modesto, Cal.	*Garth Lipsky.	1974, Jan.
Moline, Ill.	Earl Wendt, R.	1977, May
Monroe, La.	Ralph T. Troy, D.	1976, June
Montclair, N.J.	Peter Bonastia.	1976, May
Montebello, Cal.	*Roy Pederson.	1969, Jan.
Monterey Park, Cal.	*Gerald C. Weeks.	1970, Aug.
Montgomery, Ala.	Jim Robinson, N-P	1979, Oct.
Mt. Prospect, Ill.	*Robert J. Eppley.	1971, Aug.
Mt. Vernon, N.Y.	August Petrillo, R.	1979, Dec.
Mountain View, Cal.	*Richard De Long.	1973, Nov.
Muncie, Ind.	Robert Cunningham.	1979, Dec.
Mundelein, Ill.	Maurice A. Noll, N-P.	1977, Apr.
Muskegon, Mich.	*Paul F. Frederick.	1970, June
Muskogee, Okla.	*W. T. Smith.	1971, Oct.
Napa, Cal.	*Lee M. Roberts.	1952, Feb.
Nashua, N.H.	(Undecided)	
Nashville, Tenn.	Richard Fulton, D.	1979,Sept.
National City, Cal.	*Cleo Osburn.	1965, July
New Bedford, Mass.	John Markey, D.	1978, Jan.
New Britain, Conn.	Matthew Avitable, D.	1977, Nov.
New Brunswick, N.J.	*Paul Abdalla.	1975, Sept.
New Castle, Pa.	Francis J. Rogan, D.	1979, Dec.
New Haven, Conn.	Frank Logue, D.	1977, Nov.
New Kensington, Pa.	Verle N. Bevan, D.	1977, Dec.
New Orleans, La.	Moon Landrieu, D.	1978, Apr.
New Rochelle, N.Y.	*C. Samuel Kissinger.	1975, Apr.
New York, N.Y.	Abraham Beame, D.	1977, Dec.
Newark, N.J.	Kenneth Gibson, D.	1978, July
Newport, R.I.	*Vacant.	
Newport Beach, Cal.	*Robert L. Wynn.	1971, Aug.
Newport News, Va.	*W. E. Lawson Jr.	1965, Sept.
Newton, Mass.	Theodore Mann, R.	1977, Dec.
Niagara Falls, N.Y.	*Earl Lenhart Jr.	1975, June
Niles, Ill.	*Kenneth Scheel.	1973, May
Norfolk, Va.	*Julian Hirst.	1975, Apr.
Norman, Okla.	*Richard Gray.	1972, Nov.
North Charleston, S.C.	John Bourne, N-P.	1978, June
North Chicago, Ill.	Leo F. Kukla, D.	1977, Apr.
No. Little Rock, Ark.	Eddie Powell, D.	1976, Dec.
Norwalk, Cal.	*William H. Kraus.	1973, May
Norwalk, Conn.	Jennie Cave, N-P.	1977, Nov.
Norwich, Conn.	*Charles Whitty.	1973, June
Novato, Cal.	*Phillip J. Brown.	1974, May
Oak Lawn, Ill.	*Kenneth M. McDonald.	1973, Dec.
Oak Park, Ill.	*Lee A. Ellis.	1971, Sept.
Oak Park, Mich.	*James B. Thompson.	1970, Sept.
Oakland, Cal.	*Cecil S. Riley.	1972, Sept.
Oak Ridge, Tenn.	*William N. Haddock.	1974, Dec.
Oceanside, Cal.	*Lawrence M. Bagley.	1970, Apr.

City	Name	Term
Odessa, Tex.	*Ronald J. Neighbors.	1968, Nov.
Ogden, Utah	*R. L. Larsen.	1972, Feb.
Oklahoma City, Okla.	*Howard McMahon.	1974, Jan.
Omaha, Neb.	Edward Zorinsky, N-P	1977, May
Ontario, Cal.	*Roger Hughbanks.	1975, July
Orange, Cal.	*Gifford Miller.	1968, Dec.
Orange, N.J.	Carmine Capone, R.	1978, May
Orlando, Fla.	Carl Langford, D.	1976, Oct.
Oshkosh, Wis.	*Gordon Jaeger.	1970, Dec.
Overland Park, Kan.	Jack Walker.	1977, Apr.
Owensboro, Ky.	*Max N. Rhoads.	1959, Sept
Oxnard, Cal.	*Paul E. Wolven.	1953, Feb.
Pacifica, Cal.	*Donald Weidner.	1975, Oct.
Palm Springs, Cal.	William Foster, N-P	1976, Mar.
Palo Alto, Cal.	*George Sipel.	1972, Feb.
Parkersburg, W. Va.	William Nicely, R.	1977, Dec.
Parma, Ohio	John Petruska, D.	1979, Dec.
Pasadena, Cal.	*Donald F. McIntyre.	1973, June
Pasadena, Tex.	John Ray Harrison, D.	1977, Apr.
Passaic, N.J.	Gerald Goldman, R.	1977, June
Paterson, N.J.	*Larry Worth.	1974, Sept.
Pawtucket, R.I.	Dennis Lynch, D.	1978, Jan.
Pekin, Ill.	William L. Waldmeier.	1979, Apr.
Pensacola, Fla.	*Frank A. Faison.	1971, Apr.
Peoria, Ill.	*Robert O. Wright.	1970, Oct.
Perth Amboy, N.J.	*Robert J. Cabana.	1973, July
Petersburg, Va.	*Roy F. Ash.	1950, Jan.
Philadelphia, Pa.	Frank L. Rizzo, D.	1980, Jan.
Phoenix, Ariz.	*John B. Wentz.	1970, July
Pico Rivera, Cal.	*Howard Schroyer.	1970, July
Pine Bluff, Ark.	Charles Moore, N'P.	1976, Dec.
Pittsburgh, Pa.	Peter Flaherty, D.	1977, Dec.
Pittsfield, Mass.	Evan S. Dobelle.	1978, Jan.
Plainfield, N.J.	*Lawrence Bashe	1974, Mar.
Pocatello, Idaho.	*Charles W. Moss.	1970, Sept.
Pomona, Cal.	*Jerrold R. Gonce.	1973, Oct.
Pompano Bch., Fla.	*John Schoeberlein.	1975, Oct.
Pontiac, Mich.	*Frank Smiley.	1972, Jan.
Portage, Mich.	*Donald P. Ziemke.	1974, Aug.
Port Arthur, Tex.	*George E, Dibrell.	1962, Oct.
Port Huron, Mich.	*Gerald R. Bouchard.	1965, June
Portland, Me.	*John Menario.	1967, June
Portland, Ore.	Neil Goldschmidt, N-P.	1976, Dec.
Portsmouth, Oh.	*C. Scott Johnson.	1974, Feb.
Portsmouth, Va.	*Robert T. Williams.	1975, Apr.
Poughkeepsie, N.Y.	*John Geib.	1974, Oct.
Prichard, Ala.	A. J. Cooper.	1976, Oct.
Providence, R.I.	Vincent Cianci, R.	1979, Jan.
Provo, Utah.	Russell D. Grange, N-P.	1977, Dec.
Pueblo, Col.	*Fred E. Weisbroad.	1967, Feb.
Quincy, Ill.	Don Nicholson, D.	1977, May
Quincy, Mass.	(Undecided)	
Racine, Wis.	Stephen Olson, N-P	1977, Apr.
Raleigh, N.C.	*L. P. Zachary Jr.	1973, Nov.
Rapid City, S.D.	Arthur La Croix, R.	1977, May
Raytown, Mo.	Willard H. Ross, R.	1977, Apr.
Reading, Pa.	Joseph Kuzminski, D.	1980, Jan.
Redlands, Cal.	*R. P. Merritt Jr.	1964, Mar.
Redondo Beach, Cal.	*Joseph P. Leach.	1973, Feb.
Redwood City, Cal.	*James M. Fales Jr.	1971, Aug.
Reno, Nev.	*Joe Latimore.	1960, Oct.
Revere, Mass.	William Reinstein.	1980, Jan.
Richardson, Tex.	*Bob Hughey.	1974, Jan.
Richfield, Minn.	*Wayne Burggraaff.	1968, Dec.
Richmond, Cal.	*Kenneth Smith.	1967, Sept.
Richmond, Ind.	Clifford Dickman, R.	1979, Dec.
Richmond, Va.	*William J. Leidinger.	1972, June
Riverside, Cal.	*Vacant.	
Roanoke, Va.	*Byron E. Haner.	1973, Jan.
Rochester, Minn.	*Robert W. Freson.	1974, Sept.
Rochester, N.Y.	*Elisha Freedman.	1974, Jan.
Rock Hill, S.C.	*Max Holland.	1965, Mar.
Rock Island, Ill.	*Raymond P. Botch.	1961, Feb.
Rockford, Ill.	Robert McGaw, D.	1977, May
Rockville, Md.	*Larry N. Blick.	1972, Nov.
Rome, N.Y.	Wm. A. Valentine, R.	1979, Dec.
Rosemead, Cal.	*Frank Tripepi.	1975, Feb.
Roseville, Mich.	*Harvey Weatherwax.	1974, Dec.
Roseville, Minn.	*James Andre.	1974, May
Roswell, N.M.	*Robert J. Owen.	1973, Oct.
Royal Oak, Mich.	*William Baldridge.	1975, Sept.
Sacramento, Cal.	*R. L. Rathfon.	1969, Jan.

City	Name	Term
Saginaw, Mich.	*E. H Potthoff Jr.	1961, July
St. Clair Shores, Mich.	*Donald J. Harm	1962, Jan.
St. Cloud, Minn.	Alcuin Loehr	1976, Apr.
St. Joseph, Mo.	W. J. Bennett, D	1978, Apr.
St. Louis, Mo.	John Poelker, D	1977, Apr.
St. Louis Pk., Minn.	*Chris Cherches	1968, Oct.
St. Paul, Minn.	Lawrence D. Cohen.	1976, June
St. Petersburg, Fla.	*R. E. Harbaugh	1970, May
Salem, Mass.	Jean Levesque.	1978, Jan.
Salem, Ore.	*Robert S. Moore.	1968, Aug.
Salina, Kan.	*Norris D. Olson.	1964, May
Salinas, Cal.	*Robert Christofferson.	1972, Dec.
Salt Lake City, Utah.	Ted Wilson, N-P.	1980, Jan
San Angelo, Tex.	*H. D. Howard.	1958, May
San Antonio, Tex.	*Sam Granata Jr.	1973, Mar.
San Bernardino, Cal.	*Marshall Julian.	1971, Nov.
San Diego, Cal.	*Hugh McKinley.	1975, Apr.
San Francisco, Cal.	(Undecided)	
San Jose, Cal.	*Ted Tedesco	1973, Feb.
San Leandro, Cal.	*Wesley McCure.	1958, Apr.
San Mateo, Cal.	*John Lilly	1973, July
San Rafael, Cal.	*William, J. Bielser.	1973, Jan.
Sandusky, Ohio	*Frank Link	1972, Jan.
Santa Ana, Cal.	*Bruce C. Spragg.	1972, June
Santa Barbara, Cal.	*John L. Scott	1973, Mar.
Santa Cruz, Cal.	*David C. Koester.	1962, Oct.
Santa Fe, N.M.	*Philip Baca.	1972, Aug.
Santa Maria, Cal.	*Robert Grogan.	1963, Jan.
Santa Monica, Cal.	*James D. Williams.	1973, Oct.
Santa Rosa, Fla.	*Kenneth R. Blackman	1970, July
Sarasota, Fla.	*Kenneth Thompson.	1950, Feb.
Savannah, Ga.	*Arthur A. Mendonsa	1971, Sept.
Schenectady, N.Y.	*Peter Caputo.	1973, Oct.
Scottsdale, Ariz.	*Frank Aleshire.	1975, July
Scranton, Pa.	Eugene J. Peters, R.	1977, Dec.
Seattle, Wash.	Wesley C. Uhlman, N-P	1977, Dec.
Shaker Heights, Oh.	Walter C. Kelly.	1979, Dec.
Sheboygan, Wis.	Richard Suscha, R	1977, Apr.
Shreveport, La.	L. Calhoun Allen Jr., D.	1978, Nov.
Simi Valley, Cal.	*Richard Malcolm	1974, May
Sioux City, Ia.	*Gary F. Pokorny.	1974, Jan.
Sioux Falls, S.D.	Rick Knobe, R.	1979, May
Skokie, Ill.	*John N. Matzer Jr.	1970, Jan.
Somerville, Mass.	L. Lester Ralph	1978, Jan.
South Bend, Ind.	Peter J. Nemeth, D.	1979, Dec
So. Gate, Cal.	Harold Prukop, D.	1976, Mar.
So. S. F., Cal.	*Edward G. Alario.	1973, Nov.
Southfield, Mich.	*Peter Cristiano.	1968, July
Southgate, Mich.	*William Valusek.	1972, Feb.
Spartanburg, S.C.	*W. H. Carstarphen	1975, Mar.
Spokane, Wash.	*F. Sylvin Fulwiler.	1963, Aug.
Springfield, Ill.	William C. Telford, N-P.	1979, Apr.
Springfield, Mass.	William Sullivan.	1978, Jan.
Springfield, Mo.	*Don G. Busch.	1971, Oct.
Springfield, Ohio	*Alfred Strozdas.	1968, Nov.
Stamford, Conn.	Louis Clapes, R.	1977, Nov.
Sterling Hts., Mich.	*John Cartwright.	1975, May
Stillwater, Okla.	*Lawrence Gish.	1966, Aug.
Stockton, Cal.	*Elder Gunter.	1969, July
Stratford, Conn.	*Vacant.	
Sunnyvale, Cal.	*John E. Dever.	1967, Aug.
Syracuse, N.Y.	Lee Alexander, D.	1977, Dec.
Tacoma, Wash.	*Erling O. Mork	1975, June
Tallahassee, Fla.	*Daniel A. Kleman	1974, Aug.
Tampa, Fla.	William Poe, N-P.	1979, Sept.
Taunton, Mass.	Benjamin Friedman.	1977, Dec.
Taylor, Mich.	S. Richard Marshall, N-P.	1977, Dec.
Teaneck, N.Y.	*Werner H. Shmid.	1959, Mar.
Tempe, Ariz.	*Kenneth A. McDonald	1968, June
Temple, Tex.	D. M. Brady, N-P.	1976, Apr.
Terre Haute, Ind.	William Brighton, D.	1979, Dec.
Thousand Oaks, Cal.	*Glenn Kendall	1966
Titusville, Fla.	*Norman Hickey	1974, June
Toledo, Ohio.	*James B. Daken.	1971, Mar.
Topeka, Kan.	William McCormick, N-P	1977, Apr.
Torrance, Cal.	*Edward J. Ferraro	1964, Mar.
Trenton, N.J.	Arthur Holland, N-P.	1978, July
Troy, Mich.	*Frank, Gerstenecker.	1970, Feb.
Troy, N.Y.	*John P. Buckley.	1972, June
Tuscon, Ariz.	*Joel Valdez	1974, Apr.
Tulsa, Okla.	Robert La Fortune, R.	1976, May
Tuscaloosa, Ala.	C. Snow Hinton, D.	1977, Oct.
Tyler, Tex.	*Ed Wagoner.	1972, Nov.
Univ. City, Mo.	*Victor Ellman (Act.)	1975, July
Upland, Cal.	*S. Lee Travers.	1974, Oct.

City	Name	Term
Upper Arlington, O.	*H. W. Hyrne.	1968, May
Urbana, Ill.	Hiram Paley, D.	1977, May
Utica, N.Y.	Edward Hanna, N-P.	1977, Dec.
Vallejo, Cal.	*Gerald R. Davis.	1973, Aug.
Vancouver, Wash.	*Alan Harvey.	1969, May
Ventura, Cal.	*Edward E. McCombs.	1970, Mar.
Victoria, Tex.	*John Lee.	1959, Sept.
Vineland, N.J.	Joseph D'Ippolito, R.	1976, June
Virginia Beach, Va.	*George L. Hanbury.	1974, Nov.
Waco, Tex.	*David F. Smith Jr.	1971, Sept.
Walnut Creek, Cal.	*Thomas G. Dunne.	1972, Mar.
Waltham, Mass.	Arthur J. Clarke.	1980, Jan.
Warren, Mich.	Ted Bates, N-P.	1977, Nov.
Warwick, R.I.	Eugene McCaffrey	1976, Dec.
Wash., D.C.	Walter Washington, D.	1979, Jan.
Waterbury, Conn.	Edward Bergin, D.	1977, Dec.
Waterloo, Ia.	Leo Rooff, N-P	1978, Jan.
Waukegan, Ill.	Robert Sabonjian, R.	1977, Apr.
Waukesha, Wis.	Paul Vrakas, N-P.	1976, Apr.
Wauwatosa, Wis.	*J. William Little.	1972, Mar.
West Allis, Wis.	Urban Ganser, N-P	1976, Apr.
W. Covina, Cal.	*George Aiassa.	1958, May
W. Hartford, Conn.	*Richard H. Custer.	1976, Sept.
W. Have, Conn.	Robert A. Johnson, D.	1977, Dec.
W. New York, N.J.	Anthony De Fino, D.	1979, May
W. Orange, N.J.	William F. Cuozzi, D.	1978, June
W. Palm Beach, Fla.	*Richard Simmons.	1969, Sept.
Westland, Mich.	Thomas Taylor, N-P.	1977, Dec.
Westminster, Cal.	*Robert J. Huntley.	1967, July
Weymouth, Mass.	William Gunville, N-P	1976, Apr.
Wheaton, Ill.	*William Kirchhoff.	1973, May
Wheeling, W. Va.	*Charles Steele.	1973, Jan.
White Plains, N.Y.	Alfred Del Vecchio, R.	1978, Jan.
Wichita, Kan.	*Ralph Wulz.	1968, S
Wichita Falls, Tex.	*Gerald G. Fox.	1969, o.
Wilkes-Barre, Pa.	*Bernard J. Gallagher.	1972, June
Williamsport, Pa.	Daniel Kirby, D.	1980, Jan.
Wilmington, Del.	Thomas Maloney, D.	1977, Jan.
Wilmington, N.C.	*John A. Jones.	1971, Sept.
Winston-Salem, N.C.	*Orville W. Powell.	1972, Nov.
Woonsocket, R.I.	John A. Cummings, D.	1977, Nov.
Worcester, Mass.	*Francis J. McGrath.	1951, Jan.
Wyandotte, Mich.	*William Sullivan, D.	1977, Apr.
Wyoming, Mich.	*Thomas Pugh.	1974, May
Yakima, Wash.	*Craig McMicken.	1967, Sept.
Yonkers, N.Y.	*J.E. Casey.	1974, July
Youngstown, Oh.	Jack Hunter, R.	1977, Dec.
York, Pa.	John D. Krout, R.	1978, Jan.
Zanesville, Oh.	*Frank Patrizio.	1974, Sept.

Canadian Cities

City	Name	Term
Calgary, Alta.	Rod Sykes.	1976, Oct.
Dartmouth, N.S.	Eileen Stubbs.	1976, Oct.
Edmonton, Alta.	William Hawrelak.	1977, Oct.
Guelph, Ont.	N. Jary.	1976, Dec.
Halifax, N.S.	Edmund L. Morris.	1976, Oct.
Hamilton, Ont.	Victor K. Copps.	1976, Dec.
Hull, Que.	Gilles Rocheleau.	1979, Nov.
Kingston, Ont.	George N. Speal.	1976, Dec.
Kitchener, Ont.	Edith MacIntosh.	1976, Dec.
Lachine, Que.	Guy Descary.	1977, Nov.
La Salle, Que.	Gerald Raymond.	1975, Nov.
Laval, Que.	Lucien Paliement.	1977, Nov.
London, Ont.	Mrs. Jane Bigelow.	1976, Dec.
Moncton, N.B.	G. D. Wheeler.	1976, June
Montreal, Que.	Jean Drapeau.	1978, Nov.
Oshawa, Ont.	J. H. Potticary.	1976, Dec.
Ottawa, Ont.	Lorry Greenberg.	1976, Dec.
Peterborough, Ont.	James J. Behan.	1976, Dec.
Quebec, Que.	J. Gilles Lamontagne.	1977, Nov.
Regina, Sask.	Henry H. P. Baker.	1976, Dec.
St. John, N.B.	E. Flewwelling.	
Saskatoon, Sask.	Herbert S. Sears.	1976, Oct.
Sault Ste. Marie, Ont.	Nicholas Trbovich.	1976, Dec.
Sherbrooke, Que.	Marc Bureau.	1977, Nov.
Sudbury, Ont.	Joseph J. Fabbro.	1976, Dec.
Toronto, Ont.	David Crombie.	1976, Dec.
Vancouver, B.C.	Art Phillips.	
Victoria, B.C.	Peter A. Pollen.	
Waterloo, Ont.	Herbert A. Epp.	1976, Dec.
Windsor, Ont.	Bert Weeks.	1976, Dec.
Winnipeg, Man.	Stephen Juba.	1977, Oct.

PERSONAL FINANCE
Using The Consumer Price Index

To measure the impact of inflation, the indispensable tool is the Consumer Price Index (CPI) published monthly by the Bureau of Labor Statistics. The index has been specifically designed to apply to a worker family's pattern of purchases. Unless your own budget is markedly different from this norm, you should be able to employ the CPI to interpret your own affairs. The index is reported each month by most of the news media, often specifically for your own city, and what follows tells, step by step, how to employ the figures to analyze your own financial affairs.

The CPI emerges each month as a single number. In July 1975 it stood at 162.3, meaning that all the goods and services it measured cost 62.3% more that month than they did in the base year 1967. It can be considered this way: the 1967 value was 100.0%; by July 1975 another 62.3% had been added to living costs. The total comes to 162.3, the term "index" having the same sense as percent, merely omitting the percent sign.

The change in the price level for consumer goods and services can be calculated by comparing the CPI readings in one period against another. The July 1975 CPI of 162.3 may be compared to the July reading for 1974 of 148.0. Dividing 162.3 by 148.0, the excess over 1 is the percentage increase over the 12-month period; in this case, 9.66%. A similar year-to-year comparison may be made each month — indeed, these percentage changes often figure in the news releases when the month's CPI is announced.

We determined above that the CPI increased by 9.66% between July 1974 and July 1975. Did your income do the same? To make the comparison you might dig out your paycheck stubs for the same months and follow the arithmetic below.

The comparison can be made in terms of your base pay — your basic rate of earnings — or in terms of what you actually take home after standard deductions. Both gross and takehome comparisons are likely to be of interest to you, but take care to compare equals. Overtime pay should be omitted. When dealing with takehome pay, look out for changes in

Average Consumer Price Indexes

Source: Bureau of Labor Statistics, United States Department of Labor

The Consumer Price Index measures the average change in prices of goods and services purchased by urban wage-earner and clerical-worker families and single workers living alone. Data for 56 large, medium size, and small cities are combined for the all-city average.

(1967 — 100)

Year and month	All items	Food	Housing Total	Rent	Gas and electricity	Fuel and utilities	Household furnishings & operation	Apparel and upkeep	Transportation	Medical care	Personal care	Reading and recreation	Other goods and services
1970	116.3	114.9	118.9	110.1	107.3	107.6	113.4	116.1	112.7	120.6	113.2	113.4	116.0
1971	121.3	118.4	124.3	115.2	114.7	115.1	118.1	119.8	118.6	128.4	116.8	119.3	120.9
1972	125.3	123.5	129.2	119.2	120.5	120.1	121.0	122.3	119.9	132.5	119.8	122.8	125.5
1973	133.1	141.4	135.0	124.2	126.4	126.9	124.9	126.8	123.8	137.7	125.2	125.9	129.0
1974	147.7	161.7	150.6	130.6	145.8	150.2	140.5	136.2	137.7	150.5	137.3	133.8	137.2
1975 Jan	156.1	170.9	161.3	134.5	160.2	160.5	153.2	139.4	143.2	161.0	146.5	141.0	144.8
Feb	157.2	171.6	162.8	135.1	162.7	162.2	154.7	140.2	143.5	163.0	147.8	141.8	145.9
Mar	157.8	171.3	163.6	135.5	164.0	163.0	155.6	140.9	144.8	164.6	148.9	142.0	146.5
Apr	158.6	171.2	164.7	135.9	166.3	164.6	156.8	141.3	146.2	165.8	149.5	143.5	146.8
May	159.3	172.8	165.3	136.4	167.3	165.5	157.4	141.8	147.4	166.8	149.9	143.8	147.1
June	160.6	174.4	166.4	136.9	169.4	166.9	158.1	141.4	149.8	168.1	150.3	144.1	147.3
July	162.3	178.6	167.1	137.3	170.4	168.0	158.3	141.1	152.6	169.8	151.2	144.4	147.6

Indexes of Retail Prices of Foods

Source: Bureau of Labor Statistics, United States Department of Labor (1967 = 100)

Year and Month	All Food	Food Away From Home	Food Prepared at Home Food at Home	Cereals, Bakery	Beef, Veal	Pork	Other Meats	Poultry	Fish	Dairy Products	Fruits, Vegetables	Other Foods	Nonalcoholic Beverages
1969	108.9		108.2	103.3						106.7	109.3	107.9	
1970	114.9		113.7	108.9						111.8	113.4	114.1	
1971	118.4	126.1	116.4	113.9	124.9	105.0	115.6	109.0	130.2	115.3	119.1	115.9	121.6
1972	123.5	131.1	121.6	114.7	136.6	121.6	124.0	110.4	141.9	117.1	125.0	116.7	121.3
1973	141.4	141.4	141.4	127.7	161.1	161.7	154.4	154.8	162.8	127.9	142.5	130.3	130.2
1974	161.7	159.4	162.4	166.1	168.5	161.0	159.2	146.9	187.7	151.9	165.8	162.8	155.6
1975 Jan	170.9	169.0	171.4	185.3	158.5	170.0	158.2	152.8	195.7	155.2	163.5	193.4	175.3
Feb	171.6	170.5	172.0	187.3	156.6	169.6	158.3	152.0	197.2	155.6	166.7	193.1	177.0
Mar	171.3	171.3	171.4	189.1	153.3	170.5	158.8	151.8	197.1	155.4	167.4	190.1	177.8
Apr	171.2	172.2	171.0	188.9	154.6	170.0	158.6	148.9	197.3	154.8	167.8	188.3	178.0
May	171.8	172.8	171.6	187.0	166.4	175.6	160.5	149.8	199.1	153.6	169.0	182.7	175.3
June	174.4	173.1	174.9	185.2	176.6	187.9	166.4	157.7	200.4	153.3	177.4	178.7	174.9
July	178.6	174.2	179.9	184.6	186.4	204.9	170.1	172.8	202.9	153.4	188.8	177.6	174.1

46

deductions which are unrelated to inflation, such as added exemptions, credit union deductions, payroll bonds, and the like.

Measuring Your Paycheck

A. To compare the year-to-year earnings in percent form, divide your July 1975 earnings by your July 1974 earnings and express the result as a percent. If you earned the wage of the average U.S. worker, for example, your paycheck showed $164.62 per week in July 1975 as compared with $156.56 in July of 1974, an increase of 5.15%. Since prices rose by 9.66% during the same 12-month period, the average worker's pay fell 4.51% short of keeping pace with inflation.

B. Another way of dealing with the same figures takes a dollar form. For this calculation, assume your wage in July 1974 was $156.56 per week. Prices increased by 9.66% in the following 12 months, according to the CPI. To match that pace, your wage should have gone to $171.68 ($156.56 times 1.0966) by July 1975. However, if your earnings ran only $164.62 as did the average worker's, you lost $7.06 per week to inflation.

Single readings on a weekly or monthly basis could be misleading; the inflation rate changes rapidly, earnings are affected by special situations unrelated to inflation. Repeated readings over a period of months provide a broader look. For this purpose you may consider an entire year as the appropriate period for measuring the total impact of inflation on your earnings.

The CPI provides us with an index of 133.1 for the year 1973 as a whole and 147.7 for 1974. Dividing 147.7 by 133.1, we get 1.1096; the excess over 1 shows price increases of 10.96% over the year. If you compare your earnings for the same years by the methods we have described, your shortfall due to inflation can be ascertained in percent of dollar form. You can readily determine your annual earnings on your income tax return or from your W-2 statements.

The figures cited above measure an individual's progress as compared with the rate of inflation, as if matching the rate were the sole target. Nothing is said about your personal capacity for advancement. Figuring your loss to inflation is only the first step of the reckoning, a way to true up your income figures so you can check your real progress and advancement.

Savings

Less visible to the average individual than the loss on earnings is the attrition inflation brings to his savings. Narrowly considered, savings are the funds salted away in some savings institution. Although such funds earn interest, it is clear that during double-digit inflation of 10% to 12%, interest rates of 5% to 8% cause a real loss in the value of the savings.

The apparent loss in the value of savings — the amount of goods and services the funds wi' ''''mate-ly buy — should be considered in terms of a brou..... ened view of savings. In addition to funds placed at interest, savings would include the paid-up value of a home or insurance policy and the value of savings bonds. In each case the loss to inflation can be meas-

Consumer Price Indexes by Cities
(1967 = 100)

City	Annual Average All Items 1973	1974	Food 1973	1974	City	Annual Average All Items 1973	1974	Food 1973	1974
U.S. City Average	133.1	147.7	141.4	161.7	Los Angeles, Calif.	129.2	142.5	136.5	156.3
Atlanta, Georgia	133.7	148.5	144.0	165.6	Milwaukee, Wis.	131.5	144.1	138.4	158.1
Baltimore, Md.	134.9	152.4	143.8	164.4	Minneapolis, Minn.	133.0	148.3	142.0	163.6
Boston, Mass.	134.7	148.7	140.1	161.3	New York, N.Y.	139.7	154.8	145.4	166.1
Buffalo, N.Y.	134.8	149.5	141.0	160.1	Philadelphia, Pa.	135.5	151.6	142.7	165.2
Chicago, Illinois	132.0	146.1	142.7	161.6	Pittsburgh, Pa.	132.9	147.3	141.7	164.2
Cincinnati, Ohio	132.1	146.3	142.9	163.6	Portland, Oregon	127.3	142.8	133.7	154.4
Cleveland, Ohio	134.1	147.8	142.1	161.1	St. Louis, Mo.	129.3	144.2	140.2	159.7
Dallas, Texas	132.0	145.3	140.1	157.9	San Diego, Calif.	133.5	147.2	139.6	159.6
Detroit, Michigan	134.5	149.1	143.6	164.1	San Francisco, Calif.	131.5	144.4	138.0	155.6
Honolulu, Hawaii	128.3	141.8	135.2	158.7	Scranton, Pa.	134.7	151.1	141.9	161.7
Houston, Texas	132.3	147.8	143.3	164.9	Seattle, Wash.	127.5	141.5	136.3	155.8
Kansas City, Mo.	130.3	144.2	141.4	162.5	Washington, D.C.	135.0	150.0	145.5	166.9

Latest Month, 1975[1]

City	All Items (Month)	Food (July)	City	All Items (Month)	Food (July)
U.S. City Average	162.3 (7)	178.6	Los Angeles, Calif.	158.1 (7)	172.2
Atlanta, Georgia	160.9 (6)	184.8	Milwaukee, Wis.	155.4 (5)	173.0
Baltimore, Md.	164.7 (6)	182.2	Minneapolis, Minn.	161.9 (7)	180.4
Boston, Mass.	163.0 (7)	178.2	New York, N.Y.	166.6 (7)	182.9
Buffalo, N.Y.	160.4 (5)	178.9	Philadelphia, Pa.	165.0 (7)	183.5
Chicago, Illinois	158.3 (7)	176.5	Pittsburgh, Pa.	161.7 (7)	182.2
Cincinnati, Ohio	160.8 (6)	181.0	Portland, Oregon	157.1 (7)	170.5
Cleveland, Ohio	159.5 (5)	178.6	St. Louis, Mo.	156.7 (6)	179.2
Dallas, Texas	155.8 (5)	175.8	San Diego, Calif.	158.8 (5)	174.8
Detroit, Michigan	161.0 (7)	174.8	San Francisco, Calif.	158.6 (6)	175.1
Honolulu, Hawaii	153.6 (6)	177.8	Scranton, Pa.	163.1 (5)	170.9[2]
Houston, Texas	165.8 (7)	182.7	Seattle, Wash.	154.5 (5)	172.1
Kansas City, Mo.	157.2 (6)	179.9	Washington, D.C.	160.0 (5)	184.8

[1]All items indexes are computed monthly in 5 areas and on a rotating cycle in other areas: (7)=July, (6)=June, (5)=May.
[2]In May.

ured by calculating the shrinkage due to the rise of the CPI. If you had $10,000 in all forms of savings in July 1974, the buying power of such funds would decline by 9.66% by July 1975 due to inflation — that is,

by $966, to $9,034 in terms of 1974 dollars. Meanwhile you may have collected some $500 in interest, which would reduce your loss to $466. In addition you will have lost even a nominal real return on your savings.

Purchasing Power of the Dollar
Source: U.S. Department of Labor, Bureau of Labor Statistics
1967 = $1.00

Beginning 1961, wholesale prices include data for Alaska and Hawaii; and, beginning 1964, consumer prices include them. Obtained by dividing the average price index for 1967 base period (100.0) by the price index for given period and expressing the result in dollars and cents.

Year	Monthly average as measured by— Wholesale prices	Consumer prices	Year	Monthly average as measured by— Wholesale prices	Consumer prices
1940	$2.469	$2.381	1965	$1.035	$1.058
1950	1.222	1.387	1966	1.002	1.029
1955	1.139	1.247	1967	1.000	1.000
1956	1.103	1.229	1968	.976	.960
1957	1.072	1.186	1969	.939	.911
1958	1.057	1.155	1970	.906	.860
1959	1.055	1.145	1971	.878	.824
1960	1.054	1.127	1972	.840	.799
1961	1.058	1.116	1973	.744	.752
1962	1.055	1.104	1974	.625	.677
1963	1.058	1.091	1975, July	.569	.616
1964	1.056	1.076			

Average Weekly Earnings of Production Workers
Source: Bureau of Labor Statistics

Year and month	Private nonagricultural workers Spendable average weekly earnings[2]						Manufacturing workers Spendable average weekly earnings[1]					
	Gross average weekly earnings		Worker with no dependents		Worker with 3 dependents		Gross average weekly earnings		Worker with no dependents		Worker with 3 dependents	
	Current dollars	1967 dollars	Current dollars	1967 dollars	Current dollars	1967 dollars	Current dollars	1967 dollars	Current dollars	1967 dollars	Current dollars	1967 dollars
1969	114.61	104.38	90.96	82.84	99.99	91.07	129.51	117.95	101.90	92.81	111.44	101.49
1970	119.46	102.72	95.94	82.49	104.61	89.95	133.73	114.99	106.62	91.68	115.90	99.66
1971	127.28	104.93	103.78	85.56	112.41	92.67	142.44	117.43	114.97	94.78	124.24	102.42
1972	136.16	108.67	111.65	89.11	121.09	96.64	154.69	123.46	125.32	100.02	135.56	108.19
1973	145.43	109.26	117.54	88.31	127.41	95.73	165.65	124.46	132.00	99.17	142.90	107.36
1974	154.45	104.57	124.14	84.05	134.37	90.97	176.00	119.16	139.80	94.52	150.94	102.19
1975: January	157.16	100.68	126.05	80.75	136.46	87.42	179.96	115.29	142.52	91.30	154.03	98.67
February	157.44	100.15	126.24	80.31	136.67	86.94	179.80	114.33	142.40	90.59	153.90	97.90
March	158.15	100.22	126.74	80.32	137.22	86.95	182.28	115.51	144.23	91.40	155.84	98.76
April	158.51	99.94	126.99	80.07	137.50	86.70	183.22	115.52	144.92	91.37	156.57	98.72
May	160.47	100.73	131.32	82.44	145.44	91.30	184.47	115.80	147.85	92.81	153.55	102.67
June(p)	163.35	101.71	133.35	83.03	147.69	91.96	187.54	116.77	149.94	93.36	165.81	103.24
July(p)	164.62	101.43	134.24	82.71	148.68	91.61	187.85	115.74	150.16	92.52	166.04	102.30

[1]Data relate to production workers in mining and manufacturing; to construction workers in contract construction; and to nonsupervisory workers in transportation and public utilities; wholesale and retail trade; finance, insurance, and real estate; and services.
[2]Spendable average weekly earnings are based on gross average weekly earnings less the estimated amount of the worker's Federal, social security, and income taxes.   (p)—preliminary.

Productivity in the U.S. and Abroad
Indexes of output per hour, hourly pay and unit labor costs.
Source: Bureau of Labor Statistics, Monthly Labor Review, July, 1975

	Output per hour				Hourly pay				Unit labor costs in U.S. $			
	1970	1971	1972	1973	1970	1971	1972	1973	1970	1971	1972	1973
United States	107.9	115.1	121.6	128.5	122.1	130.4	137.5	147.3	113.2	113.2	113.1	114.8
Canada	115.2	122.9	128.1	133.1	124.3	133.8	143.6	155.8	111.5	116.3	122.1	126.3
Japan	146.5	151.7	163.9	193.6	153.4	189.1	218.7	272.2	112.8	129.9	159.5	188.0
Belgium	128.4	132.3	144.6	158.8	131.8	151.2	175.1	206.1	102.7	116.9	136.7	166.2
Denmark	129.3	138.8	150.0	163.9	145.0	165.4	184.3	217.8	104.4	112.4	123.4	154.0
France	121.2	127.5	136.1	144.0	134.4	150.4	168.2	191.1	98.7	105.4	120.5	147.2
Germany	116.6	122.6	130.3	139.3	133.0	151.6	169.4	191.8	124.6	141.8	162.5	207.3
Italy	117.8	123.0	133.4	146.0	141.1	167.1	191.6	236.7	119.2	137.2	153.6	173.9
Netherlands	123.5	129.2	133.3	148.0	131.8	148.1	166.7	184.6	106.2	115.9	130.8	147.9
Sweden	132.3	140.4	155.5	170.6	144.1	154.9	190.1	218.2	108.5	121.2	137.2	165.7
Switzerland	125.5	132.2	138.7	147.7	124.7	141.1	157.4	172.4	99.7	112.4	128.7	160.1
United Kingdom	109.1	114.2	118.9	127.2	132.8	151.5	171.3	194.1	106.0	117.9	181.0	136.0
11 foreign countries	123.7	129.8	138.4	151.3	138.3	157.5	177.3	205.6	111.8	125.1	143.4	170.5
9 European countries	119.2	125.5	133.7	143.0	135.0	154.2	173.3	198.1	112.7	126.0	143.1	172.9

All employed persons in the United States and Canada; wage earners only in Switzerland, and all employees in the other countries.

Inflation Raises Taxes

Spendable Income and Taxes as Per Cent of Gross Earnings

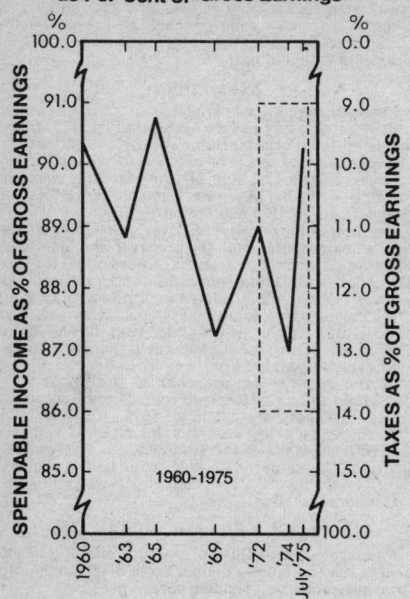

One of the least noticed but most serious effects of inflation is the unlegislated tax increase which inflation causes. As workers' wages rise to keep pace with inflation, the workers find themselves in higher tax brackets. They then have to pay more taxes on less valuable money.

In 1960, 9.6 per cent of gross income was taken for taxes, leaving the average worker with 90.4 per cent of his gross income. After a decrease to 9.2 per cent in 1965, taxes began to go up, taking as much as 13.3 per cent of the average man's income in April of 1975.

Then, with the passage of the new tax law, taxes declined sharply, amounting to 9.7 per cent of income in July, 1975.

If workers' income had been rising steadily during the period, the rising percentage for taxes would not have been so harmful. But from 1965 to April 1975, workers' real income (figured in non-inflated 1967 dollars) declined slightly.

The graphs below show the steady rise of gross income in current dollars, Line A. When adjustment is made for inflation, Line B, it becomes apparent that average gross weekly income has not increased in the last ten years.

But the average worker paid more taxes, as if his income had gone up with Line A. Line C shows average spendable income after taxes in 1967 dollars. Until the recent tax reduction, the gap between lines B and C was growing steadily wider. In fact, the April 1975 average spendable earnings of $86.70 was the lowest since 1963.

The 1975 tax cut was effective for only one year, unless Congress extended it: If it is not extended, the average worker's income will drop back immediately to 1963 levels.

Average Weekly Earnings in Current and 1967 Dollars

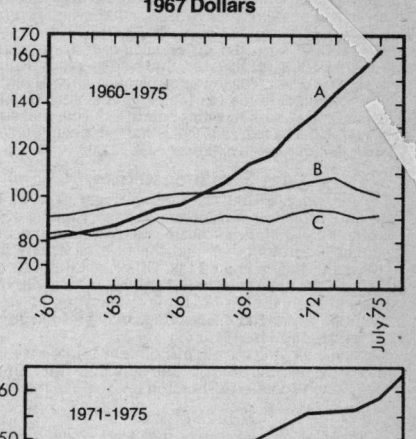

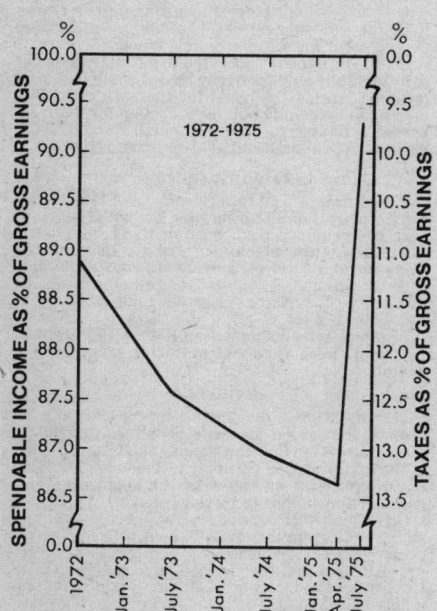

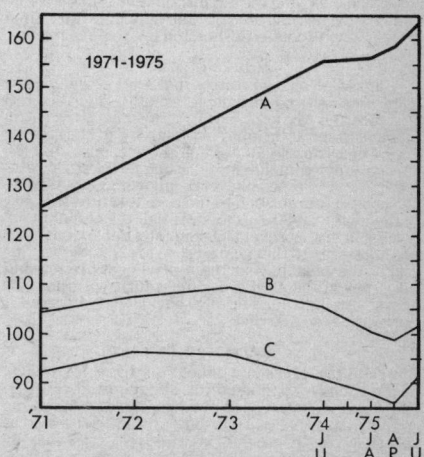

Based on gross average weekly earnings and the spendable average weekly earnings of a private nonagricultural and nonmanufacturing worker with 3 dependents. Source: Bureau of Labor Statistics, Monthly Labor Review, Sept., 1975.

Federal Individual Income Tax

Source: Tax Foundation: Internal Revenue Service, Treasury Dept.

Who Must File

Every individual under 65 years of age who resided in the United States and had a gross income of $2,350 or more during the year must file a Federal income tax return. Anyone 65 or older on the last day of the tax year is not required to file a return unless he had gross income of $3,100 or more during the year. A married couple both 65 or older, need not file unless their gross income exceeds $4,900.

A taxpayer with gross income of less than $2,350 (or less than $3,100 if 65 or older) should file a return to claim the refund of any taxes withheld, even if he is listed as a dependent by another taxpayer.

Forms to Use

A taxpayer may, at his election, file Form 1040 and let IRS compute his tax if his income is $20,000 or less and consists only of wages or salaries and tips, dividends, interest, pensions and annuities and he chooses the standard deductions.

However, a taxpayer may generally use short Form 1040A if all his income is from wages, tips, and interest income and he is taking the standard deduction.

Deductions

A taxpayer may either itemize deductions or choose one of the two types of standard deduction — the percentage standard deduction or the low-income allowance. For taxpayers with adjusted gross income of $15,000 or more, the percentage standard deduction is 16% of adjusted gross income up to a maximum of $2,600 ($1,300 for married persons filing separate returns). The low-income allowance of up to $1,900 is built into the tax tables; it is available only with adjusted gross incomes below $15,000. For single people, the percentage standard deduction is $2,300; the low income allowance is $1,600.

Dates For Filing Returns

For individuals using the calendar year, Apr. 15 is final date (unless it falls on a Saturday, Sunday or a legal holiday) for filing income tax returns and for payment of any tax due, and the first quarterly installment of the estimated tax. Other installments of estimated tax to be paid June 15, Sept. 15 and Jan. 15.

Apr. 15 is final date for filing declaration of estimated tax. Amended declarations may be filed June 15, Sept. 15, and Jan. 15.

Instead of paying the 4th installment a final income return may be filed Jan. 31. Farmers may file a final return Mar. 1 to satisfy estimated tax requirements.

Joint Return

A husband and wife may make a return jointly, even if one has no income personally. Their tax will be twice the tax imposed if the income were cut in half and taxed at the married filing separate rate.

One provision stipulates that if one spouse dies, the survivor may compute his tax using joint return rates for the first two taxable years following, provided he or she also was entitled to file a joint return the year of the death, and furnishes over half the cost of maintaining in his household a home for a dependent child or stepchild. If the taxpayer remarries before the end of the taxable year these privileges are lost but he is permitted to file a joint return with his new spouse. An individual legally separated or divorced is not considered married.

Estimated Tax

If total tax exceeds withheld tax by at least $100, declarations of estimated tax are required from (1) single individuals, heads of a household or surviving spouses, or a married person entitled to file a joint return whose spouse does not receive wages, who expects a gross income over $20,000; (2) married individuals with over $10,000 where both spouses receive wages; (3) married individuals with over $5,000 not entitled to file a joint return; and (4) individuals whose gross income can reasonably be expected to include more than $500 from sources other than wages subject to withholdings.

Exemptions

Personal exemption is $750.

Every individual has an exemption of $750, to be deducted from gross income. A husband and a wife are each entitled to a $750 exemption. A taxpayer 65 or over on the last day of the year gets another exemption of $750. A person blind on the last day of the year gets another exemption of $750.

Exemption for dependents, over one-half of whose total support comes from the taxpayer and for whom the other dependency tests have been met, is $750. This applies to a child, stepchild or adopted child as well as certain other relatives with less than $750 gross income; also to a child, stepchild, or adopted child of the taxpayer who is under 19 at the end of the year or was a full-time student during 5 months of the year even if he makes $750 or more. A dependent can be a non-relative if a member of the taxpayer's household and living there all year. There is a special $30 tax credit per dependent for 1975.

Taxpayer gets the exemption for his child who is a student regardless of the student's age or earnings, provided the taxpayer provides over half of the student's total support. If the student gets a scholarship, this is not counted as support.

Child and Disabled Dependent Care

Taxpayers with adjusted gross income of $35,000 or less may be able to deduct up to $400 per month for household and dependent care expenses.

To qualify, a taxpayer must be employed and provide over one-half the cost of maintaining a household for a dependent child under 15, a disabled dependent of any age, or a disabled spouse.

Household expenses incurred to permit a taxpayer to be gainfully employed may be deducted. Expenses incurred outside the home for the care of a child under 15 also qualify but the deduction for these expenses is limited to $200 per month for one child, $300 for two children and $400 for three or more.

Life Insurance

Life insurance paid to survivors is not taxed as income. Interest on life insurance left with the insurance company and paid to survivors at intervals is taxable when available. Surviving spouse has an exclusion of the prorata amount of principal payable at death plus up to $1,000 per year of interest earned when life insurance proceeds are payable in installments.

Regular payments under the Railroad Retirement Act, and those received as social security, are exempt.

Dividends

The first $100 in dividends can be excluded from income. If husband and wife both receive $100 on their joint return they can exclude $200.

The exclusion does not apply to dividends from tax-exempt corporations, mutual savings banks, building and loan associations and several others.

Dividends paid in stock or in stock rights are generally exempt from tax, except when paid in place of preferred stock dividends of the current or preceding year, or when the stockholder has an option to take stock or property or when the stock distribution is disproportionate.

Deductible Medical Expenses

Expenses for medical care, not compensated for by insurance or other payment for taxpayer, spouse, and dependents, in excess of 3% of adjusted gross income are deductible. This rule also applies to taxpayers 65 or over and dependent parents 65 or over. Previously these persons were not subject to the percentage limitations. There is no limit to the maximum amount of medical expense that can be deducted.

Medical care includes diagnosis, treatment and prevention of disease or for the purpose of affecting any structure or function of the body, and amounts paid for insurance to reimburse for hospitalization, surgical fees and other medical expenses.

Only medicine and drugs in excess of 1% of adjusted gross income may be included in medical expenses.

One-half the cost of medical care insurance premiums up to $150 can be deducted without regard to the 3% limitation. The other half plus any excess over $150 is included with other medical expenses subject to the 3% limit.

Medical expenses for a decedent paid by his estate within one year after his death may be treated as expenses of the decedent taxpayer.

Medical and hospital benefits provided by the employer may be exempt from individual income tax. Wages paid as "sick pay" are exempt up to $100 a week after a certain waiting period.

Deductions For Contributions

Deductions up to 50% of taxpayers' adjusted gross income may be taken for contribution to most publicly supported charitable organizations, including churches or associations of churches, tax-exempt educational institutions, tax-exempt hospitals, and medical research organizations associated with a hospital. The deduction is generally limited to 20% for such organizations as private nonoperating foundations, and certain organizations that do not qualify for the 50% limitation.

Taxpayers also are permitted to carry over for five years certain contributions, generally to publicly supported organizations, which exceed the 50% allowable deduction the year the contribution was made.

Also permissible is the deduction as a charitable contribution of unreimbursed amounts up to $50 a

1975 Income Tax Rate Schedules*

(A.) Married Individuals Filing Joint Returns and Certain Surviving Spouses.

If taxable income is: The tax is:
Not over $1,000 . . . . 14% of the taxable income.

Over	But not over			Of excess over
$1,000—	$2,000	$140,	plus 15%	$1,000
$2,000—	$3,000	$290,	plus 16%	$2,000
$3,000—	$4,000	$450,	plus 17%	$3,000
$4,000—	$8,000	$620,	plus 19%	$4,000
$8,000—	$12,000	$1,380,	plus 22%	$8,000
$12,000—	$16,000	$2,260,	plus 25%	$12,000
$16,000—	$20,000	$3,260,	plus 28%	$16,000
$20,000—	$24,000	$4,380,	plus 32%	$20,000
$24,000—	$28,000	$5,660,	plus 36%	$24,000
$28,000—	$32,000	$7,100,	plus 39%	$28,000
$32,000—	$36,000	$8,660,	plus 42%	$32,000
$36,000—	$40,000	$10,340,	plus 45%	$36,000
$40,000—	$44,000	$12,140,	plus 48%	$40,000
$44,000—	$52,000	$14,060,	plus 50%	$44,000
$52,000—	$64,000	$18,060,	plus 53%	$52,000
$64,000—	$76,000	$24,420,	plus 55%	$64,000
$76,000—	$88,000	$31,020,	plus 58%	$76,000
$88,000—	$100,000	$37,980,	plus 60%	$88,000
$100,000—	$120,000	$45,180,	plus 62%	$100,000
$120,000—	$140,000	$57,580,	plus 64%	$120,000
$140,000—	$160,000	$70,380,	plus 66%	$140,000
$160,000—	$180,000	$83,580,	plus 68%	$160,000
$180,000—	$200,000	$97,180,	plus 69%	$180,000
$200,000—		$110,980,	plus 70%	$200,000

(B.) Certain Heads of Households

Not over $1,000 . . . . 14% of the taxable income.

Over	But not over			Of excess over
$1,000—	$2,000	$140,	plus 16%	$1,000
$2,000—	$4,000	$300,	plus 18%	$2,000
$4,000—	$6,000	$660,	plus 19%	$4,000
$6,000—	$8,000	$1,040,	plus 22%	$6,000
$8,000—	$10,000	$1,480,	plus 23%	$8,000
$10,000—	$12,000	$1,940,	plus 25%	$10,000
$12,000—	$14,000	$2,440,	plus 27%	$12,000
$14,000—	$16,000	$2,980,	plus 28%	$14,000
$16,000—	$18,000	$3,540,	plus 31%	$16,000
$18,000—	$20,000	$4,160,	plus 32%	$18,000
$20,000—	$22,000	$4,800,	plus 35%	$20,000
$22,000—	$24,000	$5,500,	plus 36%	$22,000
$24,000—	$26,000	$6,220,	plus 38%	$24,000
$26,000—	$28,000	$6,980,	plus 41%	$26,000
$28,000—	$32,000	$7,800,	plus 42%	$28,000
$32,000—	$36,000	$9,480,	plus 45%	$32,000
$36,000—	$38,000	$11,280,	plus 48%	$36,000
$38,000—	$40,000	$12,240,	plus 51%	$38,000
$40,000—	$44,000	$13,260,	plus 52%	$40,000
$44,000—	$50,000	$15,340,	plus 55%	$44,000
$50,000—	$52,000	$18,640,	plus 56%	$50,000
$52,000—	$64,000	$19,760,	plus 58%	$52,000
$64,000—	$70,000	$26,720,	plus 59%	$64,000
$70,000—	$76,000	$30,260,	plus 61%	$70,000
$76,000—	$80,000	$33,920,	plus 62%	$76,000
$80,000—	$88,000	$36,400,	plus 63%	$80,000
$88,000—	$100,000	$41,440,	plus 64%	$88,000
$100,000—	$120,000	$49,120,	plus 66%	$100,000
$120,000—	$140,000	$62,320,	plus 67%	$120,000

$140,000—	$160,000	$75,720,	plus 68%	$140,000
$160,000—	$180,000	$89,320,	plus 69%	$160,000
$180,000—		$103,120,	plus 70%	$180,000

(C.) Married Individuals Filing Separate Returns

If taxable income is: The tax is:
Not over $500 . . . . 14% of the taxable income

Over	But not over			Of excess over
$500—	$1,000	$70,	plus 15%	$500
$1,000—	$1,500	$145,	plus 16%	$1,000
$1,500—	$2,000	$225,	plus 17%	$1,500
$2,000—	$4,000	$310,	plus 19%	$2,000
$4,000—	$6,000	$690,	plus 22%	$4,000
$6,000—	$8,000	$1,130,	plus 25%	$6,000
$8,000—	$10,000	$1,630,	plus 28%	$8,000
$10,000—	$12,000	$2,190,	plus 32%	$10,000
$12,000—	$14,000	$2,830,	plus 36%	$12,000
$14,000—	$16,000	$3,550,	plus 39%	$14,000
$16,000—	$18,000	$4,330,	plus 42%	$16,000
$18,000—	$20,000	$5,170,	plus 45%	$18,000
$20,000—	$22,000	$6,070,	plus 48%	$20,000
$22,000—	$26,000	$7,030,	plus 50%	$22,000
$26,000—	$32,000	$9,030,	plus 53%	$26,000
$32,000—	$38,000	$12,210,	plus 55%	$32,000
$38,000—	$44,000	$15,510,	plus 58%	$38,000
$44,000—	$50,000	$18,990,	plus 60%	$44,000
$50,000—	$60,000	$22,590,	plus 62%	$50,000
$60,000—	$70,000	$28,790,	plus 64%	$60,000
$70,000—	$80,000	$35,190,	plus 66%	$70,000
$80,000—	$90,000	$41,790,	plus 68%	$80,000
$90,000—	$100,000	$48,590,	plus 69%	$90,000
$100,000—		$55,490,	plus 70%	$100,000

(D.) Unmarried Individuals (Other Than Certain Surviving Spouse and Heads of Households).

Not over $500 . . . . 14% of the taxable income.

Over	But not over			Of excess over
$500—	$1,000	$70,	plus 15%	$500
$1,000—	$1,500	$145,	plus 16%	$1,000
$1,500—	$2,000	$225,	plus 17%	$1,500
$2,000—	$4,000	$310,	plus 19%	$2,000
$4,000—	$6,000	$690,	plus 21%	$4,000
$6,000—	$8,000	$1,110,	plus 24%	$6,000
$8,000—	$10,000	$1,590,	plus 25%	$8,000
$10,000—	$12,000	$2,090,	plus 27%	$10,000
$12,000—	$14,000	$2,630,	plus 29%	$12,000
$14,000—	$16,000	$3,210,	plus 31%	$14,000
$16,000—	$18,000	$3,830,	plus 34%	$16,000
$18,000—	$20,000	$4,510,	plus 36%	$18,000
$20,000—	$22,000	$5,230,	plus 38%	$20,000
$22,000—	$26,000	$5,990,	plus 40%	$22,000
$26,000—	$32,000	$7,590,	plus 45%	$26,000
$32,000—	$38,000	$10,290,	plus 50%	$32,000
$38,000—	$44,000	$13,290,	plus 55%	$38,000
$44,000—	$50,000	$16,590,	plus 60%	$44,000
$50,000—	$60,000	$20,190,	plus 62%	$50,000
$60,000—	$70,000	$26,390,	plus 64%	$60,000
$70,000—	$80,000	$32,790,	plus 66%	$70,000
$80,000—	$90,000	$39,390,	plus 68%	$80,000
$90,000—	$100,000	$46,190,	plus 69%	$90,000
$100,000—		$53,090,	plus 70%	$100,000

*Under the tax reform act of 1969 the maximum rate of earned income is 50% for single taxpayers earning taxable income in excess of $50,000 and for married persons filing jointly with taxable income in excess of $100,000.

school month spent to maintain an elementary or high school student, other than a dependent or relative, in taxpayer's home. There must be a written agreement between you and a qualified organization.

Deductions for Interest Paid

Interest paid by the taxpayer is deductible.

If personal property is bought under a contract providing for payment by installments, and in which carrying charges are stated but interest is not ascertainable, then subject to limitation payments are held to include interest equal to 6% on average unpaid balance.

However, the amount charged to a customer's revolving charge account is solely for the privilege of deferring payment and is interest.

Prizes and Awards

All prizes and awards must be reported in gross income, except when received without action by the recipient. To be exempt, awards must be received primarily in recognition of religious, charitable, scientific, educational, artistic, literary, or civic achievement. (Nobel and Pulitzer prizes exempt.)

Deductions for Employees

An employee may take the standard deduction and deduct as well the following if in connection with his employment: transportation, except commuting; automobile expense, including gas, oil and depreciation; however, meals and lodging are deductible as traveling expense only if the employee is away from home overnight.

An outside salesman—a salesman who works full-time outside the office, using the latter only for incidentals—may deduct both the standard deduction and all his business expenses.

An employee who is reimbursed and is required to account to his employer for his business expenses will not be required to report either the reimbursement or the expenses on his tax return. Any allowance to the employee in excess of his expenses must be included in gross income. If he claims a deduction for an excess of expenses over reimbursement he will have to report the reimbursement and claim actual expenses.

An employee who is not required to account to his employer must report on his return the total amounts of reimbursements and expenses for travel, transportation, entertainment, etc., that he incurs under a reimbursement arrangement with his employer.

The expense of moving to a new place of employment may be deducted under certain circumstances regardless of whether the taxpayer is a new or continuing employee, or whether he pays his own expenses or is reimbursed by his employer. Reimbursement must be reported as income.

Retirement Income Credit

A credit against the tax otherwise due, of 15% of retirement income up to $1,524 included in gross income, is allowed to persons 65 and over. Persons under 65 and retired under a public retirement system (firemen, policemen, teachers, federal employees) are allowed the same credit on income from pensions and annuities paid under the system, but not on dividends, interests and rent. Included in public systems are funds for members of the Armed Forces for 1955 and subsequent years. Any pension or annuity received under the Social Security Act or the Railroad Retirement Act reduces the $1,524. Compensation in excess of $900 received by an individual under 62 and compensation in excess of $1,200 for one over 62 but under 72 will reduce the $1,524 by varying amounts. No reduction if the individual is 72 or older.

Net Capital Losses

An individual taxpayer may deduct capital losses up to $1,000 against his ordinary income. ~~wever, it~~ takes $2 of net long-term capital loss to ge~~ ~~ off-set against other income. He may carry th~~ ~~ to subsequent years at the same rate, no lega~~nit on~~ the number of years.

Income Averaging

Individuals with large fluctuations in their annual income may be able to take advantage of averaging provisions available to taxpayers whose income for a particular year exceeds 120% of their average income for the prior 4 years, if the excess is more than $3,000.

Major Federal Tax Expenditures (Loopholes) Estimates
Source: Office of Management and Budget
(as of Dec. 31, 1974)

Income tax provisions resulting in tax expenditures are defined as exceptions to the "normal structure" of individual and corporate income tax. They reduce tax liabilities for particular groups of taxpayers. The normal structure is nowhere defined in the tax code. Existing rates are accepted as "normal"; when the rate structure is changed, for whatever reason, the new rate structure becomes the new norm.

The following features of the tax system are defined as part of the normal tax structure and therefore **do not result in tax expenditures**: progressive rate schedules for individual income tax; personal exemptions and the minimum standard deduction; separate schedules for single and married persons, married persons filing separately, and heads of households; deduction of business expenses; exclusion of unrealized capital gains and losses; exclusion of gifts and bequests received; exclusion of the value of government services received in kind (e.g., food stamps); foreign tax credits; treatment of individuals and corporations as separate tax paying entities; earnings of foreign corporations in operations abroad.

Expenditure	Amount (in millions) Individual	Corporate
State and local tax deductions	$6,955	$ —
Capital gains, lower tax on	6,150	745
Mortgage interest deduction	4,870	—
Pension plan payments by employers	4,790	—
Property tax deductions on homes	4,060	—
Charitable contributions deduction	3,820	290
Investment credit	880	3,690
Corporate profits, lower tax on first $25,000	—·	3,270
Social Security benefits	3,175	—
Medical care and insurance payments by employer	2,940	—
Exclusion of interest on state and local bonds	1,060	2,805
Consumer credit interest deduction	2,435	—
Medical expenses deduction	2,125	—
Mineral depletion allowances	305	1,815

	Amount (in millions) Individual	Corporate
Exclusion of interest on life insurance savings	1,420	—
Excess of percentage standard deduction over minimum	1,260	—
Financial institution excess bad debt reserve	—	1,000
Income deferral of domestic export companies	—	870
State gas tax deduction	865	—
Intangible drilling and development costs	80	750
Corporate capital gains	—	745
Group life insurance payments by employers	680	—
Parents' exemptions for students 19 and over	655	—
Armed forces benefits and allowances	650	—
Research and development expenses	—	605

Itemized Deductions by Type and Income Size

Source: Statistics of Income, 1972; Internal Revenue Service

Adjusted Gross Income	Total Itemized Deductions				Deductions for Taxes Paid					
	No. of Returns	%	Amount	%	No. of Returns	%	% of No. in AGI[1]	Amount	%	% of $ in AGI[2]
Total , all returns.......	26,980,399	100.0	46,665,330	100.0	26,835,850	100.0	99.5	36,166,086	100.0	37.4
$1.00 to 2,000	144,339	0.5	266,250	0.3	124,069	0.4	86.0	64,135	0.19	24.1
2,000 to 3,000	230,665	0.9	426,704	0.4	217,944	0.8	94.5	116,548	0.41	27.3
2,000 to 4,000	419,869	1.6	834,791	0.9	398,354	1.5	94.9	222,218	0.76	26.6
4,000 to 5,000	660,056	2.4	1,355,765	1.4	654,084	2.4	99.1	375,247	1.2	27.7
5,000 to 6,000	898,248	3.3	1,947,591	2.0	888,348	3.3	98.9	557,240	1.9	28.6
6,000 to 7,000	1,006,851	3.7	2,205,287	2.3	998,330	3.7	99.2	650,426.	2.1	29.5
7,000 to 8,000	1,354,955	5.0	3,158,341	3.3	1,350,636	5.0	99.7	939,850	2.6	29.8
8,000 to 9,000	1,601,850	5.9	3,771,334	3.9	1,598,735	6.0	99.8	1,169,952	3.6	31.0
9,000 to 10,000	1,660,487	6.1	4,194,530	4.3	1,653,798	6.2	99.6	1,342,977	3.8	32.0
10,000 to 11,000	1,672,195	6.2	4,385,146	4.5	1,667,555	6.2	99.7	1,483,436	4.0	33.8
11,000 to 12,000	1,741,482	6.5	4,937,526	5.1	1,736,985	6.5	99.7	1,654,757	4.2	33.5
12,000 to 13,000	1,599,540	5.9	4,835,328	5.0	1,594,586	5.9	99.7	1,662,352	4.1	34.4
13,000 to 14,000	1,524,537	5.7	4,819,007	5.0	1,516,335	5.7	99.5	1,698,773	4.4	35.3
14,000 to 15,000	1,409,361	5.2	4,645,631	4.8	1,404,387	5.2	99.6	1,700,015	4.0	36.6
15,000 to 20,000	5,523,687	20.5	19,770,095	20.5	5,511,910	20.5	99.8	7,754,608	17.7	39.2
20,000 to 25,000	2,588,191	9.6	10,881,500	11.3	2,581,963	9.6	99.8	4,599,122	10.6	42.3.
25,000 to 30,000	1,126,983	4.2	5,639,439	5.8	1,124,862	4.2	99.8	2,457,836	5.9	43.6
30,000 to 50,000	1,238,556	4.6	8,346,982	8.6	1,235,600	4.6	99.8	3,693,037	9.7	44.2
50,000 to 100,000	465,750	1.7	5,497,066	5.7	464,743	1.7	99.8	2,388,614	7.4	43.5
100,000 to 200,000	90,127	0.3	2,317,727	2.4	89,985	0.3	99.8	907,103	4.1	39.1
200,000 to 500,000	18,991	0.07	1,260,749	1.3	18,964	0.07	99.9	425,993	3.0	34.3
500,000 to 1,000,000	2,649	0.01	479,507	0.5	2,647	0.01	99.9	144,021	1.4	30.0
1,000,000 or more	1,030	0.004	689,034	0.7	1,030	0.004	100.0	157,826	2.9	22.9

	Deductions for Contributions						Deductions for Interest		
	No. of Returns	%	% of No. in AGI[1]	Amount	%	% of $ in AGI[2]	No. of Returns	%	% of No. in AGI[1]
Total, all returns.......	25,780,072	100.0	95.6	13,208,491	100.0	13.7	23,787,940	100.0	88.2
$1.00 to 2,000	104,860	0.14	72.6	25,978	0.19	9.8	69,058	0.29	47.8
2,000 to 3,000	188,254	0.7	81.6	54,119	0.41	12.7	118,257	0.5	51.3
3,000 to 4,000	355,543	1.4	84.7	100,777	0.76	12.1	254,432	1.1	60.6
4,000 to 5,000	589,721	2.3	89.3	159,596	1.2	11.8	463,376	1.9	70.2
5,000 to 6,000	824,406	3.2	91.8	248,915	1.9	12.8	683,951	2.9	76.1
6,000 to 7,000	923,414	3.6	91.7	278,237	2.1	12.6	788,871	3.3	78.4
7,000 to 8,000	1,260,322	4.9	93.0	344,612	2.6	10.9	1,145,075	4.8	84.5
8,000 to 9,000	1,475,827	5.7	92.1	473,168	3.6	12.5	1,391,987	5.9	86.9
9,000 to 10,000	1,584,634	6.1	95.4	505,079	3.8	12.0	1,498,442	6.3	90.2
10,000 to 11,000	1,595,955	6.2	95.4	522,603	4.0	11.9	1,515,001	6.4	90.6
11,000 to 12,000	1,674,734	6.5	96.1	559,009	4.2	11.3	1,616,505	6.8	92.8
12,000 to 13,000	1,526,613	5.9	95.4	536,353	4.1	11.1	1,503,191	6.3	93.9
13,000 to 14,000	1,476,492	5.7	96.8	575,076	4.4	11.9	1,416,385	6.0	92.9
14,000 to 15,000	1,362,699	5.3	96.8	534,298	4.0	11.5	1,329,632	5.9	94.3
15,000 to 20,000	5,399,792	20.9	97.8	2,341,722	17.7	11.8	5,150,784	21.7	93.2
20,000 to 25,000	2,542,237	9.9	98.2	1,406,391	10.6	12.9	2,347,592	9.9	90.7
25,000 to 30,000	1,108,881	4.3	98.4	781,583	5.9	13.9	986,606	4.1	87.5
30,000 to 50,000	1,217,709	4.7	98.3	1,278,427	9.7	15.3	1,044,001	4.4	84.3
50,000 to 100,000	456,994	1.8	98.1	975,514	7.4	17.7	376,301	1.6	80.8
100,000 to 200,000	88,701	0.3	98.4	538,572	4.1	23.2	70,649	0.3	78.4
200,000 to 500,000	18,649	0.07	98.2	393,182	3.0	31.6	14,875	0.06	78.3
500,000 to 1,000,000	2,614	0.01	98.7	189,132	1.4	39.4	2,134	0.008	80.6
1,000,000 or more	1,016	0.004	98.6	386,148	2.9	56.0	835	—	81.1

	Deductions for Interest			Deductions for Misc. Expenses			
	Amount	%	% of $ in AGI[2]	No. of Returns	%	% of No. in AGI[1]	Amount	%	% of $ in AGI[2]
Total, all returns.......	27,347,086	100.0	28.3	22,268,820	100.0	82.5	7,581,539	100.0	7.8
$1.00 to 2,000	54,077	0.2	20.3	70,592	0.3	48.9	19,503	0.3	7.3
2,000 to 3,000	78,508	0.3	18.4	148,354	0.7	64.3	19,754	0.3	4.6
3,000 to 4,000	165,217	0.6	19.8	293,244	1.3	69.8	44,324	0.6	5.3
4,000 to 5,000	312,147	1.1	47.3	472,789	2.1	71.6	62,228	0.8	4.6
5,000 to 6,000	441,266	1.6	22.7	656,859	2.9	73.1	107,269	1.4	5.5
6,000 to 7,000	538,700	2.0	24.4	767,751	3.4	76.3	129,510	1.7	5.9
7,000 to 8,000	858,464	3.1	27.2	1,070,290	4.8	79.0	208,936	2.8	6.6
8,000 to 9,000	4,069,750	3.9	28.4	1,351,670	6.1	84.4	315,164	4.2	8.4
9,000 to 10,000	1,255,393	4.6	30.0	1,396,737	6.3	84.0	306,771	4.0	7.3
10,000 to 11,000	1,324,400	4.8	30.2	1,422,069	6.4	85.0	346,877	4.6	7.9
11,000 to 12,000	1,529,081	5.6	31.0	1,513,853	6.8	86.9	404,928	5.3	8.2
12,000 to 13,000	1,573,497	5.8	32.5	1,377,785	6.2	86.1	406,788	5.4	8.4
13,000 to 14,000	1,508,996	5.5	31.3	1,304,538	5.9	85.6	381,238	5.0	7.9
14,000 to 15,000	1,464,178	5.4	31.5	1,197,004	5.4	84.9	353,788	4.7	7.6
15,000 to 20,000	6,062,751	22.2	30.7	4,692,870	21.1	85.0	1,494,048	19.7	7.6
20,000 to 25,000	3,141,745	11.5	28.9	2,178,246	9.8	84.2	835,412	11.0	7.7
25,000 to 30,000	1,535,066	5.6	27.2	921,982	4.1	81.8	427,486	5.6	7.6
30,000 to 50,000	2,103,204	7.7	25.2	970,689	4.4	78.4	705,362	9.3	8.5
50,000 to 100,000	1,347,443	4.9	24.5	365,088	1.6	78.4	503,644	6.6	9.2
100,000 to 200,000	540,410	2.0	23.3	75,975	0.3	84.3	249,656	3.3	10.8
200,000 to 5,000	272,906	1.0	20.9	16,979	0.08	89.4	143,875	1.9	11.3
500,000 to 1,000,000	90,930	0.3	18.9	2,488	0.01	83.8	50,279	0.7	10.5
1,000,000 or more	79,457	0.3	11.5	968	0.004	94.0	64,699	0.9	9.4

(1) Percent of returns with itemized deductions in that Adjusted Gross Income category claiming deductions of that type
(2) Percent of total deductions in that Adjusted Gross Income category which was claimed for that type of deduction.
Note: Three additional types of deductions — casualty loss, child-care, and medical are not included due to lack of space.

Canada: Taxable Returns by Income, 1972.

Source: Taxation Statistics

Total income $ 1972	Number	%	Total income (millions)	%	Taxed income (millions)	Federal Tax[1] (millions)	%
0-2,000	249,929	3.09	423.7	.67	45.1	8.8	.11
2,000-2,500	331,253	4.10	746.0	1.19	171.4	26.8	.35
2,500-3,000	378,217	4.68	1,041.6	1.66	324.7	52.1	.67
3,000-3,500	427,007	5.29	1,388.2	2.20	515.6	83.4	1.07
3,500-4,000	453,003	5.60	1,700.7	2.71	713.6	116.7	1.49
4,000-6,000	1,767,874	21.88	8,785.1	13.96	4,412.9	745.3	9.56
6,000-8,000	1,472,794	18.22	10,268.4	16.33	6,010.5	1,055.9	13.55
8,000-10,000	1,172,472	14.51	10,476.1	16.65	6,627.7	1,218.5	15.62
10,000-15,000	1,297,754	16.06	15,471.5	24.60	10,589.8	2,077.9	26.66
15,000-20,000	306,426	3.79	5,199.2	8.26	3,787.0	811.5	10.40
20,000-50,000	199,635	2.47	5,492.2	8.73	4,282.3	1,073.6	13.77
50,000-100,000	21,157	.27	1,381.7	2.20	1,192.8	369.3	4.74
100,000-200,000	3,015	.03	385.5	.61	341.8	117.3	1.51
200,000 & over	479	.01	143.5	.23	118.0	39.5	.51
Total	8,081,015	100.00	62,903.4	100.00	39,133.2	7,796.6	100.00

(1) Federal taxes include income taxes, social development tax and old age security tax.

Federal Taxes in Major Canadian Cities, 1972

Source: Taxation Statistics

City	Rank[1]	No. of Returns[2]	Average Income	Avg. Tax	City	Rank[1]	No. of Returns[2]	Average Income	Avg. Tax
Toronto	14	1,063,789	$ 8,498	$ 1,241	St. John, N.B.	80	32,518	$7,087	$ 848
Montreal	37	855,125	7,887	810	Brantford	50	31,367	7,562	985
Vancouver	18	439,253	8,285	1,150	Sault Ste. Marie	12	31,149	8,525	1,148
Winnipeg	58	235,181	7,446	947	Sarnia	5	30,356	9,097	1,284
Edmonton	28	209,721	8,028	1,077	Guelph	42	29,251	7,866	1,026
Ottawa	4	201,522	9,178	1,342	Cambridge	81	27,921	7,082	911
Hamilton	11	201,093	8,546	1,196	Peterborough	32	27,387	7,941	1,029
Calgary	17	179,529	8,303	1,137	Dartmouth	32	27,237	7,941	990
Quebec	24	106,382	8,144	1,115	Niagara Falls	44	27,129	7,833	1,006
London	6	95,772	8,897	1,204	Oakville	1	25,852	9,945	1,525
Windsor	40	90,664	7,869	1,002	Moncton	85	25,567	6,887	815
Victoria	40	90,664	7,869	1,002	New Westminister	27	23,913	8,051	1,108
Kitchener-W'loo	38	80,502	7,879	1,062	Brampton	29	23,619	8,020	1,099
Mississauga	2	67,428	9,742	1,495	Prince George	10	23,182	8,583	1,186
Halifax	35	59,296	7,891	1,035	Trois Rivieres	56	22,452	7,465	708
Regina	59	57,237	7,414	940	Chicoutimi	34	21,470	7,904	718
Sudbury	7	53,681	8,792	1,215	Kamloops	13	20,668	8,502	1,174
St. Catharines	19	50,886	8,271	1,108	Levis	66	19,152	7,312	676
Hull	52	49,173	7,545	748	Welland	41	18,983	7,868	1,017
Saskatoon	64	48,506	7,357	891	North Bay	22	18,524	8,152	1,085
Thunder Bay	26	46,064	8,101	1,084	Cornwall	67	18,149	7,302	889
Longueuil	76	40,689	7,167	664	Belleville	36	17,686	7,889	1,041
St. John's, Nfld.	70	40,026	7,280	921	Lethbridge	60	17,200	7,406	922
Oshawa	9	37,665	8,768	1,227	Chatham	15	17,178	8,356	1,132
Kingston	20	36,135	8,267	1,141	Drummondville	98	16,499	6,492	571
Sherbrooke	77	35,073	7,147	679	Barrie	23	15,841	8,149	1,098
Sydney-Glace Bay	100	34,928	6,462	681	Timmins	71	15,231	7,274	890

[1]Rank by average income among top 100 cities. [2]Taxable returns only.

City Income Tax in Cities Over 50,000

Compiled by Tax Foundation from Commerce Clearing House data and other sources.

City	Rates% 1975	Orig.	Year Start	City	Rates% 1975	Orig.	Year Start
Cities with 500,000 or more inhabitants				Toledo, Oh.	1.5	1.0	1946
Baltimore, Md.	(50% of state tax)	1.0	1966	Youngstown, Oh.	1.5	.3	1948
Cleveland, Oh.	1.0	.5	1967	**Cities with 50,000 to 99,000 inhabitants**			
Columbus, Oh.	1.5	.5	1947	Altoona, Pa.	1.0	1.0	1948
Detroit, Mich.	2.0	1.0	1965	Bethlehem, Pa.	1.0	1.0	1957
Kansas City, Mo.	1.0	.5	1964	Chester, Pa.	1.0	1.0	1956
New York, N.Y.	.7-3.5	.4-2.0	1966	Cleveland Heights, Oh.	1.0	1.0	1975
Philadelphia, Pa.	3.3125	1.5	1939	Covington, Ky.	2.5	1.0	1956
St. Louis. Mo.	1.0	.25	1948	Euclid, Oh.	1.0	.5	1967
				Gadsden, Ala.	2.0	1.0	1956
				Hamilton, Oh.	1.5	.8	1960
Cities with 100,000 to 499,000 inhabitants				Harrisburg, Pa.	1.0	1.0	1966
Akron, Oh.	1.5	1.0	1963	Kettering, Oh.	1.0	1.0	1968
Allentown, Pa.	1.0	1.0	1958	Lakewood, Oh.	1.0	1.0	1968
Birmingham, Ala.	1.0	1.0	1970	Lancaster, Pa.	1.0	.5	1959
Canton, Oh.	1.5	.6	1954	Lima, Oh.	1.0	.75	1959
Cincinnati, Oh.	2.0	1.0	1954	Lorain, Oh.	1.0	.5	1967
Dayton, Oh.	1.75	.5	1949	Pontiac, Mich.	1.0	1.0	1968
Erie, Pa.	1.0	1.0	1948	Reading, Pa.	1.0	1.0	1975
Flint, Mich.	1.0	1.0	1965	Saginaw, Mich.	1.0	1.0	1965
Grand Rapids, Mich.	1.0	1.0	1967	Springfield, Oh.	1.5	1.0	1948
Lansing, Mich.	1.0	1.0	1968	Warren, Oh.	1.0	.5	1952
Lexington, Ky.	2.0	1.0	1952	Wilkes-Barre, Pa.	0.5	1.0	1966
Louisville, Ky.	2.0	1.0	1948	York, Pa.	1.0	1.0	1965
Parma, Oh.	1.0	.5	1967	Wilmington, Del.	1.25	.5	1970
Scranton, Pa.	1.0	1.0	1948				

State Individual Income Taxes: Rates, Exemptions

Source: Office of Tax Analysis, Treasury Dept. Data as of July 1, 1975

State	Net income after pers'l. exemption	Percentage rates	Net income after pers'l. exemption	Percentage rates	Personal Exemp. Single	Married family head	Credit Depends.
Alabama[1]	First $1,000	1.5	$3,001-$5,000	4.5	$1,500	$3,000	$300
	1,001- 3,000	3	Over 5,000	5			
Alaska	Rates range from 3% on first $2,000 to 14½% over $150,001				Federal exemptions		
Arizona[1][2]	First 1,000	2	3,001- 4,000	5	1,000	2,000	600
	1,001- 2,000	3	4,001- 5,000	6			
	2,001- 3,000	4	5,001- 6,000	7	Over 6,000 8		
Arkansas[3]	First 3,000	1	9,001-15,000	4.5	17.50	35	6
	3,001- 6,000	2.5	15,001-25,000	6	(tax credit)		
	6,001- 9,000	3.5	Over 25,000	7			
California[1][2]	First 2,000	1	8,001- 9,500	6	(tax credit) 25	50	8
	2,001- 3,500	2	9,501-11,000	7			
	3,501- 5,000	3	11,001-12,500	8	Heads of households have slightly		
	5,001- 6,500	4	12,501-14,000	9	lower tax rates.		
	6,501- 8,000	5	14,001-15,500	10	Over 15,500 11		
Colorado[1][4]	First 1,000	3	6,001- 7,000	6	750	1,500	750
	1,001- 2,000	3.5	7,001- 8,000	6.5			
	2,001- 3,000	4	8,001- 9,000	7	Surtax on intangible income over $5,000,		
	3,001- 4,000	4.5	9,001-10,000	7.5	2%. A credit equal to ½ of 1% of net tax-		
	4,001- 5,000	5	Over 10,000	8	able income is allowed for income under		
	5,001- 6,000	5.5			$9,000.		
Connecticut	Capital gains	7					
Delaware[3]	First 1,000	1.6	6,001- 8,000	7.7	600	1,200	600
	1,001- 2,000	2.2	8,001-20,000	8.8			
	2,001- 3,000	3.3	20,001-25,000	9.3			
	3,001- 4,000	4.4	25,001-30,000	9.9	50,001- 75,000		15.4
	4,001- 5,000	5.5	30,001-40,000	12.1	75,001-100,000		16.5
	5,001- 6,000	6.6	40,001-50,000	13.2	Over 100,000		19.8
Dist. of Col.[1][4]	First 1,000	2	8,001-12,000	7	1,000	2,000	500
	1,001- 2,000	3	12,001-17,000	8	A tax credit is provided for low-income		
	2,001- 3,000	4	17,001-25,000	9	taxpayers (adjusted gross not over		
	3,001- 5,000	5	Over 25,000	10	$6,000) for increased sales tax on food		
	5,001- 8,000	6			($2 to $6 credit per exemption). A re-		
					fund is allowed if the credit exceeds tax		
					liability.		
Georgia[3][5]	First 750	1	5,251- 7,000	5	1,500	3,000	700
	751- 2,250	2	Over 7,000	6			
	2,251- 3,750	3			For married persons filing separately,		
	3,751- 5,250	4			rates range from 1% on the first $500 to		
			6% on $5,000 or more. For married couples filing jointly and heads of house-				
			holds, rates range from 1% on the first $1,000 to 6% on $10,000 or more.				
Hawaii[1]	First 500	2.25	5,001-10,000	8.5	750	1,500	750
	501- 1,000	3.25	10,001-14,000	9.5			
	1,001- 1,500	4.5	14,001-20,000	10			
	1,501- 2,000	5	20,001-30,000	10.5			
	2,001- 3,000	6.5	Over 30,000	11			
	3,001- 5,000	7.5			Special tax rates for heads of house-		
					holds.		
Idaho[2][3][4]	First 1,000	2	3,001- 4,000	5.5	Federal exemptions		
	1,001- 2,000	4	4,001- 5,000	6.5			
	2,001- 3,000	4.5	Over 5,000	7.5	Plus tax credit of $15 for each exemption.		
Illinois	Net taxable income	2.5			1,000	2,000	1,000
Indiana[4]	Adjusted gross	2			1,000	*2,000	500
*Lesser of $1,000 or adjusted gross income of each spouse, but not less than $500.							
Iowa[1]	First 1,000	0.5	3,001- 4,000	3.5	(Tax Credit) 15	30	10
	1,001- 2,000	1.25	4,001- 7,000	5	Incomes $4,000 or less are exempt.		
	2,001- 3,000	2.75	7,001- 9,000	6	Up to 13% over $75,000		
Kansas[1][4]	First 2,000	2	5,001- 7,000	5	600	1,200	600
	2,001- 3,000	3.5	Over 7,000	6.5			
	3,001- 5,000	4					
Kentucky[1]	First 3,000	2	4,001- 5,000	4	(Tax Credit) 20	40	20
	3,001- 4,000	3	5,001- 8,000	5	Over 8,000 6		

State	Net income after pers'l. exemption	Percentage rates	Net income after pers'l. exemption	Per-centage rates	Personal Exemp. Single	Married family head	Credit Depends.
Louisiana[2] [3]	First 10,000 10,001-50,000	2 4	Over 50,000	6	2,500	5,000	400

Credits are allowed new income which is taxed at 2%; additional $1,000 exemp. for blindness allowed for dependents.

State							
Maine	First 2,000 2,001- 5,000 5,001-10,000	1 2 3	10,001-25,000 25,000-50,000 Over 50,000	4 5 6	1,000	2,000	1,000
Maryland[1] [4]	First 1,000 1,001- 2,000	2 3	2,001- 3,000 Over 3,000	4 5	800	1,600	800

An additional exemption of $800 is allowed for each dependent 65 or over.

State							
Massachusetts[4]	Earned and business income: Interest, divs., capital gains on intangibles:	5 9			2,000	2,600-4,600	600

The exemptions shown are those allowed against business income, including salaries and wages. A specific exemption of $2,000 is allowed for each taxpayer. In addition, a dependency exemption of $600 is allowed for a dependent spouse who has income from all sources of less than $2,000. In the case of a joint return, the exemption is the smaller of (1) $4,600 or (2) $2,600 plus the income of the spouse having the smaller income.

State							
Michigan[4]			All taxable income	4.6	1,500	3,000	1,500
Minnesota[1] [4] . . .	First 500 501- 1,000 1,001- 2,000 2,001- 3,000 3,001- 4,000 4,001- 5,000	1.6 2.2 3.5 5.8 7.3 8.8	5,001- 7,000 7,001- 9,000 9,001-12,500 12,501-20,000 Over 20,000	10.2 11.5 12.8 14 15	21	42	21

An additional tax credit of $21 is allowed for each taxpayer 65 years old.

State							
Mississippi[3]	First 5,000	3	Over 5,000	4	4,500	6,500	750
Missouri[1]	First 1,000 1,001- 2,000 2,001- 3,000 3,001- 4,000 4,001- 5,000	1.5 2 2.5 3 3.5	5,001- 6,000 6,001- 7,000 7,001- 8,000 8,001- 9,000 Over 9,000	4 4.5 5 5.5 6	1,200	2,400	400

An additional $800 exemption is allowed unmarried head of household.

State							
Montana[3]	First 1,000 1,001-2,000 2,001-4,000 4,001-6,000 6,001-8,000	2 3 4 5 6	8,001-10,000 10,001-14,000 14,001-20,000 20,001-35,000 Over 35,000	7 8 9 10 11	650	1,300	650

Nebraska[3] [4]   Federal exemptions
The tax is imposed as a % of the taxpayer's Fed. income tax liability (not including surtax) before credits, with limited adjustments. For the year 1975 the rate was set at 12% by State Board of Equalization and Assessment.

State							
New Hampshire.	Interest and dividends (except interest on savings	4.25	4% commuter tax accounts).		600	600-1,200	

Joint returns are not permitted; each spouse with taxable income is allowed a $600 exemption.

State							
New Jersey[3]	First 1,000 1,001-3,000 3,001-5,000 5,001-7,000 7,001-9,000 9,001-11,000 11,001-13,000	2 3 4 5 6 7 8	13,001-15,000 15,001-17,000 17,001-19,000 19,001-21,000 21,001-23,000 23,001-25,000 Over 25,000	9 10 11 12 13 14 15	650	1,300	650

The tax is imposed on the net income derived from New York sources by New Jersey residents. The rates are the same as those in effect in New York. A surtax of 2.5% is imposed on both the regular income tax and minimum tax on tax preference items. The surtax is computed before the allowance of any applicable credits and is effective through the 1976 calendar year. The rate of tax on minimum taxable income is 6%.

State							
New Mexico[2] [3] . . .	First 500 501-1,000 1,001-1,500 1,501-2,000 2,001-3,000 3,001-4,000 4,001-5,000 5,001-6,000	0.9 1.1 1.3 1.5 1.6 1.9 2.3 2.4	6,001-7,000 7,001-8,000 8,001-10,000 10,001-12,000 12,001-20,000 20,001-50,000 50,001-100,000 Over 100,000	3.0 3.3 3.6 4.3 6.1 8.0 8.5 9.0	Federal exemptions		

The income classes reported are for individuals. For joint returns and heads of households, a separate rate schedule is provided. A credit is allowed for state and local taxes for gross income of less than $6,000.

State							
New York[1] . . .	First 1,000 1,001- 3,000 3,001- 5,000 5,001- 7,000 7,001- 9,000 9,001-11,000 11,001-13,000	2 3 4 5 6 7 8	13,001-15,000 15,001-17,000 17,001-19,000 19,001-21,000 21,001-23,000 23,001-25,000 Over 25,000	9 10 11 12 13 14 15	650	1,300	650

Tax credits of $12.50 for single persons, $12.50 for married persons filing separately, and $25 for married persons filing jointly and heads of households are allowed. Income from unincorporated business is taxed at 5½%. The following credit is allowed: $110 or less, full amount; $110 to $550, difference between $137.50 and 25% of amount of tax; $550 or more, no credit. A 2.5% surtax is imposed.

State	Net Income after pers'l. exemption	Percentage rates	Net Income after pers'l. exemption	Percentage rates	Personal Single	Exemp. Married family head	Credit Depends.
North Carolina[3]	First 2,000 2,001-4,000 4,001-6,000	3 4 5	6,001-10,000 Over 10,000	6 7	1,000	2,000	600

An additional exemption of $1,000 is allowed a married woman with a separate income; joint returns are not permitted.

State							
North Dakota[3]	First 1,000 1,001-3,000 3,001-5,000 5,001-6,000	1 2 3 5	6,001-8,000 Over 8,000	7.5 10	750	1,500	750

An additional 1% tax is imposed on net incomes of individuals, estates, trusts and corporations (minimum $20). A credit of 25% of income tax liability is allowed

State							
Ohio[4]	First 5,000 5,001-10,000 10,001-15,000	0.5 1 2	15,001-20,000 20,001-40,000 Over 40,000	2.5 3 3.5	650	1,300	650

Maximum personal exemption is $3,000 per return. Taxpayers age 65 or older are allowed a $25 credit, or if they have received a lump sum distribution from a pension, retirement or profit sharing plan during the tax year, they are allowed a credit equal to $25 times the taxpayer's expected remaining life. Credit may not exceed tax otherwise due. Credit is also allowed for an amount paid during the school year for elementary and secondary education or instruction or training of dependents who do not have a high school diploma.

State							
Oklahoma[1]	First 1,000 1,001-2,500 2,501-3,750 3,751-5,000	0.5 1 2 3	5,001-6,250 6,251-7,500 Over 7,500	4 5 6	750	1,500	750

For joint returns the rates shown apply to income classes twice as large. Rates of heads of households range from 1/2% on the first $1,500 to 6% on taxable income over $11,250. Non-residents are taxed at a flat rate of 6% of Oklahoma taxable income.

State							
Oregon[1]	First $500 501-1,000 1,001-2,000 2,001-3,000	4 5 6 7	3,001-4,000 4,001-5,000 Over 5,000	8 9 10	750	1,500	750

A credit is provided in an amount and equal to 25% of the Federal retirement income tax credit to the extent that such a credit is based on Oregon taxable income.

State							
Pennsylvania	Modified Federal taxable income 2						

Pennsylvania residents working in New Jersey are subject to a flat 2.3% commuter's tax on their New Jersey income.

State							
Rhode Island	Federal income tax liability 17						

Federal Exemptions.

State							
South Carolina[1]	First 2,000 2,001-4,000 4,001-6,000	2 3 4	6,001- 8,000 8,001-10,000 Over 10,000	5 6 7	800	1,600	800

State							
Tennessee	Interest and dividends	6					

Dividends from corporations, 75% of whose property is taxable in Tenn., are taxed at 4%.

State							
Utah[3]	First 750 751-1,500 1,501-2,250	2.5 3.5 4.5	2,251-3,000 3,001-3,750 3,751-4,500	5.5 6.5 7.5	Federal exemptions Over 4,500		8.0

Vermont...
The tax is imposed at a rate of 25% of the Fed. income tax liability of the taxpayer for the taxable year after certain credits (retirement income, investment, foreign tax and tax-free covenant bonds) but before any surtax on Fed. liability, reduced by a % equal to the % of the taxpayer's adjusted gross income for the taxable year which is not Vermont income. A 9% surcharge is imposed for 1974, and thereafter

Federal Exemptions.

State							
Virginia[3]	First 3,000 3,001-5,000	2 3	5,001-12,000 Over 12,000	5 5.75	600	1,200	600

State							
West Virginia[1]	First 2,000 2,001-4,000 4,001-6,000 6,001-8,000 8,001-10,000 10,001-12,000 12,001-14,000 14,001-16,000 16,001-18,000 18,001-20,000 20,001-22,000 22,001-26,000	2.1 2.3 2.8 3.2 3.5 4 4.6 4.9 5.3 5.4 6 6.1	26,001-32,000 32,001-38,000 38,001-44,000 44,001-50,000 50,001-60,000 60,001-70,000 70,001-80,000 80,001-90,000 90,001-100,000 100,001-150,000 150,001-200,000 Over 200,000	6.5 6.8 7.2 7.5 7.9 8.2 8.6 8.8 9.1 9.3 9.5 9.6	600	1,200	600

For joint returns and a return of a surviving spouse, a separate rate schedule is provided.

State							
Wisconsin[1][4]	First 1,000 1,001-2,000 2,001-3,000 3,001-4,000 4,001-5,000 5,001-6,000 6,001-7,000 7,001-8,000	3.1 3.4 3.6 4.8 5.4 5.9 6.5 7.6	8,001-9,000 9,001-10,000 10,001-11,000 11,001-12,000 12,001-13,000 13,001-14,000 Over 14,000	8.2 8.8 9.3 9.9 10.5 11.1 11.4	(Tax Credit) 20	40	20

(1) A standard deduction and optional tax table are provided.
(2) Community property state in which, in general, one-half of the community income is taxable to each spouse.
(3) A standard deduction is allowed.
(4) A limited tax credit is allowed for sales taxes in Colorado, the District of Columbia, Idaho, Indiana, Massachusetts, Nebraska, and Vermont; for property taxes on homesteads of the elderly in Colorado, Kansas, Michigan, Minnesota, Vermont, and Wisconsin; for income taxes in Michigan; and for personal property taxes in Maryland.
(5) Tax credits are allowed: $15 for single person or married person filing separately if AGI is $3,000 or less. (For each dollar by which the Federal AGI exceeds $3,000, the credit is reduced by $1 until no credit is allowed if Federal AGI is $3,015 or more.) $30 for heads of households or married persons filing jointly with $6,000 or less AGI. (For each dollar by which Federal AGI exceeds $6,000, credit is reduced by $1 until no credit is allowed if Federal AGI is $6,030 or more.)

State Retail Sales Taxes; Types and Rates

Source: Office of Tax Analysis, Treasury Dept. Data as of July 1, 1975

State	Tangible Personal Property	Admissions	Selected Service — Rest. Meals	Selected Service — Transient Lodging	Selected Service — Public Utilities	Rates on other services and nonretail business
Alabama[2]	4%[3] agric., mining and mfg. mach., 1.5%.	4%	4%	4%	...	Gross rcpts of amus't operators, 4%;
Arizona[2]	4	4	4	3	4	Timbering, 1.5%; storage, apt., office rental, 3%.
Arkansas[2]	3 from coin-operated dev.; repair services incl. auto and elect., 3%.	3	3	3	3	Printing, photographic services; rcpts.
California[2]	4.75[5] processing, printing, 4.75%.	...	4.75	...	[14]	Renting, leasing, producing, fabricating,
Colorado[2]	3	...	3	3[10]	3	
Connecticut	7 property items, 7%.		7[7]	7[10]	7[13]	Storing for use or consumption of personal
D. of C.	5[3] lic stenographic services, 5%; sales of food for off-premise consumption, nonprescription medicines, 2%.	5	6	6	5	Duplicating, mailing, addressing and pub-
Florida	4	4	4	4	...	Rental income of amus't. mach., 4%.
Georgia	3	3	3	3	3	Levies on amus't dev., 3%.
Hawaii[1]	4 selected businesses, 1/2%; insur. solicitors, 2%; contractors, sales rep., professions, radio stations, 4%.	4	4	4	...	Sugar processors, pineapple farmers and
Idaho[6]	3	3	3	3	...	Closed circuit tv boxing, wrestling, 5%.
Illinois[2]	4 service, 4%; remodeling, repairing and reconditioning of tangible personal property, 4%.	...	4		...	Property sold in connection with a sale of
Indiana	4	...	4	4	4	
Iowa	3 cold storage, photography, printing, repairs, barber and beauty parlor services, advt., dry cleaning equip. rentals and gross rcpts. from amus't dev., 3%.	3	3	3	3	Laundry, dry cleaning, automobile and
Kansas[2]	3 ated devices; commer. amus't, 3%.	3	3	3	3	Gross rcpts. from operation of coin-oper-
Kentucky[2]	5 photo fin., 5%; ticket sales to boxing or wrestling on closed circuit tv 5% of gross rcpts; tax also applies to pay't's for right to broadcast matches.	5	5	5	5	Storage, sewer services, photog. and
Louisiana[3]	3	3	3	3	...	Food and prescpt'n. drugs, exempt.
Maine	5	...	5	5	5	Proceeds from closed circuit tv, 5%.
Maryland[2]	4[3] that used in generation of electricity or in R.&S. sold to mfrs., 2%; watercraft, 3%.	[11]	4[7]	4	4	Farm equip., 2%; mfg. equip., including
Mass.	3	...	[7]	5[9]	...	
Michigan	4	...	4	4	4	
Minnesota[2]	4[3] coin-operated vending mach., 3% of gross sales.	4	4	4	4	Food, medicines and clothing are exempt;
Mississippi[1]	5[3] sales of meat for human consumption; 5% on beer, alc. bevs., soft drinks and motor fuel); extracting or mining of minerals, specified miscellaneous bus. incl. bowling, pool halls, warehouses, laundry and dry cleaning, pest control services, specified repair services, 5%; cotton ginning, 15c per bale; sales of materials to railroads for use in track structures, 3%; tractors, indust. fuel and mfg. mach. sales over $500, 1%.	...	5	5	5	Wholesaling, 1/8% (one-half of 1% on
Missouri[2]	3	3	3	3	3	
Nebraska[2]	2.5	2.5	2.5	2.5	2.5	
Nevada[2]	3[10]	...	3	...	...	

State	Tangible Personal Property	Admissions	Selected Service		Public Utilities	Rates on other services and nonretail business
			Rest. Meals	Trans-ient Lodging		
N.J.[1][2]	5	5[11]	5	5[9]	....	
N.M.[1-2]	4[3]	4	4	4	4	
N.Y.[2]	4	4[11]	4[7]	4[9]	4	Safe deposit rentals, 4%.
N.C.[2]	3[3]	...	3	3	...	Farm and industrial machinery, 1% ($80 max.); airplanes, boats and locomotives, 2% ($120 max.); sales of horses and mules, 1%.
N.D.	4[3]	4	4	4	4	Severance of sand or gravel from the soil, 4%.
Ohio[2]	4	...	4	4		
Okla.[2]	2[3]	2	2	2	2	Advert. (exclusive of newspapers, periodicals, billboards), printing, auto storage, gross proceeds from amusement dev., 2%.
Penn.[2]	6	...	6[7]	6	6	Cleaning, polishing, lubr. and insp. motor vehicles, rental income of coin-operated amuse. dev., 6%.
R.I.	5	...	5	5	5	
S.C.	4	...	4	4	4	
S.D.[1-2]	4[3]	3	4	3	3	Farm mach. and agric. irrigation &c., 2%; gross rcpts. from professions (other than medical), 4%.
Tenn.[2]	3.5	...	3.5	3.5	3.5	Vending machines, 1.5% (except tobacco products, 2.5%); industrial, farm equipment and machinery, 1%.
Texas[2]	4[3]		4	...	4	
Utah[2]	4	4	4	4	4	
Vt.	3	3	3[12]	3[12]	3	
Va.[2]	3[3]	...	3	3		
Wash.[1-2]	4.5	4.5	4.5	4.5		Rentals, auto, parking, other specified services, amusements, recreations, 4.5% (unless subject to county or city adm. taxes, when they remain taxable under the state business, occupation levy, 1%).
W. Va.[1]	3[3]	3	3	3	...	All services except public util. and pers. prof., 3%.
Wis.[2]	4	4[11]	4	4	4	
Wyo.[2]	3	3	3	3	3	

(1) All but a few States levy sales taxes of the single-stage retail type. Ha. and Miss. levy multiple-stage sales taxes. The N.M. and S.D. taxes have broad bases with respect to taxable services but they are not multiple-stage taxes. Wash. and W.Va. levy gross receipts taxes on all business, distinct from their sales taxes. Alaska also levies a gross receipts tax on businesses. The rates applicable to retailers, with exceptions, under these gross receipts taxes are as follows: Alaska, 1/8% on gross receipts of $20,000-$100,000 and 1/4% on gross receipts in excess of $100,000; Wash., 44/100%; and W. Va., 55/100%. N.J. imposes a tax of 1/20 of 1% on retail stores with income in excess of $150,000, and an unincorporated business tax at the rate of 1/4 of 1% if gross receipts exceed $5,000.

(2) In addition to the State tax, sales taxes are also levied by certain cities and/or counties.

(3) Motor vehicles are taxed at the general sales tax rates with the following exceptions: Ala., 1 1/2%; Miss., 3%; and N.C., 2% ($120 maximum) Motor vehicles are exempt from the general sales and use taxes but are taxed under motor vehicle tax laws in Md., 4%; Minn., 4%; N.M., 2%; N.D. 4%; Okla., 2%; S.D. and W.Va., 3%; Tex., 4%; Va., 2%; and the D.C., 4%.

(4) Ariz. and Miss. also tax the transportation of oil and gas by pipeline. Ga., Mo., Okla. and Utah do not tax transportation of property. Miss. taxes taxicab transportation at the rate of 2%. Okla. does not tax fares of 15c or less on local transportation. Utah does not tax street railway fares.

(5) "Lease" excludes the use of tangible personal property for a period of less than one day for a charge of less than $10 when the privilege of using the property is restricted to use on the premises or at a business location of the grantor.

(6) A limited credit (or refund) in the form of a flat dollar amount per personal exemption is allowed against the personal income tax to compensate for (1) sales taxes paid on food in Colo., D.C. and Neb.; and (2) all sales taxes paid in Idaho, Mass. and Vt. Low-income taxpayers (adjusted gross income not over $6,000) are allowed a credit against D.C. tax liability ranging from $2 to $6 per personal exemption, depending on taxpayer's income bracket. A refund is allowed if credit exceeds tax liability.

(7) Restaurant meals below a specified price are exempt: Conn. and Md. less than $1; N.Y. less than $1 (when alcoholic beverages are sold, meals are taxable regardless of price); and Penn., 50c or less. In Mass., restaurant meals ($1 or more) which are taxed at 8% under the meals excise tax are exempt.

(8) Conn. exempts clothing for children under 10 years of age. Penn. and Wisc. exempt clothing with certain exceptions.

(9) In Colo. and Conn., the first 30 consecutive days of rental or occupancy of rooms is taxable. Over 30 days is exempt. In Mass., transient lodging (in excess of $2 a day) is subject to a 5.7% (5% plus 14% surtax) room occupancy excise tax. In N.J. and N.Y., rooms which rent for $2 a day or less are exempt.

(10) Includes a statewide mandatory 1% county sales tax collected by the state and paid to the counties for support of local school districts.

(11) Md. taxes at 1/2 of 1% gross receipts derived from charges for rentals of sporting or recreational equipment, and admissions, cover charges for tables, services or merchandise at any roof garden or cabaret. In N.J., admissions to a place of amusement are taxable if the charge is in excess of 75c. N.Y. taxes admissions when the charge is over 10c; exempt are participating sports (such as bowling and swimming), motion picture theaters, race tracks, boxing, wrestling, and live dramatic or musical performances. In Wisc., sales of admissions to motion picture theaters costing 75c or less are exempt.

(12) Meals and rooms are exempt from sales tax, but are subject to a special excise tax of 5%.

(13) Gas, water, electricity, telephone and telegraph services provided to consumers through mains, lines or pipes are exempt. Gas and electric energy used for domestic heating are exempt. Interstate telephone calls are exempt, as are calls from coin-operated telephones.

(14) Beginning Jan. 1, 1975 a surcharge for efficiency is imposed at the rate of 1/10th mill ($0.0001) per kwh.

State Inheritance Tax Rates and Exemptions

Source: Compiled by Tax Foundation from Commerce Clearing House data
As of Sept. 1, 1975

| State (a) | Rates (per cent) (b) | | | Max. Rate applies above ($1,000) | Exemptions (c) ($1,000) | | | |
	Spouse Child or parent	Brother or sister	Other than relative		Spouse	Child or parent	Brother or sister	Other than relative
California	3-14	6-20	10-24	$400	$5 (d)	$5 (e)	$2	$.3
Colorado (f)	2-8	3-10	10-19	500	30	10(e)	2	.5 (h)
Connecticut (i)	2-8	4-10	8-14	1,000	50	10	3	.5
Delaware	1-6	5-10	10-16	200	20	3	1	None
Dist. of Col.	1-8	5-23	5-23	1,000	5	5	1	1
Hawaii	1.5-7.5	3.5-9	3.5-9	250	20	5	.5	.5
Idaho	2-15	4-20	8-30	500	10 (d, g)	4 (e)	1	None
Illinois	2-14	2-14	10-30	500	20	20	10	.1
Indiana	1-10	5-15	7-20	1,500	15	2 (e)	.5	.1
Iowa	1-8	5-10	10-15	150	80	10 (e)	None	None
Kansas	.5-5	3-12.5	10-15	500	75	15	5	.2 (h)
Kentucky	2-10	4-16	6-16	500 (j)	10 (g)	5 (e)	1	.5
Louisiana	2-3	5-7	5-10	25	5	5	1	.5
Maine	2-6	8-12	12-18	250	15	10	.5	.5
Maryland (k)	1	7.5	7.5	(l)	.15 (h)	.15 (h)	.15 (h)	.15 (h)
Massachusetts (m)	1.8-11.8	5.5-19.3	8-19.3	1,000	30 (n)	15 (n)	5 (n)	5 (n)
Michigan	2-8(o)	2-8 (o)	10-15 (o)	750	30 (e)	5	5	None
Minnesota	1.5-10	6-25	8-30	1,000	30 (g)	6 (e)	1.5	.5
Missouri	1-6	3-18	5-30	400	20 (p)	5 (e)	.5	.1 (h)
Montana	2-8	4-16	8-32	100	25	2 (e)	.5	None
Nebraska	1	1	6-18	60	10	10	10	.5
New Hampshire	(q)	15	15	(l)	(q)	(q)	None	None
New Jersey	1-16	11-16	15-16	3,200	5	5	.5 (h)	.5 (h)
North Carolina	1-12	4-16	8-17	3,000	10	2 (e)	None	None
Oregon (a)	2-10	2-10 (r)	2-10 (r)	500	(r)	(r)	3	.5
Pennsylvania	6	15	15	(l)	None (s)	None (s)	None	None
Rhode Island	2-9	3-10	8-15	1,000	10	10	5	1
South Dakota (a)	(t)	4-16	6-24	100	60	3 (e)	.5	.1
Tennessee	5.5-9.5	6.5-20	6.5-20	500	60	60	1	1
Texas	1-6	3-10	5-20	1,000	25 (d)	25	10	.5
Virginia	1-5	2-10	5-15	1,000	5	5	2	1
Washington	1-10	3-20	10-25	500	10 (d)	10	1	None
West Virginia (a)	3-13	4-18	10-30	1,000	15	5	None	None
Wisconsin	1.25-12.5	5-25	10-30	500	50	4	1	.5
Wyoming	2	2	6	(l)	10	10	10	None

(a) In addition to an inheritance tax, all states listed also levy an estate tax, generally to assure full absorption of the Federal credit. Exceptions are Ore., S. D., and W. Va.

(b) Rates generally apply to excess above graduated absolute amounts.

(c) Generally, transfers to governments or to solely charitable, educational, scientific, religious, literary, public, and other similar organizations in the U.S. are wholly exempt. Some states grant additional exemptions either for insurance, homestead, joint deposits, support allowance, disinherited minor children, orphaned, incompetent or blind children, and for previously or later taxed transfers. In many states, exemptions are deducted from the first bracket only. Adopted children generally receive the same consideration as natural children.

(d) Community property state in which, in general, either all community property to the surviving spouse is exempt, or only one-half of the community property is taxable on the death of either spouse.

(e) Exemption for child (in thousands): $15 in Iowa; and $10 in S. D. Exemption for minor child is (in thousands): $12 in Calif.; $15 in Col.; $10 in Idaho; $5 in Ind.; $10 in Ky.; $15 in Minn.; $5 in Mont.; $5 in N.C. In Mo. the exemption for an insane, blind or otherwise incapacitated lineal descendant is (thousands) $15. In Mich. a widow receives $5,000 for every minor child to whom no property is transferred in addition to the normal exemption for a spouse.

(f) Colo. imposes an additional tax of 10% upon the amount of tax computed at above rates.

(g) Exemption for widower differs in the following states (thousands): Idaho, $4; Ky., $5; Minn., $6.

(h) No exemption if share exceeds amount stated.

(i) On estates an additional inheritance tax equal to 30% of the basic tax is imposed.

(j) Estates over $3,000,000 are not subject to the inheritance tax but are subject to an estate tax equal to the amount of the Federal credit.

(k) Where property of a decedent subject to administration in Md. is $5,000 or less, no inheritance taxes are due.

(l) Rate applies to entire share.

(m) Mass. imposes a 14% surtax in addition to the inheritance tax on all property or interests.

(n) No exemption if share exceeds amount stated except that the tax shall not reduce the share below the amount of the exemption. In addition there are certain exemptions for the spouse's home.

(o) There is no tax on the share of any beneficiary if the value of the share is less than $100.

(p) In addition, an exemption of one-half of the decedent's estate, or one-third if decedent is survived by lineal descendants.

(q) Spouses, minor children and minor adopted children in the decedent's line of succession are entirely exempt. Parents have no exemption and are taxable at the flat rate of 15%.

(r) An additional tax of 2-20% is levied on all beneficiaries other than grandparents, parents, spouse, children, stepchildren or lineal descendants. These categories of beneficiaries are exempt from the additional taxes.

(s) However, the $2,000 family exemption is specifically allowed as a deduction.

(t) The rates range from 1.5-6% for a spouse or a child and from 3-12% for parents.

Federal Estate Tax

Source: Tax Foundation

An estate tax tax return must be filed for every citizen or resident of the United States whose gross estate exceeds $60,000 in value at the time of his death. In general, the tax must be paid within 9 mos. from the date of death. Extensions may be granted in hardship cases. A return must be filed for a non-resident, not a citizen, if his gross estate in the U.S. exceeds $30,000 in value.

An estate gets credit for state death taxes, according to a graduated table; also deductions for funeral expenses, administration, claims, and bequests to religious, charitable and fraternal organizations or government welfare agencies.

Life insurance payable to named beneficiaries is not to be included in the gross estate if the insured retained no incidents of ownership in the policy. A reversionary inter-est which exceeds 5 per cent of the value of the policy is considered an incident of ownership in the policy.

The marital deduction provides that the value of the tax-able estate "shall be determined by deducting from the value of the gross estate an amount equal to the value of any interest in property which passes or has passed from the decedent to his surviving spouse." Thus the deduction applies when the surviving spouse has a right to the income for life from all or only a part of the property, as well as power to appoint all, or the part in which the survivor has income rights, whether or not the property is held in trust. If the spouse has control only over part, the deduction is limited proportionately. The deduction is limited, however, to the value of one-half of the adjusted gross estate.

Estate Tax Rate

The tax is computed under the rates listed below on the net taxable estate of the decedent, citizen or resident of the United States after allowing for the specific exemption of $60,000 and deduction for debts, expenses, charitable, marital deductions. There is a credit allowance for state death taxes.

If the taxable estate is:			The tax shall be:		
Not over $5,000			3% of the taxable estate		
Over	$5,000	but not over	$10,000	$150, plus 7% of excess over	$5,000
Over	$10,000	but not over	$20,000	$500, plus 11% of excess over	$10,000
Over	$20,000	but not over	$30,000	$1,600, plus 14% of excess over	$20,000
Over	$30,000	but not over	$40,000	$3,000, plus 18% of excess over	$30,000
Over	$40,000	but not over	$50,000	$4,800, plus 22% of excess over	$40,000
Over	$50,000	but not over	$60,000	$7,000, plus 25% of excess over	$50,000
Over	$60,000	but not over	$100,000	$9,500, plus 28% of excess over	$60,000
Over	$100,000	but not over	$250,000	$20,700, plus 30% of excess over	$100,000
Over	$250,000	but not over	$500,000	$65,700, plus 32% of excess over	$250,000
Over	$500,000	but not over	$750,000	$145,700, plus 35% of excess over	$500,000
Over	$750,000	but not over	$1,000,000	$233,200, plus 37% of excess over	$750,000
Over	$1,000,000	but not over	$1,250,000	$325,700, plus 39% of excess over	$1,000,000
Over	$1,250,000	but not over	$1,500,000	$423,200, plus 42% of excess over	$1,250,000
Over	$1,500,000	but not over	$2,000,000	$528,200, plus 45% of excess over	$1,500,000
Over	$2,000,000	but not over	$2,500,000	$753,200, plus 49% of excess over	$2,000,000
Over	$2,500,000	but not over	$3,000,000	$998,200, plus 53% of excess over	$2,500,000
Over	$3,000,000	but not over	$3,500,000	$1,263,200, plus 56% of excess over	$3,000,000
Over	$3,500,000	but not over	$4,000,000	$1,543,200, plus 59% of excess over	$3,500,000
Over	$4,000,000	but not over	$5,000,000	$1,838,200, plus 63% of excess over	$4,000,000
Over	$5,000,000	but not over	$6,000,000	$2,468,200, plus 67% of excess over	$5,000,000
Over	$6,000,000	but not over	$7,000,000	$3,138,200, plus 70% of excess over	$6,000,000
Over	$7,000,000	but not over	$8,000,000	$3,838,200, plus 73% of excess over	$7,000,000
Over	$8,000,000	but not over	$10,000,000	$4,568,200, plus 76% of excess over	$8,000,000
Over	$10,000,000			$6,088,200, plus 77% of excess over	$10,000,000

State Estate Tax Rates and Exemptions*

Source: Compiled by Tax Foundation from Commerce Clearing House Data
As of Sept. 1, 1975. *See index for state inheritance tax rates and exemptions.

State (a)	Rates (on net estate after exemptions) (b)	Maximum rate applies above	Exemption	
Alabama	Maximum federal credit (c, d)	$10,040,000	$60,000	
Alaska	Maximum federal credit (c, d)	10,040,000	60,000	
Arizona	0.8% on first $50,000 to 16% (e)	10,000,000	100,000	(f, g)
Arkansas	Maximum federal credit (c, d)	10,040,000	60,000	(g)
Florida	Maximum federal credit (c, d)	10,040,000	60,000	
Georgia	Maximum federal credit (c, d)	10,040,000	60,000	
Mississippi	1% on first $60,000 to 16%	10,000,000	60,000	(f, g)
New Mexico	Maximum federal credit (c, d)	10,040,000	60,000	
New York	2% on first $50,000 to 21% (e, h)	10,100,000	(f, g, i)	
North Dakota	2% on first $25,000 to 23%	1,500,000	20,000	(g, j)
Ohio	2% on first $40,000 to 7% (e)	500,000	5,000	(g, k)
Oklahoma	1% on first $10,000 to 10% (e)	10,000,000	60,000	(g,l, m)
South Carolina	4% on first $40,000 to 6%	100,000	60,000	(g)
Utah	5% of first $35,000 to 10% (e)	85,000	60,000	(g)
Vermont	Maximum federal credit (e, n)	10,040,000	60,000	(g)

(a) Excludes states shown in table on page 60 which levy an estate tax, in addition to their inheritance taxes, to assure full absorption of the Federal credit.

(b) The rates generally are in addition to graduated absolute amounts.

(c) Maximum Federal credit allowed under the 1954 code for state estate taxes paid is expressed as a percentage of the taxable estate (after $60,000 exemption) in excess of $40,000, plus a graduated absolute amount.

(d) A tax on nonresident estates is imposed on the proportionate share of the net estate which the property located in the state bears to the entire estate wherever situated.

(e) An additional estate tax is imposed to assure full absorption of the Federal credit.

(f) Insurance receives special treatment.

(g) Transfers to religious, charitable, educational, and municipal corporations are fully exempt. Limited in Mississippi to those located in U.S.

(h) On net estate before exemption.

(i) The specific exemptions ($20,000 of the net estate transferred to spouse and $5,000 to lineal ancestors and descendants and certain other named relatives) are allowed in an amount equal to 2% of the first $50,000 and 3% of the next $100,000.

(j) A marital deduction of 50% of adjusted gross estate is allowed instead, if larger. Exemption for a lineal descendant, if a minor, is $5,000; for other lineal descendants and ancestors, $2,000.

(k) Property is exempt to the extent transferred to surviving spouse not exceeding $20,000; for a child under 18, $7,000 and for each child 18 or over, $3,000.

(l) An estate valued at $100 or less is exempt.

(m) Exemption is a total aggregate of $60,000 for father, mother, child, and other named relatives.

(n) The tax rate is 30% of the federal estate tax liability.

Savings by Individuals in the United States

Source: Federal Reserve System

(Billions of Dollars)* Indicates less than $50 million. Seasonally adjusted annual rates.

	1969	1970	1971	1972	1973	1974	1975[1]
Incr. in financial assets	61.3	79.6	99.9	124.9	132.4	129.9	205.5
Currency and demand deposits	1.6	9.6	11.0	12.9	15.1	.6	33.1
Savings accounts	6.0	44.4	70.5	75.8	67.1	59.6	95.8
Securities	29.7	-2.3	-14.7	5.1	14.2	21.3	16.2
U.S. Savings Bonds	-.4	.3	2.4	3.3	2.7	3.0	4.1
Other U.S. Treasury sec.	9.8	10.7	-11.7	1.5	7.6	0.8	-4.7
U.S.G. agency securities	2.8	2.7	-3.5	-.5	8.4	10.8	-1.5
State & local obligations	9.6	-.5	-.9	1.3	1.7	10.0	9.3
Corporation & foreign bonds	7.4	10.1	8.2	4.9	.8	-1.7	13.1
Commercial paper	4.8	-1.5	-3.9	.4	3.3	-0.5	-1.4
Investment company shares	4.8	2.6	1.2	-.6	-1.6	1.0	-1.2
Other corporate stock	-9.0	-5.2	-6.6	-5.2	-8.8	-2.0	-1.3
Private life insurance reserves	4.9	5.1	6.1	7.2	7.7	7.2	6.9
Private insured pension reserves	2.9	3.3	5.2	4.6	5.0	5.7	5.9
Private noninsured pension reserves	6.3	7.1	7.3	5.7	7.9	10.9	12.4
Government ins. & pension reserves	6.6	8.8	9.7	10.5	9.8	15.1	28.5
Miscellaneous financial assets	3.1	3.6	4.9	3.1	5.7	5.5	6.7
Gross investment in tangible assets	143.0	140.2	165.8	190.5	213.6	204.6	191.6
Nonfarm homes	22.0	19.6	26.8	34.3	40.0	32.5	27.8
Noncorporate business construction & equipment	29.2	30.4	34.3	39.5	41.7	41.2	37.0
Consumer durables	90.8	91.3	103.5	117.4	130.8	127.5	130.0
Inventories	1.1	-1.1	1.1	-.8	1.1	3.3	-3.2
Capital consumption allowances	104.5	112.4	121.3	130.6	142.0	160.3	165.3
Nonfarm homes	8.7	9.0	9.4	10.2	10.4	10.6	10.8
Noncorporate business plant and equipment	21.3	22.6	24.4	26.7	28.6	32.9	34.3
Consumer durables	74.6	80.7	87.5	93.8	103.0	116.8	120.3
Net investment in tangible assets	38.5	27.8	44.5	59.8	71.6	44.3	26.3
Nonfarm homes	13.3	10.6	17.4	24.1	29.5	21.9	17.1
Noncorporate business construction and equipment	7.9	7.7	9.9	12.8	13.1	8.4	2.7
Consumer durables	16.2	10.6	16.0	23.6	27.9	10.7	9.8
Inventories	1.1	-1.1	1.1	-.8	1.1	3.3	-3.2
Increase in debt	39.8	30.6	54.6	85.1	90.8	58.5	60.3
Mortgage debt on nonfarm homes	16.1	12.5	24.1	38.4	43.0	32.6	41.9
Noncorporate business mortgage debt	7.0	8.0	11.2	13.2	13.8	12.4	10.3
Consumer credit	10.4	6.0	11.2	19.2	22.9	9.6	2.1
Security credit	-3.4	-1.8	2.6	4.7	-4.6	-2.1	5.1
Policy loans	2.6	2.3	1.0	.9	2.1	2.7	1.1
Other debt	7.1	3.6	4.4	8.6	13.5	3.2	-.2
Individual saving	60.1	76.8	89.8	99.7	113.2	115.8	171.4
Less-Govt. ins. & pen. reserves	6.6	8.8	9.7	10.5	9.8	15.1	28.5
Net inv. in cons. dur.	16.2	10.6	16.0	23.6	27.9	10.7	9.8
Capital gains dividends from invest. cos.	2.5	.9	.8	1.4	.9	0.5	0.7
Net savings by farm crops	*	-.1	*	*	-.1	0.4	0.4
Equals pers. saving, F/F basis	34.7	56.6	63.3	64.2	74.6	89.0	132.1
Personal saving, NIA basis	38.2	56.2	60.2	49.7	54.8	77.0	114.6
Difference	-3.5	.4	3.2	14.4	19.9	12.0	17.5

(1.) Second quarter, 1975.

Federal Gift Tax

Source: Tax Foundation

Any citizen or resident who within the calendar year makes gifts in excess of $3,000 to any one individual, or any gift of a future interest regardless of value, must file a gift tax return. Since 1971, the tax has been levied quarterly on a return due one and one-half months after the end of the quarter. In addition to the annual $3,000 exclusion for each person to whom gifts are made, each donor also has a specific lifetime exemption of $30,000, and this may be taken all at one time or spread over years.

When a husband or wife transfers by gift an interest in property to his or her spouse a deduction in computing gift tax will be allowed to the extent of one-half of the value of the gift. Also gifts to a third party by either husband or wife may be treated as made one-half by each.

If the taxable gifts are:			The tax will be:	
Not over $5,000			2¼% of the taxable gifts	
Over	$5,000 but not over	$10,000	$112.50, plus 5¼% of excess over	$5,000
Over	$10,000 but not over	$20,000	$375, plus 8¼% of excess over	$10,000
Over	$20,000 but not over	$30,000	$1,200, plus 10½% of excess over	$20,000
Over	$30,000 but not over	$40,000	$2,250, plus 13½% of excess over	$30,000
Over	$40,000 but not over	$50,000	$3,600, plus 16½% of excess over	$40,000
Over	$50,000 but not over	$60,000	$5,250, plus 18¾% of excess over	$50,000
Over	$60,000 but not over	$100,000	$7,125, plus 21 % of excess over	$60,000
Over	$100,000 but not over	$250,000	$15,525, plus 22½% of excess over	$100,000
Over	$250,000 but not over	$500,000	$49,275, plus 24 % of excess over	$250,000
Over	$500,000 but not over	$750,000	$109,275, plus 26¼% of excess over	$500,000
Over	$750,000 but not over	$1,000,000	$174,900, plus 27¾% of excess over	$750,000
Over	$1,000,000 but not over	$1,250,000	$244,275, plus 29¼% of excess over	$1,000,000
Over	$1,250,000 but not over	$1,500,000	$317,400, plus 31½% of excess over	$1,250,000
Over	$1,500,000 but not over	$2,000,000	$396,150, plus 33¾% of excess over	$1,500,000
Over	$2,000,000 but not over	$2,500,000	$564,900, plus 36¾% of excess over	$2,000,000
Over	$2,500,000 but not over	$3,000,000	$748,650, plus 39¾% of excess over	$2,500,000
Over	$3,000,000 but not over	$3,500,000	$947,400, plus 42 % of excess over	$3,000,000
Over	$3,500,000 but not over	$4,000,000	$1,157,400, plus 44¼% of excess over	$3,500,000
Over	$4,000,000 but not over	$5,000,000	$1,378,650, plus 47¼% of excess over	$4,000,000
Over	$5,000,000 but not over	$6,000,000	$1,851,150, plus 50¼% of excess over	$5,000,000
Over	$6,000,000 but not over	$7,000,000	$2,353,650, plus 52½% of excess over	$6,000,000
Over	$7,000,000 but not over	$8,000,000	$2,878,650, plus 54¾% of excess over	$7,000,000
Over	$8,000,000 but not over	$10,000,000	$3,426,150, plus 57 % of excess over	$8,000,000
Over	$10,000,000 but not over		$4,566,150, plus 57¾% of excess over	$10,000,000

Social Security Programs

Source: Office of Research and Statistics, Social Security Administration, Dept. of Health, Education and Welfare

Medicare; Old-Age, Survivors and Disability Insurance; Supplemental Security Income

The Tax Reduction Act of 1975 provided for a one-time payment of $50 to every individual who received a social security benefit for March 1975. The $50 payment was received by the beneficiaries in August 1975, separate from the monthly benefit check, and was paid from general revenues, not from the social security trust funds. Railroad retirement beneficiaries and recipients of supplemental security income payments were also eligible for the $50, but only one payment was made to an individual, even for those eligible under more than one program.

The first automatic cost-of-living increase in social security monthly benefits was effective for June 1975. The 8-percent increase, reflected in the checks received early in July, applied to the benefits of all persons on the rolls except those affected by the special minimum benefit provision. The next automatic cost-of-living increase will be based on the rise in the consumer price index from the first quarter of 1975 (if there is no legislated increase) to the first quarter of 1976; if the index rises 3% or more, the benefit level will be raised as of June 1976 by the same percentage.

Under 1974 legislation, when a cost-of-living increase is established for social security benefits, Federal supplemental security income payments are raised by the same percentage; an 8-percent increase in SSI payments was therefore effective for July 1975.

Implementation of two other automatic adjustment provisions related to the increase in average taxable wages under the social security program (1) raised the maximum amount of earnings taxable and creditable for benefit purposes to $14,100 for 1975 and to $15,300 for 1976 and (2) lifted the annual exempt amount of earnings for social security beneficiaries to $2,520 in 1975 and to $2,760 in 1976.

In Medicare, following the required annual review of hospital costs under the program, increases were made in the hospital insurance deductible amount (what the patient must pay for hospital services before reimbursement can begin) and in the cost-sharing for days above the number specified in the law.

The Commissioner of Social Security is James B. Cardwell. There are 634 district offices (with 492 branches), 165 metropolitan branch offices, and 27 teleservice centers where the public may obtain information about benefit rights.

Medicare
Health Insurance for Aged and Disabled

Under Medicare, protection against the costs of hospital care is provided for social security and railroad retirement beneficiaries aged 65 and over (beginning July 1966) and, effective July 1973, for persons entitled for 24 months to receive a social security disability benefit, certain persons with chronic kidney disease and their dependents, and, on a voluntary basis with payment of a special premium, persons aged 65 and over not otherwise eligible for hospital benefits; all those eligible for hospital benefits may enroll for medical benefits and pay a monthly premium and so may persons aged 65 and over who are not eligible for hospital benefits.

Persons eligible for both hospital and medical insurance or for medical insurance only may choose to have their covered services provided through a Health Maintenance Organization (a prepaid group health or other capitation plan that meets prescribed standards).

Hospital insurance. — In the 9th year of operation (July 1974-June 1975) about $10.4 billion was withdrawn from the hospital insurance trust fund for hospital and related benefits. About 23,480,000 persons were enrolled under the program as of July 1974

— 1,880,000 of them disabled beneficiaries under age 65.

The hospital insurance program pays the cost of covered services for hospital and posthospital care as follows:

- Up to 90 days of hospital care during a benefit period (spell of illness, starting on the 1st day of care as a bed-patient is received in a hospital or skilled nursing facility and ending when the individual has not been a bed-patient for 60 consecutive days). For the first 60 days, the hospital insurance pays for all but the first $104 of expenses; for the 61st day to 90th day, the program pays all but $26 a day for covered services. In addition, each person has a 60-day lifetime reserve that can be used after the 90 days of hospital care in a benefit period are exhausted, and all but $52 a day of expenses during the reserve days are paid. Once used, the reserve days are not replaced. (Payment for care in a mental hospital is limited to 190 days.)

- Up to 100 days' care in a skilled nursing facility (skilled nursing home) in each benefit period. Hospital insurance pays for all covered services for the first 20 days and all but $13 daily for the next 80 days. At least 3 day's hospital stay must precede these services, and the skilled nursing facility must be entered within 14 days after leaving the hospital. (The 1972 law permits more than 14 days in certain circumstances).

- Up to 100 visits by nurses or other health workers (not doctors) from a home health agency in the 365 days after release from a hospital or extended-care facility.

Money to pay these benefits comes from special contributions paid by workers, their employers, and the self-employed. The 1975 rate was 0.9% on earnings up to $14,200 (the maximum taxable for that year). It is 0.9% on earnings up to $15,300 for 1976.

Medical insurance—Aged persons can receive benefits under this supplementary program only if they sign up for them and agree to a monthly premium ($6.70 to July 1975). The Federal Government pays the rest of the cost. In December of each year the Secretary of Health, Education, and Welfare announces the amount of the premium payable starting in July of the following year. The premiums are to be increased only when there is a general benefit increase in the year and it will rise no more than the percent by which the cash benefits have been increased since the last premium increase.

About 74.3 million bills were reimbursed under the medical insurance program in fiscal year 1975 for a total of $3.6 billion. As of July 1974, 23,014,000 persons were enrolled — 1,734,000 of them disabled persons under age 65.

The medical insurance program pays 80% of the reasonable charges (after the first $60 in each calendar year) for the following services:

- Physicians' surgeons' services, whether in the doctor's office, a clinic, or hospital or at home (but physician's charges for X-ray or clinical laboratory services for hospital bed-patients are paid in full and without meeting the deductible).

- Other medical and health services, such as diagnostic tests, surgical dressings and splints, and rental or purchase of medical equipment. Beginning July 1, 1973, services of a physical therapist in independent practice, furnished in his office or the patient's home. Beginning Jan. 1, 1973, a hospital or extended-care facility may provide covered outpatient physical therapy services under the medical insurance program to its patients who have exhausted their hospital insurance coverage.

- Physical therapy sevices furnished under the supervision of a practicing hospital, clinic, skilled nursing facility, or agency.

- Certain services by podiatrists.

- All outpatient services of a participating hospital (including diagnostic tests).

- Beginning Jan. 1, 1973, under the 1972 amendments, outpatient speech pathology services, under the same requirements as physical therapy.
- Services of licensed chiropractors who meet uniform standards, but only for treatment by means of manual manipulation of the spine and treatment of subluxation of the spine demonstrated by X-ray.
- Supplies related to colostomies are considered prosthetic devices and payable under the program. Home health services even without a hospital stay (up to 100 visits a year) are paid up to 100%.

To get medical insurance protection, persons approaching age 65 may enroll in the 7-month period that includes 3 months before the 65th birthday, the month of the birthday, and 3 months after the birthday, but if they wish coverage to begin in the month they reach 65 they must enroll in the 3 months **before** their birthday. Persons not enrolling within their first enrollment period may enroll later, during the first 3 months of each year but their premium is 10% higher for each 12-month period elapsed since they first could have enrolled.

The monthly premium is deducted from the cash benefit for persons receiving social security, railroad retirement, or civil service retirement benefits. Income from the medical premiums and the Federal matching payments are put in a Supplementary Medical Insurance Trust Fund, from which benefits and administrative expenses are paid.

Medicare card. Persons qualifying for hospital insurance under social security receive a health insurance card similar to cards now used by Blue Cross and other health agencies. The card indicates whether the individual has taken out medical insurance protection. It is to be shown to the hospital, skilled nursing facility, home health agency, doctor, or whoever provides the covered services.

Payments are made only in the 50 States, Puerto Rico, the Virgin Islands, Guam, and American Samoa, except that hospital services may be provided in border areas immediately outside the U.S. if comparable services are not accessible in the U. S. for a beneficiary who becomes ill or is injured in the U.S.

Old-Age Survivors, and Disability Insurance

Retired and disabled workers and their families and the survivors of deceased workers received $62.5 billion in social security cash benefits in the 12 months ended in June 1975. In that month the average benefit being received by a retired worker was about $205; for retired workers just coming on the rolls, the average benefit award was about $215. For a disabled worker, the average June check was $224 and new disabled-worker beneficiaries were awarded $245, on the average.

Old-age, survivors, and disability insurance covers almost all jobs in which people work for wages or salaries, as well as most work of self-employed persons, whether in a city job, or in business, or on a farm.

Old-age, survivors, and disability insurance is paid for by a tax on earnings (for 1975 up to $14,100 and for 1976 up to $15,300; the taxable earnings base is now subject to adjustment when cost-of-living benefit increases have been made). The employed worker and his employer share the tax equally, (cash tips count as covered wages if they amount to $20 or more from one place of employment. The worker reports them to his employer, who includes them in his social security tax reports, but only the worker pays contributions on the amount of the tips).

The employer deducts the tax each payday and sends it, with an equal amount as his own share, to the District Director of Internal Revenue. The collected taxes are deposited in the Federal Old-Age and Survivors Insurance Trust Fund and the Federal Disability Insurance Trust Fund; they can be used only to pay benefits, the costs of rehabilitation services, and administrative expenses.

Amount of Work Required

To qualify for benefits for himself and his family, the worker must have been in covered employment long enough to become insured. Just how long depends on his date of birth (or, if he dies or becomes disabled, the date of his death or disability).

A person is fully covered if he has one quarter of coverage for every year after 1950 (or year he reaches age 21) up to but not including the year in which he reaches age 62 or dies.

Certain provisions in the law permit special monthly payments under the social security program to persons aged 72 and over who are not eligible for regular social security benefits since they had little or no opportunity to earn social security work credits during their working lifetime.

To get disability benefits, the worker must also have credit for 5 out of 10 years before he becomes disabled. Persons disabled before age 31 can qualify with a briefer period of coverage.

Work Years Required

The following table shows the number of work years required to be fully insured for old-age or survivors benefits, according to the year worker reaches retirement age or dies.

Work credit for retirement benefits:

If you reach 62 in	Years you need	If you reach 62 in	Years you need
1974	6*	1979	7
1975	6	1981	7½
1976	6¼	1983	8
1977	6½	1987	9
1978	6¾	1991 or later	10

*For 1974 a woman needs only 5¾ years.

Work credit for survivors checks

Born after 1929, die at	Born before 1930, die before age 62	Years you need
28 or younger		1½
30		2
32		2½
34		3
36		3½
38		4
40		4½
42		5
44	1973	5½
45	1974	5¾
46	1975	6
48	1977	6½
50	1979	7
52	1981	7½
54	1983	8
56	1985	8½
58	1987	9
60	1989	9½
62 or older	1991 or later	10

Self-Employed

A self-employed person who has earnings of $400 or more in a year must report his earnings for income tax and social security tax purposes. If he is not a farmer he reports only net returns from his business. He need not add income from real estate, savings, dividends, loans, pensions or insurance policies if these are not part of his business.

A self-employed person who has net earnings of $400 or more in a year gets 4 quarters of coverage for that year. If his earnings are less than $400 in a year they do not count toward social security credits. The nonfarm self-employed person must make estimated payments of his social security taxes, on a quarterly basis, for taxable years after 1966, if combined estimated income tax and social security tax amount to at least $40.

The self-employed now have the option, comparable to that for farm workers, of reporting their earnings as ⅔ of their gross income from self-employment but not more than $1,600 a year. This option can be used only if actual net earnings from self-employment income is less than $1,600 and less than ⅔ of gross income and may be used only 5 times.

When a person has both taxable wages and earnings from self-employment, only as much of the self-employment income as will bring total earnings up to the current taxable maximum is subject to tax for social security purposes. A self-employed person pays the tax at a lower rate than the combined rate for an employee and his employer — about $1\frac{1}{2}$ times what the employee alone pays.

Farm Owners and Hands

Self-employed farmers whose gross annual earnings from farming are under $2,400 may report $2/3$ of their gross earnings instead of net earnings for social security purposes. Cash or crop shares received from a tenant or share farmer count if the owner participated materially in production or management. The self-employed farmer pays contributions at the same rate as other self-employed. but he may make his tax returns annually.

Farm Workers. Earnings from farm work count toward benefits (1) if the employer pays $150 or more in cash during the year; (2) if the employee works on 20 or more days for cash pay figured on a time basis. Under t.. e rules a person gets credit for one calendar quarter . each $100 in cash pay in a year but no more than four q. ters in any one year.

Foreign farm w. rs admitted to the United States on a temporary b. .. t be covered.

Household W. .. s

Anyone working as maid. cook. laundress. nursemaid. baby-sitter. chauffeur. gardener and at other household tasks in the house of another. is covered by social security if he or she earns $50 or more in cash in three months from any one employer. Room and board do not count. but carfare counts if paid in cash. The job does not have to be regular or fulltime. The employee should get a card at the social security office and show it to the employer.

The employer deducts the amount of the social security tax from the worker's pay. adds an identical amount as his own tax and sends the total amount to the Federal Government. with the number of the employee's social security card.

What Aged Workers Get

When a person has enough work in covered employment and reaches retirement age (65 for full benefit. 62 for reduced benefit). he may retire and get monthly old-age benefits. If he continues to work and has earnings of more than $2,760. $1 in benefits will be withheld for every $2 above $2,760. The amount that can be earned in a month without loss of any benefits is $230. The annual exempt amount and the monthly test will be raised automatically in the future. according to the rise in general earnings levels. The eligible worker who is 72 receives the full amount of benefit. regardless of earnings.

A worker's benefit will be raised by 1% for each year after 1970 for which the worker between 65 and 72 did not receive benefits because of earnings from work. No increases are to be paid to the worker's dependents or survivors under this provision.

A special minimum benefit is payable to persons who worked 20 or more years under social security as an alternative to the regular minimum of $93.80 if a higher amount results. The highest minimum under this provision would be $180 a month for a person ($270 for a couple) with 30 or more years of coverage.

When a person receives old-age benefits, payments can also be made to certain of his dependents. including a wife 62 or over. dependent children under 18 or who became totally disabled before age 22 or who are full-time students not yet aged 22. a wife (regardless of age) if caring for an eligible child. and a dependent husband 62 or over.

The special benefit for persons aged 72 or over who do not meet the regular coverage requirements is $69.60 a month ($104.40 for a couple if both members are eligible). Like the monthly benefits. these payments are subject to cost-of-living increases. beginning June 1975. The special payment is not made to

persons on the public assistance or supplemental security income rolls.

Social Security benefits are not subject to income taxes.

A woman worker is eligible for a full old-age benefit at age 65. but she may retire at 62 and get 80% of her full benefit for the rest of her life; the nearer she is to 65 when she begins collecting her benefit. the larger it will be. (Benefits for men retiring before 65 are reduced at the same rate as benefits for women retiring before 65.)

A child can get benefits based on his mother's earnings on the same conditions as those entitling a child to benefits based on his father's earnings record.

Benefits for Worker's Wife (or Husband)

The wife of a man who is getting social security retirement or disability payments may become entitled to wife's insurance benefits in a reduced amount when she reaches 62. or she may wait until she reaches 65 and get the entire amount of the wife's benefit. which is one-half of the husband's benefits. Benefits are also payable to the divorced wife of an insured worker if she was married to him for at least 20 years and he was contributing to or was ordered by a court to contribute to her support.

If a woman worker entitled to old-age benefit has a dependent husband aged 65 or over. he may draw a benefit similar to a wife's benefit at 65 (or a reduced benefit at age 62).

Benefits for Children of Retired or Disabled Workers

If a worker has children under 18 when he retires for age or disability they will get a benefit that is half his benefit, and so will his wife. even if she is under 62. Total benefits paid on a worker's earnings record are subject to a maximum and if the total paid to a family exceeds that maximum. the individual dependents' benefits are adjusted downward. (Total benefits paid to the family of a worker who retired in 1974 at age 65 with averaga yearly earnings of $5 838 could be no higher than $541.)

When his children reach 18. their benefits will stop. except that a child permanently and totally disabled before 22 may get a benefit as long as his disability meets the definition in the law. In addition. child's benefits are payable until the child reaches his 22nd birthday if he is attending school as a full-time student. Benefits may now be paid to a grandchild or step-grandchild of a worker or of his spouse in special circumstances.

What Disabled Worker Gets

If a worker becomes so severely disabled that he is unable to work. he may be eligible to receive a monthly disability benefit that is the same amount he would receive as an old-age benefit if he were 65 at the start of his disability. When he reaches 65. his disability benefit becomes an old-age benefit.

Benefits like those provided for dependents of retired-worker beneficiaries may be paid to dependents of disabled beneficiaries.

Survivor Benefits

If a worker should die while insured. one or more types of benefits would be payable to survivors.

1. A cash payment to cover burial expenses that amounts to 3 times the basic benefit but not more than $255 paid at the death of every insured worker.

2. A benefit for each child until the child reaches 18 (or up to age 22. if he is attending school). The monthly benefit of each child of a worker who has died is three-quarters of the amount the worker would have received if he had lived and drawn retirement benefits. A child with a permanent disability that began before age 22 may receive his benefit after that age.

3. A mother's benefit for the widow. if children under 18 are left in her care. Her benefit is 75 of the basic benefit and she draws it until the youngest child reaches 18. Payments stop then even if the

child's benefit continues because he is attending school. They will start again when she is 62 (or 60), unless she marries. If she marries and the marriage is ended, she regains benefit rights. If she has a disabled child beneficiary aged 18 or over in her care, her benefits also continue.

Disabled widows and widowers qualify for benefits at age 50 at reduced rates that depend on age at entitlement. The widow or widower must have become totally disabled before or within 7 years after the spouse's death.

4. If there are no children entitled to receive benefits, the widow will receive a benefit that is 100% of the husband's basic amount, if it is first payable when she is 65. She may choose to get her benefit when she is 60; her benefit is then reduced by 19/40 of 1% for each month it is paid before she is 65. However, for widows aged 62 and over whose husbands claimed their benefits before 65, the benefit is the reduced amount he would be getting if he were alive but not less than 82$^1/_2$% of his basic benefit. Dependent widowers aged 60 or over are entitled to survivor benefits on same basis as widows.

5. Dependent parents may be eligible for benefits if they have been receiving at least half their support

from the worker before his death, have reached age 62, and (except in certain circumstances) have not remarried since the worker's death. Each parent gets 75 of the basic benefit except that if only one parent survives the benefit is 82$^1/_2$%.

The survivors of a woman worker receive benefits on the same basis as those of men workers.

Maximum Benefits Payable

The illustrative table below shows a column heading for average earnings of $10,000, but the benefit amounts shown in the column are not in general payable yet, since it will be some time before workers can have an average that high (years when the maximum creditable amount of earnings was lower than $10,800 — the 1973 maximum — must currently be included when the average is figured). Benefit amounts larger than those shown in the table will eventually be payable to persons who raise their average yearly earnings for social security purposes by earning, for a sufficient period, the highest creditable amount in years with the higher maximums specified in the law—$14,100 in 1975 and $15,300 in 1976 (higher amounts in the future whenever the base is raised under the automatic adjustment procedure).

Examples of Monthly OASDI Cash Payments
Average yearly earnings after 1950

Benefits can be paid to:	$923 or less	$3,000	$4,000	$5,000	$6,000	$8,000	$10,000
Worker:							
Retired at 65..............................	101.40	209.70	246.80	286.10	323.40	402.00	445.40
Under 65 and disabled......................	101.40	209.70	246.80	286.10	323.40	402.00	445.40
Retired at 62.............................	81.20	167.80	197.50	228.90	258.80	321.60	356.40
Wife:							
at 65..................................	50.70	104.90	123.40	143.10	161.70	201.00	222.70
at 62, with no child......................	38.10	78.70	92.60	107.40	121.30	150.80	167.10
Under 65 and one child in her care........	50.80	111.00	175.00	242.00	270.00	301.60	334.20
Widow:							
At 65 (if worker never received reduced retirement benefits).............................	101.40	209.70	246.80	286.10	323.40	402.00	445.40
at 60 (if sole survivor)...................	74.90	150.00	176.50	204.60	231.30	287.50	318.50
at 50 and disabled (if sole survivor).......	56.80	105.00	123.50	143.10	161.80	201.10	222.80
Widowed mother (or father) caring for one child......	152.20	314.60	370.20	429.20	485.20	603.00	668.20
Maximum family payment.....................	152.20	320.60	421.80	528.10	593.30	703.60	779.60

*Generally, average earnings are figured over the period from 1951 until the worker reaches retirement age, becomes disabled, or dies. Up to 5 years of low earnings or no earnings can be excluded. The maximum earnings creditable for social security are $3,600 for 1951-1954; $4,200 for 1955-1958; $4,800 for 1959-65; $6,600 for 1966-67; $7,800 for 1968-71; $9,000 for 1972; $10,800 for 1973; $13,200 for 1974; $14,100 for 1975; and $15,300 for 1976. As the text under the heading "Maximum Benefits Payable" explains, amounts shown in the last column will generally not be payable until later. When a person is entitled to more than one benefit, the amount actually payable is limited to the larger of the benefits.

Contribution Rate for Employees, Employers, and Self-Employed
Percent of Covered Earnings

Years	Employees and employers			Self-employed		
	OASDI Benefits	Hospital Insurance	Total	OASDI Benefits	Hospital Insurance	Total
1974-77	4.95	0.90	5.85	7.0	0.90	7.90
1978-80	4.95	1.10	6.05	7.0	1.10	8.10
1981-85	4.95	1.35	6.30	7.0	1.35	8.35
1986-98	4.95	1.50	6.45	7.0	1.50	8.50
1999-2010*	4.95	(1.50)	(6.45)	7.0	(1.50)	(8.50)
2011 and thereafter	5.95	(1.50)	(7.45)	7.0	(1.50)	(8.50)

*Costs of hospital insurance estimated only through 1997.

Supplemental Security Income

On Jan. 1, 1974, the supplemental security income program established by the 1972 Social Security Act amendments replaced the former Federal grants to States for aid to the needy aged, blind, and disabled in the 50 States and the District of Columbia. The program provides both for Federal payments based on

uniform national standards and eligibility requirements and for State supplementary payments, varying from State to State. The Social Security Administration administers the Federal payments financed from general funds of the Treasury — and the State supplements as well, if the State elects to have its supplementary program federally administered. The States may supplement the Federal payment for all recipients and must supplement it for persons otherwise adversely affected by the transition from the former public assistance programs. In 1975, the number of persons receiving Federal payments and federally administered State payments was 4,240,-900, and the amount of these payments was $509,578,-000. The average amount for all types of payments (federally administered and State-administered) was $109 at the end of fiscal year 1975.

As a result of the 8-percent cost-of-living increase in social security benefits in June, 1975, the Federal SSI payment levels were raised in July, 1975, from $146 per month for an individual and $219 for a couple to $157.70 and $236, respectively.

Social Security Trust Funds
Old-Age and Survivors and Disability Insurance Trust Funds, 1937-1975
(In thousands)

| Period and fiscal year | Receipts | | Expenditures | | | |
	Net contrib. inc., transfers, and reimb. from gen. rev.	Net interest received	Cash benefit payments and rehab. services	Transfers to R.R. acct.	Adminis- trative expenses	Total assets at end of period
1937.	$ 265,000	$ 2,262	$ 27	. . . .	$ 26,840	$ 267,235
1940.	550,000	42,489	15,805	. . . .	12,288	1,744,698
1945.	1,309,919	123,854	239,834	. . . .	26,950	6,613,381
1950.	2,109,992	256,778	727,266	. . . .	56,841	12,892,612
1955.	5,087,154	438,029	4,333,147	-9,551	103,202	21,141,001
1960.	10,829,764	564,040	10,798,013	573,606	234,291	22,995,939
1965.	17,032,456	648,372	16,618,084	459,253	379,145	22,187,184
1970.	34,554,182	1,572,375	29,064,972	589,257	623,055	37,719,951
1973.	47,305,791	2,281,098	47,373,415	802,457	913,984	44,285,368
1974.	55,182,906	2,521,043	54,060,950	930,912	877,581	46,119,873
1975[1].	63,872,883	2,803,838	62,573,816	1,010,299	1,100,636	48,111,842
Cumulative to June, 1975*	527,964,316	26,005,024	485,991,379	9,380,552	10,485,567	48,111,842

(1.) Preliminary. *Cumulative totals are not totals of columns since several years are omitted.

Hospital Insurance Trust Fund: Status, 1966-75
(In thousands)

| Period | Receipts | | | | Expenditures | | Total assets |
	Net con- tribution income[1]	Transfers from gen- eral revenues[2]	Transfers from rail- road re- tirement account[3]	Net interest[4]	Net hospital and related service benefits[5]	Adminis- trative expenses[6]	
Jan. 1966-June 1975[7].	$56,009,868	$4,903,459	$585,067	$1,942,698	$52,070,915	$1,506,724	$9,864,443
Fiscal year:							
1966.	908,797			5,970		63,564	851,204
1967.	2,688,684	337,850	16,200	45,903	2,507,773	88,848	1,343,221
1968.	3,514,049	283,631	43,613	61,091	3,736,322	78,647	1,430,636
1969.	4,423,236	770,968	53,776	96,063	4,653,976	104,182	2,016,521
1970.	4,784,789	628,262	61,307	139,423	4,804,242	148,660	2,677,401
1971.	4,897,979	873,849	63,255	183,027	5,442,971	149,434	3,103,106
1972.	5,225,891	551,351	63,782	190,105	6,109,139	166,370	2,858,725
1973.	7,663,119	429,415	61,222	197,844	6,648,819	192,839	4,368,666
1974.	10,606,551	498,780	96,163	408,273	7,785,596	258,066	7,934,772
1975[7].	11,296,773	529,353	126,749	614,989	10,360,986	256,134	9,864,443

(1.)Represents amounts appropriated (estimated tax collections with suitable subsequent adjustments), after deductions for refund of estimated amount of employee-tax overpayment. (2.)Represents Federal Government transfers from general funds appropriations to meet costs of benefits for persons not insured for cash benefits under OASDHI or railroad retirement and for costs of benefits arising from military wage credits. (3.)Represents receipts under the financial interchange with railroad retirement account with respect to contributions for hospital insurance coverage of railroad workers. (4.)Represents interest and profit on investments after transfers of interest on administrative expenses reimbursed to the OASI trust fund and on amounts transferred from railroad accounts. (5.) Represents (1) payment vouchers on letters of credit issued to fiscal intermediaries under sec. 1816 and (2) direct payments to providers of services under sec. 1815 of the Social Security Act. (6.)Subject to subsequent adjustment among all 4 social security trust funds, for allocated cost of each operation. (7.)Preliminary.

Supplementary Medical Insurance Trust Fund: Status, 1966-75
(In thousands)

| Period | Receipts | | | Expenditures | | Total assets |
	Premium income[1]	Transfers from gen- eral revenues[2]	Net interest[3]	Net medical service benefits[4]	Adminis- trative expenses[5]	
Jan. 1966-June 1975[6].	$10,794,895	$11,568,981	$342,505	$18,992,734	$2,283,610	$1,430,037
Fiscal year:						
1967.	646,682	623,000	14,052	664,261	133,682	485,791
1968.	698,465	634,000	20,677	1,389,622	142,608	306,703
1969.	902,821	984,287	23,466	1,644,842	194,660	377,774
1970.	36,000	928,151	11,536	1,979,287	216,993	57,181
1972.	1,340,052	1,365,295	28,993	2,255,069	288,619	480,709
1973.	1,462,607	1,430,451	45,049	2,391,232	245,861	745,722
1974.	1,703,189	2,028,926	75,924	2,869,132	409,146	1,275,483
1975[6].	1,886,962	2,329,590	105,539	3,759,772	404,458	1,430,037

(1.)Represents voluntary premium payments from and in behalf of insured persons. (2.)Represents Federal Government transfers from general funds appropriations to match aggregate premiums paid. (3.)Represents interest and profit on investments after transfer of interest on administrative expenses reimbursed to the OASI trust fund (see footnote 5). (4.)Represents payment vouchers on letters of credit issued to carriers under section 1842 of the Social Security Act. (5.)Subject to subsequent adjustment among all 4 social security trust funds for allocated cost of each operation. (6.)Preliminary.

Employment and Training Services and Unemployment Insurance

Source: Manpower Administration, U.S. Department of Labor

The Federal-State Employment Service consists of the U.S. Employment Service and affiliated state employment services with their network of about 2,400 local offices. During fiscal year 1975, these offices made a total of 5.9 million placements, of which 4.4 million were in nonagricultural and 1.5 million in agricultural industries. Overall, 3.1 million different individuals were placed in employment.

The employment service works to refer employable applicants to job openings that use their highest skills and helps the unemployed obtain services or training to make them employable. It also provides special attention to help meet the needs of older workers, youth, minorities, the poor, handicapped workers, migrants, seasonal farmworkers, and workers who lose their jobs because of foreign trade competition. Special efforts are being made to improve services in rural areas.

The employment service helps employers find needed workers and offers many employer services, including job-related personnel assistance. To give employers a wider choice of workers and applicants access to more job openings, it has developed job banks, which provide computerized daily lists of all available jobs in a city or area. Statewide networks of job banks now serve 83% of the nation's population. Other activities include enforcing standards on housing, transportation, and other conditions for farm and woods workers recruited for jobs in other states.

Special Veterans Service

Veterans receive special services and absolute preference in placements at all employment service offices. During the year, these offices placed nearly 600,000 veterans in jobs, two-thirds of them veterans of the Vietnam era. The requirement that Federal contractors list job openings with the employment service continues to prove of particular benefit to veterans. During fiscal year 1975, these listings accounted for nearly one-fifth of the jobs in which veterans were placed. Other efforts included counseling on education, training, and job opportunities, given to 183,000 veterans.

Community Manpower System

The Comprehensive Employment and Training Act of 1973 sets up a new community manpower system to give people training and job-related services and place them in jobs. Under the new system, which replaces certain Federal manpower programs, all states and cities, counties, and combinations of local units with populations of 100,000 or more receive Federal grants to plan and run comprehensive manpower programs in their localities. The job-related services provided are much the same as those formerly offered by national programs, but they vary from one area to another, according to local decisions on the needs of the area's workers and the demands of its labor market. Among them are work experience, classroom and on-the-job training, education, job referral, and needed services such as child care and medical aid.

A major part of the community manpower system is transitional public service employment. Besides supporting public jobs provided by comprehensive manpower programs and public employment programs for areas with high jobless rates, CETA subsidizes public jobs authorized under emergency legislation enacted in December 1974. During the year, these programs created jobs for substantial numbers of unemployed workers across the country.

National Manpower Activities

The Federal role under the new system is to provide support and technical assistance to local programs; insure proper use of Federal money; and serve Indians, migrant and seasonal farmworkers, and others with particular job disadvantages. In addition, subsidized jobs for older workers are funded under the Older American Community Service Employment Act of 1973. The Federal Government also continues to administer some programs and act as the Federal partner in the employment service system and the unemployment insurance program. These responsibilities are carried out by the Department of Labor's Manpower Administration. Continuing national activities include apprenticeship, Job Corps, and the Work Incentive Program. Apprenticeship is conducted by employers, often jointly with labor unions, to train workers in a skilled trade on the job and in related classroom instruction. During the year, the Federal Government continued activities to guide, assist, and improve apprenticeship and give more minority members and women a chance to become apprentices. Job Corps, which trains disadvantaged youth largely at residential centers, introduced nontraditional training for women, including programs leading to union apprenticeship jobs in the construction trades. The Work Incentive Program provides manpower, placement, and other services to help people on Aid to Families with Dependent Children get and keep jobs. Despite a rising unemployment rate during the year, 172,000 WIN participants were placed in unsubsidized jobs.

Unemployment Insurance

Unlike old-age and survivors insurance, entirely a Federal program, the unemployment insurance program is a Federal-State system which provides insured wage earners with partial replacement of wages lost during involuntary unemployment. The program protects most workers in the industry, but few in agriculture. Some 71,300,000 jobs in commerce, industry, and government, including the Armed Forces, were covered under the Federal-State system during calendar year 1974. In addition, 594,250 railroad workers were insured against unemployment under a system administered by the Railroad Retirement Board.

Each state, as well as the District of Columbia and Puerto Rico, has its own law and operates its own program. The amount and duration of the weekly benefits are determined by state laws, based on prior wages and length of employment. States are required to extend the duration of benefits when unemployment rises to and remains above specified state or national levels; costs of extended benefits are shared by the state and Federal governments.

Under the Federal Unemployment Tax Act, as amended in 1970, the tax rate is 3.2% on the first $4,200 paid to each employee of employers with one or more employees in 20 weeks of the year or a quarterly payroll of $1,500. A credit of up to 2.7% is allowed for taxes paid under state unemployment insurance laws that meet certain criteria, leaving the Federal share at 0.5% of taxable wages, from which the Federal government pays its share of the cost of extended benefits and makes grants to the states to cover the administrative costs of the unemployment insurance and employment service programs. Grants from this source for employment service administrative costs are limited to that proportion of total employment service costs that is attributable to the covered work force.

Social Security Requirement

The Social Security Act requires, as a condition of such grants, prompt payment of due benefits. The Federal Unemployment Tax Act provides safeguards for workers' right to benefits if they refuse jobs that fail to meet certain labor standards. Through the Unemployment Insurance Service of the Manpower Administration, the Secretary of Labor determines whether states qualify for grants and for tax offset credit for employers.

Benefits are financed solely by employer contributions, except in Alaska, Alabama, and New Jersey, where employees also contribute. Benefits are paid through the public employment offices, at which unemployed workers must register for work and to which, they must report regularly for referral to a possible job during the time when they are drawing weekly benefit payments. During the 1974 calendar, year, $5.9 billion in benefits were paid under the state unemployment insurance programs to 7,730,000 beneficiaries, representing compensation for 117,615,600 weeks of unemployment. They received an average weekly payment of $64.25 for total unemployment for an average of 12.7 weeks.

Federal Worker Benefits

Title 5, chapter 85 of the U.S. Code provided unemployment insurance protection during calendar year 1973 to about 2,844,000 Federal civilian employees

and about 2,202,000 members of the Armed Forces. Benefits for unemployed Federal workers and ex-servicemen are financed through direct Federal appropriations but are paid by the state agencies as agents of the Federal government.

During calendar year 1974 a total of $148,733,228 was paid to 105,482 unemployed Federal civilian workers for a total of 2,091,089 weeks of unemployment. The average weekly payment was $65.73 and was paid for an average of 18.9 weeks. A total of $249,220,437 was paid to 248,535 unemployed ex-servicemen for 3,710,256 weeks of unemployment. The average weekly benefit was $68.15 and was paid for an average of 13.7 weeks.

Employment Security

Source: Manpower Administration, U.S. Dept. of Labor

Fiscal year 1974-75, State Program Only

State	Insured claimants[1] (1,000)	Benefici-aries[2] (1,000)	Exhaus-tions[3] (1,000)	Initial claims[4] (1,000)	Total[5] (1,000)	Avg. weekly b'fit for total unemp'ment (dollars)	Funds available for b'fits June 30, 1975[6] (millions)	Employe subj. to state law March 31, 1975 (1,000)
Alabama	219	197	40	376	$116,304	$56.70	$ 50	54
Alaska	24	22	4	47	23,532	71.93	55	8
Arizona	107	94	31	215	85,036	64.96	111	47
Arkansas	132	116	26	276	74,907	57.77	22	41
California	1,574	1,248	360	2,801	(8)	67.31	(8)	398
Colorado	88	45	16	153	56,806	79.94	67	53
Connecticut	274[7]	252	54	566	(8)	75.43	(8)	68
Delaware	42	39	10	84	39,993	72.70	14	12
District of Columbia	37	31	10	46	44,085	88.52	21	17
Florida	398	300	113	635	237,842	66.02	209	161
Georgia	383	336	96	550	188,410	58.81	339	85
Hawaii	45	36	11	57	37,758	74.46	10	17
Idaho	38	35	9	81	23,199	64.73	52	18
Illinois	575	499	117	1,022	449,619	70.24	275	192
Indiana	349	294	82	664	208,858	61.65	258	82
Iowa	101	76	20	156	61,921	69.68	94	58
Kansas	73	63	15	117	46,173	64.00	137	46
Kentucky	187	169	34	280	114,199	63.17	169	55
Louisiana	167	117	36	234	90,415	59.24	141	61
Maine	74	81	24	169	47,414	55.94	7	22
Maryland	183	166	42	371	146,610	70.58	86	67
Massachusetts	537[7]	389	142	794	434,394	71.34	—5	114
Michigan	1,326[7]	732	235	1,766	742,479	73.42	86	145
Minnesota	162	156	54	265	144,875	67.11	4	71
Mississippi	116	94	16	204	46,586	47.62	104	36
Missouri	276	237	56	622	176,023	61.12	162	85
Montana	36	28	9	63	20,955	56.51	10	19
Nebraska	64	49	16	88	37,213	63.26	41	32
Nevada	43	46	17	110	45,946	69.90	10	15
New Hampshire	89	71	3	121	35,158	59.13	39	19
New Jersey	611	536	199	986	600,292	74.91	22	142
New Mexico	35	32	8	80	23,991	53.25	37	23
New York	1,142	900	277	2,323	1,106,201	71.38	911	382
North Carolina	541	461	59	1,267	239,995	56.53	411	94
North Dakota	15	13	3	24	9,943	59.86	20	14
Ohio	616	531	91	1,186	500,630	77.50	492	179
Oklahoma	95	74	23	162	50,096	54.02	49	50
Oregon	160	142	29	373	120,824	64.23	55	50
Pennsylvania	824	698	114	1,716	769,007	77.03	199	193
Puerto Rico	150	140	78	300	89,070	(8)	8	39
Rhode Island	110[7]	88[7]	30[7]	229	78,238	66.51[7]	13	22
South Carolina	257[7]	230	37	397	130,667	60.57	135	43
South Dakota	13	13	3	23	7,883	56.86	21	15
Tennessee	325	251	55	493	160,491	55.18	247	64[7]
Texas	312	227	73	508	137,850	53.37	287	206
Utah	49	43	11	82	33,851	67.26	40	24
Vermont	38	25	7	57	24,426	65.98	2	12
Virginia	210	179	28	313	(8)	64.68	(8)	75
Washington	195	192	68	542	176,638	68.06	—50	72
West Virginia	93	85	13	157	48,916	55.84	93	27
Wisconsin	272	217	40	487	212,504	78.14	207	84
Wyoming	9	7	1	14	4,972	62.36	29	11
Total	13,789[7]	11,104[7]	2,947[7]	24,651	$8,303,296	$67.91[7]	$5,795[7]	3,920[7]

(1) Claimants whose base-period earnings or whose employment—covered by the unemployment insurance program—was sufficient to make them eligible for unemployment insurance benefits as provided by State law. (2) Based on number of first payments. (3) Based on final payments. Some claimants shown, therefore, actually experienced their final week of compensable unemployment toward the end of the previous fiscal year but received their final payments in the current fiscal year. Similarly, some claimants who served their last week of compensable unemployment toward the end of the current fiscal year did not receive their final payment in this fiscal year and hence are not shown. A final week of compensable unemployment in a benefit year results in the exhaustion of benefit rights for the benefit year. Claimants who exhaust their benefit rights in one benefit year may be entitled to further benefits in the following benefit year. (4) Excludes intrastate transitional claims to reflect more nearly instances of new unemployment. Includes claims filed by inter-state claimants in the Virgin Islands. (5) Adjusted for voided benefit checks and transfers under interstate combined wage plan. (6) Sum of balance in State clearing accounts, benefit payment accounts, and unemployment trust fund accounts maintained in the U.S. Treasury. (7) Preliminary. (8) Information not available.

How and Where to Get Help on Consumer Complaints
by Kenneth C. Johnston

Consumers complaining about faulty merchandise or shoddy repair services can get help through customer relations offices in many corporations as well as through new or expanded government agencies.

Many big businesses now provide phone numbers (some toll-free) or addresses where complainants can receive courteous consideration and have some hope of action.

New government services are also available to consumers. A new federal law, providing that guaranteed products must, if faulty, be repaired or replaced within "a reasonable time," took effect July 4, 1975, on goods made after that date. It also empowered the Federal Trade Commission to sue makers on behalf of consumers and provided for fines for repeated offenses. Congress again prepared a bill creating a federal Consumer Protection Agency but President Ford said he would veto it as such an agency would be "unnecessary and costly."

The range of services open to consumers includes Better Business Bureaus, government prosecutors, small claims courts, and local government consumer agencies.

There are also industry and trade associations and these newspapers and radio stations which intercede for readers or listeners.

What Corporations Provide

Here's what some big companies suggest you do if you can't get satisfaction from your local dealer:

Ford: Phone or write Ford Parts & Service Div., district office (see phone book or ask local Ford dealer); or phone 800 648-4848 (free call) for all vehicles made by Ford.

Chrysler: Phone or write Chrysler Corp., Customer Service (ask dealer or see phone book); or write to: Consumer Affairs, Chrysler Corp., P.M. Box 856, Detroit, Mich. 48231; include your own phone no.

General Motors: Phone or write GM zone office nearest you (listed in your owner's manual). If still unsatisfied, phone or write Divisional Owner Relations Office (also in manual).

American Motors: Phone 800 521-7500 (free call).

Volkswagen: Try Customer Assistance Dept. at Volkswagen regional office (see owner's manual); or write Customer Assistance, Volkswagen of America, Englewood Cliffs, N.J. 07632.

General Electric: Write to Manager of Customer Relations, General Electric Co., 3135 Easton Turnpike, Fairfield, Conn. 06431. But, on appliances, the warranty tells customer where to write.

Westinghouse: Phone 800 245-0600 (free call) and ask for Betty Wade, national consumer service manager.

RCA: On any RCA product, phone 212 598-4921 or write Consumer Relations, RCA Corp., 30 Rockefeller Plaza, New York, N.Y. 10020.

Panasonic: Write nearest regional office listed on card accompanying product.

Admiral Corporation: Write Customer Relations Manager, 903 Morrissey Dr., Bloomington, Ill. 61701.

Whirlpool: Round-the-clock, toll-free service through 800 253-1301.

Union Carbide: The product or the guarantee has address to write to: or write Union Carbide Corp., Consumer Information, 270 Park Ave., New York, N.Y. 10017.

Exxon: Write to John B. Boatwright, Marketing Dept., Exxon, Box 2180, Houston, Tex. 77001, on product, service, or credit card complaints.

Gulf Oil: See phone book or dealer for nearest Gulf Oil district office or write Gulf Oil Corp., 1290 Ave. of the Americas, New York, N.Y. 10019, on products or service; for credit card troubles, see address on bill.

Mobil Oil: See dealer or phone book for regional Customer Relations Dept., Mobil Oil Corp., in Chicago, Los Angeles, Philadelphia or Scarsdale, N.Y. For credit card troubles, write Mobil Oil, Credit Card Customer Relations Department, 150 E. 42d St., New York, N.Y. 10017.

Texaco: See dealer or phone book for nearest Texaco, Inc., division office; if not satisfied, write Texaco, Inc., Retail Sales Office, 135 E. 42d St., New York, N.Y. 10017.

ARCO: See phone book or dealer for Atlantic Richfield district office or write to Atlantic Richfield Co., Consumer Relations, P.O. Box 2679 T.A., Los Angeles, Cal. 90051. On credit cards, use free "800" phone no. shown on bill.

Goodyear: See dealer or phone book for Goodyear Tire & Rubber Co. customer service representative at district office, or write Director of Consumer Affairs, Goodyear Tire & Rubber Co., 1144 E. Market St., Akron, Ohio 44316.

Firestone: See dealer or phone book, under Firestone Tire & Rubber Co., for district office, contact consumer affairs representative there (in some 35 cities); or phone 800 321-9638 (free call).

Sears, Roebuck: Ask for Customer Service at the store; then, the store manager; finally, write Sears, Roebuck & Co., Customer Relations, Sears Tower, Chicago, Ill. 60684.

J. C. Penney: See store manager; if unsatisfied, write Patrick Naef, Customer Relations Dept., J. C. Penney Co., Avenue of the Americas, New York, N.Y. 10019.

Woolworth's: See store manager; if not satisfied, write F.W. Woolworth Co., 233 Broadway, New York, N.Y. 10007; Attention Consumer Relations Dept.

Kresge's: See section supervisor; then, store manager; finally, get from manager address of S.S. Kresge Co. regional office, write to Customer Relations there.

Kodak: See phone book under Eastman Kodak Co. for Kodak Consumer Center (in some 35 cities) for free minor adjustments and advice; or write Consumer Photo Information Dept., Eastman Kodak Co., 343 State St., Rochester, N.Y. 14650.

A & P: See store manager or phone book under A & P Food Stores or Great Atlantic & Pacific Tea Co. for Customer Relations Dept. (in 28 cities); finally, write Executive Office, A & P Food Stores. 2 Paragon Dr., Montvale N.J. 07645.

DuPont: See dealer or phone book under duPont de Nemours, Product Information (in 8 major cities), or write duPont Co., Wilmington, Del. 19898.

General Foods: Write to General Foods Corp., 250 North St., White Plains, N.Y. 10625.

Procter & Gamble: Write Consumer Services, P.O. Box 599, Cincinnati, Ohio 45201. If possible, include your phone number, times you can be reached and name and serial number from the product package.

United Van Lines: Call toll-free 800-325-3870, ask for Bette Malone.

Avis: Write Customer Service Dep't., Avis Rent A Car System, 900 Old Country Road, Garden City, N.Y. 11530.

Hertz: Phone 212 598-4921 or write Consumer Relations, RCA Corp., 30 Rockefeller Plaza, New York, N.Y. 10020.

Government Agencies

There are numerous government agencies which can be helpful:

Cities: Some have Offices of Consumer Complaints or Depts. of Consumer Affairs (see phone book). In N.Y. City, for example, the department will investigate the complaint, then may try to work out a settlement; it may sue on behalf of a consumer, issue violation notices, hold hearings and fine a company or revoke or suspend a company's license to operate in the city.

Many towns and counties also have consumer protection agencies.

States likewise offer aid to the unhappy consumer.

Usually, it is a part of the Attorney General's office. Write or phone the Attorney General, Attention Consumer Protection Office, in your state.

Nationally, one may write to the Bureau of Consumer Protection, Federal Trade Commission, Washington, D.C. 20580, or the nearest FTC regional office.

The Consumer Product Safety Commission, a federal agency created in 1973, offers a toll-free number, 800 638-2666, where you can find out if a particular product has been declared unsafe or complain about one you believe is hazardous. If enough complaints are received, the commission will investigate and can order the product banned.

For a complaint against an airline (fares, baggage, service, delays), write Office of the Consumer Advocate, Civil Aeronautics Board, Washington, D.C. 20428.

In **Canada,** one may write the Director, Trade Practices Branch, Dept. of Consumer and Corporate Affairs, 219 Laurier Ave. West, Ottawa, Ontario.

Other Industry Aids

Within industry groups there are industry and trade associations which may be helpful. One which claims an excellent record in handling a large number of complaints is MACAP, the **Major Appliance Consumer Action Panel,** 20 North Wacker Drive, Chicago, Ill. 60606. You may write or make a free, collect phone call to 312 236-3165, if you don't get satisfaction from a manufacturer of home laundry equipment, range, refrigerator, freezer, room air conditioner, water heater, dehumidifier, dishwasher, disposer, gas incinerator, or humidifier. Give full details.

A similar organization is CRICAP, the **Carpet and Rug Industry Consumer Action Panel,** Box 1568, Dalton, Ga. 30720. Write them, if the dealer and maker won't cooperate, giving full details and your phone number.

Among industry complaint centers sponsored by the U.S. Chamber of Commerce are:

American Apparel Manufacturers Assn., 1611 N. Kent St., Arlington, Va. 22209.

American Footwear Manufacturers Assn., 342 Madison Ave., N.Y. 10017.

Direct Mail Advertising Assn., 230 Park Ave., New York, N.Y. 10017.

Direct Selling Assn., 1730 M St. N.W., Washington, D.C. 20036. (On door-to-door sales.)

Master Photo Dealers and Finishers Assn., 603 Lansing Ave., Jackson, Mich. 49202.

Mobile Homes Manufacturing Assn., 14650 Lee Rd., Chantilly, Va. 22021.

National Assn. of Furniture Manufacturers, 8401 Connecticut Ave., Suite 911, Washington, D.C. 20015.

National Employment Assn., 2000 K St. N.W., Washington, D.C. 20006. (For employment agencies.)

National Automobile Dealers Assn., 2000 K St. N.W., Washington, D.C. 20006.

National Consumer Finance Assn., 1000 16th St. N.W., Washington, D.C. 20036.

National Institute of Drycleaning, 909 Burlington Ave., Silver Spring, Md. 20910.

The Council of Better Business Bureaus has a central office; complaints about nationwide products, especially, may be sent to it: Council of Better Business Bureaus, Trade Practices Dept., 1150 17th St. N.W., Washington, D.C. 20036. The council will seek solutions for complaints.

Don't Forget

As a complaining consumer you will find it helpful to provide whatever agency you appeal to with copies of receipts and guarantees (not the actual receipts). Be as specific as possible about the dealer's name and address, purchase date, price, name, and serial number (if any) of the product, places you may already have sought relief, with dates. Don't forget your name, address, and phone number (some companies or agencies may want to serve you as rapidly as possible and may need further information).

The consumer may even return the favor in some cases and help the manufacturer: as a Procter & Gamble spokesman points out, some manufacturers will want the consumer to hold on to the offending product so that the maker can analyze it, find out what went wrong, and try to prevent its happening again.

Consumers' Association of Canada

The Consumers' Association of Canada is a voluntary, non-profit organization, founded in 1947. CAC's aims are:

(a) to unite the strength of consumers to improve the standards of living in Canadian homes;
(b) to study consumer problems and make recommendations for their solution;
(c) to bring the views of consumers to the attention of governments, trade, and industry, and provide a channel from these to the consumer;
(d) to obtain and provide consumer information, counselling, research, and tests on consumer goods and services.

CAC publishes bi-monthly, bi-lingual magazines, Canadian Consumer and Le Consommateur Canadien, circulation 93,000, which provide test results on products, information on consumer legislation and other consumer concerns.

There are 89 local associations and consumer committees in French and English across Canada, also 2 territorial and 10 provincial branches.

Some of CAC's achievements are in the areas of packaging and labelling, hazardous products, safety standards, selling practices, and food and drug regulations.

The national office is located at 801-251 Laurier Ave. West, Ottawa, Ontario, K1P 5Z7.

Consumer Credit Statistics

Source: Federal Reserve System (Estimated amounts outstanding. In millions of dollars)

End of year or month	Total	Installment credit					Noninstallment credit			
		Total	Automobile paper	Other consumer goods paper	Repair and modernization loans	Personal loans	Total	Single payment loans	Charge Accounts	Service credit
1960......	56,141	42,968	17,658	11,545	3,148	10,617	13,173	4,507	5,329	3,337
1970......	127,163	102,064	35,184	31,465	5,070	30,345	25,099	9,675	7,968	7,456
1971......	138,394	111,295	38,664	34,353	5,413	32,865	27,099	10,585	8,350	8,164
1972......	157,564	127,332	44,129	40,080	6,201	36,922	30,232	12,256	9,002	8,974
1973......	180,486	147,437	51,130	47,530	7,352	41,425	33,049	13,241	9,829	9,979
1974......	190,121	156,124	51,689	52,009	8,162	44,264	33,997	12,979	10,134	10,884
1975, June..	186,099	152,668	50,927	49,519	7,973	44,249	33,431	12,470	9,449	11,512

Interest Laws and Consumer Finance Loan Rates

Source: Revised by Roger S. Barrett of Chicago, Editor Consumer Finance Law Bulletin

Most states have laws regulating interest rates. These laws fix a legal or conventional rate which applies when there is no contract for interest. They also fix a general maximum contract rate, but in many states there are so many exceptions that the general contract maximum actually applies only to exceptional cases.

1. Legal rate of interest. The legal or conventional rate of interest applies to money obligations when no interest rate is contracted for and also to judgments. The rate is usually 6% a year; 5% or 7% in some states.

2. General maximum contract rates. General interest laws in most states set the maximum rate between 8% and 12% per year. The general maximum is fixed by the State Constitution rather than by statute at 10% per year in Arkansas, California, Tennessee, and Texas. Loans to corporations are frequently exempted or subject to a higher maximum. In recent years, it has also been common to provide special rates for home mortgage loans. Courts generally hold that installment sale charges are not interest, but installment sale charges are limited by laws in many states.

3. Specific enabling acts. In many states special statutes permit industrial loan companies and banks to charge interest and fees without regard to installment payments which yield 1½% a month or more. Laws regulating charge accounts and credit cards generally limit charges to 1½% per month. Credit unions may generally charge 1% a month. Pawnbrokers' rates vary widely. Building and loan associations, and loans insured by the F.H.A., are also specially regulated.

4. Consumer finance loan statutes. Most consumer finance loan statutes are based on early models drafted by the Russell Sage Foundation (1916-42) to provide small loans to wage earners under license and other protective regulations. Since 1969, however, the model has frequently been the Uniform Consumer Credit Code which applies to credit sales and loans for consumer purposes up to $25,000. In general, licensed lenders may charge 2½% or 3% a month for $300 or less and reduced rates for additional amounts up to $2,000 or more. A number of states permit add-on rates of 17% to 20% ($17 to $20 per $100) a year of the original principal for $300 and lower rates for additional amounts. An add-on of 17% ($17 per $100) per year yields about 2½% per month when the loan is paid in equal monthly installments. In the table below unless otherwise stated, monthly and annual rates are based on reducing principal balances, annual add-on rates are based on the original principal for the full term, and two or more rates apply to different portions of balance or original principal.

The states with consumer finance loan laws and the rates of charge as of October 1, 1975, are as follows:

Maximum rate — Monthly unless otherwise stated — Maximum rate

- Ala. . . . Annual add-on: 15% to $500, 10% to $1,000, 8% to $2,000. Over $2,000, 8% add-on on entire balance. Higher rates for loans up to $300.
- Alas. . . . 3% to $400, 2% to $800, 1% to $1,500, 5% to $50.
- Ariz. . . . 3% to $300, 2% to $600, 1½ to $1,500, 1% to $2,500.
- Cal. . . . 2½% to $225, 2% to $625, 1½% to $1650, 1% to $10,000 (1½% min.).
- Colo. . . . 36% per annum to $300, 21% to $1,000, 15% to $25,000 (18% min.).
- Conn. . . Annual Add-on: 17% to $300, 11% to $5,000.
- Del. . . . Annual Discount: 9% for 1st 36 mos., 6% for remaining months; plus 2% fee.
- Fla. . . . 30% per annum to $300, 24% to $600, 16% to $2,500.
- Haw. . . . 3½% to $100, 2½% to $300.
- Idaho. . . 36% per annum to $390, 21% to $1,300, 15% to $32,500 (18% min.).
- Ill. . . . . 3% to $150, 2% to $300, 1% to $800.
- Ind. . . . 36% per annum to $330, 21% to $1,100, 15% to $30,000 (18% min.).
- Ia. . . . . 3% to $250, 2% to $400, 1½% to $1,000.
- Kan. . . . 36% per year to $300, 21% to $1,000, 14.45% to $25,000 (18% min.).
- Ky. . . . . 3% to $300, 2% to $1,000, 1% to $1,200; or annual add-on of 20% to $300; 16% to $800, 13% to $1,200.
- La. . . . . 36% per annum to $800, 27% to $2,000, 21% to $3,500, 15% to $25,000 (18% min.).
- Me. . . . 30% per annum to $300, 21% to $1,000, 15% to $25,000 (18% min.).
- Md. . . . 3% to $300, 2% to $500.
- Mass. . . 2½% to $200, 2% to $600; 1¾% to $1,000, ¾% to $3,000.
- Mich. . . . 2½% to $400, 1¼% to $1,500.
- Minn. . . . 2¾% to $300, 1½% to $600, 1¼% to $1200 plus fee of $1 per $100.
- Miss. . . . 36% per annum to $600, 33% to $1,800, 24% to $4,500, 12% over $4,500.
- Mo. . . . 2.218% to $500, 10% per annum on any remainder.
- Mont. . . . Annual add-on; 20% to $300, 16% to $500, 12% to $1,000, 10% to $7,500. Special rate to $90.
- Neb. . . . 30% per annum to $300, 24% to $500, 18% to $1,000, 12% to $3,000.
- Nev. . . . Annual add-on: 9% to $1,000, 8% to $2,500; monthly fee of 1% on first $200 and ½% on next $200; over $2,500 to $10,000 annual interest is 17.74%.
- N.H. . . . 2% to $600, 1½% to $1,500, 1½% on larger loans to $5,000.
- N.J. . . . 24% per annum to $500, 22% to $1,500, 18% to $2,500.
- N.M. . . . 3% to $150, 2½% to $300, 1% to $2,500 (1½% min.).
- N.Y. . . . 2½% to $100, 2% to $300, 1½% to $900, 1¼% to $2,500.
- N.C. . . . 3% to $300, 1½% to $1,500. Special rate up to $95.
- N.D. . . . 2½% to $250, 2% to $500, 1¾% to $750, 1½% to $2,500.
- Ohio . . . Annual add-on: 16% to $500, 9% to $1,000, 7% to $2,000; or equivalent simple interest rate.
- Okla. . . . 30% per annum to $300, 21% to $1,000, 15% to $25,000. Special rates to $100 (18% min.).
- Ore. . . . 3% to $300, 1¾% to $1,000, 1¼% to $5,000. Over $5,000, 1½%.
- Pa. . . . 3% to $150, 2% to $300, 1% to $600.
- P.R. . . . Annual Add-on: 20% to $300, 7% to $600.
- R.I. . . . 3% to $300, 2½% for loans between $300 and $800; 2% for larger loans to $2,500.
- S.C. . . . Annual add-on: 20% to $100, 18% to $300, 9% to $1,000; 7% for larger loans to $7,500, plus service fee. Special rate to $150.
- S.D. . . . 2½% to $300, 2% to $600, 1½% to $1,200, 1% to $2,500; $2 minimum.
- Tenn. . . . 7½% per annum discount plus fees; no size limit.
- Texas . . Annual add-on: 18% to $300, 8% to $2,500. Special rates to $100.
- Utah . . . 36% per annum to $390, 21% to $1,300, 15% to $32,500 (18% min.).
- Vt. . . . . Annual add-on of 14% to $1,500.
- Va. . . . . 2½% to $500, 1½% to $1,500; annual add-on of 17% to $500, 13% to $1,000, 11% to $1,500.
- Wash. . . 3% to $300, 1½% to $500, 1% to $1,000; $1 minimum.
- W.Va. . . 36% per year to $200, 24% to $600, 18% to $1,200.
- Wis. . . . Annual Discount: 9½% on first $1,000, 8% to $3,000 up to 36 months; 18% per annum for larger loans.
- Wyo. . . . 36% per annum to $300, 21% to $1,000, 15% to $25,000 (18% min.).

ECONOMICS

Measuring Employment and Unemployment

by Geoffrey H. Moore, former U.S.
Commissioner of Labor Statistics

During 1974 the unemployment rate averaged 5.6%, a relatively high figure by historical standards. At the same time, the percentage of the population of working age that had jobs averaged 57%, exceeding any preceding year since World War II and probably before that. According to the unemployment rate, the economy was a considerable distance away from full employment. According to the employment ratio, it was more fully employed than ever before. Which is the most appropriate guide to the hypothetical condition of full employment?

Although no categorical answer can be given, a substantial case can be made for the employment ratio on the grounds of its objectivity, its statistical reliability, and its close relation to wage and price inflation . . .

With respect to objectivity, the concept of employment is firmer than the concept of unemployment. Having a job and being paid for it is, for the most part, an observable experience . . . .

Who Is Unemployed?

The concept of unemployment is quite different. For those who have had a job and have just been laid off, the situation may be obvious. Nevertheless, unless the worker is doing something to seek work, he will not be counted as unemployed according to the definition used in the United States. Moreover, those who are unemployed because they have been laid off usually constitute less than half of the unemployed. The rest have either quit their jobs voluntarily or have not recently (or ever) had a job . . . .

Seeking a job is not as clear-cut a condition as having a job. One can seek work now and then, or systematically. One can seek a job, yet turn down one or more offers. One can set realistic or unrealistic standards for pay, hours, type of work or location. Or one can give up seeking a job because none is to be found, yet be quite ready to take one if the opportunity comes along. Indeed, not a few persons become employed without having been unemployed in the strict sense of the term.

With respect to statistical reliability, the employment figures also have an edge. Because the number of unemployed is much smaller than the number who are employed, the former is subject to a much larger sampling error than the latter. The sampling variability of the unemployment count is somewhat less than 2%; for the employment count is about one-fourth of 1%. Moreover, seasonal variations are easier to eliminate in employment than in unemployment so the results are less subject to revision . . . .

The labor force, since it includes the unemployed, is subject to many of the same problems that pertain to the identification of who is unemployed. The population figure, of course, is free of these definitional difficulties. Similarly, the labor force figure is subject to sampling error while the population figure is not . . . .

The employment ratio is quite closely related to the rate of change in the consumer price index during the same year. High employment ratios have been associated with high rates of inflation . . . There has been relatively little inflation when the percentage employed has been in the range of 53.5% to 55.5%, but higher employment ratios have been associated with increasingly sharp advances in the rate of inflation.

Moreover, the relation is reversible. Peak years in the business cycle bring forth higher employment ratios and higher inflation rates while trough years do the opposite. However, a reduction in the employment ratio during a recession is associated with a smaller reduction in inflation than an equal increase in the employment ratio during an expansion phase of the cycle. Perhaps this is an additional bit of evidence that it is harder to get rid of inflation than to generate it.

During the current recession the employment ratio declined from its all-time high, 57.7%, in October 1973 to 54.9% in March 1975 . . . Although the reduction in employment has been sharp, the percentage employed in March and April was higher than in any previous recession year, save 1970. As the historical relation would lead one to expect, the rate of increase in consumer prices has declined also . . . .

In general, rates of wage and price inflation have been far more closely correlated with the employment ratio than with the unemployment rate. The relation between inflation and unemployment is a very loose one, despite all the discussion about the trade-off. In particular, 1974 was off in a class by itself, with considerable unemployment and a great deal of inflation. What was largely overlooked was the record high employment ratio . . . .

Unemployment Rate, Employment Ratio and the Rate of Change in the Consumer Price Index

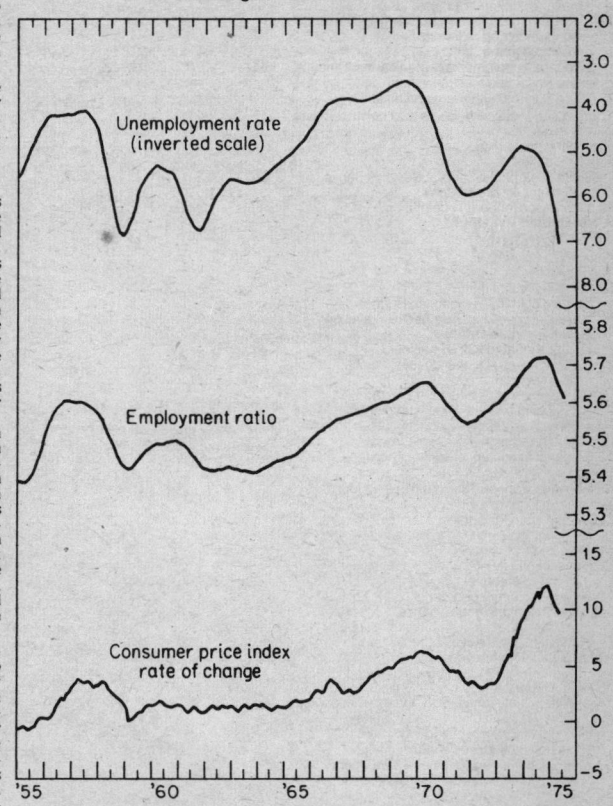

Note: The employment rate and employment ratio are 12-month moving averages; the rate of change in the Consumer Price Index is the percent change over 12 months. All series are plotted at the end of the 12-month period.

United States Budget Receipts and Outlays—1974-1975

Source: Treasury Department; each fiscal year ends June 30 (data preliminary)
(thousands of dollars)

Classification	Fiscal 1975	Fiscal 1974
Net Receipts		
Individual income taxes	122,321,565	118,951,631
Corporate income taxes	40,626,750	38,619,654
Social insurance taxes and contributions:		
Federal old-age and survivors insurance	55,206,915	47,777,693
Federal disability insurance	7,250,217	6,147,425
Federal hospital insurance	11,257,523	10,555,714
Railroad retirement taxes	1,489,201	1,411,333
Total employment taxes and contributions	**75,203,856**	**65,892,164**
Other insurance and retirement:		
Unemployment	6,764,177	6,836,546
Federal supplementary medical insurance	1,899,298	1,704,371
Federal employees retirement	2,508,918	2,302,047
Civil service retirement and disability	52,434	44,925
Total social insurance taxes and contributions	**86,428,682**	**76,780,053**
Excise taxes	16,541,971	16,843,668
Estate and gift taxes	4,589,361	5,034,641
Customs duties	3,665,929	3,334,139
Deposits of earnings-Federal Reserve Banks	5,776,550	4,845,423
Petroleum import license fees	442,615	——
All other miscellaneous receipts	527,846	523,191
Net Budget Receipts	**280,920,983**	**264,932,401**
Net Outlays		
Legislative Branch	696,279	625,341
The Judiciary	283,760	205,188
Executive Office of the President:		
Office of Management and Budget	21,715	18,271
Special Office for Drug Abuse Prevention	33,677	21,463
Total Executive Office	**92,688**	**66,065**
Funds appropriated to the President:		
Appalachian regional development	310,304	289,452
Disaster relief	224,914	250,085
Expansion of defense production	831	−155,890
Indochina postwar reconstruction	494,395	246,316
Foreign assistance-security	1,017,323	1,201,211
Foreign assistance-development	1,544,980	1,400,015
Foreign assistance-contingency fund	4,239	25,224
Miscellaneous	2,180	72,766
Total funds appropriated to the President	**3,599,166**	**3,329,180**
Agriculture Department:		
Food stamp program	5,025,901	2,844,815
Total Agriculture Department	**10,209,986**	**9,766,891**
Commerce Department	1,585,019	1,455,271
Defense Department:		
Military personnel	24,938,377	23,728,188
Retired military personnel	6,241,772	5,127,554
Operation and maintenance	26,186,535	22,478,080
Procurement	16,034,560	15,241,248
Research and development	8,865,435	8,582,286
Military construction	1,461,458	1,406,540
Family housing	1,129,608	884,322
Civil defense	86,404	75,333
Military assistance, South Vietnamese forces	402,411	——
Revolving and management funds	206,725	268,069
Corps of Engineers and other civil	2,054,622	1,681,679
Total Defense Department	**87,476,798**	**79,307,123**
Health, Education and Welfare Department:		
Old-age and survivors benefits	54,839,138	47,847,417
Public assistance	5,121,747	5,423,353
Total HEW	**112,417,309**	**93,738,362**
Housing and Urban Development Department	7,501,635	4,785,815
Interior Department	2,182,340	1,792,603
Justice Department	2,067,062	1,796,523
Labor Department	17,635,349	8,966,129
State Department	843,542	735,227
Transportation Department	9,248,535	8,104,218
Treasury Department:		
Internal Revenue Service	1,958,491	1,595,415
Interest on the public debt	32,665,000	29,318,933
Total Treasury Department	**41,188,377**	**35,992,751**
Energy Research and Development Agency	3,198,211	2,362,202
Environmental Protection Agency	2,536,179	2,032,100
General Services Administration	−617,957	−275,831
National Aeronautics and Space Administration	3,267,571	3,252,305
Veterans Administration	16,578,839	13,336,873
Independent agencies:		
Action	177,265	166,748
Arms Control and Disarmament Agency	9,726	8,893
Board for International Broadcasting	49,858	50,674
Civil Aeronautics Board	80,884	88,513
Civil Service Commission	7,036,273	5,692,360
Commission on Civil Rights	6,920	6,056
Community Services Administration	540,219	680,474
Consumer Product Safety Commission	34,211	18,709

Classification **Net Outlays (cont'd)**	Fiscal 1975	Fiscal 1974
Corporation for Public Broadcasting	62,000	47,750
District of Columbia	429,312	332,132
Emergency Loan Guarantee Board	−7,144	−4,868
Equal Employment Opportunity Commission	56,662	42,098
Federal Communications Commission	47,938	38,124
Federal Deposit Insurance Corporation	−407,682	−233,733
Federal Energy Administration	120,697	29,580
Federal Home Loan Bank Board	924,200	−369,698
Federal Maritime Commission	7,229	6,475
Federal Mediation and Conciliation Service	15,497	11,782
Federal Power Commission	34,407	26,656
Federal Trade Commission	38,714	32,339
Foreign Claims Settlement Commission	1,272	5,630
Historical and Memorial Commissions	11,441	5,241
Indian Claims Commission	1,355	1,161
Intergovernmental Agencies	177,860	173,308
International Trade Commission	8,296	7,079
Interstate Commerce Commission	43,962	37,731
National Capital Planning Commission	1,742	1,509
National Credit Union Administration	−13,236	−12,615
National Foundation on the Arts and Humanities	128,082	96,324
National Labor Relations Board	60,936	55,073
National Science Foundation	662,128	651,298
National Transportation Safety Board	8,573	8,171
Nuclear Regulatory Commission	52,792	—
Occupational Safety Commission	5,292	4,596
Postal Service payment	1,874,741	1,698,000
Railroad Retirement Board	3,082,899	2,673,100
Securities and Exchange Commission	44,395	34,516
Selective Service System	48,462	59,503
Small Business Administration	590,630	753,147
Smithsonian Institution	103,103	84,265
Temporary Study Commissions	13,610	6,631
Tennessee Valley Authority	767,225	401,105
U.S. Information Agency	239,120	214,377
U.S. Railway Association	22,700	1,200
Water Resources Council	9,417	6,788
Other independent agencies	17,850	15,106
Total independent agencies	**17,221,831**	**13,663,309**
Undistributed offsetting receipts	−14,079,865	−16,645,662
Net Budget Outlays	**325,132,657**	**268,391,983**
Less net receipts	280,920,983	264,932,401
Deficit	**−44,211,674**	**−3,459,583**

United States Net Receipts and Outlays

Source: Treasury Department; annual statements for year ending June 30

Yearly average	Re- ceipts $1,000	Expend- itures $1,000	Yearly average	Re- ceipts $1,000	Expend- itures $1,000	Yearly average	Re- ceipts $1,000	Expend- itures $1,000
1789-1800[1]	5,717	5,776	1871-1875	336,830	287,460	1911-1915	710,227	720,252
1801-1810[2]	13,056	9,086	1876-1880	288,124	255,598	1916-1920[6]	3,483,652	8,065,333
1811-1820[2]	21,032	23,943	1881-1885	366,961	257,691	1921-1925	4,306,673	3,578,989
1821-1830[2]	21,928	16,162	1886-1890	375,448	279,134	1926-1930	4,069,138	3,182,807
1831-1840[2]	30,461	24,495	1891-1895	352,891	363,599	1931-1935[3]	2,770,973	5,214,874
1841-1850[2]	28,545	34,097	1896-1900	434,877	457,451	1936-1940[4]	4,960,614	10,192,367
1851-1860	60,237	60,163	1901-1905	559,481	535,559	1941-1945[4]	25,951,137	66,037,928
1861-1865	160,907	683,785	1906-1910	628,507	639,178	1946-1950[5][7][8]	39,047,243	42,334,534
1866-1870	447,301	377,642						

Fiscal Year	Receipts	Expenditures	Fiscal Year	Receipts	Expenditures
1955	60,389,743,895	64,569,972,817	1965	93,071,796,891	96,506,904,210
1958	69,116,717,311	71,936,171,353	1968	153,675,705,000	172,803,186,000
1959	67,915,348,624	80,342,335,375	1970	193,843,791,000	194,968,258,000
1960	77,763,460,220	76,539,412,798	1971	188,332,129,000	210,652,667,000
1961	77,659,424,905	81,515,167,453	1972[9]	215,262,638,670	238,285,906,846
1962	81,409,092,072	87,786,766,580	1973	232,191,842,000	246,603,359,000
1963	86,357,020,251	92,589,764,029	1974	264,847,484,000	268,342,952,000
1964	89,458,664,071	97,684,374,794	1975	280,920,983,000	325,132,657,000

(1) Average for period March 4, 1789, to Dec. 31, 1800.
(2) Years ended Dec. 31, 1801, to 1842; average for 1841-1850 is for the period Jan. 1, 1841, to June 30, 1850.
(3) Receipts from 1937 on have deducted appropriations to Federal old-age and survivors insurance trust fund.
(4) Expenditures for years 1932 through 1946 have been revised to include Government Corps. (wholly owned) etc. (net).
(5) Effective January 3, 1949, amounts refunded by the Government, principally for the overpayment of taxes, are being reported as deductions from total receipts rather than as expenditures. Also, effective July 1, 1948, payments to the Treasury, principally by wholly owned Government corporations for retirement of capital stock and for disposition of earnings, are excluded in reporting both budget receipts and expenditures. Neither of these changes affects the size of the budget surplus or deficit. Beginning 1931 figures in each case have been adjusted accordingly for comparative purposes.
(6) Figures for 1918 through 1946 are revised to exclude statutory debt retirement (sinking fund, etc.).
(7) Excludes $3 billion transferred to Foreign Economics Corporation Trust Fund.
(8) Includes $3 billion representing expenditures made from the FEC Trust Fund.
(9) Effective fiscal year 1972 loan repayments and loan disbursements will be netted against expenditures and known as outlays.

Summary of U.S. Receipts by Source and Outlays by Function

Source: U.S. Treasury Department (June 30, 1975 preliminary)

(in thousands)

Net Receipts Fiscal Year	1975	1974	1973
Individual income taxes	$122,321,565	$118,750,071	$103,245,521
Corporation income taxes	40,626,750	38,664,197	36,152,530
Social insurance taxes and contributions:			
Employment taxes and contributions	75,203,856	65,893,961	54,876,420
Unemployment insurance	6,764,177	6,906,711	6,051,483
Contributions for other insurance and retirement	4,460,650	4,048,681	3,614,046
Excise taxes	16,541,971	16,885,403	16,259,861
Estate and gift taxes	4,589,361	5,009,320	4,917,069
Customs	3,665,929	3,334,127	3,187,980
Miscellaneous	6,746,724	5,355,013	3,920,561
Total	280,920,983	264,847,484	232,225,472
Outlays			
National defense	88,288,891	78,792,890	76,023,290
International affairs and finance	4,214,921	4,175,456	3,132,253
Space research and technology	4,156,821	3,228,146	3,311,000
Agriculture and rural development	2,008,766	5,182,770	6,051,111
Natural resources	8,020,450	-989,552	559,471
Commerce and transportation	15,545,907	12,549,002	12,505,309
Community development and housing	4,482,364	5,129,221	4,162,197
Education and manpower	15,060,808	10,574,715	10,882,340
Health	27,447,554	21,501,547	18,393,281
Income security	109,315,276	84,075,160	72,949,571
Veterans benefits and services	16,598,623	13,369,846	12,004,029
Interest	31,035,387	28,101,163	22,835,562
General government	3,582,264	6,485,062	5,519,134
General revenue sharing	6,695,095	6,105,922	6,636,369
Undistributed intrabudgetary transactions	14,079,865	-9,938,397	-8,378,934
Total	325,132,657	268,342,952	246,525,985

United States Customs and Internal Revenue Receipts

Source: Treasury Department

Gross. Not reduced by appropriations to Federal old-age and survivors insurance trust fund or refunds or receipts. Data are for fiscal years.

Year	Customs	Internal Revenue	Year	Customs	Internal Revenue	Year	Customs	Internal Revenue
1930	$587,000,903	$3,039,295,014	1962	1,171,205,973	99,440,839,244	1969	2,318,962,000	187,792,337,000
1935	343,353,034	3,277,690,028	1963	1,240,537,884	105,925,395,281	1970	2,429,799,000	193,743,251,000
1940	348,590,635	5,303,133,988	1964	1,284,176,379	112,206,115,000	1971	2,589,973,339	188,332,129,000
1945	354,775,542	43,902,001,929	1965	1,477,548,820	114,428,991,753	1972	3,284,922,000	208,595,814,000
1950	422,650,329	39,448,607,109	1966	1,811,170,211	128,842,531,268	1973	3,175,268,000	232,191,842,000
1955	606,396,634	66,288,691,586	1967	1,971,799,790	147,899,815,000	1974	3,334,127,000	264,847,484,000
1960	1,123,037,579	91,774,802,823	1968	2,113,474,950	153,675,705,000	1975	3,665,929,000	277,255,054,000

U.S. Direct Investments Abroad, Countries and Industries

Source: Bureau of Economic Analysis, U.S. Dept. of Commerce

(Millions of Dollars)

	Book Value at Year-End		Net Capital Outflows		Reinvested Earnings		Earnings		Income	
	1972	1973	1972	1973	1972	1973	1972	1973	1972	1973
Total	94,337	107,268	3,517	4,872	4,715	8,124	11,485	17,495	6,925	9,415
By area										
Developed countries	64,359	74,084	1,988	3,631	3,710	6,147	6,880	10,330	3,331	4,299
Canada	25,771	28,055	350	540	1,384	1,846	2,251	2,846	989	1,126
Europe	30,817	37,218	1,168	2,939	1,892	3,476	3,721	5,956	1,847	2,470
Japan	2,375	2,733	229	36	183	311	362	548	168	222
Australia, New Zealand and South Africa	5,395	6,079	241	116	250	514	546	981	326	481
Developing countries	25,235	27,867	1,134	1,198	894	1,510	4,110	6,538	3,195	4,932
Latin American Rep. and other Western Hemisphere	16,798	18,452	300	673	732	1,028	1,656	2,628	967	1,622
Other Africa	3,091	2,830	126	-427	99	177	504	618	410	446
Middle East	1,992	2,682	353	588	-22	108	1,391	2,277	1,418	2,172
Other Asia and Pacific	3,354	3,903	355	365	85	198	558	1,014	399	692
International and unallocated	4,743	5,317	395	43	111	467	496	627	400	185
By industry										
Mining and smelting	7,110	7,483	382	201	41	143	419	675	395	548
Petroleum	26,363	29,567	1,603	1,417	563	1,927	3,311	6,183	2,826	4,325
Manufacturing	39,716	45,791	1,100	1,820	2,991	4,408	5,172	7,286	2,144	2,757
Other	21,249	24,427	433	1,434	1,119	1,645	2,583	3,351	1,560	1,785

Public Debt of the United States
Source: Treasury Department (p preliminary subject to revision. r revised)

Fiscal Year	Gross Debt (Dollars)	Per Cap. (Dollars)	Fiscal Year	Gross Debt (Dollars)	Per Cap. (Dollars)	Fiscal Year	Gross Debt (Dollars)	Per Cap. (Dollars)
1870..	2,436,453,269	61.06	1930..	16,185,309,831	131.51	1970..	370,918,706,950(r)	1,811.12
1880..	2,090,908,872	41.60	1940..	42,967,531,038	367.48	1971..	398,129,744,455(r)	1,923.12
1890..	1,132,396,584	17.80	1950..	257,357,352,351	1,696.67	1972..	427,260,460,940(p)	2,046.00
1900..	1,263,416,913	16.60	1960..	286,330,760,848	1,584.70	1973..	458,141,605,312(p)	2,177.30
1910..	1,146,939,969	12.41	1965..	317,273,898,984	1,630.46	1974..	475,059,815,732(p)	2,241.81
1920..	24,299,321,467	228.23	1968..	347,578,406,426(r)	1,727.72	1975..	533,189,000,000(p)	2,495.84

Appropriations by the Federal Government
Source: Treasury Department (Fiscal Year)

Year	Appropriations	Year	Appropriations	Year	Appropriations	Year	Appropriations
1890..	$395,430,284.26	1940..	$13,349,202,681.73	1953..	$94,916,821,231.67	1963..	$102,149,886,566.52
1895..	492,477,759.97	1944..	118,411,173,965.24	1954..	74,744,844,304.88	1965..	107,555,087,622.62
1900..	698,912,982.83	1945..	73,067,712,071.39	1955..	54,761,172,461.58	1967..	140,861,235,376.56
1905..	781,288,215.95	1946..	76,597,999,662.67	1956..	63,857,731,203.86	1968'..	195,908,743,535.65
1910..	1,044,433,622.64	1947..	40,823,734,061.18	1957..	70,717,305,080.55	1969..	203,049,351,090.91
1915..	1,122,471,919.12	1948..	42,098,608,820.42	1958..	77,145,934,082.25	1970..	222,200,021,901.52
1920..	6,454,596,649.56	1949..	47,357,993,957.59	1959..	82,055,863,758.58	1971..	247,623,820,964.75
1925..	3,748,651,750.35	1950..	52,867,672,466.21	1960..	80,169,728,902.87	1972..	247,638,104,722.57
1930..	4,665,236,678.04	1951..	67,966,083,088.46	1961..	89,229,575,129.94	1973..	275,554,945,383.88
1935..	7,527,559,327.66	1952..	127,788,153,262.97	1962..	91,447,827,731.00	1974..	311,728,034,120.95

(1.) This appropriation for 1968 incorporates for the first time the changes in the President's Budget for 1969, in consonance with those recommendations of the President's Commission on Budget Concepts which were adopted and implemented during fiscal year 1968.

Gross National Product, National Income, and Personal Income
Source: Department of Commerce. Office of Economic Analysis
(In millions of dollars) Includes Alaska and Hawaii beginning in 1960

	1950	1960	1970	1972	1973	1974
Gross National product	284,769	503,734	977,080	1,155,155	1,294,919	1,397,400
Less: Capital consumption allowances	18,342	43,408	87,254	102,357	110,818	119,500
Equals: Net national product	266,427	460,326	889,826	1,052,798	1,184,101	1,277,900
Less: Indirect business tax and nontax liability	23,334	45,200	93,461	109,541	119,191	126,900
Business transfer payments	778	1,878	3,989	4,610	4,866	5,200
Statistical discrepancy	1,488	-1,031	-6,392	-1,481	-4,?7	400
Plus: Subsidies minus current surplus of government enterprises	247	243	1,694	1,664		-2,900
Equals: National income	241,074	414,522	800,462	941,792	1,065,590	
Less: Corporate profits and inventory valuation adjustment	37,669	49,904	69,240	91,120	105,123	?600
Contributions for social insurance	6,870	20,672	57,708	73,729	91,231	10?.?0
Wage accruals less disbursement	24	0	0	-511	-56	-5?
Plus: Government transfer payments to persons	14,294	26,609	75,119	98,343	112,977	134,60?
Net Interest paid by gov't and consumers	7,198	15,083	30,998	32,713	38,327	42,300
Dividends	8,838	13,437	24,680	26,041	29,582	32,700
Business transfer payments	778	1,878	3,989	4,610	4,866	5,200
Equals: Personal income	227,619	400,953	808,290	939,161	1,655,044	1,150,500

National Income by Type of Income
(Millions of dollars)

	1960	1965	1970	1972	1973	1974
Compensation of employees	294,226	393,844	603,869	707,052	785,983	855,800
Wage and salaries	270,844	358,885	541,976	627,334	691,620	750,700
Private	222,108	289,621	426,875	493,276	545,060	592,400
Military	9,894	12,143	19,561	20,276	20,603	21,200
Government, civilian	38,842	57,121	95,540	113,782	125,957	137,100
Supplements to wages, sal	23,382	34,959	61,893	79,718	94,363	105,100
Empl. contrib. soc. ins.	11,380	16,217	29,717	39,002	48,407	53,600
Other labor income	12,002	18,742	32,176	40,716	45,956	51,400
Empl. contrib. priv. pen.	9,684	15,623	27,214	34,672	39,161	
Other	2,318	3,119	4,962	6,044	6,795	
Proprietors' income	46,209	57,253	66,919	74,227	96,089	93,000
Business and professional	34,244	42,416	50,017	53,987	57,560	61,200
Income unincorp. enterprises	34,263	42,796	50,723	55,104	59,835	—
Inventory valuation adj.	-19	-380	-706	-1,117	-2,275	—
Farm	11,965	14,837	16,902	20,240	38,529	31,800
Rental income of persons	15,822	18,952	23,938	24,148	26,140	26,500
Corp. prof., inv. adjust.	49,904	76,070	69,240	91,120	105,123	105,600
Corp. profits before tax	49,712	77,787	74,041	98,037	122,702	140,700
Corp. profits tax liability	23,032	31,326	34,789	42,687	49,788	55,700
Corp. profits after tax	26,680	46,461	39,252	55,350	72,914	85,000
Dividends	13,437	19,808	24,680	26,041	29,582	32,700
Undistributed profits	13,243	26,653	14,572	29,309	43,332	52,400
Inventory valuation adj.	192	-1,717	-4,801	-6,917	-17,579	-35,100
Net interest	8,361	18,217	36,496	45,245	52,255	61,600
National income	414,522	564,336	800,462	941,792	1,065,590	1,142,500

National Income by Industry
Source: Department of Commerce, Bureau of Economic Analysis
(Millions of dollars)

	1960	1965	1968	1970	1971	1972	1973
Agricul., forestry, fisheries	**16,852**	**21,017**	**22,080**	**25,582**	**26,218**	**30,395**	**50,609**
Farms	15,857	19,630	20,425	23,639	24,028	27,967	47,878
Agri. services, forestry, fisheries	995	1,417	1,655	1,943	2,190	2,428	2,731
Mining	**5,732**	**6,116**	**6,702**	**7,682**	**7,012**	**8,246**	**9,397**
Metal mining	817	908	888	1,177	970	1,035	1,210
Coal mining	1,253	1,332	1,429	2,157	2,052	2,375	2,411
Crude petroleum, natural gas	2,734	2,754	3,153	3,048	2,571	3,279	4,006
Nonmetallic min. & quar.	928	1,122	1,232	1,300	1,419	1,557	1,770
Contract construction	**20,810**	**29,116**	**36,270**	**42,791**	**46,692**	**51,694**	**57,077**
Manufacturing	**125,822**	**172,572**	**212,672**	**217,505**	**226,363**	**252,589**	**287,237**
Nondurable goods	**52,208**	**66,482**	**82,069**	**88,902**	**91,828**	**99,881**	**108,895**
Food, kindred products	12,225	14,495	17,130	19,530	19,866	20,774	21,438
Tobacco manufacturers	1,017	1,111	1,359	1,738	1,770	1,805	2,010
Textile mill products	4,488	5,837	7,123	7,419	7,379	8,237	8,734
Appa'l, other fabric prod.	4,953	6,556	8,307	8,634	8,950	9,564	10,279
Paper, allied products	4,707	5,929	7,338	7,970	8,041	9,318	10,440
Ptg., pub., allied indust.	6,655	8,746	10,766	11,929	12,401	13,622	14,887
Chemicals, allied products	9,159	12,648	15,614	16,342	16,827	18,236	21,032
Petroleum refining, related ind.	4,586	5,381	6,680	7,342	7,917	8,634	9,364
Rubber, misc. plastic products	2,809	3,949	5,477	5,776	6,482	7,497	8,364
Leather, leather products	1,609	1,830	2,275	2,222	2,195	2,194	2,347
Durable goods	**73,614**	**106,090**	**130,603**	**128,603**	**134,535**	**152,708**	**178,342**
Lumber, wood, except furn.	3,255	4,212	5,035	5,135	5,705	7,109	8,740
Furniture and fixtures	2,092	2,870	3,485	3,657	3,735	4,543	4,993
Stone, clay, glass products	4,640	5,713	6,329	6,894	7,517	8,533	9,867
Primary metal industries	11,103	14,735	15,871	15,961	15,325	17,404	22,025
Fabricated metal products	8,113	11,518	14,354	14,635	15,082	17,543	20,297
Machinery, except electrical	11,861	18,357	22,891	24,296	23,596	26,585	32,489
Electrical machinery	10,469	14,850	19,772	20,327	20,614	22,539	26,928
Trans. equip. exc. autos	8,270	11,361	16,435	14,347	13,750	15,066	15,653
Motor vehicles equipment	8,532	15,432	17,156	13,801	19,454	22,555	25,387
Instruments	2,954	4,170	5,742	5,843	5,843	6,477	7,202
Misc. manufacturing	2,325	2,872	3,533	3,707	3,914	4,354	4,761
Transportation	**18,177**	**23,150**	**26,909**	**29,824**	**32,819**	**36,008**	**40,381**
Railroad	6,718	7,047	6,992	7,358	8,083	8,464	9,587
Local suburban highway pass.	1,639	1,897	2,210	2,285	2,373	2,349	2,522
Motor freight trans., warehous'g.	5,840	8,317	10,326	11,632	13,295	14,924	17,060
Water transportation	1,654	1,990	2,476	2,502	2,341	2,551	2,705
Air transportation	1,400	2,697	3,556	4,374	5,030	5,863	6,343
Pipeline transportation	355	401	414	518	524	555	695
Transportation service	571	801	935	1,155	1,173	1,302	1,469
Communication	**8,237**	**11,241**	**14,131**	**16,787**	**17,826**	**19,966**	**21,064**
Telephone and telegraph	7,304	9,991	12,594	15,074	16,026	17,907	18,821
Radio broadcasting, television	933	1,250	1,537	1,713	1,800	2,059	2,243
Electric, gas, sanitary services.	**8,934**	**11,447**	**13,391**	**14,718**	**16,462**	**18,167**	**19,077**
Wholesale and retail trade	**64,396**	**84,302**	**106,069**	**121,274**	**130,900**	**139,682**	**155,888**
Wholesale trade	23,126	30,341	38,394	44,430	46,951	50,531	58,745
Retail trade	41,270	53,961	67,675	76,844	83,949	89,151	97,143
Finance, ins. and real estate	**45,940**	**61,857**	**77,755**	**89,944**	**100,139**	**107,865**	**117,821**
Banking	7,276	8,989	12,258	16,437	16,855	18,671	20,758
Credit agencies, holding, other investment co.	—435	—505	—1,209	—1,873	—1,480	—2,448	—4,049
Security, commodity brokers	1,243	1,903	4,023	2,675	3,864	4,259	3,364
Insurance carriers	4,641	5,186	6,520	8,544	10,484	11,801	12,018
Insurance agents, brokers, service	1,948	2,671	3,299	3,871	4,334	4,700	5,305
Real estate	31,267	43,613	52,864	60,294	66,082	70,882	80,425
Services	**44,371**	**64,076**	**85,721**	**102,876**	**109,824**	**120,137**	**134,570**
Hotels, other lodging places	2,111	2,788	3,744	4,236	4,490	5,029	5,654
Personal services	4,608	5,993	7,265	7,433	7,370	7,420	7,830
Misc. business services	5,093	8,413	11,490	13,984	14,508	15,965	18,471
Automobile repair, serv., garages	1,762	2,450	3,106	3,628	4,059	4,473	5,117
Misc. repair services	1,105	1,501	1,866	2,117	2,283	2,503	2,846
Motion pictures	894	1,205	1,535	1,565	1,542	1,624	1,745
Amusement, recreation services	1,661	2,221	2,783	3,244	3,389	3,870	4,278
Medical, other health services	10,724	16,256	23,250	29,942	32,822	36,378	41,127
Legal services	2,636	4,069	5,114	6,443	7,242	8,230	9,270
Education services	2,402	4,191	5,975	7,231	7,818	8,678	9,154
Nonprofit membership org.	3,815	5,306	6,955	8,376	9,024	9,791	10,780
Misc. professional services	3,761	5,719	8,009	9,847	10,318	11,195	13,120
Private households	3,799	3,964	4,629	4,830	4,959	5,021	5,178
Govt., govt. enterprises	**52,891**	**75,233**	**104,704**	**126,850**	**138,242**	**149,507**	**164,087**
Federal	21,868	33,458	46,058	53,414	56,497	59,677	63,056
General Govt.	25,524	28,450	39,496	45,164	47,563	50,281	52,816
Govt. Enterprises	3,656	5,008	6,562	8,250	8,934	9,396	10,240
State & local.	25,615	41,775	58,646	73,436	81,745	89,830	101,031
General Govt.	27,367	39,345	55,434	69,553	77,562	85,145	95,652
Government enterprises	1,752	2,430	3,212	3,883	4,183	4,685	5,379
Rest of the world	**2,360**	**4,179**	**4,736**	**4,625**	**6,952**	**7,536**	**8,382**
All industries, total	**414,522**	**564,336**	**711,140**	**800,462**	**859,449**	**941,792**	**1,065,590**

State Finances

Revenues, Expenditures, Debts, Taxes, U.S. Aid, Military Contracts

For fiscal 1974 (year ending June 30, 1974, except: Alabama, Sept. 30; New York, Mar. 31; Texas, Aug. 31).

Sources: Census Bureau, Treasury and Defense Depts. *Military prime contracts. All figures in dollars.

State	Receipts (add 000)	Outlays (add 000)	Total Debt (add 000)	Per Cap Debt	Per Cap Taxes	Per Cap U.S. Aid	*Mltry Cntrcts (add 000)
Ala............	$2,073,443	$ 1,994,183	$ 873,184	$ 244.11	$284.42	$238	$ 336,377
Alas..........	527,045	697,584	560,820	1,664.15	368.43	772	114,733
Ariz..........	1,339,553	1,237,830	84,079	39.05	345.19	237	479,301
Ark..........	1,079,787	997,543	113,352	54.97	293.61	244	44,211
Cal..........	6,507,414	15,519,227	6,246,943	298.80	381.29	233	1,913,820
Col..........	1,641,788	1,409,801	126,663	50.75	319.55	223	239,074
Conn........	1,975,371	1,919,806	2,595,028	840.36	353.92	218	2,641,470
Del..........	502,903	496,142	555,640	969.70	537.75	212	41,980
Fla...........	4,326,520	4,084,511	1,437,955	183.93	344.45	171	790,406
Ga...........	2,748,308	2,618,445	1,073,792	219.95	310.31	242	376,871
Ha...........	989,507	990,859	1,063,947	1,256.14	584.25	316	183,447
Ida..........	535,975	503,965	37,405	46.81	320.70	260	6,336
Ill...........	7,254,548	6,523,804	2,327,347	209.09	366.81	202	456,339
Ind..........	2,734,000	2,275,371	607,338	113.95	314.11	135	747,968
Ia...........	1,786,136	1,627,392	129,242	45.27	352.03	156	157,909
Kan..........	1,234,503	1,112,219	194,785	85.81	309.56	169	296,10
Ky...........	2,075,580	1,816,615	1,858,515	553.62	329.50	256	115,4
La...........	2,606,229	2,401,410	1,214,796	322.74	350.56	258	276 6
Me...........	714,531	659,273	378,025	361.06	321.25	278	12 48
Md...........	2,782,498	2,810,456	1,759,367	429.74	385.48	189	7 ,098
Mass........	3,967,637	4,229,191	3,176,881	547.74	380.13	230	81,370
Mich........	6,674,158	6,434,408	1,437,367	157.99	404.61	203	925,012
Minn........	3,043,538	2,780,101	779,496	199.00	470.55	226	408,394
Miss........	1,470,666	1,395,240	623,647	268.35	321.20	303	899,707
Mo..........	2,261,942	2,049,510	212,955	44.58	272.23	180	1,372,585
Mon.........	545,045	476,150	88,962	121.04	299.30	301	84,721
Neb..........	754,832	698,260	73,235	47.46	262.87	180	34,190
Nev..........	502,240	420,890	55,200	96.34	438.77	256	17,323
N.H..........	467,491	452,159	195,573	242.05	204.41	201	100,348
N.J..........	4,607,734	4,389,803	3,611,221	492.66	280.53	181	967,941
N.M..........	906,143	795,143	157,819	140.66	390.08	327	102,598
N.Y..........	16,010,816	15,453,285	13,375,207	738.51	470.23	285	2,784,894
N.C..........	3,126,023	2,721,667	498,602	92.97	336.83	190	350,264
N.D..........	508,728	435,016	65,495	102.82	343.32	242	92,044
Oh...........	6,109,499	5,620,383	2,447,509	227.95	259.74	165	994,037
Okla.........	1,556,069	1,479,637	833,499	307.68	287.01	230	170,083
Ore..........	1,666,854	1,504,609	1,268,261	559.69	309.63	263	58,012
Pa...........	8,286,099	8,056,510	5,096,503	430.63	389.45	210	1,307,002
R.I...........	689,548	658,751	408,847	436.34	356.09	260	98,130
S.C..........	1,649,240	1,614,096	859,843	308.85	323.83	214	131,691
S.D..........	387,807	363,583	40,843	59.89	242.85	312	14,145
Tenn.........	2,036,318	1,910,117	690,585	167.25	264.57	216	329,000
Tex..........	5,916,788	5,027,016	1,815,507	150.66	272.86	190	1,913,820
Ut...........	812,580	745,963	87,613	74.69	309.54	259	193,277
Vt...........	424,305	416,923	413,094	878.92	382.21	338	58,237
Va...........	2,860,088	2,849,198	585,387	119.27	307.22	190	953,110
Wash........	2,849,870	2,671,746	1,160,275	333.80	391.18	227	836,671
W.Va........	1,355,948	1,293,777	927,596	517.92	340.65	337	36,472
Wis..........	3,347,687	3,223,795	945,765	207.13	445.06	182	251,365
Wy...........	309,700	270,990	75,215	209.51	346.06	355	36,488
Total or Average	**$140,751,084**	**$132,134,353**	**$65,296,227**	**$309.95**	**$352.25**		**$32,135,666**

U.S. Money in Circulation, by Denominations

Source: U.S. Mint

Outside Treasury and Federal Reserve Banks. (In millions of dollars)

End of year	Total in circulation	Coin and small denomination							Large denomination currency					
		Total	Coin	$1	$2	$5	$10	$20	Total	$50	$100	$500	$1,000	$5,000	$10,000
1950	27,741	19,305	1,554	1,113	64	2,049	5,998	8,529	8,438	2,422	5,043	368	588	4	12
1960	32,869	23,521	2,427	1,533	88	2,246	6,691	10,536	9,348	2,815	5,954	249	316	3	10
1970	57,093	39,639	6,281	2,310	136	3,161	9,170	18,581	17,454	4,896	12,084	215	252	3	4
1972	66,516	45,105	7,287	2,523	135	3,449	9,827	21,883	21,411	5,868	15,118	193	225	2	4
1973	72,497	48,288	7,759	2,639	135	3,614	10,226	23,915	24,210	6,514	17,288	185	216	2	4
1974	79,343	51,604	8,331	2,720	135	3,718	10,503	26,197	28,136	7,444	20,298	179	209	2	4

Bureau of the Mint
Source: Bureau of the Mint

The first United States Mint was established in Philadelphia, Pa., then the nation's capital, by the Act of April 2, 1792, which provided for gold, silver and copper coinage. Originally, supervision of the Mint was a function of the Secretary of State, but it became (1799) an independent agency reporting directly to the president. When the Coinage Act of 1873 was passed, all mint and assay office activities were placed under a newly organized Bureau of the Mint in the Department of the Treasury.

The Bureau of the Mint manufactures all U.S. coins and distributes them through the Federal Reserve banks and branches. The Mint also maintains physical custody of the Treasury's monetary stocks of gold and silver, and refines and processes silver bullion. Functions performed by the Mint on a reimbursable basis include: the manufacture and sale of medals of a national character, the production and sale of numismatic coins and coin sets, and, as scheduling permits, the manufacture of foreign coins.

Amendments to the Coinage Act of 1965 (Public Law 91-

607, Dec. 31, 1970) authorized the production of dollar coins and provided that the dollar and half dollar coins for general circulation be of the same nonsilver clad composition as the quarter dollars and dimes. The cladding is an alloy of 75 percent copper and 25 percent nickel, bonded to a core of pure copper. The legislation authorized the Secretary of the Treasury to mint and issue not more than 150 million one dollar pieces containing 40-percent silver, for sale to the public at premium prices. The new dollar coins bear the likeness of the late President of the United States, Dwight David Eisenhower, and a design emblematic of the symbolic eagle of the Apollo 11 landing on the moon. The silver-clad and cupronickel dollars and the cupronickel half dollars were first minted and issued during the calendar year 1971. The composition of the five cent and one cent coins remains unchanged. The five cent pieces are 75 percent copper, 25 percent nickel, while the one cent pieces are 95 percent copper and 5 percent zinc.

Calendar year 1974 coinage production for general circulation follows:

Domestic Coinage Executed During Calendar Year 1974

Denomination	Philadelphia	Denver	San Francisco	Total Value	Total Pieces
Dollars—non-silver Subsidiary	$27,366,000.00	$35,466,000.00	$ -0-	$62,832,000.00	62,832,000
Half Dollars	63,303,000.00	32,312,500.00	-0-	95,615,500.00	191,231,000
Quarter Dollars	91,361,000.00	54,806,250.00	-0-	146,167,250.00	584,669,000
Dimes	47,024,800.00	57,108,300.00	-0-	104,133,100.00	1,041,331,000
Total Subsidiary Minor	201,688,800.00	144,227,050.00	-0-	345,915,850.00	1,817,231,000
Five-cent Pieces	30,087,600.00	13,868,650.00	-0-	43,956,250.00	879,125,000
One-cent Pieces	'42,321,405.23	42,350,980.00	4,120,392.28	88,792,777.51	8,879,277,751
Total Minor	72,409,005.23	56,219,630.00	4,120,392.28	132,749,027.51	9,758,402,751
Total Domestic Coinage	$301,463,805.23	$235,912,680.00	$4,120,392.28	$541,496,877.51	$11,638,465,751

Manufactured at San Francisco Assay Office

Proof Coin Sets — 2,617,350
40% Silver Proof Dollars — 1,314,608
40% Silver Uncirculated Dollars — 1,900,000 (delivered to NYAO for packaging)[2]
(1) $1,289,575.23 Manufactured at West Point Depository included.
(2) 1,720,000 Packaged by New York Assay Office.

Coinage executed for foreign governments

Country	No. of Pieces
Honduras	4,400,000
Liberia	3,091,605
Nepal	62,237
Panama	2,114,891
Philippines	49,371,203
Taiwan	286,082,530
	345,122,466

Large Denominations of U.S. Currency Discontinued

The largest denomination of United States currency now being issued is the $100 bill. Issuance of currency in denominations of $500, $1,000, $5,000 and $10,000 has been discontinued because their use has declined sharply over the past two decades. Issuance of $2 bills has also been discontinued because of a lack of public interest.

As large denomination bills reach the Federal Reserve

Bank they are removed from circulation. Existing stocks of $2 bills in condition fit for circulation will be circulated as long as the supply lasts.

Because some of the discontinued currency is expected to be in the hands of holders for many years, the descriptions of the various denominations below is continued:

Portraits on U.S. Currency

Amt.	Portrait	Embellishment on Back	Amt.	Portrait	Embellishment on Back
$ 1	Washington	Great Seal of U.S.	$ 100	Franklin	Independence Hall
2	Jefferson	Monticello	* 500	McKinley	Ornate denominational marking
5	Lincoln	Lincoln Memorial	* 1,000	Cleveland	Ornate denominational marking
10	Hamilton	U.S. Treasury	* 5,000	Madison	Ornate denominational marking
20	Jackson	White House	* 10,000	Chase	Ornate denominational marking
50	Grant	U.S. Capitol	*100,000	Wilson	Ornate denominational marking

*For use only in transactions between Federal Reserve System and Treasury Department.

Portraits on U.S. Treasury Bills, Bonds, Notes and Savings Bonds

Denomination	Savings bonds	Treas. bills	Treas. bonds	Treas. notes
25	Washington			
50	Jefferson		Jefferson	
75	Kennedy			
100	Cleveland		Jackson	
200	F.D. Roosevelt			
500	Wilson		Washington	
1,000	Lincoln	H. McCulloch	Lincoln	Lincoln
5,000		J.G. Carlisle	Monroe	Monroe
10,000	T. Roosevelt	J. Sherman	Cleveland	Cleveland
50,000		C. Glass		
100,000		A. Gallatin	Grant	Grant
1,000,000		O. Wolcott	T. Roosevelt	T. Roosevelt
100,000,000				Madison
500,000,000				McKinley

U.S. Currency and Coin — June 30, 1975
Source: Treasury Department

Amounts Outstanding and in Circulation

	Total Currency and Coin	Total	Coin[a] Dollars	Fractional Coin
Amounts outstanding	$86,689,444,855	$9,079,635,898	[b]$862,430,898	$8,217,205,000
Less amounts held by:				
The Treasury	364,281,176	224,024,283	28,167,243	195,857,040
The Federal Reserve banks	5,128,805,945	359,201,023	18,697,096	340,503,927
Amounts in circulation	81,196,357,734	8,496,410,592	815,566,559	7,680,844,033

Currency[c]

	Total	Federal Reserve Notes[d]	United States Notes	Currency No Longer Issued
Amounts outstanding	$77,609,808,957	$77,002,467,398	$322,539,016	$284,802,543
Less amounts held by:				
The Treasury	140,256,893	139,823,925	318,221	114,747
The Federal Reserve banks	4,769,604,922	4,769,559,267	20,580	25,075
Amounts in circulation	72,699,947,142	72,093,084,206	322,200,215	284,662,721

Currency by Denominations, and Coin, in Circulation

Denomination	Total	Federal Reserve Notes[d]	United States Notes	Currency No Longer Issued
One dollar	$2,615,925,609	$2,458,924,616	$144,027	
Two dollars	135,304,692		135,291,278	13,414
Five dollars	3,570,989,100	3,410,968,550	117,592,740	42,427,810
Ten dollars	10,238,981,130	10,212,197,070	10,645	26,773,415
Twenty dollars	26,797,692,824	26,777,039,620	3,950	20,649,254
Fifty dollars	7,671,365,600	7,658,768,950	25	12,596,625
One hundred dollars	21,280,499,200	21,186,652,900	69,155,550	24,690,750
Five hundred dollars	177,074,500	176,860,500	2,000	212,000
One thousand dollars	206,309,000	206,062,000		247,000
Five thousand dollars	1,945,000	1,880,000		65,000
Ten thousand dollars	3,860,000	3,730,000		130,000
Fractional parts	487			487
Total currency	72,699,947,142	72,093,084,206	322,200,215	284,662,721
Total coin	8,496,410,592			
Total currency and coin	81,196,357,734			

Comparative Totals of Money in Circulation — Selected Dates

Date	Amounts (in millions)	Per Capita[e]	Date	Amounts (in millions)	Per Capita[e]	Date	Amounts (in millions)	Per Capita[e]
June 30, 1975	[f]$81,196.4	$380.06	June 30, 1955	30,229.3	182.90	June 30, 1930	4,522.0	36.74
June 30, 1974	73,833.1	$348.44	June 30, 1950	27,156.3	179.03	June 30, 1925	4,815.2	41.56
June 30, 1970	54,351.0	265.39	June 30, 1945	26,746.4	191.14	June 30, 1920	5,467.6	51.36
June 30, 1965	39,719.8	204.14	June 30, 1940	7,847.5	59.40	June 30, 1915	3,319.6	33.01
June 30, 1960	32,064.6	177.47	June 30, 1935	5,567.1	43.75	June 30, 1910	3,148.7	34.07

[a]Excludes coin sold to collectors at premium prices. [b]Includes $481,781,898 in standard silver dollars. [c]Excludes gold certificates, Series of 1934, which are issued only to Federal Reserve banks and do not appear in circulation. [d]Issued on and after July 1, 1929. [e]Based on Bureau of the Census estimates of population. [f]Highest amount to date. [g]Revised.

The requirement for a gold reserve against U.S. notes was repealed by Public Law 90-269 approved Mar. 18, 1968. Silver certificates issued on and after July 1, 1929, became redeemable from the general fund on June 24, 1968. The amount of security after those dates has been reduced accordingly.

*Seigniorage on Coin and Silver Bullion
Source: Fiscal Service, Dept. of Treasury
(Jan. 1, 1935, to June 30, 1974)

	Total	Potential[1]
Fiscal Year Jan. 1, 1935-June 30, 1965, cumulative	$2,525,927,763.84	[2]$ 6,560,393.72
1968	[r]383,141,339.00	759,844,047.56
1969	250,170,276.34	700,000,000.00
1970	274,217,884.01	
1971	399,652,811.18	
1972	580,586,683.00	
1973	399,799,682.00	
1974	320,706,638.49	
1975	660,898,070.69	
Cumulative Jan. 1, 1935-June 30, 1975	7,280,639,514.69	

*Seigniorage is the profit from coining money; it is the difference between the monetary value of coins and their cost, including the manufacturing expense.
(r.) Revised to include seigniorage on clad coins. (p.) Preliminary.
(1.) Not cumulative. As coinage metals held by the Teasurer of the United States changes, the potential seigniorage changes. Potential seigniorage also changes depending on the denomination of the coins manufactured.
(2.) Represents potential seigniorage as of June 30, 1965.

World Gold Production

Source: Federal Reserve Board. In millions of dollars at $35 per fine troy ounce through 1971, at $38 for 1972.

Year	estimated world prod.	Africa			North and South America					Other				
		South Africa	Ghana	Zaire	United States	Canada	Mexico	Nicaragua	Colombia	Australia	India	Japan	Philippines	All other
1960	1,175.0	748.4	30.8	11.1	58.8	162.0	10.5	7.0	15.2	38.0	5.6	11.8	14.4	61.4
1965	1,440.0	1,069.4	26.4	2.3	58.6	125.6	7.6	5.4	11.2	30.7	4.6	18.1	15.3	64.8
1966	1,445.0	1,080.8	24.0	5.6	63.1	114.6	7.5	5.2	9.8	32.1	4.2	19.4	15.8	62.9
1967	1,410.0	1,068.7	26.7	5.4	53.4	103.7	5.8	5.2	9.0	28.4	3.4	23.7	17.2	59.4
1968	1,420.0	1,088.0	25.4	5.9	53.9	94.1	6.2	4.9	8.4	27.6	4.0	21.5	18.5	61.6
1969	1,420.0	1,090.7	24.8	6.0	60.1	89.1	6.3	3.7	7.7	24.5	3.4	23.7	20.0	60.0
1970	1,450.0	1,128.0	24.8	6.2	63.5	84.3	6.9	4.0	7.1	21.7	3.7	24.8	21.1	54.1
1971p		1,098.7	24.4	6.0	52.3	79.1	5.3	3.7	6.6	23.5	4.1	27.0	22.2	
1972p		1,109.8			54.3	77.2			7.1		4.0	32.2	23.0	

(p) Preliminary.

Gold Reserves of Central Banks and Governments

Source, Federal Reserve Board

Millions of dollars; valued at $35 per ounce through 1971, at $38 for 1972, and $42.22 thereafter.

Dec.	(Est.) total world¹	Int'l Monetary Fund	United States	Canada	(Est.) rest of world	Belgium	France	Germany Fed. Rep. of	Italy	Netherlands	Switzerland	United Kingdom
1960	40,540	2,439	17,804	885	20,295	1,170	1,641	2,971	2,203	1,451	2,185	2,800
1965	43,230	1,869	13,806	1,151	27,285	1,558	4,706	4,410	2,404	1,756	3,042	2,265
1970	41,275	4,339	11,072	791	25,865	1,470	3,532	3,980	2,887	1,787	2,732	1,349
1971	41,175	4,732	10,206	792	26,235	1,544	3,523	4,077	2,884	1,909	2,909	775
1972	44,890	5,830	10,487	834	28,575	1,638	3,826	4,459	3,130	2,059	3,158	800
1973	49,850	6,478	11,652	927	30,793	1,781	4,261	4,966	3,483	2,294	3,513	886
1974	49,790	6,478	11,652	927	30,733	1,781	4,262	4,966	3,483	2,294	3,513	886

(1.) Excludes USSR, other Eastern European countries and China mainland.
Argentina 169, Australia 312, Austria 882, Brazil 56, Colombia 18, Denmark 76, Dominican Republic 4, Ecuador 16, Egypt 103, El Salvador 21, Finland 35, Greece 150, Guatemala 21, India 293, Iran 158, Iraq 173, Ireland 18, Israel 46, Japan 891, Lebanon 389, Mexico 154, Norway 41, Pakistan 67, Peru 42, Philippines 45, Portugal 1,180, South Africa 771, Spain 602, Sweden 244, Thailand 99, Turkey 151, Uruguay 148, Venezuela 472, Yugoslavia 62, B.I.S. (net) 250.

U.S. and World Silver Production

Source: Bureau of Mines

Largest production of silver in the United States in 1915—74,961,075 fine ounces. (r) revised (p) preliminary.

Year (Cal.)	United States Fine ozs.	Value	World Fine ozs.	Year (Cal.)	United States Fine ozs.	Value	World Fine ozs.
1930	50,748,127	19,538,000	248,708,426	1960	36,000,000	$33,305,858	241,300,000
1935	45,924,454	33,008,000	220,704,231	1965r	39,806,033	51,469,201	257,415,000
1940	69,585,734	49,483,000	275,387,000	1970r	45,006,000	79,697,000	310,891,000
1945	29,063,255	20,667,200	162,000,000	1972r	37,233,000	62,737,000	301,510,000
1950	43,308,739	38,291,545	203,300,000	1973r	37,827,000	96,762,000	308,927,000
1955	36,469,610	33,006,839	224,000,000	1974p	33,762,000	159,018,000	297,248,000

Bank Rates on Short-Term Business Loans

Source: Federal Reserve System

% per annum. Estimates based on reports from banks in 35 centers. Short-term loans mature within one year.

	Ave. 35 Cities	N.Y. C.	7 Other N.E.	8 No. Cent.	7 S.E.	8 S.W.	4 West	1-9	10-99	100 to 499	500 to 999	1,000 and Over
1967 Aug. 1-15	5.95	5.66	6.29	5.92	5.92	6.01	6.02	6.58	6.46	6.16	5.89	5.72
Nov. 1-15	5.96	5.71	6.29	5.91	5.94	6.03	6.03	6.60	6.48	6.17	5.90	5.73
1970 Aug. 1-15	8.50	8.24	8.89	8.47	8.49	8.53	8.54	9.15	9.07	8.75	8.46	8.25
Nov. 1-15	8.07	7.74	8.47	8.05	8.15	8.08	8.16	8.89	8.79	8.34	8.09	7.74
1971 Aug.	6.51	6.25	6.77	6.46	6.77	6.64	6.54	7.68	7.27	6.88	6.58	6.27
Nov.	6.18	5.86	6.40	6.13	6.47	6.43	6.21	7.51	7.05	6.51	6.26	5.93
1972 Aug.	5.84	5.55	6.14	5.79	6.06	6.07	5.82	7.27	6.72	6.20	5.91	5.59
Nov.	6.33	6.09	6.61	6.27	6.56	6.36	6.41	7.52	7.10	6.60	6.24	6.14
1973 Aug.	9.24	9.08	9.49	9.24	9.25	9.16	9.25	8.95	9.25	9.50	9.31	9.14
Nov.	10.08	9.90	10.51	10.02	9.96	10.08	10.04	9.80	10.14	10.43	10.18	9.95
1974 Feb.	9.91	9.68	10.28	9.98	9.80	9.93	9.78	9.86	10.09	10.28	10.06	9.75
May	11.15	11.08	11.65	11.09	10.88	10.82	11.19	10.50	11.06	11.41	11.32	11.06
1975 Feb.	9.94	9.61	10.31r	9.87	10.24	10.01	9.99	10.94	10.73	10.25	9.93	9.73
May	8.16	7.88	8.37	8.00*	8.70	8.34	8.33	9.57	9.10	8.52	8.18	7.90

NOTE:—The Quarterly Survey of Interest Rates Charged by Banks on Business Loans has been revised beginning with the survey period of February 1971. The revision incorporates a number of technical changes in coverage, sampling, and interest rate calculations. These include elimination of accounts receivable loans from the survey, shortening the sample period for respondent banks in most districts, and calculation of effective annual interest rates on discounted loans using a revised formula based on annual rather than quarterly compounding of interest. As a result of the above changes, new weights derived from this Survey have been used to calculate the weighted average rates.

U. S. Commercial Banks With Deposits Over One Billion

A compilation of the 300 largest commercial banks in the United States is made twice a year by the American Banker, daily banking newspaper, 525 W. 42 St., New York, N. Y. 10036. Of these the first 85 banks had deposits of more than $1 billion on June 30, 1975. They are listed below. (Copyright 1975, by American Banker)

Rank		Deposits	Rank		Deposits
1	Bank of America NT&SA, San Francisco.	$53,925,943,000	44	European-American B&T Co., New York.	2,019,026,000
2	First National City Bank, New York	47,115,510,000	45	Bank of New York	1,928,830,723
3	Chase Manhattan Bank NA, New York . .	34,213,967,715	46	Maryland National Bank, Baltimore.	1,914,228,900
4	Manufacturers Hanover Trust, New York.	23,181,507,000	47	First National Bank of Arizona, Phoenix . .	1,904,211,216
5	Chemical Bank, New York	19,228,462,000	48	First Wisconsin National Bank, Milwaukee	1,859,678,341
6	Morgan Guaranty Trust Co., New York . .	18,625,683,164			
7	Bankers Trust Co., New York	15,061,769,000	49	Bank of Tokyo Trust Co., New York	1,621,171,456
8	First National Bank, Chicago.	13,821,025,467	50	Hartford National Bank & Trust Co.,	
9	Continental Illinois NB&T Co., Chicago. .	13,699,126,555		Conn	1,573,906,000
10	Security Pacific Nat'l Bk., Los Angeles. . .	11,636,302,000	51	National City Bank, Cleveland.	1,525,585,000
11	Wells Fargo Bank NA, San Francisco . . .	9,381,768,000	52	Industrial NB of Rhode Island, Providence	1,509,116,000
12	Crocker National Bank, San Francisco . . .	8,647,144,000			
13	Irving Trust Co., New York	7,760,783,762	53	Marine Midl'd Bk.—West'n, Buffalo, N.Y. .	1,508,616,379
14	United California Bank, Los Angeles. . . .	7,130,916,884	54	Virginia National Bank, Norfolk	1,449,848,795
15	Mellon Bank NA, Pittsburgh	7,031,187,000	55	First Union NB of No. Carolina, Charlotte.	1,449,407,000
16	National Bank of Detroit.	6,381,271,000	56	American Fletcher NB&T Co., Ind'polis. .	1,417,975,000
17	First National Bank, Boston.	5,958,241,500	57	Equibank NA, Pittsburgh.	1,414,737,000
18	Marine Midland Bank—New York	5,604,503,000	58	Connecticut Bank & Trust Co., Hartford . .	1,403,752,228
19	First Pennsylvania Bank NA, Philadelphia	4,354,791,000	59	Central National Bank, Cleveland	1,399,337,995
			60	First National Bank, Atlanta, Ga.	1,377,534,794
20	Seattle-First National Bank	3,609,779,852	61	Mercantile Trust Co. NA, St. Louis, Mo. . .	1,360,951,747
21	Republic National Bank, Dallas.	3,113,648,171	62	Indiana National Bank, Indianapolis.	1,337,684,071
22	Union Bank, Los Angeles.	3,001,629,000	63	Michigan National Bank, Lansing.	1,301,182,210
23	First National Bank, Dallas.	2,997,353,035	64	Southeast First National Bank, Miami . . .	1,300,921,000
24	Harris Trust & Savings Bank, Chicago . . .	2,936,641,485	65	Riggs National Bank, Washington, D. C. .	1, ,297,912
25	Cleveland Trust Co.	2,893,729,511	66	First National Bank, St. Louis, Mo.	1,2 ,5, '48
26	Philadelphia National Bank	2,847,910,087	67	American National B&T Co., Chicago . . .	1,268,949,b..
27	Northern Trust Co., Chicago	2,824,896,324	68	Trust Co. Bank, Atlanta, Ga.	1,256,974,792
28	North Carolina National Bank, Charlotte .	2,699,868,000	69	Provident National Bank, Philadelphia . . .	1,229,689,000
29	Wachovia B&T NA, Winston-Salem, N.C.	2,614,578,918	70	Shawmut Bank of Boston NA, Mass.	1,214,294,000
			71	First National Bank, Minneapolis, Minn. . .	1,186,483,224
30	National Bank of No. America, New York .	2,576,790,000	72	Northwestern NB, Minneapolis, Minn. . . .	1,178,401,498
31	Girard Bank, Philadelphia	2,571,496,000	73	Manufacturers & Traders Trust Co.,	
32	Detroit Bank & Trust Co.	2,560,140,000		Buffalo N.Y.	1,151,356,711
33	Valley National Bank, Phoenix, Ariz. . . .	2,559,894,510	74	State Street Bank & Trust Co., Boston . . .	1,115,438,865
34	First City National Bank, Houston, Tex. . .	2,525,706,000	75	Lloyds Bank California, Los Angeles.	1,110,955,809
35	Manufacturers National Bank, Detroit . . .	2,363,056,000	76	First National Bank, St. Paul, Minn.	1,093,594,683
36	Citizens & Southern NB, Atlanta, Ga. . . .	2,227,119,000	77	New England Merchants NB, Boston	1,064,111,334
37	Bank of California NA, San Francisco . . .	2,181,451,000	78	Union Commerce Bank, Cleveland.	1,058,631,175
38	First National Bank of Oregon, Portland. .	2,177,565,000	79	First American Nat'l Bk., Nashville, Tenn.	1,053,296,442
39	United States NB of Oregon, Portland. . .	2,176,246,545	80	Republic National Bank of New York.	1,044,256,264
40	Pittsburgh National Bank	2,161,130,813	81	First-Citizens B&T Co., Raleigh, N.C. . . .	1,038,334,902
41	Rainier National Bank, Seattle	2,123,310,949	82	Bank of the Southwest NA, Houston, Tex..	1,025,590,580
42	Fidelity Bank, Philadelphia	2,104,446,000	83	County Trust Co., White Plains, N.Y.	1,020,226,673
43	Texas Commerce Bank NA, Houston . . .	2,086,104,000	84	American Sec. & Tr., Washington, D. C. .	1,009,758,691
			85	First & Merchants NB, Richmond, Va. . . .	1,000,140,487

Largest Bank in Each of 38 Foreign Countries

Source: 500 Largest Banks in the Free World, compiled by the American Banker, New York. (Copyright 1975) Based on deposits Jan. 1, 1975, or nearest fiscal year-end. For Canada, see Index.

(in Thousands)

Banks and Country	Deposits in U.S. $	Banks and Country	Deposits in U.S. $
Argentina, Banco de la Nacion.	2,706,170	Kuwait, National Bank of.	1,112,440
Australia, Commonwealth Bkng. Corp.	11,698,626	Luxembourg. Cie. Luxembourgeoise.	2,961,151
Austria, Creditanstalt-Bankverein.	4,954,907	Mexico, Banco de Comercio.	2,035,466
Belgium, Societe Generale de Banque	11,915,613	Netherlands, Cooperatieve Centrale	
Brazil, Banco do Brasil.	15,515,407	Raiffeisen-Boerenleenbank.	14,139,144
Denmark, Copenhagen Handelsbank.	2,387,068	New Zealand, Bank of.	1,608,545
Egypt, National Bank of Egypt	1,159,487	No. Ireland, Northern Bank Ltd.	942,863
England, Barclay's Bank.	29,263,190	Norway, Norske Creditbank.	1,608,671
Finland, Kansallis-Osake Pankki.	2,435,223	Pakistan, Habib Bank Ltd.	873,369
France, Banque Nationale de Paris	34,229,651	Peru, Banco de la Nacion	2,161,891
Germany, Deutsche Bank.	30,436,986	Portugal, Banco Portugues do Atlantico	1,912,824
Greece, National Bank of Greece	3,787,337	Scotland, Bank of.	2,748,365
Hong Kong, Hongkong & Shanghai	7,296,722	South Africa, Standard Bank of.	2,901,740
India, State Bank of India.	4,840,960	Spain, Banco Espanol de Credito	7,287,727
Iran, Bank Melli Iran.	3,705,224	Sweden, Post-Och Kreditbanken.	8,121,150
Ireland, Bank of Ireland.	2,809,445	Switzerland, Swiss Bank Corp.	14,531,536
Israel, Bank Leumi le-Israel	5,918,771	Taiwan, Bank of.	1,843,783
Italy, Banca Nazionale del Lavoro.	17,907,339	Thailand, Bangkok Bank Ltd.	1,427,143
Japan, Dai-Ichi Kangyo Bank Ltd.	23,045,859	Turkey, Cumhuriyeti Ziraat Bankasi.	1,813,820
Korea, Korea Exchange Bank.	684,270		

Federal Deposit Insurance Corporation (FDIC)

The primary purpose of the Federal Deposit Insurance Corporation (FDIC) is to insure the deposits of all banks entitled to insurance benefits under the Federal Deposit Insurance Act. The major functions of the FDIC are to pay off depositors of insured banks closed without adequate provision having been made to pay depositors' claims, to act as receiver for all national banks placed in receivership and for state banks placed in receivership when appointed receiver by state authorities, and to prevent the continuance or development of unsafe and unsound banking practices. The FDIC's entire income consists of assessments on insured banks and income from investments; it receives no appropriations from Congress. It may borrow from the U. S. Treasury not to exceed $3 billion outstanding at any one time, but has made no such borrowings since it was organized in 1933. The FDIC surplus (Deposit Insurance Fund) as of Dec. 30, 1974, was $6.2 billion.

Corporations and Stocks

Over 33 Million Persons Own Shares in U.S. Corporations

About 33 million persons owned shares in American corporations in 1975, compared to 8.63 million in 1956.

The N.Y. Stock Exchange listed 2,090 issues of 1,555 companies, for a total of 22.14 billion shares, valued Aug. 31, 1975, at $660.9 billion. Average daily trading was 20,148,610 shares through Aug. 31, compared to 13,365,138 in 1974.

The American Stock Exchange listed 1,348 issues of 1,249 companies, totaling 3.3 billion shares, valued Jan. 2, 1975, at $23.3 billion. Average daily volume through Sept. 16 was 2.32 million shares, compared to 1.87 million the previous year.

Shares traded on the NYSE in 1974 totaled 3.8 billion; on the ASE, 475 million; on other exchanges in the U.S., 542 million.

50 U.S. Companies with Largest Annual Sales or Revenues

Top listed companies on N.Y. Stock Exchange for 1974 as shown by its Research Dep't.

Company	Sales or revenues (Add 000)	Net profit (or *loss) (Add 000)	Company	Sales or revenues (Add 000)	Net profit (or *loss) (Add 000)
Exxon Corp.	$45,020,800	$3,142,200	Kresge (S. S.) Co.	5,536,300	$104,800
General Motors Corp.	31,549,500	950,100	Bethlehem Steel Corp.	5,381,000	342,000
American Tel. & Tel.	26,174,400	3,169,000	Englehard Mins. & Chem.	5,376,600	110,200
Texaco Inc.	25,417,200	1,586,400	Union Carbide Corp.	5,320,100	530,100
Ford Motor Co.	23,620,600	360,900	Goodyear Tire & Rubber.	5,256,200	157,500
Mobil Oil Corp.	20,284,000	1,047,400	Tenneco Inc.	5,001,500	321,500
Gulf Oil Corp.	17,952,000	1,065,000	Phillips Petroleum Co.	4,980,700	429,800
Standard Oil Co. of Cal.	17,924,400	970,000	Int'l Harvester Co.	4,,65,900	117,900
General Electric Co.	13,413,100	608,100	Dow Chemical Co.	4,938,500	587,400
Sears, Roebuck & Co.	13,101,200	511,400	Procter & Gamble Co.	4,912,300	316,700
Int'l Business Machines	12,675,300	1,837,600	Kroger Co.	4,782,400	45,200
Int'l Tel. & T-'	11,154,400	451,100	Union Oil Co. of Cal.	4,770,300	288,000
Ch------ --rp.	10,971,400	*52,100	LTV Corp.	4,768,000	85,700
Standard Oil Co. (Ind.).	10,024,600	970,300	Marcor Inc.	4,667,500	120,400
U.S. Steel Corp.	9,186,400	634,900	Esmark, Inc.	4,615,700	68,100
Shell Oil Co.	8,418,300	620,500	RCA Corp.	4,594,300	113,300
Safeway Stores, Inc.	8,185,200	79,200	Eastman Kodak Co.	4,583,600	629,500
Continental Oil Co.	7,279,600	327,600	Reynolds (R. J.) Inds.	4,500,900	310,700
Atlantic Richfield Co.	7,166,900	474,600	Kraftco Corp.	4,471,400	94,600
Penney (J.C.) Co.	6,935,700	125,100	Rockwell International	4,408,500	130,300
duPont de Nemours (E.I.)	6,910,100	403,500	Beatrice Foods Co.	4,191,800	134,800
Great A&P Tea Co.	6,874,600	*157,100	Woolworth (F. W.) Co.	4,177,100	64,800
Westinghouse Electric.	5,798,500	28,100	Caterpillar Tractor Co.	4,082,100	229,200
General Tel. & Electronics	5,661,500	272,700	Sun Oil Co.	3,799,600	377,700
Occidental Petroleum Corp.	5,537,500	280,700	Amerada Hess Corp.	3,744,500	201,900

30 Largest Industrial Companies Outside the U.S.

Reprinted by special permission from the Fortune Directory, as listed for 1974; © 1975, Time Inc.

Company	Sales (add 000)	Net Profit (or *loss) (add 000)	Company	Sales (add 000)	Net profit (or *loss) (add 000)
Royal Dutch Shell, N-B.	$33,037,116	$2,715,242	Daimler-Benz, G.	6,288,668	100,496
British Petroleum, B.	18,269,240	1,140,117	Montedison, It.	6,189,753	173,602
National Iranian Oil, Ir.	16,802,000	N.A.	Hitachi, J.	6,183,309	120,197
Unilever, B-N.	13,666,667	362,807	Toyota Motor, J.	5,948,335	99,997
Philips Gloeilampenfab, N.	9,422,386	273,493	ELF Group, F.	5,900,381	238,229
Cie Francaise des Petroles, F.	8,908,563	294,457	Mitsubishi Heavy Inds., J.	5,664,799	50,134
Nippon Steel, J.	8,843,550	113,099	Nestle, S.	5,603,155	250,093
August-Thyssen-Hutte, G.	8,664,021	130,025	Renault, F.	5,341,739	7,261
BASF (Badische Anilin), G.	8,497,038	201,026	British Steel, B.	5,340,909	170,455
Hoechst, G.	7,821,054	205,196	British-American Tobacco, B.	5,152,363	275,735
ENI, It.	7,172,831	*91,256	Petrobras (Brazil Oil), Br.	4,989,740	540,598
ICI (Imp Chem Inds), B.	6,911,813	567,953	Nissan Motor, J.	4,933,567	68,636
Siemens, G.	6,701,681	189,149	Matsushita Elec Ind, J.	4,837,521	178,726
Volkswagenwerk, G.	6,568,717	*312,585	Mannesmann, G.	4,717,178	87,182
Bayer, G.	6,300,940	189,388	AEG-Telefunken, G.	4,641,295	*261,721

Nation of Hqs: B, Britain; Br, Brazil; F, France; G, West Germany; Ir, Iran; It, Italy; J, Japan; N, Netherlands; S, Switzerland.

Stocks Most Widely Held by Investment Cos., Insurance Cos., Trust Funds

As listed in 1975 by the N.Y. Stock Exchange
(In order of number of institutions, etc., which held shares, 1975)

Int'l Bus. Machs.	Sears, Roebuck	duPont (E.I.) & Co.	Caterpillar Tractor	Goodyear Rub.
Exxon Corp.	Citicorp	Standard Oil (Ind.)	Kresge (S.S.)	Monsanto Co.
Eastman Kodak	Minn. Mng. Mfg.	General Tel. & Elec.	Texas Utilities	Int'l. Tel. & Tel.
General Motors	Merck & Co.	Union Carbide	Warner-Lambert	Continental Oil
General Electric	Dow Chemical Co.	Gulf Oil Corp.	Standard Oil of Cal.	Weyerhaeuser Co.
Amer. Tel. & Tel.	Ford Motor Co.	Phillips Petroleum	Westinghouse Elec.	Halliburton Co.
Xerox Corp.	Atlantic Richfield	Amer. Home Prods.	Procter & Gamble	Avon Products
Texaco Inc.	Mobil Oil Corp.	Burroughs Corp.	Pfizer Inc.	Penney (J.C.) Co.

N.Y. Stock Exchange Transactions and Seat Prices
Source: New York Stock Exchange

Year	Yearly Volumes Stock Shares	Yearly Volumes Bonds Par Values	Seat Price High	Seat Price Low	Year	Yearly Volumes Stock Shares	Yearly Volumes Bonds Par Values	Seat Price High	Seat Price Low
1900	138,981,000	$579,293,000	$47,500	$37,500	1940	207,599,749	$1,669,438,000	$60,000	$33,000
1905	260,569,000	1,026,254,000	85,000	72,000	1945	377,563,575	2,261,985,110	95,000	49,000
1910	163,705,000	634,863,000	94,000	65,000	1950	524,799,621	1,112,425,170	54,000	46,000
1915	172,497,000	961,700,000	74,000	38,000	1960	766,693,818	1,346,419,750	162,000	135,000
1920	227,636,000	3,868,422,000	115,000	85,000	1970	2,937,359,448	4,494,864,600	320,000	130,000
1925	459,717,623	3,427,042,210	150,000	99,000	1971	3,891,317,731	*6,563,822,400	300,000	145,000
1929	1,124,800,410	2,996,398,000	625,000	550,000	1972	*4,138,187,706	5,444,117,100	250,000	150,000
1930	810,632,546	2,720,301,800	480,000	205,000	1973	4,053,201,306	4,424,671,800	170,000	72,000
1935	381,635,752	3,339,458,000	140,000	65,000	1974	3,821,942,000	4,052,123,000	105,000	65,000

*Record high for trading in stocks and bonds.

American Stock Exchange Transactions and Seat Prices
Source: American Stock Exchange

Year	Yearly Volumes Stock Shares	Yearly Volumes Bonds Par Values	Seat Price High	Seat Price Low	Year	Yearly Volumes Stock Shares	Yearly Volumes Bonds Par Values	Seat Price High	Seat Price Low
1929	476,140,375	$513,551,000	$254,000	$150,000	1965	534,221,999	$146,927,000	$80,000	$55,000
1930	222,270,065	863,541,000	225,000	70,000	1970	843,116,260	641,270,000	180,000	70,000
1940	42,928,337	303,902,000	7,250	6,900	1972	1,117,989,153	728,524,000	145,000	70,000
1945	143,309,392	167,333,000	32,000	12,000	1973	759,840,245	457,940,000	100,000	27,000
1950	107,792,340	47,549,000	11,000	6,500	1974	475,297,000	256,865,000	60,000	27,000
1960	286,039,982	32,670,000	60,000	51,000					

U.S. Business Indexes
Source: Federal Reserve System

	Industrial production (Physical volume) 1967=100 Manufacturers Total	Total	Durable	Non-Durable	Mining	Utilities	Construct'n contracts (value) 1967=100 Total	Residential	All Other	Employment 1967=100 Manuf. production workers Non-agricultural	Employment	Payrolls	Prices 1967=100 Consumer	Wholesale commodity
1960.	66.2	65.4	63.3	68.6	82.7	61.8	69	77	64	82.4	88.0	78.1	88.7	94.9
1965.	89.2	89.1	88.5	90.0	93.9	86.9	93	109	84	92.3	93.9	93.6	94.5	96.6
1966.	97.9	98.3	99.0	97.3	98.4	93.6	95	91	97	97.1	99.9	97.8	97.2	99.8
1967.	100.0	100.0	100.0	100.0	100.0	100	100	100	100.0	100.0	100.0	100.0	100.0	100.0
1968.	105.7	105.7	105.5	106.0	103.9	109.4	113	117	111	103.2	101.4	106.6	104.2	102.5
1969.	110.7	110.5	110.0	111.1	107.2	19.5	124	119	126	106.9	103.2	112.7	109.8	106.5
1970.	106.6	105.2	101.4	110.6	109.7	128.3	123	115	130	107.7	98.1	114.1	116.3	110.4
1971.	106.8	105.2	99.4	113.5	107.0	133.7	145	163	134	108.1	94.2	116.3	121.2	113.9
1972.	115.2	114.0	108.4	122.1	108.8	143.4	165	N.A.	N.A.	111.9	97.6	130.2	125.3	119.8
1973.	125.6	125.1	122.0	129.7	110.3	152.6	181	N.A.	N.A.	116.7	103.1	148.9	133.1	134.7
1974.	124.8	124.4	120.7	129.7	109.3	149.9	169	N.A.	N.A.	118.9	102.1	156.6	147.7	160.1

Wholesale Price Indexes
Source: Bureau of Labor Statistics, United States Department of Labor

The Wholesale Primary Market Price Index is designed to show the rate and direction of the composite of price movements, and to measure price changes not influenced by quality, quantity, terms of sale, etc. Wholesale refers to sales in quantities, not to prices received or paid by wholesalers.

Commodity group (1967 = 100)	1975 June	1975 Jan.	1974 Avg.	1973 Avg.
All commodities	173.7	171.8	160.1	134.7
Farm products, and processed foods, and feeds	182.3	183.6	177.4	159.1
Farm products	186.2	179.9	187.7	176.3
Processed foods and feeds	179.7	186.4	170.9	148.1
All commodities except farm products	172.2	170.9	156.8	129.9
Industrial commodities	170.7	167.5	153.8	125.9
Textile products and apparel	135.9	137.5	139.1	123.8
Hides, skins, leathers and related products	148.7	142.1	145.1	143.1
Fuels and related products and power	243.0	232.2	208.3	134.3
Chemicals and allied products	181.2	176.0	146.8	110.0
Rubber and plastic products	148.6	149.6	136.2	112.4
Lumber and wood products	181.0	164.7	183.6	177.2
Pulp, paper and allied products	169.8	169.8	151.7	122.1
Metals and metal products	184.5	185.5	171.9	132.8
Machinery and equipment	161.0	156.6	139.4	121.7
Furniture and household durables	139.0	138.8	127.9	115.2
Nonmetallic mineral products	173.3	168.5	153.2	130.2
Transportation equipment (Dec. 1968 = 100)	140.1	137.1	125.5	115.1
Miscellaneous products	147.5	145.5	133.1	119.7

Assets and Liabilities of Insured Commercial Banks

Source: Federal Reserve System, Federal Deposit Insurance Corp., Comptroller of the Currency.
As of December 31, 1974 (In thousands of dollars)

State	Loans and Securities	Total Assets	Total Deposits	Total Liabilities	Reserves and Cap.Accts.	State	Loans and Securities	Total Assets	Total Deposits	Total Liabilities	Reserves and Cap.Accts.
Ala...	8,289,566	9,849,555	8,367,010	9,006,954	842,582	Neb...	5,671,312	6,791,073	5,766,599	6,231,856	559,217
Alas...	908,959	1,172,535	1,003,920	1,088,250	84,285	Nev...	1,649,063	1,997,427	1,752,424	1,835,666	161,761
Ariz...	5,956,985	7,084,402	5,710,373	6,607,644	476,758	N.H...	1,469,551	1,724,154	1,485,455	1,558,813	165,341
Ark...	5,169,244	6,287,054	5,427,786	5,771,815	515,239	N.J...	20,542,820	24,235,254	20,882,387	22,187,022	2,048,232
Cal...	77,010,633	96,897,187	79,183,770	90,615,457	6,281,582	N.M...	2,513,542	3,057,621	2,650,842	2,812,909	244,712
Colo...	6,617,883	8,336,388	6,988,495	7,662,548	673,840	N.Y...	125,922,241	171,240,561	132,714,015	157,619,618	13,620,943
Conn...	6,591,275	8,257,071	6,982,920	7,568,731	688,340	N.C...	11,674,403	14,351,291	11,894,603	13,133,114	1,218,149
Del...	2,020,924	2,351,550	1,840,146	2,158,104	193,446	N.D...	2,259,662	2,550,008	2,234,538	2,340,951	209,057
D.C...	3,505,956	4,304,038	3,585,604	3,915,676	388,362	Oh...	30,955,990	36,530,961	29,635,807	33,298,438	3,232,383
Fla...	23,174,504	28,138,333	24,094,232	25,749,927	2,388,406	Okla...	8,782,658	10,803,518	9,209,678	9,909,576	893,814
Ga...	12,463,585	15,408,747	12,156,529	14,081,516	1,327,149	Ore...	5,501,384	6,949,076	5,576,806	6,390,412	558,646
Ha...	2,386,223	2,840,178	2,443,695	2,620,237	219,941	Pa...	46,112,977	54,028,571	42,660,632	49,516,760	4,510,945
Ida...	2,317,510	2,768,851	2,432,981	2,575,466	193,385	R.I...	3,201,618	3,687,793	3,099,348	3,409,221	278,572
Ill...	60,418,558	71,631,079	58,609,992	66,245,104	5,385,935	S.C...	3,835,500	4,623,795	3,867,270	4,214,349	409,446
Ind...	16,778,302	19,908,972	16,512,921	18,413,525	1,495,433	S.D...	2,534,303	2,920,713	2,614,052	2,688,863	231,850
Ia...	10,335,146	12,110,303	10,588,706	11,127,259	982,769	Tenn...	12,031,515	14,665,861	12,287,497	13,487,427	1,178,246
Kan...	7,834,410	9,283,790	7,964,225	8,461,489	822,105	Tex...	40,244,208	50,715,192	42,515,844	46,625,773	4,088,488
Ky...	9,009,257	10,792,290	9,089,895	9,945,289	847,001	Ut...	2,759,623	3,409,757	2,958,597	3,147,430	262,210
La...	11,065,769	13,352,634	11,017,326	12,301,460	1,051,171	Vt...	1,226,620	1,388,336	1,237,236	1,271,835	116,501
Me...	1,847,447	2,136,406	1,825,104	1,953,155	183,251	Va...	13,094,922	15,543,512	13,083,867	14,278,703	1,264,597
Md...	8,123,591	9,578,209	8,011,894	8,765,376	812,833	Wash...	8,886,943	11,051,408	8,698,903	10,329,868	721,528
Mass...	14,964,491	18,450,547	14,788,448	16,909,521	1,539,619	W.Va...	5,309,101	6,063,761	4,979,614	5,545,854	517,907
Mich...	27,862,143	33,147,346	28,101,636	30,462,558	2,684,704	Wis...	13,917,488	16,389,713	13,950,902	15,090,439	1,299,250
Minn...	14,411,121	16,994,103	13,887,051	15,696,234	1,197,869	Wyo...	1,372,602	1,631,991	1,421,772	1,497,572	134,419
Miss...	4,900,609	5,901,707	5,144,397	5,396,955	504,571	*Other	4,658,240	6,144,465	4,699,673	5,873,064	271,401
Mo...	16,553,431	20,056,163	16,158,780	18,400,616	1,655,547	U.S.	739,219,055		746,412,922		171,864,152
Mon...	2,573,247	2,994,011	2,616,725	2,763,597	230,414			912,529,261		840,559,996	

*Includes Guam, Puerto Rico, and Virgin Islands.

Bank Suspensions

Source: Federal Deposit Insurance Corp. The figures for bank suspensions represent banks which, during the periods shown, closed temporarily or permanently on account of financial difficulties; does not include banks whose deposit liabilities were assumed by other banks at the time of closing (in some instances with Federal Deposit Insurance Corp. loans).

Year	Suspensions	Depo	Year	Suspensions	Depo	Year	Suspensions	Depo	Year	Suspensions	Depo
1929	659	230,643,000	1938	55	13,012,000	1954	3	2,880,000	1963	2	23,256,000
1930	1,352	853,363,000	1939	42	34,998,000	1955	4	6,498,000	1964	8	22,022,000
1931	2,294	1,690,669,000	1940	22	5,943,000	1956	3	11,881,000	1965	7	44,857,000
1932	1,456	715,626,000	1943	4	6,223,000	1957	3	12,869,000	1967	4	10,802,000
1933*	4,004	3,598,975,000	1944(a)	1	405,000	1958	8	6,287,000	1969	4	8,910,000
1934	57	36,937,000	1947	1	167,000	1959	3	2,048,000	1970	1	149,500
1935	34	10,015,000	1949	4	2,443,000	1960	2	7,987,000	1971	1	516,000
1936	44	11,306,000	1950	1	42,000	1961	9	7,527,000	1972	1	20,579
1937	59	19,723,000	1953	1	44,412,000	1962	2	1,201,000	1973	3	20,626,000
									1974	0	.....

*Figures for 1933 comprise 628 banks with deposits of $360,413,000 suspended before or after the banking holiday (the holiday began March 6 and closed March 15) or placed in receivership during the holiday; 2,124 banks with deposits of $2,520,391,000 which were not licensed following the banking holiday and were placed in liquidation or receivership; and 1,252 banks with deposits of $718,171,000 which had not been licensed by June 30, 1933. (a) No suspensions in years 1945, 1946, 1948 and 1968.

Federal Reserve System

The Federal Reserve System, central banking system of the United States, was established Dec. 23, 1913, by an Act of Congress to give the country an elastic currency, to provide facilities for discounting commercial paper, and to improve supervision of banking. Today it is generally recognized that the primary function of the System is to foster a flow of credit and money that will facilitate orderly economic growth, a stable dollar, and a long-run balance in international payments.

The Federal Reserve System consists of the (1) Board of Governors of the Federal Reserve System; (2) Federal Open Market Committee; (3) 12 Fed. Reserve Banks and 25 branches; (4) member banks, and (5) Fed. Advisory Council.

The 7 members of the Board of Governors in Washington are appointed by the President with the advice and consent of the Senate; Dr. Arthur F. Burns is chairman. One of the Board's principal functions is in the area of monetary policy. The Board has authority to approve changes in discount rates, to change member bank reserve requirements within specified limits, to set margin requirements for certain kinds of stock transactions, and to set maximum interest rates payable on member banks' savings and time deposits. Another important duty of the Board relates to supervision of Federal Reserve Banks, member banks and bank holding companies. Expenses of the Board of Governors are paid out of assessments upon the Reserve Banks.

The Federal Open Market Committee is composed of the 7 members of the Board of Governors and 5 Federal Reserve Bank representatives elected annually. The Committee establishes System open market policy for the purchases and sales of securities and for operations in foreign currencies.

Rather than having one central bank in the political capital, as in central banking systems of most countries, the Federal Reserve System is divided into 12 districts, each with a Federal Reserve Bank—in Boston, New York, Philadelphia, Cleveland, Richmond, Atlanta, Chicago, St. Louis, Minneapolis, Kansas City, Dallas, and San Francisco. Reserve Banks are operated for public service. By statute, their stock is held entirely by member banks, which include all national banks and such state banks and trust companies as have been admitted to membership. Ownership of Reserve Bank stock is in the nature of an obligation incident to membership in the System and does not carry with it the attributes of control and financial interest ordinarily attached to stock ownership in corporations that are operated for profit. The amount of stock that member banks own is specified by law and dividends are limited to 6% per annum. In case of the liquidation of any Reserve Bank, its surplus would be paid entirely to the United States. Each Reserve Bank has 9 directors, 6 of whom are chosen by member banks and 3 by the Board of Governors.

The 12-member Federal Advisory Council is composed of one member selected annually by the directors of each Federal Reserve Bank. The Council meets in Washington at least 4 times a year and advises the Board of Governors on matters within the Board's jurisdiction.

U.S. Balance of International Payments

Source: Bureau of Economic Analysis, Dept. of Commerce

(In millions of dollars. Excludes military transfers under grants. Revised. Debits—)

Exports of goods and services	1955	1960	1965	1970	1971	1972	1973	1974
	19,948	27,510	39,502	62,424	65,548	72,600	102,051	144,407
Merchandise, adjusted	14,424	19,650	26,461	42,469	43,311	49,388	71,379	98,268
Transfers under U.S. military agency sales contracts	200	335	830	1,501	1,926	1,163	2,342	2,944
Receipts of income on U.S. investments abroad	2,817	3,350	5,899	8,575	9,512	10,161	13,998	26,068
Other services	2,507	4,177	6,313	9,879	10,799	11,888	14,333	17,126
Imports of goods and services	-17,795	-23,437	-32,362	-59,458	-65,785	-78,530	-97,875	-140,833
Merchandise, adjusted	-11,527	-14,758	-21,510	-39,866	-45,579	-55,797	-70,424	-103,796
Direct defense expenditures	-2,901	-3,087	-2,952	-4,855	-4,819	-4,784	-4,658	-5,103
Payments of income on foreign investments in U.S.	-520	-1,063	-1,730	-5,056	-4,809	-5,841	-8,819	-15,946
Other services	-2,847	-4,529	-6,171	-9,683	-10,578	-12,109	-13,973	-15,988
Unilateral transfers, net	-2,498	-2,300	-2,841	-3,248	-3,642	-3,779	-3,841	-7,182
U.S. Government capital flows, net	-310	-1,100	-1,605	-1,589	-1,884	-1,568	-2,644	408
U.S. Private capital flows, net	-1,255	-3,878	-3,793	-6,920	-10,060	-8,708	-14,113	-31,719
Foreign capital flows, net	1,357	2,120	383	5,923	22,455	21,129	18,648	31,520
Transactions in U.S. official reserve assets, net	182	2,145	1,222	2,477	2,348	32	209	-1,434
Allocation of special drawing rights (SDR)	-	-	-	867	717	710	-	-
Errors and omissions, net	371	-1,060	-506	-476	-9,698	-1,884	-2,436	4,834
Balance of goods and services	2,153	4,073	7,140	2,966	-237	-5,930	4,177	3,574
Balance on goods, services, and remittances	1,556	3,445	6,107	1,455	-1,836	-7,537	2,274	1,853
Balance on current account	-345	1,774	4,299	-281	-3,879	-9,710	335	-3,608
Balance on current account and long-term capital	n.a.	-1,211	-1,829	-3,778	-10,559	-11,235	-744	
Net liquidity balance	n.a.	-3,677	-2,478	-3,851	-21,965	-13,829	-7,651	
Official reserve transactions balance	n.a.	-3,403	-1,290	-9,839	-29,753	-10,354	-5,308	-8,374
Gross Liquidity balance excluding SDR	-1,242	-3,711	-1,421	-4,466	-23,779	-15,786	-;	

Details may not add to totals because of rounding; n.a.—not available.

All Banks in United States—Number, Deposits

Source: Federal Reserve System

Comprises all national banks in the United States and all state commercial banks, trust companies, mutual and stock savings banks, private banks, and such other types of institutions that are operated as banks by the Federal bank supervisory agencies.

		Number of Banks				Total Deposits (Millions of Dollars)				
		Member Banks		Nonmember			Member		Nonmember	
Date June 30	Total All Banks	Total	Nat'l	State	Mutual Savings	Other	Total All Banks	Total	Nat'l	State	Mutual Savings	Other
1925	26,479	9,538	8,066	1,472	621	18,320	51,641	32,457	19,912	12,546	7,089	12,095
1930	23,855	8,315	7,247	1,068	604	14,936	59,828	38,069	23,235	14,834	9,117	12,642
1935	16,047	6,410	5,425	985	569	9,068	51,149	34,938	22,477	12,461	9,830	6,381
1940	14,955	6,398	5,164	1,234	551	8,008	70,770	51,729	33,014	18,715	10,631	8,410
1945	14,542	6,840	5,015	1,825	539	7,163	151,033	118,378	76,534	41,844	14,413	18,242
1950	14,674	6,885	4,971	1,914	527	7,262	163,770	122,707	82,430	40,277	19,927	21,137
1955	14,309	6,611	4,744	1,867	525	7,173	208,850	154,670	98,636	56,034	27,310	26,870
1960	14,006	6,217	4,542	1,675	513	7,276	249,163	179,519	116,178	63,341	35,316	34,328
1965	14,295	6,235	4,803	1,432	504	7,556	362,611	259,743	171,528	88,215	50,980	51,889
1970	14,167	5,803	4,637	1,166	496	7,868	502,658	346,229	254,261	91,967	69,285	87,145
1973	14,529	5,705	4,629	1,076	483	8,341	726,200	487,145	364,129	123,016	96,447	142,608
1975*	14,936	5,782	4,710	1,072	479	8,675	746,760	547,361	—	—	98,701	163,016

*Dec. 31, 1974

Bank Clearings in Chief United States Cities

Year (Cal.)	New York $1,000	Chicago $1,000	Phila. $1,000	Los Ang. $1,000	Boston $1,000	San Fran. $1,000	Detroit $1,000	Dallas $1,000
1935	181,551,008	13,194,988	16,909,000	5,852,244	10,645,822	6,478,835	4,523,167	1,969,290
1940	160,878,038	16,684,672	21,455,000	7,543,880	11,943,665	6,773,877	6,312,233	2,986,774
1945	334,432,654	27,279,588	34,710,000	17,144,078	19,589,725	15,743,086	16,472,971	6,634,514
1950	399,308,634	40,674,983	51,102,000	26,504,731	25,348,396	21,982,689	22,855,273	14,451,332
1955	530,883,498	52,815,527	59,962,000	42,818,633	32,472,726	31,492,157	36,364,754	21,678,567
1960	738,604,276	66,651,600	56,716,000	53,635,826	40,759,040	39,787,147	39,101,854	27,811,939
1965	1,280,402,568	82,507,560	69,116,728	111,587,481	60,318,717	87,095,481	56,068,833	42,414,327
1970	3,752,515,518	110,219,418	94,003,896	174,153,125	125,033,163	122,929,389	136,965,556	51,886,403
1972	6,908,405,349	126,959,884	104,819,843	222,499,794	113,535,232	155,652,822	175,620,419	63,344,639
1973	11,266,959,448	143,210,068	120,093,097	238,642,471	105,641,315	172,693,995	188,512,471	67,794,226
1974	13,163,126,958	148,493,173	129,756,288	254,091,476	117,527,838	188,674,386	212,028,019	74,039,017

Year (Cal.)	Kan. City $1,000	Houston $1,000	Pittsburgh $1,000	Cleveland $1,000	St. Louis $1,000	Minneap. $1,000	Baltimore $1,000	Atlanta $1,000
1935	4,348,113	1,420,404	5,245,718	3,417,055	3,940,654	3,044,735	2,910,637	2,204,500
1940	4,997,593	2,568,518	7,074,775	5,734,407	4,822,016	3,787,088	4,201,985	3,430,900
1945	10,856,497	5,982,318	12,978,668	11,529,428	9,723,815	8,196,274	8,315,468	8,263,900
1950	16,707,120	11,922,307	16,782,419	17,683,829	14,896,444	14,113,814	12,154,904	12,910,100
1955	20,057,800	19,199,929	21,142,527	26,426,614	18,481,105	18,496,868	17,071,914	18,597,100
1960	24,967,583	21,887,889	23,913,706	32,364,009	21,138,861	25,129,318	20,423,684	22,993,200
1965	33,936,377	33,938,170	29,070,474	44,600,090	28,399,392	34,029,120	25,893,740	34,371,000
1970	53,509,523	39,855,427	42,418,973	52,690,067	33,611,932	43,112,445	29,964,761	53,784,237
1972	56,600,642	56,312,671	48,606,390	57,634,936	40,485,176	52,798,284	32,179,679	74,959,502
1973	52,973,946	67,188,692	66,898,891	61,478,321	44,130,125	55,880,907	35,622,338	77,755,923
1974	51,771,171	80,517,773	87,752,769	69,231,013	37,993,730	61,765,880	34,858,768	80,579,538

Per Capita Personal Income, by States and Regions

Source: Department of Commerce, Bureau of Economic Analysis.

State and Region	1970	1971	1972	1973	1974	State and Region	1970	1971	1972	1973	1974
United States	3,966	4,195	4,537	5,023	5,448	Southeast	3,257	3,497	3,859	4,308	4,696
New England	4,300	4,475	4,783	5,217	5,701	Alabama	2,948	3,181	3,472	3,886	4,215
Connecticut	4,917	5,048	5,383	5,896	6,455	Arkansas	2,878	3,040	3,343	3,883	4,200
Maine	3,302	3,405	3,693	4,153	4,590	Florida	3,738	4,034	4,510	5,041	5,416
Massachusetts	4,340	4,540	4,854	5,275	5,757	Georgia	3,354	3,604	3,969	4,402	4,751
New Hampshire	3,737	3,919	4,181	4,592	4,944	Kentucky	3,112	3,314	3,607	4,009	4,442
Rhode Island	3,959	4,196	4,507	4,847	5,343	Louisiana	3,090	3,296	3,574	3,942	4,391
Vermont	3,468	3,674	3,885	4,227	4,534	Mississippi	2,626	2,846	3,187	3,542	3,803
						North Carolina	3,252	3,470	3,853	4,267	4,665
Mideast	4,471	4,720	5,044	5,470	5,973	South Carolina	2,990	3,174	3,507	3,935	4,311
Delaware	4,524	4,870	5,223	5,845	6,306	Tennessee	3,119	3,378	3,708	4,174	4,551
Dist. of Columbia	5,079	5,454	5,924	6,433	7,044	Virginia	3,712	4,001	4,400	4,874	5,339
Maryland	4,309	4,569	4,970	5,442	5,943	West Virginia	3,061	3,282	3,601	3,985	4,372
New Jersey	4,701	4,978	5,302	5,719	6,247						
New York	4,712	4,957	5,249	5,659	6,159	Southwest	3,546	3,707	4,051	4,501	4,866
Pennsylvania	3,971	4,194	4,530	4,958	5,447	Arizona	3,665	3,941	4,332	4,764	5,127
						New Mexico	3,077	3,232	3,517	3,871	4,137
Great Lakes	4,135	4,400	4,751	5,294	5,720	Oklahoma	3,387	3,551	3,834	4,252	4,581
Illinois	4,507	4,802	5,131	5,728	6,234	Texas	3,606	3,747	4,102	4,570	4,952
Indiana	3,772	4,061	4,370	4,929	5,184						
Michigan	4,180	4,499	4,950	5,506	5,883	Rocky Mountains	3,590	3,826	4,214	4,710	5,128
Ohio	4,020	4,237	4,568	5,050	5,518	Colorado	3,855	4,197	4,610	5,058	5,515
Wisconsin	3,812	3,986	4,290	4,807	5,247	Idaho	3,290	3,475	3,785	4,345	4,918
						Montana	3,500	3,576	4,070	4,742	4,956
Plains	3,751	3,947	4,318	5,077	5,260	Utah	3,227	3,437	3,740	4,137	4,473
Iowa	3,751	3,865	4,297	5,291	5,279	Wyoming	3,815	3,868	4,278	4,892	5,404
Kansas	3,853	4,084	4,539	5,224	5,500	Far West	4,374	4,593	4,924	5,393	5,929
Minnesota	3,859	4,038	4,328	5,106	5,422	California	4,493	4,711	5,044	5,491	6,032
Missouri	3,781	4,004	4,293	4,752	5,036	Nevada	4,563	4,873	5,140	5,698	6,016
Nebraska	3,789	3,974	4,442	5,187	5,278	Oregon	3,719	3,992	4,328	4,810	5,284
North Dakota	3,086	3,454	4,012	5,746	5,583	Washington	4,053	4,230	4,558	5,129	5,710
South Dakota	3,123	3,311	3,793	4,923	4,685	Alaska	4,644	4,916	5,192	5,930	7,062
						Hawaii	4,488	4,818	5,123	5,539	6,042

(1.) Per capita personal income for each state is derived by the division of total personal income by total population. Personal income is a measure of the income received from all sources during the calendar year by the residents of each state. It comprises income received by persons in the form of wages and salaries, net income of proprietors (including farmers) dividends, interest, net rents, and other items such as social insurance benefits, relief, veterans pensions and benefits, and allotment payments to dependents of military personnel.

Average Percent Increase in Earnings

Period and area Feb. 1973 to Feb. 1974	All Industries				Manufacturing			
	Office Clerical	Industrial nurses	Skilled maintenance	Unskilled plant	Office Clerical	Industrial nurses	Skilled maintenance	Unskilled plant
United States	6.2	7.2	7.7	7.1	6.3	6.8	7.5	7.7
Northeast	6.2	6.9	7.2	6.4	6.3	6.7	6.9	6.9
South	6.2	6.9	7.5	7.3	6.1	6.9	7.2	8.0
North Central	6.3	7.5	8.1	7.5	6.4	7.0	8.1	8.4
West	5.8	6.8	7.3	6.8	6.0	6.5	7.1	5.8

Indexes of Manufacturing, Industrial Countries

Source: U.S. Bureau of Labor Statistics (1967=100.0)

Output per Hour

Country	1960	1965	1969	1970	1971	1972	1973	1974
United States	79.9	98.4	107.4	107.9	115.2	121.6	128.3	129.2
11 Industrial nations	68.3	89.9	117.1	123.7	129.8	138.4	151.3	—
Canada	75.5	94.4	113.3	115.2	122.9	128.1	133.1	134.9
Japan	52.6	79.1	130.0	146.5	151.7	163.9	193.6	199.6
Belgium	70.5	88.1	117.7	128.4	132.3	144.6	158.8	—
Denmark	66.6	86.7	120.3	129.3	138.8	150.0	163.9	—
France	68.7	88.5	115.4	121.2	127.5	136.1	144.0	148.9
Germany	66.4	90.4	113.8	116.6	122.6	130.3	139.3	143.3
Italy	65.1	91.6	112.2	117.8	123.0	133.4	146.0	—
Netherlands	67.8	87.8	120.9	132.3	140.4	155.5	170.6	—
Sweden	62.3	88.6	118.2	123.5	129.2	138.3	148.0	146.6
Switzerland (wage earners only)	80.4	90.5	116.1	125.5	132.2	138.7	147.7	—
United Kingdom	76.8	92.4	108.1	109.1	114.2	118.9	127.7	127.6
9 European Countries	69.0	90.7	114.4	119.2	125.5	133.7	143.0	—
Original EEC	69.0	90.8	114.3	119.0	125.3	133.6	143.0	—

Unit Labor Costs in U.S. Dollars

Country	1960	1965	1969	1970	1971	1972	1973	1974
United States	95.8	92.6	106.1	113.2	113.2	113.1	114.7	124.8
11 Industrial nations	82.6	97.5	100.9	111.8	125.1	143.4	170.6	—
Canada	106.3	91.3	101.9	111.5	116.3	122.1	126.3	144.1
Japan	82.5	102.5	106.9	112.8	129.9	159.5	188.0	226.1
Belgium	73.9	93.8	97.9	102.7	116.9	136.7	166.2	—
Denmark	74.7	91.8	95.8	104.4	112.4	123.4	154.0	—
France	81.8	98.4	98.7	98.7	105.4	120.5	147.2	156.8
Germany	78.1	95.7	103.1	124.6	141.8	162.5	207.3	237.3
Italy	76.5	97.1	104.3	119.2	137.2	153.6	173.9	—
Netherlands	65.4	91.8	102.7	108.5	121.2	137.2	165.7	—
United Kingdom	85.7	98.6	93.0	106.0	117.9	131.0	136.0	155.5
Sweden	80.4	93.2	101.0	106.2	115.9	130.8	147.9	171.1
Switzerland (wages earned only)	71.1	95.6	97.1	99.7	112.4	128.7	160.1	—
9 European Countries	79.3	96.5	100.1	112.7	126.0	143.1	172.9	—
Original EEC	79.7	96.7	100.2	113.6	127.1	144.3	174.7	—

U. S. Labor Force, Employment and Unemployment

Source: Bureau of the Census, U. S. Dept. of Commerce; Bureau of Labor Statistics, U. S. Dept. of Labor
(Unemployment by sex, age, color and other characteristics)

	1972	1973	1974	Jan.	Feb.	Mar.	Apr.	May	June
					1975				
				(Numbers in thousands)					
U.S. Pop. (incl. armed forces overseas)	'208,842	'210,396	'211,916	212,806	212,940	213,039	213,039	213,261	N.A.
Labor Force²									
Labor force, persons 16 years of age and over . . .	88,991	91,042	93,240	93,342	93,111	93,593	93,564	93,949	96,191
Civilian labor force.	86,542	88,716	91,011	91,149	90,913	91,395	91,369	91,768	94,013
Employed, total.	81,702	84,410	85,936	82,969	82,604	83,036	83,549	84,146	85,444
Agriculture.	3,472	3,453	3,492	2,888	2,890	2,988	3,171	3,622	3,869
Nonagricultural Industries.	78,230	80,957	82,443	80,082	79,714	80,048	80,377	80,524	81,575
Unemployed	4,840	4,306	5,076	8,180	8,309	8,359	7,820	7,623	8,569
Long term, 15 weeks and over	1,158	812	937	1,554	2,031	2,553	3,054	2,923	2,852
Seasonally adjusted									
Civilian labor force	. . . . .	. . . . .	. . . .	92,091	91,511	91,829	92,262	92,940	92,340
Employed total	. . . . .	. . . . .	. . . .	84,562	84,027	83,849	84,086	84,402	84,444
Agriculture.	. . . . .	. . . . .	. . . .	3,383	3,326	3,265	3,238	3,512	3,304
Nonagricultural Industries	. . . . .	. . . . .	. . . .	81,179	80,701	80,584	80,848	80,890	81,140
Unemployed	. . . . .	. . . . .	. . . .	7,529	7,484	7,980	8,176	8,538	7,896
Long term, 15 weeks and over.	. . . . .	. . . . .	. . . .	1,537	1,822	1,991	2,403	2,643	2,887
Rates (unemployed in each group as percent of total in the group):									
All civilian workers	5.6	4.9	5.6	•	8.7	8.9	9.2	8.6	
Men, 20 years and over.	4.0	3.2	3.8	6.0	6.2	6.8	7.0	7.3	7.0
Women, 20 years and over	5.4	4.8	5.5	8.1	8.1	8.5	8.6	8.6	8.1
Both sexes, 16-19 years	16.2	14.5	16.0	20.8	19.9	20.6	20.4	21.8	19.2
White	5.0	4.3	5.0	7.5	7.4	8.0	8.1	8.5	7.9
Negro and other races	10.0	8.9	9.9	13.4	13.5	14.2	14.6	14.7	13.7
Household heads.	3.3	2.9	3.3	5.2	5.4	5.8	6.0	6.3	6.1
Married men	2.8	2.3	2.7	4.5	4.7	5.2	5.6	5.8	5.7
Occupation:									
White-collar workers	3.4	2.9	3.3	4.6	4.5	4.6	4.7	5.4	4.8
Blue-collar workers	6.5	5.3	6.7	11.0	10.9	12.5	13.0	13.0	12.6
Industry of last job (nonagricultural)									
Private wage and salary workers	5.7	4.8	•5.7	8.7	8.8	9.3	9.8	10.1	9.6
Construction.	10.3	8.8	10.6	15.0	15.9	18.1	19.3	21.8	21.0
Manufacturing	5.6	4.3	5.7	10.5	11.0	11.4	12.2	12.3	12.0
Durable goods	5.4	3.9	5.4	10.5	10.9	11.3	12.8	12.7	12.9

(1) As of July 1. (2) Effective January 1972, data reflect adjustment to the 1970 Census of Population. For exmple the civilian labor force and employment totals were increased by a little more than 300,000; unemployment levels and rates were essentially unchanged. A subsequent census adjustment, primarily affecting whites and Negroes and other race groups, was introduced into the survey for March 1973. As a result, the white labor force and employment levels were lowered by about 150,000, while Negro levels were raised by 210,000. Consequently, the overall labor force and employment showed a net increase of about 60,000. Unemployment levels and rates were not affected significantly. Comparisons with data prior to these two dates should take these adjustments into account.
N.A.—Not available.

Employed Persons by Major Occupational Groups and Sex
Source: Bureau of Labor Statistics

	Thousands of persons			Percent Distribution		
Annual Averages 1974	Both				Both	
Occupational Group	sexes	Males	Females	sexes	Males	Females
Total employed	85,936	52,519	33,417	100.0	100.0	100.0
White-collar workers	41,738	21,155	20,583	48.6	40.3	61.6
Professional and technical.	12,338	7,346	4,992	14.4	14.0	14.9
Managers and administrators, except farm.	8,941	7,291	1,650	10.4	13.9	4.9
Sales workers	5,417	3,152	2,265	6.3	6.0	6.8
Clerical workers	15,043	3,366	11,676	17.5	6.4	34.9
Blue-collar workers	29,776	24,581	5,195	34.6	46.8	15.5
Craftsmen and kindred workers	11,477	10,966	511	13.4	20.9	1.5
Operatives, except transport.	10,627	6,464	4,164	12.4	12.3	12.5
Transport equipment operatives	3,292	3,126	167	3.8	6.0	0.5
Nonfarm laborers	4,380	4,026	354	5.1	7.7	1.1
Service workers	11,373	4,218	7,156	13.2	8.0	21.4
Private household workers.	1,228	27	1,201	1.4	—	3.6
Other service workers.	10,145	4,190	5,955	11.8	8.0	17.8
Farm workers	3,048	2,564	484	3.5	4.9	1.4
Farmers and farm managers.	1,643	1,545	98	1.9	2.9	0.3
Farm laborers and foremen.	1,405	1,020	385	1.6	1.9	1.2

Employment and Unemployment in the United States

Civilian Labor Force, Persons 16 Years of Age and Over (in thousands)

Year	Civilian Labor Force	Employed	Unemployed	Year	Civilian Labor Force	Employed	Unemployed
						First Half Average	
1969	80,733	77,902	2,831				
1970	82,715	78,627	4,088	1970	81,907	78,151	3,756
1971	84,113	79,120	4,993	1971	83,165	78,064	5,101
1972	86,542	81,702	4,840	1972	85,616	80,524	5,090
1973	88,714	84,409	4,304	1974	90,022	85,234	4,788
1974	91,011	85,936	5,076	1975	91,768	83,625	8,143

Civilian Employment of the Federal Government

Source: United States Civil Service Commission, Manpower Statistics Division, data as of June 30, 1975

Agency	All Areas	United States			Outside United States		
		Total	Full-Time	Part-Time & Intermittent	Total	Territories	Foreign Countries
Total, all agencies (a)...............	2,896,952	2,771,121	2,553,752	217,369	125,831	34,577	91,254
Percent distribution........	100	96	88	8	4	1	3
Legislative Branch.................	38,531	38,458	37,672	786	73	...	73
Congress.......................	17,317	17,317	17,317	...	...	...	...
United States Senate............	6,144	6,144	6,144	...	...	...	...
House of Representatives.........	11,173	11,173	11,173	...	...	...	...
Architect of the Capitol.............	2,061	2,061	1,926	135	...	...	...
General Accounting Office..........	5,513	5,449	5,367	82	64	...	64
Government Printing Office..........	8,549	8,549	8,244	305	...	...	...
Library of Congress...............	4,649	4,640	4,407	233	9	...	9
United States Tax Court............	205	205	198	7	...	...	...
Judicial Branch....................	10,399	10,293	9,832	461	106	106	...
United States Courts...............	10,122	10,016	9,579	437	106	106	...
Supreme Court....................	277	277	253	24	...	...	...
Executive Branch..................	2,848,022	2,722,370	2,506,248	216,122	125,652	34,471	91,181
Executive Office of the President.....	1,918	1,918	1,783	135	...	...	...
White House Office..............	625	625	589	36	...	...	...
Office of the Vice President........	39	39	30	9	...	...	...
Office of Management and Budget..	673	673	659	14	...	...	...
Council of Economic Advisors.....	40	40	35	5	...	...	...
Citizens' Advisory Committee on Environmental Quality..........	1	1	1	...	...	...	...
Council on Environmental Quality...	69	69	66	3	...	...	...
Council on Wage and Price Stability .	45	45	42	3	...	...	...
Domestic Council................	34	34	34	...	...	...	...
Executive Mansion and Grounds...	81	81	81	...	...	...	...
National Commission on Productivity and Work Quality..............	40	40	23	17	...	...	...
National Security Council..........	89	89	72	17	...	...	...
Office of Special Representative for Trade Negotiations.............	49	49	46	3	...	...	...
Office of Telecommunications Policy	76	76	67	9	...	...	...
Presidential Clemency Board......	17	17	...	17	...	...	...
Executive Departments.............	1,736,872	1,638,044	1,583,493	54,551	98,828	14,433	84,395
State (b)........................	30,376	10,777	10,130	647	19,599	...	19,599
Treasury........................	121,546	120,619	117,260	3,359	927	577	350
Defense.........................	1,041,829	968,021	957,937	10,084	73,808	10,954	62,854
Office of the Secretary..........	2,189	2,152	2,051	101	37	...	37
Department of the Army..........	378,937	345,537	341,314	4,223	33,400	4,187	29,213
Department of the Navy.........	319,719	297,565	293,954	3,611	22,154	4,684	17,470
Department of the Air Force.....	268,466	251,527	249,676	1,851	16,939	1,905	15,034
Defense Supply Agency.........	53,737	53,089	52,989	100	648	64	584
Other Defense Activities........	18,781	18,151	17,953	198	630	114	516
Justice..........................	51,541	50,687	49,536	1,151	854	350	504
Interior.........................	80,198	79,789	74,231	5,558	409	350	59
Agriculture......................	120,999	119,740	98,210	21,530	1,259	630	629
Commerce.......................	36,228	35,966	31,586	4,380	262	81	181
Labor...........................	14,834	14,767	14,251	516	67	64	3
Health, Education, and Welfare.....	147,125	146,501	140,771	5,730	624	575	49
Housing and Urban Development...	17,161	16,986	16,705	281	175	175	...
Transportation...................	75,035	74,191	72,876	1,315	844	677	167
Independent agencies..............	1,109,232	1,082,408	920,972	161,436	26,824	20,038	6,786
ACTION.........................	1,864	1,265	1,184	81	599	33	566
Board of Governors, Fed. Res. Sys....	1,460	1,460	1,427	33	...	...	...
Canal Zone Government............	3,299	...	...	...	3,299	3,299	...
Civil Service Commission..........	8,157	8,136	7,021	1,115	21	21	...
Community Service Administration....	1,112	1,112	1,102	10	...	...	...
Energy Res. and Dev. Admin.........	8,262	8,250	7,983	267	12	...	12
Environmental Protection Agency.....	10,772	10,758	10,102	656	14	10	4
Federal Communication Comm......	2,137	2,130	2,108	22	7	7	...
Federal Energy Administration.......	3,257	3,257	3,203	54	...	...	...
Federal Power Commission........	1,322	1,322	1,320	2	...	...	...
Federal Trade Commission.........	1,661	1,661	1,640	21	...	...	...
General Services Administration......	39,439	39,456	38,281	1,175	83	72	11
Information Agency................	8,815	3,331	3,303	28	5,484	...	5,484
Interstate Commerce Commission....	2,115	2,115	2,102	13	...	...	...
Natl. Aero and Space Admin........	26,447	26,425	26,260	165	22	1	21
National Labor Relations Board......	2,485	2,461	2,434	27	24	24	...
Nuclear Regulatory Commission.....	2,247	2,247	2,201	46	...	...	...
Panama Canal Company...........	11,689	88	88	...	11,601	11,601	...
Securities and Exchange Comm.....	2,002	2,002	1,980	22	...	...	...
Selective Service System..........	2,257	2,215	2,081	134	42	42	...
Small Business Administration.......	4,796	4,700	4,622	78	96	96	...
Tennessee Valley Authority.........	28,423	28,318	28,110	308	5	...	5
U. S. Postal Service...............	699,174	696,300	556,947	139,353	2,874	2,874	...
Veterans Administration............	213,143	210,997	194,180	16,817	2,146	1,860	286
a-All other agencies...............	22,797	22,302	21,293	1,009	495	98	397

(a) Excludes employees of Central Intelligence Agency, National Security Agency (not reported to the Civil Service Commission) and uncompensated employees. June 1975 total includes 48,341 employees exempted from personnel ceilings in the Youth Programs and Worker Trainee Opportunities Program. (b) Includes 6,591 employees in Agency for International Development (3,102 in the Washington, D.C., metropolitan area); employees in foreign countries include 677 paid from local currency trust funds established by foreign governments.

Overseas Direct Investment in the United States
Source: U.S. Dept. of Commerce

The value of overseas direct investments in the United States increased $708,000,000 in 1972 to $14,263 billion at year-end. The increase resulted from reinvested earnings of $548 million and net capital inflows of $160 million. *Interest, dividends, and branch profits account for most of the income received by foreign owners from direct investments in the U.S.

(Millions of dollars)	Book Value	Net Cap. inflows	Total	Earnings Int.* div.	Reinv'd.
1972	14,263	383	1,202	687	496
1973 Total (prelim.)	17,748	2,537	1,843	892	945
By country					
Canada	4,003	348	332	96	233
United Kingdom	5,437	573	493	262	243
Netherlands	2,550	81	205	91	112
Switzerland	1,825	211	144	105	47
Other	3,933	1,324	669	338	310

Canadian Labor Force
Source: Statistics Canada (Apr., 1975, seasonally adjusted)
(thousands of workers)

	Can.	Nfld.	P.E.I.	N.S.	N.B.	Que.	Ont.	Man.	Sask.	Alta.	B.C.
Labor Force	9,925	189	44	302	256	2,677	3,768	425	379	778	1,109
Employed	9,208	156	40	277	227	2,435	3,540	405	369	746	1,019
Unemployed	717	33	...	25	29	242	228	20	10	32	90
Percent unemployed	7.2	17.5	..	8.3	11.3	9.0	6.1	4.7	2.6	4.1	8.1

Canada: Labor Force Characteristics
Source: Statistics Canada

	Labor force (000)	Employed (thousands)						Unemployed (000)	Unemployed %
		All workers			Paid workers				
		Total	Agriculture	Non-Agriculture	Total	Non-Agriculture			
1950	5,163	4,976	1,018	3,958	3,522	3,411		186	3.6
1955	5,610	5,364	819	4,546	4,133	4,027		245	4.4
1960	6,411	5,965	683	5,282	4,843	4,732		446	7.0
1965	7,141	6,862	594	6,268	5,760	5,655		280	3.9
1970	8,374	7,879	511	7,368	6,839	6,740		495	5.9
1971	8,631	8,079	510	7,569	7,029	6,927		552	6.4
1972	8,891	8,329	481	7,848	7,310	7,211		562	6.3
1973	9,279	8,759	467	8,292	7,757	7,661		520	5.6
1974	9,662	9,137	473	8,664	8,105	8,006		525	5.4

Average Weekly Canadian Wages and Salaries, by Province (C$)
Source: Canadian Statistical Review, Apr. 1975 (p) Preliminary

Year & Month	Canada	Nfld.	P.E.I.	N.S.	N.B.	Que.	Ont.	Man.	Sask.	Alta.	B.C.
1960	117.63	106.00	80.87	94.51	96.80	114.24	121.55	107.67	107.90	117.95	129.35
1970	126.82	117.70	83.82	104.21	104.01	122.38	131.52	115.88	114.87	128.15	137.97
1973	160.46	149.09	111.17	134.44	133.97	154.30	165.61	144.76	142.28	161.12	178.22
1974 Jan.	167.72	155.97	118.81	142.39	145.50	162.06	172.32	153.45	149.25	168.05	185.83
Apr.	172.56	161.46	123.43	145.71	148.37	166.80	176.38	158.37	155.60	171.78	193.13
Jul.	180.07	170.54	127.16	152.93	158.21	174.94	182.74	166.23	164.36	182.29	203.07
Oct. (p)	186.92	178.81	136.94	155.12	164.66	182.26	189.89	169.26	169.14	186.76	212.06

Activities of the Unemployment Insurance Commission — Canada
Source: Canadian Statistical Review — Apr., 1975

Benefits Paid (thousand dollars)

Year and Month	Claims Data Claimants[12]	Claims received (000)	Weeks paid (000)	Total[3] Paid	Benefits Paid				
					Regular	Sickness	Maternity	Retirement	Fishing
1972	804	2,470	30,462	1,871,802	1,764,030	58,855	36,431	2,440	20,404
1973	828	2,239	29,537	2,004,211	1,850,928	80,179	66,750	3,690	20,296
1974	828	2,411	28,460	2,119,213	1,924,543	98,319	81,710	4,165	22,676
Jan.	981	278	3,368	247,603	226,850	8,481	6,752	396	6,076
1975 Jan.	1,134	356	3,725	306,501	281,638	10,600	8,777	578	5,839

[1] Persons who have applied for or are in receipt of unemployment insurance benefit at the end of the month.
[2] Annual figures are average of 12 months.
[3] Includes adjustments for cancellation of warrants and collection of overpayments.

Canada: Regional Unemployment Rates, 1974-1975
Source: Statistics Canada

Region	Apr.	Mar.	Feb.	Jan.	Dec.	Nov.	Region	Apr.	Mar.	Feb.	Jan.	Dec.	Nov.
Atlantic	11.3	11.6	10.9	10.6	10.9	9.3	Prairie	4.4	4.1	3.3	3.8	4.3	5.1
Quebec	9.0	9.0	8.6	8.1	8.1	7.1	British Columbia	8.4	9.3	6.0	6.0	7.0	7.6
Ontario	6.1	6.0	5.6	6.0	4.6	4.4	Canada	7.2	7.2	6.8	6.7	6.0	5.5

Total Value of Construction Work Performed in Canada

(thousand dollars)
Source: Statistics Canada

Province	1973 New	1973 Repair	1973 Total	1974 New	1974 Repair	1974 Total
Canada	16,960,681	3,177,601	20,138,282	19,589,685	3,563,661	23,153,346
Newfoundland	418,106	53,307	471,413	452,945	60,820	513,765
Prince Edward Island	91,143	17,336	108,479	98,231	20,371	118,602
Nova Scotia	526,878	96,734	623,612	601,208	108,044	709,252
New Brunswick	404,377	89,786	494,163	517,301	103,365	620,666
Quebec	3,684,284	673,682	4,357,966	4,315,028	748,593	5,063,621
Ontario	6,086,278	1,151,244	7,237,522	6,989,776	1,290,548	8,280,324
Manitoba	745,196	143,297	888,493	800,910	169,008	969,918
Saskatchewan	534,749	171,085	705,834	590,104	189,215	779,319
Alberta	1,921,501	351,239	2,272,740	2,265,339	390,105	2,655,444
British Columbia	2,548,169	429,891	2,978,060	2,958,843	483,592	3,442,435

Includes residential, commercial, institutional, marine, road, highway and aerodrome, waterworks and sewage systems, and all other construction.

Pulpwood, Wood Pulp, and Newsprint—Canada

(thousand tons)
Source: Canadian Statistical Review, Apr. 1975

Year and Month	Pulpwood Production (thousand units[1])	Wood Pulp Production[2] Total	Wood Pulp Production[2] Mechanical	Wood Pulp Production[2] Chemical	Wood pulp Exports[3]	News-Print Production	Newsprint Shipments Total	Newsprint Shipments Domestic	Newsprint Shipments Export[4]
1972	18,805	18,593.3	7,520.8	11,033.9	6,071.2	8,660.8	8,739.4	779.7	7,959.8
1973	18,435	20,030.0	7,646.5	12,045.8	8,343.6	8,966.1	9,039.2	857.6	8,162.8
1974	21,402	21,788.6	8,224.9	12,791.5	7,056.5	9,548.0	9,596.9	886.0	8,711.1
1975									
Jan	1,728	1,753.8	683.0	1,067.1	535.7	. .	. .	. .	. .
Feb		1,647.0	645.7	998.1		. .	. .	. .	. .

(1) 100 cu. ft. of solid wood; pulpwood produced for domestic use and excluding exports, but including receipts of purchased roundwood.
(2) Total pulp production covers "screenings" which are already included in exports. "Screenings" are excluded throughout from mechanical and chemical pulp.
(3) Customs exports.
(4) Mill shipments destined for export.

Telephones in North American Cities with over 100,000 Telephones

Source: American Telephone and Telegraph Co., and Trans-Canada Telephone Systems (Jan. 1, 1974)

City	Number	City	Number	City	Number	City	Number
Akron	330,838	Evansville	112,604	Miami	924,108	St. Petersburg	262,009
Albany, N.Y.	159,111	Fayetteville	107,839	Milwaukee	766,459	Salt Lake City	384,039
Albuquerque	241,592	Flint	199,968	Minn.-St. Paul	1,427,900	San Antonio	376,422
Alexandria, Va.	210,358	Ft. Lauderdale	313,557	Mobile	185,196	San Diego (Area)	871,167
Allentown, Pa.	132,492	Fort Wayne	157,700	Monterrey, Mex.	133,455	San Francisco	744,519
Amarillo	109,630	Fort Worth	295,835	Montgomery	125,940	San Jose	474,897
Anaheim, Cal.	186,654	Fremont City	101,648	Montreal	1,106,039	San Mateo	108,764
Ann Arbor, Mich.	110,123	Fresno	209,838	Mt. Vernon, N.Y.	117,339	Santa Ana	318,981
Atlanta, Ga.	824,642	Gary	117,480	Nashville	340,178	Santa Barbara	115,805
Augusta, Ga.	116,642	Grand Rapids	259,558	New Haven	252,532	Savannah	121,575
Austin, Tex.	243,889	Greensboro	160,380	New Orleans	609,692	Schenectady	123,301
Bakersfield, Cal.	136,285	Greenville, N.C.	146,689	New York	5,952,112	Seattle	560,857
Baltimore	1,165,833	Halifax	123,316	Newark	323,290	Shreveport	174,378
Baton Rouge	216,635	Hamilton	181,570	Newport News	188,772	Skokie, Ill.	139,638
Birmingham	368,714	Harrisburg	187,023	Norfolk (Area)	394,218	South Bend	127,316
Boston	506,911	Hartford	302,706	Oklahoma City	503,603	Spokane	185,067
Bridgeport	168,013	Hayward, Cal.	124,423	Omaha	381,400	Springfield, Ill.	125,428
Buffalo	433,651	Hollywood, Fla.	184,833	Orlando	222,466	Springfield, Mass.	144,050
Calgary	305,820	Honolulu	316,203	Ottawa	369,086	Springfield, Mo.	107,497
Cambridge	106,301	Houston	1,102,855	Palo Alto	137,626	Stamford, Conn.	102,972
Canton	121,350	Huntington Beach	102,495	Passaic	132,821	Stockton, Cal.	117,890
Cedar Rapids	108,400	Huntsville, Ala.	126,424	Paterson	115,423	Syracuse	252,457
Charleston, S.C.	165,592	Indianapolis	612,108	Pensacola	127,888	Tacoma	202,862
Charlotte	292,301	Jackson, Miss.	163,895	Peoria	165,353	Tampa	330,437
Chattanooga	212,711	Jacksonville	383,833	Philadelphia	1,602,624	Toledo	291,737
Chicago	2,435,094	Jersey City	170,164	Phoenix	735,283	Topeka	101,746
Cincinnati	675,002	Kalamazoo	129,126	Pittsburgh	751,634	Toronto	763,181
Cleveland	885,518	Kansas City, Kan.	152,122	Pomona	144,828	Tucson	251,719
Colorado Springs	182,003	Kansas City, Mo.	331,955	Pompano Beach	131,431	Tulsa	334,591
Columbia, S.C.	217,512	Knoxville	177,720	Pontiac	106,144	Union City, N.J.	114,849
Columbus, Ga.	120,923	Lansing	194,528	Portland, Ore.	439,979	Vancouver	382,979
Columbus, Oh.	463,951	Las Vegas	247,002	Providence	244,182	Victoria	129,616
Corpus Christi	126,790	Lexington	135,821	Quebec City	221,805	Warren, Mich.	266,930
Covington	106,293	Lincoln	127,000	Raleigh	157,441	Washington,D.C.	970,901
Dallas	711,996	Little Rock	187,338	Reading, Pa.	148,791	Weston	193,853
Davenport	101,000	Livonia, Mich.	155,635	Reno	105,060	West Palm Beach	242,245
Dayton	363,807	London	148,858	Richmond, Va.	340,906	Wichita	197,259
Denver	986,417	Livonia, Mich.		Riverside, Cal.	130,830	Willowdale	179,006
Des Moines	244,700	Los Angeles (Area)	5,215,641	Roanoke, Va.	112,293	Wilmington, Del.	191,315
Detroit	1,437,624	Louisville	479,891	Rochester, N.Y.	353,083	Windsor	113,691
East Orange,N.J.	126,957	Lubbock, Tex.	129,783	Rockford, Ill.	163,467	Winnipeg	335,948
Edmonton	280,931	Madison, Wis.	167,529	Royal Oak, Mich.	182,230	Winston-Salem	143,371
El Paso	218,875	Memphis	506,029	Sacramento	421,961	Winter Park	103,053
Erie	129,057	Mexico City	1,013,461	Saginaw, Mich.	113,378	Worcester	128,726
Eugene, Springfield, Ore.	117,684			St. Louis	569,492	Youngstown	176,024

ENERGY

Nuclear Energy — The Balance Sheet

By Barry Youngerman

It is the year 2025. Throughout the world, thousands of clean, efficient nuclear power plants dot the landscape, churning out almost unlimited quantities of cheap energy. Forgotten are the filthy effluents that used to belch forth from coal- and oil-fired plants and from automobiles, which are now driven by cheaply-recharged batteries. Forgotten are the worldwide fuel shortages and embargoes; instead, the nations of the world share a standardized, internationally-controlled nuclear fuel and power system, and the formerly underdeveloped lands are fast catching up, thanks to the industrial and agricultural benefits of plentiful energy.

Or:

The same year. Each month brings the disclosure that another obscure tiny nation has added plutonium bombs to its arsenal. Nuclear saber-rattling is commonplace, with many thousands of effective bombs in the hands of ambitious and sometimes unstable rulers. Whole cities are paralyzed as terrorist groups threaten to release deadly radioactive materials unless their most fanatical demands are met. Cancer rates continue a long-term dramatic rise. Regions are quarantined as unacceptable radiation levels are detected in local water supplies, and thousands are reported dead from a single core-meltdown accident.

Atomic Age Arrives

Ever since the atomic age was ushered in by the destruction of Hiroshima and Nagasaki in 1945, the prospect of harnessing nuclear energy for peaceful purposes has intrigued governments, industry, and the scientific community. The needed technology was developed in the industrialized countries with relatively little public attention. In the past few years, several dozen nuclear power plants began feeding growing amounts of power into the electrical grids of the U.S., Western Europe, and the U.S.S.R.

Spurred by the oil embargo and price hikes of 1973 and 1974, the major powers announced plans for a startling expansion of this industry, and a host of secondary powers decided to join the bandwagon. But the nagging dual problems of radiation (which can cause cancer and birth defects) and atom bomb proliferation remained.

In 1975, a movement to hold back or even shut down the industry attracted vocal support among some scientists, politicians, and the general public in several countries. The outcome of the growing debate will have momentous consequences for the physical and economic well-being of mankind.

The Benefits

The benefits of atomic fission energy could be great. Oil, natural gas, and coal are all nonrenewable fuels, and economic supplies of the first might well run out within one or 2 generations. Besides, their use entails such familiar problems as strip mining, black lung disease in miners, oil spills, and air pollution. Alternative energy sources, such as the sun's rays, earth heat, ocean currents, winds, nuclear fusion, and organic wastes, may one day be exploited, but the technologies are still undeveloped.

In contrast, nuclear fission energy technology appears to have reached the point of economic viability. Costs to consumers average about 25% lower than electricity produced from coal, the cheapest of fossil fuels — a savings of about $800 million to U.S. consumers in 1975. Because of the tremendous concentration of energy in fissionable material, one kilogram (2.4 pounds) of U-235 yields as much energy as six million pounds of coal.

Besides, U.S. uranium reserves may be ample enough to fuel an advanced nuclear industry for centuries, relieving us from dependence on foreign fuel supplies. Government officials hope that nuclear reactors will increase their share of national electricity outputs from 8.5% in 1975 to 16% in 1980, 41% in 1990 and 55% in 2000, when some 2,000 plants may be in operation.

Weighed against the benefits are the risks. To understand the possible dangers, a knowledge of the basic nuclear fuel-energy cycle is helpful.

The Nuclear Cycle

Uranium is generally found in low-grade ores with about 0.2% uranium content. The ores are crushed, and the uranium chemically extracted (milling) and shipped as uranium oxide U_3O_8. The unused residues, called mill tailings, are discarded.

Natural uranium occurs in two varieties, or isotopes — U-238 and U-235. Only U-235 is fissionable. That is, its atoms tend to break down spontaneously into other elements, releasing energy in the form of heat and emitting several neutrons, sub-atomic particles that in turn cause other uranium atoms to split. But U-235 comprises only 0.7% of natural uranium, too small a proportion to sustain a chain reaction in the light-water reactors used in the U.S. Natural uranium must be upgraded in an enrichment plant, after conversion to a volatile compound, uranium hexaflouride UF_6.

The Nuclear Fuel Cycle

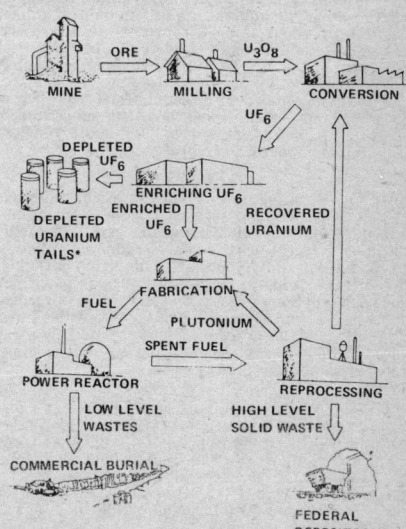

*Not required for reactor but must be stored safely.

Source: Adapted from Nuclear Industry, 1974. (U.S. Atomic Energy Commission Report No. WASH-1174-74).

The only commercially proven enrichment process is gaseous diffusion, in which the slightly lighter U-235 is gradually separated out by repeatedly forcing uranium hexaflouride gas through a series of porous barriers. The resulting uranium is composed of 2.8%-3.5% U-235. The process consumes huge amounts of energy, and may eventually be replaced by the far less energy-intensive centrifuge method, which spins off the U-235 much like a cream separator. Recent developments point to a possible laser separation method, an even less expensive and much more rapid process, which might be built on a smaller scale. In each case, quantities of slightly radioactive uranium hexaflouride which have been depleted in U-235 (enrichment tails) remain and must be stored safely.

After enrichment, the uranium undergoes *fabrication* into ceramic pellets, which are sealed into zincalloy or stainless steel tubes. In this form, the fuel is ready for insertion into the power reactor.

Most commercial reactors in operation throughout the world today are light-water reactors (LWRs). In these models, ordinary water is used as a *moderator* and a *coolant*. As a moderator, it slows down the neutrons, making them more likely to initiate additional fissions. As a coolant it absorbs the excess heat and uses it to produce steam. In some LWRs, the water is allowed to vaporize within the reactor, and is passed through tubing to turbines. In other LWRs, the water is brought under high pressure to the steam generator, and a separate tubing system leads through the turbines.

During the fission process, some U-238 atoms absorb neutrons and become plutonium, which is fissionable. About one third of the energy produced in the reactor is derived from this plutonium.

After a given period of time, the fuel mixture becomes diluted with fission products and is replaced. The spent fuel, however, contains uranium fairly high in U-238 as well as plutonium and various radioactive wastes. This material can be *reprocessed*, with the plutonium recovered and the uranium re-enriched, thereby reducing the need for natural mined uranium by about 12%. In reprocessing, the waste material is condensed to solid form, for potential long-term burial. But the high toxicity of plutonium and its bomb potential have caused the U.S. government to delay approval of commercial-sized reprocessing plants. In the meantime, the spent fuel is building up in storage, threatening some reactors with shutdown for lack of storage space.

The Risks

Each stage of the process carries risks of radiation leakage (especially for workers), as does the transport of nuclear materials between stages. The medical damage from these low-level radiation releases could develop slowly, making detection difficult. There have been proposals for nuclear parks, in which several power plants and the various processing facilities would be located at huge, isolated sites. But most countries or local regions are unlikely to be able to support a complete nuclear system, so some transport would continue to be necessary.

The U.S. Nuclear Regulatory Commission, which in 1975 assumed the regulatory functions of the old Atomic Energy Commission (AEC), announced in March 1975 that tighter procedures had been imposed on the import and export of nuclear materials. The move followed a congressional and public outcry after it was discovered that 200 pounds of plutonium was being shipped through commercial channels via Kennedy Airport in New York.

Even mining operations might be hazardous under some conditions. A report by the U.S. Environmental Protection Agency, released Aug. 18, 1975, said that "intolerable" levels of radioactive matter and of poisonous chemicals had been found during tests of drinking water in western New Mexico communities near a booming uranium mining area. (Some

naturally-occurring radiation is often found in ground water.)

But the stages with the greatest immediate safety problems, according to industry critics, are reactor operation and waste storage.

Experts agree that fears of a bomb-like explosion at a power plant are completely unfounded with current reactors, though the breeder reactors being developed may pose such a threat.

But catastrophic releases of deadly radiation are theoretically possible if a series of human or equipment failures occurred. If a major break developed in the reactor cooling system, the core could attain very high temperatures. If the emergency cooling system failed as well, the core could melt into the ground and release radiation in a hot gaseous plume that could contaminate a wide area, depending on wind currents.

A 1964 study by the Atomic Energy Commission (AEC), which was withheld from the public for several years, said that such an accident could hypothetically affect an area "the size of the state of Pennsylvania." The AEC admitted in 1973 that as many as 43,000 casualties could result from a major accident at a fairly small plant.

A more comprehensive study, commissioned by the AEC and released in 1974, sharply reduced the casualty estimates. The $3-million, 14-volume draft report was directed by Dr. Norman C. Rasmussen of the Massachusetts Institute of Technology (MIT). Using pioneering analytic tools, Rasmussen estimated that only 96 deaths and 200 acute illnesses would result from the accident foreseen in the earlier study. Furthermore, the probability of such an accident occurring was computed to be extremely remote, even taking into account the effects of earthquakes, floods, and aircraft crashes.

The final risk figures arrived at indicated that with 100 reactors in operation, the chances of an individual being killed in a nuclear reactor accident were about the same as the chances of an individual being killed by a meteorite, or one in three hundred million.

Some critics remained skeptical. Dr. Henry W. Kendall, also of MIT, noting the study's AEC sponsorship, said "I don't know how anyone could call this an independent report." Others cited the novelty of the analytic methods used, a point conceded in the report. In any case, the Rasmussen study avoided the possibility of deliberate sabotage by disgruntled or unstable employees, or by political terrorists.

A petition signed by 2,300 scientists, including some with nuclear engineering experience, called for a "drastic reduction" in new plant construction pending resolution of safety problems. The petition, sponsored by the Union of Concerned Scientists and presented to Congress and the White House Aug. 6, 1975, said that the "record to date evidences many malfunctions of major equipment, operator errors and design defects as well as a continuing weakness in the quality control practices with which nuclear plants are constructed." It should be noted that many of these defects and errors were taken into account in the Rasmussen study.

One serious mishap occurred March 22, 1975, at the Browns Ferry plant near Decatur, Ala. A fire, triggered by a worker looking for an air leak with a lighted candle, destroyed 1,600 cables, some of which controlled the emergency cooling system. Plant officials managed to devise substitute measures to flood the reactor, and no significant radiation was released. A study by a nuclear insurance consortium, reported in the Sept. 22 New York Times, found that five of 23 insured reactors needed fire prevention improvements.

Small cracks and water leaks have been detected from time to time, causing the government to order shutdowns of the plant involved and other plants using similar equipment. Twenty-three plants were ordered closed for 20-day inspections Jan. 29, 1975, by the Nuclear Regulatory Commission, after five small cracks appeared in steel tubing at one plant. Most of the same plants had suspended operations the previous September over another leak incident.

Waste Storage

Radioactive materials in spent fuel rods will remain dangerous for thousands of years. They are currently enclosed in secure containers for commercial burial, but approved storage space is shrinking. If fuel reprocessing were eventually approved on a large scale, the wastes could be condensed for long-term burial.

Of 79 million gallons of radioactive wastes from U.S. atomic bomb programs, some 400 thousand gallons leaked over a period of years from storage tanks that were designed to last 500 years. However, no injuries resulted and the tanks have since been repaired.

The government has proposed burying wastes in deep formations such as salt beds. A proposed site in Lyons, Kansas, was dropped in the face of local protests and geological doubts, but the Energy Research and Development Administration, which inherited the AEC's job of promoting the peaceful use of nuclear energy, still favors the salt bed approach.

The Union of Concerned Scientists' petition described waste disposal as "a grim legacy to future generations." On the other hand, Nobel Prize-winning physicist Dr. Hans Bethe maintained in December 1974 that "wastes from all the reactors in the world by the year 2000 can probably be stored in an area less than eight square miles, the area required for a single solar energy power plant" of 1,000 megawatts.

Breeder Reactors

Some of the dangers entailed in nuclear energy may be complicated by the development of breeder reactors. In such reactors, no moderators are present to slow down neutrons. The fast neutrons have the ability to turn U-238, the more common uranium isotope, into fissionable plutonium. If a "blanket" of U-238 is wrapped around a fast reactor core, more fuel is created than is consumed. In effect, 50% of uranium can be used as fuel, instead of 1% as at present. This would vastly extend the life of U.S. uranium resources.

But the resulting plutonium would have to be reprocessed, increasing radiation leakage risks. A minority of scientists contends that even the most minute quantities of plutonium could become embedded in lungs, causing cancer-producing lesions. But others say that no plutonium-induced cancers have been found among thousands of plutonium-handling workers observed over 30 years. Some breeder opponents also fear that the potential exists for a localized nuclear explosion within these reactors.

The government has recently drawn out the proposed construction schedule for a large-scale demonstration breeder facility at Clinch River, Tenn., which might not be completed until the end of the 1980s. The program has experienced massive cost overruns, with the Tennessee plant alone expected to cost $1.8 billion. The U.S. has so far concentrated on exhaustive testing of the individual components of the system, while France, Britain, and the USSR had already built large-scale breeder reactors by 1975.

The British and Soviet facilities reportedly had problems in the steam generators, where liquid sodium (the coolant material) must be carefully separated from water. The Soviet plant has, in fact, experienced an explosion, with a cloud of non-radioactive sodium hydroxide (lye) dispersed over the countryside. In general, Soviet nuclear power facilities incorporate far less elaborate and expensive safety features than counterparts in the West, according to American engineers who toured Soviet sites in April, 1975.

Until the past few years, the advocates of nuclear energy dominated public debate. More recently, their opponents have gained the initiative. The AEC, which had been responsible for both the promotion of nuclear energy and its regulation, was abolished by Congress in 1974. Its watchdog functions were assumed by the new Nuclear Regulatory Commission, which soon adopted a public tone of independence from the industry.

In addition, courts and state legislatures have begun to seek an enhanced regulatory role in the industry. The U.S. 7th Circuit Court of Appeals halted construction in April 1975 on a 600-megawatt reactor at Bailly, Ind. AEC regulations barred plants of that size within two miles of towns having over 25,-0000 people. Nearby Portage, Ind., was expected to surpass that population figure within a few years. At least 20 state legislatures considered legislation in 1975 tightening state control over licensing. Citizens groups were credited with delaying or defeating specific projects in the U.S., France, and West Germany.

Weapons Proliferation

All these safety issues may be resolved in the next few years by further research. There would remain the danger of the spread of nuclear weapons.

As of 1975, only six nations had exploded a nuclear device — the U.S., the USSR, Britain, France, China, and India. But several other nations were believed to possess the necessary scientific skills if nuclear explosive materials became available, and dozens more might be in the same position. Even small terrorist bands could build atom bombs, experts agree, or at least could play nuclear blackmail with contraband plutonium.

The one effective brake against proliferation is the lack of explosive material. Weapons-grade uranium is produced through the same enrichment process used for reactor fuel — the process is repeated until the U-235 proportion passes a critical level. Currently, a handful of nations has a monopoly on uranium enrichment and uranium- and plutonium-reprocessing plants. But if the worldwide nuclear industry grows as now projected, by the 1980s the present nonweapons countries could control enough plutonium to produce 2,500 bombs each year, according to the Stockholm International Peace Research Institute.

In recognition of these dangers, the 1970 Nuclear Nonproliferation Treaty provided for inspection of nuclear facilities in nonnuclear nations by the International Atomic Energy Agency (IAEA), a widely trusted United Nations-related organization. However, several major nations have not become full parties to the pact, including Brazil, Argentina, Israel, Egypt, Japan, Pakistan, Spain, and South Africa. India, a nonsignatory power, exploded a nuclear devise in 1974 with plutonium reportedly reprocessed from the residues in reactors purchased from Canada.

Proliferation fears increased when it was reported in May 1975 that West Germany had agreed to sell to Brazil a complete nuclear fuel cycle, including, eventually, enrichment and reprocessing plants. It was reported June 3 that the two countries would sign an inspection pact with the IAEA covering the facilities, and the deal was closed June 27. Later in the year, seven nuclear exporting countries — the U.S., Britain, the USSR, West Germany, Japan, France, and Canada — began talks on possible new controls.

One proposal, supported by U.S. Secretary of State Henry Kissinger in a Sept. 22, 1975, UN address, calls for multinational regional fuel cycle centers to alleviate nationalist rivalries. But as enrichment processes become simpler and less expensive, it may not be possible to restrain all prospective atom bomb countries from joining the nuclear club, even if all exports were banned.

The Choice

Every political and economic decision carries a price tag in known and unknown costs. Some opponents of atomic power seem to maintain that the possible dangers of the nuclear answer to the energy shortage are so great that we must put the program back on the shelf for the time being.

It may be safer to suggest that industry and government ought to divert more energy research dollars into nonfission alternatives. But since each of these alternatives, and even the choice of no growth, carries its own risks, a chastened and sober nuclear power industry may be here to stay.

Nuclear Power Reactors in U.S.

Source: U. S. Research and Development Administration (June 30, 1975)

State	Site	Plant Name	Capacity (kilowatts)	Utility	Commercial Operation
Alabama	Decatur	Browns Ferry Unit 1	1,065,000	Tennessee Valley Authority	1974
	Decatur	Browns Ferry Unit 2	1,065,000	Tennessee Valley Authority	1975
Arkansas	Russellville	Arkansas Unit 1	850,000	Ark. Power & Light Co.	1974
California	Eureka	Humboldt Bay Power Unit 3	65,000	Pacific Gas & Electric Co.	1963
	San Clemente	San Onofre Unit 1	430,000	So. Calif. Ed. & San Diego Gas & El. Co.	1968
	Clay Station	Rancho Seco Station	804,000	Sacramento Mun. Utility District.	1975
Colorado	Platteville	Ft. St. Vrain Station.	330,000	Public Service Co. of Ohio	1975
Connecticut	Haddam Neck	Haddam Neck.	575,000	Conn. Yankee Atomic Power Co.	1968
	Waterford	Millstone Station: Unit 1	652,100	Northeast Nuclear El. Co.	1971
	Waterford	Millstone Station: Unit 2	828,000	Northeast Nuclear El. Co.	1975
Florida	Florida City	Turkey Point Unit 3	666,000	Fla. Power & Light Co.	1972
	Florida City	Turkey Point Unit 4	666,000	Fla. Power & Light Co.	1973
	Ft. Pierce	St. Lucie Plant: Unit 1	810,000	Fla. Power & Light Co.	1975
Georgia	Baxley	Edwin I. Hatch Unit 1	786,000	Georgia Power Co.	1975
Illinois	Morris	Dresden Station: Unit 1	200,000	Commonwealth Edison Co.	1960
	Morris	Dresden Station: Unit 2	809,000	Commonwealth Edison Co.	1970
	Morris	Dresden Station: Unit 3	809,000	Commonwealth Edison Co.	1971
	Zion	Zion: Unit 1	1,050,000	Commonwealth Edison Co.	1973
	Zion	Zion: Unit 2	1,050,000	Commonwealth Edison Co.	1974
	Cordova	Quad-Cities Station: Unit 1	800,000	Comm. Ed. Co.-Ia.-Ill. Gas & Elec. Co.	1972
	Cordova	Quad-Cities Station: Unit 2	800,000	Comm. Ed. Co.-Ia.-Ill. Gas & Elec. Co.	1972
Iowa	Palo	Duane Arnold Unit 1	535,000	Iowa Electric Light and Power Co.	1975
Maine	Wiscasset	Maine Yankee Atomic Power	790,000	Me. Yankee Atomic Power Co.	1972
Maryland	Lusby	Calvert Cliffs Unit 1	845,000	Baltimore Gas and Electric Co.	1975
Massachusetts	Rowe	Yankee Station	175,000	Yankee Atomic Electric Co.	1961
	Plymouth	Pilgrim Station: Unit 1	670,000	Boston Edison Co.	1972
Michigan	Big Rock Point	Big Rock Point	75,000	Consumers Power Co.	1965
	South Haven	Palisades Station	700,000	Consumers Power Co.	1971
	Bridgman	Donald C. Cook Unit 1	1,060,000	Ind. & Michigan Electric Co.	1975
Minnesota	Monticello	Monticello	545,000	Northern States Power Co.	1971
	Red Wing	Prairie Island Unit 1	530,000	Northern States Power Co.	1973
	Red Wing	Prairie Island Unit 2	530,000	Northern States Power Co.	1975
Nebraska	Fort Calhoun	Ft. Calhoun Unit 1	457,400	Omaha Public Power District	1973
	Brownville	Cooper Station	778,000	Pub. Power Dist.-Ia. Power	1974
New Jersey	Forked River	Oyster Creek Unit 1	640,000	Jersey Central Power Co.	1969
New York	Indian Point	Indian Point Unit 1	265,000	Consolidated Edison Co.	1962
	Indian Point	Indian Point Unit 2	873,000	Consolidated Edison Co.	1973
	Indian Point	Indian Point Unit 3	965,000	Consolidated Edison Co.	1975
	Scriba	Nine Mile Point: Unit 1	610,000	Niagara Mohawk Power Co.	1969
	Ontario	R.E. Ginna Unit 1	490,000	Rochester Gas & Electric Co.	1970
	Scriba	James A. Fitzpatrick	821,000	Power Authority of State of N.Y.	1975
North Carolina	Southport	Brunswick Steam Unit 2	821,000	Carolina Power and Light Co.	1975
Pennsylvania	Peach Bottom	Peach Bottom Unit 2	1,065,000	Philadelphia Electric Co.	1974
	Peach Bottom	Peach Bottom Unit 3	1,065,000	Philadelphia Electric Co.	1974
	Shippingport	Shippingport Unit 1	90,000	Duquesne Light Co.	1957
	Shippingport	Beaver Valley: Unit 1	852,000	Duquesne Light Co.-Ohio Edison Co.	1975
	Goldsboro	Three Mile Island: Unit 1	819,000	Metropolitan Edison Co.	1974
South Carolina	Hartsville	H. B. Robinson Unit 2	700,000	Carolina Power & Light Co.	1971
	Seneca	Oconee Unit 1	871,000	Duke Power Co.	1973
	Seneca	Oconee Unit 2	871,000	Duke Power Co.	1974
	Seneca	Oconee Unit 3	871,000	Duke Power Co.	1974
Vermont	Vernon	Vermont Yankee	513,900	Vt. Yankee Nu. Power Corp.	1972
Virginia	Gravel Neck	Surry Power Unit 1	788,000	Va. Electric & Power Co.	1972
	Gravel Neck	Surry Power Unit 2	788,000	Va. Electric & Power Co.	1973
Washington	Richland	N. Reactor/WPPSS Steam	850,000	Energy Research & Devel. Admin.	1966
Wisconsin	Genoa	Genoa Station	50,000	Dairyland Power Cooperative	1971
	Two Creeks	Point Beach Unit 1	497,000	Wis. Mich. Power Co.	1970
	Two Creeks	Point Beach Unit 2	497,000	Wis. Mich. Power Co.	1972
	Carlton	Kewaunee Unit 1	541,000	Wis. Public Service Corp.	1974

Nuclear plant capacity (kilowatts): operable 36,672,400, being built 76,878,300, ordered 103,915,900, total 217,466,600.

World Nuclear Power

Source: Federal Energy Administration

Commercial capacity and generation by major non-Communist countries.

Country	Number of reactors	Capacity[1]	Generation[2] May 1975	Country	Number of reactors	Capacity[1]	Generation[2] May 1975
Canada	5	2,380	0.97	Japan	8	3,890	0.99
France	10	3,070	1.56	Spain	3	1,120	0.54
Germany, West	7	3,450	1.51[3]	Sweden	5	3,310	0.97
Great Britain	29	6,140	2.28[4]	Switzerland	3	1,050	0.69
India	3	620	0.32	United States	51	36,480	14.71
Italy	3	630	0.34	**Total**	**127**	**62,140**	**24.88**

[1]Megawatts. [2]Billion kilowatt-hours. [3]Excluding Wuergassen. [4]Four-week operating period.

Gasoline Economy, Comparative Miles per Gallon

The following are results of tests by the U.S. Environmental Protection Agency on 1976 model autos. The cars were tested on a dynamometer. simulating varied driving conditions for both city (average speed 20 mph) and highway (average 49 mph).

Combining the city and highway averages. the EPA found 3 cars tied for the best miles per gallon, overall average: the new Chevrolet Chevette. with 98 cu. in. displacement; the Datsun B-210. 85 cu. in. displacement; the Subaru. 83 cu. in. displacement. All 3 had manual shifts. In combining the city and highway mpg figures, the EPA estimated total driving includes 55% city. 45% highway.

Make & Model	Cu. In. Displcmt.	Cylinders	City mpg	Hwy mpg
AMC Gremlin	258	6	20	31
AMC Gremlin	304	8	12	19
AMC Pacer	232	6	17	25
AMC Hornet	232	6	17	25
AMC Matador	401	8	11	14
Audi Fox	97	4	24	37
Audi 100	114	4	20	30
Austin MG Midg	91	4	25	37
Bricklin	351	8	13	18
Buick Skylark	231	6	17	25
Buick Apollo. Skylrk	350	8	14	22
Buick Skyhawk	231	6	18	30
Buick Century. Regl	231	6	17	25
Buick Century. Regl	350	8	15	21
Buick LeSabre	350	8	14	18
Buick Electra	455	8	12	18
Buick Riviera	455	8	12	18
Cadillac Seville	350	8	15	21
Cadillac & Eldorado	500	8	12	16
Chevrolet Vega	140	4	22	35
Chevrolet Chevette	98	4	30	39
Chevrolet Monza	140	4	22	35
Chevrolet Monza	262	8	15	21
Chevrolet Nova	250	6	18	25
Chevrolet Nova	350	8	14	19
Chevrolet Camaro	250	6	17	25
Chevrolet Camaro	350	8	14	19
Chevrolet Chevelle	250	6	17	25
Chevrolet Chevelle	400	8	13	19
Chev Malibu Wgn	350	8	13	18
Chevrolet	350	8	13	19
Chevrolet	454	8	12	16
Chev Monte Carlo	350	8	14	18
Chev Monte Carlo	400	8	13	19
Chevrolet Corvette	350	8	14	19
Chrysler Cordoba	318	8	13	18
Chrysler Cordoba	400	8	11	16
Chrysler	360	8	13	17
Chrysler	440	8	11	16
Datsun 610 __ 710	119	4	23	33
Datsun B-210	85	4	29	41
Datsun 280 Z	168	6	17	22
Dodge Aspen	225	6	18	27

Make & Model	Cu. In. Displcmt.	Cylinders	City mpg	Hwy mpg
Dodge Aspen	360	8	13	19
Dodge Dart	225	6	19	26
Dodge Dart	360	8	13	19
Dodge Coronet	225	6	18	30
Dodge Crnt Chgr	318	8	13	18
Dodge Crnt Chgr	400	8	11	16
Dodge Monaco	318	8	13	18
Dodge Monaco	400	8	12	18
Fiat 131 Mirafiori	107	4	18	29
Fiat 124 Sport Coupe	107	4	18	31
Fiat 128	79	4	20	32
Ford Pinto	140	4	24	35
Ford Pinto	171	6	18	25
Ford Mustang II	140	4	24	34
Ford Mustang II	171	6	17	25
Ford Mustang II	302	8	15	19
Ford Maverick	200	6	22	30
Ford Maverick	302	8	14	20
Ford Granada	200	6	22	30
Ford Granada	351	8	14	18
Ford Torino, Elite	351	8	13	19
Ford	351	8	13	19
Ford & Torino	460	8	12	16
Ford Thunderbird	460	8	12	16
Jaguar XJ12	326	12	9	14
Lincoln Contntl Mk IV	460	8	12	16
Mercury Bobcat	140	4	24	34
Mercury Bobcat	171	6	17	25
Mercury Comet	200	6	22	30
Mercury Comet	302	8	14	20
Mercury Capri II	140	4	22	31
Mercury Capri II	171	6	18	28
Mercury Monarch	200	6	22	30
Mercury Monarch	351	8	14	18
Merc Montgo Cougr	351	8	13	19
Merc Montgo Cougr	400	8	12	16
Mercury	400	8	13	17
Mercury	460	8	12	16
Oldsmobile Omega	250	6	17	25
Oldsmobile Omega	350	8	14	22
Oldsmobile Starfire	231	6	18	30
Oldsmobile Cutlass	250	6	17	25
Oldsmobile Cutlass	455	8	13	19

Make & Model	Cu. In. Displcmt.	Cylinders	City mpg	Hwy mpg
Oldsmobile Delta 88	350	8	14	17
Oldsmobile Delta 88	455	8	13	18
Oldsmobile 98	455	8	13	17
Oldsmobile Toronado	455	8	12	17
Peugeot 504 Diesel	129	4	27	35
Plym Valiant Dustr	225	6	19	26
Plym Valiant Dustr	360	8	13	19
Plymouth Fury	225	6	18	30
Plymouth Fury	318	8	15	21
Plymouth Fury	400	8	11	16
Plymouth Gran Fury	318	8	13	18
Plymouth Gran Fury	400	8	12	18
Plymouth Volare	225	6	18	27
Plymouth Volare	318	8	14	22
Pontiac Astre	140	4	22	35
Pont Vtura LeMans	250	6	17	25
Pontiac Ventura	350	8	14	22
Pontiac Firebird	250	6	17	25
Pontiac Firebird	400	8	15	22
Pontiac LeMans	400	8	15	20
Pontiac Sunbird	140	4	21	35
Pontiac Sunbird	231	6	18	30
Pontiac	400	8	13	19
Pontiac	455	8	13	18
Pontiac Grand Prix	400	8	15	20
Porsche 914	120	4	20	30
Porsche 912E	120	4	19	32
Porsche 911S	164	6	12	18
Renault 5	79	4	28	40
Rolls-Royce	412	8	10	12
Subaru	83	4	29	39
Subaru	97	4	25	33
Toyota Corolla	97	4	24	36
Toyota Corolla Mk II	156	6	15	21
Toyota Corona	133	4	20	34
Toyota Celica	133	4	20	34
Toyota Corona Mk II	156	6	18	23
Triumph Spitfire	91	4	25	37
Triumph TR-6	152	6	19	25
Triumph TR-7	122	4	21	30
Volkswagen Beetle	97	4	22	34
Volkswagen Dasher	97	4	24	37
Volvo 240	130	4	18	24
Volvo 260	163	4	15	27

U.S. Petroleum and Natural Gas Production

Source: Bureau of Mines

Year	Crude oil		Natural gas liquids		Total	Natural gas	
	Production 1,000 bbls.	Value $1,000	Production 1,000 bbls.	Value $1,000	1,000 bbls.	Marketed Mil. Cu. ft.	Value $1,000
1945	1.713.655	2.094.250	112.004	187.564	1.828.539	3.944.021	191.006
1950	1.973.574	4.963.380	181.961	419.605	2.155.693	6.282.060	408.521
1955	2.484.428	6.870.380	281.371	619.006	2.766.325	9.405.351	978.357
1960	2.574.933	7.420.181	340.157	808.385	2.915.365	12.771.038	1.789.970
1965	2.848.514	8.158.298	441.556	911.603	3.290.083	16.042.753	2.494.542
1970	3.517.450	11.173.726	605.916	1.275.112	4.123.366	21.920.642	3.745.680
1971	3.453.914	11.692.998	617.815	1.386.054	4.071.729	22.493.012	4.085.482
1972	3.455.368	11.706.510	638.216	1.452.233	4.093.584	22.531.698	4.180.462
1973	3.360.903	13.057.905	634.423	1.857.073	3.995.326	22.647.549	4.894.072
1974	3.202.585	21.580.549	616.098	3.087.927	3.818.683	21.600.522	6.573.402

U. S. Crude Petroleum Production by Chief States

Source: Bureau of Mines (Figures in thousands of 42-gallon barrels)

Year	Ark.	Calif.	Ill.	Kans.	La.	Miss.	N.M.	N.D.	Okla.	Texas	Wyo.
1950	31,108	327,607	62,028	107,586	208,965	38,236	47,367		164,599	829,874	61,631
1960	30,117	305,352	77,341	113,453	400,832	51,673	107,380	21,992	192,913	927,479	133,910
1965	25,930	316,428	63,708	104,733	594,853	56,183	119,166	26,350	203,441	1,000,749	138,314
1970	18,035	372,191	43,747	84,853	906,907	65,119	128,184	21,998	223,574	1,249,697	160,345
1971	18,263	358,484	39,084	78,532	935,243	64,066	118,412	21,653	213,313	1,222,926	148,114
1972	18,519	347,022	34,874	73,744	891,827	61,100	110,525	20,624	207,633	1,301,685	140,011
1973	18,016	336,075	30,669	66,227	831,524	56,102	100,986	20,235	191,204	1,294,671	141,914
1974	16,527	323,003	27,553	61,691	737,324	50,779	98,695	19,697	177,785	1,262,126	139,997

World Production of Crude Petroleum[1]
Source: Bureau of Mines
(thousands of 42-gallon barrels)

Country	1974	1973	Percent of change
North America:			
Canada	616,532	648,348	− 4.9
Mexico[1]	238,271	191,482	+24.4
United States[1]	3,199,328	3,360,903	− 4.8
Cuba (E)	775	775	
Total	**4,054,906**	**4,201,508**	**− 3.5**
South America:			
Argentina	151,110	153,539	− 1.6
Barbados	48	10	
Bolivia	16,03	17,266	− 3.8
Brazil	64,751	62,122	+ 4.2
Chile	10,055	11,429	−12.0
Colombia	63,300	66,844	− 5.3
Ecuador	64,616	76,221	−15.2
Peru	28,069	25,767	+ 8.9
Trinidad	68,131	60,666	+12.3
Venezuela	1,086,332	1,228,594	−11.6
Total	**1,553,015**	**1,702,458**	**− 8.8**
Western Europe:			
Austria	15,609	17,982	−13.2
Denmark	689	1,460	
France	7,863	9,152	−14.1
Germany, West	44,718	47,944	− 6.7
Italy	6,956	7,082	− 1.8
Netherlands	10,906	10,169	+ 7.3
Norway	12,707	11,166	+13.8
Spain	14,334	5,932	
United Kingdom[1]	3,289	2,946	+11.6
Yugoslavia	25,613	24,680	+ 3.8
Total	**142,684**	**38,513**	**− 3.0**
Middle East:			
Bahrain	24,597	24,948	− 1.4
Iran	2,210,627	2,139,229	+ 3.3
Iraq	679,803	736,607	− 7.7
Israel[2](E)	36,500	32,193	+13.4
Kuwait	830,580	1,007,002	−17.5
Neutral Zone	198,195	190,888	+ 3.8
Oman	106,046	106,926	− 0.8
Qatar	189,348	208,152	− 9.0
Saudi Arabia	2,996,543	2,677,146	+11.9
Syria	45,352	38,170	+18.8
Turkey	24,555	24,273	+ 1.2
United Arab Emirates	616,485	559,399	+10.2
Total	**7,958,631**	**7,744,933**	**+ 2.8**

Country	1974	1973	Percent of change
Africa:			
Algeria	372,753	400,515	− 6.9
Angola	61,392	58,910	+ 4.2
Congo	22,434	12,713	+76.5
Egypt[2]	53,715	60,483	−11.2
Gabon	73,914	55,045	+34.3
Libya	555,291	793,839	−30.1
Morocco	191	320	−40.3
Nigeria	823,347	749,820	+ 9.8
Tunisia	31,841	29,828	+ 6.8
Total	**1,994,878**	**2,161,473**	**− 7.7**
Asiatic Area:			
Australia	140,890	142,277	− 1.0
Brunei	73,730	78,673	− 6.3
Burma	7,581	7,514	+ 0.9
India	54,385	55,388	− 1.8
Indonesia	501,838	488,536	+ 2.7
Japan	4,936	5,142	− 4.0
Malaysia	29,537	33,054	−10.6
New Zealand[1]	1,385	1,290	+ 7.4
Pakistan	2,923	2,871	+ 1.8
Taiwan	1,321	1,055	+25.2
Thailand (E)	42	45	− 6.7
Total	**818,568**	**815,845**	**+ 0.3**
East Europe and Peoples' Rep. of China:			
Albania	15,346	14,058	+ 9.2
Bulgaria	1,095	1,460	−25.0
Czech	1,085	1,221	−11.1
Germany, East	2,500	2,500	0.0
Hungary	15,237	15,176	+ 0.4
Peoples' Rep. of China	474,500	365,000	+30.0
Poland	4,080	2,908	+40.3
Romania	107,964	106,578	+ 1.3
U.S.S.R.[1]	3,373,650	3,094,350	+ 9.0
Total	**3,995,457**	**3,603,251**	**+10.9**
Total World	**20,518,139**	**20,367,981**	**+ 0.7**

(E) Estimate.
[1]Crude Oil and field condensate. [2]Israeli production from Sinai peninsula oilfields included with Israel rather than Egypt.

U.S. Motor Fuel Supply[1] and Demand
Source: Bureau of Mines (Figures in thousands of 42-gallon barrels)

Year	Supply Production	Supply Daily average	Demand Domestic	Demand Export	Year	Supply Production	Supply Daily average	Demand Domestic	Demand Export
1945	793,431	2,174	696,333	88,059	1969	2,057,041	5,636	2,072,144	4,468
1950	1,024,481	2,806	994,290	24,721	1970	2,135,838	5,852	2,162,439	2,956
1955	1,373,950	3,764	1,329,788	34,521	1971 (rev.)	2,231,157	6,113	2,242,921	3,104
1960*	1,522,497	4,160	1,511,670	13,456	1972	2,352,310	6,427	2,382,293	2,441
1965	1,733,258	4,749	1,750,028	6,391	1973	2,434,943	6,671	2,484,262	3,318
					1974	2,371,004	6,496	2,434,368	6,670

*Beginning with 1959 Alaska and Hawaii are included. (1.) Includes special naptha.

U. S. Total Fuel Supply and Demand[1]
In thousands of 42-gallon barrels. *Includes special naphtha production. †Includes kerosene type jet fuel.

Year	Gasoline* Production	Gasoline* Total Demand	Kerosene† Production	Kerosene† Total Demand	Distillate fuel oil Production	Distillate fuel oil Total Demand	Residual fuel oil Production	Residual fuel oil Total Demand
1950	1,024,181	1,019,011	118,512	119,922	398,912	75,435	425,217	570,021
1960[2]	1,522,497	1,525,126	136,842	133,188	667,050	695,165	332,147	577,934
1965	1,733,258	1,756,419	201,788	219,932	765,071	779,644	268,567	601,893
1970	2,135,838	2,165,395	313,544	358,025	897,097	927,211	257,510	804,288
1971	2,231,157	2,242,921	306,847	364,908	912,097	971,316	274,684	838,045
1972	2,352,310	2,382,293	313,554	379,849	963,625	1,066,049	292,519	925,647
1973	2,434,943	2,464,262	327,818	383,050	1,030,178	1,124,308	354,597	1,019,934
1974	2,371,004	2,434,368	290,780	371,759	974,025	1,072,812	390,491	957,811

(1) Demand usually exeeds the production; the difference is made up by dipping into stocks or by imports. (2) In the years prior to 1960 figures are on a 48-state basis.

U.S. Petroleum and Natural Gas Resources

(onshore and offshore to water depth of 200 meters)
Source: U. S. Geological Survey
Crude Oil — billions of barrels

Area	Cumulative[1] Production	Demonstrated Reserves Measured	Indicated	Inferred[2] Reserves	Undiscovered Recoverable Resources Statistical Mean	Estimated Range[3] (95%-5%)
Alaska onshore	0.154	9.944	0.013	6.1	12	6- 19
48 states onshore	99.892	21.086	4:315	14.3	44	29- 64
Total onshore	**100.046**	**31.030**	**4.328**	**20.4**	**56**	**37-81**
Alaska offshore	0.456	0.150	—[4]	0.1	15	3-31
Pacific offshore	1.499	0.858	0.258	0.2	3	2-5
Gulf of Mexico	4.135	2.212	0.050	2.4	5	3-8
Atlantic offshore	0.000	0.000	0.000	0.0	3	2-4[5]
Total offshore	**6.090**	**3.220**	**0.308**	**2.7**	**26**	**10-49**
Total U.S.	**106.136**	**34.250**	**4.636**	**23.1**	**82**	**50-127**
Subeconomic[6]		120 — 140				44-111

Natural Gas — trillion cubic feet

Area	Cumulative[1] Production	Measured Reserves	Inferred[2] Reserves	Undiscovered Recoverable Reserves Statistical Mean	Estimated Range[3] (95%-5%)
Alaska onshore	0.482	31.722	14.7	32	16- 57
48 states onshore	446.366	169.454	119.4	345	246-453
Total onshore	**446.848**	**201.176**	**134.1**	**377**	**264-506**
Alaska offshore	0.423	0.145	0.1	44	8- 80
Pacific offshore	1.415	0.463	0.4	3	2- 6
Gulf of Mexico	32.138	35.348	67.0	50	18- 91
Atlantic offshore	0.000	0.000	0.0	10	5- 14[6]
Total offshore	**33.976**	**35.956**	**67.5**	**107**	**42-181**
Total U.S.	**480.824**	**237.132**	**201.6**	**484**	**322-655**
Subeconomic[6]		90 — 115			40- 82

[1]To Dec. 31, 1974. [2]Based on historical data. [3]The low value of the range is associated with a 95% probability that there is at least this amount; the high value has a 5% probability that there is at least this amount. [4]Less than one million barrels. [5]Based on 75%-25% probability. [6]Recoverable with improved technology or higher prices.

U.S. Fuel Consumption—Past, Present, Future

Source: Joint Congressional Committee on Atomic Energy report, Understanding the "National Energy Dilemma," published by The Center for Strategic and International Studies, 1973.

(millions of barrels per day of oil equivalent[1])

Energy Source and Use....	1950	1960	1970	1980[2]
Natural Gas	**2.9**	**5.9**	**10.7**	**12.2**
(imported)	—	(0.1)	(0.4)	(1.9)
(from coal and oil gassification)	—	—	—	(0.3)
Electricity generation	0.3	0.8	1.9	1.6
Residential and commercial	0.8	2.0	3.5	5.0
Industrial	1.6	2.8	4.6	4.7
Transportation	0.1	0.2	0.3	0.4
Non-energy	0.2	0.2	0.5	0.5
Coal	**6.5**	**5.3**	**7.4**	**10.5**
Electricity generation	1.1	2.0	3.7	5.2
Residential and commercial	1.4	0.5	0.2	0.1
Industrial	2.8	2.3	2.5	3.5
Transportation	0.8	0.1	—	—
Non-energy	0.1	0.1	0.1	0.1
Exports	0.4	0.5	0.9	1.4
Gassification	—	—	—	0.2
Oil	**6.5**	**9.7**	**13.9**	**21.5**
(Imported)	(0.9)	(1.9)	(3.5)	(10.0)
Electricity generation	0.3	0.3	1.0	2.0
Residential and commercial	1.2	2.0	2.5	2.0
Industrial	1.0	1.3	1.6	2.7
Transportation	3.2	5.0	7.4	11.5
Non-energy	0.4	0.8	1.5	3.1
Gassification	—	—	—	0.2
Nuclear	—	—	0.1	3.6
Geothermal	—	—	0.003	0.2
Hydroelectric	0.2	0.3	0.4	0.6
TOTAL INPUT	**16.1**	**21.3**	**32.5**	**48.3[3]**

[1]All energy sources have been converted to barrels of oil equivalent (B/DOE) by determining their heat value and converting that Btu figure to barrels of oil, viz.: 5,800,000 Btu = one barrel of crude oil; 3,412 Btu = one kilowatt-hour; 1,000 Btu = 1 cu. ft. of natural gas; 26,000,000 Btu = one ton of coal. Figures may not add to totals due to

Electricity generation	1950	1960	1970	1980
Input (from above sources)	1.9	3.4	7.1	13.2
Residential and commercial	0.2	0.5	1.3	2.7
Industrial	0.2	0.7	1.2	2.0
Transportation	—	—	0.007	0.5
Conversion losses	1.4	2.3	4.6	8.1
End Use and Loss				
Residential and commercial	**3.6**	**5.0**	**7.5**	**9.9**
Used	2.7	3.5	5.6	7.3
Lost	0.9	1.5	1.9	2.6
Industrial	**5.6**	**7.1**	**9.9**	**13.0**
Used	4.2	4.9	7.4	9.6
Lost	1.4	2.1	2.4	3.4
Transportation	**4.1**	**5.3**	**7.7**	**12.0**
Used	1.0	1.2	1.9	3.0
Lost	3.1	4.0	5.8	9.0
Total Used Energy	**7.9**	**9.6**	**15.0**	**19.9**
Total lost[4]	6.8	9.9	14.7	23.3
Exports	0.7	0.7	0.9	1.4
Non-energy	0.7	1.1	1.9	3.7
TOTAL OUTPUT	**16.1**	**21.3**	**32.5**	**48.3**

rounding while converting to B/DOE.
[2]"There are many reasons for the high degree of confidence in the predictability of 1980 . . . The Nation has already ordered a large part of the electrical capacity that can be functioning commercially by the year 1980; it has already ordered every major rail-based mass transit system that can be functioning by 1980 . . ." etc.
[3]Corrected for coal and oil gassification.
[4]Including conversion loss in electricity generation and in coal and oil gassification.

Measuring Energy

Source: House Subcommittee on Energy

The following tables of equivalents contain those figures commonly used to compare different types of energy sources and their various measurements.

Btu - a British thermal unit — the amount of heat required to raise one pound of water one degree Farenheit. Equivalent to 1055 joules or about 252 gram calories. A **therm** is usually 100,000 Btu but is sometimes used to refer to other units.

Calorie - the amount of heat required to raise one gram of water one degree centigrade; abbreviated cal.; equivalent to about .003968 Btu. More common is the kilogram calorie. also called a **kilocalorie** and abbreviated Cal. or Kcal; equivalent to about 3.97 Btu. (One Kcal is equivalent to one food calorie.)

Btu Values of Energy Sources

(These are conventional or average values. not precise equivalents.)

Coal (per 2,000 lb. ton):
Anthracite	= 25.4 x 10^6 Btu
Bituminous	= 26.2 x 10^6
Sub-bituminous	= 19.0 x 10^6
Lignite	= 13.4 x 10^6

Average heating value of coal used to generate electricity in 1969 was 27.7 x 10^6 Btu.

Natural Gas (per cubic foot):
Dry	= 1.031 Btu
Wet	= 1.103
Liquid (avg.)	= 4.100

Electricity — 1 kwh = 3.413 Btu.

Petroleum (per barrel)
Crude Oil	= 5.60 x 10^6 Btu
Residual fuel oil	= 6.29 x 10^6
Distillate fuel oil	= 5.83 x 10^6
Gasoline (including av gas)	= 5.25 x 10^6
Jet fuel (kerosene)	= 5.67 x 10^6
Jet fuel (naphtha)	= 5.36 x 10^6
Kerosene	= 5.67 x 10^6

Nuclear
1 gram of fissioned U-235 — 74,000,000 Btu

The Btu. and cal.. being small amounts of energy. are usually expressed as follows when large numbers are involved:

1 x 10^3 Btu	= 1,000
1 x 10^6 Btu	= 1,000,000
1 x 10^9 Btu	= 1,000,000,000
1 x 10^{12} Btu	= 1 trillion
1 x 10^{15} Btu	= 1 quadrillion
1 x 10^{18} Btu	= 1 quintillion or 1 Q unit
One Q unit	= 38.46 billion tons of coal
	= 172.4 billion barrels of oil
	= 968.9 trillion cubic ft. of natural gas

Other Conversion Factors

Electricity — 1 kwh	= 0.88 lbs. of coal
	= 0.076 gallons of oil
	= 10.4 cu. ft. of natural gas
Natural Gas — 1 tcf (trillion cubic feet)	= 39.3x10^6 tons of coal
	= 184x10^6 barrels of oil
Coal — 1 mtce (million tons of coal equivalent	= 4.48 x 10^6 barrels of oil
	= 67 tons of oil
	= 25.19 x 10^{12} cu. ft. of natural gas
Oil — 1 million tons (6.65x10^6 barrels)	= 4x10^9 kwh of electricity (when used to generate power)
	= 12x10^9 kwh unconverted
	= 1.5 x 10^6 tons of coal
	= 41.2x10^9 cu. ft. of natural gas

Approximate Conversion Factors For Oils

To convert	Barrels to Metric tons	Metric tons to barrels	Barrels/days to tons/year	Tons/year to barrels/day
		Multiply by —		
Crude oil [1]	0.136	7.33	49.8	0.0201
Gasoline	.118	8.45	43.2	.0232
Kerosene	.128	7.80	46.8	.0214
Diesel fuel	.133	7.50	48.7	.0205
Fuel oil	.149	6.70	54.5	.0184

[1] Based on world average gravity (excluding natural gas liquids).

Coal and Coke Production in the United States

Source: Bureau of Mines

Year	Penn. Anthracite Production 1,000 net tons	Penn. Anthracite Value $1,000	Bituminous Production 1,000 net tons	Bituminous Value $1,000	Year	Penn. Anthracite Production 1,000 net tons	Penn. Anthracite Value $1,000	Bituminous Production 1,000 net tons	Bituminous Value $1,000
1965	14,866	122,021	512,088	2,276,022	1970	9,729	105,341	602,932	3,772,662
1966	12,941	100,663	533,881	2,421,293	1971	8,727	103,469	552,192	3,901,496
1967	12,256	96,160	552,026	2,555,377	1972	7,106	85,251	595,386	4,561,983
1968	11,461	97,245	545,245	2,546,340	1973	6,830	90,260	591,738	5,049,612
1969	10,473	100,769	560,505	2,795,509	1974	6,617	144,695	590,000	8,900,000

Coke Production (1,000 net tons—value in $1,000)—(1968) 63,653, $1,157,359; (1969) 64,757, $1,355,260; (1970) 66,525, $1,849,160; (1971) 57,436, $1,745,693; (1972) 60,507. $2,012,486; (1973) 64,325. $2,442,151; (1974) Not available.

Coke Exports (short tons)—(1968) 791,909; (1969) 1,629,00; (1970) 2,478,338; (1971) 1,508,639; (1972) 1231,633; (1973) 1,394,-(1974) 3,540,326.

Anthracite exports (net tons)—(1966) 766,025; (1967) 594,797; (1968) 518,159; (1969) 627,492; (1970) 789,499; (1971) 671,024; (1972) 743,451; (1973) 716,546; (1974) 735,000.

Production of Electric Energy in the U. S.

Source: The Federal Power Commission

These amounts include both the privately-owned and publicly-owned utilities.

Calendar Year	Total 1,000 Kw. hrs.	Hydro 1,000 Kw. hrs.	Steam 1,000 Kw. hrs.	Gas Turbine(a) 1,000 Kw. hrs.	Internal Comb't'n 1,000 Kw. hrs.	Coal Short tons	Oil 42 Gal. Barrels	Gas 1,000 Cu. ft.
1965	1,055,251,929	193,850,603	856,312,128		5,089,198	244,788,119	115,202,583	2,321,100,937
1968	1,329,443,027	222,490,584	1,101,767,366		5,185,000	297,779,069	188,641,862	3,147,908,961
1969	1,442,182,474	250,192,655	1,178,182,761	8,227,148	5,579,910	310,316,640	250,937,800	3,487,642,263
1970	1,531,608,921	247,456,119	1,262,358,866	15,732,082	6,061,854	320,818,141	335,503,753	3,931,996,247
1971	1,613,935,744	266,320,232	1,319,291,654	22,072,221	6,251,637	327,926,249	396,237,967	3,992,980,610
1972	1,747,322,933	272,733,504	1,438,420,059	29,493,248		351,050,000	493,930,000	3,978,700,000
1973	1,856,216,160	271,633,700	1,548,701,518	29,533,899	6,347,043	388,190,014	559,842,233	3,640,756,357
1974 (Prelim.)	1,864,961,337	300,447,428	1,526,442,169	32,082,824	5,988,916	392,345,245	536,105,244	3,429,229,964

(a) Data prior to 1969 included under steam.

World's Largest Hydroelectric Generating Plants

Source: Bureau of Reclamation
Ultimate capacity of 1,000,000 kilowatts or more.
UC—Under construction. NA—Not available. Year—Initial operation.

Name	Present Megawatts	Ultimate Megawatts	Year	Name	Present Megawatts	Ultimate Megawatts	Year
Itaipu, Brazil-Paraguay	...	10,710	U.C.	Turnut-3, Australia	750	1,500	1972
Grand Coulee, U.S.	2,161	9,780	1941	McNary, U.S.	980	1,406	1953
Guri, Venezuela	524	6,500	1967	Jupia, Brazil	600	1,400	1966
Sayansk, USSR	...	6,400	U.C.	Marimbondo, Brazil	...	1,400	U.C.
Krasnoyarsk, USSR	6,096	6,096	1968	Saratov, U.S.S.R.	...	1,359	1967
Paulo Afonso, Brazil	1,030	5,942	1955	Daniel Johnson, Canada	165	1,353	1970
Churchill Falls, Canada	1,900	5,225	1971	Hoover, U.S.	1,345	1,345	1936
Bratsk, USSR	4,500	4,600	1964	Wanapum, U.S.	831	1,330	1964
Sukhovo, USSR	...	4,500	U.C.	Zeya, USSR	...	1,290	U.C.
Ust-Illimsk, USSR	720	4,300	U.C.	Priest Rapids, U.S.	789	1,262	1959
Cabora Basa, Portugal. (Mozambique)	...	4,000	U.C.	Castaic, U.S.	...	1,250	U.C.
Inga, Zaire	350	3,700	U.C.	Keban, Turkey	620	1,240	U.C.
Chief Joseph, U.S.A.	1,024	3,642	1956	Kettle Rapids, Canada	612	1,224	1970
Ilha Soltena, Brazil	...	3,200	U.C.	Rocky Beach, U.S.	775	1,215	1961
John Day, U.S.	2,160	2,700	1968	Furnas, Brazil	900	1,200	1963
Nurek, USSR	...	2,700	U.C.	Toktogul, USSR	...	1,200	U.C.
Volga—22nd Congress, USSR.	2,543	2,560	1958	El Chocon, Argentina	...	1,200	U.C.
				Manicouagan No. 3, Canada	...	1,176	U.C.
Volga—V.I.Lenin, USSR.	2,100	2,300	1955	Sanmen-Hsia, China	...	1,100	N.A.
W.A.C. Bennett, Canada	1,816	2,270	1969	Nizhne-Kamskaya, U.S.S.R.	...	1,090	U.C.
Iron Gate, Romania-Yugo.	500	2,160	U.C.	Dworshak, U.S.A.	90	1,060	U.C.
Sir Adam Beck (No. 2), Canada.	1,224	1,224	1954	Bersimis No. 1, Canada	912	1,050	1956
Saad-El-Aali (High Aswan), Egypt	1,750	2,100	1967	Bhakra, India	450	1,050	1963
Robert Moses-Niagara, U.S.	1,950	1,950	1961	Estreito, Brazil	1,050	1,050	1969
St. Lawrence Power Dam, U.S./Canada	1,824	1,824	1958	Salto Osorio, Brazil	...	1,050	U.C.
				Lago Delio, Italy	...	1,016	U.C.
The Dalles, U.S.	1,291	1,807	1957	Manicouagan No. 2, Canada	...	1,015	1965
Mica, Canada	...	1,740	U.C.	Votkinsk, U.S.S.R.	...	1,000	1961
Kemano, Canada	813	1,670	1954	Mangla, Pakistan	300	1,000	U.C.
Beauharnois, Canada	1,021	1,670	1950	Chirkey, U.S.S.R.	...	1,000	U.C.
Cheboksary, USSR	...	1,632	U.C.	Kaniji, Nigeria	...	1,000	U.C.
Inguri, USSR	...	1,600	U.C.	Northfield Mountain, U.S.A.	...	1,000	U.C.
Kariba, Rhodesia	600	1,500	1959	Chivor, Colombia	...	1,000	U.C.
Liukiahsia, China	...	1,500	1963	Blenheim-Gilboa, U.S.A.	...	1,000	U.C.

Non-Federal Hydroelectric Plants in U.S.

Capacities of 150,000 Kilowatts or More as of Jan. 1, 1975

Auxiliary and pumped storage units are not included in hydroelectric capacities.
Source: Federal Power Commission, Bureau of Power

Plant	State	Owner	Kilowatts
Robert Moses, Niagara	N.Y.	Power Authority State of N.Y.	1,953,900
Rocky Reach	Wash.	Chelan County Dist. No. 1	1,213,100
Robert Moses, (Massena)	N.Y.	Power Authority State of N.Y.	912,000
Wanapum	Wash.	Grant County Dist. No. 2	831,250
Priest Rapids	Wash.	Grant County Dist. No. 2	788,500
Wells	Wash.	Douglas County PUD No. 1	774,300
Boundary	Wash.	Seattle Dept. of Lighting.	551,000
Conowingo	Md.	Philadelphia Electric Co.	474,480
Hells Canyon	Ore.	Idaho Power Co.	391,500
Brownlee	Idaho	Idaho Power Co.	360,400
Ross	Wash.	Seattle Dept. of Lighting Co.	360,000
Edward Hyatt	Calif.	Calif. Dept. of Water Resources.	351,000
Cowans Ford	N.C.	Duke Power Co.	350,000
Upper Smith Mt.	Va.	Appalachian Power Co.	300,200
Mossyrock	Wash.	City of Tacoma.	300,000
New Colgate	Calif.	Yuba County Water Agency.	284,400
Noxon Rapids	Mont.	The Washington Water Power Co.	282,880
Round Butte	Ore.	Portland Gen. Elec. Co.	247,050
Safe Harbor	Pa.	Safe Harbor Water Power Corp.	226,500
Walter Bouldin	Ala.	Alabama Power Co.	225,000[1]
Rock Island	Wash.	Chelan County Dist. No. 1.	212,100
Swift No. 1	Wash.	Pacific Power and Light Co.	204,000
Cabinet Gorge	Idaho	The Washington Water Power Co.	200,000
Saluda	S.C.	So. Carolina Electric and Gas Co.	197,500
Oxbow	Oreg.	Idaho Power Co.	190,000
White Rock	Calif.	Sacramento Mun. Utility Dist.	190,000
Caribou No. 1 & 2	Calif.	Pacific Gas and Electric Co.	184,800
Gaston	N.C.	Virginia Electric and Power Co	177,920
Lay Dam	Ala.	Alabama Power Co.	177,000
Osage	Mo.	Union Electric Co. of Mo.	172,000
Kerr	Mont.	The Montana Power Co.	168,000
Lewis Smith	Ala.	Alabama Power Co.	157,500
James B. Black	Calif.	Pacific Gas and Electric Co.	154,800
Martin Dam	Ala.	Alabama Power Co.	154,200

[1]Units out of service Feb. 1975 in dam failure.

World Electric Power Production

Source: United Nations Monthly Bulletin of Statistics, Aug. 1975, Federal Power Commission
million kilowatt-hours

Country	1974 Production	Country	1974 Production	Country	1974 Production
United States	1,941,084	France	179,880	Norway	76,620
USSR	975,000	Italy	142,116	Sweden	74,280
Japan	470,088	China (E)	112,000	South Africa	70,776
West Germany	311,676	Poland	91,596	Australia	69,744
Canada	279,192	Spain	81,000	India (P)	68,160
United Kingdom	273,336	East Germany	80,280	Total	5,184,828

(E) Estimate. (P) Excluding generation by industrial establishments.

MANUFACTURES AND MINERALS
General Statistics for Major Industry Groups
Source: Bureau of the Census

The estimates for 1972 in the following table are based upon reports from a representative sample of about 65,000 manufacturing establishments.

Industry	All Employees		Production Workers			Value added by mfr adj. (Millions)
	Number (1,000)	Payroll (Millions)	Number (1,000)	Man-hours (Millions)	Wages (Millions)	
Food and kindred products	1,569	$12,922	1,085	2,167	$8,007	$35,617
Tobacco manufactures	66	502	57	107	401	2,637
Textile mill products	953	6,052	836	1,726	4,807	11,718
Apparel and other textile products	1,368	7,212	1,198	2,161	5,461	13,488
Lumber and wood products	691	4,983	601	1,168	3,933	10,309
Furniture and fixtures	462	3,202	384	756	2,321	6,090
Paper and allied products	633	5,992	499	1,041	4,320	13,064
Printing and publishing	1,056	9,827	637	1,181	5,459	20,197
Chemicals and allied products	837	8,731	525	1,054	4,754	32,413
Petroleum and coal products	140	1,638	98	201	1,064	5,793
Rubber and plastics products, n.e.c.	618	5,165	487	968	3,605	11,653
Leather and leather products	273	1,589	240	449	1,231	2,917
Stone, clay, and glass products	623	5,547	493	998	4,037	12,587
Primary metal industries	1,143	12,167	923	1,850	9,202	23,258
Fabricated metal products	1,493	13,821	1,148	2,303	9,544	27,006
Machinery, except electrical	1,828	18,523	1,267	2,538	11,359	37,563
Electrical equipment and supplies	1,662	15,200	1,161	2,275	8,823	30,584
Transportation equipment	1,719	19,880	1,246	2,527	12,849	39,799
Instruments and related products	454	4,297	292	570	2,237	10,584
Miscellaneous manufacturing industries . . .	446	3,185	350	662	2,087	6,777
Administrative and auxiliary[1]	994	13,772	—	—	—	—
All industries total	**19,029**	**174,206**	**13,528**	**26,699**	**105,502**	**354,054**

(1) In addition to the employment and payroll for operating manufacturing establishments, manufacturing concerns reported separately for central administrative offices or auxiliary units (e.g., research laboratories, storage warehouses, power plants, garages, repair shops, etc.) which serve the manufacturing establishments of a company rather than the public.

Manufacturing Production Worker Statistics
Source: Bureau of Labor Statistics, U.S. Dept. of Labor (Preliminary)

Year	All Employees	Production Workers	Payroll Index 1967=100	Average Earnings	Avg. Hourly Earnings	Avg. Hrs. Weekly
1955	16,882,000	13,288,000	61.1	75.70	1.86	40.7
1960	16,796,000	12,586,000	68.9	89.72	2.26	39.7
1965	18,062,000	13,434,000	88.1	107.53	2.61	41.2
1969	20,167,000	14,767,000	116.6	129.51	3.19	40.6
1970	19,349,000	14,020,000	114.1	133.73	3.36	39.8
1971	18,572,000	13,467,000	116.7	142.44	3.57	39.9
1972	19,090,000	13,957,000	131.5	159.69	3.81	40.6
1973	20,054,000	14,752,000	149.0	165.65	4.07	40.7
1974	20,016,000	14,607,000	156.7	176.00	4.40	40.0
1975 Jan.	18,538,000	13,225,000	145.2	179.96	4.65	38.7
Feb.	18,132,000	12,851,000	140.9	179.80	4.67	38.5
Mar.	18,005,000	12,747,000	141.3	182.28	4.71	38.7
Apr.	17,967,000	12,722,000	141.9	183.22	4.71	38.9
May	18,038,000	12,799,000	143.8	184.47	4.73	39.0
June (p)	18,212,000	12,966,000	148.3	187.54	4.76	39.4
July (p)	17,948,000	12,709,000	145.5	187.85	4.78	39.3

Hourly Earnings in Manufacturing Industries
Source: Bureau of Labor Statistics, U.S. Dept. of Labor ([P] Preliminary)

Year and month (annual average)	Manufacturing		Durable goods		Nondurable goods	
	Gross	Excluding overtime	Gross	Excluding overtime	Gross	Excluding overtime
1950	$1.440	$1.39	$1.519	$1.46	$1.347	$1.31
1955	1.86	1.79	1.99	1.91	1.67	1.62
1960	2.26	2.20	2.43	2.36	2.05	1.99
1965	2.61	2.51	2.79	2.67	2.36	2.27
1969	3.19	3.06	3.38	3.24	2.91	2.79
1970	3.36	3.24	3.55	3.43	3.08	2.97
1971	3.57	3.44	3.79	3.66	3.26	3.14
1972	3.81	3.66	4.06	3.89	3.47	3.33
1973	4.07	3.89	4.33	4.13	3.68	3.53
1974	4.40	4.23	4.68	4.49	3.98	3.83
1975 Jan.	4.65	4.52	4.94	4.80	4.22	4.11
Feb.	4.67	4.54	4.96	4.82	4.24	4.13
Mar.	4.71	4.58	5.01	4.87	4.27	4.15
Apr.	4.71	4.58	5.02	4.88	4.27	4.15
May	4.73	4.60	5.04	4.91	4.29	4.16
June (p)	4.76	4.61	5.08	4.94	4.31	4.17
July (p)	4.78	4.64	5.10	4.96	4.35	4.20

General Manufacturing Statistics for States

Source: Bureau of the Census, Census of Manufacturers 1972 General Summary

Divisions, Regions and States	All employees Number (1,000)	All employees Payroll (millions)	Production workers Number (1,000)	Production workers Man-hrs. (millions)	Wages (millions)	Value added by Mfr. (millions)	Value of shipments (millions)	Capital expend. (millions)
New England Division	1,363	$11,908	942	1,853	$6,765	$22,508	$40,871	$1,244
Maine	100	699	83	162	513	1,383	2,879	139
New Hampshire	90	663	68	131	414	1,279	2,289	99
Vermont	37	311	26	52	176	576	1,229	37
Massachusetts	619	5,486	416	812	3,027	10,678	19,134	538
Rhode Island	118	888	91	174	566	1,764	3,219	101
Connecticut	399	3,860	258	521	2,069	6,828	12,121	332
Middle Atlantic Division	3,933	37,123	2,638	5,093	20,414	70,331	139,313	3,925
New York	1,679	16,222	1,076	2,068	8,174	30,404	58,559	1,506
New Jersey	836	8,107	547	1,071	4,354	16,409	32,410	940
Pennsylvania	1,418	12,794	1,015	1,954	7,886	23,519	48,345	1,479
East North Central Division	4,933	50,960	3,496	7,013	32,190	99,951	213,031	6,774
Ohio	1,346	13,810	940	1,888	8,717	27,171	55,025	1,695
Indiana	704	6,882	526	1,042	4,641	14,112	29,168	907
Illinois	1,306	12,801	901	1,780	7,675	25,849	53,553	1,564
Michigan	1,076	12,745	768	1,583	8,095	23,376	54,039	2,071
Wisconsin	501	4,722	361	721	3,063	9,443	21,246	535
West North Central Division	1,202	10,923	837	1,648	6,605	23,585	59,766	1,366
Minnesota	302	2,889	196	383	1,555	5,524	12,901	306
Iowa	216	2,039	157	311	1,355	4,758	12,600	329
Missouri	434	3,897	300	584	2,305	8,169	18,774	396
North Dakota	10	79	7	14	48	201	594	13
South Dakota	17	135	13	25	89	285	937	20
Nebraska	85	704	63	128	469	1,733	5,898	102
Kansas	137	1,181	101	203	783	2,915	8,063	199
South Atlantic Division	2,739	20,640	2,106	4,212	13,422	44,352	96,990	3,868
Delaware	69	755	38	74	304	1,292	3,388	92
Maryland	256	2,386	176	346	1,428	4,707	9,963	310
District of Columbia	19	215	9	16	92	376	617	19
Virginia	375	2,826	293	583	1,902	6,178	12,824	586
West Virginia	121	1,098	93	182	765	2,647	5,022	216
North Carolina	744	4,929	604	1,211	3,427	11,015	24,124	987
South Carolina	345	2,345	283	582	1,679	4,966	10,721	507
Georgia	468	3,336	369	738	2,243	7,386	18,374	689
Florida	343	2,750	242	482	1,581	5,787	11,958	463
East South Central Division	1,249	9,211	997	1,970	6,464	21,234	46,270	1,511
Kentucky	259	2,160	200	393	1,480	5,682	12,360	380
Tennessee	467	3,352	367	725	2,295	7,662	16,129	540
Alabama	323	2,397	262	519	1,731	5,065	11,240	355
Mississippi	200	1,302	167	332	959	2,825	6,541	236
West South Central Division	1,239	10,286	897	1,790	6,348	24,603	59,765	2,328
Arkansas	181	1,152	150	298	853	2,800	6,504	190
Louisiana	179	1,601	134	275	1,072	4,273	11,265	568
Oklahoma	143	1,188	96	186	659	2,270	5,348	224
Texas	736	6,345	517	1,031	3,763	15,259	36,648	1,346
Mountain Division	388	3,469	271	528	2,113	7,446	17,917	724
Montana	21	185	17	34	138	463	1,597	76
Idaho	43	340	34	66	245	821	2,069	75
Wyoming	7	57	5	10	39	144	451	23
Colorado	133	1,298	89	177	770	2,504	5,793	229
New Mexico	24	157	17	33	96	358	910	31
Arizona	94	855	62	121	482	1,880	4,041	198
Utah	57	486	39	74	287	1,069	2,632	68
Nevada	10	92	7	14	57	208	423	24
Pacific Division	1,983	19,685	1,345	2,594	11,182	39,986	82,611	2,338
Washington	226	2,308	160	303	1,411	4,721	10,816	354
Oregon	179	1,627	142	271	1,170	3,490	7,571	267
California	1,546	15,483	1,020	1,975	8,430	31,195	62,903	1,649
Alaska	8	75	6	12	57	170	366	22
Hawaii	25	191	18	33	114	410	956	47
Total	19,029	174,206	13,529	26,699	105,502	353,994	756,534	24,078

Employees in Non-Agricultural Establishments

Source: Bureau of Labor Statistics, U.S. Dept. of Labor (P) Preliminary

Annual Average by Industry Division
(In thousands)

Year	Total	Mining	Contract construction	Manufacturing	Trans. and public utilities	Whole., retail trade	Finance, insur., real estate	Service, miscellaneous	Government
1955	50,675	792	2,802	16,882	4,141	10,535	2,335	6,274	6,914
1960	54,234	712	2,885	16,796	4,004	11,391	2,669	7,423	8,353
1965	60,815	632	3,186	18,062	4,036	12,716	3,023	9,087	10,074
1970	70,920	623	3,536	—	4,504	15,040	3,687	11,621	12,561
1971	71,222	609	3,639	18,572	4,457	15,352	3,802	11,903	12,887
1972	73,714	625	3,831	19,090	4,517	15,975	3,943	12,392	13,340
1973	76,833	638	4,028	20,254	4,646	16,665	4,075	12,986	13,742
1974	78,334	672	3,985	20,016	4,699	17,011	4,161	13,506	14,285
1975 (July)	76,143	723	3,589	17,948	4,515	16,877	4,233	13,931	14,337

Profits of Manufacturing Corporations by Industry Groups

Source: Federal Trade Commission

Industry Group (Amounts estimated in millions of dollars)	Before Income Taxes			Profits After Taxes		
		Pct. of sales			Pct. of sales	
	1974	1974	1973	1974	1974	1973
Durable goods	**41,049**	**7.7**	**8.3**	**24,752**	**4.7**	**4.7**
Transportation equipment	4,961	4.4	7.0	3,084	2.7	3.9
Motor vehicles and equipment[1]	2,858	4.1	8.2	1,863	2.7	4.6
Electrical and electronic equipment	5,816	6.7	7.9	3,375	3.9	4.3
Machinery, except electrical	8,741	9.8	10.2	5,293	5.9	5.6
Fabricated metal products	4,861	7.9	7.3	2,822	4.6	4.0
Primary iron and steel	5,480	10.8	6.8	3,249	6.4	4.1
Primary nonferrous metals	3,100	10.7	8.0	2,035	7.0	5.4
Stone, clay, and glass products	1,895	7.1	8.1	1,183	4.4	4.8
Instruments and related products	3,001	14.9	14.9	1,857	9.2	8.4
Other durable goods	3,195	6.0	8.3	1,854	3.5	5.0
Nondurable goods	**51,113**	**9.6**	**7.7**	**34,015**	**6.4**	**4.8**
Food and kindred products	7,527	4.9	4.7	4,266	2.8	2.6
Tobacco manufactures	1,353	15.0	10.3	801	8.9	5.8
Textile mill products	1,522	4.9	5.2	795	2.5	2.8
Paper and allied products	3,692	12.0	9.4	2,183	7.1	5.4
Printing and publishing	2,980	8.5	8.6	1,642	4.7	4.8
Chemicals and allied products	11,813	13.6	11.9	7,273	8.4	6.8
Petroleum and coal products	18,153	15.5	9.8	14,743	12.6	7.6
Rubber and miscellaneous plastic products	2,271	8.5	7.1	1,339	5.0	4.0
Other nondurable products	1,799	4.5	4.2	975	2.4	2.1
All Manufacturing Corps.	**92,162**	**8.7**	**7.4**	**58,768**	**5.5**	**4.7**

[1] Included in major industry above.

Occupational Earnings in Selected Cities

Source: Bureau of Labor Statistics, Department of Labor

(Average earnings (1) for selected occupations studied in 6 broad industry divisions: Manufacturing; transportation, communication, and other public utilities; wholesale; retail; finance, insurance, and real estate; and services, March-May 1975)

Occupations (men and women combined)	Birmingham Ala.	Fort Lauderdale-Hollywood and West Palm Beach-Boca Raton, Fla.	Houston, Tex.	St. Louis, Mo.-Ill.	San Francisco-Oakland, Calif.	Toledo, O. Mich.	Worcester, Mass.
Average weekly earnings, straight-time							
Office Workers							
Accounting clerks[2]	$169.50	$157.50	$169.50	$182.50	$185.50	$183.50	$167.50
Computer operators[2]	184.00	——	226.00	222.50	234.50	198.50	202.00
Computer programmers, business[2]	260.00	——	284.00	267.00	301.50	248.50	298.50
Computer systems analysts, business[2]	——	——	361.00	346.50	337.00	322.50	314.50
Drafters[2]	238.00	244.50	273.50	269.50	262.50	279.00	244.50
File clerks[2]	138.00	——	168.50	140.50	158.50	——	——
Keypunch operators[2]	152.00	160.00	152.50	164.00	179.50	171.00	150.00
Messengers	111.50	119.50	113.50	115.00	127.00	129.50	108.00
Nurses, industrial (registered)	195.50	——	208.50	223.00	233.00	224.00	197.00
Secretaries	159.00	157.50	178.00	170.00	188.50	182.50	167.00
Stenographers, general	136.50	154.00	151.00	150.50	154.50	157.00	139.00
Typists[2]	127.50	136.50	144.00	146.50	143.00	153.00	129.50
Average hourly earnings, straight-time							
Maintenance, custodial, and material movement workers							
Carpenters	$5.95	$5.62	$6.19	$6.03	$7.10	$6.05	$5.06
Electricians	6.28	6.03	6.29	6.57	7.09	6.48	5.54
Engineers, stationary	6.12	——	5.24	6.17	7.22	6.21	5.28
Helpers, trades	5.09	3.95	4.40	5.13	5.36	5.25	3.54
Machinists	6.22	——	6.44	6.54	7.15	6.29	5.76
Mechanics, automotive	5.20	5.32	5.66	6.29	7.47	6.36	5.39
Painters	5.74	——	5.28	6.19	7.60	6.15	——
Guards and watchmen	2.54	2.55	2.64	3.04	3.11	3.03	3.14
Janitors, porters, cleaners	2.47	2.65	2.46	3.38	4.60	3.97	3.45
Laborers, material handling	3.38	3.18	3.50	4.95	5.91	5.29	3.80
Packers, shipping	4.48	3.21	3.46	4.22	4.73	4.85	4.12
Shipping clerks	5.28	——	4.13	4.91	5.38	5.16	4.01
Truckdrivers, local	4.04	4.32	4.42	6.24	6.83	5.99	5.16

1. Weekly earnings relate to regular straight-time salaries that are paid for standard workweeks. Hourly earnings exclude premium pay for overtime, weekends, holidays, or late shifts.
2. More than one skill level surveyed. Earnings are for the highest level surveyed.

Annual Rates of Profit on Stockholders' Equity

Source: Federal Trade Commission

(Each rate is the arithmetic mean of four quarterly rates, each on an annual basis.)

By industry after taxes: by percent	1950	1960	1965	1969[1]	1970	1972	1973	1974[2]
All manufacturing corporations, except newspapers	15.4	9.2	13.0	11.5	9.3	10.6	12.8	14.9
Durable goods industries	16.8	8.6	13.8	11.4	8.3	10.8	13.1	12 6
Metals and metal fabricating industries	16.9	8.6	14.2	11.2	*	*	*	*
Transportation equipment	21.5	11.7	18.5	12.0	6.3	12.5	13.1	8.0
Motor vehicles and equipment	25.2	13.5	19.5	12.6	6.1	14.6	15.1	6.9
Aircraft and parts	*	7.4	15.1	10.6	6.8	7.9	10.3	10.6
Electrical machinery, equipment and supplies	20.8	9.5	13.5	11.1	9.1	10.8	13.1	11.1
Machinery, except electrical	14.0	7.6	14.1	12.2	9.9	10.6	13.4	13.2
Metalworking machinery and equipment	*	5.3	14.4	11.6	8.3	6.5	13.5	*
Other fabricated metal products	15.9	5.6	13.2	11.3	8.6	10.8	13.9	16.6
Primary metal industries	14.5	7.2	10.6	9.5	7.0	6.0	10.1	16.4
Blast furnaces, steel works and foundries	14.3	7.2	9.8	7.6	4.3	6.0	9.5	16.8
Nonferrous metals	15.0	7.1	11.9	12.2	10.7	5.9	10.8	15.8
Other durable goods industries	16.3	8.6	12.2	12.4	*	*	*	*
Lumber and wood products, except furniture	17.4	3.6	10.0	13.2	5.9	16.2	22.4	*
Furniture and fixtures	15.1	6.5	13.3	12.6	7.9	13.3	13.2	*
Stone, clay and glass products	17.6	9.9	10.2	9.2	6.9	10.1	11.2	10.6
Instruments and related products	16.7	11.6	17.5	15.6	14.2	14.8	15.9	16.1
Miscellaneous manufacturing and ordnance	12.2	9.2	10.7	11.6	10.0	10.7	11.5	*
Nondurable goods industries	14.0	9.8	12.2	11.5	10.3	10.5	12.6	17.2
Chemicals: petroleum, rubber and plastics	15.4	10.8	13.0	12.0	*	*	*	*
Chemicals and allied products	17.8	12.2	15.2	12.8	11.5	12.8	14.8	18.2
Basic chemicals and related products	*	11.1	14.3	10.5	8.5	10.0	13.0	17.4
Drugs	*	16.8	20.3	18.4	17.6	18.4	19.0	18.8
Petroleum refining and related industries	13.8	10.1	11.8	11.7	11.0	8.7	11.6	21.0
Petroleum refining	*	10.1	11.8	11.7	11.0	8.7	11.6	*
Rubber and miscellaneous plastics products	16.7	9.1	11.7	10.4	7.1	10.8	12.1	14.4
Other nondurable goods industries	12.8	8.5	11.1	10.8	*	*	*	*
Food and kindred products	12.3	8.7	10.7	10.9	10.8	11.0	12.8	14.0
Dairy products	*	*	10.6	10.1	10.2	10.1	10.8	*
Bakery products	*	*	9.3	8.6	8.8	10.6	5.8	*
Alcoholic beverages	*	7.1	9.3	10.3	10.5	10.7	10.8	*
Tobacco manufacturers	11.5	13.4	13.5	14.4	15.7	15.4	14.8	15.6
Textile mill products	12.6	5.8	10.8	7.9	5.1	7.5	9.0	8.2
Apparel and other fabricated textile products	10.1	7.7	12.6	11.9	9.3	11.9	10.8	*
Paper and allied products	16.1	8.5	9.4	10.1	7.0	9.0	12.9	17.8
Printing and publishing, except newspapers	11.5	10.6	14.1	12.6	11.2	12.0	12.9	13.2
Leather and leather products	10.9	6.3	11.6	9.3	9.4	9.1	9.4	*

*—Not available. (1.) Includes newspapers for the first time. (2.) Profits for 1974 include equity in earnings (net of taxes) of nonconsolidated subsidiaries. In prior years this component was included in adjustment to earned surplus.

Personal Consumption Expenditures for the U.S.

Source: Bureau of Economic Analysis, U.S. Department of Commerce

(In millions of dollars)

	1950	1955	1960	1965	1970	1971	1972	1973
Food and tobacco	58,120	72,236	87,510	107,183	141,181	147,680	156,438	178,676
Clothing, accessories and jewelry	23,709	27,982	33,032	43,318	62,834	67,241	73,633	81,274
Personal care	2,438	3,461	5,324	7,578	10,420	10,621	11,443	12,315
Housing	21,286	33,738	46,305	63,509	90,926	99,117	107,895	116,367
Household operation	29,461	37,322	46,906	61,789	87,360	93,785	105,057	117,509
Medical care	8,788	12,755	19,116	28,082	47,401	51,764	57,230	62,726
Personal business	6,858	10,049	14,974	21,879	35,314	38,131	41,421	45,183
Transportation	24,672	35,574	43,134	58,154	77,776	90,489	99,949	109,228
Recreation	11,147	14,078	18,295	26,298	40,653	42,990	48,123	52,280
Private educ. and research	1,618	2,339	3,718	5,927	10,363	10,887	11,934	13,225
Religious and welfare act.	2,282	3,257	4,748	5,972	8,601	9,203	10,096	10,843
Foreign travel and remittances—net	630	1,590	2,179	3,150	4,815	5,217	5,798	5,595
Total personal consumption Expenditures	191,009	254,381	325,241	432,839	617,644	667,125	729,017	805,221

Work Stoppages (Strikes) in the United States

Source: Bureau of Labor Statistics, U. S. Department of Labor

	Number stoppages	Workers involved	Man days idle	Year	Number stoppages	Workers involved	Man days idle
Average 1935 to 1939	2,862	1,130,000	16,900,000	1969	5,700	2,481,000	42,869,000
				1970	5,716	3,305,000	66,414,000
War Period Dec. 8, 1941- Aug. 14, 1945	14,371	6,744,000	36,300,000	1971	5,138	3,280,000	47,589,000
				1972	5,010	1,714,000	27,066,000
Year				1973	5,353	2,251,000	27,948,000
1947-49	3,573	2,380,000	39,700,000	1974 (p)	5,900	2,700,000	48,000,000
1950	4,843	2,410,000	38,800,000	1975 Jan.	350	104,000	1,608,000
1955	4,320	2,650,000	28,200,000	Feb.	300	101,000	1,737,000
1960	3,333	1,320,000	19,100,000	Mar.	370	90,000	1,770,000
1965	3,963	1,550,000	23,300,000	Apr.	517	130,000	2,517,000
1968	5,045	2,649,000	49,018,000	May	619	242,000	4,930,000
				June	648	210,000	4,624,000

Retail Store Sales, by Kind of Business

Source: Bureau of the Census, U.S. Dept. of Commerce. In millions of dollars

Kinds of business	1974	1973	Kinds of business	1974	1973
All retail stores.	537,800	503,317	Nondurable goods stores .	370,500	333,042
Durable goods store.	167,300	170,275	Apparel group.	24,900	24,062
Automotive group	93,100	100,661	Men's and boys' wear stores. . .	5,700	5,609
Motor vehicle, other			Women's apparel, accessory		
automotive dealers	84,800	92,768	stores.	9,600	9,119
Tire, battery, accessory			Shoe stores	4,000	4,229
dealers.	8,300	7,895	Food group	119,800	105,731
Furniture and appliance group . . .	25,500	24,030	Grocery stores.	111,300	98,392
Furniture, home furnishings			General merchandise group		
stores.	15,400	14,290	with non stores.	89,300	83,301
Household appliance, radio			Department stores, excl.		
TV stores	8,000	7,904	mail order.	55,900	52,292
Lumber, building, hardware			Mail order (catalog sales).	5,800	5,384
group	23,500	22,766	Variety stores.	8,700	8,212
Lumber, building materials			Eating and drinking places.	41,800	37,925
dealers.	18,300	18,049	Gasoline service stations.	39,900	34,432
Hardware stores	5,200	4,717	Drug and proprietary stores	16,800	15,474
			Liquor stores.	10,300	9,602

(1) Sales by jewelry stores, other durable goods stores, other general merchandise stores, and other nondurable goods stores are not shown separately but are included in totals.

Total Retail Stores Sales (In millions of dollars) — (1955) 183,851; (1956) 189,729; (1957) 200,002; (1958) 200,353; (1959) 215,413; (1960) 219,529; (1961) 218,992; (1962) 235,563; (1963) 246,666; (1964) 261,870; (1965) 284,128; (1966) 303,956; (1967) 313,809; (1968) 341,876; (1969) 357,885; (1970) 375,527; (1971) 408,850; (1972) 448,400; (1973) 503,300; (1974) 537,800.

Cotton, Wool, Silk, and Man-Made Fibers Production

Source: Economic Research Service, U.S. Dept. of Agriculture

Cotton and wool from reports of the Dept. of Agriculture; silk, rayon and non-cellulosic man-made fibers from Textile Organon, a publication of the Textile Economics Bureau, Inc.

	Cotton[1]		Wool[2]		Silk	Man-made fibers[3]			
						Rayon & Acetate		Non-Celluosic[4]	
Year	U.S.	World	U.S.	World	World	U.S.	World	U.S.[4]	World
	Mil. Bales[5]	Mil. bales[5]	Mil. lb.	Mil. lb.	Mil. lb.	Mil. lb.	Mil. lb.	Mil.	Mil.
1940.	12.6	31.2	434.0	4,180	130	471.2	2,485.3	4.6	4.6
1950.	10.0	30.6	249.3	4,000	42	1,259.4	3,552.8	145.9	177.4
1960.	14.2	46.2	298.9	5,615	68	1,028.5	5,749.1	854.2	1,779.1
1964.	15.1	52.9	237.4	5,766	71	1,431.8	7,245.4	1,646.2	4,067.3
1965.	15.0	55.0	224.8	5,836	72	1,527.0	7,359.4	2,062.4	4,928.9
1966.	9.6	50.6	219.2	5,958	72	1,519.0	7,364.2	2,415.2	5,227.0[6]
1967.	7.4	49.5	211.4	6,040	75	1,388.1	7,297.4	2,662.1	6,013.0
1968.	10.9	54.8	197.9	6,295	82	1,594.3	7,780.2	3,632.1	7,889.0
1969.	10.0	53.2	182.8	6,261	86	1,576.2	7,835.6	4,029.3	9,207.0
1970.	10.2	53.8	176.8	6,163	90	1,373.2	7,565.2	4,053.5	10,351.0
1971.	10.5	59.2	172.2	6,033	90	1,390.9	7,613.8	4,761.0	12,335.0
1972.	13.7	61.6	168.6	5,631	93	1,394.3	7,833.1	5,927.3	13,994.0
1973[7].	13.0	62.5	153.2	5,508	97	1,357.0	8,080.0	6,997.4	16,727.0
1974.	11.5	63.1	138.6	5,758	99	1,198.8	7,700.0	6,908.5	16,400.0

(1). Year beginning Aug. 1. (2.) Grease basis. (3). Includes filament yarn and staple and tow fiber. (4). Includes textile glass fiber. (5.) 480-pound net weight bales, U.S. beginning 1960 and World beginning 1965. (6.) 1966 to date, excludes Olefin. (7.) Preliminary.

World Production of Natural Rubber

Source: Bureau of Domestic Commerce, U.S. Dept. of Commerce

Metric Tons

Year	Far East	Tropical America	Africa	Total	Year	Far East	Tropical America	Africa	Total
1940	1,379,000	26,000	16,000	1,421,000	1969	2,782,050	30,950	182,000	2,995,000
1945	173,000	49,000	54,000	276,000	1970	2,857,500	32,000	213,000	3,102,500
1950	1,771,500	27,000	55,000	1,853,500	1971	2,847,050	34,200	203,750	3,085,000
1955	1,798,000	27,500	98,500	1,924,000	1972	2,875,700	40,800	208,500	3,125,000
1960	1,825,100	29,900	148,000	2,002,000	1973	3,247,600	40,400	224,500	3,512,500
1965	2,156,950	36,300	159,250	2,352,500	1974	3,196,900	36,600	241,500	3,475,000

Full-time and Part-time Status of Civilian Labor Force

Source: Bureau of Labor Statistics, U.S. Dept. of Labor (in thousands) (Seasonally adjusted)

Employment Status Total, 16 years and over:	1974						1975					
	July	Aug.	Sept.	Oct.	Nov.	Dec.	Jan.	Feb.	Mar.	April	May	June
Full Time												
Civilian Labor Force .	77,625	77,796	78,477	78,860	78,569	78,626	78,839	78,429	78,583	78,995	79,730	78,385
Employed.	73,876	74,034	74,350	74,323	73,725	73,314	72,750	72,315	72,069	72,171	72,706	71,970
Unemployed	3,749	3,762	4,127	4,537	4,844	5,312	6,089	6,114	6,514	6,824	7,024	6,415
Unemployed rate . . .	4.8	4.8	5.3	5.8	6.2	6.8	7.7	7.8	8.3	8.6	8.8	8.2
Part Time												
Civilian Labor Force .	13,532	13,178	13,438	13,188	13,210	13,226	13,335	13,021	13,230	13,380	13,303	13,932
Employed.	12,374	12,056	12,264	12,040	11,989	11,950	11,935	11,685	11,782	11,985	11,821	12,499
Unemployed	1,158	1,122	1,174	1,148	1,221	1,276	1,400	1,336	1,448	1,395	1,482	1,433
Unemployment rate .	8.6	8.5	8.7	8.7	9.2	9.6	10.5	10.3	10.9	10.4	11.1	10.3

Labor Union Membership

Source: AFL-CIO and Dept. of Labor

AFL-CIO unions with a membership of 25,000 or over (Sept. 1975)

Union	Members	Union	Members
Actors and Artists of America, Associated	76,000	Retail Clerks International Association	602,000
Air Line Pilots Association	46,000	Retail, Wholesale and Department Store Union	117,000
Aluminum Workers International Union	27,000	Roofers, Damp & Waterproof Workers Association, United Slate, Tile & Composition	27,000
Bakery and Confectionery Workers International Union of America	123,000	Rubber, Cork, Linoleum & Plastic Workers of America, United	173,000
Barbers, Hairdressers and Cosmetologists' International Union of America, the Journeymen	42,000	Seafarers International Union of North America	80,000
Boilermakers, Iron Ship Builders, Blacksmiths, Forgers and Helpers, International Brotherhood of	123,000	Service Employees International Union, AFL-CIO	480,000
Boot and Shoe Workers' Union	34,000	Sheet Metal Workers International Association	120,000
Bricklayers, Masons, and Plasterers International Union of America	143,000	Shoe Workers of America, United	25,000
Carpenters and Joiners of America, United Brotherhood of	700,000	Stage Employes & Moving Picture Machine Operators of the United States & Canada, International Alliance of Theatrical	50,000
Chemical Workers Union, International	58,000	State, County & Municipal Employees, American Federation of	647,000
Clothing Workers of America, Amalgamated	233,000	Steelworkers of America, United	1,067
Communications Workers of America	475,000	Teachers, American Federation of	395,000
Dolls, Toys, Playthings, Novelties and Allied Products of the United States and Canada, AFL-CIO, International Union of.	29,000	Textile Workers of America, United	36,000
		Textile Workers Union of America	105,000
Electrical, Radio and Machine Workers International Union of	256,000	Tobacco Workers International Union	26,000
Electrical Workers, International Brotherhood of	856,000	Transit Union, Amalgamated	90,000
Engineers, International Union of Operating	300,000	Transport Workers Union of America	95,000
Fire Fighters, International Association of	123,000	Transportation Union, United	134,000
Firemen and Oilers, International Brotherhood of	40,000	Typographical Union, International	73,000
Furniture Workers of America, United	28,000	Upholsterers' International Union of North America	50,000
Garment Workers of America, United	32,000	Utility Workers Union of America	52,000
Garment Workers Union, International Ladies'	363,000	Woodworkers of America, International	52,000
Glass and Ceramic Workers of North America, United	28,000		
Glass Bottle Blowers' Association of the United States and Canada	75,000		
Glass Workers Union, American Flint	35,000		
Government Employees, American Federation of	252,000		
Grain Millers, American Federation of	29,00		
Graphic Arts International Union	93,000		
Hotel and Restaurant Employees' and Bartenders' International Union	421,000		
Industrial Workers of America, International Union, Allied	93,000		
Iron Workers, International Association of Bridge and Structural	160,000		
Laborers' International Union of North America	475,000		
Laundry and Dry Cleaning International Union	25,000		
Leather Goods, Plastics and Novelty Workers Union, International	39,000		
Letter Carriers, National Association of	151,000		
Longshoremen's Association, International	60,000		
Machinists and Aerospace Workers, International Association of	780,000		
Maintenance of Way Employes, Brotherhood of	71,000		
Maritime Union of America, National	35,000		
Meat Cutters and Butcher Workmen of North America, Amalgamated	451,000		
Molders and Allied Workers Union, International	50,000		
Musicians, American Federation of	215,000		
Newspaper Guild, The	27,000		
Office and Professional Employees International Union	74,000		
Oil, Chemical and Atomic Workers International Union	145,000		
Painters & Allied Trades of the United States and Canada, International Brotherhood of	160,000		
Paper Workers International Union, United	275,000		
Plasterers' & Cement Masons' International Association of the United States and Canada, Operative	55,000		
Plumbing and Pipe Fitting Industry of the United States & Canada, United Association of Journeymen & Apprentices of the	228,000		
Postal Workers Union, American	250,000		
Printing and Graphics Communications Union, International	105,000		
Railway, Airline and Steamship Clerks, Freight Handlers, Express & Station Employes, Brotherhood of	162,000		
Railway Carmen of the United States & Canada, Brotherhood	162,000		

Independent Unions
(1974)

Automobile, Aerospace and Agricultural Implement Workers of America, Intl. Union, United	1,400,000
Chemical Workers Union, Int.	86,000
Distributive Workers of America, Nat'l. Council of	40,000
Electrical, Radio and Machine Workers of America, United.	165,000
Federal Employees, Nat'l. Federation of	100,000
Government Employees, Nat'l. Assn. of	200,000
Internal Revenue Employees, Nat'l. Assn.	29,000
Letter Carriers Assn., Nat'l. Rural.	41,192
Locomotive Engineers, Brotherhood of.	39,000
Longshoremen's and Warehousemen's Union Int'l.	60,000
Mine Workers of America, United	450,000
Postal Union, National.	80,000
Postal and Federal Employees, Nat'l. Alliance of	45,000
Postal Supervisors, Nat'l. Assn. of	33,000
Postmasters, Nat'l. Assn. of.	28,273
Teamsters, Chauffeurs, Warehousemen and Helpers of America, Int'l. Brotherhood of . . .	1,973,272

CNTU Unions
(1973)

Government Employees' Union, Quebec.	30,000
Public Service Employees Inc., Federation of . .	27,555
Services, Inc., National Federation of.	58,378
Steel, Mine and Chemical Workers, Federation of.	30,641

CLC Unions
(1973)

Automobile, Aerospace and Agricultural Implement Workers of America, International Union, United	107,266
Public Employees, Canadian Union of	167,470
Public Service Alliance of Canada	133,503
Railway, Transport and General Workers, Canadian Brotherhood of.	38,296

Mineral Production in United States[1]

Source: Bureau of Mines

Mineral Fuels	1973 Quantity	1973 Value (thousands)	1974 Quantity	1974 Value (thousands)
Asphalt and related bitumens (native):				
Bituminous limestone & sandstone & gilsonite . . . . . . short tons	2,088,657	$8,464	2,021,165	$16,666
Carbon dioxide, natural (e). . . . . thousand cubic feet	1,134,986	259	966,118	237
Coal: Bituminous and lignite[2]. . . . . .thousand short tons	591,738	5,049,612	est. 590,000	est. 8,900,000
Pennsylvania anthracite. . . . . thousand short tons	6,830	90,260	6,617	144,695
Helium: Crude. . . . . million cubic feet	2,558	30,696	184	2,208
Grade A. . . . . million cubic feet	647	16,121	699	18,128
Natural gas. . . . . million cubic feet	22,647,549	4,894,072	21,600,522	6,573,402
Natural gas liquids: Gasoline products. . . . . thousand 42-gal. bbls.	187,390	668,784	168,152	1,107,158
LP gases . . . . thousand 42-gal. bbls.	447,033	1,188,289	447,946	1,980,769
Peat. . . . . thousand short tons	621	7,547	706	10,989
Petroleum (crude). . . . . .thousand 42-gal. bbls.	3,360,903	13,057,905	3,202,585	21,580,549
Total mineral fuels.	XX	25,012,000	XX	40,335,000
Non Metals (except fuels)				
Abrasive stones[3]. . . . . short tons	3,466	667	3,134	717
Asbestos. . . . . short tons	150,036	16,288	109,091	13,393
Barite. . . . . thousand short tons	1,104	16,688	1,106	16,822
Boron minerals. . . . . thousand short tons	1,225	113,648	1,185	128,306
Bromine . . . . thousand pounds	418,250	67,131	432,094	117,715
Calcium-magnesium chloride. . . . . short tons	609,300	17,581	867,100	29,189
Cement: Portland. . . . . thousand short tons	82,718	1,810,292	79,482	2,107,906
Masonry . . . . .thousand short tons	4,057	119,547	3,432	113,030
Natural and slag . . . . .thousand short tons	W	W	W	W
Clays. . . . . .thousand short tons	64,351	354,058	60,796	422,542
Diatomite . . . . short tons	608,906	36,083	664,303	50,693
Feldspar. . . . . short tons	791,900	12,830	853,702	14,482
Fluorspar . . . . short tons	248,601	17,381	201,116	14,297
Garnet (abrasive). . . . . short tons	22,772	2,381	24,684	2,550
Gem stones (e)	NA	2,739	NA	4,583
Gypsum. . . . . thousand short tons	13,558	56,650	11,999	52,894
Lime. . . . . thousand short tons	21,090	365,849	21,606	473,685
Magnesium compounds from sea water and brine				
(except for metals). . . . . short tons, MgO equivalent	853,907	77,733	907,492	96,742
Mica: Scrap. . . . . .thousand short tons	177	6,082	137	5,475
Sheet. . . . . pounds	—	—	—	7,024
Perlite. . . . . short tons	543,683	5,591	555,000	7,024
Phosphate rock. . . . . .thousand short tons	42,137	238,667	45,686	501,429
Potassium salts. . . . . thousand short tons, K₂O equivalent	2,603	112,613	2,552	158,974
Pumice. . . . . .thousand short tons	3,772	8,881	3,937	9,121
Pyrites. . . . . thousand long tons	559	4,961	424	4,238
Salt. . . . . .thousand short tons	43,910	306,103	46,536	360,763
Sand and gravel. . . . . .thousand short tons	983,629	1,359,370	978,754	1,451,071
Sodium carbonate (natural) . . . . thousand short tons	3,722	94,385	4,059	137,486
Sodium sulfate (natural). . . . . thousand short tons	672	11,597	684	16,411
Stone[4]. . . . . .thousand short tons	1,060,124	1,990,463	1,043,542	2,186,155
Sulfur: Frasch process mines. . . . . .thousand long tons	7,438	138,578	7,898	241,066
Talc, soapstone, and pyrophyllite. . . . . short tons	1,246,534	9,144	1,254,866	11,158
Tripoli. . . . . short tons	101,519	930	86,000	3,665
Vermiculite. . . . . short tons	365	9,464	341	10,120
Value of items that cannot be disclosed: Aplite, brucite, emery, graphite, iodine, kyanite, lithium minerals, magnesite, greensand marl, olivine, staurolite, wollastonite, and values of nonmetal items indicated by symbol W.		28,926	XX	20,334
Total nonmetals.	XX	7,413,000	XX	8,784,000
Metals				
Antimony ore concentrate, short tons, antimony content.	545	688	661	2,040
Bauxite. . . . . thousands long tons, dried equivalent	1,879	26,635	1,949	25,663
Beryllium concentrate. . . . . short tons, gross weight	W	W	W	W
Copper (recoverable content of ores, etc.) . . . . short tons	1,717,940	2,044,346	1,597,002	2,468,964
Gold (recoverable content of ores, etc.). . . . . troy ounces	1,175,750	115,000	1,126,886	180,009
Iron ore, (excluding iron sinter). . . . . . . thousand long tons, gr. wgt.	90,654	1,163,710	84,985	1,388,447
Lead (recoverable content of ores, etc.). . . . . short tons	603,024	196,465	663,870	298,742
Manganese ore (35% or more Mn) . . . . . . short tons, gross weight	239	W	W	W
Manganiferous ore (5 to 35% Mn) . . . . . . short tons, gross weight	203,055	W	272,908	2,323
Mercury . . . . 76-pound flasks	2,171	621	2,189	617
Molybdenum (content of concentrate). . . . . thousand pounds	135,097	217,701	118,163	234,658
Nickel (content of ore and concentrate). . . . . short tons	18,272	W	16,618	W
Rare-earth metal concentrates. . . . . short tons	31,278	13,780	35,218	15,966
Silver (recoverable content of ores, etc.). . . . . . .thousand troy ozs.	37,827	96,762	33,762	159,018
Titanium concentrate, ilmenite. . . . . . . short tons, gross weight	804,355	19,829	755,299	22,715
Tungsten ore and concentrate. . . . . thousand pounds	7,059	19,154	7,836	37,413
Uranium (Recoverable content U₃O₈). . . . . thousand pounds	25,803	167,718	23,227	243,884
Vanadium (recoverable in ore and concentrate) . . . . short tons	4,377	26,611	4,870	38,266
Zinc (recoverable content of ores, etc.). . . . . short tons	478,850	197,861	499,872	358,908
Value of items that cannot be disclosed: symbol W.	XX	55,212	XX	74,824
Total metals.	XX	4,362,000	XX	5,552,000
Grand total mineral production.	XX	36,788,000	XX	54,671,000

(e) Estimate. (R) Revised. (NA) Not available. (W) Withheld to avoid disclosing individual company confidential data; included with "Value of items that cannot be disclosed." (XX) Not applicable.
(1) Production as measured by mine shipments, sales, or marketable production (including consumption by producers).
(2) Includes a small quantity of anthracite mined in states other than Pennsylvania.
(3) Grindstones, pulpstones, grinding pebbles, sharpening stones, and tube mill liners.
(4) Excludes abrasive stone, bituminous limestone, bituminous sandstone, and soapstone, all included elsewhere.

Mineral Production in U.S.—Leading States

Source: Bureau of Mines (1973)

State	Value (thousands)	Rank	Percent of U.S. total	Principal minerals, in order of value
Texas	$8,442,494	1	22.95	Petroleum, natural gas, natural gas liquids, cement.
Louisiana	5,819,610	2	15.82	Petroleum, natural gas, natural gas liquids, sulfur.
California	2,041,686	3	5.55	Petroleum, cement, sand and gravel, natural gas.
West Virginia	1,503,045	4	4.09	Coal, natural gas, stone, cement.
Pennsylvania	1,401,900	5	3.81	Coal, cement, stone, sand and gravel.
Oklahoma	1,323,626	6	3.60	Petroleum, natural gas, nat. gas liquids, stone.
New Mexico	1,305,644	7	3.55	Petroleum, natural gas, copper, natural gas liquids.
Arizona	1,304,988	8	3.55	Copper, molybdenum, sand and gravel, cement.
Kentucky	1,164,762	9	3.17	Coal, stone, petroleum, natural gas.
Wyoming	928,105	10	2.52	Petroleum, sodium compounds, uranium, natural gas.

Value of Mineral Production in the United States[2]

Source: Bureau of Mines (r-Revised)

(In millions of dollars)

Year[1]	Fuels	Nonmetallic	Metals	Total[3]	Year[1]	Fuels	Nonmetallic	Metals	Total[3]
1930	2,500	973	501	3,980	1968	16,820	5,449	2,698	r24,966
1940	2,662	784	752	4,198	1969	17,965	5,624	3,333	26,921
1950	8,689	1,882	1,351	11,862	1970	20,152	r5,712	3,928	r29,792
1960	12,142	3,868	2,022	18,032	1971	21,247	6,058	3,403	30,708
1965	14,047	4,933	2,544	21,524	1972	22,061	6,482	3,642	32,185
1966	15,088	5,176	2,703	22,968	1973	25,012	7,413	4,362	23,788
1967	16,195	5,200	2,327	36,788	1974p	40,335	8,784	5,552	54,671

(1.) Excludes Alaska and Hawaii, 1930-53. (2.) Production as measured by mine shipments sales or marketable production. (3.) Data may not add to total because of rounding figures. (P.) Preliminary.

Copper, Lead, and Zinc Production in the U.S.

Source: Bureau of Mines

Year	Copper Mil. lbs.	$1,000	Lead[1] Short Tons	$1,000	Zinc Short tons	Mil. dol.	Year	Copper Mil. lbs.	$1,000	Lead[1] Short Tons	$1,000	Zinc Short tons	Mil. dol.
1950	1,823	379,122	418,809	113,078	591,454	167	1971	3,044	1,583,071	578,550	159,679	491,407	158
1960	2,286	733,708	228,899	53,562	334,101	87	1972	3,330	1,704,796	618,915	186,046	478,318	170
1965	2,703	957,028	301,147	93,959	611,153	178	1973	3,436	2,044,346	603,024	196,465	478,850	198
1969	3,089	1,468,400	509,013	151,635	553,124	162	1974	3,194	2,468,964	668,870	298,742	499,872	359
1970	3,439	1,984,484	571,767	178,609	534,136	164							

(1.) Production from domestic ores.

Raw Steel Production

(Thousands of Net Tons)

State	1974	State	1974
New York	5,495	Indiana	23,088
Pennsylvania	33,535	Illinois	12,939
R.I., Conn., N.J., Del., Md.	6,898	Michigan	10,459
Va., W. Va., Ga., Fla., N.C., S.C.	5,619	Minn., Mo., Okla., Texas	5,751
Kentucky	2,703	Ariz., Colo., Utah, Wash., Ore., Hawaii	4,922
Ala., Tenn., Miss., Ark.	4,767	California	4,293
Ohio	25,251	Total	145,720

United States Pig Iron and Steel Output

Source: American Iron and Steel Institute; figures show net tons

Year	Total pig iron	Pig iron and ferro-alloys	Raw steel	Year	Total pig iron	Pig iron and ferro-alloys	Raw Steel
1940	46,071,666	47,398,529	66,982,686	1969	95,017,000	97,593,000	141,262,000
1945	53,223,169	54,919,029	79,701,648	1970	91,435,000	93,851,000	131,514,000
1950	64,586,907	66,400,311	96,836,075	1971	81,299,000	83,468,000	120,443,000
1955	76,857,417	79,263,865	117,036,085	1972	88,942,000	91,338,000	133,241,000
1960	66,480,648	68,566,384	99,281,601	1973	100,837,000	103,089,000	150,799,000
1965	88,184,901	90,918,040	131,461,601	1974	95,909,000	98,175,000	145,720,000

Steel figures include only that portion of the capacity and production of steel for castings used by foundries which were operated by companies producing steel ingots.

U.S. Primary Aluminum Production

Source: The Aluminum Association

Year	Short tons	Year	Short tons	Year	Short tons	Year	Short tons
1883-1902	13,981	1930	114,518	1965	2,754,478	1971	3,925,224
1903-1912	108,412	1940	206,280	1968	3,255,042	1972	4,122,392
1913-1923	282,722	1950	718,622	1969	3,793,062	1973	4,529,117
1924-1925	145,340	1960	2,014,498	1970	3,976,148	1974	4,903,427

Estimated Markets For Total U.S. Aluminum Shipments (1972)

Market	Millions of lbs.	Percent	Market	Millions of lbs.	Percent
Building & Construction	3,074	22.6	Containers & Packaging	2,265	16.6
Transportation	2,430	17.9	Exports	944	6.9
Consumer Durables	1,155	8.5	Other	884	6.5
Electrical	1,828	13.4			
Machinery & Equipment	1,041	7.6	Total industry	13,621	100.0

TRADE AND TRANSPORTATION

Notable Steamships and Motorships

Source: Lloyd's Register of Shipping as of July 28, 1975

Gross tonnage is a measurement of enclosed space (1 gross ton = 100 cu. ft.). Deadweight tonnage is the weight (long tons) of caro, fuel, etc., which a vessel is designed to carry safely.

Oil Tankers
317,000 tons deadweight and over

Name-registry	Dwght. ton.	Lgth. Ft.	Bdth. Ft.
Nissei Maru, Jap.	484,337	1242	203
Globtik London, Br.	483,939	1243	203
Globtik Tokyo, Br.	483,664	1243	203
Ioannis Colocotronis, Gr.	386,612	1213	210
Hemland, Swed.	372,201	1193	208
Nisseki Maru, Jap.	366,813	1138	179
Al Andalus, Kuw.	362,946	1188	175
Sea Scape, Swed.	356,400	1148	196
Sea Saint, Swed.	356,400	1190	197
Sea Stratus, Swed.	356,400	1148	196
Kristine Maersk, Den.	339,090	1215	185
Katrine Maersk, Den.	333,750	1215	185
Universe Iran, Liber.	326,933	1132	175
Universe Kuwait, Liber.	326,848	1132	175
Universe Korea, Liber.	326,676	1132	175
Universe Portugal, Liber.	326,676	1132	175
Universe Ireland, Liber.	326,585	1132	175
Universe Japan, Liber.	326,562	1132	175
Venoil, Liber.	325,728	1115	175
Venpet, Liber.	325,645	1115	175
Limatula, Br.	324,789	1162	185
Lepton, Liber.	319,000	1148	180
Ocean Park, S. Kor.	317,992	1141	175
Butron, Liber.	317,985	1141	175
Arteaga, Sp.	317,985	1141	175
Liotina, W. Ger.	317,588	1153	181
Belfri, Nor.	317,500	1153	181
Lagena, W. Ger.	317,207	1153	181

Bulk, Ore, Bulk Oil & Ore Oil Carriers
168,000 tons Deadweight and over

Name-registry	Dwght. ton.	Lgth. Ft.	Bdth. Ft.
Svealand, Swed.	282,450	1109	179
Docecanyon, Liber.	271,235	1113	180
Jose Bonifacio, Braz.	270,358	1106	179
Tarfala, Swed.	265,000	1099	170
Mary R. Koch, Liber.	265,000	1099	170
Torne, Swed.	265,000	1099	170
Usa Maru, Jap.	264,523	1105	179
Nordic Conqueror, Br.	264,485	1101	176
Lauderdale, Br.	260,424	1101	176
Licorne Atlantique, Fr.	258,268	1101	176
La Loma, Br.	245,288	1069	170
Hoegh Hood, Nor.	244,677	1069	170
Hoegh Hill, Nor.	241,447	1069	170
Falkefjell, Nor.	231,045	1075	160
Berge Vanga, Liber.	227,561	1030	164
Berge Adria, Nor.	227,561	1030	164
Berge Istra, Liber.	227,556	1030	165
Havkong, Nor.	227,406	1075	161
Berge Brioni, Nor.	227,187	1030	165
Andros Atlas, Gr.	224,074	1061	158
Ambrosiana, It.	223,819	1091	149
San Giusto, It.	223,819	1091	149
Andros Antares, Liber.	223,808	1061	158
Andros Aries, Gr.	223,808	1061	158
Sysla, Nor.	223,500	1096	149
Alva Bay, Br.	222,331	1091	149
Alva Sea, Br.	221,457	1090	149
Tartar, Nor.	215,621	1075	164
Jarl Malmros, Swed.	215,500	1075	164
Tantalus, Br.	214,592	1075	164
Atsuta Maru, Jap.	214,017	1075	164
Tsurumi Maru, Jap.	213,842	1075	164
Adria Maru, Jap.	183,572	1023	156
Arafura Maru, Jap.	180,626	1023	156
Larina, Liber.	175,927	984	157
Romantic, Liber.	174,107	995	151
Rhetoric, Liber.	173,668	995	151
Sir John Hunter, Br.	171,400	965	145
Cedros, Liber.	170,418	995	142
Cetra Centaurus, Fr.	170,414	981	143
Bunga Mawar, Malaysia	169,623	967	155
Cetra Vela, Fr.	169,317	967	155

Name-registry	Dwght. ton.	Lgth. Ft.	Bdth. Ft.
Champagne, Fr.	169,300	967	155
Sir Alexander Glen, Br.	168,700	965	144

World's Largest Passenger Ships
30,000 gross tons and over

Name-registry	Gross ton.	Lgth. Ft.	Bdth. Ft.
Queen Elizabeth 2, Br.	66,852	963	105
France, Fr.	66,348	1035	110
Raffaello, It.	45,933	904	101
Michelangelo, It.	45,911	904	101
Canberra, Br.	44,807	818	102
Oriana, Br.	41,910	804	97
United States, U.S.	38,216	990	101
Rotterdam, Neth.	37,783	748	94
Windsor Castle, Br.	36,277	783	92
Leonardo Da Vinci, It.	33,340	767	92
Eugenio C., It.	30,567	713	96
S.A. Vaal, S. Afr.	30,213	760	90

Container, Liquefied Gas, Misc. Ships
32,300 gross tons and over

Name-registry	Gross ton.	Lgth. Ft.	Bdth. Ft.
Ben Franklin, Fr.	88,000	894	134
LNG Challenger, Br.	76,496	857	131
Norman Lady, Br.	76,416	818	131
Palace Tokyo, Jap.	64,378	807	131
Cardigan Bay, Br.	58,899	950	106
Kowloon Bay, Br.	58,889	950	106
Liverpool Bay, Br.	58,889	950	106
Tokyo Bay, Br.	58,889	950	106
Osaka Bay, Br.	58,889	950	106
Nedlloyd Delft, Neth.	58,716	941	106
Nedlloyd Dejima, Neth.	58,716	941	106
City of Edinburgh, Br.	58,440	950	106
Benavon, Br.	58,440	950	106
Benalder, Br.	58,440	950	106
Hamburg Express, W. Ger.	58,088	943	105
Tokio Express, W. Ger.	58,082	895	105
Bremen Express, W. Ger.	57,535	941	106
Hongkong Express, W. Ger.	57,535	941	106
Korrigan, Fr.	57,249	946	105
Esso Fuji, Panama.	55,896	807	131
Geomitra, Br.	53,128	846	114
Toyama, Nor.	52,196	902	106
Elbe Maru, Jap.	51,623	882	105
Kitano Maru, Jap.	51,159	856	105
Kurama Maru, Jap.	51,139	856	105
Kamakura Maru, Jap.	51,139	856	105
Rhine Maru, Jap.	51,085	856	105
Nihon, Swed.	50,805	902	105
Selandia, Den.	49,890	900	106
Jutlandia, Den.	49,890	900	106
Gari, Br.	48,662	842	114
Gastrana, Br.	48,662	842	114
Gadila, Br.	48,662	842	114
Gadinia, Br.	48,662	842	114
Yusho Maru, Jap.	47,783	744	114
Sun River, Jap.	45,647	734	106
Polar Alaska, Liber.	44,089	798	111
Artic Tokyo, Liber.	44,089	798	111
Nyhammer, Nor.	43,000	757	105
Remuera, Br.	42,007	824	105
Kanayama Maru, Jap.	41,939	734	113
Sea-Land Exchange, U.S.	41,555	946	105
Sea-Land Commerce, U.S.	41,127	946	105
Sea-Land Trade, U.S.	41,127	946	105
Sea-Land Market, U.S.	41,127	946	105
Sea-Land Resource, U.S.	41,127	946	105
Sea-Land Finance, U.S.	41,127	946	105
Sea-Land Galloway, U.S.	41,127	946	105
Sea-Land Mclean, U.S.	41,127	946	105
Bridgestone Maru V, Jap.	40,934	690	106
Verrazano Bridge, Jap.	39,153	867	105

Name-registry	Gross ton.	Lgth. Ft.	Bdth. Ft.	Name-registry	Gross ton.	Lgth. Ft.	Bdth. Ft.
Tokuho Maru, Jap.	39,117	705	105	Tohbei Maru, Jap.	35,491	806	105
Izumisan Maru, Jap.	38,872	705	105	Kazutama Maru, Jap.	34,529	656	103
New York Maru, Jap.	38,825	862	105	Providence Multina, Fr.	34,341	710	106
Kiso Maru, Jap.	38,540	857	105	Malmros Multina, Swed.	34,241	710	106
Svendborg Maersk, Den.	38,540	856	105	Antilla Bay, Neth.	34,015	710	105
Kurobe Maru, Jap.	37,845	854	105	Japan Ambrose, Jap.	33,287	748	105
New Jersey Maru, Jap.	37,799	863	105	Sovietskaya Rossiya, USSR.	33,154	713	94
Munchen, W. Ger.	37,134	857	105	Descartes, Fr.	32,702	721	104
Bilderdyck, Neth.	36,974	857	105	Delta Sud, U.S.	32,325	893	100
World Rainbow, Panama	36,917	734	113	Delta Mar, U.S.	32,306	893	100
Amvrosios, Liber.	36,912	734	113	Delta Norte, U.S.	32,306	893	100
Pine Queen, Liber.	36,905	734	113				
Nektar, Liber.	36,902	734	113	**Nuclear Powered Merchant Ships**			
Hongkong Container, Liber.	36,885	867	105				
Atlantic Forest, Nor.	36,870	857	106	Otto Hahn, W. Ger.	16,871	564	76
Acadia Forest, Nor.	36,862	857	106	Savannah, U.S.	15,585	595	78
World Bridgestone, Panama	36,556	690	106	Lenin, USSR	14,067	439	90
Ogden Bridgestone, Panama	36,125	690	106	Mutsu, Jap.	8,214	428	62

U.S. Exports and Imports of Leading Commodities

Source: Bureau of International Commerce, Dept. of Commerce, (Value in millions of dollars)

Commodity	Exports			Imports		
	1972	1973	1974	1972	1973	1974
Total	$48,979	$70,223	$98,506	$55,583	$69,121	$100,972
Food and live animals	5,661	11,931	13,983	6,370	7,986	9,379
Meat	252	444	381	1,223	1,668	1,344
Dairy products and eggs	143	56	67	...	...	...
Cheese	...	...	...	111	156	236
Fish	135	242	196	1,205	1,387	1,499
Grains and preparations	3,501	8,495	10,331	92	105	171
Wheat and wheat flour	1,452	4,151	4,589	...	...	...
Rice	389	541	852	...	...	...
Corn	1,241	2,837	3,772	...	...	...
Fruit and nuts	526	662	757	496	577	627
Vegetables	209	307	391	350	409	387
Sugar	...	...	...	832	918	2,256
Coffee, green	...	...	...	1,182	1,566	1,504
Beverages and Tobaccos	908	1,1008	1,247	1,009	1,213	1,321
Alcoholic beverages	...	...	...	824	996	1,028
Tobacco, unmanufactured	639	681	832	157	187	255
Crude materials, inedible other than fuels	5,030	8,384	10,934	3,860	4,988	5,915
Synthetic rubber	161	196	290	...	...	...
Ores and metal scrap	508	1,081	1,475	1,022	1,291	1,838
Coal	984	1,014	2,436	...	...	...
Petroleum and products	444	518	792	4,300	7,548	24,210
Animal and vegetable oils and fats	508	684	1,423	180	255	544
Chemicals	4,133	5,748	8,822	2,015	2,437	3,991
Medicinal and Pharmaceutical	474	626	800	149	164	214
Machinery and transport equipment	21,533	27,842	38,189	17,420	20,970	24,713
Automotive engines	485	578	673	846	983	1,013
Agricultural machinery	249	346	545	237	313	440
Tractors and parts	249	339	483	211	292	412
Metalworking machinery	410	489	639	140	188	305
Textile and leather machinery	272	375	528	638	625	609
Other nonelectrical machinery	1,040	1,300	3,541	796	1,052	1,348
Electrical apparatus	3,698	5,031	7,019	3,377	4,471	5,417
Transport equipment	7,971	10,255	13,871	9,504	10,876	12,630
New motor vehicles	2,064	2,666	3,681	5,724	6,479	7,544
Aircraft and parts	3,015	4,124	5,766	415	554	510
Other manufactured goods	8,094	11,112	16,516	18,332	21,382	27,507
Rubber manufacturers	231	308	544	...	...	...
Paper and manufactures	726	919	1,522	1,261	1,457	1,831
Diamonds excluding industrial	172	314	305	637	827	775
Metals and manufactures	828	1,111	1,665	6,004	6,885	11,383
Iron and steel-mill products	800	1,258	2,491	2,743	2,769	5,013
Nonferrous base metals	567	951	1,300	1,754	1,994	3,042
Textiles other than clothing	779	1,225	1,795	1,528	1,568	1,629
Clothing	215	254	372	1,883	2,154	2,323
Other transactions	1,560	1,844	2,587	1,598	1,790	2,252

U.S. Merchandise Exports and Imports, by Continent

Source: International Trade Analysis Division, Dept. of Commerce (Value in millions of dollars)

Year	Exports				General Imports			
	Western Hemisp.	Europe	Asia & Oceania	Africa	Western Hemisp.	Europe	Asia & Oceania	Africa
1965	9,932	9,397	7,129	1,071	9,257	6,292	4,999	867
1969	14,713	12,642	9,327	1,324	15,547	10,334	9,141	1,008
1970	15,611	14,817	11,294	1,502	16,928	11,395	10,515	1,090
1971	16,850	14,562	11,086	1,631	18,730	12,881	12,694	1,217
1972	19,694	16,180	12,407	1,500	21,930	15,744	16,279	1,578
1973	25,003	23,157	20,395	2,081	27,229	19,687	19,614	2,552
1974	35,745	30,878	28,129	3,204	40,702	24,636	29,073	6,547

United States Foreign Trade with Leading Countries

Source: Bureau of International Commerce, Dept. of Commerce
(Value in millions of dollars)

Exports from the U.S. to the following areas and countries and imports into the U.S. from those areas and countries:	Exports			Imports		
	1972	1973	1974	1972	1973	1974
Total	$49,778	$71,314	$98,506	$55,583	$69,121	$100,972
Western Hemisphere	19,694	25,003	35,745	21,930	27,229	40,702
Canada	12,415	15,073	19,932	14,927	17,670	22,282
19 American Republics	6,467	8,921	14,504	5,772	7,790	13,678
Central American Common Market	439	621	1,033	485	685	788
Latin American Free Trade Ass'n	5,576	7,708	12,571	4,949	6,668	12,199
Dominican Republic	183	229	410	232	307	471
Panama	216	286	364	55	67	108
Bahamas	144	208	253	247	286	958
Jamaica	221	268	337	181	176	233
Netherlands Antilles	122	159	193	400	733	2,018
Trinidad and Tobago	121	133	192	251	409	1,273
Europe	16,180	23,157	30,071	15,744	19,687	24,636
OECD Countries (Excludes depend and Yugo.)	15,173	21,094	28,268	15,268	18,994	23,470
Western Europe	15,361	21,361	28,639	15,423	19,167	23,745
European Economic Community	11,900	16,746	22,069	12,489	15,513	19,205
Belgium and Luxembourg	1,138	1,622	2,285	968	1,261	1,681
France	1,609	2,263	2,942	1,369	1,717	2,305
Germany, Federal Republic of	2,807	3,756	4,986	4,250	5,318	6,428
Italy	1,434	2,119	2,752	1,757	1,989	2,593
Netherlands	1,871	2,860	3,979	639	925	1,453
United Kingdom	2,658	3,563	4,574	2,987	3,642	4,021
Denmark	258	404	360	367	458	477
Ireland	125	159	193	152	202	247
European Free Trade Association	1,775	2,307	2,984	1,984	2,500	3,068
Austria	96	118	148	173	228	457
Finland	91	133	201	142	178	212
Iceland	20	26	38	59	77	75
Norway	213	297	498	241	261	307
Portugal	211	232	407	149	192	241
Sweden	472	542	908	601	753	876
Switzerland	672	960	1,150	619	811	900
Greece	250	375	488	90	92	158
Spain	930	1,319	1,899	600	761	899
Turkey	317	347	463	106	129	141
Yugoslavia	169	236	310	150	167	268
Eastern Europe	819	1,796	1,432	321	519	891
Asia	11,373	18,651	26,239	15,134	18,060	27,570
Near East	1,974	3,041	5,557	773	1,370	4,735
Egypt	76	225	455	17	26	70
Iraq	23	56	285	9	16	1
Iran	558	771	1,734	199	340	2,132
Israel	557	961	1,206	222	265	282
Jordan	65	79	105	—	—	—
Kuwait	111	119	209	49	65	13
Lebanon	130	162	287	21	32	30
Saudi Arabia	314	442	835	194	507	1,671
Japan	4,963	8,312	10,679	9,064	9,645	12,455
East and South Asia	4,373	6,609	9,196	5,264	6,979	10,264
China, Republic of (Taiwan)	628	1,168	1,427	1,293	1,772	2,108
Hong Kong	489	740	882	1,249	1,444	1,637
India	350	525	760	427	437	561
Indonesia	308	442	531	278	499	1,688
Korea, Republic of	735	1,242	1,546	708	971	1,460
Malaysia	128	162	377	301	417	773
Singapore	385	684	988	265	459	553
Pakistan	183	239	398	40	39	61
Philippines	365	495	747	491	663	1,091
Thailand	172	256	369	116	140	184
Vietnam, Republic of	318	314	675	2	3	8
Oceania	1,034	1,744	2,697	1,145	1,554	1,503
Australia	842	1,439	2,157	807	1,062	1,042
New Zealand and Western Samoa	136	249	454	277	410	348
Africa	1,500	2,081	3,204	1,578	2,552	6,547
North Africa excluding Egypt	346	504	826	309	565	1,224
Algeria	98	160	315	104	215	1,091
Ethiopia	24	25	33	58	79	64
Libya	85	104	139	116	216	1
Morocco	58	113	184	11	13	20
Tunisia	55	60	87	8	33	21
Western and Equatorial Africa	398	561	827	674	1,266	4,287
Angola	26	38	62	90	166	378
Ghana	44	63	77	80	90	126
Ivory Coast	22	69	49	92	108	95
Liberia	41	46	70	52	72	96
Nigeria	114	161	286	271	650	3,286
Central and Southern Africa	754	1,016	1,552	594	721	1,034
Kenya	24	39	49	27	26	39
South Africa, Republic of	602	746	1,160	325	374	609
Zaire	37	115	145	43	70	68

Important Waterways and Canals

The **St. Lawrence & Great Lakes Waterway**, the largest inland navigation system on the continent, extends from the Atlantic Ocean to Duluth at the western end of Lake Superior, a distance of 2,342 miles. With the deepening of channels and locks to 27 ft., ocean carriers are able to penetrate to ports in the Canadian interior and the American midwest.

The major canals are those of the St. Lawrence-Great Lakes waterway — the 3 new canals of the St. Lawrence Seaway, with their 7 locks, providing navigation for vessels of 26 foot draught from Montreal to Lake Ontario; the Welland Ship Canal by-passing the Niagara River between Lake Ontario and Lake Erie with its 8 locks, and the Sault Ste. Marie Canal and lock between Lake Huron and Lake Superior. These 16 locks overcome a drop of 580 ft. from the head of the lakes to Montreal. From Montreal to Lake Ontario the former bottleneck of narrow, shallow canals and of slow passage through 22 locks has been overcome, giving faster and safer movement for larger vessels. The new locks and linking channels now accommodate all but the largest ocean-going vessels and the upper St. Lawrence and Great Lakes are open to 80% of the world's saltwater fleet.

Subsidiary Canadian canals or branches include the St. Peters Canal between Bras d'Or Lakes and the Atlantic Ocean in Nova Scotia; the St. Ours and Chambly Canals on the Richelieu River, Quebec; the Ste. Anne and Carillon Canals on the Ottawa River; the Rideau Canal between the Ottawa River and Lake Ontario, the Trent and Murray Canals between Lake Ontario and Georgian Bay in Ontario and the St. Andrew's Canal on the Red River. The commercial value of these canals is not great but they are maintained to control water levels and permit the passage of small vessels and pleasure craft. The Canso Canal, completed 1957, permits shipping to pass through the causeway connecting Cape Breton Island with the Nova Scotia mainland.

Traffic movement on the system in 1974 encountered difficulties as a result of labor unrest in associated industries as well as an unfortunate accident on the Welland which stopped navigation for 12 days.

Cargo tonnage on the Montreal-Lake Ontario Section of the Seaway amounted to 44.1 million tons, representing a decrease of 23.4% with 16.7% less upbound and 29.5% less downbound as compared to 1973. The principal commodities carried in the Montreal-Lake Ontario Section in order of tonnage were: iron ore, wheat, manufactured iron and steel, corn, fuel oil and barley. These six items accounted for 73.4% of the total tonnage compared with 73.0% for the leading six commodities in 1973.

St. Lawrence Seaway provides a navigational channel with a minimum water depth of 27 ft. to link the Great Lakes to the Atlantic Ocean. A vessel entering the Great Lakes from the Atlantic ascends 20 ft. above sea level in the 1,000-mile long reach up the Gulf of St. Lawrence and St. Lawrence River to Montreal, Quebec. At Montreal, the vessel enters the first of 7 new locks, 5 of which are in Canadian waters and 2 within United States waters, which raise or lower shipping a total of 226 ft. in the 182-mile stretch of the St. Lawrence River between Montreal and Lake Ontario. Crossing Lake Ontario, the vessel enters Canada's 28-mile-long Welland Canal, with 8 locks to compensate for the difference in elevation of 326 ft. between Lake Ontario and Lake Erie.

The signing of the Merchant Marine Bill of 1970 removed the major obstacles to the future development of the St. Lawrence Seaway. The bill eliminated interest payments on the Seaway's debt, gave official "fourth seacoast" identity to the Great Lakes-St. Lawrence Waterway, and enabled lake shipbuilders to qualify for federal shipbuilding subsidies.

Saint Lawrence Seaway Development Corporation (U.S.), P.O. Box 520, Massena, New York, David W. Oberlin, Administrator.

St. Lawrence Seaway Authority (Canada), Ottawa, Ontario, Mr. Paul D. Normandeau, president.

The **Welland Canal** overcomes the 326-ft. drop of Niagara Falls and the rapids of the Niagara River. It has 8 locks, each 859 ft. long, 80 ft. wide and 30 ft. deep. Regulations permit ships of 730-ft. length and 75-ft. beam to transit.

The Welland Section cargo tonnage totalled 52.4 million in comparison with 67.2 million tons for 1973. The principal commodities carried in the Welland Section in order of tonnage were: iron ore, wheat, coal, corn, manufactured iron and steel, and barley. These six commodities accounted for 73.0% of the total tonnage compared with 72.1% in 1973.

Sault Ste. Marie Canal reported 110,688,294 short tons of freight passed through during the season of 1973 compared with 97,047,762 for 1972.

Panama Canal

The Panama Canal is a lock and lake canal, crossing the Isthmus of Panama from the Caribbean Sea in a southeasterly direction to the Bay of Panama of the Pacific Ocean. It is 50 mi. long from deep water to deep water, at least 500 ft. wide at the bottom of excavated channels, 110 ft. wide in lock chambers, which have a usable length of 1,000 ft. Depth varies, but is not less than 40 ft. Time in transit is 12 hours.

Gatun Dam blocks the Chagres river near its Atlantic mouth, creating Gatun lake, 23 3/4 mi. long, 85 ft. above sea level, about 45 ft. deep. Ships ascend to the lake by locks and then pass through Gaillard (formerly Culebra) Cut, 8 mi. long.

Cargo tonnage on the Panama Canal in fiscal 1974 amounted to 149.7 million compared with 127.5 million tons in 1973. Transit of oceangoing ships in fiscal 1974 totaled 14,304 compared with 14,238 in fiscal 1973 (same figure). Toll collections in fiscal 1974 were $121.3 million, $113.4 million in 1973.

Improvements have included the widening of the eight-mile long channel through Gaillard Cut from 300 to 500 feet, costing $60,000,000; illumination of Gaillard Cut and installation of new towing locomotives at the locks costing $8,000,000.

Thatcher Ferry Bridge, opened 1962, spans Panama Canal 201 ft. above the water level near Balboa. It is a steel-arch bridge, about 1 mi. long, with 3 spans and 4 lanes. It cost $20,000,000 authorized by the U.S. Congress in 1956.

Other Foreign Canals

One of the busiest canals in Europe is the Gota, in Sweden, 115 mi. long. Others: Kiel Canal, Germany, connecting the Baltic with the North Sea, 61 mi.; Elbe, Germany, 41 mi.; Amsterdam, Netherlands, 16 mi. Also the Manchester Ship Canal, England, 35.5 mi.

United States Foreign Trade, by Economic Classes

Source: International Trade Analysis Div., Dept. of Commerce. (Value in Millions of dollars)

Year (cal.)	Value of domestic exports					Value of imports				
	Crude Mater'ls	Crude Foods	Manu'd Foods	Semi Manuf's	Finish. Manuf's	Crude Mater'ls	Crude Foods	Manu'd Foods	Semi-Manuf's	Finish. Manuf's
1965.....	2,887	2,587	1,590	4,114	16,008	3,709	2,008	1,877	4,964	8,871
1970.....	4,492	2,748	1,921	6,866	26,563	4,126	2,579	3,519	7,263	22,464
1972.....	5,242	3,738	2,325	6,163	31,500	5,354	2,868	4,320	10,262	32,751
1973.....	7,826	8,804	3,524	9,250	40,820	7,795	3,552	5,494	13,043	39,238
1974.....	11,150	10,246	4,196	14,913	56,638	19,995	3,720	6,810	22,067	48,380

Total agricultural exports were valued as follows (in millions of dollars): 1965—1,942; 1968—2,177; 1969—2,057; 1970—2,524; 1971—2,884; 1972—3,325; 1973—5,290; 1974—6,981. Agricultural imports for consumption were valued as follows (in millions of dollars): 1965—864; 1968—834; 1969—909; 1970—797; 1971—685; 1972—801; 1973—1,080; 1974—1,348.

Shortest Navigable Distances Between Ports

Source: Distances Between Ports, 1965. Defense Mapping Agency Hydrographic Center.

Distances shown are in nautical miles (1,852 meters or about 6,076.115 feet).

To get statute miles, multiply by 1.15 (one statute mile equals 5280 feet).

TO	FROM	New York	Montreal	Colon[1]
Algiers, Algeria		3,617	3,600	4,745
Amsterdam, Netherlands		3,438	3,162	4,825
Baltimore, Md.		417	1,769	1,901
Barcelona, Spain		3,714	3,697	4,842
Boston, Mass.		386	1,308	2,157
Buenos Aires, Argentina		5,817	6,455	5,472
Cape Town, S. Africa[2]		6,786	7,118	6,494
Cherbourg, France		3,154	2,878	4,541
Cobh, Ireland		2,901	2,603	4,308
Copenhagen, Denmark		3,846	3,570	5,233
Dakar, Senegal		3,335	3,566	3,694
Galveston, Tex.		1,882	3,165	1,492
Gibraltar[3]		3,204	3,187	4,332
Glasgow, Scotland		3,066	2,691	4,508
Halifax, N.S.		600	895	2,295
Hamburg, W. Germany		3,674	3,398	5,061
Hamilton, Bermuda		697	1,572	1,659
Havana, Cuba		1,186	2,473	998
Helsinki, Finland		4,309	4,033	5,696
Istanbul, Turkey		5,001	4,984	6,129
Kingston, Jamaica		1,474	2,690	551
Lagos, Nigeria		4,883	5,130	5,049
Lisbon, Portugal		2,972	2,943	4,152
Marseille, France		3,891	3,874	5,019
Montreal, Quebec		1,460		3,126
Naples, Italy		4,181	4,164	5,309
Nassau, Bahamas		962	2,274	1,166
New Orleans, La.		1,708	2,991	1,389
New York, N.Y.			1,460	1,974
Norfolk, Va.		294	1,700	1,779
Oslo, Norway		3,827	3,165	5,058
Piraeus, Greece		4,688	4,671	5,816
Port Said, Egypt		5,123	5,106	6,251
Rio de Janeiro, Brazil		4,770	5,354	4,367
St. John's, Nfld.		1,093	1,043	2,695
San Juan, Puerto Rico		1,399	2,445	993
Southampton, England		3,189	2,913	4,576

TO	FROM	San Fran.	Vancouver	Panama[1]
Acapulco, Mexico		1,833	2,613	1,426
Anchorage, Alas.		1,872	1,444	5,093
Bombay, India		9,794	9,578	12,962
Calcutta, India		8,991	8,728	12,154
Colon, Panama[1]		3,298	4,076	44
Djakarta, Indonesia		7,641	7,360	10,637
Haiphong, N. Vietnam		6,496	6,231	9,673
Hong Kong		6,044	5,777	9,195
Honolulu, Hawaii		2,091	2,423	4,685
Los Angeles, Cal.		371	1,161	2,913
Manila, Philippines		6,221	5,976	9,347
Melbourne, Australia		6,970	7,343	7,928
Pusan, S. Korea		4,914	4,623	8,074
Saigon, S. Vietnam		6,878	6,664	10,017
San Francisco, Cal.			812	3,245
Seattle, Wash.		807	126	4,020
Shanghai, China		5,396	5,110	8,566
Singapore		7,353	7,078	10,505
Suva, Fiji		4,749	5,183	6,325
Valparaiso, Chile		5,140	5,915	2,616
Vancouver, B.C.		812		4,032
Vladivostok, USSR		4,563	4,378	7,741
Yokohama, Japan		4,536	4,262	7,682

TO	FROM	Port Said	Cape Town[2]	Singapore
Bombay, India		3,049	4,616	2,441
Calcutta, India		4,695	5,638	1,649
Dar es Salaam, Tanzania		3,238	2,365	4,042
Djakarta, Indonesia		5,293	5,276	525
Hong Kong		6,462	7,006	1,454
Kuwait		3,360	5,176	3,833
Manila, Philippines		6,348	6,777	1,330
Melbourne, Australia		7,842	5,963	3,844
Saigon, S. Vietnam		5,667	6,263	649
Singapore		5,018	5,614	
Yokohama		7,907	8,503	2,889

(1) Colon on the Atlantic is 44 nautical miles from Panama (port) on the Pacific. (2b2 Cape Town is 35 nautical miles northwest of the Cape of Good Hope. (3) Gibraltar (port) is 24 nautical miles east of the Strait of Gibraltar.

Mississippi River System and Gulf Intracoastal Waterway

Source: Corps of Engineers, Department of the Army.

(Note—The Mississippi River System comprises main channels and all tributaries of the Mississippi, Illinois, Missouri and Ohio Rivers. The Gulf Intracoastal Waterway, 1,137 miles long, extends from Apalachee Bay, Florida, to the Mexican border)

Port	1963 Tonnage	1972 Tonnage	1973 Tonnage
Minneapolis	825,429	1,671,323	1,849,783
St. Paul	4,210,106	5,059,621	5,080,428
Metropolitan St. Louis		*22,008,151	18,319,148
Memphis	7,024,509	10,612,101	10,392,243
Helena	1,740,938	2,672,209	3,224,197
Greenville	1,250,608	2,278,634	2,374,822

*Port limits expanded in 1972

Port	1963 Tonnage	1972 Tonnage	1973 Tonnage
Lake Providence	Not Compiled	366,387	282,022
Vicksburg	1,258,508	2,571,546	2,787,239
Natchez	582,942	898,682	501,433
Baton Rouge	30,272,282	52,903,352	53,568,530
New Orleans	79,130,710	125,719,378	136,104,315

Reach

Port	1963 Tonnage	1972 Tonnage	1973 Tonnage
Mississippi R. System	271,319,518	419,805,850	419,942,374
Minneapolis to the Gulf	157,807,291	271,980,414	276,346,896
Minneapolis to St. Louis	30,943,237	60,746,385	58,064,198
St. Louis to Cairo	35,726,911	67,545,404	63,385,876
Cairo to Baton Rouge	49,370,417	102,698,573	100,395,636

Port	1963 Tonnage	1972 Tonnage	1973 Tonnage
Baton Rouge to N. Orleans	69,913,376	163,345,088	169,849,105
New Orleans to the Gulf	99,554,315	171,370,861	182,338,659
Gulf Intracoastal Waterway	67,320,002	108,999,010	100,767,257

Ton-Mileage of Freight Carried on Inland Waterways

Source: Corps of Engineers, Department of the Army.

System	1971	1972	1973
Atlantic coast waterways	28,619,707,000	29,238,516,000	34,208,953,000
Gulf coast waterways	30,473,095,000	32,513,287,000	32,260,368,000
Pacific coast waterways	8,525,013,000	9,549,062,000	10,506,647,000
Mississippi River system, including Ohio River and tributaries	142,385,476,000	158,453,365,000	155,332,020,000
Great Lakes System includes Alaskan waterways	105,027,016,000		125,914,126,000
Total	**315,030,307,000**	**108,938,909,000**	**358,222,114,000**

Commerce at Principal North American Ports

Excluding Great Lakes Shipping
Source: Corps of Engineers, U.S. Army
Calendar Year 1973. Canadian Ports 1970. In tons of 2,000 pounds.

Ports Handling over 7,500,000 Tons

Port of New York, N.Y. and N.J.	216,896,434
New Orleans, La.	136,014,315
Houston, Texas	88,517,992
Philadelphia Harbor, Pa.	54,629,926
Norfolk Harbor, Va.	52,333,200
Baltimore Harbor and Channels, Md.	53,796,715
Baton Rouge, La.	53,568,530
Beaumont, Texas	34,490,769
Tampa Harbor, Fla.	41,923,222
Los Angeles Harbor, Calif.	25,977,491
Corpus Christi, Texas	25,899,305
Port Arthur, Texas	24,931,373
Portland Harbor, Me.	28,844,110
Paulsboro, N.J. and Vicinity	28,296,140
Mobile Harbor, Ala.	30,518,422
Boston, Mass.	27,056,868
Marcus Hook, Pa. and Vicinity	25,024,409
Huntington, W.Va.	16,657,267
Lake Charles, La.	16,505,262
Texas City, Tex.	19,959,038
Richmond Harbor, Calif.	18,259,836
Portland, Ore.	20,077,043
Clairton-Elizabeth, Pa.	8,506,379
Seattle Harbor, Wash.	17,000,178
Port of Newport News, Va.	11,491,290
Long Beach, Calif.	27,133,022
Pascagoula Harbor, Miss.	12,876,864
Penn Manor, Pa. and Vicinity	9,314,340
New Castle, Del. and Vicinity	12,695,743
New Haven Harbor, Conn.	13,709,265
Port of Metropolitan St. Louis	18,319,148
Jacksonville Harbor, Fla.	15,513,590
Cincinnati, Ohio	8,234,879
Providence River and Harbor, R.I.	10,236,062
Pittsburgh, Pa.	8,816,631
Port of Albany, N.Y.	11,328,279
Louisville, Ky.	9,148,567
Memphis, Tenn.	10,392,243
Port Everglades Harbor, Fla.	12,541,730
Vancouver, B.C.	26,517,891
Sept-Iles, P.Q.	24,240,914
Montreal, P.Q.	22,376,281
Thunder Bay, Ont.	20,754,165
Port Cartier, P.Q.	16,017,407
Hamilton, Ont.	2,881,123
Halifax, N.S.	11,072,468
Quebec, P.Q.	8,552,289
Bair Comeau, P.Q.	7,695,715

Other Ports, Maine to Washington

Searsport Harbor, Maine	1,322,686
Portsmouth Harbor, N.H.	2,314,900
Burlington Harbor, Vt.	576,533
Beverly Harbor, Mass.	255,050
Fall River Harbor, Mass.	4,625,362
Gloucester Harbor, Mass.	316,780
New Bedford, Fairhaven Harbor, Mass.	411,075
Salem Harbor, Mass.	1,800,180
Bridgeport Harbor, Conn.	3,553,980
New London Harbor, Conn.	5,580,248
Norwalk Harbor, Conn.	867,306
Stamford Harbor, Conn.	1,002,384
Hempstead Harbor, N.Y.	3,932,757
Huntington Harbor, N.Y.	471,769
Peekskill Harbor, N.Y.	214,981
Plattsburg, N.Y.	519,517
Port Chester Harbor, N.Y.	406,620
Port Jefferson Harbor, N.Y.	4,048,518
Rondout Harbor, N.Y.	861,394
Tarrytown Harbor, N.Y.	632,798
Camden-Gloucester, N.J.	9,091,162
Trenton Harbor, N.J.	1,401,832
Aliquippa-Rochester, Pa.	6,090,117
Chester, Pa.	698,441
Wilmington Harbor, Del.	4,001,816
Washington Harbor, D.C.	2,138,859
Alexandria, Va.	183,114
Port of Hopewell, Va.	1,096,964
Port of Richmond, Va.	1,930,747
Morehead City Harbor, N.C.	1,160,988
Port of Wilmington, N.C.	9,300,972
Charleston Harbor, S.C.	9,379,766
Georgetown Harbor, S.C.	1,485,731
Brunswick Harbor, Ga.	1,393,653
Savannah Harbor, Ga.	8,980,201
Canaveral Harbor, Fla.	2,362,974
Charlotte Harbor, Fla.	2,474,172
Fernandina Harbor, Fla.	386,679
Miami Harbor, Fla.	5,569,009
Palm Beach Harbor, Fla.	1,283,658
Panama City Harbor, Fla.	1,806,270
Pensacola Harbor, Fla.	2,278,755
Port St. Joe Harbor, Fla.	669,131

St. Petersburg Harbor, Fla.	680,584
Weedon Island, Fla.	436,310
Guntersville, Ala.	1,355,172
Greenville, Miss.	2,374,822
Gulfport Harbor, Miss.	988,827
Natchez, Miss.	501,433
Vicksburg, Miss.	2,787,239
Brownsville, Texas	6,010,515
Freeport Harbor, Texas	7,348,555
Galveston, Texas	6,861,741
Harbor Island, Texas	2,429,560
Orange, Texas	1,280,538
Port Isabel, Texas	366,768
Matagorda Ship Channel, Port Lavaca, Tex.	4,526,754
Sabine Pass Harbor, Texas	227,937
Victoria, Texas	3,137,397
Helena, Ark.	3,224,197
Chattanooga, Tenn.	1,701,267
Knoxville, Tenn.	422,002
Nashville, Tenn.	3,250,193
Kansas City, Mo.	1,359,888
Mount Vernon, Ind.	3,235,393
Minneapolis, Minn.	1,849,783
St. Paul, Minn.	5,080,428
Carpinteria, Calif.	430,177
Crescent City Harbor, Calif.	345,339
El Segundo, Calif.	8,678,770
Gaviota, Santa Barbara County, Calif.	116,570
Humboldt Harbor and Bay, Calif.	1,431,538
Moss Landing Harbor, Calif.	578,784
Oakland Harbor, Calif.	7,414,679
Redwood City Harbor, Calif.	467,967
San Diego Harbor, Calif.	2,063,356
San Francisco Harbor, Calif.	4,485,745
San Luis Obispo Harbor, Calif.	973,739
Stockton, Calif.	1,806,500
Ventura Harbor, Calif.	1,938,939
Astoria, Ore.	1,827,286
Coos Bay, Ore.	7,730,708
Oregon Slough (No. Portland Hbr.), Ore.	344,840
Anacortes Harbor, Wash.	2,895,947
Bellingham Bay and Harbor, Wash.	3,565,419
Everett Harbor, Wash.	4,919,930
Grays Harbor and Chehalis River, Wash. (Shelton Hbr.).	3,843,070
Hammersley Inlet, Wash.	1,067,930
Longview, Wash.	5,859,442
Olympia Harbor, Wash.	989,547
Port Angeles Harbor, Wash.	2,918,785
Port Gamble Harbor, Wash.	571,526
Port Townsend Harbor, Wash.	1,347,033
Tacoma Harbor, Wash.	9,804,752
Vancouver, Wash.	3,590,664
Willapa Riv. & Hbr., Naelle Riv., Wash.	333,448

Alaska, Hawaii, Puerto Rico

Anchorage, Alaska	2,624,763
Ketchikan Harbor, Alaska	2,167,293
Sitka Harbor, Alaska	827,774
Skagway Harbor, Alaska	1,347,761
Whittier Harbor, Alaska	392,491
Wrangell Harbor, Alaska	1,171,639
Barbers Point, Oahu, Hawaii	3,944,857
Hilo Harbor, Hawaii, Hawaii	1,041,647
Honolulu Harbor, Maui Oahu, Hawaii	8,188,466
Kahului Harbor, Maui, Hawaii	1,042,818
Kaumalapau Harbor, Lanai, Hawaii	305,555
Kaunakakai Harbor, Molokai, Hawaii	475,246
Kawaihae Harbor, Hawaii, Hawaii	385,850
Nawiliwili Harbor, Kauai, Hawaii	495,448
Pearl Harbor, Oahu, Hawaii	320,963
Wake Island Harbor	75,681
Mayaguez Harbor, P.R.	344,586
Ponce Harbor, P.R.	515,617
San Juan Harbor, P.R.	10,773,238
St. Thomas Harbor, V.I.	392,020
Guam Island, Pacific Ocean	282,765
Corner Brook, Nfld.	1,225,372
St. John's, Nfld.	794,494
Charlottetown, P.E.I.	554,399
Hantsport, N.S.	1,648,191
Sydney, N.S.	1,966,105
Saint John, N.B.	6,400,885
Port Alfred, Que.	4,973,666
Sorel, Que.	6,813,817
Trois Rivieres, Que.	4,954,649
Port Colborne, Ont.	2,259,345
Sarnia, Ont.	7,331,360
Saulte Ste. Marie, Ont.	5,753,245
Toronto, Ont.	5,162,904
Windsor, Ont.	3,550,556
Nanaimo, B.C.	2,492,110
New Westminster, B.C.	4,564,477
Powell River, B.C.	1,783,686
Victoria, B.C.	2,071,342

Commerce at Great Lakes Ports

Source: Corps of Engineers, U.S. Army
Calendar Year 1973, in tons of 2,000 pounds

Duluth-Superior Harbor, Minn. & Wis.	48,158,190	Port Dolomite, Mich.	3,711,083
Silver Bay, Minn.	12,332,073	Port Gypsum, Mich.	404,859
Taconite Harbor, Minn.	14,286,497	Port Huron, Mich.	364,264
Ashland Harbor, Wis.	369,532	Port Inland, Mich.	4,367,582
Green Bay Harbor, Wis.	2,723,596	Port of Detroit, Mich.	31,541,566
Kewaunee Harbor, Wis.	1,384,863	Presque Isle Harbor, Mich.	3,740,726
Manitowoc Harbor, Wis.	1,252,856	St. Clair, Mich.	3,338,058
Milwaukee Harbor, Wis.	5,635,524	St. Ignace, Mich.	113,080
Oak Creek, Wis.	300,738	St. Joseph Harbor, Mich.	465,417
Port Washington Harbor, Wis.	869,734	Sault Ste. Marie, Mich.	109,751
Racine Harbor, Wis.	93,443	Stoneport, Mich.	8,673,078
Sheboygan Harbor, Wis.	240,822	Traverse City Harbor, Mich.	422,447
Two Rivers Harbor, Wis.	77,380	Wells, Mich.	129,750
Alabaster, Mich.	658,997	Port of Chicago, Ill.	47,981,242
Alpena Harbor, Mich.	2,853,883	Waukegan Harbor, Ill.	590,436
Calcite, Mich.	14,985,094	Buffington Harbor, Ind.	2,365,758
Cheboygan Harbor, Mich.	135,983	Gary Harbor, Ind.	10,204,108
Detour, Mich.	221,782	Indiana Harbor, Ind.	17,897,777
Drummond Island, Mich.	2,732,803	Michigan City Harbor, Ind.	167
Escanaba, Mich.	10,250,160	Ashtabula Harbor, Ohio	10,872,484
Frankfort Harbor, Mich.	1,176,446	Cleveland Harbor, Ohio	24,828,323
Gladstone Harbor, Mich.	356,883	Conneaut Harbor, Ohio	16,731,912
Gd. Haven Harbor & Gd. River, Mich.	2,504,551	Fairport Harbor, Ohio	3,681,272
Holland Harbor, Mich.	448,314	Huron Harbor, Ohio	3,655,463
Lime Island, Mich.	62,986	Lorain Harbor, Ohio	11,584,368
Ludington Harbor, Mich.	2,541,739	Marblehead, Ohio	2,538,318
Mackinaw City, Mich.	96,967	Sandusky Harbor, Ohio	4,913,719
Manistee Harbor, Mich.	569,313	Toledo Harbor, Ohio	24,921,753
Manistique Harbor, Mich.	10,351	Erie Harbor, Pa.	1,283,342
Marquette Harbor, Mich.	773,540	Ogdensburg Harbor, N.Y.	280,039
Marysville, Mich.	606,591	Oswego Harbor, N.Y.	930,877
Menominee Harbor, Mich. & Wis.	185,827	Port of Buffalo, N.Y.	13,176,588
Muskegon Harbor, Mich.	2,922,730	Rochester (Charlotte) Harbor, N.Y.	433,948
Petoskey Penn Dixie Harbor, Mich.	534,719		

Value of U.S. Merchandise Exports and Imports

Source: International Trade Analysis Division, Dept. of Commerce
Value in Millions of dollars (Revised)

	U.S. exports					U.S. imports		
	Domestic and foreign							Gross merchandise balance[1]
Year	Total	Military aid	Excl. military aid	Domestic merchandise	Foreign merchandise	General	For consumption	
1950...	10,279	[2]282	9,997	10,146	133	8,954	8,844	1,043
1955...	15,554	1,256	14,298	15,426	128	11,566	11,519	2,732
1960...	20,608	949	19,659	20,408	201	15,073	15,069	4,586
1965...	27,521	779	26,742	27,178	343	21,427	21,345	5,315
1970...	43,224	565	42,659	42,590	634	39,952	39,756	2,707
1972...	49,778	560	49,219	48,979	800	55,583	53,310	6,384
1973...	71,314	516	70,798	70,223	1,091	69,121	68,656	1,347
1974...	98,506	599	97,907	97,143	1,363	100,972	100,126	—3,065

(1.) Balance represents exports excluding military grant-aid valued f.a.s. less imports which are valued generally at the market value in the foreign country. Export values include both commercially-financed shipments and shipments under government-financed programs. (2) Includes data from April when shipments under the program began.

Total Exports and Exports Financed by Foreign Aid

Source: Bureau of International Commerce, Dept. of Commerce

(In millions of dollars)	1965	1969	1970	1971	1972	1973	1974
Exports, total.	27,530	38,006	43,224	44,130	49,778	71,314	98,506
Agricultural commodities.	6,306	6,004	7,349	7,786	9,505	17,855	22,257
Nonagricultural commodities	20,445	31,328	35,310	35,763	39,714	52,943	75,650
Manufactured goods (domestic)	17,439	26,785	29,343	30,443	33,742	44,702	63,527
Military grant—aid.	779	674	565	581	560	516	599
Export financed under P.L. 480.	1,323	1,019	1,021	983	1,064	750	760
Sales for foreign currency	899	337	276	174	70	4	—
Donations, including disaster relief	253	256	255	291	376	209	272
Barter for strategic goods.	19	—	—	—	—	—	—
Long-term dollar credit sales.	152	426	490	518	618	537	488

Merchant Fleets of the World

Source: Maritime Administration, U.S. Dept. of Commerce

Oceangoing steam and motor ships of 1,000 gross tons and over; excludes ships operating exclusively on the Great Lakes and inland waterways and special types such as channel ships, icebreakers, cable ships, etc., and merchant ships owned by any military force. Tonnage is in thousands.

Gross tonnage is a volume measurement; each cargo gross ton represents 100 cubic ft. of enclosed space. Deadweight tonnage is the carrying capacity of a ship in long tons (2,240 lbs. ea.)

Country of Registry	Total No.	Gross Tons	Dwt. Tons	Bulk Carriers No.	Bulk Carriers Dwt.	Freighters No.	Freighters Dwt.	Tankers No.	Tankers Dwt.
Total - All Countries	22,449	306,366	503,348	4,075	139,267	11,449	93,476	5,121	261,440
United States[1]	922	12,503	17,637	19	534	539	7,261	278	9,298
Privately-owned	583	9,820	14,446	19	534	313	4,990	245	8,872
Government-owned	339	2,683	3,191	-	-	226	2,271	33	426
British Commonwealth									
United Kingdom	1,609	32,153	52,980	332	13,729	650	6,140	467	31,494
Australia	85	990	1,438	34	731	35	279	16	428
Bangladesh	14	75	109	-	-	13	107	1	2
British Colonies	96	1,745	2,705	28	888	33	228	25	1,566
Canada	76	355	459	10	98	27	103	24	241
Cyprus	601	3,552	5,193	56	724	465	3,246	61	1,131
Ghana	18	125	164	-	-	17	162	-	-
India	288	3,746	5,843	66	2,667	188	2,048	21	1,039
Malaysia	23	303	431	7	304	13	121	1	2
New Zealand	37	128	168	9	32	24	104	-	-
Nigeria	19	120	174	-	-	19	174	-	-
Pakistan	58	501	667	2	30	49	579	-	-
Singapore	346	3,296	5,119	37	1,413	228	1,714	48	1,834
Algeria	27	212	288	3	36	17	84	7	168
Argentina	160	1,305	1,795	13	218	69	599	52	840
Austria	18	74	110	2	34	16	76	-	-
Belgium	76	1,212	1,909	19	833	29	385	20	640
Brazil	257	2,558	4,039	33	1,047	155	1,151	53	1,772
Bulgaria	113	829	1,205	28	358	58	354	19	457
Chile	45	379	562	7	133	29	282	5	140
China (Taiwan)	159	1,453	2,231	30	752	96	778	15	609
*China (Communist)	335	2,285	3,211	37	484	234	2,087	38	579
Colombia	41	222	292	1	2	39	261	1	29
*Cuba	57	357	470	2	2	39	358	6	75
Czechoslovakia	12	123	181	4	126	8	55	-	-
Denmark	305	4,244	7,112	34	961	185	1,450	60	4,580
Ecuador	15	120	167	-	-	6	53	7	101
Finland	193	1,487	2,258	15	158	113	609	49	1,455
France	428	9,549	16,183	59	2,285	176	1,731	149	11,947
Gabon	5	106	183	1	15	3	28	1	140
Germany (West)	668	8,494	13,616	77	3,876	460	3,839	84	5,568
*Germany (East)	146	1,147	1,648	17	356	104	758	11	463
Greece	1,838	22,339	36,665	479	13,133	909	8,761	344	14,287
Indonesia	156	564	709	8	32	102	474	16	108
Iran	30	274	376	-	-	24	288	5	84
Iraq	13	201	317	-	-	6	71	7	246
Ireland	17	163	248	9	229	6	16	2	3
Israel	55	565	781	12	454	35	251	-	-
Italy	648	9,371	14,621	147	5,886	200	1,427	229	7,012
Ivory Coast	17	124	170	-	-	15	159	-	-
Japan	2,143	35,994	60,167	542	21,196	951	7,783	520	30,707
Korea (South)	138	1,204	2,035	21	340	85	534	29	1,146
Kuwait	37	708	1,188	-	-	31	398	6	790
Tebenon	45	136	183	4	11	37	161	-	-
Liberia	2,358	60,006	112,086	841	32,642	506	5,224	945	73,819
Libya	8	157	279	-	-	3	9	5	270
Maldives	34	91	115	1	3	29	103	-	-
Mexico	48	439	663	3	60	18	136	26	463
Nauru	6	58	74	1	32	1	14	-	-
Netherlands	434	4,697	6,972	32	780	283	2,354	82	3,664
Norway	1,028	25,095	43,306	320	15,983	313	2,643	337	24,472
Panama	1,341	11,539	18,513	183	3,621	870	5,764	222	8,828
Peru	41	350	518	8	191	28	258	5	69
Philippines	152	709	985	6	114	96	631	27	191
Poland	276	2,295	3,295	71	1,479	180	1,514	7	232
Portugal	114	1,169	1,723	6	125	65	517	25	973
*Rumania	83	657	975	15	305	56	301	6	345
Saudi Arabia	16	60	77	-	-	8	32	2	31
Somalia	251	1,873	2,739	28	630	208	1,866	12	231
South Africa	54	427	540	3	61	40	324	3	61
Spain	442	4,423	7,307	56	1,722	212	1,039	108	4,332
Sweden	330	6,761	11,230	90	4,839	134	1,186	74	4,935
Switzerland	24	211	306	3	104	18	195	1	4
Thailand	26	143	236	1	2	15	82	10	152
Turkey	102	830	1,201	7	169	61	493	19	507
United Arab Republic	49	256	347	-	-	31	130	11	177
Uruguay	17	156	240	-	-	8	47	7	180
*U.S.S.R.[2]	2,358	13,533	17,278	150	1,421	1,413	8,825	455	5,534
Venezuela	44	420	603	4	19	24	168	16	416
Yugoslavia	207	1,742	2,534	33	819	143	1,262	17	382
Zaire	7	68	92	-	-	5	68	-	-

*Source material limited. (1) Excludes 65 non-merchant type ships which are currently in the National Defense Reserve Fleet. (2) Includes U.S. Government-owned ships transferred to U.S.S.R. under lend-lease agreements, 41 of which are still under that registry.

Notable Ocean Passages by Ships

Time	From	To	Distance Naut. mi.	Date	Ship
One Hundred Years of Sailing Vessels					
16d	Liverpool.	New York	3,150	Nov. 1846	Yorkshire
76d 6h	San Francisco. . .	Boston		1853	Northern Light
12d 6h	Boston Light. . . .	Light Rock.	. . .	1854	James Baines
89d	New York.	San Francisco. . .	15,091	1854	Flying Cloud
89d 20h . . .	New York	San Francisco. . .	13,700	1860	Andrew Jackson
63d 18h 15m . .	Liverpool.	Melbourne.		1868-69	Thermopylae
13d 1h 25m . .	New York.	Liverpool.	3,150	. . . .	Red Jacket
36d	50 S. Lat.	Golden Gate	. . .	. . . .	Starr King
12d 12h	Equator.	San Francisco. . .	. . .	. . . .	Golden Fleece
12d 4h 1m . . .	Sandy Hook	England	3,013	1905	Atlantic
23d	England	Sandy Hook	3,013	1928	Atlantic
22d 6h 7m . . .	Bishop's Rock. . .	Boston Light. . . .	. . .	1936	Yankee
Atlantic Crossings by Power Vessels					
29d 4h	Savannah	Liverpool.	. . .	May 22, 1819	Savannah (Amer.) (a)
15d	Bristol.	New York	. . .	Apr. 1838	Great Western (Br.)
14d 8h	Liverpool.	New York	3,150	July 1840	Britannia (Br.) (b)
9d 13h	Liverpool.	New York	3,054	Aug. 1852	Baltic (Amer.)
8d 1h 45m . . .	Queenstown	New York	2,780	1856	Persia
8d 2h 48m . . .	Queenstown	New York	2,780	1866	Scotia
7d 4h 1m . . .	Queenstown	New York		1867	City of Paris (Br.)
7d 22h 3m . . .	Queenstown	New York	2,780	1869	City of Brussels (Br.)
7d 20h 9m . . .	Queenstown	New York	2,780	1873	Baltic (Br.)
7d 15h 48m . .	Queenstown	New York	2,780	1875	City of Berlin (Br.)
7d 11h 37m . .	Queenstown	New York	2,780	1876	Germanic (Br.)
7d 10h 53m . .	Queenstown	New York	2,780	1877	Britannic (Br.)
7d 8h 0m . . .	New York	Queenstown		1879	Arizona (Br.)
6d 7h 23m . . .	Queenstown	New York	2,780	1880	Arizona (Br.)
6d 18h 37m . .	Queenstown	New York	2,780	1882	Alaska (Br.)
6d 21h 40m . .	Queenstown	New York	2,780	1883	Alaska (Br.)
6d 10h 40m . .	New York	Queenstown	2,780	1884	Oregon (Br.)
6d 4h 34m . . .	Queenstown	New York	2,780	1887	Umbria (Br.)
5d 1h 55m . . .	Queenstown	New York	2,780	1888	Etruria (Br.)
5d 22h 50m . .	New York	Queenstown	2,780	1889	City of Paris (Br.)
5d 16h 31m . .	Queenstown	New York	2,780	1891	Teutonic (Br.)
5d 14h 24m . .	Queenstown	New York	2,780	1892	City of Paris (Br.)
5d 9h 6m	Queenstown	New York	2,780	1893	Campania (Br.)
5d 7h 23m . . .	Queenstown	New York	2,780	1894	Lucania (Br.)
5d 15h 20m . .	Southampton	New York	3,189	1898	Kaiser Wilhelm Der Grosse (Ger.)
5d 7h 38m . . .	Sandy Hook	Plymouth.	3,082	Sept. 1900	Deutschland (Ger.)
4d 11h 42m . .	Queenstown	New York	2,780	1909	Lusitania (Br.)
4d 10h 41m . .	Queenstown	New York	2,780	1910	Mauretania (Br.)
5d 6h 21m . . .	New York	Cherbourg.	3,227	Oct. 1924	Leviathan (Amer.)
4d 17h 42m . .	Cherbourg.	Ambrose Lt.	3,164	July 1929	Bremen (Ger.)*
4d 14h 30m . .	New York	Plymouth.	3,082	July 1929	Bremen (Ger.)
4d 19h 57m . .	Ambrose Lt.	Cherbourg.	3,196	June 1933	Europa (Ger.)
4d 16h 48m . .	Cherbourg.	New York	3,149	July 1933	Europa (Ger.)
4d 13h 58m . .	Gibraltar.	Ambrose Lt.	3,181	Aug. 1933	Rex (Ital.)
4d 14h 27m . .	Cherbourg.	Ambrose Lt.	3,092	Nov. 1934	Bremen (Ger.)
4d 12h 24m . .	Cherbourg.	Ambrose Lt.	3,158	May-June, 1936	Queen Mary (Br.)*
3d 23h 02m . .	Bishop's Rock . . .	Ambrose Lt.	2,906	July-Aug., 1937	Normandie (Fr.)
3d 22h 07m . .	New York	Southampton	2,936	Aug. 1937	Normandie (Fr.)
3d 20h 42m . .	Ambrose Lt.	Bishop's Rock. . .	3,120	Aug. 10-14,1938	Queen Mary (Br.)
3d 21h 48m . .	Bishop's Rock . . .	Ambrose Lt.	3,120	Aug. 1948	Queen Mary (Br.)
3d 10h40m . . .	Ambrose Lt.	Bishop's Rock. . .	2,942	July 3-7, 1952	United States (U.S.)* (e)
3d 12h 12m . .	Bishop's Rock. . .	Ambrose Lt.	2,902	July 11-14, 1952	United States (U.S.) (e)
3d 11h 24m . .	Bishop's Rock. . .	Ambrose Lt	2,912	Aug. 20, 1973	Sea-Land Exchange (U.S.) (j)
Other Ocean Passages					
3d 00h 36m . .	San Pedro.	Honolulu	2,226	June 1928	U.S.S. Lexington
86d	Halifax.	Vancouver	7,295	July-Sept. 1944	St. Roch (Can.) (c)
3d 2h 30m . . .	San Francisco. . .	Oahu, Hawaii . . .	2,091	July 16-19, 1945	U.S.S. Indianapolis (d)
4d 8h 51m . . .	Gibraltar.	Newport News . . .	3,360	Nov. 26, 1945	U.S.S. Lake Champlain
7d 18h 36m . .	Japan.	San Francisco. . .	5,000	July-Aug. 4, 1950	U.S.S. Boxer
7d 13h	Yokosuka.	Alameda	5,000	June 1-9, 1951	U.S.S. Philippine Sea
8d 11h	Nantucket	Portland, Eng	3,161	Feb. 25-Mar. 4, '58	U.S.S. Skate (f)
7d 5h	Lizard Head	Nantucket, Mass. .	. . .	Mar. 23-29, 1958	U.S.S. Skate (f)
15d	Pearl Harbor	Iceland (via N. Pole).	. . .	July 23-Aug. 7, '58	U.S.S. Nautilus (g)
84d	New London	Rehoboth, Del. . . .	41,500	Feb. 16-May 10, '60	U.S.S. Triton (h)
6d	Baffin Bay	NW Passage, Pac.	850	Aug. 15-20, 1960	U.S.S. Seadragon (i)
12d 16h 22m .	New York	Cape Town	6,786	Oct. 30-Nov. 11, '62	African Comet*
5d 6h	Kobe	Race Rock, B.C. . .	4,126	Aug. 24, 1973	Sea-Land Trade (U.S.)

*Maiden voyage. (a) The Savannah, a fully rigged sailing vessel with steam auxiliary (over 300 tons, 90.5 ft. long, beam 25.8 ft., depth 12.9 ft.), was launched in the East River in 1818. It was the first ship to use steam in crossing any ocean. It was supplied with engines and detachable iron paddle wheels. On its famous voyage it used steam 105 hours. (b) First Cunard Liner. (c) First ship to complete NW Passage in one season. (d) Carried Hiroshima atomic bomb in World War II. (e) Set world speed record; average speed eastbound on maiden voyage 35.59 knots (about 41 m.p.h.): westbound, 34.51 knots. (f) First atomic submarine to cross Atlantic both ways submerged. (g) World's first atomic submarine also first to make undersea voyage under polar ice cap, 1,830 mi. from Point Barrow, Alaska, to Atlantic Ocean, Aug. 1-4, 1958, reaching North Pole Aug. 3. Second undersea transit of the North Pole made by submarine USS Skate Aug. 11, 1958, during trip from New London, Conn., and return. (h) World's largest submarine. Nuclear-powered Triton was submerged during nearly all its voyage around the globe. It duplicated the route of Ferdinand Magellan's circuit (1519-1522) 30,708 mi., starting from St. Paul Rocks off the NE coast of Brazil, Feb. 24-Apr. 25, 1960, then sailed to Cadiz, Spain, before returning home. (i) First underwater transit of Northwest Passage. (j) Fastest freighter crossing of Atlantic.

Fastest Scheduled Train Runs in United States and Canada

Source: Donald M. Steffee; figures are based on 1975 timetables

Electric Traction-Passenger-(80 m.p.h. and over)

Railroad	Train	From	To	Dis.	Time	Speed
Amtrak	Metroliners (14)	Baltimore	Wilmington	68.4	44	93.3
Amtrak	Metroliners (11)	Wilmington	Baltimore	68.4	44	93.3
Amtrak	Metroliners (3)	Wilmington	Baltimore	68.4	45	91.2
Amtrak	Metroliner	Newark	Philadelphia	80.5	56	86.2
Amtrak	Metroliner	Newark	North Philadelphia	76.0	53	86.0
Amtrak	Metroliner	Newark	Trenton	48.1	34	84.9
Amtrak	Metroliners (2)	Metro Park	Trenton	33.9	24	84.7
Amtrak	Metroliner	Baltimore	Philadelphia	94.0	67	84.2
Amtrak	Metroliners (2)	Newark	Philadelphia	80.5	58	83.3
Amtrak	Metroliner	No. Philadelphia	Newark	76.0	55	82.9
Amtrak	Metroliners (3)	Metro Park	Philadelphia	66.3	48	82.9
Amtrak	Metroliner	Baltimore	Capital Beltway	30.3	22	82.6
Amtrak	Metroliners (2)	Trenton	Newark	48.1	35	82.4
Amtrak	Metroliners (5)	Philadelphia	Newark	80.5	59	81.9
Amtrak	Metroliner	Newark	Philadelphia	80.5	59	81.9
Amtrak	Metroliner	Philadelphia	Baltimore	94.0	69	81.7
Amtrak	Metroliner	Trenton	Metro Park	33.9	25	81.3
Amtrak	Metroliners (4)	Philadelphia	Metro Park	66.3	49	81.2
Amtrak	Metroliner	Metro Park	Philadelphia	66.3	49	81.2
Amtrak	Metroliner	New York	Trenton	58.1	43	81.1
Amtrak	Metroliner	New York	Philadelphia	90.5	67	81.0

Diesel Traction-Passenger-(75 m.p.h. and over)

Railroad	Train	From	To	Dis.	Time	Speed
Canadian National	Turbotrains(2)	Guildwood	Dorval	310.9	207	90.1
Canadian National	Turbotrains(2)	Dorval	Guildwood	310.9	210	88.8
Canadian National	Rapido	Guildwood	Belleville	100.5	72	83.7
Canadian National	Rapido	Dorval	Brockville	115.3	86	80.4
Amtrak	Southwest Limited	Dodge City	Hutchinson	120.1	90	80.1
Amtrak	Southwest Limited	Garden City	Lamar	99.9	76	78.9
Amtrak	Panama Limited; Shawnee	Champaign	Mattoon	44.6	34	78.7
Amtrak	Lone Star	Marceline	Carrollton	39.1	30	78.2
Amtrak	Panama Limited; Shawnee	Centralia	Effingham	53.2	41	77.9
Amtrak	Southwest Limited	Lamar	Garden City	99.9	77	77.8
Canadian National	Bonaventure	Cobourg	Belleville	43.3	34	76.3
Canadian National	Lakeshore	Prescott	Cornwall	45.8	36	76.3
Canadian National	Bonaventure	Belleville	Kingston	47.7	38	75.3
Amtrak	San Francisco Zephyr	Akron	McCook	143.0	114	75.3
Canadian National	Bonaventure	Brockville	Cornwall	57.6	46	75.1
Canadian National	Bonaventure	Cornwall	Brockville	57.6	46	75.1

Diesel Traction-Freight-(65 m.p.h. and over)

Railroad	Train	From	To	Dis.	Time	Speed
Santa Fe	Super C	Gallup	Winslow	127.2	105	72.7
Santa Fe	Super C	Winslow	Gallup	127.2	105	72.7
Santa Fe	Super C	Waynoka	Wellington	106.6	90	71.1
Santa Fe	Super C	Clovis	Belen	240.7	205	70.4
Santa Fe	Super C	Wellington	Waynoka	106.6	95	67.2
Santa Fe	Super C	Fort Madison	Marceline	111.8	100	67.1
Santa Fe	Super C	Marceline	Fort Madison	111.8	100	67.1
Santa Fe	Super C	Amarillo	Waynoka	205.2	185	66.6
Santa Fe	Chief	Gallup	Winslow	127.2	115	66.4
Santa Fe	Super C	Belen	Clovis	240.7	220	65.6

Date		Railroad	Run	Miles	H.	M.	S.	M.P.H.
May	1876	Pennsylvania-Chicago & Northwestern-Union Pacific-Central Pacific	Jersey City-Oakland	3310.8	83	45		39.5
July	1885	New York, West Shore & Buffalo	East Buffalo-Weehawken	422.6	9	23		45.0
Aug.	1894	Atlantic Coast Line Route	Jacksonville-Washington	780.9	15	49		49.4
Sept.	1895	New York Central	New York-Buffalo	436.32	6	51	56	63.54
Oct.	1895	Lake Shore & Michigan Southern	Chicago-Buffalo	510.1	8	1	7	63.61
May,	1905	Atlantic City	Camden—Atlantic City	55.5		42	33	78.3
July,	1905	Atchison, Topeka & Santa Fe	Los Angeles-Chicago	2244.5	44	54		50.0
April,	1911	Lake Shore & Michigan Southern	Toledo—Elkhart	133.0	1	46		75.28
Nov.,	1925	Canadian National	Montreal-Vancouver	2937.5	67	0	0	43.8
May,	1934	Chicago, Burlington & Quincy	Denver—Chicago	1015.31	13	5	44	77.6
July,	1934	Chicago, Milwaukee, St. Paul & Pac.	Chicago—Milwaukee	85.0	1	7	35	75.46
Oct.,	1934	Union Pacific	Cheyenne—Omaha	506.7	6	11	0	81.95
Oct.,	1934	Union Pacific, Chicago & Northwestern, New York Central	Los Angeles—New York	3257.6	56	55		57.2
Jan.,	1935	Pennsylvania	Philadelphia—Washington	134.2	1	50		73.2
April,	1935	New York, New Haven & Hartford	Providence—Boston	43.8		32		80.6
Oct.,	1936	Chicago, Burlington & Quincy	Chicago—Denver	1017.23	12	12	27	83.3
May,	1937	Atchison, Topeka & Santa Fe	Los Angeles—Chicago	2228.6	36	49		60.5
July,	1966	New York Central	Bryan, Ohio (MP 350-345)	5.0		1	39³/₄	181.0*
May,	1967	Pennsylvania	County Tower—Milheim Tower	21.2		11†		115.66†
Jan.,	1968	Atchison, Topeka & Santa Fe	Corwith—Hobart Yards (Super C Frgt.)	2202.1	34	35	40	63.6

*The official speed measured by ground instruments was 183.85 mph on passing mile post 347 + 13 over an accurately measured 300 feet of track. This is the highest speed on rails ever recorded in the United States. The run was made by a single Budd Rail Diesel car fitted with two turbo-jet J-47 aircraft engines mounted on forward end. †Time and speed calculated from standing start at County to passing Milheim Tower (end of test track) at 80-mph, after which the train was gradually braked down on regular track to a stop in Trenton passenger station. Between mileposts 46 and 51, speed was 150 mph or over, a momentary peak of 156 mph. was reached in the vicinity of milepost 47.

Fastest Scheduled Train Runs in European Countries

Passenger

Country	Train	From	to	Dis.	Time	Speed
France	Etendard	St. Pierre des Corps	Poitiers	62.7	37	101.5
Great Britain	18.57'/₂ train	Rugby	Watford	65.1	43¹/₂	89.8
West Germany	Adler	Hannover	Bielefeld	68.0	47	86.8
Russia	Aurora*	Moscow	Bologoe	205.5	148	83.3
Italy	Three trains	Rome	Naples	130.3	95	82.3
	Peloritano	Naples	Rome	130.3	95	82.3

Freight

Great Britain	Freightliner	Carlisle	Preeton	90.1	80	67.6
France	Freight Express	Orange	St. Rambert-d'Albon	87.6	81	64.9

*Operated during summer months only.

---

114 Japanese Trains Average over 100 Miles per Hour

Service between Tokyo and Osaka via the standard-gauged New Tokaido Line is headed by 57 "Hikari" superexpress trains daily in each direction which make the 320.1-mile run, inclusive of stops at Nagoya and Kyoto, in 3 hrs. 10 min. at average overall speed of 101.1 mph. Between Tokyo and Nagoya, 212.4 miles are covered in 121 minutes - 105.3 mph. With the extension of the New Sanyo Line westward from Okayama to Hakata in March, 1975, the runs of many "Hikari" trains were extended to provide service over the new line. Fastest time for the 664 mile run between Tokyo and Hakata is 6 hr. 56 min. - at 95.8 mph inclusive of six stops.

French Achieve 90-100 Miles per Hour Speeds on Regular Schedule

Having upgraded about 80% of its Paris to Bordeaux mainline to a 125-mile an hour standard, French National Railways has quickened the times of a number of trains between the two cities. Below are shown the fastest point-to-point timings in current French timetables.

Train	From	To	Dis.	Time	Speed
L'Etendard . . . . St. Pierre des Corps . . . Poitiers			62.7	37	101.5
L'Etendard . . . . Paris . . . . St. Pierre des Corps . . .			143.4	90	95.6
L'Etendard . . . . Angouleme Poitiers . . . . Paris			206.3	135	91.7
L'Aquitaine; Etendard . . Angouleme . . . . Poitiers			70.00	47	91.3

Iran Becomes 3d Country in the World to Schedule Trains at over 100 Miles an Hour

The Iranian State Railways have placed two French built Turbotrains in service between Teheran and Mashhad. These make the 575 mile run eastbound in 8 hours 20 minutes and westbound in 8 hours 35 minutes. The 43.4 miles between Neyshabur and Sabzevar is covered in 26 minutes—at 100.3 mph in both directions. The 77.6 miles between Sabzevar and Azadvar takes 51 minutes each way—at 91.3 mph.

American Railway Statistics

Source: Interstate Commerce Commission

Year	Mile-age Owned Miles	Miles Built Miles	Loco-mo.'es In Use No.	Freight Cars In Use No.	Pass. Cars in Use No.	Passengers No.	Freight Carried Tons	Em-ployees No.	Employees Wages Dollars
1960	217,552	21	31,178	1,690,396	25,746	327,171,745	2,409,039,608	793,071	4,956,902,360
1965	211,384	59	30,061	1,515,169	20,022	305,825,407	2,741,706,964	654,670	4,886,739,954
1970	205,782	80	29,122	1,453,708	11,378	289,468,947	2,798,324,161	577,435	5,646,480,859
1973	201,067	26	29,926	1,386,990	7,363	255,444,000	2,880,426,000	533,766	7,293,747,218

Passenger and Freight Data

Year	Passenger Revenue Dollars	Freight Revenue Dollars	Miles Trveled by Passenger Thousands	Rev. per Pas. Mile Cts.	Ave. Trip per Pas. Miles	Fre. Rev. a ton Mile Cts.	Miles Traveled by Pas. Trains Miles	Miles Traveled by Freight Trains Miles	Casualties Killed No.	Inj. No.
1960	641,495,655	8,151,706,391	21,284,084	3.01	65.05	1.42	209,676,995	411,173,556	2,248	19,577
1965	555,985,653	9,036,540,448	17,453,919	3.19	57.07	1.28	173,579,220	430,716,900	2,399	25,789
1970	423,190,535	11,124,128,498	10,785,746	3.92	37.26	1.44	93,575,236	434,584,544	2,225	21,327
1973	444,412,000	14,003,348,000	9,308,187	4.77	36.44	1.63	60,891,000	475,606,000	1,916	18,245

Revenues, Expenses and Dividends

Year	Total Operating Revenues Dollars	Operating Expenses Dollars	Tax Accurals Dollars	Net Railway Operating Income Dollars	Net Income Dollars	Dividends Declared Dollars	Ratio Oper. Exp. to Oper. Rev. Pct.
1960	9,641,592,812	7,657,328,712	1,020,471,011	594,618,250	473,174,842	411,649,958	79.42
1965	10,425,052,359	8,002,684,949	949,215,638	980,065,623	865,898,537	532,649,374	76.76
1970	12,209,237,323	9,805,555,323	1,103,988,230	505,669,405	*126,429,274	486,132,169	80.31
1973	15,243,795,000	12,067,957,000	1,416,090,000	725,047,000	*525,611,000	482,362,000	79.17

Values, Stocks, Bonds, and Capital

Year	Investment In Road and Equipment Dollars	Common Stock Outstand.[1] Dollars	Preferred Stock Outstand.[1] Dollars	Funded Debt Outstand.[1] Dollars	Tot. Railway Capital Outstand.[1] Dollars	Amount of Stock Pay Dividends Dollars
1960	35,513,350,796	6,185,117,735	1,218,060,497	8,730,551,088	16,133,729,320	5,617,239,155
1965	35,489,328,198	5,579,833,608	1,115,727,381	8,161,792,077	14,857,353,066	4,845,089,946
1970	37,918,381,770	5,604,882,147	718,205,376	8,015,822,800	14,338,910,323	3,594,834,452
1973	37,897,056,000	5,301,208,000	593,096,000	7,197,571,000	13,091,875,000	3,358,975,000

(1.) Data for Years prior to 1965 have been revised to represent amounts actually outstanding in order that they may be comparable to those shown for the year 1965. *After extraordinary and prior period time.

Major North American Turnpikes; Tolls and Speed Limits

Source: American Automobile Association, Washington, D.C. 20006

Speed limits on U.S. turnpikes 55 mph or as posted.

Airport Expressway: Miami International Airport to North—South Expressway interchange, 4.4 miles. Toll 10c per axle.

Atlantic City Expressway: N.J. Freeway at Turnersville to Atlantic City, N.J. 44 miles. Maximum toll $1.25.

Bluegrass Parkway: Fort Springs to Elizabethtown, Ky. 72 miles. Maximum toll $1.30.

Connecticut Turnpike: N.Y. State line near Greenwich, Conn. to R.I. State line at Killingly, Conn., 129 miles. Maximum toll $2.

Dallas-Ft. Worth Turnpike:. Dallas to Ft. Worth 30 miles. Maximum toll 60c.

Dallas North tollway 9.8 miles long. Max. toll 20c.

Eastern Townships Autoroute: Montreal to Sherbrooke, Quebec. 75 miles. Speed limit 70 mph. (50 minimum) car and passengers 25c at each toll gate.

Ensenada-Tijuana Tollway: Ensenada to Tijuana , Mexico, 63 miles. Speed limit 65 mph. Max. toll $2.40.

Everett Turnpike: Mass-N.H. state line to Concord, N. H. 40 miles. Toll maximum 25c.

Florida's Turnpike: Miami, Fla., to Wildwood, Fla., 265 miles. Maximum toll $4.80.

Garden State Parkway: Montvale, N.J. to Cape May, N.J. 173 miles. Max. toll $2.75.

H. E. Bailey Turnpike: Oklahoma City to Randlett, Okla., 86.4 miles. Toll max. $1.80.

Hutchinson River Parkway: N.Y.C. to Conn. state line, 15 miles. Speed limit 50 mph. Toll 25c.

Illinois Tollway: Includes Tri-State Tollway from Indiana state line to Deerfield; Northwest Tollway from the Tri-State to Wisconsin state line at So. Beloit, Ill., and East-West Tollway between Chicago and Aurora. 187 miles. Maximum tolls, Tri-State $1.80, Northwest $1.50 and East-West $1.90.

Indian Nation Turnpike: Henryetta to Hugo, Okla. 105.2 miles. Maximum toll $2.30.

Indiana Toll Road: Eastpoint (Ohio line) to Westpoint (Illinois line), 157 miles. Maximum toll $3.25.

John F. Kennedy Memorial Highway: Baltimore, Md. to Wilmington, Del., 60 miles. Maximum toll $1.00 Md., 40c Del. portion.

Kansas Turnpike: Kansas City to South Haven, Kan. 236 miles. Maximum toll $5.25.

Kentucky Turnpike: Louisville to Elizabethtown,

Ky. 40 miles. Max. toll 60c.

Maine Turnpike: York, Me., to Augusta, Me., 100 miles. Max. toll $2.15.

Massachusetts Turnpike: Downtown Boston to state line, Mass., (N. Y. border), 135 miles. Max. toll $3.30.

Merritt Parkway: New York-Conn. state line to Housatonic River, Stratford, Conn., 37½ miles. Toll 20c.

Montreal-Laurentian Autoroute: Montreal to Ste. Adele. 45 miles. Speed limit 70 mph. Toll: 25c at each gate.

Mountain Parkway: Winchester to Salyersville, Ky., 76 miles. Maximum toll $1.60.

New Hampshire Turnpike: Mass.-N. H. state line to Portsmouth, N. H., 14.7 miles. Toll 15c to 40c.

New Jersey Turnpike: Deepwater, N. J. to Ridgefield Park, N. J., 141 miles including extensions. (50 mph. on Hudson County extension). Max. toll $2.25.

New York Thruway (Thomas E. Dewey Thruway): Pennsylvania border near Erie to New York City, 559 miles including extensions. Max. toll $7.45.

Ohio Turnpike: Ohio-Pennsylvania line to Ohio-Indiana line, 241 miles. Maximum toll $3.50.

Pennsylvania Turnpike: Gateway (state line near Youngstown, Ohio) to New Jersey line at Levittown, Pa., then to Scranton, 470 miles. Maximum toll $7.10.

Richmond-Petersburg Turnpike: North of Richmond, Va., to south of Petersburg, Va., 34.7 miles. Maximum toll 95c.

Saw Mill River Parkway: New York City to Katonah, N. Y. 30 miles. Speed limit 50 mph. Maximum toll 25c. Trailers not permitted.

Seventeen-Mile Drive: Pacific Grove through Pebble Beach, Monterey, Calif. Maximum toll $3.00.

Spaulding Turnpike: Portsmouth, N. H. to Rochester, N. H. 22.8 miles. Max. toll 15c.

Turner Turnpike: Oklahoma City to Tulsa, Okla., 86 miles. Maximum toll $1.80.

Western Kentucky Parkway: Elizabethtown to Princeton, 135 miles. Maximum toll $2.20.

West Virginia Turnpike: Princeton, W. Va., to Charleston, W. Va., 88 miles. Maximum toll $3.00.

Wilbur Cross Parkway: Milford to Meriden, Conn. 29.5 miles. Maximum toll 35c.

Will Rogers Turnpike: Tulsa, Okla., to Joplin, Mo., 88 miles. Maximum toll $1.80.

Provincial Automobile Speed Limits in Canada

Source: Digest of Motor Laws; 1975

Alberta: Open highway, 60 mph, day, 50 mph, night; 4-lane highway, 70 mph day, 60 mph night, or as posted; urban areas, 30 mph or as posted; school zone, urban 20 mph, rural, 25 mph.

British Columbia: Open highway, 50 mph or as posted; residential and business districts, 30 mph; school and playground zones, 20 mph, when posted.

Manitoba: Open highway, 60 mph or as posted; urban areas 30 mph or as posted.

New Brunswick: Fixed maximum limits; residential or business districts, 30 mph; open highway, 60 mph where posted; cities and towns, local laws as posted.

Newfoundland: Reasonable and prudent not to exceed 60 mph on paved portions of trans-Canada highway. 50 mph on other paved highways; unpaved roads, 40 mph under all conditions except through settlements. 30 mph; municipalities, school zones and places of public assembly, as posted.

Nova Scotia: Reasonable and prudent with prima facie limits; residential and business districts, curves, intersections and school zones, 30 mph. Max. speed on

any highway, 60 mph or 65 mph when posted.

Ontario: Fixed maximum limits; open highway, 50 mph or as posted; cities, towns, villages and built-up areas, 30 mph or as posted; railway crossings, 20 mph; 70 mph on 4-lane highways.

Prince Edward Island: Reasonable and proper within maximum limits; open highway, 60 mph day, 55 mph night; residential and business districts, 30 mph; school zones, curves and intersections, 20 mph.

Quebec: Fixed maximum limits. Auto routes 70 mph; numbered hard-surfaced highways outside cities, towns and villages, 60 mph; hard-surfaced highways or gravel roads, outside cities, towns and villages, 50 mph; earth roads, outside cities, towns and villages, 40 mph; all speeds reduced at least 5 mph at night or in bad weather, in cities, towns, and villages, 30 mph or as posted; school zones at times when pupils enter or leave school, and at level crossing, 30 mph.

Saskatchewan: Fixed maximum limits as posted. Open highway 50 mph, or as posted. Local speeds set by municipalities.

Highway Mileage Between Selected Cities

Cities In The East*

	ALBANY, N.Y.	ATLANTA, GA.	BALTIMORE, MD.	BANGOR, ME.	BIRMINGHAM, ALA.	BOSTON, MASS.	BUFFALO, N.Y.	CHARLESTON, W. VA.	CHICAGO, ILL.	CINCINNATI, OHIO	CLEVELAND, OHIO	DETROIT, MICH.	INDIANAPOLIS, IND.	JACKSON, MISS.	JACKSONVILLE, FLA.
ALBANY		988	321	366	1091	170	283	712	807	707	466	536	766	1379	1117
ATLANTA	988		671	1315	155	1070	876	519	707	467	692	726	539	400	315
BALTIMORE	321	671		632	800	400	366	391	690	497	348	510	565	998	794
BANGOR	366	1315	632		1407	233	652	1018	1174	1094	827	892	1136	1635	1426
BIRMINGHAM	1091	155	800	1407		1210	932	589	661	499	742	743	492	243	427
BOSTON	170	1070	400	233	1210		458	781	974	861	640	707	931	1446	1201
BUFFALO	283	876	366	652	932	458		439	520	428	186	249	486	1115	1080
CHARLESTON	712	519	391	1018	589	781	439		483	202	268	357	301	786	671
CHICAGO	807	707	690	1174	661	974	520	483		294	345	269	188	747	1017
CINCINNATI	707	467	497	1094	499	861	428	202	294		244	251	104	678	783
CLEVELAND	466	692	348	827	742	640	186	268	345	244		168	300	924	971
DETROIT	536	726	510	892	743	707	249	357	269	251	168		277	931	1039
INDIANAPOLIS	766	539	565	1136	492	931	486	301	188	104	300	277		631	852
JACKSON	1379	400	998	1635	243	1446	1115	786	747	678	924	931	631		597
JACKSONVILLE	1117	315	794	1426	427	1201	1080	671	1017	783	971	1039	852	597	
LOUISVILLE	827	428	602	1198	362	964	537	266	304	108	351	363	114	573	766
MEMPHIS	1217	366	951	1594	247	1340	924	615	548	487	737	726	444	210	672
MIAMI	1468	665	1143	1773	765	1539	1431	1043	1377	1133	1322	1387	1197	920	345
NASHVILLE	1090	251	732	736	201	1126	717	409	452	289	532	544	293	375	577
NEW ORLEANS	1476	517	1153	1747	359	1556	1248	936	929	820	1060	1077	839	182	568
NEW YORK	147	863	192	450	988	211	367	566	828	635	486	626	716	1232	979
NORFOLK	560	592	249	881	753	543	561	397	874	600	531	699	698	996	661
PHILADELPHIA	233	771	99	541	897	303	360	481	758	571	425	578	639	1153	889
PITTSBURGH	457	737	230	819	763	576	220	233	459	278	127	287	355	972	893
PORTLAND, ME.	275	1185	513	128	1325	106	574	895	1089	967	752	817	1037	1552	1293
RICHMOND	472	545	144	773	697	543	473	309	786	512	443	611	620	944	646
ST. LOUIS	1016	553	804	1379	503	1188	723	538	291	338	540	513	239	505	881
TAMPA	1331	464	986	1620	552	1383	1263	884	1187	948	1166	1201	1005	678	194
TRENTON	223	783	128	520	915	289	358	513	780	590	435	594	660	1163	921
WASHINGTON	367	640	39	673	767	440	372	355	687	497	362	516	567	1000	754

	LOUISVILLE, KY.	MEMPHIS, TENN.	MIAMI, FLA.	NASHVILLE, TENN.	NEW ORLEANS, LA.	NEW YORK, N.Y.	NORFOLK, VA.	PHILADELPHIA, PA.	PITTSBURGH, PA.	PORTLAND, ME.	RICHMOND, VA.	ST. LOUIS, MO.	TAMPA, FLA.	TRENTON, N.J.	WASHINGTON, D.C.
ALBANY	827	1217	1468	1090	1476	147	560	233	457	275	472	1016	1331	223	367
ATLANTA	428	366	665	251	517	863	592	771	737	1185	545	553	464	783	640
BALTIMORE	602	951	1143	732	1153	192	249	99	230	513	144	804	986	128	39
BANGOR	1198	1594	1773	736	1747	450	881	541	819	128	773	1379	1620	520	673
BIRMINGHAM	362	247	765	201	359	988	753	897	763	1325	697	503	552	915	767
BOSTON	964	1340	1539	1126	1556	211	543	303	576	106	543	1188	1383	289	440
BUFFALO	537	924	1431	717	1248	367	561	360	220	574	473	723	1263	358	372
CHARLESTON	266	615	1043	409	936	566	397	481	233	895	309	538	884	513	355
CHICAGO	304	548	1377	452	929	828	874	758	459	1089	786	291	1187	780	687
CINCINNATI	108	487	1133	289	820	635	600	571	278	967	512	338	948	590	497
CLEVELAND	351	737	1322	532	1060	486	531	425	127	752	443	540	1166	435	362
DETROIT	363	726	1387	544	1077	626	699	578	287	817	611	513	1201	594	516
INDIANAPOLIS	114	444	1197	293	839	716	698	639	355	1037	620	239	1005	660	567
JACKSON	573	210	920	375	182	1232	996	1153	972	1552	944	505	678	1163	1000
JACKSONVILLE	766	672	345	577	568	979	661	889	893	1293	646	881	194	921	754
LOUISVILLE		365	1078	180	719	759	693	682	398	1070	575	267	865	705	605
MEMPHIS	365		1017	220	399	1142	958	1057	786	1446	845	294	782	1064	917
MIAMI	1078	1017		916	878	1327	1013	1230	1237	1649	994	1222	248	1276	1105
NASHVILLE	180	220	916		536	929	713	838	568	1232	625	295	908	853	697
NEW ORLEANS	719	399	878	536		1353	1101	1239	1113	1655	1057	699	644	1270	1150
NEW YORK	759	1142	1327	929	1353		441	91	363	317	330	961	1176	70	226
NORFOLK	693	958	1013	713	1101	441		348	400	649	88	930	859	359	195
PHILADELPHIA	682	1057	1230	838	1239	91	348		294	409	240	881	1083	32	136
PITTSBURGH	398	786	1237	568	1113	363	400	294		682	312	599	1045	205	229
PORTLAND, ME.	1070	1446	1649	1232	1655	317	649	409	682		649	1294	1488	395	549
RICHMOND	575	845	994	625	1057	330	88	240	312	649		842	842	277	107
ST. LOUIS	267	294	1222	295	699	961	930	881	599	1294	842		1030	897	804
TAMPA	865	782	248	908	644	1176	859	1083	1045	1488	842	1030		1109	947
TRENTON	705	1064	1276	853	1270	70	359	32	205	395	277	897	1109		169
WASHINGTON	605	917	1105	697	1150	226	195	136	229	549	107	804	947	169	

*Directions for Use of Mileage Charts

To measure mileage between the east and west charts there are 5 key cities: Chicago, Jackson (Miss.), Memphis, New Orleans and St. Louis.

Plot your course between the city listed nearest your home town and whichever of the 5 key cities you desire to pass through to the city of your destination.

Add the mileage shown and this will give you the approximate total mileage.

For example: The mileage between Cheyenne and Philadelphia through St. Louis: Philadelphia to St. Louis - 881 miles, St. Louis to Cheyenne - 910; the total is 1,791 miles.

Highway Mileage Between Selected Cities

Cities In The West

City	ALBUQUERQUE, N.M.	BOISE, IDAHO	CHEYENNE, WYO.	CHICAGO, ILL.	DALLAS, TEXAS	DENVER, COLO.	DES MOINES, IOWA	FARGO, N.D.	HELENA, MONT.	HOUSTON, TEXAS	JACKSON, MISS.	KANSAS CITY, MO.	LITTLE ROCK, ARK.	LOS ANGELES, CALIF.	MEMPHIS, TENN.
ALBUQUERQUE		980	545	1285	650	432	1032	1310	1111	844	1062	791	901	805	1032
BOISE	980		766	1726	1637	867	1397	1228	494	1825	2063	1446	1833	887	1913
CHEYENNE	545	766		967	880	101	632	823	700	1143	1282	657	1053	1182	1127
CHICAGO	1285	1726	967		936	1018	330	657	1478	1092	747	505	652	2106	548
DALLAS	650	1637	880	936		784	704	1110	1571	245	411	498	330	1410	468
DENVER	432	867	101	1018	784		674	901	792	1028	1219	613	962	1162	1058
DES MOINES	1032	1397	632	330	704	674		491	1162	948	828	207	581	1788	608
FARGO, N.D.	1310	1228	823	657	1110	901	491		822	1364	1271	636	1054	1935	1061
HELENA	1111	494	700	1478	1571	792	1162	822		1813	1922	1261	1666	1234	1720
HOUSTON	844	1825	1143	1092	245	1028	948	1364	1813		433	744	439	1554	572
JACKSON	1062	2063	1282	747	411	1219	828	1271	1922	433		613	257	1864	210
KANSAS CITY	791	1446	657	505	498	613	207	636	1261	744	613		409	1620	467
LITTLE ROCK	901	1833	1053	652	330	962	581	1054	1666	439	257	409		1698	139
LOS ANGELES	805	887	1182	2106	1410	1162	1788	1935	1234	1554	1864	1620	1698		1823
MEMPHIS	1032	1913	1127	548	468	1058	627	1061	1720	572	210	467	139	1823	
MILWAUKEE	1390	1763	1019	87	1063	1039	358	573	1392	1163	826	564	727	2145	632
MINNEAPOLIS	1223	1446	821	418	964	845	254	239	1056	1211	1062	461	833	1996	852
NEW ORLEANS	1145	2140	1376	929	500	1284	1028	1479	2070	358	182	846	434	1916	399
OKLAHOMA CITY	545	1489	702	826	212	616	566	900	1392	458	587	357	350	1353	482
OMAHA	892	1267	491	465	672	537	139	436	1056	917	882	208	623	1698	671
PHOENIX	449	1020	924	1753	1021	826	1449	1726	1147	1158	1456	1238	1337	389	1470
PORTLAND, ORE.	1461	435	1211	2131	2057	1285	1819	1590	657	2282	2506	1901	2284	994	2367
RENO	1036	427	995	1970	1695	1040	1638	1639	905	1888	2104	1665	2030	476	2083
ST. LOUIS	1057	1701	910	291	651	863	349	812	1498	801	505	254	357	1862	294
SALT LAKE CITY	612	363	457	1443	1262	512	1089	1215	500	1453	1685	1118	1444	730	1570
SAN FRANCISCO	1132	654	1209	2183	1773	1267	1851	1873	1134	1955	2203	1893	2032	403	2162
SEATTLE	1511	529	1279	2031	2136	1377	1766	1505	611	2354	2601	1904	2273	1177	2362
SIOUX FALLS	1082	1295	654	525	844	655	282	230	960	1110	1013	390	799	1817	858
TUCSON	454	1191	999	1739	951	845	1462	1746	1270	1070	1362	1255	1278	512	1417
WICHITA	620	1663	590	711	386	512	403	731	1241	629	733	202	472	1384	549

City	MILWAUKEE, WIS.	MINNEAPOLIS, MINN.	NEW ORLEANS, LA.	OKLAHOMA CITY, OKLA.	OMAHA, NEB.	PHOENIX, ARIZ.	PORTLAND, ORE.	RENO, NEV.	ST. LOUIS, MO.	SALT LAKE CITY, UTAH	SAN FRANCISCO, CALIF.	SEATTLE, WASH.	SIOUX FALLS, S.D.	TUCSON, ARIZ	WICHITA, KAN.
ALBUQUERQUE	1390	1223	1145	545	892	449	1461	1036	1057	612	1132	1511	1082	454	620
BOISE	1763	1446	2140	1489	1267	1020	435	427	1701	363	654	525	1295	1191	1663
CHEYENNE	1019	821	1376	702	491	924	1211	995	910	457	1209	1279	654	999	590
CHICAGO	87	418	929	826	465	1753	2131	1970	291	1443	2183	2031	525	1739	711
DALLAS	1063	964	500	212	672	1021	2057	1695	651	1262	1773	2136	844	951	386
DENVER	1039	845	1284	616	537	826	1285	1040	863	512	1267	1377	655	845	512
DES MOINES	358	254	1028	566	139	1449	1819	1638	349	1089	1851	1766	282	1462	403
FARGO, N.D.	573	239	1479	900	436	1726	1590	1639	812	1215	1873	1505	230	1746	731
HELENA	1392	1056	2070	1392	1056	1147	657	905	1498	500	1134	611	960	1270	1241
HOUSTON	1163	1211	358	458	917	1158	2282	1888	801	1453	1955	2354	1110	1070	629
JACKSON	826	1062	182	587	882	1456	2506	2104	505	1685	2203	2601	1013	1362	733
KANSAS CITY	564	461	846	357	208	1238	1901	1665	254	1118	1893	1904	390	1255	202
LITTLE ROCK	727	833	434	350	623	1337	2284	2030	357	1444	2032	2273	799	1278	472
LOS ANGELES	2145	1996	1916	1353	1698	389	994	476	1862	730	403	1177	1817	512	1384
MEMPHIS	632	852	399	482	671	1470	2367	2083	294	1570	2162	2362	858	1417	549
MILWAUKEE		334	1034	905	501	1833	2069	2003	371	1502	2203	2045	507	1819	792
MINNEAPOLIS	334		1251	818	364	1671	1721	1797	553	1246	2001	1673	221	1677	650
NEW ORLEANS	1034	1251		684	1065	1527	2591	2199	699	1773	2278	2645	1265	1436	840
OKLAHOMA CITY	905	818	648		477	989	1926	1529	523	1112	1692	1975	644	941	168
OMAHA	1501	364	1065	477		1325	1700	1500	453	955	1720	1657	187	1341	309
PHOENIX	1833	1671	1527	989	1325		1273	762	1492	688	794	1510	1481	123	1040
PORTLAND, ORE.	2069	1721	2591	1926	1700	1273		566	2113	807	669	173	1580	1396	1854
RENO	2003	1797	2199	1529	1500	762	566		1906	531	227	760	1472	912	1542
ST. LOUIS	371	553	699	523	453	1492	2113	1879		1381	2133	2102	632	1457	460
SALT LAKE CITY	1502	1246	1773	1112	953	688	807	531	1381		755	869	941	820	1020
SAN FRANCISCO	2203	2001	2278	1692	1720	794	669	227	2133	755		858	1696	921	1730
SEATTLE	2045	1673	2645	1975	1657	1510	173	760	2102	869	858		1526	1666	1842
SIOUX FALLS	507	221	1265	644	187	1481	1580	1472	632	941	1696	1526		1536	493
TUCSON	1819	1677	1436	941	1341	123	1396	912	1457	820	921	1666	1536		1074
WICHITA	792	650	840	168	309	1040	1854	1542	460	1020	1730	1842	493	1074	

Highway Mileage Between Selected Canadian and U.S. Cities

	CALGARY	EDMONTON	HALIFAX	LONDON	MONCTON	MONTREAL	OTTAWA	QUEBEC	REGINA	ST. JOHN	SAULT STE. MARIE	THUNDER BAY	TORONTO	VANCOUVER	WINNIPEG
BANGOR, ME.	2592	2595	450	762	287	310	436	241	2115	188	936	1331	651	3250	1760
BOSTON, MASS.	2620	2639	683	675	520	333	458	390	2142	421	958	1403	564	3168	1812
BUFFALO, N.Y.	2106	2125	1141	142	978	383	350	533	1628	879	532	977	102	2878	1377
BUTTE, MONT.	378	561	2950	1859	2787	2309	2033	2470	629	2739	1533	1303	1972	764	875
CALGARY, ALB.		183	3073	2246	2910	2282	2202	2432	478	2862	1601	1271	2142	659	832
DETROIT, MICH.	1915	1934	1336	122	1204	576	475	738	1437	1156	246	691	235	2505	1149
DULUTH, MINN.	1240	1243	1842	777	1679	1051	925	1199	763	1631	425	195	865	1898	408
EDMONTON, ALB.	183		3076	2249	2913	2285	2205	2435	497	2865	1632	1274	2145	842	835
FARGO, N.D.	989	1172	2092	1048	1929	1502	1175	1764	511	1881	675	445	1161	1654	233
HALIFAX, N.S.	3073	3076		1243	163	791	917	657	2596	262	1417	1812	1132	3731	2241
LONDON, ONTARIO	2246	2249	1243		1080	452	359	602	1769	1032	403	985	111	2904	1414
MONCTON, N.B.	2910	2913	163	1080		628	754	494	2433	99	1254	1649	969	3568	2078
MONTREAL, QUE.	2282	2285	791	452	628		126	150	1805	580	626	1021	341	2940	1450
OTTAWA, QUE.	2202	2205	917	359	754	126		274	1725	706	500	941	248	2860	1370
QUEBEC, QUE.	2432	2435	657	602	494	150	274		1955	446	774	1171	491	3090	1600
REGINA, SASK.	478	497	2596	1769	2433	1805	1725	1955		2385	1146	794	1665	1136	355
ST. JOHN, N.B.	2862	2865	262	1032	99	580	706	446	2385		1206	1601	921	3520	2030
SAULT STE. MARIE	1601	1632	1417	403	1254	626	500	774	1146	1206		445	440	2201	797
SEATTLE, WASH.	762	945	3494	2489	3331	2693	2577	2934	1092	3283	2077	1883	2600	146	1444
THUNDER BAY, ONT.	1271	1274	1812	985	1649	1021	941	1171	794	1601	445		881	1929	439
TORONTO, ONT.	2142	2145	1132	111	969	341	248	491	1665	921	440	881		2800	1310
VANCOUVER, B.C.	659	842	3731	2904	3568	2940	2860	3090	1136	3520	2201	1929	2800		1490
WINNIPEG, MAN.	832	835	2241	1414	2078	1450	1370	1600	355	2030	797	439	1310	1490	

Motor Bus Passenger Operations, Intercity Class I Carriers

Source: Interstate Commerce Commission

Year ended December 31	1968	1970	1972	1973	1974
Number of carriers reporting	159	71	72	71	75
Miles of line, regular route	216,668	192,130	NA	NA	NA
Regular route intercity service revenue (dollars)	484,709,405	509,753,126	534,611,714	563,466,235	639,750,810
Local and suburban revenue (dollars)	16,092,699	13,894,726	11,652,843	12,018,079	11,945,416
Charter or special service bus (dollars)	83,463,349	80,473,873	93,953,690	103,325,461	122,091,663
Total operating revenue (dollars)	685,662,405	722,174,070	768,055,522	813,396,249	916,315,874
Total expenses (dollars)	604,808,045	638,435,771	682,458,001	735,979,839	842,092,947
Net operating revenue (dollars)	80,854,360	83,738,299	85,597,521	77,416,410	74,222,927
Bus-miles in intercity line service	814,587,544	745,691,295	698,920,436	706,378,742	717,861,566
Bus-miles in local and suburban service	23,644,551	17,869,121	14,499,911	14,800,065	13,974,842
Bus-miles in charter or special service	125,941,786	111,236,118	121,363,601	127,093,013	136,622,201
Intercity revenue passengers carried	160,692,862	132,041,325	120,899,734	118,862,777	119,969,288
Local and suburban revenue passengers carried	28,871,544	21,782,439	5,500,788	14,832,110	13,403,859
Charter or special revenue passengers carried	27,086,221	19,683,951	20,389,118	22,115,336	19,413,151

Intercity Bus Operations

Source: National Association of Motor Bus Owners

	1970	1972	1973	1974*
Operating Companies	1,000	1,000	1,000	950
Buses	22,000	21,400	20,800	20,600
Miles of highway served (Dec. 31)[1]	267,000	270,000	270,000	270,000
Employees (Dec. 31)[2]	49,500	49,100	48,400	49,000
Total bus miles	1,209,000,000	1,182,000,000	1,178,000,000	1,188,000,000
Revenue passengers	401,000,000	393,000,000	381,000,000	379,000,000
Revenue passenger-miles	25,300,000,000	25,600,000,000	26,400,000,000	27,600,000,000
Operating revenue, all services	$901,400,000	974,400,000	1,022,700,000	1,144,600,000
Operating expenses	$812,200,000	882,100,000	937,900,000	1,062,000,000
Net operating rev. before inc. taxes	$89,200,000	92,300,000	84,800,000	82,600,000
Taxes assignable to operations[3]	$76,700,000	84,100,000	89,600,000	94,900,000

(1.)Includes duplication between carriers. (2).Operating companies only. (3).Excludes income taxes. (4).Preliminary.

Minimum Legal Age for Purchase of Alcoholic Beverages

In the United States and Canada

	Years		Years		Years		Years
Alabama	21	Indiana	21	New Brunswick	21	Quebec	18
Alaska	19	Iowa	18	Newfoundland	21	Rhode Island	18
Alberta	18	Kansas (c)	21	New Hampshire	18	Saskatchewan	19
Arizona	19	Kentucky	21	New Jersey	18	South Carolina (e)	21
Arkansas	21	Louisiana	18	New Mexico	21	South Dakota (g)	18
British Columbia	19	Maine	18	New York	18	Tennessee	18
California	21	Manitoba	18	North Carolina (b)	21	Texas	21
Colorado (c)	21	Maryland	21	North Dakota	21	Utah	21
Connecticut	18	Massachusetts	18	Northwest Territories	19	Vermont	18
Delaware	20	Michigan	18	Nova Scotia	19	Virginia (c)	21
Dist. of Col. (b)	21	Minnesota	21	Ohio (c)	21	Washington	21
Florida	18	Mississippi (h)	21	Oklahoma (d)	21	West Virginia	18
Georgia	18	Missouri	21	Oregon	21	Wisconsin	18
Hawaii	18	Montana	18	Ontario	18	Wyoming	19
Idaho	19	Nebraska	19	Pennsylvania	21	Yukon Territory	19
Illinois	21	Nevada	21	Prince Edward Island	18		

(b) Light wine, beer 18. (c) 3.2 beer 18. (d) 3.2 beer: male 21; female 18. (e) Beer and Wine 18. (g) 3.2 er. (h) Beer not over 4% by wt. 18.

Trucking: Employees, Payroll, Registration

Source: American Trucking Assns.; Dept. of Transportation

1973	Employees	Annual Payroll	Truck Registration 1973	1974	1973	Employees	Annual Payroll	Truck Registration 1973	1974
Alabama...	162,200	$1,300,844,000	497,825	547,364	Nebraska..	91,600	$ 714,388,400	298,986	334,457
Alaska....	14,500	189,529,500	52,471	62,181	Nevada....	42,100	393,677,100	102,615	116,875
Arizona...	114,700	1,031,726,500	354,584	389,595	N. Hamp...	28,300	226,343,400	70,400	85,214
Arkansas..	134,900	922,985,800	366,150	390,217	N. Jersey..	212,200	2,063,432,800	343,632	404,820
California..	1,185,400	13,242,103,400	2,363,897	2,498,811	N. Mexico..	56,000	459,995,200	208,792	227,403
Colorado...	146,100	1,312,854,600	426,306	462,708	New York..	408,700	4,139,722,300	697,122	787,600
Conn....	127,100	1,182,030,000	145,130	154,918	N. Carolina.	311,900	2,303,693,400	677,136	772,811
Delaware..	29,900	286,083,200	51,951	57,675	N. Dakota..	37,200	283,278,000	178,524	204,143
Dist. of Col..	15,200	173,903,200	13,527	13,894	Ohio......	331,600	3,203,256,000	788,589	846,399
Florida...	270,600	2,257,345,200	757,370	896,583	Oklahoma..	167,500	1,393,265,000	581,205	637,196
Georgia..	216,200	1,744,301,600	608,231	696,911	Oregon....	120,200	1,048,384,400	273,658	291,801
Hawaii....	21,100	194,288,800	55,678	62,890	Penna.....	453,000	4,013,580,000	873,494	927,501
Idaho.....	49,200	377,511,600	166,940	225,859	R. Island...	35,800	288,476,400	60,944	68,422
Illinois....	341,000	3,427,050,000	776,789	896,971	S. Carolina.	144,500	1,042,423,000	298,969	327,536
Indiana...	322,300	2,970,639,100	675,400	712,980	S. Dakota..	37,700	268,650,200	152,884	174,046
Iowa.....	164,600	1,343,959,000	466,896	518,331	Tenn......	143,000	1,120,119,000	499,294	572,585
Kansas...	148,200	1,195,084,800	489,722	527,887	Texas.....	677,800	5,687,419,800	1,824,967	2,019,718
Kentucky..	153,900	1,271,214,000	468,438	531,404	Utah......	59,700	484,823,700	199,836	219,829
Louisiana.	166,900	1,371,751,100	435,012	503,905	Vermont...	18,600	152,631,600	46,142	53,913
Maine.....	55,000	408,100,000	116,194	137,073	Virginia...	180,900	1,511,419,500	471,184	504,703
Maryland..	122,500	1,096,742,500	303,140	335,142	Wash.....	193,600	1,850,235,200	548,551	607,638
Mass.....	165,600	1,469,368,800	266,761	307,482	W. Va.....	87,800	794,853,400	216,217	240,581
Michigan...	316,200	3,403,260,600	750,346	850,594	Wisconsin..	155,600	1,381,261,200	381,735	436,516
Minnesota.	190,600	1,691,575,000	507,084	575,596	Wyoming...	25,000	193,075,000	102,852	116,878
Miss......	106,000	741,894,000	333,986	368,458	Total.....	9,052,400	82,207,953,100	22,175,645	24,598,284
Missouri...	241,600	2,187,204,800	627,379	673,789	1972				
Montana...	50,600	396,198,000	200,710	220,481	Totals.....	9,050,300	77,353,699,200	20,225,745	—

Intercity Truck Tonnage

Source: American Trucking Associations
Based on operations of 2,343 Class I & II intercity motor carriers. In tons.

Region	1973	1974	Commodity Class	1973	1974
New England.................	23,843,933	21,810,991	General Freight.............	257,099,421	243,618,486
Middle Atlantic.............	148,353,909	141,957,154	Household Goods............	2,817,166	2,960,766
Central...................	192,140,927	180,986,802	Heavy Machinery............	8,509,262	8,995,750
Southern.................	124,171,173	117,299,313	Liquid Petroleum............	185,126,875	176,974,945
Northwestern.............	50,976,589	47,835,346	Refrig. Solids & Liquids........	18,591,073	19,428,427
Midwestern...............	43,124,944	42,314,693	Agricultural Commodities......	12,780,505	13,018,971
Southwestern.............	71,201,527	71,098,114	Motor Vehicles..............	27,694,440	23,591,659
Rocky Mountain............	23,091,958	22,478,024	Building Materials...........	66,649,757	25,690,908
Pacific...................	61,592,822	60,754,278	All Other Classes............	199,229,283	192,254,803
United States...............	738,497,782	706,534,715	All Commodities.............	738,497,782	706,534,715

Automobile Factory Sales

Source: Motor Vehicle Manufacturers Association, Detroit, Mich.—Values, Wholesale

Year	Passenger Cars		Motor Trucks, Buses		Total	
	Number	Value	Number	Value	Number	Value
1900...........	4,192	$4,899,443	...	...	4,190	$4,899,443
1905...........	24,250	38,670,000	350	$1,330,000	187,000	225,000,000
1910...........	181,000	215,340,000	6,000	9,660,000	187,000	225,000,000
1915...........	895,930	575,978,000	74,000	125,800,000	969,930	701,778,000
1920...........	1,905,560	1,809,170,963	321,789	423,249,410	2,227,349	2,232,420,373
1925...........	3,735,171	2,458,370,026	530,659	458,400,277	4,265,830	2,916,770,303
1930...........	2,787,456	1,644,083,152	575,364	390,752,061	3,362,820	2,034,853,213
1935...........	3,273,874	1,707,836,325	697,367	380,997,330	3,971,241	2,088,833,655
1940...........	3,717,385	2,370,654,083	754,901	567,820,414	4,472,286	2,938,474,497
1945...........	69,532	57,254,655	655,683	1,181,955,532	725,215	1,239,210,187
1950...........	6,665,863	8,468,137,000	1,337,193	1,707,748,000	8,003,056	10,175,885,000
1955...........	7,920,186	12,452,871,000	1,249,106	2,020,973,000	9,169,292	14,473,844,000
1960...........	6,674,796	12,164,234,000	1,194,475	2,350,680,000	7,869,271	14,514,914,000
1965...........	9,305,561	18,380,036,000	1,751,805	3,733,664,000	11,057,366	22,113,700,000
1970...........	6,546,817	14,630,217,000	1,692,440	4,819,752,000	8,239,257	19,449,969,000
1973...........	9,657,647	26,239,996,000	2,979,688	9,544,112,000	12,637,335	35,784,108,000
1974*.........	7,331,256	21,800,000,000	2,727,313	10,100,000,000	10,058,569	31,900,000,000

After July 1, 1964 all tactical vehicles are excluded. Federal excise taxes are excluded in all years. *Preliminary.

Automotive Exports from U.S.

Source: Bureau of Economic Analysis, Dept. of Commerce
(in millions)

	Vehicles	Total Value Automotive*		Vehicles	Total Value Automotive*		Vehicles	Total Value Automotive*
1940.....	$147	$259	1965......	$739	$1,929	1970.....	$1,397	$3,652
1950.....	406	746	1967......	1,237	2,784	1972.....	2,008	5,119
1955.....	747	1,276	1968......	1,414	3,453	1973.....	2,678	6,343
1960.....	634	1,266	1969......	1,554	3,888	1974.....	3,684	8,162

*Includes new and used passenger cars and trucks, trailers, parts for assembly, and garage equipment.

Passenger Car Production, U.S. Plants

Source: Motor Vehicle Manufacturers Association of the U.S., Inc.

	1973	1974	1975 6 mos.		1973	1974	1975 6 mos.
American Motors Corp.				Lincoln	57,257	37,541	26,072
Gremlin	93,597	113,776	21,296	Mark III/IV	76,137	50,028	20,379
Hornet	114,839	127,680	34,827	**Total Lincoln**	**133,394**	**87,569**	**46,451**
Javelin/AMX	31,267	15,953	—	**Total Ford Motor**	**2,495,853**	**2,205,245**	**897,559**
Pacer	—	—	67,293	**General Motors Corp.**			
Matador	72,476	83,618	36,825	Chevrolet	866,826	472,292	155,796
Total American	**355,855**	**352,088**	**160,241**	Corvette	32,616	33,869	24,800
Chrysler Corp.				Monte Carlo	246,533	232,410	137,481
Valiant	335,816	370,316	97,732	Chevelle	314,755	292,719	114,202
Barracuda	21,338	3,939	—	Camaro	117,828	157,909	79,907
Fury (Satellite)	140,745	137,636	60,609	Nova	395,673	386,947	145,551
Gran Fury (Fury)	245,058	90,715	44,500	Vega	359,882	327,707	103,725
Total Plymouth	**742,957**	**602,606**	**202,841**	Monza Notchback	—	—	60,635
Chrysler	205,601	96,630	47,658	**Total Chevrolet**	**2,334,133**	**1,903,861**	**822,097**
Imperial	14,956	13,433	1,930	Pontiac	345,214	122,037	50,992
Total Chry.-Plym.	**963,514**	**712,669**	**252,429**	Grand Prix	168,803	78,793	43,268
Challenger	30,211	6,063	—	Le Mans	205,135	114,786	46,019
Dart	239,598	268,323	84,565	Firebird	58,296	78,919	47,173
Coronet/Charger-SE	188,584	126,432	30,797	Ventura	89,150	78,701	28,779
Dodge	134,470	63,175	29,472	Astre	—	28,847	28,526
Total Dodge	**592,863**	**463,993**	**144,834**	**Total Pontiac**	**866,598**	**502,083**	**244,757**
Total Chrysler Corp.	**1,556,377**	**1,176,662**	**397,263**	Oldsmobile	383,623	166,424	115,221
Ford Motor Co.				Toronado	56,468	19,479	9,409
Ford	752,468	283,961	103,086	Cutlass	422,477	312,004	159,210
Torino	298,545	329,607	88,579	Omega	55,551	50,751	15,946
Elite	—	73,120	44,273	**Total Oldsmobile**	**918,119**	**548,658**	**299,786**
Club Wagon	23,105	23,745	13,810	Buick	425,207	172,562	117,758
Granada	—	120,094	148,003	Riviera	29,992	17,136	6,840
Maverick	184,810	197,531	56,755	Century	311,879	158,438	95,534
Pinto	366,748	301,707	69,498	Apollo	59,128	52,126	33,336
Mustang	193,129	338,136	105,125	**Total Buick**	**826,206**	**400,262**	**253,468**
Thunderbird	90,404	49,074	15,718	Cadillac	252,767	192,729	105,459
Total Ford	**1,909,209**	**1,716,975**	**644,847**	Eldorado	54,961	37,920	22,276
Mercury	132,896	71,114	40,563	Seville	—	—	13,764
Montego	146,565	85,253	31,909	**Total Cadillac**	**307,698**	**230,649**	**141,499**
Cougar	70,514	86,641	27,689	**Total Gen. Mtrs.**	**5,252,734**	**3,585,513**	**1,761,607**
Monarch	—	47,900	48,429				
Comet	103,275	109,793	26,731	**Checkers Motors**	**6,333**	**4,996**	**1,444**
Bobcat	—	—	30,940				
Total Mercury	**453,250**	**400,701**	**206,261**	**Total Passenger Cars**	**9,667,152**	**7,324,504**	**3,218,114**

Total Road and Street Mileage in U. S.

Source: Federal Highway Administration, Dept. of Transportation 1973

State	Rural	Urban	Surfaced	Total	State	Rural	Urban	Surfaced	Total
Ala.	67,847	17,998	78,705	85,845	Neb.	91,075	6,942	78,166	98,017
Alas.	7,611	1,432	4,940	9,043	Nev.	47,738	1,921	16,163	49,659
Ariz.	44,846	6,569	23,709	51,415	N.H.	10,173	4,851	12,452	15,024
Ark.	68,339	9,749	63,514	78,088	N.J.	13,597	18,825	30,543	32,422
Cal.	122,877	46,687	124,270	169,564	N.M.	65,060	5,247	21,579	70,307
Colo.	75,707	7,879	53,183	83,586	N.Y.	56,683	51,093	103,580	107,776
Conn.	5,426	13,308	18,623	18,734	N.C.	73,366	14,556	81,021	87,922
Del.	4,348	802	5,133	5,150	N.D.	103,025	3,222	70,226	106,247
Fla.	71,774	26,355	67,256	98,129	Oh.	86,036	23,329	108,377	109,965
Ga.	85,216	15,119	69,279	100,335	Okla.	93,495	15,014	83,516	108,509
Ha.	2,652	1,014	3,504	3,666	Ore.	94,671	6,726	64,233	101,397
Ida.	52,707	3,203	30,440	55,910	Pa.	90,133	24,364	99,334	114,497
Ill.	102,487	28,007	124,159	130,494	R.I.	1,019	4,521	5,294	5,540
Ind.	75,358	15,753	87,101	91,111	S.C.	53,250	7,045	42,149	60,295
Ia.	99,080	13,864	106,884	112,944	S.D.	79,706	3,014	61,450	82,720
Kan.	123,273	11,497	101,665	134,770	Tenn.	68,575	12,081	78,936	80,656
Ky.	63,769	6,022	62,484	69,791	Tex.	198,771	52,718	189,234	251,489
La.	42,714	11,410	50,647	54,124	Ut.	43,087	4,566	23,308	47,653
Me.	18,963	2,536	20,064	21,499	Vt.	12,907	1,017	12,762	13,924
Md.	22,649	4,210	26,803	26,859	Va.	52,894	9,457	61,580	62,351
Mass.	6,150	23,661	29,453	29,811	Wash.	71,110	10,092	64,819	81,202
Mich.	98,709	19,601	101,163	118,310	W. Va.	32,678	3,645	27,069	36,323
Minn.	110,700	17,535	117,640	128,235	Wis.	89,711	14,579	98,711	104,290
Miss.	59,844	6,842	64,657	66,686	Wyo.	39,297	1,305	17,709	40,602
Mo.	99,099	15,867	108,283	114,966	D.C.	—	1,099	1,098	1,099
Mon.	75,552	2,380	44,942	77,932	**Total**	**3,175,754**	**631,129**	**3,041,618**	**3,806,883**

Car, Truck, and Bus Drivers in the U.S.

Source: Federal Highway Administration, estimated total licenses in force during 1974.

State	No. of drivers	State	No. of drivers	State	No. of drivers	State	No. of drivers
Alabama	1,902,812	Indiana	3,185,040	Nebraska	1,044,347	South Carolina	1,462,971
Alaska	179,155	Iowa	1,843,033	Nevada	398,003	South Dakota	411,283
Arizona	1,284,155	Kansas	1,641,506	New Hampshire	525,017	Tennessee	2,371,396
Arkansas	1,269,165	Kentucky	1,742,084	New Jersey	4,216,959	Texas	7,287,730
California	13,176,000	Louisiana	2,033,227	New Mexico	701,660	Utah	721,042
Colorado	1,643,451	Maine	650,462	New York	8,770,000	Vermont	302,400
Connecticut	1,784,898	Maryland	2,358,860	North Carolina	3,161,146	Virginia	2,944,068
Delaware	370,269	Massachusetts	3,567,311	North Dakota	361,720	Washington	2,122,131
Florida	4,945,289	Michigan	5,532,599	Ohio	6,781,081	West Virginia	1,221,272
Georgia	3,452,478	Minnesota	2,402,550	Oklahoma	1,711,805	Wisconsin	2,663,886
Hawaii	492,310	Mississippi	1,373,308	Oregon	1,533,153	Wyoming	257,462
Idaho	553,351	Missouri	2,908,549	Pennsylvania	6,659,977	Dist. of Col.	331,938
Illinois	6,299,774	Montana	494,640	Rhode Island	555,658	Total	125,609,381

Motor Vehicle Registrations, Taxes, Motor Fuel, Drivers' Ages

Source: Federal Highway Adm.

State	Driver's Age Jan. 1, 1975 (1) Reg-ular	Driver's Age (2) Juve-nile	Registered autos, buses & trucks est. (1974) Number	State Gas Tax per gal. (1974) Cents	Motor Fuel Gross Tax Collections $1,000 (1974)	Motor Fuel consumption (1974) Highway 1,000 Gallons	Non-Highway 1,000 Gallons	Total 1,000 Gallons
Alabama	16		2,409,744	7	145,009	2,000,126	43,654	2,043,780
Alaska	16		188,022	8	13,441	150,186	41,306	191,492
Arizona	16		1,473,935	8	95,447	1,229,138	48,089	1,277,227
Arkansas	16		1,245,543	85	107,914	1,262,652	25,999	1,288,651
California	16/18	14	13,684,399	7	743,446	10,426,956	229,519	10,656,475
Colorado	21	16	1,862,127	7	96,818	1,341,415	58,711	1,400,126
Connecticut	16/18		1,991,397	10	140,072	1,387,622	23,798	1,411,420
Delaware	16/18		343,832	9	27,545	304,854	7,666	312,520
Florida	16/18		5,616,070	8	352,997	4,342,185	123,058	4,465,243
Georgia	16		3,243,807	7.5	230,844	3,032,916	48,335	3,081,251
Hawaii	15		485,305	5	14,168	278,245	10,089	288,334
Idaho	16	14	633,103	8.5	41,368	453,666	39,525	493,191
Illinois	18	16	6,195,402	7.5	397,139	5,094,444	269,906	5,364,350
Indiana	16/21		3,268,516	8	257,484	2,976,988	98,081	3,075,069
Iowa	16/18	14	2,033,686	7	131,280	1,653,232	189,643	1,842,875
Kansas	16	14	1,785,237	7	105,605	1,317,201	128,455	1,455,656
Kentucky	16		2,164,060	9	167,099	1,780,680	31,307	1,811,987
Louisiana	17	15	2,134,526	8	151,414	1,851,456	50,734	1,902,190
Maine	15/17	15	637,155	9	50,088	551,548	10,840	562,388
Maryland	16/18		2,346,033	9	174,212	1,874,434	26,530	1,900,964
Massachusetts	18	16½	3,041,952	7.5	182,538	2,380,939	28,502	2,409,441
Michigan	16/18	14	5,400,904	9	404,467	4,599,375	155,278	4,754,653
Minnesota	16/18	15	2,532,219	7	150,559	2,034,665	158,730	2,193,395
Mississippi	15		1,341,245	9	121,045	1,293,333	28,558	1,321,891
Missouri	16		2,825,461	7	193,705	2,702,321	146,772	2,849,093
Montana	15/16		585,320	7	39,186	484,959	31,842	516,801
Nebraska	16	14	1,144,678	8.5	82,792	892,851	80,858	973,709
Nevada	16	14	456,051	6	25,893	418,361	15,332	433,693
New Hampshire	16/18	16	490,303	9	36,892	398,983	6,420	405,403
New Jersey	17	16	4,168,451	8	277,538	3,384,810	62,184	3,446,994
New Mexico	15/16		763,452	7	53,635	751,086	15,629	766,715
New York	17/18	16	7,481,022	8	507,768	5,713,265	190,649	5,903,914
North Carolina	16/18		3,569,769	9	273,127	2,971,177	78,162	3,049,339
North Dakota	16	14	526,574	7	31,359	342,292	103,561	445,853
Ohio	16/18	14	6,965,481	7	381,035	5,346,260	145,456	5,491,716
Oklahoma	16		2,040,649	6.5	109,606	1,684,312	49,438	1,733,750
Oregon	16	14	1,579,736	7	82,489	1,289,789	50,748	1,340,537
Pennsylvania	17/18	16	7,116,674	9	433,800	5,055,693	131,995	5,187,688
Rhode Island	16/18		579,350	8	31,982	380,500	11,378	391,878
South Carolina	16	15	1,671,008	8	127,068	1,557,573	34,036	1,591,609
South Dakota	16	14	506,924	7	36,107	408,256	88,546	496,802
Tennessee	16	14	2,568,381	7	172,659	2,382,234	43,325	2,425,559
Texas	16/18	15	8,053,269	5	396,610	7,592,639	167,710	7,760,349
Utah	16/17		809,625	7	46,322	660,825	19,341	680,166
Vermont	18	16	284,942	9	21,387	250,312	5,191	255,503
Virginia	16/18		3,171,744	9	250,818	2,626,012	53,137	2,679,149
Washington	16/18		2,444,446	9	163,053	1,751,500	61,946	1,813,446
West Virginia	16/18		934,617	8.5	73,237	843,001	10,282	853,283
Wisconsin	16/18	14	2,577,547	7	161,129	2,221,868	101,692	2,323,560
Wyoming	16	14	306,796	7	24,431	319,985	36,350	356,335
District of Columbia	18	16	262,598	8	18,997	251,645	4,222	255,867
Totals			**129,943,087**		**8,354,624**	**106,300,765**	**3,622,515**	**109,923,280**

(1) Unrestricted operation of private passenger car. When 2 ages are shown, license is issued at lower age upon completion of approved driver education course. (2) Juvenile license issued for use between home and school in Cal., Iowa, Kan., Me., Mich., Neb., Nev, N.H., N.D., Oreg. restricted to daylight or curfew hours in Idaho, Ill., La., Mass., Minn., N.Y., Pa., S.C., S.D., Tenn., Wisc.: hardship cases in Ohio and Texas: for agricultural pursuits in N.J. (3) Estimated.

Auto Registrations, Taxes, Gasoline, Drivers' Ages in Canada

Source: Statistics Canada and Digest of Motor Laws, 1975

	Driver's age Min.	Minor (1975)	Registered[1] autos, buses, trucks & motorcycles (1973)	Province gas tax per gal. (1973) cents	Motor fuel gross tax collect's 1,000 (1973)	Public roads & highways 1,000 gallons	Non-highway 1,000 gallons	Total[2] 1,000 gallons
Newfoundland	17	—	153,585	25	30,247	o3,825	29,271	123,095
Prince Edward Island	16	*	49,141	21	7,610	33,863	3,000	36,863
Nova Scotia	16	*	325,871	21	50,735	216,579	11,193	227,772
New Brunswick	18	16-18	256,042	20	43,923	185,589	20,440	206,029
Quebec	17	16	2,556,260	19	372,995	1,637,975	23,876	1,661,851
Ontario	16	—	3,583,379	19	547,116	2,463,796	96,991	2,560,787
Manitoba	16	*	471,507	17	56,203[4]	266,641	57,487	324,128
Saskatchewan	16	—	523,557	19	59,500	259,720	121,213	380,933
Alberta	16	14	933,673	15	100,932	556,205	131,306	687,511
British Columbia	19	16	1,281,917	15	130,913	679,086	115,517	794,603
Yukon & Northwest Territories	—	—	23,508	14	5,243	16,209	3,594	19,803
Total			**10,158,440**	**17.9**	**1,405,417**	**6,409,488**	**613,887**	**7,023,375**

(1) Registrations include: passenger automobiles 7,866,084; motor trucks and tractors 1,799,042; buses 44,265; motorcycles 287,820; other motor vehicles (includes farm tractors) 161,229. (2) Refers to gasoline sales only and excludes aviation and aviation turbo fuels. (3) Gasoline for motive purposes only. Aviation and aviation turbo fuels included but liquefied petroleum gases excluded. (4) Includes $9,938,471 revenue from "Motive Fuel Users Tax Act" which refers to diesel fuel and propane gas used in vehicles operating both on and off public highways. *No junior permit.

AGRICULTURE

Endangered: Our Daily Bread

By Hana Umlauf

At the opening session of the World Food Conference held November 1974 in Rome, Italy, U.S. Secretary of State Henry A. Kissinger stated, "within a decade no child will go to bed hungry and no family will fear for its next day's bread." A less optimistic note was sounded last June by Adeke M. Boerma at the end of his 8-year term as Secretary General of the United Nations Food and Agriculture Organization. He contended that the poorer and hungrier nations cannot achieve self-sufficiency in food within a decade.

Despite such disagreement on the long-term ramifications of the current world food shortage, there is no question that the year 1972 marked a critical change in the world food balance of supply and demand. Until 1972, food seemed to be in abundance, at least for those who could afford to buy it. Certainly people were starving in the world, but starvation due to famine, historians pointed out, had existed in isolated areas throughout history.

In fact, until 1972, the major problem facing the developed nations of the world, particularly those on the North American continent, was how to dispose of food surpluses in order to prevent prices from plummeting and ruining farmers. Although some food was used for animal feedstock at subsidized prices and some was given away or sold at very low rates to developing countries, government subsidies were paid to farmers to keep much of their cropland idle.

But in 1972, existing food surpluses were erased by deficits in expected world production of food. For the first time in 20 years, world food production fell by 5%, or 33 million tons. To satisfy the yearly increase in food demand, production should have increased by 25 million tons.

Bad Weather Devastates 1972 Crops

Poor weather worldwide in 1972 led to almost universally poor crop yields. The Soviet Union, faced by a great crop failure, decided to make up its deficit totally through imports. And inevitably, the USSR sharply cut their exports, most of which had usually gone to Eastern Europe. Consequently, combined USSR and East European imports rose to 28 million tons in 1972-73, a striking contrast to imports of 4 million tons in normal years. These imports cut deeply into reserve stocks held by the major exporting countries, chiefly the U.S. and Canada. Those reserve stocks, which had acted as a buffer against poor weather and fluctuations in the marketplace, had already been declining due to changes in agricultural policy. By 1974, world food reserves had fallen to 26 days of consumption in contrast with 95 days in 1961.

Poor crops worldwide created an immediate increase in trade volume in wheat, leading to an increase in wheat prices. From late 1972 to the end of 1973, wheat and rice prices tripled.

Simultaneously with rising food prices, the world was hit by escalating petroleum prices. Obviously, developing nations which must import both food and oil were hit hardest. Those nations lacking exportable raw materials soon used up their foreign exchange reserves and several found themselves on the verge of bankruptcy. Rising petroleum prices also drastically affected the costs of agricultural production inputs, such as fertilizer production, tractors, food transportation and processing. These rising costs pushed food prices even higher.

The 1972 events were serious in themselves. They became critical when set against the backdrop of a widening gap between the ability of developed and developing countries to maintain self-sufficiency in food output.

While developed countries, benefiting from superior technology, produced over the past decade more grain than they could consume or export, the developing countries found their ability to produce food gradually outrun by growing demand. Prior to World War II, developing countries had been net food exporters. But, given a per annum 3.5% increase in demand for food, they have become net importers of food over the past 20 years. Population increase accounted for 70% of the increase in demand. In the developed countries, in contrast, the demand for food rose by 2.5%, easily in balance with the increase in food production.

Rising affluence also contributed to rising demand. By 1972, a third of the world's annual increase in demand could be laid to more affluent diets, i.e., protein-rich meats, eggs, butter — all of which require large amounts of feedstock to produce. In the developed countries, rising affluence was met successfully by the increase in food production. In the developing countries, demand for affluent diets only exacerbated the inability of food production to keep pace with population growth.

In cold commercial terms, for developing countries the cost of food imports tripled from nearly $1 billion in 1955 to $3 billion in 1967. By 1972-73, the cost was $4 billion and was approaching $10 billion in 1973/74. During this period of increasing costs, food aid from developed countries had diminished as food reserves had decreased. From a peak of some 18 million tons in 1965/64, food aid had fallen to less than 7 million tons in 1973/74.

World Demand for Meat Rising

The increase in demand for food in the developing world reflects only one aspect of the worldwide food situation. In developed countries, increases in per capita income have spurred a rapid rise in demand for meat, followed by rising meat prices. Since large amounts of feedstock are needed to produce meat, more demand for meat has contributed to rising grain prices. A comparative look at the uses of cereals in the 2 halves of the world illuminates the situation.

Today the average North American uses as much as 5 times as many agricultural resources as the average Indian, Nigerian, or Colombian. The amount of feedstock required to nurture one pound of beef is equivalent to the grain diet of an average Indian adult for 5 days. In the U.S. and Canada, per capita cereal consumption is 1,000 kilograms, of which only 70 kilograms is consumed directly. However, in most developing countries, per capita consumption is 220 kilograms, almost all of which goes directly toward human consumption. In 1970, 1/3 of the world's population — the high-income countries — accounted for 51% of all cereal consumption for all uses. During the period 1969-71, the 372 million tons of cereal which annually fed livestock was greater than the total consumption in India and China combined. If demand for meat continues to grow in the affluent countries, cereal demand per capita would continue to grow faster than in developing countries.

Food and Agriculture Organization (FAO) projections on future food demand and supply do not bode well. In the developed world, the projected annual increase in demand should be easily met by a 2.8% annual increase in production. However, in the developing world, excluding the Asian planned economies, demand will increase by 3.4%, while food supply will

food production and to coordinate the activities of food donors.

Another major resolution called for the establishment of a Global Information and Early Warning System on Food and Agriculture and another presented by FAO called for an international study of the problem of grain reserves.

The Conference strongly emphasized the need to accelerate food production in both the developing and developed countries of the world. The group recognized that increased production would necessitate a drastic change in current farm policy. Current policy would have to be altered to one that would give farmers motivating incentives to produce more food and access to necessary but scarce resources.

Food experts agree almost universally that to reach the fullest potential for food production in developing countries reliance must be placed on the traditional or small farmers. A large international commitment of energy, technology, and resources is basic to accomplishing this goal.

Small Farmer Key to Increased Production

Noted economist Barbara Ward believes this strategy of backing the small man is the single most important long-term hope for feeding most of mankind. Evidence based on a wide variety of agricultural systems tends to show that human labor, supported by suitable inputs and drawn into the benefits of the operation, can be the strongest impetus for increasing productivity and, consequently, the best guarantor of rising food supplies.

Experts have pointed out that the low productivity now found in the poorer countries does not stem from innate backwardness of the farmers but is related to a lack of programs which would make the latest methods and equipment available. According to Nobel Peace Prize winner and father of the "Green Revolution" Dr. Norman E. Borlaug, "Almost invariably when you look at what he's doing with his land, you see he's producing the maximum under the situation he has to work with. The thing is he usually doesn't have much to work with."

Because farming has been unglamorous and of low priority in national development efforts, it did not attract the number of farmers now needed to feed a nation's population. A shift to reliance on the small farmer would improve income-distribution patterns, reduce unemployment, stem the flow of population

come to purchase modest consumer goods.

Dr. Sterling Wortman, a plant breeder and vice president of the Rockefeller Foundation, has outlined 4 prerequisites to a change-over to such a new, higher-yielding system. The farmer must have available new techniques or materials — new seed varieties with higher yields and resistance to disease, fertilizer and the know-how to use it, irrigation methods, and systems for multiple cropping or intercropping — that are demonstrably superior to existing ones. All of this, obviously, is extremely costly.

Secondly, farmers must be able to acquire and purchase, at prices they can afford, the necessary materials. Implicit is a credit system to benefit the small farmer. Previously, credit has tended to flow to the large-estate farmers.

Education or "extension" systems in the hands of skilled farmers who can command the respect of uneducated farmers are essential to communicate new methods and knowhow.

And, perhaps most importantly, the farmers must have a motivating incentive to convince them their work is worthwhile. Basically, the small farmer must be guaranteed a price which will allow him to pay back his investment and give him a profit as well. The latter may well require government regulation of marketing and distribution systems.

Given these prerequisites, numerous experts feel food production could be doubled in the developing world. The changes or structure for changes must, however, come from within the countries and evolve according to the internal dynamics and capacity of each country. The acceptance of such change may well face great political obstacles. Barbara Ward points out that neither old elites nor new ruling groups are particularly anxious to share power or reduce their standards. However, evading necessary agrarian reform could well lead to eventual economic collapse.

Population Growth Must Be Curbed

There is also no question that population growth rates in the developing world must be severely curtailed. Here again, additional funds are crucial to facilitate more fruitful research into the technology of contraceptive mechanisms and fertility control and improvement of the management of family planning programs in the developing countries.

The Most Severely Affected Countries[1]: Grain Import Requirements
(in millions of tons, estimated)
Source: Food and Agriculture Organization and International Wheat Council

Commodity	1973/74 Actual imports	Total grain import requirements	1974/75 Covered by commercial purchases	Food aid committed	Total covered
Wheat	8.6	13.7-14.5	8.8	4.1	12.9
Rice[2]	1.1	1.3	0.5	0.4	0.9
Coarse Grains	2.6	1.6	0.8	0.4	1.2
Total[3]	12.3	16.6-17.4	10.0	5.0	15.0

[1]Bangladesh, Cameroon, Central African Republic, Dahomey, El Salvador, Ethiopia, Ghana, Guinea, Guyana, Haiti, Honduras, India, Ivory Coast, Kenya, Khmer Rep., Laos, Lesotho, Madagascar, Pakistan, Rwanda, Sahel countries (Chad, Mali, Mauritania, Niger, Senegal, Upper Volta), Sierra Leone, Somalia, Sri Lanka, Sudan, Tanzania, Yemen Arab Rep., Yemen PDR. [2]Calendar years 1974 and 1975. [3]Differences are due to rounding.

from the countryside to the already crowded cities, as well as bolster national world food supplies.

In many cases, it would not be necessary, or even desirable, to transplant large-scale American machinery methods. Past experience shows that modern scientific methods can be employed successfully on small one or 2-acre farms. In countries where this has been done, South Korea and Taiwan for example, small farmers are already benefiting from a rising standard of living and beginning to earn enough income to

There is also little disagreement that an international food reserve system is desperately needed, but there is little agreement on how it should be established. Current estimates project that 50 to 80 million tons must be held in reserve to cover 95% of expected crop shortfalls.

One school favors a centrally-managed system patterned on the U. S. Commodity Credit Corporation. The body would acquire commodities when prices fell to a certain level and release stocks for emergency famine relief or when prices rose. Another possibility involves a series of independent national food reserves. Such a system would avoid issues of national sovereignty.

A last basic element in easing the world food situation is modification of the patterns of excessive food and energy consumption now prevalent in the affluent countries. Noted food expert Lester R. Brown has estimated that if total American consumption were reduced by only 10%, the savings would amount to 12 million tons of grain, a total greater than India's food deficit this year. One of the simplest ways to decrease consumption in the affluent countries is to lessen per capita consumption of red meat. This decrease would, in turn, decrease the amount of meat/grain livestock production and free land for other uses.

In the interim, however, before food production increases and population growth and food consumption in the affluent countries abates, food aid is crucial to meet immediate emergency and nutritional needs of the poorer countries. The basic obstacle is a political one — convincing the affluent nations to help out. To meet the need for aid, the World Food Conference set a yearly global food aid target of 10 million tons, double the level of international commitments at that time, to meet minimum needs.

Given the potential solutions to the imbalance in world food demand and supply, it is evident that international cooperation and interdependence are of primary importance. Lester Brown has said, "We are going to have to come to terms with this common interdependence. We're now in a situation that if some of us (in the world) eat more, others are going to eat less."

Barbara Ward looks to the past record of man's industrializing and modernizing efforts and finds hope for man's ability to cope with the present situation. At certain critical moments, she points out, "the political decision to abandon total reliance on largely automatic market mechanisms for distributing economic opportunity and income and to put in their place some system of distributive justice has given the world society the chance of a new start. It is possible that some such turning point has been reached in the larger areas of the world and, for the affluent powers and groups, the most vital issue is their ability to accept new standards of living."

Estimated World Carryover Stocks of Cereals[1]
(in millions of tons)
Source: Food and Agriculture Organization

Commodity	1970/71	1971/72	1972/73	1973/74	1974/75[3]	Commodity	1970/71	1971/72	1972/73	1973/74	1974/75[3]
Wheat	72	74	50	44	41	Total Cereals	167	183	134	116	104
Rice	24	21	13	14	13	Proportion of Total					
Coarse Grains	71	88	71	58	50	Consumption[2] 19%	22%	14%	13%	12%	

[1]Excluding China and USSR, for which no information is available [3]Forecast
[2]FAO estimates a minimum ratio of 17-18% to assure world food security

Cereals: Actual and Projected Consumption by Main Types of Use
(Source: Food and Agriculture Organization Estimates)

	Actual consumption 1970	Projected demand			Total increase		
		1980	1985	1990	1970/80	1970/85	1970/90
	Million Metric Tons				Percent		
Developed countries							
Food	160.9	163.1	164.1	164.6	1.3	2.0	2.0
Feed	371.5	467.9	522.7	565.7	25.9	40.7	52.3
Other uses	84.9	100.6	109.5	116.4	18.5	29.0	37.1
Total	617.3	731.6	796.3	846.7	18.5	29.0	37.2
	Kilograms						
Per capita	576	623	649	663	8.2	12.7	15.1
Developing Market Economies							
	Million Metric Tons						
Food	303.7	409.3	474.5	547.2	34.8	56.3	80.2
Feed	35.6	60.9	78.6	101.9	71.1	120.8	186.2
Other uses	46.4	64.1	75.4	88.5	38.1	62.5	90.7
Total	385.7	534.3	628.5	737.6	38.5	63.0	91.2
	Kilograms						
Per capita	220	233	240	246	5.9	9.1	11.8
Asian centrally planned economies							
	Million Metric Tons						
Food	164.1	200.5	215.2	225.3	22.2	31.1	37.3
Feed	15.3	38.7	48.7	61.4	152.9	218.3	301.3
Other uses	24.6	32.6	36.0	39.1	32.5	46.3	58.9
Total	204.0	271.8	299.9	325.8	33.2	47.0	59.7
	Kilograms						
Per capita	257	290	298	304	12.8	16.0	18.3
World							
	Million Metric Tons						
Food	628.7	772.9	853.8	937.1	22.9	35.8	49.1
Feed	422.4	567.5	650.0	729.0	34.4	53.9	72.6
Other uses	155.9	197.3	220.9	244.0	26.6	41.7	56.5
Total	1207.0	1537.7	1724.7	1910.1	27.4	42.9	58.3
	Kilograms						
Per capita	333	349	355	357	4.8	6.6	7.2

Chemical Fertilizer Production and Consumption

(in millions of tons)
(Source: Food and Agriculture Organization)

	Production[1]			Rate of increase 1967/68 to 1972/73	Consumption			Rate of increase 1967/68 to 1972/73
	1967/68	1971/72	1972/73		1967/68	1971/72	1972/73	
Developed market economies[2]	40.4	46.5.	48.5	3.7%	33.8	38.7	40.5	3.7%
North America	17.7	21.3	21.9	4.3%	14.5	16.5	17.2	3.5%
Western Europe	17.9	19.9	20.8	3.0%	15.1	18.1	18.8	4.6%
Oceania	1.3	1.3	1.4	2.0%	1.5	1.4	1.6	2.2%
Eastern Europe and U.S.S.R.	14.1	21.7	23.3	10.5%	12.6	18.5	20.1	9.8%
Total developed countries	54.5	68.2	71.8	5.7%	46.4	57.2	60.6	5.5%
Developing market economies[2]	2.5	5.2	6.1	19.6%	5.8	9.9	11.5	14.7%
Africa	0.3	0.8	0.9	24.9%	0.4	0.8	0.9	17.6%
Far East	1.1	2.3	2.6	18.8%	2.3	4.7	5.3	18.2%
Latin America	0.8	1.3	1.4	11.9%	2.0	3.1	3.8	13.7%
Near East	0.4	0.8	1.1	22.5%	0.8	1.3	1.5	13.4%
Asian centrally planned economies	1.9	3.5	4.0	16.1%	2.7	4.9	5.3	14.5%
Total developing countries	4.6	8.7	10.1	17.0%	8.5	14.8	16.8	14.6%
World	59.1	76.9	81.9	6.8%	54.9	72.0	77.4	7.1%

[1] Fertilizer production statistics for some countries include the production of "technicals" not used in agriculture; no account is taken for losses in storage and transit which are estimated at about 2% of total production. Making allowance for these factors, the available world supply of fertilizers is estimated to have been 73.7 million tons in 1971/72 and 78.3 million tons in 1972/73, or much closer to world consumption.

[2] Including other countries in regions not specified.

Population, Food Production and Demand Growth Rates for Selected Countries

Source: Food and Agriculture Organization

	Annual rates of growth (%)			Per Capita daily			Annual rates of growth (%)			Per Capita daily	
	Population	Food production[1]	Domestic demand for food[2]	Dietary energy supply[2,3] Kilocalories	% of requirement		Population	Food production[1]	Domestic demand for food[2]	Dietary energy supply[2,3] Kilocalories	% of requirement
Developed Countries						*Guyana	3.0	2.5	3.6	2,390	105
Australia	2.1	3.7	2.4	3,280	123	*Haiti	2.3	1.0	2.2	1,730	77
Bulgaria	0.8	4.3	2.8	3,290	132	*Honduras	3.3	4.0	4.2	2,140	94
Canada	2.2	2.2	2.5	3,180	129	*India	2.1	2.4	3.0	2,070	94
France	1.0	3.0	2.0	3,210	127	Indonesia	2.5	2.0	2.6	1,790	83
German Democratic Republic	-0.3	1.6	0.8	3,290	126	Ivory Coast	2.2	4.9	2.6	2,430	105
Germany, Federal Republic of	1.0	2.5	1.9	3,220	121	*Kenya	3.0	2.6	4.7	2,360	102
Greece	0.8	4.0	2.3	3,190	128	*Khmer Republic	2.8	3.5	4.3	2,430	109
Israel	3.4	7.7	4.9	2,960	115	*Laos	2.4	3.7	3.7	2,110	95
Japan	1.1	4.3	3.7	2,510	107	Liberia	1.5	1.1	1.8	2,170	94
Poland	1.4	3.0	2.3	3,280	125	*Madagascar	2.4	2.8	2.1	2,530	111
South Africa	2.4	3.9	3.2	2,740	112	Malaysia (West)	3.0	5.2	4.3	2,460	110
Spain	0.9	3.4	3.0	2,600	106	*Mali	2.1	1.6	4.3	2,060	88
Sweden	0.7	0.9	1.0	2,810	104	*Mauritania	2.0	2.4	3.0	1,970	85
USSR	1.5	3.9	3.0	3,280	131	Mexico	3.4	5.3	4.3	2,580	111
United Kingdom	0.5	2.8	0.7	3,190	126	Mozambique	1.7	2.7	3.2	2,050	88
United States	1.5	2.0	1.6	3,330	126	*Niger	2.8	4.1	2.2	2,080	89
Yugoslavia	1.2	4.5	2.4	3,190	125	Nigeria	2.4	2.0	3.1	2,270	96
Developing Countries						*Pakistan	3.0	3.0	4.2	2,160	93
Algeria	2.4	-0.8	3.4	1,730	72	Philippines	3.2	3.2	4.2	1,940	86
Angola	1.8	2.7	3.0	2,000	85	*Rwanda	2.6	1.8	1.9	1,960	84
*Bangladesh	3.5	1.6		1,840	80	Saudi Arabia	2.4	2.9	5.0	2,270	94
Bolivia	2.3	5.0	2.7	1,900	79	*Senegal	2.2	3.3	1.2	2,370	100
Brazil	3.0	4.4		2,620	110	*Sierra Leone	2.0	2.4	3.9	2,280	99
*Cameroon	1.8	3.3	2.5	2,410	104	*Somalia	2.2	1.1	1.5	1,830	79
*Central African Republic	1.8	2.8	1.1	2,200	98	*Sri Lanka	2.5	3.6	3.1	2,170	98
*Chad	2.1	0.9	1.2	2,110	89	*Sudan	2.9	4.3	3.9	2,160	92
China	1.7	2.3		2,170	91	*Tanzania	2.4	3.1	3.0	2,260	98
Cuba	2.2	1.1	2.0	2,700	117	Turkey	2.7	3.0	3.8	3,250	129
Cyprus	1.1	5.4	2.3	2,670	108	*Upper Volta	1.8	4.7	1.2	1,710	72
*Dahomey	2.3	1.5	0.1	2,260	98	*Yemen Arab Republic	2.4	-0.2	3.9	2,040	84
Egypt	2.6	3.4	3.8	2,500	100	*Yemen, Democratic	2.4	1.6	-1.0	2,070	86
*El Salvador	3.0	3.6	4.1	1,930	84	Zaire	2.0	0.2	2.3	2,060	93
*Ethiopia	1.8	2.3	3.0	2,160	93						
*Ghana	2.9	3.9	3.2	2,320	101						
*Guinea	2.0	2.0	3.4	2,020	88						

* Countries most severely affected by food shortages.
[1] Crop and livestock production, excluding fish.
[2] Total food, including fish.
[3] 1969-71 average.

World Wheat and Coarse Grain Production
(in millions of tons)

Source: Food and Agriculture Organization

	1973	1974	1975[1]	% change 1974 over 1975		1973	1974	1975[1]	% change 1974 over 1975
Far East	189	185	196	+6	Eastern Europe	73	76	77	+1
Near East	37	41	42	+2	USSR	212	186	202	+9
Africa	42	51	47	−8	Oceania	18	17	19	+12
Latin America	62	66	68	+3	Subtotal, above regions	722	667	735	+10
Subtotal, above regions	330	343	353	+3	World total	1,052	1,010	1,088	+8
North America	270	231	290	+26					
Western Europe	149	157	147	−6	[1] preliminary forecast, May 1975.				

Grain, Hay, Potato, Cotton, Tobacco Production
Source: Economic Research Service: Department of Agriculture (preliminary)

1973 State	Barley 1,000 bushels	Corn; grain 1,000 bushels	Cotton[1] lint 1,000 bales	All Hay 1,000 tons	Oats 1,000 bushels	Potatoes 1,000 cwt.	Rye 1,000 bushels	Tobacco 1,000 pounds	Wheat 1,000 bushels
Alabama	—	29,900	530	1,044	816	3,336	—	1,134	2,990
Alaska	—	—	—	—	—	—	—	—	—
Arizona	7,100	340	1,013	1,511	—	2,236	—	—	15,510
Arkansas	—	1,012	920	1,170	3,774	—	—	—	10,400
California	45,604	25,787	2,550	7,695	5,000	24,623	—	—	38,994
Colorado	10,710	46,000	—	2,728	2,450	10,622	114	—	67,809
Connecticut	—	—	—	173	—	598	—	8,065	—
Delaware	792	12,416	—	51	—	1,530	198	—	1,120
Florida	—	19,104	12	414	420	5,533	—	27,764	600
Georgia	360	105,280	410	1,069	4,180	—	2,070	161,420	3,680
Hawaii	—	—	—	—	—	—	—	—	—
Idaho	31,970	2,408	—	4,427	2,850	80,045	—	—	61,860
Illinois	540	830,830	—	3,154	24,480	248	361	—	53,700
Indiana	516	387,660	—	2,017	10,750	1,481	216	16,800	50,040
Iowa	—	948,000	—	6,321	88,000	660	115	—	1,230
Kansas	1,550	131,480	—	4,229	7,440	—	380	—	319,000
Kentucky	1,824	95,200	2	2,996	370	—	63	424,596	12,285
Louisiana	—	3,672	570	752	429	252	—	125	600
Maine	—	—	—	371	2,480	36,400	—	—	—
Maryland	4,500	44,940	—	621	1,378	310	253	28,800	5,328
Massachusetts	—	—	—	241	—	800	—	2,408	—
Michigan	1,020	110,410	—	2,906	19,250	9,926	625	—	37,600
Minnesota	29,564	359,900	—	7,496	96,960	17,425	1,800	—	80,862
Mississippi	—	5,904	1,640	1,128	880	190	—	—	23,888
Missouri	297	149,050	230	5,491	4,340	—	170	5,060	37,990
Montana	37,120	910	—	4,261	8,820	1,750	—	—	120,108
Nebraska	1,050	380,800	—	6,462	26,320	1,542	1,100	—	98,600
Nevada	700	—	2	913	100	3,188	—	—	946
New Hampshire	—	—	—	168	—	144	—	—	—
New Jersey	988	7,743	—	271	343	2,430	243	—	2,214
New Mexico	940	2,695	151	915	—	840	—	—	2,835
New York	528	35,200	—	5,333	21,240	13,986	416	—	8,400
North Carolina	2,760	116,180	133	530	4,770	1,790	400	789,395	10,150
North Dakota	55,385	7,301	—	4,580	40,600	22,950	2,756	—	205,062
Ohio	598	266,450	—	3,151	29,400	2,546	168	21,750	64,680
Oklahoma	3,360	8,008	300	3,087	3,920	—	765	—	134,400
Oregon	9,000	828	—	2,491	4,200	17,482	300	—	52,770
Pennsylvania	8,690	89,100	—	4,292	20,145	7,360	512	22,750	12,600
Rhode Island	—	—	—	17	—	1,034	—	—	—
South Carolina	960	31,262	280	440	3,234	—	780	172,000	3,950
South Dakota	12,800	76,890	—	5,016	78,780	371	4,242	—	57,770
Tennessee	465	34,770	310	1,818	1,110	540	54	114,305	9,425
Texas	1,350	73,600	2,647	5,106	8,100	3,206	200	—	52,800
Utah	7,205	1,680	—	1,695	636	1,481	—	—	8,814
Vermont	—	—	—	844	—	220	—	—	—
Virginia	5,250	43,320	2	1,737	1,848	4,030	416	141,328	10,175
Washington	14,720	4,128	—	2,577	2,862	41,160	200	—	122,220
West Virginia	500	5,016	—	1,007	799	323	—	2,888	561
Wisconsin	893	154,360	—	10,600	85,400	14,000	240	17,626	2,853
Wyoming	6,468	1,633	—	1,644	1,665	1,528	136	—	6,503
Total U.S.	308,077	4,651,167	11,762	126,960	620,539	340,116	19,293	1,958,214	1,793,322

Equiv. 480 lbs. [2] Estimates discontinued after 1972.

Grain Receipts at Western Grain Centers
Source: Canadian Grain Commission (In thousands of bushels)

Crop Year 1973-74 Province	Wheat	Oats	Barley	Rye	Flaxseed	Rapeseed	Total
Western Canada	536,328	39,812	235,051	7,447	15,404	43,802	877,844
Manitoba	61,349	14,057	46,065	1,391	6,158	6,402	135,423
Saskatchewan	358,594	12,488	103,352	2,464	7,046	20,005	503,949
Alberta	116,385	13,266	85,364	3,592	2,200	17,395	238,471

Production of Chief United States Crops
Source: Economic Research Service: Department of Agriculture

Year	Corn grain 1,000 bushels	Oats 1,000 bushels	Barley 1,000 bushels	Sorghums for grain 1,000 bushels	All Wheat 1,000 bushels	Rye 1,000 bushels	Flax-seed 1,000 bushels	Cotton Lint 1,000 bales	Cotton Seed 1,000 tons
1965...	4,102,867	929,554	393,055	672,698	1,315,603	33,307	35,402	14,938	6,237
1969...	4,687,057	965,863	427,055	729,919	1,442,679	30,204	34,929	9,990	4,068
1970...	4,151,938	917,159	416,139	683,571	1,351,558	36,840	29,548	10,192	4,068
1971...	5,641,112	881,227	463,601	875,752	1,617,789	49,288	18,198	10,477	4,244
1972...	5,573,320	691,973	423,461	809,264	1,544,936	29,183	13,909	13,704	5,393
1973...	5,646,806	666,867	421,527	930,012	1,705,167	26,263	16,091	12,974	4,947
1974...	4,651,167	620,539	308,077	628,081	1,793,322	19,293	13,337	11,702	4,667

Year	Tobacco 1,000 lbs.	All Hay 1,000 tons	Beans dry edible 1,000 cwt.	Peas dry field 1,000 cwt.	Peanuts 1,000	Soy-beans 1,000 bushels	Pota-toes 1,000 cwt.	Sweet Pota-toes 1,000 cwt.	Five seed crops* 1,000 lbs.
1965...	1,854,568	125,610	16,457	3,031	2,389,596	845,608	291,109	15,469	302,592
1969...	1,803,272	126,026	18,913	3,736	2,535,394	1,133,120	312,418	14,370	229,455
1970...	1,906,453	126,971	17,399	3,315	2,979,465	1,127,100	325,752	13,409	254,429
1971...	1,704,884	129,119	15,917	3,930	3,005,118	1,175,989	319,354	11,718	220,059
1972...	1,749,085	128,614	18,118	2,103	3,274,761	1,270,630	295,955	12,453	165,876*
1973...	1,742,105	134,751	16,389	1,665	3,473,837	1,547,165	299,410	12,534	172,962
1974...	1,958,214	126,960	20,805	3,228	3,679,963	1,233,425	340,116	13,360	177,351

*Five seed crops include alfalfa, red clover, sweet clover, lespedeza, and timothy. Beginning 1972 sweet clover was discontinued.

Year	Sugar and seed 1,000 tons	Syrup 1,000 gallons	Sugar 1,000 tons	Pecans 1,000 tons	Al-monds 1,000 tons	Wal-nuts 1,000 tons	Fil-berts 1,000 tons	Oranges and tan-gerines 1,000 boxes	Grape-fruit 1,000 boxes
1965.............	23,663	2,923	20,918,100	125.6	72.9	80.3	7.7	139,650	46,695
1969.............	22,615	Disc.	27,736,300	113.0	122.0	105.5	7.4	189,640	53,910
1970.............	23,996	...	26,387,000	77.6	124.0	111.8	9.3	194,790	60,560
1971.............	24,172	...	27,096,000	123.6	134.0	136.4	11.4	196,480	64,140
1972.............	28,332	...	28,410,000	91.6	125.0	116.8	10.2	229,790	65,640
1973.............	25,827	...	24,499,000	137.9	134.0	175.0	12.3	221,300	65,100
1974.............	25,760	...	22,268,000	71.7	182.0	156.0	6.7	243,300	60,700

Production of Principal Field Crops in Canada
Source: Statistic Canada

1974	Wheats 1,000 bushels	Oats 1,000 bushels	Barley 1,000 bushels	Ryes 1,000 bushels	Flaxseed 1,000 bushels
Canada¹.....................	525,513	254,745	394,286	18,914	14,300
Prince Edward Island................	444	2,805	1,048	—	—
Nova Scotia......................	120	920	271	—	—
New Brunswick..................	144	2,295	447	—	—
Quebec........................	1,535	23,810	1,650	44	—
Ontario........................	19,370	23,415	15,470	1,385	—
Manitoba.......................	63,000	43,000	53,000	2,200	7,100
Saskatchewan...................	326,000	75,000	128,000	6,930	4,700
Alberta........................	110,000	80,000	188,000	8,280	2,500
British Columbia.................	1,900	3,500	6,400	75	—

	Mixed Grains 1,000 bushels	Corn Grain 1,000 bushels	Soybeans 1,000 bushels	Rapeseed 1,000 bushels	Potatoes 1,000 c.w.t.
Canada¹.....................	80,754	101,910	11,040	52,900	53,515
Prince Edward Island................	4,358	—	—	—	10,304
Nova Scotia......................	369	—	—	—	638
New Brunswick..................	252	—	—	—	13,398
Quebec........................	4,675	11,520	—	—	8,425
Ontario........................	43,800	90,200	11,040	—	8,120
Manitoba.......................	6,000	190	—	8,500	4,900
Saskatchewan...................	6,400	—	—	24,000	530
Alberta........................	14,600	—	—	19,500	4,000
British Columbia.................	300	—	—	900	3,200

	Mustard seed 1,000 pounds	Sunflower seed 1,000 pounds	Tame hay 1,000 tons	Fodder corn 1,000 tons	Sugar beets 1,000 tons
Canada¹.....................	260,000	26,000	26,019	11,070	829
Prince Edward Island................	—	—	225	—	—
Nova Scotia....................	—	—	317	—	—
New Brunswick.................	—	—	277	—	—
Quebec........................	—	—	4,980	2,045	82
Ontario........................	—	—	6,320	8,485	—
Manitoba.......................	30,000	26,000	2,400	210	221
Saskatchewan...................	150,000	—	3,200	—	—
Alberta........................	80,000	—	6,700	—	526
British Columbia.................	—	—	1,600	330	—

(1) Excluding Newfoundland

Harvested Acreage of Principal Crops

Source: Economic Research Service: Department of Agriculture. In thousands of acres

State	1972	1973	1974	State	1972	1973	1974
Alabama	2,914	3,104	3,350	Nebraska	15,415	17,298	17,765
Arizona	1,043	1,098	5,509	Nevada	471	479	492
Arkansas	7,193	7,517	3,321	New Hampshire	111	108	108
California	5,628	5,911	6,287	New Jersey	360	390	417
Colorado	5,418	5,826	5,903	New Mexico	1,024	1,204	953
Connecticut	142	146	153	New York	3,730	3,872	4,057
Delaware	444	465	482	North Carolina	4,116	4,522	4,762
Florida	1,186	1,249	1,338	North Dakota	17,286	19,107	19,224
Georgia	4,073	4,544	4,892	Ohio	9,262	9,745	10,661
Hawaii	111	111	107	Oklahoma	8,009	9,476	10,148
Idaho	3,865	4,078	4,212	Oregon	2,438	2,476	2,688
Illinois	19,946	21,769	22,470	Pennsylvania	4,117	4,411	4,466
Indiana	10,697	11,642	12,212	Rhode Island	18	17	17
Iowa	20,916	23,606	23,833	South Carolina	2,438	2,599	2,784
Kansas	18,809	20,731	21,492	South Dakota	13,755	15,140	15,518
Kentucky	4,047	4,259	4,630	Tennessee	3,991	4,256	4,452
Louisiana	3,716	3,600	3,953	Texas	17,671	21,935	19,684
Maine	430	448	438	Utah	1,070	1,114	1,147
Maryland	1,332	1,383	1,467	Vermont	574	566	574
Massachusetts	146	151	153	Virginia	2,661	2,700	2,832
Michigan	5,533	5,785	6,214	Washington	4,189	4,431	4,803
Minnesota	17,090	19,746	20,297	West Virginia	735	764	755
Mississippi	5,194	5,223	5,469	Wisconsin	8,526	8,843	9,148
Missouri	11,486	12,302	12,852	Wyoming	1,740	1,755	1,713
Montana	8,333	8,935	8,949	**Total U. S.**	**283,458**	**310,805**	**319,210**

Crop acreages included are corn, sorghum, oats, barley, wheat, rice, rye, soybeans, flaxseed, peanuts, popcorn, cotton, all hay, dry beans, dry peas, potatoes, sweet potatoes, tobacco, sugarcane and sugar beets.

Livestock on Farms in the U.S.

Source: Economic Research Service: Dept. of Agriculture (in 1,000)

Year On Jan. 1	All Cattle	Milk Cows	All Sheep	Hogs	Horses* and Mules	Year On Jan. 1	All Cattle	Milk Cows	All Sheep	Hogs
1890	60,014	15,000	44,518	48,130	18,054	1965‡	109,000	²15,380	25,127	³50,519
1900	59,739	16,544	48,105	51,055	21,004	1966‡	108,862	14,490	24,734	³57,125
1910	58,993	19,450	50,239	48,072	24,211	1967‡	108,783	13,725	23,953	³57,125
1920	70,400	21,455	40,743	60,159	25,742	1968‡	109,371	13,115	22,223	³58,818
1925	63,373	22,575	38,543	55,770	22,569	1969‡	110,015	12,550	21,350	³60,829
1930	61,003	23,032	51,565	55,705	19,124	1970‡	112,369	12,091	20,423	³57,046
1935	68,846	26,082	51,808	39,066	16,683	1971‡	114,578	11,909	19,686	³67,433
1940	68,039	24,940	52,107	61,165	14,478	1972‡	117,862	11,778	18,710	³62,507
1945	85,573	27,770	46,520	59,373	11,950	1973‡	121,534	11,624	17,724	³59,180
1950	77,963	23,853	29,826	58,937	7,781	1974	127,540	11,286	16,394	61,106
1955	96,592	23,462	31,582	50,474	4,309	1975¹	131,826	11,217	14,538	55,062
1960	96,236	19,527	33,170	59,026	3,089					

*Discontinued in 1960. ‡Revised. (1) Total estimated value on farms as of January 1, 1975 was as follows (avg. value per head in parentheses): cattle and calves $20,963,981 ($159.00); sheep and lambs $442,271 ($30.40); hogs $2,481,644 ($45.10); chickens $652,799 ($1.71); turkeys $29,223,000 ($9.84). (2) New series, milk cows and heifers that have calved beginning 1965. (3) December 1, preceding year.

Egg Production in the U. S.

Source: Economic Research Service, Department of Agriculture (in millions of eggs)

State	1972	1973	1974	State	1972	1973	1974	State	1972	1973	1974	State	1972	1973	1974
Ala.	2,852	2,853	2,945	Ind.	3,036	2,770	2,639	Neb.	813	775	722	S.C.	1,381	1,319	1,301
Alas.	7	7	7	Ia.	2,295	2,141	2,046	Nev.	3	4	5	S.D.	814	785	770
Ariz.	164	154	149	Kan.	718	673	601	N.H.	313	320	275	Tenn.	1,113	1,088	1,026
Ark.	3,795	3,695	3,601	Ky.	537	515	527	N.J.	746	756	736	Tex.	2,685	2,496	2,276
Cal.	8,652	7,680	8,485	La.	744	665	664	N.M.	234	208	197	Ut.	295	306	311
Col.	297	317	385	Me.	1,443	1,549	1,656	N.Y.	2,271	2,052	2,030	Vt.	128	150	131
Conn.	924	932	864	Md.	334	327	335	N.C.	3,433	3,213	3,037	Va.	825	789	760
Del.	130	128	134	Mass.	535	522	510	N.D.	153	153	151	Wash.	1,035	1,063	1,089
Fla.	2,840	2,806	2,852	Mich.	1,523	1,539	1,375	Oh.	2,324	2,060	2,057	W. Va.	261	242	248
Ga.	5,465	5,534	5,827	Minn.	2,584	2,474	2,385	Okla.	502	446	428	Wis.	1,313	1,267	1,183
Ha.	204	208	207	Miss.	2,281	1,981	1,908	Ore.	554	535	543	Wy.	32	31	30
Ida.	167	197	184	Mo.	1,473	1,347	1,149	Pa.	3,599	3,576	3,492	**Total**			
Ill.	1,778	1,664	1,543	Mon.	217	215	201	R.I.	57	⁵2	66	**U.S.**	**69,879**	**66,579**	**66,045**

Gross income from farm eggs 1972, $1,799,874,000; 1973, $2,912,454,000; 1974, $2,934,542,000. Prices received by farmers per dozen eggs 1972, 30.9c; 1973, 52.5c; 1974, 53.3c. Gross income from farm chickens 1972, $106,046,000; 1973, $174,098,000; 1974. $122,618,000. Commercial broilers produced 1972, 3,074,921,000 ($1,622,638,000); 1973, 3,008,667,000 ($2,690,362,000); 1974, 2,992,844,000 ($2,437,050,000). Gross income from eggs and chickens 1972, $3,528,558,000; 1973, $5,776,914,000; 1974, $5,494,210,000.

Production and Consumption of Meat and Lard

Source: Economic Research Service: Department of Agriculture (in million lbs.)

Year	Beef Production	Beef Consumption	Veal Production	Veal Consumption	Lamb and Mutton Production	Lamb and Mutton Consumption	Pork (exclud. Lard) Production	Pork (exclud. Lard) Consumption	All Meats Production	All Meats Consumption	Lard Production	Lard Consumption
1940	7,175	7,257	981	981	876	873	10,044	9,701	19,076	18,812	2,288	1,901
1950	9,534	9,529	1,230	1,206	597	596	10,714	10,390	22,075	21,721	2,631	1,891
1960	14,753	15,147	1,109	1,093	768	852	11,607	11,566	28,237	28,658	2,562	1,358
1965	18,727	19,060	1,020	992	651	716	11,141	11,235	31,539	32,003	2,045	1,225
1970	21,685	22,926	588	581	551	657	13,436	13,391	36,260	37,555	1,913	939
1971	21,902	23,084	546	545	555	645	14,792	14,904	37,795	39,178	1,960	880
1972	22,419	23,962	459	465	543	684	13,640	13,921	37,061	39,032	1,559	796
1973	21,277	22,812	357	376	514	557	12,751	12,820	34,899	36,565	1,254	733
1974	23,017	24,372	471	476	470	489	13,688	13,845	37,646	39,182	1,350	690

Grain Storage Capacity at Principal Grain Centers in U.S. and Canada

Source: Chicago Board of Trade

United States

Cities	Capacity Bushels	Cities	Capacity Bushels
Amarillo	27,883,534	Milwaukee	5,600,000
Buffalo	16,710,000	Minneapolis-St. Paul	120,341,100
California ports	16,500,000	New Orleans area	36,698,000
Chicago	58,003,000	Omaha-Council Bluffs	35,300,000
Des Moines	9,640,000	Peoria	6,560,000
Duluth-Superior	76,221,000	Portland-Columbia R	29,500,000
Enid	66,090,000	Puget Sound	9,400,000
Fort Worth	57,600,000	Sioux City	13,756,000
Galveston-Houston	31,200,000	St. Joseph	20,600,000
Hutchinson	41,733,000	St. Louis	25,375,000
Kansas City	81,315,000	Toledo	32,200,000
Lincoln	39,592,000	Wichita	55,992,000
Lubbock	29,219,000		

Canada

Cities	Capacity Bushels	Cities	Capacity Bushels
Baie Comeau	13,778,000	Prescott, Ont.	5,500,000
Churchill, Man.	5,000,000	Prince Rupert, B.C.	2,250,000
Collingwood, Ont.	2,000,000	Quebec, Que.	8,000,000
Goderich, Ont.	4,600,000	Saint John, N.B.	500,000
Halifax, N.S.	5,152,000	Sarnia, Ont.	5,400,000
Kingston, Ont.	2,350,000	Sorel, Que.	5,230,000
Midland, Ont.	11,550,000	Three Rivers, Que.	5,880,000
Montreal, Que.	22,262,000	Thunder Bay	90,397,210
N. Vancouver, B.C.	6,972,000	Toronto, Ont.	4,000,000
Owen Sound, Ont.	4,000,000	Vancouver, B.C.	18,056,000
Port Cartier	10,462,000	Victoria, B.C.	1,040,000
Port Colborne, Ont.	5,250,000	West St. John, N.B.	2,576,000
Port McNicoll, Ont.	6,500,000		

Grain Receipts at Western Grain Centers

Source: Chicago Board of Trade (in thousands bushels)

1974	Wheat	Corn	Oats	Rye	Barley	Soybeans	Total
Chicago	19,656	92,225	707	11	132	36,244	148,975
Duluth	116,240	37,455	28,498	8,631	31,836	2,353	225,013
Enid	52,819	.....	.....	.....	.....	.....	52,819
Hutchinson	50,019	720	.....	.....	.....	.....	50,739
Kansas City	107,781	68,746	1,141	147	6	15,826	193,647
Milwaukee	690	21,607	108	2	23,570	366	46,343
Minneapolis	111,382	119,091	45,899	2,849	45,110	40,738	365,069
Omaha	14,740	47,358	263	91	.....	4,307	66,759
Peoria	151	23,181	.....	76	.....	177	23,585
Sioux City	5,281	20,662	8,113	.....	8	14,698	48,722
St. Joseph	2,727	7,040	1,207	.....	.....	2,436	13,410
St. Louis	24,306	17,035	826	49	.....	15,251	57,467
Toledo	30,335	48,302	1,884	10	.....	32,474	113,005
Wichita	41,690	3,545	6	.....	321	6,256	51,818
Total	577,817	506,927	88,652	11,866	100,983	171,126	1,457,371

Egg Production in Canada

Source: Statistics Canada
(thousand dozens)

Province	1972	1973	1974	Province	1972	1973	1974
Newfoundland	8,481	6,835	7,857	Ontario	191,091	190,718	189,323
Prince Edward Island	2,350	2,410	2,363	Manitoba	52,008	52,893	50,498
Nova Scotia	17,373	18,228	19,297	Saskatchewan	23,931	22,444	21,019
New Brunswick	9,932	10,340	8,770	Alberta	41,315	41,437	40,769
Quebec	64,490	58,518	64,613	British Columbia	57,324	56,872	54,942
				Total	**468,355**	**461,695**	**459,451**

Gross income from farm eggs (1972) $173,882,000; (1973) $255,303,000; (1974) $275,459,000. Average price of eggs sold for consumption taking the month of February (1972) $.304; (1973) $.450; (1974) $.63. Gross income from farm chickens (1972) $11,151,000; (1974) $23,784,000; $9,411,000. Gross income from eggs and chickens (included fowl) (1972) $888,771,000; (1973) $570,662,000; (1974) $620,298,000.

Canada — Production of Sawn Lumber [1]

Source: Canadian Statistical Review (July, 1975)
(million feet, board measure)

Year	Canada	N.S.	N.B.	Que.	Ont.	Sask.	Alta.	B.C.
1971	12,723.0	157.9	298.8	1,808.6	960.7	111.0	470.0	8,916.0
1972	13,887.5	179.2	313.6	2,146.9	1,082.9	135.6	580.0	9,446.9
1973	15,089.7	195.2	336.6	2,274.0	1,167.8	181.6	657.0	10,277.5
1974	13,465.5	176.4	341.7	2,206.9	1,251.8	138.6	673.4	8,750.1

(1) Excludes Newfoundland, P.E.I., Manitoba, the Yukon and the Northwest Territories which, together, account for less than 1% of the total.

Farms in United States by State — Number, Acreage and Value

Source: Bureau of the Census (Census of 1970)

State	Farms No.	Average Acreage	$ Value per Acre	2,000 Acres or more	10-49 Acres	Total Acreage
Alabama	72,491	188.3	$199.60	629	21,439	13,654,215
Alaska	322	4,831.9	12.73	35	32	1,604,211
Arizona	5,890	6,486.0	69.72	897	1,229	38,202,667
Arkansas	60,433	259.7	260.03	625	10,935	15,694,527
California	77,875	458.7	474.65	2,926	28,915	35,722,348
Colorado	27,950	1,312.9	94.58	4,166	3,048	36,697,132
Connecticut	4,490	120.5	921.19	6	1,245	541,372
Delaware	3,710	181.6	498.96	14	872	673,895
Florida	35,586	394.3	354.58	1,062	12,413	14,031,998
Georgia	67,431	234.4	234.00	693	13,737	15,805,892
Hawaii	3,896	528.2	296.82	70	1,281	2,058,087
Idaho	25,475	565.9	176.55	1,218	4,382	14,416,521
Illinois	123,565	242.0	489.52	145	13,487	29,913,190
Indiana	101,479	173.1	406.05	65	19,522	17,572,865
Iowa	140,354	239.1	391.73	84	9,586	33,569,629
Kansas	86,057	573.9	158.78	3,341	5,231	49,390,369
Kentucky	125,069	127.6	253.05	114	26,761	15,968,243
Louisiana	42,269	231.5	321.33	536	13,610	9,788,662
Maine	7,971	220.7	160.79	25	948	1,759,700
Maryland	17,181	163.1	639.63	41	3,733	2,803,442
Massachusetts	5,703	122.8	564.63	7	1,622	700,678
Michigan	77,946	152.7	326.31	43	14,334	11,900,689
Minnesota	110,747	260.4	225.76	305	6,459	28,845,240
Mississippi	72,577	221.0	233.53	894	17,060	16,039,665
Missouri	137,067	236.5	224.22	396	16,823	32,420,284
Montana	24,951	2,521.6	59.57	7,596	1,485	62,918,247
Nebraska	72,257	677.4	154.38	3,509	3,113	48,949,376
Nevada	2,112	5,070.2	53.35	333	305	10,708,346
New Hampshire	2,902	211.1	238.78	6	443	612,750
New Jersey	8,493	121.9	1,092.31	13	2,471	1,035,678
New Mexico	11,641	4,019.6	41.87	2,660	1,704	46,792,302
New York	51,909	195.5	273.13	50	6,589	10,148,359
North Carolina	119,386	106.6	333.31	205	42,911	12,733,751
North Dakota	46,381	929.6	93.82	3,157	721	43,117,831
Ohio	111,332	153.6	398.51	53	19,729	17,111,459
Oklahoma	83,037	433.6	172.58	2,024	7,655	36,007,719
Oregon	29,063	619.9	150.22	1,739	9,000	18,017,850
Pennsylvania	62,824	141.6	372.88	38	10,428	8,900,767
Rhode Island	700	98.1	733.75		235	68,720
South Carolina	39,559	176.7	261.23	286	12,129	6,991,718
South Dakota	45,726	996.9	83.69	4,148	1,402	45,584,164
Tennessee	121,406	124.0	267.50	212	35,117	15,056,907
Texas	213,550	667.6	148.49	9,941	27,315	142,566,826
Utah	13,045	867.2	91.90	849	3,159	11,312,951
Vermont	6,874	278.6	223.73	17	465	1,915,520
Virginia	64,572	164.9	286.13	206	15,169	10,649,862
Washington	34,033	515.9	223.83	1,693	10,817	17,559,187
West Virginia	23,142	187.5	135.69	67	3,808	4,340,554
Wisconsin	98,973	182.9	231.98	81	8,118	18,109,273
Wyoming	8,838	4,014.0	40.73	2,689	473	35,476,374
Total	**2,730,242**	**390.5**	**—**	**59,909**	**473,465**	**1,066,218,650**

Total Net Income Per Farm by States

Source: U.S. Department of Agriculture, Economic Research Service

State	1966	1967	1968	1969	1970	1971	1972	1973
Alabama	$ 2,296	$ 2,003	$ 2,303	$ 2,909	$ 2,703	$ 3,134	$ 4,171	$ 6,722
Alaska	2,315	1,921	4,172	2,681	4,169	3,203	3,494	1,042
Arizona	13,664	16,850	21,880	22,965	17,482	22,226	24,489	38,672
Arkansas	4,293	3,380	3,752	3,643	4,460	4,195	5,463	11,234
California	14,299	13,690	17,222	16,436	15,149	17,257	22,877	37,296
Colorado	5,184	4,384	6,114	6,442	7,570	8,491	10,158	16,052
Connecticut	7,712	5,895	7,918	8,224	9,632	9,149	8,495	12,247
Delaware	5,257	6,793	5,937	12,413	6,886	8,259	11,837	28,352
Florida	8,453	9,190	10,183	12,417	10,664	14,697	19,075	24,307
Georgia	4,017	3,845	3,477	4,528	4,215	5,126	5,508	8,818
Hawaii	12,644	9,613	11,879	9,967	10,963	14,277	17,097	16,546
Idaho	3,869	4,676	4,093	6,806	7,044	6,755	9,444	16,273
Illinois	6,337	6,029	4,457	6,159	4,644	5,756	6,172	13,224
Indiana	4,023	3,811	3,374	4,852	3,170	5,228	4,127	11,282
Iowa	7,485	6,011	5,771	7,443	7,245	5,744	8,814	19,685
Kansas	4,351	3,564	3,408	4,334	6,014	6,961	10,271	17,018
Kentucky	2,363	2,379	2,471	3,004	2,787	2,870	3,732	4,400
Louisiana	3,272	3,742	4,308	3,339	4,159	4,911	5,709	11,044
Maine	6,962	2,836	3,127	5,561	5,968	5,514	5,917	20,211
Maryland	3,108	3,938	3,725	6,015	5,575	4,316	6,505	11,552
Massachusetts	6,437	4,371	5,741	6,217	6,365	5,967	6,103	7,702
Michigan	3,240	2,561	2,719	3,377	3,185	2,862	4,365	6,171
Minnesota	4,867	4,363	4,607	5,250	6,624	5,957	7,593	19,456
Mississippi	2,920	3,308	3,232	3,127	3,489	3,907	4,806	7,606
Missouri	2,411	2,254	2,709	2,557	2,867	3,029	4,223	7,921
Montana	6,893	5,160	5,376	7,245	8,890	7,169	13,448	22,063
Nebraska	6,194	5,198	4,524	6,986	6,176	6,566	9,687	17,790
Nevada	5,251	2,892	3,944	11,739	11,300	12,197	17,353	26,853
New Hampshire	4,397	3,201	4,062	4,832	4,860	5,178	6,789	6,901
New Jersey	7,591	6,684	6,458	7,535	6,571	6,057	5,314	10,823
New Mexico	5,761	4,894	5,961	6,797	8,866	8,893	9,999	16,265
New York	5,346	4,870	5,037	5,953	5,668	5,443	4,744	7,019
North Carolina	2,997	3,003	2,643	3,696	3,768	3,688	4,860	8,288
North Dakota	5,646	4,966	4,319	6,796	5,262	7,952	13,665	35,631
Ohio	3,710	2,558	3,046	3,105	3,152	2,993	3,720	5,212
Oklahoma	2,554	2,477	1,829	2,483	3,159	2,868	3,831	7,564
Oregon	3,562	3,515	3,349	4,424	3,921	3,703	5,572	11,027
Pennsylvania	2,719	3,649	3,163	4,011	4,122	3,613	3,937	5,939
Rhode Island	6,031	3,800	5,210	6,502	8,769	7,755	7,719	5,547
South Carolina	2,677	2,789	2,146	2,733	2,710	3,036	3,670	5,766
South Dakota	6,728	5,767	6,153	6,364	6,742	7,449	11,331	22,928
Tennessee	1,653	1,459	1,477	1,704	1,730	1,686	2,188	3,426
Texas	3,390	2,505	3,094	3,182	4,114	3,300	4,605	10,235
Utah	2,293	3,071	3,315	3,829	4,171	4,472	5,892	10,408
Vermont	5,346	4,317	5,161	5,978	6,671	6,906	8,466	9,028
Virginia	1,649	2,139	1,804	2,128	2,222	1,907	2,890	4,784
Washington	5,993	5,788	5,959	7,467	5,472	7,024	10,578	19,144
West Virginia	414	769	553	773	617	596	923	1,427
Wisconsin	5,012	4,199	4,858	5,051	5,160	5,796	6,240	8,562
Wyoming	5,053	5,590	4,116	4,832	5,530	5,906	11,105	14,292
Total U.S.	**4,266**	**3,867**	**3,949**	**4,672**	**4,667**	**4,879**	**6,332**	**11,639**

Farm Income—Cash Receipts from Marketings (in $1,000)

1973 State	Crops	Live-stock	Gov't Pay'ts	Total	1973 State	Crops	Live-stock	Gov't Pay'ts	Total
Alabama	405,767	896,258	51,519	1,353,544	New Jersey	193,564	111,225	2,074	306,863
Alaska	2,059	2,987	75	5,121	New Mexico	175,111	671,776	29,365	876,252
Arizona	448,307	679,159	43,061	1,170,527	New York	391,595	963,973	14,577	1,370,145
Arkansas	1,063,741	988,856	68,228	2,120,825	North				
California	4,608,105	2,564,358	105,507	7,277,970	Carolina	1,360,905	972,971	35,866	2,369,742
Colorado	549,245	1,601,697	44,053	2,194,955	North				
Connecticut	74,614	128,621	373	203,608	Dakota	1,681,371	477,173	119,431	2,277,975
Delaware	86,695	164,923	1,124	252,742	Ohio	1,054,684	1,043,150	55,838	2,153,672
Florida	1,409,821	603,814	15,486	2,029,121	Oklahoma	689,715	1,447,517	66,869	2,204,101
Georgia	790,413	1,086,052	57,079	1,933,544	Oregon	554,826	401,928	15,284	972,038
Hawaii	211,928	55,643	9,253	276,824	Pennsylva-				
Idaho	727,018	468,656	31,931	1,227,605	nia	365,953	1,014,151	15,293	1,395,397
Illinois	2,955,932	1,923,379	138,168	5,017,479	Rhode Is-				
Indiana	1,624,458	1,308,781	76,255	3,009,494	land	11,857	10,533	26	22,416
Iowa	2,813,316	4,176,691	186,189	7,176,196	South				
Kansas	1,832,867	2,335,838	150,445	4,319,150	Carolina	414,436	297,102	36,382	747,920
Kentucky	576,373	742,452	19,328	1,338,153	South				
Louisiana	737,584	407,654	43,347	1,188,585	Dakota	665,063	1,233,787	71,353	1,970,203
Maine	198,497	227,662	560	426,719	Tennessee	502,878	640,437	41,345	1,184,660
Maryland	194,034	380,601	5,763	580,398	Texas	2,824,250	3,679,806	386,554	6,890,610
Massa-					Utah	78,020	265,477	8,009	351,506
chusetts	85,784	104,701	263	190,748	Vermont	16,067	186,573	890	203,530
Michigan	783,756	709,317	38,888	1,531,961	Virginia	397,732	509,852	12,731	920,315
Minnesota	1,876,861	2,134,619	105,044	4,116,524	Washington	1,127,071	462,402	35,137	1,624,610
Mississippi	785,105	729,103	101,263	1,615,471	West Vir-				
Missouri	1,032,653	1,535,131	94,188	2,661,972	ginia	34,873	115,826	1,571	152,270
Montana	554,885	572,107	64,990	1,191,982	Wisconsin	389,001	1,892,301	39,794	2,321,096
Nebraska	1,560,758	2,398,151	151,793	4,110,702	Wyoming	85,332	328,570	12,728	426,630
Nevada	28,097	117,665	1,690	147,452					
New Hamp-					**Total**				
shire	17,336	52,834	211	70,381	**U.S.**	**41,050,313**	**45,824,240**	**2,607,191**	**89,481,744**

Average Prices Received by U.S. Farmers

Source: Economic Research Service; Department of Agriculture

The figures represent dollars per 100 lbs. for hogs, beef cattle, veal calves, sheep, lamb and milk (wholesale); dollars per head for milk cows; cents per lb. for milk fat (in cream), chickens, broilers, turkeys and wool; cents for eggs per dozen. *Revised.

Year[1]	Hogs	Cattle (beef)	Calves (veal)	Sheep	Lambs	Cows (milk)	Milk (wholesale)	Milk fat (in cream)	Chickens (excl. broilers)	Broilers	Turkeys	Eggs	Wool
1930..	8.84	7.71	9.68	4.74	7.76	74.20	2.21	34.5	...	...	20.2	23.7	19.5
1940..	5.39	7.56	8.83	3.95	8.10	61.00	1.82	28.0	13.0	17.3	15.2	18.0	28.4
1950..	18.00	23.30	26.30	11.60	25.10	198.00	3.89	62.0	22.0	27.4	32.9	36.3	62.1
1960..	15.39	20.40	22.90	5.61	17.90	223.00	4.21	60.5	12.2	16.9	25.4	36.1	42.0
1965*	19.60	19.50	22.00	8.44	22.00	312.00	4.23	61.1	8.9	15.0	22.2	33.7	47.1
1969*	22.20	26.20	31.00	8.04	27.20	300.00	5.45	60.0	9.7	15.0	39.4	40.0	41.8
1970.	22.70	27.10	34.50	7.51	20.40	366.00	5.71	70.0	9.1	13.6	22.6	39.1	35.5
1971.	17.50	29.00	36.40	6.59	25.90	358.00	5.87	69.1	7.7	13.7	41.4	31.4	19.4
1972.	25.10	33.50	44.70	7.28	29.10	397.00	6.07	67.5	8.9	14.1	22.2	30.9	35.0
1973.	38.40	42.80	56.60	12.70	35.10	496.00	7.14	67.2	15.0	24.0	38.2	52.5	82.7
1974.	34.20	35.60	35.20	11.30	37.00	500.00	8.31	62.3	9.7	21.5	28.0	53.3	59.1

The figures represent cents per bushel for oats; cents per lb. for cotton, apples and peanuts; dollars per bushel for wheat, corn, barley and soybeans; dollars per 100 lbs. for rice, sorghum and potatoes; dollars per ton for cottonseed and baled hay.

Crop Year	Corn	Wheat	Cotton	Oats	Barley	Rice	Soy-beans	Sor-ghum	Peanuts	Cotton-seed	Hay[3]	Potatoes	Apples
1930.	.663	.550	9.46	31.1	.420	1.74	1.34	1.02	3.46	22.00	11.00	1.47	...
1940.	.674	.601	9.83	29.8	.393	1.80	.692	.873	3.33	21.70	9.78	.850	...
1950.	2.00	1.52	39.90	78.8	1.19	5.09	2.47	1.88	10.9	86.60	21.10	1.50	...
1960.	1.74	.997	30.08	59.8	.838	4.55	2.13	1.49	10.0	42.50	21.70	2.00	4.79
1965.	1.16	1.16	29.26	62.2	1.02	4.93	2.54	1.76	11.4	46.70	23.20	2.53	4.32
1969*	1.16	1.25	21.86	58.4	.885	4.95	2.35	1.91	12.3	41.10	24.70	2.24	4.06
1970	1.33	1.33	22.81	62.3	.973	5.17	2.85	2.04	12.8	56.50	26.10	1.21	4.54
1971	1.08	1.34	28.07	60.5	.993	5.34	3.03	1.88	13.6	56.80	28.10	1.90	4.92
1972	1.57	1.76	27.20	72.5	1.21	6.73	4.37	2.45	14.5	49.50	31.30	3.01	6.43
1973	2.55	3.95	44.40	118.0	2.13	13.80	5.68	3.82	16.2	100.10	41.60	4.89	8.80
1974	2.95	4.04	42.80	150.0	2.72	10.45	6.69	5.00	17.9	135.70	50.60	4.35	8.20

(1) Weighted calendar year prices for livestock and livestock products other than wool. 1943 through 1963, wool prices are weighted on marketing year basis. The marketing year has been changed (1964) from a calendar year to a Dec.-Nov. basis for hogs, chickens, broilers, eggs and eggs. (2) Weighted crop year prices. Crop years are as follows: apples, June-May; wheat, oats, barley, hay and potatoes, July-June; cotton, rice, peanuts and cottonseed, August-July; soybeans, September-August; and corn and sorghum grain, October-September. (3) Beginning 1964, 480 lb. net weight bales.

Index Numbers of Prices Received by Farmers

Source: Economic Research Service; Department of Agriculture index (1910-14 = 100 per cent)

Year	All Farm Products	All Crops	Livestock[1]	Food Grains	Feed Grains and Hay	Feed Grains	Cotton	Tobacco	Oil-bearing Crops	Fruit	Commercial Vegetables[2]	Potatoes Sweetpot[3]	Meat Animals	Dairy Products	Poultry and Eggs	Wool
1910	104	105	102	109	96	97	118	84	120	100	...	83	101	100	104	117
1920	211	235	190	249	202	209	262	233	208	188	...	294	171	202	222	214
1930	125	115	134	93	106	109	104	140	111	149	128	162	133	142	128	119
1940	100	90	109	84	85	86	83	134	103	81	122	89	108	120	09	160
1950	258	233	280	224	193	198	282	402	276	194	211	166	340	249	186	341
1960	239	222	253	203	152	151	254	500	214	244	230	203	296	259	160	235
1965	248	233	261	164	174	173	245	513	265	246	261	295	319	261	145	261
1970	280	226	326	163	177	176	183	604	266	233	294	222	405	345	151	194
1973	438	370	497	379	283	280	274	718	574	332	382	394	666	428	232	449
1974	467	483	453	530	420	428	433	821	636	349	409	566	555	489	214	327

(1.) Livestock and livestock products. (2.) For fresh market and processing beg. 1952. (3.) Including dry edible beans.

Average Farm Wages

Calendar year	Per month		Per week		Per day			Per hour	
	With house	With board & room	With board & room	Without board or room	With house	With board & room	Without board or room	With house	Without board or room
1950.	$121.00	$99.00	$23.50	$31.00	$3.50	$4.45	$4.50	$.62	$.69
1955.	154.00	123.00	29.75	38.00	4.20	5.40	5.30	.74	.82
1960.	192.00	149.00	35.50	45.75	5.30	6.50	6.60	.88	.97
1965.	223.00	171.00	40.25	51.50	6.20	7.40	7.60	1.03	1.14
1970.	328.00	251.00	60.75	78.00	9.80	10.70	11.70	1.50	1.64
1971.	340.00	263.00	64.50	81.00	10.30	11.20	12.20	1.56	1.73
1972.	361.00	280.00	67.80	85.50	11.20	12.00	13.20	1.65	1.84
1973.	393.00	309.00	74.00	94.75	12.30	13.10	14.50	1.81	2.00
1974.	423.00	334.00	80.50	102.75	13.60	14.60	16.10	2.01	2.24

Government Payments by Programs, by States

Source: Economic Research Service: Department of Agriculture (in $1,000)

1973 State	Conservation[1]	Sugar Act	Wool Act	Feed Grain Program	Wheat Program	Cotton	Cropland Adjustment	Other[2]	Total
Alabama	1,835	—	8	8,260	320	38,740	2,287	69	51,519
Alaska	21	—	54	—	—	—	—	—	75
Arizona	1,305	501	1,333	3,058	642	34,963	122	1,137	43,061
Arkansas	252	—	11	1,798	831	64,920	242	174	68,228
California	2,745	15,159	4,841	10,162	3,349	68,173	111	967	105,507
Colorado	1,471	4,998	3,401	14,725	17,406	—	795	1,257	44,053
Connecticut	150	—	9	143	1	—	67	3	373
Delaware	95	—	2	811	173	—	43	—	1,124
Florida	877	8,798	5	3,605	96	1,125	967	13	15,486
Georgia	2,643	—	12	19,837	956	29,863	3,614	154	57,079
Hawaii	99	9,154	—	—	—	—	—	—	9,253
Idaho	743	6,420	2,822	4,348	17,338	—	39	221	31,931
Illinois	2,020	—	728	121,174	13,216	87	943	—	138,168
Indiana	1,863	—	476	63,539	9,293	—	1,055	29	76,255
Iowa	1,729	61	1,820	180,649	758	—	960	212	186,189
Kansas	967	1,430	954	71,771	73,646	—	966	711	150,445
Kentucky	1,188	—	170	15,023	1,301	320	1,326	—	19,328
Louisiana	546	9,590	25	1,530	210	31,167	93	186	43,347
Maine	417	—	37	50	1	—	43	12	560
Maryland	711	—	54	4,000	917	—	80	1	5,763
Massachusetts	147	—	18	48	—	—	40	10	263
Michigan	1,018	3,394	595	21,646	9,488	—	2,530	217	38,888
Minnesota	2,142	3,472	1,353	84,337	11,201	—	2,406	133	105,044
Mississippi	817	—	13	5,137	389	94,269	538	100	101,263
Missouri	2,038	—	647	59,391	11,514	18,399	2,202	−3	94,188
Montana	2,129	1,640	3,667	10,397	45,986	—	161	1,010	64,990
Nebraska	1,124	3,647	1,018	113,107	29,679	—	2,018	1,200	151,793
Nevada	591	—	529	108	259	203	—	—	1,690
New Hampshire	157	—	13	38	—	—	2	1	211
New Jersey	195	—	23	1,375	346	—	133	2	2,074
New Mexico	1,294	28	2,282	7,173	4,635	10,519	2,852	582	29,365
New York	4,342	—	226	6,061	3,094	—	851	3	14,577
North Carolina	1,119	—	34	16,858	3,522	13,133	1,196	4	35,866
North Dakota	316	2,073	1,220	34,508	78,702	—	1,273	1,339	119,431
Ohio	1,720	1,568	1,735	37,759	11,518	—	1,528	10	55,838
Oklahoma	796	—	383	13,712	31,345	18,778	791	1,064	66,869
Oregon	1,429	1,054	2,172	2,472	7,840	—	45	272	15,284
Pennsylvania	2,740	—	426	8,249	2,722	—	953	203	15,293
Rhode Island	21	—	3	2	—	—	—	—	26
South Carolina	531	—	2	7,045	1,685	25,137	1,905	77	36,382
South Dakota	717	—	4,723	38,205	25,136	—	1,307	1,265	71,353
Tennessee	1,417	—	74	10,229	1,127	27,244	1,254	—	41,345
Texas	3,280	1,112	15,814	92,299	23,820	241,181	5,950	3,098	386,554
Utah	554	858	3,002	1,167	2,358	—	45	25	8,007
Vermont	742	—	15	90	1	—	16	26	890
Virginia	2,426	—	546	6,633	2,418	195	509	4	12,731
Washington	1,497	4,480	717	4,818	22,695	—	54	876	35,137
West Virginia	506	—	473	454	104	—	34	—	1,571
Wisconsin	2,745	—	314	33,194	332	—	2,986	223	39,794
Wyoming	715	2,246	6,160	1,053	1,924	—	52	578	12,728
Total U. S.	60,942	81,683	64,959	1,142,048	474,294	718,416	47,384	17,465	2,607,191

(1) Includes amounts paid under other similar programs not listed separately.
(2). Includes Milk Indemnity Program, Bee Keepers Indemnity Program, Hay Transportation Assistance Program, Water Bank Program, and Public Access.

Cooperative Farm Credit System

Loans outstanding to farmers and farmer's co-ops. from banks and associations supervised by the Farm Credit Admin.

Year ended Dec. 31	Farm mortgage loans Federal land banks	Farm production loans Production Credit ass'ns	Loans to co-operatives by banks for cooperatives	FICB loans and discounts other than interagency	Total
1950	946,469,000	455,472,000	344,979,000	70,020,000	1,816,940,000
1955	1,497,165,000	653,478,000	370,683,000	70,785,000	2,592,111,000
1960	2,563,772,000	1,490,138,000	648,859,000	91,951,000	4,794,720,000
1965	4,280,675,000	2,598,460,000	1,055,163,000	146,091,000	8,080,389,000
1970	7,187,139,000	5,334,495,000	2,029,864,000	222,098,000	14,773,598,000
1972	9,104,930,000	6,636,075,000	2,297,805,000	252,681,000	18,291,429,000
1973	11,073,276,000	7,859,554,000	2,576,748,000	333,207,000	21,842,785,000
1974	13,863,752,000	9,560,649,000	3,575,483,000	403,402,000	27,403,286,000

Farm Employment—Annual Averages

Source: Economic Research Service; Department of Agriculture

Yr.	Total Aver. No. (1,000)	Index %	Family Aver. No. (1,000)	Index %	Hired Aver. No. (1,000)	Index %	Yr.	Total Aver. No. (1,000)	Index %	Family Aver. No. (1,000)	Index %	Hired Aver. No. (1,000)	Index %
1920	13,432	99	10,041	99	3,391	100	1960	7,057	52	5,172	52	1,885	55
1930	12,497	92	9,307	92	3,190	94	1970	4,523	34	3,348	33	1,175	35
1940	10,979	81	8,300	82	2,679	79	1973	4,337	32	3,169	31	1,168	34
1950	9,926	73	7,597	75	2,329	69	1974	4,392	32	3,076	31	1,316	35

Index (1910-14 = 100 per cent)

Farm-Mortgage Debt Outstanding by Lender Groups

Source: National Economic Analysis Division, U.S. Department of Agriculture

Year	Total farm-mortgage debt[1] $1,000	Amounts held by principal lender groups				
		Federal land banks[1] $1,000	Farmers home adminis-tration[2] $1,000	Life in-surance com-panies[3] $1,000	All commer-cial banks[4] $1,000	Other[5] $1,000
1951	6,112,286	991,439	256,724	1,352,635	985,954	2,525,534
1952	6,662,327	1,026,906	290,529	1,541,874	1,017,360	2,785,658
1953	7,240,937	1,095,257	330,087	1,716,022	1,069,398	3,030,173
1954	7,930,931	1,187,046	352,199	1,892,773	1,091,949	3,215,964
1955	8,245,278	1,279,787	378,108	2,051,784	1,161,308	3,374,291
1956	9,012,016	1,480,204	412,670	2,271,784	1,275,429	3,571,929
1957	9,821,525	1,722,381	462,942	2,476,543	1,298,113	3,861,546
1958	10,382,475	1,897,187	540,762	2,578,958	1,315,530	4,050,038
1959	11,091,390	2,065,372	608,101	2,661,229	1,407,548	4,349,140
1960	12,082,409	2,335,124	676,224	2,819,542	1,523,051	4,728,468
1961	12,820,304	2,600,014	732,070	2,974,609	1,591,762	4,000,019
1962	13,899,105	2,803,103	948,346	3,100,191	1,710,080	5,205,100
1963	15,167,821	3,024,013	1,057,923	3,391,183	1,870,216	5,824,486
1964	16,803,505	3,281,797	1,171,373	3,780,537	2,136,571	6,433,227
1965	18,894,240	3,686,755	1,284,913	4,287,671	2,416,634	7,218,267
1966	21,186,886	4,240,227	1,497,313	4,801,677	2,607,404	8,040,265
1967	23,077,186	4,914,522	1,663,067	5,213,587	2,770,010	8,516,000
1968	25,142,401	5,563,204	1,844,046	5,539,600	3,060,551	9,135,000
1969	27,397,370	6,081,229	2,054,382	5,763,500	3,333,259	10,165,000
1970	29,182,766	6,671,222	2,279,620	5,733,900	3,545,024	10,953,000
1971	30,346,083	7,145,363	2,440,043	5,610,300	3,772,377	11,378,000
1972	32,207,666	6,879,753	2,618,131	5,564,300	4,218,482	11,927,000
1973	35,757,754	9,050,067	2,835,202	5,643,300	4,792,185	13,437,000
1974	41,252,870	10,901,352	3,013,440	5,964,800	5,458,278	15,915,000
1975[6]	46,305,473	12,402,441	3,212,389	6,316,722	5,966,282	17,407,639

(1.) Includes data for joint stock land banks and Federal Farm Mortgage Corporations.
(2.) Includes both direct and insured loans.
(3.) Taken from Life Insurance Institute Tally sheet.
(4.) FDIC number after 1973 prior to 1973 estimates reflect shift of FHA Insured loans to FHA.
(5.) Estimated by ERS, USDA 1965-73 revised June, 1974.
(6.) Preliminary.

Canadian Farm Cash Receipts[1]

Source: Statistics Canada
(in millions of dollars)

Crops

Year and quarter	Total cash receipts	Total crops	Wheat[2]	Oats[2]	Barley[2]	C.W.B. Advance pay-ments[3]	Other grains[4]	Sugar beets	Pota-toes	Fruits	Vege-tables	Tobacco	Other crops[5]
1971	4,529.76	1,713.13	721.18	33.70	208.88	−84.57	290.29	18.58	63.90	84.40	99.73	135.36	131.71
1972	5,307.43	2,081.89	948.20	31.85	221.41	−27.46	312.59	20.89	86.58	84.61	115.04	150.03	138.12
1973	6,729.25	2,623.56	1,198.83	43.58	330.57	19.90	543.38	22.29	171.18	117.57	159.86	142.82	192.24
1974 1	2,060.38	1,012.37	241.77	9.66	50.12	−5.00	148.56	4.16	71.48	6.51	12.89	129.56	37.24
2	2,628.36	1,519.21	1,063.39	10.77	225.37	−8.27	113.54	4.74	54.52	7.45	9.24	9.15	29.32
3	2,097.69	946.24	387.27	14.11	159.05	−0.51	172.45	5.76	46.71	55.74	62.10	—	43.58

Livestock and Products

Year & Quarter	Total	Cattle	Hogs	Sheep	Dairy Products	Poultry	Eggs	Other	Total forest and maple products	Dairy sup-plementary payments	Deficiency payments
1971	2,697.74	1,079.97	443.55	7.90	705.70	262.58	151.72	46.34	17.31	100.35	1.24
1972	3,076.56	1,195.84	575.71	9.06	778.82	295.85	163.77	57.31	24.46	101.41	23.10
1973	3,930.54	1,479.51	831.85	10.67	850.01	437.94	243.79	76.77	43.99	131.02	0.13
1974 1	1,012.23	400.55	217.62	3.07	200.76	98.13	70.52	21.59	2.70	30.01	3.08
2	1,038.06	391.61	169.47	2.18	287.05	108.59	67.51	11.66	17.72	41.31	12.07
3	1,057.04	322.39	187.55	3.03	315.78	148.52	62.71	17.05	7.60	82.23	11.41

[1]Cash receipts from farming operations excluding supplementary payments. Excludes Newfoundland. [2]Including particip-ation payments made by the Canadian Wheat Board direct to producers on crops delivered in previous years. [3]Net cash. [4]Includes rye, flaxseed, rapeseed, soybeans, and corn. [5]Includes clover and grass seed, hay, clover, greenhouse products, mustard seed, sunflower seed, hops, dry beans and dry peas and miscellaneous products.

Canada-Farm Cash Receipts from Farming Operations

Source: Statistics Canada
(thousands of dollars)

Province	1969	1970	1972	1973	1974
Prince Edward Island	37,870	44,533	44,017	73,520	83,286
Nova Scotia	63,380	65,855	70,147	93,281	101,580
New Brunswick	51,281	57,526	64,151	94,916	102,930
Quebec	672,495	654,285	776,678	951,583	1,107,380
Ontario	1,378,868	1,393,263	1,581,364	1,920,608	2,313,998
Manitoba	350,409	340,364	484,370	629,307	819,981
Saskatchewan	718,329	725,200	1,200,782	1,435,077	1,941,776
Alberta	729,598	715,344	921,794	1,219,505	1,609,077
British Columbia	197,589	212,004	243,447	323,477	368,132
Total	4,199,819	4,208,374	5,386,750	6,741,274	8,448,140

Farmers' Marketing, Farm Supply, Related Service Cooperatives

Source: Farmer Cooperative Service, U.S. Dept. of Agriculture (Marketing Season 1971-72[1])

A marketing season includes the period during which the farm products of a specified year are moved into the channels of trade. Marketing seasons overlap.

State	Cooperatives No.	Memberships	Net business[2] ($1,000)	State	Cooperatives No.	Memberships	Net business[2] ($1,000)
Alabama	68	70	194,082	Montana	225	81,790	130,237
Alaska	2	350	2,655	Nebraska	338	262,530	683,545
Arizona	17	85,150	133,612	Nevada	3	885	8,104
Arkansas	106	107,955	465,732	New Hampshire	5	2,830	36,927
California	293	93,675	[2]2,160,329	New Jersey	41	17,000	129,819
Colorado	87	50,145	352,376	New Mexico	22	7,325	53,221
Connecticut	13	5,470	82,595	New York	279	136,220	1,007,799
Delaware	8	13,360	21,143	North Carolina	33	147,370	332,136
Florida	90	53,735	560,199	North Dakota	668	262,855	441,629
Georgia	84	173,940	417,957	Ohio	202	220,330	756,115
Hawaii	19	1,485	[2]16,227	Oklahoma	154	137,870	356,489
Idaho	64	46,005	202,676	Oregon	71	59,415	326,235
Illinois	305	318,090	1,160,747	Pennsylvania	111	78,450	609,325
Indiana	114	412,520	689,507	Rhode Island	1	795	14,277
Iowa	468	373,230	1,487,111	South Carolina	24	38,985	112,988
Kansas	268	202,455	779,242	South Dakota	322	175,690	269,452
Kentucky	80	201,845	275,375	Tennessee	109	146,075	261,278
Louisiana	92	16,845	163,271	Texas	460	142,445	784,171
Maine	11	10,105	70,189	Utah	46	25,560	192,912
Maryland	39	47,595	193,820	Vermont	10	7,715	139,334
Massachusetts	16	10,215	118,011	Virginia	115	182,590	337,819
Michigan	147	129,655	609,514	Washington	152	109,225	519,542
Minnesota	1,095	589,960	1,436,927	West Virginia	61	50,890	57,607
Mississippi	131	126,235	361,098	Wisconsin	521	442,610	1,435,091
Missouri	165	250,165	566,212	Wyoming	31	11,255	34,157

(1) Preliminary. (2). The volume of a Hawaiian sugar coop based in Calif. is included in the dollar volume of Calif.

Food Stamps—Costs and Benefits

Source: U.S. Department of Agriculture

Fiscal Year	Average No. Persons participating per month	Value per year Total purchase	Bonus	Avg. bonus per participant per month Current $	1967$
1962	142,817	35,202,266	13,152,695	7.67	8.47
1965	424,652	85,471,989	32,505,096	6.38	6.75
1967	1,447,105	296,106,484	105,550,172	6.08	6.08
1968	2,211,474	451,800,893	173,142,015	6.52	6.26
1969	2,878,113	603,351,143	228,818,622	6.63	6.04
1970	4,340,030	1,089,960,761	549,663,811	10.55	9.07
1971	9,367,908	2,713,273,217	1,522,749,091	13.55	11.17
1972	11,109,074	3,308,647,916	1,797,285,786	13.48	10.77
1973	12,165,682	3,883,952,103	2,131,404,604	14.60	11.67
1974	12,895,709	4,724,267,407	2,714,070,651	17.54	11.87
1975 (9 mos.)	16,329,825	5,187,844,038	3,116,836,844	21.21	13.49

The Food Stamp Program enables low income families to buy more food of greater variety to improve their diets. If a household meets eligibility requirements (a family of 4 must have a net income lower than $570 per month), it is assigned an allotment of stamps based on the number of people in the household ($154 worth of stamps per month for 4 people). The family must pay a portion of the value of the stamps, but that portion must not exceed 30% of the net income ($122 if the family of 4 has a net income between $420 and $450). The value of the stamps in excess of the amount paid is the "bonus," the value of the free food.

Federal Food Program Costs, 1971-1975 (Calendar Years)

Source: U.S. Department of Agriculture, Food and Nutrition Service (millions of Dollars)

Year	Food Stamps Total Issued	Bonus Stamps[1]	Food Distribution[2] Needy Families	Supp. Food	Schools	Institutions	Child Nutrition School Lunch	School Bkfst.	Special Food	Special Milk	Total
1971	3,105	1,699	318	13	296	26	647	22	34	92	3,147
1972	3,614	1,981	271	13	282	27	807	28	43	90	3,541
1973	4,046	2,208	224	14	337	27	962	44	52	63	3,913
1974[3]	5,859	3,489	114	16	390	21	1,150	68	89	88	5,425
1975 1st Qtr.	2,002	1,228	4	4	145	6	423	27	13	38	1,888
2nd Qtr.	2,092	1,271	4	5	77	3	285	23	20	32	1,770

[1]Includes Food Certificate Program. [2]Cost of food delivered to state distribution centers. [3]Includes estimates for third and fourth quarters.

Canadian Harvested Acreage

Source: Statistics Canada

Principal Crops[1] (in thousands of acres)

Province	1971	1972	1973	1974	Province	1971	1972	1973	1974
Prince Edward Island	394	315	328	333	Manitoba	9,304	8,923	12,619	12,129
Nova Scotia	254	189	191	192	Saskatchewan	27,584	25,147	42,768	41,860
New Brunswick	373	282	288	291	Alberta	18,406	17,302	22,937	22,167
Quebec	4,728	3,889	3,910	3,941	British Columbia	871	933	976	1,031
Ontario	7,618	7,798	7,970	8,058	Total[2]	69,532	85,803	92,211	90,199

[1]Crops included are winter wheat, spring wheat, oats, barley, fall rye, spring rye, flaxseed, mixed grains, corn for grain, buckwheat, peas, dry beans, soybeans, rapeseed, potatoes, mustard seed, sunflower seed, tame hay, fodder corn, field roots, and sugar beets.
[2]Excluding Newfoundland.

Agricultural Products, Production, and Exports

Source: Foreign Agricultural Service, Dept. of Agriculture

Commodity[1]	Unit	Production U.S.	Production World	Production %U.S.	Exports U.S.	Exports World	Exports %U.S.
Wheat, grain only	Mil. M.T.	46.4	346.8	13.4	[2,3]31.2	[2,3]68.0	45.7
Oats	Mil. M.T.	6.0	53.9	11.1	[3]0.7	[2]1.7	41.2
Corn	Mil. M.T.	118.1	279.2	42.3	[2]35.0	[2]54.4	64.3
Barley	Mil. M.T.	9.2	158.1	5.8	[2]1.9	[2]12.9	14.7
Soybeans	Mil. M.T.	33.6	51.5	65.2	14.0	17.0	82.4
Rice	Mil. M.T.	[4]5.2	[4]308.7	1.7	[5]1.6	[5]11.0	14.5
Lard	1,000 M.T.	[4]568.0	[4]3,692.1	15.4	51.4	426.5	42.1
Tallow & Grease	1,000 M.T.	[4]2,412.2	[4]4,412.9	54.7	1,014.1	1,611.2	62.9
Tobacco, Unmftd	1,000 M.T.	890.0	5,170.0	17.2	254.0	1,060.0	24.0
Edible Veg. Oils[6]	Mil. M.T.	[7]8.3	29.7	28.1	[3]3.9	[9]9.8	39.8
Cotton	1,000 Bales[10]	13,332	62,370	21.4	6,119.0	19,578	31.3

[1]Crop 1973-74 as follows: wheat, oats and barley year beginning July 1; corn, October 1; soybeans, September 1, rice and cotton, August 1; other commodities on calendar year 1973 and partially estimated. Excludes Alaska, Hawaii, and Puerto Rico except for exports. [2] Fiscal year 1973-74. [3] Includes wheat flour in grain equivalent. [4] Calendar year. [5] Milled rice. [6] Includes palm oils. [7] Includes oil equivalent of exported oilseeds. [8] Excludes reexports and exports of oil produced from imported raw materials. [9] Exports from producing countries. [10] Bales of 480 pound, net weight.

Civilian Consumption of Major Food Commodities per Person

Source: Economic Research Service: Department of Agriculture

Commodity[1]	Avg. (lbs.) 1957-59	1973	1974	Commodity[1]	Avg. (lbs.) 1957-59	1973	1974
Meats (carcass wt.)	156.6	175.7	187.3	Other (exc. melons)	40.5	33.8	35.5
Beef	85.1	109.6	116.3	Processed:			
Veal	7.1	1.8	2.3	Canned fruit	22.4	21.3	19.4
Lamb and mutton	4.4	2.7	2.4	Canned juice	13.5	16.3	14.6
Pork (excl. lard)	63.0	61.6	66.3	Frozen (inc. Juices)	8.6	11.2	11.9
Fish (edible wt.)	10.5	12.7	12.0	Dried	3.3	2.8	3.0
Poultry products				Vegetables			
Eggs (farm Basis), No.	356	294	286	Fresh[2]	104.1	99.9	100.4
Chicken (ready to cook)	27.5	41.5	41.7	Canned, excl. potatoes	43.3	54.3	52.3
Turkey (ready to cook)	6.0	8.7	9.0	Frozen, excl. pot.	6.6	10.7	10.1
Dairy products				Potatoes, fresh equiv.	106.9	116.5	117.5
Cheese	7.9	13.7	14.5	Sweet potatoes, fresh	8.3	5.1	5.5
Cond. and evap. milk	14.8	6.0	5.3	Grains			
Fluid milk and cream	337	257	244	Cornmeal and flour	7.4	7.5	7.6
Ice Cream (prod. wt.)	18.4	17.5	17.6	Corn syrup	9.4	21.7	23.0
Fats and Oils-Total, fat content	45.3	54.0	52.5	Corn sugar	3.6	5.2	5.3
Butter (actual wt.)	8.2	4.8	4.5	Wheat flour[3]	120	109	106
Margarine (act. wt.)	8.9	11.3	11.3	Wheat cereals	2.8	2.9	2.9
Lard	9.3	3.4	3.2	Rice, milled	5.4	7.0	7.3
Shortening	11.4	17.3	16.5	Other			
Other edible fats and oils	10.8	21.3	20.2	Coffee (green beans)	15.7	13.7	12.8
Fruits				Tea	.58	.79	.80
Fresh	95.5	75.6	80.0	Cocoa Beans	3.5	4.2	3.7
Citrus	34.0	27.3	28.8	Peanuts (shelled)	4.6	6.6	6.4
Apples (com.)	21.0	14.5	15.7	Melons	25.1	21.8	19.1
				Sugar (refined)	96.1	102.1	97.0

[1]Quantity in pounds except for eggs. Data on calendar year basis except for dried fruits, which are on pack-year basis, fresh citrus fruits and peanuts on a crop-year basis, and rice on August 1 year. Fresh citrus year begins in previous October and rice year begins in previous August. [2]Commercial production for sale as fresh produce. [3]Includes white, whole wheat, and semolina flour.

Recommended Daily Dietary Allowances

The Recommended Daily Dietary Allowances are amounts of nutrients recommended by the Food and Nutrition Board of the National Research council as adequate for maintenance of good nutrition in healthy persons in the U.S. The minimum daily requirements for the adult man are: Vitamin A, 4,000 I.U.; thiamin 1 milligram; riboflavin 1.2 mg.; niacin 10 mg.; ascorbic acid 30 mg.; Calcium 750 mg.; iron 10 mg.

	Years From-up to	Wgt. (lbs.)	Hgt. (in.)	Calories	Protein (grams)	Calcium (grams)	Iron (mg.)	Vit. A (IU)	Thiamin (mg.)	Riboflavin (mg.)	Niacin (mg.)	Ascorbic acid (mg.)
Infants	0-1/6	9	22	lb. × 54.5	lb. × 1.0	0.4	6	1,500	0.2	0.4	5	35
	1/6-1/2	15	25	lb. × 50.0	lb. × .9	0.5	10	1,500	0.4	0.5	7	35
	1/2-1	20	28	lb. × 45.5	lb. × .8	0.6	15	1,500	0.5	0.6	8	35
Children	1-2	26	32	1,100	25	0.7	15	2,000	0.6	0.6	8	40
	2-3	31	36	1,250	25	0.8	15	2,000	0.6	0.7	8	40
	3-4	35	39	1,400	30	0.8	10	2,500	0.7	0.8	9	40
	4-6	42	43	1,600	30	0.8	10	2,500	0.8	0.9	11	40
	6-8	51	48	2,000	35	0.9	10	3,500	1.0	1.1	13	40
	8-10	62	52	2,200	40	1.0 [5]	10	3,500	1.1	1.2	15	40
Boys	10-12	77	55	2,500	45	1.2	10	4,500	1.3	1.3	17	40
	12-14	95	59	2,700	50	1.4	18	5,000	1.4	1.4	18	45
	14-18	130	67	3,000	60	1.4	18	5,000	1.5	1.5	20	55
Men	18-22	147	69	2,800	60	0.8	10	5,000	1.4	1.6	18	60
	22-35	154	69	2,800	65	0.8	10	5,000	1.4	1.7	18	60
	35-55	154	68	2,600	65	0.8	10	5,000	1.3	1.7	17	60
	55-75×	154	67	2,400	65	0.8	10	5,000	1.2	1.7	14	60
Girls	10-12	77	57	2,250	50	1.2	18	4,500	1.1	1.3	15	40
	12-14	97	61	2,300	50	1.3	18	5,000	1.2	1.4	16	45
	14-16	114	62	2,400	55	1.3	18	5,000	1.2	1.4	16	50
	16-18	119	63	2,300	55	1.3	18	5,000	1.2	1.5	15	50
Women	18-22	128	64	2,000	55	0.8	18	5,000	1.0	1.5	13	44
	22-35	128	64	2,000	55	0.8	18	5,000	1.0	1.5	13	44
	35-55	128	63	1,850	55	0.8	10	5,000	1.0	1.5	13	55
	55-75×	128	62	1,700	55	0.8	10	5,000	1.0	1.5	13	55
Pregnant				×200	65	×0.4	18	6,000	×0.1	1.8	15	60
Lactating				×1,000	75	×0.5	18	8,000	×0.5	2.0	20	60

Nutritive Value of Foods (Calories, Proteins, etc.)

Source: Home and Garden Bulletin No. 72, U. S. Department of Agriculture

Available for 75c from Supt. of Documents, U. S. Government Printing Office, Washington, D. C. 20402

Food	Measure	Water %	Food Energy (Calories)	Protein (grams)	Fat (grams)	Carbohydrate (grams)	Calcium (mg)	Iron (mg)	Vit. A (I.U.)	Thiamin (mg)	Riboflavin (mg)	Niacin (mg)	Ascorbic acid (mg)
Milk, Cream, Cheese													
Milk, fluid, whole, 3.5% fat	1 cup	87	160	9	9	12	288	0.1	350	0.07	0.41	0.2	2
Milk, fluid nonfat (skim)	1 cup	90	90	9	T	12	296	.1	10	.09	.44	.2	2
Buttermilk, fluid, cultured, made from skim milk	1 cup	90	90	9	T	12	296	.1	10	.10	.44	.2	2
Cheese, Roquefort type	1 oz.	40	105	6	9	1	89	.1	350	.01	.17	.3	0
Cheese, Cottage, creamed	12 oz.	78	360	46	14	10	320	1.0	580	.10	.85	.3	0
Cream, half-and-half	1 cup	80	325	8	28	11	261	.1	1,160	.07	.39	.1	2
Cream, heavy	1 cup	57	840	5	90	7	179	.1	3,670	.05	.26	.1	2
Custard, baked	1 cup	77	305	14	15	29	297	1.1	930	.11	.50	.3	1
Yoghurt, whole milk	1 cup	88	150	7	8	12	272	.1	340	.07	.39	.2	2
Eggs (large)													
Raw	1 egg	74	80	6	6	T	27	1.1	590	.05	.15	T	0
Scrambled (milk and fat)	1 egg	72	110	7	8	1	51	1.1	690	.05	.18	T	0
Meat, Poultry													
Bacon	2 sli.	8	90	5	8	1	2	.5	0	.08	.05	.8	...
Beef, lean and fat	3 oz.	53	245	23	16	0	10	2.9	30	.04	.18	3.5	...
Hamburger, regular	3 oz.	54	245	21	17	0	9	2.7	30	.07	.18	4.6	...
Steak, broiled, lean and fat	3 oz.	44	330	20	27	0	9	2.5	50	.05	.16	4.0	...
Corned beef	3 oz.	59	185	22	10	0	17	3.7	20	.01	.20	2.9	...
Chicken, cooked:													
Flesh only, broiled	3 oz.	71	115	20	3	0	8	1.4	80	.05	.16	7.4	...
With bone, 1/2 breast, fried	3.3 oz.	58	155	25	5	1	9	1.3	70	.04	.17	11.2	...
Chicken, potpie, baked	8 oz.	57	535	23	31	42	68	3.0	3,020	.25	.26	4.1	5
Lamb chop, thick with bone	4.8 oz.	47	400	25	33	0	10	1.5	...	.14	.25	5.6	...
Lamb, lean and fat	3 oz.	54	235	22	16	0	9	1.4	...	.13	.23	4.7	...
Liver, beef, fried	2 oz.	57	130	15	6	3	6	5.0	30,280	.15	2.37	9.4	15
Ham, light cure, lean	3 oz.	54	245	18	19	0	8	2.2	0	.40	.16	3.1	...
Boiled ham, sliced	2 oz.	59	135	11	10	0	6	1.6	0	.25	.09	1.5	...
Pork roast, lean and fat	3 oz.	46	310	21	24	0	9	2.7	0	.78	.22	4.7	...
Frankfurter, heated	2 oz.	57	170	7	15	1	3	.8	...	.08	.11	1.4	...
Veal cutlet	3 oz.	60	185	23	9	...	9	2.7	...	.06	.21	4.6	...
Veal roast	3 oz.	55	230	23	14	0	10	2.9	...	.11	.26	6.6	...
Fish													
Bluefish, baked with fat	3 oz.	68	135	22	4	0	25	.6	40	.09	.08	1.6	...
Clams, raw, meat only	3 oz.	82	65	11	1	2	59	5.2	90	.08	.15	1.1	8
Crabmeat, canned	3 oz.	77	85	15	2	1	38	.7	...	.07	.07	1.6	...
Oyster, raw, meat	1 cup	85	160	20	4	8	226	13.2	740	.33	.43	6.0	...
Salmon, pink, canned	3 oz.	71	120	17	5	0	167	.7	60	.03	.16	6.8	...
Shrimp, canned, meat	3 oz.	70	100	21	1	1	98	2.6	50	.01	.03	1.5	...
Swordfish, broiled with butter	3 oz.	65	150	24	5	0	23	1.1	1,750	.03	.04	9.3	...
Tuna, canned in oil	3 oz.	61	170	24	7	0	7	1.6	70	.04	.10	10.1	...
Nuts													
Almonds, shelled, whole	1 cup	5	850	26	77	28	332	6.7	0	.34	1.31	5.0	T
Cashew nuts, roasted	1 cup	5	785	24	64	41	53	5.3	140	.60	.35	2.5	...
Peanuts, roasted	1 cup	2	840	37	72	27	107	3.0	...	.46	.19	24.7	0
Pecans, halves	1 cup	3	740	10	77	16	79	2.6	140	.93	.14	1.0	2
Walnuts, black or native, chopped	1 cup	3	790	26	75	19	T	7.6	380	.28	.14	.9	...
Vegetables & Products													
Asparagus, cooked, spears	4 sp.	94	10	1	T	2	13	.4	540	.10	.11	.8	16
Asparagus, canned	1 cup	94	45	5	1	7	44	4.1	1,240	.15	.22	2.0	37
Beans, lima, immature, cooked	1 cup	71	190	13	1	34	80	4.3	480	.31	.17	2.2	29
Beans, snap, green, cooked	1 cup	92	30	2	T	7	63	.8	680	.09	.11	.6	15
Beans, snap, canned, green	1 cup	94	45	2	T	10	81	2.9	690	.07	.10	.7	10
Beans, snap, yellow or wax	1 cup	93	30	2	T	6	63	0.8	290	.09	.11	.6	16
Beans, sprouted mung, cooked	1 cup	91	35	4	T	7	21	1.1	30	.11	.13	.9	8
Beets, cooked	2 beets	91	30	1	T	7	14	.5	20	.03	.04	.3	6
Broccoli, cooked	1 stalk	91	45	6	1	8	158	1.4	4,500	.16	.36	1.4	162
Brussels sprouts, cooked	1 cup	88	55	7	1	10	50	1.7	810	.12	.22	1.2	135
Cabbage, raw, shredded	1 cup	92	15	1	T	4	34	.3	90	.04	.04	.2	33
Cabbage, cooked	1 cup	94	30	2	T	6	64	.4	190	.06	.06	.4	48
Carrot, raw 5 1/2 by 1 in.	One	88	20	1	T	5	18	.4	5,500	.03	.03	.3	4
Carrots, cooked, diced	1 cup	91	45	1	T	10	48	.9	15,220	.08	.07	.7	9
Cauliflower, cooked, flower buds	1 cup	93	25	3	T	5	25	.8	70	.11	.10	.7	66
Celery, raw, stalk, large	1 stalk	94	5	T	T	2	16	.1	100	.01	.01	.1	4
Corn, cooked, ear 5 x 1 3/4 in.	1 ear	74	70	3	1	16	2	.5	310	.09	.08	1.0	7
Corn, canned	1 cup	81	170	5	2	40	10	1.0	690	.07	.12	2.3	13
Cucumbers, raw, pared	10 oz.	96	30	1	T	7	35	.6	T	.07	.09	.4	23
Lettuce, Boston type	1 head	95	30	3	T	6	77	4.4	2,130	.14	.13	.6	18
Mushrooms, canned	1 cup	93	40	5	T	6	15	1.2	T	.04	.60	4.8	4
Onion, mature, raw, 2 1/2 in.	One	89	40	2	T	10	30	.6	40	.04	.04	.2	11
Peas, green, cooked	1 cup	82	115	9	1	19	37	2.9	860	.44	.17	3.7	33
Peas, green, canned	1 cup	83	165	9	1	31	50	4.2	1,120	.23	.13	2.2	22
Potato, medium, baked	One	75	90	3	T	21	9	.7	T	.10	.04	1.7	20
Potato, medium, boiled in skin	One	80	105	3	T	23	10	.8	T	.13	.05	2.0	22
Potatoes, mashed, milk added	1 cup	83	125	4	1	25	47	.8	50	.16	.10	2.0	19
Potato chips, medium	10 chips	2	115	1	8	10	8	.4	T	.04	.01	1.0	3
Sauerkraut, canned	1 cup	93	45	2	T	9	85	1.2	120	.07	.09	.4	33
Spinach, cooked	1 cup	92	40	5	1	6	167	4.0	14,580	.13	.25	1.0	50
Squash, summer, diced, cooked	1 cup	96	30	2	T	7	52	.8	820	.10	.16	1.6	21
Squash, winter, baked, mashed	1 cup	81	130	4	1	32	57	1.6	8,610	.10	.27	1.4	27
Sweet potato, baked	1	64	155	2	1	36	44	1.0	8,910	.10	.07	.7	24

Continued

Continued

Food	Measure	Water %	Food Energy (Calories)	Protein (grams)	Fat (grams)	Carbohydrate (grams)	Calcium (mg)	Iron (mg)	Vit. A (I.U.)	Thiamin (mg)	Riboflavin (mg)	Niacin (mg)	Ascorbic acid (mg)
Sweet potato, candied 3½ by 2¼ in.	1	60	295	2	6	60	65	1.6	11,030	.10	.08	.8	17
Tomato, raw, medium	1	94	40	2	T	9	24	.9	1,640	.11	.07	1.3	42
Tomato catsup, tablespoon.	1 tbsp.	69	15	T	T	4	3	.1	210	.01	.01	.2	2
Tomato juice, canned.	1 cup	94	45	2	T	10	17	2.2	1,940	.12	.07	1.9	39
Fruits and Fruit Products													
Apple, medium, raw	One	85	70	T	T	18	8	.4	50	.04	.02	.1	3
Apple, bottled or canned.	1 cup	88	120	T	T	30	15	1.5	. . .	.02	.05	.2	2
Applesauce, canned, sweetened.	1 cup	76	230	1	T	61	10	1.3	100	.05	.03	.1	3
Banana, raw 6 by 1½ in.	1	76	100	1	T	26	10	.8	230	.06	.07	.8	12
Blueberries, raw.	1 cup	83	85	1	1	21	21	1.4	140	.04	.08	.6	20
Cantaloupe, raw, medium.	½ melon	91	60	1	T	14	27	.8	6,540	.08	.06	1.2	63
Cranberry sauce, sweetened, canned	1 cup	62	405	T	1	104	17	.6	60	.03	.03	.1	6
Grapefruit, raw, medium, white.	½	89	45	1	T	12	19	.5	10	.05	.02	.2	44
Grapefruit juice, canned, unsweetened.	1 cup	89	100	1	T	24	20	1.0	20	.07	.04	.4	84
Grapes, raw, American type.	1 cup	82	65	1	1	15	15	.4	100	.05	.03	.2	3
Grapejuice, canned.	1 cup	83	165	1	T	42	28	.8	. . .	.10	.05	.5	T
Lemon, raw, medium	One	90	20	1	T	6	19	.4	10	.03	.01	.1	39
Lemon juice, raw.	1 cup	91	60	1	T	20	17	.5	50	.07	.02	.2	112
Lime juice, fresh.	1 cup	90	65	1	T	22	22	.5	20	.05	.02	.2	79
Orange, raw, 2⅝ in. diam.	One	86	65	1	T	16	54	.5	260	.13	.05	.5	66
Orange juice, frozen, undiluted.	6 oz. can	55	360	5	T	87	75	.9	1,620	.68	.11	2.8	360
Peach, raw, whole, medium.	One	89	35	1	T	10	9	.5	1,320	.02	.05	1.0	7
Peaches, canned, halves or sliced.	1 cup	79	200	1	T	52	10	.8	1,100	.02	.06	1.4	7
Pear, 3 by 2½ in.	One	83	100	1	1	25	13	.5	30	.04	.07	.2	7
Pineapple, canned, sliced.	Large sli.	80	90	T	T	24	13	.4	50	.09	.03	.2	8
Plums, raw, 2 in. diam.	1 plum	87	25	T	T	7	7	.3	140	.02	.02	.3	3
Prune juice, canned.	1 cup	80	200	1	T	49	36	10.5	. . .	.03	.03	1.0	5
Raisins, seedless, pkged. ½ oz.	1 pkg.	18	40	T	T	11	9	.5	T	.02	.01	.1	T
Strawberries, raw, capped.	1 cup	90	55	1	1	13	31	1.5	90	.04	.10	1.0	88
Watermelon, raw, wedge.	1 wedge	93	115	2	1	27	30	2.1	2,510	.13	.13	.7	30
Grain Products													
Bagel, 3 in. diam, egg.	One	32	165	6	2	28	9	1.2	30	.14	.10	1.2	0
Biscuit, baking powder.	One	27	105	2	5	13	34	.4	T	.06	.06	.1	T
Bran flakes (40% bran).	1 cup	3	105	4	1	28	25	12.3	0	.14	.06	2.2	0
Bread, cracked wheat.	1 loaf	35	1,190	40	10	236	399	5.0	T	.53	.41	5.9	0
Bread, enriched, French.	1 loaf	31	1,315	41	14	251	195	10.0	T	1.27	1.00	11.3	0
Bread, enriched, Italian.	1 loaf	32	1,250	41	4	256	77	10.0	0	1.32	.91	11.8	0
Bread, raisin, loaf.	1 loaf	35	1,190	30	13	243	322	5.9	T	.23	.41	3.2	T
Bread, American, rye.	1 loaf	36	1,100	41	5	236	340	7.3	0	.82	.32	6.4	0
Bread, white, enriched.	1 loaf	36	1,225	39	15	229	381	11.3	T	1.13	.95	10.9	0
Cake, angel food.	1 cake	34	1,645	36	1	377	603	1.9	0	.03	.70	.6	0
Cupcake, small, choc. icing.	1 cake	22	130	2	5	21	47	.3	60	.01	.04	.1	T
Cake, Boston cream pie.	1 pce.	35	210	4	6	34	46	.3	140	.02	.08	.1	T
Cake, pound.	1 loaf	17	2,430	29	152	242	108	4.1	1,440	.15	.46	1.0	0
Saltines.	4	. . .	50	1	1	8	2	.1	0	T	T	.1	0
Danish Pastry, round piece.	1 pastry	22	275	5	15	30	33	.6	200	.05	.05	T	T
Doughnut, cake type.	One	24	125	1	6	16	13	.4	30	.05	.05	.4	T
Macaroni, enriched, cooked.	1 cup	64	190	6	1	39	14	1.4	0	.23	.14	1.8	0
Noodles, enriched.	1 cup	70	200	7	2	37	16	1.4	110	.22	.13	1.9	0
Oatmeal, or rolled oats, cooked.	1 cup	87	130	5	2	23	22	1.4	0	.19	.05	.2	0
Pie, apple, ⅐ of 9-in. pie.	1 sector	48	350	3	15	51	11	.4	40	.03	.03	.5	1
Pie, custard, ⅐ of 9-in. pie.	1 sector	58	285	8	14	30	125	.8	300	.07	.21	.4	0
Pie, lemon meringue, ⅐ of 9-in. pie.	1 sector	47	305	4	12	45	17	.6	200	.04	.10	.2	4
Pie, mince, ⅐ of 9-in. pie.	1 sector	43	365	3	16	56	38	1.4	T	.09	.05	.5	1
Pie, pumpkin, ⅐ of 9-in. pie.	1 sector	59	275	5	15	32	66	.7	3,210	.04	.13	.7	T
Pizza (cheese) ⅛ of 14 in. diam.	1 sector	45	185	7	6	27	107	.7	290	.04	.12	.7	4
Popcorn, plain.	1 cup	4	25	1	1	5	1	.2	. . .	. . .	.01	.1	0
Roll, home recipe.	1 roll	26	120	3	3	20	16	.7	30	.09	.09	.8	T
Spaghetti, enriched, cooked.	1 cup	72	155	5	1	32	11	1.3	0	.20	.11	1.5	0
Fats, Oils													
Butter, regular.	½ cup	16	810	1	92	1	23	0	3,750	. . .	. . .	. . .	0
Lard.	1 cup	0	1,850	0	205	0	0	0	0	0	0	0	0
Vegetable fats.	1 cup	0	1,770	0	200	0	0	0	. . .	0	0	0	0
Margarine.	½ cup	16	815	1	92	1	23	0	3,750	. . .	. . .	. . .	0
Salad dressing, French, regular.	1 tbsp.	39	65	T	6	3	2	.1	. . .	. . .	. . .	. . .	. . .
Salad dressing, mayonnaise.	1 tbsp.	15	100	T	11	T	3	.1	40	T	.01	T	. . .
Salad dressing, 1,000 island.	1 tbsp.	32	80	T	8	3	2	.1	50	T	T	T	T
Sugars, Sweets													
Candy, milk chocolate, sweetened.	1 oz.	1	145	2	9	16	65	.3	80	.02	.10	.1	T
Candy, plain fudge.	1 oz.	8	115	1	4	21	22	.3	T	.01	.03	.1	T
Chocolate syrup, fudge type.	1 oz.	25	125	2	5	20	48	.5	60	.02	.08	.2	T
Honey, strained or extracted.	1 tbsp.	17	65	T	0	17	1	.1	0	T	.01	.1	T
Jellies.	1 tbsp.	29	50	T	T	13	4	.3	T	T	.01	T	1
Sugar, brown.	1 cup	2	820	0	0	212	187	7.5	0	.02	.07	4	0
Sugar, granulated.	1 cup	T	770	0	0	199	0	.2	0	0	0	0	0
Miscellaneous													
Barbecue sauce.	1 cup	81	230	4	17	20	53	2.0	900	.03	.03	.8	13
Beer.	12 oz.	92	150	1	0	14	18	T	. . .	.01	.11	2.2	. . .
Alcoholic beverage, 86-proof.	1½ fl. oz.	64	105	. . .	. . .	T	. . .	. . .	. . .	. . .	. . .	. . .	. . .
Cola-type beverage.	12 fl. oz.	90	145	0	0	37	. . .	. . .	0	0	0	0	0
Ginger ale.	12 fl. oz.	92	115	0	0	29	. . .	. . .	0	0	0	0	0
Soup, cream of chicken.	1 cup	85	180	7	10	15	172	.5	610	.05	.27	.7	2
Soup, tomato.	1 cup	84	175	7	7	23	168	.8	1,200	.10	.25	1.3	15
Beans with pork.	1 cup	84	170	8	6	22	63	2.3	650	.13	.08	1.0	3
Clam chowder.	1 cup	92	80	2	3	12	34	1.0	880	.02	.02	1.0	. . .

T indicates a trace.

Giant Trees of the United States

Source: The American Forestry Association

There are 865 species of trees native to the continental U.S. including a few imports that have become naturalized to the extent of reproducing themselves in the wild state.

The oldest living trees in the world are reputed to be the bristlecone pines, the majority of which are found growing on the arid crags of California's White Mts. Some of them are estimated to be more than 4,600 years old. The largest known bristlecone pine is the "Patriarch," believed to be 1,500 years old. The oldest known redwoods are about 3,500 years old.

Recognition as the National Champion of each species is determined by total mass of each tree, based on this formula: the circumference in inches as measured at a point 4½ feet above the ground plus the total height of the tree, plus ¼ of the average crown spread in feet. In case of a tie the Champion is determined on the basis of circumference. It is not possible, due to lack of space, to list all the 865 trees registered with the American Forestry Assn.

(Figure in parentheses is year tree was reported)

Species	Height (Ft.)	Location
Acacia, Koa (1969)	14	Kau, Ha.
Ailanthus, Tree-of-Heaven (1955)	60	Long Island, N.Y.
Alder, European (1974)	68	Princeton, Ill.
Apple, Southern Crab (1968)	40	Columbia, S.C.
Ash, Blue (1970)	86	Danville, Ky.
Aspen, Bigtooth (1963)	93	Walker, N.Y.
Bald cypress, Common (1950)	122	nr. Sharon, Tenn.
Basswood, American (1971)	115	Grand Traverse Cty., Mich.
Bayberry, Pacific (1961)	38	Siuslaw Natl. Forest, Ore.
Beech, American (1970)	108	Ashtabula, Oh.
Birch, River (1974)	95	Cumberland For., Va.
Blackbead, Catlaw (1972)	81	Ft. Myers, Fla.
Blackhaw, Rusty (1961)	25	Nr. Washington, Ark.
Bladdernut, American (1966)	36	nr. Utica, Mich.
Boxelder (1972)	95	Washtenaw Co., Mich.
Buckeye, Painted (1970)	144	Union County, Ga.
Buckthorn, Cascara (1945)	60	nr. Rockport, Wash.
Buckwheat tree (1967)	30	nr. Crooked Creek, Fla.
Buffaloberry, Silver (1970)	20.5	Inyo Natl. Forest, Cal.
Bumelia, Gum (1964)	52	nr. Fairfield, Tex.
Butternut (1968)	102	Portland, Ore.
Buttonbush, Common (1974)	21	San Felasco Hammock, Fla.
Button-Mangrove (1974)	52	Palm Beach, Fla.
Cajeput (1975)	66	Sarasota, Fla.
Camphor-tree (1974)	65	Mulberry, Fla.
Casuarina, Horsetail (1968)	89	Olowalo, Maui, Ha.
Catalpa, Northern (1962)	94	Lansing, Mich.
Cedar, Port-Orford (1968)	219	Siskiyou Natl. Forest, Ore.
Cercocarpus, Birchleaf (1972)	34	Central Point, Ore.
Cherry, Black (1959)	114	Lawrence, Mich.
Chestnut, American (1964)	91	Oregon City, Ore.
Chinaberry (1967)	75	Kaohe, S. Kona, Ha.
Chinkapin, Golden (1954)	127	nr. Annapolis, Calif.
Coconut (1968)	94	Hilo, Ha.
Coffeetree, Kentucky (1966)	101	Bryn Mawr. Pa.
(1973)	82	Lake County, Oh.
Chokecherry, Common (1967)	66	Ada, Mich.
Cottonwood, Black (1969)	147	Unionvalle, Ore.
Cypress, Monterey (1975)	97	Brockings, Ore.
Dahoon (1975)	72	Osceola For., Fla.
Desertwillow (1971)	40	Gila Nat'l. Forest, N.M.
Devil's-walkingstick (1974)	41	San Felasco Hammock, Fla.
Devilwood (1967)	37	Mayo, Fla.
Dogwood, Pacific (1972)	60	Keizer, Ore.
Douglas Fir (1975)	302	Coos Bay, Ore.
Doveplum (1965)	45	Miami, Fla.
Ebony, Mountain (1967)	46	Ellenton, Fla.
Elder, Blackbead (1954)	42	nr. Prescott, Ore.
Elm, American (1974)	92	White Creek, N.Y.
False-Mastic (1975)	70	Lignumvitae Key, Fla.
Fig, Florida Strangler (1973)	80	Old Cutler Hammock, Fla.
Fir, Noble (1964)	278	Gifford Pinchot Natl. Forest Wash.
Franklinia (1973)	38	McLean, Va.
Grapefruit (1967)	38	Ellenton, Fla.
Gumbo-limbo (1973)	50	Castello Hammock, Fla.
Hackberry, Common (1972)	118	Wayland, Mich.
Hawthorn (1967)	50	Glenview, Ill.
Hemlock, Western (1954)	163	Olympic Natl. Pk., Wash.
Hercules-club (1961)	38	Little Rock, Ark.
Hickory, Pignut (1970)	125	nr. Brunswick, Ga.
Holly, Tawnyberry (1973)	55	Homestead, Fla.

Species	Height (Ft.)	Location
Honeylocust, Thornless (1970)	128	Mt. Erie, Ill.
Hophornbeam, Eastern (1945)	78	nr. Winthrop, Me.
Hoptree, Common (1972)	31	Ada, Mich.
Hornbeam, American (1975)	65	Milton, N.Y.
Joshua-tree (1967)	32	San Bernardino Natl. Forest, Calif.
Juniper, Western (1945)	87	Stanislaus Natl. Forest, Calif.
Larch, Western (1945)	177	nr. Kootenai Natl. Forest, Mont.
Laurelcherry, Carolina (1970)	44	Dellwood, Fla.
Lebbek (1968)	65	Lahina, Maui, Ha.
Loblolly-Bay (1963)	84	Hugh's Island, Fla.
Locust, Black (1974)	96	Dansville, N.Y.
Lysiloma, Bahama (1955)	48	Key Largo, Fla.
Madrone, Pacific (1955)	79	Ettersburg, Cal.
Magnolia, Cucumber tree (1974)	92	Bel Air, Md.
Mangrove, Red (1973)	60	North Miami, Fla.
Maple, Red (1964)	125	nr. Armada, Mich.
Mesquite, Velvet (1949)	55	Coronado Natl. Forest, Ariz.
Mountain-Ash, Showy (1968)	58	nr. Gould City, Mich.
Mountain-Laurel (1970)	20	Chattahoochee Natl. Forest, Ga.
Mulberry, White (1970)	77	St. Joseph Co., Mich.
(1973)	68	Logan Co., Ill.
Oak, California white (1967)	120	Nr. Gridley, Calif.
Oleander, Common (1963)	22	Phoenix, Ariz.
Osage-Orange (1969)	51	Charlotte Cty., Va.
Palmetto, Cabbage (1965)	90	Highlands Hammock State Pk., Fla.
Paloverde, Blue (1967)	52	Ajo, Ariz.
Paulownia, Royal (1969)	105	Philadelphia Cty., Pa.
Pawpaw, Blue (1971)	41	nr. Smith Mills, Ky.
Pear (1966)	51	Clawson, Oakland Co., Mich.
(1972)	74	Leslie Co., Ky.
Pecan (1973)	124	Mer Rouge, La.
Peppertree (1969)	47	San Juan Capistrano, Cal.
Pinckney (1968)	21	nr. Mt. Pleasant, Fla.
Pine, ponderosa (1974)	223	Plumas, Cal.
Planertree (1967)	77	nr. Chattahoochee, Fla.
Plum, American (1972)	35	Oakland Co., Mich.
Poison Sumac (1972)	20	Robin's Island, N.Y.
Pondcypress (1969)	135	nr. Newton, Ga.
Poplar, Balsam (1969)	98	So. Egremont, Mass.
Posumhaw (1970)	25	Richland Cty., S.C.
Redbay (1971)	58	Randolph Cty., Ga.
Redwood, Coast (1966)	362	Humboldt Redwoods State Park, Calif.
Royalpalm, Florida (1973)	80	Homestead, Fla.
Sassafras (1954)	100	Owensboro, Ky.
Seagrape (1972)	57	Miami, Fla.
Sequoia, Giant (1945)	272	Sequoia Natl. Pk., Calif.
Serviceberry, Downy (1975)	50	New Philadelphia, Oh.
Silk-oak (1972)	78	nr. La Belle, Fla.
Silktree (1971)	41	Gilmer, Tex.
Silverbell, Two-wing (1971)	55	Tallahassee, Fla.
Smoketree, American (1971)	48	Lewiston, Ida.
Soapberry, Western (1969)	67	Newton County, Tex.
Sourwood (1968)	118	nr. Robbinsville, N.C.
Sparkleberry tree (1970)	29	Keltys, Texas
Spruce, Sitka (1973)	216	Seaside, Ore.

Continued

Species	Height (Ft.)	Location	Species	Height (Ft.)	Location
Sugarberry (1974)	133	Darlington, S.C.	Tupelo, Black (1969)	117	Harrison Co., Tex.
Sumac, Shining (1974)	55	Grenada, Miss.	(1971)	139	Nr. Easterly, Tex.
Sweetleak,			Wahoo, Eastern (1974)	20	Warrensburg, Mo.
Common (1967)	55	Tallahassee, Fla.	Walnut, California (1973)	116	Santa Rosa, Calif.
Sycamore, Calif. (1945)	116	nr. Santa Barbara, Calif.	Willow, Crack (1964)	112	nr. Utica, Mich.
			Winterberry,		
Tallowtree (1967	42	Polk County, Tex.	Common (1971)	40	Wildwood, Fla.
Tamarack (1966)	95	Jay, Me.	Witch-Hazel,		
Tamarisk,			Common (1967)	44	Franklin, Mich.
Five-Stamen (1967)	37	Albuquerque, N.M.	Yaupon (1964)	45	nr. Devers, Tex.
Tanoak (1969)	100	Kneeland, Calif.	Yellow-Poplar (1972)	124	Bedford, Va.
Tesota (1972)	31.6	nr. Quartzsite, Ariz.	Yellowwood (1964)	58	Morrisville, Pa.
Torreya, California (1945)	141	nr. Mendocino, Calif.	Yew, Pacific (1959)	60	nr. Mineral, Wash.
Trifoliate-Orange (1968)	26	Harrisburg, Pa.	Yucca, Aloe (1975)	29	Ormond By The Sea, Fla.

The 1973-1974 Wildfire Season

Source: Forest Service, U. S. Dept. of Agriculture
Federal, State and Private Protected Area

In 1974 one of the nation's major forest fires was caused by a careless person's campfire at Forks of the Kern River in the Sequoia National Forest California. It spread out of control for eight days, damaging 16,980 acres of watershed, golden trout habitat, and an estimated 13 million board feet of timber.

Almost 94 percent of all fires were controlled at 10 acres or less in size on the 210 million acres of Forest Service protected lands. Less than one percent were large fires burning over 300 acres. These accounted for approximately 79 percent of burned acreage. Forest fires burned .99 acres for each 1,000 acres protected.

All fires increased 7 percent over previous years. However, 13,538 fires burned only 208,721 acres. Aggressive prevention measures followed by hard-hitting attack forces reduced the potential for major conflagrations on national forests.

On federal, state, and private forest and nonforested watershed lands during 1974, a total of 145,868 fires were reported, an increase of 27,911 over the 117,957 reported during 1973. However, acreage burned on all lands totaled 2,879,095, an increase of 963,822 acres over the 1,915,273 acres burned during 1973.

Through carelessness or incendiarism, man is blamed for the largest portion of wildfires. During 1974 some 108,264 or 90 percent of the 120,875 reported as having burned on protected land were man-caused. Lightning-started fires amounted to 12,611 or 10 percent of the protected area fires. Causes of the 24,993 fires which occurred on unprotected lands are not known.

More than 708,129,000 acres of state and private forest and nonforested watershed lands are protected under the federal-state cooperative Forest Fire Control Program. Since the area qualifying for protection under the program is 771,964,000 acres, the goal of the program is to bring protection to the more than 63,835,000 acres not now receiving protection. All states participate in the cooperative forest fire protection effort. The record on state and private protected lands for 1974 follows:

Group	Number of Fires	Acres Burned
Rocky Mountain	9,827	308,948
Pacific	13,228	127,768
North Central	8,231	74,317
Southern	58,382	938,489
Eastern	16,167	61,925
Total	105,835	1,511,447

The record on state and private unprotected lands is:

Rocky Mountain	410	21,393
North Central	380	14,000
Southern	2,203	132,235
Eastern	22,000	(no data)
Total	24,993	167,618

Total Fires and Acres Burned — National Forest Protection

Calendar Year	Lightning	Man Caused	Total	Acres Burned	Calendar Year	Lightning	Man Caused	Total	Acres Burned
1967	6,790	4,981	11,771	204,106	1973	6,376	6,048	12,424	168,692
1970	7,804	7,172	14,976	519,978	1974	6,601	6,937	13,538	208,721
1971	5,876	6,363	12,239	171,867	Average				
1972	8,406	5,748	14,154	116,703	1967-74	6,365	6,050	12,415	214,141

National Forest Areas

Source: Forest Service, Dept. of Agriculture.
(In Acres) Data as of June 30, 1974

States	Area	States	Area	States	Area	States	Area
Alabama	636,517	Iowa	4,749	N. Hampshire	679,254	Tennessee	617,574
Alaska	20,715,704	Kansas	107,700	N. Mexico	9,081,531	Texas	661,518
Arizona	11,357,700	Kentucky	520,964	New York	13,232	Utah	7,991,474
Arkansas	2,459,498	Louisiana	595,321	N. Carolina	1,141,936	Vermont	250,581
California	20,046,568	Maine	40,563	N. Dakota	1,104,789	Virgin Islands	147
Colorado	13,749,403	Michigan	2,694,338	Ohio	161,956	Virginia	1,587,512
Connecticut	10	Minnesota	2,709,172	Oklahoma	244,424	Washington	9,067,271
Florida	1,082,109	Mississippi	1,135,589	Oregon	15,334,865	W. Virginia	952,625
Georgia	843,060	Missouri	1,434,330	Pennsylvania	501,898	Wisconsin	1,491,319
Idaho	20,315,266	Montana	16,709,684	Puerto Rico	27,954	Wyoming	8,679,729
Illinois	245,840	Nebraska	256,921	S. Carolina	606,825	Total	
Indiana	177,289	Nevada	5,110,634	S. Dakota	1,129,120	Acreage	184,276,463

National Forest System

Administered by the Forest Service, U. S. Dept. of Agriculture, the National Forest System is made up of 155 national forests, 19 national grasslands, 17 land utilization projects, and other minor acreages which total 187,101,120 acres in 44 states, Puerto Rico, and the Virgin Islands. All lands within the National Forest System are managed under two guiding principles; multiple use — the management of lands to make each area yield the combination of uses best suited to public needs; and sustained yield — maintenance of a continuous supply of all forest resources through wise use, management, and protection.

National forest lands which supply water for agriculture, industry, recreation, and domestic use, for example, also are managed to prevent erosion and help control floods, yet there also may be camping, skiing, and timber harvesting on the same land.

The scenic beauty and recreation opportunities available on national forests yearly draw millions of Americans to these lands to hunt, fish, camp, picnic, boat, recreational play, swim, hike, ski, and to make pack trips into the wilderness. Use reached 192,915,800 visitor days during calendar year 1974.

Giant Trees of Canada

Source: Native Trees of Canada by R. C. Hosie

(Canadian Forestry Service Dept. of Fisheries & Forestry)

There are nearly 140 species of trees native to Canada on which information is easily available. A "native" tree is defined as a single-stemmed perennial woody plant growing to a height of more than ten feet, and which is indigenous to Canada. Most of the 'giant' trees in Canada are to be found in the Forest Regions. These regions reflect differences caused by terrain, soil, and climate. The nine Forest Regions are: The Grassland, Boreal, Great Lakes-St. Lawrence, Columbia, Deciduous, Coast, Subalpine, Acadian and Montane.

It is difficult to obtain precise records of single trees of outstanding heights. Given below are several common species of trees native to Canada showing the usual or normal height of the species. But many exceptions have been noted. For example, the Douglas Fir, whose average range in height is given at 150 to 200 ft. with diameters of up to 9 ft., occasionally may attain heights above 300 ft. and diameters of 15 ft. or more. The Sitka Spruce is also known to have reached heights of at least 280 ft., and the Western White Pine is recorded as having attained 200 ft.

Species	Height (Ft.)	Forest Region
Alpine Fir	65-100	Subalpine; N.W. Boreal
Amabilis Fir	80-125	Coast & Coastal parts of Subalpine
Balsam Poplar	60-80	Boreal, Great Lakes-St. Lawrence & Acadian
Black Cottonwood	80-125	Throughout B.C. and Western Alberta
Black Maple	80-90	Ontario to Montreal Is.
Douglas-Fir	150-200	Coast
Eastern Cottonwood	75-100	Gt. Lakes-St. Lawrence
Eastern White Pine	100-175	Through east Canada
Engelmann Spruce	100-120	Southern Subalpine
Grand Fir	100-125	S. Coast & Columbia
Mockernut Hickory	75-90	Deciduous
Silver Maple	80-90	S.E. Parts of G. Lakes-St. Lawrence

Species	Height (Ft.)	Forest Region
Sitka Spruce	125-175	Coast
Sugar Maple	80-90	Gt. Lakes-St. Lawrence
Sycamore	Up to 150	Deciduous
Western Hemlock	120-160	Coast & Columbia
Western Larch	100-180	Southern part of Columbia & Montane, B.C.
Western Red Cedar	150-200	Coast & Columbia
Western White Pine	90-110	S. Coast & Columbia
White Birch	Med.-80	Throughout Canada
White Elm	60-80	G. Lakes-St. Lawrence & Acadian
White Oak	Med.-100	Southern Ontario
White Spruce	80-120	Boreal
Yellow Cypress	60-80	Coast & in coastal parts of Subalpine

The 1973 Forest Fire Season in Canada

Source: Environment Canada (Canadian Forestry Service)

Forest fire activity in 1973 was mainly concentrated in western Canada. British Columbia experienced by far the busiest fire season of any region with some 2,862 fires reported in that province alone (37% of the national total) and the Northwest Territories accounted for 2,114,595 acres or 72% of the total area burned in Canada.

However, for the second consecutive year, the total number of forest fires reported in Canada was substantially below the near record established in 1971. Indeed, there were 7,605 fire starts in 1973, compared with 8,263 in 1972 and 9,205 the previous year.

Over the year, whether through negligence or incendiarism, man has generally been blamed for the largest portion of wildland fires. This remained true in 1973, with 5,524 or 73% of all fires in Canada being of human origin. It must be pointed out, however, that man-caused fires in 1973 only accounted for 141,525 acres or less than 5% of the total area burned. Lightning — the only unpreventable cause of forest fires — was responsible for 27% of the fires but accounted for 2,785,185 acres burned or an increase of one million acres over the previous five-year average.

The total area afforded some form of organized protection in 1973 amounted to approximately 1,689,000 square miles.

Forest Fires on Provincial and Federal Protected Lands, 1973

Provincial Lands	No. of Fires	Acres Burned
Newfoundland	102	21,704
Nova Scotia	457	5,884
Prince Edward Island	40	387
New Brunswick	299	889
Quebec	506	7,492
Ontario	1,111	8,913
Manitoba	615	57,784
Saskatchewan	432	589,611
Alberta	478	26,418
British Columbia	2,862	82,508
Federal Lands		
Yukon	109	3,588
Northwest Territories	492	2,114,595
National Parks	90	6,899
Other Federal Lands	12	38
Total all lands	**7,605**	**2,926,710**

Total Fires and Acres Burned, by Causes

	Man-Caused		Lightning			Man-Caused		Lightning	
Year	No. of Fires	Acres Burned	No. of Fires	Acres Burned	Year	No. of Fires	Acres Burned	No. of Fires	Acres Burned
1968	5,917	1,904,476	1,384	307,129	1972	5,739	716,932	2,524	1,211,000
1969	5,003	809,063	1,658	1,522,641	Average				
1970	6,014	400,447	3,299	2,217,690	'68-'72	5,792	906,179	2,357	1,741,479
1971	6,287	699,978	2,918	3,448,933	1973	5,524	141,525	2,081	2,785,185

Superlative United States Statistics
Source: National Geographic Society, Washington, D.C.

Area for fifty states	Total	3,615,122 sq. mi
	Land 3,536,855 sq. mi. — Water 78,267 sq. mi.	
Largest state	Alaska	586,412 sq. mi
Smallest state	Rhode Island	1,214 sq. mi
Largest county	San Bernardino County, California	20,119 sq. mi
Smallest county	New York, New York	
Northernmost city	Barrow, Alaska	*71° 17′N.
Northernmost point	Point Barrow, Alaska	*71° 23′N.
Southernmost city	Hilo, Island of Hawaii	19° 43′N.
Southernmost town	Naalehu, Island of Hawaii	19° 03′N.
Southernmost point	Ka Lae (South Cape), Island of Hawaii	18°56′N. (155° 41′W.)
Easternmost city	Eastport Maine	66°59′W.
Easternmost town	Lubec, Maine	66° 59′W.
Easternmost point	West Quoddy Head, Maine	66° 57′W.
Westernmost city	Lihue, Island of Kauai, Hawaii	159° 22′W.
Westernmost town	Adak, Aleutians, Alaska	176° 45′W.
Westernmost point	Cape Wrangell, Attu Island, Aleutians, Alaska	172° 27′E
Highest city	Leadville, Colorado	10,200 ft.
Lowest town	Calipatria, California	−183 ft.
Highest point on Atlantic coast	Cadillac Mountain, Mount Desert Is., Maine	1,530 ft.
Largest and oldest national park	Yellowstone National Park (1872), Wyoming	3,472 sq. mi
	Montana, Idaho	
Largest national monument	Glacier Bay, Alaska	4,381 sq. mi.
Highest waterfall	Yosemite Falls—Total in three sections	2,425 ft.
	Upper Yosemite Fall	1,430 ft.
	Cascades in middle section	675 ft.
	Lower Yosemite Fall	320 ft.
Longest river	Mississippi-Missouri	3,710 mi.
Highest mountain	Mount McKinley, Alaska	20,320 ft.
Lowest point	Death Valley, California	−282 ft.
Deepest lake	Crater Lake, Oregon	1,932 ft.
Rainest spot	Mt. Waialeale, Hawaii . . . . Annual Aver. rainfall 460 inches	
Largest gorge	Grand Canyon, Colorado River, Arizona; 217 miles	
	long, 4 to 18 miles wide, 1 mile deep	
Deepest gorge	Hells Canyon, Snake River, Idaho;	7,900 ft.
Strongest surface wind	Mount Washington, New Hampshire recorded 1934	231 mph
Biggest dam	Ft. Peck, Missouri River, Montana. . . 125,628,000 cu. yds. material used	
Tallest building	Sears Tower, Chicago, Illinois.	1,454 ft.
Largest building	Boeing 747 Manufacturing Plant, Everett, Washington, 205,600,000	
	cu. ft.; covers 47 acres.	
Tallest structure	TV tower, Blanchard, North Dakota	2,063 ft.
Longest bridge span	Verrazano-Narrows, New York;	4,260 ft.
Highest bridge	Royal Gorge, Colorado; . . . . 1,053 ft. above water	
Deepest well	Gas well, Washita County, Oklahoma	31,441 ft.

The Forty-Nine States, Including Alaska

Area for forty-nine states	Total	3,608,672 sq. mi.
	Land 3,530,430 sq. mi. — Water 78,242 sq. mi.	

The Forty-Eight States

Area for forty-eight states	Total	3,022,260 sq. mi.
	Land 2,963,998 sq. mi. — Water 58,262 sq. mi.	
Largest state	Texas	267,338 sq. mi.
Northernmost town	Angle Inlet, Minnesota	49° 22′N.
Northernmost point	Northwest Angle, Minnesota	49° 23′N.
Southernmost city	Key West, Florida	24° 33′N.
Southernmost mainland city	Florida City, Florida	25° 27′N.
Southernmost point	Key West Florida	24° 33′N.
Westernmost town	La Push, Washington	124° 38′W.
Westernmost point	Cape Alava, Washington	124° 44′W.
Highest mountain	Mount Whitney, California	14,494 ft.

Note to users: The distinction between cities and towns varies from state to state. In this table the U.S. Bureau of the Census usage was followed.

Statistical Information About the United States

In the *Statistical Abstract of the United States* the Bureau of the Census of the Social and Economic Statistics Administration, U.S. Dept. of Commerce annually publishes a summary of social, political and economic information. A book of more than 1,000 pages, it presents in 33 sections comprehensive data on population, housing, health, education, employment, income, prices, business, banking, science, defense, trade, government finance, foreign country comparison and other subjects. Special features include comprehensive data for metropolitan areas and a summary of recent trends. The book is prepared under the direction of William Lerner, Data User Services Office, Bureau of the Census. Supplements to the *Statistical Abstract* are *Pocket Data Book USA, 1973, County and City Data Book, 1972; Congressional District Data Book, 93rd Congress; Historical Statistics of the United States, Colonial Times to 1970.* Information concerning these and other publications may be obtained from the Supt. of Documents, Government Printing Office, Wash., D.C. 20402, or from the U.S. Bureau of the Census, Data User Services Office, Wash., D.C. 20233.

Geodetic Datum Point of North America

The geodetic datum point of the United States is the National Ocean Survey's triangulation station Meades Ranch in Osborne County, Kansas, at latitude 39° 13′26′′, 686 N and longitude 98° 32′30′′, 506 W. (Frequently this is referred to as the geodetic center of the U.S., which has no meaning.) This geodetic datum point is a fundamental point from which all latitude and longitude computations originate for North America and Central America.

Highest and Lowest Altitudes in the United States

Source: U. S. Geological Survey. (Minus sign means below sea level; elevations are in feet.)

State	Highest Point Name	County	Elev.	Lowest Point Name	County	Elev.
Alabama	Cheaha Mountain	Cleburne	2,407	Gulf of Mexico		Sea level
Alaska	Mount McKinley		20,320	Pacific Ocean		Sea level
Arizona	Humphreys Peak	Coconino	12,633	Colorado R.	Yuma	70
Arkansas	Magazine Mountain	Logan	2,753	Ouachita R.	Ashley Union	55
California	Mount Whitney	Inyo-Tulare	14,494	Death Valley	Inyo	−282
Canal Zone	Cerro Galera	Balboa District	1,205	Atlantic Ocean		Sea level
Colorado	Mount Elbert	Lake	14,433	Arkansas R.	Prowers	3,350
Connecticut	Mount Frissell	Litchfield	2,380	L. I. Sound		Sea level
Delaware	On Ebright Road	New Castle	442	Atlantic Ocean		Sea level
Dist. of Col.	Tenleytown	N. W. part	410	Potomac R.		1
Florida	West boundary	Walton	345	Atlantic Ocean		Sea level
Georgia	Brasstown Bald	Towns-Union	4,784	Atlantic Ocean		Sea level
Guam	Mount Lamlam	Agat District	1,329	Pacific Ocean		Sea level
Hawaii	Mauna Kea	Hawaii	13,796	Pacific Ocean		Sea level
Idaho	Borah Peak	Custer	12,662	Snake R.	Nez Perce	710
Illinois	Charles Mound	Jo Daviess	1,235	Mississippi R.	Alexander	279
Indiana	Franklin Township	Wayne	1,257	Ohio R.	Posey	320
Iowa	NE of Sibley	Osceola	1,670	Mississippi R.	Lee	480
Kansas	Mount Sunflower	Wallace	4,039	Verdigris R.	Montgomery	680
Kentucky	Black Mountain	Harlan	4,145	Mississippi R.	Fulton	257
Louisiana	Driskill Mountain	Bienville	535	New Orleans	Orleans	−5
Maine	Mount Katahdin	Piscataquis	5,268	Atlantic Ocean		Sea level
Maryland	Backbone Mountain	Garrett	3,360	Atlantic Ocean		Sea level
Massachusetts	Mount Greylock	Berkshire	3,491	Atlantic Ocean		Sea level
Michigan	Mount Curwood	Baraga	1,980	Lake Erie		572
Minnesota	Eagle Mountain	Cook	2,301	Lake Superior		602
Mississippi	Woodall Mountain	Tishomingo	806	Gulf of Mexico		Sea level
Missouri	Taum Sauk Mt.	Iron	1,772	St. Francis R.	Dunklin	230
Montana	Granite Peak	Park	12,799	Kootenai R.	Lincoln	1,800
Nebraska	Johnson Township	Kimball	5,426	S.E. cor. State	Richardson	840
Nevada	Boundary Peak	Esmeralda	13,140	Colorado R.	Clark	470
New Hampshire	Mt. Washington	Coos	6,288	Atlantic Ocean		Sea level
New Jersey	High Point	Sussex	1,803	Atlantic Ocean		Sea level
New Mexico	Wheeler Peak	Taos	13,161	Red Bluff Res.	Eddy	2,817
New York	Mount Marcy	Essex	5,344	Atlantic Ocean		Sea level
North Carolina	Mount Mitchell	Yancey	6,684	Atlantic Ocean		Sea level
North Dakota	White Butte	Slope	3,506	Red River	Pembina	750
Ohio	Campbell Hill	Logan	1,550	Ohio R.	Hamilton	433
Oklahoma	Black Mesa	Cimarron	4,973	Little River	McCurtain	287
Oregon	Mount Hood	Clakamas-Hood, R.	11,235	Pacific Ocean		Sea level
Pennsylvania	Mt. Davis	Somerset	3,213	Delaware R.	Delaware	Sea level
Puerto Rico	Cerro de Punta	Ponce	4,389	Atlantic Ocean		Sea level
Rhode Island	Jerimoth Hill	Providence	812	Atlantic Ocean		Sea level
Samoa	Lata Mtn.	Tau Island	3,160	Pacific Ocean		Sea level
South Carolina	Sassafras Mountain	Pickens	3,560	Atlantic Ocean		Sea level
South Dakota	Harney Peak	Pennington	7,242	Big Stone Lake	Roberts	962
Tennessee	Clingmans Dome	Sevier	6,643	Mississippi R.	Shelby	182
Texas	Guadalupe Peak	Culberson	8,751	Gulf of Mexico		Sea level
Utah	Kings Peak	Duchesne	13,528	Beaverdam Cr.	Washington	2,000
Vermont	Mount Mansfield	Lamoille	4,393	Lake Champlain	Franklin	95
Virginia	Mount Rogers	Grayson-Smyth	5,729	Atlantic Ocean		Sea level
Virgin Islands	Crown Mt.	Is. St. Thomas	1,556	Atlantic Ocean		Sea level
Washington	Mount Rainier	Pierce	14,410	Pacific Ocean		Sea level
West Virginia	Spruce Knob	Pendleton	4,863	Potomac R.	Jefferson	240
Wisconsin	Timms Hill	Price	1,952	Lake Michigan		581
Wyoming	Gannett Peak	Fremont	13,804	B. Fourche R.	Crook	3,100

U. S. Coastline by States*

Source: NOAA, Department of Commerce

State	Coastline[1]	Shoreline[2]	State	Coastline[1]	Shoreline[2]
Atlantic Coast	2,069	28,673	Gulf coast	1,631	17,141
Connecticut	(-)	618	Alabama	53	607
Delaware	28	381	Florida	770	5,095
Florida	580	3,331	Louisiana	397	7,721
Georgia	100	2,344	Mississippi	44	359
Maine	228	3,478	Texas	367	3,359
Maryland	31	3,190	Pacific coast	7,623	40,298
Massachusetts	192	1,519	Alaska	5,580	31,383
New Hampshire	13	131	California	840	3,427
New Jersey	130	1,792	Hawaii	750	1,052
New York	127	1,850	Oregon	296	1,410
North Carolina	301	3,375	Washington	157	3,026
Pennsylvania	(-)	89	Arctic coast, Alaska	1,060	2,521
Rhode Island	40	384			
South Carolina	187	2,876	United States	12,383	88,633
Virginia	112	3,315			

*In statute miles (Apr. 1, 1961). (-) Represents zero.

(1) Figures are lengths of general outline of seacoast. Measurements were made with a unit measure of 30 minutes of latitude on charts as near the scale of 1:1,200,000 as possible. Coastline of sounds and bays is included to a point where they narrow to width of unit measure, and includes the distance across at such point.

(2) Figures obtained in 1939-40 with a recording instrument on the largest-scale charts and maps then available. Shoreline of outer coast, offshore islands, sounds, bays, rivers and creeks is included to the head of tidewater or to a point where tidal waters narrow to a width of 100 feet.

International Boundary Lines of the United States

The length of the northern boundary of the conterminous United States — the U.S.-Canadian border, excluding Alaska — is 3,987 miles according to the U.S. Geological Survey, Dept. of the Interior. The length of the Alaskan-Canadian border is 1,538 miles. The length of the U.S.-Mexican border, from the Gulf of Mexico to the Pacific Ocean, is approximately 1,933 miles (1963 boundary agreement).

States: Settled, Capitals, Entry into Union, Area, Rank

The Original Thirteen States—The 13 colonies that seceded from Great Britain and fought the War of Independence (AMERICAN Revolution) became the 13 original states. They were Massachusetts, Rhode Island, Connecticut, New Hampshire, New York, New Jersey, Pennsylvania, Delaware, Maryland, Virginia, North Carolina, South Carolina and Georgia.

State	Set-tled*	Capital	Entered Union Date	Order**	Extent in Miles Long	Wide	Area in square miles Land	Inland Water	Total	Rank in Area
Ala......	1702..	Montgomery......	Dec. 14, 1819	22	330	200	50,708	901	51,609	29
Alaska....	1784..	Juneau...........	Jan. 3, 1959	49	(a)900	800	566,432	19,980	586,412	1
Ariz.....	1848..	Phoenix..........	Feb. 14, 1912	48	390	335	113,417	492	113,909	6
Ark......	1785..	Little Rock......	Jun. 15, 1836	25	275	240	51,945	1,159	53,104	27
Cal......	1769..	Sacramento......	Sept. 9, 1850	31	770	375	156,361	2,332	158,693	3
Col......	1858..	Denver...........	Aug. 1, 1876	38	390	270	103,766	481	104,247	8
Conn....	1635..	Hartford..........	Jan. 9, 1788	5	90	75	4,862	139	5,009	48
Del....	1683..	Dover............	Dec. 7, 1787	1	110	35	1,982	75	2,057	49
D.C.		Washington.......					61	6	67	51
Fla......	1565..	Tallahassee......	Mar. 3, 1845	27	460	400	54,090	4,470	58,560	22
Ga......	1733..	Atlanta...........	Jan. 2, 1788	4	315	250	58,073	803	58,876	21
Hawaii		Honolulu..........	Aug. 21, 1959	50	...	...	6,425	25	6,450	47
Ida.....	1842..	Boise............	Jul. 3, 1890	43	490	305	82,677	880	83,557	13
Ill.....	1720..	Springfield.......	Dec. 3, 1818	21	380	205	55,748	652	56,400	24
Ind.....	1733..	Indianapolis......	Dec. 11, 1816	19	265	160	36,097	102	36,291	38
Ia......	1788..	Des Moines......	Dec. 28, 1846	29	300	210	55,941	349	56,290	25
Kan.....	1727..	Topeka..........	Jan. 29, 1861	34	400	200	81,787	477	82,264	14
Ky......	1774..	Frankfort........	Jun. 1, 1792	15	350	175	39,650	745	40,395	37
La......	1699..	Baton Rouge......	Apr. 30, 1812	18	280	275	44,930	3,593	48,523	31
Me......	1624..	Augusta..........	Mar. 15, 1820	23	235	205	30,920	2,295	33,215	39
Md......	1634..	Annapolis........	Apr. 28, 1788	7	200	120	9,891	686	10,577	42
Mass....	1620..	Boston...........	Feb. 6, 1788	6	190	110	7,826	431	8,257	45
Mich....	1668..	Lansing..........	Jan. 26, 1837	26	400	310	56,817	1,399	58,216	23
Minn....	1805..	St. Paul.........	May 11, 1858	32	400	350	79,289	4,779	84,068	12
Miss....	1699..	Jackson..........	Dec. 10, 1817	20	340	180	47,296	420	47,716	32
Mo......	1735..	Jefferson City......	Aug. 10, 1821	24	300	280	68,995	691	69,686	19
Mon.....	1809..	Helena...........	Nov. 8, 1889	41	580	315	145,587	1,551	147,138	4
Neb.....	1847..	Lincoln..........	Mar. 1, 1867	37	415	205	76,483	744	77,227	15
Nev.....	1850..	Carson City......	Oct. 31, 1864	36	485	315	109,889	651	110,540	7
N.H.....	1623..	Concord.........	Jun. 21, 1788	9	185	90	9,027	277	9,304	44
N.J.....	1664..	Trenton..........	Dec. 18, 1787	3	160	70	7,521	315	7,836	46
N.M.....	1605..	Santa Fe........	Jan. 6, 1912	47	390	350	121,412	254	121,666	5
N.Y.....	1614..	Albany...........	Jul. 26, 1788	11	320	310	47,831	1,745	49,576	30
N.C.....	1650..	Raleigh..........	Nov. 21, 1789	12	500	200	48,798	3,788	52,586	28
N.D.....	1766..	Bismarck........	Nov. 2, 1889	39	360	210	69,273	1,392	70,665	17
Oh......	1788..	Columbus........	Mar. 1, 1803	17	230	205	40,975	247	41,222	35
Okla....	1889..	Oklahoma City....	Nov.	46	585	210	68,782	1,137	69,919	18
Ore.....	1811..	Salem...........	Feb. , 1859	33	375	290	96,184	797	96,981	10
Pa......	1682..	Harrisburg.......	D. 12, 1787	2	300	180	44,966	367	45,333	33
R.I.....	1636..	Providence.......	May 29, 1790	13	50	35	1,049	165	1,214	50
S.C.....	1670..	Columbia.........	May 23, 1788	8	285	215	30,225	830	31,055	40
S.D.....	1856..	Pierre...........	Nov. 2, 1889	40	380	245	75,955	1,092	77,047	16
Tenn....	1757..	Nashville........	Jun. 1, 1796	16	430	120	41,328	916	42,244	34
Tex.....	1691..	Austin...........	Dec. 29, 1845	28	760	620	262,134	5,204	267,338(b)	2
Ut......	1847..	Salt Lake City.....	Jan. 4, 1896	45	345	275	82,906	2,820	84,916	11
Vt......	1724..	Montpelier........	Mar. 4, 1791	14	155	90	9,267	342	9,609	43
Va......	1607..	Richmond........	Jun. 25, 1788	10	425	205	39,780	1,037	40,817	36
Wash....	1811..	Olympia..........	Nov. 11, 1889	42	340	230	66,570	1,622	68,192	20
W.Va....	1727..	Charleston........	Jun. 20, 1863	35	225	200	24,070	111	24,181	41
Wis.....	1766..	Madison.........	May 29, 1848	30	300	290	54,464	1,690	56,154	26
Wy......	1834..	Cheyenne........	Jul. 10, 1890	44	365	275	97,203	711	97,914	9

*First permanent settlement. **The order for the original 13 states is the order in which they ratified the constitution. (a) Aleutian Islands and Alexander Archipelago are not considered in these lengths. (b) Total area of Texas reduced one sq. mile by Chamizal boundary solution between U.S. and Mexico. 1963.

The Continental Divide

Source: U.S. Geological Survey, Department of the Interior

Continental Divide: watershed, created by mountain ranges or table-lands of the Rocky Mountains, from which the drainage is easterly or westerly; the easterly flowing waters reaching the Atlantic Ocean chiefly through the Gulf of Mexico, and the westerly flowing waters reaching the Pacific Ocean through the Columbia River, or through the Colorado River, which flows into the Gulf of California.

The location and route of the Continental Divide across the United States may briefly be described as follows:

Beginning at point of crossing the United States-Mexican boundary, near long. 108°45'W., the Divide, in a northerly direction, crosses New Mexico along the western edge of the Rio Grande drainage basin, entering Colorado near long. 106°41'.

Thence by a very irregular route northerly across Colo-

rado along the western summits of the Rio Grande and of the Arkansas, the South Platte, and the North Platte River basins, and across Rocky Mountain National Park, entering Wyoming near long. 106°52'.

Then in a northwesterly direction, forming the western rims of the North Platte, Big Horn, and Yellowstone River basins, crossing the southwestern portion of Yellowstone National Park.

Thence in a westerly and then a northerly direction forming the common boundary of Idaho and Montana, to a point on said boundary near long. 14°00' W.

Thence northeasterly and northwesterly through Montana and the Glacier National Park, entering Canada near long. 114°04'W.

Chronological List of Territories

Name of Territory	Date of Organic Act	Organic Act Effective	Admission as State	Yrs. Terr.
Northwest Territory (a)	Jul. 13, 1787	No fixed date		
Territory south of Ohio River	May 26, 1790	No fixed date	Jun. 1, 1796b	6
Mississippi	Apr. 7, 1798	When President acted	Dec. 10, 1817	19
Indiana	May 7, 1800	Jul. 4, 1800	Dec. 11, 1816	16
Territory northwest of Ohio River	May 7, 1800	Jul. 4, 1800	Mar. 1, 1803c	2
Orleans	Mar. 26, 1804	Oct. 1, 1804	Apr. 8, 1812d	7
Michigan	Jan. 11, 1805	Jun. 30, 1805	Jan. 26, 1837	31
Louisiana-Missouri (e)	Mar. 3, 1805	Jul. 4, 1805	Aug. 10, 18211	16
Illinois	Feb. 3, 1809	Mar. 1, 1809	Dec. 3, 1813	9
Alabama	Mar. 3, 1817	When Miss. became a State	Dec. 14, 1819	2
Arkansas	Mar. 2, 1819	Jul. 4, 1819	Jun. 15, 1836	17
Florida	Mar. 30, 1822	No fixed date	Mar. 3, 1845	23
Indian (organized 1834)*				
Wisconsin	Apr. 20, 1836	Jul. 3, 1836	May 29, 1848	12
Iowa	Jun. 12, 1838	Jul. 3, 1838	Dec. 28, 1846	7
Oregon	Aug. 14, 1848	Date of act	Feb. 14, 1859	10
Minnesota	Mar. 3, 1849	Date of act	May 11, 1859	9
New Mexico	Sept. 9, 1850	On President's proclamation	Jan. 6, 1912	61
Utah	Sept. 9, 1850	Date of act	Jan. 4, 1896	44
Washington	Mar. 2, 1853	Date of act	Nov. 11, 1889	36
Nebraska	May 30, 1854	Date of act	Feb. 9, 1867	12
Kansas	May 30, 1854	Date of act	Jan. 29, 1861	6
Colorado	Feb. 28, 1861	Date of act	Aug. 1, 1876	15
Nevada	Mar. 2, 1861	Date of act	Oct. 31, 1864	3
Dakota	Mar. 2, 1861	Date of act	Nov. 2, 1889	28
Arizona	Feb. 24, 1863	Date of act	Feb. 14, 1912	49
Idaho	Mar. 3, 1863	Date of act	Jul. 3, 1890	27
Montana	May 26, 1864	Date of act	Nov. 8, 1889	25
Wyoming	Jul. 25, 1868	When officers were qualified	Jul. 10, 1890	22
Oklahoma	May 2, 1890	Date of act	Nov. 16, 1907	17
Hawaii	Apr. 30, 1900	Jun. 14, 1900	Aug. 21, 1959	59
Alaska	Aug. 24, 1912	Nov. 5, 1912	Jan. 3, 1959	47

(a) Included present Ohio, Indiana, Illinois, Michigan, Wisconsin, Eastern Minnesota; (b) as the State of Tennessee; (c) as the State of Ohio; (d) as the State of Louisiana; (e) organic act of Missouri Territory of Jun. 4, 1812, became effective Dec. 7, 1812.

*Indian Territory was set aside in 1834 for the "5 civilized Indian tribes"—Cherokee, Choctaw, Chickasaw, Creek, and Seminole. In 1889, part of it was included in the Territory of Oklahoma. In 1906, Indian Territory and the Territory of Oklahoma were merged to form the state of Oklahoma.

Geographic Centers, United States and Each State

Source: U. S. Geological Survey, Department of the Interior

United States, including Alaska and Hawaii — South Dakota; Butte County, 17 miles W of Castle Rock, 14 miles E of junction of borders of South Dakota, Montana, and Wyoming. Approx. Lat. 44°58′N, Long. 103°46′W.

Conterminous U. S. (48 States)—Near Lebanon, Smith Co., Kansas. Lat. 39°50′N, Long. 98°35′W.

North American Continent—The geographic center is in Pierce County, North Dakota, 6 miles W of Balta. Latitude 48°10′, Longitude 100°10′W.

STATES

State	County	Locality

Alabama—Chilton, 12 miles SW of Clanton.
Alaska—Lat. 63°50′N, Long. 152°00′W. Approx. 60 mi. NW of Mt. McKinley.
Arizona—Yavapai, 55 miles ESE of Prescott.
Arkansas—Pulaski, 12 miles NW of Little Rock.
California—Madera, 38 miles E of Madera.
Colorado—Park, 30 miles NW of Pikes Peak.
Connecticut—Hartford, at East Berlin.
Delaware—Kent, 11 miles S of Dover.
District of Columbia—Near Fourth and "L" Streets, NW.
Florida—Hernando, 12 miles NNW of Brooksville.
Georgia—Twiggs, 18 miles SE of Macon.
Hawaii—Hawaii, 20°15′N,156°20′W, off Maui Island.
Idaho—Custer, at Custer, SW of Challis.
Illinois—Logan, 28 miles NE of Springfield.
Indiana—Boone, 14 miles NNW of Indianapolis.
Iowa—Story, 5 miles NE of Ames.
Kansas—Barton, 15 miles NE of Great Bend.
Kentucky—Marlon, 3 miles NNW of Lebanon.
Louisiana—Avoyelles, 3 miles SE of Marksville.
Maine—Piscataquis, 18 miles north of Dover.

Maryland—Prince Georges, 4¹/₂ miles NW of Davidsonville.
Massachusetts—Worcester, north part of city.
Michigan—Wexford, 5 miles NNW of Cadillac.
Minnesota—Crow Wing, 10 miles SW of Brainerd.
Mississippi—Leake, 9 miles WNW of Carthage.
Missouri—Miller, 20 miles SW of Jefferson City.
Montana—Fergus, 12 miles west of Lewistown.
Nebraska—Custer, 10 miles NW of Broken Bow.
Nevada—Lander, 26 miles SE of Austin.
New Hampshire—Belknap, 3 miles E of Ashland.
New Jersey—Mercer, 5 miles SE of Trenton.
New Mexico—Torrance, 12 miles SSW of Willard.
New York—Madison, 12 miles S of Oneida and 26 miles SW of Utica.
North Carolina—Chatham, 10 miles NW of Sanford.
North Dakota—Sheridan, 5 miles SW of McClusky.
Ohio—Delaware, 25 miles NNE of Columbus.
Oklahoma—Oklahoma, 8 miles N of Oklahoma City.
Oregon—Crook, 25 miles SSE of Prineville.
Pennsylvania—Centre, 2¹/₂ miles SW of Bellefonte.
Rhode Island—Kent, 1 mile SSW of Crompton.
South Carolina—Richland, 13 miles SE of Columbia.
South Dakota—Hughes, 8 miles NE of Pierre.
Tennessee—Rutherford, 5 mi. NE of Murfreesboro.
Texas—McCulloch, 15 miles NE of Brady.
Utah—Sanpete, 3 miles N of Manti.
Vermont—Washington, 3 miles E of Roxbury.
Virginia—Buckingham, 5 miles SW of Buckingham.
Washington—Chelan, 10 mi. WSW of Wenatchee.
West Virginia—Braxton, 4 miles E of Sutton.
Wisconsin—Wood, 9 miles SE of Marshfield.
Wyoming—Fremont, 58 miles ENE of Lander.

There is no generally accepted definition of geographic center, and no satisfactory method for determining it. The geographic center of an area may be defined as the center of gravity of the surface, or that point on which the surface of the area would balance if it were a plane of uniform thickness.

No marked or monumented point has been established by any government agency as the geographic center of either the 50 states, the conterminous United States, or the North American continent. A monument was erected in Lebanon, Kan., conterminous U.S. center, by a group of citizens.

Origin of the Names of U.S. States

Source: State officials, the Smithsonian Institution, and the Topographic Division, U.S. Geological Survey.

Alabama—Indian for tribal town, later a tribe (Alabamas or Alibamons), of the Creek confederacy.

Alaska—Russian version of Aleutian (Eskimo) word, alakshak, for "peninsula" or "great lands."

Arizona—Spanish version of Pima Indian word for "little spring place,"or Aztec arizuma, meaning "silver-bearing."

Arkansas—French variant of Kansas, a Sioux Indian name for "south wind people."

California—Bestowed by the Spanish conquistadors (possibly by Cortez). It was the name of an imaginary island, an earthly paradise, in "Las Serges de Esplandian," a Spanish romance written by Montalvo in 1510. Baja California (Lower California, in Mexico) was first visited by Spanish in 1533. The present U.S. state was called Alta (Upper) California.

Colorado—Spanish, red, first applied to Colorado River.

Connecticut—From Mohican and other Algonquin words meaning "long river place."

Delaware—Named for Lord De La Warr, early governor of Virginia; first applied to river, then to Indian tribe (Lenni-Lenape), and the state.

District of Columbia—For Columbus, 1791.

Florida—Named by Ponce de Leon on Pascua Florida, "Flowery Easter," on Easter Sunday, 1513.

Georgia—For King George II of England by James Oglethorpe, colonial administrator, 1732.

Hawaii—Possibly derived from native word for homeland, Hawaiki or Owhyhee.

Idaho—Shoshone derivation. State calls it "light on the mountains."

Illinois—French for Illini or land of Illini, Algonquin word meaning men or warriors.

Indiana—Means "land of the Indians."

Iowa—Indian word variously translated as "one who puts to sleep" or "beautiful land."

Kansas—Sioux word for "south wind people."

Kentucky—Indian word variously translated as "dark and bloody ground," "meadow land" and "land of tomorrow."

Louisiana—Part of territory called Louisiana by LaSalle for French King Louis XIV.

Maine—From Maine, ancient French province.

Maryland—For Queen Henrietta Maria, wife of Charles I of England.

Massachusetts—From Indian tribe named after "large hill place" identified by Capt. John Smith as near Milton, Mass.

Michigan—From Chippewa words mici gama meaning "great water," after the lake of the same name.

Minnesota—From Dakota Sioux word meaning "cloudy water" or "sky-tinted water" of the Minnesota River.

Mississippi—Probably Chippewa: mici zibi, "great river" or "gathering-in of all the waters."

Missouri—Indian tribe named after Missouri River, meaning "muddy water."

Montana—Latin or Spanish for "mountainous."

Nebraska—From Omaha or Otos Indian word· meaning "broad water" or "flat river," describing the Platte River.

Nevada—Spanish, meaning snow-clad.

New Hampshire—Named 1629 by Capt. John Mason of Plymouth Council for county in England.

New Jersey—The Duke of York, 1664, gave a patent to John Berkeley and Sir George Carteret to be called Nova Caesaria, or New Jersey, after England's Isle of Jersey.

New Mexico—Spaniards in Mexico applied term to land north and west of Rio Grande in the 16th Century.

New York—For Duke of York and Albany who received patent to New Netherland from his brother Charles II and sent an expedition to capture it, 1664.

North Carolina—In 1619 Charles I gave a large patent to Sir Robert Heath to be called Province of Carolana, from Carolus, Latin name for Charles. A new patent was granted by Charles II to Earl of Clarendon and others. Divided into North and South Carolina, 1710.

North Dakota—Dakota is Sioux for friend or ally.

Ohio—Iroquois word for "beautiful river."

Oklahoma—Choctaw coined word meaning red man, proposed by Rev. Allen Wright, Choctaw-speaking Indian.

Oregon—Origin unknown.

Pennsylvania—William Penn, the Quaker, who was made full proprietor by King Charles II in 1681, suggested Sylvania, or woodland, for his tract. The king's government owed Penn's father, Admiral William Penn, £16,000, and the land being granted in part settlement, the king added the Penn to Sylvania, against the desires of the modest proprietor, in honor of the admiral.

Puerto Rico—Spanish for Rich Port.

Rhode Island—Named Roode Eylandt by Adriaen Block, Dutch explorer, because of its red clay. Name of Roger Williams' settlement was added to give the small state its long; official title: State of Rhode Island and Providence Plantations.

South Carolina—See North Carolina.

South Dakota—See North Dakota.

Tennessee—From 1784 to 1788 this was the State of Franklin, or Frankland. Tanasi was the name of Cherokee villages on the Little Tennessee River.

Texas—Variant of word used by Caddo and other Indians meaning friends or allies, and applied to them by the Spanish in eastern Texas. Also written·texias, tejas, teysas.

Utah—From a Navajo word meaning upper, or higher up, as applied to a Shoshone tribe called Ute. Spanish form is Yutta, English Uta or Utah. Proposed name Deseret, "land of honeybees," from Book of Mormon, was rejected by Congress.

Vermont—From French words Vert, green, and Mont, mountain. The Green Mountains were said to have been named by Samuel de Champlain. The Green Mountain Boys were Gen. Stark's men in the Revolution. When the state was formed, 1777, Dr. Thomas Young suggested combining vert and mont into Vermont.

Virginia—Named by Sir Walter Raleigh, who fitted out the expedition of 1584, in honor of Queen Elizabeth, the Virgin Queen of England.

Washington—Named after George Washington. When the bill creating the Territory of Columbia was introduced in the 32d Congress, the name was changed to Washington because of the existence of the District of Columbia.

West Virginia—So named when western counties of Virginia refused to secede from the United States, 1863.

Wisconsin—An Indian name, spelled Ouisconsin and Misconsing by early chroniclers. Believed to mean "grassy place" in Chippewa. Congress made it Wisconsin.

Wyoming—The word was taken from Wyoming Valley, Pa., which was the site of an Indian massacre and became widely known by Campbell's poem, Gertrude of Wyoming. In Algonquin it means "large prairie place."

Accession of Territory by The United States

Source: Statistical Abstract of the United States

Division	Yr.	Sq. mi.[1]	Division	Yr.	Sq. mi.[1]	Division	Yr.	Sq. mi.[1]
Total (1970).....		3,628,066	Texas............	1845	390,143	American Samoa...	1900	76
			Oregon..........	1846	285,580	Canal Zone[4].......	1904	550
United States.....		3,615,122	Mexican cession....	1848	529,017	Corn Islands[5]......	1914	4
Territory 1790[2]......		888,685	Gadsden Purchase..	1853	29,640	Virgin Islands......	1917	133
Louisiana Purchase.	1803	827,192	Alaska...........	1867	586,412	·Trust Territory of		
By Treaty with Spain			Hawaii..........	1898	6,450	the Pacific Is.....	1947	8,489
Florida.........	1819	58,560	The Philippines[3]....	1898	115,600	All other[6]..........	....	42
Other areas......	1819	13,443	Puerto Rico.......	1899	3,435			
			Guam...........	1899	212			

(1) Gross area (land and water), (2) Includes drainage basin of Red River on the north, south of 49th parallel, sometimes considered a part of the Louisiana Purchase, (3) Area not included in totals; became Republic of the Philippines July 4, 1946. (4) Under U.S. jurisdiction by treaty with Panama. (5) Leased from Nicaragua for 99 years but returned Apr. 25, 1971. (6) See index for Outlying Areas; U.S.

Confederate States and Secession

The American Civil War, 1861-1865, grew out of sectional disputes over the employment of slavery in the South and the contention of Southern legislators that the states retained many soverign rights, including the right to secede from the Union.

The principal product of the South was cotton, harvested by slave labor. For 50 years Northern leaders had been trying to curtail slavery, but were checkmated in Congress by Southern legislators. Extreme partisans in the North, called Abolitionists, demanded the immediate end of slavery for moral reasons.

The Southern states argued that the U.S.Constitution was a contract between sovereign states, which could withdraw (secede) when state rights were violated. This has led Southern historians to call the Civil War the War Between the States. Actually the war was not fought by state against state but by one federal regime against another, the Confederate government in Richmond assuming control over the economic, political, and military life of the South, under protest from Georgia and South Carolina.

Early Slavery Laws

Milestone U.S. laws on the slavery issue included the Missouri Compromise of 1820 which admitted Missouri as a slave state but prohibited slavery in the Louisiana Territory north of Arkansas; the Compromise of 1850, which admitted California as a free state, omitted action on slavery in organizing Utah and New Mexico as territories, ended slave trade in the District of Columbia, amended the Fugitive Slave Act to punish any who aided a fugitive, and abolished trial by jury for fugitives; Kansas-Nebraska Act, 1854, which left choice of slavery in Kansas and Nebraska to residents there (squatter sovereignty).

Harriet Beecher Stowe's *Uncle Tom's Cabin*, 1851-52, intensified feeling against slavery.

Tension increased when the Supreme Court ruled Mar. 6, 1857, that Dred Scott, a Negro, did not become free when taken to a free state and did not have rights as a citizen; also that the Missouri Compromise on slavery was unconstitutional.

John Brown's attempt to arm slaves at Harpers Ferry, Oct. 16-18, 1859, inflamed partisans.

Abraham Lincoln's stand for free soil (no slavery) in new states and territories, and his general condemnation of slavery, caused Southern fanatics to threaten secession if he were elected. When Sen. Stephen A. Douglas split the Democratic party by his stand against secession, Lincoln's election was assured. Even before inauguration Lincoln had Sen. William H. Seward (N.Y.) offer a resolution that the Constitution never be altered to interfere with slavery where established, that the Fugitive Slave Law be amended to include trial by jury, that all states repeal laws contrary to the Constitution.

Secession of States

South Carolina voted an ordinance of secession from the Union repealing its 1788 ratification of the U.S. Constitution on Dec. 20, 1860, to take effect Dec. 24. Other states seceded in 1861 and their votes in convention were:

Mississippi, Jan. 1861, by 84 to 15.
Florida, Jan. 10, 1861, by 62 to 7.
Alabama, Jan. 11, 1861, by 61 to 39.

Georgia, Jan. 19, 1861, by 208 to 89.
Louisiana, Jan. 26, 1861, by 113 to 17.
Texas, Feb. 1, 1861, by 166 to 7, ratified by popular vote Feb. 23, 1861 (for 34,794; against 11,325).

Virginia had delayed action, but when President Lincoln called for troops after Fort Sumter fell (Apr. 14, 1861), it voted for secession Apr. 17, 1861, by 88 to 55, ratified by popular vote May 23, 1861 (for secession, 128,884; against, 32,134).

Arkansas, May 6, 1861, by 69 to 1.

North Carolina, May 21, 1861, voted secession but refused by two-thirds vote to submit it to people for ratification.

Tennessee, May 7, 1861, entered a military league with the Confederacy (popular vote, June 8, for secession, 104,019; against 47,238).

Missouri Unionists stopped secession in the convention at Jefferson City Feb. 28 and at the second session in St. Louis Mar. 9. The legislature condemned secession Mar. 7. Under the protection of Confederate troops, secessionist members of the legislature adopted a resolution of secession at Neosho, Oct. 31, 1861. The Confederate Congress seated the secessionists' representatives.

Kentucky did not secede and its government remained Unionist. In a part occupied by Confederate troops, Kentuckians approved secession and the Confederate Congress admitted their representatives.

The Maryland legislature voted against secession Apr. 27, 53 to 13. Delaware did not secede. Western Virginia held conventions at Wheeling, named a pro-Union governor June 11, 1861; admitted to Union as West Virginia June 30, 1863; its constitution provided for gradual abolition of slavery.

Confederate Government

Forty-two delegates from South Carolina, Georgia, Alabama, Mississippi, Louis.... Florida met in convention at Montgomery, Ala, ... 1861. The Congress adopted a provisional constitution. f the Confederate States of America Feb. 8, 1861, and on the next day elected Jefferson Davis (Miss.), provisional president, and Alexander H. Stephens (Ga.), provisional vice president. Davis was inducted into office at Montgomery, Feb. 18, 1861.

A permanent constitution was adopted Mar. 11, 1861. It provided that the president should be elected for a single term of 6 years; it also abolished the African slave trade. The Congress moved to Richmond, Va., July 20, 1861. Jefferson Davis was elected president, October, 1861; inaugurated Feb. 22, 1862.

Jefferson Davis (1808-1889) was a West Point graduate, 1828; served in Black Hawk and Mexican Wars; senator from Mississippi, 1847-1851; secretary of war, 1853-1857; senator, 1857-1861.

The Congress adopted a flag, consisting of a red field with a white stripe in the middle third, and a blue jack with a circle of white stars, going two-thirds of the way down the flag. This flag was unfurled in Montgomery, Mar. 4, 1861. Later the more popular flag was the red field with blue diagonal cross bars that held 13 white stars, designed by Gen. P. G. T. Beauregard.

(See also Civil War, U. S., in Index)

Dixie

The name Dixie is popularly associated with the southern states of the U.S. Several possible origins have been suggested.

One is said to be the French word dix (ten) which was printed on $10 bills used in early Louisiana which were called "dixies" by Americans. Louisiana became known as "Dix's Land" or "Land of the Dixie's."

Some sources suggest that the name originated from a kind-hearted Dutch farmer, Dixie (Dixye), who unsuccessfully tried to cultivate tobacco in Harlem, N.Y. City, in the late 1700s. When he sold his slaves to a farmer in Piedmont County, S.C., they are said to have longed to return to Dixie's farm and sang of its joys.

In the South many consider Dixie a derivation from the "Mason-Dixon Line" which divided the free and slave states.

Public Lands of the United States

Source: Bureau of Land Management, U.S. Dept. of the Interior

Acquisition of the Public Domain 1781-1867

Acquisition	Area* (in Acres)	Land	Water	Total	Cost[1]
State Cessions (1781-1802)		233,415,680	3,409,920	236,825,600	[2]$6,200,000
Louisiana Purchase (1803)[3]		523,446,400	6,465,280	529,911,680	23,213,568
Red River Basin[4]		29,066,880	535,040	29,601,920	
Cession from Spain (1819)		43,342,720	2,801,920	46,144,640	6,674,057
Oregon Compromise (1846)		180,644,480	2,741,760	183,386,240	
Mexican Cession (1848)		334,479,360	4,201,600	338,680,960	16,295,149
Purchase from Texas (1850)		78,842,880	83,840	78,926,720	15,496,448
Gadsden Purchase (1853)		18,961,920	26,880	18,988,800	10,000,000
Alaska Purchase (1867)		362,516,480	12,787,200	375,303,680	7,200,000
Total		**1,804,716,800**	**33,053,440**	**1,837,770,240**	**$85,079,222**

*All areas except Alaska were computed in 1912, and have not been adjusted for the recomputation of the area of the United States which was made for the 1950 Decennial Census.

(1.)Cost data for all except "State Cessions" obtained from U.S. Geological Survey.

(2.)Paid by Federal Government for Georgia Cession, 1802 (56,689,920 acres).

(3.)Excludes areas eliminated by Treaty of 1819 with Spain.

(4.)Basin of the Red River of the North, south of the 49th parallel.

Disposition of Public Lands 1781 to 1970 (In acres)

Disposition by methods not elsewhere Classified[1]		Granted to States for:	
Granted or sold to homesteaders	303,500,000	Support of common schools	77,600,000
Granted to railroad corporations	287,500,000	Reclamation of swampland	64,900,000
Granted to veterans as military bounties	94,300,000	Construction of railroads	37,100,000
Confirmed as private land claims[2]	61,100,000	Support of misc. institutions[6]	21,700,000
Sold under timber and stone law[3]	34,000,000	Purposes not elsewhere classified[7]	117,500,000
Granted or sold under timber culture law[4]	13,900,000	Canals and rivers	6,100,000
Sold under desert land law[5]	10,900,000	Construction of wagon roads	3,400,000
	10,700,000	**Total granted to States**	**328,300,000**
		Grand Total	**1,144,200,000**

(1.) Chiefly public, private, and preemption sales, but includes mineral entries, script locations, sales of townsites and townlots.

(2.) The Government has confirmed title to lands claimed under valid grants made by foreign governments prior to the acquisition of the public domain by the United States.

(3.)The law provided for the sale of lands valuable for timber or stone and unfit for cultivation.

(4.)The law provided for the granting of public lands to settlers on condition that they plant and cultivate trees on the lands granted.

(5.)The law provided for the sale of arid agricultural public lands to settlers who irrigate them and bring them under cultivation.

(6.)Universities, hospitals, asylums, etc.

(7.) For construction of various public improvements (individual items not specified in the granting act) reclamation of desert lands, construction of water reservoirs, etc.

Land Owned by the Federal Government (In acres)

Agency (June 30, 1973)	Public Domain	Acquired	Total
Bureau of Land Management	471,631,492.0	2,363,355.7	473,994,847.7
U.S. Forest Service	160,242,696.7	26,831,497.5	187,074,194.2
U.S. Fish and Wildlife Service	24,415,715.8	3,574,742.0	27,990,457.8
U.S. Park Service	19,626,913.5	4,933,721.0	24,560,634.5
U.S. Army	7,023,022.0	3,961,389.0	10,984,411.0
Bureau of Reclamation	5,817,845.4	1,766,891.2	7,584,736.6
U.S. Air Force	6,937,192.0	1,443,707.0	8,380,899.0
Corps of Engineers	734,793.1	6,756,197.1	7,490,990.2
Bureau of Indian Affairs	4,204,849.2	769,198.6	4,974,047.8
U.S. Navy	2,155,407.5	1,435,065.6	3,590,473.1
Atomic Energy Commission	1,438,110.1	676,397.3	2,114,507.4
Other	521,846.1	1,414,342.3	1,936,188.4
Total	**704,749,883.4**	**55,926,504.3**	**760,676,387.7**

The Homestead Act; Sale of Public Land

The Homestead Act became effective Jan. 1, 1863, the same day that President Lincoln issued his Emancipation Proclamation. Its purpose was to open the vacant lands of America's vast public domain to agricultural settlement.

To qualify for a homestead a person had to be a citizen of the United States or express his intention of becoming one, be over 21 years of age or the head of a household, and own less than 160 acres of land.

To acquire title to 160 acres of public land the homesteader had to establish residence on the land and bring a portion under cultivation. After 6 months residence he could purchase the land for $1.25 per acre, or after 5 years residence he could acquire title for a $15 filing fee.

Originally passed by Congress on May 20, 1862, the Homestead Act was later amended to increase acreage limitations under certain conditions. Under the Homestead Act and its several amendments, more than a million families received title to over 248,000,000 acres of public land across the plains, prairies and mountains of western United States. But as subsequent waves of settlers moved onto vacant land the supply of arable land dwindled; by the late 1930s some homesteaders had settled on submarginal lands that would not support a farm family. In 1937 Congress passed the Bankhead-Jones Act authorizing the Government to repurchase bankrupt farms to relieve the plight of such families. Under this program about 2,000,000 acres of homestead land was returned to Federal ownership.

By the time of its 100th anniversary the Homestead Act had accomplished its purpose—the transformation of a wilderness into productive farmland. Now outdated, the Homestead Act will always be a part of the American heritage.

Public Land Sale

From time to time the Bureau of Land Management sells public land to private individuals. Public land is always sold for its fair market value as determined by public auction. The Federal Govt. offers no free land. Persons wishing to purchase public land should contact the Bureau of Land Management, Wash., D. C. 20240, or one of the Bureau's Land Offices in the public land states.

The Bureau stresses that it is the only authoritative source of information on the sale of land under its jurisdiction.

National Parks, Other Areas Administered by Nat'l Park Service

Figures given are date area was set aside by Congress or proclaimed by President, and area in acres.

National Parks

Acadia, Me. (1916) 37,005. Includes Mount Desert Island, half of Isle au Haut, Schoodic Point on mainland. Highest elevation on Eastern seaboard.

Arches, Utah (1929) 73,389. Contains giant red sandstone arches and other products of erosion.

Big Bend, Texas (1935) 709,088. On Rio Grande River.

Bryce Canyon, Utah (1923) 36,011. Spectacularly colorful and unusual display of erosion effects in Southwestern Utah.

Canyonlands, Utah (1964). At junction of Colorado and Green Rivers, extensive evidence of prehistoric Indians.

Capitol Reef, Utah (1937) 241,866. A 70-mile uplift of sandstone cliffs dissected by high-walled gorges.

Carlsbad Caverns, N.M. (1923) 46,756. Largest known underground caverns, not yet fully explored.

Crater Lake, Ore. (1902) 160,290. Extraordinary blue lake in crater of extinct volcano encircled by lava walls 500 to 2,000 feet high.

Everglades, Fla. (1934) 1,400,533. Largest remaining subtropical wilderness in Continental U.S., abundant wildlife includes rare birds.

Glacier, Mont. (1910) 1,013,599. Superb Rocky Mountain scenery, numerous glaciers and glacial lakes. Part of Waterton-Glacier International Peace Park established by U.S. and Canada in 1932.

Grand Canyon, Ariz. (1908) 1,218,275. Most spectacular part of Colorado River's greatest canyon.

Grand Teton, Wyo. (1929) 310,418. Most impressive part of the Teton Mountains, winter feeding ground of largest American elk herd.

Great Smoky Mountains, N.C.-Tenn. (1926) 517,014. Largest eastern mountain range, magnificent forests.

Guadalupe Mountains, Texas (1966) 79,972. Extensive and significant Permian limestone fossil reef; tremendous earth fault.

Haleakala, Hawaii (1960) 27,824, 10,023 foot dormant volcano on Maui.

Hawaii Volcanoes, Hawaii (1916) 229,177. Contains Kilauea and Mauna Loa, active volcanoes on the island of Hawaii.

Hot Springs, Ark. (1832) 5,779. Government supervised bath houses use waters of 45 of the 47 natural hot springs.

Isle Royale, Mich. (1931) 539,280. Largest island in Lake Superior, noted for its wilderness area and wildlife.

Kings Canyon, Calif. (1890) 460,123. Mountains wilderness, dominated by Kings River Canyons and High Sierra, contains giant sequoias.

Lassen Volcanic, Calif. (1907) 106,372. Contains Lassen Peak, most recently active volcano in continental U.S., and other volcanic phenomena.

Mammoth Cave, Ky. (1926) 52,129. 144 miles of surveyed underground passages, beautiful natural formations, river 360 feet below surface.

Mesa Verde, Colo. (1906) 52,036. Most notable and best preserved prehistoric cliff dwellings in the United States.

Mount McKinley, Alaska (1917) 1,939,493. Highest Mountain in North America, large glaciers, and unusual wildlife.

Mount Rainier, Wash. (1899) 235,404. Greatest single-peak glacial system in the U.S. radiates from this dormant volcano.

North Cascades, Wash. (1968) 504,785. Spectacular mountainous region with many glaciers, lakes, and rugged peaks.

Olympic, Wash. (1909) 897,885. Mountain wilderness containing finest remnant of Pacific Northwest rain forest, active glaciers, Pacific shoreline, rare elk.

Petrified Forest, Ariz. (1906) 94,189. Extensive petrified wood and Indian artifacts. Contains part of Painted Desert.

Platt, Okla. (1906) 912. Numerous natural springs.

Redwood, Calif. (1968) 62,304. Forty miles of Pacific coastline, virgin groves of ancient redwoods.

Rocky Mountain, Colo. (1915) 263,793. Beautiful scenery on the continental divide includes 107 named peaks over 11,000 feet.

Sequoia, Calif. (1890) 386,823. Groves of giant sequoias, largest mountain in conterminous United States — Mount Whitney (14,494 feet).

Shenandoah, Va. (1926) 190,419. Portion of the Blue Ridge Mountains; this park overlooks much of the famous Shenandoah Valley.

Virgin Islands, Virgin Islands (1956) 14,470. Covers 3/4ths of St. John Island, lush growth, lovely beaches, Indian relics, evidence of colonial Danes.

Voyageurs, Minn. (1971) 219,128. Abundant lakes, forests, wildlife, unusual recreation.

Wind Cave, S.D. (1903) 28,060. Limestone Caverns in Black Hills. Extensive wildlife includes a herd of bison.

Yellowstone, Ida., Mont., Wyo., (1872) 2,219,823. Oldest and largest National Park. World's greatest geyser area has about 3,000 geysers and hot springs; the spectacular falls and impressive canyons of the Yellowstone River are major attractions.

Yosemite, Calif. (1890) 761,094. Yosemite Valley, the nation's highest waterfall, 3 groves of giant sequoias, and mountainous terrain.

Zion, Utah (1909) 146,571. Unusual shapes and landscapes have resulted from the effects of erosion and faulting activity, Zion Canyon, with sheer walls ranging up to 2,500 feet, is readily accessible.

National Historical Parks

Appomattox Court House, Va. (1930) 995. Where Lee surrendered to Grant.

Boston, Mass. (1974) 35. Includes Faneuil Hall, Old North Church, Bunker Hill, Paul Revere House.

Chalmette, La. (1907) 142. Scene of part of the Battle of New Orleans.

Chesapeake and Ohio Canal, Md.-W. Va.-D of C. (1961) 20,239. 185 mile historic canal; D.C. to Cumberland, Md.

City of Refuge, Hawaii (1955) 181. Until 1819, a sanctuary for Hawaiians vanquished in battle, and those guilty of crimes or breaking taboos.

Colonial, Va. (1930) 9,210. Includes most of Jamestown Island, site of first successful English colony; Yorktown site of Cornwallis' surrender to George Washington; Cape Henry Memorial, approximate site of the first landing of the Jamestown colonists; and the Colonial Parkway.

Cumberland Gap, Ky.-Tenn.-Va. (1940) 20,273. Mountain pass of the Wilderness Road which carried the first great migration of pioneers into America's interior.

George Rogers Clark, Vincennes, Ind. (1966) 24. Commemorates American defeat of British in West during Revolution.

Harpers Ferry, Md., W. Va. (1944) 1,427. At the confluence of the Shenandoah and Potomac Rivers, the site of John Brown's 1859 raid on the Army arsenal. Scene of several Civil War battles.

Independence, Pa., (1948) 22. Contains several properties in Philadelphia associated with the Revolutionary War and the founding of the U.S.

Minute Man, Mass. (1959) 746. Where the colonial Minute Men battled the British, April 19, 1775. Also contains Nathaniel Hawthorne's home.

Morristown, N.J. (1933) 1,544. Sites of important military encampments during the Revolutionary War; Washington's headquarters 1777, 1779-80.

Nez Perce, Ida. (1965) 2,113. Illustrates the history and culture of the Nez Perce Indian country. 22 separate sites.

San Juan Island, Wash. (1966) 1,752. Commemorates the peaceful relations of the U.S., Canada and Great Britain since the 1872 boundary disputes at this site.

Saratoga, N.Y. (1938) 2,432. Scene of a major battle which became a turning point in the War for Independence.

Sitka, Alaska. (1910) 108. Scene of last major resistance of the Tlingit Indians to the Russians, 1804.

National Memorial Park

Theodore Roosevelt, N.D. (1947) 70,403. Part of T.R.'s Elkhorn Ranch along the Little Missouri River. Has bison and some original prairie.

National Battlefields

Big Hole, Mont. (1910) 656. Site of major battle with Nez Perce Indians.

Cowpens, S.C. (1929) 826. Revolutionary War Battlefield.

Fort Necessity, Pa. (1931) 911. First battle of French and Indian War.

Petersburg, Va. (1926) 1,516. Scene of 10-month Union campaign 1864-65.

Stones River, Tenn. (1927) 331. Civil War battle leading to Sherman's "March to the Sea."

Tupelo, Miss. (1929) 1.0 Crucial battle over Sherman's supply line.

Wilson's Creek, Mo. (1960) 1,750. Civil War battle for control of state of Missouri.

National Battlefield Parks

Kennesaw Mountain, Ga. (1917) 2,884. Two major battles of Atlanta campaign.

Manassas, Va. (1940) 3,032. Two early Civil War battles.

Richmond, Va. (1936) 746. Site of battles defending Confederate capital.

National Battlefield Sites

Antietam, Md. (1890) 1,800. End of first Confederate invasion of North.

Brices Cross Roads, Miss. (1929) 1. Civil War Battlefield.

National Military Parks

Chickamauga and Chattanooga, Ga.-Tenn. (1890) 8,089. Four Civil War Battlefields.

Fort Donelson, Tenn. (1928) 538. Site of first major Union victory.

Fredericksburg and Spotsylvania County, Va. (1927). Sites of several major Civil War battles and campaigns.

Gettysburg, Pa. (1895) 3,910. Major Confederate defeat in North.

Guilford Courthouse, N.C. (1917) 220. Revolutionary War battle.

Horseshoe Bend, Ala. (1956) 2,040. On Tallaposa River, place where Gen. Andrew Jackson broke the power of the Creek Indian Confederacy.

Kings Mountain, S.C. (1931) 3,945.Revolutionary War battle.

Moores Creek, N.C. (1926) 77. Pre-Revolutionary War battle.

Pea Ridge, Ark. (1956) 4,300. Civil War battle.

Shiloh, Tenn. (1894) 3,753. Major Civil War battle; site includes some well-preserved Indian burial mounds.

Vicksburg, Miss. (1899) 1,741. Union victory gave North control of the Mississippi and split the Confederacy in two.

Historic Area

Fort Scott, Kan. (1965) 7. Commemorates historic events in Kansas.

National Memorials

Arkansas Post, Ark. (1960) 305. First permanent French settlement in the lower Mississippi River Valley.

Chamizal, El Paso Texas (1966) 55. Commemorates 1963 settlement of 99-year border dispute with Mexico.

Coronado, Ariz.: (1952) 2,834. Commemorates first European exploration of the Southwest under Francisco Vasquez Coronado.

DeSoto, Fla. (1948) 30. Commemorates 16th-century Spanish explorations.

Federal Hall, N.Y. (1939) 0.45. First seat of U.S. government.

Fort Caroline, Fla. (1950) 129. On St. Johns River, overlooks site of second attempt by French Huguenots to colonize. N.A.

Fort Clatsop, Ore. (1958) 125. Lewis and Clark encampment 1805-06.

General Grant, N.Y. (1958) 0.76. Tombs of Gen. and wife.

Hamilton Grange, N.Y. (1962) 0.71. Home of Alexander Hamilton.

John F. Kennedy Center for the Performing Arts, D.C. (1972) 18. Memorial to late president.

Johnstown Flood, Pa. (1964) 107. Commemorates tragic flood.

Lincoln Boyhood, Ind. (1962) 200. Farm Lincoln grew up on.

Lincoln Memorial, D. of C. (1911) 164.

Lyndon B. Johnson Grove on the Potomac, D.C. (1973) 15. Memorial to late president.

Mount Rushmore, S.D. (1925) 1,278. World famous sculpture of 4 presidents.

Perry's Victory and International Peace Memorial, Ohio (1936) 26. American naval victory, War of 1812.

Roger Williams, R.I. (1965) 5. Memorial to founder of Rhode Island.

Thaddeus Kosciuszko, Pa. (1972) .01. Memorial to Polish hero of American Revolution.

Theodore Roosevelt Island, D.C. (1947) 88.5. Woods and statuary honor 25th president.

Thomas Jefferson Memorial, D. of C. (1943) 18.

Washington Monument, D. of C. (1848) 106.

Wright Brothers, N.C. (1927) 431. First powered flight.

National Historic Sites

Abraham Lincoln Birthplace, Hodgenville, Ky. (1916) 117.

Adams, Quincy, Mass. (1946) 8. Home of Presidents John Adams, John Quincy Adams, and celebrated descendants.

Allegheny Portage Railroad, Pa. (1964) 767. Part of the Pennsylvania Canal system.

Andersonville, Andersonville, Ga. (1970) 488. Noted Civil War prison.

Andrew Johnson, Greeneville, Tenn. (1935) 17. Home of the President.

Bent's Old Fort, Colo. (1960) 178. Old West fur-trading post.

Carl Sandburg Home, N.C. (1968) 247. Poet's farm home for 22 years.

Christiansted, St. Croix; Virgin Islands (1952) 28. Commemorates Danish colony.

Clara Barton, Md. (1974) 1. Home of founder of American Red Cross.

Edison, West Orange, N.J. (1955) 20. Home and laboratory.

Ford's Theatre, Washington, D.C. (1866) 0.25. Includes theater, now restored, where Lincoln was assassinated, house where he died, and Lincoln Museum.

Fort Bowie, Ariz. (1964) 970. Focal point of operations against Geronimo and the Apaches.

Fort Davis, Texas (1961) 460. Frontier outpost battled Comanches and Apaches.

Fort Laramie, Wyo. (1938) 571. Military post on Oregon Trail.

Fort Larned, Kan. (1964) 718. Military post on Sante Fe Trail.

Fort Point, San Francisco, Calif. (1970) 29. Largest West Coast fortification.

Fort Raleigh, N.C. (1941) 159. First English settlement.

Fort Smith, Ark. (1961) 19. Active post from 1817 to 1890.

Fort Union Trading Post, Mont., N.D. (1966) 400. Principal fur-trading post on upper Missouri, 1828-1867.

Fort Vancouver, Wash. (1948) 209. Hdqts. for Hudson's Bay Company in 1825. Early military and political seat of Pacific N.W.

Golden Spike, Utah (1957) 2,203. Commemorates completion of first transcontinental railroad in 1869.

Hampton, Md. (1948) 45. 18th-century Georgian mansion.

Herbert Hoover, West Branch, Iowa (1965) 187. Home of the President.

Home of Franklin D. Roosevelt, Hyde Park, N.Y. (1944) 188. Birthplace, home and "Summer White House".

Hopewell Village, Pa. (1938) 848. 19th-century iron making.

Hubbell Trading Post, Ariz. (1965) 160. Indian trading post.

Jefferson National Expansion Memorial, St. Louis, Mo. (1935) 91. Commemorates westward expansion with park and memorial arch.

John Fitzgerald Kennedy, Brookline, Mass. (1967) .09. Birthplace and childhood home of the President.

John Muir, Martinez, Calif. (1964) 9. Early conservationist and writer.

Knife River Indian Villages, N.C. (1974) 1,292. Remnants of 5 Hidatsa villages.

Lincoln Home, Springfield, Ill. (1971) 12. Residence when he was elected President, 1860.

Longfellow, Cambridge, Mass. (1972) 2. Longfellow's home, 1837-82, and Washington's hq. during Boston Siege, 1775-76. No federal facilities.

Lyndon B. Johnson, Johnson City, Texas (1969) 241. Birthplace and boyhood home of the 36th President.

Mar-A-Largo, Florida (1969) 17. Mansion expresses the affluent Palm Beach life of the 1920s.

Martin Van Buren, N.Y. (1974) 42. Lindenwald, Home of 8th President, near Kingston.

Pennsylvania Avenue, Wash. D.C. (1965) Area between the White House and the Capitol.

Puukohola Heiau, Hawaii (1972) 77. Ruins of temple built by King Kamehameha.

Sagamore Hill, Oyster Bay, N.Y. (1962) 85. Home of President Theodore Roosevelt from 1885 until his death in 1919.

Saint-Gaudens, Cornish. N.H. (1964) 86. Home, studio and gardens of American sculptor Augustus Saint-Gaudens.

Salem Maritime, Mass. (1938) 9. Only port never seized from the Patriots by the British. Major fishing and whaling port.

San Juan, Puerto Rico (1949) 53. 16th-century Spanish fortifications.

Saugus Iron Works, Mass. (1968) 9. Reconstructed 17th-century colonial ironworks.

Sewall-Belmont House, D.C. (1974) 35. National Women's Party headquarters 1929-74.

Springfield Armory, Mass. (1974) 55. Small arms center of world for nearly 200 years.

Theodore Roosevelt Birthplace, N.Y., N.Y. (1962) 0.11.

Theodore Roosevelt Inaugural, Buffalo, N.Y. (1966) 1. Wilcox House where he took oath of office, 1901.

Tuskegee Institute, Ala. (1974). College founded by Booker T. Washington in 1881 for blacks, includes student-made brick buildings.

Vanderbilt Mansion, Hyde Park, N.Y. (1940) 212. Mansion of 19th-century financier.

Whitman Mission, Wash. (1936) 98. Site where Dr. and Mrs. Marcus Whitman ministered to the Indians until slain, 1847.

William Howard Taft, Cincinnati, Ohio (1969) 0.78. Birthplace and early home of the 27th President, 1909-13; Chief Justice, 1921-30.

National Capital Parks

District of Columbia — — Maryland — Virginia (1790) 7,052. Includes 704 reservations.

White House

Washington, D.C. (1792) 18. Presidential residence since November 1800.

National Seashores

Assateague Island	Md.-Va.	1965	39,631
Canaveral	Fla.	1975	67,500
Cape Cod	Mass.	1961	44,600
Cape Hatteras	N.C.	1937	28,500
Cape Lookout**	N.C.	1966	24,500
Cumberland Island	Ga.	1972	39,494
Fire Island	N.Y.	1964	19,311

Gulf Islands, Fla.-Miss. (1971) 124,690. White sand beaches, primitive off-shore islands, historic forts

Padre Island	Texas	1962	133,918
Point Reyes	Calif.	1962	64,546

National Lakeshores

Apostle Islands, Wis. (1970) 42,826. Picturesque islands and coastal portion of Bayfield Peninsula on south shore of Lake Superior.

Indiana Dunes	Ind.	1966	8,330
Pictured Rocks	Mich.	1966	67,000

Sleeping Bear Dunes, Mich. (1970) 71,105. Notable for its beaches, massive sand dunes, forests, lakes. **Benzie and D. H. Day State Parks open to public.**

National River

Buffalo	Ark.	1972	95,840

National Scenic Riverways

Lower Saint Croix**	Minn-Wis.	1972	7,845
Ozark	Mo.	1964	82,321
Saint Croix**	Minn.-Wis.	1968	67,747

National Recreation Areas

Amistad	Texas	1965	65,000
Arbuckle	Okla.	1965	5,631
Bighorn Canyon	Mont.-Wy.	1964	140,459
Coulee Dam	Wash.	1946	100,059
Curecanti	Colo.	1965	41,572
Cuyahoga	Oh.	1974	29,112
Delaware Water Gap	N.J.-Pa.	1965	58,985
Gateway	N.Y.-N.J.	1972	26,172
Glen Canyon	Ariz.-Utah	1958	1,236,880
Golden Gate	Calif.	1972	34,202
Lake Chelan	Wash.	1968	62,000
Lake Mead	Ariz.-Nev.	1936	1,936,978
Ross Lake	Wash.	1968	107,000
Lake Meredith	Texas	1965	41,097
Shadow Mountain	Colo.	1952	18,240
Whiskeytown-Shasta-Trinity	Calif.	1962	42,445

National Scenic Trail

Appalachian	Me. to Ga.	1968	50,000

*Not open to the public **No federal facilities

National Monuments

Name	State	Year	Acreage
Agate Fossil Beds	Nebr.	1965	3,054
Alibates Flint Quarries and Texas Panhandle Pueblo Culture*	Tex.	1965	93
Aztec Ruins	N.M.	1923	27
Badlands	S.D.	1929	243,302
Bandelier	N.M.	1916	29,661
Biscayne	Fla.	1968	103,701
Black Canyon of the Gunnison	Colo.	1933	13,672
Booker T. Washington	Va.	1956	224
Buck Island Reef	Virgin Isls.	1961	850
Cabrillo	Calif.	1913	1,407
Canyon de Chelly	Ariz.	1931	83,840
Capulin Mountain	N.M.	1916	775
Casa Grande Ruins	Ariz.	1892	473
Castillo de San Marcos	Fla.	1924	20
Castle Clinton	N.Y.	1946	1
Cedar Breaks	Utah	1933	6,155
Chaco Canyon	N.M.	1907	21,510
Channel Islands	Calif.	1938	18,388
Chiricahua	Ariz.	1924	10,648
Colorado	Colo.	1911	17,669
Craters of the Moon	Idaho	1924	53,545
Custer Battlefield	Mont.	1879	765
Death Valley	Calif.-Nev.	1933	2,067,793
Devils Postpile	Calif.	1911	798
Devils Tower	Wyo.	1906	1,347
Dinosaur	Colo.-Utah	1915	211,051
Effigy Mounds	Iowa	1949	1,467
El Morro	N.M.	1906	1,279
Florissant Fossil Beds**	Colo.	1969	5,992
Fort Frederica	Ga.	1936	215
Fort Jefferson	Fla.	1935	47,125
Fort McHenry National Monument & Historic Shrine	Md.	1925	43
Fort Matanzas	Fla.	1924	299
Fort Pulaski	Ga.	1924	5,616
Fort Stanwix	N.Y.	1935	16
Fort Sumter	S.C.	1948	64
Fort Union	N.M.	1954	721
Fossil Butte	Wyo.	1972	8,178
G. Washington Birthplace	Va.	1930	456
George Washington Carver	Mo.	1943	210
Gila Cliff Dwellings	N.M.	1907	533
Glacier Bay	Alaska	1925	2,805,269
Grand Portage	Minn.	1951	710
Gran Quivira	N.M.	1909	611
Great Sand Dunes	Colo.	1932	36,667
Hohokam Pima*	Ariz.	1972	1,555
Homestead Nat'l. Monument of America	Nebr.	1936	195
Hovenweep	Colo-Utah	1923	785
Jewel Cave	S.D.	1908	1,275
John Day Fossil Beds	Ore.	1974	14,405
Joshua Tree	Calif.	1936	559,955
Katmai	Alaska	1918	2,792,137
Lava Beds	Calif.	1925	46,500
Lehman Caves	Nev.	1922	640
Montezuma Castle	Ariz.	1906	842
Mound City Group	Ohio	1923	68
Muir Woods	Calif.	1908	554
Natural Bridges	Utah	1908	7,779
Navajo	Ariz.	1909	360
Ocmulgee	Ga.	1934	683
Oregon Caves	Ore.	1909	466
Organ Pipe Cactus	Ariz.	1937	330,690
Pecos	N.M.	1965	341
Pinnacles	Calif.	1908	14,498
Pipe Spring	Ariz.	1923	40
Pipestone	Minn.	1937	282
Rainbow Bridge	Utah	1910	160
Russell Cave	Ala.	1961	310
Saguaro	Ariz.	1933	78,989
Saint Croix Island**	Me.	1949	35
Scotts Bluff	Nebr.	1919	2,988
Statue of Liberty	N.J.-N.Y.	1924	58
Sunset Crater	Ariz.	1930	3,040
Timpanogos Cave	Utah	1922	250
Tonto	Ariz.	1907	1,120
Tumacacori	Ariz.	1908	10
Tuzigoot	Ariz.	1939	58
Walnut Canyon	Ariz.	1915	2,249
White Sands	N.M.	1933	145,335
Wupatki	Ariz.	1924	35,253
Yucca House*	Colo.	1919	10

Environment

Zoo News, 1975
by Edward Ricciuti

A zoo-hopping young ape named Joe Willie and some unusual babies, very big and very small, helped enliven the zoo news during 1975.

Joe Willie, a 1½-year-old gorilla of the lowland race, left his native Bronx Zoo May 15 for a cross-country flight to California and a new home at the Los Angeles Zoo. Officials there view Joe Willie as a prospective mate for their young female, Lina.

The baby gorilla from the Bronx was named after New York Jets quarterback Joe Namath because both the ape and the athlete suffered similar shoulder injuries at about the same time. The gorilla's injury occurred while he was in a cage with his mother. Afterwards, the young ape was removed from the cage and hand-reared by a specialist assigned to the task by the zoo.

Birth Notices

The Los Angeles Zoo was also the scene of one of the most significant animal births in recent years. The new arrival, a 150-pound Asiatic elephant, was born, appropriately, Mother's Day weekend. The youngster was the first offspring of captive-born elephants in the Western Hemisphere. The baby pachyderm's parents belong to the Portland (Oregon) Zoo, but the mother was on loan to Los Angeles when the young elephant was born.

Another big zoo baby was born in May at the Philadelphia Zoo, where a pair of hippos became the parents of a youngster weighing in at 70 pounds. The parents, Jimmy and Submarie, are experienced for the job. They have had a dozen youngsters and have been made grandparents several times. Their newest offspring was born in the hippo pool outside the zoo's Pachyderm House. Baby hippos nurse underwater and learn to swim before they can walk.

Much smaller but at least as important to the zoo world were tiny twin monkeys born at the San Antonio Zoo March 31. The little monkeys, small enough to fit in the palm of a man's hand, were golden lion marmosets, a South American species threatened with extinction. The name of the species derives from its color and the ruff-like mane around its head. As an adult, the lion marmoset grows no larger than a grey squirrel.

The Bronx Zoo announced the first births there of the rare Mongolian wild horse in 46 years — not one colt but two, the first arriving June 2, the second July 2. The Mongolian wild horse, almost extinct in its native central Asia, closely resembles the horses painted on European cave walls by Stone Age artists.

Among other notable births at American zoos during the year were the arrivals of a young gorilla at the San Francisco Zoo May 1, three litters of Utah prairie dogs at the National Zoo in Washington, and 14 deadly young Australian tiger snakes, among the world's most venomous, at the San Diego Zoo in January.

As part of its program of breeding rare animals the Bronx Zoo opened up a breeding station for wild animals on St. Catherine's Island, off the coast of Georgia. Zoo officials said they plan to conduct long-term breeding of rare hoofed animals on the island. Herds of antelope — sable and gemsbok — already have been established at the station, a project funded for the zoo by the Noble Foundation.

New Exhibits

The Philadelphia Zoo, the nation's oldest, continued its modernization with the opening of the second phase of its African Plains exhibit May 17. The new phase, which cost more than $77,000, contains sections for African birds and antelopes, and for white rhinoceroses. The rhino exhibit features an artificial termite mound, which closely resembles the huge mounds made by these insects on the African savannah. The rhinos use the mound as a scratching post.

Construction of a brand-new zoo in Minnesota was begun during the year. The Minnesota State Zoo near Minneapolis, scheduled for opening in 1977, will feature animals from northern climes, including a herd of Bactrian camels, the shaggy, two-humped variety from central Asia, and Mongolian wild horses. The Minnesota Zoo, which will cost $26 million, will be one of the world's finest when completed.

The Denver Zoo completed a new building called Bird World, an 18,000-square-foot structure which houses 300 birds of 100 different species. Visitors enter the building through a hall with exhibits illustrating five different biological concepts. In one exhibit, parrots demonstrate differences in size, shape and color between birds of both sexes. In another theme exhibit, Australian kookaburra birds, noted for their cackling call, are used to illustrate facts about bird vocalization.

The main exhibit in the bird house is a tropical rain forest, 85 feet long, 40 feet wide, and 35 feet high. Visitors reach it by passing through a simulated cave. Within the forest fly 100 brightly colored jungle birds.

The Dickerson Park Zoo in Springfield, Mo., opened a natural history trail through 20 acres of undeveloped zoo property. The trail, developed by students from a local technical school, is designed to bring zoo visitors in contact with plants and animals native to the Springfield area.

In Providence, R.I., the Roger Williams Park Zoo began reconverting a city dog kennel into a breeding enclosure for birds. The Beardsley Zoo in Bridgeport, Conn. started construction of a 43,000-square-foot farmyard exhibit. It will house farm animals and a unique new building, the "Mouse House." Mice and their rodent relatives from many different types of habitats ranging from desert to the habitations of man, will be exhibited in the house.

The Lincoln Park Zoo in Chicago began construction of a major new exhibits building, which will house the great apes — chimpanzees, orangutans and gorillas — in simulated natural habitats.

Water Zoos

Aquariums kept in the news as the New England Aquarium's huge floating amphitheater, the Discovery, was towed across Boston harbor from a wharf where it had been docked temporarily, to its permanent station in the water alongside the aquarium. The Discovery, which displaces 3000 tons, houses a 1000-seat auditorium and a pool for behavioral demonstrations by dolphins and sea lions.

A Pacific bottlenose dolphin was born April 17 at San Diego's Sea World aquarium, an event that rarely occurs in captivity. Sea World also completed a trade with a Japanese aquarium by receiving two giant Chinese salamanders and eight rare pinecone fish for two alligator gars. The pinecone fish are covered with plate-like armor and produce a glowing light by means of special luminescent organs. The salamanders reach over a yard in length.

In April the Miami Seaquarium released 275 young green sea turtles from a beach at Cape Florida in hopes the young turtles will mature and return to the beach to breed. Green sea turtles, threatened with extinction, have been exterminated from many areas. They revisit the beaches on which they are hatched to lay their eggs.

Salmon Sighted
(But So Are Foreign Pests)

During the years immediately after the American Revolution, the rivers of New England were filled each spring with Atlantic salmon, swarming upstream to mate and lay their eggs, and then, unlike their Pacific relatives, returning to the sea.

Sleek and spotted, the salmon fought the current heading up waterways like the Connecticut River by the hundreds of thousands. Millworkers in riverside factories grumbled that they were fed salmon too often.

Today, because of river pollution and hydroelectric dams blocking their passage, the salmon have all but vanished, except in parts of Canada. However, this year in the Connecticut River system, there were hopeful signs that a program to reintroduce the salmon might succeed.

For several years fish and game agencies had been breeding salmon in hatcheries and releasing young in tributaries of the Connecticut River. Biologists hoped the salmon would return to the streams in which they had been released, after maturing in the sea, and breed. During 1975, fishermen began to catch adult salmon in the Connecticut system in both Massachusetts and Connecticut. The fish bore the tags that had been placed on them by biologists when, a few years before, they had been released as young.

It may take several years to determine if the reintroduction of the salmon is successful, but the outlook seems favorable. Fish ladders have been built to help the salmon negotiate dams, and the waters of the Connecticut and its tributaries are being cleansed of pollutants. If the salmon return in force, man will have corrected one of his ecological errors.

Baneful Incursions

Biologists generally view reintroduction of depleted native species as highly beneficial. This often is not the case, however, with the introduction of new animals into a region. Again and again, throughout history people have knowingly or unwittingly spread new species into regions where they cause tremendous ecological problems, and even threaten man.

The rat, which has spread some of the worst human diseases, travelled first to Europe and then to the Americas on sailing vessels. The fire ant, scourge of southeastern farmlands, arrived in the United States from South America aboard ships. Starlings, which spatter our cities with their droppings and drive out native birds, were brought to the United States by well-meaning bird fanciers. And the ill-famed Asian walking catfish was this year reported as inhabiting ten counties in southern Florida, just a few years after it escaped a pond on a tropical fish farm.

Able to breathe air and walk with its fins on land, the walking catfish has become a major pest. It competes with native sport fishes for food, and even preys on them. Biologists fear it may supplant many desirable fishes in waterways, ponds and lakes. When fish and game agents attempt to kill the catfish by poisoning their waters, the creatures simply walk overland to new homes. Ironically, the catfish are proving to be a major threat to tropical fish farms by entering ponds on these farms and killing valuable aquarium fish.

Another fish that threatens Florida is the piranha. Not long ago one of these flesh-eating South American fish was caught in a Florida waterway. Southern Florida corresponds in climate to some of South America's prime piranha country, and since the piranha was once kept as an aquarium fish by many people in this country, it could become established in the Sunshine state. Federal and state agencies, however, have taken steps to ease the threat, and keeping the fish is no longer allowed by law.

Pushy Parakeets

Controversy has mounted across the country over another introduction, the monk parakeet. This large parakeet from South America is living and breeding in places as far apart as southern California and the New York City area. Popular as a pet, the monk parakeet consumes vast amounts of fruit and grain in Argentina and other parts of South America. Biologists are not certain whether the bird will become such a pest in this country, but conceivably it could.

Flocks of monk parakeets have been reported in many states, including Michigan, New York, and California. Biologists believe that many of the parakeets escaped from pet shops and pet owners. Some of the birds are known to have escaped from shipments sent to dealers through New York City's Kennedy International Airport. Several parakeets were released by the San Diego Zoo, which claims to have recaptured all of them.

New York State has eradicated large numbers of monk parakeets, an action which many conservationists applaud, but some bird lovers protest. Biologists have warned that the parakeets could not only become a serious agricultural problem, but, because they are aggressive, could drive away native birds from backyard bird feeders, which attract many parakeets in the winter.

Victory over one invading animal was announced in the spring by the United States Department of Agriculture. The giant African land snail, which had become established in the Miami area, has been wiped out after a long campaign. The snail had escaped from a pet owner in the Miami area several years ago, and prospered, largely by consuming the paint and stucco from the walls of buildings, and feeding on shrubs and ornamental plants. The snail also is capable of transmitting a parasitic disease to man. At one time brought into the United States for the pet trade, the snail no longer may be imported.

World Pact Aids Endangered Species

An international convention to control the exploitation of rare animals, which may have dramatic long-term effects on endangered species, took effect July 1.

The result of a meeting of 80 nations in Washington, D.C. in 1973, the convention still has not been signed by the majority of governments represented at the meeting, but as the year passed the number of signatures mounted. The United States, United Arab Emirates, Chile, and Canada were among the first to sign.

The convention strictly controls commerce in more than 370 endangered species, banning shipment of these animals or their parts, unless both importing and exporting states certify that the transfer will not damage the species' chances of survival. The convention also mandates controls over the trade in more than 200 other declining creatures which are not imminently in danger of extinction.

Conservationists hope that enforcement of the treaty will curb the global trade in live endangered species, and particularly in their skins. This trade has been seen as a major factor in the decline of many species of wild animals.

Some Endangered Species in North America

Source: U.S. Fish and Wildlife Service

Common Name	Scientific Name	Range
Mammals		
Wood Bison	Bison bison athabascae	Alberta, Canada
Black-Footed Ferret	Mustela nigripes	U.S., Canada
Northern Kit Fox	Vulpus velox hebes	Canada
West Indian (Florida) Manatee	Trichechus inunguis	Caribbean (once U.S.)
Sonoran Pronghorn	Antilocapra americana sonoriensis	U.S., Mexico
Eastern Timber Wolf	Canis lupus lycaon	(endangered in U.S. only)
Northern Rocky Mountain Wolf	Canis lupus irremotus	U.S., Canada
Red Wolf	Canis rufus	U.S.
Eastern Cougar	Felis concolor cougar	U.S., Canada
Birds		
Bald Eagle	Haliaetus leucocephalus	U.S., Canada
Masked Bobwhite	Colinus virginianus ridgwayi	U.S., Mexico
California Condor	Gymnogyps californianus	Southern California
Whooping Crane	Grus americana	Canada, U.S.
Eskimo Curlew	Numenius borealis	Canada to Argentina
American Peregrine Falcon	Falco peregrinus anatum	Canada to Mexico
Arctic Peregrine Falcon	Falco peregrinus tundrius	Canada to Mexico
Aleutian Canada Goose	Branta canadensis leucopareia	U.S. to Japan
Brown Pelican	Pelecanus occidentalis	Canada to Panama
Attwater's Greater Prairie Chicken	Tympanuchus cupido attwateri	U.S.
Bachman's Warbler	Vermivora bachmani	Southeast U.S., Cuba
Kirtland's Warbler	Dendroica kirtlandi	Michigan, Bahamas
Ivory-Billed Woodpecker	Campephilus principalis	Southeast U.S., Cuba

Some Other Endangered Species in the World

Source: U.S. Fish and Wildlife Service

Common Name	Scientific Name	Range
Mammals		
Asiatic Wild Ass	Equus hemionus	Iran to Mongolia
Dugong	Dugong dugon	East Africa to Okinawa
Slender-Horned Gazelle	Gazella leptoceros	North Africa, Arabia
Mountain Gorilla	Gorilla gorilla beringei	Central Africa
Orang Utan	Pongo pygmaeus	Indonesia, Malaysia
Great Indian Rhinoceros	Rhinoceros unicornus	India, Nepal
Javan Rhinoceros	Rhinoceros sondaicus	Indonesia
Sumatran Rhinoceros	Didermocerus sumatrensis	Bangladesh to Vietnam, Indonesia
Northern White Rhinoceros	Ceratotherium simum cottoni	Sudan, Zaire, Uganda
Blue Whale	Balaenoptera musculus musculus	Oceanic
Humpback Whale	Megaptera novaeangliae	Oceanic
Birds		
Great Indian Bustard (largest land bird)	Choriotis nigriceps	India, Pakistan
Japanese Crane	Grus japonicus	Japan (once all north Asia)
Chinese Egret	Egretta eulophotes	China (once all east Asia)
Japanese Crested Ibis	Nipponia nippon	Japan (once all north Asia)

Young of Animals Have Special Names

The young of many animals, birds and fish have come to be called by special names. A young eel, for example, is an elver. Many young animals, of course, are often referred to simply as infants or babies. Some of the more distinctive names, and the animals, fish or birds of which these young are the offspring, follow.

bunny:rabbit.
calf:cattle, elephant, antelope, rhino, hippo, whale, etc.
cheeper:grouse, partridge, quail.
chick, chicken:fowl.
cockerel:rooster.
codling, sprag:codfish.
colt:horse (male).
cub:lion, bear, shark, fox, etc.
cygnet:swan.
duckling:duck.
eaglet:eagle.
elver:eel.
eyas:hawk, others.
fawn:deer.

filly:horse (female).
fingerling:fish generally.
flapper:wild fowl.
fledgling:birds generally.
foal:horse, zebra, others.
fry:fish generally.
gosling:goose.
heifer:cow.
joey:kangaroo, others.
kid:goat.
kit:fox, beaver, rabbit, cat.
kitten, kitty, catling:cats, other fur-bearers.
lamb, lambkin, cosset, hog:sheep.
leveret:hare.
nestling:birds generally.

owlet:owl.
parr, smolt, grilse:salmon.
piglet, shoat, farrow, suckling:pig.
polliwog, tadpole:frog.
poult:turkey.
pullet:hen.
pup:dog, seal, sea lion, fox.
puss, pussy:cat.
spike, blinker, tinker:mackerel.
squab:pigeon.
squeaker:pigeon, others.
whelp:dog, tiger, beasts of prey.
yearling:cattle, sheep, horse, etc.
younglet, youngling:animals generally.

Speeds of Animals

Source: *Natural History* Magazine, March 1974.
Copyright © The American Museum of Natural History, 1974.

Animals	Speeds in mph	Animals	Speeds in mph	Animals	Speeds in mph
Cheetah	70	Mongolian wild ass	40	Cat (domestic)	30
Pronghorn antelope	61	Greyhound	39.35	Man	27.89
Wildebeest	50	Whippet	35.50	Elephant	25
Lion	50	Rabbit (domestic)	35	Black mamba snake	20
Thomson's gazelle	50	Mule Deer	35	Six-lined race runner	18
Quarter horse	47.5	Jackal	35	Squirrel	12
Elk	45	Reindeer	32	Pig (domestic)	11
Cape hunting dog	45	Giraffe	32	Chicken	9
Coyote	43	White-tailed deer	30	Spider (Tegenaria atrica)	1.17
Gray fox	42	Wart hog	30	Giant tortoise	0.17
Hyena	40	Grizzly bear	30	Three-toed sloth	0.15
Zebra	40			Garden snail	0.03

Most of these measurements are for maximum speeds over approximate quarter-mile distances. Exceptions — which are included to give a wide range of animals — are the lion and elephant, whose speeds were clocked in the act of charging; the whippet, which was timed over a 200-yard course; the cheetah over a 100-yard distance; man for a 15-yard segment of a 100-yard run (of 13.6 seconds); and the black mamba, six-lined race runner, spider, giant tortoise, three-toed sloth, and garden snail, which were measured over various small distances.

Gestation, Longevity, and Incubation

Note: The figures on gestation, incubation and longevity given below are averages based on estimates by leading authorities. The potential life span of mammals is rarely attained in nature. The longevity figures for wild animals listed below were based on experience with such animals in zoos.

Animal	Gestation (Days)	Longevity (Years)	Animal	Gestation (Days)	Longevity (Years)	Animal	Gestation (Days)	Longevity (Years)
Ass	365	24	Elephant	645	47	Puma	90	11
Baboon	187	27	Elk	250	22	Rabbit	37	5
Badger	60	15	Fox	52	8	Rhinoceros	450	27
Bat		6	Giraffe	425	10	Sea Lion	350	19
Bear			Goat (dom.)	151		Sheep	154	13
Black	219	19	Goat (mtn.)	184	9	Squirrel	44	8
Grizzly	225	31	Gorilla	257	25	Tiger	105	19
Polar	240	31	Guinea Pig	68	4	Whale	365	37
Beaver	122	13	Horse	330	27	Wolf	63	12
Buffalo	278	20	Kangaroo	42	19	Zebra	365	20
Camel	406	20	Leopard	98	17			
Cat (domestic)	63	15	Lion	100	15-29	**Incubation Time**		
Chimpanzee	231	30	Monkey	164	7	Chicken	21	
Chipmunk	31	7	Moose	240	8	Duck	30	
Cow	284	18	Mouse (meadow)	21	4	Goose	30	
Deer	201	17	Opossum	14-17	4	Pigeon	18	
Dog	61	16	Pig	112	14	Turkey	26	

A Collection of Animal Collectives

The English language boasts an abundance of nouns used to describe groups of things, particularly pairs or aggregations of animals. Some of these words have fallen into comparative disuse, but many of them are still in service, helping to enrich the vocabularies of those who like their language to be precise, who tire of hearing a group referred to as "a bunch of," or who enjoy the sound of words that aren't overworked.

Here is a lexicon of some of these "collectives"

band of gorillas
bed of clams, oysters
bevy of quail, swans
brace of ducks
brood of chicks
cast of hawks
cete of badgers
charm of goldfinches
chattering of choughs
cloud of gnats
clowder of cats
clutch of chicks
clutter of cats
colony of ants
congregation of plovers
covert of coots
covey of quail, partridge

cry of hounds
down of hares
draught of fish
drift of swine
drove of cattle, sheep
exaltation of larks
flight of birds
flock of sheep, geese
gaggle of geese
gam of whales
gang of elks
grist of bees
herd of curlews, elephants
hive of bees
horde of gnats
husk of hares

kindle or kendle of kittens
knot of toads
leap of leopards
leash of greyhounds, foxes
litter of pigs
murder of crows
muster of peacocks
mute of hounds
nest of vipers
nest, nide of pheasants
pack of hounds, wolves
pair of horses
pod of whales, seals
pride of lions
school of fish
sedge or siege of cranes
shoal of fish, pilchards

skein of geese
skulk of foxes
sleuth of bears
sounder of boars, swine
span of mules
spring of teals
swarm of bees
team of ducks, horses
tribe of goats
trip of goats
troop of kangaroos, monkeys
volery of birds
watch of nightingales
wing of plovers
yoke of oxen

A Look at the Future

Source: *The Futurist*, World Future Society, Feb. 1974

The following timetable of future developments in environmental protection and management was put together by Dr. Vaclav Smil, assistant professor of geography at the University of Manitoba in Winnipeg. Dr. Smil arrived at the estimated dates by using the Delphi method, a newly developed technique for peering into the future.

Under the Delphi method, experts are interviewed separately so that they do not influence each other directly. Successive rounds of interviews, with feedback to the experts of information and opinion distilled from previous interviews, results in a relatively clear-cut and useful consensus of expert opinion.

Dr. Smil polled 40 energy and environmental experts, asking them to list major scientific, technological and management breakthroughs which they regarded as urgently needed and feasible in the next 50 years. After collating the lists, Dr. Smil asked the experts to estimate the year in which there would be a 50-50 chance of each development having occurred. The dates below are the ones which fall in the middle of the range of estimates.

1978 Environmentally motivated higher price for energy.

1978 Acceptance of the idea that all consumers share responsibility for pollution and its cost.

1980 Safe, large-scale disposal of radio-active wastes.

1980 Abolition of "growth for growth's sake" concept.

1980 Effective, harmless control of accidental oil spills.

1983 Development of waste heat utilization (desalting, heating, sewage treatment, etc.)

1983 Control of thermal pollution in water.

1983 Control of nitrogen oxides.

1985 New car (batteries, fuel cells, steam, etc.)

1985 Offshore siting of large power plants.

1986 Removal of noxious matter from fossil fuels before combustion.

1988 Establishment of worldwide environmental quality standards (air and water).

1990 Taxes to alleviate pollution problems (effluent taxes, tax incentives for dispersal of people from large cities).

1990 Establishment of worldwide environmental surveillance and warning agency.

1990 Supression of sound along highways and airways.

1992 New fast and safe mass transit systems.

1995 Coordinated international planning of energy consumption.

2000 Planned decrease of per capita energy demand and consumption.

2000 Effective population control.

2005 Conservation of fossil fuels for other future needs.

2010 Man will largely destroy his ability to survive in great numbers and in great cities.

2020 Utilization of heat sinks other than atmosphere and surface waters.

After 2020: Polar siting of large power plants.

After 2020: Elimination of all generators using fossil fuel.

Never: No private cars allowed.

Coal: Strip Mining Increase

Source: Bureau of Mines

Strip Mining by State 1973 (millions of tons)

Alabama	11.5	Kansas	1.1	Oklahoma	2.2
Alaska	.7	Kentucky	55.0	Penn.	29.8
Arizona	3.2	Maryland	1.6	Tenn.	4.2
Arkansas	.4	Missouri	4.7	Texas	6.9
Colorado	2.8	Montana	10.7	Virginia	8.7
Illinois	29.0	No. Dakota	6.9	Wash.	3.3
Indiana	24.5	New Mexico	8.3	W. Virginia	17.7
Iowa	.2	Ohio	28.5	Wyoming	14.5

Year	
1964	Total soft coal, 487,000,000 tons; Strip mined 152,000,000 tons; 31%.
1968	Total soft coal, 545,000,000 tons; Strip mined 186,000,000 tons; 34%.
1973	Total soft coal, 591,738,000 tons; Strip mined 276,645,000 tons; 47%.
1974	Not available.

Controlling Pollution

Federal Outlays Rise

The federal government spent $7 billion on protecting the environment and controlling pollution in 1975, an increase of $1.7 billion over 1974. But billions more will be needed in the coming decade to reverse the trend toward ecological decay (see next page).

Federal costs fell into three categories: understanding, describing and predicting the environment, $1,107 billion; protection and enhancement activities, $1.099 billion; pollution control and abatement (excluding construction grants), $1.908 billion; Construction grants for control and abatement came to $3.350 billion (mostly for water systems).

Inflation and more thorough research have driven up future cost estimates. Pollution control itself causes some inflation by adding to the cost of producing goods, but the Environmental Protection Agency

(EPA) says this factor will increase prices by only 0.3% to 0.5% a year. Even so, total costs should be well within the reach of government and industry, given a productive economy.

These enormous environmental outlays are expected to yield financial dividends on an equal or greater scale, apart from immeasurable benefits to physical and esthetic well-being. The President's Council on Environmental Quality estimates that by 1977, air pollution alone would be causing nearly $25 billion a year in damages to health, residential property, materials and vegetation, if no controls were enforced. Water pollution already takes a toll of over $12 billion a year, according to the EPA.

These figures do not include the benefits of an improved environment to property values, commercial fishing and recreation. In addition, billions would be saved in avoidance costs— those that people incur when they try to avoid or reduce damages, for instance, by traveling to more distant resorts to avoid polluted beaches.

Apart from financial considerations, it has been estimated by the National Academy of Sciences that 15,000 Americans die each year as a result of air pollution, while 7 million days are spent in bed by people whose chronic illnesses were aggravated by air pollution.

In sum, the balance sheet of costs and benefits of a vigorous program of environmental enhancement still points to a strong net gain.

Estimated Total Pollution Control Expenditures

(in billions of 1973 dollars)   Source: Council on Environmental Quality

Pollutant/medium	1973			Cumulative—1973-82			Incremental—1973-82[5]		
	O&M[1]	Capital Costs[2]	Total Costs	O&M[1]	Capital[2] costs	Total costs	O&M[1]	Capital[2] costs	Total costs
Air pollution									
Public.............	0.1	0.1	0.2	3.8	1.7	5.4	3.8	1.7	5.4
Private									
Mobile............	1.2	0.2	1.4	49.9	31.3	74.4	49.9	31.3	74.4
Stationary.........	1.1	1.1	2.2	35.3	21.4	62.6	31.2	16.3	53.5
Total...........	2.4	1.4	3.8	89.0	54.4	142.4	84.9	49.3	133.3
Water pollution									
Public									
Federal...........	0.2	NA	NA	NA	1.8	NA	NA	1.8	NA
State and local.....	1.4	4.1	5.4	27.4	50.6	88.5	12.8	14.8	24.4
Private									
Industrial.........	0.9	1.1	2.0	21.6	16.5	40.4	12.3	9.8	23.1
Utilities.........	NA	NA	0.01	2.2	4.4	3.5	2.2	4.4	3.5
Total...........	2.5	5.2	7.4	51.2	73.3	132.4	27.3	30.8	51.0
Noise..............	NA	0.1	NA	NA	6.0-8.7	NA	NA	6.0-8.7	NA
Radiation									
Nuclear power plants............	NA	NA	NA	0.08	0.3	0.3	0.08	0.3	0.3
Solid waste									
Public............	1.1	0.3	1.4	15.5	4.2	19.3	2.2	1.0	2.9
Private............	1.9	*	1.9	25.2	0.4	25.6	2.3	0.05	2.3
Total...........	3.0	0.3	3.3	40.7	4.6	44.9	4.5	1.0	5.2
Land reclamation									
Surface mining[3]....	0.3	0	0.3	5.0	0	5.0	5.0	0	5.0
Grand Total[4].....	8.2	6.9	14.8	185.9	132.6	325.0	121.8	81.4	194.8

(1) Operating and maintaining pollution control devices. (2) Interest and depreciation. (3) Only coal mining. (4) Excluding noise control. (5) Expenditures made pursuant to Federal environmental legislation, beyond those that would have been made in the absence of this legislation.
*Less than $50 million.

State Pollution Control Costs

Source: National Wildlife Federation

Per capita costs of state government air and water pollution control and monitoring programs. Other states unavailable.

	1973	1974	1975 est.		1973	1974	1975 est.
Alabama...............	$ .23	$ .30	$ .31	Montana................	$1.03	$1.24	$1.46
Alaska...............	1.11	1.03	1.07	Nebraska..............	.31	.65	.75
Arizona............	.60	1.18		Nevada................	.41	65	90
Arkansas............	.45	.67		New Hampshire.........	5.17	6.66	7.15
California........	1.13	1.45	NA	New Jersey............	.69	.69	.98
Colorado...........		1	1.35	New Mexico............	.88	1.05	1.34
Connecticut.........		.92	1.10	New York..............	.42	.47	NA
Delaware........		.72	1.44	North Dakota..........	.25	.27	.30
District of Columbia		.96	1.26	Oklahoma..............	.29	.39	NA
Georgia..........		.25	1.29	Oregon................	.75	1.00	1.71
Hawaii...............		.61	NA	Pennsylvania..........	2.12	2.60	2.90
Idaho...............		4.03	4.40	Rhode Island..........	.73	.78	5.61
Illinois...............		.83	.91	South Carolina........	.65	.94	1.08
Indiana...............		.40	.54	South Dakota..........	.27	.52	.53
Iowa.................	.25	.28	.28	Tennessee.............	.43	.52	.59
Kansas...............	.49	.57	.67	Texas.................	.92	1.30	1.25
Kentucky.............	.74	.90	.96	Vermont...............	1.38	2.15	2.26
Louisiana............	.28	.29	NA	Virginia..............	.95	1.28	1.13
Michigan.............	.50	.83	.93	Washington............	1.36	1.37	NA
Minnesota............	.58	.74	.94	West Virginia.........	.85	1.04	1.12
Mississippi..........	.41	.60	.64	Wisconsin.............	1.70	2.86	4.27
Missouri.............	.22	.29	.36	Wyoming...............	.82	.97	1.17

Environmental Quality Index
Source: National Wildlife Federation.
Adapted from the Feb.-Mar., 1975 issue of National Wildlife Magazine.

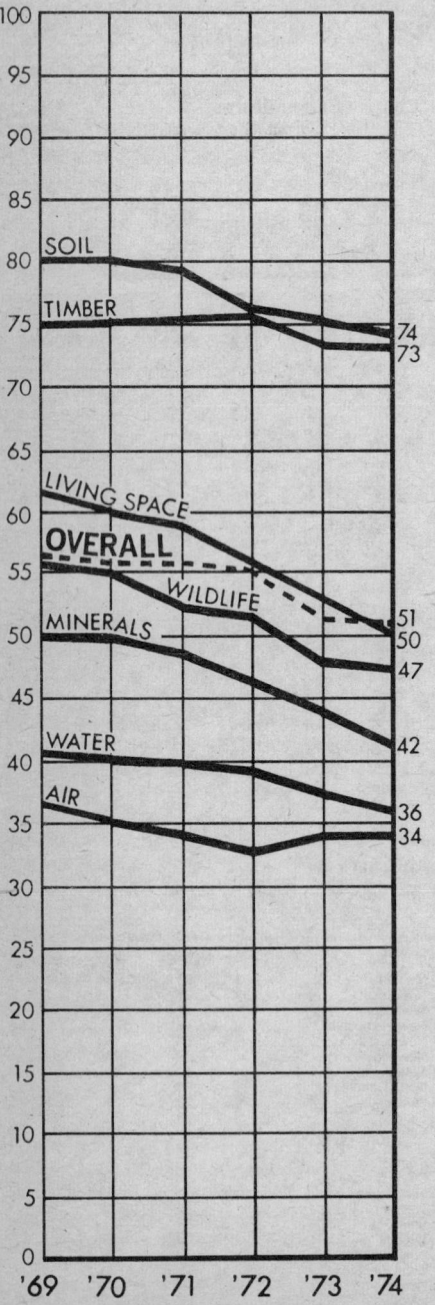

In 1969, the National Wildlife Federation began to record an index of environmental quality which measures progress or decline in 7 environmental areas. The index represents the rough, judgment of environmental protection experts and advocates influenced by very high standards of environmental quality. While their judgment is, in part, subjective and open to dispute, it does provide a relative indication of success and failure in achieving one set of goals.

Wildlife: The 1973 Endangered Species Act began to take effect, but Interior Department implementation efforts lagged; endangered species list remained at 109, though the list was said to be only 10% complete; 14 preserves were added to National Wildlife Refuge System, bringing total to 370; 5 nations ratified a pact to curb traffic in endangered plant and animal species; urbanization still removed one million acres a year from natural state.

Living space: The House of Representatives unexpectedly defeated land-use bill after the White House withdrew its backing, though the need for urban and rural planning remained great; most states enacted limited "quality of life" laws, preserving certain environmentally valuable areas; U.S. birthrate was the lowest in history, though population growth continued.

Soil: Over nine million reserve acres were plowed up in the U.S. in 1974 to meet world food needs, yet at least 23 million of total 360 million farm acres should be returned to grass or woods to prevent erosion; 4 billion tons of topsoil are eroded each year; pesticide use in general rose 40% in 1966-71, but Dieldrin and Aldrin, dangerous pesticides, were banned in 1974.

Timber: The 1974 housing recession reduced timber cut, which had increased 6% in 1973; federal funds advanced reforestation on public lands and smaller private woodlots; technology in timber and waste utilization improved; but "monoculture" (planting of one species alone) and pesticide use threatened forest ecosystems.

Minerals: An expected 60% growth in energy demand could probably be reduced by a third through conservation; also, alternate energy sources to fossil fuels are needed, as oil reserves will almost certainly decline, and coal use presents technological and environmental problems; solar energy, advanced by federal research, is emerging as a possible answer; non-fuel mineral shortages have increased, as 100% of bauxite (aluminum), chromium, and manganese is imported, as well as 90% of nickel and 50% of zinc.

Water: Funding continued to lag under 1972 Federal Water Pollution Control Act amendments, despite a Council of Environmental Quality finding that pollution control costs contribute less than one-half of one percent to U.S. inflation; 1977 clean water goals may be met by only one-third of water supplies, while some systems may not be in compliance for years; coliform bacteria and oxygen demand levels improved in 1974, but nutrient content increased, which could cause eutrophication, or accelerated aging of water bodies; in a 1975 survey, only one state reported a decline in water quality in preceding five years, but hardly any data were available to substantiate widespread improvement.

Air: Sulfur dioxide levels shot up in 1974 after earlier declines, resulting from a switch to high-sulfur fuels during Mideast oil boycott and oil price hike; a new federal law permitted the Environmental Protection Agency (EPA) to allow lower standards for power plants switching from oil to coal; the law also delayed auto emission standard enforcement, though the National Academy of Sciences reported that an $8 billion program to remove auto exhaust pollution could save $10 billion each year in medical and labor costs; the Academy also said air pollution was implicated in 15,000 U.S. urban deaths a year; a new federal EPA plan would allow states to permit some deterioration of air in rural areas, despite Supreme Court orders to the contrary; most major pollutants showed significant reductions in 1973.

EDUCATION
American Colleges and Universities

For Canadian Colleges and Universities see Index

Student and Faculty Figures for Spring Term, 1975
Source: World Almanac questionnaires and U.S. Office of Education

All coeducational unless followed by (M) for men only, or (W) for women only. Even though marked (M) or (W) some are coeducational at graduate level and in evening and summer divisions. Asterisk (*) denotes land-grant college.

Governing official is president unless otherwise designated. Year is that of founding. The word college is part of the name listed unless another designation is given.

Affiliation: C-county; D-religious denomination; Di-district; F-federal; Mu-municipal; P-private; S-state; T-territorial govt.; Y-YMCA.

Each institution listed has an enrollment of at least 200 students of college grade. Number of teachers is the total number of individuals on teaching staff. Enrollment and faculty in italics all branches and campuses.

(A) Designates colleges that have not provided up-to-date information.
(See Index for typical tuition fees)

SENIOR COLLEGES

Name	Location	Year	Governing Official and Affiliation		Students	Teachers
Abilene Christian	Abilene, Tex.	1906	John C. Stevens	P	4,479	219
Adams State	Alamosa, Col.	1925	John A. Marvel	S	2,805	119
Adelphi Univ.	Garden City, N.Y.	1896	Timothy Costello	P	8,250	350
Adrian	Adrian, Mich.	1859	John H. Dawson	P	1,032	90
Air Force Inst. of Tech.	Dayton, Oh.	1919	Maj. Gen. Simokaitis	F	428	114
Akron, Univ of	Akron, Oh.	1870	Dominic J. Guzzetta	S	21,095	1,375
Alabama A&M Univ.	Normal, Ala.	1875	Richard D. Morrison	S	4,046	234
Alabama State Univ.	Montgomery, Ala.	1874	Levi Watkins	S	3,224	193
Alabama, Univ. of.	University, Ala.	1831	David Mathews	S	15,638	1,095
At Birmingham.	Birmingham, Ala.	1966	J.F. Volker	S	10,365	902
At Huntsville.	Huntsville, Ala.	1951	Benhamin B. Graves	S	3,059	175
Alaska Methodist Univ.	Anchorage, Alas.	1957	John O. Picton	P	1,283	62
Alaska, Univ. of*.	Fairbanks, Alas.	1917	Robert W. Hiatt	S	18,254	422
Albany Coll. of Pharmacy	Albany, N.Y.	1881	Thomas Bonner, Chan	P	566	35
Albany State	Albany, Ga.	1903	Charles L. Hayes	S	1,662	143
Albertus Magnus (W)	New Haven, Conn.	1925	Sr. Francis Hefferman	D	472	61
Albion	Albion, Mich.	1835	Bernard Tagg Lomas	P	1,769	120
Albright	Reading, Pa.	1856	Arthur Schultz	P	1,419	101
Albuquerque, Univ. of	Albuquerque, N.M.	1920	Joseph Zenetti, Jr.	P	3,000	175
Alcorn State Univ.	Lorman, Miss.	1871	Walter Washington	S	2,568	125
Alderson-Broaddus	Philippi, W. Va.	1871	Richard E. Shearer	P	855	89
Alfred Univ.	Alfred, N.Y.	1857	M. Richard Rose	P	2,339	190
Allegheny	Meadville, Pa.	1815	Lawrence L. Pelletier	P	1,905	135
Allen Univ. (A).	Columbia, S.C.	1870	J. W. Hairston.	D	381	43
Alliance	Cambridge Spgs., Pa.	1912	Herman Szymanski	P	350	30
Alma	Alma, Mich.	1886	Robert D. Swanson	P	1,145	88
Alverma	Reading, Pa.	1958	Sister Mary Victorine	P	412	44
Alverno(W)	Milwaukee, Wis.	1936	Sister Joel Read	P	862	102
American Cons. of Music	Chicago, Ill.	1886	Leo Henn	P	1,900	111
American International	Springfield, Mass.	1885	Harry J. Courniotes	P	2,213	98
American Univ.	Washington, D.C.	1893	George H. Williams	P	13,000	672
Amherst	Amherst, Mass.	1821	John William Ward	P	1,276	141
Anderson	Anderson, Ind.	1917	Robert H. Reardon	P	1,726	129
Andrews Univ.	Berrien Springs, Mich.	1874	Richard Hammill	P	2,364	210
Angelo State Univ.	San Angelo, Tex.	1928	Lloyd Vincent	S	4,312	171
Anna Maria	Paxton, Mass.	1946	Sister Irene Socquet	D	663	68
Annhurst (A)	Woodstock, Conn.	1941	Sister Cecile Comtois	D	385	85
Antioch	Yellow Spgs., Oh.	1852	James P. Dixon	P	4,876	432
Appalachian Bible Inst.	Bradley, W. Va.	1950	Lester E. Pipkin	P	322	15
Appalachian State Univ.	Boone, N.C.	1899	Herbert W. Wey	S	8,014	446
Aquinas	Grand Rapids, Mich.	1940	Norbert J. Hruby	P	1,635	122
Arizona State Univ.	Tempe, Ariz.	1885	John W. Schwada	S	28,724	1,473
Arizona, Univ. of*	Tucson, Ariz.	1885	John Paul Schaefer	S	29,123	1,768
Arkansas Baptist	Little Rock, Ark.	1884	James C. Oliver	D	629	49
Arkansas College	Batesville, Ark.	1872	Dan C. West	D	483	40
Arkansas Polytechnic	Russellville, Ark.	1925	Kenneth Kersh	S	1,941	115
Arkansas State Univ.	State Univ., Ark.	1909	Carl R. Reng.	S	6,219	332
Arkansas, State Coll. of (A).	Conway, Ark.	1907	Silas D. Snow	S	4,300	275
Arkansas, Univ. of*	Fayetteville, Ark.	1871	David W. Mullins	S	23,645	1,515
At Little Rock (A).	Little Rock, Ark.	1927	Carey V. Stabler	S	4,171	148
At Pine Bluff (A)	Pine Bluff, Ark.	1873	Lawrence David	S	2,540	167
Armstrong.	Berkeley, Cal.	1918	John E. Armstrong	P	600	25
Armstrong State	Savannah, Ga.	1968	Henry L. Ashmore	S	3,300	132
Art Center Coll. of Design	Los Angeles, Cal.	1930	Donald R. Kubly	P	754	139
Asbury	Wilmore, Ky.	1890	Dennis F. Kinlaw	P	1,184	88
Ashland	Ashland, Oh.	1878	Glenn L. Clayton	D	1,904	171
Assumption	Worcester, Mass.	1904	Pasquale DiPasquale	D	2,150	150
Athenaeum of Ohio (M).	Norwood, Oh.	1829	Rev. J. Raymond Favret	D	218	50
Athens	Athens, Ala.	1822	Sidney Sandridge	D	800	53
Atlanta College of Art.	Atlanta, Ga.	1928	William Voos	P	518	29
Atlantic Christian.	Wilson, N.C.	1902	Arthur D. Wenger	D	1,710	117
Atlantic Union	So. Lancaster, Mass.	1882	W.G. Nelson	Mu	735	86
Auburn Univ. *	Auburn, Ala.	1856	Harry Philpott	S	16,013	975
Augsburg.	Minneapolis, Minn.	1869	Oscar A. Anderson	D	1,633	108

167

Name	Location	Year	Governing Official and Affiliation		Students	Teachers
Augusta	Augusta, Ga	1925	George A. Christenberry	S	3,938	133
Augustana	Rock Island, Ill	1860	J. Thomas Tredway	D	2,288	181
Augustana	Sioux Falls, S. D	1860	Charles L. Balcer	D	2,103	175
Aurora	Aurora, Ill	1897	Lloyd Richardson	D	1,056	96
Austin	Sherman, Tex	1849	John D. Moseley	D	1,073	95
Austin Peay State Univ	Clarksville, Tenn	1929	Joe Morgan	S	4,200	180
Averett	Danville, Va	1859	Conwell A. Anderson	P	1,158	45
Avila	Kansas City, Mo	1916	Sister Olive Dallavis	P	1,445	144
Azusa Pacific	Azusa, Cal	1899	Cornelius Haggard	P	1,275	76
Babson	Babson Park, Mass	1919	Ralph Sorenson	P	2,496	113
Baker Univ	Baldwin City, Kan	1858	Jerald C. Walker	D	769	72
Baldwin-Wallace	Berea, Oh	1845	A. B. Bonds, Jr	D	2,702	193
Ball State Univ	Muncie, Ind	1918	John J. Pruis	S	16,246	875
Baltimore, Univ. of	Baltimore, Md	1925	H. Mebane Turner	S	5,706	238
Baptist Bible College of Pa	Clarks Summit, Pa	1932	Ernest Pickering	D	774	49
Baptist Coll. at Charleston	Charleston, S.C	1965	John Hamrick	D	2,241	106
Barat (W)	Lake Forest. Ill	1919	Sister Margaret Burke	P	771	81
Barber-Scotia	Concord, N.C	1867	Mable McLean	P	472	38
Bard	Annandale, N.Y	1934	Leon Botstein	P	644	71
Barnard (W)	New York, N.Y	1889	Martha E. Peterson	P	1,928	200
Barrington	Barrington, R.I	1900	Louis Caister, Act	P	553	30
Barry(W)	Miami, Fla	1940	Sister M. Trinita Flood	P	1,443	125
Bates	Lewiston, Me	1864	Thomas H. Reynolds	P	1,247	97
Baylor Univ	Waco, Tex	1845	Abner V. McCall	D	8,409	441
Beaver	Glenside, Pa	1853	Edward D. Gates	P	1,157	73
Belhaven	Jackson, Miss	1883	Howard J. Cleland	D	778	47
Bellarmine	Louisville, Ky	1950	Eugene Petrik	P	1,353	88
Bellevue	Bellevue, Neb	1966	Richard Winchell	P	1,164	43
Belmont	Nashville, Tenn	1951	Herbert C. Gabhart	P	1,078	91
Belmont Abbey	Belmont, N.C	1876	Rev. John Bradley	D	688	45
Beloit	Beloit, Wis	1846	Miller Upton	P	1,600	135
Bemidji State	Bemidji, Minn	1919	Robert Decker	S	4,127	191
Benedict	Columbia, S.C	1870	Henry Ponder	P	1,286	88
Benedictine	Atchison, Kan	1971	Rev. Gerard Senecal	P	971	79
Benjamin Franklin Univ	Washington, D.C	1925	Mrs. John Kennedy	P	1,000	47
Bennett (W)	Greensboro, N.C	1873	Isaac H. Miller	D	592	61
Bennington	Bennington, Vt	1925	Gail Thain Parker	P	590	65
Bentley	Waltham, Mass	1917	Gregory Adamian	P	3,610	138
Berea	Berea, Ky	1855	W.D. Weatherford	P	1,279	130
Berry	Mount Berry, Ga	1902	John R. Bertrand	P	1,540	84
Bethany Bible	Santa Cruz, Cal	1919	C. Morse Ward	D	559	30
Bethany	Lindsborg, Kan	1881	Alvin Hahn	P	694	53
Bethany	Bethany, W.Va	1840	Cecil Underwood	P	1,092	64
Bethany Nazarene	Bethany, Okla	1899	Stephen Nease	P	1,196	72
Bethel	Mishawaka, Ind	1947	Albert Beutler	D	472	29
Bethel	North Newton, Kan	1887	Harold Schultz	P	617	52
Bethel	McKenzie, Tenn	1842	William L. Cottrell	D	400	28
Bethel	St. Paul, Minn	1947	Carl Lundquist	P	1,467	99
Bethune-Cookman(A)	Daytona Beach. Fla	1872	Richard V. Moore	D.P.	1,127	61
Biola	La Mirada, Cal	1908	J. Richard Chase	P	2,400	125
Birmingham Southern	Birmingham, Ala	1856	Ralph M. Tanner	Mu	780	70
Biscayne	Miami, Fla	1962	Rev. John McDonnell	D	14,974	83
Bishop (A)	Dallas, Tex	1881	Milton K. Curry	D	2,085	99
Black Hills State	Spearfish, S.D	1883	M. N. Freeman	S	1,736	87
Blackburn	Carlinville, Ill	1837	John Alberti	P	645	47
Bloomfield	Bloomfield, N.J	1868	Merle F. Allshouse	P	901	74
Bloomsburg State	Bloomsburg, Pa	1839	James McCormick	S	5,291	324
Blue Mountain (W)	Blue Mountain, Miss	1873	E. Harold Fisher	D	358	34
Bluefield State	Bluefield, W. Va	1895	Billy Coffindaffer	S	1,170	67
Bluffton	Bluffton, Oh	1899	Benjamin Sprunger	P	657	55
Bob Jones Univ	Greenville, S. C	1927	Bob Jones	P	4,279	281
Boca Raton	Boca Raton, Fla	1963	Donald E. Ross	P	402	33
Boise State	Boise, Ida	1932	John Barnes	S	9,757	463
Boston	Chestnut Hill, Mass	1863	Rev. J. Donald Monan	D	12,749	840
Boston State	Boston, Mass	1852	Kermit C. Morrissey	S	5,805	295
Boston Conserv. of Music	Boston, Mass	1867	George Brambilla	P	544	94
Boston Univ	Boston, Mass	1869	John Silber	P	23,581	1,197
Bowdoin	Brunswick, Me	1794	Roger Howell, Jr	P	1,356	100
Bowie State	Bowie, Md	1865	Samuel L. Myers	S	3,323	194
Bowling Green State Univ	Bowling Green, Oh	1910	Hollis A. Moore	S	15,800	725
Bradford	Haverhill, Mass	1803	Jack Armstrong	P	307	37
Bradley Univ	Peoria, Ill	1897	Martin G. Abegg	P	5,025	320
Brandeis Univ	Waltham, Mass	1948	Marver Bernstein	P	3,442	371
Brenau	Gainesville, Ga	1878	James T. Rogers	P	513	60
Brescia	Owensboro, Ky	1950	Sister Geo. Ann Cecil	P	1,008	81
Briar Cliff	Sioux City, Ia	1929	Kasper Marking	D	747	48
Briarcliff (W)	Briarcliff Manor, N.Y	1903	Josiah Bunting	P	400	58
Bridgeport Engineering Inst	Bridgeport, Conn	1924	William J. Owens	P	358	56
Bridgeport, Univ. of	Bridgeport, Conn	1927	Leland Miles	P	8,194	494
Bridgewater	Bridgewater, Va	1880	Wayne F. Geisert	P	804	63
Bridgewater State	Bridgewater, Mass	1840	Adrian Rondileau	S	7,453	296
Brigham Young Univ	Provo, Ut	1875	Dallin H. Oaks	P	25,000	1,200
Brooklyn Law School	Brooklyn, N.Y	1901	Raymond Lisle, Dean	P	1,153	43
Brooks Institute	Santa Barbara, Cal	1945	Ernest Brooks, 2d	P	650	28
Brown Univ	Providence, R.I	1764	Donald F. Hornig	P	6,758	457
Bryan	Dayton, Tenn	1930	Theodore Mercer	P	550	37
Bryant	Smithfield, R.I	1863	Harry Evarts	P	4,600	142
Bryn Mawr (W)	Bryn Mawr, Pa	1885	Harris L. Wofford, Jr	P	1,526	177
Bucknell Univ	Lewisburg, Pa	1846	C. H. Watts, 2d	P	3,148	239
Buena Vista	Storm Lake, Ia	1891	Keith G. Briscoe	P	813	57
Butler Univ	Indianapolis, Ind	1855	Alexander E. Jones	P	4,250	250
Cabrini	Radnor, Pa	1957	Sister Mary L. Sullivan	D	523	52

Name	Location	Year	Governing Official and Affiliation		Students	Teachers
Caldwell	Caldwell, N.J.	1939	Sister M. Anne John	D	805	73
California Baptist	Riverside, Cal.	1950	James R. Staples	D	729	51
Calif. Coll. of Arts and Crafts	Oakland, Cal.	1907	Harry Xavier Ford	P	1,195	135
Calif. College of Podiatric Med.	San Francisco, Cal.	1914	H. D. Bailey	P	205	45
Calif. Inst. of the Arts	Valencia, Cal.	1961	Robert Fitzpatrick	P	678	117
Calif. Inst. of Tech.	Pasadena, Cal.	1891	Harold Brown	P	1,557	264
Calif. Lutheran	Thousand Oaks, Cal.	1961	Mark Mathews	P	1,946	64
Calif. Maritime Academy	Vallejo, Cal.	1929	Joseph P. Rizza	S	360	29
Calif. State	Bakersfield, Cal.	1970	Jacob Frankel	S	2,900	190
Calif. State	California, Pa.	1859	George Roadman	S	5,174	344
Calif. State	Dominquez Hills, Cal.	1960	Leo Cain	S	5,800	350
Calif. State	Rohnert Park, Cal.	1960	Thomas McGrath	S	5,900	485
Calif. State	San Bernardino, Cal.	1965	John Pfau	S	3,500	1,210
Calif. State	Turlock, Cal.	1957	Carl Gatlin	S	2,810	178
Calif. State Polytechnic Univ.	San Luis Obispo, Cal.	1901	Robert Kennedy	S	14,434	800
Calif. State Polytechnic Univ.	Pomona, Cal.	1938	Robert C. Kramer	S	10,678	694
Calif. State Univ.	Northridge, Cal.	1958	James W. Cleary	S	25,209	950
Calif. State Univ.	Chico, Cal.	1887	Stanford Cazier	S	12,650	800
Calif. State Univ.	Fresno, Cal.	1911	Norman Baxter	S	15,400	1,000
Calif. State Univ.	Fullerton, Cal.	1957	Donald Shields	S	20,000	750
Calif. State Univ.	Long Beach, Cal.	1949	Stephen Horn	S	30,677	1,610
Calif. State Univ.	Los Angeles, Cal.	1947	J. A. Greenlee	S	24,500	1,000
Calif. State Univ.	Sacramento, Cal.	1947	James Bond	S	19,615	1,300
Calif. State Univ.	San Francisco, Cal.	1873	Paul F. Romberg	S	21,981	1,589
Calif. Univ. of*	Berkeley, Cal.	1868	David S. Saxon	S	122,436	11,758
Berkeley Campus	Berkeley, Cal.	1873	Albert H. Bowker, Chan.	S	29,730	2,384
Davis Campus	Davis, Cal.	1905	James Meyer, Chan.	S	16,239	1,513
Irvine Campus	Irvine, Cal.	1960	D.G. Aldrich, Chan.	S	8,764	701
Los Angeles Campus	Los Angeles, Cal.	1919	Charles Young, Chan.	S	31,966	3,134
Riverside Campus	Riverside, Cal.	1949	Ivan Hinderaker, Chan.	S	5,015	473
San Diego Campus	La Jolla, Cal.	1912	William D. McElroy, Chan.	S	8,875	946
San Francisco Campus	San Francisco, Cal.	1873	F. A. Sooy, Chan.	S	2,992	1,285
Santa Barbara Campus	Santa Barbara, Cal.	1891	Vernon Cheadle, Chan.	S	13,277	902
Santa Cruz Campus	Santa Cruz, Cal.	1965	M. Christensen, Chan.	S	5,578	378
Calumet	E. Chicago, Ind.	1951	Rev. James McCabe	D	1,462	80
Calvary Bible	Kansas City, Mo.	1932	Leslie Madison	P	221	16
Calvin	Grand Rapids, Mich.	1876	William Spoelhof	Mu	3,414	202
Cameron	Lawton, Okla.	1968	Don Owens	S	4,576	186
Campbell	Buies Creek, N.C.	1887	Norman A. Wiggins	D	1,820	104
Campbellsville	Campbellsville, Ky.	1906	William R. Davenport	P	678	53
Canisius	Buffalo, N.Y.	1870	V. Rev. James Demske	P	4,004	175
Capital Univ.	Columbus, Oh.	1850	Thomas H. Langevin	P	2,699	180
Cardinal Stritch	Milwaukee, Wis.	1937	Sister M. Kliebhan	D	1,109	97
Carleton	Northfield, Minn.	1866	Howard R. Swearer	P	1,636	150
Carlow	Pittsburgh, Pa.	1929	Sister Jane Scully	D	1,000	81
Carnegie-Mellon Univ.	Pittsburgh, Pa.	1900	Richard M. Cyert	D	2,990	484
Carroll	Helena, Mon.	1909	Francis Kerins	D	1,261	74
Carroll	Waukesha, Wis.	1846	Robert V. Cramer	P	1,200	94
Carson-Newman	Jefferson City, Tenn.	1851	John A. Fincher	P	1,676	112
Carthage	Kenosha, Wis.	1847	Harold H. Lentz	P	1,633	105
Case Western Reserve Univ.	Cleveland, Oh.	1880	L. A. Toepfer	P	8,843	1,500
Castleton State	Castleton, Vt.	1787	Harold Abel	S	1,831	120
Catawba	Salisbury, N.C.	1851	M.L. Shotzberger	D	1,079	88
Cathedral (M)	Douglaston, N.Y.	1947	Rev. Thomas Gradilone	D	241	44
Catholic Univ. of America (M)	Washington, D.C.	1887	Clarence C. Walton	P	6,857	583
Cath. Univ. of Puerto Rico	Ponce, Puerto Rico	1948	E. J. Carreras	P	8,247	370
Cedar Crest (W)	Allentown, Pa.	1867	Pauline Tompkins	P	668	71
Cedarville	Cedarville, Oh.	1887	James Jeremiah	D	1,050	66
Centenary	Shreveport, La.	1825	John Horton Allen	D	718	85
Central Bible	Springfield, Mo.	1922	Rev. Philip Crouch	D	1,076	42
Central	Pella, Ia.	1853	Kenneth J. Weller	P	1,349	84
Central Connecticut State	New Britain, Conn.	1849	F. Don James	S	6,908	645
Central Methodist	Fayette, Mo.	1854	Harold Hamilton	D	672	62
Central Mich. Univ.	Mt. Pleasant, Mich.	1892	William Boyd	S	14,500	628
Central Missouri State Univ.	Warrensburg, Mo.	1871	Warren C. Lovinger	S	8,760	405
Central State Univ.	Edmond, Okla.	1890	Bill Lillard	S	10,793	391
Central State Univ.	Wilberforce, Oh.	1883	Lionel H. Newsom	S	2,131	119
Central Washington State	Ellensburg, Wash.	1891	James E. Brooks	S	7,116	342
Central Wesleyan	Central, S.C.	1906	Claude Rickman	D	365	24
Centre Coll. of Kentucky	Danville, Ky.	1819	Thomas A. Spragens	P	769	81
Chadron State	Chadron, Neb.	1911	Larry Tangeman	S	1,856	129
Chaminade Col. of Honolulu	Honolulu, Ha.	1955	Robert Maguire	P	1,408	142
Charleston, Coll. of	Charleston, S.C.	1770	Theodore Stern	S	4,562	215
Chatham (W)	Pittsburgh, Pa.	1869	Edward D. Eddy	P	550	75
Chestnut Hill (W)	Philadelphia, Pa.	1924	Sister Mary Xavier Kirby	D	976	101
Cheyney State	Cheyney, Pa.	1837	Wade Wilson	S	2,400	230
Chicago Coll. (Osteopathic)	Chicago, Ill.	1913	Thaddeus Kawalek	P	374	150
Chicago State Univ.	Chicago, Ill.	1869	Benjamin Alexander	S	6,580	360
Chicago Technical (M)	Chicago, Ill.	1904	Leslie Morey	P	754	18
Chicago, Univ. of (A)	Chicago, Ill.	1891	Vacant	P	9,083	1,125
Christian Brothers	Memphis, Tenn.	1871	Rev. Bernard LoCoco	D	736	70
Cincinnati, Univ. of	Cincinnati, Oh.	1819	Warren G. Bennis	S.Mu	36,827	2,960
Citadel, The (Military) (M)	Charleston, S.C.	1842	Gen. George Seignious	S	2,967	150
Claflin	Orangeburg, S.C.	1869	Hubert V. Manning	D	895	56
Claremont Men's (M)	Claremont, Cal.	1946	Jack Lee Stark	P	819	97
Clarion State	Clarion, Pa.	1867	James Gemmell	S	4,500	310
Clark	Atlanta, Ga.	1869	Vivian Henderson	P	1,424	122
Clark Univ.	Worcester, Mass.	1887	Mortimer Apply	P	2,751	185
Clarke (W)	Dubuque, Ia.	1843	Robert Giroux	D	620	93
Clarkson Coll. of Tech.	Potsdam, N.Y.	1896	Robert A. Plane	P	2,495	178
Cleary	Ypsilanti, Mich.	1883	Lynn Brenneman, Act.	P	600	30
Clemson Univ.	Clemson, S.C.	1889	Robert C. Edwards	S	10,586	702
Cleveland Inst. of Art	Cleveland, Oh.	1882	Joseph McCullough	P	988	81
Cleveland Inst. of Music	Cleveland, Oh.	1920	Grant Johannesen	P	255	78
Cleveland State Univ.	Cleveland, Oh.	1964	Walter Waetjen	S	16,261	674
Coe	Cedar Rapids, Ia.	1853	Leo Nussbaum	P	1,162	125

Name	Location	Year	Governing Official and Affiliation		Students	Teachers
Coker	Hartsville, SC	1908	C.Womble, Jr.	P	550	43
Colby	Waterville, Me.	1813	Robert E.L. Strider	P	1,600	146
Colgate Univ.	Hamilton, N.Y.	1819	Thomas Bartlett	S	2,500	224
Colorado	Colo. Spgs. Col.	1874	Lloyd E. Werner	S	1,945	153
Colorado Sch. of Mines	Golden, Col.	1874	Guy McBride	S	1,970	188
Colorado State Univ. *	Fort Collins, Col.	1870	A.R. Chamberlain	S	16,798	1,129
Colorado, Univ. of (A)	Boulder, Col.	1876	Frederick P. Thieme	S	30,428	2,729
Colorado Springs	Colorado Springs, Col.	1965	Lawrence Silverman	S	2,525	103
Colorado Women's (W)	Denver, Col.	1888	Dumont F. Kenny	P	751	67
Columbia	Columbia, S.C.	1854	R. Wright Spears	P	940	79
Columbia	Columbia, Mo.	1851	W. Merle Hill	P	942	52
Columbia Bible	Columbia, S.C.	1923	J. Robertson McQuilkin	P	664	37
Columbia Union	Takoma Park, Md.	1904	Colin Standish	P	919	94
Columbia Univ. (A)	New York, N.Y.	1754	William McGill	P	14,475	4,500
Teachers College (A)	New York, N.Y.	1888	John H. Fischer	P	5,199	403
Columbus	Columbus, Ga.	1958	Thomas Y. Whitley	S	5,006	218
Columbus Coll. of Aryt & Design	Columbus, Oh.	1870	Joseph Canzani, Dean	P	593	54
Concord	Athens, W.Va.	1872	Billy Coffindaffer	S	1,537	96
Concordia	Bronxville, N.Y.	1881	Robert Schnabel	D	625	58
Concordia	Moorhead, Minn.	1891	Paul Dover	D	2,402	200
Concordia	St. Paul, Minn.	1893	Harvey Stegemoeller	D	614	60
Concordia Senior	Fort Wayne, Ind.	1857	Herbert Bredemeier	D	421	40
Concordia Teachers	River Forest, Ill.	1864	Paul A. Zimmerman	D	1,177	76
Concordia Teachers	Seward, Neb.	1894	W. T. Janzow	D	1,234	120
Connecticut	New London, Conn.	1911	Oakes Ames	P	1,955	184
Connecticut Univ. of*	Storrs, Conn.	1939	Glenn Fergusen	S	16,099	1,248
Converse (W)	Spartanburg, S.C.	1889	Robert T. Coleman, Jr.	P	829	72
Cooper Union	New York, N.Y.	1859	John White	P	900	160
Coppin State	Baltimore, Md.	1900	Calvin Burnett	S	2,574	217
Cornell	Mt. Vernon, Ia.	1853	Philip Secor	P	951	88
Cornell Univ.*	Ithaca, N.Y.	1865	Dale R. Corson	D	16,868	1,743
Covenant	Lookout Mt., Ga.	1955	Marion Barnes	D	538	32
Creighton Univ.	Omaha, Neb.	1878	Rev. Joseph Labaj	D	4,551	707
Culver-Stockton	Canton, Mo.	1853	Harold Doster	D	1,600	110
Cumberland	Williamsburg, Ky.	1889	J.M. Boswell	D	1,600	110
Curry	Milton, Mass.	1879	John S. Hafer	P	850	75
Dakota State	Madison, S.D.	1881	Richard Bowen	S	713	56
Dakota Wesleyan Univ.	Mitchell, S.D.	1885	Donald E. Messer	D	486	52
Dallas, Univ. of	Irving, Tex.	1956	Donald A. Cowan	D	1,717	125
Dana	Blair, Neb.	1884	Earl Mezoff	D	610	48
Daniel Payne	Birmingham, Ala.	1889	Daniel Grant	D	420	23
Dartmouth	Hanover, N.H.	1769	John George Kemeny	P	4,034	481
David Lipscomb	Nashville, Tenn.	1891	Athens C. Pullias	D	2,182	103
Davidson	Davidson, N.C.	1837	Samuel R. Spencer, Jr.	P	1,218	96
Davis and Elkins	Elkins, W. Va.	1904	G. E. Hermanson	P	790	45
Dayton Art Institute	Dayton, Oh.	1919	Sherwin Silverman (Dir.)	P	291	19
Dayton, Univ. of	Dayton, Oh.	1850	V. Rev. R. A. Roesch	D	7,843	443
Defiance	Defiance, Oh.	1850	M. Ludwig	P	571	58
Delaware State*	Dover, Del.	1891	Luna I. Mishoe	S	2,044	118
Delaware, Univ. of*	Newark, Del.	1833	E. A. Trabant	S	18,511	1,266
Del. Valley Coll. of S&A	Doylestown, Pa.	1896	James Work	P	1,357	92
Delta State Univ.	Cleveland, Miss.	1924	Aubrey K. Lucas	S	3,187	188
Denison Univ.	Granville, Oh.	1831	Joel P. Smith	P	2,127	150
Denver, Univ. of	Denver, Col.	1864	Maurice B. Mitchell	P	7,708	514
DePaul Univ.	Chicago, Ill.	1898	V. Rev. J. R. Cortelyou	P	10,010	552
DePauw Univ.	Greencastle, Ind.	1837	William E. Kerstetter	P	2,412	170
Detroit Bible	Detroit, Mich.	1945	Wendell Johnston	P	299	25
Detroit Coll. of Business	Dearborn, Mich.	1962	Frank Paone, V.P.	P	1,150	56
Detroit Coll. of Law	Detroit, Mich.	1891	G. Cameron Buchanan	P	950	45
Detroit Inst. of Technology	Detroit, Mich.	1891	Dewey F. Barich	P	1,366	112
Detroit, Univ. of	Detroit, Mich.	1877	V. Rev. M. Carron	D	8,879	678
Dickinson	Carlisle, Pa.	1773	Howard L. Rubendal	P	1,660	120
Dickinson School of Law	Carlisle, Pa.	1834	Dale F. Shughart	P	425	26
Dickinson State	Dickinson, N.D.	1918	R. C. Gilluind	S	1,001	62
Dillard Univ.	New Orleans, La.	1869	Samuel Cook	Mu	1,117	93
District of Col. Teachers (A)	Washington, D.C.	1851	Paul Cooke	Mu	2,323	127
Doane	Crete, Neb.	1872	Philip C. Heckman	P	605	50
Dr. Martin Luther	New Ulm, Minn.	1884	Rev. Conrad Frey	D	667	65
Dominican Coll. of Blauvelt	Blauvelt, N.Y.	1959	Sister Natalie Casey	P	1,112	58
Dominican Coll. of S. Rafael	San Rafael, Cal.	1889	Sister M. Samuel Conlan	D	765	95
Dordt	Sioux Center, Ia.	1955	B. J. Haan	D	990	50
Dowling	Oakdale, N.Y.	1968	Allyn Robinson	P	1,200	200
Drake Univ.	Des Moines, Ia.	1881	Wilbur C. Miller	P	6,881	341
Drew Univ.	Madison, N.J.	1866	Paul Hardin	P	3,336	317
Drexel Univ.	Philadelphia, Pa.	1891	William W. Hagerty	P	9,000	646
Drury	Springfield, Mo.	1873	William Everheart	P	2,214	156
Dubuque, Univ of (A)	Dubuque, Ia.	1852	Walter F. Peterson	P	1,004	66
Duke Univ.	Durham, N.C.	1823	Terry Sanford	P	8,923	1,000
Duquesne Univ.	Pittsburgh, Pa.	1878	V. Rev. J. McAnulty	P	8,080	484
Dyke	Cleveland, Oh.	1848	John Corfias	P	1,017	51
D'Youville	Buffalo, N.Y.	1908	Sister Mary C. Barton	P	1,021	85
Earlham	Richmond, Ind.	1847	Franklin Wallin	D	1,231	110
East Central Okla. State	Ada, Okla.	1909	Stanley Wagner	S	2,953	125
East Stroudsburg, State	E. Stroudsburg, Pa.	1891	Darrell Holmes	S	3,926	190
East Tennessee State Univ.	Johnson City, Tenn.	1911	Delos Culp	S	9,050	427
East Texas Baptist	Marshall, Tex.	1912	Howard C. Bennett	D	693	41
East Texas State Univ.	Commerce, Tex.	1889	F. H. McDowell	S	9,013	400
Eastern	St. Davids, Pa.	1952	Daniel E. Weiss	D	593	42

Name	Location	Year	Governing Official and Affiliation		Students	Teachers
Eastern Conn. State	Willimantic, Conn.	1889	Charles Richard Webb	S	2,813	150
Eastern Illinois Univ.	Charleston, Ill.	1895	Gilbert C. Fite	S	8,026	608
Eastern Kentucky Univ.	Richmond, Ky.	1906	Robert R. Martin	S	12,571	527
Eastern Mennonite	Harrisonburg, Va.	1917	Myron S. Augsburger	P	971	101
Eastern Michigan Univ.	Ypsilanti, Mich.	1849	James Brickley	S	17,422	683
Eastern Montana	Billings, Mon.	1927	Stanley Heywood	S	3,057	140
Eastern Nazarene	Quincy, Mass.	1918	Leslie Parrott	D	879	66
Eastern New Mexico Univ.	Portales, N.M.	1934	Gail Shannon, Act.	P	5,700	180
Eastern Oregon State	La Grande, Ore.	1929	Rodney A. Briggs	S	1,495	142
Easten Washington State	Cheney, Wash.	1890	Emerson C. Shuck	S	6,823	408
Eckerd	St. Petersburg, Fla.	1958	Billy O. Wireman	P	917	68
Edgecliff	Cincinnati, Oh.	1935	Sister M. A. Molitor	D	851	72
Edgewood	Madison, Wis.	1927	Sister Cecilia Carey	P	603	58
Edinboro State	Edinboro, Pa.	1857	Chester T. McNerney	S	6,689	455
Edward Waters	Jacksonville, Fla.	1866	Samuel J. Tucker	P	543	31
Eisenhower	Seneca Falls, N.Y.	1968	John Rosenkraus	P	555	64
Elizabethtown	Elizabethtown, Pa.	1899	Morely J. Mays	P	1,597	126
Elmhurst	Elmhurst, Ill.	1871	Ivan Frick	P	2,542	150
Elmira	Elmira, N.Y.	1855	J. Ralph Murray	P	3,600	131
Elon	Elon College, N.C.	1889	J. F. Young	P	2,175	94
Embry-Riddle Aero. Univ.	Daytona Beach, Fla.	1926	Jack R. Hunt	P	1,492	112
Emerson	Boston, Mass.	1880	Richard Chapin	P	1,765	137
Emmanuel (W)	Boston, Mass.	1919	Sister Mary McCarthy	P	1,176	97
Emory & Henry	Emory, Va.	1836	Thomas F. Chilcote	D	850	59
Emory Univ.	Atlanta, Ga.	1836	S. S. Atwood	D	6,995	2,179
Emporia Coll. of	Emporia, Kan.	1882	Robert Prins, Act.	D	600	25
Emporia, Kansas State	Emporia, Kan.	1863	John Visser	S	5,593	244
Erskine	Due West, S.C.	1839	M.S. Bell	D	735	59
Eureka	Eureka, Ill.	1855	Ira W. Langston	P	421	40
Evangel	Springfield, Mo.	1955	Robert Spence	D	1,165	78
Evansville, Univ. of	Evansville, Ind.	1854	Wallace B. Graves	P	4,850	250
Evergreen State Coll.	Olympia, Wash.	1967	Charles McCann	S	2,446	115
Fairfield Univ.	Fairfield, Conn.	1942	Rev. Thomas Fitzgerald	P	4,877	283
Fairleigh Dickinson Univ.	Rutherford, N.J.	1942	Jerome Pollack	P	17,594	1,999
Fairmont State (A)	Fairmont, W. Va.	1867	Eston K. Feaster	S	3,320	180
Faith Baptist Bible	Ankeny, Ia.	1924	David Nettleton	P	585	24
Federal City	Washington, D.C.	1968	Wendell P. Russell	Mu	7,563	656
Felician	Lodi, N.J.	1942	Sr. Mary Lawniczak	P	595	54
Ferris State	Big Rapids, Mich.	1884	Robert Ewigleben	S	9,264	427
Findlay	Findlay, Oh.	1882	Glen R. Rasmussen	P	928	75
Fisk Univ.	Nashville, Tenn.	1867	J. R. Lawson	P	1,489	107
Fitchburg State	Fitchburg, Mass.	1894	James Hammond	S	5,000	250
Flagler	St. Augustine, Fla.	1968	William L. Proctor	P	564	36
Florence State Univ.	Florence, Ala.	1872	Robert M. Guillot	S	3,642	162
Florida Atlantic Univ.	Boca Raton, Fla.	1961	G. L. Creech	S	7,000	350
Florida A. & M. Univ.*	Tallahassee, Fla.	1887	Benjamin Luther Perry, Jr.	S	4,871	370
Florida Inst. of Tech.	Melbourne, Fla.	1958	Jerome P. Keuper	P	2,437	200
Florida Memorial	Miami, Fla.	1879	Lester B. Brown	D	699	40
Florida Southern	Lakeland, Fla.	1885	Charles T. Thrift, Jr.	D	1,405	88
Florida State Univ.	Tallahassee, Fla.	1857	Stanley Marshall	S	21,187	1,121
Florida Technological Univ.	Orlando, Fla.	1963	Charles N. Millican	S	8,529	424
Florida, Univ. of*	Gainesville, Fla.	1853	Robert Marston	S	28,332	3,000
Fontbonne (W)	St. Louis, Mo.	1917	Sister Jane Hassett	P	619	58
Fordham Univ.	Bronx, N.Y.	1841	Rev. James C. Finley	P	14,211	799
Ft. Hays Kansas State	Hays, Kan.	1902	John W. Gustad	S	5,062	257
Ft. Lauderdale Coll. of Bus. & Fin	Ft. Lauderdale, Fla.	1962	Stanley Drake	P	500	29
Ft. Lewis	Durango, Col.	1962	Rexer Berndt	S	2,700	130
Fort Valley State*	Fort Valley, Ga.	1895	Cleveland W. Pettigrew	S	1,807	153
Ft. Wayne Art Inst	Fort Wayne, Ind.	1922	Russell Oettel	P	209	12
Fort Wayne Bible	Fort Wayne, Ind.	1904	Timothy Warner	D	626	45
Ft. Wright	Spokane, Wash.	1907	Sister Helen Volkomener	D	360	60
Framingham State	Framingham, Mass.	1839	D. Justin McCarthy	S	4,937	281
Francis Marion	Florence, S.C.	1970	Walter D. Smith	S	2,239	104
Franconia	Franconia, N.H.	1963	Leon Botstein	P	415	45
Franklin	Franklin, Ind.	1834	Wesley N. Haines	P	682	47
Franklin Univ.	Columbus, Oh.	1902	Joseph Frasen	P	3,356	120
Franklin and Marshall	Lancaster, Pa.	1787	Keith Spalding	P	2,150	153
Franklin Pierce	Rindge, N.H.	1962	Frank S. DiPietro	P	970	68
Free Will Baptist Bible	Nashville, Tenn.	1942	L. C. Johnson	D	538	30
Friends Univ.	Wichita, Kan.	1898	Harold C. Cope	D	930	63
Frostburg State	Frostburg, Md.	1898	Nelson Guild	S	3,520	171
Furman Univ.	Greenville, S.C.	1826	Gordon W. Blackwell	D	2,354	167
Gallaudet	Washington D. C.	1864	Edward C. Merrill, Jr.	P	943	126
Gannon	Erie, Pa.	1944	Rev. W. J. Nash	P	3,100	147
Gardner-Webb	Boiling Springs, NC.	1905	Ernest Eugene Poston	D	1,410	95
General Motors Institute	Flint, Mich.	1919	Harold P. Rodes	P	3,039	201
Geneva	Beaver Falls, Pa.	1848	Edwin C. Clarke	D	1,442	121
George Fox	Newberg, Ore.	1891	David La Shana	D	481	35
George Mason Univ.	Fairfax, Va.	1972	V. H. Dykstra	S	6,470	370
George Peabody Coll. for Teachers	Nashville, Tenn.	1889	John Dunworth	P	2,000	162
Geo. Washington Univ.	Washington, D.C.	1821	Lloyd H. Elliott	P	15,331	1,225
George Williams	Downers Grove, Ill	1890	Richard E. Hamlin	P	1,481	95
Georgetown	Georgetown, Ky.	1829	Robert L. Mills	P	1,057	75
Georgetown Univ.	Washington, D.C.	1789	Rev. R. J. Henle	D	10,359	1,013
Georgia	Milledgeville, Ga	1889	J. Whitney Bunting	S	3,500	172
Georgia Inst. of Technology	Atlanta, Ga.	1885	Joseph M. Pettit	S	8,000	683
Georgia Southern	Statesboro, Ga.	1906	Pope A. Duncan	S	6,125	328
Georgia Southwestern	Americus, Ga.	1906	William B. King	S	2,375	135

Name	Location	Year	Governing Official and Affiliation		Students	Teachers
Georgia State Univ.	Atlanta, Ga.	1913	Noah N. Langdale	S	19,010	864
Georgia, Univ. of*	Athens, Ga.	1786	Fred C. Davison	S	21,233	1,500
Georgian Court (W)	Lakewood, N.J.	1908	Sister Mary Stephanie	P	697	64
Gettysburg	Gettysburg, Pa.	1832	Carl Arnold Hanson	D	1,845	145
Glenville State	Glenville, W.Va.	1872	D. Banks Wilburn	S	1,469	84
Goddard	Plainfield, Vt.	1938	John Andrews, Act.	P	1,791	100
Golden Gate Univ.	San Francisco, Cal.	1901	Otto Butz	P	5,700	550
Gonzaga Univ.	Spokane, Wash.	1887	Bernard Coughlin	D	3,185	217
Gordon	Wenham, Mass.	1889	Harold J. Ockenga	P	967	50
Goshen	Goshen, Ind.	1894	J. Lawrence Burkholder	D	1,201	110
Goucher (W)	Towson, Md.	1885	Rhoda Dorsey	P	1,038	117
Governors State Univ.	Park Forest South, Ill.	1969	William Engbretson	S	2,944	217
Grace Bible Institute.	Omaha, Neb.	1943	Robert Benton	D	535	25
Graceland	Lamoni, Iowa	1895	William Higdon	P	1,295	83
Grambling State Univ.	Grambling, La.	1901	Ralph W. E. Jones	S	3,571	266
Grand Canyon	Phoenix, Ariz.	1949	William R. Hintze	P	1,036	35
Grand Valley State	Allendale, Mich.	1960	Arend Lubbers	S	6,677	357
Great Falls, Coll. of	Great Falls, Mon.	1932	Msgr. A. M. Brown	P	1,085	66
Greensboro	Greensboro, N.C.	1838	H. Wilkinson	D	526	58
Greenville	Greenville, Ill.	1892	Orley R. Herron	D	816	65
Grinnell	Grinnell, Iowa	1846	Richard Turner	P	1,187	109
Grove City	Grove City, Pa.	1884	Charles S. MacKenzie	P	2,139	119
Gulford	Greensboro, N.C.	1837	Grimsley T. Hobbs	D	1,590	100
Gulf-Coast Bible	Houston, Tex.	1953	John Conley	D	295	23
Gustavus Adolphus.	St. Peter, Minn.	1862	Vacant	D	2,040	142
Gwynedd-Mercy	Gwynedd Valley, Pa.	1948	Sister Isabelle Keiss	D	996	105
Halmemann Medical	Philadelphia, Pa.	1848	Wharton R. Shober	P	1,273	1,432
Hamilton (M)	Clinton, N.Y.	1812	J. M. Carovano, Act.	P	950	91
Hamline Univ. (A)	St. Paul, Minn.	1854	Richard Bailey	P	1,297	142
Hampden-Sydney (M)	Hampden-Sydney, Va.	1776	W. Taylor Reveley	P	716	56
Hampshire (A)	Amherst, Mass.	1965	Charles Longsworth	P	1,000	90
Hampton Institute	Hampton, Va.	1868	Roy D. Hudson	P	2,830	237
Hanover	Hanover, Ind.	1827	John E. Horner	P	1,016	80
Hardin-Simmons Univ.	Abilene, Tex.	1891	Elwin L. Skiles	P	1,636	110
Harding	Searcy, Ark.	1924	Clinton L. Ganus, Jr.	D	2,467	130
Harris Teachers.	St. Louis, Mo.	1857	Richard Stumpe	Mu	1,070	60
Hartford, Univ of	W. Hartford, Conn.	1877	A. M. Woodruff	P	8,674	523
Hartwick	Oneonta, N.Y.	1928	Adolph G. Anderson	P	1,617	127
Harvard Univ.**(1)	Cambridge, Mass.	1636	Derek Curtis Bok	P	15,730	3,090(2)
Harvey Mudd	Claremont, Cal.	1957	Joseph B. Platt	P	461	54
Hastings.	Hastings, Neb.	1882	Clyde B. Matters	P	692	58
Haverford (M)	Haverford, Pa.	1833	John R. Coleman	P	750	140
Hawaii, The Church Coll. of	Laie, Ha.	1955	Stephen Brower	P	1,008	75
Hawaii, Univ of*	Honolulu, Ha.	1907	Fujio Matsuda	S	47,214	2,302
Heald Engineering	San Francisco, Cal.	1863	James Deitz	P	1,000	70
Heidelberg	Tiffin, Oh.	1850	Leslie H. Fishel, Jr.	P	1,141	105
Henderson State	Arkadelphia, Ark.	1890	Martin Garrison	S	3,206	180
Hendrix	Conway, Ark.	1884	Roy Shilling, Jr.	D	1,058	54
High Point.	High Point, N.C.	1924	Wendell M. Patton	D	1,068	71
Hillsdale	Hillsdale, Mich.	1844	George C. Roche	P	1,025	65
Hiram	Hiram, Oh.	1850	Elmer Jagow	P	1,304	110
Hobart & William Smith.	Geneva, N.Y.	1822	Allan A. Kuusisto	P	1,795	143
Hofstra Univ.	Hempstead, N.Y.	1935	Robert J. Payton	P	11,761	693
Hollins (W)	Hollins Coll., Va.	1842	John A. Logan Jr.	P	1,028	91
Holy Cross, Coll. of the.	Worcester, Mass.	1865	Rev. John Brooks	D	2,531	198
Holy Family	Philadelphia, Pa.	1954	Sister Mary Lillian	P	1,013	90
Holy Names.	Oakland, Cal.	1868	Sister M. Irene Woodward	P	702	101
Hood	Frederick, Md.	1893	Vacant	P	840	100
Hope	Holland, Mich.	1866	Gordon Van Wylen	P	2,198	150
Houghton.	Houghton, N.Y.	1883	Wilber T. Dayton	P	1,216	86
Houston Baptist Univ.	Houston, Tex.	1963	William Hinton	D	1,206	87
Houston, Univ. of.	Houston, Tex.	1927	Philip G. Hoffman	S	34,000	1,700
Downtown College	Houston, Tex.	1948	W. I. Dykes, Chan.	S	4,250	140
Howard Payne	Brownwood, Tex.	1889	Roger L. Brooks.	D	1,392	105
Howard Univ.	Washington, D.C.	1867	James E. Cheek	P	9,505	1,600
Humboldt State Univ.	Arcata, Cal.	1913	Alistair McCrone.	S	7,500	507
Huntingdon	Montgomery, Ala.	1854	Allen Jackson	D	572	50
Huntington.	Huntington, Ind.	1897	E. DeWitt Baker.	D	522	63
Huron	Huron, S. D.	1883	Richard E. Hill.	D	313	32
Husson	Bangor, Me.	1898	Franklin Peters.	P	969	46
Huston-Tillotson.	Austin, Tex.	1876	John T. King.	D	679	41
Idaho, Coll. of.	Caldwell, Ida.	1891	William Cassell	P	849	63
Idaho State Univ.	Pocatello, Ida.	1901	William E. Davis.	S	8,172	385
Idaho, Univ of*	Moscow, Ida.	1889	Ernest W. Hartung.	S	7,138	498
Illinois.	Jacksonville, Ill.	1829	Donald Mundinger.	P	775	55
Illinois Benedictine.	Lisle, Ill.	1887	Rev. Daniel Kucera.	P	1,200	85
Illinois Coll. of Optometry	Chicago, Ill.	1872	Alfred Rosenbloom.	P	532	54
Illinois Inst. of Technology	Chicago, Ill.	1892	Thomas L. Martin.	P	6,164	726
Illinois State Univ.	Normal, Ill.	1857	Gene Budig.	S	17,362	1,002
Illinois, Univ. of*	Urbana; Champaign.	1867	John E. Corbally Jr.	S	19,393	1,098
Chicago Circle	Chicago, Ill.	1965	Warren Cheston, Chan.	S	4,311	616
Medical Center	Chicago, Ill.	1896	Joseph Begando, Chan.	S	35,045	3,636
Urbana — Champaign	Urbana, Ill.	1867	Jack W. Peliason, Chan.	S	1,620	135
Illinois Wesleyan Univ.	Bloomington, Ill.	1850	Robert Eckley.	P	1,111	139
Immaculata (W)	Immaculata, Pa.	1920	Sister Mary Antione.	P	620	69
Immaculate Heart.	Los Angeles, Cal.	1916	Sister Helen Kelley.	P	1,513	117
Incarnate Word College.	San Antonio, Tex.	1881	Sr. Margaret Slattery.	D	2,528	148
Indiana Central.	Indianapolis, Ind.	1902	Gene Sease.	P	400	34
Indiana Inst. of Tech.	Ft. Wayne, Ind.	1930	Charles W. Terrell.	P		

(1) Includes Radcliffe College. (2) Includes teaching fellows.
**oldest college in the United States.

Name	Location	Year	Governing Official and Affiliation		Stu-dents	Teach-ers
Indiana State Univ.	Terre Haute, Ind.	1865	Richard Landini	S	10,729	750
Indiana Univ.	Bloomington, Ind.	1820	John W. Ryan	S	70,286	4,500
Indiana Univ. of Penn.	Indiana, Pa.	1875	Vacant		11,006	800
Insurance, Coll. of	New York, N.Y.	1962	A. Leslie Leonard	P	1,462	139
Inter American Univ.	San Juan, P.R.	1912	Sol Luis Descartes	P	19,000	852
Iona	New Rochelle, N.Y.	1940	Rev. Bro. John Driscoll	P	4,698	224
Iowa State Univ.*	Ames, Iowa	1868	W. Robert Parks	S	19,321	1,682
Iowa, Univ. of.	Iowa City, Iowa	1847	Willard L. Boyd	S	21,271	1,193
Iowa Wesleyan	Mt. Pleasant, Iowa	1842	Louis Haselmayer	D	688	66
Ithaca	Ithaca, N.Y.	1892	Ellis L. Phillips	P	4,235	272
Jackson State Univ.	Jackson, Miss.	1877	John A. Peoples, Jr.	S	5,960	367
Jacksonville State Univ.	Jacksonville, Ala.	1883	Ernest Stone	S	5,606	242
Jacksonville Univ.	Jacksonville, Fla.	1934	Robert H. Spiro	P	2,259	125
Jamestown	Jamestown, N.D.	1883	W. S. Egekvist, Act.	P	491	53
Jarvis Christian	Hawkins, Tex.	1912	John Paul Jones	D	553	49
Jersey City State	Jersey City, N.J.	1927	W. Liggitt, Act.	S	8,200	471
John Brown Univ.	Siloam Springs, Ark.	1919	John E. Brown, Jr.	P	546	46
John Carroll Univ.	Univ. Hgts., Oh.	1886	Rev. Henry Birkenhauer	P	3,850	211
John F. Kennedy Univ.	Martinez, Cal.	1964	Robert Fisher	P	343	80
John F. Kennedy.	Wahoo, Neb.	1965	Theodore Dillow	P	238	27
John Marshall Law School.	Chicago, Ill.	1899	F. Herzog, Act. Dean	P	1,592	57
John Wesley	Owosso, Mich.	1909	Kenneth Armstrong		525	35
Johns Hopkins Univ.	Baltimore, Md.	1876	Steven Muller	P	9,849	1,506
Johnson C. Smith Univ.	Charlotte, N.C.	1867	Wilbert Greenfield	P	1,294	78
Johnson State.	Johnston, Vt.	1866	E. Elmendorf	S	1,253	100
Johnson & Wales	Providence, R.I.	1914	Morris J. Gaebe	P	5,896	278
Judson (W)	Marion, Ala.	1838	N. R. McCrummen	D	459	32
Juilliard School, The	New York, N.Y.	1906	Peter Mennin	P	1,191	180
Juniata	Huntingdon, Pa.	1876	Frederick M. Binder	P	1,150	90
Kalamazoo.	Kalamazoo, Mich.	1833	George N. Rainsford	D	1,356	74
Kan. City Art Inst.	Kansas City, Mo.	1885	John W. Lottes.	P	585	62
Kan. City Coll. of Osteop. Med.	Kansas City, Mo.	1916	Rudolph Bremen	P	543	80
Kansas Newman	Wichita, Kan.	1933	Rev. Roman S. Galiardi	P	627	52
Kansas State.	Pittsburg, Kan.	1903	George F. Budd	S	5,409	264
Kansas State Univ.*	Manhattan, Kan.	1863	James A. McCain	S	16,477	1,330
Kansas, Univ. of.	Lawrence, Kan.	1864	Archie R. Dykes	S	21,483	1,170
Kansas Wesleyan	Salina, Kan.	1886	Daniel Bratton	P	517	38
Kearney State.	Kearney, Neb.	1905	Brendon McDonald	S	5,116	231
Keene State.	Keene, N.H.	1909	Leo Redfern	S	2,998	147
Kent State Univ.	Kent, Oh.	1910	Glenn A. Olds.	S	24,850	836
Kentucky State Univ.*	Frankfort, Ky.	1886	Carl M. Hill	S	2,174	150
Kentucky, Univ. of*.	Lexington, Ky.	1865	Otis A. Singletary.	S	20,359	1,568
Kentucky Wesleyan (A).	Owensboro, Ky.	1783	William James.	P	933	71
Kenyon.	Gambier, Oh.	1824	Philip Jordon, Jr.	P	1,451	119
Keuka (W).	Keuka Park, N.Y.	1890	William Boyle.	P	586	52
King.	Bristol, Tenn.	1867	Powell A. Fraser	D	364	42
King's.	Briarcliff Manor, N.Y.	1938	Robert A. Cook.	P	783	64
King's.	Wilkes-Barre, Pa.	1946	Rev. Charles Sherrer	P	2,133	125
Kirkland (W)	Clinton, N.Y.	1968	Samuel F. Babbitt	P	625	61
Kirksville Coll. of Osteop. Med.	Kirksville, Mo.	1892	H. C. Moore.	P	472	92
Know.	Galesburg, Ill.	1837	E. Inman Fox.	P	1,253	102
Knoxville.	Knoxville, Tenn.	1875	Edward Brantley	D	794	59
Kutztown State	Kutztown, Pa.	1866	Lawrence M. Stratton.	S	3,653	330
Ladycliff	Highland Falls, N.Y.	1933	Rev. Francis J. Breidenbach.	P	460	53
Lafayette.	Easton, Pa.	1826	K. R. Bergethon	P	2,183	180
LaGrange.	LaGrange, Ga.	1831	Waights Henry, Jr.	D	698	51
Lake Erie (W).	Painesville, Oh.	1856	Paul Weaver	P	849	80
Lake Forest.	Lake Forest, Ill.	1857	Eugene Hotchkiss	P	994	90
Lakeland	Sheboygan, Wis.	1862	Ralph Mirse	D	456	41
Lake Superior State.	Sault Ste. Marie, Mich.	1946	Kenneth Shouldice.	S	2,064	118
Lamar Univ.	Beaumont, Tex.	1951	John E. Gray.	S	11,490	589
Lambuth.	Jackson, Tenn.	1843	James S. Wilder	D	850	70
Lander.	Greenwood, S.C.	1872	Larry Jackson.	S	1,314	91
Lane.	Jackson, Tenn.	1882	Herman Stone, Jr.	P	656	51
Langston Univ.*	Langston, Okla.	1897	James Mosley, Act.	S	1,024	74
LaRoche.	Pittsburgh, Pa.	1963	Sister De La Salle Mahler.	D	614	61
La Salle.	Philadelphia, Pa.	1863	Bro. Daniel Burke.	D	6,000	342
La Verne.	La Verne, Cal.	1891	Leland Newcomer	P	1,046	80
Lawrence Inst. Of Tech.	Southfield, Mich.	1932	W. H. Buell.	P	4,206	200
Lawrence Univ.	Appleton, Wis.	1847	Thomas S. Smith	P	1,374	124
Lebanon Valley.	Annville, Pa.	1866	Fredrick Sample.	D	1,284	104
Lee.	Cleveland, Tenn.	1919	Charles Conn.	Mu	1,069	72
Lehigh Univ.	Bethlehem, Pa.	1866	W. Deming Lewis.	P	6,135	598
Leland Stanford Jr. Univ.	Stanford, Cal.	1891	Richard W. Lyman	P	11,423	1,097
Le Moyne.	Syracuse, N.Y.	1946	Rev. William L. Reilly.	P	1,787	125
Le Moyne-Owen.	Memphis, Tenn.	1862	Walter Walker.	P	899	60
Lenoir Rhyne.	Hickory, N.C.	1891	Raymond Bost	D	1,333	101
Lesley (W).	Cambridge, Mass.	1909	Don A. Orton.	P	1,311	109
LeTourneau.	Longview, Tex.	1946	R. LeTourneau.	P	740	45
Lewis Univ.	Lockport, Ill.	1930	Lester Carr.	P	3,000	130
Lewis & Clark.	Portland, Ore.	1867	John R. Howard.	P	3,037	180
Limestone.	Gaffney, S.C.	1845	Jack Jones Early.	P	587	56
Lincoln Christian.	Lincoln, Ill.	1944	E. Hargrove, Chan.	D	909	58
Lincoln Memorial Univ.	Harrogate, Tenn.	1897	Frank W. Welch.	P	669	46
Lincoln Univ.	Jefferson City, Mo.	1866	James Frank.	S	2,454	165
Lincoln Univ.	Lincoln Univ., Pa.	1854	Herman Branson.	S	1,103	103
Lincoln Univ.	San Francisco, Cal.	1919	T. Kong Lee.	P	1,000	70
Lindenwood.	St. Charles, Mo.	1827	William Spencer	P	1,175	98
Linfield.	McMinnville, Ore.	1849	Cornelius Siemens.	P	936	85
Livingston Univ.	Livingston, Ala.	1835	Asa Green.	S	1,329	84
Livingstone.	Salisbury, N.C.	1879	F. George Shipman	P	816	64

Name	Location	Year	Governing Official and Affiliation		Stu-dents	Teach-ers
Lock Haven State	Lock Haven, Pa.	1870	Francis Hamblin	S	2,400	200
Lone Mountain	San Francisco, Cal.	1898	Sister Gertrude Patch	D	797	47
Long Island Univ.	Brooklyn, N.Y.	1926	E. Clark, Act.	P	7,000	400
C. W. Post	Greenvale, N.Y.	1954	Vacant.	P	9,700	331
Longwood	Farmville, Va.	1839	Henry I. Willett, Jr.	S	2,266	159
Loras	Dubuque, Iowa.	1839	Msgr. Francis P. Friedl	P	1,402	90
Los Angeles Baptist	Newhall, Cal.	1927	John Dunkin	D	305	30
Loretto Heights	Denver, Col.	1919	Ronald C. Hayes	P	726	58
Louisiana	Pineville, La.	1906	G. Earl Guinn	P	1,036	66
Louisiana Tech. Univ.	Ruston, La.	1894	F. J. Taylor	S	7,967	508
Louisiana St. Univ.*	Baton Rouge, La.	1860	Martin Woodin	S	42,650	3,870
Baton Rouge Campus	Baton Rouge, La.	1860	Paul Murrill, Chan.	S	23,667	1,257
Medical Center	New Orleans, La.	1931	Allen Copping, Chan.	S	1,785	1,617
New Orleans Campus	New Orleans, La.	1956	Homer L. Hitt, Chan.	S	12,338	449
Shreveport Campus	Shreveport, La.	1967	Donald Shipp, Chan.	S	2,921	118
Louisville, Univ. of	Louisville, Ky.	1798	James G. Miller	S	14,033	1,576
Lowell State**	Lowell, Mass.	1894	D. H. O'Leary.	S	2,193	209
Lowell Technological Inst.**	Lowell, Mass.	1895	Everett V. Olsen.	S	6,500	300

**Lowell Tech. Inst. and Lowell State College due to merge July 1, 1975 to form Univ. of Lowell.

Name	Location	Year	Governing Official and Affiliation		Stu-dents	Teach-ers
Loyola	Baltimore, Md.	1852	Rev. J. A. Sellinger.	D	4,000	203
Loyola Univ.	Chicago, Ill.	1870	Rev. R. C. Baumhart.	D	14,575	1,650
Loyola Univ.	New Orleans, La.	1904	Rev. James Carter	D	4,499	305
Loyola Marymount Univ.	Los Angeles, Cal.	1911	Rev. D. P. Merrifield.	D	5,303	335
Lubbock Christian	Lubbock, Tex.	1956	F. W. Mattox	D	1,086	76
Luther	Decorah, Iowa.	1861	Elwin D. Farwell.	P	1,898	135
Luther Rice	Alexandria, Va.	1966	Chester Bishop	P	232	33
Lycoming	Williamsport, Pa.	1812	Harold Hutson.	D	1,424	80
Lynchburg	Lynchburg, Va.	1903	Carey Brewer.	P	1,127	101
Lyndon State	Lyndonville, Vt.	1911	H. Franklin Irwin.	S	852	84
Macalester	St. Paul, Minn.	1874	C. McLarnan, Act.	P	1,748	133
MacMurray	Jacksonville, Ill.	1846	John Wittich	P	781	71
Madison	Harrisonburg, Va.	1908	Ronald Carrier	S	6,841	391
Madison Business (A)	Madison, Wis.	1856	Otto J. Madland.	P	293	19
Madonna	Livonia, Mich.	1947	Sister Mary Danatha.	P	1,780	76
Maine Maritime Academy	Castine, Me.	1941	E. A. Rodgers (Supt.)	S	500	43
Maine System, Univ. of	Bangor, Me.	1968	Stanley Freeman, Act. Chan.	S	25,696	1,115
at Augusta	Augusta, Me.	1968	Lloyd Jewett.	S	2,595	51
at Farmington	Farmington, Me.	1864	Einar Olsen.	S	1,898	95
at Ft. Kent	Ft. Kent, Me.	1878	Richard J. Spath.	S	520	26
at Machias	Machias, Me.	1909	Arthur Buswell	S	638	36
at Orono, Me.	Orono, Me.	1865	Howard Nevill.	S	10,576	579
at Portland-Gorham	Portland, Me.	1970	E. Miller.	S	8,080	263
at Presque Isle	Presque Isle, Me.	1903	Stanley Salwak.	S	1,389	65
Malone	Canton, Oh.	1892	Lon D. Randall.	D	841	61
Manchester	N. Manchester, Ind.	1889	Alfred B. Helman.	D	1,173	96
Manhattan	Bronx, N.Y.	1853	Brother Stephen Sullivan	P	4,200	285
Manhattan Sch. of Music	New York, N.Y.	1917	George Schick	P	1,000	200
Manhattanville	Purchase, N.Y.	1841	Vacant.	P	2,361	159
Mankato State	Mankato, Minn.	1867	Douglas Moore.	S	13,200	600
Mansfield State	Mansfield, Pa.	1857	Lawrence Park.	S	3,145	215
Marian	Indianapolis, Ind.	1851	Louis C. Gatto.	P	869	99
Marian Coll. of Fond du Lac	Fond du Lac, Wis.	1936	James Hanlon.	P	477	52
Marietta	Marietta, Oh.	1835	Sherrill Cleland	P	1,906	136
Marion	Marion, Ind.	1920	Woodrow Goodman	D	920	57
Marist	Poughkeepsie, N.Y.	1929	Linus Richard Foy	P	1,654	110
Marlboro	Marlboro, Vt.	1938	Thomas B. Ragle.	P	205	36
Marquette Univ.	Milwaukee, Wis.	1881	Rev. J. P. Raynor.	P	10,987	720
Mars Hill	Mars Hill, N.C.	1856	Fred Blake Bentley.	D	1,599	110
Marshall Univ.	Huntington, W. Va.	1837	John G. Barker.	S	9,041	370
Mary Baldwin	Staunton, Va.	1846	William Watkins Kelly	D	756	60
Mary Hardin Baylor	Belton, Tex.	1845	Bobby E. Parker.	D	951	63
Mary Manse	Toledo, Oh.	1922	W. Salesses.	Mu	579	38
Mary Washington	Fredericksburg, Va.	1908	Prince B. Woodward.	S	2,087	142
Marycrest	Davenport, Iowa.	1939	Sister Cathleen Real.	D	1,015	75
Marygrove	Detroit, Mich.	1910	Raymond Fleck.	D	1,700	164
Maryland Inst. of Art.	Baltimore, Md.	1826	Eugene W. Leake.	P	1,154	98
Maryland, Univ. of*	College Park, Md.	1859	Wilson Elkins.	S	34,667	5,400
Eastern Shore	Princess Anne, Md.	1886	Archie Buffkins (Chan.)	S	1,119	94
Maryhurst	Marylhurst, Ore.	1893	Sister Marian D. Robinson	D	603	46
Marymount	Salina, Kan.	1922	Emerald Dechant.	D	568	55
Marymount (W)	Tarrytown, N.Y.	1919	John Meng.	P	1,007	101
Marymount Coll. of Va.	Arlington, Va.	1951	N. Matella Berg.	P	637	57
Marymount Manhattan (W)	New York, N.Y.	1948	Sister Colette Mahoney.	D	1,572	146
Maryville	Maryville, Tenn.	1819	Joseph J. Copeland.	D	647	56
Maryville (W)	St. Louis, Mo.	1872	Sister Harriet Switzer.	P	1,041	90
Marywood (W)	Scranton, Pa.	1915	Sister M. Coleman Nee.	D	2,748	170
Massachusetts Coll. Of Art	Boston, Mass.	1873	John Nolan.	S	1,547	108
Mass. Coll. of Pharmacy	Boston, Mass.	1823	Raymond A. Gosselin.	P	1,232	100
Mass. Institute of Tech.*	Cambridge, Mass.	1861	Jerome Wiesner.	P	7,972	972
Mass. Maritime Academy (M)	Buzzards Bay, Mass.	1891	Lee Harrington.	S	1,385	108
Massachusetts, Univ. of*	Amherst, Mass.	1863	R. Bromery, Chan.	S	24,699	1,309
Boston Campus	Boston, Mass.	1964	Carlo L. Golino, Chan.	S	6,600	500
Mayville State	Mayville, N.D.	1889	James Schobel.	S	626	40
McKendree	Lebanon, Ill.	1828	Eric N. Rackham.	Mu	711	40
McMurry	Abilene, Tex.	1923	Tom K. Kim.	D	1,318	83
McNeese State Univ.	Lake Charles, La.	1939	Thomas S. Leary.	S	5,547	341
McPherson	McPherson, Kan.	1887	Galen Snell	D	794	37
Medaille	Buffalo, N.Y.	1875	Robert Hesse	P	415	37
Medical Coll. of Ga.	Augusta, Ga.	1828	William Moretz	S	2,224	440
Medical Univ. of S.C.	Charleston, S.C.	1824	William McCord	S	2,020	630
Medical Coll. of Pa.	Philadelphia, Pa.	1850	Robert J. Slater.	P	336	423
Meharry Medical	Nashville, Tenn.	1876	Lloyd C. Elam	P	735	435
Memphis Academy of Arts	Memphis, Tenn.	1936	Edwin C. Rust (Dir.).	P	225	27

Name	Location	Year	Governing Official and Affiliation		Stu-dents	Teach-ers
Memphis State Univ.	Memphis, Tenn.	1912	Billy Jones	S	21,282	716
Menlo	Menlo Park, Cal.	1915	Richard O'Brien	P	520	52
Mercer Univ.	Macon, Ga.	1833	Rufus C. Harris	D	3,480	200
Mercy	Dobbs Ferry, N.Y.	1950	Donald Grunewald	P	2,676	172
Mercy Coll. of Detroit	Detroit, Mich.	1941	Sister Agnes Mary Mansour	D	1,936	120
Mercyhurst	Erie, Pa.	1926	Marion Shane	P	1,349	95
Meredith (W)	Raleigh, N.C.	1891	John Edgar Weems	D	1,811	103
Merrimack	No. Andover, Mass.	1947	Rev. John Aherne	D	2,450	182
Mesa College	Grand Junction, Col.	1925	Carl Wahlberg	S	3,641	201
Messiah	Grantham, Pa.	1909	D. Ray Hostetter	D	945	90
Methodist	Fayetteville, N.C.	1956	Richard Pearce	P	721	57
Metropolitan State	Denver, Col.	1963	James D. Palmer	S	10,450	367
Miami Univ.	Oxford, Oh.	1809	Phillip R. Shriver	S	17,056	805
Miami, Univ. of	Coral Gables, Fla.	1925	Henry K. Stanford	P	13,213	1,279
Michigan State Univ.*	East Lansing, Mich.	1855	Clifton R. Wharton, Jr.	S	43,459	2,687
Michigan Tech. Univ.	Houghton, Mich.	1885	Raymond L. Smith	S	5,366	402
Michigan, Univ. of	Ann Arbor, Mich.	1817	Robben W. Fleming	S	44,372	5,362
Mid-America Nazarene	Olathe, Kan.	1968	R. Curtis Smith	D	975	59
Middle Tenn. State Univ.	Murfreesboro, Tenn.	1911	M. G. Scarlett	S	9,448	537
Middlebury	Middlebury, Vt.	1800	Olin Robison	P	1,896	150
Midland Lutheran	Fremont, Neb.	1883	L. Dale Lund	D	706	56
Midwestern Univ.	Wichita Falls, Tex.	1922	John Barker	S	4,200	167
Miles	Birmingham, Ala.	1905	W. Clyde Williams	P	1,103	106
Millersville State	Millersville, Pa.	1855	William Duncan	S	6,083	320
Milligan	Milligan Coll., Tenn.	1881	Jess W. Johnson	P	748	55
Millikin Univ.	Decatur, Ill.	1903	J. Roger Miller	P	1,589	127
Mills (W)	Oakland, Cal.	1885	Robert J. Wert	P	913	107
Millsaps	Jackson, Miss.	1892	Edward Collins	Mu	966	79
Milton	Milton, Wis.	1846	Joseph Kipper	P	600	70
Milwaukee Sch. of Eng.	Milwaukee, Wis.	1903	Karl O. Werwath	P	2,156	200
Minneapolis Coll. of Art & Design	Minneapolis, Minn.	1886	J. Hausman	P	1,000	73
Minnesota, Univ. of*	Minneapolis, Minn.	1851	C.P. Magrath	S	51,834	4,774
Duluth Campus	Duluth, Minn.	1947	R. W. Darland (Prov.)	S	6,768	450
Morris Campus	Morris, Minn.	1960	John Imholte (Prov.)	S	1,690	99
Minot State	Minot, N. D.	1913	Gordon Olson	S	2,200	120
Misericordia	Dallas, Pa.	1924	Sister Miriam Teresa	P	1,006	90
Mississippi	Clinton, Miss.	1826	Lewis Nobles	P	2,457	133
Mississippi Industrial	Holly Springs, Miss.	1905	E.E. Rankin	D	275	24
Miss. Univ. for Women (W)	Columbus, Miss.	1884	Charles P. Hogarth	S	2,956	175
Mississippi State Univ.*	Miss. State, Miss.	1879	William L. Giles	S	11,572	768
Mississippi Univ. of	University, Miss.	1848	P.E. Fortune, Jr. (Chan.)	S	11,000	500
Mississippi Valley State Univ.	Itta Bena, Miss.	1950	E.A. Boykins	S	2,840	146
Missouri Baptist College	St. Louis, Mo.	1968	R. Sutherland, Act.	D	355	25
Missouri Southern State	Joplin, Mo.	1938	Leon Billingsly	S	3,328	125
Missouri Univ. of*	Columbia, Mo.	1839	C. Brice Ratchford	S	49,423	2,722
At Columbia	Columbia, Mo.	1839	H.W. Schooling, Chan.	S	22,961	1,476
At Kansas City	Kansas City, Mo.	1929	James Olson, Chan.	S	11,004	514
At Rolla	Rolla, Mo.	1870	R. Bisplinghoff, Chan.	S	4,064	340
At St. Louis	St. Louis, Mo.	1963	A. Grobman, Chan.	S	11,394	383
Missouri Valley	Marshall, Mo.	1889	Donald Ziemke	D	606	42
Missouri Western State	St. Joseph, Mo.	1915	Marvin Looney	S	3,187	170
Mobile	Mobile, Ala.	1961	William K. Weaver, Jr.	P	808	35
Molloy	Rockville Ctre, N.Y.	1955	Sister Janet Fitzgerald	D	1,100	120
Monmouth	Monmouth, Ill.	1853	DeBow Freed	P	750	65
Montana Coll. of Mineral Science and Technology	Butte, Mon.	1893	Fred W. DeMoney	S	852	48
Montana State Univ.	Bozeman, Mon.	1893	Carl McIntosh	S	8,452	569
Montana, Univ. of	Missoula, Mon.	1893	Richard Bowers	S	8,566	466
Montclair State	Upper Montclair, N.J.	1908	David W. D. Dickson	S	14,000	619
Monterey Inst. of Foreign Studies	Monterey, Cal.	1955	Samson Knoll	P	350	58
Montevallo. Univ. of	Montevallo, Ala.	1896	Kermit Johnson	S	3,600	160
Moody Bible Institute	Chicago, Ill.	1886	George Sweeting	P	2,255	157
Moore Coll. of Art (W)	Philadelphia, Pa.	1844	Mayo Bryce	P	617	80
Moorhead State	Moorhead, Minn.	1885	Roland Dille	S	6,103	318
Moravian	Bethlehem, Pa.	1807	Herman E. Collier	D	1,553	125
Morehead State Univ.	Morehead, Ky.	1922	Adron Doran	S	6,765	350
Morehouse (M)	Atlanta, Ga.	1867	Hugh Gloster	P	1,230	107
Morgan State.	Baltimore, Md.	1867	T. Fraser, Act.	S	5,809	275
Morningside	Sioux City, Ia.	1894	Thomas S. Thompson	P	1,464	93
Morris College	Sumter, S.C.	1908	Luns Richardson	P	449	31
Morris Brown	Atlanta, Ga.	1881	Robert Threatt	P	1,415	94
Morris Harvey	Charleston, W. Va.	1888	Marshall Buckalew	P	2,203	150
Mt. Holyoke (W)	S. Hadley, Mass.	1837	David Bicknell	P	1,909	204
Mt. Mary	Yankton, S.D.	1936	Bruce Weier	P	578	79
Mt. Mary (W)	Milwaukee, Wis.	1929	Sister Mary Nora Barber	P	1,200	112
Mt. Mercy	Cedar Rapids, Ia.	1928	Sister Mary Hennessey	P	825	71
Mt. St. Joseph (W)	Mt. St. Joseph, Oh.	1920	Robert Wolverton	D	882	101
Mt. St. Mary (W)	Hooksett, N. H.	1934	Sister Amy Hoey	D	203	34
Mt. St. Mary	Newburgh, N. Y.	1959	William O'Hara	P	855	77
Mt. St. Mary's	Los Angeles, Cal.	1925	Sister Cecilia Louise	P	1,280	125
Mt. St. Mary's	Emmitsburg, Md.	1808	John J. Dillon	D	1,216	84
Mt. St. Vincent, Coll. of	Riverdale, N. Y.	1847	Sister Doris Smith	D	1,060	85
Mt. Senario	Ladysmith, Wis.	1962	Robert Lovett	P	238	30
Mt. Union	Alliance, Oh.	1846	Ronald Weber	P	1,185	84
Mt. Vernon	Washington, D.C.	1875	Peter Pelham	P	283	37
Mt. Vernon Nazarene	Mount Vernon, Oh.	1966	John A. Knight	D	603	43
Muhlenberg	Allentown, Pa.	1848	John H. Morey	P	1,864	162
Multnomah Sch. of the Bible	Portland, Ore.	1936	Willard M. Aldrich	P	1,421	37
Mundelein (W)	Chicago, Ill.	1930	Sister Ann Ida Gannon	P	1,024	89
Murray State Univ.	Murray, Ky.	1922	C. Curris	S	7,355	355
Muskingum	New Concord, Oh.	1837	William P. Miller	P	1,148	103
Nasson	Springvale, Me.	1912	John S. Bailey	P	661	51
Nathaniel Hawthorne	Antrim, N.H.	1962	Kenneth McLaughlin	P	506	44
National Coll. of Business	Rapid City, S.D.	1941	John Hauer	P	1,199	65
National Coll. of Chiropractic	Lombard, Ill.	1906	Joseph Janse	P	750	52
National Coll. of Education	Evanston, Ill.	1886	Calvin Gross	P	4,212	91

Name	Location	Year	Governing Official and Affiliation		Students	Teachers
Nazareth Coll. at Kalamazoo	Nazareth, Mich.	1924	T. Hamilton	P	520	66
Nazareth Coll. of Rochester	Rochester, N.Y.	1924	Alice Foley	P	2,478	132
Nebraska, Univ. of*	Lincoln, Neb.	1869	Durward Varner	S	34,512	1,850
At Omaha	Omaha, Neb.	1908	Ronald Roskens	S	14,125	430
Nebraska Wesleyan Univ.	Lincoln, Neb.	1887	Vance D. Rogers	P	1,117	94
Nevada, Univ. of*	Reno, Nev.	1874	Max Milam	S	7,556	445
At Las Vegas	Las Vegas, Nev.	1955	Donald Baepler	S	7,000	325
New	Sarasota, Fla.	1964	B. Riley	P	550	45
New England	Henniker, N.H.	1946	J. K. Cummiskey	P	1,575	95
New England Cons. of Music	Boston, Mass.	1867	Gunther Schuller	P	691	134
New Hampshire	Manchester, N.H.	1932	Edward Shapiro	P	2,100	107
New Hampshire, Univ. of*	Durham, N.H.	1923	Eugene Mills	S	9,877	803
New Haven, Univ. of*	New Haven, Conn.	1926	Phillip Kaplan	P	5,400	300
New Jersey Inst. of Tech.	Newark, N.J.	1881	Paul H. Newell	S	4,900	322
New Mexico Highlands Univ.	Las Vegas, N.M.	1893	Frank Angel, Jr.	S	2,100	134
N. Mex. Inst. of Min. & Tech.	Socorro, N.M.	1889	Glenn Ford	S	861	62
New Mexico State Univ.*	Las Cruces, N.M.	1888	Gerald W. Thomas	S	11,596	426
New Mexico, Univ. Of	Albuquerque, N.M.	1889	Ferrel Heady	S	19,019	1,322
New Rochelle, Coll. of (W)	New Rochelle, N.Y.	1904	Sister Dorothy Ann Kelly	P	2,925	168
New School for Social Research(A)	New York, N.Y.	1919	John R. Everett	P	15,000	1,000
New York, City Univ. of		1847	Robert J. Kibbee	Mu	271,930	17,542
Bernard M. Baruch	New York, N.Y.	1919	Clyde J. Wingfield	Mu	17,977	1,041
Brooklyn	Brooklyn, N.Y.	1930	John W. Kneller	Mu	37,626	2,314
City	New York, N.Y.	1847	Robert E. Marshak	Mu	20,966	1,765
Medgar Evers	Brooklyn, N.Y.	1968	Richard D. Trent	Mu	3,113	243
Hunter	New York, N.Y.	1870	Jacqueline G. Wexler	Mu	26,457	1,685
John Jay Coll. of Criminal Just.	New York, N.Y.	1964	D.H. Riddle	Mu	9,729	517
Herbert H. Lehman	Bronx, N.Y.	1931	Leonard Lief	Mu	16,279	1,172
Queens	Flushing, N.Y.	1937	Joseph Murphy	Mu	30,077	2,007
Richmond	Staten Island, N.Y.	1965	Edmond Volpe	Mu	3,976	262
York	Jamaica, N.Y.	1966	Milton G. Bassin	Mu	5,737	520
N.Y. Inst. of Technology (A)	Old Westbury, N.Y.	1955	Alexander Schure	P	4,520	200
New York Law School	New York, N.Y.	1891	E. Shapiro	P	850	56
New York Medical (A)	New York, N.Y.	1860	Frederick L. Stone	P	613	1,200
New York, State Univ. of	Albany, N.Y.	1948	Ernest L. Boyer, (Chan.)	S	161,452	9,278
State Univ.	Albany, N.Y.	1844	Louis T. Benezet	S	14,521	804
" "	Buffalo, N.Y.	1846	Robert Ketter	S	22,227	959
" "	Binghamton, N.Y.	1946	Clifford D. Clark	S	9,107	466
" "	Stony Brook, N.Y.	1957	John Toll	S	14,193	630
State Univ. Colleges	Brockport, N.Y.	1867	Albert W. Brown	S	10,668	545
" "	Buffalo, N.Y.	1867	Elbert K. Fretwell	S	12,383	587
" "	Cortland, N.Y.	1866	Richard Jones	S	6,117	325
" "	Fredonia, N.Y.	1867	Dallas Beal	S	2,242	79
" "	Geneseo, N.Y.	1867	Robert Mac Vittie	S	6,567	317
" "	New Paltz, N.Y.	1885	Stanley K. Coffman	S	8,498	400
" "	Oneonta, N.Y.	1887	Clifford Craven	S	6,806	379
" "	Oswego, N.Y.	1861	Sherwood Dunham, Act.	S	9,143	445
" "	Old Westbury, N.Y.	1965	John Maguire	S	1,390	60
" "	Plattsburgh, N.Y.	1889	George W. Angell	S	6,465	311
" "	Potsdam, N.Y.	1867	Thomas Barrington	S	5,045	293
" "	Purchase, N.Y.	1965	Abbott Kaplan	S	2,695	96
" "	Utica, N.Y.	1966	William Kunsela	S	2,198	22
" " Empire State(A)	State Springs, N.Y.	1971	James Hall	S	764	52
Buffalo Health Sciences Ctr.	Buffalo, N.Y.	1846	Clyde L. Randall, V.P.	S	2,756	425
College of Ceramics	Alfred, N.Y.	1900	W.G. Lawrence, Dean	S	550	41
Env'm't'l. Sci. & Forestry	Syracuse, N.Y.	1911	Edward Palmer	S	2,367	94
Downstate Medical Center	Brooklyn, N.Y.	1858	Calvin H. Plimpton	S	1,411	470
Health Sciences Center	Stony Brook, N.Y.	1957	Edmund Pellegrino	S	965	173
Maritime College (M)	Bronx, N.Y.	1874	Sheldon Kinney	S	884	56
Upstate Medical Center	Syracuse, N.Y.	1834	Richard P. Schmidt	S	938	263
New York Univ.	New York, N.Y.	1831	John Sawhill	P	39,676	5,373
Newark Coll. of Engineering	Newark, N.J.	1881	William Hazell	S	4,200	291
Newberry	Newberry, S.C.	1856	Fredric Brinker Irvin	D	815	65
Niagara Univ.	Niagara Un., N.Y.	1856	Rev. K.F. Slattery	P	3,755	215
Nicholls State Univ.	Thibodaux, La.	1948	Vernon Galliano	S	5,683	229
Nichols	Dudley, Mass.	1931	Darcy C. Coyle	P	627	37
Norfolk State	Norfolk, Va.	1935	Lyman Brooks	S	6,260	405
North Adams State	North Adams, Mass.	1894	James Amsler	S	2,808	150
North Carolina, Univ. of						
A.&T. State Univ.	Greensboro, N.C.	1891	Lewis Dowdy, Chan.	S	4,514	317
Appalachian State Univ.	Boone, N.C.	1899	Herbert Wey	S	8,014	446
At Asheville	Asheville, N.C.	1927	William Highsmith	S	1,506	76
At Chapel Hill	Chapel Hill, N.C.	1789	N.F. Taylor	S	19,400	2,600
At Charlotte	Charlotte, N.C.	1946	D.W. Colvard	S	6,656	438
E. Carolina Univ.	Greenville, N.C.	1907	Leo W. Jenkins, Chan.	S	12,044	679
Elizabeth City State Univ.	Elizabeth City, N.C.	1891	Marion Thorpe, Chan.	S	1,266	107
Fayetteville State Univ.	Fayetteville, N.C.	1877	Charles A. Lyons, Jr.	S	2,891	144
At Greensboro	Greensboro, N.C.	1891	J.S. Ferguson, Chan.	S	8,613	515
North Carolina Central Univ.	Durham, N.C.	1910	Albert N. Whiting	S	4,400	325
N.C. School of the Arts	Winston-Salem, N.C.	1965	Robert Suderburg	S	570	120
Pembroke State Univ.	Pembroke, N.C.	1887	English E. Jones	S	1,784	112
At Raleigh, State Univ.	Raleigh, N.C.	1889	J.T. Caldwell, Chan.	S	15,751	1,621
Western Carolina Univ.	Cullowhee, N.C.	1889	H.F. Robinson, Chan.	S	6,193	334
At Wilmington	Wilmington, N.C.	1947	Wm. H. Wagoner, Chan.	S	2,787	166
Winston-Salem State Univ.	Winston-Salem, N.C.	1892	Kenneth Williams	S	1,916	129

Name	Location	Year	Governing Official and Affiliation		Students	Teachers
North Carolina Wesleyan	Rocky Mount, N.C.	1956	Thomas A. Collins	D	535	39
North Central Bible	Minneapolis, Minn.	1930	Rev. E.M. Clark	D	532	24
North Central	Naperville, Ill.	1861	Arlo L. Schilling	D	855	57
North Dakota State Univ.	Fargo, N.D.	1890	L.D. Loftsgard	S	6,600	475
North Dakota, Univ. of.	Grand Forks, N.D.	1883	Thomas Clifford	S	8,171	428
North Georgia	Dahlonega, Ga.	1873	John H. Owen	S	1,754	92
North Park	Chicago, Ill.	1891	Lloyd Ahlem	D	1,313	109
North Texas State Univ.	Denton, Tex.	1890	C.C. Nolen	S	15,875	594
Northeast Louisiana Univ.	Monroe, La.	1931	George T. Walker	S	9,216	557
Northeast Missouri St. Univ.	Kirksville, Mo.	1867	Charles T. McClain	S	5,905	295
Northeastern Illinois Univ.	Chicago, Ill.	1961	James Mullen	S	9,800	441
Northeastern Okla. State	Tahlequah, Okla.	1846	Robert Collier	S	5,329	270
Northeastern Univ.	Boston, Mass.	1898	Asa S. Knowles	P	33,557	1,889
Northern Arizona Univ.	Flagstaff, Ariz.	1899	J.Lawrence Walkup	S	10,165	480
Northern Colorado, Univ. of	Greeley, Col.	1889	Richard R. Bond	S	10,886	600
Northern Ill. Univ.	DeKalb, Ill.	1895	Richard Nelson	S	23,270	1,171
Northern Iowa, Univ. of	Cedar Falls, Ia.	1876	John Kamerick	S	8,700	540
Northern Michigan Univ.	Marquette, Mich.	1899	John X. Jamrich	S	8,153	310
Northern Montana	Harve, Mon.	1929	Joseph R. Crowley	S	1,020	62
Northern State	Aberdeen, S.D.	1901	Norbert Baumgart	S	2,195	114
Northland	Ashland, Wis.	1892	Malcolm McLean	P	692	58
Northrop Inst. of Tech.	Inglewood, Cal.	1942	B. J. Shell	P	1,300	115
Northwest	Kirkland, Wash.	1934	D. V. Hurst	D	551	34
Northwest Christian	Eugene, Ore.	1895	Barton A. Dowdy	D	558	21
Northwest Missouri State Univ.	Maryville, Mo.	1905	Robert P. Foster	S	4,605	252
Northwest Nazarene	Nampa, Ida.	1913	Kenneth Pearsall	D	1,017	75
Northwestern	Orange City, Ia.	1928	Lars Granberg	D	698	58
Northwestern State Univ.	Natchitoches, La.	1884	Arnold R. Kilpatrick	S	6,013	335
Northwestern State	Alva, Okla.	1897	Joe Struckle	S	1,868	90
Northwestern Univ.	Evanston, Ill.	1851	Robert Henry Strotz	P	11,390	2,624
Norwich Univ.	Northfield, Vt.	1819	Loring Hart	P	1,564	140
Northwood Institute	Midland, Mich.	1959	Donald Schma	P	2,000	120
Notre Dame, Coll. of	Belmont, Cal.	1868	Sister Catharine Julie	P	1,500	109
Notre Dame	St. Louis, Mo.	1954	Sister Barbara Brumleve	D	340	35
Notre Dame	Manchester, N.H.	1950	Sister Jeannette Vezeau	D	387	50
Notre Dame	Cleveland, Oh.	1922	Sister Mary Marthe	D	507	
Notre Dame of Maryland	Baltimore, Md.	1873	Sister Kathleen Feeley	D	741	
Notre Dame, Univ. of (M).	Notre Dame, Ind.	1842	Rev. T.M. Hesburgh	D	8,800	765
Nyack	Nyack, N.Y.	1882	Harold W. Boon	D	728	62
Oakland Univ.	Rochester, Mich.	1957	Donald D. O'Dowd	S	10,216	440
Oakland City	Oakland City, Ind.	1885	James Murray	Mu	427	18
Oakwood	Huntsville, Ala.	1896	C. B. Rock	D	1,013	60
Oberlin	Oberlin, Oh.	1833	E. Danenberg	P	2,800	232
Occidental	Los Angeles, Cal.	1887	Richard C. Gilman	P	1,750	113
Oglethorpe Univ.	Atlanta, Ga.	1835	Paul K. Vonk	P	1,046	46
Ohio Dominican	Columbus, Oh.	1911	Sister M. Suzanne Uhrhane	D	959	70
Ohio Coll. of Podiatric Med.	Cleveland, Oh.	1916	Abe Rubin	P	469	72
Ohio Inst. of Technology	Columbus, Oh.	1952	Richard A. Czesmak	P	2,500	70
Ohio Northern Univ.	Ada, Oh.	1871	Samuel L. Meyer	D	2,784	168
Ohio State Univ.*	Columbus, Oh.	1870	Harold L. Enarson	S	53,514	3,619
Ohio Univ.	Athens, Oh.	1804	Harry Crewson	S	17,552	1,095
Ohio Wesleyan Univ.	Delaware, Oh.	1842	Thomas Wenzlau	P	2,280	150
Oklahoma Baptist Univ.	Shawnee, Okla.	1910	William G. Tanner	D	1,808	125
Oklahoma Christian	Oklahoma City, Okla.	1950	J. Johnson	D	1,236	50
Oklahoma City Univ.	Oklahoma City, Okla.	1904	Dolphus Whitten	P	3,010	220
Okla. Coll. of Liberal Arts	Chickasha, Okla.	1908	Roy Troutt	S	1,212	64
Oklahoma Panhandle State	Goodwell, Okla.	1909	Thomas L. Palmer	S	1,115	74
Oklahoma State Univ.*	Stillwater, Okla.	1890	Robert B. Kamm	S	19,281	1,475
Oklahoma, Univ. of	Norman, Okla.	1890	Paul F. Sharp	S	19,500	689
Old Dominion Univ.	Norfolk, Va.	1930	James Bugg	S	11,768	668
Olivet	Olivet, Mich.	1844	Ray B. Loeschner	P	805	52
Olivet Nazarene	Kankakee, Ill.	1907	Harold W. Reed	D	1,642	112
Oral Roberts Univ.	Tulsa, Okla.	1963	Oral Roberts	P	2,500	104
Oregon College of Education	Monmouth, Ore.	1856	Leonard Rice	S	3,321	237
Oregon Inst. of Technology	Klamath Falls, Ore.	1947	Winston Purvine	S	2,088	141
Oregon State Univ.*	Corvallis, Ore.	1868	R. MacVicar	S	14,300	1,520
Oregon, Univ. of	Eugene, Ore.	1876	Robert Clark	S	16,270	1,000
Osteop., Med. & Surg., Coll. of	Des Moines, Ia.	1898	J. Leonard Azneer	P	491	108
Otis Art Inst. of L.A. County	Los Angeles, Cal.	1918	G. E. Woods (Dir.)	C	498	31
Ottawa Univ.	Ottawa, Kan.	1865	Peter H. Armacost	P	661	55
Otterbein	Westerville, Oh.	1847	Thomas Jefferson Kerr	D	1,328	91
Ouachita Baptist Univ.	Arkadelphia, Ark.	1885	Daniel R. Grant	D	1,647	91
Our Lady of Angels	Aston, Pa.	1965	Sister Madonna Marie	P	467	41
Our Lady of Elms, Col. of (W)	Chicopee, Mass.	1928	Msgr. T. F. Devine	D	407	82
Our Lady of the Lake	San Antonio, Tex.	1911	Gerald Burns	D	2,083	134
Ozarks, Coll. of the	Clarksville, Ark.	1834	Robert Qualls	Mu	430	39
Ozarks, School of the	Pt. Lookout, Mo.	1906	M. Graham Clark	P	1,220	85
Pace Univ.	New York, N.Y.	1906	Edward J. Mortola	P	12,439	695
Pacific	Fresno, Cal.	1944	Arthur J. Wiebe	P	426	53
Pacific Christian	Fullerton, Cal.	1928	Medford Jones	D	500	39
Pacific Lutheran Univ.	Tacoma, Wash.	1890	Eugene Wiegman	P	3,303	240
Pacific States Univ.	Los Angeles, Cal.	1928	Steven G. Kase	P	650	50
Pacific Union	Angwin, Cal.	1882	J. W. Cassell	MU	2,069	136
Pacific Univ.	Forest Grove,Ore.	1849	James Miller	P	1,011	88
Pacific, Univ. of the	Stockton, Cal.	1851	Stanley McCaffrey	P	5,859	390
Paine	Augusta, Ga.	1882	Julius Scott	D	774	71
Palmer Coll. of Chiropractic (A)	Davenport, Iowa	1895	David Palmer	P	1,370	26
Pan American Univ.	Edinburg, Tex.	1927	Ralph Schilling	S	7,183	321
Park	Kansas City, Mo.	1875	Kenneth Beyer	P	2,500	135
Parsons School of Design	New York, N.Y.	1896	John R. Everett	P	1,000	200
Paul Quinn	Waco, Tex.	1872	S. E. Rutland	D	481	45
Peabody Cons. of Music (A)	Baltimore, Md.	1857	Richard F. Goldman	P	421	85

Name	Location	Year	Governing Official and Affiliation		Stu-dents	Teach-ers
Penn Col. of Optometry	Philadelphia, Pa.	1919	Norman F. Wallis	P	537	77
Penn. State Univ.	University Park, Pa.	1855	John Wiliswald	S	64,721	4,747
Pennsylvania, Univ. of	Philadelphia, Pa.	1740	Martin Meyerson	P	8,262	1,700
Pepperdine Univ.	Malibu, Cal.	1937	William S. Banowsky	P	6,915	478
Peru State	Peru, Neb.	1867	Douglas Pearson	S	685	46
Pfeiffer	Misenheimer, N.C.	1885	Douglas Reid Sasser	D	950	60
Phila. College of Art	Philadelphia, Pa.	1876	George D. Culler	P	1,100	142
Phila. Coll. of Bible	Philadelphia, Pa.	1913	D. B. MacCorkle	P	1,437	70
Phila. Coll. of Osteopathic Med.	Philadelphia, Pa.	1899	Thomas Rowland, Jr.	P	755	220
Phila. Coll. of Pharm. & Science	Philadelphia, Pa.	1821	John Bergen	P	1,043	80
Phila. Coll. of Textiles & Science	Philadelphia, Pa.	1884	Lawson A. Pendleton	P	1,965	84
Philander Smith	Little Rock, Ark.	1868	Walter Hazzard	D	701	52
Phillips Univ.	Enid, Okla.	1907	Thomas Broce	P	1,379	127
Piedmont	Demorest, Ga.	1897	James E. Walter	P	400	24
Piedmont Bible	Winston-Salem, N.C.	1945	Donald Drake	P	443	24
Pikeville	Pikeville, Ky.	1889	Jackson Hall	D	697	38
Pittsburgh, Univ. of	Pittsburgh, Pa.	1787	Wesley W. Posvar	S	33,299	2,671
Pitzer	Claremont, Cal.	1963	Robert Atwell	P	775	77
Plymouth State	Plymouth, N.H.	1871	Harold E. Hyde	S	2,452	123
Point Park	Pittsburgh, Pa.	1960	John Hopkins	P	1,557	101
Polytechnic Institute	Brooklyn, N.Y.	1854	George Bugliarello	P	4,500	230
Pomona	Claremont, Cal.	1887	John David Alexander	P	1,300	132
Portland State Univ.	Portland, Ore.	1968	Joseph Blumel	S	14,881	437
Portland, Univ. of	Portland, Ore.	1901	Rev. P. E. Waldschmidt	P	2,147	131
Pratt Institute	Brooklyn, N.Y.	1887	Richardson Pratt, Jr.	P	4,613	430
Prescott	Prescott, Ariz.	1966	Frank Mertz	P	421	33
Presbyterian	Clinton, S.C.	1880	Marc C. Weersing	Mu	842	68
Princeton Univ.	Princeton, N.J.	1746	William G. Bowen	P	5,727	780
Principia	Elsah, Ill.	1910	David K. Andrews	P	837	87
Providence	Providence, R.I.	1917	Rev. T. R. Peterson	P	5,123	207
Puerto Rico, Univ. of*	Rio Piedras, P.R.	1903	A. Carrion	S	52,055	3,226
Puget Sound, Univ. of	Tacoma, Wash.	1888	Philip M. Phibbs	P	4,551	256
Purdue Univ.*	Lafayette, Ind.	1869	Arthur G. Hansen	S	38,368	2,339
Queens (W)	Charlotte, N.C.	1857	Alfred Canon	D	626	59
Quincy	Quincy, Ill.	1859	Rev. Titus Ludes	D	1,446	100
Quinnipiac	Hamden, Conn.	1929	Leonard Kent	P	2,800	225
Radcliffe (W)	Cambridge, Mass.	1879	Matina Souretia Horner	P		(a)
(a) Faculty at Harvard Univ. furnishes instruction.						
Radford	Radford, Va.	1913	Donald N. Dedmon	S	4,443	277
Ramapo College of New Jersey	Mahwah, N.J.	1968	George T. Potter	S	3,963	225
Randolph-Macon	Ashland, Va.	1830	Luther W. White	P	780	72
Randolph-Macon Woman's (W)	Lynchburg, Va.	1891	William F. Quillian, Jr.	P	791	77
Redlands, Univ. of	Redlands, Cal.	1909	Eugene Dawson	P	2,407	125
Reed	Portland, Ore.	1909	Paul Bragdon	P	1,183	112
Regis	Denver, Col.	1877	Rev. David M. Clarke	D	1,150	87
Regis (W)	Weston, Mass.	1927	Sister Therese Higgins	P	800	75
Rensselaer Poly. Inst.	Troy, N.Y.	1824	Richard Grosh	P	4,815	332
Rhode Island	Providence, R.I.	1854	Charles B. Willard	S	8,650	360
R.I. School of Design	Providence, R.I.	1877	Talbot Ranfoul	P	1,350	192
Rhode Island, Univ. of	Kingston, R.I.	1892	Frank Newman	S	16,385	757
Rice Univ.	Houston, Tex.	1891	Norman Hackerman	P	3,475	408
Richmond, Univ. of	Richmond, Va.	1830	E. Bruce Heilman	P	4,353	207
Ricker	Houlton, Me.	1848	W. Abbott	P	259	24
Rider	Trenton, N.J.	1865	Frank N. Elliott	P	5,905	270
Rio Grande	Rio Grande, Oh.	1876	Alphus R. Christensen	P	747	49
Ripon	Ripon, Wis.	1851	Bernard S. Adams	P	909	82
Rivier	Nashua, N.H.	1933	Sister Doris Benoit	Mu	873	71
Roanoke	Salem, Va.	1842	Perry F. Kendig	P	1,268	70
Robert Morris	Pittsburgh, Pa.	1921	Charles Sewall	P	5,626	126
Roberts Wesleyan	Rochester, N.Y.	1866	Paul L. Adams	D	640	72
Rochester Inst. of Tech.	Rochester, N.Y.	1829	Paul A. Miller	P	11,971	942
Rochester, Univ. of	Rochester, N.Y.	1850	Robert Sproull	P	8,558	2,348
Rockford	Rockford, Ill.	1847	John A. Howard	P	1,110	106
Rockhurst	Kansas City, Mo.	1910	Rev. M.E. Van Ackeren	D	2,795	176
Rocky Mountain	Billings, Mon.	1878	B. Alton, Act.	D	505	49
Roger Williams	Bristol, R.I.	1948	Ralph Gauvey	P	2,443	176
Rollins	Winter Park, Fla.	1885	Jack Critchfield	P	3,500	200
Roosevelt Univ.	Chicago, Ill.	1945	Rolf A. Weil	P	7,340	250
Rosary	River Forest, Ill.	1901	Sister Candida Lund	P	1,314	107
Rosary Hill	Buffalo, N.Y.	1948	Robert S. Marshall	P	1,220	102
Rose-Hulman Inst. of Tech	Terre Haute, Ind.	1874	John Logan	P	960	80
Rosemont	Rosemont, Pa.	1921	Sister Ann Marie	D	654	80
Russell Sage	Troy, N.Y.	1916	Charles Walker	P	3,671	259
Rust	Holly Spgs., Miss	1866	W.A. McMillan	D	731	42
Rutgers Univ.*	New Brunswick, N.J.	1766	Edward J. Bloustein	S	44,469	3,574
Sacred Heart, Coll. of the	San Juan, P.R.	1935	Pedro Gonzalez Ramos	D	2,201	147
Sacred Heart Univ	Bridgeport, Conn.	1963	Robert Kidera	S	2,415	134
Saginaw Valley State	Univ. Center, Mich.	1963	Jack Ryder	S	2,555	142
St. Ambrose	Davenport, Iowa	1882	William Bakrow	D	1,342	95
St. Andrews Presbyterian	Laurinburg, N.C.	1958	Donald J. Hart	D	637	53
St. Anselm's	Manchester, N.H.	1889	Joseph J. Gerry	D	1,820	130
St. Augustine's	Raleigh, N.C.	1867	Prezell R. Robinson	P	1,515	78
St. Benedict, Coll. of (W)	St. Joseph, Minn.	1927	Beverly Miller	D	1,560	107
St. Bernard	St. Bernard, Ala.	1892	Rev. Aloysius Plaisance	D	393	29
St. Bonaventure Univ.	St. Bonaventure, N.Y.	1856	V. Rev. D. McElrath	P	2,291	185
St. Catherine, Coll. of (W)	St. Paul, Minn.	1905	Sister Alberta Huber	P	1,688	131
St. Cloud State	St. Cloud, Minn	1869	Charles J. Graham	S	10,463	418
St. Edward's Univ.	Austin, Tex.	1885	Bro. Stephen Walsh	P	1,410	71
St. Elizabeth, Coll. of (W)	Convent Station, N.J.	1899	Sister Eliz. Ann Maloney	D	592	77
St. Francis	Fort Wayne, Ind.	1890	Sister M. Jo Ellen Scheetz	D	1,329	75
St. Francis	Biddeford, Me.	1939	D. MacIntyre	P	475	36
St. Francis	Brooklyn, N.Y.	1858	Rev. Donald Sullivan	P	3,041	156
St. Francis	Loretto, Pa.	1847	Rev. Sean Sullivan	D	1,507	81

Name	Location	Year	Governing Official and Affiliation		Stu-dents	Teach-ers
St. Francis, Coll. of	Joliet, Ill.	1925	John Orr	D	1,137	65
St. John Coll. of Cleveland	Cleveland, Oh	1928	Rev. James McManamon	D	732	76
St. John Fisher	Rochester, N.Y.	1948	Rev. C. J. Lavery	P	1,900	110
St. John's	Annapolis, Md.	1696	Richard D. Weigle	P	855	92
St. John's Univ. (M)	Collegeville, Minn.	1869	Rev. Michael P. Blecker	P	1,888	140
St. John's Univ.	Jamaica, N.Y.	1870	V. Rev. Joseph T. Cahill	P	13,155	626
St. Joseph	West Hartford, Conn.	1932	Sr. Mary O'Connor	D	619	84
St. Joseph's	Rensselaer, Ind.	1889	Rev. Charles Banet	P	1,060	78
St. Joseph's	North Windham, Me.	1912	Bernard Currier	P	450	34
St. Joseph's	Philadelphia, Pa.	1851	Rev. Terrence Toland	D	5,834	155
St. Lawrence Univ.	Canton, N.Y.	1856	Frank Peter Piskor	P	2,289	150
St. Leo	St. Leo, Fla.	1963	Thomas Southard	P	1,034	74
St. Louis Coll. of Pharmacy	St. Louis, Mo.	1864	Charles C. Rabe	P	673	29
St. Louis Univ.	St. Louis, Mo.	1818	Rev. D. O'Connell	P	10,356	1,700
Parks Coll.	Cahokia, Ill.	1927	Leon Z. Seitzer (Dean)	P	675	56
St. Martin's	Olympia, Wash.	1895	V. Rev. Matthew Naumes	D	1,030	48
St. Mary, Coll. of (W)	Omaha, Neb.	1922	Sister Mary Angelica	D	498	80
St. Mary (W)	Leavenworth, Kan.	1923	Sister Mary Janet	D	585	66
St. Mary of the Plains	Dodge City, Kan.	1952	William V. Tucker	D	400	35
St. Mary-of-the-Woods (W)	St. Mary-of-Woods, Ind.	1840	Sister Jeanne Knoerle	D	378	58
St. Mary's (W)	Notre Dame, Ind.	1851	John Duogan	P	1,632	150
St. Mary's	Winona, Minn.	1925	Brother George Pahl	P	1,057	90
St. Mary's Coll. of Cal.	Moraga, Cal.	1863	Bro. Mel Anderson	D	1,078	97
St. Mary's Coll. of Maryland	St. Mary's City, Md	1839	J. Renwick Jackson	S	1,111	91
St. Mary's Dominican (W)	New Orleans, La.	1910	Sister Mary Eugene	D	890	66
St. Mary's Univ.	San Antonio, Tex.	1852	Rev. James Young	D	3,798	211
St. Michael's	Winooski, Vt.	1904	Rev. F. Moriarty	P	1,523	95
St. Norbert	DePere, Wis.	1898	Neil Webb	P	1,384	90
St. Olaf	Northfield, Minn.	1874	Sidney A. Rand	D	2,760	242
St. Paul Bible	Bible College, Minn.	1916	Francis W. Grubbs	D	403	31
St. Paul's	Lawrenceville, Va.	1888	James Alvin Russell Jr.	P	540	37
St. Peter's	Jersey City, N.J.	1872	V. Rev. V. R. Yanitelli	D	4,233	388
St. Rose, Coll. of	Albany, N.Y.	1920	Thomas Manion	P	1,845	112
St. Scholastica, Coll. of	Duluth, Minn.	1912	Bruce Stender	P	1,117	101
St. Theresa, Coll. of	Winona, Minn.	1911	Sister Joyce Rowland	P	1,151	132
St. Thomas Aquinas	Sparkill, N.Y.	1952	D. McNellis	P	904	57
St. Thomas, Coll. of	St. Paul, Minn.	1885	Msgr. Terrence Murphy	D	2,732	149
St. Thomas, Univ. of	Houston, Tex.	1947	Rev. Patrick Braden	P	1,648	152
St. Vincent (M)	Latrobe, Pa.	1846	Rev. Cecil Diethrich	P	1,031	79
St. Xavier	Chicago, Ill.	1847	Sister M. Irenaeus	D	1,334	126
Salem (W)	Winston-Salem N.C.	1772	John H. Chandler	P	617	72
Salem	Salem, W. Va.	1888	Dallas Bailey	P	1,290	75
Salem State	Salem, Mass.	1854	Vincent Mara	S	7,910	294
Salisbury State	Salisbury, Md.	1925	Norman Crawford	S	3,092	138
Salve Regina	Newport, R.I.	1934	Sister Lucille McKillop	D	1,485	98
Sam Houston State Univ.	Huntsville, Tex.	1879	E.T. Bowers	S	10,144	363
Samford Univ.	Birmingham, Ala.	1841	Leslie S. Wright	D	3,396	191
San Diego, Univ. of.	San Diego, Cal.	1949	Author E. Hughes	P	2,836	200
San Diego State	San Diego, Cal.	1897	Brage Golding	S	30,945	1,916
San Francisco Art Inst.	San Francisco, Cal.	1871	A. Herstand	P	907	65
San Francisco, Univ. of	San Francisco, Cal.	1855	Rev. William McInnes	P	5,970	450
Sangamon State Univ.	Springfield, Ill.	1970	Robert Spencer	S	3,446	180
San Jose State Univ.	San Jose, Cal.	1857	John H. Bunzel	S	26,000	1,600
Santa Clara, Univ. of.	Santa Clara, Cal.	1851	Rev. Thomas Terry	P	6,794	299
Sante Fe, Coll. of	Sante Fe, N.M.	1947	Bro. Cyprian Luke Roney	D	1,242	85
Sarah Lawrence	Bronxville, N.Y.	1928	Charles DeCarlo	P	996	141
Savannah State	Savannah, Ga.	1890	Prince Jackson	S	2,412	136
Scranton, Univ. of.	Scranton, Pa.	1888	Rev. E. Quary	D	3,000	150
Scripps (W)	Claremont, Cal.	1926	Mark H. Curtis	P	565	65
Seattle Pacific	Seattle, Wash.	1891	David L. McKenna	P	2,249	168
Seattle Univ.	Seattle, Wash.	1891	Edmund Ryan	P	3,736	175
Selma Univ.	Selma, Ala.	1878	Marshall C. Cleveland	D	321	23
Seton Hall Univ.	S. Orange, N.J.	1856	Msgr. Thomas G. Fahy	D	9,880	305
Seton Hill (W)	Greensburg, Pa.	1883	Sister Mary Schmidt	D	797	75
Shaw Univ.	Raleigh, N.C.	1875	J. Archie Hargraves	D	1,625	149
Shepherd	Shepherdstown, W. Va.	1871	James Butcher	S	2,248	107
Shippensburg State	Shippensburg, Pa.	1871	Gilmore B. Seavers	S	5,520	329
Shorter	Rome, Ga.	1873	Randall H. Minor	D	673	50
Siena	Loudonville, N.Y.	1937	Rev. Matthew T. Conlin	P	2,264	128
Siena Heights	Adrian, Mich.	1926	Hugh L. Thompson	D	1,013	107
Silver Lake	Manitowoc, Wis.	1939	Sister Anne Kennedy	D	410	49
Simmons (W)	Boston, Mass.	1902	William J. Holmes, Jr.	P	2,695	205
Simpson	Indianola, Ia.	1860	Richard Lancaster	P	835	77
Simpson	San Francisco, Cal.	1921	Mark W. Lee	P	418	26
Sioux Falls	Sioux Falls, S.D.	1872	Owen Halleen	D	606	49
Skidmore	Saratoga Spgs., N.Y.	1911	Joseph C. Palamoantain, Jr.	P	2,081	189
Slippery Rock State	Slippery Rock, Pa.	1893	Albert A. Watrel	S	5,500	346
Smith (W)	Northampton, Mass.	1875	Thomas C. Mendenhall	P	2,518	240
South, Univ. of the.	Sewanee, Tenn.	1857	James J. Bennett. V. Chan.	D	992	91
South Alabama, Univ. of.	Mobile, Ala.	1963	Frederick Whiddon	S	5,760	259
S. Carolina, Med. Coll. of	Charleston, S.C.	1824	William M. McCord	S	1,918	872
South Carolina St.*	Orangeburg, S.C.	1896	M. M. Nanee, Jr.	S	3,092	222
South Carolina, Univ. of	Columbia, S. C.	1801	Thomas F. Jones	S	24,859	1,200
S.D. Sch. of Mines & Tech.	Rapid City, S.D.	1885	Harvey R. Fraser	S	1,440	108
South Dakota State Univ.*	Brookings, S.D.	1881	H. M. Briggs	S	6,217	569
South Dakota, Univ. of.	Vermillion, S.D.	1882	Richard E. Bowen	S	5,154	350
South-Eastern Bible	Lakeland, Fla.	1935	Cyril Homer	D	957	25
South Florida, Univ. of.	Tampa, Fla.	1956	Maurice Mackey, Jr.	S	20,936	1,207
Southeast Missouri State Univ.	Cape Girardeau, Mo.	1873	Mark Scully	S	7,632	376
Southeastern Louisiana Univ.	Hammond, La.	1925	Clea E. Parker	S	6,410	303
Southeastern Mass. Univ.	N. Dartmouth, Mass.	1960	Donald E. Walker	S	5,912	195
Southeastern Okla. State Univ.	Durant, Okla.	1909	Leon Hibbs	S	3,543	125
Southern California	Costa Mesa, Cal.	1920	Emil Balliet	D	645	53
Southern Cal., Univ. of.	Los Angeles, Cal.	1880	John R. Hubbard	P	23,257	2,425
S. Cal. College of Optometry	Fullerton, Cal.	1904	Richard Hopping	P	300	79
Southern Coll. of Optometry	Memphis, Tenn.	1932	Spurgeon B. Eure	P	617	44
Southern Colorado State	Pueblo, Col.	1961	Harry P. Bowes	S	5,770	327
Southern Conn. State	New Haven, Conn.	1893	Manson Van B. Jennings	S	12,553	553

Name	Location	Year	Governing Official and Affiliation		Stu-dents	Teach-ers
Southern Illinois Univ.	Carbondale, Ill.	1869	David Derge	S	18,398	2,466
Southern Methodist Univ.	Dallas, Tex.	1915	Willis Tate, Chan.	P	9,448	833
Southern Missionary	Collegedale, Tenn.	1892	Frank Knittel	D	1,682	120
Southern Mississippi, U. of	Hattiesburg, Miss.	1910	William D. McCain	S	9,938	700
Southern Oregon	Ashland, Ore.	1869	James K. Sours	S	4,484	258
Southern State	Magnolia, Ark.	1909	Imon E. Bruce	S	1,721	116
Southern Univ.	Baton Rouge, La.	1880	Jesse Stone, Jr.	S	8,685	397
Southern Utah State	Cedar City, Ut.	1897	R. C. Braithwaite.	S	1,850	129
Southwest Baptist	Bolivar, Mo.	1878	James L. Sells	P	1,190	79
Southwest Minnesota State	Marshall, Minn.	1963	Jay Jones.	S	2,011	141
Southwest Missouri St. U.	Springfield, Mo.	1905	Duane Meyer	S	10,500	500
Southwest Texas State Univ.	San Marcos, Tex.	1899	Lee Smith.	S	12,363	532
Southwestern.	Winfield, Kan.	1885	Donald Ruthenberg	D	665	50
Southwestern La., Univ. of	Lafayette, La.	1898	Ray Authement	S	11,572	525
Southwestern at Memphis	Memphis, Tenn.	1848	James Daughdrill.	P	1,096	85
Southwestern Okla. State, Univ. of	Weatherford, Okla.	1901	Al Harris.	S	4,801	250
Southwestern Union	Keene, Tex.	1893	Calvin Gordon	D	673	44
Southwestern Univ.	Georgetown, Tex.	1840	Durwood Fleming.	D	905	72
Spalding	Louisville, Ky.	1920	Sister Eileen Egan	P	1,145	95
Spelman (W)	Atlanta, Ga.	1881	Albert E. Manley	P	1,155	100
Spring Arbor.	Spring Arbor, Mich.	1873	E. A. Voller	P	820	79
Spring Garden	Philadelphia, Pa.	1850	Robert H. Thompson.	P	850	60
Spring Hill.	Mobile, Ala.	1830	Rev. Paul S. Tipton.	P	1,008	60
Springfield	Springfield, Mass.	1885	Wilbert Locklin.	P	2,300	125
Stanford Univ.	Stanford, Cal.	1891	Richard W. Lyman	P	11,260	1,322
Stephen F. Austin State U.	Nacogdoches, Tex.	1923	Ralph W. Steen.	S	10,884	425
Stephens (W)	Columbia, Mo.	1833	Arland Christ-Janer	P	1,850	152
Sterling	Sterling, Kan.	1887	J. C. Schoenherr	P	458	43
Stetson Univ.	De Land, Fla.	1883	John E. Johns.	P	2,658	141
Steubenville, Coll. of.	Steubenville, Oh.	1946	Fr. M. Scanlon.	D	975	46
Stevens Inst. of Tech.	Hoboken, N.J.	1870	Kenneth C. Rogers	P	2,025	195
Stillman	Tuscaloosa, Ala.	1876	Harold N. Stinson.	D	684	45
Stockton State.	Pomona, N.J.	1971	Richard Bjork.	S	3,250	195
Stonehill	N. Easton, Mass.	1948	Rev. Ernest Bartell.	P	2,222	100
Strayer	Washington, D.C.	1904	Murray Donoho	P	1,365	124
Suffolk Univ.	Boston, Mass.	1906	Thomas Fulham	P	4,250	206
Sul Ross State Univ.	Alpine, Tex.	1919	Hugh Meredith	S	3,014	142
Susquehanna Univ.	Selinsgrove, Pa.	1858	Gustave W. Weber	D	1,439	115
Swarthmore.	Swarthmore, Pa.	1864	Theodore Friend	P	1,260	142
Sweet Briar (W)	Sweet Briar, Va.	1901	Harold B. Whiteman, Jr.	P	726	81
Syracuse Univ.	Syracuse, N.Y.	1870	M. A. Eggers (Chan.)	P	10,539	848
Tabor.	Hillsboro, Kan.	1908	Roy Just.	P	502	49
Talladega.	Talladega, Ala.	1867	Herman H. Long.	P	465	54
Tampa, Univ. of	Tampa, Fla.	1931	B. D. Owens.	P	2,001	120
Tarkio	Tarkio, Mo.	1883	Eldon E. Breazier.	P	574	39
Taylor Univ.	Upland, Ind.	1846	Milo Rediger.	P	1,437	95
Temple Univ.	Philadelphia, Pa.	1884	Marvin Wachman	S	31,387	3,057
Tennessee State Univ.	Nashville, Tenn.	1912	F. Humphries.	S	5,907	360
Tennessee Tech. Univ.	Cookeville, Tenn.	1915	Arliss Roaden.	S	7,049	291
Tennessee Temple.	Chattanooga, Tenn.	1946	Lee Roberson.	P	1,834	88
Tennessee System, Univ. of.	Knoxville, Tenn.	1968	Edward Boling	S	45,440	2,787
At Nashville.	Nashville, Tenn.	1971	Charles Smith, Act. Chan.	S	4,998	120
At Chattanooga.	Chattanooga, Tenn.	1886	James Drinnon, Chan.	S	5,034	275
At Knoxville.	Knoxville, Tenn.	1794	Jack Reese, Chan.	S	28,011	1,447
At Martin.	Martin, Tenn.	1900	Larry T. McGhee, Chan.	S	4,978	248
Ctr. for Health Sci.	Memphis, Tenn.	1911	T. Farmer, Chan.	D	2,419	690
Tennessee Wesleyan	Athens, Tenn.	1857	Vacant	D	425	40
Texas	Tyler, Tex.	1894	Allen C. Hancock.	S	536	43
Texas A & I Univ.	Kingsville, Tex.	1925	Gerald Robins.	S	6,968	300
Tex. A. & M.	College Station, Tex.	1876	Jack K. Williams	S	21,463	1,285
Prairie View A. & M. Univ.	Prairie View, Tex.	1876	Alvin Thomas .	S	4,870	255
Tarleton State Univ.	Stephenville, Tex.	1899	William O. Trogden	S	2,962	150
Texas Christian Univ.	Fort Worth, Tex.	1873	J. M. Moudy (Chan.).	P	6,132	300
Texas Lutheran	Seguin, Tex.	1891	Joe Menn.	P	1,222	76
Texas Southern Univ.	Houston, Tex.	1947	Granville Sawyer	S	7,367	348
Texas System, Univ. of.	Austin, Tex.	1883	Charles A. LeMaistre, Chan.	S	77,437	7,162
At Arlington.	Arlington, Tex.	1895	Wendell Nedderman.	S	15,434	906
At Austin.	Austin, Tex.	1883	L. Rogers, Act.	S	41,841	3,468
At Corpus Christi	Corpus Christi, Tex.	1973	D. W. Halliday	S	1,249	68
At Dallas.	Dallas, Tex.	1969	Bryce Jordan	S	850	136
El Paso	El Paso, Tex.	1913	Alkeigh Templeton	S	11,418	390
Health Science Center	Houston, Tex.	1905	Charles Berry	S	1,351	433
Medical Branch.	Galveston, Tex.	1891	William Levin.	S	1,002	354
Health Science Center	San Antonio, Tex.	1959	Frank Harrison.	S	648	327
Health Science Center	Dallas, Tex.	1943	Charles Sprague.	S	973	556
At Odessa	Odessa, Tex.	1969	V. Cardozier, Act.	S	1,352	100
At San Antonio.	San Antonio, Tex.	1969	Peter Flawn	S	1,620	81
Texas Tech. Univ.	Lubbock, Tex.	1923	Grover Murray	S	21,510	1,399
Texas Wesleyan	Fort Worth, Tex.	1891	William Pearce.	D	1,726	100
Texas Woman's Univ. (W)	Denton, Tex.	1901	John A. Guinn.	S	7,222	401
Thiel.	Greenville, Pa.	1866	Frank Bretz.	D	1,111	73
Thomas.	Waterville, Me.	1894	John L. Thomas, Jr.	P	608	25
Thomas Jefferson Univ.	Philadelphia, Pa.	1824	Peter Herbut	D	1,800	1,240
Thomas More.	Ft. Mitchell, Ky.	1921	Richard A. DeGraff.	D	1,422	115
Tiffin Univ.	Tiffin, Oh.	1918	Richard Pfeiffer.	P	785	33
Tift (W)	Forsyth, Ga.	1847	Robert W. Jackson.	P	659	35
Toccoa Falls Bible Coll.	Toccoa Falls, Ga.	1911	K. Opperman.	P	356	31
Toledo, Univ. of	Toledo, Oh.	1872	Glen R. Driscoll.	S	15,742	700
Towson State.	Baltimore, Md.	1866	James L. Fisher	S	13,041	525
Transylvania Univ.	Lexington, Ky.	1780	Irvin E. Lunger.	P	664	59
Trenton State.	Trenton, N.J.	1855	C. B. Brower.	S	8,800	546
Trevecca Nazarene	Nashville, Tenn.	1901	Mark Moore.	P	793	68
Trinity.	Hartford, Conn.	1823	Theodore Lockwood	P	2,099	148
Trinity	Deerfield, Ill.	1897	Harry Evans	D	822	60
Trinity	Burlington, Vt.	1925	Sister Elizabeth Candon.	D	483	56
Trinity	Washington, D.C.	1897	Sr. Roseanne Fleming.	D	900	109
Trinity Univ.	San Antonio, Tex.	1869	Duncan Wimpress.	P	3,393	249
Tri-State	Angola, Ind.	1884	Carl Elliott.	P	1,283	87

Name	Location	Year	Governing Official and Affiliation		Stu-dents	Teach-ers
Troy State Univ.	Troy, Ala.	1887	Ralph W. Adams	S	7,045	242
Tufts Univ.	Medford, Mass.	1852	Burton Hallowell	P	6,444	1,850
Tulane Univ.	New Orleans, La.	1834	H. E. Longenecker	P	9,038	763
Tulsa, Univ. of.	Tulsa, Okla.	1894	J. Paschal Twyman	P	5,955	350
Tusculum.	Greeneville, Tenn.	1794	Thomas Voss	P	427	35
Tuskegee Institute.	Tuskegee Inst., Ala.	1881	Luther H. Foster	P	3,196	353
Tyler State.	Tyler, Tex.	1972	James Stewart, Jr.	S	1,108	45
Union.	Barbourville, Ky.	1879	Mahlon A. Miller	D	1,041	57
Union.	Lincoln, Neb.	1891	Myrl O. Manley	D	883	76
Union.	Schenectady, N.Y.	1795	Thomas Bonner	P	3,115	190
Union Univ.	Jackson, Tenn.	1825	Robert E. Craig	D	977	60
U.S. Air Force Academy (M).	Col. Springs, Col.	1954	Maj. Gen. J. Allen, Supt.	F	4,069	540
U.S. Coast Guard Acad. (M).	New London, Conn.	1876	Rear Adm. W. Jenkins, Supt.	F	1,000	126
U.S. International Univ. (A)	San Diego, Cal.	1952	William Rust	P	5,000	260
U.S. Merch. Marine Acad.	Kings Point, N.Y.	1938	Rear Adm. A. Engel, Supt.	F	1,000	84
U.S. Military Academy (M)	West Point, N.Y.	1802	Maj. Gen. Berry, Supt.	F	4,100	626
U.S. Naval Academy (M)	Annapolis, Md.	1846	VADM. W. P. Mack, Supt.	F	4,300	525
Unity.	Unity, Me.	1966	Allan Karstetter	P	300	25
Upper Iowa.	Fayette, Ia.	1857	Aldrich Paul	P	527	45
Upsala.	E. Orange, N.J.	1893	Carl J. Fjellman	D	1,611	114
Urbana (A).	Urbana, Oh.	1850	Paul Zehner	P	650	45
Ursinus.	Collegeville, Pa.	1869	William Pettit	P	1,661	111
Ursuline.	Cleveland, Oh.	1871	Sister M. Kenan	D	425	52
Utah State Univ.*	Logan, Ut.	1888	Glen L. Taggart	S	8,900	825
Utah, Univ. of.	Salt Lake City, Ut.	1850	David P. Gardner	S	21,750	3,153
Valdosta State.	Valdosta, Ga.	1906	S. Walter Martin	S	4,994	243
Valley City State.	Valley City, N.D.	1890	Ted DeVries.	S	923	64
Valparaiso Univ.	Valparaiso, Ind.	1859	Albert Huegli	P	4,290	300
Vanderbilt Univ.	Nashville, Tenn.	1873	Alexander Heard, Chan.	P	6,923	1,540
Vassar.	Poughkeepsie, N.Y.	1861	Alan Simpson	P	2,278	216
Vermont, Univ. of*	Burlington, Vt.	1791	W. Patterson, Act.	S	10,475	988
Villa Maria (W)	Erie, Pa.	1925	Sister L. Antoun	P	502	65
Villanova Univ.	Villanova, Pa.	1842	Rev. Edward McCarthy	D	10,000	450
Virgin Islands, Coll. of the.	St. Thomas, V.I.	1962	L. C. Wanlass	S	1,698	59
Virginia Commonwealth U.	Richmond, Va.	1838	T. Temple, Act.	S	17,551	2,200
Virginia Intermont.	Bristol, Va.	1884	Floyd Turner	D	541	49
Virginia Military Inst.	Lexington, Va.	1839	Maj. Gen. Irby, Supt.	S	1,122	98
Virginia Poly. Inst. & Univ.*	Blacksburg, Va.	1872	T. Marshall Hahn, Jr.	S	18,816	1,707
Virginia State*.	Petersburg, Va.	1882	W. Quarles, Act.	S	4,176	261
Virginia, Univ. of.	Charlottesville, Va.	1819	F. Hereford, Jr.	S	14,382	1,500
Virginia Wesleyan.	Norfolk, Va.	1961	Lambuth M. Clarke.	P	634	50
Viterbo.	La Crosse, Wis.	1931	Fr. J. Thomas Finucan	P	800	97
Voorhees.	Denmark, S.C.	1897	Harry Graham.	D	855	51
Wabash (M).	Crawfordsville, Ind.	1832	Thaddeus Seymour	P	793	73
Wagner.	Staten Island, N.Y.	1883	Arthur O. Davidson.	P	2,600	125
Wake Forest Univ.	Winston-Salem, N.C.	1834	James R. Scales	D	4,195	689
Walla Walla.	College Place, Wash.	1892	Robert Reynolds.	D	1,919	140
Walsh.	Canton, Oh.	1960	Bro. Robert Francoeur.	D	771	57
Walsh Coll. of Accounting.	Troy, Mich.	1969	Jeffrey Barry.	P	757	43
Warner Pacific.	Portland, Ore.	1937	E. J. Gilliam.	D	438	40
Warren Wilson.	Swannanoa, N.C.	1894	Reuben H. Holden.	P	405	57
Wartburg.	Waverly, Ia.	1852	W. Jellema.	P	1,193	94
Washburn Univ. of Topeka.	Topeka, Kan.	1865	John W. Henderson.	C	5,033	180
Washington.	Chestertown, Md.	1782	Joseph McLain.	P	691	70
Washington and Jefferson.	Washington, Pa.	1731	Howard J. Burnett.	P	1,090	125
Washington and Lee Univ.	Lexington, Va.	1749	Robert Huntley.	P	1,618	162
Washington State Univ.	Pullman, Wash.	1890	Glenn Terrell.	S	15,613	905
Washington Univ.	St. Louis, Mo.	1853	W. H. Danforth (Chan.)	P	10,862	2,055
Washington, Univ. of.	Seattle, Wash.	1861	John R. Hogness.	S	34,504	2,383
Wayland Baptist.	Plainview, Tex.	1908	Roy C. McClung.	P	1,005	55
Wayne State.	Wayne, Neb.	1910	Lyle Seymour.	S	1,936	105
Wayne State Univ.	Detroit, Mich.	1868	George Gullen	S	34,706	2,142
Waynesburg.	Waynesburg, Pa.	1849	Joseph Marsh.	P	800	64
Weber State.	Ogden, Ut.	1889	Joseph Bishop.	S	11,320	432
Webster.	St. Louis, Mo.	1915	Leigh Gerdine	P	3,090	200
Wellesley (W)	Wellesley, Mass.	1875	Barbara W. Newell	P	2,033	245
Wells (W)	Aurora, N.Y.	1868	John Wilson	P	500	70
Wentworth Coll. of Technology	Boston, Mass.	1970	Edward Kirkpatrick	P	227	15
Wesleyan (W)	Macon, Ga.	1836	W. Earl Strickland	D	570	53
Wesleyan Univ.	Middletown, Conn.	1832	Colin G. Campbell.	P	2,289	282
West Chester State.	West Chester, Pa.	1812	Charles Mayo.	S	8,500	480
West Coast Univ.	Los Angeles, Cal.	1909	Victor Elconin	P	1,316	127
West Florida, Univ. of.	Pensacola, Fla.	1967	Harold Bryan Crosby	S	4,527	216
West Georgia.	Carrollton, Ga.	1933	Ward Pafford.	S	5,524	268
West Liberty State.	West Liberty, W. Va.	1837	James L. Chapman.	S	2,708	166
West Texas State Univ.	Canyon, Tex.	1910	Lloyd Watkins	S	6,645	250
W. Va. Inst. of Technology	Montgomery, W. Va.	1895	Leonard C. Nelson	S	2,712	145
West Virginia State.	Institute, W. Va.	1891	Harold M. McNeill.	S	3,677	167
West Virginia Univ.*	Morgantown, W. Va.	1867	James G. Harlow.	S	17,400	834
W. Virginia Wesleyan	Buckhannon, W. Va.	1890	John D. Rockefeller, IV	P	1,678	123
Western Baptist Bible.	Salem, Ore.	1946	F. R. Brock (Chan.)	D	500	30
Western, (The) (A)	Oxford, Oh.	1853	William Spencer	P	345	45
Western Conn. State.	Danbury, Conn.	1904	Ruth A. Haas.	S	5,123	259
Western Illinois Univ.	Macomb, Ill.	1889	L. Malpass	S	15,398	744
Western Kentucky Univ.	Bowling Green, Ky.	1906	Dero Downing	S	12,331	600
Western Maryland.	Westminster, Md.	1867	Ralph C. John	P	2,266	161
Western Mich. Univ.	Kalamazoo, Mich.	1903	John T. Bernhard.	S	21,113	1,034
Western Montana.	Dillon, Mon.	1893	James E. Short	S	775	46
Western New England.	Springfield, Mass.	1919	Beaumont A. Herman.	P	3,656	132
Western New Mexico Univ.	Silver City, N.M.	1893	John Snedeker	S	1,879	58
Western Washington State.	Bellingham, Wash.	1899	Paul Olscamp.	S	8,697	439
Westfield State.	Westfield, Mass.	1839	Robert L. Randolph.	S	3,900	155
Westmar.	Le Mars, Ia.	1890	Laurence Smith.	P	706	51
Westminster.	Fulton, Mo.	1851	Dale Purcell.	P	702	59
Westminster.	New Wilmington, Pa.	1852	Earland I. Carlson.	D	1,935	128
Westminster.	Salt Lake City, Ut.	1875	Manford A. Shaw.	P	851	59
Westmont.	Santa Barbara, Cal.	1940	Lyle C. Hillegas.	P	950	70
Wheaton.	Wheaton, Ill.	1860	Hudson T. Armerding.	P	2,234	163

Name	Location	Year	Governing Official and Affiliation		Students	Teachers
Wheaton (W)	Norton, Mass.	1834	William C.H. Prentice	P	1,112	117
Wheeling	Wheeling, W. Va.	1954	Rev. Charles Currie	P	637	57
Wheelock	Boston, Mass.	1889	Gordon L. Marshall	P	813	84
White Plains, College of	White Plains, N.Y.	1923	Katherine Restaino	P	675	49
Whitman	Walla Walla, Wash.	1859	Robert Skotheim	P	1,132	87
Whittier	Whittier, Cal.	1901	W. R. Newsom, Act. Pres.	P	1,661	104
Whitworth	Spokane, Wash.	1890	Edward B. Lindaman	P	2,468	147
Wichita State Univ.	Wichita, Kan.	1895	Clark Ahlberg	S	13,727	734
Wilberforce Univ. (A)	Wilberforce, Oh.	1856	Rembert E. Stokes	D	1,217	46
Widener	Chester, Pa.	1821	Clarence R. Moll	P	3,004	200
Wiley	Marshall, Tex.	1873	Robert Hayes Sr.	D	567	41
Wilkes	Wilkes-Barre, Pa.	1933	Francis Michelini	P	2,646	175
Willamette Univ.	Salem, Ore.	1842	Robert Lisensky	P	1,682	154
William Carey	Hattiesburg, Miss.	1906	J. Ralph Noonkester	P	1,259	49
William Jewell	Liberty, Mo.	1849	Thomas Field	P	1,428	114
Wm. and Mary, College of	Williamsburg, Va.	1693	Thomas A. Graves	S	5,840	430
Wm. Mitchell Coll. of Law	St. Paul, Minn.	1900	William H. Abbott	P	840	50
Wm. Paterson Coll. of N.J.	Wayne, N.J.	1855	William McKeefery	S	12,999	443
William Penn	Oskaloosa, Ia.	1873	Duane Moon	P	667	50
William Woods (W)	Fulton, Mo.	1870	Randall B. Cutlip	P	1,043	86
Williams	Williamstown, Mass.	1793	John W. Chandler	P	1,875	169
Wilmington	Wilmington, Oh.	1870	Robert E. Lucas	D	650	64
Wilmington	New Castle, Del.	1968	Donald E. Ross	P	479	34
Wilson (W)	Chambersburg, Pa.	1869	L. E. Dennis, Act.	P	392	55
Windham	Putney, Vt.	1951	Harrison Symmes	S	771	63
Winona State	Winona, Minn.	1858	Robt. DuFresne	S	4,595	186
Winthrop	Rock Hill, S.C.	1886	Charles Vail	S	3,790	227
Wisconsin, Univ. of*	Madison, Wis.	1849	Edwin Young, Chan.	S	36,915	4,624
Eau Claire	Eau Claire, Wis.	1916	Leonard Haas, Chan.	S	3,661	238
Green Bay	Green Bay, Wis.	1969	Edward W. Weidner, Chan.	S	3,661	238
La Crosse	La Crosse, Wis.	1908	Kenneth Lindner	S	7,600	400
Milwaukee	Milwaukee, Wis.	1956	John C. Weaver	S	25,421	1,157
Oshkosh	Oshkosh, Wis.	1871	Robert Birnbaum, Chan.	S	9,922	740
Platteville	Platteville, Wis.	1866	Bjarne R. Ullsvik, Chan.	S	3,941	274
River Falls	River Falls, Wis.	1874	George Field, Chan.	S	4,213	240
Stevens Point	Stevens Point, Wis.	1894	Lee S. Dreyfus, Chan.	S	8,055	560
Stout	Menomonie, Wis.	1893	Robert Swanson, Chan.	S	5,400	350
Superior	Superior, Wis.	1893	Karl W. Meyer, Chan.	S	2,592	217
Whitewater	Whitewater, Wis.	1868	James Connor, Chan.	S	8,355	453
Wittenberg Univ.	Springfield, Oh.	1845	W. A. Kinnison, Act.	P	2,343	147
Wofford	Spartanburg, S.C.	1854	J. M. Lesesne, Jr.	P	1,023	75
Woodbury	Los Angeles, Cal.	1884	Dora E. Kirby	P	1,570	68
Wooster, Coll. of	Wooster, Oh.	1866	J. G. Drushal	P	1,830	158
Worcester Polytechnic Inst.	Worcester, Mass.	1865	George W. Hazzard	P	2,761	180
Worcester State	Worcester, Mass.	1874	Robert Leestamper	S	5,174	200
Wright State Univ.	Dayton, Oh.	1967	R. J. Kegerreis	S	13,202	465
Wyoming Univ. of*	Laramie, Wy.	1887	William Carlson	S	7,621	840
Xavier Univ. of Louisiana (A)	New Orleans, La.	1925	Norman C. Francis	P	1,619	152
Xavier Univ.	Cincinnati, Oh.	1831	Rev. Robert Mulligan	P	9,661	1,261
Yale Univ.	New Haven, Conn.	1701	Kingman Brewster, Jr.	P	9,661	1,261
Yankton	Yankton, S.D.	1881	Alfred M. Gibbens	P	320	41
Yeshiva Univ.	New York, N.Y.	1886	Samuel Belkin	P	6,447	2,500
York College of Pa.	York, Pa.	1941	Ray A. Miller	P	2,982	152
Youngstown State Univ.	Youngstown, Oh.	1908	John J. Coffelt	S	13,917	760

Community and Junior Colleges

Enrollment and faculty figures in italics include all branches and campuses

Name	Location	Year	Governing Official		Students	Teachers
Adirondacks Community	Glens Falls, N.Y.	1960	Charles R. Eisenhart	S	1,565	55
Aeronautics, Academy of	Flushing, N.Y.	1932	Walter M. Hartung	P	800	42
Aims	Greeley, Col.	1967	Ed Beaty	C	2,952	200
Alabama Christian	Montgomery, Ala.	1942	E. R. Brannan	D	332	27
Alamance, Tech. Inst. of	Burlington N.C.	1959	William Taylor	S	1,169	150
Alameda, Coll. of	Alameda, Cal.	1968	Jeanette Poore	C	6,930	150
Albany Junior	Albany, Ga.	1966	B. R. Tilley	S	1,697	75
Albany, Junior Coll. of	Albany, N.Y.	1957	Charles Walker	P	680	48
Albemarle, Coll. of the	Elizabeth City, N.C.	1960	S. Bruce Petteway	S	1,006	60
Alexander City State Junior	Alexander City, Ala.	1965	W. Byron Causey	S	1,224	42
Alice Lloyd	Pippa Passes, Ky.	1923	Will Hayes	P	258	29
Allan Hancock Joint Comm.	Santa Maria, Calif.	1920	Walter E. Conrad	Di.	8,941	528
Allegany Community	Cumberland, Md.	1961	W. Ardell Haines	C	1,382	106
Allegheny Co., Comm. College of	Pittsburgh, Pa.	1966	John B. Hirt	C	15,500	1,144
Alpena Community	Alpena, Mich.	1952	Herbert N. Stoutenberg	C	1,683	115
Amarillo	Amarillo, Tex.	1929	Charles Lutz, Jr.	Mu	4,069	197
American Academy of Art	Chicago, Ill.	1923	Irving Shapiro, Dir.	P	750	19
American River	Sacramento, Cal.	1955	Kenneth Boettcher	Di	17,364	497
Anderson	Anderson, S.C.	1911	J. Cordell Maddox	D	1,168	61
Andrew	Cuthbert, Ga.	1854	J. C. Martinson, Jr.	D	300	70
Angelina	Lufkin, Tex.	1968	Jack W. Hudgins, Jr.	S	1,025	70
Anne Arundel Community	Arnold, Md.	1961	Robert P. Ludlum	CS	11,922	220
Anoka-Ramsey Comm.	Coon Rapids, Minn.	1965	H. B. Monroe	S	2,000	72
Anson Tech. Inst.	Ansonville, N.C.	1962	Ronald Denison	S	300	14
Antelope Valley	Lancaster, Cal.	1929	Clinton Stine	S	4,665	200
Aquinas Junior	Milton, Mass.	1956	Sr. Mary Morgan, Act.	D	270	21
Aquinas Junior	Nashville, Tenn.	1961	Sister Henry Suso Fletcher	D	343	38
Arapahoe Community	Littleton, Col.	1965	Joseph K. Bailey	S	3,842	174
Arizona Western	Yuma, Ariz.	1963	Robert Garin	S	4,300	70
Asheville Buncombe Tech. Inst.	Asheville, N.C.	1961	Thomas Simpson	S	1,482	122
Ashland Community	Ashland, Ky.	1957	Robert Goodpaster	S	1,253	62
Atlantic Comm.	Mays Landing, N.J.	1964	L. R. Winchell	C	4,000	120
Auburn Community	Auburn, N.Y.	1953	Albert T. Skinner	S	3,031	89
Austin Comm.	Austin, Minn.	1940	Curtis C. Mac Donald	S	852	55
Bacone	Muskogee, Okla.	1880	Charles D. Holleyman	P	540	48
Bakersfield	Bakersfield, Cal.	1913	John J. Collins	S	12,000	475

Name	Location	Year	Governing Official and Affiliation		Stu-dents	Teach-ers
Baltimore, Com. Col. of	Baltimore, Md.	1947	Harry Bard	Mu	10,000	250
Barstow Community	Barstow, Cal.	1960	R. Graham, Act.	Mu	1,688	76
Barton County Comm. Jr.	Great Bend, Kan.	1965	Paul Hines	C	1,082	68
Bay de Noc Community	Escanaba, Mich.	1962	Edwin E. Wuehle	C	996	66
Bay Path Junior	Longmeadow, Mass.	1897	Randle Elliott	P	509	34
Beal	Bangor, Me.	1891	David Tibbetts	P	268	26
Beaufort County Tech. Inst.	Washington, N.C.	1968	James P. Blanton	S	700	41
Beaver County, Com. Col. of	Monaca, Pa.	1967	Richard Adams	C	1,800	80
Becker Junior	Worcester, Mass.	1887	Lloyd H. Van Buskirk	P	628	36
Beckley	Beckley, W. Va.	1933	John Saunders	P	972	35
Bee County	Beeville, Tex.	1965	Grady C. Hogue	S	1,935	97
Bell and Howell Schools (A)	Chicago, Ill.	1969	George Doherty	P	7,200	350
Belleville Area	Belleville, Ill.	1946	William Keel	SC	8,500	390
Bellevue Community	Bellevue, Wash.	1966	Merle Landerholm	S	7,580	347
Belmont Technical	St. Clairsville, Oh.	1969	E. Earl Greer	S	422	45
Bennett	Millbrook, N.Y.	1891	J. William Nystrom	P	270	38
Bergen Community	Paramus, N.J.	1965	Sidney Silverman	C	8,000	350
Berkshire Community	Pittsfield, Mass.	1960	T. E. O'Connell	S	2,648	148
Big Bend Community	Moses Lake, Wash.	1962	Robert J. Wallenstein	S	2,030	60
Bismarck Junior	Bismarck, N.D.	1939	Ralph Werner	Mu	1,900	85
Black Hawk	Moline, Ill.	1946	Alban E. Reid	S	9,755	165
Blackhawk Technical Inst.	Janesville, Wis.	1968	O. L. Johnson (Dir.)	Di	1,562	265
Bladen Tech. Inst.	Dublin, N.C.	1967	George Ressegure	S	180	15
Blinn	Brenham, Tex.	1883	James H. Atkinson	CS	1,731	103
Bliss	Columbus, Oh.	1899	Gerald J. Wickham	P	450	25
Bluefield	Bluefield, Va.	1922	Charles L. Tyer	D	263	24
Blue Mountain Community	Pendleton, Ore.	1962	Ronald L. Daniels	S	1,050	70
Blue Ridge Comm.	Weyers Cave, Va.	1967	James A. Armstrong	S	1,346	90
Brainerd Comm.	Brainerd, Minn.	1938	William Oatey	S	500	30
Brandywine	Wilmington, Del.	1965	W. Polisbook, Act.	P	1,000	50
Brazosport	Lake Jackson, Tex.	1968	J. R. Jackson	S	2,462	125
Brevard	Brevard, N.C.	1853	Robert A. Davis	D	540	46
Brevard Community	Cocoa, Fla.	1960	Maxwell King	S	7,600	300
Brewton Parker	Mt. Vernon, Ga.	1904	J. Theodore Phillips	D	723	34
Bristol Community	Fall River, Mass.	1966	Jack Hudnall	S	5,128	319
Bronx Community	Bronx, N.Y.	1957	James A. Colston	Mu	17,489	882
Brookdale Community	Lincroft, N.J.	1967	Donald H. Smith	C	7,000	226
Broome Community	Binghamton, N.Y.	1946	Sigmund A. Smith	S	4,287	159
Broward Community	Ft. Lauderdale, Fla.	1960	Hugh Adams	S	13,585	517
Brunswick Junior	Brunswick, Ga.	1961	John W. Teel	S	1,068	54
Bryant & Stratton	Boston, Mass.	1865	L. P. White	P	367	28
Bucks County Comm.	Newtown, Pa.	1965	Charles Rollins	C	6,448	3362
Butler County Comm.	Butler, Pa.	1965	Thomas Ten Hoeve, Jr.	C	1,350	73
Butler County Comm.	El Dorado, Kan.	1927	Edwin J. Walbourn	C	1,509	85
Butte	Durham, Cal.	1968	Albert Schlueter	C	6,800	260
Cabrillo Comm.	Aptos, Cal.	1959	Robert E. Swenson	Di	7,102	241
Caldwell Comm. & Tech.	Lenoir, N.C.	1964	H. Edwin Beam	S	750	75
Camden County	Blackwood, N.J.	1967	Otto R. Mauke	S	4,800	209
Canada	Redwood City, Cal.	1968	R. Stiff, Act.	C	7,500	246
Canyons, Coll. of the	Valencia, Cal.	1969	Robert Rockwell	Di	2,584	103
Cape Cod Comm.	W. Barnstable, Mass.	1960	James F. Hall	S	3,512	150
Cape Fear Tech. Inst.	Wilmington, N.C.	1964	M. J. McLeod	S	800	60
Carl Albert Junior	Poteau, Okla.	1934	Norman McNabb	P	961	60
Carl Sandburg	Galesburg, Ill.	1967	Eltis Henson	S	2,300	120
Carteret Tech. Inst.	Morehead City, N.C.	1964	Donald Bryant	S	750	60
Casper	Casper, Wy.	1945	Tilghman Aley	C	3,460	154
Catawba Valley Tech. Inst.	Hickory, N.C.	1960	Robert E. Paap	S	1,750	100
Catonsville Community	Catonsville, Md.	1956	Robert Barringer	C	8,558	388
Cazenovia (W)	Cazenovia, N.Y.	1824	Vincent C. DeBaun	C	370	40
Cecil Community	No. East, Md.	1968	Robert L. Nash	C	1,272	80
Centenary Coll. for Women (W)	Hackettstown, N.J.	1867	Edward W. Seay	P	483	35
Central Arizona	Coolidge, Ariz.	1967	Don Pence	C	4,437	76
Central Carolina Tech. Inst.	Sanford, N.C.	1958	James F. Hockaday	C	1,194	99
Central Florida Community	Ocala, Fla.	1957	Henry E. Goodlett	C	1,750	100
Central Oregon Community	Bend, Ore.	1949	Frederick Boyle	C	1,348	65
Central Piedmont Comm.	Charlotte, N.C.	1963	Richard H. Hagemeyer	S	18,947	692
Central Nebr. Tech. Comm.	Grand Island, Neb.	1973	Chester Gausman	C	3,520	132
Central Texas	Killeen, Tex.	1967	L. M. Morton, Jr.	C	5,000	125
Central Virginia Comm.	Lynchburg, Va.	1967	Donald Puyear	S	2,676	90
Central Wyoming	Riverton, Wy.	1966	William Day	C	961	89
Central YMCA Comm.	Chicago, Ill.	1969	Donald A. Canar	S	3,756	170
Centralia	Centralia, Wash.	1925	Nels W. Hanson	S	4,109	188
Cerritos Community	Norwalk, Cal.	1956	Wilford Michael	C	21,970	562
Chabot	Hayward, Cal.	1961	Reed L. Buffington	Di	16,895	600
Chaffey	Alta Loma, Cal.	1883	T. Stanley Warburton	Di	10,750	348
Champlain	Burlington, Vt.	1878	C. Bader Brouilette	P	950	45
Charles Co. Community	La Plata, Md.	1958	J. N. Carsey	C	1,508	88
Charles S. Mott Comm.	Flint, Mich.	1923	Charles Pappas	C	9,710	430
Chattanooga St. Tech. Inst.	Chattanooga, Tenn.	1965	Charles W. Branch	S	1,322	70
Chemeketa Comm.	Salen, Ore.	1955	Donald Newport	Di	8,757	272
Chesapeake	Wye Mills, Md.	1967	George Silver	C	917	54
Chicago, City Colleges of (A)	Chicago, Ill.		Oscar Shabat	Mu	35,000	1,200
Loop College	Chicago, Ill.	1911	David Heller	S	11,202	216
Chipola Junior	Marianna, Fla.	1947	Raymond M. Deming	S	1,027	85
Chowan	Murfreesboro, N.C.	1848	Bruce E. Whitaker	I	1,014	69
Cisco Junior	Cisco, Tex.	1940	Norman Wallace	S	2,052	65
Citrus Community	Azusa, Cal.	1915	Robert Haugh	S	9,661	335
Clackamas Comm.	Oregon City, Ore.	1966	John Hakanson	C	7,118	350
Claremore Junior	Claremore, Okla.	1919	Richard Mosier	S	1,200	56
Clarendon	Clarendon, Tex.	1898	Kenneth D. Vaughan	S	478	31
Clark	Vancouver, Wash.	1933	I. S. Hakanson	S	5,755	225
Clark Tech.	Springfield, Oh.	1966	Richard Brinkman	S	1,106	66
Clarke	Newton, Miss.	1908	W. L. Compere	P	266	19
Clatsop Community	Astoria, Ore.	1962	Philip Bainer	S	1,978	73
Clayton Junior	Morrow, Ga.	1969	Harry S. Downs	S	2,871	99
Cleveland Co. Tech. Inst.	Shelby, N.C.	1965	James Petty	S	1,505	95
Cleveland State Comm.	Cleveland, Tenn.	1967	D. F. Adkisson	S	3,010	118

Name	Location	Year	Governing Official and Affiliation		Stu-dents	Teach-ers
Clinton Community	Clinton, Ia.	1946	G. Clemmensen	S	722	44
Clinton Community	Plattsburgh, N.Y.	1966	Albert B. Light	S	1,001	26
Cloud County Comm.	Concordia, Kan.	1965	Arley Bryant	C	960	40
Coahoma Junior	Clarksdale, Miss.	1949	James Earl Miller	S	986	56
Coastal Carolina Community	Jacksonville, N.C.	1963	James Henderson, Jr.	S, C	1,876	95
Cochise	Douglas, Ariz.	1964	John R. Edwards	C	2,829	200
Coffeyville Comm. Junior	Coffeyville, Kan.	1923	Russell Graham	Di	585	40
Colby Comm.	Colby, Kan.	1964	James Tangeman	S	1,254	62
Colby Women's (W)	New London, N.H.	1837	Louis Vaccaro	P	609	57
Colorado Mountain	Glenwood Spgs., Col.	1965	Elbie L. Gann	C	4,277	217
Colorado Northwestern Comm.	Rangely, Col.	1960	James H. Bos	S	813	50
Columbia Basin (A)	Pasco, Wash.	1955	Fred L. Esvelt	S	4,500	175
Columbia-Greene Comm.	Athens, N.Y.	1966	Edward Owen	S	766	23
Columbia Junior	Columbia, Cal.	1968	Harvey Rhodes	S	2,615	75
Columbia State Comm.	Columbia, Tenn.	1966	Harold S. Pryor	S	1,366	56
Columbus Tech. Inst.	Columbus, Oh.	1963	Clarence Schauer	S	2,808	214
Compton Comm.	Compton, Cal.	1927	Abel B. Sykes, Jr.	S	6,465	212
Concordia	Milwaukee, Wis.	1881	Walter W. Stuenkel	D	740	75
Concordia	St. Paul, Minn.	1893	Harvey Stegemoeller	D	629	56
Concordia Lutheran	Austin, Tex.	1926	Ray F. Martens	P	366	26
Concordia Lutheran Jr.	Ann Arbor, Mich.	1962	Rev. M. S. Pohl	P	451	34
Connors State	Warner, Okla.	1908	Melvin Self	S	1,450	41
Contra Costa (A)	San Pablo, Cal.	1948	Robert Wynne	Di	7,600	175
Coore County	Gainesville, Tex.	1924	Alton Laird	S	1,996	75
Copiah-Lincoln Junior	Wesson, Miss.	1928	Billy Thames	C	1,365	98
Corning Community	Corning, N.Y.	1956	Robert W. Frederick, Jr.	S	2,549	93
Cottey (W)	Nevada, Mo.	1884	Evelyn Milam	P	368	31
Cowley County Comm.	Arkansas City, Kan.	1922	Gwen Nelson	C	1,221	60
Craven Comm.	New Bern, N.C.	1965	Thurman E. Brock	S	844	140
Crowder	Neosho, Mo.	1964	Dell Reed	S	960	53
Cuesta	San Luis Obispo, Cal.	1965	Merlin Eisenbise	C	4,254	149
Cullman	Cullman, Ala.	1940	Sr. M. Lourdes Michel	D	185	24
Cumberland Coll. of Tenn.	Lebanon, Tenn.	1842	Ernest L. Stockton	P	321	25
Cumberland County	Vineland, N.J.	1966	William J. Sample	C	1,600	60
Curry	Milton, Mass.	1879	John S. Hafer	P	1,027	54
Cuyahoga Community	Cleveland, Oh.	1963	Nolen Ellison	C	22,416	1,114
Cypress	Cypress, Cal.	1966	Omar Scheidt	S	9,876	275
Dabney S. Lancaster Comm.	Clifton Forge, Va.	1967	John F. Backels	S	817	50
Dallas Co. Comm. Col. System (A)	Dallas, Tex.	1965	Bill J. Priest	C	16,438	412
Dalton Jr.	Dalton, Ga.	1963	Derrell Roberts	S	1,430	70
Danville Junior	Danville, Ill.	1946	William Larigas	S	3,000	100
Davenport Coll. of Business	Grand Rapids, Mich.	1866	Robert W. Sneden	P	1,311	46
Davidson County Comm.	Lexington, N.C.	1958	Grady Love	S	1,682	150
Davis Junior	Toledo, Oh.	1858	Ruth L. Davis	P	760	28
Dawson	Glendive, Mon.	1940	James Hoffman	C, S	677	38
Daytona Beach Comm.	Daytona Beach, Fla.	1958	Roy F. Bergengren	S	3,??7	144
Dean Junior	Franklin, Mass.	1865	Richard Crockford	P	200	74
De Anza	Cupertino, Cal.	1967	A. Robert DeHart	S	3,364	652
DeKalb Community	Clarkston, Ga.	1964	James H. Hinson, Jr.	C	8,483	384
Delaware Tech. & Comm. (A)	Georgetown, Del.	1967	Paul K. Weatherly	S	2,600	125
Delgado Junior	New Orleans, La.	1921	Marvin E. Thames	S	8,903	275
Del Mar	Corpus Christi, Tex.	1935	Jean Richardson	C	7,158	358
Delaware County Comm.	Media, Pa.	1967	Douglas Libby, Jr.	C	2,300	100
Delta	University Ctr., Mich.	1961	Donald Carlyon	C	10,500	482
Denver, Comm. Coll. of	Denver, Col.	1968	Leland Luchsinger	S	12,500	700
Des Moines Area Comm.	Ankeny, Ia.	1966	Paul Lowery (Supt.)	S	4,200	800
Desert, Coll. of the	Palm Desert, Cal.	1958	F. D. Stout	S	8,217	277
Diablo Valley (A)	Pleasant Hill, Cal.	1948	William P. Niland	Di	14,020	280
District One Tech. Inst.	Eau Claire, Wis.	1912	Norbert Wurtzel, Dir.	S	2,147	120
Dixie Junior (A)	St. George, Ut.	1911	Ferron C. Losee	S	1,000	65
Dodge City Community	Dodge City, Kan.	1935	Charles M. Barnes	S	990	57
Donnelly	Kansas City, Kan.	1949	Rev. John Oldfield, Act.	D	633	30
Dundalk Community	Baltimore, Md.	1970	John E. Ravekes	C	1,364	100
Du Page, Coll. of	Glen Ellyn, Ill.	1966	Rodney Berg	S	12,344	594
Durham Tech. Inst.	Durham, N.C.	1965	Harold Collins	S, C	1,604	101
Dutchess Community (A)	Poughkeepsie, N.Y.	1957	James F. Hall	S	4,857	138
Dyersburg State Comm.	Dyersburg, Tenn.	1969	Edward Eller	S	944	55
East Central Junior	Decatur, Miss.	1928	Charles V. Wright	S, C	1,300	55
East Los Angeles	Los Angeles, Cal.	1945	A. Rodriguez	Di	16,800	620
East Mississippi Junior	Scooba, Miss.	1927	William Reeves	S	987	58
Eastern Arizona	Thatcher, Ariz.	1888	Dean Curtis	S, C	2,675	174
Eastern Iowa Comm.	Davenport, Ia.	1966	Gerald Clemmensen (Supt.)	S	1,959	132
Eastern Oklahoma State	Wilburton, Okla.	1909	James Miller	S	1,705	65
Eastern Utah, Coll. Of	Price, Ut.	1938	Dean McDonald	S	800	50
Eastern Wyoming	Torrington, Wy.	1948	Charles Rogers	C	450	44
Edgecombe Tech. Inst.	Tarboro, N.C.	1968	Charles McIntyre	S	1,000	50
Edison Community	Ft. Myers, Fla.	1961	David G. Robinson	S	2,756	92
Edmunds Community	Lynnwood, Wash.	1967	James Warren	S	3,200	157
El Camino	Torrance, Cal.	1947	Stuart E. Marsee	Di	26,004	635
El Centro	Dallas, Tex.	1965	Donald T. Rippey	S	5,672	309
El Paso Comm.	Colorado Springs, Col.	1968	D. Sieck, Act.	S	5,200	259
El Paso Community	El Paso, Tex.	1969	Alfredo de Los Santos, Jr.	S	9,020	301
El Reno	El Reno, Okla.	1938	A. R. Harrison	S	605	28
Elgin Community	Elgin, Ill.	1949	Robert L. Appel, Jr.	Di	4,511	217
Elizabeth Seton	Yonkers, N.Y.	1960	Eileen Farley	P	559	34
Elizabethtown Community	Elizabethtown, Ky.	1964	James Owen	S	978	68
Ellsworth Comm.	Iowa Falls, Ia.	1890	G. P. Warford (Dean)	S	776	55
Emmanuel	Franklin Spgs., Ga.	1919	C. Y. Melton	D	361	24
Endicott Junior (W)	Beverly, Mass.	1939	Eleanor Tupper	P	725	52
Erie Community	Buffalo, N.Y.	1946	Robert H. Stausser	S	9,749	250
Essex Community	Baltimore, Md.	1957	Vernon Wanty	C	7,141	361
Essex County	Newark, N.J.	1968	J. Harry Smith	C, S	7,162	530
Everett Comm.	Everett, Wash.	1941	Nicki Haynes, Act.	S	7,500	331

Name	Location	Year	Governing Official and Affiliation		Students	Teachers
Fayetteville Tech. Inst.	Fayetteville, N.C.	1961	Howard Boudreau	S	4,188	256
Fashion Inst. of Technology	New York, N.Y.	1944	Marvin J. Feldman	S, Mu	5,895	150
Feather River	Quincy, Cal.	1968	Dale P. Wren	Di	1,001	36
Fergus Falls Comm.	Fergus Falls, Minn.	1960	W. A. Waage	S	547	37
Ferrum	Ferrum, Va.	1913	Joseph T. Hart	D	1,226	63
Finger Lakes, Comm. Coll. of	Canandaigua, N.Y.	1965	Charles Meder	S	1,796	54
Fisher Junior (W)	Boston, Mass.	1903	Scott Fisher	P	875	68
Flathead Valley Comm.	Kalispell, Mont.	1967	John Bartlett	S	1,861	120
Florida	Temple Terrace, Fla.	1946	James R. Cope	S	430	33
Florida Jr. Coll. at Jacksonville	Jacksonville, Fla.	1966	Benjamin R. Wygal	S	11,972	1,659
Florida Keys Comm.	Key West, Fla.	1965	John S. Smith	S	1,267	55
Florissant Valley Community	St. Louis, Mo.	1962	Raymond J. Stith	Di	6,869	350
Floyd Junior	Rome, Ga.	1970	David McCorkle	S	1,309	74
Foothill	Los Altos Hills, Cal.	1958	James Fitzgerald	Di	14,161	525
Forest Park Community	St. Louis, Mo.	1962	Ralph H. Lee	Di	5,828	367
Forsyth Tech. Inst.	Winston-Salem, N.C.	1964	Harley Affeldt	S	1,730	127
Fort Scott Comm.	Fort Scott, Kan.	1919	Leon Foster	C	650	30
Ft. Steilacoom Comm. (A)	Tacoma, Wash.	1967	Marion O. Oppelt	S	7,585	259
Fox Valley Tech. Inst.	Appleton, Wis.	1967	William Sirek (Dir.)	C	23,000	620
Frank Phillips	Borger, Tex.	1948	W. E. Raab	S	767	55
Franklin Inst. of Boston	Boston, Mass.	1908	L. J. Dunham Jr. (Dir.)	Mu	978	73
Freed-Hardeman	Henderson, Tenn.	1908	E. Claude Gardner	D	1,201	67
Fresno City	Fresno, Cal.	1910	Clyde McCully	S	15,729	475
Fullerton	Fullerton, Cal.	1913	John Casey	S	17,999	510
Fulton-Montgomery Community	Johnstown, N.Y.	1963	Hadley S. DePuy	S	1,478	65
Gadsden State Junior	E. Gadsden, Ala.	1965	A. D. Naylor	S	9,627	215
Gainesville Junior	Gainesville, Ga.	1964	Hugh Mills, Jr.	S	1,200	53
Galveston	Galveston, Tex.	1967	Melvin M. Plexco	S	1,700	100
Garden City Community Junior	Garden City, Kan.	1919	Raymond Wamsley	C,S	1,234	62
Garland, Junior (W)	Boston, Mass.	1872	Alice J. Thurston	P	347	31
Gaston	Dallas, N.C.	1964	W. B. Sugg	S	2,593	114
Gateway Tech. Inst.	Kenosha, Wis.	1912	Keith Stoehr	C	7,804	174
Gavilan	Gilroy, Cal.	1963	Rudy Melone	S	2,000	113
Genesee Community	Batavia, N.Y.	1966	Cornelius V. Robbins	S	2,186	92
George C. Wallace State Comm.	Dothan, Ala.	1965	Phillip J. Hamm	S	2,239	96
Germanna Comm.	Locust Grove, Va.	1970	Arnold E. Wirtala	S	913	51
Glen Oaks Comm.	Centreville, Mich.	1965	Justus Sundermann	S	900	66
Glendale	Glendale, Cal.	1927	John Grande	Mu	7,587	207
Gloucester County	Sewell, N.J.	1968	William Apetz	S	2,316	61
Gogebic Community	Ironwood, Mich.	1932	James Perry	C	1,043	50
Golden West	Huntgtn. Bch., Cal.	1966	R. Dudley Boyce	M	19,800	750
Goldey Beacom	Wilmington, Del.	1886	Paul R. Brown	P	1,747	68
Gordon Junior	Barnesville, Ga.	1852	Jerry M. Williamson	S	948	52
Grahm Junior	Boston, Mass.	1950	Arthur Griffin	P	831	72
Grand Rapids Junior	Grand Rapids, Mich.	1914	Francis McCarthy (Dean)	Mu	6,300	425
Grand View	Des Moines, Ia.	1896	K. F. Langrock	P	858	40
Grays Harbor	Aberdeen, Wash.	1930	Joseph Malik	S	3,168	165
Grayson County	Denison, Tex.	1964	Truman Webster	S	4,347	147
Greater Hartford Comm.	Hartford, Conn.	1967	Arthur C. Banks, Jr.	S	1,607	65
Green Mountain (W)	Poultney, Vt.	1834	Raymond A. Withey	P	508	49
Green River Comm.	Auburn, Wash.	1964	Melvin Lindbloom	S	6,990	215
Greenville Tech.	Greenville, S.C.	1962	Thomas Barton Jr.	S	5,152	388
Grossmont Community (A)	El Cajon, Cal.	1961	Erv. F. Metzgar	S	13,100	374
Guilford Tech. Inst.	Jamestown, N.C.	1958	Luther R. Medlin	C	2,604	90
Gulf Coast Community	Panama City, Fla.	1957	Richard E. Morley	S	2,640	109
Hagerstown Junior	Hagerstown, Md.	1946	Atlee Kepler	Di	1,744	95
Halifax County Tech. Inst.	Weldon, N.C.	1967	Phillip W. Taylor	S	750	45
Harcum Junior	Bryn Mawr, Pa.	1915	Michael A. Duzy	P	635	52
Harrisburg Area Comm.	Harrisburg, Pa.	1964	J. Odom, Jr., Act.	C	4,200	155
Hartford Community	Bel Air, Md.	1957	Kenneth Oosting	C	2,818	146
Hartford Col. for Wm. (W)	Hartford, Conn.	1939	Laura A. Johnson	P	229	28
Hartford State Tech.	Hartford, Conn.	1946	L. Barrell	S	2,227	80
Hartnell	Salinas, Cal.	1922	Gibb R. Madsen	C	6,600	230
Haskell Indian Junior	Lawrence, Kan.	1884	Wallace Galluzzi	F	1,154	104
Hawkeye Inst. of Technology	Waterloo, Ia.	1966	Travis Martin, Supt.	F	1,245	89
Haywood Tech. Inst.	Clyde, N.C.	1965	M. C. Nix	S	850	65
Hazard Community	Hazard, Ky.	1968	Marvin Jolly	S	223	22
Henderson Community	Henderson, Ky.	1960	Marshall Arnold	S	639	57
Henderson County Junior	Athens, Tex.	1946	T. M. Harvey	C	1,786	95
Henry Ford Community	Dearborn, Mich.	1938	Stuart M. Bundy	Mu	14,124	787
Herkimer County Comm.	Herkimer, N.Y.	1966	Robert McLaughlin	S	1,211	48
Hesston	Hesston, Kan.	1909	Laban Peachey	D	505	40
Hibbing Comm.	Hibbing, Minn.	1916	Jennis Bapst	S	633	39
Highland Comm.	Freeport, Ill.	1962	Howard Sims	Di	1,649	150
Highland Community Junior	Highland, Kan.	1858	T. E. Woodrum	S	367	22
Highland Park Comm. (A)	Highland Park, Mich.	1918	Thomas Lloyd (Dean)	Mu	3,748	94
Highline Comm.	Midway, Wash.	1961	Orville Carnahan	S	7,500	389
Hilbert	Hamburg, N.Y.	1957	Sister E. Paczesny	P	546	45
Hill Junior	Hillsboro, Tex.	1962	Oran Bailey	S	700	51
Hillsborough Comm.	Tampa, Fla.	1968	Morton S. Shanberg	S	8,900	436
Hinds Junior	Raymond, Miss.	1917	Robert Mayo	C,S	5,275	275
Hiwassee	Madisonville, Tenn.	1849	Horace N. Barker	D	669	31
Hocking Technical	Nelsonville, Oh.	1968	John J. Light	S	1,214	178
Holding Tech. Inst.	Raleigh, N.C.	1963	R. LeMay, Jr.	S	1,362	83
Holmes Junior	Goodman, Miss.	1925	Frank Branch	S	1,338	68
Holy Cross Junior	Notre Dame, Ind.	1966	Bro. John Driscoll	D	250	21
Holyoke Community	Holyoke, Mass.	1946	George Frost	S	4,340	250
Honolulu Comm.	Honolulu, Ha.	1920	C. Yoshioka	S	3,547	119
Hopkinsville Community	Hopkinsville, Ky.	1965	Thomas Riley	S	1,345	65
Horry — Georgetown Tech.	Conway, S.C.	1966	G. W. Dudley, Jr.	S	1,500	93
Hostos Community	Bronx, N.Y.	1968	Candido De Leon	S	2,529	147
Housatonic Comm.	Bridgeport, Conn.	1966	V. Darnowski	S	2,742	62
Houston Comm.	Houston, Tex.	1971	J. Don Boney	S	17,100	615
Howard Community	Columbia, Md.	1970	Alfred Smith, Jr.	C	1,450	69

Name	Location	Year	Governing Official and Affiliation		Students	Teachers
Howard County Jr.	Big Spring, Tex.	1946	Charles Hays	SC	1,448	98
Hudson Valley Community	Troy, N.Y.	1953	J. Fitzgibbons	S	6,571	239
Humphreys	Stockton, Cal.	1896	John Humphreys	P	265	24
Hutchinson Community Jr.	Hutchinson, Kan.	1928	A. H. Elland	C	2,138	168
Illinois Central	E. Peoria, Ill.	1967	Kenneth L. Edwards	S	10,739	400
Illinois Eastern Comm.	Olney, Ill.	1968	James Spencer, Chan.	C	5,262	88
Illinois Valley Comm.	Oglesby, Ill.	1924	Alfred Wisgoski	Mu	3,100	150
Imperial Valley	Imperial, Cal.	1922	Terrel Spencer	S	4,565	213
Independence Comm. Jr.	Independence, Kan.	1925	Neil Edds	C,S	806	33
Indian Hills Community	Ottumwa, Ia.	1966	Lyle A. Hellyer	S,C	2,365	91
Indian Valley	Novato, Cal.	1971	Ernest H. Berg	S	1,785	80
Indiana Vocational Tech.	Indianapolis, Ind.	1963	Vacant	S	8,146	570
Intl. Jr. Coll. of Business	Fort Wayne, Ind.	1889	Thomas F. Scully	P	720	25
Inver Hills Comm.	Inver Hills Hts., Minn.	1970	Curtis Johnson	S	2,500	85
Iowa Central Comm.	Ft. Dodge, Ia.	1966	Edwin Barbour, Supt.	S	17,200	140
Iowa Western Comm.	Council Bluffs, Ia.	1966	R. Looft, Supt.	S	2,298	161
Isothermal Comm.	Spindale, N.C.	1965	Fred J. Eason	S	750	40
Itasca Comm.	Grand Rapids, Minn.	1922	Harold E. Wilson	S	583	45
Itawamba Junior	Fulton, Miss.	1948	W. O. Benjamin	S	1,824	100
Jackson Comm.	Jackson, Mich.	1928	Harold Sheffer	C	4,043	211
Jackson State Comm.	Jackson, Tenn.	1967	F. E. Wright	S	2,199	89
James H. Faulkner State Jr.	Bay Minette, Ala.	1963	L. Sibert	S	2,347	78
Jamestown Community.	Jamestown, N.Y.	1950	Roger Seager	S	2,796	104
Jefferson Community	Louisville, Ky.	1967	John Smith	S	4,638	264
Jefferson Community	Watertown, N.Y.	1959	James McVean	C	1,364	45
Jefferson Davis State Jr.	Brewton, Ala.	1965	Woodfin Patterson	S	573	27
Jefferson State Jr.	Birmingham, Ala.	1965	George Layton	S	6,918	275
John A. Logan	Carterville, Ill.	1968	Thomas Deem	C	1,501	58
John C. Calhoun St. Comm.	Decatur, Ala.	1965	Carlton Kelley	S	3,659	158
John Tyler Comm.	Chester, Va.	1967	James Walpole	S	909	83
Johnson County Comm.	Overland Park, Kan.	1968	Harold Finch, Act.	C	4,474	192
Joliet Junior.	Joliet, Ill.	1901	H. D. McAninch	S	8,500	500
Jones County Junior	Ellisville, Miss.	1927	Terrell Tisdale	S	1,913	130
Kalamazoo Valley Comm.	Kalamazoo, Mich.	1966	Dale B. Lake	C	4,300	150
Kankakee Comm.	Kankakee, Ill.	1968	John Samlin	S	3,439	98
Kan. City Kan. Comm. Junior	Kansas City, Kan.	1923	Jack M. Flint	C	2,775	83
Kansas Technical Inst.	Salina, Kan.	1965	James O. Thompson, Jr.	S	335	20
Kapiolani Comm.	Honolulu, Ha.	1964	Frederick Haehnlen, Prov.	S	3,545	154
Kaskaskia.	Centralia, Ill.	1940	Ray Searby.	Di	2,000	100
Katherine Gibbs School	New York, N.Y.	1917	Fred Stapleford.	P	898	54
Kauai Community	Lihue, Ha.	1965	Edward White, Provost	S	1,128	54
Kellogg Community	Battle Creek, Mich.	1956	Richard F. Whitmore	P	6,581	180
Kendall.	Evanston, Ill.	1934	Andrew Cothran	P	1,005	36
Kennesaw Junior	Marietta, Ga.	1966	Horace W. Sturgis.	S	2,241	85
Kettering Coll. of Medical Arts	Kettering, Oh.	1967	Winton Beaven	D	322	47
Keystone Junior	La Plume, Pa.	1868	Harry K. Miller, Jr.	P	820	48
Kilgore Junior	Kilgore, Tex.	1935	Randolph C. Watson.	S	2,952	130
King's.	Charlotte, N.C.	1901	G. L. Pritchett (Dir.).	P	400	15
Kingsborough Community	Brooklyn, N.Y.	1963	Leon M. Goldstein.	Mu	9,067	280
Kirtland Comm.	Roscommon, Mich.	1966	Robert A. Stenger.	Di	861	78
Kirkwood Comm.	Cedar Rapids, Ia.	1966	Selby Ballantyne (Supt.).	C	3,445	210
Kishwaukee.	Malta, Ill.	1967	W. Lamar Fly.	C,S	3,000	141
Kittrell.	Kittrell, N.C.	1886	John Middleton	P	345	26
Labette County Community Jr.	Parsons, Kan.	1923	James J. Altendorf.	C	601	36
Lackawanna Junior.	Scranton, Pa.	1958	Stephen Budash	P	350	15
La Guardia Community	Long Island City, N.Y.	1968	Joseph Shenker	Mu	4,243	164
Lake City Comm.	Lake City, Fla.	1962	Herbert E. Phillips.	S	2,473	145
Lake County, Coll. of	Grayslake, Ill.	1968	Richard Erzen	S	7,194	335
Lakeland	Mentor, Oh.	1967	Wayne Rodehorst.	C	5,764	212
Lake Michigan	Benton Harbor, Mich.	1946	James Lehman	S	2,800	60
Lake Region Jr.	Devils Lake, N.D.	1941	Merril Berg.	S	933	45
Lake Sumter Comm.	Leesburg, Fla.	1962	Paul P. Williams	Di	1,450	80
Lakeshore Tech Inst.	Cleveland, Wis.	1912	Frederick Nierode.	Mu	1,695	84
Lakewood Comm.	White Bear L., Minn.	1967	N. Christenson, Act.	S	2,474	93
Lamar Community	Lamar, Col.	1937	Carl Westbrook.	S	485	29
Lane Community	Eugene, Ore.	1965	Eldon G. Schafer	Di	6,276	343
Lansing Community.	Lansing, Mich.	1954	Philip Gannon.	S	13,280	400
Laramie County Community	Cheyenne, Wy.	1968	H. D. Yarbrough.	C	3,076	117
Laredo Junior.	Laredo, Tex.	1946	D. Arechiga.	S	4,500	106
Lasell Junior (W)	Newton, Mass.	1851	Kenneth M. Greene.	P	592	67
Lassen.	Susanville, Cal.	1924	Robert Theiler.	Di	2,666	182
LDS Business College (A).	Salt Lake City, Ut.	1886	R. F. Kirkham.	D	754	29
Lee.	Baytown, Tex.	1934	Jim Sturgeon.	Di	5,009	169
Lees Junior (A).	Jackson, Ky.	1883	Troy R. Eslinger.	Mu	321	34
Lees-McRae.	Banner Elk, N.C.	1900	H. C. Evans, Jr.	D	717	46
Lehigh County Comm.	Schnecksville, Pa.	1966	John G. Berrier	S,Di	2,331	95
Leicester Jr.	Leicester, Mass.	1784	L. Van Burkirk.	P	209	26
Lenoir Comm. (A).	Kinston, N.C.	1960	Jesse L. McDaniel.	S	1,455	102
Lewis and Clark Community	Godfrey, Ill.	1971	Wilbur R. L. Trimpe.	S	4,153	184
Lexington Technical Inst.	Lexington, Ky.	1965	William Price	S	1,281	72
Lima Technical.	Lima, Oh.	1967	James S. Biddle (Dir.).	S	714	37
Lincoln Land Comm.	Springfield, Ill.	1967	Robert L. Poorman.	Di	4,914	198
Lincoln.	Lincoln, Ill.	1865	J. Richard Stoltz.	P	450	43
Lincoln Trail.	Robinson, Ill.	1969	Joseph Piland	S	1,033	20
Linn-Benton Comm.	Albany, Ore.	1966	Raymond J. Needham.	S	10,605	320
Lon Morris.	Jacksonville, Tex.	1873	John E. Fellers.	D	312	24
Long Beach City.	Long Beach, Cal.	1927	Frank Pearce.	Mu	29,343	1,312
Longview Community.	Lee's Summit, Mo.	1969	William D. Hatley	Di	3,370	136
Lorain County Comm.	Elyria, Oh.	1963	Omar Olsen.	S,C	4,509	176
Los Angeles City.	Los Angeles, Cal.	1929	John Anthony.	S	21,700	625
Los Angeles Harbor.	Wilmington, Cal.	1949	Eugene A. Pimentel.	Di	10,773	380
Los Angeles Pierce.	Woodland Hills, Cal.	1947	Edward Liston.	S	21,569	577
Los Angeles Southwest	Los Angeles, Cal.	1967	Franklin Turner.	S	4,777	197

Name	Location	Year	Governing Official and Affiliation	Students	Teachers
L.A. Trade Technical	Los Angeles, Cal.	1949	Fred Brinkman	Mu	18,528	945
Los Angeles Valley	Van Nuys, Cal.	1949	W. E. Lewis, Act.	Di	21,000	450
Louisburg	Louisburg, N.C.	1787	J. Allen Norris, Jr.	D	663	44
Louisiana State Univ.						
at Alexandria	Alexandria, La.	1960	Morris Abrams, Dean	S	1,147	64
at Eunice	Eunice, La.	1967	Anthony Mumphrey	S	792	38
Lower Columbia	Longview, Wash.	1934	David Story	S	3,345	163
Luzerne County Comm.	Nanticoke, Pa.	1967	Byron Rinehimer	C,S	1,673	80
Macomb County Community	Warren, Mich.	1962	J. R. Dimitry	C	21,533	615
MacCormac Junior	Chicago, Ill.	1904	Gordon Borchardt	P	235	14
Macon Junior	Macon, Ga.	1968	William Wright	S	2,185	63
Madison Area Technical	Madison, Wis.	1912	Norman P. Mitby, Dir.	Di	4,936	320
Madison Business	Madison, Wis.	1856	Otto J. Madland	P	200	16
Madisonville Community	Madisonville, Ky.	1968	Harold Massey	S	476	36
Maine, Univ. of						
at Augusta, Me.	Augusta, Me.	1965	Stanley Freeman, Act.	S	2,595	179
Mainland, Coll. of the	Texas City, Tex.	1966	Fred Taylor	Di	1,891	91
Manatee Junior	Bradenton, Fla.	1957	Samuel R. Neel	S	4,200	214
Manchester Comm. (A)	Manchester, Conn.	1963	F. W. Lowe	S	3,150	143
Manhattan Comm.	New York, N.Y.	1963	Edgar Draper	Mu	9,512	422
Manor Jr.	Jenkintown, Pa.	1948	Mother M. Olga	P	379	44
Maple Woods Community	Kansas City, Mo.	1969	John M. Garda	S	2,241	85
Maria	Albany, N.Y.	1958	Sr. Mary B. Mahoney	S	421	46
Maria Regina (W)	Syracuse, N.Y.	1963	Sr. M. Rosalie Brady	P	300	32
Maricopa Tech. County Comm.	Phoenix, Ariz.	1968	N. Bruemmer, Dean	C	7,505	367
Marin, Coll. of (A)	Kentfield, Cal.	1926	John A. Grasham	S,C	6,908	371
Marion Institute	Marion, Ala.	1842	Draper Kauffman	P	275	23
Marshalltown Community	Marshalltown, Ia.	1927	James McKinstry, Dean	Di,S	849	50
Martin	Pulaski, Tenn.	1870	Bill Starns	D	327	31
Martin Tech. Inst.	Williamston, N.C.	1968	E. M. Hunt	S,C	550	35
Mary Holmes	West Point, Miss.	1892	Joseph Gore	P	325	29
Marymount	Boca Raton, Fla.	1963	Donald E. Ross	P	464	33
Marymount Palos Verdes	Palos Verdes, Cal.	1932	Thomas D. Wood	P	250	25
Massachusetts Bay Comm.	Watertown, Mass.	1961	John McKenzie	S	1,586	106
Massasoit Comm.	Brockton, Mass.	1966	John Musselman	S	4,200	422
Mattatuck Community	Waterbury, Conn.	1967	Charles B. Kinney	S	3,062	122
Maui Community	Kahului, Ha.	1967	Sanae Moikeha, Act.	S	1,271	66
Maysville Community	Maysville, Ky.	1968	James Shires	S	317	33
McCook	McCook, Neb.	1926	John N. Harms	S	550	34
McDowell Tech. Inst.	Marion, N.C.	1964	John Price	S	395	17
McHenry County	Crystal Lake, Ill.	1967	James Davis	Di	2,446	112
McLennan Comm.	Waco, Tex.	1966	Wilbur Ball	C	2,900	125
Memphis, State Tech. Inst. at (A)	Memphis, Tenn.	1967	Charles Whitehead (Dir.)	S	1,729	135
Meramec Community	St. Louis, Mo.	1962	Glynn E. Clark	Di	7,070	378
Merced	Merced, Cal.	1963	Lowell Barker	S	7,900	320
Mercer County Comm.	Trenton, N.J.	1966	Richard Greenfield	C	6,400	134
Meridian Jr. (A)	Meridian, Miss.	1937	William F. Scaggs	Mu	1,500	90
Merritt	Oakland, Cal.	1954	Donald Godbold	Mu	9,600	250
Mesa	Gd. Junction, Col.	1925	Theodore E. Albers	S	3,573	125
Mesabi Comm.	Virginia, Minn.	1921	Gilbert Staupe	S	796	41
Metropolitan Comm.	Minneapolis, Minn.	1965	Rafael Cortada	S	2,075	100
Metropolitan Comm.	Kansas City, Mo.	1915	Ervin Harlacher, Chan.	S	13,112	577
Miami-Dade Comm.	Miami, Fla.	1960	Peter Masiko, Jr.	S	42,322	1,476
Miami-Jacobs Jr. Coll. of Bus.	Dayton, Oh.	1860	Charles P. Harbottle	P	952	37
Michael J. Owens Tech.	Perrysburg, Oh.	1967	Jacob S. See	S	1,200	75
Michigan Christian Jr.	Rochester, Mich.	1959	Don E. Gardner	D	236	31
Midland	Midland, Tex.	1972	Al G. Langford	S	1,600	101
Mid Michigan Community	Harrison, Mich.	1965	Eugene W. Gillaspy	S	2,000	80
Middle Georgia	Cochran, Ga.	1884	Louis C. Alderman Jr.	S	1,786	110
Middlesex Comm.	Middletown, Conn.	1966	Philip Wheaton	S	2,166	45
Middlesex County	Edison, N.J.	1966	Frank M. Chambers	C	8,392	400
Midlands Tech.	Columbia, S.C.	1962	Robert Grigsby	S,C	3,500	259
Midway (W)	Midway, Ky.	1847	Albert N. Cox	P	341	25
Miles Comm.	Miles City, Mont.	1939	Vernon R. Kailey	S	650	35
Milwaukee Area Technical	Milwaukee, Wis.	1911	William Ramsey (Dir)	Di	44,850	2,207
Mineral Area	Flat River, Mo.	1922	Richard Caster	Di	917	53
Mira Costa	Oceanside, Cal.	1934	John MacDonald	S	5,234	221
Mississippi Delta Jr.	Moorhead, Miss.	1926	J. T. Hall	S,C	1,306	102
Mississippi Gulf Coast Jr.	Perkinston, Miss.	1911	J. J. Hayden	S	10,834	178
Mitchell	New London, Conn.	1938	Robert D. Weller	P	772	45
Mitchell Comm.	Statesville, N.C.	1856	Charles Poindexter	S	812	60
Moberly Area Junior	Moberly, Mo.	1927	Henry T. Norris	S	800	60
Modesto Junior	Modesto, Cal.	1921	Kenneth Griffin	Di	12,883	474
Mohawk Valley Community	Utica, N.Y.	1946	G. H. Robertson	S	5,580	139
Mohegan Comm.	Norwich, Conn.	1970	Robert N. Rue	S	2,000	100
Monroe Community	Rochester, N.Y.	1961	Moses Kock	S	9,263	291
Monroe County Comm.	Monroe, Mich.	1964	Ronald Campbell	C	1,704	67
Montcalm Comm.	Sidney, Mich.	1965	C. J. Bedore	C	1,050	27
Monterey Peninsula Comm.	Monterey, Cal.	1947	George J. Faul	C	11,500	400
Montgomery Community	Rockville, Md.	1946	William Strasser	C	12,629	679
Montgomery County Comm.	Blue Bell, Pa.	1964	Leroy Brendlinger	C	5,000	250
Montreat-Anderson	Montreat, N.C.	1916	Silas M. Vaughn	D	405	27
Moorpark	Moorpark, Cal.	1967	W. Ray Hearon	C,S	10,200	513
Moraine Valley Comm.	Palos Hills, Ill.	1968	Robert E. Turner	S	4,894	238
Morgan Comm.	Ft. Morgan, Col.	1970	Robert W. Johnson	S	1,400	50
Morris, County College of (A)	Dover, N.J.	1968	Sherman H. Masten	C	5,000	120
Morton	Cicero, Ill.	1924	Vincent A. Guarna	Di	1,757	103
Motlow State Comm.	Tullahoma, Tenn.	1969	Harry D. Wagner	S	980	46
Mt. Aloysius Junior	Cresson, Pa.	1939	Sr. Mary Cecilia Meighan	P	489	48
Mt. Hood Comm.	Gresham, Ore.	1965	Earl L. Klapstein	S	10,638	620
Mt. Ida Junior	Newton, Mass.	1899	F. Roy Carlson	P	706	60
Mt. Olive	Mt. Olive, N.C.	1951	William B. Raper	D	308	26
Mt. San Antonio Comm.	Walnut, Cal.	1946	Eldon Pearce	S,Di	18,576	600
Mt. San Jacinto	San Jacinto, Cal.	1963	Milo P. Johnson	S	2,400	73
Mt. Vernon Nazarene	Mt. Vernon, Oh.	1966	John A. Knight	D	439	36
Mt. Wachusett Comm.	Gardner, Mass.	1963	Arthur F. Haley	S	2,956	149

Name	Location	Year	Governing Official and Affiliation		Stu-dents	Teach-ers
Murray State	Tishomingo, Okla.	1908	Clyde Kindell	S	708	36
Muskegon Business	Muskegon, Mich.	1885	Robert Jewell	P	500	25
Muskegon Community	Muskegon, Mich.	1926	Charles Greene	C	5,774	240
Napa	Napa, Cal.	1942	George Clark	C	5,478	243
Nash Tech. Inst.	Rocky Mount, N.C.	1968	Jack D. Ballard	S	813	35
Nassau Community	Garden City, N.Y.	1959	George Chambers	C	17,541	415
Navarro	Corsicana, Tex.	1946	Kenneth Walker	C	1,475	66
Nebraska Western	Scottsbluff, Neb.	1928	Alex Easton	Mu	761	51
Neosho County Comm. Jr.	Chanute, Kan.	1936	J. C. Sanders	C	723	42
New England Aeronautical Inst.	Nashua, N.H.	1965	W. F. Griesemer, Jr.	P	425	25
New Hampshire Tech. Inst.	Concord, N.H.	1965	D. Larrabee, Sr.	S	850	100
New Hampshire Voc. Tech.	Manchester, N.H.	1945	George C. Knox, Dir.	S	580	34
New Hampshire Voc. Tech.	Portsmouth, N.H.	1945	E. McCourt, Dir.	S	441	28
New Mexico Junior	Hobbs, N.M.	1965	Jodie Smith	S	6007	60
New Mexico Military Inst. (M)	Roswell, N.M.	1891	Col. R. Kemble	S	825	48
New River Community	Dublin, Va.	1969	W. Robert Sullins	S	1,752	85
N.Y. City Community Coll.	Brooklyn, N.Y.	1946	Herbert M. Sussman	Mu	18,077	576
New York, State Univ. of Agric. & Tech. Inst.	Alfred, N.Y.	1908	David H. Huntington	S	4,200	220
" " "	Canton, N.Y.	1906	Earl MacArthur	S	2,625	126
" " "	Cobleskill, N.Y.	1911	Walton A. Brown	S	2,659	143
" " "	Delhi, N.Y.	1913	Francis Hennessy	S	2,583	130
" " "	Farmingdale, N.Y.	1912	Charles W. Laffin	S	12,971	344
" " "	Morrisville, N.Y.	1908	Royson N. Whipple	S	2,960	141
Newton Junior	Newtonville, Mass.	1946	Charles W. Dudley	Mu	544	47
Niagara County Community	Sanborn, N.Y.	1962	Ernest Notar	S	3,928	131
Normandale Comm. (A)	Bloomington, Minn.	1968	Dale Lorenz	S	2,967	99
North Central Michigan	Petoskey, Mich.	1958	A. D. Shankland	S,C	1,189	65
North Central Tech. Inst.	Wausau, Wis.	1911	L. B. Hoyt (Dir.)	Di	2,295	132
North Country Comm.	Saranac Lake, N.Y.	1967	George Hodson	S	1,000	44
NDSU-Bottineau (A)	Bottineau, N.D.	1907	Robert Johnson (Dean)	S	539	25
N. Dak. St. Sch. of Science	Wahpeton, N.D.	1903	Clair I. Blikre	S	3,652	192
North Florida Junior	Madison, Fla.	1958	Stephen McMahon	S	870	53
North Greenville	Tigerville, S.C.	1892	Harold E. Lindsey	D	511	29
North Harris County	Houston, Tex.	1972	W. W. Thorne	S	1,500	75
North Hennepin Comm.	Brooklyn Pk., Minn.	1966	John F. Helling	S	2,849	133
North Idaho	Coeur d'Alene, Ida.	1939	Barry Schuler	C	1,233	95
North Iowa Area Comm.	Mason City, Ia.	1918	David Randall Pierce	S	2,014	90
North Platte Comm.	North Platte, Neb.	1965	John Harms	Mu	488	26
North Shore Community	Beverly, Mass.	1965	George Traicoff	S	5,500	315
Northampton County Area Comm.	Bethlehem, Pa.	1966	Richard Richardson, Jr.	C	3,008	215
Northeast Alabama State Jr.	Rainsville, Ala.	1965	E. R. Knox	S,C	1,935	75
Northeast Miss. Junior	Booneville, Miss.	1948	Harold T. White	S	1,556	95
Northeast Neb. Tech. Comm.	Norfolk, Neb.	1973	Robert P. Cox	S	1,166	91
Northeast Wisconsin Tech. Inst.	Green Bay, Wis.	1910	K. W. Hanbenschild (Dir.)	Mu	18,122	998
Northeastern Junior	Sterling, Col.	1941	Ervin S. French	S	1,712	75
Northeastern Okla. A&M	Miami, Okla.	1919	D. D. Creech	S	2,330	110
Northern Essex Comm.	Haverhill, Mass.	1961	Harold Bentley	S	5,800	435
Northern Oklahoma	Tonkawa, Okla.	1901	Edwin Vineyard	S	1,181	74
Northern Virginia Comm.	No. Springfield, Va.	1965	Richard Ernst	S	17,260	375
Northland Comm.	Thief R. Falls, Minn.	1965	Ken Wiebolt	S	504	23
Northwest Community	Powell, Wy.	1946	Sinclair Orendorff	C	956	65
Northwest Iowa Vocational (A)	Sheldon, Ia.	1966	D. W. McPherson, Supt.	Di	500	32
Northwest Miss. Junior	Senatobia, Miss.	1927	Henry B. Koon	S	1,921	130
Northwestern Conn. Comm.	Winsted, Conn.	1965	Regina Duffy	S	1,757	67
Northwestern Michigan	Traverse City, Mich.	1951	William J. Yankee	S	2,259	100
Norwalk Community	Norwalk, Conn.	1961	E. I. L. Baker	S	3,191	98
Norwalk State Tech.	Norwalk, Conn.	1961	Frank Juszli	S	2,067	103
Oakland Community	Bloomfield Hills, Mich.	1965	Joseph Hill	C	16,382	301
Oakton Comm.	Morton Grove, Ill.	1969	William Koehnline	S	15,371	671
Ocean County	Toms River, N.J.	1966	Andrew S. Moreland	C	3,922	125
Odessa	Odessa, Tex.	1946	Philip Speegle	S	3,224	188
Ohlone	Fremont, Cal.	1966	Stephen E. Epler	Di	8,305	200
Okaloosa-Walton Jr.	Niceville, Fla.	1963	J. E. McCracken	Di	2,547	151
Oklahoma City Southwestern	Oklahoma City, Okla.	1946	W. R. Corvin	P	3,024	82
Oklahoma Sch. of Business, Accountancy, Law & Finance	Tulsa, Okla.	1919	H. Everett Pope, Jr.	P	587	25
Olney Central	Olney, Ill.	1963	Gail L. Lathrop	Di	2,640	45
Olympic	Bremerton, Wash.	1946	Henry Milander	S	5,050	100
Onondaga Community	Syracuse, N.Y.	1961	Roy Price, Act.	S	5,261	160
Orange Coast	Costa Mesa, Cal.	1948	Robert Moore	C	31,261	780
Orange County Community	Middletown, N.Y.	1950	Robert T. Novak	S	4,133	141
Orangeburg Calhoun Tech.	Orangeburg, S.C.	1968	M. Rudy Groomes	S	1,800	111
Oscar Rose	Midwest City, Okla.	1970	Joe Leone	S	6,128	189
Otero Junior	La Junta, Col.	1941	William L. McDivitt	S	900	59
Ottumwa Heights	Ottumwa, Ia.	1925	Jerry Solloway	P	380	27
Paducah Comm.	Paducah, Ky.	1968	Donald J. Clemens	S	1,001	66
Palm Beach Junior	Lake Worth, Fla.	1933	Harold C. Manor	S	7,417	227
Palomar, Comm.	San Marcos, Cal.	1946	Frederick R. Huber	Mu	11,172	400
Palo Verde	Blythe, Cal.	1947	George W. Pennell	S	900	45
Panola Junior	Carthage, Tex.	1947	Arthur Johnson	S	690	34
Paris Junior	Paris, Tex.	1924	Louis B. Williams	Di	1,469	95
Parkersburg Community	Parkersburg, W.Va.	1961	Jerry Jones	S	4,009	272
Parkland	Champaign, Ill.	1967	William M. Staerkel	Di	6,000	244
Pasadena City	Pasadena, Cal.	1924	Armen Sarafian	S	18,920	440
Pasco-Hernando Comm.	Dade City, Fla.	1972	Milton O. Jones	S	1,700	150
Patrick Henry State Jr.	Monroeville, Ala.	1965	Cecil Murphy	S	713	42
Paul D. Camp Comm.	Franklin, Va.	1971	Perry Adams	S	1,100	60
Paul Smith's	Paul Smiths, N.Y.	1946	Chester L. Buxton	P	1,148	72
Peace (W)	Raleigh, N.C.	1857	S. David Frazier	Mu	465	34
Pearl River Junior	Poplarville, Miss.	1909	M. R. White	P	1,136	85
Peirce Junior	Philadelphia, Pa.	1865	Thomas M. Peirce III.	P	1,404	61

Name	Location	Year	Governing Official and Affiliation		Stu-dents	Teach-ers
Peninsula	Port Angeles, Wash.	1961	E. John Maier	S	2,500	137
Penn Valley Community	Kansas City, Mo.	1915	Thomas M. Law	Mu	5,700	210
Pensacola Jr.	Pensacola, Fla.	1948	T. Felton Harrison	S	14,396	658
Permiam Jr. Col. System (A)	Odessa, Tex.	1946	Jack Rodgers (Chan.)	C	3,549	270
Philadelphia, Comm. Coll. of	Philadelphia, Pa.	1964	Allen T. Bonnell	S	8,200	469
Phillips County Comm.	Helena, Ark.	1965	John Easley	S,C	2,741	50
Phoenix (A)	Phoenix, Ariz.	1920	William Berry (Dean)	C	10,897	350
Piedmont Tech.	Greenwood, S.C.	1966	Lex Walters	S	4,200	250
Piedmont Tech. Inst.	Roxboro, N.C.	1970	Edward W. Cox	S	905	68
Piedmont Virginia Comm.	Charlottesville, Va.	1972	Harold McGee	S	2,300	105
Pima Comm.	Tucson, Ariz.	1970	Irwin Spector	C	17,793	971
Pine Manor Junior (W)	Chestnut Hill, Mass.	1911	Donald Gordon	P	456	45
Pitt Tech. Inst.	Greenville, N.C.	1961	W. E. Fulford, Jr.	S	1,376	117
Polk Comm.	Winter Haven, Fla.	1964	Frederick T. Lenfestey	S	4,200	150
Porterville	Porterville, Cal.	1927	O. H. Shires	Di	2,488	63
Portland Community	Portland, Ore.	1961	Amo De Bernardis	S,C	28,189	1,412
Post Junior	Waterbury, Conn.	1890	F. Burton Cook	P	719	40
Potomac State	Keyser, W. Va.	1901	A. G. Slonaker (Dean)	S	835	46
Prairie State	Chicago Hts., Ill.	1958	Ashley Johnson	S	4,885	190
Pratt Community	Pratt, Kan.	1938	Norman Myers	C	688	53
Presentation	Aberdeen, S.D.	1951	Sister Francis Mary Dunn	D	368	51
Prestonsburg Community	Prestonsburg, Ky.	1964	Henry Campbell	S	481	33
Prince George's Community	Largo, Md.	1958	Robert Bickford	C	9,258	494
Puerto Rico Jr.	Rio Piedras, P.R.	1949	Jose F. Mendez	P	5,400	185
Queensborough Community	Bayside, N.Y.	1958	Kurt R. Schmeller	Mu	15,822	473
Quinebaug Valley Comm.	Danielson, Conn.	1971	Robert E. Miller	S	550	35
Quinsigamond Comm.	Worcester, Mass.	1963	Paul Preus	S	4,432	200
R. C. A. Institutes	New York, N.Y.	1909	Robert F. Adams	P	3,100	103
Randolph Tech. Inst.	Asheboro, N.C.	1962	M. H. Branson	S	702	49
Ranger Junior	Ranger, Tex.	1926	Jack Elsom	S	550	32
Rangley	Rangley, Col.	1962	James H. Bos	Di	726	35
Reading Area Comm.	Reading, Pa.	1971	Lewis Ogle	Mu	500	34
Redwoods, Coll. of the	Eureka, Cal.	1964	Donald Weichert	S,C	8,600	465
Reedley	Reedley, Cal.	1926	Clifford M. Boyer	S	2,249	125
Reinhardt	Waleska, Ga.	1883	Allen O. Jernigan	P,D	500	25
Rend Lake	Ina, Ill.	1956	James Snyder	S	1,302	76
Rhode Island Jr. (A)	Warwick, R.I.	1964	William F. Flanagan	S	4,470	286
Richland	Dallas, Tex.	1972	Ed Biggerstaff	C	8,971	403
Richmond Tech. Inst.	Hamlet, N.C.	1965	Joseph Nanney	S	881	52
Ricks	Rexburg, Ida.	1888	Henry B. Evring	D	5,469	202
Riverside City	Riverside, Cal.	1916	Kenneth Harper	C	12,300	400
Roanoke-Chowan Tech. Inst.	Ahoskie, N.C.	1967	James W. Young	S	490	35
Robeson Tech. Inst.	Lumberton, N.C.	1965	R. Craig Allen	S	1,227	45
Rochester Comm.	Rochester, Minn.	1915	Charles Hill	S	2,400	140
Rockland Community	Suffern, N.Y.	1957	Seymour Eskow	S	7,131	132
Rock Valley	Rockford, Ill.	1965	Karl Jacobs	S	4,988	531
Rockingham Comm.	Wentworth, N.C.	1966	Gerald B. James	S	1,300	60
Rogue Comm.	Grants Pass, Ore.	1970	Henry O. Pete	C,S	2,000	90
Sacramento City	Sacramento, Cal.	1916	Sam Kipp	Mu	13,617	485
St. Clair County Comm.	Pt. Huron, Mich.	1923	Richard L. Norris	C	4,100	175
St. Gregory's	Shawnee, Okla.	1915	Rev. Michael Roethler	P	375	35
St. John's	Winfield, Kan.	1893	Rev. M. J. Stelmachowicz	D	300	22
St. John's River Junior	Palatka, Fla.	1958	Robert L. McLendon	S	1,119	80
St. Mary's Jr.	Minneapolis, Minn.	1964	Sr. Anne Joachim	D	838	78
St. Mary's (W)	Raleigh, N.C.	1847	Rev. Frank W. Pisam	D	516	50
St. Petersburg Junior	St. Petersburg, Fla.	1927	Michael Bennett	S	9,759	306
Salem Community	Penns Grove, N.J.	1972	Herbert C. Donaghay	S	1,400	67
Sampson Tech Inst.	Clinton, N.C.	1965	James Vann	S	625	85
San Antonio	San Antonio, Tex.	1925	Jerome Weynand	S	19,505	824
San Bernardino Valley	San Bernardino, Cal.	1926	Arthur Jensen	Di	14,191	464
San Diego City	San Diego, Cal.	1914	Allen Repashy	S	5,250	144
San Diego, Mesa	San Diego, Cal.	1963	Ellis Bensen	Di	8,225	220
San Francisco, City Coll. of (A)	San Francisco, Cal.	1935	Harry Buttimer	C	21,374	680
San Jacinto	Pasadena, Tex.	1960	Thomas M. Spencer	S	8,443	336
San Joaquin Delta Comm.	Stockton, Cal.	1963	Joseph Blanchard	S	13,625	390
San Jose City	San Jose, Cal.	1921	Theodore Murguia	C	17,726	600
San Mateo, Coll. of	San Mateo, Cal.	1922	David H. Mertes	C	14,654	610
Sandhills Comm.	Southern Pines, N.C.	1963	Raymond A. Stone	S	1,200	160
Sanford D. Bishop Junior	Mobile, Ala.	1965	Sanford D. Bishop	S	1,068	53
Santa Ana (A)	Santa Ana, Cal.	1915	John E. Johnson	S	10,985	344
Santa Barbara City	Santa Barbara, Cal.	1908	Glenn Gooder	Di,S	7,878	270
Santa Fe Community (A)	Gainesville, Fla.	1966	Alan Robertson	S	4,054	187
Santa Monica	Santa Monica, Cal.	1929	Donald Click	Mu	15,647	532
Santa Rosa Junior	Santa Rosa, Cal.	1918	Roy Mikalson	C	15,861	560
Sauk Valley	Dixon, Ill.	1965	George Cole	S	2,200	106
Sayre Junior	Sayre, Okla.	1938	Harry Patterson	S	265	11
Schenectady County Comm.	Schenectady, N.Y.	1967	Robert Larsson	S	2,530	40
Schoolcraft	Livonia, Mich.	1964	C. Nelson Grote	S	6,816	914
Schreiner	Kerrville, Tex.	1923	Sam Junkin	D	574	30
Scottsdale Community	Scottsdale, Ariz.	1970	Ray Cattan, Exec. Dean	C	5,100	200
S.D. Bishop State Jr.	Mobile, Ala.	1937	Sanford Bishop	S	1,462	58
Seattle Central Community	Seattle, Wash.	1966	Nolen Ellison	S	3,474	189
Selma Univ.	Selma, Ala.	1878	Rev. M. Cleveland, Jr.	D	395	25
Seminole Junior	Sanford, Fla.	1966	E. S. Weldon	S	3,217	138
Sequoias, Coll. of the	Visalia, Cal.	1925	Ivan Crookshanks	Di	6,592	331
Shasta	Redding, Cal.	1950	Dale Miller	C	12,800	482
Shelby State Comm.	Memphis, Tenn.	1970	Jess Parrish	S	3,472	200
Sheldon Jackson	Sitka, Alas.	1878	Merton Munn, Act.	P	250	20
Sheridan	Sheridan, Wy.	1948	Gordon Ward	S	817	35
Shoreline Community	Seattle, Wash.	1963	Richard S. White	S	7,494	303
Shorter	Little Rock, Ark.	1886	Oley Griffin	D	201	15
Sierra	Rocklin, Cal.	1914	Marion Akers, Act.	S	7,500	270
Sinclair Community	Dayton, Oh.	1886	David Ponitz	C	9,100	435

Name	Location	Year	Governing Official and Affiliation		Students	Teachers
Siskiyous, Coll. of the	Weed, Cal.	1957	Eugene Schumacher	C	1,203	145
Skagit Valley	Mt. Vernon, Wash.	1926	Norwood Cole	S	5,188	230
Skyline (A)	San Bruno, Cal.	1969	John C. Petersen	Di	5,164	198
Snead State Jr.	Boaz, Ala.	1935	Virgil McCain	S	1,862	120
Snow	Ephraim, Ut.	1888	J.M. Higbee	S	950	46
Solano Comm.	Suisun City, Cal.	1945	N. Dallas Evans	S	9,064	292
Somerset Community	Somerset, Ky.	1965	Roscoe Kelley	S	661	54
Somerset County	Somerville, N.J.	1966	Joseph Fink	C	2,500	134
South Central Community	New Haven, Conn.	1968	W. De Homer Waller	S	1,723	35
South Georgia	Douglas, Ga.	1906	Denton Coker	S	1,244	62
South Oklahoma City Junior	Oklahoma City, Okla.	1972	Dale L. Gibson	S	2,703	94
South Plains	Levelland, Tex.	1958	Marvin L. Baker	S	2,010	101
South Texas Junior	Houston, Tex.	1948	David Royce Reagan	P	2,609	103
Southeast Community	Cumberland, Ky.	1960	Bruce Wilson	S	379	41
Southeastern Comm. (A).	Burlington, Ia.	1966	C. W. Callison, Supt.	Di	1,506	95
Southeastern Community (A)	Keokuk, Ia.	1953	C. W. Callison	C	327	28
Southeastern Community	Whiteville, N.C.	1965	W. R. McCarter	S	1,666	105
Southeastern Illinois	Harrisburg, Ill.	1960	Harry Abell	S	1,600	45
Southern Baptist	Walnut Ridge, Ark.	1941	D. W. Nicholas	D	315	25
Southern Idaho, Coll. of	Twin Falls, Ida.	1965	James L. Taylor	C	3,021	176
Southern Union State Jr.	Wadley, Ala.	1922	L. Ray Jones	S	1,527	85
Southwest Mississippi Junior (A)	Summit, Miss.	1918	Horace Holmes	S	815	45
Southwest Texas Junior	Uvalde, Tex.	1946	Wayne Matthews	S	1,680	89
Southwest Virginia Comm.	Richlands, Va.	1968	Charles King	S	1,562	100
Southwestern	Chula Vista, Cal.	1961	C. S. DeVore	S	11,600	420
Southwestern Comm.	Creston, Ia.	1966	John A. Smith	S	679	52
Southwestern Michigan	Dowagiac, Mich.	1966	R. M. Owen	C	1,260	87
Southwestern Oregon Comm.	Coos Bay, Ore.	1961	Jack E. Brookins	S	3,487	200
Spartanburg Junior	Spartanburg, S.C.	1911	James S. Barrett	D	1,008	66
Spokane Comm.	Spokane, Wash.	1963	Lloyd Stannard	S	3,600	343
Spokane Falls Community	Spokane, Wash.	1970	Gerald Saling	S	3,904	131
Spoon River	Canton, Ill.	1959	Hearl C. Bishop	S	1,044	41
Springfield Tech. Comm.	Springfield, Mass.	1967	Robert Geitz	S	5,685	300
Springfield Coll. In Illinois	Springfield, Ill.	1929	Sr. M. Patrick O'Brien	D	600	50
Stanly Tech. Inst.	Albemarle, N.C.	1972	Charles H. Byrd	S	486	40
State Fair Comm.	Sedalia, Mo.	1968	Fred E. Davis	Di	1,141	74
State Tech. Inst.	Memphis, Tenn.	1967	Charles Whitehead	S	3,598	195
Staten Island Community	Staten Island, N.Y.	1955	William M. Birenbaum	Mu	11,428	328
Sue Bennett	London, Ky.	1897	Earl F. Hays	D	165	21
Suffolk County Community	Selden, N.Y.	1959	Albert M. Ammerman	S	15,010	388
Sullins	Bristol, Va.	1870	Claude Pritchard Jr.	P	225	27
Sullivan County Community	Loch Sheldrake, N.Y.	1962	Richard F. Grego	S	1,638	63
Sumter Area Tech.	Sumter, S.C.	1962	James M. Norris	S	1,800	120
Suomi	Hancock, Mich.	1896	Ralph J. Jalkanen	P	304	21
Surry Community	Dobson, N.C.	1965	Swanson Richards	S	1,430	76
Sweetwater(A)	Chula Vista, Cal.	1960	Chester De Vore	Di	4,356	165
Tacoma Comm.	Tacoma, Wash.	1965	Thornton Ford	S	4,907	243
Taft	Taft, Cal.	1922	Garlyn A. Basham	Di	988	50
Tallahassee Community	Tallahassee, Fla.	1965	Fred W. Turner	S	2,775	107
Tarrant County Junior	Ft. Worth, Tex.	1965	Joe B. Rushing	S,C	16,307	610
Temple Junior	Temple, Tex.	1926	Marvin Felder	S	1,542	90
Texarkana	Texarkana, Tex.	1927	J.W.Cady	S	2,489	108
Thames Valley St. Tech.	Norwich, Conn.	1963	Donald Welter	S	1,100	43
Theodore Alfred Lawson St. Jr. (A)	Birmingham, Ala.	1963	Leon Kennedy	S	1,388	54
Thomas Nelson Comm.	Hampton, Va.	1968	Gerald O. Cannon	S	3,082	189
Thornton Comm. (A)	So. Holland, Ill.	1927	J. Philip Dalby	S	8,000	350
Three Rivers Community	Poplar Bluff, Mo.	1966	H. Tudor Westover	S	1,255	50
Tidewater Comm.	Portsmouth, Va.	1968	George Pass	S	8,220	378
Tomkins-Courtland Comm.	Groton, N.Y.	1967	Hushang Baheri	S	2,069	38
Tri-County Tech. Inst.	Murphy, N.C.	1964	Vincent W. Crisp	C,S	581	25
Tri-County Tech.	Pendleton, S.C.	1962	Don Garrison	S	2,203	167
Trident Tech.	Charleston, S.C.	1964	Richard Waldroup, Jr.	S	5,899	214
Trinidad State Junior	Trinidad, Col.	1925	Thomas Sullivan	S	1,410	87
Triton	River Grove, Ill.	1964	Herbert Zeitlin	Di	19,799	1,027
Truett McConnell	Cleveland, Ga.	1947	Ronald Weitman	D	561	44
Tulsa Junior	Tulsa, Okla.	1968	Alfred M. Phillips	S	5,002	225
Tunxis Community	Farmington, Conn.	1970	Benjamin G. Davis	S	2,700	150
Tyler Junior	Tyler, Tex.	1926	Harry E. Jenkins	S	5,024	193
Ulster County Community	Stone Ridge, N.Y.	1961	Robert T. Brown	S	2,308	81
Umpqua Comm.	Roseburg, Ore.	1964	I.S. Hakanson	C	7,500	165
Union	Cranford, N.J.	1933	Saul Orkin	C	4,626	225
Union County Tech. Inst.	Scotch Plains, N.J.	1960	Harvey Charles	C	2,292	107
Utica Junior	Utica, Miss.	1903	J. Louis Stokes	S	921	63
Valencia Community	Orlando, Fla.	1967	James F. Gollattscheck	S	5,482	222
Ventura	Ventura, Cal.	1926	Ray C. Loehr	C	11,616	502
Vermillion Comm.	Ely, Minn.	1922	C. Donald Miller	S	396	18
Vermont, Comm. Coll. of	Montpelier, Vt.	1970	Peter Smith	S	1,700	200
Vermont Technical	Randolph Center, Vt.	1957	Pierre Kieffer	S	526	45
Victor Valley	Victorville, Cal.	1961	B.W. Wadsworth	Di	3,252	65
Victoria	Victoria, Tex.	1925	J.D. Moore	C	1,905	70
Villa Julie	Stevenson, Md.	1952	Sister Mary Stephen	P	377	51
Vincennes Univ.	Vincennes, Ind.	1801	Isaac K. Beckes	S	3,625	167
Virginia Highlands Comm.	Abingdon, Va.	1967	Emma Schulken	S	1,153	46
Virginia Western Comm.	Roanoke, Va.	1966	Harold H. Hooper	S	4,213	117
Wabash Valley	Mt. Carmel, Ill.	1961	John Cox	Di	1,589	33
Waldorf	Forest City, Ia.	1903	Paul Mork	Mu	493	33
Walker	Jasper, Ala.	1938	David J. Rowland	P	706	48
Walla Walla Comm.	Walla Walla, Wash.	1967	Eldon Dietrich	S	3,800	100
Walters State Community	Morristown, Tenn.	1969	Jack E. Campbell	C	1,932	90
Washtenaw Comm.	Ann Arbor, Mich.	1966	David Pollock, Act.	C	5,823	330
Waterbury State Technical	Waterbury, Conn.	1964	Kenneth Fogg	S	1,234	76

Name	Location	Year	Governing Official and Affiliation		Students	Teachers
Wayne Community	Goldsboro, N.C.	1957	Clyde Erwin, Jr.	S	1,800	110
Wayne County Comm.	Detroit, Mich.	1969	Reginald Wilson	S	14,000	700
Weatherford	Weatherford, Tex.	1869	E. W. Mince	C	1,386	65
Wenatchee Valley	Wenatchee, Wash.	1939	William Steward	S	3,159	205
Wentworth Institute (A)	Boston, Mass.	1904	Edward T. Kirkpatrick	P	1,474	99
Wesley	Dover, Del.	1873	William W. Hassler	P	934	55
West Hills	Coalinga, Cal.	1932	Robert A. Annand	S	2,557	136
West Los Angeles	Culver City, Cal.	1968	Morris Heldman	Di	7,200	250
West Shore Comm.	Scottville, Mich.	1967	John Eaton	C,S	950	57
West Valley Comm. (A)	Saratoga, Cal.	1964	James P. Hardy	C	13,749	525
West Virginia North. Comm.	Wheeling, W. Va.	1972	Daniel B. Crowder	S	3,633	113
Westark Comm.	Ft. Smith, Ark.	1928	Shelby Breedlove	S	4,809	80
Westbrook	Portland, Me.	1831	James F. Dickinson	P	498	46
Westchester Community	Valhalla, N.Y.	1946	Joseph N. Hankin	S	7,301	174
Western Iowa Tech. Comm.	Sioux City, Ia.	1967	Robert Kiser	S	938	77
Western Okla. State	Altus, Okla.	1926	W. C. Burris	S	1,204	39
Western Piedmount Comm.	Morganton, N.C.	1966	Gordon Blank	S	1,655	70
Western Texas	Snyder, Tex.	1971	Robert Clinton	C	1,500	75
Western Wisc. Tech. Inst.	La Crosse, Wis.	1912	Charles Richardson, Dir.	C,Mu	3,584	175
Wharton County Junior	Wharton, Tex.	1946	Theodore Nicksick, Jr.	S	1,802	92
Wilkes Community	Wilkesboro, N.C.	1964	Howard Thompson	S	2,225	101
William Rainey Harper	Palatine, Ill.	1967	Robert E. Lahti	S	13,400	325
Williamsport Area Comm.	Williamsport, Pa.	1965	William Fedderson	S,C	2,198	155
Wilmar Comm.	Willmar, Minn.	1962	John Torgelson	S	751	33
Wilson County Tech. Inst.	Wilson, N.C.	1958	Ernest B. Parry	C	644	51
Wingate	Wingate, N.C.	1896	Thomas Corts	D	1,289	69
Worcester Junior	Worcester, Mass.	1905	Ross Dixon	P	800	40
Worthington Comm.	Worthington, Minn.	1936	W. Donald Olsen	S	500	36
Yakima Valley	Yakima, Wash.	1929	William Russell	S	4,505	140
Yavapai	Prescott, Ariz.	1969	Joseph Russo	C	4,442	
York	York, Neb.	1890	Dale Larsen	D	329	
Young Harris	Young Harris, Ga.	1886	Ray Farley	D	529	30
Yuba Comm.	Marysville, Cal.	1927	Daniel G. Walker	C,S	7,047	223

School Enrollment by Age, Sex, and Race

Source: Bureau of the Census
As of October, 1973; numbers in thousands

| | Total Population | Enrolled in School | | | | Not enrolled in School | | | |
| | | Pre-College | | College | | Hi-School Grad | | Non-Hi-School Grad | |
		Number	%	Number	%	Number	%	Number	%
White male									
5 thru 13	14,784	14,470	97.9	—	—	—	—	315	2.1
14 " 17	7,169	6,610	92.2	111	1.5	69	0.9	378	5.3
18 " 21	6,129	402	6.6	2,194	35.8	2,666	43.5	868	14.2
22 " 24	4,382	19	0.4	838	19.1	2,939	67.1	585	13.4
25 " 34	12,074	20	0.2	1,075	8.9	8,777	72.7	2,202	18.2
White female									
5 thru 13	14,167	13,902	98.1	—	—	—	—	265	1.9
14 " 17	6,928	6,245	90.1	142	2.0	124	1.8	417	6.0
18 " 21	6,573	227	3.5	1,952	29.7	3,462	52.7	934	14.2
22 " 24	4,682	12	0.3	454	9.7	3,519	75.2	698	14.9
25 " 34	12,624	23	0.2	559	4.4	9,554	75.7	2,489	19.7
Black male									
5 thru 13	2,376	2,308	97.1	—	—	—	—	67	2.8
14 " 17	1,095	1,011	92.3	7	0.6	3	0.3	75	6.8
18 " 21	854	109	12.8	189	22.1	323	37.8	235	27.5
22 " 24	580	4	0.7	77	13.3	363	62.6	136	23.4
25 " 34	1,312	2	0.2	85	6.5	803	61.2	422	32.2
Black female									
5 thru 13	2,385	2,324	97.4	—	—	—	—	60	2.5
14 " 17	1,113	989	88.9	30	2.7	22	2.0	73	6.6
18 " 21	998	86	8.6	168	16.8	466	46.7	277	27.8
22 " 24	683	12	1.8	63	9.2	428	62.7	179	26.2
25 " 34	1,623	13	0.8	64	3.9	973	60.0	573	35.3
Spanish origin male									
5 thru 13	1,022	997	95.6	—	—	—	—	24	2.3
14 " 17	412	367	89.1	11	2.7	2	0.5	32	7.8
18 " 21	355	51	14.4	76	21.4	96	27.0	133	37.5
22 " 24	270	—	—	29	10.7	147	54.4	95	35.2
25 " 34	660	4	0.6	52	7.9	259	39.2	346	52.4
Spanish origin female									
5 thru 13	990	957	96.7	—	—	—	—	32	3.2
14 " 17	474	393	82.9	5	1.0	5	1.0	72	15.2
18 " 21	382	24	6.3	77	20.2	129	33.8	152	39.8
22 " 24	276	—	—	25	9.1	131	47.5	120	43.5
25 " 34	718	3	0.4	16	2.2	308	42.9	391	54.5

Degree Granting Canadian Colleges and Universities

All coeducational unless followed by (M) for men only. Governing official is president unless otherwise designated. Year is that of founding. The word college is part of the name listed unless another designation is given. Each institution listed has an enrollment of at least 200 students of college grade. Number of teachers is the total number of individuals on teaching staff. Enrollment and faculty in italics include all branches and campuses.

Name	Location	Year	Governing Official	Students	Teachers
Acadia Univ.	Wolfville, Nova Scotia.	1838	Charles B. Huggins	2,600	180
Alberta, Univ. of	Edmonton, Calgary, Al.	1906	Harry E. Gunning	19,500	1,500
Bathurst, Le College de.	Bathurst, N. B.	1899	Leopold Lanteigne, Rector	645	35
Bishop's Univ.	Lennoxville, Que.	1843	D. Healy	929	72
Brandon Univ.	Brandon, Man.	1899	A. L. Dulmage	2,160	130
British Columbia, Univ. of.	Vancouver, B.C.	1908	Douglas T. Kenny	23,185	1,683
Brock Univ.	St. Catharines, Ont.	1964	A. J. Earp	3,980	180
Calgary, Univ. of	Calgary, Alberta.	1945	W. A. Cochrane	12,325	907
Carleton Univ.	Ottawa, Ont.	1942	Michael Oliver	14,482	525
Concordia Univ.	Montreal, Que.	1974	Henry J. Hemens	25,226	881
Dalhousie Univ.	Halifax, Nova Scotia.	1818	Henry D. Hicks	8,000	1,000
Guelph, Univ. of.	Guelph, Ont.	1964	William C. Winegard	9,768	970
King's Coll., Univ. of.	Halifax, Nova Scotia.	1789	J. G. Morgan	263	16
Lakehead Univ.	Thunder Bay, Ont.	1965	A. D. Booth	3,321	245
Laurentian Univ.	Sudbury, Ont.	1960	Edward J. Monahan	7,085	366
Laval Universite	Quebec, Que.	1852	Larkin Kerwin	17,616	2,495
Lethbridge, Univ. of.	Lethbridge, Alberta.	1967	William E. Beckel	1,700	150
Manitoba, Univ. of.	Winnipeg, Man.	1877	Ernest Sirluck	18,336	1,057
McGill Univ.	Montreal, Que.	1821	Robert E. Bell, Prin.	17,971	2,200
McMaster Univ.	Hamilton, Ont.	1887	A. N. Bourns	13,218	1,207
Moncton, Univ. of.	Moncton, N.B.	1963	Clement Cormier	5,880	389
Montreal, Universite de .	Montreal, Que.	1920	Roger Gaudry, Rector	23,055	2,000
Mount Allison Univ.	Sackville, N.B.	1840	Laurence Cragg	1,491	135
Mt. St. Vincent Univ.	Halifax, Nova Scotia.	1925	Sister Mary Albertus	1,729	150
New Brunswick, Univ. of.	Fredericton, N.B.	1785	John M. Anderson	7,227	466
Newfoundland, Mem. Univ. of.	St. John's, Newfdld.	1925	M. O. Morgan	9,935	722
Notre Dame Univ.	Nelson, B.C.	1963	Cecil L. Kaller	528	61
Nova Scotia Coll. of Arts & Design.	Halifax, Nova Scotia.	1887	Garry Neill Kennedy	485	50
Nova Scotia Technical	Halifax, Nova Scotia.	1907	Allison E. Steeves	526	63
Ontario Inst. for Studies in Education.	Toronto, Ont.	1965	Clifford C. Pitt	2,161	150
Ottawa, Univ. of	Ottawa, Ont.	1848	Rev. Roger Guindon	17,243	889
Prince Edward Island, Univ. of	Charlottetown, P.E.I.	1834	Ronald J. Baker	1,397	140
Quebec, Universite de	Montreal, Que.	1969	M. Maurice Brossard	11,447	453
Queen's Univ.	Kingston, Ont.	1841	Hon. Roland Michener	11,530	942
Regina, Univ. of.	Regina, Sask.	1974	E. C. Leslie	6,000	350
Royal Military Coll. of Canada (M).	Kingston, Ont.	1876	Hon. J. Richardson	657	110
Ryerson Polytechnical .	Toronto, Ont.	1948	Walter G. Pitman	10,000	500
St. Francis Xavier Univ.	Antigonish, Nova Scotia.	1853	Rev. M. MacDonell	2,761	161
St. Louis-Maillet.	Edmundston, N.B.	1946	Marcel Sormany	1,201	60
St. Mary's Univ.	Halifax, Nova Scotia.	1802	D. O. Carrigan	3,601	245
St. Michael's, Univ. of.	Toronto, Ont.	1851	Rev. John Kelly	2,200	180
St. Paul Univ.	Ottawa, Ont.	1866	Rev. Marcel Patry	523	106
St. Thomas Univ.	Fredericton, N.B.	1910	Rev. Msgr. Donald Duffie	900	70
Saskatchewan	Saskatoon, Sask.	1907	Hon. J. G. Diefenbaker	10,908	1,186
Sherbrooke, Univ. of.	Sherbrooke, Que.	1954	Msgr. Roger Maltais	7,624	773
Simon Fraser Univ.	Burnaby, B.C.	1965	Pauline Jewett	6,215	496
Sir George Williams Univ.	Montreal, Que.	1948	H. J. Hemens, Chan.	16,099	752
Toronto, Univ. of.	Toronto, Ont.	1827	John Robert Evans	40,131	5,141
Trent Univ.	Peterborough, Ont.	1963	T. E. W. Nind	1,980	186
Trinity.	Toronto, Ont.	1852	George Ignatieff, Provost	952	51
Victoria Univ.	Toronto, Ont.	1841	G. S. French	2,534	110
Victoria, Univ. of.	Victoria, B.C.	1963	H. E. Petch	6,968	468
Waterloo, Univ. of.	Waterloo, Ont.	1959	B. C. Matthews	13,478	838
Western Ontario, Univ. of.	London, Ont.	1878	D. C. Williams	21,000	1,250
Wilfrid Laurier Univ.	Waterloo, Ont.	1973	Frank C. Peters	6,058	200
Windsor, Univ. of.	Windsor, Ont.	1857	John Francis Leddy	11,956	550
Winnipeg, Univ. of.	Winnipeg, Man.	1871	Henry E. Duckworth	5,230	150
York Univ.	Downsview, Ont.	1959	H. Ian Macdonald	22,561	1,050

Typical Tuition Fees at Selected Canadian Colleges and Universities

Source: Association of Universities and Colleges of Canada

Institution	Cost Range	Institution	Cost Range
Alberta, The University of	$400-600	McMaster University	$585-645
British Columbia, The Univ. of	428-644	New Brunswick, University of	581
Calgary, The University of	400-800	Ottawa, University of	565-735
Carleton University, Ottawa	682-742	Queen's University of Kingston	600-725
Concordia University	450-650	Quebec, University du	500
Dalhousie University	680-822	Ryerson Polytechnical Institute	424
Guelph, University of	585-670	Saskatchewan, University of	460-555
Laval, Universite	570	Toronto, University of	559-805
Manitoba, The University of	425-625	Victoria, University of	428-506
Montreal, Universite de	495-695	Waterloo, University of	625-780
Memorial University of Newfoundland	250-300*	Western Ontario, The University of	589-774
McGill University	570-719	Windsor, University of	585-600(1)
		York University	660

Undergraduate tuition fees at Universities with enrollment of 5,000 full day-time students or more. Fee is for 1973-74 academic year.

*Per semester. (1) Excludes $100.00 for out of country students.

Typical Tuition Fees at Selected Colleges and Universities

Source: World Almanac Questionnaire

The College Entrance Examination Board has estimated that the average cost in a private college in the fall of 1975, including tuition, board, and room will be $4,391, a 6 to 8% increase over the previous year. The cost at a public college will average $2,679.

Fees for tuition charged per year by colleges and universities for courses, use of libraries, laboratories and other facilities, are a major part of student expenses. Tuition varies considerably, depending on the type of institution, its control and location. The lowest tuition fees are those of state-controlled or other public-controlled institutions for residents of their state, city, etc. Students from other states or areas have to pay more. In the following list, such state or other public institutions are shown with two figures. The lower one is the tuition fee for residents, the higher one the tuition fee for students from other states or areas.

(Tuition does not include room, board or other expenses)

School	Tuition	School	Tuition	School	Tuition
Adrian	$2,118	Holy Cross	$3,200	Pennsylvania State Univ.	$960-2,160
Akron, Univ. of	705-1,605	Houston, Univ. of	340-1,420	Peru State	588-972
Alabama, Univ. of	595-1,190	Idaho, Univ. of	400-1,400	Pittsburgh, Univ. of	1,024-2,014
Amherst	3,795	Idaho State Univ.	400-1,250	Portland, Univ. of	3,204
Anderson	1,860	Indiana Univ.	722-1,640	Princeton Univ.	4,000
Arizona, Univ. of	450-1,640	Indiana State Univ.	720-1,410	Providence	2,250
Auburn	549-1,074	Iowa, Univ. of	780-1,550	Purdue Univ.	2,020-2,970
Avila	1,700	Iowa State Univ. of Sci. & Tech.		Redlands, Univ. of	2,975
Baldwin-Wallace	2,679		720-1,584	Rhode Island, Univ. of	796-1,696
Ball State	720-1,440	Jacksonville Univ.	1,970	Rice Univ.	2,180
Baylor	1,362	John Carroll Univ.	3,200	Richmond, Univ. of	2,425
Black Hills State	574-1,142	Kansas, Univ. of	573-1,363	Roger Williams	1,015
Bob Jones	1,020	Kansas State Univ.	532-1,322	Rutgers Univ.	725-1,310
Boston	2,950	Kent State Univ.	810-2,010	St. Bonaventure Univ.	2,300
Bowdoin	3,385	Kentucky, Univ. of	480-1,210	St. Francis	2,490
Bowling Green State	780-1,959	Leland Stanford Univ.	3,810	St. Olaf	3,600
Brigham Young (a)	340	Marquette Univ.	2,450	Santa Clara, Univ. of	2,508
Brown	3,930	Maryland, Univ. of	698-1,848	Sarah Lawrence	4,150
Bryn Mawr	3,700	Memphis State Univ.	406-1,246	Seattle Univ.	2,160
Canisius	2,300	Michigan, Univ. of	800-2,600	Seton Hall Univ.	1,900
Carleton	4,600	Minnesota, Univ. of	714-1,677	Southern Calif., Univ. of	2,910
Carnegie-Mellon	2,900	Mississippi State Univ.	511-1,111	Southern Methodist Univ.	2,450
Case Western Reserve Univ.	3,120	Mississippi, Univ. of	553-1,153	Swarthmore	3,450
Clemson Univ.	640-1,340	Montana, Univ. of	529-1,501	Syracuse Univ.	3,438
Colorado, Univ. of	353-1,383	Montana State Univ.	519-1,491	Temple Univ.	525-975
Connecticut, Univ. of	765-1,815	Morgan State	701-1,151	Texas A & M Univ.	300-840
Dakota State	559-1,001	Muskingum	3,730	Tufts Univ.	3,600
Dana	2,120	Nevada, Univ. of	608-1,808	Tulane Univ.	3,000
Dayton, Univ. of	2,000	New Hampshire, Univ. of	2,472-3,772	Utah, Univ. of	480-1,245
Delaware, Univ. of	795-1,930	New Mexico, Univ. of	456-1,284	Vanderbilt Univ.	3,220
Denver, Univ. of	3,150	New York Univ.	3,300	Vassar	3,450
Doane	2,000	Niagara Univ.	2,190	Vermont, Univ. of	1,088-2,788
Drake Univ.	2,750	North Carolina, Univ. of	453-1,997	Wake Forest Univ.	2,200
Duke Univ.	2,980	North Dakota, Univ. of	527-1,255	Washburn Univ. of Topeka	700-1,134
Duquesne Univ.	2,550	North Dakota StateUniv.	435-1,164	Way College of Emporia	2,000
Evansville, Univ. of	1,995	Notre Dame, Univ. of	2,782	Wayne State Univ.	332-906
Fisk Univ.	1,950	Oberlin	3,300	Wellesley	5,150
Fordham Univ.	2,600	Ohio State Univ.	780-1,830	West Virginia Univ.	318-1,248
Furman Univ.	2,048	Oklahoma, Univ. of	445-1,245	Wyoming, Univ. of	410-1,376
Georgia, Univ. of	612-1,476	Oklahoma State Univ.	464-1,244	Yale Univ.	4,050
Gonzaga Univ.	2,100	Old Dominion Univ.	570-1,050	Youngstown State Univ.	630-1,200
Hampton Inst.	1,895	Oral Roberts Univ.	1,300	(a) Non-members of Mormon Church $360.	
Harvard Univ.	3,400	Pan American Univ.	270-1,250		
Haverford	2,975	Pennsylvania, Univ. of	3,450		

Federal Funds for Education

Source: Office of Education, Dept. of Health, Education and Welfare.
(In thousands of dollars. Includes grants, loans, and directly administered services. Estimated.)

Type of support, level, and program	1975
Total grants and loans	$14,656,322
Grants, total	14,262,241
Elementary-secondary education	4,896,057
School asst.—federally affected areas	482,060
Economic Opportunity Programs	788,194
National Defense Education Act	31,850
Supporting services	397,016
Asst. for educationally deprived children	1,859,837
Teacher Corps	43,768
Vocational education	528,177
Dependents' schools abroad	244,422
Public lands revenue for schools	110,384
Assistance in special areas	123,086

Veterans' education	44,389
Emergency school asst.	210,274
Other	32,600
Higher education	6,530,844
Basic Research	1,275,000
Research facilities	181,000
Training grants	1,115,796
Fellowships and traineeships	
Facilities and equipment	126,097
Other institutional support	355,718
Other student assistance	3,477,233
Vocational-tech. and continuing ed.	2,835,340
Vocational-technical education	2,059,673
Veterans' education	606,840
General continuing education	153,295

Continued

(continued)

Type of Support, Level, and Program	
Training State and local personnel	15,532
Loans, total	**394,081**
Student loan program, Natl. Def. Ed. Act.	404,123
College facilities loans	10,042
Other Federal funds, total	**5,722,789**
Applied research and development	1,651,000
School lunch and milk programs	1,789,243
Training of federal personnel	1,217,886
U.S. Academies	289,507
Professional training, military	900,521
Civilian education and training in non-federal facilities	27,858
Library services	**192,643**
Grants to public libraries	35,311

Type of Support, Level, and Program	
National library services	157,332
International education	**78,999**
Educational exchange program	33,859
AID Projects	17,826
Action (previously Peace Corps)	22,323
Other international educ. and training	4,991
Other	**793,018**
Agricultural extension service	206,850
Educational television facilities	42,197
Education in federal correctional inst.	11,588
Other education and training	159,578
Value of surplus property transferred: acquisition cost of personal property	345,805
Fair value of real property	27,000

Fall Enrollment and Teachers in Full Time Day Schools
Public Elementary and Secondary Day Schools Fall 1974
Source: United States Office of Education

	Pupils Enrolled[1]		Teachers[2]	1973 High School Graduates[1]	
	Elementary	Secondary		Male	Female
United States	30,700,000	14,300,000	2,362,000	1,353,000	1,377,000
Alabama	524,000	240,000	36,920	21,450	22,991
Alaska	59,000	22,000	4,120	1,974	1,996
Arizona	361,000	156,000	22,800	12,257	11,766
Arkansas	310,000	136,000	18,610	12,909	12,796
California	2,998,000	1,421,000	216,430	132,339	135,682
Colorado	387,000	181,000	28,340	16,443	16,915
Connecticut	432,000	230,000	40,540	18,296	19,575
Delaware	89,000	43,000	7,250	3,730	4,003
District of Columbia	100,000	35,000	7,910	2,076	3,137
Florida	1,044,000	480,000	73,210	40,771	41,002
Georgia	762,000	313,000	47,410	27,811	29,944
Hawaii	122,000	55,000	8,890	5,529	5,618
Idaho	124,000	63,000	8,560	6,428	6,286
Illinois	1,577,000	723,000	129,230	66,574	69,161
Indiana	817,000	379,000	56,920	37,022	36,133
Iowa	423,000	203,000	36,210	22,459	22,062
Kansas	302,000	155,000	27,240	17,110	16,831
Kentucky	484,000	219,000	34,470	20,171	20,436
Louisiana	586,000	248,000	48,010	21,848	23,856
Maine	171,000	72,000	12,800	7,174	7,203
Maryland	627,000	275,000	48,290	25,531	27,282
Massachusetts	829,000	364,000	76,280	37,186	37,186
Michigan	1,410,000	696,000	102,770	64,077	64,851
Minnesota	590,000	303,000	49,500	31,908	31,486
Mississippi	362,000	153,000	26,820	12,649	13,479
Missouri	687,000	324,000	51,420	30,516	29,552
Montana	113,000	58,000	9,220	5,266	5,266
Nebraska	216,000	105,000	19,490	11,008	11,451
Nevada	93,000	41,000	5,690	3,216	3,198
New Hampshire	118,000	52,000	9,940	4,881	4,968
New Jersey	1,008,000	460,000	90,370	45,067	46,562
New Mexico	187,000	94,000	13,290	8,627	8,621
New York	2,302,000	1,117,000	213,040	101,307	103,353
North Carolina	798,000	365,000	53,030	34,081	35,241
North Dakota	89,000	49,000	8,170	5,290	5,273
Ohio	1,585,000	773,000	118,360	76,282	76,146
Oklahoma	406,000	189,000	28,470	19,029	18,320
Oregon	315,000	157,000	23,590	15,602	15,619
Pennsylvania	1,520,000	782,000	131,010	79,279	75,321
Rhode Island	128,000	55,000	11,180	5,288	5,514
South Carolina	436,000	185,000	28,760	17,400	18,750
South Dakota	104,000	52,000	8,820	6,152	6,012
Tennessee	630,000	264,000	39,350	25,280	26,835
Texas	1,951,000	803,000	137,440	76,426	77,103
Utah	207,000	96,000	12,620	9,473	9,520
Vermont	74,000	31,000	7,100	3,096	3,207
Virginia	738,000	338,000	56,000	29,400	33,189
Washington	527,000	254,000	35,130	25,355	25,633
West Virginia	280,000	125,000	19,110	12,295	12,246
Wisconsin	642,000	337,000	56,870	35,396	35,393
Wyoming	56,000	29,000	5,000	2,872	2,781
Outlying areas	594,000	180,000	32,490	11,751	14,571
American Samoa	8,000	2,000	660	220	226
Canal Zone	8,000	4,000	650	362	377
Guam	20,000	7,000	1,420	521	535
Puerto Rico	542,000	162,000	28,420	10,648	13,433
Virgin Islands	16,000	5,000	1,340	......	......

[1]Estimated. [2]Full and part-time classroom teachers.

Public School Attendance, Teachers, Expenditures

Source: U.S. Office of Education; Salaries cover supervisors, principals, and teachers

School Year	Pop. 5 to 17 yrs.	Pupils		Teachers[1]				Total Expend.
		Enrolled	Av. daily attend.	Male	Female	Total	Salary[2]	
1900.......	21,404,322	15,503,110	10,632,772	126,588	296,474	423,062	$325	$214,964,618
1910.......	24,239,948	17,813,852	12,827,307	110,481	412,729	523,210	485	426,250,434
1920.......	27,728,788	21,578,316	16,150,035	95,654	583,648	679,302	871	1,036,151,209
1930.......	31,571,322	25,678,015	21,264,886	141,771	712,492	854,263	1,420	2,316,790,384
1940.......	29,805,259	25,433,542	22,042,151	194,725	680,752	875,477	1,441	2,344,048,927
1950.......	30,788,000	25,111,427	22,283,845	194,968	718,703	913,671	3,010	5,837,643,000
1960.......	43,881,000	36,086,771	32,477,440	392,700	962,300	1,355,000	5,174	15,613,255,000
1968 (Fall).....	52,288,000	44,961,662	41,157,000	617,805	1,324,980	1,942,785	8,200	35,511,170,000
1970 (Fall).....	52,435,000	45,909,088	42,495,346	649,250	1,411,865	2,061,115	9,570	44,423,865,000
1971 (Fall).....	52,133,000	46,081,000	42,544,000	668,000	1,395,000	2,063,000	10,100	48,513,986,000
1972 (Fall).....	51,637,000	45,744,000	42,408,000	702,000	1,400,000	2,102,000	10,608	51,905,025,000
1973.......	51,325,000	45,429,499	42,079,000	718,000	1,413,000	2,131,000	11,185	56,031,041,400
1974(P)......	50,426,000	45,056,000	41,405,000	728,000	1,431,000	2,159,000	12,070	61,629,000,000

(1.) Prior to 1954 includes other nonsupervisory instructional staff (librarians and guidance and psychological personnel)
(2.) Average annual salary per member of instructional staff. (P) Preliminary.

Cost Per Pupil by State

Source: Office of Education, Dept. HEW

Estimated expenditures per pupil in average daily attendance in public elementary and secondary day schools, by state 1973-74.

State	Expenditure per pupil				State	Expenditure per pupil			
	Total	Current	Capital outlay	Interest on school debt		Total[1]	Current	Capital outlay	Interest on school debt
United States	$1,281	$1,116	$125	$40	Nebraska.........	$1,188	$1,040	$121	$27
Alabama..........	790	716	72	3	Nevada...........	1,276	1,032	184	60
Alaska...........	2,102	1,597	407	98	New Hampshire.....	1,036	900	100	36
Arizona..........	1,439	1,153	254	33	New Jersey........	1,565	1,385	127	53
Arkansas.........	912	773	115	24	New Mexico........	1,220	1,004	205	12
California.........	1,318	1,170	104	44	New York..........	2,037	1,809	161	67
Colorado.........	1,278	1,075	169	34	North Carolina......	978	900	66	13
Connecticut.......	1,359	1,283	40	35	North Dakota......	1,101	947	132	23
Delaware.........	1,747	1,388	286	73	Ohio.............	1,120	1,009	83	28
District of Columbia..	1,827	1,523	305	..	Oklahoma.........	921	835	72	14
Florida[1].........	1,030	885	124	21	Oregon..........	1,341	1,219	100	23
Georgia..........	974	869	71	34	Pennsylvania......	1,474	1,247	143	84
Hawaii...........	1,391	1,224	160	7	Rhode Island......	1,415	1,295	78	42
Idaho...........	942	840	82	20	South Carolina.....	983	856	105	22
Illinois..........	1,425	1,228	158	38	South Dakota......	1,011	932	66	12
Indiana..........	1,152	950	159	42	Tennessee........	841	759	51	31
Iowa............	1,273	1,113	134	26	Texas...........	977	809	122	45
Kansas..........	1,114	1,043	50	21	Utah............	996	816	163	16
Kentucky.........	829	727	69	33	Vermont..........	1,308	1,109	158	40
Louisiana........	1,096	978	88	31	Virginia..........	1,142	983	125	35
Maine...........	1,033	918	87	28	Washington.......	1,136	974	124	39
Maryland.........	1,591	1,168	376	47	West Virginia......	945	871	66	8
Massachusetts.....	1,279	1,136	90	52	Wisconsin........	1,335	1,200	98	38
Michigan.........	1,459	1,260	148	50	Wyoming.........	1,301	1,232	50	19
Minnesota........	1,450	1,265	125	59	**Outlying Areas**				
Mississippi.......	858	787	62	10	American Samoa[1]...	719	653	66	..
Missouri.........	1,082	963	92	27	Canal Zone.......	1,541	1,467	73	..
Montana.........	1,248	1,186	42	20	Guam............	908	908	..	..
[1]Estimated.					Puerto Rico[1]......	483	453	30	..
					Virgin Islands......	1,387	1,387	..	..
					[1]Estimated 1972-73.				

Fall Enrollment and Teachers in Full-time Day Schools — Canada

Public Elementary and Secondary Day Schools — 1973-1974

Source: Statistics Canada

	1973-74 Enrollment			1973-74, Teachers		
	Elementary Kdgn-Gr. 8	Secondary Gr. 9 and up	Total	Elementary Kdgn-Gr. 8	Secondary Gr. 9 and up	Total
Canada.................	3,762,363	1,709,804	5,472,167	163,508	94,834	258,342
Newfoundland..........	127,555	32,276	159,831	4,855	2,000	6,855
Prince Edward Island......	21,030	8,026	29,056	1,023	535	1,558
Nova Scotia.............	153,724	53,927	207,651	6,488	3,592	10,080
New Brunswick..........	120,297	49,882	170,179	5,051	2,790	7,841
Quebec...............	940,369	524,230	1,464,599	46,800	27,900	74,700
Ontario...............	1,398,522	610,088	2,008,610	56,630	33,889	90,519
Manitoba..............	167,626	66,994	234,620	7,431	4,466	11,897
Saskatchewan..........	156,643	67,155	223,798	6,827	3,534	10,361
Alberta...............	287,605	132,132	419,737	12,400	7,953	20,353
British Columbia........	374,236	162,266	536,502	15,298	7,960	23,258
Yukon................	3,776	1,181	4,957	175	95	270
Northwest Territories.......	10,980	1,647	12,627	530	120	650

e - estimate   p - preliminary

Public Libraries in Selected North American Cities

Source: World Almanac Research
Figure in parentheses denotes number of branches.

City	No. of Volumes	Circu- lation	Cost of Operation	City	No. of Volumes	Circu- lation	Cost of Operation
Akron, Oh. (17)	777,285	1,945,499	$ 2,255,436	Montreal, Quebec (16)	1,086,252	1,135,252	$ 2,080,490
Albany, N.Y. (5)	245,439	N/A	635,917	Nashville, Tenn. (11)	432,251	1,356,925	1,744,258
Albuquerque, N.M. (6)	306,885	1,073,422	686,400	New Haven, Conn. (7)	481,234	426,980	879,747
Atlanta, Ga. (19)	784,613	2,223,997	3,757,494	New Orleans, La. (10)	723,918	1,320,500	2,081,183
Augusta, Ga. (3)	293,208	638,565	636,114	New York	17,100,215	None	15,937,000
Baltimore, Md. (19)	2,253,775	2,880,360	5,978,856	N.Y. branches (82)	6,602,604	10,552,925	20,328,713
Baton Rouge, La. (9)	292,736	829,043	886,559	Brooklyn (55)	2,926,733	7,102,336	13,657,878
Binghamton, N.Y. (5)	252,402	562,981	777,881	Queens (54)	2,699,519	6,411,386	13,296,378
Birmingham, Ala. (16)	895,823	3,377,200	1,518,042	Norfolk, Va. (9)	489,273	1,087,848	1,123,028
Boston, Mass. (29)	3,623,608	2,756,899	8,452,714	Oklahoma City, Okla. (12)	637,336	1,950,517	1,483,687
Bridgeport, Conn. (4)	448,373	430,000	981,717	Omaha, Neb. (8)	440,400	N/A	N/A
Buffalo, N. Y. (17)	2,701,424	5,817,993	7,466,232	Orlando, Fla. (10)	401,237	677,966	1,491,992
Calgary, Alberta (12)	509,471	2,187,106	2,190,236	Ottawa, Ont. (7)	451,314	1,727,618	1,762,113
Charleston, W. Va. (1)	350,932	747,767	661,280	Philadelphia, Pa. (45)	2,880,941	5,410,818	10,828,852
Charlotte, N.C. (14)	579,790	1,308,066	1,294,938	Phoenix, Ariz. (7)	893,000	2,508,000	3,394,000
Chattanooga, Tenn. (1)	245,841	482,331	606,180	Pittsburgh, Pa. (24)	2,277,503	4,361,900	5,479,240
Chicago, Ill. (48)	5,069,533	8,969,194	15,661,185	Portland, Me. (3)	230,977	323,455	549,422
Cincinnati, Oh. (38)	2,850,067	5,485,753	5,881,259	Portland, Ore. (18)	1,035,476	2,547,483	2,917,349
Cleveland, Oh. (36)	3,318,514	4,443,797	7,748,888	Providence, R.I. (9)	679,836	814,496	1,587,065
Columbus, Oh. (20)	1,104,420	2,920,780	2,892,559	Regina, Sask. (4)	249,210	1,001,765	1,264,791
Corpus Christi, Tex. (2)	305,255	682,261	447,460	Richmond, Va. (4)	481,910	975,179	1,032,348
Dallas, Tex. (12)	151,050	208,083	175,042	Roanoke, Va. (5)	271,455	364,516	486,386
Dayton, Oh. (19)	1,187,127	3,495,068	2,910,360	Rochester, N. Y. (13)	795,933	1,592,741	3,029,543
Denver, Col. (12)	1,357,395	3,045,756	4,380,387	Sacramento, Cal. (15)	847,830	3,575,269	4,198,756
Des Moines, Ia. (5)	389,144	1,073,344	1,199,030	St. Louis, Mo. (19)	1,295,726	2,772,464	5,333,950
Detroit, Mich. (29)	2,210,277	2,472,750	10,138,523	St. Paul, Minn. (10)	705,677	1,945,433	1,692,178
El Paso, Tex. (6)	428,046	949,394	878,950	St. Petersburg, Fla. (3)	315,565	1,140,009	699,251
Erie, Pa. (1)	81,308	338,082	228,306	Salt Lake City, Ut. (4)	440,820	881,415	960,307
Evansville, Ind. (8)	454,000	1,320,000	833,718	San Antonio, Tex. (8)	792,984	2,253,157	1,676,875
Halifax, Nova Scotia (1)	173,759	N/A	496,971	San Diego, Cal. (7)	1,197,690	3,673,700	3,868,975
Hamilton, Ont. (8)	667,504	1,796,639	2,351,400	San Francisco, Cal. (26)	1,443,848	3,195,475	5,501,847
Hartford, Conn. (8)	456,107	542,860	1,204,285	San Jose, Cal. (11)	625,080	2,319,169	2,970,231
Houston, Tex. (23)	1,412,927	4,119,568	3,598,480	Saskatoon, Sask. (4)	279,847	1,005,827	1,042,608
Jacksonville, Fla. (10)	884,772	1,720,792	1,922,656	Seattle, Wash. (15)	1,499,190	3,927,794	5,693,867
Kansas City, Kan. (3)	248,934	N/A	558,532	Syracuse, N. Y. (9)	384,131	1,051,382	1,092,186
Kansas City, Mo. (11)	1,221,646	2,054,672	2,342,000	Tallahassee, Fla. (2)	115,000	365,000	411,795
Kitchener, Ont.	321,407	924,548	910,488	Tampa, Fla. (7)	395,316	1,498,497	1,942,107
Knoxville, Tenn. (19)	481,538	1,349,062	1,069,023	Toledo, Oh. (18)	1,157,995	2,758,123	3,107,476
Little Rock, Ark.	254,143	456,899	420,088	Tucson, Ariz. (6)	482,576	2,198,192	2,165,885
London, Ont. (9)	436,547	1,627,893	2,361,543	Tulsa, Okla. (18)	625,402	1,483,303	1,673,203
Los Angeles, Cal. (61)	4,161,905	81,000	14,047,865	Vancouver, B. C. (11)	687,240	N/A	3,366,169
Louisville, Ky. (30)	946,009	1,542,270	N/A	Washington, D. C. (19)	2,133,102	2,050,690	7,613,800
Memphis, Tenn. (18)	1,062,029	2,452,877	3,071,276	Wichita, Kan. (8)	322,048	1,061,771	1,364,469
Miami, Fla. (17)	780,190	2,358,834	4,075,304	Winnipeg, Manitoba (7)	406,983	1,477,000	1,022,163
Milwaukee, Wis. (18)	2,214,680	3,700,914	5,396,556	Winston-Salem, N.C. (8)	300,000	900,634	1,033,580

Major American Academic Libraries

Source: World Almanac Research

Institution	No. of Volumes	Microfilm units	Enroll- ment	Expenditures
Harvard University	8,859,478	517,854	16,008	$9,752,103
Yale University	6,175,168	N/A	9,427	6,397,174
University of Illinois	4,920,183	N/A	33,857	5,785,685
Columbia University	4,473,947	N/A	15,432	6,042,529
University of California at Berkeley	4,318,214	717,091	30,061	4,359,500
Cornell University	4,092,207	482,196	16,128	5,449,500
Stanford University	3,851,260	1,072,763	11,599	7,296,130
University of Michigan	3,734,344	N/A	25,697	5,439,000
University of Chicago	3,334,152	251,612	7,550	2,584,385
University of Texas	3,330,871	346,789	39,900	5,722,674
University of California at Los Angeles	3,283,959	1,027,558	31,156	6,890,192
Princeton University	2,985,021[1]	—	5,354	3,934,862
University of Minnesota	2,902,707	608,340	49,929	3,197,494
Ohio State University	2,787,132	525,085	51,122	4,293,974
University of Wisconsin	2,654,541	791,023	32,541	2,916,791
Indiana University	2,644,460	543,223	28,034	2,555,866
Northwestern University	2,504,088	433,186	15,900	1,823,564
University of Pennsylvania	2,500,000	N/A	19,000	4,362,000
Duke University	2,438,962	225,864	8,065	3,123,329
University of North Carolina at Chapel Hill	2,386,401	492,269	19,224	2,971,366
Johns Hopkins University	2,073,777	597,802	4,748	894,000

(1.) Microfilm units included. N/A—not available.

National Spelling Bee Champions

The National Spelling Bee, conducted by Scripps-Howard Newspapers and other newspapers since 1939, was instituted by the Louisville (Ky.) Courier-Journal in 1925. Children under 16 years of age sponsored by participating newspapers are eligible to compete for the cash prizes and prize trips.

Recent winners are: **1974**—1. Julie Ann Junkin, 12, Gordo, Ala. (Birmingham Post-Herald). 2. Gail Meier, 14, Bartlett, Tenn. (Memphis Press-Scimitar). 3. Tara Farone, 14, Peninsula, Ohio (Akron Beacon Journal).

1975—1. Hugh C. Tosteson, 14, San German, Puerto Rico (San Juan Star). 2. Mark Ogle, 14, Greenwood, Ind. (Indianapolis News). 3. Diane Bryan, 14, Lubbock, Tex. (Lubbock Avalanche-Journal).

Income Discrimination: Male and Female, Black and White

Source: Bureau of the Census

Total Money Income (Includes full-and part-time workers, 25 and over, Mar. 1974)		Years of Schooling					
	Total	7 or less	8	9-11	12	13-15	18 or more
White Males with Income (1,000)	48,201	5,149	5,450	6,896	15,936	6,206	8,564
Percent	100.0	100.0	100.0	100.0	100.0	100.0	100.0
Loss to $2,999	10.3	30.2	19.0	10.1	6.0	6.2	4.5
$3,000 to $5,999	15.1	28.7	27.2	18.9	10.9	10.2	6.8
$6,000 to $7,999	10.9	14.2	14.3	13.6	11.1	9.2	5.6
$8,000 to $9,999	12.1	9.4	9.4	15.1	14.4	11.7	7.6
$10,000 to $14,999	28.3	12.0	19.0	28.7	36.2	32.3	26.0
$15,000 and over	23.2	3.9	8.7	13.5	21.5	30.2	49.6
Mean Income	$11,370	$5,874	$7,688	$9,461	$11,452	$12,836	$17,339
Black Males with Income (1,000)	$4,763	$1,472	$445	$941	$1,213	$417	$275
Percent	100.0	100.0	100.0	100.0	100.0	100.0	100.0
Loss to $2,999	25.0	46.4	27.8	17.1	12.3	12.7	6.1
$3,000 to $5,999	24.3	29.6	33.2	28.1	18.4	15.8	8.3
$6,000 to $7,999	14.5	9.8	15.7	18.9	16.7	16.1	9.7
$8,000 to $9,999	13.1	5.6	11.6	14.1	18.9	17.0	17.9
$10,000 to $14,999	17.6	6.8	8.3	17.3	28.4	26.1	30.6
$15,000 and over	5.6	1.6	3.6	3.7	5.4	12.3	27.4
Mean Income	$6,793	$4,378	$5,640	$6,712	$8,370	$8,690	$12,035
Mean Income, Full-Time Males	$13,288	$8,285	$10,144	$10,790	$12,546	$14,279	$18,738
White Females with Income (1,000)	37,654	3,942	4,278	5,865	14,618	4,455	4,496
Percent	100.0	100.0	100.0	100.0	100.0	100.0	100.0
Loss to $2,999	46.7	71.9	65.7	52.3	40.8	37.0	28.4
$3,000 to $5,999	26.3	22.9	25.2	31.0	29.0	25.5	15.5
$6,000 to $7,999	11.6	3.5	5.2	9.3	15.0	15.1	13.4
$8,000 to $9,999	7.3	1.1	2.6	4.8	8.1	10.1	14.9
$10,000 to $14,999	6.3	0.4	1.0	2.2	5.8	9.3	20.8
$15,000 and over	1.8	0.1	0.2	0.4	1.3	2.9	6.8
Mean Income	$4,328	$2,446	$2,837	$3,480	$4,490	$5,192	$7,123
Black Females with Income (1,000)	5,027	1,271	411	1,253	1,366	419	307
Percent	100.0	100.0	100.0	100.0	100.0	100.0	100.0
Loss to $2,999	51.1	80.4	64.1	51.0	31.3	27.1	14.2
$3,000 to $5,999	29.0	16.6	30.3	36.5	36.3	31.3	15.2
$6,000 to $7,999	9.9	2.1	5.1	8.5	14.0	21.7	20.8
$8,000 to $9,999	4.9	0.7	0.4	2.5	8.8	9.4	14.5
$10,000 to $14,999	4.2	0.2	—	1.1	5.4	9.7	27.0
$15,000 and over	0.7	—		0.4	0.3	0.8	8.5
Mean Income	$3,689	$2,027	$2,481	$3,294	$4,455	$5,313	$8,173
Mean Income, Full-time Females	$7,236	$4,506	$5,477	$6,923	$7,923	$10,163

(Percentages may not add to 100.0 due to rounding;—represents zero or rounds to zero.)

Explanation: The tables above demonstrate that while income tends to rise with educational attainment, it rises far less for women and blacks than for white men. For every year of schooling, the black man tends to gain less than his white counterpart. (Black women appear to improve their incomes in comparison with white women, but this is probably because more black women tend to work full-time.)

Looking at the mean incomes for full-time workers, we can see that all women tend to make only a little more than half the earnings of men with the same educational attainments.

---

100 Years of Public Schools

Source: Office of Education, Dept. of Health, Education and Welfare

Pupils and teachers (in thousands)	1869-70	1899-1900	1909-10	1919-20	1929-30	1939-40	1949-50	1959-60	1969-70	1971-72
Total U. S. population	39,818	75,995	90,492	104,512	121,770	130,880	148,665	179,323	203,212	206,217
Population 5-17 years of age	12,055	21,573	24,009	27,556	31,417	30,150	30,168	43,881	52,490	52,297
Percent aged 5-17 years	30.3	28.4	26.5	26.4	25.8	23.0	20.3	24.5	25.8	25.4
Enrollment:										
Elementary and Secondary	6,872	15,503	17,814	21,578	25,678	25,434	25,111	36,087	45,619	46,081
Percent pop. 5-17 enrolled	57.0	71.9	74.2	78.3	81.7	84.4	83.2	82.2	86.9	88.1
Percent in high schools	1.2	3.3	5.1	10.2	17.1	26.0	22.7	23.5	28.5	30.0
High school graduates		62	111	231	592	1,143	1,063	1,627	2,589	2,708
Average school term (in days)	132.2	144.3	157.5	161.9	172.7	175.0	177.9	178.0	178.9	179.3
Total instructional staff				678	880	912	962	1,464	2,253	2,322
Teachers, librarians: Men	78	127	110	93	140	195	195	402	691	737
Women	123	296	413	565	703	681	719	985	1,440	1,450
Percent men	38.7	29.9	21.1	14.1	16.6	22.2	21.3	29.0	32.4	33.7
Receipts & Expenditures (in millions)										
Total receipts		$219	$433	$970	$2,088	$2,260	$5,437	$14,746	$40,227	$50,004
Total expenditures	$63	214	426	1,036	2,316	2,344	5,837	15,613[1]	40,683	48,050
Current, elem. and secondary		179	356	861	1,843	1,941	4,687	12,329	34,218	41,818
Capital outlay		35	69	153	370	257	1,014	2,661	4,659	4,459
Interest on school debt				18	92	130	100	489	1,171	1,378
Other				3	9	13	35	132	636	395
Salaries and Pupil Cost	Data in unadjusted dollars					Data in adjusted dollars				
Average annual teacher salary[2]	$189	$325	$485	$1,554	$3,133	$3,894	$4,801	$6,651	$8,840	$10,100
Expenditure per capita total pop.	1.59	2.83	4.71	17.68	41.98	48.40	62.63	111.93	200.20	233.01
Current expenditure per pupil ADA[3]		16.67	27.85	95.15	191.27	238.05	333.06	482.24	815.98	989.67

(1) Because of a modification of the scope, "current expenditures for elementary and secondary schools" data for 1959-60 and later years are not entirely comparable with data for prior years. (2) Includes supervisors, principals, teachers and other non-supervisory instructional staff. (3) "ADA" means average daily attendance in elementary and secondary day schools.

Educational Attainment by Age, Race and Sex

Source: Bureau of the Census   (Number of Persons in thousands)

1974 Age, Race and Sex	Total Pop.	Elementary			High School				College				
		5 years	6 & 7 years	8 years	1 year	2 years	3 years	4 years	1 year	2 years	3 years	4 years	5 or more
White													
Total, 14 years and over	138,798	1,507	7,743	15,561	9,232	10,402	7,913	48,267	7,200	7,879	3,355	9,872	6,108
14 and 15 years	7,133	33	1,816	3,287	1,855	104	12	6	-	-	-	-	-
16 and 17 years	7,026	4	107	439	1,741	2,887	1,646	157	9	6	1	-	-
18 and 19 years	6,676	3	67	119	257	451	1,319	3,541	799	74	14	4	1
20 and 21 years	6,441	6	70	125	207	238	267	2,835	1,040	1,025	508	81	2
22 to 24 years	8,998	26	123	174	232	353	356	3,692	786	929	684	1,291	296
25 years and over	102,524	1,435	5,560	11,417	4,941	6,369	4,313	38,037	4,566	5,845	2,147	8,496	5,809
Male, 14 years and over	66,550	735	3,970	7,651	4,326	4,798	3,710	20,690	3,573	4,025	1,751	5,267	4,155
14 and 15 years	3,635	21	1,061	1,701	800	33	5	-	-	-	-	-	-
16 and 17 years	3,564	2	74	264	953	1,434	767	50	5	2	-	-	-
18 and 19 years	3,264	3	30	59	126	252	726	1,642	375	28	3	3	1
20 and 21 years	3,135	3	24	50	89	118	119	1,342	578	516	256	23	2
22 to 24 years	4,417	12	67	81	124	171	177	1,628	417	527	399	606	181
25 years and over	48,534	694	2,714	5,496	2,235	2,790	1,916	16,028	2,198	2,952	1,092	4,635	3,971
25 to 29 years	6,870	27	118	230	181	245	210	2,595	544	604	295	1,060	680
30 to 34 years	5,752	34	132	214	182	266	225	2,269	332	464	152	657	741
35 to 44 years	9,772	97	400	616	416	538	399	3,666	447	628	235	1,071	1,045
45 to 54 years	10,201	122	469	1,020	523	660	476	3,659	463	583	194	949	788
55 to 64 years	8,212	129	635	1,415	473	623	410	2,486	246	440	110	471	434
65 to 74 years	5,134	162	617	1,266	332	336	141	1,012	109	174	72	312	225
75 years and over	2,593	124	343	736	128	123	55	340	56	60	35	116	58
Female, 14 years and over	72,248	772	3,773	7,910	4,906	5,604	4,203	27,577	3,628	3,854	1,604	4,605	1,953
14 and 15 years	3,498	12	755	1,586	1,055	71	8	6	-	-	-	-	-
16 and 17 years	3,462	3	33	174	787	1,454	879	107	4	5	1	-	-
18 and 19 years	3,412	-	37	60	131	199	593	1,898	424	46	11	1	-
20 and 21 years	3,306	3	47	75	118	120	148	1,493	462	508	252	57	-
22 to 24 years	4,580	14	56	93	108	182	179	2,064	369	403	284	685	115
25 years and over	53,990	740	2,846	5,922	2,706	3,578	2,397	22,009	2,368	2,892	1,055	3,862	1,838
25 to 29 years	6,966	17	125	164	232	331	268	3,181	493	561	219	961	347
30 to 34 years	5,838	26	110	199	205	348	288	2,894	331	350	139	597	301
35 to 44 years	10,081	76	324	476	491	681	501	4,978	503	524	193	785	386
45 to 54 years	10,893	114	447	935	530	789	580	5,148	429	555	201	610	325
55 to 64 years	9,185	130	609	1,445	560	721	444	3,376	341	404	156	455	249
65 to 74 years	6,734	192	702	1,483	479	492	199	1,671	184	313	84	317	170
75 years and over	4,293	185	528	1,220	209	218	118	760	87	185	64	136	60
Negro & Other Races													
Total, 14 years and over	18,486	472	1,838	1,819	1,706	1,823	1,399	4,944	733	751	294	717	431
14 and 15 years	1,276	19	426	485	302	24	3	3	-	-	-	-	-
16 and 17 years	1,230	7	50	156	378	407	206	20	-	-	-	-	-
18 and 19 years	1,096	-	20	57	63	141	252	467	80	9	2	-	-
20 and 21 years	1,001	-	17	19	52	85	93	427	144	102	45	12	2
22 to 24 years	1,401	2	38	45	80	113	79	604	86	131	72	113	27
25 years and over	12,481	445	1,287	1,057	831	1,053	767	3,423	423	509	175	593	403
Male, 14 years and over	8,490	216	907	890	753	747	622	2,100	334	341	137	346	249
14 and 15 years	638	9	253	221	135	9	3	1	-	-	-	-	-
16 and 17 years	613	5	33	110	179	195	82	5	-	-	-	-	-
18 and 19 years	510	-	10	40	32	69	134	185	33	-	2	-	-
20 and 21 years	455	-	9	9	34	42	47	186	65	38	19	2	-
22 to 24 years	640	1	16	15	43	53	39	262	38	63	39	51	13
25 years and over	5,633	201	586	494	330	378	316	1,459	198	240	76	293	236
25 to 29 years	854	2	18	27	32	55	57	374	71	68	25	66	37
30 to 34 years	746	7	30	21	44	58	62	254	55	37	25	65	66
35 to 44 years	1,235	31	104	92	86	116	84	401	31	65	16	77	65
45 to 54 years	1,159	41	150	143	92	71	72	278	24	39	5	47	41
55 to 64 years	839	43	144	131	44	63	26	109	11	14	4	30	12
65 to 74 years	546	43	94	57	24	16	12	33	3	11	-	9	9
75 years and over	255	34	46	24	8	-	2	11	1	5	1	-	6
Female, 14 years and over	9,996	256	931	930	952	1,077	778	2,844	399	411	157	372	182
14 and 15 years	638	9	173	264	168	16	-	2	-	-	-	-	-
16 and 17 years	617	1	17	47	200	212	124	15	-	-	-	-	-
18 and 19 years	586	-	10	17	31	72	118	281	47	9	-	-	-
20 and 21 years	546	-	8	10	18	43	45	241	79	65	25	10	2
22 to 24 years	761	2	22	30	37	59	40	342	48	68	33	62	14
25 years and over	6,848	243	701	563	500	675	451	1,964	225	269	99	299	167
25 to 29 years	1,042	4	36	36	49	115	82	438	61	67	40	73	31
30 to 34 years	904	6	39	35	56	105	67	359	52	54	17	71	31
35 to 44 years	1,527	28	106	117	125	184	112	528	63	72	25	73	44
45 to 54 years	1,349	49	151	135	122	144	106	378	30	44	8	31	36
55 to 64 years	979	62	163	115	77	83	49	170	14	21	3	36	15
65 to 74 years	678	56	142	93	51	33	28	57	3	7	4	7	9
75 years and over	369	39	65	32	19	11	7	34	2	4	3	8	-

Education Pays — Black or White
Source: Bureau of the Census
(— represents zero or rounds to zero. B means base less than 75,000.)

Race, Age, Income, Occupation (1973)	Total (1,000)	0-8	9-11	12	13-15	16	16+	Median Years
White employed males, age 25-44	**20,336**	**934**	**2,399**	**7,797**	**3,333**	**2,599**	**2,290**	**12.8**
Under $3,000	844	57	123	243	138	85	69	12.5
$3,000-$5,999	1,835	171	333	564	238	136	136	12.3
$6,000-$9,999	5,086	335	771	2,107	795	458	259	12.5
$10,000-$14,999	7,236	262	852	3,253	1,231	809	641	12.7
$15,000 & over	5,334	109	320	1,630	931	1,111	1,186	14.8
White-collar workers	**9,523**	**103**	**391**	**2,526**	**1,962**	**2,269**	**2,200**	**15.6**
Under $6,000	791	13	58	196	183	139	178	14.7
$6,000 & over	8,732	90	333	2,330	1,779	2,130	2,022	14.8
Blue-collar workers	**9,099**	**718**	**1,820**	**4,483**	**1,081**	**221**	**57**	**12.3**
Under $6,000	1,366	154	325	446	135	55	9	12.1
$6,000 & over	7,733	564	1,495	4,037	946	166	48	12.4
Service workers	**1,077**	**49**	**119**	**518**	**227**	**67**	**24**	**12.6**
Under $6,000	237	15	37	74	35	17	14	12.1
$6,000 & over	840	34	82	444	192	50	10	12.7
Farm workers	**637**	**63**	**70**	**270**	**63**	**42**	**9**	**12.2**
Under $6,000	285	46	36	92	22	9	5	10.2
$6,000 & over	352	17	34	178	41	33	4	12.5
Black employed males, age 25-44	**1,970**	**99**	**482**	**754**	**261**	**98**	**55**	**12.2**
Under $3,000	197	15	61	49	19	—	2	10.6
$3,000-$5,999	418	36	136	118	34	8	4	11.0
$6,000-$9,999	712	40	179	305	91	36	10	12.3
$10,000-$14,999	506	7	84	241	86	33	24	12.5
$15,000 & over	137	2	22	41	31	21	15	13.0
White-collar workers	**487**	**6**	**11**	**172**	**114**	**84**	**55**	**13.3**
Under $6,000	79	—	8	38	20	5	6	(B)
$6,000 & over	409	6	33	124	94	79	49	13.3
Blue-collar workers	**1,220**	**68**	**376**	**491**	**112**	**14**	**—**	**12.0**
Under $6,000	406	35	148	100	21	3	—	10.4
$6,000 & over	814	33	228	391	91	11	—	12.3
Service workers	**217**	**17**	**49**	**88**	**35**	**—**	**—**	**12.2**
Under $6,000	84	7	25	26	14	—	—	12.2
$6,000 & over	133	10	24	62	21	—	—	12.2
Farm workers	**46**	**8**	**16**	**3**	**—**	**—**	**—**	**(B)**
Under $6,000	46	8	16	3	—	—	—	(B)
$6,000 & over	—	—	—	—	—	—	—	(B)
White employed males, age 45-64	**15,524**	**1,878**	**2,620**	**5,395**	**1,806**	**1,278**	**1,159**	**12.3**
Under $3,000	647	126	123	152	49	22	19	10.0
$3,000-$5,999	1,359	253	259	366	85	44	43	10.4
$6,000-$9,999	3,595	629	794	1,176	265	126	78	11.4
$10,000-$14,999	5,086	592	953	2,116	575	304	228	12.3
$15,000 & over	4,866	279	493	1,585	831	782	791	13.0
White-collar workers	**6,958**	**293**	**622**	**2,340**	**1,290**	**1,161**	**1,126**	**13.2**
Under $6,000	517	51	84	161	89	50	59	12.7
$6,000 & over	6,441	242	538	2,179	1,201	1,111	1,067	12.8
Blue-collar workers	**6,680**	**1,201**	**1,602**	**2,420**	**402**	**76**	**21**	**11.2**
Under $6,000	849	190	173	189	28	8	2	8.9
$6,000 & over	5,831	1,011	1,429	2,231	374	68	19	12.2
Service workers	**1,028**	**184**	**242**	**363**	**71**	**17**	**2**	**11.2**
Under $6,000	253	50	52	67	11	1	—	9.8
$6,000 & over	775	134	190	296	60	16	2	12.2
Farm workers	**888**	**201**	**155**	**272**	**43**	**23**	**10**	**10.2**
Under $6,000	387	89	73	100	6	7	2	8.9
$6,000 & over	501	112	82	172	37	16	8	12.1
Black employed males, age 45-64	**1,347**	**192**	**270**	**252**	**65**	**42**	**29**	**8.9**
Under $3,000	162	21	14	30	3	4	—	7.4
$3,000-$5,999	369	63	63	36	6	1	—	7.6
$6,000-$9,999	432	68	110	79	18	12	8	9.3
$10,000-$14,999	273	25	70	86	18	9	9	11.4
$15,000 & over	111	14	13	22	21	16	12	12.7
White-collar workers	**211**	**19**	**23**	**72**	**27**	**27**	**27**	**12.7**
Under $6,000	40	5	7	16	2	2	—	(B)
$6,000 & over	171	14	16	56	25	25	27	(B)
Blue-collar workers	**782**	**131**	**166**	**126**	**31**	**10**	**—**	**8.6**
Under $6,000	298	61	34	26	6	1	—	7.0
$6,000 & over	484	70	132	100	25	9	—	10.6
Service workers	**287**	**38**	**77**	**49**	**7**	**6**	**2**	**8.9**
Under $6,000	136	17	33	18	1	2	—	7.9
$6,000 & over	151	21	44	31	6	4	2	9.5
Farm workers	**67**	**4**	**3**	**4**	**—**	**—**	**—**	**(B)**
Under $6,000	58	2	3	4	—	—	—	(B)
$6,000 & over	9	2	—	—	—	—	—	(B)

The Principal Languages of the World

Source: Sidney S. Culbert, Assoc. Professor of Psychology, University of Washington

Total number of speakers of languages spoken by at least one million persons (Midyear 1975)
Parenthesized numbers after names of languages refer to notes below table.

	Millions		Millions		Millions
Afrikaans (S. Africa)	5	Ilocano (Philippines)	4	Pashto (see Pushtu)	
Albanian	3	Iloko (see Ilocano)		Pedi (see Sotho, Northern)	
Amharic (Ethiopia)	9	Indonesian		Persian	24
Annamese (see Vietnamese)		(see Malay-Indonesian)		Polish	35
Arabic	125	Italian	60	Portuguese	124
Armenian	4	Japanese	110	Provencal (Southern France)	6
Assamese (1) (India)	13	Javanese	44	Punjabi (1) (India; Pakistan)	55
Azerbaijani (USSR; Iran)	8	Kamba (E. Africa)	1	Pushtu (mainly Afghanistan)	15
Bahase (See Malay-Indonesian)		Kanarese (see Kannada)		Quechua (S. America)	6
Balinese	3	Kannada (1) (India)	28	Rajasthani (India)	21
Baluchi (Pakistan; Iran)	3	Kanuri (W. and Cent. Africa)	2	Romanian	22
Bashkir (USSR)	1	Kashmiri (1)	3	Rundi (S. Central Africa)	3
Batak (Indonesia)	2	Kazakh (USSR)	5	Russian (Great Russian only)	233
Bemba (S. Central Africa)	1	Khalkha (Mongolia)	1	Rwanda (S. Central Africa)	6
Bengali (1) (Bangladesh; India)	123	Kikongo (see Kongo)		Samar-Leyte (Philippines)	1
Berber (2) (N. Africa)		Kikuyu (or Gekoyo) (Kenya)	2	Sango (Central Africa)	1
Bhili (India)	4	Kimbundu (see Mbundu-Kim.)		Santali (India)	4
Bihari (India)	22	Kirghiz (USSR)	2	Sepedi (see Sotho, Northern)	
Bikol (Philippines)	2	Kituba (Congo River)	2	Serbo-Croatian (Yugoslavia)	18
Bisaya (see Cebuano, Panay-		Kongo (Congo River)	1	Shan (Burma)	1
Hiligaynon, and Samar-Leyte)		Konkani (India)	2	Shona (S.E. Africa)	4
Bugi (Indonesia)	2	Korean	52	Siamese (see Thai)	
Bulgarian	9	Kumauni (India)	1	Sindhi (India; Pakistan)	9
Burmese	23	Kurdish (S.W. of Caspian Sea)	7	Sinhalese (Sri Lanka)	10
Byelorussian (mainly USSR)	10	Kurukh (or Oraon) (India)	1	Slovak	4
Cambodian (Cambodia, Asia)	7	Lao (5) (Laos, Asia)	3	Slovene (Yugoslavia)	2
Canarese (see Kannada)		Latvian (or Lettish)	2	Somali (E. Africa)	4
Cantonese (China)	47	Lingala (see Ngala)		Sotho, Northern (S. Africa)	2
Catalan (Spain; France; Andorra)	6	Lithuanian	3	Sotho, Southern (S. Africa)	2
Cebuano (Philippines)	8	Luba-Lulua (Zaire)	3	Spanish	213
Chinese (3)		Luganda (see Ganda)		Sundanese (Indonesia)	15
Chuang (7) (China)		Luhya (or Luhia) (Kenya)	1	Swahili (E. Africa)	20
Chuvash (USSR)	2	Luo (Kenya)	1	Swedish	10
Czech	11	Luri (Iran)	1	Tagalog (Philippines)	21
Danish	5	Macedonian (Yugoslavia)	1	Tajiki (USSR)	3
Dayak (Borneo)	1	Madurese (Indonesia)	7	Tamil (1) (India; Sri Lanka)	*53
Dutch (see Netherlandish)		Makua (S.E. Africa)	2	Tatar (or Kazan-Turkic) (USSR)	6
Edo (W. Africa)	1	Malagasy (Madagascar)	8	Telugu (1) (India)	53
Efik	2	Malay-Indonesian	95	Thai (5)	30
English	358	Malayalam (1) (India)	24	Tibetan	7
Esperanto	1	Malinke-Bambara-Dyula (Africa)	5	Tigrinya (Ethiopia)	4
Estonian	1	Mandarin (China)	650	Tiv (E. Central Nigeria)	1
Ewe (W. Africa)	2	Mazandarani (Iran)	1	Tswana (S. Africa)	2
Finnish	5	Marathi (1) (India)	51	Tulu (India)	1
Flemish (see Netherlandish)		Mbundu (Umbundu group)		Turkish	39
French	90	(S. Angola)	2	Turkoman (USSR)	2
Fula (W. Africa)	7	Mbundu (Kimbundu group)		Twi-Fante (or Akan) (W. Africa)	4
Galician (Spain)	2	(Angola)	1	Uighur-(Sinkiang, China)	4
Galla (Ethiopia)	7	Mende (Sierra Leone)	1	Ukrainian (mainly USSR)	42
Ganda (or Luganda) (E. Africa)	3	Min (China)	39	Umbundu	
Georgian (USSR)	3	Moldavian (ind. w/Rumanian)		(see Mbundu-Umbundu)	
German	120	Mongolian (see Khalkha)		Urdu (1) (Pakistan; India)	57
Gilaki (Iran)	1	Mordvin (USSR)	1	Uzbek (USSR)	9
Gondi (India)	2	More (see Mossi)		Vietnamese	37
Greek	10	Mossi (W. Africa)	3	Visayan (see Cebuano, Panay-	
Guarani (mainly Paraguay)	3	Ndongo (see Mbundu-Kimbundu)		Hiligaynon, and Samar-Leyte)	
Gujarati (1) (India)	30	Nepali (Nepal; India)	10	White Russian (see Byelorussion)	
Hakka (China)	21	Netherlandish (Dutch and Flem.)	20	Wolof (W. Africa)	2
Hausa (W. and Central Africa)	18	Ngala (or Lingala) (Africa)	2	Wu (China)	42
Hebrew	3	Norwegian	4	Xhosa (S. Africa)	4
Hindi (1) (4)	209	Nyamwezi-Sukuma (S.E. Africa)	1	Yi (China)	3
Hindustani (4)		Nyanja (S.E. Africa)	2	Yiddish (6)	
Hungarian (or Magyar)	13	Oraon (see Kurukh)		Yoruba (W. Africa)	12
Ibibio (see Efik)		Oriya (1) (India)	23	Zhuang (7) (China)	
Ibo (or Igbo) (W. Africa)	10	Panay-Hiligaynon (Philippines)	4	Zulu (S. Africa)	4
Ijaw (W. Africa)		Panjabi (see Punjabi)			

(1.) One of the fourteen languages of the Constitution of India. (2.) Here considered a group of dialects. (3.) See Mandarin, Cantonese, Wu, Min, and Hakka. The "national language" (Guoyu) is a standardized form of Mandarin as spoken in the area of Peking. (4.) Hindi and Urdu are essentially the same language, Hindustani. As the official language of India it is written in the Devanagari script and called Hindi. As the official language of Pakistan it is written in a modified Arabic script and called Urdu. (5.) Thai includes Central, Southwestern, Northern and Northeastern Thai. The distinction between Northeastern Thai and Lao is political rather than linguistic. (6.) Yiddish is usually considered a variant of German, though it has its own standard grammar, dictionaries, a highly developed literature, and is written in Hebrew characters. Speakers number about 3,000,000. (7.) A group of Thai-like dialects with about 9 million speakers.

UNITED STATES POPULATION

Metropolitan Population Growth Slowing to a Stop

By Vincent P. Barabba
Director, U.S. Bureau of the Census

On January 1, 1975, the population of the United States including Armed Forces overseas was estimated at 212.8 million.

During 1974, the nation's population increased by 1.6 million, the result of 3.2 million births, 1.9 million deaths, and 360,000 added by net immigration. This compares with a net gain of 1.5 million in 1973.

Metropolitan Growth

One of the important changes since 1970 in the long-standing patterns of population and redistribution in the United States is the fact that metropolitan areas are no longer growing faster than nonmetropolitan parts of the nation. In 1974 over two-thirds of the population lived in standard metropolitan statistical areas (SMSA's), which are comprised of counties with cities of 50,000 or more inhabitants together with neighboring counties that are closely associated with them by daily commuting ties. Between 1970 and 1974, the population of SMSA's increased 3.8 percent; metropolitan population rose 5.0 percent.

The largest metropolitan areas have shown the least growth since 1970. Of the eight metropolitan areas with more than 3 million people, seven have shown little or no growth since 1970. Only the Washington, D.C., SMSA has grown significantly during this period.

The central cities of metropolitan areas have lost population since 1970. This loss is accounted for entirely by declines in the white population. The population of Negro and other races has decreased in nonmetropolitan areas, and increased in metropolitan areas since 1970. The increase among Negro and other races in central cities has been 1.9 percent per year since 1970, a lower annual increase than in the 1960's, however. At the same time, the population of Negro and other races living in the balance of SMSA's outside central cities (mostly suburban areas) grew 6 percent per year from 1970 to 1974, an annual gain greater than in the 1960's. Even so, only 26 percent of the metropolitan population of Negro and other races lived outside central cities in 1974, compared with 62 percent of their white counterparts.

The relatively high rate of growth shown by nonmetropolitan areas since 1970 represents increases in nonfarm areas but does not provide any evidence of a significant return migration by metropolitan dwellers to farm communities or pursuits. In fact, the farm population, after recording an average annual decrease of 4.8 percent during the 1960's, appears to have reached a point of stability at about 9.5 million.

Fertility

In 1974, the total fertility rate—the number of births 1,000 women would have in their lifetimes based upon the birth rates occurring in a given calendar year—was estimated to be 1.86. This compares with 1.90 in 1973. The lowest level prior to the early 1970's was 2.24 in 1935-39, and the most recent high level was 3.69 in 1955-59. The 1974 figure is the lowest level in the history of the United States. It requires 2.1 children per woman for the population to replace itself in the long run assuming there is no immigration.

Data from a special survey on the number of births expected by young wives suggest that the two-child family is becoming by far the most popular size in the U.S. In 1974, 57 percent of white wives and 42 percent of black wives 18 to 24 years old expected to have two children—no more and no fewer. This compares with an average of 2.3 children in 1973.

Marriages and Divorces

An estimated 2,223,000 marriages were contracted and 970,000 divorces granted in the United States during 1974. These figures represent a 2 percent decline in the number of marriages, and a 6 percent increase in the number of divorces from those recorded during 1973 (2,277,000 marriages and 913,000 divorces). During 1970, the total of marriages was 2,159,000, and divorces, 708,000.

The decline in marriages in 1974 came when the large number of persons born as a result of the post World War II baby boom were reaching the young adult ages. Therefore, this is a period when a great number of marriages would have ordinarily been expected.

However, there has been an increasing tendency among young men and women to postpone marriage. For all women 20 to 24 years old, the proportion single increased from about 36 percent in 1970 to 40 percent in 1974. This continues a pattern of increasing singleness among women of this age since 1960, when only about 28 percent were reported as never having been married.

The estimated median ages at first marriage for men and women in 1974 were 23.1 and 21.1 years, respectively. These figures represent an increase over the mid-1960's of about one-half year for men and one full year for women.

Whether the delay in first marriage among young adults represents a trend toward more life-long singleness, or a trend toward more careful mate selection coupled with a desire to pursue advanced educational goals or career experiences remains to be seen.

In 1974 there were 63 divorced persons for every 1,000 who were married and living with their spouse. This ratio had increased from a level of 47 per 1,000 in 1970 and 35 per 1,000 in 1960. The amount of increase was similar for both sexes as well as white persons and persons of Negro and other races.

Differences, however, existed in the level of the ratios between sex, race, and age groups. Women had higher ratios than men—77 per 1,000 compared to 44 per 1,000 in 1974—reflecting the generally higher propensity for divorced men to remarry than divorced women. Persons of Negro and other races had higher ratios than whites, 112 per 1,000 compared to 58 per 1,000 in 1974. And younger persons (under 45) had higher ratios in 1974 than older persons (45 years and over), indicating a more rapid rise in divorce among younger couples than among older couples.

Voting

The American electorate was the largest ever in 1974—141 million persons were eligible to vote on the basis of age. Ratification of the 26th Amendment to the Constitution in 1971 lowered the voting age in national elections in all states to 18 years and produced the largest 2-year increase in the size of the electorate since the enfranchisement of women in 1920.

The 1974 Congressional election produced the lowest number of voters in any Congressional election since 1966, despite an increase during the eight years of 28 million in the number of eligibles. Much of the decline in turnout resulted from diminished voter interest, as evidenced by a drop in registration from 70 to 62 percent of the eligibles, and a drop from 79 to 72 percent of the registered who reported that they had cast a ballot.

United States Population (Official Census), 1790-1880

Source: Bureau of the Census

State	1790	1800	1810	1820	1830'	1840'	1850	1860	1870	1880
Ala.	. . . . .	1,250	9,046'	127,901	309,527	590,756	771,623	964,201	996,992	1,262,505
Ariz.									9,658	40,440
Ark.	. . . . .	. . . . .	1,062	14,273	30,388	97,574	209,897	435,450	484,471	802,525
Cal.	. . . . .	. . . . .					92,597	379,994	560,247	864,694
Col.								34,277	39,864	194,327
Conn. . . .	237,946	251,002	261,942	275,248	297,675	309,978	370,792	460,147	537,454	622,700
Del.	59,096	64,273	72,674	72,749	76,748	78,085	91,532	112,216	125,015	146,608
D.C.		14,093	24,023	33,039	39,834	43,712	51,687	75,080	131,700	177,624
Fla.					34,730	54,477	87,445	140,424	187,748	269,493
Ga.	82,548	162,686	252,433	340,989	516,823	691,392	906,185	1,057,286	1,184,109	1,542,180
Ida.									14,999	32,610
Ill.			12,282	55,211	157,445	476,183	851,470	1,711,951	2,539,891	3,077,871
Ind.		5,641	24,520	147,178	343,031	685,866	988,416	1,350,428	1,680,637	1,978,301
Iowa. . . .						43,112	192,214	674,913	1,194,020	1,624,615
Kan.								107,206	364,399	996,096
Ky.	73,677	220,995	406,511	564,317	687,917	779,828	982,405	1,155,684	1,321,011	1,648,690
La.			76,556	153,407	215,739	352,411	517,762	708,002	726,915	939,946
Me.	96,540	151,719	228,705	298,335	399,455	501,793	583,169	628,279	626,915	648,936
Md.	319,728	341,548	380,546	407,350	447,040	470,019	583,034	687,049	780,894	934,943
Mass. . . .	378,787	422,845	472,040	523,287	610,408	737,699	994,514	1,231,066	1,457,351	1,783,085
Mich. . . .			4,762	8,896	31,639	212,267	397,654	749,113	1,184,059	1,636,937
Minn. . . .							6,077	172,023	439,706	780,773
Miss. . . .		8,850	40,352	75,448	136,621	375,651	606,526	791,305	827,922	1,131,597
Mo.			19,783	66,586	140,455	383,702	682,044	1,182,012	1,721,295	2,168,380
Mon.									20,595	39,159
Neb.								28,841	122,993	452,402
Nev.								6,857	42,491	62,266
N. H.	141,885	183,858	214,460	244,161	269,328	284,574	317,976	326,073	318,300	346,991
N. J.	184,139	211,149	245,562	277,575	320,823	373,306	489,555	672,035	906,096	1,131,116
N. M.							61,547	93,516	91,874	119,565
N. Y.	340,120	589,051	959,049	1,372,812	1,918,608	2,428,921	3,097,394	3,880,735	4,382,759	5,082,871
N. C.	393,751	478,103	555,500	638,829	737,987	753,419	869,039	992,622	1,071,361	1,399,750
N. D.									*2,405	36,909
Oh.		45,365	230,760	581,434	937,903	1,519,467	1,980,329	2,339,511	2,665,260	3,198,062
Okla.										
Ore.							13,294	52,465	90,923	174,768
Pa.	434,373	602,365	810,091	1,049,458	1,348,233	1,724,033	2,311,786	2,906,215	3,521,951	4,282,891
R. I.	68,825	69,122	76,931	83,059	97,199	108,830	147,545	174,620	217,353	276,531
S. C.	249,073	345,591	415,115	502,741	581,185	594,398	668,507	703,708	705,606	995,577
S. D.								*4,837	*11,776	98,268
Tenn. . . .	35,691	105,602	261,727	422,823	681,904	829,210	1,002,717	1,109,801	1,258,520	1,542,359
Tex.							212,592	604,215	818,579	1,591,749
Ut.							11,380	40,273	86,786	143,963
Vt.	85,425	154,465	217,895	235,981	280,652	291,948	314,120	315,098	330,551	332,286
Va.	821,287	880,200	974,600	1,065,366	1,211,405	1,239,797	1,421,661	1,596,318	1,225,163	1,512,565
Wash. . . .							1,201	11,594	23,955	75,116
W. Va. . . .									442,014	618,457
Wis.						30,945	305,391	775,881	1,054,670	1,315,497
Wy.									9,118	20,789
U.S.	3,929,214	5,308,483	7,239,881	9,638,453	12,866,020	17,069,453	23,191,876	31,443,321	38,558,371	50,155,783

*1860 figure is for Dakota Territory; 1870 figures are for parts of Dakota Territory.

(1.) U.S. total includes persons (5,318 in 1830 and 6,100 in 1840) on public ships in the service of the United States not credited to any region, division, or state.

U.S. Center of Population, 1790-1970

Center of population is that point which may be considered as center of population gravity of the U.S. or that point upon which the U.S. would balance if it were a rigid plane without weight and the population distributed thereon with each individual being assumed to have equal weight and to exert an influence on a central point proportional to his distance from that point.

Year	North latitude ° ' "	West longitude ° ' "	Approximate location
1790.	39 16 30	76 11 12	23 miles east of Baltimore, Md.
1800.	39 16 6	76 56 30	18 miles west of Baltimore, Md.
1810.	39 11 30	77 37 12	40 miles northwest by west of Washington, D.C. (in Va.)
1820.	39 5 42	78 33 0	16 miles east of Moorefield, W. Va.¹
1830.	38 57 54	79 16 54	19 miles west-southwest of Moorefield, W. Va.¹
1840.	39 2 0	80 18 0	16 miles south of Clarksburg, W. Va.¹
1850.	38 59 0	81 19 0	23 miles southeast of Parkersburg, W. Va.¹
1860.	39 0 24	82 48 48	20 miles south by east of Chillicothe, Oh.
1870.	39 12 0	83 35 42	48 miles east by north of Cincinnati, Oh.
1880.	39 4 8	84 39 40	8 miles west by south of Cincinnati, Oh. (in Ky.)
1890.	39 11 56	85 32 53	20 miles east of Columbus, Ind.
1900.	39 9 36	85 48 54	6 miles southeast of Columbus, Ind.
1910.	39 10 12	86 32 20	In the city of Bloomington, Ind.
1920.	39 10 21	86 43 15	8 miles south-southeast of Spencer, Owen County, Ind.
1930.	39 3 45	87 8 6	3 miles northeast of Linton, Greene County, Ind.
1940.	38 56 54	87 22 35	2 miles southeast by east of Carlisle, Haddon township, Sullivan County, Ind. . . . .
1950 (Inc. Alaska & Hawaii)	38 48 15	88 22 8	3 miles northeast of Louisville, Clay County, Ill.
1960 (Inc. Alaska & Hawaii)	38 35 58	89 12 35	6¹/₂ miles northwest of Centralia, Ill.
1970 (Inc. Alaska & Hawaii) . . . 38	27 47	89 42 22	5 miles east southeast of Mascoutah, St. Clair County, Ill.

(1) West Virginia was set off from Virginia Dec. 31, 1862, and admitted as a State June 20, 1863.

United States Population (Official Census) 1890-1970

Source: Bureau of the Census

State	1890	1900	1910	1920	1930	1940	1950	1960	1970
Ala.	1,513,401	1,828,697	2,138,093	2,348,174	2,646,248	2,832,961	3,061,743	3,266,740	3,444,165
Alaska.							226,167	302,173	
Ariz.	88,243	122,931	204,354	334,162	435,573	499,261	749,587	1,302,161	1,772,482
Ark.	1,128,211	1,311,564	1,574,449	1,752,204	1,854,482	1,949,387	1,909,511	1,786,272	1,923,295
Cal.	1,213,398	1,485,053	2,377,549	3,426,861	5,677,251	6,907,387	10,586,223	15,717,204	19,953,134
Col.	413,249	539,700	799,024	939,629	1,035,791	1,123,296	1,325,089	1,753,947	2,207,259
Conn.	746,258	908,420	1,114,756	1,380,631	1,606,903	1,709,242	2,007,280	2,535,234	3,032,217
Del.	168,493	184,735	202,322	223,003	238,380	266,505	318,085	446,292	548,104
D.C.	230,392	278,718	331,069	437,571	486,869	663,091	802,178	763,956	756,510
Fla.	391,422	528,542	752,619	968,470	1,468,211	1,897,414	2,771,305	4,951,560	6,789,443
Ga.	1,837,353	2,216,331	2,609,121	2,895,832	2,908,506	3,123,723	3,444,578	3,943,116	4,589,575
Ha.								632,772	769,913
Ida.	88,548	161,772	325,594	431,866	445,032	524,873	588,637	667,191	713,008
Ill.	3,826,352	4,821,550	5,638,591	6,485,280	7,630,654	7,897,241	8,712,176	10,081,158	11,113,976
Ind.	2,192,404	2,516,462	2,700,876	2,930,390	3,238,503	3,427,796	3,934,224	4,662,498	5,193,669
Iowa.	1,912,297	2,231,853	2,224,771	2,404,021	2,470,939	2,538,268	2,621,073	2,757,537	2,825,041
Kan.	1,428,108	1,470,495	1,690,949	1,769,257	1,880,999	1,801,028	1,905,299	2,178,611	2,249,071
Ky.	1,858,635	2,147,174	2,289,905	2,416,630	2,614,589	2,845,627	2,944,806	3,038,156	3,219,311
La.	1,118,588	1,381,625	1,656,388	1,798,509	2,101,593	2,363,880	2,683,516	3,257,022	3,643,180
Me.	661,086	694,466	742,371	768,014	797,423	847,226	913,774	969,265	993,663
Md.	1,042,390	1,188,044	1,295,346	1,449,661	1,631,526	1,821,244	2,343,001	3,100,689	3,922,399
Mass.	2,238,947	2,805,346	3,366,416	3,852,356	4,249,614	4,316,721	4,690,514	5,148,578	5,689,170
Mich.	2,093,890	2,420,982	2,810,173	3,668,412	4,842,325	5,256,106	6,371,766	7,823,194	8,875,083
Minn.	1,310,283	1,751,394	2,075,708	2,387,125	2,563,953	2,792,300	2,982,483	3,413,864	3,805,069
Miss.	1,289,600	1,551,270	1,797,114	1,790,618	2,009,821	2,183,796	2,178,914	2,178,141	2,216,912
Mo.	2,679,185	3,106,665	3,293,335	3,404,055	3,629,367	3,784,664	3,954,653	4,319,813	4,677,399
Mon.	142,924	243,329	376,053	548,889	537,606	559,456	591,024	674,767	694,409
Neb.	1,062,656	1,066,300	1,192,214	1,296,372	1,377,963	1,315,834	1,325,510	1,411,330	1,483,791
Nev.	47,355	42,335	81,875	77,407	91,058	110,247	160,083	285,278	488,738
N.H.	376,530	411,588	430,572	443,083	465,293	491,524	533,242	606,921	737,681
N.J.	1,444,933	1,883,669	2,537,167	3,155,900	4,041,334	4,160,165	4,835,329	6,066,782	7,168,164
N.M.	160,282	195,310	327,301	360,350	423,317	531,818	681,187	951,023	1,016,000
N.Y.	6,003,174	7,268,894	9,113,614	10,385,227	12,588,066	13,479,142	14,830,192	16,782,304	18,241,266
N.C.	1,617,949	1,893,810	2,206,287	2,559,123	3,170,276	3,571,623	4,061,929	4,556,155.	5,082,059
N.D.	190,983	319,146	577,056	646,872	680,845	641,935	619,636	632,446	617,761
Oh.	3,672,329	4,157,545	4,767,121	5,759,394	6,646,697	6,907,612	7,946,627	9,706,397	10,652,017
Okla.	258,657	790,391	1,657,155	2,028,283	2,396,040	2,336,434	2,233,351	2,328,284	2,559,253
Ore.	317,704	413,536	672,765	783,389	953,786	1,089,684	1,521,341	1,768,687	2,091,385
Pa.	5,258,113	6,302,115	7,665,111	8,720,017	9,631,350	9,900,180	10,498,012	11,319,366	11,793,909
R.I.	345,506	428,556	542,610	604,397	687,497	713,346	791,896	859,488	949,723
S.C.	1,151,149	1,340,316	1,515,400	1,683,724	1,738,765	1,899,804	2,117,027	2,382,594	2,509,516
S.D.	348,600	401,570	583,888	636,547	692,849	642,961	652,740	680,514	666,257
Tenn.	1,767,518	2,020,616	2,184,789	2,337,885	2,616,556	2,915,841	3,291,718	3,567,089	3,924,164
Tex.	2,235,527	3,048,710	3,896,542	4,663,228	5,824,715	6,414,824	7,711,194	9,579,677	11,196,730
Ut.	210,779	276,749	373,351	449,396	507,847	550,310	688,862	890,627	1,059,273
Vt.	332,422	343,641	355,956	352,428	359,611	359,231	377,747	389,881	444,732
Va.	1,655,980	1,854,184	2,061,612	2,309,187	2,421,851	2,677,773	3,318,680	3,966,949	4,648,494
Wash.	357,232	518,103	1,141,990	1,356,621	1,563,396	1,736,191	2,378,962	2,853,214	3,409,169
W. Va.	762,794	958,800	1,221,119	1,463,701	1,729,205	1,901,974	2,005,553	1,860,421	1,744,237
Wis.	1,693,330	2,069,042	2,333,860	2,632,067	2,939,006	3,137,587	3,434,575	3,951,777	4,417,933
Wy.	62,555	92,531	145,965	194,402	225,565	250,742	290,529	330,066	332,416
Tot. U.S.	62,947,714	75,994,575	91,972,266	105,710,620	122,775,046	131,669,275	150,697,361	179,323,175	203,235,298

Members of the Armed Forces overseas or other U.S. nationals overseas are not included.

50 Cities with the Largest Negro Population

Source: Bureau of the Census

City and State	Rank	1970 Number	%	1960 Number
New York, N. Y.	1	1,666,636	21.2	1,087,931
Chicago, Ill.	2	1,102,620	32.7	812,637
Detroit, Mich.	3	660,428	43.7	482,223
Philadelphia, Pa.	4	653,791	33.6	529,240
Washington, D.C.	5	537,712	71.1	411,737
Los Angeles, Cal.	6	503,606	17.9	334,916
Baltimore, Md.	7	420,210	46.4	325,589
Houston, Tex.	8	316,551	25.7	215,037
Cleveland, Oh.	9	287,841	38.3	250,818
New Orleans, La.	10	267,308	45.0	233,514
Atlanta, Ga.	11	255,051	51.3	186,464
St. Louis, Mo.	12	254,191	40.9	214,377
Memphis, Tenn.	13	242,513	38.9	184,320
Dallas, Tex.	14	210,238	24.9	129,242
Newark, N.J.	15	207,458	54.2	138,035
Indianapolis, Ind.	16	134,320	18.0	98,049
Birmingham, Ala.	17	126,388	42.0	135,113
Cincinnati, Oh.	18	125,070	27.6	108,754
Oakland, Cal.	19	124,710	34.5	83,618
Jacksonville, Fla.	20	118,158	22.3	105,655
Kansas City, Mo.	21	112,005	22.1	83,146
Milwaukee, Wis.	22	105,088	14.7	62,458
Pittsburgh, Pa.	23	104,904	20.2	100,692
Richmond, Va.	24	104,766	42.0	91,972
Boston, Mass.	25	104,707	16.3	63,165
Columbus, Oh.	26	99,627	18.5	77,140
San Francisco, Cal.	27	96,078	13.4	74,383
Buffalo, N.Y.	28	94,329	20.4	70,904
Gary, Ind.	29	92,695	52.8	69,123
Nashville-Davidson, Tenn.	30	87,851	19.6	76,437
Norfolk, Va.	31	87,261	28.3	78,806
Louisville, Ky.	32	86,040	23.8	70,075
Ft. Worth, Tex.	33	78,324	19.9	56,440
Miami, Fla.	34	76,156	22.7	65,213
Dayton, Oh.	35	74,284	30.5	57,288
Charlotte, N.C.	36	72,972	30.3	56,248
Mobile, Ala.	37	67,356	35.4	65,619
Shreveport, La.	38	62,152	34.1	56,607
Jackson, Miss.	39	61,063	39.7	51,556
Compton, Cal.	40	55,781	71.0	28,265
Tampa, Fla.	41	54,720	19.7	46,244
Jersey City, N.J.	42	54,595	21.0	36,692
Flint, Mich.	43	54,237	28.1	34,521
Savannah, Ga.	44	53,111	44.9	53,035
San Diego, Cal.	45	52,961	7.6	34,435
Toledo, Oh.	46	52,915	13.8	40,015
Oklahoma City, Okla.	47	50,103	13.7	37,529
San Antonio, Tex.	48	50,041	7.6	41,605
Rochester, N.Y.	49	49,647	16.8	23,586
E. St. Louis, Ill.	50	48,368	69.1	36,338

Population of the United States, 1960-70

Region, Division, and State	1970 census	1960 census	Pct. + or -	1970 Urban	1970 Rural	Pct. Urban	Rank 1970	Rank 1960
United States..............	203,235,298	179,323,175	13.3	149,324,930	53,886,996	73.5	...	...
Regions:								
Northeast.............	48,999,999	44,677,819	9.7	39,449,818	9,590,885	80.4	...	...
North Central...........	56,577,067	51,619,139	9.6	40,480,760	16,090,903	71.6	...	...
South................	62,798,347	54,973,113	14.2	40,539,961	22,255,406	64.6	...	...
West................	34,809,359	28,053,104	24.1	28,854,391	5,949,802	82.9	...	...
New England.............	11,847,186	10,509,367	12.7	9,043,517	2,798,146	76.4	...	...
Maine................	993,663	969,265	2.5	504,157	487,891	50.8	38	36
New Hampshire...........	737,681	606,921	21.5	416,040	321,641	56.4	42	45
Vermont..............	444,732	389,881	14.1	142,889	301,441	32.2	49	47
Massachusetts...........	5,689,170	5,148,578	10.5	4,810,449	878,721	84.6	10	9
Rhode Island...........	949,723	859,488	10.5	824,930	121,795	87.1	39	39
Connecticut............	3,032,217	2,535,234	19.6	2,345,052	686,657	77.4	24	25
Middle Atlantic...........	37,152,813	34,168,452	8.7	30,406,301	6,792,739	81.7	...	...
New York.............	18,241,266	16,782,304	8.4	15,602,486	2,634,481	85.6	2	1
New Jersey............	7,168,164	6,066,782	18.2	6,373,405	794,759	88.9	8	8
Pennsylvania...........	11,793,909	11,319,366	4.2	8,430,410	3,363,499	71.5	3	3
East North Central........	40,252,678	36,225,024	11.1	30,091,847	10,160,629	74.8	...	...
Ohio................	10,652,017	9,706,397	9.7	8,025,775	2,625,242	75.3	6	5
Indiana..............	5,193,669	4,662,498	11.4	3,372,060	1,821,609	64.9	11	11
Illinois.............	11,113,976	10,081,158	10.2	9,229,821	1,884,155	83.0	5	4
Michigan.............	8,875,083	7,823,194	13.4	6,553,773	2,321,310	73.8	7	7
Wisconsin.............	4,417,933	3,951,777	11.8	2,910,418	1,507,313	65.9	16	15
West North Central........	16,324,389	15,394,115	6.0	10,388,913	5,930,274	63.7	...	...
Minnesota.............	3,805,069	3,413,864	11.5	2,527,308	1,277,663	66.4	19	18
Iowa................	2,825,041	2,757,537	2.4	1,616,405	1,207,971	57.2	25	24
Missouri.............	4,677,399	4,319,813	8.3	3,277,662	1,398,839	70.1	13	13
North Dakota...........	617,761	632,446	-2.3	273,442	344,319	44.3	46	44
South Dakota...........	666,257	680,514	-2.1	296,628	368,879	44.6	45	40
Nebraska.............	1,483,791	1,411,330	5.1	912,598	570,895	61.5	35	34
Kansas...............	2,249,071	2,178,611	3.2	1,484,870	761,708	66.1	28	28
South Atlantic..........	30,671,337	25,971,732	18.1	19,523,920	11,147,417	63.7	...	...
Delaware.............	548,104	446,292	22.8	395,569	152,535	72.2	47	46
Maryland.............	3,922,399	3,100,689	26.5	3,003,935	918,464	76.6	18	21
District of Columbia.......	756,510	763,956	-1.0	756,510	....	100.0	41	...
Virginia..............	4,648,494	3,966,949	17.2	2,934,841	1,713,653	63.1	14	14
West Virginia...........	1,744,237	1,860,421	-6.2	679,491	1,064,746	39.0	34	30
North Carolina..........	5,082,059	4,556,155	11.5	2,285,168	2,796,891	45.0	12	12
South Carolina..........	2,590,516	2,382,594	8.7	1,232,195	1,358,321	47.6	26	26
Georgia..............	4,589,575	3,943,116	16.4	2,768,074	1,821,501	60.3	15	16
Florida..............	6,789,443	4,951,560	37.1	5,468,137	1,321,306	80.5	9	10
East South Central.......	12,804,552	12,050,126	6.3	6,987,943	5,815,527	54.6	...	...
Kentucky.............	3,219,311	3,038,156	6.0	1,684,053	1,534,653	52.3	23	22
Tennessee.............	3,924,164	3,567,089	10.0	2,305,307	1,618,380	58.7	17	17
Alabama..............	3,444,165	3,266,740	5.4	2,011,941	1,432,224	58.4	21	19
Mississippi............	2,216,912	2,178,141	1.8	986,642	1,230,270	44.5	29	29
West South Central.......	19,322,458	16,951,255	14.0	14,028,098	5,292,462	72.6	...	...
Arkansas.............	1,923,295	1,786,272	7.7	960,865	962,430	50.0	32	31
Louisiana.............	3,643,180	3,257,022	11.9	2,406,150	1,235,156	66.1	20	20
Oklahoma.............	2,559,253	2,328,284	9.9	1,740,137	819,092	68.0	27	27
Texas...............	11,196,730	9,579,677	16.9	8,920,946	2,275,784	79.7	4	6
Mountain................	8,283,585	6,855,060	20.8	6,054,979	2,226,583	73.1	...	...
Montana..............	694,409	674,767	2.9	370,676	323,733	53.4	44	41
Idaho................	713,008	667,191	6.9	385,434	327,133	54.1	43	42
Wyoming..............	332,416	330,066	0.7	201,111	131,305	60.5	50	48
Colorado..............	2,207,259	1,753,947	25.8	1,733,311	473,948	78.5	30	33
New Mexico............	1,016,000	951,023	6.8	708,775	307,225	69.8	37	37
Arizona..............	1,772,482	1,302,161	36.1	1,408,864	362,036	79.6	33	35
Utah................	1,059,273	890,627	18.9	851,472	207,801	80.4	36	38
Nevada..............	488,738	285,278	71.3	395,336	93,402	80.9	48	49
Pacific................	26,525,774	21,198,044	25.1	22,799,412	3,723,219	86.0	...	...
Washington............	3,409,169	2,853,214	19.5	2,476,468	932,701	72.6	22	23
Oregon..............	2,091,385	1,768,687	18.2	1,402,704	688,681	67.1	31	32
California............	19,953,134	15,717,204	27.0	18,136,045	1,817,089	90.9	1	2
Alaska..............	302,173	226,167	33.6	145,512	154,870	48.4	51	50
Hawaii..............	769,913	632,772	21.7	638,683	129,878	83.1	40	43

Urban and rural figures do not equal total 1970 population because of errors discovered by census bureau after tabulation.

Congressional Apportionment

State	1970 Census	1960 Census	State	1970 Census	1960 Census	State	1970 Census	1960 Census	State	1970 Census	1960 Census	State	1970 Census	1960 Census
Ala....	7	8	Ida.....	2	2	Minn...	8	8	N. D....	1	2	Vt.....	1	1
Alas....	1	1	Ill.....	24	24	Miss...	5	5	Oh.....	23	24	Va.....	10	10
Ariz...	4	3	Ind....	11	11	Mo....	10	10	Okla...	6	6	Wash...	7	7
Ark....	4	4	Ia.....	5	7	Mon....	2	2	Ore....	4	4	W. Va..	4	5
Cal....	43	38	Kan....	5	5	Neb....	3	3	Pa.....	25	27	Wis....	9	10
Col....	5	4	Ky.....	7	7	Nev....	1	1	R. I....	2	2	Wy.....	1	1
Conn...	6	6	La.....	8	8	N. H...	2	2	S. C....	6	6			
Del....	1	1	Me.....	2	2	N. J....	15	15	S. D....	2	2			
Fla....	15	12	Md.....	8	8	N. M...	2	2	Tenn...	8	9	Totals .	435	435
Ga.....	10	10	Mass...	12	12	N. Y...	39	41	Tex....	24	23			
Ha.....	2	2	Mich...	19	19	N. C....	11	11	Ut.....	2	2			

The chief reason why the Constitution provided for a census of the population every 10 years was to give a basis for apportionment of representatives among the states. This apportionment has largely determined the number of electoral votes allotted to each state.

The number of representatives of each state in Congress is determined by the state's population, except that each state is entitled to one representative regardless of population. A Congressional apportionment has been made after each decennial census except that of 1920.

Under provisions of a law that became effective Nov. 15, 1941, apportionment of representatives is made by the method of equal proportions. In the application of this method, the apportionment is made so that the average population per representative has the least possible variation between one state and any other. The first House of Representatives, in 1790, had 65 members, or one representative for each 30,000 of the estimated population, as provided by the Constitution. As the population grew, the number of representatives was increased but the total membership has been fixed at 435 since 1912.

Density of Population by States

By Square Mile, Land Area Only

State	1920	1960	1970	State	1920	1960	1970	State	1920	1960	1970
Ala........	45.8	64.2	67.9	Ky.........	60.1	76.2	81.2	N. D........	9.2	9.1	8.9
Alas.*.....	0.1	0.4	0.5	La.........	39.6	72.2	81.0	Oh.........	141.4	236.6	260.0
Ariz.......	2.9	11.5	15.6	Me........	25.7	31.3	32.1	Okla.......	29.2	33.8	37.2
Ark.......	33.4	34.2	37.0	Md........	145.8	313.5	396.6*	Ore.......	8.2	18.4	21.7
Cal.......	22.0	100.4	127.6	Mass......	479.2	657.3	727.0	Pa........	194.5	251.4	262.3
Col.......	9.1	16.9	21.3	Mich......	63.8	137.6	156.2	R. I.......	566.4	819.3	905.5
Conn......	286.4	520.6	623.7	Minn......	29.5	43.0	48.0	S. C.......	55.2	78.7	85.7
Del.......	113.5	225.2	276.5	Miss......	38.6	46.0	46.9	S. D.......	8.3	9.0	8.8
D. C......	7,292.9	12,523.9	12,401.8	Mo........	49.5	62.6	67.8	Tenn......	56.1	86.2	94.9
Fla.......	17.7	91.5	125.5	Mon.......	3.8	4.6	4.8	Tex.......	17.8	36.4	42.7
Ga.......	49.3	67.8	79.0	Neb.......	16.9	18.4	19.4	Ut........	5.5	10.8	12.9
Ha.*......	39.9	98.5	119.8	Nev.......	.7	2.6	4.4	Vt........	38.6	42.0	47.9
Ida........	5.2	8.1	8.6	N. H.......	49.1	67.2	81.7	Va........	57.4	99.5	116.9
Ill........	115.7	180.4	199.4	N. J.......	420.0	805.5	953.1	Wash......	20.3	42.8	51.2
Ind.......	81.3	128.8	143.9	N. M......	2.9	7.8	8.4	W. Va......	60.9	77.2	72.5
Ia........	43.2	49.2	50.5	N. Y.......	217.9	350.6	381.3	Wis.......	47.6	72.6	81.1
Kan......	21.6	26.6	27.5	N. C.......	52.5	93.2	104.1	Wy........	2.0	3.4	3.4
								U.S.......	*29.9	50.6	57.5

*For purposes of comparison, Alaska and Hawaii included in above tabulation for 1920 even though not states then.
Number of inhabitants per sq. mi. of land area in U.S. (1790) 4.5; (1800) 6.1; (1810) 4.3; (1820) 5.5; (1830) 7.4; (1840) 9.8; (1850) 7.9; (1860) 10.6; (1870) 13.0; (1880) 16.9; (1890) 21.2; (1900) 25.6; (1910) 31.0; (1920) 35.5; (1930) 41.2; (1940) 44.2; (1950) 50.7; (1960) 50.6; (1970) 57.5. (Alaska and Hawaii included in 1960 and 1970.)

United States Area and Population: 1790 to 1970

Source: Bureau of the Census

Area figures represent area on indicated date including in some cases considerable areas not then organized or settled, and not covered by the census. Area figures have been adjusted to bring them into agreement with remeasurements made in 1940. *Changes in land and water area between 1960 and 1970 due to construction of dams and reservoirs. Also total area of Texas reduced approximately one square mile in the Chamizal agreement between U.S. and Mexico.

	Area (square miles)			Population				
Census Date	Gross	Land	Water	Number	Per sq. mile of land area	No.	%
1790 (Aug. 2).............	888,811	864,746	24,065	3,929,214	4.5	(X)	(X)
1800 (Aug. 4).............	888,811	864,746	24,065	5,308,483	6.1	1,379,269	35.1
1810 (Aug. 6).............	1,716,003	1,681,828	34,175	7,239,881	4.3	1,931,398	36.4
1820 (Aug. 7).............	1,788,006	1,749,462	38,544	9,638,453	5.5	2,398,572	33.1
1830 (June 1).............	1,788,006	1,749,462	38,544	12,866,020	7.4	3,227,567	33.5
1840 (June 1).............	1,788,006	1,749,462	38,544	17,069,453	9.8	4,203,433	32.7
1850 (June 1).............	2,992,747	2,940,042	52,705	23,191,876	7.9	6,122,423	35.9
1860 (June 1).............	3,022,387	2,969,640	52,747	31,443,321	10.6	8,251,445	35.6
1870 (June 1).............	3,022,387	2,969,640	52,747	'39,818,449	'13.4	8,375,128	26.6
1880 (June 1).............	3,022,387	2,969,640	52,747	50,155,783	16.9	10,337,334	26.0
1890 (June 1).............	3,022,387	2,969,640	52,747	62,947,714	21.2	12,791,931	25.5
1900 (June 1).............	3,022,387	2,969,834	52,553	75,994,575	25.6	13,046,861	20.7
1910 (Apr. 15)............	3,022,387	2,969,565	52,822	91,972,266	31.0	15,977,691	21.0
1920 (Jan. 1).............	3,022,387	2,969,451	52,936	105,710,620	35.6	13,738,354	14.9
1930 (Apr. 1).............	3,022,387	2,977,128	45,259	122,775,046	41.2	17,064,426	16.1
1940 (Apr. 1).............	3,022,387	2,977,128	45,259	131,669,275	44.2	8,894,229	7.2
1950 (Apr. 1)²............	3,615,211	3,552,206	63,005	151,325,798	42.6	19,161,229	14.5
1960 (Apr. 1)²............	3,615,123	3,540,911	74,212	179,323,175	50.5	27,997,377	18.5
1970* (Apr. 1)²...........	3,615,122	3,536,855	78,267	203,211,926	57.5	23,888,751	13.3

(X) Not applicable. (1) Revised to include adjustments for underenumeration in Southern States; unrevised number is 38,558,371. (2) Includes Alaska and Hawaii.

Population, Urban and Rural, by Race: 1960 and 1970

Source: Bureau of the Census

In thousands. An urbanized area comprises at least 1 city of 50,000 inhabitants (central city) plus contiguous, closely settled areas (urban fringe).

YEAR AND AREA	1960			1970		
	Total	White	Negro and other	Total	White	Negro and other
Population, total...................	**179,823**	**158,832**	**20,491**	**203,212**	**177,749**	**25,463**
Urban.......................................	125,269	110,428	14,840	149,325	128,773	20,552
Inside urbanized areas...............	95,848	83,770	12,070	118,447	100,052	17,495
Central cities........................	57,975	47,627	10,348	63,922	49,547	14,375
Urban fringe.........................	37,873	36,143	1,731	54,525	51,405	3,120
Outside urbanized areas............	29,420	26,658	2,762	30,878	27,822	8,017
Rural......................................	54,054	48,403	5,651	53,887	48,976	4,911

The Poor, 1971-1974, by Family Status, Sex and Race

Source: Bureau of the Census
(numbers in thousands)

	1974 No.	1974 %*	1973 No.	1973 %*	1972 No.	1972 %*	1971 No.	1971 %*
Total Poor....................	24,260	11.6	22,973	11.1	24,460	11.9	25,559	12.5
In families..................	19,440	10.2	18,299	9.7	19,577	10.3	20,405	10.8
Head.....................	5,109	9.2	4,828	8.8	5,075	9.3	5,303	10.0
Related children.............	10,196	15.5	9,453	14.2	10,082	14.9	10,344	15.1
Other relatives.............	4,135	6.0	4,018	5.9	4,420	6.6	4,757	7.2
Unrelated individuals..........	4,820	25.5	4,674	25.6	4,883	29.0	5,154	31.6
In male-head families.........	10,877	6.5	10,121	6.0	11,463	6.8	12,608	7.5
Head.....................	2,757	5.7	2,635	5.5	2,917	6.1	3,203	6.8
Related children.............	4,809	8.7	4,282	7.6	4,988	8.6	5,494	9.3
Other relatives.............	3,310	5.2	3,204	5.1	3,558	5.7	3,910	6.3
Unrelated male individuals......	1,607	20.4	1,495	19.8	1,410	21.1	1,543	23.9
In female-head families.......	8,563	36.8	8,178	37.5	8,114	38.2	7,797	38.7
Head.....................	2,351	32.5	2,193	32.2	2,158	32.7	2,100	33.9
Related children.............	5,387	51.5	5,171	52.1	5,094	53.1	4,850	53.1
Other relatives.............	825	14.9	814	16.0	862	17.0	847	17.5
Unrelated female individuals.....	3,212	29.3	3,179	29.7	3,473	34.3	3,611	36.6
Total White Poor.............	16,290	8.9	15,142	8.4	16,203	9.0	17,780	9.9
In families..................	12,517	7.5	11,412	6.9	12,268	7.4	13,566	8.2
Head.....................	3,482	7.0	3,219	6.6	3,441	7.1	3,751	7.9
Female..................	1,297	24.9	1,190	24.5	1,135	24.3	1,191	26.5
Related children.............	6,180	11.2	5,462	9.7	5,784	10.1	6,341	10.9
Other relatives.............	2,855	4.7	2,731	4.5	3,043	5.1	3,474	5.8
Unrelated individuals..........	3,773	23.2	3,730	23.7	3,935	27.1	4,214	29.6
Total Black Poor.............	7,467	31.4	7,388	31.4	7,710	33.3	7,396	32.5
In families..................	6,506	30.3	6,560	30.8	6,841	32.4	6,530	31.2
Head.....................	1,530	27.8	1,527	28.1	1,529	29.0	1,484	28.8
Female..................	1,024	52.8	974	52.7	972	53.3	879	53.5
Related children.............	3,819	40.7	3,822	40.6	4,025	42.7	3,836	40.7
Other relatives.............	1,157	17.6	1,211	18.7	1,287	20.0	1,210	19.1
Unrelated individuals..........	961	41.0	828	37.9	870	42.9	866	46.0

*Per cent of total individuals in that classification who were poor. For example, of all black female heads of households in 1974, 52.8 per cent were poor.

Low-Income Level, 1974, by Family Size and Sex of Head

Number of family members..................	Total	Non Farm Total	Non Farm Male	Non Farm Female	Farm Total	Farm Male	Farm Female
1 member...........................	$2,487	$2,495	$2,610	$2,413	$2,092	$2,158	$2,029
Under 65 yrs.......................	2,557	2,562	2,658	2,458	2,197	2,258	2,089
65 years and over...................	2,352	2,364	2,387	2,357	2,013	2,030	2,002
2 members..........................	3,191	3,211	3,220	3,167	2,707	2,711	2,632
Head under 65 yrs...................	3,294	3,312	3,329	3,230	2,819	2,824	2,706
Head 65 & over.....................	2,958	2,982	2,984	2,966	2,535	2,535	2,533
3 members..........................	3,910	3,936	3,957	3,822	3,331	3,345	3,133
4 members..........................	5,008	5,038	5,040	5,014	4,302	4,303	4,262
5 members..........................	5,912	5,950	5,957	5,882	5,057	5,057	5,072
6 members..........................	6,651	6,699	6,706	6,642	5,700	5,700	5,702
7 or more members..................	8,165	8,253	8,278	8,079	7,018	7,017	7,066

Poverty by Age, Race and Sex
(in thousands)

Age and Sex (March, 1975)	White Total	White Number of Poor	White % of Total	Black Total	Black Number of Poor	Black % of Total
Both sexes, total.................	182,355	16,310	8.9	23,705	7,456	31.5
Under 3 years.................	7,624	1,020	13.4	1,364	544	39.9
3 to 5 years..................	8,575	1,061	12.4	1,533	604	39.4
6 to 13 years.................	25,189	2,921	11.6	4,251	1,817	42.8
14 and 15 years...............	7,142	707	9.9	1,164	461	39.6
16 to 21 years................	20,512	1,822	8.9	3,079	1,069	34.7
22 to 44 years................	55,439	3,640	6.6	6,687	1,409	21.1
45 to 54 years................	21,045	1,102	5.2	2,218	506	22.8
55 to 59 years................	9,380	704	7.5	866	203	23.5
60 to 64 years................	8,243	692	8.4	819	217	26.5
65 years and over.............	19,206	2,642	13.8	1,722	626	36.4
Male, total over 16..............	64,015	4,016	6.3	6,926	1,390	20.1
16 to 21 years................	10,193	801	7.9	1,448	496	34.3
22 to 44 years................	27,410	1,449	5.3	2,966	370	12.5
45 to 54 years................	10,194	434	4.3	1,017	165	16.2
55 to 59 years................	4,477	267	6.0	388	70	18.0
60 to 64 years................	3,848	268	7.0	379	80	21.1
65 years and over.............	7,893	797	10.1	728	209	28.7
Female, total over 16.............	69,812	6,583	9.4	8,466	2,640	31.2
16 to 21 years................	10,319	1,020	9.9	1,630	573	35.2
22 to 44 years................	28,030	2,190	7.8	3,722	1,039	27.9
45 to 54 years................	10,851	668	6.2	1,201	341	28.4
55 to 59 years................	4,903	436	8.9	479	134	28.0
60 to 64 years................	4,396	424	9.6	439	136	31.0
65 years and over.............	11,313	1,845	16.3	995	417	41.9

Welfare for Families with Dependent Children[1]

(February 1975)

Source: Social and Rehabilitation Service, Department of Health Education and Welfare

State	Number of Recipients — Number Of Families	Total (&)	Children	Payments to Recipients — Total Amount	Average Per Family	Average Per Recipient	% Change From Feb. 1974 In No. of Recip.	% Change From Feb. 1974 In Amount
Alabama	49,642	163,075	121,659	$ 4,818,100	$ 97.06	$29.55	8.0	47.2
Alaska	4,257	11,989	8,840	1,108,314	260.35	92.44	-2.7	24.7
Arizona	20,593	71,332	53,902	2,618,298	127.15	36.71	-0.6	4.0
Arkansas	31,635	102,995	76,426	4,021,091	127.11	39.04	11.7	28.3
California	440,493	1,385,601	957,269	105,028,499	238.43	75.80	3.6	18.1
Colorado	30,842[2]	98,477	69,778	6,206,569	201.24	63.03	1.5	0.2
Connecticut	38,785	126,404	92,458	10,318,986	266.06	81.63	7.1	23.0
Delaware	10,182	32,534	23,665	1,686,050	165.59	51.82	11.3	75.4
Dist. of Columbia	31,737	104,633	75,865	7,706,662	242.83	73.65	2.4	23.1
Florida	80,967	264,349	199,306	9,592,363	118.47	36.29	-9.6	5.8
Georgia	114,174	358,182	263,705	11,615,710	101.74	32.43	3.8	4.5
Hawaii	14,632	48,628	33,754	4,476,305	305.93	92.05	11.6	19.8
Idaho	6,361	19,601	13,724	1,337,584	210.28	68.24	3.0	18.5
Illinois	219,080	782,927	566,917	70,298,091	320.88	89.79	0.9	30.0
Indiana	51,810	163,151	120,124	7,759,835	149.77	47.56	-1.7	12.0
Iowa	26,747	86,002	59,683	7,518,574	281.10	87.42	7.6	54.4
Kansas	22,310	66,953	50,086	4,592,373	205.84	68.59	-0.9	13.3
Kentucky	50,980	161,993	115,892	9,145,942	179.40	56.46	8.9	63.2
Louisiana	65,965	234,864	177,209	7,943,612	120.42	33.82	-4.5	22.2
Maine	24,522[2]	83,312	58,213	4,227,085	172.38	50.74	14.0	45.4
Maryland	67,890[2]	318,564	158,321	11,470,030	168.95	52.48	-1.0	3.8
Massachusetts	108,062	255,891[2]	248,526[2]	30,629,419[2]	283.44	86.06	14.2	38.6
Michigan	198,623	655,138	462,944	53,543,860	269.58	81.73	6.2	16.8
Minnesota	43,550	127,478	90,704	10,820,452	248.46	84.88	2.1	4.3
Mississippi	53,811	186,683	144,508	2,676,474	49.74	14.34	1.3	1.3
Missouri	83,140	260,695	193,366	10,084,372	121.29	38.68	4.9	11.4
Montana	7,447	22,005	16,244	1,205,825	161.92	54.80	2.1	5.4
Nebraska	11,891	38,221	27,552	2,144,712	180.36	56.11	-0.1	20.1
Nevada	4,723	14,270	10,484	684,305	144.89	47.95	4.9	20.8
New Hampshire	8,515	26,635	18,676	2,809,008	235.94	75.43	13.4	19.3
New Jersey	130,129	443,631	318,118	35,569,059	273.34	80.18	5.6	17.5
New Mexico	18,793	61,657	45,470	2,585,024	137.55	41.93	2.6	11.8
New York	349,689	1,202,637	850,218	113,663,613	325.04	94.51	1.3	-2.7
North Carolina	58,841	176,792	129,987	9,490,653	161.29	53.68	16.1	50.8
North Dakota	4,509	13,500	9,852	900,811	199.78	66.73	-1.4	0.2
Ohio	171,870	552,165	382,559	30,035,571	174.76	54.40	11.8	17.5
Oklahoma	30,916	99,676	75,368	5,593,500	180.93	56.12	7.2	13.4
Oregon	35,704	106,354	71,124	7,243,410	202.87	68.11	14.8	20.6
Pennsylvania	182,475[2]	632,711[2]	432,053[2]	48,142,518[2]	263.83	76.09	2.9	27.7
Puerto Rico	47,561[2]	232,028[2]	169,841[2]	2,180,894[2]	45.85	9.40	-9.0	-7.6
Rhode Island	16,009	52,938	37,317	3,913,154	244.43	73.92	6.4	6.7
South Carolina	42,254	137,612	101,835	3,746,697	88.67	27.23	11.5	25.0
South Dakota	7,889	24,682	18,200	1,597,322	202.47	64.72	8.6	17.4
Tennessee	63,878	207,433	154,676	6,779,042	106.12	32.68	8.9	10.7
Texas	113,536	391,319	289,528	12,235,560	107.77	31.27	-10.3	-8.9
Utah (January)	11,865	33,782	22,772	2,606,035	219.64	77.14	—	—
Vermont	6,530	22,257	14,928	1,670,772	255.86	75.07	10.6	12.9
Virginia	56,588	176,953	126,995	10,902,453	192.66	61.61	7.0	28.1
Washington	48,937	149,546	98,260	11,457,984	234.14	76.62	0.2	1.7
West Virginia	21,210	73,635	50,455	3,696,001	174.26	50.19	9.6	32.8
Wisconsin (E)	53,702	161,417	116,179	14,263,415	265.60	88.36	11.3	15.4
Wyoming	2,320	6,931	5,122	355,153	153.08	51.24	-7.0	-11.2
Total	3,400,549	11,239,611	8,036,586	736,220,963	216.50	65.50	3.4	15.6

(1.) Includes non-medical vendor payments, unemployed father segment and AFDC-foster care data. (E) Estimated data. (&) Includes as recipients children and one or both parents or one caretaker relative other than a parent in families in which the requirements of such adults were considered in determining the amount of assistance. (2.) Does not include AFDC foster care. (—) Comparable data not available.

Recipients and Payments, 1955-1973

Category		1955, Dec.	1960, Dec.	1965, Dec.	1970, Dec.	1971, Dec.	1972, Dec.	1973, Dec.
Old-age:	Recipients	2,538,000	2,305,000	2,087,000	2,082,000	2,024,000	1,933,000	1,823,000
	Total amt	$127,003,000	$135,759,000	$131,674,000	$161,642,000	$156,585,000	$154,571,000	$138,638,000
	Avg. amt	$50.05	$58.90	$63.10	$77.65	$77.35	$79.95	$76.15
	'Avg. real $	53.50	56.70	56.85	56.05	62.85	—	—
AFDC:	Recipients[2]	2,192,000	3,073,000	4,396,000	9,660,000	10,651,000	11,069,000	10,814,000
	Total amt	$51,472,000	$87,051,000	$144,355,000	$486,232,000	$557,003,000	$598,912,000	$615,903,000
	Avg. amt	$23.50	$28.35	$32.85	$49.65	$51.65	$54.10	$56.95
	(Avg. real $	25.10	27.25	29.60	35.85	41.95	—	—
Blind:	Recipients	104,000	107,000	85,100	81,000	80,300	79,800	77,900
	Total amt	$5,803,000	$7,215,000	$6,922,000	$8,447,000	$8,548,000	$9,005,000	$8,723,000
	Avg. amt	$55.55	$67.45	$81.35	$104.35	$106.40	$112.85	$112.00
	'Avg. real $	59.40	64.95	73.25	75.35	86.45	—	—
Disabled:	Recipients	241,000	369,000	557,000	935,000	1,068,000	1,169,000	1,275,000
	Total amt	$11,750,000	$20,711,000	$37,035,000	$91,325,000	$108,947,000	$124,074,000	$139,903,000
	Avg. amt	$48.75	$56.15	$66.50	$97.65	$101.95	$106.15	$109.75
	'Avg. real $	52.15	54.05	59.95	70.50	82.80	—	—

(1) Dollar amounts adjusted to represent actual purchasing power in terms of the average value of the dollar during the period 1957-1959 based on the consumers' price index for moderate-income families in large cities maintained by the Bureau of Labor statistics. (2) Includes as recipients the children and one or both parents or one caretaker relative other than a parent in families in which the requirements of such adults were considered in determining the amount of assistance.

Rankings of U.S. Standard Metropolitan Statistical Areas

Source: Bureau of the Census

Metropolitan areas are ranked by 1970 population size based on new SMSA definitions and compared with a ranking of areas as defined in the 1970 census. Included are all of the 266 Standard Metropolitan Statistical Areas (SMSA's) as defined through May 1975 by the Office of Management and Budget. There are 27 new SMSA's since 1970. In addition, 8 existing areas were combined into 4 areas, boundary definitions were changed in 100 areas, and names were changed in 27 areas.

The four merged areas are: Dallas-Fort Worth, Texas; Raleigh-Durham, N. Car.; Salt Lake City-Ogden, Utah; and

Northeast Pennsylvania (a combination of the former Scranton and Wilkes-Barre-Hazleton SMSA's).

Nassau-Suffolk, N.Y., replaces Pittsburgh as the ninth largest metropolitan area in the new ranking. The Nassau-Suffolk SMSA was created out of the eastern Long Island counties formerly in the New York SMSA and has a population of 2.6 million.

The combined Dallas-Fort Worth SMSA now ranks 12th and has a population of 2.4 million persons. The former Dallas SMSA ranked 16th.

SMSA	1975 Rank	Pop.	1970 Rank	Pop.
New York, N.Y.-N.J.[3]	1	9,973,577		111,571,899
Los Angeles-Long Beach, Cal.	2	7,032,075	2	7,032,075
Chicago, Ill.	3	6,978,947	3	6,978,947
Philadelphia, Pa.-N.J.	4	4,817,914	4	4,817,914
Detroit, Mich.[1]	5	4,431,390	5	4,199,931
San Francisco-Oakland, Cal.	6	3,109,519	6	3,109,519
Washington, D.C.-Md.-Va.[1]	7	2,908,801	7	2,861,123
Boston, Mass.[1]	8	2,899,101	8	2,753,700
Nassau-Suffolk, N.Y.[4]	9	2,553,030		
St. Louis, Mo.-Ill.[1]	10	2,410,163	10	2,363,017
Pittsburgh, Pa.	11	2,401,245	9	2,401,245
Dallas-Fort Worth, Tex.[6]	12	2,377,979	16	1,555,950
Baltimore, Md.	13	2,070,670	11	2,070,670
Cleveland, Oh.	14	2,064,194	12	2,064,194
Newark, N.J.[1]	15	2,054,928	14	1,856,556
Houston, Tex.[1]	16	1,999,316	13	1,985,031
Minneapolis-St. Paul, Minn.-Wis.[3]	17	1,965,159	15	1,813,647
Atlanta, Ga.[1]	18	1,597,816	20	1,390,164
Seattle-Everett, Wash.	19	1,421,869	17	1,421,869
Anaheim-Santa Ana-Garden Grove, Cal.	20	1,420,386	18	1,420,386
Milwaukee, Wis.	21	1,403,688	19	1,403,688
Cincinnati, Oh.-Ky.-Ind.	22	1,384,851	21	1,384,851
San Diego, Cal.	23	1,357,854	23	1,357,854
Buffalo, N.Y.	24	1,349,211	24	1,349,211
Kansas City, Mo.-Kans.[1]	25	1,271,515	26	1,253,916
Miami, Fla.	26	1,267,792	25	1,267,792
Denver-Boulder, Col.[3]	27	1,237,208	27	1,227,529
Riverside-San Bernardino-Ontario, Cal.[2]	28	1,143,146	28	1,143,146
Indianapolis, Ind.	29	1,109,882	29	1,109,882
Tampa-St. Petersburg, Fla.[1]	30	1,088,549	32	1,012,594
San Jose, Cal.	31	1,064,714	30	1,064,714
New Orleans, La.	32	1,045,809	31	1,045,809
Columbus, Oh.[1]	33	1,017,847	35	916,228
Portland, Oreg.-Wash.	34	1,009,129	33	1,009,129
Phoenix, Ariz.	35	967,522	34	967,522
Rochester, N.Y.[1]	36	961,516	37	882,667
Providence-Warwick-Pawtucket, R.I.-Mass.[3]	37	905,558	36	910,781
San Antonio, Tex.[1]	38	888,179	38	864,014
Louisville, Ky.-Ind.[1]	39	867,330	40	826,553
Dayton, Oh.	40	850,266	39	850,266
Memphis, Tenn.-Ark.-Miss.[3]	41	834,006	42	770,120
Sacramento, Cal.[3]	42	800,592	41	800,592
Albany-Schenectady-Troy, N.Y.[1]	43	777,793	45	721,910
Birmingham, Ala.[1]	44	767,230	44	739,274
Toledo, Oh.-Mich.[1]	45	762,741	46	692,571
Norfolk-Virginia Beach-Portsmouth, Va.-N.C.[3]	46	732,600	47	680,600
Greensboro-Winston-Salem-High Point, N.C.[1]	47	723,304	56	603,895
Hartford, Conn.[1]	48	720,581	49	663,891
Salt Lake City-Ogden, Ut.[6]	49	705,458	57	557,635
Nashville-Davidson, Tenn.[3]	50	699,144	59	541,108
Oklahoma City, Okla.[1]	51	698,180	50	640,889
Akron, Oh.	52	679,239	48	679,239
Syracuse, N.Y.	53	636,507	51	636,507
Gary-Hammond-E. Chicago, Ind.	54	633,367	52	633,367
Honolulu, Ha.	55	629,176	53	629,176
Northeast Pa.[6]	56	621,830	87	342,301
Jacksonville, Fla.[1]	57	621,519	64	528,865
Fort Lauderdale-Hollywood, Fla.	58	620,100	54	620,100
Jersey City, N.J.	59	609,266	55	609,266
Allentown-Bethlehem-Easton, Pa.-N.J.[1]	60	594,124	58	543,551
New Brunswick-Perth Amboy Sayreville, N.J.[4]	61	583,813		

SMSA	1975 Rank	Pop.	1970 Rank	Pop.
Charlotte-Gastonia, N.C.[3]	62	557,785	73	409,370
Tulsa, Okla.[1]	63	550,835	68	476,945
Richmond, Va.[1]	64	542,242	65	518,319
Springfield-Chicopee-Holyoke, Mass-Con.[1]	65	541,752	63	529,922
Omaha, Neb.-Iowa	66	540,142	60	540,142
Grand Rapids, Mich.	67	539,225	61	539,225
Youngstown-Warren, Oh.	68	536,003	62	536,003
Flint, Mich.[1]	69	507,416	67	496,658
Wilmington, Del.-N.J.-Md.	70	499,493	66	499,493
Greenville-Spartanburg, S.C.[3]	71	473,226	101	299,502
Paterson-Clifton-Passaic, N.J.[1]	72	460,782	22	1,358,794
Long Branch-Asbury Park, N.J.[4]	73	459,379		
Orlando, Fla.[1]	74	453,270	69	428,003
Lansing-East Lansing, Mich.[3]	75	424,271	77	378,423
Raleigh-Durham, N.C.[6]	76	418,841	135	228,453
New Haven-West Haven, Conn.[2]	77	413,722	83	355,538
Fresno, Cal.	78	413,053	70	413,053
Tacoma, Wash.	79	411,027	71	411,027
Harrisburg, Pa.	80	410,626	72	410,626
Knoxville, Tenn.[1]	81	409,409	74	400,337
Bridgeport, Conn.[1]	82	401,752	76	389,153
Canton, Oh.[1]	83	393,789	80	372,210
Wichita, Kan.	84	389,352	75	389,352
Mobile, Ala.	85	376,690	78	376,690
Oxnard-Simi Valley-Ventura, Cal.[2]	86	376,430	79	376,430
Baton Rouge, La.[1]	87	375,628	110	285,167
Worcester, Mass.[1]	88	372,144	86	344,320
Chattanooga, Tenn.-Ga.[1]	89	370,016	97	304,927
Davenport-Rock Island-Moline, Iowa-Ill.	90	362,638	81	362,638
Fort Wayne, Ind.[1]	91	360,984	112	280,455
El Paso, Tex.	92	359,291	82	359,291
Tucson, Ariz.	93	351,667	84	351,667
West Palm Beach-Boca Raton[2]	94	384,753	85	348,753
Beaumont-Port Arthur-Orange, Tex.[1]	95	345,939	95	315,943
Peoria, Ill.	96	341,979	88	341,979
Utica-Rome, N.Y.	97	340,670	89	340,670
Charleston, N. Charleston, S.C.[3]	98	336,125	99	303,849
Shreveport, La.[1]	99	334,642	104	294,703
Albuquerque, N. Mex.[1]	100	333,266	96	315,774
Newport News-Hampton, Va.[1]	101	333,140	105	292,159
York, Pa.	102	329,540	90	329,540
Bakersfield, Cal.	103	329,162	91	329,162
Little Rock-North Little Rock	104	323,296	92	323,296
Austin, Tex.[1]	105	323,158	103	295,516
Columbia, S.C.	106	322,880	93	322,880
Lancaster, Pa.	107	319,693	94	319,693
Des Moines, Iowa[1]	108	313,533	109	286,101
Trenton, N.J.	109	303,968	98	303,968
Binghamton, N.Y.-Pa.	110	302,672	100	302,672
Reading, Pa.	111	296,382	102	296,382
Madison, Wis.	112	290,272	106	290,272
Stockton, Cal.	113	290,208	107	290,208
Spokane, Wash.	114	287,487	108	287,487
Huntington-Ashland, W. Va.-Ky.-Oh.[1]	115	286,935	123	253,743
Evansville, Ind.-Ky.[1]	116	284,959	132	232,775
Corpus Christi, Tex.	117	284,832	111	284,832
Huntsville, Ala.[1]	118	282,450	136	228,239
South Bend, Ind.	119	280,031	113	280,031
Appleton-Oshkosh, Wis.	120	276,891	114	276,891
Augusta, Ga.-S.C.[1]	121	275,757	124	253,460
Las Vegas, Nev.	122	273,288	115	273,288
Rockford, Ill.	123	272,063	116	272,063
Lexington, Ky.[1]	124	266,701	160	174,323

SMSA	1975 Rank	1975 Pop.	1970 Rank	1970 Pop.
Duluth-Superior, Minn.-Wis.	125	265,350	117	265,350
Santa Barbara-Santa Maria-Lompoc, Cal.[2]	126	264,324	118	264,324
Erie, Pa.	127	263,654	119	263,654
Johnstown, Pa.	128	262,822	120	262,822
Jackson, Miss.	129	258,906	121	258,906
Lawrence-Haverhill, Mass.-N.H.[1]	130	258,564	133	232,415
Kalamazoo-Portage, Mich.[3]	131	257,723	147	201,550
Charleston, W. Va.[1]	132	257,140	134	229,515
Lorain-Elyria, Oh.	133	256,843	122	256,843
Salinas-Seaside-Montefey, Cal.[2]	134	250,071	125	250,071
Vallejo-Fairfield-Napa, Cal.[2]	135	249,081	126	249,081
Pensacola, Fla.	136	243,075	127	243,075
New London-Norwich, Conn.-R.I.[3]	137	241,556	143	208,412
Kingsport-Bristol, Tenn.-Va.[4]	138	241,123		
Colorado Springs, Col.[1]	139	239,288	129	235,972
Columbus, Ga.-Ala.	140	238,584	128	238,584
Ann Arbor, Mich.	141	234,103	131	234,103
Melbourne-Titusville-Cocoa, Fla.[4]	142	230,006		
Lakeland-Winter Haven, Fla.[4]	143	227,222		
Macon, Ga.[1]	144	226,782	145	206,342
Hamilton-Middletown, Oh.	145	226,207	137	226,207
Montgomery, Ala.[1]	146	225,785	148	201,325
Poughkeepsie, N.Y.[4]	147	222,295		
Saginaw, Mich.	148	219,743	138	219,743
Lowell, Mass.-N.H.[3]	149	218,268	140	212,860
Waterbury, Conn.[1]	150	216,808	142	208,956
Eugene-Springfield, Ore.[2]	151	213,358	139	213,358
Fayetteville, N.C.	152	212,042	141	212,042
Lima, Oh.[1]	153	210,074	161	171,472
Savannah, Ga.[1]	154	207,938	152	187,767
Stamford, Conn.	155	206,419	144	206,419
Santa Rosa, Cal.	156	204,885	146	204,885
Roanoke, Va.[1]	157	203,153	156	181,436
Modesto, Cal.	158	194,506	149	194,506
Springfield, Oh.[1]	159	187,606	172	157,115
Salem, Ore.	160	186,658	153	186,658
Wheeling, W. Va.-Oh.	161	182,712	154	182,712
McAllen-Pharr-Edinburg, Tex.	162	181,535	155	181,535
Topeka, Kan.[1]	163	180,619	173	155,322
Battle Creek, Mich.[3]	164	180,129		
Lubbock, Tex.	165	179,295	157	179,295
Muskegon-Muskegon Heights, Mich.[1]	166	175,410	171	157,426
Terre Haute, Ind.	167	175,143	158	175,143
Atlantic City, N.J.	168	175,043	159	175,043
Springfield, Ill.[1]	169	171,020	168	161,335
Racine, Wis.	170	170,838	162	170,838
Portland, Me.[1]	171	170,081	183	141,625
Galveston-Texas City, Tex.	172	169,812	163	169,812
Fall River, Mass.-R.I.[1]	173	169,549	176	149,976
Daytona Beach, Fla.[4]	174	169,487		
Springfield, Mo.[1]	175	168,053	174	152,929
Lincoln, Neb.	176	167,972	164	167,972
Steubenville-Weirton, Oh.-W. Va.	177	165,627	165	165,627
Champaign-Urbana-Rantoul, Ill.[2]	178	163,281	166	163,281
Cedar Rapids, Ia.	179	163,213	167	163,213
New Bedford, Mass.[1]	180	161,288	175	152,642
Asheville, N.C.[1]	181	161,059	180	145,056
Fort Smith, Ark.-Okla.	182	160,421	169	160,421
Biloxi-Gulfport, Miss.[1]	183	160,070	188	134,582
Killeen-Temple, Tex.[4]	184	159,794		
Green Bay, Wis.	185	158,244	170	158,244
Brockton, Mass.[1]	186	150,416	151	189,820
Parkersburg-Marietta, W. Va.-Oh.[5]	187	148,132		
Waco, Tex.	188	147,553	177	147,553
Lake Charles, La.	189	145,415	178	145,415
New Britain, Conn.	190	145,269	179	145,269
Yakima, Wash.[4]	191	144,971		
Amarillo, Tex.	192	144,396	181	144,396
Jackson, Mich.	193	143,274	182	143,274
Brownsville-Harlingen-San Benito, Tex.	194	140,368	184	140,368
Anderson, Ind.	195	138,451	185	138,451
Provo-Orem, Ut.	196	137,776	186	137,776
Altoona, Pa.	197	135,356	187	135,356
St. Cloud, Minn.[4]	198	134,585		
Lynchburg, Va.[1]	199	133,258	196	123,474
Waterloo-Cedar Falls, Ia.[2]	200	132,916	189	132,916
Manchester, N.H.[1]	201	132,512	211	108,461
Alexandria, La.[5]	202	131,749		
Mansfield, Oh.	203	129,997	190	129,997
Wichita Falls, Tex.[1]	204	129,941	193	127,621
Muncie, Ind.	205	129,219	191	129,219
Petersburg-Colonial Heights-Hopewell, Va.[2]	206	128,809	192	128,809
Fayetteville-Springdale, Ark.[4]	207	127,846		
Norwalk, Conn.[1]	208	127,516	200	120,099
Decatur, Ill.	209	125,010	195	125,010
Anchorage, Alaska[4]	210	124,542		
Santa Cruz, Cal.[4]	211	123,790		
Abilene, Tex[1]	212	122,164	207	113,959
Vineland-Millville-Bridgeton, N.J.	213	121,374	197	121,374
Reno, Nev.	214	121,068	198	121,068
Sarasota, Fla.[4]	215	120,413		
Fargo-Moorhead, N. D.-Minn.	216	120,238	199	120,238
Clarksville-Hopkinsville, Tenn.-Ky.[4]	217	118,945		
Pueblo, Col.	218	118,238	201	118,238
Kenosha, Wis.	219	117,917	202	117,917
Florence, Ala[4]	220	117,743		
Bay City, Mich.	221	117,339	203	117,339
Sioux City, Ia.-Neb.	222	116,189	204	116,189
Tuscaloosa, Ala.	223	116,029	205	116,029
Danbury, Conn.[1]	224	115,538	235	78,405
Monroe, La.	225	115,387	206	115,387
Williamsport, Pa.[4]	226	113,296		
Texarkana, Tex.-Texarkana, Ark.[3]	227	112,392	217	101,198
Boise City, Ida.	228	112,230	208	112,230
Lafayette, La.	229	109,716	209	109,716
Lafayette-West Lafayette, Ind.	230	109,378	210	109,378
Tallahassee, Fla.[1]	231	109,355	216	103,047
Lawton, Okla.	232	108,144	212	108,144
Wilmington, N.C.	233	107,219	213	107,219
Fort Myers, Fla.[4]	234	105,216		
Gainesville, Fla.	235	104,764	214	104,764
Bloomington-Normal, Ill.	236	104,389	215	104,389
Anniston, Ala.[4]	237	103,092		
Elmira, N.Y.[4]	238	101,537		
St. Joseph, Mo.[1]	239	98,828	226	86,915
Kankakee, Ill.[4]	240	97,250		
Fitchburg-Leominister, Mass.	241	97,164	218	97,164
Tyler, Tex.	242	97,096	219	97,096
Pittsfield, Mass.[1]	243	96,817	233	79,727
Albany, Ga.[1]	244	96,683	224	89,639
Burlington, N.C.[1]	245	96,362		
Sioux Falls, S. D.	246	95,209	220	95,209
Gadsden, Ala.	247	94,144	221	94,144
Richland-Kennewick, Wash.[4]	248	93,356		
Odessa, Tex.	249	91,805	222	91,805
Dubuque, Ia.	250	90,609	223	90,609
Billings, Mon.	251	87,367	225	87,367
Nashua, N.H[1]	252	86,280	239	66,458
Pine Bluff,Ark.	253	85,329	227	85,329
Rochester, Minn.	254	84,104	228	84,104
Sherman-Denison, Tex.	255	83,225	229	83,225
Great Falls, Mon.	256	81,804	230	81,804
Columbia, Mo.	257	80,911	231	80,911
La Crosse, Wis.	258	80,468	232	80,468
Owensboro, Ky.	259	79,486	234	79,486
Laredo, Tex.	260	72,859	236	72,859
Lewiston-Auburn, Me.	261	72,474	237	72,474
San Angelo, Tex.	262	71,047	238	71,047
Bristol, Conn.[1]	263	69,878	240	65,808
Midland, Tex.	264	65,433	241	65,433
Bryan-College Station, Tex.	265	57,978	242	57,978
Meriden, Conn.[1]	266	55,959	243	55,959

(1) Change in area definition since 1970 census, without change of title.

(2) Change in title since 1970 census.

(3) Change in area definition since 1970 census, with change of title.

(4) New SMSA established since 1970 census.

(5) New SMSA established in Nov. 1971, and area definition changed in Apr. 1973.

(6) Merger of two existing SMSAs since 1970 census; rank and population given for 1970 definition refer to the larger of the two merged SMSAs.

How the Cities Grew

Source: Bureau of the Census

(Cities over 100,000 in the 1970 census)

Rank	Cities	1970	1960	1950	1900	1850	1790
1	New York, N.Y.	7,895,563	7,781,984	7,891,957	3,437,202	¹696,115	¹49,401
	Bronx boro	1,471,701	1,424,815	1,451,277	200,507	8,032	1,781
	Brooklyn boro	2,602,012	2,627,319	2,738,175	1,166,582	138,882	4,495
	Manhattan boro	1,539,233	1,698,281	1,960,101	1,850,093	515,547	33,131
	Queens boro	1,986,473	1,809,578	1,550,849	152,999	18,593	6,159
	Richmond boro	295,443	221,991	191,555	67,021	15,061	3,835
2	Chicago, Ill.	3,369,357	3,550,404	3,620,962	1,698,575	29,963	...
3	Los Angeles, Cal.	2,809,813	2,479,015	1,970,358	102,479	1,610	...
4	Phila., Pa.	1,949,996	2,002,512	2,071,605	1,293,697	121,376	28,522
5	Detroit, Mich.	1,513,601	1,670,144	1,849,568	285,704	21,019	...
6	Houston, Tex.	1,232,802	938,219	596,163	44,633	2,396	...
7	Baltimore, Md.	905,787	939,024	949,708	508,957	169,054	13,503
8	Dallas, Tex.	844,401	679,684	434,462	42,638	...	...
9	Washington, D.C.	756,510	763,956	802,178	278,718	40,001	...
10	Cleveland, Oh.	750,879	876,050	914,808	381,768	17,034	...
11	Indianapolis, Ind.	746,302	476,258	427,173	169,164	8,091	...
12	Milwaukee, Wis.	717,372	741,324	637,392	285,315	20,061	...
13	San Francisco, Cal.	715,674	740,316	775,357	342,782	²34,776	...
14	San Diego, Cal.	697,027	573,224	334,387	17,700	...	...
15	San Antonio, Tex.	654,153	587,718	408,442	53,321	3,488	...
16	Boston, Mass.	641,071	697,197	801,444	560,892	136,881	18,320
17	Memphis, Tenn.	623,530	497,524	396,000	102,320	8,841	...
18	St. Louis, Mo.	622,236	750,026	856,796	575,238	77,860	...
19	New Orleans, La.	593,471	627,525	570,445	287,104	116,375	...
20	Phoenix, Ariz.	581,562	439,170	106,818	5,544	...	...
21	Columbus, Oh.	540,025	471,316	375,901	125,560	17,882	...
22	Seattle, Wash.	530,831	557,087	467,591	80,671	...	...
23	Jacksonville, Fla.	528,865	201,030	204,517	28,429	1,045	...
24	Pittsburgh, Pa.	520,117	604,332	676,806	321,616	46,601	...
25	Denver, Col.	514,678	493,887	415,786	133,859	...	...
26	Kansas City, Mo.	507,330	475,539	456,622	163,752	...	...
27	Atlanta, Ga.	497,421	487,455	331,314	89,872	2,572	...
28	Buffalo, N.Y.	462,768	532,759	580,132	352,387	42,261	...
29	Cincinnati, Oh.	451,455	502,550	503,998	325,902	115,435	...
30	Nashville, Tenn.³	447,877	170,874	174,307	80,865	10,165	...
31	San Jose, Cal.	446,537	204,196	95,280	21,500	...	...
32	Minneapolis, Minn.	434,400	482,872	521,718	202,718	...	...
33	Fort Worth, Tex.	393,476	356,263	278,778	26,688	...	...
34	Toledo, Oh.	383,105	318,003	303,616	131,822	3,829	...
35	Newark, N.J.	381,930	405,220	438,776	246,070	38,894	...
36	Portland, Ore.	379,967	372,676	373,628	90,426	...	...
37	Oklahoma City, Okla.	368,377	324,253	243,504	10,037	...	...
38	Louisville, Ky.	361,706	390,639	369,129	204,731	43,194	200
39	Oakland, Cal.	361,561	367,548	384,575	66,960	...	...
40	Long Beach, Cal.	358,879	344,168	250,767	2,252	...	...
41	Omaha, Neb.	346,929	301,598	251,117	102,555	...	...
42	Miami, Fla.	334,859	291,688	249,276	1,681	...	...
43	Tulsa, Okla.	330,350	261,685	182,740	1,390	...	...
44	Honolulu, Ha.	324,871	294,194	248,034	39,306	...	...
45	El Paso, Tex.	322,261	276,687	130,485	15,906	...	...
46	St. Paul, Minn.	309,714	313,411	311,349	163,065	1,112	...
47	Norfolk, Va.	307,951	304,869	213,513	46,624	14,326	2,959
48	Birmingham, Ala.	300,910	340,887	326,037	38,415	...	...
49	Rochester, N.Y.	296,233	318,611	332,488	162,608	36,403	...
50	Tampa, Fla.	277,753	274,970	124,681	15,839	...	...
51	Wichita, Kan.	276,554	254,698	168,279	24,671	...	...
52	Akron, Oh.	275,425	290,351	274,605	42,728	3,266	...
53	Tucson, Ariz.	262,933	212,892	45,454	7,531	...	...
54	Jersey City, N.J.	260,350	276,101	299,017	206,433	6,856	...
55	Sacramento, Cal.	257,105	191,667	137,572	29,282	6,820	.·.
56	Austin, Tex.	251,808	186,545	132,459	22,258	629	...
57	Richmond, Va.	249,431	219,958	230,310	85,050	27,570	3,761
58	Albuquerque, N.M.	243,751	201,189	96,815	6,238	...	...
59	Dayton, Oh.	242,917	262,332	243,872	85,333	10,977	...
60	Charlotte, N.C.	241,178	201,564	134,042	18,091	1,065	...
61	St. Petersburg, Fla.	216,159	181,298	96,738	1,575	...	...
62	Corpus Christi, Tex.	204,525	167,690	108,287	4,703	...	...
63	Yonkers, N.Y.	204,297	190,634	152,798	47,931	...	...
64	Des Moines, Ia.	201,404	208,982	177,965	62,139	...	...
65	Grand Rapids, Mich.	197,649	177,313	176,515	87,565	2, 686	...
66	Syracuse, N.Y.	197,297	216,038	220,583	103,374	22,271	...
67	Flint, Mich.	193,317	196,940	163,143	13,103	...	...
68	Mobile, Ala.	190,026	194,856	129,009	38,469	20,515	...
69	Shreveport, La.	182,064	164,372	127,206	16,013	1,728	...
70	Warren, Mich.	179,260	89,246	727	350	...	...
71	Providence, R.I.	179,116	207,498	248,674	175,597	41,513	6,380
72	Fort Wayne, Ind.	178,021	161,776	133,607	45,115	4,282	...
73	Worcester, Mass.	176,572	186,587	203,486	118,421	17,049	2,095
74	Salt Lake City, Ut.	175,885	189,454	182,121	53,531	...	...
75	Gary, Ind.	175,415	178,320	133,911	...	...	...
76	Knoxville, Tenn.	174,587	111,827	124,769	32,637	2,076	...

Rank	Cities	1970	1960	1950	1900	1850	1790
77	Virginia Beach, Va..	172,106	8,091	5,390	...	...	...
78	Madison, Wis..	171,769	126,706	96,056	19,164	1,525	...
79	Spokane, Wash..	170,516	181,608	161,721	36,848	...	...
80	Kansas City, Kans..	168,213	121,901	129,553	51,418	...	...
81	Anaheim, Cal..	166,408	104,184	14,556	1,456	...	...
82	Fresno, Cal..	165,972	133,929	91,669	12,470	...	...
83	Baton Rouge, La..	165,921	152,419	125,629	11,269	3,905	...
84	Springfield, Mass..	163,905	174,463	162,399	62,059	11,766	1,574
85	Hartford, Conn..	158,017	162,178	177,397	72,850	13,555	2,683
86	Bridgeport, Conn..	156,542	156,748	158,709	70,996	6,080	...
87	Santa Ana, Cal..	155,762	100,350	45,533	4,933	...	...
88	Columbus, Ga..	155,028	116,779	79,611	17,614	5,942	...
89	Tacoma, Wash..	154,407	147,979	143,673	37,714	...	...
90	Jackson, Miss..	153,968	144,422	98,271	7,816	1,881	...
91	Lincoln, Neb..	149,518	128,521	98,884	40,159	...	...
92	Lubbock, Tex..	149,101	128,691	71,747	...	...	...
93	Rockford, Ill..	147,370	126,706	92,927	31,051	...	...
94	Paterson, N.J..	144,824	143,663	139,336	105,171	11,334	...
95	Greensboro, N.C..	144,076	119,574	74,389	10,035	...	...
96	Youngstown, Oh..	140,909	166,689	168,330	44,885	...	...
97	Riverside, Cal..	140,089	84,332	46,764	7,973	...	...
98	Fort Lauderdale, Fla..	139,590	83,648	36,328	...	...	...
99	Huntsville, Ala.	139,282	72,365	16,437	8,068	2,863	...
100	Evansville, Ind..	138,764	141,543	128,636	59,007	3,235	...
101	Newport News, Va..	138,177	113,662	42,358	19,635	...	...
102	New Haven, Conn..	137,707	152,048	164,443	108,027	20,345	4,487
103	Colorado Springs, Col.	135,060	70,194	45,472	21,083	...	...
104	Torrance, Cal..	134,968	100,991	22,241	...	...	...
105	Winston-Salem, N.C.[4]	133,683	111,135	87,811	13,650	...	...
106	Montgomery, Ala..	133,386	134,393	106,525	30,346	8,728	...
107	Glendale, Cal..	132,664	119,442	95,702	...	...	...
108	Little Rock, Ark..	132,483	107,813	102,213	38,307	2,167	...
109	Lansing, Mich..	131,403	107,807	92,129	16,485	...	...
110	Erie, Pa..	129,231	138,440	130,803	52,733	5,858	...
111	Amarillo, Tex..	127,010	137,969	74,246	1,442	...	...
112	Peoria, Ill.	126,963	103,162	111,856	56,100	5,095	...
113	Las Vegas, Nev..	125,787	64,405	24,624	...	...	...
114	South Bend, Ind..	125,580	132,445	115,911	35,999	1,652	...
115	Topeka, Kan..	125,011	119,484	78,791	33,608	...	...
116	Raleigh, N.C..	123,793	93,931	65,679	13,643	4,518	...
117	Macon, Ga..	122,423	69,764	70,252	23,272	5,720	...
118	Garden Grove, Cal..	121,357	84,238	...	...	...	...
119	Hampton, Va..	120,779	89,258	5,966	2,764	...	...
120	Springfield, Mo..	120,096	95,865	66,731	23,267	415	...
121	Chattanooga, Tenn..	119,923	130,009	131,041	30,154	...	...
122	Savannah, Ga..	118,349	149,245	119,638	54,244	15,312	...
123	Beaumont, Tex..	117,548	119,175	94,014	9,427	...	...
124	Berkeley, Cal..	116,716	111,268	113,805	13,214	...	...
125	Huntington Bch., Cal..	115,960	11,492	5,237	...	...	...
126	Albany, N.Y..	115,781	129,726	134,995	94,151	50,763	3,498
127	Columbia, S.C..	113,542	97,433	86,914	21,103	6,060	...
128	Pasadena, Cal..	112,951	116,407	104,577	3,117	...	...
129	Elizabeth, N.J..	112,654	107,698	112,817	52,130	5,583	...
130	Independence, Mo..	111,630	62,328	36,963	6,974	...	...
131	Portsmouth, Va..	110,963	114,773	80,039	17,427	8,626	...
132	Alexandria, Va..	110,927	91,023	61,787	14,528	8,734	2,748
133	Cedar Rapids, Ia..	110,642	92,035	72,296	25,656	...	...
134	Livonia, Mich..	110,109	66,702	17,534	...	...	...
135	Canton, Oh..	110,053	113,631	118,912	30,667	2,603	...
136	Stockton, Cal..	109,963	86,321	70,853	17,506	...	...
137	Allentown, Pa..	109,871	108,347	106,756	35,416	3,779	...
138	Stamford, Conn..	108,798	92,713	74,293	15,997	...	...
139	Lexington, Ky..	108,137	62,810	55,534	26,369	8,159	834
140	Waterbury, Conn..	108,033	107,130	104,477	45,859	...	...
141	Hammond, Ind..	107,885	111,698	87,594	12,376	...	...
142	Hollywood, Fla..	106,873	35,237	14,351	...	...	...
143	San Bernardino, Cal..	106,869	91,922	63,058	6,150	...	...
144	Trenton, N.J..	104,786	114,167	128,009	73,307	6,461	...
145	Dearborn, Mich..	104,199	112,007	94,994	844	...	...
146	Scranton, Pa..	103,564	111,443	125,536	102,026	...	...
147	Camden, N.J..	102,551	117,159	124,555	75,935	9,479	...
148	Hialeah, Fla..	102,452	66,972	19,676	...	...	...
149	New Bedford, Mass..	101,777	102,477	109,189	62,442	16,443	3,313
150	Fremont, Cal..	100,869	43,790	...	...	...	...
151	Duluth, Minn..	100,578	106,884	104,511	52,969	...	...
152	Cambridge, Mass..	100,361	107,716	120,740	91,886	15,215	2,115
153	Parma, Oh..	100,216	82,845	28,897	...	...	...
	San Juan, P.R..	452,749	432,377	224,767	32,048	...	...
	Bayamon, P.R..	147,552	13,109	20,171	2,218	...	...
	Ponce, P.R..	128,233	114,286	99,492	27,952	...	...

(1) Population shown for years prior to 1900 is for New York and its boroughs as constituted under the act of consolidation in 1898. (2) Population shown is for 1862 as given in State census for that year; 1850 returns for San Francisco were destoyed by fire. (3) Figure for 1970 is for the Metropolitan Government of Nashville and Davidson County; figures for previous years are for Nashville city. (4) Winston city and Salem town consolidated as Winston-Salem city between 1910 and 1920. Figure for 1900 represents combined population of Winston and Salem.

Foreign Born and 2d Generation in U.S.; Countries of Origin

Source:Bureau of the Census

The table below shows, state by state, the country of origin of U.S. residents who were either foreign born or had at least one foreign-born parent. "Mixed" means one native and one foreign-born parent.

In the table, Germany includes both East and West Germany; West Asia includes European Turkey; and China includes both the mainland and Taiwan.

	Ala.	Alaska	Ariz.	Ark.	Cal.	Col.	Conn.	Del.	D.C.	Fla.
Mixed parents..	47,742	24,842	219,830	29,269	3,234,089	219,579	708,193	48,710	39,340	695,699
Foreign Born...	15,988	7,763	76,570	8,287	1,757,990	60,311	261,614	15,648	33,562	540,284
U.K.	8,944	3,081	19,866	3,797	373,495	26,377	71,532	7,949	5,638	114,870
Ireland	1,912	804	5,670	1,056	109,888	7,804	60,366	4,244	3,553	36,389
Norway	643	2,501	4,745	408	69,278	4,787	5,513	510	504	12,288
Sweden	678	1,565	6,903	1,100	103,913	13,193	23,427	676	773	26,944
Denmark	555	632	3,180	559	61,757	5,508	5,471	231	426	9,944
Netherlands...	526	215	2,947	537	63,772	3,609	3,586	485	408	10,800
Switzerland....	408	201	1,629	989	44,483	2,419	4,291	309	533	6,909
France	1,799	630	2,972	1,010	63,449	3,695	8,388	686	1,881	14,833
Germany	12,074	3,526	25,653	9,806	360,656	43,172	60,290	5,991	5,642	123,429
Poland	2,097	765	7,930	1,331	115,833	7,882	103,820	7,263	2,787	50,591
Czecho	989	536	3,483	1,170	44,964	5,074	19,871	865	804	16,222
Austria	1,556	603	5,370	1,027	77,382	9,242	24,595	1,819	1,612	35,896
Hungary	819	169	3,144	310	58,097	3,035	21,641	952	847	23,054
Yugo	421	361	2,592	198	53,868	6,079	3,447	331	474	-5,728
USSR	1,854	679	8,812	912	221,198	28,023	48,150	3,523	5,597	81,833
Lithuania	415	169	1,591	355	22,063	1,146	20,469	487	953	8,938
Greece	2,092	208	2,009	500	43,645	3,111	10,933	1,117	1,716	11,637
Italy	5,771	866	12,498	2,284	340,675	21,411	227,782	12,112	4,657	84,881
Other Europe..	1,358	1,208	6,952	854	189,979	7,252	32,304	1,648	2,368	47,368
Western Asia..	1,753	103	2,501	672	64,565	2,272	8,655	457	1,614	13,755
China	554	282	3,162	661	136,860	1,697	2,195	523	2,099	3,110
Japan	1,392	1,203	2,310	625	144,335	6,005	1,492	516	602	4,843
Other Asia	1,797	1,808	3,488	945	222,709	4,418	6,008	1,690	4,084	10,963
Canada	5,232	6,499	26,136	3,016	439,862	21,580	126,305	4,047	3,914	114,615
Mexico	975	766	113,816	862	1,112,008	24,759	1,220	246	611	11,047
Cuba	680	56	505	86	47,699	945	5,772	483	902	252,520
Other Amer....	2,146	576	3,586	572	176,586	3,519	18,844	1,239	11,514	44,411

	Ga.	Ha.	Ida.	Ill.	Ind.	Iowa	Kan.	Ky.	La.	Me.
Mixed parents..	78,528	180,577	60,972	1,572,843	268,060	257,342	147,206	56,080	100,221	149,746
Foreign Born...	32,988	75,595	12,572	628,898	83,198	40,217	27,842	16,553	39,542	43,014
U.K.	14,517	5,114	10,406	115,891	30,039	22,008	15,986	7,619	9,252	12,073
Ireland	3,461	1,056	1,653	101,856	9,931	9,441	4,853	3,156	3,240	6,528
Norway	933	664	3,534	34,922	2,934	20,418	1,920	457	1,331	1,234
Sweden	1,641	841	5,333	98,254	8,274	21,108	9,622	817	1,284	2,740
Denmark	759	532	3,627	22,021	2,269	20,024	3,200	473	729	1,050
Netherlands...	971	355	1,568	27,189	6,760	19,213	1,692	555	1,005	448
Switzerland....	517	275	1,736	11,827	3,710	3,476	3,256	1,650	608	222
France	2,684	811	865	19,266	5,372	2,911	2,775	1,848	5,420	1,052
Germany	20,951	5,112	9,894	312,070	64,883	101,974	43,252	21,438	14,237	4,488
Poland	4,574	775	684	299,316	34,590	3,323	4,046	2,147	2,771	2,532
Czecho	1,456	385	1,118	88,259	13,681	10,995	4,978	857	977	741
Austria	2,646	746	1,091	65,026	10,441	3,347	5,581	1,627	1,751	826
Hungary	1,286	342	357	35,822	14,108	1,007	938	1,103	1,267	240
Yugo	824	198	421	59,280	14,410*	2,202	3,815	451	1,412	133
USSR	5,831	828	3,136	110,321	9,933	4,563	17,664	2,531	3,073	2,878
Lithuania	798	207	151	58,285	4,265	1,226	507	545	358	1,172
Greece	2,984	371	657	48,669	7,852	2,085	965	861	1,560	1,281
Italy	5,220	1,656	1,595	228,984	17,935	7,683	4,552	4,499	29,031	6,083
Other Europe..	3,668	8,318	3,966	67,143	15,478	6,160	3,810	2,092	4,149	2,986
Western Asia..	2,457	344	177	18,270	4,098	1,670	1,738	1,523	2,758	1,079
China	1,278	20,939	456	11,833	1,976	1,073	786	539	1,117	284
Japan	1,775	105,223	1,322	12,948	1,888	787	2,435	1,056	1,308	226
Other Asia	4,068	79,410	571	28,637	4,948	2,448	3,066	2,324	3,109	922
Canada	10,021	5,865	10,452	80,611	21,920	13,297	10,425	4,823	6,090	136,801
Mexico	1,562	1,159	5,669	117,268	18,325	4,546	13,728	692	4,865	277
Cuba	3,816	235	73	19,649	1,690	382	796	556	6,711	223
Other Amer....	3,880	1,371	371	31,276	4,208	1,538	2,011	1,998	18,235	808

	Md.	Mass.	Mich.	Minn.	Miss.	Mo.	Mon.	Neb.	Nev.	*N.H.
Mixed parents..	329,813	1,397,064	1,259,961	609,218	22,862	245,948	101,688	175,556	50,274	133,502
Foreign Born...	124,345	494,660	424,309	98,056	8,125	65,744	19,634	28,796	18,179	37,048
U.K.	40,291	152,741	148,612	25,672	3,910	23,080	11,293	11,083	6,969	14,040
Ireland	18,267	218,798	28,667	11,900	816	15,470	5,274	4,846	1,991	8,436
Norway	3,385	8,969	12,899	114,221	347	2,257	14,595	3,183	1,163	1,219
Sweden	4,546	38,753	33,639	114,512	445	6,274	6,177	17,099	1,670	2,774
Denmark	2,461	5,163	11,951	22,762	294	2,879	4,302	13,202	1,485	593
Netherlands...	3,312	5,656	72,763	13,166	237	2,425	2,731	1,754	796	616
Switzerland....	2,437	3,845	5,442	4,282	160	5,204	1,225	2,054	1,103	422
France	6,519	12,342	12,149	3,766	733	5,297	1,160	1,296	1,959	1,265
Germany	59,680	54,846	184,192	137,442	4,960	77,748	15,593	62,726	7,023	6,308
Poland	39,334	117,992	214,085	26,931	730	15,469	1,781	8,333	1,578	6,886
Czecho	11,111	6,434	32,176	17,905	377	7,504	2,171	19,551	796	428
Austria	13,516	16,898	40,730	17,266	576	11,755	3,464	3,612	1,483	1,297
Hungary	7,817	5,583	39,202	3,741	266	5,861	828	1,060	751	481
Yugo	3,148	1,776	30,375	12,266	574	6,517	3,020	1,599	957	229
USSR	46,332	104,223	65,606	18,666	534	19,127	11,365	14,160	2,247	2,982
Lithuania	9,090	32,617	16,908	2,445	152	2,168	242	1,428	282	1,929
Greece	12,508	39,669	19,519	2,833	471	4,209	541	859	1,205	5,040

Continued

Continued from previous page

	Md.	Mass.	Mich.	Minn.	Miss.	Mo.	Mon.	Neb.	Nev.	N.H.
Italy	49,619	294,318	117,064	12,910	3,957	30,114	3,415	6,414	7,927	6,465
Other Europe	15,069	117,653	94,603	41,228	954	9,085	4,157	3,823	3,645	3,952
Western Asia	8,124	27,159	31,579	2,411	1,249	3,279	377	771	633	1,281
China	5,975	11,324	5,725	1,998	1,078	2,337	245	543	811	541
Japan	3,784	3,390	4,952	2,206	394	2,618	675	1,106	1,084	370
Other Asia	13,832	10,897	12,925	4,749	945	5,301	746	1,428	2,148	662
Canada	25,300	466,942	353,154	57,604	2,496	15,532	21,106	8,247	7,587	96,834
Mexico	2,714	2,136	31,067	4,575	783	8,353	1,485	5,552	5,760	209
Cuba	4,931	6,915	3,231	765	241	1,131	45	608	1,306	195
Other Amer	19,309	27,299	13,339	3,390	1,427	3,857	426	1,017	1,147	728

	NJ.	N.M.	N.Y.	N.C.	N.D.	Ohio	Okla.	Ore.	Pa.	R.I.
Mixed parents	1,521,045	66,170	3,885,445	65,661	127,689	994,850	72,713	229,357	1,687,145	237,233
Foreign Born	634,818	22,510	2,109,776	28,620	18,437	316,496	20,160	66,149	445,895	74,374
U.K.	172,308	6,000	334,424	12,826	3,537	108,027	9,812	28,525	198,190	34,178
Ireland	122,600	1,718	386,403	2,506	1,248	37,941	2,386	7,175	118,174	21,041
Norway	17,474	872	47,605	773	38,722	4,382	901	18,085	5,251	1,093
Sweden	19,366	1,681	52,058	1,401	8,434	12,539	1,962	17,830	20,370	6,669
Denmark	11,000	721	20,911	728	3,442	4,492	1,396	8,792	4,935	574
Netherlands	28,440	655	32,043	1,444	1,120	6,539	1,101	4,776	5,691	749
Switzerland	13,219	557	23,773	678	426	12,337	1,200	6,816	8,039	522
France	22,152	1,219	56,861	1,820	402	13,640	1,669	3,263	18,484	3,261
Germany	219,178	7,438	516,216	16,614	21,004	188,386	21,475	40,242	202,611	768
Poland	217,509	1,422	557,478	3,037	1,952	116,262	2,670	4,855	243,752	13,389
Czecho	51,599	763	90,641	1,132	2,473	93,187	3,411	4,144	118,855	763
Austria	83,165	1,483	237,836	1,664	2,254	62,829	1,893	5,294	145,815	2,896
Hungary	70,424	687	115,474	1,190	1,590	82,944	793	2,298	62,014	589
Yugo	16,202	899	41,756	449	194	73,843	400	3,220	54,424	278
USSR	143,234	1,725	569,813	2,928	33,177	54,520	5,463	15,709	157,348	11,198
Lithuania	22,658	371	42,863	545	117	13,979	559	778	43,183	1,459
Greece	25,703	747	90,886	3,883	168	22,210	667	3,480	23,198	2,242
Italy	515,889	3,916	1,330,057	4,658	485	166,629	3,531	9,644	444,841	73,255
Other Europe	69,176	1,725	197,966	2,764	4,076	48,002	2,584	13,752	52,748	33,222
Western Asia	23,415	865	87,036	2,536	770	18,246	2,488	2,348	20,191	4,211
China	7,748	506	66,407	1,178	150	4,987	758	4,423	6,010	1,069
Japan	6,064	1,029	17,304	2,988	391	5,169	1,810	3,983	4,480	783
Other Asia	16,085	1,137	51,785	3,583	553	14,066	2,539	5,345	15,248	2,278
Canada	58,720	5,663	286,047	10,334	15,630	63,258	7,811	53,002	47,827	66,003
Mexico	3,301	37,822	12,249	1,770	276	13,349	6,071	7,739	4,707	407
Cuba	71,233	418	98,479	1,330	46	3,593	352	689	5,195	516
Other Amer	54,867	1,484	415,906	3,012	378	11,679	2,114	2,887	20,183	2,788

	S.C.	S.D.	Tenn.	Tex.	Ut.	Vt.	Va.	Wash.	W.Va.	Wis.
Mixed parents	35,436	98,147	49,368	889,246	102,036	62,680	179,518	481,586	57,358	617,479
Foreign born	14,364	10,899	19,024	309,772	29,573	18,482	72,281	156,020	16,662	130,669
U.K.	7,779	4,562	8,682	49,185	28,531	7,008	32,737	60,522	8,259	28,446
Ireland	1,336	1,980	2,087	12,143	1,416	3,071	10,162	13,266	1,742	9,433
Norway	392	18,898	600	5,442	4,113	651	3,077	60,427	191	52,681
Sweden	686	7,790	1,081	10,873	7,477	1,142	4,144	45,251	601	27,352
Denmark	325	6,584	630	4,801	10,464	476	2,195	14,422	170	18,959
Netherlands	516	5,126	698	4,722	7,617	518	2,690	13,297	223	15,315
Switzerland	576	950	802	4,314	3,392	529	1,640	7,675	762	14,316
France	1,069	399	1,333	8,992	1,014	759	6,210	6,145	881	4,457
Germany	9,193	26,792	11,675	104,726	14,179	4,195	32,596	71,353	6,960	234,767
Poland	1,701	1,052	2,789	16,328	904	2,797	9,423	9,821	6,360	71,534
Czecho	704	3,507	776	29,536	668	393	4,675	6,137	2,996	26,465
Austria	935	1,305	1,354	13,397	1,436	614	6,827	10,332	2,572	27,343
Hungary	479	503	995	4,852	394	602	3,814	4,269	2,931	12,448
Yugo	391	280	376	2,992	1,337	84	1,775	7,580	2,549	19,873
USSR	1,661	14,041	3,649	16,149	1,151	1,171	11,129	23,466	1,996	24,246
Lithuania	228	140	388	2,069	112	211	2,040	1,436	602	5,796
Greece	2,188	284	1,563	6,168	3,372	504	5,712	4,061	1,894	4,746
Italy	2,653	616	6,054	26,886	4,688	4,982	18,026	21,422	17,906	30,513
Other Europe	1,658	2,659	1,678	15,713	2,396	1,707	8,005	24,907	2,564	22,142
Western Asia	1,382	523	1,579	9,219	672	652	6,248	3,411	2,522	3,388
China	408	270	1,032	7,606	983	165	2,936	8,107	135	2,141
Japan	892	273	1,352	8,388	2,834	66	4,691	15,777	433	1,871
Other Asia	2,106	403	2,726	12,465	1,533	449	14,060	18,701	1,704	4,928
Canada	4,805	6,617	6,213	35,900	11,194	46,176	24,048	136,546	2,492	36,888
Mexico	668	472	1,036	711,058	7,710	111	3,167	17,892	513	9,160
Cuba	860	58	894	7,749	116	7	4,479	570	110	787
Other Amer	1,405	303	1,593	21,300	1,593	356	10,538	5,173	772	3,834

Wyoming

Mixed parents	31,014	Germany	5,721	Other Europe	1,194
Foreign born	6,989	Poland	1,033	Western Asia	177
U.K.	5,367	Czecho	824	China	177
Ireland	1,066	Austria	1,300	Japan	341
Norway	1,257	Hungary	250	Other Asia	385
Sweden	2,156	Yugo	1,263	Canada	3,069
Denmark	1,505	USSR	2,913	Mexico	2,638
Netherlands	332	Lithuania	82	Cuba	
Switzerland	563	Greece	728	Other Amer	277
France	504	Italy	1,750		

Jewish Population by Countries and Cities

Source: Jewish Statistical Bureau, Dr. H. S. Linfield, Exec. Secy. Figures are latest estimates

North America	6,145,000	Australia and New Zealand	77,000
Central and South America	787,235	Africa	177,200
Europe	4,150,750	**World Total**	**14,334,195**
Asia	2,997,010		

Europe

Albania	300	Sweden	15,000	El Salvador	300
Austria	12,000	Switzerland	21,000	Guatemala	1,900
Belgium	41,000	Turkey	30,000	Haiti	150
Bulgaria	7,000	Yugoslavia	7,000	Honduras	200
Czechoslovakia	14,000			Jamaica	600
Denmark	6,500	**North America**		Nicaragua	200
Finland	1,300	Canada	305,000	Panama	2,000
France	550,000	United States	5,800,000	Paraguay	1,200
Germany	30,000	Mexico	40,000	Peru	5,500
Gibraltar	600			Trinidad	300
Great Britain	450,000	**Central and**		Uruguay	50,000
Greece	6,500	**South America**		Venezuela	15,000
Hungary	80,000	Argentina	500,000	**Asia**	
Irish Free State	4,000	Barbados	85	Afghanistan	200
Italy	35,000	Bolivia	2,000	Burma	200
Luxembourg	1,000	Brazil	160,000	Cyprus	30
Malta	50	Chile	30,000	China	30
Netherlands	30,000	Colombia	12,000	Hong Kong	200
Norway	900	Costa Rica	2,000	India	12,000
Poland	8,000	Cuba	1,500	Indonesia	100
Portugal	600	Curacao	700	Iran	75,000
Romania	90,000	Dominican Rep.	100	Iraq	500
Soviet Union	2,700,000	Dutch Guiana	500	Israel	3,400,000[1]
Spain	9,000	Ecuador	1,000	Japan	1,000

Lebanon	2,000		
Pakistan	250		
Philippines	500		
Singapore	500		
Syria	4,000		
Yemen	500		
Africa			
Algeria	1,000		
Congo	250		
Egypt	500		
Ethiopia	12,000		
Kenya	200		
Libya	50		
Morocco	30,000		
Rhodesia	4,800		
Tunisia	8,000		
Union of South Africa	120,000		
Zambia	400		
Australia and New Zealand			
Australia	72,000		
New Zealand	5,000		

(1.) Includes about 500,000 Christians and Mohammedans.

Estimated Jewish Population in Foreign Cities

Amsterdam	15,000	Czernowitz	70,000	Manchester and	
Antwerp	13,000	Elat[1]	4,000	Salford	35,000
Ascalon[1]	46,100	Glasgow	13,500	Melbourne	34,000
Ashdod[1]	48,200	Haifa[1]	225,800	Milan	9,500
Beersheba[1]	90,400	Istanbul	22,000	Montreal	114,200
Berlin	6,000	Jerusalem[1]	326,400	Moscow	285,000
Bet Shean[1]	12,000	Johannesburg	57,500	Nazareth[1]	35,400
Birmingham	6,000	Kharkov	80,000	Nazareth Illet[1]	18,000
B'nai B'rak	79,300	Kiev	170,000	Nice	25,000
Bordeaux	6,500	Leeds	18,000	Ottawa	7,225
Brussels	24,500	Leningrad	165,000	Paris	300,000
Bucharest	40,000	Liverpool	6,500	Petach Tikvah	100,000
Budapest	65,000	Lod (Lydda)[1]	30,500	Ramath Gan[1]	121,000
Buenos Aires	350,000	London (gr.)	280,000	Rehovoth	43,300
Casablanca	30,000	Lyons	25,000	Rio de Janeiro	50,000
Copenhagen	6,500	Marseilles	65,000	Rome	13,267

Safed	14,400		
Santiago	25,000		
Sao Paulo	65,000		
Stockholm	8,000		
Strasbourg	12,000		
Sydney	25,300		
Teheran	50,000		
Tel Aviv-Jaffa[1]	367,600		
Tiberias[1]	35,300		
Toronto	97,000		
Toulouse	18,000		
Vancouver	10,815		
Vienna	9,000		
Warsaw	5,000		
Winnipeg	21,000		
Zurich	6,000		

(1.) Includes some Christians, Mohammedans

Estimated Jewish Population in Large U. S. Cities

Albany	13,500	Elizabeth*	50,000	Queens	420,000
Alexandria, Arlington & Fairfax cos., Va.	15,000	Hartford	23,000	Richmond	11,000
		Hollywood, Fla.	25,000	N.Y. City.	
		Houston	22,000	environs	
Atlanta	18,000	Jersey City	10,000	Nassau Co.	372,000
Atlantic City	10,000	Kansas City	22,000	Suffolk Co.	42,000
Baltimore	100,000	Long Beach, Cal.	16,000	Westchester Co.	131,000
Bergen County	94,000	Los Angeles*	463,000	Newark:	
Boston	180,000	Lynn	19,000	Essex Co.	95,000
Bridgeport	14,500	Miami*	200,000	Oakland:	
Buffalo	24,000	Milwaukee	24,000	Alameda and Contra Costa Co.*	21,000
Camden	21,000	Minneapolis	22,000		
Chicago	253,000	Montg'y Co., Md.	50,000	Orange Co.	
Cincinnati	30,000	New B'nswick*	18,000	Calif.	37,500
Cleveland	80,000	New Haven	20,000	Passaic	9,200
Columbus	13,000	New Orleans	10,500	Paterson*	28,000
Dallas	20,000	New York City.	1,836,000	Philadelphia*	350,000
Denver	26,000	Manhattan	250,000	Phoenix*	14,000
Detroit	80,000	Bronx	395,000		
		Brooklyn	760,000		

Pittsburgh	45,000		
Prince George County, Md.	15,000		
Providence*	22,000		
Richmond, Va.	10,000		
Rochester	21,500		
Rockland Co., N.Y.	25,000		
St. Louis	60,000		
St. Paul	10,000		
San Diego	14,000		
San Francisco*	75,000		
Seattle	12,500		
Springfield, Mass.	11,000		
Stanford	11,000		
Syracuse	11,000		
Trenton, N.J.	10,000		
Washington	113,000		
Worcester*	10,000		

*Indicates greater area.

Black Population by States

Source: Bureau of the Census (1970)

Ala.	903,467	Ill.	1,425,674	Mon.	1,995	R.I.	25,338
Alaska	8,911	Ind.	357,464	Neb.	39,911	S.C.	789,041
Ariz.	53,344	Iowa	32,596	Nev.	27,762	S.D.	1,627
Ark.	352,445	Kan.	106,977	N.H.	2,505	Tenn.	621,261
Cal.	1,400,143	Ky.	230,793	N.J.	770,292	Tex.	1,399,005
Col.	66,411	La.	1,086,832	N.M.	19,555	Ut.	6,617
Conn.	181,177	Me.	2,800	N.Y.	2,168,949	Vt.	761
Del.	78,276	Md.	699,479	N.C.	1,126,478	Va.	861,368
D.C.	537,712	Mass.	175,817	N.D.	2,494	Wash.	71,308
Fla.	1,401,651	Mich.	991,066	Oh.	970,477	W.Va.	67,342
Ga.	1,187,149	Minn.	34,868	Okla.	171,892	Wis.	128,224
Ha.	7,573	Miss.	815,770	Ore.	26,308	Wy.	2,568
Ida.	2,130	Mo.	480,172	Pa.	1,016,514	**Total**	**22,580,289**

U.S. Places of 5,000 or More Population—with ZIP Codes
Source: U.S. Bureau of the Census; U.S. Postal Service

The listings below show the official urban population of the United States. "Urban population" is defined as all persons living in (a) places of 5,000 inhabitants or more, incorporated as cities, villages, boroughs (except Alaska), and towns (except in New England, New York, New Jersey, Pennsylvania and Wisconsin), but excluding those persons living in the rural portions of extended cities; (b) unincorporated places of 5,000 inhabitants or more; and (c) other territory, incorporated or unincorporated, included in urbanized areas.

The non-urban portion of an extended city contains one or more areas, each at least 5 square miles in extent and with a population density of less than 100 persons per square mile. The area or areas constitute at least 25 percent of the legal city's land area of a total of 25 square miles or more.

In New England, New York, New Jersey, Pennsylvania, and Wisconsin, minor civil divisions called "towns" often include rural areas and one or more urban areas. Only the urban areas of these "towns" are included here, except in the case of New England where entire town populations, which may include some rural population, are shown in italics. Boroughs in Alaska may contain one or more urban areas which are included here.

Where special censuses were taken after April 1, 1970, the year appears after the name of the place.

The ZIP Code of each place appears before the name of that place, if it is obtainable.

CAUTION—Where an asterisk (*) appears before the ZIP Code, ask your local postmaster for the correct ZIP Code for a specific address within the place listed.

ZIP Code	Place	1970	1960	ZIP Code	Place	1970	1960
	Alabama			35401	Tuscaloosa	65,773	63,370
				35674	Tuscumbia	8,828	8,994
35950	Albertville	9,963	8,250	36083	Tuskegee	11,028	7,240
35010	Alexander City	12,358	13,140	35216	Vestavia Hills	8,311	4,029
36420	Andalusia	10,092	10,263	36201	West End—Cobb	5,515	5,485
36201	Anniston	31,533	33,657				
	Anniston Northwest	6,609			**Alaska**		
35611	Athens	14,360	9,330				
36502	Atmore	8,293	8,173	*99502	Anchorage	48,081	44,237
35954	Attalla	7,510	8,257	99702	Eielson	6,149	......
36830	Auburn	22,767	16,261	99506	Elmendorf	6,018	......
36507	Bay Minette	6,727	5,197	99701	Fairbanks	14,771	13,311
*35203	Birmingham	300,910	340,887	99505	Fort Richardson	10,751	......
35226	Bluff Park	12,431	......	99703	Fort Wainwright	9,097	......
35957	Boaz	5,635	4,654	99801	Juneau	6,050	6,797
36426	Brewton	6,747	6,309	99901	Ketchikan	6,994	6,483
35215	Center Point	15,675	......	99503	Spenard	18,089	9,074
36611	Chickasaw	8,447	10,002				
35045	Clanton	5,868	5,863		**Arizona**		
35055	Cullman	12,601	10,883				
36322	Daleville	5,182	693	85321	Ajo	5,881	7,049
35601	Decatur	38,044	29,217	85323	Avondale	6,626	6,151
36732	Demopolis	7,651	7,377	85603	Bisbee	8,328	9,914
36301	Dothan	36,733	31,440	85222	Casa Grande	10,536	8,311
36330	Enterprise	15,591	11,410	85224	Chandler	13,763	9,531
36027	Eufaula	9,102	8,357	85533	Clifton	5,087	4,191
35064	Fairfield	14,369	15,816	85228	Coolidge	5,314	4,990
36532	Fairhope	5,720	4,858	85607	Douglas	12,462	11,925
35630	Florence	34,031	31,649	85231	Eloy	5,381	4,899
35214	Forestdale	6,091	......	86001	Flagstaff	26,117	18,214
36201	Fort McClellan	5,334	......	85613	Fort Huachuca	6,659	......
35967	Fort Payne	8,435	7,029	*85301	Glendale	36,228	15,893
36360	Fort Rucker	14,242	......	85501	Globe	7,333	6,217
35068	Fultondale	5,163	2,001	86401	Kingman 1974	7,202	4,525
*35901	Gadsden	53,928	58,088	85301	Luke	5,047	......
35071	Gardendale	6,537	4,712	*85201	Mesa	62,853	33,772
36037	Greenville	8,033	6,894	85621	Nogales	8,946	7,286
35976	Guntersville	6,491	6,592	85253	Paradise Valley	7,155	......
35640	Hartselle	7,355	5,000	*85026	Phoenix	582,500	439,170
35209	Homewood	21,137	20,289	86301	Prescott	13,283	12,861
35020	Hueytown	8,174	5,997	85546	Safford	5,333	4,648
*35804	Huntsville	139,282	72,365	*85251	Scottsdale	67,823	10,026
36545	Jackson	5,957	4,959	85635	Sierra Vista	6,689	3,121
36265	Jacksonville	7,715	5,678	85713	South Tucson	6,220	7,004
35501	Jasper	10,798	10,799	85351	Sun City	13,670	......
36863	Lanett	6,908	7,674	*85282	Tempe	63,550	24,897
35094	Leeds	6,991	6,162	*85726	Tucson	262,933	212,892
35228	Midfield	6,340	3,556	85364	West Yuma	5,552	2,781
*36601	Mobile	190,026	194,856	86047	Winslow	8,066	8,862
*36104	Montgomery	133,386	134,393	85364	Yuma	29,007	23,974
35223	Mountain Brook	19,509	12,680				
35660	Muscle Shoals	6,907	4,084		**Arkansas**		
35476	Northport	9,435	5,245				
36801	Opelika	19,027	15,678	71923	Arkadelphia	9,841	8,069
36467	Opp	6,493	5,535	72501	Batesville	7,209	6,207
36360	Ozark	13,555	9,534	72015	Benton	16,499	10,399
35125	Pell City	5,602	4,165	72712	Bentonville, 1972	6,391	3,649
36867	Phenix City	25,281	27,630	72315	Blytheville	24,752	20,797
36272	Piedmont	5,063	4,794	72021	Brinkley	5,275	4,636
35127	Pleasant Grove	5,090	3,097	71701	Camden	15,147	15,823
36067	Prattville	13,116	6,616	72032	Conway 1973	16,772	9,791
36610	Prichard	41,578	47,371	71635	Crossett	6,191	5,370
36274	Roanoke	5,251	5,288	71730	El Dorado	25,283	25,292
35653	Russellville	7,814	6,628	72701	Fayetteville 1972	31,915	20,274
36571	Saraland	7,840	4,595	72335	Forrest City	12,521	10,544
35768	Scottsboro	9,324	6,449	72901	Fort Smith 1973	65,393	52,991
36701	Selma	27,379	28,385	72601	Harrison	7,239	6,580
35660	Sheffield	13,115	13,491	72342	Helena 1971	10,201	11,500
35150	Sylacauga	12,255	12,857	71801	Hope	8,830	8,399
35160	Talladega	17,662	17,742	71901	Hot Springs	35,631	28,337
35217	Tarrant City	6,835	7,810	72076	Jacksonville 1972	22,392	14,488
36081	Troy	11,482	10,234				

ZIP Code	Place	1970	1960
72401	Jonesboro 1974	28,962	21,418
*72201	Little Rock 1974	139,703	107,813
71753	Magnolia 1973	11,527	10,651
72104	Malvern 1974	9,848	9,566
72360	Marianna	6,196	5,134
71655	Monticello 1972	7,034	4,412
72110	Morrilton	6,814	5,997
72653	Mountain Home 1973	5,028	2,105
72112	Newport	7,725	7,007
*72114	North Little Rock	60,040	58,032
72370	Osceola	7,204	6,189
72450	Paragould	10,639	9,947
71601	Pine Bluff	57,389	44,037
72756	Rogers 1973	13,189	5,700
72801	Russellville	11,750	8,921
72143	Searcy 1973	10,867	7,272
72761	Siloam Springs	6,009	3,953
72204	Southwest Little Rock	13,231	......
72754	Springdale 1974	19,962	10,076
72160	Stuttgart	10,477	9,661
75501	Texarkana	21,682	19,788
72472	Trumann	6,023	4,511
72956	Van Buren	8,373	6,787
71671	Warren	6,433	6,752
72390	West Helena 1973	10,838	8,385
72301	West Memphis 1973	28,236	19,374
72396	Wynne 1974	7,292	4,922

California

ZIP Code	Place	1970	1960
94501	Alameda	70,968	63,855
94507	Alamo-Danville	14,059	......
94706	Albany	14,674	14,804
*91802	Alhambra	62,125	54,807
90249	Alondra Park	12,193	......
91001	Altadena	42,415	40,568
95116	Alum Rock	18,355	18,942
*92803	Anaheim	166,408	104,184
96007	Anderson	5,492	4,492
94509	Antioch	28,060	17,305
92307	Apple Valley	6,702	......
95003	Aptos	8,704	......
91006	Arcadia	45,138	41,005
95521	Arcata	8,985	5,235
95825	Arden-Arcade	82,492	73,352
93420	Arroyo Grande	7,454	3,291
90701	Artesia	14,757	9,993
93203	Arvin	5,199	......
94577	Ashland	14,810	......
93422	Atascadero	10,290	5,983
94025	Atherton	8,085	7,717
95301	Atwater	11,640	7,318
95603	Auburn	6,570	5,586
92505	August School Area	6,735	......
91746	Avocado Heights	9,810	......
91702	Azusa	25,217	20,497
*93302	Bakersfield	69,515	56,848
91706	Baldwin Park	47,285	33,951
92220	Banning	12,034	10,250
92311	Barstow	17,442	11,644
95903	Beale East	7,029	......
92223	Beaumont	5,484	4,288
90201	Bell	21,836	19,450
90706	Bellflower	51,454	45,909
90201	Bell Gardens	29,308	......
94002	Belmont	23,538	15,996
94510	Benicia	7,349	6,070
*94704	Berkeley	116,716	111,268
*90213	Beverly Hills	33,416	30,817
92314	Big Bear	5,268	1,562
92316	Bloomington	11,957	......
92225	Blythe	7,047	6,023
92227	Brawley	13,746	12,703
92621	Brea	18,447	8,487
95605	Broderick-Bryte	12,782	......
*90620	Buena Park	63,646	46,401
*91505	Burbank	88,871	90,155
94010	Burlingame	27,320	24,036
92231	Calexico	10,625	7,992
93725	Calwa	5,191	......
93010	Camarillo	19,219	......
93010	Camarillo Heights	5,892	1,704
95124	Cambrian Park	5,316	......
95008	Campbell	24,770	11,863
95010	Capitola	5,080	2,021
92007	Cardiff-by-the-Sea	5,724	3,149
92008	Carlsbad	14,944	9,253
95608	Carmichael	37,625	20,455
93013	Carpinteria	6,982	......
90744	Carson	71,150	......
94546	Castro Valley	44,760	37,120
95307	Ceres	6,029	4,406
90701	Cerritos	15,856	3,508
94541	Cherryland	9,969	......
95926	Chico	19,580	14,757
95926	Chico North	6,656	......
93555	China Lake	11,105	......
91710	Chino	20,411	10,305

ZIP Code	Place	1970	1960
*92010	Chula Vista	67,901	42,034
95610	Citrus Heights	21,760	......
91711	Claremont	23,464	12,633
93612	Clovis	13,856	5,546
92236	Coachella	8,353	4,854
93210	Coalinga	6,161	5,965
92324	Colton	20,016	18,666
*90220	Compton	78,547	71,812
90022	Commerce	10,536	9,555
*94520	Concord	85,164	36,000
93212	Corcoran	5,249	4,976
91720	Corona	27,519	13,336
92118	Coronado	20,020	18,039
94925	Corte Madera	8,464	5,962
*92626	Costa Mesa	72,660	37,550
*91722	Covina	30,395	20,124
91730	Cucamonga	5,796	......
90201	Cudahy	16,998	......
90230	Culver City	34,451	32,163
95014	Cupertino	18,216	3,664
90630	Cypress	31,569	1,753
*94017	Daly City	66,922	44,791
95616	Davis	23,488	8,910
90250	Del Aire	11,930	......
93215	Delano	14,559	11,913
91765	Diamond Bar	10,576	......
93618	Dinuba	7,917	6,103
90810	Dominguez	5,980	......
*90241	Downey	88,442	82,505
91010	Duarte	14,981	13,962
94566	Dublin	13,641	......
90220	East Compton	5,853	......
90638	East La Mirada	12,339	......
90022	East Los Angeles	105,033	104,270
94303	East Palo Alto	18,099	......
93523	Edwards	10,331	......
*92020	El Cajon	52,273	37,618
92243	El Centro 1973	21,134	16,811
94530	El Cerrito	25,190	25,437
93017	El Encanto Heights	6,225	......
91734	El Monte	69,892	13,163
93446	El Paso de Robles	7,168	6,677
93030	El Rio	6,173	6,966
90245	El Segundo	15,620	14,219
92630	El Toro	8,654	......
92709	El Toro Station	6,970	......
92024	Encinitas	5,375	2,786
96001	Enterprise	11,486	4,946
*92025	Escondido	36,792	16,377
95501	Eureka	24,337	28,137
94930	Fairfax	7,661	5,813
94533	Fairfield	44,146	14,968
95628	Fair Oaks	11,256	......
92028	Fallbrook	6,945	4,814
93015	Fillmore	6,285	4,808
94001	Florence-Graham	42,900	38,164
95828	Florin	9,646	......
95630	Folsom	5,810	3,925
92335	Fontana	20,673	14,659
94404	Foster City	9,522	......
92708	Fountain Valley	31,886	2,068
95019	Freedom	5,563	4,206
*94536	Fremont	100,869	43,790
*93706	Fresno	165,972	133,929
*92631	Fullerton	85,987	56,180
*90247	Gardena	41,021	35,943
95205	Garden Acres	7,870	......
*92640	Garden Grove	121,357	84,238
92392	George	7,404	......
95020	Gilroy	12,665	7,348
92509	Glen Avon	5,759	3,416
*91209	Glendale	132,664	119,442
91740	Glendora	31,380	20,752
92324	Grand Terrace	5,901	......
95945	Grass Valley	5,149	4,876
92041	Grossmont-Mt. Helix	8,723	......
93433	Grover City	5,939	5,210
91745	Hacienda Heights	35,969	......
93230	Hanford	15,179	10,133
90716	Hawaiian Gardens	9,052	......
90250	Hawthorne	53,304	33,035
*94544	Hayward	93,058	72,700
95448	Healdsburg	5,438	4,816
92343	Hemet	12,252	5,416
92343	Hemet East	8,598	1,936
90254	Hermosa Beach	17,412	16,115
92346	Highland	12,699	......
94010	Hillsborough	8,753	7,554
95023	Hollister	7,663	6,071
91720	Home Gardens	5,116	1,541
*92647	Huntington Beach	115,960	11,492
90255	Huntington Park	33,744	29,920
92032	Imperial Beach	20,244	17,773
92201	Indio	14,459	9,745
*90306	Inglewood	89,985	63,390
93017	Isla Vista	13,441	......
94707	Kensington	5,823	......
91011	La Canada-Flintridge	20,714	18,338

ZIP Code	Place	1970	1960	ZIP Code	Place	1970	1960
91214	La Crescenta-Montrose	19,620	......	90723	Paramount	34,734	27,249
90045	Ladera Heights	6,535	......	95823	Parkway-Sacramento So.	28,574	......
94549	Lafayette	20,484	7,114	*91109	Pasadena	112,951	116,407
*92651	Laguna Beach	14,550	9,288	92055	Pendleton North	11,803	......
92653	Laguna Hills	13,676	......	92055	Pendleton South	13,692	......
90631	La Habra	41,350	25,136	94952	Petaluma	24,870	14,035
92040	Lakeside	11,991	......	90660	Pico Rivera	54,170	49,150
*90714	Lakewood	83,025	67,126	94611	Piedmont	10,917	11,117
92041	La Mesa	39,178	30,441	94564	Pinole	13,266	6,064
90638	La Mirada	30,808	22,444	94565	Pittsburg	20,651	19,062
93241	Lamont	7,007	6,177	92670	Placentia	21,948	5,861
93534	Lancaster	32,728	26,012	95667	Placerville	5,416	4,439
90624	La Palma	9,687	622	94523	Pleasant Hill	24,610	23,844
*91747	La Puente	31,092	24,723	94566	Pleasanton	18,328	4,203
94939	Larkspur	10,487	5,710	*91766	Pomona	87,384	67,157
91750	La Verne	12,965	6,516	93257	Porterville	12,602	7,991
90260	Lawndale	24,825	21,740	93257	Porterville West	6,200	......
92045	Lemon Grove	19,690	19,348	93041	Port Hueneme	14,295	11,067
93245	Lemoore Station	9,210	......	92064	Poway	9,422	1,921
90304	Lennox	16,121	31,224	95670	Rancho Cordova	30,451	7,429
95207	Lincoln Village	6,112	......	95014	Rancho Rinconada	5,149	......
95901	Linda	7,731	6,129	96080	Red Bluff	7,676	7,202
93247	Lindsay	5,206	5,397	96001	Redding	16,659	12,773
95062	Live Oak (Santa Cruz)	6,443	3,518	92373	Redlands	36,355	26,829
94550	Livermore	37,703	16,058	*90277	Redondo Beach	57,451	46,986
95240	Lodi	28,691	22,229	*94064	Redwood City	55,686	46,290
90717	Lomita	19,784	......	93654	Reedley	8,131	5,850
93436	Lompoc	25,284	14,415	92376	Rialto	28,370	18,567
*90801	Long Beach	358,879	344,168	*94802	Richmond	79,043	71,854
90720	Los Alamitos	11,346	4,312	93555	Ridgecrest	7,6..	......
94022	Los Altos	24,726	19,696	95673	Rio Linda	...24	2,189
94022	Los Altos Hills	6,865	3,412	*92502	Riverside	1..,089	84,332
*90052	Los Angeles	2,809,813	2,479,015	94572	Rodeo	5,356	......
93635	Los Banos	9,188	5,272	94928	Rohnert Park	6,133	......
95030	Los Gatos	23,735	9,036	90274	Rolling Hills Estates	6,735	3,941
90262	Lynwood	43,354	31,614	95401	Roseland	5,105	4,510
93637	Madera	16,044	14,430	91770	Rosemead	40,972	15,476
90266	Manhattan Beach	35,352	33,934	95678	Roseville	18,221	13,421
95336	Manteca	13,845	8,242	90720	Rossmoor	12,922	......
93933	Marina	8,343	3,310	91745	Rowland Heights	16,881	......
94553	Martinez	16,506	9,604	92509	Rubidoux	13,969	......
95901	Marysville	9,353	9,553	*95813	Sacramento	257,105	191,667
95655	Mather	7,027	......	93901	Salinas	58,896	28,957
90270	Maywood	16,996	14,588	94960	San Anselmo	13,031	11,584
93023	Meiners Oaks-Mira Mone.	7,025	......	*92403	San Bernardino	106,869	91,922
94025	Menlo Park	26,826	26,957	94066	San Bruno	36,2..	29,063
95340	Merced	22,670	20,068	......	San Buenaventura (See Ventura)		
94030	Millbrae	20,792	15,873	94070	San Carlos	26,053	21,370
94941	Mill Valley	12,942	10,411	92672	San Clemente	17,063	8,527
95035	Milpitas	27,149	6,572	*92109	San Diego	697,027	573,224
91752	Mira Loma	8,482	3,982	91773	San Dimas	15,692	......
92675	Mission Viejo	11,933	......	*91340	San Fernando	16,571	16,093
*95350	Modesto	61,712	36,585	*94101	San Francisco	715,674	740,316
91016	Monrovia	30,562	27,079	91776	San Gabriel	29,336	22,561
91763	Montclair	22,546	13,546	93657	Sanger	10,088	8,072
90640	Montebello	42,807	32,097	*95101	San Jose	445,779	204,196
93940	Monterey	26,302	22,618	*94577	San Leandro	68,698	65,962
91754	Monterey Park	49,166	37,821	94580	San Lorenzo	24,633	23,773
94556	Moraga	14,205	......	93401	San Luis Obispo	28,036	20,437
95037	Morgan Hill	6,485	3,151	91108	San Marino	14,177	13,658
93442	Morro Bay	7,109	......	*94402	San Mateo	78,991	69,870
*94042	Mountain View	54,304	30,889	94806	San Pablo	21,461	19,687
92405	Muscoy	7,091	......	*94901	San Rafael	38,977	20,460
94558	Napa	35,978	22,170	*92711	Santa Ana	155,762	100,350
92050	National City	43,184	32,771	*93102	Santa Barbara	70,215	58,768
94560	Newark	27,153	9,884	*95050	Santa Clara	87,717	58,880
91321	Newhall	9,651	4,705	95060	Santa Cruz	32,076	25,596
*92660	Newport Beach	49,422	26,564	90670	Santa Fe Springs	14,750	16,342
91760	Norco	14,511	......	93454	Santa Maria	32,749	20,027
94025	North Fair Oaks	9,740	......	93454	Santa Maria South	7,129	......
95660	North Highlands	31,854	21,271	*90406	Santa Monica	88,289	83,249
92135	North Island	6,892	......	93060	Santa Paula	18,001	13,279
90650	Norwalk	91,827	88,739	*95402	Santa Rosa	50,006	31,027
94947	Novato	31,006	17,881	92071	Santee	21,107	......
95361	Oakdale	6,594	4,980	95070	Saratoga	27,110	14,861
*94615	Oakland	361,561	367,548	94965	Sausalito	6,158	5,331
92054	Oceanside	40,494	24,971	90740	Seal Beach	24,441	6,994
93308	Oildale	20,879	......	93955	Seaside	35,935	19,353
93023	Ojai	5,591	4,495	93662	Selma	7,459	6,934
95961	Olivehurst	8,100	4,835	93263	Shafter	5,327	4,576
*91761	Ontario	64,118	46,617	91024	Sierra Madre	12,140	9,732
95060	Opal Cliffs	5,425	3,825	90806	Signal Hill	5,588	4,627
*92667	Orange	77,365	26,444	*93065	Simi Valley	59,832	......
95662	Orangevale	16,493	......	92075	Solana Beach	5,023	......
93454	Orcutt	8,500	1,414	95073	Soquel	5,795	......
94563	Orinda	6,790	5,568	91733	South El Monte	13,443	4,850
95965	Oroville	7,536	6,115	90280	South Gate	56,909	53,831
92010	Otay-Castle Park	15,445	......	95705	South Lake Tahoe	12,921	......
93030	Oxnard	71,225	40,265	95350	South Modesto	7,889	5,465
94044	Pacifica	36,020	20,995	91030	South Pasadena	22,979	19,706
93950	Pacific Grove	13,505	12,121	94080	South San Francisco	46,646	39,418
93550	Palmdale	8,511	......	91770	South San Gabriel	5,051	......
92260	Palm Desert	6,171	1,295	91744	South San Jose Hills	12,386	......
92262	Palm Springs	20,936	13,468	90605	South Whittier	46,641	......
*94302	Palo Alto	55,835	52,287	95991	South Yuba	......	3,200
90274	Palos Verdes Estates	13,631	9,564	*92077	Spring Valley	29,742	......
90274	Palos Verdes Peninsula	38,914	......	94305	Stanford	8,691	......
*95969	Paradise	14,539	8,268	90680	Stanton	18,186	11,163

ZIP Code	Place	1970	1960
*95204	Stockton	109,963	86,321
92381	Sun City	5,519	
92388	Sunnymead	6,708	3,404
*94086	Sunnyvale	95,408	52,898
96130	Susanville	6,608	5,598
91780	Temple City	31,034	
*91360	Thousand Oaks	35,873	
94920	Tiburon	6,209	
*90510	Torrance	134,968	100,991
95376	Tracy	14,724	11,289
93274	Tulare	16,235	13,824
95380	Turlock	13,992	9,116
92680	Tustin	21,180	2,006
92705	Tustin-Foothills	26,598	
92277	Twentynine Palms	5,667	
92278	Twentynine Palms Base	5,647	
95482	Ukiah	10,095	9,900
94587	Union City	14,724	6,618
91786	Upland	32,551	15,918
95688	Vacaville	21,690	10,898
91744	Valinda	18,837	
94590	Vallejo	71,710	60,877
93437	Vandenburg	13,193	
*93001	Ventura	57,964	29,114
92392	Victorville	10,845	
90043	View Park-Windsor Hills	12,268	
93277	Visalia	27,268	15,791
92083	Vista	24,688	
91789	Walnut	5,992	934
*94596	Walnut Creek	39,844	9,903
94596	Walnut Creek West	8,330	
90255	Walnut Park	8,925	
93280	Wasco	8,269	6,841
95076	Watsonville	14,569	13,293
90044	West Athens	13,311	
90502	West Carson	15,918	
90247	West Compton	5,605	
*91793	West Covina	68,034	50,645
90069	West Hollywood	34,622	28,870
92683	Westminster	59,874	25,750
95351	West Modesto	6,135	1,897
90047	Westmont	29,310	
94565	West Pittsburg	5,969	5,188
91746	West Puente Valley	20,733	
95691	West Sacramento	12,002	
*90605	West Whittier-Los Nietos	20,845	
*90605	Whittier	72,863	33,663
90222	Willowbrook	32,328	
95695	Woodland	20,677	13,524
92686	Yorba Linda	11,856	
96097	Yreka City	5,394	4,759
95991	Yuba City	13,986	11,507
92399	Yucaipa	19,284	
	Colorado		
81101	Alamosa	6,985	6,205
80401	Applewood	8,214	
*80001	Arvada	49,083	19,242
80010	Aurora	74,974	48,548
*80302	Boulder	66,870	37,718
80601	Brighton	8,309	7,055
80020	Broomfield	7,261	
81212	Canon City	9,206	8,973
*80901	Colorado Springs	135,060	70,194
80022	Commerce City	17,407	8,970
81321	Cortez	6,032	6,764
*80202	Denver	514,678	493,887
80022	Derby	10,226	10,124
81301	Durango	10,333	10,530
80110	Englewood	33,695	33,398
80913	Fort Carson	19,399	
80521	Fort Collins	43,337	25,027
80701	Fort Morgan	7,594	7,379
80401	Golden	9,817	7,118
81501	Grand Junction	20,170	18,694
80631	Greeley	38,902	26,314
81050	La Junta	7,938	8,026
80215	Lakewood	92,743	
81052	Lamar	7,797	7,369
80120	Littleton	26,466	13,670
80120	Littleton Southeast	22,899	
80501	Longmont	23,209	11,489
80537	Loveland	16,220	9,734
81401	Montrose	6,496	5,044
80233	North Glenn	27,937	
81501	Orchard Mesa	5,824	4,956
*81003	Pueblo	97,453	91,181
80911	Security-Widefield	15,297	9,017
80221	Sherrewood	18,868	
80751	Sterling	10,636	10,751
80906	Stratton Meadows	6,223	
80229	Thornton	13,326	11,353
81082	Trinidad	9,901	10,691
80229	Welby	6,875	
80030	Westminster	19,432	13,850
80221	Westminster East	7,576	
80033	Wheat Ridge	29,778	

ZIP Code	Place	1970	1960
	Connecticut		
	See Note on Page 215		
06401	Ansonia	21,160	19,819
06001	Avon	8,352	5,273
06037	Berlin	14,149	11,250
06801	Bethel	10,945	8,200
06002	Bloomfield	18,301	13,613
06405	Branford	20,444	16,610
*06602	Bridgeport	156,542	156,748
06010	Bristol	55,487	45,499
06804	Brookfield	9,688	3,405
06019	Canton	6,868	4,783
06410	Cheshire	19,051	13,383
06413	Clinton	10,267	4,166
06413	Clinton Center	5,957	2,693
06415	Colchester	6,603	4,648
06340	Conning Towers-Nautilus Park	9,791	3,457
06238	Coventry	8,140	6,356
06416	Cromwell	7,400	6,780
06810	Danbury	50,781	22,928
06820	Darien	20,411	18,437
06418	Derby	12,599	12,132
06424	East Hampton	7,078	5,403
06108	East Hartford	57,583	43,977
06512	East Haven	25,120	21,388
06333	East Lyme	11,399	6,782
06016	East Windsor	8,513	7,500
06029	Ellington	7,707	5,580
06082	Enfield	46,189	31,464
06430	Fairfield	56,487	46,183
06032	Farmington	14,390	10,813
06033	Glastonbury	20,651	14,497
06035	Granby	6,150	4,968
06830	Greenwich	59,755	53,793
06351	Griswold	7,763	6,472
06340	Groton	38,244	29,937
06340	Groton Borough	8,933	10,111
06437	Guilford	2,023	7,913
06514	Hamden	49,357	41,056
*06101	Hartford	158,017	162,178
06239	Killingly	13,573	11,298
06339	Ledyard	14,837	5,395
06759	Litchfield	7,399	6,264
06443	Madison	9,768	4,567
06040	Manchester	47,994	42,102
06250	Mansfield	19,994	14,638
06450	Meriden	55,959	51,850
06762	Middlebury	5,542	4,785
06457	Middletown	36,924	33,250
06460	Milford	50,858	41,662
06468	Monroe	12,047	6,402
06353	Montville	15,662	7,759
06770	Naugatuck	23,034	19,511
*06050	New Britain	83,441	82,201
06840	New Canaan	17,455	13,466
06810	New Fairfield	6,991	3,355
*06510	New Haven	137,707	152,048
06111	Newington	26,037	17,664
06320	New London	31,630	34,182
06776	New Milford	14,601	8,318
06470	Newtown	16,942	11,373
06471	North Branford	10,778	6,771
06473	North Haven	22,194	15,935
06856	Norwalk	79,113	67,775
06360	Norwich	41,739	38,506
06475	Old Saybrook	8,468	5,274
06477	Orange	13,524	8,547
02891	Pawcatuck	5,255	4,389
06374	Plainfield	11,957	8,884
06062	Plainville	16,733	13,149
06782	Plymouth	10,321	8,981
06480	Portland	8,812	7,496
06712	Prospect	6,543	4,367
06260	Putnam	6,918	6,952
	Putnam	8,598	8,412
06875	Redding	5,590	3,359
06877	Ridgefield	5,878	2,954
	Ridgefield	18,188	8,165
06067	Rocky Hill	11,103	7,404
06483	Seymour	12,776	10,100
06484	Shelton	27,165	18,190
06070	Simsbury	17,475	10,138
06071	Somers	6,983	3,702
06488	Southbury	7,852	5,186
06489	Southington	30,946	22,797
06074	South Windsor	15,553	9,460
06075	Stafford	8,680	7,476
*06904	Stamford	108,798	92,713
06378	Stonington	15,940	13,969
06268	Storrs	10,691	6,054
06497	Stratford	49,775	45,012
06078	Suffield	8,634	6,779
06787	Thomaston	6,233	5,850
06277	Thompson	7,580	6,217
06084	Tolland	7,857	2,950
06790	Torrington	31,952	30,045
06611	Trumbull	31,394	20,379

ZIP Code	Place	1970	1960
06060	Vernon	27,237	16,961
06492	Wallingford	35,714	29,920
*06701	Waterbury	108,033	107,130
06385	Waterford	17,227	15,391
06795	Watertown	18,610	14,837
06107	West Hartford	68,031	62,382
06516	West Haven	52,851	43,002
06880	Weston	7,417	4,039
06880	Westport	27,414	20,955
06109	Wethersfield	26,662	20,561
06226	Willimantic	14,402	13,881
06897	Wilton	13,572	8,026
06094	Winchester	11,106	10,496
06280	Windham	19,626	16,973
06095	Windsor	22,502	19,467
06096	Windsor Locks	15,080	11,411
06098	Winsted	8,954	8,136
06716	Wolcott	12,495	8,889
06525	Woodbridge	7,673	5,182
06798	Woodbury	5,869	3,910

Delaware

ZIP Code	Place	1970	1960
19711	Brookside Park	7,856	
19703	Claymont	6,584	
19901	Dover	17,488	7,250
19901	Dover Base	8,106	
19805	Elsmere	8,415	7,319
19963	Milford	5,314	5,795
19711	Newark	21,298	11,404
19973	Seaford	5,537	4,430
*19899	Wilmington	80,386	95,827
19720	Wilmington Manor —Chelsea—Leedom	10,134	

District of Columbia

ZIP Code	Place	1970	1960
*20013	Washington	756,510	763,956
	Northeast	184,439	197,536
	Northwest	347,337	374,165
	Southeast	194,365	173,988
	Southwest	30,369	18,267

Florida

ZIP Code	Place	1970	1960
33821	Arcadia	5,658	5,889
33823	Auburndale	5,386	5,595
33825	Avon Park	6,712	6,073
32807	Azalea Park	7,367	
33830	Bartow	12,891	12,849
33505	Bayshore Gardens	9,255	2,297
33430	Belle Glade	15,949	11,273
33432	Boca Raton	28,506	6,961
33435	Boynton Beach	18,115	10,467
*33506	Bradenton	21,040	19,380
33511	Brandon	12,749	1,665
33314	Broadview Park-Rock Hill	6,049	
33311	Browardale	17,444	
33142	Browns Village	23,442	
33054	Bunche Park	5,773	
33904	Cape Coral	10,193	
33055	Carol City	27,361	21,749
33023	Carver Ranch Estates	5,515	
32707	Casselberry	9,438	2,463
33505	Cedar Hammock-Bradenton South	10,820	
32324	Chattahoochee	7,944	9,699
*33515	Clearwater	52,074	34,653
32922	Cocoa	16,110	12,294
32931	Cocoa Beach	9,952	3,475
32922	Cocoa West	5,779	3,975
33064	Collier Manor-Creshaven	7,202	
32809	Conway	8,642	
33134	Coral Gables	42,494	34,793
32536	Crestview	7,952	7,467
33157	Cutler Ridge	17,441	7,005
33004	Dania	9,013	7,065
33314	Davie	5,858	
*32015	Daytona Beach	45,327	37,395
33441	Deerfield Beach	16,662	9,573
32720	De Land	11,641	10,775
33444	Delray Beach	19,915	12,230
33528	Dunedin	17,639	8,444
33610	East Lake-Orient Park	5,711	
33940	East Naples	6,152	
32542	Eglin	7,769	
33614	Egypt Lake	7,556	
33533	Englewood	6,108	2,877
32726	Eustis	6,722	6,189
32034	Fernandina Beach	6,955	7,276
33030	Florida City	5,133	4,114
*33310	Fort Lauderdale	139,590	83,648
*33902	Fort Myers	27,351	22,523
33901	Fort Myers Southwest	5,086	
33450	Fort Pierce	29,721	25,256
32548	Fort Walton Beach	19,994	12,147
*32601	Gainesville	64,510	29,701

ZIP Code	Place	1970	1960
32960	Gifford	5,772	3,509
33170	Goulds	6,690	5,121
33581	Gulf Gate Estates	5,874	
33737	Gulfport	9,976	9,730
33844	Haines City	8,956	9,135
33009	Hallandale	23,849	10,483
*33010	Hialeah	102,452	66,972
32805	Holden Heights	6,206	
32017	Holly Hill	8,191	4,182
*33022	Hollywood	106,873	35,237
33030	Homestead	13,674	9,152
33030	Homestead Base	8,257	
32937	Indian Harbour Beach	5,371	
*32201	Jacksonville	528,865	201,030
33156	Kendall	35,497	
33040	Key West	29,312	33,956
32741	Kissimmee	7,119	6,845
33618	Lake Carroll	5,577	
32055	Lake City	10,575	9,465
32208	Lake Forest	5,216	
33803	Lake Holloway	6,227	3,172
*33802	Lakeland	41,550	41,350
33612	Lake Magdalene	9,266	
33403	Lake Park	6,993	3,589
33853	Lake Wales	8,240	8,346
33460	Lake Worth	23,714	20,758
33460	Lantana	7,126	5,021
33540	Largo	22,031	5,302
33313	Lauderdale Lakes	10,577	
33313	Lauderhill	8,465	132
32748	Leesburg	11,869	11,172
33614	Leto	8,458	
33064	Lighthouse Point	9,071	2,453
32060	Live Oak	6,830	6,544
32810	Lockhart	5,809	
32751	Maitland	7,157	3,570
33063	Margate	8,867	2,646
32446	Marianna	6,741	7,152
*32901	Melbourne	40,236	11,982
33314	Melrose Park	6,111	
32952	Merritt Island	29,233	3,554
*33152	Miami	334,859	291,688
33139	Miami Beach	87,072	63,145
33153	Miami Shores	9,425	8,865
33166	Miami Springs	13,279	11,229
32570	Milton	5,360	4,108
32754	Mims	8,309	1,307
33023	Miramar	23,997	5,485
32506	Myrtle Grove	16,186	
33940	Naples	12,042	4,655
33552	New Port Richey 1973	7,137	3,520
32069	New Smyrna Beach	10,580	8,781
33308	North Andrews Terrace	7,082	
33903	North Fort Myers	8,798	
33161	North Miami	34,767	28,708
33160	North Miami Beach	30,544	21,405
33408	North Palm Beach	9,035	2,684
33169	Norwood	14,973	
33308	Oakland Park	16,261	5,331
32670	Ocala	22,583	13,598
32548	Ocean City	5,267	
33054	Opa-Locka	11,902	9,810
32073	Orange Park	7,619	2,624
*32802	Orlando	99,006	88,135
32074	Ormond Beach	14,063	8,658
32074	Ormond By-The-Sea	6,002	3,476
33476	Pahokee	5,663	4,709
32077	Palatka	9,444	11,028
32905	Palm Bay	7,176	2,808
33480	Palm Beach	9,086	6,055
33403	Palm Beach Gardens	6,102	1
33561	Palmetto	7,422	5,556
33619	Palm River-Clair Mel	8,536	
32401	Panama City	32,096	33,275
33023	Pembroke Pines	15,496	1,429
*32502	Pensacola	59,507	56,752
33157	Perrine	10,257	6,424
32347	Perry	7,701	8,030
32808	Pine Hills	13,882	
33565	Pinellas Park	22,287	10,848
33566	Plant City	15,451	15,711
33314	Plantation	23,523	4,772
*33060	Pompano Beach	38,587	15,992
33064	Pompano Beach Highlands	5,014	
33950	Port Charlotte	10,769	3,197
32351	Quincy	8,334	8,874
33156	Richmond Heights	6,663	4,311
33312	Riverland Village-Lauderdale Isles	5,512	
33404	Riviera Beach	21,401	13,046
32955	Rockledge	10,523	3,481
32084	St. Augustine	12,352	14,734
32769	St. Cloud	5,041	4,353
*33730	St. Petersburg	216,159	181,298
33706	St. Petersburg Beach	8,024	6,268
32771	Sanford	17,393	19,175
*33578	Sarasota	40,237	34,083
33579	Sarasota Southeast	6,885	

ZIP Code	Place	1970	1960
32937	Satellite Beach	6,558	825
33870	Sebring	7,223	6,939
33143	South Miami	11,780	9,846
33157	South Miami Heights	10,395	......
32937	South Patrick Shores	10,313	......
32401	Springfield	5,949	4,628
33304	Sunrise 1972	11,693	......
33614	Sweetwater Creek	19,453	......
*32303	Tallahassee	72,624	48,174
33313	Tamarac	5,078	......
*33602	Tampa	277,753	274,970
33589	Tarpon Springs	7,118	6,768
33617	Temple Terrace	7,347	3,812
33905	Tice	7,254	4,377
32780	Titusville	30,515	6,410
33740	Treasure Island	6,120	3,506
33620	University (Hillsborough)	10,039	......
32580	Valparaiso	6,504	5,975
33595	Venice	6,648	3,444
32960	Vero Beach	11,908	8,849
32960	Vero Beach South	7,330	......
32507	Warrington	15,848	16,752
33505	West Bradenton	6,162	......
32446	West End	5,289	3,124
33144	West Miami	5,494	5,296
*33401	West Palm Beach	57,375	56,208
32505	West Pensacola	20,924	......
33880	West Winter Haven	7,716	5,050
33165	Westwood Lakes	12,811	22,517
33305	Wilton Manors	10,948	8,257
32787	Winter Garden	5,153	5,513
33880	Winter Haven	16,136	16,277
32789	Winter Park	21,895	17,162

Georgia

ZIP Code	Place	1970	1960
*31701	Albany	72,623	55,890
31709	Americus	16,091	13,472
30601	Athens	44,342	31,355
*30304	Atlanta	497,421	487,455
*30901	Augusta	59,864	70,626
31717	Bainbridge	10,887	12,714
31723	Blakely	5,267	3,580
31520	Brunswick	19,585	21,703
31728	Cairo	8,061	7,427
30117	Carrollton	13,520	10,973
30120	Cartersville	10,138	8,668
30125	Cedartown	9,253	9,340
30341	Chamblee	9,127	6,635
31014	Cochran	5,161	4,714
30337	College Park	18,203	23,469
*31902	Columbus	155,028	116,779
31015	Cordele	10,733	10,609
30209	Covington	10,267	8,167
30720	Dalton	18,872	17,868
31742	Dawson	5,383	5,062
*30030	Decatur	21,943	22,026
31520	Dock Junction	6,009	5,417
30340	Doraville	9,157	4,437
31533	Douglas	10,195	8,736
30134	Douglasville	5,472	4,462
31021	Dublin	15,143	13,814
31023	Eastman	5,416	5,118
30344	East Point	39,315	35,633
30635	Elberton	6,438	7,107
31750	Fitzgerald	8,187	8,781
30050	Forest Park	19,994	14,201
31905	Fort Benning	27,495	......
30905	Fort Gordon	15,589	......
31030	Fort Valley	9,251	8,310
30501	Gainesville	15,459	16,523
31408	Garden City	5,790	5,451
30223	Griffin	22,734	21,735
30354	Hapeville	9,567	10,082
31545	Jesup	9,091	7,304
30728	La Fayette	6,044	5,588
30240	La Grange	23,301	23,632
30245	Lawrenceville	5,115	3,804
*31201	Macon	122,423	69,764
30060	Marietta	27,216	25,565
31034	Midway-Hardwick	14,047	16,509
31061	Milledgeville	11,601	11,117
30655	Monroe	8,071	6,826
31768	Moultrie	14,400	15,764
30263	Newnan	11,205	12,169
31069	Perry	7,771	6,032
30161	Rome	30,759	32,226
30075	Roswell	5,430	2,983
31522	St. Simons	5,346	3,199
31082	Sandersville	5,546	5,425
*31401	Savannah	118,349	149,245
30030	Smyrna	19,157	10,157
30458	Statesboro	14,616	8,356
30747	Summerville	5,043	4,706
30401	Swainsboro	7,325	5,943
30286	Thomaston	10,024	9,336
31792	Thomasville	18,155	18,246
30824	Thomson	6,503	4,522

ZIP Code	Place	1970	1960
31794	Tifton	12,179	9,903
30577	Toccoa	6,971	7,303
31601	Valdosta	32,303	30,652
30474	Vidalia	9,507	7,569
31093	Warner Robins	33,491	18,633
31501	Waycross	18,996	20,944
30830	Waynesboro	5,530	5,359
30680	Winder	6,605	5,555
31406	Windsor Forest	7,288	......

Hawaii

ZIP Code	Place	1970	1960
96701	Aiea	12,560	11,826
96706	Ewa Beach	7,765	4,627
96701	Halawa Heights	5,809	......
96824	Hickam Housing	7,352	......
96720	Hilo	26,353	25,966
*96813	Honolulu	324,871	294,194
96732	Kahului	8,280	4,223
96734	Kailua	33,783	25,622
96744	Kaneohe	29,903	14,414
96734	Maunawili	5,303	......
96734	Mokapu	7,860	......
96792	Nanakuli	6,506	2,745
96782	Pacific Palisades	7,846	......
96782	Pearl City	19,552	......
96786	Schofield Barracks	13,516	......
96786	Wahiawa	17,598	15,512
96793	Wailuku	7,979	6,969
96797	Waipahu	24,150	......

Idaho

ZIP Code	Place	1970	1960
83221	Blackfoot	8,716	7,378
*83708	Boise City	74,990	34,481
83318	Burley	8,279	7,508
83605	Caldwell	14,219	12,230
83814	Coeur D'Alene	16,228	14,291
83401	Idaho Falls	35,776	33,161
83501	Lewiston	26,068	12,691
83843	Moscow	14,146	11,183
83647	Mountain Home 1974	6,755	5,984
83648	Mountain Home Base	6,038	......
83651	Nampa	20,768	18,897
83201	Pocatello	40,036	28,534
83440	Rexburg 1973	9,761	4,767
83301	Twin Falls	21,914	20,126

Illinois

ZIP Code	Place	1970	1960
60101	Addison 1973	25,645	6,741
60658	Alsip 1974	15,694	3,770
62002	Alton	39,700	43,047
*60004	Arlington Heights 1972	69,204	27,878
*60507	Aurora	74,182	63,715
60010	Barrington	8,674	5,434
61607	Bartonville	7,221	7,253
60510	Batavia 1974	10,816	7,496
62618	Beardstown	6,222	6,294
*62220	Belleville	41,699	37,264
60104	Bellwood 1971	21,473	20,729
61008	Belvidere	14,061	11,223
60106	Bensenville	12,956	9,141
62812	Benton	6,833	7,023
60162	Berkeley	6,152	5,792
60402	Berwyn	52,502	54,224
62010	Bethalto 1974	8,001	3,235
60108	Bloomingdale 1973	6,426	1,262
61701	Bloomington	39,992	36,271
60406	Blue Island	22,958	19,618
60439	Bolingbrook 1973	20,914	......
60914	Bourbonnais	5,909	3,336
60915	Bradley 1972	10,631	8,082
60455	Bridge View 1972	13,495	7,334
60153	Broadview 1971	9,470	8,588
60513	Brookfield	20,284	20,429
60090	Buffalo Grove 1974	18,390	1,492
60459	Burbank	29,900	......
62206	Cahokia	20,649	15,829
62914	Cairo	6,277	9,348
60409	Calumet City 1972	35,808	25,000
60643	Calumet Park	10,069	8,448
61520	Canton	14,217	13,588
62901	Carbondale	22,816	14,670
62626	Carlinville	5,675	5,440
62821	Carmi	6,033	6,152
60187	Carol Stream 1973	7,519	836
60110	Carpentersville	24,059	17,424
62801	Centralia	15,217	13,904
62206	Centreville	11,378	12,769
61820	Champaign	56,532	49,583
61920	Charleston	16,421	10,505
62233	Chester	5,310	4,460
*60607	Chicago	3,366,957	3,550,404
60411	Chicago Heights	40,900	34,331
60415	Chicago Ridge 1974	12,578	5,748
61523	Chillicothe	6,052	3,054
60650	Cicero	67,058	69,130

ZIP Code	Place	1970	1960
60514	Clarendon Hills	6,750	5,885
61727	Clinton	7,570	7,355
62234	Collinsville	17,992	14,217
60477	Country Club Hills	6,920	3,421
60525	Countryside 1973	5,434	. . . . . .
60435	Crest Hill 1973	8,322	5,887
60445	Crestwood 1973	7,557	1,213
61611	Creve Coeur 1973	6,594	6,684
60014	Crystal Lake 1972	16,049	8,314
61832	Danville	42,570	41,856
60559	Darien 1973	9,770	. . . . . .
*62521	Decatur	90,397	78,004
60015	Deerfield 1972	18,867	11,786
60115	De Kalb	32,949	18,486
*60016	Des Plaines 1973	55,594	34,886
61021	Dixon	18,147	19,565
60419	Dolton	25,937	18,746
60515	Downers Grove	32,751	21,154
62832	Du Quoin	6,691	6,558
62024	East Alton	7,309	7,630
60411	East Chicago Heights 1973	6,405	3,270
61244	East Moline	20,832	16,732
61611	East Peoria	18,455	12,310
*62201	East St. Louis	69,996	81,712
62025	Edwardsville	11,070	9,996
62401	Effingham	9,458	8,172
60120	Elgin 1972	56,937	49,447
60007	Elk Grove Village 1974	25,303	6,608
60126	Elmhurst	48,887	36,991
60635	Elmwood Park	26,160	23,866
*60204	Evanston	80,113	79,283
60642	Evergreen Park 1971	25,981	24,178
62837	Fairfield	5,897	6,362
62208	Fairview Heights	8,625	. . . . . .
62839	Flora	5,283	5,331
60422	Flossmoor	7,846	4,624
60130	Forest Park	15,472	14,452
60131	Franklin Park	20,348	18,322
61032	Freeport	27,736	26,628
60030	Gages Lake-Wildwood	5,337	. . . . . .
61401	Galesburg 1971	34,501	37,243
61254	Geneseo	5,840	5,169
60134	Geneva 1974	9,140	7,646
60022	Glencoe	10,675	10,472
60137	Glendale Heights 1973	13,494	173
60137	Glen Ellyn	21,909	15,972
60025	Glenview	24,880	18,132
60425	Glenwood 1972	9,406	882
62040	Granite City	40,685	40,073
60103	Hanover Park 1972	19,609	451
62946	Harrisburg	9,535	9,171
60033	Harvard	5,177	4,248
60426	Harvey	34,636	29,071
60656	Harwood Heights 1971	8,837	5,688
60429	Hazel Crest 1974	13,229	6,205
62948	Herrin	9,623	9,474
60457	Hickory Hills 1974	13,951	2,707
62249	Highland	5,981	4,943
60035	Highland Park	32,263	25,532
60162	Hillside 1971	9,466	7,794
60521	Hinsdale	15,918	12,859
60172	Hoffman Estates 1974	31,549	8,296
60456	Hometown	6,729	7,479
60430	Homewood 1973	20,074	13,371
60942	Hoopeston	6,461	6,606
62650	Jacksonville	20,553	21,690
62052	Jerseyville	7,446	7,420
*60431	Joliet	78,887	66,780
60458	Justice	9,473	2,803
60901	Kankakee	30,944	27,666
61109	Ken Rock	5,945	. . . . . .
61443	Kewanee	15,762	16,324
60525	La Grange	17,814	15,285
60525	La Grange Highlands	6,842	. . . . . .
60525	La Grange Park	15,459	13,793
60044	Lake Bluff	5,008	3,494
60045	Lake Forest	15,642	10,687
60047	Lake Zurich 1972	6,357	3,458
60438	Lansing 1973	28,232	18,098
61301	La Salle	10,736	11,897
62439	Lawrenceville	5,863	5,492
60439	Lemont	6,080	3,397
60048	Libertyville	11,684	8,560
62656	Lincoln	17,582	16,890
60645	Lincolnwood	12,929	11,744
60532	Lisle 1971	6,921	4,219
62056	Litchfield	7,190	7,330
60441	Lockport	9,985	7,560
60148	Lombard 1971	37,052	22,561
61111	Loves Park	12,390	9,086
60534	Lyons	11,124	9,936
60050	McHenry 1972	7,680	3,336
61455	Macomb 1973	22,304	12,135
62060	Madison	7,042	6,861
62959	Marion 1972	12,899	11,274
60426	Markham	15,987	11,704
62258	Mascoutah	5,045	3,625
61938	Mattoon 1972	19,270	19,088

ZIP Code	Place	1970	1960
60153	Maywood	29,019	27,330
*60160	Melrose Park	22,716	22,291
61342	Mendota	6,902	6,154
62960	Metropolis	6,940	7,339
60445	Midlothian 1974	14,241	6,605
61264	Milan 1972	5,053	3,065
61265	Moline	46,237	42,705
61462	Monmouth	11,022	10,372
60450	Morris 1972	8,435	7,935
61550	Morton 1973	12,217	5,325
60053	Morton Grove	26,369	20,533
62863	Mount Carmel	8,096	8,594
60056	Mount Prospect 1973	46,525	18,906
62864	Mount Vernon	16,382	15,566
60060	Mundelein 1974	17,315	10,526
62966	Murphysboro	10,013	8,673
60540	Naperville 1973	27,837	12,933
60648	Niles 1971	32,432	20,393
61761	Normal 1972	31,343	13,357
60656	Norridge 1971	18,043	14,087
60062	Northbrook	27,297	11,635
60064	North Chicago	47,275	22,938
60093	Northfield	5,010	4,005
60164	Northlake	14,212	12,318
61111	North Park	15,679	. . . . . .
60546	North Riverside 1971	7,849	7,989
60452	Oak Forest 1972	20,903	3,724
*60454	Oak Lawn 1974	62,245	27,471
*60301	Oak Park	62,511	61,093
62269	O'Fallon 1973	10,045	4,018
62450	Olney	8,974	8,780
60462	Orland Park 1973	11,219	2,592
61350	Ottawa	18,716	19,408
60067	Palatine 1973	28,807	11,504
60463	Palos Heights 1973	9,879	3,775
60465	Palos Hills 1972	9,778	3,766
62557	Pana	6,326	6,432
61944	Paris	9,971	9,823
60466	Park Forest	30,638	29,993
60068	Park Ridge	42,614	32,659
61554	Pekin 1974	32,315	28,146
*61601	Peoria	126,963	103,162
61614	Peoria Heights	7,943	7,064
61354	Peru	11,772	10,460
61764	Pontiac	10,595	8,435
60469	Posen	5,498	4,517
61356	Princeton	6,959	6,250
60070	Prospect Heights	13,333	. . . . . .
62301	Quincy	45,288	43,793
61866	Rantoul	25,562	22,116
60471	Richton Park 1973	6,551	933
60627	Riverdale	15,806	12,008
60305	River Forest	13,402	12,695
60171	River Grove	11,465	8,464
60546	Riverside	10,432	9,750
60472	Robbins	9,641	7,511
62454	Robinson	7,178	7,226
61068	Rochelle 1974	8,850	7,008
61071	Rock Falls	10,287	10,261
*61125	Rockford	147,370	126,706
61201	Rock Island	50,166	51,863
60008	Rolling Meadows 1974	19,785	10,879
60441	Romeoville 1971	15,336	3,574
60172	Roselle 1973	7,986	3,581
60073	Round Lake Beach 1974	10,525	5,011
60174	St. Charles 1974	15,144	9,269
62881	Salem 1973	6,359	6,165
60548	Sandwich	5,056	3,842
60411	Sauk	7,479	4,687
60172	Schaumburg 1974	36,944	986
60176	Schiller Park	12,712	5,687
62225	Scott	7,871	. . . . . .
61282	Silvis	5,907	3,973
60076	Skokie 1971	68,911	59,364
60473	South Holland 1972	25,220	10,412
60459	South Stickney (see Burbank)		
*62703	Springfield	91,753	83,271
61362	Spring Valley	5,605	5,371
60475	Steger 1973	9,285	6,432
61081	Sterling	16,113	15,688
60402	Stickney	6,601	6,239
60103	Streamwood	18,176	4,821
61364	Streator	15,600	16,868
60501	Summit	11,569	10,374
62221	Swansea	5,432	3,018
60178	Sycamore	7,843	6,961
62568	Taylorville	10,927	8,801
60477	Tinley Park 1974	20,782	6,392
61801	Urbana	32,800	27,294
62471	Vandalia	5,160	5,537
60181	Villa Park 1971	25,546	20,391
61571	Washington 1973	9,466	5,919
62204	Washington Park	9,524	6,601
60970	Watseka	5,294	5,219
60084	Wauconda 1974	5,662	3,227
60085	Waukegan	65,269	55,719
60153	Westchester	20,033	18,092
60185	West Chicago 1972	11,624	6,854

ZIP Code	Place	1970	1960
61120	West End.	7,554	
60558	Western Springs.	13,029	10,838
62896	West Frankfort.	8,854	9,027
60559	Westmont.	8,920	5,997
61604	West Peoria.	6,873	
60187	Wheaton 1973.	36,148	24,312
60090	Wheeling 1974.	18,106	7,169
60091	Wilmette.	32,134	28,268
60093	Winnetka.	13,998	13,368
60191	Wood Dale 1973.	10,494	3,071
60515	Woodridge 1974.	16,827	542
62095	Wood River.	13,186	11,694
60098	Woodstock.	10,226	8,897
60482	Worth 1971.	12,153	8,196
60099	Zion.	17,268	11,941

Indiana

ZIP Code	Place	1970	1960
46001	Alexandria.	5,600	5,582
*46011	Anderson.	70,787	49,061
46703	Angola.	5,117	4,746
46706	Auburn.	7,388	6,350
47421	Bedford.	13,087	13,024
46107	Beech Grove 1973.	14,651	10,973
46408	Black Oak.	9,624	
47401	Bloomington.	43,262	31,357
46714	Bluffton.	8,297	6,238
47601	Boonville.	5,736	4,801
47834	Brazil.	8,163	8,853
46112	Brownsburg.	5,751	4,478
46032	Carmel 1974.	13,484	1,442
46303	Cedar Lake.	7,589	
47111	Charlestown.	5,933	5,726
46304	Chesterton.	6,177	4,335
47130	Clarksville.	13,806	8,088
47842	Clinton.	5,340	5,843
47201	Columbus.	26,457	20,778
47331	Connersville.	17,604	17,698
47933	Crawfordsville.	13,842	14,231
46307	Crown Point 1973.	13,420	8,443
46733	Decatur.	8,445	8,327
46312	East Chicago.	46,982	57,669
46405	East Gary.	9,858	9,309
46514	Elkhart.	43,152	40,274
46036	Elwood.	11,196	11,793
*47708	Evansville.	138,764	141,543
*46802	Fort Wayne.	178,021	161,776
46041	Frankfort.	14,956	15,302
46131	Franklin.	11,477	9,453
*46401	Gary.	175,415	178,320
46933	Gas City.	5,742	4,469
46526	Goshen.	17,871	13,718
46135	Greencastle.	8,852	8,506
46140	Greenfield.	10,808	9,049
47240	Greensburg.	8,620	7,492
46142	Greenwood.	11,408	7,169
46319	Griffith 1974.	17,681	9,453
*46320	Hammond.	107,885	111,698
47348	Hartford City.	8,207	8,053
46322	Highland.	24,947	16,284
46342	Hobart.	21,485	18,680
46750	Huntington.	16,217	16,185
*46206	Indianapolis.	746,302	476,258
47546	Jasper.	8,641	6,737
47130	Jeffersonville.	20,008	19,522
46755	Kendallville.	6,838	6,765
46901	Kokomo.	44,042	47,197
*47901	Lafayette.	44,955	42,330
46350	La Porte.	22,140	21,157
46226	Lawrence.	16,917	10,103
46052	Lebanon.	9,766	9,523
47441	Linton.	5,450	5,736
46947	Logansport.	19,255	21,106
47250	Madison.	13,081	10,488
46952	Marion.	39,607	37,854
46151	Martinsville.	9,723	7,525
46410	Merrillville 1973.	25,978	
46360	Michigan City.	39,369	36,653
46544	Mishawaka.	35,517	33,361
46158	Mooresville.	5,800	3,856
47620	Mount Vernon 1974.	7,092	5,970
*47302	Muncie.	69,082	68,603
46321	Munster.	18,894	10,313
47150	New Albany.	38,402	37,812
47362	New Castle.	21,215	20,349
46774	New Haven.	5,728	3,396
46060	Noblesville.	7,548	7,664
46962	North Manchester.	5,791	4,377
46970	Peru.	14,139	14,453
46168	Plainfield.	8,211	5,460
46563	Plymouth.	7,661	7,558
46368	Portage 1973.	20,624	11,822
47371	Portland.	7,115	6,999
47670	Princeton.	7,431	7,906
47374	Richmond.	43,999	44,149
46173	Rushville.	6,686	7,264
47167	Salem.	5,041	4,546
47274	Seymour.	13,352	11,629

ZIP Code	Place	1970	1960
46176	Shelbyville.	15,094	14,317
*46624	South Bend.	125,580	132,445
46224	Speedway.	14,649	9,624
47586	Tell City 1974.	8,515	6,609
*47808	Terre Haute.	70,335	72,500
46072	Tipton.	5,313	5,604
46383	Valparaiso 1974.	20,544	15,227
47591	Vincennes.	19,867	18,046
46992	Wabash.	13,379	12,621
46580	Warsaw 1974.	9,679	7,234
47501	Washington.	11,358	10,846
46408	West Glen Park.	5,940	
47906	West Lafayette.	19,157	12,680
46394	Whiting.	7,152	8,137
47394	Winchester.	5,493	5,742

Iowa

ZIP Code	Place	1970	1960
50511	Algona.	6,032	5,702
50010	Ames.	39,505	27,003
50021	Ankeny.	9,151	2,964
50022	Atlantic.	7,306	6,890
52722	Bettendorf.	22,126	11,534
50036	Boone.	12,468	12,468
52601	Burlington.	32,366	32,430
51401	Carroll.	8,716	7,682
50613	Cedar Falls 1974.	33,154	21,195
*52401	Cedar Rapids.	110,642	92,035
52544	Centerville.	6,531	6,629
50049	Chariton.	5,009	5,042
50616	Charles City 1974.	9,119	9,964
51012	Cherokee.	7,272	7,724
51632	Clarinda.	5,420	5,901
50428	Clear Lake City 1973.	6,830	6,158
52732	Clinton.	34,719	33,589
52240	Coralville.	6,130	2,357
51501	Council Bluffs.	60,348	55,641
50801	Creston.	8,234	7,667
*52802	Davenport.	98,469	88,981
52101	Decorah.	7,458	6,435
51442	Denison.	6,218	4,930
*50318	Des Moines.	201,404	208,982
52001	Dubuque.	62,309	56,606
51334	Estherville.	8,108	7,927
50707	Evansdale.	5,038	5,738
52556	Fairfield.	8,715	8,054
50501	Fort Dodge.	31,263	28,399
52627	Fort Madison.	13,996	15,247
50112	Grinnell.	8,402	7,367
51537	Harlan.	5,049	4,350
50644	Independence.	5,910	5,498
50125	Indianola.	8,852	7,062
52240	Iowa City 1974.	47,744	33,443
50126	Iowa Falls.	6,454	5,565
52632	Keokuk.	14,631	16,316
50138	Knoxville.	7,755	7,817
51031	Le Mars.	8,159	6,767
52060	Maquoketa.	5,677	5,909
52302	Marion 1974.	18,190	10,882
50158	Marshalltown.	26,219	22,521
50401	Mason City.	30,379	30,642
52641	Mount Pleasant.	7,007	7,339
52761	Muscatine.	22,405	20,997
50208	Newton.	15,619	15,381
50662	Oelwein.	7,735	8,282
52577	Oskaloosa.	11,224	11,053
52501	Ottumwa.	29,610	33,871
50219	Pella.	6,668	5,198
50220	Perry.	6,906	6,442
51566	Red Oak.	6,210	6,421
51601	Shenandoah.	5,968	6,567
*51101	Sioux City.	85,925	89,159
51301	Spencer.	10,278	8,864
50588	Storm Lake.	8,591	7,728
50322	Urbandale.	14,434	5,821
52353	Washington.	6,317	6,037
*50701	Waterloo.	75,533	71,755
50677	Waverly.	7,205	6,357
50595	Webster City.	8,488	8,520
50265	West Des Moines.	16,441	11,949
50311	Windsor Heights.	6,303	4,715

Kansas

ZIP Code	Place	1970	1960
67410	Abilene.	6,661	6,746
67005	Arkansas City.	13,216	14,262
66002	Atchison.	12,565	12,529
67010	Augusta.	5,977	6,434
66720	Chanute.	10,341	10,849
67337	Coffeyville.	15,116	17,382
66901	Concordia.	7,221	7,022
67037	Derby.	7,947	6,458
67801	Dodge City.	14,127	13,520
67042	El Dorado.	12,308	12,523
66801	Emporia.	23,327	18,190
66205	Fairway.	5,133	5,398
66027	Fort Leavenworth.	8,060	
66701	Fort Scott.	8,967	9,410

ZIP Code	Place	1970	1960
67846	Garden City	14,790	11,811
67735	Goodland	5,510	4,459
67530	Great Bend	16,133	16,670
67601	Hays	15,396	11,947
67060	Haysville	6,483	5,836
67501	Hutchinson	36,885	37,574
67301	Independence	10,347	11,222
66749	Iola	6,493	6,885
66441	Junction City	19,018	18,700
*66110	Kansas City	168,213	121,901
66044	Lawrence	45,698	32,858
66048	Leavenworth	25,147	22,052
66206	Leawood	10,349	7,466
66215	Lenexa	5,242	2,487
67901	Liberal	13,789	13,813
67460	McPherson	10,851	9,996
66502	Manhattan	27,575	22,993
66203	Merriam	10,851	5,084
66222	Mission	8,376	4,626
67114	Newton	15,439	14,877
66442	North Fort Riley	12,469	......
66061	Olathe	17,917	10,987
66067	Ottawa	11,036	10,673
66204	Overland Park	79,034	......
67357	Parsons	13,015	13,929
66762	Pittsburg	20,171	18,678
66208	Prairie Village	28,138	25,356
67124	Pratt	6,736	8,156
66203	Roeland Park	9,974	8,949
67665	Russell	5,371	6,113
67401	Salina	37,714	43,202
*66203	Shawnee	20,482	9,072
*66603	Topeka	125,011	119,484
67152	Wellington	8,072	8,809
*67202	Wichita	276,554	254,698
67156	Winfield	11,405	11,117

Kentucky

ZIP Code	Place	1970	1960
41101	Ashland	29,245	31,283
40004	Bardstown	5,816	4,798
41073	Bellevue	8,847	9,336
40403	Berea	6,956	4,302
42101	Bowling Green	36,705	28,338
40218	Buechel	5,359	......
42718	Campbellsville	7,598	6,966
42330	Central City	5,450	3,694
40701	Corbin	7,317	7,119
*41011	Covington	52,535	60,376
41031	Cynthiana	6,356	5,641
40422	Danville	11,542	9,010
41074	Dayton	8,751	9,050
42701	Elizabethtown	11,748	9,641
41018	Elsmere	5,161	4,607
41018	Erlanger	12,676	7,072
41139	Flatwoods	7,380	3,741
41042	Florence	11,661	5,837
42223	Fort Campbell North	13,616	......
40121	Fort Knox	37,608	......
41017	Fort Mitchell	6,982	525
41075	Fort Thomas	16,338	14,896
40601	Frankfort	21,902	18,365
42134	Franklin	6,553	5,319
40324	Georgetown	8,629	6,986
42141	Glasgow	11,301	10,069
40330	Harrodsburg	6,741	6,061
41701	Hazard	5,459	5,958
42420	Henderson	22,976	16,892
42240	Hopkinsville	21,250	19,465
40299	Jeffersontown	9,701	3,431
40033	Lebanon	5,528	4,813
*40511	Lexington	108,137	62,810
*40201	Louisville	361,706	390,639
41016	Ludlow	5,815	6,233
42431	Madisonville	15,332	13,110
42066	Mayfield	10,724	10,762
41056	Maysville	7,411	8,484
40965	Middlesborough	11,878	12,607
40351	Morehead	7,191	4,170
40353	Mount Sterling	5,083	5,370
42071	Murray	13,537	9,303
*41071	Newport	25,998	30,070
40356	Nicholasville	5,829	4,275
40219	Okolona	17,643	......
42301	Owensboro	50,329	42,471
42001	Paducah	31,627	34,479
40361	Paris	7,823	7,791
41501	Pikeville	5,205	4,754
40258	Pleasure Ridge Park	28,566	10,612
42445	Princeton	6,292	5,618
40160	Radcliff	7,881	3,384
40475	Richmond	16,861	12,168
42276	Russellville	6,456	5,861
40207	St. Matthews	13,152	8,738
40216	Shively	19,139	15,155
42501	Somerset	10,436	7,112
40272	Valley Station	24,471	10,533

ZIP Code	Place	1970	1960
40383	Versailles	5,679	4,060
40391	Winchester	13,402	10,187

Louisiana

ZIP Code	Place	1970	1960
70510	Abbeville	10,996	10,414
71301	Alexandria	41,557	40,279
70714	Baker	8,281	4,823
71220	Bastrop	14,713	15,193
*70821	Baton Rouge	165,963	152,419
70360	Bayou Cane	9,077	3,173
70380	Bayou Vista	5,121	......
70427	Bogalusa	18,412	21,423
71010	Bossier City	41,595	32,776
71322	Bunkie	5,395	5,188
71101	Cooper Road	9,034	......
70433	Covington	7,170	6,754
70526	Crowley	16,104	15,617
70726	Denham Springs	6,752	5,991
70634	De Ridder	8,030	7,188
70346	Donaldsonville	7,367	6,082
70535	Eunice	11,390	11,326
71334	Ferriday	5,239	4,563
70538	Franklin	9,325	8,673
70053	Gretna	24,875	21,967
70401	Hammond	12,487	10,563
70123	Harahan	13,037	9,275
70058	Harvey	6,347	......
70360	Houma	30,922	22,561
70544	Jeanerette	6,322	5,568
70121	Jefferson Heights	16,489	19,353
70546	Jenning	11,783	11,887
71251	Jonesboro	5,072	3,848
70548	Kaplan	5,540	5,267
70062	Kenner	29,858	17,037
70501	Lafayette	68,908	40,400
70501	Lafayette Southwest	5,396	6,682
70601	Lake Charles	77,998	63,392
71254	Lake Providence	6,183	5,771
70068	Laplace	5,953	3,541
71446	Leesville	8,928	4,689
70123	Little Farms	15,713	......
71052	Mansfield	6,432	5,839
70072	Marrero	29,015	......
*70004	Metairie	136,477	......
71055	Minden	13,996	12,785
71201	Monroe	56,374	52,219
70380	Morgan City	16,586	13,540
71457	Natchitoches	15,974	13,924
70560	New Iberia	30,147	29,062
*70113	New Orleans	593,471	627,525
71459	North Fort Polk	7,955	......
71463	Oakdale	7,301	6,618
70570	Opelousas	20,387	17,417
71360	Pineville	8,951	8,636
70764	Plaquemine	7,739	7,689
70767	Port Allen	5,728	5,026
70578	Rayne	9,510	8,634
70084	Reserve	6,381	5,297
71270	Ruston	17,365	13,991
70582	St. Martinville	7,153	6,468
70807	Scotlandville	22,557	......
*71102	Shreveport	182,064	164,372
70458	Slidell	16,101	6,356
71459	South Fort Polk	15,600	......
71075	Springhill	6,496	6,437
70663	Sulphur	14,959	11,429
71282	Tallulah	9,643	9,413
71285	Terry	13,382	......
70301	Thibodaux	15,028	13,403
71373	Vidalia	5,538	4,313
70586	Ville Platte	9,692	7,512
71291	West Monroe	14,868	15,215
70094	Westwego	11,402	9,815
71483	Winnfield	7,142	7,022
71295	Winnsboro	5,349	4,437

Maine

See Note on Page 215

ZIP Code	Place	1970	1960
04210	Auburn	24,151	24,449
04330	Augusta	21,945	21,680
04401	Bangor	33,168	38,912
04530	Bath	9,679	10,717
04915	Belfast	5,957	6,140
04005	Biddeford	19,983	19,255
04412	Brewer	9,300	9,009
04011	Brunswick Center	10,867	9,444
......	Brunswick	16,195	15,797
04107	Cape Elizabeth	7,873	5,505
04736	Caribou	10,419	12,464
......	Fairfield	5,684	5,829
04105	Falmouth	6,291	5,976
......	Farmington	5,657	5,001
04345	Gardiner	6,685	6,897
......	Gorham	7,839	5,767
04730	Houlton Center	6,760	5,976
......	Houlton	8,111	8,289

ZIP Code	Place	1970	1960
.....	Kennebunk	5,646	551
03904	Kittery Center	7,363	8,051
.....	Kittery	11,028	10,689
04240	Lewiston	41,779	40,804
04750	Limestone	10,360	13,102
04250	Lisbon	6,544	5,042
04750	Loring	7,881	......
.....	Madawaska	5,585	5,507
04462	Millinocket Center	7,558	7,318
.....	Millinocket	7,742	7,453
04064	Old Orchard Beach Ctr.	5,273	4,431
.....	Old Orchard Beach	5,404	4,580
04468	Old Town	9,057	8,626
04473	Orono Center	9,146	3,234
.....	Orono	9,989	8,341
*04101	Portland	65,116	72,566
04769	Presque Isle	11,452	12,886
04841	Rockland	8,505	8,769
04276	Rumford Compact	6,198	7,233
.....	Rumford	9,363	10,005
04072	Saco	11,678	10,515
04073	Sanford Center	10,457	10,936
.....	Sanford	15,812	14,962
04074	Scarborough	7,845	6,418
04976	Skowhegan Center	6,571	6,667
.....	Skowhegan	7,601	7,661
04106	South Portland	23,267	22,788
.....	Topsham	5,022	3,818
04901	Waterville	18,192	19,001
04092	Westbrook	14,444	13,820
04082	Windham	6,593	4,498
04901	Winslow Center	5,389	3,640
.....	Winslow	7,299	5,891
03909	York	5,690	4,663

Maryland

ZIP Code	Place	1970	1960
21001	Aberdeen	12,375	9,679
21005	Aberdeen Proving Ground	7,403	......
20331	Andrews	6,418	......
*21401	Annapolis	30,095	23,385
21227	Arbutus	22,745	22,402
20853	Aspen Hill	16,823	......
20783	Avenel-Hilandale	19,520	......
21905	Bainbridge Center	5,257	......
*21233	Baltimore	905,759	939,024
21014	Bel Air	6,307	4,300
20705	Beltsville	8,912	......
20014	Bethesda	71,621	56,527
20021	Birchwood City	13,514	......
20710	Bladensburg	7,488	3,103
20715	Bowie	35,028	1,072
21225	Brooklyn	13,896	......
20705	Calverton	6,543	......
21613	Cambridge	11,595	12,239
20031	Camp Springs	22,776	......
20027	Carmody Hills-Pepper Mill	6,335	......
21228	Catonsville	54,812	37,372
20027	Chapel Oaks-Cedar Heights	6,049	......
20785	Cheverly	6,808	5,223
20015	Chevy Chase	16,424	......
20783	Chillum	35,656	......
20904	Colesville	9,455	......
20740	College Park	26,156	18,482
21043	Columbia	8,815	......
20027	Coral Hills	9,058	......
21502	Cumberland	29,724	33,415
21222	Defense Heights	6,775	......
20028	District Heights	7,659	7,524
21222	Dundalk	85,377	82,428
21601	Easton	6,809	6,337
21219	Edgemere	10,352	11,775
21040	Edgewood	8,551	1,670
21921	Elkton	5,362	5,989
*21043	Ellicott	9,435	......
21221	Essex	38,193	35,205
21061	Ferndale	9,929	......
20028	Forestville	16,188	......
20755	Fort Meade	16,699	......
21701	Frederick	23,641	21,744
21532	Frostburg	7,327	6,722
20760	Gaithersburg	8,344	3,847
21061	Glen Burnie	38,608	......
20801	Good Luck	10,584	......
20770	Greenbelt	18,199	7,479
21740	Hagerstown	35,862	36,660
21740	Halfway	6,106	4,256
20852	Halpine	6,118	......
21078	Havre De Grace	9,791	8,510
20031	Hillcrest Heights	24,037	15,295
*20780	Hyattsville	14,998	15,168
21085	Joppatowne	9,092	......
20904	Kemp Mill	10,037	......
20785	Kentland	9,849	......
20785	Landover	5,597	......
20787	Langley Park	11,564	11,510
20801	Lanham-Seabrook	13,244	......

ZIP Code	Place	1970	1960
21227	Lansdowne-Baltimore Highlands	17,770	13,134
20810	Laurel	10,525	8,503
20653	Lexington Pk.-Patuxent R.	9,136	......
21090	Linthicum	9,775	......
21093	Lutherville-Timonium	24,055	12,265
20810	Maryland City	7,102	......
21220	Middle River	19,935	10,825
20852	Montrose	5,902	......
20822	Mount Rainier	8,180	9,855
*20784	New Carrollton	14,870	3,385
20854	North Potomac	12,784	......
20012	North Takoma Park	7,373	......
21113	Odenton	5,989	1,914
21206	Overlea	13,124	10,795
21117	Owings Mills	7,360	3,810
20021	Oxon Hill	11,974	......
20785	Palmer Park	8,172	......
21234	Parkville	33,589	27,236
21128	Perry Hall	5,446	......
21208	Pikesville	25,395	18,737
20016	Potomac Valley	5,122	......
21227	Pumphrey	6,425	......
21133	Randallstown	33,683	......
20853	Randolph	13,215	......
21136	Reisterstown	12,568	4,216
20840	Riverdale	5,724	4,389
20840	Riverdale Hgts.-E. Pine	8,941	......
21122	Riviera Beach	7,464	4,902
*20850	Rockville	41,821	26,090
21237	Rosedale	19,417	......
21801	Salisbury	15,252	16,302
20027	Seat Pleasant	7,217	5,365
21146	Severna Park	16,358	3,728
*20907	Silver Spring	77,411	66,348
21061	South Gate	9,356	......
20795	South Kensington	10,289	......
20810	South Laurel	13,345	......
20023	Suitland-Silver Hills	30,355	10,300
20012	Takoma Park	18,507	16,799
21204	Towson	77,768	19,090
20601	Waldorf	7,368	1,048
20028	Walker Mill	7,103	......
21157	Westminster	7,207	6,123
20902	Wheaton	66,280	54,635
20903	White Oak	19,769	......
21207	Woodlawn-Woodmoor	28,821	......

Massachusetts

See Note on Page 215

ZIP Code	Place	1970	1960
02351	Abington	12,334	10,607
01720	Acton	14,770	7,238
02743	Acushnet	7,767	5,755
01220	Adams Center	11,256	11,949
.....	Adams	11,772	12,391
01001	Agawam	21,717	15,718
01913	Amesbury Center	10,088	9,625
.....	Amesbury	11,388	10,787
01002	Amherst Center	17,926	10,306
.....	Amherst	26,331	13,718
01810	Andover	23,695	17,134
02174	Arlington	53,534	49,953
01721	Ashland	8,882	7,779
01331	Athol Center	9,723	10,161
.....	Athol	11,185	11,637
02703	Attleboro	32,907	27,118
01501	Auburn	15,347	14,047
02322	Avon	5,295	4,301
*01432	Ayer	7,393	14,927
02630	Barnstable	19,842	13,465
01730	Bedford	13,513	10,969
01007	Belchertown	5,936	5,186
02019	Bellingham	13,967	6,774
02178	Belmont	28,285	28,715
01915	Beverly	38,348	36,108
01821	Billerica	31,648	17,867
01504	Blackstone	6,566	5,130
*02109	Boston	641,071	697,197
02532	Bourne	12,636	14,011
02184	Braintree	35,050	31,069
02324	Bridgewater	11,829	10,276
*02403	Brockton	89,040	72,813
02146	Brookline	58,886	54,044
01803	Burlington	21,980	12,852
*02138	Cambridge	100,361	107,716
02021	Canton	17,100	12,771
01824	Chelmsford	31,432	15,130
02150	Chelsea	30,625	33,749
*01021	Chicopee	66,676	61,553
01510	Clinton	13,383	12,848
02025	Cohasset	6,954	5,840
01742	Concord	16,148	12,517
01226	Dalton	7,505	6,436
01923	Danvers	26,151	21,926
02714	Dartmouth	18,800	14,607
02026	Dedham	25,938	23,869
02638	Dennis	6,454	3,727

ZIP Code	Place	1970	1960	ZIP Code	Place	1970	1960
01826	Dracut	18,214	13,674	02062	Norwood	30,815	24,898
01570	Dudley	8,087	6,510	01364	Orange	6,104	6,154
02332	Duxbury	7,636	4,727	01253	Otis	5,596	
02333	East Bridgewater	8,347	6,139	01540	Oxford Center	6,109	6,985
01027	Easthampton	13,012	12,326	......	Oxford	10,345	9,282
01028	East Longmeadow	13,029	10,294	01069	Palmer	11,680	10,358
02334	Easton	12,157	9,078	01960	Peabody	48,080	32,202
02149	Everett	42,485	43,544	02359	Pembroke	11,193	4,919
02719	Fairhaven	16,332	14,339	01463	Pepperell	5,887	4,336
*02722	Fall River	96,898	99,942	01866	Pinehurst	5,681	1,991
*02540	Falmouth Center	5,806	3,308	01201	Pittsfield	57,020	57,879
......	Falmouth	15,942	13,037	*02360	Plymouth Center	6,940	6,488
01420	Fitchburg	43,343	43,021	......	Plymouth	18,606	14,445
01433	Fort Devens	12,019		02169	Quincy	87,966	87,409
02035	Foxborough	14,218	10,136	02368	Randolph	27,035	18,900
01701	Framingham	64,048	44,526	02767	Raynham	6,705	4,150
02038	Franklin Center	8,863	6,391	01867	Reading	22,539	19,259
......	Franklin	17,830	10,530	02769	Rehoboth	6,512	4,953
01440	Gardner	19,748	19,038	02151	Revere	43,159	40,080
01833	Georgetown	5,290	3,755	02370	Rockland	15,674	13,119
01930	Gloucester	27,941	25,789	01966	Rockport	5,636	4,616
01519	Grafton	11,659	10,627	01970	Salem	40,556	39,211
01033	Granby	5,473	4,221	02563	Sandwich	5,239	2,082
01230	Great Barrington	7,537	6,624	01906	Saugus	25,110	20,666
01301	Greenfield Center	14,642	14,389	02066	Scituate	16,973	11,214
......	Greenfield	18,116	17,690	02771	Seekonk	11,116	8,399
01450	Groton	5,109	3,904	02067	Sharon	12,367	10,070
01834	Groveland	5,382	3,297	01545	Shrewsbury	19,196	16,622
01936	Hamilton	6,373	5,488	02725	Somerset	18,088	12,196
02339	Hanover	10,107	5,923	02143	Somerville	88,779	94,697
02341	Hanson	7,148	4,370	01772	Southborough	5,798	3,996
01451	Harvard	12,494	2,563	01550	Southbridge Center	14,261	15,889
02645	Harwich	5,892	3,747	......	Southbridge	17,057	16,523
01830	Haverhill	46,120	46,346	01075	South Hadley	17,033	14,956
02043	Hingham	18,845	15,378	01077	Southwick	6,330	5,139
02343	Holbrook	11,775	10,104	02664	South Yarmouth	5,380	2,029
01520	Holden	12,564	10,117	01562	Spencer Center	5,895	5,593
01746	Holliston	12,069	6,222	......	Spencer	8,779	7,838
01040	Holyoke	50,112	52,689	*01101	Springfield	163,905	174,463
01748	Hopkinton	5,981	4,932	02180	Stoneham	20,725	17,821
01749	Hudson Center	14,283	7,987	02072	Stoughton	23,459	16,328
......	Hudson	16,084	9,666	01776	Sudbury	13,506	7,447
02045	Hull	9,961	7,055	01907	Swampscott	13,578	13,294
02601	Hyannis	6,847	5,139	02777	Swansea	12,640	9,916
01938	Ipswich	5,022	4,617	02780	Taunton	43,756	41,132
......	Ipswich	10,750	8,544	01468	Templeton	5,863	5,371
02364	Kingston	5,999	4,302	01876	Tewksbury	22,755	15,902
01523	Lancaster	6,095	3,958	01983	Topsfield	5,225	3,351
*01842	Lawrence	66,915	70,933	01376	Turners Falls	5,168	4,917
01238	Lee	6,426	5,271	01569	Uxbridge	8,253	7,789
01524	Leicester	9,140	8,177	01880	Wakefield	25,402	24,295
01240	Lenox	5,804	4,253	02081	Walpole	18,149	14,068
01453	Leominster	32,939	27,929	02154	Waltham	61,582	55,413
02173	Lexington	31,886	27,691	01082	Ware Center	6,509	6,650
01773	Lincoln	7,567	5,613	......	Ware	8,187	7,517
01460	Littleton	6,380	5,109	02571	Wareham	11,492	9,461
01106	Longmeadow	15,630	10,565	02172	Watertown	39,307	39,092
*01853	Lowell	94,239	92,107	01778	Wayland	13,461	10,444
01056	Ludlow	17,580	13,805	01570	Webster Center	12,432	12,072
01462	Lunenburg	7,419	6,334	......	Webster	14,917	13,680
*01901	Lynn	90,294	94,478	02181	Wellesley	28,051	26,071
01940	Lynnfield	10,826	8,398	01581	Westborough	12,594	9,599
02148	Malden	56,127	57,676	01583	West Boylston	6,369	5,526
01944	Manchester	5,151	3,932	02379	West Bridgewater	7,152	5,061
02048	Mansfield	9,939	7,773	01085	Westfield	31,433	26,302
01945	Marblehead	21,295	18,521	01886	Westford	10,368	6,261
01752	Marlborough	27,936	18,819	02193	Weston	10,870	8,261
02050	Marshfield	15,223	6,748	02790	Westport	9,791	6,641
01754	Maynard	9,710	7,695	01089	West Springfield	28,461	24,924
02052	Medfield	9,821	6,021	02090	Westwood	12,750	10,354
02155	Medford	64,397	64,971	02188	Weymouth	54,610	48,177
02053	Medway	7,938	5,168	01588	Whitinsville	5,210	5,102
02176	Melrose	33,180	29,619	02382	Whitman	13,059	10,485
01844	Methuen	35,456	28,114	01095	Wilbraham	11,984	7,387
02346	Middleborough Center	6,259	6,003	01267	Williamstown	8,454	7,322
......	Middleborough	13,607	11,065	01887	Wilmington	17,102	12,475
01757	Milford Center	13,740	13,722	01475	Winchendon	6,635	6,237
......	Milford	19,352	15,749	01890	Winchester	22,269	19,376
01527	Millbury	11,987	9,623	02152	Winthrop	20,335	20,303
02054	Millis	5,686	4,374	01801	Woburn	37,406	31,214
02186	Milton	27,190	26,375	*01613	Worcester	176,572	186,587
01057	Monson	7,355	6,712	02093	Wrentham	7,315	6,685
01351	Montague	8,451	7,836	02675	Yarmouth	12,033	5,504
01760	Natick	31,057	28,831				
02192	Needham	29,748	25,793		**Michigan**		
*02741	New Bedford	101,777	102,477				
01950	Newburyport	15,807	14,004	49221	Adrian	20,382	20,347
02158	Newton	91,066	92,384	49224	Albion	12,112	12,749
01247	North Adams	19,195	19,905	48101	Allen Park	40,747	37,494
01060	Northampton	29,664	30,058	48801	Alma	9,611	8,978
01845	North Andover	16,284	10,908	49707	Alpena	13,805	14,682
*02760	North Attleborough	18,665	14,777	*48106	Ann Arbor	99,797	67,340
01532	Northborough	9,218	6,687	*49016	Battle Creek	38,931	44,169
01534	Northbridge	11,795	10,800	48706	Bay City	49,449	53,604
01864	North Reading	11,264	8,331	48809	Belding	5,121	4,887
02060	North Scituate	5,507	3,421	49022	Benton Central	8,067	
02766	Norton	9,487	6,818	49022	Benton Harbor	16,481	19,136
02061	Norwell	7,796	5,207	48072	Berkley	21,879	23,275

ZIP Code	Place	1970	1960	ZIP Code	Place	1970	1960
48009	Beverly Hills	13,598	8,633	49770	Petoskey	6,342	6,138
49307	Big Rapids	11,995	8,686	48170	Plymouth	11,758	8,766
*48012	Birmingham	26,170	25,525	*48053	Pontiac	85,279	82,233
49601	Cadillac	9,990	10,112	49081	Portage	33,590	......
48724	Carrollton	7,300	......	48060	Port Huron	35,794	36,084
48015	Center Line	10,379	10,164	48024	Quakertown North	7,101	......
48813	Charlotte	8,244	7,657	48218	River Rouge	15,947	18,147
48721	Cheboygan	5,553	5,859	48192	Riverview	11,342	7,237
48017	Clawson	17,617	14,795	48063	Rochester	7,054	5,431
49036	Coldwater	9,155	8,880	48066	Roseville	60,529	50,195
48041	Comstock	5,003	......	*48068	Royal Oak	86,238	80,612
49321	Comstock Park	5,766	......	48605	Saginaw	91,849	98,265
49508	Cutlerville	6,267	......	*48083	St. Clair Shores	88,093	76,657
48423	Davison	5,259	3,761	48879	St. Johns	6,672	5,629
*48120	Dearborn	104,199	112,007	49085	St. Joseph	11,042	11,755
48127	Dearborn Heights	80,069	......	49783	Sault Ste. Marie	15,136	18,722
*48233	Detroit	1,513,601	1,670,144	*48075	Southfield	69,285	31,501
49047	Dowagiac	6,583	7,208	48198	Southgate	33,909	29,404
48020	Drayton Plains	16,462	......	49090	South Haven	6,471	6,149
48021	East Detroit	45,920	45,756	*48078	Sterling Heights	61,365	......
49506	East Grand Rapids	12,565	10,924	49091	Sturgis	9,295	8,915
48823	East Lansing	47,540	30,198	48180	Taylor	70,020	......
49001	Eastwood	9,682	......	49286	Tecumseh	7,120	7,045
48229	Ecorse	17,515	17,328	49093	Three Rivers	7,355	7,092
49829	Escanaba	15,368	15,391	49684	Traverse City	18,048	18,432
48024	Farmington	10,329	6,881	48183	Trenton	24,127	18,439
48430	Fenton	8,284	6,142	48084	Troy	39,419	19,402
48220	Ferndale	30,850	31,347	49504	Walker	11,492	......
48134	Flat Rock	5,643	4,696	*48089	Warren	179,260	89,246
*48502	Flint	193,317	196,940	48184	Wayne	21,054	16,034
48433	Flushing	7,190	3,761	48185	Westland	86,749	......
48026	Fraser	11,868	7,027	49007	Westwood	9,143	......
48135	Garden City	41,864	38,017	48753	Wurtsmith	6,932	......
49837	Gladstone	5,237	5,267	*48192	Wyandotte	41,061	43,519
48439	Grand Blanc	5,132	1,565	49509	Wyoming	56,560	45,829
49417	Grand Haven	11,844	11,066	48197	Ypsilanti	29,538	20,957
48837	Grand Ledge	6,032	5,165				
*49501	Grand Rapids	197,649	177,313		**Minnesota**		
49418	Grandville	10,764	7,975				
48838	Greenville	7,493	7,440	56007	Albert Lea	19,418	17,108
48138	Grosse Ile	8,306	......	56308	Alexandria	6,973	6,713
48236	Grosse Pointe	6,637	6,631	55303	Anoka	13,295	10,562
48236	Grosse Pointe Farms	11,701	12,172	55068	Apple Valley	8,502	......
48236	Grosse Pointe Park	15,641	15,457	55112	Arden Hills	5,149	3,930
48236	Grosse Pointe Woods	21,878	18,580	55912	Austin	25,074	27,908
48212	Hamtramck	27,245	34,137	56601	Bemidji	11,490	9,958
48236	Harper Woods	20,186	19,995	55433	Blaine	20,625	7,570
49058	Hastings	6,501	6,375	55420	Bloomington	81,970	50,498
48030	Hazel Park	23,784	25,631	56401	Brainerd	11,667	12,898
48203	Highland Park	35,444	38,063	55429	Brooklyn Center	35,173	24,356
49242	Hillsdale	7,728	7,629	55429	Brooklyn Park 1972	29,945	10,197
49423	Holland	26,479	24,777	55337	Burnsville	19,940	......
48842	Holt	6,980	4,818	55316	Champlin 1972	6,298	1,271
49931	Houghton	6,067	3,393	55317	Chanhassen 1971	5,054	244
48843	Howell	5,224	4,861	55318	Chaska 1972	5,398	2,501
48070	Huntington Woods	8,536	8,746	55719	Chisholm	5,313	7,144
48141	Inkster	38,595	39,097	55720	Cloquet	8,699	9,013
48846	Ionia	6,361	6,754	55421	Columbia Heights	23,837	17,533
49801	Iron Mountain	8,702	9,299	55433	Coon Rapids	30,505	14,931
49938	Ironwood	8,711	10,265	55016	Cottage Grove	13,419	......
49849	Ishpeming	8,245	8,857	56716	Crookston	8,312	8,546
*49201	Jackson	45,484	50,720	55428	Crystal	30,925	24,283
49428	Jenison	11,266	......	56501	Detroit Lakes	5,797	5,633
*49001	Kalamazoo	85,555	82,089	*55806	Duluth	100,578	106,884
49508	Kentwood	20,310	......	56721	East Grand Forks	7,607	6,998
49788	Kincheloe	6,331	......	55343	Eden Prairie	6,938	......
49801	Kingsford	5,276	5,084	55424	Edina	44,046	28,501
49843	K.I. Sawyer	8,224	......	56031	Fairmont	10,751	9,745
48850	Lakeview	11,391	10,384	55113	Falcon Heights	5,641	5,927
48144	Lambertville	5,711	1,168	55021	Faribault	16,595	16,926
*48924	Lansing	131,403	107,807	56537	Fergus Falls	12,443	13,733
48446	Lapeer	6,314	6,160	55421	Fridley	29,233	15,173
48503	Lapeer Heights	7,130	......	55427	Golden Valley	24,246	14,559
48146	Lincoln Park	52,984	53,933	55744	Grand Rapids	7,247	7,265
*48150	Livonia	110,109	66,702	55033	Hastings	12,195	8,965
49431	Ludington	9,021	9,421	55746	Hibbing	16,104	17,731
48071	Madison Heights	38,599	33,343	55343	Hopkins	13,428	11,370
49660	Manistee	7,723	8,324	55350	Hutchinson	8,031	6,207
49855	Marquette	21,967	19,824	56649	International Falls	6,439	6,778
49068	Marshall	7,253	6,736	55075	Inver Grove Heights	12,148	......
48040	Marysville	5,610	4,065	55044	Lakeville	7,556	924
48854	Mason	5,468	4,522	55355	Litchfield	5,262	5,078
48122	Melvindale	13,862	13,089	56345	Little Falls	7,467	7,551
49858	Menominee	10,748	11,289	56001	Mankato	30,895	23,797
48640	Midland	35,176	27,779	55369	Maple Grove	6,275	2,213
48161	Monroe	23,894	22,968	55109	Maplewood	25,222	18,519
48043	Mount Clemens	20,476	21,016	56258	Marshall	9,886	6,681
48858	Mount Pleasant	20,524	14,875	55118	Mendota Heights	6,165	5,028
*49440	Muskegon	44,631	46,485	*55401	Minneapolis	434,400	482,872
49444	Muskegon Heights	17,304	19,552	55343	Minnetonka	35,737	25,037
49866	Negaunee	5,248	6,126	56265	Montevideo	5,661	5,693
49120	Niles	12,988	13,842	56560	Moorhead	29,687	22,934
48167	Northville	5,400	3,967	56267	Morris	5,366	4,199
49441	Norton Shores	22,271	......	55364	Mound	7,572	5,440
48050	Novi	9,668	6,390	55112	Mounds View	10,641	6,416
48237	Oak Park	36,762	36,632	55112	New Brighton	19,507	6,448
48864	Okemos	7,770	......	55428	New Hope	23,180	3,552
48867	Owosso	17,179	17,006	56073	New Ulm	13,051	11,114

ZIP Code	Place	1970	1960
55057	Northfield	10,235	8,707
56001	North Mankato	7,347	5,927
55109	North St. Paul	11,950	8,520
55119	Oakdale	7,304	
55391	Orono	6,787	5,643
55060	Owatonna	15,341	13,409
56164	Pipestone	5,328	5,324
55427	Plymouth	18,077	9,576
55066	Red Wing	10,441	10,528
55423	Richfield	47,231	42,523
55422	Robbinsdale	16,845	16,381
55901	Rochester	53,766	40,663
55113	Roseville	34,438	23,997
55418	St. Anthony	9,239	5,084
56301	St. Cloud	39,691	33,815
55426	St. Louis Park	48,922	43,310
*55101	St. Paul	309,714	313,411
55071	St. Paul Park	5,587	3,267
56082	St. Peter	8,339	8,484
56379	Sauk Rapids	5,051	4,038
55379	Shakopee	6,876	5,201
55112	Shoreview	10,995	7,157
55075	South St. Paul	25,016	22,032
55432	Spring Lake Park	6,417	3,260
55082	Stillwater	10,191	8,310
56701	Thief River Falls	8,618	7,151
55792	Virginia	12,450	14,034
56093	Waseca	6,789	5,898
55118	West St. Paul	18,799	13,101
55110	White Bear Lake	23,313	12,849
56201	Willmar	12,869	10,417
55987	Winona	26,438	24,895
55119	Woodbury	6,184	
56187	Worthington	9,916	9,015

Mississippi

ZIP Code	Place	1970	1960
39730	Aberdeen	6,507	6,450
38821	Amory	7,236	6,474
39520	Bay St. Louis	6,752	5,073
*39530	Biloxi	48,486	44,053
38829	Booneville	5,895	3,480
39601	Brookhaven	10,700	9,885
39046	Canton	10,503	9,707
38614	Clarksdale	21,673	21,105
38732	Cleveland	13,327	10,172
39056	Clinton	7,289	3,438
39429	Columbia	7,587	7,117
39701	Columbus	25,795	24,771
38834	Corinth	11,581	11,453
39532	D'Iberville	7,288	3,005
38701	Greenville	39,648	41,502
38930	Greenwood	22,400	20,436
38901	Grenada	9,944	7,914
39501	Gulfport	40,791	30,204
39401	Hattiesburg	38,277	34,989
38635	Holly Springs	5,728	5,621
38751	Indianola	8,947	6,714
*39025	Jackson	153,968	144,422
39090	Kosciusko	7,266	6,800
39440	Laurel	24,145	27,889
38756	Leland	6,000	6,295
39560	Long Beach	6,170	4,770
39339	Louisville	6,626	5,066
39648	McComb	11,969	12,020
39301	Meridian 1974	46,087	49,374
39563	Moss Point	19,321	6,631
39120	Natchez	19,704	23,791
38652	New Albany	6,426	5,151
39564	Ocean Springs	9,580	5,025
38655	Oxford City	13,846	5,283
39567	Pascagoula	27,264	17,155
39208	Pearl	9,623	5,081
39465	Petal	6,986	4,007
39350	Philadelphia	6,274	5,017
39466	Picayune	10,467	7,834
38671	Southaven	8,931	
39759	Starkville	11,369	9,041
38801	Tupelo	20,471	17,221
39180	Vicksburg	25,478	29,143
39501	West Gulfport	6,996	3,323
39773	West Point	8,714	8,550
38967	Winona	5,521	4,282
39194	Yazoo City	11,688	11,236

Missouri

ZIP Code	Place	1970	1960
63123	Affton	24,264	
65605	Aurora	5,359	4,683
63011	Ballwin	10,656	5,710
63137	Bellefontaine Neighbors	14,084	13,650
63133	Bel-Ridge	5,346	4,395
64012	Belton	12,179	4,897
63134	Berkeley	19,743	18,676
64015	Blue Springs	6,779	2,555
65233	Boonville	7,514	7,090
63114	Breckenridge Hills	7,011	6,299
63144	Brentwood	11,248	12,250

ZIP Code	Place	1970	1960
63044	Bridgeton	19,992	7,820
64628	Brookfield	5,491	5,694
63701	Cape Girardeau	31,282	24,947
64836	Carthage	11,035	11,264
63830	Caruthersville	7,350	8,643
63834	Charleston	5,131	5,911
64601	Chillicothe	9,519	9,236
63105	Clayton	16,100	15,245
64735	Clinton	7,504	6,925
65201	Columbia	58,812	36,650
63128	Concord	21,217	
63126	Crestwood	15,123	11,106
63141	Creve Coeur	8,967	5,122
63136	Dellwood	7,137	4,720
63020	De Soto	5,984	5,804
63131	Des Peres	5,333	4,362
63841	Dexter	6,024	5,519
64024	Excelsior Springs	9,411	6,473
63640	Farmington	6,590	5,618
63135	Ferguson	28,759	22,149
63028	Festus	7,530	7,021
*63033	Florissant	65,908	38,166
65473	Fort Leonard Wood	33,799	
65251	Fulton	12,248	11,131
64118	Gladstone	23,422	14,502
63122	Glendale	6,981	7,048
64030	Grandview	17,456	6,027
63401	Hannibal	18,698	20,028
64701	Harrisonville	5,052	3,510
*63042	Hazelwood	14,082	6,045
*64051	Independence	111,630	62,328
65101	Jefferson City	32,407	28,228
63136	Jennings	19,379	19,965
64801	Joplin	39,256	38,958
*64108	Kansas City	507,330	475,539
63857	Kennett	10,090	9,098
63140	Kinloch	5,629	6,501
63501	Kirksville	15,560	13,123
63122	Kirkwood	31,679	29,421
63124	Ladue	10,359	9,466
65536	Lebanon	8,616	8,220
64063	Lee's Summit	16,230	8,267
63125	Lemay	40,516	
64067	Lexington	5,388	4,845
64068	Liberty	13,704	8,909
63552	Macon	5,301	4,547
63863	Malden	5,374	5,007
63011	Manchester	5,031	2,021
63143	Maplewood	12,785	12,552
65340	Marshall	12,051	9,572
63043	Maryland Heights	8,805	
64468	Maryville	9,970	7,807
65265	Mexico	11,807	12,889
65270	Moberly	12,988	13,170
65708	Monett	5,937	5,359
64850	Neosho	7,517	7,452
64772	Nevada	9,736	8,416
63121	Normandy	6,236	4,452
64116	North Kansas City 1974	5,046	5,657
63366	O'Fallon	7,018	3,770
63124	Olivette	9,156	8,257
63114	Overland	24,819	22,763
63133	Pagedale	5,044	5,106
63775	Perryville	5,149	5,117
63120	Pine Lawn	5,745	5,943
63901	Poplar Bluff	16,653	15,926
64133	Raytown	33,306	17,083
63117	Richmond Heights	13,802	15,622
63124	Rock Hill	6,815	6,523
65401	Rolla	13,571	11,132
63074	St. Ann	18,215	12,155
63301	St. Charles	31,834	21,189
63114	St. John	8,960	7,342
*64501	St. Joseph	72,691	79,673
*63155	St. Louis	622,236	750,026
63126	Sappington	10,603	
65301	Sedalia	22,847	23,874
63119	Shrewsbury	5,896	4,730
63801	Sikeston	14,699	13,765
63138	Spanish Lake	15,647	
*65801	Springfield	120,096	95,865
63080	Sullivan	5,111	4,098
64683	Trenton	6,063	6,262
63084	Union	5,183	3,937
63130	University City	47,527	51,249
64093	Warrensburg	13,125	9,689
63090	Washington	8,499	7,961
64870	Webb City	6,923	6,740
63119	Webster Groves	27,457	28,990
63112	Wellston	7,050	7,979
65775	West Plains	6,893	5,836
65301	Whiteman	5,040	
63134	Woodson Terrace	5,880	6,048

Montana

ZIP Code	Place	1970	1960
59711	Anaconda	9,771	12,054

ZIP Code	Place	1970	1960
*59101	Billings	61,581	52,851
59715	Bozeman	18,670	13,361
59701	Butte	23,368	27,877
59701	Floral Park	5,113	4,079
59330	Glendive	6,305	7,058
*59401	Great Falls	60,091	55,244
59501	Havre	10,558	10,740
59601	Helena	22,730	20,227
59901	Kalispell	10,526	10,151
59457	Lewistown	6,437	7,408
59047	Livingston	6,883	8,229
59402	Malmstrom	8,374	......
59301	Miles City	9,023	9,665
59801	Missoula	29,497	27,090
59801	Missoula West	9,148	......
59701	Silver Bow Park	5,524	4,798

Nebraska

ZIP Code	Place	1970	1960
69301	Alliance	6,862	7,845
68310	Beatrice	12,389	12,132
68005	Bellevue 1974	21,145	8,831
68008	Blair	6,106	4,931
69337	Chadron	5,921	5,079
68601	Columbus	15,471	12,476
68352	Fairbury	5,265	5,572
68355	Falls City	5,444	5,598
68025	Fremont	22,962	19,698
69341	Gering	5,639	4,585
68801	Grand Island	31,269	25,742
68901	Hastings	23,580	21,412
68949	Holdrege	5,635	5,226
68847	Kearney	19,181	14,210
68128	La Vista 1974	7,840	1,004
68850	Lexington	5,654	5,572
*68501	Lincoln	149,518	128,521
69001	McCook	8,285	8,301
68137	Millard	7,460	1,014
68410	Nebraska City	7,441	7,252
68701	Norfolk	16,607	13,640
69101	North Platte	19,447	17,184
68113	Offutt East	5,195	......
68113	Offutt West	8,445	......
*68108	Omaha	346,929	301,598
68046	Papillion 1974	6,493	2,235
68048	Plattsmouth	6,371	6,244
69361	Scottsbluff	14,507	13,377
68434	Seward	5,294	4,208
69162	Sidney	6,403	8,004
68776	South Sioux City	7,920	7,200
68787	Wayne	5,379	4,217
68467	York	6,778	6,173

Nevada

ZIP Code	Place	1970	1960
89005	Boulder City	5,223	4,059
89701	Carson City	15,468	5,163
89112	East Las Vegas	6,501	......
89801	Elko	7,621	6,298
89015	Henderson	16,395	12,525
*89114	Las Vegas	125,787	64,405
89110	Nellis	6,449	......
89030	North Las Vegas	36,216	18,422
89109	Paradise	24,477	......
*89501	Reno	72,863	51,470
89431	Sparks	24,187	16,618
89110	Sunrise Manor	10,886	......
89109	Vegas Creek	8,970	......
89101	Winchester	13,981	......

New Hampshire
See note on page 215

ZIP Code	Place	1970	1960
03102	Bedford	5,859	3,636
03570	Berlin	15,256	17,821
03743	Claremont	14,221	13,563
03301	Concord	30,022	28,991
03038	Derry	6,090	4,468
03038	Derry	11,712	6,987
03820	Dover	20,850	19,131
03824	Durham	7,221	4,688
	Durham	8,869	5,504
03833	Exeter	6,439	5,896
	Exeter	8,892	7,243
03235	Franklin	7,292	6,742
03045	Goffstown	9,284	7,230
03842	Hampton	5,407	3,281
	Hampton	8,011	5,379
03755	Hanover	6,147	5,649
	Hanover	8,494	7,329
03106	Hooksett	5,564	3,713
03051	Hudson	10,638	5,876
03431	Keene	20,467	17,562
03246	Laconia	14,888	15,288
03766	Lebanon	9,725	9,299
03516	Littleton	5,290	5,003
03053	Londonderry	5,346	2,457

ZIP Code	Place	1970	1960
*03101	Manchester	87,754	88,282
03054	Merrimack	8,595	2,989
03055	Milford	6,622	4,863
03060	Nashua	55,820	39,096
03773	Newport	5,899	5,458
03076	Pelham	5,408	2,605
03801	Portsmouth	25,717	26,900
03867	Rochester	17,938	15,927
03079	Salem	20,142	9,210
03878	Somersworth	9,026	8,529

New Jersey

ZIP Code	Place	1970	1960
08201	Absecon	6,094	4,320
07401	Allendale	6,240	4,092
07712	Asbury Park	16,533	17,366
*08401	Atlantic City	47,859	59,544
07716	Atlantic Highlands	5,102	4,119
08106	Audubon	10,802	10,440
08007	Barrington	8,409	7,943
07002	Bayonne	72,743	74,215
07109	Belleville	37,629	35,005
08030	Bellmawr	15,618	11,853
07719	Belmar	5,782	5,190
07621	Bergenfield	29,000	27,203
07922	Berkeley Hts. Twp.	13,078	8,721
07924	Bernardsville	6,652	5,515
07003	Bloomfield	52,029	51,867
07403	Bloomingdale	7,797	5,293
07603	Bogota	8,960	7,965
07005	Boonton	9,261	7,981
08805	Bound Brook	10,450	10,263
08723	Brick Twp.	35,057	16,299
08302	Bridgeton	20,435	20,966
08203	Brigantine	6,741	4,201
08015	Browns Mills	7,144	......
08016	Burlington	11,991	12,687
07405	Butler	7,051	5,414
07006	Caldwell	8,677	6,942
*08101	Camden	102,551	117,159
08701	Candlewood	5,629	......
07072	Carlstadt	6,724	6,042
07008	Carteret	23,137	20,502
07009	Cedar Grove Twp.	15,582	14,603
07928	Chatham	9,566	9,517
*08002	Cherry Hill Twp.	64,395	31,522
08077	Cinnaminson Twp.	16,962	8,302
07066	Clark Twp.	18,829	12,195
08312	Clayton	5,193	4,711
07010	Cliffside Park	18,891	17,642
07721	Cliffwood-Cliffwood Beach	7,056	......
*07015	Clifton	82,437	82,084
07624	Closter	8,604	7,767
08108	Collingswood	17,422	17,370
07016	Cranford Twp.	27,391	26,424
07626	Cresskill	8,298	7,290
08075	Delran Twp.	10,065	5,327
07627	Demarest	5,133	4,231
07834	Denville Twp.	14,045	10,632
08096	Deptford Twp.	24,232	17,878
07801	Dover	15,039	13,034
07628	Dumont	20,155	18,882
08812	Dunellen	7,072	6,840
08816	East Brunswick Twp.	34,166	19,965
*07019	East Orange	75,471	77,259
07407	East Paterson	20,511	19,344
07073	East Rutherford	8,536	7,769
08520	East Windsor Twp. 1974	19,788	2,298
07724	Eatontown	14,619	10,334
08817	Edison Twp.	67,120	44,799
*07207	Elizabeth	112,654	107,698
07630	Emerson	8,428	6,849
*07631	Englewood	24,985	26,057
07632	Englewood Cliffs	5,938	2,913
08053	Evesham Twp.	13,477	4,548
08618	Ewing Twp.	32,831	26,628
07006	Fairfield	6,884	......
07701	Fair Haven	6,142	5,678
07410	Fair Lawn	37,975	36,421
07022	Fairview	10,698	9,399
07023	Fanwood	8,920	7,963
08518	Florence-Roebling	7,551	......
07932	Florham Park	8,094	7,222
08640	Fort Dix	26,290	......
07024	Fort Lee	30,631	21,815
07417	Franklin Lakes	7,550	3,316
07728	Freehold	10,545	9,140
07026	Garfield	30,797	29,253
07027	Garwood	5,260	5,426
08028	Glassboro	12,938	10,253
07028	Glen Ridge	8,518	8,322
07452	Glen Rock	13,011	12,896
08030	Gloucester City	14,707	15,511
07093	Guttenberg	5,754	5,118
*07602	Hackensack	36,008	30,521
07840	Hackettstown	9,472	5,276
08108	Haddon Twp.	18,192	17,099
08033	Haddonfield	13,118	13,201

ZIP Code	Place	1970	1960
08035	Haddon Heights	9,365	9,260
07508	Haledon	6,767	6,161
08037	Hammonton	11,464	9,854
07981	Hanover Twp.	10,700	9,329
07029	Harrison	11,811	11,743
07604	Hasbrouck Heights	13,651	13,046
07506	Hawthorne	19,173	17,735
07730	Hazlet Twp.	22,239	15,334
08904	Highland Park	14,385	11,049
08520	Hightstown	5,431	4,317
07642	Hillsdale	11,768	8,734
07205	Hillside Twp.	21,636	22,304
07030	Hoboken	45,380	48,441
07843	Hopatcong	9,052	3,391
08560	Hopewell Twp. (Mercer)	10,030	7,818
07111	Irvington	59,743	59,379
08527	Jackson Twp.	18,276	5,939
*07303	Jersey City	260,350	276,101
07734	Keansburg	9,720	6,854
07032	Kenny	37,585	37,472
08824	Kendall Park	7,412	......
07033	Kenilworth	9,165	8,379
07735	Keyport	7,205	6,440
07405	Kinnelon	7,600	4,431
07034	Lake Hiawatha	11,389	......
07871	Lake Mohawk	6,262	4,647
07054	Lake Parsippany	7,488	......
08701	Lakewood	17,874	13,004
08879	Laurence Harbor	6,715	......
07605	Leonia	8,847	8,384
07035	Lincoln Park	9,034	6,048
07036	Linden	41,409	39,931
08021	Lindenwold 1973	16,265	7,335
08221	Linwood	6,159	3,847
07424	Little Falls Twp.	11,727	9,730
07643	Little Ferry	9,064	6,176
07739	Little Silver	6,010	5,202
07039	Livingston Twp.	30,127	23,124
07644	Lodi	25,163	23,502
07740	Long Branch	31,774	26,228
07071	Lyndhurst Twp.	22,729	21,867
07940	Madison	16,710	15,122
08049	Magnolia	5,893	4,199
07430	Mahwah Twp.	10,800	7,376
08835	Manville	13,029	10,995
08052	Maple Shade Twp.	16,464	12,947
07040	Maplewood Twp.	24,932	23,977
08402	Margate City	10,576	9,474
07746	Marlboro Twp.	12,273	8,038
08053	Marlton	10,180	......
07747	Matawan	9,136	5,097
07607	Maywood	11,087	11,460
08641	McGuire	10,933	......
08619	Mercerville-Hamilton Sq.	24,465	......
08840	Metuchen	16,031	14,041
08846	Middlesex	15,038	10,520
07748	Middletown Twp.	54,623	39,675
07432	Midland Park	8,159	7,543
07041	Millburn Twp.	21,089	18,799
08850	Milltown	6,470	5,435
08332	Millville	21,366	19,096
07434	Monroe Twp. (Gloucester)	14,071	9,396
*07042	Montclair	44,043	43,129
07645	Montvale	7,327	3,699
07045	Montville Twp.	11,846	6,772
08057	Moorestown-Lenola	14,179	......
07950	Morris Plains	5,540	4,703
07960	Morristown	17,662	17,712
07092	Mountainside	7,520	6,325
08059	Mount Ephraim	5,625	5,447
08060	Mount Holly Twp.	12,713	13,271
07753	Neptune Twp.	27,863	21,487
07753	Neptune City	5,502	4,013
*07102	Newark	381,930	405,220
*08901	New Brunswick	41,885	40,139
08511	New Hanover	27,410	28,528
07646	New Milford	19,149	18,810
07974	New Providence	13,796	10,243
07724	New Shrewsbury	8,395	7,313
07860	Newton	7,297	6,563
07032	North Arlington	18,096	17,477
07047	North Bergen Twp.	47,751	42,387
08902	North Brunswick Twp.	16,691	10,099
07006	North Caldwell	6,733	4,163
08225	Northfield	8,875	5,849
07508	North Haledon	7,614	6,026
07060	North Plainfield	21,796	16,993
07647	Northvale	5,177	2,892
07110	Nutley	31,913	29,513
07755	Oakhurst	5,558	4,374
07436	Oakland	14,420	9,446
08226	Ocean City	10,575	7,618
07757	Oceanport	7,503	4,937
08857	Old Bridge	25,176	......
07649	Oradell	8,903	7,487
*07050	Orange	32,566	35,789
07650	Palisades Park	13,351	11,943
08065	Palmyra	6,969	7,036
07652	Paramus	28,381	23,238
07656	Park Ridge	8,709	6,389
*07055	Passaic	55,124	53,963
*07510	Paterson	144,824	143,663
08066	Paulsboro	8,084	8,121
08110	Pennsauken Twp.	36,394	33,771
08069	Penns Grove	5,727	6,176
08070	Pennsville	11,014	......
07440	Pequannock Twp.	14,350	10,553
*08861	Perth Amboy	38,798	38,007
08865	Phillipsburg	17,849	18,502
08021	Pine Hill	5,132	3,939
08854	Piscataway Twp.	36,418	19,890
08071	Pitman	10,257	8,644
*07061	Plainfield	46,862	45,330
08232	Pleasantville	13,778	15,172
08742	Point Pleasant	15,968	10,182
07442	Pompton Lakes	11,397	9,445
08540	Princeton	12,331	11,890
08540	Princeton North	5,488	4,506
07508	Prospect Park	5,176	5,201
*07065	Rahway	29,114	27,699
08057	Ramblewood	5,556	......
07446	Ramsey	12,571	9,527
07970	Randolph Twp.	13,296	7,295
08869	Raritan	6,691	6,137
07701	Red Bank	12,847	12,482
07657	Ridgefield	11,308	10,788
07660	Ridgefield Park	13,990	12,701
*07451	Ridgewood	27,547	25,391
07456	Ringwood	10,393	4,182
07661	River Edge	12,850	13,264
08075	Riverside Twp.	8,591	8,474
07662	Rochell Park Twp.	6,380	6,119
07866	Rockaway	6,383	5,413
07203	Roselle	22,585	21,032
07204	Roselle Park	14,227	12,546
07760	Rumson	7,421	6,405
08078	Runnemede	10,475	8,396
*07070	Rutherford	20,802	20,473
07662	Saddle Brook Twp.	15,975	13,834
08079	Salem	7,648	8,941
08872	Sayreville	32,508	22,553
07076	Scotch Plains Twp.	22,279	18,491
07094	Secaucus	13,228	12,154
08083	Somerdale	6,510	4,839
08244	Somers Point	7,919	4,504
08876	Somerville	13,652	12,458
07879	South Amboy	9,338	8,422
07079	South Orange	16,971	16,175
07080	South Plainfield	21,142	17,879
08882	South River	15,428	13,397
07871	Sparta Twp.	10,819	6,717
08884	Spotswood	7,891	5,788
08081	Springfield Twp.	15,740	14,467
08084	Stratford	9,801	4,308
07747	Strathmore	7,674	......
07901	Summit	23,620	23,677
07666	Teaneck Twp.	42,355	42,085
07670	Tenafly	14,827	14,264
08753	Toms River	7,303	6,062
07512	Totowa	11,580	10,897
*08608	Trenton	104,786	114,167
07083	Union Twp.	53,077	51,499
07735	Union Beach	6,472	5,862
07087	Union City	57,305	52,180
07458	Upper Saddle River	7,949	3,570
08406	Ventnor City	10,385	8,688
07044	Verona	15,067	13,782
08360	Vineland	47,399	37,685
07463	Waldwick	12,313	10,495
07057	Wallington	10,284	9,261
07465	Wanaque	8,636	7,126
07882	Washington	5,943	5,723
07675	Washington Twp. (Bergen)	10,577	6,654
07470	Wayne Twp.	49,141	29,353
07087	Weehawken Twp.	13,383	13,504
07006	West Caldwell	11,913	8,314
*07091	Westfield	33,720	31,447
07764	West Long Branch	6,845	5,337
07480	West Milford Twp.	17,304	8,157
07093	West New York	40,627	35,547
07052	West Orange	43,715	39,895
07424	West Paterson	11,692	7,602
08093	Westville	5,170	4,951
07675	Westwood	11,105	9,046
07885	Wharton	5,535	5,006
08610	White Horse-Yardville	18,680	......
07886	White Meadow Lake	8,499	......
08046	Willingboro Twp. 1973	44,607	11,861
08095	Winslow Twp.	11,202	9,142
07095	Woodbridge Twp.	98,944	78,846
08096	Woodbury	12,408	12,453
07675	Woodcliff Lake	5,506	2,742
07075	Wood-Ridge	8,311	7,964
07481	Wyckoff Twp.	16,039	11,205

ZIP Code	Place	1970	1960
	New Mexico		
88310	Alamogordo	23,035	21,723
*87101	Albuquerque	243,751	201,189
88210	Artesia	10,315	12,000
88101	Cannon	5,461	......
88220	Carlsbad	21,297	25,541
88101	Clovis	28,495	23,713
88030	Deming	8,343	6,764
87401	Farmington	21,979	23,786
87301	Gallup	14,596	14,089
87020	Grants	8,768	10,274
88240	Hobbs	26,025	26,275
88330	Holloman	8,001	......
88001	Las Cruces	37,857	29,367
87701	Las Vegas (city)	7,528	7,790
87701	Las Vegas (town)	6,307	6,028
87544	Los Alamos	11,310	12,584
88260	Lovington	8,915	9,660
87107	North Valley	10,366	......
88130	Portales	10,554	9,695
87740	Raton	6,962	8,146
88201	Roswell	33,908	39,593
87115	Sandia	6,867	......
87501	Santa Fe	41,167	33,394
88061	Silver City	8,557	6,972
87801	Socorro	5,849	5,271
87105	South Valley	29,389	......
88401	Tucumcari	7,189	8,143
	New York		
*12207	Albany	115,781	129,726
11507	Albertson	6,825	......
14411	Albion	5,122	5,182
11701	Amityville	9,794	8,318
12010	Amsterdam	25,524	28,772
12603	Arlington	11,203	8,317
13021	Auburn	34,599	35,249
*11702	Babylon	12,897	11,062
11510	Baldwin	34,525	30,204
13027	Baldwinsville	6,298	5,985
14020	Batavia	17,338	18,210
14810	Bath	6,053	6,166
11705	Bayport	8,232	......
11706	Bay Shore	11,119	......
11709	Bayville	6,147	3,962
12508	Beacon	13,255	13,922
11710	Bellmore	18,431	12,784
11714	Bethpage	18,555	......
*13902	Binghamton	64,123	75,941
10913	Blauvelt	5,426	......
11716	Bohemia	8,926	......
11717	Brentwood	28,327	15,387
10510	Briarcliff Manor	6,521	5,105
14420	Brockport	7,878	5,256
10708	Bronxville	6,674	6,744
*14240	Buffalo	462,768	532,759
14424	Canadaigua 1971	10,753	9,370
13032	Canastota	5,033	4,896
13617	Canton	6,398	5,046
11514	Carle Place	6,326	......
12414	Catskill	5,317	5,825
11516	Cedarhurst	6,941	6,954
11720	Centereach	9,427	8,524
11722	Central Islip	36,391	......
12065	Clifton Knolls	5,771	......
12047	Cohoes	18,653	20,129
11724	Cold Spring Harbor	5,450	1,705
12205	Colonie	8,701	6,992
11725	Commack	24,138	9,613
10920	Congers	5,928	......
11726	Copiague	19,632	14,081
14830	Corning	15,792	17,085
13045	Cortland	19,621	19,181
10520	Croton-on-Hudson	7,523	6,812
14437	Dansville	5,436	5,460
11729	Deer Park	32,274	16,726
14043	Depew	22,158	13,580
13214	DeWitt	10,032	......
11746	Dix Hills	10,050	......
10522	Dobbs Ferry	10,353	9,260
14048	Dunkirk	16,855	18,205
14052	East Aurora	7,033	6,791
10709	Eastchester	23,750	......
12302	East Glenville	5,898	......
11746	East Half Hollow Hills	9,691	......
11576	East Hills	8,624	7,184
11730	East Islip	6,861	......
11758	East Massapequa	15,926	14,779
11554	East Meadow	46,290	46,036
11743	East Neck	5,221	3,789
11731	East Northport	12,392	8,381
11772	East Patchogue	8,092	......
14445	East Rochester	8,347	8,152
11518	East Rockaway	11,795	10,721
13902	East Vestal	10,472	......
*14901	Elmira	39,945	46,517

ZIP Code	Place	1970	1960
11003	Elmont	29,363	30,138
11731	Elwood	15,031	......
13760	Endicott	16,556	18,775
13760	Endwell	15,999	......
13219	Fairmount	15,317	......
14450	Fairport	6,474	5,507
12601	Fairview	8,517	8,626
11735	Farmingdale	9,297	6,128
*11001	Floral Park	18,466	17,499
11010	Franklin Square	32,156	32,483
14063	Fredonia	10,326	8,477
11520	Freeport	40,374	34,419
13069	Fulton	14,003	14,261
11530	Garden City	25,373	23,948
11040	Garden City Park	7,488	......
14454	Geneseo	5,714	3,284
14456	Geneva	16,793	17,286
11542	Glen Cove	25,770	23,817
12801	Glens Falls	17,222	18,580
12078	Gloversville	19,677	21,741
*11022	Great Neck	10,798	10,171
11020	Great Neck Plaza	6,043	4,948
11740	Greenlawn	8,493	5,422
11746	Half Hollow Hills	12,081	......
14075	Hamburg	10,215	9,145
10528	Harrison Town	21,544	19,201
10530	Hartsdale	12,226	......
10706	Hastings-on-Hudson	9,479	8,979
11787	Hauppauge	13,957	......
10927	Haverstraw	8,198	5,771
*11551	Hempstead	39,411	34,641
13350	Herkimer	8,960	9,396
11040	Herricks	9,112	......
11557	Hewlett	6,796	......
*11802	Hicksville	49,820	50,405
10977	Hillcrest	5,357	......
11741	Holbrook-Holtsville	12,103	......
14843	Hornell	12,144	13,907
14845	Horseheads Village	7,989	7,207
12534	Hudson	8,940	11,075
12839	Hudson Falls	7,917	7,752
11743	Huntington	12,601	11,255
11746	Huntington Station	28,817	23,438
13357	Ilion	9,808	10,199
11696	Inwood	8,433	10,362
10533	Irvington	5,878	5,494
11558	Island Park	5,396	3,846
11751	Islip	7,692	......
14850	Ithaca	26,226	28,799
14701	Jamestown	39,795	41,818
10535	Jefferson Valley-Yorktown	9,008	......
11753	Jericho	14,010	10,795
13790	Johnson City	18,025	19,118
12095	Johnstown	10,045	10,390
14217	Kenmore	20,980	21,261
11754	Kings Park	5,555	4,949
11024	Kings Point	5,614	5,410
12401	Kingston	25,544	29,260
14218	Lackawanna	28,657	29,564
11755	Lake Grove	8,133	......
11552	Lakeview	5,471	......
14086	Lancaster	13,365	12,254
10538	Larchmont	7,203	6,789
12110	Latham	9,661	......
11559	Lawrence	6,566	5,907
14482	Le Roy	5,118	4,662
11756	Levittown	65,440	65,276
11757	Lindenhurst	28,359	20,905
13365	Little Falls	7,629	8,935
14094	Lockport	25,399	26,443
11791	Locust Grove	11,626	11,558
11561	Long Beach	33,127	26,473
12211	Loudonville	9,299	......
11563	Lynbrook	23,151	19,881
10541	Mahopac	5,265	1,337
12953	Malone	8,048	8,737
11565	Malverne	10,036	9,968
10543	Mamaroneck	18,909	17,673
11030	Manhasset	8,541	......
11050	Manorhaven	5,488	3,566
11758	Massapequa	26,821	32,900
11762	Massapequa Park	22,112	19,904
13662	Massena	14,042	15,478
13211	Mattydale	8,292	......
12118	Mechanicville	6,247	6,831
14103	Medina	6,415	6,681
11746	Melville	6,641	......
11566	Merrick	25,904	18,789
10940	Middletown	22,607	23,475
11501	Mineola	21,744	20,519
10952	Monsey	8,797	......
12701	Monticello	5,991	5,222
10549	Mt. Kisco	8,172	6,805
*10551	Mount Vernon	72,788	76,010
10954	Nanuet	10,447	......
11767	Nesconset	10,048	1,964
14513	Newark	11,644	12,868
12550	Newburgh	26,219	30,979

ZIP Code	Place	1970	1960
11590	New Cassel	8,721	......
10956	New City	27,344	......
11040	New Hyde Park	10,116	10,808
12561	New Paltz	6,058	3,041
*10802	New Rochelle	75,385	76,812
*12550	New Windsor	8,803	4,041
*10001	New York	7,895,563	7,781,984
*10451	Bronx	1,471,701	1,424,815
*11201	Brooklyn	2,602,012	2,627,319
*10001	Manhattan	1,539,233	1,698,281
*(Q)	Queens	1,987,174	1,809,578

(Q) There are 4 Zip Codes for Queens: 11101 for L. I. City; 11690 Far Rockaway; 11351 Flushing and 11431 Jamaica.

ZIP Code	Place	1970	1960
*10314	Richmond	295,443	221,991
*14302	Niagara Falls	85,615	102,394
13745	Nimmonsburg-Chenango Bridge	5,059	......
12309	Niskayuna	6,186	......
11701	North Amityville	11,936	......
11703	North Babylon	39,526	......
11710	North Bellmore	22,893	19,639
11713	North Bellport	5,903	......
11752	North Great River	12,080	......
11757	North Lindenhurst	11,117	......
11758	North Massapequa	23,123	......
11566	North Merrick	13,650	12,976
11040	North New Hyde Park	18,154	17,929
11772	North Patchogue	5,232	......
10803	North Pelham	5,184	5,326
11768	Northport	7,494	5,972
13212	North Syracuse	8,687	7,412
10591	North Tarrytown	8,334	8,818
14120	North Tonawanda	36,012	34,757
11580	North Valley Stream	14,881	17,239
11793	North Wantagh	15,053	......
13815	Norwich	8,843	9,175
10960	Nyack	6,659	6,062
11769	Oakdale	7,334	......
11572	Oceanside	35,372	30,448
13669	Ogdensburg	14,554	16,122
11804	Old Bethpage	7,084	......
14760	Olean	19,169	21,868
13421	Oneida	11,658	11,677
13820	Oneonta	16,030	13,412
10562	Ossining	21,659	18,662
13126	Oswego	20,913	22,155
13827	Owego	5,152	5,417
11771	Oyster Bay	6,822	......
11772	Patchogue	11,582	8,838
10965	Pearl River	17,146	......
10566	Peekskill	19,283	18,737
10803	Pelham Manor	6,673	6,114
14527	Penn Yan	5,293	5,770
11714	Plainedge	10,759	21,973
11803	Plainview	31,695	27,710
12901	Plattsburgh	18,715	20,172
12903	Plattsburgh Base	7,078	......
10570	Pleasantville	7,110	5,877
10573	Port Chester	25,803	24,960
11777	Port Jefferson	5,515	......
11776	Port Jefferson Station	7,403	1,041
12771	Port Jervis	8,852	9,268
11050	Port Washington	15,923	15,657
13676	Potsdam	10,303	7,765
*12601	Poughkeepsie	32,029	38,330
12144	Rensselaer	10,136	10,506
11901	Riverhead	7,585	5,830
*14603	Rochester	296,233	318,611
*11570	Rockville Centre	27,444	26,355
12205	Roessleville	5,476	......
13440	Rome	50,148	51,646
11779	Ronkonkoma	7,284	4,220
11575	Roosevelt	15,008	12,883
11577	Roslyn Heights	7,242	......
12303	Rotterdam	25,214	16,871
10580	Rye	15,869	14,225
11780	St. James	10,500	3,524
14779	Salamanca	7,877	8,480
11754	San Remo	8,302	3,160
12983	Saranac Lake	6,086	6,421
12866	Saratoga Springs	18,845	16,630
11782	Sayville	11,680	......
10583	Scarsdale	19,229	17,968
*12301	Schenectady	77,958	81,682
12302	Scotia	7,370	7,625
11579	Sea Cliff	5,890	5,669
11783	Seaford	17,379	14,718
11784	Selden	11,613	1,604
13148	Seneca Falls	7,794	7,439
11733	Setauket-South Setauket	6,857	......
11967	Shirley	6,280	......
14225	Sloan	5,216	5,803
13209	Solvay	8,280	8,732
11735	South Farmingdale	20,464	16,318
11741	South Holbrook	6,700	......

ZIP Code	Place	1970	1960
11746	South Huntington	9,115	7,084
14904	Southport	8,685	6,698
11790	South Stony Brook	15,329	......
11581	South Valley Stream	6,595	......
11590	South Westbury	10,978	11,977
10977	Spring Valley	18,112	6,538
11790	Stony Brook	6,391	3,548
10980	Stony Point	8,270	3,330
10901	Suffern	8,273	5,094
11791	Syosset	10,084	......
*13201	Syracuse	197,297	216,038
10983	Tappan	7,424	......
10591	Tarrytown	11,115	11,109
10594	Thornwood	6,874	......
14150	Tonawanda	21,898	21,561
12180	Troy	62,918	67,492
*10707	Tuckahoe	6,236	6,423
11553	Uniondale	22,077	20,041
*13503	Utica	91,340	100,410
10989	Valley Cottage	6,007	......
*11580	Valley Stream	40,413	38,629
11731	Vernon Valley	7,925	5,998
13850	Vestal-Twin Orchards	8,303	......
10901	Viola	5,136	......
12586	Walden	5,277	4,851
11793	Wantagh	21,873	34,172
12590	Wappingers Falls	5,607	4,447
13165	Waterloo	5,418	5,098
13601	Watertown	30,787	33,306
12189	Watervliet	12,404	13,917
14892	Waverly	5,261	5,950
14580	Webster	5,037	3,060
14895	Wellsville	5,815	5,967
11758	West Amityville	6,424	......
11704	West Babylon	12,893	......
11590	Westbury	15,362	14,757
14905	West Elmira	5,901	5,763
10993	West Haverstraw	8,558	5,020
11552	West Hempstead	20,375	......
11795	West Islip	17,374	......
12203	Westmere	6,364	......
10994	West Nyack	5,510	......
11796	West Sayville	7,386	......
13219	Westvale	7,253	......
*10602	White Plains	50,346	50,485
14221	Williamsville	6,835	6,316
11596	Williston Park	9,154	8,255
11598	Woodmere	19,831	14,011
*11798	Wyandanch	15,716	......
11980	Yaphank	5,460	......
*10701	Yonkers	204,297	190,634
10598	Yorktown Heights	6,805	2,478

North Carolina

ZIP Code	Place	1970	1960
27910	Ahoskie	5,105	4,583
28001	Albemarle	11,126	12,261
27203	Asheboro	10,797	9,449
*28801	Asheville	57,681	60,192
28012	Belmont	5,054	5,007
28607	Boone	8,754	3,686
28712	Brevard	5,243	4,857
27215	Burlington	35,930	33,199
28542	Camp Le Jeune Central	34,549	......
28716	Canton	5,158	5,068
27510	Carrboro	5,058	1,997
27511	Cary	7,435	3,356
27514	Chapel Hill	25,537	12,573
*28202	Charlotte	241,178	201,564
28533	Cherry Point	12,029	......
28021	Cherryville	5,258	3,607
28328	Clinton	7,157	7,461
28025	Concord	18,464	17,799
28334	Dunn	8,302	7,566
*27701	Durham	95,438	78,302
27288	Eden	15,871	......
27909	Elizabeth City	14,381	14,062
*28302	Fayetteville	53,510	47,106
28043	Forest City	7,179	6,556
28307	Fort Bragg	46,995	......
28052	Gastonia	47,142	37,276
27530	Goldsboro	26,810	28,873
27253	Graham	8,172	7,728
*27420	Greensboro	144,076	119,574
27834	Greenville	29,063	22,860
28532	Havelock	5,283	2,433
27536	Henderson	13,896	12,740
28739	Hendersonville	6,443	5,911
28601	Hickory	20,569	19,328
*27260	High Point	63,259	62,063
28540	Jacksonville	16,289	13,491
28081	Kannapolis	36,293	34,647
28086	Kings Mountain	8,465	8,008
28501	Kinston	23,020	24,819
28352	Laurinburg	8,859	8,242

ZIP Code	Place	1970	1960
28645	Lenoir	14,705	10,257
27292	Lexington	17,205	16,093
28092	Lincolnton	5,293	5,699
28358	Lumberton	16,961	15,305
28110	Monroe	11,282	10,882
28115	Moorsville	8,808	6,918
28557	Morehead City	5,233	5,583
28655	Morganton	13,625	9,186
27030	Mount Airy	7,325	7,055
28120	Mount Holly	5,107	4,037
28560	New Bern	14,660	15,717
28540	New River Gieger	8,699	......
28658	Newton	7,857	6,658
28012	North Belmont	10,672	8,328
27565	Oxford	7,178	6,978
*27611	Raleigh	123,793	93,931
27320	Reidsville	13,636	14,267
27870	Roanoke Rapids	13,508	13,320
28379	Rockingham	5,852	5,512
27801	Rocky Mount	34,284	32,147
27573	Roxboro	5,370	5,147
28144	Salisbury	22,515	21,297
27330	Sanford	11,716	12,253
27530	Seymour-Johnson	8,172	......
28150	Shelby	16,328	17,698
27577	Smithfield	6,677	6,117
28387	Southern Pines	5,937	5,198
28677	Statesville	20,007	19,844
27886	Tarboro	9,425	8,411
27360	Thomasville	15,230	15,190
27889	Washington	8,961	9,939
28786	Waynesville	6,488	6,159
28025	West Concord	5,347	5,510
27892	Williamston	6,570	6,924
28401	Wilmington	46,169	44,013
27893	Wilson	29,347	28,753
*27102	Winston-Salem	133,683	111,135

North Dakota

ZIP Code	Place	1970	1960
58501	Bismarck	34,703	27,670
58301	Devils Lake 1974	7,354	6,299
58601	Dickinson	12,405	9,971
58102	Fargo	53,365	46,662
58237	Grafton, 1973	5,931	5,885
58201	Grand Forks, 1971	40,060	34,451
58201	Grand Forks Base	10,474	......
58401	Jamestown, 1971	15,078	15,163
58554	Mandan, 1973	11,400	10,525
58701	Minot	32,290	30,604
58701	Minot Base	12,077	......
58072	Valley City	7,843	7,809
58075	Wahpeton	7,076	5,876
58078	West Fargo, 1972	6,437	3,328
58801	Williston	11,280	11,866

Ohio

ZIP Code	Place	1970	1960
45810	Ada	5,309	3,918
*44309	Akron	275,425	290,351
44601	Alliance	26,547	28,362
44001	Amherst	9,902	6,750
44805	Ashland	19,872	17,419
44004	Ashtabula	24,313	24,559
45701	Athens	24,168	16,470
44202	Aurora	6,549	4,049
44515	Austintown	29,393	......
44011	Avon	7,214	6,002
45404	Avondale	5,240	......
44012	Avon Lake	12,261	9,403
44203	Barberton	33,052	33,805
44140	Bay Village	18,163	14,489
44122	Beachwood	9,631	6,089
44146	Bedford	17,552	15,223
44146	Bedford Heights	13,063	5,275
43906	Bellaire	9,655	11,502
43311	Bellefontaine	11,255	11,424
44811	Bellevue	8,604	8,286
45714	Belpre	7,189	5,418
44017	Berea	22,465	16,592
43209	Bexley	14,888	14,319
43004	Blacklick Estates	8,351	......
45242	Blue Ash	8,324	8,341
44512	Boardman	30,852	......
43402	Bowling Green	21,760	13,574
44141	Brecksville	9,137	5,435
45211	Bridgetown	13,352	......
44141	Broadview Heights	11,463	6,209
44144	Brooklyn	13,142	10,733
44142	Brook Park	30,774	12,856
44212	Brunswick	15,852	11,725
43506	Bryan	7,008	7,361
44820	Bucyrus	13,111	12,276
43725	Cambridge	13,656	14,562
44405	Campbell	12,577	13,406
*44711	Canton	110,053	113,631
45822	Celina	8,072	7,659

ZIP Code	Place	1970	1960
45459	Centerville	10,333	3,490
45211	Cheviot	11,135	10,701
45601	Chillicothe	24,842	24,957
44505	Churchill	7,457	......
*45234	Cincinnati	451,455	502,550
43113	Circleville	11,687	11,059
*44101	Cleveland	750,879	876,050
44118	Cleveland Heights	60,767	61,813
43410	Clyde	5,503	4,826
*43216	Columbus	540,025	471,316
44030	Conneaut	14,552	10,557
43812	Coshocton	13,747	13,106
45238	Covedale	6,639	......
44827	Crestline	5,947	5,521
45341	Crystal Lakes	5,851	1,569
*44222	Cuyahoga Falls	49,678	47,922
*45401	Dayton	242,917	262,332
45236	Deer Park	7,415	8,423
43512	Defiance	16,281	14,553
43015	Delaware	15,008	13,282
45833	Delphos	7,608	6,961
44622	Dover	11,516	11,300
44112	East Cleveland	39,600	37,991
44094	Eastlake	19,690	12,467
43920	East Liverpool	20,020	22,306
43920	East Liverpool North	6,223	......
44413	East Palestine	5,604	5,232
45320	Eaton	6,020	5,034
*44035	Elyria	53,427	43,782
45322	Englewood	7,885	1,515
44117	Euclid	71,552	62,998
45324	Fairborn	32,267	19,453
45014	Fairfield	14,680	9,734
44313	Fairlawn	6,102	......
44126	Fairview Park	21,681	14,624
45840	Findlay	35,800	30,344
45405	Forest Park	15,139	......
45426	Fort McKinley	11,536	......
44830	Fostoria	16,037	15,732
45005	Franklin	10,075	7,917
43420	Fremont	18,490	18,767
43230	Gahanna	12,400	2,717
44833	Galion	13,123	12,650
45631	Gallipolis	7,490	8,775
44125	Garfield Heights	41,417	38,455
44041	Geneva	6,449	5,677
44420	Girard	14,119	12,997
45237	Golf Manor	5,170	4,648
43212	Grandview Heights	8,460	8,270
45218	Greenhills	6,092	5,407
45331	Greenville	12,380	10,585
43123	Grove City	13,911	8,107
*45012	Hamilton	67,865	72,354
43055	Heath	6,768	2,426
44124	Highland Heights	5,926	2,929
43026	Hilliard	8,369	5,633
45133	Hillsboro	5,584	5,474
44425	Hubbard	8,583	7,137
45424	Huber Heights	18,943	......
44839	Huron	6,896	5,197
44131	Independence	7,034	6,868
45243	Indian Hill	5,651	4,526
45638	Ironton	15,030	15,745
45640	Jackson	6,843	6,980
44240	Kent	28,183	17,836
45236	Kenwood	8,315	8,747
43326	Kenton	8,315	8,747
45429	Kettering	71,864	54,462
44094	Kirtland	5,530	......
45432	Knollwood	5,353	......
44107	Lakewood	70,173	66,154
43130	Lancaster	32,911	29,916
45036	Lebanon	7,934	5,993
*45802	Lima	53,734	51,037
45215	Lincoln Heights	6,099	7,798
43228	Lincoln	11,215	......
43217	Lockbourne Base	5,623	......
45215	Lockland	5,288	5,292
43138	Logan	6,269	6,417
43140	London	6,481	6,379
*44052	Lorain	78,185	68,932
44641	Louisville	6,298	5,116
45140	Loveland	7,144	5,008
44124	Lyndhurst	19,749	16,805
44056	Macedonia	6,375	......
45243	Madeira	6,713	6,744
44057	Madison North	6,882	......
*44901	Mansfield	55,047	47,325
44137	Maple Heights	34,093	31,667
45750	Marietta	16,861	16,847
43302	Marion	38,646	37,079
43935	Martins Ferry	10,757	11,919
43040	Marysville	5,744	4,952
45040	Mason	5,677	4,727
44646	Massillon	32,539	31,236
43537	Maumee	15,937	12,063
44124	Mayfield Heights	22,139	13,478
44256	Medina	10,913	8,235

ZIP Code	Place	1970	1960
44060	Mentor	36,912	4,354
44060	Mentor-on-the-Lake	6,517	3,290
45342	Miamisburg	14,797	9,893
44017	Middleburg Heights	12,367	7,282
45042	Middletown	48,767	42,115
43938	Mingo Junction	5,278	4,987
45242	Montgomery	5,683	3,075
45231	Mount Healthy	7,446	6,553
43050	Mount Vernon	13,373	13,284
43545	Napoleon	7,791	6,739
43055	Newark	41,836	41,790
45344	New Carlisle	6,112	4,107
44663	New Philadelphia	15,184	14,241
44444	Newton Falls	5,378	5,038
44446	Niles	21,581	19,545
44720	North Canton	15,228	7,727
45239	North College Hill	12,363	12,035
44070	North Olmsted	34,861	16,290
45414	Northridge	10,084	
44039	North Ridgeville	13,152	8,057
44133	North Royalton	12,807	9,290
44203	Norton	12,308	
44857	Norwalk	13,386	12,900
45212	Norwood	30,420	34,580
45873	Oakwood City	10,095	10,493
44074	Oberlin	8,761	8,198
43616	Oregon	16,563	13,319
44667	Orrville	7,408	6,511
45431	Overlook-Page Manor	19,719	
45056	Oxford	15,868	7,828
44077	Painesville	16,536	16,116
44077	Painesville Southwest	5,461	
44129	Parma	100,216	82,845
44130	Parma Heights	27,192	18,100
44124	Pepper Pike	5,382	3,217
43551	Perrysburg	7,693	5,519
45356	Piqua	20,741	19,219
43452	Port Clinton	7,202	6,870
45662	Portsmouth	27,633	33,637
44266	Ravenna	11,780	10,918
45215	Reading	14,617	12,832
43068	Reynoldsburg	13,921	7,793
44143	Richmond Heights	9,220	5,068
44270	Rittman	6,308	5,410
44116	Rocky River	22,958	18,097
43460	Rossford	5,302	4,406
45217	St. Bernard	6,080	6,778
45885	St. Marys	7,699	7,737
44460	Salem	14,186	13,854
44870	Sandusky	32,674	31,989
44870	Sandusky South	8,501	4,724
44131	Seven Hills	12,700	5,708
43947	Shadyside	5,070	5,028
44120	Shaker Heights	36,306	36,460
45241	Sharonville	11,393	3,890
44054	Sheffield Lake	8,734	6,884
44875	Shelby	9,847	9,106
44878	Shiloh	11,368	
45365	Sidney	16,332	14,663
45236	Silverton	6,588	6,682
44139	Solon	11,519	6,333
44121	South Euclid	29,579	27,569
45246	Springdale	8,127	3,556
*45501	Springfield	81,941	82,723
43952	Steubenville	30,771	32,495
44224	Stow	19,847	12,194
44240	Streetsboro	7,966	
44136	Strongsville	15,182	8,504
44471	Struthers	15,343	15,631
43560	Sylvania	12,031	5,187
44278	Tallmadge	15,274	10,246
44883	Tiffin	21,596	21,478
45371	Tipp City	5,090	4,267
*43601	Toledo	383,105	318,003
43964	Toronto	7,705	7,780
45067	Trenton	5,278	3,064
45426	Trotwood	6,997	4,992
45373	Troy	17,186	13,685
44087	Twinsburg	6,432	4,098
44683	Uhrichsville	5,731	6,201
44118	University Heights	17,055	16,641
43221	Upper Arlington	38,727	28,486
43351	Upper Sandusky	5,645	4,941
43078	Urbana	11,237	10,461
45377	Vandalia	10,796	6,342
45891	Van Wert	11,320	11,323
44089	Vermilion	9,872	4,785
44281	Wadsworth	13,142	10,635
45895	Wapakoneta	7,324	6,756
*44481	Warren	63,494	59,648
44122	Warrensville Heights	18,925	10,609
43160	Washington	12,495	12,388
45692	Wellston	5,410	5,728
43968	Wellsville	5,891	7,117
45449	West Carrollton	10,748	4,749
43081	Westerville	12,530	7,011
44145	Westlake	15,689	12,906
43213	Whitehall	25,263	20,818
44092	Wickliffe	21,354	15,760
44890	Willard	5,510	5,457
44094	Willoughby	18,634	15,058
44094	Willoughby Hills	5,247	4,241
44094	Willowick	21,237	18,749
45177	Wilmington	10,051	8,915
44691	Wooster	18,703	17,046
43085	Worthington	15,326	9,239
45433	Wright-Patterson	10,151	
45215	Wyoming	9,089	7,736
45385	Xenia	25,373	20,445
*44501	Youngstown	140,909	166,689
43701	Zanesville	33,045	39,077

Oklahoma

ZIP Code	Place	1970	1960
74820	Ada	14,859	14,347
73521	Altus	23,302	21,225
73717	Alva	7,440	6,258
73005	Anadarko	6,682	6,299
73401	Ardmore	20,881	20,184
74003	Bartlesville	29,683	27,893
73008	Bethany	22,694	12,342
74631	Blackwell	8,645	9,588
74012	Broken Arrow	11,787	5,928
73018	Chickasha	14,194	14,866
74017	Claremore	9,084	6,639
73601	Clinton	8,513	9,617
74023	Cushing	7,529	8,619
73115	Del City	27,133	12,934
73533	Duncan	19,718	20,009
74701	Durant	11,118	10,467
73034	Edmond	16,633	8,577
73644	Elk City	7,323	8,196
73036	El Reno	14,510	11,015
73701	Enid	44,986	38,859
73503	Fort Sill	21,217	
73542	Frederick	6,132	5,879
73044	Guthrie	9,575	9,502
73942	Guymon	7,674	5,760
74437	Henryetta	6,430	6,551
74848	Holdenville	5,181	5,712
74743	Hugo	6,585	6,287
74745	Idabel	5,946	4,967
73501	Lawton	74,470	61,697
74501	McAlester	18,802	17,419
74354	Miami	13,880	12,869
73110	Midwest City	48,212	36,058
73060	Moore	18,761	1,783
74401	Muskogee	37,331	38,059
73069	Norman	52,117	33,412
*73125	Oklahoma City	368,377	324,253
74447	Okmulgee	15,180	15,951
73075	Pauls Valley	5,769	6,856
73077	Perry	5,341	5,210
74601	Ponca City	25,940	24,411
74953	Poteau	5,500	4,428
74361	Pryor	7,057	6,476
74063	Sand Springs	10,565	7,754
74066	Sapulpa	15,159	14,282
74868	Seminole	7,878	11,464
74801	Shawnee	25,075	24,326
74074	Stillwater	31,126	23,965
73086	Sulphur	5,158	4,737
74464	Tahlequah	9,254	5,840
73120	The Village	13,695	12,118
*74101	Tulsa	330,350	261,685
74301	Vinita	5,847	6,027
73132	Warr Acres	9,887	7,135
73096	Weatherford	7,959	4,499
74884	Wewoka	5,284	5,954
73801	Woodward	9,412	7,747
73099	Yukon	8,411	3,076

Oregon

ZIP Code	Place	1970	1960
97321	Albany	18,181	12,926
97601	Altamont	15,746	10,811
97520	Ashland	12,342	9,119
97103	Astoria	10,244	11,239
97814	Baker	9,354	9,986
97005	Beaverton	18,577	5,937
97701	Bend	13,710	11,936
97420	Coos Bay	13,466	7,084
97330	Corvallis	35,056	20,669
97424	Cottage Grove	6,004	3,895
97338	Dallas	6,361	5,072
*97401	Eugene	79,028	50,977
97116	Forest Grove	8,275	5,628
97301	Four Corners	5,823	4,743
97027	Gladstone	6,254	3,854
97526	Grants Pass	12,455	10,118
97030	Gresham	10,030	3,944
97303	Hayesville	5,518	4,568
97123	Hillsboro	14,675	8,232
97303	Keizer	11,405	5,288
97601	Klamath Falls	15,775	16,949
97850	La Grande	9,645	9,014

ZIP Code	Place	1970	1960
97034	Lake Oswego	14,615	8,906
97355	Lebanon	6,636	5,858
97128	McMinnville	10,125	7,656
97501	Medford	28,454	24,425
97222	Milwaukie	16,444	9,099
97361	Monmouth	5,237	2,229
97132	Newberg	6,507	4,204
97365	Newport	5,188	5,344
97459	North Bend	8,553	7,512
97914	Ontario	6,523	5,101
97045	Oregon City	9,176	7,996
97801	Pendleton	13,197	14,434
*97208	Portland	379,967	372,676
97470	Roseburg	14,461	11,467
97051	St. Helens	6,212	5,022
*97301	Salem	68,480	49,142
97477	Springfield	26,874	19,616
97058	The Dalles	10,423	10,493
97223	Tigard	5,302	......
97068	West Linn	7,091	3,933
97071	Woodburn	7,495	3,120

Pennsylvania

ZIP Code	Place	1970	1960
19001	Abington	8,594	......
19018	Aldan	5,001	4,324
15001	Aliquippa	22,277	26,369
*18101	Allentown	109,527	108,347
*16603	Altoona	63,115	69,407
19002	Ambler	7,800	6,765
15003	Ambridge	11,324	13,865
18403	Archbald	6,118	5,642
19003	Ardmore	5,131	......
15068	Arnold	8,174	9,437
15202	Avalon	7,010	6,859
15005	Baden	5,536	6,109
19004	Bala-Cynwyd	6,483	......
15234	Baldwin	26,729	24,489
18013	Bangor	5,425	5,766
15009	Beaver	6,100	6,160
15010	Beaver Falls	14,375	16,240
16823	Bellefonte	6,828	6,088
15202	Bellevue	11,586	11,412
18603	Berwick	12,274	13,353
15102	Bethel Park	34,791	23,650
*18016	Bethlehem	72,686	75,408
18447	Blakely	6,391	6,374
17815	Bloomsburg	11,652	10,655
15104	Braddock	8,795	12,337
16701	Bradford	12,672	15,061
19406	Brandywine	11,411	......
15227	Brentwood	13,732	13,706
19405	Bridgeport	5,630	5,306
15017	Bridgeville	6,717	7,112
19007	Bristol	12,085	12,364
19015	Brookhaven 1973	7,262	5,280
19010	Bryn Mawr	5,815	......
16001	Butler	18,691	20,975
15419	California	6,635	5,978
17011	Camp Hill	9,931	8,559
15317	Canonsburg	11,439	11,877
18407	Carbondale	12,808	13,595
17013	Carlisle	18,079	16,623
15106	Carnegie	10,864	11,887
15108	Carnot-Moon	13,093	......
15234	Castle Shannon	11,899	11,836
18032	Catasauqua	5,702	5,062
19095	Cedarbrook-Melrose Park	9,980	......
19428	Cedar Heights	6,326	......
17201	Chambersburg	17,315	17,670
15022	Charleroi	6,723	8,148
19380	Chatwood	7,168	3,621
*19003	Chester	56,331	63,658
15025	Clairton	15,051	18,389
16214	Clarion	6,095	4,958
18411	Clarks Summit	5,376	3,693
16830	Clearfield	8,176	9,270
19018	Clifton Heights	8,348	8,005
19320	Coatesville	12,331	12,971
19023	Collingdale	10,605	10,268
17512	Columbia	11,237	12,075
15425	Connellsville	11,643	12,814
19428	Conshohocken	10,195	10,259
15108	Coraopolis	8,435	9,643
16407	Corry	7,435	7,744
15205	Crafton	8,233	8,418
17821	Danville	6,176	6,889
19023	Darby	13,729	14,059
18519	Dickson City	7,698	7,738
15033	Donora	8,825	11,131
15216	Dormont	12,856	13,098
19335	Downingtown	7,437	5,598
18901	Doylestown	8,270	5,917
15801	Du Bois	10,112	10,667
18512	Dunmore	17,300	18,917
15110	Duquesne	11,410	15,019
18642	Duryea	5,264	5,626

ZIP Code	Place	1970	1960
18042	Easton	29,450	31,955
18301	East Stroudsburg	7,894	7,674
15005	Economy 1973	7,605	5,925
15218	Edgewood	5,138	5,124
18704	Edwardsville	5,633	5,711
17022	Elizabethtown	8,072	6,780
16117	Ellwood City	10,857	12,413
18049	Emmaus	11,511	10,262
17522	Ephrata	9,662	7,688
*16501	Erie	129,231	138,440
15223	Etna	5,819	5,519
16121	Farrell	11,022	13,793
19031	Flourtown	9,149	......
19032	Folcroft	9,610	7,013
15221	Forest Hills	9,561	8,796
18704	Forty Fort	6,114	6,431
18015	Fountain Hill	5,384	5,428
17931	Frackville	5,445	5,654
16323	Franklin	8,629	9,586
15143	Franklin Park	5,310	......
18052	Fullerton	7,908	......
19004	General Wayne	5,368	......
17325	Gettysburg	7,275	7,960
15045	Glassport	7,450	8,418
19036	Glenolden	8,697	7,249
19038	Glenside	17,353	......
15601	Greensburg	17,077	17,383
15220	Green Tree	6,441	5,226
16125	Greenville	8,704	8,765
16127	Grove City	8,312	8,368
17331	Hanover	15,623	15,538
*17105	Harrisburg	68,061	79,697
19040	Hatboro	8,880	7,315
19044	Hatboro West	13,542	......
18201	Hazelton	30,426	32,056
18055	Hellertown	6,615	6,716
17033	Hershey	7,407	6,851
18042	Highland Park (Northampton)	5,500	......
16648	Hollidaysburg	6,262	6,475
16001	Homeacre-Lyndora	8,415	......
15120	Homestead	6,309	7,502
18431	Honesdale	5,224	5,569
16652	Huntingdon	6,987	7,234
15701	Indiana	16,100	13,005
15644	Jeannette	15,209	16,565
15344	Jefferson	8,512	8,280
19401	Jefferson-Trooper	13,022	......
19046	Jenkintown	5,990	5,017
17740	Jersey Shore	5,322	5,613
18229	Jim Thorpe	5,456	5,945
*15901	Johnstown	42,476	53,949
16735	Kane	5,001	5,380
18704	Kingston	18,325	20,261
16201	Kittanning	6,231	6,793
19444	Lafayette Hills-Plymouth Meeting	8,275	......
*17604	Lancaster	57,690	61,055
19446	Lansdale	18,451	12,612
19050	Lansdowne	14,090	12,601
18232	Lansford	5,168	5,958
15650	Latrobe	11,749	11,932
17042	Lebanon	28,572	30,045
18235	Lehighton	6,095	6,318
17837	Lewisburg	6,376	5,523
17044	Lewistown	11,098	12,640
17543	Lititz	7,072	5,987
17745	Lock Haven	11,427	11,748
15068	Lower Burrell	13,654	11,952
*15134	McKeesport	37,977	45,489
15136	McKees Rocks	11,901	13,185
17948	Mahanoy City	7,257	8,536
17545	Manheim	5,434	4,790
16335	Meadville	16,573	16,671
17055	Mechanicsburg	9,385	8,123
*19063	Media	6,444	5,803
19066	Merion	5,686	......
17057	Middletown	9,080	11,182
15059	Midland	5,271	6,425
17551	Millersville	6,396	3,883
15209	Millvale	5,815	6,624
17847	Milton	7,723	7,972
17954	Minersville	6,012	6,606
15061	Monaca	7,486	8,394
15062	Monessen	15,216	18,424
15063	Monongahela	7,113	8,388
15146	Monroeville	29,011	22,446
17754	Montoursville	5,985	5,211
19067	Morrisville	11,309	7,790
17851	Mount Carmel	9,317	10,760
17552	Mount Joy	5,041	3,292
15210	Mount Oliver	5,487	5,980
15666	Mount Pleasant	5,895	6,107
15120	Munhall	16,574	17,312
18634	Nanticoke	14,632	15,601
19072	Narberth	5,151	5,109
18064	Nazareth	5,815	6,209
15066	New Brighton	7,637	8,397
*16101	New Castle	38,559	44,790

ZIP Code	Place	1970	1960
17070	New Cumberland	9,803	9,257
15068	New Kensington	20,312	23,485
*19401	Norristown	38,169	38,925
18067	Northampton	8,389	8,866
19003	North Ardmore	5,856	......
15104	North Braddock	10,838	13,204
19038	North Hills-Ardsley	13,096	......
19074	Norwood	7,229	6,729
19126	Oak Lane	6,192	......
15139	Oakmont	7,550	7,504
19117	Ogontz	5,463	2,254
16301	Oil City	15,033	17,692
18518	Old Forge	9,522	8,928
18447	Olyphant	5,422	5,864
19075	Oreland	9,261	......
18071	Palmerton	5,620	5,942
17078	Palmyra	7,615	6,999
19301	Paoli	5,835	......
17331	Parkville	5,120	4,516
19004	Pencoyd	6,650	......
19401	Penn Sq.-Plymouth Valley	20,238	......
19151	Penn Wynne	6,038	......
18944	Perkasie	5,451	4,650
*19104	Philadelphia	1,949,996	2,002,512
19460	Phoenixville	14,823	13,797
*15219	Pittsburgh	520,117	604,332
*18640	Pittston	11,113	12,407
18705	Plains	6,606	......
15236	Pleasant Hills	10,409	8,573
15239	Plum	21,932	10,241
18651	Plymouth	9,536	10,401
15133	Port Vue	5,862	6,635
19464	Pottstown	25,355	26,144
17901	Pottsville	19,715	21,659
19076	Prospect Park	7,250	6,596
15767	Punxsutawney	7,792	8,805
18951	Quakertown	7,276	6,305
*19603	Reading	87,643	98,177
17356	Red Lion	5,645	5,594
15853	Ridgway	6,022	6,387
19078	Ridley Park	9,025	7,387
19001	Roslyn	18,380	......
19046	Rydal	5,083	......
15857	St. Marys	7,470	8,065
18840	Sayre	7,473	7,917
17972	Schuylkill Haven	6,125	6,470
15683	Scottdale	5,818	6,244
*18503	Scranton	103,564	111,443
17870	Selinsgrove	5,116	3,948
15143	Sewickley	5,660	6,157
17872	Shamokin	11,719	13,674
16146	Sharon	22,653	25,267
19079	Sharon Hill	7,464	7,123
15215	Sharpsburg	5,453	6,096
16150	Sharpsville	6,126	6,061
17976	Shenandoah	8,287	11,073
19607	Shillington	6,249	5,639
17257	Shippensburg	6,536	6,138
15501	Somerset	6,269	6,347
18964	Souderton	6,366	5,381
17701	South Williamsport	7,153	6,972
15144	Springdale	5,202	5,602
16801	State College	33,778	22,409
17113	Steelton	8,556	11,266
18360	Stroudsburg	5,451	6,070
16323	Sugar Creek	5,944	......
17801	Sunbury	13,025	13,687
19081	Swarthmore	6,156	5,753
15218	Swissvale	13,819	15,089
18704	Swoyersville	6,786	6,751
18252	Tamaqua	9,246	10,173
15084	Tarentum	7,379	8,232
18517	Taylor	6,977	6,148
16354	Titusville	7,331	8,356
15145	Turtle Creek	8,308	10,607
16686	Tyrone	7,072	7,792
15401	Uniontown	16,282	17,942
15690	Vandergrift	7,889	8,742
16365	Warren	12,998	14,505
15301	Washington	19,827	23,545
17268	Waynesboro	10,011	10,427
15370	Waynesburg	5,152	5,188
19380	West Chester	19,301	15,705
18201	West Hazleton	6,059	6,278
15122	West Mifflin	28,070	27,289
15905	Westmont	6,673	6,573
18643	West Pittston	7,074	6,998
15229	West View	8,312	8,079
17404	West York	5,314	5,526
18052	Whitehall	16,551	16,075
15131	White Oak	9,304	9,047
*18701	Wilkes-Barre	58,856	63,551
15221	Wilkinsburg	26,780	30,066
17701	Williamsport	37,918	41,967
19090	Willow Grove	16,494	......
15025	Wilson	8,406	8,465
15963	Windber	6,332	6,994

ZIP Code	Place	1970	1960
19610	Wyomissing	7,136	5,044
19050	Yeadon	12,136	11,610
*17405	York	50,335	54,504

Rhode Island

See Note on Page 215

ZIP Code	Place	1970	1960
02806	Barrington	17,554	13,826
02809	Bristol	17,860	14,570
02830	Burrillville	10,087	9,119
02863	Central Falls	18,716	19,858
02816	Coventry	22,947	15,432
02910	Cranston	74,287	66,766
02864	Cumberland	26,605	18,792
02818	East Greenwich	9,577	6,100
02914	East Providence	48,207	41,955
02814	Glocester	5,160	3,397
02833	Hopkinton	5,392	4,174
02919	Johnston	22,037	17,160
02881	Kingston	5,601	2,616
02865	Lincoln	16,182	13,551
02840	Middletown	29,290	12,675
02882	Narragansett	7,138	3,444
02840	Newport	34,562	47,049
02843	Newport East	10,285	2,643
02852	North Kingstown	29,793	18,977
02908	North Providence	24,337	18,220
02876	North Smithfield	9,349	7,632
*02860	Pawtucket	76,984	81,001
02871	Portsmouth	12,521	8,251
*02904	Providence	179,116	207,498
02857	Scituate	7,489	5,210
02917	Smithfield	13,468	9,442
02879	South Kingstown	16,913	11,942
02878	Tiverton	12,559	9,461
*02880	Wakefield-Peacedale	6,331	5,569
02885	Warren	10,523	8,750
*02887	Warwick	83,694	68,504
02891	Westerly Center	13,654	9,698
02891	Westerly	17,248	14,267
02893	West Warwick	24,323	21,414
02895	Woonsocket	46,820	47,080

South Carolina

ZIP Code	Place	1970	1960
29620	Abbeville	5,515	5,436
29801	Aiken	13,436	11,243
29621	Anderson	27,556	41,316
29407	Avondale-Moorland	5,236	......
29902	Beaufort	9,434	6,298
29627	Belton	5,257	5,106
29512	Bennettsville	7,468	6,963
29611	Berea	7,186	......
29020	Camden	8,532	6,842
29033	Cayce	9,967	8,517
*29401	Charleston	66,945	65,925
29404	Charleston Base	6,238	......
29408	Charleston Yard	13,565	......
29520	Cheraw	5,627	5,171
29706	Chester	7,045	6,906
29631	Clemson	5,578	1,587
29325	Clinton	8,138	7,937
*29201	Columbia	113,542	97,433
29526	Conway	8,151	8,563
29532	Darlington	6,990	6,710
29536	Dillon	6,391	6,173
29640	Easley	11,175	8,283
29501	Florence	25,997	24,722
29206	Forest Acres	6,808	3,842
29340	Gaffney	13,253	10,435
29605	Gantt	11,386	......
29440	Georgetown	10,449	12,261
*29602	Greenville	61,436	66,188
29646	Greenwood	21,069	16,644
29651	Greer	10,642	8,967
29410	Hanahan	8,376	......
29550	Hartsville	8,017	6,392
29560	Lake City	6,247	6,059
29720	Lancaster	9,186	7,999
29360	Laurens	10,298	9,598
29571	Marion	7,435	7,174
29662	Mauldin 1973	5,480	1,462
29464	Mount Pleasant	6,879	5,116
29574	Mullins	6,006	6,299
29577	Myrtle Beach	9,035	7,834
29108	Newberry	9,218	8,208
29841	North Augusta	12,883	10,348
29115	Orangeburg	13,252	13,852
29905	Parris Island	8,868	......
29730	Rock Hill	33,846	29,404
29407	St. Andrews	9,202	......
29678	Seneca	6,382	5,227
29150	Shannontown	7,491	7,064
29152	Shaw	5,819	......
*29301	Spartanburg	44,546	44,352
29150	Sumter	24,555	23,062
29687	Taylors	6,831	1,071

ZIP Code	Place	1970	1960
29379	Union	10,775	10,191
29607	Wade-Hampton	17,152	......
29488	Walterboro	6,257	5,417
29169	West Columbia	7,838	6,410
29745	York	5,081	4,758

South Dakota

ZIP Code	Place	1970	1960
57401	Aberdeen	26,476	23,073
57006	Brookings	13,717	10,558
57706	Ellsworth	6,207	......
57350	Huron	14,299	14,180
57754	Lead	5,420	6,211
57042	Madison	6,315	5,420
57301	Mitchell	13,425	12,555
57501	Pierre	9,699	10,088
57701	Rapid City	43,836	42,399
*57101	Sioux Falls	72,488	65,466
57069	Vermilion	9,128	6,102
57201	Watertown	13,388	14,077
57078	Yankton	11,919	9,279

Tennessee

ZIP Code	Place	1970	1960
37701	Alcoa	7,739	6,395
37303	Athens	11,790	12,103
38008	Bolivar	6,674	3,338
37620	Bristol	20,064	17,582
38012	Brownsville	7,011	5,424
*37401	Chattanooga	119,923	130,009
37040	Clarksville	31,719	22,021
37311	Cleveland	20,651	16,196
38401	Columbia	21,471	17,624
38501	Cookeville	14,270	7,805
38019	Covington	5,801	5,298
38555	Crossville	5,381	4,668
37055	Dickson	5,665	5,028
38024	Dyersburg	14,523	12,499
37801	Eagleton Village	5,345	5,068
37412	East Ridge	21,799	19,570
37643	Elizabethton	12,269	10,896
37334	Fayetteville	7,030	6,804
42223	Fort Campbell South	9,279	......
37064	Franklin 1974	11,298	6,977
37066	Gallatin	13,253	7,901
37075	Greater Hendersonville	11,996	......
37743	Greeneville	13,722	11,759
37748	Harriman	8,734	5,931
37343	Hixson	6,188	......
38343	Humboldt	10,066	8,482
38301	Jackson	39,996	34,376
37760	Jefferson City	5,124	4,550
37601	Johnson City	33,770	31,187
*37662	Kingsport	31,938	26,314
37665	Kingsport North	13,118	......
*37901	Knoxville	174,587	111,827
37766	La Follette	6,902	6,204
37416	Lake Hills-Murray Hills	7,806	......
38464	Lawrenceburg	8,889	8,042
37087	Lebanon	12,492	10,512
37771	Lenoir City	5,324	4,979
37091	Lewisburg	7,207	6,338
38351	Lexington	5,024	3,943
37110	Mc Minnville	10,662	9,013
37355	Manchester	6,208	3,930
38237	Martin	7,781	4,750
37801	Maryville	13,808	10,348
*38101	Memphis	623,530	497,524
38358	Milan	7,313	5,208
38053	Millington	21,177	6,059
37814	Morristown	20,318	21,267
37130	Murfreesboro	26,360	18,991
*37202	Nashville-Davidson	**447,877	170,874
37821	Newport	7,328	6,448
37830	Oak Ridge	28,319	27,169
38242	Paris	9,892	9,325
38478	Pulaski	6,989	6,616
37415	Red Bank	12,715	10,777
37854	Rockwood	5,259	5,345
38372	Savannah	5,576	4,315
37160	Shelbyville	12,262	10,466
37167	Smyrna	5,698	3,612
37379	Soddy-Daisy	7,569	......
37311	South Cleveland	5,070	1,512
37172	Springfield	9,720	9,221
37388	Tullahoma	15,311	12,242
38261	Union City	11,925	8,837
37398	Winchester	5,256	4,760

**Comprises the Metropolitan Government of Nashville and Davidson County.

Texas

ZIP Code	Place	1970	1960
*79604	Abilene	89,653	90,368
78209	Alamo Heights	6,933	7,552
78332	Alice	20,121	20,861
79830	Alpine	5,971	4,740
77511	Alvin	10,671	5,643
*79105	Amarillo	127,010	137,969
79714	Andrews	8,625	11,135
77515	Angleton	9,770	7,312
78336	Aransas Pass	5,813	6,956
*78010	Arlington	90,032	44,775
75751	Athens	9,582	7,086
77551	Atlanta	5,007	4,076
*78710	Austin	251,808	186,545
75149	Balch Springs	10,464	6,821
77414	Bay City	13,445	11,656
77520	Baytown	43,980	28,159
*77704	Beaumont	117,548	119,175
76021	Bedford	10,049	2,706
78102	Beeville	13,506	13,811
77401	Bellaire	19,009	19,872
76704	Bellmead	7,698	5,127
76513	Belton	8,696	8,163
76126	Benbrook	8,169	3,254
79720	Big Spring	28,735	31,230
75418	Bonham	7,698	7,357
79007	Borger	14,195	20,911
76230	Bowie	5,185	4,566
76825	Brady	5,557	5,338
76024	Breckenridge	5,944	6,273
77833	Brenham	8,922	7,740
77611	Bridge City	8,164	4,677
79316	Brownfield	9,647	10,286
78520	Brownsville	52,522	48,040
76801	Brownwood	17,368	16,974
77801	Bryan	33,719	27,542
76354	Burkburnett	9,230	7,621
76028	Burleson	7,713	2,345
76520	Cameron	5,546	5,640
79015	Canyon	8,333	5,864
78834	Carrizo Springs	5,374	5,699
75006	Carrollton	13,855	4,242
75633	Carthage	5,392	5,262
78213	Castle Hills	5,311	2,624
79201	Childress	5,408	6,399
76031	Cleburne	16,015	15,381
77327	Cleveland	5,627	5,838
77531	Clute City	6,023	4,501
76834	Coleman	5,608	6,371
77840	College Station	17,676	11,396
79512	Colorado City	5,227	6,457
75428	Commerce	9,534	5,789
77301	Conroe	11,969	9,192
76522	Copperas Cove	10,818	4,567
*78408	Corpus Christi	204,525	167,690
75110	Corsicana	19,972	20,344
75835	Crockett	6,616	5,356
78839	Crystal City	8,104	9,101
77954	Cuero	6,956	7,338
79022	Dalhart	5,705	5,160
*75260	Dallas	844,401	679,684
77536	Deer Park	12,773	4,865
78840	Del Rio	21,330	18,612
75020	Denison	24,923	22,748
76201	Denton	39,874	26,844
75115	De Soto	6,617	1,969
77539	Dickinson	10,776	4,715
78537	Donna	7,365	7,522
79029	Dumas	9,771	8,477
75116	Duncanville	14,105	3,774
78852	Eagle Pass	15,364	12,094
78539	Edinburg	17,163	18,706
77957	Edna	5,332	5,038
77437	El Campo	9,332	7,700
*79910	El Paso	322,261	276,687
75119	Ennis	11,046	9,347
76039	Euless	19,316	4,263
78855	Falfurrias	6,355	6,515
75234	Farmers Branch	27,492	13,441
76119	Forest Hill	8,236	3,221
79906	Fort Bliss	13,288	......
76544	Fort Hood	32,597	......
78234	Fort Sam Houston	10,553	......
79735	Fort Stockton	8,283	6,373
*76101	Fort Worth	393,476	356,268
78624	Fredericksburg	5,326	4,629
77541	Freeport	11,997	11,619
77546	Friendswood	5,675	......
76240	Gainesville	13,830	13,083
77547	Galena Park	10,479	10,852
77550	Galveston	61,809	67,175
*75040	Garland	81,437	38,501
78626	Georgetown	6,395	5,218
75647	Gladewater	5,574	5,742
78629	Gonzales	5,854	5,829
76046	Graham	7,477	8,505
75050	Grand Prairie	50,904	30,386
76051	Grapevine	7,023	2,821
75401	Greenville	22,043	19,087
77619	Groves	18,067	17,304
76117	Haltom City	28,127	23,133
78550	Harlingen	33,503	41,207
75652	Henderson	10,187	9,666
79045	Hereford	13,414	7,652

ZIP Code	Place	1970	1960
75205	Highland Park	10,133	10,411
76645	Hillsboro	7,224	7,402
77563	Hitchcock	5,565	5,216
78861	Hondo	5,487	4,992
*77013	Houston	1,232,802	938,219
77340	Huntsville	17,610	11,999
76053	Hurst	27,215	10,165
76367	Iowa Park	5,796	3,295
*75061	Irving	97,260	45,985
77029	Jacinto City	9,563	9,547
75766	Jacksonville	9,734	9,590
75951	Jasper	6,251	4,889
79745	Kermit	7,884	10,465
78028	Kerrville	12,672	8,901
75662	Kilgore	9,495	10,092
76541	Killeen	35,507	23,377
78363	Kingsville	28,915	25,297
78236	Lackland	19,141	
77566	Lake Jackson	13,376	9,651
77568	La Marque	16,131	13,969
79331	Lamesa	11,559	12,438
76550	Lampasas	5,922	5,061
75146	Lancaster	10,522	7,501
77571	La Porte	7,149	4,512
78040	Laredo	69,024	60,678
77573	League City	10,818	
79336	Levelland	11,445	10,153
75067	Lewisville	9,264	3,956
77575	Liberty	5,591	6,127
79339	Littlefield	6,738	7,236
78644	Lockhart	6,489	6,084
75601	Longview	45,547	40,050
*79408	Lubbock	149,101	128,691
75901	Lufkin	23,049	17,641
78501	McAllen	37,636	32,728
75069	McKinney	15,193	13,763
76661	Marlin	6,351	6,918
75670	Marshall	22,937	23,846
78368	Mathis	5,351	6,075
78570	Mercedes	9,355	10,943
75149	Mesquite	55,131	27,526
76667	Mexia	5,943	6,121
79701	Midland	59,463	62,625
76067	Mineral Wells	18,411	11,053
78572	Mission	13,043	14,081
79756	Monahans	8,333	8,567
75455	Mount Pleasant	9,459	8,027
75961	Nacogdoches	22,544	12,674
77868	Navasota	5,111	4,937
77627	Nederland	16,810	12,036
78130	New Braunfels	17,859	15,631
76118	North Richland Hills	16,514	8,662
*79760	Odessa	78,380	80,338
77630	Orange	24,457	25,605
75801	Palestine	14,525	13,974
79065	Pampa	21,726	24,664
75460	Paris	23,441	20,977
*77501	Pasadena	89,277	58,737
77581	Pearland	6,444	1,497
78061	Pearsall	5,545	4,957
79772	Pecos	12,682	12,728
79070	Perryton	7,810	7,903
78577	Pharr	15,829	14,106
79072	Plainview	19,096	18,735
75074	Plano	17,872	3,695
78064	Pleasanton	5,407	3,467
77640	Port Arthur	57,371	66,676
78374	Portland	7,302	2,538
77979	Port Lavaca	10,491	8,864
77651	Port Neches	10,894	8,696
75475	Randolph	5,329	
78580	Raymondville	7,987	9,385
75080	Richardson	48,582	16,810
76118	Richland Hills	8,865	7,804
77469	Richmond	5,777	3,668
78582	Rio Grande City	5,676	5,835
77019	River Oaks	8,193	8,444
78380	Robstown	11,217	10,266
77471	Rosenberg	12,098	9,698
76901	San Angelo	63,884	58,815
*78284	San Antonio	654,153	587,718
78586	San Benito	15,176	16,422
78589	San Juan	5,070	4,371
78666	San Marcos	18,860	12,713
78155	Seguin	15,934	14,299
79360	Seminole	5,007	5,737
75090	Sherman	29,061	24,988
77656	Silsbee	7,271	6,277
78387	Sinton	5,563	6,008
79364	Slaton	6,583	6,568
79549	Snyder	11,171	13,850
77587	South Houston	11,527	7,523
76401	Stephenville	9,277	7,359
75482	Sulphur Springs	10,642	9,160
79556	Sweetwater	12,020	13,914
76574	Taylor	9,616	9,434
76501	Temple	33,431	30,419
75160	Terrell	14,182	13,803

ZIP Code	Place	1970	1960
78209	Terrell Hills	5,225	5,572
75501	Texarkana	30,497	30,218
77590	Texas City	38,908	32,065
79088	Tulia	5,294	4,410
75701	Tyler	57,770	51,230
78148	Universal City	7,613	
76308	University Park	23,498	23,202
78801	Uvalde	10,764	10,293
76384	Vernon	11,454	12,141
77901	Victoria	41,349	33,047
77662	Vidor	9,738	
*76701	Waco	95,326	97,808
75165	Waxahachie	13,452	12,749
76086	Weatherford	11,750	9,759
78596	Weslaco	15,313	15,649
77005	West University Place	13,317	14,628
77488	Wharton	7,881	5,734
76108	White Settlement	13,449	11,513
*76307	Wichita Falls	96,265	101,724
77995	Yoakum	5,755	5,761

Utah

ZIP Code	Place	1970	1960
84003	American Fork	7,713	6,373
84010	Bountiful	27,751	17,039
84302	Brigham City	14,007	11,728
84720	Cedar City	8,946	7,543
84015	Clearfield	13,316	8,833
84121	Cottonwood	8,431	
84109	East Millcreek	26,579	
84119	Granger-Hunter	9,029	
84106	Granite Park	9,573	
84117	Holladay	23,014	
84037	Kaysville	6,192	3,608
84118	Kearns	17,247	17,172
84041	Layton	13,603	9,027
84321	Logan	22,333	18,731
84044	Magna	5,509	6,442
84047	Midvale	7,840	5,802
84117	Mount Olympus	5,909	
84107	Murray	21,206	16,806
84404	North Ogden	5,257	2,621
*84401	Ogden	69,478	70,197
84057	Orem	25,729	18,394
84062	Pleasant Grove	5,327	4,772
84501	Price	6,218	6,802
84601	Provo	53,131	36,047
84067	Roy	14,356	9,239
84770	St. George	7,097	5,130
*84101	Salt Lake City	175,885	189,454
84070	Sandy City	6,438	3,322
84403	South Ogden	9,991	7,405
84115	South Salt Lake	7,810	9,520
84660	Spanish Fork	7,284	6,472
84663	Springville	8,790	7,913
84015	Sunset	6,268	4,235
84074	Tooele	12,539	9,133
84403	Washington Terrace	7,241	6,441
74070	White City	6,402	

Vermont

See Note on Page 215

ZIP Code	Place	1970	1960
05641	Barre	10,209	10,387
	Barre	6,509	4,580
05201	Bennington	14,586	13,002
	Bennington	7,950	8,023
05301	Brattleboro	9,055	9,315
	Brattleboro	12,239	11,734
05401	Burlington	38,633	35,531
05446	Colchester	8,776	4,718
05451	Essex	10,951	7,090
05452	Essex Junction	6,511	5,340
05047	Hartford	6,477	6,355
05753	Middlebury	6,532	5,305
05602	Montpelier	8,609	8,782
05101	Rockingham	5,501	5,704
05701	Rutland	19,293	18,325
05478	St. Albans	8,082	8,806
05819	St. Johnsbury	8,409	8,869
05401	South Burlington	10,032	6,903
05156	Springfield	5,632	6,600
	Springfield	10,063	9,934
05401	Williston Road Section	5,376	3,259
05404	Winooski	7,309	7,420

Virginia

ZIP Code	Place	1970	1960
*22313	Alexandria	110,927	91,023
22003	Annandale	27,405	
*22210	Arlington	174,284	163,401
22041	Bailey's Crossroads	7,295	
24523	Bedford	6,011	5,921
22307	Belleview	8,299	
24060	Blacksburg	9,384	7,070
24605	Bluefield	5,286	4,235
23235	Bon Air	10,771	
24201	Bristol	14,857	17,144
24416	Buena Vista	6,425	6,300

ZIP Code	Place	1970	1960
*22906	Charlottesville	38,880	29,427
*23320	Chesapeake	89,580	
23831	Chester	5,556	1,290
24073	Christiansburg	7,857	3,653
24422	Clifton Forge	5,501	5,268
24078	Collinsville	6,015	3,586
23834	Colonial Heights	15,097	9,587
24426	Covington	10,060	11,062
22701	Culpeper	6,056	2,412
22191	Dale	13,857	
24541	Danville	46,391	46,577
23847	Emporia	5,300	5,535
22030	Fairfax	21,970	13,585
*22046	Falls Church	10,772	10,192
22060	Fort Belvoir	14,591	
22308	Fort Hunt	10,415	
23801	Fort Lee	12,435	
23851	Franklin	6,880	7,264
22401	Fredericksburg	14,450	13,639
22630	Front Royal	8,211	7,949
24333	Galax	6,278	5,254
22306	Groveton	11,761	
*23360	Hampton	120,779	89,258
22801	Harrisonburg	14,605	11,916
23075	Highland Springs	7,345	
23860	Hopewell	23,471	17,895
22303	Huntington	5,559	
22042	Jefferson	25,432	
22041	Lake Barcroft	11,605	
23228	Lakeside	11,137	
24450	Lexington	7,597	7,537
22312	Lincolnia	10,761	
22030	Long Branch	21,634	
*24505	Lynchburg	54,083	54,790
22110	Manassas	9,164	3,555
22110	Manassas Park	6,844	5,342
22030	Mantua	6,911	
24354	Marion	8,158	8,385
24112	Martinsville	19,653	18,798
22101	McLean	17,698	
23111	Mechanicsville	5,189	
*23607	Newport News	138,177	113,662
*23501	Norfolk	307,951	304,869
22151	North Springfield	8,631	
23803	Petersburg	36,103	36,750
23662	Poquoson	5,441	4,278
*23705	Portsmouth	110,963	114,773
24301	Pulaski	10,279	10,469
22134	Quantico Station	6,213	
24141	Radford	11,596	9,371
22070	Reston	5,723	
*23232	Richmond	249,431	219,958
*24001	Roanoke	92,115	97,110
24281	Rose Hill	14,492	
24153	Salem	21,982	16,058
22044	Seven Corners	5,590	
24592	South Boston	6,889	5,974
*22150	Springfield	11,613	10,783
24401	Staunton	24,504	22,232
22170	Sterling Park	8,321	
23434	Suffolk	9,858	12,609
22180	Vienna	17,146	11,440
24179	Vinton	6,347	3,432
*23458	Virginia Beach	172,106	8,091
22980	Waynesboro	16,707	15,694
22152	West Springfield	14,143	
23185	Williamsburg	9,069	6,832
22601	Winchester	14,643	15,110
22191	Woodbridge-Marumsco	25,412	
24382	Wytheville	6,069	5,634

Washington

ZIP Code	Place	1970	1960
98520	Aberdeen	18,489	18,741
98221	Anacortes	7,701	8,414
98002	Auburn	21,653	11,933
*98009	Bellevue	61,196	12,809
98225	Bellingham	39,375	34,688
98011	Bothell	5,420	2,237
98310	Bremerton	35,307	28,922
98607	Camas	5,790	5,666
98531	Centralia	10,054	8,586
98532	Chehalis	5,727	5,199
99004	Cheney	6,358	3,173
99403	Clarkston	6,312	6,209
99213	Dishman	9,079	
98020	Edmonds	23,998	8,016
98926	Ellensburg	13,568	8,625
98823	Ephrata	5,255	6,548
*98201	Everett	53,622	40,304
99011	Fairchild	6,754	
98466	Fircrest	5,651	3,565
98433	Fort Lewis	38,054	
98550	Hoquiam	10,466	10,762
98626	Kelso	10,296	8,379
99336	Kennewick	15,212	14,244
98031	Kent	16,596	9,017
98033	Kirkland	14,970	6,025

ZIP Code	Place	1970	1960
98503	Lacey	9,696	
98499	Lakes District	48,195	
98632	Longview	28,373	23,349
98036	Lynwood	16,919	7,207
98438	McChord	6,515	
98040	Mercer Island	19,047	
98837	Moses Lake	10,310	11,299
98043	Mountlake Terrace	16,600	9,122
98273	Mount Vernon	8,804	7,921
98277	Oak Harbor	9,167	3,942
*98501	Olympia	23,296	18,273
99214	Opportunity	16,604	12,465
98444	Parkland	21,012	
99301	Pasco	13,920	14,522
98362	Port Angeles	16,367	12,653
98368	Port Townsend	5,241	5,074
99163	Pullman	20,509	12,957
98371	Puyallup	14,742	12,063
98052	Redmond	11,020	1,426
98055	Renton	25,878	18,453
99352	Richland	26,290	23,548
*98109	Seattle	530,831	557,087
98584	Shelton	6,515	5,651
98290	Snohomish	5,174	3,894
98387	Spanaway	5,768	
*99210	Spokane	170,516	181,608
98944	Sunnyside	6,751	6,208
*98402	Tacoma	154,407	147,979
98948	Toppenish	5,744	5,667
99268	Town and Country	6,484	
98502	Tumwater	5,373	3,885
98406	University Place	13,230	
*98660	Vancouver	41,859	32,464
99362	Walla Walla	23,619	24,536
98801	Wenatchee	16,912	16,726
*98901	Yakima	45,588	43,284

West Virginia

ZIP Code	Place	1970	1960
25801	Beckley	19,884	18,642
24701	Bluefield	15,921	19,256
26201	Buckhannon	7,261	6,386
*25301	Charleston	71,505	85,796
26301	Clarksburg	24,864	28,112
25064	Dunbar	9,151	11,006
26241	Elkins	8,287	8,307
26554	Fairmont	26,093	27,477
26354	Grafton	6,433	5,791
*25701	Huntington	74,315	83,627
26726	Keyser	6,586	6,192
25401	Martinsburg	14,626	15,179
26505	Morgantown	29,431	22,487
26041	Moundsville	13,560	15,163
26155	New Martinsville	6,528	5,607
25143	Nitro	8,019	6,894
26105	Parkersburg	44,208	44,797
25550	Point Pleasant	6,122	5,785
24740	Princeton	7,253	8,393
25177	St. Albans	14,356	15,103
25303	South Charleston	16,333	19,180
26101	Vienna	11,549	9,381
26062	Weirton	27,131	28,201
26452	Weston	7,323	8,754
26505	Westover	5,086	4,749
26003	Wheeling	48,188	53,400
25661	Williamson	5,831	6,746

Wisconsin

ZIP Code	Place	1970	1960
54301	Allouez	13,753	
54409	Antigo	9,005	9,691
54911	Appleton	56,377	48,411
54806	Ashland	9,615	10,132
54304	Ashwaubenon	9,323	
53913	Baraboo	7,931	7,660
53916	Beaver Dam	14,265	13,118
53511	Beloit	35,729	32,846
54923	Berlin	5,338	4,838
53005	Brookfield	32,140	19,812
53209	Brown Deer	12,582	11,280
53105	Burlington	7,479	5,856
53012	Cedarburg	7,697	5,191
54729	Chippewa Falls	12,351	11,708
53110	Cudahy	22,078	17,975
53115	Delavan	5,526	4,846
54115	De Pere	13,309	10,045
54701	Eau Claire	44,619	37,987
53122	Elm Grove	7,201	4,994
54935	Fond Du Lac	35,515	32,719
53538	Fort Atkinson	9,164	7,908
53217	Fox Point	7,939	7,315
53132	Franklin	12,247	10,006
53022	Germantown	6,974	622
53209	Glendale	13,426	9,537
53024	Grafton 1973	7,169	3,748
*54305	Green Bay	87,809	62,888
53129	Greendale	15,089	6,843
53220	Greenfield	24,424	17,636

ZIP Code	Place	1970	1960
53130	Hales Corners	7,771	5,549
53027	Hartford	6,499	5,627
54016	Hudson 1973	5,322	4,325
53545	Janesville	46,426	35,164
53549	Jefferson	5,429	4,548
54130	Kaukauna	11,308	10,096
53140	Kenosha	78,805	67,899
54136	Kimberly	6,131	5,322
54601	La Crosse	51,153	47,575
54140	Little Chute	5,522	5,099
*53701	Madison 1974	168,671	126,706
54220	Manitowoc	33,430	32,275
54143	Marinette	12,696	13,329
54449	Marshfield	15,619	14,153
54952	Menasha	14,836	14,647
53051	Menomonee Falls	31,697	18,276
54751	Menomonie	11,275	8,624
53092	Mequon	12,150	8,543
54452	Merrill	9,502	9,451
53562	Middleton	8,286	4,410
*53203	Milwaukee	717,372	741,324
53716	Monona	10,420	8,178
53566	Monroe	8,654	8,050
53150	Muskego	11,573	
54956	Neenah	22,902	18,057
53151	New Berlin	26,910	15,788
54961	New London	5,801	5,288
53154	Oak Creek	13,928	9,372
53066	Oconomowoc	8,741	6,682
54901	Oshkosh	53,082	45,110
53511	Perry Go Place	5,912	4,475
53818	Platteville	9,599	6,957
53073	Plymouth	5,810	5,128
53901	Portage	7,821	7,822
53074	Port Washington	8,752	5,984
53821	Prairie Du Chien	5,540	5,649
*53401	Racine	95,162	89,144
54501	Rhinelander	8,218	8,790
54868	Rice Lake	7,278	7,303
53581	Richland Center	5,086	4,746

ZIP Code	Place	1970	1960
54971	Ripon	7,053	6,163
54022	River Falls	7,238	4,857
53207	St. Francis	10,489	10,065
54166	Shawano	6,488	6,103
53081	Sheboygan	48,484	45,747
53211	Shorewood	15,576	15,990
53172	South Milwaukee	23,297	20,307
54656	Sparta	6,258	6,080
54481	Stevens Point	23,479	17,837
53589	Stoughton	6,096	5,555
54235	Sturgeon Bay 1973	7,202	7,353
53590	Sun Prairie	9,935	4,008
54880	Superior	32,237	33,563
54660	Tomah	5,647	5,321
54241	Two Rivers 1974	13,243	12,393
53094	Watertown	15,683	13,943
53186	Waukesha	39,695	30,004
53963	Waupun	7,946	7,935
54401	Wausau	32,806	31,943
54401	Wausau West	6,399	4,105
53213	Wauwatosa	58,676	56,923
53214	West Allis	71,649	68,157
53095	West Bend	16,555	9,969
53217	Whitefish Bay	17,402	18,390
53190	Whitewater	12,038	6,380
54494	Wisconsin Rapids	18,587	15,042

Wyoming

ZIP Code	Place	1970	1960
82601	Casper	39,361	38,930
82001	Cheyenne	40,914	43,505
82414	Cody	5,161	4,838
82716	Gillette	7,194	3,580
82520	Lander	7,125	4,182
82070	Laramie	23,143	17,520
82301	Rawlins	7,855	8,968
82501	Riverton	7,995	6,845
82901	Rock Springs	11,657	10,371
82801	Sheridan	10,856	11,651
82401	Worland	5,055	5,806

1970 Census & Areas of Counties and States

WITH NAMES OF COUNTY SEATS OR COURT HOUSES; LAND AREA IN SQUARE MILES
Source: Bureau of the Census

County	Pop. Apr. 1, 1970	County Seat or Court House	Land Area Sq. Mi.
Alabama			
(67 counties, 50,708 sq. mi. land; pop. 3,444,165)			
Autauga	24,460	Prattville	599
Baldwin	59,382	Bay Minette	1,578
Barbour	22,543	Clayton	891
Bibb	13,812	Centreville	625
Blount	26,853	Oneonta	639
Bullock	11,824	Union Springs	615
Butler	22,007	Greenville	773
Calhoun	103,092	Anniston	611
Chambers	36,356	Lafayette	597
Cherokee	15,606	Centre	556
Chilton	25,180	Clanton	699
Choctaw	16,589	Butler	911
Clarke	26,724	Grove Hill	1,232
Clay	12,636	Ashland	603
Cleburne	10,996	Heflin	574
Coffee	34,872	Elba	677
Colbert	49,632	Tuscumbia	596
Conecuh	15,645	Evergreen	850
Coosa	10,662	Rockford	650
Covington	34,079	Andalusia	984
Crenshaw	13,188	Luverne	611
Cullman	52,445	Cullman	730
Dale	52,938	Ozark	559
Dallas	55,296	Selma	978
De Kalb	41,981	Fort Payne	778
Elmore	33,661	Wetumpka	624
Escambia	34,912	Brewton	962
Etowah	94,144	Gadsden	555
Fayette	16,252	Fayette	627
Franklin	23,933	Russellville	644
Geneva	21,924	Geneva	577
Greene	10,650	Eutaw	627
Hale	15,888	Greensboro	662
Henry	13,254	Abbeville	554
Houston	56,574	Dothan	575
Jackson	39,202	Scottsboro	1,079
Jefferson	644,991	Birmingham	1,115
Lamar	14,335	Vernon	605
Lauderdale	68,111	Florence	662
Lawrence	27,281	Moulton	685
Lee	61,268	Opelika	612
Limestone	41,699	Athens	546
Lowndes	12,897	Hayneville	715
Macon	24,841	Tuskegee	616
Madison	186,540	Huntsville	803
Marengo	23,819	Linden	978
Marion	23,788	Hamilton	743
•Marshall	54,211	Guntersville	571
Mobile	317,308	Mobile	1,240
Monroe	20,883	Monroeville	1,032
Montgomery	167,790	Montgomery	790
Morgan	77,306	Decatur	570
Perry	15,388	Marion	734
Pickens	20,326	Carrollton	887
Pike	25,038	Troy	673
Randolph	18,331	Wedowee	581
Russell	45,394	Phenix City	627
St. Clair	27,956	Ashville & Pell City	640
Shelby	38,037	Columbiana	798
Sumter	16,974	Livingston	915
Talladega	65,280	Talladega	750
Tallapoosa	33,840	Dadeville	704
Tuscaloosa	116,029	Tuscaloosa	1,333
Walker	56,246	Jasper	805
Washington	16,241	Chatom	1,066
Wilcox	16,303	Camden	899
Winston	16,654	Double Springs	615

Alaska

(29 divisions, 566,432 sq. mi. land; pop. 302,173)

Census Division	Pop. Apr. 1, 1970	Land Area Sq. Mi.
Aleutian Islands	8,057	14,583
Anchorage	126,385	927
Angoon	503	2,825
Barrow	2,663	57,587

Census Division	Pop. Apr. 1, 1970	Land Area Sq. Mi.
Bethel	7,767	19,642
Bristol Bay Borough	1,147	531
Bristol Bay	3,485	36,565
Cordova-McCarthy	1,857	15,481
Fairbanks	45,864	7,074
Haines	1,504	2,128
Juneau	13,556	1,286
Kenai-Cook Inlet	14,250	12,474
Ketchikan	10,041	1,345
Kobuk	4,434	42,978
Kodiak	9,409	5,375
Kuskokwim	2,306	56,562
Matanuska-Susitna	6,509	25,730
Nome	5,749	24,968
Outer Ketchikan	1,676	3,762
Prince of Wales	2,106	3,485
Seward	2,336	3,727
Sitka	6,106	2,296
Skagway-Yakutat	2,157	8,646
Southeast Fairbanks	4,179	17,713
Upper Yukon	1,684	84,142
Valdez-Chitina-Whittier	3,098	18,619
Wade Hampton	3,917	16,770
Wrangell-Petersburg	4,913	6,178
Yukon-Koyukuk	4,758	73,053

Arizona

(14 counties, 113,417 sq. mi. land; pop. 1,772,482) ·

County	Pop. Apr. 1, 1970	County Seat or Court House	Land Area Sq. Mi.
Apache	32,304	Saint Johns	11,171
Cochise	61,918	Bisbee	6,256
Coconino	48,326	Flagstaff	18,540
Gila	29,255	Globe	4,748
Graham	16,578	Safford	4,618
Greenlee	10,330	Clifton	1,879
Maricopa	968,487	Phoenix	9,155
Mohave	35,714	Kingman	13,217
Navajo	47,559	Holbrook	9,910
Pima	351,667	Tucson	9,240
Pinal	68,579	Florence	5,364
Santa Cruz	13,966	Nogales	1,246
Yavapai	37,005	Prescott	8,091
Yuma	60,827	Yuma	9,983

Arkansas

(75 counties, 51,945 sq. mi. land; pop. 1,923,295)

County	Pop. Apr. 1, 1970	County Seat or Court House	Land Area Sq. Mi.
Arkansas	23,347	DeWitt & Stuttgart	1,015
Ashley	24,976	Hamburg	928
Baxter	15,319	Mountain Home	537
Benton	50,476	Bentonville	851
Boone	19,073	Harrison	586
Bradley	12,778	Warren	651
Calhoun	5,573	Hampton	629
Carroll	12,301	Berryville and Eureka Sprg	626
Chicot	18,164	Lake Village	643
Clark	21,537	Arkadelphia	878
Clay	18,771	Corning; Piggott	639
Cleburne	10,349	Heber Springs	554
Cleveland	6,605	Rison	601
Columbia	25,952	Magnolia	768
Conway	16,805	Morrilton	561
Craighead	52,068	Jonesboro and Lake City	716
Crawford	25,677	Van Buren	596
Crittenden	48,106	Marion	608
Cross	19,783	Wynne	625
Dallas	10,022	Fordyce	672
Desha	18,761	Arkansas City	736
Drew	15,157	Monticello	832
Faulkner	31,578	Conway	641
Franklin	11,301	Charleston and Ozark	613
Fulton	7,699	Salem	608
Garland	54,131	Hot Spgs. Nat'l Pk.	658
Grant	9,711	Sheridan	631
Greene	24,765	Paragould	579
Hempstead	19,308	Hope	726
Hot Spring	21,963	Malvern	621
Howard	11,412	Nashville	569
Independence	22,723	Batesville	574
Izard	7,381	Melbourne	574
Jackson	20,452	Newport	629
Jefferson	85,329	Pine Bluff	873
Johnson	13,630	Clarksville	673
Lafayette	10,018	Lewisville	523

County	Pop. Apr. 1, 1970	County Seat or Court House	Land Area Sq. Mi.
Lee	18,884	Marianna	608
Lincoln	12,913	Star City	563
Little River	11,194	Ashdown	486
Logan	16,789	Booneville & Paris	718
Lonoke	26,249	Lonoke	796
Madison	9,453	Huntsville	832
Marion	7,000	Yellville	584
Miller	33,385	Texarkana	623
Mississippi	62,060	Blytheville and Osceola	904
Monroe	15,657	Clarendon	607
Montgomery	5,821	Mount Ida	775
Nevada	10,111	Prescott	616
Newton	5,844	Jasper	822
Ouachita	30,896	Camden	736
Perry	5,634	Perryville	551
Phillips	40,046	Helena	686
Pike	8,711	Murfreesboro	600
Poinsett	26,843	Harrisburg	760
Polk	13,297	Mena	859
Pope	28,607	Russellville	812
Prairie	10,249	Des Arc and De Valls Bluff	661
Pulaski	287,189	Little Rock	765
Randolph	12,645	Pocohontas	647
St. Francis	30,799	Forest City	635
Saline	36,107	Benton	724
Scott	8,207	Waldron	898
Searcy	7,731	Marshall	664
Sebastian	79,237	Fort Smith; Greenwood	527
Sevier	11,272	De Queen	522
Sharp	8,233	Ash Flat	581
Stone	6,838	Mountain View	608
Union	45,428	El Dorado	1,050
Van Buren	8,275	Clinton	699
Washington	77,370	Fayetteville	958
White	39,253	Searcy	1,041
Woodruff	11,566	Augusta	591
Yell	14,208	Danville and Dardanelle	929

California

(58 counties, 156,361 sq. mi. land; pop. 19,953,134)

County	Pop. Apr. 1, 1970	County Seat or Court House	Land Area Sq. Mi.
Alameda	1,073,184	Oakland	733
Alpine	484	Markleeville	727
Amador	11,821	Jackson	583
Butte	101,969	Oroville	1,645
Calaveras	13,585	San Andreas	1,024
Colusa	12,430	Colusa	1,152
Contra Costa	555,805	Martinez	735
Del Norte	14,580	Crescent City	1,007
El Dorado	43,833	Placerville	1,715
Fresno	413,329	Fresno	5,966
Glenn	17,521	Willows	1,314
Humboldt	99,692	Eureka	3,586
Imperial	74,492	El Centro	4,241
Inyo	15,571	Independence	10,130
Kern	329,281	Bakersfield	8,152
Kings	66,717	Hanford	1,396
Lake	19,548	Lakeport	1,261
Lassen	16,796	Susanville	4,561
Los Angeles	7,040,697	Los Angeles	4,069
Madera	41,519	Madera	2,145
Marin	206,758	San Rafael	520
Mariposa	6,015	Mariposa	1,453
Mendocino	51,101	Ukiah	3,511
Merced	104,629	Merced	1,958
Modoc	7,469	Alturas	4,097
Mono	4,016	Bridgeport	3,027
Monterey	247,450	Salinas	3,324
Napa	79,140	Napa	787
Nevada	26,346	Nevada City	973
Orange	1,420,676	Santa Ana	782
Placer	77,632	Auburn	1,431
Plumas	11,707	Quincy	2,566
Riverside	459,074	Riverside	7,176
Sacramento	634,190	Sacramento	975
San Benito	18,226	Hollister	1,396
San Bernardino	682,233	San Bernardino	20,117
San Diego	1,357,854	San Diego	4,261
San Francisco	715,674	San Francisco	45
San Joaquin	289,564	Stockton	1,412
San Luis Obispo	105,690	San Luis Obispo	3,183
San Mateo	556,605	Redwood City	447
Santa Barbara	264,324	Santa Barbara	2,737
Santa Clara	1,066,174	San Jose	1,300
Santa Cruz	123,790	Santa Cruz	440
Shasta	77,640	Redding	3,788
Sierra	2,365	Downieville	958
Siskiyou	33,225	Yreka	6,262
Solano	171,989	Fairfield	823
Sonoma	204,885	Santa Rosa	1,604
Stanislaus	194,506	Modesto	1,511

County	Pop. Apr. 1, 1970	County Seat or Court House	Land Area Sq. Mi.
Sutter	41,935	Yuba City	603
Tehama	29,517	Red Bluff	2,982
Trinity	7,615	Weaverville	3,173
Tulare	188,322	Visalia	4,812
Tuolumne	22,169	Sonora	2,252
Ventura	378,497	Ventura	1,863
Yolo	91,788	Woodland	1,028
Yuba	44,736	Marysville	639

Colorado

(63 counties, 103,766 sq. mi. land; pop. 2,207,259)

County	Pop. Apr. 1, 1970	County Seat or Court House	Land Area Sq. Mi.
Adams	185,789	Brighton	1,237
Alamosa	11,422	Alamosa	719
Arapahoe	162,142	Littleton	797
Archuleta	2,733	Pagosa Springs	1,364
Baca	5,674	Springfield	2,563
Bent	6,493	Las Animas	1,519
Boulder	131,889	Boulder	748
Chaffee	10,162	Salida	1,038
Cheyenne	2,396	Cheyenne Wells	1,772
Clear Creek	4,819	Georgetown	394
Conejos	7,846	Conejos	1,268
Costilla	3,091	San Luis	1,213
Crowley	3,086	Ordway	802
Custer	1,120	Westcliffe	737
Delta	15,286	Delta	1,154
Denver	514,678	Denver	95
Dolores	1,641	Dove Creek	1,026
Douglas	8,407	Castle Rock	843
Eagle	7,498	Eagle	1,681
Elbert	3,903	Kiowa	1,864
El Paso	235,972	Colorado Springs	2,157
Fremont	21,942	Canon City	1,561
Garfield	14,821	Glenwood Springs	2,996
Gilpin	1,272	Central City	148
Grand	4,107	Hot Sulphur Springs	1,854
Gunnison	7,578	Gunnison	3,220
Hinsdale	202	Lake City	1,054
Huerfano	6,590	Walsenburg	1,574
Jackson	1,811	Walden	1,622
Jefferson	235,300	Golden	783
Kiowa	2,029	Eads	1,767
Kit Carson	7,530	Burlington	2,171
Lake	8,282	Leadville	379
La Plata	19,199	Durango	1,683
Larimer	89,900	Fort Collins	2,611
Las Animas	15,744	Trinidad	4,794
Lincoln	4,836	Hugo	2,593
Logan	18,852	Sterling	1,822
Mesa	54,374	Grand Junction	3,301
Mineral	786	Creede	921
Moffat	6,525	Craig	4,743
Montezuma	12,952	Cortez	2,094
Montrose	18,366	Montrose	2,238
Morgan	20,105	Fort Morgan	1,278
Otero	23,523	LaJunta	1,254
Ouray	1,546	Ouray	540
Park	2,185	Fairplay	2,162
Phillips	4,131	Holyoke	680
Pitkin	6,185	Aspen	973
Prowers	13,258	Lamar	1,621
Pueblo	118,238	Pueblo	2,405
Rio Blanco	4,842	Meeker	3,263
Rio Grande	10,494	Del Norte	915
Routt	6,592	Steamboat Spgs.	2,330
Saguache	3,827	Saguache	3,144
San Juan	831	Silverton	391
San Miguel	1,949	Telluride	1,283
Sedgwick	3,405	Julesburg	544
Summit	2,665	Breckenridge	604
Teller	3,316	Cripple Creek	553
Washington	5,550	Akron	2,526
Weld	89,297	Greeley	4,002
Yuma	8,544	Wray	2,379

Connecticut

(8 counties, 4,862 sq. mi. land; pop. 3,032,217)

County	Pop. Apr. 1, 1970	County Seat or Court House	Land Area Sq. Mi.
Fairfield	792,814	Bridgeport	626
Hartford	816,737	Hartford	739
Litchfield	144,091	Litchfield	925
Middlesex	115,018	Middletown	372
New Haven	744,948	New Haven	604
New London	230,654	Norwich	667
Tolland	103,440	Rockville	416
Windham	84,515	Putnam	514

Delaware

(3 counties, 1,982 sq. mi. land; pop. 548,104)

County	Pop. Apr. 1, 1970	County Seat or Court House	Land Area Sq. Mi.
Kent	81,892	Dover	594
New Castle	385,856	Wilmington	438
Sussex	80,356	Georgetown	950

District of Columbia

(61 sq. mi. land; pop. 756,510)

Florida

(67 counties, 54,090 sq. mi. land; pop. 6,789,443)

County	Pop. Apr. 1, 1970	County Seat or Court House	Land Area Sq. Mi.
Alachua	104,764	Gainesville	916
Baker	9,242	Macclenny	585
Bay	75,283	Panama City	747
Bradford	14,625	Starke	294
Brevard	230,006	Titusville	1,011
Broward	620,100	Fort Lauderdale	1,219
Calhoun	7,624	Blountstown	561
Charlotte	27,559	Punta Gorda	703
Citrus	19,196	Inverness	560
Clay	32,059	Green Cove Spgs.	593
Collier	38,040	Naples	2,006
Columbia	25,250	Lake City	784
Dade	1,267,792	Miami	2,042
De Soto	13,060	Arcadia	648
Dixie	5,480	Cross City	692
Duval	528,865	Jacksonville	766
Escambia	205,334	Pensacola	665
Flagler	4,454	Bunnell	487
Franklin	7,065	Apalachicola	536
Gadsden	39,184	Quincy	512
Gilchrist	3,551	Trenton	346
Glades	3,669	Moore Haven	753
Gulf	10,096	Port St. Joe	565
Hamilton	7,787	Jasper	514
Hardee	14,889	Wauchula	629
Hendry	11,859	La Belle	1,187
Hernando	17,004	Brooksville	484
Highlands	29,507	Sebring	997
Hillsborough	490,265	Tampa	1,038
Holmes	10,720	Bonifay	482
Indian River	35,992	Vero Beach	506
Jackson	34,434	Marianna	935
Jefferson	8,778	Monticello	605
Lafayette	2,892	Mayo	549
Lake	69,305	Tavares	961
Lee	105,216	Fort Myers	785
Leon	103,047	Tallahassee	670
Levy	12,756	Bronson	1,083
Liberty	3,379	Bristol	839
Madison	13,481	Madison	703
Manatee	97,115	Bradenton	739
Marion	69,030	Ocala	1,600
Martin	28,035	Stuart	556
Monroe	52,586	Key West	1,034
Nassau	20,626	Fernandina Beach	650
Okaloosa	88,187	Crestview	944
Okeechobee	11,233	Okeechobee	777
Orange	344,311	Orlando	910
Osceola	25,267	Kissimmee	1,313
Palm Beach	348,993	West Palm Beach	2,023
Pasco	75,955	Dade City	742
Pinellas	522,329	Clearwater	265
Polk	228,026	Bartow	1,858
Putnam	36,424	Palatka	779
St. Johns	31,035	Saint Augustine	605
St. Lucie	50,836	Fort Pierce	584
Santa Rosa	37,741	Milton	1,032
Sarasota	120,413	Sarasota	587
Seminole	83,692	Sanford	305
Sumter	14,839	Bushnell	555
Suwannee	15,559	Live Oak	686
Taylor	13,641	Perry	1,051
Union	8,112	Lake Butler	241
Volusia	169,487	De Land	1,062
Wakulla	6,308	Crawfordville	601
Walton	16,087	De Funiak Springs	1,053
Washington	11,453	Chipley	585

Georgia

(159 counties, 58,073 sq. mi. land; pop. 4,589,575)

County	Pop. Apr. 1, 1970	County Seat or Court House	Land Area Sq. Mi.
Appling	12,726	Baxley	513
Atkinson	5,879	Pearson	318
Bacon	8,233	Alma	293
Baker	3,875	Newton	355
Baldwin	34,240	Milledgeville	255
Banks	6,833	Homer	231
Barrow	16,859	Winder	171
Bartow	32,911	Cartersville	461
Ben Hill	13,171	Fitzgerald	255
Berrien	11,556	Nashville	468

County	Pop. Apr. 1, 1970	County Seat or Court House	Land Area Sq. Mi.	County	Pop. Apr. 1, 1970	County Seat or Court House	Land Area Sq. Mi.
Bibb	143,418	Macon	254	Oconee	7,915	Watkinsville	186
Bleckley	10,291	Cochran	219	Oglethorpe	7,598	Lexington	435
Brantley	5,940	Nahunta	447	Paulding	17,520	Dallas	318
Brooks	13,743	Quitman	491	Peach	15,990	Fort Valley	151
Bryan	6,539	Pembroke	443	Pickens	9,620	Jasper	225
Bulloch	31,585	Statesboro	685	Pierce	9,281	Blackshear	342
Burke	18,255	Waynesboro	831	Pike	7,316	Zebulon	230
Butts	10,560	Jackson	185	Polk	29,656	Cedartown	312
Calhoun	6,606	Morgan	289	Pulaski	8,066	Hawkinsville	253
Camden	11,334	Woodbine	653	Putnam	9,394	Eatonton	339
Candler	6,412	Metter	250	Quitman	2,180	Georgetown	156
Carroll	45,404	Carrollton	495	Rabun	8,327	Clayton	368
Catoosa	28,271	Ringgold	167	Randolph	8,734	Cuthbert	436
Charlton	5,680	Folkston	796	Richmond	162,437	Augusta	323
Chatham	187,816	Savannah	445	Rockdale	18,152	Conyers	128
Chattahoochee	25,813	Cusseta	253	Schley	3,097	Ellaville	162
Chattooga	20,541	Summerville	317	Screven	12,591	Sylvania	651
Cherokee	31,059	Canton	415	Seminole	7,059	Donalsonville	246
Clarke	65,177	Athens	116	Spalding	39,514	Griffin	201
Clay	3,636	Fort Gaines	200	Stephens	20,331	Toccoa	173
Clayton	98,126	Jonesboro	149	Stewart	6,511	Lumpkin	452
Clinch	6,405	Homerville	797	Sumter	26,931	Americus	488
Cobb	196,793	Marietta	343	Talbot	6,625	Talbotton	390
Coffee	22,828	Douglas	612	Taliaferro	2,423	Crawfordville	195
Colquitt	32,298	Moultrie	563	Tattnall	16,557	Reidsville	490
Columbia	22,327	Appling	290	Taylor	7,865	Butler	403
Cook	12,129	Adel	233	Telfair	11,394	McRae	440
Coweta	32,310	Newnan	442	Terrell	11,416	Dawson	329
Crawford	5,748	Knoxville	315	Thomas	34,562	Thomasville	541
Crisp	18,087	Cordele	292	Tift	27,288	Tifton	266
Dade	9,910	Trenton	168	Toombs	19,151	Lyons	368
Dawson	3,639	Dawsonville	211	Towns	4,565	Hiawassee	166
Decatur	22,310	Bainbridge	575	Treutlen	5,647	Soperton	194
De Kalb	415,387	Decatur	269	Troup	44,466	La Grange	415
Dodge	15,658	Eastman	498	Turner	8,790	Ashburn	293
Dooly	10,404	Vienna	395	Twiggs	8,222	Jeffersonville	364
Dougherty	89,639	Albany	324	Union	6,811	Blairsville	309
Douglas	28,659	Douglasville	202	Upson	23,505	Thomaston	334
Early	12,682	Blakely	524	Walker	50,691	La Fayette	445
Echols	1,924	Statenville	425	Walton	23,404	Monroe	330
Effingham	13,632	Springfield	480	Ware	33,525	Waycross	912
Elbert	17,262	Elberton	358	Warren	6,669	Warrenton	284
Emanuel	18,357	Swainsboro	686	Washington	17,480	Sandersville	674
Evans	7,290	Claxton	186	Wayne	17,858	Jesup	645
Fannin	13,357	Blue Ridge	394	Webster	2,362	Preston	195
Fayette	11,364	Fayetteville	199	Wheeler	4,596	Alamo	306
Floyd	73,742	Rome	514	White	7,742	Cleveland	243
Forsyth	16,928	Cumming	219	Whitfield	55,108	Dalton	281
Franklin	12,784	Carnesville	263	Wilcox	6,998	Abbeville	383
Fulton	607,592	Atlanta	530	Wilkes	18,184	Washington	468
Gilmer	8,956	Ellijay	439	Wilkinson	9,393	Irwinton	458
Glascock	2,280	Gibson	143	Worth	14,770	Sylvester	579
Glynn	50,528	Brunswick	412				
Gordon	23,570	Calhoun	358				
Grady	17,826	Cairo	466				
Greene	10,212	Greensboro	403				
Gwinnett	72,349	Lawrenceville	437				
Habersham	20,691	Clarkesville	282				
Hall	59,405	Gainesville	378				
Hancock	9,019	Sparta	478				
Haralson	15,927	Buchanan	285				
Harris	11,520	Hamilton	465				
Hart	15,814	Hartwell	231				
Heard	5,354	Franklin	297				
Henry	23,724	McDonough	331				
Houston	62,924	Perry	380				
Irwin	8,036	Ocilla	372				
Jackson	21,093	Jefferson	346				
Jasper	5,760	Monticello	373				
Jeff Davis	9,425	Hazlehurst	331				
Jefferson	17,174	Louisville	530				
Jenkins	8,332	Millen	351				
Johnson	7,727	Wrightsville	313				
Jones	12,218	Gray	402				
Lamar	10,688	Barnesville	181				
Lanier	5,031	Lakeland	177				
Laurens	32,738	Dublin	810				
Lee	7,044	Leesburg	355				
Liberty	17,569	Hinesville	514				
Lincoln	5,895	Lincolnton	193				
Long	3,746	Ludowici	402				
Lowndes	55,112	Valdosta	508				
Lumpkin	8,728	Dahlonega	292				
McDuffie	15,276	Thomson	253				
McIntosh	7,371	Darien	426				
Macon	12,933	Oglethorpe	403				
Madison	13,517	Danielsville	281				
Marion	5,099	Buena Vista	365				
Meriwether	19,461	Greenville	499				
Miller	6,424	Colquitt	287				
Mitchell	18,956	Camilla	510				
Monroe	10,991	Forsyth	398				
Montgomery	6,099	Mount Vernon	237				
Morgan	9,904	Madison	356				
Murray	12,986	Chatsworth	342				
Muscogee	167,377	Columbus	220				
Newton	26,282	Covington	271				

Hawaii

(4 counties, 6,425 sq. mi. land; pop. 769,913)

County	Pop. Apr. 1, 1970	County Seat or Court House	Land Area Sq. Mi.
Hawaii	63,468	Hilo	4,037
Honolulu	630,528	Honolulu	596
Kauai	29,761	Lihue	619
Maui*	46,156	Wailuku	1,173

*Includes population of Kalawao County (279) shown separately in 1960 but included with Maui County in 1970.

Idaho

(44 counties, 82,677 sq. mi. land; pop. 713,008)

County	Pop. Apr. 1, 1970	County Seat or Court House	Land Area Sq. Mi.
Ada	112,230	Boise	1,043
Adams	2,877	Council	1,371
Bannock	52,200	Pocatello	1,122
Bear Lake	5,801	Paris	984
Benewah	6,230	Saint Maries	788
Bingham	29,167	Blackfoot	2,084
Blaine	5,749	Hailey	2,647
Boise	1,763	Idaho City	1,910
Bonner	15,560	Sandpoint	1,733
Bonneville	52,457	Idaho Falls	1,836
Boundary	5,484	Bonners Ferry	1,275
Butte	2,925	Arco	2,239
Camas	728	Fairfield	1,054
Canyon	61,288	Caldwell	578
Caribou	6,534	Soda Springs	1,746
Cassia	17,017	Burley	2,544
Clark	741	Dubois	1,751
Clearwater	10,871	Orofino	2,521
Custer	2,967	Challis	4,929
Elmore	17,479	Mountain Home	3,048
Franklin	7,373	Preston	664
Fremont	8,710	Saint Anthony	1,864
Gem	9,387	Emmett	555
Gooding	8,645	Gooding	720
Idaho	12,891	Grangeville	8,516
Jefferson	11,740	Rigby	1,096
Jerome	10,253	Jerome	595

County	Pop. Apr. 1, 1970	County Seat or Court House	Land Area Sq. Mi.
Kootenai	35,332	Coeur d'Alene	1,249
Latah	24,898	Moscow	1,090
Lemhi	5,566	Salmon	4,580
Lewis	3,867	Nezperce	476
Lincoln	3,057	Shoshone	1,203
Madison	13,452	Rexburg	473
Minidoka	15,731	Rupert	750
Nez Perce	30,376	Lewiston	844
Oneida	2,864	Malad City	1,191
Owyhee	6,422	Murphy	7,641
Payette	12,401	Payette	402
Power	4,864	American Falls	1,413
Shoshone	19,718	Wallace	2,609
Teton	2,351	Driggs	457
Twin Falls	41,807	Twin Falls	1,947
Valley	3,609	Cascade	3,676
Washington	7,633	Weiser	1,462

Illinois

(102 counties, 55,748 sq. mi. land; pop. 11,113,976)

County	Pop. Apr. 1, 1970	County Seat or Court House	Land Area Sq. Mi.
Adams	70,861	Quincy	862
Alexander	12,015	Cairo	229
Bond	14,012	Greenville	378
Boone	25,440	Belvidere	283
Brown	5,586	Mount Sterling	306
Bureau	38,541	Princeton	866
Calhoun	5,675	Hardin	247
Carroll	19,276	Mount Carroll	456
Cass	14,219	Virginia	371
Champaign	163,281	Urbana	1,000
Christian	35,948	Taylorville	709
Clark	16,216	Marshall	505
Clay	14,735	Louisville	464
Clinton	28,315	Carlyle	434
Coles	47,815	Charleston	506
Cook	5,493,766	Chicago	954
Crawford	19,824	Robinson	443
Cumberland	9,772	Toledo	347
De Kalb	71,654	Sycamore	636
De Witt	16,975	Clinton	399
Douglas	18,997	Tuscola	420
Du Page	490,822	Wheaton	331
Edgar	21,591	Paris	628
Edwards	7,090	Albion	225
Effingham	24,608	Effingham	481
Fayette	20,752	Vandalia	703
Ford	16,382	Paxton	488
Franklin	38,329	Benton	434
Fulton	41,900	Lewiston	877
Gallatin	7,418	Shawneetown	328
Greene	17,014	Carrollton	543
Grundy	26,535	Morris	432
Hamilton	8,665	McLeansboro	435
Hancock	23,664	Carthage	797
Hardin	4,914	Elizabethtown	183
Henderson	8,451	Oquawka	376
Henry	53,217	Cambridge	826
Iroquois	33,532	Watseka	1,122
Jackson	55,008	Murphysboro	605
Jasper	10,741	Newton	495
Jefferson	31,848	Mount Vernon	573
Jersey	18,492	Jerseyville	376
Jo Daviess	21,766	Galena	606
Johnson	7,550	Vienna	345
Kane	251,005	Geneva	520
Kankakee	97,250	Kankakee	678
Kendall	26,374	Yorkville	320
Knox	60,939	Galesburg	728
Lake	382,638	Waukegan	457
La Salle	111,409	Ottawa	1,150
Lawrence	17,522	Lawrenceville	374
Lee	37,947	Dixon	728
Livingston	40,690	Pontiac	1,043
Logan	33,538	Lincoln	622
McDonough	36,653	Macomb	582
McHenry	111,555	Woodstock	610
McLean	104,389	Bloomington	1,173
Macon	125,010	Decatur	578
Macoupin	44,557	Carlinville	872
Madison	250,911	Edwardsville	733
Marion	38,986	Salem	579
Marshall	13,302	Lacon	391
Mason	16,180	Havana	541
Massac	13,889	Metropolis	245
Menard	9,685	Petersburg	312
Mercer	17,294	Aledo	556
Monroe	18,831	Waterloo	382
Montgomery	30,260	Hillsboro	705
Morgan	36,174	Jacksonville	561
Moultrie	13,263	Sullivan	326
Ogle	42,867	Oregon	758
Peoria	195,318	Peoria	623
Perry	19,757	Pinckneyville	439
Piatt	15,509	Monticello	437
Pike	19,185	Pittsfield	828
Pope	3,857	Golconda	381
Pulaski	8,741	Mound City	204
Putnam	5,007	Hennepin	160
Randolph	31,379	Chester	594
Richland	16,829	Olney	364
Rock Island	166,734	Rock Island	424
St. Clair	285,199	Belleville	673
Saline	25,721	Harrisburg	383
Sangamon	161,335	Springfield	879
Schuyler	8,135	Rushville	434
Scott	6,096	Winchester	251
Shelby	22,589	Shelbyville	752
Stark	7,510	Toulon	291
Stephenson	48,861	Freeport	568
Tazewell	118,649	Pekin	652
Union	16,071	Jonesboro	416
Vermilion	97,047	Danville	899
Wabash	12,841	Mt. Carmel	222
Warren	21,595	Monmouth	541
Washington	13,780	Nashville	564
Wayne	17,004	Fairfield	715
White	17,312	Carmi	502
Whiteside	62,877	Morrison	687
Will	247,825	Joliet	847
Williamson	49,021	Marion	429
Winnebago	246,623	Rockford	519
Woodford	28,012	Eureka	528

Indiana

(92 counties, 36,097 sq. mi. land; pop. 5,193,669)

County	Pop. Apr. 1, 1970	County Seat or Court House	Land Area Sq. Mi.
Adams	26,871	Decatur	345
Allen	280,455	Fort Wayne	671
Bartholomew	57,022	Columbus	402
Benton	11,262	Fowler	409
Blackford	15,888	Hartford City	167
Boone	30,870	Lebanon	427
Brown	9,057	Nashville	319
Carroll	17,734	Delphi	374
Cass	40,456	Logansport	415
Clark	75,876	Jeffersonville	384
Clay	23,933	Brazil	364
Clinton	30,547	Frankfort	407
Crawford	8,033	English	312
Daviess	26,602	Washington	430
Dearborn	29,430	Lawrenceburg	306
Decatur	22,738	Greensburg	370
De Kalb	30,837	Auburn	366
Delaware	129,219	Muncie	396
Dubois	30,934	Jasper	433
Elkhart	126,529	Goshen	468
Fayette	26,216	Connersville	215
Floyd	55,622	New Albany	149
Fountain	18,257	Covington	397
Franklin	16,943	Brookville	394
Fulton	16,984	Rochester	368
Gibson	30,444	Princeton	498
Grant	83,955	Marion	421
Greene	26,894	Bloomfield	549
Hamilton	54,532	Noblesville	401
Hancock	35,096	Greenfield	305
Harrison	20,423	Corydon	479
Hendricks	53,974	Danville	417
Henry	52,603	New Castle	400
Howard	83,198	Kokomo	293
Huntington	34,970	Huntington	369
Jackson	33,187	Brownstown	520
Jasper	20,429	Rensselaer	562
Jay	23,575	Portland	386
Jefferson	27,006	Madison	366
Jennings	19,454	Vernon	377
Johnson	61,138	Franklin	315
Knox	41,546	Vincennes	516
Kosciusko	48,127	Warsaw	540
Lagrange	20,890	Lagrange	381
Lake	546,253	Crown Point	513
La Porte	105,342	La Porte	607
Lawrence	38,038	Bedford	459
Madison	138,522	Anderson	453
Marion	793,769	Indianapolis	392
Marshall	34,986	Plymouth	443
Martin	10,969	Shoals	345
Miami	39,246	Peru	377
Monroe	85,221	Bloomington	386
Montgomery	33,930	Crawfordsville	507
Morgan	44,176	Martinsville	406
Newton	11,606	Kentland	413
Noble	31,382	Albion	412
Ohio	4,289	Rising Sun	87
Orange	16,968	Paoli	405
Owen	12,163	Spencer	390
Parke	14,600	Rockville	445
Perry	19,075	Cannelton	384
Pike	12,281	Petersburg	335
Porter	87,114	Valparaiso	425
Posey	21,740	Mount Vernon	412

County	Pop. Apr. 1, 1970	County Seat or Court House	Land Area Sq. Mi.
Pulaski	12,534	Winamac	433
Putnam	26,932	Greencastle	490
Randolph	28,915	Winchester	457
Ripley	21,138	Versailles	442
Rush	20,352	Rushville	409
St. Joseph	245,045	South Bend	466
Scott	17,144	Scottsburg	193
Shelby	37,797	Shelbyville	409
Spencer	17,134	Rockport	396
Starke	19,280	Knox	310
Steuben	20,159	Angola	309
Sullivan	19,889	Sullivan	457
Switzerland	6,306	Vevay	221
Tippecanoe	109,378	Lafayette	500
Tipton	16,650	Tipton	261
Union	6,582	Liberty	168
Vanderburgh	168,772	Evansville	241
Vermillion	16,793	Newport	263
Vigo	114,528	Terre Haute	415
Wabash	35,553	Wabash	398
Warren	8,705	Williamsport	368
Warrick	27,972	Boonville	391
Washington	19,278	Salem	516
Wayne	79,109	Richmond	405
Wells	23,821	Bluffton	368
White	20,995	Monticello	497
Whitley	23,395	Columbia City	337

Iowa

(99 counties; 55,941 sq. mi. land; pop. 2,825,041)

County	Pop. Apr. 1, 1970	County Seat or Court House	Land Area Sq. Mi.
Adair	9,487	Greenfield	569
Adams	6,322	Corning	426
Allamakee	14,968	Waukon	636
Appanoose	15,007	Centerville	523
Audubon	9,595	Audubon	448
Benton	22,885	Vinton	718
Black Hawk	132,916	Waterloo	568
Boone	26,470	Boone	573
Bremer	22,737	Waverly	439
Buchanan	21,762	Independence	568
Buena Vista	20,693	Storm Lake	572
Butler	16,953	Allison	582
Calhoun	14,292	Rockwell City	571
Carroll	22,912	Carroll	574
Cass	17,007	Atlantic	559
Cedar	17,655	Tipton	585
Cerro Gordo	49,223	Mason City	575
Cherokee	17,269	Cherokee	573
Chickasaw	14,969	New Hampton	505
Clarke	7,581	Oscea	429
Clay	18,464	Spencer	580
Clayton	20,606	Elkader	779
Clinton	56,749	Clinton	693
Crawford	19,116	Denison	716
Dallas	26,085	Adel	597
Davis	8,207	Bloomfield	509
Decatur	9,737	Leon	530
Delaware	18,770	Manchester	572
Des Moines	46,982	Burlington	408
Dickinson	12,565	Spirit Lake	380
Dubuque	90,609	Dubuque	612
Emmet	14,009	Estherville	394
Fayette	26,898	West Union	728
Floyd	19,860	Charles City	503
Franklin	13,255	Hampton	586
Fremont	9,282	Sidney	524
Greene	12,716	Jefferson	569
Grundy	14,119	Grundy Center	501
Guthrie	12,243	Guthrie Center	596
Hamilton	18,383	Webster City	577
Hancock	13,506	Garner	570
Hardin	22,248	Eldora	574
Harrison	16,240	Logan	696
Henry	18,114	Mount Pleasant	440
Howard	11,442	Cresco	471
Humboldt	12,519	Dakota City	435
Ida	9,283	Ida Grove	431
Iowa	15,419	Marengo	584
Jackson	20,839	Maquoketa	644
Jasper	35,425	Newton	731
Jefferson	15,774	Fairfield	436
Johnson 1974	75,025	Iowa City	619
Jones	19,868	Anamosa	585
Keokuk	13,943	Sigourney	579
Kossuth	22,937	Algona	979
Lee	42,996	Fort Madison and Keokuk	527
Linn	163,213	Cedar Rapids	717
Louisa	10,682	Wapello	403
Lucas	10,163	Chariton	434
Lyon	13,340	Rock Rapids	588
Madison	11,558	Winterset	564
Mahaska	22,177	Oskaloosa	572
Marion	26,352	Knoxville	498
Marshall	41,076	Marshalltown	574
Mills	11,832	Glenwood	447
Mitchell	13,108	Osage	467
Monona	12,069	Onawa	699
Monroe	9,357	Albia	435
Montgomery	12,781	Red Oak	422
Muscatine	37,181	Muscatine	443
O'Brien	17,522	Primghar	575
Osceola	8,555	Sibley	398
Page	18,537	Clarinda	535
Palo Alto	13,289	Emmetsburg	561
Plymouth	24,322	Le Mars	863
Pocahontas	12,793	Pocahontas	581
Polk	286,130	Des Moines	578
Pottawattamie	86,991	Council Bluffs	963
Poweshiek	18,803	Montezuma	589
Ringgold	6,373	Mount Ayr	538
Sac	15,573	Sac City	578
Scott	142,687	Davenport	454
Shelby	15,528	Harlan	587
Sioux	27,996	Orange City	766
Story	62,783	Nevada	568
Tama	20,147	Toledo	720
Taylor	8,790	Bedford	528
Union	13,557	Creston	425
Van Buren	8,643	Keosauqua	487
Wapello	42,149	Ottumwa	437
Warren	27,432	Indianola	558
Washington	18,967	Washington	568
Wayne	8,405	Corydon	532
Webster	48,391	Fort Dodge	718
Winnebago	12,990	Forest City	401
Winneshiek	21,758	Decorah	688
Woodbury	103,052	Sioux City	871
Worth	8,984	Northwood	400
Wright	17,294	Clarion	577

Kansas

(105 counties, 81,787 sq. mi. land; pop. 2,249,071)

County	Pop. Apr. 1, 1970	County Seat or Court House	Land Area Sq. Mi.
Allen	15,043	Iola	505
Anderson	8,501	Garnett	577
Atchison	19,165	Atchison	427
Barber	7,016	Medicine Lodge	1,146
Barton	30,663	Great Bend	894
Bourbon	15,215	Fort Scott	639
Brown	11,685	Hiawatha	577
Butler	38,658	El Dorado	1,442
Chase	3,408	Cottonwood Falls	774
Chautauqua	4,642	Sedan	647
Cherokee	21,549	Columbus	586
Cheyenne	4,256	Saint Francis	1,027
Clark	2,896	Ashland	983
Clay	9,890	Clay Center	635
Cloud	13,466	Concordia	711
Coffey	7,397	Burlington	617
Comanche	2,702	Coldwater	800
Cowley	35,012	Winfield	1,136
Crawford	37,850	Girard	598
Decatur	4,988	Oberlin	899
Dickinson	19,993	Abilene	855
Doniphan	9,107	Troy	388
Douglas	57,932	Lawrence	471
Edwards	4,581	Kinsley	617
Elk	3,858	Howard	647
Ellis	24,730	Hays	900
Ellsworth	6,146	Ellsworth	717
Finney	19,029	Garden City	1,301
Ford	22,587	Dodge City	1,091
Franklin	20,007	Ottawa	577
Geary	28,111	Junction City	374
Gove	2,940	Gove	1,070
Graham	4,751	Hill City	891
Grant	5,961	Ulysses	571
Gray	4,516	Cimarron	872
Greeley	1,819	Tribune	783
Greenwood	9,141	Eureka	1,133
Hamilton	2,747	Syracuse	992
Harper	7,871	Anthony	801
Harvey	27,236	Newton	540
Haskell	3,672	Sublette	580
Hodgeman	2,662	Jetmore	860
Jackson	10,342	Holton	656
Jefferson	11,945	Oskaloosa	510
Jewell	6,099	Mankato	910
Johnson	220,073	Olathe	476
Kearny	3,047	Lakin	855
Kingman	8,886	Kingman	864
Kiowa	4,088	Greensburg	720
Labette	25,775	Oswego	654
Lane	2,707	Dighton	720
Leavenworth	53,340	Leavenworth	466
Lincoln	4,582	Lincoln	725
Linn	7,770	Mound City	606
Logan	3,814	Oakley	1,073

County	Pop. Apr. 1, 1970	County Seat or Court House	Land Area Sq. Mi.	County	Pop. Apr. 1, 1970	County Seat or Court House	Land Area Sq. Mi.
Lyon	32,071	Emporia	841	Grayson	16,445	Leitchfield	496
McPherson	24,778	McPherson	896	Green	10,350	Greensburg	282
Marion	13,935	Marion	945	Greenup	33,192	Greenup	351
Marshall	13,139	Marysville	883	Hancock	7,080	Hawesville	187
Meade	4,912	Meade	979	Hardin	78,421	Elizabethtown	616
Miami	19,254	Paola	592	Harlan	37,370	Harlan	469
Mitchell	8,010	Beloit	714	Harrison	14,158	Cynthiana	308
Montgomery	39,949	Independence	628	Hart	13,980	Munfordville	420
Morris	6,432	Council Grove	697	Henderson	36,031	Henderson	433
Morton	3,576	Elkhart	728	Henry	10,910	New Castle	289
Nemaha	11,825	Seneca	708	Hickman	6,264	Clinton	246
Neosho	18,812	Erie	587	Hopkins	38,167	Madisonville	553
Ness	4,791	Ness City	1,081	Jackson	10,005	McKee	337
Norton	7,279	Norton	872	Jefferson	695,055	Louisville	375
Osage	13,352	Lyndon	707	Jessamine	17,430	Nicholasville	177
Osborne	6,416	Osborne	886	Johnson	17,539	Paintsville	264
Ottawa	6,183	Minneapolis	723	Kenton	129,440	Independence	165
Pawnee	8,484	Larned	755	Knott	14,698	Hindman	356
Phillips	7,888	Phillipsburg	897	Knox	23,689	Barbourville	373
Pottawatomie	11,755	Westmoreland	820	Larue	10,672	Hodgenville	260
Pratt	10,056	Pratt	729	Laurel	27,386	London	446
Rawlins	4,393	Atwood	1,078	Lawrence	10,726	Louisa	425
Reno	60,765	Hutchinson	1,260	Lee	6,587	Beattyville	210
Republic	8,498	Belleville	718	Leslie	11,623	Hyden	409
Rice	12,320	Lyons	725	Letcher	23,165	Whitesburg	339
Riley	56,788	Manhattan	597	Lewis	12,355	Vanceburg	486
Rooks	7,628	Stockton	886	Lincoln	16,663	Stanford	340
Rush	5,117	LaCrosse	724	Livingston	7,596	Smithland	311
Russell	9,428	Russell	867	Logan	21,793	Russellville	563
Saline	46,592	Salina	720	Lyon	5,562	Eddyville	216
Scott	5,606	Scott City	724	McCracken	58,281	Paducah	250
Sedgwick	350,694	Wichita	1,007	McCreary	12,548	Whitley City	418
Seward	16,062	Liberal	646	McLean	9,062	Calhoun	257
Shawnee	155,322	Topeka	548	Madison	42,730	Richmond	446
Sheridan	3,859	Hoxie	893	Magoffin	10,443	Salyersville	303
Sherman	7,792	Goodland	1,055	Marion	16,714	Lebanon	343
Smith	6,757	Smith Center	893	Marshall	20,381	Benton	303
Stafford	5,943	Saint John	795	Martin	9,377	Inez	231
Stanton	2,287	Johnson	676	Mason	17,273	Maysville	238
Stevens	4,198	Hugoton	731	Meade	18,796	Brandenburg	305
Sumner	23,553	Wellington	1,186	Menifee	4,050	Frenchburg	210
Thomas	7,501	Colby	1,070	Mercer	15,960	Harrodsburg	256
Trego	4,436	Wakeeney	901	Metcalfe	8,177	Edmonton	296
Wabaunsee	6,397	Alma	792	Monroe	11,642	Tompkinsville	334
Wallace	2,215	Sharon Springs	911	Montgomery	15,364	Mount Sterling	204
Washington	9,249	Washington	891	Morgan	10,019	West Liberty	369
Wichita	3,274	Leoti	724	Muhlenberg	27,537	Greenville	481
Wilson	11,317	Fredonia	574	Nelson	23,477	Bardstown	437
Woodson	4,789	Yates Center	497	Nicholas	6,508	Carlisle	204
Wyandotte	186,845	Kansas City	152	Ohio	18,790	Hartford	596
				Oldham	14,687	La Grange	184

Kentucky

(120 counties, 39,650 sq. mi. land; pop. 3,219,311)

County	Pop. Apr. 1, 1970	County Seat or Court House	Land Area Sq. Mi.
Owen	7,470	Owenton	351
Owsley	5,023	Booneville	197
Pendleton	9,949	Falmouth	279
Perry	26,259	Hazard	341
Pike	61,059	Pikeville	782
Powell	7,704	Stanton	173
Pulaski	35,234	Somerset	653
Robertson	2,163	Mount Olivet	101
Rockcastle	12,305	Mount Vernon	311
Rowan	17,010	Morehead	290
Russell	10,542	Jamestown	238
Scott	17,948	Georgetown	284
Shelby	18,999	Shelbyville	383
Simpson	13,054	Franklin	239
Spencer	5,488	Taylorsville	193
Taylor	17,138	Campbellsville	277
Todd	10,823	Elkton	376
Trigg	8,620	Cadiz	408
Trimble	5,349	Bedford	146
Union	15,882	Morganfield	340
Warren	57,884	Bowling Green	546
Washington	10,728	Springfield	307
Wayne	14,268	Monticello	440
Webster	13,282	Dixon	339
Whitley	24,145	Williamsburg	459
Wolfe	5,669	Campton	227
Woodford	14,434	Versailles	193

County	Pop. Apr. 1, 1970	County Seat or Court House	Land Area Sq. Mi.
Adair	13,037	Columbia	370
Allen	12,598	Scottsville	351
Anderson	9,358	Lawrenceburg	206
Ballard	8,276	Wickliffe	259
Barren	28,677	Glasgow	468
Bath	9,235	Owingsville	287
Bell	31,121	Pineville	370
Boone	32,812	Burlington	249
Bourbon	18,476	Paris	300
Boyd	52,376	Catlettsburg	159
Boyle	21,861	Danville	183
Bracken	7,227	Brooksville	204
Breathitt	14,221	Jackson	494
Breckinridge	14,789	Hardinsburg	554
Bullitt	26,090	Shepherdsville	300
Butler	9,723	Morgantown	443
Caldwell	13,179	Princeton	357
Calloway	27,692	Murray	384
Campbell	88,704	Alexandria	149
Carlisle	5,354	Bardwell	195
Carroll	8,523	Carrollton	130
Carter	19,850	Grayson	397
Casey	12,930	Liberty	435
Christian	56,224	Hopkinsville	725
Clark	24,090	Winchester	259
Clay	18,481	Manchester	474
Clinton	8,174	Albany	190
Crittenden	8,493	Marion	365
Cumberland	6,850	Burkesville	310
Daviess	79,486	Owensboro	462
Edmonson	8,751	Brownsville	298
Elliott	5,933	Sandy Hook	240
Estill	12,752	Irvine	260
Fayette	174,323	Lexington	280
Fleming	11,366	Flemingsburg	350
Floyd	35,889	Prestonsburg	399
Franklin	34,481	Frankfort	211
Fulton	10,183	Hickman	203
Gallatin	4,134	Warsaw	100
Garrard	9,457	Lancaster	236
Grant	9,999	Williamstown	249
Graves	30,939	Mayfield	60

Louisiana

(64 parishes, 44,930 sq. mi. land; pop. 3,643,180)

County	Pop. Apr. 1, 1970	County Seat or Court House	Land Area Sq. Mi.
Acadia	52,109	Crowley	663
Allen	20,794	Oberlin	774
Ascension	37,086	Donaldsonville	301
Assumption	19,654	Napoleonville	356
Avoyelles	37,751	Marksville	832
Beauregard	22,888	De Ridder	1,181
Bienville	16,024	Arcadia	832
Bossier	63,703	Benton	849
Caddo	230,184	Shreveport	899
Calcasieu	145,415	Lake Charles	1,105
Caldwell	9,354	Columbia	551
Cameron	8,149	Cameron	1,441
Catahoula	11,769	Harrisonburg	742

County	Pop. April 1, 1970	County Seat or Court House	Land Area Sq. Mi.
Claiborne	17,024	Homer	763
Concordia	22,578	Vidalia	718
De Soto	22,764	Mansfield	894
East Baton Rouge	285,167	Baton Rouge	459
East Carroll	12,884	Lake Providence	436
East Feliciana	17,657	Clinton	454
Evangeline	31,932	Ville Platte	669
Franklin	23,946	Winnsboro	648
Grant	13,671	Colfax	670
Iberia	57,397	New Iberia	589
Iberville	30,746	Plaquemine	627
Jackson	15,963	Jonesboro	582
Jefferson	338,229	Gretna	369
Jefferson Davis	29,554	Jennings	658
Lafayette	111,643	Lafayette	283
Lafourche	68,941	Thibodaux	1,141
La Salle	13,295	Jena	643
Lincoln	33,800	Ruston	469
Livingston	36,511	Livingston	654
Madison	15,065	Tallulah	661
Morehouse	32,463	Bastrop	804
Natchitoches	35,219	Natchitoches	1,292
Orleans	593,471	New Orleans	197
Ouachita	115,387	Monroe	638
Plaquemines	25,225	Pointe a la Hache	1,030
Pointe Coupee	22,002	New Roads	563
Rapides	118,078	Alexandria	1,318
Red River	9,226	Coushatta	406
Richland	21,774	Rayville	576
Sabine	18,638	Many	873
St. Bernard	51,185	Chalmette	514
St. Charles	29,550	Hahnville	294
St. Helena	9,937	Greensburg	420
St. James	19,733	Convent	253
St. John The Baptist	23,813	Edgard	227
St. Landry	80,364	Opelousas	932
St. Martin	32,453	Saint Martinville	736
St. Mary	60,752	Franklin	624
St. Tammany	63,585	Covington	887
Tangipahoa	65,875	Amite	808
Tensas	9,732	Saint Joseph	626
Terrebonne	76,049	Houma	1,368
Union	18,447	Farmerville	885
Vermilion	43,071	Abbeville	1,205
Vernon	53,794	Leesville	1,351
Washington	41,987	Franklinton	665
Webster	39,939	Minden	615
West Baton Rouge	16,864	Port Allen	203
West Carroll	13,028	Oak Grove	356
West Feliciana	11,376	Saint Francisville	405
Winn	16,369	Winnfield	950

Maine

(16 counties, 30,920 sq. mi. land; pop. 993,663)

County	Pop. April 1, 1970	County Seat or Court House	Land Area Sq. Mi.
Androscoggin	91,279	Auburn	474
Aroostook	94,078	Houlton	6,821
Cumberland	192,528	Portland	879
Franklin	22,444	Farmington	1,709
Hancock	34,598	Ellsworth	1,536
Kennebec	95,306	Augusta	872
Knox	29,013	Rockland	369
Lincoln	20,537	Wiscasset	454
Oxford	43,457	South Paris	2,080
Penobscot	125,393	Bangor	3,390
Piscataquis	16,285	Dover-Foxcroft	3,892
Sagadahoc	23,452	Bath	257
Somerset	40,597	Skowhegan	3,894
Waldo	23,328	Belfast	737
Washington	29,859	Machias	2,554
York	111,576	Alfred	1,001

Maryland

(23 cos., 1 ind. city, 9,891 sq. mi. land; pop. 3,922,399)

County	Pop. April 1, 1970	County Seat or Court House	Land Area Sq. Mi.
Allegany	84,044	Cumberland	428
Anne Arundel	298,042	Annapolis	423
Baltimore	620,409	Towson	598
Calvert	20,682	Prince Frederick	217
Caroline	19,781	Denton	321
Carroll	69,006	Westminster	456
Cecil	53,291	Elkton	362
Charles	47,678	La Plata	459
Dorchester	29,405	Cambridge	594
Frederick	84,927	Frederick	665
Garrett	21,476	Oakland	659
Harford	115,378	Bel Air	453
Howard	62,394	Ellicott City	251
Kent	16,146	Chestertown	281
Montgomery	522,809	Rockville	495
Prince Georges	661,082	Upper Marlboro	485
Queen Annes	18,422	Centreville	375
St. Marys	47,388	Leonardtown	373
Somerset	18,924	Princess Anne	339
Talbot	23,682	Easton	261
Washington	103,829	Hagerstown	459
Wicomico	54,236	Salisbury	381
Worcester	24,442	Snow Hill	479
Baltimore	905,787	....	78

Massachusetts

(14 counties; 7,826 sq. mi. land; pop. 5,689,170)

County	Pop. Apr. 1, 1970	County Seat or Court House	Land Area Sq. Mi.
Barnstable	96,656	Barnstable	393
Berkshire	149,402	Pittsfield	941
Bristol	444,301	Taunton	554
Dukes	6,117	Edgartown	104
Essex	637,887	Salem	494
Franklin	59,210	Greenfield	708
Hampden	459,050	Springfield	619
Hampshire	123,981	Northampton	529
Middlesex	1,397,465	Cambridge	825
Nantucket	3,774	Nantucket	46
Norfolk	604,854	Dedham	394
Plymouth	333,314	Plymouth	654
Suffolk	735,190	Boston	56
Worcester	637,037	Worcester	1,509

Michigan

(83 counties; 56,817 sq. mi. land; pop. 8,875,083)

County	Pop. Apr. 1, 1970	County Seat or Court House	Land Area Sq. Mi.
Alcona	7,113	Harrisville	678
Alger	8,568	Munising	905
Allegan	66,575	Allegan	826
Alpena	30,708	Alpena	565
Antrim	12,612	Bellaire	476
Arenac	11,149	Standish	367
Baraga	7,789	L'Anse	901
Barry	38,166	Hastings	554
Bay	117,339	Bay City	447
Benzie	8,593	Beulah	316
Berrien	163,940	Saint Joseph	580
Branch	37,906	Coldwater	506
Calhoun	141,963	Marshall	709
Cass	43,312	Cassopolis	491
Charlevoix	16,541	Charlevoix	414
Cheboygan	16,573	Cheboygan	721
Chippewa	32,412	Sault Sainte Marie	1,590
Clare	16,695	Harrison	571
Clinton	48,492	Saint Johns	572
Crawford	6,482	Grayling	561
Delta	35,924	Escanaba	1,177
Dickinson	23,753	Iron Mountain	757
Eaton	68,892	Charlotte	571
Emmet	18,331	Petoskey	461
Genesee	445,589	Flint	642
Gladwin	13,471	Gladwin	503
Gogebic	20,676	Bessemer	1,107
Grand Traverse	39,175	Traverse City	462
Gratiot	39,246	Ithaca	566
Hillsdale	37,171	Hillsdale	600
Houghton	34,652	Houghton	1,017
Huron	34,083	Bad Axe	819
Ingham	261,039	Mason	559
Ionia	45,848	Ionia	575
Iron	13,813	Crystal Falls	1,171
Isabella	44,594	Mount Pleasant	572
Jackson	143,274	Jackson	698
Kalamazoo	201,550	Kalamazoo	562
Kalkaska	5,272	Kalkaska	566
Kent	411,044	Grand Rapids	857
Keweenaw	2,264	Eagle River	538
Lake	5,661	Baldwin	571
Lapeer	52,361	Lapeer	658
Leelanau	10,872	Leland	345
Lenawee	81,951	Adrian	753
Livingston	58,967	Howell	572
Luce	6,789	Newberry	906
Mackinac	9,660	Saint Ignace	1,014
Macomb	625,309	Mount Clemens	480
Manistee	20,393	Manistee	553
Marquette	64,686	Marquette	1,828
Mason	22,612	Ludington	490
Mecosta	27,992	Big Rapids	560
Menominee	24,587	Menominee	1,038
Midland	63,769	Midland	520
Missaukee	7,126	Lake City	565
Monroe	119,172	Monroe	557
Montcalm	39,660	Stanton	712
Montmorency	5,247	Atlanta	555
Muskegon	157,426	Muskegon	501
Newaygo	27,992	White Cloud	849
Oakland	907,871	Pontiac	867
Oceana	17,984	Hart	536
Ogemaw	11,903	West Branch	571

Nebraska

(93 counties, 76,483 sq. mi. land; pop., 1,483,791)

County	Pop. Apr. 1 1970	County Seat or Court House	Land Area Sq. Mi.
Adams	30,553	Hastings	562
Antelope	9,047	Neligh	853
Arthur	606	Arthur	704
Banner	1,034	Harrisburg	738
Blaine	847	Brewster	710
Boone	8,190	Albion	683
Box Butte	10,094	Alliance	1,065
Boyd	3,752	Butte	538
Brown	4,021	Ainsworth	1,216
Buffalo	31,222	Kearney	949
Burt	9,247	Tekamah	483
Butler	9,461	David City	582
Cass	18,076	Plattsmouth	555
Cedar	12,192	Hartington	742
Chase	4,129	Imperial	890
Cherry	6,846	Valentine	5,966
Cheyenne	10,778	Sidney	1,186
Clay	8,266	Clay Center	570
Colfax	9,498	Schuyler	406
Cuming	12,034	West Point	571
Custer	14,092	Broken Bow	2,558
Dakota	13,137	Dakota City	255
Dawes	9,761	Chadron	1,386
Dawson	19,771	Lexington	975
Deuel	2,717	Chappell	436
Dixon	7,453	Ponca	475
Dodge	34,782	Fremont	528
Douglas	389,455	Omaha	335
Dundy	2,926	Benkelman	921
Fillmore	8,137	Geneva	577
Franklin	4,566	Franklin	578
Frontier	3,982	Stockville	962
Furnas	6,897	Beaver City	722
Gage	25,731	Beatrice	858
Garden	2,929	Oshkosh	1,678
Garfield	2,411	Burwell	569
Gosper	2,178	Elwood	464
Grant	1,019	Hyannis	764
Greeley	4,000	Greeley	570
Hall	42,851	Grand Island	537
Hamilton	8,867	Aurora	537
Harlan	4,357	Alma	556
Hayes	1,530	Hayes Center	711
Hitchcock	4,051	Trenton	712
Holt	12,933	O'Neil	2,405
Hooker	939	Mullen	722
Howard	6,807	Saint Paul	564
Jefferson	10,436	Fairbury	577
Johnson	5,743	Tecumseh	377
Kearney	6,707	Minden	512
Keith	8,487	Ogallala	1,032
Keya Paha	1,340	Springview	768
Kimball	6,009	Kimball	953
Knox	11,723	Center	1,107
Lancaster	167,972	Lincoln	845
Lincoln	29,538	North Platte	2,522
Logan	991	Stapleton	570
Loup	854	Taylor	574
McPherson	623	Tryon	856
Madison	27,402	Madison	572
Merrick	8,751	Central City	480
Morrill	5,813	Bridgeport	1,402
Nance	5,142	Fullerton	439
Nemaha	8,976	Auburn	400
Nuckolls	7,404	Nelson	579
Otoe	15,576	Nebraska City	619
Pawnee	4,473	Pawnee City	433
Perkins	3,423	Grant	885
Phelps	9,553	Holdrege	544
Pierce	8,493	Pierce	573
Platte	26,544	Columbus	667
Polk	6,468	Osceola	432
Red Willow	12,191	McCook	686
Richardson	12,277	Falls City	550
Rock	2,231	Bassett	1,009
Saline	12,809	Wilber	575
Sarpy	66,200	Papillion	239
Saunders	17,108	Wahoo	759
Scotts Bluff	36,432	Gering	726
Seward	14,460	Seward	571
Sheridan	7,285	Rushville	2,462
Sherman	4,725	Loup City	567
Sioux	2,034	Harrison	2,063
Stanton	5,758	Stanton	431
Thayer	7,779	Hebron	577
Thomas	954	Thedford	716
Thurston	6,942	Pender	388
Valley	5,783	Ord	569
Washington	13,310	Blair	386
Wayne	10,400	Wayne	443
Webster	5,396	Red Cloud	575
Wheeler	1,051	Bartlett	576
York	13,685	York	577

Nevada

(16 cos. 1 ind. city, 109,889 sq. mi. land; pop., 488,738)

County	Pop. Apr. 1 1970	County Seat or Court House	Land Area Sq. Mi.
Churchill	10,513	Fallon	4,883
Clark	273,288	Las Vegas	7,874
Douglas	6,882	Minden	703
Elko	13,958	Elko	17,162
Esmeralda	629	Goldfield	3,570
Eureka	948	Eureka	4,182
Humboldt	6,375	Winnemucca	9,702
Lander	2,666	Austin	5,621
Lincoln	2,557	Pioche	10,649
Lyon	8,221	Yerington	2,030
Mineral	7,051	Hawthorne	3,765
Nye	5,599	Tonopah	18,064
Pershing	2,670	Lovelock	6,001
Storey	695	Virginia City	262
Washoe	121,068	Reno	6,366
White Pine	10,150	Ely	8,904
Independent City			
Carson City	15,468	Carson City	150

New Hampshire

(10 counties, 9,027 sq. mi. land; pop., 737,681)

County	Pop. Apr. 1 1970	County Seat or Court House	Land Area Sq. Mi.
Belknap	32,367	Laconia	400
Carroll	18,548	Ossipee	938
Cheshire	52,364	Keene	715
Coos	34,291	Lancaster	1,820
Grafton	54,914	Woodsville	1,732
Hillsborough	223,941	Nashua	887
Merrimack	80,925	Concord	930
Rockingham	138,951	Exeter	691
Strafford	70,431	Dover	376
Sullivan	30,949	Newport	539

New Jersey

(21 counties, 7,521 sq. mi. land; pop. 7,168,164)

County	Pop. Apr. 1 1970	County Seat or Court House	Land Area Sq. Mi.
Atlantic	175,043	Mays Landing	569
Bergen	897,148	Hackensack	234
Burlington	323,132	Mount Holly	819
Camden	456,291	Camden	221
Cape May	59,554	Cape May Court House	267
Cumberland	121,374	Bridgeton	500
Essex	932,526	Newark	130
Gloucester	172,681	Woodbury	329
Hudson	607,839	Jersey City	47
Hunterdon	69,718	Flemington	423
Mercer	304,116	Trenton	228
Middlesex	583,813	New Brunswick	312
Monmouth	461,849	Freehold	476
Morris	383,454	Morristown	468
Ocean	208,470	Toms River	642
Passaic	460,782	Paterson	192
Salem	60,346	Salem	365
Somerset	198,372	Somerville	307
Sussex	77,528	Newton	527
Union	543,116	Elizabeth	103
Warren	73,960	Belvidere	362

New Mexico

(32 counties, 121,412 sq. mi. land; pop., 1,016,000)

County	Pop. Apr. 1 1970	County Seat or Court House	Land Area Sq. Mi.
Bernalillo	315,774	Albuquerque	1,169
Catron	2,198	Reserve	6,897
Chaves	43,335	Roswell	6,084
Colfax	12,170	Raton	3,764
Curry	39,517	Clovis	1,403
De Baca	2,547	Fort Sumner	2,356
Dona Ana	69,773	Las Cruces	3,804
Eddy	41,119	Carlsbad	4,167
Grant	22,030	Silver City	3,970
Guadalupe	4,969	Santa Rosa	2,998
Harding	1,348	Mosquero	2,134
Hidalgo	4,734	Lordsburg	3,447
Lea	49,554	Lovington	4,393
Lincoln	7,560	Carrizozo	4,858
Los Alamos	15,198	Los Alamos	108
Luna	11,706	Deming	2,957
McKinley	43,208	Gallup	5,454
Mora	4,673	Mora	1,940
Otero	41,097	Alamogordo	6,638
Quay	10,903	Tucumcari	2,875
Rio Arriba	25,170	Tierra Amarilla	5,843
Roosevelt	16,479	Portales	2,454
Sandoval	17,492	Bernalillo	3,714
San Juan	52,517	Aztec	5,500
San Miguel	21,951	Las Vegas	4,741
Santa Fe	54,774	Santa Fe	1,902
Sierra	7,189	Truth or Consequences	4,166
Socorro	9,763	Socorro	6,603
Taos	17,516	Taos	2,256

County	Pop. Apr. 1, 1970	County Seat or Court House	Land Area Sq. Mi.
Torrance	5,290	Estancia	3,346
Union	4,925	Clayton	3,816
Valencia	40,576	Los Lunas	5,656

New York

(62 counties, 47,831 sq. mi. land; pop., 18,241,266)

County	Pop. Apr. 1, 1970	County Seat or Court House	Land Area Sq. Mi.
Albany	286,742	Albany	526
Allegany	46,458	Belmon	1,047
Bronx	1,471,701	Bronx	41
Broome	221,815	Binghamton	714
Cattaraugus	81,666	Little Valley	1,318
Cayuga	77,439	Auburn	698
Chautauqua	147,305	Mayville	1,081
Chemung	101,537	Elmira	415
Chenango	46,368	Norwich	903
Clinton	72,934	Plattsburgh	1,059
Columbia	51,519	Hudson	645
Cortland	45,894	Cortland	502
Delaware	44,718	Delhi	1,443
Dutchess	222,295	Poughkeepsie	813
Erie	1,113,491	Buffalo	1,058
Essex	34,631	Elizabethtown	1,823
Franklin	43,931	Malone	1,671
Fulton	52,637	Johnstown	498
Genesee	58,722	Batavia	501
Greene	33,136	Catskill	653
Hamilton	4,714	Lake Pleasant	1,735
Herkimer	67,633	Herkimer	1,435
Jefferson	88,508	Watertown	1,294
Kings	2,602,012	Brooklyn	70
Lewis	23,644	Lowville	1,291
Livingston	54,041	Geneseo	638
Madison	62,864	Wampsville	661
Monroe	711,917	Rochester	675
Montgomery	55,883	Fonda	408
Nassau	1,428,838	Mineola	289
New York	1,539,233	New York	23
Niagara	235,720	Lockport	532
Oneida	273,037	Utica	1,223
Onondaga	472,835	Syracuse	794
Ontario	78,849	Canandaigua	651
Orange	221,657	Goshen	833
Orleans	37,305	Albion	396
Oswego	100,897	Oswego	964
Otsego	56,181	Cooperstown	1,013
Putnam	56,696	Carmel	231
Queens	1,987,174	Jamaica	108
Rensselaer	152,510	Troy	665
Richmond	295,443	Saint George	58
Rockland	229,903	New City	176
St. Lawrence	112,309	Canton	2,768
Saratoga	121,764	Ballston Spa	818
Schenectady	161,078	Schenectady	207
Schoharie	24,750	Schoharie	624
Schuyler	16,737	Watkins Glen	330
Seneca	35,083	Ovid & Waterloo	330
Steuben	99,546	Bath	1,410
Suffolk	1,127,030	Riverhead	929
Sullivan	52,580	Monticello	980
Tioga	46,513	Owego	524
Tompkins	77,064	Ithaca	482
Ulster	141,241	Kingston	1,141
Warren	49,402	Lake George	887
Washington	52,725	Hudson Falls	836
Wayne	79,404	Lyons	606
Westchester	894,406	White Plains	443
Wyoming	37,688	Warsaw	598
Yates	19,831	Penn Yan	343

North Carolina

(100 counties, 48,798 sq. mi. land; pop., 5,082,059)

County	Pop. Apr. 1, 1970	County Seat or Court House	Land Area Sq. Mi.
Alamance	96,362	Graham	428
Alexander	19,466	Taylorsville	259
Alleghany	8,134	Sparta	225
Anson	23,488	Wadesboro	533
Ashe	19,571	Jefferson	426
Avery	12,655	Newland	245
Beaufort	35,980	Washington	826
Bertie	20,528	Windsor	698
Bladen	26,477	Elizabethtown	883
Brunswick	24,223	Southport	856
Buncombe	145,056	Asheville	657
Burke	60,364	Morganton	511
Cabarrus	74,629	Concord	363
Caldwell	56,699	Lenoir	469
Camden	5,453	Camden	239
Carteret	31,603	Beaufort	536
Caswell	19,055	Yanceyville	428
Catawba	90,873	Newton	394
Chatham	29,554	Pittsboro	709
Cherokee	16,330	Murphy	452
Chowan	10,764	Edenton	173

County	Pop. Apr. 1, 1970	County Seat or Court House	Land Area Sq. Mi.
Clay	5,180	Hayesville	209
Cleveland	72,556	Shelby	468
Columbus	46,937	Whiteville	945
Craven	62,554	New Bern	699
Cumberland	212,042	Fayetteville	654
Currituck	6,976	Currituck	246
Dare	6,995	Manteo	391
Davidson	95,627	Lexington	549
Davie	18,855	Mocksville	265
Duplin	38,015	Kenansville	815
Durham	132,681	Durham	295
Edgecombe	52,341	Tarboro	510
Forsyth	215,118	Winston-Salem	419
Franklin	26,820	Louisburg	491
Gaston	148,415	Gastonia	356
Gates	8,524	Gatesville	337
Graham	6,562	Robbinsville	292
Granville	32,762	Oxford	537
Greene	14,967	Snow Hill	267
Guilford	288,645	Greensboro	655
Halifax	53,884	Halifax	734
Harnett	49,667	Lillington	603
Haywood	41,710	Waynesville	551
Henderson	42,804	Hendersonville	378
Hertford	23,529	Winton	353
Hoke	16,436	Raeford	389
Hyde	5,571	Swanquarter	613
Iredell	72,197	Statesville	572
Jackson	21,593	Sylva	491
Johnston	61,737	Smithfield	797
Jones	9,779	Trenton	467
Lee	30,467	Sanford	256
Lenoir	55,204	Kinston	400
Lincoln	32,682	Lincolnton	297
McDowell	30,648	Marion	436
Macon	15,788	Franklin	513
Madison	16,003	Marshall	450
Martin	24,730	Williamston	455
Mecklenburg	354,656	Charlotte	530
Mitchell	13,447	Bakersville	215
Montgomery	19,267	Troy	488
Moore	39,048	Carthage	704
Nash	59,122	Nashville	544
New Hanover	82,996	Wilmington	185
Northampton	24,009	Jackson	536
Onslow	103,126	Jacksonville	765
Orange	57,707	Hillsboro	400
Pamlico	9,467	Bayboro	338
Pasquotank	26,824	Elizabeth City	228
Pender	18,149	Burgaw	871
Perquimans	8,351	Hertford	246
Person	25,914	Roxboro	401
Pitt	73,900	Greenville	655
Polk	11,735	Columbus	239
Randolph	76,358	Asheboro	798
Richmond	39,889	Rockingham	475
Robeson	84,842	Lumberton	949
Rockingham	72,402	Wentworth	569
Rowan	90,035	Salisbury	523
Rutherford	47,337	Rutherfordton	563
Sampson	44,954	Clinton	945
Scotland	26,929	Laurinburg	319
Stanly	42,822	Albemarle	398
Stokes	23,782	Danbury	457
Surry	51,415	Dobson	536
Swain	8,835	Bryson City	524
Transylvania	19,713	Brevard	382
Tyrrell	3,806	Columbia	390
Union	54,714	Monroe	639
Vance	32,691	Henderson	249
Wake	229,006	Raleigh	858
Warren	15,810	Warrenton	424
Washington	14,038	Plymouth	343
Watauga	23,404	Boone	317
Wayne	85,408	Goldsboro	557
Wilkes	49,524	Wilkesboro	757
Wilson	57,486	Wilson	375
Yadkin	24,599	Yadkinville	336
Yancey	12,629	Burnsville	312

North Dakota

(53 counties, 69,273 sq. mi. land; pop., 617,761)

County	Pop. Apr. 1, 1970	County Seat or Court House	Land Area Sq. Mi.
Adams	3,832	Hettinger	989
Barnes	14,669	Valley City	1,479
Benson	8,245	Minnewaukan	1,403
Billings	1,198	Medora	1,139
Bottineau	9,496	Bottineau	1,677
Bowman	3,901	Bowman	1,170
Burke	4,739	Bowbells	1,119
Burleigh	40,714	Bismarck	1,628
Cass	73,653	Fargo	1,749
Cavalier (1973)	10,977	Langdon	1,512
Dickey	6,976	Ellendale	1,143
Divide	4,564	Crosby	1,300

County	Pop. Apr. 1, 1970	County Seat or Court House	Land Area Sq. Mi
Dunn	4,895	Manning	1,992
Eddy	4,103	New Rockford	635
Emmons	7,200	Linton	1,503
Foster	4,832	Carrington	645
Golden Valley	2,611	Beach	1,014
Grand Forks	61,102	Grand Forks	1,438
Grant	5,009	Carson	1,666
Griggs	4,184	Cooperstown	710
Hettinger	5,075	Mott	1,134
Kidder	4,362	Steele	1,358
La Moure	7,117	La Moure	1,136
Logan	4,245	Napoleon	1,001
McHenry	8,977	Towner	1,879
McIntosh	5,545	Ashley	992
McKenzie	6,127	Watford City	2,735
McLean	11,251	Washburn	2,065
Mercer	6,175	Stanton	1,042
Morton	20,310	Mandan	1,920
Mountrail	8,437	Stanley	1,819
Nelson	5,807	Lakota	995
Oliver	2,322	Center	721
Pembina	10,728	Cavalier	1,124
Pierce	6,323	Rugby	1,038
Ramsey	12,915	Devils Lake	1,248
Ransom	7,102	Lisbon	861
Renville	3,828	Mohall	886
Richland	18,089	Wahpeton	1,449
Rolette	11,549	Rolla	913
Sargent	5,937	Forman	853
Sheridan	3,232	McClusky	989
Sioux	3,632	Fort Yates	1,103
Slope	1,484	Amidon	1,225
Stark	19,613	Dickinson	1,316
Steele	3,749	Finley	710
Stutsman	23,550	Jamestown	2,264
Towner	4,645	Cando	1,043
Traill	9,571	Hillsboro	861
Walsh	16,251	Grafton	1,286
Ward	58,560	Minot	2,044
Wells	7,847	Fessenden	1,299
Williams	19,301	Williston	2,064

Ohio

(88 counties, 40,975 sq. mi. land; pop., 10,652,017)

County	Pop. Apr. 1, 1970	County Seat or Court House	Land Area Sq. Mi
Adams	18,957	West Union	587
Allen	111,144	Lima	410
Ashland	43,303	Ashland	424
Ashtabula	98,237	Jefferson	700
Athens	55,747	Athens	504
Auglaize	38,602	Wapakoneta	400
Belmont	80,917	Saint Clairsville	534
Brown	26,635	Georgetown	490
Butler	226,207	Hamilton	471
Carroll	21,579	Carrollton	390
Champaign	30,491	Urbana	432
Clark	157,115	Springfield	402
Clermont	95,887	Batavia	458
Clinton	31,464	Wilmington	410
Columbiana	108,310	Lisbon	534
Coshocton	33,486	Coshocton	562
Crawford	50,364	Bucyrus	404
Cuyahoga	1,720,835	Cleveland	456
Darke	49,141	Greenville	605
Defiance	36,949	Defiance	412
Delaware	42,908	Delaware	450
Erie	75,909	Sandusky	264
Fairfield	73,301	Lancaster	505
Fayette	25,461	Washington, C. H.	404
Franklin	833,249	Columbus	538
Fulton	33,071	Wauseon	407
Gallia	25,239	Gallipolis	471
Geauga	62,977	Chardon	407
Greene	125,057	Xenia	415
Guernsey	37,665	Cambridge	528
Hamilton	923,205	Cincinnati	414
Hancock	61,217	Findlay	532
Hardin	30,813	Kenton	467
Harrison	17,013	Cadiz	401
Henry	27,058	Napoleon	416
Highland	28,996	Hillsboro	549
Hocking	20,322	Logan	421
Holmes	23,024	Millersburg	424
Huron	49,587	Norwalk	497
Jackson	27,174	Jackson	419
Jefferson	96,193	Steubenville	411
Knox	41,795	Mount Vernon	531
Lake	197,200	Painesville	231
Lawrence	56,868	Ironton	456
Licking	107,799	Newark	686
Logan	35,072	Bellefontaine	460
Lorain	256,843	Elyria	495
Lucas	483,594	Toledo	343
Madison	28,318	London	463
Mahoning	304,545	Youngstown	415
Marion	64,724	Marion	405

County	Pop. Apr. 1, 1970	County Seat or Court House	Land Area Sq. Mi
Medina	82,717	Medina	425
Meigs	19,799	Pomeroy	436
Mercer	35,558	Celina	444
Miami	84,342	Troy	407
Monroe	15,739	Woodsfield	456
Montgomery	608,413	Dayton	459
Morgan	12,375	McConnelsville	420
Morrow	21,348	Mount Gilead	403
Muskingum	77,826	Zanesville	651
Noble	10,428	Caldwell	398
Ottawa	37,099	Port Clinton	261
Paulding	19,329	Paulding	417
Perry	27,434	New Lexington	410
Pickaway	40,071	Circleville	504
Pike	19,114	Waverly	443
Portage	125,868	Ravenna	495
Preble	34,719	Eaton	427
Putnam	31,134	Ottawa	486
Richland	129,997	Mansfield	496
Ross	61,211	Chillicothe	687
Sandusky	60,983	Fremont	409
Scioto	76,951	Portsmouth	608
Seneca	60,696	Tiffin	551
Shelby	37,748	Sidney	408
Stark	372,210	Canton	576
Summit	553,371	Akron	408
Trumbull	232,579	Warren	608
Tuscarawas	77,211	New Philadelphia	569
Union	23,786	Marysville	434
Van Wert	29,194	Van Wert	409
Vinton	9,420	McArthur	411
Warren	85,505	Lebanon	408
Washington	57,160	Marietta	641
Wayne	87,123	Wooster	561
Williams	33,669	Bryan	421
Wood	89,722	Bowling Green	619
Wyandot	21,826	Upper Sandusky	406

Oklahoma

(77 counties, 68,782 sq. mi. land; pop., 2,559,253)

County	Pop. Apr. 1, 1970	County Seat or Court House	Land Area Sq. Mi
Adair	15,141	Stillwell	570
Alfalfa	7,224	Cherokee	868
Atoka	10,972	Atoka	991
Beaver	6,282	Beaver	1,790
Beckham	15,754	Sayre	907
Blaine	11,794	Watonga	917
Bryan	25,552	Durant	889
Caddo	28,931	Anadarko	1,272
Canadian	32,245	El Reno	897
Carter	37,349	Ardmore	830
Cherokee	23,174	Tahlequah	756
Choctaw	15,141	Hugo	778
Cimarron	4,145	Boise City	1,843
Cleveland	81,839	Norman	527
Coal	5,525	Coalgate	526
Comanche	108,144	Lawton	1,084
Cotton	6,832	Walters	651
Craig	14,722	Vinita	764
Creek	45,532	Sapulpa	936
Custer	22,665	Arapaho	980
Delaware	17,767	Jay	707
Dewey	5,656	Taloga	1,018
Ellis	5,129	Arnett	1,242
Garfield	56,343	Enid	1,054
Garvin	24,874	Pauls Valley	814
Grady	29,354	Chickasha	1,096
Grant	7,117	Medford	1,007
Greer	7,979	Mangum	633
Harmon	5,136	Hollis	545
Harper	5,151	Buffalo	1,041
Haskell	9,578	Stigler	602
Hughes	13,228	Holdenville	807
Jackson	30,902	Altus	810
Jefferson	7,125	Waurika	780
Johnston	7,870	Tishomingo	638
Kay	48,791	Newkirk	950
Kingfisher	12,857	Kingfisher	904
Kiowa	12,532	Hobart	1,027
Latimer	8,601	Wilburton	737
Le Flore	32,137	Poteau	1,560
Lincoln	19,482	Chandler	973
Logan	19,645	Guthrie	751
Love	5,637	Marietta	513
McClain	14,157	Purcell	573
McCurtain	28,642	Idabel	1,800
McIntosh	12,472	Eufaula	608
Major	7,529	Fairview	963
Marshall	7,682	Madill	366
Mayes	23,302	Pryor	648
Murray	10,669	Sulphur	423
Muskogee	59,542	Muskogee	818
Noble	10,043	Perry	743
Nowata	9,773	Nowata	537
Okfuskee	10,683	Okemah	637
Oklahoma	527,717	Oklahoma City	700

County	Pop. Apr. 1, 1970	County Seat or Court House	Land Area Sq. Mi.
Okmulgee	35,358	Okmulgee	700
Osage	29,750	Pawhuska	2,272
Ottawa	29,800	Miami	464
Pawnee	11,338	Pawnee	61
Payne	50,654	Stillwater	694
Pittsburg	37,521	McAlester	1,241
Pontotoc	27,867	Ada	714
Pottawatomie	43,134	Shawnee	794
Pushmataha	9,385	Antlers	1,420
Roger Mills	4,452	Cheyenne	1,140
Rogers	28,425	Claremore	685
Seminole	25,144	Wewoka	630
Sequoyah	23,370	Sallisaw	696
Stephens	35,902	Duncan	891
Texas	16,352	Guymon	2,062
Tillman	12,901	Frederick	901
Tulsa	399,982	Tulsa	573
Wagoner	22,163	Wagoner	563
Washington	42,302	Bartlesville	424
Washita	12,141	Cordell	1,009
Woods	11,920	Alva	1,298
Woodward	15,537	Woodward	1,251

Oregon

(36 counties, 96,184 sq. mi. land; pop., 2,091,385)

County	Pop. Apr. 1, 1970	County Seat or Court House	Land Area Sq. Mi.
Baker	14,919	Baker	3,068
Benton	53,776	Corvallis	668
Clackamas	166,088	Oregon City	1,884
Clatsop	28,473	Astoria	805
Columbia	28,790	Saint Helens	639
Coos	56,515	Coquille	1,604
Crook	9,985	Prineville	2,975
Curry	13,006	Gold Beach	1,627
Deschutes	30,442	Bend	3,031
Douglas	71,743	Roseburg	5,063
Gilliam	2,342	Condon	1,208
Grant	6,996	Canyon City	4,530
Harney	7,215	Burns	10,166
Hood River	13,187	Hood River	523
Jackson	94,533	Medford	2,812
Jefferson	8,548	Madras	1,793
Josephine	35,746	Grants Pass	1,625
Klamath	50,021	Klamath Falls	5,970
Lake	6,343	Lakeview	8,231
Lane	215,401	Eugene	4,552
Lincoln	25,755	Newport	986
Linn	71,914	Albany	2,283
Malheur	23,169	Vale	9,859
Marion	151,309	Salem	1,166
Morrow	4,465	Heppner	2,060
Multnomah	554,668	Portland	423
Polk	35,349	Dallas	736
Sherman	2,139	Moro	830
Tillamook	18,034	Tillamook	1,115
Umatilla	44,923	Pendleton	3,227
Union	19,377	La Grande	2,032
Wallowa	6,247	Enterprise	3,178
Wasco	20,133	The Dalles	2,381
Washington	157,920	Hillsboro	716
Wheeler	1,849	Fossil	1,707
Yamhill	40,213	McMinnville	711

Pennsylvania

(67 counties, 44,966 sq. mi. land; pop., 11,793,909)

County	Pop. Apr. 1, 1970	County Seat or Court House	Land Area Sq. Mi.
Adams	56,937	Gettysburg	526
Allegheny	1,605,133	Pittsburgh	728
Armstrong	75,590	Kittanning	652
Beaver	208,418	Beaver	440
Bedford (1973)	43,278	Bedford	1,018
Berks	296,382	Reading	862
Blair	135,356	Hollidaysburg	530
Bradford	57,962	Towanda	1,148
Bucks	416,728	Doylestown	614
Butler	127,941	Butler	794
Cambria	186,785	Ebensburg	692
Cameron	7,096	Emporium	401
Carbon	50,573	Jim Thorpe	404
Centre	99,267	Bellefonte	1,115
Chester	277,746	West Chester	761
Clarion	38,414	Clarion	597
Clearfield	74,619	Clearfield	1,139
Clinton	37,721	Lock Haven	889
Columbia	55,114	Bloomsburg	484
Crawford	81,342	Meadville	1,012
Cumberland	158,177	Carlisle	555
Dauphin	223,713	Harrisburg	518
Delaware	601,715	Media	184
Elk	37,770	Ridgeway	807
Erie	263,654	Erie	813
Fayette	154,667	Uniontown	802
Forest	4,926	Tionesta	419
Franklin	100,833	Chambersburg	754
Fulton	10,776	McConnellsburg	435
Greene	36,090	Waynesburg	578
Huntingdon	39,108	Huntingdon	895
Indiana	79,451	Indiana	825
Jefferson	43,695	Brookville	652
Juniata	16,712	Mifflintown	386
Lackawanna	234,107	Scranton	454
Lancaster	320,079	Lancaster	946
Lawrence	107,374	New Castle	367
Lebanon	99,665	Lebanon	363
Lehigh	255,304	Allentown	348
Luzerne	342,329	Wilkes-Barre	886
Lycoming	113,296	Williamsport	1,216
McKean	51,915	Smethport	992
Mercer	127,225	Mercer	670
Mifflin	45,268	Lewistown	431
Monroe	45,422	Stroudsburg	611
Montgomery	623,956	Norristown	496
Montour	16,508	Danville	130
Northampton	214,545	Easton	376
Northumberland	99,190	Sunbury	453
Perry	28,615	New Bloomfield	551
Philadelphia	1,949,996	Philadelphia	129
Pike	11,818	Milford	542
Potter	16,395	Coudersport	1,092
Schuylkill	160,089	Pottsville	784
Snyder	29,269	Middleburg	327
Somerset	76,037	Somerset	1,078
Sullivan	5,961	Laporte	478
Susquehanna	34,344	Montrose	833
Tioga	39,691	Wellsboro	1,146
Union	28,603	Lewisburg	318
Venango	62,353	Franklin	678
Warren	47,682	Warren	905
Washington	210,876	Washington	857
Wayne	29,581	Honesdale	741
Westmoreland	376,935	Greensburg	1,024
Wyoming	19,082	Tunkhannock	398
York	272,603	York	909

Rhode Island

(5 counties, 1,049 sq. mi. land; pop., 949,723)

County	Pop. Apr. 1, 1970	County Seat or Court House	Land Area Sq. Mi.
Bristol	45,937	Bristol	25
Kent	142,382	East Greenwich	173
Newport	94,228	Newport	115
Providence	581,470	Providence	416
Washington	85,706	West Kingston	321

South Carolina

(46 counties, 30,225 sq. mi. land; pop., 2,590,516)

County	Pop. Apr. 1, 1970	County Seat or Court House	Land Area Sq. Mi.
Abbeville	21,112	Abbeville	506
Aiken	91,023	Aiken	1,087
Allendale	9,783	Allendale	418
Anderson	105,474	Anderson	749
Bamberg	15,950	Bamberg	395
Barnwell	17,176	Barnwell	553
Beaufort	51,136	Beaufort	579
Berkeley	56,199	Moncks Corner	1,110
Calhoun	10,780	Saint Matthews	377
Charleston	247,650	Charleston	939
Cherokee	36,791	Gaffney	394
Chester	29,811	Chester	584
Chesterfield	33,667	Chesterfield	790
Clarendon	25,604	Manning	599
Colleton	27,622	Walterboro	1,049
Darlington	53,442	Darlington	543
Dillon	28,838	Dillon	407
Dorchester	32,276	Saint George	569
Edgefield	15,692	Edgefield	482
Fairfield	19,999	Winnsboro	696
Florence	89,636	Florence	805
Georgetown	33,500	Georgetown	812
Greenville	240,774	Greenville	792
Greenwood	49,686	Greenwood	446
Hampton	15,878	Hampton	562
Horry	69,992	Conway	1,154
Jasper	11,885	Ridgeland	652
Kershaw	34,727	Camden	781
Lancaster	43,328	Lancaster	502
Laurens	49,713	Laurens	711
Lee	18,323	Bishopville	409
Lexington	89,012	Lexington	717
McCormick	7,955	McCormick	360
Marion	30,270	Marion	487
Marlboro	27,151	Bennettsville	483
Newberry	29,273	Newberry	635
Oconee	40,728	Walhalla	654
Orangeburg	69,789	Orangeburg	1,106
Pickens	58,956	Pickens	492
Richland	233,868	Columbia	748
Saluda	14,528	Saluda	458
Spartanburg	173,724	Spartanburg	831
Sumter	79,425	Sumter	672
Union	29,230	Union	514

County	Pop. Apr. 1, 1970	County Seat or Court House	Land Area Sq. Mi.
Williamsburg	34,243	Kingstree	935
York	85,216	York	684

South Dakota
(67 counties, 75,955 sq. mi. land; pop., 666,257)

County	Pop. Apr. 1, 1970	County Seat or Court House	Land Area Sq. Mi.
Aurora	4,183	Plankinton	709
Beadle	20,877	Huron	1,259
Bennett	3,088	Martin	1,181
Bon Homme	8,577	Tyndall	560
Brookings	22,158	Brookings	800
Brown	36,920	Aberdeen	1,674
Brule	5,870	Chamberlain	818
Buffalo	1,739	Gannvalley	482
Butte	7,825	Belle Fourche	2,250
Campbell	2,866	Mound City	732
Charles Mix	9,994	Lake Andes	1,097
Clark	5,515	Clark	964
Clay	12,923	Vermillion	405
Codington	19,140	Watertown	687
Corson	4,994	McIntosh	2,470
Custer	4,698	Custer	1,557
Davison	17,319	Mitchell	432
Day	8,713	Webster	1,030
Deuel	5,686	Clear Lake	639
Dewey	5,170	Timber Lake	2,351
Douglas	4,569	Armour	435
Edmunds	5,548	Ipswich	1,154
Fall River	7,505	Hot Springs	1,743
Faulk	3,893	Faulkton	996
Grant	9,005	Milbank	681
Gregory	6,710	Burke	997
Haakon	2,802	Philip	1,816
Hamlin	5,520	Hayti	511
Hand	5,883	Miller	1,432
Hanson	3,781	Alexandria	430
Harding	1,855	Buffalo	2,682
Hughes	11,632	Pierre	748
Hutchinson	10,379	Olivet	815
Hyde	2,515	Highmore	863
Jackson	1,531	Kadoka	808
Jerauld	3,310	Wessington Spgs.	527
Jones	1,882	Murdo	973
Kingsbury	7,657	De Smet	818
Lake	11,456	Madison	567
Lawrence	17,453	Deadwood	800
Lincoln	11,761	Canton	576
Lyman	4,060	Kennebec	1,683
McCook	7,246	Salem	575
McPherson	5,022	Leola	1,147
Marshall	5,965	Britton	848
Meade	17,020	Sturgis	3,465
Mellette	2,420	White River	1,306
Miner	4,454	Howard	570
Minnehaha	95,209	Sioux Falls	813
Moody	7,622	Flandreau	523
Pennington	59,349	Rapid City	2,779
Perkins	4,769	Bison	2,860
Potter	4,449	Gettysburg	869
Roberts	11,678	Sisseton	1,108
Sanborn	3,697	Woonsocket	570
Shannon	8,198	(Attached to Fall River)	2,100
Spink	10,595	Redfield	1,505
Stanley	2,457	Fort Pierre	1,414
Sully	2,362	Onida	1,004
Todd	6,606	(Attached to Tripp)	1,388
Tripp	8,171	Winner	1,620
Turner	9,872	Parker	612
Union	9,643	Elk Point	452
Walworth	7,842	Selby	718
Washabaugh	1,389	(Attached to Jackson)	1,061
Yankton	19,039	Yankton	519
Zeibach	2,221	Dupree	1,981

Tennessee
(95 counties, 41,328 sq. mi. land; pop., 3,924,164)

County	Pop. Apr. 1, 1970	County Seat or Court House	Land Area Sq. Mi.
Anderson	60,300	Clinton	335
Bedford	25,039	Shelbyville	482
Benton	12,126	Camden	392
Bledsoe	7,643	Pikeville	404
Blount	63,744	Maryville	575
Bradley	50,686	Cleveland	334
Campbell	26,045	Jacksboro	451
Cannon	8,467	Woodbury	271
Carroll	25,741	Huntingdon	596
Carter	42,259	Elizabethton	348
Cheatham	13,199	Ashland City	305
Chester	9,927	Henderson	285
Claiborne	19,420	Tazewell	444
Clay	6,624	Celina	233
Cocke	25,283	Newport	424
Coffee	32,572	Manchester	434

County	Pop. Apr. 1, 1970	County Seat or Court House	Land Area Sq. Mi.
Crockett	14,402	Alamo	269
Cumberland	20,733	Crossville	678
Davidson	447,877	Nashville	508
Decatur	9,457	Decaturville	337
De Kalb	11,151	Smithville	278
Dickson	21,977	Charlotte	485
Dyer	30,427	Dyersburg	529
Fayette	22,692	Somerville	704
Fentress	12,593	Jamestown	498
Franklin	27,289	Winchester	553
Gibson	47,871	Trenton	607
Giles	22,138	Pulaski	619
Grainger	13,948	Rutledge	282
Greene	47,630	Greeneville	613
Grundy	10,631	Altamont	358
Hamblen	38,696	Morristown	155
Hamilton	255,077	Chattanooga	550
Hancock	6,719	Sneedville	230
Hardeman	22,435	Bolivar	656
Hardin	18,212	Savannah	587
Hawkins	33,757	Rogersville	480
Haywood	19,596	Brownsville	519
Henderson	17,360	Lexington	515
Henry	23,749	Paris	567
Hickman	12,096	Centerville	610
Houston	5,853	Erin	201
Humphreys	13,560	Waverly	530
Jackson	8,141	Gainesboro	323
Jefferson	24,940	Dandridge	274
Johnson	11,569	Mountain City	293
Knox	276,293	Knoxville	508
Lake	8,074	Tiptonville	167
Lauderdale	20,271	Ripley	477
Laarence	29,097	Lawrenceburg	634
Lewis	6,761	Hohenwald	285
Lincoln	24,318	Fayetteville	580
Loudon	24,266	Loudon	237
McMinn	35,462	Athens	432
McNairy	18,369	Selmer	569
Macon	12,315	Lafayette	304
Madison	65,774	Jackson	560
Marion	20,577	Jasper	506
Marshall	17,319	Lewisburg	377
Maury	44,(.3	Columbia	614
Meigs	5,219	Decatur	191
Monroe	23,475	Madisonville	660
Montgomery	62,721	Clarksville	539
Moore	3,568	Lynchburg	124
Morgan	13,619	Wartburg	539
Obion	30,247	Union City	556
Overton	14,866	Livingston	441
Perry	5,238	Linden	411
Pickett	3,774	Byrdstown	158
Polk	11,669	Benton	434
Putnam	35,487	Cookeville	405
Rhea	17,202	Dayton	312
Roane	38,881	Kingston	350
Robertson	29,102	Springfield	476
Rutherford	59,428	Murfreesboro	612
Scott	14,762	Huntsville	544
Sequatchie	6,331	Dunlap	273
Sevier	28,241	Sevierville	597
Shelby	722,111	Memphis	755
Smith	12,509	Carthage	325
Stewart	7,319	Dover	470
Sullivan	127,329	Blountville	413
Sumner	56,266	Gallatin	534
Tipton	28,001	Covington	459
Trousdale	5,155	Hartsville	114
Unicoi	15,254	Erwin	185
Union	9,072	Maynardville	212
Van Buren	3,758	Spencer	254
Warren	26,972	McMinnville	439
Washington	73,924	Jonesboro	323
Wayne	12,365	Waynesboro	739
Weakley	28,827	Dresden	576
White	16,329	Sparta	382
Williamson	34,423	Franklin	593
Wilson	36,999	Lebanon	567

Texas
(254 counties, 262,134 sq. mi. land; pop., 11,196,730)

County	Pop. Apr. 1, 1970	County Seat or Court House	Land Area Sq. Mi.
Anderson	27,789	Palestine	1,072
Andrews	10,372	Andrews	1,504
Angelina	49,349	Lufkin	738
Aransas	8,902	Rockport	275
Archer	5,759	Archer City	913
Armstrong	1,895	Claude	907
Atascosa	18,696	Jourdanton	1,206
Austin	13,831	Bellville	663
Bailey	8,487	Muleshoe	835
Bandera	4,747	Bandera	763
Bastrop	17,297	Bastrop	890
Baylor	5,221	Seymour	845
Bee	22,737	Beeville	842

County	Pop. Apr. 1, 1970	County Seat or Court House	Land Area Sq. Mi.	County	Pop. Apr. 1, 1970	County Seat or Court House	Land Area Sq. Mi.
Bell	124,483	Belton	1,047	Hood	6,368	Granbury	426
Bexar	830,460	San Antonio	1,246	Hopkins	20,710	Sulphur Springs	793
Blanco	3,567	Johnson City	719	Houston	17,855	Crockett	1,237
Borden	888	Gail	907	Howard	37,796	Big Spring	911
Bosque	10,966	Meridian	990	Hudspeth	2,392	Sierra Blanca	4,554
Bowie	67,813	Boston	891	Hunt	47,948	Greenville	826
Brazoria	108,312	Angleton	1,423	Hutchinson	24,443	Stinnett	875
Brazos	57,978	Bryan	586	Irion	1,070	Mertzon	1,073
Breaster	7,780	Alpine	6,204	Jack	6,711	Jacksboro	945
Briscoe	2,794	Silverton	874	Jackson	12,975	Edna	850
Brooks	8,005	Falfurrias	904	Jasper	24,692	Jasper	907
Brown	25,877	Brownwood	938	Jeff Davis	1,527	Fort Davis	2,259
Burleson	9,999	Caldwell	670	Jefferson	246,402	Beaumont	951
Burnet	11,420	Burnet	996	Jim Hogg	4,654	Hebbronville	1,143
Caldwell	21,178	Lockhart	544	Jim Wells	33,032	Alice	845
Calhoun	17,831	Port Lavanca	527	Johnson	45,769	Cleburne	740
Callahan	8,205	Baird	856	Jones	16,106	Anson	956
Cameron	140,368	Brownsville	896	Karnes	13,462	Karnes City	758
Camp	8,005	Pittsburg	192	Kaufman	32,392	Kaufman	815
Carson	6,358	Panhandle	900	Kendall	6,964	Boerne	670
Cass	24,133	Linden	941	Kenedy	678	Sarita	1,394
Castro	10,394	Dimmitt	880	Kent	1,434	Jayton	880
Chambers	12,187	Anahuac	616	Kerr	19,454	Kerrville	1,101
Cherokee	32,008	Rusk	1,049	Kimble	3,904	Junction	1,274
Childress	6,605	Childress	699	King	464	Guthrie	944
Clay	8,079	Henrietta	1,102	Kinney	2,006	Brackettville	1,393
Cochran	5,326	Morton	783	Kleberg	33,166	Kingsville	851
Coke	3,087	Robert Lee	911	Knox	5,972	Benjamin	851
Coleman	10,288	Coleman	1,280	Lamar	36,062	Paris	984
Collin	66,920	McKinney	836	Lamb	17,770	Littlefield	1,022
Collingsworth	4,755	Wellington	894	Lampasas	9,323	Lampasas	726
Colorado	17,638	Columbus	949	La Salle	5,014	Cotulla	1,500
Comal	24,165	New Braunfels	567	Lavaca	17,903	Hallettsville	975
Comanche	11,898	Comanche	944	Lee	8,048	Giddings	637
Concho	2,937	Paint Rock	1,004	Leon	8,738	Centerville	1,102
Cooke	23,471	Gainesville	985	Liberty	33,014	Liberty	1,180
Coryell	35,311	Gatesville	1,043	Limestone	18,100	Groesbeck	931
Cottle	3,204	Paducah	900	Lipscomb	3,486	Lipscomb	934
Crane	4,172	Crane	795	Live Oak	6,697	George West	1,055
Crockett	3,885	Ozona	2,794	Llano	6,979	Llano	941
Crosby	9,085	Crosbyton	911	Loving	164	Mentone	648
Culberson	3,429	Van Horn	3,851	Lubbock	179,295	Lubbock	893
Dallam	6,012	Dalhart	1,494	Lynn	9,107	Tahoka	915
Dallas	1,327,695	Dallas	859	McCulloch	8,571	Brady	1,066
Dawson	16,604	Lamesa	902	McLennan	147,553	Waco	1,000
Deaf Smith	18,999	Hereford	1,510	McMullen	1,095	Tilden	1,159
Delta	4,927	Cooper	276	Madison	7,693	Madisonville	480
Denton	75,633	Denton	911	Marion	8,517	Jefferson	380
Dewitt	18,660	Cuero	910	Martin	4,774	Stanton	911
Dickens	3,737	Dickens	931	Mason	3,356	Mason	935
Dimmit	9,039	Carrizo Springs	1,344	Matagorda	27,913	Bay City	1,157
Donley	3,641	Clarendon	905	Maverick	18,093	Eagle Pass	1,289
Duval	11,722	San Diego	1,814	Medina	20,249	Hondo	1,352
Eastland	18,092	Eastland	952	Menard	2,646	Menard	914
Ector	91,805	Odessa	907	Midland	65,433	Midland	939
Edwards	2,107	Rocksprings	2,076	Milam	20,028	Cameron	1,028
Ellis	46,638	Waxahachie	940	Mills	4,212	Goldthwaite	734
El Paso	359,291	El Paso	1,057	Mitchell	9,073	Colorado City	920
Erath	18,141	Stephenville	1,085	Montague	15,326	Montague	932
Falls	17,300	Marlin	764	Montgomery	49,479	Conroe	1,090
Fannin	22,705	Bonham	905	Moore	14,060	Dumas	909
Fayette	17,650	La Grange	934	Morris	12,310	Daingerfield	260
Fisher	6,344	Roby	904	Motley	2,178	Matador	980
Floyd	11,044	Floydada	993	Nacogdoches	36,362	Nacogdoches	902
Foard	2,211	Crowell	676	Navarro	31,150	Corsicana	1,070
Fort Bend	52,314	Richmond	869	Newton	11,657	Newton	949
Franklin	5,291	Mount Vernon	293	Nolan	16,220	Sweetwater	922
Freestone	11,116	Fairfield	865	Nueces	237,544	Corpus Christi	841
Frio	11,159	Pearsall	1,116	Orchiltree	9,704	Perryton	907
Gaines	11,593	Seminole	1,489	Oldham	2,258	Vega	1,478
Galveston	169,812	Galveston	399	Orange	71,170	Orange	359
Garza	5,289	Post	914	Palo Pinto	28,962	Palo Pinto	948
Gillespie	10,553	Fredericksburg	1,055	Panola	15,894	Carthage	869
Glasscock	1,155	Garden City	863	Parker	33,888	Weatherford	903
Goliad	4,869	Goliad	871	Parmer	10,509	Farwell	859
Gonzales	16,375	Gonzales	1,056	Pecos	13,748	Fort Stockton	4,740
Gray	26,949	Pampa	934	Polk	14,457	Livingston	1,100
Grayson	83,225	Sherman	940	Potter	90,511	Amarillo	898
Gregg	75,929	Longview	282	Presidio	4,842	Marfa	3,892
Grimes	11,855	Anderson	801	Rains	3,752	Emory	210
Guadalupe	33,554	Seguin	714	Randall	53,885	Canyon	914
Hale	34,137	Plainview	979	Reagan	3,239	Big Lake	1,132
Hall	6,015	Memphis	885	Real	2,013	Leakey	622
Hamilton	7,198	Hamilton	844	Red River	14,298	Clarksville	1,033
Hansford	6,351	Spearman	907	Reeves	16,526	Pecos	2,608
Hardeman	6,795	Quanah	687	Refugio	9,494	Refugio	774
Hardin	29,996	Kountze	897	Roberts	967	Miami	899
Harris	1,741,912	Houston	1,723	Robertson	14,389	Franklin	877
Harrison	44,841	Marshall	894	Rockwall	7,046	Rockwall	147
Hartley	2,782	Channing	1,488	Runnels	12,108	Ballinger	1,058
Haskell	8,512	Haskell	877	Rusk	34,102	Henderson	939
Hays	27,642	San Marcos	650	Sabine	7,187	Hemphill	456
Hemphill	3,084	Canadian	904	San Augustine	7,858	San Augustine	473
Henderson	26,466	Athens	943	San Jacinto	6,702	Coldspring	624
Hidalgo	181,535	Edinburg	1,543	San Patricio	47,288	Sinton	685
Hill	22,596	Hillsboro	1,010	San Saba	5,540	San Saba	1,120
Hockley	20,396	Levelland	908	Schleicher	2,277	Eldorado	1,331

County	Pop. Apr. 1, 1970	County Seat or Court House	Land Area Sq. Mi.
Scurry	15,760	Snyder	904
Shackelford	3,323	Albany	887
Shelby	19,672	Center	778
Sherman	3,657	Stratford	916
Smith	97,096	Tyler	934
Somervell	2,793	Glen Rose	197
Starr	17,707	Rio Grande City	1,211
Stephens	8,414	Breckenridge	899
Sterling	1,056	Sterling City	914
Stonewall	2,397	Aspermont	926
Sutton	3,175	Sonora	1,493
Swisher	10,373	Tulia	896
Tarrant	716,317	Fort Worth	861
Taylor	97,853	Abilene	912
Terrell	1,940	Sanderson	2,391
Terry	14,118	Brownfield	899
Throckmorton	2,205	Throckmorton	920
Titus	16,702	Mount Pleasant	418
Tom Green	71,047	San Angelo	1,500
Travis	295,516	Austin	1,012
Trinity	7,628	Groveton	707
Tyler	12,417	Woodville	919
Upshur	20,976	Gilmer	584
Upton	4,697	Rankin	1,312
Uvalde	17,348	Uvalde	1,588
Val Verde	27,471	Del Rio	3,241
Van Zandt	22,155	Canton	845
Victoria	53,766	Victoria	892
Walker	27,680	Huntsville	790
Waller	14,285	Hempstead	509
Ward	13,019	Monahans	827
Washington	18,842	Brenham	594
Webb	72,859	Laredo	3,306
Wharton	36,729	Wharton	1,076
Wheeler	6,434	Wheeler	914
Wichita	120,563	Wichita Falls	611
Wilbarger	15,355	Vernon	952
Willacy	15,570	Raymondville	591
Williamson	37,305	Georgetown	1,104
Wilson	13,041	Floresville	802
Winkler	9,640	Kermit	887
Wise	19,687	Decatur	922
Wood	18,589	Quitman	721
Yoakum	7,344	Plains	830
Young	15,400	Graham	888
Zapata	4,352	Zapata	957
Zavala	11,370	Crystal City	1,291

Utah

(29 counties, 82,096 sq. mi. land; pop. 1,059,273)

County	Pop. Apr. 1, 1970	County Seat or Court House	Land Area Sq. Mi.
Beaver	3,800	Beaver	2,584
Box Elder	28,129	Brigham City	5,603
Cache	42,331	Logan	1,174
Carbon	15,647	Price	1,476
Daggett	666	Manila	682
Davis	99,028	Farmington	297
Duchesne	7,299	Duchesne	3,255
Emery	5,137	Castle Dale	4,439
Garfield	3,157	Panguitch	5,158
Grand	6,688	Moab	3,682
Iron	12,177	Parowan	3,300
Juab	4,574	Nkephi	3,412
Kane	2,421	Kanab	3,904
Millard	6,988	Fillmore	6,793
Morgan	3,983	Morgan	603
Piute	1,164	Junction	754
Rich	1,615	Randolph	1,023
Salt Lake	458,607	Salt Lake City	764
San Juan	9,606	Monticello	7,707
Sanpete	10,976	Manti	1,597
Sevier	10,103	Richfield	1,929
Summit	5,879	Coalville	1,849
Tooele	21,545	Tooele	6,923
Uintah	12,684	Vernal	4,487
Utah	137,776	Provo	2,014
Wasatch	5,863	Heber City	1,191
Washington	13,669	Saint George	2,427
Wayne	1,483	Loa	2,486
Weber	126,278	Ogden	581

Vermont

(14 counties, 9,267 sq. mi. land; pop. 444,732)

County	Pop. Apr. 1, 1970	County Seat or Court House	Land Area Sq. Mi.
Addison	24,266	Middlebury	784
Bennington	29,282	Bennington	672
Caledonia	22,789	Saint Johnsbury	612
Chittenden	99,131	Burlington	533
Essex	5,416	Guildhall	663
Franklin	31,282	Saint Albans	660
Grand Isle	3,574	North Hero	83
Lamoille	13,309	Hyde Park	474
Orange	17,676	Chelsea	690
Orleans	20,153	Newport	715
Rutland	52,637	Rutland	927
Washington	47,659	Montpelier	707

County	Pop. Apr. 1, 1970	County Seat or Court House	Land Area Sq. Mi.
Windham	33,476	Newfane	784
Windsor	44,082	Woodstock	962

Virginia

(96 cos., 38 ind. cities, 39,780 sq. mi.; pop. 4,648,494)

County	Pop. Apr. 1, 1970	County Seat or Court House	Land Area Sq. Mi.
Accomack	29,004	Accomac	476
Albemarle	37,780	Charlottesville	740
Alleghany	12,461	Covington	444
Amelia	7,592	Amelia, C. H.	366
Amherst	26,072	Amherst	470
Appomattox	9,784	Appomattox	345
Arlington	174,284	Arlington	26
Augusta	44,220	Staunton	986
Bath	5,192	Warm Springs	540
Bedford	26,728	Bedford	727
Bland	5,423	Bland	369
Botetourt	18,193	Fincastle	548
Brunswick	16,172	Lawrenceville	579
Buchanan	32,071	Grundy	508
Buckingham	10,597	Buckingham	582
Campbell	43,319	Rustburg	529
Caroline	13,925	Bowling Green	545
Carroll	23,092	Hillsville	494
Charles City	6,158	Charles City	181
Charlotte	12,366	Charlotte Courthouse	470
Chesterfield	77,045	Chesterfield	442
Clarke	8,102	Berryville	174
Craig	3,524	New Castle	336
Culpeper	18,218	Culpeper	389
Cumberland	6,179	Cumberland	291
Dickenson	16,077	Clintwood	332
Dinwiddie	25,046	Dinwiddie	507
Essex	7,099	Tappahannock	250
Fairfax	455,032	Fairfax	399
Fauquier	26,375	Warrenton	660
Floyd	9,775	Floyd	383
Fluvanna	7,621	Palmyra	288
Franklin	28,163	Rocky Mount	716
Frederick	28,893	Winchester	405
Giles	16,741	Pearisburg	363
Gloucester	14,059	Gloucester	228
Goochland	10,069	Goochland	289
Grayson	15,439	Independence	452
Greene	5,248	Stanardsville	153
Greensville	9,604	Emporia	299
Halifax	30,076	Halifax	796
Hanover	37,479	Hanover	465
Henrico	154,364	Richmond	229
Henry	50,901	Martinsville	381
Highland	2,529	Monterey	416
Isle of Wight	18,285	Isle of Wight	317
James City	17,853	Williamsburg	152
King and Queen	5,491	King and Queen	318
King George	8,039	King George	176
King William	7,497	King William	278
Lancaster	9,126	Lancaster	137
Lee	20,321	Jonesville	438
Loudoun	37,150	Leesburg	517
Louisa	14,004	Louisa	517
Lunenburg	11,687	Lunenburg	442
Madison	8,638	Madison	327
Mathews	7,168	Mathews	89
Mecklenburg	29,426	Boydton	612
Middlesex	6,295	Saluda	130
Montgomery	47,157	Christiansburg	394
*Nansemond	35,166	Suffolk	408
Nelson	11,702	Lovingston	471
New Kent	5,300	New Kent	210
Northampton	14,442	Eastville	220
Northumberland	9,239	Heathsville	190
Nottoway	14,260	Nottoway	308
Orange	13,792	Orange	355
Page	16,581	Luray	316
Patrick	15,282	Stuart	464
Pittsylvania	58,789	Chatham	1,001
Powhatan	7,696	Powhatan	260
Prince Edward	14,379	Farmville	357
Prince George	29,092	Prince George	276
Prince William	111,102	Manassas	347
Pulaski	29,564	Pulaski	328
Rappahannock	5,199	Washington	267
Richmond	6,504	Warsaw	190
Roanoke	67,339	Salem	262
Rockbridge	16,637	Lexington	601
Rockingham	47,890	Harrisonburg	865
Russell	24,533	Lebanon	483
Scott	24,376	Gate City	539
Shenandoah	22,852	Woodstock	507
Smyth	31,349	Marion	435
Southampton	18,582	Courtland	602
Spotsylvania	16,424	Spotsylvania	409
Stafford	24,587	Stafford	270
Surry	5,882	Surry	277
Sussex	11,464	Sussex	494
Tazewell	39,816	Tazewell	522

County	Pop. Apr. 1, 1970	County Seat or Court House	Land Area Sq. Mi.	County	Pop. Apr. 1, 1970	County Seat or Court House	Land Area Sq. Mi.
Warren	15,301	Front Royal	219	Boone	2,118	Madison	501
Washington	40,835	Abingdon	574	Braxton	12,666	Sutton	511
Westmoreland	12,142	Montross	229	Brooke	29,685	Wellsburg	88
Wise	35,947	Wise	412	Cabell	106,918	Huntington	279
Wythe	22,139	Wytheville	460	Calhoun	7,046	Grantsville	281
York	33,203	Yorktown	129	Clay	9,330	Clay	343

*1/1/74 merged with ind. city of Suffolk.

County	Pop. Apr. 1, 1970	County Seat or Court House	Land Area Sq. Mi.	County	Pop. Apr. 1, 1970	County Seat or Court House	Land Area Sq. Mi.
Independent Cities				Doddridge	6,389	West Union	319
Alexandria	110,927		15	Fayette	49,332	Fayetteville	663
Bedford	6,011		7	Gilmer	7,782	Glenville	339
Bristol	14,857		4	Grant	8,607	Petersburg	478
Buena Vista	6,425		3	Greenbrier	32,090	Lewisburg	1,026
Charlottesville	38,880		10	Hampshire	11,710	Romney	639
Chesapeake	89,580		341	Hancock	39,749	New Cumberland	83
Clifton Forge	5,501		4	Hardy	8,855	Moorefield	585
Colonial Heights	15,097		8	Harrison	73,028	Clarksburg	418
Covington	10,060		4	Jackson	20,903	Ripley	461
Danville	46,391		17	Jefferson	21,280	Charles Town	211
Emporia	5,300		2	Kanawha	229,515	Charleston	907
Fairfax	21,970		6	Lewis	17,847	Weston	392
Falls Church	10,772		2	Lincoln	18,912	Hamlin	438
Franklin	6,880		4	Logan	46,269	Logan	456
Fredericksburg	14,450		6	McDowell	50,666	Welch	533
Galax	6,278		7	Marion	61,356	Fairmont	311
Hampton	120,779		55	Marshall	37,598	Moundsville	304
Harrisonburg	14,605		6	Mason	24,306	Point Pleasant	433
Hopewell	23,471		9	Mercer	63,206	Princeton	417
Lexington	7,597		3	Mineral	23,109	Keyser	330
Lynchburg	54,083		25	Mingo	32,780	Williamson	423
Martinsville	19,653		11	Monongalia	63,714	Morgantown	365
Newport News	138,177		69	Monroe	11,272	Union	473
Norfolk	307,951		53	Morgan	8,547	Berkeley Springs	233
Norton	4,172		4	Nicholas	22,552	Summersville	642
Petersburg	36,103		8	Ohio	64,197	Wheeling	106
Portsmouth	110,963		29	Pendleton	7,031	Franklin	695
Radford	11,596		5	Pleasants	7,274	St. Marys	129
Richmond	249,431		60	Pocahontas	8,870	Marlinton	943
Roanoke	92,115		27	Preston	25,455	Kingwood	645
Salem	21,982		14	Putnam	27,625	Winfield	348
South Boston	6,889		5	Raleigh	70,080	Beckley	605
Staunton	24,504		9	Randolph	24,596	Elkins	1,036
Suffolk	9,858		2	Ritchie	10,145	Harrisville	452
Virginia Beach	172,106		259	Roane	14,111	Spencer	486
Waynesboro	16,707		7	Summers	13,213	Hinton	350
Williamsburg	9,069		5	Taylor	13,878	Grafton	174
Winchester	14,643		3	Tucker	7,447	Parsons	421

Washington

(39 counties, 66,570 sq. mi. land; pop., 3,409,169)

County	Pop. Apr. 1, 1970	County Seat or Court House	Land Area Sq. Mi.	County	Pop. Apr. 1, 1970	County Seat or Court House	Land Area Sq. Mi.
Adams	12,014	Ritzville	1,894	Tyler	9,929	Middlebourne	256
Asotin	13,799	Asotin	633	Upshur	19,092	Buckhannon	352
Benton	67,540	Prosser	1,722	Wayne	37,581	Wayne	513
Chelan	41,103	Wenatchee	2,918	Webster	9,809	Webster Springs	551
Clallam	34,770	Port Angeles	1,753	Wetzel	20,314	New Martinsville	363
Clark	128,454	Vancouver	627	Wirt	4,154	Elizabeth	235
Columbia	4,439	Dayton	853	Wood	86,818	Parkersburg	368
Cowlitz	68,616	Kelso	1,144	Wyoming	30,095	Pineville	504
Douglas	16,787	Waterville	1,831				
Ferry	3,655	Republic	2,202				
Franklin	25,816	Pasco	1,253				
Garfield	2,911	Pomeroy	709				
Grant	41,881	Ephrata	2,675				
Grays Harbor	59,553	Montesano	1,910				
Island	27,011	Coupeville	212				
Jefferson	10,661	Port Townsend	1,805				
King	1,159,375	Seattle	2,128				
Kitsap	101,732	Port Orchard	393				
Kittitas	25,039	Ellensburg	2,317				
Klickitat	12,138	Goldendale	1,908				
Lewis	45,467	Chehalis	2,423				
Lincoln	9,572	Davenport	2,306				
Mason	20,918	Shelton	962				
Okanogan	25,867	Okanogan	5,301				
Pacific	15,796	South Bend	908				
Pend Oreille	6,025	Newport	1,402				
Pierce	411,027	Tacoma	1,676				
San Juan	3,856	Friday Harbor	179				
Skagit	52,381	Mount Vernon	1,735				
Skamania	5,845	Stevenson	1,672				
Snohomish	265,236	Everett	2,098				
Spokane	287,487	Spokane	1,758				
Stevens	17,405	Colville	2,481				
Thurston	76,894	Olympia	714				
Wahkiakum	3,592	Cathlamet	261				
Walla Walla	42,176	Walla Walla	1,262				
Whatcom	81,950	Bellingham	2,126				
Whitman	37,900	Colfax	2,153				
Yakima	144,971	Yakima	4,268				

Wisconsin

(72 counties, 54,464 sq. mi. land, pop., 4,417,933)

County	Pop. Apr. 1, 1970	County Seat or Court House	Land Area Sq. Mi.
Adams	9,234	Friendship	646
Ashland	16,743	Ashland	1,038
Barron	33,955	Barron	864
Bayfield	11,683	Washburn	1,460
Brown	158,244	Green Bay	524
Buffalo	13,743	Alma	711
Burnett	9,276	Grantsburg	840
Calumet	27,604	Chilton	322
Chippewa	47,717	Chippewa Falls	1,018
Clark	30,361	Neillsville	1,221
Columbia	40,150	Portage	776
Crawford	15,252	Prairie du Chien	568
Dane	290,272	Madison	1,198
Dodge	69,004	Juneau	899
Door	20,106	Sturgeon Bay	492
Douglas	44,657	Superior	1,305
Dunn	29,154	Menomonie	853
Eau Claire	67,219	Eau Claire	647
Florence	3,298	Florence	487
Fond Du Lac	84,567	Fond du Lac	725
Forest (1973)	8,265	Crandon	1,007
Grant	48,398	Lancaster	1,147
Green	26,714	Monroe	585
Green Lake	16,878	Green Lake	354
Iowa	19,306	Dodgeville	762
Iron	6,533	Hurley	747
Jackson	15,325	Black River Falls	999
Jefferson	60,060	Jefferson	564
Juneau	18,455	Mauston	774
Kenosha	117,917	Kenosha	272
Kewaunee	18,961	Kewaunee	330
La Crosse	80,468	La Crosse	451
Lafayette	17,456	Darlington	643
Langlade	19,220	Antigo	856
Lincoln	23,499	Merrill	892
Manitowoc	82,294	Manitowoc	590

West Virginia

(55 counties, 24,070 sq. mi. land; pop., 1,744,237)

County	Pop. Apr. 1, 1970	County Seat or Court House	Land Area Sq. Mi.
Barbour	14,030	Philippi	341
Berkeley	36,356	Martinsburg	316

County	Pop. Apr. 1, 1970	County Seat or Court House	Land Area Sq. Mi.	County	Pop. Apr. 1, 1970	County Seat or Court House	Land Area Sq. Mi.
Marathon	97,457	Wausau	1,586	Waupaca	37,780	Waupaca	751
Marinette	35,810	Marinette	1,378	Waushara	14,795	Wautoma	627
Marquette	8,865	Montello	455	Winnebago	129,946	Oshkosh	448
Menominee	2,607	Keshena	360	Wood	65,362	Wisconsin Rapids	807
Milwaukee	1,054,249	Milwaukee	237				
Monroe	31,610	Sparta	915				
Oconto	25,553	Oconto	1,001				
Oneida	24,427	Rhinelander	1,112				
Outaramie	119,398	Appleton	634				
Ozaukee	54,461	Port Washington	236	Albany	26,431	Laramie	4,248
Pepin	7,319	Durand	235	Big Horn	10,202	Basin	3,157
Pierce	26,652	Ellsworth	590	Campbell	12,957	Gillette	4,756
Polk	26,666	Balsam Lake	931	Carbon	13,354	Rawlins	7,905
Portage	47,541	Stevens Point	806	Converse	5,938	Douglas	4,281
Price	14,520	Phillips	1,260	Crook	4,535	Sundance	2,882
Racine	170,838	Racine	337	Fremont	28,352	Lander	9,106
Richland	17,079	Richland Center	583	Goshen	10,885	Torrington	2,228
Rock	131,970	Janesville	721	Hot Springs	4,952	Thermopolis	2,022
Rusk	14,238	Ladysmith	906	Johnson	5,587	Buffalo	4,175
St. Croix	34,354	Hudson	734	Laramie	56,360	Cheyenne	2,703
Sauk	39,057	Baraboo	841	Lincoln	8,640	Kemmerer	4,085
Sawyer	9,670	Hayward	1,259	Natrona	51,264	Casper	5,342
Shawano	32,650	Shawano	919	Niobrara	2,924	Lusk	2,614
Sheboygan	96,660	Sheboygan	505	Park	17,752	Cody	6,959
Taylor	16,958	Medford	975	Platte	6,486	Wheatland	2,086
Trempealeau	23,344	Whitehall	735	Sheridan	17,852	Sheridan	2,532
Vernon	24,557	Viroqua	802	Sublette	3,755	Pinedale	4,851
Vilas	10,958	Eagle River	867	Sweetwater	18,391	Green River	10,429
Walworth	63,444	Elkhorn	557	Teton	4,823	Jackson	4,000
Washburn	10,601	Shell Lake	817	Uinta	7,100	Evanston	2,086
Washington	63,839	West Bend	429	Washakie	7,569	Worland	2,262
Waukesha	231,338	Waukesha	554	Weston	6,307	Newcastle	2,407

Wyoming

(23 counties, 97,203 sq. mi. land; pop., 332,416)

1970 Population of Outlying Areas

Source: Bureau of the Census

Puerto Rico

Zip Code	Municipios	Pop. April 1	Land Area Sq. Mile	Zip Code	Municipios	Pop. April 1	Land Area Sq. Mile	Zip Code	Municipios	Pop. April 1	Land Area Sq. Mile
00601	Adjuntas	18,691	66	00653	Guanica	14,889	37	00720	Orocovis	20,201	63
00602	Aguada	25,658	30	00654	Guayama	36,249	65	00723	Patillas	17,828	48
00603	Aguadilla	51,355	36	00656	Guayanilla	18,144	42	00724	Penuelas	15,973	44
00607	Aguas Buenas	18,600	30	00657	Guaynabo	67,042	27	00731	Ponce	158,981	116
00609	Aibonito	20,044	31	00658	Gurabo	18,289	28	00742	Quebradillas	15,582	23
00610	Anasco	19,416	40	00659	Hatillo	21,913	42	00743	Rincon	9,094	14
00612	Arecibo	73,468	127	00660	Hormigueros	10,827	11	00745	Rio Grande	22,032	61
00615	Arroyo	13,033	15	00661	Humacao	36,023	45	00747	Sabana Grande	16,343	37
00617	Barceloneta	20,792	34	00662	Isabela	30,430	56	00751	Salinas	21,837	69
00618	Barranquitas	20,118	33	00664	Jayuya	11,588	39	00753	San German	27,990	54
00619	Bayamon	156,192	44	00665	Juana Diaz	36,270	61	*00936	San Juan	463,242	47
00623	Cabo Rojo	26,060	72	00666	Juncos	21,814	26	00754	San Lorenzo	27,755	53
00625	Caguas	95,661	58	00667	Lajas	16,545	60	00755	San Sebastian	30,157	71
00627	Camuy	19,922	46	00669	Lares	25,263	62	00757	Santa Isabel	16,056	34
00630	Carolina	107,643	48	00670	Las Marias	7,841	44	00758	Toa Alta	18,964	27
00632	Catano	26,459	5	00671	Las Piedras	18,112	33	00759	Toa Baja	46,384	24
00633	Cayey	38,432	50	00672	Loiza	39,062	53	00760	Trujillo Alto	30,669	21
00635	Ceiba	18,312	27	00673	Luquillo	10,390	26	00761	Utuado	35,494	115
00638	Ciales	15,595	66	00701	Manati	30,559	46	00762	Vega Alta	22,810	28
00639	Cidra	23,892	36	00706	Maricao	5,991	37	00763	Vega Baja	35,327	47
00640	Coamo	26,468	77	00707	Maunabo	10,792	21	00765	Vieques	7,767	52
00642	Comerio	18,819	28	00708	Mayaguez	85,857	77	00766	Villalba	18,733	37
00643	Corozal	24,545	42	00716	Moca	22,361	51	00767	Yabucoa	30,165	55
00645	Culebra	732	10	00717	Morovis	19,059	39	00768	Yauco	35,103	68
00646	Dorado	17,388	23	00718	Naguabo	17,996	52	Total		2,712,033	3,421
00648	Fajardo	23,032	31	00719	Naranjito	19,913	28				

Zip Code	Area	Pop. April 1	Land Area Sq. Mile		Area	Pop. April 1	Land Area Sq. Mile	Zip Code	Area	Pop. April 1	Land Area Sq. Mile
	American Samoa				Dededo	10,780	30		**Virgin Islands**		
96920	American Samoa	27,159	76		Inarajan	1,897	19		St. Croix	31,779	80
					Mangilao	3,228	10	00830	St. John	1,729	20
	Canal Zone				Merizo	1,529	6	00801	St. Thomas	28,960	32
	Canal Zone	44,198	362		Mongmong-Too-Maite	6,057	2	00801	Charlotte Amalie	12,220	
	Balboa	32,552	222		Piti	1,284	7	00820	Christiansted	3,020	
	Cristobal	11,646	140		Santa Rita	8,109	17	00840	Frederiksted	1,531	
					Sinajana	3,506	1		Total	62,468	132
	Guam				Talofofo	1,935	17				
96910	Guam	84,996	209		Tamuning	10,218	6		**Trust Territory of Pacific Islands**		
	Agana	2,119	1		Umatac	813	6		Mariana district	9,640	184
	Agana Hts.		1		Yigo	11,542	35		Marshall district	22,888	70
	Agat	4,308	10		Yona	2,599	20		Palau district	11,210	192
	Asan	2,629	6						Ponape district	18,536	176
	Barrigada	6,356	9						Truk district	21,041	49
	Chalan-Pago-Ordot	2,931	6						Yap district	7,625	46
									Total	90,940	717

International Women's Year
Mexico Conference Approves 10-Year Action Plan
By Hana Umlauf

As 1,221 delegates to the UN-sponsored International Women's Conference met in Mexico City for 2 weeks in June, the city played host to a startling diversity of styles, political philosophies, and goals.

The setting in Mexico, still a stronghold of "machismo," provided a constant reminder of the equality gap between men and women. The men smacked their lips and made crude propositions as the delegates, especially those who were bra-less and clad in tight T-shirts, passed by. Furthermore, the Mexican government overlooked the activist wife of its president to elect a man, Attorney General Pedro Ojeda, as president of the women's assembly. And, at the conference's end, the Mexican government presented gifts of dolls in wicker baskets to the female, but not the male, participants.

Sharp political differences among the 133 nations represented emerged as a split between nations of the developed and developing world. Delegates from developing nations argued that a new world economic order must be the basis for transforming women's role in society. Delegates from industrialized nations maintained that such a focus diverted attention from the real issues at stake, such as equality, education, and career choices. Carole de Saram, the president of the New York chapter of NOW, argued early in the conference: "The true issues, the problems of women, are being forgotten here. Instead, this conference is concentrating on political issues that represent the male mentality. The direction here is not coming from women, it's coming from men."

The delegates from the communist nations took still another point of view, maintaining women in their own countries had already achieved equality. Cuba's Vilma Espin, the wife of Raul Castro, stated: "We have already obtained for our women what the conference is asking for. What we can do here is tell other women of our own experiences, and help them that way."

Poor Nations vs. Rich Nations

The ideological split between the developing and developed nations had emerged early in the 2-week conference. On the first day of the meeting, Mexican Pres. Luis Echeverria Alvarez called for a redistribution of the world's wealth as a prerequisite to female equality: "Only a critical, radical effort will make possible the true liberation of women. That is, the liberation of humanity and the transformation of the world economic order. Anything else is but a phase of ideological or moral integration and adaptation to the positions of the ruling class."

The U. S. delegation was conspicuous in not applauding Echeverria's plea. Chief of U. S. delegate Patricia Hutar expressed the view that women must participate along with men in fighting for social and economic betterment: "Women cannot wait with arms folded for men to achieve a new order before women can achieve equality. On the contrary, women must continue their work already begun to achieve a truly equal partnership. Women must be in decision-making positions in the power structure along with men to build a more just world order." Chief British delegate Dr. Shirley Summerskill went a step further. While agreeing there cannot be advancement for women, let alone equality, without development, she argued: "However, if the real advancement of women requires greater economic prosperity, it does

not necessarily follow from it. There is evidence that women have not always benefited from changes introduced in the name of development and, indeed, that their position in relation to men has sometimes deteriorated."

However, as the conference progressed, the U. S. position gradually moved closer to that of the third world nations. Midway through the meeting, Patricia Hutar issued a new U. S. position paper: "We in the United States are committed to pursuit of the combined International Women's Year goal of equality and development although recognizing that achieving this long-run goal implies, for us as no doubt for others, modifications in many existing economic and social structures."

10-Year Plan of Action

Despite the divergent points of view represented at the conference, in the meeting's 11th hour, the delegates unanimously approved a 49-page 10-year Plan of Action. Along with it, the conference voted to issue a shorter, politically-oriented statement, the Declaration of Mexico. The latter, which called for a new world economic order to benefit the poorer nations, also stated: "International cooperation and peace require the achievement of national liberation and independence, the elimination of colonialism and neo-colonialism, foreign occupation, Zionism, apartheid, racial discrimination in all its forms as well as the recognition of the dignity of peoples and their rights to self-determination." Two nations, the United States and Israel, voted against the document and 18 nations abstained.

The official document, the Plan of Action, which is not legally binding on any government, covered almost all issues relating to women, basically calling for elimination of discrimination against women in all the nations of the world.

In its introduction, the plan reflected the conference's long debate between western and third world nations. Without offering a means of achievement, the plan stated that a new economic order was necessary because of "uneven development which prevails in international economic relations, three-quarters of humanity is faced with urgent and pressing social and economic problems."

In specifics, the action plan, containing 219 items, called for improving women's health and nutrition, housing, literacy and means of rescuing rural women from the drudgery of their daily lives. For the benefit of women in the industrialized world, the delegates approved provisions calling for an end to stereotyped sex roles, for the recognition of women as wives, mothers, and job holders, for legal status equal with men, and for equal access to policy-making roles in the professional world.

Although the conference failed to approve a U. S.-backed amendment to give women complete freedom to "control their fertility," it did include a controversial item calling for the right of individuals and couples "freely and responsibly to determine the number and spacing of their children and to have the information and means to do so." Another item, in the family section, called for the abolition of child marriages, recommended that unwed mothers have "full-fledged status" as parents, and demanded the same status and privileges for children born out of wedlock as those born in wedlock.

To insure and sustain national and international action in the prescribed areas, the conference called on the United Nations to proclaim the decade 1975-1985 the UN Decade for Women and Development.

As a monitoring system for implementation of the plan, interim goals in specific areas were set for 1980 when another international women's conference will be held in Iran. Specific areas included literacy, equal access to education at every level, increased employment opportunities, and equality in civic, social, and political rights.

Conference Evaluated

Evaluations of the Plan of Action and the conference varied considerably. Conference Secretary General Helvi Sipila was optimistic: "This plan is only the beginning of a new world. The women who have been here say they are not the same persons anymore." On the other hand, Australian delegate Elizabeth Reid felt the plan would probably "wind up in the bottom drawer of government" because few delegates attending had represented the higher echelons of their governments. "This conference," she said, "could easily lead only to token gestures, hollow promises, and for women, a series of unfulfilled hopes and expectations."

And, while chief U. S. delegate Patricia Hutar called the document "very historic," U. S. congresswoman Bella Abzug hit at the problem now facing women: "But the realism is that we have to put teeth in the plan ourselves and the teeth are the women who are going to change the power structure of their governments."

France's Secretary of State for the Condition of Women, Francoise Giroud, declared the conference a "total failure" because political discussions had diverted attention from issues uniquely concerning women. Early in the conference, Giroud had charged these discussions had enunciated policies set by men: "Throughout our history men have got women to fight their revolutions, but once the fight is terminated, the women return to making coffee. And International Women's Year will have been one more trick if it's subtly deviated toward political goals, national or international, no matter how urgent, respectable or noble."

This and other charges that men had manipulated the conference were not unfounded. Reporters noted that many women did not speak without consulting the men right behind them. Speaking at the official conference, New York State Lt. Gov. Mary Anne Krupsak used that very point in an attempt to convince delegates to focus on basic women's issues. "The women who are delegates here were all handpicked by men," she told the conference. "That's the status of women today, and if we start by admitting that, then we have a common denominator here."

The effectiveness of the conference cannot be evaluated for several years. Most experts feel it will take at least that long before the provisions of the plan filter down through government agencies and private organizations to benefit women. However, in the short run, the conference was valuable in itself as a forum. As Bella Abzug aptly summed up the 2 weeks: "Perhaps this conference was intended as a sop. But we did get here, we did talk about issues, and the world was focused on this issue. I believe deeply that we accomplished something here."

Equal Rights Amendment Falters in 1975

Following elections in November, 1974, when many women and backers of the Equal Rights Amendment won seats in crucial state legislatures, prospects for ratification of the 27th amendment in 1975 looked bright. By April, women's rights advocates conceded there was no chance for the amendment in 1975. The amendment would bar discrimination based on sex by action of federal, state, or local governments.

During March and April, legislatures in North Carolina, Indiana, Missouri, Florida, Illinois, and South Carolina defeated the amendment. The status remained unchanged from several months before: 34 states had approved the amendment. And, of those 34 states, 2 states had rescinded ratification, thus making it necessary for 4 or 6 more states, depending on court tests of recision, to ratify the ERA.

The reasons behind the current setback were many. ERA backers feel many church groups, most notably those holding fundamentalist views on women's role in society, took a more active and effective role in opposition by promoting rejection on religious grounds. Also, certain segments of the Catholic church, ERA advocates contend, opposed passage for fear the amendment would affect institutions maintaining separate facilities for boys and girls.

Also noteworthy is the fact that early ratification came in the large, industrial states; ERA is now faltering in rural states where traditional sex roles might have greater social relevance.

Staunch ERA opponent Phyllis Schlafly maintained the amendment had been rejected "where full debate and discussion had occurred." However, ERA advocates maintained that ERA opponents had used emotional scare tactics to convince women passage would mean abortion on demand, legalization of homosexual marriages, sex-integrated prisons and reform schools.

Fredi Wechsler, of the National Political Women's Caucus, said fear of change had influenced would-be male supporters: "Women's liberation is threatening to a lot of men and women. ERA has become a focal point of that fear. They see a society where women have become freer to choose a career and life style. This, simply, is a threat."

The Fight Continues

Refusing to admit defeat, the National Women's Political Caucus, meeting in June for its biennial convention, went on the offensive and adopted an "elective strategy" for ratification of the ERA. Pointing out that ratification had failed in 5 states by extremely narrow margins, Caryl Stewart, head of the ERA ratification strategy for the caucus, described the outlook as much better then most people imagined.

The group's newly adopted "elective strategy" means the caucus will concentrate its efforts in 1976 to defeat state legislators who had voted against the amendment. Crucial states include Florida and Nevada where only 3 votes have to be changed, Indiana and Missouri where 4 legislators must be ousted, and Illinois where 6 must be defeated. However, adoption of the new strategy signals publicly that ratification will not be possible before 1977. The deadline for ratification is 1979.

Women's rights advocates, however, could take some consolation from the results of a Gallup Poll released in March. Although the poll showed support for ratification of the ERA was weakest in the Midwest and South where most of the nonratifying states are located, overall, 58% of those questioned expressed support for the amendment, 24% were opposed, and 18% had no opinion.

Hispanic Americans

Hispanic Americans, Americans of Spanish descent or origin, now constitute approximately 5% of the U.S. population. The over 11 million people in this group form the second largest minority in the United States today. Twenty-five years ago the two largest Hispanic groups, Mexican-Americans and Puerto Ricans, were concentrated in the border areas of the southwest and the New York City metropolitan area, respectively. Today, however, the ranks of the Hispanic Americans have been swollen by the immigration of hundreds of thousands of Cubans and Dominicans as well as large numbers from every Central and South American nation and they have spread out from the two traditional areas to cover the entire nation.

Still the largest of the Hispanic groups, the Mexican-Americans account for over 50% of the total Hispanic population. In this group are included Americans of Mexican birth as well as descent, also known as Chicanos. The vast majority of Mexican-Americans still live in the southwestern United States from Texas to California.

Mexican-American History

In the early 1600s, before the English arrived on the Eastern seaboard, the first Spanish settlements in what later became the United States had sprung up near Sante Fe, New Mexico. The movement north into California was slow until the expeditions of Jose de Galvez and Padre Junipero Serra in 1769.

After Mexico declared its independence from Spain in 1821 the northern Mexican colonies languished. The Mexican War of 1846-48 was settled by the Treaty of Guadalupe Hidalgo in 1848, which assured all the conquered Mexicans who chose to become American citizens all the rights guaranteed to all other Americans under the United States Constitution.

California entered the Union in 1850 as a bilingual state. Its constitution required that all laws would be published in both Spanish and English. Colorado and New Mexico adopted similar provisions.

Apart from many Hispanic contributions to the English language, including lariat, rodeo, mesa, savvy, and the geographical names of the West, the U.S. owes a political debt to the early Mexican leaders who served as a bridge between the two cultures. Mariano Guadalupe Vallejo and Pablo de la Guerra were among the leaders of the Constitutional Convention at Monterey in 1848 who helped dissuade California from joining the Confederacy. Along with Jose Antonio Carrillo, Manuel Dominguez, Miguel de Pedrorena, Antonia M. Pico and Jacinto Rodriguez, they set the stage for civil rights for all minorities.

Between 1910 and 1930, during the Mexican Revolution and boom times in the U.S., nearly 2,000,000 Mexicans emigrated permanently to this country. It was during this latter period, that the term "Chicano," a shortened version of "Mexicano," became the Mexican-American community's term of derision and exasperated sympathy for the new arrivals. "Chicano" is now the "in" word for those fighting to reassert racial and cultural pride in the community.

Puerto Ricans

The second largest Hispanic group in the U.S., Puerto Ricans number about 1,376,275 (1970 census), with nearly 70% living in the New York City Metropolitan Statistical Area.

Puerto Rico, ceded to the U.S. by Spain in 1898, is a free commonwealth with its own government, and all Puerto Ricans are U.S. citizens.

Although Puerto Ricans in the U.S. numbered only 1,500 in 1910, their contribution to New York City and State has brought many to the fore in business, education, government and the arts.

Cubans

Cubans constitute the third largest Hispanic group in the U.S. The vast majority came to the U.S. as exiles after 1959 when Fidel Castro took over the Cuban government. The 1970 census counted 639,374 persons who were either born in Cuba or had at least one parent born there. Nearly 40% of Cubans live in Florida, primarily in the Miami area.

Education

The principal language of the majority of Hispanic Americans is Spanish. It is the language used at home and in everyday affairs. In a great many cases, however, it is the only language known and used. This presents a great problem in the education of the children of such Hispanic families. Until recently, relatively few schools, even in areas of high Hispanic population, were equipped to provide the specialized instruction in Spanish that these children needed. Now several areas with large Hispanic communities have provided for extensive bi-lingual education in all classes beginning with the very earliest grades.

Employment

The employment status of Hispanic Americans is yet another area that points out the difficult circumstances these people face. Over two-thirds of the Hispanic workers that are employed are holding down "blue collar", service or farm jobs. Only three in ten have "white collar" jobs and half of those are clerical rather than sales or management positions. These figures, though similar to those for black laborers, fall far short of those for white workers, of whom half hold "white collar" jobs. At the same time, the unemployment rate of Hispanic men in the prime working ages of 25 to 54 is twice that of white workers.

Another interesting characteristic of the Hispanic labor force is the extremely high representation of teenagers, aged 16 to 19, who themselves have an unemployment rate of about 20%. The situation becomes even more bleak if the figures for Hispanic women are isolated.

Employment by Occupational Groups, 1974
Source: Bureau of Labor Statistics

Occupation	Total	White	Black	Spanish origin
Total employed (thousands)..	85,936	76,620	8,112	3,609
Percent...................	100.0	100.0	100.0	100.0
White collar workers.......	48.6	50.6	28.9	31.5
Professional and technical..	14.4	14.8	8.8	7.0
Managers and administrators, except farm...........	10.4	11.2	3.4	5.7
Sales workers..........	6.3	6.8	1.9	3.5
Clerical workers.........	17.5	17.8	14.8	15.3
Blue collar workers........	34.7	33.9	42.1	47.6
Craft and kindred workers..	13.4	13.8	9.5	12.4
Operatives..........	16.2	15.5	23.2	26.7
Nonfarm laborers.........	5.1	4.6	9.4	8.5
Service workers...........	13.2	12.0	26.3	16.5
Farm workers.............	3.5	3.6	2.8	4.5

Illegal Aliens

In the past year yet another situation has come to public attention that has been associated with Hispanic Americans. This is the problem of illegal immigration. At a time when national unemployment was near the 10% level, perhaps one million jobs were held by illegal aliens. The Hispanic Americans tend to carry this burden more heavily than others for two reasons. First, it is the "blue collar", service or farm jobs upon which the Hispanics so heavily depend that are most likely to be held by illegal aliens. Second, because the majority of the illegal aliens are also of Hispanic stock, the two groups are closely associated and identified with each other.

Federal and State Indian Reservations

Source: U. S. Dept. of Commerce (data as of circa Dec., 1972)

State	No. of Reservations	Tribally-owned Acreage[1]	Alloted Acreage[1]	No. of Tribes[5]	No. of Persons[4]	Avg. Unemp. Rate%[5]	Major Tribes
Alaska	13[2]	(2)	(2)	6	35,817	NA	Eskimo, Tlingit, Haida, Aleut, Athapascan[6]
Arizona	17	23,467,727	892,917	13	173,412	41	Navaho, Apache, Papago, Hopi, Pima
California	76	386,954	67,390	(7)	6,905	45	Quechan, Hoopa, Paiute, mission bands[7]
Colorado	2	888,155	14,425	1	2,144	37	Ute
Connecticut	4	795	—	3	25	NA	Pequot, Mohegan[8]
Florida	5	183,319	—	2	1,511	31	Seminole, Miccosukee[9]
Idaho	4	274,428	36,723	5	4,849	36	Shoshone, Bannock, Nez Perce
Iowa	1	3,476	—	1	561	35	Sac and Fox[10]
Kansas	4	2,436	24,030	5	3,009	10	Potawatomi, Kickapoo, Iowa
Louisiana	1	262	—	1	268	NA	Chitimacha
Maine	3	27,546	—	2	1,077	45	Passamaquoddy, Penobscot
Massachusetts	1	12	—	1	1	0	Hassanamisco-Nipmuk[11]
Michigan	5	4,425	12,210	2	2,069	38	Chippewa, Potawatami
Minnesota	11	682,534	50,935	2	10,739	40	Chippewa, Sioux
Mississippi	1	17,381	209	1	3,294	10	Choctaw
Montana	7	1,792,383	3,279,926	10	24,137	38	Blackfeet, Sioux, Crow, Assiniboine, Cheyenne
Nebraska	3	27,193	45,467	3	2,601	62	Omaha, Winnebago, Santee Sioux
Nevada	23	1,133,529	32,691	3	4,784	46	Paiute, Shoshone, Washoe
New Mexico	24	3,329,270	119,877	7	30,125	43	Keresan, Zuni, Apache, Tanoan, Navajo[12]
New York	9	88,158	—	7	11,616	27	Seneca, Mohawk, Onondaga, Oneida[13]
North Carolina	1	56,573	—	1	4,880	21	Cherokee
North Dakota	4	375,936	996,744	5	16,735	41	Chippewa, Sioux, Mandan, Arikara, Hidatsa
Oklahoma[14]	(14)	56,741	991,715	27	80,994	24	Cherokee, Creek, Choctaw, Chicasaw, Cheyenne, Arapaho[14]
Oregon	4	495,842	165,778	8	2,718	41	Warm Springs, Wasco, Piaute, Umatilla
South Dakota	8	1,807,623	2,371,427	1	29,119	37	Sioux
Texas	2	4,400	—	3	1,000	30	Tigua (Pueblo), Alabama, Coushatta
Utah	4	1,095,531	48,095	3	1,961	36	Ute, Southern Paiute, Goshute
Virginia	2	925	—	1	110	NA	Algonquian
Washington	22	1,920,850	537,876	20	18,138	45	Yakima, Confederated, Lummi, Quinault
Wisconsin	10	61,911	82,977	6	7,497	38	Chippewa, Oneida, Winnegabo
Wyoming	1	1,776,136	109,344	2	4,435	47	Shoshone, Arapaho

[1]Approximations. Ownership of reservation land is very complex. Most tribally-owned land listed here is owned by tribal organizations, but some of it is held in trust by the government and some is leased to or occupied by non-Indians. Government-owned land, even that held for the exclusive use of Indians, and non-Indian land formally included in reservations is not counted here.
Alloted land was land held by Indian individuals or families. The Department of Commerce data is not clear on whether all land listed as alloted is still securely held by Indians.

[2]Alaskan Indian affairs are handled under the Native Claims Settlement Act (Dec. 18, 1971). The act provides for the establishment of regional and village corporations to conduct business for profit. There are 12 regional corporations. Within each regional corporation, village corporations must be organized. These village corporations then receive title to lands previously held in reservations. There were approximately 2.5 million acres in reservations subject to the Settlement Act. Another 86,471 acres remain outside the Act in Annette Island Reserve. Latest figures show that 5,687 acres have been assigned to village corporations, while an additional 13,490 acres have been surveyed but not yet assigned.

[3]The concept of "tribe" is, in many cases, a white man's invention and, at first, was used to define loosely associated Indians with cultural similarities. Today, "tribe" is a formal status of Indians organized by law. Some present day "tribes", such as the Blackfeet are really confederacies of smaller groups. The Alaskan natives are organized, on paper, into general linguistic groups.

[4]Number of Indians living on or adjacent to reservations. When these figures are compared to 1970 census figures, it appears that nearly 64% of Indians are living on or near reservations.

[5]Unemployment rate of Indian labor force living on or adjacent to reservations.

[6]Aleuts and Eskimos are racially and linguistically related. Athapascans are related to the Navaho and Apache Indians.

[7]Many California Indians are historically associated with groups which settled near Spanish missions where much of the traditional culture was destroyed. Many of these bands, however, still retain some of their Indian language and customs. Excluding the bands, there are 22 tribes represented on California reservations.

[8]The Mohegan or Mohican are a branch of the Pequot.

[9]"Seminole" means "runaways" and these Indians from various tribes were originally refugees from whites in the Carolinas and Georgia. Later joined by runaway slaves, the Seminole were united by their hostility to the United States. Formal peace with the Seminoles in Florida was not achieved until 1934. The Miccosukee are a branch of the Seminole; they retain their Indian religion and have not made formal peace with the U.S.

[10]Once two tribes, the Sac and Fox formed a political alliance in 1734.

[11]Reservation prior to 1728 consisted of 8,000 acres. The land was sold to whites who put the Indians' money in a bank. Over the years the money was "lost" or "borrowed." In 1848, the state granted 11.9 acres to one Indian family of which there are about 20 direct descendants today.

[12]Tanoan, Keresan, and Zuni are all pueblo-dwelling Indians.

[13]These 4 tribes along with the Cayuga and Tuscarora made up the Iroquois League, which ruled large portions of New York, New England, and Pennsylvania and ranged into the Mid-West and South. The Onondaga, who traditionally provide the president of the League, maintain that they are a foreign nation within New York and the U.S.

[14]Indian land status in Oklahoma is unique and there are no reservations in the sense that the term is used elsewhere in the U.S. Likewise, many of the Oklahoma tribes are unique in their high degree of assimilation to the white culture.

Legal or Public Holidays

Technically there are no national holidays in the United States; each state has jurisdiction over its holidays, which are designated by legislative enactment or executive proclamation. In practice, however, most states observe the Federal legal public holidays, even though the President and Congress can legally designate holidays only for the District of Columbia and for Federal employees.

Federal legal public holidays are New Year's, Washington's Birthday, Memorial Day, Independence Day, Labor Day, Columbus Day, Veterans Day, Thanksgiving and Christmas.

1976

Chief Legal or Public Holidays

When a holiday falls on a Sunday it is usually observed on the following Monday. For some holidays, government and business closing practices vary.

Jan. 1 (Thursday) — New Year's Day. All the states.

Feb. 12 (Thursday) — Lincoln's Birthday. Alas., Ariz., Cal., Col., Conn., Ill., Ind., Kan., Md., Mich., Mo., Mon., Neb., N.J., N.M., N.Y., N.C., Pa., Ut., Vt., Wash., W.Va.

Feb. 16 (Third Monday in Feb.) — Washington's Birthday. All the states. In Ha. and Minn. known as President's Day; in Oh., S.D., Tex., Wis., and Wy. known as Lincoln-Washington Day.

Apr. 16 — Good Friday. Observed in all the states. A legal holiday in Conn., Del., Ha., Ind., Ia., La., Md., N.J., N.D., Pa., Tenn. Partial holiday in Ky., N.M. and Wis.

May 31 (Last Monday in May) — Memorial Day. All the states except Ala., Miss., S.C. (Confederate Memorial Day in Virginia). Observed on May 30 in Ill., Ky., La., Me., Md., Mich., Minn., N.H., N.M., Nev., N.C., Pa., S.D., Tenn., Va., Wash., W.Va., Wy.

July 4 (Sunday) — Independence Day. All the states.

Sept. 6 (First Monday in Sept.) — Labor Day. All the states.

Oct. 11 (Second Monday in Oct.) — Columbus Day. All the states except Alas., Ark., Fla., Ia., Ky., Miss., Nev., Okla., S.C., S.D. (Discoverer's Day in Hawaii; Landing Day in Wis.).

Nov. 2 (First Tuesday after first Monday in Nov.) — General Election Day. All the states except Ala., Alas., Ark., Conn., Fla., Ga., Id., Ia., Kan., Ky., Mass., Minn., Neb., N.M., Nev., N.D., Oh., Okla., Ore., S.C., S.D., Ut. (Observed usually only when presidential or general elections are held. Primary election days are observed as holidays or part holidays in some states.)

Nov. 11 (Thursday) — Armistice Day (Veterans Day). All the states.

Nov. 25 (Fourth Thursday in Nov.) — Thanksgiving Day. All the states. Fla. and Okla. also observe the day after Thanksgiving.

Dec. 25 (Saturday) — Christmas. All the states.

Other Legal or Public Holidays

Jan. 8 — Battle of New Orleans. In Louisiana.

Jan. 19 — Robert E. Lee's Birthday. Ark., Ga., La.; In Ala. and Miss. observed on third Monday in Jan.

Jan. 19 — Lee-Jackson Day (third Monday in January). In Virginia.

Jan. 19 — Confederate Heroes Day. In Texas.

Jan. 20 — Inauguration Day. In the District of Columbia; observed every fourth year.

Feb. 14 — Admission Day. In Arizona.

March 2 — Mardi Gras (Shrove Tuesday). Ala., La.

March 2 — Texas Independence Day. In that state.

March 2 — Town Meeting Day (first Tuesday in March). In Vermont.

March 17 — Evacuation Day. In Boston and Suffolk County, Mass.

March 25 — Maryland Day. In that state.

March 26 — Kuhio Day. In Hawaii.

March 29 — Seward's Day. In Alaska.

April 13 — Thomas Jefferson's Birthday. In Alabama.

April 19 — Easter Monday. In North Carolina.

April 19 — Patriot's Day (third Monday in April). Me. and Mass.

April 21 — San Jacinto Day. In Texas.

April 22 — Arbor Day. In Nebraska.

April 26 — Fast Day. In New Hampshire.

April 26 — Confederate Memorial Day. In Georgia.

April 30 — Arbor Day (last Friday in April). In Utah.

April 30 — Confederate Memorial Day (last Monday in April). Alabama and Miss.

May 8 — Harry Truman's Birthday. In Missouri.

May 10 — Confederate Memorial Day. In South Carolina.

June 3 — Birthday of Jefferson Davis. Ala., Ga.; in Ala., Miss., S.C., observed on first Monday in June.

June 3 — Confederate Memorial Day. In Louisiana.

June 11 — Kamehameha Day. In Hawaii.

June 14 — Flag Day. In Pennsylvania.

June 20 — West Virginia Day. In that state.

July 24 — Pioneer Day. In Utah.

Aug. 2 — Colorado Day (first Monday in August). In that state.

Aug. 9 — VJ Day (second Monday in August). In Rhode Island.

Aug. 16 — Bennington Battle Day. In Vermont.

Aug. 20 — Admission Day (third Friday in August). In Hawaii.

Aug. 27 — Lyndon Johnson's Birthday. In Texas.

Aug. 30 — Huey Long's Birthday. In Louisiana.

Sept. 9 — Admission Day. In California.

Sept. 12 — Defenders Day. In Maryland.

Oct. 11 — Pioneers Day (second Monday in Oct.). In So. Dakota.

Oct. 18 — Alaska Day. In that state.

Oct. 31 — Nevada Day. In that state.

Nov. 1 — All Saints' Day. In Louisiana.

Dec. 10 — Wyoming Day. In that state.

Days Usually Observed

Not legal or public holidays:

American Indian Day (Sept. 24 in 1976). Always fourth Friday in September.

Arbor Day. Tree-planting day. First observed April 10, 1872, in Nebraska. Now observed in every state in the Union except Alaska (often on the last Friday in April). A legal holiday in Utah (always last Firday in April), and in Nebraska (April 22)

Armed Forces Day (May 17 in 1976). Always third Saturday in that month, by presidential proclamation. Replaced Army, Navy and Air Force Days.

Bill of Rights Day, Dec. 15. By Act of Congress. Bill of Rights took effect Dec. 15, 1791.

Bird Day. Often observed with Arbor Day.

Child Health Day (Oct. 4 in 1976). Always first Monday in October, by presidential proclamation.

Citizenship Day, Sept. 17. President Truman, Feb. 29, 1952, signed bill designating Sept. 17 as annual Citizenship Day. It replaced I Am An American Day, formerly 3rd Sunday in May and Constitution Day, formerly Sept. 17.

Easter Sunday (April 18 in 1976).

Elizabeth Cady Stanton Day, Nov. 12. Birthday of pioneer leader for equal rights for women.

Father's Day (June 20, in 1976). Always third Sunday in that month.

Flag Day, June 14. By presidential proclamation. It is a legal holiday in Pennsylvania.

Forefathers' Day, Dec. 21. Landing on Plymouth Rock, in 1620. Is celebrated with dinners by New England societies, especially "Down East."

Frances Willard Day, Sept. 28. Observed in Minnesota.

Nathan Bedford Forrest's Birthday, July 13. In Tennessee.

Four Chaplains Memorial Day, February 3.

Gen. Douglas MacArthur Day, Jan. 26. A memorial day in Arkansas.

Gen. Pulaski Memorial Day, Oct. 11. Native of Poland and Revolutionary War hero; died (Oct. 11, 1779) from wounds received at the siege of Savannah, Ga.

Gen. von Steuben Memorial Day, Sept. 17. By presidential proclamation.

Georgia Day, Feb. 12. In that state.

Groundhog Day, Feb. 2. A popular belief is that if the groundhog sees his shadow this day he returns to his burrow and winter continues 6 weeks longer.

Halloween, Oct. 31. The evening before All Saints or All-Hallows Day. Informally observed in the United States with masquerading and pumpkin-decorations. Traditionally an occasion for children to play harmless pranks.

Andrew Jackson's Birthday, Mar. 15. In Tennessee.

Leif Ericsson Day, Oct. 9. Observed in Minnesota.

Loyalty Day, May 1. By act of Congress.

Martin Luther King's Birthday, Jan. 15. Observed by many schools and black groups.

May Day. Popularly given to May 1st.

Minnesota Day, May 11. In that state.

Mother's Day (May 9 in 1976). Always second Sunday in that month.

National Aviation Day, Aug. 19. By presidential proclamation.

National Day of Prayer. By presidential proclamation each year on a day other than a Sunday.

National Freedom Day, February 1. To commemorate the signing of a document abolishing slavery, Feb. 1, 1865. By presidential proclamation.

National Maritime Day, May 22. First proclaimed 1935 in commemoration of the departure of the SS Savannah, from Savannah, Ga., on May 22, 1819, on the first successful transatlantic voyage under steam propulsion. By presidential proclamation.

Pan American Day, April 14. In 1890 the First International Conference of American States, meeting in Washington, was held on that date. A resolution was adopted which resulted in the creation of the organization known today as the Pan American Union. By presidential proclamation.

Poetry Day, Oct. 15.

Primary Election Day. Observed usually only when presidential or general elections are held.

Reformation Day, Oct. 31. Observed by Protestant groups.

Sadie Hawkins Day, first Saturday after November 11.

St. Patrick's Day, March 17. Observed by Irish Societies and with parades.

St. Valentine's Day, Feb. 14. Festival of a martyr beheaded at Rome under Emperor Claudius. Association of this day with lovers has no connection with the saint and probably had its origin in an old belief that on this day birds begin to choose their mates.

Susan B. Anthony Day, Feb. 15. Birthday of a pioneer crusader for equal rights for women.

United Nations Day, Oct. 24. By presidential proclamation, to commemorate founding of United Nations.

Verrazano Day, April 17. Observed by New York State, to commemorate the probable discovery of New York harbor by Giovanni da Verrazano in April, 1524.

Will Rogers Day, Nov. 4. In Oklahoma.

Wright Brothers Day, Dec. 17. By presidential designation, to commemorate first successful flight by Orville and Wilbur Wright, Dec. 17, 1903.

Youth Honor Day, Oct. 31. Iowa day of observance.

Weeks and Months

The following list contains special weeks and months designed to call to the attention of the public an event of importance. The dates usually change each year at the discretion of the sponsoring organization. Among the Weeks observed each year are American Art Week, American Education Week, American Heart Month, American Red Cross Fund Drive, Boy Scout Week, Brotherhood Week, Camp Fire Girls Birthday Week, Cancer Control Month, Christmas Seal Sale (sponsored by National Tuberculosis Association), Constitution Week, Earth Week, Fire Prevention Week, Girl Scout Week, Human Rights Week, Jewish Youth Week, March of Dimes (sponsored by National Foundation), National Allergy Month, National Bible Week, National Boys' Club Week (sponsored by Boys Clubs of America), National Crime Prevention Week, National Drum Corps Week, National Employ the Physically Handicapped Week, National Heart Month, National Farm Safety Week, National 4-H Club Week, National Garden Week, National Highway Week, National Hospital Week, National Library Week, National Safe Boating Week, National Salvation Army Week, National Stamp Collecting Week, National Transportation Week, National Wildlife Week (sponsored by National Wildlife Federation), Poppy Week (sponsored by Veterans of Foreign Wars of the U. S.), Red Cross Month, Save Your Vision Week, United Nations Week, United States-Canada Good Will Week (sponsored by the Kiwanis International), World Trade Week, and Youth Week (sponsored by United Christian Youth Movement).

Revolutionary Calendar, 1776

1776 Jan.	**1**	Washington raises flag of the United Colonies at Cambridge
Jan.	**10**	Thomas Paine publishes his pamphlet, Common Sense
Mar.	**17**	British and Loyalists evacuate Boston
April	**6**	Ports opened to all nations except Britain
April	**17**	Continental Navy captures its first ship, the Edward
June	**3**	Washington authorized to use Indian troops
June	**10**	France lends colonies one million livres
June	**11**	Continental Congress names committee to draft a Declaration of Independence
June	**12**	Virginia Convention adopts Declaration of Rights
June	**28**	British repulsed at Charleston
July	**4**	Congress approves Declaration of

Independence, and the United States of America is born

July	**10**	Statue of George III overturned in Bowling Green, New York City
Aug.	**27**	Americans lose Battle of Long Island
Sept.	**9**	Congress authorizes use of name United States on all commissions
Sept.	**15**	British occupy New York
Sept.	**22**	Nathan Hale is executed as an American spy
Sept.	**27**	Benjamin Franklin, Silas Deane, Arthur Lee commissioned to the Court of France
Oct.	**13**	Americans defeated at Lake Champlain
Oct.	**18**	Thaddeus Kosciuszko commissioned as Colonel of Engineers
Nov.	**13**	John Paul Jones captures the Mellish
Dec.	**26**	Washington crosses Delaware River, defeats Hessians at Trenton

"THE RIGHT OF THE PEOPLE"

The American Revolution

By Don Oakley

(Italics indicate sites worth a visit today.)

"The Revolution was effected before the war commenced," John Adams wrote more than four decades after the first American and British blood was shed at Lexington and Concord. "The Revolution was in the minds and hearts of the people."

The origins of that momentous upheaval, which was to culminate in the birth of a new nation, can be traced to the first settlement of the North American continent, when men and women fled the religious, political and economic oppression of the Old World for freedom and opportunity in the New. Distance alone, given the primitive communications of the day, ensured that the ties between the two worlds, between ruler and subjects, must inevitably weaken as the vitality of the colonies grew stronger.

It was in the aftermath of the French and Indian War (in Europe, the Seven Years' War), however, that factors theretofore operating almost unconciously in the "minds and hearts" of the colonists — they hardly yet thought of themselves as "Americans" — began to find expression.

At the conclusion of the struggle with France in 1763, Great Britain found herself mistress of vast new territories added to her empire, but also saddled with an enormously magnified public debt. Since the war had been fought in defense of the colonies, to ordinary Briton and king's minister alike it seemed only just that the colonies, which had profited greatly from the war while contributing precious little to it, should share in paying for it. An end to a long period of "salutary neglect" was in order. For years, a host of laws governing colonial trade and manufacture, embodying the mercantilist philosophy that colonies exist for the benefit of the mother country, had been honored more in the breach than the observance.

Yet every attempt by Britain to tax the colonists, either directly or indirectly, or to tighten up colonial administration, under which the colonies enjoyed virtual self-government, was to prove but one more spur goading the colonies to open rebellion.

Colonial land speculators as well as would-be emigrants chafed under the Proclamation of 1763, aimed at preserving the rich fur trade with the Indians and placing trans-Allegheny lands out of bounds for settlement. The Sugar Act of 1764, placing duties on lumber, foodstuffs, molasses and rum, merely encouraged an already flourishing smuggling trade. The Stamp Act of 1765 required revenue stamps on documents to help defray the cost of royal troops stationed in the colonies. In reaction, the colonists organized Sons of Liberty groups and boycotted British goods. Nine colonies convened a Stamp Act Congress in New York on Oct. 7 and adopted a declaration of rights opposing taxation without representation and trial without jury in admiralty courts. In the Virginia House of Burgesses, Patrick Henry warned King George III of the consequences, declaring, "If this be treason make the most of it." Parliament repealed the Stamp Act on Mar. 17, 1766.

An ensuing era of good feeling between crown and colonies lasted only briefly. The Townshend Acts of 1767 levied taxes on glass, painters' colors, paper and tea. In 1770, again because of colonial resistance, all duties except the tax on tea were repealed but the principle of Parliament's right to tax the colonies was maintained. On Mar. 5, 1770, British troops in Boston fired into a mob killing 5, including Crispus Attucks, a black, reportedly leader of the group. It became known as the Boston Massacre. On June 9, 1772, the grounded revenue cutter Gaspe was burned by a mob near Providence, R.I. Political agitator Samuel Adams devised the scheme of Committees of Correspondence to rally the people against oppression.

Parliament's most fatal step was the granting of a monopoly in the tea trade to the British East India Co. in 1773. Tea ships were turned back at Boston, New York and Philadelphia in May. On Dec. 16 colonists disguised as Indians staged the Boston Tea Party, throwing overboard a cargo of tea valued at 15,000 pounds. An outraged Parliament ordered 4 regiments to Boston and passed the "Coercive" or "Intolerable" Acts closing the port until the tea was paid for and suppressing town meetings and elective representation in Massachusetts.

Virginia called for the first Continental Congress, which met in *Philadelphia* Sept. 5-Oct. 26, 1774, and issued a "Declaration of American Rights and Grievances" denouncing the "Intolerable" Acts and asserting the rights of the colonists to "life, liberty and property" and the exclusive power of legislation in their provincial assemblies. In Richmond, Mar. 23, 1775, Patrick Henry roused the colonies by crying: "Give me liberty or give me death!"

Although even then — and later — the majority of colonists affirmed their loyalty to the king and claimed they were only defending their rights as British subjects, the stage was set for revolution. And as John Adams was also to write later, "Revolutions are no trifles." The dispute between colonists and Parliament became a war, in many ways a civil war, that was eventually to involve the powers of Europe and be fought around the globe.

1775 — The Appeal to Arms

On the night of Apr. 18, Paul Revere, William Dawes and Samuel Prescott rode to alert Samuel Adams and John Hancock at Lexington and others that 700 British were proceeding to Concord to destroy arms. At *Lexington* on the morning of Apr. 19, Minutemen confronted the British. Both sides later claimed the other fired first. The Americans lost 8 killed, 10 wounded. On the return from *Concord* the harassed British suffered 273 casualties. Only the dispatch of a relief column from *Boston* by Gen. Thomas Gage saved the British force from annihilation.

Col. Ethan Allen, joined by Col. Benedict Arnold, captured *Ft. Ticonderoga*, N.Y., May 10; also *Crown Point*. On May 25, British Maj. Gens. Howe, Clinton and Burgoyne landed in Boston with reinforcements. The colonials, who had fortified *Bunker* and *Breed's Hills* overlooking Charlestown, twice repulsed attacks led by Gen. William Howe before retreating June 17. British casualties in the Battle of Bunker Hill were 1,054, nearly 50 per cent.

On June 14 the second Continental Congress had voted to raise 20,000 men and two days later named

George Washington commander-in-chief of the Continental Army; he took command at Cambridge July 3.

In September, to secure the northern route into New England, two American forces moved into Canada. One, under Maj. Gen. Richard Montgomery, marched via New York and captured Montreal Nov. 13. The second, led by Arnold, undertook an arduous crossing of the Maine wilderness. On Dec. 31 their combined assault on Quebec was repulsed; Montgomery was killed. The first American invasion of Canada in the war ended in retreat.

The Northern Theater (I)
1776 — Year of Glory and Defeat

In January, publication of Thomas Paine's pamphlet "Common Sense," setting forth the arguments for independence, electrified Americans. The arrival of 53 pieces of artillery at the Siege of Boston, hauled by Gen. Henry Knox from Ticonderoga, made the British position untenable; they evacuated the city Mar. 17. Also in March, Congress sent Silas Deane as secret emissary to France.

By April, North Carolina, Rhode Island and Virginia had declared for independence. In the Continental Congress June 7, Richard Henry Lee of Virginia moved "that these united colonies are and of right ought to be free and independent states." John Adams, Benjamin Franklin and Thomas Jefferson were appointed to draw up the document of independence. Congress adopted Lee's resolution July 2, then debated and revised Jefferson's draft. On July 4, the Declaration of Independence was proclaimed.

In June, a second invasion of Canada under Gen. John Sullivan was forced back by Guy Carleton and Burgoyne. In the South on June 28, Col. Moultrie's batteries repulsed a British sea attack on *Charleston*, S.C. The British fleet sailed north to New York to await a massive expeditionary force under the command of Adm. Richard Howe and his brother, Gen. Howe. British strategy was to seize New York, gateway to the Hudson, and by simultaneously striking down from Canada, seal off rebellious New England from the rest of the colonies.

On July 3, Gen. Howe landed some 30,000 troops on Staten Island unopposed. He was sympathetic to the Americans, but his peace overtures were rejected and on Aug. 27 he delivered a stunning defeat to Washington in the Battle of *Long Island*. Mindful of the price paid at Bunker Hill, he did not press home an attack against fortified positions on *Brooklyn Heights* and thus lost the best opportunity of the war to wipe out the American army. Washington was able to carry off a brilliant withdrawal to *Manhattan*. Nevertheless, because of British control of the sea, New York could not be held. The British landed at Kip's Bay (near present 34th Street) Sept. 15 and routed and panicked Americans. Howe's leisurely pursuit again allowed the Americans to evacuate. A large part of New York was later destroyed, Sept. 19-20, in a fire of unknown origin.

Nathan Hale, 21, was executed as a spy, without trial, by the British on Manhattan Sept. 22.

Washington threw Howe back at *Harlem Heights* Sept. 16, but the danger of being outflanked forced him to retreat to *White Plains*, where an indecisive battle was fought Oct. 28.

Brig. Gen. Arnold's Lake Champlain fleet was defeated at *Valcour Island* Oct. 11, but the British invasion force returned to Canada. The Americans lost

3,000 men captured at Ft. Washington, Manhattan, Nov. 16; British occupied Ft. Lee, N.J., on the opposite side of the Hudson Nov. 18. The Americans retreated across New Jersey into Pennsylvania.

In December, Thomas Paine's "The Crisis" called for American resolve in "the times that try men's souls." Washington, faced with the expiration of militia enlistments at year's end and the complete dissolution of what remained of his dispirited army, determined on a bold stroke. On Christmas night he crossed the Delaware and surprised the Hessians in *Trenton* Dec. 26, killing 106 and taking 900 prisoners out of a force of 1,400.

The Northern Theater (II)
1777 — The Turning Point

Despite the success at Trenton, the American cause faced disaster as the New Year began. Washington successfully appealed to the militiamen to serve beyond their enlistments and at *Princeton*, N.J., Jan. 3, defeated Cornwallis. The wounded British gave up their attempts to corner the elusive American army and Washington went into winter quarters at *Morristown*.

The Continental Congress adopted a vague description of a Stars and Stripes flag June 14.

In a second attempt to divide the colonies, Maj. Gen. John Burgoyne moved from Canada with 8,000 men and captured Ft. Ticonderoga July 2. Gen. Nicholas Herkimer, to raise St. Leger's siege of *Ft. Stanwix*, N.Y., routed Indian allies of the British at *Oriskany*. Aug. 6. Burgoyne's Hessians were defeated by Gen. John Stark and the Green Mountain Boys at *Bennington*, Vt., Aug. 16 and Arnold forced St. Leger to retreat from Ft. Stanwix Aug. 23.

Congress commissioned Marquis de Lafayette, aged 20, major general July 31; Count Pulaski was commissioned brigadier general Sept. 15.

Howe defeated Washington near *Brandywine Creek* in Pennsylvania, Sept. 11, and occupied Philadelphia; Congress fled to Lancaster. An inconclusive battle was fought at *Germantown*, Pa., Oct. 4.

On Sept. 19 Burgoyne attacked Americans massed at Bemis Heights on the Hudson River under Maj. Gen. Horatio Gates. At Freeman's Farm nearby, Gen. Arnold and Col. Daniel Morgan's riflemen repulsed the British and inflicted great losses. Gen. Henry Clinton moved north from New York and took Fts. *Clinton* and *Montgomery* below *West Point* Oct. 6, but did not support Burgoyne. The Americans beat back Burgoyne at Bemis Heights Oct. 7 and cut off the British escape route. Burgoyne surrendered 5,000 men at *Saratoga*, N.Y. (now Schuylersville) Oct. 17.

Articles of Confederation and Perpetual Union were adopted by Congress Nov. 15.

In December, Washington took up winter quarters at *Valley Forge*, Pa., where the army suffered great privations. Prussian Baron von Steuben trained the Americans in discipline and maneuver. Although neither side knew it at the time, the series of battles around Saratoga was the turning point in the war. News of the victory convinced Louis XVI of France to support American independence.

1778-79 — A Continent Aflame

On Feb. 6, 1778, France recognized the United States and signed a treaty of alliance; the American Revolution entered a new phase. The opening of French ports to American ships enabled John Paul

Jones and other raiders to carry the war to England's own shores.

The British evacuated Philadelphia June 18 and headed across New Jersey to New York City. Washington harassed them at *Monmouth Court House*, N.J., June 28 in what was to be the last major battle in the North. During the fighting, "Molly Pitcher" (Mary Ludwig Hayes, wife of a Pennsylvania private) carried water to the thirsty troops.

The Wyoming Massacre of settlers in Western Pennsylvania was carried out July 3 by Tory rangers under Col. John Butler and Indians led by Mohawk chief Joseph Brant.

The French fleet under Adm. d'Estaing entered Narragansett Bay in July, but the first combined American-French military operation resulted in the abortive Battle of Rhode Island, Aug. 29.

In the West, in one of the most far-reaching campaigns of the Revolution, though little appreciated at the time, George Rogers Clark led a tiny army down the Ohio River and across Illinois country, taking the former French outposts of Cahokia, Kaskaskia and *Vincennes* (Ind.) in July. In January 1779, a force of British from Detroit under Gen. Henry Hamilton reoccupied the latter post, which Clark had left. On Feb. 20 Clark retook Vincennes and captured Hamilton without the loss of a man. By virtue of his exploit the United States was later to lay claim to the vast Midwest.

Punitive expeditions against the Six Nations in retaliation for the Wyoming Massacre were led by Sullivan, May-Nov., 1779, and Broadhead, Aug.-Sept. Spain entered the war in June, seized Natchez and Baton Rouge and began the siege of Gibraltar. D'Estaing took the British West Indies islands of St. Vincent, June 16, and Grenada, July 4.

John Paul Jones in the *Bonhomme Richard* defeated the *Serapis* on the Atlantic Sept. 23. Americans under Maj. Gen. Benjamin Lincoln were repulsed at the siege of *Savannah*, Ga., Sept. 23-Oct. 9; Pulaski was killed.

The Southern Theater
1780-81 — The Road to Yorktown

On May 12, Gen. Henry Clinton delivered a stunning reversal to the Americans by taking Charleston. S.C. Congress appointed Gates to succeed Lincoln as commander in the South.

In July, a French expeditionary army of 6,000 men under the Comte de Rochambeau landed at Newport, R.I. The British now turned their efforts toward conquering the South before French aid could become effective. In another setback, one of the worst of the war, Cornwallis defeated Gates at *Camden*, S.C., Aug. 16. Cornwallis launched an invasion of North Carolina but turned back when American frontiersmen wiped out a force of Loyalists under Maj. Patrick Ferguson at *Kings Mountain*, S.C., Oct. 7. Partisans led by Thomas Sumter and Francis Marion harassed British outposts and supply routes.

In August, the brilliant but overambitious Benedict Arnold was appointed to command of the Hudson highlands and West Point. On Sept. 23, Continental soldiers captured Maj. John Andre, adjutant general of the British army, in disguise at Tarrytown, N. Y., finding papers on him betraying West Point. Before Arnold's involvement in the plot was realized he escaped aboard the British sloop Vulture on the Hudson. Andre was found guilty and hanged Oct. 2.

What was to prove to be the last year of the war began inauspiciously for the Americans. In January, 1781, mutinies broke out among Pennsylvania and New Jersey troops demanding their back pay from Congress. Arnold, now a brigadier general in the British army, plundered Richmond, Va.

Elsewhere, however, the British southern strategy began unraveling. *Cowpens*, S.C., Jan. 17 was an American victory and *Guilford Court House*, N.C., Mar. 15, while a British gain, was a costly one. Unable to score a decisive victory, Cornwallis retired to Wilmington, N.C., and from there to Yorktown, Va., in August. Hobkirk's Hill, S.C., Apr. 25, was another British victory; nevertheless British operations in the South continued to be checked throughout 1781 by Maj. Gen. Nathanael Green and Brig. Gen. Daniel Morgan. Inconclusive battles were fought at *Fort Ninety-Six*, S.C., in June and *Eutaw Springs*, S.C., in September.

The actors began assembling for the last act in the Revolution. While Lafayette waited near Yorktown, Adm. de Grasse landed 3,000 French troops and then routed Adm. Graves' British fleet off the Chesapeake Capes Sept. 5; without the support of the fleet, Cornwallis' doom was sealed. Washington and Rochambeau combined their forces and, leaving 2,000 men to mislead Clinton in New York, proceeded to Yorktown, arriving Sept. 26.

The siege of *Yorktown* began Oct. 6. Slowly Washington tightened the noose around the British. An attempt by Cornwallis to evacuate on the night of Oct. 16 was thwarted by a storm. Too late, Clinton decided to relieve him. Clinton arrived off the peninsula with 7,000 troops Oct. 24, but Cornwallis had surrendered Oct. 19.

1782-83 — The Winding Down

Militarily the Revolution was ended at Yorktown, but peace negotiations were to continue for another year. In March 1782 a new British cabinet agreed to recognize the independence of the former colonies. Holland recognized the United States Apr. 19.

The British evacuated Savannah in July and Charleston in December but still occupied New York. Also in December, the French army embarked from Boston.

In the West, Delawares and Shawnees wiped out an invading American army near Upper Sandusky (Ohio) in June, burning its leader, Col. William Crawford, at the stake, and laid siege to Ft. Henry (Wheeling, W. Va.) in August in the last battle of the Revolution in which the British flag was flown. (The British were to continue to support the Indians against the Americans in the Ohio country for another 10 years, until the Jay Treaty of 1794 finally ended hostilities in the West.)

Preliminary articles of peace were signed in Paris, Nov. 30, 1782.

Sweden and Denmark recognized U.S. independence, Feb. 1783. Congress proclaimed a cessation of hostilities Apr. 11 and ratified the preliminary treaty Apr. 15. The definitive treaty of peace was signed Sept. 3, but not ratified by Congress until Jan. 14, 1784.

Congress disbanded the American army on Oct. 18, 1783, and the British evacuated New York Nov. 25. There, at *Fraunces Tavern*, Washington bade farewell to his officers on Dec. 4. He resigned his commission Dec. 23 and returned to his home at *Mount Vernon*, Va.

Declaration of Independence

The Declaration of Independence was adopted by the Continental Congress in Philadelphia, on July 4, 1776. John Hancock was president of the Congress and Charles Thomson was secretary. A copy of the Declaration, engrossed on parchment, was signed by members of Congress on and after Aug. 2, 1776. On Jan. 18, 1777, Congress ordered that "authenticated copies, with the names of the members of Congress subscribed the same, be sent to each of the United States, and that they be desired to have same put upon record." Authenticated copies were printed in broadside form in Baltimore, where the Continental Congress was then in session. The following text is that of the original printed by John Dunlap at Philadelphia for the Continental Congress.

IN CONGRESS, July 4, 1776.
A DECLARATION
By the REPRESENTATIVES of the
UNITED STATES OF AMERICA,
In GENERAL CONGRESS assembled

When in the Course of human Events, it becomes necessary for one People to dissolve the Political Bands which have connected them with another, and to assume among the Powers of the Earth, the separate and equal Station to which the Laws of Nature and of Nature's God entitle them, a decent Respect to the Opinions of Mankind requires that they should declare the causes which impel them to the Separation.

We hold these Truths to be self-evident, that all Men are created equal, that they are endowed by their Creator with certain unalienable Rights, that among these are Life, Liberty, and the Pursuit of Happiness—That to secure these Rights, Governments are instituted among Men, deriving their just Powers from the Consent of the Governed, that whenever any Form of Government becomes destructive of these Ends, it is the Right of the People to alter or to abolish it, and to institute new Government, laying its Foundation on such Principles, and organizing its Powers in such Form, as to them shall seem most likely to effect their Safety and Happiness. Prudence, indeed, will dictate that Governments long established should not be changed for light and transient Causes; and accordingly all Experience hath shewn, that Mankind are more disposed to suffer, while Evils are sufferable, than to right themselves by abolishing the Forms to which they are accustomed. But when a long Train of Abuses and Usurpations, pursuing invariably the same Object, evinces a Design to reduce them under absolute Despotism, it is their Right, it is their Duty, to throw off such Government, and to provide new Guards for their future Security. Such has been the patient Sufferance of these Colonies; and such is now the Necessity which constrains them to alter their former Systems of Government. The History of the present King of Great-Britain is a History of repeated Injuries and Usurpations, all having in direct Object the Establishment of an absolute Tyranny over these States. To prove this, let Facts be submitted to a candid World.

He has refused his Assent to Laws, the most wholesome and necessary for the public Good.

He has forbidden his Governors to pass Laws of immediate and pressing Importance, unless suspended in their Operation till his Assent should be obtained; and when so, suspended, he has utterly neglected to attend to them.

He has refused to pass other Laws for the Accommodation of large Districts of People, unless those People would relinquish the Right of Representation in the Legislature, a Right inestimable to them, and formidable to Tyrants only.

He has called together Legislative Bodies at Places unusual, uncomfortable, and distant from the Depository of their public Records, for the sole Purpose of fatiguing them into Compliance with his Measures.

He has dissolved Representative Houses repeatedly, for opposing with manly Firmness his Invasions on the Rights of the People.

He has refused for a long Time, after such Dissolutions, to cause others to be elected; whereby the Legislative Powers, incapable of Annihilation, have returned to the People at large for their exercise; the State remaining in the mean time exposed to all the Dangers of Invasion from without, and Convulsions within.

He has endeavoured to prevent the Population of these States; for that Purpose obstructing the Laws for Naturalization of Foreigners; refusing to pass others to encourage their Migrations hither, and raising the Conditions of new Appropriations of Lands.

He has obstructed the Administration of Justice, by refusing his Assent to Laws for establishing Judiciary Powers.

He has made Judges dependent on his Will alone, for the Tenure of their Offices, and the Amount and payment of their Salaries.

He has erected a Multitude of new Offices, and sent hither Swarms of Officers to harrass our People, and eat out their Substance.

He has kept among us, in Times of Peace, Standing Armies, without the consent of our Legislatures.

He has affected to render the Military independent of and superior to the Civil Power.

He has combined with others to subject us to a Jurisdiction foreign to our Constitution, and unacknowledged by our Laws; giving his Assent to their Acts of pretended Legislation:

For quartering large Bodies of Armed Troops among us:

For protecting them, by a mock Trial, from Punishment for any Murders which they should commit on the Inhabitants of these States:

For cutting off our Trade with all Parts of the World:

For imposing Taxes on us without our Consent:

For depriving us, in many Cases, of the Benefits of Trial by Jury:

For transporting us beyond Seas to be tried for pretended Offences:

For abolishing the free System of English Laws in a neighbouring Province, establishing therein an arbitrary Government, and enlarging its Boundaries, so as to render it at once an Example and fit Instrument for introducing the same absolute Rule into these Colonies:

For taking away our Charters, abolishing our most valuable Laws, and altering fundamentally the Forms of our Governments:

For suspending our own Legislatures, and declaring themselves invested with Power to legislate for us in all Cases whatsoever.

He has abdicated Government here, by declaring us out of his Protection and waging War against us.

He has plundered our Seas, ravaged our Coasts, burnt our towns, and destroyed the Lives of our People.

He is, at this Time, transporting large Armies of foreign Mercenaries to compleat the works of Death, Desolation, and Tyranny, already begun with circumstances of Cruelty and Perfidy, scarcely paralleled in the most barbarous Ages, and totally unworthy the Head of a civilized Nation.

He has constrained our fellow Citizens taken Captive on the high Seas to bear Arms against their Country, to become the Executioners of their Friends and Brethren, or to fall themselves by their Hands.

He has excited domestic Insurrections amongst us, and has endeavoured to bring on the Inhabitants of our Frontiers, the merciless Indian Savages, whose known Rule of Warfare, is an undistinguished Destruction, of all Ages, Sexes and Conditions.

In every stage of these Oppressions we have Petitioned for Redress in the most humble Terms: Our repeated Petitions have been answered only by repeated Injury. A Prince, whose Character is thus marked by every act which may define a Tyrant, is unfit to be the Ruler of a free People.

Nor have we been wanting in Attentions to our British Brethren. We have warned them from Time to Time of Attempts by their Legislature to extend an unwarrantable Jurisdiction over us. We have reminded them of the Circumstances of our Emigration and Settlement here. We have appealed to their native Justice and Magnanimity, and we have conjured them by the Ties of our common Kindred to disavow these Usurpations, which, would inevitably interrupt our Connections and Correspondence. They too have been deaf to the Voice of Justice and of Consanguinity. We must, therefore, acquiesce in the Necessity, which denounces our Separation, and hold them, as we hold the rest of Mankind, Enemies in War, in Peace, Friends.

We, therefore, the Representatives of the UNITED STATES OF AMERICA, in General Congress, Assembled, appealing to the Supreme Judge of the World in the Rectitude of our Intentions, do, in the Name, and by Authority of the good People of these Colonies, solemnly Publish and Declare, That these United Colonies are, and of Right ought to be, Free and Independent States; that they are absolved from all Allegiance to the British Crown, and that all political Connection between them and the State of Great-Britain, is and ought to be totally dissolved; and that as Free and Independent States, they have full Power to levy War, conclude Peace, contract Alliances, establish Commerce, and to do all other Acts and Things which Independent States may of right do. And for the support of this declaration, with a firm Reliance on the Protection of divine Providence, we mutually pledge to each other our lives, our Fortunes, and our sacred Honor.

JOHN HANCOCK, President.

Attest.

CHARLES THOMSON, Secretary.

Signers of the Declaration of Independence

Delegate and State	Vocation	Birthplace	Born		Died	
Adams, John (Mass.)	Lawyer	Braintree (Quincy), Mass.	1735, Oct.	30	1826, July	4
Adams, Samuel (Mass.)	Political Leader	Boston, Mass.	1722, Sept.	27	1803, Oct.	2
Bartlett, Josiah (N. H.)	Physician, Jurist	Amesbury, Mass.	1729, Nov.	21	1795, May	19
Braxton, Carter (Va.)	Farmer	King & Queen C.H., Va.	1736, Sept.	10	1797, Oct.	10
Carroll, Chas. of Carrollton (Md.)	Lawyer	Annapolis, Md.	1737, Sept.	19	1832, Nov.	14
Chase, Samuel (Md.)	Jurist	Princess Anne, Md.	1741, Apr.	17	1811, June	19
Clark, Abraham (N. J.)	Surveyor	Elizabeth, N. J.	1726, Feb.	15	1794, Sept.	15
Clymer, George (Pa.)	Merchant	Philadelphia, Pa.	1739, Mar.	16	1813, Jan.	23
Ellery, William (R. I.)	Jurist	Newport, R.I.	1727, Dec.	22	1820, Feb.	15
Floyd, William (N. Y.)	Soldier	Brookhaven, N. Y.	1734, Dec.	17	1821, Aug.	4
Franklin, Benjamin (Pa.)	Printer, Publisher	Boston, Mass.	1706, Jan.	17	1790, Apr.	17
Gerry, Elbridge (Mass.)	Merchant	Marblehead, Mass.	1744, July	17	1814, Nov.	23
Gwinnett, Button (Ga.)	Merchant	Down Hatherly, England	1732		1777, May	19
Hall, Lyman (Ga.)	Physician	Wallingford, Conn.	1724, Apr.	12	1790, Oct.	19
Hancock, John (Mass.)	Merchant	Braintree (Quincy), Mass.	1737, Jan.	12	1793, Oct.	8
Harrison, Benjamin (Va.)	Farmer	Berkeley, Va.	1726, Apr.	5	1791, Apr.	24
Hart, John (N. J.)	Farmer	Stonington, Conn.	(1707-1711?)		1779, May	11
Hewes, Joseph (N. C.)	Merchant	Kingston, N. J.	1730, Jan.	23	1779, Nov.	10
Heyward, Thos. Jr. (S. C.)	Lawyer, Farmer	St. Luke's Parish, S. C.	1746, July	28	1809, Mar.	6
Hooper, William (N. C.)	Lawyer	Boston, Mass.	1742, June	28	1790, Oct.	14
Hopkins, Stephen (R. I.)	Jurist, Educator	Providence, R. I.	1707, Mar.	7	1785, July	13
Hopkinson, Francis (N. J.)	Jurist, Author	Philadelphia, Pa.	1737, Sept.	21	1791, May	9
Huntington, Samuel (Conn.)	Jurist	Windham County, Conn.	1731, July	3	1796, Jan.	5
Jefferson, Thomas (Va.)	Lawyer	Old Shadwell, Va.	1743, Apr.	13	1826, July	4
Lee, Richard Henry (Va.)	Farmer	Stratford, Va.	1732, Jan.	20	1794, June	19
Lee, Francis Lightfoot (Va.)	Farmer	Stratford, Va.	1734, Oct.	14	1797, Jan.	11
Lewis, Francis (N. Y.)	Merchant	Landaff, Wales	1713, Mar.		1803, Dec.	30
Livingston, Philip (N. Y.)	Merchant	Albany, N. Y.	1716, Jan.	15	1778, June	12
Lynch, Thomas Jr. (S. C.)	Farmer	Winyah, S. C.	1749, Aug.	5	1779, (at sea)	
McKean, Thomas (Del.)	Lawyer	New London, Pa.	1734, Mar.	19	1817, June	24
Middleton, Arthur (S. C.)	Farmer	Charleston, S. C.	1742, June	26	1787, Jan.	1
Morris, Lewis (N.Y.)	Farmer	Morisania, N. Y. (N.Y.C.)	1726, Apr.	8	1798, Jan.	22
Morris, Robert (Pa.)	Merchant	Liverpool, England	1734, Jan.	20	1806, May	9
Morton, John (Pa.)	Jurist	Ridley, Pa.	1724		1777, Apr.	
Nelson, Thos. Jr. (Va.)	Farmer	Yorktown, Va.	1738, Dec.	26	1789, Jan.	4
Paca, William (Md.)	Jurist	Abingdon, Md.	1740, Oct.	31	1799, Oct.	23
Paine, Robert Treat (Mass.)	Jurist	Boston, Mass.	1731, Mar.	11	1814, May	12
Penn, John (N. C.)	Lawyer	Near Port Royal, Va.	1741, May	17	1788, Sept.	14
Read, George (Del.)	Jurist	Near North East, Md.	1733, Sept.	18	1798, Sept.	21
Rodney, Caesar (Del.)	Jurist	Dover, Del.	1728, Oct.	7	1784, June	29
Ross, George (Pa.)	Jurist	New Castle, Del.	1730, May	10	1779, July	14
Rush, Benjamin (Pa.)	Physician	Byberry, Pa. (Philadelphia)	1745, Dec.	24	1813, April	19
Rutledge, Edward (S.C.)	Lawyer	Charleston, S. C.	1749, Nov.	23	1800, Jan.	23
Sherman, Roger (Conn.)	Lawyer	Newton, Mass.	1721 Apr.	19	1793, July	23
Smith, James (Pa.)	Lawyer	Dublin, Ireand	1713		1806, July	11
Stockton, Richard (N. J.)	Lawyer	Near Princeton, N. J.	1730, Oct.	1	1781, Feb.	28
Stone, Thomas (Md.)	Lawyer	Charles County, Md.	1743		1787, Oct.	5
Taylor, George (Pa.)	Ironmaster	Ireland	1716		1781, Feb.	23
Thornton, Matthew (N. H.)	Physician	Ireland	1714		1803, June	24
Walton, George (Ga.)	Jurist	Prince Edward County, Va.	1741		1804, Feb.	2
Whipple, William (N. H.)	Merchant, Jurist	Kittery, Me.	1730, Jan.	14	1785, Nov.	28
Williams, William (Conn.)	Merchant	Lebanon, Conn.	1731, Apr.	23	1811, Aug.	2
Wilson, James (Pa.)	Jurist	Carskerdo, Scotland	1742, Sept.	14	1798, Aug.	28
Witherspoon, John (N. J.)	Educator	Gifford, Scotland	1723, Feb.	5	1794, Nov.	15
Wolcott, Oliver (Conn.)	Jurist	Windsor, Conn.	1726, Dec.	1	1797, Dec.	1
Wythe, George (Va.)	Lawyer	Elizabeth City, Va.	1726		1806, June	8

How the Declaration of Independence Was Adopted

On June 7, 1776, Richard Henry Lee, who had issued the first call for a congress of the colonies, introduced in the Continental Congress at Philadelphia a resolution declaring "that these United Colonies are, and of right ought to be, free and independent states, that they are absolved from all allegiance to the British Crown, and that all political connection between them and the state of Great Britain is, and ought to be, totally dissolved."

The resolution, seconded by John Adams on behalf of the Massachusetts delegation, came up again June 10 when a committee of 5, headed by Thomas Jefferson, was appointed to express the purpose of the resolution in a declaration of independence. The others on the committee were John Adams, Benjamin Franklin, Robert R. Livingston, and Roger Sherman.

Drafting the Declaration was assigned to Jefferson, who worked on a portable desk of his own construction in a room at Market and 7th Sts. The committee reported the result June 28, 1776. The members of the Congress suggested a number of changes, which Jefferson called "deplorable." They didn't approve Jefferson's arraignment of the British people and King George III for encouraging and fostering the slave trade, which Jefferson called "an execrable commerce." They made 86 changes, eliminating 480 words and leaving 1,337. In the final form capitalization was erratic. Jefferson had written that men were endowed with "inalienable" rights; in the final copy it came out as "unalienable" and has been thus ever since.

The Lee-Adams resolution of independence was adopted by 12 yeas July 2 — the actual date of the act of independence. The Declaration, which explains the act, was adopted July 4, in the evening.

After the Declaration was adopted, July 4, 1776, it was turned over to John Dunlap, printer, to be printed on broadsides. The original copy was lost and one of his broadsides was attached to a page in the journal of the Congress. It was read aloud July 8 in Philadelphia, Easton, Pa., and Trenton, N. J. On July 9 at 6 p.m. it was read by order of Gen. George Washington to the troops assembled on the Common in New York City (City Hall Park).

The Continental Congress on July 19, 1776, adopted the following resolution:

"Resolved, That the Declaration passed on the 4th, be fairly engrossed on parchment with the title and stile of 'The unanimous Declaration of the thirteen united States of America' and that the same, when engrossed, be signed by every member of Congress."

Not all delegates who signed the engrossed Declaration were present on July 4. Robert Morris (Pa.), William Williams (Conn.) and Samual Chase (Md.) signed on Aug. 2. Oliver Wolcott (Conn.), George Wythe (Va.), Richard Henry Lee (Va.) and Elbridge Gerry (Mass.) signed in August and September. Matthew Thornton (N. H.) joined the Congress Nov. 4 and signed later. Thomas McKean (Del.) rejoined Washington's Army before signing and said later that he signed in 1781.

Charles Carroll of Carrollton was appointed a delegate by Maryland on July 4, 1776, presented his credentials July 18, and signed the engrossed Declaration Aug. 2. Born Sept. 19, 1737, he was 95 years old and the last surviving signer when he died Nov. 14, 1832.

Two Pennsylvania delegates who did not support the Declaration on July 4 were replaced.

The 4 New York delegates did not have authority from their state to vote on July 4. On July 9 the New York state convention authorized its delegates to approve the Declaration and the Congress was so notified on July 15, 1776. The 4 signed the Declaration on Aug. 2.

The original engrossed Declaration is preserved in the National Archives Building in Washington.

Independence Hall, American Patriotic Shrine

Independence Hall is the central and main building of a group in Philadelphia, located in Independence Square and facing Chestnut St. It is connected by arcades with 2 buildings, the East and West Wings, and 2 separate corner buildings. Of the latter, Congress Hall is at Sixth St., and Old City Hall at Fifth St.

Independence Hall originally was the State House. It was begun in 1732, and completed in 1759. The East and West Wings were intended to house offices. Tower and spire were completed by June 1753.

The Pennsylvania Assembly occupied Assembly Hall in 1735, before the whole structure was completed. In 1775 it gave the use of the room to the Second Continental Congress. Here, on June 16, 1775, George Washington accepted command of the Continental Army. Here the Declaration of Independence was adopted on July 4, 1776; the Articles of Confederation and Perpetual Union were signed beginning on July 9, 1778, and the Constitution of the United States was framed by the Constitutional Convention in 1787.

Congress Hall, at the west end of the group, was erected in 1787 and was the seat of the United States Congress from 1790 to 1800, when the Congress moved to Washington, D.C. The Court House, or Old City Hall, at the east end, was built in 1790 for the municipal courts, and was the first seat of the United States Supreme Court.

Independence Hall and the other buildings in Independence Square form the nucleus around which has been developed the Independence National Historical Park, established in 1956. Much restoration work has been done.

The Liberty Bell; Its History and Significance

The Liberty Bell, in Independence Hall, Philadelphia, is an object of great reverence to Americans because of its association with the historic events of the War of Independence.

The original Province bell, ordered to commemorate the 50th anniversary of the Commonwealth of Pennsylvania, was cast by Thomas Lister, Whitechapel, London, and reached Philadelphia in Aug. 1752. It bore an inscription from Leviticus XXV. 10: "Proclaim liberty throughout all the land unto all the inhabitants thereof."

The bell was cracked by a stroke of its clapper in Sept. 1752 while it hung on a truss in the State House yard for testing. Pass & Stow, Philadelphia founders, recast the bell, adding 1½ ounces of copper to a pound of the original metal to reduce brittleness. It was found that the bell contained too much copper, injuring its tone, so Pass & Stow recast it again, this time successfully.

In June 1753 the bell was hung in the wooden steeple of the State House, erected on top of the brick tower. In use while the Continental Congress was in session in the State House, it rang out in defiance of British tax and trade restrictions, and proclaimed the Boston Tea Party and the first public reading of the Declaration of Independence.

On Sept. 18, 1777, when the British Army was about to occupy Philadelphia, the bell was moved in a baggage train of the American Army to Allentown, Pa., where it was hidden in the Zion Reformed Church until June 27, 1778. It was moved back to Philadelphia after the British left.

In July 1781 the wooden steeple became insecure and had to be taken down. The bell was lowered into the brick section of the tower. Here it was hanging in July, 1835, when it cracked while tolling for the funeral of John Marshall, chief justice of the United States. Because of its association with the War of Independence it was not recast but remained mute in this location until 1846, the year of the Mexican War, when it was placed on exhibition in the Declaration Chamber of Independence Hall.

In 1876, when many thousands of Americans visited Philadelphia for the Centennial Exposition, it was placed in its old walnut frame in the tower hallway. In 1877 it was hung from the ceiling of the tower by a chain of 13 links. It was returned again to the Declaration Chamber and in 1896 taken back to the tower hall, where it occupied a glass case. In 1915 the case was removed so that the public might touch it. It remains there today.

The measurements of the bell follow: circumference around the lip, 12 ft.; circumference around the crown, 7 ft. 6 in.; lip to the crown, 3 ft.; height over the crown, 2 ft. 3 in.; thickness at lip, 3 in.; thickness at crown, 1¼ in.; weight, 2080 lbs.; length of clapper, 3 ft. 2 in.; cost, £60 14s 5d.

State American Revolution Bicentennial Commission Addresses

Alabama ARBC
State Office Building, Rm. 509
Montgomery, Alabama 36104

Alaska ARBC
840 MacKay Building
338 Denali Street
Anchorage, Alaska 99501

Arizona Bicentennial Commission
1807 North Central Avenue
Suite 108
Phoenix, Arizona 85004

Arkansas Bicentennial Celebration Committee
Old State House
300 West Markham Street
Little Rock, Arkansas 72201

ARBC of California
1501 Eighth Street
Sacramento, California 95814

Colorado Centennial-Bicentennial Commission
Colorado County Penthouse
901 Sherman
Denver, Colorado 80203

Connecticut ARBC
59 South Prospect Street
Hartford, Connecticut 06106

Delaware ARBC
P. O. Box 2476
Wilmington, Delaware 19899

D.C. Bicentennial Commission
1025 15th St., N.W.
Washington, D.C. 20004

Florida Bicentennial Commission
504 East Jefferson Street
Tallahassee, Florida 32301

Georgia Commission for the
National Bicentennial Celebration
1776 Peachtree, N.W.
Suite 520, South Wing
Atlanta, Georgia 30309

Hawaii Bicentennial Commission
P. O. Box 2359
Honolulu, Hawaii 96804

Idaho ARBC
210 Main Street
Boise, Idaho 83702

Illinois Bicentennial Commission
410 North Michigan Avenue
Room 1044
Chicago, Illinois 60611

Indiana State Bicentennial Commission
State Office Building
Room 504
Indianapolis, Indiana 46204

Iowa ARBC
State House
Des Moines, Iowa 50319

Kansas ARBC
1518 North Broadway
Wichita, Kansas 67214

Kentucky Historical Events
Celebration Commission
Capitol Plaza Towers
Room 1005
Frankford, Kentucky 40601

Louisiana ARBC
P. O. Box 44343
Baton Rouge, Louisiana 70804

Maine State ARBC
State House
Augusta, Maine 04330

Maryland Bicentennial Commission
2525 Riva Road
Annapolis, Maryland 21401

Massachusetts Revolutionary
War Bicentennial Commission
10 Tremont Street, Room 64
Boston, Massachusetts 02108

Michigan Bicentennial Commission
T.M.L. Building, Suite #7
6425 South Pennsylvania Avenue
Lansing, Michigan 48910

Minnesota ARBC
The State Capitol
St. Paul, Minnesota 55101

Mississippi ARBC
Department of Archives and History
P. O. Box 571
Jackson, Mississippi 39205

ARBC of Missouri
P. O. Box 1776
Jefferson City, Missouri, 65101

Montana ARBC
Montana Historical Society
225 North Roberts Street
Helena, Montana 59601

Nebraska ARBC
Radisson Cornhusker Hotel
13th and M Streets
Lincoln, Nebraska 68508

Nevada ARBC
Capitol Building
Carson City, Nevada 89701

New Hampshire Bicentennial Commission
37 Pleasant Street
Concord, New Hampshire 03301

New Jersey ARB Celebration Commission
379 West State Street
Trenton, New Jersey 08618

New Mexico ARBC
141 East de Vargas
Santa Fe, New Mexico 87501

New York State ARBC
Office of State History
State Education Department
99 Washington Avenue
Albany, New York 12210

North Carolina ARBC
Department of Art, Culture and History
109 East Jones Street
Raleigh, North Carolina 27601

North Dakota Bicentennial Commission
State Capitol Building, Rm. 206
Bismarck, North Dakota 58501

Ohio American Revolution
Bicentennial Advisory Commission
Ohio Historical Center
Columbus, Ohio 43211

Oklahoma ARBC
4040 North Lincoln Boulevard
Suite 107
Oklahoma City, Oklahoma 73105

ARBC of Oregon
P. O. Box 1399
Portland, Oregon 97207

Pennsylvania Bicentennial Commission
Wm. Penn Memorial Museum
5th Floor
Harrisburg, Pennsylvania 17108

Rhode Island Bicentennial Commission
Capitol Industrial Center Building
289 Promenade Street
Providence, Rhode Island 02908

South Carolina ARBC
P. O. Box 1976
Columbia, South Carolina 29202

South Dakota ARBC
State Capitol
Pierre, South Dakota 57501

Tennessee ARBC
102 Capitol Towers
Nashville, Tennessee 37219

ARBC of Texas
Executive Offices
210 University Hall
University of Texas at Arlington
Arlington, Texas 76019

Utah ARBC
State Capitol Building
Suite 403
Salt Lake City, Utah 84114

Vermont Bicentennial Commission
Box 195
Saxtons River, Vermont 05154

Virginia Independence
Bicentennial Commission
Drawer JF
Williamsburg, Virginia 23185

Washington ARBC
c/o Washington State Historical Society
315 North Stadium Way
Tacoma, Washington 98403

West Virginia ARBC
1900 Washington Street, East
Charleston, West Virginia 25305

Wisconsin ARBC
816 State Street
Madison, Wisconsin 53706

Wyoming Bicentennial Commission
c/o State Archives and Historical Dept.
Wyoming State Office Building
Cheyenne, Wyoming 82001

Estimated Population of American Colonies: 1760 to 1780

Source: U.S. Bureau of the Census, Historical Statistics

Colony	1780	1770	1760
White and Negro			
Total........	2,780,369	2,148,076	1,593,625
Maine (counties)[1]..	49,133	31,257	—
New Hampshire...	87,802	62,396	39,093
Vermont........	47,620	10,000	—
Massachusetts[1]...	268,627	235,308	222,600
Rhode Island.....	52,946	58,196	45,471
Connecticut......	206,701	183,881	142,470
New York.......	210,541	162,920	117,138
New Jersey......	139,627	117,431	93,813
Pennsylvania.....	327,305	240,057	183,703
Delaware........	45,385	35,496	33,250
Maryland........	245,474	202,599	162,267
Virginia.........	538,004	447,016	339,726
North Carolina....	270,133	197,200	110,442
South Carolina....	180,000	124,244	94,074
Georgia.........	56,071	23,375	9,578
Kentucky........	45,000	15,700	—
Tennessee.......	10,000	1,000	—

Colony	1780	1770	1760
Negro			
Total........	575,420	459,822	325,806
Maine (counties)[1]..	458	475	—
New Hampshire...	541	654	600
Vermont........	50	25	—
Massachusetts[1]...	4,822	4,754	4,866
Rhode Island....	[2]2,671	3,761	3,468
Connecticut......	[2]5,885	5,698	3,783
New York.......	21,054	19,112	16,340
New Jersey......	10,460	8,220	6,567
Pennsylvania.....	7,855	5,761	4,409
Delaware........	2,996	1,836	1,733
Maryland........	80,515	63,818	49,004
Virginia.........	220,582	187,605	140,570
North Carolina....	91,000	69,600	33,554
South Carolina....	97,000	75,178	57,334
Georgia.........	20,831	10,625	3,578
Kentucky........	7,200	2,500	—
Tennessee.......	1,500	200	—

[1]For 1760, Maine Counties included with Massachusetts. [2]Includes some Indians.

Percent Distribution of the White Population, by Nationality: 1790

Source: U.S. Bureau of the Census, Historical Statistics

Area	Total	English	Scotch	Irish Ulster	Irish Free State	German	Dutch	French	Swedish	Unassigned
Total colonies..............	100.0	60.9	8.3	6.0	3.7	8.7	3.4	1.7	0.7	5.6
Maine......................	100.0	60.0	4.5	8.0	3.7	1.3	0.1	1.3	—	21.1
New Hampshire..............	100.0	61.0	6.2	4.6	2.9	0.4	0.1	0.7	—	24.1
Vermont....................	100.0	76.0	5.1	3.2	1.9	0.2	0.6	0.4	—	12.6
Massachusetts..............	100.0	82.0	4.4	2.6	1.3	0.3	0.2	0.8	—	8.4
Rhode Island...............	100.0	71.0	5.8	2.0	0.8	0.5	0.4	0.8	0.1	18.6
Connecticut................	100.0	67.0	2.2	1.8	1.1	0.3	0.3	0.9	—	26.4
New York..................	100.0	52.0	7.0	5.1	3.0	8.2	17.5	3.8	0.5	2.9
New Jersey.................	100.0	47.0	7.7	6.3	3.2	9.2	16.6	2.4	3.9	3.7
Pennsylvania...............	100.0	35.3	8.6	11.0	3.5	33.3	1.8	1.8	0.8	3.9
Delaware...................	100.0	60.0	8.0	6.3	5.4	1.1	4.3	1.6	8.9	4.4
Maryland and District of Columbia..	100.0	64.5	7.6	5.8	6.5	11.7	0.5	1.2	0.5	1.7
Virginia and West Virginia........	100.0	68.5	10.2	6.2	5.5	6.3	0.3	1.5	0.6	0.9
North Carolina..............	100.0	66.0	14.8	5.7	5.4	4.7	0.3	1.7	0.2	1.2
South Carolina.............	100.0	60.2	15.1	9.4	4.4	5.0	0.4	3.9	0.2	1.4
Georgia....................	100.0	57.4	15.5	11.5	3.8	7.6	0.2	2.3	0.6	1.1
Kentucky and Tennessee........	100.0	57.9	10.0	7.0	5.2	14.0	1.3	2.2	0.5	1.9

News Traveled . . . Slowly

The Declaration of Independence, dated July 4, 1776, was printed in colonial newspapers on the following dates.

July 6   Philadelphia, *Pennsylvania Evening Post*
July 8   Philadelphia, *Dunlap's Pennsylvania Packet*
July 9   Philadelphia, *Pennsylvanischer Staatsbote*
July 9   Baltimore, *Dunlap's Maryland Gazette*
July 10   Philadelphia, *Pennsylvania Gazette*
July 10   Philadelphia, *Pennsylvania Journal*
July 10   Baltimore, *Maryland Journal*
July 10   New York, *Constitutional Gazette*
July 11   *New York Packet*
July 11   *New York Journal*
July 11   Annapolis, *Maryland Gazette*
July 12   New London, *Connecticut Gazette*
July 13   Philadelphia, *Pennsylvania Ledger*
July 13   *Providence Gazette*
July 15   *New York Gazette*
July 15   Hartford, *Connecticut Courant*

July 15   *Norwich Packet*
July 16   Exeter, *New Hampshire Gazette, Extraordinary*
July 16   Salem, *American Gazette*
July 17   Worcester, *Massachusetts Spy*
July 17   New Haven, *Connecticut Journal*
July 18   Boston, *Continental Journal*
July 18   Boston, *New England Chronicle*
July 18   *Newport Mercury, Extraordinary*
July 19   Newburyport, *Essex Journal*
July 19   Williamsburg, *Virginia Gazette* (Purdie) extract; in full July 26
July 20   Williamsburg, *Virginia Gazette* (Dixon & Hunter)
July 20   Portsmouth, *Freeman's Journal*
July 22   Watertown, *Boston Gazette*

The Declaration was briefly mentioned in the *London Chronicle* Aug. 13, 1776, and printed in full Aug. 17.

Value and Quantity of Articles Exported From British Continental Colonies, by Destination: 1770

Source: U.S. Bureau of the Census, Historical Statistics

Value in pounds sterling, quantities in units as indicated.   For year ending January 4 of following year.
Includes Newfoundland, Bahamas and Bermuda.

[1] Fractional quantities have been dropped; therefore, total may not equal sum of components.   [2] Information needed to provide totals is not available.   [3] Except for a few items where value is shown.

Article	Value, total	Quantity shipped[3]					
		Total	Great Britain	Ireland	Southern Europe	West Indies	Africa
Total	**3,437,715**						
Potash . . . . tons	35,192	1,173	1,173	—	—	—	—
Pearlash . . . . do	29,469	737	737	—	—	—	—
Spermaceti candles . . . . . . lb	23,688	379,012	4,865	450	14,167	351,625	7,905
Tallow candles . . . . do	1,238	59,420	—	—	1,630	57,550	240
Coal . . . . chaldrons	25	20	—	—	—	20	—
Castorium . . . . lb	1,680	7,465	7,465	—	—	—	—
Fish, dried . . . . quintala	375,394	660,003	22,086	450	431,386	206,081	—
Fish, pickled . . . . bbl	22,551	30,068	123	25	307	29,582	31
Flaxseed . . . . bu	35,169	312,612	6,780	305,083	749	—	—
Indian corn . . . . do	43,376	578,349	—	150	175,221	402,958	20
Oats . . . . do	1,243	24,859	—	—	3,421	21,438	—
Wheat . . . . do	131,467	[4]751,240	11,739	149,985	588,561	955	—
Peas and beans . . . . do	10,077	50,383	—	—	1,046	49,337	—
Ginseng . . . . lb	1,243	74,604	74,604	—	—	—	—
Hemp . . . . cwt	130	86	86	—	—	—	—
Iron, pig . . . . tons	30,089	6,017	5,747	267	—	—	—
Iron, bar . . . . do	36,961	[4]2,470	2,102	85	10	273	—
Iron, cast . . . . do	33	2	—	—	—	2	—
Iron, wrought . . . . tons	167	8	—	—	—	8	—
Indigo . . . . lb	131,552	584,672	584,593	—	—	83	—
Whale oil . . . . tons	85,013	5,667	5,202	22	175	268	—
Whale fins . . . . lb	19,121	112,971	112,971	—	—	—	—
Linseed oil . . . . tons	488	168	161	—	—	7	—
Copper ore . . . . do	854	41	41	—	—	—	—
Lead ore . . . . do	83	6	6	—	—	—	—
Bread and flour . . . . do	504,553	45,868	263	3,583	18,501	23,449	72
Meal . . . . bu	443	4,430	—	—	—	4,430	—
Potatoes . . . . do	127	3,382	—	—	—	3,382	—
Beef and pork . . . . bbl	66,035	[2]	—	—	244	[4]2,870	439
Butter . . . . lb	3,492	167,613	—	—	—	167,313	300
Cheese . . . . do	933	55,997	—	—	—	55,997	—
New England rum . . . . gal	21,836	[4]349,381	600	7,931	45,310	2,574	292,966
Rice . . . . bbl	340,693	[4]151,418	74,073	—	36,296	[4]40,932	117
Rough rice . . . . bu	615	8,200	—	—	—	8,200	—
American loaf sugar . . . . . . lb	333	10,648	—	—	600	8,548	1,500
Raw silk . . . . do	542	541	541	—	—	—	—
Soap . . . . do	2,165	86,585	—	—	550	85,035	1,000
Shoes . . . . pairs	394	3,149	—	—	—	3,149	—
Ship stuff . . . . bbl	9,959	7,964	—	—	7,327	640	—
Onions . . . . value	6,495	[2]	—	—	117	6,379	—
Pitch . . . . bbl	3,200	9,144	8,265	—	—	822	57
Tar, common . . . . do	24,427	81,422	78,115	—	—	3,173	134
Tar, green . . . . do	261	653	653	—	—	—	—
Turpentine . . . . do	6,806	17,014	15,125	—	—	1,807	82
Rosin . . . . do	279	223	195	—	—	28	—
Oil of turpentine . . . . do	103	41	11	—	—	30	—
Masts, yards, etc . . . . tons	16,630	3,045	3,043	—	—	2	—
Walnut wood . . . . value	115	[2]	106	9	—	—	—
Pine, oak, cedar boards . . . . ft	58,618	42,756,306	6,013,519	329,741	486,078	35,922,168	4,800
Pine timber . . . . tons	4,405	11,011	10,582	50	64	315	—
Oak timber . . . . do	3,487	3,874	3,710	10	10	144	—
Houses framed . . . . . number	3,260	163	—	—	—	163	—
Staves and heading . . . . . . do	61,619	20,546,326	4,921,020	2,828,762	1,680,403	11,116,141	—
Hoops . . . . do	8,668	3,852,383	18,912	—	7,072	3,817,899	8,500
Shook hogsheads . . . . do	7,835	62,678	—	—	549	62,099	30
Cattle . . . . do	14,328	3,184	—	—	—	3,184	—
Horses . . . . do	60,228	6,692	—	—	—	6,692	—
Sheep and hogs . . . . do	4,479	12,797	—	—	—	12,797	—
Poultry . . . . doz	1,177	2,615	—	—	—	2,615	—
Furs . . . . value	91,486	[2]	91,486	—	—	—	—
Deer skins . . . . lb	57,750	799,807	799,622	185	—	—	—
Tobacco . . . . value	906,638	[2]	904,982	—	—	1,569	87
Tallow and lard . . . . lb	3,857	185,143	800	—	—	183,893	450
Beeswax . . . . do	6,426	128,523	62,794	10,980	50,529	1,820	2,400

Give Me Liberty . . .

Besides, sir, we shall not fight our battles alone. There is a just God who presides over the destinies of nations, and who will raise up friends to fight our battles for us. The battle, sir, is not to the strong alone; it is to the vigilant, the active, the brave. Besides, sir, we have no election. If we were base enough to desire it, it is now too late to retire from the contest. There is no retreat but in submission and slavery! Our chains are forged. Their clanking may be heard on the plains of Boston! The war is inevitable — and let it come!! I repeat it, sir, let it come!!!

It is vain, sir, to extenuate the matter. Gentlemen may cry, peace, peace; but there is no peace. The war is actually begun! The next gale that sweeps from the north will bring to our ears the clash of resounding arms! Our brethren are already in the field! Why stand we here idle? What is it that gentlemen wish? What would they have? Is life so dear or peace so sweet as to be purchased at the price of chains and slavery? Forbid it, Almighty God — I know not what course others may take; but as for me, give me liberty, or give me death!

> — Patrick Henry
> from Speech to Virginia
> Assembly, 1775

The cause of America is in great measure the cause of all mankind. Many circumstances hath, and will arise, which are not local, but universal, and through which principles of all Lovers of Mankind are affected, and in the Event of which, their Affections are interested. The laying a Country desolate with Fire and Sword 'declaring war against natural rights of all Mankind, and extirpating the Defenders thereof from the Fa e of the Earth, is the Concern of every Man to whom Nature hath given the Power of feeling; of which Class, regardless of Party Censure, is the
> Author.

It is repugnant to reason, to the universal order of things, to all examples from former ages, to suppose, that this continent can longer remain subject to any external power. The most sanguine in Britain does not think so. The utmost stretch of human wisdom cannot, at this time, compass a plan short of separation, which can promise the continent even a year's security. Reconciliation is now a fallacious dream.

As to government matters, it is not in the power of Britain to do this continent justice: The business of it will soon be too weighty, and intricate, to be managed with any tolerable degree of convenience, by a power so distant from us, and so very ignorant of us; for if they cannot conquer us, they cannot govern us. To be always running three or four thousand miles with a tale or a petition, waiting four or five months for an answer, which when obtained requires five or six more to explain it in, will in a few years be looked upon as folly and childishness — There was a time when it was proper, and there is a proper time for it to cease . . . .

To talk of friendship with those in whom our reason forbids us to have faith, and our affections wounded through a thousand pores instruct us to detest, is madness and folly. Every day wears out the little remains of kindred between us and them, and can there be any reason to hope, that as the relationship expires, the affection will increase, or that we shall agree better, when we have ten times more and greater concerns to quarrel over than ever?

Ye that tell us of harmony and reconciliation, can ye restore to us the time that is past? Can ye give to prostitution its former innocence? Neither can ye reconcile Britain and America. The last cord is now broken, the people of England are presenting addresses against us. There are injuries which nature cannot forgive; she would cease to be nature if she did. As well can the lover forgive the ravisher of his mistress, as the continent forgive the murders of Britain. The Almighty hath implanted in us these unextinguishable feelings for good and wise purposes. They are the guardians of his image in our hearts. They distinguish us from the herd of common animals. The social compact would dissolve, and justice be extirpated the earth, or have only a casual existence were we callous to the touches of affection. The robber, and the murderer, would often escape unpunished, did not the injuries which our tempers sustain, provoke us into justice.

O ye that love mankind! Ye that dare oppose, not only the tyranny, but the tyrant, stand forth! Every spot of the old world is overrun with oppression. Freedom hath been hunted round the globe. Asia, and Africa, have long expelled her — Europe regards her like a stranger, and England hath given her warning to depart. O! Receive the fugitive, and prepare in time an asylum for mankind.

> —Thomas Paine
> Common Sense, 1776

These are the times that try men's souls: The summer soldier and the sunshine patriot will, in this crisis, shrink from the service of his country; but he that stands it NOW, deserves the love and thanks of man and woman. Tyranny, like hell, is not easily conquered; yet we have this consolation with us, that the harder the conflict, the more glorious the triumph. What we obtain too cheap, we esteem too lightly: 'Tis dearness only that gives every thing its value. Heaven knows how to put a proper price upon its goods; and it would be strange indeed, if so celestial an article as FREEDOM should not be highly rated. Britain, with an army to enforce her tyranny, has declared that she has a right (not only to TAX) but "to BIND us in ALL CASES WHATSOEVER," and if being bound in that manner, is not slavery, then is there not such a thing as slavery upon earth. Even the expression is impious, for so unlimited a power can belong only to GOD.

> —Thomas Paine
> The Crisis, 1776

DECLARATION OF RIGHTS made by the representatives of the good people of Virginia, assembled in full and free convention; which rights do pertain to them and their posterity, as the basis and foundation of government.

1. That all men are by nature equally free and independent, and have certain inherent rights, of which, when they enter into a state of society, they cannot, by any compact, deprive or divest their posterity; namely, the enjoyment of life and liberty, with the means of acquiring and possessing property, and pursuing and obtaining happiness and safety.

2. That all power is vested in, and consequently derived from, the people; that magistrates are their trustees and servants, and at all times amenable to them.

3. That government is, or ought to be, instituted for

the common benefit, protection, and security of the people, nation, or community; of all the various modes and forms of government, that is best which is capable of producing the greatest degree of happiness and safety, and is most effectually secured against the danger of maladministration; and that when any government shall be found inadequate or contrary to these purposes, a majority of the community hath an indubitable right to reform, alter, or abolish it, in such manner as shall be judged most conducive to the public weal.

> — From the Virginia Bill of Rights, 1776, drafted by George Mason

We must all hang together, or assuredly we shall all hang separately.

> — Benjamin Franklin At the signing of the Declaration of Independence, 1776

Canada and the American Revolution

Of all the American events that have influenced the course of Canadian life, America's War of Independence had an impact on Canadian history unsurpassed by any other event.

The revolution split the people in the 13 colonies on the aims, philosophy, and the necessity of the revolution. Those who were not merely opposed to the principle of independence but wanted to remain under the British crown were called Tories or Loyalists. As the war gained momentum and the revolutionary forces scored successive victories, the Tories were proscribed. Many thousands fled north to the British colonies in Canada which had been captured from the French only 13 years before.

Following the signing of the Treaty of Versailles in 1783, despite British attempts to secure the safety and property of its loyal supporters in America, the new republic failed to implement the terms of the treaty calling for restitution of confiscated Loyalist property during the war and the cessation of any further persecution or prosecution of Loyalists. The British arranged for the transportation of its supporters to Canada and provided grants of land and other benefits. These factors led to another wave of immigrants into Canada in the aftermath of the war.

In Canada a distinction was made in 1789 between the first wave of Loyalists consisting of those who joined the Royal Standard in America before the Treaty of Separation in the year 1783 and those who were dispossessed at the end of the war and fled to Canada after the signing of the treaty. Those in the first group received the official designation "United Empire Loyalists" and were entitled to affix the letters U.E.L. after their names.

By all accounts it would seem that Loyalists who entered Canada numbered a little more than 50,000. Of these, 4,487 settled on the St. Lawrence; 28,347 in Nova Scotia, the River St. John, New Brunswick, and Prince Edward Island; 3,150 in Cape Breton; 5,628 settled about Montreal, Chambly, St. John's, and the Bay of Chaleurs; and an estimated 10,000 settled in Ontario.

An immediate consequence of the Loyalist migration was the alteration of existing provincial boundaries. In the Maritimes, the settlement of Loyalists in Nova Scotia occasioned local resentment. The ruling elite in that province was disinclined to share its power and influence with the new group, so a portion of Nova Scotia north of the Bay of Fundy was severed and given to the Loyalists. In 1784 this area became a distinct province, New Brunswick.

Again, the arrival and settlement of thousands of Loyalists in predominantly French-speaking Canada led to the partition of the province into Upper and Lower Canada by the Constitutional Act of 1791. Lower Canada, present day Quebec, remained primarily French-speaking and Roman Catholic. Upper Canada, which later became Ontario, was predominantly (and until recently almost exclusively) English-speaking and Protestant. This division along ethnic or racial lines, coinciding with religious, language, and cultural differences, continues to pose the gravest challenge to national unity in Canada.

During the War of Independence, the American revolutionaries invaded Canada in 1775. This act estranged several generations of Canadians from their American neighbors.

Loyalists also affected the development of Canadian attitudes and feelings towards Americans. The Loyalists, who played a prominent role in shaping Canada, carried deep scars from the revolution and held an unfriendly, if not hostile, posture towards their neighbors to the south.

For nearly a century, until at least 1871, animosity between the two nations continued unabated. Continual threats of war strengthened anti-American sentiments in Canada. The War of 1812 between Britain and the United States and the Fenian raids carried out in 1866 against Canada roused the passion of Canadians against the American nation. (Members of the Fenian Brotherhood were devoted to the overthrow of the British in North America as a means of liberating their Irish homeland.)

When the American Civil War came to a close there developed a renewed American interest in the vast unsettled lands to the north, to the west of the British North American colony. Fear of a U.S. takeover of this territory and, perhaps, of Canada itself prompted Canadians to strive towards union. Following the Fenian raid of 1866 Canadians reached a common agreement that the united force of all the British North American colonies was needed to stem American aggressiveness. The slogan "In Union is Strength" reflected the spirit of the day. In this wave of national feeling fostered by anti-Americanism, the new Dominion of Canada was born in 1867.

In shaping the structure of their new political institutions, Canadians remained loyal to the institutions of the mother country. The institution of the American Presidency was felt to be definitely inferior to the system of parliamentary government. Canadians were also highly critical of the power entrusted to the individual American states and sought to remove this weakness in strengthening the power of the Canadian federal government. Except in Quebec, the Canadian judicial system was also patterned on the English system of Common Law.

The early history of Canada-United States relations was one of hostilities, aggression, and mutual distrust. Nonetheless, with the passage of time the two nations moved closer together, cooperating in many areas of mutual interest to both countries. Bi-lateral trade agreements have created greater interdependence between the two economies. The U.S. absorbs two-thirds of all Canadian exports. International agreements such as NATO and NORAD have brought the two nations together for their joint protection and defense. The free movement of people across the Canada-U.S. border is an indication of warm relations between the two countries.

In sharp contrast to the early years, Canada-United States relations must be described as good, if not excellent. But slight traces of anti-Americanism linger. Fear of U.S. economic strangulation stemming from excessive American investment which could lead to the peaceful takeover of the Canadian economy is strong in some areas of central Canada. There is, also, a growing fear of cultural domination by the U.S. These misgivings have been echoed by the Prime Minister of Canada when he compared Canadian-American relations to a mouse sleeping with an elephant.

Who's Who in the American Revolution

Adams, John, 1735-1826; American writer and lawyer defended the British soldiers accused of murder in the "Boston Massacre;" urged action in the Continental Congress that led to the separation from Britain; drafter of the Declaration of Independence; commissioner to France, 1777; signatory to the Treaty of Paris.

Adams, Samuel, 1722-1803; leading publicist and agitator preceding the Revolution; helped organize the Sons of Liberty, and the Committees of Correspondence.

Alexander, William (Lord Stirling), 1726-1783; American general engaged at Long Island, Brandywine, Monmouth.

Amherst, Jeffrey, 1717-1797; British general in the French and Indian war; refused command of British forces in America because of unwillingness to fight against his old American comrades-in-arms.

Andre, John, 1751-1780; British major negotiated the aborted surrender of West Point with Benedict Arnold; caught behind enemy lines and hanged.

Arnold, Benedict, 1741-1801; American general, traitor; engaged at Ticonderoga, Quebec; hero of the Battle of Saratoga; began treasonable correspondence, 1779; arranged the surrender of West Point, 1780; fought for the British in Virginia.

Attucks, Crispus, 1723-1770; a leader of the mob that precipitated the "Boston Massacre;" one of 5 killed in the incident.

Bancroft, Edward, 1744-1821; American spy, turned double agent; betrayed American secrets to the British during the war.

Barry, John, 1745-1803; American naval captain made the first capture of a British ship by an American ship, 1776.

Brant, Joseph (Thayendanegea), 1742-1807; Mohawk Indian war chief supported the British during the war; led war parties against American-held towns and villages.

Burgoyne, John, 1722-1792; British general commanded expedition from Canada; defeated at the Battle of Saratoga.

Burr, Aaron, 1756-1836; American officer served in the Quebec expedition, and the Battle of Long Island.

Carleton, Guy, 1724-1808; British administrator of Canada; commanded forces that repelled the attack of Montgomery and Arnold on Quebec.

Clark, George Rogers, 1752-1818; American military leader won victories over the British and their Indian allies in the Illinois country northwest of the Ohio River; captured Vincennes.

Clinton, George, 1739-1812; American public official influenced the politics of the revolutionary and early national periods.

Clinton, Henry, 1738-1795; British general fought in battles of Bunker Hill and Long Island; commander of British forces in North America, 1778-81.

Clinton, James, 1733-1812; American general defeated at Ft. Clinton, 1777; defeated Loyalists and Indians at Elmira, N.Y.

Conway, Thomas, 1735-1800?; American general engaged at Brandywine; forced to resign because of the "Conway Cabal," a plot to have Gates replace Washington as commander-in-chief; actually played a minor role in the incident.

Corbin, Margaret (Captain Molly), 1751-1800; American heroine replaced fallen husband as a cannoneer during attack on Ft. Washington, 1776.

Cornwallis, Charles, 1738-1805; British general engaged at Brandywine, Monmouth; surrendered at Yorktown.

Dawes, William, 1745-1799; rode with Paul Revere to warn of the British advance.

Deane, Silas, 1737-1789; first American diplomat abroad, France, 1776.

Delancey, Oliver, 1718-1785; senior Loyalist officer in the British army during the war.

Dickinson, John, 1732-1808; American political theorist; urged conciliation with England, but later fought in Revolution; a framer of the Constitution.

Dickinson, Philemon, 1739-1809; headed New Jersey militia that retarded the British retreat toward New York prior to the Battle of Monmouth.

Erskine, Robert, 1735-1780; American geographer and surveyor produced maps that contributed to Washington's operations.

d'Estaing, Charles, 1729-1794; French admiral aided the Americans in the unsuccessful attack on Savannah.

Ferguson, Patrick, 1744-1780; British officer invented a breech-loading rifle used against the Americans at Brandywine.

Francisco, Peter, 1760-1831; American soldier famed for his strength and bravery at Brandywine, Guilford Courthouse and Yorktown.

Franklin, Benjamin, 1706-1790; American statesman helped draft the Declaration of Independence; helped win French recognition of the American cause; negotiated the Treaty of Paris.

Gage, Thomas, 1721-1787; British general and governor of Massachusetts; sent troops to seize colonial arms precipitating the battles of Lexington and Concord.

Gates, Horatio, 1728-1806; American general led forces at the Battle of Saratoga; defeated at Camden, S.C., 1780.

George 3rd, King, 1738-1820; British monarch supported policies that led to the American Revolution.

de Grasse, Francois, 1722-1788; French admiral repulsed the British at Chesapeake Bay, insuring the American victory at Yorktown.

Greene, Nathaniel, 1742-1786; American general with Washington at Trenton, Brandywine, Valley Forge; resigned as quartermaster general after criticism by Congress, 1780; drove the British out of Georgia and the Carolinas, 1782.

Hale, Nathan, 1755-1776; American officer captured as spy behind British lines on Long Island; hanged the following morning.

Hamilton, Alexander, 1755-1804; served as secretary and aide-de-camp to Washington during the war.

Hancock, John, 1737-1793; pre-Revolution agitator; president of the Continental Congress, 1775-77; first signer of the Declaration of Independence.

Henry, Patrick, 1736-1799; American statesman led militant anti-crown faction in Virginia.

Herkimer, Nicholas, 1728-1777; American general routed Indian allies of the British at Oriskany; died from wounds suffered in the battle.

Hopkins, Esek, 1718-1802; American naval commander-in-chief, 1775; censured by the Continental Congress and dismissed, 1777.

Howe, Richard, 1726-1799; British admiral, brother of Gen. William Howe and naval commander-in-chief, 1776-78.

Howe, William, 1729-1814; British general led forces at Bunker Hill; won the Battle of Long Island, occupied New York City; victorious at Brandywine, Germantown.

Hutchinson, Thomas, 1711-1780; royal governor of Massachusetts, 1771-74.

Jay, John, 1745-1829; president of the Continental Congress, 1778-79; helped negotiate the Treaty of Paris.

Jefferson, Thomas, 1743-1826; drafted the Declaration of Independence.

Jones, John Paul, 1747-1792; most successful of American naval officers; captured many ships; raided the British coast.

de Kalb, Johann, 1721-1780; German officer served in the American army.

Knox, Henry, 1750-1806; American artillery officer served throughout the war as close friend and advisor to Washington; took part in all notable engagements.

Kosciusko, Thaddeus, 1746-1817; Polish officer served in the American army throughout the war.

de Lafayette, Marquis, 1757-1834; French officer joined the American army, 1777; with Washington at Brandywine, Valley Forge; advanced the American cause in France, 1778-80; engaged at Yorktown.

Lee, Henry (Light-Horse Harry), 1756-1818; American cavalry commander covered Greene's retreat in North Carolina, 1781.

Lee, Richard Henry, 1732-1794; American statesman opposed the Stamp and Townshend acts; signed the Declaration of Independence.

Lincoln, Benjamin, 1733-1810; American general defeated at Charleston, 1779; served in the Yorktown campaign.

Ludington, Sybil; American heroine rode through Connecticut countryside rallying the militia to repel a British raid on Danbury, 1777.

Marion, Francis, 1732-1795; American partisan leader famed for guerrilla warfare.

Mason, George, 1725-1792; American statesman opposed the Stamp and Townshend acts.

Montgomery, Richard, 1738-1775; American general captured Montreal, 1775; killed in the Quebec campaign.

Morgan, Daniel, 1736-1802; American general engaged in the Quebec campaign; commanded troops in the Carolina campaign; defeated the British at Cowpens.

Morris, Gouverneur, 1752-1816; American statesman prominent in financial, military, and diplomatic affairs.

Morris, Robert, 1734-1806; American merchant; finance director of the Revolution.

Moultrie, William, 1730-1805; American general repulsed the British at Charleston harbor, 1776.

Muhlenberg, Peter, 1746-1807; American clergyman, general; engaged at Brandywine, Monmouth.

Murphy, Timothy, 1751-1818; American war hero and legendary marksman; distinguished at Saratoga, elsewhere.

North, Lord (Frederick), 1732-1792; British prime minister, 1770-82.

Otis, James, 1725-1783; pre-Revolution leader in Massachusetts.

Paine, Thomas, 1737-1809; political philosopher and author whose "Common Sense," 1776, influenced sentiment for immediate independence, and "Crisis," 1776-83, boosted patriot morale.

Parker, Peter, 1721-1811; British admiral aided Howe in capture of New York.

Pickens, Andrew, 1739-1817; American partisan leader fought at Cowpens, Augusta, and Eutaw Springs, 1781.

Pitcher, Molly, 1754-1832; American heroine memorialized in poem by Whittier.

Poor, Salem, American black soldier cited for his leadership and bravery at Bunker Hill.

Prescott, Dr. Samuel, 1751-1777; American patriot rode and was captured with Paul Revere; escaped and carried the warning to Concord.

Prescott, William, 1726-1795; American militia officer; a hero at Bunker Hill.

Pulaski, Casimer, 1748-1779; Polish cavalry officer served in the American army at Brandywine; killed leading cavalry charge at Siege of Savannah.

Putnam, Israel, 1718-1790; American general distinguished himself at Bunker Hill.

Quincy, Josiah, 1744-1775; American lawyer chosen by the Continental Congress to plead the American cause in London, 1774.

Randolph, Peyton, 1721-1775; Virginia politician; first president of the Continental Congress.

Revere, Paul, 1735-1818; American silversmith, engraver, and patriot; famed for ride to warn the Massachusetts countryside of the approach of the British; designed the first issue of Continental money, and the first official seal of the colonies.

de Rochambeau, Jean Baptiste, 1725-1807; French general commanded French forces at Yorktown.

Ross, Betsy, 1752-1836; American flagmaker of myth; the story of her designing and making the first stars and stripes is without validity.

St. Clair, Arthur, 1736-1818; American general fought at Trenton, Princeton; surrendered Ticonderoga, 1777.

St. Leger, Barry, 1737-1789; British officer defeated at Oriskany, 1777.

Salomon, Haym, 1740-1785; American merchant, banker; raised money to help finance the American army.

Sampson, Deborah, 1760-1827; American heroine masqueraded as a man, joined the army, and was wounded. Awarded a pension by Congress as an invalided soldier.

Schuyler, Philip, 1733-1804; American general in charge of northern New York; replaced after the surrender of Ticonderoga, 1777.

Shays, Daniel, 1747-1825; American soldier fought at Bunker Hill, Ticonderoga, and Saratoga; led an insurrection in Massachusetts against constituted authority, 1786-87.

Stark, John, 1728-1822; American general served at Bunker Hill, and in the Quebec campaign; won the Battle of Bennington.

Von Steuben, Friedrich, 1730-1794; Prussian officer re-organized and trained the American army; engaged at Monmouth, Yorktown.

Sullivan, John, 1740-1795; American general served through the siege of Boston; defeated the British at Staten Island, 1777; defeated Indian-Loyalist contingent near Elmira, N.Y., 1779.

Sumter, Thomas, 1734-1832; American partisan leader in the Carolina campaign.

Townshend, Charles, 1725-1767; British cabinet minister imposed taxes on imports into the American colonies (Townshend Acts), causing colonial unrest.

Trumbull, John, 1756-1843; American artist and officer; aide to Washington, and Gates; famed for paintings depicting the major events of the war.

de Vergennes, Charles, 1717-1787; French foreign minister whose hatred for England led to French support of the American cause.

Warner, Seth, 1743-1784; American colonel captured Crown Point, 1775; led regiment at the Battle of Bennington.

Warren, Joseph, 1741-1775; American physician; pre-Revolution agitator; drafted "Suffolk Resolves;" dispatched Paul Revere on his famous ride; fought at Lexington and Concord; killed at Bunker Hill.

Washington, George, 1732-1799; commander-in-chief of the American army throughout the war.

Wayne, "Mad" Anthony, 1745-1796; American general engaged at Brandywine; captured Stony Point, N.Y., 1779; active in the Yorktown campaign.

Origin of the Constitution

The War of Independence was conducted by delegates from the original 13 states, called the Congress of the United States of America and generally known as the Continental Congress. In 1777 the Congress submitted to the legislatures of the states the Articles of Confederation and Perpetual Union, which were ratified by New Hampshire, Massachusetts, Rhode Island, Connecticut, New York, New Jersey, Pennsylvania, Delaware, Virginia, North Carolina, South Carolina, and Georgia, and finally, in 1781, by Maryland.

The first article of the instrument read: "The stile of this confederacy shall be the United States of America." This did not signify a sovereign nation, because the states delegated only those powers they could not handle individually, such as power to wage war, establish a uniform currency, make treaties with foreign nations and contract debts for general expenses, such as paying the army. Taxes for the payment of such debts were levied by the individual states. The president under the Articles signed himself "President of the United States in Congress assembled," but here the United States were considered in the plural, a cooperating group. Canada was invited to join the union on equal terms but did not act.

When the war was won it became evident that a stronger federal union was needed to protect the mutual interests of the states. The Congress left the initiative to the legislatures. Virginia in Jan. 1786 appointed commissioners to meet with representatives of other states, with the result that delegates from Virginia, Delaware, New York, New Jersey, and Pennsylvania met at Annapolis. Alexander Hamilton prepared their call asking delegates from all states to meet in Philadelphia in May 1787 "to render the Constitution of the Federal government adequate to the exigencies of the union." Congress endorsed the plan Feb.

21, 1787. Delegates were appointed by all states except Rhode Island.

The convention met May 14, 1787. George Washington was chosen president (presiding officer). The states certified 65 delegates, but 10 did not attend. The work was done by 55, not all of whom were present at all sessions. Of the 55 attending delegates, 16 failed to sign, and 39 actually signed Sept. 17, 1787, some with reservations. Some historians have said 74 delegates were named and 19 failed to attend. These 9 additional persons refused the appointment, were never delegates and never counted as absentees. Washington sent the Constitution to Congress with a covering letter and that body, Sept. 28, 1787, ordered it sent to the legislatures, "in order to be submitted to a convention of delegates chosen in each state by the people thereof."

The Constitution was ratified by votes of state conventions as follows: Delaware, Dec. 7, 1787, unanimous; Pennsylvania, Dec. 12, 1787, 43 to 23; New Jersey, Dec. 18, 1787, unanimous; Georgia, Jan. 2, 1788, unanimous; Connecticut, Jan. 9, 1788, 128 to 40; Massachusetts, Feb. 6, 1788, 187 to 168; Maryland, Apr. 28, 1788, 63 to 11; South Carolina, May 23, 1788, 149 to 73; New Hampshire, June 21, 1788, 57 to 46; Virginia, June 25, 1788, 89 to 79; New York, July 26, 1788, 30 to 27. Nine states were needed to establish the operation of the Constitution "between the states so ratifying the same" and New Hampshire was the 9th state. The government did not declare the Constitution in effect until the first Wednesday in Mar. 1789 which was Mar. 4. After that North Carolina ratified it Nov. 21, 1789, 197 to 77; and Rhode Island May 29, 1790, 34 to 32. Vermont in convention ratified it Jan. 10, 1791, and by act of Congress approved Feb. 19, 1791, was admitted into the Union as the 14th state, Mar. 4, 1791.

Constitution of the United States

The Original Seven Articles

PREAMBLE

We, the people of the United States, in order to form a more perfect Union, establish justice, insure domestic tranquility, provide for the common defense, promote the general welfare, and secure the blessings of liberty to ourselves and our posterity, do ordain and establish this Constitution for the United States of America.

ARTICLE 1.

Section 1—Legislative powers; in whom vested:

All legislative powers herein granted shall be vested in a Congress of the United States, which shall consist of a Senate and House of Representatives.

Section 2—House of Representatives, how and by whom chosen. Qualifications of a Representative. Representatives and direct taxes, how apportioned. Enumeration. Vacancies to be filled. Power of choosing officers, and of impeachment.

1. The House of Representatives shall be composed of members chosen every second year by the people of the several States, and the electors in each State shall have the qualifications requisite for electors of the most numerous branch of the State Legislature.

2. No person shall be a Representative who shall not have attained to the age of twenty-five years, and been seven years a citizen of the United States, and who shall not, when elected, be an inhabitant of that State in which he shall be chosen.

3. (Representatives and direct taxes shall be apportioned among the several States which may be included within this Union, according to their respective numbers, which shall be determined by adding to the whole number of free persons, including those bound to service for a term of years, and excluding Indians not taxed, three-fifths of all other persons.) ((The previous sentence was superseded by Amendment XIV, section 2.) The actual enumeration shall be made within three years after the first meeting of the Congress of the United States, and within every subsequent term of ten years, in such manner as they shall by law direct. The number of Representatives shall not exceed one for every thirty thousand, but each State shall have at least one Representative; and until such enumeration shall be made, the State of New Hampshire shall be entitled to choose three, Massachusetts eight, Rhode Island and Providence Plantations one, Connecticut five, New York six, New Jersey four, Pennsylvania eight, Delaware one, Maryland six, Virginia ten, North Carolina five, South Carolina five, and Georgia three.

4. When vacancies happen in the representation from any State, the Executive Authority thereof shall issue writs of election to fill such vacancies.

5. The House of Representatives shall choose their Speaker and other officers; and shall have the sole power of impeachment.

Section 3—Senators, how and by whom chosen. How classified. Qualifications of a Senator. President of the Senate, his right to vote. President pro tem., and other officers of the Senate, how chosen. Power to try impeachments. When President is tried, Chief Justice to preside. Sentence.

1. The Senate of the United States shall be composed of two Senators from each State, (chosen by the Legislature thereof.) (The preceding five words were superseded by Amendment XVII, section 1.) for six years; and each Senator shall have one vote.

2. Immediately after they shall be assembled in consequence of the first election, they shall be divided as equally as may be into three classes. The seats of the Senators of the first class shall be vacated at the expiration of the second year, of the second class at the expiration of the fourth year, and of the third class at the expiration of the sixth year, so that one-third may be chosen every second year;

(and if vacancies happen by resignation, or otherwise, during the recess of the Legislature of any State, the Executive thereof may make temporary appointments until the next meeting of the Legislature, which shall then fill such vacancies.) (The words in parenthesis were superseded by Amendment XVII, section 1.)

3. No person shall be a Senator who shall not have attained to the age of thirty years, and been nine years a citizen of the United States, and who shall not, when elected, be an inhabitant of that State for which he shall be chosen.

4. The Vice President of the United States shall be President of the Senate, but shall have no vote, unless they be equally divided.

5. The Senate shall choose their other officers, and also a President pro tempore, in the absence of the Vice President, or when he shall exercise the office of President of the United States.

6. The Senate shall have the sole power to try all impeachments. When sitting for that purpose, they shall be on oath or affirmation. When the President of the United States is tried, the Chief Justice shall preside; and no person shall be convicted without the concurrence of two-thirds of the members present.

7. Judgment in cases of impeachment shall not extend further than to removal from office, and disqualification to hold and enjoy any office of honor, trust or profit under the United States; but the party convicted shall nevertheless be liable and subject to indictment, trial, judgment and punishment, according to law.

Section 4—Times, etc., of holding elections, how prescribed. One session in each year.

1. The times, places and manner of holding elections for Senators and Representatives, shall be prescribed in each State by the Legislature thereof; but the Congress may at any time by law make or alter such regulations, except as to the places of choosing Senators.

2. The Congress shall assemble at least once in every year, and such meeting shall (be on the first Monday in December.) (The words in parenthesis were superseded by Amendment XX, section 2.) unless they shall by law appoint a different day.

Section 5—Membership, quorum, adjournments, rules. Power to punish or expel. Journal. Time of adjournments, how limited, etc.

1. Each House shall be the judge of the elections, returns and qualifications of its own members, and a majority of each shall constitute a quorum to do business; but a smaller number may adjourn from day to day, and may be authorized to compel the attendance of absent members, in such manner, and under such penalties as each House may provide.

2. Each House may determine the rules of its proceedings, punish its members for disorderly behavior, and, with the concurrence of two-thirds, expel a member.

3. Each House shall keep a journal of its proceedings, and from time to time publish the same, excepting such parts as may in their judgment require secrecy; and the yeas and nays of the members of either House on any question shall, at the desire of one-fifth of those present, be entered on the journal.

4. Neither House, during the session of Congress, shall, without the consent of the other, adjourn for more than three days, nor to any other place than that in which the two Houses shall be sitting.

Section 6—Compensation, privileges, disqualifications in certain cases.

1. The Senators and Representatives shall receive a compensation for their services, to be ascertained by law, and paid out of the Treasury of the United States. They shall in all cases, except treason, felony and breach of the peace, be privileged from arrest during their attendance at the session of their respective Houses, and in going to and returning from the same; and for any speech or debate in

either House, they shall not be questioned in any other place.

2. No Senator or Representative shall, during the time for which he was elected, be appointed to any civil office under the authority of the United States, which shall have been created, or the emoluments whereof shall have been increased during such time; and no person holding any office under the United States, shall be a member of either House during his continuance in office.

Section 7—House to originate all revenue bills. Veto. Bill may be passed by two-thirds of each House, notwithstanding, etc. Bill, not returned in ten days, to become a law. Provisions as to orders, concurrent resolutions, etc.

1. All bills for raising revenue shall originate in the House of Representatives; but the Senate may propose or concur with amendments as on other bills.

2. Every bill which shall have passed the House of Representatives and the Senate, shall, before it become a law, be presented to the President of the United States; if he approve he shall sign it, but if not he shall return it, with his objections to that House in which it shall have originated, who shall enter the objections at large on their journal, and proceed to reconsider it. If after such reconsideration two-thirds of that House shall agree to pass the bill, it shall be sent, together with the objections, to the other House, by which it shall likewise be reconsidered, and if approved by two-thirds of that House, it shall become a law. But in all such cases the votes of both Houses shall be determined by yeas and nays, and the names of the persons voting for and against the bill shall be entered on the journal of each House respectively. If any bill shall not be returned by the President within ten days (Sundays excepted) after it shall have been presented to him, the same shall be a law, in like manner as if he had signed it, unless the Congress by their adjournment prevent its return, in which case it shall not be a law.

3. Every order, resolution, or vote to which the concurrence of the Senate and House of Representatives may be necessary (except on a question of adjournment) shall be presented to the President of the United States; and before the same shall take effect, shall be approved by him, or being disapproved by him, shall be repassed by two-thirds of the Senate and House of Representatives, according to the rules and limitations prescribed in the case of a bill.

Section 8—Powers of Congress.

The Congress shall have power

1. To lay and collect taxes, duties, imposts and excises, to pay the debts and provide for the common defense and general welfare of the United States; but all duties, imposts and excises shall be uniform throughout the United States;

2. To borrow money on the credit of the United States;

3. To regulate commerce with foreign nations, and among the several States, and with the Indian tribes;

4. To establish a uniform rule of naturalization, and uniform laws on the subject of bankruptcies throughout the United States;

5. To coin money, regulate the value thereof, and of foreign coin, and fix the standard of weights and measures;

6. To provide for the punishment of counterfeiting the securities and current coin of the United States;

7. To establish post-offices and post-roads;

8. To promote the progress of science and useful arts, by securing for limited times to authors and inventors the exclusive right to their respective writings and discoveries;

9. To constitute tribunals inferior to the Supreme Court;

10. To define and punish piracies and felonies committed on the high seas, and offenses against the law of nations;

11. To declare war, grant letters of marque and reprisal, and make rules concerning captures on land and water;

12. To raise and support armies, but no appropriation of money to that use shall be for a longer term than two years;

13. To provide and maintain a navy;

14. To make rules for the government and regulation of the land and naval forces;

15. To provide for calling forth the militia to execute the laws of the Union, suppress insurrections and repel invasions;

16. To provide for organizing, arming, and disciplining the militia, and for governing such part of them as may be employed in the service of the United States, reserving to the States respectively, the appointment of the officers, and the authority of training the militia according to the discipline prescribed by Congress;

17. To exercise exclusive legislation in all cases whatsoever, over such district (not exceeding ten miles square) as may, by cession of particular States, and the acceptance of Congress, become the seat of the Government of the United States, and to exercise like authority over all places purchased by the consent of the Legislature of the State in which the same shall be, for the erection of forts, magazines, arsenals, dockyards, and other needful buildings; — And

18. To make all laws which shall be necessary and proper, for carrying into execution the foregoing powers, and all other powers vested by this Constitution in the Government of the United States, or in any department or officer thereof.

Section 9—Provision as to migration or importation of certain persons. Habeas corpus, bills of attainder, etc. Taxes, how apportioned. No export duty. No commercial preference. Money, how drawn from Treasury, etc. No titular nobility. Officers not to receive presents, etc.

1. The migration or importation of such persons as any of the States now existing shall think proper to admit, shall not be prohibited by the Congress prior to the year one thousand eight hundred and eight, but a tax or duty may be imposed on such importation, not exceeding ten dollars for each person.

2. The privilege of the writ of habeas corpus shall not be suspended, unless when in cases of rebellion or invasion the public safety may require it.

3. No bill of attainder or ex post facto law shall be passed.

4. No capitation, or other direct, tax shall be laid, unless in proportion to the census or enumeration herein before directed to be taken. (Modified by Amendment XVI.)

5. No tax or duty shall be laid on articles exported from any State.

6. No preference shall be given by any regulation of commerce or revenue to the ports of one State over those of another: nor shall vessels bound to, or from, one State, be obliged to enter, clear, or pay duties in another.

7. No money shall be drawn from the Treasury, but in consequence of appropriations made by law; and a regular statement and account of the receipts and expenditures of all public money shall be published from time to time.

8. No title of nobility shall be granted by the United States: and no person holding any office of profit or trust under them, shall, without the consent of the Congress, accept of any present, emolument, office, or title, of any kind whatever, from any king, prince, or foreign state.

Section 10—States prohibited from the exercise of certain powers.

1. No State shall enter into any treaty, alliance, or confederation; grant letters of marque and reprisal; coin money; emit bills of credit; make anything but gold and silver coin a tender in payment of debts; pass any bill of attainder, ex post facto law, or law impairing the obligation of contracts, or grant any title of nobility.

2. No State shall, without the consent of the Congress, lay any imposts or duties on imports or exports, except what may be absolutely necessary for executing its inspection laws: and the net produce of all duties and imposts, laid by any State on imports or exports, shall be for the use of the Treasury of the United States; and all such laws shall be subject to the revision and control of the Congress.

3. No State shall, without the consent of Congress, lay any duty of tonnage, keep troops, or ships of war in time of peace, enter into any agreement or compact with another State, or with a foreign power, or engage in war, unless actually invaded, or in such imminent danger as will not admit of delay.

ARTICLE II.

Section 1—President: his term of office. Electors of President; number and how appointed. Electors to vote on same day. Qualification of President. On

whom his duties devolve in case of his removal, death, etc. President's compensation. His oath of office.

1. The Executive power shall be vested in a President of the United States of America. He shall hold his office during the term of four years, and together with the Vice President, chosen for the same term, be elected as follows

2. Each State shall appoint, in such manner as the Legislature thereof may direct, a number of electors, equal to the whole number of Senators and Representatives to which the State may be entitled in the Congress: but no Senator or Representative, or person holding an office of trust or profit under the United States, shall be appointed an elector.

(The electors shall meet in their respective States, and vote by ballot for two persons, of whom one at least shall not be an inhabitant of the same State with themselves. And they shall make a list of all the persons voted for, and of the number of votes for each; which list they shall sign and certify, and transmit sealed to the seat of the Government of the United States, directed to the President of the Senate. The President of the Senate shall, in the presence of the Senate and House of Representatives, open all the certificates, and the votes shall then be counted. The person having the greatest number of votes shall be the President, if such number be a majority of the whole number of electors appointed; and if there be more than one who have such majority, and have an equal number of votes, then the House of Representatives shall immediately choose by ballot one of them for President; and if no person have a majority, then from the five highest on the list the said House shall in like manner choose the President. But in choosing the President, the votes shall be taken by States, the representation from each State having one vote; a quorum for this purpose shall consist of a member or members from two-thirds of the States, and a majority of all the States shall be necessary to a choice. In every case, after the choice of the President, the person having the greatest number of votes of the electors shall be the Vice President. But if there should remain two or more who have equal votes, the Senate shall choose from them by ballot the Vice President.)

(This clause was superseded by Amendment XII.)

3. The Congress may determine the time of choosing the electors, and the day on which they shall give their votes; which day shall be the same throughout the United States.

4. No person except a natural born citizen, or a citizen of the United States, at the time of the adoption of this Constitution, shall be eligible to the office of President; neither shall any person be eligible to that office who shall not have attained to the age of thirty-five years, and been fourteen years a resident within the United States.
(For qualification of the Vice President, see Amendment XII.)

5. In case of the removal of the President from office, or of his death, resignation, or inability to discharge the powers and duties of the said office, the same shall devolve on the Vice President, and the Congress may by law provide for the case of removal, death, resignation or inability, both of the President and Vice President, declaring what officer shall then act as President, and such officer shall act accordingly, until the disability be removed, or a President shall be elected.

(This clause has been modified by Amendment XX, sections 3 and 4).

6. The President shall, at stated times, receive for his services, a compensation, which shall neither be increased nor diminished during the period for which he shall have been elected, and he shall not receive within that period any other emolument from the United States, or any of them.

7. Before he enter on the execution of his office, he shall take the following oath or affirmation:

"I do solemnly swear (or affirm) that I will faithfully execute the office of President of the United States, and will to the best of my ability, preserve, protect and defend the Constitution of the United States."

Section 2—President to be commander-in-chief. He may require opinions of cabinet officers, etc., may pardon. Treaty-making power. Nomination of certain officers. When President may fill vacancies.

1. The President shall be Commander-in-Chief of the Army and Navy of the United States, and of the militia of the several States, when called into the actual service of the United States; he may require the opinion, in writing, of the principal officer in each of the executive departments, upon any subject relating to the duties of their respective offices, and he shall have power to grant reprieves and pardons for offenses against the United States, except in cases of impeachment.

2. He shall have power, by and with the advice and consent of the Senate, to make treaties, provided two-thirds of the Senators present concur; and he shall nominate, and by and with the advice and consent of the Senate, shall appoint ambassadors, other public ministers and consuls, judges of the Supreme Court, and all other officers of the United States, whose appointments are not herein otherwise provided for, and which shall be established by law: but the Congress may by law vest the appointment of such inferior officers, as they think proper, in the President alone, in the courts of law, or in the heads of departments.

3. The President shall have power to fill up all vacancies that may happen during the recess of the Senate, by granting commissions, which shall expire at the end of their next session.

Section 3—President shall communicate to Congress. He may convene and adjourn Congress, in case of disagreement, etc. Shall receive ambassadors, execute laws, and commission officers.

He shall from time to time give to the Congress information of the state of the Union, and recommend to their consideration such measures as he shall judge necessary and expedient; he may, on extraordinary occasions, convene both Houses, or either of them, and in case of disagreement between them, with respect to the time of adjournment, he may adjourn them to such time as he shall think proper; he shall receive ambassadors and other public ministers; he shall take care that the laws be faithfully executed, and shall commission all the officers of the United States.

Section 4—All civil offices forfeited for certain crimes.

The President, Vice President, and all civil officers of the United States, shall be removed from office on impeachment for, and conviction of, treason, bribery, or other high crimes and misdemeanors.

ARTICLE III.

Section 1—Judicial powers, Tenure. Compensation.

The judicial power of the United States, shall be vested in one Supreme Court, and in such inferior courts as the Congress may from time to time ordain and establish. The judges, both of the Supreme and inferior courts, shall hold their offices during good behavior, and at stated times, receive for their services, a compensation, which shall not be diminished during their continuance in office.

Section 2—Judicial power; to what cases it extends. Original jurisdiction of Supreme Court; appellate jurisdiction. Trial by jury, etc. Trial, where.

1. The judicial power shall extend to all cases, in law and equity, arising under this Constitution, the laws of the United States, and treaties made, or which shall be made, under their authority; to all cases affecting ambassadors, other public ministers and consuls; to all cases of admiralty and maritime jurisdiction; to controversies to which the United States shall be a party; to controversies between two or more States; between a State and citizens of another State; between citizens of different States, between citizens of the same State claiming lands under grants of different States, and between a State, or the citizens thereof, and foreign states, citizens, or subjects.
(This section is modified by Amendment XI.)

2. In all cases affecting ambassadors, other public ministers and consuls, and those in which a State shall be party, the Supreme Court shall have original jurisdiction. In all the other cases before mentioned, the Supreme Court shall have appellate jurisdiction, both as to law and fact, with such exceptions, and under such regulations as the Congress shall make.

3. The trial of all crimes, except in cases of impeachment, shall be by jury; and such trial shall be held in the State where the said crimes shall have been committed; but when not committed within any State, the trial shall be at such place or places as the Congress may by law have directed.

Section 3—Treason Defined. Proof of. Punishment of.

1. Treason against the United States, shall consist only in levying war against them, or in adhering to their enemies, giving them aid and comfort. No person shall be convicted of treason unless on the testimony of two witnesses to the same overt act, or on confession in open court.

2. The Congress shall have power to declare the punishment of treason, but no attainder of treason shall work corruption of blood, or forfeiture except during the life of the person attainted.

ARTICLE IV.

Section 1—Each State to give credit to the public acts, etc., of every other State.

Full faith and credit shall be given in each State to the public acts, records, and judicial proceedings of every other State. And the Congress may by general laws prescribe the manner in which such acts, records and proceedings shall be proved, and the effect thereof.

Section 2—Privileges of citizens of each State. Fugitives from justice to be delivered up. Persons held to service having escaped, to be delivered up.

1. The citizens of each State shall be entitled to all privileges and immunities of citizens in the several States.

2. A person charged in any State with treason, felony, or other crime, who shall flee from justice, and be found in another State, shall on demand of the Executive authority of the State from which he fled, be delivered up, to be removed to the State having jurisdiction of the crime.

(3. No person held to service or labor in one State, under the laws thereof, escaping into another, shall in consequence of any law or regulation therein, be discharged from such service or labor, but shall be delivered up on claim of the party to whom such service or labor may be due.) (This clause was superseded by Amendment XIII.)

Section 3—Admission of new States. Power of Congress over territory and other property.

1. New States may be admitted by the Congress into this Union; but no new State shall be formed or erected within the jurisdiction of any other State; nor any State be formed by the junction of two or more States, or parts of States, without the consent of the Legislatures of the States concerned as well as of the Congress.

2. The Congress shall have power to dispose of and make all needful rules and regulations respecting the territory or other property belonging to the United States; and nothing in this Constitution shall be so construed as to prejudice any claims of the United States, or of any particular State.

Section 4—Republican form of government guaranteed. Each State to be protected.

The United States shall guarantee to every State in this Union a Republican form of government, and shall protect each of them against invasion; and on application of the Legislature, or of the Executive (when the Legislature cannot be convened) against domestic violence.

ARTICLE V

Constitution: how amended; proviso.

The Congress, whenever two-thirds of both Houses shall deem it necessary, shall propose amendments to this constitution, or, on the application of the Legislatures of two-thirds of the several States, shall call a convention for proposing amendments, which, in either case, shall be valid to all intents and purposes, as part of this Constitution, when ratified by the Legislatures of three-fourths of the several states, or by conventions in three-fourths thereof, as the one or the other mode of ratification may be proposed by the Congress; provided that no amendment which may be made prior to the year one thousand eight hundred and eight shall in any manner affect the first and fourth clauses in the Ninth Section of the First Article; and that no State, without its consent, shall be deprived of its equal suffrage in the Senate.

ARTICLE VI.

Certain debts, etc., declared valid. Supremacy of Constitution, treaties, and laws of the United States. Oath to support Constitution, by whom taken. No religious test.

1. All debts contracted and engagements entered into, before the adoption of this Constitution, shall be as valid against the United States under this Constitution, as under the Confederation.

2. This Constitution, and the laws of the United States which shall be made in pursuance thereof; and all treaties made, or which shall be made, under the authority of the United States, shall be the supreme law of the land; and the judges in every State shall be bound thereby, any thing in the Constitution or laws of any State to the contrary notwithstanding.

3. The Senators and Representatives before mentioned, and the members of the several State Legislatures, and all executive and judicial officers, both of the United States and of the several States, shall be bound by oath or affirmation, to support this Constitution; but no religious test shall ever be required as a qualification to any office or public trust under the United States.

ARTICLE VII.

What ratification shall establish Constitution.

The ratification of the Conventions of nine States, shall be sufficient for the establishment of this Constitution between the States so ratifying the same.

Done in convention by the unanimous consent of the States present the Seventeenth day of September in the year of our Lord one thousand seven hundred and eighty seven, and of the independence of the United States of America the Twelfth. In witness whereof we have hereunto subscribed our names.

George Washington, President and deputy from Virginia.
New Hampshire—John Langdon, Nicholas Gilman.
Massachusetts—Nathaniel Gorham, Rufus King.
Connecticut—Wm. Saml. Johnson, Roger Sherman.
New York—Alexander Hamilton.
New Jersey—Wil: Livingston, David Brearley, Wm. Paterson, Jona: Dayton.
Pennsylvania—B. Franklin, Thomas Mifflin, Robt. Morris, Geo. Clymer, Thos. FitzSimons, Jared Ingersoll, James Wilson, Gouv. Morris.
Delaware—Geo: Read, Gunning Bedford Jun., John Dickinson, Richard Bassett, Jaco: Broom.
Maryland—James McHenry, Daniel of Saint Thomas Jenifer, Danl. Carroll.
Virginia—John Blair, James Madison Jr.
North Carolina—Wm. Blount, Rich'd. Dobbs Spaight, Hugh Williamson.
South Carolina—J. Rutledge, Charles Cotesworth Pinckney, Charles Pinckney, Pierce Butler.
Georgia—William Few, Abr. Baldwin.
Attest: William Jackson, Secretary.

Ten Original Amendments—The Bill of Rights

In Force Dec. 15, 1791

(The First Congress, at its first session in the City of New York, Sept. 25, 1789, submitted to the states 12 amendments to clarify certain individual and state rights not named in the Constitution. They are generally called the Bill or Rights.

(Influential in framing these amendments was the Declaration of Rights of Virginia, written by George Mason (1725-1792) in 1776. Mason, a Virginia delegate to the Constitutional Convention, did not sign the Constitution and opposed its ratification on the ground that it did not sufficiently oppose slavery or safeguard individual rights.

(In the preamble to the resolution offering the proposed amendments, Congress said: "The conventions of a number of the States having at the time of their adopting the Constitution, expressed a desire, in order to prevent misconstruction or abuse of its powers, that further declaratory and restrictive clauses should be added, and as extending the ground of public confidence in the government will best insure the beneficent ends of its institution, be it resolved," etc.

(Ten of these amendments now commonly known as one to 10 inclusive, but in reality 3 to 12 inclusive, were ratified by the states as follows: New Jersey, Nov. 20, 1789; Maryland, Dec. 19, 1789; North Carolina, Dec. 22, 1789; South Carolina, Jan. 19, 1790; New Hampshire, Jan. 25, 1790; Delaware, Jan. 28, 1790; New York, Feb. 24, 1790; Pennsylvania, Mar. 10, 1790; Rhode Island, June 7, 1790; Vermont, Nov. 3, 1791; Virginia, Dec. 15, 1791; Massachusetts, Mar. 2, 1939; Georgia, Mar. 8, 1939; Connecticut, Apr. 19, 1939. These original 10 ratified amendments follow as Amendments I to X inclusive.

(Of the two original proposed amendments which were not ratified by the necessary number of states, the first related to apportionment of Representatives; the second, to compensation of members.)

AMENDMENT I.

Religious establishment prohibited. Freedom of speech, of the press, and right to petition.

Congress shall make no law respecting an establishment of religion, or prohibiting the free exercise thereof; or abridging the freedom of speech, or of the press; or the right of the people peaceably to assemble, and to petition the Government for a redress of grievances.

AMENDMENT II.

Right to keep and bear arms.

A well-regulated militia, being necessary to the security of a free State, the right of the people to keep and bear arms, shall not be infringed.

AMENDMENT III.

Conditions for quarters for soldiers.

No soldier shall, in time of peace be quartered in any house, without the consent of the owner, nor in time of war, but in a manner to be prescribed by law.

AMENDMENT IV.

Right of search and seizure regulated.

The right of the people to be secure in their persons, houses, papers, and effects, against unreasonable searches and seizures, shall not be violated, and no warrants shall issue, but upon probable cause, supported by oath or affirmation, and particularly describing the place to be searched, and the persons or things to be seized.

AMENDMENT V

Provisions concerning prosecution. Trial and punishment—private property not to be taken for public use without compensation.

No person shall be held to answer for a capital, or otherwise infamous crime, unless on a presentment or indictment of a Grand Jury, except in cases arising in the land or naval forces, or in the militia, when in actual service in time of war or public danger; nor shall any person be subject for the same offense to be twice put in jeopardy of life or limb; nor shall be compelled in any criminal case to be a witness against himself, nor be deprived of life, liberty, or property, without due process of law; nor shall private property be taken for public use without just compensation.

AMENDMENT VI.

Right to speedy trial, witnesses, etc.

In all criminal prosecutions, the accused shall enjoy the right to a speedy and public trial, by an impartial jury of the State and district wherein the crime shall have been committed, which district shall have been previously ascertained by law, and to be informed of the nature and cause of the accusation; to be confronted with the witnesses against him; to have compulsory process for obtaining witnesses in his favor, and to have the assistance of counsel for his defense.

AMENDMENT VII.

Right of trial by jury.

In suits at common law, where the value in controversy shall exceed twenty dollars, the right of trial by jury shall be preserved, and no fact tried by a jury shall be otherwise reexamined in any court of the United States, than according to the rules of the common law.

AMENDMENT VIII.

Excessive bail or fines and cruel punishment prohibited.

Excessive bail shall not be required, nor excessive fines imposed, nor cruel and unusual punishments inflicted.

AMENDMENT IX.

Rule of construction of constitution.

The enumeration in the Constitution, of certain rights, shall not be construed to deny or disparage others retained by the people.

AMENDMENT X.

Rights of States under Constitution.

The powers not delegated to the United States by the Constitution, nor prohibited by it to the States, are reserved to the States respectively, or to the people.

Amendments Since the Bill of Rights

AMENDMENT XI.

Judicial powers construed.

The judicial power of the United States shall not be construed to extend to any suit in law or equity, commenced or prosecuted against one of the United States by citizens of another State, or by citizens or subjects of any foreign state.

(This amendment was proposed to the Legislatures of the several States by the Third Congress on March 4, 1794, and was declared to have been ratified in a message from the President to Congress, dated Jan. 8, 1798.

(It was on Jan. 5, 1798, that Secretary of State Pickering received from 12 of the States authenticated ratifications, and informed President John Adams of that fact.

(As a result of later research in the Department of State, it is now established that Amendment XI became part of the Constitution on Feb. 7, 1795, for on that date it had been ratified by 12 States as follows:

(1. New York, Mar. 27, 1794. 2. Rhode Island, Mar. 31, 1794. 3. Connecticut, May 8, 1794. 4. New Hampshire, June 16, 1794. 5. Massachusetts, June 26, 1794. 6. Vermont, between Oct. 9, 1794, and Nov. 9, 1794. 7. Virginia, Nov. 18, 1794. 8. Georgia, Nov. 29, 1794. 9. Kentucky, Dec. 7, 1794. 10. Maryland, Dec. 26, 1794. 11. Delaware, Jan. 23, 1795. 12. North Carolina, Feb. 7, 1795.

(On June 1, 1796, more than a year after Amendment XI had become a part of the Constitution (but before anyone was officially aware of this), Tennessee had been admitted as a State; but not until Oct. 16, 1797, was a certified copy of the resolution of Congress proposing the amendment sent to the Governor of Tennessee (John Sevier) by Secretary of State Pickering, whose office was then at Trenton, New Jersey, because of the epidemic of yellow fever at Philadelphia; it seems, however, that the Legislature of Tennessee took no action on Amendment XI, owing doubtless to the fact that public announcement of its adoption was made soon thereafter.

(Besides the necessary 12 States, one other, South Carolina, ratified Amendment XI, but this action was not taken until Dec. 4, 1797; the two remaining States, New Jersey and Pennsylvania, failed to ratify.)

AMENDMENT XII.

Manner of choosing President and Vice-President.

(Proposed by Congress Dec. 9, 1803; ratification completed June 15, 1804.)
The Electors shall meet in their respective States and vote by ballot for President and Vice-President, one of whom, at least, shall not be an inhabitant of the same State with themselves; they shall name in their ballots the person voted for as President, and in distinct ballots the person voted for as Vice-President, and they shall make distinct lists of all persons voted for as President, and of all persons voted for as Vice-President, and of the number of votes for each, which lists they shall sign and certify, and transmit sealed to the seat of the Government of the United States, directed to the President of the Senate; the President of the Senate shall, in the presence of the Senate and House of Representatives, open all the certificates and the votes shall then be counted;—The person having the greatest number of votes for President, shall be the President, if such number be a majority of the whole number of Electors appointed; and if no person have such majority, then from the persons having the highest numbers not exceeding three on the list of those voted for as President, the House of Representatives shall choose immediately, by ballot, the President. But in choosing the President, the votes shall be taken by States, the representation from each State having one vote; a quorum for this purpose shall consist of a member or members from two-thirds of the States,

and a majority of all the States shall be necessary to a choice. *(And if the House of Representatives shall not choose a President whenever the right of choice shall devolve upon them, before the fourth day of March next following, then the Vice-President shall act as President, as in case of the death of other constitutional disability of the President.) (The words in parentheses were superseded by Amendment XX, section 3.)* The person having the greatest number of votes as Vice-President, shall be the Vice-President, if such number be a majority of the whole number of Electors appointed, and if no person have a majority, then from the two highest numbers on the list, the Senate shall choose the Vice-President; a quorum for the purpose shall consist of two-thirds of the whole number of Senators, and a majority of the whole number shall be necessary to a choice. But no person constitutionally ineligible to the office of President shall be eligible to that of Vice-President of the United States.

THE RECONSTRUCTION AMENDMENTS

(Amendments XIII, XIV, and XV are commonly known as the Reconstruction Amendments, inasmuch as they followed the Civil War, and were drafted by Republicans who were bent on imposing their own policy of reconstruction on the South. Post-bellum legislatures there—Mississippi, South Carolina, Georgia, for example—had set up laws which, it was charged, were contrived to perpetuate Negro slavery under other names.)

AMENDMENT. XIII.

Slavery abolished.

(Proposed by Congress Jan. 31, 1865; ratification completed Dec. 6, 1865. The amendment, when first proposed by a resolution in Congress, was passed by the Senate, 38 to 6, on Apr. 8, 1864, but was defeated in the House, 95 to 66 on June 15, 1864. On reconsideration by the House, on Jan. 31, 1865, the resolution passed, 119 to 56. It was approved by President Lincoln on Feb. 1, 1865, although the Supreme Court had decided in 1798 that the President has nothing to do with the proposing of amendments to the Constitution, or their adoption.)
1. Neither slavery nor involuntary servitude, except as a punishment for crime whereof the party shall have been duly convicted, shall exist within the United States or any place subject to their jurisdiction.
2. Congress shall have power to enforce this article by appropriate legislation.

AMENDMENT XIV.

Citizenship rights not to be abridged.

(The following amendment was proposed to the Legislatures of the several states by the 39th Congress, June 13, 1866, and was declared to have been ratified in a proclamation by the Secretary of State, July 28, 1868.
(The 14th amendment was adopted only by virtue of ratification subsequent to earlier rejections. Newly constituted legislatures in both North Carolina and South Carolina (respectively July 4 and 9, 1868), ratified the proposed amendment, although earlier legislatures had rejected the proposal. The Secretary of State issued a proclamation, which, though doubtful as to the effect of attempted withdrawals by Ohio and New Jersey, entertained no doubt as to the validity of the ratification by North and South Carolina. The following day (July 21, 1868), Congress passed a resolution which declared the 14th Amendment to be a part of the Constitution and directed the Secretary of State so to promulgate it. The Secretary waited, however, until the newly constituted Legislature of Georgia had ratified the amendment, subsequent to an earlier rejection, before the promulgation of the ratification of the new amendment.)
1. All persons born or naturalized in the United States, and subject to the jurisdiction thereof, are citizens of the

United States and of the State wherein they reside. No State shall make or enforce any law which shall abridge the privileges or immunities of citizens of the United States; nor shall any State deprive any person of life, liberty, or property, without due process of law; nor deny to any person within its jurisdiction the equal protection of the laws.

2. Representatives shall be apportioned among the several States according to their respective numbers, counting the whole number of persons in each State, excluding Indians not taxed. But when the right to vote at any election for the choice of Electors for President and Vice-President of the United States, Representatives in Congress, the executive and judicial officers of a State, or the members of the Legislature thereof, is denied to any of the male inhabitants of such State, being twenty-one years of age, and citizens of the United States, or in any way abridged, except for participation in rebellion, or other crime, the basis of representation therein shall be reduced in the proportion which the number of such male citizens shall bear to the whole number of male citizens twenty-one years of age in such State.

3. No person shall be a Senator or Representative in Congress, or Elector of President and Vice-President, or hold any office, civil or military, under the United States, or under any State, who, having previously taken an oath, as a member of Congress, or as an officer of the United States, or as a member of any State Legislature, or as an executive or judicial officer of any State, to support the Constitution of the United States, shall have engaged in insurrection or rebellion against the same, or given aid or comfort to the enemies thereof. But Congress may by a vote of two-thirds of each House, remove such disability.

4. The validity of the public debt of the United States, authorized by law, including debts incurred for payment of pensions and bounties for services in suppressing insurrection or rebellion, shall not be questioned. But neither the United States nor any State shall assume or pay any debt or obligation incurred in aid of insurrection or rebellion against the United States, or any claim for the loss or emancipation of any slave; but all such debts, obligations and claims, shall be held illegal and void.

5. The Congress shall have power to enforce, by appropriate legislation, the provisions of this article.

AMENDMENT XV.

Race no bar to voting rights.

(The following amendment was proposed to the legislatures of the several States by the 40th Congress, Feb. 26, 1869, and was declared to have been ratified in a proclamation by the Secretary of State, Mar. 30, 1870.)

1. The right of citizens of the United States to vote shall not be denied or abridged by the United States or by any State on account of race, color, or previous condition of servitude.

2. The Congress shall have power to enforce this article by appropriate legislation.

AMENDMENT XVI.

Income taxes authorized.

(Proposed by Congress July 12, 1909; ratification completed Feb. 3, 1913.)

The Congress shall have power to lay and collect taxes on incomes, from whatever sources derived, without apportionment among the several States, and without regard to any census or enumeration.

AMENDMENT XVII.

United States Senators to be elected by direct popular vote.

(Proposed by Congress May 13, 1912; ratification completed Apr. 8, 1913.)

1. The Senate of the United States shall be composed of two Senators from each State, elected by the people thereof, for six years; and each Senator shall have one vote. The electors in each State shall have the qualifications requisite

for electors of the most numerous branch of the State Legislatures.

2. When vacancies happen in the representation of any State in the Senate, the executive authority of such State shall issue writs of election to fill such vacancies: Provided, That the Legislature of any State may empower the Executive thereof to make temporary appointments until the people fill the vacancies by election as the Legislature may direct.

3. This amendment shall not be so construed as to affect the election or term of any Senator chosen before it becomes valid as part of the Constitution.

AMENDMENT XVIII.

Liquor prohibition amendment.

(Proposed by Congress Dec. 18, 1917; ratification completed Jan. 16, 1919. Repealed by Amendment XXI, effective Dec. 5, 1933.)

(1. After one year from the ratification of this article the manufacture, sale, or transportation of intoxicating liquors within, the importation thereof into, or the exportation thereof from the United States and all territory subject to the jurisdiction thereof for beverage purposes is hereby prohibited.

(2. The Congress and the several States shall have concurrent power to enforce this article by appropriate legislation.

(3. This article shall be inoperative unless it shall have been ratified as an amendment to the Constitution by the Legislatures of the several States, as provided in the Constitution, within seven years from the date of the submission hereof to the States by the Congress.)

(The total vote in the Senates of the various States was 1,310 for, 237 against — 84.6% dry. In the lower houses of the States the vote was 3,782 for, 1,035 against — 78.5% dry.

(The amendment ultimately was adopted by all the States except Connecticut and Rhode Island.)

AMENDMENT XIX.

Giving nationwide suffrage to women.

(Proposed by Congress June 4, 1919; ratification certified by Secretary of State Aug. 26, 1920.)

1. The right of citizens of the United States to vote shall not be denied or abridged by the United States or by any State on account of sex.

2. Congress shall have power to enforce this Article by appropriate legislation.

AMENDMENT XX.

Terms of President and Vice President to begin on Jan. 20; those of senators, representatives, Jan. 3.

(Proposed by Congress Mar. 2, 1932; ratification completed Jan. 23, 1933.)

1. The terms of the President and Vice President shall end at noon on the 20th day of January, and the terms of Senators and Representatives at noon on the 3rd day of January, of the years in which such terms would have ended if this article had not been ratified; and the terms of their successors shall then begin.

2. The Congress shall assemble at least once in every year, and such meeting shall begin at noon on the 3rd day of January, unless they shall by law appoint a different day.

3. If, at the time fixed for the beginning of the term of the President, the President elect shall have died, the Vice President elect shall become President. If a President shall not have been chosen before the time fixed for the beginning of his term, or if the President elect shall have failed to qualify, then the Vice President elect shall act as President until a President shall have qualified; and the Congress may by law provide for the case wherein neither a President elect nor a Vice President shall have qualified, declaring who shall then act as President, or the manner in which one who is to act shall be selected, and such person shall act accordingly until a President or Vice President shall have qualified.

4. The Congress may by law provide for the case of the death of any of the persons from whom the House of Repre-

sentatives may choose a President whenever the right of choice shall have devolved upon them, and for the case of the death of any of the persons from whom the Senate may choose a Vice President whenever the right of choice shall have devolved upon them.

5. Sections 1 and 2 shall take effect on the 15th day of October following the ratification of this article (Oct., 1933).

6. This article shall be inoperative unless it shall have been ratified as an amendment to the Constitution by the Legislatures of three-fourths of the several States within seven years from the date of its submission.

AMENDMENT XXI.

Repeal of Amendment XVIII.

(Proposed by Congress Feb. 20, 1933; ratification completed Dec. 5, 1933.)

1. The eighteenth article of amendment to the Constitution of the United States is hereby repealed.

2. The transportation or importation into any State, Territory, or Possession of the United States for delivery or use therein of intoxicating liquors, in violation of the laws thereof, is hereby prohibited.

3. This article shall be inoperative unless it shall have been ratified as an amendment to the Constitution by conventions in the several States, as provided in the Constitution, within seven years from the date of the submission hereof to the States by the Congress.

AMENDMENT XXII.

Presidential vote for District of Columbia.

(Proposed by Congress June 17, 1960; ratification completed Mar. 29, 1961.)

1. No person shall be elected to the office of the President more than twice, and no person who has held the office of President, or acted as President, for more than two years of a term to which some other person was elected President shall be elected to the office of the President more than once. But this Article shall not apply to any person holding the office of President when this Article was proposed by the Congress, and shall not prevent any person who may be holding the office of President, or acting as President, during the term within which this Article becomes operative from holding the office of President or acting as President during the remainder of such term.

2. This article shall be inoperative unless it shall have been ratified as an amendment to the Constitution by the Legislatures of three-fourths of the several States within seven years from the date of its submission to the States by the Congress.

AMENDMENT XXIII.

Presidential vote for District of Columbia.

(Proposed by Congress June 17, 1960; ratification completed Mar. 29, 1961.)

1. The District constituting the seat of Government of the United States shall appoint in such manner as the Congress may direct:

A number of electors of President and Vice President equal to the whole number of Senators and Representatives in Congress to which the District would be entitled if it were a State, but in no event more than the least populous State; they shall be in addition to those appointed by the States, but they shall be considered, for the purposes of the election of President and Vice President, to be electors appointed by a State; and they shall meet in the District and perform such duties as provided by the twelfth article of amendment.

2. The Congress shall have power to enforce this article by appropriate legislation.

AMENDMENT XXIV.

Barring poll tax in federal elections.

(Proposed by Congress Aug. 27, 1962; ratification completed Jan. 23, 1964.)

1. The right of citizens of the United States to vote in any primary or other election for President or Vice President, for electors for President or Vice President, or for Senator or Representative in Congress, shall not be denied or abridged by the United States or any State by reason of failure to pay any poll tax or other tax.

2. The Congress shall have power to enforce this article by appropriate legislation.

AMENDMENT XXV.

Presidential disability and succession.

(Proposed by Congress July 6, 1965; ratification completed Feb. 10, 1967.)

1. In case of the removal of the President from office or of his death or resignation, the Vice President shall become President.

2. Whenever there is a vacancy in the office of the Vice President, the President shall nominate a Vice President who shall take office upon confirmation by a majority vote of both houses of Congress.

3. Whenever the President transmits to the President pro tempore of the Senate and the Speaker of the House of Representatives his written declaration that he is unable to discharge the powers and duties of his office, and until he transmits to them a written declaration to the contrary, such powers and duties shall be discharged by the Vice President as Acting President.

4. Whenever the Vice President and a majority of either the principal officers of the executive departments or of such other body as Congress may by law provide, transmit to the President pro tempore of the Senate and the Speaker of the House of Representatives their written declaration that the President is unable to discharge the powers and duties of his office, the Vice President shall immediately assume the powers and duties of the office as Acting President.

Thereafter, when the President transmits to the President pro tempore of the Senate and the Speaker of the House of Representatives his written declaration that no inability exists, he shall resume the powers and duties of his office unless the Vice President and a majority of either the principal officers of the executive department or of such other body as Congress may by law provide, transmit within four days to the President pro tempore of the Senate and the Speaker of the House of Representatives their written declaration that the President is unable to discharge the powers and duties of his office. Thereupon Congress shall decide the issue, assembling within forty-eight hours for that purpose if not in session. If the Congress, within twenty-one days after receipt of the latter written declaration, or, if Congress is not in session, within twenty-one days after Congress is required to assemble, determines by two-thirds vote of both houses that the President is unable to discharge the powers and duties of his office, the Vice President shall continue to discharge the same as Acting President; otherwise, the President shall resume the powers and duties of his office.

AMENDMENT XXVI.

Lowering voting age to 18 years.

(Proposed by Congress Mar. 23, 1971; ratification completed June 30, 1971.)

1. The right of citizens of the United States, who are 18 years of age or older, to vote shall not be denied or abridged by the United States or any state on account of age.

2. The Congress shall have the power to enforce this article by appropriate legislation.

PROPOSED EQUAL RIGHTS AMENDMENT

(Proposed by Congress Mar. 22, 1972; ratification completed, as of Apr. 25, 1975, by 34 states, rejected by 11; needs total of 38 for adoption.)

1. Equality of rights under the law shall not be denied or abridged by the United States or by any State on account of sex.

2. The Congress shall have the power to enforce, by appropriate legislation, the provisions of this article.

3. This amendment shall take effect two years after the date of ratification.

Statue of Liberty National Monument

Since 1886, the Statue of Liberty Enlightening the World has stood as a symbol of freedom in New York harbor. It also commemorates French-American friendship for it was given by the people of France, designed by Frederic Auguste Bartholdi (1834-1904). A $2.5 million building housing the American Museum of Immigration was opened by Pres. Nixon Sept. 26, 1972, at the base of the statue. Exhibit halls, a library, and study rooms as well as a hall of records will be grouped within the star-shaped Fort Wood which contains the museum. The statue is a National Monument, administered by the National Park Service.

Edouard de Laboulaye, French historian and admirer of American political institutions, suggested that the French present a monument to the United States, the latter to provide pedestal and site. Bartholdi visualized a colossal statue at the entrance of New York harbor, welcoming the peoples of the world with the torch of liberty.

The French approved the idea and formed the Franco-American Union to raise funds, which eventually reached $250,000. Bartholdi began work about 1874 in Paris. He made several models and one, 36 ft. tall, enabled him to compute the statue in sections. Wooden battens were made and sheets of copper 3/32 of an inch thick were hammered into shape by hand. A framework of 4 steel supports was designed by Gustave Eiffel, creator of the Eiffel Tower.

On Washington's birthday, Feb. 22, 1877, Congress approved the use of a site on Bedloe's Island suggested by Bartholdi. This island of 12 acres had been owned in the 17th century by a Walloon named Isaac Bedloe, who came to New Amsterdam in 1639. He died in 1673 and his wife sold the island for £ 80. In later years it was owned by the City of New York and the U.S. Government. It was called Bedloe's until Aug. 3, 1956, when President Eisenhower approved a resolution of Congress changing the name to Liberty Island.

The hand of the statue holding aloft the torch was exhibited at the Centennial Exposition in Philadelphia in 1876 and later in Madison Square.

The head was shown at the Paris exposition of 1878. When framework and base were put in place in Paris the American minister, Levi P. Morton, drove the first rivet on Oct. 24, 1881, in honor of the centennial of the battle of Yorktown, in which the French and Americans were allies.

The statue was finished May 21, 1884, and formally presented to U.S. Minister Morton July 4, 1884, by Ferdinand de Lesseps, head of the Franco-American Union, promoter of the Panama Canal, and builder of the Suez Canal.

On Aug. 5, 1884, the Americans laid the cornerstone for the pedestal. This was to be built on the foundations of Fort Wood, which had been erected by the Government in 1811. The American committee had raised $125,000, but when the pedestal was 15 ft. high, this was found to be inadequate. Joseph Pulitzer, owner of the New York World, appealed on Mar. 16, 1885, for general donations. By Aug. 11, 1885, he had raised $100,000. The pedestal was made of concrete with granite facing and steel girders were built into it to connect with framework of the statue.

The statue arrived dismantled, in 214 packing cases, in the steamship Isere, which reached New York from Rouen, France, in June, 1885. The last rivet of the statue was driven Oct. 28, 1886, when President Grover Cleveland dedicated the monument. The total cost of statue and pedestal was estimated at $500,000.

Funds for permanently lighting the statue were raised by the World in 1916 and President Wilson turned on the lights Dec. 2, 1916.

At the celebration of the statue's 50th anniversary, in 1936, President Franklin D. Roosevelt said: "The realization that we are all bound together by hope of a common future rather than by reverence for a common past has helped us to build upon this continent a unity unapproached in any similar area or similar size population in the whole world. For all our millions of people, there is a unity in language and speech, in law and economics, in education and in general purpose which nowhere finds its match.

"It was the hope of those who gave us this statue and the hope of the American people in receiving it that the Goddess of Liberty and the Goddess of Peace were the same."

The statue weighs 450,000 lbs. or 225 tons. The copper sheeting weighs 200,000 lbs. There are 167 steps from the land level to the top of the pedestal, 168 steps inside the statue to the head, and 54 rungs on the ladder leading to the arm that holds the torch. Visitors may enter the head, which holds from 30 to 40 persons, but not the torch. The statue is open daily.

Dimensions of the Statue	Ft.	In.
Height from base to torch (45.3 meters)	151	1
Foundation of pedestal to torch (91.5 meters)	305	1
Heel to top of head	111	1
Length of hand	16	5
Index finger	8	0
Circumference at second joint	3	6
Size of finger nail 13x10 in.		
Head from chin to cranium	17	3
Head, thickness from ear to ear	10	0
Distance across the eye	2	6
Length of nose	4	6
Right arm, length	42	0
Right arm, greatest thickness	12	0
Thickness of waist	35	0
Width of mouth	3	0
Tablet, length	23	7
Tablet, width	13	7
Tablet, thickness	2	0

Emma Lazarus' Famous Poem

A poem by Emma Lazarus is graven on a tablet within the pedestal on which the statue stands:

The New Colossus

Not like the brazen giant of Greek fame,
With conquering limbs astride from land to land;
Here at our sea-washed, sunset gates shall stand
A mighty woman with a torch, whose flame
Is the imprisoned lightning, and her name
Mother of Exiles. From her beacon-hand
Glows world-wide welcome; her mild eyes command
The air-bridged harbor that twin cities frame.
"Keep ancient lands, your storied pomp!" cries she
With silent lips. "Give me your tired, your poor,
Your huddled masses yearning to breathe free,
The wretched refuse of your teeming shore.
Send these, the homeless, tempest-tost to me,
I lift my lamp beside the golden door!"

Nearby Ellis Island, abandoned as an immigration center in 1954 after serving as the gateway to America for 16 million, was proclaimed by President Johnson in 1965 part of the Statue of Liberty National Monument.

The National Anthem — The Star-Spangled Banner

The Star-Spangled Banner was ordered played by the military and naval services by President Woodrow Wilson in 1916. It was designated the National Anthem by Act of Congress, Mar. 3, 1931. It was written by Francis Scott Key, of Georgetown, D. C., during the bombardment of Fort McHenry, Baltimore, Md., Sept. 13-14, 1814. Key was a lawyer, a graduate of St. John's College, Annapolis, and a volunteer in a light artillery company. When a friend, Dr. Beanes, a physician of Upper Marlborough, Md., was taken aboard Admiral Cockburn's British squadron for interfering with ground troops, Key and J. S. Skinner, carrying a note from President Madison, went to the fleet under a flag of truce on a cartel ship to ask Beanes' release. Admiral Cockburn consented, but as the fleet was about to sail up the Patapsco to bombard Fort McHenry he detained them, first on H. M. S. Surprise, and then on a supply ship.

Key witnessed the bombardment from his own vessel. It began at 7 a.m., Sept. 13, 1814, and lasted, with intermissions, for 25 hours. The British fired over 1,500 shells, each weighing as much as 220 lbs. They were unable to approach closely because the Americans had sunk 22 vessels in the channel. Only four Americans were killed and 24 wounded. A British bomb-ship was disabled.

During the bombardment Key wrote a stanza on the back of an envelope. Next day at Indian Queen Inn, Baltimore, he wrote out the poem and gave it to his brother-in-law, Judge J. H. Nicholson. Nicholson suggested the tune, Anacreon in Heaven, and had the poem printed on broadsides, of which two survive. On Sept. 20 it appeared in the Baltimore American. Later Key made 3 copies; one is in the Library of Congress and one in the Pennsylvania Historical Society.

The copy that Key wrote in his hotel Sept. 14, 1814, remained in the Nicholson family for 93 years. In 1907 it was sold to Henry Walters of Baltimore. In 1934 it was bought at auction in New York from the Walters estate by the Walters Art Gallery, Baltimore, for $26,400. The Walters Gallery in 1953 sold the manuscript to the Maryland Historical Society for the same price.

The flag that Key saw during the bombardment is preserved in the Smithsonian Institution, Washington. It is 30 by 42 ft., and has 15 alternate red and white stripes and 15 stars, for the original 13 states plus Kentucky and Vermont. It was made by Mary Young Pickersgill. The Baltimore Flag House, a museum, occupies her premises, which were restored in 1953.

The Star-Spangled Banner

I

Oh, say can you see by the dawn's early light
  What so proudly we hailed at the twilight's last gleaming?
Whose broad stripes and bright stars thru the perilous fight.
  O'er the ramparts we watched were so gallantly streaming?
And the rocket's red glare, the bombs bursting in air.
  Gave proof through the night that our flag was still there.
Oh, say does that star-spangled banner yet wave
  O'er the land of the free and the home of the brave?

II

On the shore, dimly seen through the mists of the deep,
  Where the foe's haughty host in dread silence reposes,
What is that which the breeze, o'er the towering steep,
  As it fitfully blows, half conceals, half discloses?
Now it catches the gleam of the morning's first beam,
  In full glory reflected now shines on the stream:
'Tis the star-spangled banner! O long may it wave
  O'er the land of the free and the home of the brave!

III

And where is that band who so vauntingly swore
  That the havoc of war and the battle's confusion,
A home and a country should leave us no more!
  Their blood has washed out their foul footsteps' pollution.
No refuge could save the hireling and slave
  From the terror of flight, or the gloom of the grave:
And the star-spangled banner in triumph doth wave
  O'er the land of the free and the home of the brave!

IV

Oh! thus be it ever, when freemen shall stand
  Between their loved homes and the war's desolation!
Blest with victory and peace, may the heav'n rescued land
  Praise the Power that hath made and preserved us a nation.
Then conquer we must, when our cause it is just,
  And this be our motto: "In God is our trust."
And the star-spangled banner in triumph shall wave
  O'er the land of the free and the home of the brave!

Yankee Doodle

The first known American printing of the popular song "Yankee Doodle" was as part of Benjamin Carr's *Federal Overture* in Baltimore in 1795. The origin of the song is unknown but it is believed to have been composed in the 1750s and used to deride the colonies. It became instead a patriotic American air. Some of the verses are:

Father and I went down to camp
Along with Captain Gooding,
And there we saw the men and boys
As thick as hasty pudding.

Yankee Doodle keep it up
Yankee Doodle Dandy,
Mind the music and the step,
And with the girls be handy.

There was Captain Washington
Upon a slapping stallion
A-giving orders to his men—
There must have been a million.

There I saw a wooden keg
With heads made out of leather;
They knocked upon it with some sticks
To call the folks together.

Then they'd fife away like fun
And play on cornstalk fiddles,
And some had ribbons red as blood
All bound around their middles.

I can't tell you all I saw—
They kept up such a smother.
I took my hat off, made a bow,
And scampered home to mother.

Code of Etiquette for Display and Use of the U.S. Flag

Although the Stars and Stripes originated in 1777, it was not until 146 years later that there was a serious attempt to establish a uniform code of etiquette for the United States flag. The War Department issued Feb. 15, 1923, a circular on the rules of flag usage. These were adopted almost in their entirety Jun. 14, 1923, by a conference of 68 patriotic organizations in Washington. Finally, on Jun. 22, 1942, a joint resolution of Congress codified "existing rules and customs pertaining to the flag for civilians."

When to Display the Flag—The flag should be displayed on all days when the weather permits, especially on legal holidays and other special occasions, on official buildings when in use, in or near polling places on election days, and in or near schools when in session. A citizen may fly the flag at any time he wishes. It is customary to display the flag only from sunrise to sunset on buildings and on stationary flagstaffs in the open. However, it may be displayed at night on special occasions, preferably lighted. In Washington, the flag now flies over the White House both day and night. It flies over the Senate wing of the Capitol when the Senate is in session and over the House wing when that body is in session. It flies day and night over the east and west fronts of the Capitol, without floodlights at night but receiving light from the illuminated Capitol Dome. It flies 24 hours a day at several other places, including the Fort McHenry Nat'l. Monument in Baltimore, where it inspired Francis Scott Key to write The Star Spangled Banner.

How to Fly the Flag—The flag should be hoisted briskly and lowered ceremoniously, and should never be allowed to touch the ground or the floor. When hung over a sidewalk from a rope extending from a building to a pole, the union should be away from the building. When hung over the center of a street it should have the union to the north in an east-west street and to the east in a north-south street. No other flag may be flown above or, if on the same level, to the right of the United States flag, except that at the United Nations Headquarters the UN flag may be placed above flags of all member nations and other national flags may be flown with equal prominence or honor with the flag of the United States. At services by Navy chaplains at sea, the church pennant may be flown above the flag.

When two flags are placed against a wall with crossed staffs, the U.S. flag should be at right—its own right, and its staff should be in front of the staff of the other flag; when a number of flags are grouped and displayed from staffs, it should be at the center and highest point of the group.

Church and Platform Use—In an auditorium, the flag may be displayed flat, above and behind the speaker. If on a staff in a church chancel or on a speaker's platform, it should be in the position of honor at the clergyman's or speaker's right as he faces the congregation or audience. Any other flag in the chancel or on the platform should be displayed at the clergyman's or speaker's left. If elsewhere than in chancel or on platform, the flag should be displayed at the right of the congregation or audience as they face the speaker.

When the flag is displayed horizontally or vertically against a wall, the stars should be at the observer's left.

When to Salute the Flag—All persons present should face the flag, stand at attention and salute on the following occasions: (1) When the flag is passing in a parade or in a review, (2) During the ceremony of hoisting or lowering, (3) When the National Anthem is played and the flag is dis-

played, and (4) During the Pledge of Allegiance. Those present in uniform should render the military salute. When not in uniform, men should remove the hat with the right hand holding it at the left shoulder, the hand being over the heart. Men without hats should salute in the same manner. Aliens should stand at attention. Women should salute by placing the right hand over the heart.

On Memorial Day, the flag should fly at half-staff until noon, then be raised to the peak.

As provided by Presidential proclamation the flag should fly at half-staff for 30 days from the day of a death of a president or former president; for 10 days from the day of death of a vice president, chief justice or retired chief justice of the U.S., or speaker of the House of Representatives; from day of death until burial of an associate justice of the Supreme Court, cabinet member, former vice president, or Senate president pro tempore, majority or minority Senate leader, or majority or minority House leader; for a U.S. senator, representative, territorial delegate, or the resident commissioner of Puerto Rico, on day of death and the following day within the metropolitan area of the District of Columbia and from day of death until burial within the decedent's state, congressional district, territory or commonwealth; and for the death of the governor of a state, territory, or possession of the U.S., from day of death until burial within that state, territory, or possession.

When used to cover a casket, the flag should be placed so that the union is at the head and over the left shoulder. It should not be lowered into the grave nor touch the ground.

Prohibited Uses of the Flag—The flag should not be dipped to any person or thing. It should never be displayed with the union down save as a distress signal. It should never be carried flat or horizontally, but always aloft and free.

It should not be displayed on a float, motor car or boat except from a staff.

It should never be used as a covering for a ceiling, nor have placed upon it any word, design, or drawing. It should never be used as a receptacle for carrying anything. It should not be used to cover a statue or a monument.

The flag should never be used for advertising purposes, nor be embroidered on such articles as cushions or handkerchiefs, printed or otherwise impressed on boxes or used as a costume or athletic uniform. Advertising signs should not be fastened to its staff or halyard.

The flag should never be used as drapery of any sort, never festooned, drawn back, nor up, in folds, but always allowed to fall free. Bunting of blue, white and red always arranged with the blue above and the white in the middle, should be used for covering a speaker's desk, draping the front of a platform, and for decoration in general.

An Act of Congress approved Feb. 8, 1917, provided certain penalties for the desecration, mutilation or improper use of the flag within the District of Columbia. A 1968 federal law provided penalties of up to a year's imprisonment or a $1,000 fine or both, for publicly burning or otherwise desecrating any flag of the United States. In addition, many states have laws against flag desecration.

How to Dispose of Worn Flags—The flag, when it is in such condition that it is no longer a fitting emblem for display, should be destroyed in a dignified way, preferably by burning in private.

Pledge of Allegiance to the Flag

I pledge allegiance to the flag of the United States of America and to the republic for which it stands, one nation under God, indivisible, with liberty and justice for all.

This, the current official version of the Pledge of Allegiance, has developed from the original pledge, which was first published in the Sept. 8, 1892, issue of the Youth's Companion, a weekly magazine then published in Boston. The original pledge contained the phrase "my flag," which was changed more than 30 years later to "flag of the United States of America." An act of Congress in 1954 added the words "under God."

The authorship of the pledge has been in dispute for

many years. The Youth's Companion stated in 1917 that the original draft was written by James B. Upham, an executive of the magazine who died in 1910. A leaflet circulated by the magazine later named Upham as the originator of the draft "afterwards condensed and perfected by him and his associates of the Companion force."

Francis Bellamy, a former member of the Youth's Companion editorial staff, publicly claimed authorship of the pledge in 1923. The United States Flag Assn., acting on the advice of a committee named to study the controversy, upheld in 1939 the claim of Bellamy, who had died 8 years earlier. The Library of Congress issued in 1957 a report attributing the authorship to Bellamy.

The Flag of the United States—The Stars and Stripes

The 50-star flag of the United States was raised for the first time officially at 12:01 a.m. on Jul. 4, 1960, at Fort McHenry National Monument in Baltimore, Md. The 50th star had been added for Hawaii; a year earlier the 49th, for Alaska. Before that, no star had been added since 1912, when N. M. and Ariz. were admitted to the Union.

History of the Flag

The true history of the Stars and Stripes has become so cluttered by a volume of myth and tradition that the facts are difficult, and in some cases impossible, to establish. For example, it is not certain who designed the Stars and Stripes, who made the first such flag, or even whether it ever flew in any sea fight or land battle of the American Revolution. Historians disagree on many details of the history of the Stars and Stripes and the flags that preceded it.

One thing all agree on is that the Stars and Stripes originated as the result of a resolution offered by the Marine Committee of the Second Continental Congress at Philadelphia and adopted Jun. 14, 1777. It read:

Resolved: that the flag of the United States be thirteen stripes, alternate red and white; that the union be thirteen stars, white in a blue field, representing a new constellation.

Congress gave no hint as to the designer of the flag, no instructions as to the arrangement of the stars, and no information on its appropriate uses. Historians have been unable to find the original flag law.

The resolution establishing the flag was not even published until Sept. 2, 1777, more than 11 weeks after its passage. Despite repeated requests by the American commander, Gen. George Washington, for the "Standard of the United States" for his army, he did not get the flags until 1783, after the Revolutionary War was over. And there is no certainty that they were the Stars and Stripes.

Early Flags

Although it was never officially adopted by the Continental Congress, many historians consider the first flag of the United States to have been the Grand Union (sometimes called Great Union) flag. This was a modification of the British Meteor flag, which had the red cross of St. George and the white cross of St. Andrew combined in the blue canton. For the Grand Union flag, 6 horizontal stripes were imposed on the red field, dividing it into 13 alternate red and white stripes. On Jan. 1, 1776, when the Continental Army came into formal existence, this flag was unfurled on Prospect Hill, Somerville, Mass. Washington wrote that "we hoisted the Union Flag in compliment to the United Colonies."

One of several flags about which controversy has raged for years is at Easton, Pa. Containing the devices of the national flag in reversed order, this has been in the public library at Easton for over 150 years. Supporters of the movement contend that this flag was actually the first Stars and Stripes, and that it was first displayed on Jul. 8, 1776, on the occasion of the public reading of the Declaration of Independence at the court house in Easton. This flag has 13 red and white stripes in the canton, 13 white stars centered in a blue field.

A flag was hastily improvised from garments by the defenders of Fort Schuyler at Rome, N.Y., Aug. 3-22, 1777, and this has led to the assumption that it was the Stars and Stripes. Historians believe it was the Grand Union Flag.

The Sons of Liberty had a flag of 9 red and white stripes, to signify 9 colonies, when they met in New York in 1765 to oppose the Stamp Tax. By 1775, the flag had grown to 13 red and white stripes, with a rattlesnake on it.

At Concord, Apr. 19, 1775, the minute men from Bedford, Mass., are said to have carried a flag having a silver arm with sword on a red field.

At Cambridge, Mass., the Sons of Liberty used a plain red flag with a green pine tree on it.

In June 1775, Washington went from Philadelphia to Boston to take command of the army, escorted to New York by the Philadelphia Light Horse Troop. It carried a yellow flag which had an elaborate coat of arms — the shield charged with 13 knots, the motto "For These We Strive" — and a canton of 13 blue and silver stripes.

In Feb., 1776, Col. Christopher Gadsden, member of the Continental Congress, gave the South Carolina Provincial Congress a flag "such as is to be used by the commander-in-chief of the American Navy." It had a yellow field, with a rattlesnake about to strike and the words Don't Tread on Me. Benjamin Franklin's paper, the Pennsylvania Gazette, had suggested sending a cargo of rattlesnakes to London parks to retaliate for British injustice.

At the battle of Bennington, Aug. 16, 1777, patriots used a flag of 7 white and 6 red stripes with a blue canton extending down 9 stripes and showing an arch of 11 white stars over the figure 76 and a star in each of the upper corners. The stars are seven-pointed. This flag is preserved in the Historical Museum at Bennington, Vt.

At the Battle of Cowpens, Jan. 17, 1781, the 3d Maryland Regt. is said to have carried a flag of 13 red and white stripes, with a blue canton containing 12 stars in a circle around one star.

Legends about the Flag

Who Designed the Flag? No one knows for a certainty. Francis Hopkinson, a signer of the Declaration of Independence and designer of seals for the State Department, the Treasury Board, and of a naval flag, declared he also had designed the flag and in 1781 asked Congress to reimburse him for his services. Congress did not do so. Dumas Malone of Columbia Univ. wrote: "This talented man . . . designed the American flag."

Who Called the Flag Old Glory? — The flag is said to have been named Old Glory by William Driver, a sea captain of Salem, Mass. One legend has it that when he raised the flag on his brig, the Charles Doggett, in 1824, he said: "I name thee Old Glory." But his daughter, who presented the flag to the Smithsonian Institution, said he named it at his 21st birthday celebration Mar. 17, 1824, when his mother presented the homemade flag to him.

Washington Coat-of-Arms Legend — The idea that the flag was suggested by Washington's coat of arms was publicized by Martin F. Tupper, an English writer, in a play in the 1870s. It rests on a coincidence and has no validity.

Washington's Invocation Legend — Circulation has been given to this speech attributed to General Washington: "We take the stars from heaven, the red from our mother country, separating it by white stripes, thus showing that we have separated from her, and the white stripes shall go down to posterity representing liberty." There is no proof that Washington ever said this.

The Betsy Ross Legend — The widely publicized legend that Mrs. Betsy Ross made the first Stars and Stripes in June 1776, at the request of a committee composed of George Washington, Robert Morris, and George Ross, an uncle, was first made public in 1870, by a grandson of Mrs. Ross. Historians have been unable to find a historical record of such a meeting or committee. Dr. Milo Milton Quaife wrote: "No record has ever been found of the creation by Mrs. Ross of the first Stars and Stripes." The New Century Cyclopedia of Names (1954) says: "There is documentary evidence that she was paid in May, 1777, for 'making ships' colours, etc.' but no direct documentary evidence has been found to link her with the flag adopted by the Continental Congress on June 14, 1777, as the national emblem, and most historians now doubt if she made it."

Adding New Stars

The flag of 1777 was used until 1795. Then, on the admission of Vermont and Kentucky to the Union, Congress passed and President Washington signed an act that after May 1, 1795, the flag should have 15 stripes, alternate red and white, and 15 white stars on a blue field in the union.

When new states were admitted it became evident that the flag would become burdened with stripes. Congress thereupon ordered that after Jul. 4, 1818, the flag should have 13 stripes, symbolizing the 13 original states; that the union have 20 stars, and that whenever a new state was admitted a new star should be added on the Jul. 4 following admission. No law designates the permanent arrangement of the stars. However, since 1912 when a new state has been admitted, the new design has been announced by executive order. No star is specifically identified with any state.

British Red Ensign. This "Meteor" flag, in common use from 1707, flew on British Royal Navy ships.

Great Union Flag. Flown Jan. 1, 1776, on Prospect Hill in Somerville, Mass., in celebration of formal existence of Continental Army.

Pine Tree Flag. First naval ensign, made at request of George Washington's military secretary in autumn of 1775 for fleet of armed schooners.

Moultrie Flag. Designed in 1776 by Col. William Moultrie, flew over Ft. Sullivan in Charleston Harbor, S.C.

Bunker Hill Flag. From a John Turnbull painting, one of 2 flags believed to have been flown at Battle of Bunker Hill on June 17, 1775.

Gadsden Rattler. Emblem of Col. Christopher Gadsden, South Carolina delegate to Continental Congress; Commodore Hopkins' personal standard on 1776 voyage to Bahamas Is.

Navy Jack. In common use at sea for many years and known as American Stripes, flag recorded in history as First Navy Jack.

Betsy Ross. According to legend now discredited, flag made by Betsy Ross of Philadelphia, Pa., in May or June 1776 following a sketch by Washington.

Bennington Flag. According to tradition, raised by Bennington militia at Battle of Bennington on Aug. 16, 1777. Possibly the oldest stars and stripes now in existence.

Serapis. According to a reliable sketch by a Dutch artist, flag flown by Serapis, British ship captured by John Paul Jones as his flagship in sea battle Sept. 1779.

3rd Maryland Regiment. Another early stars and stripes believed to be banner flown by 3rd Maryland Regiment on Jan. 17, 1781, at Battle of Cowpens, in South Carolina.

Yorktown Flag. Based on Lt. Col. John Graves Simcoe's watercolor, flag believed to have flown when Gen. Cornwallis surrendered at Yorktown, Va.

North Carolina Militia Flag. Another claimant for first stars and stripes honors, flag was supposedly carried by N.C. militiamen at Guilford Courthouse, Mar. 15, 1781.

Alliance. According to a reliable sketch by a Dutch artist, stars and stripes flown by Alliance, American ship which sailed with Serapis.

Boston Flag. Generally classed as garrison rather than battle flag; supposed to have flown over Ft. Independence at Boston, Mass., in 1871.

Probable Hopkinson. Stars and stripes design claimed, in 1870, by Francis Hopkinson, signer of Declaration of Independence. Claim never recognized.

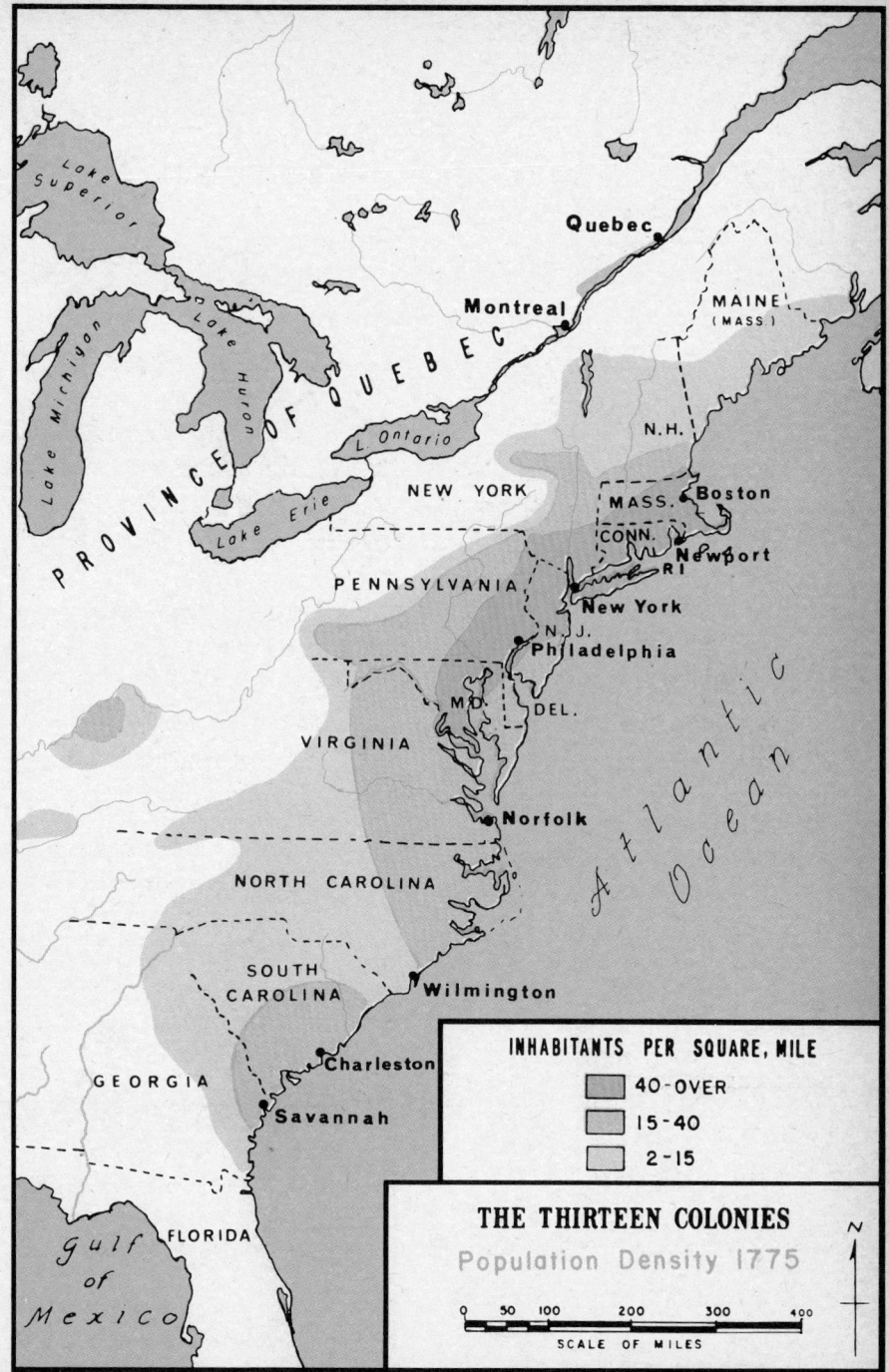

Lake Superior

Lake Michigan

Lake Huron

L. Ontario

Lake Erie

PROVINCE OF QUEBEC

Quebec

Montreal

MAINE
(MASS.)

N.H.

NEW YORK

MASS. Boston

CONN.

Newport

R.I.

PENNSYLVANIA

New York

N.J.

Philadelphia

MD.

DEL.

VIRGINIA

Norfolk

NORTH CAROLINA

SOUTH
CAROLINA

Wilmington

GEORGIA

Charleston

Savannah

FLORIDA

Atlantic Ocean

Gulf
of
Mexico

INHABITANTS PER SQUARE, MILE

40-OVER

15-40

2-15

THE THIRTEEN COLONIES

Population Density 1775

N

0   50   100   200   300   400

SCALE OF MILES

Maps pages 291-299 by Edward J. Krasnoborski in Dave R. Palmer's *Early American Wars and Institutions*.
West Point, 1974. Reprinted by permission of the Professor and Head, Department of History, U.S. Military Academy.

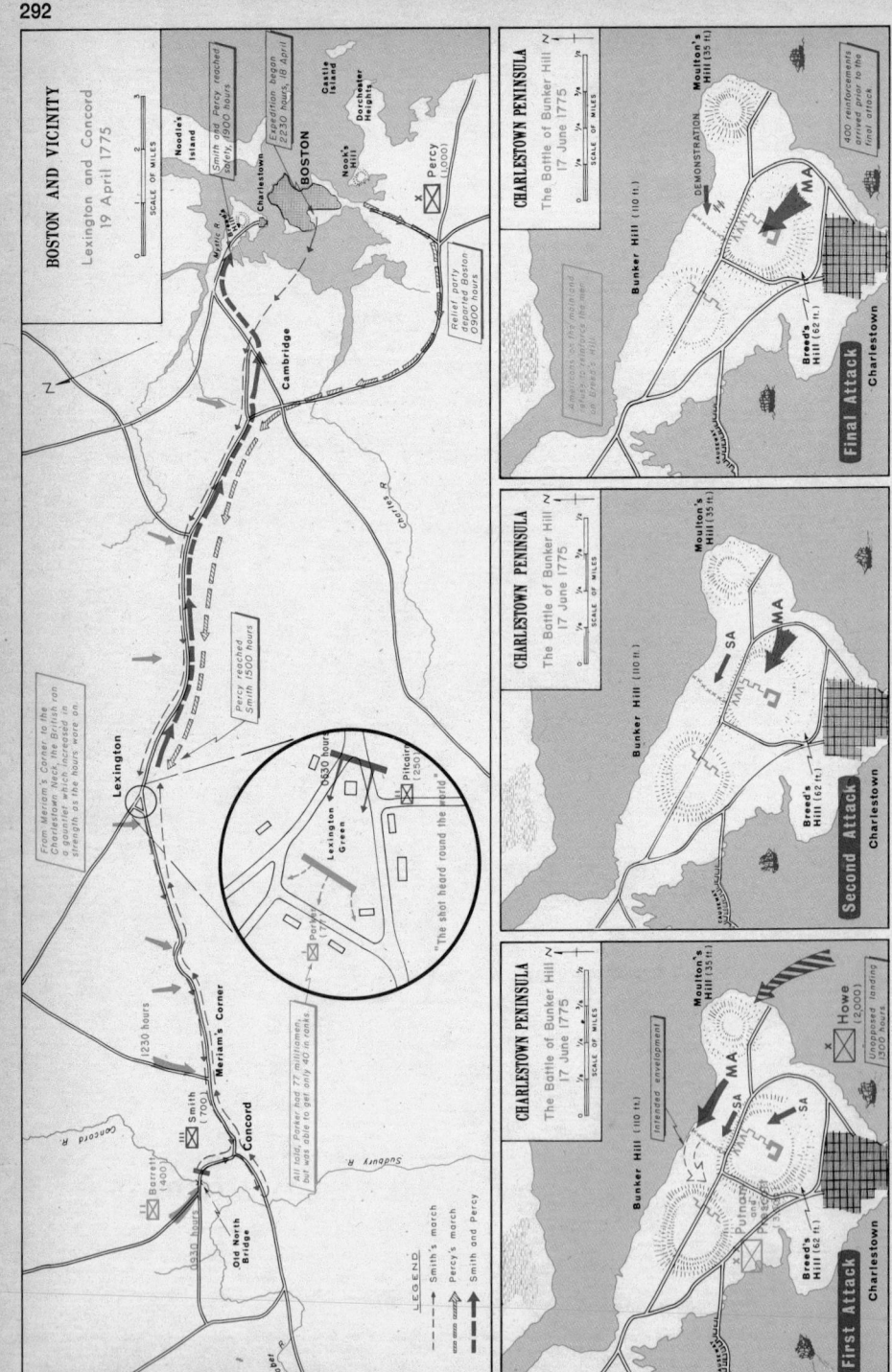

BOSTON AND VICINITY

Lexington and Concord
19 April 1775

SCALE OF MILES
0 — 3

Needle's Island

Smith and Percy reached
Safety, 1900 hours

Charlestown

Expedition began
2230 hours, 18 April

BOSTON

Noah's Hill

Castle Island

Dorchester Heights

Percy
(1,000)

Relief party
departed Boston
0900 hours

Cambridge

Charles R.

From Meriam's Corner to the
Charlestown Neck, the British ran
a gauntlet which increased in
strength as the hours wore on

Percy reached
Smith 1500 hours

Lexington

0630 hours

Pitcairn
(250)

Lexington Green

Percy
(1,?)

"The shot heard round the world"

1230 hours

Meriam's Corner

Concord

Alt told, Parker had 77 militiamen,
but was able to get only 40 in ranks.

Smith
(700)

Concord R.

Berrett
(400)

Old North Bridge

0930 hours

Sudbury R.

Assabet R.

LEGEND

Smith's march
Percy's march
Smith and Percy

CHARLESTOWN PENINSULA

The Battle of Bunker Hill
17 June 1775

N

SCALE OF MILES

Moulton's Hill (35 ft.)

DEMONSTRATION

MA

Bunker Hill (110 ft.)

Americans to the mainland
while maintaining their rear
on Breed's Hill

Breed's Hill (62 ft.)

Charlestown

400 reinforcements
arrived prior to the
final attack

Final Attack

CHARLESTOWN PENINSULA

The Battle of Bunker Hill
17 June 1775

N

SCALE OF MILES

Moulton's Hill (35 ft.)

SA

MA

Bunker Hill (110 ft.)

Breed's Hill (62 ft.)

Charlestown

Second Attack

CHARLESTOWN PENINSULA

The Battle of Bunker Hill
17 June 1775

N

SCALE OF MILES

Moulton's Hill (35 ft.)

Howe
(2,000)

SA

MA

SA

Intended envelopment

Bunker Hill (110 ft.)

SA

Putnam

Prescott

Breed's Hill (62 ft.)

Unopposed landing
1300 hours

Charlestown

First Attack

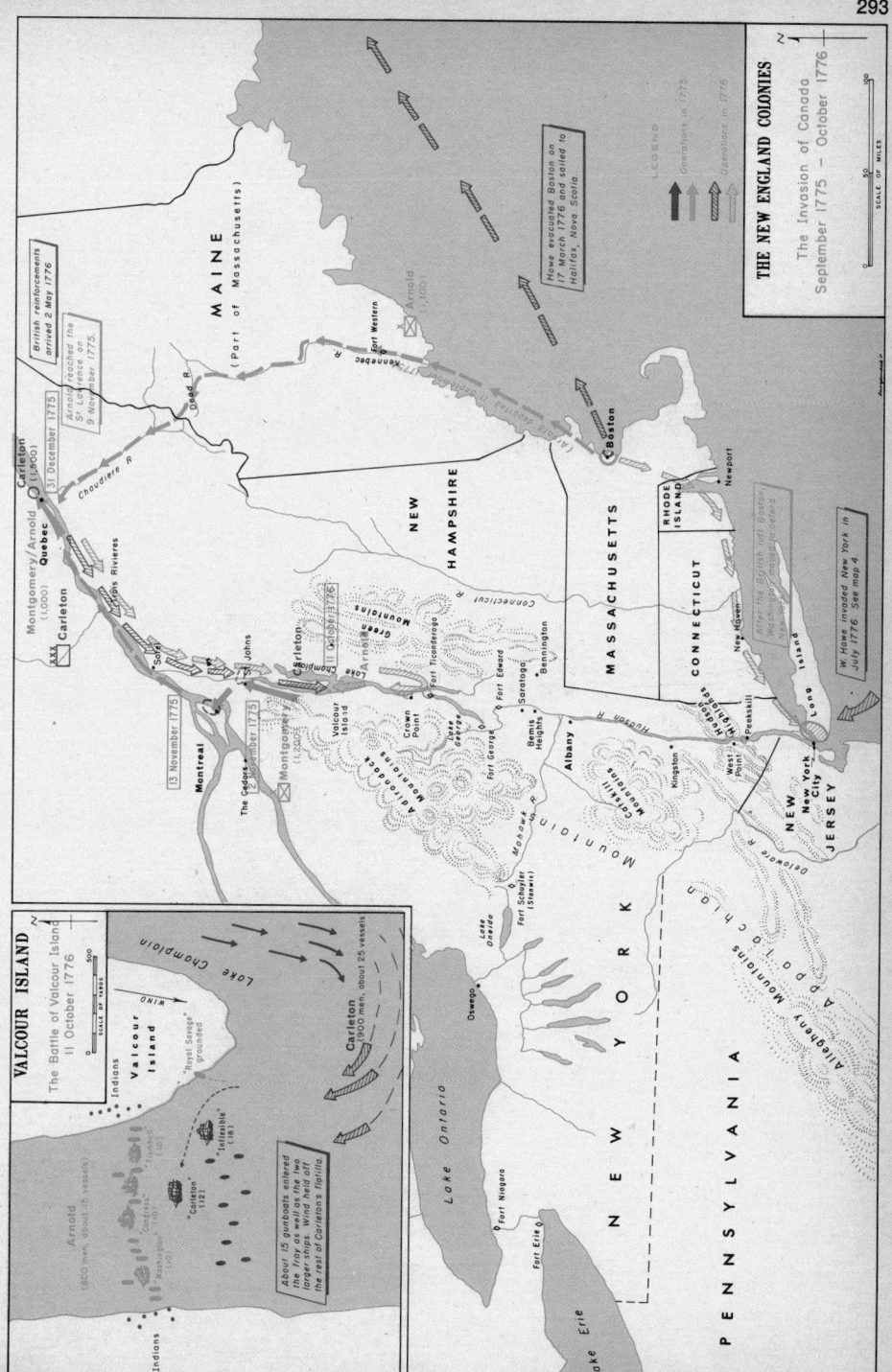

THE NEW ENGLAND COLONIES

The Invasion of Canada
September 1775 – October 1776

LEGEND

Operations in 1775

Operations in 1776

Howe evacuated Boston on
17 March 1776 and sailed to
Halifax, Nova Scotia

SCALE OF MILES

MAINE
(Part of Massachusetts)

British reinforcements
arrived 2 May 1776

Arnold reached the
St Lawrence on
9 November 1775.

Arnold
(1,100)

Fort Western

Kennebec R.

Dead R.

Chaudiere R.

31 December 1775
Montgomery/Arnold   Carleton
Quebec (1,000)   (1,900)

Carleton

Trois Rivieres

XXX Carleton

Sorel

St Johns

Carleton
October 1776

13 November 1775

Montreal

The Cedars

Montgomery
(2,000)
17 November 1775

NEW
HAMPSHIRE

Connecticut R.

Green
Mountains

Lake
Champlain

Valcour Island

Crown Point

Lake George

Fort Ticonderoga

Fort Edward

Saratoga

Bennington

Bemis
Heights

Albany

Adirondack
Mountains

Mohawk R.

Fort Schuyler
(Stanwix)

Lake
Oneida

Oswego

Lake Ontario

Fort Niagara

Fort Erie

Lake Erie

NEW   YORK

PENNSYLVANIA

Allegheny Mountains

Appalachian

Catskill
Mountains

Kingston

West
Point

Peekskill

Hudson R.

Delaware R.

NEW
JERSEY

New York
City

Long Island

MASSACHUSETTS

CONNECTICUT

New Haven

Stamford

RHODE
ISLAND

Newport

Boston

After the British left Boston,
Washington marched
to New York

W. Howe invaded New York in
July 1776. See map 4.

VALCOUR ISLAND

The Battle of Valcour Island
11 October 1776

SCALE OF YARDS

WIND

Lake Champlain

Indians

Valcour
Island

"Royal Savage" grounded

Arnold
(800 men, about 15 vessels)

"Congress" (10)

"Trumbull" (10)

Inflexible (18)

"Carleton" (12)

"Washington" (10)

Carleton
(900 men, about 25 vessels)

Indians

About 15 gunboats entered
the fray as well as the two
larger ships. Wind held off
the rest of Carleton's flotilla.

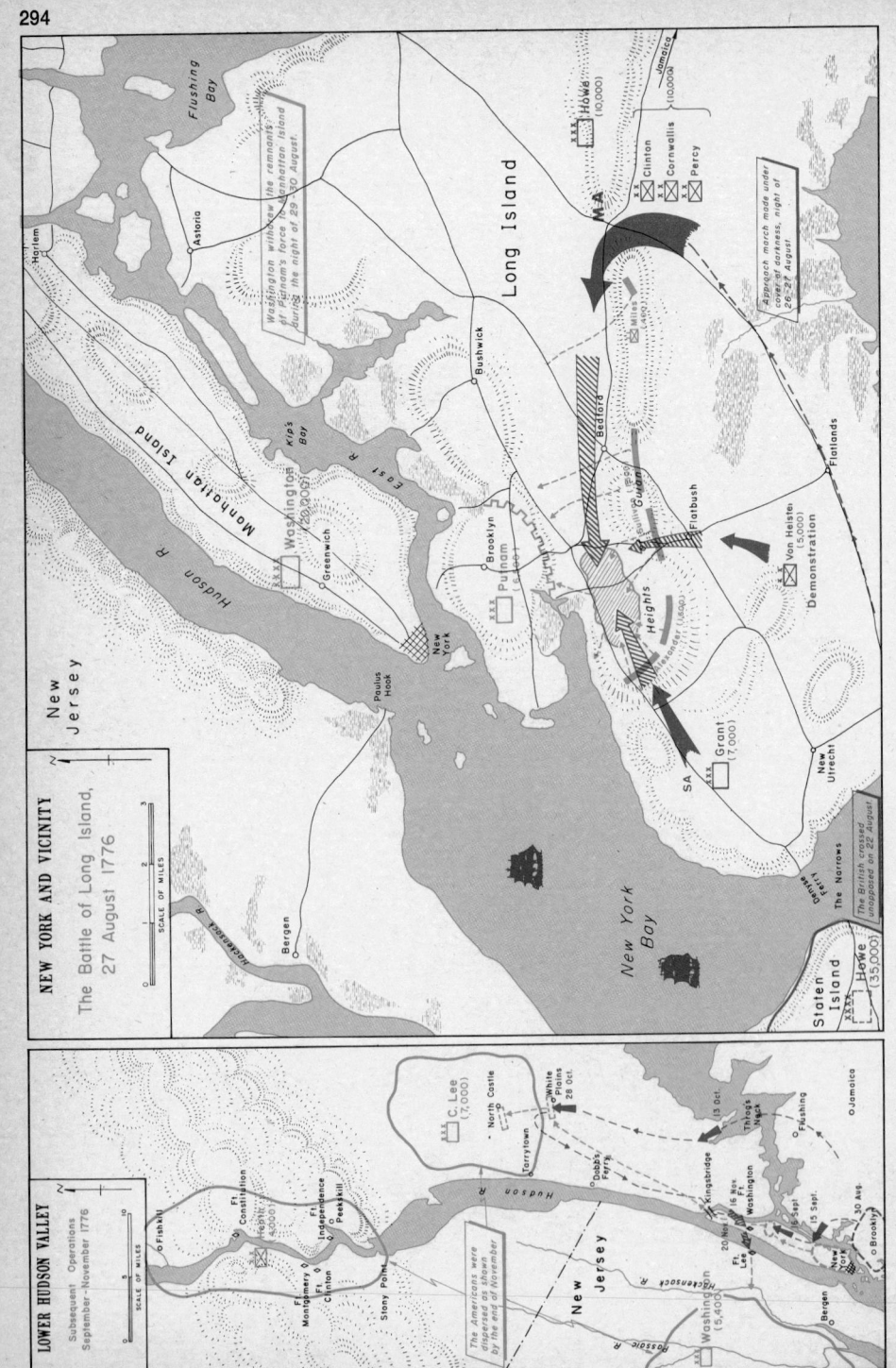

NEW YORK AND VICINITY

The Battle of Long Island,
27 August 1776

SCALE OF MILES
0   1   2   3

LOWER HUDSON VALLEY

Subsequent Operations
September–November 1776

SCALE OF MILES
0   5   10

New Jersey

Long Island

Manhattan Island

Flushing Bay

Hudson R.

East R.

Kip's Bay

New York Bay

Staten Island

The Narrows

Flatlands

Flatbush

New Utrecht

New York

Brooklyn

Heights

Bushwick

Bedford

Jamaica

Astoria

Harlem

Greenwich

Paulus Hook

Bergen

Washington (20,000)

Howe (35,000)

Howe (10,000)

Clinton   Cornwallis   Percy

Von Heister (5,000)

Grant (7,000)

Putnam (8,000)

Sullivan (1,600)

Miles (1,400)

Stirling (1,600)

Demonstration

Washington withdrew the remnants of Putnam's force to Manhattan Island during the night of 29–30 August.

Approach march made under cover of darkness, night of 26–27 August.

The British crossed unopposed on 22 August.

C. Lee (7,000)

North Castle

White Plains 28 Oct.

Tarrytown

Dobb's Ferry

Kingsbridge

Throg's Neck

Flushing

Jamaica

Brooklyn

New York

Bergen

Ft. Constitution

Ft. Independence

Peekskill

Ft. Montgomery

Ft. Clinton

Stony Point

Ft. Lee

Ft. Washington (5,400)

Washington (5,400)

Fishkill

Highlands (4,000)

Hudson R.

Hackensack R.

Passaic R.

New Jersey

13 Oct.

9 Nov.

12 Nov.

20 Nov.

16 Nov.

15 Sept.

30 Aug.

The Americans were dispersed as shown by the end of November.

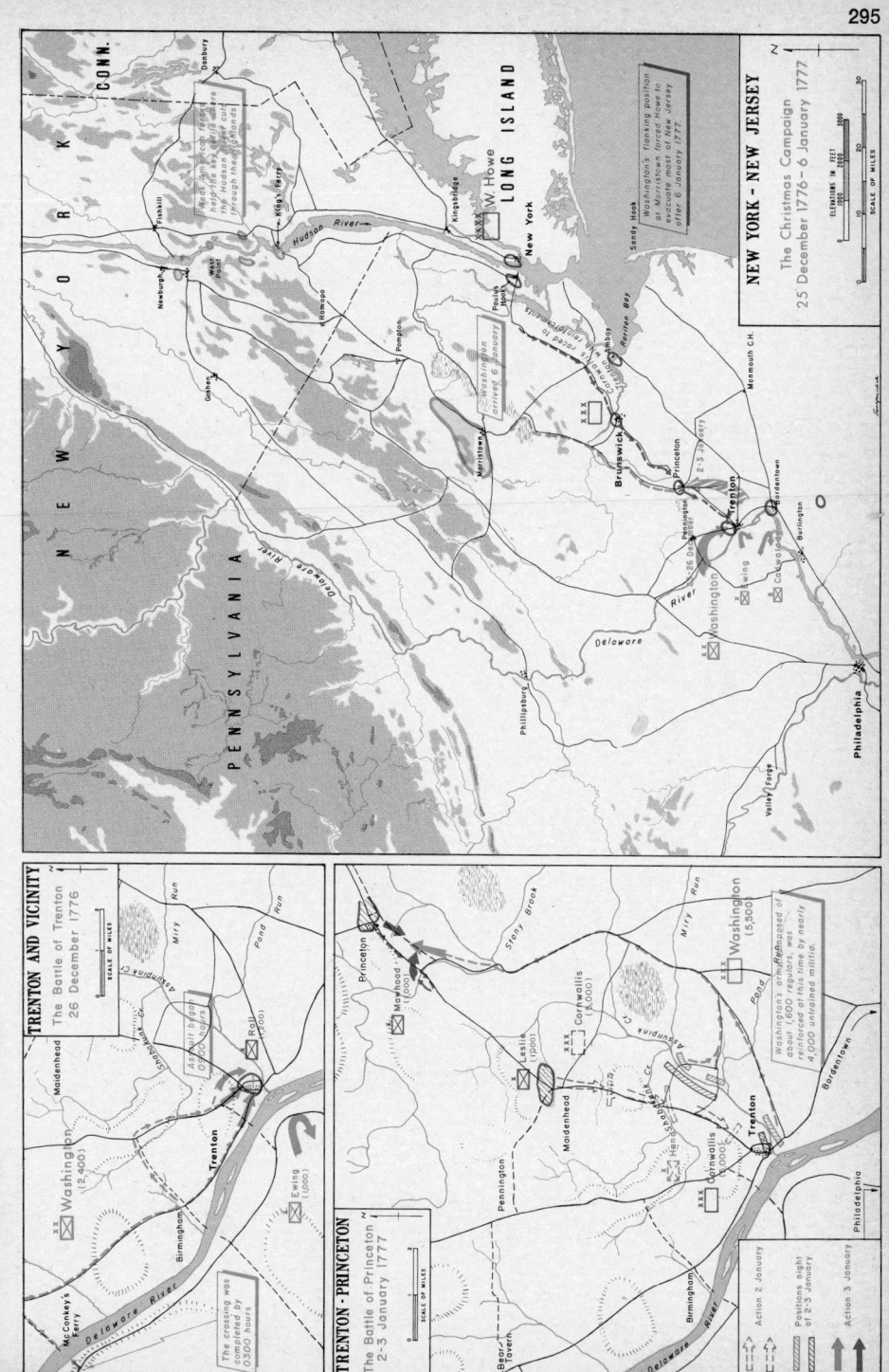

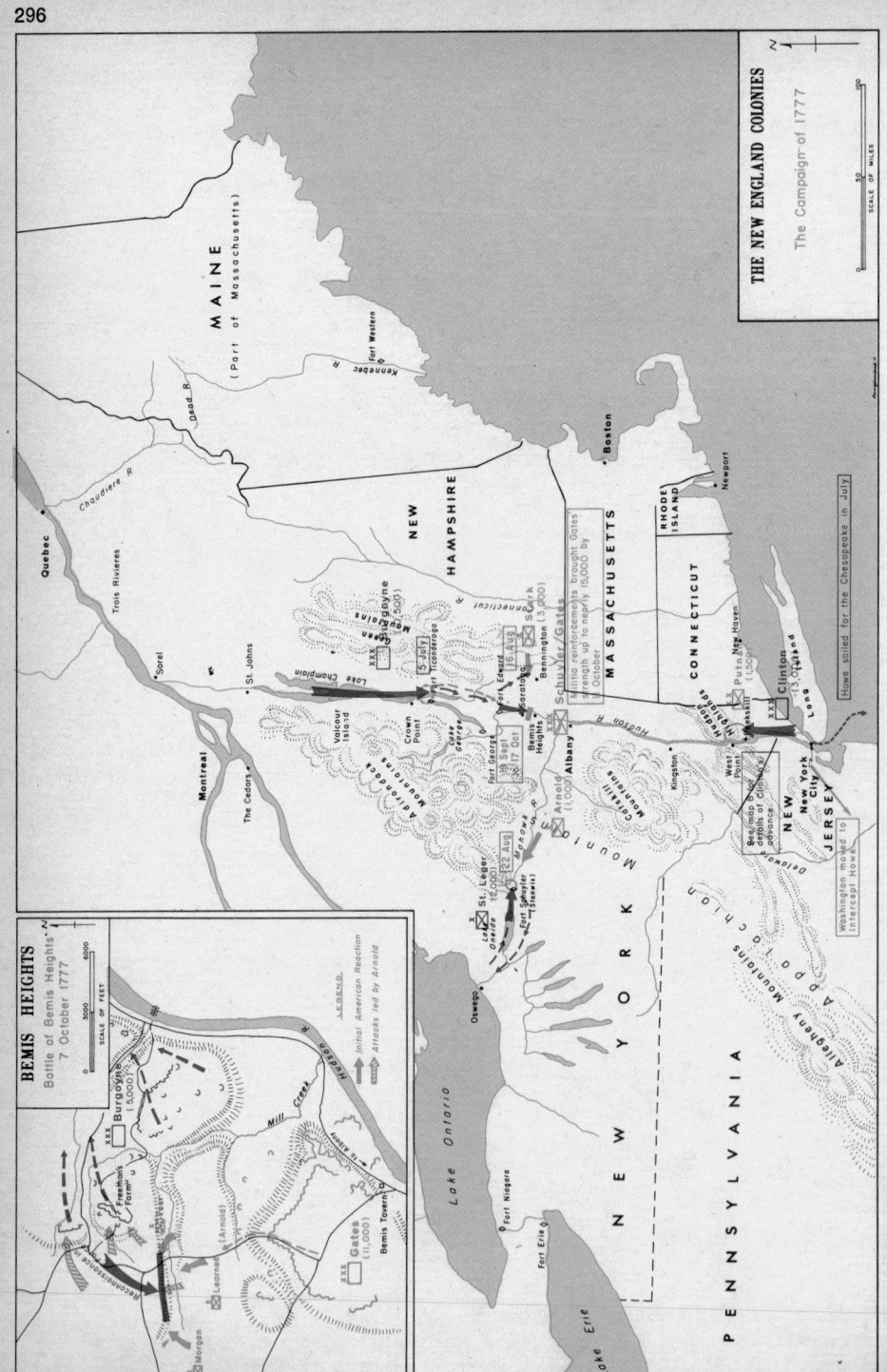

THE NEW ENGLAND COLONIES

The Campaign of 1777

BEMIS HEIGHTS

Battle of Bemis Heights
7 October 1777

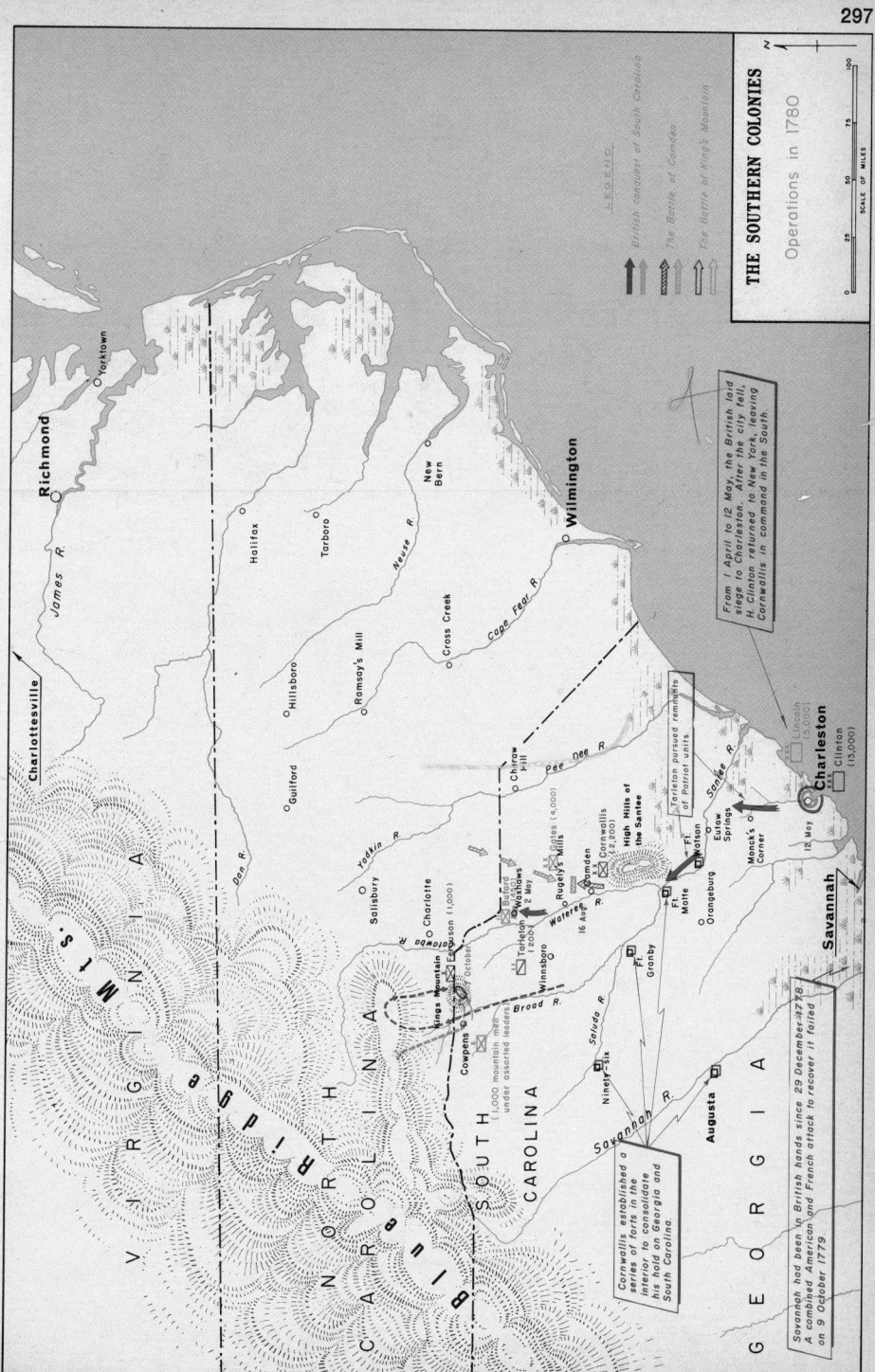

THE SOUTHERN COLONIES

Operations in 1780

LEGEND

British conquest of South Carolina

The Battle of Camden

The Battle of King's Mountain

SCALE OF MILES
0   25   50   75   100

From 1 April to 12 May, the British laid siege to Charleston. After the city fell, H. Clinton returned to New York, leaving Cornwallis in command in the South.

Cornwallis had been in British hands since 29 December 1778. A combined American and French attack to recover it failed on 9 October 1779.

Cornwallis established a series of forts in the interior to consolidate his hold on Georgia and South Carolina.

Tarleton pursued remnants of Patriot units.

Richmond
Yorktown
Charlottesville
Wilmington
New Bern
Tarboro
Halifax
Cross Creek
Ramsoy's Mill
Hillsboro
Guilford
Salisbury
Charlotte
Winnsboro
Kings Mountain
Cowpens
Ninety-Six
Augusta
Savannah
Charleston
Clinton (10,000)
Lincoln (5,000)
Camden
Cornwallis (2,200)
Gates (4,000)
Rugely's Mills
Ft. Watson
Ft. Motte
Orangeburg
Granby
Monck's Corner
Eutaw Springs
High Hills of the Santee
Waxhaws
Buford
Tarleton
Ferguson (1,000)
1,000 mountain men under assorted leaders

James R.
Neuse R.
Cape Fear R.
Pee Dee R.
Yadkin R.
Dan R.
Catawba R.
Broad R.
Saluda R.
Santee R.
Savannah R.
Wateree R.
Chiraw Hill

VIRGINIA
NORTH CAROLINA
SOUTH CAROLINA
GEORGIA
Blue Ridge Mts.

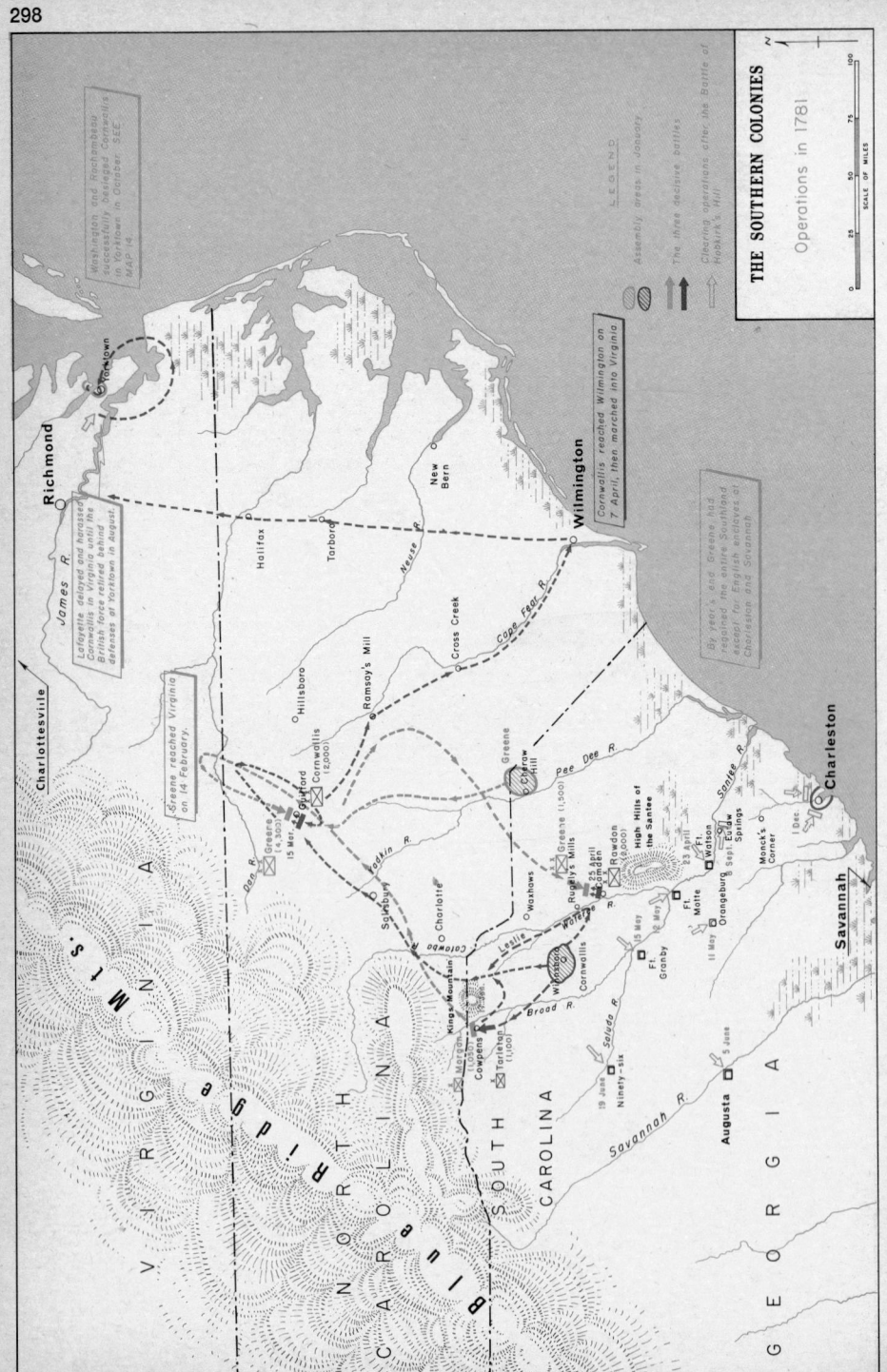

THE SOUTHERN COLONIES

Operations in 1781

LEGEND

Assembly area in convoy

The three decisive battles

Clearing operations after the Battle of Hobkirk's Hill

SCALE OF MILES
0   25   50   75   100

Washington and Rochambeau successfully besieged Cornwallis in Yorktown in October. SEE MAP 14.

Lafayette delayed and harassed Cornwallis in Virginia until the British force retired behind the defenses of Yorktown in August.

Greene reached Virginia on 14 February.

Cornwallis reached Wilmington on 7 April, then marched into Virginia.

By year's end Greene had regained the entire Southland except for the British enclaves at Charleston and Savannah.

Richmond

James R.

Yorktown

Charlottesville

VIRGINIA

Blue Ridge Mts.

Halifax

Tarboro

New Bern

Wilmington

Neuse R.

Cross Creek

Cape Fear R.

Hillsboro

Ramsoy's Mill

Greene (2,000)

Guilford

Cornwallis (2,000)

15 Mar

Greene (4,300)

Dan R.

NORTH CAROLINA

Yadkin R.

Salisbury

Charlotte

Catawba R.

Leslie

Kings Mountain

Wilmington

Cornwallis

Broad R.

Cowpens

Tarleton (1,100)

Ninety-Six

19 June

Saluda R.

Waxhaws

Rugeley's Mills

Camden

Rawdon (8,000)

Greene (1,500)

Snow Hill

Pee Dee R.

Charleston

Savannah R.

GEORGIA

Augusta

5 June

Ft. Granby

15 May

Ft. Motte

11 May

Orangeburg

Watboo R.

High Hills of the Santee

Eutaw Springs 8 Sep

23 April

Monck's Corner

Santee R.

Ft. Watson

Charleston

Savannah

N

SOUTH CAROLINA

ATLANTIC SEABOARD
The Yorktown Campaign
Washington's March and the
Naval Actions, 20 August –
26 September 1781

YORKTOWN AND VICINITY
The Yorktown Campaign
The Siege 6-20 October 1781

**European
Exploration and Settlement**

OHIO 1669	Earliest Exploration in Vicinity
Akron 1779	First Settlement of Immediate Area

MAINE 1498

N.H. 1603

VT. 1609

MASS. 1602

CONN. 1614

NEW YORK 1609

PENNSYLVANIA 1615

N.J.

MD.

WEST VIRGINIA 1669

VIRGINIA 1585

NORTH CAROLINA 1524

S. CAROLINA 1525

GEORGIA 1540

FLORIDA 1513

MICHIGAN 1621

MICH. 1621

WISCONSIN 1634

ILLINOIS 1673

INDIANA 1673

OHIO 1669

KENTUCKY 1654

TENNESSEE 1540

ALABAMA 1505

MISSISSIPPI 1540

MINNESOTA 1679

IOWA 1673

MISSOURI 1673

ARKANSAS 1541

LOUISIANA 1519

NORTH DAKOTA 1738

SOUTH DAKOTA 1743

NEBRASKA 1541

KANSAS 1541

OKLAHOMA 1541

TEXAS 1519

MONTANA 1743

WYOMING 1743

COLORADO 1598

NEW MEXICO 1531

IDAHO 1805

UTAH 1776

ARIZONA 1539

WASHINGTON 1774

OREGON 1543

NEVADA 1775

CALIFORNIA 1542

ALASKA 1741

HAWAII 1778

Biographies of U.S. Presidents

George Washington

George Washington, first president, was born Friday, Feb. 22, 1732 (Feb. 11, 1731, Old Style), the son of Augustine Washington and Mary Ball, at Wakefield on Pope's Creek, Westmoreland Co., Va. Col. John Washington, George's great-grandfather, came from Northamptonshire in 1657 or 1658; in 1665 he and an associate named Spencer bought 5,000 acres on the Potomac. George's father took the north 2,500 acres near Hunting Creek in 1735 and built a house in which George lived from 3 to 6 years of age; then the family moved to Ferry farm, near Fredericksburg. His father died in 1743 when George was 11. He studied mathematics and surveying and when 16 went to live with his half brother Lawrence, who had inherited the Potomac farm and built Mount Vernon, the original house having burned. George surveyed the lands of William Fairfax on the Shenandoah, keeping a diary. He accompanied Lawrence to Barbados, West Indies, contracted small pox, and was deeply scarred. Lawrence died in 1752 and George acquired his property by inheritance and purchase and added the 2,500 acres held by the Spencers. He valued land and when he died owned 70,000 acres in Virginia and 40,000 acres on the Great Kanawha in what is now West Virginia.

Washington's military service began in 1753 when Gov. Dinwiddie of Virginia made him lieutenant-colonel of militia. He clashed with the French and had to surrender Fort Necessity July 3, 1754. He was an aide to Braddock and helped organize the retreat after the fatal ambuscade of July 9, 1755. He helped take Fort DuQuesne from the French in 1758.

After his marriage to Martha Dandridge Custis, widow, 1759, Washington lived at Mount Vernon, bred horses and cattle, raised fruit and practiced crop rotation. During the Stamp Act agitation, 1765, he supported the protesting Virginians. Although not at first for independence, he stood out against British exactions and took charge of the Virginia troops before war broke out. He was made commander-in-chief by the Continental Congress June 15, 1775, and took command at Cambridge July 3.

The successful issue of a war filled with hardships was largely due to his leadership. He was resourceful, a stern disciplinarian, and the one strong, dependable force for unity. He favored a federal government and became chairman of the Constitutional Convention of 1787. He helped get the Constitution ratified and was unanimously elected president by the Electoral College and inaugurated, Apr. 30, 1789, on the balcony of New York's Federal Hall at Broad and Wall Sts., now marked by his statue. His pew in St. Paul's Chapel is preserved.

His birthplace, Wakefield, was burned in 1780. On Feb. 22, 1932, a new Wakefield, built by donations, was dedicated as the George Washington Birthplace Monument, administered by the National Parks Service. The older Washingtons are buried there. It is 34 mi. from Fredericksburg, Va., and 5 mi. from Stratford Hall, birthplace of Robert E. Lee.

Although a Federalist, Washington made Thomas Jefferson secretary of state (resigned 1793). He was reelected 1792, but refused to consider a 3d term and retired to Mount Vernon, 1797. He suffered acute laryngitis after a ride in snow and rain around his estate, was bled profusely, and died Dec. 14, 1799, aged 67. He was mourned here and abroad as one of the great men of his time. He was buried in a vault at Mount Vernon. (See article on Mount Vernon.) He willed Mount Vernon to his nephew, Bushrod Washington (1762-1829), associate justice, U. S. Supreme Court.

John Adams

John Adams, 2d president, Federalist, was born in Braintree (Quincy), Mass., Oct. 30, 1735 (Oct. 19, O.S.), the son of John Adams, a farmer, and Susanna Boylston of Brookline. He was a great-grandson of Henry Adams who came from England in 1636. He was graduated from Harvard, 1755, taught school, studied law. In 1765 he argued against taxation without representation before the royal governor. In 1770 he defended the British soldiers, who fired on civilians in the "Boston Massacre." He took part in the Provincial Congress of Massachusetts and the Continental Congress, seconded the independence resolution presented by Richard Henry Lee and with his cousin, Samuel Adams, signed the Declaration of Independence. He was a commissioner to France, 1778, with Benjamin Franklin and Arthur Lee; won recognition of the United States by The Hague, 1782; was first American minister to England, 1785-1788, and elected vice president with Washington, 1788 and 1792.

In 1796 Adams was chosen president by the electors, 71 to 68, so that opponents called him "president by 3 votes." The candidate with the second highest number of votes became vice president; this was Thomas Jefferson, his opponent. Intense antagonism to America by France caused agitation for war, led by Alexander Hamilton. Adams, breaking with Hamilton, opposed war but put the navy on a fighting basis. The U.S.S. Constitution, the United States, both 44 guns, and the Constellation, 36 guns, and armed merchantmen bagged 84 French ships in an undeclared war. To fight alien influence and muzzle criticism Adams supported the Alien and Sedition laws of 1798, which led to his defeat for reelection. He died July 4, 1826, on the same day as Jefferson, and was buried in the First Unitarian Church in Quincy, Mass.

Adams married Abigail Smith, 1764. They had 2 daughters and 3 sons, one of whom, John Quincy Adams, became the 6th president.

Thomas Jefferson

Thomas Jefferson, 3d president, was born Apr. 13, 1743 (Apr. 2, O. S.), at Shadwell, Va., the son of Peter Jefferson, a civil engineer of Welsh descent who raised tobacco, and Jane Randolph. Jefferson was an agrarian and an expansionist. Because he opposed the Federalists and centralization he was called a Republican, now synonymous with Democrat. His father died when he was 14, leaving him 2,750 acres and his slaves. Jefferson attended the college of William and Mary, 1760-1762, read classics in Greek and Latin and played the violin. In 1769 he was elected to the House of Burgesses. In 1770 he began building Monticello, near Charlottesville. In 1772 he married Martha Wayles Skelton. He was a member of the Virginia Committee of Correspondence and the Continental Congress and denied Britain's right to tax. Named a member of the committee to draw up a Declaration of Independence, he wrote the basic draft, 1776. He was a member of the Virginia House of Delegates, 1776-79, elected governor to succeed Patrick Henry, 1779, reelected 1780, resigned June 1781, amid charges of ineffectual military preparation. During his term he wrote the statute on religious freedom. In the Continental Congress, 1783, he drew up an ordinance for the Northwest Territory, forbidding slavery after 1800; its terms were put into the Ordinance of 1787. He was sent to Paris with Benjamin Franklin and John Adams to negotiate treaties of commerce, 1784; made minister to France, 1785. He made treaties with France and Prussia, studied architecture, gardening, and the French Revolution, whose leaders consulted him.

Washington appointed him secretary of state, 1789. Jefferson's strong faith in the consent of the governed; as opposed to executive control favored by Hamilton, secretary of the treasury, often led to conflict: Dec. 31, 1793, he resigned. He was the Republican candidate for president in 1796; beaten by John Adams, he became vice president. He opposed Adams' alien and sedition laws with the Kentucky and Virginia resolutions, reiterating the basic rights of states. In 1800 Jefferson and Aaron Burr received equal votes for president, so the House of Representatives, with Hamilton's help, elected Jefferson, the first president to be inaugurated in Washington. Adams left town before the ceremony, but when Jefferson was reelected in 1804 he voted for him. Jefferson canceled levees and titles and ignored diplomatic precedence. He turned Federalists out of office. He opposed a strong navy. By fighting those who feared to give power to the people he made democracy work. He considered John Marshall's Supreme Court reactionary. Big events of his administration were the Louisiana Purchase, 1803, and the Lewis and Clark Expedition. He established the University of Virginia and designed its buildings. After the Library of Congress was burned by the British he sold Congress some 6,000 vols. for $23,950. He was 6 ft. 2, temperate in debate, a deist in religion. He died July 4, 1826, on the same day as John Adams and was buried at Monticello, which, after various vicissitudes, passed to the Thomas Jefferson Memorial Foundation in 1923.

He married Martha Wayles Skelton, a widow, Jan. 1, 1872. They had one son and 5 daughters.

James Madison

James Madison, 4th president, Republican, was born Mar. 16, 1751 (Mar. 5, 1750, O. S.) at Port Conway, King George Co., Va., the eldest of 12 children of James Madison and Eleanor Rose Conway. His great-grandfather, James Taylor (1674-1729), was also the great-grandfather of Zachary Taylor. Madison was graduated from Princeton, 1771; studied theology, 1772; sat in the Virginia Constitutional Convention, 1776, where his resolution on religious freedom was voted down. He was a member of the Continental Congress and of the Annapolis Convention, 1786, where he and Alexander Hamilton proposed the Constitutional Convention. He was chief recorder at that convention in 1787, and supported ratification in the Federalist papers, written with Hamilton and John Jay. In 1785 he carried Jefferson's statute on religious liberty through the Virginia Assembly. He was elected to the House of Representatives in 1789, helped adopt the Bill of Rights and fought John Adams' alien and sedition laws. He favored agrarian policies with Jefferson and in 1801 became Jefferson's secretary of state. In 1803, when the Louisiana Purchase was consummated, he insisted on free navigation of the Mississippi, which he had already urged on Jay in 1780.

Elected president in 1808, Madison was a "strict constructionist," opposed to the free interpretation of the Constitution by the Federalists; he vetoed federal funds for state improvements, but changed in his second term. Madison inherited the conflict with Britain over its orders in council and its impressment of American seamen, which had led to Jefferson's embargo act and injured American commerce. He was reelected in 1812 by the votes of the agrarian South and recently admitted western states. Caught between British and French maritime restrictions, Madison drifted into war, declared June 18, 1812, unaware that Britain had canceled the orders 2 days before. While the war was inconclusive, it opened the way to peaceful negotiations. Madison successfully advocated a tariff to protect industry, a national system of roads and canals and a strong military organization. He retired in 1817 to his estate at Montpelier in Orange County, Va., built 1760, with a portico suggested by Jefferson. There he edited his famous papers on the Constitutional Convention. He became rector of the University of Virginia, 1826. He died June 28, 1836, and was buried near his home.

Madison married Dorothea "Dolley" Payne Todd, a widow, Sept. 15, 1794.

James Monroe

James Monroe, 5th president, Republican, was born Apr. 28, 1758, in Westmoreland Co., Va., the son of Spence Monroe and Eliza Jones, who were of Scottish and Welsh descent, respectively. He attended the College of William and Mary, fought in the 3d Virginia Regiment at White Plains, Brandywine, Monmouth, and was wounded at Trenton. He studied law with Thomas Jefferson, 1780, was a member of the Virginia House of Delegates and of Congress, 1783-86. He opposed ratification of the Constitution because it lacked a bill of rights; was U.S. senator, 1790; minister to France, 1794-96, during which he improved relations with France, Spain, and Algiers; 4 times governor of Virginia, 1799-1802, and 1811. Jefferson sent him to France as minister, 1803, to join R. R. Livingston in buying the Isle of New Orleans from France and East and West Florida from Spain. Exceeding instructions, he signed a treaty for all of Louisiana. He was also sent to Madrid, 1804, and London, 1805, to settle disputes. He ran against Madison for president in 1808. He was chosen member of the Virginia Assembly, 1810-1811; secretary of state under Madison, 1811-1817; also secretary of war, Sept. 1814-Mar., 1815.

In 1816 Monroe was elected president; in 1820 reelected with all but one vote, this being cast for John Quincy Adams by William Plumer Sr. of New Hampshire. Although many historians have held that Plumer withheld his vote from Monroe so that only Washington would have been elected unanimously, Plumer himself said he voted for Adams because he had "discovered a want of foresight" in Monroe. Monroe's administration became the "Era of Good Feeling." He obtained the Floridas from Spain and suppressed the Seminoles; settled boundaries with Canada and eliminated border forts; supported the anti-slavery position that led to the Missouri Compromise. (In 1801 he had proposed settling Negro slaves in Africa. Monrovia, Liberia, was named for him.) In July, 1823, the U.S. served notice on Russia that it would oppose any Russian colony on this continent, after Russia had prohibited fishing on the northwest coasts. On Dec. 2, 1823, Monroe announced the doctrine that the U. S. would consider its safety endangered if European powers had authority on this hemisphere or attempted colonization. First half had been suggested by George Canning, British foreign minister, to curb Spain; U. S., rejecting proposal for joint declaration, issued it also as warning to Russia. Monroe owned Ash Lawn, 5 mi. from Charlottesville, Va., 1799-1825; inherited Oak Hill, Loudon Co., Va., from his uncle Joseph Jones, 1806. The mansion, replacing Jones' cottage, was designed by Jefferson and executed by James Hoban, White House architect.

Monroe married Elizabeth Kortwright in 1786. They had a son who died in infancy and 2 daughters. Mrs. Monroe died in 1830 and he and the daughters moved to New York, where he died July 4, 1831.

John Quincy Adams

John Quincy Adams, 6th president, independent Federalist, was born July 11, 1767, at Braintree (Quincy), Mass., the son of John and Abigail Adams. His father was the 2d president. He was educated in Paris, Leyden, and Harvard, graduating in 1787. He served as American minister in the Netherlands, Berlin, St. Petersburg, and London and helped draft the peace treaty of 1814. He had served as senator from 1803 to 1808 and his support of the Republican administration alienated the Federalists. President Monroe made him secretary of state, 1817, and he negotiated the cession of the Floridas from Spain, supported exclusion of slavery in the Missouri Compromise, and laid the base for the Monroe Doctrine, of which he, as much as Monroe, was the creator. In 1824 he was elected president by the House after he failed to win an Electoral College majority over Henry Clay and Andrew Jackson. His expansion of executive powers was strongly opposed and he was beaten in 1828 by Jackson. In 1831 he was sent to Congress as representative and served 9 terms with distinction and independence. He fought slavery, opposed the annexation of Texas and the war with Mexico; was responsible for the Smithsonian Institution. He had a stroke in the House and died in the Speaker's room, Feb. 23, 1848.

Adams married Louise Catherine Johnson on July 26, 1797. They had 3 sons and a daughter.

Andrew Jackson

Andrew Jackson, 7th president, originally a Jeffersonian-Republican, later a Democrat, was born in the Waxhaws district, New Lancaster Co., S. C., Mar. 15, 1767, the posthumous son of Andrew Jackson, who came from County Antrim, Ireland, with his wife, Elizabeth Hutchinson, and 2 sons, in 1765. At 13 young Andrew joined the militia in the Revolution and was captured; a British officer struck him with his sword when the boy refused to shine his boots. He read law in Salisbury, N. C., moved to Nashville, Tenn., speculated in land, married, and raised cotton at the Hermitage, originally a log house. In 1796 he helped draft the Constitution of Tennessee and for one year occupied its one seat in the national House. He was in the Senate in 1797, and again in 1823. He defeated the Creek Indians at Horseshoe Bend, Ala., 1814, and, as major general, drove the British out of Pensacola. With 6,000 backwoods fighters he defeated Packenham's 12,000 British troops at Chalmette, outside New Orleans, Jan. 8, 1815, losing only 7 to the British loss of 2,000. In 1818 he briefly invaded Spanish Florida to quell Seminoles and outlaws who harassed frontier settlements. In 1824 he ran for president against John Quincy Adams and won the most votes in the Electoral College, but not a majority; the election was decided by the House, which chose Adams. In 1828 he carried everything, the West rising to support "Old Hickory" and a liberal land policy. He was a noisy debater and a duelist and introduced rotation in office called the "spoils system." He was suspicious of privilege; ruined the Bank of the United States by depositing federal funds with state banks. Though "Let the people rule" was his slogan, he at times supported strict constructionist policies against the expansionist West. He killed the Congressional caucus for nominating presidential candidates and substituted the national convention, 1832, when he was reelected, with Martin Van Buren vice president. When South Carolina refused to collect imports under its protective tariff he ordered army and naval forces to Charleston. At the Jefferson Day dinner, 1830, he offered the toast: "Our Federal Union; it must be preserved." Vice President John C. Calhoun, exponent of state sovereignty, gave in reply the toast: "The Union — next to our liberty, most dear." Jackson recognized the Republic of Texas, 1836.

In 1791 Jackson married Rachel Donelson Robards who believed she had been divorced by Capt. Lewis Robards. But he did not actually obtain a divorce until 1793, after which the Jacksons were remarried. Mrs. Jackson died in 1828, shortly after Jackson's first election. He died at the Hermitage, June 8, 1845, and is buried there.

Martin Van Buren

Martin Van Buren, 8th president, Democrat, was born Dec. 5, 1782, at Kinderhook, N. Y., the son of Abraham Van Buren, a Dutch farmer, and Mary Hoes. He was surrogate of Columbia County, N.Y., state senator and attorney general and a law partner of Benjamin F. Butler in Albany. He was U. S. senator

1821, reelected, 1827, elected governor of New York, 1828. He helped swing eastern support to Andrew Jackson in 1828 and was his secretary of state 1829-31. In 1832 he was elected vice president. He was a consummate politician, known as "the little magician," and influenced Jackson's policies. In 1836 he defeated William Henry Harrison for president by 170 to 73 electoral votes. He inaugurated the independent treasury system, and was the first advocate of mutual insurance of deposits by banks. He urged tariffs for revenue only and opposed internal improvements at national expense. His refusal to spend land revenues led to his defeat by Harrison in 1840. He lost the Democratic nomination of 1844 to Polk because he opposed annexation of Texas. In 1848 he ran for president on the Free Soil ticket and lost. He died July 24, 1862, at Kinderhook.

Van Buren married Hannah Hoes, a cousin, in 1807; she died in 1819. One of their sons, Abraham, was secretary to the president. Abraham's wife Angelica Singleton, a cousin of "Dolley" Madison, was White House hostess during Van Buren's term.

William Henry Harrison

William Henry, Harrison, 9th president, Whig, who served only 31 days, was born in Berkeley, Charles City Co., Va., Feb. 9, 1773, the third son of Benjamin Harrison, signer of the Declaration of Independence. Educated at Hampden Sydney College, he later studied medicine under Dr. Benjamin Rush. Commissioned by Washington, he fought under Gen. Anthony Wayne at Fallen Timbers, 1794. He was secretary of the Northwest Territory, 1798; its delegate in Congress, 1799; first governor of Indiana Territory, and superintendent of Indian affairs. With 900 men he routed Tecumseh's Indians at Tippecanoe, Nov. 7, 1811. A major general, he defeated British and Indians at Battle of the Thames, Oct. 5, 1813. He served Ohio in Congress, 1816; as senator, 1824; was minister to Colombia. In 1840, when 68, he was elected president with John Tyler, 234 to 60, on a "log cabin and hard cider" slogan. He caught pneumonia during the inauguration and died Apr. 4, 1841. He was buried in North Bend, Oh.

Harrison married Anna Symmes in 1795. They had 6 sons. A grandson, Benjamin Harrison, became the 23d president.

John Tyler

John Tyler, 10th president, Independent Whig, was born Mar. 29, 1790, in Greenway, Charles City Co., Va., son of John Tyler and Mary Armistead. His father was governor of Virginia, 1808-11. Tyler was graduated from William and Mary, 1807; member of the House of Delegates, 1811; in Congress, 1816-21; in Virginia legislature, 1823-25; governor of Virginia, 1825-26; U. S. senator, 1827-36. In 1840 he was elected vice president and, on President Harrison's death, succeeded him. He favored pre-emption, allowing settlers to get government land; rejected a new bank bill and thus alienated Whig supporters except Daniel Webster, his secretary of state; refused to honor the spoils system. He signed the resolution annexing Texas, Mar. 1, 1845. He accepted renomination, 1844, but withdrew before election. He condemned South Carolina's nullification and secession and, as Virginia's commissioner to Buchanan, tried to keep Fort Sumter neutralized. He was president of the peace congress called in Washington by Virginia, 1861. After its failure he supported secession, sat in the provisional Confederate Congress, became a member of the Confederate House, but died, Jan. 18, 1862, before it met. He was buried in Richmond.

Tyler first married Letitia Christian, in 1813; they had 3 sons and 4 daughters; she died in 1842. He married Julia Gardiner, of Gardiner's Is., N.Y., in 1844. They had 5 sons and 2 daughters.

James Knox Polk

James Knox Polk, 11th president, Democrat, was born in Mecklenburg Co., N. C., Nov. 2, 1795, the son of Samuel Polk, farmer and surveyor of Scotch-Irish descent, and Jane Knox. He went to Maury Co., Tenn., 1806; was graduated from the University of North Carolina, 1818; member of the Tennessee state legislature, 1823-25, known as "Napoleon of the Stump." He served in Congress 1825-39 and as speaker 1835-39. He supported Jackson and Van Buren, but was always expansionist. He was governor of Tennessee 1839-41, being defeated 1841 and 1843. In 1844, when both Clay and Van Buren announced opposition to annexing Texas, the Democrats made Polk the first dark horse nominee because he demanded control of all Oregon and annexation of Texas. James Buchanan was his secretary of state. Polk re-established the independent treasury system originated by Van Buren. His expansionist policy was opposed by Clay, Webster, Calhoun; he sent Zachary Taylor and an army to the Mexican border and when Mexicans attacked declared war existed. Abraham Lincoln, a Whig in Congress, opposed his war policy. Polk approved the acquisition of California, Utah and New Mexico (522,568 square miles) as part of America's "manifest destiny," but opposed retaining Mexico by force. He compromised on the Oregon boundary ("54-40 or fight!") by accepting the 49th parallel and giving Vancouver to the British. The Wilmot Proviso, outlawing slavery in new states, was debated in his term. Polk died in Nashville, June 15, 1849, and was buried on the capitol grounds there.

Polk married Sarah Childress on Jan. 1, 1824. They had no children.

Zachary Taylor

Zachary Taylor, 12th president, Whig, who served only 16 months, was born Nov. 24, 1784, in Orange Co., Va., the son of Richard Taylor, later collector of the port of Louisville, Ky. His grandfather and James Madison's paternal grandmother were brother and sister. Taylor enlisted 1806; was commissioned lieutenant by Jefferson, 1808; fought in the War of 1812, the Black Hawk War, 1832, and the Seminole war, 1837. He became known as Old Rough and Ready. He settled on a plantation near Baton Rouge, La. In 1845 Polk sent him to the Rio Grande; when the Mexicans attacked him, Polk declared war. Taylor was successful at Palo Alto and Resaca de la Palma, May 8 and 9, 1846; occupied Monterey. Polk made him major general but gave many of his troops to Gen. Winfield Scott at Veracruz. Taylor, with 5,000 men, defeated Santa Anna's 20,000 at Buena Vista, Feb. 22, 1847. He defeated Scott at the Whig convention, 1848; was elected president over Martin Van Buren with Millard Fillmore vice president. He resumed the spoils system and though once a slave-holder worked to 'have California admitted as a free state. He died of typhus July 9, 1850, and was buried near Louisville.

Taylor married Margaret Smith in 1810. They had one son and 5 daughters, one of whom, Sarah, married Jefferson Davis in 1835; she died a few months later.

Millard Fillmore

Millard Fillmore, 13th president, Whig, was born Jan. 7, 1800, in a log cabin on a Cayuga Co., N. Y., farm cleared in 1795 by his father, Nathaniel. He was apprenticed to a fuller and dyer; bought his freedom for $30 to study and became a teacher and postmaster in Buffalo, N. Y. He was counselor of the state Supreme Court, 1829; in the state Assembly, 1829-32; in Congress, 1833-35 and again 1837-43. He opposed the entrance of Texas as slave territory and voted for a protective tariff. He supported the appropriation of $30,000 for Morse's telegraph. In 1844 he was defeated for governor of New York. In 1848 he was elected vice president and succeeded as president July 10,

1850, after Taylor's death. Fillmore favored the Compromise of 1850 and signed the Fugitive Slave Law. His policies pleased neither expansionists nor slaveholders and he was not renominated in 1852. In 1856 he was nominated by the American (Know-Nothing) party and accepted by the Whigs, but defeated by Buchanan. He was chancellor of the University of Buffalo. He died in Buffalo, Mar. 8, 1874.

Fillmore first married Abigail Powers, in 1826, and they had one son and one daughter. Abigail died in 1853 and Fillmore married Caroline Carmichael McIntosh, a widow, in 1858. They had no children.

Franklin Pierce

Franklin Pierce, 14th president, Democrat, was born in Hillsboro, N. H., Nov. 23, 1804, the son of Benjamin Pierce, veteran of the Revolution and governor of New Hampshire, 1827. He attended Exeter and was graduated from Bowdoin, 1824. A lawyer, he served in the New Hampshire House, 1829-32; in Congress, supporting Jackson, 1833; U.S. senator, 1837-42. He enlisted in the Mexican War, became brigadier general of volunteers and was wounded at Contreras. In 1852 Pierce was nominated on the 49th ballot over Cass, Douglas, and Buchanan, and defeated Gen. Winfield Scott, Whig. Though against slavery, Pierce was influenced by southern pro-slavery men (Jefferson Davis was his secretary of war) but he ignored the Ostend Manifesto that the U.S. either buy or take Cuba. He approved the Kansas-Nebraska Act, leaving slavery to popular vote ("squatter sovereignty"), 1854, and named a pro-slavery governor of Kansas. He signed a reciprocity treaty with Canada and approved the Gadsden Purchase from Mexico, 1853. He supported Commodore Matthew Perry's opening of Japan, 1854. Pierce died at Concord, N.H., Oct. 8, 1869.

Pierce married Jane Means Appleton in 1834. They had 3 children; all died in childhood.

James Buchanan

James Buchanan, 15th president, Federalist, later Democrat, was born of Scottish descent near Mercersburg, Pa., Apr. 23, 1791. He was a volunteer in the War of 1812; graduated from Dickinson, 1809; member, Pennsylvania legislature, 1814-16, Congress, 1820-31; Jackson's minister to Russia, 1831-33; U.S. senator 1834-45. As Polk's secretary of state, 1845-49, he ended the Oregon dispute with Britain, supported the Mexican War and annexation of Texas. As minister to Britain, 1853, he signed the Ostend Manifesto, 1854, urging the U. S. to take Cuba. Nominated by Democrats over Pierce and Stephen A. Douglas, he was elected, 1856, over John C. Fremont (Republican) and Millard Fillmore (American Know-Nothing and Whig tickets). On slavery he favored popular sovereignty and choice by state constitutions; he accepted the pro-slavery Dred Scott decision as binding. His support of the pro-slavery Lecompton constitution for Kansas caused a break with Douglas Democrats. He denied the right of states to secede but wanted U. S. constitutional recognition of property rights in slaves and Federal action against fugitives. Buchanan refused demands of South Carolina for Federal property, but also refused to reinforce forts there until too late to help Fort Sumter. A strict constructionist, he desired to keep peace and found no authority for using force. He died at Wheatland, near Lancaster, Pa., June 1, 1868, aged 77.

Buchanan was a bachelor. The mistress of the White House was the daughter of Buchanan's sister Jane, Harriet Lane, whose parents had died when she was a child.

Abraham Lincoln

Abraham Lincoln, 16th president, Republican, was born Feb. 12, 1809, in a log cabin on a farm then in Hardin Co., Ky., now in Larue. He was the son of

Thomas Lincoln (1778-1851), a descendant of Samuel Lincoln, who came from Hingham, England, 1637, settled at Salem and Hingham, Mass., and had 11 children. Thomas Lincoln, a carpenter, married Nancy Hanks, June 12, 1806. Nancy has been long believed to have been illegitimate, the "natural" daughter of Lucy Hanks. But recent research by David S. Keiser of Elkins Park, Pa., strongly suggests that Nancy was not illegitimate but was actually the daughter of Mary Berry, who Keiser says was the wife of Thomas Hanks. Mary died when Nancy was 2 years old, Keiser says, and Lucy Hanks, Thomas' sister, then took on the task of bringing up little Nancy.

Abraham had a sister, Sarah, born 1807, died 1828, and a brother Thomas, who died in infancy.

The Lincolns moved to Spencer Co., Ind., near Gentryville, when Abe was 7. Nancy died Oct. 5, 1818, aged 35. His father married Mrs. Sarah Bush Johnston, 1819; she had a favorable influence on Abe. In 1830 the family moved to Macon Co., Ill., where Abe and a cousin split 3,000 fence rails. In 1831 they moved to Coles Co. In New Salem, 1831-1837, Lincoln lost election to the Illinois General Assembly, 1832, but later won 4 times, beginning in 1834. He enlisted in the militia for the Black Hawk War, 1832. In New Salem he ran a store, 1833; surveyed land, 1834-36, and was postmaster, 1833-36.

In 1837 Lincoln was admitted to the bar and became partner in a Springfield, Ill., law office. He began practice in the 8th Judicial Circuit, 1839. He was a presidential elector, 1839, 1844, 1852, 1856. He failed of nomination for representative, 1843, but was elected to the 30th Congress, 1847. He opposed the Mexican War. He stumped New England for Zachary Taylor, 1848. He refused offices of secretary and governor of Oregon Territory, 1849. He opposed the Kansas-Nebraska Act and extension of slavery 1854. When elected to the Illinois legislature, 1854, he declined in order to try for the Senate, but failed of election, 1855. He was proposed but not chosen for vice president at the first Republican convention 1856 and he made 50 speeches for John C. Fremont, presidential nominee.

In 1858 Lincoln had Republican support in the Illinois legislature for the Senate but was defeated by Stephen A. Douglas, Dem., who had sponsored the Kansas-Nebraska Act. The issues were debated by Lincoln and Douglas Aug. 21-Oct. 15 at Ottawa, Freeport, Jonesboro, Charleston, Galesburg, Quincy, and Alton, Ill.

Lincoln was nominated for president by the Republican party on an anti-slavery platform, at Chicago, May 18, 1860. He ran against Stephen A. Douglas, northern Democrat; John C. Breckinridge, southern pro-slavery Democrat; John Bell, Constitutional Union party. Lincoln got only 40% of the votes, but 180 electoral votes to 123. South Carolina seceded from the Union Dec. 20, 1860, followed in 1861 by 10 southern states.

Lincoln was inaugurated Mar. 4, 1861. Fort Sumter was attacked Apr. 12-14, and surrendered. Lincoln called for 75,000 volunteers Apr. 15, and 500,000 May 3. On Sept. 22, 1862, 5 days after the battle of Antietam, he announced that slaves in territory then in rebellion would be free Jan. 1, 1863, date of the Emancipation Proclamation. He reached high degrees of moving eloquence in his Gettysburg and Inaugural Addresses and other speeches.

Lincoln was reelected, 1864, over Gen. Geo. B. McClellan, Democrat. Lee surrendered Apr. 9, 1865. On Apr. 14 (Good Friday) Lincoln was shot by actor John Wilkes Booth in Ford's Theater, Washington. He died the next day. His body lay in state in New York, Chicago, and other cities before burial in Springfield, Ill. His estate reached $110,974, most of it saved from his annual salary of $25,000. His humanity, lofty concept of office and generous spirit made him the hero of the common man the world over.

Lincoln married Mary Todd in Springfield, Nov. 4, 1842; they had 4 sons.

Andrew Johnson

Andrew Johnson, 17th president, Democrat, was born in Raleigh, N. C., Dec. 29, 1808, the son of Jacob Johnson, porter at an inn and church sexton, and Mary McDonough Johnson, who had been a maid at the inn. His father died when he was 5. At 10 he was apprenticed to a tailor. At 16 he ran off to Greenville, Tenn. He became an alderman, 1828; mayor, 1830; state representative and senator, 1835-43; member of Congress, 1843-53; governor of Tennessee, 1853-57; U.S. senator, 1857-62. He supported John C. Breckinridge against Lincoln in 1860. He had held slaves, but opposed secession and refused to follow Tennessee out of the Union. In Mar. 1862, Lincoln appointed him military governor of occupied Tennessee. In 1864 he was nominated for vice president with Lincoln on the National Union ticket to win Democratic support. He succeeded Lincoln as president April 15, 1865. In a controversy with Congress over the president's power over the South, he proclaimed, May 26, 1865, an amnesty to all Confederates except certain leaders if they would abolish slavery and ratify the 13th Amendment. States doing so added anti-Negro provisions that enraged Congress, which intended to enfranchise all Negroes and disenfranchise former Confederates. Congress restored military control over the South. When Johnson removed Edwin M. Stanton, secretary of war, without notifying the Senate, thus repudiating the Tenure of Office Act, the House impeached him for this and other reasons. He was tried by the Senate, which voted 35 for conviction, 19 for acquittal, lacking the two-thirds necessary to convict, May 26, 1868. He was a candidate before the next Democratic convention, but not nominated. He returned to the Senate in 1875, and in a strong speech defended his course. He supported the Lincoln policies, but his conciliatory attitude toward the South was fought by the radical Republicans. Johnson died July 31, 1875, and was buried at Greenville (now Greeneville), where his log cabin tailor shop and home are museums.

Johnson married Eliza McArdle in 1827. They had 3 sons and 2 daughters.

Ulysses S. Grant

Ulysses Simpson Grant, 18th president, Republican, was born at Point Pleasant, Oh., Apr. 27, 1822, son of Jesse R. Grant, a tanner. The next year the family moved to Georgetown, Oh. Grant's mother was Hannah Simpson. Grant was named Hiram Ulysses, but on entering West Point, 1839, his name was entered as Ulysses Simpson and he adopted it. He was graduated in 1843; and was first lieutenant and captain under Gens. Taylor and Scott in the Mexican War; resigned, 1854; worked in St. Louis until 1860, then went to Galena, Ill., where his father sold leather and hardware. He became colonel of the 21st Illinois Vols., 1861, then brigadier general; took Forts Henry and Donelson; was made major general of volunteers; fought at Shiloh. Took Vicksburg, became major general USA, and in March 1864, lieutenant general. He accepted Lee's surrender at Appomattox. In 1866 he was named a full general. President Johnson appointed Grant secretary of war when he suspended Stanton in defiance of the Senate, but Grant was not confirmed. He was nominated on the first ballot, May 30, 1868, and elected over Horatio Seymour, Democrat, 214 vs. 80 electoral votes. The 15th Amendment, amnesty bill, and civil service reform were events of his administration. The Liberal Republicans opposed him with Horace Greeley, also Democratic nominee, 1872, but he was reelected. An attempt by the Stalwarts (Old Guard) to nominate him in 1880 failed. In 1884 the collapse of Grant & Ward, investment house, left him penniless. He began his Personal Memoirs, writing while ill of cancer and completing them 4 days before his death at

Mt. McGregor, N.Y., July 23, 1885. The book realized over $450,000. Grant was buried in an imposing tomb on Riverside Drive, New York, where his wife also lies.

Grant married Julia Dent in 1848. They had 3 sons and one daughter.

Rutherford Birchard Hayes

Rutherford Birchard Hayes, 19th president, Republican, was born in Delaware, Oh., Oct. 4, 1822, the posthumous son of Rutherford Hayes, a farmer, and Sophia Birchard. He was descended from George Hayes, a Scot, who reached Windsor, Conn., in 1680. He was raised by his uncle Sardis Birchard, educated in Norwalk, Oh!, and Middletown, Conn., and graduated from Kenyon College, 1842, and Harvard Law School, 1845. He practiced law in Lower Sandusky, Oh., now Fremont; was city solicitor of Cincinnati, 1858-61. He was major of the 23d Ohio Vols., wounded at South Mountain; became brigadier general and major general by brevet, 1864. He served in Congress 1864-67, supporting Reconstruction and Johnson's impeachment. He was elected governor of Ohio, 1867 and 1869; beaten for Congress 1872; reelected governor, 1875. He supported the merit principle in appointments, economy, prison reform, and public libraries. In 1876 he was nominated for president over James G. Blaine and believed he had lost· to Samuel J. Tilden, Democrat, 184 to 163 electoral votes. But Zachariah Chandler, chairman of the Republican National Committee, relying on Republican domination of the South, urged the validity of contesting 22 electoral returns from Florida, South Carolina, Louisiana, and Oregon. Frauds in Louisiana injuring Tilden were permitted to stand. Promises to withdraw troops from the South were reported used to suborn Democrats. An Electoral Commission, appointed by Congress, 8 Republicans and 7 Democrats, awarded all disputed votes to Hayes. The Electoral College vote then became 185 for Hayes, 184 for Tilden. The withdrawal of troops followed, but handicapped Republican rule, and as Hayes proceeded to reform civil service he alienated political spoilsmen. He advocated repeal of the Tenure of Office Act that had led to Johnson's impeachment. He supported sound money and specie payments. Hayes died in Fremont, Oh., Jan. 17, 1893.

Hayes married Lucy Webb in 1852. They had 7 sons and one daughter.

James Abram Garfield

James A. Garfield, 20th president, Republican, was born Nov. 19, 1831, in a log cabin at Orange, Cuyahoga Co., Oh., the son of Abram and Eliza Ballou Garfield. His father, a canal contractor and farmer from New York, was descended from Edward Garfield, who reached Massachusetts Bay Colony in 1630 and helped found Watertown, Mass. James was the youngest of 4 children; his father died in 1833 and his mother supported them. He worked as a canal bargeman, farmer, and carpenter; attended Western Reserve Eclectic, later Hiram College, and was graduated from Williams in 1856. He became professor of ancient languages and literature at Hiram, then principal. He was in the Ohio Senate in 1859. Anti-slavery and anti-secession, he volunteered for the war, became colonel of the 42d Ohio Infantry and brigadier in 1862. He fought at Shiloh, was chief of staff for Rosecrans and was made major general for gallantry at Chickamauga. He entered Congress as a radical Republican in 1863; supported specie payment as against paper money (greenbacks). On the electoral commission in 1876 he voted for Hayes against Tilden on strict party lines. He was senator-elect in 1880 when he became the Republican nominee for president. He was chosen on the 36th ballot as a compromise over Gen. Grant, James G. Blaine, and John Sherman. This alienated the Grant following but Garfield was elected and Blaine became his secretary of state. On July 2, 1881, Garfield was shot by an unbalanced office-seeker, Charles J. Guiteau, while entering the old Baltimore & Potomac station in Washington. He died Sept. 19, 1881, at Elberon, N.J., and was buried in Cleveland, Oh. Guiteau was hanged June 30, 1882.

Garfield married Lucretia Rudolph in 1858. They had 4 sons and one daughter.

Chester Alan Arthur

Chester A. Arthur, 21st president, Republican, was born at Fairfield, Vt., Oct. 5, 1829, the son of the Rev. William Arthur, from County Antrim, Ireland, and Malvina Stone Arthur, member of a New Hampshire family. He graduated at Union College, 1848, taught school at Pownall, Vt., studied law in New York. In 1853 he argued in a fugitive slave case that slaves transported through N.Y. State were thereby freed; in 1855 he obtained a ruling that negroes were to be treated the same as whites on street cars. He helped organize the N.Y. State Militia, 1861; was made quartermaster general and equipped troops for the front. He was made collector of the Port of New York, 1871. In 1877 President Hayes, reforming the civil service, ordered Arthur's resignation; he refused because he was not personally culpable, but was removed, 1879. This made Senators Conkling, Platt, and the New York machine stalwarts enemies of Hayes. Arthur and the stalwarts tried to nominate Grant, for a third term, 1880; when Garfield was nominated, Arthur received second place in the interests of harmony. On Sept. 19, 1881, Garfield died and Arthur became president. He supported civil service reform and the tariff of 1883; arranged an unratified canal treaty with Nicaragua. He was defeated for renomination by James G. Blaine, 1884, but supported Blaine. He died Nov. 18, 1886, and was buried in Albany, N. Y.

Arthur married Ellen Lewis Herndon in 1859. They had 2 sons and one daughter.

Grover Cleveland

(According to a ruling of the State Dept. Grover Cleveland is both the 22d and the 24th president, because his 2 terms were not consecutive. By individuals, he is only the 22d.)

Grover Cleveland, 22d and 24th president, Democrat, was born in Caldwell, N. J., Mar. 18, 1837, the son of Richard F. Cleveland, a Presbyterian minister, and Ann Neale, daughter of a Baltimore merchant who had come from Ireland. The future president was named Stephen Grover, but dropped the Stephen. He clerked in Clinton and Buffalo, N. Y., taught in the N.Y. City Institution for the Blind; was admitted to the bar in Buffalo, 1859; became assistant district attorney 1863; sheriff 1869; mayor, 1881; governor of New York, 1882. He was an independent, honest administrator who hated corruption. He was nominated for president over Tammany Hall opposition, 1884, defeating James G. Blaine, 219 to 182. He enlarged the civil service, vetoed many pension raids on the Treasury. In 1888 he was defeated by Benjamin Harrison, although his popular vote was larger. Reelected over Harrison, 1892, by 277 to 145, he faced a money crisis brought about by lowering of the gold reserve, circulation of paper and exorbitant silver purchases under the Sherman Act; he obtained repeal of the latter and a reduced tariff. An income tax was passed but declared unconstitutional by the Supreme Court, 1895. A severe depression and labor troubles racked his administration but he refused to interfere in business matters and rejected, as crackpot theory, Jacob Coxey's demand for work ·relief on $20 million monthly. He broke the Pullman strike with troops to move the mail, 1894. He rejected the platform of W. J. Bryan's silver Democrats, 1896, and supported the gold Democrats, Palmer and Buckner. He died in Princeton, N.J., June 24, 1908.

Cleveland married Frances Folsom in the White House, June 2, 1886. They had 2 sons and 3 daughters.

Cleveland married Frances Folsom in the White House, Jun. 2, 1886. They had 2 sons and 3 daughters.

Benjamin Harrison

Benjamin Harrison, 23d president, Republican, was born at North Bend, Oh., Aug. 20, 1833. His great-grandfather, Benjamin Harrison, was a signer of the Declaration of Independence; his grandfather, William Henry Harrison, was 9th president; his father, John Scott Harrison, was a member of Congress, 1853-57. His mother was Elizabeth F. Irwin. He attended school in a log cabin on his father's farm; graduated from Miami University, 1852; was admitted to the bar, 1853, and practiced in Indianapolis, Ind. As a second lieutenant, he raised recruits and became colonel of the 70th Indiana Volunteer Infantry. He fought at Kenesaw Mountain, Peachtree Creek, Nashville, and in the Atlanta campaign. In 1865 he was made a brigadier general by brevet. He failed to be elected governor of Indiana, 1876; but became senator, 1881, and worked for the G. A. R. pensions vetoed by Cleveland. In 1888 he defeated Cleveland for president 233 to 168. He expanded the pension list greatly; suppressed the Louisiana lottery; signed the McKinley high tariff bill and the Sherman silver purchase act. He helped the admission of North and South Dakota, Montana, Washington, Idaho, and Wyoming, Republican states. He was defeated for reelection, 1892. He represented Venezuela in arbitration with Great Britain in Paris, 1899. He died at Indianapolis, Mar. 13, 1901, and was buried there.

Harrison married Caroline Lavinia Scott in 1853; they had one son and one daughter. The first Mrs. Harrison died in 1892 and in 1896 Harrison married her niece, Mary Scott Lord Dimmock, a widow. They had one daughter.

William McKinley

William McKinley, 25th president, Republican, was born in Niles, Oh., Jan. 29, 1843, the son of William McKinley, an iron manufacturer, and Nancy Allison McKinley, and was the 7th of 9 children. His father's family was Scotch-Irish from County Antrim, Ireland; his great-grandfather fought in the American Revolution. McKinley attended school in Poland, Oh., and Alleghany College, Meadville, Pa., and enlisted for the Civil War at 18 in the 23d Ohio, in which Rutherford B. Hayes was a major. He was a commissary sergeant at Antietam. He rose to captain and in 1865 was made major by brevet. He studied law in the Albany, N.Y., law school; opened an office in Canton, Oh., in 1867, and campaigned for Grant and Hayes. From 1876 to 1890, excepting 1882, he served in the House of Representatives and led the fight for a high tariff to protect "infant industries" and with reciprocal trade agreements (McKinley bill, enacted Oct. 1, 1890). Defeated on the issue in 1890, he was elected governor of Ohio, 1891 and 1893. He received 182 ballots for president in the Republican convention that nominated Benjamin Harrison in 1892. In 1896 he was elected president on a protective tariff, sound money (gold standard) platform over William Jennings Bryan, Democratic proponent of free silver. Chief factor was the astute vote-getting of Senator Marcus S. Hanna. McKinley was reluctant to intervene in Cuba on grounds of humanity, but the loss of the battleship Maine at Havana crystallized opinion. He demanded Spain's withdrawal from Cuba; Spain agreed to arbitration and armistice but Congress announced state of war as of Apr. 21. (Peace signed Dec. 10). In the 1900 campaign he defeated Bryan's anti-imperialist arguments with the prestige of prosperity, "the full dinner pail" and the vigorous campaigning of Theodore Roosevelt, vice presidential nominee. McKinley was a Methodist, beloved for his conciliatory nature, but conservative on business issues. He abhorred violence. On Sept. 6, 1901, while welcoming citizens at the Pan-American Exposition, Buffalo, N.Y., he was shot by Leon Czolgosz, an anarchist. He died Sept. 14. His last words were: "It is God's way. His will, not ours, be done." McKinley, his wife, and infant daughters rest in an imposing tomb in Canton. His favorite flower, the red carnation, was made the state flower.

McKinley married Ida Saxton in 1871. They had 2 daughters; both died in childhood.

Theodore Roosevelt

Theodore Roosevelt, 26th president, Republican was born in N.Y. City, Oct. 27, 1858, the son of Theodore Roosevelt, collector of the port, and Martha Bulloch, daughter of Maj. J. S. Bulloch, Roswell, Ga. Roosevelt was descended from Claes Martenszan van Rosenvelt, and his wife Janett, who reached New Netherland from Holland about 1650. Theodore was a fifth cousin of Franklin D. Roosevelt and an uncle of Mrs. Eleanor Roosevelt. His mother was of Scotch-Irish, Huguenot stock and a southern sympathizer. Roosevelt was graduated from Harvard, 1880, attended Columbia Law School briefly; sat in the N.Y. State Assembly, 1882-84; ranched in North Dakota, 1884-86; failed election as mayor of N.Y. City, 1886; member of U.S. Civil Service Commission, 1889; president, N.Y. Police Board, 1895, supporting the merit system; assistant secretary of the Navy under McKinley, Apr. 19, 1897 — May 10, 1898, during which he instituted naval target practice and instructed Commodore George Dewey to take Manila in the event of war with Spain. He organized the 1st U.S. Volunteer Cavalry (Rough Riders) as lieutenant colonel; led the charge up Kettle Hill at San Juan and was made colonel by brevet. Elected governor, New York, 1898-1900, he fought the spoils system and achieved taxation of corporation franchises. Drafted for vice president, 1900, he became nation's youngest president at 42 years, 10 mos., 18 days, when McKinley died at Buffalo, Sept. 14, 1901. As president he fought corruption of politics by big business; dissolved Northern Securities Co. and others for violating anti-trust laws; intervened in coal strike on behalf of the public, 1902; instituted the old Dept. of Commerce and Labor; obtained Elkins Law forbidding rebates to favored corporations, 1903; Hepburn Law regulating railroad rates, 1906; Pure Food and Drugs Act, 1906, Reclamation Act and employers' liability laws. He organized conservation, mediated the peace between Japan and Russia, 1905; won the Nobel Peace Prize. He was the first to use the Hague Court of International Arbitration. By recognizing the new Republic of Panama he made Panama Canal possible, appointed Col. George W. Goethals head commissioner and began canal. He was reelected 1904, with 336 electoral votes. vs. 140.

In 1908 he obtained the nomination of William H. Taft, who was elected. Later, considering Taft inimical to liberal policies, he organized the Progressive Party, June 22, 1912, and ran for president against Taft and Woodrow Wilson, splitting the Republicans and causing Wilson's election. He was shot during the campaign but recovered. He advocated recall of elected officials, referendum on legislation, and recall of judicial decisions, which alienated conservatives. In 1916 he left the Progressives and supported Charles E. Hughes, Republican. A strong friend of Britain, he fought American isolation. In 1917 President Wilson refused to let him organize a division. He wrote on many topics—his *Winning of the West* is best known—was a naturalist and hunter and traced the River of Doubt in Brazil, 1913-14, now Rio Roosevelt. He died Jan. 6, 1919, at Sagamore Hill, Oyster Bay, N. Y., now a national shrine, and was buried near the Roosevelt bird refuge there.

Roosevelt's first marriage, in 1880, was to Alice

Hathaway Lee, who died in 1884; they had one daughter. In 1886, he married Edith Kermit Carow; they had one daughter and 4 sons. All 4 served in World War I; one was killed and 2 wounded. The 3 left all served in World War II; 2 died of natural causes while on active duty.

William Howard Taft

William Howard Taft, 27th president, Republican, was born in Cincinnati, Oh., Sept. 15, 1857, the son of Alphonso Taft and Louisa Maria Torrey. His father was secretary of war and attorney general in Grant's cabinet; minister to Austria and Russia under Arthur. Taft was graduated from Yale, 1878; Cincinnati Law School, 1880; became law reporter for Cincinnati newspapers; was assistant prosecuting attorney, 1881-83; assistant county solicitor, 1885; judge, Superior Court, 1887; U.S. solicitor-general, 1890; federal circuit judge, 1892. In 1900 he became head of the U.S. Philippines Commission and was first civil governor of the Philippines, 1901-04; secretary of war, 1904; provisional governor of Cuba, 1906. He was groomed for president by Theodore Roosevelt as an exemplary public servant and elected over W. J. Bryan, 1908. His administration dissolved Standard Oil and tobacco trusts; instituted Department of Labor; drafted direct election of senators and income tax amendments. His tariff and conservation policies angered progressives; though renominated he was fought by Theodore Roosevelt; the result was Wilson's election. Taft was president of the League to Enforce Peace, supporting the League of Nations. He was professor of constitutional law, Yale, 1913-21; Chief Justice of the United States, 1921-30; illness forced him to resign. He died in Washington, Mar. 8, 1930, and was buried in Arlington National Cemetery.

Taft married Helen Herron in 1886; they had 2 sons and a daughter.

Woodrow Wilson

Woodrow Wilson, 28th president, Democrat, was born at Staunton, Va., Dec. 28, 1856, as Thomas Woodrow Wilson, son of a Presbyterian minister, the Rev. Joseph Ruggles Wilson and Janet (Jessie) Woodrow, daughter of a Presbyterian minister. He was a grandson of James Wilson, a Presbyterian of Ulster who reached Philadelphia in 1807, became a printer and in 1808 married an Ulster Presbyterian girl, a shipmate. In his youth Wilson lived in Augusta, Ga., Columbia, S. C., and Wilmington, N. C. He attended Davidson College, 1873-74; was graduated from Princeton, A.B., 1879; A. M., 1882; read law at the University of Virginia, 1881; practiced law, Atlanta, 1882-83; Ph.D., Johns Hopkins, 1886. He taught history and political economy at Bryn Mawr, 1885-88; at Wesleyan, 1888-90; was professor of jurisprudence and political economy at Princeton, 1890-1910; president of Princeton, 1902-1910, during which he tried to introduce innovations of organization that were fought by the graduate dean and alumni; governor of New Jersey, 1911-13, during which he obtained a primary election law, an employers' liability law and other reforms . In 1912 he was nominated for president with the aid of William Jennings Bryan, who sought to block James "Champ" Clark and Tammany Hall. Wilson won the election because the Republican vote for Taft was split by the Progressives under Theodore Roosevelt.

Wilson protected American interests in revolutionary Mexico and fought for American rights on the high seas as the first World War opened. His sharp warnings to Germany led to the resignation of his secretary of state, Bryan, a pacifist, while his protests against British interference with American ships disturbed the Allies. In 1916 he was re-elected by a slim margin with the slogan, "He kept us out of war," over Charles Evans Hughes, who was strongly supported by Theodore Roosevelt. Wilson's offer to mediate in the war (Dec. 18, 1916) was rejected. When the Germans started unrestricted submarine warfare, contrary to pledges, he broke diplomatic relations. After 4 American ships had been sunk he asked a declaration of war against Germany; it was voted Apr. 6, 1917.

Wilson kept tight personal control over all phases of diplomatic and military activity. He relied more on reports of his confidential agent in Europe, Col. E. M. House, than on Secretary of State Robert Lansing and the U.S. ambassadors. However, he backed Gen. John J. Pershing, U.S. commander in chief, Herbert Hoover, food administrator, and others who had his confidence.

Wilson proposed peace Jan. 8, 1918, on the basis of his Fourteen Points, a state paper with worldwide influence. Basic was his doctrine of self-determination, or consent of the governed, in which he opposed handing peoples from one sovereignty to another. He also demanded a league to enforce peace. The Germans overturned their monarchy and a new republic accepted his terms and an armistice, Nov. 11. But at the November elections, the Democrats lost control of Congress.

Wilson went to Paris to help negotiate the peace treaty, the crux of which he considered the League of Nations, also urged by ex-President Taft and Elihu Root. In the U.S. Senate, Henry Cabot Lodge, William E. Borah, and Hiram Johnson demanded reservations that would not make the United States subordinate to the votes of other nations in case of war. Wilson refused to consider any reservations and toured the country to get support. At Pueblo, Col., Sept. 25, 1919, he broke down and several days later suffered a stroke. An invalid for months, he clung to his executive powers while his wife and doctor sought to shield him from affairs which would tire him.

He was awarded the 1919 Nobel Peace Prize, but the treaty was rejected by the Senate, Mar. 1920, by 49 to 35 (29 being sufficient to kill it). He made a public appearance on the day of Harding's inauguration in 1921, and formed a law partnership with Bainbridge Colby, but did not practice. He died Feb. 3, 1924, and was buried in Washington Cathedral.

Wilson's first marriage, in 1885, was to Ellen Louise Axson, who died in 1914. They had 3 daughters. Wilson married Edith Bolling Galt, a widow, in 1915; they had no children.

Warren Gamaliel Harding

Warren Gamaliel Harding, 29th president, Republican, was born near Corsica, now Blooming Grove, Oh., Nov. 2, 1865, the son of Dr. George Tyron Harding, a country physician, and Phoebe Elizabeth Dickerson. He attended Ohio Central College, Iberia, Oh., 1879-82; worked on the Star, Marion, Oh., 1884 and a few years later bought the paper with a friend's help for a reported $300. He was state senator, 1900-04; lieutenant governor, 1904-06; defeated for governor, 1910; chosen U.S. Senator, 1915. He was a regular, "Old Guard" Republican; supported Taft, opposed federal control of food and fuel; voted for anti-strike legislation, woman's suffrage, and the Volstead prohibition enforcement act over President Wilson's veto; and opposed the League of Nations. In 1920 he was nominated for president on the 10th ballot with Calvin Coolidge. The Republicans capitalized on war weariness and fear that Wilson's League of Nations would curtail U.S. sovereignty. They defeated the Democrats, James M. Cox and Franklin D. Roosevelt, 16,152,000 to 9,147,000. Harding stressed a return to "normalcy"; worked for tariff revision and repeal of excess profits and high income taxes. On announcing ratification of treaties with Germany, Austro-Hungary, Nov. 14, 1921, he declared war officially ended July 2, 1921. His cabinet included Charles Evans Hughes (state); Herbert Hoover (commerce); Andrew

S. Mellon (treasury). Two appointees, Albert B. Fall (interior) and Harry Daugherty (attorney general), became involved in the Teapot Dome scandal that embittered Harding's last days. He called the International Conference on Limitation of Armaments, 1921-22. Returning from a trip to Alaska he became ill and died in San Francisco, Aug. 2, 1923. He was buried in Marion, Oh.

In 1891 Harding married Florence Kling De Wolfe, who had divorced her first husband. The Hardings had no children.

Calvin Coolidge

Calvin Coolidge, 30th president, Republican, was born in Plymouth, Vt., July 4, 1872, the son of John Calvin Coolidge, a storekeeper, and Victoria J. Moor, and named John Calvin Coolidge. His paternal ancestors came from England to Watertown, later Cambridge, Massachusetts Bay Colony, in 1630. Coolidge was graduated at Amherst, 1895; admitted to the bar in Northampton, 1897; became city councilman, 1889; city solicitor, 1900-01; clerk of the courts, 1904; member of the lower Massachusetts house, 1907-08; mayor of Northampton, 1910-11; state senator, 1912-15; and president of Senate, 1914-15; lieutenant governor, 1916-18; governor, 1919; reelected, 1920. In Sept., 1919, Coolidge attained national prominence by his action in the Boston police strike during which he declared: "There is no right to strike against the public safety by anybody, anywhere, anytime." This brought his name before the Republican convention of 1920, where he received 34 votes for president and was nominated for vice president by 674¼ votes. He succeeded to the presidency on Harding's death, Aug. 2, 1923, the oath being administered by his father, a justice of the peace, in his home in Plymouth, Aug. 3, and again Aug. 17 before Justice A. A. Hoehling of the Supreme Court of the District of Columbia. He opposed the League of Nations; approved the World Court; vetoed the soldiers' bonus bill, which was passed over his veto. In 1924 he was reelected by a huge majority with 15,725,016 over John W. Davis, Democrat, 8,385,586, and Robert M. LaFollette, Progressive, 4,822,856. He reduced the national debt by $2 billion in 3 years. He opposed the McNary-Haugen farm bill and price fixing, and supported his secretary of state, Frank B. Kellogg, in the Kellogg-Briand treaties outlawing war. His dry, laconic remarks are often quoted; opposing Europe's war debt, "They hired the money, didn't they?" With Republicans eager to renominate him he announced, Aug. 2, 1927: "I do not choose to run for president in 1928." He became a life insurance director and wrote syndicated articles. He died of a heart attack in Northampton, Mass., Jan. 5, 1933. He was buried on a Plymouth hillside.

Coolidge married Grace Ann Goodhue in 1905; they had 2 sons.

Herbert Hoover

Herbert Clark Hoover, 31st president, Republican, was born at West Branch, Ia., Aug. 10, 1874, son of Jesse Clark Hoover, a blacksmith (1847-1880), and Hulda Randall Minthorn (1848-83). Ancestor Andrew Hoover came to Pennsylvania from the West German Palatinate, 1738. Hoover grew up in Indian Territory and Oregon, won A.B. in engineering at Stanford, 1891. Briefly with U.S. Geological Survey and western mines; then mining engineer in western Australia, Asia, Europe, Africa, America. While chief engineer, imperial mines, China, he directed food relief for victims of Boxer Rebellion, 1900. He became a world figure in relief work, distributing over $5 billion worth during 1914-1923. He directed American Relief Committee, London, 1914-15; U.S. Comm. for Relief in Belgium, 1915-1919; U.S. Food Administrator, 1917-1919; American Relief Administrator, 1918-1923, feeding children in defeated nations; Russian Relief, 1918-1923; Interallied Food Council; Supreme Economic Council. As secretary of commerce, 1921-28, he began regulation of radio and aviation, pushed research program for National Academy of Science; organized 7-state pact for Colorado River irrigation and Hoover (Boulder) Dam. Elected president over Alfred E. Smith, 1928, he started White House Conferences on child health and protection, and housing; supported conservation of forests, oil, resources; initiated Naval Conference, 1930; organized RFC, Home Loan Banks, expanded Farm Loan Banks. He gave his official salary to charities and underpaid help. President Truman made him coordinator of European Food Program, 1947, chairman of the Commission for Reorganization of the Executive Branch, 1947-49, and chairman of the 2d Commission on Reorganization, 1953-55. He founded the Hoover Institution on War, Revolution, and Peace at Stanford University. He died in N.Y. City, Oct. 20, 1964, and was buried at West Branch, Ia., where his birthplace is now a memorial.

Hoover married Lou Henry in 1899. They had 2 sons.

Franklin D. Roosevelt

Franklin Delano Roosevelt, 32d president, Democrat, was born near Hyde Park, N.Y., Jan. 30, 1882, the son of James Roosevelt (died 1900) and Sara Delano (died 1941). His ancestor, Claes Martenszan van Rosenvelt, came to New Amsterdam from Holland about 1650. Claes' son Nicholas, a New York alderman in 1700 and 1715, had a son Johannes, from whom Theodore Roosevelt was descended, and a son Jacobus, from whom Franklin D. Roosevelt was descended. Franklin was graduated at Harvard, 1904; attended Columbia Law School, was admitted to the bar. He went to the New York Senate from his Dutchess County district, 1910 and 1913. He voted for Woodrow Wilson at the 1912 Democratic convention; in 1913 Wilson made him assistant secretary of the navy.

Roosevelt ran for vice president, 1920, with James Cox and was defeated. From 1920 to 1928 he was a New York lawyer and vice president of Fidelity & Deposit Co. In Aug., 1921, polio paralyzed his legs. He learned to walk with leg braces and a cane and established the Warm Springs, Ga., Foundation, for helping other victims.

Roosevelt presented the name of Alfred E. Smith to the Democratic conventions of 1924 in New York and 1928 in Houston, calling Smith the Happy Warrior. Smith was nominated in 1928 and defeated. Roosevelt was elected governor of New York, 1928 and 1930. In 1932 at Chicago W. G. McAdoo, pledged to John N. Garner, threw his votes to Roosevelt, who was nominated, alienating Smith. The financial crash, unemployment, and the Democratic promise to repeal prohibition made his victory inevitable. He asked emergency powers, proclaimed the New Deal, and put into effect a vast number of administrative changes. Foremost was "pump priming," or use of public funds for relief and public works, resulting in deficit financing. He greatly expanded the controls of the central government over business, and by an excess profits tax and pyramiding income taxes produced a redistribution of earnings on an unprecedented scale. The Wagner Act gave labor many advantages in organizing and collective bargaining. He was the last president inaugurated on Mar. 4 (1933) and the first inaugurated on Jan. 20 (1937).

Roosevelt was a tremendous worker and traveler despite physical handicaps. He was the first president to use radio for "fireside chats." When the Supreme Court nullified some New Deal laws, he sought power to "pack" the court with additional justices, but Congress refused to give him the authority. Court resignations soon enabled him to replace conservatives who had opposed him. He was the first president to break the 3d term tradition and was elected to a 4th term, 1944, despite failing health. The culminating event of his career was World War II. He was openly hostile to fascist governments before the war and gave Britain substantial support, such as exchanging 50 destroyers for air bases, before Pearl Harbor made the United States a belligerent. He wrote the principles of fair dealing into the Atlantic Charter, Aug. 14, 1941, (with Winston Churchill) and in the Four Freedoms (freedom of speech, of worship, from want, from fear) Jan. 6, 1941. He conferred with allied heads of state at Casablanca, Jan., 1943; Quebec, Aug., 1943; Teheran, Nov.-Dec., 1943; Cairo, Dec., 1943; Yalta, Feb., 1945. He died at Warm Springs, Ga., Apr. 12, 1945, aged 63, and was buried on his Hyde Park estate, where his house and library are in the national care.

Roosevelt married Anna Eleanor Roosevelt (a 5th cousin who was a niece of Theodore Roosevelt) in 1905. They had 4 sons and one daughter and a child that died in infancy.

Harry S. Truman

Harry S. Truman, 33d president, Democrat, was born at Lamar, Mo., May 8, 1884, the son of John Anderson Truman and Martha Ellen Young. Four grandparents were born in Kentucky and moved to Missouri in the 1840s. The Trumans came from England, the president's mother's grandmother from Northern Ireland, while an ancestor of his maternal grandfather, Solomon Young, came from Germany. A family disagreement on whether Harry Truman's middle name was Shippe or Solomon, after names of two grandfathers, resulted in his using only S. for his middle initial.

He attended public schools in Independence, Mo., worked for the Kansas City Star, 1901, and as railroad timekeeper, and helper in Kansas City banks up to 1905. He joined the Missouri National Guard, 1905, and was rejected by West Point for defective eyesight. He ran his family's farm, 1906-17. He entered the Field Artillery School at Fort Sill, Okla., 1917; became first lieutenant, Battery F, and captain, Battery D, 129th Field Artillery, 35th Div., AEF. He served in the Vosges, Meuse-Argonne, and St. Mihiel actions in World War I and was discharged as major, 1919. After the war he ran a haberdashery, became judge of Jackson Co. Court, 1922-24; attended Kansas City School of Law, 1923-25. He was defeated, then elected presiding judge.

Truman was elected U.S. Senator in 1934; reelected 1940. In 1944 with President Roosevelt's approval he was nominated for vice president and elected. On Roosevelt's death Apr. 12,1945, Truman was sworn in as president by Chief Justice Harlan F. Stone. In 1948 he was elected president as polls predicted his defeat.

Truman authorized the first use of the atomic bomb (Hiroshima and Nagasaki, Aug. 6 and 9, 1945), bringing World War II to a rapid end. He was responsible for creating NATO, the Marshall Plan (to restore Western Europe economically) and for what came to be called the Truman Doctrine (to aid nations such as Greece and Turkey, threatened by Russian or other communist takeover). He broke a Russian blockade of East Berlin with a massive airlift, 1948-49. When communist North Korea invaded South Korea, June 1950, he won UN approval for a " "police action" and sent in forces under Gen. Douglas MacArthur. When MacArthur sought to pursue North Koreans into Communist China, Truman removed him from command.

On the domestic front, Truman was responsible for higher-minimum-wage, increased-social-security, and aide-for-housing laws. His 1952 seizure of the nation's steel mills to avert a strike was ruled illegal by the Supreme Court; a strike followed but was settled in 3 weeks. Truman died Dec. 26, 1972, at his Independence, Mo., home at the age of 88.

He married Elizabeth Virginia Wallace in 1919. They had one daughter, Margaret.

Dwight David Eisenhower

Dwight David Eisenhower, 34th president, Republican, was born Oct. 14, 1890, at Denison, Tex., the son of David Jacob Eisenhower and Ida Elizabeth Stover Eisenhower. His paternal grandfather was descended from German Mennonites who left the Rhineland for Pennsylvania in the 1730s, moved to Kansas in 1878. His father met his mother at Lane University, a United Brethren college at Lecompton, Kan. When Dwight was one year old his parents moved to Abilene, Kan. He attended high school and, in 1915 was graduated at West Point. He was a lieutenant colonel in charge of a tank corps at Camp Colt, Gettysburg, Pa., in 1918. He was in the office of the chief of staff, 1933-35. He was on the American Military Mission to the Philippines, 1935-39 and during 4 of those years on the staff of Gen. MacArthur. He was chief of staff, 3d Army, 1941, as brigadier general. After the Louisiana maneuvers he was made chief of the War Plans Div., War Dept. General Staff, and then became assistant chief of staff, Operations Div., and in June, 1942, lieutenant general. He was made commander of allied forces landing in North Africa Nov. 8, 1942, and advanced to full general in Feb., 1943, and commander in chief of allied forces in North Africa. He became supreme commander, allied expeditionary forces Dec. 31, 1943, and as such led the Normandy invasion June 6, 1944. He was given the temporary rank of general of the army Dec. 19, 1944, which was made permanent in 1946. On May 7, 1945, he received the surrender of the Germans at Rheims. He was in command of the U.S. Occupation Force in Germany in 1945, and returned to serve as chief of staff, Nov. 19, 1945, to Feb. 7, 1948. From June 7, 1948, to Jan. 19, 1953, he was president of Columbia University, but he took leave of absence Dec. 16, 1950, to serve as supreme allied commander in Europe to organize NATO forces.

Eisenhower resigned from the army in June, 1952, and was nominated for president by the Republicans at Chicago, July 11, 1952. He defeated Adlai E. Stevenson by 442 to 89 electoral votes, was inaugurated Jan. 20, 1953. He was renominated unanimously in San Francisco, Aug. 22, 1956, and defeated Stevenson by 457 to 74. He called himself a moderate, favored "free market system" vs. government price and wage controls; kept government out of labor disputes; reorganized defense establishment; promoted missile programs, including Polaris. With strong aid of John Foster Dulles, his secretary of state, he continued foreign aid; demanded unification of Germany by free elections; sped end of Korean fighting; supplied planes to anti-communist Guatemalan government; endorsed Formosa and SE Asia defense treaties; backed UN in condemning Anglo-French raid on Egypt; advocated "open skies" policy of mutual inspection to USSR. He sent U.S. troops into Little Rock, Ark., Sept., 1957, during the segregation crisis and ordered Marines into Lebanon July-Aug., 1958.

In 1948, Eisenhower published *Crusade in Europe*, his war memoirs, which quickly became a best seller. His other published works included *Mandate for Change* (1962), *Waging Peace* (1965), *The White House Years*, and *At Ease: Stories I Tell My Friends* (1967). He was an enthusiastic golfer and painter.

During his retirement at his farm near Gettysburg, Pa., Eisenhower took up the role of elder statesman, counseling his 3 successors in the White House. He was hospitalized in early 1968 after his 4th heart attack and died Mar. 28, 1969, in Washington. He was buried in Abilene, Kan.

Eisenhower married Mamie Geneva Doud, July 1, 1916. They had 2 sons; the first died at age 4.

John F. Kennedy

John Fitzgerald Kennedy, 35th president, Democrat, was born May 29, 1917, in Brookline, Mass., the second of 9 children of Joseph P. Kennedy, financier, who later became ambassador to Great Britain, and Rose Fitzgerald Kennedy. He entered Harvard, attended the London School of Economics briefly in 1935, received a B.S., *cum laude* from Harvard in 1940. He served in the U. S. Navy, 1941-1945, commanded a PT boat in the Solomons and won the Navy and Marine Corps medal and Purple Heart. He covered the Potsdam Conference and the start of the UN at San Francisco for International News Service. He served as representative in Congress from Massachusetts, 1947-1953, defeated Henry Cabot Lodge for the Senate in 1952, was reelected 1958. He nearly won the vice presidential nomination in 1956.

Kennedy won the Democratic nomination for president at Los Angeles, July 14, 1960, Sen. Lyndon B. Johnson (Tex.), was named for vice president. Kennedy defeated Richard M. Nixon, Republican, by the slim margin of 118,550 popular votes and an electoral vote of 303 to 219. He was the first Roman Catholic to be elected president.

President Kennedy's most important act was his successful demand Oct. 22, 1962, that the Soviet Union dismantle all missile bases in Cuba. He established a quarantine of arms shipments to Cuba and continued surveillance by air. He defied Soviet attempts to force the Allies out of Berlin. He made the steel industry rescind a price rise. He backed civil rights, a mental health program, arbitration of railroad disputes, and expanded medical care for the aged. Astronaut flights and satellite orbiting were greatly developed during his less than 3 years tenure. He wrote *Profiles in Courage*, which won a Pulitzer Prize, and *Why England Slept*. He turned the White House spotlight on the cultural arts.

On Nov. 22, 1963, Kennedy was assassinated in Dallas, Tex. On Nov. 25, a national day of mourning, he was buried in Arlington National Cemetery.

Kennedy married Jacqueline Lee Bouvier Sept. 12, 1953. They had one daughter and one son; a second son died a few hours after birth.

Lyndon Baines Johnson

Lyndon Baines Johnson, 36th president, Democrat, was born on a farm near Stonewall, Tex., Aug. 27, 1908, son of Sam Ealy and Rebekah Baines Johnson. His father and grandfather had served in the Texas legislature. His family moved to Johnson City in 1913, where he was graduated from the high school in 1924. He received a B.S. degree at Southwest Texas State Teachers College, 1930, attended Georgetown Univ., Law School, Washington, 1935. He taught public speaking in Houston High School, 1930-32; served as secretary to Rep. R. M. Kleberg, 1932-35. In 1935 President Roosevelt appointed Johnson Texas state administrator of the National Youth Administration. In 1937 Johnson won a contest to fill the vacancy caused by the death of a representative and in 1938 was elected to the full term, after which he returned for 4 terms. A member of the naval reserve, he was a lieutenant commander, U.S. Navy, 1941-42, winning the Silver Star for a flight over Japanese positions at New Guinea. He was elected U.S. senator 1948 by Texas; in 1954 he was reelected by a large majority. He became Democratic whip, 1951, and leader, 1953. At 44, Johnson was Texas' favorite son for the Democratic presidential nomination in 1956 and had strong support in the 1960 convention, when the nominee, John F. Kennedy, asked him to run for vice president. His campaigning helped overcome religious bias against Kennedy in the South.

Johnson took the oath of office as president at 2:30 p.m., CST, on Nov. 22, 1963, 99 min. after the death of President Kennedy. In filling out the Kennedy term Johnson worked hard for welfare legislation and signed acts for civil rights, anti-poverty, and tax reduction and averted strikes on railroads. He was nominated for president and elected Nov. 3, 1964, by 486 electoral votes to 52. Overshadowing other developments during Johnson's first full term in the White

House were the expansion of the war in Vietnam, the committing of more than 500,000 American servicemen to conflict, intensive bombing by U.S. planes, and mounting U.S. casualties.

In face of increasing division in the nation and in his own party over his conduct of the war, Johnson announced, on Mar. 31, 1968, "I shall not seek, and I will not accept the nomination of my party for another term as your president." Near the end of his tenure, he indicated that he felt his greatest achievement was the passage of the Voting Rights Act of 1965; his biggest disappointment was that "peace has eluded me."

Retiring to his LBJ Ranch near Johnson City, Tex., the former president wrote his memoirs, *The Vantage Point* (1971), and oversaw the construction of the Lyndon Baines Johnson Library on the campus of the University of Texas in Austin. President Johnson died of a heart attack on Jan. 22, 1973. He was buried on his ranch near the Pedernales River.

Johnson married Claudia Alta (Lady Bird) Taylor on Nov. 17, 1934. They had 2 daughters.

Richard Milhous Nixon

Richard Milhous Nixon, 37th president, Republican, was the only president to voluntarily resign without completing his elected term. He was born in the small farming community of Yorba Linda, Cal., Jan. 9, 1913, the 2d of the 5 sons of Francis Anthony and Hannah Milhous Nixon. In 1922, the family moved to Whittier, Cal., where the future president graduated from Whittier College in 1934. He attended Duke University Law School. After practicing law in Whittier and serving briefly in the Office of Price Administration in 1942, he entered the navy, serving in the South Pacific, and was discharged as a lieutenant commander.

Nixon was elected to the House of Representatives from California's 12th Congressional District in 1946 and reelected in 1948. He achieved prominence as the House Un-American Activities Committee member who forced the showdown that resulted in the Alger Hiss perjury conviction. In 1950 Nixon moved to the Senate by defeating Democrat Helen Gahagan Douglas in a bitter campaign in which he accused her of being "soft on communism."

Elected vice president in the Eisenhower landslides of 1952 and 1956, Nixon achieved more prominence in that position than had his predecessors.

With Eisenhower's endorsement, Nixon won the Republican presidential nomination in 1960. He was defeated by Democrat John F. Kennedy, returned to California, and 2 years later was defeated in his race for governor against Democratic incumbent Pat Brown.

Taking the "long hard road" of the presidential primaries in 1968, he won the presidential nomination easily on the first ballot and went on to defeat Democrat Hubert H. Humphrey.

The 1969-73 Nixon Administration saw remarkable developments in international affairs as Nixon became the first U.S. president to visit China and Russia. He and his foreign affairs advisor, Dr. Henry A. Kissinger, achieved a detente with China and a partial strategic arms limitation agreement with the Soviet Union. In addition, Nixon brought an end to the U.S. ground combat role in South Vietnam.

These diplomatic triumphs did not, however, overshadow the serious economic difficulties which confronted the nation. In Aug., 1971, faced with alarming trade and balance of payments deficits and continuing inflation, Nixon announced a "new economic policy," with wage and price controls at home and negotiations abroad leading to the devaluation of the dollar.

In the field of law, Nixon appointed 4 new Supreme Court Justices, including the chief justice, thus altering the court's balance in favor of a more conservative view. A conservative trend on issues of public order was also observed.

By the summer of 1972, the peace movement had

cooled, the economy showed signs of healthy growth, and a period of normal relations among the superpowers seemed at hand. On Aug. 22, a confident Republican party nominated Nixon for election to a 2d term as president.

Reelected in a massive landslide in 1972, Nixon soon secured a cease-fire agreement in Vietnam and completed the withdrawal of all U.S. troops in spite of heavy fighting and U.S. bombing in Cambodia and continued sporadic conflict in South Vietnam.

On, Jan. 11, 1973, the Nixon administration ended most mandatory wage and price controls and on Feb. 12 announced a further devaluation of the dollar. Inflation, however, continued at peak levels and the dollar came under heavy pressure in the world's gold markets.

Nixon's 2d term was cut short by "The Watergate Affair," a series of scandals beginning with the espionage burglary of Democratic party national headquarters in the Watergate office complex on June 17, 1972. The break-in was led by employees of Nixon's reelection campaign committee and former White House staff members. Investigations and press revelations exposed the existence of secret wiretapping and political espionage by White House aides dating back to May 1969, as well as an organized attempt to frustrate any investigation of these activities or of the Watergate break-in.

From the beginning, Nixon denied any White House involvement in the Watergate break-in. When White House personnel were implicated in the spring of 1973, Nixon denied personal knowledge of either that involvement or of the subsequent cover-up.

On July 16, 1973, a White House aide, under questioning by the Senate Select Committee on Presidential Campaign Activities, revealed that most of Nixon's office conversations and telephone calls had been recorded by an automatic taping system. The ensuing year saw the most severe constitutional confrontation in the nation's history as the president claimed executive privilege to keep the tapes secret and the courts and Congress sought the tapes for the prosecution of criminal indictments against former White House aides and for a House inquiry into possible impeachment proceedings against Nixon.

The confrontation reached its first climax Oct. 10, 1973, in the "Saturday Night Massacre" when Nixon fired the special prosecutor assigned to Watergate matters and accepted the resignations of the attorney general and his deputy when they refused to go along with the firing. The public outcry which followed caused Nixon to appoint a new special prosecutor and to turn over to the courts a number of subpoenaed tape recordings. Public reaction also brought the initiation of a formal inquiry into possible impeachment by the House of Representatives.

The second climax came on July 24, 1974, when the Supreme Court ruled unanimously that Nixon's claim of executive privilege must fall before the special prosecutor's subpoenas of tapes relevant to criminal trial proceedings. At the same time, the court refused to rule on Nixon's claim that a grand jury erred in naming him an "unindicted co-conspirator" in the Watergate cover-up.

Later the same day, the House Judiciary Committee opened a public, televised debate on whether to recommend that the full House impeach the president. By July 30, the 38-member committee had recommended House adoption of 3 articles charging obstruction of justice (21 Dems., 6 Reps. voting in favor), abuse of power (21 Dems., 7 Reps.), and contempt of Congress for refusing to respond to committee subpoenas (19 Dems., 2 Reps.).

On Aug. 5, under pressure from his special legal counsel, Nixon released transcripts of 3 recordings of conversations held on Jun. 23, 1972, 6 days after the Watergate break-in. These transcripts showed that Nixon had known of, approved, and directed Watergate cover-up activities.

As his defenders in the House and Senate withdrew their support, Nixon's aides and top Republican leaders publicly and privately urged him to resign. He announced his resignation on nationwide television on Aug. 8 and left office at noon on Aug. 9. He retired to San Clemente, Cal. One month later, Sept. 8, his chosen successor, Gerald Ford, granted Nixon an unconditional pardon for all federal crimes he "committed or may have committed" while president.

Nixon married Thelma Catherine Patricia "Pat" Ryan on Jun. 21, 1940. They had 2 daughters.

(See Chronology for further developments.)

Gerald Rudolph Ford

Gerald Rudolph Ford, 38th president, Republican, was born July 14, 1913, in Omaha, Neb., son of Leslie and Dorothy Gardner King, and was named Leslie Jr. When he was 2, his parents were divorced and his mother moved with the boy to Grand Rapids, Mich. There she met and married Gerald R. Ford, head of a paint company, who formally adopted the boy and gave him his own name.

In high school, young Gerald became a star football center, named to all-city and all-state teams; at the University of Michigan he played on the undefeated 1932 and 1933 teams and was named most valuable player on the 1934 team. He turned down a Green Bay Packers professional football bid and went to Yale Law School, working part-time as assistant football coach, boxing coach, and professional model. He graduated in the top third of the 1941 law class.

He began practicing law in Grand Rapids, but in 1942, shortly after U.S. entry into World War II, he joined the navy and served 47 months in the Pacific, leaving the service in 1946 as a lieutenant commander.

Back in Grand Rapids, he resumed his law practice and won several Chamber of Commerce awards for community work. Entering the 1948 GOP primary, he upset the incumbent congressman in Michigan's 5th District and won the November election. He continued to win elections, spending 25 years in the House of Representatives, 8 of them as Republican leader. He also served on the Warren Commission, which investigated the assassination of President Kennedy, and was co-author of a book on the commission's work.

As congressman and GOP leader, he was consistently conservative, opposing much social welfare legislation but giving support to final passage of civil rights bills. His colleagues described him as dogged, sincere, a man of modest tastes.

On Oct. 12, 1973, after Vice President Spiro T. Agnew pleaded "no contest" to charges of income tax fraud and resigned his high office, House Minority Leader Ford was nominated by President Nixon to become the new vice president. It was the first use of the procedures set out in the 25th Amendment. The Senate approved the appointment Nov. 27 by a 92-3 vote; The House followed suit, 387-35, on Dec. 6 and Ford was sworn in as the nation's 40th vice president that same day. As vice president, he spent much of his time on speaking tours, seeking to soothe the divisiveness which gripped the nation in the wake of the Watergate scandals.

When President Nixon, facing probable impeachment, resigned Aug. 9, 1974, Ford was sworn in as president, the first to serve without being chosen by the American people in a national election. On Sept. 8 he pardoned Nixon for any federal crimes he might have committed as president. During his first year in office, Ford sought to increase domestic oil production by urging an end to oil price controls; he vetoed, as too costly, a farm-price support bill and a $5.3 billion bill to create jobs, and 2 bills to regulate stripmining lest they cut coal production. The Democratic Congress failed to override him.

On Oct. 18, 1948, Ford married Elizabeth Bloomer Warren, whose first marriage had ended in divorce. The Fords had 3 sons and one daughter.

(See Chronology for further developments.)

Presidents of the United States

No.	Name	Politics	Native State	Date Born	Inaug. at Age	Date of Death	Age at Death
1.	George Washington	Fed.	Va.	1732, Feb. 22	1789 . . . 57	1799, Dec. 14	67
2.	John Adams	Fed.	Mass.	1735, Oct. 30	1797 . . . 61	1826, July 4	90
3.	Thomas Jefferson	Dem.-Rep.	Va.	1743, Apr. 13	1801 . . . 57	1826, July 4	83
4.	James Madison	Dem.-Rep.	Va.	1751, Mar. 16	1809 . . . 57	1836, June 28	85
5.	James Monroe	Dem.-Rep.	Va.	1758, Apr. 28	1817 . . . 58	1831, July 4	73
6.	John Quincy Adams	Dem.-Rep.	Mass.	1767, July 11	1825 . . . 57	1848, Feb. 23	80
7.	Andrew Jackson	Dem.	S.C.	1767, Mar. 15	1829 . . . 61	1845, June 8	78
8.	Martin Van Buren	Dem.	N.Y.	1782, Dec. 5	1837 . . . 54	1862, July 24	79
9.	William Henry Harrison	Whig	Va.	1773, Feb. 9	1841 . . . 68	1841, Apr. 4	68
10.	John Tyler	Whig	Va.	1790, Mar. 29	1841 . . . 51	1862, Jan. 18	71
11.	James Knox Polk	Dem.	N.C.	1795, Nov. 2	184 . . . 49	1849, June 15	53
12.	Zachary Taylor	Whig	Va.	1784, Nov. 24	1849 . . . 64	1850, July 9	65
13.	Millard Fillmore	Whig	N.Y.	1800, Jan. 7	1850 . . . 50	1874, Mar. 8	74
14.	Franklin Pierce	Dem.	N.H.	1804, Nov. 23	1853 . . . 48	1869, Oct. 8	64
15.	James Buchanan	Dem.	Pa.	1791, Apr. 23	1857 . . . 65	1868, June 1	77
16.	Abraham Lincoln	Rep.	Ky.	1809, Feb. 12	1861 . . . 52	1865, Apr. 15	56
17.	Andrew Johnson	(see note)*	N.C.	1808, Dec. 29	1865 . . . 56	1875, Jul. 31	66
18.	Ulysses Simpson Grant	Rep.	Oh.	1822, Apr. 27	1869 . . . 46	1885, Jul. 23	63
19.	Rutherford Birchard Hayes	Rep.	Oh.	1822, Oct. 4	1877 . . . 54	1893, Jan. 17	70
20.	James Abram Garfield	Rep.	Oh.	1831, Nov. 19	1881 . . . 49	1881, Sept. 19	49
21.	Chester Alan Arthur	Rep.	Vt.	1830, Oct. 5	1881 . . . 50	1886, Nov. 18	56
22.	Grover Cleveland	Dem.	N.J.	1837, Mar. 18	1885 . . . 47	1908, June24˙	71
23.	Benjamin Harrison	Rep.	Oh.	1833, Aug. 20	1889 . . . 55	1901, Mar. 13	67
24.	Grover Cleveland	Dem.	N.J.	1837, Mar. 18	1893 . . . 55	1908, June 24	71
25.	William McKinley	Rep.	Oh.	1843, Jan. 29	1897 . . . 54	1901, Sept. 14	58
26.	Theodore Roosevelt	Rep.	N.Y.	1858, Oct. 27	1901 . . . 42	1919, Jan. 6	60
27.	William Howard Taft	Rep.	Oh.	1857, Sept. 15	1909 . . . 51	1930, Mar. 8	72
28.	Woodrow Wilson	Dem.	Va.	1857, Dec. 28	1913 . . . 56	1924, Feb. 3	67
29.	Warren Gamaliel Harding	Rep.	Oh.	1865, Nov. 2	1921 . . . 55	1923, Aug. 2	57
30.	Calvin Coolidge	Rep.	Vt.	1872, July 4	1923 . . . 51	1933, Jan. 5	60
31.	Herbert Clark Hoover	Rep.	Ia.	1874, Aug. 10	1929 . . . 54	1964, Oct. 20	90
32.	Franklin Delano Roosevelt	Dem.	N.Y.	1882, Jan. 30	1933 . . . 51	1945, Apr. 12	63
33.	Harry S. Truman	Dem.	Mo.	1884, May 8	1945 . . . 60	1972, Dec. 26	88
34.	Dwight David Eisenhower	Rep.	Tex.	1890, Oct. 14	1953 . . . 62	1969, Mar. 28	78
35.	John F. Kennedy	Dem.	Mass.	1917, May 29	1961 . . . 43	1963, Nov. 22	46
36.	Lyndon Baines Johnson	Dem.	Tex.	1908, Aug. 27	1963 . . . 55	1973, Jan. 22	64
37.	Richard Milhous Nixon**	Rep.	Cal.	1913, Jan 9	1969 . . . 56	. . . .	. . .
38.	Gerald R. Ford	Rep.	Neb.	1913, July 14	1974 . . . 61		

*Andrew Johnson — a Democrat, nominated vice president by Republicans and elected with Lincoln on National Union ticket. **Resigned Aug. 9, 1974.

Presidents, Vice Presidents, Congresses

	President		Service					Vice President	Congress
1	George Washington	Apr.	30,	1789-Mar.	3,	1797	1	John Adams	1, 2, 3, 4
2	John Adams	Mar.	4,	1797-Mar.	3,	1801	2	Thomas Jefferson	5, 6
3	Thomas Jefferson	Mar.	4,	1801-Mar.	3,	1805	3	Aaron Burr	7, 8
	"	Mar.	4,	1805-Mar.	3,	1809	4	George Clinton	9, 10
4	James Madison	Mar.	4,	1809-Mar.	3,	1813		"(1)	11, 12
	"	Mar.	4,	1813-Mar.	3,	1817	5	Elbridge Gerry(2)	13, 14
5	James Monroe	Mar.	4,	1817-Mar.	3,	1825	6	Daniel D. Tompkins	15, 16, 17, 18
6	John Quincy Adams	Mar.	4,	1825-Mar.	3,	1829	7	John C. Calhoun	19, 20
7	Andrew Jackson	Mar.	4,	1829-Mar.	3,	1833		"(3)	21, 22
	"	Mar.	4,	1833-Mar.	3,	1837	8	Martin Van Buren	23, 24
8	Martin Van Buren	Mar.	4,	1837-Mar.	3,	1841	9	Richard M. Johnson	25, 26
9	William Henry Harrison (4)	Mar.	4,	1841-Apr.	4,	1841	10	John Tyler	27
10	John Tyler	Apr.	6,	1841-Mar.	3,	1845			27, 28
11	James K. Polk	Mar.	4,	1845-Mar.	3,	1849	11	George M. Dallas	29, 30
12	Zachary Taylor (4)	Mar.	5,	1849-July	9,	1850	12	Millard Fillmore	31
13	Millard Fillmore	July	10,	1850-Mar.	3,	1853			31, 32
14	Franklin Pierce	Mar.	4,	1853-Mar.	3,	1857	13	William R. King (5)	33, 34
15	James Buchanan	Mar.	4,	1857-Mar.	3,	1861	14	John C. Breckinridge	35, 36
16	Abraham Lincoln	Mar.	4,	1861-Mar.	3,	1865	15	Hannibal Hamlin	37, 38
	"(4)	Mar.	4,	1865-Apr.	15,	1865	16	Andrew Johnson	39
17	Andrew Johnson	Apr.	15,	1865-Mar.	3,	1869			39, 40
18	Ulysses S. Grant	Mar.	4,	1869-Mar.	3,	1873	17	Schuyler Colfax	41, 42
	"	Mar.	4,	1873-Mar.	3,	1877	18	Henry Wilson (6)	43, 44
19	Rutherford B. Hayes	Mar.	4,	1877-Mar.	3,	1881	19	William A. Wheeler	45, 46
20	James A. Garfield (4)	Mar.	4,	1881-Sept.	19,	1881	20	Chester A. Arthur	47
21	Chester A. Arthur	Sept.	20,	1881-Mar.	3,	1885			47, 48
22	Grover Cleveland (7)	Mar.	4,	1885-Mar.	3,	1889	21	Thomas A. Hendricks (8)	49, 50
23	Benjamin Harrison	Mar.	4,	1889-Mar.	3,	1893	22	Levi P. Morton	51, 52
24	Grover Cleveland (7)	Mar.	4,	1893-Mar.	3,	1897	23	Adlai E. Stevenson	53, 54
25	William McKinley	Mar.	4,	1897-Mar.	3,	1901	24	Garret A. Hobart (9)	55, 56
	"(4)	Mar.	4,	1901-Sept.	14,	1901	25	Theodore Roosevelt	57
26	Theodore Roosevelt	Sept.	14,	1901-Mar.	3,	1905			57, 58
	"	Mar.	4,	1905-Mar.	3,	1909	26	Charles W. Fairbanks	59, 60
27	William H. Taft	Mar.	4,	1909-Mar.	3,	1913	27	James S. Sherman (10)	61, 62
28	Woodrow Wilson	Mar.	4,	1913-Mar.	3,	1921	28	Thomas R. Marshall	63, 64, 65, 66
29	Warren G. Harding (4)	Mar.	4,	1921-Aug.	2,	1923	29	Calvin Coolidge	67
30	Calvin Coolidge	Aug.	3,	1923-Mar.	3,	1925			68
	"	Mar.	4,	1925-Mar.	3,	1929	30	Charles G. Dawes	69, 70
31	Herbert C. Hoover	Mar.	4,	1929-Mar.	3,	1933	31	Charles Curtis	71, 72

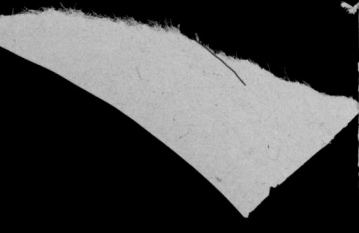

32	Franklin D. Roosevelt	Mar.	4,	1933-Jan.	20,	1941	32	John N. Garner	73, 74, 75, 76
	"	Jan.	20,	1941-Jan.	20,	1945	33	Henry A. Wallace	77, 78
	"(4).	Jan.	20,	1945-Apr.	12,	1945	34	Harry S. Truman	79
33	Harry S. Truman	Apr.	12,	1945-Jan.	30,	1949			79, 80
	"	Jan.	20,	1949-Jan.	20,	1953	35	Alben W. Barkley	81, 82
34	Dwight D. Eisenhower	Jan.	20,	1953-Jan.	20,	1961	36	Richard M. Nixon	83, 84, 85, 86
35	John F. Kennedy (4)	Jan.	20,	1961-Nov.	22,	1963	37	Lyndon B. Johnson	87, 88
36	Lyndon B. Johnson	Nov.	22,	1963-Jan.	20,	1965			88
	"	Jan.	20,	1965-Jan.	20,	1969	38	Hubert H. Humphrey	89, 90
37	Richard M. Nixon	Jan.	20,	1969-Jan.	20,	1973	39	Spiro T. Agnew (11)	91, 92 93
	"(12)	Jan.	20,	1973-Aug.	9,	1974	40	Gerald R. Ford (13)	93
38	Gerald R. Ford (14)	Aug.	9,	1974			41	Nelson A. Rockefeller (15)	93, 94

(1) Died Apr. 20, 1812. (2) Died Nov. 23, 1814. (3) Resigned Dec. 28, 1832, to become U. S. Senator. (4) Died in office. (5) Died Apr. 18, 1853. (6) Died Nov. 22, 1875. (7) Terms not consecutive. (8) Died Nov. 25, 1885. (8) Died Nov. 21, 1899. (10) Died Oct. 30, 1912. (11) Resigned Oct, 10, 1973. (12) Resigned Aug. 9, 1974. (13) First non-elected vice president, chosen under 25th amendment procedure. (14) First non-elected president. (15) 2d non-elected vice presient.

The Presidents of the Continental Congresses

Congress President	Date Elected	Meeting Place	Term
Peyton Randolph, Va. (1)	Sept. 5, 1774	Philadelphia	Sept. 5 to Oct. 26, 1774
Henry Middleton, S.C.	Oct. 22, 1774		
Peyton Randolph, Va.	May 10, 1775	Philadelphia	May 10, 1775 to Dec. 12, 1776
John Hancock, Mass.	May 24, 1775	Baltimore	Dec. 20, 1776 to Mar. 4, 1777
		Philadelphia	Mar. 5 to Sept. 18, 1777
		Lancaster, Pa.	Sept. 27, 1777 (one day)
Henry Laurens, S.C.	Nov. 1, 1777(4)	York, Pa.	Sept. 30, 1777 to June 27, 1778
John Jay, N.Y.	Dec. 10, 1778	Philadelphia	July 2, 1778 to June 21, 1783
Samuel Huntington, Conn.	Sept. 28, 1779		
Thomas McKean, Del.	July 10, 1781		
John Hanson, Md. (2)	Nov. 5, 1781		
Elias Boudinot, N.J.	Nov. 4, 1782	Princeton, N.J.	June 30 to Nov. 4, 1783
Thomas Mifflin, Pa.	Nov. 3, 1783	Annapolis, Md.	Nov. 26, 1783 to June 3, 1784
Richard Henry Lee, Va.	Nov. 30, 1784	Trenton, N.J.	Nov. 1 to Dec. 24, 1784
		New York City	Jan. 11 to Nov. 4, 1785
John Hancock, Mass. (3)	Nov. 23, 1785	"	Nov. 7, 1785 to Nov. 3, 1786
Nathaniel Gorham, Mass.	June 6, 1786	"	Nov. 6, 1786 to Oct. 30, 1787
Arthur St. Clair, Pa.	Feb. 2, 1787	"	Nov. 5, 1787 to Oct. 21, 1788
Cyrus Griffin, Va.	Jan. 22, 1788	"	Nov. 3, 1788 to Mar. 2, 1789

(1) Resigned Oct. 2, 1774.
(2) Titled "President of the United States in Congress Assembled," John Hanson is considered by some to be the first U.S. President as he was the first to serve under the Articles of Confederation. He was, however, little more than presiding officer of the Congress, which retained full executive power. He could be considered the head of government, but not head of state.
(3) Resigned May 29, 1786, without serving, because of illness.
(4) Articles of Confederation agreed upon, Nov. 15, 1777; last ratification from Maryland, Mar. 1 1781.

Longevity of Presidents of the U. S.
Source: Statistical Bulletin, Metropolitan Life

	Year of Birth	Age, 1st Inauguration	Age at Death	Expectancy After 1st Inaugural	Years Lived After First Inaugural		
					Actual	Above Expected	Below Expected
George Washington	1732	57	67	17.1	10.6		6.5
John Adams	1735	61	90	14.4	29.3	14.9	
Thomas Jefferson	1743	57	83	16.4	25.3	8.9	
James Madison	1751	57	85	16.3	27.3	11.0	
James Monroe	1758	58	73	15.7	14.3		1.3
John Quincy Adams	1767	57	80	16.3	23.0	6.7	
Andrew Jackson	1767	61	78	13.5	16.3	2.7	
Martin Van Buren	1782	54	79	17.2	25.4	8.2	
William H. Harrison†	1773	68	68	.1	.1		9.3
John Tyler	1790	51	71	19.2	20.8	1.6	
James K. Polk	1795	49	53	21.5	4.3		17.2
Zachary Taylor†	1784	64	65	12.8	1.3		11.5
Millard Fillmore	1800	50	74	20.7	23.7	2.9	
Franklin Pierce	1804	48	64	22.0	16.6		5.4
James Buchanan	1791	65	77	11.9	11.3		.6
Abraham Lincoln‡	1809	52	56	19.8	4.1		15.6
Andrew Johnson	1808	56	66	17.2	10.3		6.9
Ulysses S. Grant	1822	46	63	22.8	16.4		6.4
Rutherford B. Hayes	1822	54	70	18.0	15.9		2.1
James A. Garfield‡	1831	49	49	21.2	.5		20.7
Chester A. Arthur	1830	50	56	20.1	5.2		15.0
Grover Cleveland	1837	47	71	22.1	23.3	1.2	
Benjamin Harrison	1833	55	67	17.2	12.0		5.2
William McKinley‡	1843	54	58	18.2	4.5		13.6
Theodore Roosevelt	1858	42	60	26.1	17.3		8.8
William H. Taft	1857	51	72	20.3	21.0	.8	
Woodrow Wilson	1856	56	67	17.1	10.9		6.2
Warren G. Harding†	1865	55	57	18.1	2.4		15.6
Calvin Coolidge	1872	51	60	21.4	9.4		12.0

Herbert C. Hoover	1874	54	90	19.0	35.6	16.7
Franklin D. Roosevelt†	1882	51	63	21.7	12.1	9.6
Harry S. Truman	1884	60	88	15.3	27.7	12.4
Dwight D. Eisenhower	1890	62	78	14.7	16.2	1.4
John F. Kennedy‡	1917	43	46	28.5	2.8	25.7
Lyndon B. Johnson	1908	55	64	19.3	9.2	10.1
Richard M. Nixon	1913	56		18.8		

†Died during tenure. ‡Assassinated.

Cabinets of the United States

Secretaries of State

The Department of Foreign Affairs was created by act of Congress Jul. 27, 1789, and the name changed to Department of State on Sept. 15.

President	Secretary	Home	Apptd.	President	Secretary	Home	Apptd.
Washington	Thomas Jefferson	Va.	1789	Arthur	James G. Blaine	Me.	1881
"	Edmund Randolph	"	1794	"	F. T. Frelinghuysen	N. J.	1881
"	Timothy Pickering	Pa.	1795	Cleveland			1885
J. Adams	"	"	1795	"	Thomas F. Bayard	Del.	1885
"	John Marshall	Va.	1800	B. Harrison		"	1889
Jefferson	James Madison	"	1801	"	James G. Blaine	Me.	1889
Madison	Robert Smith	Md.	1809	"	John W. Foster	Ind.	1892
"	James Monroe	Va.	1811	Cleveland	Walter Q. Gresham	Ill.	1893
Monroe	John Quincy Adams	Mass.	1817	"	Richard Olney	Mass.	1895
J. Q. Adams	Henry Clay	Ky.	1825	McKinley			1897
Jackson	Martin Van Buren	N.Y.	1829	"	John Sherman	Oh.	1897
"	Edward Livingston	La.	1831	"	William R. Day	"	1898
"	Louis McLane	Del.	1833	"	John Hay	D. C.	1898
"	John Forsyth	Ga.	1834	T. Roosevelt	"	"	1901
Van Buren	"	"	1837	"	Elihu Root	N. Y.	1905
W. H. Harrison	Daniel Webster	Mass.	1841	"	Robert Bacon	"	1909
Tyler	"	"	1841	Taft	"	"	1909
"	Abel P. Upshur	Va.	1843	"	Philander C. Knox	Pa.	1909
"	John C. Calhoun	S. C.	1844	Wilson	"	"	1913
Polk	"	"	1845	"	William J. Bryan	Neb.	1913
"	James Buchanan	Pa.	1845	"	Robert Lansing	N. Y.	1915
Taylor	"	"	1849	"	Bainbridge Colby	"	1920
"	John M. Clayton	Del.	1849	Harding	Charles E. Hughes	"	1921
Fillmore	"	"	1850	Coolidge	"	"	1923
"	Daniel Webster	Mass.	1850	"	Frank B. Kellogg	Minn.	1925
"	Edward Everett	"	1852	Hoover	"	"	1929
Pierce	William L. Marcy	N. Y.	1853	"	Henry L. Stimson	N. Y.	1929
Buchanan	"	"	1857	F. D. Roosevelt	Cordell Hull	Tenn.	1933
"	Lewis Cass	Mich.	1857	"	E. R. Stettinius Jr.	Va.	1944
"	Jeremiah S. Black	Pa.	1860	Truman	"	"	1945
Lincoln	"	"	1861	"	James F. Byrnes	S. C.	1945
"	William H. Seward	N. Y.	1861	"	George C. Marshall	Pa.	1947
Johnson, A.	"	"	1865	"	Dean G. Acheson	Conn.	1949
Grant	Elihu B. Washburne	Ill.	1869	Eisenhower	John Foster Dulles	N. Y.	1953
"	Hamilton Fish	N. Y.	1869	"	Christian A. Herter	Mass.	1959
Hayes	"	"	1877	Kennedy	Dean Rusk	N. Y.	1961
"	William M. Evarts	"	1877	Johnson, L. B.	"	"	1963
Garfield	"	"	1881	Nixon	William P. Rogers	N. Y.	1969
"	James G. Blaine	Me.	1881	"	Henry A. Kissinger	D.C.	1973
				Ford	"	"	1974

Secretaries of the Treasury

The Treasury Department was organized by act of Congress on Sept. 2, 1789.

President	Secretary	Home	Apptd.	President	Secretary	Home	Apptd.
Washington	Alexander Hamilton	N. Y.	1789	Taylor	William M. Meredith	Pa.	1849
"	Oliver Wolcott	Conn.	1795	Fillmore	Thomas Corwin	Oh.	1850
J. Adams	"	"	1797	Pierce	James Guthrie	Ky.	1853
"	Samuel Dexter	Mass.	1801	Buchanan	Howell Cobb	Ga.	1857
Jefferson	"	"	1801	"	Phillip F. Thomas	Md.	1860
"	Albert Gallatin	Pa.	1801	"	John A. Dix	N. Y.	1861
Madison	"	Pa.	1809	Lincoln	Salmon P. Chase	Oh.	1861
"	George W. Campbell	Tenn.	1814	"	William P. Fessenden	Me.	1864
"	Alexander J. Dallas	Pa.	1814	"	Hugh McCulloch	Ind.	1865
"	William H. Crawford	Ga.	1816	Johnson, A.	"	"	1865
Monroe	"	"	1817	Grant	George S. Boutwell	Mass.	1869
J. Q. Adams	Richard Rush	Pa.	1825	Grant	William A. Richardson	Mass.	1873
Jackson	Samuel D. Ingham	Pa.	1829	"	Benjamin H. Bristow	Ky.	1874
"	Louis McLane	Del.	1831	"	Lot M. Morrill	Me.	1876
"	William J. Duane	Pa.	1833	Hayes	John Sherman	Oh.	1877
"	Roger B. Taney	Md.	1833	Garfield	William Windom	Minn.	1881
"	Levi Woodbury	N. H.	1834	Arthur	Charles J. Folger	N. Y.	1881
Van Buren	"	"	1837	"	Walter Q. Gresham	Ind.	1884
W. H. Harrison	Thomas Ewing	Oh.	1841	"	Hugh McCulloch	"	1884
Tyler	"	"	1841	Cleveland	Daniel Manning	N. Y.	1885
"	Walter Forward	Pa.	1841	"	Charles S. Fairchild	"	1887
"	John C. Spencer	N. Y.	1843	B. Harrison	William Windom	Minn.	1889
"	George M. Bibb	Ky.	1844	"	Charles Foster	Oh.	1891
Polk	Robert J. Walker	Miss.	1845	Cleveland	John G. Carlisle	Ky.	1893

President	Secretary	Home	Apptd.
McKinley	Lyman J. Gage	Ill.	1897
T. Roosevelt	"	"	1901
"	Leslie M. Shaw	Iowa	1902
"	George B. Cortelyou	N.Y.	1907
Taft	Franklin MacVeagh	Ill.	1909
Wilson	William G. McAdoo	N.Y.	1913
"	Carter Glass	Va.	1918
"	David F. Houston	Mo.	1920
Harding	Andrew W. Mellon	Pa.	1921
Coolidge	"	"	1923
Hoover	"	"	1929
"	Ogden L. Mills	N.Y.	1932
F. D. Roosevelt	William H. Woodin	"	1933
"	Henry Morgenthau Jr.	"	1934
Truman	Fred M. Vinson	Ky.	1945
"	John W. Snyder	Mo.	1946
Eisenhower	George M. Humphrey	Oh.	1953
"	Robert B. Anderson	Conn.	1957
Kennedy	C. Douglas Dillon	N.J.	1961
Johnson, L. B.	"	"	1963
"	Henry H. Fowler	Va.	1965
"	Joseph W. Barr	Ind.	1968
Nixon	David M. Kennedy	Ill.	1969
"	John B. Connally	Tex.	1970
"	George P. Shultz	Ill.	1972
"	William E. Simon	N.J.	1974
Ford	"	"	1974

Attorneys General

The office of attorney general was organized by act of Congress Sept. 24, 1789. The attorney general was made a member of the cabinet in 1814. The Dept. of Justice was created Jun. 22, 1870.

President	Attorney General	Home	Apptd.
Washington	Edmund Randolph	Va.	1789
"	William Bradford	Pa.	1794
"	Charles Lee	Va.	1795
J. Adams	Charles Lee	Va.	1797
Jefferson	Levi Lincoln	Mass.	1801
"	John Breckenridge	Ky.	1805
Jefferson	Caesar A. Rodney	Del.	1807
Madison	"	"	1809
"	William Pinkney	Md.	1811
"	Richard Rush	Pa.	1814
Monroe	"	"	1817
"	William Wirt	Va.	1817
J. Q. Adams	"	"	1825
Jackson	John McP. Berrien	Ga.	1829
"	Roger B. Taney	Md.	1831
"	Benjamin F. Butler	N.Y.	1833
Van Buren	"	"	1837
"	Felix Grundy	Tenn.	1838
"	Henry D. Gilpin	Pa.	1840
W. H. Harrison	John J. Crittenden	Ky.	1841
Tyler	"	"	1841
"	Hugh S. Legare	S.C.	1841
"	John Nelson	Md.	1843
Polk	John Y. Mason	Va.	1845
"	Nathan Clifford	Me.	1846
"	Isaac Toucey	Conn.	1848
Taylor	Reverdy Johnson	Md.	1849
Fillmore	John J. Crittenden	Ky.	1850
Pierce	Caleb Cushing	Mass.	1853
Buchanan	Jeremiah S. Black	Pa.	1857
"	Edwin M. Stanton	Pa.	1860
Lincoln	Edward Bates	Mo.	1861
"	James Speed	Ky.	1864
Johnson, A.	"	Ky.	1865
"	Henry Stanbery	Oh.	1866
"	William M. Evarts	N.Y.	1868
Grant	Ebenezer R. Hoar	Mass.	1869
"	Amos T. Akerman	Ga.	1870
"	George H. Williams	Ore.	1871
"	Edwards Pierrepont	N.Y.	1875
"	Alphonso Taft	Oh.	1876
Hayes	Charles Devens	Mass.	1877
Garfield	Wayne MacVeagh	Pa.	1881
Arthur	Benjamin H. Brewster	"	1881
Cleveland	Augustus Garland	Ark.	1885
B. Harrison	William H. H. Miller	Ind.	1889
Cleveland	Richard Olney	Mass.	1893
"	Judson Harmon	Oh.	1895
McKinley	Joseph McKenna	Cal.	1897
"	John W. Griggs	N.J.	1898
"	Philander C. Knox	Pa.	1901
T. Roosevelt	"	"	1901
"	William H. Moody	Mass.	1904
"	Charles J. Bonaparte	Md.	1906
Taft	George W. Wickersham	N.Y.	1909
Wilson	J. C. McReynolds	Tenn.	1913
"	Thomas W. Gregory	Tex.	1914
"	A. Mitchell Palmer	Pa.	1919
Harding	Harry M. Daugherty	Oh.	1921
Coolidge	"	"	1923
"	Harlan F. Stone	N.Y.	1924
"	John G. Sargent	Vt.	1925
Hoover	William D. Mitchell	Minn.	1929
F. D. Roosevelt	Homer S. Cummings	Conn.	1933
"	Frank Murphy	Mich.	1939
"	Robert H. Jackson	N.Y.	1940
"	Francis Biddle	Pa.	1941
Truman	Tom C. Clark	Tex.	1945
"	J. Howard McGrath	R.I.	1949
"	J. P. McGranery	Pa.	1952
Eisenhower	H. Brownell Jr.	N.Y.	1953
"	William P. Rogers	Md.	1957
Kennedy	Robert F. Kennedy	Mass.	1961
Johnson, L. B.	"	"	1963
"	N. de B. Katzenbach	Ill.	1965
"	Ramsey Clark	Tex.	1967
Nixon	John N. Mitchell	N.Y.	1969
"	Richard G. Kleindienst	Ariz.	1972
"	Elliot L. Richardson	Mass.	1973
"	William B. Saxbe	Oh.	1974
Ford	"	"	1974
"	Edward H. Levi	Ill.	1975

Secretaries of Agriculture

The Department of Agriculture was created by act of Congress May 15, 1862. On Feb. 8, 1889, its commissioner was renamed secretary of agriculture and became a member of the cabinet.

President	Secretary	Home	Apptd.
Cleveland	Norman J. Colman	Mo.	1889
B. Harrison	Jeremiah M. Rusk	Wis.	1889
Cleveland	J. Sterling Morton	Neb.	1893
McKinley	James Wilson	Ia.	1897
T. Roosevelt	"	"	1901
Taft	"	"	1909
Wilson	David F. Houston	Mo.	1913
"	Edward T. Meredith	Ia.	1920
Harding	Henry C. Wallace	Ia.	1921
Coolidge	"	"	1923
"	Howard M. Gore	W. Va.	1924
"	W. M. Jardine	Kan.	1925
Hoover	Arthur M. Hyde	Mo.	1929
F. D. Roosevelt	Henry A. Wallace	Ia.	1933
"	Claude R. Wickard	Ind.	1940
Truman	Clinton P. Anderson	N.M.	1945
"	Charles F. Brannan	Col.	1948
Eisenhower	Ezra Taft Benson	Ut.	1953
Kennedy	Orville L. Freeman	Minn.	1961
Johnson, L. B.	"	"	1963
Nixon	Clifford M. Hardin	Ind.	1969
"	Earl L. Butz	Ind.	1971
Ford	"	"	1974

Secretaries of the Interior

The Department of Interior was created by act of Congress Mar. 3, 1849.

President	Secretary	Home	Apptd.	President	Secretary	Home	Apptd.
Taylor	Thomas Ewing	Oh.	1849	T. Roosevelt	Ethan A. Hitchcock	Mo.	1901
Fillmore	Thomas M. T. McKennan	Pa.	1850	"	James R. Garfield	Oh.	1907
"	Alex H. H. Stuart	Va.	1850	Taft	Richard A. Ballinger	Wash.	1909
Pierce	Robert McClelland	Mich.	1853	"	Walter L. Fisher	Ill.	1911
Buchanan	Jacob Thompson	Miss.	1857	Wilson	Franklin K. Lane	Cal.	1913
Lincoln	Caleb B. Smith	Ind.	1861	"	John B. Payne	Ill.	1920
"	John P. Usher	"	1863	Harding	Albert B. Fall	N. M.	1921
A. Johnson	"	"	1865	"	Hubert Work	Col.	1923
"	James Harlan	Ia.	1865	Coolidge	"	"	1923
"	Orville H. Browning	Ill.	1866	"	Roy O. West	Ill.	1929
Grant	Jacob D. Cox	Oh.	1869	Hoover	Ray Lyman Wilbur	Cal.	1929
"	Columbus Delano	"	1870	F. D. Roosevelt	Harold L. Ickes	Ill.	1933
"	Zachariah Chandler	Mich.	1875	Truman	"	"	1945
Hayes	Carl Schurz	Mo.	1877	"	Julius A. Krug	Wis.	1946
Garfield	Sam. J. Kirkwood	Ia.	1881	"	Oscar L. Chapman	Col.	1950
Arthur	Henry M. Teller	Col.	1882	Eisenhower	Douglas McKay	Ore.	1953
Cleveland	Lucius Q. C. Lamar	Miss.	1885	"	Fred A. Seaton	Neb.	1956
"	William F. Vilas	Wis.	1888	Kennedy	Stewart L. Udall	Ariz.	1961
B. Harrison	John W. Noble	Mo.	1889	L.B. Johnson	"	"	1963
Cleveland	Hoke Smith	Ga.	1893	Nixon	Walter J. Hickel	Alas	1969
"	David R. Francis	Mo.	1896	"	Rogers C. B. Morton	Md.	1971
McKinley	Cornelius N. Bliss	N. Y.	1897	Ford	"	"	1974
"	Ethan A. Hitchcock	Mo.	1898	"	Stanley K. Hathaway	Wyo	1975
				"	Vacant		

Secretaries of Health, Education, and Welfare

The Department of Health, Education, and Welfare was created by act of Congress Apr. 11, 1953.

President	Secretary	Home	Apptd.	President	Secretary	Home	Apptd.
Eisenhower	Oveta Culp Hobby	Tex.	1953	Johnson, L. B.	Wilbur J. Cohen	Mich.	1968
"	Marion B. Folsom	N. Y.	1955	Nixon	Robert H. Finch	Cal.	1969
"	Arthur S. Flemming	Oh.	1958	"	Elliot L. Richardson	Mass.	1970
Kennedy	Abraham A. Ribicoff	Conn.	1961	"	Caspar W. Weinberger	Cal.	1973
"	Anthony J. Celebrezze	Oh.	1962	Ford	"	"	1974
Johnson, L.B.	"	"	1963	"	Forrest D. Mathews	Ala.	1975
"	John W. Gardner	N. Y.	1965				

Secretaries of Housing and Urban Development

The Department of Housing and Urban Development was created by act of Congress Sept. 9, 1965.

President	Secretary	Home	Apptd.	President	Secretary	Home	Apptd.
Johnson, L. B.	Robert C. Weaver	Wash.	1966	Nixon	James T. Lynn	Oh.	1973
"	Robert C. Wood	Mass.	1968	Ford	"	"	1974
Nixon	George W. Romney	Mich.	1969	"	Carla Anderson Hills	Cal.	1975

Secretaries of Defense

The Department of Defense, originally designated the National Military Establishment, was created Sept. 18, 1947. It is headed by the secretary of defense, who is a member of the president's cabinet.

The departments of the army, of the navy, and of the air force function within the Department of Defense, and their respective secretaries are no longer members of the president's cabinet.

President	Secretary	Home	Apptd.	President	Secretary	Home	Apptd.
Truman	James V. Forrestal	N. Y.	1947	Kennedy	Robert S. McNamara	Mich.	1961
"	Louis A. Johnson	W. Va.	1949	Johnson, L. B.	"	"	1963
"	George C. Marshall	Pa.	1950	"	Clark M. Clifford	Md.	1968
"	Robert A. Lovett	N. Y.	1951	Nixon	Melvin R. Laird	Wis.	1969
Eisenhower	Charles E. Wilson	Mich.	1953	"	Elliot L. Richardson	Mass.	1973
"	Neil H. McElroy	Oh.	1957	"	James R. Schlesinger	Va.	1973
"	Thomas S. Gates Jr.	Pa.	1959	Ford	"	"	1974

Not Members of the President's Cabinet

The Dept. of Defense, created Sept. 18, 1947, consolidated the navy, army, air force into a single department.

Secretary of the Air Force	Appointed		
W. Stuart Symington	Sept. 18, 1947	Gordon Gray*	June 20, 1949
Thomas K. Finletter	Apr. 24, 1950	Frank Pace Jr.	Apr. 12, 1950
Harold E. Talbot	Feb. 4, 1953	Earl D. Johnson (Acting)	Jan. 20, 1953
Donald A. Quarles	Aug. 12, 1965	Robert T. Stevens	Feb. 4, 1953
James H. Douglas	Mar. 26, 1957	Wilber M. Brucker	July 21, 1955
Dudley C. Sharpe	Dec. 10, 1959	Elvis J. Stahr Jr.	Jan. 23, 1961
Eugene M. Zuckert	Jan. 23, 1961	Cyrus R. Vance	May 21, 1962
Dr. Harold Brown	July 10, 1965	Stephen Ailes	Jan. 20, 1964
Robert C. Seamans Jr.	Jan. 20, 1969	Stanley R. Resor	June 17, 1965
John L. McLucas	July 19, 1973	Robert F. Froehlke	June 15, 1971
		Howard H. Callaway	May 2, 1973
Secretary of the Army		Norman R. Augustine (acting)	July 3, 1975
Kenneth C. Royall	Sept. 18, 1947		

Martin R. Hoffman...................... July 31, 1975
*In addition, Gordon Gray was acting secretary of the army from Apr. 28, 1949, and under secretary from May 25, 1949, until June 20, 1949.

Secretary of the Navy	Appointed
John L. Sullivan	Sept. 18, 1947
Francis P. Matthews	May 25, 1949
Dan A. Kimball	July 31, 1951
Robert B. Anderson	Feb. 4, 1953

Secretary of the Navy (cont.)

Charles S. Thomas	May 3, 1954
Thomas S. Gates Jr.	Apr. 1, 1957
William B. Franke	June 1, 1958
John B. Connally Jr.	Jan. 23, 1961
Fred Korth	Dec. 11, 1961
Paul H. Nitze	Oct. 14, 1963
John T. McNaughton	June 6, 1967
Paul R. Ignatius	Aug. 4, 1967
John H. Chafee	Jan. 20, 1969
John W. Warner	Apr. 7, 1972
J. William Middendorf 2d	June 10, 1974

Secretaries of War

The War (and Navy) Department was created by act of Congress Aug. 7, 1789, and Gen. Henry Knox was commissioned secretary of war under that act Sept. 12, 1789.

President	Secretary	Home	Apptd.
Washington	Henry Knox	Mass.	1789
"	Timothy Pickering	Pa.	1795
"	James McHenry	Md.	1796
J. Adams	"	"	1797
J. Adams	Samuel Dexter	Mass.	1800
Jefferson	Henry Dearborn	"	1801
Madison	William Eustis	Mass.	1809
"	John Armstrong	N.Y.	1813
"	James Monroe	Va.	1814
"	William H. Crawford	Ga.	1815
Monroe	John C. Calhoun	S.C.	1817
J. Q. Adams	James Barbour	Va.	1825
"	Peter B. Porter	N.Y.	1828
Jackson	John H. Eaton	Tenn.	1829
"	Lewis Cass	Oh.	1831
"	Benjamin F. Butler	N.Y.	1837
Van Buren	Joel R. Poinsett	S.C.	1837
W. H. Harrison	John Bell	Tenn.	1841
Tyler	"	"	1841
Tyler	John C. Spencer	N.Y.	1841
"	James M. Porter	Pa.	1843
"	William Wilkins	"	1844
Polk	William L. Marcy	N.Y.	1845
Taylor	George W. Crawford	Ga.	1849
Fillmore	Charles M. Conrad	La.	1850
Pierce	Jefferson Davis	Miss.	1853
Buchanan	John B. Floyd	Va.	1857
"	Joseph Holt	Ky.	1861
Lincoln	Simon Cameron	Pa.	1861
"	Edwin M. Stanton	Pa.	1862
Johnson, A.	"	"	1865
"	John M. Schofield	Ill.	1868
Grant	John A. Rawlins	Ill.	1869
"	William T. Sherman	Oh.	1869
"	William W. Belknap	Ia.	1869
"	Alphonso Taft	Oh.	1876
"	James D. Cameron	Pa.	1876
Hayes	George W. McCrary	Ia.	1877
"	Alexander Ramsey	Minn.	1879
Garfield	Robert T. Lincoln	Ill.	1881
Arthur	"	"	1881
Cleveland	William C. Endicott	Mass.	1885
B. Harrison	Redfield Proctor	Vt.	1890
"	Stephen B. Elkins	W. Va.	1891
Cleveland	Daniel S. Lamont	N.Y.	1893
McKinley	Russel A. Alger	Mich.	1897
"	Elihu Root	N.Y.	1899
T. Roosevelt	"	"	1901
"	William H. Taft	Oh.	1904
"	Luke E. Wright	Tenn.	1908
Taft	Jacob M. Dickinson	"	1909
"	Henry L. Stimson	N.Y.	1911
Wilson	Lindley M. Garrison	N.J.	1913
"	Newton D. Baker	Oh.	1916
Harding	John W. Weeks	Mass.	1921
Coolidge	"	"	1923
"	Dwight F. Davis	Mo.	1925
Hoover	James W. Good	Ill.	1929
"	Patrick J. Hurley	Okla.	1929
F. D. Roosevelt	George H. Dern	Ut.	1933
"	Harry H. Woodring	Kan.	1937
"	Henry L. Stimson	N.Y.	1940
Truman	Robert P. Patterson	N.Y.	1945
"	*Kenneth C. Royall	N.C.	1947

Secretaries of the Navy

The Navy Department was created by act of Congress Apr. 30, 1798.

President	Secretary	Home	Apptd.
J. Adams	Benjamin Stoddert	Md.	1798
Jefferson	"	"	1801
"	Robert Smith	"	1801
Madison	Paul Hamilton	S.C.	1809
"	William Jones	Pa.	1813
"	Benjamin Williams Crowninshield	Mass.	1814
Monroe	"	"	1817
"	Smith Thompson	N.Y.	1818
"	Samuel L. Southard	N.J.	1823
J. Q. Adams	"	"	1825
Jackson	John Branch	N.C.	1829
"	Levi Woodbury	N.H.	1831
"	Mahlon Dickerson	N.J.	1834
Van Buren	"	"	1837
"	James K. Paulding	N.Y.	1838
W. H. Harrison	George E. Badger	N.C.	1841
Tyler	"	"	1841
"	Abel P. Upshur	Va.	1841
"	David Henshaw	Mass.	1843
"	Thomas W. Gilmer	Va.	1844
"	John Y. Mason	"	1844
Polk	George Bancroft	Mass.	1845
"	John Y. Mason	Va.	1846
Taylor	William B. Preston	"	1849
Fillmore	William A. Graham	N.C.	1850
"	John P. Kennedy	Md.	1852
Pierce	James C. Dobbin	N.C.	1853
Buchanan	Isaac Toucey	Conn.	1857
Lincoln	Gideon Welles	Conn.	1861
Johnson, A.	"	"	1865
Grant	Adolph E. Borie	Pa.	1869
"	George M. Robeson	N.J.	1869
Hayes	Richard W. Thompson	Ind.	1877
"	Nathan Goff Jr.	W. Va.	1881
Garfield	William H. Hunt	La.	1881
Arthur	William E. Chandler	N.H.	1882
Cleveland	William C. Whitney	N.Y.	1885
B. Harrison	Benjamin F. Tracy	N.Y.	1889
Cleveland	Hilary A. Herbert	Ala.	1893
McKinley	John D. Long	Mass.	1897
T. Roosevelt	"	"	1901
"	William H. Moody	"	1902
"	Paul Morton	Ill.	1904
"	Charles J. Bonaparte	Md.	1905
"	Victor H. Metcalf	Cal.	1906
"	Truman H. Newberry	Mich.	1908
Taft	George von L. Meyer	Mass.	1909
Wilson	Josephus Daniels	N.C.	1913
Harding	Edwin Denby	Mich.	1921
Coolidge	"	"	1923
"	Curtis D. Wilbur	Cal.	1924
Hoover	Charles Francis Adams	Mass.	1929
F. D. Roosevelt	Claude A. Swanson	Va.	1933
"	Charles Edison	N.J.	1940
"	Frank Knox	Ill.	1940
"	*James V. Forrestal	N.Y.	1944
Truman	"	"	1945

*Last members of Cabinet. The War Dept. became the Dept. of the Army and it and the Navy Dept. became branches of the Dept. of Defense, created Sept. 18, 1947.

Secretaries of Commerce and Labor

The Dept. of Commerce & Labor, created by Congress Feb. 14, 1903, was divided by Congress Mar. 4, 1913, into separate Depts. of Commerce and Labor. The secretary of each was made a cabinet member.

Secretaries of Commerce and Labor

President	Secretary	Home	Apptd.
T. Roosevelt	Geo. B. Cortelyou	N. Y.	1903
"	Victor H. Metcalf	Cal.	1904
"	Oscar S. Straus	N. Y.	1906
Taft	Charles Nagel	Mo.	1909

Secretaries of Labor

President	Secretary	Home	Apptd.
Wilson	William B. Wilson	Pa.	1913
Harding	James J. Davis	Pa.	1921
Coolidge	"	"	1923
Hoover	"	"	1929
"	William N. Doak	Va.	1930
F. D. Roosevelt	Frances Perkins	N. Y.	1933
Truman	L. B. Schwellenbach	Wash.	1945
"	Maurice J. Tobin	Mass.	1949
Eisenhower	Martin P. Durkin	Ill.	1953
"	James P. Mitchell	N. J.	1953
Kennedy	Arthur J. Goldberg	Ill.	1961
"	W. Willard Wirtz	Ill.	1962
Johnson, L. B.	W. Willard Wirtz	Ill.	1963
Nixon	George P. Shultz	Ill.	1969
"	James D. Hodgson	Cal.	1970
"	Peter J. Brennan	N. Y.	1973
Ford	"	"	1974
"	John T. Dunlop	Cal.	1975

Secretaries of Commerce

President	Secretary	Home	Apptd.
Wilson	William C. Redfield	N. Y.	1913
"	Josh. W. Alexander	Mo.	1919
Harding	Herbert C. Hoover	Cal.	1921
Coolidge	"	"	1923
"	William F. Whiting	Mass.	1928
Hoover	Robert P. Lamont	Ill.	1929
"	Roy D. Chapin	Mich.	1932
F. D. Roosevelt	Daniel C. Roper	S. C.	1933
"	Harry L. Hopkins	N. Y.	1939
"	Jesse Jones	Tex.	1940
"	Henry A. Wallace	Ia.	1945
Truman	"	"	1945
Truman	W. Averell Harriman	N. Y.	1947
"	Charles Sawyer	Oh.	1948
Eisenhower	Sinclair Weeks	Mass.	1953
"	Lewis L. Strauss	N. Y.	1958
"	Frederick H. Mueller	Mich.	1959
Kennedy	Luther H. Hodges	N. C.	1961
Johnson, L. B.	John T. Connor	N. J.	1965
"	Alex B. Trowbridge	N. J.	1967
"	C. R. Smith	N. Y.	1968
Nixon	Maurice H. Stans	Minn.	1969
"	Peter G. Peterson	Ill.	1972
"	Frederick B. Dent	S. C.	1973
Ford	"	"	1974
"	Rogers C. B. Morton	Md.	1975

Secretaries of Transportation

The Department of Transportation was created by act of Congress Oct. 15, 1966.

President	Secretary	Home	Apptd.
Johnson, L. B.	Alan S. Boyd	Fla.	1966
Nixon	John A. Volpe	Mass.	1969
"	Claude S. Brinegar	Cal.	1973

President	Secretary	Home	Apptd.
Ford	Claude S. Brinegar	Cal.	1974
"	William T. Coleman Jr.	Pa.	1975

Law on Succession to the Presidency

If by reason of death, resignation, removal from office, inability, or failure to qualify there is neither a president nor vice president to discharge the powers and duties of the office of president, then the speaker of the House of Representatives shall upon his resignation as speaker and as representative, act as president. The same rule shall apply in the case of the death, resignation, removal from office, or inability of an individual acting as president.

If at the time when a speaker is to begin the discharge of the powers and duties of the office of president there is no speaker, or the speaker fails to qualify as acting president, then the president pro tempore of the Senate, upon his resignation as president pro tempore and as senator, shall act as president.

An individual acting as president shall continue to act until the expiration of the then current presidential term, except that (1) if his discharge of the powers and duties of the office is founded in whole or in part in the failure of both the president-elect and the vice president-elect to qualify, then he shall act only until a president or vice president qualifies, and (2) if his discharge of the powers and duties of the office is founded in whole or in part on the inability of the president or vice president, then he shall act only until the removal of the disability of one of such individuals.

If, by reason of death, resignation, removal from office, or failure to qualify, there is no president pro tempore to act as president, then the officer of the United States who is highest on the following list, and who is not under disability to discharge the powers and duties of president, shall act as president: the secretaries of state, treasury, defense; attorney general; secretaries of interior, agriculture, commerce, labor; health, education and welfare; housing and urban development; transportation.

(Legislation approved July 18, 1947; amended Sept. 9, 1965, and Oct. 15, 1966.)

Presidents' Original Paternal Ancestry

Dutch: Van Buren, Theodore Roosevelt, Franklin D. Roosevelt. **German:** Eisenhower. **Swiss and Palatinate German:** Hoover.

English: Washington, John Adams, Madison, John Quincy Adams, William Henry Harrison, Tyler, Taylor, Fillmore, Pierce, Lincoln, Andrew Johnson, Grant, Garfield, Cleveland, Benjamin Harrison, Taft, Harding, Coolidge. **English-French-German:** L. B. Johnson. **English-Scottish-Irish:** Truman.

Irish: Kennedy, Nixon. **Scottish:** Monroe, Hayes, **Scottish-Irish:** Jackson, Polk, Buchanan, Arthur, McKinley, Wilson. **Welsh:** Jefferson (according to family tradition).

Wives and Children of the Presidents

President*	Wife's Name	State	Born	Married	Died	Sons	Daughters
Washington	Martha (Dandridge) Custis	Va.	1732	1759	1802		
John Adams	Abigail Smith	Mass.	1744	1764	1818	3	2
Jefferson	Martha (Wayles) Skelton	Va.	1748	1772	1782	1	5
Madison	Dorothea "Dolley" (Payne) Todd	N. C.	1768	1794	1849		
Monroe	Elizabeth Kortwright (1)	N. Y.	1768	1786	1830		
J. Q. Adams	Louisa Catherine Johnson (2)	Md.	1775	1797	1852	3	1
Jackson	Rachel (Donelson) Robards	Va.	1767	1791	1828		
Van Buren	Hannah Hoes	N. Y.	1783	1807	1819	4	
William H. Harrison	Anna Symmes	N. J.	1775	1795	1864	6	4
Tyler	Letitia Christian	Va.	1790	1813	1842	3	4
"	Julia Gardiner	N. Y.	1820	1844	1889	5	2
Polk	Sarah Childress	Tenn.	1803	1824	1891		
Taylor	Margaret Smith	Md.	1788	1810	1852	1	5
Fillmore	Abigail Powers	N. Y.	1798	1826	1853	1	1
"	Caroline (Carmichael) McIntosh	N. J.	1813	1858	1881		
Pierce	Jane Means Appleton	N. H.	1806	1834	1863	3	
Lincoln	Mary Todd	Ky.	1818	1842	1882	4	
Johnson, Andrew	Eliza McCardle	Tenn.	1810	1827	1876	3	2
Grant	Julia Dent	Mo.	1826	1848	1902	3	1
Hayes	Lucy Ware Webb	Oh.	1831	1852	1889	7	1
Garfield	Lucretia Rudolph	Oh.	1832	1858	1918	4	1
Arthur	Ellen Lewis Herndon	Va.	1837	1859	1880	2	1
Cleveland	Frances Folsom	N. Y.	1864	1886	1947	2	3
Benjamin Harrison	Caroline Lavinia Scott	Oh.	1832	1853	1892	1	1
"	Mary Scott (Lord) Dimmock	Pa.	1858	1896	1948		1
McKinley	Ida Saxton	Oh.	1847	1871	1907		2
Theodore Roosevelt	Alice Hathaway Lee	Mass.	1861	1880	1884		1
"	Edith Kermit Carow	Conn.	1861	1886	1948	4	1
Taft	Helen Herron	Oh.	1861	1886	1943	2	1
Wilson	Ellen Louise Axson	Ga.	1860	1885	1914		3
"	Edith (Bolling) Galt	Va.	1872	1915	1961		
Harding	Florence (Kling) De Wolfe	Oh.	1860	1891	1924		
Coolidge	Grace Anna Goodhue	Vt.	1879	1905	1957	2	
Hoover	Lou Henry	Ia.	1875	1899	1944	2	
F. D. Roosevelt	Anna Eleanor Roosevelt (1)	N. Y.	1884	1905	1962	4	1
Truman	Bess Wallace	Mo.	1885	1919			1
Eisenhower	Mamie Geneva Doud (1)	Ia.	1896	1916	1916	1	
Kennedy	Jacqueline Lee Bouvier (1)	N. Y.	1929	1953		1	1
Johnson, Lyndon	Claudia Alta Taylor	Tex.	1912	1934			2
Nixon	Thelma Catherine Patricia Ryan	Nev.	1912	1940			2
Ford	Elizabeth Bloomer Warren	Ill.	1918	1948		3	1

*James Buchanan, 15th president, was unmarried. (1) Plus one infant, deceased. (2) Born London, father a Maryland citizen.

Religious Background of Presidents

Baptist: Harding, Truman.
Christian Church (Disciples of Christ): Garfield, Lyndon B. Johnson.
Congregationalist: Coolidge.
Episcopalian: Washington, Madison, Monroe, William Henry Harrison, Tyler, Taylor, Pierce, Arthur, Franklin D. Roosevelt, Ford.
Jefferson, an Episcopal Church member, later became a deist, said he was a "disciple of the doctrines of Jesus," and commended Unitarianism.
Friends (Quakers): Hoover, Nixon.

Methodist: Polk, Andrew Johnson, Grant, McKinley. Hayes attended the Methodist Church, but never joined.
Presbyterian: Jackson, Buchanan, Cleveland, Benjamin Harrison, Wilson, Eisenhower.
Lincoln attended Presbyterian services in Washington but was not a member.
Reformed Dutch: Van Buren, Theodore Roosevelt.
Roman Catholic: Kennedy.
Unitarian: John Adams, John Quincy Adams, Fillmore, Taft.

Burial Places of the Presidents

G. Washington	1732-1799	Mt. Vernon, Va.
John Adams	1735-1826	Quincy, Mass.
T. Jefferson	1743-1826	Charlottesville, Va.
James Madison	1751-1836	Montpelier Station, Va.
James Monroe	1758-1831	Richmond, Va.
John Q. Adams	1767-1848	Quincy, Mass.
Andrew Jackson	1767-1845	Nashville, Tenn.
M. Van Buren	1782-1862	Kinderhook, N.Y.
W. H. Harrison	1773-1841	North Bend, Oh.
John Tyler	1790-1862	Richmond, Va.
James Knox Polk	1795-1849	Nashville, Tenn.
Zachary Taylor	1784-1850	Louisville, Ky.
Millard Fillmore	1800-1874	Buffalo, N.Y.
Franklin Pierce	1804-1869	Concord, N.H.
James Buchanan	1791-1868	Lancaster, Pa.
A. Lincoln	1809-1865	Springfield, Ill.
Andrew Johnson	1808-1875	Greeneville, Tenn.
Ulysses S. Grant	1822-1885	New York City
R. B. Hayes	1822-1893	Fremont, Oh.
J. A. Garfield	1831-1881	Cleveland, Oh.
C. A. Arthur	1830-1886	Albany, N. Y.
Grover Cleveland	1837-1908	Princeton, N.J.
B. Harrison	1833-1901	Indianapolis, Ind.
W. McKinley	1843-1901	Canton, Oh.
T. Roosevelt	1858-1919	Oyster Bay, N.Y.
William H. Taft	1857-1930	Arlington Nat'l. Cem'y.
Woodrow Wilson	1856-1924	Washington Cathedral
W. G. Harding	1865-1923	Marion, Oh.
Calvin Coolidge	1872-1933	Plymouth, Vt.
Herbert Hoover	1874-1964	West Branch, Ia.
F. D. Roosevelt	1882-1945	Hyde Park, N.Y.
Harry S. Truman	1884-1972	Independence, Mo.
D. D. Eisenhower	1890-1969	Abilene, Kan.
J. F. Kennedy	1917-1963	Arlington Nat'l. Cem'y.
Lyndon B. Johnson	1908-1973	Stonewall, Tex.

Election Statistics

Popular and Electoral Vote for President 1972

Compiled by The World Almanac from official returns of the States.
Blank and void ballots are excluded from all totals.

States	Electoral Vote Nixon	Electoral Vote McGovern	Republican Nixon	Democrat McGovern	American Schmitz	Soc. Labor Fisher	Soc. Worker Jenness or Reed	Communist Hall	Others**	Total
Ala......	9	....	728,701	256,923	11,918	....	....	....	8,551	1,006,093
Alas....	3	....	55,349	32,967	6,903	....	....	....	....	95,219
Ariz....	6	....	402,812	198,540	21,208	....	30,945 †	....	....	653,505
Ark......	6	....	445,751	198,899	3,016	....	....	....	....	647,666
Cal.....	45	....	4,602,096	3,475,847	232,554	197	574	373	56,218	8,367,859
Col......	7	....	597,189	329,980	17,269	4,361	666	432	3,981	953,878
Conn....	8	....	810,763	555,498	17,239	....	....	....	777	1,384,277
Del.....	3	....	140,357	92,298	2,638	....	....	....	238	235,516
D.C.....		3	35,226	127,627	....	....	316	252	....	163,421
Fla.....	17	....	1,857,759	718,117	....	....	....	....	7,407	2,583,283
Ga......	12	....	881,496	289,529	2,288	3	....	....	1,456	1,174,722
Ha......	5	....	168,865	101,409	....	....	....	....	....	270,274
Ida.....	4	....	199,384	80,826	28,869	....	397	....	903	310,379
Ill......	26	....	2,788,179	1,913,472	2,471	1,344	....	4,541	2,229	4,723,236
Ind.....	13	....	1,405,154	708,568	....	1,688	5,575	....	4,544	2,125,529
Ia......	8	....	706,207	496,206	22,056	195	488	272	520	1,225,944
Kan....	7	....	619,812	270,287	21,808	....	....	....	4,188	916,095
Ky......	9	....	676,446	371,159	17,627	....	685	464	1,118	1,067,499
La......	10	....	686,852	298,142	52,099	....	14,398	....	....	1,051,491
Me......	4	....	256,458	160,584	....	....	....	....	229	417,271
Md......	10	....	829,305	505,781	18,726	....	....	....	....	1,353,812
Mass....		14	1,112,078	1,332,540	22,877	129	10,600	46	486	2,458,756
Mich.....	21	....	1,961,721	1,459,435	63,381	2,437	1,603	1,210	....	3,489,727
Minn.....	10	....	898,269	802,346	31,407	4,261	940	662	3,767	1,741,652
Miss.....	7	....	505,125	126,782	11,598	....	2,458	....	....	645,963
Mo......	12	....	1,154,058	698,531	....	....	....	....	....	1,852,589
Mon.....	4	....	183,976	120,197	13,430	....	....	....	....	317,603
Neb.....	5	....	406,298	169,991	....	....	....	....	817	577,225
Nev.....	3	....	115,750	66,016	....	....	....	....	....	181,766
N.H.....	4	....	213,724	116,435	3,386	....	368	....	142	334,055
N.J.....	17	....	1,845,502	1,102,211	34,378	4,544	2,233	1,263	7,098	2,997,229
N.M.....	4	....	235,606	141,084	8,767	....	474	....	....	385,931
N.Y......	41	....	4,192,778	2,951,084	....	4,530	7,797	5,641	....	7,161,830
N.C.....	13	....	1,054,889	438,705	25,018	....	....	....	1,51,612	1,51,612
N.D.....	3	....	174,109	100,384	5,646	....	288	87	....	280,514
Oh......	25	....	2,441,827	1,558,889	80,067	7,107	....	6,437	460	4,094,787
Okla.....	8	....	759,025	247,147	23,728	....	....	....	....	1,029,900
Ore.....	6	....	486,686	392,760	46,211	....	....	....	2,289	927,946
Pa......	27	....	2,714,521	1,796,951	70,953	....	4,639	2,686	2,715	4,592,105
R.I......	4	....	218,290	191,981	....	....	729	....	....	411,000
S.C......	8	....	477,044	186,824	10,075	....	....	....	17	673,960
S.D......	4	....	166,476	139,945	....	....	994	....	....	307,415
Tenn....	10	....	813,147	357,293	30,373	....	....	....	369	1,201,182
Tex......	26	....	2,298,896	1,154,289	6,039	....	8,664	....	3,393	3,471,281
Ut......	4	....	323,643	126,284	28,549	....	....	....	....	478,476
Vt......	3	....	117,149	68,174	....	....	296	....	1,328	186,947
Va.*....	11	....	988,493	438,887	19,721	9,918	....	....	....	1,457,019
Wash....	9	....	837,135	568,334	58,906	1,102	623	566	4,181	1,470,847
W. Va...	6	....	484,964	277,435	....	....	....	....	....	762,399
Wis......	11	....	989,430	810,174	47,525	998	506	663	3,594	1,852,890
Wy......	3	....	100,464	44,358	748	....	....	....	....	145,570
Total U.S.....	**520**	**17**	**47,165,234**	**29,168,110**	**1,101,052**	**53,814**	**97,256**	**25,595**	**123,015**	**77,734,195**

*One elector in Virginia for John Hospers and Theodora Nathan.
**Dr. Benjamin Spock, People's Party: Cal. 55,167. Col. 2,403. Ida. 903. Ind. 4,544. Ky. 1,118. Mass. 101. Minn. 2,805. N. J. 5,355. Wash. 2,644. Wis. 2,701. Total 77,741. In Vermont, under label of Liberty Party, 1,010. John Mahalchik, America First New Jersey 1,743. Earle H. Munn, Prohibition: Ala. 8,551. Cal. 50. Col. 467. Del. 238. Kan. 4,188. Total 13,494 John Hospers, Libertarian: Cal. 980. Col. 1,111. Mass. 43. Wash. 1,537. Total 3,671. Gabriel Green, Universal Party: Cal. 21. Ia. 199. Total 220. Scattered: Conn. 777. Fla. 7,407. Ga. 1,456. Ill. 2,229. Ia. 32. Me. 229. Minn. 962. Neb. 817. N. H. 142. Oh. 460. Ore. 2,289. Pa. 2,715. S. C. 17. Tenn. 369. Tex. 3,393. Vt. 318. Wis. 893. Total 25,136.
†Due to a confused ballot, thousands of Arizonians mistakenly voted for two candidates.

Major Parties' Popular and Electoral Vote for President

(F) Federalist; (D) Democrat; (R) Republican; (DR) Democrat Republican; (NR) National Republican;
(W) Whig; (P) People's; (PR) Progressive; (SR) States' Rights; Asterisk (*)—See notes below.

Year	President Elected	Popular	Elec.	Losing Candidate	Popular	Elec.
1789	George Washington (F)......	Unknown	69	No opposition.............................		
1792	George Washington (F)......	Unknown	132	No opposition.............................		
1796	John Adams (F).............	Unknown	71	Thomas Jefferson (DR)......	Unknown	68
1800	Thomas Jefferson (DR)......	Unknown	73	Aaron Burr (DR)..........,.	Unknown	73
	Elected by House of Representatives (due to tie vote)					
1804	Thomas Jefferson (DR)......	Unknown	162	Charles Pinckney (F).......	Unknown	14
1808	James Madison (DR)........	Unknown	122	Charles Pinckney (F).......	Unknown	47
1812	James Madison (DR)........	Unknown	128	DeWitt Clinton (F)..........	Unknown	89
1816	James Monroe (DR).........	Unknown	183	Rufus King (F).............	Unknown	34
1820	James Monroe (DR).........	Unknown	231	John Quincy Adams (DR)....	Unknown	1
1824	John Quincy Adams (NR)....	105,321	84	Andrew Jackson (D)........	155,872	99
	Elected by House of Representatives (no			Henry Clay (DR)...........	46,587	37
	candidate having polled a majority)			William H. Crawford (DR)...	44,282	41
1828	Andrew Jackson (D)........	647,231	178	John Quincy Adams (NR)....	509,097	83
1832	Andrew Jackson (D)........	687,502	219	Henry Clay (DR)...........	530,189	49
	First national Presidential convention					
1836	Martin Van Buren (D)......	762,678	170	William H. Harrison (W).....	548,007	73
1840	William H. Harrison (W).....	1,275,017	234	Martin Van Buren (D).......	1,128,702	60
1844	James K. Polk (D)..........	1,337,243	170	Henry Clay (W)............	1,299,068	105
1848	Zachary Taylor (W)........	1,360,101	163	Lewis Cass (D)............	1,220,544	127
1852	Franklin Pierce (D).........	1,601,474	254	Winfield Scott (W).........	1,386,578	42
1856	James C. Buchanan (D)......	1,927,995	174	John C. Fremont (R)........	1,391,555	114
1860	Abraham Lincoln (R)........	1,866,352	180	Stephen A. Douglas (D)....	1,375,157	12
				John C. Breckinridge (D)....	845,763	72
				John Bell (Const. Union).....	589,581	39
1864	Abraham Lincoln (R)........	2,216,067	212	George McClellan (D).....	1,808,725	21
1868	Ulysses S. Grant (R).·......	3,015,071	214	Horatio Seymour (D).......	2,709,615	80
1872*	Ulysses S. Grant (R).........	3,597,070	286	Horace Greeley (D-T)......	2,834,079	....
1876*	Rutherford B. Hayes (R).....	4,033,950	185	Samuel J. Tilden (D).......	4,284,757	184
1880	James A. Garfield (R).......	4,449,053	214	Winfield S. Hancock (D).....	4,442,030	155
1884	Grover Cleveland (D).......	4,911,017	219	James G. Blaine (R).......	4,848,334	182
1888*	Benjamin Harrison (R)......	5,444,337	233	Grover Cleveland (D).......	5,540,050	168
1892	Grover Cleveland (D).......	5,554,414	277	Benjamin Harrison (R)......	5,190,802	145
				James Weaver (P).........	1,027,329	22
1896	William McKinley (R).......	7,035,638	271	William J. Bryan (D-P)......	6,467,946	176
1900	William McKinley (R).......	7,219,530	292	William J. Bryan (D).......	6,358,071	155
1904	Theodore Roosevelt (R)......	7,628,834	336	Alton B. Parker (D).........	5,084,491	140
1908	William H. Taft (R)........	7,679,006	321	William J. Bryan (D).......	6,409,106	162
1912	Woodrow Wilson (D)........	6,286,214	435	Theodore Roosevelt (PR).....	4,216,020	88
				William H. Taft (R)	3,483,922	8
1916	Woodrow Wilson (D)........	9,129,606	277	Charles E. Hughes (R).......	8,538,221	254
1920	Warren G. Harding (R)......	16,152,200	404	James M. Cox (D).........	9,147,353	127
1924	Calvin Coolidge (R)........	15,725,016	382	John W. Davis (D).........	8,385,586	136
				Robert M. LaFollette (PR)....	4,822,856	13
1928	Herbert Hoover (R)........	21,392,190	444	Alfred E. Smith (D)........	15,016,443	87
1932	Franklin D. Roosevelt (D)....	22,821,857	472	Herbert Hoover (R)........	15,761,841	59
				Norman Thomas (Socialist)..	884,781	....
1936	Franklin D. Roosevelt (D)....	27,751,597	523	Alfred Landon (R)..........	16,679,583	8
1940	Franklin D. Roosevelt (D)....	27,243,466	449	Wendell Willkie (R).......	22,304,755	82
1944	Franklin D. Roosevelt (D)....	25,602,505	432	Thomas E. Dewey (R).......	22,006,278	99
1948	Harry S. Truman (D)........	24,105,812	303	Thomas E. Dewey (R).......	21,970,065	189
				J. Strom Thurmond (SR).....	1,169,021	39
				Henry A. Wallace (PR)......	1,157,172	....
1952	Dwight D. Eisenhower (R)....	33,936,252	442	Adlai E. Stevenson (D)......	27,314,992	89
1956*	Dwight D. Eisenhower (R)....	35,585,316	457	Adlai E. Stevenson (D)......	26,031,322	73
1960*	John F. Kennedy (D).......	34,227,096	303	Richard M. Nixon (R)........	34,108,546	219
1964	Lyndon B. Johnson (D)......	43,126,506	486	Barry M. Goldwater (R).....	27,176,799	52
1968	Richard M. Nixon (R)........	31,785,480	301	Hubert H. Humphrey (D)....	31,275,166	191
				George C. Wallace (3d party).	9,906,473	46
1972*	Richard M. Nixon (R)........	47,165,234	520	George S. McGovern........	29,168,110	17

1872 — Greeley died Nov. 29, 1872. His electoral votes were split among 4 individuals.
1876 — Fla., La., Ore., and S. C. election returns were disputed. Congress in joint session (Mar. 2, 1877) declared Hayes and Wheeler elected President and Vice-President.
1888 — Cleveland had more votes than Harrison but the 233 electoral votes cast for Harrison against the 168 for Cleveland elected Harrison president.
1956 — Democrats elected 74 electors but one from Alabama refused to vote for Stevenson.
1960 — Sen. Harry F. Byrd (D-Va.) received 15 electoral votes.
1972 — John Hospers of Cal. and Theodora Nathan of Ore. received one vote from an elector of Virginia.

Electoral Votes for President, 1956-72

The Constitution, Article 2, Section 1 (consult index), provides for the appointment of electors, the counting of the electoral ballots and the procedure in the event of a tie. (See *Electoral College*.)

State	1956 R	1956 D	1960 R	1960 D	1964 R	1964 D	1968 R	1968 D	1968 3d	1972 R	1972 D
Ala.		'11		²5	10				10	9	
Alas.				³3	3		3			3	
Ariz.	4		4		5		5			6	
Ark.		8		8		6			6	6	
Cal.	32		32			40	40			45	
Col.	6		6			6	6			7	
Conn.	8			8		8		8		8	
Del.	3			3		3	3			3	
D.C.						³3		3			3
Fla.	10		10		14		14			17	
Ga.		12		12	12				12	12	
Ha.				³3		4		4		4	
Ida.	4		4		4		4			4	
Ill.	27		27			26	26			26	
Ind.	13		13			13	13			13	
Ia.	10		10			9	9			8	
Kan.	8		8		7		7			7	
Ky.	10		20			9	9			9	
La.	10			10	10				10	10	
Me.	5		5			4		4		4	
Md.	9			9		10		10		10	
Mass.	16			16		14		14			14
Mich.	20			20		21		21		21	
Minn.	11			11		10		10		10	
Miss.		8		(²)	7				7	7	
Mo.		13		13		12	12			12	
Mon.	4		4			4	4			4	
Neb.	6		6		5		5			5	

State	1956 R	1956 D	1960 R	1960 D	1964 R	1964 D	1968 R	1968 D	1968 3d	1972 R	1972 D
Nev.	3		3			3	3			3	
N.H.	4		4			4	4			4	
N.J.	16			16		17	17			17	
N.M.	4			4		4	4			4	
N.Y.	45			45		43		43		41	
N.C.		14		14		13	12		⁴1	13	
N.D.	4		4			4	4			3	
Oh.	25		25			26	26			25	
Okla.	8		⁷7		8		8			8	
Ore.	6		6			6	6			6	
Pa.	32			32		29		29		27	
R.I.	4			4		4		4		4	
S.C.		8		8	8		8			8	
S.D.	4		4			4	4			4	
Tenn.	11		11			11	11			10	
Tex.	24			24		25		25		26	
Ut.	4		4			4	4			4	
Vt.	3		3			3	3			3	
Va.	12		12			12	12			⁵11	
Wash.	9			9		9		9		9	
W. Va.	8			8		7		7		6	
Wis.	12		12			12		12		11	
Wy.	3		3			3	3			3	
Totals	457	'74	219	303	52	486	301	191	46	520	17
Plurality	383			²84		434	110			²503	

(1.) In 1956 in Alabama one Democratic elector refused to vote for Stevenson and cast his ballot for Walter B. Jones, making the Democratic total actually 73.
(2.) In 1960 Sen. Harry F. Byrd (D.-Va.) got 15 electoral votes, including those of 8 unpledged Mississippi Democratic electors, 6 unpledged Alabama Democrats, and one Oklahoma Republican.
(3.) First Presidential election.
(4.) In 1968 in North Carolina one Republican elector cast his ballot for Wallace.
(5.) In 1972 one Republican elector in Virginia cast his ballot for John Hospers.

Presidential Election Returns by States

Compiled by the World Almanac from official state returns.

Alabama

1932 (Pres.), Roosevelt, Dem., 207,910; Hoover, Rep., 34,675; Foster, Com., 406; Thomas, Soc., 2,030; Upshaw, Proh., 13.
1936 (Pres.), Roosevelt, Dem., 238,195; Landon, Rep., 35,358; Colvin, Proh., 719; Browder, Com., 679; Lemke, Union, 549; Thomas, Soc., 242.
1940 (Pres.), Roosevelt, Dem., 250,726; Willkie, Rep., 42,174; Babson, Proh., 698; Browder, Com., 509; Thomas, Soc., 100.
1944 (Pres.), Roosevelt, Dem., 198,918; Dewey, Rep., 44,540; Watson, Proh., 1,095; Thomas, Soc., 190.
1948 (Pres.), Thurmond, States' Rights, 171,443; Dewey, Rep., 40,930; Wallace, Prog., 1,522; Watson, Proh., 1,085.
1952 (Pres.), Eisenhower, Rep., 149,231; Stevenson, Dem., 275,075; Hamblen, Proh., 1,814.
1956 (Pres.), Stevenson, Dem., 290,844; Eisenhower, Rep., 195,694; Independent electors, 20,323.
1960 (Pres.), Kennedy, Dem., 324,050; Nixon, Rep., 237,981; Faubus, States' Rights, 4,367; Decker, Proh., 2,106; King, Afro-Americans, 1,485; scattering, 236.
1964 (Pres.), Dem., 209,848 (electors unpledged); Goldwater, Rep., 479,085; scattering, 105.
1968 (Pres.), Nixon, Rep., 146,923; Humphrey, Dem., 196,579; Wallace, 3d party, 691,425; Munn, Proh., 4,022.
1972 (Pres.), Nixon, Rep., 728,701; McGovern, Dem., 219,108 plus 37,815 Natl. Demo. Party of Alabama; Schmitz, Conservative, 11,918; Munn, Proh., 8,551.

Alaska

1960 (Pres.), Kennedy, Dem., 29,809; Nixon, Rep., 30,953.
1964 (Pres.), Johnson, Dem., 44,329; Goldwater, Rep., 22,930.
1968 (Pres.), Nixon, Rep., 37,600; Humphrey, Dem., 35,411; Wallace, 3d party, 10,024.
1972 (Pres.), Nixon, Rep., 55,349; McGovern, Dem., 32,967; Schmitz, American, 6,906.

Arizona

1932 (Pres.), Roosevelt, Dem., 79,264; Hoover, Rep., 36,104; Thomas, Soc., 2,030; Foster, Com., 406.
1936 (Pres.), Roosevelt, Dem., 86,722; Landon, Rep., 33,433; Lemke, Union, 3,307; Colvin, Proh., 384; Thomas, Soc., 317.
1940 (Pres.), Roosevelt, Dem., 95,267; Willkie, Rep., 54,030; Babson, Proh., 742.
1944 (Pres.), Roosevelt, Dem., 80,826; Dewey, Rep., 56,287; Watson, Proh., 421.

1948 (Pres.), Truman, Dem., 95,251; Dewey, Rep., 77,-597; Wallace, Prog., 3,310; Watson, Proh., 786; Teichert, Soc. Lab., 121.

1952 (Pres.), Eisenhower, Rep., 152,042; Stevenson, Dem., 108,528.

1956 (Pres.), Eisenhower, Rep., 176,990; Stevenson, Dem., 112,880; Andrews, Ind. 303.

1960 (Pres.), Kennedy, Dem., 176,781; Nixon, Rep., 221,241; Haas, Soc. Lab., 469.

1964 (Pres.), Johnson, Dem., 237,753· Goldwater, Rep. 242,535; Haas. Soc. Labor. 482.

1968 (Pres.), Nixon, Rep., 266,721; Humphrey, Dem., 170,514; Wallace, 3d party, 46,573; McCarthy, New Party, 2,751; Halstead, Soc. Worker, 85; Cleaver, Peace and Freedom, 217; Blomen, Soc. Labor, 75.

1972 (Pres.), Nixon, Rep., 402,812; McGovern, Dem., 198,540; Schmitz, American, 21,208; Soc. Worker, 30,945. Due to ballot peculiarities in 3 counties (particularly Pima), thousands of voters cast ballots for the Socialist Workers Party and one of the major candidates. Court ordered both votes counted as official.

Arkansas

1932 (Pres.), Roosevelt, Dem., 189,602; Hoover, Rep., 28,467; Thomas, Soc., 1,269; Harvey, Ind., 1,049; Foster, Com., 175.

1936 (Pres.), Roosevelt, Dem., 146,765; Landon, Rep., 32,039; Thomas, Soc., 446; Browder, Com., 164; Lemke, Union, 4.

1940 (Pres.), Roosevelt, Dem., 158,622; Willkie, Rep.,42,121; Babson, Proh., 793; Thomas, Soc., 305.

1944 (Pres.), Roosevelt, Dem., 148,965; Dewey, Rep., 63,551; Thomas, Soc. 438.

1948 (Pres.), Truman, Dem., 149,659; Dewey, Rep., 50,959; Thurmond, States' Rights, 40,068; Thomas, Soc., 1,037; Wallace, Prog., 751; Watson, Proh., 1.

1952 (Pres.), Eisenhower, Rep., 177,155; Stevenson, Dem., 226,300; Hamblen, Proh., 886; MacArthur, Christian Nationalist. 458; Haas. Soc. Lab., 1.

1956 (Pres.), Stevenson, Dem., 213,277; Eisenhower, Rep., 186,287; Andrews, Ind., 7,008.

1960 (Pres.), Kennedy, Dem., 215,049; Nixon, Rep., 184,508; National States' Rights, 28,952.

1964 (Pres.), Johnson, Dem., 314,197; Goldwater, Rep., 243,264; Kasper, Nat'l. States Rights, 2,965.

1968 (Pres.), Nixon, Rep., 189,062; Humphrey, Dem., 184,901; Wallace, 3d party, 235,627.

1972 (Pres.), Nixon, Rep. 445,751; McGovern, Dem., 198,899; Schmitz, Amer. Party, 3,016.

California

1932 (Pres.), Roosevelt, Dem., 1,324,157; Hoover, Rep., 847,902; Thomas, Soc,, 63,299; Upshaw, Proh., 20,637; Harvey, Liberty, 9,827; Foster, Com., 1,023.

1936 (Pres.), Roosevelt, Dem., 1,766,836; Landon, Rep., 836,431; Colvin, Proh., 12,917; Thomas, Soc., 11,325; Browder, Com., 10,877.

1940 (Pres.), Roosevelt, Dem., 1,877,618; Willkie, Rep., 1,351,419; Thomas, Prog., 16,506; Browder, Com., 13,586; Babson, Proh., 9,400.

1944 (Pres.), Roosevelt, Dem., 1,988,564; Dewey, Rep., 1,512,965; Watson, Proh., 14,770; Thomas, Soc., 3,923; Teichert, Soc. Lab., 327.

1948 (Pres.), Truman, Dem., 1,913,134; Dewey, Rep., 1,895,269; Wallace, Prog., 190,381; Watson, Proh., 16,926; Thomas, Soc., 3,459; Thurmond, States' Rights, 1,228; Teichert, Soc. Lab., 195; Dobbs, Soc. Wkr., 133.

1952 (Pres.), Eisenhower, Rep., 2,897,310; Stevenson, Dem., 2,197,548; Hallinan, Prog., 24,106; Hamblen, Proh., 15,653; MacArthur, (Tenny Ticket) 3,326; (Kellems Ticket) 178; Haas, Soc. Lab., 273; Hoopes, Soc.,206; Scattered, 3,249.

1956 (Pres.), Eisenhower, Rep., 3,027,668; Stevenson,

Dem., 2,420,136; Holtwick, Proh., 11,119; Andrews, Constitution, 6,087; Haas, Soc. Lab., 300; Hoopes, Soc., 123; Dobbs, Soc. Workers. 96; Smith, Christian Nat'l., 8.

1960 (Pres.), Kennedy, Dem., 3,224,099; Nixon, Rep., 3,259,722; Decker, Proh., 21,706; Haas, Soc. Lab., 1,051.

1964 (Pres.), Johnson, Dem., 4,171,877; Goldwater, Rep., 2,879,108; Haas, Soc. Labor, 489; DeBerry, Soc. Worker, 378; Munn, Proh., 305; Hensley, Universal, 19.

1968 (Pres.), Nixon, Rep., 3,467,664; Humphrey, Dem., 3,244,318; Wallace, 3d party, 487,270; Peace and Freedom party, 27,707; McCarthy, Alternative, 20,721; Gregory, write-in, 3,230; Mitchell, Communist, 260; Munn, Prohibition, 59; Blomen, Socialist, 341; Soeters, Defense, 17.

1972 (Pres.), Nixon, Rep., 4,602,096; McGovern, Dem., 3,475,847; Schmitz, Amer., 232,554; Spock, Peace and Freedom, 55,167; Hall, Communist, 373; Hospers, Libertarian, 980; Munn. Prohibition, 53; Fisher, Soc. Labor, 197; Jenness, Soc. Workers, 574; Green, Universal, 21.

Colorado

1932 (Pres.), Roosevelt, Dem., 250,877; Hoover, Rep., 189,617; Thomas, Soc., 14,018; Upshaw, Proh., 1,928.

1936 (Pres.), Roosevelt, Dem., 295,081; Landon, Rep., 18,267; Lemke, Union, 9,962; Thomas, Soc., 1,593; Browder, Com., 497; Aiken, Soc. Labor, 336.

1940 (Pres.), Roosevelt, Dem., 265,554; Willkie, Rep., 279,576; Thomas, Soc., 1,899; Babson, Proh., 1,597; Browder, Com., 378.

1944 (Pres.), Roosevelt, Dem., 234,331; Dewey, Rep., 268,731; Thomas, Soc., 1,977.

1948 (Pres.), Truman, Dem., 267,288; Dewey, Rep., 239,714; Wallace, Prog., 6,115; Thomas, Soc., 1,678; Dobbs, Soc. Workers, 228; Teichert, Soc. Lab., 214.

1952 (Pres.), Eisenhower, Rep., 379,782; Stevenson, Dem., 245,504; MacArthur, Constitution, 2,181; Hallinan, Prog., 1,919; Hoopes, Soc., 365; Haas, Soc. Lab., 352.

1956 (Pres.), Eisenhower, Rep., 394,479; Stevenson, Dem., 263,997; Haas, Soc. Lab., 3,308; Andrews, Ind., 759; Hoopes, Soc., 531.

1960 (Pres.), Kennedy, Dem., 330,629; Nixon, Rep., 402,242; Haas, Soc. Lab., 2,803; Dobbs, Soc. Workers, 572.

1964 (Pres.), Johnson, Dem., 476,024; Goldwater, Rep., 296,767; Haas. Soc. Labor, 302; DeBerry, Soc. Worker, 2,537; Munn, Proh., 1,356.

1968 (Pres.), Nixon, Rep., 409,345; Humphrey, Dem., 335,174; Wallace, 3d party, 60,813; Blomen, Soc., 3,016; Gregory, New-party, 1,393; Munn, Proh., 275; Halstead, Soc. Work., 235.

1972 (Pres.), Nixon, Rep., 597,189; McGovern, Dem., 329,980; Fisher, Soc. Labor, 4,361; Hospers, Libertarian, 1,111; Hall, Com., 432; Jenness, Soc. Wrks., 666; Munn, Proh., 467; Schmitz, American, 17,269; Spock, Peoples, 2,403.

Connecticut

1932 (Pres.), Roosevelt, Dem., 281,632; Hoover, Rep., 288,420; Thomas, Soc., 22,767.

1936 (Pres.), Roosevelt, Dem., 382,129; Landon, Rep., 278,685; Lemke, Union, 21,805; Thomas, Soc., 5,683; Browder, Com., 1,193.

1940 (Pres.), Roosevelt, Dem., 417,621; Willkie, Rep., 361,021; Browder, Com., 1,091; Aiken, Soc. Lab., 971; Willkie, Union, 798.

1944 (Pres.), Roosevelt, Dem., 435,146; Dewey, Rep., 390,527; Thomas, Soc., 5,097; Teichert, Soc. Lab., 1,220.

1948 (Pres.), Truman, Dem., 423,297; Dewey, Rep., 437,754; Wallace, Prog., 13,713; Thomas, Soc.,

6,964; Teichert, Soc. Lab., 1,184; Dobbs, Soc. Workers, 606.

1952 (Pres.), Eisenhower, Rep., 611,012; Stevenson, Dem., 481,649; Hoopes, Soc., 2,244; Hallinan, Peoples, 1,466; Haas, Soc. Lab., 535; write-in, 5.

1956 (Pres.), Eisenhower, Rep., 711,837; Stevenson, Dem., 405,079; scattered, 205.

1960 (Pres.), Kennedy, Dem., 657,055; Nixon, Rep., 565,813.

1964 (Pres.), Johnson, Dem., 826,269; Goldwater, Rep., 390,996; scattered, 1,313.

1968 (Pres.), Nixon, Rep., 556,721; Humphrey, Dem., 621,561; Wallace, 3d party, 76,650; scattered, 1,300.

1972 (Pres.), Nixon, Rep., 810,763; McGovern, Dem., 555,498; Schmitz, Amer. Party, 17,239; scattered, 777

Delaware

1932 (Pres.), Hoover, Rep., 57,074; Roosevelt, Dem., 54,319; Thomas, Soc., 1,376; Foster, Com., 133.

1936 (Pres.), Roosevelt, Dem., 69,702; Landon, Rep., 54,014; Lemke, Union, 442; Thomas, Soc., 179; Browder, Com., 52.

1940 (Pres.), Roosevelt, Dem., 74,599; Willkie, Rep., 61,440; Babson, Proh., 220; Thomas, Soc., 115.

1944 (Pres.), Roosevelt, Dem., 68,166; Dewey, Rep., 56,747; Watson, Proh., 294; Thomas, Soc., 154.

1948 (Pres.), Truman, Dem., 67,813; Dewey, Rep., 69,688; Wallace, Prog., 1,050; Watson, Proh., 343; Thomas, Soc., 250; Teichert, Soc. Lab., 29.

1952 (Pres.), Eisenhower, Rep., 90,059; Stevenson, Dem., 83,315; Haas, Soc. Lab., 242; Hamblen, Proh., 234; Hallinan, Prog., 155; Hoopes, Soc., 20.

1956 (Pres.), Eisenhower, Rep., 98,057; Stevenson, Dem., 79,421; Holtwick, Proh., 400; Haas, Soc. Lab., 110.

1960 (Pres.), Kennedy, Dem., 99,590; Nixon, Rep., 96,373; Faubus, States' Rights, 354; Decker, Proh., 284; Haas, Soc. Lab., 82.

1964 (Pres.), Johnson, Dem., 122,704; Goldwater, Rep., 78,078; Haas, Soc. Lab., 113; Munn, Proh., 425.

1968 (Pres.), Nixon, Rep., 96,714; Humphrey, Dem., 89,194; Wallace, 3d party, 28,459.

1972 (Pres.), Nixon, Rep., 140,357; McGovern, Dem., 92,283; Schmitz, Amer. Party, 2,638; Munn, Proh., 238.

District of Columbia

1964 (Pres.), Johnson, Dem., 169,796; Goldwater, Rep., 28,801.

1968 (Pres.), Nixon, Rep., 31,012; Humphrey, Dem., 139,566.

1972 (Pres.), Nixon, Rep., 35,226; McGovern, Dem., 127,627; Reed, Soc. Worker, 316; Hall, Communist, 252.

Florida

1932 (Pres.), Roosevelt, Dem., 206,307; Hoover, Rep., 69,170; Thomas, Soc., 775.

1936 (Pres.), Roosevelt, Dem., 249,117; Landon, Rep., 78,248; Thomas, Soc., 775.

1940 (Pres.), Roosevelt, Dem., 359,334; Willkie, Rep., 126,158.

1944 (Pres.), Roosevelt, Dem., 339,377; Dewey, Rep., 143,215.

1948 (Pres.), Truman, Dem., 281,988; Dewey, Rep., 194,280; Thurmond, States' Rights, 89,755; Wallace, Prog., 11,620.

1952 (Pres.), Eisenhower, Rep., 544,036; Stevenson, Dem., 444,950; scattered, 351.

1956 (Pres.), Eisenhower, Rep., 643,849; Stevenson, Dem., 480,371.

1960 (Pres.), Kennedy, Dem., 748,700; Nixon, Rep., 795,476.

1964 (Pres.), Johnson, Dem., 948,540; Goldwater, Rep., 905,941.

1968 (Pres.), Nixon, Rep., 886,804; Humphrey, Dem., 676,794; Wallace, 3d party, 624,207.

1972 (Pres.), Nixon, Rep., 1,857,759; McGovern, Dem., 718,117; scattered 7,407.

Georgia

1932 (Pres.), Roosevelt, Dem., 234,118; Hoover, Rep., 19,863; Upshaw, Proh., 1,125; Thomas, Soc., 461; Foster, Com., 23.

1936 (Pres.), Roosevelt, Dem., 255,364; Landon, Rep., 36,942; Colvin, Proh., 660; Lemke, Union, 141; Thomas, Soc., 68.

1940 (Pres.), Roosevelt, Dem., 265,194; Willkie, Rep., 23,934; Ind. Dem., 22,428; total, 46,362; Babson, Proh., 983.

1944 (Pres.), Roosevelt, Dem., 268,187; Dewey, Rep., 56,506; Watson, Proh., 36.

1948 (Pres.), Truman, Dem., 254,646; Dewey, Rep., 76,691; Thurmond, States' Rights, 85,055; Wallace, Prog., 1,636; Watson, Proh., 732.

1952 (Pres.), Eisenhower, Rep., 198,979; Stevenson, Dem., 456,823; Liberty Party, 1.

1956 (Pres.), Stevenson, Dem., 444,388; Eisenhower, Rep., 222,778; Andrews, Ind., write-in, 1,754.

1960 (Pres.), Kennedy, Dem., 458,638; Nixon, Rep., 274,472; write-in 239.

1964 (Pres.), Johnson, Dem., 522,557; Goldwater, Rep., 616,600.

1968 (Pres.), Nixon, Rep., 380,111; Humphrey, Dem., 334,440; Wallace, 3d party, 535,550; write-in vote, 162.

1972 (Pres.), Nixon, Rep., 881,496; McGovern, Dem., 289,529; Schmitz, Amer. Party, 2,288; scattered 1,459.

Hawaii

1960 (Pres.), Kennedy, Dem., 92,410; Nixon, Rep., 92,295.

1964 (Pres.), Johnson, Dem., 163,249; Goldwater, Rep., 44,022.

1968 (Pres.), Nixon, Rep., 91,425; Humphrey, Dem., 141,324; Wallace, 3d party, 3,469.

1972 (Pres.), Nixon, Rep., 168,865; McGovern, Dem., 101,409.

Idaho

1932 (Pres.), Roosevelt, Dem., 109,479; Hoover, Rep., 71,312; Harvey, Lib., 4,712; Thomas, Soc., 526; Foster, Com., 491.

1936 (Pres.), Roosevelt, Dem., 125,683; Landon, Rep., 66,256; Lemke, Union, 7,684.

1940 (Pres.), Roosevelt, Dem., 127,842; Willkie, Rep., 106,553; Thomas, Soc., 497; Browder, Com,, 276.

1944 (Pres.), Roosevelt, Dem., 107,399; Dewey, Rep., 100,137; Watson, Proh., 503; Thomas, Soc., 282.

1948 (Pres.), Truman, Dem., 107,370; Dewey, Rep., 101,514; Wallace, Prog., 4,972; Watson, Proh., 628; Thomas, Soc., 332.

1952 (Pres.), Eisenhower, Rep., 180,707; Stevenson, Dem., 95,081; Hallinan, Prog., 443; write-in, 23.

1956 (Pres.), Eisenhower, Rep., 166,979; Stevenson, Dem., 105,868; Andrews, Ind., 126; write-in, 16.

1960 (Pres.), Kennedy, Dem., 138,853; Nixon, Rep., 161,597.

1964 (Pres.), Johnson, Dem., 148,920; Goldwater, Rep., 143,557.

1968 (Pres.), Nixon, Rep., 165,369; Humphrey, Dem., 89,273; Wallace, 3d party, 36,541.

1972 (Pres.), Nixon, Rep., 199,384; McGovern, Dem., 80,826; Schmitz, American, 28,869; Spock, Peoples, 903; Jenness, Soc. Worker, 397.

Illinois

1932 (Pres.), Roosevelt, Dem., 1,882,304; Hoover, Rep., 1,432,756; Thomas, Soc., 67,258; Foster, Com., 15,582; Upshaw, Proh., 6,388; Reynolds, Soc. Lab., 3,638.
1936 (Pres.), Roosevelt, Dem., 2,282,999; Landon, Rep., 1,570,393; Lemke, Union, 89,439; Thomas, Soc., 7,530; Colvin, Proh., 3,439; Aiken, Soc. Lab., 1,921.
1940 (Pres.), Roosevelt, Dem., 2,149,934; Willkie, Rep., 2,047,240; Thomas, Soc., 10,914; Babson, Proh., 9,190.
1944 (Pres.), Roosevelt, Dem., 2,079,479; Dewey, Rep., 1,939,314; Teichert, Soc. Lab., 9,677; Watson, Proh., 7,411; Thomas, Soc., 180.
1948 (Pres.), Truman, Dem., 1,994,715; Dewey, Rep., 1,961,103; Watson, Proh., 11,959; Thomas, Soc., 11,-522; Teichert, Soc. Lab., 3,118.
1952 (Pres.), Eisenhower, Rep., 2,457,327; Stevenson, Dem., 2,013,920; Haas, Soc. Lab., 9,363; write-in, 448.
1956 (Pres.), Eisenhower, Rep., 2,623,327; Stevenson, Dem., 1,775,682; Haas, Soc. Lab., 8,342; write-in, 56.
1960 (Pres.), Kennedy, Dem., 2,377,846; Nixon, Rep., 2,368,988; Haas, Soc. Lab., 10,560; write-in, 15.
1964 (Pres.), Johnson, Dem., 2,796,833; Goldwater, Rep., 1,905,946; write-in, 62.
1968 (Pres.), Nixon, Rep., 2,174,774; Humphrey, Dem., 2,039,814; Wallace, 3d party, 390,958; Blomen, Soc. Labor, 13,878; write-in, 325.
1972 (Pres.), Nixon, Rep., 2,788,179; McGovern, Dem., 1,913,472; Fisher, Soc. Labor, 12,344; Schmitz, Amer., 2,471; Hall, Communist, 4,541; others, 2,229.

Indiana

1932 (Pres.), Roosevelt, Dem., 862,054; Hoover, Rep., 677,184; Thomas, Soc., 21,388; Upshaw, Proh., 10,-399; Foster, Com., 2,187; Reynolds, Soc. Lab., 2,070.
1936 (Pres.), Roosevelt, Dem., 943,974; Landon, Rep., 691,570; Lemke, Union, 19,407; Thomas, Soc., 3,856; Browder, Com., 1,090.
1940 (Pres.), Roosevelt, Dem., 874,063; Willkie, Rep., 899,466; Babson, Proh., 6,437; Thomas, Soc., 2,075; Aiken, Soc. Lab., 706.
1944 (Pres.), Roosevelt, Dem., 781,403; Dewey, Rep., 875,891; Watson, Proh., 12,574; Thomas, Soc., 2,223.
1948 (Pres.), Truman, Dem., 807,833; Dewey, Rep., 821,079; Watson, Proh., 14,711; Wallace, Prog., 9,649; Thomas, Soc., 2,179; Teichert, Soc. Lab., 763.
1952 (Pres.), Eisenhower, Rep., 1,136,259; Stevenson, Dem., 801,530; Hamblen, Proh., 15,335; Hallinan, Prog., 1,222; Haas, Soc. Lab., 979.
1956 (Pres.), Eisenhower, Rep., 1,182,811; Stevenson, Dem., 783,908; Holtwick, Proh., 6,554; Haas, 1,334.
1960 (Pres.), Kennedy, Dem., 952,358; Nixon, Rep., 1,175,120; Decker, Proh., 6,746; Haas, Soc. Lab., 1,136.
1964 (Pres.), Johnson, Dem., 1,170,848; Goldwater, Rep., 911,118; Munn, Proh., 8,266; Haas, Soc. Lab., 1,374.
1968 (Pres.), Nixon, Rep., 1,067,885; Humphrey, Dem., 806,659; Wallace, 3d party, 243,108; Munn, Prohibition, 4,616; Halstead, Soc. Worker, 1,293; Gregory, 36.
1972 (Pres.), Nixon, Rep., 1,405,154; McGovern, Dem., 708,568; Reed, Soc. Worker, 5,575; Fisher, Soc. Labor, 1,688; Spock, Peace & Freedom, 4,544.

Iowa

1932 (Pres.), Roosevelt, Dem., 598,019; Hoover, Rep., 414,433; Thomas, Soc., 20,467; Upshaw, Proh., 2,111; Coxey, Farm-Lab., 1,094; Foster, Com., 559. (Pres.).
1936 (Pres.), Roosevelt, Dem., 621,756; Landon, Rep., 487,977; Lemke, Union, 29,687; Thomas, Soc.,

1,373; Colvin, Proh., 1,182; Browder, C., 506; Aiken, Soc. Lab., 252.
1940 (Pres.), Roosevelt, Dem., 578,800; Willkie, Rep., 632,370; Babson, Proh., 2,284; Browder, Com., 1,524; Aiken, Soc. Lab., 452.
1944 (Pres.), Roosevelt, Dem., 499,876; Dewey, Rep., 547,267; Watson, Proh., 3,752; Thomas, Soc., 1,511; Teichert, Soc. Lab., 193.
1948 (Pres.), Truman, Dem., 522,380; Dewey, Rep., 494,018; Wallace, Prog., 12,125; Teichert, Soc. Lab., 4,274; Watson, Proh., 3,382; Thomas, Soc., 1,829; Dobbs, Soc. Workers, 26.
1952 (Pres.), Eisenhower, Rep., 808,906; Stevenson, Dem., 451,513; Hallinan, Prog., 5,085; Hamblen, Proh., 2,882; Hoopes, Soc., 219; Haas, Soc. Lab., 139; scattering 29.
1956 (Pres.), Eisenhower, Rep., 729,187; Stevenson, Dem., 501,858; Andrews (A.C.P. of Iowa), 3,202; Hoopes, Soc., 192; Haas, Soc. Lab., 125.
1960 (Pres.), Kennedy, Dem., 550,565; Nixon, Rep., 722,381; Haas, Soc. Lab., 230; write-in, 634.
1964 (Pres.), Johnson, Dem., 733,030; Goldwater, Rep., 449,148; Haas, S. L., 182; DeBerry, S. W., 159; Munn, Proh., 1,902.
1968 (Pres.), Nixon, Rep., 619,106; Humphrey, Dem., 476,699; Wallace, 3d party, 66,422; Munn, Proh., 362; Halstead, Soc. Worker, 3,377; Cleaver, Peace and Freedom, 1,332; Blomen, S. L., 241.
1972 (Pres.), Nixon, Rep., 706,207; McGovern, Dem., 496,206; Schmitz, American, 22,056; Jenness, Soc. Worker, 488; Fisher, Soc. Labor, 195; Hall, Communist, 272; Green, Universal, 199; scattered, 321.

Kansas

1932 (Pres.), Roosevelt, Dem., 424,204; Hoover, Rep., 349,498; Thomas, Soc., 18,276.
1936 (Pres.), Roosevelt, Dem., 464,520; Landon, Rep., 397,727; Thomas, Soc., 2,766; Lemke, Union, 494.
1940 (Pres.), Roosevelt, Dem., 364,725; Willkie, Rep., 489,169; Babson, Proh., 4,056; Thomas, Soc., 2,347.
1944 (Pres.), Roosevelt, Dem., 287,458; Dewey, Rep., 442,096; Watson, Proh., 2,609; Thomas, Soc., 1,613.
1948 (Pres.), Truman, Dem., 351,902; Dewey, Rep., 423,039; Watson, Proh., 6,468; Wallace, Prog., 4,603; Thomas, Soc., 2,807.
1952 (Pres.), Eisenhower, Rep., 616,302; Stevenson, Dem., 273,296; Hamblen, Proh., 6,030; Hoopes, Soc., 530.
1956 (Pres.), Eisenhower, Rep., 566,878; Stevenson, Dem., 296,317; Holtwick, Proh., 3,048.
1960 (Pres.), Kennedy, Dem., 363,213; Nixon, Rep., 561,474; Decker, Proh., 4,138.
1964 (Pres.), Johnson, Dem., 464,028; Goldwater, Rep., 386,579; Munn, Proh., 5,393; Haas, Soc. Labor, 1,901.
1968 (Pres.), Nixon, Rep., 478,674; Humphrey, Dem., 302,996; Wallace, 3d, 88,921; Munn, Proh., 2,192.
1972 (Pres.), Nixon, Rep., 619,812; McGovern, Dem., 270,287; Schmitz, Cons., 21,808; Munn, Proh., 4,188.

Kentucky

1932 (Pres.), Roosevelt, Dem., 580,574; Hoover, Rep., 394,716; Upshaw, Proh., 2,252; Thomas, Soc., 3,853; Reynolds, Soc. Lab., 1,396; Foster, Com., 272.
1936 (Pres.), Roosevelt, Dem., 541,944; Landon, Rep., 369,702; Lemke, Union, 12,501; Colvin, Proh., 929; Thomas, S., 627; Aiken, S. L., 294; Browder, Com., 204.
1940 (Pres.), Roosevelt, Dem., 557,222; Willkie, Rep., 410,384; Babson, Proh., 1,443; Thomas, Soc., 1,014.
1944 (Pres.), Roosevelt, Dem., 472,589; Dewey, Rep., 392,448; Watson, Proh., 2,023; Thomas, Soc., 535; Teichert, Soc. Lab., 326.
1948 (Pres.), Truman, Dem., 466,756; Dewey, Rep., 341,210; Thurmond, States' Rights, 10,411; Wallace, Prog., 1,567; Thomas, Soc., 1,284; Watson, Proh., 1,245; Teichert, Soc. Lab., 185.

1952 (Pres.), Eisenhower, Rep., 495,029; Stevenson, Dem., 495,729 Hamblen, Proh., 1,161; Haas, Soc. Lab., 893; Hallinan, Prog., 336.
1956 (Pres.), Eisenhower, Rep., 572,192; Stevenson, Dem., 476,453; Byrd, States' Rights, 2,657; Holtwick, Proh., 2,145; Haas, Soc. Lab., 358.
1960 (Pres.), Kennedy, Dem., 521,855; Nixon, Rep., 602,607.
1964 (Pres.), Johnson, Dem., 669,659; Goldwater, Rep., 372,977; John Kasper, Nat'l. States Rights, 3,469.
1968 (Pres.), Nixon, Rep., 462,411; Humphrey, Dem., 397,547; Wallace, 3d p., 193,098; Halstead, S. W., 2,843.
1972 (Pres.), Nixon, Rep., 676,446; McGovern, Dem., 371,159; Schmitz, Amer., 17,627; Jenness, Soc. Worker, 685; Hall, Comm., 464; Spock, Peoples, 1,118.

Louisiana

1932 (Pres.), Roosevelt, Dem., 249,418; Hoover, Rep., 18,863.
1936 (Pres.), Roosevelt, Dem., 292,894; Landon, Rep., 36,791.
1940 (Pres.), Roosevelt, Dem., 319,751; Willkie, Rep., 52,446.
1944 (Pres.), Roosevelt, Dem., 281,564; Dewey, Rep., 67,750.
1948 (Pres.), Thurmond, States' Rights, 204,290; Truman, Dem., 136,344; Dewey, Rep., 72,657; Wallace, Prog., 3,035.
1952 (Pres.), Eisenhower, Rep., 306,925; Stevenson, Dem., 345,027.
1956 (Pres.), Eisenhower, Rep., 329,047; Stevenson, Dem., 243,977; Andrews, States' Rights, 44,520.
1960 (Pres.), Kennedy, Dem., 407,339; Nixon, Rep., 230,890; States' Rights (unpledged) 169,572.
1964 (Pres.), Johnson, Dem., 387,068; Goldwater, Rep., 509,225.
1968 (Pres.), Nixon, Rep., 257,535; Humphrey, Dem., 309,615; Wallace, 3d party, 530,300.
1972 (Pres.), Nixon, Rep., 686,852; McGovern, Dem., 298,142; Schmitz, American, 52,099; Jenness, Soc. Worker, 14,398.

Maine

1932 (Pres.), Roosevelt, Dem., 128,907; Hoover, Rep., 166,631; Thomas, Soc., 2,439; Reynolds, Soc. Lab., 255; Foster, Com., 162.
1936 (Pres.), Landon, Rep., 168,823; Roosevelt, Dem., 126,333; Lemke, Union, 7,581; Thomas, Soc., 783; Colvin, Proh., 334; Browder, Com., 257; Aiken, Soc. Lab., 129.
1940 (Pres.), Roosevelt, Dem., 156,478; Willkie, Rep., 165,951; Browder, Com., 411.
1944 (Pres.), Roosevelt, Dem., 140,631; Dewey, Rep., 155,434; Teichert, Soc. Lab., 335.
1948 (Pres.), Truman, Dem., 111,916; Dewey, Rep., 150,234; Wallace, Prog., 1,884; Thomas, Soc., 547; Teichert, Soc. Lab., 206.
1952 (Pres.), Eisenhower, Rep., 232,353; Stevenson, Dem., 118,806; Hallinan, Prog., 332; Haas, Soc. Lab., 156; Hoopes, Soc., 138; scattered, 1.
1956 (Pres.), Eisenhower, Rep., 249,238; Stevenson, Dem., 102,468.
1960 (Pres.), Kennedy, Dem., 181,159; Nixon, Rep., 240,608.
1964 (Pres.), Johnson, Dem., 262,264; Goldwater, Rep., 118,701.
1968 (Pres.), Nixon, Rep., 169,254; Humphrey, Dem., 217,312; Wallace, 3d party, 6,370.
1972 (Pres.), Nixon, Rep., 256,458; McGovern, Dem., 160,584; scattered, 229.

Maryland

1932 (Pres.), Roosevelt, Dem., 314,314; Hoover, Rep.,

184,184; Thomas, Soc., 10,489; Reynolds, Soc. Lab., 1,036; Foster, Com., 1,031.
1936 (Pres.), Roosevelt, Dem., 389,612; Landon, Rep., 231,435; Thomas, Soc., 1,629; Aiken, Soc. Lab., 1,305; Browder, Com., 915.
1940 (Pres.), Roosevelt, Dem., 384,546; Wilkie, Rep., 269,534; Thomas, Soc., 4,093; Browder, Com., 1,274; Aiken, Soc. Lab., 657.
1944 (Pres.), Roosevelt, Dem., 315,490; Dewey, Rep., 292,949.
1948 (Pres.), Truman, Dem., 286,521; Dewey, Rep., 294,814; Wallace, Prog., 9,983; Thomas, Soc., 2,941; Thurmond, States' Rights, 2,476; Wright, write-in, 2,294.
1952 (Pres.), Eisenhower, Rep., 499,424; Stevenson, Dem., 395,337; Hallinan, Prog., 7,313.
1956 (Pres.), Eisenhower, Rep., 559,738; Stevenson, Dem., 372,613.
1960 (Pres.), Kennedy, Dem., 565,800; Nixon, Rep., 489,538.
1964 (Pres.), Johnson, Dem., 730,912; Goldwater, Rep., 385,495; write-in, 50.
1968 (Pres.), Nixon, Rep., 517,995; Humphrey, Dem., 538,310; Wallace, 3d party, 178,734.
1972 (Pres.), Nixon, Rep., 829,305; McGovern, Dem., 505,781; Schmitz, American Party, 18,726.

Massachusetts

1932 (Pres.), Roosevelt, Dem., 800,148; Hoover, Rep., 736,959; Thomas, Soc., 34,305; Foster, Com., 4,821; Reynolds, Soc. Lab., 2,668; Upshaw, Proh., 1,142.
1936 (Pres.), Roosevelt, Dem., 942,716; Landon, Rep., 768,613; Lemke, Union, 118,639; Thomas, Soc., 5,111; Browder, Com., 2,930; Aiken, Soc. Lab., 1,305; Colvin, Proh., 1,032.
1940 (Pres.), Roosevelt, Dem., 1,076,522; Willkie, Rep., 939,700; Thomas, Soc., 4,091; Browder, Com., 3,806; Aiken, Soc. Lab., 1,492; Babson, Proh., 1,370.
1944 (Pres.), Roosevelt, Dem., 1,035,296; Dewey, Rep., 921,350; Teichert, Soc. Lab., 2,780; Watson, Proh., 973.
1948 (Pres.), Truman, Dem., 1,151,788; Dewey, Rep., 909,370; Wallace, Prog., 38,157; Teichert, Soc. Lab., 5,535; Watson, Proh., 1,663.
1952 (Pres.), Eisenhower, Rep., 1,292,325; Stevenson, Dem., 1,083,525; Hallinan, Prog., 4,636; Haas, Soc. Lab., 1,957; Hamblen, Proh., 886; scattered, 69; blanks, 41,150.
1956 (Pres.), Eisenhower, Rep., 1,393,197; Stevenson, Dem., 948,190; Haas, Soc. Lab., 5,573; Holtwick, Proh., 1,205; others, 341.
1960 (Pres.), Kennedy, Dem., 1,487,174; Nixon, Rep., 976,750; Haas, Soc. Lab., 3,892; Decker, Proh., 1,633; others, 31; blank and void, 26,024.
1964 (Pres.), Johnson, Dem., 1,786,422; Goldwater, Rep., 549,727; Haas, Soc. Lab., 4,755; Munn, Proh., 3,735; scattered, 159; blank, 48,104.
1968 (Pres.), Nixon, Rep., 766,844; Humphrey, Dem., 1,469,218; Wallace, 3d party, 87,088; Blomen, Soc. Labor, 6,180; Munn, Prohibition, 2,369; scattered, 53; blanks, 25,394.
1972 (Pres.), Nixon, Rep., 1,112,078; McGovern, Dem., 1,332,540; Jenness, Soc. Worker, 10,600; Fisher, Soc. Labor, 129; Schmitz, American, 2,877; Spock, Peoples, 101; Hall, Communist, 46; Hospers, Libertarian, 43; scattered, 342.

Michigan

1932 (Pres.), Roosevelt, Dem., 871,700; Hoover, Rep., 739,894; Thomas, Soc., 39,025; Foster, Com., 9,318; Upshaw, Proh., 2,893; Reynolds, Soc. Lab., 1,041; Harvey, Lib., 217.
1936 (Pres.), Roosevelt, Dem., 1,016,794; Landon, Rep., 699,733; Lemke, Union, 75,795; Thomas, Soc., 8,208; Browder, Com., 3,384; Aiken, Soc. Lab., 600; Colvin, Proh., 579.
1940 (Pres.), Roosevelt, Dem., 1,032,991; Willkie,

Rep., 1,039,917; Thomas, Soc., 7,593; Browder, Com., 2,834; Babson, Proh., 1,795; Aiken, Soc. Lab., 795.
1944 (Pres.), Roosevelt, Dem., 1,106,899; Dewey, Rep., 1,084,423; Watson, Proh., 6,503; Thomas, Soc., 4,598; Smith, America First, 1,530; Teichert, Soc. Lab., 1,264.
1948 (Pres.), Truman, Dem., 1,003,448; Dewey, Rep., 1,038,595; Wallace, Prog., 46,515; Watson, Proh., 13,052; Thomas, Soc., 6,063; Teichert, Soc. Lab., 1,263; Dobbs, Soc. Workers, 672.
1952 (Pres.), Eisenhower, Rep., 1,551,529; Stevenson, Dem., 1,230,657; Hamblen, Proh., 10,331; Hallinan, Prog., 3,922; Haas, Soc. Lab., 1,495; Dobbs, Soc. Workers, 655; scattered, 3.
1956 (Pres.), Eisenhower, Rep., 1,713,647; Stevenson, Dem., 1,359,898; Holtwick, Proh., 6,923.
1960 (Pres.), Kennedy, Dem., 1,687,269; Nixon, Rep., 1,620,428; Dobbs, Soc. Workers, 4,347; Decker, Proh., 2,029; Daly, Tax Cut, 1,767; Haas, Soc. Lab., 1,718; Ind. American 539.
1964 (Pres.), Johnson, Dem., 2,136,615; Goldwater, Rep., 1,060,152; DeBerry, Soc. Workers, 3,817; Haas, Soc. Lab., 1,704; Proh. (no candidate listed), 699; scattering, 145.
1968 (Pres.), Nixon, Rep., 1,370,665; Humphrey, Dem., 1,593,082; Wallace, 3d party, 331,968; Halstead, Soc. Worker, 4,099; Blomen, Soc. Labor, 1,762; Cleaver, New Politics, 4,585; Munn, Prohib., 60; scattering, 29.
1972 (Pres.), Nixon, Rep., 1,961,721; McGovern, Dem., 1,459,435; Schmitz, Amer., 63,321; Fisher, Soc. Labor, 2,437; Jenness, Soc. Worker, 1,603; Hall, Communist, 1,210.

Minnesota

1932 (Pres.), Roosevelt, Dem., 600,806; Hoover, Rep., 363,959; Thomas, Soc., 25,476; Foster, Com., 6,101; Coxey, Farm.-Lab., 5,731; Reynolds, Ind., 770.
1936 (Pres.), Roosevelt, Dem., 698,811; Landon, Rep., 350,461; Lemke, Union, 74,296; Thomas, Soc., 2,872; Browder, Com., 2,574; Aiken, Soc., 961.
1940 (Pres.), Roosevelt, Dem., 644,196; Willkie, Rep., 596,274; Thomas, Soc., 5,454; Browder, Com., 2,711; Aiken, Ind., 2,553.
1944 (Pres.), Roosevelt, Dem., 589,864; Dewey, Rep., 527,416; Thomas, Soc., 5,073; Teichert, Ind. Gov't., 3,176.
1948 (Pres.), Truman, Dem., 692,966; Dewey, Rep., 483,617; Wallace, Prog., 27,866; Thomas, Soc., 4,646; Teichert, Soc. Lab., 2,525; Dobbs, Soc. Workers, 606.
1952 (Pres.), Eisenhower, Rep., 763,211; Stevenson, Dem., 608,458; Hallinan, Prog., 2,666; Haas, Soc. Lab., 2,383; Hamblen, Proh., 2,147; Dobbs, Soc. Workers, 618.
1956 (Pres.), Eisenhower, Rep., 719,302; Stevenson, Dem., 617,525; Haas, Soc. Lab. (Ind. Gov.), 2,080; Dobbs, Soc. Workers, 1,098.
1960 (Pres.), Kennedy, Dem., 779,933; Nixon, Rep., 757,915; Dobbs, Soc. Workers, 3,077; Industrial Gov., 962.
1964 (Pres.), Johnson, Dem., 991,117; Goldwater, Rep., 559,624; DeBerry, Soc. Workers, 1,177; Haas, Industrial Gov., 2,544.
1968 (Pres.), Nixon, Rep., 658,643; Humphrey, Dem., 857,738; Wallace, 3d party, 68,931; scattered, 2,443; Halstead, Soc. Worker, 808; Blomen, Ind. Gov't., 285; Mitchell, Communist, 415; Cleaver, Peace 935; McCarthy, write-in, 585; scattered 170.
1972 (Pres.), Nixon, Rep. 898,269; McGovern, Dem., 802,346; Schmitz, American, 31,407; Spock, Peoples, 2,805; Fisher, Soc. Labor, 4,261; Jenness, Soc. Worker, 940; Hall, Communist, 662; scattered 962.

Mississippi

1932 (Pres.), Roosevelt, Dem., 140,168; Hoover, Rep.,

5,180; Thomas, Soc., 686.
1936 (Pres.), Roosevelt, Dem., 157,318; Landon, Rep., Howard faction, 2,760; Rowlands faction, 1,675 total, 4,435; Thomas, Soc., 329.
1940 (Pres.), Roosevelt, Dem., 168,252; Willkie, Ind. Rep., 4,550; Rep., 2,814; total, 7,364; Thomas, Soc., 103.
1944 (Pres.), Roosevelt, Dem., 158,515; Dewey, Rep., 3,742; Reg. Dem., 9,964; Ind. Rep., 7,859.
1948 (Pres.), Thurmond, States' Rights, 167,538; Truman, Dem., 19,384; Dewey, Rep., 5,043; Wallace, Prog., 225.
1952 (Pres.), Eisenhower, Ind. vote pledged to Rep. candidate, 112,966; Stevenson, Dem., 172,566.
1956 (Pres.), Stevenson, Dem., 144,498; Eisenhower, Rep., 56,372; Black and Tan Grand Old Party, 4,313; total, 60,685; Byrd, Independent, 42,966.
1960 (Pres.), Democratic unpledged electors, 116,248; Kennedy, Dem., 108,362; Nixon, Rep., 73,561. Mississippi's victorious slate of 8 unpledged Democratic electors cast their votes for Sen. Harry F. Byrd (D-Va.).
1964 (Pres.), Johnson, Dem., 52,618; Goldwater, Rep., 356,528.
1968 (Pres.), Nixon, Rep., 88,516; Humphrey, Dem., 150,644; Wallace, 3d party, 415,349.
1972 (Pres.), Nixon, Rep., 505,125; McGovern, Dem., 126,782; Schmitz, American, 11,598; Jenness, Soc. Worker, 2,458.

Missouri

1932 (Pres.), Roosevelt, Dem., 1,025,406; Hoover, Rep., 564,713; Thomas, Soc., 16,374; Upshaw, Proh., 2,429; Foster, Com., 568; Reynolds, Soc. Lab., 404.
1936 (Pres.), Roosevelt, Dem., 1,111,403; Landon, Rep., 697,891; Lemke, Union, 14,630; Thomas, Soc., 3,454; Colvin, Proh., 908; Browder, Com., 417; Aiken, Soc. Lab., 292.
1940 (Pres.), Roosevelt, Dem., 958,476; Willkie, Rep., 871,009; Thomas, Soc., 2,226; Babson, Proh., 1,809; Aiken, Soc. Lab., 209.
1944 (Pres.), Roosevelt, Dem., 807,357; Dewey, Rep., 761,175; Thomas, Soc., 1,750; Watson, Proh., 1,175; Teichert, Soc. Lab., 221.
1948 (Pres.), Truman, Dem., 917,315; Dewey, Rep., 655,039; Wallace, Prog., 3,998; Thomas, Soc., 2,222.
1952 (Pres.), Eisenhower, Rep., 959,429; Stevenson, Dem., 929,830; Hallinan, Prog., 987; Hamblen, Proh., 885; MacArthur, Christian Nationalist, 302; America First, 233; Hoopes, Soc. 227; Haas, Soc.-Lab., 169.
1956 (Pres.), Stevenson, Dem., 918,273; Eisenhower, Rep., 914,299.
1960 (Pres.), Kennedy, Dem., 972,201; Nixon, Rep., 962,221.
1964 (Pres.), Johnson, Dem., 1,164,344; Goldwater, Rep., 653,535.
1968 (Pres.), Nixon, Rep., 811,932; Humphrey, Dem., 791,444; Wallace, 3d party, 206,126.
1972 (Pres.), Nixon, Rep., 1,154,058; McGovern, Dem., 698,531.

Montana

1924 (Pres.), Coolidge, Rep., 74,138; LaFollette, Prog., 61,105; Davis, Dem., 33,805; Foster, Workers, 357; Johns, Soc., Lab., 247.
1928 (Pres.), Hoover, Rep., 113,300; Smith, Dem., 78,-578; Thomas, Soc., 1,667; Foster, Com., 563.
1932 (Pres.), Roosevelt, Dem., 127,286; Hoover, Rep., 78,078; Thomas, Soc., 7,891; Foster, Com., 1,775; Harvey, Lib., 1,449.
1936 (Pres.), Roosevelt, Dem., 159,690; Landon, Rep., 63,598; Lemke, Union, 5,549; Thomas, Soc., 1,066; Browder, Com., 385; Colvin, Proh., 224.
1940 (Pres.), Roosevelt, Dem., 145,698; Willkie, Rep., 99,579; Thomas, Soc., 1,443; Babson, Proh., 664; Browder, Com., 489.

1944 (Pres.), Roosevelt, Dem., 112,556; Dewey, Rep., 93,163; Thomas, Soc., 1,296; Watson, Proh., 340.

1948 (Pres.), Truman, Dem., 119,071; Dewey, Rep., 96,770; Wallace, Prog., 7,313; Thomas, Soc., 695; Watson, Proh., 429.

1952 (Pres.), Eisenhower, Rep., 157,394; Stevenson, Dem., 106,213; Hallinan, Prog., 723; Hamblen, Proh., 548; Hoopes, Soc., 159.

1956 (Pres.), Eisenhower, Rep., 154,933; Stevenson, Dem., 116,238.

1960 (Pres.), Kennedy, Dem., 134,891; Nixon, Rep., 141,841; Decker, Proh., 456; Dobbs, Soc. Workers, 391.

1964 (Pres.), Johnson, Dem., 164,246; Goldwater, Rep., 113,032; Kasper, Nat'l States Rights, 519; Munn, Proh., 499; DeBerry, Soc. Worker, 332.

1968 (Pres.), Nixon, Rep., 138,835; Humphrey, Dem., 114,117; Wallace, 3d party, 20.015; Halstead, Soc. Worker, 457; Munnn Prohibition, 510; Caton, New Reform, 470.

1972 (Pres.), Nixon, Rep., 183,976; McGovern, Dem., 120,197; Schmitz, American, 13,430.

Nebraska

1932 (Pres.), Roosevelt, Dem., 359,082; Hoover, Rep., 201,177; Thomas, Soc., 9,876.

1936 (Pres.), Roosevelt, Dem., 347,454; Landon, Rep., 248,731; Lemke, Union, 12,847.

1940 (Pres.), Roosevelt, Dem., 263,677; Willkie, Rep., 352,201.

1944 (Pres.), Roosevelt, Dem., 233,246; Dewey, Rep., 329,880.

1948 (Pres.), Truman, Dem., 224,165; Dewey, Rep., 264,774.

1952 (Pres.), Eisenhower, Rep., 421,603; Stevenson, Dem., 188,057.

1956 (Pres.), Eisenhower, Rep., 378,108; Stevenson, Dem., 199,029.

1960 (Pres.), Kennedy, Dem., 232,542; Nixon, Rep., 380,553.

1964 (Pres.), Johnson, Dem., 307,307; Goldwater, Rep., 276,847.

1968 (Pres.), Nixon, Rep., 321,163; Humphrey, Dem., 170,784; Wallace, 3d party, 44,904.

1972 (Pres.), Nixon, Rep., 406,298; McGovern, Dem., 169,991; scattered, 817.

Nevada

1932 (Pres.), Roosevelt, Dem., 28,756; Hoover, Rep., 12,674.

1936 (Pres.), Roosevelt, Dem., 31,925; Landon, Rep., 11,923.

1940 (Pres.), Roosevelt, Dem., 31,945; Willkie, Rep., 21,229.

1944 (Pres.), Roosevelt, Dem., 29,623; Dewey, Rep., 24,611.

1948 (Pres.), Truman, Dem., 31,291; Dewey, Rep., 29,-357; Wallace, Prog., 1,469.

1952 (Pres.), Eisenhower, Rep., 50,502; Stevenson, Dem., 31,688.

1956 (Pres.), Eisenhower, Rep., 56,049; Stevenson, Dem., 40,640.

1960 (Pres.), Kennedy, Dem., 54,880; Nixon, Rep., 52,387.

1964 (Pres.), Johnson, Dem., 79,339; Goldwater, Rep., 56,094.

1968 (Pres.), Nixon, Rep., 73,188; Humphrey, Dem., 60,598; Wallace, 3d party, 20,432.

1972 (Pres.), Nixon, Rep., 115,750; McGovern, Dem., 66,016.

New Hampshire

1932 (Pres.), Roosevelt, Dem., 100,680; Hoover, Rep., 103,629; Thomas, Soc., 947; Foster, Com., 264.

1936 (Pres.), Roosevelt, Dem., 108,640; Landon, Rep., 104,642; Lemke, Union, 4,819; Browder, Com., 193.

1940 (Pres.), Roosevelt, Dem., 125,292; Willkie, Rep.,

110,127.

1944 (Pres.), Roosevelt, Dem., 119,663; Dewey, Rep., 109,916; Thomas, Soc., 46.

1948 (Pres.), Truman, Dem., 107,995; Dewey, Rep., 121,299; Wallace, Prog., 1,970; Thomas, Soc., 86; Teichert, Soc. Lab., 83; Thurmond, States' Rights, 7.

1952 (Pres.), Eisenhower, Rep., 166,287; Stevenson, Dem., 106,663.

1956 (Pres.), Eisenhower, Rep., 176,519; Stevenson, Dem., 90,364; Andrews, Const., 111.

1960 (Pres.), Kennedy, Dem., 137,772; Nixon, Rep., 157,989.

1964 (Pres.), Johnson, Dem., 182,065; Goldwater, Rep., 104,029.

1968 (Pres.), Nixon, Rep., 154,903; Humphrey, Dem., 130,589; Wallace, 3d party, 11,173; New Party, 421; Halstead, Soc. Worker, 104.

1972 (Pres.), Nixon, Rep., 213,724; McGovern, Dem., 116,435; Schmitz, American, 3,386; Jenness, Soc. Worker, 368; scattered, 142.

New Jersey

1932 (Pres.), Roosevelt, Dem., 806,630; Hoover, Rep., 775,684; Thomas, Soc., 42,998; Foster, Com., 2,915; Reynolds, Soc. Lab., 1,062; Upshaw, Proh., 774.

1936 (Pres.), Roosevelt, Dem., 1,083,549; Landon, Rep., 719,421; Lemke, Union, 9,405; Thomas, Soc., 3,895; Browder, Com., 1,590; Colvin, Proh., 916; Aiken, Soc. Lab., 346.

1940 (Pres.), Roosevelt, Dem., 1,016,404; Willkie, Rep., 944,876; Browder, Com., 8,814; Thomas, Soc., 2,823; Babson, Proh., 851; Aiken, Soc. Lab., 446.

1944 (Pres.), Roosevelt, Dem., 987,874; Dewey, Rep., 961,335; Teichert, Soc. Lab., 6,939; Watson, Nat'l Proh., 4,255; Thomas, Soc., 3,385.

1948 (Pres.), Truman, Dem., 895,455; Dewey, Rep., 981,124; Wallace, Prog., 42,683; Watson, Proh., 10,-593; Thomas, Soc., 10,521; Dobbs, Soc. Workers, 5,825; Teichert, Soc. Lab., 3,354.

1952 (Pres.), Eisenhower, Rep., 1,373,613; Stevenson, Dem., 1,015,902; Hoopes, Soc., 8,593; Haas, Soc. Lab., 5,815; Hallinan, Prog., 5,589; Krajewski, Poor Man's, 4,203; Dobbs, Soc. Workers, 3,850; Hamblen, Proh., 989.

1956 (Pres.), Eisenhower, Rep., 1,606,942; Stevenson, Dem., 850,337; Holtwick, Proh., 9,147; Haas, Soc. Lab., 6,736; Andrews, Conservative, 5,317; Dobbs, Soc. Workers, 4,004; Krajewski, American Third Party, 1,829.

1960 (Pres.), Kennedy, Dem., 1,385,415; Nixon, Rep., 1,363,324; Dobbs, Soc. Workers, 11,402; Lee, Conservative, 8,708; Haas, Soc. Lab., 4,262.

1964 (Pres.), Johnson, Dem., 1,867,671; Goldwater, Rep., 963,843; DeBerry, Soc. Workers, 8,181; Haas, Soc. Labor, 7,075,

1968 (Pres.), Nixon, Rep., 1,325,467; Humphrey, Dem., 1,264,206; Wallace, 3d party, 262,187; Halstead, Soc. Worker, 8,667; Gregory, Peace Freedom, 8,084; Blomen, Soc. Labor, 6,784.

1972 (Pres.), Nixon, Rep., 1,845,502; McGovern, Dem., 1,102,211; Schmitz, American, 34,378; Spock, Peoples, 5,355; Fisher, Soc. Labor, 4,544; Jenness, Soc. Worker, 2,233; Mahalchik, Amer. First, 1,743; Hall, Communist, 1,263.

New Mexico

1932 (Pres.), Roosevelt, Dem., 95,089; Hoover, Rep., 54,217; Thomas, Soc., 11,776; Harvey, Lib., 389; Foster, Com., 135.

1936 (Pres.), Roosevelt, Dem., 105,838; Landon, Rep., 61,710; Lemke, Union, 942; Thomas, Soc., 343; Browder, Com., 43.

1940 (Pres.), Roosevelt, Dem., 103,699; Willkie, Rep., 79,315.

1944 (Pres.), Roosevelt, Dem., 81,389; Dewey, Rep., 70,688; Watson, Proh., 148.

1948 (Pres.), Truman, Dem., 105,464; Dewey, Rep.,

80,303; Wallace, Prog., 1,037; Watson, Proh., 127;
Thomas, Soc., 83; Teichert, Soc. Lab., 49.
1952 (Pres.), Eisenhower, Rep., 132,170; Stevenson,
Dem., 105,661; Hamblen, Proh., 297; Hallinan, Ind.
Prog., 225; MacArthur, Christian National, 220;
Haas, Soc. Lab., 35.
1956 (Pres.), Eisenhower, Rep., 146,788; Stevenson,
Dem., 106,098; Holtwick, Proh., 607; Andrews, Ind.,
364; Haas, Soc. Lab., 69.
1960 (Pres.), Kennedy, Dem., 156,027; Nixon, Rep.,
153,733; Decker, Proh., 777; Haas, Soc. Lab., 570.
1964 (Pres.), Johnson, Dem., 194,017; Goldwater,
Rep., 131,838; Haas, Soc. Labor, 1,217; Munn, Proh.,
543.
1968 (Pres.), Nixon, Rep., 169,692; Humphrey, Dem.,
130,081; Wallace, 3d party, 25,737; Chavez, 1,519;
Halstead, Soc. Worker, 252.
1972 (Pres.), Nixon, Rep., 235,606; McGovern, Dem.,
141,084; Schmitz, Amer., 8,767; Jenness, Soc.
Worker, 474.

New York

1932 (Pres.), Roosevelt, Dem., 2,534,959; Hoover,
Rep., 1,937,963; Thomas, Soc., 177,397; Foster,
Com., 27,956; Reynolds, Soc. Lab., 10,339.
1936 (Pres.), Roosevelt, Dem., 3,018,298; American
Lab., 274,924; total, 3,293,222; Landon, Rep., 2,180,-
670; Thomas, Soc., 86,879; Browder, Com., 35,609.
1940 (Pres.), Roosevelt, Dem., 2,834,500; American
Lab., 417,418; total 3,251,918; Willkie, Rep., 3,027,-
478; Thomas, Soc., 18,950; Babson, Proh., 3,250.
1944 (Pres.), Roosevelt, Dem., 2,478,598; American
Lab., 496,405; Liberal, 329,325; total, 3,304,238;
Dewey, Rep., 2,987,647; Teichert, Ind. Gov't., 14,-
352; Thomas, Soc., 10,553.
1948 (Pres.), Truman, Dem., 2,557,642; Liberal, 222,-
562; total, 2,780,204; Dewey, Rep., 2,841,163;
Wallace, Amer. Lab., 509,559; Thomas, Soc., 40,879;
Teichert, Ind. Gov't., 2,729; Dobbs, Soc. Workers,
2,675.
1952 (Pres.), Eisenhower, Rep., 3,952,815; Stevenson,
Dem., 2,687,890, Liberal, 416,711; total, 3,104,601;
Hallinan, American Lab., 64,211; Hoopes, Soc.,
2,664; Dobbs, Soc. Workers, 2,212; Haas, Ind.
Gov't., 1,560; scattering, 178; blank and void,
87,813.
1956 (Pres.), Eisenhower, Rep., 4,340,340; Stevenson,
Dem., 2,458,212; Liberal, 292,557; total, 2,750,769;
write-in votes for Andrews, 1,027; Werdel, 492;
Haas, 150; Hoopes, 82; others, 476.
1960 (Pres.), Kennedy, Dem., 3,423,909; Liberal, 406,-
176; total, 3,830,085; Nixon, Rep., 3,446,419; Dobbs,
Soc. Workers, 14,319; scattering, 256; blank and
void, 88,896.
1964 (Pres.), Johnson, Dem., 4,913,156; Goldwater,
Rep., 2,243,559; Haas, Soc. Labor, 6,085; DeBerry,
Soc. Workers, 3,215; scattering, 188; blank and
void, 151,383.
1968 (Pres.), Nixon, Rep., 3,007,932; Humphrey,
Dem., 3,378,470; Wallace, 3d party, 358,864;
Blomen, Soc. Labor, 8,432; Halstead, Soc. Worker,
11,851; Gregory, Freedom and Peace, 24,517;
blank, void, and scattering, 171,624.
1972 (Pres.), Nixon, Rep., 3,824,642; Conservative,
368,136; McGovern, Dem., 2,767,956; Liberal, 183,-
128; Reed, Soc. Worker, 7,797; Fisher, Soc. Labor,
4,530; Hall, Communist, 5,641; blank, void, or scattered, 161,641.

North Carolina

1932 (Pres.), Roosevelt, Dem., 497,566; Hoover, Rep.,
208,344; Thomas, Soc., 5,591.
1936 (Pres.), Roosevelt, Dem., 616,141; Landon, Rep.,
223,283; Thomas, Soc., 21; Browder, Com., 11;
Lemke, Union, 2.
1940 (Pres.), Roosevelt, Dem., 609,015; Willkie, Rep.,
213,633.
1944 (Pres.), Roosevelt, Dem., 527,399; Dewey, Rep.,
263,155.
1948 (Pres.), Truman, Dem., 459,070; Dewey, Rep.,

258,572; Thurmond, States' Rights, 69,652; Wallace,
Prog., 3,915.
1952 (Pres.), Eisenhower, Rep., 558,107; Stevenson,
Dem., 652,803.
1956 (Pres.), Eisenhower, Rep., 575,062: Stevenson,
Dem., 590,530.
1960 (Pres.), Kennedy, Dem., 713,136; Nixon, Rep.,
655,420.
1964 (Pres.), Johnson, Dem., 800,139; Goldwater,
Rep., 624,844.
1968 (Pres.), Nixon, Rep., 627,192; Humphrey, Dem.,
464,113; Wallace, 3d party, 496,188.
1972 (Pres.), Nixon, Rep., 1,054,889; McGovern, Dem.,
438,705; Schmitz, American, 25,018.

North Dakota

1932 (Pres.), Roosevelt, Dem., 178,350; Hoover, Rep.,
71,772; Harvey, Lib., 1,817; Thomas, Soc., 3,521;
Foster, Com., 830.
1936 (Pres.), Roosevelt, Dem., 163,148; Landon, Rep.,
72,751; Lemke, Union, 36,708; Thomas, Soc., 552;
Browder, Com., 360; Colvin, Proh., 197.
1940 (Pres.), Roosevelt, Dem., 124,036; Willkie, Rep.,
154,590; Thomas, Soc., 1,279; Knuttson, Com., 545;
Babson, Proh., 325.
1944 (Pres.), Roosevelt, Dem., 100,144; Dewey, Rep.,
118,535; Thomas, Soc., 943; Watson, Proh., 549.
1948 (Pres.), Truman, Dem., 95,812; Dewey, Rep.,
115,139; Wallace, Prog., 8,391; Thomas, Soc., 1,000;
Thurmond, States' Rights, 374.
1952 (Pres.), Eisenhower, Rep., 191,712; Stevenson,
Dem., 76,694; MacArthur, Christian Nationalist,
1,075; Hallinan, Prog., 344; Hamblen, Proh., 302.
1956 (Pres.), Eisenhower, Rep., 156,766; Stevenson,
Dem., 96,742; Andrews, American, 483.
1960 (Pres.), Kennedy, Dem., 123,963; Nixon, Rep.,
154,310; Dobbs, Soc. Workers, 158.
1964 (Pres.), Johnson, Dem., 149,784; Goldwater,
Rep., 108,207; DeBerry, Soc. Worker, 224; Munn,
Proh., 174.
1968 (Pres.), Nixon, Rep., 138,669; Humphrey, Dem.,
94,769; Wallace, 3d party, 14,244; Halstead, Soc.
Worker, 128; Munn, Prohibition, 38; Troxell, Ind.,
34.
1972 (Pres.), Nixon, Rep., 174,109; McGovern, Dem.,
100,384; Jenness, Soc. Worker, 288; Hall, Communist, 87; Schmitz, American, 5,646.

Ohio

1932 (Pres.), Roosevelt, Dem., 1,301,695; Hoover,
Rep., 1,227,679; Thomas, Soc., 64,094; Upshaw,
Proh., 7,421; Foster, Com., 7,221; Reynolds, Soc.
Lab., 1,968.
1936 (Pres.), Roosevelt, Dem., 1,747,122; Landon,
Rep., 1,127,709; Lemke, Union, 132,212; Browder,
Com., 5,251; Thomas, Soc., 117; Aiken, Soc. Lab.,
14.
1940 (Pres.), Roosevelt, Dem., 1,733,139; Willkie,
Rep., 1,586,773.
1944 (Pres.), Roosevelt, Dem., 1,570,763; Dewey, Rep.,
1,582,293.
1948 (Pres.), Truman, Dem., 1,452,791; Dewey, Rep.,
1,445,684; Wallace, Prog., 37,596.
1952 (Pres.), Eisenhower, Rep., 2,100,391; Stevenson,
Dem., 1,600,367.
1956 (Pres.), Eisenhower, Rep., 2,262,610; Stevenson,
Dem., 1,439,655.
1960 (Pres.), Kennedy, Dem., 1,944,248; Nixon, Rep.,
2,217,611.
1964 (Pres.), Johnson, Dem., 2,498,331; Goldwater,
Rep., 1,470,865.
1968 (Pres.), Nixon, Rep., 1,791,014; Humphrey,
Dem., 1,700,586; Wallace, 3d party, 467,495; Gregory, 372; Munn, Prohibition, 19; Blomen, Soc. Labor,
120; Halstead, Soc. Worker, 69; Mitchell, Communist, 23.
1972 (Pres.), Nixon, Rep., 2,441,827; McGovern, Dem.,
1,558,889; Fisher, Soc. Labor, 7,107; Hall, Communist, 6,437; Schmitz, American, 80,067; Wallace,
Ind., 460.

Oklahoma

1932 (Pres.), Roosevelt, Dem., 515,468; Hoover, Rep., 188,165.

1936 (Pres.), Roosevelt, Dem., 501,069; Landon, Rep., 245,122; Thomas, Soc., 2,221; Colvin, Proh., 1,328.

1940 (Pres.), Roosevelt, Dem., 474,313; Willkie, Rep., 348,872; Babson, Proh., 3,027.

1944 (Pres.), Roosevelt, Dem., 401,549; Dewey, Rep., 319,424; Watson, Proh., 1,663.

1948 (Pres.), Truman, Dem., 452,782; Dewey, Rep., 268,817.

1952 (Pres.), Eisenhower, Rep., 518,045; Stevenson, Dem., 430,939.

1956 (Pres.), Eisenhower, Rep., 473,769; Stevenson, Dem., 385,581.

1960 (Pres.), Kennedy, Dem., 370,111; Nixon, Rep., 533,039.

1964 (Pres.), Johnson, Dem., 519,834; Goldwater, Rep. 412,665.

1968 (Pres.), Nixon, Rep., 449,697; Humphrey, Dem., 301,658; Wallace, 3d party, 191,731.

1972 (Pres.), Nixon, Rep., 759,025; McGovern, Dem., 247,147; Schmitz, American, 23,728.

Oregon

1932 (Pres.), Roosevelt, Dem., 213,871; Hoover, Rep., 136,019; Thomas, Soc., 15,450; Reynolds, Soc. Lab., 1,730; Foster, Com., 1,681.

1936 (Pres.), Roosevelt, Dem., 266,733; Landon, Rep., 122,706; Lemke, Union, 21,831; Thomas, Soc., 2,143; Aiken, Soc. Lab., 500; Browder, Com., 104; Colvin, Proh., 4.

1940 (Pres.), Roosevelt, Dem., 258,415; Willkie, Rep., 219,555; Aiken, Soc. Lab., 2,487; Thomas, Soc., 398; Browder, Com., 191; Babson, Proh., 154.

1944 (Pres.), Roosevelt, Dem., 248,635; Dewey, Rep., 225,365; Thomas, Soc., 3,785; Watson, Proh., 2,362.

1948 (Pres.), Truman, Dem., 243,147; Dewey, Rep., 260,904; Wallace, Prog., 14,978; Thomas, Soc., 5,051.

1952 (Pres.), Eisenhower, Rep., 420,815; Stevenson, Dem., 270,579; Hallinan, Ind., 3,665.

1956 (Pres.), Eisenhower, Rep., 406,393; Stevenson, Dem., 329,204.

1960 (Pres.), Kennedy, Dem., 367,402; Nixon, Rep., 408,060.

1964 (Pres.), Johnson, Dem., 501,017; Goldwater, Rep., 282,779; write-in, 2,509.

1968 (Pres.), Nixon, Rep., 408,433; Humphrey, Dem., 358,866; Wallace, 3d party, 49,683; write-in, McCarthy, 1,496; N. Rockefeller, 69; others, 1,075.

1972 (Pres.), Nixon, Rep., 486,686; McGovern, Dem., 392,760; Schmitz, American, 46,211; write-in, 2,289.

Pennsylvania

1932 (Pres.), Roosevelt, Dem., 1,295,948; Hoover, Rep., 1,453,540; Thomas, Soc., 91,119; Upshaw, Proh., 11,319; Foster, Com., 5,658; Cox, Jobless, 725; Reynolds, Indust., 659.

1936 (Pres.), Roosevelt, Dem., 2,353,788; Landon, Rep., 1,690,300; Lemke, Royal Oak, 67,467; Thomas, Soc., 14,375; Colvin, Proh., 6,691; Browder, Com., 4,060; Aiken, Ind., Lab., 1,424.

1940 (Pres.), Roosevelt, Dem., 2,171,035; Willkie, Rep., 1,889,848; Thomas, Soc., 10,967; Browder, Com., 4,519; Aiken, Ind. Gov., 1,518.

1944 (Pres.), Roosevelt, Dem., 1,940,479; Dewey, Rep., 1,835,054; Thomas, Soc., 11,721; Watson, Proh., 5,750; Teichert, Ind. Gov., 1,789.

1948 (Pres.), Truman, Dem., 1,752,426; Dewey, Rep., 1,902,197; Wallace, Prog., 55,161; Thomas, Soc., 11,-325; Watson, Proh., 10,338; Dobbs, Militant Workers, 2,133; Teichert, Ind. Gov., 1,461.

1952 (Pres.), Eisenhower, Rep., 2,415,789; Stevenson, Dem., 2,146,269; Hamblen, Proh., 8,771; Hallinan, Prog., 4,200; Hoopes, Soc., 2,684; Dobbs, Militant Workers, 1,502; Haas, Ind. Gov., 1,347; scattered, 155.

1956 (Pres.), Eisenhower, Rep., 2,585,252; Stevenson,

Dem., 1,981,769; Haas, Soc. Lab., 7,447; Dobbs, Militant Workers, 2,035.

1960 (Pres.), Kennedy, Dem., 2,556,282; Nixon, Rep., 2,439,956; Haas, Soc. Lab., 7,185; Dobbs, Soc. Workers, 2,678; scattering, 440.

1964 (Pres.), Johnson, Dem., 3,130,954; Goldwater, Rep., 1,673,657; DeBerry, Soc. Worker, 10,456; Haas, Soc. Labor, 5,092; scattering, 2,531.

1968 (Pres.), Nixon, Rep., 2,090,017; Humphrey, Dem., 2,259,405; Wallace, 3d party, 378,582; Blomen, Soc. Labor, 4,977; Halstead, Soc. Worker, 4,862; Gregory, 7,821; others, 2,264.

1972 (Pres.), Nixon, Rep., 2,714,521; McGovern, Dem., 1,796,951; Schmitz, American, 70,593; Jenness, Soc. Worker, 4,639; Hall, Communist, 2,686; others 2,715.

Rhode Island

1932 (Pres.), Roosevelt, Dem., 146,604; Hoover, Rep., 115,266; Thomas, Soc., 3,138; Foster, Com., 546; Reynolds, Soc. Lab., 433; Upshaw, Proh., 183.

1936 (Pres.), Roosevelt, Dem., 165,238; Landon, Rep., 125,031; Lemke, Union, 19,569; Aiken, Soc. Lab., 929; Browder, Com., 411.

1940 (Pres.), Roosevelt, Dem., 182,182; Willkie, Rep., 138,653; Browder, Com., 239; Babson, Proh., 74.

1944 (Pres.), Roosevelt, Dem., 175,356; Dewey, Rep., 123,487; Watson, Proh., 433.

1948 (Pres.), Truman, Dem., 188,736; Dewey, Rep., 135,787; Wallace, Prog., 2,619; Thomas, Soc., 429; Teichert, Soc. Lab., 131.

1952 (Pres.), Eisenhower, Rep., 210,935; Stevenson, Dem., 203,293; Hallinan, Prog., 187; Haas, Soc. Lab., 83.

1956 (Pres.), Eisenhower, Rep., 225,819; Stevenson, Dem., 161,790.

1960 (Pres.), Kennedy, Dem., 258,032; Nixon, Rep., 147,502.

1964 (Pres.), Johnson, Dem., 315,463; Goldwater, Rep., 74,615.

1968 (Pres.), Nixon, Rep., 122,359; Humphrey, Dem., 246,518; Wallace, 3d party, 15,678; Halstead, Soc. Worker, 383.

1972 (Pres.), Nixon, Rep., 220,383; McGovern, Dem., 194,645; Jenness, Soc. Worker, 729.

South Carolina

1932 (Pres.), Roosevelt, Dem., 102,347; Hoover, Rep., 1,978; Thomas, Soc., 82.

1936 (Pres.), Roosevelt, Dem., 113,791; Landon, Rep., Tolbert faction 953, Hambright faction 693, total, 1,646.

1940 (Pres.), Roosevelt, Dem., 95,470; Willkie, Rep., 1,727.

1944 (Pres.), Roosevelt, Dem., 90,601; Dewey, Rep., 4,547; Southern Democrats, 7,799; Watson, Proh., 365; Rep. Tolbert faction, 63.

1948 (Pres.), Thurmond, States' Rights, 102,607; Truman, Dem., 34,423; Dewey, Rep., 5,386; Wallace, Prog., 154; Thomas, Soc., 1.

1952 (Pres.), Eisenhower ran on two tickets. Under State law vote cast for two Eisenhower slates of electors could not be combined. Eisenhower, Ind., 158,289; Rep., 9,793; total 168,082; Stevenson, Dem., 173,004; Hamblen, Proh., 1.

1956 (Pres.), Stevenson, Dem., 136,372; Byrd., Ind., 88,509; Eisenhower, Rep., 75,700; Andrews, Ind., 2.

1960 (Pres.), Kennedy, Dem., 198,129; Nixon, Rep., 188,558; write-in, 1.

1964 (Pres.), Johnson, Dem., 215,700; Goldwater, Rep., 309,048; write-ins: Nixon, 1; Wallace, 5; Powell, 1; Thurmond, 1.

1968 (Pres.), Nixon, Rep., 254,062; Humphrey, Dem., 197,486; Wallace, 3d party, 215,430.

1972 (Pres.), Nixon, Rep., 477,044; McGovern, Dem., 184,559, United Citizens, 2,265; Schmitz, American, 10,075; write-in, 17.

South Dakota

1932 (Pres.), Roosevelt, Dem., 183,515; Hoover, Rep., 99,212; Harvey, Lib., 3,333; Thomas, Soc., 1,551;

Upshaw, Proh., 463; Foster, Com., 364.
1936 (Pres.), Roosevelt, Dem., 160,137; Landon, Rep., 125,977; Lemke, Union, 10,338.
1940 (Pres.), Roosevelt, Dem., 131,862; Willkie, Rep., 177,065.
1944 (Pres.), Roosevelt, Dem., 96,711; Dewey, Rep., 135,365.
1948 (Pres.), Truman, Dem., 117,653; Dewey, Rep., 129,651; Wallace, Prog., 2,801.
1952 (Pres.), Eisenhower, Rep., 203,857; Stevenson, Dem., 90,426.
1956 (Pres.), Eisenhower, Rep., 171,569; Stevenson, Dem., 122,288.
1960 (Pres.), Kennedy, Dem., 128,070; Nixon, Rep., 178,417.
1964 (Pres.), Johnson, Dem., 163,010; Goldwater, Rep., 130,108.
1968 (Pres.), Nixon, Rep., 149,841; Humphrey, Dem., 118,023; Wallace, 3d party, 13,400.
1972 (Pres.), Nixon, Rep., 166,476; McGovern, Dem., 139,945; Jenness, Soc. Worker, 994.

Tennessee

1932 (Pres.), Roosevelt, Dem., 259,817; Hoover, Rep., 126,806; Upshaw, Proh., 1,995; Thomas, Soc., 1,786; Foster, Com., 234.
1936 (Pres.), Roosevelt, Dem., 327,083; Landon, Rep., 146,516; Thomas, Soc., 685; Colvin, Proh.', 632; Browder, Com., 319; Lemke, Union, 296.
1940 (Pres.), Roosevelt, Dem., 351,601; Willkie, Rep., 169,153; Babson, Proh., 1,606; Thomas, Soc., 463.
1944 (Pres.), Roosevelt, Dem., 308,707; Dewey, Rep., 200,311; Watson, Proh., 882; Thomas, Soc., 892.
1948 (Pres.), Truman, Dem., 270,402; Dewey, Rep., 202,914; Thurmond, States' Rights, 73,815; Wallace, Prog., 1,864; Thomas, Soc., 1,288.
1952 (Pres.), Eisenhower, Rep., 446,147; Stevenson, Dem., 443,710; Hamblen, Proh., 1,432; Hallinan, Prog., 885; MacArthur, Christian Nationalist, 379.
1956 (Pres.), Eisenhower, Rep., 462,288; Stevenson, Dem., 456,507; Andrews, Ind., 19,820; Holtwick, Proh., 789.
1960 (Pres.), Kennedy, Dem., 481,453; Nixon, Rep., 556,577; Faubus, States' Rights, 11,304; Decker, Proh., 2,458.
1964 (Pres.), Johnson, Dem., 635,047; Goldwater, Rep., 508,965; write-in, 34.
1968 (Pres.), Nixon, Rep., 472,592; Humphrey, Dem., 351,233; Wallace, 3d party, 424,792.
1972 (Pres.), Nixon, Rep., 813,147; McGovern, Dem., 357,293; Schmitz, American, 30,373; write-in. 369.

Texas

1924 (Pres.), Davis, Dem., 484,605; Coolidge, Rep., 130,023; LaFollette, Prog., 42,881.
1928 (Pres.), Hoover, Rep., 367,036; Smith, Dem., 341,032; Thomas, Soc., 722; Foster, Com., 209.
1932 (Pres.), Roosevelt, Dem., 760,348; Hoover, Rep., 97,959; Thomas, Soc., 4,450; Harvey, Lib., 324; Foster, Com., 207; Jackson Party, 104.
1936 (Pres.), Roosevelt, Dem., 734,485; Landon, Rep., 103,874; Lemke, Union, 3,281; Thomas, Soc., 1,075; Colvin, Proh., 514; Browder, Com., 253.
1940 (Pres.), Roosevelt, Dem., 840,151; Willkie, Rep., 199,152; Babson, Proh., 925; Thomas, Soc., 728; Browder, Com., 212.
1944 (Pres.), Roosevelt, Dem., 821,605; Dewey, Rep., 191,425; Texas Regulars, 135,439; Watson, Proh., 1,017; Thomas, Soc., 594; America First, 250.
1948 (Pres.), Truman, Dem., 750,700; Dewey, Rep., 282,240; Thurmond, States' Rights. 106,909; Wallace, Prog., 3,764; Watson, Proh., 2,758; Thomas, Soc., 874.
1952 (Pres.), Eisenhower, Rep., 1,102,878; Stevenson, Dem., 969,228; Hamblen, Proh., 1,983; MacArthur, Christian Nationalist, 833; MacArthur, Constitution, 730; Hallinan, Prog., 294.
1956 (Pres.), Eisenhower, Rep., 1,080,619; Stevenson, Dem., 859,958; Andrews, Ind., 14,591.
1960 (Pres.), Kennedy, Dem., 1,167,932; Nixon, Rep.,

1,121,699; Sullivan, Constitution, 18,169; Decker, Proh., 3,870; write-in, 15.
1964 (Pres.), Johnson, Dem., 1,663,185; Goldwater, Rep., 958,566; Lightburn, Constitution, 5,060.
1968 (Pres.), Nixon, Rep., 1,227,844; Humphrey, Dem., 1,266,804; Wallace, 3d party, 584,269; write-in, 489.
1972 (Pres.), Nixon, Rep., 2,298,896; McGovern, Dem., 1,154,289; Schmitz, American, 6,039; Jenness, Soc. Worker, 8,664; others, 3,393.

Utah

1924 (Pres.), Coolidge, Rep., 77,327; Davis, Dem., 47,-001; LaFollette, Prog., 33,662.
1928 (Pres.), Hoover, Rep., 94,618; Smith, Dem., 80,-985; Thomas, Soc., 954; Foster, Com., 47.
1932 (Pres.), Roosevelt, Dem., 116,750; Hoover, Rep., 84,795; Thomas, Soc., 4,087; Foster, Com., 947.
1936 (Pres.), Roosevelt, Dem., 150,246; Landon, Rep., 64,555; Lemke, Union, 1,121; Thomas, Soc., 432; Browder, Com., 280; Colvin, Proh., 43.
1940 (Pres.), Roosevelt, Dem., 154,277; Willkie, Rep., 93,151; Thomas, Soc., 200; Browder, Com., 191.
1944 (Pres.), Roosevelt, Dem., 150,088; Dewey, Rep. 97,891; Thomas, Soc., 340.
1948 (Pres.), Truman, Dem., 149,151; Dewey, Rep., 124,402; Wallace, Prog., 2,679; Dobbs, Soc. Workers, 73.
1952 (Pres.), Eisenhower, Rep., 194,190; Stevenson, Dem., 135,364.
1956 (Pres.), Eisenhower, Rep., 215,631; Stevenson, Dem., 118,364.
1960 (Pres.), Kennedy, Dem., 169,248; Nixon, Rep., 205,361; Dobbs, Soc. Workers, 100.
1964 (Pres.), Johnson, Dem., 219,628; Goldwater, Rep., 181,785.
1968 (Pres.), Nixon, Rep., 238,728; Humphrey, Dem., 156,665; Wallace, 3d party, 26,906; Halstead, Soc. Worker, 89; Peace and Freedom, 180.
1972 (Pres.), Nixon, Rep., 323,643; McGovern, Dem., 126,284; Schmitz, American, 28,549.

Vermont

1932 (Pres.), Roosevelt, Dem., 56,266; Hoover, Rep., 78,984; Thomas, Soc., 1,533; Foster, Com., 195.
1936 (Pres.), Landon, Rep., 81,023; Roosevelt, Dem., 62,124; Browder, Com., 405.
1940 (Pres.), Roosevelt, Dem., 64,269; Willkie, Rep., 78,371; Browder, Com., 411.
1944 (Pres.), Roosevelt, Dem., 53,820; Dewey, Rep., 71,527.
1948 (Pres.), Truman, Dem., 45,557; Dewey, Rep., 75,-926; Wallace, Prog., 1,279; Thomas, Soc., 585.
1952 (Pres.), Eisenhower, Rep., 109,717; Stevenson, Dem., 43,355; Hallinan, Prog., 282; Hoopes, Soc., 185.
1956 (Pres.), Eisenhower, Rep., 110,390; Stevenson, Dem., 42,549; scattered, 39.
1960 (Pres.), Kennedy, Dem., 69,186; Nixon, Rep., 98,131.
1964 (Pres.), Johnson, Dem., 107,674; Goldwater, Rep., 54,868.
1968 (Pres.), Nixon, Rep., 85,142; Humphrey, Dem., 70,255; Wallace, 3d party, 5,104; Halstead, Soc. Worker, 295; Gregory, New Party, 579.
1972 (Pres.), Nixon, Rep., 117,149; McGovern, Dem., 68,147; Spock, Liberty Union, 1,010; Jenness, Soc. Worker, 296; scattered, 318.

Virginia

1932 (Pres.), Roosevelt, Dem., 203,979; Hoover, Rep., 89,637; Thomas, Soc., 2,382; Upshaw, Proh., 1,843; Foster, Com., 86; Cox, Ind., 15.
1936 (Pres.), Roosevelt, Dem., 234,980; Landon, Rep., 98,366; Colvin, Proh., 594; Thomas, Soc., 313; Lemke, Union, 233; Browder, Com., 98.
1940 (Pres.), Roosevelt, Dem., 235,961; Willkie, Rep., 109,363; Babson, Proh., 882; Thomas, Soc., 282; Browder, Com., 71; Aiken, Soc. Lab., 48.
1944 (Pres.), Roosevelt, Dem., 242,276; Dewey, Rep.,

145,243; Watson, Proh., 459; Thomas, Soc., 417; Teichert, Soc. Lab., 90.
1948 (Pres.), Truman, Dem., 200,786; Dewey, Rep., 172,070; Thurmond, States' Rights, 43,393; Wallace, Prog., 2,047; Thomas, Soc., 726; Teichert, Soc. Lab., 234.
1952 (Pres.), Eisenhower, Rep., 349,037; Stevenson, Dem., 268,677; Haas, Soc. Lab., 1,160; Hoopes, Social Dem., 504; Hallinan, Prog., 311.
1956 (Pres.), Eisenhower, Rep., 386,459; Stevenson, Dem., 267,760; Andrews, States' Rights, 42,964; Hoopes, Soc. Dem., 444; Haas, Soc. Lab., 351.
1960 (Pres.), Kennedy, Dem., 362,327; Nixon, Rep., 404,521; Coiner, Conservative, 4,204; Haas, Soc. Lab., 397.
1964 (Pres.), Johnson, Dem., 558,038; Goldwater, Rep., 481,334; Haas, Soc. Lab., 2,895.
1968 (Pres.), Nixon, Rep., 590,319; Humphrey, Dem., ·442,387; Wallace, 3d party, *320,272; Blomen, Soc. Labor, 4,671; Munn, Prohibition, 601; Gregory, Peace and Freedom, 1,680.
*10,561 votes for Wallace were omitted in the count.
1972 (Pres.), Nixon, Rep., 988,493; McGovern, Dem., 438,887; Schmitz, American, 19,721; Fisher, Soc. Labor, 9,918.

Washington

1932 (Pres.), Roosevelt, Dem., 353,260; Hoover, Rep., 208,645; Harvey, Lib., 30,308; Thomas, Soc., 17,080; Foster, Com., 2,972; Upshaw, Proh., 1,540; Reynolds, Soc. Lab., 1,009.
1936 (Pres.), Roosevelt, Dem., 459,579; Landon, Rep., 206,892; Lemke, Union, 17,463; Thomas, Soc., 3,496; Browder, Com., 1,907; Pellsy, Christian, 1,598; Colvin, Proh., 1,041; Aiken, Soc. Lab., 362.
1940 (Pres.), Roosevelt, Dem., 462,145; Willkie, Rep., 322,123; Thomas, Soc., 4,586; Browder, Com., 2,626; Babson, Proh., 1,686; Aiken, Soc. Lab., 667.
1944 (Pres.), Roosevelt, Dem., 486,774; Dewey, Rep., 361,689; Thomas, Soc., 3,824; Watson, Proh., 2,396; Teichert, Soc. Lab., 1,645.
1948 (Pres.), Truman, Dem., 476,165; Dewey, Rep., 386,315; Wallace, Prog., 31,692; Watson, Proh., 6,117; Thomas, Soc., 3,534; Teichert, Soc. Lab., 1,133; Dobbs, Soc. Workers, 103.
1952 (Pres.), Eisenhower, Rep., 599,107; Stevenson, Dem., 492,845; MacArthur, Christian Nationalist, 7,290; Hallinan, Prog., 2,460; Haas, Soc. Lab., 633; Hoopes, Soc., 254; Dobbs, Soc. Workers, 119.
1956 (Pres.), Eisenhower, Rep., 620,430; Stevenson, Dem., 523,002; Haas, Soc. Lab., 7,457.
1960 (Pres.), Kennedy, Dem., 599,298; Nixon, Rep., 629,273; Haas, Soc. Lab., 10,895; Curtis Constitution, 1,401; Dobbs, Soc. Workers, 705.
1964 (Pres.), Johnson, Dem., 779,699; Goldwater, Rep., 470,366; Haas, Soc. Labor, 7,772; DeBerry, Freedom Soc., 537.
1968 (Pres.), Nixon, Rep., 588,510; Humphrey, Dem., 616,037; Wallace, 3d party, 96,990; Blomen, Soc. Labor, 488; Cleaver, Peace and Freedom, 1,609; Halstead, Soc. Worker, 270; Mitchell, Free Ballot, 377.
1972 (Pres.), Nixon, Rep., 837,135; McGovern, Dem., 568,334; Schmitz, American, 58,906; Spock, Ind., 2,644; Fisher, Soc. Labor, 1,102; Jenness, Soc. Worker, 623; Hall, Communist, 566; Hospers, Libertarian, 1,537.

West Virginia

1932 (Pres.), Roosevelt, Dem., 405,124; Hoover, Rep., 330,731; Thomas, Soc., 5,133; Upshaw, Proh., 2,342; Foster, Com., 444.
1936 (Pres.), Roosevelt, Dem., 502,582; Landon, Rep., 325,358; Colvin, Proh., 1,173; Thomas, Soc., 832.
1940 (Pres.), Roosevelt, Dem., 495,662; Willkie, Rep., 372,414.
1944 (Pres.), Roosevelt, Dem., 392,777; Dewey, Rep., 322,819.

1948 (Pres.), Truman, Dem., 429,188; Dewey, Rep., 316,251; Wallace, Prog., 3,311.
1952 (Pres.), Eisenhower, Rep., 419,970; Stevenson, Dem., 453,578.
1956 (Pres.), Eisenhower, Rep., 449,297; Stevenson, Dem., 381,534.
1960 (Pres.), Kennedy, Dem., 441,786; Nixon, Rep., 395,995.
1964 (Pres.), Johnson, Dem., 538,087; Goldwater, Rep., 253,953.
1968 (Pres.), Nixon, Rep., 307,555; Humphrey, Dem., ,374,091; Wallace, 3d party, 72,560.
1972 (Pres.), Nixon, Rep., 484,964; McGovern, Dem., 277,435.

Wisconsin

1932 (Pres.), Roosevelt, Dem., 707,410; Hoover, Rep., 347,741; Thomas, Soc., 53,379; Foster, Com., 3,112; Upshaw, Proh., 2,672; Reynolds, Soc., Lab., 494.
1936 (Pres.), Roosevelt, Dem., 802,984; Landon, Rep., 380,828; Lemke, Union, 60,297; Thomas, Soc., 10,- 626; Browder, Com., 2,197; Colvin, Proh., 1,071; Aiken, Soc. Lab., 557.
1940 (Pres.), Roosevelt, Dem., 704,821; Willkie, Rep., 679,260; Thomas, Soc., 15,071; Browder, Com., 2,394; Babson, Proh., 2,148; Aiken, Soc. Lab., 1,882.
1944 (Pres.), Roosevelt, Dem., 650,413; Dewey, Rep., 674,532; Thomas, Soc., 13,205; Teichert, Soc. Lab., 1,002.
1948 (Pres.), Truman, Dem., 647,310; Dewey, Rep., 590,959; Wallace, Prog., 25,282; Thomas, Soc., 12,- 547; Teichert, Soc. Lab., 399; Dobbs, Soc. Workers, 303.
1952 (Pres.), Eisenhower, Rep., 979,744; Stevenson, Dem., 622,175; Hallinan, Ind., 2,174; Dobbs, Ind., 1,350; Hoopes, Ind., 1,157; Haas, Ind., 770.
1956 (Pres.), Eisenhower, Rep., 954,844; Stevenson, Dem., 586,768; Andrews, Ind., 6,918; Hoopes, Soc., 754; Haas, Soc. Lab., 710; Dobbs, Soc. Workers, 564.
1960 (Pres.), Kennedy, Dem., 830,805; Nixon, Rep., 895,175; Dobbs, Soc. Workers, 1,792; Haas, Soc. Lab., 1,310.
1964 (Pres.), Johnson, Dem., 1,050,424; Goldwater, Rep., 638,495; DeBerry, Soc. Worker, 1,692; Haas, Soc. Lab., 1,204.
1968 (Pres.), Nixon, Rep., 809,997; Humphrey, Dem., 748,804; Wallace, 3d party, 127,835; Blomen, Soc. Labor, 1,338; Halstead, Soc. Worker, 1,222; scattered, 2,342.
1972 (Pres.), Nixon, Rep., 989,430; McGovern, Dem., 810,174; Schmitz, American, 47,525; Spock, Ind., 2,701; Fisher, Soc. Labor, 998; Hall, Communist, 663; Reed, Ind., 506; scattered, 893.

Wyoming

1932 (Pres.), Roosevelt, Dem., 54,370; Hoover, Rep., 39,583; Thomas, Soc. 2,829; Foster, Com., 180.
1936 (Pres.), Roosevelt, Dem., 62,624; Landon, Rep., 38,739; Lemke, Union, 1,653; Thomas, Soc., 200; Browder, Com., 91; Colvin, Proh., 75.
1940 (Pres.), Roosevelt, Dem., 59,287; Willkie, Rep., 52,633; Babson, Proh., 172; Thomas, Soc., 148.
1944 (Pres.), Roosevelt, Dem., 49,419; Dewey, Rep., 51,921.
1948 (Pres.), Truman, Dem., 52,354; Dewey, Rep., 47,- 947; Wallace, Prog., 931; Thomas, Soc., 137; Teichert, Soc. Lab., 56.
1952 (Pres.), Eisenhower, Rep., 81,047; Stevenson, Dem., 47,934; Hamblen, Proh., 194; Hoopes, Soc., 40; Haas, Soc. Lab., 36.
1956 (Pres.), Eisenhower, Rep., 74,573; Stevenson, Dem., 49,554.
1960 (Pres.), Kennedy, Dem., 63,331; Nixon, Rep., 77,451.
1964 (Pres.), Johnson, Dem., 80,718; Goldwater, Rep., 61,998.
1968 (Pres.), Nixon, Rep., 70,927; Humphrey, Dem., 45,173; Wallace, 3d party, 11,105.
1972 (Pres.), Nixon, Rep., 100,464; McGovern, Dem., 44,358; Schmitz, American, 748.

United States Government

The Ford Administration
As of July 20, 1975

Terms of office of the President and Vice President, from Jan. 20, 1973, to Jan. 20, 1977. No person may be elected President of the United States for more than two four-year terms.

PRESIDENT — Gerald R. Ford of Michigan. Receives salary of $200,000 a year taxable, and in addition an expense allowance, also taxable, of $50,000 to assist in defraying expenses resulting from his official duties. Also there may be expended not exceeding $100,000, non-taxable, a year for travel expenses and official entertainment. Congress has provided lifetime pensions of $60,000 a year, free mailing privileges, free office space, and up to $90,000 a year for office help for ex-Presidents and $20,000 annually for their widows.

VICE PRESIDENT — Nelson A. Rockefeller, N. Y., salary $62,500 a year and $10,000 for expenses, all of which is taxable.

For succession to presidency, see Succession in Index.

The Cabinet
(Salaries $60,000 each)

Secretary of State — Henry A. Kissinger, Wash., D.C.
Secretary of Treasury — William E. Simon, N.J.
Secretary of Defense — James R. Schlesinger, Va.
Attorney General — Edward H. Levi, Ill.
Secretary of Interior — Stanley K. Hathaway, Wy.
Secretary of Agriculture — Earl L. Butz, Ind.
Secretary of Commerce — Rogers C. B. Morton, Md.
Secretary of Labor — John T. Dunlop, Cal.
Secretary of Health, Education and Welfare — Forrest D. Mathews, Ala., designate.
Secretary of Housing and Urban Development — Carla Anderson Hills, Cal.
Secretary of Transportation — William T. Coleman, Pa.

The White House Staff
1600 Pennsylvania Ave. NW 20500

Counselor to the President — Robert Hartmann.
Assistant to the President — Donald Rumsfeld.
Press Secretary to the President — Ronald H. Nessen.
Counsel to the President — Philip Buchen.
Personal Assistant to the President — Mildred Leonard.
Press Secretary to the First Lady — Sheila Weidenfeld.
Physician to the President — Rear Adm. William M. Lukash, USN.
Chief Usher — Rex W. Scouten.

Executive Agencies

National Security Council — Assistant to the President for Natl. Security Affairs — Henry A. Kissinger.
Council of Economic Advisers — Alan Greenspan.
Council on Environmental Quality — Dr. Russell W. Peterson, chairman.
Central Intelligence Agency — William Colby, director.
Office of Management and Budget — James T. Lynn, director.
Special Representative for Trade Negotiations — Frederick B. Dent.

Department of State
2201 C St. NW 20520

Secretary of State — Henry A. Kissinger.
Deputy Secretary — Robert S. Ingersoll.
Under Sec. for Political Affairs — Joseph J. Sisco.
Under Sec. for Security Assistance — Carlisle E. Maw.
Deputy Under Secretaries — Charles W. Robinson (for economic affairs), Lawrence S. Eagleburger (for management).
Ambassadors at Large — U. Alexis Johnson, Ellsworth Bunker, Robert J. McCloskey.
Counselor — Helmut Sonnenfeldt.
Legal Advisor — Monroe Leigh.
Director of Policy Planning Staff — Winston Lord.
Assistant Secretaries for:
Administration — John M. Thomas.
African Affairs — Edward W. Mulcahy (acting).

Congressional Relations — Robert J. McCloskey.
Economic Affairs — Thomas O. Enders.
Educational & Cultural Affairs — John Richardson.
European Affairs — Arthur A. Hartman.
East Asian & Pacific Affairs — Philip C. Habib.
Internatl. Organization Affairs — William B. Buffum.
Inter-American Affairs — William D. Rogers.
Near-Eastern & S. Asian Affairs — Alfred L. Atherton Jr.
Public Affairs — Carol C. Laise.
Bureau of Security & Consular Affairs — Leonard F. Walentynowicz, administrator.
Inspector General, Foreign Assistance — Webster B. Todd Jr.
Chief of Protocol — Ambassador Henry E. Catto.
Dir. General, Foreign Service — Nathaniel Davis.
Dir. of Intelligence & Research — William G. Hyland.
Bureau of Oceans and Internat'l. Environmental and Scientific Affairs — Assistant Sec. Dixy Lee Ray.
Dir. of Politico-Military Affairs — George S. Vest.
Insp. Gen. Foreign Service — vacant.
Foreign Service Inst. — Howard E. Sollenberger, director.
Agency for Internatl. Development — Daniel Parker, administrator.
Advisory Committee on Voluntary Foreign Aid — Margaret Hickey.
Action — Michael P. Balzano.
U.S. Rep. to the UN and Rep. in the Security Council — Daniel P. Moynihan, ambassador.

Treasury Department
15th St. & Pennsylvania Ave. NW 20220

Secretary of the Treasury — William E. Simon.
Deputy Sec. of the Treasury — Stephen S. Gardner.
Under Sec. for Monetary Affairs — vacant.
Under Secretary — Edward C. Schmults.
General Counsel — Richard Albrecht.
Assistant Secretaries: — Frederic W. Hickman, Charles Cooper, David R. Macdonald, Warren F. Brecht, John M. Hennessy, John K. Carlock, Gerald L. Parsky, Frederick L. Webber, Sidney L. Jones.
Special Assistants to the Secretary: — James N. Sites (public affairs), William N. Morell (national security).
Bureaus:
Alcohol, Tobacco and Firearms — Rex D. Davis, director.
Consolidated Federal Law Enforcement Training Center — William B. Butler, director.
Comptroller of the Currency — James E. Smith.
Customs — Vernon D. Acree, commissioner.
Engraving & Printing — James A. Conlon, director.
Internal Revenue Service — Donald C. Alexander, commissioner.
Mint — Mrs. Mary T. Brooks, director.
Public Debt — H. J. Hintgen, commissioner.
Treasurer of the U. S. — Francine I. Neff.
U. S. Savings Bonds — Francine I. Neff, national director.
U. S. Secret Service — H. Stuart Knight, director.

Department of Defense
The Pentagon 20301

Secretary of Defense — James R. Schlesinger.
Deputy Sec. of Defense — William P. Clements Jr.
Dir. of Def. Research and Engineering — Dr. Malcolm R. Currie.
Asst. Secretaries of Defense:
Comptroller — Terrence E. McClary.
Health and Environment — James R. Cowan, M.D.
Installations & Logistics — vacant.
Intelligence — Albert C. Hall.
Internatl. Security — Robert Ellsworth.
Legislative Affairs — John M. Maury.
Manpower & Reserve — William K. Brehm.
Program Analysis & Evaluation — Leonard Sullivan Jr.
Public Affairs — Joseph Laitin.
General Counsel — Martin R. Hoffmann.
Joint Chiefs of Staff, chairman — Gen. George S. Brown, USAF.

Department of the Army
The Pentagon 20310

Secretary of the Army — Martin R. Hoffmann, designate.
Under Secretary — Norman R. Augustine.
Assistant Secretaries for:
  Finance Management — Hadlai A. Hull.
  Civil Works — Victor V. Veysey.
  Installations & Logistics — Harold L. Browman.
  Research & Development — vacant.
  Manpower & Reserve Affairs — Donald G. Brotzman.
Chief of Public Information — Maj. Gen. L. Gordon Hill Jr.
Chief of Staff — Gen. Fred C. Weyand.
Comptroller of the Army — Lt. Gen. John A. Kjellstrom.
Surgeon General — Lt. Gen. Richard R. Taylor.
Adjutant General and Auditor — Maj. Gen. Verne L. Bowers
Inspector General — Lt. Gen. Herron N. Maples.
Judge Advocate General — Brig. Gen. Wilton B. Persons Jr.
Deputy Chiefs of Staff:
  Logistics — Lt. Gen. Fred Kornet Jr.
  Operations & Plans — Lt. Gen. D. H. Cowles.
  Research, Development, Acquisition — Lt. Gen. Howard H. Cooksey.
  Intelligence — Maj. Gen. Harold R. Aaron.
Chief of Engineers — Lt. Gen. W.C. Gribble Jr.
U.S. Women's Army Corps. — Brig. Gen. Mildred C. Bailey.
Nat. Guard Bureau — Maj. Gen. LaVern E. Weber.
Chief Army Reserve — Maj. Gen. Henry Mohr.
U. S. Army Materiel Command — Gen. John R. Deane Jr.
U. S. Army Forces Command — Gen. Bernard W. Rogers.
U.S. Army Training and Doctrine Command — Gen. William E. DePuy.
Commanding Generals, U. S. Armies:
  1st, Fort Meade Md. — Lt. Gen. James G. Kalergis.
  5th, Ft. Sam Houston Tex. — Lt. Gen. Allen M. Burdette.
  6th Presidio of San Francisco Cal. — Lt. Gen. Edward M. Flanagan Jr.
  Military Dist. of Washington—Maj. Gen. Ronald J. Fairfield.

Department of the Navy
The Pentagon 20360

Secretary of the Navy — J. William Middendorf 2d.
Under Secretary — D. S. Potter.
Assistant Secretaries for:
  Financial Management — Gary D. Penisten.
  Installations & Logistics — Jack L. Bowers.
  Manpower & Reserve Affairs — Joseph T. McCullen Jr..
  Research & Development — H. Tyler Marcy.
Judge Advocate General — R. Adm. H. B. Robertson Jr.
Chief of Naval Operations — Adm. James L. Holloway 3d.
Chief of Naval Materiel — Adm. I. C. Kidd Jr.
Bureau Chiefs:
  Medicine & Surgery — V. Adm. Donald Custis.
  Naval Personnel — V. Adm. J. D. Watkins.
Military Sealift Command — R. Adm. Sam H. Moore.
U. S. Marine Corps:
  Commandant — Gen. Louis H. Wilson.
  Asst. Commandant — Gen. Samuel Jaskilka.
  Chief of Staff — Lt. Gen. Leslie E. Brown.
Dir. of Women Marines — Col. Margaret A. Brewer.
Commandants, Naval Districts:
  1st, Boston — R. Adm. Roy D. Snyder Jr.
  3d, New York — R. Adm. Frank D. Guest.
  4th, Philadelphia — R. Adm. Joseph L. Coleman.
  5th, Norfolk — R. Adm. Richard E. Rumble.
  6th, Charleston — R. Adm. Julian T. Burke Jr.
  8th New Orleans — R. Adm. George L. Cassel.
  9th, Great Lakes — R. Adm. Warren H. O'Neil.
  10th, Roosevelt Roads — R. Adm. James D. Ramage.
  11th, San Diego — R. Adm. Fillmore B. Gilkeson.
  12th, San Francisco — R. Adm. Martin D. Carmody.
  13th, Seattle — R. Adm. Lando W. Zech Jr.
  14th, San Francisco — R. Adm. Richard A. Paddock.
  15th, Balboa — R. Adm. Richard H. Blount.
Naval District, Wash., D. C. — R. Adm. Arthur G. Esch.

Department of the Air Force
The Pentagon 20330

Secretary of the Air Force — Dr. John L. McLucas.
Under Secretary of the Air Force — James W. Plummer.
Deputy Under Secretary for Space Systems — Dr. Charles W. Cook.
Assistant Secretaries for:

Financial Management — vacant.
Research and Development — Walter B. LaBerge.
Installations and Logistics — Frank A. Shrontz.
Manpower and Reserve Affairs — David P. Taylor.
General Counsel — Jack L. Stempler.
Director of Information — Maj. Gen. Guy E. Hairston Jr.
Director of Space Systems — Col. Harold P. Wheeler.
Chief of Staff — Gen. David C. Jones.
Vice Chief of Staff — Gen. William V. McBride.
Chief, National Guard Bureau — Maj. Gen. LaVern Weber (U. S. Army).
Chief of Air Force Reserves — Maj. Gen. William Lyon.
Surgeon General — Lt. Gen. George E. Schafer.
Judge Advocate — Maj. Gen. H. R. Vague.
Inspector General — Lt. Gen. Donald G. Nunn.
Deputy Chiefs of Staff:
  Systems and Logistics — Lt. Gen. Robert E. Hails.
  Programs and Resources — Lt. Gen. James A. Hill.
  Personnel — Lt. Gen. (nominee) Kenneth L. Tallman
  Research and Development — Lt. Gen. (nominee) Alton D. Slay.
  Plans and Operations — Lt. Gen. John W. Pauly.
Major Air Commands:
  NORAD/ADCOM — Gen. (nominee) Daniel James Jr.
  AF Logistics Command — Gen. (nominee) Felix M. Rogers.
  AF Systems Command — Gen. (nominee) William J. Evans.
  Air Training Command — Lt. Gen. John W. Roberts
  Air University — Lt. Gen. (nominee) Raymond B. Furlong.
  Headquarters Command — Brig. Gen. William C. Norris.
  Military Airlift Command — Gen. Paul K. Carlton.
  Strategic Air Command — Gen. Russell E. Dougherty
  Tactical Air Command — Gen. Robert J. Dixon.
  Alaskan Air Command — Lt. Gen. James E. Hill.
  USAF Southern Command — Maj. Gen. James M. Breedlove.
  Pacific Air Forces — Gen. Louis L. Wilson Jr.
  USAF Europe — Gen. Richard H. Ellis.
  USAF Security Service — Col. Kenneth D. Burns.
  AF Communications Service — Brig. Gen. Rupert H. Burris.

Department of Justice
Constitution Ave. & 10th St. NW 20530

Attorney General — Edward H. Levi.
Deputy Attorney General — Laurence H. Silberman.
Solicitor General — Robert H. Bork.
Assistant Attorneys General:
  Antitrust Division — Thomas E. Kauper.
  Civil Division — Rex E. Lee.
  Civil Rights Division — J. Stanley Pottinger.
  Criminal Division — vacant.
  Drug Enforcement Admin. — Henry Dogin, acting admin.
  Land & Natural Resources Division — Wallace Johnson.
  Legal Counsel — Antonin Scalia.
  Office of Legislative Affairs — A. Mitchell McConnell Jr. (acting).
  Office of Management & Finance — Glen E. Pommerening.
  Public Information — Robert Havel, director.
  Tax Division — Scott P. Crampton.
Fed. Bureau of Investigation — Clarence M. Kelley.
Board of Immigration Appeals — David L. Mil-Hollan, chairman.
Board of Parole — Maurice H. Sigler.
Bureau of Prisons — Norman A. Carlson.
Community Relations Ser. — Benjamin Holman, dir.
Immigration and Naturalization Service — Leonard F. Chapman Jr., commissioner.
Law Enforcement Assistance Admin. — Richard W. Velde.
Pardon Attorney — Lawrence M. Traylor.

Department of the Interior
C St. between 18th & 19th Sts. NW 20240

Secretary of the Interior — Stanley K. Hathaway.
Under Secretary — vacant.
Assistant Secretaries for:
  Fish, Wildlife and Parks — Nathaniel P. Reed.
  Energy & Minerals — Jack W. Carlson.
  Land and Water Resources — Jack O. Horton.
  Program Development & Budget — Royston C. Hughes.
  Management — James T. Clarke.
  Congressional & Legislative Affairs — John H. Kyl.

Commissioner of Indian Affairs — Morris Thompson.
Bureau of Land Management — Curtis J. Berklund.
Bureau of Mines — Dr. Thomas V. Falkie.
Bureau of Outdoor Recreation — James W. Watt.
Bureau of Reclamation — Gilbert G. Stamm.
Bureau of Sport Fisheries & Wildlife — Lynn Greenwalt.
Geological Survey — V.E. McKelvey.
National Park Service — Gary E. Everhardt.
Office of Communications — Samuel Marler, director designate.
Office of Water Research and Technology — Warren Hall, director.
Office of Solicitor — Kent Frizzell.

Department of Agriculture
14th St. & Independence Ave. SW 20250

Secretary of Agriculture — Earl L. Butz.
Under Secretary — J. Phil Campbell.
Conservation, Research, & Education — Robert W. Long.
Internatl. Affairs & Commodity Programs — vacant.
Marketing & Consumer Services — Richard L. Feltner.
Rural Development — William Erwin.
Agricultural Economics — Don Paarlberg.
Public Affairs — vacant.
Intergovernmental Affairs — R. B. Wilson.
Agric. Mktg. Service — vacant.
Agric. Stabilization & Conserv. Service — Kenneth Frick, administrator.
Animal & Plant Health Inspection Ser. — F. J. Mulhern.
Cooperative State Research Ser. — R. L. Lovvorn.
Econ. Research Service — Quentin M. West, admin.
Extension Service — Edward Kirby, admin.
Farmer Coop. Service — Ronald D. Knutson, admin.
Farmers Home Admin. — Frank B. Elliott, admin.
Fed. Crop Insurance Corp. — Melvin R. Peterson.
Food & Nutrition Ser. — Edward J. Hekman, admin.
Foreign Agric. Service — David L. Hume.
Forest Service — John R. McGuire, chief.
General Counsel — James D. Keast.
Office of Investigation — John V. Graziano, dir.
Packers & Stockyards Admin — Marvin McLain.
Rural Electrific. Admin. — David Hamil, admin.
Soil Conservation Service — Ronello M. Davis, admin.
Statistical Reporting Service — Harry C. Trelogan.

Department of Commerce
14th St. between Constitution & E St. NW 20230

Secretary of Commerce — Rogers C. B. Morton.
Under Secretary — vacant.
Asst Secretaries — Robert J. Blackwell, Betsy Ancker-Johnson, James L. Pate.
General Counsel — Karl E. Bakke.
Bureau of the Census — Vincent R. Barabba.
Bureau of Economic Analysis — George Jaszi.
Bureau of Internatl. Commerce — Charles W. Hostler.
Bureau of East-West Trade — Arthur Downey.
Bureau of Domestic Commerce — Samuel B. Sherwin.
Natl. Oceanic & Atmospheric Admin. — Robert M. White, administrator.
Natl. Technical Info. Service — William T. Knox, director.
Economic Develop. Admin. — Wilbur Mizell.
Natl. Bureau of Standards — Dr. Richard Roberts.
Office of Minority Business Enterprise — Alex M. Armendaris, director.
Office of Product Standards — Frank LaQue.
Office of Telecommunications — John M. Richardson, acting director.
Office of Textiles — Arthur Garel, director.
Social & Economic Statistics Admin. — Edward D. Failor, administrator.
U.S. Patent Office — vacant.
U.S. Travel Service — C. Langhorne Washburn.

Department of Labor
14th St. & Constitution Ave. NW 20210

Secretary of Labor — John T. Dunlop.
Under Secretary — vacant.
Executive Assistant-Counselor — John C. Read.
Asst. Secretary for Manpower — William H. Kolberg.
Asst. Secretary for Labor-Management Relations — Paul J. Fasser Jr.
Asst. Secretary for Occupational Safety & Health — John H. Stender.
Asst. Secretary for Employment Standards — Bernard E. DeLury.

Women's Bureau — Carmen R. Maymi, director.
Asst. Secretary for Policy, Evaluation & Research — Abraham Weiss.
Solicitor of Labor — William J. Kilberg.
Bureau of Labor Statistics — Julius Shiskin.
Dep. Under Secy. for Internatl. Affairs — Joel Segall.
Dep. Under Secy. for Legislative Affairs — James Hogue.
Asst. Secretary for Admin. & Management — Fred G. Clark.
Director of Public Affairs — Richard Lukstat.
Office of Information, Publications & Reports — John W. Leslie, director.

Department of Health, Education, and Welfare
330 Independence Ave. SW 20201

Secretary of HEW — Forrest David Mathews.
Under Secretary — vacant.
Assistant Secretaries for:
    Administration and Management — John R. Ottina.
    Public Affairs — Lewis M. Helm.
    Health — Dr. Theodore Cooper.
    Planning and Evaluation — William Morrill.
    Education — Virginia Y. Trotter.
    Human Development — Stanley B. Thomas.
    Legislation — Stephen Kurzman.
    Comptroller — John D. Young.
General Counsel — John B. Rhinelander.
Surgeon General, Public Health Ser. — vacant.
Center for Disease Control — Dr. David J. Sencer, dir.
Alcohol, Drug Abuse and Mental Health Admin. — James D. Isbister (acting).
Health Resources Admin. — Dr. Kenneth Endicott.
Health Services Admin. — Dr. Robert Van Hoek (acting).
Office for Civil Rights — Peter E. Holmes, director.
Social and Rehabilitation Serv. — John A. Svahn (acting).
Commissioners of:
    Education — Terrel H. Bell.
    Social Security — James B. Cardwell.
    Food and Drug Admin. — Dr. Alexander M. Schmidt.
National Institutes of Health — Dr. Donald S. Frederickson.
National Institute of Education — Harold L. Hodgkinson.

Department of Housing and Urban Development
451 7th St SW 20410

Secretary of Housing & Urban Development — Carla Anderson Hills.
Under Secretary — vacant.
Assistant Secretaries:
    Administration — Thomas G. Cody.
    Community Planning & Development — David O. Meeker Jr.
    Fair Housing and Equal Opportunity — James H. Blair
    Housing Management — H. R. Crawford.
    Housing Production & Mortgage Credit — David M. DeWilde (acting).
    Policy Development & Research — Michael H. Moskow.
    Legislative Affairs — Sol Mosher.
President, Govt. Natl. Mortgage Assn. — Daniel P. Kearney.
Office of Public Affairs — Ronald E. Weber (acting).
Office of International Affairs — L. Wayne Gertmenian.
General Counsel — Robert R. Elliott.
Federal Insurance Administrator — J. Robert Hunter Jr. (acting).
Office of Interstate Land Sales Registration — John R. McDowell, administrator (acting).
Inspector General — Charles G. Haynes.

Department of Transportation
400 7th St. SW 20590

Secretary — William T. Coleman.
Deputy Secretary — John W. Barnum.
Assistant Secretaries — Benjamin O. Davis Jr., William S. Heffelfinger, W. E. Stoney (acting), John W. Snow (acting).
National Highway Traffic Safety Admin. — Dr. James B. Gregory.
U. S. Coast Guard Commandant — Adm. Owen W. Siler.
Federal Aviation Admin. — James E. Dow (acting).
Federal Highway Admin. — Norbert T. Tiemann.
Federal Railroad Admin. — Asph H. Hall (acting).
Urban Mass Transportation Admin. — Frank C. Herringer.
St. Lawrence Seaway Development Corp. — David W. Oberlin, administrator.

Judiciary of the United States

Data as of July 15, 1975

Justices of the United States Supreme Court

The Supreme Court comprises the Chief Justice of the United States and 8 Associate Justices, all appointed by the President with advice and consent of the Senate. Salaries: Chief Justice $62,500 annually, Associate Justice $60,000.

Name; apptd from *Chief Justices in italics*	Service Term	Yrs.	Born	Died
John Jay, N. Y.	1789-1795	5	1745	1829
John Rutledge, S. C.	1789-1791	1	1739	1800
William Cushing, Mass.	1789-1810	20	1732	1810
James Wilson, Pa.	1789-1798	8	1742	1798
John Blair, Va.	1789-1796	6	1732	1800
James Iredell, N. C.	1790-1799	9	1751	1799
Thomas Johnson, Md.	1791-1793	1	1732	1819
William Paterson, N. J.	1793-1806	13	1745	1806
John Rutledge, S. C.	1795(a)	—	1739	1800
Samuel Chase, Md.	1796-1811	15	1741	1811
Oliver Ellsworth, Conn.	1796-1800	4	1745	1807
Bushrod Washington, Va.	1798-1829	31	1762	1829
Alfred Moore, N. C.	1799-1804	4	1755	1810
John Marshall, Va.	1801-1835	34	1755	1835
William Johnson, S. C.	1804-1834	30	1771	1834
Henry B. Livingston, N.Y.	1806-1823	16	1757	1823
Thomas Todd, Ky.	1807-1826	18	1765	1826
Joseph Story, Mass.	1811-1845	33	1779	1845
Gabriel Duval, Md.	1811-1835	22	1752	1844
Smith Thompson, N. Y.	1823-1843	20	1768	1843
Robert Trimble, Ky.	1826-1828	2	1777	1828
John McLean, Oh.	1829-1861	32	1785	1861
Henry Baldwin, Pa.	1830-1844	14	1780	1844
James M. Wayne, Ga.	1835-1867	32	1790	1867
Roger B. Taney, Md.	1836-1864	28	1777	1864
Philip P. Barbour, Va.	1836-1841	4	1783	1841
John Catron, Tenn.	1837-1865	28	1786	1865
John McKinley, Ala.	1837-1852	15	1780	1852
Peter V. Daniel, Va.	1841-1860	19	1784	1860
Samuel Nelson, N. Y.	1845-1872	27	1792	1873
Levi Woodbury, N. H.	1845-1851	5	1789	1851
Robert C. Grier, Pa.	1846-1870	23	1794	1870
Benjamin R. Curtis, Mass.	1851-1857	6	1809	1874
John A. Campbell, Ala.	1853-1861	8	1811	1889
Nathan Clifford, Me.	1858-1881	23	1803	1881
Noah H. Swayne, Oh.	1862-1881	18	1804	1884
Samuel F. Miller, Ia.	1862-1890	28	1816	1890
David Davis, Ill.	1862-1877	14	1815	1886
Stephen J. Field, Cal.	1863-1897	34	1816	1899
Salmon P. Chase, Oh.	1864-1873	8	1808	1873
William Strong, Pa.	1870-1880	10	1808	1895
Joseph P. Bradley, N. J.	1870-1892	21	1813	1892
Ward Hunt, N. Y.	1872-1882	9	1810	1886
Morrison R. Waite, Oh.	1874-1888	14	1816	1888
John M. Harlan, Ky.	1877-1911	34	1833	1911
William B. Woods, Ga.	1880-1887	6	1824	1887
Stanley Matthews, Oh.	1881-1889	7	1824	1889
Horace Gray, Mass.	1881-1902	20	1828	1902
Samuel Blatchford, N.Y.	1882-1893	11	1820	1893
Lucius Q.C. Lamar, Miss.	1888-1893	5	1825	1893
Melville W. Fuller, Ill.	1888-1910	21	1833	1910
David J. Brewer, Kan.	1889-1910	20	1837	1910
Henry B. Brown, Mich.	1890-1906	15	1836	1913
George Shiras Jr., Pa.	1892-1903	10	1832	1924
Howell E. Jackson, Tenn.	1893-1895	2	1832	1895
Edward D. White, La.	1894-1910	16	1845	1921

Name; apptd from *Chief Justices in italics*	Service Term	Yrs.	Born	Died
Rufus W. Peckham, N.Y.	1895-1909	13	1838	1909
Joseph McKenna, Cal.	1898-1925	26	1843	1926
Oliver W. Holmes, Mass.	1902-1932	29	1841	1935
William R. Day, Oh.	1903-1922	19	1849	1923
William H. Moody, Mass.	1906-1910	3	1853	1917
Horace H. Lurton, Tenn.	1909-1914	4	1844	1914
Charles E. Hughes, N.Y.	1910-1916	5	1862	1948
Willis Van Devanter, Wy.	1910-1937	26	1859	1941
Joseph R. Lamar, Ga.	1910-1916	5	1857	1916
Edward D. White, La.	1910-1921	10	1845	1921
Mahlon Pitney, N. J.	1912-1922	10	1858	1924
Jas. C. McReynolds, Tenn.	1914-1941	26	1862	1946
Louis D. Brandeis, Mass.	1916-1939	22	1856	1941
John H. Clarke, Oh.	1916-1922	5	1857	1945
William H. Taft, Conn.	1921-1930	8	1857	1930
George Sutherland, Ut.	1922-1938	15	1862	1942
Pierce Butler, Minn.	1922-1939	16	1866	1939
Edward T. Sanford, Tenn.	1923-1930	7	1865	1930
Harlan F. Stone, N. Y.	1925-1941	16	1872	1946
Charles E. Hughes, N.Y.	1930-1941	11	1862	1948
Owen J. Roberts, Pa.	1930-1945	15	1875	1955
Benjamin N. Cardozo, N.Y.	1932-1938	6	1870	1938
Hugo L. Black, Ala.	1937-1971	34	1886	1971
Stanley F. Reed, Ky.	1938-1957	19	1884	—
Felix Frankfurter, Mass.	1939-1962	23	1882	1965
William O. Douglas, Conn.	1939 —	—	1898	—
Frank Murphy, Mich.	1940-1949	9	1890	1949
Harlan F. Stone, N.Y.	1941-1946	5	1872	1946
James F. Byrnes, S. C.	1941-1942	1	1879	1972
Robert H. Jackson, N.Y.	1941-1954	12	1892	1954
Wiley B. Rutledge, Ia.	1943-1949	6	1894	1949
Harold H. Burton, Oh.	1945-1958	13	1888	1964
Fred M. Vinson, Ky.	1946-1953	7	1890	1953
Tom C. Clark, Tex.	1949-1967	18	1899	—
Sherman Minton, Ind.	1949-1956	7	1890	1965
Earl Warren, Cal.	1953-1969	16	1891	1974
John Marshall Harlan, N. Y.	1955-1971	16	1899	1971
William J. Brennan Jr., N.J.	1956 —	—	1906	—
Charles E. Whittaker, Mo.	1957-1962	5	1901	—
Potter Stewart, Oh.	1958 —	—	1906	—
Byron R. White, Col.	1962 —	—	1917	—
Arthur J. Goldberg, Ill.	1962-1965	3	1908	—
Abe Fortas, Tenn.	1965-1969	4	1910	—
Thurgood Marshall, N.Y.	1967 —	—	1908	—
Warren E. Burger, Va.	1969 —	—	1907	—
Harry A. Blackmun, Minn.	1970 —	—	1908	—
Lewis F. Powell Jr., Va.	1961 —	—	1907	—
William H. Rehnquist, Ariz.	1971 —	—	1924	—

(a) Rejected Dec. 15, 1795.

U.S. Court of Customs and Patent Appeals

Washington, D.C. 20439 (Salaries, $42,500)
Chief Judge — Howard T. Markey.
Associate Judges — Giles S. Rich, Phillip B. Baldwin, Donald E. Lane, Jack R. Miller.

United States Court of Claims

Washington, D.C. 20005 (Salaries, $42.500)
Chief Judge — Wilson Cowen.
Associate Judges — Oscar H. Davis, Shiro Kashiwa, Robert L. Kunzig, Marion T. Bennett, Byron G. Skelton, Philip Nichols Jr.

United States Custom Court

New York, N.Y. 10007 (Salaries, $40,000)
Chief Judge — Nils A. Boe.
Judges — Morgan Ford, Scovel Richardson, Frederick Landis, James L. Watson, Herbert N. Maletz, Bernard Newman, Edward D. Re, Paul P. Rao.

United States Tax Court

Washington, D.C. 20004 (Salaries, $40,000)
Chief Judge — Arnold Raum, Bruce M. Forrester, Irene F. Scott, William M. Fay, William M. Drennen, Austin Hoyt, Theodore Tannenwald Jr., Charles R. Simpson, C. Moxley Featherston, Leo H. Irwin, Samuel B. Sterrett, William Quealy, William A. Goffe, Cynthia H. Hall, Darrell D. Wiles.

U.S. Courts of Appeals
(Salaries, $42,500. CJ means Chief Judge)

District of Columbia — David L. Bazelon, CJ; J. Skelly Wright, Carl McGowan, Edward Allen Tamm, Harold Leventhal, Spottswood W. Robinson III, Roger Robb, George E. MacKinnon, Malcolm Richard Wilkey; Clerk's office, Washington, D.C. 20001.

First Circuit (Me., Mass., N.H., R.I., Puerto Rico) — Frank M. Coffin, CJ; Edward M. McEntee, Levin H. Campbell; Clerk's Office, Boston, Mass. 02109.

Second Circuit (Conn., N.Y., Vt.) — Irving R. Kaufman, CJ; Wilfred Feinberg, Walter R. Mansfield, William H. Mulligan, James L. Oakes, William H. Timber, Murray I. Gurfein, Ellsworth Van Graafeiland; Clerk's Office, New York, N.Y. 10007.

Third Circuit (Del., N.J., Pa., Virgin Is.) — Collins J. Seitz, CJ; Francis L. Van Dusen, Ruggero J. Aldisert, Arlin M. Adams, John J. Gibbons, Max Rosenn, James Hunter 3d, Joseph F. Weis Jr., Leonard I. Garth; Clerk's Office, Philadelphia, Pa. 19107.

Fourth Circuit (Md., N.C., S.C., Va., W.Va.) — Clement F. Haynsworth Jr., CJ; Harrison L. Winter, J. Braxton Craven Jr., John D. Butzner Jr., Donald Russell, John A. Field Jr., H. Emory Widener Jr.; Clerk's Office, Richmond, Va. 23219.

Fifth Circuit (Ala., Fla., Ga., La., Miss., Tex., Canal Zone) — John R. Brown, CJ; John Minor Wisdom, Walter Pettus Gewin, Griffin B. Bell, Homer Thornberry, James P. Coleman, Irving L. Goldberg, Robert A. Ainsworth Jr., John C. Godbold, David W. Dyer, Bryan Simpson, Lewis R. Morgan, Charles Clark, Thomas G. Gee, Paul H. Roney; Clerk's Office, New Orleans, La. 70130.

Sixth Circuit (Ky., Mich., Ohio, Tenn.) — Harry Phillips, CJ; Paul C. Weick, George Clifton Edwards Jr., Anthony J. Celebrezze, John W. Peck, Wade H. McCree Jr., William E. Miller, Albert J. Engel, Pierce Lively; Clerk's Office, Cincinnati, Oh. 45202.

Seventh Circuit (Ill., Ind., Wis.) — Thomas E. Fairchild, CJ; Luther M. Swygert, Walter J. Cummings, Wilbur F. Pell Jr., John Paul Stevens, Robert A. Sprecher, Philip W. Tone; Clerk's Office, Chicago 60604.

Eighth Circuit (Ark., Ia., Minn., Mo., Neb., N.D., S.D.) — Floyd R. Gibson, CJ; Donald P. Lay, Gerald W. Heaney, Myron H. Bright, Donald R. Ross, Roy L. Stephenson, William H. Webster; Clerk's Office, St. Louis 63101.

Ninth Circuit (Ariz., Cal., Ida., Mont., Nev., Ore., Wash., Alaska, Ha., Guam) — Richard H. Chambers, CJ; M. Oliver Koelsch, James R. Browning, Ben Cushing Duniway, Walter Ely, Shirley M. Hufstedler, Eugene A. Wright, Ozell M. Trask, Joseph T. Sneed, Herbert Y. C. Choy, J. Clifford Wallace, Alfred T. Goodwin; Clerk's Office, San Francisco 94101.

Tenth Circuit (Col., Kan., N.M., Okla., Ut., Wy.) — David T. Lewis, CJ; Delmas C. Hill, Oliver Seth, William J. Holloway Jr., Robert H. McWilliams, James E. Barrett, William E. Doyle; Clerk's Office, Denver, Col. 80202.

U.S. District Courts
(Salaries, $40,000. CJ means Chief Judge)

Alabama — Northern: Frank H. McFadden, CJ; Sam C. Pointer Jr., James Hughes Hancock, J. Foy Guin Jr.; Clerk's Office, Birmingham 35203. **Middle:** Frank M. Johnson Jr., CJ; Robert E. Varner: Clerk's Office, Montgomery 36101. **Southern:** Virgil Pittman, CJ; William Brevard Hand; Clerk's Office, Mobile 36602.

Alaska — James A. Von der Heydt, CJ; James M. Fitzgerald; Clerk's Office, Anchorage 99510.

Arizona — Walter Early Craig, CJ; James A. Walsh, C. A. Muecke, William P. Copple, William C. Frey; Clerk's Office, Phoenix 85025.

Arkansas — Eastern: J. Smith Henley, CJ; Oren Harris, Garnett Thomas Eisele; Clerk's Office, Little Rock 72203. **Western:** Paul X. Williams, CJ; Oren Harris, J. Smith Henley; Clerk's Office, Fort Smith 72902.

California—Northern: Oliver J. Carter, CJ; Albert C. Wollenberg, Lloyd H. Burke, Alfonso J. Zirpoli, Stanley A. Weigel, Robert F. Peckham, Robert H. Schnacke, Samuel Conti, Spencer M. Williams, Charles B. Renfrew; William H. Orrick Jr.; Clerk's Office, San Francisco 94102. **Eastern:** Thomas J. MacBride, CJ; M. D. Crocker, Philip C. Wilkins; Clerk's Office, Sacramento 95814. **Central:** Albert Lee Stephens Jr., CJ; Jesse W. Curtis, E. Avery Crary, Francis C. Whelan, Irving Hill, A. Andrew Hauk, William P. Gray, Warren J. Ferguson, Manuel L. Real, Harry Pregerson, David W. Williams, Robert J. Kelleher, Wm. Matthew Byrne Jr., Lawrence T. Lydick, Malcolm M. Lucas, Robert

Firth; Clerk's Office, Los Angeles 90012. **Southern:** Edward J. Schwartz, CJ; Howard B. Turentine, Gordon Thompson Jr., Leland C. Nielsen, William B. Enright; Clerk's Office, San Diego 92101.

Colorado — Alfred A. Arraj, CJ; Fred M. Winner, Sherman G. Finesilver, Richard P. Matsch; Clerk's Office, Denver 80201.

Connecticut —T. Emmet Clarie, CJ; M. Joseph Blumenfeld; Robert C. Zampano, Jon O. Newman; Clerk's Office, New Haven 06505.

Delaware — James L. Latchum, CJ; Walter K. Stapleton, Murray M. Schwartz; Clerk's Office, Wilmington 19899.

District of Columbia —George L. Hart Jr., CJ; John J. Sirica, William B. Jones, Howard F. Corcoran, Oliver Gasch, William B. Bryant, John Lewis Smith Jr., Aubrey E. Robinson Jr., Joseph C. Waddy, Gerhard A. Gesell, John H. Pratt, June L. Green, Barrington D. Parker, Charles R. Richey, Thomas A. Flannery; Clerk's Office, Washington 20001.

Florida—Northern: Winston E. Arnow, CJ; Clerk's Office, Tallahassee 32302. **Middle:** George C. Young, CJ; Charles R. Scott, Ben Krentzman, Gerald B. Tjoflat, William Terrell Hodges, John A. Reed Jr.; Clerk's Office, Jacksonville 32201. **Southern:** Charles B. Fulton, CJ; William O. Mehrtens, C. Clyde Atkins, Joe Eaton, Peter T. Fay, James Lawrence King, Norman C. Roettger Jr.; Clerk's Office, Miami 33101.

Georgia — Northern: Newell Edenfield, CJ; Albert J. Henderson Jr., William C. O'Kelley, Charles A. Moye Jr., Richard C. Freeman, James C. Hill; Clerk's Office, Atlanta 30301. **Middle:** J. Robert Elliott, CJ; Wilbur D. Owens Jr.; Clerk's Office, Macon 31202. **Southern:** Alexander A. Lawrence, CJ; Anthony A. Alaimo; Clerk's Office, Savannah 31402.

Hawaii — Samuel P. King, CJ; Clerk's Office, Honolulu 96801.

Idaho — Ray McNichols, CJ; J. Blaine Anderson; Clerk's Office, Boise 83702.

Illinois — Northern: Edwin A. Robson, CJ; Richard B. Austin, James B. Parsons, Hubert L. Will, Bernard M. Decker, Abraham L. Marovitz, William J. Lynch, Frank J. McGarr, Thomas R. McMillen, Richard W. McLaren, Prentice H. Marshall, Joel M. Flaum, Alfred Y. Kirkland; Clerk's Office, Chicago 60604. **Eastern:** Henry S. Wise, CJ; James L. Foreman; Clerk's Office, Danville 61832. **Southern:** Robert D. Morgan, CJ; Harlington Wood Jr.; Clerk's Office, Peoria 61601.

Indiana — Northern: Jesse E. Eschbach, CJ; Allen Sharp; Clerk's Office, Hammond 46325. **Southern:** William E. Steckler, CJ; Cale J. Holder, S. Hugh Dillin, James E. Noland; Clerk's Office, Indianapolis 46204.

Iowa — Northern: Edward J. McManus, CJ; William C. Hanson; Clerk's Office, Cedar Rapids 52401. **Southern:** William C. Hanson, CJ; William C. Stuart; Clerk's Office, Des Moines 50309.

Kansas — Wesley E. Brown, CJ; Frank G. Theis, Earl E. O'Connor; Clerk's Office, Wichita 67201.

Kentucky — Eastern: Bernard T. Moynahan Jr., CJ; Howard David Hermansdorfer; Clerk's Office, Lexington 40501. **Western:** James F. Gordon, CJ; Rhodes Bratcher, Charles M. Allen; Clerk's Office, Louisville 40202.

Louisiana — Eastern: Frederick J. R. Heebe, CJ; Herbert W. Christenberry, Edward J. Boyle Sr., Lansing L. Mitchell, Fred J. Cassibry, Alvin B. Rubin, James A. Comiskey, R. Blake West, Jack M. Gordon; Clerk's Office, New Orleans 70130. **Middle:** E. Gordon West; Clerk's Office, Baton Rouge 70801. **Western:** Edwin F. Hunter Jr., CJ; Richard J. Putnam, Nauman S. Scott, Tom Stagg; Clerk's Office, Shreveport 71161.

Maine — Edward Thaxter Gignoux; Clerk's Office, Portland 04112.

Maryland — Edward S. Northrop, CJ; Frank A. Kaufman, Alexander Harvey 2d, James R. Miller Jr., Joseph Young, Herbert F. Murray, C. Stanley Blair; Clerk's Office, Baltimore 21202.

Massachusetts — Andrew A. Caffrey, CJ; W. Arthur Garrity Jr., Frank J. Murray, Frank H. Freedman, Joseph L. Tauro, Walter Jay Skinner; Clerk's Office, Boston 02109.

Michigan — Eastern: Frederick W. Kaess, CJ; Damon J. Keith, Lawrence Gubow, Cornelia G. Kennedy, John Feikens, Philip Pratt, Robert E. deMascio, Charles W. Joiner,

James Harvey; Clerk's Office, Detroit 48226. **Western:** Noel P. Fox, CJ; Wendell A. Miles; Clerk's Office, Grand Rapids 49502.

Minnesota — Edward J. Devitt, CJ; Earl R. Larson, Miles W. Lord, Donald D. Alsop; Clerk's Office, St. Paul 55101.

Mississippi — **Northern:** William C. Keady, CJ; Orma R. Smith; Clerk's Office, Oxford 38655. **Southern:** Dan M. Russell Jr., CJ; William Harold Cox, Walter L. Nixon Jr.; Clerk's Office, Jackson 39205.

Missouri — **Eastern:** James H. Meredith, CJ; John K. Regan, William R. Collinson, H. Kenneth Wangelin, John F. Nangle; Clerk's Office, St. Louis 63101. **Western:** William H. Becker, CJ; John W. Oliver, William R. Collinson, Elmo B. Hunter, H. Kenneth Wangelin; Clerk's Office, Kansas City 64106.

Montana — Russell E. Smith, CJ; James F. Battin; Clerk's Office, Great Falls 59401.

Nebraska — Warren K. Urbom, CJ; Robert V. Denney, Albert G. Schatz; Clerk's Office, Omaha 68101.

Nevada — Roger D. Foley, CJ; Bruce R. Thompson; Clerk's Office, Las Vegas 89101.

New Hampshire — Hugh H. Bownes; Clerk's Office, Concord 03301.

New Jersey — Lawrence A. Whipple, CJ; James A. Coolahan, George H. Barlow, Clarkson S. Fisher, Frederick B. Lacey, Vineent P. Biunno, Herbert J. Stern, H. Curtis Meanor, John F. Gerry; Clerk's Office, Trenton 08605.

New Mexico — H. Vearle Payne, CJ; Howard C. Bratton, Edwin L. Mechem; Clerk's Office, Albuquerque 87103.

New York — **Northern:** James T. Foley, CJ; Edmund Port; Clerk's Office, Albany 12201. **Eastern:** Jacob Mishler, CJ; John F. Dooling Jr., Jack B. Weinstein, Orrin G. Judd, Mark A. Costantino, Edward R. Neaher, Thomas C. Platt Jr., Henry Bramwell; Clerk's Office, Brooklyn 11201. **Southern:** David N. Edeistein, CJ; Edward Weinfeld, Charles M. Metzner, Lloyd F. MacMahon, Dudley B. Bonsal, Harold R. Tyler Jr., Inzer B. Wyatt, John M. Cannella, Charles H. Tenney, Marvin E. Frankel, Constance Baker Motley, Milton Pollack, Morris E. Lasker, Lawrence W. Pierce, Lee P. Gagliardi, Charles L. Brieant Jr., Whitman Knapp, Charles E. Stewart Jr., Thomas P. Griesa, Robert L. Carter, Robert J. Ward, Kevin Thomas Duffy, William C. Conner, Richard Owen, Henry F. Werker; Clerk's Office, N. Y. City 10007. **Western:** John T. Curtin, CJ; Harold P. Burke, John T. Elfvin; Clerk's Office, Buffalo 14202.

North Carolina — **Eastern:** Algernon L. Butler, CJ; John D. Larkins Jr., Franklin T. Dupree Jr.; Clerk's Office, Raleigh 27611. **Middle:** Eugene A. Gordon, CJ; Hiram H. Ward; Clerk's Office, Greensboro 27402. **Western:** Woodrow Wilson Jones, CJ; James B. McMillan; Clerk's Office, Asheville 28802.

North Dakota — Paul Benson, CJ; Bruce M. Van Sickle; Clerk's Office, Bismarck 58501.

Ohio — **Northern:** Frank J. Battisti, CJ; Ben C. Green, Don J. Young, William K. Thomas, Thomas D. Lambros, Robert B. Krupansky, Nicholas J. Walinski, Leroy J. Contie Jr.; Clerk's Office, Cleveland 44114. **Southern:** Joseph P. Kinneary, CJ; Timothy S. Hogan, Davis S. Porter, Carl B. Rubin, Robert M. Duncan; Clerk's Office, Columbus 43215.

Oklahoma — **Northern:** Allen E. Barrow, CJ; Frederick A. Daugherty, H. Dale Cook; Clerk's Office, Tulsa 74103. **Eastern:** Frederick A. Daugherty, CJ; Joseph W. Morris, H. Dale Cook; Clerk's Office, Muskogee 74402 **Western:** Frederick A. Daugherty, CJ; Stephen S. Chandler, Luther B. Eubanks, H. Dale Cook; Clerk's Office, Oklahoma City 73102.

Oregon — Robert C. Belloni, CJ; James M. Burns, Otto R. Skopil Jr.; Clerk's Office, Portland 97207.

Pennsylvania — **Eastern:** John S. Lord 3d, CJ; Alfred L. Luongo, A. Leon Higginbotham Jr., John P. Fullam, Charles

R. Weiner, E. Mac Troutman, John B. Hannum, Daniel H. Huyett 3d, Donald W. VanArtsdalen, J. William Ditter Jr., Edward R. Becker, James H. Gorbey, Raymond J. Broderick, Clarence C. Newcomer, Clifford Scott Green, Louis Charles Bechtle, Herbert A. Fogel, Joseph L. McGlynn Jr., Edward N. Cahn; Clerk's Office, Philadelphia 19107. **Middle:** Michael H. Sheridan, CJ; William J. Nealon Jr., R. Dixon Herman, Malcolm Muir; Clerk's Office, Scranton 18501. **Western:** Rabe Ferguson Marsh, CJ; Herbert P. Sorg, Edward Dumbauld, Louis Rosenberg, Gerald, J. Weber, William W. Knox, Hubert I. Teitelbaum, Barron P. McCune, Ralph F. Scalera, Daniel J. Snyder Jr.; Clerk's Office, Pittsburgh 15230.

Rhode Island — Raymond J. Pettine, CJ; Edward William Day; Clerk's Office, Providence 02901.

South Carolina — J. Robert Martin Jr., CJ; Robert W. Hemphill, Charles E. Simons Jr., Solomon Blatt Jr., Robert F. Chapman; Clerk's Office, Columbia 29202.

South Dakota — Fred J. Nichol, CJ; Andrew W. Bogue; Clerk's Office, Sioux Falls 57102.

Tennessee — **Eastern:** Frank W. Wilson, CJ; Robert L. Taylor, C. G. Neese; Clerk's Office, Knoxville 37901. **Middle:** Frank Gray Jr., CJ; L. Clure Morton; Clerk's Office, Nashville 37203. **Western:** Bailey Brown, CJ; Robert M. McRae Jr., Harry W. Wellford; Clerk's Office, Memphis 38103.

Texas — **Northern:** William M. Taylor Jr., CJ; Sarah T. Hughes, Halbert O. Woodward, Eldon B. Mahon, Robert M. Hill, Robert W. Porter; Clerk's Office, Dallas 75202. **Southern:** Reynaldo G. Garza, CJ; Allen B. Hannay, James Noel Jr., John V. Singleton Jr., Woodrow B. Seals, Carl O. Bue Jr., Owen D. Cox; Clerk's Office, Houston 77208. **Eastern:** Joe J. Fisher, CJ; William Wayne Justice, William M. Steger; Clerk's Office, Beaumount 77704. **Western:** Adrian A. Spears, CJ; Dorwin W. Suttle, Jack Roberts, William S. Sessions, John H. Wood Jr.; Clerk's Office, San Antonio 78298.

Utah — Willis W. Ritter, CJ; Aldon J. Anderson; Clerk's Office, Salt Lake City 84101.

Vermont — James S. Holden, CJ; Albert W. Coffrin; Clerk's Office, Burlington 05401.

Virginia — **Eastern:** Richard B. Kellam, CJ; Robert R. Merhige Jr., John A. MacKenzie, Albert V. Bryan Jr., D. Dortch Warriner, J. Calvitt Clarke; Clerk's Office, Norfolk 23501. **Western:** James C. Turk, CJ; Ted Dalton; Clerk's Office, Roanoke 24006.

Washington — **Eastern:** Marshall A. Neill, CJ; William N. Goodwin; Clerk's Office, Spokane 99210. **Western:** William N. Goodwin, CJ; Walter T. McGovern, Morell E. Sharp, Donald S. Voorhees; Clerk's Office, Seattle 98104.

West Virginia — **Northern:** Robert Earl Maxwell, CJ; Clerk's Office, Elkins 26241. **Southern:** Dennis Raymond Knapp, CJ; Kenneth K. Hall; Clerk's Office, Charleston 25329.

Wisconsin — **Eastern:** John W. Reynolds, CJ; Myron L. Gordon, Robert W. Warren; Clerk's Office, Milwaukee 53202. **Western:** James E. Doyle; Clerk's Office, Madison 53701.

Wyoming — Ewing T. Kerr; Clerk's Office, Cheyenne 82001.

U.S. Territorial District Courts

Canal Zone — Guthrie F. Crowe; Clerk's Office, Ancon.

Guam — Cristobal C. Duenas; Clerk's Office, Agana, 96910.

Puerto Rico — Jose V. Toledo, CJ; Hernan G. Pesquera, Juan R. Torruella; Clerk's Office, San Juan 00904.

Virgin Islands — Almeric L. Christian, CJ; Warren H. Young; Clerk's Office, Charlotte Amalie, St. Thomas 00801.

The Federal Judicial System

The federal judicial system begins with the District Court. There are 94 of these courts, at least one in each state, in Washington, D.C., and in certain territories. Called courts of general jurisdiction, they have power to determine the facts and pass judgement in criminal cases involving violations of federal law and in civil cases where the amount of the suit is $10,000 or more and the contending parties reside in different states. Other types of cases handled by District Courts include suits in admiralty (maritime matters involving navigational waters), bankruptcy, patents, trademarks, and copyrights.

Equal to the District Courts are special courts which handle only certain issues: the U.S. Customs Court, the Tax Court, and the Court of Claims, which hears suits against the U.S. government.

These trial courts are responsible for finding the facts in

a case and for applying the law to the facts found. Appellate courts, theoretically, do not review the trial court's findings of fact. The job of the appellate court is to decide whether the trial judge applied the law properly. If an appellate court decides that there was error in the application of the law, it can simply reverse the lower court's decision and end the case there. But it can also send the case back to the lower court for retrial or for other proceedings that may be appropriate.

The District Courts and special courts are trial courts. Above them are several levels of appellate courts. The U.S. Courts of Appeals, often called circuit courts, sit in 10 judicial circuits and Washington, D.C. It hears appeals from the District Courts and the Tax Court, and will review decisions of federal administrative agencies if it appears that such decisions may be unreasonable or arbitrary. The U.S. Court of Customs and Patent Appeals hears appeals from the Customs Court.

Ultimately, all decisions of these courts can be reviewed by the U.S. Supreme Court, which is also the first court of appeal from the U.S. Court of Claims. Besides reviewing federal court decisions, the Supreme Court is empowered to hear suits between the states and to review state supreme court decisions if an issue of federal law or the Constitution is involved.

Presidents Pro Tempore of the Senate

Until 1890, presidents "pro tem" were named "for the occasion only." Beginning with that year, they have served "until the Senate otherwise ordered." Sen. John J. Ingalls, chosen under the old rule in 1887, was again elected, under the new rule, in 1890. Party designations are D, Democrat; R, Republican.

Name	Party	State	Elected	Name	Party	State	Elected
John J. Ingalls	R	Kan.	Apr. 3, 1890	George H. Moses	R	N.H.	Mar. 6, 1925
Charles F. Manderson	R	Neb.	Mar. 2, 1891	Key Pittman	D	Nev.	Mar. 9, 1933
Isham G. Harris	D	Tenn.	Mar. 22, 1893	William H. King	D	Ut.	Nov. 19, 1940
Matt W. Ransom	D	N.C.	Jan. 7, 1895	Pat Harrison	D	Miss.	Jan. 6, 1941
Isham G. Harris	D	Tenn.	Jan. 10, 1895	Carter Glass	D	Va.	July 10, 1941
William P. Frye	R	Me.	Feb. 7, 1896	Kenneth McKellar	D	Tenn.	Jan. 6, 1945
Charles Curtis	R	Kan.	Dec. 4, 1911	Arthur H. Vandeberg	R	Mich.	Jan. 4, 1947
Augustus O. Bacon	D	Ga.	Jan. 15, 1912	Kenneth McKellar	D	Tenn.	Jan. 3, 1949
Jacob H. Gallinger	R	N.H.	Feb. 12, 1912	Styles Bridges	R	N.H.	Jan. 3, 1953
Henry Cabot Lodge	D	Mass.	Mar. 25, 1912	Walter F. George	D	Ga.	Jan. 5, 1955
Frank R. Brandegee	R	Conn.	May 25, 1912	Carl Hayden	D	Ariz.	Jan. 3, 1957
James P. Clarke	D	Ark.	Mar. 23, 1915	Richard B. Russell	D	Ga.	Jan. 3, 1969
Willard Saulsbury	D	Del.	Dec. 14, 1916	Allen J. Ellender	D	La.	Jan. 22, 1971
Albert B. Cummins	R	Ia.	May 19, 1919	James O. Eastland	D	Miss.	July 28, 1972

Speakers of the House of Representatives

Party designations: A, American; D, Democratic; DR, Democratic Republican; F, Federalist; R, Republican; W, Whig. *Served only one day.

Name	Party, State	Tenure	Name	Party, State	Tenure
Frederick A. C. Muhlenberg	F, Pa.	1789–1791	Galusha A. Grow	R, Pa.	1861–1863
Jonathan Trumbull	F, Conn.	1791–1793	Schuyler Colfax	R, Ind.	1863–1869
Frederick A. C. Muhlenberg	F, Pa.	1793–1795	*Theodore M. Pomeroy	R, N.Y.	1869–1869
Jonathan Dayton	F, N.J.	1795–1799	James G. Blaine	R, Me.	1869–1875
Theodore Sedgwick	F, Mass.	1799–1801	Michael C. Kerr	D, Ind.	1875–1876
Nathaniel Macon	DR, N.C.	1801–1807	Samuel J. Randall	D, Pa.	1876–1881
Joseph B. Varnum	DR, Mass.	1807–1811	Joseph W. Keifer	R, Oh.	1881–1883
Henry Clay	DR, Ky.	1811–1814	John G. Carlisle	D, Ky.	1883–1889
Langdon Cheves	DR, S.C.	1814–1815	Thomas B. Reed	R, Me.	1889–1891
Henry Clay	DR, Ky.	1815–1820	Charles F. Crisp	D, Ga.	1891–1895
John W. Taylor	DR, N.Y.	1820–1821	Thomas B. Reed	R, Me.	1895–1899
Philip P. Barbour	DR, Va.	1821–1823	David B. Henderson	R, Ia.	1899–1903
Henry Clay	DR, Ky.	1823–1825	Joseph G. Cannon	R, Ill.	1903–1911
John W. Taylor	D, N.Y.	1825–1827	Champ Clark	D, Mo.	1911–1919
Andrew Stevenson	D, Va.	1827–1834	Frederick H. Gillett	R, Mass.	1919–1925
John Bell	D, Tenn.	1834–1835	Nicholas Longworth	R, Oh.	1925–1931
James K. Polk	D, Tenn.	1835–1839	John N. Garner	D, Tex.	1931–1933
Robert M. T. Hunter	D, Va.	1839–1841	Henry T. Rainey	D, Ill.	1933–1935
John White	D, Ky.	1841–1843	Joseph W. Byrns	D, Tenn.	1935–1936
John W. Jones	D, Va.	1843–1845	William B. Bankhead	D, Ala.	1936–1940
John W. Davis	D, Ind.	1845–1847	Sam Rayburn	D, Tex.	1940–1947
Robert C. Winthrop	W, Mass.	1847–1849	Joseph W. Martin Jr.	R, Mass.	1947–1949
Howell Cobb	D, Ga.	1849–1851	Sam Rayburn	D, Tex.	1949–1953
Linn Boyd	D, Ky.	1851–1855	Joseph W. Martin Jr.	R, Mass.	1953–1955
Nathaniel P. Banks	A, Mass.	1856–1857	Sam Rayburn	D, Tex.	1955–1961
James L. Orr	D, S.C.	1857–1859	John W. McCormack	D, Mass.	1962–1971
William Pennington	R, N.J.	1860–1861	Carl Albert	D, Okla.	1971-

National Political Parties

As of July, 1975

Democratic Party Officers

Chairman—Robert S. Strauss.
Vice Chairmen—Basil Paterson, Caroline Wilkins.
Secretary—Dorothy V. Bush.
Treasurer—Edward Bennett Williams.
National Headquarters—1625 Massachusetts Ave., N.W., Washington, D.C. 20036.

Republican Party Officers

Chairman—Mrs. Mary Louise Smith

Co-Chairman—Richard D. Obenshain.
Vice Chairmen—Ray C. Bliss, Mrs. Hope McCormick, Bernard M. Shanley, Mrs. J. William Marriott, Robert J. Shaw, Mrs. Paula F. Hawkins, George P. Stadelman, Mrs. Isabel C. Moberly.
Secretary—Mrs. Estelle Stacy Carrier.
Treasurer—O. C. Carmichael, Jr.
General Counsel—William C. Cramer.
National Headquarters—310 First St., S. E., Washington, D.C. 20003.

Other Major Political Organizations

American Party
(PO Box 1098, Pigeon Forge, TN 37863)
Chairman—Thomas J. Anderson

Americans For Democratic Action
(1424 16th St., N.W., Washington, DC 20036)
President—Donald M. Fraser
National Director—Leon Shull
Chairperson Exec. Comm.—Cushing Dolbeare

Comm. on Political Education, AFL-CIO
(AFL-CIO Building, 815 16th St., Wash., DC 20006)
Chairman—George Meany
Secretary-Treasurer—Lane Kirkland
National Director—Alexander E. Barkan

Conservative Party of the State of N.Y.
(468 Park Ave. So., New York, NY 10016)
Chairman—J. Daniel Mahoney
Executive Director—Serphin R. Maltese
Secretary—Henry S. Jorin Jr.
Treasurer—James E. O'Doherty

Liberal Party of New York State
(1560 Broadway, New York, NY 10036)
Chairman—Donald S. Harrington

First Vice Chairman—David Dubinsky
Secretary & Exec. Director—Ben Davidson
Treasurer—Bernice Benedick

National States' Rights Party
(P.O. Box 1211, Marietta, GA 30061)
Chairman—J. B. Stoner
Secretary—Edward R. Fields
Treasurer—Peter Xavier

Prohibition National Committee
(P.O. Box 2635, Denver, CO 80201)
National Chairman—Charles Wesley Ewing
Executive Secretary—Earl F. Dodge
National Secretary—Roger C. Storms

Socialist Labor Party
In Minnesota: Industrial Gov't. Party
(914 Industrial Ave., Palo Alto, CA 94303)
National Secretary—Nathan Karp

Socialist Workers Party
(14 Charles Lane, New York, NY 10014)
National Secretary—Jack Barnes
Organization Secretary—Barry Sheppard

America's Third Parties

Since 1860, there have been only 4 presidential elections in which all third parties together polled more than 10% of the vote: the Populists (James Baird Weaver) in 1892, the National Progressives (Theodore Roosevelt) in 1912, the La Follette Progressives in 1924, and George Wallace's American Party in 1968. In 1948, the combined third parties (Henry Wallace's Progressives, Strom Thurmond's States' Rights party or Dixiecrats, Prohibition, Socialists, and others) received only 5.75% of the vote In most elections since 1860, fewer than one vote in 20 has been cast for a third party. The only successful third party in American history was the Republican party in the election of Abraham Lincoln in 1860.

Major Third Parties

Party	Presidential Nominee	Election	Issues	Strength in
Anti-Masonic	William Wirt	1832	Against secret societies and oaths	Pennsylvania, Vermont
Free Soil	Martin Van Buren	1848	Anti-slavery	New York, Ohio
American (Know Nothing)	Millard Fillmore	1856	Anti-immigrant	Northeast, South
Greenback	Peter Cooper	1876	For "cheap money," labor rights	National
Greenback	James B. Weaver	1880		
Prohibition	(numerous)	1872-	Anti-liquor	National
Populist	James B. Weaver	1892	For "cheap money," end of national banks	South, West
Socialist	Eugene V. Debs	1900-20	For public ownership	National
Socialist	Norman Thomas	1928-48		
Progressive (Bull Moose)	Theodore Roosevelt	1912	Against high tariffs	Midwest, West
Progressive	Robert M. LaFollette	1924	Farmer & labor rights	Midwest, West
States Rights	Strom Thurmond	1948	For segregation	South
Progressive	Henry Wallace	1948	Anti-cold war	New York, California
American	George Wallace	1968	For states' rights	South
American	John G. Schmitz	1972	For "law and order"	California, Ohio

The Electoral College

The president and the vice president of the United States are the only elective federal officials not elected by direct vote of the people. They are elected by the members of the Electoral College, an institution that has survived since the founding of the nation despite repeated attempts in Congress to alter or abolish it. In the elections of 1824, 1876 and 1888 the presidential candidate receiving the largest popular vote failed to win a majority of the electoral votes.

On presidential election day, the first Tuesday after the first Monday in November of every 4th year, each state chooses as many electors as it has senators and representatives in Congress. In 1964 for the first time, as provided by the 23d Amendment to the Constitution, the District of Columbia voted for 3 electors. Thus, with 100 senators and 435 representatives, there are 538 members of the Electoral College, with a majority of 270 electoral votes needed to elect the president and vice president.

Political parties customarily nominate their lists of electors at their respective state conventions. An elector cannot be a member of Congress or any person holding federal office.

Some states print the names of the candidates for president and vice president at the top of the ballot while others list only the names of the electors. In either case, the electors of the party receiving the highest vote are elected. The electors will meet on the first Monday after the 2d Wednesday in December in their respective state capitals or in some other place prescribed by state legislatures. By long-established custom they vote for their party nominee, thus giving all the state's electoral votes to him, although the Constitution does not require them to do so. The only Constitutional requirement is that at least one of the persons each elector votes for shall not be an inhabitant of that elector's home state.

Certified and sealed lists of the votes of the electors in each state are mailed to the president of the U.S. Senate. He opens them in the presence of the members of the Senate and House of Representatives in a joint session held on Jan. 6 (the next day if that falls on a Sunday), and the electoral votes of all the states are then counted. If no candidate for president has a majority, the House of Representatives chooses a president from among the 3 highest candidates, with all representatives from each state combining to cast one vote for that state. If no candidate for vice president has a majority, the Senate chooses from the top 2, senators voting as individuals.

United States Government Independent Agencies

Source: General Services Administration

Address: Washington, D.C. Location and zip codes of agencies in parentheses, as of June 15, 1975

ACTION — Director: Michael P. Balzano, Jr. (806 Connecticut Ave., NW, 20525).

Administrative Conference of the United States — Chmn Robert A Anthony (2120 L St., NW, 20037).

American Battle Monuments Commission — Chmn., Mark Clark (Forrestal Bldg., 20314).

American Revolution Bicentennial Administration — Administrator: John W. Warner (2401 E St. NW, 20276).

Appalachian Regional Commission — Federal co-chairman: Donald W. Whitehead, state co-chairman: Gov. Julian M. Carroll (1666 Connecticut Ave. NW. 20235).

Arms Control & Disarmament Agency — Director: Fred C. Ikle (Department of State Bldg. 20451).

Central Intelligence Agency — William Colby, director, (Wash., D.C. 20505).

Civil Aeronautics Board — Chairman: John E. Robson. (1825 Connecticut Ave. NW, 20428).

Civil Service Commission — Robert E. Hampton, chmn.; Jayne B. Spain, vice chmn. (1900 E. St. NW, 20415).

Commission on Civil Rights — Chmn.: Arthur S. Flemming. (1121 Vermont Ave., NW, 20425).

Commission of Fine Arts — J. Carter Brown, chmn. (708 Jackson Pl., NW, 20006).

Community Services Administration — Director: Bert Gallegos (1200 19th St. NW, 20506).

Consumer Product Safety Commission — Chairman: Richard O. Simpson (1750 K St. NW, 20207).

Energy Research and Development Administration — Administrator: Robert C. Seamans, Jr. (Washington, D. C. 20545).

Environmental Protection Agency — Administrator: Russell E. Train. (401 M St., SW, 20460).

Equal Employment Opportunity Commission — Lowell Perry, chmn. (2401 E NW, 20506).

Export-Import Bank of the United States — William J. Casey, pres. and chmn., (811 Vermont Ave. NW, 20571).

Farm Credit Administration — Kenneth N. Probasco, chmn. (490 L'Enfant Plaza West, SW).

Federal Communications Commission — Richard Wiley, chmn. (1919 M St. NW, 20554).

Federal Deposit Insurance Corporation — Chairman: Frank Wille. (550 17th St., NW 20429).

Federal Election Commission — Chairman: Thomas B. Curtis (1325 K St. NW).

Federal Energy Administration — Administrator: Frank G. Zarb. (12th St. and Pennsylvania Ave. NW, 20461).

Federal Home Loan Bank Board — Chairman: Thomas R. Bomar. (320 First St. NW, 20552).

Federal Maritime Commission — Helen D. Bentley, chmn. (1100 L St. NW, 20573).

Federal Mediation and Conciliation Service — Director: W. J. Usery (Dept. of Labor Bldg., 20427).

Federal Power Commission — John N. Nassikas, chmn., Don S. Smith, vice chmn. (825 N. Capital St., NW, 20426).

Federal Reserve System — Chairman, board of governors: Arthur F. Burns. (20th St. & Constitution Ave., NW, 20551).

Federal Trade Commission — Commissioners: Lewis A. Engman, chmn., Paul Rand Dixon, Mayo J. Thompson, M. Elizabeth Hanford, Stephen Nye. (Pennsylvania Ave. at 6th St., NW).

Foreign Claims Settlement Comm. of the U.S. — J. Raymond Bell, chmn. (1111 20th St., NW, 20579).

General Accounting Office — Comptroller general of the U.S.; Elmer B. Staats. (441 G St., NW, 20548).

General Services Administrat. on — Administrator: Arthur F. Sampson, (18th & F Sts., NW, 20405).

Government Printing Office — Public printer:

Thomas F. McCormick (North Capitol and H Sts., NW, 20401).

Indian Claims Commission — Jerome K. Kuykendall, chmn. (1730 K St., NW, 20006).

Inter-American Foundation — Chmn., Augustin S. Hart, Jr. (1515 Wilson Blvd., Rosslyn, Va., 22209).

Interstate Commerce Commission — George M. Stafford, chmn. (12th St. and Constitution Ave., NW, 20423).

Library of Congress — Vacancy, Librarian (10 First St., SE, 20540).

National Academy of Sciences — **National Academy of Engineering** — **National Research Council** — **Institute of Medicine** — President: Philip Handler, (2101 Constitution Ave., NW, 20418).

National Aeronautics and Space Administration — Administrator, James C. Fletcher. (Washington, D.C. 20546).

National Credit Union Administration — Herman Nickerson, Jr., administrator. (2025 M St., NW, 20456).

National Foundation on the Arts and Humanities — Nancy Hanks, chmn. (arts). Ronald S. Berman, chmn. (humanities) (806 15th St., NW, 20506).

National Labor Relations Board — Chairman: Betty Southard Murphy. (1717 Pennsylvania Ave., NW, 20570).

National Mediation Board — George S. Ives, chmn. (1230 16th St., NW, 20036).

National Science Foundation — Director: Norman Hackerman. (1800 G St., NW, 20550).

National Transportation Safety Board — Chairman: John H. Reed (800 Independence Ave. SW, 20594).

Nuclear Regulatory Commission — Chairman: William A. Anders (Washington, D.C. 20555).

Occupational Safety and Health Review Commission — Chmn., Robert D. Moran (1825 K St., NW, 20006).

Overseas Private Investment Corporation — President, Marshall T. Mays. (1129 20th St., NW, 20527).

Pension Benefit Guaranty Corporation — Executive Director: Steven E. Schanes, Acting (P.O. Box 7119, 20044).

Postal Rate Commission — Chairman: Clyde S. DuPont (2000 L St., NW, 20268).

Railroad Retirement Board — Chairman: James L. Cowen. (Rm. 444, 425 13th St. NW, 20004), Main Office (844 Rush St., Chicago, Ill. 60611).

Renegotiation Board — Chairman: Rex M. Mattingly, Acting. (2000 M St., NW, 20446).

Securities and Exchange Commission — Commissioners: Ray Garrett Jr., chmn.; A. A. Sommer Jr., Irving M. Pollack, Philip Loomis Jr., John R. Evans. (500 N. Capitol St., 20549).

Selective Service System — Director: Byron V. Pepitone. (1724 F St., NW, 20435).

Small Business Administration — Administrator: Thomas S. Kleppe, (1441 L St., NW, 20416).

Smithsonian Institution — S. Dillon Ripley, secy. (1000 Jefferson Drive, SW, 20560).

Tennessee Valley Authority — Chairman, board of directors: Aubrey J. Wagner. (New Sprankle Bldg., Knoxville, Tenn. 37901 and Woodward Bldg. 15th and H Sts., NW, Washington, D.C. 20444).

United States Information Agency — Director: James Keogh. (1750 Pennsylvania Ave., NW, 20547).

United States International Trade Commission — Chairman: Catherine Bedell (8th and E Sts. NW, 20436).

United States Postal Service — Benjamin F. Bailar, postmaster general (475 L'Enfant Plaza West, SW 20260).

Veterans Administration — Administrator: Richard L. Roudebush. (Vermont Ave. at H. St., NW, 20420).

The Ninety-Fourth Congress
With Official 1974 Election Results

The Senate

Terms are for 6 years and end January 3 of the year preceding name. Annual salary $42,500. To be eligible for the U.S. Senate a person must be at least 30 years of age, a citizen of the United States for at least 9 years, and a resident of the state from which he is chosen. The Congress must meet annually on Jan. 3, unless it has, by law, appointed a different day.

Senate officials: Pres. Pro Tempore, James O. Eastland; Secretary, Francis R. Valeo; Sgt. at Arms, Willam H. Wannall; Chaplain, L. R. Elson, S.T.D.

Dem., 61; Rep., 37; Ind., 1; Con., 1. Total, 100. * Star designates senior senator.

Term Ends	Senator (Party, Home)	1974 Election	Term Ends	Senator (Party, Home)	1974 Election
	Alabama				
				Hawaii	
1979	John Sparkman* (D, Huntsville).				
1981	James B. Allen (D, Gadsden).	501,541	1977	Hiram L. Fong* (R, Honolulu).	
	A. Abercrombie (Prohibition).	21,749	1981	Daniel K. Inouye (D, Honolulu).	207,454
				J. D. Kimmel (Prohibition).	42,767
	Alaska				
				Idaho	
1979	Ted Stevens* (R, Anchorage).				
1981	Mike Gravel (D, Anchorage).	54,361	1979	James A. McClure (R, Payette).	
	C. R. Lewis (R).	38,914	1981	Frank Church* (D, Boise).	145,140
				Bob Smith (R).	109,072
	Arizona				
				Illinois	
1977	Paul J. Fannin* (R, Phoenix).				
1981	Barry M. Goldwater (R, Scottsdale).	320,396	1979	Charles H. Percy* (R, Kenilworth).	
	Jonathan Marshall (D). . . . . , . . .	229,523	1981	Adlai E. Stevenson 3d (D, Chicago).	1,811,496
				Geo. M. Burditt (R).	1,084,884
	Arkansas			E. T. Heisler (SW)	12,413
1977	John L. McClellan* (D, Little Rock).			**Indiana**	
1981	Dale Bumpers (D, Charleston).	461,056	1977	Vance Hartke* (D, Evansville).	
	John Harris Jones (R)	82,026	1981	Birch Bayh (D, Indianapolis).	889,269
				Richard Lugar (R).	814,117
	California			Don L. Lee (Am.).	49,592
1977	John V. Tunney (D, Riverside)				
1981	Alan Cranston* (D, Palm Springs).	3,639,334		**Iowa**	
	H. L. Richardson (R).	2,176,315	1979	Dick Clark* (D, Marion)	
	Jack McCoy (Am. Ind.).	100,111	1981	John C. Culver (D, Cedar Rapids).	426,947
	Gayle M. Justice (P&F)	95,394		David Stanley (R).	420,546
	Colorado				
				Kansas	
1979	Floyd K. Haskell* (D, Denver).		1979	James B. Pearson* (R, Prairie Village) . . .	
1981	Gary Hart (D, Denver).	471,688	1981	Robert J. Dole (R, Russell).	403,983
	Peter H. Dominick (R)	325,526		Bill Roy (D).	390,451
	John M. King (Ind.).	16,131			
				Kentucky	
	Connecticut		1979	Walter Huddleston* (D, Elizabethtown). . .	
			1981	Wendell H. Ford (D, Owensboro)	398,887
1977	Lowell P. Weicker Jr. (R, Greenwich). . . .			Marlow W. Cook (R).	328,260
1981	Abraham R. Ribicoff* (D, Hartford).	690,820		W. E. Parker (Am.).	17,551
	James H. Brannen III (R).	372,055			
	A. F. Capozzi Jr. (Wallace).	19,184		**Louisiana**	
			1979	J. Bennett Johnston Jr. (D, Shreveport) . .	
	Delaware		1981	Russell B. Long* (D, Baton Rouge).	434,643
				unopposed	
1977	William V. Roth Jr.* (R, Wilmington).				
1979	Joseph R. Biden Jr. (D, Faulkland).			**Maine**	
			1977	Edmund S. Muskie* (D, Waterville).	
	Florida		1979	William D. Hathaway (D, Auburn).	
1977	Lawton Chiles* (D, Lakeland)				
1981	Richard Stone (D, Tallahassee).	781,031		**Maryland**	
	Jack Eckerd (R).	736,674	1977	J. Glenn Beall Jr. (R, Frostburg).	
	John Grady (Am.).	282,659	1981	Charles McC. Mathias* (R, Frederick) . . .	503,223
				Barbara A. Mikulski (D)	374,563
	Georgia				
				Massachusetts	
1979	Sam Nunn (D, Perry).		1977	Edward M. Kennedy* (D, Boston).	
1981	Herman E. Talmadge* (D, Lovejoy).	627,376	1979	Edward W. Brooke (R, Newton Center). . .	
	Jerry R. Johnson (R)	246,866			

Term Ends	Senator (Party, Home)	1974 Election
	Michigan	
1977	Philip A. Hart* (D, Mackinac Is.).......	
1979	Robert P. Griffin (R, Traverse City).....	
	Minnesota	
1977	Hubert Humphrey (D, Waverly).......	
1979	Walter F. Mondale* (D, Minneapolis)....	
	Mississippi	
1977	John Stennis (D, DeKalb)............	
1979	James O. Eastland* (D, Doddsville).....	
	Missouri	
1977	Stuart Symington* (D, St. Louis).......	
1981	Thomas F. Eagleton (D, St. Louis)......	735,433
	Thomas B. Curtis (R)............	480,900
	Montana	
1977	Mike Mansfield* (D, Missoula).........	
1979	Lee Metcalf (D, Helena).............	
	Nebraska	
1977	Roman L. Hruska* (R, Omaha).........	
1979	Carl T. Curtis (R, Minden)............	
	Nevada	
1977	Howard W. Cannon* (D, Las Vegas).....	
1981	Paul Laxalt (R, Carson City)..........	79,605
	Harry Reid (D)...................	78,981
	J. C. Doyle (Ind. Am.)...............	10,887
	New Hampshire	
1979	Thomas J. McIntyre* (D, Laconia).......	
1981	†John A. Durkin (D), Manchester).......	140,273
	Louis C. Wyman (R.)..............	113,004
	New Jersey	
1977	Harrison Williams Jr. (D, Westfield)......	
1979	Clifford P. Case* (R, Rahway).........	
	New Mexico	
1977	Joseph M. Montoya* (D, Sante Fe)......	
1979	Pete V. Domenici (R, Albuquerque).....	
	New York	
1977	James L. Buckley (C, New York)........	
1981	Jacob K. Javits* (R, L, New York).......	2,340,188
	Ramsey Clark (D)................	1,973,781
	Barbara A. Keating (C)..............	822,584
	North Carolina	
1979	Jesse A. Helms* (R, Raleigh).........	
1981	Robert Morgan (D, Lillington)..........	633,775
	Wm. E. Stevens (R)...............	377,618
	North Dakota	
1977	Quentin N. Burdick (D, Fargo).........	
1981	Milton R. Young* (R, La Moure)........	114,852
	Wm. L. Guy (D)..................	114,675

Term Ends	Senator (Party, Home)	1974 Election
	Ohio	
1977	Robert Taft Jr.* (R, Cincinnati).........	
1981	John Glenn (D, Columbus)............	1,930,670
	Ralph J. Perk (R)................	918,133
	K. G. Harroff (Ind.).................	76,882
	R. B. Kay (Ind.)....................	61,921
	Oklahoma	
1979	Dewey F. Bartlett (R, Tulsa)...........	
1981	Henry Bellmon* (R, Red Rock).........	390,997
	Ed Edmondson (D)................	387,162
	P. E. Trent (Ind.)..................	13,650
	Oregon	
1979	Mark O. Hatfield# (R, Salem)...........	
1981	Robert W. Packwood (R, Lake Oswego)..	420,984
	Betty Roberts (D)..................	338,591
	Pennsylvania	
1977	Hugh Scott* (R, Philadelphia)..........	
1981	Richard S. Schweicker (R, Worcester)...	1,843,317
	Pete Flaherty (D).................	1,596,121
	G. W. Shankey Jr. (Constit.)..........	38,004
	Rhode Island	
1977	John O. Pastore* (D, Providence).......	
1979	Claiborne Pell (D, Newport)...........	
	South Carolina	
1979	Strom Thurmond* (R, Aiken)...........	
1981	Ernest F. Hollings (D, Columbia)........	356,126
	Gwen Bush (R)...................	146,645
	South Dakota	
1979	James Abourezk (D, Rapid City)........	
1981	George McGovern* (D, Mitchell)........	147,929
	Leo K. Thorsness (R)...............	130,955
	Tennessee	
1977	William E. Brock, 3d (R, Chattanooga)...	
1979	Howard H. Baker Jr.* (R, Knoxville).....	
	Texas	
1977	Lloyd M. Bentsen (D, Houston).........	
1979	John G. Tower* (R, Wichita Falls).......	
	Utah	
1977	Frank E. Moss* (D, Salt Lake City)......	
1981	Jake Garn (R, Salt Lake City)..........	210,299
	Wayne Owens (D).................	185,377
	K. R. Larsen (Am.).................	24,966
	Vermont	
1977	Robert T. Stafford* (R, Rutland)........	
1981	Patrick J. Leahy (D., I.V., Burlington).....	70,629
	R. W. Mallory (R).................	66,223
	Virginia	
1977	Harry F. Byrd Jr.* (Ind., Winchester).....	
1979	William Lloyd Scott (R, Fairfax).........	

†1975 special election, September 16. The 1974 election remained undecided as each man received approximately 110,925 votes.

(Am. Ind. — American Independent; P&F — Peace and Freedom; Wallace — George Wallace party; Am. — American; SW — Socialist Workers; C — Conservative; Constit. — Constitutional; L — Liberal; I.V. — Independent Vermonters. Only candidates receiving 10,000 votes or more are listed.)

Term Ends	Senator (Party, Home)	1974 Election	Term Ends	Senator (Party, Home)	1974 Election
	Washington			**Wisconsin**	
1977	Henry M. Jackson (D, Everett)		1977	William Proxmire* (D, Madison)	
1981	Warren G. Magnuson* (D, Seattle)	611,811	1981	Gaylord A. Nelson (D, Madison)	740,700
	Jack Metcalf (R)	363,626		Thomas E. Petri (R)	429,327
	Gene Goosman (Am. Ind.)	19,871		G. L. McFarren (Am.)	24,003
	West Virginia			**Wyoming**	
1977	Robert C. Byrd (D, Sophia)		1977	Gale W. McGee* (D. Laramie)	
1979	Jennings Randolph* (D, Elkins)		1979	Clifford P. Hansen (R, Jackson)	

The House of Representatives

Members' terms to Jan. 3, 1977. Annual salary $42,500; House Speaker $62,500 and $10,000 expenses, all taxable. To be eligible for membership, a person must be at least 25, a U.S. citizen for at least 7 years, and a resident of the state from which he is chosen.

94th Congress House Officials

Parliamentarian, Lewis Deschler; chaplain, Rev. Edward G. Latch; sergeant at arms, Kenneth Harding; clerk, W. Pat Jennings; doorkeeper, William M. Miller; postmaster, Robert V. Rota.

Democrats, 291; Republicans, 144; Total 435.
(Those marked * served in the 93rd Congress.)

Dist.	Representative (Party, Home)	1974 Election	Dist.	Representative (Party, Home)	1974 Election
	ALABAMA		9.	**Fortney H. Stark*** (D,Danville)	87,854
				Edson Adams (R)	36,522
1.	**Jack Edwards*** (R,Mobile)	60,170	10.	**Don Edwards*** (D,San Jose)	86,014
	Augusta E. Wilson (D)	37,718		John M. Enright (R)	25,678
2.	**William L. Dickinson*** (R,Montgomery)	54,089	11.	**Leo J. Ryan*** (D,S.San Francisco)	106,075
	Clair Chisler (D)	27,729		B.G. Merdinger (R)	29,783
3.	**Bill Nichols*** (D,Sylacauga)	63,582	12.	**Paul N. McCloskey Jr.*** (R,Menlo Park)	103,228
4.	**Tom Bevill*** (D,Jasper)	77,925		Gary G. Gillmor (D)	46,197
5.	**Bob Jones*** (D,Scottsboro)	56,375	13.	**Norman Y. Mineta** (D,San Jose)	78,649
6.	**John H. Buchanan Jr.*** (R,Birmingham)	54,505		George W. Milias (R)	63,381
	Nina Miglionico (D)	39,444	14.	**John J. McFall*** (D,Manteca)	101,932
7.	**Walter Flowers*** (D,Tuscaloosa)	73,203		Charles M. Gibson (R)	34,679
			15.	**B.F. Sisk*** (D,Fresno)	80,205
	ALASKA - At Large			Carol O. Harner (R)	31,361
	Don Young* (R,Fort Yukon)	51,641	16.	**Burt L. Talcott*** (R,Salinas)	76,084
	William L. Hensley (D)	44,280		Julian Camacho (D)	74,018
			17.	**John Krebs** (D,Fresno)	66,082
	ARIZONA			Bob Mathias* (R)	61,242
1.	**John J. Rhodes*** (R,Mesa)	63,847	18.	**William M. Ketchum*** (R,Bakersfield)	66,603
	Patricia M. Fullinwider (D)	52,897		George A. Seielstad (D)	59,931
2.	**Morris K. Udall*** (D, Tucson)	84,491	19.	**Robert J. Lagomarsino*** (R,Ojai)	84,849
	Keith Dolgaard (R)	51,886		James D. Loebl (D)	65,334
3.	**Sam Steiger*** (R,Prescott)	71,497	20.	**Barry M. Goldwater Jr.*** (R,Burbank)	96,324
	Pat Bosch (D)	68,424		Arline Mathews (D)	61,119
4.	**John B. Conlan*** (R,Paradise Valley)	78,887	21.	**James C. Corman*** (D,Reseda)	86,778
	Byron T. Brown (D)	63,677		Mel Nadell (R)	31,365
			22.	**Carlos J. Moorhead*** (R,Glendale)	78,983
	ARKANSAS			Richard Hallin (D)	62,770
1.	**Bill Alexander*** (D,Osceola)	104,247	23.	**Thomas M. Rees*** (D,Beverly Hills)	119,239
	James Lawrence Dauer (R)	10,821		Jack E. Roberts (R)	47,615
2.	**Wilbur D. Mills*** (D,Kensett)	80,296	24.	**Henry A. Waxman** (D,Los Angeles)	85,343
	Judy Petty (R)	56,038		Elliott Stone Graham (R)	43,680
3.	**J.P. Hammerschmidt*** (R,Harrison)	89,324	25.	**Edward R. Roybal*** (D,Los Angeles)	43,998
	Bill Clinton (D)	83,303	26.	**John Rousselot*** (R,San Marino)	80,782
4.	**Ray Thornton*** (D,Sheridan)	(1)		Paul A. Conforti (D)	56,487
			27.	**Alphonzo Bell*** (R,Marina Del Ray)	99,645
	CALIFORNIA			John Dalessio (D)	50,919
1.	**Harold T. Johnson*** (D,Roseville)	137,849	28.	**Yvonne Brathwaite Burke*** (D,Los Angeles)	86,743
	Dorothy D. Paradis (Am. Ind.)	22,628		Tom Neddy (R)	21,308
2.	**Don H. Clausen*** (R,Crescent City)	95,508	29.	**Augustus F. Hawkins*** (D,Los Angeles) . . .	45,977
	Oscar Klee (D)	76,951	30.	**George E. Danielson*** (D,Monterey Park) . . .	66,074
3.	**John E. Moss*** (D,Sacramento)	121,842		John J. Perez (R)	22,928
	Ivaldo Lenci (R)	46,585	31.	**Charles H. Wilson*** (D,Hawthorne)	60,560
4.	**Robert L. Leggett*** (D,Suison City)	100,934		Norman A. Hodges (R)	23,039
5.	**John Burton*** (D,San Francisco)	87,323	32.	**Glenn M. Anderson*** (D,Harbor City)	82,485
	Thomas Caylor (D)	55,881		Virgil V. Badalich (Am. Ind.)	8,710
6.	**Phillip Burton*** (D,San Francisco)	84,585	33.	**Del Clawson*** (R,Downey)	71,054
	Tom Spinosa (R)	25,721		Robert E. White (D)	57,423
7.	**George Miller** (D,Martinez)	82,765	34.	**Mark W. Hannaford** (D,Lakewood)	78,345
	Gary Fernandez (R)	66,115		Bill Bond (R)	72,967
8.	**Ronald V. Dellums*** (D,Berkeley)	93,016	35.	**Jim Lloyd** (D,W. Covina)	60,709
	Jack Redden (R)	65,432		Victor V. Veysey* (R)	60,102
			36.	**George E. Brown Jr.*** (D,Colton)	69,615
				Jim Osgood (R)	35,858

Dist.	Representative (Party, Home)	1974 Election

CALIFORNIA
(Continued)

37.	Shirley N. Pettis* (R,Loma Linda)[2]	50,103
	·Ron Pettis (D)	12,920
38.	Jerry M. Patterson (D,Santa Ana)	67,209
	David Rehmann (R)	51,509
39.	Charles E. Wiggins* (R,Fullerton)	87,995
	William E. Farris (D)	64,375
40.	Andrew Hinshaw* (R,Newport Beach)	114,895
	Roderick J. Wilson (D)	56,195
41.	Bob Wilson* (R, San Diego)	93,461
	Colleen M. O'Connor (D)	73,954
42.	Lionel Van Deerlin* (D, Chula Vista)	66,746
	Wes Marden (R)	30,058
43.	Clair W. Burgener* (R,Rancho Santa Fe)	114,102
	Bill Bandes (D)	74,905

COLORADO

1.	Pat Schroeder* (D,Denver)	94,583
	Frank Southworth (R)	66,046
2.	Timothy E. Wirth (D,Denver)	93,827
	Donald G. Brotzman* (R)	86,818
3.	Frank E. Evans* (D,Beulah)	91,783
	E. Keith Records (R)	43,298
4.	James P. Johnson* (R,Fort Collins)	82,982
	John Carroll (D)	76,452
5.	William L. Armstrong* (R,Aurora)	85,326
	Ben Galloway (D)	56,888

CONNECTICUT

1.	William R. Cotter* (D,Hartford)	117,038
	Francis M. Buckley (R)	67,080
2.	Christopher J. Dodd (D, N.Stonington)	104,436
	Samuel B. Hellier (R)	69,380
3.	Robert Giaimo* (D,North Haven)	114,316
	James Altham Jr. (R)	55,177
4.	Stewart B. McKinney* (R,Fairfield)	83,630
	James G. Kellis (D)	71,047
5.	Ronald A. Sarasin* (R,Beacon Falls)	94,998
	William Ratchford (D)	90,407
6.	Anthony Moffett (D,Unionville)	122,785
	Patsy J. Piscopo (R)	69,942

DELAWARE-At Large

| | Pierre S. du Pont 4th* (R,Wilmington) | 93,826 |
| | James R. Soles (D) | 63,490 |

FLORIDA

1.	Bob Sikes* (D,Crestview)	(1)
2.	Don Fuqua* (D,Altha)	(1)
3.	Charles E. Bennett* (D,Jacksonville)	(1)
4.	Bill Chappell Jr.* (D,Ocala)	74,720
	Warren Hauser (R)	34,867
5.	Richard Kelly (R,Holiday)	74,954
	JoAnn Saunders (D)	63,610
6.	C.W. Bill Young* (R,St. Petersburg)	109,302
	Mickey Monrose (D)	34,886
7.	Sam M. Gibbons* (D,Tampa)	(1)
8.	James A. Haley* (D,Sarasota)	63,283
	Joe Z. Lovingood (R)	48,240
9.	Lou Frey Jr.* (R,Winter Park)	86,226
	William D. Rowland (D)	26,255
10.	L.A.Bafalis* (R,Ft. Myers Beach)	117,368
	Evelyn Tucker (D)	41,925
11.	Paul G. Rogers* (D,W. Palm Beach)	(1)
12.	J. Herbert Burke* (R,Hollywood)	61,191
	Charles Friedman (D)	58,899
13.	William Lehman* (D,N. Miami)	(1)
14.	Claude Pepper* (D,Miami Beach)	45,479
	Michael A. Carricarte (R)	20,383
15.	Dante B. Fascell* (D,Miami)	68,064
	S. Peter Capua (R)	28,444

GEORGIA

1.	Bo Ginn* (D,Millen)	64,958
	Bill Gowan (R)	10,485
2.	Dawson Mathis* (D,Albany)	59,514
3.	Jack Brinkley* (D,Columbus)	67,438
	Carl P. Savage Jr. (R)	9,453
4.	Elliott H. Levitas (D,Atlanta)	61,211
	Ben B. Blackburn* (R)	49,922
5.	Andrew Young* (D,Atlanta)	69,221
	Wyman C. Lowe (R)	27,397
6.	John J. Flynt Jr.* (D,Griffen)	49,082
	Newt Gingrich (R)	46,308
7.	Larry McDonald (D,Marietta)	47,993
	Quincy Collins (R)	47,450
8.	W.S. Stuckey Jr.* (D,Eastman)	59,182
9.	Phil Landrum* (D,Jasper)	64,096
	Ronald D. Reeves Sr. (R)	21,540
10.	Robert G. Stephens Jr.* (D,Athens)	45,843
	Gary Pleger (R)	21,214

HAWAII

1.	Spark M. Matsunaga* D,Honolulu)	71,552
	William B. Paul (R)	49,065
2.	Patsy Takemoto Mink* (D,Waipahu)	86,916
	Carla W. Coray (R)	51,984

IDAHO

1.	Steven D. Symms* (R,Caldwell)	75,404
	J. Ray Cox (D)	54,001
2.	George Hansen (R,Pocatello)	67,274
	Max Hanson (D)	53,599

ILLINOIS

1.	Ralph H. Metcalfe* (D,Chicago)	75,206
	Oscar H. Haynes (R)	4,399
2.	Morgan F. Murphy* (D,Chicago)	65,812
	James J. Ginderske (R)	9,386
3.	Martin A. Russo (D,Calumet Park)	65,336
	Robert P. Hanrahan* (R)	58,891
4.	Edward J. Derwinski* (R,Flossmoor)	68,428
	Ronald A. Rodger (D)	47,096
5.	John C. Kluczynski* (D,Chicago)	93,069
	William H.G. Toms (R)	15,108
6.	Henry J. Hyde (R,Port Ridge)	66,027
	Edward V. Hanrahan (D)	57,654
7.	Cardiss Collins* (D,Chicago)	63,962
	Donald L. Metzger (R)	8,800
8.	D.D. Rostenkowski* (D,Chicago)	75,011
	Salvatore E. Oddo (R)	11,664
9.	Sidney R. Yates* (D,Chicago)	93,864
10.	Abner J. Mikva (D,Evanston)	83,457
	Samuel H. Young*(R)	80,597
11.	Frank Annunzio* (D,Chicago)	102,541
	Mitchell G. Zadrozny (R)	39,182
12.	Philip M. Crane* (R,Mount Prospect)	70,731
	Betty C. Spence (D)	45,049
13.	Robert McClory* (R,Lake Bluff)	51,405
	Stanley W. Beetham (D)	42,903
14.	John N. Erlenborn* (R,Glen Ellyn)	77,718
	Robert H. Renshaw (D)	38,981
15.	Tim L. Hall (D,Dwight)	61,912
	Clifford D. Carlson (R)	54,278
16.	John B. Anderson* (R,Rockford)	65,175
	Marshall Hungness (D)	33,724
	W. John Schade Jr. (Ind.)	18,580
17.	George M. O'Brien* (R,Joliet)	59,984
	John J. Houlihan (D)	56,541
18.	Robert H. Michel* (R,Peoria)	71,681
	Steven L. Nordvall (D)	59,225
19.	Tom Railsback* (R,Moline)	84,049
	Jim Gende (D)	44,677
20.	Paul Findley* (R,Pittsfield)	84,426
	Peter F. Mack (D)	69,551
21.	Edward R. Madigan* (R,Lincoln)	78,640
	Richard N. Small (D)	40,896

Dist.	Representative (Party, Home)	1974 Election

ILLINOIS
(Continued)

22.	George E. Shipley* (D,Olney)	97,921
	William A. Young (R)	65,731
23.	Melvin Price* (D,E.St.Louis)	78,347
	Scott Randolph (R)	18,987
24.	Paul Simon (D,Carbondale)	108,417
	Val Oshel (R)	73,634

INDIANA

1.	Ray J. Madden* (D,Gary)	71,759
	Joseph D. Harkin (R)	32,793
2.	Floyd J. Fithian (D,Lafayette)	101,856
	Earl F. Landgrebe* (R)	64,950
3.	John Brademas* (D,South Bend)	89,306
	Virginia R. Black (R)	50,116
4.	J. Edward Roush* (D,Huntington)	83,604
	Walter P. Helmke (R)	75,031
5.	Elwood H. Hillis* (R,Kokomo)	95,331
	William T. Sebree (D)	73,239
6.	David Walter Evans (D,Indianapolis)	78,414
	William B. Bray* (R)	71,134
7.	John T. Myers* (R,Covington)	100,128
	Elden Creasy Tipton (D)	73,802
8.	Philip H. Hayes (D,Evansville)	100,121
	Roger H. Zion* (R)	87,296
9.	Lee H. Hamilton* (D,Columbus)	117,648
	Delson Cox Jr. (R)	47,881
10.	Philip R. Sharp (D,Muncie)	85,418
	David W. Dennis* (R)	71,701
11.	Andrew Jacobs Jr. (D,Indianapolis)	81,508
	William H. Hudnut 3d* (R)	73,793

IOWA

1.	Edward Mezvinsky* (D,Iowa City)	75,687
	James A S. Leach (R)	63,540
2.	Michael T. Blouin (D,Dubuque)	73,416
	Tom Riley (R)	69,088
3.	Charles E. Grassley (R,New Hartford)	77,468
	Stephen J. Rapp (D)	74,895
4.	Neal Smith* (D,Altoona)	96,755
	Chuck Dick (R)	53,756
5.	Tom Harkin (D,Ames)	81,146
	Bill Scherle* (R)	77,683
6.	Berkley Bedall (D,Spirit Lake)	86,315
	Wiley Mayne* (R)	71,695

KANSAS

1.	Keith J. Sebelius* (R,Norton)	101,565
	Don Smith (D)	57,326
2.	Martha Keyes (D,Manhattan)	84,864
	John C. Peterson (R)	67,650
3.	Larry Winn Jr.* (R,Overland Park)	89,694
	Samuel J. Wells (D)	49,976
4.	Garner E. Shriver* (R,Wichita)	70,401
	Bert Chaney, (D)	61,210
5.	Joe Skubitz* (R,Pittsburg)	88,646
	Frank Gaines (D)	72,024

KENTUCKY

1.	Carroll Hubbard Jr. (D,Mayfield)	70,723
	C.T. Banken Jr. (R)	16,937
2.	William H. Natcher* (D,Bowling Green)	56,502
	Art Eddleman (R)	18,312
3.	Romano L. Mazzoli* (D,Louisville)	75,571
	Vincent N. Barclay (R)	28,813
4.	Marion Gene Snyder* (R,Brownsboro Farms)	63,845
	Kyle T. Hubbard (D)	59,539
5.	Tim Lee Carter* (R,Tompkinsville)	66,709
	Lyle L. Willis (D)	28,706
6.	John Breckinridge* (D,Lexington)	63,010
	Thomas F. Rogers 3d (R)	21,039
7.	Carl D. Perkins* (D,Hindman)	71,221
	Granville Thomas (R)	22,982

Dist.	Representative (Party, Home)	1974 Election

LOUISIANA

1.	F. Edward Hebert* (D,New Orleans)	48,452
2.	Lindy (Mrs. Hale) Boggs* (D,New Orleans)	53,802
	Diane Morphos (R)	9,632
3.	David C. Treen* (R,Metairie)	55,574
	Charles Grisbaum Jr. (D)	39,412
4.	Joe D. Waggonner Jr.* (D,Plain Dealing)	47,371
5.	Otto E. Passman* (D,Monroe)	43,068
6.	W. Henson Moore (R,Baton Rouge)	73,802
	Jeff La Caze (D)	63,366
7.	John B. Breaux* (D,Crowley)	59,406
	Jeremy J. Millett (Ind.)	7,131
8.	Gillis W. Long* (D,Alexandria)	41,704

MAINE

1.	David F. Emery* (R,Rockland)	94,203
	Peter N. Kyros (D)	93,524
2.	William S. Cohen* (R,Bangor)	118,154
	Markham L. Gartley (D)	47,399

MARYLAND

1.	Robert E. Bauman* (R,Easton)	59,570
	Thomas J. Hatem (D)	52,853
2.	Clarence D. Long* (D,Towson)	103,222
	John M. Seney (R)	30,639
3.	Paul S. Sarbanes* (D,Baltimore)	93,218
	William H. Mathews (R)	17,967
4.	Marjorie S. Holt* (R,Severna Park)	61,208
	Fred L. Wineland (D)	44,059
5.	Gladys Noon Spellman (D,Laurel)	45,211
	John B. Burcham Jr. (R)	40,805
6.	Goodloe E. Byron* (D,Frederick)	90,882
	Elton R. Wampler (R)	32,416
7.	Parren J. Mitchell* (D,Baltimore)	43,252
8.	Gilbert Gude* (R,Bethesda)	104,675
	Sidney Kramer (D)	54,112

MASSACHUSETTS

1.	Silvio O. Conte* (R,Pittsfield)	107,285
	Thomas R. Manning (D)	43,524
2.	Edward P. Bowland* (D,Springfield)	105,763
3.	Joseph D. Early (D,Worcester)	78,244
	David J. Lionett (R)	60,717
	Douglas J. Rowe (Ind.)	19,018
4.	Robert F. Drinan* (D,Newton)	77,286
	Jon Rotenberg (Ind.)	52,785
	Alvin Mandell (R)	21,922
5.	Paul E. Tsongas (D,Lowell)	99,518
	Paul W. Cronin* (R)	64,596
6.	Michael J. Harrington* (D,Beverly)	119,278
7.	Torbert H. Macdonald* (D,Malden)	122,165
	James J. Murphy (Ind.)	30,959
8.	Thomas P. O'Neill Jr.* (D,Cambridge)	107,042
9.	John Joseph Moakley* (D,Boston)	94,804
	L.R. Sherman (U.S. Labor)	11,344
10.	Margaret M. Heckler* (R,Wellesley)	99,993
	Barry F. Monahan (D)	55,871
11.	James A. Burke* (D,Milton)	125,978
12.	Gerry E. Studds* (D,Cohasset)	138,779
	J. Alan MacKay (R)	46,787

MICHIGAN

1.	John Conyers Jr.* (D,Detroit)	97,620
	Walter F. Girardot (R)	9,358
2.	Marvin L. Esch* (R,Ann Arbor)	72,245
	John S. Reuther (D)	62,755
3.	Garry Brown* (R,Schoolcraft)	70,157
	Paul H. Todd Jr. (D)	65,212
4.	Edward Hutchinson* (R,St. Joseph)	64,751
	Richard E. Daugherty (D)	55,469
5.	Richard F. Vander Veen* (D,Grand Rapids)	80,778
	Paul G. Goebel Jr. (R)	66,659

Dist.	Representative (Party, Home)	1974 Election
	MICHIGAN	
	(Continued)	
6.	**Bob Carr** (D,E. Lansing)	73,956
	Clifford W. Taylor (R)	73,309
7.	**Donald W. Riegle Jr.*** (D,Flint)	81,014
	Robert E. Eastman (R)	41,603
8.	**Bob Traxler*** (D,Bay City)	77,705
	James M. Sparling Jr. (R)	61,578
9.	**Guy A. Vander Jagt*** (R,Luther)	87,551
	Norm Halbower (D)	65,235
10.	**Elford A. Cederberg*** (R,Midland)	77,118
	Samuel D. Marble (D)	69,246
11.	**Philip E. Ruppe*** (R,Houghton)	83,293
	Francis D. Brouillette (D)	79,793
12.	**James G. O'Hara*** (D,Utica)	89,822
	Eugene J. Tyza (R)	34,250
13.	**Charles C. Diggs Jr.*** (D,Detroit)	63,246
	George E. McCall (R)	8,036
14.	**Lucien N. Nedzi*** (D,Detroit)	93,973
	Herbert O. Steiger (R)	35,723
15.	**William D. Ford*** (D,Taylor)	86,601
	Jack A. Underwood (R)	23,028
16.	**John D. Dingell*** (D,Trenton)	95,834
	Wallace D. English (R)	25,248
17.	**William M. Brodhead** (D,Detroit)	94,242
	Kenneth C. Gallagher (R)	39,856
18.	**James J. Blanchard** (D,Pleasant Ridge)	83,523
	Robert J. Huber* (R)	57,133
19.	**William S. Broomfield*** (R,Birmingham)	86,846
	George F. Montgomery (D)	50,924
	MINNESOTA	
1.	**Albert H. Quie*** (R,Dennison)	95,138
	Ulric Scott (D)	56,868
2.	**Tom Hagedorn** (R,Truman)	88,071
	Steve Babcock (D)	77,780
3.	**Bill Frenzel*** (R,Golden Valley)	83,325
	Bob Riggs (D)	54,630
4.	**Joseph E. Karth*** (D,St. Paul)	95,437
	J.A. Rheinberger (R)	30,083
5.	**Donald M. Fraser*** (D,Minneapolis)	90,012
	Phil Ratte (R)	30,146
6.	**Richard Nolan** (D,Waite Park)	96,465
	Jon Grunseth (R)	77,797
7.	**Bob Bergland*** (D,Roseau)	129,207
	Dan Reber (R)	43,054
8.	**James L. Oberstar** (D,Chisholm)	104,740
	Jerome Arnold (R)	44,298
	W.R.Ojala (Economic Justice)	16,932
	MISSISSIPPI	
1.	**James L. Whitten*** (D,Charleston)	39,158
	Jack Benney (Ind.)	5,250
2.	**David R. Bowen*** (D,Cleveland)	37,909
	Ben F. Hilburn Jr. (R)	15,876
3.	**G.V. Montgomery*** (D,Meridian)	43,020
4.	**Thad Cochran*** (R, Jackson)	62,634
	Kenneth L. Dean (D)	25,699
5.	**Trent Lott*** (R,Pascagoula)	52,489
	W.W. Murphy (D)	10,333
	MISSOURI	
1.	**Willian Clay*** (D,St. Louis)	61,933
	Arthur O. Martin (R)	28,707
2.	**James W. Symington*** (D,Ladue)	85,977
	Howard C. Ohlendorf (R)	55,026
3.	**Leonor K. Sullivan*** (D,St. Louis)	96,201
	Jo Ann P. Raisch (R)	31,489
4.	**William J. Randall*** (D,Independence)	82,447
	Claude Patterson (R)	39,055
5.	**Richard Bolling*** (D,Kansas City)	57,081
	John McDonough (R)	24,669
6.	**Jerry Litton*** (D,Chillicothe)	101,609
	Grover H. Speers (R)	27,147
7.	**Gene Taylor*** (R,Sarcoxie)	79,787
	Richard L. Franks (D)	72,653
8.	**Richard H. Ichord*** (D,Houston)	86,595
	James A. Noland Jr. (R)	37,369

Dist.	Representative (Party, Home)	1974 Election
9.	**William L. Hungate*** (D,Troy)	87,546
	Milton Bischof Jr. (R)	44,318
10.	**Bill D. Burlison*** (D,Cape Girardeau)	77,677
	Truman Farrow (R)	29,050
	MONTANA	
1.	**Max S. Baucus** (D,Missoula)	74,304
	Dick Shoup* (R)	61,309
2.	**John Melcher*** (D,Forsyth)	74,680
	John J. McDonald (R)	43,853
	NEBRASKA	
1.	**Charles Thone*** (R,Lincoln)	82,353
	Hess Dyas (D)	72,099
2.	**John Y. McCollister*** (R,Omaha)	72,731
	Daniel C. Lynch (D)	59,142
3.	**Virginia Smith** (R,Chappel)	80,992
	Wayne W. Ziebarth (D)	80,255
	NEVADA - At Large	
	Jim Santini (D,Las Vegas)	93,665
	David Towell* (R)	61,182
	NEW HAMPSHIRE	
1.	**Norman E. D'Amours** (D,Manchester)	58,388
	David A. Banks (R)	53,610
2.	**James C. Cleveland*** (R,New London)	69,068
	Helen L. Bliss (D)	38,463
	NEW JERSEY	
1.	**James J. Florio** (D,Camden)	80,768
	John E. Hunt * (R)	54,069
2.	**William J. Hughes** (D,Ocean City)	109,763
	Charles W. Sandman Jr.* (R)	79,064
3.	**James J. Howard*** (D,Spring Lake Hts.)	105,979
	Kenneth W. Clark (R)	45,932
4.	**Frank Thompson Jr.*** (D,Trenton)	82,195
	Henry J. Keller (R)	40,797
5.	**Millicent Fenwick** (R,Bernardsville)	81,498
	Frederick M. Bohen (D)	66,380
6.	**Edwin B. Forsythe*** (R,Moorestown)	81,190
	Charles B. Yates (D)	70,353
7.	**Andrew Maguire** (D,Ridgewood)	79,808
	William B. Widnall* (R)	71,377
8.	**Robert A. Roe*** (D,Wayne)	83,724
	Herman Schmidt (R)	27,839
9.	**Henry Helstoski*** (D,Rutherford)	99,592
	Harold A. Pareti (R)	50,859
10.	**Peter Rodino Jr.*** (D,Newark)	53,094
	John R. Taliaferro (R)	9,936
11.	**Joseph G. Minish*** (D, W.Orange)	98,957
	William B. Grant (R)	42,036
12.	**Matthew J. Rinaldo*** (R,Union)	92,829
	Adam K. Levin (D)	46,246
13.	**Helen S. Meyner** (D,Phillipsburg)	86,043
	Joseph J. Maraziti* (R)	64,166
14.	**Dominick V. Daniels*** (D,Union City)	85,438
	Claire J. Sheridan (R)	17,231
15.	**Edward J. Patten*** (D,Perth Amboy)	92,593
	Ernest J. Hammefahr (R)	35,875
	NEW MEXICO	
1.	**Manuel Lujan Jr.*** (R,Albuquerque)	106,268
	Robert A. Mondragon (D)	71,968
2.	**Harold Runnels*** (D,Lovington)	90,127
	Donald W. Trubey (R)	43,045
	NEW YORK³	
1.	**Otis G. Pike*** (D,Riverhead)	101,130
	Donald R. Sallah (R)	44,513
2.	**Thomas J. Downey** (D,W. Islip)	58,289
	James R. Grover, Jr.* (R)	53,344
3.	**Jerome Ambro Jr.** (D.E. Northport)	76,383
	Angelo D. Roncallo* (R,C)	67,986

Dist.	Representative (Party, Home)	1974 Election
	NEW YORK (Continued)	
4.	**Norman F. Lent*** (R,L,C,Baldwin)	89,648
	Franklin Ornstein (D)	69,556
5.	**John W. Wydker*** (R,L,C,Mineola)	96,520
	Allard K. Lowenstein (D)	72,513
6.	**Lester L. Wolff*** (D,Great Neck)	92,582
	Edythe Layne (R,L,C)	59,183
7.	**Joseph P. Addabbo*** (D,L,R,Ozone Park)	83,972
8.	**Benjamin S. Rosenthal*** (D,Flushing)	78,396
	Albert Lemishow (R,L,C)	35,784
9.	**James J. Delaney*** (D,R,C, L.I. City)	92,231
10.	**Mario Biaggi*** (D,R,Bronx)	75,375
	Francis L. McHugh (C)	10,250
11.	**James H. Scheuer** (D,Floral Park)	62,388
	Edward G. Desborough (R)	12,297
12.	**Shirley A. Chisholm*** (D,L,Brooklyn)	26,446
	Francis J. Voyticky (R)	4,577
13.	**Stephen J. Solarz** (D,Brooklyn)	91,008
	Jack N. Dobosh (R,C)	20,229
14.	**Frederick W. Richmond** (D,Brooklyn)	33,195
	Michael Carbajal, Jr. (R)	5,360
	Donald H. Elliott (L)	6,186
15.	**Leo C. Zeferetti** (D,Brooklyn)	45,855
	Austen D. Canade (R)	34,814
	Herbert M. Feinsod (L,C)	11,253
16.	**Elizabeth Holtzman*** (D,L,Brooklyn)	74,010
	Joseph L. Gentili (R,C)	19,806
17.	**John M. Murphy*** (D,Staten Island)	63,805
	Frank J. Biondolillo (R)	28,269
	Jerome Kretchmer (L)	10,622
18.	**Edward I. Koch*** (D,L,N.Y. City)	91,885
	John Boogaerts Jr. (R)	22,560
19.	**Charles B. Randel*** (D,R,L,N.Y. City)	63,146
20.	**Bella S. Abzug*** (D,L,N.Y. City)	76,074
	Stephen Posner (R)	15,053
21.	**Herman Badillo*** (D,L,Bronx)	28,025
22.	**Jonathan B. Bingham*** (D,Bronx)	69,449
	Robert Black (R)	8,142
	John DiGiovanni (C,L)	13,041
23.	**Peter A. Peyser*** (R,C,Irvington)	80,361
	William Greenawalt (D,L)	59,108
24.	**Richard L. Ottinger** (D,Pleasantville	82,542
	Charles Stephens (R,C)	60,180
25.	**Hamilton Fish Jr.*** (R,C,Millbrook)	103,799
	Nicholas Angell (D)	53,357
26.	**Benjamin A. Gilman*** (R,Middletown)	81,562
	John Dow (D,L)	58,161
27.	**Matthew F. McHugh** (D,L,Ithaca)	83,562
	Alfred J. Libous (R)	68,273
28.	**Samuel S. Stratton*** (D,Amsterdam)	156,439
	Wayne E. Wagner (R)	33,493
29.	**Edward W. Pattison** (D,L,W. Sand Lake)	99,324
	Carleton J. King* (R,C)	83,768
30.	**Robert C. McEwen*** (R,C,Ogdensburg)	78,117
	Roger W. Tubby (D)	63,893
31.	**Donald J. Mitchell*** (R,C,Herkimer)	94,319
	Donald J. Reile (D)	59,639
32.	**James M. Hanley*** (D,Syracuse)	88,660
	William E. Bush (R,C)	61,379
33.	**William F. Walsh*** (R,Syracuse)	97,380
	Robert H. Bockman (D)	45,043
34.	**Frank Horton*** (R,Rochester)	105,585
	Irene Gossin (D,L)	45,408
35.	**Barber B. Conable Jr.*** (R,Alexander)	90,269
	Margaret Costanza (D)	63,012
36.	**John J. LaFalce** (D,L,Kenmore)	90,498
	Russell A. Rourke (R,C)	61,442
37.	**Henry J. Nowak** (D,L,Buffalo)	84,064
	Joseph R. Bala (R,C)	27,531
38.	**Jack F. Kemp*** (R,C,Hamburg)	126,687
	Barbara C. Wicks (D,L)	49,929
39.	**James F. Hastings*** (R,Caneadea)	87,321
	William L. Parment (D,L)	53,866
	NORTH CAROLINA	
1.	**Walter B. Jones*** (D,Farmville)	55,323
	Harry McMullan (R)	16,098

Dist.	Representative (Party, Home)	1974 Election
2.	**L. H. Fountain*** (D,Tarboro)	52,786
3.	**David N. Henderson*** (D,Wallace)	50,931
4.	**Ike Andrews*** (D,Siler City)	62,600
	Ward Purrington (R)	33,521
5.	**Stephen L. Neal** (D,Winston-Salem)	64,634
	Wilmer Mizell* (R)	59,182
6.	**Richardson Preyer*** (D,Greensboro)	56,507
	R. S. Ritchie (R)	31,906
7.	**Charles Rose*** (D,Fayetteville)	49,780
8.	**W.G. Hefner** (D,Concord)	61,591
	Earl B. Ruth* (R)	46,500
9.	**James G. Martin*** (R,Davisson)	51,032
	Milton Short (D)	41,387
10.	**James T. Broyhill*** (R,Lenoir)	63,382
	Jack L. Rhyne (D)	53,131
11.	**Roy A. Taylor*** (D,Asheville)	89,163
	Albert F. Gilman (R)	45,983
	NORTH DAKOTA - At Large	
	Mark Andrews* (R,Mapleton)	130,184
	Byron Dorgan (D)	103,504
	OHIO	
1.	**Willis D. Gradison Jr.** (R,Cincinnati)	70,284
	Thomas A. Luken (D	67,685
2.	**Donald D. Clancy*** (R,Cincinnati)	71,512
	Edward W. Wolterman (D)	62,530
3.	**Charles W. Whalen Jr.*** (R,Dayton)	82,159
4.	**Tennyson Guyer*** (R,Findlay)	81,674
	James L. Gehrlich (D)	51,065
5.	**Delbert L. Latta*** (R,Bowling Green)	89,161
	Bruce Edwards (D)	53,391
6.	**William H. Harsha*** (R,Portsmouth)	93,400
	Lloyd Allan Wood (D)	42,316
7.	**Clarence J. Brown*** (R,Urbana)	73,503
	Patrick L. Nelson (D)	34,828
	Dorothy Franke (Ind.)	13,088
8.	**Thomas N. Kindness** (R,Hamilton)	51,097
	T. Edward Strinko (D)	45,701
	Don Gingerich (Ind.)	23,616
9.	**Thomas Ludlow Ashley*** (D,Maumee)	64,831
	Carleton S. Finkbeiner Jr. (R)	57,892
10.	**Clarence E. Miller*** (R,Lancaster)	100,521
	H. Kent Bumpass (D)	42,333
11.	**J. William Stanton*** (R,Painesville)	79,756
	Michael D. Coffey (D)	52,017
12.	**Samuel L. Devine*** (R,Columbus)	73,303
	Fran Ryan (D)	70,818
13.	**Charles A. Mosher*** (R,Oberlin)	72,881
	Fred M. Ritenauer (D)	53,766
14.	**John F. Seiberling*** (D,Akron)	93,931
	Mark Figetakis (R)	30,603
15.	**Chalmers P. Wylie*** (R,Worthington)	79,376
	M. L. McGee (D)	49,683
16.	**Ralph S. Regula*** (R,Navarre)	92,986
	John G. Freedom (D)	48,754
17.	**John M. Ashbrook*** (R,Johnstown)	70,708
	David D. Noble (D)	63,342
18.	**Wayne L. Hays*** (D,Flushing)	90,447
	Ralph H. Romig (R)	47,385
19.	**Charles J. Carney*** (D,Youngstown)	97,709
	James L. Ripple (R)	36,649
20.	**James V. Stanton*** (D,Cleveland)	86,405
	Robert A. Frantz (R)	12,991
21.	**Louis Stokes*** (D,Cleveland)	58,969
	Bill Mack (R)	12,986
22.	**Charles A. Vanik*** (D,Euclid)	112,671
	William J. Franz (R)	30,585
23.	**Ronald M. Mottl*** (D,Parma)	53,338
	George E. Mastics (R)	46,810
	Dennis J. Kucinich (Ind.)	45,186
	OKLAHOMA	
1.	**James R. Jones*** (D,Tulsa)	88,159
	George Alfred Mizer Jr. (R)	41,697

Dist.	Representative (Party, Home)	1974 Election

OKLAHOMA
(Continued)

2. **Theodore M. Risenhoover** (D,Tahlequah). . | 78,046
   Ralph F. Keen (R). . . . . | 54,110
3. **Carl Albert*** (D,McAlester) . . . . | (1)
4. **Tom Steed*** (D,Shawnee) . . . . | (1)
5. **John Jarman*** (D,Oklahoma City). . . . . | 52,107
   M. H. Edwards (R). . . . . | 48,705
6. **Glenn English** (D,Cordell). . . . . | 76,302
   John N. Camp* (R). . . . . | 63,731

OREGON

1. **Les AuCoin** (D,Forest Grove). . . . . | 114,629
   Diarmuid O'Scannlain (R). . . . . | 89,848
2. **Al Ullman*** (D,Baker). . . . . | 140,963
   Kenneth Brown (R). . . . . | 39,441
3. **Robert Duncan** (D,Gresham). . . . . | 129,290
   John Piacentini (R). . . . . | 54,080
4. **James Weaver** (D,Eugene). . . . . | 97,580
   John Dellenback* (R). . . . . | 86,950

PENNSYLVANIA

1. **William A. Barret*** (D,Philadelphia). . . . . . . | 96,988
   Russel M. Nigro (R). . . . . | 29,772
2. **Robert N. C. Nix*** (D,Philadelphia). . . . . . . | 75,033
   Jesse W. Woods Jr. (R). . . . . | 26,353
3. **William J. Green*** (D,Philadelphia). . . . . . . | 84,675
   Richard P. Colbert (R). . . . . | 27,692
4. **Joshua Eilberg*** (D,Philadelphia). . . . . | 123,952
   Isadore Einhorn (R). . . . . | 50,688
5. **Richard T. Schulze** (R,Malvern). . . . . | 83,526
   Leo D. McDermott (D). . . . . | 56,626
6. **Gus Yatron*** (D,Reading). . . . . | 111,127
   Stephen Postupack (R). . . . . | 35,805
7. **Robert W. Edgar** (D,Broomhall). . . . . | 89,680
   Stephen J. McEwen Jr. (R). . . . . | 70,894
8. **Edward G. Biester Jr.*** (R,Furlong). . . . . . | 75,313
   William B. Moyer (D). . . . . | 54,815
9. **E. G. Shuster*** (R,Everett). . . . . | 73,881
   Robert D. Ford (D). . . . . | 56,844
10. **Joseph M. McDade*** (R,Scranton). . . . . . . | 100,793
    Thomas J. Hanlon (D). . . . . | 54,401
11. **Daniel J. Flood*** (D,Wilkes-Barre). . . . . . . | 111,572
    Richard A. Muzyka (R). . . . . | 38,106
12. **John P. Murtha*** (D,Johnstown). . . . . | 89,193
    Harry M. Fox (R). . . . . | 64,416
13. **Lawrence Coughlin*** (R,Villanova). . . . . . . | 98,985
    Lawrence H. Curry (D). . . . . | 59,433
14. **William S. Moorhead*** (D, Pittsburgh). . . . . | 93,169
    Zachary T. Davis (R). . . . . | 27,116
15. **Fred B. Rooney*** (D,Bethlehem). . . . . | 85,905
16. **Edwin D. Eshleman*** (R,Lancaster). . . . . . | 73,130
    Michael J. Minney (D). . . . . | 40,273
17. **Herman T. Schneebeli*** (R,Williamsport). . . | 70,274
    Peter C. Wambach (D). . . . . | 64,576
18. **H. John Heinz, 3d*** (R,Pittsburgh). . . . . . . | 107,723
    Francis J. McArdle (D). . . . . | 41,706
19. **William F. Goodling*** (R. Jacobus). . . . . . . | 66,417
    Arthur L. Berger (D). . . . . | 61,414
20. **Joseph M. Gaydos*** (D,McKeesport). . . . . . | 112,237
    Joseph J. Anderko (R). . . . . | 25,129
21. **John H. Dent*** (D,Ligonier). . . . . | 88,701
    Charles L. Sconing (R). . . . . | 38,111
22. **Thomas E. Morgan*** (D,Fredericktown). . . . | 83,654
    James R. Montgomery (R). . . . . | 41,706
23. **Albert W. Johnson*** (R,Smethport). . . . . . . | 67,192
    Yates Mast (D). . . . . | 60,211
24. **Joseph P. Vigorito*** (D,Erie). . . . . | 76,920
    Clement R. Scalzitti (R). . . . . | 54,277
25. **Gary A. Myers** (R,Butler). . . . . | 74,645
    Frank M. Clark* (D). . . . . | 64,049

RHODE ISLAND

1. **Fernand J. St. Germain*** (D,Woonsocket). . | 105,288
   Ernest Barone (R). . . . . | 39,096

Dist.	Representative (Party, Home)	1974 Election

2. **Edward P. Beard** (D,Cranston). . . . . | 124,759
   Vincent J. Rotondo (R) . . . . | 34,728

SOUTH CAROLINA

1. **Mendel J. Davis*** (D,Charleston). . . . . | 63,111
   George B. Rast (R). . . . . | 22,450
2. **Floyd Spence*** (R,Lexington). . . . . | 58,936
   Matthew J. Perry (D). . . . . | 45,205
3. **Butler Derrick** (D,Edgefield). . . . . | 55,120
   Marshall J. Parker (R). . . . . | 34,046
4. **James R. Mann*** (D,Greenville). . . . . | 45,070
   Robert L. Watkins (R). . . . . | 26,185
5. **Kenneth L. Holland** (D,Camden) . . . . | 47,614
   Len Phillips (R). . . . . | 29,294
6. **John W. Jenrette Jr.** (D, N.Myrtle Beach) . . . | 45,396
   Edward L. Young* (R) . . . . | 41,982

SOUTH DAKOTA

1. **Larry Pressler** (R,Humboldt). . . . . | 78,266
   Frank E. Denholm* (D). . . . . | 63,339
2. **James Abdnor*** (R,Kennebec). . . . . | 88,746
   Jack M. Weiland (D). . . . . | 42,119

TENNESSEE

1. **James H. Quillen*** (R,Kingsport). . . . . | 76,394
   Lloyd Blevins (D). . . . . | 42,523
2. **John Duncan*** (R,Knoxville). . . . . | 87,419
   Jesse James Brown (D). . . . . | 35,920
3. **Marilyn Lloyd** (D,Chattanooga). . . . . | 61,926
   LaMar Baker* (R). . . . . | 55,580
4. **Joe E. Evins*** (D,Smithville). . . . . | 94,847
5. **Richard Fulton*** (D,Goodlettsville). . . . . . . | 88,206
6. **Robin Beard*** (R,Brentwood). . . . . | 76,928
   Tim Schaeffer (D). . . . . | 58,824
7. **Ed Jones*** (D,Yorkville). . . . . | 83,231
8. **Harold E. Ford** (D,Memphis). . . . . | 67,925
   Dan Kuykendall* (R). . . . . | 67,181

TEXAS

1. **Wright Patman*** (D,Texarkana) . . . . | 49,426
   James W. Farris (R). . . . . | 22,619
2. **Charles Wilson*** (D,Lufkin). . . . . | 57,096
3. **James M. Collins*** (R,Dallas). . . . . | 63,489
   Harold Collum (D). . . . . | 34,623
4. **Ray Roberts*** (D,McKinney). . . . . | 48,209
   Dick LeTourneau (R). . . . . | 16,113
5. **Alan Steelman*** (R,Dallas). . . . . | 28,446
   Mike McKool (D). . . . . | 26,190
6. **Olin E. Teague*** (D,College Station). . . . . . | 53,345
   Carl A. Nigliazzo (R). . . . . | 10,908
7. **Bill Archer*** (R,Houston). . . . . | 70,363
   Jim Brady (D). | 18,524
8. **Bob Eckhardt*** (D,Houston). . . . . | 30,158
   Donald D. Whitefield (R). . . . . | 11,605
9. **Jack Brooks*** (D,Beaumont). . . . . | 37,275
   Coleman R. Ferguson (R). . . . . | 22,935
10. **J. J. Pickle*** (D,Austin). . . . . | 76,240
    Paul A. Weiss (R). . . . . | 18,560
11. **W. R. Poage*** (D,Waco). . . . . | 46,828
    Don Clements (R). . . . . | 9,883
12. **James C. Wright Jr.*** (D,Ft. Worth). . . . . . . | 42,632
    James S. Garvey (R). . . . . | 11,543
13. **Jack Hightower*** (D,Vernon). . . . . | 53,094
    Bob Price (R). | 39,087
14. **John Young*** (D,Corpus Christi). . . . . | 41,066
15. **E. de la Garza*** (D,Mission). . . . . | 42,567
16. **Richard C. White*** (D,El Paso). . . . . | 42,880
17. **Omar Burleson*** (D,Anson). . . . . | 64,595
18. **Barbara Jordan*** (D,Houston). . . . . | 36,597
    Robbins Mitchell (R). . . . . | 6,053
19. **George Mahon*** (D,Lubbock). . . . . | 49,619
20. **Henry B. Gonzalez*** (D,San Antonio). . . . . | 39,538
21. **Robert Krueger** (D,New Braunfels). . . . . . . | 53,543
    Douglas S. Harlan (R). . . . . | 45,959
22. **Bob Casey*** (D,Pasadena). . . . . | 47,783
    Ron Paul (R). | 19,483
23. **Abraham Kazen Jr.*** (D,Laredo). . . . . | 47,249
24. **Dale Milford*** (D,Grand Prairie). . . . . | 36,085
    Joseph Beaman Jr. (R). . . . . | 9,698

Dist.	Representative (Party, Home)	1974 Election
	UTAH	
1.	**K. Gunn McKay*** (D,Huntsville)	124,793
	Ronald W. Inkley (R)	62,807
2.	**Allan T. Howe** (D,Salt Lake City)	105,739
	Stephen Harmsen (R)	100,259
	VERMONT - At Large	
	James M. Jeffords (R. Montpelier)	74,561
	Francis J. Cain (D)	53,701
	VIRGINIA	
1.	**Thomas N. Downing*** (D,Newport News)	58,338
2.	**G. William Whitehurst*** (R,Norfolk)	49,369
	Robert Richards (D)	32,923
3.	**David E. Satterfield 3d*** (D,Richmond)	64,627
	Alan Robert Ogden (Ind.)	7,574
4.	**Robert W. Daniel Jr.*** (R. Spring Grove)	48,032
	Lester E. Schlitz (D)	36,489
	Curtis W. Harris (Ind.)	17,224
5.	**W. D. Daniel*** (D,Danville)	52,459
6.	**M. Caldwell Butler*** (R,Roanoke)	45,805
	Paul J. Pluckett (D)	27,350
	Warren D. Saunders (Ind.)	26,466
7.	**J. Kenneth Robinson*** (R,Winchester)	54,267
	George H. Gilliam (D)	48,611
8.	**Herbert E. Harris 2d** (D,Alexandria)	53,074
	Stanford E. Parris* (R)	38,997
9.	**William C. Wampler*** (R,Bristol)	68,183
	Charles J. Horne (D)	65,783
10.	**Joseph L. Fisher** (D,Arlington)	67,184
	Joel T. Broyhill* (R)	56,649
	WASHINGTON	
1.	**Joel Pritchard*** (R,Seattle)	108,391
	W. R. Knedlik (D)	44,655
2.	**Lloyd Meeds*** (D.Everett)	81,565
	Ronald C. Reed (R)	53,157
3.	**Don Bonker** (D,Ridgefield)	93,980
	A. Ludlow Kramer (R)	58,774
4.	**Mike McCormack*** (D,Richland)	84,949
	Floyd Paxton (R)	59,249
5.	**Thomas S. Foley*** (D,Spokane)	87,959
	Gary G. Gage (R)	48,739

Dist.	Representative (Party, Home)	1974 Election
6.	**Floyd V. Hicks*** (D,Tacoma)	95,354
	George M. Nalley (R)	37,400
7.	**Brock Adams*** (D,Seattle)	85,593
	Raymond Pritchard (R)	34,847
	WEST VIRGINIA	
1.	**Robert H. Mollohan*** (D,Fairmont)	72,457
	Joe Laurita Jr. (R)	48,966
2.	**Harley O. Staggers*** (D,Keyser)	73,683
	William H. Loy (R)	40,779
3.	**John M. Slack*** (D,Charleston)	77,586
	William L. Larcamp (R)	33,623
4.	**Ken Hechler*** (D,Huntington)	66,420
	WISCONSIN	
1.	**Les Aspin*** (D,Racine)	81,902
	Leonard W. Smith (R)	34,288
2.	**Robert W. Kastenmeier*** (D,Sun Prairie)	93,561
	Elizabeth T. Miller (R)	50,890
3.	**Alvin Baldus** (D,Menominie)	76,668
	Vernon W. Thomson* (R)	71,171
4.	**Clement J. Zablocki*** (D,Milwaukee)	84,768
	Lewis H. Collison (R)	27,818
5.	**Henry S. Reuss*** (D,Milwaukee)	65,060
	Mildren A. Morries (R)	16,293
6.	**William A. Steiger*** (R,Oshkosh)	86,652
	Nancy J. Simenz (D)	51,571
7.	**David R. Obey*** (D,Wausau)	104,468
	Josef Burger (R)	43,558
8.	**Robert J. Cornell** (D,DePere)	79,923
	Harold V. Froelich* (R)	66,889
9.	**Robert W. Kasten Jr.** (R,Milwaukee)	77,733
	Lynn S. Adelman (D)	66,071
	WYOMING - At Large	
	Teno Roncalio* (D,Cheyenne)	69,434
	Tom Stroock (R)	57,499

Non-Voting Delegates

District of Columbia	Walter E. Fauntroy*
Guam	Antonio Borja Won Pat* (Sumay)
Virgin Islands	Ron deLugo* (St. Croix)

Puerto Rico

Resident Commissioner	Jaime Benitez (San Juan)

1) Arkansas, Florida and Oklahoma laws do not require a tally for unopposed candidates.
2) Unofficial returns in Apr. 29. 1975 special election. In 1974, Ms. Pettis' husband, Jerry L., won the election over B. R. Vincent (D) 88,548 to 46,449; he was killed in an airplane crash Feb. 14. 1975.
3) Representatives and candidates supported by coalitions claim membership in the first party indicated after their names.

Longevity of Male Government Officials to End of 1968

By period of initial entry into office (Compared to white males in U.S. population)
Source: Statistical Bulletin. Metropolitan Life Ins. Co.

Period of 1st Entry to Office	Number at Entry	Avg. Age at Entry	No. Died By end of 1968	Avg. Years Lived From Entry to End '68 or Prior Death	Differentials
		Representatives			
1861-1900	2,434	45.4	2,434	23.8	0.1
1901-1930	1,582	46.1	1,520	24.6	0.4
1931-1968	1,659	45.7	585	17.0	-0.2
		Senators			
1861-1900	392	49.5	392	21.7	0.8
1901-1930	319	52.3	310	21.0	1.1
1931-1968	339	51.5	148	15.7	0.4
		State Governors			
1901-1930	415	49.5	412	22.1	0.7
1931-1968	441	49.6	179	15.5	0.5
		Cabinet Officers			
1789-1860	118	47.8	118	21.4	-0.2
1861-1900	108	53.1	108	20.0	1.4
1901-1930	73	52.9	73	21.1	1.8
1931-1968	92	52.7	38	12.2	-0.7
		Supreme Court Justices			
1789-1900	57	51.2	57	20.2	0.2
1901-1968	39	54.3	25	17.2	1.4

*The difference between (a) the average number of years actually lived from entry into office to end of 1968 or prior death and (b) the average life expectancy of contemporaneous cohorts of white males in the general population of the United States observed for the same periods.

Political Divisions of the U.S. Senate and House of Representatives from 1885 (34th Cong.) to 1975-77 (94th Cong.)

Source: Clerk of the House of Representatives

Congress	Years	Senate					House of Representatives				
		Number of Senators	Democrats	Republicans	Other parties	Vacant	Number of Representatives	Democrats	Republicans	Other parties	Vacant
34th	1855-57	62	42	15	5		234	83	108	43	
35th	1857-59	64	39	20	5		237	131	92	14	
36th	1859-61	66	38	26	2		237	101	113	23	
37th	1861-63	50	11	31	7	1	178	42	106	28	2
38th	1863-65	51	12	39			183	80	103		
39th	1865-67	52	10	42			191	46	145		
40th	1867-69	53	11	42			193	49	143		1
41st	1869-71	74	11	61		2	243	73	170		
42d	1871-73	74	17	57			243	104	139		
43d	1873-75	74	19	54		1	293	88	203		2
44th	1875-77	76	29	46		1	293	71	107	3	2
45th	1877-79	76	36	39	1		293	156	137		
46th	1879-81	76	43	33			293	150	128	14	1
47th	1881-83	76	37	37	2		293	130	152	11	
48th	1883-85	76	36	40			325	200	119	6	
49th	1885-87	76	34	41		1	325	182	140	2	1
50th	1887-89	76	37	39			325	170	151	4	
51st	1889-91	84	37	47			330	156	173	1	
52d	1891-93	88	39	47	2		333	231	88	14	
53d	1893-95	88	44	38	3	3	356	220	126	10	
54th	1895-97	88	39	44	5		357	104	246	7	
55th	1897-99	90	34	46	10		357	134	206	16	1
56th	1899-1901	90	26	53	11		357	163	185	9	
57th	1901-3	90	29	56	3	2	357	153	198	5	1
58th	1903-5	90	32	58			386	178	207		1
59th	1905-7	90	32	58			386	136	250		
60th	1907-9	92	29	61		2	386	164	222		
61st	1909-11	92	32	59		1	391	172	219		
62d	1911-13	92	42	49		1	391	228	162	1	
63d	1913-15	96	51	44	1		435	290	127	18	
64th	1915-17	96	56	39	1		435	231	193	8	3
65th	1917-19	96	53	42	1		435	[1]210	216	9	
66th	1919-21	96	47	48	1		435	191	237	7	
67th	1921-23	96	37	59			435	132	300	1	2
68th	1923-25	96	43	51	2		435	207	225	3	
69th	1925-27	96	40	54	1	1	435	183	247	5	
70th	1927-29	96	47	48	1		435	195	237	3	
71st	1929-31	96	39	56	1		435	163	267	1	4
72d	1931-33	96	47	48	1		435	[2]216	218	1	
73d	1933-35	96	59	36	1		435	313	117	5	
74th	1935-37	96	69	25	2		435	322	103	10	
75th	1937-39	96	75	17	4		435	333	89	13	
76th	1939-41	96	69	23	4		435	262	169	4	
77th	1941-43	96	66	28	2		435	267	162	6	
78th	1943-45	96	57	38	1		435	222	209	4	
79th	1945-47	96	57	38	1		435	243	190	1	
80th	1947-49	96	45	51			435	188	246	1	
81st	1949-51	96	54	42			435	263	171	1	
82d	1951-53	96	48	47	1		435	234	199	2	
83d	1953-55	96	46	48	2		435	213	221	1	
84th	1955-57	96	48	47	1		435	232	203		
85th	1957-59	96	49	47			435	234	201		
86th	1959-61	98	64	34			[3]436	283	153		
87th	1961-63	100	64	36			[4]437	262	175		
88th	1963-65	100	67	33			435	258	176		1
89th	1965-67	100	68	32			435	295	140		
90th	1967-69	100	64	36			435	248	187		
91st	1969-71	100	58	42			435	243	192		
92d	1971-73	100	54	44	2		435	255	180		
93d	1973-75	100	56	42	2		435	242	192	1	
94th	1975-77	100	61	37	2		435	291	144		

[1] Democrats organized House with help of other parties. [2] Democrats organized House due to Republican deaths. [3] Proclamation declaring Alaska a State issued Jan. 3, 1959. [4] Proclamation declaring Hawaii a State issued Aug. 21, 1959.

NATIONAL DEFENSE

Data as of July, 1975

Chairman, Joint Chiefs of Staff
George S. Brown (USAF)

Army

General of the Army	Date of Rank
Bradley, Omar N.	Sept. 20, 1950

Generals

Davison, Michael S.	May	26, 1971
Deane, John R.	Feb.	12, 1975
DePuy, William E.	July	1, 1973
Haig, Alexander	Mar.	18, 1974
Hennessey, John J.	Nov.	8, 1974
Kerwin, Walter T., Jr.	Feb.	1, 1973
Rogers, Bernard W.	Nov.	7, 1974
Rosson, William B.	May	15, 1969
Stilwell, Richard G.	July	31, 1973
Weyand, Frederick C.	Oct.	31, 1970
Zais, Melvin	Aug.	1, 1973

Air Force

Chief of Staff—David C. Jones

Generals

Carlton, Paul K.	Oct.	9, 1972
Clay, Lucius D., Jr.	Sept.	1, 1970
Dixon, Robert J.	Oct.	1, 1973
Dougherty, Russell E.	May	5, 1972
Eade, George J.	Apr.	18, 1973
Ellis, Richard H.	Sept.	30, 1973
McBride, William V.	Sept.	1, 1974
Phillips, Samuel C.	Aug.	1, 1973
Seith, Louis T.	Aug.	1, 1974

Vogt, John W., Jr.	Apr.	7, 1972
Wilson, Louis L., Jr.	July	1, 1974

Navy

Chief of Naval Operations
Admiral James L. Holloway III (Aviation)

Admirals

Bagley, David H.	May	21, 1975
Gayler, Noel A.M. (Aviation)	Sept.	1, 1972
Johnson, Means, Jr.	Nov.	25, 1973
Kidd, Isaac C., Jr.	Dec.	1, 1971
Michaelis, Frederick H. (Aviation)	Apr.	19, 1975
Shear, Harold E.	May	24, 1974
Weinel, John P.	Aug.	2, 1974
Weisner, Maurice F. (Aviation)	Sept.	1, 1972

Marine

Corps Commandant, with rank of General

Louis H. Wilson	July	1, 1975

Asst. Commandant with rank of General

Samuel Jaskilka	July	1, 1975

Coast Guard

Commandant, with rank of Admiral

Owen W. Siler	June	1, 1974

Vice Commandant, with rank of Vice Admiral

Ellis L. Perry	July	1, 1974

United States Unified and Specified Commands

Alaskan Command — Lt. Gen. James E. Hill, USAF.

Atlantic Command — Adm. Ralph Cousins, USN.

North American Air Defense Command & Continental Air Defense Command — Gen. Lucius D. Clay Jr., USAF.

European Command — Gen. Alexander Haig Jr., USA.

Pacific Command — Adm. Noel A. M. Gayler, USN.

Southern Command — Gen. William B. Rosson, USA.

Strat. Air Command — Gen. Russell E. Dougherty, USAF

U.S. Readiness Command — Gen. John J. Hennessey, USA.

North Atlantic Treaty Organization International Commands

Supr. Allied Commander, Europe (SACEUR) — Gen. Alexander Haig Jr., USA.

Deputy SACEUR — Gen. Sir John Mogg (UK).

C-in-C, Allied Forces, Northern Europe — Gen. Sir John Sharp (UK).

C-in-C, Allied Forces, Central Europe — Gen. Ernst Ferber (Germany).

C-in-C, Allied Forces, Southern Europe — Adm. Stanfield Turner, USN.

Cmdr. Naval Forces, Southern Europe — Adm. L. Tomasulo (Italy).

Supr. Allied Cmdr. Atlantic (SACLANT) — Adm. Issac Kidd, USN.

Deputy SACLANT — Adm. James Jungius (UK).

Cmdr. Striking Fleet Atlantic — V. Adm. John J. Shanahan, USN.

Allied Cmdr. in Chief, Channel — Adm. Sir Edward Ashmore (UK).

Primary U.S. Military Training Centers

Army

Name, P.O. Address	Zip	Nearest City	Name, P.O. Address	Zip	Nearest City
Aberdeen Proving Ground, MD.	21005	Aberdeen	Fort Jackson, SC.	29207	Columbia
Carlisle Barracks, PA.	17013	Carlisle	Fort Knox, KY.	40121	Louisville
Fort Belvoir, VA.	22060	Alexandria	Fort Leavenworth, KS.	66027	Leavenworth
Fort Benning, GA.	31905	Columbus	Fort Lee, VA.	23801	Petersburg
Fort Bliss, TX.	79906	El Paso	Fort McClellan, AL.	36201	Anniston
Fort Bragg, NC.	28307	Fayetteville	Fort Monmouth, NJ.	07703	Red Bank
Fort Devens, MA.	01433	Ayer	Fort Ord, CA.	93941	Seaside
Fort Dix, NJ.	08640	Trenton	Fort Polk, LA.	71459	Leesville
Fort Eustis, VA.	23604	Newport News	Fort Rucker, AL.	36362	Dothan
			Fort Sill, OK.	73503	Lawton
Fort Gordon, GA.	30905	Augusta	Fort Leonard Wood, MO.	65473	Rolla
Fort Wadsworth, NY.	10305	Staten Island	Redstone Arsenal, AL.	35809	Huntsville
Fort Benjamin Harrison, IN.	46216	Indianapolis	Rock Island Arsenal, IL.	61202	Rock Island
Fort Sam Houston, TX.	78234	San Antonio	The Judge Advocate.		Charlottes-
Fort Huachuca, AZ.	85613	Sierra Vista	General School, VA.	22901	ville

Navy

Name, P.O. Address	Zip	Nearest City	Name, P.O. Address	Zip	Nearest City
Great Lakes, IL.	60088	Waukegan	Orlando, FL.	32813	Orlando
San Diego, CA.	92133	San Diego			

353

Marine Corps

Name, P.O. Address	Zip	Nearest City	Name, P.O. Address	Zip	Nearest City
Camp Lejeune, N.C.	28542	Jacksonville, N.C.	Marine Corps Development		
Marine Corps Air Station, NC	28533	Cherry Point, N.C.	& Educ. Command, Va.	22134	Quantico
Marine Corps Air Station, SC	29902	Beaufort	Parris Island, S.C.	29905	Beaufort
Marine Corps Air Station, CA	92630	El Toro	Camp Pendleton, Calif.	92055	Oceanside
Marine Corps Air Station, AZ	85364	Yuma	San Diego, Calif.	92140	San Diego

Air Force

Name, P.O. Address	Zip	Nearest City	Name, P.O. Address	Zip	Nearest City
Chanute AFB, Ill.	61866	Rantoul	Maxwell AFB, Ala.	36112	Montgomery
Columbus AFB, Miss.	39701	Columbus	Moody AFB, Ga.	31601	Valdosta
Craig AFB, Ala.	36701	Selma	Nellis AFB, Nev.	89110	Las Vegas
Fairchild AFB, Wash.	99011	Spokane	Randolph AFB, Texas	78148	San Antonio
Keesler AFB, Miss.	39534	Biloxi	Reese AFB, Tex.	79489	Lubbock
Lackland AFB, Texas	78236	San Antonio	Sheppard AFB, Tex.	76311	Wichita Falls
Laughlin AFB, Tex.	78840	Del Rio	Vance AFB, Okla.	73701	Enid
Lowry AFB, Colo.	80230	Denver	Webb AFB, Texas	79720	Big Spring
Mather AFB, Calif.	95655	Sacramento	Williams AFB, Ariz.	85224	Chandler

Personal Salutes and Honors

The United States national salute, 21 guns, is also the salute to a national flag. The independence of the United States is commemorated by the salute to the union — one gun for each state — fired at noon on July 4 at all military posts provided with suitable artillery.

A 21-gun salute on arrival and departure, with 4 ruffles and flourishes, is rendered to the President of the United States, to an ex-President and to a President-elect. The national anthem or *Hail to the Chief*, as appropriate, is played for the President, and the national anthem for the others. A 21-gun salute on arrival and departure, with 4 ruffles and flourishes, also is rendered to the sovereign or chief of state of a foreign country or a member of a reigning royal family; the national anthem of his or her country is played. The music is considered an inseparable part of the salute and will immediately follow the ruffles and flourishes without pause.

Rank	Salute—guns		Ruffles flour- ishes	Music
	Arrive	Leave		
Vice President of United States	19		4	Hail Columbia
Speaker of House	19		4	March
American or foreign ambassador	19		4	Nat. anthem of official
Premier or prime minister	19		4	Nat. anthem of official
Secretary of Defense, Army, Navy or Air Force	19	19	4	March
Other Cabinet members, Senate President pro tempore, Governor, or Chief Justice of U.S.	19		4	March
Chairman, Joint Chiefs of Staff	19	19	4	
Army Chief of Staff, Chief of Naval Operations, Air Force Chief of Staff, Marine Commandant	19	19	4	General's or
General of the Army; General of the Air Force; Fleet Admiral	19	19	4	Admiral's March
Generals, Admirals	17	17	4	
Assistant Secretaries of Defense, Army, Navy or Air Force	17	17	4	March
Chairman of a Committee of Congress	17		4	March

Other salutes (on arrival only) include 15 guns for American envoys or ministers and foreign envoys or ministers accredited to the United States; 15 guns for a lieutenant general or vice admiral; 13 guns for a major general or rear admiral (upper half); 13 guns for American ministers resident and ministers resident accredited to the U.S.; 11 guns for a brigadier general or rear admiral (lower half); 11 guns for American charges d'affaires and like officials accredited to U.S.; and 11 guns for consuls general accredited to U.S.

Military Units, U.S. Army and Air Force

Army units. Squad. In infantry usually ten men under a staff sergeant. **Platoon.** In infantry 4 squads under a lieutenant. **Company.** Headquarters section and 4 platoons under a captain. (Company in the artillery is a battery; in the cavalry, a troop). **Battalion.** Hdqts. and 4 or more companies under a lieutenant colonel. (Battalion size unit in the cavalry is a squadron.) **Brigade.** Hdqts. and 3 or more battalions under a colonel. **Division.** Hdqts. and 3 brigades with artillery, combat support and combat service support units under a major general. **Army Corps.** Two or more divisions with corps troops under a lieutenant general. **Field Army.** Hdqts. and two or more corps with field Army troops under a general.

Air Force Units. Flight. Small components of a squadron organized for special purpose such as medical evacuation flights. **Squadron.** The basic organized unit of the Air Force, used by operational as well as support forces but not limited by numbers of personnel assigned; two to three tactical squadrons are assigned to a tactical wing. **Group.** Terminologyy used for special tactical forces and for many support elements. They do not necessarily have subordinate units assigned. **Wing.** Used for tactical and support forces. A tactical wing usually has two to three operational squadrons assigned. **Division.** An organizational component of operational numbered Air Forces consisting of two to three wings, also used to designate numerous support and research components. **Air Force.** An intermediate echelon of command directly under the headquarters of a large operational command, usually with four to seven subordinate divisions. **Major command.** A major subdivision of the Air Force that is assigned a major segment of the USAF mission, usually two or four subordinate Air Force elements.

Armed Services Senior Enlisted Adviser

The U.S. Army, Navy and Air Force in 1966-67 each created a new position of senior enlisted adviser whose primary job is to represent the point of view of his services' enlisted men and women on matters of welfare, morale and any problem concerning enlisted personnel. The senior adviser will have direct access to the military chief of his branch of service and policy-making bodies.

The senior enlisted adviser for each Dept. is:

Army-Sgt. Major of the Army William G. Bainbridge.

Navy-Master Chief Petty Officer of the Navy John D. Whittet.

Air Force-Chief Master Sgt. of the Air Force Thomas N. Barnes.

Marines-Sgt. Major of the Marine Corps Henry H. Black.

U. S. Army Insignia and Chevrons

Source: Department of the Army

Grade	Insignia

General of the Armies
(General John J. Pershing, the only person to have held this rank, was authorized to prescribe his own insignia, but never wore in excess of four stars. The rank originally was established by Congress for George Washington in 1799, but no record has been found to show that the appointment was made.)

General of the Army . . . Five silver stars fastened together in a circle and the coat of arms of the United States in gold color metal with shield and crest enameled.
General . . . . Four silver stars
Lieutenant General . . . . . . .Three silver stars
Major General . . . . .Two silver stars
Brigadier General . . . . .One silver star
Colonel . . . . .Silver eagle
Lieutenant Colonel . . . . . . .Silver oak leaf
Major . . . . .Gold oak leaf
Captain . . . . .Two silver bars
First Lieutenant . . . . .One silver bar
Second Lieutenant . . . . . . .One gold bar

Warrant officers
Grade Four—Silver bar with 4 enamel black bands.
Grade Three—Silver bar with 3 enamel black bands.
Grade Two—Silver bar with 2 enamel black bands.
Grade One—Silver bar with 1 enamel black band.

Non-Commissioned officers
Sergeant Major of the Army (E-9). Same as Command Sergeant Major (below). Also wears distinctive red and white shield on lapel.
Command Sergeant Major (E-9). Three chevrons above three arcs with a 5-pointed star with a wreath around the star between the chevrons and arcs.
Sergeant Major (E-9). Three chevrons above three arcs with a five-pointed star between the chevrons and arcs.
First Sergeant (E-8). Three chevrons above three arcs with a lozenge between the chevrons and arcs.
Master Sergeant (E-8). Three chevrons above three arcs.
Platoon Sergeant or Sergeant First Class (E-7). Three chevrons above two arcs.
Staff Sergeant (E-6). Three chevrons above one arc.
Sergeant (E-5). Three chevrons.
Corporal (E-4). Two chevrons

Specialists
Specialist Seven (E-7). Three arcs above the eagle device.
Specialist Six (E-6). Two arcs above the eagle device.
Specialist Five (E-5). One arc above the eagle device.
Specialist Four (E-4). Eagle device only.

Other Enlisted
Private First Class (E-3). One chevron above one arc.
Private (E-2). One chevron.
Private (E-1). None.

United States Army

Source: Department of the Army

Army Military Personnel on Active Duty (a)

June 30 (b)	Total strength	Commissioned officers Total	Male	Female (c)	Warrant officers Male (d)	Female	Enlisted personnel Total	Male	Female
1940	267,767	17,563	16,624	939	763.	—	249,441	249,441	———
1942	3,074,184	203,137	190,662	12,475	3,285	—	2,867,762	2,867,762	—
1943	6,993,102	557,657	521,435	36,222	21,919	0	6,413,526	6,358,200	55,325
1944	7,992,868	740,077	692,351	47,726	36,893	10	7,215,888	7,144,601	71,287
1945	8,266,373	835,403	772,511	62,892	56,216	44	7,374,710	7,283,930	90,780
1946	1,889,690	257,300	240,643	16,657	9,826	18	1,622,546	1,605,847	16,699
1950	591,487	67,784	63,375	4,409	4,760	22	518,921	512,370	6,551
1955	1,107,606	111,347	106,173	5,174	10,552	48	985,659	977,943	7,716
1960	871,348	91,056	86,832	4,224	10,141	39	770,112	761,833	8,279
1961	856,853	90,066	85,853	4,213	9,817	38	756,932	748,372	8,560
1962	1,064,647	105,225	100,920	4,305	10,777	48	948,597	939,876	8,721
1963	974,070	98,622	94,810	3,812	9,640	40	865,768	857,476	8,292
1964	971,384	100,640	96,905	3,735	10,193	37	860,514	852,556	7,958
1965	967,049	101,812	98,029	3,783	10,285	23	854,929	846,409	8,520
1966	1,197,468	106,468	102,347	4,121	11,296	22	1,079,682	1,070,503	9,179
1967	1,440,120	127,393	122,685	4,708	16,090	34	1,296,603	1,286,862	9,741
1968	1,567,900	145,988	140,919	5,069	20,158	27	1,401,727	1,391,016	10,711
1969	1,509,637	148,836	143,699	5,137	23,734	20	1,337,047	1,316,326	10,721
1970	1,319,735	143,704	138,469	5,235	23,005	13	1,153,013	1,141,537	11,476
1971	1,120,822	130,261	125,240	5,021	18,670	19	971,872	960,047	11,825
1972	807,985	105,364	100,961	4,403	15,907	19	686,695	674,346	12,349
1973	798,177	101,194	96,936	4,258	14,990	21	681,972	665,515	16,457
1974	780,464	91,873	87,504	4,369	14,106	19	674,466	648,138	26,328
1975 (Jan. 1) . . .	772,763	89,816	85,187	4,629	13,400	NA	665,517	631,972	33,545

(a)Represents strength of the active Army, including Philippine Scouts, retired Regular Army personnel on extended active duty, and National Guard and Reserve personnel on extended active duty; excludes U. S. Military Academy cadets, contract surgeons, and National Guard and Reserve personnel not on extended active duty.
(b)Data for 1940 to 1947 include personnel in the Army Air Forces and its predecessors (Air Service and Air Corps).
(c)Includes: Women Doctors, Dentists and Medical Service Corps Officers for 1946 and subsequent years, women in the Army Nurse Corps for all years, and the Women's Army Corps and Women's Medical Specialists Corps (dieticians, physical therapists and occupational specialists) for 1943 and subsequent years.
(d)Act of Congress approved April 27, 1926, directed the appointment as warrant officers, of field clerks still in active service. Includes Flight Officers as follows: 1943, 5,700, 1944, 13,615, 1945, 31,117, 1946, 2,580.

Army Expenditures for Military Functions (1)

(in millions of dollars)

Fiscal Year	Amount	Fiscal Year	Amount	Fiscal Year	Amount	Fiscal Year	Amount
1942	14,805	1953	16,337	1961	10,131	1968	25,223
1943	42,573	1954	12,910	1962	11,427	1969	25,035
1944	49,289	1955	8,899	1963	11,499	1970	24,749
1945	49,750	1957	9,063	1964	12,050	1971	23,077
1946	27,176	1958	9,051	1965	11,600	1972	22,556
1947	8,027	1959	9,468	1966	11,832	1973	20,576
1950	3,985	1960	9,392	1967	21,010	1974	21,649

(1)Excludes expenditures for all civil functions as defined in "The Budget of the United States Government." Data for fiscal years to 1947 include all Army Air Force expenditures.

U.S. Navy Insignia

Navy
Stripes and corps device are of gold embroidery.

Stripes

Fleet Admiral . . . . 1 two inch with 4 one-half inch.
Admiral . . . . 1 two inch with 3 one-half inch.
Vice Admiral . . . . 1 two inch with 2 one-half inch.
Rear Admiral . . . . 1 two inch with 1 one-half inch.
Commodore
  (war time only) . . . . . 1 two inch.
Captain . . . . 4 one-half inch.
Commander . . . . 3 one-half inch.
Lieut. Commander. . . . 2 one-half inch, with 1 one-quarter
                               inch between.
Lieutenant . . . . .2 one-half inch.
Lieutenant (j.g.). . . . . . .1 one-half inch with 1 one-quarter
                               inch above.
Ensign . . . . 1 one-half inch.
Warrant Officers—One $\frac{1}{2}''$ ($\frac{1}{2}''$ for warrant officer W-1)
broken with $\frac{1}{8}''$ intervals of blue as follows:
Chief Warrant Officer W-4—1 break
Chief Warrant Officer W-3—2 breaks, 2″ apart

Chief Warrant Officer W-2—3 breaks, 2″ apart
The breaks are symmetrically centered on outer face of the
sleeve.
Enlisted personnel (non-commissioned petty officers) . . . A
rating badge worn on the upper left arm, consisting of a
spread eagle, appropriate number of chevrons and centered specialty mark.

Marine Corps
Marine Corps and Army officer insignia are similar Marine Corps and Army enlisted insignia, although basically
similar, differ in color, design, and few Marine Corps
subdivisions. The Marine Corps' distinctive cap and collar
ornament is a combination of the American eagle, globe
and anchor.

Coast Guard
Coast Guard insignia follow Navy custom, with certain
minor changes such as the officer cap insignia. The Coast
Guard shield is worn on both sleeves of officers and on the
right sleeve of all enlisted men.

United States Naval Budget Outlays
Source: Department of the Navy

Fiscal year	Total amount expended	Shipbuilding conversion and modernizations	Aircraft and missile procurement	Military construction	All other expenditures
1940.	$885,769,794	$328,819,394	$24,011,998	$72,503,151	$460,435,251
1945.	29,380,421,832	7,228,192,871	3,541,009,589	1,576,096,922	17,035,122,450
1950.	4,065,484,778	281,328,056	452,723,233	86,054,932	3,245,378,557
1955.	9,637,637,835	903,303,717	1,834,511,038	238,631,005	6,661,192,075
1960.	11,848,690,002	1,380,031,231	2,027,098,025	284,928,383	8,228,632,362
1967.	19,291,496,288	1,398,414,838	3,006,902,022	522,638,470	14,363,540,958
1968.	22,106,320,837	1,355,850,877	3,642,007,920	92,966,944	17,015,495,096
1970.	2,501,628,282	2,065,660,211	3,183,464,921	333,271,852	16,919,231,298
1971.	22,046,000,000	2,592,000,000	3,273,000,000	327,000,000	15,854,000,000
1972.	24,100,000,000	3,010,000,000	3,983,000,000	353,000,000	16,754,000,000
1973.	25,425,000,000	2,962,000,000	3,673,000,000	486,000,000	18,122,000,000
1974.	26,800,000,000	3,509,000,000	3,744,000,000	612,000,000	18,935,000,000
1975 (Plan).	28,100,000,000	3,175,000,000	3,515,000,000	624,000,000	20,786,000,000

United States Navy Personnel on Active Duty
Source: DOD Comptroller

June 30	Officers[1]	Nurses	Enlisted[2]	Off. Cand.	Total
1940.	13,162	442	144,824	2,569	160,997
1945.	320,293	11,086	2,988,207	61,231	3,380,817
1950.	42,687	1,954	331,860	5,037	381,538
1955.	72,423	2,104	579,864	6,304	660,695
1960.	67,456	2,103	544,040	4,385	617,984
1965.	75,996	1,870	587,183	6,399	671,448
1970.	78,488	2,273	605,899	6,000	692,660
1972.	71,041	2,114	510,669	4,219	588,043
1973.	68,432	2,134	490,009	3,959	564,534
1974.	67,200	—	478,700	—	545,900
1975.	65,900	—	483,500	—	549,400

(1.) Nurses are included after 1973. (2.) Officer candidates are included after 1973

Marine Corps Personnel On Active Duty
Source: DOD Comptroller

Yr.	Officers	Enl.	Total	Yr.	Officers	Enl.	Total	Yr.	Officers	Enl.	Total
1955. . .	18,417	186,753	205,170	1965. . .	17,258	172,955	190,213	1974. . .	18,700	170,100	188,800
1960. . .	16,203	154,408	170,621	1970. . .	24,941	234,796	259,737	1975. . .	18,100	174,100	192,200

The Federal Service Academies

U.S. Military Academy, West Point, N.Y. Founded
1802. Awards B.S. degree and Army commission
for a 5-year service obligation. For admissions
information, write Admissions Office, USMA, West
Point, N.Y. 10996.

U.S. Naval Academy, Annapolis, Md. Founded 1845.
Awards B.S. degree and Navy or Marine Corps
commission for a 5-year service obligation. For
admissions information, write Dean of Admissions,
Naval Academy, Annapolis, Md. 21402.

U.S. Air Force Academy, Colorado Springs, Colo.
Founded 1954. Awards B.S. degree and Air Force
commmission for a 5-year service obligation. For
admissions information, write Registrar, U.S. Air
Force Academy, Colo. 80840.

U.S. Coast Guard Academy, New London, Conn.
Founded 1876. Awards B.S. degree and Coast
Guard commission for a 5-year service obligation.
For admissions information, write Admissions Of-
fice, Coast Guard Academy, New London, Conn.
06320.

U.S. Merchant Marine Academy, Kings Point, N.Y.
Founded 1943. Awards B.S. degree, a license as a
deck or engineer officer, and a U.S. Naval Reserve
commission. Service obligations vary according to
options taken by the graduating ensign. For admissions information, write Admission Office, U.S.
Merchant Marine Academy, Kings Point, N.Y.
11024.

United States Air Force
Source: Department of the Air Force

The Army Air forces were started Aug. 1, 1907, as the Aeronautical Division of the Signal Corps, U.S. Army. The division consisted of one officer and two enlisted men, and it was more than a year before it carried out its first mission in an airplane of its own. When the U.S. entered World War I (April 6, 1917), the Aviation Service, as it was called then, had 55 planes and 65 officers, only 35 of whom were fliers. On the day the Japanese struck at Pearl Harbor

(Dec. 7, 1941), the Army Air Forces, as they had been renamed six months previously, had 10,329 planes, of which only 2,846 were suited for combat service. But when the Army's air arm reached its peak during World War II (in July, 1944), it had 79,908 of all types of aircraft and (in May, 1945) 43,248 combat aircraft and (in March, 1944) 2,411,294 officers and enlisted men. The Air Force was established under the Armed Services Unification Act of July 26, 1947.

USAF Personnel at Home and Overseas — Officers and Enlisted Men

June 30	Continental U. S.	Overseas	Total	June 30	Continental U. S.	Overseas	Total
1940	40,229	10,936	51,165	1967	617,632	279,862	897,494
1945	1,153,373	1,128,886	2,282,259	1968	616,163	285,035	901,198
1950	317,816	93,461	411,277	1969	566,475	291,936	858,411
1955	689,635	270,311	959,946	1970	531,386	255,819	787,205
1957*	651,674	268,161	919,835	1971	528,493	222,586	751,079
1960[1]	607,383	207,369	814,752	1972	529,672	191,776	721,449
1965	635,430	189,232	824,662	1973	515,439	171,399	686,838
				1974	472,415	171,380	643,795

*Since 1957 continental U.S. includes Air Force Academy Cadets as follows: (1957) 504; (1960) 1,949; (196) 2,660; (1964) 2,838; (1965) 2,907; (1966) 3,152; (1967) 3,361; (1968) 3,652; (1969) 3,941; (1970) 4,144; (1971) 2,997; (1972) 2,885; (1973) 4,356; (1974) 4,412.
(1.) Since 1960 Overseas includes Alaska and Hawaii. All figures include Mobilized Personnel. Officers 292, airmen 1,323.

USAF Military Personnel

June 30	Officers & Airmen	Male Commissioned Officers				Total Warrant Officers
		USAF (Reg.) & RA	USAFR & ORC	ANG & NG	AFUS & AUS	
1950	411,277	19,735	33,585	14	55	2,085
1955	959,946	23,463	105,587	984	2	3,961
1960	814,752	49,584	72,115	248	3	4,069
1965	824,662	62,076	62,537	280	54	2,532
1970	787,205	63,678	65,852	168	105	639
1971	624,980	63,903	61,817	154	45	398
1972	721,448	61,045	54,549	146	30	238
1973	686,838	60,456	49,568	146	37	114
1974	643,795[1]	60,835	9,425[2]	....	27	67

(1.) Includes 4,412 USAF Academy cadets. (2.) Selected Reserves only.

Female Commissioned Officers, and Enlisted Personnel

June 30	Female commissioned officers				Female	Enlisted personnel		
	Total	WAF	Nurses	WMSC	WO	Total	Male	Female
1950	1,525	303	1,143	79	7	354,271	350,489	3,782
1960	3,858	679	3,020	159	5	685,063	679,412	5,651
1965	4,099	708	3,185	206	1	690,177	685,436	4,741
1970	4,667	1,072	3,407	188	....	657,402	648,415	8,987
1971	4,718	1,157	3,383	178	....	625,160	615,028	10,132
1972	4,766	1,214	3,391	161	....	599,774	588,049	11,725
1973	4,727	1,241	3,304	182	....	571,790	556,767	15,023
1974	4,767	1,488	3,083	196	....	533,479	514,014	19,465

Those Who Served in United States' Wars
Source: Veterans Administration

Revolution (1775-1784)
Participants 290,000
Deaths in Service 4,000
Last Veteran Died April 5, 1869 .... Age 109
War of 1812 (1812-1815)
Participants 287,000
Deaths in Service 2,000
Last Veteran Died May 13, 1905 .... Age 105
Mexican War (1846-1848)
Participants 79,000
Deaths in Service 13,000
Last Veteran Died September 3, 1929 ... Age 98
Civil War (1861-1865) (Union Forces Only)
Participants 2,213,000
Deaths in Service 364,000
Last Veteran Died August 2, 1956 .... Age 109
Indian Wars (Approx. 1817-1898)
Participants 106,000
Deaths in Service 1,000
Last Veteran Died June 18, 1973 .... Age 101
Spanish-American War (1898-1902)
Participants 392,000
Deaths in Service 11,000
Living Veterans 1,196
World War I (1917-1918)
Participants 4,744,00
Deaths in Service 116,000
Living Veterans 1,020,000

World War II (1940-1947)
Participants .... [1]16,535,000
Deaths in Service 406,000
Living Veterans 13,654,000
Korean Conflict (June 27, 1950-Jan. 31, 1955)
Participants .... [2]6,807,000
Deaths in Service 55,000
Living Veterans 5,969,000
Service Between Korean Conflict and Vietnam Era (Jan. 31, 1955 — Aug. 5, 1964)
Participants 3,195,000
Deaths in Service 20,000
Living Veterans 3,095,000
Vietnam Era (Active duty service after Aug. 4, 1964)
Participants .... [2]9,712,000
On Active Duty 2,150,000
America's Wars
Total through January 1, 1975
Participants* 44,360,000
Deaths in Service 1,093,000
Living Veterans 29,381,000
*Persons who served in more than one war period are counted as participants in each.
1. Includes 1,476,000 who served in both World War II and the Korean Conflict.
2. Includes 1,252,000 who served in both the Vietnam Era and the Korean Conflict.

The Medal of Honor

The Medal of Honor is the highest military award for bravery that can be given to any individual in the United States. The first Army Medals were awarded on March 25, 1863, and the first Navy Medals went to sailors and Marines on April 3, 1863.

The Medal of Honor, established by Joint Resolution of Congress, 12 July 1862 (amended by Act of 9 July 1918 and Act of 25 July 1963) is awarded in the name of Congress to a person who, while a member of the Armed Forces, distinguishes himself conspicuously by gallantry and intrepidity at the risk of his life above and beyond the call of duty while engaged in an action against any enemy of the United States; while engaged in military operations involving conflict with an opposing foreign force; or while serving with friendly foreign forces engaged in an armed conflict against an opposing armed force in which the United States is not a belligerent party. The deed performed must have been one of personal bravery or self-sacrifice so conspicuous as to clearly distinguish the individual above his comrades and must have involved risk of life. Incontestable proof of the performance of service is exacted and each recommendation for award of this decoration is considered on the standard of extraordinary merit.

Prior to World War I, the 2,625 Army Medal of Honor awards up to that time were reviewed to determine which past awards met new stringent criteria. The Army removed 911 names from the list, most of them former members of a volunteer infantry group during the Civil War who had been induced to extend their enlistments when they were promised the Medal.

Since that review Medals of Honor have been awarded in the following numbers:

World War I	124	Korean War	131
World War II	431	Vietnam (to date)	231

(For names of Vietnam winners of the Medal of Honor, see the 1972 and 1973 editions of the World Almanac.)

American Military Action, 1900-1973

1900—Occupation of Puerto Rico (ceded to U.S., 1899).
1900—500 Marines, 1,500 Army troops help relieve Peking in Boxer Rebellion.
1900-1902—Occupation of Cuba.
1900-1902—Guerrilla war in Philippines.
1903—Sailors and Marines from U.S.S. Nashville stop Colombian Army at Panama.
1904—Brief intervention in Dominican Republic.
1906-1909—Intervention in Cuba.
1909—Brief intervention in Honduras.
1910, 1912-1913—Intervention in Nicaragua.
1911—Intervention (to collect customs) in Honduras, Nicaragua, Dominican Republic.
1912-1917—Intervention in Cuba.
1914—Intervention in Dominican Republic.
1914—April 21 to Nov. 23. Marines in Vera Cruz; also Atlantic fleet and Brig. Gen. Fredk. Funston.
1914—Navy and Marines enter Haiti, stay until 1934
1916—Gen. John J. Pershing and 10,000 into Northern Mexico to stop raids by Villa, Mar. 15-Nov. 24.
1916-1924—Marines in Dominican Republic.
1917—Apr. 6 to Nov. 11, 1918. War with Germany, Austria-Hungary.
1918-1920—Expeditions into North Russia, Siberia.
1918-1923—Occupation of Germany.
1922-24—Marines in Nicaragua.
1926-33—Marines in Nicaragua.
1927—1,000 U.S. Marines in China.

1941-1945—War with Japan, Germany, Italy and allies. Army units posted in Japan and West Germany.
1950-1953—U.S. and other UN countries aid the Republic of Korea to repel North Korean invaders; U.S. Navy protects Taiwan.
1956—U.S. Fleet evacuates U.S. nationals during Suez crisis.
1957—U.S. Fleet to Near East during Jordan crisis.
1958—Navy, Marines and Army units support Lebanon.
1960—Navy patrol in Caribbean to protect Guatemala and Nicaragua.
1961—Army units to Vietnam.
1962—Units of U.S. Navy on Cuban quarantine duty. Marines in Thailand.
1962-65—U.S. Military Assistance Command, Vietnam; units of U.S. Army, Navy, Air Force, Marine Corps, Coast Guard.
1965—Navy, Marines, U.S. Army units to Dominican Republic.
1965—American commanders in Vietnam authorized to send U.S. Armed Force into combat.
1969—President Nixon announces, June 8, first phase of withdrawal of U.S. troops from Vietnam.
1970—Army units participate in Cambodian sanctuary operations, Apr. 29-June 30.
1973—Last U.S. troops leave Vietnam, U.S. Military Assistance Command deactivated, March 29.
1973—End of all U.S. bombing operations over Indochina, Aug. 15.

Adjutant General's Figures of Civil War Deaths

Figures reported from the Adjutant General's Office previous to the above revision, and accepted for many years, are as follows:

Union Army, according to records in the office of the Adjutant General of the War Department in Washington — killed or died of wounds, 110,070 (6,365 officers, 103,705 men); died of disease, 224,586 (2,795 officers, 221,791 men); other deaths, 24,872 (424 officers, 24,448 men). Totals, 359,528 (9,584 officers, 349,944 men).

Confederate Army, estimated, no official records in the office of the Adjutant General of the War Department in Washington — killed in battle, 52,954 (2,086 officers, 50,868 men); died of wounds, 21,570 (1,246 officers, 20,324 men); died of disease, 59,297 (1,294 officers, 58,003 men). Total, 133,821 (4,626 officers, 129,195 men).

World War II Merchant Marine Casualties
Source: U.S. Coast Guard

Died from direct causes while serving on American flag ships, 845; died in prisoner-of-war camps, 37; listed as missing, 4,780.

There were 572 released prisoners of war, and one prisoner unaccounted for. Another 500 men died while serving on foreign flag ships under U.S. control.

The number of U.S. flag ships lost was 605 of 6,000,000 deadweight tons.

How the Military Hand Salute Originated

Hand-raising as a formal greeting originated with the cavemen, who wanted to prove to one another that they carried no weapons, according to the National Georgraphic Society. Later an armored knight raised his right arm to lift his helmet visor and to show friendship by keeping his sword hand away from the weapon. Before the 19th Century, British soldiers saluted by tipping their hats. In the modern U.S. military salute the right hand is raised smartly so the forefinger touches the forehead just above and to the right of the right eye, thumb and fingers extended, forearm and wrist at a 45-degree angle. This salute, with variations, is common among military forces around the world.

Veterans Administration Expands Services As Rolls Grow

Source: Veterans Administration, Richard L. Roudebush, Administrator, Washington, D. C.

Despite the cessation of hostilities in the Far East and the subsequent reduction in numbers of men and women being released from the armed forces, Veterans Administration operations continued expanding in 1975.

There were 29.4 million living veterans. With their 66 million family members and 4 million survivors of deceased veterans they make up nearly one-half the population of the U.S.

The $16.4 billion FY 1976 VA budget is the highest in history. Most of that — 76 per cent — goes for paying benefits such as pensions, G.I. Bill education, etc. The VA medical system with its 171 hospitals and 215 clinics uses 23 per cent, or $3.8 billion. This budget permits the VA to pay $4.6 billion in compensation benefits to 2.6 million veterans with service-connected disabilities and to survivors of deceased veterans. VA sends more than $2.7 billion in pension checks to 2.2 million veterans and survivors of veterans in financial need. Some 2.6 million veterans' children, wives and widows of veterans are provided $4.1 billion in education and training assistance. The budget allows VA to guarantee more than $10 billion in G.I. Home Loans for nearly 370,000 veterans, most of whom were Vietnam veterans. VA also administers $98.4 billion in life insurance protection for 8.2 million veterans and service people on active duty. Although it employs 196,000 persons, VA's operating expenses are held to 2.7 per cent of the entire budget.

G.I. Bill education and training programs broke all records in 1975. After a slow start, Vietnam Era veterans began taking advantage of the school and college education and enrolled in gradually increasing numbers until 2.37 million — or 58 per cent — were on the rolls.

The VA's Department of Medicine & Surgery (DM&S) continued its expansion in 1975 with the opening of the new Audie L. Murphy Memorial Veterans Hospital (named after WW II's most-decorated soldier) and the acquisition of the old U.S. Naval Hospital at St. Albans, N.Y.; new buildings at White River Junction, Vt., and Hampton, Va., and increasing nursing homes to 85, VA upped its total bed capacity to 1,115,032. In addition VA treated 14.75 million outpatients.

Some VA investigators participated in 5,688 research projects in 1975 at a cost of $97 million.

The agency had 71 alcoholic treatment centers in operation in 1975. Using a combination of new and old treatment techniques, drying out periods followed by group therapy and social counseling, the incidence of recovery of alcoholics rose rapidly. VA doctors have reported 42 per cent recovery of alcoholics — a figure regarded as impossible just a few years ago.

VA's care of paraplegics, in the midst of remarkable new techniques, was watched by the scientific world. A few years ago, paraplegics were given a maximum life span of 15 years. Now the span has no such limit. In addition to treating the paralyzed veteran for his physical problems, VA has opened new centers (Boston and Brockton, Mass.) to treat his mind, eliminate his feelings of helplessness and through therapy return him to a place in the community with a meaningful and rewarding job.

In previous years, the VA had been criticised because many veterans in school were not receiving their G.I. Bill allowance checks on time.

Innovations in handling the checks were made including sending the checks first and then checking later. The most important development in solving this check and other related problems was the forming of the corps of VET-REPS—1,300 VA counselors right on college campuses to give personal aid.

VA, in 1975, continued its *Outreach* programs. This massive project was designed to contact—personally or by telephone or letter—America's 7.5 million Vietnam Era veterans and tell them about their benefits.

The selection of four new National Cemeteries (Patterned after Arlington) continued to be the biggest task of the National Cemetery System which was taken over from the Army and Interior in 1973. In all, 10 new national cemeteries are planned with four already authorized. The Arlington, Va., National Cemetery is still operated by the Army.

Nearly 800,000 Vietnam Era veterans have received VA-guaranteed home loans valued at almost $17 billion. Since 1944, when the G.I. Home Loan program began, 9 million loans with a face value of $112 billion have been guaranteed by the VA. The recent changes in the legislation affecting the VA home loan program increased the maximum that VA can guarantee from $12,500 to $17,500 and the limit on the amount of the whole loan was eliminated.

With the nation at peace, expectations that VA activity would lessen in the near future were dispelled. World War II veterans are getting to the age where they require more medical and hospital treatment. More and more former servicemen are going back to school.

Veteran Population, April 1975

1.	Veterans in civil life, end of month — Total	29,400,000
2.	War Veterans — Total	26,308,000
3.	Vietnam Era — Total(a)	7,520,000
4.	And service in Korean Conflict	498,000
5.	No service in Korean Conflict	7,022,000
6.	Korean Conflict — Total (includes line 4)(b)	5,967,000
7.	And service in WW II	1,248,000
8.	No service in WW II	4,719,000
9.	World War II (includes line 7)	13,582,000
10.	World War I	984,000
11.	Spanish-American War	1,000
12.	Service between Korean Conflict (January 31, 1955) and Vietnam (August 5, 1964) Only (c)	3,092,000

(a) Service after Aug. 4, 1964; (b) includes 2,385,000 veterans who also served after the end of the Korean Conflict (Jan. 31, 1955); (c) excludes men who served on active duty for training only.

Fiscal year	Living veteran cases No.	Deceased veteran cases No.	Total cases No.	Total disbursement Dollars	Fiscal year	Living veteran cases No.	Deceased veteran cases No.	Total cases No.	Total disbursement Dollars
1890	415,654	122,290	537,944	106,093,850	1965	3,204,275	1,277,009	4,481,284	3,901,598,010
1900	752,510	241,019	993,529	138,462,130	1967	3,130,390	1,334,634	4,465,024	4,284,265,036
1910	602,622	318,461	921,083	159,974,056	1968	3,112,038	1,389,379	4,501,417	4,406,319,385
1920	419,627	349,916	769,543	316,418,029	1969	3,107,162	1,443,367	4,550,529	4,722,489,826
1930	542,610	298,223	840,833	418,432,808	1970	3,127,338	1,487,176	4,614,514	5,113,649,490
1940	610,122	239,176	849,298	429,138,465	1971	3,222,394	1,584,167	4,806,561	5,726,485,000
1950	2,368,238	658,123	3,026,361	2,009,462,298	1972	3,268,826	1,641,370	4,910,196	6,045,214,000
1955	2,668,786	808,303	3,477,089	2,634,292,537	1973	3,256,746	1,654,287	4,911,033	6,426,647,000
1960	3,008,935	950,802	3,959,737	3,314,761,383	1974	3,241,263	1,627,482	4,868,745	6,615,599,000

The Nuclear Debate

The Jargon

Since the dawn of the nuclear era, the basic policy of defense has been **deterrence** — discouraging the opponents' use of nuclear weapons by maintaining sufficient nuclear forces to cause unacceptable, massive damage to the opponent's population and economy even if he should strike first. This policy led to the **mutual assured destruction** (MAD) policy of both the USSR and the U.S.

Deterrence works only if each side's forces have **credibility**: each side must be convinced that the opponent is ready and willing to use nuclear weapons in certain circumstances and that those weapons are secure from attack and will be devastatingly effective.

The security of nuclear forces is based on **redundancy**: a land-based nuclear force, protected in underground silos (**hard sites**), is duplicated by an almost untrackable submarine missile force and by an airborne force already aloft or on constant standby.

The effectiveness of nuclear forces depends on missile thrusting power (**throw-weight**), the number of warheads, the explosive **yield** of warheads, and the accuracy of the missiles and the delivery vehicles they carry.

At present, the Soviet Union has a slight lead in throw-weight, yield and number, while U.S. missiles are 3 to 5 times more accurate at greater ranges than Soviet missiles. If missiles are targeted against other missiles in silos, accuracy is 10 to 25 times more effective than yield. When Soviet missiles achieve the same accuracy as U.S. missiles, that advantage in throw-weight will enable the Soviet Union to launch many more warheads with more explosive power.

The effectiveness of both Soviet and U.S. missile forces has been questioned because of the newly-raised **fratricide** problem — that is, the atmospheric havoc created by the first explosion of a nuclear warhead may deflect, damage or destroy a second warhead aimed into the same area.

Nuclear warheads can be aimed at industrial and civilian targets (**countervalue targeting**) or at military command centers, bases and missile sites (**counterforce targeting**). Counterforce targeting can range from an ability to destroy some bases and a small percentage of the opponent's missiles up to an ability to destroy most of an opponent's missiles and, therefore, his ability to retaliate effectively. In the latter case, counterforce targeting — from the opponent's point of view — looks exactly like a **first-strike capability** — the ability to attack first with little fear of an effective response. One response to an opponent's first-strike capability would be to adopt a **launch-on-warning** system that would immediately (and perhaps automatically) launch retaliatory missiles at the first sign that the other side had fired first.

Since the mid-1960s, U.S. policy has favored targeting against industrial and population centers as the best deterrent. However, in January 1974, Defense Secretary Schlesinger announced the flexible re-targeting of some missiles so they could strike at military installations as well as cities. The wisdom of this change is still under debate.

The Issues

1. Should the U.S. work toward achieving maximum targeting flexibility?
YES — The president should not be limited to a choice between surrender and slaughter.
— Because there is uncertainty about how a nuclear war might start, a wide range of possible responses should be available.
— A properly limited response to a small scale nuclear attack would not only not invite escalation, but would provide incentives against it.
NO — If nuclear war becomes more manageable, it will also become more likely.
— In a crisis, a variety of military options might cause leaders to overlook some diplomatic possibilities.

2. Is there a difference between a counterforce capability and a disarming first-strike capability?
YES — A disarming first-strike is not possible because of redundancy of missile forces.
— Destroying hard-sited missiles is more difficult than supposed because of the fratricide problem.
NO — As technology improves, counterforce targeting will inevitably result in first strike capability.
— In spite of one side's good intentions, the other side might launch a preemptive attack to destroy first-strike missiles.
— Fear of a first-strike could lead to a launch-on-warning doctrine, increasing the possibility that a nuclear war might begin by accident or miscalculation.

3. Can improvement of counterforce capability be kept from provoking an uncontrollable arms race?
YES — Even if an arms race does develop, that is better than falling behind the other side.
— Technology and bureaucracy influence weapons development more than do the actions of the other side.
— If only minor improvements are made, an arms race can be avoided.
NO — The early 60's arms race came when the U.S. pursued a counterforce capability.
— Increase in types and numbers of weapons would increase problems of negotiations to limit weapons and make verification more difficult.

4. Is limited nuclear warfare possible?
YES — There is nothing inevitable about escalation or mass destruction of population.
— The kinds of weapons available and the way they are used can limit deaths and forestall escalation.
— Small, accurate, clean weapons directed against military targets can limit civilian casualties.
— Targeting can concentrate on military sites far removed from large populations.
NO — Many important military targets are in or near large population centers.
— The number of casualties resulting from even a small attack would be so large that retaliation against urban industrial targets would be almost inevitable.

5. Would an American lack of targeting flexibility and limited war options lead our allies to doubt that we would come to their defense?
YES — The idea that the U.S. would risk a major nuclear exchange to defend West Germany, for example, is not really believable. No one believes that U.S. decision makers are prepared to sacrifice Houston to save Munich.
NO — Rough equality of nuclear forces is important, but diplomacy and economics, not nuclear strength, are the real bonds between the U.S. and its allies.
— Maintainance of U.S. forces in Europe and Asia and U.S. preparedness to involve and defend those forces are guarantees enough.
— U.S. allies are relatively unaware of and unmoved by details of U.S. strategic planning.

6. Does the U.S. have to follow suit if the Soviet Union develops great targeting flexibility and counterforce capability?
YES — Deterrence works only if the U.S. is genuinely the equal of the Soviet Union in capability. If the U.S. does not have similar options, the deterrent against limited nuclear attacks in a political crisis would be weakened.
NO — U.S. aims differ from those of the Soviet Union, so U.S. strategy need not ape the Soviets.
— Improving counterforce capability is expensive, probably ineffective, and would lead to an arms race.

Strategic Nuclear Armaments: United States and Soviet Union

Source: International Institute for Strategic Services, London

United States

Type		Range[2] (statute miles)	Estimated warhead yield[3]	Deployed (July 1974)
Land-based Missiles[1]				
ICBM	Titan 2	7,250	5-10 MT	54
	Minuteman 1	7,500	1 MT	21
	Minuteman 2	8,000	1-2 MT	450
	Minuteman 3	8,000	3x200 KT	529
IRBM		—	—	—
MRBM		—	—	—
Sea-based Missiles				
SLBM	UGM-27C			
(nuclear	Polaris A3	2,880	3x200 KT	304
subs)	UGM-73A			
	Poseidon	2,880	10x50 KT	352
SLBM				
(diesel				
subs)		—	—	—

Soviet Union

Type		Range[2] (statute miles)	Estimated warhead yield[3]	Deployed (July 1974)
Land-based Missiles[1]				
ICBM	SS-7 Saddler	6,900	5 MT	209
	SS-8 Sasin	6,900	5 MT	
	SS-9Scarp	7,500	20-25 MT[4]	288
	SS-11	6,500	1-2 MT[5]	1,018
	SS-13 Savage	5,000	1 MT	60
IRBM	SS-5 Skean	2,300	1 MT	100
MRBM	SS-4Sandal	1,200	1 MT	500
Sea-based Missiles				
SLBM	SS-N-5 Serb	750	MT range	24
(nuclear	SS-N-6-Sawfly	1,750	MT range	528
subs)	SS-N-8	4,800	MT range	108
SLBM				
(diesel	SS-N-4 Sark	350	MT range	27
subs)	SS-N-5 Serb	750	MT range	33

United States

Type		Range[7] (statute miles)	Weapons load (lb)	Deployed (July 1974)
Aircraft[6]				
Long-range	B-52D-F	11,500	60,000 }	437[8]
	B-52G/H	12,500	75,000	
Medium range	FB-111A	3,800	37,500	66
strike aircraft;	F-105D	2,100	16,500	
land-based	F-4	2,300	16,000 }	1,600[9]
	F-111A/E	3,800	25,000	
	A-7D	3,400	15,000	
Strike aircraft	A-4	2,055	10,000	
carrier-based	A-6A	3,225	18,000 }	1,000[9]
	A-7A/B/E	3,400	15,000	
	F-4	1,997	1,600	

Soviet Union

Type		Range[7] (statute miles)	Weapons load (lb)	Deployed (July 1974)
Aircraft[6]				
	Tu-95 Bear	7,800	40,000	100
	Mya-4 Bison	6,050	20,000	40
	Tu-16 Badger	4,000	20,000	800
	Il-28 Beagle	2,500	4,850	
	Su-7 Fitter	900	4,500	
	Tu-22 Blinder	1,400	12,000	
	Yak-28 Brewer	1,750	4,400 }	1,300[9]
	MiG-21 Fishbed J	1,150	2,000	
	MiG-23 Flogger	1,800	N.A.	

(1) ICBM = intercontinental ballistic missile. IRBM = intermediate-range ballistic missile. MRBM = medium-range missile. SLBM = submarine-launched ballistic missile. (2) Operation range depends upon the payload carried; use of maximum payload may reduce missile range by up to 25%. (3) MT = megaton = 1,000,000 tons of TNT equivalent (MT range = 1 MT or over); KT = kiloton = 1,000 tons of TNT equivalent (KT range = less than 1 MT). (4) Some SS-9 missiles carry 3 warheads of 4-5 MT each. (5) Some SS-11 missiles may carry 3xKT warheads. (6) All aircraft listed are dual-capable and many, especially in the categories of strike aircraft, would be more likely to carry conventional than nuclear weapons. (7) Theoretical maximum range, with internal fuel only, at optimum altitude and speed. Ranges for strike aircraft assume no weapons load. Especially in the case of strike aircraft, therefore, range falls sharply for flights at lower altitude, at higher speed or with full weapons load. (8) Including approximately 40 B-52 D-F aircraft in active storage. (9) These aircraft are nuclear capable but may not have a nuclear role.

Women In The Armed Forces

Women are now eligible for 93% of all military job classifications and enlistments are coming in at a rate that strains the capacity of the armed forces to handle them. The services had planned on having 88,000 women in uniform by 1977. With enlistments coming in at 100% of the goals the services set themselves, there are plans to increase barracks space and other facilities to accommodate 120,000 by that date—double the present number.

Women's Army Corps — Brig. Gen. Mary E. Clark, WAC Director, Dept. of Army, Pentagon, Washington, D.C.; 1,466 officers, 35,656 enlisted women; wide variety of assignments, world-wide; subsidizes some college training.

Army Nurse Corps — Brig. Gen. Lillian Dunlap, Chief, Office of the Surgeon General, Dept. of Army, Washington, D.C. 20314; 2,907 officers; nursing and supervision assignments, world-wide; subsidizes some training; includes men.

Navy — Fully integrated, no commander; for information: Commander, Naval Recruiting, Dept. of Navy, Washington, D.C. 22203; 3,722 officers, 15,114 enlisted women; variety of assignments.

Navy Nurse Corps — Rear Adm. Maxine Conder, Director, Navy Nurse Corps, Bureau of Medicine and Surgery, Navy Dept. Washington, D.C.; 2,134 officers; nursing and supervision assignments at U.S. and foreign bases, and shipboard; subsidizes some training.

Air Force —Colonel Bianca D. Trimeloni, Director, WAF, Hq. USAF, Pentagon, Washington, D.C. 20330; 1,400 officers, 16,500 enlisted women; variety of assignments, world-wide.

Air Force Nurse Corps — Brig. Gen. Claire M. Garrecht, Chief, Office of the Surgeon General, USAF, Washington, D.C. 20333; 3,295 officers; nursing and supervision assignments, world-wide; subsidizes some training; includes men.

Women Marines — Col. Margaret A. Brewer, Director, Headquarters, Marine Corps, Washington, D.C. 20380; 354 officers, 2,767 enlisted women.

Coast Guard Women — Fully integrated, no commander. U.S. Coast Guard, Washington, D.C. 20590; 32 officers, 420 enlisted women.

Monthly Pay Scale of the

Commissioned Officers

Pay grade	Army or Air Force rank	Navy rank	Under 2	Over 2	Over 3	Over 4	Over 6	Over 8
0-10[1]	Chief of Staff*		$3,000.00	$3,000.00	$3,000.00	$3,000.00	$3,000.00	$3,000.00
0-10	General*	Admiral	2,705.70	2,800.80	2,800.80	2,800.80	2,800.80	2,908.20
0-9	Lieutenant General	Vice Admiral	2,397.90	2,461.20	2,513.40	2,513.40	2,513.40	2,577.00
0-8	Major General	Rear Admiral (up. half)	2,172.00	2,237.10	2,290.20	2,290.20	2,290.20	2,461.20
0-7	Brigadier General	Rear Admiral (low.-half)	1,804.50	1,927.80	1,927.80	1,927.80	2,013.60	2,013.60
0-6	Colonel	Captain	1,337.70	1,470.00	1,565.70	1,565.70	1,565.70	1,565.70
0-5	Lieutenant Colonel	Commander	1,069.80	1,256.70	1,343.10	1,343.10	1,343.10	1,343.10
0-4	Major	Lieutenant Comdr	902.10	1,097.70	1,171.80	1,171.80	1,192.80	1,245.90
0-3	Captain	Lieutenant	838.20	936.90	1,001.40	1,108.20	1,161.00	1,203.00
0-2	First Lieutenant	Lieutenant (J.G.)	730.50	798.30	958.80	990.80	1,011.60	1,011.60
0-1	Second Lieutenant	Ensign	634.20	660.30	798.30	798.30	798.30	798.30

Commissioned officers with over 4 years service as enlisted members

Pay grade	Army or Air Force rank	Navy rank	Under 2	Over 2	Over 3	Over 4	Over 6	Over 8
0-3	Captain	Lieutenant				1,108.20	1,161.00	1,203.00
0-2	First Lieutenant	Lieutenant (J.G.)				990.90	1,011.60	1,043.70
0-1	Second Lieutenant	Ensign				798.30	852.30	884.10

Warrant Officers

Pay grade	Army or Air Force rank	Navy rank	Under 2	Over 2	Over 3	Over 4	Over 6	Over 8
W-4	Chief Warrant	Comm. Warrant	853.80	915.90	915.90	936.90	979.80	1,022.70
W-3	Chief Warrant	Comm. Warrant	776.40	842.10	842.10	852.30	862.50	925.80
W-2	Chief Warrant	Comm. Warrant	679.80	735.00	735.00	756.60	798.30	842.10
W-1	Warrant Officer	Warrant Officer	566.40	649.50	649.50	703.50	735.00	767.10

Enlisted Personnel[2]

Pay grade	Army or Air Force rank	Navy rank	Under 2	Over 2	Over 3	Over 4	Over 6	Over 8
E-9[3]	Sergeant Major**	Master C. P. O.						813.90
E-8[3]	Master Sergeant	Senior C. P. O.						
E-7	Sgt. 1st Class	Chief Petty Officer	568.20	613.20	636.00	658.20	681.00	702.30
E-6	Staff Sergeant	Petty Officer 1st Class	490.80	535.20	557.40	580.50	602.70	624.90
E-5	Sergeant	Petty Officer 2nd Cl.	438.80	469.20	491.70	513.00	546.60	568.80
E-4	Corporal	Petty Officer 3rd Cl.	414.30	437.40	462.90	499.20	518.70	518.70
E-3	Private 1st Class	Seaman	398.40	420.30	437.10	454.20	454.20	454.20
E-2	Private	Seaman Apprentice	383.40	383.40	383.40	383.40	383.40	383.40
E-1	Private	Seaman Recruit	344.10	344.10	344.10	344.10	344.10	344.10

The pay scale also applies to: Coast Guard and Marine Corps, Coast and Geodetic Survey, Public Health Service, National Guard, and the Organized Reserves.

*Four star General or Admiral—personal money allowances of $2,200 per annum, or $4,000 if Chief of Staff or Chief of Naval Operations. Three star General or Admiral—personal money allowance of $500 per annum.

**A new title of Chief Master Sergeant created in 1965 rates E-9 classification.

(1) While serving as Chairman of Joint Chiefs of Staff, Chief of Staff of the Army, Chief of Naval Operations, Chief of Staff of the Air Forces, or Commandant of the Marine Corps, basic pay for this grade is $4 195.80 regardless of years of service.

(2) Air Force enlisted personnel pay grades, E-9, Chief Master Sergeant; E-8, Sr. Master Sergeant; E-7, Master Sergeant; E-6, Technical Sergeant; E-5, Staff Sergeant; E-4, Sergeant; E-3, Airman 1st Class; E-2, Airman; E-1, Basic Airman.

Marine Corps enlisted ranks are as follows: E-9, Sergeant Major and Master Gunnery Sergeant; E-8, First Sergeant and Master Sergeant; E-7 Gunnery Sergeant; E-6, Staff Sergeant; E-5, Sergeant; E-4, Corporal; E-3, Lance Corporal; E-2, Private, First Class Marine; E-1 Private.

Marine Corps officer ranks are same as Army and AF.

(3) While serving as Sergeant Major of the Army, Master Chief Petty Officer of the Navy, Chief Master Sergeant of the A.r Force or Sergeant Major of the Marine Corps, basic pay for this grade is $1,518.60 regardless of years of service.

Hazardous Duty

Flying Duty (enlisted crew member) and Submarine Duty Additional Monthly Pay

	Under 2 yrs.	Over 2 yrs.	Maximum Over—Amt.
O-10	$165	$165	$165
O-9	165	165	165
O-8	155	155	165
O-7	150	150	160
O-6	200	200	18 yrs. —245
O-5	190	190	18 " —245
O-4	170	170	18 " —240
O-3	145	145	14 " —205
O-2	115	125	14 " —185
O-1	100	105	14 " —170
W-4	115	*	18 " —165
W-3	110	115	14 " —140
W-2	105	110	14 " —135
W-1	100	105	12 " —130
E-9	105	105	105
E-8	105	105	105
E-7	80	85	12 yrs. —105
E-6	70	75	14 " —100
E-5	60	70	12 " — 95
E-4	55	65	8 " — 80
E-3	55	60	2 " — 60
E-2	50	60	2 " — 60
E-1	50	55	2 " — 55

Aviation Cadet under 2 years $50.
*W-4 Under 6 years receives $115.

Incentive Pay

Officers and Warrant Officers	$110.00
Enlisted men	55.00

Types of duties for which these flat rates are payable are as follows—(1) Frequent and regular aerial flights not as a crew member. (2) Parachute jumping as an essential part of military duty. (3) Duty involving intimate contact with leprosy. (4) Duty involving demolition of explosives. (5, 6) Special pay is authorized for diving duty. Pay varies with rank and type of duty. (7) Human acceleration or deceleration duty. (8) High-or-low pressure chamber duty. (9) Thermal stress duty. (10) Training for assignment to submarines of advanced design or for positions of increased responsibility aboard a submarine. Rates payable for this category are the same as those paid flying crew members listed under Hazardous Duty. (11) Flight Deck Duty.

Sea and Foreign Duty

Defense Secretary designates places where special duty pay may be awarded.

E-9	$22.50	E-4	13.00
E-8	22.50	E-3	9.00
E-7	22.50	E-2	8.00
E-6	20.00	E-1	8.00
E-5	16.00		

Uniformed Services (1975)

Commissioned Officers

		Cumulative years of service						Basic allowances for quarters	
Over 10	Over 12	Over 14	Over 16	Over 18	Over 20	Over 22	Over 26	Without Dependents $	With Dependents $
$3,000.00	$3,000.00	$3,000.00	$3,000.00	$3,000.00	$3,000.00	$3,000.00	$3,000.00		
2,908.20	3,131.10*	3,131.10*	3,335.20*	3,335.20*	3,579.30*	3,579.30*	3,802.50*	243.00	303.90
2,577.00	2,684.10	2,684.10	2,908.20	2,908.20	3,131.10*	3,131.10*	3,355.20*	243.00	303.90
2,461.20	2,577.00	2,577.00	2,684.10	2,800.80	2,908.20	3,024.90*	3,024.90*	243.00	303.90
2,130.90	2,130.90	2,237.10	2,461.20	2,630.40	2,630.40	2,630.40	2,630.40	243.00	303.90
1,565.70	1,565.70	1,618.80	1,875.00	1,971.00	2,013.60	2,130.90	2,310.60	223.50	272.70
1,384.20	1,458.00	1,555.50	1,672.20	1,768.20	1,821.30	1,885.50	1,885.50	209.10	252.00
1,330.50	1,405.80	1,470.00	1,533.90	1,576.50	1,576.50	1,576.50	1,576.50	188.70	227.40
1,267.50	1,330.50	1,363.20	1,363.20	1,363.20	1,363.20	1,363.20	1,363.20	167.10	206.40
1,011.60	1,011.60	1,011.60	1,011.60	1,011.60	1,011.60	1,011.60	1,011.60	146.40	185.40
798.30	798.30	798.30	798.30	798.30	798.30	798.30	798.30	114.90	149.40
1,267.50	1,330.50	1,384.20	1,384.20	1,384.20	1,384.20	1,384.20	1,384.20	167.10	206.40
1,097.70	1,140.30	1,171.80	1,171.80	1,171.80	1,171.80	1,171.80	1,171.80	146.40	185.40
915.90	948.00	990.90	990.90	990.90	990.90	990.90	990.90	114.90	149.40

Warrant Officers

Over 10	Over 12	Over 14	Over 16	Over 18	Over 20	Over 22	Over 26	Without Dependents	With Dependents
1,065.30	1,140.30	1,192.80	1,235.10	1,267.50	1,309.50	1,353.00	1,458.00	182.10	219.30
979.80	1,011.60	1,043.70	1,074.90	1,108.20	1,150.80	1,192.80	1,235.10	164.10	202.20
873.60	905.40	936.90	969.60	1,001.40	1,033.20	1,074.90	1,074.90	144.60	183.30
798.30	831.00	862.50	894.60	925.80	958.80	958.80	958.80	130.80	169.80

Enlisted Personnel[2]

Over 10	Over 12	Over 14	Over 16	Over 18	Over 20	Over 22	Over 26	Without Dependents	With Dependents
969.90	992.10	1,014.60	1,038.00	1,060.80	1,081.80	1,138.80	1,249.20	138.00	194.40
836.70	858.90	881.40	904.20	925.50	948.30	1,003.80	1,116.00	128.70	181.80
724.50	747.30	781.20	803.10	825.60	836.70	892.80	1,003.80	110.40	170.40
647.40	681.00	702.30	724.50	735.90	735.90	735.90	735.90	101.10	158.40
591.60	613.20	624.90	624.90	624.90	624.90	624.90	624.90	97.80	146.40
518.70	518.70	518.70	518.70	518.70	518.70	518.70	518.70	86.10	128.10
454.20	454.20	454.20	454.20	454.20	454.20	454.20	454.20	76.20	110.70
383.40	383.40	383.40	383.40	383.40	383.40	383.40	383.40	67.50	110.70
344.10	344.10	344.10	344.10	344.10	344.10	344.10	344.10	63.30	110.70

*Limited under existing law to $3,000

Basic Allowances for Subsistence

This allowance, the quarters allowance, and any other allowance are not subject to income tax.

Officers — Subsistence (food) is paid to all officers regardless of rank .... $50.52 per month
Enlisted members: When rations in kind are not available .... $2.71 per day
When assigned to duty under emergency conditions where
no government messing facilities are available .... $3.61 per day (maximum rate)

Family Separation Allowance

Under certain conditions of family separation of more than 30 days, members in Pay Grades E-4 (with over 4 years' service) and above will be allowed $30 a month in addition to any other allowances to which he is entitled. When separated from family and required to maintain a home for his family and one for himself, the member is entitled to an additional monthly basic allowance for quarters at the "without dependents" rate for his grade.

Uniform Allowance

Enlisted personnel receive an initial uniform allowance valued at about $250 with variations between services. After 6 months and up to the 36th month maintenance allowance of $5.70 is paid. After 36 months the monthly allowance is $8.40. An officer is entitled to an initial allowance of not more than $300.00.

Enlistment Bonus

DOD currently authorizes a bonus of up to $2,500 for a four-year enlistment in certain skills designated as critical.

Reenlistment Bonuses

All reenlistees who were on active duty on June 1, 1974, are entitled to a bonus for reenlisting (Regular Reenlistment Bonus, Selective Reenlistment Bonus, or a combination thereof) of at least $2,000 during a 20-year career. A member who is eligible for both the Regular Reenlistment Bonus and the Selective Reenlistment Bonus may elect to receive either bonus. However, once an individual receives $2,000 in reenlistment bonuses his entitlement to the Regular Bonus terminates.

Members serving in critical military specialties may, as a special incentive, receive the Selective Reenlistment Bonus. This retention incentive is paid to individuals designated as having a critical military specialty who reenlist for at least 3 years between 21 months and 10 years of service. Maximum allowable Selective Reenlistment Bonus is $15,000 based upon multiples (1 through 6) of monthly basic pay multiplied by years (not to exceed 6) of additional obligated service.

Special Pay

Members of the uniformed services entitled to receive basic pay shall, in addition thereto, be entitled to receive incentive pay for the performance of hazardous duty required by competent orders. The President, may in time of war, suspend the payment of hazardous duty incentive pay. Officers receive no additional pay for overseas or sea duty.

Duty Subject to Hostile Fire

Except in time of war declared by the Congress, a special pay of $65 a month is authorized for any member of the Uniformed Services during any month in which he was subject to hostile fire.

Medical and Dental Corps

Commissioned officers in the Medical and Dental Corps of the Army, Navy and Air Force and commissioned medical, dental, and veterinary officers of the Regular Corps of the Public Health Service receive special pay based on cumulative years of service (0-2 years, $100; 2 to 6 years, $150; 6 to 10 years, $250; over 10 years, $350 for dental officers; and 0-2 years, $100; 2 or more years, $350 for medical officers). In addition to basic pay and allowance Optometrists and Veterinary Corps Officers receive $100 per month extra.

Casualties in Principal Wars of the United States

Data on Revolutionary War casualties is from **The Toll of Independence**, Howard H. Peckham, ed., U. of Chicago Press, 1974.

Data prior to World War I are based upon incomplete records in many cases. Casualty data are confined to dead and wounded personnel and therefore exclude personnel captured or missing in action who were subsequently returned to military control. Dash (—) indicates information is not available.

Wars	Branch of service	Number serving	Casualties			
			Battle deaths	Other deaths	Wounds not mortal	Total
Revolutionary War	Total	—	6,824	18,500	8,445	33,769
1775-1783	Army	184,000	5,992	—	7,988	13,980
	Navy &	to	—	—	—	—
	Marines	250,000	832	—	457	1,289
War of 1812	Total	⁹286,730	2,260	—	4,505	6,765
1812-1815	Army	—	1,950	—	4,000	5,950
	Navy	—	265	—	439	704
	Marines	—	45	—	66	111
Mexican War	Total	⁹78,718	1,733	11,550	4,152	17,435
1846-1848	Army	—	1,721	11,550	4,102	17,373
	Navy	—	1	—	3	4
	Marines	—	11	—	47	58
Civil War	Total	⁹2,213,363	140,414	224,097	281,881	646,392
(Union forces only)	Army	2,128,948	138,154	221,374	280,040	639,568
1861-1865	Navy	—	2,112	2,411	1,710	6,233
	Marines	84,415	148	312	131	591
Confederate forces	Total	—	⁷4,524	59,297	—	133,821
(estimate)[1]	Army	600,000	—	—	—	—
1863-1866	Navy	to	—	—	—	—
	Marines	1,500,000	—	—	—	—
Spanish-American	Total	306,760	385	2,061	1,662	4,108
War	Army[4]	280,564	369	2,061	1,594	4,024
1898	Navy	22,875	10	0	47	57
	Marines	3,321	6	0	21	27
World War I	Total	4,743,826	53,513	63,195	204,002	320,710
April 6, 1917-	Army[5]	4,057,101	50,510	55,868	193,663	300,041
Nov. 11, 1918	Navy	599,051	431	6,856	819	8,106
	Marines	78,839	2,461	390	9,520	12,371
	Coast Gd.	8,835	111	81	—	192
World War II	Total	16,353,659	292,131	115,185	670,846	1,078,162
Dec. 7, 1941-	Army[6]	11,260,000	234,874	83,400	565,861	884,135
Dec. 31, 1946[2]	Navy[7]	4,183,466	36,950	25,664	37,778	100,392
	Marines	669,100	19,733	4,778	67,207	91,718
	Coast Gd.	241,093	574	1,343	—	1,917
Korean War	Total	5,764,143	33,629	20,617	103,284	157,530
June 25, 1950-	Army	2,834,000	27,704	9,429	77,596	114,729
July 27, 1953[3]	Navy	1,177,000	458	4,043	1,576	6,077
	Marines	424,000	4,267	1,261	23,744	29,272
	Air Force	1,285,000	1,200	5,884	368	7,452
	Coast Gd.	44,143	—	—	—	—
Vietnam (preliminary)[10]	Total	8,744,000	46,397	10,346	153,311	210,048
Aug. 4,1964-	Army	4,368,000	30,667	7,186	96,811	134,664
Jan. 27, 1973	Navy	1,842,000	1,505	880	4,178	6,563
	Marines	794,000	12,980	1,682	51,389	66,051
	Air Force	1,740,000	1,245	592	933	2,770

[1] Authoritative statistics for the Confederate Forces are not available. An estimated 26,000-31,000 Confederate personnel died in Union prisons.

[2] Data are for the period Dec. 1, 1941 through Dec. 31, 1946 when hostilities were officially terminated by Presidential Proclamation, but few battle deaths or wounds not mortal were incurred after the Japanese acceptance of Allied peace terms on Aug. 14, 1945. Numbers serving from Dec. 1, 1941-Aug. 31, 1945 were: Total—14,903,213; Army—10,420 - 000; Navy—3,883,520; and Marine Corps—599,693.

[3] Tentative final data based upon information available as of Sept. 30, 1954, at which time 24 persons were still carried as missing in action.

[4] Number serving covers the period April 21-Aug. 13, 1898, while dead and wounded data are for the period May 1-Aug. 31, 1898. Active hostilities ceased on Aug. 13, 1898, but ratifications of the treaty of peace were not exchanged between the United States and Spain until April 11, 1899.

[5] Includes Air Service. Battle deaths and wounds not mortal include casualties suffered by American forces in Northern Russia to Aug. 25, 1919 and in Siberia to April 1, 1920. Other deaths covered the period April 1, 1917-Dec. 31, 1918.

[6] Includes Army Air Forces.

[7] Battle deaths and wounds not mortal include casualties incurred in Oct. 1941 due to hostile action.

[8] Marine Corps data for World War II, the Spanish-American War and prior wars represent the number of individuals wounded, whereas all other data in this column represent the total number (incidence) of wounds.

[9] As reported by the Commissioner of Pensions in his Annual Report for Fiscal Year 1903.

[10] Number serving covers the period 4 August 1964-27 January 1973 (date of ceasefire). Number of casulties incurred in connection with the conflict in Vietnam from 1 January 1961-27 January 1973. Wounds not mortal exclude 150,332 persons not requiring hospital care.

American Military Cemeteries and Memorials on Foreign Soil

Administered by the American Battle Monuments Commission, Washington, D.C. 20314
(Numbers of graves, and numbers of commemorated missing in parentheses)

World War I Cemeteries

Aisne-Marne, near Belleau (Aisne) France (2,288-1,060)
Brookwood (Surrey) England (468-563)
Flanders Field, Waregem, Belgium (368-43)
Meuse-Argonne, Romagne (Meuse), France (14,246-954)
Oise-Aisne, Seringes (Aisne), near Fere-en-Tardenois (Aisne), France (6,012-241)
St. Mihiel, Thiaucourt (M. et M.), France (4,153-284)
Somme, Bony (Aisne), France (1,844-284)
Suresnes (Seine), France (1,541-974). In this cemetery rest also 24 of our unknown dead of World War II. The World War I chapel was, by the addition of two loggias, converted into a shrine to commemorate our dead of both wars. Senior representatives of the American and French governments assemble here on ceremonial occasions to pay homage to our military dead of these wars.

Henri-Chapelle, near Henri-Chapelle, Belgium (7,989-450)
Lorraine. St. Avold (Moselle), France (10,489-444)
Luxembourg. Hamm, Luxembourg (5,076-370)
Manila, near Manila. Rep. of the Philippines (17,208-36,279)
Netherlands, Margraten. Holland (8,301-1,722)
Normandy, near St. Laurent (Calvados), Fr. (9,386-1,557)
North Africa, Carthage, Tunisia (2,840-3,724)
Rhone, Draguignan (Var), France (861-293)
Sicily-Rome, Nettuno, Italy (7,862-3,094)

World War I Monuments

Audenarde, Belgium.
Bellicourt (Aisne), France.
Brest (Finistere), France.
Cantigny (Somme), France.
Chateau-Thierry (Aisne), Fr.
Gibraltar.
Kemmel, near Ypres, Belgium.
Montfaucon (Meuse), France.
Montsec (Meuse), France.
Sommepy (Marne), France.
Tours (Indre et Loire), France.

World War II Cemetery Memorials

Ardennes, near Neuville-en-Condroz, Belgium (5,313-462)
Brittany, near St. James (Manche), France (4,410-498)
Cambridge, near Cambridge, England, (3,811-5,125)
Epinal, near Epinal (Vosges), France (5,255-424)
Florence, near Florence (Tuscany), Italy (4,402-1,409)

World War II Memorials

To commemorate those who met their deaths in the American coastal waters of the Atlantic and Pacific Oceans the commission has erected a memorial in Battery Park. New York City, on which are inscribed 4,596 names, and at the Presidio of San Francisco, California, which carries 412 names. At the Honolulu Cemetery a memorial was erected which records the names of 18,093 missing of World War II and 8,194 missing resulting from the Korean operations.

The commission also maintains a cemetery in Mexico City where the remains of 750 Americans who gave their lives in the Mexican War (1846-1848) are buried.

Services

The commission provides the following services: exact location and other information concerning place of interment or memorialization; best routes and modes of travel in-country to the cemeteries and memorials; escort service within the cemetery memorials for next-of-kin and members of their immediate families; letters authorizing "non-fee" passports for members of the immediate families; color lithographs of World War I and II cemeteries together with black-and-white photographs of the appropriate gravesite or section of the Tablets of the Missing; and arrangements for floral decorations of gravesites or the Tablets of the Missing.

Veterans Administration National Cemeteries (with ZIP Code)

Alabama
Mobile Natl. Cemetery
  Mobile 36604
Arizona
Prescott Natl. Cemetery
  Prescott 86301
Arkansas
Fayetteville Natl.
  Cemetery
  Fayetteville 72701
Fort Smith Natl. Cemetery
  Fort Smith 72901
Little Rock Natl. Cemetery
  Little Rock 72206
California
Fort Rosecrans Natl.
  Cemetery
  San Diego 92106
Golden Gate Natl.
  Cemetery
  San Bruno 94066
Los Angeles Natl.
  Cemetery
  Los Angeles 90049
San Francisco Natl.
  Cemetery
  Presidio 94129
Colorado
Fort Logan Natl. Cemetery
  Denver 80235
Fort Lyon Natl. Cemetery
  Fort Lyon 81038
Florida
Barrancas Natl.
  Cemetery
  Pensacola 32508
Bay Pines Natl.
  Cemetery
  Bay Pines 33504
St. Augustine Natl.
  Cemetery
  St. Augustine 32084
Georgia
Marietta Natl. Cemetery
  Marietta 30060
Hawaii

Natl. Memorial Cemetery
  of the Pacific
  Honolulu 96813
Illinois
Alton Natl. Cemetery
  Alton 62003
Camp Butler Natl.
  Cemetery
  Springfield 62707
Danville Natl. Cemetery
  Danville 61832
Mound City Natl. Cemetery
  Mound City 62963
Quincy Natl. Cemetery
  Quincy 62301
Rock Island Natl. Cemetery
  Rock Island 61201
Indiana
Crown Hill Natl.
  Cemetery
  Indianapolis 46208
Marion Natl. Cemetery
  Marion. 46952
New Albany Natl.
  Cemetery
  New Albany 47150
Iowa
Keokuk Natl. Cemetery
  Keokuk 52632
Kansas
Fort Leavenworth Natl.
  Cemetery
  Fort Leavenworth 66027
Fort Scott Natl. Cemetery
  Fort Scott 66701
Leavenworth Natl.
  Cemetery
  Leavenworth 66048
Kentucky
Camp Nelson Natl.
  Cemetery
  Nicholasville 40356
Cave Hill Natl. Cemetery
  Louisville 40204
Danville Natl. Cemetery
  Danville 40442

Lebanon Natl. Cemetery
  Lebanon 40033
Lexington Natl. Cemetery
  Lexington 40508
Mill Springs Natl.
  Cemetery
  Nancy 42544
Perryville Natl. Cemetery
  Perryville 40468
Zachary Taylor Natl.
  Cemetery
  Louisville 40207
Louisiana
Alexandria Natl.
  Cemetery
  Pineville 71360
Baton Rouge Natl.
  Cemetery
  Baton Rouge 70806
Port Hudson Natl.
  Cemetery
  Zachary 70791
Maine
Togus Natl. Cemetery
  Togus 04330
Maryland
Annapolis Natl. Cemetery
  Annapolis 21401
Baltimore Natl. Cemetery
  Baltimore 21228
Loudon Park Natl.
  Cemetery
  Baltimore 21229
Minnesota
Fort Snelling Natl.
  Cemetery
  St. Paul 55111
Mississippi
Biloxi Natl. Cemetery
  Biloxi 39531
Corinth Natl. Cemetery
  Corinth 38834
Natchez Natl. Cemetery
  Natchez 39120
Missouri
Jefferson Barracks Natl.

Cemetery
  St. Louis 63125
Jefferson City Natl.
  Cemetery
  Jefferson City 65101
Springfield Natl. Cemetery
  Springfield 65804
Nebraska
Fort McPherson Natl.
  Cemetery
  Maxwell 69151
New Jersey
Beverly Natl. Cemetery
  Beverly 08010
Finn's Point Natl.
  Cemetery
  Salem 08079
New Mexico
Fort Bayard Natl.
  Cemetery
  Fort Bayard 88036
Santa Fe Natl. Cemetery
  Sante Fe 87501
New York
Bath Natl. Cemetery
  Bath 14810
Cypress Hills Natl.
  Cemetery
  Brooklyn 11208
Long Island Natl. Cemetery
  Farmingdale 11735
Woodlawn Natl. Cemetery
  Elmira 14901
North Carolina
New Bern Natl. Cemetery
  New Bern 28560
Raleigh Natl. Cemetery
  Raleigh 27610
Salisbury Natl. Cemetery
  Salisbury 28144
Wilmington Natl. Cemetery
  Wilmington 28401
Ohio
Dayton Natl. Cemetery
  Dayton 45428

Oklahoma
Fort Gibson Natl. Cemetery
  Fort Gibson 74434
Oregon
Roseburg Natl. Cemetery
  Roseburg 97470
White City Natl. Cemetery
  White City 97501
Willamette Natl.
  Cemetery
  Portland 97266
Pennsylvania
Philadelphia Natl.
  Cemetery
  Philadelphia 19138
Puerto Rico
Puerto Rico Natl. Cemetery
  Bayamon 00619
South Carolina
Beaufort Natl. Cemetery
  Beaufort 29902
Florence Natl. Cemetery
  Florence 29501

South Dakota
Black Hills Natl. Cemetery
  Sturgis 57785
Fort Meade Natl. Cemetery
  Fort Meade 57741
Hot Springs Natl. Cemetery
  Hot Springs 57747
Tennessee
Chattanooga Natl.
  Cemetery
  Chattanooga 37404
Knoxville Natl. Cemetery
  Knoxville 37917
Memphis Natl. Cemetery
  Memphis 38122
Mountain Home Natl.
  Cemetery
  Mountain Home 37684
Nashville Natl. Cemetery
  Madison 37115
Texas
Fort Bliss Natl. Cemetery
  Fort Bliss 79906

Fort Sam Houston Natl.
  Cemetery
  San Antonio 78209
Houston Natl. Cemetery
  Houston 77088
Kerrville Natl. Cemetery
  Kerrville 78028
San Antonio Natl.
  Cemetery
  San Antonio 78202
Virginia
Alexandria Natl. Cemetery
  Alexandria 22314
Balls Bluff Natl. Cemetery
  Leesburg 22075
City Point Natl. Cemetery
  Hopewell 23860
Cold Harbor Natl.
  Cemetery
  Mechanicsville 23111
Culpeper Natl. Cemetery
  Culpeper 22701
Danville Natl. Cemetery

Danville 24541
Fort Harrison Natl.
  Cemetery
  Richmond 23231
Glendale Natl. Cemetery
  Richmond 23231
Hampton Natl. Cemetery
  Hampton 23369
Richmond Natl. Cemetery
  Richmond 23231
Seven Pines Natl.
  Cemetery
  Sandston 23150
Staunton Natl. Cemetery
  Staunton 24401
Winchester Natl. Cemetery
  Winchester 22601
West Virginia
Grafton Natl. Cemetery
  Grafton 26354
Wisconsin
Wood Natl. Cemetery
  Wood 53193

Department of the Army

District of Columbia
Soldiers Home National
  Cemetery
  Washington, D. C. 20011

Virginia
Arlington National Cemetery
  Arlington 22211

Department of the Interior

District of Columbia
Battleground National
  Cemetery
  Washington, D. C. 20012
Georgia
Andersonville National
  Historic Site
  Andersonville 31711
Louisiana
Chalmette National Histor-
  ical Park

Arabi 70032
Maryland
Antietam National Battle-
  field Site and Cemetery
  Sharpsburg 21782
Mississippi
Vicksburg National
  Military Park and Ceme-
  tery
  Vicksburg 39180
Montana

Custer Battlefield National
  Monument
• Crow Agency 59022
Pennsylvania
Gettysburg National Mili-
  tary Park and Cemetery
  Gettysburg 17325

Tennessee
Andrew Johnson National
  Historic Site
  Greeneville 37743
Fort Donelson National
  Military Park and Ceme-
  tery
  Dover 37058
Shiloh National Military
  Park and Cemetery
  Shiloh 38376

Stones River National Bat-
  tlefield and Cemetery
  Murfreesboro 37131
Virginia
Fredericksburg and Spot-
  sylvania County Battle
  Memorial
  National Military Park
  and Cemetery
  Fredericksburg 22401
Poplar Grove National
  Cemetery
Petersburg National Bat-
  tlefield
  Petersburg 23803
Yorktown Battlefield
  Colonial National Histor-
  ical Park
  Yorktown 23490

Debt Owed U.S. Arising from World War I

Source: Treasury Department (Dec. 31, 1974)

Country	Original Indebtedness	Interest thru Dec. 31, 1974	Cumulative Payments Principal	Interest	Unmatured Principal	Principal and Interest due and unpaid
Armenia.....	$ 11,959,917.49	$ 32,871,322.91	$ 32.49	$	,.....,.	$ 44,831,207.91
Austria[1]....	26,843,148.66	44,058.93	862,668.00	......	......	26,024,539.59
Belgium.....	419,837,630.37	381,254,720.47	19,157,630.37	33,033,642.87	139,180,000.00	609,721,077.60
Cuba.......	10,000,000.00	2,286,751.58	10,000,000.00	2,286,751.58	......	......
Czechoslova-kia.........	185,071,023.07	145,162,058.73	19,829,914.17	304,178.09	60,595,000.00	249,503,989.54
Estonia......	16,466,012.87	26,163,755.01	10.66	1,248,432.07	5,680,000.00	35,701,325.15
Finland......	8,999,999.97	12,510,133.46	6,030,999.97	12,510,133.46	2,969,000.00	......
France......	4,089,689,588.18	4,248,573,343.39	226,039,588.18	260,036,302.82	1,283,158,102.73	6,569,028,937.84
Great Britain..	4,802,181,641.56	8,119,381,958.11	434,181,641.56	1,590,672,656.18	1,539,000,000.00	9,357,709,301.93
Greece......	34,319,843.67	5,553,381.77	1,472,946.85	4,956,395.30	19,565,975.33	13,877,907.96
Hungary[4]....	1,982,555.50	3,273,194.87	73,995.50	482,924.26	719,355.00	3,979,475.61
Italy.......	2,042,364,319.28	474,346,720.22	37,464,319.28	63,365,560.88	846,900,000.00	1,568,981,159.34
Latvia.......	6,888,664.20	11,044,795.91	9,200.00	752,349.07	2,402,900.00	14,769,011.04
Liberia......	26,000.00	10,471.56	26,000.00	10,471.56	......	......
Lithuania....	6,432,465.00	10,228,869.13	234,783.00	1,003,173.58	2,294,652.00	13,128,725.55
Nicaragua[5]...	141,950.36	26,625.58	141,950.36	26,625.58	......	......
Poland......	207,344,297.37	333,185,614.38	1,287,297.37[n]	21,359,000.18	70,756,000.00	447,127,614.20
Rumania.....	68,359,192.45	64,875,061.85	4,498,632.02[7]	292,375.20[7]	18,100,000.00	110,343,247.08
Russia......	192,601,297.37	548,315,165.96	......	8,750,311.88[8]	......	732,166,151.45
Yugoslavia...	63,577,712.55	42,001,840.42	1,952,712.55	636,059.14	25,655,000.00	77,335,781.28
Totals....	**12,195,087,259.92**	**14,461,109,844.14**	**763,264,322.33**	**2,001,727,343.60**	**4,016,975,985.06**	**19,874,229,453.07**

(1.) The Federal Republic of Germany has recognized liability for securities falling due between March 12, 1938 and May 8, 1945.
(2.) $8,840,090.26 has been made available for educational exchange programs with Finland pursuant to 22 U.-S.C. 2455 (e).
(3.) Includes $13,155,921.00 refunded by the agreement of May 28, 1964. The agreement was ratified by Congress November 5, 1966.
(4.) Interest payments from December 15, 1932 to June 15, 1937 were paid in pengo equivalent.
(5.) The indebtedness of Nicaragua was canceled pursuant to the agreement of April 14, 1938.
(6.) Excludes claim allowance of $1,813,428.69 dated December 15, 1969.
(7.) Excludes payment of $100,000.00 on June 14, 1940 as a token of good faith.
(8.) Principally proceeds from liquidation of Russian assets in the United States.
(9.) Includes $12,813,601.32 on agreement of May 28, 1964.

STATES AND OTHER AREAS OF THE U.S.

Their Resources, Histories, Industries, Agriculture, Mineral Products, Tourist Attractions, Nicknames, State Symbols

Areas of the states are total land and water areas reported by the Geography Division, Bureau of the Census; populations are July 1, 1974, estimates by the Bureau of the Census, including armed forces personnel in each state but excluding such personnel stationed overseas; agricultural figures are based on reports of the Dept. of Agriculture and state agencies; mineral statistics are those reported by the Bureau of Mines; manufacturing statistics are from the Bureau of the Census. Per capita income figures are preliminary.

For maps and for descriptive articles on cities, see Index.

Alabama

Heart of Dixie, Cotton State

AREA: 51,609 sq. mi.; rank, 29th. POPULATION (U.S. est. 1974): 3,577,000; rank, 21st. CAPITAL: Montgomery. MOTTO: We Dare Defend Our Rights. FLOWER: Camellia. BIRD: Yellowhammer. TREE: Southern pine. SONG: Alabama. ENTERED UNION: Dec. 14, 1819; rank, 22d.

Alabama lies in the cotton belt of the Old South but introduction of new and diversified industries has given the state a more balanced economy. Natural wealth includes coal, which underlies about 7,000 sq. mi. in the northern Appalachian region; iron, bauxite and timber.

Cheaha Mtn., 2,407 ft., is the state's highest point.

Abundant water for hydroelectric power and river shipping has contributed to the growth of Alabama's economy. Three Tennessee Valley Authority dams and a large nuclear power plant are in the northern part of the state. Historic sites, fishing and hunting are among its attractions.

With two-thirds of the state's land area in timber, Alabama is a leading producer of pulp, paper, plywood, and paperboard.

Iron and steel production is the most important of Alabama's manufacturing industries; there is also a large segment of manufacturing devoted to primary metal products of wide diversity, particularly structural steel. Other important industry groupings include chemicals and fertilizers, textile mill products and apparel, processing of foods, stone-clay-glass products, transportation equipment, electrical and other machinery. Value added by manufacture is over $4.5 billion a year.

Industrial growth in 1974 saw a record $2.01 billion invested in 662 new or expanded plants, providing 17,836 new jobs. Per capita personal income was $4,198 in 1974 (U. S. average was $5,434).

Birmingham, center of the steel industry, has long been known as "the Pittsburgh of the South."

At Huntsville is the George C. Marshall Space Flight Center of NASA and a space and rocket museum.

Agriculture remains a vital part of the economy. Cotton has long been king among Alabama's crops but is rivaled by corn, soybeans, pecans, and peanuts. Among the states, Alabama ranked 3d in production of pecans in 1973, 2d in peanuts. Also important are potatoes, watermelons, tobacco, and peaches.

Livestock, especially poultry, has grown in importance. Alabama was 5th among the states in number of chickens in 1975. Farm receipts for livestock and livestock products in 1974 totaled $778 million; for crops, the total was $605 million. Forest product sales totaled $157 million.

Alabama ranks 2d behind Arkansas in production of bauxite and is the 2d largest producer of asphalt and mica. But bituminous coal accounts for over 50% of the value of its total mineral production, which in 1974 rose 50% to an estimated $619 million. Also important are cement, stone and petroleum.

There are 56 institutions of higher education. Per pupil expenditure in public schools in 1974-75 was $871, ranking 47th among the states.

Earliest traces of mankind in the area date to 10,-000 years ago. First Europeans were Spanish explorers in the early 1500's. The French made the first permanent settlement, on Mobile Bay, 1701-02; later, English settled in the northern areas. France ceded the entire region to England at the end of the French and Indian War, 1763, but Spanish Florida claimed the Mobile Bay area until U. S. troops took it, 1813. Gen. Andrew Jackson broke the power of the Creek Indians, 1814, and they were removed to Oklahoma.

The Confederate States were organized at Montgomery, Feb. 4, 1861, and Jefferson Davis took the oath as president at State Capital there Feb. 18. Davis' "first White House" now is a state shrine; others include the house in Tuscumbia where Helen Keller was born June 27, 1880; Statue of Vulcan near Birmingham.

Tourists spent an estimated $718 million in Alabama in 1974.

At Russell Cave National Monument, near Bridgeport, may be seen a detailed record of occupancy by humans from about 7000 B.C. to 1650 A.D., including tools, weapons and pottery. The exhibit is free.

The George Washington Carver Museum at Tuskegee Institute, Tuskegee, contains records of the famous black scientist's contributions to agronomy and dioramas of achievements by blacks.

The University of Alabama Museum of Natural History, in Tuscaloosa, displays Alabama fossils, shells and aboriginal materials and collections. Mound State Monument, Moundville, an adjunct of the museum, shows aboriginal burials.

Famous Alabamians include Gov. George Wallace, Hank Aaron, Willie Mays, Tallulah Bankhead, Nat King Cole, Hank Williams, Jesse Owens, Helen Keller, Harper Lee, Joe Louis, George Washington Carver.

(See also Index for Birmingham, Mobile, Montgomery.)

Alaska

No official nickname

AREA: 585,412 sq. mi.; rank, 1st. POPULATION: 337,000 (U. S. est. 1974); rank, 50th. CAPITAL: Juneau. FLOWER: Forget-me-not. BIRD: Willow ptarmigan. TREE: Sitka spruce. SONG: Alaska's Flag. FISH: King salmon. MOTTO: North to the Future. ENTERED UNION: Jan. 3, 1959; rank, 49th.

Alaska became the 49th state Jan. 3, 1959. Largest political division of the U.S., it is two and one-fifth times the size of Texas. Alaska occupies the NW part of North America, separated from the rest of the continental U.S. by Canada's British Columbia. Alaska's general coastline runs 6,640 mi.; including all its islands, 33,904 mi. It has mountain ranges, volcanoes, fjords and glaciers.

About one-sixth of the population are Eskimos and Indians.

Pt. Barrow in Arctic Alaska is the northernmost spot in the state. The Yukon River flows E to W 1,200 mi. through Central Alaska, from the Canadian border to the Bering Sea. In South Central Alaska stands Mt. McKinley, 20,320 ft., highest point in North America.

In west central Alaska, off the tip of the Seward Peninsula, lies Little Diomede Is., only 2.4 mi. from the Big Diomede Is., owned by the USSR. The Alaska Peninsula and the Aleutian Islands into which it tapers, extends SW and W for 1,200 mi., with numerous volcanoes; at the base of the peninsula is Katmai National Monument, containing the Valley of 10,000

Smokes, scene of a 1912 eruption.

Alaska's Panhandle stretches SE; it is a narrow strip of mainland and islands, with fjords and Glacier Bay National Monument (containing the Muir Glacier, 2 mi. wide and 250 ft. high), facing the Pacific, W of British Columbia.

Vitus Bering, a Danish explorer working for Russia, was the first European to land in Alaska, 1741. Alexander Baranov, first governor of Russian America, set up headquarters at Archangel, near present Sitka, in 1799. Secretary of State William H. Seward in 1867 bought Alaska from Russia for $7,200,000, a bargain which some called "Seward's Folly." In 1896, gold was discovered and the famed Gold Rush was on. Many of the fortune hunters settled in Alaska as farmers or traders. It was not until 1959 that Alaska became a state.

Resources and Industries. Principal income is from fisheries, minerals (esp. oil), wood products, tourism and furs. Salmon, halibut, herring, cod, and shellfish are frozen or canned; Alaska is a leader in value of its commercial catch, about $141 million in 1974.

Processing of fish and other foods is the largest manufacturing industry, followed by forest products.

Spruce, yellow cedar, and hemlock are plentiful; there also are red cedar, and birch. Commercial timberland of Alaska's vast forest totals 28 million acres. The forest products industry in SE is expanding as pulp mills increase. Timber products value is over $134 million yearly.

Furs produced are those of the seal, sable, ermine, wolverine, land otter, muskrat, beaver, mink, red fox, blue fox, lynx, marten. Wildlife includes the gray wolf, moose, caribou, and 5 kinds of bear: black, grizzly, polar, Kodiak, and glacier. There are plenty of sea fowl, but whales, walrus, sea lion, and sea otter have diminished.

The seal herd on the Pribilof Islands is owned by the federal government and seal harvesting is managed by the U.S. Commerce Dept. Reindeer herds are multiplying and their meat is marketed.

Oil production, mainly from offshore fields in Cook Inlet, had an est. value of $246 million in 1973. Total mineral production value was est. at $303 million.

Sale of leases for the vast North Slope oil discovery area at Prudhoe Bay brought the state $900 million in 1969. After long delay caused by ecological controversy, Congress in Nov. 1973 authorized construction of a $6-billion, 796-mi., trans-Alaska pipeline to carry oil from Prudhoe Bay to the south Alaska port of Valdez. Oil was to start flowing by mid-1977.

The value of gold production in 1973 was $1.3 million. Alaska also has natural gas, tin, bituminous coal, and mercury.

Principal ports are in the Panhandle where Juneau, the capital, is on the mainland shore; N of it is Skagway, historic entry to Klondike gold fields via Chiloot Pass and White Pass. Sitka, Wrangell, and Ketchikan (center of salmon industry), are on islands of the Alexander group.

At the head of Cook Inlet, in S Central Alaska, is the state's largest city, Anchorage. Seward, S of Anchorage, is the terminus for the government-owned Alaska Railroad, which runs N to Fairbanks. Nine domestic airlines serve Alaska. International lines flying via Arctic routes make stops. Ships transport 90% of the goods and foods to and from Alaska linking some 50 Alaskan ports with Seattle, etc.

More than 235,000 tourists visit Alaska annually, spending some $72 million.

There are 2 motor routes to Alaska. The newer is by-way of Marine Highway, a 450-mile ferry route from Prince Rupert, B.C., to Skagway, Alaska. Motorists leaving the ferry at Haines may drive to Fairbanks. Anchorage, etc., with part of the route passing through Canada. The older route is the Alaska Highway, from British Columbia. Fairbanks, largest city in Central Alaska, has the northernmost international airport on the continent. Nearby is Eielson AFB.

There are 9 institutions of higher education.

Pay of public school teachers, $16,053 in 1973, is the highest in the 50 states. Average per capita income was $7,023 in 1974, highest in the U.S.

The Alaska State Museum in Juneau features Eskimo and Indian exhibits, mounted wildlife specimens, rocks and minerals and historical exhibits.

The University of Alaska Museum, in College, near Fairbanks, maintains cultural and natural history collections for research and for the public.

Famous Alaskans include pioneer pilot Carl Eielson, prospector Joe Juneau, painter Sydney Laurence, former Gov. Ernest Gruening, Congressman James Wickersham.

(See also Index for Anchorage.)

Arizona
Grand Canyon State

AREA: 113,809 sq. mi.; rank, 6th. POPULATION (U.S. est. 1974): 2,153,000; rank, 33d. CAPITAL: Phoenix. MOTTO: Ditat Deus, God Enriches. FLOWER: Giant cactus or saguaro. BIRD: Cactus wren. TREE: Paloverde. SONG: Arizona. ENTERED UNION: Feb. 14, 1912, rank, 48th.

Arizona leads the nation in copper production with half of the total U.S. output, but its rapidly-growing manufacturing industries, such as machinery, aerospace, and electronics, form the largest source of income. Agriculture and tourism are also important.

Loads of sunshine and a wealth of scenic attractions give Arizona a mounting tourist business; 12 million out-of-staters spent an est. $690 million in 1974.

The climate is dry in southern regions and the northern plateau, but high mountains and forests in central areas have heavy snows in winter. Highest point is Humphreys Peak, 12,633 ft. Over 44% of the land is U.S. owned.

The only point in the U.S. at which 4 states meet is the juncture of Arizona, Utah, Colorado and New Mexico.

Arizona is noted for the Grand Canyon of the Colorado, an immense, vari-colored fissure 217 mi. long, 4 to 13 mi. wide at the brim, 4,000 to 5,500 ft. deep. Hoover Dam (formerly Boulder), in Black Canyon of the Colorado, is 726 ft. high, 660 ft. wide at base, 1,244 ft. long at top, creating Lake Mead.

Nature has given Arizona the Painted Desert, extending for 30 mi. along U.S. 66; the Petrified Forest; Canyon Diablo, 225 ft. deep and 500 ft. wide, and Meteor Crater, 4,150 ft. across, 570 ft. deep, made by a prehistoric meteor. The state has 17 national monuments, 2 national parks. Rodeos and historic sites of Indian and Spanish eras are other attractions.

Copper is king among Arizona's many minerals and the state normally produces a half or more of the nation's copper output. The 1974 est. value of the state's copper production was $1.3 million. Arizona also ranks high among the states in pumice, silver, molybdenum, and gold. Total value of mineral production in 1974 was est. at $1.5 billion.

Cotton is a major crop; Arizona's harvest ranked 4th among the states in 1974. Cash receipts for all crops in 1974 were $603 million; receipts from livestock and livestock products, $628 million. The state ranks 10th in number of sheep. Fruit production is important; Arizona ranks high in lemons, oranges, grapefruit, and grapes. Lettuce, melons, and alfalfa are valuable crops.

Manufacturing has made large strides in recent years. Value added by manufacture is over $1.9 billion a year. Electrical machinery, including electronic components, accounts for over $335 million of this total; other machinery is also highly important.

Federal spending on defense contracts, construction projects, air bases, etc., is an important factor in Arizona's economy. Per capita personal income was $4,989 in 1974.

Schools include the Univ. of Arizona at Tucson, Arizona State Univ. at Tempe, and Northern Arizona Univ. at Flagstaff. The new observatory of the National Science Foundation is located on Kitt Peak near Tucson. Taliesin West is the Frank Lloyd Wright architectural school near Phoenix.

Marcos de Niza, a Franciscan, and Estevan, a black slave, explored the Arizona area in 1539. Eusebio Francisco Kino, Jesuit missionary, taught Indians Christianity and farming, 1690-1711, and left a chain of missions. Spain ceded Arizona to Mexico, 1821. The U. S. took over at the end of the Mexican War, 1848. The area below the Gila River was obtained from Mexico in the Gadsden Purchase, 1854. Long Apache wars did not end until 1886, with Geronimo's surrender.

Museums include Arizona State Museum, Tucson, which stresses the archeology and ethnology of the Southwest. The Museum of Northern Arizona, 3 mi. N of Flagstaff, has exhibits illustrating the geology and paleontology of the area.

The Southwestern Arboretum, on U.S. 60 and 70 near Superior, has over 6,000 plants and trees from arid regions of the world, from lowly cactus to lofty boojum tree. The Phoenix Zoo is one of the nation's largest. The Arizona-Sonora Desert Museum, near Tucson, displays animals and plants of the desert.

Famous Arizonans include Cochise, Geronimo, Helen Jacobs, Zane Grey, Barry Goldwater, Percival Lowell, Stewart Udall, Frank Lloyd Wright, William H. Pickering, George W. P. Hunt.

(See also Index for Phoenix and Tucson.)

Arkansas
Land of Opportunity

AREA: 53,104 sq. mi.; rank, 27th. POPULATION (U.S. est. 1974): 2,062,000; rank, 32d. CAPITAL: Little Rock. MOTTO: Regnat Populus, Let the People Rule. FLOWER: Apple blossom. BIRD: Mockingbird. TREE: Pine. SONG: Arkansas. ENTERED UNION: June 15, 1836; rank, 25th.

Arkansas is an important agricultural state with growing industries, has valuable mineral production and thermal springs and is popular with sportsmen. Highest point is Magazine Mtn., 2,753 ft.

First European explorers were Hernando de Soto, 1541; Louis Jolliet, 1673; La Salle, 1682. First settlement was by the French under Henri de Tonty, 1686, at Arkansas Post. In 1762 the area was ceded by France to Spain, then back again in 1800 and was part of the Louisiana Purchase by the U. S. in 1803. Arkansas seceded from the Union in 1861, only after the Civil War began, and many Arkansans (over 10,000) fought on the Union side. The state rejoined the Union in 1868.

Manufacturing is growing in importance with a 64% increase in employees in a 10-year period. New and expanded factories provided 13,000 new jobs in 1974. Per capita income was $4,280 in 1974. Lumber, petroleum, bauxite, and cotton are major products.

The $1.2 billion Arkansas River program, involving navigation, flood control, and power developments and construction of 17 dams and locks in Arkansas and Oklahoma, was completed to Catoosa, near Tulsa, Okla., in 1971 and provided an important boost to the area's economy.

The state has 18.5 million acres of oak, hickory, gum, cypress, and pine, and forest industries have a $500 million annual payroll. Cotton accounts for 48% of farm income and Arkansas ranked 5th in cotton production in the U.S. in 1974. It was 4th in rice. It was 3d in number of chickens, 6th in turkeys.

Arkansas accounts for by far the greatest amount of bauxite (aluminum ore) produced in the U.S. It has the only diamond field in the U.S., ranks 1st in bromine and vanadium.

But petroleum is the state's main mineral product; 1974 output was valued at $115 million; that of bauxite was $26.5 million. Natural gas and stone were also important. Total value of mineral production was est. at $356 million, up 30% from the record 1973 figure.

Arkansas has 24 institutions of higher learning.

Fresh-water fishing, duck-hunting in southeast lowlands, and recreation areas in 21 state parks and 3 national forests attract visitors. There are several reservoir-recreation areas, as at Norfork, Bull Shoals, Nimrod and Dardanelle, and others are being created. There are 47 hot springs in government-operated Hot Springs National Park, which entirely surrounds the city of Hot Springs, about 50 mi. SW of Little Rock. Spring water ranges from 95° to 147°F. and is piped in insulated conduits for baths and drinking. The state has 93 airports.

Out-of-state visitors spent more than $623 million in Arkansas in 1973.

Historic attractions in Little Rock include the Territorial Capital Restoration, a block of 13 original frame and brick buildings, furnished as in 1820-36, including the governor's home and an early print shop of the Arkansas Gazette, oldest newspaper west of the Mississippi. The Old State House in Little Rock was the state capitol 1836-1912; it houses many historical exhibits.

The Little Rock Museum of Science and Natural History occupies the building where Gen. Douglas MacArthur was born; also in MacArthur Park is the Arkansas Museum of Fine Arts.

Famous Arkansans include Hattie Caraway, "Dizzy" Dean, Orval Faubus, James W. Fulbright, Douglas MacArthur, John L. McClellan, Winthrop Rockefeller, Edward Durell Stone, Thyra Samter Winslow, Opie Read, Archibald Yell.

(See also Index for Little Rock.)

California
Golden State

AREA: 158,693 sq. mi.; rank, 3d. POPULATION (U. S. est. 1974): 20,907,000; rank, 1st. CAPITAL: Sacramento. MOTTO: Eureka, I Have Found It. FLOWER: California poppy. BIRD: Valley quail. TREE: Redwood. SONG: I Love You, California. ENTERED UNION: Sept. 9, 1850; rank 31st.

California is the leading state in agriculture, manufacturing, and population.

Third largest in area, California also has, within only 85 mi. of each other, the highest and lowest points in the conterminous 48 states; Mt. Whitney, 14,494 ft., and Death Valley, 282 ft. below sea level.

The U.S. Bureau of the Census estimated California's population as of July 1, 1964, at 18,084,000 and New York's at 17,915,000, giving California 1st place; New York had been in 1st place from 1820 through the census of 1960. In the 1970 census, New York had 18,241,266; California, 19,953,134. California also has the most dogs and cats — an est. 50 million.

Among scenic regions are the Yosemite Valley, Lassen and Sequoia-King Canyon national parks, Lake Tahoe, the Mojave and Colorado deserts, San Francisco Bay, and Monterey Peninsula. National forests cover one-fifth of the state.

Oldest living trees on earth are believed to be a stand of Bristlecone pine in the Inyo National Forest, est. to be 4,600 years old.

The world's tallest tree, the Howard Libbey redwood, 362 ft. with a girth of 44 ft., stands on Redwood Creek, Humboldt County.

California's huge fruit and vegetable production is fed by large irrigation systems. Receipts from crops in 1974 totaled $5.5 billion (tops in U.S.); from livestock, $2.7 billion (3d in U.S.); total receipts were $8.2 billion (most in U.S.).

The state ranked 1st in numbers of chickens, 2d in turkeys, 3d in sheep, 7th in cattle, as of Jan. 1, 1975.

California produces the most apricots, avocados, grapes and raisins, peaches, persimmons, pomegranates, plums, prunes, lemons, nectarines, olives, dates, almonds, walnuts, and sugar beets. Its total vegetable crop is the largest; it ranks 2d to Florida in oranges and was also 2d in cotton and barley, 3d in rice and grapefruit.

It was 2d to Alaska in commercial fishing in 1974 with a catch valued at $130 million.

The state's giant aerospace industries employ a

third of all its manufacturing employees. Value added by manufacture is over $31 billion (1972); transportation equipment, especially aircraft and missiles, led; food products, particularly frozen and canned foods, were 2d; electrical machinery, including electronic components, was 3d followed by ordnance, other machinery, metal products. Per capita income was $5,997 in 1974, $247 lower than in New York.

Gold, discovered at Sutter's sawmill Jan. 24, 1848, set off the historic Gold Rush and gave initial impetus to California's development, but petroleum is the leading mineral product today.

Oil output in 1974 was valued at an est. $1.7 billion, over half the state's total mineral production value, $2.8 billion, up 40% and 3d highest in the U.S. after Texas and Louisiana. Ranking 3d in oil production, California is a leader in output of asbestos, cement, boron, gypsum, and tungsten.

The Oroville Dam, main unit in the world's largest water project — the $2.8 billion Feather River Project -- was dedicated May 4, 1968, N of Sacramento; electric power and water for irrigation were flowing even before completion.

Tourists spend about $4.8 billion a year in California.

There are some 200 institutions of higher learning. Three of the world's largest observatories are located on Palomar Mtn., Mt. Hamilton, and Mt. Wilson.

The Tournament of Roses and the Rose Bowl football game at Pasadena are held annually on Jan. 1. Winter sports are featured in many mountain areas.

Vandenberg AFB, 170 mi. NW of Los Angeles, is center of an interservice missile range.

First European visitors were Juan Rodriguez Cabrillo, 1542, and Francis Drake, 1579. First settlement was the Spanish Alta California mission at San Diego, 1769, first in a string founded by Franciscan Father Junipero Serra. U. S. traders and settlers arrived in the 19th Century and staged the abortive Bear Flag Revolt, 1846; the Mexican War began later in 1846 and U.S. forces occupied California; Mexico ceded the province to the U.S. in 1848, the same year the Gold Rush began. By 1964 California was the most populous state in the U.S.

Among museums the Pasadena Art Museum has collections of modern German painting, American painting, Oriental art and prints. The Santa Barbara Museum of Art has exhibits of Greek and Roman sculpture, Oriental art, old master and modern paintings, primitive arts, American paintings, and old and modern European drawings. The Santa Barbara Historical Society Museum displays and interprets objects of state and local history and operates the Gledhill Library for historical research. In Sacramento, the Crocker Art Gallery has collections of paintings, drawings, prints, sculpture, and crafts representing all European schools, American glass, and pottery from 5th Century B.C. to contemporary American.

The J. Paul Getty Museum in Malibu opened in 1974 with collections of Greek and Roman antiquities, 18th Century French furniture and Western European paintings.

Famous Californians include Luther Burbank, W. R. Hearst, Joe DiMaggio, Jack London, Richard Nixon, Herbert Hoover, William Saroyan, Earl Warren, John Steinbeck, Gertrude Atherton, Bret Harte.

(See also Index for Bakersfield, Fresno, Los Angeles, Oakland, Orange County, Sacramento, San Diego, San Bernardino, San Francisco, San Jose.)

Colorado
Centennial State

AREA: 104,247 sq. mi.; rank, 8th. POPULATION (U.S. est. 1974): 2,496,000; rank, 30th. CAPITAL: Denver. MOTTO: Nil Sine Numine, Nothing Without Deity. FLOWER: Columbine. BIRD: Lark bunting. TREE: Colorado blue spruce. ANIMAL: Big horn sheep. SONG: Where the Columbines Grow. ENTER-

ED UNION: Aug. 1, 1876; rank, 38th.

Once primarily a mining and grazing state, Colorado now draws the largest segment of its income from manufacturing, followed by agriculture, tourism, and mining. Its snow-capped peaks, ski centers, ghost towns and health spas make it a popular vacation-recreation area.

Early civilization centered around Mesa Verde 2,000 years ago. The U. S. acquired eastern Colorado in the Louisiana Purchase, 1803; Lt. Zebulon M. Pike explored the area, 1806, discovering the peak that bears his name. After the Mexican War, 1846-48, U.S. immigrants settled in the east, former Mexicans in the south. Gold was discovered, 1858, bringing more immigrants. By mid-20th century, Colorado's economy was based on manufacturing, agriculture, tourism and mining, in that order.

The total of value added by Colorado's varied manufacturing industries is over $3 billion yearly. Important industry groups are processing of meat, dairy and other food products, as well as machinery, electronics, metals, and stone-clay-glass products. Research and aerospace industries are growing. Per capita income was $5,343 in 1974.

Farm receipts in 1974 totaled $2 billion, about 70% from livestock and livestock products. Colorado ranked 4th among the states in the number of sheep in 1975, 11th in cattle. Its sugar beet crop is the 2d largest in the U.S. Other important crops are wheat, corn, barley, alfalfa, potatoes, apples, peaches, pears.

Gold was discovered on the Platte in 1858 and at Leadville in 1860.

Climax, near Leadville, now produces most of the world's molybdenum. Colorado produces a rich variety of minerals and is a leader among the states in output of tin, vanadium, tungsten, carbon dioxide, uranium, lead, zinc, and pyrites. Total 1974 mineral production was valued at $737 million, up 38% from 1973; petroleum accounted for $277 million of the total, up 78%.

With Utah and Wyoming, Colorado shares the world's richest oil shale deposits, still to be developed.

Colorado is the highest state in the Union, with an average altitude of 6,800 ft. It has 54 of the nation's highest mountains and 1,500 peaks over 10,000 ft. Highest is Mt. Elbert, 14,433 ft. Frozen Lake, altitude 12,940 ft., is the highest lake in the 48 conterminous states.

Six major rivers—the Colorado, Rio Grande, Arkansas, North Platte, South Platte, and Republican — rise in Colorado, supply water to 19 states. The western rivers have cut great canyons; the Black Canyon of the Gunnison and the Royal Gorge of the Arkansas, 1,000 to 1,500 ft. deep. One of the world's highest bridges crosses the Arkansas 1,053 ft. above the river at Royal Gorge.

The Federal Government owns 36.4% of the land, including 2 National Parks, 6 monuments, 2 Recreation Areas, 12 forests, 2 Indian reservations, 7 major military reservations.

Colorado has 29 institutions of higher education.

Colorado was the 1st of several states which in 1966 liberalized its abortion laws.

Attractions for an annual 8 million tourists include Rocky Mountain National Park, Garden of the Gods, Great Sand Dunes and Dinosaur National Monuments, Pikes Peak and Mt. Evans Highways, Mesa Verde National Park (pre-historic cliff dwellings). The Grand Mesa tableland comprises Grand Mesa Forest, 659,584 acres, with 200 lakes stocked with trout. Other attractions include the U.S. Air Force Academy near Colorado Springs, Denver Western Stock Show, Colorado State Fair, horse, dog, and auto races, rodeos, and pioneer celebrations. Thirty-nine major ski areas operate from November to May. Tourists spend some $678 million a year.

Big game include deer, bear, elk, mountain lion, gray wolf, coyote. There are thousands of miles of trout streams and 2,000 fishing lakes.

The old mining towns of Aspen and Central City have become cultural centers.

Museums include the Colorado Springs Fine Arts Center which has paintings, prints and drawings by contemporary artists, exhibits of the cultural history of the SW and Latin America, and the John F. Huckel collection of 112 Navajo sand painting reproductions. The University of Colorado Museum, in Boulder, has more than a million objects in its exhibits of rocks, plants and early peoples as well as an art gallery.

Famous Coloradans include Lowell Thomas, Paul Whiteman, William N. Byers, Frederick Bonfils, Harry Tammen, Jack Dempsey, Douglas Fairbanks, Ralph Edwards, Byron R. White, M. Scott Carpenter.

(See also Index for Denver.)

Connecticut
Constitution State

AREA: 5,009 sq. mi.; rank 48th. POPULATION (U.S. est. 1974): 3,088,000; rank, 24th. CAPITAL: Hartford. MOTTO: Qui Transtulit, Sustinet; He Who Transplanted, Sustains. FLOWER: Mountain laurel. BIRD: American robin. TREE: White oak. Fifth of the 13 original states to ratify the Constitution, Jan. 9, 1788.

Connecticut's heavily industrialized cities are in sharp contrast to its picturesque New England villages and scenic countryside. Despite its small size, the state has large and diverse manufacturing industries, mainly of high-value specialty products. Per capita income was $6,471 in 1974, 2d only to Alaska.

It is a leading maker of jet engines, helicopters, nuclear subs, pins and needles, silverware, hardware, cutlery, and ball bearings. Ranking 48th in area, it is 16th in value added by manufacturing, a total of over $6.05 billion annually. Its factories employ over 34% of the working force. Hartford is headquarters for many of the nation's largest insurance companies.

Poultry and dairy products account for the largest part of farm receipts, which totaled $200 million in 1974. Much of the soil is stony, but tobacco, potatoes, fruits, and vegetables are grown. Greenhouse, nursery, and forest products are valued at over $21 million annually.

The vacation-recreation industry is important. Attractions include historic sites, charming villages, the American Shakespeare Festival in Stratford, Mystic Seaport and Marine Museum, trolley museums, skiing, boating on Long Island Sound.

There are 85 state parks, 29 state forests, recreation areas, and historic sites, covering 163,000 acres.

Tourism brings Connecticut about $425 million a year from out-of-state vacationers.

Mineral production is mostly of sand, stone, and gravel for construction of roads and buildings. Total value for 1974 was $39.7 million.

Adriaen Block, Dutch explorer, was the first European visitor, 1614. By 1633, settlers from Plymouth Bay started colonies along the Connecticut River and in 1637 defeated the Pequot Indians, opening the area to more settlements. In the Revolution, Connecticut men fought in most major campaigns and beat off British raids on Danbury and other towns. Connecticut privateers captured British merchant ships; the state was nicknamed "The Provision State" for the large amount of food it furnished the Continental Army.

Free public schools were established in New Haven, 1642, Hartford, 1643. Compulsory education in elementary and Latin grammar schools was established in 1650.

There are 49 institutions of higher education.

Museums include the P. T. Barnum Museum, Bridgeport; American Clock and Watch Museum, Bristol; trolley museums, East Haven and Warehouse Point; Hill-Stead Museum, a country house with paintings by famous impressionists, Farmington; Museum of American Art, New Britain; Old Lighthouse, Stonington; Lyman Allyn Museum, New London; Bruce Museum, Greenwich; Wadsworth Atheneum, Hartford.

In New Haven, museums include the Winchester Gun Museum, with 5,000 items from the 15th century to present. The Yale University Art Gallery's collections range from ancient to modern. The Peabody Museum at Yale has collections in paleontology, mineralogy, zoology and, archeology.

Mystic Seaport, Mystic, is a recreated 19th Century village, including smithy, chapel, and schoolhouse. At the docks lie the wooden whaleship, Charles W. Morgan, the squarerigger, Joseph Conrad; the Gloucester fishing schooner, L. A. Dunton.

Famous "Nutmeggers" include Phineas T. Barnum, Ethan Allen, Walter Camp, Samuel Colt, Nathan Hale, Isaac Hull, J. Pierpont Morgan, Abraham Ribicoff, Harriet Beecher Stowe, Mark Twain, Noah Webster, Emma Hart Willard.

(See also Index for Bridgeport, Hartford, New Haven.)

Delaware
First State, Diamond State

AREA: 2,057 sq. mi.; rank, 49th. POPULATION: (U.S. est. 1974); 573,000; rank, 46th. CAPITAL: Dover. MOTTO: Liberty and Independence. FLOWER: Peach blossom. BIRD: Blue hen chicken. TREE: American holly, SONG: Our Delaware. First of original 13 states to ratify the Constitution, Dec. 7, 1787.

Delaware occupies part of the Delmarva Peninsula, so-called because Delaware and parts of Maryland and Virginia share the peninsula separating Delaware and Chesapeake Bays. Delaware is 96 mi. long and from 9 to 35 mi. wide. The land slopes from rolling hills (442 ft. highest elevation) in the N to a near sea-level plain.

Second smallest of the states in area, Delaware has a high per capita income, $6,227 in 1974, with large chemical and other industries, the hqs. of many large corporations, prosperous farms, and important shellfish production.

Important in Delaware's total of value added by manufacture are canned and frozen foods, leather and metal products, textiles and machinery. Total value added by manufacture is over $1.28 billion.

Broiler chickens are the largest item of farm income. Farm receipts for 1974 were $257 million.

Mineral production is mainly sand, gravel, and stone used for construction. Total value in 1974 was est. at $3.3 million. There is also a sizable commercial fishing catch, valued at $1.9 million in 1974.

Delaware's major tourist attractions include several famed beaches, racetracks, and historic sites and museums. Annual value of tourism is about $300 million.

The Dutch first settled in Delaware near present Lewes, 1631, but were wiped out by Indians. Swedes settled at present Wilmington, 1638; Dutch settled anew, 1651, near New Castle and seized the Swedish settlement, 1655, only to lose all Delaware to the British, 1664. Delaware troops served in Washington's New Jersey campaigns and at the Brandywine, near home, where Washington suffered defeat. Delaware troops also fought in the southern campaigns and, finally, at Yorktown. In the Civil War, over 10% of Delaware's total population served in the Union Army.

Fort Christina Monument marks the site of founding of New Sweden. Holy Trinity (Old Swedes) Church erected 1698 is the oldest Protestant church in the U.S. still in use. Center New Castle comprises a unique survival of a colonial capital nearly in its late 18th Century form. The home of John Dickinson, "Penman of the Revolution," and drafter of the Articles of Confederation, has been restored near Dover.

Museums include the Delaware Art Center in Wilmington which has collections of Pre-Raphaelite English paintings and American paintings. The Henry Francis du Pont Winterthur Museum, at Winterthur near Wilmington, has 100 American period rooms from 17th to early 19th Centuries (reservations are required to visit some of them). The Hagley

Museum at Wilmington includes many of the old du Pont powder mills and other exhibits illustrating the development of American industry. The Delaware Museum of Natural History is in Greenville.

The Delaware State Museum, Dover, has varied exhibits on Delaware history and life and a collection on the development of the Victor Talking Machine and related sound recording.

Delaware has 7 institutions of higher education.

Famous Delawareans include E. I. du Pont, Caesar Rodney, Howard Pyle, Henry Seidel Canby, John P. Marquand.

(See also Index for Wilmington.)

Florida
Sunshine State

AREA: 58,560 sq. mi.; rank, 22d. POPULATION: (U.S. est. 1974): 8,090,000; rank, 9th. CAPITAL: Tallahassee. MOTTO: In God We Trust. FLOWER: Orange blossom. BIRD: Mockingbird. TREE: Sabal palm. SONG: Old Folks at Home. ENTERED UNION: Mar. 3, 1845; rank 27th.

Florida's many miles of beaches and other resort areas offer fun in the sun to millions of vacationers. The state also has a tremendous agricultural output, producing 80% of the nation's citrus fruits and ranking 2d only to California in production of vegetables. Its growing and diversified manufacturing industries provide even more income than its agriculture. Per capita income was $5,235 in 1974.

The Florida peninsula juts southward 500 mi. between the Atlantic and the Gulf of Mexico; Cuba is only 90 mi. from its southern tip. It has some 30,000 lakes; Okeechobee, covering 700 sq. mi., is the 4th largest natural lake inside the U.S. Highest elevation in the state is 345 ft., in the NW.

First European to see Florida was Ponce de Leon, 1513. France established a colony, Fort Caroline, on the St. Johns River, 1564; Spain settled St. Augustine, 1565, and Spanish troops massacred most of the French. Britain's Francis Drake burned St. Augustine, 1586. Britain held the area briefly, 1763-83, returning it to Spain. After Andrew Jackson led a U.S. invasion, 1818, Spain ceded Florida to the U.S., 1819. The Seminole War, 1835-42, resulted in removal of most Indians to Oklahoma. Florida seceded from the Union, 1861, was readmitted, 1868.

Tourism is a major industry; about 24.5 million visitors spend some $6.7 billion annually in Florida. It offers a wide variety of tourist attractions in addition to climate, resorts, and water sports.

Many tourists have become permanent residents.

Major tourist objectives are metropolitan Miami, with the nation's greatest concentration of luxury hotels at Miami Beach; Palm Beach; St. Augustine, oldest city in U.S.; Daytona Beach, Fort Lauderdale, all on the E coast; Sarasota, Tampa, Key West, St. Petersburg on the W; Walt Disney World, an entertainment and vacation development near Orlando.

Everglades National Park, 3d largest of U.S. national parks, preserves the beauty of the vast Everglades swamp. Castillo de San Marcos (St. Augustine), Fort Matanzas, Fort Jefferson (Dry Tortugas), De Soto National Memorial (Bradenton), and Fort Caroline (Jacksonville) are national monuments.

The John F. Kennedy Space Center is another big tourist attraction. From it the nation's first earth satellite was launched Jan. 31, 1958; first U.S. manned space flight, May 5, 1961; first manned orbital flight, Feb. 20, 1962 (Col. John H. Glenn), as well as the first man-on-the-moon launch, July 16, 1969.

Key West became the 1st U.S. city to get its fresh water from the sea when a desalting plant, capable of producing 3.5 million gallons a day, opened 1967.

Florida produces most of the nation's oranges and grapefruit; 1974 output was an est. 7.4 million tons of oranges and 2 million tons of grapefruit, both several times the amount produced by California. It also produces vegetables, avocados, watermelons, limes, tangerines, sugarcane, peanuts, cotton, tobacco,

strawberries. Florida also ranks high in chickens.

The cattle industry has grown in importance. Crop and livestock receipts for 1974 totaled $2 billion.

Manufacturing has made great gains and provides payrolls totaling $2.28 billion. Leading industries, in terms of value added by manufacturing, are food processing, chemicals, electrical equipment, transportation equipment, metal products, paper.

Florida leads the U.S. in production of phosphate rock and is 2d to New York in titanium. Total mineral production value in 1974 was est. at $984.7 million, up 64% from 1973, with most of the increase due to raised petroleum prices.

The commercial catch of fish and shellfish is worth over $66 million a year, high among the states.

Florida has 17 airports with scheduled service, 62 scheduled airlines, and 5 major railroads. There are 14 deepwater ports which handle domestic and foreign trade valued at $1.8 billion a year.

Florida has 66 institutions of higher learning.

Florida has no state income tax.

Museums include the Florida State Museum in Gainesville, with exhibits in archeology, ethnology, paleontology, ornithology, history, and industry. Castillo de San Marcos in St. Augustine is a Spanish fort built 1672-1696 which is now a national monument. Marineland of Florida, 18 mi. S of St. Augustine, has some 2,500 marine specimens ranging from sharks and porpoises to tiny tropical fish; trained porpoises and pilot whales perform in shows. Miami's Seaquarium and Orlando's Sea World have similar shows.

At Pensacola is the Naval Aviation Museum, with exhibits tracing flight development into the space age; Fort Pickens, built 1829, where Geronimo was imprisoned; the T. T. Wentworth Museum, with exhibits of local historical interest; the Pensacola Historical Museum and Spanish Village Museum.

At Lake Wales are the 205-ft. Singing Tower with a carillon of 53 bells (the largest weighs 11 tons) and Mountain Lake Sanctuary, with trails and picnic area, given "to the American people" by publisher Edward Bok in thanks for "the successful life they gave" him.

In Sarasota, the John and Mable Ringling Museum of Art, willed to the state, contains works by Rembrandt, Rubens, Hals, Tiepolo, Velasquez, Murillo, Gainsborough, Reynolds, and other masters. The Ringling Museum of the Circus includes elaborately decorated wagons, costumes, and printed bills showing performers at fairs and circuses from the 16th to 20th centuries: the Asolo Theater presents operas.

Also in Sarasota, the Circus Hall of Fame gives circus acts and puppet shows, displays mementos such as a coach given Tom Thumb by Queen Victoria, a sleigh P. T. Barnum gave Jenny Lind.

Famous Floridians include Henry M. Flagler, Rex Beach, Irving Bacheller, James Weldon Johnson, Marjorie Kinnan Rawlings, MacKinlay Kantor, Gen. Joseph W. Stilwell.

(See also Index for Jacksonville, Miami, Orlando, Pensacola, St. Petersburg, Tallahassee, Tampa, West Palm Beach.)

Georgia
Empire State of the South, Peach State

AREA: 58,876 sq. mi.; rank, 21st. POPULATION (U.S. est. 1974): 4,882,000; rank 15th. CAPITAL: Atlanta. MOTTO: Wisdom, Justice, Moderation. FLOWER: Cherokee rose. BIRD: Brown thrasher. TREE: Live oak. SONG: Georgia. Fourth of the 13 original states to ratify the Constitution, Jan. 2, 1788.

Largest in area of the states east of the Mississippi, Georgia is rich in a number of natural resources and in its growing, diversified industries.

There are large deposits of marble in the mountainous N, along with fertile plains and industry centers in the NW. The central Georgia Piedmont plateau boasts rich farmlands and a flourishing textile industry. The SE coastal plain produces pecans and peanuts and its forests yield a wealth of pulpwood and turpentine. Off its 100-mi. Atlantic coast lie its famed Golden Isles. The state also has large deposits of clay, limestone, and talc.

Okefenokee in the SE is one of the largest swamps in the U.S., a wetland wilderness and peat bog covering 660 sq. mi. A large part of it is a National Wildlife Refuge, a home for wild birds, alligators, bear, deer.

Highest point in the state is Brasstown Bald in the NE, 4,784 ft.; Stone Mtn., near Atlanta, is 1,686 ft.

Manufacturing production has increased many times over since World War II, but the textile industry remains the largest, both in terms of number of workers and value added by manufacture. Also of great importance are paper products, transportation equipment, apparel, food products, and chemicals. Value added by manufacture totals over $6.5 billion a year. Per capita income was $4,662 in 1974.

Georgia ranks high among the states in forest products, particularly in pulpwood and turpentine.

Georgia is by far the nation's largest producer of peanuts, harvesting 800,000 tons in 1974, more than twice that of any other state. It is among the leading growers of pecans, peaches, and rye.

It ranked 2d among the states in numbers of chickens, about 35 million in 1974, and also had a large hog production. Farm receipts totaled over $2.2 billion in 1974, more than half from livestock.

Georgia is also a leader in production of marble, zirconium, bauxite, and kyanite. Total value of mineral production in 1974 was an est. $348 million.

Savannah and Brunswick are the main ports. The state is served by 6 major railroads and 10 airlines.

Notable among attractions are the Little White House in Warm Springs where President Franklin D. Roosevelt died Apr. 12, 1945, the 2,500-acre Callaway Gardens, Jekyll Island State Park, the restored 1850s farming community of Westville; Dahlonega, site of America's first gold rush; Helen, a mountain village with Alpine motif, Stone Mountain and Six Flags over Georgia.

Georgia has also become a sports center, with professional baseball, basketball, football, hockey.

Andersonville Prison Park and National Cemetery are on the site of the Confederate prison camp in which a total of 50,000 Union soldiers were confined, Feb. 1864 to Apr. 1865.

There are 62 institutions of higher learning.

Gen. James Oglethorpe established the first settlements, 1733, for poor and religiously-persecuted Englishmen. Oglethorpe defeated a Spanish army from Florida at Bloody Marsh, 1742. In the Revolution, Georgians siezed the Savannah armory, 1775, and sent the munitions to the Continental Army. Led by Light-Horse Harry Lee, Elijah Clarke, Andrew Pickens and Anthony Wayne, Georgians fought see-saw campaigns with Cornwallis' British troops, twice liberating Augusta and forcing final evacuation by the British from Savannah, 1782.

Famous Georgians include Ty Cobb, Margaret Mitchell, Erskine Caldwell, Joel Chandler Harris, Laurence Stallings, John C. Fremont, James Bowie, Joseph Wheeler, Lucius D. Clay.

(See also Index for Atlanta, Augusta, Columbus, Macon, Savannah.)

Hawaii
Aloha State

AREA: 6,450 sq. mi.; rank, 47th. **POPULATION** (U.S. est. 1974): 847,000; rank, 40th. **CAPITAL:** Honolulu. **MOTTO:** The Life of the Land Is Perpetuated in Righteousness. **FLOWER:** Hibiscus. **BIRD:** Nene (Hawaiian goose). **TREE:** Kukui (candlenut). **SONG:** Hawaii Ponoi. **ENTERED UNION:** Aug. 21, 1959, rank, 50th.

Hawaii, prosperous paradise of the Pacific, became the 50th state Aug. 21, 1959, and the 50-star U. S. flag became official the following July 4.

The Hawaiian Islands lie in the North Pacific, 2,397 mi. from San Francisco (5 hrs. by commercial jet). They consist of 8 major islands (7 inhabited) and 124 minor islands.

The principal islands are Hawaii, the largest; Oahu, on which are Honolulu and Pearl Harbor; Lanai, Maui, Molokai, Kauai, Niihau and Kahoolawe.

The islands are volcanic. Highest point is Mauna Kea, on Hawaii, an extinct volcano 13,796 ft. above sea level. Its twin is Mauna Loa, about 100 ft. lower but an active volcano. Average annual rainfall is 22 inches at Honolulu Airport, 136.6 inches in Hilo, and 486 inches atop Waialeale, a mountain on Kauai. Honolulu is subtropical (all-time range, 57° to 88°) but Mauna Kea is often snowcapped.

Lake Waiau, at 13,020 ft. near the summit of Mauna Kea, is the highest lake in the U.S.

Ka Lae, or South Cape, on the island of Hawaii, is the southernmost point in the 50 states.

Polynesians from islands 2,000 mi. to the south settled the Hawaiian Islands, probably about 700 A.D. First European visitor was British Capt. James Cook, 1778. Missionaries arrived, 1820, taught religion, reading and writing. King Kamehameha III and his chiefs created the first Constitution and a Legislature which set up a public school system. Sugar production began in 1835; it became the dominant industry. In 1893, Queen Liliuokalani was deposed, followed, 1894, by a republic headed by Sanford B. Dole. Annexation by the U.S. came in 1898. Attempts to attain statehood did not succeed until 1959.

Hawaii has a very heterogeneous population with Americans of Polynesian, Asian, European, and African extraction.

Many of the Polynesians intermarried with the other racial groups, which arrived mainly in the 19th Century.

The 1970 Census gave as racial origins: Japanese, 28.3%; Caucasian, 39.2%; the remainder, Hawaiian, Chinese, Filipino, Korean, etc., with many of mixed racial descent.

Major sources of income are tourism, defense expenditures, sugar and pineapple production, in that order. Visitors totaled 2.6 million in 1974, with an average 59,400 present daily.

Value added by manufacturing, led by food processing, was $412 million in 1973. There were 4,100 farms, with a total of 2.3 million acres; farm receipts for 1974 were $205 million. The commercial fishing catch was valued at $5.5 million in 1974.

Mineral production, mostly cement and stone for construction, was valued at $43 million in 1974.

Per capita income was $5,882 in 1974.

More than 7,400 ships put into Honolulu in 1973. Honolulu International Airport has an average of over 300,000 arrivals and departures annually.

A marine exposition is scheduled for 1978, bicentennial of Capt. Cook's arrival in the islands.

There are 13 institutions of higher education.

Famous Hawaiians include Duke Kahanamoku, Don Ho, Patsy Mink, Daniel K. Inouye, Father Joseph Damien, Bette Midler.

(See also Index for Honolulu.)

Idaho
Gem State

AREA: 83,557 sq. mi.; rank, 13th. **POPULATION** (U.S. est. 1974): 799,000; rank, 43d. **CAPITAL:** Boise. **MOTTO:** Esto Perpetua, Let It Be Forever. **FLOWER:** Lewis mock orange (syringa). **BIRD:** Mountain bluebird. **TREE:** Western white pine. **SONG:** Here We Have Idaho. **ENTERED UNION:** July 3, 1890; rank, 43d.

A land of rugged grandeur, Idaho nevertheless ranks high in agricultural production.

Exploration of the Idaho area began with Lewis and Clark, 1805; they returned through Idaho, 1806. Next came fur traders, setting up posts, 1809-34, and missionaries, establishing missions, 1830s-1850s. Mormons made their first permanent settlement at Franklin, 1860. Idaho's Gold Rush began that same year, and brought thousands of permanent settlers. Strangest of the Indian Wars was the 1,300-mi. trek of Chief Joseph and the Nez Perce tribe, pursued by troops that caught them a few miles short of the

Canadian border. By 1890, Idaho adopted a progressive Constitution and became a state that year.

Idaho was chiefly a farming, grazing, timber, and mineral state for many years, but manufacturing has recently become second in importance to agriculture. There are rugged mountains, beautiful valleys, plateau regions, and extensive lava fields. Mt. Borah, in the Sawtooth Mts., is the highest peak, 12,662 ft.

The Snake River runs through Hells Canyon, which averages 5,510 ft. in depth for 40 mi., at one point 7,900 ft., exceeding Grand Canyon, and is 10 mi. from rim to rim at widest point. The Snake has several noted waterfalls: Shoshone, Twin, American.

Idaho is the nation's leading potato producer, growing about 80 million cwt. annually. It ranks high in sugar beets, barley, wheat, hops, and apples.

It ranks high in wool production and was 8th among the states in number of sheep in 1974 with 595,000. Farm marketing receipts in 1974 totaled $1.4 million, more than half from crops, the rest from livestock.

Manufacturing's gains were mainly in processing of potatoes and other foods, phosphates, paper, etc. Total value added by manufacturing was est. at over $775 million. Per capita income was $4,734 in 1974.

Discovery of silver in 1884 at Coeur d'Alene caused a stampede; Idaho still leads the nation in production of that metal. It also ranks high among the states in antimony, lead, cobalt, garnet, phosphate rock, vanadium, zinc, and mercury. Total mineral production in 1974 was estimated at $196 million, up 44%.

With 39% of its area in forests, Idaho produces much lumber, with the world's largest white pine lumber mill at Lewiston. Yellow pine, Douglas fir, white spruce, larch, hemlock abound; the DeVoto Grove has cedars 1,000 years old. Total value of forest products is more than $153 million a year.

Hells Canyon, Brownlee, and Oxbow Dams are 3 recent hydro-electric projects on the Snake River. The National Reactor Testing Station of the AEC on Upper Snake River Plains has more than a score of reactors in operation.

Tourism brings in an est. $200 million or more annually, making it an important industry.

The state offers excellent hunting and fishing and Lake Pend Oreille, which has a 111-mile shoreline, is home of the world's largest trout, Kamloop rainbow.

Craters of the Moon National Monument, 18 mi. W of Arco, is a jagged landscape; lava covers the area.

The Nez Perce National Historic Park, in northern Idaho, includes many sites visited by the Lewis and Clark Expedition. The State Historical Museum in Boise has displays of early Idaho Indian life, the fur trade, mining, farm and pioneer mementos.

There are 9 institutions of higher education.

Famous Idahoans include William E. Borah, Fred T. Dubois, Chief Joseph and Sacajawea, girl guide for Lewis and Clark.

(See also Index for Boise.)

Illinois
The Inland Empire

AREA: 56,400 sq. mi.; rank, 24th. **POPULATION:** (U.S. est. 1974): 11,131,000, rank, 5th. **CAPITAL:** Springfield. **MOTTO:** State Sovereignty, National Union. **FLOWER:** Native violet. **BIRD:** Cardinal. **TREE:** White oak. Song: Illinois. **SLOGAN: Land of Lincoln. ENTERED UNION: Dec. 3, 1818; rank, 21st.**

Illinois ranks high among the states as both an agricultural and industrial empire. It is rich in coal and oil reserves and boasts highly developed rail, water, and air transportation facilities.

The soil is rich and level, with the high point, Charles Mound near the Wisconsin line, only 1,235 ft.

Fur traders were the first Europeans in Illinois, followed shortly, 1673, by Louis Jolliet and Father Jacques Marquette, and, 1680, La Salle, who built a fort near present Peoria. First settlements were French, at Fort St. Louis on the Illinois River, 1692, and Kaskaskia, 1700. France ceded the area to Britain, 1763, and in 1778 American Gen. George Rogers

Clark took it from the British without a shot. Defeat of Indian tribes in Black Hawk War, 1832, inspired new immigration, as did railroads in 1850s.

Illinois ranks 4th highest among the states in terms of value added by manufacture with a total of close to $25.8 billion. Manufacturing payrolls total $12.9 billion.

Major manufacturing lines are machinery (particularly construction and farm), processing of food products (especially grain, beverages and bakery), electrical machinery (communications, electronic components and appliances), primary metals (mainly iron and steel), transportation equipment (for railroads, aircraft, and cars) and chemicals. Rockford is one of the nation's machine-tool centers; Peoria is a distilling center. Per capita income was $6,337 in 1974.

In 1974 Illinois ranked 2d to California in receipts from farm crops, $4.4 billion. It stood 8th in receipts for livestock and livestock products and was 3d in total cash farm receipts, $6.3 billion.

Illinois and Iowa vie closely with each other for the largest corn crop. Illinois produces the most soybeans; in 1975 it ranked 2d to Iowa in number of hogs and stood high in cattle and milk cows.

The state has large coal and oil reserves. It ranks high among the states in annual bituminous coal production, est. at $606 million in 1974. Petroleum production, 2d in value to coal, was est. to be worth $211 million. The state is a leader in output of fluorspar, tripoli, stone, and peat. Total 1974 minerals were valued at $1.1 billion.

A major research and development installation of the Atomic Energy Commission is the Argonne National Laboratory, Lemont, Ill., directed by the Univ. of Chicago, which also operates the Argonne Cancer Research Hospital in Chicago. At Batavia, W of Chicago, the AEC completed the nation's largest atomsmasher in 1971.

Illinois has 138 institutions of higher education.

The Illinois State Fair is held annually in August in Springfield. More than 37,000 entries compete for more than $270,000 in cash awards. Attendance is over 700,000.

State forests, parks, and conservation areas cover 283,430 acres. Some are associated with the history of the Middle West, including Lincoln's home and tomb in Springfield; the restored Fort de Chartres, seat of French 18th Century authority; old settlements such as Kaskaskia.

The Illinois State Museum in Springfield has large collections of local art and archeology; art of the ancient Near East, and antique furnishings.

Located in Springfield is a state memorial including Abraham Lincoln's tomb and the Lincoln home which the family occupied 1844-1860. The Old State Capitol Building has been restored.

New Salem State Park, 20 mi. NW of Springfield, contains the restored pioneer village of New Salem where Lincoln lived as storekeeper, surveyor, and postmaster, 1831-37. Annual performances are staged of Robert Sherwood's Abe Lincoln in Illinois.

Famous Illinoisans include Abraham Lincoln, William Jennings Bryan, Jane Addams, Adlai Stevenson, Carl Sandburg, Mary Garden, Ernest Hemingway, James T. Farrell, Frank Lloyd Wright.

(See also Index for Bloomington, Chicago, Springfield.)

Indiana
Hoosier State

AREA: 36,291 sq. mi.; rank, 38th. **POPULATION** (U.S. est. 1974): 5,330,000; rank, 11th. **CAPITAL:** Indianapolis. **MOTTO: Cross-roads of America. FLOWER:** Peony. **BIRD:** Cardinal. **TREE:** Tulip (yellow poplar). **SONG: On the Banks of the Wabash. ENTERED UNION: Dec. 11, 1816; rank, 19th.**

Indiana is heavily industrialized, yet is also important among the states for its agricultural output. It ranks among the top states in production of both steel and corn; it quarries much of the building limestone used in the U.S. and is a large producer of coal.

Pre-Indian Mound Builders of 1,000 years ago were the earliest known inhabitants. French explorer La Salle visited the present South Bend area, 1679 and 1681. A French trading post was built, 1731-32, at Vincennes. France ceded the area to Britain, 1763. During the Revolution, American Gen. George Rogers Clark captured Vincennes, 1778, and defeated British forces 1779; at war's end Britain ceded the area to the U.S. Miami Indians defeated U.S. troops twice, 1790, but were beaten, 1794, at Fallen Timbers by Gen. Anthony Wayne. At Tippecanoe, 1811, Gen. William H. Harrison defeated Tecumseh's Indian confederation.

There are sand dunes and lakes in the N, a level plain through most of the central area, and hills in the S. Highest point is 1,257 ft. in Wayne Co.

The Calumet region in the state's NW corner, including Gary, Hammond, East Chicago, and Whiting, has one of the world's greatest concentrations of heavy industry, especially steel, cement, and oil-refining plants. Gary was a sand dune in 1906 when U.S. Steel began constructing mills there; in 1970 it had a pop. of 175,415.

Per capita income was $5,263 in 1974.

Another vast steel complex has been developed further E along Lake Michigan, including a deep-water port at Burns Harbor in the famed Dunes area, a large plant of the Midwest Steel Div. of the National Steel Corp., plus Bethlehem Steel Corp. works.

While steel and other metal industries are responsible for $1.8 billion of the $12 billion in value added annually by manufacture, electrical machinery, including television sets and household appliances, is a close 2d with $1.9 billion. Auto parts, aircraft and other transportation equipment is next, with $1.6 billion; farm and other machinery, 4th; chemicals, 5th; processing of food products, 6th.

Indiana is a leader in production of pre-fabricated wood products, mobile homes, and band instruments. Furniture is manufactured in over 40 cities.

Corn is the principal crop and much of it goes to fatten the hogs. Among the states, Indiana ranks 3d in hogs and soybeans, 3d in corn, 7th in chickens. Farm marketing receipts for 1973 totaled $2.8 billion, 8th highest among the states.

Coal accounts for over a third of the value of mineral production which in 1974 totaled $411 million. Portland cement, petroleum, limestone, clay, and gypsum are also important.

Indiana limestone, from vast quarries in the southern part of the state, sheathes tens of thousands of buildings, including the Empire State, Rockefeller Center, the United Nations, the Pentagon, the National Cathedral and many federal and state buildings.

Spending by out-of-state tourists is est. at $500 million a year.

Indiana has 27 state parks and recreation areas, including Dunes State Park on Lake Michigan; prehistoric Indian mounds; over 1,000 lakes; French Lick and other mineral spas; Wyandotte Cave, 3d largest in the U.S.; the Indianapolis 500-mile auto race, and the famous post office, Santa Claus.

Lincoln's boyhood home in Spencer County and the grave of his mother, Nancy Hanks Lincoln, are part of the Lincoln Boyhood National Memorial. State memorials commemorate the capture of Vincennes by George Rogers Clark in the Revolution, the defeat of Indian forces at Tippecanoe, and the Rappite and Robert Owen communities at New Harmony.

Spring Mill, Conner Prairie, and Billie Creek are restored pioneer settlements. The restored White-water Canal is at Brookville.

There are 45 institutions of higher education.

Famous "Hoosiers" include Wendell L. Willkie, Wilbur Wright, Lew Wallace, Cole Porter, Hoagy Carmichael, James Whitcomb Riley, Ernie Pyle, Booth Tarkington, Gene Stratton Porter, George Jean Nathan.

(See also Index for Evansville, Fort Wayne,

Indianapolis.)

Iowa
Hawkeye State

AREA: 56,290 sq. mi.; rank, 25th. POPULATION (U.S. est. 1974): 2,855,000: rank, 25th. CAPITAL: Des Moines. MOTTO: Our Liberties We Prize and Our Rights We Will Maintain. FLOWER: Wild rose. BIRD: Eastern goldfinch. TREE: Oak. SONG: Iowa. ENTERED UNION: Dec. 28, 1846; rank, 29th.

Iowa, the heart of the rich Midwest farm belt, is one of the nation's wealthiest agricultural states, but its industrial buildup has been so great that the value of its manufacturing output is more than twice that of its farms.

Many industries process farm products or produce farm implements. However, the fast-growing industrial economy includes a wide variety of manufacturing plants, with electronic items, home appliances, tires, railway equipment, furnaces, automobile accessories, chemicals and fertilizers, vending machines, office furniture, and gypsum wallboard among the diversified products. Value added by manufacture is over $4.7 billion a year. Per capita income was $5,302 in 1974.

Iowa's broad plains contain much of the finest soil in the world. Its huge harvests support the nation's richest livestock industry. Iowa had by far the most hogs, 13.4 million in 1975, twice as many as Illinois, the next largest raiser. In cattle, with 7.4 million, Iowa was 2d only to Texas. It also had large numbers of chickens, turkeys, and sheep.

In field crops, Iowa ranked first in corn, 2d in soybeans, and 4th in alfalfa.

Receipts for livestock and livestock products totaled $3.8 billion in 1974, tops in the nation. In receipts for crops, Iowa stood 3d. Its total farm receipts were $7.7 billion, 2d only to California.

Iowa's forests produce hardwood lumber.

Mineral production was valued at $159 million in 1974. Products, in order of value, were cement, limestone, sand and gravel, gypsum, and coal.

Visitors from other states add more than $400 million to Iowa's economy annually.

Tourist attractions include the Herbert Hoover birthplace and library near West Branch, tulip festivals at Pella and Orange City in May, Iowa State Fair at Des Moines in August, several rodeos, the National Hot Air Balloon Races. The Little Brown Church in the Vale, near Nashua, inspired a well-known hymn. There are 91 state parks and other recreation areas. Effigy Mounds National Monument at Marquette is a prehistoric Indian burial site.

The Davenport Municipal Art Gallery has a collection of paintings and memorabilia of the Iowa painter Grant Wood, as well as other American, Mexican, Haitian, and European paintings. The State Historical Building, Des Moines, has Indian artifacts.

In Decorah, the Norwegian-American Museum preserves homes of pioneers from Norway.

Waterloo's Museum of History and Science has exhibits on Iowa history, pioneer life, Indian lore, and earth sciences, and a planetarium.

Iowa has 55 institutions of higher education.

A thousand years ago several groups of pre-Indian Mound Builders dwelt on Iowa's fertile plains. Father Jacques Marquette and Louis Jolliet gave France its claim to the area, 1673. It became U.S. territory through the 1803 Louisiana Purchase. Indian tribes were moved into the area from states further east, but by mid-19th Century were forced to move on to Kansas. Before and during the Civil War, Iowans strongly supported Abraham Lincoln and became traditional Republicans.

Famous Iowans include Herbert Hoover, Buffalo Bill Cody, Billy Sunday, Susan Glaspell, Harry Hansen, Marquis Childs, James Norman Hall, Carl Van Vechten, Margaret Wilson, Grant Wood, Meredith Willson.

(See also Index for Des Moines.)

Kansas
Sunflower State

AREA: 82,264 sq. mi.; rank, 14th. POPULATION (U.S. est. 1974): 2,270,000; rank, 28th. CAPITAL: Topeka. MOTTO: Ad Astra per Aspera, To the Stars through Difficulties. FLOWER: Sunflower. BIRD: Western meadowlark. TREE: Cottonwood. SONG: Home on the Range. ENTERED UNION: Jan. 29, 1861; rank, 34th.

Rolling fields of wheat, clusters of oil well derricks, great herds of cattle, and towering grain storage elevators feature the landscape of Kansas, the geographical center of the 48 conterminous states. The land rises from broad plains in the E, 680 ft. above sea level, to slightly over 4,000 ft. in the W.

Manufacturing, farming, and mining (especially petroleum and natural gas) are major factors in the Kansas economy. Large industry fields include transportation equipment, food processing, machinery, and chemicals. Value added by manufacture is $2.5 billion a year. Per capita income was $5,446 in 1974.

Most of the land of Kansas is devoted to agriculture, and much of that to growing wheat. Kansas ranked first among the states in its wheat crop in 1974, 2d in sorghum, 6th in cattle. Total farm receipts for 1974 were $4.3 billion, 6th highest in the U. S. Forest products, particularly walnut lumber are valued at about $14 million a year.

Wichita ranks first in the nation in production of private aircraft.

Kansas stands high in petroleum production and has large reserves of natural gas and helium. It ranks first among the states in helium production.

Petroleum production in 1974 was valued at an est. $465 million, almost half the total mineral production value, $946 million, up $300 million. Also important are natural gas and salt.

Coronado marched through the Kansas area, 1541; French explorers came next. The U.S. took over in the Louisiana Purchase, 1803. In the pre-war North-South struggle over slavery, so much violence swept the area it was called Bleeding Kansas; it was deeply involved in the Civil War. Railroad construction after the war made Abilene and Dodge City terminals of large cattle drives from Texas. Sale of alcoholic beverages was prohibited from 1880 to 1948.

In Abilene, the boyhood home of the late President Dwight D. Eisenhower, is the Eisenhower Center, with the Eisenhower Home, Museum, and Library. Near them, in a chapel named "Place of Meditation," the 34th president was buried Apr. 2, 1969.

The Agricultural Hall of Fame and National Center, 14 mi. W of Kansas City, Kan., displays farm equipment of the past such as a wooden-wheeled corn planter, anvils, wheat drills, etc. In Dodge City are extensive reproductions of the original Front Street, saloons, and Boot Hill cemetery.

The Wichita Art Museum has works by many modern artists. The Kansas State Historical Society in Topeka has displays and period rooms of Midwest history.

In Lawrence, the Univ. of Kansas has a Museum of Natural History which presents a panorama of North American mammals from the Arctic to the tropics; a Museum of Art, with European and American painting and sculpture and European and Oriental decorative arts; and the Snow Entomological Museum, with over 2 million insects.

It is estimated that tourists spend over $527 million a year in the state.

Kansas has 53 institutions of higher learning.

Kansas has developed an extensive recreation system around its reservoirs, lakes, and roadside parks.

Famous Kansans include John Brown, Dwight D. Eisenhower, Gen. Hugh Johnson, Walter P. Chrysler, Amelia Earhart, Osa Johnson, Brock Pemberton, Walter Johnson, Alf M. Landon.

(See also Index for Wichita.)

Kentucky
Blue Grass State

AREA: 40,395 sq. mi.; rank, 37th. POPULATION (U.S. est. 1974): 3,357,000; rank, 23d. CAPITAL: Frankfort. MOTTO: United We Stand, Divided We Fall. FLOWER: Goldenrod. BIRD: Cardinal. SONG: My Old Kentucky Home. TREE: Tulip tree. ENTERED UNION: June 1, 1792; rank, 15th.

Kentucky was the first area west of the Alleghenies settled by American pioneers. First permanent settlers were led by James Harrod at Harrodsburg, 1774. Daniel Boone blazed the Wilderness Trail through the Cumberland Gap and founded Boonesboro, 1775. Indian attacks, spurred by the British, were unceasing until, during the Revolution, Gen. George Rogers Clark, leading Kentucky volunteers, captured British forts in Indiana and Illinois, 1778; Boone, captured by Indians, escaped and warned Boonesboro of a coming Indian attack, which was repulsed. In 1792, after Virginia dropped its claims to the region, Kentucky became the 15th state.

Kentucky rises from an elevation of less than 260 ft., at the Mississippi, to over 4,000 ft. in the Cumberland and Pine mountains. Over 42% of the state is forested, and lumbering, particularly of hardwoods, is an important industry. Forest products are valued at over $50 million a year.

Manufacturing has shown important gains but agriculture and mining remain vital parts of Kentucky's economy.

Tobacco is the principal crop, 2d only to that of North Carolina. Corn, soybeans, wheat, fruit, hogs, and cattle, especially milk cows, are also important. Farm receipts in 1974 totaled $669 million from livestock, $917 million from crops.

In 1974 Kentucky produced more tons of coal than West Virginia but was 2d in terms of its value. Kentucky also produces important amounts of petroleum, natural gas, fluorspar, clay, and stone. But coal accounts for 90% of the total mineral value, est. at $2 billion for 1974, up 87% from 1973.

In 1966 Kentucky enacted a law requiring surface and strip miners of coal to restore and regrade earth removed by their operations, but problems have remained.

Manufacturing has shown needed growth and diversity. Leading fields are food processing and beverages (including liquor), tobacco products, machinery, chemicals, transportation equipment and apparel. Value added by manufacture is over $5.8 billion a year. Per capita income was $4,470 in 1974.

Tourists bring in an est. $575 million a year. There are 48 state and national parks and shrines.

Two of the largest man-made lakes in the world, Kentucky Lake and Lake Barkley, parallel each other in Western Kentucky, creating a 170,000-acre isthmus called the Land Between the Lakes National Recreation Area.

Lexington, heart of the Bluegrass country, has the University of Kentucky and Transylvania, oldest college west of the Alleghenies (1780), and a large tobacco market, and holds annual trotting and running races and a horse show. The Kentucky Derby is run annually at Churchill Downs, Louisville.

Fort Knox, repository of the nation's gold reserve, also contains the George S. Patton Jr. Military Museum of World War II equipment.

Mammoth Cave, 40 mi. from Bowling Green, is in a national park. Discovered 1799, it has 150 mi. of passageways, rooms with 200-ft. ceilings, blind fish, and an Echo River 360 ft. below ground.

Old Fort Harrod State Park, Harrodsburg, contains the reconstructed fort with stockade, blockhouses, the log cabin in which Thomas Lincoln and Nancy Hanks, Abraham Lincoln's parents, were married, and a museum with relics of Shakertown, Ky.

Abraham Lincoln Birthplace National Historic Site, 3 mi. from Hodgenville, contains the original Thomas Lincoln farm and cabin.

My Old Kentucky Home, one mi. E of Bardstown,

was the home of John Rowan, senator and state chief justice. Stephen Foster, a relative, visited the Rowan family in 1852 and is said to have written My Old Kentucky Home on a desk preserved in the house.

Kentucky has 36 institutions of higher learning.

Famous Kentuckians include Abraham Lincoln, Vice Presidents Adlai Stevenson and Alben Barkley, Henry Clay, Jefferson Davis, Louis D. Brandeis, Kit Carson, Irvin S. Cobb, Elizabeth Madox Roberts, John Fox Jr., Robert Penn Warren.

(See also Index for Louisville.)

Louisiana
Pelican State

AREA: 48,523 sq. mi.; rank 31st. **POPULATION** (U.S. est. 1974): 3,764,000; rank, 20th. **CAPITAL:** Baton Rouge. **MOTTO:** Union, Justice, Confidence.· **FLOWER:** Southern magnolia. **BIRD:** Eastern brown. pelican. **SONG:** Give Me Louisiana. **TREE:** Bald cypress. **ENTERED UNION:** Apr. 30, 1812; rank, 18th.

Louisiana blends a wealth of historic charm, rich natural resources, and giant modern industries. Fertile soil, huge mineral deposits and over 7,000 mi. of navigable waterways linking the nation's heart with deepsea ports are factors basic to the state's wealth.

Mardi Gras and other festivals, the beat of Dixieland jazz in the land of its origin, and the nostalgic relics of the days of French and Spanish rule and the prosperous pre-Civil War era are among the attractions which bring Louisiana an est. $508 million a year in tourist revenues.

In total value of its 1974 mineral output, $8.7 billion (up 52%), Louisiana was 2d only to Texas among the 50 states. It was first in value of its natural gas and salt production, 2d in petroleum and sulphur. Much of the oil and sulphur comes from offshore deposits.

The lush Louisiana land produces one of the nation's largest crops of sweet potatoes. It is 2d to Texas in rice, 3d in sugarcane. Also important are pecans, soybeans, cotton, and corn.

Farm receipts in 1974 included $897 million from crops, $360 million from livestock.

Total value added by manufacture is over $4.4 billion annually. Per capita income was $4,310 in 1974.

Leading manufacturing industries include chemicals, food processing, petroleum and coal products (especially oil refining), paper (particularly paperboard), lumber and wood products, transportation equipment, stone clay-glass products, apparel.

With 7,409 sq. mi. under water, Louisiana marshes supply most of the nation's muskrat fur; there are also opossum, raccoon, mink, otter and large numbers of game birds. The annual catch of fresh and salt water fish, shrimp, and oyster is valued at about $86 million. Lake Pontchartrain covers 630 sq. mi.

Much of the land is a rich alluvial plain; there are also rolling hills, bluffs on the Mississippi, and coastal marshes. The elevation ranges from 5 ft. below sea level, protected by vast levees, to 535 above.

Louisiana is rich in historical relics and traditions. The area was first visited, 1530, by Cabeza de Vaca and Panfilo de Narvaez. The region was claimed for France by LaSalle, 1682. First permanent settlement was by French at Fort St. Jean Baptiste (now Natchitoches), 1717. France ceded the region to Spain, 1762, took it back, 1800, and sold it to the U.S., 1803, in the Louisiana Purchase. During the Revolution, Spanish Louisiana aided the Americans. Admitted to statehood, 1812, Louisiana was the scene of the Battle of New Orleans, 1815. The state seceded from the Union, 1861, was readmitted, 1868.

Louisiana Creoles are descendants of early French and/or Spanish settlers. About 4,000 Acadians, French settlers in Nova Scotia, Canada, were forcibly transported by the British to Louisiana in 1755 (an event commemorated in Longfellow's Evangeline) and settled near Bayou Teche; their descendants became known as Cajuns. Another group, the Islenos, were descendants of Canary Islanders brought to Louisiana by a Spanish governor in 1770. Traces of

Spanish and French survive in local dialects.

Louisiana has 25 institutions of higher education.

Famous Louisianians include Zachary Taylor, Leonidas K. Polk, Braxton Bragg, Judah P. Benjamin, Pierre Beauregard, Huey Long, Grace King.

(See also Index for Baton Rouge, New Orleans, Shreveport.)

Maine
Pine Tree State

AREA: 33,215 sq. mi.; rank, 39th. **POPULATION** (U.S. est. 1974): 1,047,000; rank, 38th. **CAPITAL:** Augusta. **MOTTO:** Dirigo, I Direct. **FLOWER:** Pine cone and tassel. **BIRD:** Chickadee. **TREE:** Eastern white pine. **SONG:** State of Maine Song. **ENTERED UNION:** Mar. 15, 1820; rank, 23d.

Maine is noted for its scenic and vacation attractions, lobsters, potatoes, poultry, and forest products, fishing and hunting.

Largest of the 6 New England states, it is the farthest NE and borders on only one other state, New Hampshire. Its rugged coast, because of deep indentations, measures 3,478 mi. Tides are often high; in Passamaquoddy Bay they average 20 ft.

Mt. Cadillac, on Mt. Desert Is., 1,532 ft., is the highest Atlantic seacoast point N of Brazil; West Quoddy Head, Long 66° 57′ W. is the farthest east point on the U.S. Atlantic coast. Lubec is the most easterly town on the U.S. mainland.

Maine's rocky coast was explored by John and Sebastian Cabot, 1498-99. French settlers arrived, 1604, at the St. Croix River; English, 1607, on the Kennebec. In 1691, Maine was made part of Massachusetts. Joining that colony's protests against Britain, Maine staged its own Tea Party at York. In the Revolution, a Maine regiment fought at Bunker Hill; a British fleet destroyed Falmouth (now Portland), 1775; but the British ship Margaretta was captured near Machiasport. In 1820, Maine broke off from Massachusetts, became a separate state.

Maine's coastal waters produce an annual 20 million lbs. of lobsters, 75% of the nation's total, and 50% of its soft-shelled clams. The state packs over 150 million cans of sardines a year, tops among the states. The fish and shellfish catch is worth $40 million annually to the fisherman.

Maine grows about 12% of the nation's potatoes; 2d to Idaho, and is the leading supplier of seed potatoes. It produces 90% of the nation's low bush blueberries. Also grown are apples, sweet corn, peas, beans. Farm income totaled $465 million in 1974, with poultry and eggs the largest item.

With more than 80% of its area forested, Maine turns out wood products from boats to toothpicks, paper, lumber, and Christmas trees. Over 98% of the forest land is privately owned. Forest products are valued at over $700 million a year. Spruce, white pine, and birch are the most important woods. Also vital to Maine's economy are processed foods, shoes, and textiles. Boatyards build fishing and sailing craft.

Per capita income was $4,439 in 1974.

Granite, cement, and feldspar account for much of the 1974 value of mineral products, $38.5 million.

Maine's scenic seacoast, beaches, lakes, mountains, and resorts make it a popular vacationland; tourism is a $500 million-a-year industry. There are 26 state parks, including Baxter, where Mt. Katahdin, tallest of the state's 10 mountains over 4,000 ft., rises 5,268 ft. Maine has over 2,500 lakes, 1,300 wooded islands and 5,000 streams. Moosehead Lake is 40 mi. long and 2 to 10 mi. wide. Deer, grouse, black bear abound; game fish include salmon, tuna, trout, bass. There are over 45 public skiing facilities. Acadia National Park and Bar Harbor are on Mt. Desert Island.

Museums include the Bowdoin College Museum, Brunswick, which has portraits by American masters; also Assyrian, Greek, and Roman sculpture.

The Colby College Art Museum, Waterville, has paintings by classic and contemporary Europeans and Americans.

The Farnsworth Library and Museum, Rockland, has 19th and 20th Century American fine art.

The Portland Museum of Art comprises the Sweat Museum of American Art and the Sweat Mansion, a Federal-style house built in 1800. Other historic homes in Portland are the Tate House, 1755, and the Victoria Mansion, 1859.

There are 18 institutions of higher learning.

Famous "Down Easters" include Longfellow, Kenneth Roberts, Edna St. Vincent Millay, Kate Douglas Wiggin, Ben Ames Williams, James G. Blaine, Hiram and Hudson Maxim, Cyrus H. K. Curtis.

(See also Index for Portland.)

Maryland

Old Line State, Free State

AREA: 10,577 sq. mi.; rank, 42d. POPULATION (U.S. est. 1974): 4,094,000; rank, 21st. CAPITAL: Annapolis. MOTTO: Fatti Maschi, Parole Femine; Manly Deeds, Womanly Words. FLOWER: Black-eyed Susan. BIRD: Baltimore oriole. TREE: White oak. SONG: Maryland, My Maryland. Seventh of the original 13 states to ratify Constitution; Apr. 28, 1788.

Maryland stretches from the Atlantic Ocean to the Allegheny Mountains with 2 major interruptions, Chesapeake Bay, and the District of Columbia. Both contribute importantly to the state's economy.

The bay cuts off the low coastal plain of the Eastern Shore from the rest of the state, provides both commercial and sports fishing and leads to the port of Baltimore, which handles some $3 billion in imports and exports a year. The 7.11-mi. Chesapeake Bay Highway Bridge spans the bay near Annapolis.

The national capital area provides a market for much of Maryland's produce as well as adding to the crowds which enjoy its recreational facilities.

Backbone Mtn. in the far W part of the state is its highest point, 3,360 ft.

Virginia's Capt. John Smith first explored Maryland, 1608. William Claiborne set up a trading post on Kent Is. in Chesapeake Bay, 1631. Britain granted land to Lord Baltimore (Cecilius Calvert), 1632; his brother Leonard Calvert led 200 settlers to St. Marys River, 1634. An informal Maryland Convention, 1774, headed pre-Revolutionary agitation. The bravery of Maryland troops in the Revolution, as at the Battle of Long Island, won the state its nickname, The Old Line State. In the War of 1812, when a British fleet tried to take Fort McHenry, Marylander Francis Scott Key wrote The Star-Spangled Banner.

Maryland has a diversified economy. Leading industries in number of workers are wholesale and retail trade, government, services, manufacturing. Value added by manufacture totals over $4.6 billion annually. Important manufacturing industries are food products, primary metals, electrical equipment, printing and publishing, apparel, machinery. Per capita income was $5,881 in 1974.

Almost half of the land area is covered with forests. About 40% of timber cut is softwood. Stone and cement are leading mineral products; mineral output was valued at $145 million in 1974.

Seafood is an important industry. In a typical year, the fish and shellfish catch has a value of about $20 million. Striped bass is the principal contributor to the fin fish revenues, while oysters account for about 60% of the shellfish, followed by soft-shelled clams.

Many of Maryland's farms are fertile though not extensive. The state's largest cash crops are tobacco, corn, soybeans, apples, and tomatoes. Commercial broilers and dairy products are important.

The first U.S. steam locomotive, Peter Cooper's Tom Thumb, was built in Baltimore and made its first run on the tracks of the Baltimore & Ohio R.R., 1830.

There are 47 institutions of higher education.

Famous racing events include the Preakness, at Pimlico track, Baltimore; the International at Laurel Race Course, and John B. Campbell Handicap at Bowie. Annapolis is a center for yacht races. Ocean City is a popular summer resort.

Famous historic sites include Fort McHenry, Baltimore, restored, where in 1814 waved the flag that inspired Francis Scott Key to write the Star-Spangled Banner; Antietam Battlefield near Hagerstown (1862); South Mountain Battlefield (1862); Edgar Allan Poe house, Baltimore. The State House, Annapolis (1772), is the oldest still in use in the U.S.

The U.S. Frigate Constellation, which was launched at Baltimore in 1797, has been made a National Historic Landmark in Baltimore.

The Chesapeake Bay Maritime Museum in St. Michael's exhibits the last surviving oyster sloop, a cottage-type lighthouse and models of Baltimore clippers, log canoes, bugeyes and skipjacks.

Tourism is valued at $500 million a year.

Famous Marylanders include Upton Sinclair, H.L. Mencken, James M. Cain, Benjamin Banneker.

Massachusetts

Bay State, Old Colony

AREA: 8,257 sq. mi.; rank, 45th. POPULATION (U.S. est. 1974): 5,800,000; rank, 10th. CAPITAL: Boston. MOTTO: Ense Petit Placidam sub Libertate Quietem: By the Sword We Seek Peace, but Peace Only under Liberty. FLOWER: Mayflower. BIRD: Chickadee. TREE: American elm. SONG: All Hail to Massachusetts. Sixth of the original 13 states to ratify Constitution, Feb. 6, 1788.

Massachusetts has played important roles in the political, intellectual, and economic development of the U.S. Here the Pilgrims, seeking religious freedom, founded Plymouth Colony in 1620.

The Pilgrims made their first settlement at Plymouth, 1620. French and Indian wars destroyed frontier settlements but Massachusetts troops captured France's Fortress Louisburg, Nova Scotia, 1745. British restrictions brought on the "Boston Massacre," 1770; Boston "tea party," 1773; British dissolution of the legislature, 1774. First bloodshed of the Revolution was at Lexington, 1775. At Bunker Hill, 1775, the British suffered a Pyrrhic victory. The 19th Century saw an intellectual renaissance, growth of the abolition movement, great industrial expansion.

The state became the home of great universities such as Harvard and Massachusetts Institute of Technology.

In Massachusetts ports, a great shipping industry, including the famed China trade, developed, along with vast whaling and fishing interests. Abundant waterpower helped create a variety of industries.

Religious freedom, at first restricted by the Puritans, was eventually achieved. In 1867, Mary Baker Eddy founded Christian Science in Lynn. Heavy immigration of Irish, Italians, Poles, Czechs, and French Canadians increased number of Catholics.

The first free American public school, the Mathws founded in Dorchester (Boston) in 1639. The state has 122 institutions of higher learning.

Commercial fishing, in the rich waters off Massachusetts and the Grand Banks off Newfoundland, was one of the area's earliest industries. Whalers sailed the oceans around the world. Modern trawlers with huge nets help bring in a catch valued at about $61 million in 1974, ranking high among the states.

Massachusetts was a pioneer in the manufacture of textiles and shoes and in creation of specialized machinery for them. The Bay State remains one of the top producers of shoes. A power loom, perfected by Francis Cabot Lowell in 1822, launched cotton manufacturing in Lowell.

Production of electrical machinery, including electronics and communications equipment, has become the leading manufacturing division, in terms of numbers of employees and value added by manufacture. Also important are apparel, metal and food products, and plastics.

Total value added by manufacture is over $10.7 billion a year, placing Massachusetts, despite its relatively small size, 11th among the states. A third of the state's workers are employed in manufacturing. Per capita income was $5,731 in 1974.

Massachusetts' cranberry crop is the nation's largest. Also important are dairy and poultry products, cigar wrapper tobacco, apples, peaches, maple syrup. Farm receipts totaled $194 million in 1974. Mineral production for that year was valued at an est. $70.4 million, mostly of stone, sand, and gravel.

Because of the state's numerous recreational areas and historic landmarks, tourism has become an important factor in the economy of the state. Tourists generate an est. $2.19 billion annually.

Cape Cod has summer theaters, sports, and an artists' colony at Provincetown. Tanglewood, in the Berkshires, has the summer concerts of the Boston Symphony Orchestra.

In New Bedford, the Old Dartmouth Historical Society and Whaling Museum has a large and unique collection of whaling implements, scrimshaw, and logbooks as well as furniture, costumes, and firearms. In Old Deerfield are Memorial Hall (1799), Hall Tavern (1765), Parson Ashley House (1732).

In Pittsfield, the Berkshire Athenaeum has memorabilia of Herman Melville, who lived there while writing Moby Dick; a scrimshaw and whaling collection, and a large library. The Berkshire Museum, Pittsfield, has paintings by Rubens, Van Dyck, Reynolds, Murillo, the Hudson River artists, etc.; mineral and animal rooms; one of the sledges with which Robert E. Peary reached the North Pole.

In Plymouth, Pilgrim Hall contains relics of the Mayflower Pilgrims, including swords of Myles Standish, Bibles of Gov. William Bradford and John Alden, and the cradle of Peregrine White, first child born in the colony.

Old Sturbridge Village, in Sturbridge, is a recreated early New England village of 35 authentic homes and shops, shown functioning.

The Sterling and Francine Clark Art Institute, Williamstown, displays 14th-17th Century European paintings, a large collection of Impressionists, sculpture, silver, and drawings.

The Worcester Art Museum presents a survey of art through 50 centuries, stressing early American painting, pre-Columbian, and contemporary arts. Also in Worcester, the John W. Higgins Armory displays medieval armor, and the American Antiquarian Society has a collection of early printing.

Famous "Bay Staters" include Samuel, John, and John Quincy Adams, Hancock, Revere, Bryant, Emerson, Hawthorne, Holmes, Whittier, Poe, Thoreau, Alger, James, Emily Dickinson, Louisa May Alcott, Lucy Stone, Clara Barton, Whistler, Sargent, Homer, Morse, Elias Howe.

(See also Index for Boston, Springfield.)

Michigan

Great Lake State, Wolverine State

AREA: 58,216 sq. mi.; rank, 23d. **POPULATION (U.S. est. 1974):** 9,098,000; rank, 7th. **CAPITAL:** Lansing. **MOTTO:** Si Quaeris Peninsulam Amoenam Circumspice, If You Seek a Pleasant Peninsula, Look about You. **FLOWER:** Apple blossom. **BIRD:** Robin. **TREE:** White pine. **SONG (unofficial):** Michigan, My Michigan. **ENTERED UNION:** Jan. 26, 1837; rank, 26th.

Bordering on 4 of the 5 Great Lakes, Michigan is divided into an Upper and Lower Peninsula by the Straits of Mackinac, which link Lakes Michigan and Huron. The 2 parts of the state are connected by the Mackinac Bridge, which has the 3d largest suspension span in the U. S. To the N, separating Michigan from Canada, is the Sault Ste. Marie (Soo) Ship Canal, one of the world's most heavily used waterways.

Michigan contains the world's greatest concentration of automobile manufacturers; its rich orchards near the shores of Lake Michigan grow large fruit crops; the Upper Peninsula produces important amounts of iron, copper, and other minerals, and the

state's lakes and forests make it a highly popular vacationland. The highest point is Mt. Curwood, 1,980 ft., in the Upper Peninsula.

While Michigan ranks first among the states in production of motor vehicles and parts, it is also a leader in many other lines including prepared cereals, machine tools, hardware, steel springs, furniture, padding and upholstering, industrial patterns, nonferrous castings, industrial leather belts, paperboard mills, and gray iron foundries.

The state ranked 6th in the U. S. in terms of value added by manufacture, $23.3 billion. Motor vehicles and equipment accounted for $8.3 billion of that and also provided the most jobs, almost 400,000. Other major industry groups were primary metals and metal products, machinery, food, and chemicals. Per capita income was $5,924 in 1974.

Tourist attractions are many and an est. 9 million out-of-staters visit each year. The state has 36,000 mi. of streams, over 11,000 lakes and the longest freshwater shoreline (facing 4 of the Great Lakes). Water sports, music festivals, skiing, winter carnivals, fishing, and hunting are among attractions.

There are 5 national forests, 78 state parks and recreational areas, and numerous canoe trails.

Farm receipts in 1974 totaled $1.7 billion, more than half from livestock products. The state ranked 6th in the U.S. in number of milk cows. It grew the most tart and sweet cherries and ranked high in apples, pears, grapes, and sugar beets. Truck farm vegetables were valued at $160 million; forest products at $1.75 billion.

Iron ore is the largest source of Michigan's income from minerals. With continued depletion of high-grade iron ore deposits, production of high-grade pellets from low-grade taconite iron ore has increased, amounting to over 85% of the ore total.

Michigan was 2d only to Minnesota among the states in value of iron ore output, $210 million in 1974. It was also a leading producer of gypsum, peat, iodine, bromine, salt, magnesium compounds, lime, gravel, cement. Total output was est. at $953 million.

There are some 88 institutions of higher education.

French fur traders and missionaries visited the region, 1616, set up a mission at Sault Ste. Marie, 1641, and a settlement there, 1668. The whole region went to Britain, 1763. During the Revolution, the British led attacks from the area on American settlements to the south until Anthony Wayne defeated their Indian allies at Fallen Timbers, Ohio, 1794. The British returned, 1812, seized Fort Mackinac and Detroit. Oliver H. Perry's Lake Erie victory and William H. Harrison's troops, who carried the war to the Thames River in Canada, 1813, freed Michigan once more.

Famous Michiganders include Henry Ford, Robert Ingersoll, Thomas Dewey, Milton A. McRae, James Oliver Curwood, Stewart Edward White, Paul de Kruif, Gen. George Custer, Edgar Guest, Ellen Burstyn, Betty Hutton, Diana Ross, Mike Marshall, Danny Thomas.

(See Index for Detroit and Kalamazoo.)

Minnesota

North Star State, Gopher State

AREA: 84,068 sq. mi.; rank, 12th. **POPULATION (U.S. est. 1974):** 3,917,000; rank, 19th. **CAPITAL:** St Paul. **MOTTO:** L'Etoile du Nord, Star of the North. **FLOWER:** Showy lady's-slipper. **BIRD:** Loon. **TREE:** Red (Norway) pine. **SONG:** Hail! Minnesota. **ENTERED UNION:** May 11, 1858; rank, 32d.

Minnesota is a land rich in natural resources. Its fertile prairies support large crops and an important dairy industry, its mines yield most of the iron ore produced in the U.S., its forests produce mountains of pulpwood, its manufacturing is varied and vigorous, its thousands of lakes and other attractions lure millions of sportsmen and vacationers.

Known as the "land of 10,000 lakes," Minnesota actually has 15,291 larger than 10 acres each. Lake Itaska is the source of the Mississippi River. Two-thirds of the state is rolling prairie. Highest point is

Eagle Mt. in the NE, 2,301 ft.

Fishing, hunting, water sports, and winter sports are among attractions for more than 5.5 million vacationers who spend some $940 million yearly.

Minnesota produces about 63% of the iron ore mined in the U.S., despite depletion of the high-grade ore in the famed Mesabi and other ranges in the NE part of the state. Lost production from the huge open pit and underground mines is being replaced by high-grade pellets refined from low-grade taconite iron ore. By 1974, shipments of taconite pellets comprised about 68% of the total iron ore value.

One taconite company, Reserve Mining, was enjoined in 1974 from polluting Lake Superior drinking waters but won a stay of the court order.

Iron ore production in 1974 was valued at $857 million, the major part of the total mineral production value, $920 million.

Manufacturing has shown both growth and diversity. Largest industries are food processing and machinery. Also important are electrical machinery, chemicals, paper, stone-clay-glass products, apparel, lumber, fabricated metal products. Value added by manufacture is $5.6 billion.

Per capita income was $5,450 in 1974.

Much of the land is richly fertile. With $4.7 billion in farm receipts for 1974, Minnesota ranked 7th among the states. About 55% of that income was from livestock products, the rest from crops. Ranking 3d in number of milk cows in 1974, the state was the leader in butter; also in turkeys.

Minnesota's farms grew the most oats and it ranked among the top states in spring wheat, corn, rye, alfalfa, and sugar beets.

Forest products have a yearly estimated value of over $500 million, most of it in pulpwood.

Nationally known is the Mayo Clinic at Rochester, founded by Drs. William J. and Charles H. Mayo.

Minnesota has 57 institutions of higher learning.

The Minnesota Orchestra, the Tyrone Guthrie Theater in Minneapolis, and the St. Olaf College Choir in Northfield are widely known.

Minnesota has many state parks and recreation areas. Minnehaha Falls in Minneapolis became famous in Longfellow's "Song of Hiawatha."

Other attractions are the St. Paul Winter Carnival, Minneapolis Aquatennial, and State Fair.

Fur traders and missionaries from French Canada opened the region in the 17th Century. Britain took the area east of the Mississippi, 1763. The U.S. took over that portion after the Revolution and in 1803 bought the western area as part of the Louisiana Purchase. The U.S. built present Fort Snelling, 1820, bought lands from the Indians, 1837. In the Civil War, Minnesota was first to offer troops to the Union. Sioux Indians staged a bloody uprising, 1862, and were driven from the state.

Famous Minnesotans include Hubert Humphrey, Charles Lindbergh, Sinclair Lewis, F. Scott Fitzgerald, Thorstein Veblen, Cass Gilbert, Paul Manship, E. G. Marshall, Blanche Yurka, Lew Ayres.

(See also Index for Minneapolis and St. Paul.)

Mississippi
Magnolia State

AREA: 47,716 sq. mi.; rank, 32d. POPULATION (U.S. est. 1974): 2,324,000; rank, 29th. CAPITAL: Jackson. MOTTO: Virtute et Armis, By Valor and Arms. FLOWER: Magnolia. TREE: Magnolia. BIRD: Mockingbird. SONG: Go, Mississippi! ENTERED UNION: Dec. 10, 1817; rank, 20th.

Mississippi's economy, long based on one crop, "King Cotton," has become balanced and diversified, thanks to promotion of industry, other crops, tourism, and federal agency installations.

The land slopes from the NE hills, where the high point is Woodall Mt. (806 ft.), to the Delta, a cotton-producing alluvial plain in the W and NW lying between the Yazoo River and the Mississippi, which flows along the state's western border. The land also slopes to the S where the sandy beaches on the Gulf of Mexico have created a popular vacationland.

Hernando de Soto explored the area, 1540, discovered the Mississippi River, 1541. La Salle traced the river from Illinois to its mouth and claimed the entire valley for France, 1682. First settlement was the French Fort Maurepas, near Biloxi, 1699. The area was ceded to Britain, 1763; American settlers followed. During the Revolution, Spain seized part of the area and refused to leave even after the U.S. acquired title at the end of the Revolution, finally moving out, 1798. Mississippi seceded 1861. Union forces captured Corinth and Vicksburg and destroyed Jackson and much of Meridian.

Soybeans have taken over as Mississippi's largest crop; the state ranks 3d in cotton production. Other important farm products include large crops of pecans and sweet potatoes; other crops include rice and sugarcane. Poultry and eggs are also important. Farm receipts totaled $1.6 billion in 1974.

Biloxi has a large seafood industry, operating deep-sea trawlers for shrimp and oysters. Value of the catch is over $16 million a year. Home-pond catfish production was valued at $26 million in 1973.

With more than 50% of the land classified as forest, timber products yielded over $1 billion in 1974.

The state produces the most hardwood pulpwood, much hardwood lumber, and slashpine products, including fiberboard, kraft paper, newsprint.

Petroleum production was valued at $339 million for 1974, up 60% in price although total oil production was down 10%. Natural gas output was valued at $25 million; total value of mineral production was est. at $423 million, up 50%.

Mississippi has achieved considerable industrial expansion. The main fields have been lumber, along with furniture and paper, food processing, apparel, chemicals, electronics, machinery.

Per capita income was $3,764 in 1974, lowest in the nation. Annual pay for public school teachers was $7,854 in 1973, also the nation's lowest. But the legislature provided 25% increases in 1975.

A $250 million NASA space installation is used as a center for International Earth Sciences by NOAA and NASA. There are 42 institutions of higher learning.

Mississippi became the last state to abandon prohibition, adopting a local-option law May 21, 1966.

Tourism is of growing economic importance. It is estimated that out-of-state tourists spend over $460 million a year in the state.

Gulfport holds an annual yacht regatta and a fishing rodeo in July, Biloxi has a Mardi Gras, Pass Christian has a tarpon rodeo. A dozen cities sponsor pilgrimages each spring featuring visits to ante-bellum mansions.

In Vicksburg National Military Park, visitors may see remains of forts, trenches, and other works which featured the 1863 siege of the city.

The Old Court House Museum in Vicksburg, built in 1858 by slave labor, has a museum with relics of the siege of Vicksburg, including flags, weapons, newspapers printed on the back of wallpaper, etc.

The Lauren Rogers Library and Museum of Art in Laurel contains works of 19th and early 20th Century Americans and Europeans, local artifacts and an unusual basket collection (about half of them Indian).

Famous Mississippians include Jefferson Davis, James Street, William Faulkner, Eudora Welty, Dana Andrews, B. B. King, Bobby Gentry.

Missouri
Show Me State

AREA: 69,686 sq. mi.; rank, 19th. POPULATION (U.S. est. 1974): 4,777,000; rank, 13th. CAPITAL: Jefferson City. MOTTO: Salus Populi Suprema Lex Esto, The Welfare of the People Shall Be the Supreme Law. FLOWER: Hawthorn. BIRD: Eastern bluebird. TREE: Dogwood. SONG: Missouri Waltz. ENTERED UNION: Aug. 10, 1821; rank, 24th.

The gateway through which the pioneers passed on their way West, Missouri today is a leading manufacturing state, with aerospace and a wide variety of other industries; it is the nation's largest producer of lead; it ranks high among the states in agricultural products; its areas of scenic and historic interest attract over 28 million vacationers each year.

Gently rolling hills in the N and W produce large crops, and support cattle, sheep, and hogs. The Ozark highlands in the S are famed for fishing, hunting, and rugged scenery, including numerous caves and springs. The "delta" area in the SE produces soybeans, cotton, and melons.

The Mississippi forms the state's boundary on the E; the Missouri forms part of the boundary in the W, then flows across the state to join the Mississippi above St. Louis. Highest point in the state is Taum Sauk Mt., 1,772 ft., in the E central area.

Missouri has endeared itself to generations of Americans with its river lore, folk tales, and especially the writings of Mark Twain (Samuel L. Clemens). Statues of 2 of his creations, Tom Sawyer and Huckleberry Finn, stand in Hannibal, his boyhood home. His birthplace near Florida, Mo., has been enshrined in Mark Twain State Park.

The farm birthplace of notorious bandit Jesse James (1847-1882) is near Excelsior Springs. A log cabin built by U.S. Grant is near St. Louis. The farm where George Washington Carver, agricultural scientist, was born near Diamond is now a National Monument. The Harry S. Truman Library, near Independence, contains presidential papers and memorabilia. Mr. Truman, who died Dec. 26, 1972, is buried in the library courtyard.

The St. Joseph Museum in St. Joseph stresses the natural history and wildlife of the region and has exhibits on Indian tribes from Alaska to Florida. Also in St. Joseph is the Pony Express Museum.

Manufacturing, paced by the state's large aerospace industries, is the top income producer and employs more persons than any other segment of the economy. Value added by manufacture is over $8.1 billion yearly. Transportation equipment, including space capsules, rocket engines, aircraft, and auto assemblies, ranks first, followed by food processing, esp. meat packing, grain milling, beer, and other beverages. Also important are chemicals, printing, metal products, machinery, shoes. Corncob pipes and charcoal are well-known products.

Agriculture is also an important income producer. Farm receipts in 1974 totaled $2.8 billion, two-thirds from livestock products. Missouri ranked 4th among the states in hogs, cattle, and turkeys. It has large soybean, corn, and clover crops. Also important are winter wheat, tobacco, apples, peaches, alfalfa, popcorn.

Per capita income was $5,636 in 1974.

Tourism, described as the 3d largest industry, produces $2 billion annually. There is a wide variety of vacation facilities; large resort areas include Lake of the Ozarks, Lake Taneycomo and Table Rock Lake.

Missouri is rich in minerals. Its output of lead, valued at $259 million for 1974, was the largest in the U.S. Total mineral production value was worth $667 million, up 30%. It was also a leader in barite and lime. Other products include cement, coal, iron ore, copper, zinc, asphalt.

There are 7 institutions of higher learning. The nation's first Journalism School, founded 1908, is at the University of Missouri in Columbia.

DeSoto visited the area, 1541. French hunters and lead miners made the first settlement, c. 1735, at Ste. Genevieve. The U.S. acquired Missouri as part of the Louisiana Purchase, 1803. The fur trade and the Santa Fe Trail provided prosperity and adventure; St. Louis became the "jump-off" point for pioneers on their way West. Pro-and anti-slavery forces staged guerrilla raids during the Civil War.

Famous Missourians include Harry Truman, John J. Pershing, Omar Bradley, Mark Twain, Zoe Akins, Sara Teasdale, T. S. Eliot, Luman H. Long, George Washington Carver, Shelley Winters, Gladys Swarthout, Helen Traubel, Thomas Hart Benton, Ken Holtzman, Mel Stottlemyre, Bernarr Macfadden.

(See also Index for Kansas City and St. Louis.)

Montana

Treasure State

AREA: 147,138 sq. mi.; rank, 4th. POPULATION (U.S. est. 1974): 735,000; rank, 43d. CAPITAL: Helena. MOTTO: Oro y Plata, Gold and Silver. FLOWER: Bitterroot. TREE: Ponderosa pine. BIRD: Western meadowlark. SONG: Montana. ENTERED UNION: Nov. 8, 1889; rank, 41st.

The Rocky Mountains, with snow-capped peaks, forested slopes, broad valleys, and many lakes, cover the western 40% of Montana; the rest is High Plains country devoted to grazing and farming. Montana is rich in minerals, hydroelectric power, and impressive scenery. Highest mountain is Granite Peak, 12,-799 ft.

Agriculture plays a vital role in Montana's economy, along with manufacturing, mining, tourism, recreation. Per capita income was $4,776, 1974.

Oceans of grain cover much of Montana's plains; it ranks high among the states in wheat and barley output. Also grown are rye, oats, flaxseed, sugar beets, and potatoes. Montana ranks 6th in sheep and high in cattle. Farm receipts totaled over $1.2 billion in 1974, more than half from livestock.

Manufacturing industries have grown, with value added by manufacture over $450 million a year. Processing of forest products and primary metal industries are most important and have the most employees, followed by food processing. Wood products include pulp, plywood, and lumber. The state ships more than 3 million Christmas trees annually.

Total mineral production for 1974 was est. at $576 million, up 50% from 1973, with petroleum accounting for $202 million and copper $212 million. Other products include silver, gold, natural gas. In 1973, 10 million tons of coal were strip-mined.

Out-of-state tourists spend an est. $166 million annually. Tourist attractions include hunting, fishing, skiing, dude ranching.

Hunters annually take about 100,000 deer, 11,000 antelope, 10,000 elk, 1,100 black bear, 500 moose.

Glacier National Park, on the Continental Divide, is a scenic and recreational wonderland, with 60 glaciers, 200 lakes and many trout streams.

Flathead Lake, in the NW, covers 189 sq. mi. Fort Peck Reservoir, in the NE, covers 382.8 sq. mi.

French explorers, the Verendrye brothers, visited the region, 1742. The U.S. acquired the area, partly through the Louisiana Purchase, 1803, and partly through the explorations of Lewis and Clark, 1805-06. Fur traders and missionaries established posts in the early 19th Century. Indian uprisings hit their highwater mark in the Battle of the Little Big Horn, in which Col. George Custer and his 264 men were wiped out, 1876. The coming of the Northern Pacific Railway, 1883, spurred farming, cattle raising and mining and brought population growth.

Important historical site is Custer Battlefield National Cemetery, in Big Horn County (near Hardin).

There are 7 Indian reservations, covering over 5 million acres; tribes are Blackfeet, Crow, Confederated Salish & Kootenai, Assiniboine, Gros Ventre, Sioux, Northern Cheyenne, Chippewa, Cree. Population of the reservations is approximately 25,500.

The Museum of the Plains Indian, on the Blackfeet Reservation near Browning, features exhibits of historic and contemporary arts and crafts of the Northern Plains Indians and an Indian craft shop.

The Historical Society of Montana, in Helena, has paintings, dioramas, and other exhibits of Montana's Indian and buffalo days, mining camps, frontier settlements, cattle roundups. Outstanding is the collection of nearly 100 Charles M. Russell paintings.

Famous Montanans include Gary Cooper, Myrna Loy, Mike Mansfield, Chet Huntley, Charles M. Russell, Will James, Jeannette Rankin.

There are 12 colleges and universities.

(See also Index for Billings.)

Nebraska
Cornhusker State

AREA: 77,227 sq. mi.; rank, 15th. **POPULATION** (U.S. est. 1974): 1,543,000; rank, 35th. **CAPITAL:** Lincoln. **MOTTO: Equality Before the Law. FLOWER:** Goldenrod. **TREE:** Cottonwood. **BIRD: Western meadowlark. SONG: Beautiful Nebraska. ENTERED UNION:** Mar. 1, 1867; rank, 37th.

Fields of corn, wheat, and sorghum cover the Nebraska plain, sloping gently toward the Missouri River, the eastern border of the state; vast herds of cattle roam the grassy sandhills which rise to the W, ending in the broken tablelands which mark the foothills of the Rockies. Highest point, 5,426 ft., is in the far SW corner.

With more than 23 million acres under cultivation, Nebraska is an agricultural stronghold, an important grain and livestock producer. Many of its manufacturing industries are agriculture-related.

But manufacturing has also become diversified, broadening the state's economic base. Firms making electronic components, auto accessories, pharmaceuticals, and other sophisticated products have joined the older industries.

Processing of meat, grain, and dairy products is by far the largest manufacturing field, accounting for more than a third of the total value added by manufacture, which is estimated at almost $1.8 billion, as well as for the largest number of workers.

Other important manufacturing fields are electrical machinery and other machinery, especially farm equipment; chemicals, metal products, transportation equipment, instruments, and related products. Per capita income was $4,877 in 1974.

Nebraska ranked 7th among the states in total farm receipts for 1974; $4 billion, with the larger part coming from livestock products. Its cattle herds ranked 3d among the states; it had 6.9 million cattle in 1975. It ranked 6th in hogs. Nebraska was also a leader in sorghum, winter wheat, corn, and rye. Also important are soybeans, sugar beets, and oats.

Mineral production in Nebraska was valued at $99.3 million for 1974. Oil continued to be the most important product, valued at $44 million. The value of fuel production increased over 50% although production declined. Other products included cement, lime, pumice, sand, and gravel.

Nebraska has a unicameral or one-house legislature with 49 members elected on a non-partisan ballot. All electric power facilities are state or municipally owned.

Nebraska has 27 institutions of higher education.

Arbor Lodge State Park at Nebraska City is a memorial to J. Sterling Morton, founder of Arbor Day, which is observed as a legal holiday on his birthday, Apr. 22. Boys Town is just west of Omaha.

The Sheldon Memorial Art Gallery at the Univ. of Nebraska, Lincoln, in a building designed by Philip Johnson, has works by many leading modern artists.

The Joslyn Art Museum, Omaha, has works by Titian, El Greco, Rembrandt, Goya, Renoir, etc.; exhibits of furniture, the early West, fur trade, Indian art.

Pioneer Village, Minden, has some 30,000 items of Americana displayed in a rural schoolhouse, depot, general store, fort, fire house, sod house, Pony Express station, etc. The Stuhr Museum of the Prairie Pioneer has 57 original 19th Century buildings near Grand Island.

The House of Yesterday, Hastings, has exhibits of pioneer days and natural science and the J. M. McDonald Planetarium. The Strategic Aerospace Museum is in Bellevue.

Spanish and French explorers and fur traders visited the area prior to the 1803 Louisiana Purchase. Lewis and Clark passed through, 1804-06. First permanent settlement was Bellevue, near Omaha, 1823. Many Civil War veterans settled under free land terms of the 1862 Homestead Act; struggles followed between homesteaders and ranchers. Under Gov. Charles W. Bryan, farm mortgage moratoriums

were declared, 1933, during the Depression.

Famous Nebraskans include William Jennings and Charles W. Bryan, the Rev. Edward J. Flanagan, Willa Cather, Mignon Eberhart, Rollin Kirby, Clare Briggs, Gen. Alfred Gruenther, Roscoe Pound, Darryl Zanuck, Susette (Bright Eyes) La Flesche.

(See also Index for Omaha)

Nevada
Sagebrush State, Battle Born State

AREA: 110,540 sq. mi.; rank, 7th. **POPULATION** (U.S. est. 1974): 573,000; rank, 47th. **CAPITAL:** Carson City. **MOTTO: All for Our Country. FLOWER:** Sagebrush. **BIRD: Mountain bluebird. TREE: Single-leaf pinon. SONG: Home Means Nevada. ENTERED UNION:** Oct. 31, 1864; rank, 36th.

Nevada lies mostly in the Great Basin, a rugged plateau region broken by mountain chains running N-S. It is enclosed on the E by the Rockies and the Wasatch Range in Utah, and on the W by California's Sierra Nevada and Cascade Ranges which rob the clouds of moisture, making Nevada's climate extremely dry. Boundary Peak, near the SW border with California, is the state's highest point, 13,140 ft.

One of the smallest states in population, Nevada has attracted large numbers of outsiders, starting with the famed rush to the Comstock Lode (1859) and other gold and silver mines. Today, the attractions are legalized gambling, highly-developed entertainment and recreation facilities, and lenient divorce laws requiring only 6-weeks residence.

Spending by visitors is the biggest factor in Nevada's economy. More than 12 million from out of state, about 50 times the state population, visit annually.

Tourist-connected industries—hotels, casinos, amusement and recreation facilities—make up the largest employment category. Per capita income was $6,073 in 1974.

State collections from gaming were $74,370,654 in 1973-74, up $12,126,654 from 1972-73. This income provides about 41% of the state's revenue. Gross gambling receipts for 1974 were $1.004 billion.

There are big resort areas, with skiing as well as sunbathing, near Lake Tahoe, Reno, Las Vegas. Ghost towns, rodeos, trout fishing, water skiing, and deer hunting are other attractions.

Large recreation areas include those at Pyramid Lake, wholly within the state; Lake Tahoe, partly in California; Lake Mead, formed by Hoover Dam, and Lake Mohave, formed by Davis Dam, both in Lake Mead National Recreation Area, shared with Arizona.

Mineral production value for 1974 was est. at $248 million with copper accounting for $125 million. Nevada is also a leader in gold, mercury, lithium, barite, and silver. With rising prices, old gold mines have reopened.

Nevada is the largest manufacturer of gaming devices. Also important are electronic devices, chemicals, forest products, suntan lotion, stone-clay-glass products. About $161 million is the est. value added annually by growing manufacturing industries.

Farm receipts totaled $140 million for 1974, more than 80% from livestock products. The dry climate makes much of the state more suitable for grazing than for crops, although large-scale irrigation has expanded the growing areas.

The Nevada Test Site, NW of Las Vegas, is a proving ground for various atomic devices.

Nevada has 6 institutions of higher learning.

The Nevada State Museum, Carson City, occupies a former U.S. Mint, and exhibits coins, habitat groups of mammals and birds of the Great Basin area, Indian baskets, full-scale replicas of underground mining operations, and thousands of arrowheads.

Nevada was first explored by Spaniards in 1776. Fur trader Peter Skene Ogden trapped the region, 1825 and 1828; Jedediah Smith, another trader, crossed the state, 1826 and 1827. The area was acquired by the U.S., 1848, at the end of the Mexican

War. First settlement, Mormon Station, was established 1849. In the early 20th Century, Nevada adopted progressive measures such as the initiative, referendum, recall and woman suffrage.

Famous Nevadans include Dr. Robert C. Lynch, Sarah Winnemucca Hopkins, Pat McCarran, Walter Van Tilburg Clark.

(See also Index for Las Vegas, Reno.)

New Hampshire

Granite State

AREA: 9,304 sq. mi.; rank, 44th. POPULATION (U.S. est. 1974) 808,000; rank, 41st. CAPITAL: Concord. MOTTO: Live Free or Die. FLOWER: Purple lilac. BIRD: Purple finch. TREE: Paper (white) birch. SONG: Old New Hampshire. Ninth of the original 13 states to ratify the Constitution, June 21, 1788.

One of the 6 New England states, New Hampshire is a land of impressive mountains, picturesque lakes, swift rivers, and, in the north, thick forests. Mountain slopes provide excellent ski trails. Numerous lakes and streams afford fishing for trout, bass, pickerel, perch, whitefish.

Abundant water power early turned New Hampshire into an industrial state, with manufacturing the principal source of income. Soil and climate have curtailed agricultural growth, but scenic and recreation resources have been developed and the tourist-vacation business, over $400 million a year, ranks 2d in its contribution to the state's economy. Per capita income was $5,143 in 1974.

In 1964, to raise funds to support education, the state ran the first legal sweepstakes lottery in the U.S. since 1894 (in that year, a lottery in Louisiana was outlawed). Profits from the state lottery are turned over to local school districts.

Most important industrial products are shoes and boots, electrical and other machinery, wool and other textiles, and paper.

Most factories are concentrated along the Merrimack and Connecticut Rivers, and in the seacoast area. Manufacturing employs about 100,000 workers. Value added by manufacture is $1.09 billion a year.

Farm receipts for 1974 totaled $74 million, about 55% from dairy and poultry products. Crops include apples, peaches, and maple syrup, in which it is No. 1.

Mineral products, mainly sand, gravel, and stone for construction, were valued at $14 million for 1974.

Recreation and vacation attractions include Lake Winnipesaukee, largest of 1,300 lakes and ponds; the White Mountains, with skiing and scenic beauty; beaches on the Atlantic Coast, and historic sites.

One-third of the state is over 2,000 ft. above sea level. Highest land in Northeast U.S. is the Presidential Range of the White Mountains, with Mt. Washington, 6,288 ft. (first cog railway in world opened 1869). National forests cover 677,559 acres; 142 state forests and parks, 63,805 acres.

State-owned parks include areas in Crawford and Franconia Notches; the latter includes the Old Man of the Mountains, described by Nathaniel Hawthorne as the Great Stone Face.

Portsmouth is the state's only port. Manchester is the largest city.

First explorers to visit the New Hampshire area were England's Martin Pring, 1603, and Samuel Champlain, 1605. First settlement was Little Harbor, near Rye, 1623. Indian raids were halted, 1759, by Robert Rogers' Rangers. Before the Revolution, New Hampshire men seized a British fort at Portsmouth, 1774, and drove the royal governor out, 1775. Three regiments served in the Continental Army and scores of privateers raided British shipping. Industry, roads, schools and railroads were built early in the 19th Century.

New Hampshire shared the educational pioneering of Massachusetts Bay from 1642; it established its first free public library at Dublin, 1822.

There are 25 institutions of higher education.

The MacDowell colony at Peterborough, established in 1908 in honor of Edward MacDowell, is a summer haven for writers, composers, artists.

The Currier Gallery of Art, Manchester, exhibits silver by Paul Revere, textiles, hooked rugs, pewter, and glass, and works by old and modern masters.

The New Hampshire Historical Society, Concord, has a museum displaying New Hampshire furniture, silver, pewter, glass, china, quilts, costumes, etc.

Famous men and women included Daniel Webster, Salmon P. Chase, Franklin Pierce, Robert Frost, Charles A. Dana, Horace Greeley, Sarah Buell Hale, Mary Baker Eddy, Ralph Adams Cram, Daniel Chester French, Augustus Saint-Gaudens.

New Jersey

Garden State

AREA: 7,836 sq. mi.; rank, 46th. POPULATION (U.S. est. 1974): 7,330,000; rank, 8th. CAPITAL: Trenton. MOTTO: Liberty and Prosperity. FLOWER: Purple violet. BIRD: Eastern goldfinch. TREE: Red oak. SONG: New Jersey Loyalty Song. Third of the original 13 states to ratify the Constitution, Dec. 18, 1787.

Smallest of the Middle Atlantic states, New Jersey has the heaviest pop. per sq. mi. of the 50 states, ranks near the top in manufacturing, is rich in poultry and vegetable production, and has a flourishing resort industry.

There are vast shipping facilities, and New Jersey divides authority over important airports, harbors, tunnels, and bridges with the Port Authority of N.Y. and N.J. and the states of Delaware and Pennsylvania.

About 63% of the state's land area is in farms and forests. Highest point is High Point, Sussex County, 1,803 ft.

Small in area, New Jersey has a heavy concentration of factories, highways, railroads, and farms, and is a leader in many fields.

It also has the greatest population density among the 50 states, reaching that status in 1965, when it passed Rhode Island. In the 1970 Census, New Jersey had 953.1 persons per sq. mi., Rhode Island had 905.5.

Per capita income was $6,384 in 1974.

Highly industrialized, New Jersey ranks 7th among the states in value added by manufacture, over $16 billion annually. It ranks 1st among the states in chemical products, having large pharmaceutical, basic chemical, and paint industries.

It is also a leader in other manufacturing lines: apparel, food processing, electrical and other machinery, stone-clay-glass products, printing, rubber and plastics, petroleum products, leather products. It has a large concentration of research installations.

New Jersey also ranks high in the U. S. in gross income per farm acre. Chief crops are tomatoes, corn, asparagus, apples, cranberries, peaches, spinach. Poultry and dairy products are also important.

Total farm receipts in 1974 were $341 million, more than half from crops.

Mineral production is mostly stone, sand, and gravel, mainly for construction work. Zinc, peat, and clays among other products. Total value was $134 million in 1974.

Large refineries, which process oil from out of state, have a total crude capacity of more than 500,000 barrels a day.

The commercial fishing catch is valued at over $16 million a year.

There are 61 institutions of higher learning.

Atlantic City, Ocean City, Cape May, Asbury Park, Point Pleasant, Wildwood, are among more than 100 resorts. The resort industry generates over $3.7 billion in business annually. There are 40 state parks with 55,717 acres. The 10 state forests comprise 176,652 acres. There are several historic sites relating to the Revolutionary War period.

In Camden, the Walt Whitman House, home of the poet from 1884 until his death, Mar. 26, 1892, contains books, mementos, and furnishings used by Whitman. The U. S. Army Signal Corps Museum, Fort Monmouth, contains communications equipment from the earliest visual methods to modern satellites.

The Montclair Art Museum exhibits art of many periods and lands, emphasizing the American. The Newark Museum is a museum of art, science and industry, including American paintings and sculpture; Chinese, Japanese and Tibetan art; collections of birds, insects, minerals, shells, glass, ceramics, and jewelry. The New Jersey Historical Society Museum, Newark, has old New Jersey rooms and collections of New Jersey furniture, paintings, china, costumes, etc.

The Garden State Arts Center is an amphitheater for concerts and stage shows at Telegraph Hill Park.

The Johnston Historical Museum, adjacent to the national hq. of the Boy Scouts of America, New Brunswick, depicts Scouting history, has a weather station, ham radio station, and 22-acre Outdoor Museum of Nature and Conservation.

The Edison National Historic Site, West Orange, displays Thomas Alva Edison's chemical laboratory, machine shop, and library; a reproduction of the "Black Maria," Edison's first movie studio; originals or replicas of his phonograph, incandescent lamp, and movie camera. In South Orange, the New Jersey Fire Museum displays 19th Century hand-pumpers, hose carts, helmets, etc.

In Trenton, the New Jersey State Museum displays the state's achievements in the arts, sciences, history, technology, and industry, and has a planetarium.

The New Jersey Meadowlands, lying close to the state's northeastern metropolitan centers, are the target of new development plans, including a New Jersey Sports Complex with a football stadium and race track. The N.Y. Giants plan to play their 1976 or 1977 football season in the stadium.

The state's network of modern highways gives New Jersey more miles of roads per sq. mi. of area than any other state.

There are 16 airlines and 17 railroads. New Jersey has the most rail trackage per sq. mi. in the U.S.

The Lenni Lenapé (Delaware) Indians had mostly peaceful relations with European colonists who arrived after the explorers Verrazano, 1524, and Henry Hudson, 1609. The Dutch were first. When the British took New Netherland, 1664, the area between the Delaware and Hudson Rivers was given to Lord John Berkeley and Sir George Carteret. New Jersey was the scene of nearly 100 battles, large and small, during the Revolution, including Trenton, 1776, Princeton 1777, Monmouth, 1778. The state abolished slavery, 1846.

Famous New Jerseyites include Cleveland, Wilson, Hamilton, Paine, Burr, Molly Pitcher, Gen. George McClellan, Edison, Whitman, James Fenimore Cooper, George Inness, Paul Robeson, Alexander Woolcott, Joyce Kilmer, Stephen Crane.

(See also Index for Newark.)

New Mexico
Land of Enchantment

AREA: 121,666 sq. mi.; rank, 5th. **POPULATION** (U.S. est. 1974): 1,122,000; rank, 30th. **CAPITAL:** Santa Fe. **MOTTO:** Crescit Eundo, It Grows as it Goes. **FLOWER:** Yucca. **BIRD:** Roadrunner. **TREE:** Pinon (nut pine). **SONGS:** O, Fair New Mexico, Asi Es Nuevo Mejico. **ENTERED UNION:** Jan. 6, 1912; rank, 47th.

New Mexico is a land of contrasts, presenting remnants of old Indian and Spanish cultures along with nuclear and space research centers; mountains over 13,000 ft., and a cavern 829 ft. below ground; ski slopes, and desert vistas.

Vast areas are made fertile by irrigation through dams and reservoirs on the Rio Grande, San Juan, Pecos, Canadian, Cimarron, Gila, and San Francisco Rivers. Wheeler Peak, 13,161 ft., is highest point.

The climate is dry and invigorating; annual rainfall is 7″ to 16″; mean temperature is 50°, reaching 100° on the plains in summer.

National forests cover 13,281 sq. mi. Douglas fir, Ponderosa pine, and spruce are cut for timber. Almost 34% of the land is federally owned.

Minerals are New Mexico's richest natural resource, and the state leads the U.S. in output of uranium and potassium salts.

Mineral production reached a total value of $2 billion in 1974, up 48%. Petroleum accounted for the largest single part of this, $698 million, followed by natural gas, $385 million, and copper, $309 million. Also high in value were potassium salts and uranium. New Mexico ranks high among the states in perlite, and carbon dioxide. Its rich variety of minerals also includes gold, silver, zinc, lead, molybdenum.

Farm receipts accounted for $732 million for 1974, more than two-thirds from livestock products. New Mexico ranked 9th among the states in number of sheep. Cotton, pecans, and sorghum are the most important field crops. Also grown are corn, peanuts, beans, onions, and lettuce.

Manufacturing industries have grown and diversified. Principal lines are food products, chemicals, ordnance, and transportation equipment, lumber, electrical machinery, stone-clay-glass products. Value added by manufacture is over $366 million annually.

Federal government activities, especially nuclear and space research and testing, have played a large role in New Mexico's economic growth. Nuclear and space centers are at Los Alamos, White Sands, Holloman, Kirtland, and Sandia.

Per capita income was $4,137 in 1974.

About 22 million tourists visit per year.

New Mexico's most awe-inspiring natural wonder, Carlsbad Caverns, has more than a half-million visitors annually. A national park, the caverns are on 3 levels and have the largest natural cave "room" in the world, 1,500 by 300 ft., 300 ft. high.

There are 4 large Indian reservations and 19 inhabited pueblos, including Acoma, the "sky city," built atop a 357-ft. mesa. There are pueblo ruins from 1000 A.D. in Chaco Canyon.

Skiing, hunting, fishing, ghost towns, and dude ranches help tourism show steady gains. Visitors spend more than $350 million in the state annually.

Franciscan Marcos de Niza and his black slave Estevan explored the area, 1539, seeking gold. First settlements were at San Juan Pueblo, 1598, and Santa Fe, 1599. Settlers alternately traded and fought with the Apaches, Comanches and Navahos. Trade on the Santa Fe Trail to Missouri started 1821. In the Mexican War, Gen. Stephen Kearney took Santa Fe, 1846. In the 1870s, cattlemen staged the famed Lincoln County War in which Billy (the Kid) Bonney played a leading role. Pancho Villa raided Columbus, 1916.

There are 13 institutions of higher education.

Santa Fe (c. 1609) is the 2d oldest city in the U.S. It and Taos have large artist colonies. Albuquerque (1706) is the state's largest city.

The Museum of Navaho Ceremonial Art, Santa Fe, housed in a modernized version of a ceremonial hogan, has over 600 sandpaintings, recordings of 2,000 Navaho chants; books, manuscripts, baskets, blankets.

The Museum of New Mexico, Santa Fe, maintains the oldest public building in the U.S., the Palace of the Governors (built 1610), a hall of modern Indian culture, collected works of artists of the SW, folk art exhibits.

The Roswell Museum and Art Center, Roswell, has 19th and 20th Century art collections, archeology and geology exhibits, the Robert H. Goddard rocket collection.

Famous New Mexicans include Kit Carson, Archbishop John Lamy, Billy (the Kid) Bonney, Pat Garrett, Lew Wallace, Peter Hurd, Bill Mauldin, Kim Stanley.

(See also Index for Albuquerque.)

New York
Empire State

AREA: 49,576 sq. mi.; rank, 30th. POPULATION (U.S. est. 1974): 18,111,000; rank, 2d. Capital: Albany. MOTTO: Excelsior, Ever Upward. FLOWER: Rose. BIRD: Bluebird. TREE: Sugar maple. Eleventh of the original 13 states to ratify the Constitution, July 26, 1788.

New York is the nation's leading manufacturing state and within its borders are the financial capital of the nation, the largest city and port, the headquarters of the United Nations, the head offices of many of the greatest national corporations and insurance companies, and a great variety of industries.

New York's manufacturing industries outrank those of all other states in number, employees, and payrolls, but are 2d to California in value added by manufacture ($30.4 billion, 1972).

Value added by manufacture in New York exceeded that of every other state in apparel ($3.2 billion), printing and publishing ($4.2 billion), instruments ($3.5 billion), paper and paper products ($855 million), and in the miscellaneous group, which includes jewelry, silverware, toys and sporting goods, pens and pencils, etc. ($1.2 billion).

The state produces more than 33% of the nation's instruments, 29% of apparel, 23% of printing and publishing, 21% of the miscellaneous category. It is the largest producer of both leather and paper products.

Average employment for 1974 was 7 million. Wages and salaries totaled nearly $60 billion.

The bi-state Port Authority of New York and New Jersey handled 20% of the nation's foreign trade (by value) in 1973 by U.S. Commerce Dept. figures. The 3 Customs Districts (New York, Buffalo, and Ogdensburg) handled 28% of U.S. exports and imports by value in 1973.

Kennedy International Airport in N.Y. City handled about 50% of the nation's overseas air travel and is the nation's largest air cargo center, handling half of export-import air tonnage (by value).

The state Barge Canal System is 800 mi. long. There are 34 railroads and 526 landing facilities, including 27 seaplane bases and 77 heliports. The Verrazano-Narrows Bridge has the world's longest suspension span.

The Dewey Thruway runs from N.Y. City to the Pennsylvania border on Lake Erie, 559 mi.; 90% of the state's 1,441-mi. portion of the Interstate Highway System was completed by 1973.

Tourism and business travel provide $4 billion a year to businesses in the state. Major vacation areas include the Adirondack and Catskill Mtns., Finger Lakes, Great Lakes, Thousand Islands, Long Island, N.Y. City, and Niagara Falls.

Rich, rolling farmlands support a large agricultural output. New York usually ranks 1st among the states in production of clover and timothy and ice cream; it is 2d to Washington in apples and 2d to California in grapes (it has large wine and grape juice industries).

It is also a leader in milk production, with the 2d largest number of milk cows in the U.S., and is high in vegetables and melons, sweet and tart cherries, pears, and potatoes. Also important are corn, oats, wheat, peaches, peas, beans, beets, onions, cauliflower, cabbages. Poultry and egg production is also high. Farm production supports large canning and freezing industries in the state.

Farm receipts for 1974 were est. at $1.5 billion, with more than two-thirds of the total from livestock and dairy products. Commercial fishing produced $25 million in 1974.

The state has a rich and varied mineral industry, normally ranking 1st in the U.S. in talc, titanium, emery, abrasive garnet, and wollastonite, and among the leaders in salt and zinc. Other products include lead, gypsum, petroleum, clay, stone, iron. Total value for 1974 was $437 million.

Per capita income was $6,244 in 1974, $247 higher than in California.

Highest point in the state is Mt. Marcy in the Adirondacks, 5,344 ft. The 128 state parks are visited annually by over 45 million persons.

There are 259 institutions of higher education, most in any state. Expenditure per pupil in public schools is highest of any state, $1,809 in 1974.

New York was the nation's most populous state from 1820 through 1964. As of July 1, 1964, the U.S. Census Bureau estimated California's pop. reached 18,084,000. New York's 17,915,000 (including Armed Forces stationed in the 2 states; without them, New York still led 17,870,000 to 17,749,000). By July 1, 1965, the Bureau estimated California led in both categories. In the 1970 census, California had 19,953,134; New York had 18,241,266.

In 1609 Henry Hudson discovered the river that bears his name and Samuel de Champlain explored the lake, far upstate, which was named for him. In 1614 and 1624, the Dutch built posts near Albany; in 1626 they settled Manhattan. A British fleet seized New Netherland, 1664. In New York, 92 of the 300 or more engagements of the Revolution were fought, including the Battle of Bemis Heights-Saratoga, a turning point of the war.

Sunnyside, the home of Washington Irving, "as full of angles and corners as an old cocked hat," is in Tarrytown. The Dutch Church of Sleepy Hollow (1697), North Tarrytown, overlooks a bridge commemorating Irving's story of the "headless horseman"; Irving is buried close by in Sleepy Hollow Cemetery. Also in Tarrytown is Lyndhurst, 19th century mansion of Jay Gould, maintained by the National Trust for Historic Preservation.

The Franklin D. Roosevelt National Historic Site, in Hyde Park, includes the graves of President and Mrs. Roosevelt, the home occupied by the Roosevelt family from 1867, greenhouse, etc. The Roosevelt Library has historic papers, trophies, and ship models.

Philipsburg Manor, in North Tarrytown, a trading center of the early 1700s, includes the restored Frederick Philipse home, a dam, and grist mill. Van Cortlandt Manor, Croton-on-Hudson, has the restored Van Cortlandt home and ferry house.

In Kingston, the Senate House, seat of the first Senate of the state, exhibits early historical objects; its museum has works by John Vanderlyn, local historical painter. In Newburgh, Washington's Hq., the Jonathan Hasbrouck House has Revolutionary relics.

The Suffolk Museum and Carriage House, Stony Brook, L. I., has early American paintings and furniture, apothecary shop, tavern, Wells Fargo, Conestoga, and gypsy wagons, etc.

In Cooperstown are the National Baseball Hall of Fame and Museum with a wide collection of mementos of the national game; nearby is Abner Doubleday Field, said to be where baseball originated in 1839. Near Cooperstown are Fenimore House, hq. of the State Historical Society, with collections including James Fenimore Cooper memorabilia and an art gallery; the Farmers' Museum; the Village Crossroads, with blacksmith shop, etc; the Carriage and Harness Museum.

The restored Fort Ticonderoga, overlooking the waters connecting Lakes George and Champlain, has relics of the French and Indian War and the Revolution in which the fort played important roles.

The New York State Museum in Albany has exhibits of natural resources, Indian life, Louis Agassiz Fuertes' paintings of birds, colonial housewares, etc.

The Corning Glass Center, Corning, has a museum and the Steuben factory, where visitors may see crystal glass formed and engraved. Also in the Finger Lakes area are the Curtiss Museum of aviation and the Wine Museum at Hammondsport and several wineries which offer tours to visitors. In Binghamton, the Roberson Center for the Arts and Sciences has art and historical collections.

In Utica, the Munson-Williams-Proctor Institute has a museum of 19th and 20th Century art and Fountain Elms, a restored mid-19th Century home.

The Remington Art Memorial Museum, Ogdensburg, has paintings and bronzes by Frederic Remington (1861-1909), born in nearby Canton.

Famous New Yorkers include Van Buren, Fillmore, Theodore and Franklin Roosevelt, Alfred E. Smith, Charles Evans Hughes, Julia Ward Howe, Elizabeth Cady Stanton, Melville, Whitman, Henry and William James, Peter Cooper, George Eastman.

(See also index for Albany, Binghamton, Buffalo, N.Y. City, Rochester, Schenectady, Syracuse, Troy.)

North Carolina

Tar Heel State, Old North State

AREA: 52,586 sq. mi.; rank, 28th. POPULATION (U.S. est. 1974): 5,363,000; rank, 12th. CAPITAL: Raleigh. MOTTO: Esse Quam Videri; To Be, Rather Than to Seem. FLOWER: Dogwood. BIRD: Cardinal. TREE: Pine. SONG: The Old North State. Twelfth of the original 13 states to ratify the Constitution, Nov. 21, 1789.

From a low coastal plain, with Capes Hatteras, Lookout, and Fear jutting into the Atlantic, North Carolina rises to a central Piedmont plateau region and, in the W, to the scenic Blue Ridge and Great Smoky Mountains. Mt. Mitchell, 6,684 ft., is the highest peak E of the Mississippi.

Modernization of production methods has brought North Carolina increasing prosperity from its factories. Per capita personal income was $4,612 in 1974.

The state leads the U.S. in production of textiles, bricks, and household furniture, and in both tobacco grown and cigarettes made.

In 1974, 85 new industrial plants opened and 147 expanded their facilities, creating an est. 18,778 new jobs through an investment of $872 million.

About 771,500 are employed in factories. The textile industry is the state's largest, with shipments valued at about $23.8 billion annually.

North Carolina ranks 1st among the states in tobacco production; in 1974 it totaled 394,682 tons. It was 2d in sweet potatoes, 3d in peanuts. Other large crops are cotton, corn, and soybeans. Also grown are wheat, oats, barley, peaches, apples. In crop receipts the state ranked 10th in 1974 with $1.7 million; for livestock receipts were $900 million.

There is a large poultry products business. The state ranked 3d in turkeys, 4th in chickens in 1974.

Mineral production value was est. at $144 million for 1974. North Carolina ranked 1st in mica, feldspar, and lithium; it was also a leader in talc and asbestos.

Tourism is important; in 1974 travelers spent an est. $980 million in the state. Sports include year-round golfing, skiing at mountain resorts, fishing in both fresh and salt water, hunting.

Among attractions are the Great Smoky Mtns. (half in Tennessee), the Blue Ridge Parkway (partly in Virginia) and the Cape Hatteras and Cape Lookout National Seashores.

Other attractions include the restored Fort Raleigh National Historic Site, Roanoke Is., where Virginia Dare, first child of English parents in the New World, was born Aug. 18, 1587; Wright Brothers National Memorial near Kitty Hawk with aviation exhibits and a reproduction of the plane in which Wilbur and Orville Wright made their first flights, 1903; Guilford Court House and Moore's Creek parks, sites of Revolutionary battles. The battleship North Carolina, a war memorial, is berthed at Wilmington.

In Asheville is one of the world's largest rayon plants as well as Biltmore Industries, native craft plants set up by Mrs. George W. Vanderbilt in 1901 to continue handweaving traditions of the area. Just S of Asheville is the 19th Century Biltmore mansion of the Vanderbilts, which has a large collection of paintings, antiques, and Ming china. Also in Asheville, the Thomas Wolfe Memorial was the home of the author.

Bennett Place, 6 mi. NW of Durham, is the site where Gen. Joseph E. Johnston surrendered the last Confederate army to Gen. William Sherman.

The Mint Museum of Art, Charlotte, has collections of paintings, sculpture, and ceramics. The North Carolina Museum of Art, Raleigh, exhibits American and European paintings, sculpture and decorative art. Tryon Palace, New Bern, is the reconstructed colonial capitol of 1770-1794.

Old Salem, in Winston-Salem, includes buildings erected by the Moravians from 1766 on. The R.J. Reynolds Tobacco Co. welcomes visitors at its plant.

There are 99 institutions of higher education.

The first English colony in America was the first of 2 established by Sir Walter Raleigh on Roanoke Is., 1585 and 1587. The first group returned to England, the second, the "Lost Colony," disappeared without trace. Permanent settlers came from Virginia, c. 1660. Roused by British repressions, the colonists drove out the royal governor, 1775; the province's Congress was the first to vote for independence. Ten regiments were furnished to the Continental Army. Cornwallis' forces were defeated at Kings Mountain, 1780, and forced out after Guilford Courthouse, 1781.

Famous men and women included Virginia Dare, James K. Polk, Andrew Johnson, Dolley Madison, Gaylord and Jim Perry, Jim (Catfish) Hunter and Enos Slaughter.

(See also Index for Charlotte, Raleigh, and Winston-Salem.)

North Dakota

Sioux State, Flickertail State

AREA: 70,665 sq. mi.; rank, 17th. POPULATION (U.S. est. 1974): 637,000; rank, 45th. CAPITAL: Bismarck. MOTTO: Liberty and Union, Now and Forever, One and Inseparable. FLOWER: Wild prairie rose. BIRD: Western meadowlark. TREE: American elm. SONG: North Dakota Hymn. ENTERED UNION: Nov. 2, 1889; rank, 39th or 40th, with South Dakota.

The eastern plains of North Dakota are rich in vast fields of grain and support large numbers of livestock, in sharp contrast to the rough, colorful Badlands in the West which have elements of scenic beauty and include Theodore Roosevelt National Memorial Park. Highest point is White Butte, 3,506 ft., in the SW.

North Dakota's economy is based on agriculture and mining; but manufacturing industries, especially processing of food, have grown in number and size. Most of the usable land is in farms and ranches.

North Dakota led the other states in production of spring and durum wheat, barley, and flaxseed in 1974. It was also a leader in rye, oats, sugar beets, and potatoes. Farm receipts for 1974 totaled $2.4 billion, more than half from its large grain crops. In 1975 there were 2.6 million cattle in the state.

Mineral production in 1974 was valued at $180 million, up 61% from 1973. The larger part of this was from petroleum. Other products include natural gas, natural gas liquids, coal (lignite), salt, peat.

Tourism brings in over $58 million a year.

Per capita income was $5,547 in 1974.

There are 65 state parks and historic sites. The International Peace Garden, on a 2,200-acre tract extending across the border into Manitoba, commemorates the friendly relations between the U.S. and Canada. The state is known for its waterfowl, grouse, and deer hunting, bass, trout, and northern pike fishing. Lake Sakakawea, formed by the Garrison Dam across the Missouri River, is 609 sq. mi. in area.

A museum with exhibits of pioneer life, the Northern Plains Indians and natural history of the area, is maintained by the State Historical Society on the State Capitol grounds, Bismarck.

Pierre La Verendrye was the first (1738) French fur trader in the area, followed later by English traders. The U.S. acquired half the territory in the Louisiana Purchase, 1803. Lewis and Clark built Fort Mandan, spent the winter of 1804-05 there. In 1818, American ownership of the other half was confirmed by agreement with Britain. First permanent settlement was at Pembina, 1812. Missouri River steamboats reached the area, 1832; the first railroad, 1873, bringing many homesteaders. The state was first to hold a presidential primary, 1912; other progressive measures were the referendum and recall.

There are 12 institutions of higher learning.

Famous North Dakotans include Vilhjalmur Stefansson, Maxwell Anderson, and Eric Sevareid.

(See also Index for Bismarck.)

Ohio
Buckeye State

AREA: 41,222 sq. mi.; rank, 35th. POPULATION (U.S. est. 1974): 10,737,000; rank, 6th. CAPITAL: Columbus. MOTTO: With God, All Things Are Possible. FLOWER: Scarlet carnation. BIRD: Cardinal. TREE: Ohio buckeye. SONG: Beautiful Ohio. ENTERED UNION: Mar. 1, 1803; rank, 17th.

Ohio is the nation's 3d greatest industrial state; it ranks among the wealthier states in livestock and crop receipts, and is a leader in output of lime, coal, and coke.

Ohio leads the U.S. in a wide variety of products: tires, machine tools, playing cards, business machines, glassware, cutlery, dishwashers, clay, and metal products.

Per capita income was $5,549 in 1974.

Total value added by manufacture was $23.1 billion. Of this, autos, aircraft, boats, and parts accounted for $2.9 billion; iron, steel, and other metals, $2.9 billion; machinery, especially industrial, $3.4 billion; electrical machinery, especially household appliances, $2.4 billion. Also important are metal products, chemicals, rubber and plastic products, food processing.

Farm receipts for 1974 totaled over $2.7 billion, 10th among the states, with more than half of it from livestock products. Ohio has large numbers of milk cows, hogs, and sheep; it ranks high in milk production. It is also a large producer of corn, grapes, clover, popcorn, oats, soybeans, and other crops.

Mineral production was valued at a total $992 million for 1974, with the largest item being bituminous coal. Ohio was the top state in lime production and one of the leaders in clays, salt, sand, and gravel. Other important products include petroleum, cement, gypsum, and natural gas.

It was estimated that the value of the tourist industry was more than $3.8 billion for 1974.

There are 64 state parks, over 300 roadside parks, and many historic memorials including Fallen Timbers Battlefield, prehistoric Indian mounds, and the restored first settlement, Schoenbrunn (1772).

The National Rifle and Pistol Matches are held at Camp Perry and the Grand American Trapshoot at Vandalia.

Unusual museums include the Air Force Museum and Paul Lawrence Dunbar House, Dayton; Dental Museum, Bainbridge; Auto-Aviation Museum, Cleveland; Ohio Historical Museum, Columbus.

In Canton, the Pro Football Hall of Fame has a museum and daily movies; the Stark County Historical Soc'ety has industry and historical museums.

The state is served by 27 railroads and 21 scheduled airlines. It has busy ports on Lake Erie and the Ohio River. Highest point is Campbell Hill, 1,550 ft., in the W. central area.

There are 104 institutions of higher education.

LaSalle visited the Ohio area, 1669; American fur-traders arrived, beginning 1685; the French and Indians sought to drive them out. During the Revolution, Virginians defeated the Indians, 1774, but hostilities were renewed, 1777. The region became U.S. territory after the Revolution. First organized settlement was at Marietta, 1788. Indian warfare ended with Anthony Wayne's victory at Fallen Timbers, 1794. In the War of 1812, Oliver H. Perry's victory on Lake Erie and William H. Harrison's invasion of Canada, 1813, ended British incursions.

Famous Ohioans include Grant, Hayes, Garfield, William H. and Benjamin Harrison, McKinley, Taft, Harding, Sherman, Rickenbacker, Edison, Orville Wright, George Bellows, Ambrose Bierce, Paul Lau-

rence Dunbar, Sherwood Anderson.

(See also index for Akron, Cincinnati, Cleveland, Columbus, Dayton, Toledo, Youngstown.)

Oklahoma
Sooner State

AREA: 69,919 sq. mi.; rank, 18th. POPULATION (U.S. est. 1974): 2,709,000; rank, 27th. CAPITAL: Oklahoma City. MOTTO: Labor Omnia Vincit, Labor Conquers All Things. FLOWER: Mistletoe. BIRD: Scissortailed flycatcher. TREE: Redbud. SONG: Oklahoma! ENTERED UNION: Nov. 16, 1907; rank, 46th.

Most of Oklahoma is a great, rolling plain sloping S and E with a mean altitude of 1,300 ft. There are 4 mountainous areas; the Ozark Plateau in the NE, the Ouachitas in the SE, the Arbuckles in the S central and the Wichitas in the SW. In the western Panhandle, the land rises toward the Rockies with Black Mesa, 4,973 ft., the highest point.

Oil, wheat, and cattle are the basic ingredients of Oklahoma's economy, but manufacturing industries have gained increasing importance. Per capita income was $4,566 in 1974.

The $1.2 billion Arkansas River Navigation System, involving shipping, flood control, and power dams, was completed to Catoosa, near Tulsa, in 1971. It made Catoosa a "seaport," with barge shipping to the Mississippi and beyond.

The state's output of petroleum was valued at $1.3 billion for 1974, up 67.3% from 1973 despite a cut in production, accounting for much of the total value of mineral production, $2.1 billion. The state is one of the leaders in the U.S. in petroleum production, and in total mineral production.

Natural gas was 2d most important among minerals; production was valued at $427 million. Other minerals include helium, in which the state is a leader, gypsum, zinc, cement, coal, copper, silver.

Oklahoma's rich plains produced the nation's 2d largest winter wheat crop in 1974 as well as large crops of sorghum, other grains, and peanuts. Its cattle herd was the 5th largest in the U.S. Total farm receipts were $1.9 billion, more than half from livestock products.

While much of Oklahoma's manufacturing industry is based on processing of the state's own meat, wheat, and oil, other lines have become important rivals. Value added by manufacture exceeds $1.7 billion annually. Important lines include food processing, machinery (especially construction and oil equipment), transportation equipment, metal products, petroleum, and coal products.

There are 41 institutions of higher education.

Total tourist revenues are estimated at more than $615 million annually. Attractions include 30 state parks, large lakes and reservoirs such as Eufaula (102,500 acres) and Lake Texoma (93,080 acres); Ouachita National Forest (176,000 acres), rodeos, Indian powwows, the National Cowboy Hall of Fame, and Western Heritage Center in Oklahoma City, bass fishing, and quail hunting.

The Will Rogers Memorial, Claremore, has collections of the great humorist's saddles and ropes, as well as trophies; his ashes lie also there. In Anadarko, the Southern Plains Indian Museum and Crafts Center exhibits Indian arts and has a crafts sales shop. The Woolaroc Museum near Bartlesville has 55,000 exhibits in a panorama of New World history, and a collection of paintings of the West.

The restored Fort Gibson Stockade, with many of the original buildings, near Muskogee, was erected 1824 and was the army's largest outpost in the Indian lands.

Near Tahlequah is the Cherokee Cultural Center with a restored 1700 Cherokee village and a spring and summer pageant.

The first permanent white settlement in the area was made in 1796 by Maj. Jean Pierre Chouteau on the site of present-day Salina, Okla.

Part of the Louisiana Purchase, 1803, Oklahoma

was known as Indian Territory (but was not given territorial government) after it became the home of the "Five Civilized Tribes"—Cherokee, Choctaw, Chickasaw, Creek, and Seminole—1828-1846. The land was also used by Comanche, Osage, and other Plains Indians. As white settlers pressed west, land was opened for homesteading by runs and lottery, a run being a race for a claim at a specific time. The first run took place Apr. 22, 1889; the most famous was the run to the Cherokee Outlet, 1893. The portion thus opened was organized as a Territory; this and Indian Territory were joined by Congress in the State of Oklahoma, admitted to the Union Nov. 16, 1907. Oklahoma's Indian population (1970 Census) was 97,-731, largest in the U.S.

Famous Oklahomans include Will Rogers, Gen. Patrick J. Hurley, Jim Thorpe, Maria Tallchief, Kay Starr, Mickey Mantle, Allie Reynolds, Johnny Bench.

(See also Index for Oklahoma City and Tulsa.)

Oregon
Beaver State

AREA: 96,981 sq. mi.; rank, 10th. POPULATION (U.S. est. 1974): 2,266,000; rank, 31st. CAPITAL: Salem. MOTTO: The Union. FLOWER: Oregon grape. BIRD: Western meadowlark. ANIMAL: Beaver. TREE: Douglas fir. SONG: Oregon, My Oregon. ENTERED UNION: Feb. 14, 1859; rank, 33d.

Oregon is rich in timber, fish and wildlife, water power, and scenic beauty, with lofty mountain ranges, deep river gorges, and broad, fertile valleys.

Half of Oregon, or about 30 million acres, is thickly forested and the state leads the nation in value of forest products, over $3 billion a year. Production of lumber, furniture, paper, and other forest products provides jobs for about 75,000 workers and is a major factor in the state's economy.

Also important are food processing, transportation equipment, machinery, fabricated metal. Total value added by manufacture is over $3.4 billion a year.

Per capita income was $5,270 in 1974.

Oregon's agriculture is rich and varied. While farmers grow fair-sized crops of wheat, oats, potatoes, and other staples, the state is a leader in production of berries, pears, cherries, filberts, walnuts, vegetables. It also ranks high in number of turkeys and of sheep. Farm receipts for 1974 were $1.1 billion, half from crops, the rest livestock.

Stone, nickel, cement, lime are important in mineral production, valued at $91 million for 1974.

Hydroelectric power, from both privately-owned and publicly-owned utilities, is abundant. A federal agency, the Bonneville Power Administration, markets electric power, much of it from a series of great dams across the Columbia River, to many of the utilities and to large industrial plants. Among users are plants for the refining and processing of metals from out of state, including aluminum.

The commercial fish catch, including salmon, tuna, halibut, sole, cod, and shellfish, was worth over $34 million in 1974.

Tourism is also an important industry, est. at over $588 million annually. There are 237 state parks, and both state and national forests. Crater Lake, a national park, is a body of sapphire blue water in a former volcano, 6 mi. in diameter and 1,932 ft. deep—deepest lake in the U.S. Oregon Dunes National Recreation Area was created in 1972.

Fort Clatsop National Memorial includes a replica of the fort in which the Lewis and Clark expedition spent the winter of 1805-06. Oregon Caves National Monument contains stone waterfalls. Skiing and the annual Pendleton Round-Up are other attractions.

A summer Shakespearean Festival is staged annually in Ashland.

Snow-capped Mt. Hood, which rises 11,235 ft., is the highest point in the state; nearby are scenic recreation areas.

The Columbia River brings ocean shipping to Portland, 100 mi. inland but one of the Pacific Coast's principal ports, and to other river ports.

Oregon has 40 institutions of higher education.

The Univ. of Oregon in Eugene has a Museum of Art with oriental, Pacific Northwest and other art collections. It also has a Museum of Natural History.

American Capt. Robert Gray discovered and sailed into the Columbia River, 1792; Lewis and Clark, traveling overland, wintered at the mouth of the river, 1805-06. Fur traders followed. Settlers arrived in the Willamette Valley, 1834. In 1843 the first large wave of settlers arrived via the Oregon Trail. After a period of hostilities, which followed a mining boom, Indians were placed on reservations, 1858. Early in the 20th Century, the "Oregon System," reforms which included the initiative, referendum, recall, direct primary, and woman suffrage, was adopted.

Famous Oregonians include Edwin Markham, Ernest Haycox, Stewart Holbrook, John Reed, Childe Hassam, Ernest Bloch, Dr. Marcus Whitman, Chief Joseph, Mickey Lolich.

(See also Index for Portland.)

Pennsylvania
Keystone State

AREA: 45,333 sq. mi.; rank, 33d. POPULATION (U.S. est. 1974): 11,835,000; rank, 3d. CAPITAL: Harrisburg. MOTTO: Virtue, Liberty and Independence. FLOWER: Mountain laurel. BIRD: Ruffed grouse. TREE: Eastern hemlock. Second of the original 13 states to ratify the Constitution, Dec. 12, 1787.

Pennsylvania has extensive mineral resources and fertile farmlands, is a leader in manufacturing, and boasts a wealth of historic landmarks and scenic attractions.

Roughly rectangular in shape, Pennsylvania has prosperous farmlands in the SE and the W. Through the center, running NE-SW, are parallel mountain ridges with valleys between. Highest point is Mt. Davis in the SW, 3,213 ft.

Many of the nation's largest steel plants are in Pennsylvania, with the greatest concentration in the Pittsburgh area. Pennsylvania ranks 1st among the states in steel wire and structural metal.

Mill and factory products are many and varied; value added by manufacture is over $23.2 billion. Primary metals are the most important, over $3.6 billion. Other large lines are machinery and electrical machinery, food processing, chemicals, metal products, women's dresses, and men's suits.

Per capita income was $5,490 in 1974.

Pennsylvania produces almost all of the nation's anthracite coal; it ranked 3d in 1973 in output of bituminous coal. Also important are cement, stone, petroleum, lime, clays, zinc, iron. Mineral production value, 1974, was $2.3 billion, up 63.4%.

Prosperous farms, such as those in the Pennsylvania Dutch country in the SE, brought in total livestock and crop receipts for the state of $1.5 billion in 1974, much of it from dairy and poultry products. The state ranked high in number of cows, chickens, turkeys.

The state ranks high in its output of grapes, peaches, apples, and cherries. It claims 1st place in scrapple, pretzels, mushrooms, and plantation-grown Christmas trees. It also ranks high in ice cream. Forest products are valued at over $7 billion annually.

Pennsylvania is among the leading states in hunting, fishing, golf, and winter sports. Tourism reportedly produces sales of $5.4 billion a year.

There are more than 100 state and federal parks, recreation areas, and historic sites. Scenic attractions include the Delaware Water Gap in the east and the 1,000-ft. deep Pine Creek Gorge in the north. Dutch folk festivals, country fairs, and fall foliage in the Poconos draw many visitors.

Washington Crossing State Park, where Continental troops crossed the Delaware to attack Hessian-British forces in Trenton, Christmas Night 1776, has restored buildings and picnic areas.

Longwood Gardens, near Kennett Square, include conservatories and rock, heather, flower, and water gardens; arboretum, illuminated fountains, open-air theater; open every day of the year.

Lancaster County and nearby areas in the southeast are known as Pennsylvania Dutch Country. Descendants of early German (Deutsch) and Swiss settlers still maintain many of the early customs and "old world" culture which make their farms, festivals, and market places attractive to tourists.

The William Penn Memorial Museum, Harrisburg, has collections of folk art, ironwork, glass, pewter, china, textiles, stage coaches, sleighs; replicas of artisans' shops, period rooms; fine arts, planetarium.

There are 146 institutions of higher learning.

First settlers were Swedish, 1643, on Tinicum Is. In 1655 the Dutch seized the settlement but lost it to the British, 1664. The region was given by Charles II to William Penn, 1681. Philadelphia (brotherly love) was the capital of the colonies during most of the Revolution, and of the U.S., 1790-1800. Pennsylvanians aided in the siege of Boston; Philadelphia was taken by the British, 1777; Washington's troops encamped at Valley Forge in the bitter winter of 1777-78. The Declaration of Independence, 1776, and the Constitution, 1787, were signed in Philadelphia.

Famous Pennsylvanians include Betsy Ross, Benjamin Franklin, Robert E. Peary, Andrew Carnegie, George C. Marshall, Stephen Foster, Marion Anderson, Mary Roberts Rinehart, Maxwell Anderson, Stan Musial.

(See also Index for Allentown, Erie, Philadelphia, Pittsburgh.)

Rhode Island
Little Rhody, Ocean State

AREA: 1,214 sq. mi.; rank, 50th. POPULATION (U.S. est. 1974): 937,000; rank, 39th. CAPITAL: Providence. MOTTO: Hope. FLOWER: Violet. BIRD: Rhode Island red (hen). TREE: Red maple. SONG: Rhode Island. Thirteenth of original 13 states to ratify the Constitution; May 29, 1790.

Rhode Island is the smallest of the 50 states but has the longest official name: State of Rhode Island and Providence Plantations. It is not an island, although its Narragansett Bay, extending from the Atlantic 28 mi. inland, contains many islands, the largest of which is named Rhode Is. Highest point, Jerimoth Hill in Providence County, is 812 ft.

Tiny Rhode Island is densely populated and highly industrialized. It is 2d to New Jersey in population density. The 1970 Census showed New Jersey averaging 953.1 persons per sq. mi.; Rhode Island 905.5.

Industries show more than $1.7 billion in value added annually by manufacturing. Until 1940, textile mills, dating back to a 1793 cotton mill, employed more workers than all other Rhode Island industries put together. Employment in the mills fell off sharply but jobs in other fields increased.

The state also pioneered in the manufacture of jewelry and silverware and remains tops in the U.S. Other leading industry groups are primary metal processing, metal products, machinery, rubber, and plastics, food processing, chemicals, apparel. The tourist industry produces over $100 million annually.

Per capita income was $5,376 in 1974.

Only 1% of the labor force is engaged in farming, and farm receipts in 1974 totaled $25 million. Dairy and poultry (notably Rhode Island reds) are the most important lines; potatoes and apples are principal crops. The fish and shellfish catch is valued at over $15 million annually.

There are 13 institutions of higher education.

Rhode Island is distinguished historically for its battle for freedom of conscience and action, begun by Roger Williams, founder of Providence, who was exiled from Massachusetts Bay Colony in 1636, and Anne Hutchinson, exiled in 1638. The first Baptist church in the U.S. was founded in Providence in 1638. Rhode Island gave protection to Quakers in 1657 and to Jews from Holland in 1658.

In the French and Indian wars, colonists broke the power of the Narragansetts in the Great Swamp Fight, 1675. British trade restrictions angered the colonists and they burned the British revenue cutter Gaspee, 1772. The colony declared its independence May 4, 1776. Gen. John Sullivan and Lafayette won a partial victory, 1778, but failed to oust the British.

Providence is a major manufacturing and educational center, and a port handling over 9 million tons of cargo per year.

The Rhode Island Historical Society in Providence occupies the historic John Brown House, with rooms containing furniture by 18th Century cabinet makers. Also in Providence, the Rhode Island School of Design has collections of classic art, 18th Century American furniture, 19th Century paintings, etc.

Newport became famous as the summer capital of society in the mid-19th Century. Touro Synagogue (1763) is the oldest in the U.S. and is a national historic site.

The Newport Historical Society has a marine museum; extensive exhibits of silver, furniture, china, etc.; a grist mill, several forts, a Seventh Day Baptist meeting house built 1729.

In Pawtucket, the Old Slater Mill Museum is a restored 1793 cotton mill, considered the first to spin yarn successfully in this country; it has demonstrations of hand spinning and weaving.

Famous Rhode Islanders include Nathanael Greene, Gilbert Stuart, Oliver and Matthew C. Perry, Jabez Gorham, George M. Cohan, Nelson Eddy, Ambrose Burnside, Oliver and Christopher La Farge.

(See also Index for Providence.)

South Carolina
Palmetto State

AREA: 31,055 sq. mi.; rank, 40th. POPULATION (U.S. est. 1940): 2,784,000; rank, 26th. CAPITAL: Columbia. MOTTO: Dum Spiro, Spero, While I Breathe, I Hope; and Animis Opibusque Parati, Prepared in Spirit and Resources. FLOWER: Carolina (yellow) jessamine. BIRD: Carolina wren. SONG: Carolina. TREE: Palmetto. Eighth of the original 13 states to ratify the Constitution, May 23, 1788.

In South Carolina, the land slopes from the Blue Ridge Mountains in the NW, through thick pine forests and fertile farmlands with great fields of tobacco and cotton, to semi-tropic beaches and busy ports on the Atlantic. Deep-sea and inland fishing, hunting, the charm of antebellum houses, public gardens, and famed shore resorts are among the state's attractions. Highest point is Sassafras Mtn. in NW, 3,560 ft.

Efforts to diversify industry and expand foreign trade and tourism have been highly successful. Per capita income was $4,248 in 1974.

Manufacturing is by far the major source of income; value added by manufacture is over $4.2 billion annually. The textile industry is still the most important, comprising about 40% of the value of all manufactured products, and employing the most workers. The mills rank high in cotton goods, and are a major producer of synthetic and woolen goods.

Other important manufacturing lines are chemicals, apparel, paper, lumber, food processing, machinery, and stone-clay-glass products.

In 1974, new industrial investment was valued at $666 million; it was estimated this would provide 12,-654 jobs. Major areas of expansion were in chemical, textile, and metal-working fields.

Farms have become fewer but larger. South Carolina grows more peaches than any other state except California; it ranks 3d in tobacco. Also grown are cotton, peanuts, sweet potatoes, pecans, etc. Poultry and eggs are important revenue producers; the state has large sales of chickens and turkeys.

Total farm receipts for 1974 were $907 million.

The state's mineral production value for 1974 was est. at $109 million. It is a leader in production of vermiculite, used in insulation, and of kyanite and kaolin used in ceramics. Also produced are mica, cement, and stone, including Winnsboro blue granite. Lumber for pulp and saw-timber is a major resource, especially the loblolly pine.

Income from tourism has risen; 28.6 million out-of-state visitors spent an est. $659 million in 1974.

Attractions include state parks, famed gardens, historic sites, coastal islands, shore resorts such as Myrtle Beach, fishing, and quail hunting.

There are many historic churches and white-pillared houses in Charleston, Columbia, and Beaufort. Gardens near Charleston include Middleton Place, Magnolia, and Cypress; Brookgreen, south of Myrtle Beach, has 340 outdoor statues; other gardens are Edisto, at Orangeburg; Glencairn, at Rock Hill.

Fort Sumter National Monument is in Charleston Harbor. Charleston Museum, estab. 1773, has exhibits of interior paneling, furniture, arts, crafts, and utensils from early South Carolina days.

The first English colonists settled, 1670, on the Ashley River, moved to the site of Charleston, 1680. The colonists seized the government, 1775, and the royal governor fled. In 1780 the British took Charleston, but British troops were defeated at Kings Mountain that year, and at Cowpens and Eutaw Springs, 1781. In the 1830s, South Carolinians, angered by Federal protective tariffs, adopted the Nullification Doctrine, holding a state can void an act of Congress. The state was the first to secede and, in 1861, fired on and forced the surrender of U.S. troops at Fort Sumter.

There are 47 institutions of higher education.

Famous South Carolinians include Andrew Jackson, John C. Calhoun, Francis Marion, James F. Byrnes, Julia Peterkin, DuBose Heyward.

(See also Index for Columbia.)

South Dakota
Coyote State, Sunshine State

AREA: 77,047 sq. mi.; rank, 16th. POPULATION (U.S. est. 1974): 682,000; rank, 44th. CAPITAL: Pierre. MOTTO: Under God, the People Rule. FLOWER: American pasque. BIRD: Ringnecked pheasant. SONG: Hail, South Dakota. TREE: Black Hills spruce. ENTERED UNION: Nov. 2, 1889; rank, 39th or 40th, entered at same time as North Dakota.

South Dakota is a rectangle split down the middle by the Missouri R. and a chain of huge lakes formed behind dams on the river. In the E are rich farmlands which produce large crops of rye, oats, and other grains. In the W are rolling grasslands which support millions of cattle and sheep, as well as vast acreages of wheat. In the far W are the Black Hills with Harney Peak, 7,242 ft., the highest point E of the Rockies.

With more than 43,000 farms and ranches, occupying most of the land area, agriculture is South Dakota's basic industry. Its livestock and livestock products account for three-quarters of farm income. Mining and lumbering are large natural resource industries. Per capita income was $4,218 in 1974.

The state normally ranks first in the U.S. in size of its rye crop and high in spring wheat, flaxseed, oats, barley. In 1974 South Dakota ranked 5th in sheep, 8th in cattle, and 10th in hogs. Total farm receipts for 1974 were $1.9 billion.

Large areas are reclaimed by irrigation and plans were under way for additional hundreds of thousands of acres to be fed from the Oahe Reservoir.

South Dakota leads the nation in gold production; the Homestake Mine in Lawrence County is the largest in the U.S. Gold accounted for $35 million of the state's total mineral production value which was $118 million for 1974, up 45%, mostly in gold despite a drop in production. The state was also a leader in production of beryllium. Other products include silver, petroleum, uranium, cement.

Processing of foods produced by farms and ranches is the largest of South Dakota's manufacturing industries. Also important are lumber and wood products, and machinery, including farm equipment. Total value added by manufacture is over $272.5 million.

South Dakota has 8,400 sq. mi. of Indian Reservations. The Indians, mostly Sioux, are est. at 32,365.

There are 16 institutions of higher education and

12 state parks, 35 recreation areas, and 49 roadside parks. Pheasant, duck, and geese are abundant. There are large herds of deer and elk and about 5,000 bison in state and private herds.

Mount Rushmore, in the Black Hills, has an altitude of 6,200 ft. Sculptured on its granite face are the heads of Washington, Jefferson, Lincoln, and Theodore Roosevelt. These busts by Gutzon Borglum are proportionate to men 465 ft. tall. Rushmore is visited by about 2 million persons annually.

Other tourist attractions include Custer State Park, with the world's largest herd of bison, the Black Hills Passion Play, staged from June to Sept. in an amphitheater at Spearfish.

The "Great Lakes of South Dakota" are 4 reservoirs created behind Oahe, Big Bend, Fort Randall, and Gavins Point Dams on the Missouri River with total water surface area of 571,000 acres.

Nine million out-of-state tourists, it is estimated, spend more than $250 million a year in South Dakota.

Fort Sisseton State Park, 18 mi. SE of Britton, is a restored army frontier post of 1864. The Sioux Indian Museum in Rapid City features historic and contemporary arts of the Sioux, and an Indian craft shop.

The French Verendrye brothers explored the region, 1742-43. Lewis and Clark passed through the area, 1804, and recrossed it on their return from the Pacific, 1806. First American settlement was at Sioux Falls, 1857, but there were few other settlements until after gold was discovered, 1874, on the Sioux Reservation. Miners rushed in; the U.S. first tried to stop them, then relaxed its opposition. Custer's defeat by the Sioux followed, and in 1877 the Sioux relinquished the land and the "great Dakota Boom" began. Miners and settlers poured in. A new Indian uprising came in 1890, climaxed by the massacre of Indian families at Wounded Knee.

Famous South Dakotans include Sakajawea, Sitting Bull, Crazy Horse, Gutzon Borglum, Dr. Ernest O. Lawrence.

(See also Index for Sioux Falls.)

Tennessee
Volunteer State

AREA: 42,244 sq. mi.; rank, 34th. POPULATION (U.S. est. 1974): 4,129,000; rank, 17th. CAPITAL: Nashville. MOTTO: Agriculture, Commerce. FLOWER: Iris. BIRD: Mockingbird. TREE: Tulip poplar. SONG: Tennessee Waltz. ENTERED UNION: June 1, 1796; rank, 16th.

Eastern Tennessee is rugged country with the Great Valley separating the Great Smoky Mtns., on the state's E border, from the Cumberland Mtns.; the Central Basin is a rolling area containing the famed Bluegrass country; from there the state slopes W to the bottom lands of the Mississippi. Clingman's Dome, in the Great Smokies, is the highest point, 6,643 ft.

Manufacturing has taken the top place in Tennessee's economy; products are many and varied. Among the most important are chemicals (especially plastic fibers), textiles, apparel, electrical machinery. Other important lines are food processing, furniture, lumber, paper, metal products, leather.

Value added by manufacture is over $7.7 billion annually. Per capita income was $4,484 in 1974.

There are 24 research centers including Oak Ridge, TVA, and Arnold Engineering Development Center for rocket research.

Tennessee ranks among the top states in tobacco production. Farm receipts for 1974 totaled $1.1 billion, more than half of it from livestock, the rest from crops. It has large numbers of hogs and cattle.

Forest products are also important, providing full-time jobs to 40,000 persons and contributing over $500 million annually to the economy. The state is known as the U.S. hardwood flooring center.

Tennessee produces a wide range of minerals and leads the other states in zinc. Other products include silver, cement, copper, coal. Total mineral production was valued at $383 million for 1974.

Tourism is of increasing importance; tourists spend

about $750 million annually in Tennessee. Folk music and the "Nashville sound" have made that city a leading recording center.

With 6 other states, Tennessee shares in federal reservoir developments on the Tennessee and Cumberland River systems. The Tennessee Valley Authority built Norris Dam on the Clinch River and operates a number of other dams in the state. Their reservoirs cover 756,321 acres.

Tennessee has a number of natural wonders—Reelfoot Lake, the reservoir basin of the Mississippi River formed by an earthquake (1811); Lookout Mountain, a rock-faced promontory carved by the currents of the Tennessee River and overlooking Moccasin Bend, at Chattanooga; Fall Creek Falls, 256 ft. high; and the west half of Great Smoky Mountains National Park.

The American Museum of Atomic Energy in Oak Ridge has displays, models, lectures. The Hermitage, 13 mi. E of Nashville, home of Andrew Jackson, contains furniture and personal effects of the president. The Ancestral Home of James K. Polk, in Columbia, has portraits, furniture, and various articles used by President Polk in the White House. The home, tailor shop, and grave of President Andrew Johnson are a national monument at Greeneville. The Parthenon, in Centennial Park, Nashville, is a full-size replica of the Parthenon of Athens. There are 26 state parks.

There are 62 institutions of higher education.

Spanish explorers first visited the area, 1541. English traders crossed the Great Smokies from the east while France's Marquette and Jolliet sailed down the Mississippi on the west, 1673. First permanent settlement was by Virginians on the Watauga River, 1769. During the Revolution, these colonists helped win the Battle of Kings Mountain, N.C., 1780, and joined other eastern campaigns. In the Civil War, hundreds of engagements were fought in the state. It seceded from the Union 1861, but of a total of 145,000 Tennessean soldiers, 30,000 fought for the Union.

Famous Tennesseans include Jackson, Johnson, Polk, Crockett, Houston, Farragut, Cordell Hull, Grace Moore, Pat Boone, Dinah Shore.

(See also Index for Chattanooga, Knoxville, Memphis, Nashville.)

Texas
Lone Star State

AREA: 267,338 sq. mi.; rank, 2d. POPULATION (U.S. est. 1974): 12,050,000; rank, 4th. CAPITAL: Austin. MOTTO: Friendship (Carrying out meaning of Indian word, Tejas—Friends). FLOWER: Bluebonnet. TREE: Pecan. BIRD: Mockingbird. SONG: Texas, Our Texas. ENTERED UNION: Dec. 29, 1845; rank, 28th.

Texas leads all other states in many categories, among them oil, cattle, sheep, and cotton. While these are basic to the Texas economy, manufacturing, as measured in terms of value added, makes an even greater contribution than either mineral output or farm receipts. It is 2d only to Alaska in area.

Texas normally produces a third of the nation's total petroleum output. The state's 1974 petroleum production was valued at $8.8 billion, nearly double the 1973 figure, although the amount produced was less. Texas is also the leading producer of asphalt, graphite, natural gas liquids, and magnesium chloride; Louisiana and Texas are the leading producers of natural gas. Texas ranks first among the states in output of sulphur, 2d in salt, helium, and bromine, and 3d in cement and clays.

The total value of the state's annual mineral production is by far the greatest of any state, $13.8 billion in 1974, a 63.7% increase over 1973.

Texas ranked 4th among the states in 1974 in cash receipts for crops, $2.9 billion; 2d for livestock products, $3 billion; 3d in total farm receipts, $5.9 billion.

It led all states in number of cattle, 16.6 million (giving the state more cattle than people), and in sheep, 2.7 million; it ranked 5th in turkeys and 9th in chickens. It grew the largest crops of rice, pecans, sorghum, and cotton, and ranked high in peanuts. It

also grows large amounts of vegetables and melons; its varied output includes sweet potatoes, oranges, grapefruit, peaches, and roses. Irrigation has reclaimed large arid areas in the west.

The largest of its many livestock expositions are held annually in Fort Worth, San Antonio, Houston, and El Paso; the largest cattle auction in Amarillo.

Manufacturing industries have shown tremendous growth. Value added by manufacture was over $13.7 billion a year. About 20% of the total value is in chemicals, the largest manufacturing industry. Other important lines are petroleum refining, processing of foods, transportation equipment, machinery, primary metals. Per capita income was $4,790 in 1974.

Texas ranks high among the states in commercial fishing with the 1974 catch valued at over $72 million.

About 18 million tourists spend over 2.3 billion dollars annually in Texas. There are 70 state parks, recreation areas, and historic sites; Big Bend and Guadalupe Mtns. National Parks, Padre Is. National Seashore, and Fort Davis National Historic Site. Named for President Lyndon B. Johnson, who died Jan. 22, 1973, are a National Historic Site, a National Park and a State Park, marking his birthplace, boyhood home, and ranch, all near Johnson City.

In 1974, Texas listed 376 museums; included were renowned art and historical collections.

Texas has 136 institutions of higher education.

Texas is the only state that was an independent republic, recognized by the U.S., before annexation. Over it have flown the flags of Spain, France, Mexico, the Lone Star Flag of the Republic, the Confederate States, and the U.S.

Alonso de Pineda sailed along the Texas coast, 1519; Cabeza de Vaca and Coronado visited the interior, 1541. Spaniards made the first settlement at Ysleta, near El Paso, 1682. Americans moved into the vast, empty land early in the 19th Century. Mexico, of which Texas was a part, won independence from Spain, 1821; Santa Anna became dictator, 1835; Texans rebelled, Santa Anna wiped out defenders of the Alamo, 1836; Sam Houston's Texans defeated Santa Anna at San Jacinto and independence was proclaimed the same year. In 1845, Texas was admitted to the Union; it seceded, 1861.

Famous Texans include Stephen Austin, James Bowie, J. Frank Dobie, Katharine Ann Porter, Dwight Eisenhower, Lyndon Johnson, Chester Nimitz, Frank Robinson.

(See also Index for Amarillo, Austin, Corpus Christi, Dallas, El Paso, Fort Worth, Houston, Lubbock, San Antonio.)

Utah
Beehive State

AREA: 84,916 sq. mi.; rank, 11th. POPULATION (U.S. est. 1974): 1,173,000; rank, 36th. CAPITAL: Salt Lake City. MOTTO: Industry. FLOWER: Sego lily. BIRD: California gull. TREE: Blue spruce. EMBLEM: Beehive. SONG: Utah, We Love Thee. ENTERED UNION: Jan. 4, 1896; rank, 45th.

Wrested from the wilderness by Mormon settlers in the mid-19th Century, Utah is for the most part a mountainous area, broken by fertile irrigated valleys, several deserts and 2 large lakes, Great Salt Lake in the N and Lake Powell in the S.

Great Salt Lake is 4,200 ft. above sea level, but has no known outlet. Its salt density varies from 20 to 25%, 2d only to that of the Dead Sea; it covers more than 1,500 sq. mi.; it is crossed by a 13-mi., rock-fill railroad causeway. Highest point in Utah is Kings Peak in the NE, 13,528 ft.

Manufacturing has become the state's major industry, well ahead of mining, agriculture, and tourism. Value added by manufacture in 1974 was an est. $1.5 billion. Transportation equipment was the most important line, followed by food products, machinery, metal products, printing-publishing, and electrical equipment. Per capita income was $4,452 in 1974.

Utah is an important center for research on, and production of, intercontinental missiles, rocket engines, solid fuel propellants, supersonic engines, aircraft navigational systems, and military computer components.

Utah is a rich storehouse of a wide variety of minerals. Among the states, it is a leading producer of copper, gold, silver, asphalt, molybdenum, lead, vanadium, and potassium salts.

Copper has by far the greatest value among Utah's mineral products. In 1974, copper production was valued at $357 million, 2d only to Arizona's, and total mineral production value was $942 million, up 40%.

The nation's largest open-pit copper mine at Bingham Canyon normally employs about 7,000 persons and produces about 20% of the newly-mined copper in the U.S. There are large smelters and refineries.

Petroleum has also been a large product; 1973 production was valued at $101 million. With Colorado and Wyoming, Utah shares what have been called the world's richest oil shale deposits.

Utah ranked 7th among the states in number of sheep in 1974 with 697,000. It also raises large flocks of turkeys. It is a leader in apricots and cherries. Other crops include barley, sugar beets, alfalfa, winter wheat, potatoes. Farm receipts for 1974 included $237 million from livestock, $93 million from crops.

Over 66% of the land is owned by the U.S.

Tourists spend about $190 million a year in Utah.

Utah is a great recreational area, with 11,000 mi. of fishing streams and 147,000 acres of lakes and reservoirs, numerous winter sports areas, and camp grounds. Natural wonders may be seen at Zion, Canyonlands, Bryce Canyon, Arches, and Capitol Reef National Parks, and Dinosaur, Rainbow Bridge, Timpanogas Cave and Natural Bridges National Monuments. The Lake Powell Recreation Area and Flaming Gorge Dam are other attractions.

Works by Utah artists, and archeological, botanical, mineral, and fossil collections may be seen at the Brigham Young University Collections in Provo.

In 1776, when the American colonies were declaring independence, 2 Spanish Franciscans visited the Utah area, the first white men to do so. American fur traders followed. Permanent settlement began with the arrival of the Mormons, 1847. They made the arid land bloom and created a prosperous economy; in 1849 they organized the State of Deseret and asked admission to the Union. This was not achieved until 1896, after a long period of controversy over the Mormon Church's doctrine of polygamy, which it discontinued in 1890.

Mormons comprise 72% of the population.

Famous Utahans include Brigham Young, George Romney, Ivy Baker Priest, Philo Farnsworth, John Browning, Maude Adams, Laraine Day, Loretta Young.

(See also Index for Salt Lake City.)

Vermont
Green Mountain State

AREA: 9,609 sq. mi.; rank, 43d. **POPULATION** (U.S. est. 1974): 470,000; rank, 48th. **CAPITAL:** Montpelier. **MOTTO:** Freedom and Unity. **FLOWER:** Red clover. **TREE:** Sugar maple. **BIRD:** Hermit thrush. **SONG:** Hail, Vermont. **ENTERED UNION:** Mar. 4, 1791; rank, 14th.

Vermont, first state to join the Union after the original 13, was the home of the Green Mountain Boys who played heroic roles in several victories of the American Revolution. They took their name from the Green Mountains which form the N-S backbone of the state. There are rich marble quarries in the western part of the state and large granite beds in the E. The Connecticut River runs along the E boundary, Lake Champlain forms much of the W line; among the many lakes is Memphremagog which lies partly in Canada to the N. Seven peaks rise over 4,000 ft. with Mt. Mansfield, 4,393 ft., the highest.

Vermont has long been known for its stoneworking, forest, and dairy industries. Tourism is the 2d industry, attracting 6 million visitors annually. Per capita income was $4,588 in 1974.

Principal manufactured goods are machine tools, computer components, stone, and clay products, lumber, furniture, and paper. Value added by manufacture is over $579 million a year.

Tourism is important; the accent is on recreation, which produces more than $250 million a year. Skiing has accounted for a tremendous growth. There are more than 95 miles of ski lifts in the state and many ski areas, including Stowe, Killington, Mt. Snow, Stratton, Bromley, Jay Peak, and Sugarbush.

Vermont has 72 state parks and forests covering 130,000 acres. The Long Trail is popular for hiking and camping. There is fishing for trout, salmon, bass, muskellunge; hunting for deer and game birds.

Large milk and butter production accounts for most of the total value of farm receipts which was $217 million for 1974. For its small size, Vermont has a large number of milk cows.

The state ranks high in output of marble, granite, limestone; it is a leader in asbestos and talc.

The Shelburne Museum, 7 mi. S of Burlington, preserves 35 early American buildings, including furnished homes, doctor's and dentist's offices, stagecoach inn; covered bridge, side-wheeler, old trains, folk art, etc.; Webb gallery of paintings by Rembrandt, Goya, Corot, Manet, Cassatt.

The Bennington Museum displays early American glass, furniture, pottery, and what is said to be the oldest Stars and Stripes flag in existence.

Champlain explored the lake that bears his name and separates Vermont from New York, 1609. First American settlement was Fort Dummer, 1724, near Brattleboro. With the Revolution, Ethan Allen and Benedict Arnold captured Fort Ticonderoga and Seth Warner took Crown Point, both in N.Y., 1775. Britain's Burgoyne recaptured them, 1777, but John Stark defeated part of Burgoyne's forces near Bennington. In the War of 1812, Thomas MacDonough defeated a British fleet on Champlain off Plattsburgh, 1814. In the Civil War, Confederate soldiers, operating from Canada, robbed St. Albans banks.

Vermont has 20 institutions of higher learning.

Famous Vermonters include Chester Arthur, Calvin Coolidge, Stephen A. Douglas, Adm. George Dewey, Dorothy Canfield Fisher, John Dewey.

Virginia
Old Dominion

AREA: 40,817 sq. mi.; rank, 36th. **POPULATION** (U.S. est. 1974): 4,908,000; rank, 14th. **CAPITAL:** Richmond. **MOTTO:** Sic Semper Tyrannis, Thus Ever to Tyrants. **FLOWER:** American dogwood. **BIRD:** Cardinal. **TREE:** American dogwood. **SONG:** Carry Me Back to Old Virginia. Tenth of the original 13 states to ratify the Constitution; June 26, 1788.

The Commonwealth of Virginia is famed for its colonial heritage, for the statesmen it produced, its historic homes and estates, and great battlefields on which the fate of the nation was decided in both the 18th and 19th Centuries.

Virginia's coastal plain, the Tidewater, consists mostly of 4 peninsulas formed by Chesapeake Bay and the Potomac, Rappahannock, York, and James Rivers. The central Piedmont plateau rises, toward the W, to the Blue Ridge Mtns. Beyond the Blue Ridge and between it and the Alleghenies on the W border lies the Shenandoah Valley, a rich farming region. Highest point is Mt. Rogers in the SW, 5,729 ft.

Virginia's manufacturing industries have grown steadily and are diversified. They provide jobs for 401,000, over 5 times the number employed in agriculture. Total value added by manufacture is more than $6 billion, with payrolls totaling $2.8 billion; value of shipments was estimated at $12.8 billion.

Largest lines were chemicals, textiles, food products, and clothing. Other important lines were lumber, furniture, paper, electrical machinery, transportation equipment, cigarettes, metal products, stone-clay-glass products, shipbuilding.

The federal government is a major employer with

military installations at Hampton Roads and U.S. agencies near Washington, D.C.

Per capita income was $5.265 in 1974.

Hampton Roads is the major port, a leader in bulk export tonnage.

Agriculture remains a vital factor in the economy. Virginia ranks among the leaders in the U.S. in its crops of tobacco, peanuts, apples, and sweet potatoes. Other important crops are corn, vegetables, barley, peaches. It has large numbers of turkeys; its Smithfield hams are famous. Farm receipts for 1974 totaled $1.03 billion, more than half from livestock.

Coal is Virginia's leading mineral commodity, in terms of both tonnage and value, and usually accounts for about 70% of the value of total mineral production. Also important are lime, zinc, stone, cement. Total mineral production for 1974 was valued at $1.03 billion, up 90% from 1973.

The fish catch was worth $33 million, 1974.

With its wealth of historical attractions and recreational facilities such as Shenandoah National Park in the Blue Ridge Mts. and Virginia Beach, the state drew 25 million out-of-state travelers who spent about $662 million in 1973.

Virginia was the birthplace of 8 presidents. It has many historic shrines, including Washington's birthplace, Wakefield; his home and grave at Mount Vernon; Jefferson's Monticello, near Charlottesville and the Univ. of Virginia he designed; Robert E. Lee's birthplace, Stratford Hall, and grave at Lexington.

Colonial Williamsburg is a restoration of the 18th Century buildings and living conditions in what was the capital of Virginia when Washington, Jefferson, Patrick Henry, and George Mason were young men. There are over 800 buildings, some the originals.

At Jamestown, first permanent English settlement, are foundations and ruins of early buildings, relics, statues and monuments.

At Yorktown, where the surrender of British Gen. Cornwallis to American and French forces virtually ended the American Revolution, may be seen colonial buildings, earthworks and cannons.

In Fredricksburg, the James Monroe Law Office and Museum is the original building in which President Monroe practiced law in the 1780s, containing the desk at which he signed the Monroe Doctrine.

Appomattox Court House National Monument includes the rebuilt Wilmer McLean house in which Gen. Lee surrendered.

Fort Monroe Casement Museum has relics of the imprisonment in the fort of Jefferson Davis and Chief Black Hawk, and of the battle between the Monitor and Merrimac. The Quartermaster Museum, Fort Lee, exhibits clothing, saddles, etc., of American soldiers from the Revolution on. The War Memorial Museum of Virginia, in Newport News, displays World War I and II weapons and equipment.

In Lexington are Washington and Lee University and Virginia Military Institute, both closely linked with leaders and action in the Civil War. Also in Lexington is the George C. Marshall Research Library and Museum with displays of the life of the famed World War II general and statesman.

At Staunton is the Woodrow Wilson birthplace, with memorabilia of his family. The Gen. Douglas MacArthur Memorial in Norfolk contains the general's sarcophagus, flags of 30 units he commanded, documents, and murals of events in his life.

English settlers founded Jamestown, 1607. British repression led to calls for independence; royal Gov. Dunmore had to flee, 1775. In the Revolution, George Rogers Clark freed the Ohio-Indiana-Illinois area. Benedict Arnold burned Richmond and Petersburg, 1781. That same year, Britain's Cornwallis was trapped at Yorktown and surrendered. Though a slave state, Virginia was one of the last to secede; 1861. It was the scene of major battles, ending with Robert E. Lee's surrender at Appomattox, April 9, 1865.

There are 70 institutions of higher education.

Famous Virginians include Washington, Jefferson, Madison, Monroe, William Harrison, Tyler, Taylor, Wilson, Patrick Henry, John Marshall, Joseph E. Johnston, Poe, Cabell, Cather, Ellen Glasgow, Booker T. Washington, Lewis and Clark, Richard E. Byrd.

(See also Index for Norfolk, Richmond, Roanoke.)

Washington
Evergreen State

AREA: 68,192 sq. mi.; rank, 20th. POPULATION (U.S. est. 1974): 3,476,000; rank, 22d. CAPITAL: Olympia. MOTTO: Al-Ki, By and By. FLOWER: Coast rhododendron. TREE: Western hemlock. BIRD: Willow goldfinch. SONG: Washington, My Home. ENTERED UNION: Nov. 11, 1889; rank, 42d. Nickname: Evergreen State.

The state of Washington in the Pacific Northwest is a leader in many ways — in lumber, in fruit and other crops, and in aircraft production; its ports on Puget Sound are gateways to Alaska and the Far East; the great dams on the Columbia River provide power for production of aluminum and irrigation for the rich Columbia Basin.

The lofty Cascade Range splits the state, running N-S. To the W, the Puget Sound lowlands support dairy, poultry, and truck-farming. On the E slopes of the Cascades are great fruit orchards; further E, plateau country provides sheep and cattle lands and a rich wheat belt. Highest peak is Mt. Rainier in the Cascades, 14,410 ft.

The Columbia River cuts a zig-zag course across Washington from the NE, then flows W along the Oregon border to the Pacific.

Puget Sound has many deep harbors beside which Seattle, Tacoma, Everett, and other great cities have grown. Foreign trade, mainly with Japan and Canada, has increased greatly.

Manufacturing industries employ 252,400 workers with payrolls of $2.7 billion and value added by manufacture over $4.6 billion a year. Transportation equipment, mostly aircraft, but including ships and trucks, accounts for $1.13 billion.

Other important manufacturing lines are lumber, food processing, paper, metal products, chemicals, machinery. The Atomic Energy Commission plant at Hanford produces nuclear fuels and electricity. Per capita income was $5,651 in 1974.

Washington's large production of fruits, berries, and other crops places it first among the states in apples, blueberries, hops, and red raspberries; it is among the top producers of potatoes, winter wheat, pears, grapes, apricots, filberts, cranberries, cherries, asparagus, strawberries. It ranks 3d in winter wheat. Farm receipts for 1974 totaled $1.8 billion, over half from crops, the rest from livestock.

The commercial fishing catch is valued at over $59 million a year. Salmon accounts for half the total, followed by halibut, and bottomfish.

Mineral production in 1974 was valued at an est. $132 million. Sand and gravel, silver, cement, zinc, and lead were the most important products.

Large aluminum reduction plants, using refined ore from out-of-state and hydro-electric power, have expanded. Aluminum output is 25% of U.S. total.

A series of great dams on the Columbia, including the massive Grand Coulee in the NE, and Bonneville on the Oregon border, provide power and irrigation.

More than half the state is in forests; one-sixth of the nation's standing sawtimber is in Washington. Towering Douglas firs and Ponderosa pines, western hemlocks, and red cedars are among commercially important trees; income, $1.4 billion a year.

There are 43 institutions of higher education.

Spain's Bruno Hezeta sailed the coast, 1775; American Capt. Robert Gray sailed up the Columbia River, 1792. Canadian fur traders set up Spokane House, 1810; Americans under John Jacob Astor established a post at Fort Okanogan, 1811. Missionary Marcus Whitman settled near Walla Walla, 1836. Final agreement on the border of Washington and Canada was made with Britain, 1846, and gold was discovered in the state's northeast, 1855, bringing new settlers. World Wars brought great industrial expansion.

The state has 3 national parks, Mt. Rainier, North Cascades, and Olympic National Park. Its state parks and national forests of nearly 10 million acres have large hunting, fishing, and recreation areas.

The Washington State Historical Society, Tacoma, has exhibits of the fur trade, Indian, and Eskimo arts, and pioneer cabins, schoolhouse, and covered wagon.

Tourists, it has been estimated, spend about $1 billion annually in the state.

Famous Washingtonians include Bing Crosby, Patrice Munsel, Eric Johnston, Guthrie McClintic, Upton Close, Audrey Wurdemann.

(See also Index for Seattle, Yakima.)

West Virginia
Mountain State

AREA: 24,181 sq. mi.; rank, 41st. **POPULATION** (U.S. est. 1974): 1,791,000; rank, 34th. **CAPITAL:** Charleston. **MOTTO:** Montani Semper Liberi, Mountaineers Always Free. **FLOWER:** Rhododendron maximum. **BIRD:** Cardinal. **TREE:** Sugar maple. **SONGS: The West Virginia Hills, This Is My West Virginia,** and **West Virginia, My Home, Sweet Home. ENTERED UNION: June 20, 1863; rank, 35th.**

West Virginia's fortunes have long been based on those of the bituminous coal industry; the state usually is first in coal production with about 20% of the U.S. total. Increased output of coal and natural gas, plus growth in the chemical, steel, glass, and tourist industries, have aided the economy.

The terrain is mountainous, with the Alleghenies running NE-SW in the eastern half of the state; the western half is a plateau sloping down to the Ohio River which forms most of the boundary on the W. Highest point is Spruce Knob in the NE, 4,863 ft.

Early explorers included George Washington, 1753, and Daniel Boone. The area became part of Virginia and often objected to rule by the eastern part of the state. When Virginia seceded, 1861, the first Wheeling Convention repudiated the act; the second later created a new state, Kanawha, subsequently changed to West Virginia. It was admitted to the Union as such, 1863. In the late 19th and early 20th Centuries, the state was torn by industrial warfare. In recent years, it has battled economic troubles.

Coal accounts for more than 91% of the total value of mineral production. In 1974 production was valued at an est. $2.4 billion. Coal output fell 10% but its value rose 64%. Kentucky had a slight lead in tonnage, but West Virginia led in its value.

West Virginia produces and markets more natural gas than any other state east of the Mississippi. Also important are petroleum, salt, stone, cement, lime.

Production of a wide variety of chemicals, based in the state's resources of salt brine, gas, oil, and coal, and including synthetic fibers and plastics, dominates the manufacturing field, accounting for about 36% of the $2.6 billion in value added annually by manufacture. Large plants are in the Ohio and Kanawha valleys, where electric power is abundant. The state is also a major producer of steel, glass, pottery.

Farm receipts totaled $152 million for 1974; the hilly terrain is not conducive to large-scale agriculture. Poultry, dairy products, cattle, and sheep accounted for most receipts. Apples and peaches are profitable. About 79% of the state is forested.

Per capita income was $4,390 in 1974; the national average was $5,434.

Tourism is being promoted and an est. 10 million visitors spend over $600 million annually. More than a million acres have been set aside for recreation in 34 state parks, 9 state forests; Monongahela, George Washington, and part of Jefferson National Forests.

Attractions include Harpers Ferry National Historical Park, mineral water resorts at White Sulphur, and Berkeley Springs, trout fishing, turkey, deer, and bear hunting.

Part of the town of Harpers Ferry has been restored to its condition in 1859, when John Brown seized the U.S. Armory. Still standing is the fire-engine

house in which Brown and a score of followers were besieged and captured by a force of U.S. Marines under Robert E. Lee, then a U.S. colonel.

The State Museum in Charleston displays local relics and artifacts from prehistoric cultures (as early as 8,000 B.C.), Indians, and pioneers.

The Huntington Galleries, Huntington, has collections of 19th and 20th Century European and American paintings, furniture, and decorative arts. The Oglebay Mansion-Museum displays colonial furniture and 19th Century glassware.

There are 25 institutions of higher education.

Famous West Virginians include Stonewall Jackson, Dwight Morrow, Michael Owens, John W. Davis, Newton D. Baker, Pearl Buck, Eleanor Steber.

(See also Index for Charleston, Huntington.)

Wisconsin
Badger State

AREA: 56,154 sq. mi.; rank, 26th. **POPULATION** (U.S. est. 1974): 4,566,000; rank, 16th. **CAPITAL:** Madison. **MOTTO:** Forward. **FLOWER:** Butterfly violet. **BIRD:** Robin. **TREE:** Sugar maple. **ANIMAL:** Badger. **FISH:** Muskellunge. **SONG: On, Wisconsin! ENTERED UNION: May 29, 1848; rank, 30th.**

Known as America's Dairyland, Wisconsin produces more milk and cheese than any other state and agriculture is a vital part of the state's economy. However, manufacturing, including processing of foods, has become the state's largest employer and biggest income producer.

Mining has declined with the near-cessation in 1965 of iron mining, but output of several other minerals has increased. Reforestation has kept the paper and wood product industries important. There are 14 ports on Lakes Michigan and Superior. Per capita income was $5,210 in 1974.

The state has an abundance of recreation resources; water and winter sports, hunting and fishing are among its attractions. Vacationers, it is estimated, spend over $1 billion a year.

Highest point is Timms Hill in the N, 1,952 ft.

Wisconsin's rolling pasturelands and large crops support the nation's largest herd of milk cows, about 1.8 million; 80% of its farms are dairy farms.

The state produces the most milk, cheese, hay, and alfalfa in the U.S. It ranks 3d in oats. It is also a leading producer of butter, corn, cranberries, and maple syrup. In addition to cattle, it also has large numbers of hogs and turkeys.

Farm receipts for 1974 totaled $2.5 billion, 11th highest among the states, most of it from livestock.

About 40% of income produced in Wisconsin comes from manufacturing and, with over 500,000 factory employees, the state ranks among the top 12. Value added by manufacturing is over $10 billion a year.

Most important products, in terms of value added, are: machinery, especially engines, turbines, industrial, and construction; food products, including dairy, meat and beer; transportation equipment, especially motor vehicle parts and equipment, and mobile homes; iron and steel, metal products, paper.

Mineral production for 1974 was valued at $123 million. Zinc, lime, cement, and stone are important.

Most of Wisconsin's timber production goes into pulp and paper, but the state is also a leading producer of hardwood plywood and veneer.

Wisconsin has over 8,500 lakes, of which Winnebago is the largest, and fronts on both Lakes Michigan and Superior. Water sports, ice-boating, and fishing for trout, bass, and muskellunge are popular, as are skiing and hunting for deer, bear, and wildfowl. Public parks and forests take up one-seventh of the land area; there are 49 state parks, 9 state forests, 2 national forests. Wisconsin produces 900,000 mink pelts per year, one-third the U.S. total.

Other attractions include small towns which preserve Swiss, Scandinavian, German, and other European cultures, visits to breweries and cheese factories, Indians festivals, and the Dells (scenic gorges) of the Wisconsin River.

The Circus World Museum in Baraboo has over 100 circus wagons and other displays, and presents circus shows daily, early May-early Sept.

There are 59 institutions of higher learning.

Jean Nicolet was the first European to see the Wisconsin area, arriving in Green Bay, 1634. French missionaries and fur traders followed; the British took over, 1763. Thanks to the Revolution, the U.S. won the land but the British were not ousted until after the War of 1812. Lead miners came next and then farmers. Railroads were started in 1851, serving growing wheat harvests and iron mines. In the 20th Century, Wisconsin became an industrial state and also took the lead in dairy products.

Famous Wisconsinites include Robert and Philip LaFollette, Joseph R. McCarthy, Marc Mitscher, Thorstein Veblen, Zona Gale, Thornton Wilder, Edna Ferber, Alfred Lunt, Frank Lloyd Wright, Harry Houdini.

(See also Index for Madison, Milwaukee.)

Wyoming
Equality State

AREA: 97,914 sq. mi.; rank, 9th. POPULATION (U.S. est. 1974): 359,000; rank, 49th. CAPITAL: Cheyenne. MOTTO: Equal Rights. FLOWER: Indian paintbrush. BIRD: Western meadowlark. TREE: Plains cottonwood. SONG: Wyoming State Song. ENTERED UNION: July 10, 1890; rank, 44th.

Wyoming's towering mountains and rolling plains provide spectacular scenery, grazing ranges for sheep and cattle, and a wealth of mineral resources.

Ranges of the Rockies cover the western two-thirds of the state; the eastern third is Great Plains country. Highest point is Gannett Peak in the W, 13,804 ft. The spectacular Teton Mtns. lie S of Yellowstone National Park, mostly carved out of Wyoming's NW corner.

The most important industry is mining, particularly of oil and natural gas. Agriculture, especially livestock, runs 2d. Tourism and manufacturing are growing. Per capita income was $5,156 in 1974.

Wyoming has large reserves of coal, oil, gas, oil shale, iron ore, and gypsum.

Production of petroleum in 1974 was valued at $983 million, up 81% from 1973. Total mineral production value for the year was est. at $1.5 billion. The state ranked first in the U.S. in sodium carbonate production, 2d in uranium. Also important are coal, natural gas, clays, and iron ore.

Wyoming is 2d among the states in wool production, and in 1975 its sheep numbered 1.5 million, exceeded only by Texas; it also had 1.7 million cattle. Principal crops include wheat, oats, sugar beets, corn, potatoes, barley, and alfalfa. Livestock receipts for 1974 totaled $244 million; crops, $115 million.

Much of Wyoming's manufacturing is based on its mining and agricultural products. Leading lines include petroleum and coal products, processed foods, timber, and wood, construction materials, iron and steel, electronic components. Value added by manufacture is about $119 million annually.

Wyoming is a main source for 3 important river systems; the Missouri, Colorado, and Columbia. Both power and irrigation are provided by a growing number of dams and reservoirs. Tourism produces an est. annual $190 million from 9 million visitors.

The French explorers, Francois and Louis Verendrye, were the first European visitors, 1743. John Colter, American, was first to traverse Yellowstone Park, 1807-08. Trappers and fur traders followed in the 1820s. Forts Laramie and Bridger became important stops on the pioneer trail to the West Coast. Indian wars followed massacres of army detachments in 1854 and 1866. Population grew after the Union Pacific crossed the state, 1869. Mining is the largest industry but the state ranks 2d in wool production. Women won the vote, for the first time in the U.S., from the Territorial Legislature, 1869.

Grand Teton National Park, with mountains 13,000 ft. high, comprises 299,326 acres; the National Elk Refuge covers 25,000 acres. Devils Tower, a cluster of rock columns 865 ft. high, became the first National Monument in the U.S. in 1906. Fort Laramie, partly preserved, partly restored, is a National Historic Site. The annual Cheyenne Frontier Days Celebration, last full week in July, is the state's largest rodeo. Hunting, fishing, and skiing are other attractions.

The Buffalo Bill Historical Center in Cody has a museum with personal effects of William F. Cody (Buffalo Bill), as well as the Whitney Gallery of Modern Art with Indian art and paintings by Frederic Remington, Charles M. Russell, George Catlin, etc.

The Bradford Brinton Memorial Ranch, near Big Horn, has collections of western painting and sculpture, antiques, Indian arts, hunting trophies.

There are 8 institutions of higher education.

Famous Wyomingites include Jim Bridger, Nellie Tayloe Ross, Buffalo Bill Cody.

(See Index for Yellowstone National Park.)

District of Columbia

AREA: 67 sq. mi. POPULATION (U.S. est. 1974): 728,000. MOTTO: Justitia omnibus, Justice for all. FLOWER: American beauty rose. TREE: Scarlet oak. BIRD: Wood thrush. The city of Washington is coextensive with the District of Columbia.

The District of Columbia is the seat of the federal government of the United States. It lies on the west central edge of Maryland on the Potomac River, opposite Virginia. Its area was originally 100'sq. mi. taken from the sovereignty of Maryland and Virginia. Virginia's portion south of the Potomac was given back to that state in 1846.

The 23d Amendment, ratified in 1961, granted residents of the District the right to vote for president and vice president for the first time and gave it 3 members in the Electoral College. Residents cast the first such votes in Nov. 1964.

Congress governed the District 1878-1967 through 3 commissioners appointed by the president. The Reorganization Plan of 1967 substituted a single commissioner (also called mayor) and assistant, and a 9-member City Council; funds were still appropriated by Congress; residents had no vote in local government (except to elect school board members).

In Sept. 1970, Congress approved legislation giving the District one delegate to the House of Representatives. The delegate could vote in committee but not on the House floor. The first was elected 1971.

In May 1974 voters approved a charter giving them the right to elect their own mayor and a 13-member city council in Nov. 1974. It took office Jan. 1, 1975. The district won the right to levy its own taxes but Congress retained power to kill council actions.

Proposals for a "federal town" for the deliberations of the Continental Congress were made in 1783, 4 years before the adoption of the Constitution that gave the Confederation a national government. Rivalry between northern and southern delegates over the site appeared in the First Congress, meeting in New York in 1789. John Adams, presiding officer of the Senate, cast the deciding vote of that body for Germantown, Pa. In 1790 Congress compromised by making Philadelphia the temporary capital for 10 years. The Virginia members of the House wanted a capital on the eastern bank of the Potomac; they were defeated by the Northerners, while the Southerners defeated the Northern attempt to have the nation assume the war debts of the 13 original states, the Assumption Bill fathered by Alexander Hamilton. Hamilton and Jefferson arranged a compromise: the Virginia men voted for the Assumption Bill, and the Northerners conceded the capital to the Potomac. President Washington chose the site in Oct. 1790 and persuaded landowners to sell their holdings to the government at £25, then about $66, an acre. The capital was named Washington.

Washington appointed Pierre Charles L'Enfant, a French engineer who had come over with Lafayette, to plan the capital on an area not over 10 mi. square. The L'Enfant plan was considered grandiose, for streets 100 to 110 feet wide and one avenue 400 feet wide and a mile long on the Potomac pastures seemed foolhardy. But Washington endorsed his plans. When L'Enfant ordered a wealthy landowner to remove his new manor house because it obstructed a vista, and demolished it when the owner refused, Washington stepped in and dismissed L'Enfant. The official map was completed by Andrew Ellicott, surveyor, and Benjamin Banneker, black mathematician.

On Sept. 18, 1793, the cornerstone of the north wing of the Capitol was laid by President Washington. The occasion was expected to drum up sales of city lots, but there were few purchasers. Washington bought several lots. In the next few years Robert Morris and others invested. By 1799 the Senate wing of the Capitol had been roofed, the walls of the President's house were up and the Treasury building was ordered. On June 3, 1800, President John Adams moved to Washington and on June 10, Philadelphia ceased to be the temporary capital. The City of Washington was incorporated in 1802; the District of Columbia was created as a municipal corporation in 1871, embracing Washington, Georgetown, and Washington County.

(See also Index for Washington, D. C.)

Outlying U. S. Areas

Commonwealth of Puerto Rico

Estado Libre Asociado de Puerto Rico

AREA: 3,435 sq. mi. POPULATION (est.): 2,794,-000. CAPITAL: San Juan. SONG: La Borinquena. TREE: Flamboyant. BIRD: Reinita. FLOWER: Hibiscus.

Puerto Rico is a hilly, tropical island lying between the Atlantic to the N and the Caribbean to the S; it is the easternmost of the West Indies group called the Greater Antilles, of which Cuba, Hispaniola and Jamaica are the larger units. It lies about 1,600 mi. SE of New York, 500 mi. N of Venezuela. It is roughly rectangular, 105 mi. long by 35 wide. Numerous small islands include Vieques, Culebra, and Mona.

The soil of the coast plain is fertile and there are many lush valleys, but there are dry areas in the S which need irrigation and an extensive system has been constructed by the government. The climate is mild, with a mean temperature of 76°; the mean maximum is 82°, and the mean minimum 73°. Highest point is Cerro de Punta, 4,389 ft.

President Truman, on Aug. 5, 1947, signed an act giving Puerto Rico the right to choose its chief executive by popular vote. An act of 1950, affirmed by special election, June 4, 1951, permitted Puerto Rico to draft its own constitution. One similar to that of the U. S. was approved in a convention Feb. 4, 1952, and ratified by a popular vote March 3, 1952. President Truman signed, July 3, 1952, a Congressional resolution approving the new constitution, elevating Puerto Rico to the status of a free commonwealth associated with the U. S., effective July 25, 1952.

In a July 23, 1967, referendum, Puerto Ricans strongly favored continuation of commonwealth status. The vote was: commonwealth, 425,081; statehood, 273,315; independence, 4,205.

The Legislative Assembly consists of a Senate and House of Representatives, elected by direct vote every 4 years. Eight senatorial districts elect 2 senators each; 40 representative districts one member each; also 11 senators and 11 representatives at large. Its directly elected resident commissioner in the U.S. Congress has only committee voting privileges. Puerto Ricans were granted American citizenship under the Organic Act of 1917. They do not vote for president unless they move to the U.S., where they come under local laws.

Executive power is vested in a governor elected by direct vote. There are 12 executive departments each headed by a secretary. The judiciary is vested in a Supreme Court and lower courts.

The Commonwealth's "Operation Bootstrap" program for economic development has radically raised the standard of living; per capita income for 1974 was $1,913, up $1,011 from 1969.

Puerto Rico derives its largest income from manufacturing, $1.83 billion in 1974. Products include textiles and apparel, electrical and electronic equipment, plastics, chemicals, petrochemicals, petroleum products, processed foods, metal, leather.

Gross capital investment in 1974 reached $1.63 billion; gross product was $6.81 billion.

Mineral production is mainly of construction materials, with cement accounting for a large part of the value; total value for 1974 was $114 million.

Agriculture, a large source of income, rose in 1974 to $230 million. Income from dairy and livestock products has surpassed that from sugar. Also important are tobacco, coffee, pineapples, coconuts, fruits, garden truck, rum, molasses.

Off-island trade is chiefly with the United States.

	Imports	Exports
1973	$3,496,000,000	$2,465,000,000
1974	$4,262,000,000	$3,339,000,000

The flow of migrants to mainland U.S. after 1945 was reversed in 1963, reversed again in 1970, and in 1974 there was an excess of 18,378 arrivals over departures. These changes are caused mainly by employment conditions, mainland and Puerto Rican. Unemployment on the island is usually over 12%.

San Juan, with its international airport and resort hotels, is the center of the tourism industry. Visitors totaled 1,441,002 in 1974, up from 1,322,258 in 1973, and their spending rose to $360.3 million, up from $317.3 million.

Spanish is the official language but most persons also speak English. Public school education is free and compulsory at the elementary school level; English is taught as a secondary language and is compulsory in all 8 grades. Chief religion is Roman Catholicism.

Puerto Rico (or Borinquen, after the original Arawak Indian name Boriquen) was discovered by Columbus, Nov. 19, 1493. Ponce de Leon conquered it for Spain, 1509, and established the first settlement at Caparra, across the bay from San Juan.

Sugarcane was introduced, 1515, and slaves imported 3 years later. Gold mining petered out, 1570. Spaniards fought off a series of British and Dutch attacks; slavery was abolished, 1873.

Famous Puerto Ricans include Luis Munoz Marin, Dona Felisa Rincon de Gautier, Pablo Casals, Roberto Clemente, Orlando Cepeda, Jose Ferrer, Rita Moreno, Jose Feliciano.

(See also Index for San Juan.)

Canal Zone and Panama Canal

For Panama Canal cargo traffic see Index.

The Canal Zone has been, in effect, a U. S. Government reservation. It is a strip of land extending 5 mi. on each side of the axis of the Canal, under jurisdiction of the U.S. by treaty with the Republic of Panama.

Efforts to change the zone's status have been made by both nations for several years.

The canal connects the Caribbean with the Bay of Panama on the Pacific. Because of the geographic loop made by the Isthmus of Panama, the Caribbean end of the canal, which could be called the eastern end, is actually further west than the Pacific end.

The zone has an area of 553 sq. mi. of which 371 are land. Population (1971 est.) was 45,000. About 11,000 U.S. army, air force, and navy personnel are normally stationed in the zone.

The Canal Zone government and the Panama Canal Co. are the 2 operating agencies, both headed by an individual who acts as governor of the Canal Zone and president of the company. The governor is appointed by the president of the U.S. As governor he reports directly to the secretary of the army. As president of the company he reports to its board of directors, appointed by the secretary of the army. The Canal Zone government maintains civil government. The company operates the canal, the Panama Railroad, and a ship between New Orleans and the Canal Zone.

A French syndicate under Ferdinand de Lesseps failed to complete a canal, 1880-89, and a second French company failed in 1899. The U. S. bought their rights and offered Colombia compensation for a canal zone, but Colombia failed to ratify the treaty, Oct. 1903. Panama declared itself independent of Colombia Nov. 3, 1903, and was recognized by President Theodore Roosevelt Nov. 6. American naval forces discouraged· action by Colombia. On Nov. 18 Panama granted the canal strip to the U.S. by treaty, ratified Feb. 26, 1904, compensation $10 million, with annual payments of $250,000 after 9 years, and a guarantee of Panama independence.

Under terms of the 1903 treaty, Panama granted the U.S. perpetual sovereignty over the Canal Zone.

The canal was opened to traffic Aug. 15, 1914. In 1922, Colombia accepted $25 million from the U. S. plus special land transportation privileges, and agreed to recognize Panama. The U. S. increased its annual payment to Panama to $430,000 and withdrew its guarantee of independence.

A further treaty regulating relations between the U. S. and Panama was signed Jan. 25, 1955, increasing the annuity paid Panama to $1.9 million, increasing it to $2.3 million because of devaluation of the U.S. dollar. In addition, the U. S. gave Panama $28 million worth of real estate and buildings no longer needed by the Canal Zone administration. U. S. citizen and non-citizen employees were guaranteed equality of pay and opportunity. In addition, the U. S. agreed to build the high level bridge over the Pacific entrance to the canal, opened Oct. 12, 1962, as a link in the Inter-American Highway.

Negotiations for a new treaty began after Panamanian riots protesting the 1903 and 1955 treaties caused the death of 21 Panamanians and 3 U. S. soldiers, Jan. 9, 1964. Preliminary agreement was reached in 1967, but in 1970, after a change of government, Panama declared the proposal unacceptable.

In Mar. 1973, the U. S. vetoed a Panama-backed resolution in the UN Security Council which called on the U. S. and Panama to negotiate a new treaty to "guarantee full respect for Panama's effective sovereignty over all its territory." The U. S. said it wished to negotiate with Panama "without outside pressure."

In Feb. 1974, U. S. and Panama representatives agreed on principles for negotiating a new treaty which would set a date for giving Panama jurisdiction over the canal area but give the U. S. the right to operate and protect the canal for a certain period, with Panama sharing in the revenues, until a date set for final transfer to Panama.

Virgin Islands

CAPITAL: Charlotte Amalie, on St. Thomas Is. AREA: 133 sq. mi. POPULATION: (1975 est.) 100,000. FLOWER: Yellow cedar.

The Virgin Islands of the United States, an unincorporated territory administered by the Interior Dept., lie to the E of Puerto Rico at the western end of the Lesser Antilles, 1,629 mi. SE of New York. There are about 100 islands in the Virgins, of which more than 50 islands and islets in the western area belong to the U.S.; the remainder are the British Virgin Islands.

The 3 largest and most populous of the U.S. islands are St. Croix, St. Thomas, and St. John. Formerly the Danish West Indies, the islands were purchased by the U.S. from Denmark for $25 million (effective Mar. 31, 1917) for defense purposes. The islands were discovered by Columbus in 1493. About 80% of the population is of Negro descent.

Mean winter temperature is 78°; summer, 82°.

Virgin Islands National Park occupies about three-fourths of St. John, smallest of the 3 principal islands.

The inhabitants have been citizens of the U.S. since 1927. Legislation originates in a unicameral house of 15 senators, elected for 2 years.

The governor, formerly appointed by the president of the U.S., was elected for the first time under a 4-year term in Nov. 1970 and took office Jan. 4, 1971. In 1972 a U.S. law gave the Virgin Islands one delegate to the U.S. House of Representatives; the delegate may vote in committee but not on the House floor.

Tourism is the largest industry, but it was hurt by a series of murders in 1973 and early 1974. Principal exports are watch movements, jewelry, rum, wool textile products, thermometers, bay rum.

Minor Caribbean Islands

Quita Sueno Bank, Roncador Cay, Serrana Bank and Seranilla Bank lie in the Caribbean between Nicaragua and Jamaica. They are uninhabited. They were to be turned over to Colombia under a 1972 agreement, but this still awaited U.S. Senate ratification in mid-1975.

Navassa lies between Jamaica and Haiti, covers about 2 sq. mi., is reserved by the U.S. for a lighthouse and is uninhabited.

American Samoa

CAPITAL: Pago Pago, Island of Tutuila. AREA: 76 sq. mi. POPULATION: (1974 est.) 30,000. MOTTO: Samoa Muamua Le Atua — In Samoa, God Is First.

Blessed with spectacular scenery and delightful South Seas climate, American Samoa is the most southerly of all lands under U. S. ownership. It is an unincorporated territory consisting of 6 small islands of the Samoan group: Tutuila (where Pago Pago, the capital, lies by a crescent bay beneath tall mountains), Aunuu, the Manua Islands (Tau, Olosega and Ofu), and Rose. Also administered as part of American Samoa is Swain's Is., 210 mi. to the NW, acquired by the U.S. in 1925. The islands are 2,300 mi. SW of Hawaii.

American Samoa became U. S. territory by a treaty with the United Kingdom and Germany in 1899, confirmed by local chiefs in 1900 and 1904. Pago Pago had been a U.S. navy coaling station under an 1872 commercial treaty.

Western Samoa, comprising the larger islands of the Samoan group, was a New Zealand mandate and UN Trusteeship until it became an independent nation Jan. 1, 1962. (See Index.)

Tutuila has an area of 52 sq. mi. Tau has an area of 17 sq. mi., and the islets of Ofu and Olosega 5 sq. mi., with a population of a few thousand. Swain's Island has nearly 2 sq. mi. and about 100 population. Highest peak is Lata, on Tau Is., 3,056 ft.

About 70% of the land is forest. Chief products and exports are fish products, copra, and handicrafts. Taro, bread-fruit, yams, coconuts, pineapples, oranges, and bananas are also produced.

Formerly under jurisdiction of the navy, since July 1, 1951, it has been administered by the Interior Dept., which appoints a governor and a lieutenant governor. It has a bicameral legislature and an elected delegate to represent the territory before U.S. agencies in Washington.

The American Samoans are of Polynesian origin. They are nationals of the U. S.

Wake, Midway, Other Islands

Wake Island, and its sister islands, Wilkes and Peale, lie in the Pacific Ocean on the direct route from Hawaii to Hong Kong, about 2,000 mi. W of Hawaii and 1,290 mi. E of Guam. The group is 4.5 mi. long, 1.5 mi. wide, and totals less than 3 sq. mi. Population (1970 census) was 1,647.

The U.S. flag was hoisted over Wake Island, July 4, 1898, by Gen. F. V. Greene, commanding 2d Detachment, Philippine Expedition. Formal possession was taken Jan. 17, 1899; Wake has been administered by the U.S. air force since 1972.

The **Midway Islands,** acquired in 1867, consist of 2, **Sand** and **Eastern,** in the North Pacific 1,150 mi. NW of Hawaii, with area of about 2 sq. mi., administered by the Navy Dept. Population (1970 census) was 2,220.

Johnston Atoll, SW of Hawaii, is under air force control, and **Kingman Reef,** S of Hawaii, is under navy control.

Howland, Jarvis, and **Baker Islands** south of the Hawaiian group, uninhabited since World War II, are under the Interior Dept.

Palmyra is an atoll SW of Hawaii, 4 sq. mi. Privately-owned, it has been under the Interior Dept. since 1961.

Guam

The World Almanac is sponsored on Guam by the Pacific Daily News, 90 O'Hara St., Agana, GU 96910; phone 777-9711; successor in 1970 to Guam Daily News; circulation throughout Micronesia, 20,350; a Gannett newspaper; president and publisher Robert E. Udick, editor Joe Murphy, managing editor George Blake.

CAPITAL: Agana. AREA: 212 sq. mi. POPULA-TION: (1974 est.) 100,000.

Guam, the largest of the Mariana Islands, now an unincorporated territory, was ceded to the U.S. by Spain in the treaty of Paris, Dec. 10, 1898. It is 30 mi. long and 4 to 8½ mi. wide. Distance from Manila, 1,499 mi.; from San Francisco, 5,053 mi. Mean annual temp. is 81°, average annual rainfall, July to Sept., 70 in. The island is volcanic and mountains rise 700 to 1,329 ft. Highest peak is Mt. Lamlam.

Magellan discovered the group of islands, Mar. 6, 1521, and called them the Ladrones (thieves). They were colonized in 1668 by Spanish missionaries who renamed them the Mariana Islands in honor of Maria Anna, queen of Spain.

When Spain ceded Guam to the U. S., it sold the other Marianas to Germany. Japan obtained a League of Nations mandate over the German islands in 1919; in Dec. 1941 it seized Guam; the island was retaken by the U. S. in July 1944. Guam has navy and air force bases.

Guam is under the jurisdiction of the Dept. of the Interior. It is administered under the Organic Act of 1950, which provides for a governor, a 21-member unicameral legislature, elected biennially by the residents, who are American citizens but do not vote for president.

Beginning in Nov. 1970, Guamanians elected their own governor, previously appointed by the U.S. president. He took office in Jan. 1971. In 1972 a U.S. law gave Guam one delegate to the U.S. House of Representatives; the delegate may vote in committee but not on the House floor.

School attendance is compulsory. The University of Guam provides higher education. English is the official language. Chief religion is Roman Catholicism.

The Guamanians are of primarily Chamorro (Micronesian) stock, with some of mixed Spanish or Filipino descent.

Copra, fish, and handicraft products are exported. Tourism has become a major aspect of Guam's economy. Over 125,000 tourists, most from Japan, visit annually.

Islands Under Trusteeship
Carolines, Marianas, Marshalls

The U. S. Trust Territory of the Pacific Islands, also called Micronesia, includes 3 major archipelagoes; the **Caroline Islands, Marshall Islands,** and **Mariana Islands** (except **Guam:** see above). There are 2,141 islands, 98 of them inhabited; land area total 717 sq. mi. but the islands are scattered over 3 million sq. mi. of Micronesia in the western Pacific N of the Equator and E of the Philippines. Total pop. est. (1974) at 115,000.

In 1885, many of the islands were claimed by Germany. Others, held by Spain, were sold to Germany at the time of the Spanish-American War, 1898. After the outbreak of World War I, Japan took over the islands and, after that war, League of Nations mandates over them were awarded to Japan.

After World War II, the United Nations assigned them (1947) as a Trust Territory to be administered by the U.S. They were placed under administration of the U.S. Interior Dept. in 1951.

There is a high commissioner, appointed by the U.S. president. Saipan is the headquarters of the administration. The Congress of Micronesia, an elected legislature with limited powers, held its first meeting in 1965. It has a Senate of 12 members and a House of Representatives of 21.

In 1969, a commission of the Congress of Micronesia recommended that Micronesia be given internal self-government in free association with the U.S.

A U.S. offer of commonwealth status, similar to Puerto Rico's, was rejected by Micronesian leaders in 1970.

In 1974 talks, tentative agreement was reached on parts of a U. S. plan for self-government for the Marshalls and Carolines in free association with the U. S. (which would be responsible for foreign affairs and defense).

The people of the "northern" Mariana Islands (all except Guam) voted June 17, 1975, to become a commonwealth of the U.S., 78.5% approving the step and asking the U.S. Congress to agree. It would give the islands federal aid benefits, and military bases for the U.S. The 14 islands comprise 246 sq. mi.; population in 1972 was 13,381, mostly Roman Catholic Micronesians.

Among the noted islands are: **Saipan** and **Tinian** in the Marianas, scene of bitter fighting when they were taken by the U. S. from Japan in World War II; the former Japanese strongholds of **Palau, Peleliu, Truk** and **Yap** in the Carolines; **Bikini** and **Eniwetok,** where U.S. nuclear tests were staged, and **Kwajalein,** another World War II battle scene, all in the Marshalls.

Many of the islands are volcanic with luxuriant vegetation; others are of coral formation. Only a few are self-sustaining. Principal exports are copra, trochus shells, fish products, handicrafts, and vegetables.

Disputed Pacific Islands

In the central Pacific, S and SW of Hawaii, lie 25 islands and atolls claimed by the U.S.; 18 of them are also claimed by the United Kingdom, and 7 by New Zealand. All are S of the Equator except Christmas Island.

Those claimed by the UK are:

The **Line Islands,** S of Hawaii, including Christmas, Flint, Malden, Starbuck, and Vostok Islands and Caroline Atoll; only Christmas is inhabited. All are administered by the UK

Also, the **Phoenix Islands,** SW of Hawaii, including Canton and Enderbury Islands, and Birnie, Gardner, Hull, McKean, Sydney, and Phoenix Atolls. All are inhabited and administered by the UK except for Canton and Enderbury which are under joint U.S. and UK administration. A U.S. missile-tracking station on Canton was discontinued in Dec. 1967.

Also, the **Ellice Islands,** further to the SW, including Funafuti, Nukufetau and Nukulailai Atolls and Nurakita; all inhabited and all administered by the UK.

Those claimed by New Zealand are:

The **Tokelau (Union) Islands,** S of the Phoenix group, including Nukunono, Atafu, and Fakaofu Atolls. All are inhabited and administered by New Zealand.

Also, the **Northern Cook Islands,** E of the Tokelaus, including Danger, Manahiki, Rakahanga, and Penrhyn (Tongareva) Atolls. All are inhabited and administered by New Zealand.

NORTH AMERICAN CITIES

Their History, Business and Industry, Educational Facilities, Cultural Advantages, Tourist Attractions and Transportation

Akron, Ohio

The World Almanac is sponsored in the Akron area by the Akron Beacon Journal, 44 E. Exchange St., Akron, OH 44328; (216) 375-8111; founded 1809; circulation 172,971 daily, 211,833 Sunday; John S. Knight, president and editorial chairman; Ben Maidenburg, publisher; Mark Ethridge, vice president and editor; Robert Giles, exec. editor; William Ott, vice president and general manager.

Population: 277,650 (city); 716,710 (metro), 5th in state; total employed, 270,000; 1974 average metro household buying income, $14,138.

Area: 56 sq. mi. (city), 413 sq. mi. (metro); on Ohio Canal 30 mi. south of Lake Erie; founded 1825; Summit County seat.

Industry: approx. $2 billion value added by Akron area mfg. industry in 1974; home plants of Firestone, Goodyear, Goodrich, General and many smaller rubber firms employ 37,000, use 40% of entire world rubber supply; other products mfd. in area include auto bodies, salt, clay, matches, rubber toys, road building equipment, missile components.

Transportation: Akron-Canton Airport served by 3 major carriers; Akron Muni Airport; 9 rail and trunk lines; birthplace of trucking industry, served by 113 motor carriers and 58 contract carriers; metro transit system; Greyhound and Continental Trailways services on interstate highway systems.

Communications: 5 TV, one cablevision and 5 radio stations.

New construction: new $16 million Ohio Edison Co. headquarters and $80 million Innerbelt Freeway system.

Federal facilities: new $17 million downtown Federal

Office Bldg.; Army Reserve Center; Navy-Marine Reserve Center.

Medical facilities: 7 major hospitals including specialized children's treatment center; State of Ohio Fallsview Mental Health Center.

Education: University of Akron, Kent State University, Firestone Conservatory of Music.

Sports: NBA Cleveland Cavaliers, WHA Crusaders and WTT Nets in nearby Richfield Township; Firestone Country Club, home of the World Series of Golf, American Golf Classic and site of the 1975 PGA championship; 35,000-seat Akron Rubber Bowl; Derby Downs, home of the All-American Soap Box Derby.

Cultural attractions: E. J. Thomas Performing Arts Center; Blossom Music Center; Stan Hywet mansion; Akron Art Institute; Akron Symphony Orchestra.

Other attractions: Children's Zoo; John Brown Home; Simon Perkins Mansion; Railway Museum.

Accommodations: Nearly 2,000 rooms in downtown hotels and motels.

Further information: Akron Regional Development Board, Delaware Bldg., 44308, or Akron Convention Bureau Inc., 2600 First National Tower, 44308.

Albany, New York

The World Almanac is sponsored in the Albany-Schenectady-Troy area by The Times-Union and Knickerbocker News-Union Star, 645 Albany-Shaker Road, Albany, N.Y. 12201; (518) 453-5454; Times-Union founded 1856; Knickerbocker News 1843; Union-Star 1855; circulation Times-Union (morn) 77,373, Sunday Times-Union 140,-865, Knickerbocker News-Union Star (aft) 65,241, publisher Robert J. Danzig.

Population: 115,781 (city), 286,742 (county); total employed 99,047.

Area: 19.6 sq. mi. on west bank of Hudson River, 150 miles north of New York City; state capital and Albany County seat.

Industry: chief products are felts, woolen goods, meat products, paper products, iron and brass castings, drugs and medicines; 295 manufacturing firms.

Commerce: 5 savings banks, 9 commercial banks.

Transportation: 2 major freight lines; 4 airlines at Albany County Airport; New York State Thruway, Adirondack Northway; Port of Albany.

Communications: 4 TV and 11 radio stations.

Medical facilities: 5 major hospital complexes including a Veteran's Administration installation.

Cultural facilities: Albany Symphony Orchestra, art museum, 90 church buildings, city libraries.

Educational facilities: Albany Law School, Albany College of Pharmacy, Albany Medical College, the State University of New York at Albany, Siena College, Saint Rose College, Albany Junior College and Maria College; 24 elementary schools, 2 senior high schools, 25 private and parochial schools.

New construction: Albany is in the midst of a major revamping of its downtown area. The $1-billion South Mall includes a 44-story state office tower, 4 large state agency buildings, as well as cultural buildings.

Recreational facilities: municipal golf course, private clubs, 2 large city parks with tennis, baseball, swimming facilities.

Other attractions: Dudley Observatory, Fort Crailo in Rensselaer, Joseph Henry Memorial Building, Ten Broeck Mansion, First Church in Albany (Reformed), Schuyler Mansion, State Capitol.

Government: 2d only to Washington, Albany is the most important governmental city in the U.S.; home city of the governor, state officials and 30,000 state employees.

History: founded 1609 when Henry Hudson terminated his voyage in the Half Moon at the location where Albany was later settled by the Dutch.

Bicentennial plans: parade, June 12, 1976; Tulip Festival May 8, 1976; State Barge visitation, July 1-4, 1976.

Further information: Albany Chamber of Commerce, 508 Broadway, Albany, N.Y. 12207.

Albuquerque, New Mexico

The World Almanac is sponsored in the Albuquerque area by the Albuquerque Tribune, 701 Silver Ave. SW, Albuquerque, N.M. 87103; (505) 842-2300; founded June 22, 1922, by Carl Magee; a Scripps-Howard Newspaper since Sept. 24, 1923; circulation 41,450; editor Ralph Looney; sponsors Tribune Annual Spelling Bee.

Population: 286,300 (city), 361,400 (metro area); first in state, 58th in nation; total employed, 159,200.
Area: 81 sq. mi. on Rio Grande and U.S. 66. Bernalillo County seat.
Industry: electronics with Singer, GTE-Lenkurt, Gulton, Sparton Sandia Laboratories, General Electric; clothing with Levi Strauss, Pioneer Wear; movie production center.
Commerce: retail sales $1.35 billion; per capita income $4,374; bank resources $1.39 billion in 10 banks.
Transportation: Santa Fe Railway, Amtrak, Continental Trailways and Greyhound bus lines; Albuquerque Intl. Airport, hub for 7 airlines, average 594 air movements daily.
Communications: 4 TV and 18 radio stations.
Federal facilities: Kirtland AF Base, Air Force Special Weapons Center, Air Force Weapons Laboratory; Bureau of Indian Affairs, Forest Service, Social Security.
Medical facilities: 9 major hospitals.

Cultural facilities: symphony orchestra, 26 art galleries, 4 museums, 8 library branches.
Educational facilities: Univ. of N.M., Univ. of Albuquerque, 117 public schools.
Recreational facilities: Sandia Peak Ski Area with longest tramway in North America; 80 city parks, 16 swimming pools, 9 golf courses, 83 tennis courts; Cibola National Forest; Rio Grande Zoo.
Convention facilities: $9.2 million convention center with underground parking facility and 300-room hotel; 118 motels and hotels.
Sports: Dukes AAA baseball.
History: founded Feb. 7, 1706; named for Duke of Albuquerque, viceroy of New Spain.
Bicentennial plans: Heritage '76 program to rediscover New Mexico's history; dramatic historical presentations; musical festival; new center for performing arts and recreation.
Further information: Chamber of Commerce, 401 Second NW.

Allentown, Pennsylvania

The World Almanac is sponsored in the Allentown-Bethlehem-Easton area by Call-Chronicle Newspapers, 101 N. 6th St., Allentown, 18105; (215) 433-4241; Call founded 1883, daily circulation 103,000, Sunday 149,000; Chronicle founded 1870, circulation 23,000; publisher Donald P. Miller, executive editor Edward D. Miller; sponsors Park & Shop, housing development, newspaper-in-the-classroom, newsprint recycling.

Population: Allentown 109,871; Bethlehem 72,686; Easton 30,256; metro area 543,620, 3d in state; total employed 229,934.
Area: 5,000 sq. mi. (metro) in eastern Pa. at Lehigh and Delaware rivers; Lehigh County seat.
Industry: Bethlehem Steel Corp., 2d largest in U.S.; home offices for Mack Truck Inc., Air Products & Chemicals, New Jersey Zinc Co., Allen Products (ALPO); area leads in textile production; transistor developed in Western Electric here.
Commerce: retail center for east-central Pa.; retail sales (1972) $970 million; average family buying power $11,647.
Transportation: 3 major rail lines, 5 bus lines; 9 federal and state highways intersect area; jet airport averages 335 movements per day on 6 airlines.
Communications: 3 TV and 12 radio stations.
Medical facilities: 6 major hospitals.
Cultural facilities: Allentown Art Museum (including Kress Renaissance and Baroque collection), Bethlehem Bach Choir, Allentown Symphony, 7 theater groups (plus 4 summer); Allentown Band is oldest

continuing concert band in U.S.; 10 colleges including Lehigh Univ., Muhlenberg, Cedar Crest and Lafayette serve 12,000 students.
Other attractions: center of "Pennsylvania Dutch" area, covered bridges; 1,400-acre park system; 1,170-acre game preserve, pre-Cambrian mountain range, access to Appalachian Trail, many historic houses, Allentown Fair, folk festivals, Liberty Bell Shrine.
Sports: fishing, small game hunting, auto racing at Pocono Raceway, Allentown Jets basketball.
History: settled in 1600s by Germans seeking religious freedom; Allentown founded 1762; hiding place for Liberty Bell during Revolutionary War; GAR founded Flag Day here 1906; Allentown one of 5 First Defender Companies in Civil War.
Bicentennial plans: Festival of Bands Feb. 23; 13 Colonies Band Contest June 14-18; re-enactment of Liberty Bell trek from Philadelphia in 1777, Sept. 19-25.
Further information: Chambers of Commerce in Allentown: 462 Walnut St. (18105); Bethlehem: 11 W. Market St. (18018); Easton: 157 S. 4th St. (18042).

Amarillo, Texas

The World Almanac is sponsored in the Amarillo area by the Amarillo Globe-News, 900 S. Harrison, Amarillo, Tex., 79166, (806) 376-4488; a division of Southwestern Newspapers Corp., and publisher of Daily News, Globe-Times and Sunday News-Globe; daily circulation, 76,210; Sunday 71,190; James L. Whyte, vice president and general manager; Jerry Huff, executive editor.

Population: 142,548 city; 161,959 metro area; 11th in state; total employed 70,140.
Area: 68.98 sq. mi. in Central Texas Panhandle at junction of Interstates 40 and 27 in Potter and Randall counties. Potter County seat.
Industry: 3-state hub of $8 billion agribusiness market including wheat, beef and produce, value $20 million; American Smelting & Refining copper plant; Santa Fe rail welding plant; Bell Helicopter, Levi Strauss, Iowa Beef Processors, oil and gas, coal-burn-

ing power plants.
Commerce: wholesale-retail center for 5-state area; retail sales $494.5 million 1974; bank resources $622.9 million, 9 banks, 5 savings and loan associations; 104th in wholesale sales ($729.9 million) among 230 metro areas.
Transportation: served by 5 airlines; 3 railroads, 4 bus lines, 22 truck lines; 2 interstate, 4 federal and one state highway intersect Amarillo.
Communications: 4 TV, 6 radio stations.

Medical: 5 hospitals in metro area including VA facility, mental health centers.

Culture, recreation: Amarillo Symphony; Fine Arts Complex; Civic Center complex; summer musical, "Texas"; area historical museum; Discovery Center; Worlds of Nature zoological-botanical gardens; 46 parks, 3 colleges.

Sports: drag racing, college and high school football,

basketball.

History: settled 1887 as railroad crew camp, incorporated 1892; named for yellow lake clay.

Bicentennial plans: area-wide festival series, June 11-July 4, 1976.

Further information: Amarillo Chamber of Commerce, Amarillo Bldg., 301 Polk, Amarillo, Tex. 79101.

Anchorage, Alaska

The World Almanac is sponsored in the Anchorage area by the Anchorage Daily Times, 820 W. 4th Avenue, Ancrage, AK 99510; (907) 279-5622; founded 1915; circulation 45,000; editor-publisher Robert B. Atwood; sponsors Spelling Bee, Airline Ski Races, Kodak Photo Contest.

Population: 84,290 (1975), largest in state; 168,500 in Greater Anchorage, nearly half of Alaska's population.

Area: 927 sq. mi. (census district), at head of Cook Inlet on south central coast.

Industry and commerce: business center for most of Alaska; aviation, oil companies, railroading, shipping and national defense activities are largest elements in area's economy; headquarters for construction of $4.5 billion trans-Alaska oil pipeline.

Transportation: Anchorage International Airport is major refueling stop on transpolar flights; thousands of small planes make city one of country's busiest air traffic centers with 5 airports and 25% of world's seaplanes in area; headquarters of Alaska Railroad; $10 million port.

Communications: 4 TV and 7 radio stations; 2 daily newspapers.

Medical facilities: 5 hospitals.

Cultural facilities: Annual Festival of Music; 4 theater groups; fine arts museum; community concert organization, opera company, civic symphony.

Educational facilities: 56 elementary and secondary schools enroll 35,600; Univ. of Alaska, Alaska Methodist Univ.

Recreation: 2 major ski areas; cross-country skiing and bicycling; annual Fur Rendezvous with dogsled races; Iditarod dogsled race to Nome; Chugach National Forest.

Convention facilities: 5 major hotels and motels offer facilities for over 1,000 persons.

History: founded 1915 as headquarters for Alaska Railroad; twice winner of All America city award, for coping with rapid growth, and for swift recovery from catastrophic 1964 earthquake.

Further information: Chamber of Commerce, 612 F St. (99501).

Bicentennial plans: community cultural complex; Far North Bicentennial Park; erection of statue of Capt. James Cook, explorer.

Atlanta, Georgia

Population: 474,600 (city), 1,732,500 (metro), first in state, 18th in nation; total employed, 756,400 (metro).

Area: 136 sq. mi. in north central Georgia, on Piedmont plateau of Blue Ridge foothills, 1,050 ft. above sea level; 4,326 sq. mi. in 15-county metro area.

Industry: over 2,000 manufacturers produce more than 3,500 commodities; 432 of Fortune 500 firms operate in Atlanta; Ford assembly plant, 2 GM assembly plants, Lockheed-Ga. Co.; home base for Coca-Cola, Fuqua Ind., Delta Air Lines, Retail Credit, Scripto, Genuine Parts.

Commerce: financial, retail, wholesale center of Southeast; annual metro retail sales over $4.7 billion (1974); massive Merchandise Mart; 6th Federal Reserve District hdqtrs.; 83 banks, 263 branches with resources of $8.7 billion (metro); 23 savings and loan associations with assets of $3.2 billion.

Transportation: founded as railroad center, now served by 6 systems; Greyhound and Trailways bus terminals used by 5 companies carrying over 14,000 passengers daily; 9 passenger airlines, 3 commuter carriers, one freight-only carrier; more than 1,100 scheduled flights daily; non-stop service to 93 cities from Hartsfield International Airport, 25,605,742 passengers (1974); approved rapid transit system to have 50 mi. of high speed rail, 14 mi. of busways coordinated with street bus operations; 6 legs of 3 interstate highways intersect 100-acre downtown interchange; 63 mi. highway encircles city.

Communications: 7 TV stations; 43 radio stations; Protestant Radio and TV Center; largest Bell system toll-free dialing area; one of nation's 5 TV and radio network control centers; 9 daily newspapers.

New construction: boom in luxury hotels, office towers and parks; condominiums; total value 1974 city building permits $164.2 million; metro private construction, $649.7 million.

Medical facilities: 58 hospitals (metro), VA hospital; National Center for Disease Control, National Cancer Center at Emory Univ. Medical School.

Federal facilities: 27,600 federal employees; Ft. McPherson, hdqtrs. U.S. Army Forces Command; Ft. Gillem; Dobbins A.F. Base; NAS Atlanta.

Cultural facilities: Memorial Arts Center with museum, symphony orchestra, ballet, School of Art; Civic Center with auditorium-theater-exhibition hall; 24 degree-granting schools including Ga. Tech., Ga. State Univ., Emory Univ., Atlanta Univ.

Sports: NBA Hawks; NFL Falcons; NL Braves; NHL Flames; Stadium seats 52,000, Omni arena, 16,500.

Convention facilities: 568,000 delegates attended 713 conventions in 1974.

History: named 1845, chartered 1847; burned by Gen. Wm. Sherman 1864.

Further information: Chamber of Commerce, 1300 Commerce Building, Atlanta, 30303.

Augusta, Georgia

The World Almanac is sponsored in the Augusta area by The Chronicle-Herald, 725 Broad St., 30903; (404) 724-0851; Chronicle established in 1785, circulation 50,000; Herald 20,000; Sunday, 72,000; William S. Morris III publisher, E.B. Skinner general manager, L.C. Harris editor, David L. Playford managing editor Herald, W.H. Eanes, managing editor Chronicle.

Population: 55,600 (city), 277,200 (metro area); total employed, 101,300 (metro).

Area: 1,713 sq. mi. (metro: Richmond, Columbia

counties, Ga.; Aiken County, S.C.) straddling Savannah River; Augusta County Seat.

Industry: diversified; Continental Can, Du Pont,

Procter & Gamble, Lily-Tulip, Olin, Dymo, Monsanto.
Commerce: wholesale, retail center of 17 counties in
2 states; 1974 retail sales, $658,873,000; per capita income, $3,638; per family income, $12,178; effective
buying income. $1,008,317; 4 banks, 3 savings-loan
assns.; distribution center.

Transportation: 5 railroads, 26 truck lines, 3 airlines
at modern airport and in-city field for executive
planes; Interstate 20, other federal highways; river
shipping.

Communications: 3 TV and 10 radio stations.
Medical facilities: 5 major hospitals, including Eisen-

hower Memorial at Ft. Gordon, Medical College of
Georgia.
Federal facilities: Ft. Gordon and Savannah River
(AEC) Plant.
Cultural facilities: Augusta College, Paine College;
museum, art gallery, arts council with 25 affiliates.
Recreational facilities: hunting, fishing, boating,
camping; 7 golf courses; home of Masters Golf
Tournament.
History: founded as fort 1717; named for wife of
Prince of Wales 1735; capital of Georgia, 1778.
Further information: Chamber of Commerce of
Greater Augusta, 624 Greene St., Augusta, Ga. 30902.

Austin, Texas

The World Almanac is sponsored in the Austin area by The Austin American-Statesman, 308 Guadalupe St.,
Austin, Texas, 78701; (512) 476-2661; Statesman founded 1871; American 1914; combined 1924; published by
Newspapers, Inc.; circulation, American-Statesman (morn.) 70,874. American-Statesman (aft.) 38,320. American-
Statesman (Sunday) 115,248. Harlon M. Fentress chairman of the board emeritus, Pat Taggart chairman of the
board, Richard F. Brown president and publisher, Tim Brown executive vice president, Sam Wood editor, Bill Mero-
ney general manager.

Population: 283,700 (city), 334,000 (metro area), 6th
in state, 56th in nation; total employed 158,500.
Area: 91 sq. mi. in mid-Texas on Colorado River.
Industry: electronics — Texas Instruments, IBM,
Motorola, Tracor; Glastron (Conroy) boats, Westing-
house Electric; county has 360 manufacturing firms.
Commerce: wholesale, retail center for 10 counties
(750,000 pop.) in triangle of Dallas-Fort Worth, San
Antonio, Houston; retail sales (1972) $616,000,000;
bank assets $1.4 billion in 14 banks; 7 savings associa-
tions with assets $442 million; 33 insurance home of-
fices.
Transportation: 3 airlines; 3 railroads, Amtrak; 4 bus
lines; 13 motor freight carriers; U.S. Interstate 35,
State 71, 79, 183, 290.
Communications: 4 TV and cable, 12 radio stations.
Medical facilities: 7 hospitals, 1,032 beds; 389 physi-
cians; 174 dentists.
Federal facilities: Bergstrom AFB; Internal Revenue
Service center with 3,300 employees.
Cultural facilities: University of Texas System & UT
at Austin; Lyndon Baines Johnson Library dedicated

1971 with 1,700,000 visitors in 2 years; other libraries; Texas Memorial & Art Museums; 85,000-seat
stadium; law and other graduate schools; 4 small colleges. O. Henry Home, Laguna Gloria, Elizabet Ney &
French Legation museums; 4 local theater companies, Austin Symphony, 2 ballet companies; City library, branches and mobile service. Austin public
school district, 76 schools, 55,000 students.
State facilities: Capitol and office building complex;
5 special schools for handicapped; psychiatric hospital, 36,578 employes.
Convention facilities: city center seats 5,000.
Recreational facilities: 2 lakes; 7,000 acres of parks,
pools, 6 golf courses, tennis courts; 3 annual fiestas:
Aqua (motor boat racing), Laguna Gloria, and Highland Lakes arts and crafts.
Bicentennial plans: Horizon 76 Program, a plan to
preserve, restore and enhance the waterways of Aus-
tin.
Further information: Chamber of Commerce, 901 W.
Riverside Dr., Austin, Texas 78701.

Bakersfield, California

The World Almanac is sponsored in the Bakersfield and Kern County area by The Bakersfield Californian (eves. and
Sunday), 1707 Eye Street, Bakersfield, Cal. 93302, phone 805-323-7631; founded 1866 as Havilah Courier, christened
The Bakersfield Californian 1897; circulation 54,970 daily, 59,150 Sunday; president Berenice Fritts Koerber, publisher
Donald H. Fritts, executive director Alfred T. Fritts, managing editor James E. Griffith.

Population: 76,200 city, 192,350 metro, 345,800 Kern
County.
Area: approximately 8,060 square miles in Kern
County of which Bakersfield is county seat; in Cali-
fornia's San Joaquin Valley.
Industry: oil, gas, agriculture, military; oil valuation
$350,300,000; total agriculture production $706,685,-
000; Edwards AFB and China Lake Naval Test
Station in eastern Kern County.
Commerce: retail sales in Kern $976,510,000; total
bank deposits $634,797,000.

Transportation: 2 railroads, 3 airlines, 2 bus lines,
Interstate 5, Highway 99.
Communications: 3 TV and 8 radio stations.
Cultural facilities: symphony orchestra, Cunningham
Art Gallery; 4-year state college, city college; community theater.
History: Kern County organized April 2, 1866, from
portions of Los Angeles and Tulare counties. Discovery of gold on Kern River in 1851 brought influx of
settlers. Oil discovered in 1865, with major boom in
1909. Gold mining town of Havilah first county seat,
moved to Bakersfield in 1875.

Baltimore, Maryland

The World Almanac is sponsored in the Baltimore area by the Baltimore News American, 301 E. Lombard St.,
Baltimore, Md. 21203; (301) 752-1212; founded in 1773 as the Maryland Journal and Baltimore Advertiser; Balti-
more American founded 1799; Baltimore Evening News founded 1872; adopted present name 1964; daily circula-
tion, 202,895; Sunday 275,679; publisher Mark F. Collins; general manager Roy W. Anderson; executive editor
Thomas J. White; American Medical Association Award and Albert Lasker Award; sponsors I Am An American Day
Parade.

Population: 862,620 (city), 2,114,230 (metro), 1st in state, 7th in U.S.; total employment 308,000 (city), 851,000 (metro).

Area: 91 sq. mi. (city), 2,225 sq. mi. (metro); on Patapsco River, a tributary of Chesapeake Bay.

Industry: highly diversified, none dominating; most important are steel fabricating, shipbuilding and repairing; manufacture of electrical equipment and food containers; food processing, sugar, petroleum, chemicals, copper; added value of manufacturing in 1974 was $3.8 billion.

Commerce: metro area consists of city and 5 adjacent counties; estimated buying income $4,182 per capita; retail sales about $5 billion in 1974, ranked 16th in metro areas nationally; area has 209 shopping centers with 3,591 stores; home ownership 57%.

Transportation: 3 railroads including Amtrak; Baltimore-Washington International Airport, used by 11 lines, served 2,798,000 passengers in 1974; 150 certified truck lines; tunnel carries motor traffic through city under the harbor; buses operated by state authority carry 410,000 passengers daily.

Port facilities: 120 steamship lines serve port, the nation's 4th largest and the farthest inland on the Atlantic Coast; in 1974, a record 4,193 ships moved 43.4 million tons of international cargo; port was 2d largest container cargo port on the Atlantic and Gulf Coasts; leading cargos are petroleum products, ores, grain, coal, bananas.

Communications: 3 daily newspapers in city, 2 more in metro area; 3 VHF TV stations, 2 UHF public broadcast stations; 25 radio stations.

Cultural facilities: Enoch Pratt Free Library with 31 agencies and 2.2 million volumes; metro county libraries have 28 branches; Baltimore Symphony Orchestra; Maryland Ballet Co.; Baltimore Opera Co.; Walters Art Gallery, Peale Museum, Carroll Mansion, Md. Academy of Sciences, Morris A. Mechanic Theater, and Center Stage.

Educational facilities: 30 colleges and 9 junior colleges, including Johns Hopkins Univ. and medical institutions, Univ. of Md. (downtown and county campuses), Loyola, Goucher, and Towson State colleges, Morgan State Univ.; Peabody Conservatory of Music;

Md. Inst. College of Art; St. Mary's Seminary and Univ.; Ner Israel Rabbinical College.

Medical facilities: 26 general hospitals, with 8,664 beds in metro area, including the renowned Johns Hopkins and the Univ. of Md. and its Institute for Emergency Medicine.

Sports: Memorial Stadium, home of football Colts and baseball Orioles; horse racing, including Preakness at Pimlico, and the International Race at Laurel, Bowie and Timonium tracks nearby. Chesapeake Bay's 1,700 sq. mi. of open water are noted for fishing, boating, and waterfowl hunting; ocean and ski resorts within 3 hours drive.

Convention facilities: Civic Center, 45 meeting rooms, 87,160 sq. ft. of exhibition space; 7 hotels downtown and over 100 motels in or near the city.

Other attractions: Fort McHenry Historic Shrine where Francis Scott Key wrote "The Star Spangled Banner"; U.S. frigate Constellation; the Flag House; Baltimore and Ohio transportation museum; Edgar Allan Poe's home and grave; Babe Ruth's home; annual Preakness Festival Week in May, Mother Seton House, Most of the central business district rebuilt in last 15 years; Inner Harbor project will provide World Trade Center, Academy of Science Building, restoration of early 19th century rowhouses, a floating restaurant, a marina, aquarium, and new hotels. Many old neighborhoods are experiencing a revival with early townhouses being preserved.

History: founded 1729 by act of the Provincial Assembly of the Maryland Colony which was established by members of the Calvert family, the Lords of Baltimore; early economy based on shipment of tobacco, grain, flour, and on shipbuilding; privateering in the War of 1812 tempted British to try to capture the American "nest of pirates." When economic growth was threatened by completion of the Erie Canal, the city's business leaders countered by building the nation's first railroad, the Baltimore and Ohio.

Bicentennial information: Independence Day Festival; Operation Sail Ships featuring sailing vessels July 10 to 14; annual City Fair Sept. 17-19.

Further information: Chamber of Commerce Metro Baltimore, 22 Light St.; Baltimore Promotion Council, 102 St. Paul St., 21202.

Baton Rouge, Louisiana

The World Almanac is sponsored in the Baton Rouge area by the Morning Advocate and State-Times, 525 Lafayette St., B.R., La. 70821; (504) 383-1111; founded 1842; combined daily circ., 106,660; Sunday, 100,713; pres., Charles P. Manship Jr.; publisher, Douglas L. Manship; production dir., Richard Palmer; bus. mgr., Charles Garvey; MEs, Edwin Price Jr. (MA); Jim Hughes (ST).

Population: 165,963 (city); 392,400 (metro); total 1974 city-parish employment, 168,475.

Area: city, 42.83 sq. mi.; parish, 407.01 sq. mi.; on east bank of Mississippi River, 80 mi. northeast of New Orleans; state capital, East Baton Rouge Parish seat.

Industry: northern anchor of 100-mi. long petrochemical complex along Mississippi River.

Commerce: marketing center for major trade area of 400,000; bank resources, $1.6 billion; 6 banks, 7 savings and loan associations.

Transportation: major transfer point on southern federal interstate system; 2 airports with 4 airlines; 2 bus lines; 4 railroad trunk lines; Port of Baton Rouge handled over 55 million tons in 1974.

Communications: 4 TV and 9 radio stations.

Cultural facilities: 6 museums, 4 theaters, symphony, planetarium, 5 art galleries.

Educational facilities: Louisiana State Univ., founded

1860, center of 8-campus system; Southern Univ., largest Negro land-grant college in U.S., center of 3-college system.

Sports: LSU Tigers and Southern Jaguars home stadia, football, basketball, track.

Other attractions: state capitol; city-parish zoo and arboretum, 67 parks; major recreational lakes.

History: first noted by French explorer Iberville in 1699, Baton Rouge (French: red stick) was already occupied by the Istrouma (also translates red stick) Indians; Louisiana's capital since 1836; government structure is a city-parish combination with a mayor-president and city-parish council.

Bicentennial plans: opening of Civic Center and Plaza, food fest, costume ball, parade, entertainment.

Further information: Chamber of Commerce, P.O. Box 1868, Baton Rouge, 70821; Louisiana Tourist Commission, P.O. Box 44291, Capitol Station, Baton Rouge, 70804.

Billings, Montana

The World Almanac is sponsored in the Billings area by the Billings Gazette, 401 N. Broadway, Billings, Mont., 59101; telephone (406) 245-3071; founded 1885; member of Lee Enterprises Inc., since 1960; circulation daily 56,598, Sunday; 57,758; publisher J. S. Hilleboe, editor William N. Roesgen.

Population: 70,666 (city), 85,889 (metro area), first in state; total employed 41,800 (non-agri).

Area: south central Montana on Yellowstone River, 125 mi. from Yellowstone Park, Yellowstone County seat.

Industry: 3 oil refineries, beet sugar refinery, 2 packing plants, 3d largest livestock auction yards in U.S., center for Northern Great Plains coal industry.

Commerce: wholesale-retail center for eastern Montana, northern Wyoming; retail sales (1973) $247 million; bank debits (1974) $4.5 billion; 6 banks, 2 savings and loan associations, 274 wholesale firms, 804 retail firms; per capita income $3,545.

Transportation: 3 airlines, one railroad, 2 bus lines, 98 motor carriers, Interstates 90 and 94.

Communications: 2 TV and 5 radio stations, one weekly, one daily newspaper.

Medical facilities: 2 hospitals, 400 beds, 11 clinics, 128 doctors, 40 dentists.

Cultural facilities: 3 art galleries, symphony orchestra, 2 western museums, studio theater, liberal arts college, business college, private (church-related) college, 2 nursing schools, voc-tech program; 30 public, 8 parochial schools.

New construction: $24 million shopping center, $10 million auditorium, $11 million hospital expansion.

Other attractions: big game hunting, fishing, boating, skiing, within hour's drive; 21 city parks, 3,200 hotel-motel rooms, convention facilities for 5,000.

History: founded 1882 with arrival of Northern Pacific Railroad, named after Frederic Billings, then NP president; now largest city in 500-mile radius.

Further information: Tourist Information Bureau, Billings Chamber of Commerce, P.O. Box 2519, Billings, 59103.

Binghamton, New York

The World Almanac is sponsored in the Binghamton area by The Evening Press and The Sunday Press, Vestal Parkway East, Binghamton, N.Y. 13902; (607) 798-1234; founded 1904; circulation daily 75,529, Sunday 81,144; president and publisher Robert R. Eckert, editor Laurence S. Hale, managing editor George R. Venizelos.

Population: 60,800 (city), 303,500 (metro area), 12th in state; total employed 119,300.

Area: 10.98 sq. mi. at junction of Chenango and Susquehanna Rivers. Broome County seat.

Industry: GAF, second largest producer of film in country; computers, IBM; electronics & simulators, Singer Co.; shoes, Endicott Johnson Corp.; a major railroad center.

Commerce: wholesale-retail center of area producing $490 million a year; 5 banks; national headquarters of Security Mutual Life Insurance Co.

Transportation: 3 airlines, major being Allegheny, out of Broome County Airport; intersection Interstates 81 & 88 and Route 17; Erie-Lackawanna and Delaware and Hudson freight rail carriers.

Communications: 3 TV and 4 radio stations.

Medical facilities: 2 major hospitals.

Cultural facilities: Roberson Center Arts & Sciences; State Univ. at Binghamton; Broome County College; Tri-Cities Opera Co.; symphony orchestra; public library; Civic Theater.

Other attractions: municipal parks zoo; major state park on outskirts; new Veterans Memorial Arena.

Sports: Dusters pro-hockey team.

History: Settled 1800; became rail center by 1848, with roads replacing old Chenango Canal that fed Erie Canal; named for Philadelphia patriot and multi-millionaire William Bingham.

Birmingham, Alabama

The World Almanac is sponsored in the Birmingham area by The Birmingham Post-Herald, 2200 Fourth Ave., N. Birmingham, Ala. 35202; telephone (205) 325-2222; Post founded 1921 by Scripps-Howard Newspaper; Herald founded 1887; circulation, 75,630; editor Duard LeGrand, vice president W. H. Metz, managing editor George Cook; major public service projects include Goodfellow Christmas Fund, Alabama Favorite Teacher selection.

Population: 308,600 (city, 1972 est.), 778,500 (metro area), employment 323,500 (metro).

Area: 82 sq. mi. in north central Alabama; state's largest city; Jefferson County seat.

Industry: heavy manufacturing in metals; U.S. Steel is area's largest employer; U.S. Pipe and Foundry and American Cast Iron Pipe Co. are in top 10 employers; South Central Bell's 5-state headquarters located in city.

Commerce: wholesale-retail center for Alabama; retail sales, (1974) $2.092 billion; bank debits (1974) $55.3 billion; 12 banks (county); 6 bank holding companies; 7 savings and loan assns.

Transportation: 5 major rail freight lines, Amtrak; Greyhound and Continental Trailways bus lines; Eastern, Delta, United, and Southern air lines with modern airport terminal completed in 1973; 75 truck line terminals; 3 interstate highways, I-65, I-59 and I-20 all under construction.

Communications: 3 commercial TV stations, 1 PBS TV outlet and 15 radio stations.

Medical facilities: Univ. of Alabama in Birmingham Medical Center covers 60 sq. blocks; heart surgery team brings patients from all over the world; Veterans Administration hospital, in same complex, is the base of organ transplant program; Baptist Medical Centers have 2 major hospitals; 13 other hospitals.

Cultural facilities: symphony orchestra, Oscar Wells Museum of Art with more than $4 million in assets; Civic Opera; 4 resident civic theaters; 2 resident ballet companies.

Education: Samford Univ., Birmingham-Southern, Miles, and Daniel Payne Colleges; Jefferson State and Lawson State Junior Colleges.

Convention facilities: civic center with exhibition hall, theater and music hall; coliseum under construction; several new convention motels in civic center area.

Sports: Birmingham Vulcans (WFL); nicknamed "Football Capital of the South" for Univ. of Alabama and Auburn Univ. games played at municipal stadi-um, Legion Field; Birmingham A's, farm club of Oakland A's.

Other attractions: world's second largest cast iron statue, Vulcan, mythical god of the forge, overlooks Birmingham from Red Mountain as a symbol of the steel industry; Arlington Shrine, antebellum home that housed federal troops during Civil War; Botanical Gardens complex with Japanese Garden; Jimmie Morgan Zoo; extensive city park system.

History: chartered 1871; soon became known as the "Magic City" because of its rapid growth brought on by the presence of the 3 ingredients in steelmaking — coal, iron ore, and lime; mining died out in recent years and most iron ore is now imported by ship and barge to Birmingham on Warrior River from South America; coal mining, in decline since the 1940s, is on the upswing.

Bicentennial plans: military history exhibit, Festival of Arts, Freedom Train visit, coliseum dedication, special art exhibits.

Bismarck, North Dakota

The World Almanac is sponsored in western North Dakota by The Bismarck Tribune, 222 Fourth St., Bismarck, N.D., 58501; (701) 223-2500; founded 1873 as weekly, became daily 1881; circ. 26,400; publisher A. G. Sorlie, editor John O. Hjelle, advertising director J. Joe Miller; major awards include Pulitzer Prize Gold Medal, 1937.

Population: 37,700, 3d in state; total employed 18,270.

Area: 11 sq. mi. on Missouri River; state capital and Burleigh County seat.

Industry: agriculture, printing, trucking, farm machinery, state government, electric power, manufacturing, concrete products, railroad, insurance, livestock sales rings.

Commerce: retail trade area radius 100 miles, serving 150,000 people; retail sales (1974) $127.2 million; bank deposits (1974) $397.8 million; 4 banks, 4 building and loan associations.

Transportation: 2 railroad trunk lines, one transcontinental; airport, hub for 3 airlines; 13 truck lines; 4 bus lines; U.S. Highways 10, 83 and I-94.

Communications: one daily newspaper; 3 AM, 2 FM radio stations; 2 TV stations.

New construction: 1974 building permits, $22.6 million.

Medical facilities: 2 hospitals, 500 bed capacity, served by 70 M.D.s.

Cultural facilities: Bismarck Junior College; Mary College; Civic Center; 67,000-volume public library; state library.

Recreation: 20 parks with over 1,250 acres; indoor artificial ice arena; YMCA; duck and goose hunting, fishing.

Other attractions: Dakota Zoo; Garrison Dam.

History: founded 1872 as Edwinton, a rail town; name changed to Bismarck in 1873 to bring in German investment capital.

Further information: Chamber of Commerce, 412 Sixth St., Bismarck, 58501.

Bloomington, Illinois

The World Almanac is sponsored in Bloomington-Normal and central Illinois by The Daily Pantagraph, 301 W. Washington St., Bloomington, Ill. 61701; (309) 829-9411; founded 1837 by Jesse W. Fell; circulation 51,747; president and publisher Davis U. Merwin; editor Harold Liston; general manager William Diesel; managing editor Gene F. Smedley.

Population: 77,367 Bloomington-Normal, 114,192 (metro area) McLean County; mid-way between Chicago and St. Louis in central Illinois.

Industry: over 50 industries in county, ranks 9th in insurance cities in U.S., home offices of State Farm, Country Companies, Union Auto; uniform diversity of non-agricultural employment in all major work force areas; leads nation in corn and soybean production with 2,316 farms in county.

Commerce: 1974 metro retail sales $310.6 million; per household income $14,263; per household retail sales, 48th in nation, $8,799.

Transportation: new terminal at B-N Airport, 3 bus lines; 6 federal and state highways, 4 railroads, Amtrak, 35 interstate and 23 intrastate motor carriers, Ozark Airlines.

Communications: 6 radio stations.

Medical facilities: 3 hospitals; Watson-Gailey Foundation Eye Bank.

Cultural facilities: Illinois Wesleyan Univ., 1,650 in Bloomington; Illinois State Univ., 19,000, in Normal; 49 churches; home of American Passion Play; B-N Symphony, community players, amateur musical.

History: incorporated 1850; site of A. Lincoln's "Lost Speech", and David Davis mansion, state historical shrine; city's Stevenson family has produced 3 generations of leadership; vice president Adlai E.; governor, presidential candidate and UN Ambassador, Adlai E. II; and U.S. Senator Adlai E. III.

Bicentennial plans: McLean County Bicentennial Arts Festival in June, 1976.

Further information: Association of Commerce and Industry of McLean County, 210 S. East St., Bloomington, Ill. 61701.

Boise, Idaho

The World Almanac is sponsored in the Boise area by the Idaho Statesman, 1200 N. Curtis Road, Boise, Idaho 83704; (208) 376-2121; founded 1864 as Tri-Weekly; daily circulation 60,282; Sunday 68,764; publisher Robert B. Miller Jr., general manager C. Ralph Guilieri, managing editor Richard P. Hronek; a Gannett newspaper.

Population: 86,800 (city), 120,200 (metro area), 1st in state, 224th in nation; total employed 76,848.
Area: 1,054 sq. mi. on Boise River at foot of Salmon River Mountains. State capital and Ada County seat.
Industry: mobile home and recreational trailers produced $150 million in 1973; world headquarters Boise Cascade Corp., Morrison-Knudsen Co., and Albertson Food Stores.
Commerce: wholesale and retail center for southwest Idaho; retail sales $299.5 million (1974); bank resources $6,980 million in 16 banks with 16 branches; 4 saving and loan associations, and 7 insurance company offices.
Transportation: 2 major airlines, 2 feeder airlines, 1 rail freight line, 4 bus lines, 17 common carrier truck lines.

Communications: 4 TV and 9 radio stations.
Medical facilities: 3 major hospital complexes including a Veteran's Administration facility.
Cultural facilities: Boise Philharmonic Orchestra, art gallery, state museum, Boise Little Theatre, new $1.4 million public library, Boise State University.
Other attractions: 33 parks, Southwestern Idaho Fairgrounds, 2 major recreational lakes, scenic mountain areas.
History: founded 1863; name derived from "les bois" (the trees), a description for area used by French fur trappers in 1811.
Further Information: Boise Chamber of Commerce, P.O. Box 2368, 83701, or Department of Commerce & Development, Idaho Statehouse, 83701.

Boston, Massachusetts

The World Almanac is sponsored in the Boston area by The Boston Globe, a wholly-owned subsidiary of Affiliated Publications, Inc., 135 Morrissey Blvd., Boston, MA 02107; (617) 929-2000; established 1872; combined daily circulation 475,346; Sunday 583,787. Chairman of the board and publisher Wm. Davis Taylor, president William O. Taylor, editor Thomas L. Winship. Four Pulitzer prizes including gold medal for meritorious public service in 1966 and 1975; Sigma Delta Chi; Sidney Hillman; AP Managing Editors meritorious public service award; UPI, University of Missouri and Sevellon Brown memorial (1969, 1974 and 1975) awards. Sponsors Mass. Drama Festival; High School Art Competition, Science Fair, Photo Competition, Newspaper in the Classroom program and Boston Globe Book Festival. In-town offices in historic Old Corner Bookstore, one of locations on Boston's Freedom Trail.

Population: 641,071 (city); 2,899,401 (metro area of 92 cities and towns around Boston); 6th largest metro area in nation; total employed, 266,505.
Area: 50 sq. mi. on Massachusetts Bay; state capital and Suffolk County seat.
Commerce: northeast center for finance and insurance; home for 50 insurance companies and regional hqs. for most U.S. and foreign companies; banking center for New England with total deposits of $12.264 billion (1972); birthplace of mutual fund, accounts for 35% of the nation's mutual fund holdings; retail center for northern New England; median family income $8,133 (city), $11,449 (metro); major electronics industry and publishing center.
Transportation: terminating point for 2 railroads, Penn Central and Boston & Maine; Logan International Airport, operated by Mass. Port Authority, terminal for 38 scheduled airlines, including 10 commuter lines, 8th busiest in world, served 10,750,000 passengers in 1973; Volpe International terminal; 5 interstate highways.
Communications: 2 newspapers; 7 TV and 31 radio stations.
New Construction: John Hancock Tower, Blue Cross-Blue Shield, Mass. Hqs.; Stone & Webster Engineering Hqs.; Federal Reserve Tower; major addition to Sheraton-Boston Hotel; Faneuil Hall Market Area; National Shawmut Bank; West End Residential-Office Complex, Atlantic Ave. waterfront.
Medical Facilities: in terms of dollars invested, health care is Boston's largest industry. Major institutions: Mass. General, Children's & New England Medical Centers, Boston City, Beth Israel, Deaconess Hospitals; Harvard, Boston Univ. & Tufts Medical Schools; Lahey Clinic.
Federal facilities: 50 federal agencies employ 45,700 (military facilities not included.)
Cultural facilities: the "Athens of America"; Boston Public Library includes capacity for 500,000 books on

open shelf, plus large lecture hall; Boston Symphony Orchestra; Boston Pops; Opera Company; Boston Ballet; Museums of Fine Art, of Science, and Hayden Planetarium; New England Aquarium.
Educational facilities: 16 degree-granting institutions in the city and 47 in the metro area, including Harvard, Boston College, Boston Univ., Tufts, M.I.T., Brandeis, Univ. of Mass., Suffolk, Emanuel, Simmons, and Wentworth Inst.
Recreation: 2,327 acres of city recreation area, includes historic Boston Common and Public Garden; Metropolitan District Commission provides extensive facilities, including beaches and harbor islands.
Convention facilities: 49 hotels equipped to handle conventions; exhibition halls include Commonwealth Pier Exhibition Hall with 168,000 sq. ft. and John B. Hynes Veterans Auditorium in Prudential Center with 154,000 sq. ft. and auditorium seating 5,800.
Sports: pro teams include Red Sox (baseball), Celtics (basketball), New England Patriots (football), Bruins (hockey), Astros and Minutemen (soccer) and Lobsters (tennis.)
Other attractions: "The Freedom Trail," a 1½ mile walk through historic Boston; Beacon Hill and Back Bay historical districts; U. S. S. Constitution, "Old Ironsides," oldest commissioned ship in U. S. Navy; reconstruction of Boston Tea Party ship, the "Beaver"
Bicentennial plans: "Citygame," walking tours of historic areas of the city; special audio-visual presentations and attractions.
Nicknames: The Hub (of the Universe), Bean Town.
History: capital city of Commonwealth, founded 1630; from 1770, Boston was scene of many events leading to American Revolution, including Boston Tea Party on Dec. 16, 1773; incorporated Feb. 23, 1822.
Further information: Boston 200 Corp., P. O. Box 1773, Boston 02114, and Boston Chamber of Commerce, 125 High Street, Boston.

Bridgeport, Connecticut

The World Almanac is sponsored in the Bridgeport area by The Bridgeport Post (evening), The Bridgeport Telegram (morning) and The Bridgeport Sunday Post, published by The Post Publishing Co., 410 State Street, Bridgeport, Conn. 06602; (203) 333-0161; circulation Post, 78,574, Telegram, 12,028, Sunday Post, 88,209; John E. Pfriem president and general manager, Leonard E. Gilbert managing editor.

Population: 152,900 (State Health Dept. estimate 1974), 2d in state; planning region, 314,500; 8-town district labor force, 178,500.

Area: 17.5 sq. mi. on north shore of Long Island Sound at mouth of the Pequonnock River.

Industry: "Industrial Capital of Connecticut"; products include tools, metallic cartridges, wiring devices, brass goods, valves, corsets, electrical apparatus and appliances; nearby are Sikorsky Aircraft and Avco Lycoming; General Electric has new corporate headquarters in Fairfield, one mile from city line.

Commerce: retail sales, $406,751,000 (1974); downtown renewal includes completed complex with Gimbels and Sears stores, mall, 2,000-car parking garage, U.S. courthouse; also, 2 new bank buildings, major addition to another; new state courthouse; construction started on downtown residential project.

Transportation: $3 million railroad station opened in 1975, to be connected with planned $7 million multi-transportation center with bus terminal, 1,500-car parking garage. City served by Conn. Turnpike (Interstate 95); historic U.S. 1 (Boston Post Road); 3 airlines at municipal Sikorsky Memorial Airport; Penn Central RR; 2 national bus lines; summer ferry to Port Jefferson, L.I.

Medical facilities: 3 general hospitals, state mental health center; work nearing completion on $5.5 million municipal convalescent hospital, only one of kind in state.

Cultural facilities: Univ. of Bridgeport, Fairfield Univ., Sacred Heart Univ., Housatonic Community College; Museum of Art, Science, Industry; P. T. Barnum museum; symphony orchestra; American Shakespeare theater in adjoining town of Stratford.

Recreational facilities: "The Park City" has 1,200 acres of parks, including Seaside with 2-mile shoreline; zoo; municipal indoor ice-skating rink.

Bicentennial plans: Barnum Festival honoring former mayor and founder of circus, an annual 2-week celebration with largest July 4 weekend parade in the nation, will be a focal point.

Further information: Bridgeport Area Chamber of Commerce, Stratfield Motor hotel, Chapel Street, Bridgeport, 06604.

Buffalo, New York

The World Almanac is sponsored in the Buffalo area by The Courier-Express, 785 Main St., Buffalo, NY 14240; (716) 847-5353; founded 1926, as merger of Courier and Express by William J. Conners Sr.; circulation mornings 127,648, Sunday 278,112; publisher William J. Conners III, asst. to publisher Howard W. Clother; treasurer R. C. Lyons, gen. mgr. Donald J. Maul; sponsors hole-in-one tournament, learn to swim program, ski school, Goodfellows.

Population: 1,349,211 (metro area), 462,768 (city) 2d in state; metro area 24th in U.S.; employment about 500,000 (metro); hub of broad 8 county area with population of 1,758,000.

Area: 49.6 sq. mi. city, 1,567 sq. mi. metro; at western end of N.Y. State on Lake Erie, Niagara River, and U.S.-Can. boundary. Metro area includes cities of Niagara Falls, Lockport, Tonawanda, N. Tonawanda, Lackawanna.

Industry: 1,602 manufacturing establishments, highly diversified; headquarters for National Gypsum, Carborundum, Buffalo Forge, Trico Products, Fisher-Price Toys; large plants for Bethlehem Steel, Chevrolet, Ford, Westinghouse, Union Carbide.

Commerce: wholesale and financial center for western N.Y. area; distribution center for northeastern U.S. and Canada; $6.5 billion in trade between U.S. and Canada handled each year; 9 commercial banks, 3 savings banks, 17 savings and loans.

Transportation: Greater Buffalo Int. Airport served by 4 scheduled airlines with 2.7 million passengers, 141,544 scheduled and non-scheduled flights in 1974; 6 major railroads, 10 freight terminals; about 150 motor carriers; highway system includes New York State Thruway. Direct highway and rail service to all parts of Canada; direct water service to entire Great Lakes-St. Lawrence Seaways system, overseas, and Atlantic seaboard.

Communications: 2 newspapers, 3 additional dailies and one Sunday in surrounding cities; 5 TV and 20 AM and FM radio stations; 5 cable systems.

Cultural facilities: Buffalo Philharmonic in Kleinhans Music Hall; Albright-Knox Art Gallery; Studio Arena theater; Museum of Science; Historical Museum; Zoological Gardens (23 acres); Shaw Festival at Niagara-on-the-Lake, Ontario; Performing Arts Center (Artpark) in Lewiston.

Educational facilities: State Univ. at Buffalo (now building $650 million new campus), State College at Buffalo, Niagara University, Canisius College; 5 other colleges; several 2-year institutions.

Convention facilities: newly rebuilt Memorial Auditorium seats up to 17,000; new Niagara Falls Convention Center seats up to 12,000; additional facilities available at several hotels and motels.

Sports attractions: Bills football (AFL), Sabres hockey (NHL), Braves basketball (NBA); Rich Stadium.

Recreation: abundant facilities for water and winter sports and activities; near to both U.S. and Canada vacationlands.

Other attractions: Niagara Falls and river areas from Buffalo to Lake Ontario; Robert Moses and Adam Beck hydro stations, St. Lawrence Seaway, Welland Canal Locks, Ceramics Center (Niag. Falls), Aquarium (Niag. Falls), Our Lady of Victory Basilica (Lackawanna); Old Fort Niagara; Letchworth and Allegany State Parks.

Bicentennial plans: many interrelated events and exhibits throughout western New York.

Further information: Chamber of Commerce, 238 Main, Buffalo 14202.

Calgary, Alberta, Canada

The World Almanac is sponsored in the Calgary and southern Alberta area by the Calgary Albertan, 830 Tenth Ave., S.W., Calgary, Alberta, T2R OB1; (403) 263-7730; founded 1902; circulation 34,441; publisher Bruce L. Rudd; managing editor Les Buhasz; business manager Al Vogt.

Population: 448,295.
Area: 157 sq. mi., one of Canada's highest cities (elevation 3,440 feet); in foothills of Rocky Mountains, 150 miles north of the Montana-Alberta border.
Industry: over 400 firms directly connected with the oil industry have headquarters in Calgary; also chemical, fertilizer and supply industries, and older agricultural industries; assistance in locating industrial information is provided by Ken Ford, Director, Industrial Development, City Hall, Calgary, Alberta.
Transportation: 2 railways; Greyhound Bus Lines; International Airport served by 6 airlines.
Communications: 3 TV and 6 radio stations; 2 cable TV channels.
Medical facilities: 6 major hospital complexes.
New construction: building permits in 1974 totaled $275,871,730.
Cultural facilities: 2,700-seat auditorium, Glenbow Museum; Allied Arts Centre; centennial planetari-

um; symphony orchestra, live theatre; University of Calgary enrolls over 12,290.
Other attractions: Calgary Exhibition and Stampede in July; Heritage Park reconstructs life in early days; Calgary Zoo and Natural History Park show life-size dinosaurs; 626 ft. rotating Calgary Tower gives panoramic view of city, seats 200 for dining and 300 in observation area.
Sports: every active sport; facilities for hockey, football and curling; Stampeders of Canadian Football League; Cowboys (WHA).
History: began as Mounted Police Outpost; as early as 1885, when the railway arrived, had a population of 1,800; discovery of oil in 1914 at Turner Valley contributed to Calgary's present prominence.
Further information: Chamber of Commerce, 300 Canada Permanent Building, 315 Eighth Ave., S.W.; Calgary Tourist and Convention Bureau, Mewata Park, 1300 Sixth Ave., S.W.

Charleston, West Virginia

The World Almanac is sponsored in the Charleston area by The Charleston Gazette, 1001 Virginia St., E., Charleston, W. Va. 25330; (304) 348-5140; founded 1873 as the Kanawha Chronicle, became The Charleston Gazette 1898; W. E. Chilton III publisher; Harry G. Hoffmann editor; Dallas C. Higbee executive editor.

Population: 71,505 (city), 229,500 (Kanawha County), most populous county in state; county labor force, 85,800.
Area: 29.3 sq. mi. at meeting place of Elk and Kanawha rivers; state capital.
Industry: diversified industrial complex, with coal and chemicals dominating; center for production of limestone, lumber, salt brines, vitreous clays and natural gas; also glass, petroleum products, alloys.
Commerce: Wholesale, retail center for central and southern West Virginia; county retail sales, $713,622,000; average family income, $11,500.
Transportation: 2 rail freight lines, Amtrak, bus lines, state's busiest airport; barge lines, 3 interstate highways.
Communications: 3 TV and 7 radio stations.
Medical facilities: 6 hospitals, 2 of them major complexes.

Cultural facilities: modern civic center and auditorium, Sunrise Cultural and Art Center, symphony orchestra, Community Music Assn., Light Opera Guild, Kanawha Players, State Museum, Morris Harvey College, W. Va. Univ. Graduate Center.
Other attractions: Coonskin Park, Kanawha State Forest, 6 golf courses, public tennis, International League baseball.
History: first settlement, Fort Lee, 1788; Virginia Assembly established Charles Town 1794; named, Charleston 1818.
Bicentennial plans: week-long Downtown Festival, Bicentennial Park along Elk River, new amphitheater in Cato Park; historical and architectural survey by Kanawha Valley Historical Society.
Further information: Chamber of Commerce, 818 Virginia St., East, Charleston, W. Va. 25301.

Charlotte, North Carolina

The World Almanac is sponsored in the Charlotte area by The Charlotte Observer, 600 S. Tryon St., Charlotte, N.C. 28233; (704) 374-7070; founded 1886 as Charlotte Chronicle, changed to Charlotte Daily Observer March, 1892; sold to Knight Newspapers Inc. 1955; circulation 175,755 daily, 221,613 Sunday; president and publisher James L. Knight; vice-president and general manager Erwin R. Potts; editor C. A. McKnight; executive editor James K. Batten.

Population: 305,500 (city), 394,050 (Mecklenburg County), 604,900 (metro), 66th in nation; labor force 304,800.
Area: 530 sq. mi. in Piedmont section of N.C., a plateau extending from the Appalachians to the Coastal Plains.
Industry: electronic data processing, industrial chemicals, textiles, food products, machinery, printing & publishing; over 600 manufacturing companies.
Commerce: major distribution center: 1,400 wholesale firms with $6.7 billion sales; retail sales (SMSA 1975) $1.8 billion; EBI per household $14,982; 16 banks, 11 mortgage banks, 5 building and loan associations.
Transportation: 3 major railway lines; 4 bus lines; 5 airlines with 189 air movements per day; 115 trucking firms.

Communications: 5 TV and 12 radio stations.
Medical facilities: outstanding center in southeast, 7 hospitals including 3 large general.
Cultural facilities: Opera Assn.; symphony orchestra; Oratorio Society; Mint Museum (art); Coliseum Auditorium, Civic Center; Johnson C. Smith Univ.; Univ. of N.C. — Charlotte; Davidson College; Queens College; Central Piedmont Community College; Kings College; Biscayne-Southern College.
Sports: Charlotte Checkers (Southern Hockey League); Charlotte Motor Speedway (NASCAR) with World 600 and National 500 races; Kemper Open golf tournament; Charlotte Hornets (WFL); NCNB Tennis Classic.
Other attractions: 2 major recreational lakes; nature museum; Carowinds, a family entertainment park.
History: Incorporated 1768; named for Queen Char-

lotte of England; played major part in American Revolution; county was the gold mining capital of the country before 1849; U.S. Mint was built in Charlotte in 1836 to serve the gold mining industry.
Further information: Chamber of Commerce, P.O. Box 1867, Charlotte, N.C. 28233.

Chattanooga, Tennessee

The World Almanac is sponsored in the Chattanooga area by the Chattanooga News-Free Press, 400 E. 11th St., Chattanooga, Tenn., 37401; (615) 266-0171, circulation 63,000 daily and Sunday; publisher Roy McDonald, president Frank McDonald, senior vice president Everett Allen, vice president and editor Lee Anderson, secretary J. W. Hoback, treasurer Clifford Welch.

Population: 169,952 (city), 370,857 (metro area); 4th in state, 89th in nation; 168,400 employed.
Area: 2,109.8 sq. mi. Metropolitan shopping area at juncture of Tennessee River and North Georgia boundary line.
Industry: over 600 manufacturers employ 55,000; receipts added by manufacture in 1973, $754 million; agriculture grossed $19 million in 1973.
Commerce: wholesale and retail center; wholesale sales (1973), $721 million; bank assets, $1.29 billion; 9 banks, 2 mortgage banks, 4 savings and loan assns., 3 major life insurance companies.
Transportation: 2 major freight lines, 2 bus lines, 13 federal and state highways; modern municipal airport serves 4 airlines.
New construction: development underway on Twin Tower Complex to feature two 21-story towers.
Communications: 5 TV, 20 radio stations, and 2 newspapers.

Medical facilities: speech and hearing rehabilitation center; children and adults rehabilitation and education center; 11 major hospital complexes including psychiatric hospital.
Cultural facilities: Univ. of Tenn. at Chattanooga; 3 liberal arts colleges; state tech community college; state vocational-tech school; symphony orchestra, opera assn., civic chorus.
Other attractions: multi-million dollar vacation complex; Chattanooga Choo-Choo, in one of the world's largest restaurants, in restored railroad terminal; recreational lakes, mountains, museums.
History: explored by DeSoto 1540, settled 1828 at Ross' landing, incorporated 1839.
Bicentennial plans: construction of $5 million Bicentennial Library; series of outdoor symphony concerts.
Further information: Chattanooga Convention and Visitors Bureau, Memorial Auditorium.

Chicago, Illinois

The World Almanac is sponsored in the Chicago area by the Chicago Tribune, 435 N. Michigan Ave., Chicago, Ill., 60611; (312) 222-3232; founded 1847 by Joseph Medill; circulation daily 806,083; Sunday 1,112,638; publisher Stanton R. Cook; editor Clayton Kirkpatrick; major awards include 7 Pulitzer prizes won by staff members; sponsors college-pro All Star football game, academic honors dinner, Nutcracker Ballet, Golden Gloves, Silver Skates Derby and Chicago Tribune swimming meet. Co-sponsors Coho Fishing Derby; Golden Helmet Awards; Golden Basketball Awards.

Population: est. 3,291,900 (city), 2d largest in nation; est. 7,737,200 (8-county metro area in Illinois and Indiana); est. 1,185,300 households in city and est. 2,552,600 in metro area; total employed 3,138,000.
Area: 227 sq. mi. on s.w. shore of Lake Michigan.
Industry: metro area is leading producer of steel, telephone equipment, radios, TV sets, confectionery products, household products, diesel engines, and frozen and canned foods. Largest industry is primary metals worth $9.9 billion; food and related products follow at $8.1 billion; then come metal products, electrical equipment, non-electrical machinery, chemicals, printing and publishing, petroleum, and transportation equipment. Chicago accounts for 5% of the gross national product.
Commerce: 14,318 manufacturers have sales of $41 billion in metro area; 54,000 retailers do a $21 billion business; wholesale sales are estimated at $65 billion. Average spendable family income $15,508. Midwest Stock Exchange markets stocks and bonds; 7th Federal Reserve District Bank; world's leading grain futures market; Chicago Board of Trade; Mercantile Exchange.
Transportation: 3 major airports with 27 commercial airlines handled 37,650,000 passengers in 1974; O'-Hare is world's largest and busiest commercial airport. Lake, ocean and river shipping makes city link between Mississippi River and St. Lawrence Seaway; Chicago handles one-third of Seaway cargo; 1974 overseas tonnage totaled more than 2,000,000 tons. Amtrak rail system headquarters. Over 12 major highways, expressways, tollways.
New Construction: total industrial construction, development and investment for 1974, $452.4 million; total commercial construction for 1974, $822 million, of which total shopping center construction accounted for $120 million.
Convention facilities: 1,266 trade shows and conventions in 1974 attended by over 2,000,000 people.
Educational facilities: 95 institutions of higher learning, include University of Chicago, Illinois Institute of Technology, Northwestern University; 6 medical schools; 3 dental colleges and one college of pharmacy and osteopathy.
Medical facilities: over 150 hospitals.
Recreation: 548 parks with an area of 6,505 acres; 103 swimming pools; baseball diamonds, golf courses, bicycle paths, handball courts, etc.

Cultural facilities: Art Institute; Museum of Contemporary Art; Museum of Science and Industry; Field Museum of Natural History; Shedd Aquarium is largest in world; Adler Planetarium; Lincoln Park and Brookfield Zoos; museums of Academy of Science and Historical Society.
Sports: NFL Bears, WFL Winds, American (baseball) League White Sox, National (baseball) League Cubs,

NHL Black Hawks, NBA Bulls, N.A. Soccer League Sting, American Soccer League Cats.
History: Indians named area Checagou after area's strong-smelling wild onions; incorporated 1837 with population of 4,170.
Further information: Visitors Bureau and Information Center, Association of Commerce and Industry, 130 South Michigan Avenue, Chicago, 60603.

Cincinnati, Ohio

The World Almanac is sponsored in the Cincinnati area by The Post, a Scripps-Howard Newspaper, 800 Broadway, Cincinnati, Ohio 45202; (513) 721-1111; founded 1881 by Alfred and Walter Wellman; evening circulation 216,713; editor Walter Friedenberg; business manager Earl Brown.

Population: 443,600 (city), 1,400,000 (metro area), 3d in state, 21st in nation; total employed 554,900 (March '75).
Area: 2,150 sq. mi. (metro) in s.w. Ohio; s.e. Indiana and 3 north central counties in Ky.
Industry: home of Proctor and Gamble, Federated Department Stores, Kroger Foods, Armco Steel, U.S. Shoe, Western-Southern Life Insurance, Baldwin Piano and Organ, Cincinnati Milacron; also the home of GM, Ford, and GE plants; production of jet engines, playing cards, cosmetics, chemicals, machine tools, printing and publishing.
Commerce: retail sales ('75 E&P est.) $4.175 billion; bank assets and deposits ('73 figure) $3.950 billion (metro area) with 44 banks with 170 branches; 71 savings and loan associations in metro area.
Transportation: 7 truck lines and Amtrak; 101 common motor carriers; Greater Cincinnati Airport with 300 incoming-outgoing flights daily serving 7 airlines; Lunken Airport with 4 hard surface runways and FAA control tower; Port of Cincinnati with 100 barge lines, making up 6.1% of total Ohio River traffic of 136 million tons; 2 major transcontinental bus lines; city-owned local bus lines; metro freeway.
Communications: 5 TV, 12 AM, 22 FM radio stations; 2 daily newspapers.
New construction: Greater Cincinnati Airport $46 million expansion program; Riverfront Sports Arena; I-75 link to Ky.; $37 million Cincinnati Bell expansion; $20 million Environmental Protection Ag-

ency Research Center; Queensgate housing development.
Medical facilities: 27 hospitals with over 8,824 beds; 88.3 physicians per 100,000 population; UC Medical Center where Sabin oral vaccine was discovered; Burn Institute and VA Hospital.
Cultural facilities: Art Museum, Historical Society, symphony orchestra, Krohn Conservatory, Lloyd Library, May Festival, Taft Museum, Summer Opera, Museum of Natural History, Shubert Theater, Contemporary Arts Center, UC Observatory, Playhouse in the Park.
Eucational facilities: Cincinnati, Xavier Univs.; Edgecliff, Mt. St. Joseph, Hebrew Union, Thomas More, Bible Seminary colleges; 8 technical and 2-year colleges; 47 vocational schools.
Convention facilities: numerous hotels and restaurants, Convention and Exposition Center, Cincinnati Gardens, Emery Auditorium, Taft Auditorium and Music Hall.
Other attractions: zoo, Reds baseball, Bengals football, Swords and Stingers ice hockey, Fountain Square Plaza, River Downs Race Track, Kings Island Amusement Park, Delta Queen Riverboat.
Bicentennial plans: riverfront parks, riverfront village, carillon tower, Spirit '76 Park, Bicentennial Grove, Bicentennial riverboat paddlewheel.
Further information: Chamber of Commerce, 120 W. Fifth St., 45202.

Cleveland, Ohio

The World Almanac is sponsored in the Cleveland area by The Cleveland Press, 901 Lakeside Ave., Cleveland, Ohio 44114; (216) 623-1111; founded 1878 by E. W. Scripps; circulation 357,147; managing editor Richard R. Campbell; business manager Robert H. Hartmann; major awards include Pulitzer Prize, Lasker Award.

Population: 690,774 (city), 2,018,200 (metro area), first in state, total employed 857,000 (non-agricultural).
Area: 1,519 sq. mi., SMSA 4 county area; along southern shore of Lake Erie, east and west of Cuyahoga River.
Industry: city has been described as "an industrial powerhouse"; bills itself "The Best Location in the Nation." Within 500 miles are: more than 50% of populations of the U.S. and Canada, more than 55% of U.S. manufacturing plants, more than 50% of retail sales in the U.S. and more than 60% of U.S. product value. No single industry dominates economy — steel and metal products are mainstays; manufacturing complex occupied essentially with primary metals, fabricated metal products, machinery, tools, automotive products. Important industries include making of electric motors, products of petroleum, rubber, plastic, stone, clay and glass, chemicals, paints, wearing apparel, measuring instruments, electronic components, food products, and publishing-printing. Value of products is $15 billion a year. Retail sales are almost $5 billion with average family spending about $6,000 on retail merchandise. More than 50% of families earn more than $10,000 a year.
Transportation: Hopkins Airport with more than 5 million passengers each year; Burke Lakefront Air-

port, 5 minutes from Public Square and capable of handling intermediate jets; Port of Cleveland visited by more than 50 overseas steamship lines and Great Lakes fleet; largest city on Lake Erie and 3d largest on Great Lakes. Cleveland is only U.S. city with airport-to-downtown rail service. Ride takes 20 minutes and costs about $10 less than a cab ride.
Communications: Cleveland Press, evening daily; Cleveland Plain Dealer, morning daily plus Sunday; numerous foreign language newspapers; 6 TV stations; 12 AM and 14 FM radio stations.
New construction: under construction are 2 hotels, a parking garage, a $61 million justice center, and others. Projects on the drawing boards include a 32-acre complex of offices, stores and apartments, and a gateway and jetport on Lake Erie.
Cultural facilities: Cleveland Orchestra; Play House, nation's oldest and largest resident professional theater; Museum of Art; Karamu House for interracial arts; Western Reserve Historical Society; Health Museum; Natural Science Museum; Cultural Gardens; zoo; Blossom Music Center; Salvador Dali Museum; Garden Center; Sea World; aquarium.
Educational facilities: Case Western Reserve Univ., Baldwin-Wallace College, Cleveland State Univ., Cuyahoga Community College, John Carroll Univ.; Notre Dame, and Ursuline Colleges.

Sports attractions: NFL Browns, American League Indians, WHA Crusaders, NBA Cavaliers, and World Team Tennis Nets; also golfing, horse and car racing, boating.

Other attractions: downtown Convention Center is largest city-owned convention facility in U.S.; public library is 2d in size of book collection to New York. Public Square, hub of city, marked by 52-story Terminal Tower. "The Forest City" is encircled by "Emerald Necklace," 18,000 acres of metropolitan parks. Cleveland Clinic, known for medical research, attracts patients from throughout the world.

History: settlement established in summer, 1796 by Gen. Moses Cleaveland, was capital of the Western Reserve, became a city in 1836.

Bicentennial plans: A Bicentury of Progress Showcase showing Cleveland's contribution to the country's industry, culture, recreation, etc.

Further information: Greater Cleveland Growth Assn., 690 Union Commerce Bldg., Cleveland 44115.

Columbia, South Carolina

The World Almanac is sponsored in the Columbia area by Columbia Newspapers, Inc., P.O. Box 1333, Columbia, S.C. 29202; phone (803) 771-6161; circulation The State (am) 103,903; The Columbia Record (pm) 31,915; The State (Sun.) 121,635 (ABC 3/31/75); Ambrose G. Hampton, publisher; Ben R. Morris, co-publisher; Arthur D. Cooper, associate publisher, president and general manager; James W. Holton, Jr., assistant general manager and advertising director; William E. Rone, editorial page editor (The State); Thomas N. McLean, editor, The Columbia Record.

Population: 113,542 (1970 census), city corporate limits; 2-county metro area (Richland and Lexington) estimated 360,000 (Fed-State Co-op '75).

Area: 105 sq. mi. (Richland County); 1,525 sq. mi. (metro); center of South Carolina, at confluence of Broad and Saluda Rivers (at Columbia).

Government: state capital with about 100 agencies (state); 19 (federal) agencies: government employees total more than 25,000; Fort Jackson Military Post numbers over 25,000 personnel.

Industry: more than 50 national firms such as General Electric, Allied Chemical, Continental Can, Burlington, Litton, Bendix, M. Lowenstein, Rockwell Int., Square D, Westinghouse, Colite Ind., Tamper, Shakespeare, Allis-Chalmers; fibres, heavy equipment, electronics, textiles, fertilizer, and cement products.

Commerce: retail sales (metro) $807 million ('74); consumer spendable income $1,250 billion; median household income (metro) $13,200; 9 commercial (main) banking institutions.

Transportation: Metropolitan Airport with 4 major airlines and freight service; 3 rail freight lines, Amtrak; 44 motor freight companies; 3 interstate, 6 federal, and 5 state highways.

Communications: 4 TV and 8 radio stations.

Medical facilities: 6 general hospitals, including modern Richland Memorial; William S. Hall Psychiatric Institute; 2 state mental hospitals.

Cultural facilities: Town Theatre, the oldest continuous community theater in nation; 3 other theaters; Museum of Art and Sciences; Gibbes Planetarium; Township Auditorium, home of Artist Series; Dreher Auditorium with Philharmonic Orchestra, City Ballet, Lyric Theatre and Choral Society; Fraser Hall.

Recreation facilities: 13 golf courses; city park system; 2 municipal pools; wide range of hunting activities; Riverbanks Zoological Park, part of 135-acre complex; Lake Murray, water sports.

Sports: Williams-Brice Stadium, home of Univ. of South Carolina Fighting Gamecock football team; Carolina Coliseum for basketball, conventions.

Educational facilities: 20,000-student Univ. of South Carolina; 4 private colleges; Technical Education Center; Lutheran Seminary.

History: established 1786 as state capital; burned in 1865 by Union General Sherman.

Further information: Chamber of Commerce, 1308 Laurel St., Columbia, S.C. 29202.

Bicentennial plans: publication of a book on South Carolina's history.

Columbus, Georgia — Phenix City, Alabama

The World Almanac is sponsored in the Columbus, Ga. - Phenix City, Ala., area by the Columbus Enquirer and the Columbus Ledger, 17 W. 12th Street, Columbus, GA 31902; phone (404) 322-8831; combined daily circulation 64,662; Sunday 59,128. Enquirer founded 1828, awarded Pulitzer Prize 1926; Ledger founded 1886, awarded Pulitzer Prize 1955. Published by The R. W. Page Corporation; M.R. Ashworth, president; Glenn Vaughn, vice-president and general manager; J. Carrol Dadisman, vice-president and executive editor. Owned by Knight-Ridder Newspaper Inc.

Population: 164,900 (Columbus); 29,200 (Phenix City); 224,700 (metro); 75.4 thousand employed (metro).

Area: 1,100 sq. miles (metro: Muscogee and Chattahoochee counties, Ga.; Russell County, Ala.) straddling the Chattahoochee River.

Industry: major textile production center: Swift, Fieldcrest, Cartersville, Columbus Mills, Bibb Mfg., Reeves Bros., West Point Pepperell. International hqs. Tom's Foods Ltd. and Burnham Van Lines; lumber products, beverages, concrete, bakery goods and paper.

Commerce: center of west Georgia—east Alabama finance, agriculture, textiles, hydroelectric power; metro retail sales $559.2 million; avg. household buying income $11.087; 9 banks, 6 savings and loan associations.

Federal facilities: Ft. Benning, world's largest infantry school, $244 million annual disbursements.

Transportation: 2 rail lines, 2 bus lines; Delta, Eastern, Southern airlines; 33 truck lines; Chattahoochee is navigable river.

Communications: 3 TV and 10 radio stations.

New construction: Peachtree Mall, Columbus East Industrial Park, Fieldcrest Mills.

Medical facilities: 4 hospitals, one under construction.

Cultural facilities: Museum of Arts and Crafts, Springer Theater (state theater of Georgia), Three Arts Theater, Bradley Memorial Library; Columbus College, Chattahoochee Valley Community College.

Sports: Astros, Southern baseball league.

History: Columbus founded 1828; gained early prominence as shipping center for cotton, fish; birthplace of Coca-Cola formula. Phenix City founded 1883, growing from a Creek Indian trading post.

Bicentennial plans: redevelopment of city's birth-

place. along the Chattahoochee River — the Chatta-hoochee Promenade.
Further information: Columbus Chamber of Commerce, P.O. Box 1200, Columbus, GA 31902. or Phenix City-Russell County Chamber of Commerce, P.O. Box 1326. Phenix City, AL 36867.

Columbus, Ohio

The World Almanac is sponsored in the Columbus area by the Columbus Citizen-Journal, 34 S. Third St., Columbus, Oh. 43216; (614) 461-5000; Citizen founded 1899, Journal 1811; circ. 113,752 a.m. daily except Sun.; owned by E. W. Scripps Co.; editor Charles Egger, business manager Gregory A. Dembski, managing editor Jack Keller.

Population: 576,100 (city), 1,107,000 (metro area). 1975 ests.; 2d in state, 33d in nation, total employed 475,300.
Area: 168.8 sq. mi., central Ohio, state capital, Franklin County seat.
Industry: diversified; 1019 manufacturers including General Motors, Rockwell International, Western Electric, Westinghouse, Borden (natl. hqs.); planes, missiles, refrigerators, mining machinery, telephones, glass products, auto parts; 1973 manufacturing payroll $851 million; home office of Battelle Memorial Institute with world-wide research laboratories.
Commerce: wholesale, retail center for central, southern Ohio, parts of W. Va., Ky. Retail sales: $1,881,551,000; bank assets; $9.2 billion, 7 banks; 20 savings & loan assns.; 39 insurance co. home offices, assets $3.7 billion. Per capita income: $5,031. Defense Construction Supply Center, world's largest; 21% of employment is government.
Transportation: 87 truck lines, 6 intercity bus lines, 4 railroads, 8 airlines using Port Columbus International with 750 air movements daily; 11 major highways.

Communications: 4 TV stations. 15 radio stations.
Medical facilities: 18 hospitals, medical centers; Children's Hospital leads nation in children admitted; Ohio State Univ. School of Medicine.
Cultural facilities: Ohio Theatre; symphony orchestra, public library with 22 branches; art museums, Center of Science and Industry, Ohio Historical Center with recreated early 19th Century village.
Other attractions: 104 parks, Park of Roses world's largest; Ohio Railway Museum; zoo, boating.
Educational facilities: Ohio State, Capital, Franklin Univ., Ohio Dominican College, Columbus College of Art & Design, Columbus Technical Institute.
Sports: Ohio Stadium; Owls (hockey), Beulah Park (thoroughbreds), Scioto Downs (harness).
History: founded 1812 as state capital, named for Christopher Columbus.
Bicentennial plans: 4-hour Birthday-of-the-United-States-of-America Party on the eve of the 4th of July in St. John Arena on the Ohio State Univ. campus with celebrities helping Columbusites celebrate.
Further information: Chamber of Commerce, P. O. Box 1527, Columbus, Oh. 43216.

Corpus Christi, Texas

The World Almanac is sponsored in the Corpus Christi area by The Caller-Times, P.O. Box 9136, Corpus Christi, Tex. 78408; Caller (a.m.) founded 1883; Times (p.m.) founded 1911; merged 1929. Caller circ. 62,525; Times 31,-865; Sunday 86,055; publisher Edward H. Harte; editor Gregory E. Favre; president Allan P. Johnson III; managing editor John. B. Anderson; associate editor; editorial page John L. Stallings.

Population: 220,000 (est.); labor force 94,000.
Area: 328 sq. mi. (226 water), 210 miles SW of Houston on Corpus Christi Bay. Nueces County seat.
Industry: oil refineries and chemical, petrochemical, synthetics, aluminum, and zinc plants.
Commerce: Port of Corpus Christi handled 40.9 million tons in 1974; 72-foot-deep superport proposed for 1977; economic hub of South Texas; farming, ranching, oil and gas production, commercial fishing, tourist trade; 13 banks have deposits in excess of $644 million; personal income $1.2 billion.
Transportation: 3 airlines, 2 bus lines; 3 railroads but no passenger service.
Medical facilities: 9 hospitals, including a children's center, with 1,497 beds.
Federal facilities: Corpus Christi Naval Air Station is headquarters for Naval Air Training Command; Corpus Christi Army Depot is Army's only complete helicopter overhaul plant; combined payroll more than $100 million.
Cultural facilities: science museum, Art Museum of

South Texas, Japanese art museum, symphony, little theatre, Del Mar College, Texas A&I Univ. at Corpus Christi.
Recreation: public beaches and fishing piers on the Bay and along Gulf of Mexico on Mustang Island, and in 88-mile-long Padre Island National Seashore; surf and charter boat fishing, sailing, city marina with public launching ramps, large public tennis center, 3 private tennis clubs, 5 golf courses.
History: Spanish explorer Alonzo de Pineda discovered Corpus Christi Bay in 1519. Blas Maria de la Garza Falcon established San Petronilla Ranch on Petronilla Creek about 1765; city grew from a frontier trading post est. in 1839; city incorporated Feb. 16, 1852.
Bicentennial plans: over 3,000 Girl Scouts from 23 counties will participate in "Festival of American Heritage" on March 14, 1976; the symphony will produce 3 half-hour TV shows.
Further information: Corpus Christi Chamber of Commerce, P. O. Box 640, Corpus Christi, 78403.

Dallas, Texas

The World Almanac is sponsored in Dallas by The Dallas Morning News, Communications Center, Dallas, Tex. 75222; telephone (214) 745-8222; published by the oldest business in Texas, the News was founded in 1842 by Samuel Bangs; circulation, 314,588 Sunday, 259,276 daily, President Joe M. Dealey, executive editor Tom J. Simmons. Winner of numerous national awards including Freedoms Foundation and National Headliner; Sponsors Teen-age Citizenship Tribute, Fly-the-Flag program, Spelling Bee, Sports Show, Involved Citizen Award, etc.

Population: city, 870,400 (8th in nation); county 1,395,200; Dallas-Fort Worth metro area, 2,524,100
(10th in nation); total employed, 1,103,500 with 5.2% unemployment.

Area: 900 sq. mi. astride Trinity River in North Texas, about 75 miles south of Oklahoma border; elevation from 450 to 750 feet.

Industry: banking and insurance capital of the Southwest, Dallas ranks 3d among U.S. cities in the number of million-dollar-net-worth companies with 672 such firms. Manufacturing accounts for one-fourth of employment, about evenly divided between durable (including electronics, aviation, aerospace, and machinery) and non-durable (including food products, apparel, and printing-publishing).

Commerce: a $2.5 billion wholesale market ($5 billion retail), Dallas ranks first nationally in giftware, home furnishing and floor covering wholesaling, 2d in apparel. Metro retail sales totaled $8 billion in 1974, while estimated buying income reached $12.7 billion and bank deposits $13.6 billion.

Transportation: Dallas-Fort Worth Airport is the world's largest. In 1974, it was the nation's 5th busiest with 309,018 total operations; 6,791,000 passengers enplaned there. City is served by 10 major commercial and 4 commuter air lines, 8 railroads, 2 transcontinental bus lines, 78 motor freight lines, 2 taxicab companies with 570 cabs. Dallas Transit System serves 125,000 people daily on 97 lines, 481 route miles.

Communications: 2 metropolitan daily newspapers, numerous suburban dailies, 4 commercial VHF TV stations, public television, 1 UHF station, 17 AM and 20 FM radio stations, 2 city magazines.

New construction: $712 million in building permits in 1974 ($356 nonresidential); projects include 300-acre, $300 million office park and $210 million Union Terminal area redevelopment.

Medical facilities: 57 hospitals with 9,364 beds, 500 bassinets. Baylor University Medical Center was recently chosen No. 4 among the country's top 13 "super hospitals."

Culture: symphony orchestra, civic opera, summer musicals, civic ballet, Sunday Concert series — among others — offer varied programs; drama at Dallas Theater Center, Theater Three, National Children's Theater, Repertory Theater and 4 dinner theaters; 7 museums; SMU's Owens Fine Arts Center with a collection of paintings and sculpture; numerous art galleries.

Education: 123,998 students attend 28 colleges and universities within 50 miles of Dallas; Southern Methodist Univ., the Univ. of Texas at Dallas, Univ. of Dallas, North Texas State, Univ. of Texas at Arlington, Baylor Univ. College of Dentistry, Southwestern Medical School; the Dallas Community College System with 36,000 students on 4 campuses and 3 more planned.

Convention facilities: 3 major convention centers, including expanded Dallas Convention Center with more combined meeting-exhibit space (611,000 sq. ft.) than any other in U.S.; 26,000 air-conditioned hotel rooms. Dallas consistently ranks in top 5 convention cities. In 1974, 1,152,000 people attended 743 conventions.

Sports attractions: professional sports include football, baseball, tennis, golf, hockey, soccer, and rodeo. Cotton Bowl is site of annual New Year's Day football game and SMU home games.

Other attractions: Six Flags Over Texas, Dallas Zoo, Seven Seas, Lion Country Safari. Fair Park is home of State Fair of Texas 16 days each October; museums of fine arts, health and science, natural history; Hall of State; Garden Center, and Music Hall; excellent lakes, golf courses, parks, luxury hotels, and restaurants.

History: first settler was Tennessee frontiersman John Neely Bryan who established a trading post and plotted the townsite in 1844; incorporated 1856; named for Vice-President George Millifin Dallas. Since 1931, the city has had council-manager form of government. Spectacular population growth began after World War II, when aircraft manufacturing augmented an economy that had been built first on cotton, then on oil, banking, and insurance. Diversified economic expansion fed the growth of the 1960s.

Bicentennial plans: dedication of 2 parks, and an air show among many events.

Further information: Dallas Chamber of Commerce, Fidelity Union Tower, Dallas, 75201.

Dayton, Ohio

The World Almanac is sponsored in the Dayton area by The Journal Herald, 37 South Ludlow St., Dayton, Oh. 45401; (513) 223-1111; founded as Dayton Repertory; circulation, 111,502; Editor Dennis Shere, Managing editor Ralph Langer, editorial page editor Alvin P. Sanoff, Modern Living department editor Virginia Hunt.

Population: 239,700 (city), 862,700 (metro), 4th in state, 43d in nation; total employed 345,000 (1974).

Area: 43.64 sq. mi. (1975) at junction of Miami, Mad, and Stillwater rivers.

Industry: NCR Corp., McCall Printing Co., General Motors Corp. (Delco Moraine, Delco Products, Delco-Air, Inland Mfg. and Frigidaire); more than 800 other manufacturing facilities.

Commerce: retail sales (1973), 2.107 billion; average effective buying household income, $14,331.

Transportation: 2 airports, 6 airlines, 4 trunk rail systems, 6 bus lines, Dayton Regional Transit Authority.

Communications: 4 TV and 10 radio stations.

Medical facilities: 10 hospitals, including a Veterans Administration facility.

Federal facilities: Wright Patterson AFB, headquarters for the Air Force Logistics Command and Aeronautical Systems Division; Defense Electronics Supply Center.

Convention facilities: new downtown convention and exhibition center.

New construction: transportation center, 2 bank towers, hi-rise senior citizen apts., federal building, Courthouse Sq. Plaza (incl. new dept. store), Stouffer hotel.

Educational facilities: Univ. of Dayton, Wright State Univ.; 2 junior colleges — Sinclair downtown campus, Miami Jacobs (business); United Theological Seminary.

Cultural facilities: Dayton Art Institute, Philharmonic Orchestra, opera, ballet, 4 amateur theatrical groups, 2 professional companies; Diehl Memorial band shell, Deed's carillon, 3 new dinner theaters.

Sports attractions: Dayton Gems (IHL); Amateur Trapshoot Headquarters; college sports, DABC (1975).

Other attractions: Air Force Museum, Carillon Park, Paul Lawrence Dunbar home, Wright Bros. Memorial, Aviation Hall of Fame, Old Courthouse Museum.

Bicentennial plans: Dayton is focusing on its heritage of "The Birthplace of Aviation".

Further information: Dayton Area Chamber of Commerce, 111 West First St., Dayton 45402.

Denver, Colorado

The World Almanac is sponsored in the Denver area by the Rocky Mountains News, 400 W. Colfax Ave., Denver, Col. 80201; (303) 892-5000; founded 1859 by William N. Byers; circulation daily 219,341, Sunday 244,428; editor

Michael Balfe Howard, business manager William W. Fletcher; sponsors Colorado-Wyoming spelling bee, Golden Wedding party, Huck Finn Day, Showagon.

Population: 529,700 (city), 1,506,800 (metro area), first in state, 26th in nation; total employed 669,300.
Area: 116.4 sq. mi. on S. Platte River at edge of Great Plains near Rocky Mountains. State capital.
Industry: Gates Rubber Co. is world's largest maker of v-belts and hose, 6th largest U.S. rubber company; Samsonite Corp. is world's largest luggage manufacturer, also makes furniture; Adolph Coors Co. is nation's 4th largest brewer of beer; center for smokeless industry with 1,500 manufacturing firms.
Commerce: largest distribution center in region embracing one-third of U.S. geographical area; retail sales, $7.8 billion (1974); bank deposits $4.432 billion, 89 banks, 16 savings and loan associations and 45 insurance company home offices; per capita income, $4,728.
Transportation: 6 major rail freight lines, Amtrak; Continental and Greyhound bus lines; 3 interstate highways intersect city; Stapleton International Airport is nation's 10th largest, with 620 daily flights, hub for 6 trunk airlines; Frontier Air Lines; United Air Lines Flight Training Center.
Communications: 5 TV and 32 radio stations.
Medical facilities: largest medical center between Kansas City and San Francisco; one of 17 regional comprehensive cancer centers with operations to begin in 1976; Univ. of Colorado Medical Center, National Jewish Hospital, Children's Asthma Research Institute and Hospital (CARIH); 22 major hospitals.
Federal facilities: largest complex of federal offices

outside Washington, D.C., with 37,700 federal employes; site of Energy Research and Development Administration's Rocky Flats plant, U.S. Mint, Lowry AFB, Air Force Accounting and Finance Center, Fitzsimons Army Medical Center, Army's Rocky Mountain Arsenal.
Cultural facilities: symphony orchestra, 3 nonprofessional orchestras, 2 choral groups, Denver Art Museum, 3 theater companies; 3-sq.-block convention center; 12,000-seat Red Rocks outdoor theater.
Educational facilities: Univ. of Denver, Colorado School of Mines; Colorado Women's, Metropolitan State, Loretto Heights and Regis colleges; Univ. of Colorado School of Medicine, Iliff School of Theology.
Recreational facilities: 150 parks, 8,030 acres of mountain parks, 34 golf courses in metro area, City Park Zoo, 2 amusement parks; many ski areas.
Sports: pro teams include Broncos, NFL; Bears, baseball, American Assn.; Nuggets, ABA; Dynamos, NASL; Spurs, WHA.
Other attractions: Museum of Natural History, Botanic Gardens, State Historical Museum.
History: founded 1858 with discovery of gold, fast became supply center for mountain mining camps; named for territorial governor.
Bicentennial plans: only state with Centennial in 1976; folk arts festival, June, 1976; Night in Old Denver.
Further information: Denver Chamber of Commerce, 1301 Welton St., Denver 80204; Hospitality Center, 280 14th St., Denver 80202.

Des Moines, Iowa

The World Almanac is sponsored in Iowa by the Des Moines Register and Tribune, 715 Locust St., Des Moines Ia. 50304; (515) 284-8000; founded 1849; circulation evening Tribune 101,891, morning Register 242,166, Sunday Register 459,525; president and publisher David Kruidenier, editor Kenneth MacDonald, executive editor Michael Gartner, business manager Louis Norris; sales director J. Robert Hudson.

Population: 201,404 (city, 1970), 326,500 (1974 SMSA).
Area: 66 sq. mi., at juncture of Raccoon and Des Moines rivers, south central Iowa. State capital and Polk County seat.
Industry: considered to be 2d largest insurance center in nation (56 home companies) and 2d largest tire center with Firestone, Armstrong plants; publishing center — Meredith Co., Better Homes and Gardens, Wallace-Homestead, others; farm implements — North American headquarters and plant of Massey-Ferguson, John Deere; lawn and garden equipment, sporting goods, food products, cosmetics, dental equipment, automotive accessories, concrete forms, nozzles, tools; 700 wholesale and jobbing firms; Standard Oil credit card center.
Commerce: retail sales in metro area, $788,097,000 (1974); per capita income, $4,988 (1973); bank deposits, $1.2 billion (1975).
Transportation: newly enlarged in-city airport, 3 major airlines; 4 bus lines; 6 railroads; 69 truck lines, Interstate Highways 80 and 35.
New Construction: 2 large shopping centers, major additions 2 hospitals, $75 million dam and 5,400-acre

reservoir.
Communications: 13 radio, 4 TV, cablevision.
Medical facilities: 11 hospitals with 2,500 beds.
Cultural facilities: Art Center, Center of Science and Industry, Community Playhouse, Drama Workshop, Drake University, symphony orchestra; Grand View Junior, Area Community, and 2 bible colleges; College of Osteopathic Medicine and Surgery, civic ballet.
Recreation: 1,400 acres of parks, 9 public golf courses, 11 public pools, tennis, YMCA; two huge reservoirs.
Other attractions: AAA baseball, pro hockey, Drake Relays, Missouri Valley and Big Eight (Iowa State U.) conferences; 15,000-seat auditorium; boys and girls state basketball tournaments, State Fair, Living History Farm, Children's Zoo, 36-story Ruan Center, tallest in Iowa, Terrace Hill.
History: founded 1843 as a fort to protect rights of Indians; incorporated 1853, became Iowa capital 1857.
Bicentennial plans: major 18th Century Art Exhibit, Natl. Science Foundation Display, State Fair.

Detroit, Michigan

The World Almanac is sponsored in the Detroit area by The Detroit News, 615 Lafayette, Detroit, Mich. 48231 (313) 222-2000; founded 1873 by James E. Scripps; circulation (D) 684,852 (S) 847,045; president and publisher Peter B. Clark Sr., v.p. R.M. Spitzley, v.p. and gen. mgr. J. T. Dorris, v.p. and editor Martin S. Hayden; major awards won include Pulitzer Prize, Nat'l Headliners; 66 community projects include NCAA Indoor Track Championships, Policeman and Fire Fighter of the Month, Science Fair, Scholastic Writing and Art Awards, Spelling Bee.

Population: 1,500,000 (city), 4,250,000 (metro area), (1972); first in state, 5th in U.S.
Area: 139.6 sq. mi. on the Detroit River, a Great

Lakes connecting link and the world's busiest inland waterway.
Industry: "The Motor City"; area plants produce 25%

of the nation's cars and trucks, employing more than 206,000. Nonautomotive manufacturing and nonmanufacturing firms employ more than 1.4 million. Other products are machine tools, iron products, metal stampings, hardware, industrial chemicals, drugs, paint, wire products.

Commerce: total metro personal income per household was $14,111 (1971); area retail sales were $8.6 billion.

Transportation: served by 5 railroads, over 200 intercity truck lines, 19 airlines, and 31 scheduled steamship lines serving more than 40 countries.

Communications: 9 TV and 18 radio stations.

New construction: $500 million riverfront development, Renaissance Center, will be built on east side waterfront area, incorporating living units, business offices and hotels; other projects include 660-acre, $284 million downtown residential developments, and a 235-acre, $500 million mid-town medical center.

Cultural facilities: symphony orchestra, International Institute, Meadow Brook music and drama programs, Institute of Arts, concert band, and the annual Freedom Festival, celebrating Canada's Dominion Day, July 1, and U.S. Independence Day, July 4.

Educational facilities: 11 colleges and universities are located in the metro area, including Wayne State Univ., Univ. of Detroit, and branches of the Univ. of Michigan and Michigan State Univ.

Convention facilities: 75-acre, $100 million Civic Center, including Cobo Hall and Convention Arena with 400,000 sq. ft. of exhibit space, more than 24,000 rooms in 250 hotels and motels.

Sports: Tigers baseball (American League), NFL Lions, NHL Red Wings, NBA Pistons; 6 winter skiing areas within short driving distance.

Other attractions: Chrysler, Ford, and General Motors auto plants; Henry Ford Museum and Greenfield Village historical displays, Cranbrook Institute (science museum and arts), Belle Isle (1,000-acre park), zoo, public library, Historical Museum, and Fort Wayne Military Museum.

History: founded 1701 by the Frenchman Cadillac as a strategic frontier fort and trading post, ceded to the British in 1763 and turned over to the U.S. in 1796 as a village of 2,500; reoccupied by the British for a year in the War of 1812. Completion of the Erie Canal in 1825 opened a cheap water transport route from New York to the Northwest and made Detroit an important commercial center. R. E. Olds built Detroit' first auto factory in 1899; and Henry Ford, who hand-built his first car in 1896, formed his first company in 1899, and the present Ford Motor Co. in 1903. The area's industries made it the "Arsenal of Democracy" in World War II.

Bicentennial plans: historic sites restoration; large ethnic festivals; performing arts, cultural events.

Further information: Greater Detroit Chamber of Commerce, 150 Michigan Ave., 48226; Cities Reporting and Information Dept., City-County Bldg., 48226; Detroit Convention Bureau, 1400 Book Bldg., 48226.

Edmonton, Alberta, Canada

The World Almanac is sponsored in central and nothern Alberta by the Edmonton Journal, 10006-101 St., Edmonton, Alberta, T5J2S6; telephone (403) 425-9120; founded November 11, 1903. A division of Southam Press Limited; circulation 171,600. Publisher Ross Munro; editor Andrew Snaddon. Sponsor Learn to Ski, Curl, Play Golf, Tennis, and Fitness Finders programs; Literary Awards, Newspaper in the Classroom.

Population: (est.) 451,635 (city), 543,000 (metro), capital and largest Alberta city, 5th in Canada; total employed 218,775.

Area: 122.6 square miles on North Saskatchewan River.

Industry: 2d largest refining center in Canada. 7,000 producing wells; petrochemical industries include plastics, fertilizers, man made fibers, steel tube mills; 2d largest meat processing center in Canada; prosperous mixed farming.

Commerce: major supply center for Northwest Territories, Yukon, northeastern B.C. and Canadian Arctic; originating terminus of 5 oil and natural gas pipelines east and west from Alberta, Alaska and the Canadian north; retail sales (est. 1974) $1 575 billion; mfg. shipments $1.32 billion; trading area population (est.) 1,097,496.

Transportation: Alaska and Mackenzie Highways; Canadian National, Canadian Pacific, Pacific Northern, Great Slave, and Alberta Resources railroads; 4 airports, 6 airlines, 169,892 itinerant movements in 1974, 5th busiest in Canada.

Communications: 3 TV, 3 cable TV and 8 radio stations.

Medical facilities: 5 general and 5 auxiliary hospitals, 2 rehabilitation centers, 9 nursing homes.

Cultural facilities: Edmonton Symphony Orchestra, Edmonton Art Gallery, Centennial Library, Provincial Museum and Archives, Univ. of Alberta, Northern Alberta Institute of Technology, Grant McEwan Community College, Alberta and Edmonton ballet companies, Canada's most active professional theatre, Edmonton Opera, Northern Alberta Jubilee Auditorium, Queen Elizabeth Planetarium.

Other attractions: Klondike Days annual celebration of the 1898 Yukon gold rush is held in mid-July; Valley Zoo, Fort Edmonton, Mayfair Park, Alberta Game Farm, Elk Island Park; many lakes nearby.

Sports: CFL Eskimos, WHA Oilers, Western Major Fastball League Monarchs; 16,000 seat Coliseum, 40,-000 seat sport complex being built for the 1978 Commonwealth Games; Speedway, one of the top auto race tracks on continent; Kinsmen Field House indoor track.

History: Fort Edmonton built in 1795, named after a town now a borough of London, England; oil discovered at Leduc (20 miles south) in 1947.

El Paso, Texas

The World Almanac is sponsored in the El Paso area by the El Paso Herald-Post, 401 Mills Ave., El Paso, Tex. 79999; (915) 532-1661; Herald founded 1881, Post 1922, merged (under Scripps-Howard) 1931; circulation 40,-735. Robert W. Lee, editor; Robert McBrinn, managing editor.

Population: 359,302 (city); with twin city, Juarez, Mexico, 847,026; 5th in state, 45th in nation; total employed, 146,100.

Area: 159,781 sq. mi., western tip of Texas where Rio Grande cuts boundaries of Texas, New Mexico, and Mexico; includes Franklin Mtns.

Industry: manufacturing payroll, $180.6 million (1974), manufacturing employment, 30,683; clothing largest employer including Farah and Mann. Juarez-El Paso border in-bond industries at 90 and 17,907 employed since 1967, many in electronics including RCA, GE and Sylvania; home of El Paso Natural Gas,

American Smelting & Refining, Phelps Dodge, Standard and Texaco refineries; also leather goods, dairies, processed Mexican foods, meat packing, nut processing, cattle, agriculture.

Commerce: wholesale-retail center for west Texas, New Mexico, northern Mexico; retail sales 1973, $973 million; bank deposits (1974) $978 million; bank clearings, $6.7 billion; 17 banks, 6 savings and loan associations.

Transportation: 4 major rail lines, Amtrak; 8 bus lines, 29 truck lines, 5 major highways, gateway to Mexico; international airport, 4 airlines with 129,336 (1974) flights and 1,116,403 passengers, freight 11,403 tons.

Communications: 4 TV and 14 radio stations.

New construction: 1974 building permits totaled $166,520,862.

Medical facilities: 14 hospitals with 1,951 beds; area

cancer treatment center; El Paso School of Nursing.

Federal facilities: Ft. Bliss (U.S. Army Air Defense Center, Allied Students Missile Center, Sgts. Major Academy), William Beaumont Medical Center; near McGregor and White Sands Missile Range, N.M.

Cultural facilities: University of Texas at El Paso, El Paso Community College, El Paso Symphony, Museum of Art, University ballet, opera companies, theater groups; $20 million civic-convention center; public libraries.

Other attractions: annual Sun Carnival-Sun Bowl, Chamizal Park, Tigua Indian community, historic missions, horse and dog races, Cavalry Museum, zoo, nearby Juarez, Mexico.

Bicentennial Plans: open $1.5 million amphitheater with Southwest history outdoor drama; restoration of old buildings, horsedrawn parade; purchase Gilbert Stuart's portrait of George Washington.

Erie, Pennsylvania

The World Almanac is sponsored in the Erie area by the Erie Daily Times, 205 W. 12th Street, Erie, Pa., 16501; (814) 456-8531; founded in 1888; circulation 74,000 daily, 92,000 Sunday; president Edward M. Mead, executive editor Joseph Meagher, managing editor Len Kholos.

Population: 129,231 (city), 186,652 (metro area), 3d in state; total employed, 51,175.

Area: 19.53 sq. mi. at tip of northwestern Pa.

Commerce: Erie County, pop. 220,000, produces $133 million in exports, highest per capita export in U.S.; tourism — 5 miles of beaches, good fishing, boating, winter sports; seaport — 60 or more oceangoing vessels each year; over 506 industrial plants producing machinery and parts; iron and steel forgings, hardware, meters, plastics, paper (Hammermill), furniture, and toys; General Electric producing Amtrak passenger trains.

New construction: main street transformed into pedestrian walkway; 200-room Hilton Hotel; "Mid City Towers," a 14-story apt. bldg.; $32 million Saint Vincent Health Center building project; $36 million Hamot Medical Center building project; Millcreek

shopping mall, $65 million, largest single-design shopping center under one roof in U.S.

Special awards: All America City through 1974.

Transportation: 4 railroads, Boston-Chicago Amtrak line; airport; 35 trucking companies, 4 bus lines.

Cultural facilites: Penn State Univ. extension, Gannon, Mercyhurst, and Villa Maria colleges; Philharmonic Society, Council of the Arts, theatre groups; new field house for plays, entertainment, sports.

History: Named after Eriez Indians; site of building of ship Niagara with which Oliver Hazard Perry defeated British in 1813 in Lake Erie battle.

Bicentennial plans: restoration of Old Land Lighthouse, first lighthouse beacon on Great Lakes; restoration of Old Custom House.

Further information: Chamber of Commerce, 1006 State, 16501.

Evansville, Indiana

The World Almanac is sponsored in southwestern Indiana, western Kentucky and southeastern Illinois by the Evansville Press, 201 N.W. Second Street, Evansville, Ind. 47701; (812) 424-7711; founded July 2, 1906, by E. W. Scripps and J. C. Harper; circulation, 47,000; editor, Michael Grehl; managing editor, William R. Burleigh

Population: 138,764 (city), 287,600 (metro area), 4th in state.

Area: 47 sq. mi. at bend of Ohio River in southwest corner of state; Vanderburgh County seat.

Industry: Whirlpool Corp. plants (refrigeration and air conditioning); Mead Johnson & Co. (pharmaceutical division of Bristol-Myers Co.); Alcoa Warrick Operations (aluminum) just east of city; 22 plastics firms, 303 manufacturing firms.

Commerce: retail sales, $767,758,000 (1974); effective buying income per household, $11,967, (1974); home offices of CrediThrift of America, Inc.; 5 banks, 7 savings and loan associations.

Transportation: world headquarters of Atlas Van Lines; 4 railroads; 5 commercial barge lines; 4 interstate bus lines; Allegheny, Delta, Eastern air lines.

Communications: 2 daily newspapers; 4 TV and 6 radio stations.

Medical facilities: 5 general and mental hospitals; branch of Indiana University Medical School.

Cultural facilities: Philharmonic Orchestra, Museum of Arts and Science, Mesker Zoo, Univ. of Evansville, Indiana State Univ. Evansville; national headquarters of Phi Mu Alpha music fraternity. Abraham Lincoln boyhood home nearby.

Sports: Evansville Triplets baseball; site of NCAA college division basketball tournament.

Bicentennial plans: Freedom Festival, late June and early July; Ohio River Arts Festival, May.

Further information: Chamber of Commerce, Southern Securities Building, Evansville, Ind. 47708.

Fort Wayne, Indiana

The World Almanac is sponsored in the Fort Wayne area by The Journal-Gazette, 600 W. Main St., Fort Wayne, Ind., 46802; (219) 423-3311; established June 14, 1899, by consolidation of The Journal and The Daily Gazette;

circulation daily 66,035, Sundays 108,354; president-publisher Richard G. Inskeep; secretary-treasurer Naomi Erb; editor Larry W. Allen; managing editor James P. Lovette.

Population: 184,700 (city); 378,300 (metro area); total employed 168,600.

Area: 50.4 sq. mi. at confluence of St. Joseph, St. Mary's and Maumee rivers. Allen County seat.

Industry: General Electric and International Harvester largest employers; Magnavox, Essex International and Central Soya home offices; several firms manufacture about 85% of world's diamond wire dies.

Commerce: wholesale and retail center for northeastern Indiana, southeastern Michigan, northwestern Ohio; retail sales (metro) over $1 billion; bank deposits $1,386 billion; 5 banks, 4 savings-and-loan; 6 life insurance companies, including Lincoln National Life, based here.

Transportation: 2 major rail freight lines; Amtrak; 56 motor freight lines including home-based North American Van, Elway Express, Scott and Transport Motor; I-69 connects city with Indianapolis and Indiana Toll Road; U.S. 30 dual lane to Chicago; municipal airport; hq. for 122nd Tactical Fighter Wing, Indiana Air National Guard.

Communications: 7 radio, 3 TV stations.

Medical facilities: 4 hospitals including VA.

Cultural facilities: Philharmonic Orchestra; Fine Arts and Performing Arts complex; 9 universities and colleges; 3 museums.

Sports: Komet Hockey Team (IHL) plays at Allen Co. War Memorial Coliseum.

Other attractions: children's zoo; 70 parks and playgrounds; 11 golf courses; 36 shopping centers.

History: first white settlement in Indiana (circa 1692).

Bicentennial plans: reconstruction of old Fort.

Further information: Chamber of Commerce, 826 Ewing St.

Fort Worth, Texas

The World Almanac is sponsored in the Fort Worth area by the Fort Worth Star-Telegram, 400 West Seventh, Fort Worth, Texas 76101 (817) 336-9271. Established in 1906. Publisher Amon G. Carter, Jr.; Editor, Jack Butler; vice-president and general manager Jack W. Campbell.

Population: 401,000 (city, 1975 est.); metro area 842,-000 (1975 est.); 4th largest Texas city; work force of 360,150 (1974 avg.), unemployment 5.1%.

Area: 233 sq. mi. on the Trinity River in North Central Texas, Tarrant County seat.

Commerce: all types of manufacturing; wholesale and retail center for large area including West Texas; retail sales $2.2 billion (1974 est.); effective buying income $4.1 billion (1974 est.); bank deposits $2.9 billion (65 area banks); over 60 mortgage institutions, insurance companies and savings and loans associations.

Transportation: Dallas-Fort Worth Regional Airport, 17 miles from downtown; Meacham Field, general aviation airport, many smaller airports; 9 railroads, Amtrak, 38 motor carriers, and 5 bus companies.

Communications: 2 TV and 18 area radio stations; 1 daily newspaper, several weekly and monthly publications.

Medical facilities: over 20 hospitals.

Federal facilities: 14 federal agencies and Carswell Air Force Base; reserve training centers.

Cultural: Casa Manana, America's first permanent musical arena theater; symphony, opera, Van Cliburn Piano Competition; museums include Kimball Art Museum, Amon Carter Museum of Western Art, and others.

Educational facilities: 3 campuses of Tarrant County Junior College; Texas Christian Univ., Univ. of Texas at Arlington, Texas Wesleyan College, Southwestern Baptist Seminary; Texas Woman's Univ.; and other technical and vocational schools.

Recreation: 6 Flags over Texas and Seven Seas in Arlington; Forest Park and Fort Worth Zoological Park; several other parks.

Convention facilities: Tarrant County Convention Center, Will Rogers Memorial Center.

Sports attractions: Texas Rangers baseball, Fort Worth Texans in hockey, Colonial National Golf Tournament; TCU football, other college and semi-pro teams.

Other attractions: Fat Stock Show and Rodeo; Miss Texas Pageant.

History: founded 1849 as a frontier Army post on the Chisholm Trail; became major railhead.

Bicentennial plans: Rename Main Street "Bicentennial Avenue" until 1977.

Further Information: Chamber of Commerce, 700 Throckmorton St., Fort Worth, 76102.

Fresno, California

The World Almanac is sponsored in the Fresno area by The Fresno Bee, 1626 E Street, Fresno, Cal. 93721; phone (209) 268-5221; founded 1922; circulation daily 139,507, Sunday 112,265; president Eleanor McClatchy, editor C. K. McClatchy, managing editor George Gruner.

Population: 175,900 (city), 439,200 (county); total employed 192,400.

Area: one of largest counties in the state, 3,819,456 acres; located in geographical center of the state midway between San Francisco and Los Angeles.

Agriculture: leading county in U. S. in annual value of agricultural production; state's leading county in production of grapes, barley, figs, turkeys, nectarines, cantaloupes, alfalfa seed, peaches, cotton lint; 2d leading county in plums, naval/misc. oranges, pomegranates, sweet potatoes, processing tomatoes, safflower, sheep, lambs.

Industry: 475 diversified manufacturing establishments; food processing is major industry; 2d in importance is production of beverages, primarily wine, brandy and spirits; metro retail sales (1973) 1.2 billion.

Transportation: airports, daily service by 5 airlines; freeways connect to all major metropolitan areas in California; served by 23 common truck carriers, 2 interstate bus lines and 2 mainline railroads with freight handling facilities.

Communications: 5 TV and 16 radio stations.

Medical facilities: 6 general hospitals, including a Veterans Administration installation.

Cultural facilities: Community and Convention Center; community philharmonic, opera, ballet and theater; California State Univ.-Fresno, Pacific College, 3 community colleges.

Recreation: golf courses; tennis courts; swimming pools; 3 national parks; Yosemite, Sequoia and Kings Canyon with groves of giant Sequoia trees plus facilities for boating, sailing, hunting, fishing, skiing, hiking, pack trips and camping.

Other attractions: City Zoo, nationally famous rodeo, county fair, underground gardens, Kearney museum; downtown malls with one of the best outdoor art displays in the West.

History: area explored by the Spaniards in the early 1800s and visited by fur trappers before 1840; settlement began when gold miners came in the 1850s; county created Apr. 19, 1856, from parts of Mariposa, Merced and Tulare counties.

Halifax, Nova Scotia, Canada

The World Almanac is sponsored in Nova Scotia by The Chronicle-Herald and The Mail-Star, 1650 Argyle Street, Halifax; phone (902) 426-2811; circulation Chronicle (morning) 67,115, Mail-Star (aft.) 48,602; publisher and president Graham W. Dennis, chairman of the board Ira B. MacCallum, general-manager Fred G. Mounce, managing editor Alvin M. Savage, secretary-treasurer W. D. Coleman.

Population: 122,035 (1971); labor force 57,305; employed 53,170.

Area: 24.19 sq. mi. of land, on the southeast coast of the province; capital city.

Industry: leading industrial area in Atlantic provinces; establishments include oil refineries, electronic equipment manufacturers, ship yards, car assembly plant, plastic fabricators, metal works, breweries, and fish processing; 3d largest and one of Canada's most diversified scientific research centers.

Commerce: financial center of region, regional head offices for all major banks and investment houses; retail sales over $320 million annually in Halifax County; average income $8,396 (1971); all three levels of government constitute employment for 12,000; armed forces have over 14,000 stationed in city.

Transportation: 2 major passenger-freight rail lines, 11 container lines call regularly at eastern-most commercial port on mainland North America; only Canadian container port with 3 sea-shore cranes; handled 166,000, 20-foot equivalent containers (1974), over 650,000 tons break bulk general cargo; international airport.

Communication: 5 radio and 2 TV stations.

New construction: building permits issued for $54.7 million worth of construction last year.

Education: 6 degree-granting universities, 79 common and 3 private schools, one technical institute.

Medical facilities: 9 hospitals (3 teaching).

Cultural facilities: Atlantic Symphony Orchestra, 2 professional live theatres and one amateur, 2 public libraries.

Parks: 3 major parks (403 acres).

Sports: home of Halifax Voyageurs of the AHL.

History: founded in 1749; meeting place of first legislative assembly in Canada (1758).

Hamilton, Ontario, Canada

The World Almanac is sponsored in Hamilton and the Niagara Peninsula by The Spectator (a division of Southam Press Ltd.), 115 King Street East, Hamilton, Ontario; phone (416) 522-8642; founded in 1846; circulation 137,226; publisher John D. Muir, business manager James S. Thomson, executive editor Gordon Bullock, managing editor Paul Warnick.

Population: 306,462 (city), 401,421 (Hamilton-Wentworth region); 3d in province, 6th in Canada; total work force, 260,000 (1974 region).

Area: 54.4 sq. mi. (city), 426 sq. mi. (region), at the west end of Lake Ontario.

Industry: 56.5% of Canada's steel is produced at the Steel Company of Canada and Dominion Foundaries and Steel Limited; city ranks 3d in Canada in industrial production; about 2,000 plants in the region, manufacturing iron and steel products, electrical apparatus, agricultural equipment, tires, food products, wire, heavy machinery, chemicals and textiles.

Commerce: retail sales (1973) $952 million; average weekly wage (1974) $192.42; 7th in Canada in total retail sales, 6th in annual wage.

Transportation: Hamilton Street Railway, Canadian National and Canadian Pacific railways, as well as the Toronto, Hamilton, and Buffalo line; western terminus for GO Transit (provincial rapid transit system); provincial highways through Toronto to Windsor and Buffalo pass through region; city airport 9 miles south at Mount Hope.

Communications: one TV, one community programming cable station, 4 radio stations.

New construction: Plans call for a 15,000-seat hockey arena; convention center slated for 1978; $5.2 million art gallery under construction.

Medical facilities: 5 major hospitals including medical center at McMaster Univ.; Hamilton Psychiatric Hospital; St. Peter's Centre for chronically ill and geriatric patients.

Educational facilities: McMaster Univ., Mohawk College of Applied Arts and Technology.

Cultural facilities: Hamilton Place, theater-auditorium; Hamilton Art Gallery; Hamilton Philharmonic Orchestra; Hamilton Players Guild; Multicultural Centre.

Sports: Hamilton Tiger-Cats, football; 2 municipal golf courses; Hamilton Fincups, hockey; Royal Hamilton Yacht Club.

Convention facilities: convention center slated for 1978, will have 17 meeting rooms, banquet space for up to 2,300 people in one room, 15-story office tower; 590 hotel rooms between 3 hotels in downtown core; banquet facilities for up to 700.

Other attractions: Dundurn Castle, restored prime minister's residence circa 1850; Whitehearn, restored Victorian home; Royal Botanical Gardens; Canadian Football League Hall of Fame; one of the largest park systems per capita in Canada; Hess Village, boutiques and restaurants in old restored homes; Bruce Trail winds through region along the Niagara Escarpment.

History: explorer Sieur de La Salle discovered Hamilton area in 1669; city takes name from George Hamilton, who laid out streets on part of the farm he bought in 1813.

Further information: Hamilton and District Visitors and Convention Bureau, 58 Jackson Street West; Hamilton; District Chamber of Commerce, 155 James St. South.

Hartford, Connecticut

The World Almanac is sponsored in the Hartford area by The Hartford Times, 10 Prospect St., Hartford, Conn. 06101; phone (203) 249-8211; founded 1817 by Frederick D. Bolles and John M. Niles; circulation 85,000 afternoons and Sunday; publisher Lionel S. Jackson, editor Charles A. Betts, Pulitzer citation as a newspaper; sponsor of Times Farm Camp for less privileged children, Learn-to-swim, Learn-to-ski.

Population: 156,500 (city), 823,200 (county); total employed greater Hartford, 335,500.

Area: 17.2 sq. miles.

Industry: "Insurance City", headquarters for 33 insurance firms employing 39,950; East Hartford is home office of United Technologies, one of the world's largest aircraft firms, manufacturers of Pratt & Whitney jet engines, employer of 52,000.

Commerce: total retail sales (county, 1973) $2.12 billion; per household consumer spendable income (1973) $14,628.

Transportation: intersection of highways 84 and 91; Amtrak, Penn Central Railroad; Bradley International Airport with 8 scheduled airlines, several providing cargo service.

New construction: Hartford Civic Center complex, including $18 million Aetna Life & Casualty shopping arcade, 20-story Sheraton Hotel, 10,000 seat coliseum, 70,000 sq. ft. exhibition hall, and 17,000 sq. ft. assembly hall.

Communications: 6 radio and 4 TV stations.

Educational facilities: Trinity College, Univ. of Hartford, Graduate Center of Rensselaer Polytechnic Institute, St. Joseph College, Hartford Seminary Foundation, Univ. of Connecticut Law School, Greater Hartford Community College.

Cultural facilities: Wadsworth Atheneum, the oldest public art museum in America; Mark Twain House; symphony orchestra; Conn. Opera Association; Stage Company; Mark Twain Masques; ballet company.

Sports: Greater Hartford Open (golf), Aetna World Cup (tennis); Bicentennials, Yankees (soccer); New England Whalers (hockey).

History: founded 1636 by Thomas Hooker and company of settlers from Newtown (Cambridge), Mass.; became Connecticut's capital city 1665.

Further information: Chamber of Commerce, 250 Constitution Plaza, Hartford, Conn. 06103.

Honolulu, Hawaii

The World Almanac is sponsored in Hawaii by The Honolulu Advertiser, P.O. Box 3110, Honolulu, Ha., 96802; (808) 537-2977; founded July 2, 1856, as Pacific Commercial Advertiser by Henry M. Whitney; circulation 76,196 mornings, 184,528 Sunday; president and publisher Thurston Twigg-Smith, editor-in-chief George Chaplin, executive editor Buck Buchwach, managing editor Mike Middlesworth; awards from American Political Science Assn., American Assn. for the Advancement of Science, others.

Population: 691,200 (metro); 1st in state; total employed, 269,110.

Area: 595 sq. mi., encompassing Oahu Island.

Commerce: major destination for U.S., Japanese tourists; persons staying a night or more, 2.8 million in 1974, up from 564,000 a decade earlier, tourist spending, $1 billion in 1974, up from $205 million 10 years earlier; visitor dollars top military spending, which totaled $897.9 million in 1974; sugarcane and pineapple major agriculture export crops; retail sales (statewide) $3 billion, per capita income $5,882, total income $4.9 billion; Pacific Basin business and financial center.

Transportation: dependent on ships, planes for most goods; passengers arrive mostly by air; ocean liners seldom call; 21 airlines serve airport: 8 domestic trunk carriers, 11 foreign, 2 inter-island; airport 13th busiest in nation.

Communications: 5 TV, 32 radio stations.

Medical facilities: 18 hospitals, including U.S. Army Tripler Hospital; Univ. of Hawaii School of Medicine. Research labs specialize in tropical diseases.

Cultural facilities: 10-campus, University of Hawaii with 56,500 students; main campus at Manoa in Honolulu, 21,526 students; university stresses oceanography, geophysics, Asian studies, tropical agriculture; U.S. State Department co-sponsors East-West Center at Manoa, attracts international student body; Bernice Pauahi Bishop Museum is center for studies of Pacific cultures, houses artifacts, maintains floating square-rigger Falls of Clyde, plus branch museum in Waikiki.

Other attractions: Waikiki Beach, extinct volcano Diamond Head, balmy weather, tradewinds, multiracial population, racial tolerance, Polynesian heritage.

History: Honolulu ("sheltered bay" in Hawaiian) was a small village when first Westerners called aboard 2 British ships in 1786, 8 years after Capt. James Cook became first known European to find Hawaiian Islands.

Bicentennial plans: include experimental outrigger canoe voyage between Hawaii and Tahiti using ancient navigation and sailing techniques with crew of 20.

Houston, Texas

The World Almanac is sponsored in the Southwest by The Houston Post, 47447 Southwest Freeway, Houston, Tex., 77001. Tel: (713) 621-7000; founded 1836; Oveta Culp Hobby, chairman of the board and editor; William P. Hobby, president. Circulation; daily 294,556; Saturday 330,032; Sunday 349,068. Awards include Pulitzer Prize, Grand Prix, Editor & Publisher. Community events sponsored; Science Fair, Spring Art Festival, travel fairs, charity football, others.

Population: 1,430,000 (city) 6th in nation; 2,274,000 (metro); total employed (1974) 1,018,600; total wages, salaries (metro 1974) $11.2 billion.

Area: 507 sq. mi. (city) on upper center Gulf Coast prairies, 41 ft. above sea level; Harris County seat; connected to Gulf of Mexico by 50-mile inland waterway, the Ship Channel.

Industry. major petroleum refining complex; Houston with Gulf Coast area has refining capacity of 3.4 million barrels per day of refined products (1974); nation's largest mfgr.-distributor petroleum equipment, pipeline transmissions; nation's greatest concentration of chemical/petrochemical industries; 3,096 mfg. firms (Dec. 1974 metro). Continually expanding complex of more than 1200 miles of product pipelines connect over 100 chemical plants, refineries, salt domes, and gasoline processing plants; metals industries have aggregate sales of over $2 billion annually, total metals payroll $537.8 million per year; nation's leading supplier of agricultural chemicals, fertilizers, and fuels; 1974 agric. income $52.6 million.

Commerce: metro retail sales $5.8 billion; 179 banks in metro area with 1974 resources of $13.5 billion, deposits of $11.4 billion. Average spendable family income (metro) $13,668.

Transportation: Port of Houston (3d largest in nation) moved almost 84 million tons of cargo in 1974; over 100 steamship lines; inland waterway 1974 tonnage exceeded 25 million short tons; 9 common carrier lines, 20 contract and specialized operators; 2 airports, 6 international airlines, 5 domestic airlines, one intrastate airline; 2 cargo carriers; 6 major rail systems moved 22 million short tons in 1974; 391 miles of freeways; 4 intercity bus lines; 400-bus local transit system.

Communications: 2 daily newspapers; 29 radio stations; 5 commercial, one educational TV station.
New construction: non-residential contract awards (1974) $1.1 billion; residential units completed value $713.3 million (1974).
Medical facilities: Texas Medical Center coordinates health education, research, patient care, 25 bldgs. on 200 acres; 58 hospitals including.VA hospital (metro), over 13,000 beds.
Federal facilities: Lyndon B. Johnson Space Center, $202 million manned-spacecraft center.
Cultural facilities: Houston Symphony Orchestra; Grand Opera Assn.; Houston Chorale; Alley Theatre; Miller Outdoor Theatre; 25 major art institutes; Natural Science Museum & Planetarium; 27-branch library system; Museum of Fine Arts, Contemporary Arts Museum.
Educational facilities: 7th largest school district in nation; more than 500,000 public school students in 54 districts (metro); 25 colleges and universities in area, including Univ. of Houston, Rice Univ.; 6 medical schools.
Recreational facilities: 258 parks and playgrounds; 5 municipal golf courses; 34 municipal swimming pools; Astroworld 60-acre amusement park; botanical garden, arboretum, Hermann Park & Zoo; 50 community centers; 28 Harris County parks; 70 miles of Gulf beaches in one hour's driving distance.

Convention facilities: world's largest single facility Astrohall and Abercrombie Arena, 991,000 sq. ft., next to Astrodome with its 60,000-seat capacity for conventions; downtown locations include Albert Thomas Convention Center (300,000 sq. ft.); Coliseum (50,000 sq. ft.) 11,500 seats; adjoining Music Hall seats 3,036; Exposition Hall, 83,000 sq. ft. exhibit area.
Sports: pro teams Astros baseball, Oilers football, Aeros hockey, Rockets basketball; sports events centers are Astrodome and Summit.
Climate: temperatures moderated by winds from the Gulf of Mexico; 1974 rainfall 49.3 in.; average yearly temps. 68.9° with highs in 90's, lows in 40's; avg. humidity in 70's.
History: founded 1836 by J. K. and A. C. Allen; city eventually encompassed Old Harrisburgh which was an 1826 townsite laid out by John Harris; named for Gen. Sam Houston, commander of the Texas Army which won independence from Mexico for the Republic of Texas Apr. 21, 1836; Houston was first president of the Republic, later governor of the state of Texas; both Houston and Harrisburg were for brief periods capitals of the Republic.
Bicentennial plans: beautification of Tranquility Park, Buffalo Bayou, Allen's Landing; establishment of Houston Metropolitan Archives and Research Center.
Further information: Houston Convention & Visitors Council, 10006 Main, Houston, 77002.

Huntington, West Virginia

The World Almanac is sponsored in the Huntington-Ashland-Ironton area by The Herald-Dispatch (morn.), and The Huntington Advertiser (aft.), Huntington Publishing Company, 946 Fifth Avenue, Huntington, West Virginia 25720, member of the Gannett Group; circulation 62,934, Sunday 54,918. Publisher and president N. S. Hayden, business manager James D. Hoffman, executive editor John H. McMillan; managing editors, C. Donald Hatfield (Advertiser), and Donald G. Mayne (Herald-Dispatch).

Population: 74,315 (city), 297,200 (5-county metro area); largest city in the state.
Area: 15.86 sq. mi., on Ohio River near where West Virginia, Ohio, and Kentucky meet.
Industry: center for coal transport and for handcrafted glass; leading industries are Ashland Oil, Armco Steel Co., Huntington Alloys Division of International Nickel Co.
Commerce: largest port for inland vessels in U.S. handles nearly 20,000,000 tons of materials per year, moved by 7 freight companies; 1974 total retail sales in metro area, $665 million.
Transportation: Tri-State Airport, with the longest runway in the state, is served by 2 airlines, 500 air

movements a month; 18 truck lines; urban bus transport system; 2 interstate bus lines.
Communications: 4 TV and 11 radio stations.
Cultural facilities: Marshall University; Ashland Community College (University of Kentucky); The Huntington Galleries of art.
Medical facilities: 5 general hospitals with 1,076 total beds; 3 specialty hospitals including a VA hospital.
New construction: $32,000,000 renewal program calls for large shopping mall, riverfront marina, civic auditorium, and additional convention facilities.
Further information: Group 2000, Prichard Bldg., Huntington, 25701; Chamber of Commerce, 522 Ninth Street, Huntington, 25701.

Indianapolis, Indiana

The World Almanac is sponsored in the Indianapolis area by The Indianapolis Star, The Indianapolis News, 307 N. Pennsylvania St., Indianapolis, IN 46206; (317) 633-1240. News founded 1869, Star 1903; circ. Star 217,901; News 161,751; Sunday Star 357,834; president-publisher Eugene C. Pulliam, asst. publ. Eugene S. Pulliam, Star editor Frank Crane, news editor Dr. Harvey Jacobs; Pulitzer Prizes—News, Star; Nat'l Headliners first prize—Star.

Population: 745,739 (consolidated city 1970), nation's 11th largest; 1,111,173 (metro 1970); total employed 500,000.
Area: 379.4 sq. mi., geographic center of state; state capital and Marion County seat.
Industry: over 1,400 diversified manufacturers including plane and auto engines and parts, electronics, pharmaceutical, machinery; 1974 manufacturing payroll over $1.3 billion.
Commerce: commercial center for Indiana; retail sales 3.2 billion; per capita personal income $5,300; 6 banks with resources over $5.2 billion; home offices of over 60 insurance companies.
Transportation: 9 airlines; 5 rail freight lines, Amtrak; 2 interstate bus lines, 67 truck lines, 7 interstate freeway routes.
New construction: projects totaling over $389 million under construction in 1975.
Communications: 6 TV and 18 radio stations.
Medical facilities: 16 hospitals, over 7,700 beds.
Federal facilities: Fort Harrison incl. Army Finance

and Acctng. Center, U.S.A. Admin. Center.
Cultural facilities: Museum of Art and Oldfields Museum of Decorative Arts; Indiana State Museum; Children's Zoo; Children's Museum; Conner Prairie Pioneer Settlement and Museum of Indian Heritage; Clowes Hall, home of symphony orch.; Civic Theatre, oldest U.S. amateur theatrical group; Repertory Theatre.
Education facilities: Butler Univ., Indiana Central Univ., Marion College, Christian Theological and St. Mauer's seminaries, Indiana Univ., Purdue Univ. at Indianapolis, with nation's largest medical school.
Recreational facilities: 9,000 park acres, 16 swimming pools, 10 municipal golf courses; pro basketball and hockey in 18,000-seat domed sports arena, home of the Pacers, ABA; Racers, WHA; minor league baseball, football.
Other attractions: Indianapolis 500, Yankee 300; annual National Drag Racing championships.
History: sesquicentennial in 1971; important before

Civil War, with nation's first union railway station (1853); home of James Whitcomb Riley, Booth Tarkington and President Benjamin Harrison.
Bicentennial plans: community efforts in city beauti-fication, neighborhood improvement, restoration areas, festival, and pride in cultural heritage.
Additional information: Indianapolis Chamber of Commerce, 320 N. Meridian St., 46204, (317) 635-4747.

Jacksonville, Florida

The World Almanac is sponsored in the Jacksonville area by The Florida Times-Union and The Jacksonville Journal, One Riverside Ave. 32202; phone (904) 791-4111; circulation, Times-Union 147,769, Journal 57,966, combined Sunday 178,351, president Robert R. Feagin, vice president John A. Tucker, executive editor John S. Walters; Journal won Pulitzer Prize for photography in 1967.

Population: 528,865 (1970); total employment, 264,-600 at end of 1974.
Area: 827 sq. mi., including nearly all of Duval Co. in northeast Fla.; largest incorporated developed area in Western Hemisphere.
Industry: 500 industries, added value total of $290 million annually; Offshore Power Systems investing $250 million in floating nuclear power plant production facility to employ 10,000 when completed.
Commerce: emphasis on finance, distribution; home or regional headquarters for 34 insurance companies; 1973 retail sales, $1.773 billion; effective buying income per household in 1973, $11,357.
Transportation: 3 major railroads and Amtrak; 16 major truck lines; 6 airlines averaging 130 air movements daily; 2 interstate bus lines; port handled 15.5 million tons in 1973.
Communications: 4 TV and 14 radio stations.
New construction: $232.6 million in building permits issued in 1974; 37-story Independent Life building, tallest in Florida.
Medical facilities: 10 general hospitals and one naval hospital with total of 3,158 beds.
Federal facilities: 2 naval air stations, one naval station add $400 million yearly to economy.
Cultural facilities: Cummer Art Gallery, Jacksonville Art Museum, Children's Museum; Jacksonville Symphony, Ballet Guild, 4 community theaters.
Education: Univ. of North Florida, Jacksonville Univ., Edward Waters College, Florida Jr. College.
Sports: Gator Bowl; Greater Jacksonville Open, $165,000 PGA tournament; World Football League "Express."
Other attractions: Civic Auditorium, Coliseum, Jacksonville Zoo, Fort Caroline, Kingsley Plantation; 8 miles of public beaches.
History: founded in 1822 by Isaiah Hart, named for Andrew Jackson; fire in 1901 destroyed 2,368 buildings, left 10,000 homeless; city and county governments merged in 1968 after referendum.
Further information: Chamber of Commerce, 604 Hogan St., or Convention & Visitors Bureau, Hemming Park, Jacksonville, 32202.

Kalamazoo, Michigan

The World Almanac is sponsored in the Kalamazoo area by The Kalamazoo Gazette, 401 S. Burdick, Kalamazoo, Mich. 49003; telephone (616) 345-3511, founded 1833; circulation daily 57,202, Sunday 61,178; owned and operated by Booth Newspapers Inc.; president James E. Sauter, editor Daniel M. Ryan, manager Ralph H. Bastien Jr.

Population: 78,152 (city), 200,879 (county); total employed in county, 89,575.
Area: located equidistant to the 3d and 5th largest metro areas in nation — Chicago and Detroit, 140 miles away.
Industry: paper-making is the traditional industry, with 5 large plants. Checker Motors Corp. manufactures cars; large Fisher Body Division body stamping plant; Upjohn Company, pharmaceuticals.
Commerce: shopping center for large part of Southwestern Michigan. In 1959, city became first in country to close downtown streets and create a pedestrian mall; now known as "Mall City". Retail sales (1974) $622 million; 4 banks had combined assets in 1974 of $766,146,472, 3 savings and loan associations have assets of over $200,000,000.
Transportation: 2 railroads provide freight service, Amtrak passenger service; 33 general carriers provide trucking services; airport with freight and passenger service; 3 bus lines.
Cultural facilities: 4 auditoriums offering music and theatrical performances, 6 live arts theaters, an art center, symphony orchestra, Kalamazoo Civic Players.
Educational facilities: 3 colleges and one university with combined student enrollment over 27,000.
Other attractions: Kalamazoo Nature Center, 83 lakes (county), National Junior Tennis Championships, 2 major hospitals, Kalamazoo Hotel-Business-Convention Center, IHL Kalamazoo Wings.
Bicentennial plans: 2-day Freedom Train stop.
Further information: Kalamazoo County Chamber of Commerce, 500 W. Crosstown, Kalamazoo, 49008, telephone (616) 381-4000.

Kansas City, Missouri

The World Almanac is sponsored in the Kansas City area by The Kansas City Star, 1729 Grand Ave., Kansas City, Mo. 64108; telephone (816) 421-1200; founded by William Rockhill Nelson; circulation morning 332,629, evening 310,779, Sunday 404,051; president and editor W. W. Baker, executive assistant to the president George Burg, general manager Frank S. McKinney, executive editor Cruise Palmer, advertising director W. W. Meyer.

Population: 511,600 (city); 1,307,800 (metro area), 27th in nation; total employed, 592,200.
Area: 316.3 sq. mi., at confluence of Missouri and Kansas rivers.
Industry: 2d in nation in automotive assembly; first in production of vending machines, greeting cards, underground freezer space, and winter wheat trading. Top employers: U.S. government, General Motors, TWA, Bendix, Western Electric, Ford. Presently Kansas City is a leading hard wheat center, stocker and feeder market, and is among the top 5 cities in flour production and grain elevator capacity.
Commerce: Total retail sales in 1973, $3.874 billion;
the center of a 7-county metro area: Jackson, Clay, Platte, Cass, and Ray counties in Missouri; Johnson and Wyandotte counties in Kansas.
Transportation: 9 airlines with 400 scheduled arrivals and departures daily at Kansas City International Airport; 169 truck lines and 4 barge companies; city is one of the nation's major rail centers.
New construction: $250,000,000 Crown Center business and apartment complex covers 25 square blocks; new medical center of University of Missouri; American Royal Arena; Mercantile Bank Building; United Missouri Bank headquarters; 30-story office and retail building downtown. Worlds of Fun recreation

center. More than 6 large hotels and several hospital additions.

Cultural facilities: Starlight Theater, nation's 2d largest outdoor theater; William Rockhill Nelson Gallery of Art, among the 10 top American museums with the 3d largest Oriental collection outside China; Performing Arts Foundation formed in 1965 to present festival events; University of Missouri at Kansas City; Rockhurst College; Kansas City Art Institute; University of Kansas Medical Center. Within commuting distance are University of Kansas, Park College, William Jewell College, Truman Library in Independence. Linda Hall Library of Science and Technology is one of the largest privately endowed technical reference libraries in the nation.

Recreational facilities: more than 100 parks cover

5,345 acres, including Swope Park, 2d largest in nation, with fine zoo.

Sports: The American Royal Livestock and Horse Show each fall attracts entries from throughout the country; home of the Chiefs of the NFL, Royals, American League baseball, Kings, NBA, and the Scouts, NHL.

History: Kansas City's beginnings can be traced to a trading post of French fur trappers about 1826. It became an important trade and transportation center as the overland routes of the Oregon and Santa Fe Trails spread westward. As agricultural production boomed, it became an important market and distribution center for crops from throughout the Middle West.

Further information: Chamber of Commerce of Greater Kansas City, 920 Main, Kansas City, Missouri.

Kitchener-Waterloo, Ontario, Canada

The World Almanac is sponsored in the Kitchener-Waterloo area by the Kitchener-Waterloo Record, 225 Fairway Road, Kitchener, Ont.; phone (519) 579-2231; founded 1878, circulation 63,788, president John E. Motz, publisher K. A. Baird.

Population: 126,162 (Kitchener) and 45,349 (Waterloo), 277,284 (metro area); total employed 93,100.

Area: 48.85 sq. mi. (Kitchener) and 25.47 sq. mi. (Waterloo), 65 miles west of Toronto.

Industry: highly diversified industry (519 companies), rubber, plastics, electronics, metal fabrication, brewing, distilling, meat packing, footwear, furniture, food processing, automotive components; Budd Automotive Co., largest autoframe manufacturer in Canada; Deilcraft furniture plant is the largest under one roof in North America.

Agricultural: beef and dairy area; Waterloo County's 1,537 farms accounted for $78 million production in 1974.

Commerce: wholesale and retail center for area; metro retail sales (1974) $471.8 million; 6 banks, 61 branches; 6 trust companies, 18 branches; 36 life insurance offices, 21 other insurance offices; Waterloo, "The Hartford of Canada," head office for 6 insurance companies.

Transportation: 2 major rail lines, 34 truck lines, on Ontario's key highway 401; Waterloo-Wellington Airport; 45 mi. from Toronto International.

Communications: one TV and 4 radio stations.

Medical facilities: 2 major hospitals.

Cultural facilities: symphony orchestra, Kitchener-Waterloo Art Gallery, Doon Pioneer Village; 28 mi. from famed Stratford Festival Theatre.

Educational facilities: Univ. of Waterloo, Wilfrid Laurier Univ., Conestoga College.

Other attractions: nationally-known farmers market; Canada's largest annual Oktoberfest celebration; Woodside, national historic park, boyhood of W. L. Mackenzie King, Canadian prime minister 22 years.

History: founded 1807 by German settlers; retains strong Germanic flavor.

Further information: Kitchener Chamber of Commerce, 68 King East; Waterloo Chamber of Commerce, Waterloo Square.

Knoxville, Tennessee

The World Almanac is sponsored in the Knoxville area by The Knoxville News-Sentinel, 204 West Church Ave., Knoxville, TN 37901. Sentinel founded in 1886; News in 1921 by Scripps-Howard Newspapers; Sentinel purchased by Scripps-Howard in 1926 and combined with News. Circulation 108,253 daily; 162,458 Sunday; editor Ralph L. Millett Jr., managing editor Harold E. Harlow.

Population: 180,447 (city), 308,797 (county), 452,281 (metro area); 3d in state; total employed metro area, 178,000.

Area: city 77.6 sq. mi., county 528 sq. mi., located almost in exact center of that portion of United States lying east of the Mississippi River and south of Great Lakes.

Industry: major-manufacturing industries are primary metals and chemicals; nearly 500 plants representing 51 diversified major industries (coal and zinc mining, marble quarrying, meat packing, steel fabrication, industrial controls eqpt., furniture, auto safety eqpt., refuse eqpt., apparel) with Aluminum Co. of America, Union Carbide Corp. Nuclear Div. at Oak Ridge, included in Knoxville market.

Commerce: wholesale and retail trade center of a multi-county area in East Tennessee, Virginia, Kentucky, N. Carolina; county retail sales (1974) $895 million.

Transportation: 2 rail lines, 5 airlines, 2 inter-state bus lines, 25 motor freight carriers; interstate Highways I-40 and I-75 intersect in heart of city.

New construction: $32 million City-County bldg. to house both Knoxville and Knox County governmental offices; downtown redevelopment.

Cultural facilities: Univ. of Tennessee, Knoxville College, Knoxville Symphony Orchestra, 10 museums, art gallery, auditorium-coliseum, city-county library (496,879 book volume), Zoological Park; University-community theater, Choral Society, opera workshop.

Sports: Univ. of Tennessee Vols football; Knoxville Sox, farm club of Chicago White Sox.

Other attractions: Great Smoky Mountains National Park, 39 miles from Knoxville, offers year-round scenic beauty, skiing in season; within 30 miles of Knoxville, 6 TVA lakes offer 2,320 miles of shoreline providing fishing, boating, swimming. Oak Ridge, known for its nuclear developments, 22 miles from Knoxville; American Museum of Atomic Energy.

Bicentennial plans: development of Bicentennial Riverfront Park.

Further information: Chamber of Commerce, 301 E. Church Ave., Knoxville, 37902 or Tourist Bureau, 811 Henley St., Knoxville, 37902.

Las Vegas, Nevada

The World Almanac is sponsored in the Las Vegas area by the Las Vegas Review-Journal, 1111 W. Bonanza, Las Vegas, 89101; phone (702)385-4241; founded as a weekly 1909; purchased 1956 by Donald W. Reynolds, present publisher; member Donrey Media Group; circulation 67,355 weekdays, 71,434 Sundays; general manager Wm. Wright; editor Don Digilio.

Population: 334,192 greater Las Vegas (1974); 1974 total employment 139,400.

Area: southern Nevada, 7,927 sq. miles, 283 miles NW of Phoenix, 289 miles NE of Los Angeles.

Industry: 24-hour tourism; hotel/gaming/recreation payroll $392.3 million; 1974 tourist volume 8.6 million; convention and tourist revenue $1.2 billion, gaming revenue $684 million.

Commerce: 6 banks total resources over $992 million, 5 savings & loans, resources $472 million; retail sales $1 billion, average spendable family income $10,345.

Transportation: McCarran Int'l Airport, total 5.9 million yearly passengers, 7 major airlines, plus foreign carriers, U.S. Customs Port of Entry, 3 bus lines, daily auto traffic entering area 14 thousand.

Communications: 5 TV stations, 12 radio stations, 3 newspapers.

Medical facilities: 8 hospitals, 8 convalescent homes, acupuncture clinics.

Federal facilities: Nellis Air Force Base, 7,000 military, 1,100 civilian personnel, $72 million annual federal payroll.

Cultural facilities: cultural arts; arts & crafts; centers for cultural & athletic programs; drama theatre; music; dance; beautification; museum, educational displays, historical societies, collectors organizations, libraries.

Education: enrollment (public & private) 82,153; Univ. of Nevada Las Vegas; community college.

Recreation: Lake Mead recreation area, Hoover Dam; Mt. Charleston, Lee & Kyle Canyons, skiing; Valley of Fire, Lost City Museum, one-day drive to ghost towns; Death Valley.

Convention facilities: Las Vegas Convention Center 45 acres, 50,000 sq. ft. under roof, 330,000 sq. ft. exhibit area; 7,500 seat rotunda, 10 hotels with convention facilities; over 365 conventions in city each year.

Sports: 12 golf courses, 125 tennis courts, 16,000-seat Las Vegas Stadium; Casinos, pro football; Gamblers, hockey; UNLV basketball, baseball & football.

History: First recorded group to enter the Las Vegas Valley was Antonio Armijo's party in early 1839. Las Vegas, Spanish for "The Meadows," first settled by Europeans in June of 1855, by a 30-man Mormon group under William Bringhurst. City of Las Vegas founded May 15, 1905, as a result of public land auction by the railroad.

Bicentennial plans: 2 major projects under heritage theme; preservation of old Mormon fort; remodeling of Reed Whiple center into 800 seat Cultural Arts Center.

Further information: Las Vegas Chamber of Commerce, 2301 East Sahara, Las Vegas, 89105.

Lethbridge, Alberta

The World Almanac is sponsored in the Lethbridge area by The Lethbridge Herald, 504 7th St. S., Lethbridge, Alberta; phone (403) 328-4411; founded as weekly in 1907; circulation, weekdays, 23,932, Saturdays, 25,600; editor and publisher Cleo W. Mowers, general manager Donald Doram, managing editor Donald H. Pilling.

Population: 44,377, 3d in province.

Area: 22 square miles; located on Oldman River 60 miles north of Montana border, 125 miles south of Calgary.

Industry: heavily dependent on agriculture; federally-inspected packing plants slaughtered 27% of cattle slaughtered in Alberta in 1974; large dryland grain growing, ranching area and extensive irrigation district; brewery, distillery, flour mill, foundry, oilseed processing.

Commerce: 1974 retail sales of $187.5 million, 35% more than 1973; 5 banks; 4 trust companies, 11 finance companies.

Transportation: CP Rail; 2 bus lines; depots for 50 trucking firms; regional airline flies out of Lethbridge Airport.

New construction: Building permits valued at $42.5 million in 1974, compared with $28.7 in 1973.

Communications: 2 radio, 2 TV stations.

Medical facilities: 2 general hospitals, one long-term care hospital, 4 nursing homes for aged.

Cultural facilities: Canada agriculture research station, Univ. of Lethbridge, Lethbridge Community College, Alexander Galt Museum, Nikka Yuko Centennial Japanese Garden, symphony orchestra and chorus, local theatre groups.

Other attractions: 2 major parks, 4 artificial ice arenas, Stewart Game Farm.

Sports: Expos, Montreal Expos farm team; Broncos, Western Canada Hockey League.

History: early coal-mining town, named Lethbridge Oct. 16, 1885, after a coal executive. A whisky traders' depot, Fort Whoop-Up was booming, 5 miles southwest of what is now Lethbridge, in the 1860's. First settlers in area came 15 years later, many from United States.

Little Rock, Arkansas

The World Almanac is sponsored in Arkansas by the Arkansas Gazette, 112 West Third Street, Little Rock 72203, phone (501) 376-6161; founded 1819 at Arkansas Post, A. T., by Wm. E. Woodruff, moved to Little Rock 1821; circulation 121,135 daily, 143,635 Sunday; Hugh B. Patterson Jr., publisher and president; J. O. Powell, editorial director; Robert R. Douglas, managing editor; J. R. Williamson, executive vice president-general manager.

Population: 169,398 (city), 344,600 (metro); 152,500 employed.

Area: 110 sq. mi. at point where Ozarks-Ouachita highlands meet central coastal plain at geographical center of state.

Industry: 378 manufacturing plants, employing 31,500 persons, and including Allis-Chalmers, Armstrong Rubber Co., Timex, AMF Cycle Division, Remington Arms, Jacuzzi Bros., Teletype, and Westinghouse, among others.

Commerce: Retail sales (estimated 1974) $818,936,000; bank resources $1.435 billion; building permits (1974) $76,571,780; 11 banks, 6 building & loan associations, 4 old line insurance companies.

Transportation: 3 trunkline railroads, 5 federally certified airlines, 8 bus lines, 14 common carrier barge lines.

Communications: 3 commercial TV; one ETV, 12 radio stations.

Medical facilities: 10 hospitals including UA Medical Center, 2 VA hospitals, and Ark. State Hospital for Nervous Diseases.

Federal facilities: Little Rock Air Force Base (LRAFB), Military Airlift (MAC) Command; Camp Joseph T. Robinson, Arkansas National Guard headquarters and training center; U.S. National Guard Bureau's Non-Commissioned Officers Institute.

Cultural facilities: Univ. of Arkansas at Little Rock with Schools of Law, Medicine, Nursing, and Pharmacy; UA School of Graduate Technology; Philander Smith, Shorter, and Arkansas Baptist colleges;

Arkansas State Symphony, Arkansas Arts Center, 3 major public libraries, convention center-auditorium-hotel.

History: French explorer Bernard de la Harpe noted "le petit roche" on his map of the Arkansas River Valley in 1722.

Further information: Chamber of Commerce, Continental Bldg., Markham & Main Streets; Arkansas Parks & Tourist Dept., State Capitol — both Little Rock 72201.

Los Angeles, California

Population: 2.82 million (1974, city), 7.1 million (county); first in state, 3d in nation; total civilian employed 2.9 million (county, 1974); labor force 3.2 million (county, 1974).

Area: 463.7 sq. mi. on Pacific, 418 mi. south of San Francisco, 145 mi. north of Mexico. Los Angeles county seat, one of 77 cities in county.

Industry: leading aerospace industry with 17 of top 100 defense contractors in nation located in southern California; center of entertainment industry with more than 600 firms in movie work; women's clothing, sports wear, electronics, rubber, tires, printing, furniture, paper, autos, auto parts, chemicals; manufacturing work force 837,300; trade 698,100; services 625,600, government 447,300. Among nation's leaders in agriculture; farm income $136.8 million (1973), cattle slaughter 1.5 million (1972), 219,500 tons sea fish harvested (1974).

Commerce: total taxable sales by retail stores $12.7 billion (county, 1974); median family income $10,251; average per capita income $4,967 (county); personal income $41.3 billion (county, 1973); approximately 90 commercial banks, 80 savings and loans; bank deposits over $5 billion (city, 1974); S&L savings over $17.6 billion (county); bank clearings 1974 $558.8 billion. International trade through Los Angeles customs district $8.9 billion; imports $5.65 billion, exports $3.3 billion (1973).

Transportation: Santa Fe, Union Pacific, Southern Pacific railroads, Amtrak; 6 major bus lines; largest concentration of trucks in western U.S., 58,000; more than 3.9 million private cars; 143.7 mi. freeway in city, 463.2 mi. in county; 36 domestic and international airlines serving L.A. International Airport handling 460,713 landings and takeoffs; 23.6 million passengers; 1.5 billion pounds cargo (1974); more than 46 miles of commercial waterfront in Los Angeles-Long Beach harbor which served 5,702 ships, 57 million tons of cargo, including 35.7 million tons petroleum products (1974).

Communications: 11 TV stations, over 60 radio stations, more than 25 daily publications in English and foreign languages in county.

New construction: building permits $2.2 billion (county, 1973), including $1.1 billion residential, 43,-107 new housing units (1973).

Medical facilities: 90 hospitals, 16,799 beds (city); 204 hospitals, 43,560 beds (county).

Educational facilities: 436 elementary schools; 75 junior high schools; 54 high schools, more than 150 private schools; 150 libraries; UCLA; Univ. of Southern California; Cal. Institute of Technology, Loyola Marymount Univ., Claremont Colleges, Whittier College, Pepperdine Univ., regional campuses of State University and Colleges at L.A., Northridge, Long Beach, Domingues.

Cultural facilities: 1,600 churches, Huntington Art Gallery and Library; Hollywood Bowl; Greek Theater; Griffith Park Planetarium; Mt. Wilson and Mt. Palomar Observatories; Los Angeles Museum, Music Center, County Art Museum; UCLA Botanical Gardens, Southwest Museum.

Recreational facilities: more than 200 parks and playgrounds, 6 public golf courses, 15 public beaches within 35 miles of downtown; mountains, lakes, skiing, deserts, Disneyland, Marineland, Knott's Berry Farm, and Magic Mountain within 2 hours drive.

Convention facilities: large convention center; over 50,000 rooms.

Sports: pro teams in baseball (Dodgers, Angels in Anaheim), football (Rams); basketball (Lakers); hockey (Kings); Santa Anita and Hollywood Park thoroughbred racing; collegiate basketball and football; Rose Bowl.

History: discovered 1542 by Portuguese navigator Juan Rodriguez Cabrillo. Mission San Gabriel founded Sept. 1771; city formally founded Sept. 4, 1781, by Spanish colonial governor as El Pueblo de Nuestra Senora la Reina de los Angeles de Porciuncula, Inc. Apr. 4, 1850.

Bicentennial plans: cultural festival June-Sept.; festival of faiths, Feb.; music festival Jan.-Feb.

Further information: Chamber of Commerce, P.O. Box 3696 Terminal Annex, Los Angeles, 90051.

Louisville, Kentucky

The World Almanac is sponsored in Kentucky and Southern Indiana by The Courier-Journal and The Louisville Times, 525 West Broadway, Louisville, Kentucky 40202; (502) 582-4011; Courier-Journal founded 1868; Times 1884; Courier circulation 227,463; Times, 173,165; Sunday 361,996; chairman of the board Barry Bingham Sr., editor and publisher Barry Bingham Jr.; major awards include 5 Pulitzer Prizes.

Population: 346,500 (city), 898,400 (metro area); 1st in state; total employed 366,700.

Area: 65.2 sq. mi. (city), 1,392 sq. mi. (metro); on southern bank of Ohio River.

Industry and commerce: one of top 20 industrial markets; famous for baseball bats, cigarettes, railroad repair shops, electrical appliances, farm machinery, motor vehicles, plumbing fixtures and whiskey; 900 manufacturing firms in area; estimated retail sales, Jefferson County (1974), $2.243 billion.

Transportation: 6 trunk-line railroads, 2 terminal railroads; 87 inter-city truck lines; 5 barge lines; 4 bus lines; 7 airlines, and 2 municipal airports.

Communications: 14 radio, 4 TV stations, one educational.

Medical facilities: 21 hospitals, 5,811 total beds.

Cultural facilities: Louisville Orchestra, Kentucky Opera Association, Art Center Association, J. B. Speed Art Museum; 20 private art galleries, Macauley Theatre, Actors Theatre, The Children's Theatre, Louisville Civic Ballet, Louisville-Jefferson County Youth Orchestra, The Louisville Free Public Library (29 branches); 678 churches, 46 denominations.

Education: 11 colleges and universities, 4 business colleges and technical schools in area.

Recreation: 147 public parks, covering 7,000 acres.

Convention facilities: Kentucky Fair & Exposition Center, largest multi-purpose exposition building in U.S. with 22 acres under one roof, 20,000-plus seating, parking for 27,000 cars; Convention Center, downtown, handles up to 7,000; new 400,000 sq. ft. exhibition hall and convention center in downtown Louisville under construction.

Sports: Kentucky Derby, held annually at Churchill Downs since 1875, attended annually by over 125,000; Commonwealth Racecourse; Louisville Downs (harness racing); Kentucky Colonels, ABA.

Other attractions: Belle of Louisville excursion steamboat; Churchill Downs Museum; Louisville Zoo; American Printing House for the Blind; Kentucky Railway Museum.

History: founded by explorer George Rogers Clark, in 1778; named after King Louis XVI of France.

Further information: Louisville Area Chamber of Commerce, 300 West Liberty, Louisville, 40202.

Lubbock, Texas

The World Almanac is sponsored in the Lubbock area by the Lubbock Avalanche-Journal, 8th St. and Ave. J., Lubbock, Texas, 79408; (806) 762-8844; founded 1900 as Leader, became Avalanche 1908, daily 1921; Plains Journal weekly founded 1923; consolidated 1926; circulation (morn) 58,285, (eve) 15,779, (Sat) 69,014, (Sun) 76,-453; member Southwestern Newspaper Corp.; general manager Robert R. Norris; editor Jay Harris.

Population: 171,100 (city), 201,200 (metro area), 8th in state; total employed 79,770.
Area: 82.2 sq. mi.; center of South Plains territory of northwest Texas.
Industry: vegetable oils, cotton, cotton seed flour, grain sorghum, livestock, petroleum, sand and gravel; 228 manufacturing companies.
Commerce: wholesale and retail center for west Texas and eastern New Mexico; retail sales $499 million; bank resources: $679 million; 8 banks and 6 savings and loan associations.
Transportation: 12 motor freight carriers; 2 major railroads, and 3 bus lines; Lubbock Regional Airport, 3 major airlines averaging 60 air movements per day; 6 major federal and state highways.
Communications: 4 TV and 9 radio stations.
Medical facilities: 8 hospitals, Lubbock State School for Mentally Retarded; medical school being constructed on Texas Tech campus, County Teaching Hospital under construction.
Federal facilities: Reese AFB, Federal Building, Federal Aviation Admin., and National Weather

Service, U.S. Customs Port of Entry.
Cultural facilities: symphony orchestra, Theatre Centre; Museum of Texas Tech Univ., Moody Planetarium; Ranch Headquarters (authentic ranch houses dating to 1835); Lubbock Christian College; Memorial Convention Center under construction; Texas Tech Univ., Lubbock Cultural Affairs Council, and Lubbock Garden & Arts Center.
Recreational facilities: 39 city parks, 1,750 acres; Mackenzie State Park, state's largest, with Prairie Dog Town, Buffalo Lakes; Municipal Auditorium, 3,200 seats; Municipal Coliseum, 10,000 capacity; annual Panhandle South Plains Fair.
Sports: Texas Tech, and Christian College sports; Tech Jones Stadium, site of annual Coaches All-American football game; indoor Rodeos.
Bicentennial plans: completion of Ranch Headquarters, and Memorial Civic Center; landscaping drive to connect points of interest in Lubbock to be called The Bicentennial Trail.
Further information: Chamber of Commerce, 902 Texas Avenue, Lubbock, Tex. 79401.

Macon, Georgia

The World Almanac is sponsored in the Macon area by The Macon Telegraph & News, 120 Broadway, Macon, Ga. 31208; phone (912) 743-2621; acquired by Knight-Ridder Newspapers Inc., 1969; circulation, Telegraph (morn) 50,294, News (eve) 20,941, Sat. 64,911, Sun. 77,811; general manager Bert Struby, executive editor Don Carter, News editor Joseph Parham.

Population: 122,423 (city), 226,782 (metro), 3d in state; labor force, 93,470.
Area: 52 sq. mi., 6 miles northwest of geographic center of Georgia; Bibb County seat.
Industry: textiles; Bibb Company, longtime industry leader, headquartered in area; 2 textile-related plants — YKK Zipper Co. of Japan, and Texprint, Inc.; forestry; Armstrong Cork Co. acoustical tile plant is area's largest; pulpwood also is used to manufacture cardboard, packaging; tobacco, Brown & Williamson Tobacco Corp. to open $200 million cigarette plant in 1976; Kaolin (clay) deposits are mined in area and processed in numerous ways; Government Employees Insurance Co. regional office.
Federal Facilities: Warner Robins Air Logistics

Center and Robins Air Force Base, 16 miles from Macon, are area's largest employers.
Educational facilities Wesleyan College, nation's oldest college for women, and Mercer Univ. with law school; Macon Jr. College.
Other attractions: Ocmulgee National Monument displays archeological remains of 3 prehistoric Indian civilizations; $4.5 million coliseum seats 10,000.
History: settled when U. S. established Fort Hawkins in 1806; chartered in 1823, named for Nathaniel Macon of North Carolina.
Bicentennial plans: Freedom Rally July 4, 1976, with political, religious speakers; monument unveiled.
Further information: Chamber of Commerce, 305 Coliseum Drive, Macon, Ga. 31201.

Madison, Wisconsin

The World Almanac is sponsored in Madison by Madison Newspapers, Inc., publisher of the Capital Times and Wisconsin State Journal, 115 S. Carroll St., Madison, Wis., 53701; (608) 256-5511; circulation, State Journal (morn) 76,000, Capital Times (eve) 46,100, Sunday Journal 121,446.

Population: 171,169 (city), 290,272 (county), 2d in state; metro work force 150,500.
Area: 52 sq. mi. (city), 1,194 sq. mi. (county), in south-central Wisconsin, state capital and Dane County seat.
Commerce: home office of 29 insurance firms; 375 industrial firms; 26 banks, 7 savings and loans; retail sales $568,165,000 (city), $850,493,000 (county); average spendable family income, $14,686.
Transportation: Dane County regional airport, 3 airlines; 3 railroads, Amtrak, major Interstate highway system; 5 bus lines; 30 truck lines; city owned bus system.
Communications: 4 TV, 2 cable, 6 AM and 8 FM radio stations.
Medical facilities: 9 hospitals, including U.W. hospital

and V.A.; 20 major clinics, 600 physicians.
Federal facilities: Forest Products Laboratory.
Cultural facilities: Dane County Coliseum; 2 art centers, ballet company, 11 drama groups, 7 music organizations; 15 Catholic, 150 Protestant, one Greek Orthodox church, 2 synagogues.
Education: Univ. of Wis., and 3 colleges; 35 elementary, 10 middle, 5 high schools; 15 parochial, one vocational-technical, 63 specialized schools; 7 city and 32 university libraries.
Recreation: 5 lakes with total of 18,000 acres of water surface; 4,300 acres of parks.
Convention facilities: 12 hotels with large convention facilities.
Sports: Blues, hockey; Univ. of Wis. in Big Ten.
Bicentennial plans: special weeks for individual ob-

servances of historical events of nation, state, and city.

Further information: Greater Madison Chamber of Commerce, 615 E. Washington Ave. 53701.

Memphis, Tennessee

The World Almanac is sponsored in the Memphis area by The Memphis Press-Scimitar, 495 Union Ave., Memphis, Tenn., 38101; phone (901) 526-2141; Scimitar founded 1880 by G. P. M. Turner; Press 1906 by Scripps-McRae League, predecessor of Scripps-Howard Newspapers; circulation 123,362; editor Charles H. Schneider, managing editor Ed Ray.

Population: 675,000 (city), 863,600 (metro area); first in state, 16th in nation; 330,400 employed.
Area: 274 sq. mi., Shelby County seat, on east bank Mississippi River.
Industry: a major hardwood lumber center; manufacture of furniture and flooring; extensive cotton marketing-warehousing and processing of cotton seed into vegetable oil products; headquarters of Holiday Inns Inc., Cook Industries (cotton and grain), and Conwood Corp. (tobacco and food products). Other large industries include Schering-Plough (drugs), International Harvester (cotton pickers, hay balers), and Firestone (tires).
Commerce: wholesale-retail center for large parts of Tennessee, Arkansas and Mississippi; retail sales (1973) $2.2 billion; bank deposits $2.1 billion; 17 banks, 7 savings-loan assns. Per capita personal income $4,166 (1972).
Transportation: 10 airlines, 150 arrivals a day; 7 trunk line railroads, 82 motor freight lines, 6 barge lines; river port handled 10.4 million tons of freight in 1972.
Communications: 4 TV and 21 radio stations.
Medical facilities: Univ. of Tennessee medical units and a Veterans Administration hospital in complex with public hospital; 3 private general hospitals and St. Jude Hospital, research center for childhood illnesses, particularly leukemia.
Federal facilities: Naval Air Station, Naval Air Technical Training Center, Defense Depot Memphis and Air Forces's 164th Air Transport Group.
Cultural facilities: symphony orchestra, Opera Theater, Little Theater, Brooks Art Gallery, museum; annual performances of Metropolitan Opera.
Educational facilities: Memphis State Univ., Southwestern College, LeMoyne-Owen College, Christian Brothers College, Univ. of Tennessee medical units, Shelby State Community College, State Technical Institute, Southern College of Optometry, Mid-South Bible College.
Recreational facilities: Meeman-Shelby Forest state park, 12,500 acres; also 137 other parks.
Convention facilities: $27 million Cook Convention Center, 1.3 million sq. ft., seating 16,500.
Sports: Memorial Stadium, home of Southmen of World Football League and Memphis State University football team; Mid-South Coliseum, home of MSU's basketball team and Memphis Sounds of the ABA; also Memphis Blues, International Baseball League (AAA), and Danny Thomas Memphis Classic golf tournament.
Other attractions: Cotton Carnival each May; Mid-South Fair each September; Beale Street, home of the blues, where composer W. C. Handy lived.
History: DeSoto, exploring Mississippi River, stopped here in 1541; Ft. Adams established in 1797; Memphis incorporated in 1826. Yellow fever in 1878 nearly depopulated city, but its population grew back to 64,589 in 1890.
Bicentennial plans: grand opening of Libertyland; half-time heritage program at Liberty Bowl football game.
Further information: Memphis Area Chamber of Commerce, 42 S. 2d St., Memphis, 38103.

Mexico City (Ciudad de Mexico), Mexico

Population: 2,902,969 (1970).
Area: About 53 sq. mi. within the 573 sq. mi. Federal District (Distrito Federal; population, 1975 est. 9 million); in central Mexico at an altitude of 7,349 ft.
Industry and commerce: capital of Mexico; the political and economic hub of the nation; manufactures include steel, automobiles, appliances, textiles, rubber goods, furniture, and electrical equipment; marketing center of Mexico.
Transportation: center of modern highway and rail system; 25-mi. subway system; served by most international air lines. Mexico City is 4 hrs. by jet from New York and 3 hrs. from Los Angeles.
Communications: major media center for Mexico and parts of Latin America; major film center.
Cultural facilities: Palace of Fine Arts and Ballet Folklorico; National Palace (Diego Rivera murals); National University with over 90,000 students; National Museum of Anthropology; city itself is an architectural exhibit of Aztec ruins, baroque cathedrals, and ultra-modern buildings.
Other attractions: Xochimilco with the "floating gardens" and gondolas; Chapultepec Castle, palace of the French-supported Emperor and Empress of Mexico, Maximilian and Carlota; 22-ton Aztec Calendar Stone; 2 volcanoes, Popocatepetl (17,887 ft.) and Iztaccihuatl (17,343 ft.); sports centers.
History: traditionally founded 1321 by Aztecs, city was called Tenochtitlan; captured by Spanish under Cortez in 1519 and again in 1521; occupied by U. S. in 1847 and by the French from 1863 to 1867.
Further information: Mexican National Tourist Council, Mariano Escobedo 726, Mexico, D.F., or 677 5th Ave., New York 10022; or 9445 Wilshire Blvd., Beverly Hills, Cal. 90212.

Miami, Florida

The World Almanac is sponsored in the Miami area by The Miami Herald, 1 Herald Plaza, Miami, Fla. 33101; phone (305) 350-2111; founded Dec. 1 1910, by Frank B. Shutts; circulation 477,061 daily, 507,777 Sunday; editorial chairman John S. Knight, editor Don Shoemaker, executive editor Larry Jinks, managing editor Ron Martin; newspaper or staff writers have won or shared in 4 Pulitzer prizes, the latest in 1973, and numerous other honors.

Population: 350,000 (city), 1,350,000 (metro); 1st in state, 24th in nation; total employed in metro area, 673,000.
Area: 53.8 sq. mi., land and water, on Biscayne Bay at mouth of Miami River in southeast Florida; Dade County seat.
Industry: 4,900 light manufacturing plants; tourism and aviation are mainstays of economy; 1,000 hotels and motels employ 50,000 and handle 12 million visitors a year; aviation accounts for 80,000 jobs; Eastern (largest industrial employer), National, and Pan American operate bases; winter agriculture center.
Commerce: center of Pan-American finance and commerce, with 76 banks, 15 savings and loan associ-

ations, Federal Reserve Bank branch; retail sales (1974) $4.27 billion; Port of Miami busy in waterborne commerce as well as Caribbean cruise center, with 20 cruise sailings weekly.

Transportation: Miami International, served by 105 air carriers, handled 12.4 million travelers in 1974; Seaboard Coast Line, Amtrak, and all-freight Fla. East Coast Railroads operate in Miami, as do Greyhound and Trailways buses; 39 truck lines.

Communications: 5 commercial and 5 educational or closed-circuit TV stations, 36 radio stations.

New construction: major new office buildings downtown, topped by 40-story One Biscayne Tower, in a $500 million building surge; ground broken at $75 million Omni International Miami "megastructure" with shops, a hotel, restaurants, and entertainment.

Medical facilities: 38 hospitals, 9,296 beds; over 13,-000 beds at 54 nursing and convalescent homes in metro area; 2,800 members of Dade County Medical Association; Jackson Memorial Hospital one of area's leading research facilities.

Federal facilities: Homestead Air Force Base south of Miami with 8,900 men and women; Federal Aviation Administration; Coast Guard bases; 2 federal hospitals; oceanographic center; 12,400 U.S. employees.

Cultural facilities: Philharmonic, Opera Guild, and other musical groups perform regularly; 18 auditoriums, including new downtown Gusman Hall; resident and touring theatrical productions; 6 major art museums; 7 playhouses, and 55 night clubs and theater restaurants, some in major hotels.

Educational facilities: 8 colleges and universities, plus 3 campuses of Miami-Dade Community College, total enrollment of 62,000; Univ. of Miami is largest independent institution of higher learning in southeast; Florida International Univ. public school system with 244,565 students.

Recreational facilities: 14 miles of public beach on ocean and bay; 297 parks and playgrounds, 11 stadiums and grandstands; resort-oriented, Miami offers 42 golf courses and 57 marinas for boaters, with 43,-000 pleasure craft registered; 72 movie houses.

Convention facilities: newly expanded Miami Beach Convention Hall can handle largest conventions; 695 conventions brought 370,000 delegates to Miami Beach in 1974; 204 brought 83,910 delegates to Miami proper.

Sports: pro football Miami Dolphins and U. of Miami play in Orange Bowl, which seats 80,050; stadium also hosts Orange Bowl game, Orange Blossom classic, North-South All-Star Shrine Game; parimutuel wagering at 5 horse and greyhound tracks, jai-alai fronton.

Other attractions: balmy subtropical climate, with mean annual temperature of 75.3 degrees; 532 Protestant, 49 Catholic churches, and 41 Jewish synagogues; city is bilingual with 400,000 Latin American residents; one of nation's largest Jewish communities; marine stadium features powerboat and regatta racing, twilight concerts; Everglades National Park, 40 miles south of Miami, is virgin wilderness.

History: America's newest big city, Miami had only 3 houses in 1895 in a community called Fort Dallas. Julia Tuttle persuaded Henry M. Flagler to extend his railroad south from West Palm Beach to stimulate Miami development. City was incorporated in 1896, when railroad arrived.

Bicentennial Plans: Third Century Inc., a non-profit community organization, expects to mobilize 15,000 volunteers for a year-long countywide observance.

Further information: Miami-Metro Department of Publicity and Tourism, 499 Biscayne Blvd., Miami, Fla., 33132.

Milwaukee, Wisconsin

The World Almanac is sponsored in the Milwaukee area by The Milwaukee Journal, Journal Square, Milwaukee, Wis. 53201; telephone (414) 224-2000; founded 1882 by Lucius W. Nieman; circulation 347,364 daily, 537,612 Sunday; chairman of the board Irwin Maier; publisher Donald B. Abert; president of The Journal Co. Donald B. Abert; editor Richard H. Leonard; major awards include 2 Pulitzer Prizes to the newspaper and 2 to staff members.

Population: 667,671 (city); 1,435,400 (metro area); city 12th and metro area 19th in U.S.; total employment 602,800 (metro area).

Area: 95.8 sq. mi. on shore of Lake Michigan, Milwaukee County seat.

Industry: largest U.S. producer of diesel and gasoline engines, outboard motors, motorcycles, tractors, padlocks, beer; 4th largest U.S. automaking center; graphic arts and food processing are largest nondurable goods employers; location for 10 "Fortune 500" industries.

Commerce: wholesale and retail trade center for Wisconsin, upper Michigan; total retail sales $2.9 billion; wholesale trade $4 billion. Average household spendable income $12,601; 79 banks with $4.7 billion deposits; 53 savings and loan associations with $2.7 billion deposits.

Transportation: 4 major rail lines; Amtrak. 5 major airlines provide direct service to East and West coasts, south, southeast, and Florida for 2 million users of Gen. Mitchell field; 30 U.S. and foreign-flag ship lines use Milwaukee's St. Lawrence seaway port, handling nearly 3.5 million tons annually including 533,000 tons overseas cargo; port of Milwaukee gateway for 350 cities in 31 states and overseas ports. Wisconsin ranks 11th in foreign trade-exports and imports; 4 inter-city bus lines, 68 motor freight carriers; I-94, 5 federal and 14 state highways intersect Milwaukee.

Communications: morning, evening, and Sunday metropolitan newspaper; 4 commercial, 2 educational TV stations; 28 AM and FM radio stations.

Medical facilities: 21 major hospitals and medical centers, including 600 bed VA hospital.

Cultural facilities: Milwaukee Symphony, Repertory Theater, 2 opera and one operetta companies; Mid-America Ballet; Milwaukee Art Center; Milwaukee museum; University of Wisconsin, Marquette University, Medical College of Wisconsin, 8 other colleges and vocational schools enroll over 45,000 annually; new $13 million Performing Arts Center; $15.9 million exhibition addition to convention-arena-auditorium complex; Mitchell Park Conservatory and Milwaukee County Zoo are parts of 13,000 acre county park system.

Sports: baseball, Brewers; basketball, Marquette Univ., Univ. Wisconsin-Milwaukee, Bucks (NBA); football, Green Bay Packers (NFL) play 5 of 11 home games in Milwaukee.

History: founded by Solomon Juneau, (1818), one of many French trappers in area in early 1800s; incorporated as town 1837; as city 1846.

Bicentennial plans: restoration of the 1846 Jeremiah Curtain house; survey of historic buildings; Summerfest.

Further information: Metropolitan Milwaukee Association of Commerce, 828 N. Broadway, Milwaukee, Wis. 53202.

Minneapolis, Minnesota

Population: 424,362 (city), 1,181,074 (metro); 1st in state, 17th in nation; total employed (city, non-agricultural, 1974) 303,914.

Area: 59 sq. mi. (city), 4,000 sq. mi. (10-county metro area) around St. Anthony Falls near junction of Minnesota and Mississippi Rivers.

Industry: diverse; major electronics-computer manufacturing center, including Honeywell, Control Data, Medtronics; headquarters for nation's 4 largest grain millers, including General Mills, Pillsbury, and International Multifoods.
Commerce: $11,583 median household income; $3.2 billion total retail sales metro area (1974); 24 commercial banks, 6 savings and loan associations; headquarters for Ninth Federal Reserve District; world trade center, 12th among U.S. metro areas in exports.
Transportation: Amtrak regional terminal, 5 trunk railroads; 150 trucking firms; 5 major barge lines headquartered in city; Mpls.-St. Paul International Airport, 650 flights daily.
Communications: 4 commercial, 2 educational TV stations; 39 radio stations.
Medical facilities: 21 hospitals, including a leading heart hospital at Univ. of Minn.
Federal facilities: Farm Credit Administration regional office; FBI regional office, Environmental Protection Agency district office.
Cultural facilities: Minnesota Orchestra, 7 art galleries-museums, Tyrone Guthrie Theatre, Walker Art Center, Univ. of Minnesota.
Sports: Minnesota Twins (American League), Minnesota Vikings (NFL), Minnesota North Stars (NHL).
Other attractions: 153 parks, 22 lakes; 57-story IDS Tower; Mpls. Aquatennial celebration in July; average yearly snowfall, 41 inches.
History: first visited in 1680s by Fr. Louis Hennepin who discovered and named St. Anthony Falls on the Mississippi River; French fur traders used the area in 18th century; incorporated 1871. Falls became power source for lumber and milling operations in 19th century.
Bicentennial plans: Riverfront development project.
Further information: Greater Minneapolis Chamber of Commerce Information, 15 S. 5th St., Minneapolis 55402.

Mobile, Alabama

The World Almanac is sponsored in the Mobile area by The Mobile Press Register, 304 Government St., 36630; phone (205) 433-1441; circulation, Register (morn) 45,500, Press (eve) 56,600, combined (Sat., Sun.) 95,750; Register founded 1813, Press 1928; William J. Hearin publisher and president, Fallon Trotter executive editor, John Fay associate executive editor.

Population: 190,026 (city), 376,690 (metro), 2d city in state, 68th in nation; total employed (metro), 125,000.
Area: 142 sq. mi., at head of Mobile Bay.
Industry: home of Alabama State Docks, a $225 million complex where 33 ocean-going ships can be docked at one time; over $835 million is invested in diversified industry, including paper and paper products, forest products, shipbuilding, chemicals, roofing, paints, alumina, oil, aircraft engines and metals.
Commerce: wholesale-retail center for large portion of southwest Alabama and southeast Mississippi; Mobile County retail sales (1974), $678,166,000.
Transportation: served by 4 major railroads, one of the great river systems, 3 major airlines, 55 truck lines and about 100 steamship lines.
Communications: 2 TV and 12 radio stations.
Medical facilities: Univ. of South Alabama Medical College and 5 modern hospitals.
Cultural facilities: Municipal Auditorium-Theater complex seats 16,000; art gallery, museum, amateur dramatic theater, public library and branches; Univ. of South Alabama, Spring Hill, Mobile Colleges, and Bishop State Junior College.
Annual attractions: America's Junior Miss Pageant, Senior Bowl Football Game, and Mardi Gras.
History: founded in 1702 by Jean Baptiste Le Moyne; 6 flags have flown over the city since then.
Bicentennial plans: restoration of Fort Conde, original site of city.
Further information: Chamber of Commerce, Commercial Guaranty Bank Bldg.

Montgomery, Alabama

The World Almanac is sponsored in the Montgomery area by the Advertiser-Journal, 200 Washington Street, Montgomery AL 36102; phone: (205) 262-1611; Advertiser founded 1828, Journal 1881; circulation Advertiser (morn) 54,884, Journal (eve) 26,523; combined Sunday 77,579; publisher Harold Martin, managing editor Ben R. Davis.

Population: 142,500 (city), 240,300 (metro); 147th in nation; total employed, 101,400.
Area: 50.34 sq. mi. (city), 442 sq. mi. (county).
Industry: machinery manufacture, glass products, textiles, refrigeration equipment, axles, furniture, food products, paper, and fertilizers; over 250 industries.
Commerce: wholesale-retail center for 13 counties in central Alabama; retail trade area sales (1974), $1 billion; 7 banks, 3 savings & loans associations, 6 insurance company home offices; state capital
Transportation: 5 railroads, 3 airlines, 2 national bus lines; Interstates 65 and 85 intersect in the city; Alabama River navigable to the Gulf of Mexico.
Medical facilities: 6 general hospitals and a VA hospital; over 2,000 beds.
Military: Home of Maxwell Air Force Base, The Air University and Gunther Field.
Cultural Facilities: Art Guild, Civic Ballet, Little Theater, and a Community Concert Series; Museum of Fine Arts; 5 major colleges and universities.
Sports: Rebels, farm team of Detroit; Blue-Gray Football Classic; Southeastern Championship Rodeo.
History: incorporated 1819; Jefferson Davis inaugurated president of the Confederate States of America, Feb. 18, 1861, in Montgomery.
Bicentennial plans: Blue-Gray Football halftime show, national TV, Dec. 1975; Martin Luther King Birthday celebration; Statewide Forest Festival, May 7-8; Broadway Musical "1976."

Montreal, Quebec, Canada

The World Almanac is sponsored in the Montreal area by The Gazette, a Southam newspaper, 1000 St. Antoine Street, Montreal H3C 3R7, Quebec, Canada; phone (514) 861-1111; founded 1778 by Fleury Mesplet; circulation 123,937 daily; publisher Mark Farrell; editorial page editor Tim Creery; executive editor R. Lindsay Crysler; managing editor Brodie Snyder; sponsors Christmas fund; 5 National Newspaper Awards in last 2 years.

Population: 1,214,300 (city), 2,761,000 (metro); after Paris, the 2d largest French-speaking city in the world, 67% French origin, 12% Anglo-Saxon, 21% other origins; Canada's largest urban center.

Area: some 68 sq. mi. on an island of 190 sq. mi. in the St. Lawrence River where the Ottawa and Richelieu Rivers flow into it at the head of the St. Lawrence Seaway. The metropolitan area extends more than 1,000 sq. mi. Except for the 769 ft. Mount Royal mountain, the island is flat and averages 100 ft. above sea level.

Industry: Canada's industrial hub ($6.9 billion, value of shipments of goods of own manufacture), petroleum refining, women's and men's clothing, slaughtering and meat packing, tobacco products, brewing, foods, and primary metal industries.

Commerce: headquarters of many of the largest financial institutions in Canada, and home of the Montreal and Canadian Stock Exchanges; about 75% of countries having official representation in Canada have a consulate or representative in Montreal; $4.1 billion total retail sales.

Transportation: St. Lawrence Seaway, a $1-billion Canadian-U.S. waterway and power project which runs 1,300 miles to the Great Lakes in the heart of North America, has helped Montreal, 1,000 miles from the sea, become the world's 2d greatest inland port, after Rotterdam; harbor extends 42 miles. Air capital of the world, headquarters of the International Civil Aviation Organization and the International Air Transport Association; some 30 airlines serve

Dorval International airport; a new $500 million airport, Mirable, has been completed north of Montreal Island. Canadian National and Canadian Pacific Railways maintain head offices and terminals in Montreal. The Metro, Montreal's $225,000,000 16-mile subway system, the 8th largest in the world, opened in 1966; system is being extended in all directions to be completed before Montreal hosts the 1976 Summer Olympic Games.

Cultural facilities: a major cultural center; Place des Arts, a 3,000-seat concert hall and 2 theaters, home of the Symphony Orchestra, attracts the finest in drama, opera, ballet, and music; Museum of Fine Arts, the Musee de l'Art Contemporain. Some of the continent's most beautiful churches, including the Roman Catholic Mary Queen of The World Basilica, a half-size replica of St. Peter's in Rome; McGill Univ. and l'Universite de Montreal.

Sports: NHL Canadiens, the Canadian Football League Alouettes, the Expos of baseball's National League, and Les Quebecois of the National Lacrosse League.

History: first visited by Jacques Cartier in 1535; founded under the name of Ville Marie in 1642. Old Montreal, some 1,000 acres in all, is the largest such area undergoing restoration in North America and retains the general atmosphere of the 18th century.

Nashville, Tennessee

The World Almanac is sponsored in Nashville by The Tennessean, 1100 Broadway, 37202; phone (615) 255-1221; founded as The Tennessean in 1907 but incorporated publications date to 1812; circulation daily 134,700, Sunday 236,-400; president Amon Carter Evans, publisher John Seigenthaler; 3 Pulitzer prizes, 8 Headliner awards, 3 Sigma Delta Chi Awards.

Population: 470,000 (in unified Metro government). 2d in state; labor force 238,400.

Area: 533 sq. mi., straddling Cumberland River, in north central part of state.

Industry: music, 52% of U.S. singles are recorded in 35 studio complexes; clothing, headquarters of Genesco, world's largest and most diversified clothing and footwear manufacturer; insurance, 2 of largest U.S. companies located here; world's largest auto glass plant; chemicals, printing (especially religious materials), aerostructures, tires, heating equipment.

Commerce: retail center for middle Tennessee, south Kentucky; retail sales (1974) $1,694 million; per capita income (1972), $4,508; bank resources, over $3.9 billion in 13 banks, 115 branches.

Transportation: 9 U.S. highways and 6 branches of the interstate system radiate from Nashville; 9 commercial airlines with 174 daily flights; 2 railroads, Amtrak; bus service, 73 motor freight lines.

Communications: 5 TV stations (one public), and 22 AM and FM radio stations.

Medical facilities: 18 hospitals (6,019 beds), 2 medical schools, VA hospital, speech-hearing center.

Cultural: symphony orchestra; replica of Parthenon with art gallery; public and state libraries; botanic garden and art center, 3 community theaters.

Educational facilities: 15 colleges and universities; 137 public schools, 39 private schools.

Convention facilities: 10,000-seat auditorium; Opryland convention center under construction.

Other attractions: Grand Ole Opry, Opryland U.S.A. ($32 million theme park featuring music); Country Music Hall of Fame; Hermitage (home of Andrew Jackson); Belle Meade antebellum mansion.

Recreation facilities: water sports, outdoor activity on Old Hickory and Percy Priest lakes.

History: settled in 1780 as a fort in then western North Carolina; incorporated, 1784, with first written charter west of Alleghenies.

Bicentennial plans: new performing arts center.

Further information: Chamber of Commerce, 161 4th Ave. N., Nashville, TN 37203.

New Haven, Connecticut

The World Almanac is sponsored in the greater New Haven area by the New Haven Register (founded 1812) and the New Haven Journal-Courier (founded 1755); circulation Register (eve.) 106,712, Sunday 126,859; Journal-Courier (morn.) 32,165; president and publisher Lionel S. Jackson, vp and general manager Donald A. Spargo, vp and treasurer George S. Stearns Jr., vp and editor Robert J. Leeney.

Population: 135,500 (city), 360,400 (metro); 3d in state.

Area: 21.1 sq. mi. southern coast of Conn. on north shore of Long Island Sound; county seat.

Industry: 1,000 firms in immediate area; principal products are guns, hardware, rubber goods, paper products, machinery, and tools.

Commerce: wholesale-retail center for southern Conn.; retail city sales (1974), 336.5 million, highest in Conn.; serves 850,000 people within a radius of 25

miles; busy harbor, particularly with cargo ships delivering oil.

Transportation: Penn Central, Amtrak Cosmopolitan turbotrain; 25 major truck lines; 14 federal and state highways; Tweed-New Haven Airport served by 3 airlines; limo service to N. Y. airports, 2 bus lines.

Communications: VHF, 2 UHF TV stations, and 6 radio stations.

Medical facilities: Yale Medical Center; Yale-New Haven Hospital; Hospital of St. Raphael.

Cultural facilities: Yale Univ. Library with over 6,000,000 books one of the world's largest collections; Yale's Peabody Museum of Natural History, Art Gallery and Beinecke Rare Book Library; New Haven Historical Society; Cultural Center; 2 legitimate theaters, and The New Haven Symphony.

Educational facilities: Yale Univ. and graduate schools; Albertus Magnus, Southern Conn. State, South Central Community, Quinnipiac Colleges; Univ. of New Haven.

Recreational facilities: Yale Bowl, Woolsey Hall, Ingalls Rink, the Coliseum, 15 parks, including Frederick Brewster's estate, East and West Rock scenic drives, 50 playgrounds, West Rock Nature Center; 7

golf courses, 30 tennis courts, 6 skating rinks.

Convention facilities: Coliseum-convention center with a 19-story hotel nearby.

Sports attractions: AHL Nighthawks; NFL New York Giants use Yale Bowl for home games.

History: founded 1638 by Puritans; named after Newhaven in England; incorporated 1638, became a part of Conn. 1662; first mayor was Roger Sherman, signer of Declaration of Independence.

Bicentennial plans: Exhibitions, theatrical productions, and pageantry spotlighting ethnic-cultural backgrounds over the past 2 centuries.

Further information: New Haven Chamber of Commerce, 152 Temple St., New Haven, 06510.

New Orleans, Louisiana

The World Almanac is sponsored in the New Orleans area by The States-Item, 3800 Howard Ave., New Orleans, La. 70140; phone (504) 586-3560; founded Jan. 3, 1880, by Maj. Henry J. Hearsey, circulation 130,188 daily, 117,-130 Saturday; editor Walter G. Cowan, associate editor Charles A. Ferguson, city editor William U. Madden; sponsors Women Against Crime Crusade and Football Fund for Underprivileged.

Population: 593,471 (city), 1,034,316 (metro area); first in state; total employed, 434,200.

Area: 363.5 sq. mi. of which 199.4 are land.

Industry: Port of New Orleans, second largest in nation, handled 33 million tons of cargo valued at $8.2 billion in 1974.

Commerce: trade center for lower Mississippi valley. Bank resources $4.6 billion.

Transportation: rail hub for north, east and westbound commerce. Amtrak passenger service to Chicago, New York, Los Angeles. New Orleans International Airport serves major airlines; Lakefront Airport private aviation.

New construction: hotel building booming with Dome opening and popularity of annual Mardi Gras festival; tallest building, 51-story One Shell Square.

Communications: 4 commercial TV stations and educational channel.

Medical facilities: major medical center with Charity Hospital, 2 schools of medicine and one of dentistry; Oschner Clinic, Touro Infirmary.

Cultural facilities: new Center for the Performing Arts seats 2,317 for operas, concerts; museums in-

clude Louisiana State Museum, Isaac Delgado Museum of Art, the Middle American Research Institute of Tulane University and many small galleries.

Educational facilities: Tulane Univ., Louisiana State Univ. in New Orleans, Loyola, Dillard, Southern Univ. in New Orleans, Xavier, St. Mary's Dominican.

Other attractions: Louisiana Superdome seats 80,000 for major events; French Quarter remains major historic tourist attraction.

Sports: New Orleans Saints (NFL), New Orleans Jazz (NBA). Sugar Bowl is major college attraction.

History: named after the Duke of Orleans, founded on the edge of a swamp within crescent of the Mississippi River 100 miles upstream from the Gulf of Mexico by Jean Baptiste Le Moyne, Sieur de Bienville; became capital of Louisiana Territory in 1722, when Adrien de Pauger laid out what is now the French Quarter; became part of U. S. with signing of Louisiana Purchase in 1803.

Bicentennial plans: France-Louisiana Festival July 4-14, 1976, tying together two major national holidays, Independence Day and Bastille Day; restoration of historic Lafayette Square.

New York City, New York

The World Almanac is sponsored in the greater New York City metropolitan area by the Daily News and Sunday News, 220 E. 42d St., New York, N.Y. 10017, phone (212) MU 2-1234; New York News Inc., founded June 26, 1919, by Joseph Medill Patterson; circulation daily 1,967,116; Sunday 2,827,760; president and publisher W.H. James, editor Michael J. O'Neill, managing editor William J. Brink, treasurer Robert J. Rohrbach, general manager Valfrid E. Palmer; Pulitzer Prizes for news photography, cartoon, editorial writing and international and local investigative reporting; sponsors Golden Gloves, National Spelling Bee championships for New York City, Long Island, Westchester, and other major school events as community service programs.

Population: 7,895,563 (city), 15,495,683 (consolidated area); 1st in state and nation; total employed 3,378,-700; per capita personal income $5,662.

Area: 300 sq. mi. at mouth of Hudson River; embraces 5 boroughs — Manhattan, Bronx, Brooklyn, Queens, and Staten Island.

Industry: nation's leader in manufacturing and service industries; produces 25.3% of America's apparel, 18.2% of printing and publishing; 22,500 manufacturing establishments (Sept. 1974).

Commerce: nation's richest port, handling annual 216,896,434 tons of maritime cargo; Wall Street, world's largest financial center, with New York and American Stock exchanges; wholesale-retail center for New York, New Jersey and southwestern Connecticut, retail sales $15.8 billion (1974); 33 commercial banks, resources $143.7 billion; 43 savings banks, resources $46.2 billion; World Trade Center, twin

110-story towers, cost $850 million.

Transportation: Kennedy International Airport handles 42% of nation's overseas air travel and 51% of export-import air tonnage, served by 57 scheduled air carriers; LaGuardia Airport served by 15 domestic airlines; 4 heliports. Penn Central Railroad, Amtrak; 2 major rail terminals, Pennsylvania and Grand Central stations; 41 interstate bus lines; subway network covers every borough except Staten Island; ferry and the 4,260-ft. Verrazano-Narrows Bridge (world's longest suspension span) link Staten Island to Manhattan and Brooklyn; 18 bridges connect Manhattan with other boroughs, George Washington Bridge over the Hudson connects New Jersey; 5 tunnels under the Hudson and East Rivers.

Communications: 13 TV stations (6 commercial, 2 educational, 1 municipal, 2 Spanish, 2 CATV); 39 AM and FM radio stations; WPIX-TV and WPIX-FM are broadcast affiliates of The News.

Medical facilities: 116 hospitals (17 municipal, 33 private, 66 voluntary non-profit); 5 major medical research centers specialize in cancer, heart diseases, sickle cell anemia and other research; Sloan-Kettering Institute for Cancer Research; 4 VA hospitals.

Federal facilities: Fort Wadsworth, Staten Island; Governors Island; many federal agencies represented in buildings at Federal Plaza and 90 Church St.

Educational facilities: 6 universities, 23 colleges, including 5 medical colleges, 4 law schools, 3 colleges of pharmacy, 2 colleges of dentistry, 2 institutes of art and architecture; 976 schools in the public school system; more than 1,000 private schools; public libraries total 199.

Cultural facilities: Lincoln Center for the Performing Arts (Philharmonic, Ballet Company, Metropolitan Opera and other theatrical arts), Carnegie Hall, Brooklyn Academy of Music. Broadway and Off-Broadway alliance for varied theatrical productions; Shakespeare Festival at Delacorte Theatre; 42 museums including American Museum of Natural History, Metropolitan Museum of Art, Museum of the Performing Arts, Museum of Modern Art, Whitney Museum, and South Street Seaport Museum.

Other attractions: United Nations; botanic gardens in the Bronx and Brooklyn; Central Park and Prospect Park; Bronx Zoo and 4 other zoos; 13 municipal golf courses, 520 tennis courts, 37 outdoor swimming pools.

Sports: NBA Knicks, NHL Rangers and Islanders; NL Mets and NFL Jets play in Shea Stadium; AL Yankees will play in Shea during Yankee Stadium renovations; for 1975-1976, NFL Giants play in Yale Bowl in New Haven, Conn.; tennis WTT Sets; soccer NASL Cosmos.

History: discovered by Giovanni da Verrazano in 1524; in 1626 Peter Minuit bought the island from the Manhattan Indians for about $24 in goods and trinkets; settlement named New Amsterdam. In 1664, British troops occupied city without resistance and named it New York in honor of the Duke of York, brother of the King. On Jan. 1, 1898, Manhattan and large areas to the NE, E and S were consolidated into one City of New York.

Bicentennial plans: numerous special events planned throughout city by civic and veterans organizations, municipal agencies, community groups, etc.

Further information: N. Y. City Bicentennial Corp., 331 Madison Ave.; Department of Commerce and Industry, 225 Broadway; Convention and Visitors Bureau, 90 East 42d St.

Newark, New Jersey

Population: 390,300; first in state, swells on weekdays with non-residents working and attending school; 1,876,500 (metro area) including Essex, Morris and Union counties; 135,169 employed (city, nonagricultural).

Area: 25.4 sq. mi. (city), 15 miles SW of New York City.

Industry: wide diversity of manufacturers, fine craftsmanship; more than 10,000 businesses, major banking and insurance center. Headquarters for several national firms.

Transportation: international airport; major port; 5 railroads; world's largest privately owned bus system; one of world's largest truck terminals; world's largest containerized shipping center.

Communication: 5 radio stations and one VHF public TV station.

Medical facilities: 6 major hospitals with new home of the College of Medicine and Dentistry under construction; Beth Israel Medical Center.

Federal facilities: new federal building; old federal courthouse.

Cultural facilities: museum, library, New Jersey Historical Society, New Jersey Symphony Orchestra, Opera Theater of N.J., Garden State Ballet, and Symphony Hall.

Educational facilities: New Jersey College of Medicine and Dentistry; Rutgers Univ.; Seton Hall Univ. Law School; New Jersey Institute of Technology; Essex County College.

Recreational facilities: parks cover 783.97 acres; 7 swimming pools, 74 playgrounds, 2 ice skating rinks and 2 lakes.

Convention facilities: large hotel and 2 large motor inns, with others under construction.

Other attractions: 7 famous works of sculpture, including 'John F. Kennedy' by Jacques Lipchitz; Sacred Heart, one of the largest Gothic cathedrals in the world, and the historic Plume House, built in 1710.

History: founded in 1666, incorporated 1836; British troops ravaged the town during the Revolution.

Bicentennial plans: historical map, chronology of Newark events during the Revolution, and a compilation of colonial documents.

Further information: Greater Newark Chamber of Commerce, 1180 Raymond Blvd., Newark, 07102.

Norfolk, Virginia

The World Almanac is sponsored in the Norfolk metro. area by The Virginian-Pilot and Ledger-Star, 150 W. Brambleton Av., Norfolk, Va. 23501; phone (804) 446-2000; Va. founded 1865, Ledger, 1876; circulation: LS (even) 100,685; VP (morn) 129,128; VP (Sun) 188,361; Frank Batten publisher, Derek Dunn-Rankin president & general manager, Perry Morgan exec. editor, Robert H. Mason VP editor, George J. Hebert LS editor.

Population: 297,200 (city), 715,700 (metro); 1st in state; civilian employed, 241,600; military pop., 84,600.

Area: 915 sq. mi. in SE Virginia.

Industry: General Electric, Ford Motor Co., Norfolk Shipbuilding & Drydock Corp.

Commerce: retail sales (1973) $1.6 billion; average household income, $12,053.

Transportation: Port of Hampton Roads, world's finest natural harbor, ranks first in export tonnage (48,699,000 tons handled 1973) among Atlantic ports; biggest coal port in world; Regional Airport, 4 major airlines; Chesapeake Bay Bridge-Tunnel supplies direct north highway route; 8 trunk line railroads, 50 common carrier trucking companies, 2 bus companies.

Communications: 5 TV, 13 AM, 9 FM stations.

Medical facilities: 11 hospitals including oldest and 2d largest naval hospital in U.S.

Federal facilities: greatest concentration of naval installations in world; 36 major commands include Atlantic Fleet, Second Fleet, NATO Supreme Allied Command Atlantic (SACLANT), Armed Forces Staff College and Commandant 5th Naval Dist.

Cultural facilities: symphony orchestra, Feldman Chamber Quartet, repertory theater, dinner and little theaters, civic and univ. ballet; Chrysler Museum collection; yearly Festival of the Arts.

Educational facilities: Old Dominion Univ., Norfolk State, Virginia Wesleyan, and Tidewater Community Colleges; Eastern Va. Medical School.
Recreational facilities: General Douglas MacArthur Memorial, Adam Thoroughgood House (1636), Gardens-by-the-sea; Dismal Swamp located in Chesapeake; resort city of Virginia Beach offers 38 mi. of swimming, fishing and surfing; camping facilities at Seashore State Park.

Seashore State Park.
Convention facilities: Scope, $30 million cultural and convention center.
Sports: Squires (ABA), Red Wings (AHL), Tidewater Tides (International League).
Climate: Average temp.: 67° to 41°.
Further information: Chamber of Commerce, 475 St. Paul Blvd., Norfolk, 23501.

Oakland, California

Population: 336,000.
Area: 53.4 sq. mi.; seat of Alameda County.
Industry: food processing, fabricated metal products, transportation equipment, chemicals and paint; Port of Oakland is 2d in containerized cargo; home base for Kaiser Industries.
Commerce: 8,146 retail outlets with taxable sales (Jan. 1975) of 1.1 billion; effective buying income for family, $8,959 per annum.
Transportation: western terminus for Southern Pacific, Santa Fe, and Western Pacific Railroads; International Airport is major airfreight terminal and center for supplemental air carriers; headquarters for Bay Area Rapid Transit, underground, underwater 75-mile subway connecting 15 communities.
Medical facilities: 9 hospitals include Children's Hospital Medical Center, Kaiser Foundation and the Veteran's Administration.
New construction: major downtown redevelopment with $100 million invested in construction.
Cultural facilities: museum, half garden, half gallery design, has divisions of Natural Science, History and Art; symphony, Chinese Community Cultural Center.

Educational facilities: Univ. of California at Berkeley, Mills College, College of Holy Names, Cal State, Hayward, Chabot, California College of Arts and Crafts, Peralta Community College.
Recreational facilities: 26,000 acre Regional Park System serving the East Bay; zoo in 100-acre Knowland State Park has large collection of gibbons and aerial tram; Lake Merritt Park includes botanical garden, wildfowl refuge, natural science center, and Children's Fairyland.
Sports: Raiders (football), Athletics (baseball), Seals (hockey), Golden State Warriors (basketball).
Other attractions: Oakland Coliseum, over 50,000 capacity, for theatrical entertainment, exhibits, conventions and circus; Jack London Square.
History: area explored in 1772, settled in 1850; incorporated as town in 1852, as city in 1854.
Bicentennial plans: restore Cameron-Stanford House; art festival and parade; build a pavillion center which will be used as a permanent meeting hall.
Further information: Chamber of Commerce, 1320 Webster St., Oakland, 94612.

Oklahoma City, Oklahoma

The World Almanac is sponsored in the Oklahoma City area by The Daily Oklahoman and Oklahoma City Times, Oklahoma City, Okla. 73125; phone (405) 232-3311; The Oklahoman founded in 1894; Times in 1888; Oklahoma Publishing Co. acquired The Oklahoman 1903 and the Times 1916; circulation Oklahoman 174,000; Times 99,000; Sunday, 295,000; editor and publisher E. L. Gaylord, executive editor Charles L. Bennett.

Population: 368,856 (city), 669,092 (metro); largest in state; labor force 346,700.
Area: city area, among nation's largest, is 647.5 sq. mi.; metro area, 3,491 sq. mi.; located in state's center on Canadian River.

Industry: oil, with about 1,800 producing wells in metro area, employs about 30,000; Tinker AFB, one of world's largest air depots, employs 22,000 civilians and 2,500 military on $100 million installation; FAA and other aviation employ some 37,000, with annual payroll of $300 million; agricultural and ranching area; manufactured goods include aircraft, telephone equipment, oil field machinery, oil and greases, building materials, feed, flour, meat, and tires.

Commerce: regional, national and international marketing center; effective buying income, $10,839 per household, consumer sales near $1.8 billion.

Transportation: 5 passenger airlines; 4 primary federal and 3 major state highways, with I-40 and I-35 intersecting the city; fully planned urban expressway system, major bus, truck, and rail lines.

Medical facilities: Oklahoma Univ. Health Sciences Center and 25 hospitals and clinics.
Cultural facilities: symphony and junior symphony; Oklahoma Art Center; Lyric Theater at Oklahoma City Univ.; Warehouse Theater; Oklahoma Theater Center; Southwest Repertory Theater, Univ. of Oklahoma.
Education: Univ. of Oklahoma, Oklahoma City Univ., Central State Univ.
Convention facilities: $23 million Myriad Convention Center, seating 15,000 in the center of a downtown redevelopment project, hosts 350 conventions yearly with more than 150,000 delegates.
Other attractions: National Cowboy Hall of Fame; 130 municipal parks; major college sports; pro sports: Oklahoma City 89ers, American Assn. baseball; International Softball headquarters.
History: founded by land run, Apr. 22, 1889.
Bicentennial plans: a $100,000 Oklahoma City heritage plaza in downtown Civic Center Park.
Further information: Chamber of Commerce, 1 Santa Fe Plaza, Oklahoma City, 73102.

Omaha, Nebraska

The World Almanac is sponsored in Nebraska by The Omaha World-Herald, World-Herald Square, Omaha, Neb. 68102; phone (402) 444-1000; Evening World, founded 1885 by G. M. Hitchcock, acquired Daily Herald, founded 1865; adopted present name 1889; circulation 247,728 daily, 282,206 Sunday; president Harold W. Andersen, executive editor Louis G. Gerdes; 3 Pulitzer Prizes; sponsors Midwest Spelling Bee, Newspapers in the Classroom, Music in the Parks, Show Wagon, Good Fellows charities, college scholarships.

Population: 375,800 (city), 583,600 (metro) (1974 est.) first in state, 67th in U.S.; 252,660 employment.

Area: eastern Nebraska, 83 sq. mi. of rolling hills on Missouri River; Douglas County seat.

Industry: manufacturing shipments valued at $2.1 billion annually; 600 plants employ 40,000; food processing, meatpacking, metals; 2d in frozen food production; 3d largest livestock market in salable receipts.

Commerce: major trade center; 1,000 wholesale firms, $1.5 billion retail sales, 33d in buying income per household ($15,341); 28 banks, $2 billion deposits; 11 savings and loans, $2 billion assets; 4th largest insurance center in U.S. (36 home offices, including Mutual of Omaha). Also headquarters Union Pacific; Northern Natural Gas, Northwestern Bell, ConAgra.

Transportation: 6 major airlines; 4th largest rail center, 75 trains daily, Amtrak, 122 truck lines, Interstates 80 and 29, bus, 3 barge lines; 2.6 million tons carried on Missouri River annually; port of entry, foreign trade zone.

Communications: Nebraska's largest daily newspaper, 5 TV, 17 radio stations.

Medical facilities: 16 hospitals, 4,680 beds; 2 medical schools (Nebraska U., Creighton U.), 8 nursing schools, Eppley Institute for Cancer Research.

Federal facilities: Strategic Air Command's global headquarters at Offutt Air Base; Missouri River Division of the U.S. Army Corps of Engineers.

Cultural facilities: Orpheum performing arts center, symphony orchestra, opera company, ballet society; 10 live theatre groups, 7 art galleries, 5 museums, Joslyn Art Museum's $20 million collection.

Educational facilities: 3 universities, 3 colleges educate 21,000 students; 30 adult education schools.

Recreation: 5,000 acres of parks, 20 public pools, 100 tennis courts, 8 public golf courses; 1,200-acre Fontenelle Forest, Henry Doorly Zoo, Boys Town; pro baseball, hockey; Ak-Sar-Ben horseracing, NCAA College World Series; 10th of top 50 cities in quality of life, (January 1975 Harper's magazine).

History: Lewis and Clark, 1804; Indian trading post, 1825; Mormon settlement, 1846; Omaha (named after Indian tribe) laid out when Nebraska Territory opened, 1854; chartered as city, 1867.

Further information: Chamber of Commerce, 1620 Dodge St., Omaha, 68102.

Orange County, California

The World Almanac is sponsored in Orange County by The Register, 625 N. Grand, Santa Ana, Cal. 92711; telephone (714) 835-1234; circulation combined daily 195,152, Sunday 220,345; purchased in 1935 by late R.C. Hoiles, president-founder Freedom Newspapers Inc., now headed by son, Clarence H. Hoiles, also publisher of The Register. General manager Richard Wallace, executive editor Jim Dean, managing editor Mike Maloney, research and promotion dir. Jim Lyons Sr.

Population: estimated 1,705,300, up 19% since 1970 in shift from fastest growing U.S. metropolitan area by rate to fastest numerically; compares with 212,364 in 1950, 2.5 million projected 1990. 2d most populous county in Cal. Encompasses 26 cities; Anaheim 187,-400 population, county seat Santa Ana 170,500, Huntington Beach 143,600, Garden Grove 121,500.

Area: 511,040 acres in so. Cal. from Pacific Ocean 25 miles inland to Cleveland National Forest; 42-mile coastline stretches from Long Beach past Huntington Beach surfing, Newport Beach yacht harbor, Laguna Beach art colony, Dana Point small-craft harbor to San Clemente and Camp Pendleton. County lies at center of developing San Diego-to-Santa Barbara megalopolis.

Industry and Commerce: median family income $16,-139 in 1974; $5,255 billion in retail sales; spendable income est. at $10.3 billion in 1975; employment (1975) 716,400, with 149,300 in manufacturing, 141,-600 trade, 110,400 services, 94,100 government, 30,-900 insurance, finance and real estate, 23,000 construction, 17,500 transportation and communications, and 10,800 in an agriculture industry which had 1974 output of $142.8 million; biggest manufacturing employer Rockwell International's Autonetics, Minuteman missiles and electronic calculators, sewing and reading machines firm; RI's Space Division built Apollo moon rocket 2d stage; McDonnell Douglas Astronautics, Apollo 3d stage and Skylab. Other major employers include corporate or major unit headquarters for international firms such as Hughes, Philco-Ford Aeronutronics, Beckman Instruments, Fluor Corp., AMF-Voit, Hunt-Wesson Foods; county is center for such industries as tourism, sailboat construction, fiberglass products, glass containers, food processing, computers, and agriculture, with strawberries a $20.3 million crop in 1974 and oranges $15.5 million.

Transportation: 6 major freeways, including main Los Angeles-San Diego artery; nation's 2d busiest airport with 605,530 tower operations in 1974; transit district. countywide bus network, including freeway commuter buses and Dial-A-Ride in some areas.

New construction: Newport Beach financial center; 2 enclosed shopping malls; 6 hotels opened over past year.

Communications: 13 TV, over 40 radio stations.

Federal facilities: Marine Corps Air Station at El Toro, Los Alamitos Naval Air Station, Seal Beach Naval Weapons Station, Santa Ana Marine Corps Lighter-Than-Air (Helicopter) Station; federal building in Santa Ana, General Services Administration building in Laguna Niguel; Cleveland National Forest; Marine Corps' Camp Pendleton nearby.

Recreation: 781 acres of beaches, 141 scenic sea cliffs, 3 yacht basins, 2 fishing lakes, wilderness campgrounds, many golf courses.

Other attractions: Disneyland, 9.7 million visitors in 1974; Knott's Berry Farm; Lion Country Safari; Movieland Wax Museum and Cars of Stars; air and car museums; Los Alamitos Racetrack; auto races. Mediterranean climate attracts new residents, development and visitors.

Convention facilities: Anaheim Convention Center; hotels in Anaheim, Buena Park, Irvine, Newport Beach offer convention facilities.

Sports attractions: AL Angels, WFL California Sun, school sports.

Cultural facilities: 2 major tax-supported universities, 4 private liberal arts colleges, 6 community colleges, multiple trade and special interest schools; over 50 high schools; 52 city and county libraries, symphony orchestra, 2 master chorales, light opera, 6 ballet companies, 32 community theater groups, 6 performing art support groups, 4 major art museums, art associations.

Orlando, Florida

The World Almanac is sponsored in the Orlando area by the Sentinel Star, 633 N. Orange Ave., Orlando, Fla.-32802; phone (305) 423-4411; Sentinel and Evening Star founded as dailies in 1913; merged 1931; acquired by Tribune Co. of Chicago in 1965; combined to create "all'day" newspaper in 1973; circulation, 181,914 weekdays, 174,929 Saturday, 213,403 Sunday; editor-publisher William G. Conomos.

Population: 117,435 (city), 598,692 (metro); 247,200 employed (metro).
Area: 30.1 sq. mi. in east central Florida: 52 lakes inside city limits; avg. temperature 72.1°.
Industry: center of citrus belt; 6 regional home and 10 national home insurance company offices; Martin Marietta Co., aerospace division; General Electric plant; Westinghouse Electric Co., minicomputer division; 12 industrial parks; naval training center (only one training women recruits), over 30,000 recruits trained annually.
Commerce: 52 commercial banks; total deposits, $1.4 billion; 7 savings and loan assns.; 30 major shopping centers; retail sales, $1.9 billion.
Transportation: 7 airlines serving jetport at McCoy, about 85 scheduled flights daily; Seaboard Coastline Railroad, Amtrak; 9 intercity bus lines, 195 common carrier truck lines and 7 freight forwarding services; every major Florida market less than 4 hours by highway.
Communications: 16 radio and 6 TV stations.
Medical facilities: 15 hospitals in metro area.
Cultural facilities: Florida Symphony Orchestra; Loch Haven Art Center, John Young Museum and Planetarium, Central Florida Civic Theater; Rollins College and Florida Tech Univ., 2 junior colleges.
Other attractions: Walt Disney World, 18 miles from downtown Orlando; Sea World; Circus World Preview Center; Church Street Station, renovated area in downtown Orlando; Stars Hall of Fame, wax museum.
Convention facilities: 29,026 rooms; through June, 1975, 411 conventions attended by 146,000.
Sports: Minnesota Twins spring training site; Tangerine Bowl Sports Week; 2 pro golf tournaments, $200,-000 Florida Citrus Invitational; $200,000 Walt Disney World Tournament; Ben White Raceways, training ground for trotters; Seminole Turf Club, harness racing; Sanford-Orlando Kennel Club; Jai-Alai Fronton.
Bicentennial plans: (Orlando's 100th anniversary) Central Florida Fair, Feb. 24-Mar. 6; bicentennial concert, Mar. 20; Dimensions '76, music and arts festival, May 1-9; Picnic in Park, July 4; performance of Handel's "Messiah", Dec. 5; American Freedom Train, Dec. 14-16.
Additional information: Orlando Area Chamber of Commerce. P.O. Box 1913, Orlando, 32802.

Ottawa, Ontario, Canada

Population: 303,000 (city), 619,000 (metro region including greater Ottawa and Hull, Que.); Canada's 5th largest city, linked with neighboring city of Hull (pop. 130,000) by 5 bridges.

Area: 30,481 acres (city), 1,100 sq. mi. (region) on Ontario-Quebec border at the Chaudiere Falls on the Ottawa River.

National Capital Region: Ottawa and Hull, occupying 1800 square miles of eastern Ontario and western Quebec, form the National Capital Region of Canada; it includes 24 municipalities and 2 regional governments.

Industry: major employer is the federal government; E.B. Eddy Co. largest private employer.

Commerce: capital city of Canada with a large tourist business and developing convention capacity; some 57 hotels and motels, 5,180 rooms.

Transportation: 45 miles of parkways and bicycle paths in and around the city; Canadian Pacific and Canadian National Railways; International Airport, nation's 5th busiest, more than 85 scheduled flights daily by 5 airlines.

Cultural facilities: $45 million National Arts Centre with 2,300-seat opera house-concert hall, a theatre and an experimental studio; Ottawa Little Theatre.
National museums: National Gallery of Canada, Museum of Man, Museum of Natural Sciences, Museum of Science and Technology, Canadian War Museum, National Aeronautical Collection.
Other attractions: Gothic-style Parliament buildings, housing Canada's House of Commons and Senate; Peace Tower, memorial to Canada's war dead; Central Canada Exhibition; Ottawa's oldest building, the Bytown Museum; Royal Mint; Rideau Canal provides boating facilities in summer, skating in winter; the experimental farm, 1,300 working acres in the heart of Ottawa; Winter Fair; 80 camping and trailer parks, 7 city beaches; mountain lake recreation facilities.
Sports: Ottawa Rough Riders, CFL; Ottawa 67's, hockey.
History: founded 1827 as Bytown, incorporated as Ottawa 1855; named after Outaouac (or Outaouais Indian tribe); became capital of Canada 1857.
Further information: Canada's Capital Visitors and Convention Bureau, 251 Laurier Ave. West, Ottawa, Ont., K1P-5J6.

Pensacola, Florida

The World Almanac is sponsored in the Pensacola area by the Pensacola News-Journal, 101 E. Romana St., Pensacola, Fla. 32501; (904) 433-0041; predecessor The Floridian founded 1821, first daily News 1899, Journal 1898; merged 1924; combined circulation daily 86,204, Sunday 71,612; member Gannett Group; publisher James H. Jesse, editor J. Earle Bowden.

Population: 60,705 (city), 295,159 (county), 450,000 (primary trade area).
Area: southern end of 759 sq. mi. Escambia County at westernmost edge of Florida Panhandle.
Industry: U.S. Navy employs 15,200 military, 5,000 civilian personnel; major manufacturers are Monsanto, St. Regis Paper, Armstrong Cork, Tenneco, West-inghouse, Air Products and Chemical, American Cyanamid, Vanity Fair; major industries are food and kindred products, lumber, printing and stone, clay, glass, and concrete.
Commerce: wholesale, retail center for 4 counties in west Florida, one in Alabama; effective buying income $1.662 billion; retail sales 1973 $834.694 mil-

lion; 17 banks, 5 savings and loan banks, 26 mortgage firms; tourist industry $60 million, and farm and forest income $18.33 million annually.

Transportation: 2 railways, 2 airlines, 2 bus lines, 16 truck lines; 3 U.S. highways, Interstate 10.

Communications: one TV, 9 radio stations.

Medical facilities: 5 hospitals in addition to the U.S. Naval Aviation Medical Center.

Cultural facilities: public library; 5 museums: Historical Museum, T. T. Wentworth Museum, Hispanic Museum, Transportation Museum, Museum of Naval

Aviation; little theater; symphony orchestra; Art Association; Arts Council, Inc.; Oratorio Society.

Other attractions: historic forts, Pensacola Beach, Gulf Islands National Seashore, Seville Quarter.

Sports: Monsanto Open PGA tournament, Falstaff Classic Amateur Golf Classic, intercollegiate basketball.

History: colonized in 1559, failed; city founded in 1698, existing under 5 flags until ceded by Spain to U.S. in 1813.

Bicentennial plans: year long celebration, including historical restoration of buildings.

Philadelphia, Pennsylvania

The World Almanac is sponsored in the Philadelphia area by The Philadelphia Inquirer, 400 N. Broad St., Philadelphia, Pa. 19101; phone (215) 854-2000; established 1829, lineage traced to Pennsylvania Packet, founded 1771; circulation 436,800 daily, 831,600 Sunday; Pulitzer Prize 1975; published by Philadelphia Newspapers, Inc.; president Frederick Chait; vice president and general manager Sam S. McKeel; executive editor Eugene L. Roberts Jr.; editor Creed C. Black; managing editor Gene Foreman; sponsors Delaware Valley Science Fair, Book & Author Luncheons. PNI also publishes the Philadelphia Daily News, an afternoon tabloid, at same address; founded 1925; circulation 256,100; editor Rolfe Neill; managing editor David Lawrence; senior vice president Natt Getlin; sponsors annual Circus Party for disadvantaged children, Secret Witness rewards.

Population: 1,881,300 (4th in U.S.); 4,819,200 (metro: 5 counties in Pa., 3 in N.J.); employment: 1,848,100 (metro).

Area: 130 sq. mi. (city); 3,575 sq. mi. (metro area); city located in southeastern Pa. on Delaware and Schuylkill rivers; 90 mi. from N.Y.C., 136 mi. from Wash., D.C., 60 mi. from Atlantic City.

Industry: diversified, with over 90% of all U.S. basic industries represented; major center for textiles and apparel, food processing, petroleum (largest oil refining region on East Coast), printing and publishing, instruments, chemicals and pharmaceuticals; companies headquartered in metro area include Sun Oil, Campbell Soup, American Stores, Scott Paper, Leeds & Northrup, Smithkline, Rohm & Haas, Food Fair, Crown Cork & Seal, Pennwalt.

Commerce: 17 commercial banks, over $18 billion deposits; 4 mutual savings banks, over $6 billion; retail sales (1974 metro), $11.2 billion; average household income, $14,133.

Transportation: largest fresh-water port in world (50 mi. of waterfront); 1974 leader in foreign trade with 80.8 million tons; 2 new marine terminals for containerized cargo; rail service provided by Penn Central, Reading, B&O, and Amtrak; over 200 truck lines, vast highway network, 5 bridges in metro area for motor traffic between Pa. and N.J.; International Airport's $174 million terminal expansion, set for completion in spring 1976, will double number of passengers handled in 1974 (7.9 million); Cargo City, $50 million air freight facility; area transit (SEPTA) conveyed 293 million passengers on subway, el, rail commuter, bus and streetcar lines in 1974.

Communications: 3 major daily newspapers: Inquirer, Bulletin and News; 23 AM, 23 FM, 6 commercial TV stations; cable TV.

New construction: Market St. East, $300 million reconstruction of major retail area; Franklin Town, privately financed $400 million redevelopment of 50-acre midcity site (will provide 4,000 residential units, employment for 20,000); Penn's Landing, $120 million waterfront development.

Medical facilities: 97 hospitals with 23,000 beds.

Federal facilities: Phila. Naval Base; Defense Industrial Supply Center; Defense Personnel Support Center; U.S. Naval Publications and Forms Center;

U.S. Mint; Frankford Arsenal.

Cultural facilities: Phila. Orchestra; Pa. Ballet; Opera Co. of Phila.; Acad. of Music; Museum of Art; Franklin Inst.; Pa. Acad. of the Fine Arts; Rodin Museum; University Museum; Acad. of Natural Sciences; Barnes Foundation; Robin Hood Dell; Walnut St. Theater (oldest in America); Shubert, Forrest, and New Locust theaters; community and summer theaters.

Educational facilities: 54 colleges and universities within 25 mi. of City Hall; 6 medical schools in city; University City Science Center.

Convention facilities: Civic Center has 321,000 sq. ft. of exhibit space, 57 meeting rooms incl. 12,500-seat Convention Hall; 296 hotels/motels, 18,000 first-class rooms.

Recreational facilities: over 8,000 acres of parks incl. 4,079-acre Fairmount Park; hundreds of playgrounds, swimming pools, golf courses, tennis courts, ice-skating rinks; close to seashore, mountains.

Sports: NL Phillies, NFL Eagles, Atoms soccer, NHL Flyers, NBA 76ers, Wings lacrosse; WFL Bell, and Penn Relays; Army-Navy Football game; horse racing.

Other attractions: City Hall; restored Society Hill area; Elfreth's Alley; zoo (nation's first); Longwood Gardens; Mummers Parade (Jan. 1); Freedom Week (June 27-July 4).

History: Wm. Penn founded his "Greene Countrie Towne" as Quaker colony in 1682; gave it name that means "City of Brotherly Love"; national capital 1790-1800; historical shrines include Independence Hall, Liberty Bell, Carpenters' Hall, Betsy Ross House, Gloria Dei Church, Christ Church, USS Olympia, Fort Mifflin.

Bicentennial plans: focal point of nation's 1976 celebration; major project is $11.6 million center where history will come to life on giant IMAX screen (70'x100'), other multi-media exhibits; many preserved, restored or reconstructed historic bldgs.; Liberty Bell in new home; July 4 visit by President Ford; centers of attraction will be famed historic district and tree-lined Benj. Franklin Parkway.

Further information: City Representative, 1660 Municipal Services Bldg., Phila., Pa. 19107.

Phoenix, Arizona

The World Almanac is sponsored in the Phoenix area by The Phoenix Gazette, 120 East Van Buren Street, Phoenix, Arizona 85004; phone (602) 271-8000; founded Oct. 28, 1880, as Arizona Gazette by Charles H. McNeil;

circulation 105,728; publisher Eugene C. Pulliam, managing editor Alan D. Moyer; sponsors Christmas Fund Drive, Music Memory Programs, Science Fair, Phoenix Suns Christmas Day Basketball Game, Family Symphony Concerts, and other events.

Population: 766,000 (city), 1,304,000 (metro); capital and largest city in state, 15th (city) in nation; total employed 484,100.
Area: 269.3 sq. mi. (city), 9,155 sq. mi. (metro), in south central Arizona.
Industry: electronic equipment manufacturers, Honeywell Information Systems, and Motorola, Inc. each employ more than 2,500; aircraft and parts manufacturers, AiResearch, a division of The Garrett Corp., and Sperry Flight Systems each employ more than 2,500; other major employers are E. L. Gruber (apparel), Goodyear Aerospace, General Electric, Western Electric Cable, Reynolds Metals, Marathon Steel, Arizona Public Service, Salt River Project, Mountain Bell, Amerco, Greyhound, American Express, and Phoenix Newspapers.
Commerce: wholesale-retail center for state; retail sales (1974) $4.0 billion; effective household buying income, $12,787; bank and S&L assets $9.4 billion; 12 banks with 211 area offices, 5 S&Ls with 79 offices in metro area.
Transportation: transportation center of the Southwest; Sky Harbor International Airport served by 10 airlines, 3,948,569 passengers (1974); 2 railroads; 2 transcontinental buslines; 10 transcontinental truck lines; 25 transcontinental heavy equipment haulers; 34 interstate and 39 intrastate truck lines.
Communications: 6 TV and 32 radio stations.
New construction: In 1974, 19,707 new residential building units were permitted; total value all types of building permits, $690 million.

Medical facilities: Barrow Neurological Institute; 20 general care hospitals, Veterans' Hospital; other special service facilities.
Cultural facilities: art museum, public library, symphony orchestra, Indian museums, zoo, botanical gardens, community and professional theaters; Civic Plaza convention center; Gammage Auditorium.
Educational facilities: Arizona State Univ. American Graduate School of International Management; 4 community colleges; Maricopa Technical College (vocational); 56 public and parochial high schools.
Sports: 50 golf courses and $150,000 Phoenix Open; inland surfing beach; ice skating rinks; amusement park; pro hockey, basketball, baseball teams; auto racing, greyhound and horse racing; annual Fiesta Bowl (holiday football game).
Other attractions: Frank Lloyd Wright's Taliesin West; Paolo Soleri's Arcosanti; Firebird Festival of the Arts; Dons' Club guided tours of Arizona; full calendar of events including state and county fairs and rodeos, horse shows, regattas, polo tournaments.
History: founded 1870, on site of ancient Indian settlement; the Hohokam tribe, which flourished ca. 500-1200 A.D., developed an intricate system of irrigation canals which form the base of the canal system in use today.
Bicentennial plans: Heritage Days in the Park; Masque of the Yellow Moon; U.S.S. Arizona (sunk at Pearl Harbor) anchor sited and dedicated; theme of Fiesta Bowl activities.

Pittsburgh, Pennsylvania

The World Almanac is sponsored in the Pittsburgh area by The Pittsburgh Press, 34 Blvd. of the Allies, Pittsburgh, Pa. 15222; phone (412) 263-1100; founded June 23, 1884, as Evening Penny Press by Thomas J. Keehan; circulation 283,017 daily, 676,136 Sunday; editor John Troan, business manager Barney G. Cameron, executive editor Leo Koeberlein; managing editor Ralph Brem; sponsors Press Old Newsboys Fund for Children's Hospital which raised $430,200 in 1974.

Population: 520,117 (city), 2,401,245 (4-county metro area), 2d in state and 24th in nation; metro area labor force of 997,300 is 6th in nation.
Area: 55.5 sq. mi. at juncture of Allegheny and Monongahela rivers which form Ohio River; Allegheny County seat; altitude, 702 feet.
Industry: one-fifth of nation's steelmaking capacity concentrated in metro area; western Pennsylvania mines produce 44 million tons of bituminous coal annually; 6,000 different products made in area; home of world's first full-scale nuclear power plant, world's largest manufacturers of aluminum, steel rolls, rolling mill machinery, air brakes, plate and window glass and safety equipment; 3d largest headquarters city in nation.
Commerce: retail sales (1974), $6.1 billion; exports abroad totaled over $370 million (1973) while river tonnage totaled 70 million tons, more than any other inland area; average household effective buying income, $12,666.
Transportation: 7 scheduled airlines handled 7,473,-670 passengers on 101,780 flights at International Airport (1974) where $250 million expansion is underway; 19 railroads; Continental Trailways and Greyhound bus lines; over 400 common carriers; Port Authority Transit vehicles carried 104.6 million passengers (1974) over 165 bus routes, 5 trolley lines; 9 major highways serve city; rapid and mass transit plan under development.
Communications: 2 daily newspapers; 5 TV (including country's first educational station) and 27 radio stations.
New construction: twin-tower 34-story Equibank

Bldg.; $32 million, 140,000 sq. ft. convention center underway for completion in 1978.
Medical facilities: 21 hospitals include Univ. of Pittsburgh Health and Medical complex where Dr. Jonas Salk developed polio vaccine; VA installation.
Federal facilities: Federal Building contains scores of U.S. government offices (information center: 412/644-3456); Army base at Oakdale; Air Force base.
Cultural facilities: Heinz Hall is home of the opera co., ballet, Civic Light Opera, Youth Symphony and symphony orchestra; 3 community and 2 legitimate theaters; Frick Art Museum; Carnegie Museum and Art Gallery, home of the triennial Carnegie International; American Wind Symphony.
Educational facilities: Univ. of Pittsburgh, Duquesne Univ.; Point Park, Chatham, Carlow, Robert Morris and La Roche Colleges, Carnegie-Mellon Univ., Community College of Allegheny Co.; 18 Carnegie public libraries, 3 bookmobiles, community libraries.
Sports: NL Pirates, NFL Steelers, NHL Penguins; World Team Tennis Triangles.
Other attractions: Highland Park Zoo, children's zoo, Twilight Zoo, aquarium, aviary, Buhl Planetarium, Allegheny Observatory, Phipps Conservatory, Fort Pitt Museum; 4 amusement parks; 2 operating passenger inclines; folk festival; Three Rivers Arts Festival every June; harness racing; river cruises; Civic Arena; Three Rivers Stadium.
History: first hunters and trappers came through in 1714; city dates from Nov. 25, 1758, when English forces under Brig. Gen. John Forbes occupied the ruins of Fort Duquesne, which French soldiers had burned and abandoned, and built a new and bigger

fortress called Fort Pitt. When incorporated in 1816, it already had a reputation as a "Smoky City" from factories and coal-burning homes. Massive "Renaissance Plan" has cleared the skies and rebuilt the heart of the city during the past 25 years.

Bicentennial plans: neighborhood festivals in spring and summer of 1976, featuring art, history, culture, and ethnic foods, culminating in city-wide fall festival.

Further information: Chamber of Commerce, 411 Seventh Ave.; Convention and Visitors Bureau, 3001 Jenkins Arcade; both Pittsburgh, PA 15222.

Portland, Maine

The World Almanac is sponsored in the Portland area by the Maine Sunday Telegram, 390 Congress, Portland, Me, 04104; phone (207) 775-5811; published by Guy Gannett Publishing Co., founded 1921; circulation 107,838; president Jean Gannett Hawley; editor Ernest Chard; also publishes morning Press Herald, circulation 53,483, and Evening Express, 29,590.

Population: 66,500 (city), 164,000 (metro area), 1st in state; total employed, 26,959 (1970).

Area: 21.6 sq. mi.; peninsula on Casco Bay; Cumberland County seat.

Industry: Atlantic Coast's 2d busiest oil shipping center, east terminus Montreal pipeline; fishing fleet base, seafood shipping center; landbased products: printed materials, clothing, metal, processed food, electronic parts, wooden goods.

Commerce: tourist center, regional retail-wholesale hub, large shopping complex, 1,000 retail, 350 wholesale, 600 service enterprises; retail sales (1972), $247,156,000; median family income (1970), $8,456.

Transportation: municipal jetport, Delta airline; 3 rail freight lines, integrated bus system, Greyhound, Continental bus terminals, 25 truck lines; Maine Turnpike, Interstate 95 and 295 highways connect to all New England; deep water anchorage, auto cruise ferries year round to Yarmouth, Nova Scotia.

Communications: 3 TV, 5 AM, 4 FM stations.

New construction: Cumberland County Civic Center, vocational school, telephone complex, bank, condominiums.

Medical facilities: medical center, 2 hospitals.

Cultural facilities: symphony orch., Kotzschmar organ, one of world's largest; public, historical libraries; Victorian art museums; Henry Longfellow home (1785); branch Univ. of Maine, Westbrook College, art, vocational, and business schools; Portland Headlight, oldest lighthouse in country.

Recreation: 18-hole municipal golf course, 9 others in area; scenic cruises; swimming, tennis, fishing within easy travel; scenic parks.

Convention facilities: 2 large assembly halls, meeting rooms in modern hotels and motels. Tourist Bureau: 142 Free St.

Bicentennial plans: art festival; local history, cultural and ethnic group projects.

Portland, Oregon

The World Almanac is sponsored in the Portland area by The Oregon Journal, 1320 SW Broadway, Portland, Ore. 97201; phone (503) 221-8275; founded Mar. 1902; circulation 124,392; editor Donald J. Sterling Jr.; managing editor Edward F. O'Meara.

Population: 371,800 (city), 1,080,500 (metro) in 1974; 1st in state; 30th in nation; total employed, 485,000.

Area: 80 sq. mi., at juncture of Columbia and Willamette rivers.

Industry: electrical and electronic industries along with lumber and wood products, food, and paper; ranks first in manufacture of logging, lumbering equipment; home of Georgia-Pacific, Louisiana-Pacific (forest products), Tektronix (oscilloscopes), Omark (saw cutting chain), Hyster (lifts, hoists, lumber handling), White Stag, Pendleton, Jantzen (clothing).

Commerce: wholesale-retail center for large part of Oregon, SW Washington; retail sales metro area (1974), $3.04 billion. There are 16 banks, 11 savings and loan associations.

Transportation: 4 major rail freight lines, Amtrak, Greyhound, Trailways buses; 10th largest freshwater port in U.S., with 27-mile frontage, 29 marine berths; 11 million tons of cargo pass over docks annually; more than 1,000 ships visit annually, most active harbor in U.S.; hub for 9 airlines, flights to all parts of world.

Communications: 5 TV and 19 radio stations.

Medical facilities: 17 major hospitals, Univ. of Oregon Medical School, VA Hospital.

Cultural facilities: Art Museum, Oregon Symphony Orchestra, Opera Association, Oregon Historical Society, Portland State Univ., Univ. of Portland, and Lewis & Clark, Reed, and Concordia Colleges.

Other attractions: annual Rose Festival, Rose Show; park system includes Washington Park, Hoyt Arboretum International Rose Test Garden, Portland Zoo, Oregon Museum of Science and Industry; Forest Park is largest forest area in a U.S. city's limits; sports events and other attractions are presented in Memorial Coliseum.

History: chartered 1851 with population of 821; named after Portland, Me., rather than Boston, Mass., on flip of coin by 2 early citizens.

Bicentennial plans: overall theme of entire 1976 Rose Festival.

Further information: Chamber of Commerce, 824 SW 5th, Portland, Oregon 97204.

Providence, Rhode Island

The World Almanac is sponsored in the Providence area by The Providence Journal-Bulletin, 75 Fountain St., Providence, R.I. 02902; phone (401) 277-7000; Journal founded 1829, Bulletin 1863, Sunday Journal 1883; circulation, Journal (morn) 67,250, Bulletin (eve) 145,408, Sunday Journal 205,588; publisher John C. A. Watkins, president Michael P. Metcalf, v.p. and asst. publ. Edwin P. Young, v.p.-admin. Charles P. O'Donnell, v.p. and exec. editor Charles McC.Hauser.

Population: 177,500 (city), 981,000 (metro); total employed 115,835.
Area: 18.91 sq. mi., at the head of Narragansett Bay.
Industry: jewelry, silverware, plated ware, costume jewelry are largest industries; Textron is based in Providence; 1,271 manufacturing companies in the city.
Commerce: wholesale-retail center for entire state; retail sales $2.5 billion (metro); consumer spendable income per household $13,037 (metro); Allendale Insurance, world's largest mutual insurer of industrial firms, is based outside of city in Johnston; home of Narragansett Capital, largest small business investment company in nation; 2 savings and loan assns., 2 mutual savings banks, one cooperative bank, 6 commercial banks.
Transportation: Penn Central Railroad, fast "Turbo-Liner" passenger service between Boston, Providence, and N.Y.; 5 bus lines; 45 locally-based common carriers and contract truckers; 9 major highways link Providence to every corner of R.I.; 6 major airlines out of T. F. Green Airport in Warwick (15 min. away); port is 3d largest in New England with 25 wharves and docks, 10.5 miles of commercial waterfront on the bay.
Communications: 3 TV and 8 radio stations.
Medical facilities: 7 hospitals; one VA hospital.

Cultural facilities: Trinity Square Repertory Co., R. I. Philharmonic, R. I. School of Design Museum.
Education: Brown University, founded 1764, is 7th oldest college in nation; 7-year M.D. program inaugurated 1973; Providence and R. I. Colleges, and R.I. School of Design.
Recreation: one of America's most attractive recreational areas centers around Providence: 69 salt water beaches, 25 fresh water beaches, 49 golf and country clubs, 4 ski areas, 26 yacht clubs, 23 parks, all within 45 minutes of city.
Convention facilities: R.I. Civic Center (seats 12,000).
Sports: America's Cup races since 1930; Newport-Bermuda race starts at Newport every other year; Reds (hockey), Oceaneers (soccer).
Other attractions: largest collection of original early American homes of any city; located along Benefit St., they have been preserved by the Providence Preservation Society.
History: founded 1636 by Roger Williams; incorporated 1832; official state name is "Rhode Island and Providence Plantations."
Bicentennial plans: between 50-80 of the world's biggest sail-powered ships will visit Newport, July, 1976.
Further information: Chamber of Commerce, 10 Dorrance St. or R. I. Tourist/Travel Assn., Turks Head Bldg., both Providence, R. I. 02903.

Quebec City, Quebec, Canada

Population: 186,088 (city), 480,500 (metro); oldest city in Canada (1608) and the capital city of the Province of Quebec.
Area: 30 sq. mi.; natural citadel on north shore of St. Lawrence River at confluence with St. Charles River; 400 miles from Gulf of St. Lawrence; 167 miles east of Montreal; older part is built on a cliff 360 ft. above the St. Lawrence.
Industry: some 300 industrial firms, ranging from primary industry products to a variety of consumer products, employ over 16,000 people; food and beverage, leather footwear and leather products, textiles, apparel, wood products, pulp and paper, printing and publishing, iron and steel products, non-ferrous metal and chemical products.
Commerce: Quebec harbor, one of the busiest seaports of Canada, accommodates the largest ocean-going vessels with year-round facilities, an important container terminal on the North Atlantic coast; Provincial Government, with more than 15,000 employees, is the largest single employer and consumer in the city.
Transportation: Canadian Pacific, and Canadian National railroads; Air Canada, Quebecair, Nordair; major bus center.
Communications: 3 TV stations (2 French, 1 bilingual); 5 radio stations (4 French, 1 English).
Medical facilities: 5 large general hospitals, many

smaller ones.
Cultural facilities: historic character, cultural appeal and natural beauty make tourism important area of economic activity; annual "Carnaval" in Feb. is internationally known; annual summer Festival (July) changes the city into an open theater for numerous artistic events; Expo-Quebec, an annual provincial exhibition (industrial, commercial and agricultural), draws over 500,000 people a year.
Educational facilities: Laval University, the first in North America; Quebec University; 3 colleges for general and vocational training, numerous private schools.
Sports: Home of WHA Nordiques, and Les Caribous of the National Lacrosse League.
Other attractions: only walled city in North America with fortifications standing today as they were 125 years ago; the Citadel, built from 1823-1832, contains within its walls 25 buildings, including the summer residence of Governor-General of Canada, Parliament buildings (1886), Quebec Museum, Battlefield Park, Ursulines Museum, Seminary (1663), Talon cellars, Notre Dame des Victoires Church, and Tresor Street.
History: founded 1608 by French explorer Samuel de Champlain; cradle of French civilization in America; once the key to the interior of the North American continent.

Raleigh, North Carolina

The World Almanac is sponsored in eastern North Carolina by The News & Observer and The Raleigh Times, 215 S. McDowell St., Raleigh, NC 27602, (919) 821-1234; circulation N&O (morn) 129,000, Times (eve) 33,000, N&O Sunday 160,231; publisher Frank Daniels Jr., editorial director Claude Sitton, editor Times A. C. Snow, managing editor N&O Bob Brooks, Times Mike Yopp.

Population: 150,000 (city), 275,000 (county), 500,000 (metro area); 4th in state; 200,000 employed (metro area).
Area: 45 sq. mi. in geographical center of state where

piedmont joins coastal plain; alt. 363 ft.; state capital and Wake Co. seat.

Industry: major industry is government, employing

25% of work force; also electrical machinery, foods and textiles.

Commerce: financial, retail center of eastern N.C.; retail sales (1974) $994 million; 13 banks with $40 billion debits; income average per household $15,000.

Education: 6 colleges; N.C. State Univ. largest, with Univ. of N.C. (Chapel Hill), and Duke Univ. (Durham) within 30 mi. form Research Triangle; 5,000 acre Triangle Park employs 10,000 in drug, fiber, biomedical and engineering research.

Transportation: 3 rail and 3 bus lines; airport has 4 airlines and 46 flights daily.

Communications: 4 TV and 13 radio stations.

New construction: $50 million (1974).

Medical facilities: 3 hospitals, 818 beds; major mental hospital, 2,765 beds; 350 doctors.

Convention facilities: 30 motels, 4,000 rooms.

Cultural facilities: 3 museums, state fairgrounds; Dorton Arena seats 9,111, Memorial Auditorium 3,000, and Reynolds Coliseum 12,000.

Recreation: 4,200-acre Umstead Park; Carter Stadium; 100 city parks.

Sports: one pro golf meet; college sports.

History: founded 1792; Andrew Johnson birthplace.

Further information: Chamber of Commerce, 411 S. Salisbury St., Raleigh, NC 27602.

Regina, Saskatchewan, Canada

The World Almanac is sponsored in southern Saskatchewan by The Leader-Post, 1964 Park St., Regina, Sask., phone (306) 527-8511; founded 1885 by Nicholas Flood Davin; circulation 66,336; president Michael Sifton, Toronto; executive vice-president Max Macdonald; editor W. Ivor Williams; managing editor C.E.W. Bell; business manager William Duffus; advertising manager George Crawford; MacLaren Trophy for editorial page reproduction excellence.

Population: 148,200, first in province, 17th in nation; labor force, 60,985.

Area: 30.98 sq. mi., 100 miles north of Canada-U.S. border; provincial capital.

Industry: over 250 manufacturing industries; gross production value (1974) $274.2 million, 37% of Saskatchewan total.

Commerce: service center for oil, potash; grain production area; retail sales (1974) $420 million, 24.2% of province.

Transportation: 2 rail lines, 2 airlines, 3 bus lines, and 80 trucking companies; main Trans-Canada highway bisects; city-run transit system, including Telebus, hybrid system with demand/response taxi service and mass transit, provides to-and-from service to user's home.

Communications: 2 TV and 6 radio stations.

Medical facilities: 4 major hospitals, 1,483 beds.

Cultural facilities: Saskatchewan Centre of Arts, multi-purpose theater-convention center with: Jubi-

lee theater (seats 450) stage, ballroom, reception hall and dining room; Centennial theater (seats 2,029); Hanbidge Hall convention area, 12,200 square feet, 9 meeting rooms, seats 1,600, serves 1,200. Regina Symphony; Globe Repertory; Museum Natural History; Norman Mackenzie Art Gallery; RCMP Museum.

Educational facilities: Regina University; 13 collegiates; 78 elementary; Wascana Institute of Applied Arts and Sciences.

Recreation facilities: Saskatchewan Roughriders (Canadian pro football); 96 parks and playgrounds; 9 golf courses; 6 swimming pools; 6 indoor ice rinks.

Other attractions: Wascana Centre, 2,000-acre development, with man-made lake, public buildings, parks, recreation in heart of city.

History: founded 1882, and since that time headquarters for RCMP training depot.

Further information: Regina Chamber of Commerce, 2145 Albert Street, Regina, Saskatchewan.

Reno, Nevada

The World Almanac is sponsored in the northern Nevada area by the Nevada State Journal and the Reno Evening Gazette, 401 West 2d St., Reno, Nev. 89504; phone (702) 786-8989; Journal founded 1870; Gazette 1876; combined daily circulation 48,632, Sunday 38,563; publisher Richard J. Schuster, executive editor Warren L. Lerude.

Population: estimated 1974 pop. of 86,178 (city), 149,-300 (county including Sparks with 33,462); 2d largest in the state; 1974 labor force, 78,900.

Area: 36.8 sq. mi. (including Stead annexation), in northwestern part of state at the eastern foot of the Sierra Nevada; Washoe County seat.

Industry: gross gaming revenue for county, $170.4 million (1974) netted state taxes of $13.1 million; 69,-010 delegates attended 229 conventions, staying in 11,408 rooms, paying $1.7 million in room taxes; warehousing continues to grow because of Nevada's liberal free port law with 8 million sq. ft. in the county; marriages (33,933) outnumbered divorces (3,461).

Commerce: taxable sales in metro area (including Sparks) for Jan.-Oct., 1974, $564.9 million; assessed valuation (city) $433.3 million; median household income $9,492; bank resources, $1.7 billion.

Transportation: 12 motor freight lines, 3 freight railroads, Amtrak, and 3 commercial airlines; airport handled 1,053,789 passengers (1974) as international

port of entry; U.S. 395 and Interstate 80.

Communications: 3 TV, 10 radio stations; one CTV.

Medical facilities: 3 hospitals, including VA.

Educational facilities: Univ. of Nevada, Reno, 8,434 enrollment; community college; public school enrollment, 30,686, parochial, 1,059.

Sports: semi-pro Aces hockey, Silver Sox baseball.

Cultural facilities: 1,428 seat Pioneer Theater Auditorium and 8,000 seat Centennial Coliseum; Fleischman Atmospherium Planetarium, and 180,000-volume library; national air races; rodeo; little theater.

Recreation: 21 ski resorts within a 2-hour drive; Lake Tahoe and Pyramid Lake offer fishing, boating, and sun-bathing; medium game hunting.

History: established 1868 with public auction of land by Central Pacific RR; named after Civil War hero Gen. Jesse L. Reno.

Further information: Chamber of Commerce, P.O. Box 3499, Reno, Nev. 89505.

Richmond, Virginia

The World Almanac is sponsored in the Richmond area by the Richmond Times-Dispatch and News Leader, 333 E. Grace St., Richmond, Va. 23213; (804) 649-6000; Times-Dispatch founded 1950 by James A. Cowardin, circulation 132,367 daily, 196,510 Sunday; News Leader founded 1896 by Joseph Bryan, circulation 113,669; publisher D. Tennant Bryan; president Alan S. Donnahoe, executive editor John E. Leard, Times-Dispatch managing editor Alf Goodykoontz, News Leader managing editor J. A. Finch.

Population: 230,400 (city), 529,400 (metro area), total employed (non-agricultural) 278,600.
Area: 62.5 sq. mi. (city), located at fall line of James River, 90 miles from Atlantic Ocean.
Industry: tobacco, with 9,300 workers, and chemicals, with 8,400 are leaders in employment; Philip Morris cigarette plant which began production in 1974 is world's largest and most modern; printing, publishing, manufacture of paper and allied products, and food.
Commerce: wholesale-retail center for central Virginia; retail sales $1.4 billion in 1974, per capita income $5,068, family $11,660, total income $2.88 billion.
Transportation: 4 major railroads, 5 intercity bus lines, 3 commercial air lines, one commuter air line, 50 motor truck lines; 3 interstate, 6 U. S., and 9 state highways; deepwater terminal accessible to ocean-going ships.
Communications: 4 TV, 16 radio stations.
Medical facilities: Medical College of Virginia known worldwide for heart and kidney transplants, medical research; 21 other hospitals, including McGuire VA Hospital.
Federal facilities: Defense General Supply Center, Fifth Federal Reserve Bank, U. S. Fourth Circuit Court, Ft. Lee (Quartermaster Corps).
Cultural facilities: Va. Museum and Theater with professional artists make city a center for dramatic,

other performing arts; variety of other drama groups; symphony orchestra.
Educational facilities: Virginia Commonwealth Univ. has state's largest enrollment; Univ. of Richmond, Virginia Union Univ., Union Theological Seminary (Presbyterian), Randolph-Macon College.
Recreational facilities: Coliseum for athletic, entertainment events; city-owned Mosque auditorium. Parker Field, City Stadium, numerous parks.
Convention facilities: large downtown hotels near Mosque and Coliseum.
Sports: Braves (IL baseball), Robins (hockey), national ranked track and tennis events; Russian-American indoor track meets.
Other attractions: St. John's Church, scene of Patrick Henry's "Liberty or Death" speech; Virginia Capitol, designed by Thomas Jefferson; White House of the Confederacy; Civil War battlefields.
History: exploration here in 1607 by Capt. John Smith, first settlement 1609, incorporated as town 1742, made Va. capital 1780, Confederate Capital 1861-65; burned 1781 by Benedict Arnold, and 1865 when cotton, tobacco stockpiles fire set by fleeing Confederates spread to city; damaged by floods 1771, 1969, 1972.
Further information: Chamber of Commerce, 201 E. Franklin St., Richmond, Va. 23219.
Bicentennial plans: commemorative events, public programs, film slide shows.

Roanoke, Virginia

The World Almanac is sponsored in the Roanoke area by The Roanoke Times and The World-News, 201-203 Campbell Avenue, Roanoke, Va. 24010, telephone (703) 981-3000; Times founded 1886, World-News founded 1889; Richard F. Barry III, president; Barton W. Morris Jr., publisher; circulation combined daily, 113,454; Sunday 111,674.

Population: 109,500 (City, Jan. 1, 1976), 214,300 (metro area); labor force 102,750.
Area: 43.25 sq. mi.; Metro SMSA includes Roanoke City, Salem City, Roanoke, Craig, Botetourt Counties; located at southern extremity of Shenandoah Valley midway between Maryland and Tennessee.
Industry: 21% of work force in manufacturing. Leading firms are General Electric, Eaton Corp., ITT, Singer, Burlington Industries, Mohawk Rubber, Ingersoll Rand.
Commerce: headquarters Shenandoah Life Ins. Co., Estate Life Ins. Co., Appalachian Power Co., Advance Stores, Mick or Mack Groceries; Retail Center for 20 counties and parts of West Virginia and North Carolina.
Transportation: Norfolk & Western Railway Co. headquarters. 2 airlines; Trailways and Greyhound buses; Amtrak east-west route Norfolk to Cincinnati. 30 interstate trucking firms with terminals; Highways Interstate 81, Spur 581, US 11, US 460, US 220, US 221, Blue Ridge Parkway.
Communications: 3 TV and 12 radio stations.

Medical facilities: 4 general, 2 specialty hospitals, VA facility; state hospital.
Cultural facilities: 2 civic centers with auditorium, coliseums and exhibit halls, symphony orchestra, art center, theaters, Roanoke College, Hollins College, Virginia Western Community College, National Business College; concert and lecture series.
Other attractions: Mill Mt. Park rising 1,000 ft. in center of city; children's zoo; Transportation and Historical Museum; Smith Mt.; Fairy Stone and Claytor Lakes state parks; Natural Bridge, Dixie Caverns, Peaks of Otter.
Sports: professional ice hockey, baseball; school sports, winter skiing nearby, public recreation and parks programs.
History: formerly named Big Lick, Roanoke, an Indian word for shell money, became a city in 1884 with the linking of the Shenandoah Valley Railroad with Norfolk and Western Railroad.
Further information: Roanoke Valley Chamber of Commerce, 14 West Kirk Avenue, P.O. Box 20, Roanoke, 24001.

Rochester, New York

The World Almanac is sponsored in the Rochester area by Gannett Rochester Newspapers, 55 Exchange St., Rochester, N. Y. 14614; phone (716) 232-7100; circulation, Democrat and Chronicle (morn) 137,887; Times-Union (eve), 142,661; Democrat and Chronicle, (Sun.) 230,713; publisher Eugene C. Dorsey; executive editor Stuart Dunham; director of advertising James E. McKearney, Jr.; Times-Union reporters awarded a 1972 Pulitzer Prize.

Population: 295,011 (1970 adj.); 5-county metro area 990,400 (1973 est.); 420,900 employed; unemployment 6.8%.
Area: 675 sq. mi. (Monroe County) straddling Genesee River, on Lake Ontario; 2,966 sq. mi. (metro); Monroe County seat.
Industry: world leader in production of photographic optical, and scientific instruments, with Eastman Kodak (48,775 employees), Xerox (15,000), and Bausch & Lomb (5,000), all founded in Rochester, the most prominent; other fields include machinery, food products, apparel, printing and publishing; industrial wage increase, 41% since 1969.
Commerce: retail sales (1973 est.) over $2 billion; 20 commercial and savings banks, with assets of $5.8 billion; 1973 median household income (Monroe County) $12,423, (metro area) $10,242, 32d in nation.
Transportation: Monroe County Airport, with 3 major airlines and several freight companies; rail freight service by 4 lines, Amtrak; port of Rochester; over 75 motor freight firms.
Communications: 4 TV and 15 radio stations.
New construction: First Federal Bldg., 22 story office tower.
Medical facilities: one of the nation's most advanced health care centers: 8 general hospitals, including Strong Memorial Hospital.
Cultural facilities: Eastman Theater, part of Univ. of Eastman School of Music, and home of the Philharmonic Orchestra; Memorial Art Gallery; Museum and Science Center, including Strasenburgh Planetarium; George Eastman House of Photography; 3 resident theatre companies.
Educational facilities: 8 private and 2 public 4-year colleges; 3 community colleges.
Recreational facilities: Finger Lakes area, with 13 parks, summer and winter sports, golf, tennis, bowling; 16-park Monroe County system, including Seneca Park Zoo, Highland Park, with Lilac Festival (May).
Convention facilities: 2d largest site in N.Y.; War Memorial, 7,500 cap., Dome Arena, 5,000 cap.; 4,600 rms. available.
Sports: International League Red Wings, top Baltimore Orioles farm team; AHL Amerks, North American Soccer League Lancers, National Lacrosse League Griffins; thoroughbred racing and Finger Lakes Race Track, (Canandaigua).
Further information: Chamber of Commerce, 55 St. Paul St., 14604; or Convention and Publicity Bureau, 100 Exchange St., 14614.

Sacramento, California

The World Almanac is sponsored in the Sacramento area by The Sacramento·Bee, 21st & Q, Sacramento, Cal. 95816; telephone (916) 442-5011; founded 1857; circulation daily 170,025, Sunday 200,370; president Eleanor McClatchy, editor C. K. McClatchy, managing editor Frank McCulloch.

Population: 262,100 (city), 690,900 (county), 889,000 (metro); total employed (metro) 332,600.
Area: 94 sq. mi. (city), 997 sq. mi. (county) in Sacramento Valley, 85 mi. northeast of San Francisco.
Industry: 475 manufacturing plants including Campbell Soup, Procter and Gamble, Libby McNeil and Libby, California Almond Growers Exchange, Del Monte, Teichert Construction, and Aerojet-General.
Commerce: state capital; wholesale-retail center for large area of Sacramento Valley; retail sales (1973), $1.8 billion; bank debits, $7.1 billion (city).
Transportation: 3 county operated airports, including metropolitan airport, plus numerous private airports; $55-million Port of Sacramento gives access to the Pacific; 2 mainline transcontinental rail carriers; junction 4 major highways.
Communications: 6 TV and 21 radio stations.
New construction: downtown Mall; Old Sacramento being restored as state and federal historical project; Rancho Seco Atomic Power Plant; regional sewage treatment plant; 2 major hotels.
Medical facilities: 10 major hospitals, Univ. of California Medical School in nearby Davis.
Federal facilities: 2 large Air Force bases, Army depot, many regional federal offices.
Cultural facilities: Sacramento Earl Warren Community Center complex; Eagle Theater; symphony orchestra; ballet; Civic Theater; Crocker Art Gallery; California State Univ., Sacramento; McGeorge College of Law; Lincoln Univ. Law School, and 3 community colleges.
Other attractions: zoo, 95 public parks; 74 playgrounds; 12 public and 4 private golf courses, Sutter's Fort, State Capitol, Stanford Home, Pony Express Terminal, Fairytale Town, and Governor's Mansion; fishing, hunting, boating, camping, hiking and skiing in nearby high Sierras; annual State Fair at Cal Expo.
History: founded by John Augustus Sutter in 1839; James Marshall discovered gold at Sutter's Mill, in 1848, 35 miles northeast, gateway to Mother Lode Country; Pony Express and Central Pacific Railroad which crossed the Sierra Nevada were part of early history.

St. Louis, Missouri

The World Almanac is sponsored in the St. Louis area by the Post-Dispatch, 900 N. 12th Blvd., 63101; telephone (314) 621-1111; founded Dec. 12, 1878 by Joseph Pulitzer; circulation, 297,634 daily, 491,407 Sunday; editor and publisher Joseph Pulitzer Jr., managing editor Evarts A. Graham Jr., general manager Alex T. Primm, director of promotion and public affairs William J. Isam; major awards include 5 Pulitzer Prizes to the newspaper and 11 to staff members.

Population: 591,000 (city), 994,000 (county), 2,481,000 (metro), 11th in nation in payroll employment (859,600 in March 1975).
Area: 4,935 sq. mi. (metro) just south of confluence of Missouri and Mississippi rivers.
Industry: 2d to Detroit in auto assembly with Ford, GM and Chrysler plants; McDonnell Douglas headquarters, aerospace manufacturer; other headquarters include nation's largest shoemaker, Interco; Anheuser-Busch, world's largest brewer; Monsanto, General Dynamics, Ralston-Purina, Pet, Inc., grain market with 44.9 million bushel annual yield; 3,215 manufacturing concerns employing 226,500 persons.
Commerce: $6.2 billion retail sales (est. 1975, metro); $13,492 median family income; 173 banking institutions, total deposits $7.5 billion (1974).

Transportation: 10 major airlines with 6.3 million passenger movements (1974); 2d largest rail center in the nation, 14 trunk line railroads; largest inland river port in nation; 9 major highways; 14 motor-bus lines; 350 motor freight lines.

Communications: 6 TV and 18 radio stations.

New construction: industrial and commercial contracts totaled $339 million (1974); residential, $257 million; Mercantile Center, $150 million office, store and hotel complex; work progressing on $28 million Convention Center.

Medical facilities: 67 hospitals with 16,170 beds; Washington Univ. and St. Louis Univ. medical schools and affiliated hospitals provide specialized treatment in many areas.

Federal facilities: Military Personnel Records Center, Defense Mapping Agency Aerospace Center, Army Mobility Equipment Command, Scott Air Force Base.

Cultural facilities: Art Museum; Museum of Science and Natural History; restored historic homes; symphony orchestra; Mississippi River Festival near Edwardsville in summer; Municipal Theatre (Muny Opera) offers Broadway shows in big outdoor theater in Forest Park.

Educational facilities: 4 major universities: Washington, St. Louis, Univ. of Missouri at St. Louis, and Southern Illinois Univ. at Edwardsville; private colleges; 3-branch junior college system.

Recreational facilities: Jefferson National Expansion Memorial with 630-foot Gateway Arch on the river-front; 1,326-acre Forest Park with 3 golf courses, ball fields, floral displays, zoo and, McDonnell Planetarium; National Museum of Transport; Six Flags Over Mid-America; Grant's Farm with President Grant's cabin, and animal displays; Missouri Botanical Gardens with advanced research-display greenhouse, the Climatron.

Convention facilities: 12,000 hotel rooms; largest exhibit space is 90,000 sq. ft. in Kiel Auditorium.

Sports attractions: Busch Stadium home of the Cardinals baseball and football teams; St. Louis Blues (NHL); Spirits of St. Louis (ABA); soccer Stars.

Other attractions: climate has 4 distinct seasons; spring and autumn warm, winters mild, summers hot with 90-degree temperatures; average temperature is 54.1 degrees; average precipitation 35.3 inches; downtown area contains significant architecture such as Eads Bridge, Old Post Office, Old Courthouse, Old Cathedral, Spanish International Pavilion, and Louis Sullivan's Wainwright Building.

History: named for French King Louis IX by fur trapper Pierre Laclede whose trading post became major fur market and gateway to the West; starting point of Lewis and Clark expedition and other explorations.

Bicentennial plans: Bicentennial Horizons of American Music & Performing Arts, June 14-July 4; Freedom Train, March 30-April 12.

Further information: Convention and Tourist Board, 500 N. Broadway, or Commerce and Growth Assoc., 10 S. Broadway.

St. Paul, Minnesota

The World Almanac is sponsored in the St. Paul area by the St. Paul Dispatch and Pioneer Press, 55 E. 4th St., St. Paul, Minn. 55101; phone (612) 222-5011; founded 1849 as Minnesota Pioneer by James Goodhue; circulation, Pioneer Press (morn) 109,186, Dispatch (eve) 127,077, Sunday Pioneer Press 239,477. Bernard H. Ridder Jr., president, Ridder Pub., Inc. and vice-chairman Knight-Ridder Inc., publisher Thomas L. Carlin, executive editor John R. Finnegan, editor William G. Sumner.

Population: 304,651 (city); 1,999,200 (metro), 2d in state, 46th in nation; total employed (city, non-agricultural) (1974) 191,452.

Area: 55 sq. mi. in eastern Minnesota on banks of Mississippi River close to Minnesota and Wisconsin vacationlands, state capital and Ramsey County seat.

Industry: West Publishing, world's largest law book publisher; international center for electronics and computer technology; Union Stockyards is largest livestock center in nation (3,561,626 head in 1974). Headquarters 3M Co., Am. Hoist & Derrick Co., Burlington Northern RR, Univac, Brown & Bigelow, Whirlpool, Economics Laboratory, Hoerner-Waldorf Corp., St. Paul Companies (insurance).

Commerce: retail sales (1974) $1.7 billion (metro); median household income, $11,822; 25 banks and 6 savings and loan associations.

Transportation: 5 major and 2 regional rail lines, Amtrak; 21 intercity truck firms, 37 terminals; 3 interstate bus lines; 730-mile public transit system; metropolitan airport, hub of 8 commercial airlines, headquarters for Northwest and North Central airlines, averages 824 air movements per day; Downtown Airport; 60 firms operate barges on Mississippi River, using a 9-foot channel downtown.

Communications: 4 commercial TV and 2 educational stations; 29 radio stations.

Medical facilities: 12 private hospitals; a 611 bed community hospital and research center: Ramsey Hospital.

Federal facilities: Ft. Snelling; area headquarters for HUD, HEW; district headquarters for IRS, FCC, Immigration and Naturalization Service; U.S. District Court.

Cultural facilities: Minnesota Symphony Orchestra; Univ. of Minnesota Institute of Agriculture, Hamline Univ., St. Thomas, St. Catherine, Bethel, Concordia, and Macalester Colleges, and William Mitchell College of Law; $66 million city school system with 80 public schools and 61 private schools.

Recreation facilities: more than 900 lakes in metro area, 438 tennis courts, 148 swimming beaches, 513 parks, 50 golf courses, 27 ski centers; 52 neighborhood recreation centers, 35 miles of parkways, 100 miles of hiking and biking trails.

Convention facilities: Civic Center complex with 101,000 sq. ft. exhibit space, seating for 35,000 in 4 main buildings, 15 meeting halls; 50 hotels and motels.

Other attractions: Winter Carnival, Minnesota State Fair, Como Park Zoo and Conservatory; onyx statue of Indian God of Peace in City Hall, Minnesota Historical Society Museums, Arts & Science Center, Fort Snelling State Park, Fighting Saints (WHL).

History: once called "Pig's Eye" for first settler, Pierre "Pig's Eye" Parrant; changed to St. Paul when Father Lucien Galtier built St. Paul's Chapel 1841; became town 1847, city 1854.

Bicentennial plans: 4-day city-county Landmark Festival — art competition, exhibitions and a ball.

Further information: St. Paul Area Chamber of Commerce, Osborn Bldg., St. Paul, 55102.

St. Petersburg, Florida

The World Almanac is sponsored in Florida's Suncoast area by The St. Petersburg·Times and Evening Independent, 490 1st Ave. S., St. Petersburg, Fla. 33701; phone (813) 893-8111. Times founded 1884, Independent 1906; circulation, Times (morn) 185,837; Independent (evening) 32,633; Sunday Times 228,917; Nelson Poynter, chairman of the board, The Times Publishing Co.; Eugene C. Patterson, editor of The Times and president of The Times Publishing Co.; Robert Stiff, editor, The Independent; John B. Lake, publisher, The Times Publishing Co.

Population: 259,500 (city), 665,200 (Pinellas County), 1,369,400 (metro); Pinellas County April 1975 employment 244,200; unemployment 10.7%.

Area: 58 sq. mi., midway on Florida's West Coast between Tampa Bay and Gulf of Mexico; over 100 mi. of shoreline.

Industry and commerce: tourism, over 3½ million visited county in 1974, spending about $1 billion; industries include General Electric, Honeywell, Sperry, Milton Roy Co., Eckerd Drugs, Jim Walter Research, All-State Insurance regional office, U.S. Homes headquarters; Morgan Yacht; county retail sales (1974) over $2.15 billion.

Transportation: U.S. 19, 41, and 98 link city to rest of Gulf Coast Florida; Interstates 275, 75, and 4 link St. Petersburg with Tampa, Orlando, and east coast; Tampa International Airport 25 minutes from downtown St. Petersburg; other airports are St. Petersburg-Clearwater International, and Albert Whitted; Amtrak, Seaboard Coast Line railroads; Greyhound and Trailways bus lines.

Communications: 6 TV and 46 radio stations.

Convention and tourist facilities: Over 52,000 units can house 160,000 visitors; Bayfront Center seats 9,400 in arena, 2,200 in auditorium. Pinellas restaurants can serve 90,000 people at one time. Major attractions within easy driving distance.

Medical facilities: 7 major hospitals; Bay Pines Veterans complex; All Children's Hospital.

Cultural facilities: Museum of Fine Arts, Gulf Coast Symphony, Historical Museum, community theatres, Eckerd College Free Institutions Forums; varied musical, dancing, and theatrical events at Bayfront Center Complex.

Educational facilities: Univ. of South Fla., Bayboro Campus; Stetson College of Law, Eckerd College, St. Petersburg Jr. College.

Recreational facilities: 76 parks on 1,800 acres of land, many with recreational buildings, pools, tennis courts, boat ramps, and picnic areas; municipal and private marinas; deep sea fishing, golf courses, baseball fields.

Sports: Cardinals and Mets spring training; spectator sports include greyhound racing, baseball, jai alai, horse racing, NFL football, basketball, pro tennis, boat racing, soccer.

Bicentennial plans: waterfront historical pageant; ethnic Folk Fair.

Additional information: St. Petersburg Chamber of Commerce, 225 4th St. S., St. Petersburg, Fla. 33701.

Salt Lake City, Utah

The World Almanac is sponsored in the Salt Lake City area by the Salt Lake Tribune, 143 S. Main St., Salt Lake City, Utah 84110; phone (801) 524-4545; founded Apr. 15, 1871; circulation, 102,951 daily, 173,232 Sunday; publisher, John W. Gallivan; executive editor, Arthur C. Deck; 1957 Pulitzer Prize; civic projects: statewide civic beautification awards, Sub for Santa program, living Community Christmas Tree, Arbor Day tree plantings; Spring Garden Festival; Ski Race; No Champs Tennis Tourn.

Population: (1974 est.) 182,900 (city); 493,100 (county); 765,700 (metro); 1st in state, 48th in nation; 53% of state pop. lives within 30 miles; state capital and Salt Lake County seat.

Area: nestled in a vast valley (elev. 4,327 ft.) surrounded by Wasatch and Oquirrh Mountains.

Industry: labor force, 229,430; effective buying income, $2.8 billion (1974), per family income, $12,483; 55% of state construction in county; total construction value, $202 million (1974 record high); major employers are Hill Air Force Base (30 miles north), local defense industries, and Kennecott Copper; metro area becoming major center for electronics, apparel manufacturing; mining, smelting, refining; distribution, warehousing center of West.

Commerce: trade center of Mountain West.

Transportation: 6 air lines, customs office, International Airport; geographic center of 11 Western states; hub of central transcontinental highway system; 3 railroads, all major western truck, bus lines.

Communications: 2 daily newspapers; 3 commercial and 2 public TV, 18 radio stations.

New construction: downtown ZCMI Mall, 70 shops, 27-story office bldg.

Medical facilities: 10 hospitals, including Univ. of Utah Medical Center, major research in transplant surgery.

Cultural facilities: Utah Symphony Orchestra among 12 best in U.S.; Mormon Tabernacle Choir, Ballet West, Repertory Dance Theatre.

Other Attractions: Temple Square, home of 3.5 million member Church of Jesus Christ of Latter Day Saints; Salt Palace Civic Auditorium; 700 acres in 22 parks, 25 playgrounds, 10 golf courses, 85 tennis courts; near Great Salt Lake (7 times more salty than ocean); Hogle Zoological Gardens, Kennecott Copper's Bingham Mine.

Sports: 9 major ski resorts; Utah Stars (ABA), Golden Eagles (Central Hockey League), Salt Lake Gulls, baseball; Bonneville Salt Flats.

Education: Univ. of Utah, Westminster College.

Other: 4 well-defined seasons, mean annual temperature is 50.9°F.

History: founded July 24, 1847, By Brigham Young and contingent of pioneers.

Bicentennial plans: plant 1 million trees for 1 million pop.; major Tribune Old-Fashioned July 4th celebration; Tribune Bicentennial writing, Historic Documents contest.

Further Information: Chamber of Commerce, 19 E. 2d So.; Utah Travel Council, Council Hall, Salt Lake City.

San Antonio, Texas

The World Almanac is sponsored in the San Antonio area by the S. A. Express (morning) and S. A. News (evening), P. O. Box 2171, San Antonio, Tex. 78297; tel. (512) 225-7411; circulation daily, Express 80,839, News 72,612, Sunday Express-News 158,236; chairman K. Rupert Murdoch, publisher and editor Charles O. Kilpatrick; Sunday Express-News 158,236; chairman K. Rupert Murdoch, publisher and editor Charles O. Kilpatrick; Express-News Corp. is a division of News America, Inc.

Population: 771,361 city; 896,785 metro area. Total employed, 318,700.

Area: Bexar County, 1,247 sq. mi., 2½ hours from Gulf Coast and Mexican border.

Industry: 5 military bases include Kelly AFB, largest employer; fast-growing medical industry; diverse manufacturing, tourism, construction, trade, and service industries.

Commerce: center for 50-county retail trade area, truck crops, livestock production; retail sales (1974), $2,528,567,000.

Federal facilities: Kelly AFB, hq. AF Air Security Service; Randolph AFB, hq. AF Air Training Command & AF Personnel Center; Brooks AFB, hq. AF Aerospace Medical Division; Lackland AFB with Wilford Hall USAF Medical Center; Fort Sam Houston, hq. Fifth Army, & Army Health Services Command, Brooke Army Medical Center.

Medical facilities: University of Texas Medical, Dental, Nursing Schools; Audie Murphy VA Hospital; Southwest Research Institute; Southwest Foundation

of Research and Education.

Transportation: International Airport, 6 major airlines; 3 rail freight, 2 Amtrak lines.

Education facilities: Univ. of Texas at San Antonio; Trinity, St. Mary's Universities; Our Lady of the Lake, Incarnate Word Colleges; 2 jr. colleges, San Antonio College, St. Philip's College; permanent extension of National University of Mexico.

Convention facilities: Convention Center with large arena, theater, exhibit, meeting space.

Cultural facilities: symphony orchestra; Institute of Texan Cultures, Mexican Cultural Institute, Witte Museum, McNay Art Institute.

Other attractions: historic Alamo, old Spanish missions of San Jose, Concepcion, Capistrano, Espada; Hemis Fair Plaza with 622-foot observation tower-restaurant; downtown River Walk; zoo; annual events: Fiesta San Antonio, Livestock Show & Rodeo, Folklife Festival; pro. sports: Spurs (ABA); Wings (WFL); Thunder (NASL); minor league baseball, Brewers.

Bicentennial plans: special events and projects.

San Bernardino, California

The World Almanac is sponsored in the San Bernardino area by the Sun-Telegram, 399 North D St., San Bernardino, Cal. 92401, phone (714) 889-9666; Telegram founded 1873, Sun 1894; daily circulation 84,080, Sunday 87,-208; member Gannett chain; editor-publisher James Geehan, vice president-operations Paul Balosso, managing editor Ted Warmbold.

Population: 100,479 (city), 1,225,300 (2-county metro area); 43d in state, 149 in nation; total employed 41,-221.

Area: 47.22 sq. mi. at base of Cajon Pass, 58 miles east of Los Angeles; county seat.

Industry: 165 business and industrial firms including Culligan, Edginton Oil, Fleetwood Enterprises, Hanford Foundry, Knudsen Dairy, Mode O'Day, Pepsi Cola and Seven-Up bottling plants, Santa Fe Railway, TRW Systems.

Commerce: trading center for 20,189 sq. mi. San Bernardino county, largest in the nation; retail sales (1974) $504,399,000; 7 banks, 22 branches; 8 savings and loan associations; 2 major shopping center complexes, each parking over 5,000 cars.

Transportation: Santa Fe, Southern Pacific, and Union Pacific rail lines, Amtrak; Greyhound and Continental bus lines; major interstate highways leading from Mexico to Canada and West to East Coast; municipal airport and nearby Ontario International Airport, over 1,250,000 passengers (1974).

Communications: 15 radio and one VHF educational TV station, access to 5 Los Angeles channels.

Medical facilities: 3 major hospitals with 995 beds; major research and training center for heart surgery and hip and knee replacement surgery.

Federal facilities: Norton Air Force Base.

Cultural facilities: symphony orchestra, Civic Light Opera, nearby Redlands Bowl (summer concerts); National Orange Show with orange festival every spring; Convention Center-Exhibit Hall complex.

Educational facilities: California State College, junior college, 3 major universities nearby.

History: founded 1852 by Mormons who purchased land from Spanish grant holders.

Bicentennial plans: July 4 pageant in new 10,000-seat ampitheater; year-long art, opera, theater expo.

Further information: Chamber of Commerce, 546 West 6th St., San Bernardino, Cal. 92401.

San Diego, California

The World Almanac is sponsored in San Diego by The San Diego Union and Evening Tribune (Copley Newspapers), P.O. Box 191, San Diego 92112; (714) 299-3131; Union founded 1868 (pioneer daily of Southwest); circulation, Union (morn) 180,417, Tribune (eve) 128,089, Sunday Union 290,231; publisher Helen K. Copley, general manager Al De Bakcsy, director of editorial and news policy Victor Krulak, Union Exec. editor Ed. Nichols, Tribune editor Fred Kinne.

Population: 772,591 (1975, city); 1,537,717 (county); 11th in U.S. (official state estimate); total civilian employment, 587,400.

Area: (county) 4,255 sq. mi.; 70 mi. Pacific Coast, San Clemente to Mexican border.

Industry: tourism, manufacturing, military, and agriculture; manufactured products earn $2.3 billion a year; non-military payroll $3.7 billion, military $823.2 million; tourist spending over $400 million; corporations with bases or divisions include Bendix, Burroughs, Control Data, Cubic, General Dynamics, Gulf, Honeywell, International Harvester's Solar division, NCR Corp., Pacific Southwest Airlines, Rohr, Sea World, Teledyne Ryan, TraveLodge, Wickes; aerospace, rapid transit design and manufacture; oceanography; nuclear energy, medicine important; also shipbuilding, tuna fishing, clothing, ocean shipping; among top 20 counties in farm products (avocados, cut flowers, eggs); Marine Corps Recruit Depot, Naval Training Center, North Island and Miramar Naval Air Stations, Naval Electronics Lab and Undersea Center, Marine Corps base at Camp Pendleton.

Transportation: freeway system state's 2d largest; urban transit service, 25-cent fare, Mexican border to 35 miles north; Amtrak, 9 airlines, bus lines; primary airport Lindbergh Field.

Communications: Some 30 TV and radio stations.

Medical facilities: Salk Institute for Biological Studies, Scripps Clinic & Research Foundation; Naval Hospital; many hospitals.

Educational and cultural facilities: San Diego State Univ., U.S. International Univ., Univ. of San Diego; Univ. of California, San Diego (3 colleges and Scripps Institution of Oceanography), Point Loma College; symphony; Old Globe Theatre (functioning reproduction of Shakespeare's Globe Theatre); opera; ballet; Fine Arts and Timken Galleries; La Jolla Museum of Contemporary Art.

Other attractions: world famous zoo and wild animal park; Balboa Park, central 1,400 acres containing museums, Zoo, Fleet Space Theatre (computerized planetarium), many other attractions; Mission Bay Park includes Sea World; "Old San Diego" State Historical Park; "Star of India" ship-museum; visits to neighboring Mexico (Tijuana); 70 miles of beaches.

Sports: NFL Chargers, NL Padres, ABA Conquistadors, WHA Mariners; racing at Del Mar, Caliente.

History: area discovered 1542 by Cabrillo, founded in 1769 by Father Serra.

Other attractions: climate sunny; summer and winter resort; average temp. 68° in summer, 57° in winter, rainfall mainly December to March; famous "place names" include La Jolla (part of city of San Diego); 70 golf courses, including Torrey Pines; large convention facilities; off-shore "whale watching."

San Francisco, California

The World Almanac is sponsored in the San Francisco-Oakland area by the San Francisco Examiner, P. O. Box 3100, Rincon Annex, S.F., Cal. 94119 (415) 781-2424; founded June 12, 1865; circulation daily Examiner, 176,286; Sunday Examiner & Chronicle, 667,121; president and editor, R.A. Hearst; executive editor Thomas Eastham; general manager, Wells Smith; major awards: Pulitzer Prize, Freedoms Foundation; Examiner sponsors Examiner Games, Golden Gloves, Distinguished Ten, Bay to Breakers Race.

Population: 681,200, 3d in state, 13th in nation; total employed: 737,700.

Area: 44.6 sq. mi. on the northern tip of a peninsula. San Francisco County seat.

Industry: food products, printing, publishing, fabricated metal products; West's financial capital and administrative center for many of the nation's leading corporations; West Coast operations' headquarters for a majority of the federal agencies; finance, insurance, and real estate; chief port of the Pacific Coast.

Commerce: wholesale-retail trade employment, 286,-000; services 264,600; manufacturing 187,100 (Apr. 1975); total retail outlets 20,465; taxable sales 2.8 billion; 40 banks with 157 branches; 25 savings and loans with 39 branches; total deposits in banks 12.5 billion (May 1975).

Transportation: 26 major airlines serve the Bay Area; International Airport processed 17,410,644 passengers, 710,431,949 lbs. of freight (1974); Municipal Railway (intra-city); AC-Transit and Bay Area Rapid Transit System (BART) to East Bay cities; Greyhound bus and Southern Pacific Railroad to Peninsula areas; Golden Gate Bridge District Bus and Ferry service to Marin County; Port of San Francisco services available: LASH, BULK, general cargo, containerization and barge service.

Communications: 2 major newspapers; 118 others serving the Bay Area; 45 radio stations, 7 TV channels received directly, one TV cable system.

Medical facilities: 21 general hospitals with over 6,516 total beds; and 5 specialty hospitals with over 1,935 beds; 3,033 physicians/surgeons and 772 dentists; Univ. of Cal. Medical Center, with 42 buildings, is a general teaching and research institute and is the largest kidney transplant center in the world.

Cultural facilities: San Francisco Opera, Spring Opera, Western Opera Theater, symphony, ballet, Civic Light Opera, American Conservatory Theater, Japanese Cultural Center, Chinese Cultural Center, International Film Festival, 3 museums, 29 libraries, and 540 churches.

Educational facilities: 103 public elementary schools with a total enrollment of 35,439 and 11 junior high, and 18 high schools with a combined enrollment of 38,859 students; Univ. of California, San Francisco; California State Univ., Univ. of San Francisco, Lone Mountain College, and City College of San Francisco.

Recreational facilities: 120 parks and many mini-parks, 78 playgrounds, 6 golf courses, numerous tennis courts, 10 swimming pools, 5 1/2 miles of ocean beach, 1 lake, 1 fishing pier, Marina small craft harbor and 3 yacht clubs.

Convention facilities: 124 hotels and motels.

Sports: Candlestick Park, home of the NL Giants and the NFL 49ers.

Other attractions: zoo and 1,013-acre Golden Gate Park containing the California Academy of Sciences, De Young Museum, Japanese Tea Garden, and Arboretum; cable cars, Fisherman's Wharf, Chinatown, the Ferry Building, Coit Tower, the Palace of Fine Arts, and Grace Cathedral.

History: San Francisco Bay discovered 1769 by Sgt. Jose Ortega; pueblo of Yerba Buena established 1834, renamed San Francisco on January 3, 1847; incorporated April 15, 1850.

Bicentennial plans: sports competitions, neighborhood improvement projects, restoration of historical monuments and landmarks, re-enactments of historical events. A contemporary opera, "Angle of Repose," commissioned by the S.F. Opera; the Symphony has commissioned special Bicentennial works.
Further information: Chamber of Commerce, 465 California St., San Francisco, 94104.

San Jose, California

The World Almanac is sponsored in the San Jose area by The Mercury and News, 750 Ridder Pk. Dr., San OSE, Cal. 95190; (408) 289-5000; Mercury founded June 20, 1851; News July 23, 1883; combined daily circulation, 204,-412; Sunday Mercury-News; 221,109; publisher Joseph B. Ridder; general manager P. A. Ridder; business manager W. H. Lindsay; executive editor Paul Conroy.

Population: 527,500 (city), 1,178,900 (metro area coextensive with Santa Clara County); total employed 531,000 (metro).
Area: broad alluvial 832,256-acre valley at south end of San Francisco Bay.

Industry: largest county in northern California for manufacturing employment and total wages; called "Silicone Valley" due to high technology semi-conductor and other electronics firms: IBM, Fairchild-Semi-conductor, Hewlett-Packard, Varien Associates, Intel Corp., National Semi-conductor; diversity shown by Ford Motor Co., Lockheed Missiles & Space, FMC Corp., Syntex Laboratories; county a major producer of cut flowers.

Commerce: leading retail trade center of northern California, $3.11 billion in sales; 135 shopping centers; 3d nationally in median household income, 65% of households earn $10,000 & over annually, 36% over $15,000 (metro).

Transportation: Municipal Airport served by 9 airlines; highway system interconnected with interstate in north—south, east—west directions; Southern Pacific and Western Pacific railroads.
Education: San Jose State, Santa Clara, and Stanford universities, plus community colleges have total enrollments of 106,400; 37% of adult pop. is college educated (metro).

Cultural facilities: symphony, First State Capital Museum, Rosicrucian Egyptian Temple, Science Museum and Planetarium, De Saisset Gallery & Museum, Villa Montalvo estate and arboretum, City Gallery, Triton Museum of Art, New Almaden Museum.

Sports: Earthquakes (soccer); Bees, farm club for KC Royals; 8 reservoirs with boat ramps, 2 with camping; outlet to S.F. Bay for ocean sports.
Other attractions: Japanese Tea Gardens, Lick Observatory, Winchester Mystery House (St. Monument).

History: founded 1777, first civil settlement in California; county is one of the original 27 in California; first public school in California, San Jose Granary, 1795; first California state capitol Dec. 15, 1849.
Bicentennial plans: San Jose celebrating its 200th anniversary along with nation with more than 30 events and projects.

Further information: Chamber of Commerce Metro-San Jose, 165 W. San Carlos 95113, (408) 998-7000.

San Juan, Puerto Rico

The World Almanac is sponsored in Puerto Rico by the San Juan Star, GPO Box 4187, San Juan, Puerto Rico 00936; telephone (809) 782-4200; founded Nov. 2, 1959; circulation 42,000 daily, 43,000 Sunday; president and general manager John A. Zerbe, Jr.; vice president and editor Andrew T. Viglucci; major awards include 1961 Pulitzer Prize for editorial writing; APME citations 1960, 1965; staff awards include 1970 LAPA Mergenthaler Award, 1972 Overseas Press Club Award; National Spelling Bee 1975 champion.

Population: 463,244 (city), 936,700 (metro area) first in commonwealth.

Area: 47 sq. mi. in Caribbean, capital city.

Industry: seat of Puerto Rico's tourism industry with 19 luxury hotels and several dozen high rise condominiums. City is also the commercial and shipping hub of the island and is a major stop for cruise ships plying the Caribbean. Major industries are electronics, pharmaceuticals, and an expanding petrochemical industry serviced by 3 major refineries. Petrochemical industry represents $1.5 billion in investments. Center of island's rum industry with the Bacardi distillery on San Juan Bay, the largest in the world. More than 75 per cent of all rum sold in U.S. is Puerto Rican rum.

Transportation: San Juan International Airport handles more than 500,000 passengers monthly with 4 major U.S. airlines and 10 foreign lines. Isla Grande Airport handles small aircraft traffic.

Education: seat of the Rio Piedras campus of the University of Puerto Rico, the public university system, InterAmerican University, College of the Sacred Heart, UPR Medical Sciences campus and UPR Law School, World University, and several junior and regional colleges.
Cultural facilities and events: The Casals Festival, guided for 15 years by the late Maestro Casals, is an annual June event bringing together some of the world's finest musicians; The Puerto Rico Institute of Culture is housed in a restored Dominican convent; El Morro, the Spanish-built fortress that guards the entrance to San Juan Harbor; numerous art museums in Old San Juan; the Puerto Rico Symphony Orchestra in concerts spread over the year; the Capitol building and governor's mansion.

New construction: Old City restoration program, Riomar Hotel, Ramada Inn; new banking district located in Hato Rey.

Sports: Hiram Bithorn Stadium, winter baseball, track, and outdoor events; Roberto Clemente Coliseum, basketball, boxing, and indoor events; soccer, cockfighting arenas (legal); preparations for 1979 PanAm Games.
History: Discovered by Columbus on his second voyage to the New World in 1493, colonized by Juan Ponce de Leon, Puerto Rico's first Spanish governor; since 1952 a commonwealth freely associated with the United States. Free market with U.S. and same currency, common citizenship.

Santa Ana, California

See Orange County, California

Saskatoon, Saskatchewan, Canada

The World Almanac is sponsored in northern Saskatchewan by the Saskatoon Star-Phoenix, 204 Fifth Ave. North, Saskatoon, Sask., S7K 2P1; (306) 652-9200; Daily Star and Phoenix, founded in 1906 and 1902 respectively, merged in 1928 into the Star-Phoenix; circulation daily, 50,491; publisher Michael C. Sifton, executive vice president James K. Struthers.

Population: 136,000, 2d in prov., 17th in nation.
Area: 38.5 sq. mi. land, 1.5 sq. mi. water, on S. Sask. River, center of agricultural province.
Commerce: retail, wholesale, service, distribution hub for 400,000 in 100-mi. radius trading area; world's richest, largest potash reserves; meat packing, grain milling dominant; garment and electronics newest; base for northern mineral explorations; retail sales (1974) $328 million.
Transportation: 2 railways, 2 airlines, 2 bus lines, air and bus terminals on Yellowhead Highway, easiest access through Rockies from prairies to West Coast ports.
Communications: One daily, 2 TV, 5 radio stations, one farm weekly, one community weekly.
Medical facilities: 3 major hospitals, 6 nursing homes; Univ. hospital known for kidney transplants, open-heart surgery; $26 million expansion planned.

Cultural facilities: $7 million, 2,000-seat Centennial Auditorium, convention facilities for over 1,800; Mendel Art Gallery/Civic Conservatory; Western Development Museum houses N. America's largest display of antique cars, farm implements and 1910 Pioneer Village; theme pavilion for summer fair.
Education: Univ. of Sask. (17,500 students), famed for agriculture, space, Arctic, physics, medicine, veterinary college; Kelsey Institute for Applied Arts and Science (4,700 students); School for Deaf.

Recreation: 1,456 acres parkland; wild animal farm; man-made ski mountain; camping, fishing.

History: founded 1883 as temperance colony; incorporated 1906; battle sites of 1885 Riel Rebellion nearby.

Further information: Board of Trade, Bessborough Hotel, Saskatoon, Sask. S7K 3GB.

Savannah, Georgia

The World Almanac is sponsored in the Savannah area by the Savannah News-Press, 111 W. Bay St., Savannah, Ga. 31401, phone (912) 236-9511, publisher of the Savannah Morning News and Savannah Evening Press; combined daily circulation 75,900; Sunday 67,274. Donald E. Harwood, general manager; Wallace M. Davis Jr., executive editor.

Population: 119,100 (city), 213,800 (metro).
Area: 37 sq. mi. on Savannah River 18 miles from Atlantic Ocean.
Industry: world's largest pulpwood-to-paper container plant owned by Union Camp Corp; Savannah Sugar Refining Corp., nation's 3d largest seller; jet aircraft manufacture (Grumman American Aviation), tea packaging (Tetley), fertilizer materials, ship repair, titanium dioxide production (American Cyanamid).
Commerce: hub of "Coastal Empire," economic center of 8 Georgia and 3 South Carolina counties; Southeast's leading foreign trade port, 86 steamship lines, 40 deep water terminals; retail sales (1974) $510.2 million; 6 commercial banks, resources (1974) $8.6 billion; 3 savings and loan associations.
Transportation: 2 rail freight lines, Amtrak; Grey-

hound, Trailways bus lines; 70 truck lines; Delta, National Air Lines.
Communications: 4 TV and 13 radio stations.
Medical facilities: 6 hospitals.
Cultural facilities: symphony orchestra, ballet guild, dance theater, little theater, Telfair Academy of Arts and Sciences; maritime museum, science museum, military museum; $10.4 million Civic Center; Savannah State, Armstrong State Colleges.
Sports: Savannah Braves, Southern League.
History: founded 1733 by Gen. James Oglethorpe, first planned U.S. city; much of old city is national Historic Landmark, largest in country.
Bicentennial plans: development of a park on the site of the Battle of Savannah.
Further information: Chamber of Commerce, P.O. Box 530, Savannah, Georgia 31402.

Schenectady, New York

Population: 77,958; total employed, 38,000.
Area: 11.3 sq. mi., 13 miles northwest of Albany.
Industry: General Electric, employing about 27,000, is largest employer. Other firms manufacture industrial chemicals, pollution control and measuring devices, and military vehicles.
Commerce: there are 2,100 retail establishments with net sales of over $200,000,000; 9 banks with total deposits over $500 million.
Cultural facilities: Union College, 66 homes and

buildings built between 1700-1850; the Schenectady Museum and County Historical Society.
Other attractions: 5 hospitals, 87-acre Industrial Park; 65 schools; 175 churches; 25 parks, 5 golf courses, 30 tennis courts, 18 playgrounds; Schenectady Community College.
Bicentennial plans: Colonial Fair, May 29-31, 1976; State Barge visitation, July 28-31, 1976.
Further information: Schenectady County Chamber of Commerce, 101 State St., Schenectady, 12305.

Seattle, Washington

The World Almanac is sponsored in the Seattle area by The Seattle Times, Fairview Ave. N. & John St., P.O. Box 70, Seattle, Wash. 98111; phone (206) MA 2-0300; founded 1896 by Alden J. Blethen; circulation 226,773 daily, 299,721 Sunday; publisher John A. Blethen; president W. J. Pennington; vice president and general manager Harold G. Fuhrman.

Population: 515,000 (city), 1,424,611 (metro): first in state, 17th in nation; total employed (metro) 600,800.

Area: 91.6 sq. mi. between Puget Sound and Lake Washington; King County seat.

Industry: headquarters for Boeing, 51,000 employes, world's largest manufacturer of commercial jet aircraft; Port of Seattle has $370 million in facilities, nation's 4th largest containerized-shipping seaport; area has 1,630 manufacturers; major industries are transportation products, retail trade, shipbuilding, wood products, and food products.

Commerce: business center for western Wash. and Alaska; major import-export center for Far East; principal supply point for construction of Trans-Alaska oil pipeline; total retail sales (1974) $4.11 billion; per capita income (1974) $5,516; 29 commercial banks.

Transportation: 3 transcontinental railroads, Amtrak; International Airport served by 12 scheduled airlines, 6 commuter airlines, handled 5.79 million passengers (1974); ferries serve Puget Sound, Canada and Alaska.

Communications: 3 daily newspapers in metro area; 5 TV, 18 AM and 15 FM stations.

Medical facilities: 26 hospitals, including Univ. of Wash. Health Sciences Center and Fred Hutchinson Cancer Research Center, which is under construction.

Educational facilities: Three 4-year colleges: Univ. of Wash., Seattle Univ., and Seattle Pacific College; 7 community colleges.

Cultural facilities: symphony orchestra, opera association, art museum and 10 other museums, 2 professional theater companies.

Recreation: major boating center; several nearby ski areas; Mt. Rainier, North Cascades, and Olympic National Parks within 2-hour drive.

Sports: NBA SuperSonics; Sounders, North American Soccer League; Totems, Central Hockey League; Rainiers, Northwest League (baseball); National Football League and National Hockey League teams to begin play in 1976. 65,000-seat King County domed stadium to open in 1976.

Other attractions: $50 million Seattle Center, site of 1962 world's fair, has 14,000-seat Coliseum, Opera House, Playhouse, Arena, Space Needle and Pacific Science Center.

History: settled 1851, named for an Indian chief who befriended the settlers; virtually destroyed by fire in 1889, quickly rebuilt; Alaska Gold Rush of 1897 spurred economic and population growth and propelled Seattle toward its status as the Northwest's principal city.

Bicentennial plans: some 200 events, projects, and festivals planned.

Further information: Chamber of Commerce, 215 Columbia St., or Convention and Visitors Bureau, 1815 7th Ave.

Shreveport, Louisiana

The World Almanac is sponsored in the Shreveport area by the Shreveport Journal (eves. except Sunday), 222 Lake St., Shreveport, La. 71130; phone (318) 424-0373; founded 1895 as The Judge, given present name in 1897; circulation 50,000; president Douglas F. Attaway, vice-president D. Wesley Attaway, editor Stanley R. Tiner.

Population: 193,745 (special 1974 census); total employed approximately 125,000.

Area: 80.286 sq. mi., on Red River in Caddo Parish, northwest Louisiana.

Industry: oil, gas, timber, agriculture, largest manufacturer of telephones in the world, steel products, glassware, car batteries; Barksdale Air Force Base across Red River in Bossier Parish.

Commerce: wholesale-retail center for Ark-La-Tex area; retail sales (1974) over one billion dollars; total bank deposits $1.1 billion; 8 banks, 2 savings and loan companies.

Transportation: 6 railroads, 4 airlines, one busline, 16 motor-freight lines; Interstate Hwy. 20; north-south toll road and Red River barge traffic proposed for 1980s.

Communications: 3 TV and 9 radio stations.

Cultural facilities: State Exhibit Museum and Planetarium, 2 art galleries; Norton Arts Gallery and Barnwells Memorial Garden and Arts Center, symphony orchestra, civic opera, 5 colleges, 5 community theaters, headquarters for the American Rose Society, garden center and conservatory, world famous Men's Camellia Club.

Other attractions: Shreve Square, restoration project downtown on riverfront; Louisiana State Fair; Holiday-in-Dixie spring festival; 12 hospitals, LSU Medical School, speech and hearing center.

Sports: college basketball (Centenary College); Steamer team in WFL, Louisiana Downs Race Track across Red River in Bossier Parish, 7 golf courses, Cross Lake 8,960 acres, boating-fishing waters, skiing, and yacht club.

History: founded 1836 as Shreve Town, named for riverboat Capt. Henry M. Shreve who cleared massive logjam on river; starting point for the Texas Trail during westward expansion; Louisiana capital for 2 years during Civil War; second largest city in Louisiana.

Sioux Falls, South Dakota

The World Almanac is sponsored in the Sioux Falls area by the Sioux Falls Argus-Leader, 200 S. Minnesota Ave., Sioux Falls, S.D. 57102, tel. (605) 336-1130; a Speidel newspaper; founded 1885; circulation 49,256 daily,

...ʊitor Anson Yeager.

Population: 72,444 (city), 95,209 (metro area) according to 1970 census; largest in state.

Area: 27 square miles in southeastern South Dakota at junction of interstates 29 and 90; Minnehaha County seat.

Federal facilities: Earth Resources Observation Systems Data Center of the U.S. Dept. of Interior is nearby.

Industry & commerce: located in the nation's breadbasket, Sioux Falls Stockyards is the 4th largest public market in the U.S. John Morrell & Co. is the largest of 170 manufacturers. There are 22 banks with clearings in excess of $1.3 billion and 3 savings and loan associations. Wholesale and retail center for South Dakota, parts of Minnesota and Iowa; yearly retail sales over $300 million, wholesale over $500 million.

Transportation: served by 4 major rail lines, 4 bus lines, 5 major highways. Joe Foss Field with modern terminal is within 2 miles of business district, has 3 major airlines offering 35 daily flights.

Medical facilities: 4 hospitals including Royal C. Johnson Veterans Hospital and Crippled Children's Hospital and School.

Communications: 3 TV and 9 radio stations.

Culture & Education: public library, convention center, Civic Fine Arts Center, Sioux Falls Symphony, Community Playhouse. Augustana College, Sioux Falls College, North American Baptist Seminary, the South Dakota School For the Deaf, a vocational school, business college, 2 nurses training schools, 3 high schools, 29 public, 8 parochial schools, 89 churches.

Bicentennial plans: tour of a 100-acre pioneer homestead farmed by horsepower.

Springfield, Illinois

The World Almanac is sponsored in the Springfield area by The State Journal-Register (morn and eve), oldest newspaper in Illinois, 313 S. 6th St., Springfield, Ill. 62701; (217) 544-5711; circulation, 73,163; John P. Clarke, publisher; Edward H. Armstron, editor; Patrick Coburn, managing editor.

Population: 94,800 (city), 166,800 (metro), 4th in state; total employed, 78,775.

Area: 41.72 sq. mi. on Sangamon River in center of state; state capital and Sangamon County seat.

Commerce: state and federal offices; 11 banks; 6 savings and loan assns.; 8 insurance company home offices; 129 state orgs.; 5 national orgs.; 27 civic clubs; 36 social service orgs.; 167 women's orgs.; annual retail sales of $529.8 million.

Transportation: 5 railroads; 38 truck carriers; one airport; nearby barge facilities.

Communications: one TV and 6 radio stations.

Medical facilities: 2 hospitals with 1,200 beds, one 200-bed hospital under construction; 290 doctors; 9 clinics; 18 nursing homes.

Cultural facilities: municipal band, opera, symphony, chorus; Theatre Guild; museum; Lincoln Historical Sites; New Salem State Park; Old State Capitol; art assns.; summer theater; Illinois Country Opry; Clay-ville renovated Stagecoach Stop, arts & crafts festivals.

Education: Sangamon State Univ.; Lincoln Land Community College; Springfield College; Southern Illinois School of Medicine; Concordia Theological Seminary.

Recreation: 25 district parks; swimming, boating, skiing at 6 parks on Lake Springfield; public golf, tennis.

Special events: Ill. State Fair; Old Capitol Art Fair; NCAA College Division World Series; International Carillon Festival; Midwest Horse Show.

History: settled 1818-1819; became county seat 1823; incorporated as town 1832; chartered as city 1840; selected as state capital 1837.

Bicentennial plans: ethnic festivals, arts projects and original colonies celebrations; on July 4, 1976, the opening of a Visitors' Orientation Center at the Lincoln Home National Historic Site, and the premiere of the $600,000 sound and light spectacular show at the Old State Capitol.

Springfield, Massachusetts

The World Almanac is sponsored in the Springfield area by The Springfield Union, Sunday Republican, and Daily News, 1860 Main St., Springfield, Ma. 01101; phone (413) 787-2411. Union founded 1864; Republican 1824; Daily News 1880; circulation, Union, 76,172; Republican, 135,439; Daily News, 82,744; publisher Sidney R. Cook; Union-Republican editor Joseph W. Mooney; Daily News, Richard C. Garvey.

Population: 169,027 (city); 529,922 (metro); 2d in state (city-metro), 4th in New England, 84th in U.S.; 66,233 employed.

Area: 33.1 sq. mi. in S.W. part of state; I-91 skirts city.

Industry: 227 manufacturing plants produce boxes, childrens' games, wallets, auto tires, handguns, plastics, envelopes, hair shampoo, chemicals, paper; major employers Monsanto, Milton Bradley, Smith & Wesson, Breck.

Commerce: retail sales, $1.4 billion; avg. household spendable income $12,800; Mass Mutual Life Ins. Co., number 10 in U.S.; Baystate West, a combined highrise shopping mall, office-hotel complex.

Transportation: Amtrak, 2 rail lines, 5 bus lines, Bradley International Airport (Hartford-Springfield) 18 miles south, major truck depot.

Communications: 3 TV, 9 radio stations.

Medical facilities: 8 major hospital complexes.

Educational facilities: College belt of N.E.; North Adams State, Williams, Smith, Hampshire, Amherst, Univ. of Massachusetts at Amherst, Mount Holyoke, Our Lady of the Elms, American International, Springfield, Western New England and Law School, Westfield State, Greenfield and Holyoke Community Colleges, Springfield Technical Community College.

Cultural facilities: symphony; Stage/West theater; quadrangle complex— 2 museums of art; library, natural history museum including planetarium; 143 churches and 7 synagogues; Tanglewood festival, 155 parks; civic center.

Sports: Indians (AHL) hockey; Basketball Hall of Fame.

History: founded 1636 by William Pynchon; first U.S. musket developed at city's armory (now a U.S. landmark) 1795; Springfield rifle developed in 1903 and produced here as was the Garand, M-1 rifle.

Bicentennial plans: history program in schools; restoration of colonial documents; walking tour of underground railroad; riverfront park.

Further information: Chamber of Commerce, 1500 Main St.; Bicentennial Committee, 284 State St.

Syracuse, New Y...

The World Almanac is sponsored in the Syracuse area by the Herald-Journal, Clinton Square, Syracuse, N.Y. 13201; telephone (315) 473-7700; founded Jan. 15, 1877, by Arthur Jenkins; circulation 123,899 daily, 240,526 Sunday Herald-American Post-Standard; publisher, Stephen Rogers; editor, William D. Cotter; sponsors college scholarship fund for police.

Population: 197,297 (city), 636,507 (metro), 5th in state, 66th in nation; 254,200 employed.
Area: 25.82 sq. mi. near center of state; Interstate Routes 90 and 81 intersect at Syracuse.
Industry: some 500 manufacturing plants produce electrical and non-electrical machinery, primary metals, food, transportation equipment, chemicals, pharmaceuticals, paper, candles, china; new $100 million Schlitz brewery, world's largest ever built at one time, under construction in suburban Lysander; major Miller brewery being built north of city; major employers: General Electric, Carrier Corp., Crucible Steel, Crouse-Hinds, Allied Chemical.
Commerce: retail sales (1974 est.) $1.7 billion; average household spendable income (1974 est.) $12,620.
Transportation: 2 rail freight lines, Amtrak; 3 bus lines, 190 truck lines; 3 airlines.

Communications: 4 TV, 14 radio stations.
Medical facilities: 4 major hospital complexes.
Cultural facilities: Syracuse Univ., State Univ. College of Environmental Science and Forestry, and Le Moyne, Maria Regina, and Onondaga Community Colleges; Everson Museum of Art; symphony; $22 million county office-cultural center.
Sports: Syracuse Univ. football; Chiefs (baseball).
History: first explored 1615 by French; salt deposits led to area development, known as "Salt City"; "crossroads" since Indian days; became city 1847.

Bicentennial plans: Everson Museum community project to buy a Gilbert Stuart portrait of George Washington.

Further information: Chamber of Commerce, One MONY Plaza, Syracuse, N.Y. 13202.

Tallahassee, Florida

The World Almanac is sponsored in the north Florida-south Georgia panhandle area by The Tallahassee Democrat, 277 N. Magnolia Drive, Tallahassee, Florida 32302; (904) 599-2100; founded 1905; circulation 41,079 (eve), 43,492 Sunday; member Knight-Ridder Newspapers, Inc., Alvah H. Chapman, president; W. H. Harwell Jr., v.p. and general manager; Malcolm B. Johnson, v.p. and editor.

Population: 84,969 (city), 129,588 (metro); total employment 63,900.
Area: 26.14 sq. mi. between Gulf of Mexico and Georgia line; state capital and Leon County seat.
Commerce: 44% of economic base is state government; small manufacturers; agriculture only 1.1% of economic base; retail-wholesale center serving 17 county area; 2 shopping malls and 10 shopping centers containing 232 outlets; retail sales (1973) $382,546,000; effective buying income per household is $12,648, 3d highest in state; 15 commercial banks (resources, $360,383,274) and 3 savings & loan (resources $188,633,429).
Transportation: 3 major airlines, 2 commuter flight services, one railroad, and 5 motor carriers.
Communications: 8 radio, 9 TV stations by cable.
Medical facilities: one major hospital, a retardation hospital, and a university hospital.
Recreational facilities: 5 recreation centers, 10 play-grounds, 45 ball fields, 21 tennis courts; salt water fishing, bass fishing in Lake Jackson; deer, dove, quail, duck, geese hunting; 4 golf courses, PGA Tallahassee Open Invitational.
Other attractions: college athletic events at Florida State Univ., and Florida A&M; symphony, ballet, repertory theater, opera, touring plays, and art exhibits; 1845 historic capitol and other historic sites; Apalachicola National Forest; Junior Museum; Wakulla Springs, Maclay Gardens State Park, Le-Moyne Art Gallery, Natural Bridge State Historic Memorial, and Florida State Univ. "Flying High" Circus.
History: established as state capital 1823; Tallahassee means "old town" or "deserted fields" in Creek; area prospered with large plantations and antebellum mansions, many still standing.
Further information: Chamber of Commerce, P.O. Box 1639, Tallahassee, Florida 32302. (904) 224-8116.

Tampa, Florida

The World Almanac is sponsored in the Tampa Bay area by The Tampa Tribune and The Tampa Times, 507 E. Kennedy Blvd., Tampa, Fla., 33602; (813) 224-7711; Times founded 1893, Tribune 1894; comb. cir. 195,566; A.S. Donnahoe, pres.; J. Clendinen, chmn. of editorial board; R. F. Pittman Jr., v.p./gen. mgr.; J. S. Bryan III, exec. v.p.; J. Urbanski , bus. mgr.; P. Hogan, Tribune mgr. ed.; B. Witwer, Times mgr. ed.

Population: 303,900 (city), 562,200 (co.); 3d in state, 47th in nation; total employed in county, 215,000.
Area: 84.45 sq. mi., halfway between the northern edge of Florida and southern tip; Hillsborough County seat.
Industry: port ranks 8th in the nation; principal export cargo, phosphate; Ybor City section well-known for cigar manufacturing.
Commerce: retail sales (1974) $1.844 billion; 39 banks, resources $2.069 billion, 8 savings & loan assns.
Transportation: 22 freight lines, Amtrak; 5 bus lines;
city-owned bus system; 48 truck lines; junction of I-75 & I-4; Intl. Airport, 9 major airlines.
Communications: 6 TV and 19 radio stations.
New construction: Univ. Square; Tampa Cultural Center; Univ. of So. Fla. expansion; Tampa Medical Center; Tribune Co. Bldg.; East Lake Square Mall; expansion of Busch Gardens; General Telephone; Univ. Community Hosp.; Tampa Bay Regional Mall; Westinghouse Electric expansion; Medical Office Bldg.; Jim Walters Office Tower; Founders Life Insurance Bldg.
Medical facilities: 6 major hospital complexes.
Federal facilities: MacDill AFB., U.S. Federal Bldg.

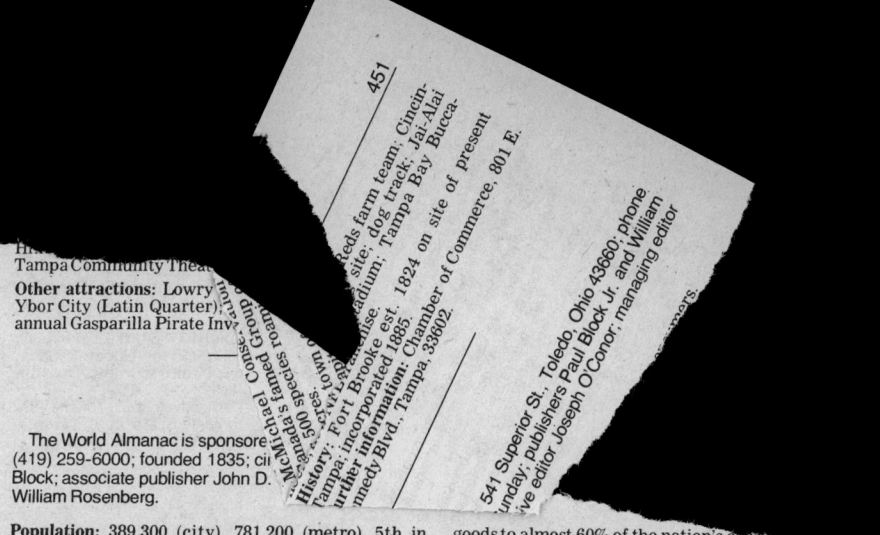

451

Reds farm team: Cincin- site; dog track; Jai-Alai ... Tampa Bay Buca-

Tampa Community Thea...
Other attractions: Lowry ...
Ybor City (Latin Quarter); ...
annual Gasparilla Pirate Inv...

McMichael Conser... Group... Canada's famed roa... 500 species ... Town house est... **History:** Fort Brooke est. 1824 on site of present Tampa; incorporated 1885. ... **urther information:** Chamber of Commerce, 801 E. ... mmerly Blvd. Tampa, 33602.

541 Superior St., Toledo, Ohio 43660; phone ... unday; publishers Paul Block Jr. and William ... ve editor Joseph O'Conor; managing editor

The World Almanac is sponsore... (419) 259-6000; founded 1835; ci... Block; associate publisher John D. ... William Rosenberg.

Population: 389,300 (city), 781,200 (metro), 5th in state, 45th in nation; total employed, 298,000.
Area: 85.3 sq. mi. at juncture of Maumee River and Lake Erie, in northwestern Ohio.
Industry: glass, headquarters for Owens-Illinois, Owens Corning & Libbey-Owens-Ford; automotive parts, largest producer in nation, home of American Motors Jeep, Toledo Scale, and Haughton Elevator; largest petroleum refining center between Chicago and the East Coast.
Commerce: growing port on Great Lakes, annual overseas cargo runs to 500,000 tons; 2d in international tonnage, 3d in total tonnage, 11th among all ports, only inland foreign trade zone in the nation; total retail sales $2.03 billion; spendable income per household: $14,841.
Transportation: 9 railroads, 4 major airlines, 120 motor freight lines, 2 interstate bus lines; 13 major highways converge here, permitting the rapid flow of goods to almost 60% of the nation's consu...
Communications: 4 TV, 15 radio stations and one cablevision company.
Medical facilities: 12 major hospital complexes, including the Medical College of Ohio Hospital.
Cultural facilities: Museum of Art with largest display of antique glass in the world; Peristyle used for the performing arts; symphony, Opera Society.
Education: Univ. of Toledo and its Community and Technical College; Michael J. Owens Technical College; Mary Manse College; Bowling Green State Univ.
Other attractions: Municipal Zoo among top 10 in the nation; modern 2,500 seat Masonic Auditorium with a Great Hall annex.
Sports: Mud Hens, farm club of the Philadelphia Phillies, at the Lucas County Recreation Center.
History: founded in 1835; took its name from sister city, Toledo, Spain.

Toronto, Ontario, Canada

The World Almanac is sponsored in the Metropolitan Toronto area by The Toronto Star, One Yonge St., Toronto, Ontario, M5E 1E6; (416) 367-2000; established 1892, Joseph E. Atkinson, publisher, 1899-1948; circulation daily 496,645; Saturday, 779,172; president and publisher, Beland H. Honderich; senior vice-president, Burnett M. Thall; editor-in-chief, Martin Goodman; Canada's largest newspaper in circulation, display and classified advertising linage; winner of 31 national newspaper awards and sponsor of the Santa Claus Fund and Fresh Air Fund.

Population: 720,000 (city), 2,300,000 (metro); 2d largest city in Canada, 15th in North America; total employment: 1.25 million.
Area: 241 sq. mi., on northwest shore of Lake Ontario; provincial capital.
Industry: Canada's leading commercial and industrial center; 6300 manufacturing establishments; value of 1974 factory shipments, $13 billion; principal industries: slaughtering and meat packing, clothing, printing and publishing, machinery, electrical goods, furniture, food products, rubber goods, sheet metal products.
Commerce: retail sales (1975 est.) $6.7 billion; headquarters for Eaton's, and Simpson's, Canada's largest department store and mail order firms; head offices of 12 trust companies and 4 of 10 federally chartered banks; value of checks cashed (1974), $719.5 billion; Toronto Stock Exchange, 4th in North America, traded shares worth $4.5 billion in 1974; per capita disposable incomes, $4,770.
Transportation: 10 railway lines carry 300 freight and passenger trains daily; 9,000 trucks use 12 major highways; Transit Commission carries 348 million passengers annually on 696 miles of routes; 6.5 miles of line now under construction will extend subways to 33 miles in 1977; 2.9 million tons of cargo unloaded (1974) at this major Great Lakes port; 24 airlines handle 9.3 million passengers annually at International Airport.
Communications: 6 TV stations including educational and French-language channels; 10 AM and 4 FM radio stations; 3 daily newspapers; 42 foreign language newspapers.
New construction: value of building permits (1974) $1.1 billion; $40 million CN Tower, world's tallest free-standing structure.
Medical facilities: 27 active-treatment hospitals including renowned Hospital for Sick Children; special treatment centers: Clarke Institute for Psychiatry, Addiction Research Centre, Ontario Crippled Children's Centre.
Cultural facilities: 20 local groups offer experimental, repertory, and revue theatre; National Ballet of Canada and Canadian Opera Company perform in 3,200-seat O'Keefe Centre; symphony orchestra and Mendelssohn Choir at Massey Hall; original and touring productions at Royal Alexandra Theatre; 79 public libraries; Royal Ontario Museum; $40-million collection of Henry Moore sculptures housed in Art Gallery of Ontario.
Educational facilities: 2 universities, York and Toronto, Canada's largest (1974-75 enrollment: 45,288); Ryerson Polytechnical Institute, 4 colleges of applied arts and technology, 2 teachers' colleges,

...da;
Collection of works by
... Seven painters; Metro Zoo
... g 5 continental areas covering

... York founded 1793 on site of French
...al of British colony of Upper Canada;
...ated as city 1834; named Toronto from. In-
...ord for meeting place.
Further information: Convention and Tourist Bureau, 85 Richmond St. West, Suite 300, Toronto, Ontario, M5H 1H9.

Troy, New York

Population: 62,918.
Area: 9.8 sq. mi., 8 miles northeast of Albany.
Industry: known for manufacture of collars and shirts; military equipment, precision machines, automobile parts, abrasive materials, metals.
Commerce: 7 banks.
Cultural facilities: Rensselaer Polytechnic Institute Fieldhouse (seating 7,500); Troy Music Hall, Junior Museum, Historical Society.

Other attractions: 21 playgrounds, 3 hospitals, Russell Sage College, Hudson Valley Community College, Emma Willard School for Girls, 31 public and parochial schools.
Bicentennial plans: Burden Sound and Light Show, July 4, 1976; Flag Day Parade, June 13, 1976.

Further information: Greater Troy Chamber of Commerce, 28 Second St., Troy, 12180.

Tucson, Arizona

The World Almanac is sponsored in the Tucson area by The Arizona Daily Star, 4850 S. Park Ave., Tucson 85726:(602)294-4433; founded 1877 as a weekly. Michael E. Pulitzer, editor and publisher; Frank E. Johnson, managing editor; Abe Chanin, editorial section director; Frank Delehanty, business manager; William Waters, public affairs editor; sponsors Sportsmen's Fund for less-chance youngsters.

Population: 262,933 within city limits, 360,000 in Pima County (US Census, 1970).
Area: Sonoran Desert of southern Arizona, elev. 2,500 ft.; Santa Catalina Mts. immediately N and E reach 9,000 ft.; Pima County seat.
Industry: Hughes Aircraft, various aircraft-reclamation plants handling surplus craft from Davis-Monthan AFB; electronics, light manufacturing, and tourism; center of the "copper circle" — hundreds of millions of development dollars have been invested in the area by Anaconda, Duval, American Smelting and Refining, Kennecott, Magma, Pima and other mining operations.

Transportation: International Airport served by AeroMexico and Hughes AirWest (to and from Mexico), most major airlines nationally and Cochise Airlines within Arizona; 3 smaller airports; 2 national, one local bus line; Southern Pacific Railroad; trucks.
Communications: 2 newspapers; 5 TV and 18 radio stations.
Medical facilities: 10 hospitals, including Arizona Medical Center, which contains teaching hospital.

Climate: mild, dry; rare freezing temperatures in winter; summer brings some rain, mostly after July 1, and temperatures of about 100°F.
Culture: Univ. of Arizona; Tucson Museum of Art; Tucson Symphony; Arizona Civic Theater; Tucson Civic Ballet; many musical, drama, and dance groups; Tucson Boys Chorus, Los Changuitos Feos mariachi group provide local flavor.
Convention facilities: convention center accommodates 10,000 theater-style in arena; sit-down functions 5,000; meeting-rooms 1,000 theater-style; music hall, 2,300; contiguous exhibit space 64,000 sq. ft.
Sports: Toros, farm club of Oakland Athletics; Cleveland Indians spring training site; Dean Martin Tucson Open golf tournament; American Airlines Tennis; collegiate athletics.
History: Presidio of Tucson est. 1775; Mission San Xavier del Bac founded nearby by Rev. Eusebio Francisco Kino, S. J., who first visited area in 1692.
Bicentennial plans: fiestas, parades, commemorative publications with "Colonial heritage" theme.
Further information: Tucson Chamber of Commerce, P.O. Box 991, Tucson, 85702.

Tulsa, Oklahoma

The World Almanac is sponsored in the Tulsa area by The Tulsa Tribune, 315 So. Boulder, Tulsa, Oklahoma, 74102; phone (918) 582-1101; founded 1904 as The Tulsa Democrat, renamed The Tulsa Tribune in 1920; circulation, 87,332; editor Jenkin Lloyd Jones; managing editor Gordon Fallis; executive editor Jenkin Lloyd Jones Jr.

Population: 347,600 (city), 492,200 (metro); 252,300 employed.
Area: 175 sq. mi., on Arkansas River at 96th meridian.
Industry: petroleum, 30,000 employed by 825 oil and oil-related firms with $185 million annual payroll, Sun Oil and Texaco refineries; aviation, 15,000 in

aviation and aerospace industries, including Rockwell International, McDonnell Douglas, and American Airlines; world's largest manufacturer of industrial heaters and winches; 1,200 diversified manufacturing plants.
Commerce: retail sales (1974): $1.222 billion; 17 banks (resources $1.721 billion), 10 savings and loan

firms and holding companies.

Commerce: port is major auto importing center; retail sales (SMSA 1974) $1.5 billion, est. 1975 personal income in SMSA $3.8 billion, est. personal income per household $21,859. State has 12 state-chartered commercial banks, 19 state-chartered savings and loans, 5 national banks, 2 mutual savings banks, 2 federally chartered savings and loans, 1 non-deposit trust company.

Transportation: 3 major railway lines, 3 bus lines, more than 60 trucking firms.

Communications: 1 public TV station; 7 radio stations.

Medical facilities: Wilmington Medical Center (4 divisions); 2 private hospitals; Alfred I. du Pont Institute.

Cultural attractions: Grand Opera House; Winterthur Museum; Hagley Museum; Delaware Art Museum; Old Brandywine Village; Fort Christina Park; Wilmington Symphony Orchestra; Wilmington Opera Society; Wilmington Drama League; Museum of Natural History; University of Delaware (Newark); Delaware State College (Dover); Delaware Technical and Community College.

Sports: Delaware Park; Brandywine Raceway; Dover Downs (Dover); Harrington Raceway (Harrington); Univ. of Delaware football.

Other attractions: Rehoboth Beach (100 mi.); Longwood Gardens, and Brandywine River Museum (both in nearby PA); several state parks and recreation areas; historic old New Castle; Hillendale Museum.

History: founded as Fort Christina in 1638; named for Queen of Sweden; name changed to Willington in 1731, and then to Wilmington 1739 in honor of the Earl of Wilmington; it is the first city in the first state of the union.

Further information: Delaware State Chamber of Commerce, 1102 West St., Wilmington, 19801.

Windsor, Ontario, Canada

The World Almanac is sponsored in Windsor and a large part of Southwestern Ontario including Essex, Kent and Lambton Counties, by The Windsor Star (cir. 84,013), 167 Ferry St., Windsor 12, Ontario; a division of Southam Press Ltd.; published daily since 1890 (present name since 1957); publisher J. Patrick O'Callaghan, general manager A. H. Fast, editor R. M. Pearson.

Population: 198,086 (city); 266,000 (metro); 539,700 (tri-county); 10th in nation; total employed 113,000.

Area: 50 sq. mi., one-half mile across Detroit River from Detroit, Mich.; largest Canadian city on U.S.-Canada border.

Industry: autos and feeder plants, more than 25% national production (Chrysler, Ford, GM); tool and die shops; alcoholic beverages (home office Hiram Walker and Sons); food processing (H. J. Heinz, Green Giant); salt mining; zinc and plastic die-casting; pharmaceuticals; agriculture (rich producer early vegetables) tomatoes, corn, soybeans, peaches, tobacco; tourism (largest port of entry in nation for U.S. visitors).

Commerce: retail sales $518.8 million (6% above national average); personal disposable income $1.149 billion (1.34% Canadian total); average weekly income $207.98 (12% above national average); 6 banks, 7 loan companies, 65 branches.

Transportation: 7 rail lines; 2 airlines; linked to Detroit by suspension bridge and underwater tunnel; western terminus Highway 401; major harbor terminal (deep water port); private marinas; yacht club; municipal bus line.

Communications: 6 radio, 1 TV outlets; access to Detroit's 50 radio and 6 TV outlets; 1 monthly magazine; 1 daily newspaper.

Medical facilities: 5 major hospitals including large hospital complex for chronically ill, and burn unit.

Cultural facilities: Univ. of Windsor; St. Clair Community College; symphony orchestra; Light Opera Association; new art gallery; Hiram Walker Museum; public libraries; Cleary Auditorium and convention center.

Other attractions: 60 parks and playgrounds, sunken gardens; close access to Great Lakes resort areas; site of International Freedom Festival.

Winnipeg, Manitoba, Canada

The World Almanac is sponsored in the Winnipeg area by the Winnipeg Free Press, 300 Carlton St., Winnipeg, Man., Canada; phone (204) 943-9331; founded 1872; daily circulation 136,663; publisher Richard C. Malone; president R. H. Shelford; editor Peter McLintock; managing editor Albert Boothe; the newspaper and its staff have received numerous awards for outstanding journalism.

Population: 577,923, 1st in province; capital of Manitoba.

Area: 220 sq. mi., junction Red and Assiniboine rivers, near center of North America.

Industry: manufacturing is single largest source of jobs; 1,055 establishments, 43,300 employees; value of factory shipments, $1.525 billion.

Commerce: retail sales over $1.215 billion; Winnipeg Commodity Exchange is only gold futures market in Canada; headquarters Canada Grains Council, Canadian Grain Commission, Canadian International Grains Institute, Canadian Wheat Board.

Transportation: International Airport, Canada's 4th busiest, served by 6 airlines; 2 national rail lines and freight link to U. S.; 5 national and regional bus lines; major trucking hub.

Communications: 4 TV and 5 radio stations.

New construction: valued at $225 million (1974) compared with $173 million (1973).

Medical facilities: one of Canada's largest medical teaching centers; research in immunology, transplant-tissue rejection problems; of Manitoba's 85 active treatment hospitals, 13 are in Winnipeg, including 2 major teaching centers.

Cultural facilities: Art Gallery, Royal Winnipeg Ballet, contemporary dancers, symphony orchestra, Manitoba Theatre Centre, Manitoba Opera Association, Cercle Moliere, Museum of Man and Nature plus over 20 amateur theater groups.

Educational facilities: Univ. of Manitoba with 4 affiliated colleges, Univ. of Winnipeg, and Red River Community College.

Sports attractions: Blue Bombers (Canadian Football League), Jets (World Hockey Assn.).

Other attractions: major zoo; Red River Exhibition and multi-cultural Folklorama festival in summer; French Canadian festival in winter; museums and planetarium.

History: first colony, Lord Selkirk Settlers, 1812; incorporated Nov. 8, 1873; on Jan. 1, 1972, amalgamated city government replaced 7 cities, 4 urban

municipalities, one town and a metropolitan government.
Additional information: Chamber of Commerce, 177

Lombard Ave.; Tourist Information: 101 Legislative Bldg.; and Tourist and Convention Assn. of Manitoba, 400-365 Hargrave St.

Winston-Salem, North Carolina

The World Almanac is sponsored in the Piedmont Triad area by the Winston-Salem Journal and the Twin City Sentinel, 416-20 Marshall St., Winston-Salem, N.C. 27102; phone (919) 725-2311; Sentinel founded 1856, Journal 1897; brought under one ownership in 1927; now an affiliate of Media General; Charles W. Crowder, publisher-general manager.

Population: 147,400 (city), 223,500 (Forsyth County); 1975 estimates.
Area: 58.57 square miles (city), 419 square miles (county) in north central North Carolina.
Industry: R. J. Reynolds Industries, with diversified interests in tobacco, food, shipping, oil, packaging; Western Electric; Jos. Schlitz Brewery; Westinghouse; Hanes Corp.; Hanes Dye and Finishing; Duplan; Brenner Industries; Bahnson; Graveley Corp.; Hennis Inc.; Wachovia Corp.
Commerce: total retail sales (city 1975) nearly $850 million; part of Piedmont Triad which, with Greensboro and High Point, comprise a rapidly-growing industrial and business area.
Transportation: headquarters for Piedmont Airlines at Smith Reynolds Airport; city also served by regional airport with 4 airlines; 2 bus lines; 54 motor-freight carriers.
Communication: 4 TV and 9 radio stations.
Medical facilities: Bowman Gray School of Medicine

of Wake Forest Univ.; Baptist, Forsyth Memorial, Medical Park, and Reynolds hospitals.
Cultural facilities: one of the nation's first arts councils, formed in 1949; N. C. School of the Arts; Wake Forest Univ., Salem College, and Winston-Salem State Univ.; Old Salem, restoration of colonial town.
Convention facilities: Hyatt House hotel complex sits across from the Benton Convention Center; hotels and motels offer 2,600 rooms.
Recreation: more than 50 public parks, 10 community centers, 10 swimming centers; fishing and boating on Winston and Salem lakes; 17 golf courses, including Tanglewood.
Sports: Polar Twins, Southern Hockey League; Red Sox, Carolina League farm club of Boston Red Sox; stock car racing; Wake Forest football at Groves Stadium, basketball at Memorial Coliseum.
History: Salem founded 1766 by members of the Moravian Church; Winston founded 1849; merged in 1913.

Yakima, Washington

The World Almanac is sponsored in the Yakima area by the Yakima Herald-Republic (eves, except Saturday and Sunday), 114 N. 4th St., Yakima, Wash. 98901; phone (509) 248-1251; founded 1903 as The Yakima Republic, given present name in 1970; circulation 38,958 (daily) and 43,056 (Sunday); publisher James E. Tonkin, editorial page editor J. M. (Tom) Thomas, managing editor Alan K. Hooper.

Population: 46,300 (1974 census); total employed, approximately 35,000.
Area: 11.78 sq. mi., on Yakima River east of Cascade Mountains in southcentral Washington; county seat of Yakima County.
Industry: agriculture, timber, fisheries; ranks first in the nation in the production of apples, hops and mint and in the number of all fruit trees.
Commerce: wholesale-retail center for the Yakima Valley area; retail sales (1974) over $200 million; total bank deposits, over $356 million; 4 banks, 3 savings and loan associations and 2 mutual savings banks; per capita income, $3,261 (1973).
Transportation: 2 airlines, 3 railroads (including Amtrak), 40 motor freight lines, 1 bus line, 1 city bus line, Interstate 82, State Highway 24, U.S. Highways 12

and 97.
Communications: 4 TV stations, 8 radio stations, 1 daily newspaper, 1 weekly newspaper.
Medical facilities: 3 hospitals, 130 MD's.
Cultural facilities: art galleries, The Warehouse Little Theatre, Yakima Valley College, symphony orchestra, Allied Arts Council, Yakima Valley Regional Library, Capitol Theatre.
Recreation: 5 theatres, 6 drive-in theatres, 2 private golf courses, 2 public golf courses, 23 city parks; pari-mutuel horse racing at Yakima Meadows; Central Washington State Fair; Yakima Sunfair celebration.
Convention facilities: Bicentennial Pavilion (under construction); over 1,254 hotel and motel units.
History: founded Jan. 27, 1886, as "North Yakima" on route of Northern Pacific railroad.

Youngstown, Ohio

The World Almanac is sponsored in the Youngstown area by The Vindicator, Vindicator Sq., Youngstown, O. 4501; phone (216) 747-1471; founded 1863 by J. H. Odell; Wm. F. Maag began daily Sept. 25, 1889; daily circulation 103,094, Sunday 160,004; president, publisher, general manager William J. Brown; advertising manager William Mittler; managing editor Irving L. Mansell.

Population: 140,909 (city) Ohio's 7th largest; 536,836 (metro) 63d largest in U. S.; Mahoning County seat.
Area: 35 sq. mi. in northeastern Ohio at juncture of Ohio Turnpike, I-80, Ohio Rt. 11.
Industry: historically a strong iron and steel center, still important producer with Youngstown Sheet & Tube, Republic Steel, and U. S. Steel; local steel supplied to big nearby plants of General Motors-Packard Electric Div. in Warren and GMAD plant in Lordstown, where Chevrolet Vegas and trucks are made; GF Business Equipment sells office furnishings worldwide; Commercial Shearing does worldwide tunnel frame and hydraulics business; other fabricators use local steel, rubber.
Commerce: wholesale-retail center for large area of northeast Ohio and western Penn.; retail sales for

metro area (est.) over $1 billion; estimated value added by mfg. $1.7 billion.
Transportation: rail and truck transport center with 7 railroads and 92 motor freight terminals; airport served by 2 major airlines, headquarters for Beckett Aviation, largest fleet of executive aircraft in U. S.
Communications: 3 TV, 5 radio stations.
Medical facilities: 6 large hospitals in area.
Cultural facilities: symphony orchestra with downtown bldg.; ballet guild; Youngstown Playhouse in own modern bldg.; Butler Institute of American Art.
Educational facilities: Youngstown State Univ. with over 15,500 students and graduate program; medical college being established; 55 public and parochial schools; branches of Kent State Univ.
Recreational facilities: 10 parks, 44 playgrounds, golf course, 6 swim pools; Mill Creek Park, 2,383 acres.

Washington, Capital of the United States

The Capitol

The Capitol (building) since 1961 has presented an entirely new east central front, the central portion having been reconstructed and extended. It was moved forward 32½ ft. The former facade of Virginia sandstone was reproduced in Georgia marble, the original wall becoming an interior wall. The new section added 78 offices and other important facilities. The cost of the extension project was $11.4 million; improved illumination and other work brought the total to $24 million.

The original plan for the Capitol was drawn by Dr. William Thornton, of Tortola, West Indies, and accepted April 5, 1793. It had a central section, nearly square, a low dome and rectangular buildings north and south, 126 by 120 ft. The southeast cornerstone of the north section was laid by President Washington with Masonic ceremonies Sept. 18, 1793. Sandstone from Aquia Creek, Va., was used. The northern wing was completed first. The Congress occupied it in Nov. 1800. The Supreme Court met there in Feb. 1801, and other local courts also used the Capitol. In charge of early construction were architects Stephen H. Hallet, Geo. Hadfield, and James Hoban, who was architect of the White House. Benjamin H. Latrobe was architect of the South or House wing which was occupied in 1807, but not completed until 1811. All the interiors were burned by the British in 1814. Latrobe had charge of the rebuilding until 1818 when Charles Bulfinch became the architect for 11 years. Congress reoccupied the Capitol in 1819 and the central rotunda area was finished in 1829.

The present Senate and House wings were designed and constructed under the architect Thomas U. Walter from 1851 to 1863. The wing extensions are white marble from Lee, Mass., and the columns are from Maryland. Daniel Webster spoke at the laying of the cornerstone.

The House moved in Dec. 16, 1857; the Senate Jan. 4, 1859. In 1860 the Supreme Court moved into the former Senate Chamber, and in 1864 the old Hall of the House was designated Statuary Hall. The court moved into its own building in 1935.

The original dome of the Capitol, wood covered with copper, was replaced, 1856, by the present dome of cast iron, completed 1865. Its greatest exterior diameter is 135 ft. 5 in. The rotunda is 96 ft. in diameter; height from floor to base of lantern is 180 ft. 3 in. In the "eye" of the dome is a fresco by Constantino Brumidi, the "Apotheosis of Washington." Below the dome runs a 300-ft. frieze in fresco, portraying American history from Columbus, 1492, to Kitty Hawk, 1903. Brumidi painted part of it by 1880. Costaggini added panels by 1888. Allyn Cox completed the frieze in 1953 and it was dedicated in 1954.

The Statue of Freedom on the dome, 19½ ft. tall, is of bronze and weighs 14,985 pounds. At its base are the words "E Pluribus Unum" (Out of Many One). It was modeled in plaster by Thomas Crawford in Rome and cast in bronze. It cost $23,796, exclusive of erection.

Inaugurations of presidents and vice presidents are usually held on a platform erected over the great steps on the east front. The oath of office of the president is usually given by the chief justice of the United States.

Prayer Room

A nondenominational room for meditation and prayer is located off the rotunda. Decorated in blue, it has a white oak altar with an open Bible and candelabra, 10 seats, and 2 kneeling benches.

National Statuary Hall

Statuary Hall was created in 1864 to occupy the former Hall of the House of Representatives. States were invited to contribute not more than two statues of distinguished persons judged worthy of national commemoration by the States. In 1933 the number of statues in Statuary Hall was limited to one statue from each state, others to be placed in other parts of the Capitol. To date 91 statues have been contributed by 50 states. The statues in Statuary Hall:

Alabama—Gen. Jos. Wheeler, U.S.A., C.S.A.
Arizona—John C. Greenway, U.S.A.
Arkansas—Uriah M. Rose, jurist.
California—Junipero Serra, mission founder.
Colorado—Dr. Florence Rena Sabin, scientist.
Connecticut—Roger Sherman, statesman.
Delaware—Caesar Rodney, statesman.
Florida—Dr. John Gorrie, inventor.
Georgia—Alex H. Stephens, statesman.
Hawaii—King Kamehameha I, uniter of islands.
Idaho—Geo. L. Shoup, first governor.
Illinois—Francis E. Willard, WCTU head.
Indiana—Lew Wallace, U.S.A., author.
Iowa—Saml. J. Kirkwood, governor.
Kansas—John J. Ingalls, senator.
Kentucky—Henry Clay, statesman.
Louisiana—Huey P. Long, senator.
Maine—Hannibal Hamlin, vice president.
Maryland—Charles Carroll, signer, D. of I.
Massachusetts—Samuel Adams, statesman.
Michigan—Lewis Cass, statesman.
Minnesota—Henry M. Rice, senator.
Mississippi—Jefferson Davis, statesman.
Missouri—Thos. H. Benton, senator.
Montana—Charles Marion Russell, artist.
Nebraska—Wm. Jennings Bryan, statesman.
Nevada—Patrick A. McCarran, senator.
New Hampshire—Daniel Webster, statesman.
New Jersey—Richard Stockton, statesman.
New York—Robt. R. Livingston, statesman.
North Carolina—Zebulon B. Vance, governor.
North Dakota—John Burke, U.S. treasurer.
Ohio—William Allen, senator, governor.
Oklahoma—Sequoyah, Cherokee leader.
Oregon—Rev. Jason Lee, pioneer.
Pennsylvania—Robert Fulton, inventor.
Rhode Island—Roger Williams, founder.
South Carolina—John C. Calhoun, statesman.
South Dakota—Gen. W.H.H. Beadle, educator.
Tennessee—John Sevier, first governor.
Texas—Sam Houston, pioneer leader.
Utah—Brigham Young, Mormon leader.
Vermont—Ethan Allen, Revolutionary leader.
Virginia—Robt. E. Lee, U.S.A., C.S.A.
Washington—Dr. Marcus Whitman, pioneer.
West Virginia—Francis H. Pierpont, statesman.
Wisconsin—Robt. M. La Follette Sr., statesman.
Wyoming—Esther Hobart Morris, suffragette.

Located Elsewhere

Alaska—E. L. "Bob" Bartlett, senator.
New Mexico—Dennis Chavez, senator.

Under the dome in the **Great Rotunda** are statues and busts of Washington (Va.), Lincoln, Jefferson, Hamilton, Jackson (Tenn.), Lafayette, Grant, Garfield (Ohio), and Edward Dickinson Baker.

Adjoining it, the **South Small Rotunda** has statues of George Clinton (N.Y.), Stephen F. Austin (Tex.), and John Peter Muhlenberg (Pa.). The corridor leading from Statuary Hall to the House has statues of Jonathan Trumbull (Conn.), Wm. King (Me.), Father Jacques Marquette (Wis.), Wade Hampton (S.C.), Will Rogers (Okla.), E. L. "Bob" Bartlett (Alaska), and Dr. John McLoughlin (Ore.).

In the foyer of the former Senate and Supreme Court Chamber are statues of John Stark (N.H.), Dennis Chavez (N.M.), and Nathanael Greene (R.I.). In the corridor leading to the Senate wing are statues of Dr. Ephraim McDowell (Ky.), and Dr. Crawford W. Long (Ga.), first to use ether as anaesthetic, John Hanson (Md.), 9th president of the Continental Congress, and John M. Clayton (Del.), secy. of state, Wm. E. Borah (Ida.), Edward D. White (La.), and Maria L. Sanford (Minn.).

In the **Hall of Columns** on the first floor, House wing, are statues of E. Kirby Smith (Fla.), Zachariah Chandler (Mich.), Jas. Harlan (Ia.), Francis P. Bair Jr. (Mo.), Gen. Philip Kearny (N.J.), Gen. Jas. Shields (Ill.), John Winthrop (Mass.), Oliver P. Morton (Ind.), J. Sterling Morton (Neb.), Rev. Thos. Starr King (Cal.), J. L. McCurry (Ala.), J. P. Clarke (Ark.), Geo. W. Glick (Kan.), Jas. Z. George (Miss.), Chas. B. Aycock (N.C.), Jacob Collamer (Vt.), John E. Kenna (W. Va.), Joseph Ward (S.D.), Eusebio F. Kino, S. J. (Ariz.), and Father Damien (Ha.).

Office Buildings for Members

Members of Congress meet constituents and transact other business in five office buildings on Capitol Hill, two for the Senate and three for the House.

The original Senate building, now named the Richard Brevard Russell Office Building, was completed in 1909, enlarged in 1933; the second Senate building, now named the Everett McKinley Dirksen Office Building, was constructed in 1958. A subway connects both with the Capitol.

The original House building (1908) was named for former Speaker Joseph G. Cannon (R. Ill.), the second (1933) for former Speaker Nicholas Longworth (R. Oh.), and the third (1964) for former Speaker Sam Rayburn (D. Tex.). The Rayburn Building has underground transportatioon to the Capitol.

Also on Capitol Hill is the bell tower and statue memorial to Sen. Robert A. Taft of Ohio (1889-1953). It was erected by popular subscription and dedicated Apr. 14, 1959, by President Eisenhower.

Hours for Visiting

The Capitol is normally open from 9 a.m. to 4:30 p.m. daily. The Capitol is closed Christmas, New Year's Day, and Thanksgiving Day. Should either the House or the Senate remain in session beyond closing time, the wing of the Capitol in use stays open until the session closes.

Tours, through the Capitol, including the House and Senate Galleries, are conducted from 9 a.m. to 4 p.m. without charge. It is not necessary to take a tour to see the Capitol. Visitors desiring to hear debate in either chamber for a longer period than the tour allows must obtain a visitor's card from their Senator or Representative.

The White House

The White House, the president's residence, stands on 18 acres on the south side of Pennsylvania Avenue, between the Treasury and the Executive Office Building. The main building, 170 by 85 ft., has 6 floors, with the East Terrace, 135 by 35 ft., leading to the East Wing, a 3-story building, 139 by 82 ft., used for offices and as an entrance for official functions. The West Terrace, 174 by 35 ft., contains offices and new press facilities above the boarded over swimming pool, and leads to the Executive Office, 3 stories high, 148 by 98 ft., erected in 1902 and enlarged several times since.

The White House was designed by James Hoban, an Irishborn architect, in a competition that paid $500. The main facade resembles the Duke of Leinster's house in Dublin. President Washington chose the site, which was included on the plan of the Federal City prepared by the French engineer, Major Pierre L'Enfant. The cornerstone was laid Oct. 13, 1792. President Washington never lived in the house. President John Adams entered in Nov. 1800, and Mrs. Adams hung her washing in the uncompleted East Room.

The walls are of sandstone, quarried at Aquia Creek, Va. The exterior walls were painted during the course of construction, causing the building to be termed the "White House." For many years, however, it was generally referred to as the "President's House" or the "President's Palace." Thos. Jefferson developed the east and west terraces and built one-story offices, woodsheds, and a wine cellar. On Aug. 24, 1814, during Madison's administration, the house was burned by the British. James Hoban completed rebuilding by Dec. 1817, and President Monroe moved in.

The south portico was added in 1824 and the north colonnade and porch in 1829 by Benjamin Latrobe, surveyor of public buildings, based on sketches by Hoban, approved by Jefferson. In 1948 President Truman had a second-floor balcony built into the south portico. In 1948 he had Congress authorize complete rebuilding because the White House was unsafe. During its reconstruction he lived in Blair House, 1651 Pennsylvania Ave.

Reconstruction cost $5,761,000. The interior was completely removed, new underpinning 24 ft. deep was placed under the outside walls and a steel frame was built to support the interior. All original trim and metal work were preserved.

The Green Room, used for informal receptions, is in American Sheraton style, with green silk moire on the walls, a white marble fireplace, and white enamel wainscoting and door trim. On the west wall hangs a portrait of Benjamin Franklin, painted in 1767. Most of the furniture now in the room was made in New York City about 1815-1825 by Duncan Phyfe or his contemporaries.

The Blue Room, an oval drawing room, is the main reception room. The parquet floor is exposed; the walls are covered with wallpaper reproduced from a French document of 1800. Portraits of Washington, Adams, Jefferson, Jackson, Monroe, Taylor, and Tyler, as well as two seascapes by Fitz Hugh Lane of Boston harbor and Baltimore harbor decorate the walls. Seven chairs and a French clock from Monroe's original 1817 furnishings remain in the room.

The Red Room, used as a parlor, is furnished in the Empire period, hung in red twill satin with gold scroll borders. There are a Savonnerie carpet of the period and a marble-topped gueridon labeled by Charles Honore Lannuier. There are portraits of Pierce, Polk, T. Roosevelt, Abigail Adams, Dolley Madison, Angelica Van Buren, Audubon, and Alexander Hamilton in the room. Also there is a marble bust of Martin Van Buren by Hiram Powers.

The State Dining Room has a large chief table. Other tables are brought in for large dinners but do not remain there. Centerpiece of the main table is a French bronzedore plateau purchased by Monroe in 1817. China in use was ordered during the Lyndon B. Johnson Administration. Chairs are in Queen Anne style. The room is paneled in oak with Corinthian pilasters, painted white.

The Family Dining Room, used for breakfasts and luncheons, has a portrait of Mrs. Theodore Roosevelt by Theobold Chartran.

The President's Dining Room is on the second floor. It has scenic wallpaper and is furnished with American Federal furniture, an 18th Century chandelier, and blue silk window hangings. There is a mahogany sideboard once owned by Daniel Webster.

The Diplomatic Reception Room, an oval room on the ground floor, is used as the entrance to the mansion at state functions. It has scenic wallpaper based on 1820 engravings, and a new Aubusson style rug with seals of the 50 states, installed in June 1971.

The Library, on the ground floor, has the painted decor of an early American room. In Aug. 1963, 2,780 titles were selected to be placed in the library. All but a few are by American authors. They were chosen by a committee headed by the late James T. Babb, librarian emeritus of Yale University.

The Lincoln Bedroom which contains an ornately carved bed and furniture of his period, is at the east end of the second floor. It served as Lincoln's cabinet room and in it he signed the Emancipation Proclamation of Jan. 1, 1863. A portrait of Jackson, admired by Lincoln, hangs there today. Seven pieces of furniture have Lincoln associations. The bed was used in the State Bedroom during the Lincoln administration. In the room is a copy of the Gettysburg Address, written out by Lincoln and donated to the White House by the will of Oscar B. Cintas, one-time Cuban ambassador, who died in 1957.

The Treaty Room, one door removed from Lincoln's cabinet room was used by Andrew Johnson as his cabinet room, and so used until 1902, when it became a sitting room. Here in 1899 was signed the peace protocol, a forerunner to the final treaty of peace with Spain. It is now a waiting or meeting room for the President and contains some of the original Victorian furniture. There are portraits of Presidents A. Johnson, Grant, and Taylor and paintings of McKinley observing the signing of the treaty, and of Lincoln and Grant in conference.

The Queen's Bedroom is assigned to distinguished women guests, and has sheltered five queens — Queen Mother Elizabeth and Queen Elizabeth II of Britain, Wilhelmina and Juliana of the Netherlands, Queen Mother Frederika of Greece. The English overmantel mirror was presented by Princess Elizabeth in 1951.

The Yellow Oval Room, directly above the Blue Room, is used as a private sitting room by the President and First Lady.

The Map Room, on the ground floor, a top-secret war room during World War II, was redecorated in 1970 at the request of President and Mrs. Nixon. Furnished in American Chippendale style, it contains 4 American landscape paintings and a portrait of Benjamin Franklin which was taken from Franklin's Philadelphia home by a British officer quartered there during the American Revolution.

The President's Office, oval in form, is in the West Wing and looks out on the rose garden. The office was added in 1909 to the West Wing, which had been built 7 years earlier by Theodore Roosevelt. The West Wing also contains the Roosevelt Room and the Cabinet Room.

Visiting Hours

The White House is open from 10 a.m. to 12 noon, Tuesday through Friday, except on holidays. Also Saturdays, 10 a.m. to 2 p.m. Jun. 1 through Labor Day, and 10 a.m. to noon Labor Day through May 31. Only the public rooms in the basement and the first floor rooms may be visited. No permit is required.

President's Guest House

Blair House, the President's Guest House, fronts on Pennsylvania Ave., northwest of the White House grounds. It is supervised by the Dept. of State and is the official residence of heads of state who visit Washington. Built 1824, it was the home of Francis Preston Blair (1791-1876), political leader and Lincoln advisor. President Truman lived there 1948-1952 during rebuilding of the White House, and 2 Puerto Rican fanatics tried to shoot their way in Nov. 1, 1950, killing one guard and wounding 2 others.

Restoration and refurnishing began in 1963 and the house was reopened Jan. 14, 1964, on the occasion of the visit of President Antonio Segni of the Italian Republic. The Blair House Fine Arts Committee continues to provide for the house.

Other Centers of Interest

Arlington National Cemetery

Arlington National Cemetery, on the former Custis-Lee estate in Virginia, is the site of the **Tomb of the Unknown Soldier** and the final resting place of John Fitzgerald Kennedy, president of the United States, who was buried there Nov. 25, 1963. A torch burns day and night over his grave. The remains of his brother Sen. Robert F. Kennedy (N.Y.) were interred on June 8, 1968, in an area adjacent. Many other famous Americans also are buried at Arlington, as well as American soldiers from every major war.

Arlington National Cemetery, administered by the Department of the Army, was established June 15, 1864, on land originally the estate of George Washington Parke Custis. The land was part of the District of Columbia from 1791 until 1847, when Arlington County was returned to Virginia.

The Unknown Soldier of World War I was entombed on the east front of the Arlington Memorial Amphitheater Nov. 11, 1921, in the presence of President Warren G. Harding. The tomb is inscribed: *Here rests in honored glory an American soldier known but to God.* The body had been chosen at Chalons-sur-Marne from unidentified dead in Europe. On Memorial Day, May 30, 1958, two unidentified servicemen, one of whom died in World War II and one in the Korean War, were placed in crypts beside the first, in ceremonies led by President Eisenhower and Vice President Nixon. The president placed the Medal of Honor on each of the two coffins.

As of Mar. 31, 1975, a total of 165,142 interments had been made in Arlington National Cemetery. Among the unknown dead are 2,111 who died on the battlefields of Virginia in the Civil War and 167 who lost their lives when the battleship Maine was blown up in Havana Harbor Feb. 15, 1898. The total of unknown dead interred in Arlington National Cemetery is 4,724.

Arlington House, The Robert E. Lee Memorial

On a hilltop above the cemetery, stands Arlington House, the Robert E. Lee Memorial, which from 1955 to 1972 was officially called the Custis-Lee Mansion. The house has a portico 60 ft. wide, with 8 Doric columns, and faces the Potomac. With its two wings the house extends 140 ft. It was built by George Washington Parke Custis, grandson of Martha Washington and father of Mary Ann Randolph Custis, who married Lee in this house in 1831. Here Lee wrote his resignation from the U.S. Army, Apr. 20, 1861. The house became a military hq. and was confiscated by the government. The U.S. Supreme Court restored it to the legal heir, George Washington Custis Lee, grandson of the builder, who sold the entire estate (including the mansion)

to the Government in 1883 for $150,000.

The mansion and grounds are administered by the National Park Service of the Dept. of the Interior.

U.S. Marine Corps War Memorial

North of the National Cemetery, approximately 350 yards, stands the bronze statue of the raising of the United States flag on Iwo Jima, executed by Felix de Weldon from the photograph by Joe Rosenthal, and presented to the nation by members and friends of the U.S. Marine Corps, at a cost of $850,000. It was dedicated Nov. 10, 1954, and is under the administration of the Dept. of the Interior, National Park Service.

Folger Shakespeare Library

The Folger Shakespeare Library on Capitol Hill, Washington, D. C., is a research institution devoted to the advancement of learning in the background of Anglo-American civilization in the 16th and 17th centuries and in most aspects of the continental Renaissance. It has the largest collection of Shakespeareana in the world, with 79 copies of the First Folio. Its collection of English books printed before 1640 is the largest in the Western Hemisphere. It also has extensive source materials for the history of theatre and drama from the Middle Ages to the end of the 19th century, both English and American. The library owns approximately 250,000 books and manuscripts, about half of them, rare.

The library was founded and endowed by Henry Clay Folger, a former president of the Standard Oil Co. of New York, and his wife, Emily Jordan Folger. He left its administration to the trustees of his alma mater, Amherst College. The exhibition gallery and replica Elizabethan Theatre are open free 10 a.m. to 4:30 p.m. daily; closed federal holidays and on Sundays after Labor Day to April 15.

Library of Congress

Established by and for Congress in 1800, the Library of Congress has extended its services over the years to other Government agencies and other libraries, to scholars, and to the general public, and it now serves as the national library. Two buildings, an ornate Italian Renaissance structure (1897) and a modern annex (1939), cover 6 acres of the 15³/₄-acre library site and contain 35 acres of floor space. In addition, the library occupies 10 other buildings dispersed throughout the Metropolitan area. In Oct. 1965 Congress passed a law authorizing construction of a third library building, the James Madison Memorial Building; completion is expected in 1977.

L. Quincy Mumford, the 11th Librarian of Congress, retired Dec. 31, 1974. John G. Lorenz is serving as Acting Librarian of Congress.

The library had over 3,000 volumes when it was destroyed in the burning of the Capitol, Aug. 24-25, 1814. In Jan. 1815 Congress bought Thomas Jefferson's library of some 6,000 volumes. In 1851 fire destroyed about half the collections. In 1866 the science library of the Smithsonian Institution was transferred to the library, and in 1870 the library became the repository for materials deposited for copyright. Today the library's collections contain almost 74 million items, including more than 16 million volumes and pamphlets.

In addition to providing a variety of reference and bibliographic services to other government agencies, the Library of Congress serves as a cataloging and bibliographic center for libraries throughout the country. Its cataloging data is available on printed cards (a service offered since 1901), on magnetic tapes for libraries using computers, and in book catalogs. A recent program called Cataloging in Publication makes cataloging information available in books themselves so that they can be processed and put into circulation almost immediately after their delivery to libraries.

The library's exhibit halls are open to the public. Guided tours are given on the hour from 9 to 4 Monday through Friday; arrangements for groups should be made in advance with the Tour Coordinator. Many of the library's treasures are on exhibit — the Gutenberg Bible, the first and second drafts of the Gettysburg Address, Jefferson's so-called "rough draft" of the Declaration of Independence, and many items from the Presidential Papers collection. Changing exhibits feature interesting selections from the library's collection of photographs, rare books, music, maps, and manuscripts. These are sometimes seen outside Washington as well, as traveling exhibits circulated by the Library of Congress to libraries and museums elsewhere in the country. The library's resources are also made available to the public through publication of guides, bibliographies, catalogs, and facsimiles. An annual list of **Publications in Print** is available free of charge from Central Services Division, Library of Congress, Washington, DC 20540. A monthly **Calendar of Events** listing exhibits currently on view, literary programs, chamber music, and concerts scheduled is also available from the same address. Information about the Library of Congress, publications, posters, and greeting and postal cards are available at the Information Counter, in the west entrance ground floor lobby of the Main Building.

Thomas Jefferson Memorial

The **Thomas Jefferson Memorial** stands on the south shore of the Tidal Basin in West Potomac park. It is a circular stone structure, with Vermont marble on the exterior and Georgia white marble inside, and combines architectural elements of the dome of the Pantheon in Rome and the rotunda designed by Jefferson for the University of Virginia. The central circular chamber, 86¹/₄ ft. in diameter, is dominated by a 19-ft. tall full-length figure of Thomas Jefferson by the American sculptor Rudulph Evans. The architects were John Russell Pope and his associates Otto R. Eggers and Daniel P. Higgins. The Memorial was dedicated by President F. D. Roosevelt Apr. 13, 1943, the 200th anniversary of Jefferson's birth.

On the pediment over the portico is a sculptured group by Adolph A. Weinman showing Jefferson standing before the committee appointed by the Continental Congress to draft the Declaration of Independence. On the interior walls are four panels with inscriptions from Jefferson's writings. On the frieze of the main entablature are Jefferson's lines: "I have sworn upon the altar of God eternal hostility against every form of tyranny over the mind of man."

The memorial is open daily from 8 a.m. to midnight, except Christmas Day.

John F. Kennedy Center

John F. Kennedy Center for the Performing Arts, designated by Congress as the National Cultural Center and the official memorial in Washington to President Kennedy, was opened September 8, 1971. The white marble building, designed by Edward Durell Stone, houses a 2,300-seat Opera House, a 2,750-seat Concert Hall, the 1,150-seat Eisenhower Theater, the 224-seat American Film Institute Theater, an unfinished 500-seat studio theater, and 3 restaurants. All facilities are in full operation throughout the year. Tours are available daily, free of charge, between 10:00 a.m. and 1:15 p.m.

Lincoln Memorial

The **Lincoln Memorial**, in West Potomac Park, on the axis of the Capitol and the Washington Monument, consists of a large marble hall enclosing a heroic statue of Abraham Lincoln in meditation, sitting on a large armchair. It was dedicated on Memorial Day, May 30, 1922. The Memorial was designed by Henry Bacon. The statue was made by Daniel Chester French. Murals and ornamentation on the bronze ceiling beams are by Jules Guerin.

The memorial, built on bedrock, is of white Colorado-Yule marble. There are 2 Doric columns at the entrance, and 36 others in the colonnade. The frieze above the 36 columns bears the names of the 36 states existing at the time of Lincoln's death. On the attic parapet are recorded names of the 48 states existing in 1922.

Inside are 3 memorials to Lincoln. The seated figure of Lincoln is 19 ft. from head to foot and the classic armchair is 12¹/₂ ft. tall. Over the back of the chair a flag is draped in marble. The statue was fashioned out of 28 blocks of Georgia white marble. On the north wall is inscribed the Second Inaugural Address. On the south wall is the Gettysburg Address.

The walls of the interior are Indiana limestone. The panels between the overhead girders are of Alabama marble saturated with melted beeswax to produce translucency. The interior floor and the wall base are of pink Tennessee marble. The cost of the Memorial was $2,957,000 and of the statue $88,400.

The memorial is open daily from 8 a.m. to midnight, except Christmas Day.

Mount Vernon

Mount Vernon, on the south bank of the Potomac, 16 miles below Washington, D.C., is part of a large tract of land in northern Virginia which was originally included in a royal grant made to Lord Culpepper, who in 1674 granted 5,000 acres to Nicholas Spencer and John Washington. The division between Spencer and Washington put John Washington's son Lawrence in possession of the Washington half in 1690. Later it became the property of Lawrence Washington's son Augustine, the father of George Washington.

The present house is an enlargement of one apparently built on the site of an earlier one by Augustine Washington, who lived there 1735-1738. His son Lawrence came there in 1743, when he renamed the plantation Mount Vernon in honor of Admiral Vernon under whom he had served in the West Indies. Lawrence Washington died in 1752 and was succeeded as proprietor of Mount Vernon by his half-brother, George Washington.

To Mount Vernon in 1759 Washington brought his wife, Martha Dandridge Custis, having previously enlarged the house from 1¹/₂ to 2¹/₂ stories. Just before the Revolution he planned additions, and when he was called away to war his kinsman Lund Washington supervised the work, which was completed after Washington returned in 1783. During the Revolution Washington visited Mount Vernon only twice, on the way to and from Yorktown in 1781. In 1789 he left to become president and lived in New York and Philadelphia, with brief visits to the plantation. He came back in 1797 and died in Mount Vernon Dec. 14, 1799. He was buried in the old family vault. He had made plans for a new burial vault and this was built in 1831. Both his remains and those of Martha, who died in 1802, were transferred there.

Mount Vernon was left to Washington's nephew, U.S. Supreme Court Justice Bushrod Washington, and by him to his nephew, John Augustine Washington, whose son, John A. Washington Jr., was the last private owner. In 1853 Miss Ann Pamela Cunningham of South Carolina organized the

Mount Vernon Ladies' Assn., which bought the mansion and 200 acres, since extended to just under 500 acres. The Association reassembled original Washington furniture and repaired the buildings. It restored the kitchen garden, flower garden and experimental botanical garden, reconstructed the greenhouse, and built a museum. Several trees planted by Washington still exist, and the boxwood dates from 1798.

The Association preserves house and tomb with the visitor's fee. The regent of the Mount Vernon Ladies' Association is Mrs. Thomas Turner Cooke. About 31 states are represented by vice regents. The Resident Director is Chas. C. Wall.

National Arboretum

The National Arboretum, established in 1927 for the study of trees and plants, has become one of Washington's great show places. Occupying 415 acres of rolling land along the Anacostia River in the northeastern section of the city, it is administered by the secretary of agriculture through the Plant Science Research Division of the Agricultural Research Service.

The Arboretum is open every day of the year except Christmas. The visiting hours are as follows: April through October—8 a.m. to 7 p.m. Monday through Friday; 10 a.m. to 7 p.m. Saturdays and Sundays. November through March —8 a.m. to 5 p.m. Monday through Friday; 10 a.m. to 5 p.m. Saturdays and Sundays.

National Archives

The Declaration of Independence, the Constitution of the United States and the Bill of Rights are on permanent display in the National Archives Exhibition Hall. They are sealed in glass-and-bronze cases filled with inert helium gas. They can be lowered at a moment's notice into a large shockproof and fireproof safe.

The National Archives holds the permanently valuable federal records of the United States government, 1774 to the present. As a research institution, it is designed to preserve these records and make them available to government agencies, scholars, students, writers, and the general public.

The National Archives and Records Service is a part of the General Services Administration. Through the Presidential Libraries Office it administers the Franklin D. Roosevelt Library at Hyde Park, N. Y., the Harry S. Truman Library at Independence, Mo., the Dwight D. Eisenhower Library at Abilene, Kan., the Herbert Hoover Library at West Branch, Iowa, the Lyndon Baines Johnson Library at Austin, Tex., and the John Fitzgerald Kennedy Library, temporarily at Waltham, Mass.

The National Archives and Records Service is headed by Dr. James B. Rhoads, archivist of the United States, Pennsylvania Ave. and 8th St. N.W. For research information, call 202-963-6411. For visitor information, call 202-962-2000.

National Gallery of Art

The National Gallery of Art, situated in an area bounded by Constitution Avenue and the Mall, between Third and Seventh Streets, was established by Joint Resolution of Congress Mar. 24, 1937, and opened Mar. 17, 1941. Although technically a bureau of the Smithsonian Institution, the gallery is an autonomous organization governed by its own board of trustees. The chairman of the board is the Chief Justice of the United States. Other members are the Secretaries of State and of the Treasury, the Secretary of the Smithsonian Institution, and five distinguished private citizens.

The collections comprise gifts of over 200 donors (none of the works were acquired with Government funds) and cover more than a dozen schools in the history of western art from the 13th century to the present.

The building was erected with funds given by Andrew W. Mellon, who also gave his collection, consisting of 126 paintings and 26 pieces of sculpture, the latter largely from the Dreyfus Collection. The paintings cover the various European schools from the 13th century to the 19th, and include such masterpieces as Raphael's Alba Madonna, the Niccolini-Cowper Madonna, and St. George and the Dragon; van Eyck's Annunciation; Botticelli's Adoration of the Magi; and 9 Rembrandts. Twenty-one paintings came from the Hermitage in Leningrad. Also in this collection are the Vaughan Portrait of George Washington, by Gilbert Stuart, and The Washington Family, by Edward Savage.

The Samuel H. Kress Collection includes the great tondo of the Adoration of the Magi by Fra Angelico and Fra Filippo Lippi, the Laocoon by El Greco, and fine examples by Giorgione, Titian, Grunewald, Durer, Memling, Bosch, Juan de Flandes, Francois Clouet, Poussin, Watteau, Chardin, Boucher, Fragonard, David, and Ingres. Also included are a number of masterpieces of sculpture, especially of the Italian and French schools.

The Widener Collection of over 100 paintings includes 14 Rembrandts, 8 Van Dycks, 2 Vermeers, and examples of Italian, Spanish, English, and French painting; also Renaissance and French sculpture and examples of the decorative arts.

The Chester Dale Collection includes masterpieces by Manet, Cezanne, Renoir, Toulouse-Lautrec, Monet, Modigliani, Pissarro, Degas, van Gogh, Gauguin, Matisse, Picasso, Braque, and a group of American paintings.

Major works of art by some of the most important artists of the last hundred years, including Picasso, Cezanne, Gauguin, and the American painter, Walt Kuhn, have been given to the gallery by the W. Averell Harriman Foundation in memory of Marie N. Harriman.

Pictures to round out the collection have been bought with funds provided by the late Ailsa Mellon Bruce, daughter of Andrew W. Mellon. Preeminent among them is the portrait of Ginevra de' Benci, the only generally acknowledged painting by Leonardo da Vinci outside Europe; Georges de la Tour's Repentant Magdalen, one of the rarest paintings of the 17th Century; and Pablo Picasso's Femme Nue, the key work of the artist's analytical cubist period. Among others are: Rubens' Daniel in the Lions' Den; Claude Lorrain's Judgment of Paris; Saint George and the Dragon, attributed to van der Weyden; and a number of American paintings, including Cole's second set of The Voyage of Life.

Cezanne's great early portrait of his father and 351 paintings by George Catlin, mostly of North and South American Indians, are among recent acquisitions given by Paul Mellon, president of the gallery and son of Andrew Mellon. A fine collection of French Impressionist pictures are on loan to the gallery from Mr. and Mrs. Mellon.

The National Gallery's rapidly expanding graphic arts holdings, in great part given by Lessing J. Rosenwald, number about 30,000 items and date from the 12th century to the present. Mr. Rosenwald's gift, one of the world's great collections of prints and drawings, forms the nucleus of the gallery's holdings in this field.

The Index of American Design contains over 17,000 watercolor renderings and 5000 photographs of American crafts and folk arts.

The gallery's Education Department gives daily talks on the collections in the galleries. The Extension Service lends films, slide programs, and slide sets to schools, colleges, and civic groups in some 4000 communities in the United States and Canada. Nearly all of the gallery's services are available to the public free of charge.

Construction is in progress for the expansion of the National Gallery in the block immediately east of the present building. Funds for this project have come from the Mellon family. The architect is I. M. Pei. Expected to open in stages, the first of which — a connecting link with major new restaurant facilities — will open in 1976, the East Building will provide space for temporary exhibitions, for the National Gallery's growing collection of 20th-century paintings and sculpture, for a Center for Advanced Study in the Visual Arts, and for a greatly expanded library and photographic archive.

Open daily except Christmas and New Year's. Hours: 10 a.m. to 5 p.m. weekdays, noon to 9 p.m. Sundays. During the summer open weekdays 10 a.m. to 9 p.m., noon to 9 p.m. Sundays.

National Geographic Society

The National Geographic Society, founded in 1888 "for the increase and diffusion of geographic knowledge," is the world's largest nonprofit scientific and educational institution. The Society produces the illustrated monthly *National Geographic*, books, maps, globes, atlases, other educational materials, and television programs. Its activities are supported by the dues of 9,000,000 members.

The society's 10-story headquarters building in Washington, D. C., was dedicated by President Lyndon B. Johnson in 1964. It attracts many thousands of visitors, including members of the Society from all over the world. Explorers Hall offers exhibits, artifacts, and mementos depicting the organization's research and exploration activities.

In 1968 the society occupied its new Membership Center Building on a 100-acre tract near Gaithersburg, Md. The building accommodates 1,200 employees charged with handling membership files, correspondence, changes of address, and other clerical operations.

Executive officers are: Melvin M. Payne, president of the society; Gibert M. Grosvenor, vice president and editor; Melville Bell Grosvenor, editor-in-chief and chairman of the board of trustees; Thomas W. McKnew, advisory chairman of the board; Robert E. Doyle, vice president and secretary; Thomas M. Beers, vice president and associate secretary; Hilleary F. Hoskinson, treasurer.

The Pentagon

The Pentagon, headquarters of the Department of Defense, is the world's largest office building, twice as large as the Merchandise Mart in Chicago and with 3 times the floor space of the Empire State Building in New York. Situated on the Virginia side of the Potomac River, it houses 26,000 employees in offices that occupy 3,707,745 square feet.

The Pentagon was completed Jan. 15, 1943, at a cost of about $83,000,000. It covers 34 acres and has 204 acres of lawns and terraces. It is 5 stories high and consists of 5 rings of buildings connected by 10 corridors, with a 5-acre pentagonal court in the center. Each of the outer-most sides of the building is 921 ft. long and the perimeter is seven-eighths of a mile. Total length of corridors is 17$^1/_2$ miles. There is a partial mezzanine below the first floor and a partial basement below that.

Smithsonian Institution

The Smithsonian Institution is one of the world's great historical, scientific, educational, and cultural establishments. It comprises numerous facilities, mostly in the metropolitan Wash., D.C., area. It was founded by an Act of Congress in 1846, pursuant to a bequest of James Smithson, a British scholar-scientist, to the United States to found at Washington "an establishment for the increase and diffusion of knowledge among men." The Smithsonian, ever since its founding, has been a center for basic scientific research; it engages in programs of education and it is also the largest museum-gallery complex in the world. About 20 million persons visit its halls annually. S. Dillon Ripley became the 8th secretary of the Smithsonian Feb. 1, 1964.

The Anacostia Neighborhood Museum opened in 1967 as a satellite museum located in a low-income urban setting. The first of its kind in the nation, it provides an environment for open, nondirected learning through actual contact with real things, for adults and children who rarely, if ever, use existing museums and other cultural resources. Its programs include exhibits drawn from Smithsonian collections in art, history, and science; workshops, clubs, and classes related to the exhibits; and exhibits assembled or made by the residents of the neighborhood. A mobile unit brings small portable exhibitions to the schools and street corners of the Anacostia community.

The Freer Gallery of Art, the gift of Detroit industrialist Charles Lang Freer, is an outstanding museum and re-

search center in art of the Far and Near East. The gallery also houses the Whistler Peacock Room and his etchings and paintings.

The Joseph H. Hirshhorn Museum and Sculpture Garden, opened in 1974, houses works in the Hirshhorn collection which were donated in 1966 to the people of the United States. Primary emphasis is on art of the 20th century although the sculpture section ranges from antiquity to works of the most significant European and American contemporaries.

The National Museum of History and Technology has exhibits illustrating American culture, civil and military history, and the history of science and technology. The museum consists of 3 floors of exhibitions, and food facilities for its visitors. In the rotunda the visitor will find the original Star-Spangled Banner and a Foucault pendulum demonstrating the earth's rotation. Other major exhibits feature gowns of the first ladies, the Petroleum Hall, the history of transportation, American political and military history, numismatics, philately, ceramics and glass, musical instruments, timekeeping, physical and medical sciences, graphic arts, electricity, photography, and news reporting. National treasures on display include the desk on which Thomas Jefferson drafted the Declaration of Independence and Samuel Morse's first telegraph. A popular attraction is an authentic 19th century country store-post office where mail is hand-stamped with a "Smithsonian Station" postmark.

The National Museum of Natural History serves as a national and international center for the natural sciences. It maintains the largest reference collection in the nation and conducts a broad program of basic research on man, plants, animals, fossil organisms, rocks, minerals, and materials from outer space. Exhibits show aspects of life and cultures in Asia, Africa, and the Pacific. Other exhibits include fossil plants and invertebrate animals, fishes, amphibians, dinosaurs, primitive reptiles and archaeology of the Americas, osteology, physical anthropology, geology, the World of Mammals, the Hall of Birds, the Fenykovi Elephant, and the Hall of Gems and Minerals, including the 44$^1/_2$-carat blue Hope diamond and the largest gem emerald on public exhibit, the 858-carat Gachala emerald.

The National Air and Space Museum. Pending new construction, the Arts and Industries building and the temporary Air and Space building house the historic Wright Brothers' airplanes, Charles A. Lindbergh's "Spirit of St. Louis," spacecrafts of John Glenn and Alan Shepard, the Apollo 11 command module which carried Armstrong, Collins and Aldrin to the moon and back, and other significant air and space artifacts. The Arts and Industries building housing famous air and space firsts will be closed after Labor Day 1975 for renovation. When it reopens in the spring of 1976, it will house items of the Centennial Exhibition of 1876 era. The new Air and Space building is due to open July 4, 1976, between 5th and 7th Streets on the Mall.

The National Collection of Fine Arts opened its doors in 1968 in the renovated Old Patent Office Building, noted for its classical Greek architecture. In addition to its Two-Century Survey of American Art, there are special and loan exhibits of American sculpture, painting, and graphics. **The Renwick Gallery,** a division of the National Collection of Fine Arts, is a new national showcase for creativity in design, crafts, and the decorative arts. Two permanent public rooms, restored and furnished in styles of the post-Civil War period, and special temporary exhibitions can be seen in the renovated building.

The National Portrait Gallery, also located in the Old Patent Office Bldg., exhibits the likenesses of persons who have made significant contributions to the history, development, and culture of the people of the United States.

The National Zoological Park is noted for its outstanding collections including two giant pandas from China. Its research includes investigation in animal behavior, ecology, nutrition and reproduction physiology, pathology, and clinical medicine. Conservation-oriented studies cover maintenance of wild population and long-term captive breeding and care of endangered species.

The Smithsonian Associates was founded to stimulate interest and active participation in the Smithsonian's work. Its membership programs for adults and young people include seminars, lectures, workshops, demonstrations, concerts, theater, exhibition previews, dramas, films, tours, and field and camping trips. *Smithsonian*, a monthly magazine of the arts, sciences, and history is available to members of the Associates.

The Smithsonian Institution Traveling Exhibition Service (SITES) organizes and circulates exhibitions for art and science museums, colleges, and other educational institutions around the United States and Canada. More than one hundred twenty-five exhibitions are on continuous tour, with fifty or sixty openings of these shows occurring monthly across the country.

Washington National Monument

The Washington National Monument is a tapering shaft or obelisk of white marble, 555 ft., 5 1/8 inches in height and 55 ft., 1 1/2 inches square at base. Eight small windows, 2 on each side, are located at the 500-ft. level, where Washington points of interest are indicated.

The capstone weighs 3,300 lbs. and was placed Dec. 6, 1884. The monument was dedicated Feb. 21, 1885, and opened Oct. 9, 1888. It weighs 81,120 tons. It is dressed with white Maryland marble in 2-ft. courses. The first 150 ft. are backed by rubble masonry. From that point to 452 ft. Maine granite was used as backing, and above 452 ft. marble was used. The face of the monument is primarily marble from Maryland. Set into the interior wall are 190 memorial stones from states, foreign countries, and organizations. An iron stairway has 50 landings and 898 steps. A modern elevator takes sightseers to the 500-ft. level in one minute, compared with 12 "precarious minutes" in 1888.

The erection of the monument by the Washington National Monument society with funds obtained by popular subscription was authorized by Congress in 1848. The cornerstone was laid July 4 of the same year. Work progressed slowly until 1854 when $300,000 had been subscribed and 152 ft. of the shaft erected. In that year the enterprise became controversial and contributions ceased. Work was resumed in 1880 at government expense by the Corps of Engineers.

The Monument is open 7 days a week, 9 a.m. to 5 p.m. Extended summer hours are 8 a.m. to 12 midnight. It is closed Christmas Day.

Famous Churches

The National Shrine of the Immaculate Conception, at Fourth St. and Michigan Ave., NE, Washington, D. C. is the largest Catholic church in the United States and one of the largest in the world. Built by all the bishops and Catholics of the U.S. it honors the Blessed Virgin Mary as Patroness of the United States. The Shrine is impressive not only in size but also in beauty, its blue and gold dome and soaring bell-tower having become Washington landmarks. Open daily from 7 a.m. to 8 p.m., Sunday masses, 7, 8, 9, 10, 11 a.m. and noon, 1:15 and 4:30 p.m. Free guided tours 9 a.m. to 5 p.m. daily; Sunday tours 2 p.m. to 4 p.m. Carillon concerts on Sundays and preceding organ and choral concerts. Organ recitals every Sun. at 7:00 p.m. (June through August) and 4th Friday organ recitals (Sept. through May).

Washington Cathedral, Massachusetts and Wisconsin Aves., NW, is atop Mt. Saint Alban, the highest point in Washington, D.C. It is the seat of the Presiding Bishop of the Episcopal Church and of the Bishop of Washington. Started in 1907, the cathedral is nearly complete. The nave will be finished and opened in 1976, with a festive dedicatory ceremony to take place June 6, Pentecost Sunday. The west facade will be completed by 1980. When complete it will be the 6th largest cathedral in the world. Notables buried in the cathedral include Woodrow Wilson, Adm. George Dewey, Cordell Hull, and Frank B. Kellogg. The cathedral is considered one of the finest examples of Gothic architecture in the country.

Several Protestant churches commemorate the association of presidents with their congregations. **St. John's Episcopal Church,** across Lafayette Sq. from the White House, designed by Benj. Latrobe in 1815, was regularly attended by Madison and F. D. Roosevelt and at times by other presidents. **New York Ave. Presbyterian Church,** 1313 New York Ave., NW, preserves the pew in which Lincoln sat, also an original manuscript of the first draft of his first proposal to abolish slavery. The church was rebuilt on same site in 1950-51.

The new National Presbyterian Church, on a 13-acre tract, at Nebraska Ave. and Van Ness St., NW, was dedicated on May 10, 1970. The Church traces its origin to a group of stonemasons who met in a carpenter's shop in the grounds of the White House in 1795, later becoming the First Presbyterian Church in the District of Columbia. The Church of the Covenant, founded in 1883, united with the original Presbyterian body in 1930 to become the congregation of the National Presbyterian Church. President Eisenhower was baptized by the pastor, Dr. Edward L. R. Elson, and became a member of the Church on Feb. 1, 1953. He laid the cornerstone of the new Church on his 77th birthday, Oct. 14, 1967, and the Chapel of the Presidents is dedicated to him. The Chapel of the Presidents contains the Eisenhower pew, and pews representing 16 additional presidents who worshipped with the congregation. The oldest president's pew, occupied by Jackson, Polk, Pierce, Buchanan and Cleveland, is on view together with much historic memorabilia.

The Islamic Center, 2551 Massachusetts Ave, NW, a magnificent monument of Islamic culture and outstanding landmark for visitors, a mosque for worship, and an institute for study of Islamic culture.

Cherry Blossom Time

Cherry blossom time in Washington is looked upon as the opening of spring. The famous cherry trees encircle the Tidal Basin in West Potomac Park and for 2 miles line the roadside in East Potomac Park. A gift by the Mayor of Tokyo to the city of Washington, the original 3,000 trees were propagated from the trees on the Arawaka River in a suburb of Tokyo. The first trees were planted by Mrs. William Howard Taft, wife of the president, and by Viscountess Chinda, wife of the Japanese Ambassador, Mar. 27, 1912. Today many of the 650 trees around the Tidal Basin have white blossoms, while some have pink; deep pink blossoms are in East Potomac Park. The trees usually are in full blossom the first week in April, but no precise date can be given earlier than 10 days prior to full blossom, which lasts about one week.

Other Points of Interest

Pan American Union Building, 17th St. and Constitution Ave., NW, houses the General Secretariat of the Organization of American States, the oldest major international organization in the world, representing 24 countries of the western hemisphere. Of traditional Spanish architecture with a tropical garden courtyard, the building is one of the more gracious sights in Washington. It contains the Hall of the Americas assembly room, permanent and temporary exhibits of Latin American art, the Columbus Memorial Library, and behind the building, the Aztec Gardens.

National Society, Daughters of the American Revolution on a block bounded by 17th and 18th Sts., and C and D Sts. NW.

American National Red Cross, 17th and D Sts. NW, occupies three white marble buildings of neoclassic design, embellished with a Corinthian portico, colonnades, and bronze doors. The Red Cross Museum is in the east building.

Federal Reserve Building, Constitution Ave., between 20th and 21st Sts. NW, is a 4-story white marble building of Georgian design, with formal gardens and fountains, and tasteful but relatively simple interiors, built 1937. An annex, the William McChesney Martin Building, was occupied in 1974.

The Corcoran Gallery of Art, 17th St. between New York Ave., and E St. NW, Washington, was donated by William Wilson Corcoran in 1859. Other donors, including Sen. W. A. Clark, have augmented its collection. The gallery is open 11 a.m. to 5 p.m. Tuesday through Sunday; closed Mondays, and on Jan. 1, July 4, Thanksgiving, and Dec. 24, 25, and 31. Admission is $1.00; free on Tues. and Weds. and at all times to senior citizens, children under 12 accompanied by an adult, and clergy; 50 cents to students with I.D., and military, EA rank and below.

New York City Museums, Libraries, Centers of Interest

See Index for Statue of Liberty

The New York Aquarium, in Coney Island, exhibits marine life from all climes, with over 3,000 live specimens including whales, sharks, seals, sea lions, fish, penguins; whale and dolphin training sessions.

The New York Botanical Garden occupies 230 acres in the Bronx. An 11-greenhouse Main Conservatory features seasonal shows and permanent exhibits of palms, tropical and temperate plants, ferns, orchids. There are specialized gardens, a museum of plant evolution and uses, and a botanical library.

The New York Cultural Center, Columbus Circle, features exhibitions of painting, sculpture, photography, and documentary work, changed periodically. The building was designed by Edward Durrell Stone.

The Frick Collection, 1 E. 70th St., was founded by Henry Clay Frick (1849-1919). The principal part of the collection consists of 14th-19th Century paintings as well as sculpture.

The Solomon R. Guggenheim Museum, 5th Ave. and 89th St.; permanent collection contains over 3,000 paintings, drawings, sculptures, and graphic works by 19th and 20th Century artists. The museum's unique spiral building was designed by Frank Lloyd Wright.

The Hayden Planetarium, facing 81st St. near Central Park W., presents dramatic representations of the skies inside a large hemispheric dome with a Zeiss planetarium projector and other instruments; about 9,000 stars are shown. Also: astronomy, space, weather, time exhibits; Guggenheim Space Theater.

The Hispanic Society of America is a free public museum and reference library devoted to the art and literature of Spain and Portugal. It is on Audubon Terrace, between 155th and 156th Sts., west of Broadway. Collections run from ancient to modern.

The Jewish Museum, 5th Ave. at 92d St., offers exhibitions of Jewish art and ceremonial objects and exhibits of Jewish interest. The permanent collection of Judaica is considered the most comprehensive in the world. There are lectures and a book and print shop.

The Metropolitan Museum of Art, 5th Ave. at 82d St. With over 1 million works of art, the museum's collection is the largest of its kind in the Western Hemisphere. Great masters of all the ages of art are included in the collections; Egyptian, Greek, Roman, Ancient Near Eastern, Islamic, Far Eastern, Medieval, Arms and Armor, European, Pre-Columbian, American, Contemporary Arts, Musical Instruments, Costume Institute, and Junior Museum. A new American Bicentennial Wing is to be completed in 1976.

The Cloisters, in Manhattan's Fort Tryon Park, is a branch of the Metropolitan devoted to Medieval art and architecture in 5 cloisters and other early European structures.

The Museum of the American Indian, Heye Foundation, Broadway at 155th St., maintains the world's largest collection of American Indian materials, extensive archeological and ethnological displays from North, Central, and South America, as well as study and photographic facilities.

The Museum of Modern Art, 11 W. 53d St., est. 1929, presents 20th Century painting, sculpture, drawings, prints, architectural and industrial design, photography, and film. A library contains about 30,-000 vols. and a reference collection of more than 100,-000 photographs. The film department has more than 12 million ft. of film. Bookstore, restaurant, and gift shop.

The American Museum of Natural History occupies a group of buildings at Central Park West between 77th and 81st Sts. There are large exhibits of man and beast from the most primitive times to the present,

with extensive reconstruction of fossilized remains, dioramas of men and animals in their natural settings, dinosaurs, birds, Indians, Eskimos, and glass models of protozoa, rotifers, and coelenerates. The collections of gems and ocean life are famous. Visitors may handle artifacts in the People Center.

The Museum of the City of New York on 5th Ave. at 104th St., illustrates the history and life of the city. Its collections include dioramas, paintings, prints, maps, photographs, portraits, miniatures, vehicles, ship models, costumes, silver, furniture, theatrical and musical memorabilia, toys, and rare books.

The New-York Historical Society, founded 1804, is at 170 Central Park W. between 76th and 77th Sts. The society maintains a museum devoted to Americana; a large gallery of American portrait, landscape, and genre paintings; a reference library of American, and especially New York, history; manuscripts from all periods of the nation's past; maps, prints, broadsides, and photographs. Of special interest are the original weater color drawings by John James Audubon for his *Birds of America*. Also, fire engine, carriage, toy collections.

The American Numismatic Society, founded 1858, maintains a museum of coins and other currency, ancient and modern medals, and decorations at Broadway and 156th St.

The New York Public Library: In 1974, its resources were placed at more than 34.5 million items of which over 9 million were books, over 10 million manuscripts, over 6 million pictures, 3.5 million posters, photographs, and broadsides, 6 million pamphlets, scrapbooks, and clippings. Of this total, 4 million books and the pictures are in the collections of the Branch Libraries which are maintained by N.Y. City and which operate 83 branch libraries in Manhattan, the Bronx and Staten Island and 6 bookmobiles. The Research Libraries, based at 5th Ave. and 42d St., include the Performing Arts Research Center, in Lincoln Center, and the Schomburg Center for Research in Black Culture, 103 W. 135th St.

Seamen's Church Institute, facing Manhattan's Battery Park, has dining room, cafeteria, collections of ships' bells and models, marine paintings, gym, sauna, and showers, all open to public.

South Street Seaport Museum, on the East River waterfront in lower Manhattan, is a growing restoration of earlier eras of New York's port. At piers off South St. at Fulton, the museum has 8 ships, including an iron-hulled windjammer, a Hudson River steamboat, and the original Ambrose Lightship. Ashore on Fulton St. are museum galleries, a 19th Century printshop, and a bookshop. Special features include puppet and craft shows, songfests, plays for children and adults, and seminars on nautical subjects. Restorations will include 100 early buildings with art shops, apartments, offices, restaurants.

The Staten Island Institute of Arts and Sciences, founded 1881, has a museum of art, natural science, conservation, and Indian life at 75 Stuyvesant Pl., St. George, S.I., and library at 51 Stuyvesant Pl. It offers lectures and classes for children and adults.

Whitney Museum of American Art, Madison Ave. at 75th St., holds exhibitions of group and individual artists, historical and contemporary. Comprehensive permanent collection of American art.

Zoos. One of the world's largest zoos is the N.Y. Zoological Park (the Bronx Zoo), Pelham Parkway and Southern Blvd., the Bronx. About 3,000 mammals, birds, reptiles are displayed in its 252 acres, including African Plains exhibit, World of Birds, Children's Zoo. The city's Parks Administration runs the Central Park Zoo and the adjoining Children's Zoo at 5th Ave. and 64th St. in Manhattan, the Prospect Park Zoo and Children's Farmyard in Brooklyn, and the Queens Zoo and Children's Farm in Flushing Meadows-Corona Park, Queens. The Staten Island Zoological Society operates the Staten Island Zoo and Children's Zoo in Barrett Park, West New Brighton.

Brooklyn Centers

Brooklyn Academy of Music, 30 Lafayette Ave., presents a Sept.-through-May program of music, dance, theater, and film.

Brooklyn Botanic Garden, Eastern Parkway, Washington and Flatbush Aves., has 50 acres of gardens, including rose, herb, wild flower, and Japanese, and a fragrance garden for the blind.

The Brooklyn Museum, Eastern Parkway and Washington Ave., estab. 1897, has comprehensive exhibitions in all major fields of art. An Outdoor Sculpture Garden contains ornaments from razed N.Y. area buildings.

The Brooklyn Public Library occupies the Ingersoll Building, Grand Army Plaza, and 57 branches. The Ingersoll Building has 5 major-subject divisions and Periodicals Division, Audio-Visual section, children's room, and telephone reference service.

Houses of Worship

Central Synagogue (Reform), Lexington Ave. at 55th St., is the oldest Jewish house of worship in N.Y. State (1870), and combines 2 earlier congregations founded in 1839 and 1846. Its modern community house, 123 E. 55th St., includes a religious school, chapel, meeting rooms. Since 1934, the synagogue has presented the weekly Message of Israel program on a nationwide radio network.

John Street United Methodist Church, 44 John St., erected 1841, on site of Wesley Chapel of 1768, "first Methodist preaching-house in America," houses oldest Methodist Society, formed 1766. Has noontime services for office workers, and a museum.

Marble Collegiate Church (Collegiate Reformed Protestant Dutch), 5th Ave. and W. 29th St., erected 1854, is notable for the preaching by Dr. Norman Vincent Peale.

Plymouth Church of the Pilgrims (Congregational), Orange St., Brooklyn, is a National Historic Site, built 1847, present structure 1849. Has windows illustrating Puritan influence on America and pew where Lincoln sat to hear Henry Ward Beecher, the first minister. In 1860 Beecher raised funds at an auction here to purchase the freedom of a slave girl, Pinky.

Riverside Church (Interdenominational-American Baptist and United Church of Christ), Riverside Drive and W. 122d St. The chief donor was John D. Rockefeller Jr. The tower, reminiscent of Chartres, is 100 ft. square, rises 392 ft.

Russian Orthodox Cathedral of the Transfiguration (Orthodox Church in America), 228 N. 12th St., Brooklyn, is of a design similar to Moscow's Cathedral of the Assumption, with 5 onion-shaped domes. A screen of icons includes one from the 13th Century.

Cathedral of St. John the Divine on Morningside Heights, Amsterdam Ave. and W. 112th St. (Episcopal), was begun 1892 as a Romanesque building; the design was changed to Gothic. The church is 601 ft. long, 146 ft. wide at nave, and will be 330 ft. wide at transept. Two front towers will rise to over 250 ft.

St. Mark's-in-the-Bowery (Episcopal), 2d Ave. and E. 10th St., originally a chapel built on the farm of Director General Peter Stuyvesant in 1660, rebuilt in 1799. A statue of Stuyvesant in the churchyard was presented by Queen Wilhelmina of the Netherlands in 1915. The church has a modern theater and poetry center.

St. Patrick's Cathedral (Roman Catholic) occupies a block facing 5th Ave., between E. 50th and E. 51st Sts., opposite Rockefeller Center. It was begun in 1858 in granite and marble in a Gothic revival style designed by James Renwick. It was opened in part in 1877 and dedicated May 25, 1879. It has 2 spires, 330 ft. tall, and a 26-ft. rose window. St. Patrick's is the cathedral church of the Archdiocese of N.Y.

St. Paul's Chapel of Trinity Parish (Episcopal), Broadway and Vesey St., is the oldest colonial church edifice in Manhattan. It was opened Oct. 30, 1766. Much of the interior decoration was by L'Enfant, who laid the plans for Washington, D.C. There is a unique collection of 14 Waterford Irish cut glass chandeliers.

St. Peter's Church (Roman Catholic), Barclay and Church Sts., has the form of a Greek temple with large porch, wide steps, granite pillars, erected 1836-38 to replace the original church of 1785 of the first Catholic parish of New York.

St. Thomas Church (Episcopal), 5th Ave. at 53d St., is the 4th church building, consecrated 1916, of a parish founded in 1823. The limestone Gothic edifice was designed by architects Bertram G. Goodhue and Ralph Adams Cram. It has 2 organs; recitals are given Thursdays at noon. It also has the only church-affiliated boarding choir school in the U.S.; choir recitals are given Wednesdays at noon.

St. Vartan Armenian Cathedral (Armenian Church of America), 2d Ave. and 35th St. Steel arches support a gilded, conic dome.

Temple Emanu-El, 5th Ave. and 65th St., was erected 1929 by Congregation Emanu-El (Reform), which dates from 1845. It was built of limestone in early Romanesque style, its auditorium 77 ft. wide by 150 ft. long and 103 ft. high, one of the largest temples in the world. Noteworthy are the high arch at the entrance, the rose window, mosaics, and 6 bronze doors.

Trinity Church (Episcopal) faces Broadway at the head of Wall St. It was built 1841-46 of brown sandstone in perpendicular Gothic, designed by Richard Upjohn, is 78 ft. wide by 202 ft. long. The first church was opened in 1698. In the churchyard are buried Alexander Hamilton, Robert Fulton, Capt. James Lawrence, and Revolutionary soldiers who died in British prisons.

Historic Sites

Castle Clinton, Battery Park, lower Manhattan, is an 1811 fort, restored 1975; historical exhibits.

Edgar Allan Poe Cottage, Grand Concourse and Kingsbridge Rd., Bronx, is a restored cottage, built 1812, in which Poe lived 1846-49, and in which his wife, Virginia Clem, died, 1847.

Federal Hall National Memorial, Wall and Nassau Sts., is a Greek Revival structure of 1842, originally the Custom House, later the U.S. Sub-Treasury. On the site stood the Colonial City Hall and later Federal Hall, where the Stamp Act Congress, Continental and U.S. Congresses met, and George Washington took the oath of office as president.

Fraunces Tavern, Broad and Pearl Sts., was erected 1719 as the DeLancey mansion, acquired 1762 by Samuel Fraunces and operated as the Queen's Head Tavern. The Long Room was the scene of Washington's farewell to his officers, Dec. 4, 1783. It was restored by the Sons of the Revolution in the State of New York and is their headquarters. It contains a Revolutionary War museum and art gallery, free to the public.

General Grant National Memorial (Grant's Tomb), Riverside Dr. and W. 122d St., is a formal Roman-style mausoleum in which Gen. U. S. Grant, 18th president, and Mrs. Grant are buried. The tomb is 165 ft. tall.

The Jumel Mansion, W. 160th St. and Edgecombe Ave., is a 3-story colonial mansion with 4-pillared portico built in 1765 by Col. Roger Morris of the British Army. From Sept. 15-Oct. 19, 1776, it was the headquarters of Gen. George Washington. In 1810 Stephen Jumel bought 63 acres of the property. In 1833, the widowed Mrs. Jumel married Aaron Burr. He lived there briefly.

Washington Square, at the foot of 5th Ave., is the best known landmark of **Greenwich Village,** a colorful community and tourist attraction. Facing the lower end of 5th Ave. is the marble **Washington Arch,** designed by Stanford White to commemorate the centenary of the first inauguration and completed in 1895.

Important Buildings

Battery Park City. On a mile-long, 100-acre site reclaimed from the Hudson River, running north from Battery Park in lower Manhattan, buildings will provide 16,000 housing units, 6 million sq. ft. of office space, a hotel, and entertainment, cultural, shopping, and recreational facilities. Occupancy to begin in 1977.

City Hall, headquarters of the mayor, the City Council, and the Board of Estimate of the City of New York, is in City Hall Park (the original Common), bounded by Broadway, Park Row, and Chambers St. Erected 1803-1812, it is an adaptation of French Renaissance with clock cupola surmounted by a figure of Justice.

The Colisuem, facing Columbus Circle between W. 58th and W. 60th Sts., is New York's principal center for national and international exhibitions. Opened Apr. 28, 1956, it cost about $35 million. The Coliseum has over 320,000 sq. ft. of exhibition space.

Empire State Building, 5th Ave., between W. 33d and 34th Sts., is one of the world's tallest buildings (see also World Trade Center, below), 1,250 ft. high plus a 222-ft. television and FM radio transmitting tower. The building was completed May 1, 1931. More than 1.5 million persons annually visit the 86th and 102d floor observatories. On a clear day viewers can see a distance of 80 mi.

Lincoln Center for the Performing Arts was opened Sept. 23, 1962, with a concert in Philharmonic (later renamed Avery Fisher) Hall. The center is located between W. 62d and 66th Sts., Amsterdam and Columbus Aves. It is a private, nonprofit, tax-exempt corporation of 8 constituent organizations. The New York State Theater opened in 1964; the Vivian Beaumont Theater, for repertory, and the Library-Museum of the Performing Arts, 1965; the Metropolitan Opera House, 1966; the Juilliard School of Music, including Alice Tully Hall, 1969.

Madison Square Garden Center, Pennsylvania Plaza (7th-8th Aves., 31st-33d Sts.), opened in the 1967-68 season. The huge development, above the modernized underground Pennsylvania RR station, includes a 29-story office building and the Sports and Entertainment Center which has the Garden Arena seating over 20,000, the 5,000-seat Felt Forum, 48 bowling lanes, the National Art Museum of Sport, an Exposition Rotunda for trade and walk-around shows, and 500-seat Cinema.

Pan Am Building, north of Grand Central Station, is one of the world's largest commercial office build-

ings. It has 59 floors rising 808 ft., with provision for a rooftop heliport, and was erected over the tracks of Grand Central Terminal. It covers a ground area of 3½ acres. Estimated office population is 17,000.

Rockefeller Center, the largest privately-owned business and entertainment center in America was started Sept., 1931. Its area includes the 3 blocks from 48th to 51st Sts. between 5th Ave. and the Ave. of the Americas, a large portion of the 51st-52d St. block and 4 blockfronts on the west side of the Ave. of the Americas between 47th and 51st Sts. There are 21 buildings. It has 175,000 daily visitors; over 66,000 work there.

The surface area of Rockefeller Center covers 24 acres; almost one half are leased for a long period from Columbia University. Rockefeller Center pays Columbia an annual rental of nearly $4 million. The lease with options for renewal runs until 2069.

The part of Rockefeller Center comprising theaters and radio and television studios is often referred to as Radio City. Studios of the National Broadcasting Co. are located in the 70-story RCA building (850 ft. tall). There is an observation roof on the 70th Floor.

Radio City Music Hall, Ave. of the Americas and W. 50th St., largest indoor theater in the world, seats 6,000 people. Its stage, 144 ft. wide by 67 ft. deep, has a proscenium arch 60 ft. high and 100 ft. wide. Has first-run films and stage spectacles with the Rockettes, Symphony Orchestra, and guest artists, plus concerts and other special events.

New York Stock Exchange, visitors' entrance 20 Broad St., has visitors' gallery, films, guided tours, Mon. through Fri., 10 a.m. to market closing.

American Stock Exchange, visitors' entrance 78 Trinity Pl., has visitors' gallery, guides, films and other exhibits, Mon. through Fri. during trading hours.

United Nations Headquarters occupies over 16 acres between 1st Ave. and F.D.R. (East River) Drive, E. 42d and E. 48th Sts. Most unusual is the Secretariat Bldg., 505 ft. high at front entrance, 286 ft. long and only 72 ft. wide. The 2 sides have 5,400 windows; the end walls are of 2,000 tons of Vermont marble. General Assembly Bldg. has a hall 165 ft. long, 115 ft. wide. Conference Bldg. houses 3 Council chambers, etc. There are guided tours daily.

World Trade Center, dedicated Apr. 4, 1973, on Manhattan's lower west side, has twin towers of 110 stories, 1,350 ft. each (2d in height to Chicago's Sears Tower) and 4 other buildings. In 1974, over 28,000 of an eventual 50,000 persons worked in trade firms in the North and South Towers. Construction of this office complex for international trade, a Port Authority of N.Y. and N.J. facility, is to be completed in 1977.

A Guide to Avenue Addresses in New York City

To find the location of a number on the following avenues of Manhattan, cancel the last figure of the number, divide the remainder by 2 and add the given key number. Thus: Where is 596 7th Ave.? Divide 59 by 2 equals 30, plus 12 equals 42d St.

Ave. A......... add	4	Up to 600.... add	18	8th Ave........ add	9	Lenox Ave....... add	110
Ave. B......... add	3	Up to 775.... add	20	9th Ave........ add	13	Lexington Ave... add	22
Ave. C......... add	3	From 775 to 1286		10th Ave........ add	13	Madison Ave..... add	27
Ave.D.......... add	3	see exception below		11th ave........ add	15	Manhattan Ave... add	100
1st Ave........ add	4	Up to 1500... add	45	Amsterdam Ave.. add	59	Park Ave........ add	34
2d Ave......... add	3	Above 2,000... add	24	Audubon Ave.... add	165	Pleasant Ave..... add	101
3d Ave......... add	10	Ave. of Americas (6th Ave.)		Columbus Ave.... add	60	St. Nicholas Ave.. add	110
4th Ave......... add	8	subtract 12 or 13		Convent Ave..... add	127	Wadsworth Ave.. add	175
5th ave. to 200... add	13	7th Ave......... add	12	Edgecomb Ave.... add	134	West End Ave.... add	59
Up to 400.... add	16	Above 1800.. add	20	Ft. Wash. Ave.... add	158		

Exceptions

Broadway: Up to 754 below East 8th St.
Above 754, apply above rule but deduct following key numbers:
From 754 to 858 deduct 29.
From 857 to 958 deduct 25.
Above 1000 deduct 31.

Riverside Drive: Below 567, drop last figure, add 75, do not divide by 2.
Above 577, drop last figure, add 78.
Central Park West: Drop last figure, add 60.
5th Ave.: From 775 to 1286, drop last figure and deduct 18 from remainder.

Street Addresses

From Washington Square north most crosstown streets have 100 numbers to the block. Numbering of these streets starts east and west from 5th Ave.

Notable Tall Buildings in North American Cities

Height from sidewalk to roof, including penthouse and tower if enclosed as integral part of structure; actual number of stories beginning at street level. Asterisks (*) denote buildings still under construction Jan. 1976.

City	Hgt. ft.	Stories
New York City		
World Trade Center (2 towers)	1,350	110
Empire State, 34th St. & 5th Ave	1,250	102
TV tower, 222 ft., makes total	1,472	. .
Chrysler, Lexington Ave. & 43d St.	1,046	77
60 Wall Tower, 70 Pine St	950	67
40 Wall Tower	927	71
Bank of Manhattan	900	71
RCA, Rockefeller Center	850	70
Chase Manhattan Bldg.	813	60
Pan Am Bldg., 200 Park Ave.	808	59
Woolworth, 233 Broadway	792	60
1 Penn Plaza	764	57
U.S. Steel, 165 Broadway	743	50
Citibank	741	57
Exxon, 1251 Ave. of the Americas	735	54
One Astor Plaza	730	54
9 W. 57th St.	725	50
Union Carbide Bldg., 270 Park Ave.	707	52
General Motors Bldg.	705	50
Metropolitan Life, 1 Madison Ave.	700	50
500 5th Ave.	697.	60
Chem. Bank, N.Y. Trust Bldg.	687	50
55 Water St.	686	53
Chanin, Lexington Ave. & 42d St.	680	56
Gulf & Western Bldg., 15 Columbus Circle	679	44
Marine Midland Bldg., 140 Bway.	677	52
McGraw Hill, 1221 Ave. of the Am.	674	51
Lincoln, 60 E. 52d Street	673	53
1633 Broadway	670	50
American Brands, 245 Park Ave.	648	47
Irving Trust, 1 Wall St.	640	50
345 Park Ave.	634	44
Monsanto Bldg., 1114 Ave. of the Am.	630	50
1 New York Plaza	630	50
Home Insurance Co. Bldg.	630	44
1 Dag Hammarskjold Plaza	628	50
Waldorf-Astoria, 301 Park Ave.	625	47
Burlington House, 1345 Ave. of Am.	625	50
Olympic Tower, 643 5th Ave.	620	50
10 E. 40th St.	620	48
General Electric, Lexington Ave.	616	50
New York Life, 51 Madison Ave.	615	40
Penney Bldg., 1301 6th Ave.	609	46
Celanese Bldg., 1211 Ave. of the Am.	592	45
U.S. Court House, 505 Pearl St.	590	37
Federal Bldg., Foley Square	587	41
Time & Life, 1271 Ave. of the Am.	587	47
Cooper Bregstein Bldg., 1250 Bway.	580	40
1185 Ave. of the Americas	580	42
Municipal, Park Row & Centre St.	580	34
1 Madison Square Plaza	576	42
Westvaco Bldg., 299 Park Ave.	574	42
Socony Mobil Bldg., East 42d St.	572	45
Sperry Rand Bldg., 1290 Ave. of Am.	570	43
600 3d Ave.	570	42
N.Y. General, 230 Park Ave.	565	35
1 Bankers Trust Plaza	565	40
30 Broad St.	562	48
Sherry-Netherland, 5th Ave. & 59th St.	560	40
Continental Can, 633 3d Ave.	557	39
Sperry & Hutchinson, 330 Madison	555	39
Galleria, 117 E. 57th St.	552	57
Interchem Bldg., 1133 Ave. of Am.	552	44
919 3d Ave.	550	47
Burroughs Bldg., 605 3d Ave.	550	44
Bankers Trust, 33 E. 48 St.	547	41
Transportation Bldg., 225 Bway.	546	45
Equitable Life, 1285 Ave. of the Am.	540	42
Ritz Tower, Park Ave. & 57th St.	540	41
Bankers Trust, 6 Wall St.	540	39
1166 Ave. of the Americas	540	44
Equitable, 120 Broadway	538	42
1700 Broadway	533	41
Downtown Athletic Club, 19 West St.	530	45
Nelson Towers, 7th Ave. & 34th St.	525	45
Hotel Pierre, 5th Ave. & 61st St.	525	44
House of Seagram, 375 Park Ave.	525	38
Random House, 825 3d Ave.	522	40
3 Park Ave.	522	42
Du Mont Bldg., 515 Madison Ave.	520	42

City	Hgt. ft.	Stories
26 Broadway	520	31
Newsweek Bldg., 444 Madison Ave.	518	43
Sterling Drug Bldg., 90 Park Ave.	515	41
First National City Bank	515	41
Bank of New York, 48 Wall St.	513	32
Navarre, 512 7th Ave.	513	43
Williamsburg Savings Bank, Bklyn.	512	42
ITT—American, 437 Madison Ave.	512	40
International, Rockefeller Center.	512	41
1407 Broadway Realty Corp.	512	44
United Nations, 405 E. 42 St.	505	39
2 New York Plaza	504	40
22 E. 40th St.	503	43
60 Broad St.	503	39
Americana Hotel	501	51
World Apparel Center, 1411 Bway.	501	42
Akron, Ohio		
First National Tower Bldg.	330	28
Cascade, 10 W. Bowery	316	24
Albany, N.Y.		
Office Tower, So. Mall	589	44
State Office Building	388	34
Agency (four bldgs.), So. Mall.	310	23
University Towers	286	22
Atlanta, Ga.		
Peachtree Center Plaza Hotel	721	71
First National Bank, 2 Peachtree	556	44
Equitable Building, 100 Peachtree.	453	34
101 Marietta Tower, 101 Marietta St.	446	36
National Bank of Georgia, 34 Peachtree	439	32
Peachtree Summit #1	406	31
Atlanta Hilton Hotel, 255 Courtland St.	404	30
Tower Place, 3361 Piedmont Road	401	29
Peachtree Center Harris Bldg.	382	31
Southern Bell Telephone.	380	. . .
Trust Company Bank	377	28
Coastal States Insurance, 260 Peachtree	377	27
Peachtree Center Cain Building.	376	30
Peachtree Center Building, 230 Peachtree	374	31
Life of Georgia Tower	371	29
Peachtree Center South, 225 Peachtree	332	27
Gas Light Tower, 235 Peachtree	331	27
Hyatt Regency Hotel, 265 Peachtree.	330	23
100 Colony Square, 1175 Peachtree	328	25
Georgia Power Building, 270 Peachtree	318	22
Fairmont Hotel, 180 14th St.	310	28
400 Colony Square, 1201 Peachtree.	308	23
Atlanta Center Building, 260 Piedmont Ave.	301	23
Merchandise Mart, 240 Peachtree.	300	22
Austin, Tex.		
Austin National Bank	327	26
American Bank	313	21
State Capitol	309	. . .
Univ. of Texas Admin. Bldg.	307	29
J. Frank Dobie Univ. Center.	299	29
Westgate Bldg.	261	24
Baltimore, Md.		
U.S. Fidelity & Guaranty Co.	529	40
Maryland National Bank Bldg.	509	34
World Trade Center Bldg.	405	32
Saint-Paul Apartments Bldg.	385	37
Arlington Federal Savings and Loan Assn. Bldg.	370	28
Blaustein Bldg.	370	30
Charles Plaza Apts. So.	350	31
Charles Center South	330	26
Tower Bldg.	330	16
Baltimore Arts Tower	319	15
First National Bank of Maryland.	315	22

City	Hgt. ft.	Stories
Lord Baltimore Hotel	315	24
Mercantile-Safe Deposit and Trust Co..	315	21
Charles Plaza Apts. No.	315	28
Baltimore Hilton Hotel.	302	29
One Charles Center Bldg.	301	24
Baltimore Gas and Electric Co. Bldg...	300	22
Chesapeake & Potomac Telephone Co..	300	16

Baton Rouge, La.

State Capitol	460	34
American Bank Bldg.	310	25
Hilton Hotel	290	28
La. Natl. Bank Bldg.	277	21

Birmingham, Ala.

First Natl. Southern Natural Bldg....	390	30
South Central Bell Hdqts. Bldg.	390	30
City Federal Bldg.	325	27
Cabana Motel	287	21
Daniel Bldg.	283	20

Boston, Mass.

John Hancock Tower	790	60
Prudential Tower.	750	52
Boston Co. Bldg., Court St.	601	41
First National Bank of Boston.	591	37
Employers Commercial Union Co's...	507	40
New England Merch. Bank Bldg	500	40
U.S. Custom House.	496	32
John Hancock Bldg.	495	26
State St. Bank Bldg.	477	34
Keystone Custodian Funds.	400	32
State Office Bldg.	350	22
Federal Bldg. & Post Office.	345	22
Suffolk County Courthouse.	330	19
Sheraton-Boston Hotel.	310	29
State Service Center.	300	23

Buffalo, N.Y.

Marine Midland, Main St.	529	40
City Hall.	378	32
Rand Bldg., not incl. 40-ft. beacon	351	29
Erie County Savings Bank, Main St...	350	26
Manuf. & Trades Trust Co.	317	21
Liberty Bank.	305	23
Electric Tower.	294	18

Calgary, Alta.

Calgary Tower.	626	...
Sun Oil Bldg.	397	32
Capitol Plaza.	389	40
Western Centre.	385	40
Two Bow Valley Square.	378	39
Mobil Tower.	362	32
One Palliser Square.	350	28
Place Concorde.	339	37
Mount Royal House.	330	32
International Hotel	321	36
Standard Life Bldg.	316	27
Penthouse Towers.	312	34
Two Calgary Place .	300	28

Charlotte, N.C.

NCNB Plaza, 101 S. Tryon.	503	40
Jefferson First Union Tower	433	32
Wachovia Center, 400 S. Tryon.	420	32
Southern National Center, 1200 S. College	300	22
NCNB Bldg., 200 S. Tryon.	299	18
Bank of NC Bldg., 112 S. Tryon.	280	20

Chicago, Ill.

Sears Tower (World's Tallest).	1,454	110
Standard Oil (Indiana).	1,136	80
John Hancock Center	1,127	100
*Water Tower Plaza.	850	74
First Natl. Bank.	850	60
IBM Bldg.	695	52
Civic Center (City Hall)	662	31
Lake Point Tower.	645	70
Board of Trade, incl. 81 ft. statue	605	44
Prudential Bldg., 130 E. Randolph....	601	41
Antenna tower, 311 ft., makes total	912	...
1000 Lake Shore Plaza Apts.	590	55
Marina City Apts., 2 buildings.	588	61
Mid Continental Plaza.	580	50
Pittsfield, 55 E. Washington St.	557	38

City	Hgt. ft.	Stories
Kemper Insurance Bldg.	555	45
Newberry Plaza, State & Oak	553	56
Harbor Point.	550	54
LaSalle Natl. Bank, 135 S. LaSalle St...	535	44
One LaSalle Street.	530	49
111 E. Chestnut St.	529	56
Pure Oil, 35 E. Wacker Drive.	523	40
United Ins. Bldg., 1 E. Wacker Dr.	522	41
Lincoln Tower, 75 E. Wacker Dr.	519	42
Carbide & Carbon, 230 N. Mich.	503	37
Walton Colonnade.	500	44
Edgewater Beach Apts., 5445 Sheridan	449	39
LaSalle-Wacker, 221 N. LaSalle St.	491	41
Amer. Nat'l. Bank, 33 N. LaSalle St...	479	40
Bankers, 105 W. Adams St.	476	41
Brunswick Bldg.	475	37
Continental Companies.	475	45
American Furniture Mart.	474	24
Sheraton Hotel, 505 N. Mich. Ave.	471	42
Playboy Bldg., 919 N. Mich. Ave.	468	37
188 Randolph Tower.	465	45
Tribune Tower, 435 N. Mich. Ave.	462	36
Equitable Life, 401 N. Michigan	457	35
Roanoke, 11 S. LaSalle St.	452	37

Cincinnati, Ohio

Carew Tower.	574	48
Central Trust Tower.	495	34
Dubois Tower, 5th & Walnut.	423	32
Kroger Bldg.	345	25
U. of Cinn., Sander Hall.	297	27
Terrace Hilton Hotel.	273	19

Cleveland, Ohio

Terminal Tower.	708	52
Erieview Plaza Tower.	529	40
Federal Bldg.	419	32
Cleveland Trust Tower # 1.	383	29
Ohio-Bell Telephone.	365	22
Park Centre.	320	26
Central Natl. Bank Bldg.	305	23
Diamond Shamrock Bldg.	300	23
CEI Bldg.	300	22
Union Commerce Bldg.	289	21
Standard Bldg.	282	21
Crystal Tower.	280	26
East Ohio Bldg.	275	21
Bond Court, 1300 E. 9th.	270	20

Columbus, Ohio

State Office Tower, 30 E. Broad	624	41
LeVeque-Lincoln Tower, 50 W. Broad.	555	47
*Nationwide Plaza.	485	40
Borden Building, 180 E. Broad.	438	34
Columbus Center, 100 E. Broad.	357	26
Ohio Bell Building, 150 E. Gay St.	348	26
*Ohio National Plaza, E. Broad.	317	25
Motorists Building, 471 E. Broad.	297	21
Midland Building, 250 E. Broad.	278	21

Dallas, Tex.

First International Bldg.	710	56
First National Bank	625	52
Republic Bank Tower.	598	50
Southland Life Tower.	550	42
2001 Bryan St.	512	40
Republic Bank Bldg., not incl. 150-ft. ornamental tower	452	36
One Main Place.	445	34
Ling-Tempco-Vought Tower.	434	31
Mercantile Natl. Bank Bldg., not incl. 115-ft. weather beacon.	430	31
Mobil Bldg.	430	31
Fidelity Union Tower.	400	33
Southwestern Bell Toll Bldg.	372	22
Court House & Fedl. Office Bldg.	362	16
Mercantile Dallas Bldg.	360	22
Sheraton Hotel.	352	38
Elm Place, 1005-09 Elm St.	341	22
Main Tower.	336	26
Park Central # 3	327	20
Adolphus Tower.	327	27
Bell Telephone Bldg.	326	23
Davis Bldg.	323	21
Manor House, Bank of Service & Trust.	319	26
Preston Tower.	316	29
Tower Petroleum Bldg.	315	23
Adolphus Hotel.	312	25

City	Hgt. ft.	Stories
Fairmont Hotel.	308	24
Baptist Annuity Center	303	17
Life Bldg.	302	22
Santa Fe Bldg. (1st unit).	300	20

Dayton, Ohio

City	Hgt. ft.	Stories
Winters Bank Bldg.	404	30
Hulman Bldg.	295	23
Knott Bldg.	297	21
Grant-Deneau Bldg.	290	22

Denver, Colo.

City	Hgt. ft.	Stories
Brooks Towers, 1020 15th St.	504	42
First of Denver Plaza.	415	32
Colorado Nat'l. Bank, 17th & Curtis.	389	26
First National Bank	385	28
Security Life Bldg.	384	33
Lincoln Center.	367	30
Western Fed. Savings.	354	27
Colorado State Bank	352	27
Brooks Tower Annex	350	30
D&F Tower	330	20
Prudential Tower Plaza.	322	26
Denver Club Building.	277	23

Des Moines, Iowa

City	Hgt. ft.	Stories
Ruan Center.	457	36
Financial Center, 7th & Walnut.	345	25
Equitable Bldg.	318	19
State Capitol.	275	4

Detroit, Mich.

City	Hgt. ft.	Stories
Detroit Plaza Hotel	748	70
City Natl. Bank Bldg., 637 Griswold.	557	47
Guardian, 500 Griswold.	485	40
*Renaissance Center (4 bldgs.)	479	39
Book Tower, 1227 Wash. Blvd.	472	35
Cadillac Tower, 51 Cadillac Sq.	437	40
David Stott, 1150 Griswold.	436	38
Mich. Cons. Gas Co. Bldg.	430	32
Fisher, W. Grand Blvd. & 2d St.	420	28
J. L. Hudson Bldg.	397	28
McNamara Federal Office Bldg.	393	27
Detroit Bank & Trust Bldg.	370	28
Walker Cisler	365	25
David Broderick Tower	358	34
Buhl, 535 Griswold.	350	26
Michigan Bell Telephone	340	19
1st Federal Savings & Loan Assn.	338	23
Pontchartrain Motor Hotel	336	23
Michigan Bell Telephone.	327	17
Commonwealth Bldg.	325	25
1300 Lafayette East.	325	30
First National Bldg.	319	25
City-County Bldg.	317	20
The Executive Plaza, 1200 6th Ave.	313	21
Sheraton Cadillac Hotel	310	28
Mich. Blue Cross/Blue Shield.	307	22
The Jeffersonian	305	29

Edmonton, Alta.

City	Hgt. ft.	Stories
AGT Tower, 10020-100 St.	441	34
Edmonton House.	402	45
CN Tower, 1004-104 Ave.	365	26
Edmonton Centre, Tower One.	325	25
Imperial Oil, 10025 Jasper Ave.	272	24

Fort Wayne, Ind.

City	Hgt. ft.	Stories
Ft. Wayne Natl. Bank.	339	26
Lincoln Natl. Bank.	312	23

Fort Worth, Tex.

City	Hgt. ft.	Stories
Ft. Worth Natl. Bank.	454	37
Continental Natl. Bank Bldg.	380	30
Continental Life Ins. Bldg.	282	23
Electric Service Bldg., 800 Main St.	275	20
W. T. Waggoner Bldg.	270	22
Service Life Center.	270	19

Halifax, N.S.

City	Hgt. ft.	Stories
Fenwick Towers.	300	31

Harrisburg, Pa.

City	Hgt. ft.	Stories
State Capitol.	272	6
Presbyterian Apts., 322 N. 2nd Ave.	260	23

Hartford, Conn.

City	Hgt. ft.	Stories
Travelers Ins. Co. Bldg.	527	34
Hartford Plaza.	420	22
Hartford Natl. Bank & Trust.	360	26
One Financial Plaza, 755 Main.	335	26

Honolulu, Hawaii

City	Hgt. ft	Stories
Ala Moana Hotel.	390	38
Pacific Trade Center.	360	30
*Discovery Bay.	350	42
Hemmeter Center.	350	39
Regency Tower, 2525 Date St.	350	42
Yacht Harbor Towers.	350	40
Chateau Waikiki.	349	39
Rainbow Plaza.	348	37
*Royal Kuhio.	346	39
Waipuna.	343	38
The Villa on Eaton Square.	335	37
*Kukui Plaza.	333	33
The Skyrise.	333	38
Diamond Head Vista.	322	35
Reed & Martin Apt. Bldg.	321	36
1350 Ala Moana	309	33
*Mott-Smith Laniloa.	303	34
Ala Moana Bldg.	300	23

Houston, Tex.

City	Hgt. ft	Stories
One Shell Plaza.	714	50
1100 Milam Bldg.	651	47
Exxon Bldg.	606	44
2 Houston Center	570	40
Dresser Tower.	550	40
Pennzoil, 700 Milam	523	36
Entex Bldg.	518	35
Tenneco Bldg.	502	33
Conoco Bldg.	465	32
One Allen Center.	452	34
Gulf Bldg.	428	37
First City Natl. Bank.	410	32
Houston Lighting & Power.	410	27
Neils Esperson Bldg.	409	31
Regency Hyatt Hotel.	401	34
Houston Natural Gas Bldg.	386	28
Bank of the Southwest.	369	24
Sheraton-Lincoln Hotel.	352	28
Two Shell Plaza.	341	26
American General Life.	337	25
Transco.	333	25
609 Fannin Bldg.	325	22
Holiday Inn.	325	30
Capitol Natl. Bank.	320	21
Post Oak Central.	318	25
St. Luke's Hospital.	316	26
500 Jefferson Bldg.	316	21
Marathon Manufacturing Co. Bldg.	313	21
Sterling Bldg.	312	22
Melrose Bldg.	308	21
Chamber of Commerce Bldg.	306	22
Control Data Center.	303	22
First National Life Bldg.	302	22
Prudential Bldg.	300	21
Kellogg Bldg.	300	22

Indianapolis, Ind.

City	Hgt. ft	Stories
Indiana Natl. Bank Tower.	504	37
City-County Bldg.	377	26
Indiana Bell Telephone.	320	20
Blue Cross-Blue Shield Bldg.	302	18
Riley Towers (2 bldgs.).	294	30
Indiana Bell "220" Bldg.	284	20
Monument Circle.	284	
Market Square Office Bldg.	283	20

Jacksonville, Fla.

City	Hgt. ft	Stories
Independent Life & Accident Ins. Co.	535	37
Gulf Life Ins. Co. Bldg.	432	28
Prudential Ins. Co. of America	295	22
Blue Cross-Blue Shield.	287	20
Atlantic National Bank.	278	19

Jersey City, N.J.

Medical Center
(5 bldgs.; 332 ft., 294 ft., 274 ft., (2) 273 ft.)

Kansas City, Mo.

City	Hgt. ft	Stories
Kansas City Power and Light Bldg.	476	32
City Hall.	443	29
Federal Office Bldg.	413	35
Commerce Tower.	402	32

City	Hgt. ft.	Stories
Southwest Bell Telephone Bldg.	394	27
A. T. & T. Long Line Bldg.	331	20
Bryant Bldg.	319	26
Federal Reserve Bldg.	311	21
Holiday Inn	300	28

Las Vegas, Nev.

Las Vegas Hilton	346	30
Landmark Hotel	308	27
Sahara Hotel	294	24
Dunes Hotel	277	24

Little Rock, Ark.

First National Bank	454	33
Worthen Bank & Trust	375	28
Union National Bank	331	24
Tower Bldg.	300	18

Los Angeles, Calif.

United Cal.Bank	858	62
Security Pacific Natl. Bank	738	55
Atlantic Richfield Plaza (2 bldgs.)	699	52
Crocker-Citizen Plaza	620	42
Theme Towers (2 Bldgs.)	571	44
Union Bank Square	516	41
City Hall	454	28
Equitable Life Bldg.	454	34
Occidental Life Bldg.	452	32
Mutual Benefit Life Ins. Bldg.	435	31
Broadway Plaza	414	33
1900 Ave. of Stars	398	27
1 Wilshire Bldg.	395	28
Calif. Fed. Savings & Loan Bldg.	363	28
Century City Office Bldg.	363	24
Bunker Hill Towers	349	32
International Industries Plaza	347	24
City Natl. Bank Bldg.	344	24
Wilshire West Plaza	327	24
Luxury Towers	316	27
Getty Realty Bldg.	312	22
Water & Power Bldg.	310	20
6312 Wilshire Office Bldg.	307	21
Los Angeles Fed. Savings Bldg.	306	22
Barrington Plaza Bldg.	300	25

Louisville, Ky.

First Natl. Bank	512	40
Citizen's Plaza	420	30
Galt House	325	25
Louisville Trust Bldg.	312	24
800 Apartments Bldg.	290	29

Memphis, Tenn.

100 N. Main Bldg.	430	37
Commerce Square	396	31
Sterick Bldg.	365	31
Clark, 5100 Poplar	365	32
First Natl. Bank Bldg.	332	25
Lowenstein's Towers	296	25
Lincoln American Life Tower	290	22
White Station Tower	280	24

Miami, Fla.

One Biscayne Corp.	456	40
First Federal Savings & Loan	375	32
Dade County Court House	357	28
Ferre Bldg.	340	30
Flagler Center Bldg.	318	25
Brickell Bay Club	286	29
Palm Bay Club	279	24
Wimbledon Racquet Club	275	24

Milwaukee, Wis.

First Wisc. Center & Office Tower	625	42
City Hall	350	9
Wisconsin Telephone Co.	313	19
Marine Plaza Bldg.	288	22
Allen-Bradley Co.	280	17
Marshall & Ilsley Bank	277	21
Regency House Apts.	274	27
Prospect Towers Apts.	268	23
Juneau Village Apts.	265	28
Marc Plaza Hotel	265	24
Carl Sandburg Dorm. (U. of Wisc.)	264	26
Locust Court Apts.	262	24

City	Hgt. ft.	Stories
Minneapolis, Minn.		
IDS Center	772	57
Foshay Tower, not including 163-ft. antenna tower	447	32
Hennepin County Government Center	403	24
First Natl. Bank Bldg.	366	28
Municipal Building	355	14
North Western Bell Telephone	350	26
Cedar-Riverside	337	39
Dane Tower	311	26
Midwest Federal Savings & Loan	276	20
Batzli Apts.	266	23
River Towers Apts.	260	27

Montreal, Que.

Place Victoria	624	47
Place Ville Marie	616	49
Canadian Imperial Bank of Commerce	580	45
Le Complexe Desjardins		
La Tour du Sud	498	40
La Tour du L'Est	428	32
La Tour du Nord	355	27
Chateau Champlain	480	38
CIL House	429	32
Royal Bank	397	22
Sun Life	390	26
Banque Canadienne National	390	32
Place du Canada	372	33
Alexis Nihon Plaza	331	33
Bell Telephone	324	22
Le Cartier Apts.	320	32

Nashville, Tenn.

Natl. Life & Acc. Ins. Co.	452	31
Nashville Life & Casualty Tower	409	30
First American Natl. Bank	354	28
Hyatt Regency	300	28
Third Natl. Bank Bldg.	292	20
Andrew Jackson State Office Bldg.	286	17

Newark, N. J.

National Newark & Essex Bank	465	36
Raymond-Commerce	448	36
Prudential Corporate Bldg.	369	27
Western Electric Bldg.	359	31
Gateway 1, tower	355	30
Prudential Insurance Company	353	21
American Insurance Company	326	21
N. J. Bell Telephone Co.	275	21
Gateway 2, Western Electric	272	20
Mutual Benefit Life Ins. Co.	271	18

New Haven, Conn.

Knights of Columbus Hqs.	320	24

New Orleans, La.

One Shell Square	697	51
Plaza Tower	531	45
Marriott Hotel	450	42
Bank of New Orleans	438	31
Int'l. Trade Mart Bldg.	407	33
225 Baronne St.	362	28
Hibernia Bank Bldg.	355	23
American Bank Bldg.	330	23
Canal LaSalle Bldg.	288	24
Charity Hospital of Louisiana	279	19
Lykes Center, 300 Poydras	276	22

Oakland, Cal.

Ordway Bldg., 2150 Valdez St.	404	28
Kaiser Bldg.	390	28
Clorox Bldg.	330	24
City Hall	319	15
Tribune Tower	305	21
United Calif. Bank Bldg.	297	18
Blue Cross Bldg.	296	21
Telephone Bldg.	289	15
565 Bellevue Apts.	270	25

Oklahoma City, Okla.

Liberty Tower	500	36
First National Bank	493	33
City National Bank Tower	440	32
Kerr-McGee Center	393	30
Fidelity Plaza	310	15
Southwestern Bell Telephone	303	15
Hotel Oklahoma	298	24
The Regency Tower	288	25

City	Hgt. ft.	Stories
Omaha, Neb.		
Woodmen Tower	469	30
Northwestern Bell Telephone Hdqrs...	334	16
Masonic Manor	320	22
First Natl. Bank	295	22
Mutual of Omaha	269	13
Ottawa, Ont.		
Place de Ville, Tower C	368	29
Place Bell Canada	318	26
DBS Tower	308	26
Holiday Inn	308	28
Parliament Bldgs., Peace Tower	291	
Skyline Hotel	286	25
Dept. of National Defense	261	22
Philadelphia, Pa.		
City Hall Tower, incl. 37-ft.		
statue of Wm. Penn	548	7
1818 Market St.	500	40
Fidelity Mutual Life Ins. Bldg.	490	38
Phila. Saving Fund Society	490	39
Central Penn Natl. Bank	490	36
Center Square	490	38, 40
Industrial Valley Bank Bldg.	482	32
Philadelphia National Bank	475	25
2000 Market St. Bldg.	435	29
Fidelity Bank Bldg.	410	30
Two Girard Plaza	404	30
Lewis Tower, 15th & Locust	397	33
Fifteen Hundred Locust	390	44
Philadelphia Electric Co.	384	27
Penn Mutual Life	375	20
The Drake, 15th & Spruce	375	33
Medical Tower, 255 So. 17th	364	33
State Bldg., 1400 Spring Garden	351	18
Packard, 15th & Chestnut	340	25
Inquirer Building	340	18
Dorchester	339	32
Transportation Centre	336	18
Land Title, Broad & Chestnut	331	22
Suburban Station Bldg.	330	21
Edison, 9th & Sansom	325	23
Penn Towers	320	31
1 East Penn Square	319	24
Architects, 17th & Sansom	316	24
1500 Walnut Street	313	23
Rittenhouse Towers	312	28
Society Hill Towers	309	32
1616 Walnut Street	309	25
Sheraton Hotel, (incl. tower)	307	21
Kennedy House	306	29
Mutual Benefit Bldg.	304	20
Hopkinson House	301	35
1528 Walnut St.	300	21
Phoenix, Ariz.		
Valley National Bank	483	40
Arizona Bank Downtown	407	31
First National Bank	372	27
First Federal Savings Bldg.	341	26
Regency Apts.	297	21
*Hyatt-Regency Hotel.	281	21
Del Webb TowneHouse	280	23
United Bank Square	272	20
Del Webb Bldg.	271	17
Pittsburgh, Pa.		
U.S. Steel Bldg.	841	64
Gulf, 7th Ave. and Grant St.	582	44
University of Pittsburgh	535	42
Mellon Bank Bldg.	520	41
1 Oliver Plaza	511	39
Grant, Grant St. at 3rd Ave.	485	40
Koppers, 7th Ave. and Grant.	475	34
Equibank Bldg.	445	34
Pittsburgh National Bldg.	424	30
Alcoa Bldg., 425 Sixth Ave.	410	30
Westinghouse Bldg.	355	23
Oliver, 535 Smithfield St.	347	25
Gateway Bldg. No. 3	344	24
Smithfield Plaza	341	26
Federal Bldg., 1000 Liberty Ave.	340	23
Bell Telephone, 416 7th Ave.	339	21
Hilton Hotel	333	22
Frick, 437 Grant St.	330	20

City	Hgt. ft.	Stories
301 Fifth Ave.	322	24
Washington Plaza Apts.	300	23
Commonwealth, 316 Fourth Ave.	300	21
Portland, Ore.		
First Natl. Bank of Oregon	538	41
Georgia Pacific Bldg.	367	27
Providence, R.I.		
Industrial National Bank	420	26
Rhode Island Hospital Trust Tower	408	30
First Hartford Realty Corp.	301	23
Richmond, Va.		
First & Merchants Natl. Bank	313	26
City Hall	310	18
Central National Bank Bldg.	282	24
First National Bank Bldg.	262	19
Fidelity Bankers Life	261	23
Rochester, N.Y.		
Xerox Tower	443	30
Lincoln First Tower	390	26
Eastman Kodak Bldg.	360	19
First Federal Bank Bldg.,		
28 E. Main St.	305	22
Marine Midland Bank Bldg.	280	22
St. Louis, Mo.		
Gateway Arch	630	
Mercantile Trust Bldg.	485	35
Laclede Gas. Bldg., 8th & Olive.	400	34
S. W. Bell Telephone Bldg.	398	31
Civil Courts	387	13
Queeny Tower	321	19
Counsil House Plaza	320	27
Park Plaza Hotel	310	30
Pierre Laclede Tower	309	24
Riverfront Inn, 3rd St.	301	30
Pet, Inc. Bldg.	300	22
Riverfront Holiday Inn	290	28
Mansion House	285	28
500 Broadway	282	22
Inn of the Spanish Pavilion	280	23
Continental Bldg.	277	23
Railroad Exchange Bldg.	277	21
University Club Bldg.	276	23
77 Bonhomme Bldg.	275	25
Boatman's Bank Tower	275	22
Equitable Bldg.	275	21
Lennox Hotel	275	25
Boatmen's Tower	275	22
Park Tower Apts.	270	24
St. Paul, Minn.		
First Natl. Bank Bldg., incl.		
100-ft. sign	517	32
Osborn Bldg.	368	20
Kellogg Square Apts.	366	32
Northwestern Bell Telephone Bldg.	340	15
American National Bank Bldg.	335	25
St. Paul Cathedral	307	
U.S. Post Office Bldg.	274	12
St. Paul Hilton Hotel.	273	24
City Hall & Court House	261	18
Salt Lake City, Utah		
L.D.S. Church Office Bldg.	420	30
Beneficial Life Tower	351	27
City & County Bldg.	290	
State Capitol	285	
Univ. Club Bldg.	277	24
Kennecott Bldg.	267	18
San Antonio, Tex.		
Tower of the Americas	622	
Tower Life	404	30
Nix Professional Bldg.	375	23
Natl. Bank of Commerce	310	24
First Natl. Bank Tower.	302	20
Frost Bank Tower	300	21
Alamo National Bldg.	288	23
Milam Bldg.	280	20
San Diego, Cal.		
So. Calif. First Natl. Bank Bldg.	388	27
Crocker Natl. Bank Bldg.	340	25

City	Hgt. ft.	Stories
Financial Square	339	24
*Central Federal	320	22
Union Bank	320	22
Little America Westgate Hotel	303	19
San Diego Gas & Electric Bldg.	293	21
Charter Oil Bldg.	281	23
Security Pacific Natl. Bank Bldg.	278	18
Home Tower	278	18

San Francisco, Cal.

City	Hgt. ft.	Stories
Transamerica Pyramid	853	48
Bank of America	778	52
Spear St. Tower	580	46
Security Pacific Bank	569	45
Wells Fargo Bldg.	561	43
Standard Oil, 575 Market St.	551	39
Aetna Life	529	38
First & Market Bldg.	529	38
Metropolitan Life	524	38
Hilton Hotel	493	46
Pacific Gas & Electric	492	34
Union Bank	487	37
Pacific Insurance	476	34
Hartford Bldg.	465	33
Mutual Benefit Life	438	32
Russ Bldg.	435	31
Telephone Bldg.	435	26
*Embarcadero Center, No. 3	412	31
Levi Strauss	412	31
Calif. State Automobile Assn.	399	29
Alcoa Bldg.	398	27
St. Francis Hotel	395	32
Steuart St. Tower	393	31
Shell Bldg.	386	29
Great Western Savings	359	26
Union Square Hyatt House Hotel	355	35
Equitable Life Bldg.	355	25
Fox Plaza	354	29
International Bldg.	350	22
450 Sutter Street	343	26
Cathedral Apartments	340	21
Royal Towers	330	24
Fairmont Hotel	330	29
Bechtel Bldg.	327	23
Standard Oil Bldg.	327	22

Seattle, Wash.

City	Hgt. ft.	Stories
Seattle-1st Natl. Bank Bldg.	609	50
Space Needle	605	
Bank of Calif., 900 4th Ave.	536	42
Rainer Bank Tower, 4th & Univ.	536	40
L. C. Smith Bldg.	500	42
Federal Office Bldg.	487	37
Pacific Northwest Bell	480	33
Washington Plaza Hotel	397	40
Financial Center	389	40
Safeco Ins. Co. of America	325	22
Northern Life Tower	314	27
Norton Bldg.	310	21
Pacific Bldg.	298	22
Washington Bldg.	289	21
Exchange Bldg.	275	23
IBM Bldg.	272	20
Park Place	270	21
Plaza 600	270	20

Syracuse, N.Y.

City	Hgt. ft.	Stories
State Tower	315	22
Mony Office Bldg.	268	19
Carrier Tower	268	19

Tampa, Fla.

City	Hgt. ft.	Stories
First Financial Tower	458	36
Exchange Natl. Bldg.	280	22

Toledo, Ohio

City	Hgt. ft.	Stories
Owens-Corning Fiberglas Tower	400	30
Owens Illinois Bldg.	368	27
Toledo Trust Bldg.	288	23

Toronto, Ont.

City	Hgt. ft.	Stories
CN Tower, world's tallest self-supporting structure	1815	. . .
First Canadian Place	935	72
Commerce Court	784	57
Toronto-Dominion Bank Tower (TD Centre)	740	56
Royal Trust Tower (TD Centre)	600	46
Manufacturers Life Centre	545	51
Royal Bank Plaza—South Tower	480	41
Bank of Commerce	476	34
Four Seasons-Sheraton Hotel	470	43
Simpson Tower	470	33
390 Bay St.	452	33
Two Bloor St. West	450	34
Two Bloor St. East	440	37
Harbour Castle Hotel	438	38
Commercial Union Tower (TD Centre)	420	32
Royal York Hotel	407	28
Harbour Square Apts.	403	34
Leaside Towers Apts.	387	43
Yonge-Eglinton Centre	380	30
100 Bloor St. West	370	29
Hyatt Regency Hotel	365	31
York Centre	360	27
Summerhill Square Apts.	354	37
Hotel Toronto	350	28
Bloor-Islington Square	350	23
MacDonald Block	349	24
Sutton Place Hotel	340	32
Richmond-Adelaide Centre	340	26

Tulsa, Okla.

City	Hgt. ft.	Stories
National Bank of Tulsa	667	50
1st National Tower	516	41
4th Natl. Bank of Tulsa	412	32
National Bank of Tulsa	400	24
Cities Service Bldg.	388	28
Univ. Club Tower	377	32
Philtower	343	23

Vancouver, B.C.

City	Hgt. ft.	Stories
Vancouver Square	586	32
Royal Bank Centre	468	37
Scotiabank Bldg.	462	36
T-D Bank Tower	410	31
200 Granville Square	403	30
Sheraton-Landmark Hotel	394	41
First Bank Tower	386	30
*Oceanic Plaza	359	26
Hyatt Regency Hotel	357	36
Hotel Vancouver	352	22
Board of Trade Tower	342	26
MacMillan-Bloedel Bldg.	340	28
Guinness Tower	328	23
Marine Bldg.	321	21
Four Seasons Hotel	305	30
Martello Tower	300	31

Wilmington, Del.

City	Hgt. ft.	Stories
Hercules Tower	287	23
American Life Ins. Co. Bldg.	282	21

Winnipeg, Man.

City	Hgt. ft.	Stories
Richardson Bldg., 1 Lombard Place	439	34
55 Nassau St.	354	39
North Star Inn	300	30
1 Evergreen Place	294	32

Winston-Salem, N.C.

City	Hgt. ft.	Stories
Wachovia Bldg.	410	30
Reynolds Bldg.	315	21

Tall Buildings In Other Cities

Figures denote number of stories. Height in feet is in parentheses.

Cape Canaveral, Fla., Vehicle Assembly Bldg., 40 (552); Albuquerque, N.M., National Bldg., 18 (272); Allentown, Pa., Power & Light Bldg., 23 (320); Amarillo, Texas, American Natl. Bank, 33 (374); Bethlehem, Pa., Martin Tower, 21 (332); Charleston, W. Va., Kanawha Valley Bldg., 20 (384); Cuyahoga Falls, Ohio, Cathedral Tower Restaurant, 60 (554); Frankfort, Ky., Capital Plaza Office Tower, 28 (338); Galveston, Tex., American National Ins.,20 (358); Greenville, S.C., Daniel Bldg., 22 (305); Lansing, Mich., Michigan Natl. Tower, 25 (300, not including antenna tower); Lincoln, Neb., State Capital (432); Long Beach, Ca. International Tower, 27 (277); Mobile, Ala., First Natl. Bank, 33 (420); Niagara Falls, Ont., Skylon (520); Norfolk, Va., Va. Natl. Bank, 23 (304); Reading, Pa., Berks County Courthouse (280); So. Bend, Indiana, American National Bank Bldg., 25 (312); Springfield, Mass., Valley Bank Tower (370); Tacoma, Wash., Washington Plaza, 23 (290).

United States—Associations and Societies

Source: World Almanac Questionnaire

- Arranged according to key words in titles. Last figure indicates membership.

— A —

Aaron Burr Association (1946), Tremont, Inca Rd., Linden, A 22642; 600.

Abortion, Assn. for the Study of (1964), 120 W. 57th St., Y., NY 10019; 22,000.

Abortion Rights Action League, Natl. (1969), 250 W. 57th t., N.Y., NY 10019; 10,000.

Accountants, Amer. Institute of Certified Public (1887), 11 Ave. of the Americas, N.Y., NY 10036; 103,863.

Accountants, Natl. Assn. of (1919), 919 Third Ave., N.Y., NY 0022; 71,000.

Accountants, Natl. Society of Public (1945), 1717 Pennsylnia Ave., NW, Wash., DC 20006; 15,000.

Acoustical Society of America (1929), 335 E. 45 St., N.Y., √ 10017; 5,000.

Actors' Equity Assn. (1913), 1500 Broadway, N.Y., NY 036; 18,500.

Actors' Fund of America (1882), 1501 Broadway, N.Y., NY 036; 2,852.

Actuaries, Society of (1949), 208 S. La Salle St., Chicago, IL 604; 5,040.

Acupuncture Foundation of America (1972), Box 1424, antucket, MA 02554.

Adirondack Mountain Club (1922), 172 Ridge St., Glens lls, NY 12801; 9,000.

Administrative Management Society (1919), Maryland Rd., /illow Grove, PA 19090; 15,500.

Adult Education Assn. of the U.S.A. (1951), Office of ducation, 810 18th St., NW, Wash., DC 20006; 6,500.

Advertisers, Assn. of National (1910), 155 E. 44th St., N.Y., Y 10017; 440 cos.

Advertising Agencies, American Assn. of (1917), 200 Park ve., N.Y., NY 10017; 390 agencies.

Aeronautic Assn., Natl. (1922), 806 15th St., NW, Wash., DC 005; 150,000.

Aeronautics and Astronautics, Amer. Institute of (1963), 290 Ave. of the Americas, N.Y., NY 10019; 25,000.

Aerospace Industries Assn. of America (1919), 1725 De- ales St., NW, Wash., DC 20036; 49 cos.

Aerospace Medical Association (1929), Washington Na- onal Airport, Wash., DC 20001; 4,064.

African Violet Society of America (1946), 706 Hamilton ank Blvd., Knoxville, TN 37901; 14,000.

Afro-American Life and History, Assn. for the Study of 915), 1407 14th St., Wash., DC 20005; 20,000.

Aging Assn., American (1970), Univ. of Neb. Medical Cntr., 2d & Dewey Ave., Omaha, NE 68105; 500.

Agricultural Chemicals Assn., Natl. (1933), 1155 15th St., W, Wash., DC 20005; 121 companies.

Agricultural Economics Assn., American (1910), Univ. of entucky, Lexington, KY 40506; 4,500.

Agricultural Engineers, Amer. Society of (1907), 2950 iles Rd., St. Joseph, MI 49085; 6,800.

Agricultural History Society (1919), U. S. Dept. of Agricul- re, Rm. 146, 500 12th St., SW, Wash., DC 20250; 800.

Agronomy, American Society of (1907), 677 S. Segoe Rd., ladison, WI 53711; 8,075.

Ahepa, Order of (1922), 1422 K St., NW, Wash., DC 20005; 5,000.

Air, Citizens for Clean (1965), 572 Madison Ave., N.Y., NY 0022; 3,000.

Air Force Aid Society (1942), 1117 N. 19th St., Arlington, VA 2209; 23,700.

Air Force Association (1946), 1750 Pennsylvania Ave., NW, lash., DC 20006; 130,000.

Air Force Sergeants Assn. (1961), 4235 28th Ave., Marlow eights, MD 20031; 34,000.

Air Line Employees Assn. (1952), 5600 S. Central Ave., hicago, IL 60638; 10,000.

Air Line Pilots Assn. (1931), 1625 Massachusetts Ave., /ash., DC 20036; 30,000 pilots.

Air Pollution Control Assn. (1907), 4400 Fifth Ave., Pitts- urgh, PA 15213; 6,700.

Air Transport Assn. of America (1936), 1709 New York ve., NW, Wash., DC 20006; 26 airlines.

Air Transport Assn. Internatl. (1945), 1155 Mansfield St., ontreal P.Q., Canada H38 4A4; 111 airlines.

Aircraft Owners and Pilots Assn. (1939), 7315 Wisconsin ve., Bethesda, MD 20014; 180,000.

Airport Operators Council International. (1948), 1700 K St., W, Wash., DC 20006; 160.

Alcohol Problems, Amer. Council on (1964), 119 Constitu- n Ave., NE, Wash., DC 20002.

Alcoholics Anonymous, Box 459, N.Y., NY 10017; 650,000.

Alcoholism, Natl. Council on (1944), 2 Park Ave., N.Y., NY 10016; 180 affiliates.

Allergy, American Academy of (1943), 225 E. Michigan St., Milwaukee, WI 53202; 2,400.

Allied Youth (1936), 933 N. Kenmore St., Arlington, VA 22201; 15,000.

Alpine Club, American (1902), 113 E. 90th St., N.Y., NY 10028; 1,200.

Altrusa International (1917), 332 S. Michigan Ave., Chicago, IL 60604; 17,950.

Aluminum Assn. (1933), 750 Third Ave., N.Y., NY 10017; 70 cos.

Alumni Council, American (1913), One Dupont Circle, Wash., DC 20036; 1,600 schools.

American Federation of Labor & Congress of Industrial Organizations (AFL-CIO) (1955), by merging **American Feder- ation of Labor** estab. 1881 and **Congress of Industrial Organ- izations** estab. 1935, 815 16th St. NW, Wash., DC 20006; 14,300,000.

American Field Service (1947), 313 E. 43d St., N.Y., NY 10017; 110,000.

American Indian Affairs, Assn. on (1923), 432 Park Ave. S., N.Y., NY 10016; 75,000.

American Legion, The (1919), 700 N. Pennsylvania St., Indi- anapolis, IN 46206; 2,700,000.

American Legion Auxiliary (1919), 777 N. Meridian St., Indi- anapolis, IN 46204; 900,000.

American Veterans of World War II, Korea & Vietnam (AMVETS), (1947), 1710 Rhode Island Ave., NW, Wash., DC 20036; 200,000. **AMVETS Auxiliary** (1946), Saco Rd., Old Or- chard Beach, ME 04064; 25,000.

Americans for Freedom (1960), 1221 Massachusetts Ave., Wash., DC 20005; 70,000.

Amputation Foundation, National, (1949), 12-45 150th St., Whitestone, NY 11357; 2,000.

Animal Protection Institute (1968), 5894 S. Land Park Dr., Sacramento, CA 95822; 46,000.

Animal Welfare Institute (1951), P.O. Box 3650, Wash., DC 20007; 4,000.

Animals, Amer. Society for Prevention of Cruelty to (ASP- CA) (1866), 441 E. 92d St., N.Y., NY 10028; 2,000.

Animals, Friends of (1957), 11 W. 60th St., N.Y., NY 10023; 60,000.

Animals, The Fund for (1967), 140 W. 57th St., N.Y., NY 10019; 65,000.

Anthropological Assn., American (1904), 1703 New Hamp- shire Ave., NW, Wash., DC 20009; 9,150.

Anti-Vivisection Society, American (1883), 1903 Chestnut St., Phila., PA 19103; 15,000.

Antiquarian Society, American (1812), 185 Salisbury St., Worcester, MA 01609; 280.

Antique Automobile Club of America (1935), 501 W. Governor Rd., Hershey, PA 17033; 36,000.

Appalachian Mountain Club (1876), 5 Joy St., Boston, MA 02108; 22,000.

Appalachian Trail Conference (1925), Box 236, Harpers Ferry, WV 25425; 75,000.

Appraisers, Amer. Society of (1952), Dulles International Airport, P.O. Box 17265, Wash., DC 20041; 4,600.

Arbitration Association, Amer. (1926), 140 W. 51st St., N.Y., NY 10020; 3,000.

Archaeological Institute of America (1879), 260 W. Broad- way, N.Y., NY 10013; 6,000.

Archers Assn., Professional (1961), G-6299 Fenton Rd., Flint, MI 48507; 275.

Archery Assn. of the U.S., Natl. (1879), 1951 Geraldson Dr., Lancaster, PA 17601; 4,000.

Architects, American Institute of (1857), 1735 New York Ave., NW, Wash., DC 20006; 25,000.

Architectural Historians, Society of (1940), 1700 Walnut St., Phila., PA 19103; 4,200.

Archivists, Society of American (1936), P.O. Box 8198, Univ. of Illinois, Chicago, IL 60680; 2,700.

Armed Forces Communications and Electronics Assn. (1945), Skyline Center, 5205 Leesburg Pike, Falls Church, VA 22041; 11,000.

Army and Navy Union, U.S.A. (1886), 1391 Main St., Lake- more, OH 44250; 12,000.

Art, Natl. Assn. of Schools of (1944), 11250 Roger Bacon Dr., No. 5, Reston, VA 22090; 75 schools.

Arthritis Foundation (1948), 475 Riverside Dr., N.Y., NY 10027; 73 chapters.

Artists of America, Allied (1914), 1083 Fifth Ave., N.Y., NY 10028; 375.

Arts, American Federation of (1909), 41 E. 65th St., N.Y., NY 10021; 3,000.

Arts, Associated Councils of the (1965), 1564 Broadway, N.Y., NY 10036; 800.

Arts, Natl. Endowment for the (1965), 2401 E. St., NW, Wash., DC 20506.

Arts and Letters, American Academy of (1904), 633 W. 155th St., N.Y., NY 10032; 47.

Arts and Letters, Natl. Institute of (1898), 633 W. 155th St., N.Y., NY 10032; 231.

Arts and Sciences, American Academy of (1780), 165 Allandale St., Jamaica Plain, MA 02130; 2,244.

Assistance League, National (1935), 5627 Fernwood Ave., Hollywood, CA 90028; 11,000.

Associated Press (1848), 50 Rockefeller Plaza, N.Y., NY 10020.

Astrologers, Amer. Federation of (1938), 6 Library Ct., SE, Wash., DC 20003; 3,000.

Astronautical Society, American (1953), 6060 Duke St., Alexandria, VA 22304; 500.

Astronomical Society, American (1899), 211 FitzRandolph Rd., Princeton, NJ 08540; 3,044.

Atheist Assn. (1925), Box 2832, San Diego, CA 92112; 200.

Athletic Associations, Natl. Federation of State High School (1920), 400 Leslie St., Elgin, IL 60120; 50 states.

Athletic Conference, Eastern College (1938), 1311 Craigville Beach Rd., Centerville, MA 02632; 211 schools.

Athletic Union of the U.S., Amateur (1888), 3400 W. 86th St., Indianapolis, IN 46268; 235,000 athletes.

Attorneys General, National Assn. of (1907), P.O. Box 11910, Iron Work Pike, Lexington, KY 40511; 54.

Audit Bureau of Circulations (1914), 123 N. Wacker Dr., Chicago, IL 60606; 3950 companies.

Audubon Society, National (1905), 950 Third Ave., N.Y., NY 10022; 335,000.

Authors and Composers, American Guild of (1931), 40 W. 57th St., N.Y., NY 10019; 2,500.

Authors League of America (1912), 234 W. 44th St., N.Y., NY 10036; 6,500.

Automobile Assn., American (1902), 8111 Gatehouse Rd., Falls Church, VA 22042; 16,000,000.

Automobile Club, National (1924), 65 Battery St., San Francisco, CA 94111; 360,000.

Automobile Dealers Assn., National (1917), 1640 Westpark Dr., McLean, VA 22101; 22,200.

Automobile License Plate Collectors' Assn. (1954), Box 399; Brattleboro, VT 05301; 1073.

Automotive Booster Clubs (1921), 1803 S. Busse Rd., Mt. Prospect, IL 60056; 2,985.

Automotive Engineers, Society of (1909), 2 Pennsylvania Plaza, N.Y., NY 10001; 26,221.

Automotive Organization Team (1939), P.O. Box 1742, Midland, MI 48640; 2,500.

Aviation Historical Society, American (1956), P. O. Box 99, Garden Grove, CA 92642; 4,500.

— B —

Badminton Assn., American (1936), 1330 Alexandria Dr., San Diego, CA 92107; 3,000.

Ball Players of America, Assn. of Professional (1924), 530 E. Wardlow Rd., Long Beach, CA 90807; 10,000.

Banker Assn., Internatl. (1968), 422 Washington Bldg., Wash., DC 20005; 1,500.

Bankers Assn., American (1875), 1120 Connecticut Ave. NW, Wash., DC 20036; 18,398 banks, branches.

Bankers Assn. of America, Independent (1930), 1168 S. Main St., Sauk Centre, MN 56378; 7,323 banks.

Bar Association, American (1878), 1155 E. 60th St., Chicago, IL 60637; 179,000.

Bar Assn., Federal (1920), 1815 H Street, NW, Wash., DC 20006; 14,000.

Barber Shop Quartet Singing in America, Society for the Preservation & Encouragement of (1938), 6315 Third Ave., Kenosha, WI 53141; 35,508.

Barbers and Beauticians of America, Associated Master (1924), 219 Greenwich Rd., Charlotte, NC 28211; 10,000.

Baseball Congress, American Amateur (1935), 212 Plaza Bldg., 2855 W. Market St., P.O. Box 5322 Akron, OH 44313.

Baseball Congress of America, Natl. (1931), 338 S. Sycamore, Wichita, KS 67213; 15,000.

Basketball Assn., American (1967), 1700 Broadway, N.Y., NY 10019; 10 teams.

Basketball Assn., Natl. (1946), 2 Penn Plaza, N.Y., NY 10001; 17 teams.

Baton Twirling Assn., Internatl. (1967), Box 234, Waldwick, NJ 07463; 2,900.

Battleship Assn., American (1963), P.O. Box 11247, San Diego, CA 92111; 2,000.

Beta Sigma Phi (1931), 1800 W. 91st Pl., Kansas City, MO 64114; 225,000.

Bible Society, American (1816), 1865 Broadway, N.Y., NY 10023; 440,000.

Biblical Literature, Society of (1880), Harvard Divinity School, 45 Francis Ave., Cambridge, MA 02138; 3,200.

Bibliographical Society of America (1904), P. O. Box 397, Grand Central Sta., N.Y., NY 10017; 1,625.

Bicycle Institute of America (1937), 122 E. 42d St., New York, N.Y 10017; 250.

Bide-A-Wee Home Assn. (1903), 410 E. 38th St., N.Y., NY 10016; 21,500.

Big Brothers of America (1946), 220 Suburban Station Bldg., Phila., PA 19103; 275 agencies.

Billiard Congress of America (1948), 717 N. Michigan Ave., Chicago, IL 60611; 625.

Biological Chemists, American Society of (1906), 9650 Rockville Pike, Bethesda, MD 20014; 3,900.

Biological Sciences, Amer. Institute of (1947), 1401 Wilson Blvd., Arlington, VA 22209; 11,500.

Blind, American Foundation for the (1921), 15 W. 16th St., N.Y., NY 10011.

Blind, National Federation of the (1940), 218 Randolph Hotel, Des Moines, IA 50309; 50,000.

Blind & Visually Handicapped, Natl. Accreditation Council for Agencies Serving the (1967), 79 Madison Ave., N.Y., NY 10016; 14 agencies.

Blinded Veterans Assn. (1945), 1735 DeSales St., NW, Wash., DC 20036; 1,800.

Blindness, Natl. Society for the Prevention of (1908), Madison Ave., N.Y., NY 10016; 343.

Blindness, Research to Prevent (1960), 598 Madison Ave., N.Y., NY 10022; 1,500.

Blizzard Club, January 12th, 1888 (1940), c/o Historian, 4827 Hillside Ave., Lincoln, NE 68506; 70.

Blood Banks, American Assn. of (1947), 1818 L St., NW, Wash., DC 20036; 6,517.

Blue Cross Assn. (1948), 840 N. Lake Shore Dr., Chicago, 60611; 74 plans.

Blue Shield Plans, Natl. Assn. of (1946), 211 E. Chicago Ave., Chicago, IL 60611; 72 plans.

Blueberry Council, North American (1966), P. O. Box 166, Marmora, NJ 08223; 6,000.

B'nai B'rith (1843), 1640 Rhode Island Ave., NW, Wash., DC 20036; 500,000. Component units include: **B'nai B'rith Hillel Foundations** (1923); **B'nai B'rith Youth Organization** (1924) Other units: **B'nai B'rith Women, Anti-Defamation League of B'nai B'rith, B'rith Vocational Service.**

Board of Trade, World (1973), 295 Fifth Ave., N.Y., NY 10016.

Boat Owners Assn. of the U.S. (1966), 5261 Port Royal Rd., Springfield, VA 22151; 33,000.

Book Manufacturers Institute (1933), Box 368, Ridgefield, CT 06877; 100 companies.

Booksellers Assn., American (1900), 800 Second Ave., N.Y., NY 10017; 4,500.

Botanical Gardens & Arboreta, Amer. Assn. of (1940), Dept. of Horticulture, New Mexico State Univ., Las Cruces, N 88003; 115 institutions.

Botanical Society of America (1906), Univ. of Texas, Austin, TX 78703; 4,400.

Bottle Clubs, Federation of Historical (1969), c/o Corresponding Secty., 5001 Queen Avenue, N., Minneapolis, MN 55430; 120 clubs.

Bowling Congress, American (1895), 5301 S. 76th St., Greendale, WI 53129; 4.2 million male bowlers.

Bowling Congress, Women's International (1916), 5301 S. 76th St., Greendale, WI 53129; 3,343,965.

Boy Scouts of America (1910), N. Brunswick, NJ 08902; 6,405,225 scouts & leaders.

Boys' Brigades of America, United (1893), P. O. Box 840, Baltimore, MD 21234.

Boys' Clubs of America (1860), 771 First Ave., N.Y., NY 10017; 1,000,000.

Brand Names Foundation (1943), 477 Madison Ave., N.Y., NY 10022; 600.

Brewers Assn., U.S. (1862), 1750 K St., Wash., DC 20006.

Brick Institute of America (1934), 1750 Old Meadow Rd., McLean, VA 22101; 110 Cos.

Brith Sholom (1905), 1235 Chestnut Street, Philadelphia, PA 19107; 20,000.

Broadcasters, Natl. Assn. of (1922), 1771 N St., NW, Washington, DC 20036; 4,908.

Burroughs, Edgar Rice, Bibliophiles (1960), 454 Elaine Dr., Pittsburgh, PA 15236; 875.

Business Bureaus, Council on Better (1970), 845 Third Ave., N.Y., NY 10022; 137.

Business Clubs, Natl. Assn. of American (1922), 3315 North Main St., High Point, NC 27262; 5,000.

Business Communication Assn., American (1935), 317-B David Kinley Hall, Urbana, IL 61801; 1,060.

Business Education Assn., Natl. (1898), 1906 Association Drive, Reston, VA 22091; 24,000.

Business Law Association, American (1923), Colorado State Univ., Ft. Collins, CO 80521; 700.

Business Press Editors, Amer. Society of (1964), 2550 Green Bay Rd., Evanston, IL 60201; 300.

Button Society Natl. (1938), 353 Stockton St., Hightstown, NJ 08520; 2,250.

— C —

Camp Fire Girls (1910), 1740 Broadway, N.Y., NY 10019; 500,000.

Campers & Hikers Assn., Natl. (1954), 7172 Transit Rd., Buffalo, NY 14221; 61,000 families.

Camping Assn., American (1910), Bradford Woods, Martinsville, IN 46151; 7,000.

Cancer Council, United (1963), 1803 N. Meridian St., Indianapolis, IN 46202; serves 27,500,000 people.

Cancer Society, American (1913), 219 E. 42d St., N.Y., NY 10017; 233.

Candy Brokers Assn. of America, P.O. Box 34236 Wash., DC 20034; 200.

Canners Assn., National (1907), 1133 20th St., NW, Wash., DC 20036; 500 companies.

Captive European Nations, Assembly of (1954), 29 W. 57th St., N.Y., NY 10019; 9 national committees.

CARE (Cooperative For American Relief Everywhere) (1945), 660 First Ave., N.Y., NY 10016; 25 agencies.

Carillonneurs in North America, Guild of (1936), c/o Secty., 3718 Settle Rd., Cincinnati, OH 45227; 315.

Carl Schurz Assn., Natl. (1930), 339 Walnut St., Phila., PA 19106; 2,766.

Carnegie Hero Fund Commission (1904), 1932 Oliver Bldg., Pittsburgh, PA 15222.

Cartoonists Society, Natl. (1946), 9 Ebony Court, Brooklyn, NY 11229; 450.

Casting Assn., American (1906), P. O. Box 51, Nashville, TN 37202; 2,500.

Catch Society (1968), Dept. of English, SUNY—Fredonia, NY, 14063; 300.

Catholic Bishops, Natl. Conference of—U.S. Catholic Conference (1966), 1312 Massachusetts Ave., NW, Wash., DC 20005; 300.

Catholic Charities, Natl. Conference of (1910), 1346 Connecticut Ave., NW, Wash., DC 20036; 3,000.

Catholic Church Extension Society (1905), 1307 S. Wabash Ave., Chicago, IL 60605; 36,645.

Catholic Daughters of America (1903), 10 W. 71st St., N.Y., NY 10023; 182,985.

Catholic Educational Assn., Natl. (1904), One Dupont Circle, Suite 350, NW, Wash., DC 20036; 14,000.

Catholic Hospital Assn. (1915), 1438 S. Grand Blvd., St. Louis, MO 63104; 879.

Catholic Press Assn. (1911), 432 Park Ave. S., N.Y., NY 10016; 400.

Catholic Rural Life Conference, National (1923), 3801 Grand Ave., Des Moines, IA 50312; 3,400.

Catholic War Veterans of U.S.A. (1935), 2 Massachusetts Ave., NW, Wash., DC 20001; 75,000.

Cemetery Assn., American (1887), 250 E. Broad St., Columbus, OH 43215; 1,200

Ceramic Society, American (1899), 65 Ceramic Drive, Columbus, OH 43214; 7,300

Cerebral Palsy Association, United (1948), 66 E. 34th St., New York, NY 10016; 308.

Chamber of Commerce of the U.S. (1912), 1615 H St., NW, Wash., DC 20006; 36,000.

Chartered Life Underwriters, Amer. Society of (1928), 270 Bryn Mawr Ave., Bryn Mawr, PA 19010; 20,100.

Chartered Property & Casualty Underwriters, Society of (1944), P. O. Box 566, Media, PA 19063; 7,500.

Chautauqua Institution (1874), Box 28, Chautauqua, NY 14722.

Chemical Engineers, American Institute of (1908), 345 E. 47th St., N.Y., NY 10017; 38,800.

Chemical Society, American (1876), 1155 16th St., NW, Wash., DC 20036; 110,000.

Chemists, Amer. Institute of (1923), 7315 Wisconsin Ave., Washington, DC 20014; 7,300.

Chemists and Chemical Engineers, Assn. of Consulting (1928), 50 E. 41st St., N.Y., NY 10017; 120

Chess Federation, U.S. (1939), 479 Broadway, Newburgh, NY 12550; 57,493.

Chief Warrant and Warrant Officers' Assn., USCG (1930), 955 L'Enfant Plaza N., SW, Wash., DC 20024; 2,981.

Child Study Assn. of America (1888), 50 Madison Ave., N.Y., NY 10010; 2,500.

Child Welfare League of America (1920), 67 Irving Place, N.Y., NY 10003; 400 agencies.

Childbirth Without Pain Leagues (1964), P.O. Box. 1403, Colton, CA 92324; 600.

Children of the American Revolution, Natl. Society (1895), 1776 D St., NW, Wash., DC 20006; 13,000.

Children's Aid Society (1853), 105 E. 22d St., N.Y., NY 10010.

Children's Book Council (1945), 175 Fifth Ave., N.Y., NY 10010; 63.

Chinese Women's Association (1932), 54-32 152d St., Flushing, NY 11355; 374.

Chiropractic Association, American (1964), 2200 Grand Ave., Des Moines, IA 50312; 9,630.

Chiropractors Association, International (1926), 741 Brady St., Davenport, IA 52808; 6,000.

Christian Anti-Defamation League (1956), P. O. Box 714, Mt. Vernon, NY 10551; 120,000.

Christian Laymans Counseling Board (1970), 5901 Plainfield Drive, Charlotte, NC 28215; 3,248,389.

Christians and Jews, Natl. Conference of (1928), 43 W. 57th St., N.Y., NY 10019; 200,000.

Churches of City of N.Y., Council of (1815), 475 Riverside Drive, N.Y., NY 10027; 1,700 churches.

Cincinnati, Society of the (1783), 2118 Massachusetts Ave., NW, Wash., DC 20008; 2,650.

Circus Fans Assn. of America (1926), P. O. Box 605, Aurora, IL 60507; 2,000.

Circus Historical Society (1939), 1325 Commercial St., Atchison, KS 66002; 1,300.

Cities, Natl. League of (1924), 1620 Eye St., NW, Wash., DC 20006; 15,000 municipalities.

City Management Assn., International (1914), 1140 Connecticut Ave., NW, Wash., DC 20036; 5,821.

Civil Engineers, American Society of (1852), 345 E. 47th St., N.Y., NY 10017; 69,576.

Civil Liberties Union, American (1920), 22 E. 40th St., N.Y., NY 10016; 275,000.

Civil Service League, Natl. (1881), 917 15th St., NW, Wash., DC 20005; 1,000.

Civitan International (1920), 115 N. 21st St., Birmingham, AL 35203; 53,500.

Classical League, American (1919), Miami Univ., Oxford, OH 45056; 3,500.

Clinical Pastoral Education, Assn. for (1967), 475 Riverside Drive, N.Y., NY 10027; 4,000.

Clinical Pathologists, American Society of (1922), 2100 W. Harrison, Chicago, IL 60612; 20,000.

Coal Association, National (1917), 1130 17th St., NW, Wash., DC 20036; 200 companies.

Cocoa Exchange, New York (1925), 127 John St., N.Y., NY 10038; 183.

Coffee and Sugar Exchange, New York (1882), 79 Pine St., N.Y., NY 10005; 342.

Collectors Assn., American (1939), 4040 W. 70th St., Minneapolis, MN 55435; 2,550 firms.

College Entrance Examination Board (1900), 888 Seventh Ave., N.Y., NY 10019; 2,000 institutions.

College Physical Education Assn. for Men, Natl. (1897), 108 Cooke Hall, Univ. of Minn., Minneapolis, MN 55455; 1,500.

College Placement Council (1956), 65 E. Elizabeth Ave., Bethlehem, PA 18018; 1,650.

College Public Relations Assn., American (1917), One Dupont Circle, NW, Wash., DC 20036; 1,314.

Colleges, Assn. of American (1915), 1818 R St., NW, Wash., DC 20007; 741 colleges.

Collegiate Athletic Assn., National (1906), Highway 50 & Nall Ave., Mission, KS 66222; 811.

Collegiate Schools of Business, Amer. Assembly of (1916), 760 Office Parkway, St. Louis, MO 63141; 604 schools.

Colonial Dames of America (1890), 421 E. 61 St., N.Y., NY 10021; 2,000.

Colonial Dames XVII Century, Natl. Society (1915), 1300 New Hampshire Ave., NW, Wash., DC 20036; 7,500.

Colonial Wars, General Society of (1892), c/o Lawson Whitesides, 840 Woodbine Ave., Glendale, OH 45246; 4,400.

Colored Women's Clubs, Natl. Assn. of (1896), 5808 16th St., NW, Wash., DC 20011; 40,000.

Columbia Assns. in Civil Service, Grand Council of (1938), 299 Broadway, N.Y., NY 10007; 80,000.

Commercial Law League of America (1895), 222 W. Adams St., Chicago, IL 60606; 5,400.

Common Cause (1970), 2030 M St., NW, Wash., DC 20036; 300,000.

Composers, Authors & Publishers, American Society of (ASCAP) (1914), One Lincoln Plaza, N.Y., NY 10023; 23,000.

Composers and Conductors, Natl. Assn. for American (1933), 133 W. 69th St., N.Y., NY 10023; 850.

Computing Machinery, Assn. for (1947), 1133 Ave. of Americas, N.Y., NY 10036; 26,406.

Concern, Project (1961), 3802 Houston St., San Diego, CA 92110.

Concrete Institute, American (1905), Box 19150, Detroit, MI 48219; 16,126.

Conference Board (1916), 845 Third Ave., New York, NY 10022; 4,000.

Congress of Racial Equality (1942), 200 W. 135th St., New York, NY 10030.

Conscientious Objectors, Central Committee for (1948), 2016 Walnut St., Philadelphia, PA 19103.

Conservation Engineers, Assn. of (1961), Mo. Dept. of Conservation, P. O. Box 180, Jefferson City, MO 65101; 161.

Conservation Foundation (1948), 1717 Massachusetts Ave., NW, Wash., DC 20036.

Conservation & Trustees of the Universe, Citizens for (1953), 1013 S. Washington Ave., Lansing, MI 48910.

Construction Industry Manufacturers Assn. (1922), 111 E. Wisconsin Ave., Milwaukee, WI 53202; 200 companies.

Construction Specifications Institute (1948), 1150 17th Street, NW, Wash., DC 20036; 10,700.

Consumer Credit Assn., International (1912), 375 Jackson Ave., St. Louis, MO 63130; 50,000.

Consumer Federation of America (1967), 1012 14th St., NW, Wash., DC 20005; 200 organizations.

Consumer Interests, American Council on (1953), 238 Stanley Hall, Univ. of Mo., Columbia, MO 65201; 3,000.

Consumer Protection Council, Natl. Student (1971), Villanova Univ., Bartley Hall, Rm. 328, Villanova, PA 19085; 500.

Consumers League, Natl. (1899), 1785 Massachusetts Ave., NW, Wash., DC 20036; 25,000.

Consumers Union of the U.S. (1936), 256 Washington St., Mount Vernon, NY 10550; 308,059.

Consumers Unions, Internatl. Organization of (1960), 9 Emmastraat, The Hague, Netherlands; 100 national organizations.

Contract Bridge League, Amer. (1937), 2200 Democrat Rd., Memphis, TN 38116; 192,115.

Cooperative League of the U.S.A. (1916), 1828 L St., NW, Wash., DC 20036.

Corporate Responsibility, Project Center on (1970), 1712 N St., NW, Wash., DC 20036; 5,000.

Correctional Administrators, Assn. of State (1955), 36 W. 44th St., N.Y., NY 10036; 56.

Correctional Assn., American (1870), 4321 Hartwick Rd., College Park, MD 20740; 10,000.

Cosmopolitan International (1919), 7341 W. 80th St., Overland Park, KS 66204; 4,000.

Cotton Council of America, Natl. (1938), 1918 North Parkway, Memphis, TN 38112; 282.

Country Music Assn. (1958), 700 16th Ave. S., Nashville, TN 37203; 4,000.

Credit Management, National Assn. of (1896), 475 Park Ave. S., N.Y., NY 10016; 39,000.

Credit Unions, World Council of (1971), 1617 Sherman Ave., Madison, WI 53701; 48,000,000.

Crime and Delinquency, Natl. Council on (1907), 411 Hackensack Ave., Hackensack, NJ 07601; 60,000.

Criminology, American Assn. of (1953), Box 321, Harvard Square Sta., Cambridge, MA 02138; 2,500.

Crop Science Society of America (1955), 677 S. Segoe Rd., Madison, WI 53711; 3,517.

Cryptogram Assn., American (1932), 9504 Forest Rd., Bethesda, MD 20014; 1,000.

Customs Brokers & Forwarders Assn. of America, Natl. (1897), One World Trade Center, N.Y., NY 10048; 500.

Cyprus, Sovereign Order of (1192; in U. S. 1964), 853 Seventh Ave., N.Y., NY 10019; 414.

— D —

Dairy Council, Natl. (1915), 111 N. Canal St., Chicago, IL 60606; 1,000.

Dairy and Food Industries Supply Assn. (1912), 5530 Wisconsin Ave., Wash., DC 20015; 400 organizations.

Dairy Goat Assn., Amer. (1904), P.O. Box 186, Spindale, NC 28160; 6,100.

Dairy Science Assn., American (1906), 113 N. Neil St., Champaign, IL 61820; 2,600.

Dairylea Cooperative (1919), One Blue Hill Plaza, Pearl River, NY 10965; 8,600.

Data Processing Management Assn. (1951), 505 Busse Highway, Park Ridge, IL 60068; 24,500.

Daughters of the American Revolution, Natl. Society (1890), 1776 D St., NW, Wash., DC 20006; 196,000.

Daughters of the Confederacy, United (1894), 328 North Blvd., Richmond, VA 23220; 35,000.

Daughters of the Union Veterans of the War 1861-1865 (1885), 503 S. Walnut St., Springfield, IL 62704; 15,000.

Deaf, Alexander Graham Bell Assn. for the (1890), 3417 Volta Place, NW, Wash., DC 20007; 7,000.

Deaf, Conference of Executives of American Schools for the (1868), 5034 Wisconsin Ave., NW, Wash., DC 20016; 350.

Deaf, Convention of Amer. Instructors of the (1850), 5034 Wisconsin Ave., NW, Wash., DC 20016; 3,800.

Deaf, National Assn. of the (1880), 814 Thayer Ave., Silver Spring, MD 20910; 1,700.

Defense Preparedness Assn., Amer. (1919), 819 Union Trust Bldg., Wash., DC 20005; 29,000.

Delta Kappa Gamma Society (1929), 416 W. 12th St., Austin, TX 78701; 131,000.

DeMolay, Order of (1919), 201 E. Armour Blvd., Kansas City, MO 64111; 2,800,000.

Dental Association, American (1859), 211 E. Chicago Ave., Chicago, IL 60611; 122,500.

Dental Assn., Natl. (1918), P. O. Box 197, Charlottesville, VA 22902; 800.

Descendants of the Colonial Clergy, Society of the (1933), 255 Madison St., Dedham, MA 02026; 925.

Descendants of the Signers of the Declaration of Independence (1907), 1300 Locust St., Phila., PA 19107; 721.

Desert Protective Council (1954), Box 4294, Palm Springs, CA 92262; 450.

Diabetes Assn., American (1940), One W. 48th St., N.Y., NY 10020; 3,147.

Dialect Society, American (1889), 1611 N. Kent St., Arlington, VA 22209; 1,000.

Dietetic Assn., American (1917), 620 N. Michigan Ave., Chicago, IL 60611; 24,970.

Directors Guild of America (1936), 9750 Sunset Blvd., Los Angeles, CA 90046; 4,200.

Disabled American Veterans (1921), P.O. Box 14301, Cincinnati, OH 45214; 475,000.

Disabled Officers Assn. (1919), 1612 K St., NW, Wash., DC 20006; 5,500.

Divorce Reform, United States (1961), P. O. Box 243, Kenwood, CA 95452; 6,000.

Dowsers, American Society of (1961), 957 Norwood Ave., Schenectady, NY 12303; 1,400.

Drug, Chemical and Allied Trades Assn. (1890), 350 Fifth Ave., N.Y., NY 10001; 450 firms.

Drum Corps International (1971), P.O. Box 192, Villa Park, IL 60181; 3,100.

Duckpin Bowling Congress, Natl. (1927), 711 14th St., NW, Wash., DC 20005; 250,000.

Ducks Unlimited (1937), P.O. Box 66300; Chicago, IL 60666; 125,000.

Dulcimer Assn., Appalachian (1974), Rte. 1, Box 473, Helena, AL 35080; 77.

Duodecimal Society of America (1944), 4728 Cielo Dr., Huntington Beach, CA 92649; 120.

Dutch Settlers Soc. of Albany (1924), 1088 Cortland St., Albany, NY 12203; 275.

— E —

Eagles, Fraternal Order of (1898), 2401 W. Wisconsin Ave., Milwaukee, WI 53233; 850,000.

Earth, Friends of the (1969), 529 Commercial St., San Francisco, CA 94111; 20,000.

Easter Seal Society for Crippled Children and Adults, Natl. (1921), 2023 W. Ogden Ave., Chicago, IL 60612.

Eastern Star, Order of the (1876), 1618 New Hampshire Ave., Wash., DC 20009; 3,000,000.

Ecological Society of America (1915), c/o Frank McCormick, Univ. of N. C., Chapel Hill, NC 27514; 5,000.

Economic Assn., American (1885), 1313 21st Ave., S., Nashville, TN 37212; 25,092.

Economic Development, Committee for (1942), 477 Madison Ave., N.Y., NY 10022; 200 trustees.

Edison Electric Institute (1933), 90 Park Ave., New York, NY 10016.

Education, American Council on (1918), One Dupont Circle, NW, Wash., DC 20036; 1,600 schools.

Education, Council for Basic (1956), 725 15th St., NW, Wash., DC 20005; 4,350.

Education, Natl. Society for the Study of (1902), 5835 Kimbark Ave., Chicago, IL 60637; 4,600.

Education, Society for the Advancement of (1939),1860 Broadway, N.Y., NY 10023; 2,500.

Education Assn., Natl. (1857), 1201 16th St., NW, Wash., DC 20036; 1,500,000.

Education Society, Comparative and International (1956), Grad. School of Education, Univ. of Cal., 405 Hilgard Ave., Los Angeles, CA 90024; 2,500.

Education of Young Children, Natl. Assn. for the (1926), 1834 Connecticut Ave., NW, Wash., DC 20009; 23,000.

Educational Broadcasters, Natl. Assn. of (1925), 1346 Connecticut Ave., NW, Wash., DC 20036; 3,000.

Educational Exchange, Council on Internatl. (1947), 777 UN Plaza, N.Y., NY 10017; 184 schools.

Educational Research Assn., American (1915), 1126 16th St., NW, Wash., DC 20036; 11,875.

Educators for World Peace, Internatl. Assn. of(1969), P.O. Box 3282, Blue Springs Sta., Huntsville, AL 35810; 8,500.

Electric Railroaders Assn.(1934), 145 Greenwich St., New York, NY 10006; 3,000.

Electrical and Electronics Engineers, Institute of(1884), 345 E. 47th St., N.Y., NY 10017; 170,000.

Electrical Manufacturers Assn., Natl.(1926), 155 E. 44th St., N.Y., NY 10017; 550 companies.

Electrochemical Society(1902), P. O. Box 2071, Princeton, NJ 08540; 4,150.

Electronic Industries Assn.(1924), 2001 Eye St., NW, Washington, DC 20006; 200 firms.

Electronic Technicians, Internatl. Society of Certified(1971), 1715 Expo Lane, Indianapolis, IN 46224; 1,000.

Electroplaters' Society, American(1909), 56 Melmore Gardens, E. Orange, NJ 07017; 7,500.

Elks, Benevolent and Protective Order of(1868), 2750 N. Lakeview Ave., Chicago, IL 60614; 1,558,772.

Elks, Improved Benevolent Protective Order of(1898), 1522 N. 16th St., Phila., PA 19121; 450,000.

Engine and Boat Manufacturers, Natl. Assn. of(1904), 666 Third Ave., N.Y., NY 10017; 400 firms.

Engineering, Natl. Academy of(1964), 2101 Constitution Ave., NW, Wash., DC 20418; 587.

Engineering Education, Amer. Society for(1893), One Dupont Circle, NW, Wash., DC 20036; 13,000.

Engineering Technicians, Amer. Society of Certified(1964), 2029 K St., NW, Wash., DC 20006; 7,500.

Engineering Trustees, United(1904), 345 East 47th St., N.Y., NY 10017; 5 societies.

Engineers, American Institute of Consulting(1910), 345 East 47th St., N.Y., NY 10017; 425.

Engineers, Natl. Society of Professional(1934), 2029 K St., NW, Wash., DC 20006; 70,000.

Engineers Joint Council(1945), 345 E. 47th St., N.Y., NY 10017; 500,000.

English Association, College(1939), Oakland Univ., Rochester, MI 48063; 3,000.

English-Speaking Union(1920), 16 E. 69th St., N.Y., NY 10021; 35,000.

Entomological Society of America(1889), 4603 Calvert Rd., College Park, MD 20740; 6,600.

Environmental Defense Fund(1967), 162 Old Town Rd., East Setauket, NY 11733; 54,000.

Epilepsy Foundation of America(1968), 1828 L St., NW, Wash., DC 20036; 40,000.

Esperanto Assn., Internatl. Catholic(1910), Limbiate, Italy; U.S. Rep., 7605 Winona Ln., Sebastopol, CA 95472; 1,100.

Esperanto Assn. of North America(1905), 1837 NE 49th Ave., Portland, OR 97213; 306.

Esperanto League for North America(1952), P.O. Box 508, Burlingame, CA 94010; 800.

Evangelicals, Natl. Assn. of(1942), 350 S. Main Pl., Box 28, Wheaton, IL 60187; 3,500,000.

Evangelism Crusades, International(1959), 7970 Woodman Ave., Van Nuys, CA 91402; 5,000.

Exchange Club, National(1917), 3050 Central Ave., Toledo, OH 43606; 50,000.

Executives' Secretaries(1938), 2188 Highland Dr., Salt Lake City, UT 84106; 3,500.

Experiment in International Living(1932), Kipling Rd., Brattleboro, VT 05301; 60,000.

Eye-Bank Assn. of America(1961), 3195 Maplewood Ave., Winston-Salem, NC 27103; 64.

Eye-Bank for Sight Restoration(1945), 3195 Maplewood Ave., Winston-Salem, NC 27103.

—F—

Fairs & Expositions, International Assn. of(1919), 500 Ashland Ave., Chicago Heights, IL 60411; 1,100.

Family Physicians, Amer. Academy of(1947), 1740 W. 92d St., Kansas City, MO 64114; 37,000.

Family Service Assn. of America(1911), 44 E. 23d St., N.Y., NY 10010; 310 agencies.

Farm Bureau Federation, American(1919), 225 Touhy Ave., Park Ridge, IL 60068; 2,393,731 families.

Farmer Cooperatives, Natl. Council of(1929), 1129 20th St., NW, Washington, DC 20036; 145 firms.

Farmers of America, Future(1928), 563 Mt. Vernon Hwy., Alexandria, VA 22309; 465,180.

Farmers Educational and Co-Operative Union of America (1902), 12025 E. 45th Ave., Denv., CO 80201; 250,000 families.

Federal Employees, Natl. Federation of(1957), 1737 H St., NW, Wash., DC 20006; 80,000.

Federal Employes Veterans Assn.(1957), 124 Union Ave., Bala Cynwyd, PA 19004; 574.

Federally Employed Women(1968), 1249 National Press Bldg., Wash., DC 20045; 78 Chapters.

Feline Society, American(1938), 41 Union Sq. W., N.Y., NY 10003; 650.

Feminists for Life (1972), P.O. Box 5631, Columbus, OH 43221; 5,000.

Fencers League of America, Amateur(1891), 249 Eton Place, Westfield, NJ 07090; 7,000.

Film Library Assn., Educational (1943), 17 W. 60th St., N.Y., NY 10023; 1,800.

Financial Analysts Federation (1947), 219 E. 42d St., N.Y., NY 10017; 1,400.

Financial Executives Institute (1932), 633 Third Ave., N.Y., NY 10017; 8,500.

Fire Chiefs, International Assn. of (1873), 1725 K St., NW, Wash., DC 20006; 7,600.

Fire Fighters, International Assn. of (1918), 905 16th St., NW, Wash., DC 20006; 155,000.

Fire Marshals Assn. of N. America (1906), 470 Atlantic Ave., Boston, MA 02210; 950.

Fire Protection Assn., Natl. (1896), 470 Atlantic Ave., Boston, MA 02210; 33,000.

Fire Protection Engineers, Society of (1950), 60 Batterymarch St., Boston, MA 02110; 1,809.

Fisheries Society, Amer. (1870), 1319 18th St., NW, Wash., DC 20036; 6,161.

Fishing Institute, Sport (1949), 608 13th St., NW, Wash., DC 20005; 24,500.

Fishing Tackle Manufacturers Assn., Amer. (1933), 20 No. Wacker Dr., Chicago, IL 60606; 329.

Flag Day Assn., American (1888), P.O. Box, 1121, Denver, CO 80201.

Flag Foundation, U.S. (1948), 115 E. 86th St., N.Y., NY 10028; 1,000.

Flat Earth Research Society, International, Box 2533, Lancaster, CA 93534.

Florists, Society of American (1884), 901 N. Washington St., Alexandria, VA 22314; 5,800.

Fluid Power Society (1968), 432 E. Kilbourn Ave., Milwaukee, WI 53202; 3,500.

Folklore Society, American (1888), Center for Folklore & Ethnomusicology — SWB 306, Univ. of Texas, Austin, TX 78712; 2,800.

Food Processing Machinery and Supplies Assn. (1885), 7758 Wisconsin Ave., Wash., DC 20014; 325 firms.

Footwear Industries Assn., Amer. (1869), 1611 N. Kent St., Arlington, VA 22209; 384.

Foreign Policy Assn. (1918), 345 E. 46th St., N.Y., NY 10017.

Foreign Press Assn. (1918), 866 Second Ave., N.Y., NY 10017; 350.

Foreign Relations, Council on (1921), 58 E. 68th St., N.Y., NY 10021; 1,600.

Foreign Student Affairs, Natl. Assn. for (1948), 1860 19th St., NW, Wash., DC 20009; 2,500.

Foreign Study, Amer. Institute for (1964), 102 Greenwich Ave., Greenwich, CT 06830; 50,000.

Foreign Trade Council, Natl. (1914), 10 Rockefeller Plaza, N.Y., NY 10020; 600 companies.

Forensic League, Natl. (1925), Ripon College, Ripon, WI 54971; 270,000.

Forensic Sciences, American Academy of (1948), 11400 Rockville Pike, Rockville, MD 20852; 1,534.

Forest Institute, American (1941), 1619 Massachusetts Ave., NW, Wash., DC 20036; 200.

Forest Products Assn., Natl. (1902), 1619 Massachusetts Ave., NW, Wash., DC 20036; 29 assns.

Forest Products Research Society (1947), 2801 Marshall Ct., Madison, WI 53705; 4,200.

Foresters, Society of American (1900), 1010 16th St., NW, Wash., DC 20036; 20,000.

Forestry Assn., American (1875), 1319 18th St., NW, Wash., DC 20036; 80,000.

Foster Parents Plan (1937), 170 Service Road, Warwick, RI 02886; 30,000.

Founders & Patriots of America, Order of the (1896), 53 State St., Boston, MA 02109; 1,000.

Foundrymen's Society, Amer. (1896), Golf & Wolf Rds., Des

Plaines, IL 60016; 14,000.

4-H Clubs (betw. 1901-05), Federal Extension Service, Dept. of Agric., Wash., DC 20250; 5,000,000.

French Institute (1911), 22 E. 60th St. N.Y. NY 10022; 6500.

French Legion of Honor, Amer. Society of the (1922), 22 E. 60th St., N.Y., NY 10022; 440.

Friends Service Committee, Amer. (1917), 1501 Cherry St., Phila., PA 19102.

—G—

Game Fish Assn., International (1939), 3000 E. Las Olas Blvd., Ft. Lauderdale, FL 33316; 10,000 clubs.

Garden Club of America(1913), 598 Madison Ave., N.Y., NY 10022; 12,750.

Garden Clubs of America, Men's(1932), 5560 Merle Hay Rd., Des Moines, IA 50323; 10,000.

Garden Clubs, Natl. Council of State(1929), 4401 Magnolia Ave., St. Louis, MO 63110; 500,000.

Gas Appliance Manufacturers Assn.(1935), 1901 N. Ft. Myer Drive, Arlington, VA 22209; 340 companies.

Gas Assn., American(1918), 1515 Wilson Blvd., Arlington, VA 22209; 5,000.

Genealogical Society, National(1903), 1921 Sunderland Pl., NW, Wash., DC 20036; 2,700.

Genealogical Society, New England Historic (1845), 101 Newbury St., Boston, MA 02114; 4,000.

General Contractors of America, Associated(1918), 1957 E St., NW, Wash., DC 20006; 8,400.

Genetic Assn., American(1903), 1028 Connecticut Ave., NW, Wash., DC 20036; 1,550.

Geographers, Assn. of American(1904), 1710 16th St., NW, Wash., DC 20009; 6,500.

Geographic Education, Natl. Council for(1914), 115 N. Marion St., Oak Park, IL 60301; 6,000.

Geographic Society, National(1888), 17th & M Sts., NW, Wash., DC 20036; 8,900,000.

Geographical Society, American(1852), Broadway at 156th St., New York, NY 10032; 2,367.

Geolinguistics, Amer. Society of(1964), Bronx Community Coll., 120 E. 184th St., Bronx, NY 10468; 100.

Geological Institute, American(1948), 5205 Leesburg Pike, Falls Church, VA 22041; 18 societies.

Geological Society of America(1888), 3300 Penrose Place, Boulder, CO 80301; 12,101.

Geologists, Assn. of Engineering(1957), 8310 San Fernando Way, Dallas, TX 75218; 2,200.

Geophysical Union, American(1919), 1707 L St., NW, Wash., DC 20036; 11,000.

Geophysicists, Society of Exploration(1930), 3707 E. 51st St., Tulsa, OK 74135; 8,800.

Geriatrics Society, American(1942), 10 Columbus Circle, N.Y., NY 10019; 7,000.

Gideons International (1899), 2900 Lebanon Rd., Nashville, TN 37214; 43,000.

Gifted Children, American Assn. for(1946), 15 Gramercy Park, N.Y., NY 10003; 200.

Gifted Children, Natl. Assn. for(1954), 8080 Springvalley Dr., Cincinnati, OH 45236; 2,000.

Girl Scouts of the U.S.A.(1912), 830 Third Ave., N.Y., NY 10022; 2,953,000 girls, 585,000 adults.

Girls Clubs of America (1945), 133 E. 62d St., N.Y., NY 10021; 164,000.

Gladiolus Council, North American(1945), 11345 Moreno Ave., Lakeside, CA 92040; 2,000.

Gold Star Mothers, American(1928), 2128 Leroy Pl., NW, Washington, DC 20008; 15,000.

Golf Association, U.S.(1894), Golf House, Far Hills, NJ 07931; 4,362 clubs.

Goose Island Bird & Girl Watching Society(1960), 301 Arthur Ave., Park Ridge, IL 60068; 878.

Gospel Music Assn.(1964), 816 19th Ave., S. Nashville, TN 37202; 2,000.

Governmental Research Assn.(1914), P.O. Box 387, Ocean Gate, NJ 08740; 450.

Graduate Schools in the U.S., Council of(1961), One Dupont Circle, NW. Wash., DC 20036; 334 institutions.

Grandmother Clubs of America, Natl. Federation of(1938), 203 N. Wabash Ave., Chicago 60601; 18,000.

Grange, National(1867), 1616 H St., NW, Wash., DC 20006; 600,000.

Graphic Artists, Society of American(1877), 1083 Fifth Ave., N.Y., NY 10028; 232.

Graphic Arts, American Institute of(1914), 1059 Third Ave., N.Y., NY 10021; 1,750.

Grocery Manufacturers of America(1908), 1425 K St., Wash., DC 20005; 150 firms.

Guide Dog Foundation for the Blind(1946), 109-19 72d Ave., Forest Hills, NY 11375; 25,000.

Gyro International(1912), 1096 Mentor Ave., Painesville, OH 44077; 5,600.

—H—

Hadassah (Women's Zionist Organization of America) (1912), 65 E. 52d St., N.Y., NY 10022; 335,000.

Handball Assn., U.S.(1950), 4101 Dempster St., Skokie, IL 60076; 14,000.

Handicapped, Federation of the(1935), 211 W. 14th St., N.Y., NY 10011; 1,000.

Handicapped, Natl. Assn. of the Physically(1958), 6473 Grandville, Detroit, MI 48228; 35 chapters.

Hang Gliding Assn., U.S.(1973), 11312¹/₂ Venice Blvd., Los Angeles, CA 90066; 8,000.

Health Assn., Amer. Social (1912), 1740 Broadway, N.Y., NY 10019; 1,900.

Health Council, Natl. (1921), 1740 Broadway, N.Y., NY 10019; 70 agencies.

Health Insurance Assn. of America (1956), 1701 K St., NW, Wash., DC 20006; 325 companies.

Health Insurance Institute (1956), 277 Park Ave., N.Y., NY 10017; 326 companies.

Health, Physical Education & Recreation, Amer. Alliance for (1885), 1201 16th St., Wash., DC 20036; 45,000.

Hearing Aid Society, Natl. (1951), 20361 Middlebelt Rd., Livonia, MI 48152; 2,300.

Hearing and Speech Action, Natl. Assn. for (1919), 814 Thayer Ave., Silver Spring, MD 20910; 12,000.

Heart Association, Amer. (1924), 44 E. 23d St., N.Y., NY 10010; 105,000.

Heating, Refrigerating & Air Conditioning Engineers, Amer. Society of (1894), 345 E. 47th St., N.Y., NY 10017; 30,000.

Helicopter Assn. of America (1948), 1156 15th St., NW, Wash., DC 20005; 508.

Helicopter Society, American (1943), 30 E. 42d St., N.Y., NY 10017; 3,000.

HIAS (Hebrew Immigrant Aid Society) (1884), 200 Park Ave., S., N.Y., NY 10003; 15,000.

High Twelve International (1921), 3681 Lindell Blvd., St. Louis, MO 63108; 20,500.

Historians, Organization of Amer. (1907), 112 N. Bryan St., Bloomington, IN 47401; 12,000.

Historians, The Society of Amer. (1939), 706 Hamilton Hall, Columbia Univ., N.Y., NY 10027; 250.

Historic Preservation, National Trust for (1948), 740-748 Jackson Place, NW, Wash., DC 20006; 75,000.

Historical Assn., American (1884), 400 A St., SE, Wash., DC 20003; 18,000.

Historical Research Associates, Western (1971), 415 5th Road N., Nampa, ID 83651; 115.

Hockey Assn. of the U.S., Amateur (1935), Broadmoor Hotel, Colorado Springs, CO 80906; 10,298 teams, 6,000 referees.

Hockey League, National (1917), 920 Sun Life Bldg., Montreal, Quebec, Canada H3B 2W2; 18 clubs.

Holiday Institute of Yonkers (1969), 82 Borcher Ave., Yonkers, NY 10704.

Holy Cross of Jerusalem, Order of (1965), 853 Seventh Ave., N.Y., NY 10019; 1,053.

Home Builders, Natl. Assn. of (1942), 15th & M Sts., NW, Wash., DC 20005; 77,000.

Home Economics Assn., American (1909), 2010 Massachusetts Ave., NW, Wash., DC 20036; 52,000.

Home Improvement Council, Natl. (1956), 11 E. 44th St., New York, NY 10017; 1,500.

Homemakers of America, Future (1945), 2010 Massachusetts Ave. NW, Wash., DC 20036; 450,000.

Homoeopathy, Amer. Foundation for (1924), 910 17th St., NW, Wash., DC 20006; 500.

Homoeopathy, Amer. Institute of (1844), 910 17th St., NW, Wash., DC 20006; 105.

Horatio Alger Society (1961), 4907 Allison Dr., Lansing, MI 48910; 238.

Horse Show Assn. of America Ltd., Natl. (1883), Empire Hotel, 44 W. 63d St., N.Y., NY 10023; 14.

Horse Shows Assn., American (1917), 527 Madison Ave., N.Y., NY 10022; 17,000.

Horticultural Society, American (1922), Mount Vernon, VA 22121; 20,000.

Hospital Assn., American (1898), 840 N. Lake Shore Dr., Chicago, IL 60611; 21,000.

Hospital Public Relations of the AHA/Amer. Society for (1965), 840 N. Lake Shore Dr., Chicago, IL 60611; 850.

Hot Rod Assn., Natl. (1951), 10639 Riverside Dr., N. Hollywood, CA 91602; 40,000.

Hotel & Motel Assn., American (1911), 888 Seventh Ave.,

N.Y., NY 10019; 8,000 hotels & motels.

Humane Assn., American (1877), P. O. Box 1266, Denver, CO 80201, 2,000,000 in 1,050 societies.

Humane Legislation, Committee for (1967), 910 16th Street, NW, Wash., DC 20006; 20,000.

Humane Society of the U.S. (1954), 2100 L Street, NW, Wash., DC 20037; 50,000.

Humanics, American (1948), 912 Baltimore Ave., Kansas City, MO 64105; 800.

Humanist Assn., American (1941), 602 Third St., San Francisco, CA 94107; 5,500.

Humanities, Natl. Endowment for the (1965), 806 15th St., NW, Wash., DC 20506.

— I —

Iceland Veterans (1946), 2101 Walnut St., Phila., PA 19103; 1,580.

Identification, International Assn. for (1915), P. O. Box 139, Utica, NY 13503; 2,000.

Illuminating Engineering Society (1906), 345 E. 47th St., N.Y., NY 10017; 10,000.

Illustrators, Society of (1901), 128 E. 63d St., N.Y., NY 10021; 575.

Immigration and Nationality Lawyers, Assn. of (1946), 50 Court St., Brooklyn, NY 11201; 600.

Imperial Order of the Dragon (1900-1901), Temple of Agriculture, P.O. Box 1707, San Francisco, CA 94101.

Indian Rights Assn. (1882), 1505 Race St., Phila., PA 19102; 2,500.

Indoor Sports Club (1930), 1145 Highland St., Napoleon, OH 43545; 2,300.

Industrial Advertisers, Assn. of (1922), 41 E. 42d St., N.Y., NY 10017; 3,000.

Industrial Democracy, League for (1905), 112 E. 19th St., N.Y., NY 10003; 2,000.

Industrial Engineers, Amer. Institute of (1948), 25 Technology Park, Norcross, GA 30071; 20,000.

Industrial Health Foundation (1935), 5231 Centre Ave., Pittsburgh, PA 15232; 136 companies.

Industrial Management Society (1938), 570 Northwest Highway, Des Plaines, IL 60018; 750.

Infant Survival, Internatl. Guild for (1964), 7501 Liberty Rd., Baltimore, MD 21207; 700 families.

Information Industry Assn. (1969), 4720 Montgomery Lane, Bethesda, MD 20014; 70 companies.

Instrument Society of America (1945), 400 Stanwix St., Pittsburgh, PA 15222; 20,136.

Insurance Assn., American (1866), 85 John St., N.Y., NY 10038; 138 companies.

Intercollegiate Athletics, Natl. Assn. of (1940), 1205 Baltimore St., Kansas City, MO 64105; 555 schools.

Intercollegiate (Big Ten) Conference (1896), c/o Sheraton-Chicago Hotel, Chicago IL 60611; 10 univ.

Interfraternity Conference, Natl. (1909), P.O. Box 40368, Indianapolis, IN 46240; 46 fraternities.

Interior Designers, Amer. Society of (Jan. 1, 1975, by merger of Amer. Inst. of Interior Designers and Natl. Soc. of Interior Designers), 730 5th Ave., N.Y., NY 10019; 10,000.

International Education, Institute of (1919), 809 United Nations Plaza, N.Y., NY 10017.

International Law, Amer. Society of (1906), 2223 Massachusetts Ave., Wash., DC 20008, 5,500.

Investment Clubs, Natl. Assn. of (1951), 1515 E. Eleven Mile Rd., Royal Oak, MI 48067; 100,000.

Iron Founders' Society, Gray and Ductile (1928), 20611 Center Ridge Rd., Rocky River, OH 44116; 220 firms.

Iron and Steel Engineers, Assn. of (1907), Three Gateway Center, Pittsburgh, PA 15222; 12,000.

Iron and Steel Institute, American (1908), 150 E. 42d St., N.Y., NY 10017; 2,500.

Italian Historical Society of America (1949), 111 Columbia Heights, Brooklyn, NY 11201; 2,177.

Italy-America Chamber of Commerce (1887), 350 Fifth Ave., N.Y., NY 10001; 950.

Izaak Walton League of America (1922), 1800 N. Kent St., Arlington, VA 22304; 56,000.

— J —

Jamestowne Society (1936), P. O. Box 7389, Richmond, VA 23221; 1,850.

Japanese American Citizens League (1930), 1765 Sutter St., San Francisco, CA 94115; 28,727.

Jaycees, United States (1920), P.O. Box 7, 4 West 21st St., Tulsa, OK 74102; 325,000.

Jewish Appeal, United (1939), 1290 Ave. of the Americas, N.Y., NY 10019.

Jewish Center Workers, Assn. of (1918), 15 E. 26th St., N.Y., NY 10010, 850.

Jewish Committee, American (1906), 165 E. 56th St., New York, NY 10022; 40,000.

Jewish Community Centers, World Federation of (1946), 15 E. 96th St., N.Y., NY 10010.

Jewish Congress, American (1918), 15 E. 84th St., New York, NY 10028.

Jewish Federations and Welfare Funds, Council of (1932), 315 Park Ave. S., N.Y., NY 10010; 235 agencies.

Jewish Historical Society, American (1892), 2 Thornton Rd., Waltham, MA 02154; 3,200.

Jewish War Veterans of the U.S.A. (1896), 1712 New Hampshire Ave., NW, Wash., DC 20009; 100,000.

Jewish Welfare Board, National (1917), 15 E. 26th St., N.Y., NY 10010; serves 1,000,000.

Jewish Women, National Council of (1893), W. 47th St., N.Y., NY 10036; 100,000.

Job's Daughters, Internatl. Order of (1921), 1820 Douglas, Masonic Temple, Omaha, NE 68102; 88,000.

Jockey Club (1894), 300 Park Ave., N.Y., NY 10022; 73.

John Birch Society (1958), 395 Concord Ave., Belmont, MA 02178; 60,000 to 100,000.

Journalists, Society of Professional, Sigma Delta Chi (1909), 35 E. Wacker Dr., Chicago, IL 60601; 60,000.

Judaism, American Council for (1943), 309 Fifth Ave., N.Y., NY 10016; 15,000.

Judicature Society, American (1913), 200 W. Monroe, Chicago, IL 60602; 47,000.

Junior Achievement (1919), 909 Third Ave., N.Y., NY 10022; 160,000 children, 23,225 advisers.

Junior College Athletic Assn., Natl. (1938) 12 East 2d, Hutchinson, KS 67501; 561 colleges.

Junior Colleges, American Assn. of Community and (1920), One Dupont Circle, NW, Wash., DC 20036; 905 colleges.

Junior Leagues, Assn. of (1921), 825 Third Ave., N.Y., NY 10022; 113,000.

Jurists, Amer. Justinian Society of (1966), 31 Chambers St., N.Y., NY 10009; 685.

— K —

Kailtone Adventure Society (1970), P. O. Box 233, Dayton, NV 89403; 106.

Kennel Club, American (1884), 51 Madison Ave., N.Y., NY 10010; 400 clubs.

Key Club International (1925), 101 E. Erie St., Chicago, IL 60611; 78,000.

Kindergarten Assn., National (1909), 23 E. 16th St., N.Y., NY 10003.

Kiwanis International (1915), 101 E. Erie St., Chicago, IL 60611; 279,221.

Knights of Columbus (1882), One Columbus Plaza, New Haven, CT 06507; 1,988,460.

Knights of Equity (1895), 278 Howland Ave., Rochester, NY 14620; 1,500.

Knights of Pythias (1864), 47 N. Grant St., Rm. 201, Stockton, CA 95202; 165,865.

Knights Templar, Grand Encampment, of the U.S.A. (1816), 14 E. Jackson Blvd., Suite 1700, Chicago, IL 60604; 362,414.

— L —

La Leche League Internatl. (1956), 9616 Minneapolis Ave., Franklin Park, IL 60131; 30,000.

La Societe de Femme (1963), 777 N. Meridian St., Indianapolis, IN 46204; 2,100.

Lacrosse Foundation (1959), Newton H. White Athletic Ctr., Homewood, Baltimore, MD 21218; 124.

Lambs, The (1874), 131 W. 56th St., N.Y., NY 10019; 400.

Landscape Architects, American Society of (1899), 1750 Old Meadow Rd., McLean, VA 22101; 4,500.

Language Teachers Associations, Natl. Federation of Modern (1916), 400 Wilkeson Quad., SUNY-Buffalo, Buffalo, NY 14261.

Law, Ralph Nader Center for Study of Responsive (1968), P.O. Box 19367, Wash., DC 20036.

Law Institute, American (1923), 4025 Chestnut St., Phila., PA 19104; 2,035.

Law Libraries, American Assn. of (1906), 53 W. Jackson Blvd., Chicago, IL 60604; 1,950.

Law and Social Policy, Center for (1969), 1751 N St., Wash., DC 20036.

Lawn Bowls Assn., American (1915), 10337 Cheryl Dr., Sun City, AZ 85351; 6,200.

Lawn Tennis Assn., U.S. (1881), 51 E. 42d St., N.Y., NY 10017; 85,000.

Learned Societies, American Council of (1919), 345 E. 46th St., N.Y., NY 10017; 41 societies.

Legal Aid and Defender Assn., National (1911), 1155 E. 60th St., Chicago, IL 60637; 3,000.

Legal Secretaries, Natl. Assn. of (1949), 3005 E. Skelly Dr., Tulsa, OK 74105; 22,000.

Legalized Murder, Citizens Against (1966), P.O. Box 24, N.Y., NY 10024; 6,000.

Legion of Valor of the U.S.A. (1890), 621 S. Taylor St., Arlington, VA 22204; 875.

Leonard Wood Memorial (American Leprosy Foundation) (1928), 2430 Pennsylvania Ave., NW, Wash., DC 20037.

Leprosy Missions, American (1917), 297 Park Ave. S., N.Y., NY 10010.

Letter Carriers National Assn. of (1889), 100 Indiana Ave., NW, Wash., DC 20001; 230,086.

Leukemia Society of America (1949), 211 E. 43d St., N.Y., NY 10017; 1,267 trustees.

Liberty Lobby (1955), 300 Independence Ave., SE, Wash., DC 20003; 23,000.

Libraries Association, Special (1909), 235 Park Ave., S., N.Y., NY 10003; 9,300.

Library Association, American (1876), 50 E. Huron St., Chicago, IL 60611; 30,000.

Library Assn., Home and School (1938), 500 Wallace Ave., Covington, KY 41014.

Library Assn., Medical (1902), 919 N. Michigan Ave., Chicago, IL 60611; 3,600.

Life Insurance, Institute of (1939), 277 Park Ave., N.Y., NY 10017; 164 companies.

Life Insurance Assn. of Amer. (1973), 1730 Pennsylvania Ave., NW, Wash., DC 20006; 365 companies.

Life Insurance Marketing & Research Assn. (1916), 170 Sigourney St., Hartford, CT 06105; 560.

Life Office Management Assn. (1924), 100 Park Ave., N.Y., NY 10017; 480 companies.

Life Underwriters, National Assn. of (1890), 1922 F St., NW, Wash., DC 20006; 130,000.

Lifespan (formerly, **People Taking Action Against Abortion**) (1970), 4274 N. Woodward, Royal Oak, MI 48073; 15,000.

Lighter-Than-Air Society (1952), 1800 Triplett Blvd., Akron, OH 44306; 1,200.

Lions Clubs, Internatl. Assn. of (1917), York & Cermak Rds., Oak Brook, IL 60521; 1,036,802.

Little League Baseball (1939), P. O. Box 1127, Williamsport, PA 17701; 9,841 chartered leagues, 54,000 teams.

Log Rolling Assn., International (1926), R.R. # 1, Shawnigar Lake, British Columbia, VOR 2WO, Canada; 186.

Lone Indian Fellowship (1926), 1010 Huron Ave., Sheboygan, WI 53081; 800.

Lubrication Engineers, Amer. Society of (1945), 838 Busse Highway, Park Ridge, IL 60068; 3,000.

Lung Association, American (formerly, **Natl. Tuberculosis & Respiratory Disease Assn.**) (1904), 1740 Broadway, N.Y., NY 10019; 2,000.

Lutheran Education Assn. (1942), 7300 Augusta St., River Forest, IL 60305; 2,750.

— M —

Macaroni Manufacturers Assn., Natl. (1904), 19 S. Bothwell, Box 336, Palatine, IL 60067; 130 firms.

Magazine Publishers Assn. (1919), 575 Lexington Ave., N.Y., NY 10022; 130 companies.

Magazine Writers, Society of (1948), c/o Overseas Press Club, 123 W. 43d St., N.Y., NY 10036; 360.

Magicians Guild of America (1941), 20 W. 40th St., N.Y., NY 10018; 78.

Magicians, Society of Amer. (1902), 66 Marked Tree Rd., Needham, MA 02192; 3,500.

Mail and Marketing Assn., Direct (1917), 6 E. 43d St., N.Y., NY 10017; 2,769.

Mammalogists, Amer. Society of (1919), c/o Museum, Oklahoma State Univ., Stillwater, OK 74074; 3,800.

Management, American Institute of (1948), 125 E. 38th St., New York, NY 10016; 5,000.

Management Assn., American (1923), 135 W. 50th St., N.Y., NY 10020; 50,000.

Management Assn., National (1925), 2210 Arbor Blvd., Dayton, OH 45439; 70,000.

Management Consultants, Institute of (1968), 347 Madison Ave., N.Y., NY 10017; 720.

Management Engineers, Assn. of Consulting (1933), 347 Madison Ave., N.Y., NY 10017; 52 firms.

Management Information Systems, Society for (1968), 10 W. 31st St., Chicago, IL 60616; 1,000.

Manufacturers, Natl. Assn. of (1895), 1776 F St., NW, Washington, DC 20006; 12,100.

Manufacturers' Agents National Assn. (1947), 3130 Wilshire Blvd., Los Angeles, CA 90010; 4,400.

Manufacturing Chemists Assn. (1872), 1825 Connecticut Ave., NW, Wash., DC 20009; 196 companies.

Manufacturing Engineers, Society of (1932), 20501 Ford Rd., Dearborn, MI 48128; 40,000 in 35 countries.

Manuscript Society (1948), 120 Prospect Ave., Princeton, NJ 08540; 1,150.

Marathon Swimming Federation, World Professional (1963), 10295 Windstream Dr., Columbia, MD 21044; 135.

March of Dimes, Natl. Foundation (1938), 1275 Mamaroneck Ave., White Plains, NY 10605; 2,300 chapters.

Marine Corps Combat Correspondents Assn. (1943), 663 Fifth Ave., N.Y., NY 10022; 1,400.

Marine Corps League (1923), 933 N. Kenmore St., Arlington, VA 22201; 20,000.

Marine Society of the City of N. Y. (1770), 80 Broad St., N.Y., NY 10004; 236.

Marine Surveyors, Natl. Assn. of (1960), P.O. Box 55, Peck Slip Station, N.Y., NY 10038; 299.

Marine Technology Society (1963), 1730 M St., NW, Wash., DC 20036; 3,400.

Marine Underwriters, Amer. Institute of (1898), 99 John St., N.Y., NY 10038; 120.

Marketing Assn., American (1937), 222 S. Riverside Plaza, Chicago, IL 60606; 17,689.

Masonic Relief Assn. of U.S. and Canada (1885), 415 S. Main Ave., Sioux Falls, SD 57102; 2,956,585.

Masonic Service Assn. of the U.S. (1919), 8120 Fenton St., Silver Spring, MD 20910; 44 lodges.

Masons, Ancient and Accepted Scottish Rite, Northern Masonic Jurisdiction, Supreme Council 33° (1813), 33 Marrett Rd., Lexington, MA 02173; 511,000.

Masons, Ancient and Accepted Scottish Rite, Southern Jurisdiction, Supreme Council (1801), 1733 16th St., NW, Wash., DC 20009; 626,000.

Masons, Royal Arch, General Grand Chapter (1797), P.O. Box 5320, Lexington, KY 40505; 500,000.

Masons of the State of N.Y., Grand Lodge of Free & Accepted (1781), 71 W. 23d St., N.Y., NY 10010; 229,896.

Mathematical Assn. of America (1915), 1225 Connecticut Ave., Wash., DC 20036; 19,000.

Mathematical Society, American (1888), 201 Charles St., Providence, RI 02904; 16,630.

Mathematical Statistics, Institute of (1937), 1367 Laurel, San Carlos, CA 94070; 3,000.

Mathematics, Society for Industrial and Applied (1952), 33 S. 17th St., Phila., PA 19103; 3,800.

Mattachine Society (1953), 59 Christopher St., N.Y., NY 10014; 500.

Mayflower Descendants, General Society of (1897), P.O. Box 297, Plymouth, MA. 02360; 16,192.

Mayors, U.S. Conference of (1932), 1620 Eye St., NW, Wash., DC 20006; 500 cities.

Mechanical Engineers, Amer. Society of (1880), 345 E. 47th St., New York, NY 10017; 69,325.

Mechanics, Assn. of Chairmen of Departments of (1969), Dept. of Applied Mechanics, Sch. of Engineering, Stanford Univ., Stanford, CA 94305; 105 institutions.

Mechanics, Junior Order of United Amer. (1853), 170 Railway Rd., Grafton, VA 23692; 1,020.

Mediaeval Academy of America (1925), 1430 Massachusetts Ave., Cambridge, MA 02138; 3,660.

Medical Assn., American (1847), 535 N. Dearborn St., Chicago, IL 60610; 210,000.

Medical Association, National (1895), 2109 E St., NW, Wash., DC 20037; 3,000.

Medical Colleges, Assn. of American (1876), One Dupont Circle, NW, Wash., DC 20036; 2,900.

Medical Record Assn., Amer. (1928), 875 N. Michigan Ave., Chicago, IL 60611; 13,688.

Medical Technologists, American (1939), 710 Higgins Rd., Park Ridge, IL 60068; 11,641.

Medical Technologists, Amer. College of (1942), 5608 Lane, Raytown, MO 64133; 368.

Medical Women's Association, Amer. (1915), 1740 Broadway, N.Y., NY 10019; 6,000.

Medicine, New York Academy of (1847), 2 E. 103d St., N.Y., NY 10029; 2,830.

Men Voters of the U. S., League of (1969), 88 Arbol, Oroville, CA 95965.

Mensa (1946), 50 East 42d St., N.Y., NY 10017; 12,500.

Mental Health, Natl. Assn. for (1909), 1800 N. Kent St., Arlington, VA 22209; 1,000,000.

Mental Health Program Directors, Natl. Assn. of State (1963), 15 E St., NW, Wash., DC 20001; 50.

Merchant Marine Library Assn., Amer. (1921), One World Trade Center, Suite 2601, N.Y., NY 10048; 4,160.

Metal Finishers, Natl. Assn. of (1955), 22 S. Park St., Montclair, NJ 07042; 1,000 cos.

Metals, American Society for (1913), Metals Park, OH 44073; 36,059.

Meteorological Society, American (1919), 45 Beacon St., Boston, MA 02108; 9,000.

Metric Assn. U.S. (1916), Sugarloaf Star Rte., Boulder, CO 80302; 5,500.

Microbiology, American Society for (1899), 1913 Eye St., NW, Wash., DC 20006; 21,000.

Microfilm Assn., Natl. (1943), 8728 Colesville Rd., Silver Spring, MD 20910; 7,000.

Middle East, American Friends of the (1951), 1717 Massachusetts Ave., NW, Wash., DC 20036; 300.

Military Chaplains Assn. of the U.S.A. (1925), 7758 Wisconsin Ave., Wash., DC 20014; 2,900.

Military Engineers, Society of Amer. (1920), 740 15th St., NW, Wash., DC 20005; 21,364.

Military Institute, American (1933), P.O. Box 568, Benj. Franklin Sta., Wash., DC 20044; 950.

Military Order of the Carabao (1900, in Manila), 4829 Fairmont Ave., Bethesda, MD 20014; 1,250.

Military Order of the Loyal Legion of the U. S. A. (1865), 1805 Pine St., Phila., PA 19103; 1,100.

Military Order of the Purple Heart (1782, by Gen. George Washington; reactivated Feb. 22, 1932, by President Herbert Hoover and Chief of Staff Douglas MacArthur), P.O. Box 1901; Wash., DC 20013; 15,000.

Military Order of the World Wars (1919), 1100 17th St., NW, Wash., DC 20036; 11,500

Military Surgeons of the U.S., Assn. of (1891), 8502 Connecticut Ave., Chevy Chase, MD 20015; 9,559.

Mining, Metallurgical and Petroleum Engineers, Amer. Institute of (1871), 345 E. 47th St., N.Y., NY 10017; 49,726.

Mining and Metallurgical Society of America (1908), 299 Park Ave., N.Y., NY 10017; 307.

Ministerial Assn., American (1929), 446 Salem Ave., P. O. Box 1252, York, PA 17405; 7,178.

Minute Men of America (1918), P. O. Box 505, Stuart, FL 33494; 16,000.

Model Railroad Assn., Natl. (1935), P.O. Box 1328 Sta. C, Canton, OH 44708; 26,000.

Modern Language Assn. of America (1883), 62 Fifth Ave., N.Y., NY 10011; 30,000.

Moose, Loyal Order of (1888), Mooseheart, IL 60539; 1,396,409.

Mothers Committee, American (1935), Waldorf Astoria, N.Y., NY 10022; 3,000.

Motion Picture Arts & Sciences, Academy of (1927), 8949 Wilshire Blvd., Beverly Hills, CA 90211; 3,700.

Motion Picture Assn. of America (1922), 522 Fifth Ave., N.Y., NY 10036.

Motion Picture & Television Engineers, Society of (1913) 862 Scarsdale Ave., Scarsdale, NY 10583; 7,500.

Motion Pictures, Natl. Board of Review of (1909), 210 E. 68th St., N.Y., NY 10021.

Motor Bus Owners, Natl. Assn. of (1926), 1025 Connecticut Ave., Wash., DC 20036; 600.

Motor Vehicle Administrators, Amer. Assn. of (1933), 1201 Connecticut Ave., NW, Wash., DC 20036; 130.

Motor Vehicle Manufacturers Assn. (1913), 320 New Center Building, Detroit MI 48202; 125.

Motorcycle Assn., American (1924), 33 Collegeview Ave., Westerville, OH 43081; 150,000.

Motoress Aid (1970), 28671 Northwestern Hwy., Southfield, MI 48075; 5,000.

Multiple Sclerosis Society, National (1946), 257 Park Ave. S., N.Y., NY 10010; 182,000.

Municipal Finance Officers Assn. of the U. S. & Canada (1906), 1313 E. 60th St., Chicago, IL 60637; 5,500.

Municipal League, National (1894), 47 E. 68th St., N.Y., NY 10021; 6,400.

Mural Painters, Natl. Society of (1895), 41 E. 65th St., N.Y., NY 10021; 150.

Muscular Dystrophy Assn. (1950), 810 Seventh Ave., N.Y., NY 10019; 79 corporate members.

Museums, American Assn. of (1906), 2233 Wisconsin Ave., NW, Wash., DC 20007; 5,970.

Music, Natl. Assn. of Schools of (1924), 11250 Roger Bacon Drive, Reston, VA 22090; 429 institutions.

Music Center, American (1940), 250 W. 57th St., N.Y., NY 10019; 750.

Music Clubs, Natl. Federation of (1898), Suite 1215, 600 S. Michigan Ave., Chicago, IL 60605; 500,000.

Music Conference, American (1947), 150 E. Huron St., Chicago, IL 60611; 250 cos.

Music Council, National (1940), 250 W. 57th St., N.Y., NY 10019; 60 org.

Music Educators National Conference (1907), 1902 Association Dr., Reston, VA 22091; 62,000.

Music Players, Amateur Chamber (1948), Box 66A, Vienna, VA 22180; 6,500.

Music Publishers' Assn., Natl. (1917), 110 E. 59th St., N.Y., NY 10022; 80.

Music Teachers National Assn. (1876), 408 Carew Tower, Cincinnati, OH 45202; 14,500.

Musicians, American Federation of (1896), 1500 Broadway, N.Y., NY 10036; 332,894.

Musicological Society, American (1934), 201 S. 34th St., Phila., PA 19174; 3,200.

Mutual Savings Banks, National Assn. of (1920), 200 Park Ave., N.Y., NY 10017; 485 banks.

Mystic Seaport (1929), 30 Greenmanville Ave., Mystic, CT 06355; 12,812.

— N —

NAACP (Natl. Assn. for the Advancement of Colored People) (1909), 1790 Broadway, N.Y., NY 10019; 412,000

NAAFA (Natl. Assn. to Aid Fat Americans) (1969), P.O. Box 475, Westbury, NY 11590; 1,000.

Name Society, American (1951), SUNY-Potsdam, Potsdam, NY 13676; 980.

NAPAN (Natl. Assn. for the Prevention of Addiction to Narcotics) (1960), 175 Fifth Ave., N.Y., NY 10010; 125.

NASCAR (Natl. Assn. for Stock Car Auto Racing) (1948), 1801 Speedway Blvd., Daytona Beach, FL 32015; 17,000.

National Guard Assn. (1878), One Massachusetts Ave., Wash., DC 20001; 50,000.

Nationalities Service, American Council for (1958), 20 W. 40th St., N.Y., 10018.

Natural Science for Youth Foundation (1961), 763 Silvermine Rd., New Canaan, CT 06840; 400.

Naturalists, Assn. of Interpretive (1961), 6700 Needwood Rd., Derwood, MD 20855; 1,000.

Nature Conservancy (1950), 1800 N. Kent St., Arlington, VA 22314; 25,000.

Nature & Natural Resources, Internatl. Union for Conservation of (1948), 1110 Morges, Switzerland; 35 countries.

Nature Study Society, Amer. (1908), R.D. 1, Homer, NY 13077; 850.

Naval Architects & Marine Engineers, Society of (1893), 74 Trinity Pl., N.Y., NY 10006; 10,000.

Naval Cadets of America, Junior (1958), 117 Bridge St., Groton, CT 06340; 2,500.

Naval Engineers, American Society of (1888), 1012 14th St. NW, Wash., DC 20005; 4,000.

Naval Institute, U.S. (1873), U.S. Naval Academy, Annapolis, MD 21402; 60,000.

Naval Reserve Assn. (1954), 1913 Eye St., NW, Wash., DC 20006; 17,000.

Navigation, Institute of (1945), 815 15th St., NW, Wash., DC 20005; 3,000.

Navy Club of the U. S. A. (1940), 1602 Wells St., Fort Wayne, IN 46801; 3,000. **Navy Club of the U. S. A. Auxiliary** (1940), 418 W. Pontiac St., Fort Wayne, IN 46807; 1,000.

Navy League of the U. S. (1902), 818 18th St., NW, Wash., DC 20006; 49,556.

Navy Mother's Clubs of America (1930), P. O. Drawer E, Fremont, NE 68025; 25,000.

Needlework Guild of America (1885), 1736 Pine St., Phila., PA 19103; 400,000.

Negro Business and Professional Women's Clubs, Natl. Assn. of (1935), 3411 Lynchester Rd., Baltimore, MD 21215; 2,000.

Negro College Fund, United (1944), 500 E. 62d St., N.Y., NY 10021; 41 colleges.

Newspaper Editors, American Society of (1922), 1350 Sullivan Trail, Easton, PA 18042; 800.

Newspaper Promotion Assn., International (1931), 11600 Sunrise Valley Dr., Reston, VA 22070; 1,150.

Newspaper Publishers Assn., American (1887), 11600 Sunrise Valley Dr., Reston, VA 22070; 1,080 firms.

Newspaper Publishers Assn., Natl. (1940), 2400 S. Michigan Ave., Chicago, IL 60616; 80.

Ninety-Nines (1929), P. O. Box 59964; Will Rogers World Airport, Oklahoma City, OK 73159; 4,600.

Non-Commissioned Officers Assn. of the U. S. A. (1960), Box 2268, San Antonio, TX 78298; 168,000.

Norway, Sons of (1895), 1455 W. Lake St., Minneapolis, MN 55408; 84,000.

Notaries, American Society of (1965), 810 18th St., NW, Wash., DC 20006; 5,154.

Nuclear Society, American (1954), 244 E. Ogden Ave., Hinsdale, IL 60521; 11,000.

Numismatic Assn., American (1891), 818 N. Cascade, Colorado Springs, CO 80903; 32,177.

Numismatic Society, American (1858), Broadway bet. 155th & 156 Sts., N.Y., NY 10032; 1,745.

Nurse Education and Service, Natl. Assn. for Practical (1941), 122 E. 42d St., N.Y., NY 10017; 33,000.

Nurses' Assn., American (1896), 2420 Pershing Rd., Kansas City, MO 64108; 200,000.

Nurses, Natl. Federation of Licensed Practical (1949), 250 W. 57th St., N.Y., NY 10019; 26,548.

Nursing, Natl. League for (1952), 10 Columbus Circle, N.Y., NY 10019; 14,773.

Nutrition, American Institute of (1928), 9650 Rockville Pike, Bethesda, MD 20014; 1,550.

—O—

Occupational Therapy Assn., American (1917), 6000 Executive Blvd., Rockville, MD 20852; 19,000.

Odd Fellows, Independent Order of (1819), 16 W. Chase St., Baltimore, MD 21201; 1,250,000.

Old Crows, Assn. of (1964), 2361 S. Jefferson Davis Highway, Arlington, VA 22202; 8,000.

Olympic Committee, U. S. (1950), 57 Park Ave., N.Y., NY 10016.

Optical Society of America (1916), 2000 L St., NW, Wash., DC 20036; 7,000.

Optimist International (1919), 4494 Lindell Blvd., St. Louis, MO 63108; 112,538.

Optometric Assn., American (1898), 7000 Chippewa St., St. Louis, MO 63119; 19,071.

Oral Surgeons, American Society of (1918), 211 E. Chicago Ave., Chicago, IL 60611; 2,929.

Order of the Rainbow for Girls, Supreme Assembly Internatl. (1922), 315 Carl Albert Parkway, McAlester, OK 74501; 1,000,000.

Organists, American Guild of (1896), 630 Fifth Ave., N.Y., NY 10020; 16,000.

Organization of American States (1890), Pan American Union, 17th & Constitution Ave., NW, Wash., DC 20006; 24 nations.

Oriental Society, American (1840), 329 Sterling Memorial Library, New Haven, CT 06520; 1,850.

Ornithologists' Union, American (1883), c/o National Museum of Natural History, Smithsonian Institution, Wash., DC 20560; 3,400.

ORT Federation, Amer. (Organization for Rehabilitation through Training) (1972), 817 Broadway, N.Y., NY 10013; 120,000.

Osteopathic Assn., American (1901), 212 E. Ohio St., Chicago, IL 60611; 11,453.

Overeaters Anonymous (1960), 3730 Motor Ave., Los Angeles, CA 90034.

—P—

Paleontological Research Institution (1932), 1259 Trumansburg Rd., Ithaca, NY 14850; 492

Paper Institute, American (1964), 260 Madison Ave., N.Y., NY 10016; 200 cos.

Paper Stationery & Tablet Manufacturers Assn. (1934), 1916 Massachusetts Ave., NW, Wash., DC 20036; 25 cos.

Parasitologists, Amer. Society of (1914), 1041 New Hampshire St., Box 368, Lawrence, KS 66044; 1,800.

Parents & Teachers, Natl. Congress of (1897), 700 N. Rush St., Chicago, IL 60611; 7,658,014.

Parents Without Partners (1957), 7910 Woodmont Ave., Wash., DC 20014; 105,000.

Parking Assn., Natl. (1951), 1101 17th St., NW, Wash., DC 20036; 1,500.

Parkinson's Disease Foundation (1957), 640 W. 168th St., N.Y., NY 10032.

Parks & Conservation Assn., National (1919), 1701 18th St., NW, Wash., DC 20009; 50,000.

Pathologists & Bacteriologists, Amer. Assn. of (1900), Dept. of Pathology, Box 3712, Duke Univ. Medical Center, Durham, NC 27710; 1,271.

Pay Toilets in America, Committee to End (1969), Box 71, 118 W. Third St., Dayton, OH 45402; 1,600

Pedestrian Assn., American (1949), 170 Broadway, N.Y., NY 10038; 106.

P.E.N. American Center (1922), 156 Fifth Ave., N.Y., NY 10010; 1,600.

Pen Women, Natl. League of American (1897), 1300 17th St., NW, Wash., DC 20036; 6,000.

Pennsylvania Society (1899), Suite 594, Walfdorf-Astoria Hotel, 301 Park Ave., N.Y., NY 10022; 2,450.

P.E.O. Sisterhood (1869), 3700 Grand Ave., Des Moines, IA 50312; 187,000.

Performance Improvement, Amer. Society for (formerly, Amer. Society for Zero Defects) (1966), 790 Broad St., Newark, NJ 07102; 250.

Personnel Administration, Amer. Society for, (1948), 19 Church St., Berea, OH 44017; 15,000.

Personnel & Guidance Assn., Amer. (1952), 1607 New Hampshire Ave., NW, Wash., DC 20009; 34,000.

Personnel Women, Internatl. Assn. (1950), 358 Fifth Ave., N.Y., NY 10001; 1,000

Petroleum Geologists, American Assn. of (1917), Box 979, 1444 S. Boulder, Tulsa, OK 74101; 16,983.

Petroleum Institute, American (1919), 1801 K St., NW, Wash., DC 20006; 7,000.

Petroleum Landmen, Amer. Assn. of (1955), 2404 Continental Life Bldg., Fort Worth, TX 7610; 4,200.

Pharmaceutical Assn., American (1852), 2215 Constitution Ave., NW, Wash., DC 20037; 52,000.

Philatelic Americans, Society of (1894), P. O. Box 42060, Cincinnati, OH 45242; 7,000.

Philatelic Society, American (1886), P. O. Box 800, 336 S. Fraser St., State College, PA 16801; 34,683.

Philaticians, Society of (1972), P. O. Box 150, Salt Point Tpke., Clinton Corners, NY 12514; 200.

Philharmonic Symphony Society of New York (1928 by merger of **Philharmonic Soc. of N. Y.,** estab. 1842, and **Symphony Soc. of N.Y.,** estab. 1887), Avery Fisher Hall, Lincoln Center, N.Y., NY 10023; 5,000.

Philological Assn., American (1869), 431-432 N. Burrowes, Penn. State Univ., University Park, PA 16802; 2,500.

Philosophical Assn., American (1901), Hamilton College, Clinton, NY 13323; 4,800.

Philosophical Society, American (1743), 104 S. 5th St., Philadelphia, PA 19106; 483.

Photographers of America, Professional (1880), 1090 Executive Way, Des Plaines, IL 60018; 16,578.

Photographers in Communications, Society of (1944), 60 E. 42d St., N.Y., NY 10017; 950.

Photographic Society of America (1934), 2005 Walnut St., Phila., PA 19103; 17,200.

Physical Society, American (1899), 335 E. 45th St., N.Y., NY 10017; 29,000.

Physical Therapy Assn., Amer. (1921), 1156 15th St., NW, Wash., DC 20005; 31,932.

Physicians, American College of (1915), 4200 Pine St., Phila., PA 19104; 20,000.

Physics, American Institute of (1931), 335 E. 45th St., N.Y., NY 10017; 50,000.

Physiological Society, American (1887), 9650 Rockville Pike, Bethesda, MD 20014; 4,500.

Pilgrim Society (1818), 75 Court St., Plymouth, MA 20360; 700.

Pilgrims of the United States (1903), 74 Trinity Pl., N.Y., NY 10006; 1,000.

Pilot Club International (1921), 244 College St., Macon, GA 31201; 18,000.

Pioneer Women (1925), 315 Fifth Ave., N.Y., NY 10016; 50,000.

Planned Parenthood Federation of America (1922), 810 Seventh Ave., N.Y., NY 10019; 190 affiliates.

Planners, Amer. Institute of (1917), 1776 Massachusetts Ave., NW, Wash., DC 20036; 11,118.

Planning Assn., Natl. (1934), 1606 New Hampshire Ave., NW, Wash., DC 20009; 3,500.

Planning Officials, Amer. Society of (1934), 1313 E. 60th St., Chicago, IL 60637; 11,000.

Plastics Engineers, Society of (1942), 656 W. Putnam Ave., Greenwich, CT 06830; 18,000.

Plastics Industry, Society of (1937), 250 Park Ave., N.Y., NY 10017; 1,200 cos.

Platform Assn., Internatl. (1826), 2564 Berkshire Rd., Cleveland Heights, OH 44106; 11,000.

Podiatry Assn., American (1912), 20 Chevy Chase Circle, NW, Wash., DC 20015; 6,200.

Poetry Day Committee, Natl. (1947), 1110 N. Venetian Dr., Miami Beach, FL 33139; 12,000.

Poetry Society of America. (1910), 15 Gramercy Park, N.Y., NY 10003; 700.

Poets, Academy of American (1934), 1078 Madison Ave., N.Y., NY 10028; 81.

Polar Society, American (1934), c/o Secretary, 98-20 62d Dr., Apt. 7H, Rego Park, NY 11374; 2,500.

Police, Amer. Federation of (1966), 1100 NE 125th St., N. Miami, FL 33161; 33,000.

Police, International Assn. of Chiefs of (1893), 11 Firstfield Rd., Gaithersburg, MD 20760; 10,700.

Police, Natl. Assn. of Special and Reserve (1965), Box 45, Bay Sta., Brooklyn, NY 11235; 1,000.

Police Reserve Officers Assn. Natl. (1967), 14600 S. Trail, Venice, FL 33595; 21,000.

Polish Army Veterans Assn. of America (1921), 17 Irving Pl., N.Y., NY 10003; 9,762.

Polish Cultural Society of America (1940), 55 W. 42d St., N.Y., NY 10036; 21,651.

Polish Legion of American Veterans (1921), 3024 N. Laramie Ave., Chicago, IL 60641; 20,000.

Political Items Collectors, Amer. (1945), 66 Golf St., Newington, CT 06111; 2,000.

Political Science, Academy of (1880), 2852 Broadway, N.Y., NY 10025; 11,000.

Political Science Assn., American (1903), 1527 New Hampshire Ave., NW, Wash., DC 20036; 12,000.

Political & Social Science, Amer. Academy of (1889), 3937 Chestnut St., Phila., PA 19104; 18,500.

Polo Association, U.S. (1890), 1301 W. 22d St., Oak Brook, IL 60521; 2,000.

Population Assn. of America (1932), Box 14182, Benjamin Franklin Sta., Wash., DC 20044; 2,500.

Portuguese Continental Union of the U.S.A. (1925), 899 Boylston St., Boston, MA 02115; 9,350.

Postal Clerks, United Federation of (1906), 817 14th St., NW, Wash., DC 20005; 285,000.

Postmasters of the U.S., Natl. Assn. of (1898), 490 L'Enfant Plaza E., SW, Wash., DC 20024; 28,010.

Postmasters of the U.S., Natl. League of (1904), 955 L'Enfant Plaza, SW, Wash., DC 20024; 17,000.

Poultry Science Assn. (1908), c/o Dr. C. B. Ryan, Texas A & M Univ., College Station, TX 77843; 1,500.

Power Boat Assn., American (1903), 22811 Greater Mack, St. Clair Shores, MI 48080; 7,514.

Power Conference, American (1938), Illinois Inst. of Technology, 10 W. 32d St., Chicago, IL 60616.

Power Engineers, Natl. Assn. of (1882), 176 W. Adams St., Chicago, IL 60603; 12,296.

Power Squadron, U.S. (1914), 50 Craig Rd., Montvale, NJ 07645; 88,000.

Precancel Collectors, Natl Assn. of (1950), 5121 Park Blvd., Wildwood, NJ 08260; 6,000.

Press Club, Natl. (1908), 529 14th St., NW, Wash., DC 20045; 5,000.

Press Institute, International (1951), Munstergasse 9, CH-8001 Zurich, Switzerland; 1,900.

Press and Radio Club (1948), P.O. Box 7023, Montgomery, AL 36107; 691.

Press Women, Natl. Federation of (1937), 1105 Main St., Blue Springs, MD 64015.

Production & Inventory Control Society, Amer. (1957), 2600 Virginia Ave., NW, Wash., DC 20037; 12,100.

Propeller Club of the U.S. (1927), 1730 M St., NW, Wash., DC 20036; 13,000.

Psychiatric Assn., American (1844), 1700 18th St., NW, Wash., DC 20009; 21,364.

Psychical Research, Amer. Society of (1885), 5 W. 73d St., N.Y., NY 10023; 2,500.

Psychoanalytic Assn., American (1911), One E. 57th St., N.Y., NY 10022; 2,090.

Psychological Assn., American (1892), 1200 17th St., NW, Wash., DC 20036; 39,000.

Psychological Assn. for Psychoanalysis, Natl. (1946), 150 W. 13th St., N.Y., NY 10011; 165.

Psychological Minorities, Society for the Aid of (1968), 42-25 Hampton St., Elmhurst, NY 11373; 500.

Psychotherapy Assn., Amer. Group (1942), 1865 Broadway, N.Y., NY 10023; 3,000.

Public Health Assn., American (1872), 1015 18th St., NW, Wash., DC 20036; 50,000.

Public Relations Society of America (1948), 845 Third Ave., N.Y., NY 10022; 7,200.

Public Welfare Assn., American (1936), 1313 E. 60th St., Chicago, IL 60637; 7,900.

Publishers, Assn. of American (1970), One Park Ave., N.Y., NY 10016; 260 cos.

— Q & R —

Quality Control, Amer. Society for (1946), 161 W. Wisconsin Ave., Milwaukee, WI 53203; 22,300.

Quint-A (1954), 23219 Lincolnshire Dr., Bay Village, OH 44140; 6,881.

Racing Commissioners, National Assn. of State (1934), P.O. Box 4216, Lexington, KY 40504; 650.

Racquetball Assn., Natl. (1974), 4101 Dempster St., Skokie, IL 60076; 10,000.

Radio Free Europe (1949), 2 Park Ave., N.Y., NY 10016.

Radio Liberty (1951), 30 E. 42d St., N.Y., NY 10017.

Radio Relay League, Amer. (1914), 225 Main St., Newington, CT 06111; 108,191.

Radio and Television Society, International (1939), 420 Lexington Ave., N.Y., NY 10017; 1,200.

Radio Union, International Amateur (1925), 225 Main St., Newington, CT 06111; 86 societies.

Radiological Society of N. America (1915), One MONY-Plaza, Syracuse, NY 13202; 7,560.

Railroad Passengers, Natl. Assn. of (1967), 417 New Jersey Ave., SE, Wash., DC 20003; 4,800.

Railroads, Assn. of American (1943), 1920 L St., NW, Wash., DC 20036; 167 railroads.

Railway Engineering Assn., American (1899), 59 E. Van Buren St., Chicago, IL 60605; 3,400.

Railway Historical Society, Natl. (1935), P.O. Box 2051, Phila., PA 19013; 8,900.

Railway Progress Institute (1908), 801 N. Fairfax St., Alexandria, VA 22314; 145 cos.

Range Management, Society for (1948), 2120 S. Birch St., Denver, CO 80222; 5,000.

Real Estate Investment Funds, Natl. Assn. of (1960), 1101 17th St., NW, Wash., DC 20036; 310.

Realtors, Natl. Assn. of (1908), 155 E. Superior St., Chicago, IL 60611; 350,000.

Reconciliation, Fellowship of (1915), 523 N. Broadway, Nyack, NY 10960; 23,500.

Recording Industry Assn. of America (1952), One E. 57th St., N.Y., NY 10022; 50 firms.

Records Management Assn., American (1956), Suite 823, 24 N. Wabash Av., Chicago, IL 60602; 2,400.

Recreation and Park Assn., Natl. (1965), 1601 N. Kent St., Arlington, VA 22209; 18,000.

Red Cross, American National (1881), 17th & D Sts., NW, Wash., DC 20006; 30,867,850.

Red Men, Improved Order of (1765), 1525 W. Ave., Box 683, Waco, TX 76707; 67,000.

Regional Plan Assn. (1929), 235 E. 45th St., N.Y., NY 10027; 3,000.

Rehabilitation Assn., Natl. (1925), 1522 K St., NW, Wash., DC 20005; 35,000.

Religion, Amer. Academy of (1896), Dept. of Religion, Florida State Univ., Tallahassee, FL 32306; 4,058.

Renaissance Society of America (1954), 1161 Amsterdam Ave., N.Y., NY 10027; 3,300.

Rescue Committee, Internatl. (1933), 386 Park Ave., S., N.Y., NY 10010; 62 directors.

Reserve Officers Assn. of the U.S. (1920), One Constitution Ave., NE, Wash., DC 20002; 95,300.

Responsible Patriotism, Natl. Committee for (1967), Commodore Hotel, 109 E. 42d St., N.Y., NY 10017; 150.

Restaurant Assn., Natl. (1919), IBM Plaza, Chicago, IL 60611; 125,000.

Retail Druggists, National Assn. of (1898), One E. Wacker Dr., Chicago, IL 60601; 32,000.

Retail Merchants, Natl. Assn. (1911), 100 W. 31st St., N.Y., NY 10001; 30,000.

Retarded Citizens, Natl. Assn. for (1950), 2709 Ave. E. East., Arlington, TX 76011; 250,000.

Retired Assn. for the Uniformed Services (1970), 1701 21st Ave. S., Nashville, TN 37212; 24,788.

Retired Federal Employees, Natl. Assn. of (1921), 1533 New Hampshire Ave., NW, Wash., DC 20036; 216,000.

Retired Officers Assn. (1929), 1625 Eye St., NW, Wash., DC 20006; 210,000.

Retired Persons, Amer. Assn. of (1958), 1909 K St., NW, Wash., DC 20049; 7,500,000.

Retired Teachers Assn., Natl. (1947), 1909 K St., NW, Wash., DC 20049; 420,000.

Retreads (of World War I & II) (1947), 40-07 154th St., Flushing, NY 11354; 1,500.

Revolver Assn., U.S. (1900), 59 Alvin St., Springfield, MA 01104; 1,250.

Rhodes Scholars, Assn. of American (1907), 1100 Philadelphia Natl. Bank Bldg., Phila., PA 19107; 1,493.

Rifle Assn. of America, Natl. (1871), 1600 Rhode Island Ave., NW, Wash., DC 20036; 1,000,000.

Road Builders' Assn., American (1902), 525 School St., SW, Wash., DC 20024; 5,000.

Rocketry, National Assn. of (1956), P.O. 178, McLean, VA 22101; 5,000.

Rodeo Cowboys Assn., Professional (1954), 2929 W. 19th Ave., Denver, CO 80204; 8,000.

Roller Skating Assn., U.S. Amateur (1942), 152 W. 42d St., N.Y., NY 10036; 11,000.

Roller Skating Confederation, U.S.A. (1973), 7700 A St., Lincoln, NE 68510; 25,000.

Roller Skating Rink Operators Assn. (1937), 7700 A St., Lincoln, NE 68510; 970 rinks.

Rose Society, American (1889), P.O. Box 30,000, Shreveport, LA 71130; 18,000.

Rosicrucian Fraternity (1614 in Germany, 1861 in U.S.), Beverly Hall, Quakertown, PA 18951.

Rosicrucian Order, AMOCR (1915), Rosicrucian Park, San Jose, CA 95151; 120,000.

Rosicrucians, Society of (1909), 321 W. 101st St., N.Y., NY 10025.

Rotary International (1905), 1600 Ridge Ave., Evanston, IL 60201; 768,250.

Round Table International (1923), 61 E. Colorado Blvd., Pasadena, CA 91101; 866.

Rowing Assn., Intercollegiate (1895), Hotel Manhattan, 8th Ave. at 44th St., N.Y., NY 10036; 5 colleges.

Royal Arcanum, Supreme Council of the (1877), 61 Batterymarch St., Boston, MA 02110; 30,918.

Rubber Manufacturers Assn. (1915), 444 Madison Ave., N.Y., NY 10022; 200 firms.

Ruritan National (1928), Box 487, Dublin, VA 24084; 37,121.

Russian Orthodox Clubs, Federated (1927), 84 E. Market St., Wilkes-Barre, PA 18701; 4,500.

—S—

Safety Council, National (1913), 425 N. Michigan Ave., Chicago, IL 60611; 16,000.

Safety Engineers, Amer. Society of (1911), 850 Busse Hwy., Park Ridge, IL 60068; 13,000.

St. Paul, National Guilds of (1937), 601 Hill 'N Dale, Lexington, KY 40503; 13,275.

Salt Institute (1914), 206 N. Washington St., Alexandria, VA 22314; 25 cos.

Salvation Army (1865 in England, 1880 in U.S.), 120 W. 14th St., N.Y., NY 10011; 361,571.

Sane World, A Citizen's Organization for a (1957), 318 Massachusetts Ave., NE, Wash., DC 20002; 20,000.

Save-the-Redwoods League (1920), 114 Sansome St., San Francisco, CA 94104; 55,000.

Savings & Loan League, Natl. (1943), 1101 15th St., NW, Wash., DC 20005; 500.

School Administrators, American Assn. of (1865), 1801 N. Moore St., Arlington, VA 22209; 20,000.

School Boards Assn., Natl. (1940), State Natl. Bank Plaza, P. O. Box 1496, Evanston, IL 60204; 53 assns.

School Counselor Assn., American (1952), 1607 New Hampshire Ave., NW, Wash., DC 20009; 14,100.

School Principals, Natl. Assn. of Secondary (1916), 1904 Association Dr., Reston, VA 22091; 30,000.

Schools & Colleges, Amer. Council on (1927), 446 Salem Ave., P.O. Box 1252, York, PA 17405; 123 schools.

Schweitzer, Albert, Fellowship (1939), 866 United Nations Plaza, N.Y., NY 10017.

Schweitzer, Albert, Friendship House (1967), Hurburt Rd., Great Barrington, MA 01230; 70,000.

Science, Amer. Assn. for the Advancement of (1848), 1515 Massachusetts Ave., NW, Wash., DC 20005; 120,458.

Science Service (1921), 1719 N St., NW, Wash., DC 20036.

Science Teachers Assn., Natl. (1944), 1742 Connecticut Ave., NW, Wash., DC 20009; 21,000.

Science Writers, Natl. Assn. of (1934), Box H, Sea Cliff, NY 11579; 950.

Sciences, National Academy of (1863), 2101 Constitution Ave., NW, Wash., DC 20418; 1,054.

Sciences, New York Academy of (1818), 2 E. 63d St., N.Y., NY 10021; 25,000.

Scientific Apparatus Makers Assn. (1918), 1140 Connecticut Ave., NW, Wash., DC 20036; 222 cos.

Scientists, Federation of American (1946), 307 Massachusetts Ave., NE, Wash., DC 20002; 6,500.

Scottish Clans, Order of (1878), 111 Washington St., Brookline, MA 02146; 10,000.

Screen Actors Guild (1933), 7750 Sunset Blvd., Hollywood, CA 90046; 29,000.

Sculpture Society, Natl. (1893), 75 Rockefeller Plaza, N.Y., N.Y. 10019; 350.

Seamen's Service, United (1942), 17 Battery Place, N.Y., NY 10004.

Secularists of America, United (1947), 377 Vernon St., Oakland, CA 94610; 900.

Securities Industry Assn. (1972), 20 Broad St., N.Y., NY 10005; 850 firms.

Security Industrial Assn., National (1944), 740 15th St., NW, Wash., DC 20005; 350.

Seeing Eye, The (1929), Morristown, NJ 07960; 26,000.

Semantics, Institute of General (1938), White Hollow Rd., Lime Rock, CT 06039; 1,000.

Separation of Church & State, Americans United for (1947), 8120 Fenton St., Silver Spring, MD 20910; 122,000.

Separationists, Society of (1963), P.O. Box 2117, Austin, TX 78767; 28,000 families.

Sertoma International (1912), 1900 E. Meyer Blvd., Kansas City, MO 64132; 30,104.

Settlements & Neighborhood Centers, Natl. Federation of (1911), 232 Madison Ave., N.Y., NY 10016; 2,500.

Sex Information & Education Council of the U.S. (SIECUS) (1964), 1855 Broadway, N.Y., NY 10023; 50.

Shade Tree Conference, Internatl. (1924), P.O. Box 71, 3 Lincoln Sq., Urbana, IL 61801; 3,000.

Sheriff's Assn., Natl. (1940), 1250 Connecticut Ave., NW, Wash., DC 20036; 41,000.

Shipbuilders Council of America (1921), Watergate 600, Wash., DC 20037; 37 cos.

Shoe Retailers Assn., Natl. (1912), 200 Madison Ave., N.Y., NY 10016; 3,500.

Shore & Beach Preservation Assn., Amer. (1926), 10 Flickenbacker Causeway, Miami, FL 33149; 600.

Shorthand Reporters Assn., Natl. (1899), 2361 S. Jefferson Davis Hwy., Arlington, VA 22202.

Showmen's League of America (1913), 300 W. Randolph St., Chicago, IL 60606; 1,650.

Shrine, Imperial Council of the A. A. Order of Nobles of

the Mystic (1872), 323 N. Michigan Ave., Chicago, IL 60601; 896,750.

Shut-In Day Society, Natl. (1970), 237 Franklin St., Reading, PA 19602; 5,000.

Sierra Club (1892), 220 Bush St., San Francisco, CA 94104; 145,000.

Silurians, Society of the (1924), 45 John St., N.Y., NY 10038; 700.

Skating Union of the U. S., Amateur (1927), 4423 W. Deming Pl., Chicago, IL 60639; 2,100

Skeet Shooting Assn., Natl. (1946), P.O. Box 28188, San Antonio, TX 78228; 19,500.

Ski Assn., U.S. (1904), 1726 Champa St., Denver CO 80202; 110,000.

Small Business, Amer. Federation of (1963), 407 S. Dearborn, Chicago, IL 60605; 5,000.

Small Business Assn., Natl. (1937), 1225 19th St., NW, Wash., DC 20036; 40,000.

Smoking & Health, Natl. Clearinghouse for (1965), 5401 Westbard Ave., Bethesda, MD 20016.

Soaring Society of America (1932), 3200 Airport Ave., Santa Monica, CA 90405; 13,567.

Soccer Federation, U.S. (1913), 350 Fifth Ave., N.Y., NY 10001; 41 assns.

Social Biology, Society for the Study of (1972), 722 W. 168th St., N.Y., NY 10032; 475.

Social Health Assn., American (1912), 1740 Broadway, N.Y., NY 10019; 1,200.

Social Science Research Council (1924), 605 Third Ave., N.Y., NY 10016; 30.

Social Sciences, Natl. Institute of (1865), 545 Madison Ave., N.Y., NY 10022; 675.

Social Welfare, Internatl. Council on (1928), 345 E. 46th St., N.Y., NY 10017; 70 natl. committees.

Social Welfare, Natl. Conference on (1873), 22 W. Gay St., Columbus, OH 43215; 7,000.

Social Work Education, Council on (1952), 345 E. 46th St., N.Y., NY 10017; 4,800.

Social Workers, National Assn. of (1955), 1425 H St., NW, Wash., DC 20005; 62,640.

Sociological Assn., American (1905), 1722 N St., NW, Wash., DC 20036; 14,000.

Soft Drink Assn., National (1919), 1101 16th St., NW, Wash., DC 20006; 1,896.

Softball Assn., Amateur (1933), 2801 N.E. 50th St., Oklahoma City, OK 73111; 1,500,000.

Softball League, Cinderella (1958), 34 E. Market St., Corning, NY 14830; 50,000.

Soil Conservation Society of America (1945), 7515 N.E. Ankeny Rd., Ankeny, IA 50021; 14,500.

Sojourners, National (1919), 4600 Duke St., Alexandria, VA 22304; 10,000.

Soldier's, Sailor's and Airmen's Club (1919), 283 Lexington Ave., N.Y., NY 10016.

Sons of the American Legion (1932), 700 N. Pennsylvania St., Indianapolis, IN 46204; 21,000.

Sons of the American Revolution, Natl. Society (1889), 2412 Massachusetts Ave., Wash., DC 20008; 20,000.

Sons of Confederate Veterans (1896), Southern Sta., Box 1, Hattiesburg, MS 39401; 4,000.

Sons of Italy in America, Order (1905), 1226 S. Broad St., Phil., PA 19146; 250,000.

Sons of Poland, Assn. of the (1903), 655 Newark Ave., Jersey City, NJ 07306; 16,000.

Sons of the Revolution in the State of New York (1876), Fraunces Tavern, 54 Pearl St., N.Y., NY 10004; 1,500.

Sons of St. Patrick, Society of the Friendly (1784), 80 Wall St., N.Y., NY 10005; 1,300.

Sons of Union Veterans of the Civil War (1881), Box 24, Federal Bldg., Gettysburg, PA 17325; 3,500.

Soroptimist Federation of the Americas (1921), 1616 Walnut St., Phila., PA 19103; 30,000.

Southern Christian Leadership Conference (1957), 334 Auburn Ave., NE, Atlanta, GA 30303; 243 affiliate orgs.

Southern Regional Council (1944), 52 Fairlie St., NW, Atlanta, GA 30303; 110.

Spanish War Veterans, United (1904), 810 Vermont Ave., NW, Wash., DC 20420; 450.

Speech Communication Assn. (1914), Statler Hilton Hotel, N.Y., NY 10001; 6,730.

Speech & Hearing Assn., American (1925), 9030 Old Georgetown Rd., Wash., DC 20014; 20,000.

Speleological Society of America (1964), 1124 100th Ave. NE, Bellevue, WA 98004; 3,627.

Speleological Society, Natl. (1941), Cave Ave., Huntsville, AL 35810; 4,500.

Spelling Council, Phonemic (1971), 521 W. 120th St., N.Y., NY 10027; 100.

Sports Car Club of America (1944), 1562 S. Parker Rd., Denver, CO 80231; 22,000.

Stamp Dealers' Assn., American (1914), 595 Madison Ave., N.Y., NY 10022; 1,000.

Standards Institute, Amer. National (1918), 1430 Broadway, N.Y., NY 10018; 1,032 orgs.

State Communities Aid Assn. (1872), 105 E. 22d St., N.Y., NY 10010; 285.

State Governments, Council of (1933), Iron Works Pike, Lexington, KY 40511.

State High School Assns., Natl. Federation of (1920), 400 Leslie St., Elgin, IL 60120; 50 states, 10 provinces.

State & Local History, American Assn. for (1940), 1400 8th Ave., So., Nashville, TN 37203; 4,300.

State Parks, Natl. Conference on (1921), 1601 N. Kent St., Arlington, VA 22209; 657.

State Universities & Land-Grant Colleges, Natl. Assn. of (1871), One Dupont Circle, NW, Wash., DC 20036.

Statistical Assn., American (1839), 806 15th St., NW, Wash., DC 20005; 10,800.

Steamship Historical Society of America (1935), 414 Pelton Ave., Staten Island, NY 10310; 1,903.

Steel Construction, American Institute of (1921), 101 Park Ave., N.Y., NY 10017; 944.

Steel Founders' Society of America (1902), 20611 Center Ridge Rd., Rocky River, OH 44116; 115 companies.

Steeplechase and Hunt Assn., Natl. (1895), Box 308, Elmont, NY 11003; 3,000.

Sterilization, Assn. for Voluntary (1943), 708 Third Ave., N.Y., NY 10017; 5,000.

Steuben Society of America (1919), 369 Lexington Ave., N.Y., NY 10017.

Stock Exchange, American (1908), 86 Trinity Pl., N.Y., NY 10006; 650.

Stock Exchange, New York (1792), 11 Wall St., N.Y., NY 10005; 1,366.

Stock Exchange, Philadelphia-Baltimore-Washington (1790), 17th St., Stock Exchange Pl., Phila., PA 19103; 448.

Student Assn., U.S. Natl. (1947), 2115 S. St., NW, Wash., DC 20008; 500 schools.

Student Councils, Natl. Assn. of (1916), 1904 Association Dr., Reston, VA 22091; 7,000.

Students of German, Natl. Federation of (1968), 339 Walnut St., Phila., PA 19106; 25,000.

Sugar Association (1949), 254 W. 31st St., N.Y., NY 10001; 24.

Sugar Brokers Assn., National (1903), 76 Beaver St., N.Y., NY 10005; 278.

Sunday League (1933), 279 Highland Ave., Newark, NJ 07104; 25,000.

Surgeons, American College of (1913), 55 E. Erie St., Chicago, IL 60611; 35,500.

Surgeons, International College of (1935), 1516 N. Lake Shore Dr., Chicago, IL 60610; 12,000.

Surveying & Mapping, Amer. Congress on (1941), 733 15th St., NW, Wash., DC 20005; 6,450.

Symphony Orchestra League, Amer. (1942), P. O. Box 66, Vienna, VA 22180; 2,563.

Systems Management, Assn. for (1947), 24587 Bagley Rd., Cleveland, OH 44138; 9,940.

— T —

Table Tennis Assn., U.S. (1933), Box 815, Orange, CT 06477; 5,000

Tattoo Club of America (1974), 112 W. First St., Mt. Vernon, NY 10550; 3,500.

Tax Accountants, Natl. Assn. of Enrolled Federal (1960), 6108 N. Harding Ave., Chicago, IL 60659; 500.

Tax Administrators, Federation of (1937), 1313 E. 60th St., Chicago, IL 60637.

Tax Assn., Natl.-Tax Institute of America (1907), 21 E. State St., Columbus, OH 43215; 2,500.

Tax Foundation (1937), 50 Rockefeller Plaza, N.Y., NY 10020; 2,000.

Tea Assn. of the U.S.A. (1899), 230 Park Ave., N.Y., NY 10017; 250.

Teachers, American Federation of (1916), 1012 14th St., NW, Wash., DC 20005; 450,000.

Teachers' Agencies, Natl. Assn. of (1915), 1825 K St., NW, Wash., DC 20006; 60.

Teachers of English, Natl. Council of (1911), 1111 Kenyon Rd., Urbana, IL 61801; 100,000.

Teachers of French, Amer. Assn. of (1927), 57 E. Armory Ave., Champaign, IL 61820; 11,100.

Teachers of German, Amer. Assn. of (1930), 339 Walnut St., Phila., PA 19106; 8,500.

Teachers of Singing, Natl. Assn. of (1944), 250 W. 57th St., N.Y., NY 10019; 2,700.

Teachers of Spanish & Portuguese, Amer. Assn. of (1917), Holy Cross Coll., Worcester, MA 01601; 14,500.

Technical Communication, Society for (1953), 1010 Vermont Ave., NW, Wash., DC 20005; 3,000.

Television Arts & Sciences, Natl. Academy of (1948), 291 S. La Cienega, Beverly Hills, CA 90211; 9,889.

Television & Radio Arts, Amer. Federation of (1937), 1350 Ave. of Americas, N.Y., NY 10019; 29,000.

Telluride Assn. (1911), 217 West Ave., Ithaca, NY 14850; 75.

Tennis League, Youth (1968), 1701 Vandalia, Collinsville, IL 62234; 850.

Testing & Materials, Amer. Society for (1898), 1916 Race St., Phila., PA 19103; 24,000.

Textile Assn., Northern (1854), 211 Congress St., Boston, MA 02110; 150 cos.

Textile Manufacturers Institute, Amer. (1949), 1501 Johnston Bldg., Charlotte, NC 28281.

Theatre & Academy, American National (1935), 245 West 52d St., N.Y., NY 10019; 800.

Theatre Assn., American (1936), 1317 F St., NW, Wash., DC 20004; 6,000.

Theatre Organ Society, Amer. (1955), P.O. Box 1002, Midleburg, VA 22117; 5,300.

Theatre Owners, Natl. Assn. of (1924), 1501 Broadway, N.Y., NY 10036; 8,000.

Theodore Roosevelt Assn. (1919), P.O. Box 720, Oyster Bay, NY 11771; 300.

Theological Library Assn., Amer. (1947), Lutheran Theological Seminary, 7301 Germantown Ave., Phila., PA 19119; 559.

Theological Schools, Amer. Assn. of (1936), P.O. Box 396, Vandalia, OH 45377; 198 schools.

Theosophical Society (1875), 1926 N. Main St., Wheaton, IL 60187; 5,500.

Thoreau Society (1941), SUNY-Geneseo, Geneseo, NY 14454; 1,200.

Thoroughbred Racing Assn. (1942), 522 Fifth Ave., N.Y., NY 10036; 56 Race Tracks.

Titanic Historical Society (1963), P.O. Box 53, Indian Orchard, MA 01051; 612.

Toastmistress Clubs, Internatl. (1938), 9068 E. Firestone Blvd., Downey, CA 90241; 23,000.

Topical Assn., American (1949), 3306 N. 50th St., Milwaukee, WI 53216; 10,881.

Torch Clubs, Internatl. Assn. of (1924), Box 8670, University Sta., Knoxville, TN 37916; 5,200.

Trade Relations Council (1885), 1001 Connecticut Ave., NW, Wash., DC 20036; 50 cos.

Traffic Engineers, Institute of (1930), 1815 N. Ft. Myer Dr., Arlington, VA 22209; 4,246.

Traffic and Transportation, Amer. Society of (1946), 547 W. Jackson Blvd., Chicago, IL 60606; 2,717.

Training Corps, American (1961), 107-12 Jamaica Ave., Richmond Hill, NY 11418; 650.

Training & Development, Amer. Society for (1943), P.O. Box 5307, Madison, WI 53705; 10,000.

Transit Assn., Amer. Public (1882), 1100 17th St., NW Wash., DC 20036; 590.

Transportation Assn. of America (1935), 1100 17th St., NW, Wash., DC 20036; 650 cos.

Trapshooting Assn., Amateur (1899), 601 W. National Rd., Vandalia, OH 45377; 70,000.

Travel Agents, American Society of (1931), 360 Lexington Ave., N.Y., NY 10017; 13,000.

Travel Organizations, Discover America (1969), 1100 Connecticut Ave., NW, Wash., DC 20036; 1,000.

Traveleers International (1943), P.O. Box 1017, Chandler, AZ 85224; 16,688.

Travelers Aid-Internatl. Social Service of America (1972), E. 46th St., N.Y., NY 10017.

Trotting Assn., U.S. (1932), 750 Michigan Ave., Columbus, OH 43215; 35,000.

Trucking Assns., American (1933), 1616 P St., NW, Wash., DC 20036; 51 assns.

True Sisters, United Order (1846), 150 W. 85th St., N.Y., NY 10024; 11,000.

Turners, American (1848), 1550 Clinton Ave., N. Rochester, NY 14621; 17,000.

— U —

UNICEF, U.S. Committee for (1947), 331 E. 38th St., N.Y., NY 10016; 3,000,000 volunteers.

Unidentified Flying Objects, Natl. Investigations Committee on (1967), 7970 Woodman Ave., Van Nuys, CA 91402; 1,000.

Uniformed Services, Natl. Assn. for (1968), 956 N. Monroe St., Arlington, VA 22201; 25,000.

United Nations, U.S. People for (1967), 777 United Nations Pl., N.Y., NY 10017; 30,000.

United Nations Assn. of the U.S.A. (1923, as **League of Nations Assn.**), 345 E. 46th St., N.Y., NY 10017; 31,928.

United Press International (1907, formerly **United Press Assn.**; renamed 1958 after merger with **International News**

Service), 220 E. 42d St., N.Y., NY 10017.

United Service Organizations (1941), 237 E. 52d St., N.Y., NY 10022; 90,000.

United States Army, Assn. of the (1950), 1529 18th St., NW, Wash., DC 20036; 81,247.

United Way of America (1918), 801 N. Fairfax St., Alexandria, VA 22314; 1,119.

Universities, Assn. of American (1900), One Dupont Circle, Wash., DC 20036; 48 universities.

Universities & Colleges, Assn. of Governing Boards of (1963), One Dupont Circle, NW, Wash., DC 20036; 14,000.

University Extension Assn., Natl. (1915), One Dupont Circle, Wash., DC, 20036; 1,200.

University Foundation Internatl. (1973), 501 E. Armour Blvd., Kansas City, MO 64109.

University Professors, American Assn. of (1915), One Dupont Circle, NW, Wash., DC 20036; 75,069.

University Women, Amer. Assn. of (1882), 2401 Virginia Ave., NW, Wash., DC 20037; 185,000.

Up With People (1965), 3103 N. Campbell, Tucson, AZ 85719.

Urban Coalition, National (1968), 1201 Connecticut Ave., NW, Wash., DC 20036.

Urban League, National (1910), 55 E. 52d St., N.Y., NY 10022; 12,000.

Utility Commissioners, Natl. Assn. of Regulatory (1889), 1102 Interstate Commerce Comm. Bldg., Box 684, Wash., DC 20044; 66 agencies.

— V —

Variety Clubs International (1928), 7210 Red Rd., S. Miami, FL 33143; 10,000.

Vegetable Growers Assn. of America (1908), 1616 H. St., NW, Wash., DC 20006; 1,100.

Veteran Motor Car Club of America (1938), 105 Elm St., Andover, MA 01810; 4,075.

Veterans Committee, Amer. (1946), 1333 Connecticut Ave., NW, Wash., DC 20036.

Veterans of Foreign Wars of the U.S. & Ladies Auxiliary (1899), VFW Bldg., 34th St., Kansas City, MO 64111; 2,300,000.

Veterans of World War I of the U.S.A. (1958), 916 Prince St., Alexandria, VA 22314; 150,000.

Veterinary Medical Assn., Amer. (1863), 930 N. Meachan Rd., Schaumburg, IL 60172; 25,136.

Victorian Society in America (1966), The Athenaeum, 219 S. 6th St., Phila., PA 19106; 2,200.

Vocational Assn., American (1925), 1510 H St., NW, Wash., DC 20005; 55,000.

Volleyball Assn., U.S. (1928), 557 Fourth St., San Francisco, CA 94107; 8,000.

— W —

Walther League (1893), 119 W. Locust St., Chicago, IL 60610.

War of 1812, Society of (1814), 1307 New Hampshire Ave., NW, Wash., DC 20036; 1,000.

War Mothers, Amer. (1917), 2615 Woodley Pl. NW, Wash., DC 20008; 14,000.

Watch & Clock Collectors, Natl. Assn. of (1943), NAWCC Bldg., 514 Popular St., Columbia, PA 17512; 42,000.

Water Pollution Control Federation (1928), 3900 Wisconsin Ave., NW, Wash., DC 20016; 25,000.

Water Resources Assn., American (1964), Mississippi River at 3d Ave., SE Minneapolis, MN 55414; 2,400.

Water Ski Assn., Amer. (1939), 7th St. & Ave. G, SW, Winter Haven, FL 33880; 11,500.

Water Well Assn., Natl. (1948), 88 E. Broad St., Columbus, OH 43215; 4,000.

Water Works Assn., Amer. (1881), 6666 W. Quincy Ave., Denver, CO 80235; 23,000.

Welding Society, Amer. (1919), 2501 NW 7th St., Miami, FL 33125; 22,995.

Wheelchair Athletic Assn., Natl. (1957), 40-24 62d St., Woodside, NY 11377; 1,600.

Wilderness Society (1935), 1901 Pennsylvania Ave. NW, Wash., DC 20006; 90,000.

Wildlife, Defenders of (1925), 2000 N. St., NW, Wash., DC 20036; 32,000.

Wildlife Federation, Natl. (1936), 1412 16th St., NW, Wash., DC 20036; 3,500,000.

Wildlife Foundation, N. American (1935), 709 Wire Bldg., 100 Vermont Ave. NW, Wash., DC 20005.

Wildlife Fund, World (1961), 910 17th St., NW, Wash., DC 20006; 28 national chapters.

Wildlife Management Institute (1946), 1000 Vermont Ave., NW, Wash., DC 20005.

Wildlife Society (1937), S-176, 3900 Wisconsin Ave., NW

Wash., DC 20016; 7,732.

William Penn Assn. (1886), 429 Forbes Ave., Pittsburgh, PA 15219; 68,004.

Wireless Pioneers, Society of (1967), P.O. Box 530, 3366 Mendocino Ave., Santa Rosa, CA 95402; 2,059.

Woman's Assn., American 19 W. 44th St., N.Y., NY 10036.

Woman's Christian Temperance Union, Natl. (1874), 1730 Chicago Ave., Evanston, IL 60201; 250,000.

Women, Natl. Organization for (NOW) (1966), 5 S. Wabash, Chicago, IL 60603; 52,000.

Women Artists, Natl. Assn. of (1889), 156 Fifth Ave., N.Y., NY 10010; 700.

Women Engineers, Society of (1950), 345 E. 47th St., N.Y., NY 10017; 2,900.

Women Geographers, Society of (1925), 1619 New Hampshire Ave., NW, Wash., DC 20009; 450.

Women Marines Assn. (1960), c/o President, 1415 Springdale Ave., McLean, VA 22065; 3,500.

Women Strike for Peace (1961), 145 S. 13th St., Phila., PA 19107.

Women of the U.S., Natl. Council of (1888), 345 E. 46th St., N.Y., NY 10017; 1,500.

Women Voters of the U.S., League of (1920), 1730 M St., NW, Wash., DC 20036; 145,000.

Women World War Veterans (1919), 237 Madison Ave., N.Y., NY 10016; 160,000.

Women's Army Corps Veterans Assn. (1946), 6049 Amboy Rd., Dearborn Heights, MI 48127; 1,500.

Women's Clubs, General Federation of (1890), 1734 N St., NW, Wash., DC 20036; 621,000.

Women's Clubs, Natl. Federation of Business & Professional (1919), 2012 Massachusetts Ave., NW, Wash., DC 20036; 170,000.

Women's Educational & Industrial Union (1877), 264 Boylston St., Boston, MA 02116; 2,300.

Women's Internatl. League for Peace & Freedom (1915), 1213 Race St., Phila., PA 19107; 10,000.

Women's Overseas Service League (1921), 2456 20th St., NW, Wash., DC 20009; 1,550.

Women's Veterinary Medical Assn. (1947), c/o Dr. Bonnie Beaver, Coll. of Veterinary Medicine, Texas A&M, College Sta., TX 77843; 250.

Woodmen of America, Modern (1883), 1710 First Ave., Rock Island, IL 61201; 495,000.

Woodmen of the World (1890), 1450 Speer Blvd., Denver, CO 80204; 29,925.

Wool Growers Assn., Natl. (1865), 600 Crandall Bldg., Salt Lake City, UT 84101; 22 assns.

Workmen's Circle (1900), 45 E. 33d St., N.Y., NY 10016; 55,000.

World Federalists, World Assn. of (1946), Leliegracht 21, Amsterdam, Netherlands; 40,000.

World Future Society (1967), 4916 St. Elmo Ave., Bethesda, MD 20014; 16,500.

World Health Organization, U.S. Committee for (1951), 777 United Nations Plaza, N.Y., NY 10017; 2,245.

World Ship Society (1946), c/o Dudley Thickens, 3319 Sweet Dr., Lafayette, CA 94549; 3,600.

Wrestling Foundation, U.S. Amateur (1959), 620 N. 48th St., Lincoln, NE 68504; 300.

Writers Assn. of America, Outdoor (1927), 4141 W. Bradley Rd., Milwaukee, WI 53209; 1,375.

— Y & Z —

Yeomen F, National (1926), 11104 Haines Ave. NE, Albuquerque, NM 87112; 1,100.

Young Americans for Freedom (1960), Woodland Rd., Sterling, VA 22176; 100,000.

Young Men's Christian Assns., Natl. Council of (1844 in London, 1851 in U.S.), 291 Broadway, N.Y., NY 10007; 8,000,000.

YM-YWHAs of Greater New York, Assoc. (1957), 130 E. 59th St., N.Y., NY 10022; 55,000.

Young Women's Christian Assn. of the U.S.A. (1855 in England; 1858 in U.S.), 600 Lexington Ave., N.Y., NY 10022; 2,400,000 in the U.S.

Youth Hostels, American (1934), Natl. Campus, Delaplane, VA 22025; 80,000.

Zero Population Growth (1968), 1346 Connecticut Ave., NW, Wash., DC 20036; 10,000.

Ziegfeld Club (1936), 55 W. 42d St., N.Y., NY 10036; 341.

Zionist Organization of America (1897), 4 E. 34th St., N.Y., NY 10016; 110,000.

Zonta International (1919), 59 E. Van Buren St., Chicago, IL 60605; 23,500.

Zoological Parks & Aquariums, Amer. Assn. of (1924), Oglebay Park, Wheeling, WV 26003; 1,500.

Zoologists, American Society of (1890), Box 2739 California Lutheran College, Thousand Oaks, CA 91360; 4,100.

RELIGIOUS INFORMATION

Census of Religious Bodies in the United States

Source: THE WORLD ALMANAC Questionnaire and 1975 Yearbook of American Churches

Membership figures in the following table are the latest available. Some denominations submitted carefully compiled data while others approached the task more casually. Some membership figures were obtained by WORLD ALMANAC Questionnaire, others from the 1975 Yearbook of American Churches. The number of churches is given in parentheses.

Denomination	Members
Adventist Bodies:	**496,413**
Advent Christian Church (382)	31,586
Primitive Advent Christian Ch. (10)	551
Seventh-day Adventists (3,301)	464,276
Amana Church Society (7)	**1,500**
American Rescue Workers (21)	**1,880**
Anglican Orthodox Church (37)	**2,630**
Apostolic Faith (45)	**4,100**
Armenian Church of America (58)	**372,000**
Assemblies of God (9,019)	**785,348**
Baptist Bodies:	**27,705,529**
American Baptist Assn. (3,500)	786,536
American Baptist Churches in U.S.A. (6,005)	1,579,029
Baptist General Conference (632)	111,093
Baptist Missionary Assn. of Amer. (1,450)	203,903
Christian Unity Baptist Assn. (5)	345
Conserv. Baptist Assn. of Amer. (1,120)	300,000
Duck River (and Kindred) Assns. of Baptists (86)	8,909
Free Will Baptists, Natl. Assn. of (2,500)	235,000
Gen. Assn. of General Baptists (790)	67,390
Gen. Assn. of Regular Baptist Chs. (1,495)	225,000
General Baptists (834)	70,000
General Six-Principle Baptist (8)	308
Natl. Baptist Conv. of Amer. (11,398)	2,668,799
Natl. Baptist Conv., U.S.A. (27,396)	6,487,003
Natl. Primitive Baptist Convention (2,198)	1,645,000
N. Amer. Baptist Gen. Conf. (245)	41,437
Progressive Natl. Baptist Conv. (655)	521,692
Regular Bap. Chs., Gen. Assn. of (1,495)	225,463
Separate Baptists in Christ (84)	7,496
Seventh Day Bapt. Gen. Conf. (68)	5,284
Southern Baptist Convention (34,275)	12,515,842
Berean Fundamental Church (50)	**2,350**
Bethel Ministerial Association (25)	**4,000**
Bible Protestant Church (42)	**2,254**
Bible Way Churches of Our Lord Jesus Christ World Wide (350)	**30,000**
Brethren (German Baptist):	**233,429**
Brethren Ch. (Ashland, Oh.) (119)	16,357
Brethren Churches, Natl. Fellowship of (243)	33,514
Church of the Brethren (1,035)	179,333
Old German Baptist Brethren (54)	4,225
Brethren, Plymouth (690)	**40,000**
Brethren (River):	**10,754**
Brethren in Christ Church (156)	9,877
United Zion Church (16)	877
Buddhist Churches of America (60)	**60,000**
Christadelphians (850)	**15,800**
Christian Catholic Church (6)	**2,000**
Christian Church of N. Amer., Gen. Council (110)	**8,500**
Christian Church (Disciples of Christ) (4,524)	**1,312,326**
Christian & Missionary Alliance (1,261)	**153,105**
Christian Nation Church, U.S.A. (16)	**2,000**
Christian Union (108)	**5,301**
Church of Christ (Holiness) U.S.A. (159)	**9,289**
Church of Christ, Scientist (2,350) (membership not recorded)	
Church of Christ (32)	**2,400**
The Church of God (2,035)	**75,890**
Church of God in Christ (4,500)	**425,000**
Church of Illumination (14)	**9,000**
Church of the Nazarene (4,727)	**430,128**
Church of Revelation (10)	**750**
Churches of Christ (18,000)	**2,400,000**
Chs. of Christ in Christian Union (216)	**8,771**

Denomination	Members
Churches of God:	**675,625**
Ch. of God (Anderson, Ind.) (2,235)	157,828
Ch. of God (Cleveland, Tenn.) (4,270)	313,332
Church of God of Prophecy (1,711)	59,535
Ch. of God, Seventh Day (7)	2,000
Ch. of God, Seventh Day (Denver) (56)	5,500
Churches of God, Gen. Conference (351)	37,040
The Church of God (2,035)	75,890
The (Original) Ch. of God (70)	20,000
The Church of God by Faith (105)	4,500
Churches of the Living God:	**47,670**
Church of the Living God (276)	45,320
House of God, Which is the Church of the Living God, the Pillar and Ground of the Truth (107)	2,350
Church of New Jerusalem, Gen. (33)	**2,143**
Congregational Christian Churches, Natl. Assn. of (350)	**100,000**
Congregational Holiness Ch. (147)	**4,859**
Conservative Cong. Christian Conf. (126)	**21,014**
Eastern Orthodox Churches:	**4,070,015**
Albanian Orthodox Archdio. in Amer. (15)	40,000
Albanian Orthodox Diocese of Amer. (10)	5,150
American Carpatho-Russian Orthodox Greek Catholic Church (70)	100,000
American Catholic Church (Syro-Antiochian) (5)	495
Antiochian Orthodox Archdiocese of Toledo, Oh. (16)	15,000
Antiochian Orthodox Christian Archdio. (100)	100,000
Armenian Apostolic Ch. of America (29)	125,000
Armenian Church of Amer. Diocese of the (49)	10,000
Bulgarian Eastern Orthodox Ch. (11)	3,000
Church of the East (Assyrians) (12)	5,000
Greek Archdio. of N. and S. America (510)	2,000,000
Holy Orthodox Church in America (Eastern Cath. & Apostolic) (4)	260
Holy Ukrainian Autocephalic Orthodox Ch. in Exile (15)	4,800
Orthodox Church in America (483)	1,000,000
Romanian Orthod. Episc. of Amer. (34)	40,000
Russian Orthodox Church in the U.S.A., Patriarchal Parishes (41)	51,000
Russian Orthodox Church Outside Russia (117)	60,000
Serbian Eastern Orthodox Church (56)	350,000
Syrian Orthodox Church of Antioch (Archdio. of the U.S.A. & Canada) (10)	50,000
Ukrainian Orthodox Ch. of the U.S.A. (95)	79,000
Ukrainian Orthodox Church in Amer. (Ecumenical Patriarchate) (23)	30,000
Ethical Union, American (23)	**5,000**
Evangelical Christian Churches California Synod (121)	**23,419**
Evangelical Congregational Ch. (160)	**29,331**
Evangelical Covenant Ch. of America (524)	**69,922**
Evangelical Free Ch. of America (562)	**70,490**
Evangelistic Associations:	**73,410**
Apostolic Christian Chs. of Amer. (78)	9,500
Apostolic Christian Ch. (Nazarean) (41)	3,720
The Christian Congregation (363)	55,090
Pillar of Fire (61)	5,100
Free Christian Zion Ch. of Christ (742)	**22,260**
Friends:	**70,552**
Friends United Meeting (515)	68,717
Religious Society of Friends (Conservative) (61)	1,835
Holiness Church of God (28)	**927**

Denomination	Members
Independent Fundamental Churches of Amer. (624).	**77,079**
Internatl. Church of the Foursquare Gospel (763).	**113,607**
Jehovah's Witnesses (6,542).	**554,257**
Jewish Congregations:	**6,215,000**
Union of Amer. Hebrew Cong. (715)	1,100,000
Union of Orthodox Jewish Cong. of Amer. (3,000)	3,000,000
United Synagogue of Amer. (824)	1,500,000
Latter-Day Saints:	**2,367,645**
Church of Jesus Christ (Bickertonites) (50)	2,469
Church of Jesus Christ of Latter-Day Saints (Mormon) (5,162)	2,208,045
Reorganized Church of Jesus Christ of Latter-Day Saints (1,023)	157,131
Lutheran Bodies:	**8,248,534**
Lutheran Church-Mo. Synod (5,777)	2,776,104
The American Lutheran Church (4,805)	2,437,862
The Lutheran Ch. in America (5,738)	3,006,846
Other Lutheran Churches:	**429,048**
Church of the Lutheran Brethren of Amer. (100)	9,000
Church of the Lutheran Confession (68)	9,616
Evangelical Lutheran Synod (Norwegian Synod) (98)	17,804
Protestant Conference (Lutheran) (7)	2,600
Wis. Evangelical Lutheran Synod (1,037)	390,028
Mennonite Bodies:	**172,056**
Beachy Amish Mennonite Ch. (62)	3,699
Ch. of God in Christ (Mennonite) (38)	6,204
Evangelical Mennonite Brethren (32)	3,874
Evangelical Mennonite Church (20)	3,131
Gen. Conference Mennonite Ch. (189)	36,129
Hutterian Brethren (29)	3,405
Mennonite Church (1,063)	92,390
Old Order Amish Church (368)	14,720
Old Order (Wisler) Mennonite Ch. (38)	8,000
Reformed Mennonite Church (12)	500
Methodist Bodies:	**13,191,322**
African Meth. Episcopal Ch. (4,500)	1,500,000
African M.E. Zion Church (5,994)	1,024,974
Christian Meth. Episcopal Ch. (2,598)	466,718
Evangelical Methodist Church (143)	10,519
Free Methodist Ch. of N. Amer. (1,046)	65,209
Fundamental Methodist Church (14)	724
The United Methodist Church (39,195)	10,063,046
Primitive Method. Ch. U.S.A. (86)	11,945
Reformed Meth. Union Episc. Ch. (18)	2,192
Reformed Zion Union Apostolic Ch. (50)	16,000
Southern Methodist Church (150)	9,917
Missionary Church, The (273)	20,078
Moravian Bodies:	**62,776**
Moravian Ch. in Amer., North Prov. (107)	34,954
Moravian Ch. in Amer., South Prov. (51)	21,680
Unity of the Brethren (32)	6,142

Denomination	Members
New Apostolic Church of N. Amer. (289).	**22,608**
Old Catholic Churches:	**67,023**
American Catholic Church, N.Y. Archdio. (4)	200
N. Amer. Old R.C. Church (25)	1,290
Old Roman Catholic Ch. (English Rite) (186)	65,128
Open Bible Standard Churches (275).	**25,000**
Pentecostal Assemblies:	**528,088**
Elim Fellowship (70)	5,000
Internatl. Pentecostal Assemblies (55)	10,000
Pentecostal Church of Christ (45)	1,435
Pentecostal Ch. of God of Amer. (1,350)	127,000
Pentecostal Fire-Baptized Holiness Ch. (41)	545
Pentecostal Free Will Baptist Ch. (126)	10,000
Pentecostal Holiness Church (1,340)	74,108
United Pentecostal Church (2,650)	300,000
Polish Natl. Catholic Ch. of Amer. (162).	**282,411**
Presbyterian Bodies:	**3,786,763**
Associate Reformed Presbyt. Church (General Synod) (152)	31,347
Cumberland Presbyterian Ch. (828)	87,490
Orthodox Presbyterian Ch. (123)	14,871
Presbyterian Ch. in the U.S. (4,131)	902,366
Reformed Presbyterian Ch., Evangelical Synod (150)	22,452'
Reformed Presbyterian Church of N. Amer. (68)	5,560
United Presbyt. Ch. in the U.S.A. (8,675)	2,723,565
Protestant Episcopal Church (7.074).	**2.917.111**
Reformed Bodies:	**435,235**
Christian Reformed Church (525)	206,000
Hungarian Reformed Ch. in Am. (27)	11,250
Reformed Church in America (925)	213,977
Reformed Church in the U.S. (24)	4,008
Reformed Episcopal Church (69).	**6,444**
Roman Catholic Church (18,515).	**48,701,835**
Salvation Army (1,104).	**361,571.**
The Schwenkfelder Church (5).	**2,250**
Social Brethren (33).	**1,699**
Spiritualists:	
Int. Gen. Assembly of Spiritualists (43)	8,500
Natl. Spiritual Alliance of the U.S.A. (34)	3,230
Natl. Spiritualist Assn. of Chs. (204)	4,962
Triumph the Church and Kingdom of God in Christ (495).	**54,307**
Unitarian Universalist Assn. (1,019).	**210,648**
United Brethren:	**26,757**
United Brethren in Christ (285)	26,335
United Christian Church (12)	422
United Church of Christ (6,581).	**1,841,312**
United Holy Ch. of America (470).	**28,980**
Vedanta Society of New York (13).	**1,000**
Volunteers of America (583).	**31,440**
Wesleyan Church, The (1,828).	**94,215**

Religious Population of the World

Source: The 1975 Encyclopaedia Britannica Book of the Year.

Religion	N. America[1]	S. America	Europe[2]	Asia	Africa	Oceania[3]	Total
Total Christian	225,504,750	161,583,500	352,597,100	86,811,000	100,465,100	17,104,000	944,065,450
Roman Catholic	128,884,000	151,600,000	171,748,500	45,122,000	32,039,500	3,188,000	532,582,000
Eastern Orthodox	4,115,000	54,000	65,534,600	1,835,000	17,410,000	353,000	89,301,600
Protestant[4]	92,505,750	9,929,500	115,314,000	39,854,000	51,015,600	13,563,000	322,181,850
Jewish	6,346,525	678,700	3,960,700	3,026,150	299,465	75,000	14,386,540
Muslim	235,000	191,200	8,730,000	422,208,000	97,678,500	66,000	529,108,700
Zorastian	250	. . . .	. . . .	224,650	475	. . . .	225,375
Shinto	55,000	90,000	. . . .	62,004	. . . .	. . . .	62,149,000
Taoist[5]	16,000	12,000	. . . .	31,360,700	. . . .	. . . .	31,388,700
Confucian[5]	96,000	83,000	30,000	205,725,700	500	41,500	205,976,700
Buddhist	148,000	180,300	220,000	247,951,500	2,000	15,000	248,516,800
Hindu	70,000	502,000	350,000	512,418,000	463,400	629,000	514,432,400
Totals	232,471,525	163,320,700	365,887,800	1,571,729,700	198,909,440	17,930,500	2,550,249,665

(1) Includes Central America and the West Indies. (2) Includes the USSR where it is difficult to determine religious affiliation. (3) Includes Australia, New Zealand, and islands of the South Pacific. (4) Protestant figures include "full members" rather than all baptized persons and are not comparable to those of ethnic religions or churches counting all adherents. (5) Statistics for Confucianism and Taoism are undeterminable in China since the Cultural Revolution.

Headquarters of U.S. Religious Bodies

(Year organized in parentheses)

Advent Christian Church (1854)—Pres., Rev. Joe Tom Tate. Exec. V.P., Rev. Adrian B. Shepard. Box 23152, Charlotte. NC 28212.

Adventists, Seventh-day General Conference of (1863)—Pres., Robert H. Pierson. Sec., C.O. Franz, 6840 Eastern Ave., NW Takoma Park, Wash., DC 20012.

African Methodist Episcopal Zion Church (1796)—Senior Bishop, Herbert Shaw. Sec., Board of Bishops, Bishop Charles H. Foggie, 1200 Windermere Dr., Pittsburgh, PA 15218.

Antiochian Orthodox Archdiocese of Toledo, Ohio (1936)—Archbishop Metropolitan Michael G. Shaheen, 2656 Pemberton Dr., Toledo, OH 43606.

Antiochian Orthodox Christian Archdiocese (formerly **Syrian Antiochian Orthodox Church**) (1894)—Head of Archdiocese Metropolitan, Archbishop Philip (Saliba), 358 Mountain Rd., Englewood, NJ 07631.

Armenian Church of America, Diocese (1889)—Primate, Most Rev. Archbishop Torkom Manoogian. Sec., Very Rev. Zaven Arzoumanian, 630 Second Ave., N.Y., NY 10016.

Assemblies of God (1914)—Gen. Supt., Thomas F. Zimmerman. Gen. Sec., Bartlett Peterson, 1445 Boonville Ave., Springfield, MO 65802.

Augustana Evangelical Lutheran Church. See The Lutheran Church in America.

Baha'i Faith—About 5,500 communities, groups and isolated centers in the U.S. Sec., Natl. Spiritual Assembly, Glenford E. Mitchell, 536 Sheridan Rd., Wilmette, IL 60091.

Baptist Association, American (1905)—Pres., Dr. Roy M. Reed. Sec., Dr. L. Chester Guinn, 4605 N. State Line, Texarkana, TX 75501.

Baptist Association of America, Conservative (1947)—Pres., Rev. Robert P. Dugan, Jr. Sec., Rev. Charles W. Jewitt. P.O. Box 66, Wheaton, IL 60187.

Baptist Churches in the U.S.A., Amer. (1907)—Pres., Dr. Peter H. Armacost. Gen. Sec., Rev. Dr. Robert Campbell, Valley Forge, PA 19481.

Baptist Convention, Southern (1845)—Pres., Jaroy Weber. Exec. Sec., Dr. Porter Routh, 460 James Robertson Parkway, Nashville, TN 37219.

Baptist Churches, Unified Free Will (1964)—President Bishop Caldwell Thomas. Exec. Sec., Ernest Leonard, P.O. Box 4255, Newark, N.J. 07112.

Baptists, General (1611)—Moderator, Rev. Cecil Robertson. Clerk, Vern Whitten, 1629 Stinson Ave., Evansville, IN 47712.

Baptist General Conference (1879)—Gen. Sec., Warren Magnuson, 1233 Central St., Evanston, IL 60201.

Baptist General Conference, North American (1865)—Moderator, Delmar Wesseler. Exec. Sec., Dr. G. K. Zimmerman, 7308 Madison St., Forest Park, IL 60130.

Baptist, Natl. Assn. of Free Will (1727)—Moderator, Dr. J. D. O'Donnell. Exec. Sec., Rufus Coffey, P.O. Box 1088, Nashville, TN 37202.

Baptist Missionary Assn. of America (formerly **North American Baptist Assn.**) (1950)—Pres. Rev. Kenneth Bobo. Gen. Sec., Craig Branham, 720 Main St., Little Rock, AR 72201.

Buddhist Churches of America (1914)—Bishop Kenryu Takashi Tsuji, 1710 Octavia St., San Francisco, CA 94109.

Bulgarian Eastern Orthodox Church (1909)—Most Rev. Joseph Metropolitan, 312 West 101st St., N.Y., NY 10025.

Calvary Grace Christian Churches of Faith (1898)—Internatl. Gen. Supt., Rev. Dr. Herman Keck Jr., P.O. Box 14576, Ft. Lauderdale, FL 33302.

Calvary Grace Church of Faith (1874)—Rev. A. C. Spern, Internatl. Gen. Supt., P.O. Box 333, Rillton, PA 15678.

Christian Church (Disciples of Christ) (1809)—Gen. Minister and Pres., Dr. Kenneth L. Teegarden, Box 1986, Indianapolis, IN 46206.

Christian Endeavor, International Society of (1881)—Pres., Dr. LaVerne H. Boss. Gen. Sec., Rev. Charles W. Barner, 1221 East Broad St., P.O. Box 1110, Columbus, OH 43216.

Christian and Missionary Alliance (1887)—Pres., Dr. Nathan Bailey. Sec., Dr. R. W. Battles, 350 N. Highland Ave., Nyack, NY 10960.

Christian Reformed Church (1857)—Stated Clerk, Rev. William P. Brink, 2850 Kalamazoo Ave., SE, Grand Rapids, MI 49508.

Church of the Brethren (1719)—Gen. Sec., General Board, S. Loren Bowman, 1451 Dundee Ave., Elgin, IL 60120.

Church of Christ, Scientist (1879)—Christian Science Mother Church. The First Church of Christ, Scientist, in Boston, Mass. Pres., Jules Cern. First Reader, Clem W. Collins. Second Reader, Jane O. Robbins. Clerk, George W. Ledbetter. Christian Science Center, Boston, MA 02115.

Church of God (Anderson, Ind.) (1880)—Exec. Sec., W. E. Reed, Box 2420, Anderson, IN 46011.

Church of God, The (1903)—General Overseer, Bishop Voy M. Bullen, 2504 Arrow Wood Dr., SE, Huntsville, AL 35803.

Church of Jesus Christ of Latter Day Saints (Mormon) (1830)—Pres., Spencer W. Kimball. Pres. of the Council of Twelve Apostles, Ezra Taft Benson, 47 E. South Temple St., Salt Lake City, UT 84111.

Church of Jesus Christ of Latter Day Saints, Reorganized (1830)—Pres., W. Wallace Smith. Comm. of Communications, Elroy Hanton, Saints Auditorium, Independence, MO 64051.

Church of the Nazarene (1908)—Gen. Sec., B. Edgar Johnson, 6401 The Paseo, Kansas City, MO 64131.

Churches of Christ—No central organization. B. C. Goodpasture, editor, the Gospel Advocate, 1006 Elm Hill Rd., Nashville, TN 37210.

Churches of God, Gen. Conference (1825)—Pres., Dr. K. E. Boldosser. Sec., Rev. Harry G. Cadamore, 1210 Carlisle St., Natrona Heights, PA 15065.

Congregational Christian Churches, General Council. See United Church of Christ.

Congregational Christian Churches, Natl. Assn. of (1955)—Moderator, Rev. Raymond A. Waser. Exec., Rev. John H. Alexander, P.O. Box 1620, Oak Creek, WI 53154.

Ethical Union, American (Ethical Culture Movement)—Pres., Paul Gellert. Exec. Dir., Jean S. Kotkin, 2 W. 64th St., N.Y., NY 10023. Member of Internatl. Humanist and Ethical Union.

Evangelical Christian Churches (1966)—Pres., Dr. Kenneth T. Giles, P.O. Box 174, Jacksonville, FL 32219.

Evangelical Lutheran Synod (Norwegian Synod) (1918)—Pres., Rev. G.,M. Orvick. Sec., Rev. Alf Merseth, 106 13th St., S., Northwood, IA 50459.

Evangelical Methodist Church (1946)—Gen. Supt., Rev. Lloyd H. Garrett. Gen. Sec., Rev. R. D. Driggers, 3036 N. Meridan, Wichita, KS 67204.

Evangelical and Reformed Church. See United Church of Christ.

Finnish Evangelical Lutheran Church (Suomi Synod). See Lutheran Church in America.

Foursquare Gospel, International Church of the (1927)—Pres., Dr. Rolf K. McPherson. Sec., Dr. Leland B. Edwards, 1100 Glendale Blvd., Los Angeles, CA 90026.

Free Methodist Church of North America (1860)—Sec., Board of Bishops, 901 College, Winona Lake, IN 46590.

Friends, General Conference of the Religious Society of (1900)—Chmn., C. Lloyd Bailey. Gen. Sec., Howard W. Bartram, 1520 Race St., Philadelphia, PA 19102.

Friends United Meeting (formerly Five Years Meeting of Friends) (1902)—Presiding Clerk, Thomas R. Bodine. Gen. Sec., Lorton Heusel, 101 Quaker Hill Dr., Richmond, IN 47374.

Greek Orthodox Church of North and South America (1864)—Primate, the Most Rev. Archbishop Iakovos. Chan., Very Rev. George J. Bacopulos, 10 E. 79th St., N.Y., NY 10021.

Hebrew Congregations, Union of American—Pres., Rabbi Alexander M. Schindler, 838 Fifth Ave., N.Y., NY 10021.

Independent Fundamental Churches of America (1930)—Pres., Rev. Robert L. Gray. Exec. Dir., Rev. Bryan J. Jones, Box 242, Westchester, IL 60153.

Jehovah's Witnesses (1884)—Pres., Nathan H. Knorr, 124 Columbia Heights, Brooklyn, NY 11201.

Jewish Congregations of America, Union of Orthodox—Pres., Harold M. Jacobs. Natl. Dir., Rabbi David Cohen, 116

East 27th St., N.Y., NY 10016.

Latter-Day Saints. See Church of Jesus Christ.

Lutheran Church, The American (1961) — Pres., Dr. David W. Preus. Sec., A. R. Mickelson, 422 S. 5th St., Minneapolis, MN 55415.

Lutheran Church in America, The (estab. June 28, 1962 by consolidating Amer. Evangelical Lutheran Ch., Augustana Evangelical Lutheran Ch., Finnish Evangelical Lutheran Ch., and The United Lutheran Ch. in Amer.) — Pres., Rev. Robert J. Marshall. Sec., Rev. James R. Crumley, Jr., 231 Madison Ave., N.Y., NY 10016.

Lutheran Church-Missouri Synod (1847)—Pres., Dr. J. A. O. Preus. Sec., Rev. Herbert A. Mueller, 500 N. Broadway, St. Louis, MO 63102.

Lutheran World Federation, U.S.A. National Committee of the (formed Jan. 1, 1967, former National Lutheran Council)—Gen. Sec., Rev. Paul A. Wee, 315 Park Ave. South, N.Y., NY 10010.

Mennonite Church (1863)—Moderator, Edward B. Stoltzfus. Sec., Paul N. Kraybill, 528 East Madison St., Lombard, IL 60148.

Methodist Church, The United (1784)—Council of Bishops Pres., Bishop W. Ralph Ward. Sec., Bishop Ralph T. Alton, 1100 W. 42nd St., Indianapolis, IN 46208.

Moravian Church (Unitas Fratrum) (1740)—**Northern Province:** Hq., 69 West Church St., P.O. Box 1245, Bethlehem, PA 18018; Pres., Provincial Elders' Conf., Dr. J. S. Groenfeldt. **Southern Province:** Hq., 459 S. Church St., Winston-Salem, NC 27101; Pres., Provincial Elders' Conf., Dr. Richard F. Amos.

New Jerusalem in the U.S.A., General Convention of the (1782)—Pres., Rev. Eric J. Zacharias. Rec. Sec., Mrs. Wilfred G. Rice, 194 Sylvan St., Malden, MA 02194.

Open Bible Standard Churches (1919)—Gen. Supt., Raymond E. Smith. Sec.-Treas., O. Ralph Isbill, P.O. Box 1737, Des Moines, IA 50306.

Orthodox Church in America (formerly Russian Orthodox Catholic Ch. of Amer.) (1794)—Primate, Metropolitan Archbishop Ireney. Chancellor, Very Rev. Daniel Hubiak, Rte. 25A, P.O. Box 675, Syosset, NY 11791.

Pentecostal Church of God of America (1919)—Gen. Supt., Dr. R. D. Heard, 211 Main St., Joplin, MO 64801.

Pentecostal Church, United (1945)—Gen. Supt., Stanley W. Chambers. Gen. Sec., Cleveland M. Becton, 8855 Dunn Rd., Hazelwood, MO 63042.

Presbyterian Church, Cumberland (1810)—Moderator, David A. Brown. Stated Clerk, H. Shaw Scates, Box 4149, Memphis, TN 38104.

Presbyterian Church in the U.S. (1861)—Moderator, Rev. Lawrence W. Bottom. Stated Clerk, Rev. James E. Andrews, 341 Ponce de Leon Ave., NE, Atlanta, GA 30308.

Presbyterian Church in the U.S.A., United (formed 1958 through merger of the Presbyterian Ch. in the U.S.A. and the United Presbyt. Ch. of N. America)—Moderator, Robert C. Lamar. Stated Clerk, Ruling Elder William P. Thompson, 475 Riverside Dr., N.Y., NY 10027.

Protestant Episcopal Church, The (1789)—Presiding Bishop, Pres. of Exec. Council, Rt. Rev. John M. Allin, 815 Second Ave., N.Y., NY 10017.

Rabbinical Alliance of America—Pres., Rabbi David B. Hollander, 156 5th Ave., N.Y., NY 10010.

Rabbinical Assembly, The—Pres., Rabbi Mordecai Waxman. Exec. V.P., Rabbi W. Kelman, 3080 Broadway, N.Y., NY 10027.

Rabbinical Council of America—Pres., Rabbi Fabian Schonfeld. Exec. V.P., Rabbi Israel Klavan, 220 Park Ave. South, N.Y., NY 10003.

Rabbis, Central Conference of American—Pres., Arthur J. Lelyveld. Exec. V.P., Rabbi Joseph B. Glaser, 790 Madison Ave., N.Y., NY 10021.

Reformed Church in America (1628)—Pres., Rev. Bert Van Soest. Gen. Sec., Rev. Marion de Velder, D.D., 475 Riverside Dr., N.Y., NY 10027.

Reformed Episcopal Church (1873)—Pres. and Presiding Bishop, Rev. Theophilus J. Herter. Sec., Rev. D. Ellsworth Raudenbush, 560 Fountain St., Havre de Grace, MD 21078.

Reformed Presbyterian Church, Evangelical Synod (Apr. 6, 1965, union of the Reformed Presbyterian Ch., General Synod and the Evangelical Presbyterian Ch.)—Moderator, Rev. Paul H. Alexander. Stated Clerk, Dr. Paul R. Gilchrist, 107 Hardy Rd., Lookout Mountain, TN 37350.

Regular Baptist Churches, General Assn. of (1932)—Natl. Rep., Dr. Joseph M. Stowell, 180 Oakton Boulevard, Des. Plaines, IL 60018.

Romanian Orthodox Episcopate of America (1929)— Bishop, His Grace Valerian D. Trifa. Sec., Rev. Eugene Lazar, 2522 Grey Tower Rd., Jackson, MI 49201.

Russian Orthodox Church Outside Russia (1920)—Pres., Council of Bishops, Most Rev. Metropolitan Philaret, 75 East 93rd St., N.Y., NY 10028.

Salvation Army, The (1865 in Eng., 1880 in America)— Natl. Cmdr., William E. Chamberlain. Natl. Chief Sec., Col. W.R.H. Goodier. Natl. Hq., 120-130 W. 14th St., N.Y., NY 10011.

Seamen's Church Institute of N.Y. (1834)—Dir., Rev. John M. Mulligan. Sec., Alfred Lee Loomis III, 15 State St., N.Y., NY 10004.

Serbian Eastern Orthodox Church —Diocese for U.S., Canada and Europe. Bishops: Most Rev. Dionisije and Iriney. Sec., Very Rev. Aleksandar Ivanovich, St. Sava Monastery, Libertyville, IL 60048.

Serbian Eastern Orthodox Church in U.S. and Canada— Bishops: Rt. Rev. Bishop Firmilian, Midwest Diocese, 5701 N. Redwood Dr., Chicago, IL 60631. Rt. Rev. Gregory, Western Diocese, 2511 W. Garvey Ave., Alhambra, CA 91803. Rev. Sava, Eastern U.S. and Canadian Diocese, Way Hollow Rd., Edgeworth, PA 15143.

Spiritualists, International General Assembly of (1936)— Pres., Fred Jordan. Sec., Charles Doyle, 1809 E. Bayview Blvd., Norfolk, VA 23503.

Synagogue Council of America—Pres., Joseph H. Lookstein. Exec. V.P., Rabbi Henry Siegman, 432 Park Ave. South, N.Y., NY 10016.

Ukrainian Orthodox Church of the U.S.A. (1919)—Metropolitan Most Rev. Mstyslav S. Skrypnyk, Box 495, South Bound Brook, NJ 08880.

Unitarian Universalist Assn. (formed May 11, 1961 by merger of the American Unitarian Assn. and the Universalist Church of America)—Pres., Rev. Robert Nelson West. Moderator, Dr. Joseph L. Fisher. Sec., Russel F. Benson, 25 Beacon St., Boston, MA 02108.

United Church of Christ (formed June 25, 1957 through union of the General Council of the Congregational Christian Churches with the Evangelical and Reformed Ch.)— Pres., Rev. Dr. Robert V. Moss Jr. Sec., Rev. Dr. Joseph H. Evans, 297 Park Ave. South, N.Y., NY 10010.

United Sons & Daughters of True Holiness Assn. (1912)— Gen. Sec., Elder B.W. Shoffner, 109 Daniel St., Greensboro, NC 27401.

United Synagogue of America—Pres., Arthur Levine. V.P., Dr. Bernard Segal, 3080 Broadway, N.Y., NY 10027.

Volunteers of America (1896)—Commander-in-chief, Gen. John F. McMahon. Natl. Field Sec., Lt. Colonel Belle Leach. Hq., 340 West 85th St., N.Y., NY 10024.

Wesleyan Church, The (1968) (organized through the merger of the Pilgrim Holiness Ch. and the Wesleyan Methodist Ch. of America)—Gen. Superintendents, Dr. Robert W. McIntyre, Dr. M.H. Snyder, Dr. J.D. Abbott, Dr. V.A. Mitchell. Sec., D. Wayne Brown, Box 2000, Marion, IN 46952.

Wesleyan Methodist Church of America, The (1893)—See Wesleyan Church.

Wisconsin Evangelical Lutheran Synod (1850)—Pres., Rev. Oscar Naumann. Sec., Prof. Heinrich J. Vogel, 11757 N. Seminary Drive 65W, Mequon, WI 53092.

World Council of Churches, U.S. Conference for the— Chmn., Dr. Robert J. Marshall. Exec. Sec., Rev. Charles H. Long Jr. 475 Riverside Dr., N.Y., NY 10027.

National Council of Churches

The National Council of the Churches of Christ in the U.S.A. is a cooperative federation of 31 Protestant and Orthodox churches which seeks to advance programs and policies of mutual interest to its members. The NCC was formed in 1950 by the merger of 12 inter-denominational agencies. The Council's member churches now have an aggregate membership totaling approximately 42,000,000. The NCC is not a governing body and has no control over the policies or operations of any church belonging to it. The work of the Council is divided into 3 divisions — Church and Society, Education and Ministry, Overseas Ministries, and 5 commissions on Faith and Order, Regional and Local Ecumenism, Communication, Stewardship, and Justice, Liberation and Human Fulfillment. The chief administrative officer of the NCC is Dr. Claire Randall, 475 Riverside Drive, N.Y., NY 10027.

Leading Protestant Bodies in the United States

Baptists

The Baptist church was formed in England in 1609 as part of the separatist movement from the Church of England.

The first Baptist Church in America was founded in 1638 in Providence, R.I., by Roger Williams. National organization began in 1814, and a Missionary Convention was formed to permit followers to express themselves in terms of missionary activities. Baptist bodies throughout the United States have a membership of 27,705,520.

American Baptist Churches in the U.S.A. (formerly Northern Baptist Convention, renamed American Baptist Convention in 1950, and renamed American Baptist Churches in the U.S.A. in 1973) was organized in 1907. Churches, 6,005, membership, 1,579,029. Headquarters at Valley Forge, Pa. 19481. Agencies operating under this convention of Baptists include the American Baptist Board of International Ministries, American Baptist Board of National Ministries, American Baptist Board of Educational Ministries, and the Ministers and Missionaries Benefit Board, all at Valley Forge, Pa. 19481.

National Baptist Convention of America, organized 1880. Churches, 11,398; membership, 2,668,799. Consists of the General Organization and 9 others. Pres., Dr. James C. Sams, 1724 Jefferson St., Jacksonville, Fla. 32290.

National Baptist Convention, U.S.A., Inc., founded in 1880, in Montgomery, Ala., is the oldest and parent convention of Negro Baptists. Churches, 27,396; membership, 6,487,003. Pres., Dr. J. H. Jackson; Sec., Rev. T. J. Jemison, 915 Spain St., Baton Rouge, La. 70802.

Southern Baptist Convention. In 1845 Southern Baptists withdrew from the General Missionary Convention over the question of slavery and other matters and formed the Southern Baptist Convention, largest of Baptist bodies. Churches in all 50 states are related to the Convention, 2,534 missionaries serve in 77 countries. Churches, 34,643; membership, 12,515,-842. Executive Committee, 460 James Robertson Parkway, Nashville, Tenn. 37219. Pres., Jaroy Weber, Exec. Sec., Porter Routh. Boards include Sunday Board, Nashville, Tenn.; Foreign Mission Board, Richmond, Va.; Home Mission Board, Atlanta, Ga.; Annuity Board, Dallas, Tex.

Church of Christ, Scientist

First organized in 1879, under the direction of Mary Baker Eddy, The Christian Science Church took its present form in 1892 as the Mother Church, the First Church of Christ, Scientist, in Boston, Mass. Today there are about 3,200 branches in 54 countries. There are 2,350 Christian Science churches in the United States. Membership figures are not recorded. Christian Science regards the Bible as its ultimate authority and includes spiritual healing as part of its teachings.

The denomination supports radio and television programs, charitable institutions, and a world-wide Board of Lectureship. It also maintains the Christian Science Publishing Society which publishes the Christian Science Monitor and various religious periodicals. The affairs of the denomination are administered by the Christian Science Board of Directors, Christian Science Center, Boston, Mass. 02115. Pres., Mrs. Georgina Tennant.

Disciples of Christ

The Christian Church (Disciples of Christ) is an American communion arising out of a concern for Christian unity expressed by Barton W. Stone in 1804 and by Thomas Campbell and his son Alexander, in 1809. The first churches were Cane Ridge in Kentucky and Brush Run near Washington, Pa. The "Christians" of Kentucky and the "Disciples" of Pennsylvania and Virginia united in 1832. The first General Convention was held in 1849. The church is thoroughly ecumenical in stance, and is congregational in government. Congregations in the U.S. and Canada number 4,524; membership is 1,312,326. The communion is served by the General Office of the Christian Church (Disciples of Christ), 17 general units, 37 regional bodies, and 32 educational institutions. General Minister and Pres., Dr. Kenneth L. Teegarden, Box 1986, Indianapolis, Ind. 46206.

Evangelical Churches

The Evangelical and Reformed Church. See United Church of Christ.

The Evangelical United Brethren Church. See United Methodist Church.

Latter-Day Saints

The churches of the Latter-Day Saints do not consider themselves Protestants because they had no part in the 16th century Protestant Reformation and consider themselves to be the "restored" Church of Jesus Christ.

The Church of Jesus Christ of Latter-Day Saints, often called the "Mormon" church, regards the Bible, the Book of Mormon, the Doctrine and Covenants, and the Pearl of Great Price as the word of God. The church was organized Apr. 6, 1830, at Fayette, N.Y., by Joseph Smith, first president. After settling in Kirtland, Oh., and Independence, Mo., the members located in Nauvoo, Ill., in 1839 to escape persecution. Attacks by a mob led to the fatal shooting of Joseph Smith and his brother Hyrum while they were in the Carthage, Ill., jail for protection from the mob, Jun. 27, 1844. Beginning in 1847 most members, under the leadership of Brigham Young, moved by covered wagons across the Great Plains to Utah.

The church is divided into stakes, wards, branches, and missions. Highest authority is the First Presidency, consisting of the president and 2 counselors, assisted by 12 apostles. Spencer W. Kimball is the 12th and current president. Churches, 5,612; membership, 2,208,045. Hq. at 47 East South Temple St., Salt Lake City, Ut. 84111.

The Reorganized Church of Jesus Christ of Latter-Day Saints was founded Apr. 6, 1830, by Joseph Smith Jr. and reorganized under the leadership of the founder's son, Joseph Smith 3d, in 1860. The church is established in 25 countries, the U.S., and Canada. Membership is 157,131 in 1,023 churches. Headquarters is at Saints Auditorium, Independence, Mo. 64051.

Lutherans

The church was started in Europe during the Protestant Reformation by the followers of Martin Luther.

Lutheranism was introduced into the United States by Dutch colonists on Manhattan, later by Swedes on the Delaware, by Palatines in Pennsylvania and New York, and by Salzburgers in Georgia.

The American Lutheran Church was organized during a constituting convention at Minneapolis, Minn., in Apr. 1960, merging the American Lutheran Church, The Evangelical Lutheran Church, and United Evangelical Lutheran Church. The merger brought together Lutherans of Danish, German, and Norwegian heritage. A fourth body, The Lutheran Free Church, joined with The American Lutheran Church in Feb. 1963. The American Lutheran Church has 2,465,584 members. Headquarters at 422 S. 5th

St., Minneapolis, Minn. Rev. David W. Preus is president. The 4,822 congregations are divided territorially into districts in the U.S. The foreign mission program involves 424 missionaries (including wives) on 13 fields in South America, Africa, and Asia. The church's Board of Publication operates the Augsburg Publishing House, 422 S. 5th St., Minneapolis, Minn. 55415.

Augustana Evangelical Lutheran Church. See The Lutheran Church in America.

The Lutheran Church-Missouri Synod was organized in 1847. It is the leader in the conservative group among the Lutherans with 5,777 churches and a membership of 2,776,104. The Synod is divided into 40 districts (35 in the U.S., 3 in Canada, 2 in South America). The Synod conducts a world-wide mission program and fosters a system of 16 ministerial and teacher training colleges to staff its congregations and its 1,239 parochial schools. Affiliated are the Lutheran Laymen's League, Lutheran Women's Missionary League, and Walther League (a young people's organization). Valparaiso University, Valparaiso, Ind., is supported and controlled by the Lutheran University Assn. Hq. for the Synod: 500 N. Broadway, St. Louis, Mo. 63102.

The Lutheran Church in America was organized Jun. 28, 1962, by the consolidation of the American Evangelical Lutheran Church, the Augustana Evangelical Lutheran Church, the Finnish Evangelical Lutheran Church and the United Lutheran Church in America. With 3,006,846 baptized members, the body is the largest of the Lutheran churches in the United States. The Lutheran Church in America has 5,738 congregations, organized in 33 synods in the U.S., Canada, Puerto Rico, and the Virgin Islands. The headquarters of the denomination is at 231 Madison Ave., N.Y., N.Y. 10016, and principal agencies are located at 2900 Queen Lane, Philadelphia, Pa.; 327 South LaSalle St., Chicago, Ill.; and 608 Second Ave. S., 2d floor, Minneapolis, Minn.

Wisconsin Evangelical Lutheran Synod was organized in 1850. It has 1,037 congregations, 390,028 members. Formerly the second largest body of the Synodical conference, Wisconsin withdrew from the Conference in Aug. 1963.

Methodists

The name Methodist was originally given to Charles and John Wesley and several other Oxford students, in 1729. It is thought that the term was selected due to the exact and "methodical" manner in which they performed various engagements which a sense of Christian duty induced them to undertake. The Methodist movement was carried to America in 1760, by emigrants from Ireland. Methodist bodies in the United States have a membership of 13,191,322.

The United Methodist Church has 39,195 churches and 10,063,046 members. The present organization of The United Methodist Church was formed Apr. 23, 1968, in Dallas, Tex., by the union of The Methodist Church and The Evangelical United Brethren Church.The two churches shared a common historical and spiritual heritage. The Methodist Church resulted in 1939 from the unification of 3 branches of Methodism — the Methodist Episcopal Church, the Methodist Episcopal Church, South, and the Methodist Protestant Church. The Methodist movement began in 18th century England under the preaching of John Wesley, but the so-called Christmas Conference of 1784 in Baltimore is regarded as the date on which the organized Methodist Church was founded as an ecclesiastical organization. It was there that Francis Asbury was elected the first bishop in this country. The Evangelical United Brethren Church was formed in 1946 with the merger of the Evangelical Church and the Church of the United Brethren in Christ, both of which had their beginnings in Pennsylvania in the evangelistic movement of the 18th and early 19th centuries. Philip William Otterbein and Jacob Albright were early leaders of this movement among German-speaking settlers of the Middle Colonies.

The supreme policy-making body of The United Methodist Church is the quadrennial General Conference. Principal agencies are in the following cities: New York, N.Y.; Evanston, Ill.; Nashville, Tenn.; Washington, D. C.; Dayton, Oh.; and Lake Janaluska, N.C.

African Methodist Episcopal Church, incorporated 1816 under Pennsylvania laws, is second largest of the Methodist bodies. Churches, 4,500; membership, 1,500,000. Pres., Board of Bishops, Bishop Hubert N. Robinson, 951 Old Grove Manor, Jacksonville, Fla. 32207.

Presbyterians

Presbyterianism is a system of representative church governed by presbyters, or elders. John Calvin (1509-1564) has been regarded as the founder of Presbyterianism. Presbyterians were among the earliest colonists of America. Their first church was established about 1640 and the first presbytery in 1706. Nine Presbyterian bodies in the United States have a membership of 3,786,763.

The United Presbyterian Church in the U.S.A., largest of the Presbyterian bodies, was formed on May 28, 1958, by a merger of the Presbyterian Church in the U.S.A. and the United Presbyterian Church of North America. It has 8,675 churches and 2,723,565 members. Offices of the General Assembly, General Assembly's Mission Council, Support Agency, Program Agency, and Vocations Agency: 475 Riverside Dr., N.Y., N.Y. 10027.

Presbyterian Church in the United States, which established a separate existence in 1861, is sometimes miscalled the Southern Church. Churches, 4,131, membership, 902,366. Office of the Gen. Assembly, 341 Ponce de Leon Ave., NE, Atlanta, Ga. 30308. Moderator, Rev. Lawrence W. Bottom. Stated Clerk, Rev. James E. Andrews.

Protestant Episcopal Church

An American religious denomination directly descended from the Church of England. Brought to America by the Jamestown colonists in 1607. Separated from English church and adopted present name in 1789. Alternate name, "The Episcopal Church" was adopted in 1967. Churches, 7,074. membership, 2,917,111. Headquarters of the Exec. Council, 815 Second Ave., N.Y., N.Y. 10017. Presiding Bishop Rt. Rev. John M. Allin; Interim Exec. Officer of General Convention, Rt. Rev. Scott Field Bailey.

United Church of Christ

Formed in 1957 by a union of the General Council of the Congregational Christian Church and the Evangelical and Reformed Church. It is the first union in the United States of churches with different forms of church government — congregational and modified presbyterian — and different historical backgrounds. Congregationalism was brought to America by both the Pilgrims of the "Mayflower" and the Puritans of the Massachusetts Bay Colony. Eventually it became the dominant form of church organization in New England. The Evangelical and Reformed Church was started in 1934 with the union of the Evangelical Synod of North America and the Reformed Church in the U.S.

A constitution for the United Church of Christ was declared in force in Jul. 1961. The denomination has 1,841,312 members in 6,581 local congregations. The United Church Board of World Ministries has 251 missionaries and other personnel at work in 30 countries. In the United States, the United Church of Christ is active in Christian education church extension, health and welfare, mass communication, race relations, and social action. Headquarters of United Church of Christ, 297 Park Ave. S., N.Y., N.Y. 10010; Office of Communication, 289 Park Ave. S., N.Y. N.Y. United Church Board for Homeland Ministries, 287 Park Ave., S., N.Y., N.Y. 10010. United Church Board for World Ministries, 475 Riverside Dr., N.Y., N.Y. 10027.

Leading Protestant Denominations in Canada

Source: Yearbook of American and Canadian Churches and Ontario Bible College

Anglicans

The Anglican Church of Canada was established in the early 1700s, and its first bishop Charles Inglis was appointed in 1787. The General Synod, created in 1893, acts to co-ordinate the various activities of the Church, and usually meets biennially. It is made up of the Church's archbishops and bishops together with the elected clerical and lay representatives from the 28 dioceses and one Episcopal district. The Anglican Church has 1,704 churches, and an inclusive membership of 1,048,261.

Baptists

The two largest Baptist churches are the Federation of Canada and the Fellowship of Evangelical Baptist Churches. The Federation has about 131,757 members in 4 subdivisions: the Baptist Convention of Ontario and Quebec; the Baptist Union of Western Canada; the United Baptist Convention of the Atlantic Provinces; and the French Baptist Union. Other large Baptist organizations are the Baptist General Conference, the North American Baptist Conference, and the Canadian Southern Baptist Conference.

Lutherans

The first large settlement of Lutherans in Canada was in Halifax in 1749. There are 3 main Lutheran bodies: the Evangelical Lutheran Church of Canada, the Lutheran Church-Canada (Missouri Synod), and the Lutheran Church in America-Canada Section. These bodies cooperate through the Lutheran Council in Canada. The Lutheran churches of Canada have 300,540 members.

Presbyterians

The Presbyterian Church in Canada is connected historically to the Church of Scotland. It is organized into 8 synods and 44 presbyteries, and has an inclusive membership of 179,267.

United Church

The United Church of Canada is the largest Protestant denomination in Canada with an inclusive membership of 993,190. It was established in 1925 as a result of a merger among the Methodist Church, the Congregational Churches, and 70% of the Presbyterian Church. The Canada Conference of the Evangelical United Brethren Church joined this union in 1968. The highest policy making body of the United Church of Canada is the General Council which meets biennially.

Headquarters of Religious Bodies in Canada

Source: Yearbook of American and Canadian Churches and Ontario Bible College.

(Year organized in parentheses)

Anglican Church of Canada (creation of General Synod 1893)—Primate, Most Rev. E.W. Scott, Gen. Sec. of the General Synod, The Ven. E.S. Light, 600 Jarvis St., Toronto, Ontario, M4Y 2I6

Antiochian Orthodox Christian Church (Syrian)—Rev. Father E. Hanna, 555-575 Jean Talon E., Montreal 328.

Apostolic Church of Pentecost of Canada (Inc. 1904). — Pres., Rev. D.S. Morris, 388 Gerald St., La Salle, Que.

Associated Gospel Churches (1922)—Pres., Rev. L.K. Redinger. Sec.-Tres., Rev. J.L. Hockney, 280 Plains Rd. W., Burlington, Ontario L7T 1G4.

Association of Regular Baptist Churches (Canada), — Pres., Dr. H.C. Slade, 337 Jarvis St., Toronto, Ont. M5B 2C7.

Baptist Federation of Canada—Gen. Sec.-Treasurer, Rev. R. Fred Bullen, 91 Queen St., Box 1298 Brantford, Ontario, N3T 3B7.

Baptist General Conference—Exec. Sec., D.L. Clink, 421 Berkley St. N., Winnipeg, Manitoba R3R 1J7

Brethren in Christ Church, Canada Conference — Mod. Bishop R.V. Sider, Box 65, Sherkston, Ontario.

British Israel World Federation—Office Manager and Secretary, Mrs. S. Cunningham, 313 Sherbourne St., Toronto, 2 Ontario.

Buddhist Churches of Canada—Bishop, Rev. Neuton Isiura, 918 Bathurst St., Toronto, Ontario

Byelorussian Autocephalic Orthodox Church Abroad —Rt. Rev. Bishop Mikalay, 524 St. Clarens Ave., Toronto 172, Ontario.

Canadian Council of Churches, The (1938)—Pres. Rev. Dr. A.B.B. Moore, 40 St. Clair Ave. E., Toronto 7.

Canadian Jewish Congress (1919)—Exec. Vice-Pres., Saul Hayes, Q.C., 1590 McGregor Ave., Montreal 109, Quebec.

Christian and Missionary Alliance in Canada, The (1897)—2026 Yonge St., Toronto, Ontario. M4S 1Z9; Pres., Rev. W.J. Newell, 125 Panin Rd., Burlington, Ont.

Christian Church (Disciples of Christ) (All Canada Committee formed 1922)—39 Arkell Rd., R.R. 2, Guelph, Ont., N1H 6H8; Pres., Mrs. K. McNeill, R.R. 2, Springfield, Ont., N0L 2J0.

Christian Reformed Churches, The Canadian Council of—Rev. John Van Harmelen, R.R. 8, London, Ont.

Christian Science in Canada—Mr. J.D. Fulton 696 Yonge St., Ste. 403, Toronto, Ont. M4Y 2A7.

Church of Jesus Christ of Latter Day Saints (Mormons), (1830)—Pres., Alberta Stake, Mr. F.N. Spackman, Cardston, Alberta; Pres., Toronto Stake, Mr. W. M. Davies, 139 Richland Cres., Etobicoke, Ont.; Pres., Vancouver Stake, Mr. K. M. Humphreys, 1677 Davenport Pl., N. Vancouver, B.C.

Church of the Nazarene (1902)—Dist. Superintendent of Canada Central District, Rev. N. Hightower, 38 Riverhead Drive, Rexdale, Ont., Chairman of Exec. Board, Dr. Herman L.G. Smith, 2236 Capitol Hill Crescent, N.W., Calgary, Alta. T2M 4B9

Evangelical Mennonite Conference, (1812)—Conf. Mod., H. Kornelsen, R.R. 1, Giroux, Man. R0A 0N0.

Fellowship of Evangelical Baptist Churches in Canada (merging of Union of Regular Baptist Churches of Ontario and Quebec, and Fellowship of Independent Baptist Churches) (1953)—Gen. Sec., Dr. J. H. Watt, 74 Sheppard Ave. W., Willowdale, Ontario.

Free Methodist Church in Canada (1880)—Pres., Rev. E.S. Bull, 40 Glen Rd., Belleville, Ont. K8P 4G1.

Gospel Missionary Assn., The (1951)—Pres., Rev. W.J. Laing, c/o Bethel Baptist Church, 830 7th Ave., S.W., Calgary, Alberta T2P 0Z9.

Greek Orthodox Church—Ninth Archdiocese District, Canada, Titular Bishop of Ancona, His Grace Theodosios, 27 Teddington Park Ave., Toronto M4N 2C4

Independent Holiness Church (merger of former Holiness Movement of Canada with The Free Methodist Church in 1958)—Pres., Rev. Murdo Campbell, 5861 Berwick St., Burnaby, B.C.

Italian Pentecostal Church of Canada, The (Incorp. 1959)—Gen. Supt. Rev. D. Ippolito, 384 Sunnyside Ave., Toronto M6R ZS1

Jehovah's Witnesses (Branch Office established, in Winnipeg 1918)—Presiding Minister, Mr. Kenneth A. Little, 150 Bridgeland Ave., Toronto Ontario M6A 1Z5

Lutheran Church of Canada, The Evangelical—Pres., Dr. S.T. Jacobson, 212 Wiggins Ave., Saskatoon, Sask. S7N 1K4

Lutheran Church-Canada (1959)—Pres., Rev. Louis Scholl, 3500 Askin, Windsor, Ont. N9E 3J9.

Lutheran Church in America—Canada Section— Pres. Dr. Otto A. Olson Jr., 211-228 Portage Ave., Winnipeg, Man. R3J 0M1.

Lutheran Council in Canada—a joint body of the three main churches, Gen. Sec., Dr. J.M. Zimmerman, 9901-107 St., Edmonton, Alta.

Mennonite Brethren Churches of North America, Canadian Conference (Inc. 1945)—159 Henderson Hwy., Winnipeg, Manitoba R2L 1L4; Mod Herbert J. Branot, 1020 No. 5 Rd., Richmond, B.C.

Mennonites in Canada, Conference of—Moderator, Rev. Jacob Tilitzky, 2201 Queen Rd., R.R. 1, Abbotsford, B.C.

Mennonite Church, The (Old)—First Mennonite Church, Chmn., Newton L. Gingrich, Travistock, Ont. N0B.

Missionary Church, The—(an Anabaptist body)—Dist. Supt. (Ontario) Rev. Grant Sloss, Ste. 203, Federick St. Plaza, Kitchener, Ont. N2H 2P2.

Moravian Church in America, Northern Province, Canadian District of the—Pres., and Corr. Sec., D.H. Laverty, 5719-114A St., Edmonton, Alberta T6H 3M8.

National Spiritual Assembly of the Baha'is of Canada (incorporated 1949)—Gen. Sec. J.D. Martin, 7290 Leslie St., Thornhill, Ont.

Old German Baptist Brethren in Canada—c/o Elder Amos Baker, Gormley, Ont.

Northern Canada Evangelical Mission—58 18th St., Prince Albert, Sask.

Overseas Missionary Fellowship (1887)—Gen. Dir., Mr. Michael C. Griffiths, 1058 Avenue Road, Toronto 12, Ontario.

Pentecostal Assemblies of Canada, The (incorporated 1919)—Gen. Supt., Rev. Robert W. Tartinger, 10 Overlea Blvd., Toronto, Ontario M4H 1A5.

Pentecostal Holiness Church in Canada—Gen. Supt., Rev. G.H. Nunn, 4 Hobart Dr. S., Willowdale, Ont. M2J 2J5.

Polish National Catholic Church of Canada (1967)—The Rt. Rev. Joseph Nieminski, Bishop of the Canadian Diocese, 186 Cowan Ave., Toronto, Ont. M6K 2N6.

Presbyterian Church in Canada, The (1875)—50 Wynford Dr., Don Mills, Ont.; Moderator, Rev. A.H. Johnston, Thunder Bay, Ont.; Treasurer, R.R. Merifield, Q.C. Clerks of Assembly: Rev. L.H. Fowler; Rev. D.C. MacDonald.

Religious Society of Friends (Quakers), (Canadian Yearly Meeting of the Religious Society of Friends formed 1955)—Presiding Clerk, Burton Hill, Box 33, Rockwood, Ont.; Secretary of Yearly Meeting, Ms. Dorothy Mums, 60 Lowther Ave., Toronto 180, Ont.

Reorganized Church of Jesus Christ of Latter Day Saints, The (1830)—P.O. Box 38, Guelph, Ontario.

Roman Catholic Church in Canada—Apostolic Pro Nuncio, His Excellency the Most Reverend Guido Del Mestri, Apostolic Nunciature, 724 Manor Ave., Rockcliffe Park, Ottawa, Ontario K1M 0E3.

Salvation Army, The (1882)—Territorial Commander, Commissioner Clarence D. Wiseman, 20 Albert St., Toronto, Ontario M5G 1A6.

Seventh-day Adventist Church in Canada—Pres., Pastor J. W. Bothe, 1148 King St. E., Oshawa, Ontario L1H 1H8.

Ukrainian Greek Orthodox Church in Canada—Presidium, Chmn., V. Rev. D. Luchak, 7 St. John's Ave., Winnipeg, Manitoba R2W 1G8.

Union of Spiritual Communities of Christ (Orthodox Doukhobors in Canada) (1938)—Honorary Chmn. of the Exec. Comm., John J. Verigin, Box 760, Grand Forks, B.C.

Unitarian Church, Canadian (1842)—Pres. Mr. C. Peterson, 175 St. Clair Ave. W., Toronto, 7 Ont.

United Church of Canada, The (1925)—Mod. Rt. Rev. N. Bruce McLeod; Sec. of General Council, Rev. G. Morrison, 85 St. Clair Ave. E., Toronto, Ontario M4T 1M8.

Protestant Episcopal Calendar and Altar Colors

White — from the First Service (First Vespers) of Christmas Day to the Octave of Epiphany, inclusive (except on the Feasts of Martyrs); on Maundy Thursday (for the celebration); from the First Service of Easter Day to the Vigil of Pentecost (except on Feasts of Martyrs and Rogation Days); on Trinity Sunday, Conversion of St. Paul, Purification, Annunciation, St. John Baptist, St. Michael, All Saints, Saints not Martyrs, and Patron Saints (Transfiguration and Dedication of Church.

Red — from First Vespers of Pentecost to the First Vespers of Trinity Sunday (which includes Ember Days); Holy Innocents, and Feasts of all Martyrs, Apostles and Evangelists.

Violet — from Septuagesima to Maundy Thursday; Easter Even; Advent Sunday to Christmas Eve, Vigils, Ember Days (except in Whitsun Week); and Rogation Days.

An alternate Lenten color scheme: **Violet** — from Septuagesima to the Tuesday before Ash Wednesday; **Lenten White** — from Ash Wednesday to the Saturday after Fourth Lent; and **Crimson** — from Passion Sunday (Fifth Lent) to Easter Even (all inclusive).

Black — Good Friday and at funerals. **Green** — all other days.

Days, Etc.	1973	1974	1975	1976	1977	1978	1979
Golden Number	17	18	0	1	2	3	4
Sunday Letter	G	F	E	DC	B	A	G
Sundays after Epiphany	6	4	2	5	4	2	5
Septuagesima*	Feb. 18	Feb. 10	Jan. 26	Feb. 14	Feb. 6	Jan. 22	Feb. 11
Ash Wednesday	Mar. 7	Feb. 27	Feb. 12	Mar. 3	Feb. 23	Feb. 8	Feb. 28
First Sunday in Lent	Mar. 11	Mar. 3	Feb. 16	Mar. 7	Feb. 27	Feb. 12	Mar. 4
Passion Sunday*	Apr. 8	Mar. 31	Mar. 16	Apr. 4	Mar. 27	Mar. 12	Apr. 1
Palm Sunday	Apr. 15	Apr. 7	Mar. 23	Apr. 11	Apr. 3	Mar. 19	Apr. 8
Good Friday	Apr. 20	Apr. 12	Mar. 28	Apr. 16	Apr. 8	Mar. 24	Apr. 13
Easter Day	Apr. 22	Apr. 14	Mar. 30	Apr. 18	Apr. 10	Mar. 26	Apr. 15
Rogation Sunday*	May 27	May 19	May 4	May 23	May 15	Apr. 30	May 20
Ascension Day	May 31	May 23	May 8	May 27	May 19	May 4	May 24
Whitsunday	Jun. 10	Jun. 2	May 18	Jun. 6	May 29	May 14	Jun. 3
Trinity Sunday	Jun. 17	Jun. 9	May 25	Jun. 13	Jun. 5	May 21	Jun. 10
Sundays after Trinity**	23	24	26	23	24	27	24
First Sunday in Advent	Dec. 2	Dec. 1	Nov. 30	Nov. 28	Nov. 27	Dec. 3	Dec. 2

In the Protestant Episcopal Church the days of fasting are Ash Wednesday and Good Friday. Other days of abstinence are the 40 days of Lent, the Ember Days, and all Fridays of the year except Christmas Day and the Epiphany and any Friday which may fall between them. Ember Days (12 annually at about the beginning of the four seasons) are days of abstinence and prayer for ordinands and the increase of the ministry. They fall on the Wednesday, Friday, and Saturday after the first Sunday in Lent, the Feast of Pentecost (Whitsunday), Sept. 14, and Dec. 13. Rogation Days are the three days from Rogation Sunday (the fifth after Easter) to Ascension Day, and are days of solemn supplication for God's blessing upon the fields and harvests of the world.

The Episcopal Church is studying, and trying out, a revised calendar of the Church Year. If adopted, the following changes in the foregoing list will obtain: *These Sundays will no longer be observed. **This listing will carry the title "Sundays after Pentecost".

Ash Wednesday and Easter Sunday

Year	Ash Wed.	Easter Sunday	Year	Ash Wed.	Easter Sunday	Year	Ash Wed.	Easter Sunday	Year	Ash Wed.	Easter Sunday
1901	Feb. 20	Apr. 7	1951	Feb. 7	Mar. 25	2001	Feb. 28	Apr. 15	2051	Feb. 15	Apr. 2
1902	Feb. 12	Mar. 30	1952	Feb. 27	Apr. 13	2002	Feb. 13	Mar. 31	2052	Mar. 6	Apr. 21
1903	Feb. 25	Apr. 12	1953	Feb. 18	Apr. 5	2003	Mar. 5	Apr. 20	2053	Feb. 19	Apr. 6
1904	Feb. 17	Apr. 3	1954	Mar. 3	Apr. 18	2004	Feb. 25	Apr. 11	2054	Feb. 11	Mar. 29
1905	Mar. 8	Apr. 23	1955	Feb. 23	Apr. 10	2005	Feb. 9	Mar. 27	2055	Mar. 3	Apr. 18
1906	Feb. 28	Apr. 15	1956	Feb. 15	Apr. 1	2006	Mar. 1	Apr. 16	2056	Feb. 16	Apr. 2
1907	Feb. 13	Mar. 31	1957	Mar. 6	Apr. 21	2007	Feb. 21	Apr. 8	2057	Mar. 7	Apr. 22
1908	Mar. 4	Apr. 19	1958	Feb. 19	Apr. 6	2008	Feb. 6	Mar. 23	2058	Feb. 27	Apr. 14
1909	Feb. 24	Apr. 11	1959	Feb. 11	Mar. 29	2009	Feb. 25	Apr. 12	2059	Feb. 12	Mar. 30
1910	Feb. 9	Mar. 27	1960	Mar. 2	Apr. 17	2010	Feb. 17	Apr. 4	2060	Mar. 3	Apr. 18
1911	Mar. 1	Apr. 16	1961	Feb. 15	Apr. 2	2011	Mar. 9	Apr. 24	2061	Feb. 23	Apr. 10
1912	Feb. 21	Apr. 7	1962	Mar. 7	Apr. 22	2012	Feb. 22	Apr. 8	2062	Feb. 8	Mar. 26
1913	Feb. 5	Mar. 23	1963	Feb. 27	Apr. 14	2013	Feb. 13	Mar. 31	2063	Feb. 28	Apr. 15
1914	Feb. 25	Apr. 12	1964	Feb. 12	Mar. 29	2014	Mar. 5	Apr. 20	2064	Feb. 20	Apr. 6
1915	Feb. 17	Apr. 4	1965	Mar. 3	Apr. 18	2015	Feb. 18	Apr. 5	2065	Feb. 11	Mar. 29
1916	Mar. 8	Apr. 23	1966	Feb. 23	Apr. 10	2016	Feb. 10	Mar. 27	2066	Feb. 24	Apr. 11
1917	Feb. 21	Apr. 8	1967	Feb. 8	Mar. 26	2017	Mar. 1	Apr. 16	2067	Feb. 16	Apr. 3
1918	Feb. 13	Mar. 31	1968	Feb. 28	Apr. 14	2018	Feb. 14	Apr. 1	2068	Mar. 7	Apr. 22
1919	Mar. 5	Apr. 20	1969	Feb. 19	Apr. 6	2019	Mar. 6	Apr. 21	2069	Feb. 27	Apr. 14
1920	Feb. 18	Apr. 4	1970	Feb. 11	Mar. 29	2020	Feb. 26	Apr. 12	2070	Feb. 12	Mar. 30
1921	Feb. 9	Mar. 27	1971	Feb. 24	Apr. 11	2021	Feb. 17	Apr. 4	2071	Mar. 4	Apr. 19
1922	Mar. 1	Apr. 16	1972	Feb. 16	Apr. 2	2022	Mar. 2	Apr. 17	2072	Feb. 24	Apr. 10
1923	Feb. 14	Apr. 1	1973	Mar. 7	Apr. 22	2023	Feb. 22	Apr. 9	2073	Feb. 8	Mar. 26
1924	Mar. 5	Apr. 20	1974	Feb. 27	Apr. 14	2024	Feb. 14	Mar. 31	2074	Feb. 28	Apr. 15
1925	Feb. 25	Apr. 12	1975	Feb. 12	Mar. 30	2025	Mar. 5	Apr. 20	2075	Feb. 20	Apr. 7
1926	Feb. 17	Apr. 4	1976	Mar. 3	Apr. 18	2026	Feb. 18	Apr. 5	2076	Mar. 4	Apr. 19
1927	Mar. 2	Apr. 17	1977	Feb. 23	Apr. 10	2027	Feb. 10	Mar. 28	2077	Feb. 24	Apr. 11
1928	Feb. 22	Apr. 8	1978	Feb. 8	Mar. 26	2028	Mar. 1	Apr. 16	2078	Feb. 16	Apr. 3
1929	Feb. 13	Mar. 31	1979	Feb. 28	Apr. 15	2029	Feb. 14	Apr. 1	2079	Mar. 8	Apr. 23
1930	Mar. 5	Apr. 20	1980	Feb. 20	Apr. 6	2030	Mar. 6	Apr. 21	2080	Feb. 21	Apr. 7
1931	Feb. 18	Apr. 5	1981	Mar. 4	Apr. 19	2031	Feb. 26	Apr. 13	2081	Feb. 12	Mar. 30
1932	Feb. 10	Mar. 27	1982	Feb. 24	Apr. 11	2032	Feb. 11	Mar. 28	2082	Mar. 4	Apr. 19
1933	Mar. 1	Apr. 16	1983	Feb. 16	Apr. 3	2033	Mar. 2	Apr. 17	2083	Feb. 17	Apr. 4
1934	Feb. 14	Apr. 1	1984	Mar. 7	Apr. 22	2034	Feb. 22	Apr. 9	2084	Feb. 9	Mar. 26
1935	Mar. 6	Apr. 21	1985	Feb. 20	Apr. 7	2035	Feb. 7	Mar. 25	2085	Feb. 28	Apr. 15
1936	Feb. 26	Apr. 12	1986	Feb. 12	Mar. 30	2036	Feb. 27	Apr. 13	2086	Feb. 13	Mar. 31
1937	Feb. 10	Mar. 28	1987	Mar. 4	Apr. 19	2037	Feb. 18	Apr. 5	2087	Mar. 5	Apr. 20
1938	Mar. 2	Apr. 17	1988	Feb. 17	Apr. 3	2038	Mar. 10	Apr. 25	2088	Feb. 25	Apr. 11
1939	Feb. 22	Apr. 9	1989	Feb. 8	Mar. 26	2039	Feb. 23	Apr. 10	2089	Feb. 16	Apr. 3
1940	Feb. 7	Mar. 24	1990	Feb. 28	Apr. 15	2040	Feb. 15	Apr. 1	2090	Mar. 1	Apr. 16
1941	Feb. 26	Apr. 13	1991	Feb. 13	Mar. 31	2041	Mar. 6	Apr. 21	2091	Feb. 21	Apr. 8
1942	Feb. 18	Apr. 5	1992	Mar. 4	Apr. 19	2042	Feb. 19	Apr. 6	2092	Feb. 13	Mar. 30
1943	Mar. 10	Apr. 25	1993	Feb. 24	Apr. 11	2043	Feb. 11	Mar. 29	2093	Feb. 25	Apr. 12
1944	Feb. 23	Apr. 9	1994	Feb. 16	Apr. 3	2044	Mar. 2	Apr. 17	2094	Feb. 17	Apr. 4
1945	Feb. 14	Apr. 1	1995	Mar. 1	Apr. 16	2045	Feb. 22	Apr. 9	2095	Mar. 9	Apr. 24
1946	Mar. 6	Apr. 21	1996	Feb. 21	Apr. 7	2046	Mar. 7	Mar. 25	2096	Feb. 29	Apr. 15
1947	Feb. 19	Apr. 6	1997	Feb. 12	Mar. 30	2047	Feb. 27	Apr. 14	2097	Feb. 13	Mar. 31
1948	Feb. 11	Mar. 28	1998	Feb. 25	Apr. 12	2048	Feb. 19	Apr. 5	2098	Mar. 5	Apr. 20
1949	Mar. 2	Apr. 17	1999	Feb. 17	Apr. 4	2049	Mar. 3	Apr. 18	2099	Feb. 25	Apr. 12
1950	Feb. 22	Apr. 9	2000	Mar. 8	Apr. 23	2050	Feb. 23	Apr. 10	2100	Feb. 10	Mar. 28

A lengthy dispute over the date for the celebration of Easter was settled by the first Council of the Christian Churches at Nicaea, in Asia Minor, in 325 A.D. The Council ruled that Easter would be observed on the first Sunday following the 14th day of the Paschal Moon, referred to as the Paschal Full Moon. The Paschal Moon is the first moon whose 14th day comes on or after March 21. Dates of the Paschal Full Moon, which are not necessarily the same as those of the real or astronomical full moon, are listed in the table below with an explanation of how to compute the date of Easter.

If the Paschal Full Moon falls on a Sunday, then Easter is the following Sunday. The earliest date on which Easter can fall is March 22; it fell on that date in 1761 and 1818 but will not do so in the 20th or 21st century. The latest possible date for Easter is April 25; it fell on that date in 1943 and will again in 2038.

Lent begins on Ash Wednesday, which comes 40 days before Easter Sunday, not counting Sundays.

Originally it was a period of but 40 hours. Later it comprised 30 days of fasting, omitting all the Sundays and also all the Saturdays except one. Pope Gregory added Ash Wednesday to the fast, together with the remainder of that week.

The last seven days of Lent constitute Holy Week, beginning with Palm Sunday. Passion Week precedes Holy Week. The last Thursday — Maundy Thursday — commemorates the institution of the Eucharist. The following day, Good Friday, commemorates the day of the crucifixion.

Easter is the chief festival of the Christian year, commemorating the resurrection of Christ. It occurs about the same time as the ancient Roman celebration of the Vernal Equinox, the arrival of Spring. In the second century, A.D., Easter Day among Christians in Asia Minor was the 14th Nisan, the seventh month of the Jewish calendar. The Christians in Europe observed the nearest Sunday.

Date of Paschal Full Moon, 1900-2199

The Golden Number, used in the table, is greater by unity (one) than the remainder obtained upon dividing the given year by 19. For example, when dividing 1976 by 19, one obtains a remainder of 0. Adding 1 gives 1 as the Golden Number for the year 1976. From the table then the date of the Paschal Full Moon is Apr. 14, 1976. This being a Wednesday, the date of Easter is the following Sunday Apr.18.

Golden Number	Date	Golden Number	Date	Golden Number	Date	Golden Number	Date
1	April 14	6	Apr. 18	11	Mar. 25	16	Mar. 30
2	Apr. 3	7	Apr. 8	12	Apr. 13	17	Apr. 17
3	Mar. 23	8	Mar. 28	13	Apr. 2	18	Apr. 7
4	Apr. 11	9	Apr. 16	14	Mar. 22	19	Mar. 27
5	Mar. 31	10	Apr. 5	15	Apr. 10		

Roman Catholic Hierarchy

Source: Apostolic Delegation, Washington, D.C.

Supreme Pontiff

At the head of the Roman Catholic Church is the Supreme Pontiff, Paul VI, Giovanni Battista Montini, born at Concesio, Italy, Sept. 26, 1897, ordained priest May 29, 1920, enthroned archbishop of Milan Jan. 6, 1955, proclaimed cardinal Dec. 15, 1958; elected Pope as successor of John XXIII, Jun. 21, 1963; crowned Jun. 30, 1963.

Cardinals

		Nationality	Born	Chosen
Alfrink: Bernard	Archbishop of Utrecht	Dutch	1900	1960
Antonelli: Ferdinando		Italian	1896	1973
Aponte Martinez: Luis	Archbishop of San Juan in Puerto Rico	American	1922	1973
Arns: Paulo	Archbishop of Sao Paulo	Brazilian	1921	1973
Baggio: Sebastiano	Prefect of the Sacred Congregation for the Bishops	Italian	1913	1969
Barbieri: Antonio Maria	Archbishop of Montevideo	Uruguayan	1892	1958
Bengsch: Alfred	Archbishop-Bishop of Berlin	German	1921	1967
Bertoli: Paolo		Italian	1908	1969
Biayenda: Emile	Archbishop of Brazzaville	Congolese	1927	1973
Brandao Vilela: Avela	Archbishop of Sao Salvador da Bahia	Brazilian	1912	1973
Bueno y Monreal: Jose M	Archbishop of Seville	Spanish	1904	1958
Caggiano: Antonio	Archbishop of Buenos Aires	Argentinian	1889	1946
Carberry: John	Archbishop of St. Louis	American	1904	1969
Carpino: Francesco		Italian	1905	1967
Casariego: Mario	Archbishop of Guatemala	Guatemalan	1909	1969
Cerejeira: Manuel Goncalves		Portuguese	1888	1929
Cody: John P	Archbishop of Chicago	American	1907	1967
Colombo: Giovanni	Archbishop of Milan	Italian	1902	1965
Concha: Luis		Colombian	1891	1961
Confalonieri: Carlo		Italian	1893	1958
Conway: William	Archbishop of Armagh	Irish	1913	1965
Cooke: Terence	Archbishop of New York	American	1921	1969
Cooray: Thomas B	Archbishop of Colombo in Ceylon	Ceylonese	1901	1965
Cordeiro: Joseph	Archbishop of Karachi	Pakistan	1918	1973
da Costa Nunes: Jose		Portuguese	1880	1962
Darmojuwono: Justin	Archbishop of Semarang	Indonesian	1914	1967
De Araujo Sales: Eugenio	Archbishop of St. Sebastian di Rio de Janeiro	Brazilian	1920	1969
Dearden: John	Archbishop of Detroit	American	1907	1969
de Furstenberg: Maximilian		Belgian	1904	1967
Di Jorio: Alberto		Italian	1884	1958
Doepfner: Julius	Archbishop of Munich	German	1913	1958
Duval: Leon-Etienne	Archbishop of Algiers	Algerian	1903	1965
Enrique y Tarancon: Vincenzo	Archbishop of Madrid	Spanish	1907	1969
Felici: Pericle	President of Pontifical Commission for the Revision of Code of Canon Law	Italian	1911	1967
Feltin: Maurice		French	1883	1953
Flahiff: George	Archbishop of Winnipeg	Canadian	1905	1969
Florit: Ermenegildo	Archbishop of Florence	Italian	1901	1965
Forni: Efrem		Italian	1889	1962
Freeman: James	Archbishop of Sydney	Australian	1907	1973
Frings: Joseph		German	1887	1946
Garrone: Gabriele M	Prefect of the Sacred Congregation for Catholic Education	French	1901	1967
Gilroy: Norman		Australian	1896	1946
Gonzalez Martin: Marcelo	Archbishop of Toledo	Spanish	1918	1973
Gouyon: Paul	Archbishop of Rennes	French	1910	1969
Gracias: Valerian	Archbishop of Bombay	Indian	1900	1953
Grano: Carlo		Italian	1887	1967
Gray: Gordon	Archbishop of St. Andrews and Edinburgh	Scottish	1910	1969
Guerri: Sergio	Pro-President of the Pontificial Comm. for Vatican City State	Italian	1905	1969
Guyot: Louis	Archbishop of Toulouse	French	1905	1973
Heenan: John	Archbishop of Westminster	English	1905	1965
Hoffner: Joseph	Archbishop of Cologne	German	1906	1969
Jubany Arnau: Narciso	Archbishop of Barcelona	Spanish	1913	1973
Kim Sou Hwan: Stephan	Archbishop of Seoul	Korean	1922	1969
Knox, James	Prefect ot the Sacred Congregations of the Sacraments and of Divine Worship	Australian	1914	1973
Koenig: Franz	Archbishop of Vienna	Austrian	1905	1958
Krol: John	Archbishop of Philadelphia	American	1910	1967
Landazuri: Ricketts Juan	Archbishop of Lima	Peruvian	1913	1962
Leger: Paul		Canadian	1904	1953
Lercaro: Giacomo		Italian	1891	1953
Luciani: Albino	Patriarch of Venice	Italian	1912	1973

Continued

Cardinals

		Nationality	Born	Chosen
Malula: Joseph	Archbishop of Kinshasa	Congolese	1917	1969
Manning: Timothy	Archbishop of Los Angeles	American	1909	1973
Marella: Paolo		Italian	1895	1959
Martin: Joseph		French	1891	1965
Marty: Francis	Archbishop of Paris	French	1904	1969
Maurer: Jose	Archbishop of Sucre	Bolivian	1900	1967
McCann: Owen	Archbishop of Cape Town	S. African	1907	1965
McIntyre: James		American	1886	1953
Medeiros: Humberto	Archbishop of Boston	American	1915	1973
Meouchi: Paul	Maronite Patriarch of Antioch	Lebanese	1894	1965
Miranda y Gomez: Miguel	Archbishop of Mexico	Mexican	1895	1969
Motta: Carlos Carmelo de Vasconcellos	Archbishop of Aparecida	Brazilian	1890	1946
Mozzoni: Umberto		Italian	1904	1973
Munoz Duque: Anibal	Archbishop of Bogota	Colombian	1908	1973
Munoz Vega: Paolo	Archbishop of Quito	Ecuadorian	1903	1969
Nasalli Rocca: Mario		Italian	1903	1969
O'Boyle: Patrick		American	1896	1967
Oddi: Silvio		Italian	1910	1969
Ottaviani: Alfredo		Italian	1890	1953
Otunga: Maurice	Archbishop of Nairobi	Kenyan	1923	1973
Palazzini: Pietro		Italian	1912	1973
Pappalardo: Salvatore	Archbishop of Palermo	Italian	1918	1973
Parecattil: Joseph	Archbishop of Ernakulam	Indian	1912	1969
Parente: Pietro		Italian	1891	1967
Paupini: Giuseppe	Grand Penitentiary	Italian	1907	1969
Pellegrino: Michele	Archbishop of Turin	Italian	1903	1967
Philippe: Paul	Prefect of the Sacred Congregation for the Oriental Churches	French	1905	1973
Pignedoli: Sergio	President of the Secretariat for Non-Christians	Italian	1910	1973
Poletti: Ugo	Vicar General of His Holiness for the City of Rome	Italian	1914	1973
Poma: Antonio	Archbishop of Bologna	Italian	1910	1969
Primatesta: Francisco	Archbishop of Cordova	Argentinian	1919	1973
Quintero: Jose	Archbishop of Caracas	Venezuelan	1902	1961
Rakotomalala: Jerome	Archbishop of Tananarive	Madagascar	1913	1969
Renard: Alexandre	Archbishop of Lyon	French	1906	1967
Ribeiro: Antonio	Patriarch of Lisbon	Portuguese	1928	1973
Roberti: Francesco		Italian	1889	1958
Rosales: Julio	Archbishop of Cebu	Filipino	1906	1969
Rossi: Agnelo	Prefect of the Sacred Congregation for the Evangelization of Peoples	Brazilian	1913	1965
Roy: Maurice	Archbishop of Quebec	Canadian	1905	1965
Rugambwa: Laurean	Archbishop of Dar es Salaam	Tanzania	1912	1960
Salazar Lopez: Jose	Archbishop of Guadalajara	Mexican	1910	1973
Samore: Antonio	Archivist of Holy Roman Church	Italian	1905	1967
Scherer: Alfredo	Archbishop of Porto Alegre	Brazilian	1903	1969
Seper: Franjo	Prefect of Sacred Congregation for the Doctrine of the Faith	Yugoslav	1905	1965
Shehan: Lawrence		American	1898	1965
Sidarouss: Stephanos	Coptic Patriarch of Alexandria	United Arab Republic	1904	1965
Silva Henriquez: Raul	Archbishop of Santiago	Chilean	1907	1962
Siri: Giuseppe	Archbishop of Genoa	Italian	1906	1953
Slipyj: Josyf	Ukrainian Archbishop of Lwow	Ukrainian	1892	1965
Staffa: Dino	Prefect of Supreme Tribunal of Apostolic Signatura	Italian	1906	1967
Suenens: Leo	Archbishop of Malines Brussels	Belgian	1904	1962
Tabera Araoz: Arturo	Prefect of the Sacred Congregation for Religious and Secular Institutes	Spanish	1903	1969
Taguchi: Paul	Archbishop of Osaka	Japanese	1902	1973
Taofinu'u: Pio	Bishop of Apia	Samoan	1923	1973
Tragliac: Luigi		Italian	1895	1960
Ursi: Corrado	Archbishop of Naples	Italian	1908	1967
Vagnozzi: Egidio	Pres. of the Prefecture of the Holy See's Economic Affairs	Italian	1906	1967
Villot: Jean	Secretary of State of His Holiness	French	1905	1965
Violardo: Giacomo		Italian	1898	1969
Volk: Hermann	Bishop of Mainz	German	1903	1973
Willebrands: John	President of Secretariat for the Union of Christians	Dutch	1909	1969
Wojtyla: Karol	Archbishop of Krakow	Polish	1920	1967
Wright: John	Prefect of the Sacred Congregation for the Clergy	American	1909	1969
Wyszynski: Stefan	Archbishop of Gniezno-Warsaw	Polish	1901	1953
Yu Pin: Paul	Archbishop of Nanking	Chinese	1901	1969
Zoungrana: Paul	Archbishop of Ouagadougou	Upper Volta	1917	1965

Jewish Holidays, Festivals and Fasts

Source: Synagogue Council of America

All Jewish holidays, etc., begin at sunset on the day previous. *Also observed the following day.

+Hebrew date varies to avoid conflict with Sabbath.

Festivals and Fasts	Hebrew Date		1975-1976 (5736)		1976-1977 (5737)		1977-1978 (5738)		1978-1979 (5739)	
Rosh Hashana (New Year)*	Tishri	1	Sept. 6	Sa.	Sept. 25	Sa	Sept. 13	Tu	Oct. 2	Mo
Fast of Gedalia	Tishri	3	Sept. 8	Mo	Sept. 27	Mo	Sept. 15	Th	Oct. 4	We
Fast of Gedalia	Tishri	4	. . . . .		. . . . .		. . . . .		. . . . .	
Yom Kippur (Day of Atonement)	Tishri	10	Sept. 15	Mo	Oct. 4	Mo	Sept. 22	Th	Oct. 11	We
Sukkoth (Feast of Tabernacles), 1st Day*	Tishri	15	Sept. 20	Sa	Oct. 9	Sa	Sept. 27	Tu	Oct. 16	Mo
Sukkoth, 8th Day (Shemim Atzereth)	Tishri	22	Sept. 27	Sa .	Oct. 16	Sa	Oct. 4	Tu	Oct. 23	Mo
Simchat Torah (Rejoicing of the Law)	Tishri	23	Sept. 28	Su	Oct. 17	Su	Oct. 5	We	Oct. 24	Tu
Chanukah (Feast of Lights)	Kislev	25	Nov. 29	Sa	Dec. 17	Fr	Dec. 5	Mo	Dec. 25	Mo
Fast of Tebet +	Tebet	10	Dec. 14	Su	Dec. 31	Fr	Dec. 20	Tu	Jan. 9	Tu
Fast of Esther+	Adar	13	. . . . .		Mar. 3	Th	. . . . .		Mar. 12	Mo
Fast of Esther+	Adar II	13	Mar. 15	Mo	. . . . .		Mar. 22	We-	. . . . .	
Purim (Feast of Lots)	Adar	14	. . . . .		Mar. 4	Fr	. . . . .		Mar. 13	Tu
Purim	Adar II	14	Mar. 16	Tu	. . . . .		Mar. 23	Tu	. . . . .	
Pesach (Passover), 1st Day*	Nisan	15	Apr. 15	Th	Apr. 3	Su	Apr. 22	Sa	Apr. 12	Th
Pesach, 7th Day*	Nisan	21	Apr. 21	We	Apr. 9	Sa	Apr. 28	Fr	Apr. 18	We
Lag B'Omer	Iyar	18	May 18	Tu	May 6	Fr	May 25	Th	May 15	Tu
Shavuoth (Feast of Weeks)*	Sivan	6	Jun. 4	Fr	May 23	Mo	Jun. 11	Su	Jun. 1	Fr
Fast of Tammuz+	Tammuz	17	Jul. 15	Th	Jul. 3	Su	Jul. 23	Su	Jul. 12	Th
Tisha B'Av (Fast of Av)+	Av	9	Aug. 5	Th	Jul. 24	Su	Aug. 13	Su	Aug. 2	Th

The months of the Jewish year are: 1 Tishri; 2 Chesvan (also Marchesvan); 3 Kislev; 4 Tebet (also Tebeth); 5 Sebat (also Shebhat); 6 Adar; 6a, added month some years, Adar Sheni (II); 7 Nisan; 8 Iyar; 9 Sivan; 10 Tammuz, 11 Av (also Abh); 12 Elul.

Greek Orthodox Church Calendar, 1976

		Holy Days			Holy Days
Jan.	1	The Circumcision of Christ—The Feast day of St. Basil—New Year's Day	Jun.	22	Sunday of Pentecost
Jan.	6	The Epiphany—The Baptism of Jesus . Christ—The Sanctification of the Waters	Jun.	29	Feast day of Saints Peter and Paul
			Jun.	30	Feast day of the Twelve Holy Apostles
Jan.	7	Feast day of St. John the Baptist	Aug.	6	The Transfiguration
Jan.	30	Feast day of Three Hierarchs: St. Basil, St. Gregory, and St. John Chrysostom	Aug.	15	The Dormition of the Virgin Mary
			Aug.	29	Beheading of St. John The Baptist
Feb.	2	Presentation of Jesus in the Temple	Sept.	1	Beginning of the Church Year
Mar.	8	Easter Lent begins	Sept.	8	Nativity of the Virgin Mary
Mar.	14	Sunday of Orthodoxy (1st Sun. of Lent)	Sept.	14	The Elevation of the Holy Cross
Mar.	25	The Annunciation of the Virgin Mary	Oct.	23	The Feast of James (Iakovos)
Apr.	18	Palm Sunday	Oct.	26	Feast day of St. Demetrios the Martyr
Apr.	18-24	Holy Week	Nov.	15	The beginning of the Christmas Lent
Apr.	23	Good Friday—The Burial of Christ	Nov.	21	Presentation of Blessed Virgin Mary
Apr.	25	Easter Sunday	Nov.	30	The Feast of St. Andrew, Founder Ecumenical Patriarchate of ·Constantinople
Apr.	26	Feast day of St. George	Dec.	6	Feast day of St. Nicholas, Bishop of Myra
Jun.	12	The Ascension	Dec.	25	Christmas Day: The Birth of Jesus Christ

The dates above are according to the Gregorian calendar. adopted by the Greek Church in 1923. First Greek Orthodox church in U. S. founded 1864, in New Orleans, La.

Islamic (Moslem) Calendar 1976-1977

The Islamic calendar, often referred to as Mohammedan, is a lunar reckoning from the year of the hegira, 622 A.D., when Mohammed moved to Medina from Mecca. It runs in cycles of 30 years, of which the second, 5th, 7th, 10th, 13th, 16th, 18th, 21st, 24th, 26th and 29th are leap years. Common years have 354 days, leap years 355, the extra day being added to the last month, Zu'lhijjah. Except for this case, the 12 months beginning with Muharram have alternately 30 and 29 days. The month begins at sunset on the day before that given in the tables.

Year	Name of Month	Month Begins	Year	Name of Month	Month Begins
1396	Muharram (New Year)	Jan. 3, 1976	1397	Muharram (New Year)	Dec. 23, 1976
1396	Safar	Feb. 2, 1976	1397	Safar	Jan. 22, 1977
1396	Rabia I	Mar. 2, 1976	1397	Rabia I	Feb. 20, 1977
1396	Rabia II	Apr. 1, 1976	1397	Rabia II	Mar. 22, 1977
1396	Jumada I	Apr. 29, 1976	1397	Jumada I	Apr. 20, 1977
1396	Jumada II	May 30, 1976	1397	Jumada II	May 20, 1977
1396	Rajab	Jun. 28, 1976	1397	Rajab	Jun. 18, 1977
1396	Shaban	Jul. 28, 1976	1397	Shaban	Jul. 18, 1977
1396	Ramadan	Aug. 26, 1976	1397	Ramadan	Aug. 16, 1977
1396	Shawwai	Sept. 25, 1976	1397	Shawwai	Sept. 15, 1977
1396	Zu'lkadah	Oct. 24, 1976	1397	Zu'lkadah	Oct. 14, 1977
1396	Zu'lhijjah	Nov. 23, 1976	1397	Zu'lhijjah	Nov. 13, 1977

NOTED PERSONALITIES
American Statesmen of the Past

(Excluding Presidents, Vice Presidents, Sup. Ct. Justices, and most signers of the Declaration of Independence; listed elsewhere.)

Born	Died	Name	Born	Died	Name	Born	Died	Name
1893	1971	Acheson, Dean	1813	1861	Douglas, Stephen A.	1863	1941	McAdoo, William G.
1807	1886	Adams, Charles Francis	1888	1959	Dulles, John Foster	1874	1944	McNary, Charles L.
1841	1915	Aldrich, Nelson W.	1794	1865	Everett, Edward	1891	1967	Morgenthau, Henry, Jr.
1793	1836	Austin, Stephen	1808	1893	Fish, Hamilton	1752	1816	Morris, Gouverneur
1887	1962	Austin, Warren R.	1892	1949	Forrestal, James V.	1873	1931	Morrow, Dwight W.
1871	1937	Baker, Newton D.	1706	1790	Franklin, Benjamin	1900	1974	Morse, Wayne
1874	1940	Bankhead, William B.	1813	1890	Fremont, John C.	1861	1944	Norris, George W.
1870	1965	Baruch, Bernard M.	1761	1849	Gallatin, Albert	1757	1824	Pinckney, Charles
1797	1869	Bell, John	1805	1879	Garrison, William Lloyd	1746	1825	Pinckney, Charles C.
1772	1858	Benton, Thomas Hart	1858	1946	Glass, Carter	1753	1813	Randolph, Edmund
1830	1893	Blaine, James G.	1757	1804	Hamilton, Alexander	1773	1833	Randolph, John
1821	1875	Blair, Francis P., Jr.	1737	1793	Hancock, John	1721	1775	Randolph, Peyton
1835	1899	Bland, Richard P.	1838	1905	Hay, John	1880	1973	Rankin, Jeannette
1865	1940	Borah, William E.	1736	1799	Henry, Patrick	1882	1961	Rayburn, Sam
1760	1806	Breckinridge, John	1895	1967	Herter, Christian A.	1872	1937	Robinson, Joseph T.
1860	1925	Bryan, William Jennings	1890	1946	Hopkins, Harry L.	1884	1962	Roosevelt, Eleanor
1891	1967	Bullitt, William C.	1895	1972	Hoover, J. Edgar	1845	1937	Root, Elihu
1904	1971	Bunche, Ralph	1858	1938	House, Edward M.	1829	1906	Schurz, Carl
1887	1966	Byrd, Harry F.	1793	1863	Houston, Samuel	1733	1804	Schuyler, Philip J.
1836	1926	Cannon, Joseph G.	1871	1955	Hull, Cordell	1801	1872	Seward, William H.
1808	1873	Chase, Salmon P.	1874	1952	Ickes, Harold L.	1873	1944	Smith, Alfred E.
1799	1859	Choate, Rufus	1866	1945	Johnson, Hiram W.	1814	1869	Stanton, Edwin M.
1850	1921	Clark, Champ	1874	1956	Jones, Jesse H.	1812	1883	Stephens, Alexander H.
1777	1852	Clay, Henry	1903	1963	Kefauver, Estes	1900	1949	Stettinius, Edward R., Jr.
1769	1828	Clinton, DeWitt	1856	1937	Kellogg, Frank B.	1900	1965	Stevenson, Adlai E.
1829	1888	Conkling, Roscoe	1925	1968	Kennedy, Robert F.	1867	1950	Stimson, Henry L.
1877	1963	Connally, Tom	1755	1827	King, Rufus	1889	1953	Taft, Robert A.
1870	1957	Cox, James M.	1874	1944	Knox, Frank	1884	1968	Thomas, Norman M.
1787	1863	Crittenden, John J.	1855	1925	La Follette, Robert M.	1814	1886	Tilden, Samuel J.
1862	1948	Daniels, Josephus	1878	1963	Lehman, Herbert H.	1890	1961	Tydings, Millard E.
1808	1889	Davis, Jefferson	1850	1924	Lodge, Henry Cabot	1884	1951	Vandenberg, Arthur H.
1873	1955	Davis, John W.	1786	1857	Marcy, William L.	1877	1953	Wagner, Robert F.
1855	1926	Debs, Eugene V.	1880	1959	Marshall, George C.	1782	1852	Webster, Daniel
1902	1971	Dewey, Thomas E.	1884	1968	Martin, Joseph W.	1892	1961	Welles, Sumner
1896	1969	Dirksen, Everett M.				1892	1944	Willkie, Wendell L.

American Business Leaders, Philanthropists

Born	Died	Name	Born	Died	Name	Born	Died	Name
1884	1966	Arden, Elizabeth	1837	1904	Hanna, Marcus A.	1875	1970	Neiman, Abraham
1832	1901	Armour, Phillip D.	1874	1940	Harkness, Edward S.	1887	1963	Olds, Irving S.
1764	1848	Astor, John Jacob	1848	1909	Harriman, Edward	1795	1869	Peabody, George
1875	1967	Babson, Roger	1865	1957	Hartford, Geo. L.A.	1887	1973	Post, Marjorie Merriweather
1894	1968	Bache, Harold L.	1838	1916	Hill, James J.	1839	1937	Rockefeller, John D.
1853	1924	Belmont, August	1795	1873	Hopkins, Johns	1874	1960	Rockefeller, J. D., Jr.
1786	1844	Biddle, Nicholas	1889	1974	Hunt, H.L.	1862	1932	Rosenwald, Julius
1835	1919	Carnegie, Andrew	1821	1900	Huntington, C.P.	1740	1785	Salomon, Haym
1821	1905	Cooke, Jay	1882	1967	Kaiser, Henry J.	1891	1971	Sarnoff, David
1791	1883	Cooper, Peter	1888	1969	Kennedy, Joseph P.	1847	1920	Schiff, Jacob H.
1834	1928	Depew, Chauncey M.	1876	1958	Kettering, Charles F.	1875	1966	Sloan, Alfred P.
1806	1893	Drexel, Anthony J.	1879	1948	Knudsen, Wm. K.	1845	1912	Straus, Isidor
1856	1925	Duke, James B.	1867	1966	Kresge, S. S.	1848	1931	Straus, Nathan
1739	1817	duPont, Pierre S.	1863	1955	Kress, Samuel H.	1839	1903	Swift, Gustavus
1890	1962	Fairless, Benjamin	1870	1948	Lamont, Thomas W.	1794	1877	Vanderbilt, Cornelius
1835	1906	Field, Marshall	1880	1952	Lasker, Albert D.	1843	1899	Vanderbilt, Cornelius
1860	1937	Filene, Edward A.	1891	1969	Lehman, Robert	1849	1920	Vanderbilt, Wm. K.
1894	1970	Folsom, Frank M.	1903	1972	Litton, Charles	1835	1900	Villard, Henry
1863	1947	Ford, Henry	1831	1902	Mackay, John W.	1838	1922	Wanamaker, John
1846	1927	Gary, Elbert H.	1855	1937	Mellon, Andrew W.	1896	1969	Warburg, James P.
1898	1974	Gerber, Daniel	1899	1970	Mellon, Richard K.	1888	1974	Whitney, Richard
1870	1949	Giannini, Amadeo Peter	1884	1968	Mennen, William G.	1841	1904	Whitney, Wm. C.
1885	1966	Gimbel, Bernard F.	1825	1910	Mills, Darius	1886	1972	Wilson, Charles E.
1836	1892	Gould, Jay	1837	1913	Morgan, J. Pierpont	1890	1961	Wilson, Chas. Erwin
1834	1916	Green, Henrietta (Hetty)	1868	1943	Morgan, J. P., Jr.	1879	1969	Wood, Robert E.
1828	1905	Guggenheim, Meyer	1875	1973	Mott, Charles Stewart	1852	1919	Woolworth, Frank

American Explorers, Naturalists of the Past

Explorers

Born	Died	Name	Born	Died	Name	Born	Died	Name
			1775	1813	Colter, John	1774	1809	Lewis, Meriwether
1884	1960	Andrews, Roy C.	1865	1940	Cook, Frederick A.	1902	1974	Lindbergh, Charles A.
1778	1838	Ashley, William Henry	1898	1970	Cruzen, Richard H.	1784	1864	Long, Stephen H.
1875	1946	Bartlett, Robert A.	1844	1881	De Long, G. W.	1874	1970	Macmillan, Donald
1790	1847	Bent, Charles	1877	1948	Dickey, H.S.	1799	1877	Palmer, Nathaniel
1875	1956	Bingham, Hiram	1880	1951	Ellsworth, Lincoln	1856	1920	Peary, Robert E.
1796	1878	Bonneville, Benjamin	1799	1854	Fitzpatrick, Thomas	1779	1813	Pike, Zebulon M.
1734	1820	Boone, Daniel	1813	1890	Fremont, John C.	1834	1902	Powell, John W.
1796	1836	Bowie, James	1844	1935	Greely, Adolphus W.	1793	1864	Schoolcraft, Henry R.
1804	1881	Bridger, James	1821	1871	Hall, Charles F.	1849	1892	Schwatka, Frederick
1888	1957	Byrd, Richard E.	1884	1937	Johnson, Martin	1785	1843	Stuart, Robert
1809	1868	Carson, Kit	1894	1953	Johnson, Osa	1799	1845	Sublette, William L.
1770	1838	Clark, William	1820	1857	Kane, Elisha K.	1798	1876	Walker, Joseph R.

499

Born	Died	Name	Born	Died	Name	Born	Died	Name
1802	1847	Whitman, Marcus	1780	1851	Audubon, John J.	1838	1914	Muir, John
1798	1877	Wilkes, Charles	1650	1941	Beard, Daniel C.	1887	1969	Osborn, Fairfield
1787	1849	Williams, W. S. (Old Bill)	1849	1926	Burbank, Luther	1817	1862	Thoreau, Henry D.
		Naturalists	1837	1921	Burroughs, John	1766	1813	Wilson, Alexander
1864	1926	Akeley, Carl Ethan						

American Military Leaders of the Past
All Army unless marked (N) Navy; (M) Marine; (AF) Air Force.

Born	Died	Name	Born	Died	Name	Born	Died	Name
1914	1974	Abrams, Creighton	1883	1959	Halsey, William F. (N)	1825	1875	Pickett, George E.
1737	1789	Allen, Ethan	1818	1902	Hampton, Wade	1822	1892	Pope, John
1741	1801	Arnold, Benedict	1728	1777	Herkimer, Nicholas	1813	1891	Porter, David D. (N)
1886	1950	Arnold, Henry F.	1825	1865	Hill, Ambrose P.	1905	1970	Power, Thomas S. (AF)
		(Hap) (AF)	1892	1966	Hobbs, Leland	1809	1867	Price, Stirling
1816	1894	Banks, Nathaniel	1870	1937	Hobson, Richmond (N)	1896	1973	Radford, Arthur (N)
1745	1803	Barry, John (N)	1887	1966	Hodges, Courtney	1890	1973	Rickenbacker, Edward (AF)
1818	1893	Beauregard, Pierre	1814	1879	Hooker, Joseph	1819	1892	Rodgers, C. R. P. (N)
1853	1930	Bliss, Tasker H.	1831	1879	Hood, John B.	1773	1838	Rodgers, John (N)
1878	1967	Bloch, Claude C. (N)	1773	1843	Hull, Isaac (N)	1819	1898	Rosecrans, William S.
1817	1876	Bragg, Braxton	1824	1863	Jackson, Thomas	1736	1818	St. Clair, Arthur
1775	1828	Brown, Jacob J.			(Stonewall)	1840	1903	Sampson, William T. (N)
1888	1950	Buchanan, Pat (N)	1803	1862	Johnston, Albert S.	1831	1906	Schofield, John
1823	1914	Buckner, Simon B.	1807	1891	Johnston, Joseph	1786	1866	Scott, Winfield
1886	1945	Buckner, Simon, Jr.	1747	1792	Jones, John Paul (N)	1835	1906	Shafter, William R.
1826	1863	Buford, John	1814	1862	Kearny, Philip	1831	1888	Sheridan, Phillip
1861	1947	Bullard, Robert L.	1794	1848	Kearny, Stephen	1896	1951	Sherman, Forrest P. (N)
1824	1881	Burnside, Ambrose	1879	1956	King, Ernest J. (N)	1820	1891	Sherman, William T.
1818	1893	Butler, Benjamin F.	1781	1813	Lawrence, James (N)	1858	1936	Sims, William S. (N)
1817	1873	Canby, Edward	1843	1899	Lawton, Henry	1780	1867	Sloat, John D. (N)
1884	1970	Cates, Clifton B. (M)	1875	1959	Leahy, William D. (N)	1882	1967	Smith, Holland M. (M)
1772	1840	Chauncey, Isaac (N)	1756	1818	Lee, Henry	1895	1961	Smith, W. Bedell
1842	1914	Chaffee, Adna R.	1807	1870	Lee, Robert E.	1891	1974	Spaatz, Carl A. (AF)
1890	1958	Chennault, Claire (AF)	1907	1975	Lincoln, George A.	1886	1969	Spruance, Raymond (N)
1752	1818	Clark, George Rogers	1821	1904	Longstreet, James	1728	1822	Stark, John
1786	1836	Crockett, David	1818	1861	Lyon, Nathaniel	1883	1946	Stilwell, Joseph W.
1819	1893	Crittenden, Thomas L.	1845	1912	MacArthur, Arthur	1726	1783	Stirling, Lord (Alexander)
1828	1890	Crook, George	1880	1964	MacArthur, Douglas	1890	1969	Stratemeyer, George (AF)
1842	1874	Cushing, William B. (N)	1733	1795	Marion, Francis	1833	1864	Stuart, J. E. B.
1839	1876	Custer, George	1806	1873	Maury, Matthew F. (N)	1740	1795	Sullivan, John
1779	1820	Decatur, Stephen (N)	1826	1885	McClellan, George B.	1822	1880	Sykes, George
1837	1917	Dewey, George (N)	1818	1885	McDowell, Irvin	1784	1850	Taylor, Zachary
1857	1927	Dickman, Joseph T.	1828	1864	McPherson, James	1827	1890	Terry, Alfred H.
1879	1951	Drum, Hugh A.	1815	1872	Meade, George	1816	1870	Thomas, George H.
1816	1894	Early, Jubal A.	1839	1925	Miles, Nelson A.	1884	1955	Towers, John H. (N)
1886	1961	Eichelberger, R. L.	1879	1936	Mitchell, Billy	1899	1954	Vandenberg, Hoyt (AF)
1890	1969	Eisenhower, Dwight D.	1887	1947	Mitscher, Marc A. (N)	1883	1953	Wainwright, Jonathan
1846	1912	Evans, Robley D. (N)	1736	1775	Montgomery, Richard	1889	1950	Walker, Walton H.
1817	1872	Ewell, Richard	1736	1802	Morgan, Daniel	1732	1799	Washington, George
1801	1870	Farragut, David G. (N)	1730	1805	Moultrie, William	1745	1796	Wayne, Anthony
1806	1863	Foote, Andrew (N)	1885	1966	Nimitz, Chester (N)	1836	1906	Wheeler, Joseph
1821	1877	Forrest, Nathan B.	1906	1971	O'Donnell, Emmett	1837	1925	Wilson, James H.
1865	1917	Funston, Frederick			(Rosy) (AF)	1860	1927	Wood, Leonard
1728	1806	Gates, Horatio	1896	1959	Parks, Floyd L.	1818	1897	Worden, John L. (N)
1805	1877	Goldsborough, L. M. (N)	1885	1945	Patton, George S.	1820	1899	Wright, Horatio G.
1822	1885	Grant, Ulysses S.	1814	1881	Pemberton, J. C.	1898	1969	Wyman, Willard G.
1742	1786	Greene, Nathaniel	1785	1819	Perry, Oliver H. (N)	1876	1959	Yarnell, Hy. E. (N)
1896	1970	Groves, Leslie R.	1860	1948	Pershing, John J.	1887	1964	York, Alvin C. (Sgt.)
1815	1872	Halleck, Henry	1739	1817	Pickens, Andrew			

American Scientists, Physicians, Engineers of the Past

Born	Died	Name	Born	Died	Name	Born	Died	Name
1838	1916	Abbe, Cleveland	1884	1967	Funk, Casimir	1868	1953	Millikan, Robert
1872	1973	Abbot, Charles Greeley	1903	1973	Gibbon, John H.	1866	1945	Morgan, Thomas H.
1876	1945	Albee, Fred H.	1839	1903	Gibbs, Josiah W.	1819	1868	Morton, W. T. G.
1807	1873	Agassiz, Louis	1858	1928	Goethals, George W.	1890	1967	Muller, Hermann J.
1823	1887	Baird, Spencer	1874	1929	Goldberger, Joseph	1904	1967	Oppenheimer, J. Robert
1839	1883	Beard, George Miller	1854	1920	Gorgas, William C.	1883	1962	Papanicolaou, George N.
1785	1853	Beaumont, William	1863	1914	Hall, Charles M.	1903	1967	Pincus, Gregory
1889	1967	Bigelow, Henry B.	1896	1965	Hench, Philip S.	1851	1902	Reed, Walter S.
1899	1964	Blalock, Alfred	1883	1964	Hess, Victor F.	1846	1927	Remsen, Ira
1773	1838	Bowditch, Nath.	1889	1953	Hubble, Edwin P.	1871	1910	Ricketts, Howard T.
1882	1961	Bridgman, Percy W.	1865	1958	Jackson, Chevalier	1806	1869	Roebling, John A.
1848	1908	Brooks, William K.	1905	1973	Kuiper, Gerard	1879	1970	Rous, Peyton
1890	1974	Bush, Vannevar	1834	1906	Langley, Samuel P.	1745	1813	Rush, Benjamin
1868	1939	Cabot, Richard C.	1881	1957	Langmuir, Irving	1877	1967	Schick, Bela
1873	1944	Carrel, Alexis	1884	1964	Lanza, Anthony J.	1885	1972	Shapley, Harlow
1864	1943	Carver, George W.	1901	1958	Lawrence, Ernest O.	1813	1883	Sims, James M.
1887	1968	Cobb, Stanley	1815	1878	Long, Crawford	1859	1934	Smith, Theobald
1892	1962	Compton, Arthur H.	1855	1916	Lowell, Percival	1865	1923	Steinmetz, Charles
1877	1954	Compton, Karl T.	1806	1873	Maury, Matthew F.	1915	1974	Sutherland, Earl W.
1901	1974	Condon, Edward	1865	1939	Mayo, Charles H.	1898	1964	Szilard, Leo
1869	1939	Cushing, Harvey W.	1898	1968	Mayo, Charles W.	1899	1972	Theiler, Max
1927	1961	Dooley, Thomas	1861	1939	Mayo, William J.	1888	1973	Waksman, Selman
1901	1965	Du Mont, Allen	1845	1913	McBurney, Charles	1886	1973	White, Paul Dudley
1820	1887	Eads, James P.	1909	1968	McLean, John Milton	1894	1964	Wiener, Norbert
1879	1955	Einstein, Albert	1899	1966	Menninger, William C.	1844	1930	Wiley, Harvey W.
1706	1790	Franklin, Benjamin	1852	1931	Michelson, Albert A.	1856	1931	Williams, Daniel Hale
1895	1974	Fremont-Smith, Frank	1903	1966	Millikan, Clark	1898	1974	Zwicky, Fritz

American Inventors of the Past

Born	Died	Name
1891	1954	Armstrong, Edwin
1847	1922	Bell, Alex. Graham
1890	1970	Bell, Herbert A.
1851	1929	Berliner, Emile
1857	1898	Burroughs, William
1906	1968	Carlson, Chester F.
1876	1950	Carrier, Willis
1873	1975	Coolidge, William D.
1874	1961	De Forrest, Lee
1862	1938	Duryea, Charles E.
1870	1967	Duryea, J. Frank
1854	1932	Eastman, George
1847	1931	Edison, Thomas A.
1803	1889	Ericcson, John

Born	Died	Name
1743	1798	Fitch, John
1765	1815	Fulton, Robert
1818	1903	Gatling, Richard J.
1882	1945	Goddard, Robert H.
1800	1860	Goodyear, Charles
1803	1855	Gorrie, John
1835	1901	Gray, Elisha
1797	1878	Henry, Joseph
1812	1886	Hoe, Richard M.
1819	1867	Howe, Elias
1866	1945	Lake, Simon
1881	1957	Langmuir, Irving
1826	1886	Loomis, Mahlon
1809	1884	McCormick, Cyrus H.
1854	1899	Mergenthaler, Ottmar

Born	Died	Name
1791	1872	Morse, S. F. B.
1811	1861	Otis, Elisha
1831	1897	Pullman, George M.
1894	1974	de Seversky, Alexander P.
1889	1972	Sikorsky, Igor
1894	1970	Spencer, Percy L.
1860	1930	Sperry, Elmer A.
1856	1943	Tesla, Nikola
1853	1937	Thomson, Elihu
1846	1914	Westinghouse, George
1765	1825	Whitney, Eli
1900	1975	Williams, David M.
1871	1948	Wright, Orville
1867	1912	Wright, Wilbur

American Educators and Religious Leaders

Educators

Born	Died	Name
1897	1967	Allport, Gordon
1829	1916	Angell, James B.
1870	1949	Angell, James R.
1811	1900	Barnard, Henry
1827	1911	Bascom, John
1862	1947	Butler, Nich. Murray
1807	1874	Cornell, Ezra
1862	1948	Cross, Wilbur
1859	1952	Dewey, John
1868	1963	DuBois, William E. B.
1834	1926	Eliot, Charles W.
1863	1940	Finley, John H.
1903	1967	Gassner, John W.
1831	1908	Gilman, Daniel C.
1906	1963	Griswold, A. Whitney
1844	1924	Hall, G. Stanley
1856	1906	Harper, William R.
1802	1887	Hopkins, Mark
1842	1910	James, William
1882	1974	Kallen, Horace M.
1880	1968	Keller, Helen
1797	1849	Lyon, Mary
1800	1873	McGuffey, William H.
1796	1859	Mann, Horace
1872	1964	Meiklejohn, Alexander
1818	1901	Muhlenberg, Fred. A.
1869	1946	Neilson, William A.
1909	1969	Northrop, Eugene P.
1827	1908	Norton, Chas. Eliot
1855	1902	Palmer, Alice Freeman

Born	Died	Name
1804	1894	Peabody, Elizabeth P.
1870	1964	Pound, Roscoe
1855	1916	Royce, Josiah
1885	1963	Seymour, Charles
1779	1864	Silliman, Benjamin
1917	1969	Smith, Courtney C.
1840	1910	Sumner, Wm. Graham
1893	1969	Tannenbaum, Frank
1858	1915	Washington, Booker T.
1832	1918	White, Andrew D.
1787	1870	Willard, Emma

Religious Leaders

Born	Died	Name
1835	1922	Abbott, Lyman
1745	1816	Asbury, Francis
1813	1887	Beecher, Henry Ward
1775	1863	Beecher, Lyman
1835	1893	Brooks, Phillips
1582	1658	Bulkeley, Peter
1802	1867	Bushnell, Horace
1780	1842	Channing, Wm. Ellery
1584	1652	Cotton, John
1895	1970	Cushing, Richard
1752	1817	Dwight, Timothy
1821	1910	Eddy, Mary Baker
1703	1758	Edwards, Jonathan
1902	1973	Eisendrath, Maurice N.
1900	1968	Fry, Franklin C.
1834	1921	Gibbons, James
1867	1938	Hayes, Patrick J.

Born	Died	Name
1748	1830	Hicks, Elias
1879	1964	Holmes, John Haynes
1590	1643	Hutchinson, Anne
1883	1968	Jones, Bob
1884	1973	Jones, E. Stanley
1843	1926	Kohler, Kaufmann
1866	1949	Manning, William T.
1663	1728	Mather, Cotton
1873	1970	McKay, David O.
1890	1944	McPherson, Aimee Semple
1837	1899	Moody, Dwight L.
1711	1787	Muhlenberg, H. M.
1891	1963	Oxnam, G. Bromley
1810	1860	Parker, Theodore
1913	1969	Pike, James A.
1884	1968	Poling, Daniel A.
1729	1796	Seabury, Samuel
1774	1821	Seton, Elizabeth
1886	1969	Sheil, Bernard J.
1882	1968	Shipler, Guy E.
1881	1968	Silver, Eliezer
1805	1844	Smith, Joseph
1876	1972	Smith, Joseph Fielding
1889	1970	Sockman, Ralph W.
1889	1967	Spellman, Francis
1863	1935	Sunday, Wm. (Billy)
1886	1965	Tillich, Paul
1862	1969	Welch, Herbert
1599	1683	Williams, Roger
1874	1949	Wise, Stephen S.
1801	1877	Young, Brigham

American Reformers, Social-Economic Leaders of the Past

Born	Died	Name
1860	1935	Addams, Jane
1909	1972	Alinsky, Saul O.
1847	1902	Altgeld, Peter
1820	1906	Anthony, Susan B.
1891	1969	Arnold, Thurman W.
1867	1961	Balch, Emily G.
1821	1912	Barton, Clara H.
1818	1895	Bloomer, Amelia J.
1809	1890	Brisbane, Albert
1800	1859	Brown, John
1859	1947	Catt, Carrie Chapman
1855	1926	Debs, Eugene
1802	1887	Dix, Dorothea
1817	1895	Douglass, Frederick
1805	1879	Garrison, Wm. L.

Born	Died	Name
1887	1940	Garvey, Marcus
1839	1897	George, Henry
1837	1927	Gerry, Elbridge T.
1850	1924	Gompers, Samuel
1873	1952	Green, William
1887	1975	Hansen, Alvin
1887	1946	Hillman, Sidney
1801	1876	Howe, Samuel G.
1929	1968	King, Martin Luther
1855	1925	LaFollette, Robt. M.
1880	1969	Lewis, John L.
1793	1880	Mott, Lucretia
1886	1952	Murray, Phillip
1846	1911	Nation, Carry
1811	1886	Noyes, John H.
1801	1877	Owen, Robt. Dale

Born	Died	Name
1842	1933	Parkhurst, Charles H.
1811	1884	Phillips, Wendell
1849	1914	Riis, Jacob A.
1816	1906	Sage, Russell
1828	1918	Sage, Margaret Olivia
1883	1967	Sanger, Margaret
1747	1825	Shays, Daniel
1797	1874	Smith, Gerrit
1816	1902	Stanton, Eliz. Cady
1818	1893	Stone, Lucy
1867	1960	Townsend, Francis E.
1893	1955	White, Walter
1931	1973	Wiley, George
1839	1898	Willard, Frances E.
1921	1971	Young, Whitney M.

American Sculptors of the Past

Born	Died	Name
1878	1949	Aitken, Robert I.
1887	1964	Archipenko, Alexander
1819	1911	Ball, Thomas
1863	1938	Barnard, George Grey
1865	1925	Bartlett, Paul W.
1867	1915	Bitter, Karl T.
1913	1969	Boehm, Edward M.
1871	1941	Borglum, Gutzon
1868	1922	Borglum, Solon H.
1814	1886	Brown, Henry K.
1898	1970	Bufano, Benjamino
1870	1945	Calder, Alexander S.
1814	1857	Crawford, Thomas
1861	1944	Dallin, Cyrus
1884	1952	Davidson, Jo
1844	1917	Ezekiel, Moses Jacob

Born	Died	Name
1869	1943	Farnham, Sally James
1895	1942	Flannagan, John
1877	1953	Fraser, James E.
1790	1852	Frazee, John
1850	1931	French, Daniel C.
1805	1852	Greenough, Horatio
1887	1967	Hoffman, Malvina
1830	1908	Hosmer, Harriet
1847	1914	Hoxie, Vinnie Ream
1825	1879	Jackson, John Adams
1868	1925	Jaegers, Albert
1892	1969	Jones, Thomas H.
1863	1947	Kitson, Henry Hudson
1871	1932	Kitson, Theo Alice
1882	1935	Lachaise, Gaston
1877	1954	Laessle, Albert

Born	Died	Name
1877	1963	Lawrie, Lee
1871	1935	Lukeman, Henry A.
1863	1937	MacMonnies, Fred W.
1885	1966	Manship, Paul
1879	1947	McCartan, Edward
1876	1916	Mears, Helen F.
1883	1962	Mestrovic, Ivan
1817	1904	Palmer, Erastus Dow
1805	1873	Powers, Hiram
1867	1917	Pratt, Bela
1868	1929	Quinn, Edmond T.
1816	1879	Rimmer, William
1825	1874	Rinehart, William H.
1829	1904	Rogers, John
1825	1892	Rogers, Randolph
1879	1922	Rumsey, Charles Cary

Born	Died	Name	Born	Died	Name	Born	Died	Name
1756	1833	Rush, William	1906	1965	Smith, David	1870	1952	Weinman, Adolph A.
1848	1907	St. Gaudens, Augustus	1819	1895	Story, William W.	1877	1942	Whitney, Gertrude
1871	1922	Shrady, Henry M.	1860	1936	Taft, Lorado	1877	1957	Young, Mahonri M.
1839	1913	Simmons, Franklin	1830	1910	Ward, J. O. A.	1887	1966	Zorach, William

American Painters of the Past

Born	Died	Name	Born	Died	Name	Born	Died	Name
1852	1911	Abbey, Edwin A.	1792	1866	Harding, Chester	1778	1860	Peale, Rembrandt
1779	1843	Allston, Washington	1848	1892	Harnett, William M.	1851	1914	Pearce, Charles S.
1785	1851	Audubon, John James	1868	1933	Hart, George O.	1884	1970	Peirce, Waldo
1893	1965	Avery, Milton C.	1877	1943	Hartley, Marsden	1912	1956	Pollock, Jackson
1912	1963	Baziotes, William	1859	1935	Hassam, Childe	1823	1879	Powell, William H.
1863	1942	Beaux, Cecelia	1813	1894	Healy, George P. A.	1861	1924	Prendergast, Maurice B.
1882	1925	Bellows, George W.	1865	1929	Henri, Robert	1853	1911	Pyle, Howard
1889	1975	Benton, Thomas Hart	1780	1849	Hicks, Edward	1801	1881	Quidor, John
1885	1974	Biddle, George	1823	1890	Hicks, Thomas	1861	1909	Remington, Frederic
1830	1902	Bierstadt, Albert	1880	1966	Hofmann, Hans	1838	1905	Richards, William T.
1811	1879	Bingham, George Caleb	1836	1910	Homer, Winslow	1903	1970	Rothko, Mark
1856	1943	Birch, Reginald B.	1882	1967	Hopper, Edward	1847	1917	Ryder, Albert P.
1848	1936	Blashfield, Edwin H.	1824	1879	Hunt, William M.	1856	1925	Sargent, John Singer
1847	1927	Bridgman, Frederic A.	1801	1846	Inman, Henry	1898	1969	Shahn, Ben
1855	1941	Brush, George de Forest	1825	1894	Inness, George	1883	1965	Sheeler, Charles
1893	1967	Burchfield, Charles E.	1843	1942	Jackson, William H.	1876	1953	Shinn, Everett
1845	1926	Cassatt, Mary	1824	1906	Johnson, Eastman	1871	1951	Sloan, John
1796	1872	Catlin, George	1838	1911	Keith, William	1883	1962	Speicher, Eugene E.
1849	1916	Chase, William M.	1818	1872	Kensett, John F.	1880	1946	Stella, Joseph
1826	1900	Church, Frederic	1880	1949	Kuhn, Walt	1755	1828	Stuart, Gilbert
1801	1848	Cole, Thomas	1835	1910	La Farge, John	1783	1872	Sully, Thomas
1737	1815	Copley, John S.	1873	1939	Lawson, Ernest	1861	1930	Symons, Gardner
1856	1919	Cox, Kenyon	1816	1868	Leutze, Emanuel	1849	1921	Thayer, Abbott H.
1843	1909	Currier, J. Frank	1867	1933	Luks, George B.	1848	1933	Tiffany, Louis C.
1897	1946	Curry, John Steuart	1866	1912	MacCameron, Robert L.	1756	1843	Trumbull, John
1862	1928	Davies, Arthur B.	1872	1953	Marin, John	1849	1925	Tryon, Dwight N.
1894	1964	Davis, Stuart	1898	1954	Marsh, Reginald	1853	1902	Twachtman, John H.
1883	1935	Demuth, Charles	1836	1897	Martin, Homer	1776	1852	Vanderlyn, John
1884	1958	Du Bois, Guy Pene	1813	1884	Matteson, Tompkins H.	1836	1923	Vedder, Elihu
1796	1886	Durand, Asher Brown	1868	1932	Maurer, Alfred H.	1858	1933	Vonnoh, Robert W.
1848	1919	Duveneck, Frank	1860	1932	Melchers, Gari	1843	1929	Walker, Henry Oliver
1844	1916	Eakins, Thomas	1858	1925	Metcalf, Willard L.	1881	1961	Weber, Max
1751	1801	Earle, Ralph	1829	1901	Moran, Edward	1841	1926	Weir, John F.
1871	1956	Feininger, Lyonel	1837	1926	Moran, Thomas	1852	1919	Weir, Julian Alden
1822	1884	Fuller, George	1860	1961	Moses, Grandma	1803	1889	Weir, Robert W.
1870	1938	Glackens, William J.	1807	1868	Mount, William S.	1738	1820	West, Benjamin
1904	1948	Gorky, Arshile	1867	1940	Myers, Jerome	1834	1903	Whistler, James A. M.
1903	1974	Gottlieb, Adolph	1741	1827	Peale, Charles W.	1820	1910	Whittredge, Worthington
1893	1959	Grosz, George	1749	1831	Peale, James	1891	1942	Wood, Grant
1866	1946	Guerin, Jules	1774	1825	Peale, Raphaelle	1836	1892	Wyant, Alexander H.

Noted American Cartoonists

Charles Addams, b. 1912. Noted for macabre cartoons.

Peter Arno, 1904-1968. Noted for urban characterizations.

George Baker, 1915-1975. The Sad Sack.

Jim Berry, b. 1932. Berry's World.

Clare Briggs, 1875-1930. Mr. & Mrs.

Milton Caniff, b. 1907. Terry & the Pirates; Steve Canyon.

Al Capp, b. 1909. Li'l Abner.

Roy Crane, b. 1901. Captain Easy; Buzz Sawyer.

Jay N. Darling (Ding), 1876-1962. Political cartoonist won 2 Pulitzer Prizes.

Rudolph Dirks 1877-1968. The Katzenjammer Kids.

Alan Dunn, 1900-1974. Cartoonist for The New Yorker.

Bud Fisher, 1885-1954. Mutt & Jeff.

Fontaine Fox, 1884-1964. Toonerville Folks.

Rube Goldberg, 1883-1970. Boob McNutt. Famed for cartoons of mechanical contrivances whose humor is derived from their absurd, unnecessary complexity.

Chester Gould, b. 1900. Dick Tracy.

Harold Gray, 1894-1968. Little Orphan Annie.

John Held, Jr., 1889-1958. His cartoons epitomized the spirit of the "jazz age" of the 20s.

Herb Block, (Herblock), b. 1909; Leading political cartoonist.

George Herriman, 1881-1944. Krazy Kat.

Harry Hershfield, 1885-1974. Cartoonist, raconteur.

Helen Hokinson, 1900-1949. Known for satirical drawings of plump, bewildered suburban matrons and clubwomen.

Walt Kelly, 1913-1973. Pogo.

Hank Ketcham, b. 1920. Dennis the Menace.

Ted Key, b. 1912. Hazel.

Frank King, 1883-1969. Gasoline Alley.

Rollin Kirby, 1875-1952. Political cartoonist won 3 Pulitzer Prizes.

Bill Mauldin, b. 1921. Depicted squalid life of the G.I. in WW II.

Winsor McCay, 1872-1934. Little Nemo.

John T. McCutcheon, 1870-1949. Noted for cartoons of midwestern rural life.

George McManus, 1884-1954. Bringing Up Father (Maggie & Jiggs).

Bob Montana, 1920-1975. Archie.

Thomas Nast, 1840-1902. His political cartoons were instrumental in breaking the corrupt Boss Tweed ring in N.Y. Created the donkey and elephant to represent the Democratic and Republican parties.

Frederick Burr Opper, 1857-1937. Happy Hooligan.

Richard Outcault, 1863-1928. Yellow Kid; Buster Brown.

Art Sansom, b. 1920. The Born Loser.

Charles Schulz, b. 1922. Peanuts.

Elzie C. Segar, 1894-1938. Popeye.

Sydney Smith, 1887-1935. The Gumps.

Otto Soglow, 1900-1975. The Little King; The Canyon Kiddies

James Swinnerton, 1875-1974. Little Jimmy.

Mort Walker, b. 1923. Beetle Bailey.

Russ Westover, 1887-1966. Tillie the Toiler.

J. R. Williams, 1888-1957. The Willets Family; Out Our Way.

Art Young, 1866-1943. Political radical and satirist.

Chic Young, 1901-1973. Blondie.

Modern American Playwrights and Some of Their Plays

George Abbott, b. 1887. Co-author Three Men on a Horse, The Boys from Syracuse, Damn Yankees.

Edward F. Albee, b. 1928. Who's Afraid of Virginia Woolf?, Tiny Alice, A Delicate Balance, Seascape.

William Alfred, b. 1922. Hogan's Goat.

Maxwell Anderson, (1888-1959). What Price Glory?, Winterset, Saturday's Children; High Tor, Key Largo.

Philip Barry, (1886-1949). The Animal Kingdom, Holiday, The Philadelphia Story.

Abe Burrows, b. 1910. Co-author Guys and Dolls, How to

Succeed in Business Without Really Trying.

Mary C. Chase, b. 1907. Harvey.

Paddy Chayefsky, b. 1923. Middle of the Night, The Tenth Man, Gideon, The Passions of Josef D.

Marc Connelly, b. 1890. The Green Pastures.

Russell Crouse, (1893-1966). Co-author State of the Union, Life With Father, Call Me Madam, The Sound of Music, Mr. President.

Edna Ferber, (1885-1968). Co-author Dinner at Eight, Stage Door.

Paul Foster, b. 1932. Tom Paine.

Jack Gelber, b. 1932, The Connection, The Cuban Thing.

William Gibson, b. 1914. Two for the Seesaw, The Miracle Worker.

Frank D. Gilroy, b. 1915. The Subject Was Roses, The Only Game in Town.

Charles Gordone, b. 1925. No Place to Be Somebody.

Paul Green, b. 1894. In Abraham's Bosom, Wilderness Road.

William Hanley, b. 1931. Slow Dance on the Killing Ground.

Lorraine Hansberry, (1930-1965). A Raisin in the Sun.

Moss Hart, (1904-1961). Co-author Once in a Lifetime, You Can't Take it With You.

Ben Hecht, (1884-1964). Co-author The Front Page.

Lillian Hellman, b. 1907. The Children's Hour, The Little Foxes, Watch on the Rhine.

Sidney Howard, (1881-1939). The Silver Cord, Yellow Jack, They Knew What They Wanted.

William Inge, (1913-1973). Come Back Little Sheba, Picnic, Bus Stop, The Dark at the Top of the Stairs, A Loss of Roses.

LeRoi Jones (Imamu Amini Baraka), b. 1934. Dutchman, The Slave.

George S. Kaufman, (1889-1961). Co-author Dinner at Eight, Stage Door, You Can't Take It With You, The Man Who Came to Dinner.

George Kelly, (1887-1974). The Show-off, Craig's Wife.

Jean Kerr, b. 1923, Mary, Mary; Poor Richard; Finishing Touches.

Joseph Kesselring, (1902-1967). Arsenic and Old Lace.

Sidney Kingsley, b. 1906. Men in White, The Patriots, Dead End, Darkness at Noon.

Arthur Kopit, b. 1937. Oh Dad, Poor Dad, Mamma's Hung You in a Closet and I'm Feelin' So Sad.

Howard Lindsay, (1889-1968). Co-author State of the Union, Life With Father, Call Me Madam, The Sound of Music, Mr. President.

Charles MacArthur, (1895-1956). Co-author The Front Page.

Archibald MacLeish, b. 1892, J. B.

Terrence McNally, b. 1939. And Things That Go Bump in the Night, Sweet Eros.

Arthur Miller, b. 1915. All My Sons, Death of a Salesman, Crucible, View from the Bridge, After the Fall, Incident at Vichy, The Price.

Anne Nichols, (1891-1966). Abie's Irish Rose.

Clifford Odets, (1906-1963). Waiting for Lefty, Awake and Sing, Golden Boy, The Country Girl.

Eugene O'Neill, (1888-1953). The Long Voyage Home, The Emperor Jones, Anna Christie, Desire Under the Elms, Strange Interlude, Mourning Becomes Electra; Ah, Wilderness; The Iceman Cometh, Long Day's Journey Into Night.

John Patrick, b. 1905. The Hasty Heart, Teahouse of the August Moon.

Elmer Rice, (1892-1967). The Adding Machine, Street Scene, Counsellor-at-Law, Dream Girl.

Howard Sackler, b. 1930. The Great White Hope.

William Saroyan, b. 1908. My Heart's in the Highlands, The Time of Your Life.

Dore Schary, b. 1905. Sunrise at Campobello.

Murray Schisgal, b. 1926. The Typists and the Tiger, Luv.

Robert Sherwood, (1896-1955). Reunion in Vienna, The Petrified Forest, Idiot's Delight, There Shall Be No Night, Abe Lincoln in Illinois.

Neil Simon, b. 1927. Sweet Charity, Plaza Suite, The Odd Couple, Barefoot in the Park, Last of the Red Hot Lovers, The Gingerbread Lady, The Prisoner of Second Avenue, The Sunshine Boys, The Good Doctor.

Samuel A. Taylor, b. 1912. The Happy Time, The Pleasure of His Company, co-author Sabrina Fair and No Strings.

John Van Druten, (1901-1957). The Voice of the Turtle; I Remember Mama; Bell, Book and Candle; I Am a Camera.

Thornton Wilder, b. 1897. Our Town, The Skin of Our Teeth, The Matchmaker.

Tennessee Williams, b. 1914. The Glass Menagerie, A Streetcar Named Desire, Cat on a Hot Tin Roof, The Night of the Iguana, The Milk Train Doesn't Stop Here Anymore, Camino Real.

American Writers of the Past

Novelists, Poets, Historians, Journalists, Publishers, Biographers

A

Charles Francis Adams, biographer, diplomat, 1807-1886.

Charles Francis Adams, historian, lawyer, 1835-1915.

Franklin P. Adams, journalist, 1881-1960.

Henry Adams, historian, philosopher, 1838-1918.

James Truslow Adams, historian, 1878-1949.

George Ade, humorist, dramatist, 1866-1944.

Conrad Aiken, poet, critic, 1889-1973.

Louisa May Alcott, novelist, 1832-1889. Little Women.

Thomas Bailey Aldrich, author, editor, 1836-1907.

Henry M. Alden, editor, 1836-1919. Harper's Magazine.

Horatio Alger, author of "rags-to-riches" boys' books, 1832-1899.

James Lane Allen, novelist, 1849-1925.

Stewart Alsop, political columnist, writer, 1914-1974.

Charlotte Armstrong, mystery writer, 1905-1969.

Hamilton Fish Armstrong, journalist and editor of Foreign Affairs, 1893-1973.

Gertrude Atherton, novelist, 1857-1948. Black Oxen.

Mary Austin, novelist, playwright, 1868-1934.

B

Irving Bacheller, novelist, journalist, 1859-1950. Eben Holden.

Arthur (Bugs) Baer, humorous columnist, 1886-1969.

Ray Stannard Baker, biographer, historian, 1870-1946.

George Bancroft, historian, diplomat, 1800-1891.

Margaret Ayer Barnes, novelist, 1886-1967. Years of Grace.

John Bartlett, publisher, 1820-1905. Familiar Quotations.

Bruce Barton, author, businessman, 1875-1967. The Man Nobody Knows.

Charles A. Beard, historian, 1874-1948.

Mary Ritter Beard, historian, 1876-1958.

Lucius M. Beebe, journalist, author, 1902-1966. N. Y. Herald Tribune.

Edward Bellamy, novelist, 1850-1898. Looking Backward: 2000-1887.

Robert C. Benchley, humorist, journalist, 1889-1945.

Stephen Vincent Benet, poet, novelist, 1898-1943.

William Rose Benet, poet, novelist, 1886-1950.

James Gordon Bennett, journalist, 1795-1872. Founded N. Y. Herald.

James Gordon Bennett, Jr., journalist, 1841-1918. N. Y. Herald, Evening Telegram.

William Benton, publisher, 1900-1973. Encyclopaedia Britannica.

John Berryman, poet, 1914-1972.

Ambrose Bierce, short-story writer, journalist, 1842-1914.

Earl Derr Biggers, novelist, 1884-1933. Created Charlie Chan.

Josh Billings (H. W. Shaw), humorist, 1818-1885.

Louise Bogan, lyric poet, 1897-1970.

Samuel Bowles II, editor, 1826-1878. Springfield Republican.

Gamaliel Bradford, biographer, 1863-1932.

Anne Bradstreet, poet, 1612-1672.

William Cowper Brann, iconoclast, editor, reformer, 1855-1898.

Arthur Brisbane, journalist, 1864-1936. N. Y. Sun, Evening Sun, World.

Louis Bromfield, novelist, essayist, 1896-1956.

Van Wyck Brooks, historian, critic, 1886-1963.

Heywood Broun, journalist, 1888-1939. N. Y. Tribune, World.

John Mason Brown, drama, literary critic, 1900-1969.

Orestes Brownson, author, editor, clergyman, 1803-1876.

William Cullen Bryant, poet, editor, 1794-1878.

Pearl Buck, author, won the Pulitzer and Nobel Prizes, 1892-1973. The Good Earth.

Henry C. Bunner, journalist, poet, 1855-1896. Editor of Puck.

Ned Buntline, wrote dime novels, 1823-1886. Nicknamed "Buffalo Bill" Cody.

Edgar Rice Burroughs, novelist, 1875-1950. Tarzan of the Apes.

C

George W. Cable, novelist, essayist, 1844-1925.

Henry Seidel Canby, editor, critic, 1878-1961. Saturday Review of Literature.

Jimmy Cannon, sports columnist, 1909-1973.

Will Carleton, poet, journalist, 1845-1912. Over the Hill to the Poorhouse.

Rachel Carson, marine biologist, author, 1907-1964. Silent Spring.

Alice Cary, novelist, 1820-1871.

Phoebe Cary, poet, 1824-1871. One Sweetly Solemn Thought.

Willa Cather, novelist, essayist, 1876-1947. O Pioneers!, My Antonia.

Robert W. Chambers, novelist, artist,

1865-1933. The Rogue's Moon.
Raymond Chandler, wrote detective fiction, 1888-1959. Philip Marlowe series.
Winston Churchill, novelist, 1871-1947. The Crisis.
Raymond Clapper, journalist, 1892-1944.
Walter Van Tilburg Clark, novelist, 1909-1972. The Ox-Bow Incident.
Irvin S. Cobb, humorist, journalist, 1876-1944.
James Fenimore Cooper, novelist, 1789-1851. Leather-Stocking Tales.
Royal Cortissoz, journalist, author, 1869-1948. N. Y. Herald Tribune.
Thomas B. Costain, novelist, journalist, 1885-1965. The Black Rose.
Hart Crane, poet, 1899-1932.
Stephen Crane, novelist, 1871-1900. The Red Badge of Courage.
Francis Marion Crawford, novelist, 1854-1909. .
Countee Cullen, poet, 1903-1946. The Black Christ.
E. E. Cummings, poet, 1894-1962.
Cyrus H. K. Curtis, magazine, newspaper publisher, 1850-1933.
George William Curtis, journalist, author, 1824-1892.

D

Charles A. Dana, editor, 1819-1897. New York Sun.
Richard H. Dana, author, lawyer, 1815-1882. Two Years Before the Mast.
Josephus Daniels, journalist, statesman, 1862-1948. Raleigh News & Observer.
Elmer Davis, journalist, radio commentator, 1890-1958.
Richard Harding Davis, journalist, novelist, 1864-1916.
Ludwell Denny, journalist, 1894-1970. Scripps-Howard Newspapers.
Bernard De Voto, historian, editor, 1897-1955.
Michael H. De Young, newspaper editor, 1849-1925. San Francisco Chronicle.
Emily Dickinson, poet, 1830-1886.
Thomas Dixon, novelist, clergyman, 1865-1946. The Clansman.
J. Frank Dobie, author, educator, 1888-1964.
Hilda Doolittle (H.D.), poet, 1886-1961.
John Dos Passos, author, 1896-1970. U.S.A., Midcentury.
Joseph Rodman Drake, poet, 1795-1820.
Theodore Dreiser, novelist, 1871-1945. An American Tragedy.
Orvil E. Dryfoos, newspaper publisher, 1912-1963. New York Times.
Paul L. Dunbar, poet, novelist, 1872-1906.

E

Edward Eggleston, novelist, clergyman, 1837-1902.
Ralph Waldo Emerson, poet, essayist, 1803-1882.
John Erskine, novelist, educator, 1879-1951. The Private Life of Helen of Troy.

F

Martha Farquharson, author of juveniles, 1828-1909. Elsie Dinsmore series.
John C. Farrar, publisher, editor, 1896-1974.
William Faulkner, novelist, 1897-1962. Sanctuary, Light in August.
Edna Ferber, novelist, 1885-1968. Show Boat, Saratoga Trunk, Giant.
Arthur D. Ficke, poet, novelist, 1883-1945.
Eugene Field, poet, journalist, 1850-1895. Little Boy Blue; Wynken, Blynken and Nod.
James T. Fields, editor, author, 1817-

1881. Atlantic Monthly.
Louis Fischer, historian, 1896-1970. The Life of Lenin.
Dorothy Canfield Fisher, novelist, writer of juveniles, 1879-1958.
John Fiske, historian, philosopher, 1842-1901.
F. Scott Fitzgerald, novelist, short-story writer, 1896-1940. The Great Gatsby.
John Gould Fletcher, poet, critic, 1886-1950.
F.M. Flynn, publisher, N.Y. Daily News, 1903-1975.
Kathryn Forbes, novelist, 1909-1966. Mama's Bank Account.
Paul Leicester Ford, novelist, historian, 1865-1902.
Gene Fowler, journalist, author, 1890-1960. Good Night, Sweet Prince.
John W. Fox, Jr., novelist, 1863-1919. The Little Shepherd of Kingdom Come.
Douglas S. Freeman, historian, editor, 1886-1953. Richmond News Leader.
Mary E. W. Freeman, short-story writer, 1852-1930.
Philip Freneau, poet, journalist, 1752-1832.
Robert Frost, poet, 1874-1963.

G

Zona Gale, novelist, dramatist, 1874-1938.
Frank E. Gannett, newspaper publisher, 1876-1957. Gannett Newspapers.
Erle Stanley Gardner, author, lawyer, 1889-1970. Perry Mason series.
Hamlin Garland, novelist, 1860-1940. Main-Traveled Roads.
Floyd Gibbons, journalist, radio personality, 1887-1939.
Ellen Glasgow, novelist, 1873-1945.
Susan Glaspell, novelist, dramatist, 1882-1948.
Edwin L. Godkín, journalist, 1831-1902. Founded The Nation.
Henry W. Grady, journalist, orator, 1850-1889. Atlanta Constitution.
Horace Greeley, journalist, politician, 1811-1872. N. Y. Tribune.
Abel Green, journalist, editor, 1900-1973. Variety.
Zane Grey, writer of western stories, 1875-1939.
Gilbert H. Grosvenor, editor, geographer, 1875-1966. National Geographic.
Edgar A. Guest, poet, 1881-1959. A Heap of Livin'.
Louis I. Guiney, poet, essayist, 1861-1920.
Arthur Guiterman, poet, 1871-1943.
John Gunther, journalist, author, 1901-1970. Inside U.S.A., Inside Europe.

H

Edward Everett Hale, author, clergyman, 1822-1909. The Man Without a Country.
James Norman Hall, novelist, 1887-1951. Co-author Mutiny on the Bounty.
Dashiell Hammett, writer of detective fiction, 1894-1961. Created Sam Spade.
Norman Hapgood, magazine editor, author, 1868-1937.
Joel Chandler Harris, short-story writer, 1848-1908. Uncle Remus series.
Bret Harte, short-story writer, poet, 1836-1902. The Luck of Roaring Camp.
George B. M. Harvey, journalist, diplomat, 1864-1928.
Cameron Hawley, novelist, 1905-1969. Executive Suite.
Nathaniel Hawthorne, novelist, 1804-1864. The Scarlet Letter.
John M. Hay, historian, diplomat, 1838-1905. Abraham Lincoln: A History.
Lafcadio Hearn, author, 1850-1904.
Gabriel Heatter, radio commentator, 1890-1972.
William Randolph Hearst, newspaper

publisher, 1863-1951.
Ben Hecht, novelist, playwright, journalist, 1894-1964.
Ernest Hemingway, novelist, short-story writer, 1899-1961. A Farewell to Arms.
Burton J. Hendrick, biographer, journalist, 1871-1949.
O. Henry (W. S. Porter), short-story writer, 1862-1910. The Gift of the Magi.
William M. (Bill) Henry, journalist, radio analyst, 1890-1970. Los Angeles Times.
Joseph Hergesheimer, novelist, 1880-1954. Java Head.
Marguerite Higgins, journalist, 1920-1966.
Robert Hillyer, poet, novelist, 1895-1962.
Alice Tisdale Hobart, novelist, 1882-1967. Oil for the Lamps of China.
Samuel Hoffenstein, poet. 1890-1947.
Charles Fenno Hoffman, poet, editor, 1806-1884.
Richard Hofstadter, historian, 1916-1970. The Age of.Reform.
Oliver Wendell Holmes, poet, novelist, 1809-1894. .
Roy W. Howard, newspaper publisher, editor, 1883-1964. Scripps-Howard Newspapers.
Ed Howe, journalist, author, 1853-1937.
Mark DeWolfe Howe, historian, 1906-1967.
Julia Ward Howe, poet, reformer, 1819-1910. The Battle Hymn of the Republic.
William Dean Howells, novelist, critic, 1837-1920.
Elbert Hubbard, author, editor, 1856-1915. A Message to Garcia.
Langston Hughes, poet, playwright, 1902-1967.
Rupert Hughes, novelist, playwright, 1872-1956.
Frazier (Spike) Hunt, journalist, war correspondent, 1885-1967. .
Chet Huntley, TV newscaster, 1911-1974.
Fannie Hurst, novelist, 1889-1968. Back Street, Lummox.

I

Washington Irving, essayist, author, 1783-1859. Rip Van Winkle.
Wallace Irwin, journalist, humorist, 1876-1959.
Will Irwin, journalist, author, 1873-1948.

J

Charles Jackson, novelist, 1887-1968. The Lost Weekend.
Henry James, novelist, critic, 1843-1916.
Robinson Jeffers, poet, dramatist, 1887-1962.
Sarah Orne Jewett, novelist, short-story writer, 1849-1909.
James Weldon Johnson, author, poet, 1871-1938.

K

H. V. Kaltenborn, editor, radio commentator, 1878-1965.
Clarence Budington Kelland, novelist, short-story writer, 1881-1964.
Jack Kerouac, author, 1922-1969. On the Road.
Francis Scott Key, poet, 1779-1843. The Star-Spangled Banner.
Frances Parkinson Keyes, author, editor, 1885-1970. Dinner at Antoine's.
Dorothy Kilgallen, journalist, radio-TV personality, 1913-1965.
Bernard Kilgore, journalist, 1908-1967. Wall Street Journal.
Joyce Kilmer, poet, 1886-1918. Trees.
Willard M. Kiplinger, journalist, 1891-1967. Changing Times.
Arthur Krock, journalist, 1887-1974. N. Y. Times.

Joseph Wood Krutch, author, naturalist, 1885-1970. The Measure of Man.

L

Oliver La Farge, novelist, 1901-1963. Laughing Boy.
William M. Laffan, publisher, 1848-1900. New York Sun, N. Y. Evening Sun.
Rose Wilder Lane, novelist, 1887-1968. Let the Hurricane Roar.
Sidney Lanier, poet, critic, 1842-1881.
Ring Lardner, short-story writer, journalist, 1885-1933.
David Lawrence, journalist, founder and editor of U. S. News & World Report, 1888-1973.
Emma Lazarus, poet, essayist, 1849-1887. The New Colossus.
Margaret Leech, author, historian, 1893-1974.
Charles Godfrey Leland, author, journalist, 1824-1903.
William Ellery Leonard, poet, 1876-1944.
Fulton Lewis, Jr., radio news commentator, 1903-1966.
Oscar Lewis, author, anthropologist, 1914-1970. La Vida.
Sinclair Lewis, novelist, playwright, 1885-1951. Babbitt, Arrowsmith, Dodsworth.
Ludwig Lewisohn, novelist, critic, 1882-1955.
Willy Ley, science writer, 1906-1969.
Vachel Lindsay, poet, 1879-1931.
Walter Lippmann, dean of American political journalism, 1889-1974.
Louis Lomax, author, 1922-1970. The Negro Revolt.
Jack London, novelist, journalist, 1876-1916. The Call of the Wild.
Henry Wadsworth Longfellow, poet, 1807-1882. The Wreck of the Hesperus, Evangeline, The Song of Hiawatha.
Benson John Lossing, historian, artist, 1813-1891. Pictorial Field Book of the Revolution.
Elijah P. Lovejoy, journalist, abolitionist, 1802-1837.
Amy Lowell, poet, critic, 1874-1925.
James Russell Lowell, poet, editor, 1819-1891.
Jim Lucas, journalist, 1914-1970. Scripps-Howard Newspapers.
Henry R. Luce, publisher, 1898-1967. Time, Life, Fortune magazines.

M

Edwin Markham, poet, 1852-1940. The Man with the Hoe.
John P. Marquand, novelist, 1893-1960. The Late George Apley.
Don Marquis, humorist, journalist, 1878-1937. The Old Soak.
Edgar Lee Masters, poet, biographer, 1869-1950. Spoon River Anthology.
James McClatchy, publisher, editor, 1824-1883. McClatchy Newspapers.
S. S. McClure, editor, publisher, 1857-1949.
Joseph Medill McCormick, journalist, politician, 1887-1925. Chicago Tribune.
Robert R. McCormick, editor, publisher, 1880-1955. Chicago Tribune.
Carson McCullers, novelist, 1917-1967. The Heart is a Lonely Hunter.
Ralph E. McGill, editor, publisher, Atlanta Constitution. 1898-1969.
John B. McMaster, historian, 1852-1932.
Joseph Medill, journalist, 1823-1899. Chicago Tribune.
Herman Melville, novelist, poet, 1819-1891. Moby Dick.
Henry L. Mencken, editor, author, philologist, 1880-1956. Baltimore Sun, American Mercury.
Thomas Merton, poet, religious writer, 1915-1968. Seven Storey Mountain.
Edna St. Vincent Millay, poet, 1892-1950.

Joaquin Miller poet, 1839-1913.
Max Miller, novelist, 1889-1967. I Cover the Waterfront.
Margaret Mitchell, novelist, 1900-1949. Gone With the Wind.
William Vaughn Moody, poet, dramatist, 1869-1910.
Clement C. Moore, poet, educator, 1779-1863. A Visit from Saint Nicholas.
Marianne Moore, poet, 1887-1972.
Christopher Morley, journalist, novelist, 1890-1957. Kitty Foyle.
John L. Motley, historian, diplomat, 1814-1877.
Willard Motley, novelist, 1912-1966. Knock on Any Door.
Edward R. Murrow, radio-TV commentator, 1908-1965.

N

Ogden Nash, poet, 1902-1971.
William Rockhill Nelson, journalist, 1841-1915. Kansas City Star.
Allan Nevins, historian, biographer, 1890-1971.
John G. Nicolay, biographer, 1832-1901. Abraham Lincoln: A History.
Charles B. Nordhoff, novelist, 1887-1947. Co-author Mutiny on the Bounty.
Frank Norris, novelist, journalist, 1870-1902. The Pit.
Kathleen Norris, novelist, 1880-1966.
Frank B. Noyes, newspaper executive, 1863-1948. Associated Press.

O

Edwin G. O'Connor, novelist, 1918-1968. Edge of Sadness, The Last Hurrah.
Adolph S. Ochs, newspaper publisher, 1858-1935, The New York Times.
John O'Hara, novelist, 1905-1970. Butterfield 8, Ten North Frederick.
Fremont Older, journalist, 1856-1935. San Francisco Call-Bulletin.
James Oppenheim, poet, novelist, 1882-1932.

P

Thomas (Tom) Paine, author, political theorist, 1737-1809, Common Sense.
Frederick Palmer, war correspondent, 1873-1958.
Dorothy Parker, poet, short-story writer, 1893-1967.
Francis Parkman, historian, 1823-1893.
James K. Pauling, poet, novelist, 1778-1860.
John Howard Payne, poet, dramatist, 1791-1852. Home, Sweet Home.
Alicia Patterson, journalist, 1906-1963. Newsday.
Eleanor Medill Patterson, journalist, 1884-1948. Washington Times-Herald.
Joseph Medill Patterson, publisher, 1879-1946. Founded N. Y. Daily News.
Josephine P. Peabody, poet, dramatist, 1874-1922.
Drew Pearson, newspaper columnist, 1897-1969.
Westbrook Pegler, newspaper columnist, 1894-1969.
David G. Phillips, journalist, novelist, 1867-1911.
Egar Allan Poe, poet, short-story writer, critic, 1809-1849.
Ernest Poole, novelist, journalist, 1880-1950.
Ezra Pound, poet, 1885-1972.
William H. Prescott, historian, 1796-1859.
Joseph Pulitzer, journalist, 1847-1911. St. Louis Post-Dispatch, N. Y. World.
Joseph Pulitzer, journalist, 1885-1955. St. Louis Post-Dispatch.
Ralph Pulitzer, journalist, 1879-1939. St. Louis Post-Dispatch, N. Y. World.
Ernie Pyle, journalist, war correspondent, 1900-1945.

R

James G. Randall, historian, 1881-1953.
Burton Rascoe, journalist, author, 1892-1957.
Marjorie Kinnan Rawlings, novelist, 1896-1953. The Yearling.
Thomas Buchanan Read, poet, painter, 1822-1872. Sheridan's Ride.
Lizette Woodworth Reese, poet, 1856-1935.
Ogden M. Reid, journalist, 1882-1947. N. Y. Herald Tribune.
Whitelaw Reid, journalist, diplomat, 1837-1912. N. Y. Tribune.
Erich Maria Remarque, novelist, 1898-1970. All Quiet on the Western Front.
Quentin Reynolds, journalist, author, 1902-1965.
James Ford Rhodes, historian, 1848-1927.
Alice Hegan Rice, novelist, 1870-1952. Mrs. Wiggs of the Cabbage Patch.
Cale Young Rice, poet, novelist, 1872-1943.
Grantland Rice, journalist, 1880-1954.
Conrad M. Richter, novelist, 1890-1968. The Town.
James Whitcomb Riley, poet, 1849-1916.
Mary Roberts Rinehart, mystery writer, 1876-1958. The Circular Staircase, The Bat.
Elizabeth Madox Roberts, poet, novelist, 1886-1941.
Kenneth Roberts, novelist, 1885-1957. Northwest Passage.
Roy A. Roberts, journalist, 1887-1967. Kansas City Star.
Edwin Arlington Robinson, poet, 1869-1935.
Theodore Roethke, poet, 1908-1963.
Robert Ruark, journalist, author, 1915-1965. Something of Value.
Damon Runyon, short-story writer, journalist, 1884-1946. Guys and Dolls.
Cornelius Ryan, novelist, 1920-1974. The Longest Day.

S

Carl Sandburg, poet, biographer, 1878-1967.
George Santayana, poet, essayist, philosopher, 1863-1952.
Lew Sarett, poet, 1888-1954.
Max L. Schuster, editor, publisher, 1897-1970. Simon & Schuster.
Edward W. Scripps, newspaper publisher, 1854-1926.
Robert P. Scripps, newspaper publisher, 1895-1938. Scripps-Howard Newspapers.
Alan Seeger, poet, 1888-1916. I Have a Rendezvous with Death.
Gilbert Seldes, author, critic, 1893-1970. The 7 Lively Arts, The Great Audience.
Ernest Thompson Seton, author, naturalist, 1860-1946. Wild Animals I Have Known.
Anne Sexton, poet, won Pulitzer Prize, 1928-1974.
Vincent Sheean, foreign correspondent, 1899-1975.
Frank Dempster Sherman, poet, educator, 1860-1916.
Lydia H. Sigourney, poet, 1791-1865.
Edward Rowland Sill, poet, educator, 1841-1887.
Upton Sinclair, novelist, 1878-1968. The Jungle, Dragon's Teeth.
Betty Smith, novelist, 1896-1972. A Tree Grows in Brooklyn.
Lillian Smith, novelist, 1897-1966. Strange Fruit.
Merriman Smith, newspaper correspondent, 1913-1970. UPI.
Samuel Francis Smith, poet, clergyman, 1808-1895. America.
Jared Sparks, historian, educator, 1789-1866.

Burt L. Standish (Gilbert Patten), author, 1866-1945. Frank Merriwell series.

Frank L. Stanton, poet, journalist, 1857-1927. Mighty Lak' a Rose.

Edmund C. Stedman, poet, critic, 1833-1908.

Lincoln Steffens, editor, author, 1866-1936. The Shame of the Cities.

Gertrude Stein, author, 1874-1946. Three Lives.

John Steinbeck, novelist, 1902-1968. Of Mice and Men, The Grapes of Wrath.

George Sterling, poet, 1869-1926.

Wallace Stevens, poet, 1879-1955.

Frank R. Stockton, novelist, short-story writer, 1834-1902. The Lady or the Tiger?

Melville E. Stone, journalist, 1848-1929. Associated Press.

Harriet Beecher Stowe, novelist, 1811-1896. Uncle Tom's Cabin.

Edward Stratemeyer, author, 1862-1930. Creator of such series as the Rover Boys, Bobbsey Twins, Tom Swift.

Gene Stratton-Porter, novelist, 1863-1924. A Girl of the Limberlost.

Anna Louise Strong, journalist, 1885-1970.

Mark Sullivan, journalist, author, 1874-1952.

Arthur Hays Sulzberger, publisher, 1891-1968. The New York Times.

Jacqueline Susann, novelist, 1921-1974. Valley of the Dolls.

Herbert Bayard Swope, journalist, 1882-1958. N. Y. World.

T

John B. Tabb, poet, 1845-1909.

Genevieve Taggard, poet, 1894-1948.

Ida M. Tarbell, editor, author, 1857-1944. The History of the Standard Oil Company.

Booth Tarkington, novelist, 1869-1946. Seventeen, Alice Adams.

Bayard Taylor, poet, novelist, 1825-1878. The Bedouin Love Song.

Edward Taylor, poet, c. 1642-1729.

Sara Teasdale, poet, 1884-1933.

Albert Payson Terhune, novelist, journalist, 1872-1942. Lad: A Dog.

Dorothy Thompson, journalist, author, 1894-1961.

Henry D. Thoreau, essayist, naturalist, 1817-1862. Walden.

James Thurber, humorist, artist, 1894-1961. The New Yorker. .

Eunice Tietjens, poet, novelist, 1884-1944.

Ridgely Torrence, poet, dramatist, 1875-1950.

Charles Hanson Towne, poet, editor, 1877-1949.

George A. Townsend, journalist, war correspondent, 1841-1914.

Frederick J. Turner, historian, educator, 1861-1932.

Mark Twain (Samuel Clemens), novelist, humorist, 1835-1910. The Adventures of Huckleberry Finn, Tom Sawyer.

V

Carl Van Doren, historian, critic, educator, 1885-1950.

Mark Van Doren, poet, author, critic, 1894-1972.

Henry Van Dyke, poet, educator, essayist, 1852-1933.

Hendrik Willem van Loon, historian, journalist, 1882-1944.

Carl Van Vechten, novelist, music critic, 1880-1964.

Oswald G. Villard, editor, author, 1872-1949. The Nation.

W

Lew Wallace, novelist, diplomat, 1827-1905. Ben Hur.

Artemus Ward (Charles F. Browne), humorist, 1834-1867.

Henry Watterson, editor, author, 1840-1921. Louisville Courier-Journal.

Nathanael West, novelist, 1903-1940.

Edith Wharton, novelist, 1862-1937. The Age of Innocence.

Steward Edward White, novelist, 1873-1946.

William Allen White, editor, author, 1868-1944. Emporia (Kan.) Gazette.

Walt Whitman, poet, 1819-1892. Leaves of Grass.

John Greenleaf Whittier, poet, journalist, 1809-1892.

Kate Douglas Wiggin, children's author, educator, 1856-1923. Rebecca of Sunnybrook Farm.

Ella Wheeler Wilcox, poet, 1850-1919.

Robert Wilder, novelist, 1901-1974. Written on the Wind.

Ben Ames Williams, novelist, 1889-1953.

William Carlos Williams, poet, physician, 1883-1963.

Nathaniel P. Willis, journalist, author, 1806-1867.

Edmund Wilson, author, literary and social critic, 1895-1972.

Lyle C. Wilson, journalist, 1899-1967. United Press International.

Walter Winchell, Broadway columnist, 1897-1972.

P.G. Wodehouse, novelist, playwright, 1881-1975.

Thomas Wolfe, novelist, 1900-1938. Look Homeward, Angel.

Frederick E. Woltman, journalist, 1907-1970. N. Y. World-Telegram & Sun.

Samuel Woodworth, poet, dramatist, 1784-1842.

Alexander Woollcott, journalist, critic, 1887-1943.

Harold Bell Wright novelist, 1872-1944. The Shepherd of the Hills.

Richard Wright, novelist, 1908-1960. Native Son.

Elinor Wylie, poet, novelist, 1885-1928.

Philip Wylie, author, 1902-1971. Generation of Vipers.

Z

John Peter Zenger, journalist, printer, 1697-1746. N. Y. Weekly Journal.

American Architects and Some of Their Achievements

Max Abramovitz, b. 1908. Avery Fisher Hall at Lincoln Center, N.Y.C.

Henry Bacon, (1866-1924) Lincoln Memorial.

Pietro Belluschi, b. 1899. Julliard School of Music, Lincoln Center, N.Y.C.

Marcel Breuer, b. Pecs, Hungary, 1902. Whitney Museum of American Art, N.Y.C. (with Hamilton Smith).

Charles Bulfinch, (1763-1844) State House, Boston; Capitol, Washington, (part).

Daniel H. Burnham, (1846-1912) Union Station, Washington; Flatiron, N.Y.C.

Ralph Adams Cram, (1863-1942) Cathedral of St. John the Divine, New York; U.S. Military Academy (part).

Alexander J. Davis, (1803-1892) Sub-treasury, N.Y.C.; capitols of Ind., N. C., Ill., Ohio.

R. Buckminster Fuller, b. 1895. U.S. Pavilion, Expo 67, Montreal (geodesic domes).

William F. Gibbs, (1886-1967) Designed liner United States.

Cass Gilbert, (1859-1934) Custom House, Woolworth Bldg., N.Y.C.; Capitol, St. Paul.

Bertrand Goldberg, b. 1913. Marina City Towers, Chicago.

Bertram G. Goodhue, (1869-1924) Capitol, Lincoln, Neb.; St. Thomas, St. Bartholomew, N.Y.C.

Walter Gropius, (1883-1969) Pan Am Building, N.Y.C. (with Pietro Belluschi).

Wallace K. Harrison, b. 1895. Metropolitan Opera House at Lincoln Center, N.Y.C.

Thomas Hastings, (1860-1929) Public Library, Frick Mansion, N.Y.C.

James Hoban, (1762-1831) The White House.

Raymond Hood, (1881-1934) Rockefeller Center, N.Y.C. (part); Daily News, N.Y.C.; Tribune, Chicago.

Richard M. Hunt, (1828-1896) Metropolitan Museum, N.Y.C. (part); The Breakers, Newport.

William Le Baron Jenney, (1832-1907) Home Insurance, Chicago (demolished).

Philip C. Johnson, b. 1906. N.Y. State Theater at Lincoln Center, N.Y.C.

Albert Kahn, (1869-1942) Athletic Club Bldg., General Motors Bldg., N.Y.C.

Louis Kahn, (1901-1974), Salk Laboratory, La Jolla, Cal.; Yale Art Gallery.

Christopher Grant LaFarge, (1862-1938) Chapel, West Point; Cathedral, Seattle.

Benjamin H. Latrobe, (1764-1820) U.S. Capitol (part).

William Lescaze, (1896-1969) Philadelphia Savings Fund Society; Borg-Warner Bldg., Chicago.

Theodore C. Link, (1850-1923) Union Station, St. Louis.

Charles F. McKim, (1847 1909) Public Library, Boston; Columbia Univ., N.Y.C. (part).

Charles M. McKim, b. 1920. KUHT-TV Transmitter Building, Houston; Lutheran Church of the Redeemer, Houston.

Milton B. Medary, (1874-1929) Bok Carillon Tower, Mountain Lake, Fla.

Ludwig Mies van der Rohe, (1886-1969). Seagram Building, N.Y.C. (with Philip C. Johnson); National Gallery, Berlin.

Robert Mills, (1781-1855) Washington Monument.

Richard J. Neutra, (1892-1970). Mathematics Park, Princeton; Orange Co. Courthouse, Santa Ana, Cal.

Frederick L. Olmsted, (1822-1903) Central Park, N.Y.C.; Fairmount Park, Philadelphia.

Ieoh Ming Pei, b. Canton, China, 1917. Kips Bay Plaza, N.Y.C.; Earth Sciences Building (M.I.T.) Cambridge, Mass.; National Center for Atmospheric Research, Boulder, Col.

John Russell Pope, (1874-1937) National Gallery.

John Portman, b. 1924. Peachtree Center, Atlanta.

James Renwick, Jr., (1818-1895) Grace Church, St. Patrick's Cathedral, N.Y.C.; Smithsonian, Corcoran Galleries, Wash., D.C.

Henry H. Richardson, (1838-1886) Trinity, Boston.

Kevin Roche, b. 1922. Oakland Cal. Museum; Fine Arts Center, U. of Mass.

James Gamble Rogers, (1867-1947) Columbia-Presbyterian Medical Center, N.Y.C.; Northwestern Univ., Chicago.

John Weldon Root, b. 1887. Palmolive Building, Chicago; Hotel Statler, Washington; Hotel Tamanaco, Caracas.

Paul Rudolph, b. 1918. Jewitt Art Center, Wellesley College; Art & Architecture Bldg., Yale.

Eero Saarinen, (1910-1961) Gateway to the West arch, St. Louis; Trans World Flight Center, N.Y.C.
Louis Skidmore, (1897-1962) AEC town site, Oak Ridge, Tenn.; Terrace Plaza Hotel, Cincinnati.
Clarence S. Stein, b. 1882. Temple Emanu-El, N.Y.C.
Edward Durell Stone, b. 1902. U.S. Embassy, New Delhi, India; (H. Hartford) Gallery of Modern Art, N.Y.C.
Louis H. Sullivan, (1856-1924) Auditorium, Chicago.
Richard Upjohn, (1802-1878) Trinity Church, N.Y.C.
Ralph T. Walker, (1889-1973), N.Y. Telephone Hdqrs.,

N.Y.C.; IBM Research Lab., Poughkeepsie, N.Y.
Roland A. Wank, (1898-1970) Cincinnati Union Terminal; head architect TVA, 1933-44.
Stanford White, (1853-1906) Washington Arch; first Madison Square Garden, N.Y.C.
Frank Lloyd Wright, (1869-1959) Imperial Hotel, Tokyo; Guggenheim Museum, N.Y.C.
William Wurster, b. 1895. Ghirardelli Sq., San Francisco; Cowell College, U. Cal., Berkeley.
Minoru Yamasaki, b. 1912, World Trade Center, N.Y.C.

The Hall of Fame for Great Americans

The Hall of Fame for Great Americans was a gift to the American people by Mrs. Helen Gould Shepard. New York University acts as Trustee for the Shrine for the nation. Busts and tablets are donated. The Americans honored since 1900 are:

1900	1905	1920	1950
John Adams	John Quincy Adams	Samuel Langhorne Clemens	Susan B. Anthony
John James Audubon	James Russell Lowell	(Mark Twain)	Alexander Graham Bell
Henry Ward Beecher	Mary Lyon	James Buchanan Eads	Josiah Willard Gibbs
William Ellery Channing	James Madison	Patrick Henry	William Crawford Gorgas
Henry Clay	Maria Mitchell	William Thomas Green	Theodore Roosevelt
Peter Cooper	William Tecumseh Sherman	Morton	Woodrow Wilson
Jonathan Edwards	John Greenleaf Whittier	Alice Freeman Palmer	
Ralph Waldo Emerson	Emma Willard	Augustus Saint-Gaudens	**1955**
David Glasgow Farragut	**1910**	Roger Williams	Thomas Jonathan Jackson
Benjamin Franklin	George Bancroft	**1925**	George Westinghouse
Robert Fulton	Phillips Brooks	Edwin Booth	Wilbur Wright
Ulysses Simpson Grant	William Cullen Bryant	John Paul Jones	**1960**
Asa Gray	James Fenimore Cooper	**1930**	Thomas A. Edison
Nathaniel Hawthorne	Oliver Wendell Holmes	Matthew Fontaine Maury	Edward A. MacDowell
Washington Irving	Andrew Jackson	James Monroe	Henry David Thoreau
Thomas Jefferson	John Lothrop Motley	James Abbott McNeil	
James Kent	Edgar Allan Poe	Whistler	**1965**
Robert Edward Lee	Harriet Beecher Stowe	Walt Whitman	Jane Addams
Abraham Lincoln	Frances Elizabeth Willard	**1935**	Oliver Wendell Holmes, Jr.
Henry Wadsworth Longfellow	**1915**	Grover Cleveland	Sylvanus Thayer
Horace Mann	Louis Agassiz	Simon Newcomb	Orville Wright
John Marshall	Daniel Boone	William Penn	
Samuel Finley Breese Morse	Rufus Choate	**1940**	**1970**
George Peabody	Charlotte Saunders Cushman	Stephen Collins Foster	Albert Abraham Michelson
Joseph Story	Alexander Hamilton	**1945**	Lillian D. Wald
Gilbert Charles Stuart	Joseph Henry	Sidney Lanier	**1973**
George Washington	Mark Hopkins	Thomas Paine	Louis Dembitz Brandeis
Daniel Webster	Elias Howe	Walter Reed	George Washington Carver
Eli Whitney	Francis Parkman	Booker T. Washington	Franklin Delano Roosevelt
			John Philip Sousa

Noted Black Americans — Past and Present

(Names of black athletes and entertainers are not included here as they are well known and are listed elsewhere in The World Almanac.)

Explorers and Settlers

Pedro Alonzo Nino, navigator of the Nina, one of Christopher Columbus' three ships on his first voyage of discovery to the New World, 1492.
Estevanico (also called Esteban) led the first Spanish explorations into the Arizona and New Mexico area, 1539.
Jean Baptiste Point du Sable, fur trader and first settler of Chicago, 1779.
James P. Beckwourth (1798-c.1867) western fur-trader, scout, after whom Beckwourth Pass in northern California is named.
Matthew A. Henson (1866-1955), with Robert E. Peary and 4 Eskimos, discovered the North Pole, 1909; Henson planted the U.S. flag at the Pole.

Soldiers, Patriots

Crispus Attucks (c. 1723-1770), leader of a group fired on by British soldiers and one of the 5 slain in the "Boston Massacre," Mar. 5, 1770.
Peter Salem, one of the defenders at the Battle of Bunker Hill, June 17, 1775, shot and killed Maj. John Pitcairn, one of the British commanders.
(About 5,000 blacks served in the Continental Army, mostly in integrated units, some in all-black combat outfits.)
Harriet Tubman, after escaping from slavery made repeated trips to the South and led more than 300 slaves to freedom as an Underground Railroad conductor; served as nurse and spy for Union Army in the Civil War.

(Some 200,000 blacks served in the Union Army during the Civil War; 38,000 gave their lives; 22 won the Medal of Honor, the nation's highest award.)
Isaiah Dorman (19th Century), U.S. Army interpreter, killed with Custer at Battle of the Little Big Horn (1876).
Henry O. Flipper, first black to graduate from West Point (1877).
Pvt. Henry Johnson of Albany, N.Y., the first American decorated by France in World War I with the Croix de Guerre.
(Of 367,000 blacks in the Armed Forces in World War I, 100,000 served in France.)
Dorie Miller of Waco, Tex., a Navy mess attendant on the battleship Arizona during the Pearl Harbor attack, took over an anti-aircraft gun from a dying white sailor and shot down 4 Japanese bombers, Dec. 7, 1941; awarded the Navy Cross by President Franklin D. Roosevelt.
(More than 1,000,000 blacks served in the U.S. Armed Forces in World War II; all-black fighter and bomber AAF units and infantry divisions gave distinguished service. In 1954 the policy of all-black units was finally abolished.)
Brig. Gen. Benjamin O. Davis Sr., born 1877, first black general (1940) in U.S. Army, rose through ranks to inspector general, retired 1948.
Lt. Gen. Benjamin O. Davis Jr., b. 1912, West Point (1936), first Negro Air Force general (1954), had distinguished service as pilot and commander in World War II, retired 1970.

Admiral Samuel L. Gravely, Jr., first black admiral (1971), served in World War II, Korea, and Vietnam.

Scientists, Inventors

Benjamin Banneker (1731-c. 1806), author of annual almanacs (1791-1802), served on commission which surveyed and helped lay out the future city of Washington, D. C.

Henry Blair (19th century), obtained patent (believed the first issued to a black) for a corn-planter (1834) and for a cotton-planter (1836).

Norbert Rillieux (1806-1894), invented a vacuum pan evaporator which revolutionized the sugar-refining industry (1846).

Lewis H. Latimer (1848-1928), associate of Thomas Edison, wrote textbook on the Edison Co. lighting system in New York City; supervised installation of first electric street lighting in New York.

Jan Matzeliger (1852-1889), invented lasting machine which cut shoe industry costs in half and brought higher wages to shoe workers.

Dr. Daniel Hale Williams (1856-1931), performed one of first two open-heart operations (1893); founded Provident, Chicago's first Negro hospital; first black elected a fellow of the American College of Surgeons.

Granville T. Woods (1856-1910), invented the third-rail system now used in subways and a complex railway telegraph device that helped reduce train accidents.

George Washington Carver (c. 1864-1943), agricultural scientist, philanthropist; brought about an agricultural revolution in the South, finding ways to enrich the soil, adding to its one-crop cotton economy not only emphasis on peanuts, sweet potatoes, and soybeans, but discovering some 300 industrial uses for byproducts he synthesized from them.

Dr. William A. Hinton (1883-1959), developed the Hinton and Davies-Hinton tests for detection of syphilis; first black professor at Harvard Medical School (1949).

Dr. Charles Richard Drew (1904-1950), pioneer in development of blood banks; director of American Red Cross blood donor project in World War II.

Writers, Educators

Jupiter Hammon (c.1720-1800), a Long Island, N. Y. poet, the first black American to have his works published.

Phillis Wheatley (c.1753-1784), poet, second American woman and first black woman to have her works published; b. in Senegal, enslaved, taken to Boston, freed 1773.

John B. Russwurm (1799-1851) with **Samuel E. Cornish** (1793-1858), founded the nation's first black newspaper, Freedom's Journal (1827) in N. Y. City.

William Wells Brown (1815-1884), b. a slave, first American black to publish a novel (Clotel), as well as a drama, a travel book, 3 histories.

Frederick Douglass (1717-1895), author, editor, orator, diplomat; a runaway slave (b. Frederick Bailey), edited the abolitionist weekly, The North Star, in Rochester, N. Y., before the Civil War, became U. S. Minister and Consul General to Haiti.

Edward Bouchet (1852-1918), first black to earn a Ph.D. at a U. S. university (Yale, 1876); first to be elected to Phi Beta Kappa.

Booker T. Washington (1856-1915), founder and first president of Tuskegee Institute (1871); author of a dozen books including Up From Slavery; social reformer.

Charles Waddell Chestnutt (1858-1932), novelist; best-known for his short stories including The Conjure Woman.

William Edward Burghardt Du Bois (1868-1963), historian, sociologist, a founder of the NAACP (1909) and founding editor of its magazine The Crisis; author of The Souls of Black Folk (1903) and other books.

James Weldon Johnson (1871-1938), poet, song-lyricist, novelist; first black admitted to Florida bar; a U. S. consul in Venezuela and Nicaragua.

Paul Laurence Dunbar (1872-1906), poet, novelist; won fame with Lyrics of Lowly Life (1896).

Dr. Carter G. Woodson (1875-1950), historian; founded Journal of Negro History and Assn. for Study of Negro Life and History (1915).

Langston Hughes (1902-1967), a major American poet; also author of stories and song lyrics.

Countee Cullen (1903-1946), poet, winner of numerous literary prizes.

Richard Wright (1908-1960), best-selling novelist; Native Son (1940), Black Boy (1945), etc.

Willard Motley (1912-1965), novelist; wrote Knock on Any Door (1947).

Ralph Ellison, b. 1914, novelist, winner of 1952 National Book Award for Invisible Man.

Frank Yerby, b. 1916, most successful of American black novelists; some 19 novels with over 20,000,000 copies sold, including The Foxes of Harrow, Vixen.

Gwendolyn Brooks, b. 1917, poet, novelist; first black to win a Pulitzer Prize (1950), for Annie Allen.

Wilson C. Riles, b. 1917, elected California State Superintendent of Public Instruction (1970).

James Baldwin, b. 1924, best-seller author, playwright; Another Country (1962), The Fire Next Time (1963).

Charles Gordone, b. 1925, won 1970 Pulitzer Prize for Drama with play, No Place to Be Somebody.

Lorraine Hansberry (1930-1965), playwright; won N. Y. Drama Critics Circle Award with Raisin in the Sun (1959).

Imamu Amiri Baraka, b. LeRoi Jones, 1934; poet, playwright, community leader in Newark, N. J.

Public Officials

Hiram R. Revels (1822-1901), first black U. S. Senator, elected in Mississippi, served 1870-1871.

Joseph H. Rainey (1832-1887), first black elected to House of Representatives (1869-79) (from South Carolina).

Dr. Mary McCleod Bethune (1875-1955), adviser to Presidents Franklin D. Roosevelt and Harry Truman; division administrator in National Youth Administration (1935); founder, president of Bethune-Cookman College.

William L. Dawson (1886-1970), congressman from Illinois, first black chairman of a major House of Representatives committee.

William H. Hastie, b. 1904, first black Federal Judge (appointed 1937); Governor of Virgin Islands (1946-1949); Judge, U. S. Circuit Court of Appeals (1949).

Dr. Ralph Bunche (1904-1971), first black to win the Nobel Peace Prize (1950); became undersecretary of the United Nations (1950).

Dr. Robert C. Weaver, b. 1907, first black member of the U. S. Cabinet; secretary of the Department of Housing & Urban Development (1966).

Adam Clayton Powell (1908-1972), early civil rights leader (1930's), congressman (1945-1969); as head of House Committee on Education and Labor (1960-1967) was responsible for 48 major pieces of social legislation.

Thurgood Marshall, b. 1908, first black U. S. solicitor general (1965); first black to be made a justice of the U. S. Supreme Court (1967); as a lawyer led the legal battery which won the historic decision from the Supreme Court declaring segregation of public schools unconstitutional (1954).

Edward W. Brooke, b. 1919; attorney general of Massachusetts (1962); first black elected to U.S. Senate since 19th Century Reconstruction (1967).

Mrs. Shirley Chisholm, b. 1924, first black woman elected to House of Representatives (Brooklyn, N. Y. 1968).

Louis Stokes (Dem., Oh.), chairman of Black Caucus of the 13 black members of the House.

Carl T. Rowan, b. 1925, prize-winning journalist; public official; director of the U. S. Information Agency (1964), making him the first black to sit on the National Security Council; U. S. ambassador to Finland (1963).

Benjamin Hooks, first black appointed to the Federal Communications Commission (1972).

Andrew F. Brimmer, b. 1926, first black member (1966) of the Federal Reserve Board, the U. S. central banking facility.

Robert C. Henry, elected mayor of Springfield, Oh. (1965), first black mayor of a moderate-sized city in the 20th century.

Thomas Bradley, b. 1917, elected mayor of Los Angeles (1973).

Coleman Young, elected mayor of Detroit (1973).

Maynard Jackson, elected mayor Atlanta (1973).

(As of May, 1975, there were 66 black mayors, 1,237 city councilmen, 305 county officers, 53 state senators, 223 state representatives, one U.S. senator, and 17 U.S. representatives. There are now 3,503 blacks holding elected office in the United States, an increase of 17% over the previous year, according to a survey by the Joint Center for Political Studies, Washington, D.C.

Labor, Civil Rights Leaders

Sojourner Truth (1797-1883), born Isabella Baumfree; preacher, abolitionist; raised funds for Union in Civil War; worked for black educational opportunities.

Nat Turner (1800-1831), leader of the most significant of over 200 slave revolts in U. S. history, in Southhampton, Va.; he and 16 others were hanged.

Marcus Garvey (1887-1940), founded Universal Negro Improvement Assn. (1911), sought to promote a Back to Africa movement.

Willard Townsend (1895-1957), organized (1935) the United Transport Service Employees (redcaps, etc.); vice president of AFL-CIO.

Bishop Stephen Spottswood (1897-1974), board chairman of NAACP since 1966.

Elijah Muhammad (1897-1975), founded the Nation of Islam or Black Muslims (1931),

A. Philip Randolph, b. 1889, organized the Brotherhood of Sleeping Car Porters (1925); organizer of 1941 and 1963 March on Washington movements; vice president of AFL-CIO.

Walter White (1893-1955), executive secretary, NAACP, (1931-1955).

Roy Wilkins, b. 1901, became executive secretary, NAACP in 1955.

Bayard Rustin, b. 1910, an organizer of the 1963 March on Washington; executive director of the A. Philip Randolph Institute.

The Rev. Dr. Ralph David Abernathy, b. 1916, an organizer (1957) of the Southern Christian Leadership Conference; its president (1968).

James Farmer, b. 1920, a founder of the Congress of Racial Equality (1942); asst. secretary of H.E.W. (1969).

Whitney M. Young Jr. (1921-1971), executive director of the National Urban League (1961); author, lecturer, newspaper columnist.

Floyd McKissick, b. 1922, national director of CORE (1966).

Malcolm X (1925-1965), founded the Organization of Afro-American Unity (1963), a leading spokesman for black pride.

The Rev. Dr. Martin Luther King Jr. (1929-1968), led 382-day, Montgomery, Ala., boycott which brought 1956 U. S. Supreme Court decision holding segregation on buses unconstitutional; founder and president of the Southern Christian Leadership Conference (1957); leader of rights marches; won Nobel Peace Prize (1964).

Dr. George A. Wiley (1934-1973), executive director of National Welfare Rights Organization (founded 1966).

Roy Innis, b. 1934, national director of CORE (1963).

Eldridge Cleaver, b. 1935, former Black Panther party leader, author of Soul on Ice.

Bobby G. Seale, national chairman, Black Panther party.

The Rev. Jesse Jackson, national director, Operation Bread Basket, and major community leader in Chicago.

John Lewis, former chairman of Student Nonviolent Coordinating Committee, leader of Voter Education Project in the South.

Widely Known Americans of the Present

Statesmen, Authors, Military Men and Other Prominent Persons Not Listed in Other Categories.

Name Birthplace	Birthdate
Abernathy, Ralph (Linden, Ala.)	3/11/26
Abzug, Bella (New York, N.Y.)	7/24/20
Agnew, Spiro (Baltimore, Md.)	11/9/18
Albee, Edward (Washington, D.C.)	3/12/28
Albert, Carl (McAlester, Okla.)	5/10/08
Aldrin, Edwin E. (Buzz) (Glen Ridge, N.J.)	1/20/30
Ali, Muhammad (Louisville, Ky.)	1/18/42
Alioto, Joseph (San Francisco, Cal.)	2/12/16
Alsop, Joseph W., Jr. (Avon, Conn.)	10/11/10
Alston, Walter (Butler Co., Oh.)	12/1/11
Anderson, Jack (Long Beach, Cal.)	10/19/22
Arcaro, Eddie (Cincinnati, Oh.)	2/19/16
Armstrong, Neil (Wapakoneta, Oh.)	8/5/30
Ashe, Arthur (Richmond, Va.)	7/10/43
Askew, Reubin (Muskogee, Okla.)	9/11/28
Bailey, F. Lee (Waltham, Mass.)	1933
Baker, Howard (Huntsville, Tenn.)	11/15/25
Baker, Russell (Loudoun Co., Va.)	8/14/25
Baldwin, Faith (New Rochelle, N.Y.)	10/1/93
Baldwin, James (New York, N.Y.)	8/2/24
Ball, George (Des Moines, Iowa)	12/21/09
Barth, John (Cambridge, Md.)	5/27/30
Bayh, Birch (Terre Haute, Ind.)	1/22/28
Beame, Abraham (London, Eng.)	3/20/06
Belli, Melvin (Sonora, Cal.)	7/29/07
Bellow, Saul (Quebec, Canada)	7/10/15
Bentsen, Lloyd (Mission, Texas)	2/11/21
Bishop, Jim (Jersey City, N.J.)	11/21/07
Blackmun, Harry (Nashville, Ill.)	11/12/08
Bok, Derek (Ardmore, Pa.)	3/22/30
Bond, Julian (Nashville, Tenn.)	1/14/40
Borman, Frank (Gary, Ind.)	3/14/28
Bowles, Chester (Springfield, Mass.)	4/5/01
Bradley, Omar N. (Clark, Mo.)	2/12/93
Bradley, Thomas (Calvert, Tex.)	12/29/17
Braun, Wernher von (Wirsitz, Germany)	3/23/12
Brennan, William J. (Newark, N.J.)	4/25/06
Breslin, Jimmy (Jamaica, L.I., N.Y.)	10/17/30
Brewster, Kingman (Longmeadow, Mass.)	6/17/19
Brinkley, David (Wilmington, N.C.)	7/10/20
Brooke, Edward (Washington, D.C.)	10/26/19
Buchanan, Patrick (Washington, D.C.)	11/2/38
Buchwald, Art (Mt. Vernon, N.Y.)	10/20/25
Buckley, James (New York, N.Y.)	3/9/23
Buckley, William F. (New York, N.Y.)	11/24/25
Burns, Arthur F. (Stanislau, Aust.)	4/27/04
Bundy, McGeorge (Boston, Mass.)	3/30/19
Burger, Warren (St. Paul, Minn.)	9/17/07
Bush, George (Milton, Mass.)	6/12/24
Butz, Earl (Albion, Ind.)	7/3/09
Byrd, Robert (N. Wilkesboro, N.C.)	1/15/18
Caldwell, Erskine (Coweta Co., Ga.)	12/17/03
Capote, Truman (New Orleans, La.)	9/30/24
Carey, Hugh (Brooklyn, N.Y.)	4/11/19
Case, Clifford (Franklin Park, N.J.)	4/16/04
Celler, Emmanuel (Brooklyn, N.Y.)	5/6/88
Chamberlain, Wilt (Philadelphia, Pa.)	8/21/36

Name Birthplace	Birthdate
Chancellor, John (Chicago, Ill.)	7/14/27
Chavez, Cesar (Yuma, Ariz.)	3/31/27
Chisholm, Shirley (Brooklyn, N.Y.)	11/30/24
Church, Frank (Boise, Ida.)	7/25/24
Clark, Ramsey (Dallas, Tex.)	12/18/27
Clay, Lucius D. (Marietta, Ga.)	4/23/97
Colby, William (St. Paul, Minn.)	1/4/20
Conant, James B. (Dorchester, Mass.)	3/26/93
Connally, John B. (Floresville, Tex.)	2/28/17
Considine, Bob (Washington, D.C.)	11/4/06
Cooke, Terence (New York, N.Y.)	3/1/21
Cooper, John Sherman (Somerset, Ky.)	8/23/01
Cousins, Norman (Union Hill, N.J.)	6/24/12
Cox, Archibald (Plainfield, N.J.)	5/17/12
Cranston, Alan (Palo Alto, Cal.)	6/19/14
Cronkite, Walter (St. Joseph, Mo.)	11/4/16
Daley, Richard (Chicago, Ill.)	5/15/02
Davis, Angela (Birmingham, Ala.)	1/26/44
Dempsey, Jack (Manassa, Col.)	6/24/95
Dickey, James (Atlanta, Ga.)	2/2/23
DiMaggio, Joe (Martinez, Cal.)	11/25/14
Dole, Robert (Russell, Kan.)	7/22/23
Doolittle, James H. (Alameda, Cal.)	12/14/96
Douglas, William O. (Maine, Minn.)	10/16/98
Drury, Allan (Houston, Tex.)	9/2/18
Dubinsky, David (Brest-Litovsk, Poland)	2/22/92
Durocher, Leo (West Springfield, Mass.)	7/27/06
Eagleton, Thomas (St. Louis, Mo.)	9/4/29
Ehrlichman, John (Tacoma, Wash.)	3/20/25
Eisenhower, Mamie (Boone, Ia.)	11/14/96
Eisenhower, Milton S. (Abilene, Kan.)	9/15/99
Ervin, Sam (Morganton, N.C.)	9/27/96
Farley, James A. (Grassy Point, N.Y.)	5/30/88
Farmer, James (Marshall, Tex.)	1/12/20
Finch, Robert (Tempe, Ariz.)	10/9/25
Fischer, Bobby (Chicago, Ill.)	3/9/43
Fong, Hiram (Honolulu, Ha.)	10/1/07
Ford, Gerald R. (Omaha, Neb.)	7/14/13
Ford, Elizabeth(Mrs. Gerald) (Chicago, Ill.)	4/8/18
Friedman, Milton (Brooklyn, N.Y.)	7/31/12
Fulbright, J. William (Sumner, Mo.)	4/9/05
Galbraith, John Kenneth (Ontario, Can.)	10/15/08
Gardner, John (Los Angeles, Cal.)	10/8/12
Gavin, James (New York, N.Y.)	3/22/07
Getty, J. Paul (Minneapolis, Minn.)	12/15/92
Glenn, John (Cambridge, Oh.)	7/18/21
Goldberg, Arthur J. (Chicago, Ill.)	8/8/08
Goldwater, Barry M. (Phoenix, Ariz.)	1/1/09
Graham, Billy (Charlotte, N.C.)	11/7/18
Grange, Red (Forksville, Pa.)	6/13/04
Grasso, Ella (Windsor Locks, Conn.)	5/10/19
Gravel, Mike (Springfield, Mass.)	5/13/30
Griffin, Robert P. (Traverse City, Mich.)	11/6/23
Haig, Alexander (Philadelphia, Pa.)	12/2/24

Name	Birthplace	Birthdate
Harriman, W. Averell (New York, N.Y.)		11/15/91
Hart, Phillip A. (Bryn Mawr, Pa.)		12/10/12
Hatfield, Mark O. (Dallas, Ore.)		7/12/22
Hayakawa, S. I. (Vancouver, B.C.)		7/18/06
Heller, Walter (Buffalo, N.Y.)		8/27/15
Helms, Richard (St. Davids, Pa.)		3/30/13
Hogan, Ben (Dublin, Tex.)		8/13/12
Hughes, Harold (Ida Grove, Ia.)		2/10/22
Hughes, Howard (Houston, Tex.)		12/24/05
Humphrey, Hubert (Wallace, S.D.)		5/27/11
Inouye, Daniel (Honolulu, Ha.)		9/7/24
Jackson, Henry (Everett, Wash.)		5/31/12
Jackson, Jesse (Greenville, N.C.)		10/8/41
Javits, Jacob K. (New York, N.Y.)		5/18/04
Johnson, Luci Baines (Mrs. Patrick Nugent)		7/2/47
Johnson, Lynda Bird (Mrs. Charles Robb)		3/19/44
Johnson, Mrs. Lyndon B. (Karnack, Tex.)		12/22/12
Jones, James (Robinson, Ill.)		11/6/21
Kelley, Clarence M. (Kansas City, Mo.)		10/24/11
Kennedy, Edward M. (Brookline, Mass.)		2/22/32
Kennedy, Rose (Mrs. Joseph P.) (Boston)		1890
Kerr, Walter (Evanston, Ill.)		7/8/13
Kheel, Theodore (New York, N.Y.)		5/9/14
Kissinger, Henry (Fuerth, Germany)		5/27/23
Klein, Herbert (Los Angeles, Cal.)		4/1/28
Kleindienst, Richard (Winslow, Ariz.)		8/5/23
Koufax, Sandy (Brooklyn, N.Y.)		12/30/35
Kuhn, Bowie (Tacoma Park,, Mo.)		10/28/26
Laird, Melvin (Omaha, Neb.)		9/1/22
Landon, Alfred (West Middlesex, Pa.)		9/9/87
Lemnitzer, Lyman L. (Honesdale, Pa.)		8/29/99
Levi, Edward (Chicago, Ill.)		6/26/11
Lindbergh, Ann Morrow (Englewood, N.J.)		1906
Lindsay, John V. (New York, N.Y.)		11/24/21
Lodge, Henry Cabot (Nahant, Mass.)		7/5/02
Long, Russell B. (Shreveport, La.)		11/3/18
Louis, Joe (Lafayette, Ala.)		5/13/14
Lowell, Robert (Boston, Mass.)		3/1/17
Lowenstein, Allard (Newark, N.J.)		1/16/29
Luce, Clare Boothe (New York, N.Y.)		4/10/03
MacGregor, Clark (Minneapolis, Minn.)		7/12/22
MacLeish, Archibald (Glencoe, Ill.)		5/7/92
Maddox, Lester (Atlanta, Ga.)		9/30/15
Mailer, Norman (Long Branch, N.J.)		1/31/23
Mansfield, Mike (New York, N.Y.)		3/16/03
Mantle, Mickey (Spavinaw, Okla.)		10/20/31
Marshall, Thurgood (Baltimore, Md.)		7/2/08
Mays, Willie (Fairfield, Ala.)		5/6/31
McCarthy, Eugene (Watkins, Minn.)		3/29/16
McCormack, John W. (Boston, Mass.)		12/21/91
McGinley, Phyllis (Ontario, Ore.)		3/21/05
McClellan, John J. (Sheridan, Ark.)		2/25/96
McCloskey, Paul (San Bernardino, Cal.)		9/29/27
McGovern, George (Avon, S.D.)		7/19/22
McNamara, Robert S. (San Francisco, Cal.)		6/9/16
Mead, Margaret (Philadelphia, Pa.)		12/16/01
Meany, George (New York, N.Y.)		8/16/94
Menotti, Gian-Carlo (Cadegliano, Italy)		7/7/11
Michener, James A. (New York, N.Y.)		2/3/07
Miller, Arthur (New York, N.Y.)		10/17/15
Millett, Kate (St. Paul, Minn.)		9/14/34
Milliken, William (Traverse City, Mich.)		3/26/22
Mills, Wilbur (Kensett, Ark.)		5/24/09
Mitchell, John (Detroit, Mich.)		9/15/13
Mondale, Walter (Ceylon, Minn.)		1/5/28
Morton, Rogers (Louisville, Ky.)		9/19/14
Morton, Thruston (Louisville, Ky.)		8/19/07
Moses, Robert (New Haven, Conn.)		12/18/88
Moynihan, Daniel P. (Tulsa, Okla.)		3/16/27
Musial, Stan (Donora, Pa.)		11/21/20
Muskie, Edmund (Rumford, Me.)		3/28/14
Nader, Ralph (Winsted, Conn.)		2/27/34
Nesson, Ron (Washington, D.C.)		5/25/34
Nicklaus, Jack (Columbus, Oh.)		1/21/40
Nixon, Julie (Mrs. David Eisenhower) (Wash., D.C.)		7/5/48
Nixon, Mrs. Richard (Ely, Nevada)		3/16/12
Nixon, Richard (Yorba Linda, Cal.)		1/9/13
Nixon, Tricia (Mrs. Edward Cox) (Cal.)		2/21/46
Nizer, Louis (London, England)		2/6/02
Oates, Joyce Carol (Lockport, N.Y.)		6/16/38
O'Brien, Lawrence F. (Springfield, Mass.)		7/7/17

Name	Birthplace	Birthdate
Onassis, Jacqueline (Southampton, N.Y.)		7/28/29
Paley, William S. (Chicago, Ill.)		9/28/01
Palmer, Arnold (Youngstown, Pa.)		9/10/29
Pauling, Linus (Portland, Ore.)		2/28/01
Patterson, Floyd (Waco, N.C.)		1/4/35
Peale, Norman Vincent (Bowersville, Oh.)		5/31/98
Percy, Charles H. (Pensacola, Fla.)		9/27/19
Perelman, S. J. (Brooklyn, N.Y.)		2/1/04
Porter, Katherine Ann (Indian Creek, Tex.)		5/15/94
Powell, Lewis F. (Suffolk, Va.)		9/19/07
Proxmire, William (Lake Forest, Ill.)		1/11/15
Rand, Ayn, (St. Petersburg, Russia)		1905
Randolph, A. Philip (Crescent City, Fla.)		4/15/89
Reagan, Ronald (Tampico, Ill.)		2/6/11
Reasoner, Harry (Dakota City, Ia.)		4/17/23
Rehnquist, William (Milwaukee, Wis.)		10/1/24
Reston, James (Clydebank, Scotland)		11/3/09
Rhodes, John (Council Grove, Kan.)		9/18/16
Ribicoff, Abe (New Britain, Conn.)		4/9/10
Richardson, Elliot L. (Boston, Mass.)		7/20/21
Rickover, Hyman (Makowa, Poland)		1/27/00
Robertson, Oscar (Charlotte, Tenn.)		11/24/38
Rockefeller, David (New York, N.Y.)		6/12/15
Rockefeller, John D. 3rd (New York, N.Y.)		3/21/06
Rockefeller, Laurance S. (New York, N.Y.)		5/26/10
Rockefeller, Nelson A. (Bar Harbor, Me.)		7/8/08
Rockwell, Norman (New York, N.Y.)		2/3/94
Rodino, Peter (Newark, N.J.)		6/7/09
Rogers, William P. (Norfolk, N.Y.)		6/23/13
Romney, George W. (Chihuahua, Mexico)		7/8/07
Roosevelt, Elliot (New York, N.Y.)		9/23/10
Roosevelt, Franklin D., Jr. (Canada)		8/17/14
Roth, Philip (Newark, N.J.)		3/19/33
Rozelle, Pete (South Gate, Cal.)		3/1/26
Ruckelshaus, William (Indianapolis, Ind.)		7/24/32
Rusk, Dean (Cherokee Co., Ga.)		2/9/09
Ryun, Jim (Wichita, Kan.)		4/29/47
Safire, William (New York, N.Y.)		12/17/29
Salinger, J. D. (New York, N.Y.)		1/1/19
Salinger, Pierre (San Francisco, Cal.)		6/14/25
Salk, Jonas (New York, N.Y.)		10/28/14
Samuelson, Paul A. (Gary, Ind.)		5/15/15
Scali, John (Canton, Oh.)		4/27/18
Schlesinger, Arthur Jr. (Columbus, Oh.)		10/15/17
Schlesinger, James (New York, N.Y.)		2/15/29
Scott, Hugh (Fredericksburg, Va.)		11/11/00
Scranton, William W. (Madison, Conn.)		7/19/17
Seaborg, Glenn T. (Ishpeming, Mich.)		4/19/12
Sevareid, Eric (Velva, N.D.)		11/26/12
Sheen, Fulton J. (El Paso, Ill.)		5/8/95
Shirer, William L. (Chicago, Ill.)		2/23/04
Shoemaker, Willie (Fabens, Tex.)		8/19/31
Shor, Toots (Philadelphia, Pa.)		5/6/05
Shriver, Sargent (Westminster, Md.)		11/9/15
Shultz, George (New York, N.Y.)		12/13/20
Simon, Neil (New York, N.Y.)		7/4/27
Simon, William (Paterson, N.J.)		1927
Smith, H. Allen (McLeansboro, Ill.)		12/19/06
Smith, Howard K. (Ferriday, La.)		5/12/14
Smith, Margaret Chase (Skowhegan, Me.)		12/14/97
Sorenson, Theodore (Lincoln, Neb.)		5/8/28
Spillane, Mickey (Brooklyn, N.Y.)		3/9/18
Spock, Benjamin (New Haven, Conn.)		5/2/03
Stassen, Harold (West St. Paul, Minn.)		4/13/07
Steinem, Gloria (Toledo, Oh.)		3/25/36
Stengel, Casey (Kansas City, Mo.)		7/30/91
Stevenson 3rd, Adlai (Chicago, Ill.)		10/10/30
Stewart, Potter (Jackson, Mich.)		1/23/15
Stokes, Carl (Cleveland, Oh.)		6/21/27
Stone, Irving (San Francisco, Cal.)		7/14/03
Symington, Stuart (Amherst, Mass.)		6/26/01
Taft, Robert, Jr. (Cincinnati, Oh.)		2/26/17
Talmadge, Herman (Lovejoy, Ga.)		8/9/13
Taylor, Maxwell D. (Keytesville, Mo.)		8/26/01
Thomas, Lowell (Woodington, Oh.)		4/6/92
Thurmond, J. Strom (Edgefield, S.C.)		12/5/02
Tower, John (Houston, Tex.)		9/29/25
Truman, Mrs. Harry (Independence, Mo.)		2/13/85
Truman, Margaret (Mrs. Clifton Daniel) (Independence, Mo.)		2/17/24
Tuchman, Barbara (New York, N.Y.)		1/30/12
Tunney, Gene (New York, N.Y.)		5/25/98
Tunney, John V. (New York, N.Y.)		6/26/34
Udall, Morris K. (St. Johns, Ariz)		6/15/22
Unitas, John (Pittsburgh, Pa.)		5/7/33

Name	Birthplace	Birthdate	Name	Birthplace	Birthdate
Vanderbilt, Alfred G. (London, England)	9/22/12		Westmoreland, William (Spartanburg, S.C.)	3/26/14
Van Buren, Abigail (Sioux City, Ia.)	7/4/18		White, Byron R. (Ft. Collins, Col.)	6/8/17
Veeck, Bill (Chicago, Ill.)	2/9/14		White, Theodore (Boston, Mass.)	5/6/15
Vidal, Gore (West Point, N.Y.)	10/3/25		Wicker, Tom (Hamlet, N.C.)	6/18/26
Volpe, John (Wakefield, Mass.)	12/8/08		Wilder, Thornton (Madison, Wis.)	4/17/97
Vonnegut, Kurt, Jr. (Indianapolis, Ind.)	11/11/22		Wilkins, Roy (St. Louis, Mo.)	8/30/01
			Williams, Edward Bennett (Hartford, Conn.)	5/31/20
Wagner, Robert F. (New York, N.Y.)	4/20/10		Williams, Ted (San Diego, Cal.)	8/30/18
Walcott, Jersey Joe (Merchantville, N.J.)	1/31/14		Williams, Tennessee (Columbus, Miss.)	3/26/14
Wallace, George (Clio, Ala.)	8/25/19		Woodcock, Leonard (Providence, R.I.)	2/15/11
Wambaugh, Joseph (E. Pittsburgh, Pa.)	1/22/37		Wouk, Herman (New York, N.Y.)	5/27/15
Warren, Robert Penn (Guthrie, Ky.)	4/24/05			
Weicker, Lowell (Paris, France)	5/16/31		Yorty, Sam (Lincoln, Neb.)	10/1/09
Weinberger, Casper (San Francisco, Cal.)	8/18/17		Ziegler, Ronald (Covington, Ky.)	5/12/39

British

Poets, Dramatists, Essayists, Historians, Novelists

Born	Died	Name	Born	Died	Name	Born	Died	Name
1672	1719	Addison, Joseph	1834	1896	Du Maurier, Geo. L.	1838	1923	Morley, John
1805	1882	Ainsworth, W. H.	1819	1880	Eliot, George	1870	1916	Munro, H. H. (Saki)
1904	1966	Allingham, Margery	1888	1965	Eliot, T. S.	1880	1958	Noyes, Alfred
1832	1904	Arnold, Edwin	1620	1706	Evelyn, John	1903	1950	Orwell, George
1822	1888	Arnold, Matthew	1707	1754	Fielding, Henry	1839	1894	Pater, Walter
1775	1817	Austen, Jane	1809	1883	Fitzgerald, Edward	1785	1866	Peacock, Thomas L.
1561	1626	Bacon, Francis	1908	1964	Fleming, Ian	1632	1703	Pepys, Samuel
1214	1294	Bacon, Roger	1873	1939	Ford, Ford Madox	1688	1744	Pope, Alexander
1762	1851	Baillie, Joanna	1889	1966	Forester, C. S.	1900	1969	Potter, Stephen
1860	1937	Barrie, James M.	1879	1970	Forster, E. M.	1664	1721	Prior, Matthew
1584	1616	Beaumont, Francis	1908	1967	Frankau, Pamela	1863	1944	Quiller-Couch, Arthur T.
673	735	Bede, the Venerable	1867	1933	Galsworthy, John	1552	1618	Raleigh, Sir Walter
1872	1956	Beerbohm, Max	1685	1732	Gay, John	1814	1884	Reade, Charles
1870	1953	Belloc, Hilaire	1737	1794	Gibbon, Edward	1882	1957	Richardson, Dorothy
1867	1931	Bennett, Arnold	1857	1903	Gissing, George	1689	1761	Richardson, Samuel
1748	1832	Bentham, Jeremy	1728	1774	Goldsmith, Oliver	1819	1900	Ruskin, John
1662	1742	Bentley, Richard	1716	1771	Gray, Thomas	1872	1970	Russell, Bertrand
1869	1951	Blackwood, Algernon	1840	1928	Hardy, Thomas	1886	1967	Sassoon, Siegfried
1740	1795	Boswell, James	1831	1923	Harrison, Frederic	1893	1957	Sayres, Dorothy L.
1844	1930	Bridges, Robert	1778	1830	Hazlitt, William	1771	1832	Scott, Sir Walter
1816	1855	Bronte, Charlotte	1849	1903	Henley, Wm. Ernest	1564	1616	Shakespeare, William
1818	1848	Bronte, Emily	1591	1674	Herrick, Robert	1856	1950	Shaw, G. Bernard
1806	1861	Browning, Elizabeth B.	1588	1679	Hobbes, Thomas	1797	1851	Shelley, Mary W.
1812	1889	Browning, Robert	1770	1835	Hogg, James	1792	1822	Shelley, Percy Bysshe
1628	1688	Bunyan, John	1799	1845	Hood, Thomas	1751	1816	Sheridan, Richard B.
1729	1797	Burke, Edmund	1859	1936	Housman, Alfred E.	1554	1586	Sidney, Sir Phillip
1759	1796	Burns, Robert	1711	1776	Hume, David	1887	1964	Sitwell, Edith
1788	1824	Byron, Lord Geo. Gordon	1894	1963	Huxley, Aldous	1892	1969	Sitwell, Osbert
1777	1844	Campbell, Thomas	1825	1895	Huxley, Thos. H.	1771	1845	Smith, Sydney
1795	1881	Carlyle, Thomas	1709	1784	Johnson, Samuel	1721	1771	Smollett, Tobias
1832	1898	Carroll, Lewis	1573	1637	Jonson, Ben	1774	1843	Southey, Robert
1888	1957	Cary, Joyce	1795	1821	Keats, John	1552	1599	Spenser, Edmund
1340	1400	Chaucer, Geoffrey	1896	1967	Kennedy, Margaret	1672	1729	Steele, Richard
1694	1773	Chesterfield, Earl of	1819	1875	Kingsley, Charles	1713	1768	Sterne, Laurence
1874	1936	Chesterton, G. K.	1865	1936	Kipling, Rudyard	1850	1894	Stevenson, Robert Louis
1911	1968	Churchill, Randolph	1775	1834	Lamb, Charles	1880	1932	Strachey, Lytton
1762	1835	Cobbett, William	1332	1400	Langland, William	1667	1745	Swift, Jonathan
1772	1834	Coleridge, S. T.	1885	1930	Lawrence, David H.	1837	1909	Swinburne, Algernon C.
1824	1889	Collins, Wilkie	1838	1903	Lecky, W. E. H.	1809	1892	Tennyson, Alfred
1670	1729	Congreve, William	1866	1947	LeGallienne, Richard	1811	1863	Thackeray, W. M.
1857	1924	Conrad, Joseph	1894	1957	Lewis, Wyndham	1914	1953	Thomas, Dylan
1878	1957	Coppard, A. E.	1895	1970	Liddell Hart, Basil	1892	1973	Tolkien, J.R.R.
1864	1924	Corelli, Marie	1632	1704	Locke, John	1876	1962	Trevelyan, Geo. M.
1731	1800	Cowper, William	1800	1859	Macaulay, Thomas B.	1815	1882	Trollope, Anthony
1908	1973	Creasey, John	1863	1947	Machen, Arthur	1884	1941	Walpole, Hugh
1809	1882	Darwin, Charles	1888	1923	Mansfield, Katherine	1593	1683	Walton, Izaak
1660	1731	Defoe, Daniel	1564	1593	Marlowe, Christopher	1851	1920	Ward, Mrs. Humphry
1873	1956	De la Mare, Walter	1897	1969	Martin, Kingsley	1674	1748	Watts, Isaac
1785	1859	De Quincey, Thomas	1878	1967	Masefield, John	1903	1966	Waugh, Evelyn
1812	1870	Dickens, Charles	1583	1640	Massinger, Phillip	1866	1946	Wells, H. G.
1573	1631	Donne, John	1874	1965	Maugham, W. Somerset	1906	1964	White, T. H.
1868	1952	Douglas, Norman	1828	1909	Meredith, George	1861	1947	Whitehead, Alfred N.
1867	1900	Dowson, Ernest	1806	1873	Mill, John Stuart	1854	1900	Wilde, Oscar
1859	1930	Doyle, Arthur Conan	1882	1956	Milne, A. A.	1770	1850	Wordsworth, William
1563	1631	Drayton, Michael	1608	1674	Milton, John	1882	1941	Woolf, Virginia
1631	1700	Dryden, John				1640	1715	Wycherly, William

British Painters and Sculptors

Born	Died	Name	Born	Died	Name	Born	Died	Name
1872	1898	Beardsley, Aubrey	1866	1934	Fry, Roger E.	1834	1896	Morris, William
1757	1827	Blake, William	1727	1788	Gainsborough, Thos.	1878	1931	Orpen, William
1833	1898	Burne-Jones, Edward	1648	1721	Gibbons, Grinling	1756	1823	Raeburn, Henry
1896	1967	Charoux, Siegfried	1903	1975	Hepworth, Barbara	1723	1792	Reynolds, Joshua
1776	1837	Constable, John	1697	1764	Hogarth, William	1734	1802	Romney, George
1803	1902	Cooper, Thos. Sidney	1758	1810	Hoppner, John	1828	1882	Rossetti, D. G.
1782	1842	Cotman, John S.	1827	1910	Hunt, W. Holman	1891	1959	Spencer, Stanley
1793	1865	Eastlake, Charles L.	1646	1723	Kneller, Godfrey	1775	1851	Turner, J. M. W.
1880	1959	Epstein, Jacob	1856	1941	Lavery, John	1817	1904	Watts, George
1787	1849	Etty, William	1769	1830	Lawrence, Thomas	1785	1841	Wilkie, David
1755	1826	Flaxman, John	1806	1870	Maclise, Daniel	1713	1782	Wilson, Richard
			1829	1896	Millais, John			

British Army (A), Navy (N), Air Force (F), Explorers (E)

Born	Died	Name	Born	Died	Name	Born	Died	Name
1891	1969	Alexander, Harold R. (A)	1710	1759	Forbes, John (A)	1871	1951	Maurice, Frederick (A)
1861	1936	Allenby, Edmund (A)	1786	1847	Franklin, John (E)	1867	1948	Milne, George (A)
1717	1797	Amherst, Jeffrey (A)	1535	1594	Frobisher, Martin (E)	1894	1967	Morgan, Frederick (A)
1584	1622	Baffin, William (E)	1721	1787	Gage, Thomas (A)	1782	1853	Napier, Charles J. (A)
1871	1936	Beatty, David (N)	1833	1885	Gordon, Chas. G. (A)	1810	1890	Napier, Robert C. (A)
1873	1967	Boyle, Wm. H. D. (N)	1541	1591	Grenville, Richard (N)	1758	1805	Nelson, Horatio (N)
1695	1755	Braddock, Edward (A)	1861	1928	Haig, Douglas (A)	1696	1785	Oglethorpe, James (A)
1839	1908	Buller, Redvers (A)	1853	1947	Hamilton, Ian (A)	1895	1968	Robb, James (F)
1723	1792	Burgoyne, John (A)	1795	1857	Havelock, Henry (A)	1832	1914	Roberts, Frederick (A)
1663	1733	Byng, George (N)	1745	1792	Hearne, Samuel (E)	1719	1792	Rodney, George (N)
1675	1726	Cadogan, Wm. (A)	1536	1624	Howard, Charles (N)	1800	1862	Ross, James C. (E)
1593	1676	Cavendish, Wm. (A)	1726	1799	Howe, Richard (N)	1893	1969	Scobie, Ronald M. (A)
1873	1967	Chatfield, Alfred (N)	1729	1814	Howe, William (A)	1868	1912	Scott, Robert F. (E)
1738	1795	Clinton, Henry (A)	1575	1611	Hudson, Henry (E)	1874	1922	Shackleton, Ernest (E)
1770	1851	Codrington, Ed. (N)	1883	1966	Humphrey, Noel (E)	1891	1970	Slim, Wm. Joseph (A)
1727	1779	Cook, James (E)	1880	1959	Ironside, Wm. E. (A)	1841	1904	Stanley, Henry M. (E)
1738	1805	Cornwallis, Chas. (A)	1859	1935	Jellicoe, John (N)	1869	1951	Swinton, Ernest (A)
1550	1605	Davis, John (E)	1715	1774	Johnson, Wm. (A)	1890	1967	Tedder, Arthur W. (F)
1896	1969	Dempsey, Miles (A)	1872	1945	Keyes, Roger (N)	1757	1798	Vancouver, George (E)
1883	1970	Dowding, Hugh C. (F)	1850	1916	Kitchener, H. H. (A)	1883	1950	Wavell, Archibald (A)
1540	1596	Drake, Francis (N)	1888	1935	Lawrence, T. E. (A)	1787	1834	Weddell, James (E)
1877	1967	Ellington, Edward (F)	1650	1722	Marlborough, Duke of (A)	1769	1852	Wellington, Duke of (A)
1841	1920	Fisher, John A. (N)				1727	1759	Wolfe, James (A)

British Statesmen

Born	Died	Name	Born	Died	Name	Born	Died	Name
1852	1928	Asquith, Herbert H.	1869	1940	Chamberlain, Neville	1863	1935	Henderson, Arthur
1879	1964	Astor, Viscountess	1874	1965	Churchill, Winston	1889	1969	Horsbrugh, Florence
1883	1967	Atlee, Clement	1725	1774	Clive, Robert	1858	1923	Law, Andrew Bonar
1867	1947	Baldwin, Stanley	1889	1952	Cripps, Stafford	1863	1945	Lloyd George, David
1848	1930	Balfour, Arthur J.	1599	1658	Cromwell, Oliver	1866	1937	MacDonald, J. Ramsay
1879	1964	Beaverbrook, Lord	1859	1925	Curzon of Kedleston	1854	1925	Milner, Alfred
1897	1960	Bevan, Aneurin	1804	1881	Disraeli, Benjamin	1732	1792	North, Frederick
1881	1951	Bevin, Ernest	1749	1806	Fox, Charles James	1784	1865	Palmerston, Viscount
1838	1922	Bryce, James	1906	1963	Gaitskell, Hugh	1788	1850	Peel, Robert
1884	1968	Cadogan, Alexander	1809	1898	Gladstone, Wm. E.	1759	1806	Pitt, William (Younger)
1770	1827	Canning, George	1764	1845	Grey, Charles	1708	1778	Pitt, W. (Chatham)
1769	1822	Castlereagh, Robert	1862	1933	Grey, Edward	1853	1902	Rhodes, Cecil
1864	1958	Cecil, Edgar	1594	1643	Hampden, John	1792	1878	Russell, John
1863	1937	Chamberlain, Austen	1732	1818	Hastings, Warren	1830	1903	Salisbury, Robert
1836	1914	Chamberlain, Joseph				1676	1745	Walpole, Robert

British Scientists, Engineers, Physicians

Born	Died	Name	Born	Died	Name	Born	Died	Name
1813	1898	Bessemer, Henry	1849	1945	Fleming, Ambrose	1831	1879	Maxwell, James Clerk
1897	1974	Blackett, Patrick	1898	1968	Florey, Howard W.	1642	1727	Newton, Isaac
1899	1966	Cameron, Roy	1892	1964	Haldane, J. B. S.	1903	1969	Powell, Cecil F.
1881	1966	Campbell, Donald F.	1578	1657	Harvey, William	1733	1804	Priestley, Joseph
1731	1810	Cavendish, Henry	1792	1871	Herschel, John	1886	1975	Robinson, Robert
1891	1974	Chadwick, James	1738	1822	Herschel, William	1857	1932	Ross, Ronald
1905	1967	Cockcroft, John	1897	1967	Hinshelwood, Cyril	1871	1937	Rutherford, Ernest
1832	1919	Crookes, William	1861	1947	Hopkins, Frederick	1624	1689	Sydenham, Thomas
1875	1968	Dale, Henry H.	1887	1975	Huxley, Julian	1824	1907	Thomson, Wm. (Kelvin)
1766	1844	Dalton, John	1749	1823	Jenner, Edward	1823	1913	Wallace, Alf. Russell
1809	1882	Darwin, Charles	1815	1898	Jenner, William	1892	1973	Watson-Watt, Robert
1791	1867	Faraday, Michael	1827	1912	Lister, Jos.	1736	1819	Watt, James E.
1881	1955	Fleming, Alexander				1802	1875	Wheatstone, Chas.

British Religious Leaders

Born	Died	Name	Born	Died	Name	Born	Died	Name
1117	1170	Becket, Thomas a	1860	1954	Inge, William Ralph	1613	1667	Taylor, Jeremy
1685	1753	Berkeley, George	1874	1966	Johnson, Hewlett	1484	1536	Tyndale, William
1829	1912	Booth, William B.	1505	1572	Knox, John	1703	1791	Wesley, John
1566	1644	Brewster, William	1491	1555	Latimer, Hugh	1714	1770	Whitefield, Geo.
1489	1556	Cranmer, Thos.	1813	1873	Livingston, David	1802	1865	Wiseman, Nicholas
1624	1691	Fox, George	1808	1892	Manning, Henry E.	1475	1530	Wolsey, Thomas
1554	1600	Hooker, Richard	1801	1890	Newman, John H.	1324	1384	Wycliffe, John

Poets Laureate of England

·There is no authentic record of the origin of the office of Poet Laureate of England. According to Warton, there was a Versificator Regis, or Kings's Poet, in the reign of Henry III (1216-1272), and he was paid 100 shillings a year. Geoffrey Chaucer (1340-1400) assumed the title of Poet Laureate, and in 1389 got a royal grant of a yearly allowance of wine. In the reign of Edward IV (1461-1483), John Kay held the post. Under Henry VII (1485-1509), Andrew Bernard was the Poet Laureate, and was succeeded under Henry VIII (1509-1547) by John Skelton. Next came Edmund Spenser, who died in 1599; then Samuel Daniel, who died in 1619, and then Ben Jonson (appointed 1619). Sir William D'Avenant was appointed in 1638. He was a godson of William Shakespeare.

Others were John Dryden, 1670-1688; Thomas Shadwell, 1689; Nahum Tate, 1692; Nicholas Rowe, 1715; the Rev. Laurence Eusden, 1718; Colly Cibber, 1730; William Whitehead, 1758, on the refusal of Gray; Rev. Thomas Warton, 1785, on the refusal of Mason; Henry J. Pye, 1790; Robert Southey, 1813, on the refusal of Sir Walter Scott; William Wordsworth, 1843; Alfred Tennyson, 1850; Alfred Austin, 1896; Robert Bridges, 1913 (died 1930); John Masefield, 1930 (died 1967); Cecil Day Lewis (died May 22, 1972); Sir John Betjeman, 1972.

Canadian

Born	Died	Name
		Statesmen
1821	1893	Abbott, John
1878	1943	Aberhart, William
1804	1858	Baldwin, Robert
1912	1970	Beaudoin, Louis Rene
1870	1957	Bennett, Richard B.
1833	1912	Blake, Edward
1854	1937	Borden, Robert
1823	1917	Bowell, Mackenzie
1884	1969	Bracken, John
1818	1880	Brown, George
1875	1940	Buchan, John
1814	1873	Cartier, Georges
1890	1959	Duplessis, Maurice
1896	1969	Dupuy, Pierre
1895	1973	Frost, Leslie
1817	1893	Galt, Alexander T.
1869	1953	Hepburn, Mitchell F.
1804	1873	Howe, Joseph
1874	1950	King, W. Mackenzie
1841	1919	Laurier, Wilfrid
1815	1891	Macdonald, John A.
1795	1861	Mackenzie, Wm. Lyon
1887	1967	Massey, Vincent
1822	1905	McDougall, William
1825	1868	McGee, Thomas D'Arcy
1874	1960	Meighen, Arthur
1897	1972	Pearson, Lester B.
1904	1968	Robertson, Norman A.
1820	1914	Strathcona (Smith)
1844	1894	Thompson, John
1855	1927	Tupper, Charles H.
1888	1967	Vanier, George P.
1892	1969	Wilgress, Dana
		Authors
1913	1966	Allen, Ralph
1748	1784	Alline, Henry
1850	1931	Beauchemin, Neree
....	1931	Beck, L. Adams
1861	1924	Blake, W. H.
1868	1952	Bourassa, Henri
1840	1901	Buies, Arthur
1861	1918	Campbell, W. Wilfred
1861	1929	Carman, W. Bliss
1831	1904	Casgrain, Henri R.
1858	1946	Chapais, Thomas
1850	1917	Chapman, William
1820	1890	Chauveau, Pierre
1885	1953	Chopin, Rene
1850	1887	Crawford, Isabella
1827	1879	Cremazie, Octave
1831	1904	Cosgrain, Abbe R.
1866	1944	Dafoe, John Wesley
1865	1945	Dantin, Louis
1895	1958	Dawson, R. MacGregor
1848	1917	Dionne, Narcisse
....	1936	Doughty, Arthur G.
1854	1907	Drummond, W. H.
1862	1932	Duncan, Sara J.
1864	1922	Edwards, Robert (Bob)
1799	1870	Faillon, Etienne
1805	1865	Ferland, Jean
1860	1936	Fraser, Alexander
1839	1908	Frechette, Louis H.
1809	1866	Garneau, Francis X.
1786	1871	Gaspe, Philippe de
1824	1882	Gerin-Lajoie, Antoine
1871	1918	Gill, Charles
1860	1937	Gordon, Chas. W.
		(Ralph Connor)
1878	1967	Groulx, Lionel A.
1871	1948	Grove, Frederick
1796	1865	Haliburton, Thos. C.
1842	1910	Hannay, James
1816	1876	Heavysege, Charles

Born	Died	Name
1880	1913	Hemon, Louis
1766	1844	Heriot, George
1894	1952	Innis, H. A.
1881	1943	Kennedy, W. P. M.
1859	1931	Kingsford, William
1817	1906	Kirby, William
1862	1913	Johnson, Pauline
1871	1960	Laberge, Albert
1861	1899	Lampman, Archibald
1871	1936	Laut, Agnes
1869	1944	Leacock, Stephen
1841	1907	Legendre, Napoleon
1837	1918	Lemay, Pamphile
1857	1954	Lighthall, William
1909	1957	Lowry, Malcolm
1878	1924	Lozeau, Albert
1853	1931	Lucas, L. P.
1874	1942	Macdonald, Lucy M.
1876	1951	Mac Innes, Tom
1862	1933	MacMechan, Archibald
1840	1927	Mair, Charles
1844	1895	Marmette, Joseph
1864	1936	Marquis, Thomas
1882	1958	Martin, Chester
1872	1918	McCrae, John
1820	1907	McMullen, John
1865	1944	Miner, John T. (Jack)
1874	1942	Montgomery, Lucy
1803	1885	Moodie, Susanna
1889	1963	Morin, Paul
1879	1941	Nelligan, Emile
1737	1818	Odell, Jonathan
1895	1960	Panneton, Philippe
1862	1932	Parker, Gilbert
1887	1970	Phelps, Arthur L.
1883	1922	Pickthall, Marjorie
1883	1964	Pratt, Edwin J.
1749	1809	Quesnel, Joseph
1796	1852	Richardson, John
1860	1943	Roberts, Chas. G. D.
1885	1961	Roche, Mazo de la
1839	1920	Routhier, Adoph
1870	1943	Roy, Camille
1858	1913	Roy, Joseph E.
1822	1893	Sangster, Charles
1862	1944	Scott, Duncan C.
1874	1958	Service, Robert W.
1859	1931	Short, Adam
1878	1941	Skelton, O. D.
1823	1910	Smith, Goldwin
1841	1923	Sulte, Benjamin
1888	1951	Trotter, R. G.
1856	1926	Weir, R. Stanley
1860	1948	Wrong, George M.
		Painters and Sculptors
1863	1936	Ahrens, Carl
1876	1955	Allward, Walter S.
1759	1830	Baillarge, Francois
1740	1794	Beaucort, Francois
1905	1960	Borduas, Paul-Emile
1827	1916	Bourassa, Napoleon
1855	1925	Brymner, William
1871	1945	Carr, Emily
1866	1934	Cullen, Maurice
1769	1819	Field, Robert
1810	1894	Fowler, Daniel
1881	1942	Gagnon, Clarence
1817	1870	Hamel, Theophile
1885	1870	Harris, Lawren Stewart
1849	1919	Harris, Robert
1850	1917	Hebert, Louis P.
1882	1974	Jackson, Alexander Y
1812	1901	Jacobi, Otto
1852	1908	Julien, Henri
1810	1871	Kane, Paul

Born	Died	Name
1815	1872	Krieghoff, Cornelius
1873	1939	Lawson, Ernest
1864	1955	Leduc, Ozias
1795	1855	Legare, Joseph
1887	1968	Loring, Ernest
1847	1939	MacCarthy, Hamilton
1873	1932	MacDonald, J. E. H.
1882	1953	Milne, David
1865	1924	Morrice, James Wilson
1832	1899	O'Brien, Lucius Richard
1860	1892	Peel, Paul
1802	1895	Plamondon, Antoine S.
1739	1819	Ranvoyze, Francois
1816	1853	Ritter, Henry
1869	1937	Suzor-Cote, Aurele de Foy
1877	1918	Thomson, Tom
1798	1849	Valentine, William
1881	1969	Varley, F. H.
1858	1938	Walker, Horatio
1855	1936	Watson, Homer
1903	1966	Wood, Elizabeth Wynn
1881	1968	Wyle, Florence
		Science, Industry
1859	1942	Adams, Frank D.
1810	1882	Allan, Hugh
1891	1941	Banting, Fredk. G.
1877	1943	Beatty, Edward W.
1889	1966	Hilton, Hugh G.
1798	1875	Logan, William
1849	1919	Osler, William
1876	1935	Macleod, John J. R.
1863	1892	Stairs, Wm. Grant
1902	1967	Zimmerman, Adam
		Anthropologists, Geologists, and Naturalists
1876	1961	Anderson, Rudolph M.
1883	1969	Barbeau, Charles M.
1888	1938	Belaney, George Stansfeld (Grey Owl)
1841	1917	Bell, Robert
1820	1876	Billings, Elkanah
1874	1935	Brock, Reginald Walter
1878	1937	Collins, William Henry
1876	1957	Currelly, Charles Trick
1849	1901	Dawson, George Mercer
1846	1925	Dionne, Charles Eusibe
1817	1896	Hale, Horatio
1859	1944	Hill-Tout, Charles
1826	1892	Hunt, Thomas Sterry
1886	1969	Jenness, Diamond
1833	1881	LaRue, Francois A. H.
1798	1875	Logan, Sir William E.
1861	1942	Low, A. P.
1862	1920	Macoun, James Melville
1831	1920	Macoun, John
1869	1933	Macoun, William Tyrell
1885	1944	Marie-Victorin, frere
1867	1947	Massicotte, Edouard Z.
1857	1942	McConnell, Richard G.
1820	1892	Provancher, Leon, abbe
1905	1970	Rousseau, Jacques
1891	1957	Rowan, William
1870	1953	Roy, Pierre Georges
1867	1937	Saunders, Sir Charles E.
1836	1914	Saunders, William
1824	1902	Selwyn, Alfred R. C.
1860	1946	Seton, Ernest Thompson
1872	1940	Smith, Harlan I.
1875	1947	Taverner, Percy A.
1863	1945	Tyrrell, James Williams
1858	1957	Tyrrell, Joseph Burr
1872	1924	Waugh, Fredrick W.
1881	1964	Wilson, Alice Evelyn
1876	1941	Wintemberg, William J.

French

French Scientists, Physicians

Born	Died	Name
1775	1836	Ampere, Andre-Marie
1788	1878	Becquerel, A. C.
1852	1908	Becquerel, H. A.
1813	1878	Bernard, Claude
1827	1907	Berthelot, Marcelin
1872	1936	Bleriot, Louis

Born	Died	Name
1825	1893	Charcot, Jean M.
1746	1823	Charles, Jacques
1786	1889	Chevreul, Michel
1867	1934	Curie, Marie
1859	1906	Curie, Pierre
1890	1967	Danjon, Andre

Born	Died	Name
1678	1761	Fauchard, Pierre
1842	1925	Flammarion, Camille
1778	1850	Gay-Lussac, Joseph
1900	1958	Joliot-Curie, Frederic
1897	1956	Joliot-Curie, Irene
1781	1826	Laennec, Rene

Born	Died	Name	Born	Died	Name	Born	Died	Name
1736	1813	Lagrange, Joseph	1862	1954	Lumiere, Auguste	1647	1714	Papin, Denis
1744	1829	Lamarck, Jean B.	1864	1948	Lumiere, Louis	1510	1590	Pare, Ambroise
1749	1827	Laplace, Pierre S.	1852	1907	Moissan, Henri	1822	1895	Pasteur, Louis
1743	1794	Lavoisier, Antoine	1807	1873	Nelaton, Auguste	1854	1912.	Poincare, Henri
1822	1900	Lenoir, Etienne	1863	1933	Painleve, Paul	1850	1935	Richet, Charles
1811	1877	LeVerrier, Urbain				1875	1965	Schweitzer, Albert

French Military Leaders and Explorers

Born	Died	Name	Born	Died	Name	Born	Died	Name
1769	1821	Bonaparte, Napoleon	1753	1800	Kleber, Jean-Bapt.	1769	1851	Soult, Nicolas J.
1753	1823	Carnot, Lazare	1757	1834	La Fayette, Marquis de	1611	1675	Turenne, Vicomte de
1877	1969	Catroux, Georges	1902	1947	Leclerc, Jacques P.			
1519	1572	Coligny, Gasp. de	1854	1934	Lyautey, Louis H.			**Explorers**
1621	1686	Conde, Prince de	1756	1817	Massena, Andre	1658	1730	Cadillac, Antoine
1881	1942	Darlan, Jean F.	1712	1759	Montcalm, Louis de	1491	1557	Cartier, Jacques
1722	1788	DeGrasse, Francois	1763	1813	Moreau, Jean V.	1567	1635	Champlain, Sam'l de
1739	1823	Dumouriez, Chas. F.	1767	1815	Murat, Joachim	1867	1936	Charcot, Jean B.
1897	1975	Ely, Paul	1769	1815	Ney, Michel	1868	1969	David-Neel, Alexandra
1851	1929	Foch, Ferdinand	1856	1951	Petain, Henri Philippe	1640	1701	Hennepin, Louis
1849	1916	Gallieni, Jos. S.	1725	1807	Rochambeau, Jean-Bapt.	1645	1700	Jolliet, Louis
1879	1949	Giraud, Henri H.	1579	1638	Rohan, Henri	1643	1687	LaSalle, Robt. de
1852	1931	Joffre, Jos.	1696	1750	Saxe, Maurice de	1637	1675	Marquette, Jacques

French Political Leaders

Born	Died	Name	Born	Died	Name	Born	Died	Name
1884	1966	Auriol, Vincent	1620	1698	Frontenac, Louis de	1749	1791	Mirabeau, Honore
1872	1950	Blum, Leon	1838	1882	Gambetta, Leon	1860	1934	Poincare, Raymond
1862	1932	Briand, Aristide	1872	1957	Herriot, Edouard	1911	1974	Pompidou, Georges
1841	1929	Clemenceau, Georges	1889	1975	Laniel, Joseph	1884	1970	Queuille, Henri
1619	1683	Colbert, Jean-Bapt.	1883	1945	Laval, Pierre	1878	1966	Reynaud, Paul
1884	1970	Daladier, Edouard	1871	1950	Lebrun, Albert	1585	1642	Richelieu, Cardinal de
1759	1794	Danton, Georges	1744	1793	Marat, Jean-Paul	1758	1794	Robespierre, Max.
1890	1970	DeGaulle, Charles	1602	1661	Mazarin, Jules	1208	1265	Simon de Montfort
1760	1794	Desmoulins, Camille				1754	1838	Talleyrand, Chas. de

French Painters and Sculptors

Born	Died	Name	Born	Died	Name	Born	Died	Name
1834	1904	Bartholdi, Frederic	1880	1954	Derain, Andre	1884	1920	Modigliani, Amadeo
1848	1884	Bastien-Lepage, Jules	1807	1876	Diaz de la Pana, N. V.	1840	1926	Monet, Claude
1822	1899	Bonheur, Rosa	1877	1953	Dufy, Raoul	1824	1898	Moreau, Gustave
1867	1947	Bonnard, Pierre	1811	1889	Dupre, Jules	1830	1903	Pissarro, Camille
1703	1770	Boucher, Francois	1732	1806	Fragonard, Jean	1594	1665	Poussin, Nicolas
1825	1905	Bouguereau, W.	1820	1876	Fromentin, Eugene	1758	1823	Prudhon, Pierre
1876	1957	Brancusi, Constantin	1848	1903	Gauguin, Paul	1824	1898	Puvis de Chavannes, P. C.
1882	1963	Braque, Georges	1770	1837	Gerard, Francois	1840	1916	Redon, Odilon
1851	1933	Carrier-Belleuse, P.	1791	1824	Gericault, J. L. A. T.	1841	1919	Renoir, Pierre
1839	1906	Cezanne, Paul	1628	1715	Girardon, Fr.	1840	1917	Rodin, Auguste
1699	1779	Chardin, Jean-Bapt.	1725	1805	Greuze, J. B.	1871	1958	Rouault, Georges
1600	1682	Claude Lorrain	1741	1828	Houdon, J. A.	1812	1867	Rousseau, P. E. T.
1796	1875	Corot, J. B. C.	1780	1867	Ingres, J. A. D.	1859	1891	Seurat, Georges
1819	1877	Courbet, Gustave	1887	1965	Le Corbusier	1863	1935	Signac, Paul
1817	1878	Daubigny, C. F.	1891	1973	Lipchitz, Jacques	1839	1899	Sisley, Alfred
1808	1879	Daumier, Honore	1861	1944	Maillol, Aristide	1900	1955	Tanguy, Yves
1748	1825	David, Louis J.	1832	1883	Manet, Edouard	1864	1901	Toulouse-Lautrec
1783	1856	David d'Angers, P. J.	1869	1954	Matisse, Henri	1883	1955	Utrillo, Maurice
1834	1917	Degas, H. G. E.	1815	1891	Meissonier, J. L. E.	1876	1958	Vlaminck, Maurice
1799	1863	Delacroix, Eugene	1815	1875	Millet, J. F.	1868	1940	Vuillard, Edouard
1797	1856	Delaroche, Paul				1684	1721	Watteau, Antoine

French Authors, Dramatists, Historians, Religionists

Born	Died	Name	Born	Died	Name	Born	Died	Name
1079	1142	Abelard, Pierre	1541	1603	Charron, Pierre	1333	1400	Froissart, Jean
1717	1783	Alembert, Jean d'	1768	1848	Chateaubriand, Francois	1811	1872	Gautier, Theophile
1885	1969	Allain, Marcel	1762	1794	Chenier, Andre	1869	1951	Gide, Andre
1880	1918	Apollinaire, Guillaume	1895	1969	Chevallier, Gabriel	1882	1944	Giraudoux, Jean
1820	1889	Augier, (Emile)	1889	1963	Cocteau, Jean	1816	1882	Gobineau, Comte de
1902	1967	Ayme, Marcel	1873	1954	Colette, Sidonie	1822	1896	Goncourt, Edmond de
1799	1850	Balzac, Honore de	1445	1509	Comines, Philippe de	1830	1870	Goncourt, Jules de
1823	1891	Banville, Theodore de	1798	1857	Comte, Auguste	1787	1874	Guizot, Francois
1873	1935	Barbusse, Henri	1743	1794	Condorcet, Marquis de	1842	1905	Heredia, Jose-Maria de
1862	1923	Barres, Maurice	1767	1830	Constant, Benjamin	1857	1915	Hervieu, Paul
1821	1867	Baudelaire, Charles	1842	1908	Coppee, Francois	1802	1885	Hugo, Victor
1732	1799	Beaumarchais, Pierre	1845	1875	Corbiere, Tristan	1848	1907	Huysmans, Joris-Karl
1837	1899	Becque, Henry	1606	1684	Corneille, Pierre	1876	1944	Jacob, Max
1780	1857	Beranger, Pierre	1854	1928	Curel, Francois de	1868	1938	Jammes, Francis
1859	1941	Bergson, Henri	1840	1897	Daudet, Alphonse	1412	1431	Joan of Arc
1888	1948	Bernanos, Georges	1596	1650	Descartes, Rene	1815	1888	Labiche, Eugene
1866	1947	Bernard, Tristan	1902	1969	De Vilmorin, Louise	1645	1696	La Bruyere, Jean de
1876	1953	Bernstein, Henri	1713	1784	Diderot, Denis	1621	1695	La Fontaine, Jean de
1876	1967	Birot, Pierre A.	1881	1958	Du Gard, Roger M.	1860	1887	Laforgue, Jules
1636	1711	Boileau, Nicolas	1803	1870	Dumas, Alexandre	1790	1869	Lamartine, Alphonse de
1627	1704	Bossuet, Jacques	1824	1895	Dumas (fils). Alexandre	1846	1870	Lautreamont, Comte de
1852	1935	Bourget, Paul	1926	1967	Fall, Bernard B.	1818	1894	Leconte de Lisle
1858	1932	Brieux, Eugene	1651	1715	Fenelon, Francois de	1853	1914	Lemaitre, Jules
1707	1788	Buffon, Georges	1821	1880	Flaubert, Gustave	1668	1747	Lesage, Alain-Rene
1509	1564	Calvin, John	1886	1914	Fournier, Alain	1850	1923	Loti, Pierre (J. Viaud)
1913	1960	Camus, Albert	1844	1924	France, Anatole	1889	1973	Marcel, Gabriel

Born	Died	Name	Born	Died	Name	Born	Died	Name
1842	1898	Mallarme, Stephane	1495	1553	Rabelais, Francois	1791	1861	Scribe, Eugene
1882	1973	Maritain, Jacques	1639	1699	Racine, Jean	1626	1696	Sevigne, (Mme. de)
1688	1763	Marivaux, Pierre	1864	1936	Regnier, Henri de	1875	1959	Siegfried, Andre
1850	1893	Maupassant, Guy de	1823	1892	Renan, Ernest	1766	1817	Stael, (Mme. de)
1885	1967	Maurois, Andre	1854	1891	Rimbaud, Arthur	1783	1842	Stendhal, (Beyle)
1803	1870	Merimee, Prosper	1866	1944	Rolland, Romain	1839	1907	Sully-Prudhomme, Rene
1798	1874	Michelet, Jules	1524	1585	Ronsard, Pierre de	1828	1893	Taine, Hippolyte
1622	1673	Moliere, Jean-Baptiste	1868	1918	Rostand, Edmond	1795	1856	Thierry, Augustin
1533	1592	Montaigne, Michel de	1712	1778	Rousseau, Jean-Jacques	1805	1859	Tocqueville, A. C. de
1689	1755	Montesquieu, Charles de	1610	1703	Saint-Evremond, de	1871	1945	Valery, Paul
1810	1857	Musset, Alfred de	1900	1944	Saint-Exupery, Ant. de	1844	1896	Verlaine, Paul
1394	1465	Orleans, Charles d'	1675	1755	Saint-Simon, Duc de	1828	1905	Verne, Jules
1895	1974	Pagnol, Marcel	1804	1869	Sainte-Beuve, Charles A.	1797	1863	Vigny, Alfred de
1623	1662	Pascal, Blaise	1567	1622	Sales (Saint Francois de)	1838	1889	Villiers de l'Isle-Adam
1873	1914	Peguy, Charles	1804	1876	Sand, George (Lucile	1431	1484	Villon, Francois
1697	1763	Prevost (L'Abbe)			Dupin)	1694	1778	Voltaire, (Arouet)
1871	1922	Proust, Marcel	1831	1908	Sardou, Victorien	1840	1902	Zola, Emile

German

German Artists: Painters, Sculptors, Architects

Born	Died	Name	Born	Died	Name	Born	Died	Name
1480	1538	Altdorfer, Albrecht	1829	1880	Feuerbach, Anselm	1847	1935	Liebermann, Max
1476	1545	Baldung, Hans	1774	1840	Friedrich, Caspar	1880	1916	Marc, Franz
1870	1938	Barlach, Ernst	1480	1528	Grunewald, Mathias	1837	1887	Marees, Hans v.
1884	1950	Beckmann, Max	1847	1921	Hildebrand, Adolf v.	1815	1905	Menzel, Adolf v.
1726	1801	Chodowiecki, Dan'l	1460	1524	Holbein, Hans (Sr.)	1803	1884	Richter, Ludwig
1858	1925	Corinth, Lovis	1497	1543	Holbein, Hans (Jr.)	1764	1850	Schadow, Johann
1783	1867	Cornelius, Peter	1877	1947	Kolbe, Georg	1781	1841	Schinkel, Karl
1472	1553	Cranach, Lucas	1867	1945	Kollwitz, Kaethe	1839	1924	Thoma, Hans
1471	1528	Durer, Albrecht				1455	1529	Vischer, Peter

German Authors, Dramatists, Essayists, Religionists

Born	Died	Name	Born	Died	Name	Born	Died	Name
1769	1860	Arndt, Ernest Moritz	1862	1946	Hauptmann, Gerhart	1796	1835	Platen, August v.
1886	1956	Benn, Gottfried	1813	1863	Hebbel, Friedrich	1795	1886	Ranke, Leopold v.
1898	1956	Brecht, Bertolt	1770	1831	Hegel, Georg W. F.	1810	1874	Reuter, Fritz
1778	1842	Brentano, Clemens	1797	1856	Heine, Heinrich	1763	1825	Richter, (Jean Paul)
1491	1551	Bucer, Martin	1744	1803	Herder, Johann v.	1875	1926	Rilke, Rainer Maria
1740	1815	Claudius, Matthias	1877	1962	Hesse, Hermann	1899	1966	Ropke, Wilhelm
1863	1920	Dehmel, Richard	1878	1945	Kaiser, Georg	1788	1866	Rueckert, Friedrich
1788	1857	Eichendorff, Josef v.	1724	1804	Kant, Immanuel	1494	1576	Sachs, Hans
1820	1895	Engels, Friedrich	1896	1966	Kasack, Hermann	1775	1854	Schelling, Friedrich v.
1886	1933	Ernst, Paul	1777	1811	Kleist, Heinrich v.	1759	1805	Schiller, Friedrich
1170	1220	Eschenbach, Wolfram v.	1724	1803	Klopstock, Friedr.	1767	1845	Schlegel, Aug. W.
1884	1958	Feuchtwanger, Lion	1875	1967	Kolb, Annette	1772	1829	Schlegel, Friedrich v.
1762	1814	Fichte, Johann G.	1646	1716	Leibnitz, Gottfried	1768	1834	Schleiermacher, Friedrich
1869	1966	Foerster, Friedrich	1729	1781	Lessing, Gotthold	1788	1860	Schopenhauer, Arthur
1819	1898	Fontane, Theodor	1844	1909	Liliencron, Detlev v.	1817	1888	Storm, Theodor
1816	1895	Freytag, Gustav	1881	1948	Ludwig, Emil	1857	1928	Sudermann, Hermann
1868	1933	George, Stefan	1483	1546	Luther, Martin	1893	1939	Toller, Ernst
1749	1832	Goethe, Johann W. v.	1871	1950	Mann, Heinrich	1834	1896	Treitschke, Heinrich v.
1785	1863	Grimm, Jakob	1875	1955	Mann, Thomas	1787	1862	Uhland, Ludwig
1786	1859	Grimm, Wilhelm	1804	1875	Moerike, Eduard	1873	1934	Wassermann, Jakob
1890	1941	Hasenclever, Walter	1817	1903	Mommsen, Theodor	1733	1813	Wieland, Chris. M.
			1844	1900	Nietzsche, Friedrich			

German Engineers, Naturalists, Scientists, Industrialists

Born	Died	Name	Born	Died	Name	Born	Died	Name
1840	1905	Abbe, Ernst	1882	1964	Franck, James	1848	1896	Lilienthal, Otto
1902	1958	Adler, Kurt	1400	1468	Gutenberg, Johannes	1734	1815	Mesmer, Franz
1193	1280	Albertus Magnus	1834	1919	Haeckel, Ernst	1899	1968	Nordhoff, Heinrich
1844	1929	Bénz, Carl	1879	1968	Hahn, Otto	1787	1854	Ohm, Geo. S.
1882	1970	Born, Max	1755	1843	Hahnemann, Samuel	1853	1932	Ostwald, Wilhelm
1874	1940	Bosch, Karl	1821	1894	Helmholtz, Hermann v.	1858	1947	Planck, Max
1811	1899	Bunsen, Robert	1857	1894	Hertz, Heinrich	1875	1951	Porsche, Ferdinand
1834	1900	Daimler, Gottlieb	1769	1859	Humboldt, Alex. v.	1632	1694	Pufendorf, Samuel
1858	1913	Diesel, Rudolf	1859	1935	Junkers, Hugo	1845	1923	Roentgen, Wilhelm
1895	1964	Domagk, Gerhard	1571	1630	Kepler, Johannes	1822	1890	Schliemann, Heinrich
1884	1969	Dornier, Claude	1843	1910	Koch, Robert	1816	1892	Siemens, Ernst Werner v.
1861	1935	Duisberg, Carl	1812	1887	Krupp, Alfred	1842	1926	Thyssen, Aug.
1868	1954	Eckener, Hugo	1907	1967	Krupp, Alfried	1821	1902	Virchow, Rudolf
1854	1915	Ehrlich, Paul	1900	1967	Kuhn, Richard	1883	1970	Warburg, Otto
1686	1736	Fahrenheit, Gabriel	1646	1716	Leibnitz, Gottfried v.	1866	1925	Wassermann, Aug. v.
1852	1919	Fischer, Emil	1803	1873	Liebig, Justus v.	1838	1917	Zeppelin, Ferd. v.

German Political and Military Leaders; Economists

Born	Died	Name	Born	Died	Name	Born	Died	Name
1876	1967	Adenauer, Konrad	1863	1931	Hipper, Franz v.	1879	1969	Papen, Franz v.
1856	1921	Bethmann-Hollweg, T. v.	1889	1945	Hitler, Adolf	1876	1960	Raeder, Erich
1815	1898	Bismarck, Otto v.	1887	1960	Kesselring, Albert	1867	1922	Rathenau, Walter
1742	1819	Bluecher, Gebhart v.	1871	1919	Liebknecht, Karl	1891	1944	Rommel, Erwin
1885	1970	Bruning, Heinrich	1886	1966	Luckner, Felix v.	1876	1953	Rundstedt, Karl v.
1849	1929	Bulow, Bernard v.	1865	1937	Ludendorff, Erich	1877	1970	Schacht, Hjalmar
1780	1831	Clausewitz, Karl v.	1880	1919	Luxemburg, Rosa	1865	1939	Scheidemann, Philipp
1875	1921	Erzberger, Matthias	1849	1945	Machensen, August v.	1833	1913	Schlieffen, Alfred v.
1760	1831	Gneisenau, August	1818	1883	Marx, Karl	1878	1929	Stresemann, Gustav
1893	1946	Goering, Hermann	1800	1891	Moltke, Helmuth von	1849	1930	Tirpitz, Alf. v.
1847	1934	Hindenburg, Paul v.	1848	1916	Moltke, Helmuth von	1893	1973	Ulbricht, Walter

Italian

Authors, Dramatists, Poets, Philosophers, Historians

Born	Died	Name	Born	Died	Name	Born	Died	Name
1749	1803	Alfieri, Vittorio	1863	1938	D'Annunzio, Gabriele	1785	1873	Manzoni, Alessandro
1846	1908	Amicis, Edmond de	1265	1321	Dante, Alighieri	1805	1872	Mazzini, Giuseppe
1227	1274	Aquinas, Thomas	1875	1936	Deledda, Grazia	1698	1782	Metastasio (P. Trapassi)
1492	1556	Aretino, Pietro	1817	1883	De Sanctis, Francesco	1672	1750	Muratori, Ludovico
1474	1533	Ariosto, Ludovico	1909	1967	Emanuelli, Enrico	1848	1923	Pareto, Vilfredo
1829	1907	Ascoli, Graziadio	1842	1911	Fogazzaro, Antonio	1855	1912	Pascoli, Giovanni
1791	1863	Belli, Giuseppe	1778	1827	Foscolo, Ugo	1788	1854	Pellico, Silvio
1313	1375	Boccaccio, Giovanni	1875	1944	Gentile, Giovanni	1304	1374	Petrarca, Francesco
1441	1494	Boiardo, Matteo Maria	1809	1850	Giusti, Giuseppe	1867	1936	Pirandello, Luigi
1548	1599	Bruno, Giordano	1707	1793	Goldoni, Carlo	1432	1484	Pulci, Luigi
1568	1639	Campanella, Tommaso	1713	1786	Gozzi, Gaspare	1901	1968	Quasimodo, Salvatore
1835	1907	Carducci, Giosue	1483	1540	Guicciardini, Francesco	1626	1698	Redi, Francesco
1725	1798	Casanova, Giacomo	1798	1837	Leopardi, Giacomo	1544	1595	Tasso, Torquato
1478	1529	Castiglione, Baldassarre	1836	1909	Lombroso, Cedare	1888	1970	Ungaretti, Giuseppe
1884	1966	Cecchi, Emilio	1469	1527	Machiavelli, Niccolo	1840	1922	Verga, Giovanni
1866	1952	Croce, Benedetto	1898	1957	Malaparte, Curzio	1668	1744	Vico, Giambattista
			1449	1515	Manuzio, Aldo (Aldus)			

Italian Painters, Sculptors, and Architects

Born	Died	Name	Born	Died	Name	Born	Died	Name
1404	1472	Alberti, Leon Battista	1500	1571	Cellini, Benvenuto	1480	1528	Palma, Jacopo
1512	1572	Alessi, Galeazzo	1240	1302	Cimabue, Giovanni	1445	1523	Perugino, Pietro
1447	1522	Amadeo, Giovanni	1489	1534	Correggio, Antonio da	1720	1778	Piranesi, Giovanni
1387	1455	Angelico, Fra	1462	1521	Cosimo, Piero di	1454	1513	Pinturicchio
1591	1666	Barbieri, Giovanni	1486	1531	Del Sarto, Andrea	1483	1520	Raphael (Raffaelo)
1475	1517	Bartolomeo, Fra	1386	1466	Donatello, Donato	1575	1642	Reni, Guido
1426	1507	Bellini, Gentile	1378	1455	Ghiberti, Lorenzo	1400	1482	Robbia, Luca della
1428	1516	Bellini, Giovanni	1449	1494	Ghirlandaio, Domenico	1615	1673	Rosa, Salvator
1400	1470	Bellini, Jacopo	1477	1510	Giorgione	1460	1529	Sansovino, Andrea
1467	1516	Beltraffio, Giovanni	1260	1336	Giotto di Bondone	1486	1570	Sansovino, Jacopo
1562	1629	Bernini, Gian Lor.	1420	1497	Gozzoli, Benozzo	1858	1899	Segantini, Giovanni
1598	1680	Bernini, Pietro	1902	1975	Levi, Carlo	1883	1966	Severini, Gino
1445	1510	Botticelli, Sandro	1406	1469	Lippi, Fra Filippo	1696	1770	Tiepolo, Giambattista
1444	1514	Bramante, Donato	1459	1504	Lippi, Filippino	1518	1594	Tintoretto, Jacopo
1377	1446	Brunelleschi, Filippo	1431	1506	Mantegna, Andrea	1477	1576	Titian (Tiziano)
1697	1768	Canaletto (Canale)	1401	1428	Masaccio, Tommaso	1397	1475	Uccello, Paolo
1757	1822	Canova, Antonio	1827	1887	Mengoni, Giuseppe	1511	1574	Vasari, Giorgio
1570	1610	Caravaggio, Merisi	1475	1564	Michelangelo Buonarroti	1528	1588	Veronese, Paolo
1450	1522	Carpaccio, Vittore	1826	1901	Morelli, Domenico	1435	1488	Verrocchio, Andrea
1881	1966	Carra, Carlo	1518	1580	Palladio, Andrea	1452	1519	Vinci, Leonardo da

Italian Explorers, Scientists, Political Leaders

Born	Died	Name	Born	Died	Name	Born	Died	Name
1776	1856	Avogadro, Amedeo	1847	1897	Ferraris, Galileo	1859	1953	Nitti, Francesco
1738	1794	Beccaria, Cesare	1564	1642	Galileo (G. Galilei)	1254	1324	Polo, Marco
1835	1900	Beltrami, Eugenio	1737	1798	Galvani, Luigi	1626	1698	Redi, Francesco
1476	1507	Borgia, Cesare	1807	1882	Garibaldi, Giuseppe	1878	1970	Ruini, Meuccio
16th	Cen	Cabot, John (Caboto)	1882	1955	Graziani, Rodolfo	1835	1910	Schiaparelli, Giovanni
1826	1910	Cannizzaro, Stanislao	1483	1540	Guicciardini, Francesco	1818	1878	Secchi, Angelo
1810	1861	Cavour, Camillo Benso	1628	1694	Malpighi, Marcello	1872	1952	Sforza, Carlo
1451	1506	Columbus, Christopher	1874	1937	Marconi, Guglielmo	1729	1799	Spallanzani, Lazzaro
1830	1903	Cremona, Luigi	1389	1464	Medici, Cosimo de' (1)	1608	1647	Torricelli, Evangelista
1881	1954	De Gasperi, Alcide	1519	1574	Medici, Cosimo de' (2)	1485	1533	Verrazano, Giovanni
1466	1560	Doria, Andrea	1449	1492	Medici, Lorenzo de'	1454	1512	Vespucci, Amerigo
1901	1954	Fermi, Enrico	1846	1910	Mosso, Angelo	1745	1827	Volta, Alessandro
			1883	1945	Mussolini, Benito			

Russian

Authors—Poets

Born	Died	Name
1888	1966	Akhmatova, Anna A.
1791	1859	Aksakov, Sergei
1878	1927	Artsibashev, Mikhail
1894	1941	Babel, Isaac
1811	1848	Belinsky, Vissarion
1880	1921	Blok, Aleksandr
1891	1940	Bulgakov, Mikhail
1870	1953	Bunin, Ivan
1860	1904	Chekhov, Anton
1821	1881	Dostoyevsky, Fyodor
1891	1967	Ehrenburg, Ilya G.
1809	1852	Gogol, Nicholas V.
1812	1891	Goncharov, Ivan A.
1868	1936	Gorky, Maxim
1886	1921	Gumilev, Nikolai
1812	1870	Herzen, Aleksandr
1853	1921	Korolenko, Vladimir
1768	1844	Krylov, Ivan
1870	1938	Kuprin, Aleksandr
1814	1841	Lermontov, Mikhail
1831	1895	Leskov, Nikolai
1891	1938	Mandelstam, Osip
1893	1930	Mayakovsky, Vladimir

Born	Died	Name
1821	1877	Nekrasov, Nikolai
1823	1886	Ostrovsky, Aleksandr
1890	1960	Pasternak, Boris
1799	1837	Pushkin, Aleksandr
1856	1919	Rozanov, Vasili
1820	1879	Soloviev, Sergei
1883	1945	Tolstoy, Alexei
1828	1910	Tolstoy, Lev
1892	1941	Tsvetaeva, Marina
1818	1883	Turgenev, Ivan
1895	1925	Yesenin, Sergei

Artists

Born	Died	Name
1866	1924	Bakst, Leon S.
1866	1944	Kandinsky, Vasili
1783	1836	Kiprensky, Orest
1878	1927	Kustodiev, Boris
1861	1900	Levitan, Isaak
1844	1918	Repin, Ilya
1865	1911	Serov, Valentin
1842	1904	Vereshchagin, Vasili
1865	1910	Vrubel, Mikhail
1890	1967	Zadkine, Ossip

Scientists

Born	Died	Name
1877	1968	Arbuzov, Aleksandr
1898	1967	Balandin, Aleksei
1857	1927	Bekhterev, Vladimir
1908	1968	Landau, Lev D.
1711	1765	Lomonosov, Mikhail
1909	1967	Maltsev, Anatoli
1834	1907	Mendeleyev, Dmitri
1845	1916	Metchnikov, Elie
1905	1970	Mikoyan, Artem I.
1849	1936	Pavlov, Ivan
1859	1905	Popov, Aleksandr
1907	1966	Sisakian, Norayr M.
1891	1969	Stechkin, Boris S.
1857	1935	Tsiolkovsky, Konstantin E.

Political Leaders

Born	Died	Name
1899	1953	Beria, Lavrenti
1814	1876	Bakunin, Mikhail
1888	1938	Bukharin, Nikolai
1895	1975	Bulganin, Nikolai. A.
1875	1946	Kalinin, Mikhail
1883	1936	Kamenev, Lev

Born	Died	Name
1881	1970	Kerensky, Aleksandr
1842	1921	Kropotkin, Pyotr
1870	1924	Lenin, Vladmir
1877	1952	Litvinov, Maxim
1857	1918	Plekhanov, Georgi
1739	1791	Potemkin, Grigori
1772	1839	Speransky, Mikhail
1879	1953	Stalin, Josef
1863	1911	Stolypin, Pyotr

Born	Died	Name
1879	1940	Trotsky, Leon
1849	1915	Witte, Sergei
1883	1936	Zinoviev, Grigori

Military Leaders

Born	Died	Name
1883	1973	Budenny, Semyon
1872	1947	Denikin, Anton
1874	1920	Kolchak, Aleksandr

Born	Died	Name
1897	1973	Konev, Ivan
1870	1918	Kornilov, Lavr
1745	1813	Kutuzov, Mikhail
1902	1974	Kuznetzov, Nikolai
1859	1914	Samsonov, Aleksandr
1729	1800	Suvorov, Aleksandr
1895	1970	Timoshenko, Semyon
1881	1969	Voroshilov, Klimenti Y
1895	1974	Zhukov, Georgi K.

Additional Foreign Personalities of the Past

S. Y. Agnon, Israeli novelist, 1888-1970.
Emilio Aguinaldo, Filipino revolutionary, 1869-1964.
Roald Amundsen, Norwegian explorer, 1872-1928.
Hans Christian Andersen, Danish writer, 1805-1875.
Julius Andrassy, Hungarian statesman, 1823-1890.
Ivo Andric, Yugoslav novelist, 1892-1975.
Pedro Aramburu, Argentine statesman, 1903-1970.
Sholem Asch, Polish-born Yiddish writer, 1880-1957
Miguel Angel Asturias, Guatemalan novelist, 1899-1974.
Kemal Ataturk, Turkish statesman, 1881-1938.

Vasco Nunez de Balboa, Spanish explorer, 1475-1519.
Karl Barth, Swiss theologian, 1889-1966.
Brendan Behan, Irish playwright, 1923-1964.
Bjarni Benediktson, Icelandic statesman, 1908-1970.
Eduard Benes, Czech. statesman, 1884-1948.
David Ben-Gurion, first Israeli premier, 1886-1973.
Vitus J. Bering, Danish explorer, 1681-1741.
Folke Bernadotte, Swedish statesman, 1895-1948.
Vicente Blasco-Ibarrez, Spanish novelist, 1867-1928.
Arnold Boecklin, Swiss painter, 1827-1901.
Niels Bohr, Danish physicist, 1885-1962.
Simon Bolivar, South American revolutionary, 1783-1830.
Jose Bonifacio, Brazilian statesman, 1763-1838.
Louis Botha, South African statesman, 1862-1919.
Emil Brunner, Swiss theologian, 1889-1966.
Martin Buber, Austrian-born Jewish philosopher, 1878-1965.

Plutarco Calles, Mexican statesman, 1877-1945.
Constantine Canaris, Greek statesman, 1790-1877.
Karel Capek, Czech. writer, 1890-1938.
Lazaro Cardenas, Mexican statesman, 1895-1970.
Venustiano Carranza, Mexican political leader, 1859-1920.
Roger Casement, Irish revolutionary, 1864-1916
Humberto Castelo Branco, Brazilian political leader, 1900-1967
Miguel de Cervantes Saavedra, Spanish novelist, 1547-1616.
Chiang Kai-shek, president of Nationalist China, 1886-1975
Henri Christophe, Haitian revolutionary, 1767-1820.
Nicholas Copernicus, Polish astronomer, 1473-1543.
Hernando Cortez, Spanish conqueror of Mexico, 1485-1547.
Marie Sklodowska Curie, Polish chemist, 1867-1934.

Hernando De Soto, Spanish explorer, 1500-1543.
Jean J. Dessalines, Haitian emperor, 1758-1806.
Porfirio Diaz, Mexican statesman, 1830-1915.
Ngo Dinh Diem, South Vietnamese president, 1901-1963.
Isak Dinesen, Danish author, 1885-1962.
Engelbert Dollfuss, Austrian statesman, 1892-1934.
Christian Doppler, Austrian physicist, 1803-1853.

Robert Emmet, Irish patriot, 1778-1803.
Enver Pasha, Turkish political leader, 1881-1922.
Erasmus Desiderius, Dutch author 1466-1536.
Levi Eshkol, Israeli statesman, 1895-1969.

Manuel de Falla, Spanish composer, 1876-1946.
Ragnar Frisch, Norwegian economist, 1895-1973.

Vasco da Gama, Portuguese explorer, 1469-1524.
Mohandas K. Gandhi, Indian political leader, 1869-1948.
Alberto Giacometti, Swiss sculptor, 1901-1966.
Vincent van Gogh, Dutch painter, 1853-1890.
Francisco Goya y Lucientes, Spanish painter, 1746-1828.
El Greco, Greek painter in Spain, 1541-1614.
Lady Augusta Gregory, Irish dramatist, 1859-1932.
Edvard Grieg, Norwegian composer, 1843-1907.

Franz Hals, Dutch painter, 1584-1666.
Dag Hammarskjold, Swedish statesman, 1905-1961.
Theodor Herzl, Hungarian founder of modern Zionism, 1860-1904.
Ho Chi Minh, North Vietnamese president, 1890-1969.
Andreas Hofer, Austrian patriot, 1767-1810.

Nicholas Horthy, Hungarian statesman, 1868-1957.
Mikhailo Hrushevsky, Ukrainian statesman, 1866-1934.
Jan Hus, Czech, religionist, 1369-1415.

Henrik Ibsen, Norwegian playwright, 1828-1906.

James Joyce, Irish author, 1882-1941.
Benito Juarez, Mexican statesman, 1806-1872.
Franz Kafka, Czech.-born Austrian author, 1883-1924.
Joseph Kasavubu, Congolese political leader, 1910-1969.
Abdul Karim Kassem, Iraqi politician, 1914-1963.
Yasunari Kawabata, Japanese novelist, 1899-1972.
Elizabeth (Sister) Kenny, Australian nurse, 1886-1952.
Paul Klee, Swiss painter, 1879-1940.
Thaddeus Kosciusko, Polish general, 1746-1817.
Paul Kruger, South African statesman, 1825-1904.
Mikola Kulish, Ukrainian dramatist, 1892-1934.
Frank Kupka, Czech. painter, 1871-1957.

Par Lagerkrist, Swedish novelist, 1891-1974.
Selma Lagerlof, Swedish writer, 1858-1940.
Wanda Landowska, Polish harpsichordist, 1879-1959.
Francisco Largo Caballero, Spanish statesman, 1869-1946.
Trygve Lie, Norwegian statesman, 1896-1968.
Patrice E. Lumumba, Congolese political leader, 1925-1961.
Albert J. Luthuli, South African political leader, 1899-1967.

Francisco I. Madera, Mexican statesman, 1873-1913.
Maurice Maeterlinck, Belgian dramatist, 1862-1949.
Ferdinand Magellan, Portuguese explorer, 1480-1521.
Carl Gustav Mannerheim, Finnish statesman, 1867-1951.
Jose Marti, Cuban patriot, 1853-1895.
Jan Masaryk, Czech. statesman, 1886-1948.
Thomas Masaryk, Czech. statesman, 1850-1937.
Tom Mboya, Kenyan political leader, 1930-1969.
Lise Meitner, Austrian mathematician, 1878-1968.
Gregor J. Mendel, Austrian botanist, 1822-1884.
John Metaxas, Greek statesman, 1871-1941.
Clemens W. N. L. Metternich, Austrian statesman, 1773-1859.
Draja Mikhailovich, Yugoslav soldier, 1893-1946.
Carl Milles, Swedish sculptor, 1875-1955.
Jozef Cardinal Mindszenty, Roman Catholic primate of Hungary, 1892-1975.
Yukio Mishima, Japanese author, 1925-1970.
Vilhelm Moberg, Swedish novelist, 1898-1973.
Ferenc Molnar, Hungarian dramatist, 1878-1952.
George Moore, Irish novelist, 1852-1933.
Thomas Moore, Irish poet, 1779-1852.
Jose M. Morelos y Pavon, Mexican revolutionary leader, 1765-1815.
Mohammed Mossadegh, Iranian statesman, 1880-1967.
Bartolome E. Murillo, Spanish painter, 1618-1682.

Imre Nagy, Hungarian statesman, 1895-1958.
Fridtjof Nansen, Norwegian explorer, 1861-1930.
Juan Negrin, Spanish statesman, 1891-1956.
Jawaharlal Nehru, Indian statesman, 1889-1964.
Florence Nightingale, English nurse, 1820-1910.
Alfred Nobel, Swedish philanthropist, 1833-1898.

Alvaro Obregon, Mexican statesman, 1880-1928.
Sean O'Casey, Irish dramatist, 1884-1964.
Daniel O'Connell, Irish political leader, 1775-1847.
Frank O'Connor, Irish writer, 1903-1966.
Thomas P. O'Connor, Irish journalist, 1848-1929.
Bernardo O'Higgins, Chilean revolutionary, 1776-1842.
Aristotle Onassis, Greek shipping magnate, 1900-1975.

George Papandreou, Greek statesman, 1888-1968.
Charles Stewart Parnell, Irish nationalist, 1846-1891.
Juan Peron, president of Argentina, 1895-1974.
Pablo Picasso, Spanish artist & sculptor, 1881-1973.
Joseph Pilsudski, Polish statesman, 1867-1935.
Miguel Primo de Rivera, Spanish dictator, 1870-1930.

Adam Rapacki, Polish statesman, 1910-1970.
Fritz Reiner, Austrian orchestra conductor, 1888-1963.
Rembrandt van Rijn, Dutch painter, 1605-1669.
Syngman Rhee, South Korean president, 1875-1965.
Jose Rizal, Filipino patriot, 1861-1896.
Peter Paul Rubens, Flemish painter, 1577-1640.

Antonio de O. Salazar, Portuguese statesman, 1899-1970.
Jose de San Martin, South American revolutionary, 1778-1850.
Antonio L. de Santa Anna, Mexican general, 1794-1876.
Francisco de Paula Santander, Colombian politician, 1792-1840.
Arthur Schnitzler, Austrian dramatist, 1862-1931.
Dudley Senanayake, Ceylon statesman, 1911-1973.
David Alfaro Siqueiros, Mexican artist, 1898-1974.
Moshe Sharett, Israeli statesman, 1894-1965.
Richard B. Sheridan, Irish author, 1751-1816.
Taras Shevchenko, Ukrainian poet, 1814-1861.
Frans E. Sillanpaa, Finnish novelist, 1888-1964.
Jan C. Smuts, South African statesman, 1870-1950.
Paul Henri Spaak, Belgian statesman, 1899-1972.
Baruch Spinoza, Dutch philosopher, 1632-1677.
Antonio Stradivari, Italian violin-maker, 1644-1737.
August Strindberg, Swedish writer, 1849-1912.
Sun Yat-Sen, Chinese statesman, 1866-1925.
Otto Sverdrup, Norwegian explorer, 1854-1930.
Emanuel Swedenborg, Swedish scientist, scholar, 1688-1772.

John M. Synge, Irish author, 1871-1909.

Rabindranath Tagore, Indian poet, 1861-1941.
Vaino A. Tanner, Finnish statesman, 1881-1966.
U Thant, Burmese statesman, 1909-1974.
Hideki Tojo, Japanese political & military leader, 1884-1948.
Rafael L. Trujillo Molina, Dominican dictator, 1891-1961.
Moise K. Tshombe, Congolese leader, 1919-1969.

Lesia Ukrainka, Ukrainian writer, 1871-1913.
Sigrid Undset, Norwegian author, 1882-1949.

Anthony Van Dyck, Flemish painter, 1599-1641.
Getulio D. Vargas, Brazilian statesman, 1883-1954.
Diego Velazquez, Spanish painter, 1599-1660.
Eleutherios Venizelos, Greek statesman, 1864-1936.
Jan Vermeer, Dutch painter, 1632-1675.
Hendrik F. Verwoerd, South African prime minister, 1901-1966.
Vladimir Vinnichenko, Ukrainian novelist, 1880-1951.
Artturi Virtanen, Finnish chemist, 1895-1973.

Franz Werfel, Austrian author, 1890-1945.
Chaim Weizmann, first Israeli president, 1874-1952.

William Butler Yeats, Irish poet, 1865-1939.

Emiliano Zapata, Mexican revolutionary, 1879-1919.
Stefan Zweig, Austrian author, 1881-1942.

Composers of the Western World

Carl Philipp Emanuel Bach, 1714-1788. (G.) Prussian and Wurtembergian Sonatas.
Johann Christian Bach, 1735-1782. (G.) Concertos; sonatas.
Johann Sebastian Bach, 1685-1750. (G.) St. Matthew Passion, The Well-Tempered Clavichord.
Samuel Barber, b. 1910 (U.S.) Adagio for Strings, Vanessa.
Bela Bartok, 1881-1945. (Hung.) Concerto for Orchestra, The Miraculous Mandarin.
Ludwig Van Beethoven, 1770-1827. (G.) Concertos (Emperor); sonatas (Moonlight, Pastorale, Pathetique); symphonies (Eroica).
Vincenzo Bellini, 1801-1835. (It.) La Sonnambula, Norma, I Puritani.
Alban Berg, 1885-1935. (Aus.) Wozzeck, Lulu.
Hector Berlioz, 1803-1869. (F.) Damnation of Faust, Symphonie Fantastique, Requiem.
Leonard Bernstein, b. 1918. (U.S.) Jeremiah, West Side Story.
Georges Bizet, 1838-1875. (F.) Carmen, Pearl Fishers.
Ernest Bloch, 1880-1959. (Swiss) Schelomo, Voice in the Wilderness, Sacred Service.
Luigi Boccherini, 1743-1805 (It.) Cello Concerto in B Flat, Symphony in C.
Alexander Borodin, 1834-1887. (R.) Prince Igor, in the Steppes of Central Asia.
Johannes Brahms, 1833-1897. (G.) Liebeslieder Waltzes, Rhapsody in E Flat Major, Opus 119 for Piano, Academic Festival Overture; symphonies; quartets.
Benjamin Britten, b. 1913 (Br.) Peter Grimes, Turn of the Screw, Ceremony of Carols.
Anton Bruckner, 1824-1896, (Aus.) Symphonies (Romantic), Intermezzo for String Quintet.
Ferruccio Busoni, 1866-1924. (It.) Doctor Faust, Comedy Overture.
Dietrich Buxtehude, 1637-1707. (G.) Cantatas, Trio sonatas.
William Byrd, 1543-1623 (Br.) Masses, Sacred Songs.
Alexis Emmanuel Chabrier, 1841-1894. (Fr.) Le Roi Malgre Lui, Espana.
Gustave Charpentier, 1860-1956. (F.) Louise.
Frederic Chopin, 1810-1849. (P.) Concertos, Polonaise No. 6 in A Flat Major (Heroic); sonatas.
Aaron Copland, b. 1900. (U.S.) Appalachian Spring.
Claude Achille Debussy, 1862-1918. (F.) Pelleas et Mellisande, La Mer, Prelude to the Afternoon of a Faun.
C. P. Leo Delibes, 1836-1891, (F.) Lakme, Coppelia, Sylvia.
Norman Dello Joio, b. 1913. (U.S.), Triumph of St. Joan, Psalm of David.
Gaetano Donizetti, 1797-1848. (It.) Elixir of Love, Lucia de Lammermoor, Daughter of the Regiment.
Paul Dukas, 1865-1935. (Fr.) Sorcerer's Apprentice.
Antonin Dvorak, 1841-1904. (C.) Symphony in E Minor (from the New World).
Edward Elgar, 1857-1934. (Br.) Pomp and Circumstance.
Manuel de Falla, 1876-1946. (Sp.) La Vide Breve, El Amor Brujo.
Gabriel Faure, 1845-1924. (Fr.) Requiem, Ballade.
Friedrich von Flotow, 1812-1883. (G.) Martha.
Cesar Franck, 1822-1890. (Belg.) D Minor Symphony.

George Gershwin, 1898-1937. (U.S.) Rhapsody in Blue, American in Paris, Porgy and Bess.
Umberto Giordano, 1867-1948 (It.) Andrea Chenier.
Alex K. Glazunoff, 1865-1936. (R.) Symphonies, Stenka Razin.
Mikhail Glinka, 1857-1904. (R.) Ruslan & Ludmilla.
Christoph W. Gluck, 1714-1787. (G.) Alceste, Iphigenie en Tauride.
Charles Gounod, 1818-1893. (F.) Faust, Romeo and Juliet.
Edvard Grieg, 1843-1907. (Nor.) Peer Gynt Suite, Concerto in A Minor.
George Frederick Handel, 1685-1759. (G.-Br.) Messiah, Xerxes, Berenice.
Howard Hanson, b. 1896. (U.S.) Symphonies No. 1 (Nordic) and 2 (Romantic).
Roy Harris, b. 1898. (U.S.) Symphonies, Amer. Portraits.
Joseph Haydn, 1732-1809. (Aus.) Symphonies (Clock); oratorios; chamber music.
Paul Hindemith, 1895-1963. (U.S.) Das Marienleben; Mathis Der Maler.
Gustav Holst, 1874-1934. (Br.) The Planets, The Hymn of Jesus.
Arthur Honegger, 1892-1955. (Swiss) Judith, Le Roi David, Pacific 231.
Alan Hovhaness, b. 1911. (U.S.) Symphonies, Magnificat.
Engelbert Humperdinck, 1854-1921. (G.) Hansel and Gretel.
Charles Ives, 1874-1954. (U.S.) Third Symphony.
Aram Khachaturian, b. 1903. (R.) Gayane (ballet), symphonies.
Zoltan Kodaly, 1882-1967. (Hung.) Hary Janos, Psalmus Hungaricus.
Fritz Kreisler, 1875-1962. (Aus.) Caprice Viennois, Tambourin Chinois.
Rodolphe Kreutzer, 1766-1831. (F.) 40 etudes for violin.
Edouard V. A. Lalo, 1823-1892. (F.) Fiesque, Symphonie Espagnole.
Ruggiero Leoncavallo, 1858-1919, (It.) I Pagliacci.
Franz Liszt, 1811-1886. (Hung.) 20 Hungarian Rhapsodies; symphonic poems.
Edward MacDowell, 1861-1908. (U.S.) To a Wild Rose.
Gustav Mahler, 1860-1911. (Aus.) Symphonies, Lied von der Erde.
Pietro Mascagni, 1863-1945. (It.) Cavalleria Rusticana.
Jules Massenet, 1842-1912. (F.) Manon, Le Cid, Thais, Don Quixote.
Mendelssohn-Bartholdy, 1809-1847. (G.) Midsummer Night's Dream, Songs Without Words.
Gian-Carlo Menotti, b. 1911. (It.-U.S.) The Medium, The Consul, Amahl and the Night Visitors.
Claudio Monteverdi, 1567-1643. (It.) Opera; masses; madrigals.
Wolfgang Amadeus Mozart, 1756-1791. (Aus.) Magic Flute, Marriage of Figaro; concertos; symphonies, etc.
Modest Moussorgsky, 1835-1881. (R.) Boris Godunov, Pictures at an Exhibition.
Jacques Offenbach, 1819-1880. (F.) Tales of Hoffman (operetta).
Karl Orff, b. 1895 (G.) Carmina Burana.
Ignace Paderewski, 1860-1941 (P.) Minuet in G.

Giovanni P. da Palestrina, 1524-1594. (It.) Masses; madrigals.

Amilcare Ponchielli, 1834-1886. (It.) La Gioconda.

Francis Poulenc, 1899-1963. (F.) La voix humaine, Les animaux modeles.

Serge Prokofiev, 1891-1953. (R.) Love for Three Oranges, Lt. Kije, Peter and the Wolf.

Giancomo Puccini, 1858-1924, (It.) La Boheme, Manon Lescaut, Tosca, Madame Butterfly.

Sergei Rachmaninov, 1873-1943. (R.) Prelude in C Sharp Minor.

Maurice Ravel, 1875-1937. (Fr.) Bolero, Daphne et Chloe. Rapsodie Espagnole.

Nikolai Rimsky-Korsakov, 1844-1908. (R.) Golden Cockerel, Cappriccio Espagnol, Scheherazade, Russian Easter Overture.

Gioacchino Rossini, 1792-1868. (It.) Barber of Seville, Semiramide, William Tell.

Chas. Camille Saint-Saens, 1835-1921. (F.) Samson and Delilah, Danse Macabre.

Alessandro Scarlatti, 1659-1725. (It.) Cantatas; concertos.

Arnold Schoenberg, 1874-1951. (Aus.) Pelleas and Melisande, Transfigured Night, De Profundis.

Franz Schubert, 1797-1828. (A.) Lieder; symphonies (Unfinished); overtures (Rosamunde).

William Schuman, b. 1910. (U.S.) Credendum, New England Triptych.

Robert Schumann, 1810-1856. (G.) Symphonies, songs.

Aleksandr Scriabin, 1872-1915. (R.) Prometheus.

Jean Sibelius, 1865-1957, (Finn.) Finlandia, Karelia.

Dimtri Shostakovich, 1906-1975. (R) Symphonies, Lady Macbeth of Minsk, The Nose.

Bedrich Smetana, 1824-1884. (C.). The Bartered Bride.

Karlheinz Stockhausen, b. 1928. (G.) Kontrapunkte, Kontakte.

Richard Strauss, 1864-1949. (G.) Salome, Elektra, Der Rosenkavalier, Thus Spake Zarathustra.

Igor F. Stravinsky, 1882-1971. (R.-U.S.) Oedipus Rex, Le Sacre du Printemps, Petrushka.

Peter I. Tchaikovsky, 1840-1893. (R.) Nutcracker Suite, Swan Lake, Eugen Onegin.

Ambroise Thomas, 1811-1896. (F.) Mignon.

Ralph Vaughan Williams, 1872-1958, (Br.) Job, London Symphony, Symphony No. 7 (Antarctica).

Giuseppe Verdi, 1813-1901. (It.) Aida, Rigoletto, Don Carlo, Il Trovatore, La Traviata, Falstaff, Macbeth.

Hector Villa Lobos, 1887-1959. (Brazil) Choros.

Antonio Vivaldi, 1669-1741. (It.) Operas and cantatas.

Richard Wagner, 1813-1883. (G.) Rienzi, Tannhauser, Lohengrin, Tristan und Isolde.

Karl Maria von Weber, 1786-1826. (G.) Der Freischutz.

Concert Violinists of the Past

Born	Died	Name	Born	Died	Name	Born	Died	Name
1856	1943	Adamowski, T. . . . . Pol.	1875	1962	Kreisler, Fritz. . . . . Aus.	1815	1894	Sivori, Ern. . . . . . . Ital.
1845	1930	Auer, Leopold. . . . Hung.	1880	1940	Kubelik, Jan. . . . . . Boh.	1888	1953	Spalding, Albert. . . U.S.
1795	1876	Boehm, Jos. . . . . . Czech.	1790	1861	Lipinski, Karl. . . . . . Pol.	1784	1859	Spohr, Ludwig. . . . Ger.
1810	1880	Bull, Ole. . . . . Nor.	1840	1927	Lotto, Isidor. . . . . . . Pol.	1892	1973	Szigeti, Joseph. . . Hung.
1653	1713	Corelli, Arcangelo. Ital.	1722	1793	Nardini, Pietro. . . . . Ital.	1692	1770	Tartini, Gius. . . . . . Ital.
1891	1967	Elman, Mischa. . . . U.S.	1908	1974	Oistrakh, David. . . Rus.	1876	1975	Tertis, Lionel. . . . . Brit.
1881	1955	Enesco, Georges . Rum.	1782	1840	Paganini, Nicolo. . Ital.	1880	1953	Thibaud, Jacq. . . . . Fr.
1667	1762	Geminiani, F. . . . . . Ital.	1868	1920	Powell, Maud. . . . . U.S.	1820	1881	Vieuxtemps, H. . . . Belg.
1716	1796	Giardini, F. di . . . . . Ital.	1830	1898	Remenyi, Edw. . . . Hung.	1753	1824	Viotti, Giovanni. . . . Ital.
1858	1937	Hubay, Jeno. . . . . Hung.	1892	1936	Rigo, Jancsi. . . . . . Hung.	1675	1741	Vivaldi, Antonio . . . Ital.
1882	1947	Huberman, B. . . . . . Pol.	1774	1830	Rode, Jacques . . . . Fr.	1835	1880	Wieniawski, H. . . . . Pol.
1831	1907	Joachim, Joseph . Hung.	1863	1946	Rose, Arnold . . . . . Aus.	1845	1908	Wilhelmj, Aug. . . . . Ger.
1889	1934	Kichanski, Paul. . . Pol.	1844	1908	Sarasate, P.M. . . . . Span.	1858	1931	Ysaye, Eugene. . . Belg.

Composers of Operettas, Musicals and Popular Music

Leroy Anderson, 1908-1975. (U.S.) Syncopated Clock, Typewriter Serenade.

Harold Arlen, b. 1905. (U.S.) Stormy Weather, Over the Rainbow, Blues in the Night, That Old Black Magic.

Burt Bacharach, b. 1928. (U.S.) Raindrops Keep Fallin' on My Head, Walk on By, What the World Needs Now is Love.

Ernest Ball, 1878-1927. (U.S.) Mother Machree, When Irish Eyes are Smiling.

Irving Berlin, b. 1888. (U.S.) Ziegfield Follies; Face the Music; As Thousands Cheer; This is the Army; Annie Get Your Gun; Call Me Madam; God Bless America; White Christmas.

Jerry Bock, b. 1928. (U.S.) Mr. Wonderful; Fiorello; Fiddler on the Roof; The Rothschilds.

Carrie Jacobs Bond, 1862-1946. (U.S.) I Love You Truly.

George M. Cohan, 1878-1942. (U.S.) Give My Regards to Broadway, You're A Grand Old Flag, Over There.

Sherman Edwards, b. 1919. (U.S.) See You in September; Wonderful! Wonderful!

Stephen Collins Foster, 1826-1864. (U.S.) My Old Kentucky Home, Old Folks At Home.

Rudolf Friml, 1879-1972. (naturalized U.S.) The Firefly; Rose Marie; Vagabond King; Bird of Paradise.

John Gay, 1685-1732. (Br.) The Beggar's Opera.

Edwin F. Goldman, 1878-1956. (U.S.) Marches.

Percy Grainger, 1882-1961. (Br.) Country Gardens.

Ferde Grofe, 1892-1972. (U.S.) Grand Canyon Suite.

W. C. Handy, 1873-1958. (U.S.) St. Louis Blues.

Victor Herbert, 1859-1924. (Ir.-U.S.) Mlle. Modiste; Babes in Toyland; The Red Mill; Naughty Marietta; Sweethearts.

Jerry Herman, b. 1932. (U.S.) Milk and Honey; Hello Dolly; Mame; Dear World.

Scott Joplin, 1868-1917 (U.S.) Maple Leaf Rag; Treemonisha.

Jerome Kern, 1885-1945. (U.S.) Sally; Sunny; Show Boat; Cat and the Fiddle; Music in the Air; Roberta.

Burton Lane, b. 1912. (U.S.) Three's a Crowd; Finnian's Rainbow; On A Clear Day You Can See Forever.

Franz Lehar, 1870-1948. (Hung.) Merry Widow.

Mitch Leigh, b. 1928. (U.S.) Man of La Mancha.

Frank Loesser, 1910-1969. (U.S.) Guys and Dolls; Where's Charley?; The Most Happy Fella.

Frederick Loewe, b. 1901. (Aust.-U.S.) The Day Before Spring; Brigadoon, Paint Your Wagon; My Fair Lady; Camelot.

Henry Mancini, b. 1924. (U.S.) Moon River, Days of Wine and Roses, Pink Panther Theme.

Cole Porter, 1893-1964. (U.S.) Anything Goes; Jubilee; Du-Barry Was a Lady; Panama Hattie; Mexican Hayride; Kiss Me Kate; Can Can; Silk Stockings.

Andre Previn, b. 1929. (U.S.) Coco.

Richard Rodgers, b. 1902. (U.S.) Garrick Gaieties; Connecticut Yankee; America's Sweetheart; On Your Toes; Babes in Arms; The Boys from Syracuse; Oklahoma!; Carousel; South Pacific; The King and I; Flower Drum Song; The Sound of Music.

Sigmund Romberg, 1887-1951. (Hung.) Maytime; The Student Prince; Desert Song; Blossom Time.

Harold Rome, b. 1908. (U.S.) Pins and Needles; Call Me Mister; Wish You Were Here; Fanny; Destry Rides Again.

Harry Ruby, 1895-1974. (U.S.) Three Little Words; Who's Sorry Now?

Arthur Schwartz, b. 1900. (U.S.) The Band Wagon, Inside U.S.A., A Tree Grows in Brooklyn.

Stephen Sondheim, b. 1930, (U.S.) Follies; A Little Night Music.

John Philip Sousa, 1854-1932. (U.S.) The Smuggler; Desiree; Queen of Hearts; El Capitan;·The Bride-Elect.

Oley Speaks, 1875-1948. (U.S.) The Road to Mandalay.

Oskar Straus, 1870-1954. (Aus.) Chocolate Soldier.

Johann Strauss, 1825-1899. (Aus.) Gypsy Baron, Die Fledermaus, Waltzes; Blue Danube, Artist's Life.

Charles Strouse, b. 1928. (U.S.) Bye Bye, Birdie; All American; Golden Boy; Applause.

Jule Styne, b. 1905. (b. London-U.S.) Gentlemen Prefer Blondes; Bells Are Ringing; Gypsy; Funny Girl.

Arthur S. Sullivan, 1842-1900. (Br.) H.M.S. Pinafore, Pirates of Penzance. The Mikado (with W. S. Gilbert, 1836-1911, librettist).

Deems Taylor, 1885-1966, (U.S.) Peter Ibbetson.

James Van Heusen, b. 1913. (U.S.) Moonlight Becomes You, Swinging on a Star.

Harry Warren, b. 1893. (U.S.) You're My Everything, We're in the Money, I Only Have Eyes for You, September in the Rain.

Kurt Weill, 1900-1950. (G.-U.S.) Three-Penny Opera; Down in the Valley; Lady in the Dark; Knickerbocker Holiday; One Touch of Venus; Lost in the Stars.

Meredith Willson, b. 1902. (U.S.) The Music Man.

Vincent Youmans, 1898-1946. (U.S.) Two Little Girls in Blue; Wildflower; No, No, Nanette; Hit the Deck; Rainbow; Smiles; Through the Years; Take A Chance.

Entertainment Personalities — Where and When Born

Actors. Actresses, Composers, Dancers, Musicians, Producers, Radio-TV Performers, Singers

Name	Birthplace	Born
A		
Abbott, George	Forestville, N.Y.	1887
Abel, Walter	St. Paul, Minn.	1898
Abner (Norris Goff)	Cove, Ark.	1906
Ackermann, Bettye	Cottageville, S.C.	1928
Acuff, Roy	Maynardsville, Tenn.	1903
Adams, Don	New York, N.Y.	1927
Adams, Edie	Kingston, Pa.	1929
Adams, Joey	New York, N.Y.	1911
Adams, Julie	Waterloo, Iowa	1926
Addams, Dawn	Suffolk, England.	1930
Adler, Kurt H.	Vienna, Austria	1905
Adler, Larry	Baltimore, Md.	1914
Adler, Luther	New York, N.Y.	1903
Agar, John	Chicago, Ill.	1921
Aherne, Brian	Worcestershire, Eng.	1902
Aimee, Anouk	Paris, France	1932
Akins, Claude	Bedford, Ind.	1918
Albanese, Licia	Bari, Italy.	1913
Alberghetti, Anna	Pesaro, Italy.	1936
Albert, Eddie	Rock Island, Ill.	1908
Albertson, Jack	Malden, Mass.	1910
Albright, Lola	Akron, Ohio.	1925
Alda, Alan	New York, N.Y.	1936
Alda, Robert	New York, N.Y.	1914
Alexander, Jane	Boston, Mass.	1939
Alexander, Katherine	Arkansas.	1901
Allan, Elizabeth	England	1910
Allbritton, Louise	Oklahoma City, Okla.	1920
Allen, Mel	Birmingham, Ala.	1913
Allen, Steve	New York, N.Y.	1921
Allen, Woody	Brooklyn, N.Y.	1935
Allison, Fran	LaPorte City, Ia.	—
Allyson, June	Lucerne, N.Y.	1923
Alpert, Herb	Los Angeles, Cal.	1935
Ameche, Don	Kenosha, Wis.	1908
Ames, Ed	Boston, Mass.	1929
Ames, Leon	Portland, Ind.	1903
Ames, Nancy	Washington, D.C.	1937
Amos (F. F. Gosden)	Richmond, Va.	1904
Amos, John	Newark, N.J.	—
Amsterdam, Morey	Chicago, Ill.	1914
Anderson, Judith	Adelaide, Australia.	1898
Anderson, Lynn	Grand Forks, N.D.	1947
Anderson, Marian	Philadelphia, Pa.	1902
Anderson, Mary	Birmingham, Ala.	1922
Anderson, Michael, Jr.	London, England.	1943
Anderson, Warner	Brooklyn, N.Y.	1911
Andersson, Bibi	Stockholm, Sweden.	1935
Andress, Ursula	Switzerland.	1938
Andrews, Dana	Collins, Miss.	1909
Andrews, Edward	Griffin, Ga.	1915
Andrews, Julie	Walton, England	1935
Andrews, Maxene	Minneapolis, Minn.	1918
Andrews, Patty	Minneapolis, Minn.	1920
Angel, Heather	Oxford, England.	1909
Anka, Paul	Ottawa, Canada.	1941
Ann-Margret	Stockholm, Sweden.	1941
Annabella	Paris, France	1912
Ansara, Michael	Lowell, Mass.	1927
Archer, John	Osceola, Neb.	1915
Arden, Eve	Mill Valley, Cal.	1912
Arkin, Alan	New York, N.Y.	1934
Arlen, Richard	Charlottesville, Va.	1900
Arnaz, Desi	Santiago, Cuba.	1917
Arnaz, Desi Jr.	Los Angeles, Cal.	1953
Arnaz, Lucie	Hollywood, Cal.	1951
Arness, James	Minneapolis, Minn.	1923
Arnold, Eddy	Henderson, Tenn.	1918
Arrau, Claudio	Chillau, Chile.	1903
Arroyo, Martina	New York, N.Y.	1937
Arthur, Beatrice	New York, N.Y.	1924
Arthur, Jean	New York, N.Y.	1908
Ashley, Elizabeth	Ocala, Fla.	1941
Asner, Edward	Kansas City, Kan.	1929
Astaire, Fred	Omaha, Neb.	1899
Astin, John	Baltimore, Md.	1930
Astor, Mary	Quincy, Ill.	1906
Atkins, Chet	Luttrell, Tenn.	1924
Attenborough, Richard	Cambridge, Eng.	1923
Aumont, Jean-Pierre	Paris, France	1913
Autry, Gene	Tioga, Texas	1907
Avalon, Frankie	Philadelphia, Pa.	1940

Name	Birthplace	Born
Ayres, Lew	Minneapolis, Minn.	1908
Aznavour, Charles	Paris, France	1924
B		
Bacall, Lauren	New York, N.Y.	1924
Backus, Jim	Cleveland, Ohio.	1913
Baer, Max Jr.	Oakland, Cal.	1937
Baez, Joan	Staten Island, N.Y.	1941
Bailey, Pearl	Newport News, Va.	1918
Bailey, Raymond	San Francisco, Cal.	1904
Bain, Barbara	Chicago, Ill.	1934
Baird, Bill	Grand Island, Neb.	1904
Baker, Carroll	Johnstown, Pa.	1931
Baker, Diane	Hollywood, Cal.	1938
Baker, Kenny	Monrovia, Cal.	1912
Baker, Stanley	Glamorgan, Wales.	1928
Bakewell, William	Hollywood, Cal.	1908
Balanchine, George	St. Petersburg, Russia.	1904
Ball, Lucille	Jamestown, N.Y.	1911
Ballard, Kay	Cleveland, Ohio.	1926
Balsam, Martin	New York, N.Y.	1919
Bampton, Rose	Cleveland, Ohio.	1909
Bancroft, Anne	New York, N.Y.	1931
Bannon, Ian	Airdrie, Scotland.	1928
Barber, Red	Columbus, Miss.	1908
Bardot, Brigitte	Paris, France	1934
Bari, Lynn	Roanoke, Va.	1917
Barnett, Vincent	Pittsburgh, Pa.	1902
Barrault, Jean-Louise	Le Vesinet, France.	1910
Barrett, Sheila	Washington, D. C.	1909
Barrie, Mona	London, Eng.	1909
Barrie, Wendy	Hong Kong, China.	1913
Barry, Gene	New York, N.Y.	1922
Barry, Jack	Lindenhurst, N.Y.	1918
Barrymore, John, Jr.	Beverly Hills, Cal.	1932
Bartholomew, Freddie	London, England.	1924
Bartok, Eva	Budapest, Hungary.	1929
Basehart, Richard	Zanesville, Ohio.	1914
Basie, Count (Wm.)	Red Bank, N.J.	1904
Bassey, Shirley	Cardiff, Wales.	1937
Bates, Alan	Allestree, Eng.	1934
Baum, Kurt	Cologne, Germany.	1908
Bavier, Frances	New York, N.Y.	1905
Baxter, Anne	Michigan City, Ind.	1923
Beal, John	Joplin, Mo.	1909
Bean, Orson	Cambridge, Mass.	1928
Beatty, Robert	Hamilton, Ont.	1909
Beatty, Warren	Richmond, Va.	1938
Becker, Sandy	New York, N.Y.	1922
Bedelia, Bonnie	New York, N.Y.	1948
Beery, Noah, Jr.	New York, N.Y.	1916
Belafonte, Harry	New York, N.Y.	1927
Bel Geddes, Barbara	New York, N.Y.	1922
Bellamy, Ralph	Chicago, Ill.	1904
Belmondo, Jean-Paul	Neuilly-sur-Seine, Fr.	1933
Benjamin, Dick	New York, N.Y.	1939
Bennett, Joan	Palisades, N.J.	1910
Bennett, Tony	Astoria, N.Y.	1926
Bentley, John	Warwickshire, England	1916
Bergen, Candice	Beverly Hills, Cal.	1946
Bergen, Edgar	Chicago, Ill.	1903
Bergen, Polly	Knoxville, Tenn.	1930
Berger, Senta	Vienna, Austria	1941
Bergerac, Jacques	France	1927
Bergman, Ingmar	Uppsala, Sweden.	1918
Bergman, Ingrid	Stockholm, Sweden.	1915
Bergner, Elisabeth	Vienna, Austria	1900
Berkeley, Busby	Los Angeles, Cal.	1895
Berle, Milton	New York, N.Y.	1908
Berlinger, Warren	Brooklyn, N.Y.	1937
Berman, Shelley	Chicago, Ill.	1926
Bernardi, Hershel	New York, N.Y.	1923
Bernstein, Elmer	New York, N.Y.	1922
Bernstein, Leonard	Lawrence, Mass.	1918
Berry, Ken	Moline, Ill.	—
Bessell, Ted	Flushing, N.Y.	1935
Bikel, Theodore	Vienna, Austria	1924
Birney, David	Washington, D.C.	
Bishop, Joey	Bronx, N.Y.	1918
Bisset, Jacqueline	Weybridge, England	1944
Bixby, Bill	San Francisco, Cal.	1934
Black, Karen	Park Ridge, Ill.	1942
Blaine, Vivian	Newark, N.J.	1924
Blair, Janet	Altoona, Pa.	1921
Blair, Linda	Westport, Conn.	1959

Name	Birthplace	Born	Name	Birthplace	Born
Blake, Robert	Nutley, N.J.	1938	Cannon, Dyan	Tacoma, Wash.	1937
Blanc, Mel	San Francisco, Cal.	1908	Canova, Judy	Jacksonville, Fla.	1916
Bloch, Ray	Alsace-Lorraine	1902	Cantinflas	Mexico City, Mex.	1917
Blondell, Joan	New York, N.Y.	1912	Cantrell, Lana	Sydney, Aust.	1944
Bloom, Claire	London, England	1931	Capra, Frank	Palermo, Italy	1897
Blyth, Ann	Mt. Kisco, N.Y.	1928	Cardinale, Claudia	Tunisia	1939
Bottoms, Timothy	Santa Barbara, Cal.	1951	Carey, Macdonald	Sioux City, Ia.	1913
Boehm, Karl	Graz, Austria	1894	Carey, Phil	Hackensack, N.J.	1925
Bogarde, Dirk	London, England	1921	Carle, Frankie	Providence, R.I.	1903
Bolger, Ray	Boston, Mass.	1904	Carlisle, Kitty	New Orleans, La.	1915
Bonaduce, Danny	Philadelphia, Pa.	1959	Carlson, Richard	Alberta Lea, Minn.	1914
Bond, Sheila	New York, N.Y.	1928	Carmichael, Hoagy	Bloomington, Ind.	1899
Bondi, Beulah	Chicago, Ill.	1892	Carmichael, Ian	Hull, England	1920
Bono, Sonny	Detroit, Mich.	1940	Carne, Judy	Northampton, England.	1939
Boone, Pat	Jacksonville, Fla.	1934	Carney, Art	Mt. Vernon, N.Y.	1918
Boone, Richard	Los Angeles, Cal.	1917	Carnovsky, Morris	St. Louis, Mo.	1897
Booth, Shirley	New York, N.Y.	1909	Caron, Leslie	Boulogne, France	1931
Borge, Victor	Copenhagen, Denmark.	1909	Carpenter, Karen	New Haven, Conn.	1950
Borgnine, Ernest	Hamden, Conn.	1917	Carpenter, Richard	New Haven, Conn.	1946
Bosley, Tom	Chicago, Ill.	1927	Carr, Vicki	El Paso, Tex.	1942
Boswell, Connee	New Orleans, La.	—	Carradine, David	Hollywood, Cal.	1945
Bowman, Lee	Cincinnati, Ohio	1914	Carradine, John	New York, N.Y.	1906
Boyd, Stephen	Belfast, Ireland	1928	Carroll, Diahann	Bronx, N.Y.	1935
Boyer, Charles	Figeac, France	1899	Carroll, Madeleine	W. Bromwich, England.	1906
Bracken, Eddie	Astoria, N.Y.	1920	Carroll, Pat	Shreveport, La.	1927
Brand, Neville	Kewanee, Ill.	1921	Carson, Jeannie	Yorkshire, England	1929
Brando, Marlon	Omaha, Neb.	1924	Carson, Johnny	Corning, Ia.	1925
Brasselle, Keefe	Elyria, Ohio	1923	Carson, Mindy	New York, N.Y.	1927
Brazzi, Rossano	Bologna, Italy	1916	Carter, Jack	New York, N.Y.	1923
Brennan, Eileen	Los Angeles, Cal.	1937	Casadesus, Gaby	Marseilles, France	1902
Brent, Evelyn	Tampa, Fla.	1899	Cash, Johnny	Kingsland, Ark.	1932
Brent, George	Dublin, Ireland	1904	Cass, Peggy	Boston, Mass.	1926
Brewer, Teresa	Toledo, Ohio	1931	Cassavetes, John	New York, N.Y.	1929
Brian, David	New York, N.Y.	1914	Cassidy, David	New York, N.Y.	1950
Bridges, Beau	Hollywood, Cal.	1941	Cassidy, Jack	New York, N.Y.	1927
Bridges, Lloyd	San Leandro, Cal.	1913	Cassidy, Ted	Pittsburgh, Pa.	1932
Britton, Barbara	Long Beach, Cal.	1923	Castellano, Richard	New York, N.Y.	1933
Brolin, James	Los Angeles, Cal.	1942	Caulfield, Joan	West Orange, N.J.	1922
Bronson, Charles	Scooptown, Pa.	1921	Cavallaro, Carmen	New York, N.Y.	1913
Brooks, Louise	Cherryvale, Kansas	1906	Cavett, Dick	Kearny, Neb.	1937
Brooks, Mel	New York, N.Y.	1926	Chamberlain, Richard	Beverly Hills, Cal.	1935
Brooks, Stephen	Columbus, Ohio	1942	Champion, Gower	Geneva, Ill.	1921
Brothers, Joyce	New York, N.Y.	1928	Champion, Marge	Los Angeles, Cal.	1926
Brown, James	Augusta, Ga.	1934	Channing, Carol	Seattle, Wash.	1923
Brown, Jimmy	St. Simons Island, Ga.	1936	Chaplin, Charles	London, England.	1889
Brown, Les	Reinerton, Pa.	1912	Chaplin, Geraldine	Santa Monica, Cal.	1944
Brown, Tom	New York, N.Y.	1913	Chaplin, Sydney	Beverly Hills, Cal.	1926
Brown, Vanessa	Vienna, Austria	1928	Charisse, Cyd	Amarillo, Tex.	1923
Brubeck, Dave	Concord, Cal.	1920	Charles, Ray	Albany, Ga.	1930
Bruce, Carol	Great Neck, N.Y.	1919	Chase, Ilka	New York, N.Y.	1905
Bruce, Virginia	Minneapolis, Minn.	1910	Checker, Chubby	Philadelphia, Pa.	1941
Bryant, Anita	Barnsdale, Okla.	1940	Cher	El Centro, Cal.	1946
Brynner, Yul	Sakhalin, Japan	1920	Christian, Linda	Tampico, Mexico.	1924
Bubbles, John	Louisville, Ky.	1903	Christie, Audrey	Chicago, Ill.	1912
Buchanan, Edgar	Humansville, Mo.	1903	Christie, Julie	Chukur, India	1940
Bucholz, Horst	Berlin, Germany.	1933	Christopher, Jordon	Youngstown, Ohio	1941
Bujold, Genevieve	Canada	1942	Christy, June	Springfield, Ill.	1925
Burke, Paul	New Orleans, La.	1926	Cilento, Diane	Queensland, Australia	1933
Burnett, Carol	San Antonio, Tex.	1936	Claire, Ina	Washington, D.C.	1892
Burns, George	New York, N.Y.	1896	Clark, Dane	New York, N.Y.	1913
Burr, Raymond	New Westminster, B.C.	1917	Clark, Dick	Mt. Vernon, N.Y.	1929
Burrows, Abe	New York, N.Y.	1910	Clark, Petula	Ewell, Surrey, England.	1934
Burstyn, Ellen	Detroit, Mich.	1932	Clark, Roy	Meherrin, Va.	1933
Burton, Richard	South Wales	1925	Clayton, Jan	Tularosa, N. M.	1925
Bushell, Anthony	Kent, England	1904	Cliburn, Van	Shreveport, La.	1934
Buttons, Red	New York, N.Y.	1919	Clooney, Rosemary	Maysville, Ky.	1928
Buzzell, Eddie	Brooklyn, N.Y.	1897	Cobb, Lee J.	New York, N.Y.	1911
Buzzi, Ruth	Westerly, R.I.	1936	Coburn, James	Laurel, Neb.	1928
			Coca, Imogene	Philadelphia, Pa.	1920
			Coco, James	New York, N.Y.	1929
C			Cohen, Myron	Grodno, Poland.	1902
			Colbert, Claudette	Paris, France	1907
Caan, James	New York, N.Y.	1940	Cole, Dennis	Detroit, Mich.	1943
Cabot, Sebastian	London, England.	1918	Cole, Michael	Madison, Wis.	1945
Caesar, Sid	Yonkers, N.Y.	1922	Cole, Tina	Hollywood, Cal.	1943
Cagney, James	New York, N.Y.	1899	Collins, Dorothy	Windsor, Ontario.	1926
Caine, Michael	London, England.	1933	Collins, Joan	London, England.	1933
Caldwell, Zoe	Melbourne, Australia.	1933	Collins, Judy	Seattle, Wash.	1939
Calhoun, Rory	Los Angeles, Cal.	1922	Colonna, Jerry	Boston, Mass.	1903
Callahan, James	Grand Rapids, Mich.	1930	Como, Perry	Canonsburg, Pa.	1912
Callan, Michael	Philadelphia, Pa.	1935	Conklin, Peggy	Dobbs Ferry, N.Y.	1912
Callas, Maria	New York, N.Y.	1923	Conley, Eugene	Lynn, Mass.	1908
Calloway, Cab	Rochester, N.Y.	1907	Conner, Nadine	Compton, Cal.	1913
Calvert, Phyllis	London, England.	1917	Connery, Sean	Edinburgh, Scotland	1930
Calvet, Corinne	Paris, France	1926	Conniff, Ray	Attleboro, Mass.	1916
Cambridge, Godfrey	New York, N.Y.	1933	Connors, Chuck	Brooklyn, N.Y.	1921
Cameron, Rod	Calgary, Canada.	1912	Connors, Michael	Fresno, Cal.	1925
Campbell, Glen	Billstown, Ark.	1936	Conrad, Robert	Chicago, Ill.	1935
Canary, David	Elwood, Ind.	1938	Conrad, William	Louisville, Ky.	1920

Name	Birthplace	Born
Conried, Hans	Baltimore, Mo.	1917
Considine, Tim	Los Angeles, Cal.	1940
Converse, Frank	St. Louis, Mo.	1938
Conway, Gary	Boston, Mass.	1938
Conway, Shirl	Franklinville, N.Y.	1916
Conway, Tim	Chagrin Falls, Ohio	1933
Coogan, Jackie	Los Angeles, Cal.	1914
Cook, Barbara	Atlanta, Ga.	1927
Cooke, Alistair	England	1908
Cooper, Jackie	Los Angeles, Cal.	1922
Corey, Jeff	New York, N.Y.	1914
Cornell, Don	New York, N.Y.	1921
Cortez, Ricardo	Vienna, Austria	1899
Cosby, Bill	Philadelphia, Pa.	1937
Cosell, Howard	Winston-Salem, N.C.	1920
Costello, Dolores	Pittsburgh, Pa.	1905
Cotsworth, Staats	Oak Park, Ill.	1908
Cotten, Joseph	Petersburg, Va.	1905
Courtenay, Tom	Hull, England	1937
Crabbe, Buster	Oakland, Cal.	1907
Crain, Jeanne	Barstow, Cal.	1925
Crane, Bob	Waterbury, Conn.	1928
Crane, Les	New York, N.Y.	1934
Crawford, Broderick	Philadelphia, Pa.	1911
Crawford, Joan	San Antonio, Tex.	1908
Crawford, Michael	Salisbury, England	1942
Crenna, Richard	Los Angeles, Cal.	1927
Cristal, Linda	Argentina	1936
Cronyn, Hume	London, Ontario	1911
Crosby, Bing (Harry)	Tacoma, Wash.	1904
Crosby, Bob	Spokane, Wash.	1913
Crowley, Pat	Scranton, Pa.	1929
Cruz, Brandon	Bakersfield, Cal.	1962
Cugat, Xavier	Barcelona, Spain	1900
Cullen, Bill	Pittsburgh, Pa.	1920
Cullum, John	Knoxville, Tenn.	1930
Culp, Robert	Berkeley, Cal.	1930
Cummings, Constance	Seattle, Wash.	1910
Cummings, Robert	Joplin, Mo.	1910
Cummins, Peggy	Prestatyn, N. Wales	1925
Curtin, Phyllis	Clarksburg, W. Va.	1930
Curtis, Ken	Lamar, Col.	1916
Curtis, Tony	New York, N.Y.	1925
Cusack, Cyril	Durban, So. Africa	1910
Cushing, Peter	Surrey, England	1913

D

Name	Birthplace	Born
Dagmar (Egnor)	Huntington, W.Va.	1926
Dahl, Arlene	Minneapolis, Minn.	1927
Dailey, Dan	New York, N.Y.	1917
Dalrymple, Jean	Morristown, N.J.	1910
Dalton, Abby	Las Vegas, Nev.	1935
Daly, James	Wisconsin Rapids, Wis.	1918
Daly, John	Johannesburg, S. Africa	1914
Damita, Lili	Paris, France	1907
Damone, Vic	Brooklyn, N.Y.	1928
Dana, Bill	Quincy, Mass.	1924
Dangerfield, Rodney	Babylon, N.Y.	1921
Daniels, William	Brooklyn, N.Y.	1927
Danilova, Alexandra	Peterhof, Russia	1907
Danton, Ray	New York, N.Y.	1931
Darby, Kim	Hollywood, Cal.	1948
Darcel, Denise	Paris, France	1925
Darren, James	Philadelphia, Pa.	1936
Darrieux, Danielle	Bordeaux, France	1917
Darrow, Henry	New York, N.Y.	1933
Da Silva, Howard	Cleveland, Ohio	1909
Dassin, Jules	Middletown, Conn.	1911
Dauphin, Claude	Corbeil, France	1905
Davidson, John	Pittsburgh, Pa.	1941
Davis, Ann B.	Schenectady, N.Y.	1926
Davis, Bette	Lowell, Mass.	1908
Davis, Clifton	Chicago, Ill.	1945
Davis, Miles	Alton, Ill.	1927
Davis, Sammy, Jr.	New York, N.Y.	1925
Davis, Ossie	Cogdell, Ga.	1917
Dawn, Hazel	Ogden, Utah	1898
Day, Dennis	New York, N.Y.	1917
Day, Doris	Cincinnati, Ohio	1924
Day, Laraine	Roosevelt, Ut.	1920
Dean, Jimmy	Plainview, Tex.	1928
De Camp, Rosemary	Prescott, Ariz.	1913
De Carlo, Yvonne	Vancouver, B. C.	1924
Dee, Frances	Los Angeles, Cal.	1907
Dee, Joey	Passaic, N.J.	1940
Dee, Ruby	Cleveland, Ohio	1924
Dee, Sandra	Bayonne, N.J.	1942
DeFore, Don	Cedar Rapids, Ia.	1917

Name	Birthplace	Born
DeHaven, Gloria	Los Angeles, Cal.	1925
deHavilland, Olivia	Tokyo, Japan	1916
Dell, Gabriel	Brooklyn, N.Y.	1921
Della Chiese, Vivienna	Chicago, Ill.	1920
Delon, Alain	France	1935
DeLuise, Dom	Brooklyn, N.Y.	1933
Del Rio, Dolores	Durango, Mexico	1905
Demarest, William	St. Paul, Minn.	1892
De Mille, Agnes	New York, N.Y.	1905
Dempster, Carol	Duluth, Minn.	1901
Deneuve, Catherine	Paris, France	1943
Denning, Richard	Poughkeepsie, N.Y.	1914
Dennis, Sandy	Hastings, Neb.	1937
Denver, Bob	New Rochelle, N.Y.	1935
Derek, John	Hollywood, Cal.	1926
Dern, Bruce	Chicago, Ill.	1936
Desmond, Johnny	Detroit, Mich.	1921
Devine, Andy	Flagstaff, Ariz.	1905
Dewhurst, Colleen	Montreal, Canada	1926
Diamond, Neil	Brooklyn, N.Y.	1941
Dickinson, Angie	Kulm, N. D.	1936
Dietrich, Marlene	Berlin, Germany	1901
Diller, Phyllis	Lima, Ohio	1917
Dillman, Bradford	San Francisco, Cal.	1930
Dixon, Ivan	New York, N.Y.	1931
Domino, Fats	New Orleans, La.	1928
Donahue, Troy	New York, N.Y.	1936
Donald, James	Aberdeen, Scotland	1917
Donald, Peter	Bristol, England	1918
Donnelly, Ruth	Trenton, N.J.	1896
Donovan	Glasgow, Scotland	1946
Dors, Diana	Swindon, England	1931
d'Orsay, Fifi	Montreal, Canada	1908
Douglas, Donna	Baywood, La.	1939
Douglas, Kirk	Amsterdam, N.Y.	1918
Douglas, Melvyn	Macon, Ga.	1901
Douglas, Michael	New Brunswick, N.J.	1945
Douglas, Mike	Chicago, Ill.	1925
Downey, Morton	Wallingford, Conn.	1902
Downs, Hugh	Akron, Ohio	1921
Dragonette, Jessica	Calcutta, India	—
Drake, Alfred	Bronx, N.Y.	1914
Drake, Betsy	Paris, France	1923
Drew, Ellen	Kansas City, Mo.	1915
Dreyfuss, Richard	Brooklyn, N.Y.	—
Dru, Joanne	Logan, W.Va.	1923
Drury, James	New York, N.Y.	1934
Duchin, Peter	New York, N.Y.	1937
Duff, Howard	Bremerton, Wash.	1917
Duke, Patty	New York, N.Y.	1946
Dullea, Keir	Cleveland, Ohio	1936
Dunaway, Faye	Bascom, Fla.	1941
Duncan, Sandy	Henderson, Texas	1946
Duncan, Todd	Danville, Ky.	1900
Duncan, Vivian	Los Angeles, Cal.	1902
Dunham, Katherine	Chicago, Ill.	1910
Dunne, Irene	Louisville, Ky.	1904
Dunnock, Mildred	Baltimore, Md.	1906
Durante, Jimmy	New York, N.Y.	1893
Durbin, Deanna	Winnipeg, Canada	1922
Duvall, Robert	San Diego, Cal.	1931
Dvorak, Ann	New York, N.Y.	1912
Dylan, Bob	Duluth, Minn.	1941

E

Name	Birthplace	Born
Eastwood, Clint	San Francisco, Cal.	1930
Eaton, Shirley	London, England	1937
Ebsen, Buddy	Belleville, Ill.	1908
Eckstine, Billy	Pittsburgh, Pa.	1914
Edelman, Herb	Brooklyn, N.Y.	1933
Eden, Barbara	Tucson, Ariz.	1934
Edwards, Ralph	Merino, Col.	1913
Edwards, Vincent	Brooklyn, N.Y.	1928
Egan, Richard	San Francisco, Cal.	1923
Eggar, Samantha	London, England	1939
Eggerth, Marta	Budapest, Hungary	1916
Ekberg, Anita	Malmo, Sweden	1931
Ekland, Britt	Stockholm, Sweden	1942
Elam, Jack	Phoenix, Ariz.	—
Eldridge, Florence	Brooklyn, N.Y.	1901
Elgart, Larry	New London, Conn.	1922
Elgart, Les	New Haven, Conn.	1918
Elliott, Bob	Boston, Mass.	1923
Emerson, Faye	Elizabeth, La.	1917
Erickson, Leif	Alameda, Cal.	1911
Esmond, Jill	London, England	1908
Etting, Ruth	David City, Neb.	1896
Evans, Dale	Uvalde, Tex.	1912

Name	Birthplace	Born
Evans, Dame Edith	London, England	1888
Evans, Maurice	Dorchester, England	1901
Everett, Chad	South Bend, Ind.	1937
Evers, Jason	New York, N.Y.	1927
Ewell, Tom	Owensboro, Ky.	1909

F

Name	Birthplace	Born
Fabares, Shelley	Santa Monica, Cal.	1944
Fabian (Forte)	Philadelphia, Pa.	1943
Fabray, Nanette	San Diego, Cal.	1920
Fadiman, Clifton	Brooklyn, N.Y.	1904
Fairbanks, Doug, Jr.	New York, N.Y.	1909
Faith, Percy	Toronto, Ontario.	1908
Falk, Peter	New York, N.Y.	1927
Falkenburg, Jinx	Barcelona, Spain	1919
Farber, Barry	Baltimore, Md.	1930
Farentino, James	Brooklyn, N.Y.	1938
Fargo, Donna	Mt. Airy, N.C.	1945
Farr, Felicia	Westchester, N.Y.	1932
Farrell, Charles	Onset Bay, Mass.	1901
Farrell, Eileen	Willimantic, Conn.	1920
Farrow, Mia	Los Angeles, Cal.	1946
Faye, Alice	New York, N.Y.	1915
Feld, Fritz	Berlin, Germany	1900
Feldon, Barbara	Pittsburgh, Pa.	1941
Feliciano, Jose	Puerto Rico	1945
Fellini, Federico	Rimini, Italy	1920
Fellows, Edith	Boston, Mass.	1923
Feldman, Marty	England	1933
Ferrer, Jose	Santurce, P.R.	1912
Ferrer, Mel	Elberon, N.J.	1917
Ferris, Barbara	London, England.	1942
Fetchit, Stepin	Key West, Fla.	1902
Fiedler, Arthur	Boston, Mass.	1894
Field, Sally	Pasadena, Cal.	1946
Fields, Gracie	Rochdale, England	1898
Fields, Totie	Hartford, Conn.	1931
Finch, Peter	London, England.	1916
Finney, Albert	Salford, England	1936
Firkusny, Rudolf	Napajedla, Czechoslovakia	1912
Fisher, Eddie	Philadelphia, Pa.	1928
Fisher, Gail	Orange, N.J.	—
Fitzgerald, Ella	Newport News, Va.	1918
Fitzgerald, Geraldine	Dublin, Ireland.	1914
Fitzgerald, Pegeen	Norcatur, Kan.	1910
Fix, Paul	Dobbs Ferry, N.Y.	1902
Flack, Roberta	Black Mountain, N.C.	1940
Flatt, Lester	Overton County, Tenn.	1914
Fleming, Rhonda	Hollywood, Cal.	1923
Foch, Nina	Leyden, Netherlands.	1924
Fonda, Henry	Grand Island, Neb.	1905
Fonda, Jane	New York, N.Y.	1937
Fonda, Peter	New York, N.Y.	1939
Fontaine, Frank	Cambridge, Mass.	1920
Fontaine, Joan	Tokyo, Japan	1917
Fontanne, Lynn	London, England.	1887
Fonteyn, Margot	Reigate, England	1919
Foran, Dick	Flemington, N.J.	1910
Forbes, Bryan	London, England.	1926
Ford (Tenn.), Ernie	Bristol, Tenn.	1919
Ford, Glenn	Quebec, Canada.	1916
Ford, Paul	Baltimore, Md.	1901
Ford, Ruth	Hazelhurst, Miss.	1915
Forrest, Sally	San Diego, Cal.	1928
Forrest, Steve	Huntsville, Tex.	1925
Forster, Robert	Rochester, N.Y.	1942
Forsythe, John	Penns Grove, N.J.	1918
Fosse, Bob	Chicago, Ill.	1927
Foster, Phil	Brooklyn, N.Y.	1914
Fountain, Pete	New Orleans, La.	1930
Fox, James	London, England.	1939
Foxx, Redd	St. Louis, Mo.	1922
Foy, Eddie, Jr.	New Rochelle, N.Y.	1905
Francescatti, Zino	Marseilles, France	1904
Franciosa, Anthony	New York, N.Y.	1928
Francis, Arlene	Boston, Mass.	1908
Francis, Connie	Newark, N.J.	1938
Franciscus, James	Clayton, Mo.	1934
Frankenheimer, John.	Malba, N.Y.	1930
Franklin, Aretha	Memphis, Tenn.	1942
Franklin, Joe	New York, N.Y.	1926
Franz, Arthur	Perth Amboy, N.J.	1920
Freberg, Stan	Pasadena, Cal.	1926
Freed, Bert	New York, N.Y.	1919
Freeman, Mona	Baltimore, Md.	1926
Froman, Jane	St. Louis, Mo.	1911
Frost, David	Tenterden, England.	1939

Name	Birthplace	Born
Frye, David	Brooklyn, N.Y.	1934
Funicello, Annette	Utica, N.Y.	1942
Funt, Allen	New York, N.Y.	1914
Furness, Betty	New York, N.Y.	1916

G

Name	Birthplace	Born
Gabel, Martin	Philadelphia, Pa.	1912
Gabin, Jean	Villette, Paris, France.	1904
Gabor, Eva	Hungary	1921
Gabor, Zsa Zsa	Hungary	1919
Gahagan, Helen	Boonton, N.J.	1900
Galloway, Don	Brooksville, Ky.	1937
Gam, Rita	Pittsburgh, Pa.	1929
Gambling, John	New York, N.Y.	1930
Garagiola, Joe	St. Louis, Mo.	1926
Garbo, Greta	Stockholm, Sweden.	1905
Gardenia, Vincent	Naples, Italy	1922
Gardiner, Reginald	Wimbledon, England.	1903
Gardner, Ava	Smithfield, N.C.	1922
Gardner, Hy	New York, N.Y.	1908
Gargan, William	Brooklyn, N.Y.	1905
Garfunkel, Art	New York, N.Y.	1941
Garland, Beverly	Santa Cruz, Cal.	1930
Garner, Erroll	Pittsburgh, Pa.	1923
Garner, James	Norman, Okla.	1928
Garner, Peggy Ann	Canton, Ohio.	1932
Garrett, Betty	St. Joseph, Mo.	1919
Garroway, Dave	Schenectady, N.Y.	1913
Garson, Greer	Co. Down, N. Ireland.	1908
Garver, Kathy	Long Beach, Cal.	1948
Gary, John	Watertown, N.Y.	1932
Gavin, John	Los Angeles, Cal.	1932
Gaynor, Janet	Philadelphia, Pa.	1906
Gaynor, Mitzi	Chicago, Ill.	1931
Gazzara, Ben	New York, N.Y.	1930
Gedda, Nicolai	Sweden.	1925
Geer, Will	Frankfort, Ind.	1902
Geeson, Judy	Sussex, England.	1948
Genevieve (G. Auger).	Paris, France	1930
Genn, Leo	London, England.	1905
Gennaro, Peter	Metairie, La.	1924
Gentry, Bobby	Chickasaw Co., Miss.	1944
Getz, Stan	Philadelphia, Pa.	1927
Ghostley, Alice	Eve, Mo.	1926
Gibson, Henry	Germantown, Pa.	1935
Gielgud, John	London, England.	1904
Gifford, Frank	Santa Monica, Cal.	1930
Gilford, Jack	New York, N.Y.	1907
Gillespie, Dizzy	Cheraw, N.C.	1917
Gillette, Anita	Baltimore, Md.	1936
Gingold, Hermione	London, England.	1897
Gish, Lillian	Springfield, Ohio	1896
Givot, George	Omaha, Neb.	1903
Gleason, Jackie	Brooklyn, N.Y.	1916
Gobel, George	Chicago, Ill.	1919
Godard, Jean Luc	Paris, France	1930
Goddard, Paulette	Great Neck, N.Y.	1911
Godfrey, Arthur	New York, N.Y.	1903
Goldsboro, Bobby	Marianne, Fla.	1941
Goodman, Benny	Chicago, Ill.	1909
Gordon, Gale	New York, N.Y.	1906
Gordon, Max	New York, N.Y.	1892
Gordon, Ruth	Wollaston, Mass.	1896
Gorin, Igor	Ukraine, Russia	1909
Gorme, Eydie	Bronx, N.Y.	1932
Gorshin, Frank	Pittsburgh, Pa.	1935
Gortner, Marjoe	Long Beach, Cal.	1945
Gould, Elliot	Brooklyn, N.Y.	1938
Gould, Morton	Richmond Hill, N.Y.	1913
Goulding, Ray	Lowell, Mass.	1922
Goulet, Robert	Lawrence, Mass.	1933
Gowdy, Curt	Green River, Wy.	1919
Grady, Don	San Diego, Cal.	1944
Graham, Martha	Pittsburgh, Pa.	1902
Graham, Virginia	Chicago, Ill.	1913
Grahame, Gloria	Los Angeles, Cal.	1929
Grahame, Margot	Canterbury, England.	1911
Granger, Farley	San Jose, Cal.	1925
Granger, Stewart	London, England.	1913
Granville, Bonita	New York, N.Y.	1923
Grant, Cary	Bristol, England.	1904
Grant, Kathryn	Houston, Tex.	1933
Grant, Lee	New York, N.Y.	1927
Grauer, Ben	New York, N.Y.	1908
Graves, Peter	Minneapolis, Minn.	1926
Gray, Coleen	Staplehurst, Neb.	1922
Gray, Dolores	Chicago, Ill.	1924
Grayson, Kathryn	Winston-Salem, N.C.	1923
Graziano, Rocky	New York, N.Y.	1922

Name	Birthplace	Born
Greco, Buddy	Philadelphia, Pa.	1926
Greco, Jose	Abruzzi, Italy	1918
Greco, Juliette	Paris, France	—
Greene, Lorne	Ottawa, Canada	1915
Greenwood, Charlotte	Philadelphia, Pa.	1893
Greenwood, Joan	London, England.	1921
Greer, Jane	Washington, D.C.	1924
Gregory, Dick	St. Louis, Mo.	1933
Grey, Joel	Cleveland, Ohio	1932
Griffin, Merv	San Mateo, Cal.	1925
Griffith, Andy	Mount Airy, N.C.	1926
Griffith, Hugh	Wales.	1912
Grimes, Tammy	Lynn, Mass.	1936
Grizzard, George	Roanoke Rapids, N.C.	1928
Guardino, Harry	New York, N.Y.	1925
Guinness, Alec	London, England.	1914
Gunn, Moses	St. Louis, Mo.	1929
Guthrie, Arlo	New York, N.Y.	1947

H

Name	Birthplace	Born
Hackett, Buddy	Brooklyn, N.Y.	1924
Hackett, Joan	New York, N.Y.	1933
Hackman, Gene	San Bernardino, Cal.	1931
Hagen, Uta	Gottingen, Germany	1919
Haggard, Merle	Bakersfield, Cal.	1937
Hagman, Larry	Ft. Worth, Tex.	1931
Hale, Barbara	DeKalb, Ill.	1922
Haley, Jack	Boston, Mass.	1899
Hall, Huntz	New York, N.Y.	1920
Hall, Monty	Winnipeg, Canada	1923
Hall, Tom T.	Olive Hill, Ky.	1936
Hamilton, George	Memphis, Tenn.	1939
Hamilton, Margaret	Cleveland, Ohio	1902
Hamilton, Neil	Lynn, Mass.	1899
Hampshire, Susan	London, England.	1941
Hampton, Lionel	Birmingham, Ala.	1914
Hampton, Ruth	Throop, Pa.	1932
Hanley, Bridget	Minneapolis, Minn.	1943
Hanson, Howard	Wahoo, Neb.	1896
Harding, Ann	Ft. Sam Houston, Tex.	1904
Harper, Ron	Turtle Creek, Pa.	1935
Harper, Valarie	Suffern, N.Y.	—
Harrington, Pat, Jr.	New York, N.Y.	1929
Harris, Barbara	Evanston, Ill.	1935
Harris, Julie	Grosse Pte. Park, Mich.	1925
Harris, Phil	Linton, Ind.	1906
Harris, Richard	Co. Limerick, Ireland.	1933
Harris, Rosemary	Ashby, England.	1930
Harrison, George	Liverpool, England.	1943
Harrison, Noel	London, England.	1933
Harrison, Rex	Huyton, England	1908
Hartman, David	Pawtucket, R.I.	1935
Hartman, Elizabeth	Boardman, Ohio.	1943
Hartman, Paul	San Francisco, Cal.	1904
Hasso, Signe	Stockholm, Sweden.	1915
Haver, June	Rock Island, Ill.	1926
Havoc, June	Vancouver, Canada.	1916
Hawn, Goldie	Washington, D.C.	1945
Haworth, Jill	Sussex, England.	1945
Hayden, Melissa	Toronto, Canada.	1928
Hayden, Russell	Chico, Cal.	1912
Hayden, Sterling	Montclair, N.Y.	1916
Haydon, Julie	Oak Park, Ill.	1910
Hayes, Helen	Washington, D.C.	1900
Hayes, Isaac	Covington, Tenn.	1942
Hayes, Peter Lind	San Francisco, Cal.	1915
Hayes, Roland	Curryville, Ga.	1887
Haymes, Dick	Buenos Aires, Argentina	1918
Haynes, Lloyd	South Bend, Ind.	1934
Hayward, Louis	Johannesburg, S. Africa.	1909
Hayworth, Rita	New York, N.Y.	1918
Healy, Mary	New Orleans, La.	1918
Heatherton, Joey	Rockville Centre, N.Y.	1944
Heckart, Eileen	Columbus, Ohio.	1919
Hefner, Hugh	Chicago, Ill.	1926
Heifetz, Jascha	Vilna, Russia.	1901
Helmore, Tom	London, England.	1912
Helpmann, Robert	Mt. Gambier, Australia.	1909
Henderson, Florence	Dale, Ind.	1934
Henderson, Marcia	Andover, Mass.	1932
Henderson, Skitch	Halstad, Minn.	1918
Henning, David	Guildford, England.	1941
Henning, Linda Kaye	Toluca Lake, Cal.	1944
Henreid, Paul	Trieste, Italy	1908
Hepburn, Audrey	Brussels, Belgium	1929
Hepburn, Katharine	Hartford, Conn.	1909
Herbert, Evelyn	Philadelphia, Pa.	1898
Herlie, Eileen	Glasgow, Scotland.	1920
Herman, Woody	Milwaukee, Wis.	1913

Name	Birthplace	Born
Heston, Charlton	Evanston, Ill.	1923
Heywood, Anne	Birmingham, England	1937
Hickman, Darryl	Los Angeles, Cal.	1931
Hickman, Dwayne	Los Angeles, Cal.	1934
Hildegarde	Adell, Wis.	1906
Hill, Arthur	Melfort, Sask., Canada	1922
Hiller, Wendy	Stockport, England	1912
Hines, Earl (Fatha)	Duquesne, Pa.	1905
Hines, Jerome	Hollywood, Cal.	1921
Hines, Mimi	Vancouver, B.C.	1933
Hingle, Pat	Denver, Col.	1924
Hirt, Al	New Orleans, La.	1922
Hitchcock, Alfred	London, England.	1899
Ho, Don	Kakaako, Oahu, Hawaii	1930
Hobart, Rose	New York, N.Y.	1906
Hoffman, Dustin	Los Angeles, Cal.	1937
Holbrook, Hal	Cleveland, Ohio	1925
Holden, William	O'Fallon, Ill.	1918
Holder, Geoffrey	Trinidad.	1930
Holloway, Stanley	London, England.	1890
Holloway, Sterling	Cedartown, Ga.	1905
Holm, Celeste	New York, N.Y.	1919
Holtz, Lou	San Francisco, Cal.	1893
Homeier, Skip	Chicago, Ill.	1930
Homolka, Oscar	Vienna, Austria	1903
Hooks, Robert	Washington, D.C.	1937
Hope, Bob	London, England.	1903
Hopkin, Mary	Wales.	1950
Hopper, Dennis	Dodge City, Kan.	1936
Horne, Lena	Brooklyn, N.Y.	1917
Horowitz, Vladimir	Kiev, Russia.	1904
Horton, Robert	Los Angeles, Cal.	1924
Howard, Clint	Burbank, Cal.	1959
Howard, Ron	Duncan, Okla.	1954
Howard, Trevor	Kent, England	1916
Howes, Sally Ann	London, England.	1934
Hudson, Rock	Winnetka, Ill.	1925
Hull, Henry	Louisville, Ky.	1890
Humperdinck, Engelbert	Madras, India	1937
Hunnicutt, Arthur	Gravelly, Ark.	1911
Hunt, Lois	York, Pa.	1925
Hunt, Marsha	Chicago, Ill.	1917
Hunter, Ian	Cape Town, S. Africa	1900
Hunter, Kim	Detroit, Mich.	1922
Hunter, Tab	New York, N.Y.	1931
Hussey, Olivia	Buenos Aires, Argentina	1952
Hussey, Ruth	Providence, R.I.	1917
Huston, John	Nevada, Mo.	1906
Hutchinson, Josephine	Seattle, Wash.	1916
Hutton, Betty	Battle Creek, Mich.	1921
Hutton, Ina Ray	Chicago, Ill.	1918
Hutton, Lauren	Charleston, S.C.	1944
Hyde-White, Wilfrid	England	1903
Hyer, Martha	Fort Worth, Tex.	1929
Hyland, Diana	Cleveland Hts., Ohio	1937
Hyman, Earle	Rocky Mt., N.C.	1926

I

Name	Birthplace	Born
Inescort, Frieda	Edinburgh, Scotland	1901
Ingels, Marty	Brooklyn, N.Y.	1936
Ireland, John	Vancouver, B.C.	1915
Iturbi, Jose	Valencia, Spain.	1895
Ives, Burl	Hunt, Ill.	1909

J

Name	Birthplace	Born
Jackson, Anne	Allegheny, Pa.	1926
Jackson, Glenda	Cheshire, England	1937
Jaeckel, Richard	Long Beach, Cal.	1926
Jaffe, Sam	New York, N.Y.	1891
Jagger, Dean	Columbus Grove, Ohio	1905
Jagger, Mick	Dartford, England.	1944
James, Dennis	Jersey City, N.J.	1917
James, Harry	Albany, Ga.	1916
Janney, William	New York, N.Y.	1908
Janssen, David	Naponee, Neb.	1930
Jason, Rick	New York, N.Y.	1926
Jeanmaire, Renee	Paris, France	1925
Jeffreys, Anne	Goldsboro, N.C.	1923
Jeffries, Fran	San Jose, Cal.	1939
Jeffries, Lionel	England	1926
Jennings, Waylon	Littlefield, Tex.	1937
Jepson, Helen	Titusville, Pa.	1907
Jeritza, Maria	Brunn, Austria	1887
Jessel, George	New York, N.Y.	1898
John, Elton	Middlesex, England	1947
Johns, Glynis	Durban, S. Africa.	1923
Johnson, Ben	Pawhuska, Okla.	1919
Johnson, Richard	Essex, England.	1927
Johnson, Van	Newport, R.I.	1916
Johnston, Johnny	St. Louis, Mo.	1916

Name	Birthplace	Born
Lom, Herbert	Prague, Czechoslovakia	1917
Lombardo, Guy	London, Ont., Canada	1902
London, Julie	Santa Rosa, Cal.	1926
Longet, Claudine	France	1942
Lopez, Trini	Dallas, Tex.	1937
Lopez, Vincent	Brooklyn, N.Y.	1895
Lord, Jack	New York, N.Y.	1930
Loren, Sophia	Rome, Italy	1934
Loring, Gloria	New York, N.Y.	1946
Losch, Tilly	Vienna, Austria	1902
Loudon, Dorothy	Boston, Mass.	1932
Louise, Tina	New York, N.Y.	1934
Love, Bessie	Midland, Tex.	1898
Loy, Myrna	Helena, Mon.	1905
Lucas, Nick	New Jersey	1897
Ludwig, Christa	Berlin, Germany	1928
Luke, Keye	Canton, China	1904
Lulu	Glasgow, Scotland	1948
Lum (Chester Lauck)	Allene, Ark.	1902
Lumet, Sidney	Philadelphia, Pa.	1924
Lund, John	Rochester, N.Y.	1913
Lundigan, William	Syracuse, N.Y.	1914
Lunt, Alfred	Milwaukee, Wis.	1892
Lupino, Ida	London, England	1918
Lynde, Paul	Mt. Vernon, Ohio	1926
Lynley, Carol	New York, N.Y.	1942
Lynn, Jeffrey	Auburn, Mass.	1909
Lynn, Loretta	Butcher Hollow, Ky.	—
Lyon, Ben	Atlanta, Ga.	1901
Lyon, Sue	Davenport, Ia.	1946

M

Name	Birthplace	Born
MacArthur, James	Los Angeles, Cal.	1937
MacGraw, Ali	Pound Ridge, N.Y.	1939
Mack, Ted	Greeley, Col.	1904
MacKenzie, Gisele	Winnipeg, Man., Canada	1927
MacKay, Jim	Philadelphia, Pa.	1921
MacLaine, Shirley	Richmond, Va.	1934
MacMurray, Fred	Kankakee, Ill.	1908
MacRae, Gordon	East Orange, N.J.	1921
MacRae, Meredith	Houston, Tex.	1945
MacRae, Sheila	London, England	1924
Macy, Bill	Revere, Mass.	1922
Madison, Guy	Bakersfield, Cal.	1922
Malbin, Elaine	New York, N.Y.	1932
Malden, Karl	Gary, Ind.	1914
Malone, Dorothy	Chicago, Ill.	1925
Malone, Nancy	New York, N.Y.	1935
Mancini, Henry	Cleveland, Ohio	1924
Mann, Herbie	New York, N.Y.	1930
Manning, Irene	Cincinnati, Ohio	1918
Mantovani, Annuzio	Venice, Italy	1905
Marceau, Marcel	France	1923
Margo	Mexico City, Mexico	1918
Margolin, Janet	New York, N.Y.	1943
Markova, Alicia	London, England	1910
Marlowe, Hugh	Philadelphia, Pa.	1914
Marshall, Brenda	Philippines	1915
Marshall, E. G.	Owatonna, Minn.	1919
Marshall, Everett	Lawrence, Mass.	1901
Marshall, William	Chicago, Ill.	1917
Martin, Dean	Steubenville, Ohio	1917
Martin, Dick	Detroit, Mich.	1928
Martin, Mary	Weatherford, Tex.	1913
Martin, Ross	Poland	1920
Martin, Tony	San Francisco, Cal.	1913
Martini, Nino	Verona, Italy	1905
Marvin, Lee	New York, N.Y.	1924
Marx, Herbert (Zeppo)	New York, N.Y.	1901
Marx, Julius (Groucho)	New York, N.Y.	1890
Mason, Jackie	Sheboygan, Wis.	1931
Mason, James	Huddersfield, England	1909
Mason, Marsha	St. Louis, Mo.	—
Mason, Pamela	Westgate, England	1918
Massey, Curt	Midland, Tex.	—
Massey, Raymond	Toronto, Canada	1896
Massine, Leonide	Moscow, Russia	1896
Mastroianni, Marcello	Italy	1924
Mathis, Johnny	San Francisco, Cal.	1935
Matthau, Walter	New York, N.Y.	1920
Mature, Victor	Louisville, Ky.	1916
May, Billy	Pittsburgh, Pa.	1916
May, Elaine	Philadelphia, Pa.	1932
Mayehoff, Eddie	Baltimore, Md.	1914
Mayo, Virginia	St. Louis, Mo.	1920
Mazurki, Mike	Austria	1909
McBride, Mary Marg.	Paris, Mo.	1899
McCaffery, J.K.M.	Moscow, Ida.	1913

Name	Birthplace	Born
McCallum, David	Glasgow, Scotland	1933
McCambridge, Mercedes	Joliet, Ill.	1918
McCarthy, Kevin	Seattle, Wash.	1915
McCartney, Paul	Liverpool, England	1942
McClure, Doug	Glendale, Cal.	1935
McCord, Kent	Los Angeles, Cal.	1942
McCoy, Tim	Saginaw, Mich.	1891
McCrary, Tex (John)	Calvert, Tex.	1910
McCrea, Joel	Los Angeles, Cal.	1905
McDowall, Roddy	London, England	1928
McDowell, Malcolm	Leeds, England	1943
McEachin, James	Pennert, N.C.	1930
McFarland, George	Dallas, Tex.	1928
McGavin, Darren	San Joaquin, Cal.	1922
McGee, Fibber	Peoria, Ill.	1896
McGiver, John	New York, N.Y.	1913
McGoohan, Patrick	Astoria, N.Y.	1928
McGuire Sisters:		
Christine	Middletown, Ohio	1928
Dorothy	Middletown, Ohio	1930
Phyllis	Middletown, Ohio	1931
McGuire, Dorothy	Omaha, Neb.	1919
McHugh, Frank	Homestead, Pa.	1899
McIntyre, John	Spokane, Wash.	1907
McKay, Scott	Pleasantville, Ia.	1915
McKenna, Siobhan	Belfast, Ireland	1923
McKuen, Rod	San Francisco, Cal.	1933
McLean, Don	New Rochelle, N.Y.	1945
McLerie, Allyn	Grand Mere, Que., Canada	1926
McMahon, Ed	Detroit, Mich.	1923
McNair, Barbara	Chicago, Ill.	1939
McQueen, Butterfly	Tampa, Fla.	1911
McQueen, Steve	Indianapolis, Ind.	1930
Meadows, Audrey	Wu Chang, China	1929
Meadows, Jayne	Wu Chang, China	1926
Meara, Ann	New York, N.Y.	1929
Medford, Kay	New York, N.Y.	1920
Meeker, Ralph	Minneapolis, Minn.	1920
Melton, Sid	Brooklyn, N.Y.	1920
Menuhin, Yehudi	New York N.Y.	1916
Mercer, Johnny	Savannah, Ga.	1909
Mercouri, Melina	Athens, Greece	1929
Meredith, Burgess	Cleveland, Ohio	1909
Merkel, Una	Covington, Ky.	1903
Merman, Ethel	Astoria, N.Y.	1909
Merrick, David	Hong Kong	1911
Merrill, Dina	New York, N.Y.	1925
Merrill, Gary	Hartford, Conn.	1915
Merrill, Robert	Brooklyn, N.Y.	1919
Middleton, Guy	Hove, England	1907
Middleton, Ray	Chicago, Ill.	1907
Midler, Bette	Honolulu, Hawaii	—
Mielziner, Jo	Paris, France	1901
Milanov, Zinka	Zagreb, Yugoslavia	1908
Miles, Sarah	Ingatestone, England	1941
Miles, Vera	near Boise City, Okla.	1930
Milland, Ray	Neath, Wales	1908
Miller, Ann	Houston, Tex.	1923
Miller, Cheryl	Sherman Oaks, Cal.	1943
Miller, Jason	Scranton, Pa.	1940
Miller, Mitch	Rochester, N.Y.	1911
Miller, Roger	Erick, Okla.	1936
Mills, Hayley	London, England	1946
Mills, John	Suffolk, England	1908
Mills, Juliet	London, England	1941
Milner, Martin	Detroit, Mich.	1937
Milstein, Nathan	Odessa, Russia	1904
Mimieux, Yvette	Hollywood, Cal.	1942
Minnelli, Liza	Los Angeles, Cal.	1946
Mineo, Sal	New York, N.Y.	1939
Mitchell, Cameron	Dallastown, Pa.	1918
Mitchell, Guy	Detroit, Mich.	1925
Mitchell, Joni	Alberta, Canada	1943
Mitchum, Robert	Bridgeport, Conn.	1917
Moffo, Anna	Wayne, Pa.	—
Montalban, Ricardo	Mexico City, Mexico	1920
Montand, Yves	Monsummano, Italy	1921
Montgomery, Eliz.	Hollywood, Cal.	1933
Montgomery, George	Brady, Mon.	1916
Montgomery, Robert	Beacon, N.Y.	1904
Moore, Colleen	Port Huron, Mich.	1902
Moore, Constance	Sioux City, Ia.	1922
Moore, Dickie	Los Angeles, Cal.	1925
Moore, Garry	Baltimore, Md.	1915
Moore, Mary Tyler	Brooklyn, N.Y.	1937
Moore, Melba	New York, N.Y.	1945
Moore, Roger	London, England	1928
Moore, Terry	Los Angeles, Cal.	1932

Name	Birthplace	Born
Moran, Lois.	Pittsburgh, Pa.	1907
Moreau, Jeanne.	Paris, France.	1929
Moreno, Rita.	Humacao, P.R.	1931
Morgan, Dennis.	Prentice, Wis.	1910
Morgan, Harry.	Detroit, Mich.	1915
Morgan, Henry.	New York, N.Y.	1915
Morgan, Jane.	Boston, Mass.	1920
Morgana, Nina.	Buffalo, N.Y.	1895
Morini, Erika.	Vienna, Austria	1910
Morison, Patricia.	New York, N.Y.	1915
Morley, Robert.	Wiltshire, England.	1908
Morris, Greg	Cleveland, Ohio	1934
Morris, Howard.	New York, N.Y.	1919
Morrow, Vic.	Bronx, N.Y.	1932
Morse, Robert.	Newton, Mass.	1931
Moss, Arnold.	Brooklyn, N.Y.	1910
Mostel, Zero (Sam).	Brooklyn, N.Y.	1915
Muir, Gavin.	Chicago, Ill.	1909
Muir, Jean.	New York, N.Y.	1911
Mulhall, Jack.	Wappingers Falls, N.Y.	1894
Mulhare, Edward	Ireland.	1923
Mundy, Meg.	London, England.	—
Munsel, Patrice.	Spokane, Wash.	1925
Murphy, George.	New Haven, Conn.	1902
Murray, Arthur.	New York, N.Y.	1895
Murray, Don.	Hollywood, Cal.	1929
Murray, Jan.	New York.	1917
Murray, Kathryn.	Jersey City, N.J.	1906
Murray, Ken.	New York, N.Y.	1903

N

Name	Birthplace	Born
Nabors, Jim.	Sylacauga, Ala.	1933
Namath, Joe.	Beaver Falls, Pa.	1943
Nardini, Tom.	Los Angeles, Cal.	1945
Natwick, Mildred.	Baltimore, Md.	1908
Neal, Patricia.	Packard, Ky.	1926
Neff, Hildegarde.	Ulm, Germany.	1925
Negri, Pola.	Lipno, Poland.	1899
Nelson, Barry.	Oakland, Cal.	1920
Nelson, David.	New York, N.Y.	1936
Nelson, Ed.	New Orleans, La.	1928
Nelson, Gene.	Seattle, Wash.	1920
Nelson, Harriet (Hilliard)	Des Moines, Ia.	1914
Nelson, Ricky.	Teaneck, N.J.	1940
Nero, Peter.	New York, N.Y.	1934
Nesbit, Cathleen.	Cheshire, England	1889
Newhart, Bob.	Oak Park, Ill.	1929
Newley, Anthony.	Hackney, England.	1931
Newman, Barry.	Boston, Mass.	1938
Newman, Paul.	Cleveland, Ohio	1925
Newman, Phyllis	Jersey City, N.J.	1935
Newmar, Julie.	California	1935
Newton, Wayne.	Roanoke, Va.	1942
Newton-John, Olivia.	England	1949
Nicholas, Denise.	Detroit, Mich.	—
Nichols, Mike.	Berlin, Germany.	1931
Nicholson, Jack.	Neptune, N.J.	1937
Nielson, Leslie.	Regina, Canada.	1926
Nilsson, Birgit.	W. Karop, Sweden.	1918
Nimoy, Leonard.	Boston, Mass.	1931
Niven, David.	Kirriemuir, Scotland	1910
Noble, Ray.	Sussex, England.	1908
Nolan, Doris.	New York, N.Y.	1916
Nolan, Jeannette.	Los Angeles, Cal.	1911
Nolan, Kathy.	St. Louis, Mo.	1934
Nolan, Lloyd.	San Francisco, Cal.	1902
North, Jay.	Hollywood, Cal.	1953
North, John Ringling.	Baraboo, Wis.	1903
North, Sheree.	Los Angeles, Cal.	1933
Norton, Judy.	Santa Monica, Cal.	1958
Novak, Kim.	Chicago, Ill.	1933
Nugent, Edward.	New York, N.Y.	1904
Nugent, Elliott.	Dover, Ohio.	1899
Nureyev, Rudolf.	Russia.	1938
Nuyen, France.	Marseilles, France	1939

O

Name	Birthplace	Born
Oakie, Jack.	Sedalia, Mo.	1903
Oberon, Merle.	Tasmania, Australia	1911
O'Brian, Hugh.	Rochester, N.Y.	1930
O'Brien, Edmond.	New York, N.Y.	1915
O'Brien, George.	San Francisco, Cal.	1900
O'Brien, Margaret.	San Diego, Cal.	1937
O'Brien, Pat.	Milwaukee, Wis.	1899
Ochs, Phil.	El Paso, Tex.	1940
O'Connell, Arthur.	New York, N.Y.	1908
O'Connell, Helen.	Lima, Ohio.	1920
O'Connor, Carroll.	New York, N.Y.	1925

Name	Birthplace	Born
O'Connor, Donald.	Chicago, Ill.	1925
Odetta.	Birmingham, Ala.	1930
O'Driscoll, Martha.	Tulsa, Okla.	1922
O'Hara, Jill.	Warren, Pa.	1947
O'Hara, Maureen.	Dublin, Ireland.	1920
O'Herlihy, Dan.	Wexford, Ireland.	1919
O'Keefe, Walter.	Hartford, Conn.	1907
Olivier, Laurence.	Dorking, England	1907
O'Malley, J. Pat.	Burnley, England	1901
O'Neal, Patrick.	Ocala, Fla.	1927
O'Neal, Ryan.	Los Angeles, Cal.	1941
O'Neill, Jennifer.	Brazil.	1948
Opatoshu, David.	New York, N.Y.	1918
Orbach, Jerry.	New York, N.Y.	1935
Orlando, Tony.	New York, N.Y.	1944
Ormandy, Eugene.	Budapest, Hungary.	1899
O'Sullivan, Maureen.	Boyle, Ireland.	1911
O'Toole, Peter.	Connemara, Ireland.	1934
Owens, Buck.	Sherman, Tex.	1929

P

Name	Birthplace	Born
Paar, Jack.	Canton, Ohio.	1918
Pacino, Al.	New York, N.Y.	1939
Page, Geraldine.	Kirksville, Mo.	1924
Page, Patti.	Claremore, Okla.	1927
Paige, Janis.	Tacoma, Wash.	1923
Paige, Robert.	Indianapolis, Ind.	1910
Palance, Jack.	Lattimer, Pa.	1920
Palmer, Betsy.	East Chicago, Ind.	1929
Palmer, Gregg.	San Francisco, Cal.	1927
Palmer, Lili.	Posen, Germany.	1914
Papas, Irene.	Greece.	1926
Parker, Eleanor.	Cedarville, Ohio.	1922
Parker, Fess.	Ft. Worth, Tex.	1925
Parker, Frank.	New York, N.Y.	1906
Parker, Jean.	Deer Lodge, Mon.	1916
Parker, Suzy.	New York, N.Y.	1934
Parkins, Barbara.	Vancouver, Canada.	1942
Parks, Bert.	Atlanta, Ga.	1914
Parsons, Estelle.	Lynn, Mass.	1927
Parton, Dolly.	Sevier County, Tenn.	1946
Pasternak, Joseph.	Hungary.	1901
Paterson, Pat.	Bradford, England.	1911
Patterson, Melody.	Los Angeles, Cal.	1947
Patterson, Neva.	Nevada, Ia.	1922
Paulsen, Pat.	South Bend, Wash.	—
Pavan, Marisa.	Cagliari, Sardinia	1932
Payne, John.	Roanoke, Va.	1912
Pearl, Jack.	New York, N.Y.	1895
Pearl, Minnie.	Centerville, Tenn.	1912
Peck, Gregory.	La Jolla, Cal.	1916
Peerce, Jan.	New York, N.Y.	1904
Penn, Arthur.	Philadelphia, Pa.	1922
Peppard, George.	Detroit, Mich.	1933
Perkins, Anthony.	New York, N.Y.	1932
Persoff, Nehemiah.	Jerusalem.	1920
Peters, Bernadette.	Queens, N.Y.	1944
Peters, Brock.	New York, N.Y.	1927
Peters, Jean.	Canton, Ohio.	1926
Peters, Roberta.	New York, N.Y.	1930
Petit, Pascale.	France.	1937
Pettet, Joanna.	London, England.	1944
Piatigorsky, Gregor.	Russia.	1903
Piazza, Ben.	Little Rock, Ark.	1934
Piazza, Marguerite.	New Orleans, La.	1926
Pickens, Jane.	Macon, Ga.	—
Pickens, Slim.	Kingsberg, Cal.	1919
Pickford, Mary.	Toronto, Canada.	1894
Picon, Molly.	New York, N.Y.	1898
Pidgeon, Walter.	E. St. John, N.B.	1898
Piston, Walter.	Rockland, Me.	1894
Pleasance, Donald.	Worksop, England	1919
Pleshette, Suzanne.	New York, N.Y.	1937
Plimpton, George.	New York, N.Y.	1927
Plowright, Joan.	Brigg, England.	1929
Plummer, Christopher.	Toronto, Canada.	1929
Poitier, Sidney.	Miami, Fla.	1927
Pollard, Michael.	Passaic, N.J.	1939
Pons, Lily.	Cannes, France	1904
Ponselle, Carmela.	Schenectady, N.Y.	1892
Ponselle, Rosa.	Meriden, Conn.	1897
Ponti, Carlo.	Milan, Italy.	1913
Poston, Tom.	Columbus, Ohio.	1927
Powell, Eleanor.	Springfield, Mass.	1912
Powell, Jane.	Portland, Ore.	1929
Powell, William.	Pittsburgh, Pa.	1892
Powers, Mala.	San Francisco, Cal.	1931
Powers, Stefanie.	Hollywood, Cal.	1942

Name	Birthplace	Born	Name	Birthplace	Born
Preminger, Otto	Vienna, Austria	1906	Roman, Ruth	Boston, Mass.	1924
Prentiss, Paula	San Antonio, Tex.	1939	Romero, Cesar	New York, N.Y.	1907
Presley, Elvis	Tupelo, Miss.	1935	Rooney, Mickey	Brooklyn, N.Y.	1922
Preston, Robert	Newton, Mass.	1918	Rose Marie	New York, N.Y.	—
Previn, Andre	Berlin, Germany	1929	Ross, David	St. Paul, Minn.	1924
Price, Leontyne	Laurel, Miss.	1927	Ross, Diana	Detroit, Mich.	1944
Price, Ray	Perryville, Tex.	1926	Ross, Katharine	Hollywood, Cal.	1942
Price, Roger	Charleston, W. Va.	1920	Ross, Lanny	Seattle, Wash.	1906
Price, Vincent	St. Louis, Mo.	1911	Ross, Shirley	Omaha, Neb.	1909
Pride, Charlie	Sledge, Miss.	1938	Roth, Lillian	Boston, Mass.	1910
Prima, Louis	New Orleans, La.	1912	Roundtree, Richard	New Rochelle, N.Y.	1942
Prince, William	Nichols, N.Y.	1913	Rowan, Dan	Beggs, Okla.	1922
Prinze, Freddie	New York, N.Y.	1954	Rowlands, Gena	Cambria, Wis.	1936
Provine, Dorothy	Deadwood, S. D.	1937	Rubin, Benny	Boston, Mass.	1899
Prowse, Juliet	Bombay, India	1937	Rubinoff, David	Grodno, Russia.	1897
Pyle, Denver	Bethune, Col.	1920	Rubinstein, Artur	Lodz, Poland.	1889
			Rudolf, Max	Frankfurt, Germany.	1902
Q			Rule, Janice	Norwood, Ohio.	1931
Qualen, John	Vancouver, B.C.	1899	Rush, Barbara	Denver, Col.	1930
Quayle, Anthony	Lancashire, England	1913	Russell, Jane	Bemidji, Minn.	1921
Quillan, Eddie	Philadelphia, Pa.	1907	Russell, Ken	Southampton, England	1927
Quinn, Anthony	Chihuahua, Mexico	1916	Russell, Nipsy	Atlanta, Ga.	1924
			Russell, Rosalind	Waterbury, Conn.	1911
R			Rutherford, Ann	Toronto, Canada.	1924
Raft, George	New York, N.Y.	1895	Rydell, Bobby	Philadelphia, Pa.	1942
Rainer, Luise	Vienna, Austria	1912			
Raines, Ella	Snoqualmie Falls, Wash.	1921	**S**		
Raitt, John	Santa Ana, Cal.	1917	Sahl, Mort	Montreal, Que., Canada.	1927
Ralston, Esther	Bar Harbor, Me.	1902	Saint, Eva Marie	E. Orange, N.J.	1924
Ralston, Vera	Prague, Czechoslovakia	1921	Sainte-Marie, Buffy	Craven, Sask.	1941
Randall, Tony	Tulsa, Okla.	1920	St. James, Susan	Los Angeles, Cal.	1946
Rawls, Lou	Chicago, Ill.	1935	St. John, Jill	Los Angeles, Cal.	1940
Ray, Aldo	Pen Argyl, Pa.	1926	Sales, Soupy	Franklinton, N.C.	1926
Ray, Johnnie	Dallas, Ore.	1927	Sand, Paul	Los Angeles, Cal.	1941
Rayburn, Gene	Christopher, Ill.	1917	Sands, Tommy	Chicago, Ill.	1937
Raye, Martha	Butte, Mont.	1916	Sargent, Dick	Carmel, Cal.	1933
Raymond, Gene	New York, N.Y.	1908	Sarnoff, Dorothy	New York, N.Y.	1919
Reddy, Helen	Melbourne, Australia	1942	Sarrazin, Michael	Quebec City, Quebec.	1940
Redford, Robert	Santa Monica, Cal.	1937	Saunders, Lori	Kansas City, Mo.	1941
Redgrave, Lynn	London, England.	1943	Savalas, Telly	Garden City, N.Y.	1924
Redgrave, Michael	Bristol, England.	1908	Saxon, John	Brooklyn, N.Y.	1935
Redgrave, Vanessa	London, England.	1937	Sayao, Bidu	Rio de Janeiro, Brazil.	1908
Redman, Joyce	Co. Mayo, Ireland.	1918	Schallert, William	Los Angeles, Cal.	1925
Reed, Donna	Denison, Ia.	1921	Schary, Dore	Newark, N.J.	1905
Reed, Jerry	Atlanta, Ga.	1937	Schell, Maria	Vienna, Austria	1926
Reed, Robert	Highland, Park, Ill.	1932	Schell, Maximilian	Vienna, Austria	1930
Reese, Della	Detroit, Mich.	1932	Schenkel, Chris	Bippus, Ind.	1924
Regan, Phil	Brooklyn, N.Y.	1906	Scherman, Thomas	New York, N.Y.	1917
Reilly, Charles Nelson	New York, N.Y.	—	Schippers, Thomas	Kalamazoo, Mich.	1930
Reiner, Carl	Bronx, N.Y.	1922	Schneider, Alexander	Vilna, Poland.	1908
Reiner, Rob	Bronx, N.Y.	1946	Schneider, Romy	Austria	1938
Remick, Lee	Boston, Mass.	1937	Schuman, William	New York, N.Y.	1910
Renaldo, Duncan	Camden, N.J.	1904	Schwarzkopf, Elisabeth	Jarotschin, Poland	1915
Resnik, Regina	New York, N.Y.	1923	Scofield, Paul	Hurst, Pierpont, England.	1922
Reynolds, Burt	Georgia	1935	Scott, George C.	Wise, Va.	1927
Reynolds, Debbie	El Paso, Tex.	1932	Scott, Hazel	Trinidad.	1920
Reynolds, Marjorie	Buhl, Ida.	1921	Scott, Lizabeth	Scranton, Pa.	1923
Reynolds, William	Los Angeles, Cal.	1931	Scott, Martha	Jamesport, Mo.	1916
Rhodes, Hari	Cincinnati, Ohio	1932	Scott, Randolph	Orange Co., Va.	1903
Rich, Buddy	New York, N.Y.	1917	Scourby, Alexander	New York, N.Y.	1913
Rich, Charlie	Forest City, Ark.	1932	Sebastian, John	New York, N.Y.	1944
Rich, Irene	Buffalo, N.Y.	1897	Seberg, Jean	Marshalltown, Ia.	1938
Richardson, Ralph	Cheltenham, England	1902	Seeger, Pete	New York, N.Y.	1919
Richardson, Tony	Shipley, England.	1929	Segal, George	Great Neck, N.Y.	1934
Rickles, Don	New York, N.Y.	1926	Segal, Vivienne	Philadelphia, Pa.	1897
Riddle, Nelson	Hackensack, N.J.	1921	Sellers, Peter	Southsea, England.	1925
Rigg, Diana	England	1938	Serkin, Rudolf	Eger, Austria	1903
Ritchard, Cyril	Sydney, Australia.	1898	Severinsen, Doc	Arlington, Ore.	1927
Ritz, Harry	Newark, N.J.	1908	Shankar, Ravi	India.	1920
Ritz, Jimmy	Newark, N.J.	1905	Sharif, Omar	Alexandria, Egypt.	1932
Rivers, Joan	Brooklyn, N.Y.	1935	Shatner, William	Montreal, Canada.	1931
Robards, Jason, Jr.	Chicago, Ill.	1922	Shaw, Artie	New York, N.Y.	1910
Robbins, Jerome	New York, N.Y.	1918	Shaw, Reta	S. Paris, Me.	1912
Robbins, Marty	Glendale, Ariz.	1925	Shaw, Robert	Red Bluff, Cal.	1916
Robertson, Cliff	La Jolla, Cal.	1925	Shaw, Robert	West Houghton, England.	1927
Robertson, Dale	Oklahoma City, Okla.	1923	Shaw, Winfred	San Francisco, Cal.	1899
Robeson, Paul	Princeton, N.J.	1898	Shearer, Moira	Scotland.	1926
Robinson, Jay	New York, N.Y.	1930	Shearer, Norma	Montreal, Canada	1904
Robson, Flora	South Shields, England.	1902	Shearing, George	London, England.	1920
Rochester (E. Anderson)	Oakland, Cal.	1905	Shepherd, Cybill	Memphis, Tenn.	1955
Rockwell, Geo. (Doc.)	Providence, R.I.	1889	Shepherd, Jean	Chicago, Ill.	1929
Rodgers, Jimmie	Camas, Wash.	1933	Sherman, Bobby	Santa Monica, Cal.	1945
Rodriquez, Johnny	Sabinal, Tex.	1951	Sherwood, Roberta	St. Louis, Mo.	1913
Rogers, Chas. (Buddy)	Olathe, Kan.	1904	Shirley, Ann	New York, N.Y.	1918
Rogers, Ginger	Independence, Mo.	1911	Shore, Dinah	Winchester, Tenn.	1920
Rogers, Roy	Cincinnati, Ohio	1912	Sidney, Sylvia	New York, N.Y.	1910
Roland, Gilbert	Juarez, Mexico.	1905	Siepi, Cesare	Milan, Italy.	1923
Rolle, Esther	Pompano Beach, Fla.	—	Signoret, Simone	Wiesbaden, Germany	1921

Name	Birthplace	Born	Name	Birthplace	Born
Sills, Beverly	Brooklyn, N.Y.	1929	Swayze, John Cameron.	Wichita, Kan.	1906
Silvers, Phil	Brooklyn, N.Y.	1912	Sweet, Blanche	Chicago, Ill.	1896
Sim, Alastair	Edinburgh, Scotland	1900	Swenson, Inga	Omaha, Neb.	1934
Simmons, Jean	London, England.	1929	Swit, Loretta	Passaic, N.J.	—
Simon, Paul	New York, N.Y.	1940			
Simon, Simone	Marseilles, France	1914	**T**		
Simone, Nina	Tyron, N.C.	1933	Talbot, Lyle	Pittsburgh, Pa.	1902
Sinatra, Frank	Hoboken, N.J.	1915	Talbot, Nita	New York, N.Y.	1930
Sinatra Jr., Frank	Jersey City, N.J.	1944	Tallchief, Maria	Fairfax, Okla.	1925
Sinatra, Nancy	Jersey City, N.J.	1940	Tamblyn, Russ	Los Angeles, Cal.	1935
Skelton, Red (Richard)	Vincennes, Ind.	1913	Tandy, Jessica	London, England.	1909
Skinner, Cornelia Otis.	Chicago, Ill.	1903	Taylor, Billy	Greenville, N.C.	1921
Slezak, Walter	Vienna, Austria	1902	Taylor, Elizabeth	London, England.	1932
Slick, Grace	Chicago, Ill.	1939	Taylor, James	Boston, Mass.	1948
Smith, Alexis	Penticton, Canada	1921	Taylor, Kent	Nashua, Ia.	1907
Smith, Bob	Buffalo, N.Y.	1917	Taylor, Rod	Sydney, Australia.	1930
Smith, Connie	Elkhart, Ind.	1941	Tebaldi, Renata	Pesaro, Italy.	1922
Smith, Ethel	Pittsburgh, Pa.	1921	Temple, Shirley	Santa Monica, Cal.	1928
Smith, Kate	Greenville, Va.	1909	Terris, Norma.	Columbus, Kan.	1904
Smith, Keely	Norfolk, Va.	1935	Terry-Thomas	London, England.	1911
Smith, Loring	Stratford, Conn.	1900	Teyte, Maggie	Wolverhampton, England .	1889
Smith, Maggie	Ilford, England.	1934	Thaxter, Phillis	Portland, Me.	1921
Smith, Roger	South Gate, Cal.	1934	Thebom, Blanche	Monessen, Pa.	1919
Smothers, Dick	New York, N.Y.	1939	Thibault, Conrad.	Northbridge, Mass.	1898
Smothers, Tom.	New York, N.Y.	1937	Thinnes, Roy	Chicago, Ill.	1938
Snodgress, Carrie.	Park Ridge, Ill.	1945	Thomas, B.J.	Houston, Tex.	1942
Snow, Hank	Nova Scotia, Canada	1914	Thomas, Danny	Deerfield, Mich.	1914
Somes, Michael	nr. Stroud, England.	1917	Thomas, Lowell	Woodrington, Ohio.	1892
Sommer, Elke	Berlin, Germany.	1941	Thomas, Marlo	Detroit, Mich.	1938
Sorvino, Paul	Brooklyn, N.Y.	1939	Thomas, Richard	New York, N.Y.	1951
Sothern, Ann.	Valley City, N.D.	1912	Thompson, Marshall	Peoria, Ill.	1926
Specht, Bobby	Superior, Wis.	1921	Thompson, Sada	Des Moines, Ia.	1929
Spewack, Bella.	Hungary.	1899	Thorndike, Sybil.	Gainsborough, England.	1882
Spivak, Lawrence	Brooklyn, N.Y.	1900	Thulin, Ingrid.	Sweden.	1929
Stack, Robert.	Los Angeles, Cal.	1919	Tierney, Gene.	Brooklyn, N.Y.	1920
Stafford, Jo	Coalinga, Cal.	1918	Tierney, Lawrence	Brooklyn, N.Y.	1919
Stamp, Terence	London, England.	1940	Tiffin, Pamela.	Oklahoma City, Okla.	1942
Stang, Arnold.	Chelsea, Mass.	1925	Tillstrom, Burr	Chicago, Ill.	1917
Stanley, Kim	Tularosa, N.M.	1925	Tiny Tim	New York, N.Y.	—
Stanley, Pat	Cincinnati, Ohio	1931	Tobias, George	New York, N.Y.	1901
Stanwyck, Barbara	Brooklyn, N.Y.	1907	Todd, Richard.	Dublin, Ireland.	1919
Stapleton, Jean.	New York, N.Y.	1923	Tomkins, Angel	Albany, Cal.	1943
Stapleton, Maureen	Troy, N.Y.	1925	Tomlin, Lili	Detroit, Mich.	1940
Starr, Kay.	Dougherty, Okla.	1924	Tomlinson, David	Scotland.	1917
Starr, Ringo	Liverpool, England.	1940	Toomey, Regis	Pittsburgh, Pa.	1902
Steber, Eleanor	Wheeling, W. Va.	1916	Torme, Mel	Chicago, Ill.	1925
Steele, Bob.	Pendleton, Ore.	1907	Torn, Rip.	Temple, Tex.	1931
Steele, Karen	Hawaii.	1934	Totter, Audrey	Joliet, Ill.	1923
Steele, Ted	Hartford, Conn.	1917	Tracy, Arthur	Philadelphia, Pa.	1903
Steele, Tommy	London, England.	1937	Travers, Mary	Louisville, Ky.	1936
Steiger, Rod.	W. Hampton, N.Y.	1925	Treacher, Arthur	Brighton, England.	1894
Steinberg, David	Winnipeg, Canada	1942	Trevor, Claire.	New York, N.Y.	1909
Sterling, Jan.	New York, N.Y.	1923	Truffaut, Francois	Paris, France	1932
Sterling, Robert.	New Castle, Pa.	1917	Tryon, Tom.	Hartford, Conn.	1926
Stern, Isaac	Kreminisey, Russia.	1920	Tucker, Forrest	Plainfield, Ind.	1919
Stevens, Cat	London, England.	1948	Tucker, Orrin.	St. Louis, Mo.	1911
Stevens, Connie	Brooklyn, N.Y.	1938	Tucker, Tanya	Seminole, Tex.	1958
Stevens, Kaye	Pittsburgh, Pa.	1935	Tucker, Tommy	Souris, N.D.	1907
Stevens, Mark.	Cleveland, Ohio	1922	Turner, Lana	Wallace, Ida.	1921
Stevens, Onslow.	Los Angeles, Cal.	1902	Tushingham, Rita	Liverpool, England.	1942
Stevens, Rise	New York, N.Y.	1913	Twiggy (Leslie Hornby).	London, England.	1949
Stevens, Stella.	Yazoo City, Miss.	1938	Tyrell, Susan.	New Canaan, Conn.	1946
Stewart, Elaine	Montclair, N.J.	1929			
Stewart, James	Indiana, Pa.	1908	**U**		
Stewart, Rod.	London, England.	1944	Uggams, Leslie	New York, N.Y.	1943
Stickney, Dorothy	Dickinson, N.D.	1903	Ullman, Liv.	Tokyo, Japan.	1939
Stockwell, Dean.	Hollywood, Cal.	1936	Umeki, Miyoshi	Hokkaido, Japan.	1929
Stokowski, Leopold.	London, England.	1882	Ustinov, Peter.	London, England.	1921
Stone, Carol.	New York, N.Y.	1916			
Stone, Dorothy.	Bensonhurst, N.Y.	1905	**V**		
Stone, Ezra.	New Bedford, Mass.	1917	Vaccaro, Brenda.	Brooklyn, N.Y.	1939
Stone, Milburn	Burton, Kan.	1904	Vale, Jerry	New York, N.Y.	1931
Stone, Paula.	New York, N.Y.	1916	Valente, Caterina	Italy.	1931
Storch, Larry	New York, N.Y.	1925	Valentine, Karen	Santa Rosa, Cal.	1947
Storm, Gale	Bloomington, Tex.	1922	Vallee, Rudy	Island Pond, Vt.	1901
Storrs, Suzanne.	Salt Lake City, Ut.	1934	Valli, Alida	Pola, Italy.	1921
Straight, Beatrice	Old Westbury, N.Y.	1918	Vance, Vivian.	Cherryvale, Kan.	1912
Strasberg, Susan.	New York, N.Y.	1938	Van Cleef, Lee.	Somerville, N.J.	1925
Streisand, Barbra.	Brooklyn, N.Y.	1942	Van Doren, Mamie.	Rowena, S.D.	1933
Stritch, Elaine	Detroit, Mich.	1925	Van Dyke, Dick.	West Plains, Mo.	1925
Strode, Woody.	Los Angeles, Cal.	1914	Van Dyke, Jerry	Danville, Ill.	1932
Struthers, Sally	Portland, Ore.	1948	Van Fleet, Jo.	Oakland, Cal.	1922
Sullivan, Barry	New York, N.Y.	1912	Vandervere, Trish	Tenafly, N.J.	1945
Sumac, Yma.	Ichocan, Peru.	1928	Varnay, Astrid.	Stockholm, Sweden.	1918
Susskind, David.	New York, N.Y.	1920	Varsi, Diane.	San Francisco, Cal.	1938
Sutherland, Donald.	New Brunswick, Canada.	1934	Vaughn, Robert	New York, N.Y.	1932
Sutherland, Joan	Sydney, Australia	1926	Vaughn, Sarah.	Newark, N.J.	1924
Suzuki, Pat	Cressey, Cal.	1931	Venuta, Benay.	San Francisco, Cal.	1911
Swanson, Gloria	Chicago, Ill.	1899			

Name	Birthplace	Born
Vera-Ellen	Cincinnati, Ohio	1926
Verdon, Gwen	Los Angeles, Cal.	1926
Vernon, Jackie	New York, N.Y.	1929
Vidor, King Louis	Galveston, Tex.	1895
Vinson, Helen	Beaumont, Tex.	1907
Vinton, Bobby	Canonsburg, Pa.	1935
Vogel, Mitch	Alhambra, Cal.	1956
Voight, Jon	Yonkers, N.Y.	1938
Von Furstenberg, Betsy	Westphalia, Germany	1931
Von Sydow, Max	Lund, Sweden	1929
Von Zell, Harry	Indianapolis, Ind.	1906
Voorhees, Donald	Allentown, Pa.	1903

W

Name	Birthplace	Born
Waggoner, Lyle	Kansas City, Kan.	1935
Wagner, Robert	Detroit, Mich.	1930
Wain, Bea	Bronx, N.Y.	1917
Waite, Ralph	White Plains, N.Y.	1928
Walker, Clint	Hartford, Ill.	1927
Walker, Nancy	Philadelphia, Pa.	1922
Wallace, Mike	Brookline, Mass.	1918
Wallach, Eli	Brooklyn, N.Y.	1915
Wallenstein, Alfred	Chicago, Ill.	1898
Wallis, Hal	Chicago, Ill.	1899
Walston, Ray	New Orleans, La.	1918
Walters, Barbara	Boston, Mass.	1931
Ward, Burt	Los Angeles, Cal.	1946
Warden, Jack	Newark, N.J.	1920
Warfield, William	Helena, Ark.	1920
Warhol, Andy	Cleveland, Oh.	1931
Waring, Fred	Tyrone, Pa.	1900
Warner, David	Manchester, England	1941
Warwicke, Dionne	E. Orange, N.J.	1941
Waters, Ethel	Chester, Pa.	1900
Watts, Andre	Germany	1946
Wayne, David	Traverse City, Mich.	1914
Wayne, John	Winterset, Ia.	1907
Weaver, Dennis	Joplin, Mo.	1924
Weaver, Fritz	Pittsburgh, Pa.	1926
Webb, Alan	York, England	1906
Webb, Jack	Santa Monica, Cal.	1920
Weissmuller, Johnny	Windber, Pa.	1904
Welch, Raquel	La Jolla, Cal.	1942
Weld, Tuesday	New York, N.Y.	1943
Welk, Lawrence	Near Strasburg, N.D.	1903
Welles, Orson	Kenosha, Wis.	1915
Wells, Kitty	Nashville, Tenn.	1919
Werner, Oskar	Vienna, Austria	1922
West, Adam	Walla Walla, Wash.	1929
West, Mae	Brooklyn, N.Y.	1892
Whitaker, Johnny	Van Nuys, Cal.	1959
White, Jesse	Buffalo, N.Y.	1919
Whiting, Margaret	Detroit, Mich.	1924
Whitman, Stuart	San Francisco, Cal.	1936
Whitmore, James	White Plains, N.Y.	1921
Widmark, Richard	Sunrise, Minn.	1914
Wilcoxon, Henry	British West Indies	1905
Wilde, Cornel	New York, N.Y.	1918
Wilder, Billy	Vienna, Austria	1906
Wilder, Gene	Milwaukee, Wis.	1934
Wilding, Michael	Essex, England	1912

Name	Birthplace	Born
Williams, Andy	Wall Lake, Ia.	1930
Williams, Clarence	New York, N.Y.	1946
Williams, Emlyn	Mostyn, Wales	1905
Williams, Esther	Los Angeles, Cal.	1923
Williams, Joe	Cordele, Ga.	1918
Williams, Mason	Abilene, Tex.	1938
Williams, Paul	Omaha, Neb.	1940
Williams, Roger	Omaha, Neb.	1926
Williamson, Fred	Gary, Ind.	1937
Williamson, Nicol	Hamilton, Scotland	1936
Wills, Chill	Seagoville, Tex.	1903
Wilson, Demond	Valdosta, Ga.	—
Wilson, Dolores	Philadelphia, Pa.	1929
Wilson, Don	Lincoln, Neb.	1900
Wilson, Flip	Jersey City, N.J.	1933
Wilson, Julie	Omaha, Neb.	1924
Wilson, Nancy	Chillicothe, Oh.	1937
Winchell, Paul	New York, N.Y.	1922
Windom, William	New York, N.Y.	1923
Winters, Jonathan	Dayton, Ohio	1925
Winters, Shelley	St. Louis, Mo.	1922
Winwood, Estelle	Lee, England	1884
Wiseman, Joseph	Montreal, Canada	1918
Withers, Jane	Atlanta, Ga.	1927
Wood, Helen	Clarksville, Tenn.	1937
Wood, Natalie	San Francisco, Cal.	1938
Wood, Peggy	Brooklyn, N.Y.	1892
Woodward, Joanne	Thomasville, Ga.	1930
Wonder, Stevie	Detroit, Mich.	1951
Worley, Jo Anne	Lowell, Ind.	1937
Wray, Fay	Alberta, Canada	1907
Wright, Martha	Seattle, Wash.	1926
Wright, Teresa	New York, N.Y.	1919
Wrightson, Earl	Baltimore, Md.	1916
Wyatt, Jane	Campgaw, N.J.	1912
Wyler, William	Mulhouse, France	1902
Wyman, Jane	St. Joseph, Mo.	1914
Wynette, Tammy	Red Bay, Ala.	1942
Wynn, Keenan	New York, N.Y.	1916
Wynter, Dana	London, England	1930

Y

Name	Birthplace	Born
Yarborough, Glenn	Milwaukee, Wis.	1930
Yarrow, Peter	New York, N.Y.	1938
York, Dick	Ft. Wayne, Ind.	1928
York, Michael	Fulmer, England	1942
York, Susannah	London, England	1942
Young, Alan	Northumberl'd, England	1919
Young, Gig	St. Cloud, Minn.	1917
Young, Loretta	Salt Lake City, Ut.	1913
Young, Robert	Chicago, Ill.	1907
Young, Stephen	Toronto, Canada	1939
Youngman, Henny	Liverpool, England	1906

Z

Name	Birthplace	Born
Zanuck, Darryl F.	Wahoo, Neb.	1902
Zimbalist, Efrem	Rostov, Russia	1889
Zimbalist, Efrem, Jr.	New York, N.Y.	1923
Zimmer, Norma	Larsen, Ida.	—
Zorina, Vera	Berlin, Germany	1917
Zukor, Adolph	Ricse, Hungary	1873

Entertainment Personalities of the Past

Born	Died	Name
		A
1896	1974	Abbott, Bud
1872	1953	Adams, Maude
1931	1968	Adams, Nick
1855	1926	Adler, Jacob P.
1858	1953	Adler, Sarah Levitzka
1898	1933	Adoree, Renee
1909	1964	Albertson, Frank
1885	1952	Alda, Frances
1894	1956	Allen, Fred
1906	1964	Allen, Gracie
1883	1950	Allgood, Sara
1882	1971	Anderson, Gilbert (Bronco Billy)
1886	1954	Anderson, John Murray
1859	1940	Anderson, Mary
1915	1967	Andrews, Laverne
1933	1971	Angeli, Pier
1876	1958	Anglin, Margaret

Born	Died	Name
1887	1933	Arbuckle, Fatty (Roscoe)
1868	1946	Arliss, George
1900	1971	Armstrong, Louis
1890	1956	Arnold, Edward
1905	1975	Arquette, Cliff (Charlie Weaver)
1885	1946	Atwill, Lionel
1845	1930	Auer, Leopold
1905	1967	Auer, Mischa
1900	1972	Austin, Gene
1898	1940	Ayres, Agnes
		B
1864	1922	Bacon, Frank
1903	1951	Bailey, Mildred
1893	1968	Bainter, Fay
1895	1957	Baker, Belle
1906	1975	Baker, Josephine
1898	1963	Baker, Phil

Born	Died	Name
1882	1956	Bancroft, George
1903	1968	Bankhead, Tallulah
1890	1952	Banks, Leslie
1897	1950	Banks, Monty
1890	1955	Bara, Theda
1810	1891	Barnum, Phineas T.
1879	1959	Barrymore, Ethel
1882	1942	Barrymore, John
1878	1954	Barrymore, Lionel
1848	1905	Barrymore, Maurice
1897	1963	Barthelmess, Richard
1891	1962	Barton, James
1873	1951	Bauer, Harold
1893	1951	Baxter, Warner
1880	1928	Bayes, Nora
1904	1965	Beatty, Clyde
1904	1962	Beavers, Louise
1887	1955	Beecher, Janet
1884	1946	Beery, Noah

Born	Died	Name
1889	1949	Beery, Wallace
1901	1970	Begley, Ed.
1903	1931	Beiderbecke, Bix
1854	1931	Belasco, David
1906	1968	Benaderet, Bea
1906	1964	Bendix, William
1905	1965	Bennett, Constance
1873	1944	Bennett, Richard
1894	1974	Benny, Jack
1924	1970	Benzell, Mimi
1867	1944	Beresford, Harry
1899	1966	Berg, Gertrude
1863	1927	Bernard, Sam
1844	1923	Bernhardt, Sarah
1893	1943	Bernie, Ben
1889	1967	Bickford, Charles
1911	1960	Bjoerling, Jussi
1898	1973	Blackmer, Sidney
1882	1951	Blaney, Charles E.
1900	1943	Bledsoe, Jules
1928	1972	Blocker, Dan
1888	1959	Blore, Eric
1901	1975	Blue, Ben
1899	1957	Bogart, Humphrey
1885	1965	Boland, Mary
1897	1969	Boles, John
1903	1960	Bond, Ward
1833	1893	Booth, Edwin
1796	1852	Booth, Junius Brutus
1894	1953	Bordoni, Irene
1888	1960	Bori, Lucrezia
1867	1943	Bosworth, Hobart
1905	1965	Bow, Clara
1874	1946	Bowes, Maj. Edward
1895	1972	Boyd, William
1893	1939	Brady, Alice
1871	1936	Breese, Edmund
1898	1964	Brendel, El
1901	1948	Breneman, Tom
1894	1974	Brennan, Walter
1875	1948	Brian, Donald
1891	1951	Brice, Fanny
1891	1959	Broderick, Helen
1898	1965	Brokenshire, Norman
1904	1951	Bromberg, J. Edward
1892	1973	Brown, Joe E.
1926	1966	Bruce, Lenny
1895	1953	Bruce, Nigel
1891	1957	Buchanan, Jack
1886	1957	Buck, Gene
1904	1965	Bunce, Alan
1863	1915	Bunny, John
1886	1970	Burke, Billie
1912	1967	Burnette, Smiley
1896	1956	Burns, Bob
1902	1971	Burns, David
1882	1941	Burr, Henry
1883	1966	Bushman, Francis X.
1896	1946	Butterworth, Charles
1893	1971	Byington, Spring

C

Born	Died	Name
1905	1972	Cabot, Bruce
1895	1956	Calhern, Louis
1858	1942	Calve, Emma
1865	1940	Campbell, Mrs. Patrick
1892	1964	Cantor, Eddie
1878	1947	Carey, Harry
1876	1941	Carle, Richard
1897	1954	Carney, "Uncle Don"
1880	1961	Carrillo, Leo
1892	1972	Carroll, Leo G.
1905	1965	Carroll, Nancy
1910	1963	Carson, Jack
1862	1937	Carter, Mrs. Leslie
1873	1921	Caruso, Enrico
1876	1973	Casals, Pablo
1894	1969	Castle, Irene
1887	1918	Castle, Vernon
1889	1960	Catlett, Walter
1874	1944	Cavalieri, Lina
1887	1950	Cavanaugh, Hobart
1873	1938	Chaliapin, Feodor
1919	1961	Chandler, Jeff
1883	1930	Chaney, Lon
1906	1973	Chaney, Jr., Lon
1893	1940	Chase, Charlie
1893	1961	Chatterton, Ruth
1888	1971	Chevalier, Maurice

Born	Died	Name
1888	1960	Clark, Bobby
1914	1968	Clark, Fred
1887	1950	Clayton, Lou
1920	1966	Clift, Montgomery
1932	1963	Cline, Patsy
1900	1937	Clive, Colin
1892	1967	Clyde, Andy
1877	1961	Coburn, Charles
1887	1934	Cody, Lew
1878	1942	Cohan, George M.
1876	1916	Cohan, Josephine
1919	1965	Cole, Nat (King)
1878	1955	Collier, Constance
1866	1944	Collier, William, Sr.
1891	1958	Colman, Ronald
1908	1934	Columbo, Russ
1907	1944	Compton, Betty
1887	1940	Connolly, Walter
1855	1909	Conried, Henrich
1890	1964	Conroy, Frank
1918	1975	Conte, Richard
1904	1967	Conway, Tom
1901	1961	Cook, Donald
1890	1959	Cook, Joe
1893	1958	Cook, Phil
1901	1961	Cooper, Gary
1891	1971	Cooper, Gladys
1896	1973	Cooper, Melville
1914	1968	Corey, Wendell
1893	1974	Cornell, Katherine
1890	1972	Correll, Charles
1876	1951	Cossart, Ernest
1904	1957	Costello, Helene
1906	1959	Costello, Lou
1877	1950	Costello, Maurice
1899	1973	Coward, Noel
1890	1950	Cowl, Jane
1924	1973	Cox, Wally
1847	1924	Crabtree, Lotta
1875	1945	Craven, Frank
1916	1944	Cregar, Laird
1880	1942	Crews, Laura Hope
1880	1974	Crisp, Donald
1943	1973	Croce, Jim
1910	1960	Cromwell, Richard
1897	1975	Cross, Milton
1893	1966	Crouse, Russell
1878	1968	Currie, Finlay
1909	1953	Curtis, Alan

D

Born	Died	Name
1924	1965	Dandridge, Dorothy
1869	1941	Danforth, William
1894	1963	Daniel, Henry
1901	1971	Daniels, Bebe
1860	1935	Daniels, Frank
1936	1973	Darin, Bobby
1921	1965	Darnell, Linda
1894	1967	Darwell, Jane
1866	1949	Davenport, Harry
1900	1961	Davies, Marion
1908	1961	Davis, Joan
1931	1955	Dean, James
1881	1950	DeCordoba, Pedro
1905	1968	Dekker, Albert
1898	1965	Demarco, Tony
1881	1959	DeMille, Cecil B.
1891	1967	Denny, Reginald
1902	1975	DeSica, Vittorio
1878	1949	Desmond, William
1878	1930	Destinn, Emmy
1942	1972	De Wilde, Brandon
1916	1974	De Wolfe, Billy
1865	1950	De Wolfe, Elsie
1879	1947	Digges, Dudley
1890	1944	Dinehart, Alan
1901	1966	Disney, Walt
1895	1949	Dix, Richard
1856	1924	Dockstader, Lew
1892	1941	Dolly, Jennie
1892	1970	Dolly, Rosie
1905	1958	Donat, Robert
1903	1972	Donlevy, Brian
1904	1957	Dorsey, Jimmy
1905	1956	Dorsey, Tommy
1907	1959	Douglas, Paul
1889	1956	Draper, Ruth
1881	1965	Dresser, Louise
1869	1934	Dressler, Marie

Born	Died	Name
1820	1897	Drew, Mrs. John
1853	1927	Drew, John (son)
1879	1920	Drew, Sydney
1909	1951	Duchin, Eddy
1940	1971	Duel, Peter
1900	1964	Dumke, Ralph
1890	1965	Dumont, Margaret
1877	1927	Duncan, Isadora
1905	1967	Dunn, James
1873	1947	Dupree, Minnie
1907	1968	Duryea, Dan
1859	1924	Duse, Eleanora

E

Born	Died	Name
1894	1929	Eagles, Jeanne
1896	1930	Eames, Clare
1865	1952	Eames, Emma
1901	1967	Eddy, Nelson
1894	1971	Edwards, Cliff
1879	1945	Edwards, Gus
1899	1974	Ellington, Duke
1941	1974	Elliot, Cass
1871	1940	Elliott, Maxine
1891	1967	Elman, Mischa
1883	1941	Eltinge, Julian
1881	1951	Errol, Leon
1903	1967	Erwin, Stuart
1913	1967	Evelyn, Judith

F

Born	Died	Name
1883	1939	Fairbanks, Douglas
1915	1970	Farmer, Frances
1870	1929	Farnum, Dustin
1876	1953	Farnum, William
1882	1967	Farrar, Geraldine
1904	1971	Farrell, Glenda
1868	1940	Faversham, William
1861	1939	Fawcett, George
1897	1960	Fay, Frank
1895	1962	Fazenda, Louise
1903	1971	Fernandel
1905	1950	Field, Sidney
1867	1941	Fields, Lew
1879	1946	Fields, W. C.
1911	1975	Fine, Larry
1865	1932	Fiske, Minnie Maddern
1888	1961	Fitzgerald, Barry
1874	1941	Fitzgerald, Cissy
1895	1962	Flagstad, Kirsten
1900	1971	Flippen, Jay C.
1909	1959	Flynn, Errol
1925	1974	Flynn, Joe
1880	1942	Fokine, Michel
1910	1968	Foley, Red
1905	1951	Forbes, Ralph
1853	1937	Forbes-Robertson
1887	1970	Ford, Ed (Senator)
1895	1973	Ford, John
1899	1965	Ford, Wallace
1806	1872	Forrest, Edwin
1904	1970	Foster, Preston
1854	1928	Foy, Eddie
1905	1968	Francis, Kay
1893	1966	Frawley, William
1885	1938	Frederick, Pauline
1870	1955	Friganza, Trixie
1890	1958	Frisco, Joe
1860	1915	Frohman, Charles
1851	1940	Frohman, Daniel
1885	1947	Fyffe, Will

G

Born	Died	Name
1901	1960	Gable, Clark
1889	1963	Galli-Curci, Amelita
1877	1967	Garden, Mary
1913	1952	Garfield, John
1922	1969	Garland, Judy
1893	1963	Gaxton, Wm.
1904	1954	George, Gladys
1879	1961	George, Grace
1892	1962	Gibson, Hoot
1890	1957	Gigli, Beniamino
1894	1971	Gilbert, Billy
1897	1936	Gilbert, John
1855	1937	Gillette, William
1867	1943	Gillmore, Frank
1879	1939	Gilpin, Charles
1898	1968	Gish, Dorothy
1886	1959	Gleason, James

Born	Died	Name
1884	1938	Gluck, Alma
1874	1955	Golden, John
1882	1974	Goldwyn, Samuel
1917	1969	Gorcey, Leo
1884	1940	Gordon, C. Henry
1887	1948	Gordon, Vera
1869	1944	Gottschalk, Ferdinand
1829	1869	Gottschalk, Louis
1916	1973	Grable, Betty
1901	1959	Gray, Gilda
1879	1954	Greenstreet, Sydney
1874	1948	Griffith, David Wark
1885	1957	Guitry, Sacha
1912	1967	Guthrie, Woody
1875	1959	Gwenn, Edmund

H

Born	Died	Name
1888	1942	Hackett, Charles
1902	1958	Hackett, Raymond
1870	1943	Haines, Robert T.
1892	1950	Hale, Alan
1847	1919	Hammerstein, Oscar
1895	1960	Hammerstein, Oscar, 2d
1879	1955	Hampden, Walter
1873	1958	Handy, W. C.
1924	1964	Haney, Carol
1893	1964	Hardwicke, Sir Cedric
1892	1957	Hardy, Oliver
1883	1939	Hare, T. E. (Ernie)
1911	1937	Harlow, Jean
1872	1946	Harned, Virginia
1844	1911	Harrigan, Edward
1895	1943	Hart, Lorenz
1870	1946	Hart, William S.
1907	1955	Hartman, Grace
1928	1973	Harvey, Laurence
1876	1945	Harwood, John
1910	1973	Hawkins, Jack
1890	1973	Hayakawa, Sessue
1885	1969	Hayes, Gabby
1902	1971	Hayward, Leland
1919	1975	Haywood, Susan
1896	1937	Healy, Ted
1910	1971	Heflin, Van
1879	1936	Heggie, O. P.
1873	1918	Held, Anna
1903	1947	Hellinger, Mark
1885	1955	Hempel, Frieda
1943	1970	Hendrix, Jimi
1913	1969	Henie, Sonja
1879	1942	Herbert, Henry
1887	1951	Herbert, Hugh
1886	1956	Hersholt, Jean
1895	1942	Hibbard, Edna
1857	1927	Hillard, Robert C.
1865	1929	Hitchcock, Raymond
1914	1955	Hodiak, John
1876	1957	Hofmann, Josef
1894	1973	Holden, Fay
1919	1959	Holliday, Billie
1923	1965	Holliday, Judy
1888	1951	Holt, Jack
1871	1947	Homer, Louise
1858	1935	Hopper, DeWolf
1874	1959	Hopper, Edna Wallace
1890	1966	Hopper, Hedda
1916	1970	Hopper, William
1888	1970	Horton, Edward Everett
1874	1926	Houdini, Harry
1881	1965	Howard, Eugene
1867	1961	Howard, Joe
1893	1943	Howard, Leslie
1905	1975	Howard, Moe
1886	1955	Howard, Tom
1886	1949	Howard, Willie
1914	1972	Hudson, Rochelle
1886	1957	Hull, Josephine
1907	1967	Hume, Benita
1895	1958	Humphrey, Doris
1895	1945	Hunter, Glenn
1925	1969	Hunter, Jeffrey
1901	1962	Husing, Ted
1884	1950	Huston, Walter

I

Born	Died	Name
1892	1950	Ingram, Rex
1895	1969	Ingram, Rex
1838	1905	Irving, Henry
1871	1944	Irving, Isabel

Born	Died	Name
1872	1914	Irving, Laurence
1862	1938	Irwin, May

J

Born	Died	Name
1875	1942	Jackson, Joe
1911	1972	Jackson, Mahalia
1889	1956	Janis, Elsie
1886	1950	Jannings, Emil
1829	1905	Jefferson, Joseph
1859	1923	Jefferson, Thomas
1900	1974	Jenkins, Allen
1862	1930	Jewett, Henry
1892	1962	Johnson, Chic
1878	1952	Johnson, Edward
1888	1850	Jolson, Al
1899	1940	Jones, Billy
1889	1942	Jones, Buck
1911	1965	Jones, Spike
1943	1970	Joplin, Janis
1897	1961	Jordan, Marian (Molly McGee)
1890	1955	Joyce, Alice

K

Born	Died	Name
1878	1965	Kaltenborn, Hans V.
1910	1966	Kane, Helen
1887	1969	Karloff, Boris
1893	1970	Karns, Roscoe
1811	1868	Kean, Charles
1806	1880	Kean, Mrs. Charles
1787	1833	Kean, Edmund
1895	1966	Keaton, Buster
1858	1929	Keenan, Frank
1830	1873	Keene, Laura
1841	1898	Keene, Thomas W.
1899	1960	Keith, Ian
1894	1973	Kellaway, Cecil
1899	1956	Kelly, Paul
1873	1939	Kelly, Walter C.
1909	1968	Kelton, Pert
1823	1895	Kemble, Agnes
1775	1854	Kemble, Charles
1809	1893	Kemble, Fannie
1848	1935	Kendal, Dame Madge
1843	1917	Kendal, Wm. H.
1926	1959	Kendall, Kay
1890	1948	Kennedy, Edgar
1885	1965	Kennedy, Tom
1886	1945	Kent, William
1880	1947	Kerrigan, J. Warren
1886	1956	Kibbee, Guy
1902	1966	Kiepura, Jan
1888	1964	Kilbride, Percy
1913	1965	Kilgallen, Dorothy
1863	1933	Kilgour, Joseph
1899	1965	King, Alexander
1894	1944	King, Charles
1897	1971	King, Dennis
1889	1938	Kohler, Fred
1897	1957	Korngold, Erich W.
1919	1962	Kovacs, Ernie
1885	1974	Kruger, Otto
1909	1973	Krupa, Gene

L

Born	Died	Name
1913	1964	Ladd, Alan
1895	1967	Lahr, Bert
1919	1973	Lake, Veronica
1904	1948	Landi, Elissa
1919	1948	Landis, Carole
1904	1972	Landis, Jessie Royce
1884	1944	Langdon, Harry
1856	1929	Langtry, Lillian
1921	1959	Lanza, Mario
1881	1958	Lasky, Jesse L.
1870	1950	Lauder, Harry
1899	1962	Laughton, Charles
1890	1965	Laurel, Stan
1892	1954	Laurie, Joe, Jr.
1898	1952	Lawrence, Gertrude
1890	1929	Lawrence, Margaret
1907	1952	Lee, Canada
1914	1970	Lee, Gypsy Rose
1848	1929	Lehmann, Lilli
1896	1950	Lehr, Lew
1913	1967	Leigh, Vivien
1852	1908	Leighton, Margaret
1894	1931	Leitzel, Lillian
1831	1905	Lemoyne, W. J.

Born	Died	Name
1870	1941	Leonard, Eddie
1911	1973	Leonard, Jack E.
1906	1972	Levant, Oscar
1881	1955	Levy, Ethel
1902	1971	Lewis, Joe E.
1891	1971	Lewis, Ted
1874	1944	Lhevinne, Josef
1889	1952	Lincoln, Elmo
1820	1887	Lind, Jenny
1889	1968	Lindsay, Howard
1869	1952	Lipman, Clara
1889	1971	Lloyd, Harold
1876	1922	Lloyd, Marie
1891	1957	Lockhart, Gene
1913	1969	Logan, Ella
1876	1943	Loftus, Cissie (Marie)
1909	1942	Lombard, Carole
1927	1975	Long, Richard
1890	1950	Lord, Pauline
1888	1968	Lorne, Marion
1904	1964	Lorre, Peter
1917	1970	Louise, Anita
1914	1962	Lovejoy, Frank
1892	1971	Lowe, Edmund
1892	1947	Lubitsch, Ernst
1885	1956	Lugosi, Bela
1895	1971	Lukas, Paul
1902	1947	Lunceford, Jimmy
1853	1932	Lupino, George
1893	1942	Lupino, Stanley
1897	1957	Lyman, Abe
1926	1971	Lynn, Diana
1885	1954	Lytell, Bert
1867	1936	Lytton, Henry

M

Born	Died	Name
1907	1965	MacDonald, Jeanette
1902	1969	MacLane, Barton
1909	1973	Macready, George
1861	1946	Macy, George Carleton
1908	1973	Magnani, Anna
1896	1967	Mahoney, Will
1890	1975	Main, Marjorie
1933	1967	Mansfield, Jayne
1857	1907	Mansfield, Richard
1897	1975	March, Fredric
1920	1970	March, Hal
1865	1950	Marlowe, Julia
1890	1966	Marshall, Herbert
1864	1943	Marshall, Tully
1885	1969	Martinelli, Giovanni
1887	1961	Marx, Leonard (Chico)
1888	1964	Marx, Arthur (Harpo)
1862	1951	Maude, Cyril
1922	1972	Maxwell, Marilyn
1879	1948	May, Edna
1885	1957	Mayer, Louis B.
1895	1973	Maynard, Ken
1884	1945	McCormack, John
1907	1962	McCormick, Myron
1888	1931	McCoy, Bessie
1883	1936	McCullough, Paul
1895	1952	McDaniel, Hattie
1924	1965	McDonald, Marie
1879	1949	McIntyre, Frank J.
1857	1937	McIntyre, James
1879	1937	McKinley, Mabel
1886	1959	McLaglen, Victor
1907	1971	McMahon, Horace
1880	1946	Meek, Donald
1879	1936	Meighan, Thomas
1861	1931	Melba, Nellie
1890	1973	Melchior, Lauritz
1904	1961	Melton, James
1890	1963	Menjou, Adolphe
1902	1966	Menken, Helen
1882	1939	Mercer, Beryl
1880	1946	Merivale, Phillip
1904	1944	Miller, Glenn
1860	1926	Miller, Henry
1898	1936	Miller, Marilyn
1895	1927	Mills, Florence
1903	1955	Minnevitch, Borrah
1917	1955	Miranda, Carmen
1875	1957	Mitchell, Grant
1892	1962	Mitchell, Thomas
1880	1940	Mix, Tom
1845	1909	Modjeska, Helena
1926	1962	Monroe, Marilyn

Born	Died	Name		Born	Died	Name		Born	Died	Name
1883	1953	Werrenrath, Reinald		1867	1918	Williams, Evan		1886	1966	Wynn, Ed
1879	1942	Westley, Helen		1923	1953	Williams, Hank		1906	1964	Wynyard, Diana
1895	1968	Wheeler, Bert		1917	1972	Wilson, Marie				**Y**
1889	1938	White, Pearl		1884	1969	Winninger, Charles				
1890	1967	Whiteman, Paul		1904	1959	Withers, Grant		1891	1960	Young, Clara Kimball
1882	1943	Whiting, George		1881	1931	Wolheim, Louis		1887	1953	Young, Roland
1865	1948	Whitty, Dame May		1907	1961	Wong, Anna May		1900	1956	Young, Victor
1906	1966	Whorf, Richard		1888	1963	Woolley, Monty				**Z**
1895	1948	William, Warren		1889	1938	Woolsey, Robert				
1877	1922	Williams, Bert		1881	1956	Wycherly, Margaret		1869	1932	Ziegfeld, Florenz

Rulers of England and Great Britain

England
Saxons and Danes

Name		Began	Died	Age	Rgd
Egbert	King of Wessex, won allegiance of all English	827	839	—	12
Ethelwulf	Son, King of Wessex, Sussex, Kent, Essex	839	858	—	19
Ethelbald	Son of Ethelwulf, displaced father in Wessex	858	860	—	2
Ethelbert	2d son of Ethelwulf, united Kent and Wessex	858	866	—	8
Ethelred	3d son, King of Wessex, defeated Danes	866	871	—	5
Alfred	The Great, 4th son, fought Danes, fortified London	871	901	52	30
Edward	The Elder, Alfred's son, united English, claimed Scotland	901	925	55	24
Athelstan	The Glorious, Edward's son, King of Mercia, Wessex	925	940	45	15
Edmund	3d son of Edward, King of Wessex, Mercia	940	946	25	6
Edred	4th son of Edward	946	955	32	9
Edwy	The Fair, eldest son of Edmund, King of Wessex	955	959	18	3
Edgar	The Peaceful, son of Edmund, ruled all English	959	975	32	17
Edward	The Martyr, son of Edgar, murdered by stepmother	975	978	17	4
Ethelred II	The Unready, son of Edgar, married Emma of Normandy	978	1016	48	37
Edmund	Ironside, son of Ethelred II, King of London	1016	1016	27	0
Canute	The Dane, gave Wessex to Edmund, married Emma	1017	1035	40	18
Harold I	Harefoot, natural son of Canute	1035	1040	—	5
Hardicanute	Son of Canute by Emma; Danish King	1040	1042	24	2
Edward	The Confessor, son of Ethelred II (Canonized 1161)	1042	1066	62	24
Harold II	Edward's brother-in-law, last Saxon King	1066	1066	44	0

House of Normandy

Name		Began	Died	Age	Rgd
William I	The Conqueror, defeated Harold at Hastings	1066	1087	60	21
William II	Rufus, 3d son of William I, killed by arrow	1087	1100	43	13
Henry I	Beauclerc, youngest son of William I	1100	1135	67	35

House of Blois

Name		Began	Died	Age	Rgd
Stephen	Son of Adela, 4th dau. of William I, and Count of Blois	1135	1154	50	19

House of Plantagenet

Name		Began	Died	Age	Rgd
Henry II	Son of Goeffrey Plantagenet (Angevin) by Matilda, dau. of Henry I	1154	1189	56	35
Richard I	Coeur de Lion, son of Henry II, crusader	1189	1199	42	10
John	Lackland, son of Henry II, signed Magna Carta, 1215	1199	1216	50	17
Henry III	Son of John, acceded at 9, under regency until 1227	1216	1272	65	56
Edward I	Longshanks, son of Henry III	1272	1307	68	35
Edward II	Son of Edward I, deposed by Parliament, 1327	1307	1327	43	20
Edward III	Of Windsor, son of Edward II	1327	1377	65	50
Richard II	Grandson of Edw. III, minor until 1389, deposed 1399	1377	1400	34	22

House of Lancaster

Name		Began	Died	Age	Rgd
Henry IV	Son of John of Gaunt, Duke of Lancaster, son of Edw. III	1399	1413	47	13
Henry V	Son of Henry IV, victor of Agincourt	1413	1422	34	9
Henry VI	Son of Henry V deposed 1461, died in Tower	1422	1471	49	39

House of York

Name		Began	Died	Age	Rgd
Edward IV	Great-great-grandson of Edward III, son of Duke of York	1461	1483	41	22
Edward V	Son of Edward IV, murdered in Tower of London	1483	1483	13	0
Richard III	Crookback, bro. of Edward IV, fell at Bosworth Field	1483	1485	35	2

House of Tudor

Name		Began	Died	Age	Rgd
Henry VII	Son of Edmund Tudor, Earl of Richmond, whose father had married the widow of Henry V; descended from Edward III through his mother, Margaret Beaufort via John of Gaunt. By marriage with dau. of Edward IV he united Lancaster and York	1485	1509	53	24
Henry VIII	Son of Henry VII *See memorable dates*	1509	1547	56	38
Edward VI	Son of Henry VIII, by Jane Seymour, his 3d queen. Ruled under regents. Was forced to name Lady Jane Grey his successor. Council of State proclaimed her queen Jul. 10, 1553. Mary Tudor won Council, was proclaimed queen Jul. 19, 1553. Mary had Lady Jane Grey beheaded for treason, Feb., 1554	1547	1553	16	6
Mary I	Daughter of Henry VIII, by Catharine of Aragon	1553	1558	43	5
Elizabeth I	Daughter of Henry VIII, by Anne Boleyn, *Designated Elizabeth I in 1952*	1558	1603	69	44

Great Britain
House of Stuart

Name		Began	Died	Age	Rgd
James I	James VI of Scotland, son of Mary, Queen of Scots. *First to call himself King of Great Britain. This became official with the Act of Union, 1707.*	1603	1625	59	22
Charles I	Only surviving son of James I: beheaded Jan. 30, 1649	1625	1649	48	24

Commonwealth, 1649-1660
Council of State, 1649: Protectorate, 1653

Name		Began	Died	Age	Rgd
The Cromwells	Oliver Cromwell, Lord Protector	1653	1658	59	—
	Richard Cromwell, Lord Protector, resigned May 25, 1659	1658	1712	86	—

House of Stuart (Restored)	Began	Died	Age	Rgd
Charles II.........Eldest son of Charles I, died without issue.....................	1660	1685	55	25
James II..........2d son of Charles I. Deposed 1688. Interregnum Dec. 11, 1688, to Feb. 13, 1689...	1685	1701	68	3
William III.........Son of William, Prince of Orange, by Mary, dau. of Charles I......	1689	1702	51	13
and Mary II Eldest daughter of James II and wife of William III................		1694	33	6
Anne.............2d daughter of James..................................	1702	1714	49	12
House of Hanover				
George I..........Son of Elector of Hanover, by Sophia, grand-dau. of James I.........	1714	1727	67	13
George II.........Only son of George I, married Caroline of Brandenburg.............	1727	1760	77	33
George III.........Grandson of George II, married Charlotte of Mecklenburg...........	1760	1820	81	59
George IV.........Eldest son of George III, Prince Regent, from Feb., 1811...........	1820	1830	67	10
William IV........3d son of George III, married Adelaide of Saxe-Meiningen..........	1830	1837	71	7
Victoria..........Dau. of Edward, 4th son of George III; married (1840) Prince Albert of Saxe-Coburg and Gotha, who became Prince Consort...........	1837	1901	81	63
House of Saxe-Coburg and Gotha				
Edward VII........Eldest son of Victoria, married Alexandria, Princess of Denmark.....	1901	1910	68	9
House of Windsor				
Name Adopted Jul. 17, 1917				
George V.........2d son of Edward VII, married Princess Mary of Teck..............	1910	1936	70	25
Edward VIII.......Eldest son of George V; acceded Jan. 20, 1936, abdicated Dec. 11...	1936	1972	77	1
George VI.........2d son of George V; married Lady Elizabeth Bowes-Lyon..........	1936	1952	56	15
Elizabeth II.......Elder daughter of George VI, acceded Feb. 6, 1952..............	1952	—	—	—

Rulers of Scotland

The Romans gave the name of Caledonia to present-day Scotland and called the people Caledonians. The Scots, a Celtic race that spoke Gaelic, came from Ireland, then called Scotia.

Kenneth I (S. C. MacAlpin) was the first Scot to rule both Scots and Picts, 843 A.D.

Duncan I was the first general ruler, 1034. Macbeth seized the kingdom 1040, was slain by Duncan's son, Malcolm Canmore (Malcolm III), 1058.

Malcolm married Margaret, English princess who had fled from the Normans. Queen Margaret introduced English language and English monastic customs. She was canonized. Her son Edgar, 1097, moved the court to Edinburgh. His brothers Alexander I and David I succeeded. Malcolm IV, grandson of David I, 1153, was followed by his brother, William the Lion, 1165, whose son was Alexander II, 1214. The latter's son, Alexander III, defeated the Norse and regained the Hebrides. When he died, 1286, his granddaughter, Margaret, child of Eric of Norway and grandniece of Edward I of England, known as the Maid of Norway, was chosen ruler, but died on the way, 1290.

John Baliol, 1292-1296. (Interregnum, 10 years).

Robert Bruce (The Bruce), 1306-1329, victor at Bannockburn, 1314.

David II only son of Robert Bruce ruled 1329-1371.

Robert II, 1371-1390, grandson of Robert Bruce, son of Walter, the Steward of Scotland, was called The Steward, first of the so-called Stuart line.

Robert III, son of Robert II, 1390-1406.

James I, son of Robert III, 1406-1437.

James II, son of James I, 1437-1460.

James III, 1460-1488, eldest son of James II.

James IV, 1488-1513, eldest son of James III.

James V, 1513-1542, eldest son of James IV.

Mary, daughter, born 1542, became queen when 1 week old; was crowned 1543. Married, 1558, Francis, son of Henry II of France, who became king 1559, died 1560. Mary ruled Scots 1561 until abdication, 1567. She also married (2) Henry Stewart, Lord Darnley, and (3) James, Earl of Bothwell. Imprisoned by Elizabeth I; beheaded 1587.

James VI, 1567-1625, son of Mary and Lord Darnley, became King of England on death of Elizabeth in 1603. Although the thrones were thus united, the legislative union of Scotland and England was not effected until the act of Union, May 1, 1707.

Rulers of France: Kings, Queens, Presidents

Caesar to Charlemagne

Julius Caesar subdued the Gauls, native tribes of Gaul (France) 57 to 52 B.C. The Romans ruled 500 years. The Franks, a Teutonic tribe, reached the Somme from the East ca. 250 A.D. By the 5th Century the Merovingian Franks ousted the Romans. In 451 A.D., with the help of Visigoths, Burgundians and others, they defeated Attila and the Huns at Chalons-sur-Marne.

Childeric I became leader of the Merovingians 458 A.D. His son Clovis I (Chlodwig, Ludwig, Louis), crowned 481, founded the dynasty. After defeating the Alemanni (Germans) 496, he was baptized a Christian and made Paris his capital. His line ruled until Childeric III was deposed, 742.

The West Merovingians were called Neustrians, the eastern Austrasians. Pepin of Herstal (687-714) major domus, or head of the palace, of Austrasia, took over Neustria as dux (leader) of the Franks. Pepin's son, Charles, called Martel (the Hammer) defeated the Saracens at Tours-Poitiers, 732; was succeeded by his son, Pepin the Short, 741, who deposed Childeric III and ruled as king until 768.

His son, Charlemagne, or Charles the Great (742-814) became king of the Franks, 768, with his brother Carloman, who died 771. He ruled France, Germany, parts of Italy, Spain, Austria and enforced Christianity. Crowned Emperor of the Romans by Pope Leo III in St. Peter's, Rome, Dec. 25, 800 A.D. Succeeded by son, Louis the Pious, 814. At death, 840, Louis left empire to sons, Lothair (Roman emperor); Pepin I (king of Aquitaine); Louis II (of Germany); Charles the Bald (France). They quarreled and by the peace of Verdun, 843, divided the empire.

A.D. Name and Year of Accession

The Carolingians

840 Charles I, the Bald, Roman Emperor, 875
877 Louis II, the Stammerer, son
879 Louis III (died 882) and Carloman (bro.)
884 Charles II, the Fat; Roman Emperor, 881
888 Eudes (Odo) elected by nobles. Ceded land to
898 Charles III, the Simple, son of Louis II, defeated by
922 Robert, brother of Eudes, killed in war
923 Rodolph (Raoul) Duke of Burgundy
936 Louis IV, son of Charles III
954 Lothair, son, aged 13, defeated by Capet
986 Louis V, the Sluggard, left no heirs

The Capets

987 Hugh Capet, son of Hugh the Great
996 Robert (the Wise), his son
1031 Henry I, his son, last Norman
1060 Philip I (the Fair), son, king at 14
1108 Louis VI (the Fat), son
1137 Louis VII (the Younger), son
1180 Philip II (Augustus), son, crowned at Reims
1223 Louis VIII (the Lion), son
1226 Louis IX, son, crusader; Louis IX (1214-1270) reigned 44 years, arbitrated disputes with English King Henry III; led crusades, 1248 (captured in Egypt 1250) and 1270, when he died of plague in Tunis. Canonized 1297 as St. Louis.
1270 Philip III (the Hardy), son
1285 Philip IV (the Fair), son, king at 17
1314 Louis X (the Headstrong), son. His posthumous son, John I, lived only 7 days
1316 Philip V (the Tall), brother of Louis X

1322   Charles IV (the Fair), brother of Louis X

House of Valois

1328   Philip VI (of Valois), grandson of Philip III
1350   John II (the Good), his son, retired to England
1364   Charles V (the Wise), son
1380   Charles VI (the Beloved), son
1422   Charles VII (the Victorious), son. In 1429 Joan of Arc (Jeanne d'Arc) promised Charles to oust the English, who occupied northern France. Joan won at Orleans and Patay and had Charles crowned at Reims July 17, 1429. Joan was captured May 24, 1430, and executed May 30, 1431, at Rouen for heresy. Charles ordered her rehabilitation, effected 1455.
1461   Louis XI (the Cruel), son, civil reformer
1483   Charles VIII (the Affable), son
1498   Louis XII, great grandson of Charles V
1515   Francis I, of Angouleme, nephew, son-in-law. Francis I (1494-1547) reigned 32 years, fought 4 big wars, was patron of the arts, aided Cellini, del Sarto, Leonardo da Vinci, Rabelais. Embellished Fontainebleau
1547   Henry II, son, killed at a joust in a tournament. He was the husband of Catherine de Medici (1519-1589) and the lover of Diane de Poitiers (1499-1566). Catherine was born in Florence, daughter of Lorenzo de Medici. By her marriage to Henry II she became the mother of Francis II, Charles IX, Henry III and Queen Margaret (Reine Margot) wife of Henry IV. She persuaded Charles IX to order the massacre of Huguenots on the Feast of St. Bartholomew, Aug. 24, 1572, the day her daughter was married to Henry of Navarre.
1559   Francis II, son of Henry II. In 1548, Mary, Queen of Scots since infancy, was betrothed when 6 to Francis, aged 4. They were married 1558. Francis died 1560, aged 16; Mary ruled Scotland, abdicated 1567.
1560   Charles IX, brother of Francis II
1574   Henry III, brother, assassinated

House of Bourbon

1589   Henry IV, of Navarre, assassinated. Henry IV made enemies when he gave tolerance to Protestants by Edict of Nantes, 1598. He was grandson of Queen Margaret of Navarre, literary patron. He married Margaret of Valois, Catherine de Medici's daughter; was divorced; in 1600 married Marie de Medicis, who was Regent of France, 1610-17 for her son, Louis XIII, and was exiled by Richelieu
1610   Louis XIII (the Just), son, Louis XIII (1610-1643) married Anne of Austria. His ministers were Cardinals Richelieu and Mazarin
1643   Louis XIV (The Grand Monarch), son, Louis XIV was king 72 years. He exhausted a prosperous country in wars for thrones and territory. By revoking the Edict of Nantes (1685) he caused the emigration of the Huguenots. He said: "I am the state." His mistresses were Louise de la Valliere, Madame de Montespan and Madame de Maintenon
1715   Louis XV, great grandson. Louis XV (1710-1774) married a Polish princess. Lost Canada to the English. His favorites, Mme. Pompadour and Mme. Du Barry influenced policies. Noted for saying: Apres moi; le deluge. (After me, the deluge)

1774   Louis XVI, grandson; married Marie Antoinette, dau. of Empress Maria Therese of Austria. King and queen beheaded by Revolution, 1793. Their son, called Louis XVII, died in prison, never ruled.

First Republic

1792   National Convention of the French Revolution
1795   Directory, under Barras and others
1799   Consulate, Napoleon Bonaparte, First Consul. In 1802 elected Consul for life

First Empire

1804   Napoleon I, Emperor. Josephine (de Beauharnais) Empress, 1804-09; Marie Louise, Empress, 1810-1814. Her son, Francois (1811-1832) titular King of Rome, later Duke de Reichstadt and "Napoleon II," never ruled. Napoleon abdicated 1814, died 1821.

Bourbons Restored

1814   Louis XVIII king; brother of Louis XVI.
1824   Charles X, brother; reactionary, deposed by the July Revolution, 1830.

House of Orleans

1830   Louis Philippe, the Citizen King

Second Republic

1848   Louis Napoleon. President, nephew of Napoleon I. He became:

Second Empire

1852   Napoleon III, Emperor, Eugenie (de Montijo) Empress. Lost Franco-Prussian war, deposed 1870. Son, Prince Imperial (1856-79), died in Zulu War. Eugenie died 1920.

Third Republic—Presidents

1871   Thiers, Louis Adolphe (1797-1877), historian
1873   MacMahon, Marshal Patrice M. (1808-1893)
1879   Grevy, Paul J. (1807-1891), resigned
1887   Sadi-Carnot, M. (1837-1894), assassinated
1894   Casimir-Pernier, Jean P. P. (1847-1907), resigned
1895   Faure, Francois Felix (1841-1899)
1899   Loubet, Emile (1838-1929)
1906   Fallieres, Armand (1841-1931)
1913   Poincare, Raymond (1860-1934)
1920   Deschanel, Paul (1856-1922), resigned
1920   Millerand, Alexandre (1859-1943), resigned
1924   Doumergue, Gaston (1863-1937)
1931   Doumer, Paul (1857-1932), assassinated
1932   Lebrun, Albert (1871-1950), resigned 1940

1940   Vichy govt. under German armistice: Henri Phillipe Petain (1856-1951) Chief of State, 1940-1944.
Provisional govt. after liberation: Chas. De Gaulle (1890-1970) Oct. 1944-Jan. 21, 1946; Felix Gouin (1884-   ) Jan. 23, 1946; Georges Bidault (1899-   ) June 24, 1946.

Fourth Republic—Presidents

1947   Auriol, Vincent (1884-1966)
1954   Coty, Rene (1882-1962)

Fifth Republic—Presidents

1958   De Gaulle, Charles Andre M. J. (1890-1970)
1969   Pompidou, Georges J. R. (1911-1974)
1974   Giscard d'Estaing, Valery (1926-   )

Rulers of Middle Europe; Rise and Fall of Dynasties

Carolingian Dynasty

Charles the Great, or Charlemagne, ruled France, Italy, and Middle Europe; established Ostmark (later Austria); crowned Roman emperor by pope in Rome, 800 A. D. Died 814.
Louis I (Ludwig) the Pious, son; crowned by Charlemagne 813, d. 840.
Louis the German, son, succeeded to East Francia (Germany) 843-876.
Charles the Fat, son, inherited East Francia and West Francia (France) 876, reunited empire, crowned emperor by pope, 881, deposed 887.
Arnulf, nephew, 887-899. Partition of empire.
Louis the Child, 900-911, last direct descendant of Charlemagne.
Conrad I, duke of Franconia, first elected German king, 911-918, founded House of Franconia.

Saxon Dynasty; First Reich

Henry I, the Fowler, duke of Saxony, 919-936.
Otto I, the Great, 936-973, son; crowned Holy Roman Emperor by pope, 962.
Otto II, 973-983, son; failed to oust Greeks and Arabs from Sicily.
Otto III, 983-1002, son. Crowned emperor at 16.
Henry II, duke of Bavaria, 1002-1024, great grandson of Henry the Fowler.

House of Franconia

Conrad II, 1024-1039, son-in-law of Otto I.
Henry III, 1039-1056, son; deposed 3 popes; annexed Burgundy.
Henry IV, 1056-1106, son; regency by his mother, Agnes of Poitou. Banned by Pope Gregory VII, he did penance at Canossa.
Henry V, 1106-1125, son; last of Salic House.
Lothair, duke of Saxony, 1125-1137. Crowned emperor in Rome, 1134.

House of Hohenstaufen

Conrad III, duke of Suabia, 1138-1152. In 2d Crusade.
Frederick I, Barbarossa, 1152-1190; son of Conrad's brother; in 3d Crusade.
Henry VI, 1190-1196, took lower Italy from Normans. Son became king of Sicily.
Philip of Suabia, 1198-1208, son of Frederick I.
Otto IV, of House of Welf, 1198-1215; deposed.
Frederick II, 1215-1250, son of Henry VI; king of Sicily; crowned king of Jerusalem in 5th Crusade.
Conrad IV, 1250-1254, son, lost lower Italy to Charles of Anjou.
Conradin, son, king of Jerusalem and Sicily, was beheaded. Last Hohenstaufen.

Interregnum, 1250-1273, Rise of the Electors.

Transition

Rudolph of Hapsburg, 1273-1291, defeated King Ottocar II of Bohemia. Bequeathed duchy of Austria to eldest son, Albert.

Adolphus, count of Nassau, 1291-1298, killed in war with Albert of Austria.

Albert I, German king, 1298-1308.

Henry VII, of Luxemburg, 1308-1313, crowned emperor in Rome. Seized Bohemia, 1310.

Louis IV of Bavaria (Wittelsbach), 1314-1347. Also elected was Frederick of Austria, 1314-1330 (Hapsburg). Abolition of papal sanction for election of Holy Roman Emperor.

Charles IV, of Luxemburg, 1347-1378, grandson of Henry VII, German emperor and king of Bohemia, Lombardy, Burgundy; took Mark of Brandenburg.

Wenceslaus, 1378-1400, deposed.

Rupert, Duke of Palatine, 1400-1410.

Hungary

Stephen I, house of Arpad, 907-1038. Crowned king by Pope Silvester II, 1001 A. D., converted Magyars. After several centuries of feuds Charles Robert of Anjou became Charles I, 1308-1342.

Louis I, the Great, son, 1342-1382, joint ruler of Poland with Casimir III, 1370. Defeated Turks.

Mary, daughter, 1385-1395, ruled with husband. Sigismund of Luxemburg, 1387-1437, also king of Bohemia. As bro. of Wenceslaus he succeeded Rupert as Holy Roman Emperor, 1410.

Albert II, 1438-1439, son-in-law of Sigismund; also Roman emperor. *See under Hapsburg.*

Ulaszlo I of Poland, died in battle, 1444.

Ladislaus V, child. John Hunyadi (Hunyadi Janos) guardian, fought Turks, Czechs; died 1456.

Matthias I (Corvinus) son of Hunyadi, 1458-1490. Shared rule of Bohemia, captured Vienna, 1485, annexed Austria, Styria, Carinthia.

Ulaszlo II (King of Bohemia) 1490-1516.

Louis II, son, aged 10. 1516-1526. Wars with Suleiman, Turk. In 1527 Hungary was split between Ferdinand I, Archduke of Austria, bro.-in-law of Louis II, and John Zapolya, of Transylvania. After Turkish invasion, 1547, Hungary was split between Ferdinand, Prince John Sigismund (Transylvania) and the Turks.

House of Hapsburg

Albert V of Austria, Hapsburg, crowned king of Hungary, Jan. 1438, Roman emperor, March, 1438, as Albert II; died 1439.

Frederick III, cousin, 1430-1493. Fought Turks.

Maximilian I, son, 1493-1519. Assumed title of Holy Roman emperor (German), 1493.

Charles V, grandson, 1519-1556. King of Spain with mother co-regent; crowned Roman emperor at Aix 1520. Confronted Luther at Worms; attempted church reform and religious conciliation. Abdicated 1556.

Ferdinand I, king of Bohemia, 1526, of Hungary, 1527; disputed. German king, 1531. Crowned Roman emperor on abdication of Charles V, 1556.

Maximilian II, son, 1564-1576; Rudolph II, son, 1576-1612.

Matthias, brother, 1612-1619, king of Bohemia and Hungary.

Ferdinand II, of Styria, king of Bohemia, 1617, of Hun-gary, 1618, Roman emperor, 1619. Bohemian Protestants deposed him, elected Frederick V of Palatine, starting Thirty Years War.

Ferdinand III, son, king of Hungary, 1625, Bohemia, 1627, Roman emperor, 1637. Peace of Westphalia, 1648, ended war. Leopold I, 1658-1705; Joseph I, 1705-1711; Charles VI, 1711-1740.

Maria Theresa, daughter, 1740-1780; Archduchess of Austria, queen of Hungary; ousted pretender, Charles VII, crowned 1742; in 1745 obtained election of her husband Francis I as Roman emperor and co-regent (d. 1765). Fought Seven Years' War with Frederick II (the Great) of Prussia. Mother of Marie Antoinette, Queen of France.

Joseph II, son 1765-1790, Roman emperor, reformer; powers restricted by Empress Maria Theresa until her death, 1780. First partition of Poland. Leopold II, 1790-1792.

Francis II, 1792-1835. Fought Napoleon. Proclaimed first hereditary emperor of Austria, 1806. Forced to abdicate as Roman emperor, 1806, last use of title. Ferdinand I, son, 1835-1848, abdicated during revolution.

Austro-Hungarian Monarchy

Francis Joseph I, nephew, 1848-1916, emperor of Austria, king of Hungary. Dual monarchy of Austria-Hungary formed, 1867. After assassination of heir, Archduke Francis Ferdinand, June 28, 1914, Austrian diplomacy precipitated World War I.

Charles I, grand-nephew, 1916-1918, last emperor of Austria and king of Hungary. Abdicated Nov. 11-13, 1918, died 1922.

Rulers of Prussia

Nucleus of Prussia was the Mark of Brandenburg. First margrave was Albert the Bear (Albrecht), 1134-1170. First Hohenzollern margrave was Frederick, burggrave of Nuremberg, 1415-1440.

Frederick William, 1640-1688, the Great Elector, son, Frederick III, 1688-1713, was crowned king Frederick of Prussia, 1701.

Frederick II, the Great, 1740-1786, annexed Silesia part of Austria.

Frederick William II, nephew, 1786-1797.

Frederick William III, 1797-1840. Napoleonic wars.

Frederick William IV, 1840-1861. Uprising of 1848 and first parliament and constitution.

Second and Third Reich

William I, 1861-1888, brother. Annexation of Schleswig and Hanover; Franco-Prussian war, 1870-71, proclamation of German Reich, Jan. 18, 1871, at Versailles; William, German emperor (Deutscher Kaiser), Bismarck, chancellor.

Frederick III, son, 1888.

William II, son 1888-1918. Led Germany in World War I, abdicated as German emperor and king of Prussia, Nov. 9, 1918. Died in exile in Netherlands June 4, 1941. Minor rulers of Bavaria, Saxony, Wurttemberg also abdicated.

Germany proclaimed a republic at Weimar, July 1, 1919. Presidents: Frederick Ebert, 1919-1925, Paul von Hindenburg-Beneckendorff, 1925, reelected 1932, d. Aug. 2, 1934. Adolf Hitler, chancellor, chosen successor as Leader-Chancellor (Fuehrer & Reichskanzler) of Third Reich. Annexed Austria, March, 1938. Precipitated World War II, 1939-1945. Committed suicide April 30, 1945.

Rulers of Denmark, Sweden, Norway

Denmark

Earliest rulers invaded Britain; King Canute, who ruled in London 1017-1035, was most famous. The Valdemars furnished kings until the 15th century. In 1282 the Danes won the first national assembly, Danehof, from King Erik.

Most redoubtable medieval character was Margaret, daughter of Valdemar IV, born 1353, married at 10 to King Haakon VI of Norway. In 1375 she had her first infant son Olaf made king of Denmark. After his death, 1387, she was regent of Denmark and Norway. In 1388 Sweden accepted her as sovereign. In 1389 she made her grand-nephew, Duke Erik of Pomerania, titular king of Denmark, Sweden and Norway, with herself as regent. In 1397 she effected the Union of Kalmar of the three kingdoms and had Erik crowned. In 1439 the three kingdoms deposed him and elected Christopher of Bavaria king (Christopher III). On his death, 1448, the union broke up.

Succeeding rulers were unable to enforce their claims as rulers of Sweden until 1520, when Christian II conquered Sweden. He was thrown out 1522, and in 1523 Gustavus Vasa united Sweden. Denmark continued to dominate Norway until the Napoleonic wars, when Frederick VI joined the Napoleonic cause after Britain had destroyed the Danish fleet (1807). In 1814 he was forced to cede Norway to Sweden and Helgoland to Britain, receiving Lauenburg. Successors: 1839—Christian VIII; 1848—Frederick VII; 1863-Christian IX; 1906—Frederick VIII; 1912—Christian X; 1947—Frederick IX; 1972—Queen Margrethe.

Sweden

Early kings ruled at Uppsala, but did not dominate the country. Sverker (1134-1156) united the Swedes and Goths. In 1435 Sweden obtained the Riksdag, or parliament. After the Union of Kalmar, 1379, the Danes either ruled or harried the country until Christian II of Denmark conquered it anew, 1520. This led to a rising under Gustavus Vasa, who ruled Sweden 1523-1560, and established an independent kingdom. Charles IX (1594-1611, crowned 1607), conquered Moscow. Gustavus II Adolphus (1611-1633) was called the Great. Later rulers, 1633—Christina; 1654—Charles X; 1660—Charles XI; 1697—Charles XII (invader of Russia and Poland, defeated at Poltava, June 28, 1709);

1718—his sister, Unrika Eleanora, elected queen; 1720—her husband, Frederick I (of Hesse); 1751—Adolphus Frederick; 1771—Gustavus III; 1792—Gustavus IV; 1809—Charles XIII. (Union with Norway began, 1814). 1818—Charles XIV. He was Jean Bernadotte, Napoleon's Prince of Ponte Corvo, elected 1810 to succeed Charles XIII. He founded the present dynasty. 1844—Oscar I; 1859—Charles XV; 1872—Oscar II; 1907—Gustavus V; 1950—Gustav VI Adolf; 1973—Carl XVI Gustaf.

Norway

Overcoming many rivals, Harald Haarfager (872-930) conquered Norway, Orkneys and Shetlands; Olaf, great-grandson (995-1000) brought Christianity into Norway, Iceland, Greenland. In 1035 Magnus the Good also became king of Denmark. Haakon V (1299-1319) had married his daughter to Erik of Sweden. Their son, Magnus, became ruler of Norway and Sweden at 6. His son, Haakon VI, married Margaret of Denmark; their son Olaf became king of Norway and Denmark, followed by Margaret's regency and the Union of Kalmar, 1397.

In 1450 Norway became subservient to Denmark. Christian IV (1588-1648) founded Christiania, now Oslo. After Napoleonic wars, when Denmark ceded Norway to Sweden, a strong nationalist movement forced recognition of Norway as an independent kingdom united with Sweden under the Swedish kings, 1814-1905. In 1905 the union was dissolved and Prince Carl of Denmark became Haakon VII. He died Sept. 21, 1957, aged 85; succeeded by son, Olav V. b. July 2, 1903.

Rulers of the Netherlands and Belgium

The Netherlands (Holland)

William Frederick, Prince of Orange, led a revolt against French rule, 1813, and was crowned King of the Netherlands, 1815. Belgium seceded Oct. 4, 1830, after a revolt, and formed a separate government. The change was ratified by the two kingdoms by treaty Apr. 19, 1839.

(1840) William II; (1849) William III; (1890) Wilhelmina (daughter of William III and his second wife Princess Emma of Waldeck); Wilhelmina abdicated Sept. 4, 1948, in favor of daughter Juliana, 39.

Belgium

A national congress elected Prince Leopold of Saxe-Coburg King; he took the throne July 21, 1831, as Leopold I. (1865) Leopold II; (1909) Albert I, nephew of Leopold II; (1934) Leopold III, son of Albert; (1944) Prince Charles, Regent, Leopold returned, 1950, yielded powers to son Baudouin, Prince Royal, Aug. 6, 1950, abdicated Jul. 16, 1951. Baudouin I took throne July 17, 1951.

For political history prior to 1830 see articles on the Netherlands and Belgium.

Rulers of Modern Spain

From 8th to 11th centuries Spain was dominated by the Moors (Arabs and Berbers). The Christian reconquest established small competing kingdoms of the Asturias, Aragon, Castile, Catalonia, Leon, Navarre, and Valencia. In 1474 Isabella (Isabel) b. 1451, became Queen of Castile & Leon. Her husband, Ferdinand, b. 1452, inherited Aragon 1474, with Catalonia, Valencia and the Balearic Islands, became Ferdinand V of Castile. By Isabella's request Pope Sixtus IV established the Inquisition, 1478. Last Moorish kingdom, Granada, fell 1492. Columbus opened New World of colonies, 1492. Isabella died 1504, succeeded by her daughter, Juana "the Mad," but Ferdinand ruled until his death 1516.

Charles I, b. 1500, son of Juana and grandson of Ferdinand and Isabella and of Maximilian I of Hapsburg; succeeded later as Holy Roman Emperor, Charles V, 1520. Abdicated 1556. Philip II, son, 1556-1598, inherited only Spanish throne; conquered Portugal, fought Turks, persecuted non-Catholics, sent Armada vs. England. Was briefly married to Mary I of England, 1554-1558. Succession: Philip III, 1598-1621; Philip IV, 1621-1665; Charles II, 1665-1700, left Spain to Philip of Anjou, grandson of Louis XIV, who as Philip V, 1700-1746, founded Bourbon dynasty. Ferdinand IV, 1746-1759; Charles III, 1759-1788; Charles IV, 1788-1808, abdicated.

Napoleon now dominated politics and made his brother Joseph King of Spain but the Spanish ousted him finally in 1813. Ferdinand VII, 1814-1833, lost American colonies; succeeded by daughter Isabella II, aged 3, with wife Maria Christina of Naples regent until 1843. Isabella deposed by revolution 1868. Prince Amadeo of Savoy, 1870-1873. First republic, 1873-1874. Alphonso XII 1875-1885. His posthumous son was Alphonso XIII, with his mother, Queen Maria Christina regent; Spanish-American war, Spain lost Cuba, gave up Puerto Rico, Philippines, Sulu Is., Marianas, Alphonso took throne 1902, aged 16, married British Princess Victoria Eugenia of Battenberg. The dictatorship of Primo de Rivera, 1923-30, precipitated the revolution of 1931. Alphonso agreed to leave without formal abdication. The monarchy was abolished and the second republic established, with strong socialist backing. Presidents were Niceto Alcala Zamora, to 1936, when Manuel Anzana was chosen.

In July, 1936, the army in Morocco revolted against the government and General Francisco Franco led the troops into Spain. The revolution succeeded by Feb., 1939, when Anzana resigned. Franco became chief of state, with provisions that if he is incapacitated the Regency Council by two-thirds vote may propose a king to the Cortes, which must have a two-thirds majority to elect him.

Alphonso XIII, died in Rome Feb. 28, 1941, aged 54. His property and citizenship had been restored.

A succession law theoretically restoring the monarchy was approved in a 1947 referendum. A new Constitution, approved by referendum Dec. 14, 1966, affirmed Spain's status as a monarchy under a king or a regent. Prince Juan Carlos was designated by Franco and the Cortes in 1969 as the future king and chief of state. Juan Carlos is the son of the pretender to the throne, Don Juan of Bourbon.

Leaders in the South American Wars of Liberation

Simon Bolivar (1783-1830), Jose Francisco de San Martin (1783-1850) and Francisco Antonio Gabriel Miranda (1750-1816) are among the heroes of the early 19th century struggles of South American nations to free themselves from Spain. All three, and their contemporaries, operated in periods of intense factional strife, during which soldiers and civilians suffered.

Miranda, a Venezuelan, who had served with the French in the American Revolution and commanded parts of the French Revolutionary armies in the Netherlands, attempted to start a revolt in Venezuela in 1806 and failed. In 1810, with British and American backing, he returned and was briefly a dictator, until the British withdrew their support. In 1812 he was overcome by the royalists in Venezuela and taken prisoner, dying in a Spanish prison in 1816.

San Martin was born in Argentina and during 1789-1811 served in campaigns of the Spanish armies in Europe and Africa. He first joined the independence movement in Argentina in 1812 and then in 1817 invaded Chile with 4,000 men over the high mountain passes. Here he and General Bernardo O'Higgins (1778-1842) defeated the Spaniards at Chacabuco, 1817, and O'Higgins was named Liberator and became first dictator of Chile, 1817-1823. In 1821 San Martin occupied Lima and Callao, Peru, and became Protector of Peru.

Bolivar, the greatest leader of South American liberation from Spain, was born in Venezuela, the son of an aristocratic family. His organizing and administrative abilities were superior and he foresaw many of the political difficulties of the future. He first served under Miranda in 1812 and in 1813 captured Caracas, where he was named Liberator. Forced out next year by civil strife, he led a campaign that captured Bogota in 1814. In 1817 he was again in control of Venezuela and was named dictator. He organized Nueva Granada with the help of General Francisco de Paula Santander (1792-1840). By joining Nueva Granada, Venezuela and the present terrain of Panama and Ecuador, the republic of Colombia was formed with Bolivar president. After numerous setbacks he decisively defeated the Spaniards in the second battle of Carabobo, Venezuela, June 24, 1821.

In May, 1822, Gen. Antonio Jose de Sucre, Bolivar's trusted lieutenant, took Quito. Bolivar went to Guayaquil to confer with San Martin, who resigned as Protector of Peru and withdrew from politics. With a new army of Colombians and Peruvians Bolivar defeated the Spaniards in a saber battle at Juin in 1824 and cleared Peru.

De Sucre organized Charcas (Upper Peru) as Republica Bolivar (now Bolivia) and acted as president in place of Bolivar, who wrote its constitution. Sucre defeated the Spanish faction of Peru at Ayacucho, Dec. 19, 1824.

Continued civil strife finally caused the Colombian federation to break apart. Santander turned against Bolivar, but the latter defeated him and banished him. In 1828 Bolivar gave up the presidency he had held precariously for 14 years. He became ill from tuberculosis and died Dec. 17, 1830. He was honored as the great liberator and is buried in the national pantheon in Caracas.

Ancient Greeks and Latins

B. C. years are in black type; A. D. years in light. Herodotus believed Homer lived c. 850 B. C.

Greeks

Born	Died	Name	Subj.	Born	Died	Name	Subj.	Born	Died	Name	Subj.
389	314	Aeschines	Orat.	450	...	Empedocles	Philos.	582	500	Pythagoras	Philos.
525	456	Aeschylus	Dram.	55	135	Epictetus	Pilos.	600	...	Sappho	Poet
...	550	Aesop	Tales	342	270	Epicurus	Philos.	556	469	Simonides	Poet
563	478	Anacreon	Poet	480	406	Euripides	Dram.	469	399	Socrates	Philos.
500	428	Anaxagoras	Philos.	576	480	Heraclitus	Philos.	495	405	Sophocles	Dram.
287	212	Archimedes	Physt.	484	424	Herodotus	Hist.	63	24	Strabo	Geog.
448	380	Aristophanes	Dram.	...	735	Hesiod	Poet	600	540	Thales	Philos.
384	322	Aristotle	Philos.	460	377	Hippocrates	Medic.	530	460	Themistocles	Philos.
...	194	Athenaeus	Antiq.	...	...	Homer	Poet	...	255	Theocritus	Poet
460	370	Democritus	Philos.	342	292	Menander	Dram.	382	287	Theophrastus	Philos.
310	240	Callimachus	Poet	522	443	Pindar	Poet	471	401	Thucydides	Hist.
382	322	Demosthenes	Orat.	429	347	Plato	Philos.	280	...	Timon	Philos.
50	13	Diodorus	Hist.	49	120	Plutarch	Biog.	430	357	Xenophon	Hist.
...	7	Dionysius	Hist.	207	122	Polybius	Hist.	490	...	Zeno	Philos.

Latins

Born	Died	Name	Subj.	Born	Died	Name	Subj.	Born	Died	Name	Subj.
330	390	Ammianus	Hist.	59	17	Livy	Hist.	35	95	Quintilian	Critic
125	200	Apuleius	Satir.	38	65	Lucan	Poet	86	34	Sallust	Hist.
130	175	Aulus Gellius	Satir.	180	103	Lucilius	Satir.	5	65	Seneca	Moral.
475	524	Boethius	Philos.	96	52	Lucretius	Philos.	25	100	Silius	Poet
100	44	Caesar, Julius	States.	43	104	Martial	Poet	61	96	Statius	Poet
234	149	Cato (Elder)	Orat.	100	30	Nepos	Hist.	70	150	Suetonius	Biog.
87	54	Catullus	Poet	43	18	Ovid	Poet	55	117	Tacitus	Hist.
107	43	Cicero	Orat.	34	62	Persius	Satir.	185	159	Terence	Dram.
365	408	Claudian	Poet	254	184	Plautus	Dram.	54	18	Tibullus	Poet
65	8	Horace	Poet	23	79	Pliny	Natur.	70	19	Virgil	Poet
60	140	Juvenal	Satir.	62	113	Pliny (Younger)	Letters	70	16	Vitruvius	Arch.

Roman Rulers

From Romulus to the end of the Empire in the West. Rulers of the Roman Empire in the East sat in Constantinople and for a brief period in Nicaea, until the capture of Constantinople by the Turks in 1453, when Byzantium was succeeded by the Ottoman Empire.

B.C.	Name
	The Kingdom
753	Romulus (Quirinus)
716	Numa Pompilius
673	Tullus Hostilius
640	Ancus Marcius
616	L. Tarquinius Priscus
578	Servius Tullius
534	L. Tarquinius Superbus
	The Republic
509	Consulate established
509	Quaestorship instituted
498	Dictatorship introduced
494	Plebeian Tribunate created
494	Plebeian Aedileship created
444	Consular Tribunate organized
435	Censorship instituted
366	Praetorship established
366	Curule Aedileship created
362	Military Tribunate elective
326	Proconsulate introduced
311	Naval Duumvirate elective
217	Dictatorship of Fabius Maximus
133	Tribunate of Tiberius Gracchus
123	Tribunate of Gaius Gracchus
82	Dictatorship of Sulla
60	First Triumvirate formed (Caesar, Pompeius, Crassus)
46	Dictatorship of Caesar
43	Second Triumvirate formed (Octavianus, Antonius, Lepidus)
	The Empire
27	Augustus (Gaius Julius Caesar Octavianus)
A.D.	
14	Tiberius I
37	Gaius (Caligula)
41	Claudius I
54	Nero
68	Galba
69	Galba; Otho; Vitellius
69	Vespasianus

A.D.	Name
79	Titus
81	Domitianus
96	Nerva
98	Trajanus
117	Hadrianus
138	Antoninus Pius
161	Marcus Aurelius and Lucius Verus
169	Marcus Aurelius (alone)
180	Commodus
193	Pertinax; Julianus I
193	Septimius Severus
211	Caracalla and Geta
212	Caracalla (alone)
217	Macrinus
218	Elagabalus (Heligabalus)
222	Alexander Severus
235	Maximinusi (the Thracian)
238	Gordianus I and Gordianus II; Pupienus and Balbinus
238	Gordianus III
244	Philippus (the Arabian)
249	Decius
251	Gallus and Volusianus
253	Aemilianus
253	Valerianus and Gallienus
258	Gallienus (alone)
268	Claudius II (the Goth)
270	Quintillus
270	Aurelianus
275	Tacitus
276	Florianus
276	Probus
282	Carus
283	Carinus and Numerianus
284	Diocletianus
286	Diocletianus and Maximianus
305	Galerius and Constantius I
306	Galerius, Maximinus II, Severus II
307	Galerius, Maximinus II, Constantinus I, Licinius, Maxentius
311	Maximinus II, Constantinus I, Licinius, Maxentius
312	Maximinus II, Constantinus I, Licinius

A.D.	Name
314	Constantinus I and Licinius
324	Constantinus I (the Great)
337	Contantinus II, Constans I, Constantius II
340	Constantius II and Constans I
350	Constantius II
360	Julianus II (the Apostate)
363	Jovianus
	West (Rome) and East (Constantinople)
364	Valentinianus I (West) and Valens (East)
367	Valentinianus I with Gratianus (West) and Valens (East)
375	Gratianus with Valentinianus II (West) and Valens (East)
378	Gratianus with Valentinianus II (W) Theodosius I (E)
383	Valentinianus II (West) and Theodosius I (East)
394	Theodosius I (the Great)
395	Honorius (West) and Arcadius (East)
408	Honorius (West) and Theodosius II (East)
423	Valentinianus III (West) and Theodosius II (East)'
450	Valentinianus III (West) and Marcianus (East)
455	Maximus (West); Avitus (West); Marcianus (East)
456	Avitus (W); Marcianus (E)
457	Majorianus (W), Leo I (E)
461	Severus II (W), Leo I (E)
467	Anthemius (W), Leo I (E)
472	Olybrius (W), Leo I (E)
473	Glycerius (W), Leo I (E)
474	Julius Nepos (W), Leo II (E)
475	Romulus Augustulus (West) and Zeno (East)
476	End of Empire in West; Odovacar, King, drops title of Emperor; murdered by King Theodoric of Ostrogoths 493 A. D.

Chronological List of Popes

Source: Annuario Pontifici Table lists year of coronation of each Pope.

The Roman Catholic Church names the Apostle Peter as founder of the Church in Rome. He arrived there c. 42, was martyred there c. 67, and raised to sainthood.

The Pope's temporal title is: Sovereign of the State of Vatican City.

The Pope's spiritual titles are: Bishop of Rome, Vicar of Jesus Christ, Successor of St. Peter, Prince of the Apostles, Supreme Pontiff of the Universal Church, Patriarch of the West, Primate of Italy, Archbishop and Metropolitan of the

Roman Province and Sovereign of the State of Vatican City.
Anti-Popes are in *Italics*. Anti-Popes were illegitimate claimants of or pretenders to the papal throne.

Year	Name of Pope	Year	Name of Pope	Year	Name of Pope	Year	Name of Pope
See above.	St. Peter	615	St. Deusdedit	974	Benedict VII	1305	Clement V
67	St. Linus		or Adeodatus I	983	John XIV	1316	John XXII
76	St. Anacletus	619	Boniface V	985	John XV	1328	*Nicholas V*
	or Cletus	625	Honorius I	996	Gregory V	1334	Benedict XII
88	St. Clement I	640	Severinus	*997*	*John XVI*	1342	Clement VI
97	St. Evaristus	640	John IV	999	Sylvester II	1352	Innocent VI
105	St. Alexander I	642	Theodore I	1003	John XVII	1362	Urban V
115	St. Sixtus I	649	St. Martin I	1004	John XVIII	1370	Gregory XI
125	St. Telesphorus	654	St. Eugene I	1009	Sergius IV	1378	Urban VI
136	St. Hyginus	657	St. Vitalian	1012	Benedict VIII	*1378*	*Clement VII*
140	St. Pius I	672	Adeodatus II	*1012*	*Gregory*	1389	Boniface IX
155	St. Anicetus	676	Donus	1024	John XIX	*1394*	*Benedict XIII*
166	St. Soter	678	St. Agatho	1032	Benedict IX	1404	Innocent VII
175	St. Eleutherius	682	St. Leo II	1045	Sylvester III	1406	Gregory XII
189	St. Victor I	684	St. Benedict II	1045	Benedict IX	*1409*	*Alexander V*
199	St. Zephyrinus	685	John V	1045	Gregory VI	*1410*	*John XXIII*
217	St. Callistus I	686	Conon	1046	Clement II	1417	Martin V
217	*St. Hippolytus*	687	Theodore	1047	Benedict IX	1431	Eugene IV
222	St. Urban I	*687*	*Paschal*	1048	Damasus II	*1440*	*Felix V*
230	St. Pontian	687	St. Sergius I	1049	St. Leo IX	1447	Nicholas V
235	St. Anterus	701	John VI	1055	Victor II	1455	Callistus III
236	St. Fabian	705	John VII	1057	Stephen IX	1458	Pius II
251	St. Cornelius	708	Sisinnius	*1058*	*Benedict X*	1464	Paul II
251	*Novatian*	708	Constantine	1059	Nicholas II	1471	Sixtus IV
253	St. Lucius I	715	St. Gregory II	1061	Alexander II	1484	Innocent VIII
254	St. Stephen I	731	St. Gregory III	*1061*	*Honorius II*	1492	Alexander VI
257	St. Sixtus II	741	St. Zachary	1073	St. Gregory VII	1503	Pius III
259	St. Dionysius	752	Stephen II	*1080*	*Clement III*	1503	Julius II
269	St. Felix I	757	St. Paul I	1086	Victor III	1513	Leo X
275	St. Eutychian	*767*	*Constantine*	1088	Urban II	1522	Adrian VI
283	St. Caius	*768*	*Philip*	1099	Paschal II	1523	Clement VII
296	St. Marcellinus	768	Stephen III	*1100*	*Theodoric*	1534	Paul III
308	St. Marcellus I	772	Adrian I	*1102*	*Albert*	1550	Julius III
309	St. Eusebius	795	St. Leo III	*1105*	*Sylvester IV*	1555	Marcellus II
311	St. Melchiades	816	Stephen IV	1118	Gelasius II	1555	Paul IV
314	St. Sylvester I	817	St. Paschal I	*1118*	*Gregory VIII*	1559	Pius IV
336	St. Mark	824	Eugene II	1119	Callistus II	1566	St. Pius V
337	St. Julius I	827	Valentine	1124	Honorius II	1572	Gregory XIII
352	Liberius	827	Gregory IV	*1124*	*Celestine II*	1585	Sixtus V
355	*Felix II*	*844*	*John*	1130	Innocent II	1590	Urban VII
366	St. Damasus I	844	Sergius II	*1130*	*Anacletus II*	1590	Gregory XIV
366	*Ursinus*	847	St. Leo IV	*1138*	*Victor IV*	1591	Innocent IX
384	St. Siricius	855	Benedict III	1143	Celestine II	1592	Clement VIII
399	St. Anastasius I	*855*	*Anastasius*	1144	Lucius II	1605	Leo XI
401	St. Innocent I	858	St. Nicholas I	1145	Eugene III	1605	Paul V
417	St. Zozimus	867	Adrian II	1153	Anastasius IV	1621	Gregory XV
418	St. Boniface I	872	John VIII	1154	Adrian IV	1623	Urban VIII
418	*Eulalius*	882	Marinus I	1159	Alexander III	1644	Innocent X
422	St. Celestine I	884	St. Adrian III	*1159*	*Victor IV*	1655	Alexander VII
432	St. Sixtus III	885	Stephen V	*1164*	*Paschal III*	1667	Clement IX
440	St. Leo I	891	Formosus	*1168*	*Callistus III*	1670	Clement X
461	St. Hilary	896	Boniface VI	*1179*	*Innocent III*	1676	Innocent XI
468	St. Simplicius	896	Stephen VI	1181	Lucius III	1689	Alexander VIII
483	St. Felix III or II	897	Romanus	1185	Urban III	1691	Innocent XII
492	St. Gelasius I	897	Theodore II	1187	Gregory VIII	1700	Clement XI
496	Anastasius II	898	John IX	1187	Clement III	1721	Innocent XIII
498	St. Symmachus	900	Benedict IV	1191	Celestine III	1724	Bennedict XIII
498	*Lawrence*	903	Leo V	1198	Innocent III	1730	Clement XII
	(501-505)	*903*	*Christopher*	1216	Honorius III	1740	Benedict XIV
514	St. Hormisdas	904	Sergius III	1227	Gregory IX	1758	Clement XIII
523	St. John I	911	Anastasius III	1241	Celestine IV	1769	Clement XIV
526	St. Felix IV or III	913	Landus	1243	Innocent IV	1775	Pius VI
530	Boniface II	914	John X	1254	Alexander IV	1800	Pius VII
530	*Dioscorus*	928	Leo VI	1261	Urban IV	1823	Leo XII
533	John II	928	Stephen VII	1265	Clement IV	1829	Pius VIII
535	St. Agapitus	931	John XI	1271	Gregory X	1831	Gregory XVI
536	St. Silverius	936	Leo VII	1276	Innocent V	1846	Pius IX
537	Vigilius	939	Stephen VIII	1276	Adrian V	1878	Leo XIII
556	Pelagius I	942	Marinus II	1276	John XXI	1903	St. Pius X
561	John III	946	Agapitus II	1277	Nicholas III	1914	Benedict XV
575	Benedict I	955	John XII	1281	Martin IV	1922	Pius XI
579	Pelagius II	963	Leo VIII	1285	Honorius IV	1939	Pius XII
590	St. Gregory	964	Benedict V	1288	Nicholas IV	1958	John XXIII
604	Sabinian	965	John XIII	1294	St. Celestine V	1963	Paul VI
607	Boniface III	973	Benedict VI	1294	Boniface VIII		
608	St. Boniface IV	*974*	*Boniface VII*	1303	Benedict XI		

Rulers of Modern Italy

After the fall of Napoleon in 1814, the Congress of Vienna, 1815, restored Italy as a political patchwork, comprising the Kingdom of Naples and Sicily, the Papal States, and smaller units. Piedmont and Genoa were awarded to Sardinia, ruled by King Victor Emmanuel I of Savoy.

United Italy emerged under the leadership of Camillo, Count di Cavour (1810-1861), Sardinian prime minister. Agitation was led by Giuseppe Mazzini (1805-1872) and Giuseppe Garibaldi (1807-1882), soldier. Victor Emmanuel I abdicated 1821. After a brief regency for a brother, Charles Albert was King 1831-1849, abdicating when defeated by the Austrians at Novara. Succeeded by Victor Emmanuel II (1820-1878).

In 1859 France forced Austria to cede Lombardy to Sardinia, which gave rights to Savoy and Nice to France. In 1860 Garibaldi led 1,000 volunteers in a spectacular campaign, took Sicily and expelled the King of Naples. In 1860 the House of Savoy annexed Tuscany, Parma, Moderna, Romagna, the Two Sicilies, the Marches, and Umbria. Victor Emmanuel assumed the title of King of Italy at Turin Mar. 17, 1861. In 1866 he joined Prussia and Austria in the Triple Alliance and received Venetia from Austria. On Sept. 20, 1870, his troops under Gen. Raffaele Cardorna entered Rome and took over the Papal States, ending the temporal power of the Roman Catholic Church.

Succession: Humbert I, 1878, assassinated 1900; Victor

Emmanuel.III, 1900, abdicated 1946, died 1947; Humbert II, 1946, ruled a month. In 1921 Benito Mussolini (1883-1945) formed the Fascist party and became prime minister Oct. 31, 1922. He made the King Emperor of Ethiopia, 1937; entered World War II as ally of Hitler. He was deposed Jul. 25, 1943.

At a plebiscite Jun. 2, 1946, Italy voted for a republic, Premier Alcide de Gasperi became Chief of State June 13, 1946. On Jun. 28, 1946, the Constituent Assembly elected Enrico de Nicola, Liberal, Provisional President of the Republic of Italy. Luigi Einaudi was elected President May 11, 1948. Giovanni Gronchi was elected Apr. 29, 1955, inaugurated May 11, 1955. Antonio Segni elected May 6, 1962, Giuseppe Saragat Dec. 28, 1964; Giovanni Leone Dec. 29, 1971.

Rulers of Russia; Premiers of the USSR

First ruler to consolidate Slavic tribes was Rurik, leader of the Russians who established himself at Novgorod A. D. 862. He and his immediate successors had Scandinavian affiliations. They moved to Kiev after 972 A. D. and ruled as Dukes of Kiev. In 988 Vladimir was converted and adopted the Byzantine Greek service, later modified by Slav influences. Important as organizer and lawgiver was Yaroslav, 1018-1054, whose daughters married kings of Norway, Hungary and France. His grandson, Vladimir II (Monomachos) 1113-1125, was progenitor of several rulers, but in 1169 Andrew Bogolubski overthrew Kiev and began the line known as Grand Dukes of Vladimir.

Of the Grand Dukes of Vladimir, Alexander Nevsky, 1245-1263, had a son, Daniel, first to be called Duke of Muscovy (Moscow) who ruled 1294-1303. His successors became Grand Dukes of Muscovy. After Demetrius III, Donskol, in 1380 defeated the Tartars, they also became Grand Dukes of all Russia. Independence of the Tartars and considerable territorial expansion were achieved under Ivan III, 1462-1505.

Czars of Muscovy—Ivan III was referred to in church ritual as Czar. He married Sofia, niece of the last Byzantine emperor. His successor, Basil, died in 1533 when Basil's son Ivan was only 3. He became Ivan IV, "the Terrible," crowned 1547 as Czar of all the Russians, ruled till 1584. Under the weak rule of his son, Theodore, Boris Godunov had control. The dynasty died, and after years of tribal strife and intervention by Polish and Swedish armies, the Russians united under 17-year-old Michael Romanov, distantly related to the first wife of Ivan IV. The fourth ruler after Michael was Peter I.

Czars, or Emperors of Russia (Romanovs)—Peter I, 1682-1725, known as Peter the Great, took title of Emperor in 1721. His successors and dates of accession were: Catherine, his widow, 1725, Peter II, his grandson, 1727, d. 1730; Anne, Duchess of Courtland, 1730, daughter of Peter the Great's brother, Czar Ivan; Ivan VI, 1740-1741, great grandson of Ivan V, child, kept in prison and

murdered 1764; Elizabeth, daughter of Peter I, 1741; Peter III, grandson of Peter I, 1761, deposed 1762 for his consort, Catherine II, former princess of Anhalt Zerbst (German) who is known as Catherine the Great, 1762-1796; Paul I, her son, 1796, killed 1801. Alexander I, son of Paul, 1801-1825, defeated Napoleon; Nicholas I, his brother, 1825; Alexander II, son of Nicholas 1855, assassinated 1881 by terrorists; Alexander III, son, 1881-1894.

Nicholas II, son, 1894-1917, last Czar of Russia, was forced to abdicate by the Revolution that followed defeat by Germany. The Czar, the Czarina, the Czarevitch (Crown Prince) and the Czar's 4 daughters were murdered by the Bolshevists in Ekaterinburg, July 17, 1918.

Provisional Government—Prince Georgi Lvov and Alexander Kerensky, premiers, 1917.

Union of Soviet Socialist Republics

Bolshevist Revolution, Nov. 7, 1917, displaced Kerensky; Council of People's Commissars formed, Nicolai Lenin, premier. Lenin died Jan. 21, 1924. Alexei Rykov (executed 1938) and V. M. Molotov held the office, but actual ruler was Joseph Stalin (Joseph Vissarionovich Djugashvili), general secretary of the Central Committee of the Communist Party. Stalin became president of the Council of Ministers (premier) May 7, 1941, died Mar. 5, 1953. Succeeded by Georgi M. Malenkov, as head of the Council and premier and Nikita S. Khrushchev, first secretary of the Central Committee. Malenkov resigned Feb. 8, 1955, became deputy premier, was dropped Jul. 3, 1957. Marshal Nikolai A. Bulganin became premier. Marshal Georgi K. Zhukov became minister of defense, was dropped Nov. 1, 1957. Bulganin was demoted and Khrushchev became premier Mar. 27, 1958, Khrushchev was ousted Oct. 14-15, 1964, replaced by Leonid I. Brezhnev as first secretary of the party and by Aleksei N. Kosygin as premier.

The Dynasties of China

(Until 221 B.C. and frequently thereafter, China was not a unified state. Where dynastic dates overlap, the rulers or events referred to appeared in different areas of China.)

Hsia	c.2000B.C. -	c.1500B.C.
Shang	c.1500B.C. -	c.1000B.C.
Western Chou	c.1000B.C. -	771B.C.
Eastern Chou	770B.C. -	256B.C.
Warring States	403B.C. -	222B.C.
Ch'in (first unified empire)	221B.C. -	206B.C.
Han	202B.C. -	220A.D.
Western Han (expanded Chinese state beyond the Yellow and Yangtze River valleys)	202B.C. -	9A.D.
Hsin (Wang Mang, usurper)	9A.D. -	23A.D.
Eastern Han (expanded Chinese state into Indo-China and Turkestan)	25A.D. -	220A.D.
Three Kingdoms (Wei, Shu, Wu)	220 -	264
Chin (western)	265 -	317
(eastern)	317 -	420
Northern Dynasties (followed several short-lived governments by Turks, Mongols, etc.)	386 -	581
Southern Dynasties (capital: Nanking)	420 -	589
Sui (reunified China)	581 -	618
T'ang (a golden age of Chinese culture; capital: Sian)	618 -	907
Five Dynasties (Yellow River basin)	907 -	959
Ten Kingdoms (southern China)	907 -	979
Liao (Khitan Mongols; capital: Peking)	947 -	1125
Sung	960 -	1279
Northern Sung (reunified central and southern China)	960 -	1127
Western Hsai (non-Chinese rulers in northwest)	990 -	1227
Chin (Tartars; drove Sung out of central China)	1114 -	1234
Southern Sung (capital: Hangchow)	1127 -	1379
Yuan (Mongols; Kublai Khan made Peking his capital in 1267)	1271 -	1368
Ming (China reunified under Chinese rule; capital: Nanking, then Peking in 1420)	1368 -	1644
Ch'ing (Manchus, descendants of Tartars)	1644 -	1912
Republic (disunity: provincial rulers, warlords)	1912 -	1949

Awards — Medals — Prizes
The Alfred B. Nobel Prize Winners

Alfred B. Nobel, inventor of dynamite, bequeathed $9,000,000, the interest to be distributed yearly to those who had most benefited mankind in physics, chemistry, medicine-physiology, literature, and peace. The first Nobel Prize in Economics was awarded in 1969. No awards given for years omitted. In 1974, each prize was worth $124,000.

Physics

1974 Martin Ryle, British
   Antony Hewish, British
1973 Ivar Giaever, American
   Leo Esaki, American
   Brian D. Josephson, British
1972 John Bardeen, American
   Leon N. Cooper, American
   John R. Schrieffer, American
1971 Dennis Gabor, British
1970 Louis Neel, French
   Hannes Alfven, Swedish
1969 Murray Gell-Mann, American
1968 Luis W. Alvarez, American
1967 Hans A. Bethe, American
1966 Alfred Kastler, French
1965 Richard P. Feynman, American
   Julian S. Schwinger, American
   Shinichiro Tomanaga, Japanese
1964 Nikolai G. Basov, Russian
   Aleksander M. Prochorov, Russ.
   Charles H. Townes, American
1963 Maria Goeppert-Mayer, Am.
   J. Hans D. Jensen, German
   Eugene P. Wigner, American
1962 Lev. D. Landau, Russian
1961 Robert Hofstadter, American
   Rudolf L. Mossbauer, German
1960 Donald A. Glaser, American
1959 Owen Chamberlain, American
   Emillo G. Segre, American
1958 Paval Cerenkov, Ilya Frank,
   Igor J. Tamm, all Russian
1957 Tsung-Dao Lee,
   Chen Ning Yang, both Am.
1956 John Bardeen, American

Walter H. Brattain, American
   William Shockley, American
1955 Polykarp Kusch, American
   Willis E. Lamb, American
1954 Max Born, British
   Walter Bothe, German
1953 Frits Zernike, Dutch
1952 Felix Bloch, American
   Edward M. Purcell, American
1951 Sir John D. Cockroft, British
   Ernest T. S. Walton, Irish
1950 Cecil F. Powell, British
1949 Hideki Yukawa, Japanese
1948 Patrick M. S. Blackett, British
1947 Sir Edward V. Appleton, British
1946 Percy Williams Bridgman, Am.
1945 Wolfgang Pauli, American
1944 Isidor Isaac Rabi, American
1943 Otto Sern, American
1939 Ernest O. Lawrence, American
1938 Enrico Fermi, American
1937 Clinton J. Davisson, American
   George P. Thomson, British
1936 Carl D. Anderson, American
   Victor F. Hess, Austrian
1935 James Chadwick, British
1933 Paul A. M. Dirac, British
   Erwin Schrodinger, Austrian
1932 Werner Heisenberg, German
1930 Sir Chandrasekhara V. Raman,
   Indian
1929 Prince Louis-Victor de Broglie,
   French
1928 Owen W. Richardson, British
1927 Arthur H. Compton, American

Charles T. R. Wilson, British
1926 Jean B. Perrin, French
1925 James Franck,
   Gustav Hertz, both German
1924 Karl M. G. Siegbahn, Swedish
1923 Robert A. Millikan, American
1922 Niels Bohr, Danish
1921 Albert Einstein, American
1920 Charles E. Guillaume, French
1919 Johannes Stark, German
1918 Max K. E. L. Planck, German
1917 Charles G. Barkla, British
1915 Sir William H. Bragg, British
   William L. Bragg, British
1914 Max von Laue, German
1913 Heike Kamerlingh-Onnes, Dutch
1912 Nils G. Dalen, Swedish
1911 Wilhelm Wein, German
1910 Johannes D. van der Waals, Dutch
1909 Carl F. Braun, German
   Guglielmo Marconi, Italian
1908 Gabriel Lippmann, French
1907 Albert A. Michelson, American
1906 Sir Joseph J. Thomson, British
1905 Philipp E. A. von Lenard, Ger.
1904 Rayleigh, Lord (John W. Strutt),
   British
1903 Antoine Henri Becquerel, Fr.
   Marie Curie, French
   Pierre Curie, French
1902 Hendrik A. Lorentz,
   Pieter Zeeman, both Dutch
1901 Wilhelm C. Rontgen, German

Chemistry

1974 Paul J. Flory, American
1973 Ernst Otto Fischer, W. German
   Geoffrey Wilkinson, British
1972 Christian B. Anfinsen, Am.
   Stanford Moore, American
   William H. Stein, American
1971 Gerhard Herzberg, Canadian
1970 Luis A. Leloir, Arg.
1969 Derek H. R. Barton, British
   Odd Hassel, Norwegian
1968 Lars Onsager, American
1967 Manfred Eigen, German
   Ronald G. W. Norrish, British
   George Porter, British
1966 Robert S. Mulliken, American
1965 Robert B. Woodward, American
1964 Dorothy C. Hodgkin, British
1963 Giulio Natta, Italian
   Karl Ziegler, German
1962 John C. Kendrew, British
   Max F. Perutz, British
1961 Melvin Calvin, American
1960 Willard F. Libby, American
1959 Jaroslav Heyrovsky, Czech
1958 Frederick Sanger, British
1957 Sir. Alexander R. Todd, British
1956 Sir Cyril N. Hinshelwood, British
   Nikolai N. Semenov, Russian
1955 Vincent du Vigneaud, American

1954 Linus C. Pauling, American
1953 Hermann Staudinger, German
1952 Archer J. P. Martin, British
   Richard L. M. Synge, British
1951 Edwin M. McMillan, American
   Glenn T. Seaborg, American
1950 Kurt Adler, German
   Otto P. H. Diels, German
1949 William F. Glauque, American
1948 Arne W. K. Tiselius, Swedish
1947 Sir Robert Robinson, British
1946 James B. Sumner, John H.
   Northrop, Wendell M. Stanley, all
   Am.
1945 Artturi I. Virtanen, Finnish
1944 Otto Hahn, German
1943 Georg de Hevesy, Hungarian
1939 Adolf F. J. Butenandt, German
   Leopold Ruzicka, Swiss
1938 Richard Kuhn, German
1937 Walter N. Haworth, British
   Paul Karrer, Swiss
1936 Peter J. W. Debye, Dutch
1935 Frederic Joliot-Curie, French
   Irene Joliot-Curie, French
1934 Harold C. Urey, American
1932 Irving Langmuir, American
1931 Friedrich Bergius, German
   Carl Bosch, German

1930 Hans Fischer, German
1929 Arthur Harden, British
   Hans von Euler-Chelpin, Swed.
1928 Adolf O. R. Windaus, German
1927 Heinrich O. Wieland, German
1926 Theodor Svedberg, Swedish
1925 Richard A. Zsigmondy, German
1923 Fritz Pergl, Austrian
1922 Francis W. Aston, British
1921 Frederick Soddy, British
1920 Walther H. Nernst, German
1918 Fritz Haber, German
1915 Richard M. Willstatter, German
1914 Theodore W. Richards, Am.
1913 Alfred Werner, Swiss
1912 Victor Grignard, French
   Paul Sabatier, French
1911 Marie Curie, French
1910 Otto Wallach, German
1909 Wilhelm Ostwald, German
1908 Ernest Rutherford, British
1907 Eduard Buchner, German
1906 Henri Moissan, French
1905 Adolf von Baeyer, German
1904 Sir William Ramsay, British
1903 Svante A. Arrhenius, Swedish
1902 Emil Fischer, German
1901 Jacobus H. van't Hoff, Dutch

Physiology or Medicine

1974 Albert Claude, Lux.-Amer.; George
   Emil Palade, Rom.-Am.; Christian
   Rene de Duve, Belg.
1973 Karl von Frisch, Konrad Lorenz,
   both Ger.; Nikolaas Tinbergen,
   Brit.
1972 Gerald M. Edelman, American
   Rodney R. Porter, British
1971 Earl W. Sutherland Jr., American
1970 Julius Axelrod, American

Sir Bernard Katz, British
   Ulf von Euler, Swedish
1969 Max Delbruck,
   Alfred D. Hershey,
   Salvador Luria, all American
1968 Robert W. Holley,
   H. Gobind Khorana,
   Marshall W. Nirenberg, all Am.
1967 Ragnar Granit, Swedish
   Haldan Keffer Hartline, Am.

George Wald, American
1966 Charles B. Huggins,
   Francis Peyton Rous, both Am.
1965 Francois Jacob, Andre Lwoff,
   Jacquest Monod, all French
1964 Konrad E. Bloch, American
   Feodor Lynen, German
1963 Sir John C. Eccles, Australian
   Alan L. Hodgkin, British
   Andrew F. Huxley, British

1962 Francis H. C. Crick, British
James D. Watson, American
Maurice H. F. Wilkins, British
1961 Georg von Bekesy, American
1960 Sir F. MacFarlane Burnet, Australian
Peter B. Medawar, British
1959 Arthur Kornberg, American
Severo Ochoa, American
1958 George W. Beadle, American.
Edward L. Tatum, American
Joshua Lederberg, American
1957 Daniel Bovet, Italian
1956 Andre F. Cournand, American
Werner Forssmann, German
Dickinson W. Richards, Jr., Am.
1955 Alex H. T. Theorell, Swedish
1954 John F. Enders,
Frederick C. Robbins,
Thomas H. Weller, all American
1953 Hans A. Krebs, British
Fritz A. Lipmann, American
1952 Selman A. Waksman, American
1951 Max Theiler, American
1950 Philip S. Hench,
Edward C. Kendall, both Am.
Tadeus Reichstein, Swiss
1949 Walter R. Hess, Swiss

1974 Eyvind Johnson, Harry Edmund Martinson, both Swedish
1973 Patrick White, Australian
1972 Heinrich Boll, W. German
1971 Pablo Neruda, Chilean
1970 Aleksandr I. Solzhenitsyn, Russ.
1969 Samuel Beckett, Irish
1968 Yasunari Kawabata, Japanese
1967 Miguel Angel Asturias, Guate.
1966 Samuel Joseph Agnon, Israeli
Nelly Sachs, Swedish
1965 Mikhail Sholokhov, Russian
1964 Jean Paul Sartre, French (Prize declined)
1963 Giorgos Seferis, Greek
1962 John Steinbeck, American
1961 Ivo Andric, Yugoslavian
1960 Saint-John Perse, French
1959 Salvatore Quasimodo, Italian
1958 Boris L. Pasternak, Russian (Prize declined)
1957 Albert Camus, French
1956 Juan Ramon Jimenez, Puerto Rican
1955 Halldor K. Laxness, Icelandic

1974 Eisaku Sato, Jap., Sean MacBride, Irish
1973 Henry Kissinger, American
Le Duc Tho, N. Vietnamese
1971 Willy Brandt, W. German
1970 Norman E. Borlaug, American
1969 Intl. Labor Organization
1968 Rene Cassin, French
1965 U.N. Children's Fund (UNICEF)
1964 Martin Luther King, Jr., Am.
1963 International Red Cross,
League of Red Cross Societies
1962 Linus C. Pauling, American
1961 Dag Hammarskjold, Swedish
1960 Albert J. Luthuli, South African
1959 Philip J. Noel-Baker, British
1958 Georges Pire, Belgian
1957 Lester B. Pearson, Canadian
1954 Office of the UN High Commissioner for Refugees
1953 George C. Marshall, American
1952 Albert Schweitzer, French
1951 Leon Jouhaux, French
1950 Ralph J. Bunche, American
1949 Lord John Boyd Orr of Brechin, British

1974 Gunnar Myrdal, Swed., Friedrich A. von Hayek, Austrian
1973 Wassily Leontief, American

Antonio Moniz, Portuguese
1948 Paul H. Muller, Swiss
1947 Carl F. Cori,
Gerty T. Cori, both American
Bernardo A. Houssay, Arg.
1946 Hermann J. Muller, American
1945 Ernst B. Chain, British
Sir Alexander Fleming, British
Sir Howard W. Florey, British
1944 Joseph Erlanger, American
Herbert S. Gasser, American
1943 Henrik C. P. Dam, Danish
Edward A. Doisy, American
1939 Gerhard Domagk, German
1938 Corneille J. F. Heymans, Belg.
1937 Albert Szent-Gyorgyi, American
1936 Sir Henry H. Dale, British
Otto Loewi, American
1935 Hans Spemann, German
1934 George R. Minot, Wm. P. Murphy, G. H. Whipple, all Am.
1933 Thomas H. Morgan, American
1932 Edgard D. Adrian, British
Sir Charles S. Sherrington, Brit.
1931 Otto H. Warburg, German
1930 Karl Landsteiner, American
1929 Christiaan Eijkman, Dutch
Sir Frederick G. Hopkins, British

Literature

1954 Ernest Hemingway, American
1953 Sir Winston Churchill, British
1952 Francois Mauriac, French
1951 Par F. Lagerkvist, Swedish
1950 Bertrand Russell, British
1949 William Faulkner, American
1948 T. S. Eliot, British
1947 Andre Gide, French
1946 Hermann Hesse, Swiss
1945 Gabriela Mistral, Chilean
1944 Johannes V. Jensen, Danish
1939 Frans. E. Sillanpaa, Finnish
1938 Pearl S. Buck, American
1937 Roger Martin du Gard, French
1936 Eugene O'Neill, American
1934 Luigi Pirandello, Italian
1933 Ivan A. Bunin, French
1932 John Galsworthy, British
1931 Erik A. Karlfeldt, Swedish
1930 Sinclair Lewis, American
1929 Thomas Mann, German
1928 Sigrid Undset, Norwegian
1927 Henri Bergson, French
1926 Grazia Deledda, Italian
1925 George Bernard Shaw, British

Peace

1947 Friends Service Council, Brit.
Amer. Friends Service Com.
1946 Emily G. Balch,
John R. Mott, both American
1945 Cordell Hull, American
1944 International Red Cross
1938 Nansen International Office for Refugees
1937 Viscount Cecil of Chelwood (Lord Edgar A. R. G. Cecil), Brit.
1936 Carlos de Saavedra Lamas, Arg.
1935 Carl von Ossietzky, German
1934 Arthur Henderson, British
1933 Sir Norman Angell, British
1931 Jane Addams, American
Nicholas Murray Butler, Amer.
1930 Nathan Soderblom, Swedish
1929 Frank B. Kellogg, American
1927 Ferdinand E. Buisson, French
Ludwig Quidde, German
1926 Aristide Briand, French
Gustav Stresemann, German
1925 Sir J. Austen Chamberlain, Brit.
Charles G. Dawes, American
1922 Fridtjof Nansen, Norwegian
1921 Karl H. Branting, Swedish

Economics

1972 Kenneth J. Arrow, American
John R. Hicks, British
1971 Simon Kuznets, American

1928 Charles J. H. Nicolle, French
1927 Julius Wagner-Jauregg, Aus.
1926 Johannes A. G. Fibiger, Danish
1924 Willem Einthoven, Dutch
1923 Frederick G. Banting, Canadian
John J. R. Macleod, Canadian
1922 Archibald V. Hill, British
Otto F. Meyerhof, German
1920 Schack A. S. Krogh, Danish
1919 Jules Bordet, Belgian
1914 Robert Barany, Hungarian
1913 Charles R. Richet, French
1912 Alexis Carrel, American
1911 Allvar Gullstrand, Swedish
1910 Albrecht Kossel, German
1909 Emil T. Kocher, Swiss
1908 Paul Ehrlich, German
Elie Metchnikoff, French
1907 Charles L. A. Laveran, French
1906 Camillo Golgi, Italian
Santiago Roman y Cajal, Sp.
1905 Robert Koch, German
1904 Ivan P. Pavlov, Russian
1903 Niels R. Finsen, Danish
1902 Sir Ronald Ross, British
1901 Emil A. von Behring, German

1924 Wladyslaw S. Reymont, Polish
1923 William Butler Yeats, Irish
1922 Jacinto Benavente, Spanish
1921 Anatole France, French
1920 Knut Hamsun, Norwegian
1919 Carl F. G. Spitteler, Swiss
1917 Karl A. Gjellerup, Danish
Henrik Pontoppidan, Danish
1916 Verner von Heidenstam, Swed.
1915 Romain Rolland, French
1913 Rabindranath Tagore, Indian
1912 Gerhart Hauptmann, German
1911 Maurice Maeterlinck, Belgian
1910 Paul J. L. Heyse, German
1909 Selma Lagerlof, Swedish
1908 Rudolf C. Eucken, German
1907 Rudyard Kipling, British
1906 Giosue Carducci, Italian
1905 Henryk Sienkiewicz, Polish
1904 Frederic Mistral, French
Jose Echegaray, Spanish
1903 Bjornsterne Bjornson, Norw.
1902 Theodor Mommsen, German
1901 Rene F. A. Sully Prudhomme, French

Christian L. Lange, Norwegian
1920 Leon V. A. Bourgeois, French
1919 Woodrow Wilson, American
1917 International Red Cross
1913 Henri La Fontaine, Belgian
1912 Elihu Root, American
1911 Tobias M. C. Asser, Dutch
Alfred H. Fried, Austrian
1910 Permanent International Peace Bureau
1909 Auguste M. F. Beernaert, Belg.
Paul H. B. B. d'Estournelles de Constant, French
1908 Klas P. Arnoldson, Swedish
Fredrik Bajer, Danish
1907 Ernesto T. Moneta, Italian
Louis Renault, French
1906 Theodore Roosevelt, American
1905 Baroness Bertha von Suttner, Austrian
1904 Institute of International Law
1903 Sir William R. Cremer, British
1902 Elie Ducommun,
Charles A. Gobat, both Swiss
1901 Jean H. Dunant, Swiss
Frederic Passy, French

1970 Paul A. Samuelson, American
1969 Ragnar Frisch, Norwegian
Jan Tinbergen, Netherlandish

Pulitzer Prizes in Journalism, Letters, and Music

The Pulitzer Prizes were endowed by Joseph Pulitzer (1847-1911), publisher of The World, New York, N. Y., in a bequest to Columbia University, New York, N. Y., and are awarded annually by the president of the university on recommendation of the Advisory Board on Pulitzer Prizes for work done during the preceding year. Secretary of the Advisory Board is John Hohenberg of Columbia Univ. All prizes are $1,000 (originally $500) in each category, except Meritorious Public Service for which a gold medal is given. No awards given for years omitted.

Pulitzer Prizes in Journalism
Meritorious Public Service

For disinterested and meritorious public service by a United States newspaper.

1918—New York Times. Also special award to Minna Lewinson and Henry Beetle Hough.
1919—Milwaukee Journal.
1921—Boston Post.
1922—New York World.
1923—Memphis (Tenn.) Commercial Appeal.
1924—New York World.
1926—Enquirer-Sun, Columbus, Ga.
1927—Canton (Oh.) Daily News.
1928—Indianapolis Times.
1929—Evening World, New York.
1931—Atlanta (Ga.) Constitution.
1932—Indianapolis (Ind.) News.
1933—New York World-Telegram.
1934—Medford (Ore.) Mail-Tribune.
1935—Sacramento (Cal.) Bee.
1936—Cedar Rapids (Ia.) Gazette.
1937—St. Louis Post-Dispatch.
1938—Bismarck (N. D.) Tribune.
1939—Miami (Fla.) Daily News.
1940—Waterbury (Conn.) Republican and American.
1941—St. Louis Post-Dispatch.
1942—Los Angeles Times.
1943—Omaha World Herald.
1944—New York Times.
1945—Detroit Free Press.
1946—Scranton (Pa.) Times.
1947—Baltimore Sun.
1948—St. Louis Post-Dispatch.
1949—Nebraska State Journal.
1950—Chicago Daily News; St. Louis Post-Dispatch.
1951—Miami (Fla.) Herald and Brooklyn Eagle.
1952—St. Louis Post-Dispatch.
1953—Whiteville (N. C.) News Reporter; Tabor City (N. C.) Tribune.
1954—Newsday (Long Island, N.Y.).
1955—Columbus (Ga.) Ledger and Sunday Ledger-Enquirer.
1956—Watsonville (Cal.) Register-Pajaronian.
1957—Chicago Daily News.
1958—Arkansas Gazette, Little Rock.
1959—Utica (N. Y.) Observer-Dispatch and Utica Daily Press.
1960—Los Angeles Times.
1961—Amarillo (Tex.) Globe-Times.
1962—Panama City (Fla.) News-Herald.
1963—Chicago Daily News.
1964—St. Petersburg (Fla.) Times.
1965—Hutchinson (Kan.) News.
1966—Boston Globe.
1967—The Louisville Courier-Journal and The Milwaukee Journal.
1968—Riverside (Cal.) Press-Enterprise.
1969—Los Angeles Times.
1970—Newsday (Long Island, N.Y.).
1971—Winston Salem (N.C.) Journal & Sentinel.
1972—New York Times.
1973—Washington Post.
1974—Newsday (Long Island, N.Y.).
1975—Boston Globe.

Reporting

This category originally embraced all fields, local, national, and international. Later separate categories were created for the different fields of reporting.

1917—Herbert Bayard Swope, New York World.
1918—Harold A. Littledale, New York Evening Post.
1920—John J. Leary, Jr., New York World.
1921—Louis Seibold, New York World.
1922—Kirke L. Simpson, Associated Press.
1923—Alva Johnston, New York Times.
1924—Magner White, San Diego Sun.
1925—James W. Mulroy and Alvin H. Goldstein, Chicago Daily News.
1926—William Burke Miller, Louisville Courier-Journal.
1927—John T. Rogers, St. Louis Post-Dispatch.

1929—Paul Y. Anderson, St. Louis Post-Dispatch.
1930—Russell D. Owens, New York Times. Also $500 to W. O. Dapping, Auburn (N. Y.) Citizen.
1931—A. B. MacDonald, Kansas City (Mo.) Star.
1932—W. C. Richards, D. D. Martin, J. S. Pooler, F. D. Webb, J. N. W. Sloan, Detroit Free Press.
1933—Francis A. Jamieson, Asssociated Press.
1934—Royce Brier, San Francisco Chronicle.
1935—William H. Taylor, New York Herald Tribune.
1936—Lauren D. Lyman, New York Times.
1937—John J. O'Neill, N. Y. Herald Tribune; William L. Laurence, N. Y. Times; Howard W. Blakeslee, A. P.; Gobind Behari Lal, University Service; and David Dietz, Scripps-Howard Newspapers.
1938—Raymond Sprigle, Pittsburgh Post-Gazette.
1939—Thomas L. Stokes, Scripps-Howard Newspaper Alliance.
1940—S. Burton Heath, New York World-Telegram.
1941—Westbrook Pegler, New York World-Telegram.
1942—Stanton Delaplane, San Francisco Chronicle.
1943—George Weller, Chicago Daily News.
1944—Paul Schoenstein, N. Y. Journal-American.
1945—Jack S. McDowell, San Francisco Call-Bulletin.
1946—William L. Laurence, New York Times.
1947—Frederick Woltman, N. Y. World-Telegram.
1948—George E. Goodwin, Atlanta Journal.
1949—Malcolm Johnson, New York Sun.
1950—Meyer Berger, New York Times.
1951—Edward S. Montgomery, San Francisco Examiner.
1952—Geo. de Carvalho, San Francisco Chronicle.

(1) to meet a deadline; (2) free of deadline.

1953—(1) Providence (R.I.) Journal and Evening Bulletin; (2) Edward J. Mowery, N.Y. World-Telegram & Sun.
1954—(1) Vicksburg (Miss.) Sunday Post-Herald; (2) Alvin Scott McCoy, Kansas City (Mo.) Star.
1955—(1) Mrs. Caro Brown, Alice (Tex.) Daily Echo; (2) Roland K. Towery, Cuero (Tex.) Record.
1956—(1) Lee Hills, Detroit Free Press; (2) Arthur Daley, New York Times.
1957—(1) Salt Lake Tribune, Salt Lake City, Ut.; (2) Wallace Turner and William Lambert, Portland Oregonian.
1958—(1) Fargo (N. D.) Forum; (2) George Beveridge, Evening Star, Washington, D. C.
1959—(1) Mary Lou Werner, Washington Evening Star; (2) John Harold Brislin, Scranton (Pa.) Tribune, and The Scrantonian.
1960—(1) Jack Nelson, Atlanta Constitution; (2) Miriam Ottenberg, Washington Evening Star.
1961—(1) Sanche de Gramont, N. Y. Herald Tribune; (2) Edgar May, Buffalo Evening News.
1962—(1) Robert D. Mullins, Deseret News, Salt Lake City; (2) George Bliss, Chicago Tribune.
1963—(1) Shared by Sylvan Fox, William Longgood, and Anthony Shannon, N. Y. World-Telegram & Sun; (2) Oscar Griffin, Jr., Pecos (Tex.) Independent and Enterprise.

(1) General Reporting; (2) Special Reporting.

1964—(1) Norman C. Miller, Wall Street Journal; (2) Shared by James V. Magee, Albert V. Gaudiosi, and Frederick A. Meyer, Philadelphia Bulletin.
1965—(1) Melvin H. Ruder, Hungry Horse News (Columbia Falls, Mon.); (2) Gene Goltz, Houston Post.
1966—(1) Los Angeles Times Staff; (2) John A. Frasca, Tampa (Fla.) Tribune.
1967—(1) Robert V. Cox, Chambersburg (Pa.) Public Opinion; (2) Gene Miller, Miami Herald.
1968—Detroit Free Press Staff; (2) J. Anthony Lukas, N. Y. Times.
1969—(1) John Fetterman, Louisville Courier-Journal and Times; (2) Albert L. Delugach, St. Louis Globe Democrat, and Denny Walsh, Life.
1970—(1) Thomas Fitzpatrick, Chicago Sun-Times; (2) Harold Eugene Martin, Montgomery Advertiser & Alabama Journal.
1971—(1) Akron Beacon Journal Staff; (2) William Hugh Jones, Chicago Tribune.
1972—(1) Richard Cooper and John Machacek, Rochester (N.Y.) Times-Union; (2) Timothy Leland, Gerard M. O'Neill, Stephen A. Kurkjian and Anne De Santis, Boston Globe.

1973—(1) Chicago Tribune; (2) Sun Newspapers of Omaha.
1974—(1) Hugh F. Hough, Arthur M. Petacque, Chicago Sun-Times; (2) William Sherman, N.Y. Daily News.
1975—(1) Xenia (Oh.) Daily Gazette; (2) Indianapolis Star.

Criticism or Commentary

(1) Criticism; (2) Commentary

1970—(1) Ada Louise Huxtable, N.Y. Times; (2) Marquis W. Childs, St. Louis Post-Dispatch.
1971—(1) Harold C. Schonberg, N.Y. Times; (2) William A. Caldwell, The Record, Hackensack, N.J.
1972—(1) Frank Peters Jr., St. Louis Post-Dispatch; (2) Mike Royko, Chicago Daily News.
1973—(1) Ronald Powers, Chicago Sun-Times; (2) David S. Broder, Washington Post.
1974—(1) Emily Genauer, Newsday, (N.Y.); (2) Edwin A. Roberts, Jr., National Observer.
1975—(1) Roger Ebert, Chicago Sun Times; (2) Mary McGrory, Washington Star.

National Reporting

1942—Louis Stark, New York Times.
1944—Dewey L. Fleming, Baltimore Sun.
1945—James B. Reston, New York Times.
1946—Edward A. Harris, St. Louis Post-Dispatch.
1947—Edward T. Folliard, Washington Post.
1948—Bert Andrews, New York Herald Tribune; Nat S. Finney, Minneapolis Tribune.
1949—Charles P. Trussell, New York Times.
1950—Edwin O. Guthman, Seattle Times.
1952—Anthony Leviero, New York Times.
1953—Don Whitehead, Associated Press.
1954—Richard Wilson, Cowles Newspapers.
1955—Anthony Lewis, Washington Daily News.
1956—Charles L. Bartlett, Chattanooga Times.
1957—James Reston, New York Times.
1958—Relman Morin, AP; Clark Mollenhoff, Des Moines Register & Tribune.
1959—Howard Van Smith, Miami (Fla.) News.
1960—Vance Trimble, Scripps-Howard, Washington, D. C.
1961—Edward R. Cony, Wall Street Journal.
1962—Nathan G. Caldwell and Gene S. Graham, Nashville Tennessean.
1963—Anthony Lewis, New York Times.
1964—Merriman Smith, UPI.
1965—Louis M. Kohlmeier, Wall Street Journal.
1966—Haynes Johnson, Washington Evening Star.
1967—Monroe Karmin and Stanley Penn, Wall Street Journal.
1968—Howard James, Christian Science Monitor; Nathan K. Kotz, Des Moines Register.
1969—Robert Cahn, Christian Science Monitor.
1970—William J. Eaton, Chicago Daily News.
1971—Lucinda Franks & Thomas Powers, UPI.
1972—Jack Anderson, United Features.
1973—Robert Boyd and Clark Hoyt, Knight Newspapers.
1974—James R. Polk, Washington Star-News; Jack White, Providence Journal-Bulletin.
1975—Donald L. Barlett and James B. Steele, Philadelphia Inquirer.

International Reporting

1942—Laurence Edmund Allen, Associated Press.
1943—Ira Wolfert, No. Am. Newspaper Alliance.
1944—Daniel DeLuce, Associated Press.
1945—Mark S. Watson, Baltimore Sun.
1946—Homer W. Bigart, New York Herald Tribune.
1947—Eddy Gilmore, Associated Press.
1948—Paul W. Ward, Baltimore Sun.
1949—Price Day, Baltimore Sun.
1950—Edmund Stevens, Christian Science Monitor.
1951—Keyes Beech and Fred Sparks, Chicago Daily News; Homer Bigart and Marguerite Higgins, New York Herald Tribune; Relman Morin and Don Whitehead, AP.
1952—John M. Hightower, Associated Press.
1953—Austin C. Wehrwein, Milwaukee Journal.
1954—Jim G. Lucas, Scripps-Howard Newspapers.
1955—Harrison Salisbury, New York Times.
1956—William Randolph Hearst, Jr., Frank Conniff, Hearst Newspapers; Kingsbury Smith, INS.
1957—Russell Jones, United Press.
1958—New York Times.
1959—Joseph Martin and Philip Santora, N.Y. News.
1960—A. M. Rosenthal, New York Times.
1961—Lynn Heinzerling, Associated Press.
1962—Walter Lippmann, N.Y. Herald Tribune Synd.
1963—Hal Hendrix, Miami (Fla.) News.

1964—Malcolm W. Browne, AP; David Halberstam, N. Y. Times.
1965—J. A. Livingston, Philadelphia Bulletin.
1966—Peter Arnett, AP.
1967—R. John Hughes, Christian Science Monitor.
1968—Alfred Friendly, Washington Post.
1969—William Tuohy, L. A. Times.
1970—Seymour M. Hersh, Dispatch News Service.
1971—Jimmie Lee Hoagland, Washington Post.
1972—Peter R. Kann, Wall Street Journal.
1973—Max Frankel, N.Y. Times.
1974—Hedrick Smith, N.Y. Times.
1975—William Mullen and Ovie Carter, Chicago Tribune.

Correspondence

For Washington or foreign correspondence. Category was merged with those in national and international reporting in 1948.

1929—Paul Scott Mowrer, Chicago Daily News.
1930—Leland Stowe, New York Herald Tribune.
1931—H. R. Knickerbocker, Philadelphia Public Ledger and New York Evening Post.
1932—Walter Duranty, New York Times, and Charles G. Ross, St. Louis Post-Dispatch.
1933—Edgar Ansel Mowrer, Chicago Daily News.
1934—Frederick T. Birchall, New York Times.
1935—Arthur Krock, New York Times.
1936—Wilfred C. Barber, Chicago Tribune.
1937—Anne O'Hare McCormick, New York Times.
1938—Arthur Krock, New York Times.
1939—Louis P. Lochner, Associated Press.
1940—Otto D. Tolischus, New York Times.
1941—Bronze plaque to commemorate work of American correspondents on war fronts.
1942—Carlos P. Romulo, Philippines Herald.
1943—Hanson W. Baldwin, New York Times.
1944—Ernest Taylor Pyle, Scripps-Howard Newspaper Alliance.
1945—Harold V. (Hal) Boyle, Associated Press.
1946—Arnaldo Cortesi, New York Times.
1947—Brooks Atkinson, New York Times.

Editorial Writing

The test of excellence is clearness of style, moral purpose, sound reasoning and power to influence public opinion.

1917—New York Tribune.
1918—Louisville (Ky.) Courier-Journal.
1920—Harvey E. Newbranch, Omaha Evening World-Herald.
1922—Frank M. O'Brien, New York Herald.
1923—William Allen White, Emporia Gazette.
1924—Frank Buxton, Boston Herald. Special Prize. Frank I. Cobb, New York World.
1925—Charleston (S. C.) News and Courier.
1926—Edward M. Kingsbury, N. Y. Times.
1927—F. Lauriston Bullard, Boston Herald.
1928—Grover C. Hall, Montgomery Advertiser.
1929—Louis Isaac Jaffe, Norfolk Virginian-Pilot.
1931—Chas. Ryckman, Fremont (Neb.) Tribune.
1933—Kansas City (Mo.) Star.
1934—E. P. Chase, Atlantic (Ia.) News Telegraph.
1936—Felix Morley, Washington Post, George B. Parker, Scripps-Howard Newspapers.
1937—John W. Owens, Baltimore Sun.
1938—W. W. Waymack, Des Moines (Ia.) Register and Tribune.
1939—Ronald G. Callvert, Portland Oregonian.
1940—Bart Howard, St. Louis Post-Dispatch.
1941—Reuben Maury, Daily News, N. Y.
1942—Geoffrey Parsons, New York Herald Tribune.
1943—Forrest W. Seymour, Des Moines (Ia.) Register and Tribune.
1944—Henry J. Haskell, Kansas City (Mo.) Star.
1945—George W. Potter, Providence (R. I.) Journal-Bulletin.
1946—Hodding Carter, Greenville (Miss.) Delta Democrat-Times.
1947—William H. Grimes, Wall Street Journal.
1948—Virginius Dabney, Richmond (Va.) Times-Dispatch.
1949—John H. Crider, Boston (Mass.) Herald, Herbert Elliston, Washington Post.
1950—Carl M. Saunders, Jackson (Mich.) Citizen-Patriot.
1951—William H. Fitzpatrick, New Orleans States.
1952—Louis LaCoss, St. Louis Globe Democrat.
1953—Vermont C. Royster, Wall Street Journal.
1954—Don Murray, Boston Herald.
1955—Royce Howes, Detroit Free Press.
1956—Lauren K. Soth, Des Moines (Ia.) Register and Tribune.

1957—Buford Boone, Tuscaloosa (Ala.) News.
1958—Harry S. Ashmore, Arkansas Gazette.
1959—Ralph McGill, Atlanta Constitution.
1960—Lenoir Chambers, Norfolk Virginian-Pilot.
1961—William J. Dorvillier, San Juan (Puerto Rico) Star.
1962—Thomas M. Storke, Santa Barbara (Cal.) News-Press.
1963—Ira B. Harkey, Jr., Pascagoula (Miss.) Chronicle.
1964—Hazel Brannon Smith, Lexington (Miss.) Advertiser.
1965—John R. Harrison, The Gainesville (Fla.) Sun.
1966—Robert Lasch, St. Louis Post-Dispatch.
1967—Eugene C. Patterson, Atlanta Constitution.
1968—John S. Knight, Knight Newspapers.
1969—Paul Greenberg, Pine Bluff (Ark.) Commercial.
1970—Philip L. Geyelin, Washington Post.
1971—Horance G. Davis, Jr., Gainesville (Fla.) Sun.
1972—John Strohmeyer, Bethlehem (Pa.) Globe-Times.
1973—Roger B. Linscott, Berkshire Eagle, Pittsfield, Mass.
1974—F. Gilman Spencer, Trenton (N.J.) Trentonian.
1975—John D. Maurice, Charleston (W. Va.) Daily Mail.

Editorial Cartooning

1922—Rollin Kirby, New York World.
1924—Jay N. Darling, New York Herald Tribune.
1925—Rollin Kirby, New York World.
1926—D. R. Fitzpatrick, St. Louis Post-Dispatch.
1927—Nelson Harding, Brooklyn Eagle.
1928—Nelson Harding, Brooklyn Eagle.
1929—Rollin Kirby, New York World.
1930—Charles Macauley, Brooklyn Eagle.
1931—Edmund Duffy, Baltimore Sun.
1932—John T. McCutcheon, Chicago Tribune.
1933—H. M. Talburt, Washington Daily News.
1934—Edmund Duffy, Baltimore Sun.
1935—Ross A. Lewis, Milwaukee Journal.
1937—C. D. Batchelor, New York Daily News.
1938—Vaughn Shoemaker, Chicago Daily News.
1939—Charles G. Werner, Daily Oklahoman.
1940—Edmund Duffy, Baltimore Sun.
1941—Jacob Burck, Chicago Times.
1942—Herbert L. Block, Newspaper Enterprise Assn.
1943—Jay N. Darling, New York Herald Tribune.
1944—Clifford K. Berryman, Washington Star.
1945—Bill Mauldin, United Feature Syndicate.
1946—Bruce Alexander Russell, Los Angeles Times.
1947—Vaughn Shoemaker, Chicago Daily News.
1948—Reuben L. (Rube) Goldberg, N. Y. Sun.
1949—Lute Pease, Newark (N. J.) Evening News.
1950—James T. Berryman, Washington Star.
1951—Reginald W. Manning, Arizona Republic.
1952—Fred L. Packer, New York Mirror.
1953—Edward D. Kuekes, Cleveland Plain Dealer.
1954—Herbert L. Block. Washington Post & Times-Herald.
1955—Daniel R. Fitzpatrick, St. Louis Post-Dispatch.
1956—Robert York, Louisville (Ky.) Times.
1957—Tom Little, Nashville Tennessean.
1958—Bruce M. Shanks, Buffalo Evening News.
1959—Bill Mauldin, St. Louis Post-Dispatch.
1961—Carey Orr, Chicago Tribune.
1962—Edmund S. Valtman, Hartford Times.
1963—Frank Miller, Des Moines Register.
1964—Paul Conrad, Denver Post.
1966—Don Wright, Miami News.
1967—Patrick B. Oliphant, Denver Post.
1968—Eugene Gray Payne, Charlotte Observer.
1969—John Fischetti, Chicago Daily News.
1970—Thomas F. Darcy, Newsday.
1971—Paul Conrad, L. A. Times.
1972—Jeffrey K. MacNelly, Richmond News-Leader.
1974—Paul Szep, Boston Globe.
1975—Gary Trudeau, Universal Press Syndicate.

Spot News Photography

1942—Milton Brooks, Detroit News.
1943—Frank Noel, Associated Press.
1944—Frank Filan, AP; Earle L. Bunker, Omaha World-Herald.
1945—Joe Rosenthal, Associated Press, for photograph of planting American flag on Iwo Jima.
1947—Arnold Hardy, amateur, Atlanta, Ga.
1948—Frank Cushing, Boston Traveler.
1949—Nathaniel Fein, New York Herald Tribune.
1950—Bill Crouch, Oakland (Cal.) Tribune.
1951—Max Desfor, Associated Press.
1952—John Robinson and Don Ultang, Des Moines Register and Tribune.
\53—William M. Gallagher, Flint (Mich.) Journal.

1954—Mrs. Walter M. Schau, amateur.
1955—John L. Gaunt, Jr., Los Angeles Times.
1956—New York Daily News.
1957—Harry A. Trask, Boston Traveler.
1958—William C. Beall, Washington Daily News.
1959—William Seaman, Minneapolis Star.
1960—Andrew Lopez, UPI.
1961—Yasushi Nagao, Mainichi Newspapers, Tokyo.
1962—Paul Vathis, Associated Press.
1963—Hector Rondon, La Republica, Caracas, Venezuela.
1964—Robert H. Jackson, Dallas Times-Herald.
1965—Horst Faas, Associated Press.
1966—Kyoichi Sawada, UPI.
1967—Jack R. Thornell, Associated Press.
1968—Rocco Morabito, Jacksonville Journal.
1969—Edward Adams, A.P.
1970—Steve Starr, A.P.
1971—John Paul Filo, Valley Daily News & Daily Dispatch of Tarentum & New Kensington, Pa.
1972—Horst Faas and Michel Laurent, AP.
1973—Huynh Cong Ut, AP.
1974—Anthony K. Roberts, AP.
1975—Gerald H. Gay, Seattle Times.

Feature Photography

1968—Toshio Sakai, UPI.
1969—Moneta Sleet, Jr., Ebony.
1970—Dallas Kinney, Palm Beach Post.
1971—Jack Dykinga, Chicago Sun-Times.
1972—Dave Kennerly, UPI.
1973—Brian Lanker, Topeka Capitol-Journal.
1974—Slava Veder, AP.
1975—Matthew Lewis, Washington Post.

Special Citation

1938—Edmonton (Alberta) Journal, bronze plaque.
1941—New York Times.
1944—Byron Price and Mrs. William Allen White. Also to Richard Rodgers and Oscar Hammerstein 2d, for musical, Oklahoma!
1945—Press cartographers for war maps.
1947—(Pulitzer centennial year.) Columbia Univ. and the Graduate School of Journalism, and St. Louis Post-Dispatch.
1948—Dr. Frank Diehl Fackenthal.
1951—Cyrus L. Sulzberger, New York Times.
1952—Max Kase, New York Journal-American.
1953—The New York Times; Lester Markel.
1957—Kenneth Roberts, for his historical novels.
1958—Walter Lippmann, New York Herald Tribune.
1960—Garrett Mattingly, for The Armada.
1961—American Heritage Picture History of the Civil War.
1964—The Gannett Newspapers.
1973—James T. Flexner, for "George Washington," a four-volume biography.

Pulitzer Prizes in Letters
Fiction

For fiction in book form by an American author, preferably dealing with American life.
1918—Ernest Poole, His Family.
1919—Booth Tarkington, The Magnificent Ambersons.
1921—Edith Wharton, The Age of Innocence.
1922—Booth Tarkington, Alice Adams.
1923—Willa Cather, One of Ours.
1924—Margaret Wilson, The Able McLaughlins.
1925—Edna Ferber, So Big.
1926—Sinclair Lewis, Arrowsmith. (Refused prize.)
1927—Louis Bromfield, Early Autumn.
1928—Thornton Wilder, Bridge of San Luis Rey.
1929—Julia M. Peterkin, Scarlet Sister Mary.
1930—Oliver LaFarge, Laughing Boy.
1931—Margaret Ayer Barnes, Years of Grace.
1932—Pearl S. Buck, The Good Earth.
1933—T. S. Stribling, The Store.
1934—Caroline Miller, Lamb in His Bosom.
1935—Josephine W. Johnson, Now in November.
1936—Harold L. Davis, Honey in the Horn.
1937—Margaret Mitchell, Gone With the Wind.
1938—John P. Marquand, The Late George Apley.
1939—Marjorie Kinnan Rawlings, The Yearling.
1940—John Steinbeck, The Grapes of Wrath.
1942—Ellen Glasgow, In This Our Life.
1943—Upton Sinclair, Dragon's Teeth.
1944—Martin Flavin, Journey in the Dark.
1945—John Hersey, A Bell for Adano.
1947—Robert Penn Warren, All the King's Men.

1948—James A. Michener, Tales of the South Pacific.
1949—James Gould Cozzens, Guard of Honor.
1950—A. B. Guthrie, Jr., The Way West.
1951—Conrad Richter, The Town.
1952—Herman Wouk, The Caine Mutiny.
1953—Ernest Hemingway, The Old Man and the Sea.
1955—William Faulkner, A Fable.
1956—MacKinlay Kantor, Andersonville.
1958—James Agee, A Death in the Family.
1959—Robert Lewis Taylor, The Travels of Jaimie McPheeters.
1960—Allen Drury, Advise and Consent.
1961—Harper Lee, To Kill a Mockingbird.
1962—Edwin O'Connor, The Edge of Sadness.
1963—William Faulkner, The Reivers.
1965—Shirley Ann Grau, The Keepers of the House.
1966—Katherine Anne Porter, Collected Stories of Katherine Anne Porter.
1967—Bernard Malamud, The Fixer.
1968—William Styron, The Confessions of Nat Turner.
1969—N. Scott Momaday, House Made of Dawn.
1970—Jean Stafford, Collected Stories.
1972—Wallace Stegner, Angle of Repose.
1973—Eudora Welty, The Optimist's Daughter.
1975—Michael Shaara, The Killer Angels.

Drama

For an American play, preferably original and dealing with American life.

1918—Jesse Lynch Williams, Why Marry?
1920—Eugene O'Neill, Beyond the Horizon.
1921—Zona Gale, Miss Lulu Bett.
1922—Eugene O'Neill, Anna Christie.
1923—Owen Davis, Icebound.
1924—Hatcher Hughes, Hell-Bent for Heaven.
1925—Sidney Howard, They Knew What They Wanted.
1926—George Kelly, Craig's Wife.
1927—Paul Green, In Abraham's Bosom.
1928—Eugene O'Neill, Strange Interlude.
1929—Elmer Rice, Street Scene.
1930—Marc Connelly, The Green Pastures.
1931—Susan Glaspell, Alison's House.
1932—George S. Kaufman, Morrie Ryskind and Ira Gershwin, Of Thee I Sing.
1933—Maxwell Anderson, Both Your Houses.
1934—Sidney Kingsley, Men in White.
1935—Zoe Akins, The Old Maid.
1936—Robert E. Sherwood, Idiot's Delight.
1937—George S. Kaufman and Moss Hart, You Can't Take It With You.
1938—Thornton Wilder, Our Town.
1939—Robert E. Sherwood, Abe Lincoln in Illinois.
1940—William Saroyan, The Time of Your Life.
1941—Robert E. Sherwood, There Shall Be No Night.
1943—Thornton Wilder, The Skin of Our Teeth.
1945—Mary Chase, Harvey.
1946—Russel Crouse and Howard Lindsay, State of the Union.
1948—Tennessee Williams, A Streetcar Named Desire.
1949—Arthur Miller, Death of a Salesman.
1950—Richard Rodgers, Oscar Hammerstein 2d, and Joshua Logan, South Pacific.
1952—Joseph Kramm, The Shrike.
1953—William Inge, Picnic.
1954—John Patrick, Teahouse of the August Moon.
1955—Tennessee Williams, Cat on a Hot Tin Roof.
1956—Frances Goodrich and Albert Hackett, The Diary of Anne Frank.
1957—Eugene O'Neill, Long Day's Journey Into Night.
1958—Ketti Frings, Look Homeward, Angel.
1959—Archibald MacLeish, J. B.
1960—George Abbott, Jerome Weidman, Sheldon Harnick and Jerry Bock, Fiorello.
1961—Tad Mosel, All the Way Home.
1962—Frank Loesser and Abe Burrows, How To Succeed In Business Without Really Trying.
1965—Frank D. Gilroy, The Subject Was Roses.
1967—Edward Albee, A Delicate Balance.
1969—Howard Sackler, The Great White Hope.
1970—Charles Gordone, No Place to Be Somebody.
1971—Paul Zindel, The Effect of Gamma Rays on Man-in-the-Moon Marigolds.
1973—Jason Miller, That Championship Season.
1975—Edward Albee, Seascape.

History

1917—J. J. Jusserand, With Americans of Past and Present Days.

1918—James Ford Rhodes, History of the Civil War.
1920—Justin H. Smith, The War with Mexico.
1921—William Sowden Sims, The Victory at Sea.
1922—James Truslow Adams, The Founding of New England.
1923—Charles Warren, The Supreme Court in United States History.
1924—Charles Howard McIlwain, The American Revolution: A Constitutional Interpretation.
1925—Frederick L. Paxton, A History of the American Frontier.
1926—Edward Channing, The History of the U. S.
1927—Samuel Flagg Bemis, Pinckney's Treaty.
1928—Vernon Louis Parrington, Main Currents in American Thought.
1929—Fred A. Shannon, The Organization and Administration of the Union Army, 1861-65.
1930—Claude H. Van Tyne, The War of Independence.
1931—Bernadotte E. Schmitt, The Coming of the War, 1914.
1932—Gen. John J. Pershing, My Experiences in the World War.
1933—Frederick J. Turner, The Significance of Sections in American History.
1934—Herbert Agar, The People's Choice.
1935—Charles McLean Andrews, The Colonial Period of American History.
1936—Andrew C. McLaughlin, The Constitutional History of the United States.
1937—Van Wyck Brooks, The Flowering of New England.
1938—Paul Herman Buck, The Road to Reunion, 1865-1900.
1939—Frank Luther Mott, A History of American Magazines.
1940—Carl Sandburg, Abraham Lincoln: The War Years.
1941—Marcus Lee Hansen, The Atlantic Migration, 1607-1860.
1942—Margaret Leech, Reveille in Washington.
1943—Esther Forbes, Paul Revere and the World He Lived In.
1944—Merle Curti, The Growth of American Thought.
1945—Stephen Bonsal, Unfinished Business.
1946—Arthur M. Schlesinger, Jr., The Age of Jackson.
1947—James Phinney Baxter 3d, Scientists Against Time.
1948—Bernard De Voto, Across the Wide Missouri.
1949—Roy F. Nichols, The Disruption of American Democracy.
1950—O. W. Larkin, Art and Life in America.
1951—R. Carlyle Buley, The Old Northwest: Pioneer Period 1815-1840.
1952—Oscar Handlin, The Uprooted.
1953—George Dangerfield, The Era of Good Feelings.
1954—Bruce Catton, A Stillness at Appomattox.
1955—Paul Horgan, Great River: The Rio Grande in North American History.
1956—Richard Hofstadter, The Age of Reform.
1957—George F. Kennan, Russia Leaves the War.
1958—Bray Hammond, Banks and Politics in America—From the Revolution to the Civil War.
1959—Leonard D. White and Jean Schneider, The Republican Era; 1869-1901.
1960—Margaret Leech, In the Days of McKinley.
1961—Herbert Feis, Between War and Peace: The Potsdam Conference.
1962—Lawrence H. Gibson, The Triumphant Empire: Thunderclouds Gather in the West.
1963—Constance McLaughlin Green, Washington: Village and Capital, 1800-1878.
1964—Sumner Chilton Powell, Puritan Village: The Formation of A New England Town.
1965—Irwin Unger, The Greenback Era.
1966—Perry Miller, Life of the Mind in America.
1967—William H. Goetzmann, Exploration and Empire: the Explorer and Scientist in the Winning of the American West.
1968—Bernard Bailyn, The Ideological Origins of the American Revolution.
1969—Leonard W. Levy, Origin of the Fifth Amendment.
1970—Dean Acheson, Present at the Creation: My Years in the State Department.
1971—James McGregor Burns, Roosevelt: The Soldier of Freedom.
1972—Carl N. Degler, Neither Black Nor White.
1973—Michael Kammen, People of Paradox: An Inquiry Concerning the Origins of American Civilization.
1974—Daniel J. Boorstin, The Americans: The Democratic Experience.
1975—Dumas Malone, Jefferson and His Time.

Biography or Autobiography

For a distinguished biography or autobiography by an American author, preferably on an American subject.

1917—Laura E. Richards and Maude Howe Elliott, assisted by Florence Howe Hall, Julia Ward Howe.
1918—William Cabell Bruce, Benjamin Franklin, Self-Revealed.
1919—Henry Adams, The Education of Henry Adams.
1920—Albert J. Beveridge, The Life of John Marshall.
1921—Edward Bok, The Americanization of Edward Bok.
1922—Hamlin Garland, A Daughter of the Middle Border.
1923—Burton J. Hendrick, The Life and Letters of Walter H. Page.
1924—Michael Pupin, From Immigrant to Inventor.
1925—M. A. DeWolfe Howe, Barrett Wendell and His Letters.
1926—Harvey Cushing, Life of Sir William Osler.
1927—Emory Holloway, Whitman: An Interpretation in Narrative.
1928—Charles Edward Russell, The American Orchestra and Theodore Thomas.
1929—Burton J. Hendrick, The Training of an American: The Earlier Life and Letters of Walter H. Page.
1930—Marquis James, The Raven. (Sam Houston).
1931—Henry James, Charles W. Eliot.
1932—Henry F. Pringle, Theodore Roosevelt.
1933—Allan Nevins, Grover Cleveland.
1934—Tyler Dennett, John Hay.
1935—Douglas Southall Freeman, R. E. Lee.
1936—Ralph Barton Perry, The Thought and Character of William James.
1937—Allan Nevins, Hamilton Fish: The Inner History of the Grant Administration.
1938—Divided between Odell Shepard, Pedlar's Progress: Marquis James, Andrew Jackson.
1939—Carl Van Doren, Benjamin Franklin.
1940—Ray Stannard Baker, Woodrow Wilson, Life and Letters.
1941—Ola Elizabeth Winslow, Jonathan Edwards.
1942—Forrest Wilson, Crusader in Crinoline.
1943—Samuel Eliot Morison, Admiral of the Ocean Sea (Columbus).
1944—Carleton Mabee, The American Leonardo: The Life of Samuel F. B. Morse.
1945—Russell Blaine Nye, George Bancroft: Brahmin Rebel.
1946—Linny Marsh Wolfe, Son of the Wilderness.
1947—William Allen White, The Autobiography of William Allen White.
1948—Margaret Clapp, Forgotten First Citizen: John Bigelow.
1949—Robert E. Sherwood, Roosevelt and Hopkins.
1950—Samuel Flag Bemis, John Quincy Adams and the Foundations of American Foreign Policy.
1951—Margaret Louise Coit, John C. Calhoun: American Portrait.
1952—Merlo J. Pusey, Charles Evans Hughes.
1953—David J. Mays, Edmund Pendleton, 1721-1803.
1954—Charles A. Lindbergh, The Spirit of St. Louis.
1955—William S. White, The Taft Story.
1956—Talbot F. Hamlin, Benjamin Henry Latrobe.
1957—John F. Kennedy, Profiles in Courage.
1958—Douglas Southall Freeman (decd. 1953), George Washington, Vols. I-VI; John Alexander Carroll and Mary Wells Ashworth, vol. VII.
1959—Arthur Walworth, Woodrow Wilson: American Prophet.
1960—Samuel Eliot Morison, John Paul Jones.
1961—David Donald, Charles Sumner and The Coming of the Civil War.
1963—Leon Edel, Henry James: Vol. II, The Conquest of London, 1870-1881; Vol. III, The Middle Years, 1881-1895.
1964—Walter Jackson Bate, John Keats.
1965—Ernest Samuels, Henry Adams.
1966—Arthur M. Schlesinger, Jr., A Thousand Days.
1967—Justin Kaplan, Mr. Clemens and Mark Twain.
1968—George F. Kennan, Memoirs (1925-1950).
1969—B. L. Reid, The Man from New York: John Quinn and his Friends.
1970—T. Harry Williams, Huey Long.
1971—Lawrence Thompson, Robert Frost: The Years of Triumph, 1915-1938.
1972—Joseph P. Lash, Eleanor and Franklin.
1973—W. A. Swanberg, Luce and His Empire.
1974—Louis Sheaffer, O'Neill, Son and Artist.
1975—Robert A. Caro, The Power Broker: Robert Moses and the Fall of New York.

American Poetry

Before this prize was established in 1922, the following awards were made from gifts provided by the Poetry Society. 1918—Love Songs, by Sara Teasdale. 1919—Old Road to Paradise, by Margaret Widdemer; Corn Huskers, by Carl Sandburg.

1922—Edwin Arlington Robinson, Collected Poems.
1923—Edna St. Vincent Millay, The Ballad of the Harp-Weaver; A Few Figs from Thistles; Eight Sonnets in American Poetry, 1922; A Miscellany.
1924—Robert Frost, New Hampshire: A Poem with Notes and Grace Notes.
1925—Edwin Arlington Robinson, The Man Who Died Twice.
1926—Amy Lowell, What's O'Clock.
1927—Leonora Speyer, Fiddler's Farewell.
1928—Edwin Arlington Robinson, Tristram.
1929—Stephen Vincent Benet, John Brown's Body.
1930—Conrad Aiken, Selected Poems.
1931—Robert Frost, Collected Poems.
1932—George Dillon, The Flowering Stone.
1933—Archibald MacLeish, Conquistador.
1934—Robert Hillyer, Collected Verse.
1935—Audrey Wurdemann, Bright Ambush.
1936—Robert P. Tristram Coffin, Strange Holiness.
1937—Robert Frost, A Further Range.
1938—Marya Zaturenska, Cold Morning Sky.
1939—John Gould Fletcher, Selected Poems.
1940—Mark Van Doren, Collected Poems.
1941—Leonard Bacon, Sunderland Capture.
1942—William Rose Benet, The Dust Which Is God.
1943—Robert Frost, A Witness Tree.
1944—Stephen Vincent Benet, Western Star.
1945—Karl Shapiro, V-Letter and Other Poems.
1947—Robert Lowell, Lord Weary's Castle.
1948—W. H. Auden, The Age of Anxiety.
1949—Peter Viereck, Terror and Decorum.
1950—Gwendolyn Brooks, Annie Allen.
1951—Carl Sandburg, Complete Poems.
1952—Marianne Moore, Collected Poems.
1953—Archibald MacLeish, Collected Poems.
1954—Theodore Roethke, The Waking.
1955—Wallace Stevens, Collected Poems.
1956—Elizabeth Bishop, Poems, North and South.
1957—Richard Wilbur, Things of This World.
1958—Robert Penn Warren, Promises: Poems 1954-1956.
1959—Stanley Kunitz, Selected Poems 1928-1958.
1960—W. D. Snodgrass, Heart's Needle.
1961—Phyllis McGinley, Times Three: Selected Verse from Three Decades.
1962—Alan Dugan, Poems.
1963—William Carlos Williams, Pictures From Breughel.
1964—Louis Simpson, At the End of the Open Road.
1965—John Berryman, 77 Dream Songs.
1966—Richard Eberhart, Selected Poems.
1967—Anne Sexton, Live or Die.
1968—Anthony Hecht, The Hard Hours.
1969—George Oppen, Of Being Numerous.
1970—Richard Howard, Untitled Subjects.
1971—William S. Merwin, The Carrier of Ladders.
1972—James Wright, Collected Poems.
1973—Maxine Winokur Kumin, Up Country.
1974—Robert Lowell, The Dolphin.
1975—Gary Snyder, Turtle Island.

General Non-Fiction

For best book by an American, not eligible in any other category.

1962—Theodore H. White, The Making of the President 1960.
1963—Barbara W. Tuchman, The Guns of August.
1964—Richard Hofstadter, Anti-Intellectualism in American Life.
1965—Howard Mumford Jones, O Strange New World.
1966—Edwin Way Teale, Wandering Through Winter.
1967—David Brion Davis, The Problem of Slavery in Western Culture.
1968—Will and Ariel Durant, Rousseau and Revolution.
1969—Norman Mailer, The Armies of the Night; and Rene Jules Dubos, So Human an Animal: How We Are Shaped by Surroundings and Events.
1970—Eric H. Erikson, Gandhi's Truth.
1971—John Toland, The Rising Sun.
1972—Barbara W. Tuchman, Stilwell and the American Experience in China, 1911-1945.

1973—Frances FitzGerald. Fire in the Lake: The Vietnamese and the Americans in Vietnam; and Robert Coles. Children of Crisis. Volumes II and III.
1974—Ernest Becker. The Denial of Death.
1975—Annie Dillard. Pilgrim at Tinker Creek.

Pulitzer Prize in Music

For composition in the larger forms of chamber, orchestral or choral music or for an operatic work including ballet, performed or published by a composer resident in the United States.

1943—William Schuman. Secular Cantata No. 2. A Free Song.
1944—Howard Hanson. Symphony No. 4, Op. 34.
1945—Aaron Copland. Appalachian Spring.
1946—Leo Sowerby. The Canticle of the Sun.
1947—Charles E. Ives. Symphony No. 3.
1948—Walter Piston, Symphony No. 3.
1949—Virgil Thomson, Louisiana Story.
1950—Gian-Carlo Menotti. The Consul.
1951—Douglas Moore, Giants in the Earth.
1952—Gail Kubik. Symphony Concertante.
1954—Quincy Porter. Concerto for Two Pianos and Orchestra.
1955—Gian-Carlo Menotti. The Saint of Bleecker Street.
1956—Ernest Toch. Symphony No. 3.
1957—Norman Dello Joio. Meditations on Ecclesiastes.
1958—Samuel Barber. Vanessa.
1959—John La-Montaine. Concerto for Piano and Orchestra.
1960—Elliott Carter. Second String Quartet.
1961—Walter Piston. Symphony No. 7.
1962—Robert Ward. The Crucible.
1963—Samuel Barber. Piano Concerto No. 1.
1966—Leslie Bassett, Variations for Orchestra.
1967—Leon Kirchner, Quartet No. 3.
1968—George Crumb, Echoes of Time and the River.
1969—Karel Husa. String Quartet No. 3.
1970—Charles W. Wuorinen, Time's Encomium.
1971—Mario Davidovsky. Synchronisms No. 6.
1972—Jacob Druckman. Windows.
1973—Elliott Carter. String Quartet No. 3.
1974—Donald Martino, Notturno. (Special citation) Roger Sessions.
1975—Dominick Argento. From the Diary of Virginia Woolf.

Special Awards
Awarded in 1975 unless otherwise designated
Books, Allied Arts

American Library Association Awards. for distinguished books for children. Newberry Medal: Virginia Hamilton for M. C. Higgins, the Great: Caldecott Medal: Gerald McDermott. Arrow to the Sun: A Pueblo Indian Tale.

Bancroft Prizes. by Columbia Univ. for books in American history. diplomacy. and international relations. $4,000 each: Stanley L. Engerman. Robert W. Fogel. Time on the Cross: Eugene D. Genovese. Roll. Jordan. Roll: The World The Slaves Made: Alexander L. George. Richard Smoke. Deterrence in American Foreign Policy: Theory and Practice.

Batchelder Award, by American Library Association. for translation of children's book: Crown Publishers for An Old Tale Carved Out of Stone by A. Linevsky. trans. Maria Polushkin.

B'nai B'rith Book Award, $500: Arnost Lustig for A Prayer for Katerina Horovitzova.

Bollingen Prize in Poetry by Yale University Library. $5,000: Archie Randolph Ammons. for Sphere: The Form of a Motion.

The Canadian Governor General's Literary Awards, to Canadian writers of outstanding literary merit. $2,500: Ralph Gustafson for Fire on Stone; Margaret Laurence for The Diviners; Charles Ritchie for The Siren Years; Victor-Levy Beaulieu for Don Quichotte de la demanche; Nicole Brossard for Mecanique jongleuse suivi de Masculin grammaticale (Hexagone) and Louise Dechene for Habitants et marchands de Montreal au XVII siecle (Plon).

Carey-Thomas Award for creative publishing project: Ladislao Reti for Madrid Codices of Leonardo da Vinci and The Unknown Leonardo.

Children's Book Award of the Child Study Association of America: Eleanor Clymer for Luke Was There.

Children's Science Book Awards, by New York Academy of Sciences: junior: Roger Duvoisin for See What I Am: senior: Ruth Kirk for Hunters of the Whale.

Edgar Awards, by Mystery Writers of America: best novel: Jon Cleary for Peter's Pence; Grand Master Award: Eric Ambler; first novel: Gregory McDonald, Fletch; fact crime book: Vincent Bugiosi, Curt Gentry, Helter Skelter; criticism and scholarship: Howard Haycraft, Frances M. Nevins, Jr.; short story: Ruth Rendell, "The Fallen Curtain"; juvenile: Jay Bennett, The Dangling Witness; paperbound novel: Roy Winsor. The Corpse that Walked.

Emerson-Thoreau Medal, by American Academy of Arts and Sciences: Robert Penn Warren.

English-Speaking Union of U.S., award for English belles lettres by non-native speaker of English from Africa or Asia. $2,000: R.K. Narayan for My Days.

R. T. French National Tastemaker Award. best overall: Richard Olney for Simple French Food.

Geographic Society of Chicago Publication Award: Walter Sullivan for Continents in Motion: The New Earth Debate.

International Reading Assoc. Children's Book Award, $1,000: T. Degens for Transport 7-41-R.

James Russell Lowell Prize, by the Modern Language Assn. of America. $1,000: Josephine Miles, for Poetry and Change.

Melcher Award, by the Unitarian Universalist Assn. for best book on religious liberalism. $1,000: Eugene Genovese. Roll. Jordan. Roll: The World The Slaves Made.

National Book Awards, for distinguished books by American authors. $1,000 for each award: Fiction (tie): Robert Stone. Dog Soldiers and Thomas Williams. The Hair of Harold Roux; Poetry: Marilyn Hacker. Presentation Piece; History: Bernard Bailyn. The Ordeal of Thomas Hutchinson; Children's Book: Virginia Hamilton. M. C. Higgins, the Great; Philosophy and Religion: Robert Nozick. Anarchy, State and Utopia; Sciences: Silvano Arieti. Interpretation of Schizophrenia; Contemporary Affairs: Theodore Rosengarten. All God's Dangers. The Life of Nate Shaw; Translation: Anthony Kerrigan. The Agony of Christianity by Miguel De Unamuno; Arts and Letters (tie): Roger Shattuck, Marcel Proust and Lewis Thomas. The Lives of a Cell; Biography: Richard B. Sewall. The Life of Emily Dickinson.

National Institute of Arts and Letters Awards, Literature. $3,000 each: William S. Burroughs. J. P. Donleavy. John Gardner. William H. Gass. Terrence McNally. Tillie Olsen. John Peck. Mark Strand. Colin M. Turnbull. Helen Hennessy Vendler; Award of Merit Medal. Poetry. $2,000: Galway Kinnell; E. M. Forster Award. $5,000: Seamus Heaney; Rosenthal Award. $2,500: Ishmael Reed; Zabel Award. $2,500: Charles Newman; Howells Medal: Thomas Pynchon for Gravity's Rainbow; Gold Medal for Belles Lettres: Kenneth Burke.

National Jewish Book Awards, by the Jewish Book Council. $500 each. Fiction: Jean Karsavina. *White Eagle, Dark-Skies;* History: Solomon Zeitlin; Juvenile: Bea Stadtler. *The Holocaust; A History of Courage and Resistance;* Poetry: Reuven Ben-Yosef. *Metim ve-Ohavim;* Holocaust: Isaiah Trunk, *Judenrat: The Jewish Councils in Eastern Europe Under Nazi Occupation;* Israel: Arnold Krammer. *The Forgotten Friendship: Israel and the Soviet Bloc, 1947-53;* Jewish Thought: Eliezer Berkovits, *Major Themes in Modern Philosophies of Judaism.*

Pacific Northwest Booksellers Awards; non-fiction: Justice William O. Douglas for *Go East, Young Man;* fiction: Ursula K. LeGuin for *The Dispossessed;* poetry: James Masao Mitsui for *Journal of the Sun;* children's: Barbara Corcoran for *A Dance to Still Music.*

Francis Parkman Prize by the Society of American Historians: Robert A. Caro for *The Power Broker: Robert Moses and the Fall of New York.*

P.E.N. American Center Awards; Translation Prize. $1,000 (sponsored by Book-of-the-Month Club): Helen R. Lane for *Count-Julian* by Juan Goytisolo: Goethe House Prize. $500: Peter Sander for *Ice Age* by Tankred Dorst; Lucille J. Medwick Memorial Award. $500: Grace Schulman. poet and translator.

Poetry Society of America Awards, Alice Fay di Castagnola Award, $2,000: Philip Appleman; Shelley Memorial Award, $1,500: Edward Field; Melville Cane Award, $500: Richard B. Sewall for *The Life of Emily Dickinson;* other awards, $500: Philip Appleman, Gail Trebbe; Florence B. Jacobs, Violette New-

ton; $300: Sarah Singer. Hulda Weber. Ruth Lisa Schechter; $250: Florence Trefethen and Ruth Whitman.

Academy of American Poets Awards: Copernicus Award, $10,000: Kenneth Rexroth; Academy Fellowship, $10,000: Leonie Adams; Poe Award. poet under 45. $5,000: Charles Simic: Lamont Selection. publication of first book: John Balaban. *After Our War:* Whitman Award, $1,000 and publication of first book: Reg Saner. *Climbing into the Roots.*

Political Book Awards, by the Washington Monthly: Robert A. Caro-for *The Power Broker: Robert Moses and the Fall of New York;* David R. Mayhew for *Congress: The Electoral Connection.*

Skinner Award by Women's National Book Association: Margaret K. McElderry. editor and publisher.

Watumull Prize, by the American Historical Association for book on history of India: Leonard A. Gordon, for *Bengal: The Nationalist Movement, 1876-1940.*

Western Heritage Award, by National Cowboy Hall of Fame; novel: James Michener for *Centennial;* nonfiction: Benjamin Capps for *The Warren Wagontrain Raid;* regional history: Margaret Sanborn for *The American;* local history: Harold Davidson for *Edward Borein, Cowboy Artist.*

Laura Ingalls Wilder Award, by American Library Association for lasting contribution to children's literature: Beverly Cleary.

Journalism Awards

Heywood Broun Award, by the Newspaper Guild, $1,000: Selwyn Raab, N.Y. Times.

Sevellon Brown Memorial Award, by New England Associated Press News Executives Association, for public service: The Boston Globe, integration coverage.

National Cartoonists Society, Reuben Award: Dick Moores, Gasoline Alley; other awards: Advertising and Illustration: Bill Kresse, N.Y. News; Editorial Cartoons: Pat Oliphant, Washington Star; Special Features: Burne Hogarth, Jungle Tales of Tarzan; Sports Cartoons: Murray Olderman, Newspaper Enterprise Association; Syndicated Panels. Bill Keane. Family Circus; Animation: Jim Logan, Fritz the Cat; Silver T-Square: Jack Rosen.

Roy W. Howard Public Service Award, by the Scripps-Howard Foundation: Seven Milwaukee Journal newswomen and men ($2,500); WABC-TV, New York ($2,500); Dolores Katz. Detroit Free Press ($1,000); Bette Orsini. St. Petersburg Times ($500); KNXT-TV. Los Angeles ($500); WNEW. New York ($500).

A.J. Liebling Award for reportorial excellence: Studs Terkel.

Edward J. Meeman Awards, by the Scripps-Howard Foundation for work in the field of conservation: David Johnston, Detroit Free Press ($2,500); Gene Cunningham, Stuart Wilk. Milwaukee Sentinel ($1,750); Don Wright, Miami News ($1,500); Gordon Bishop, Newark Star-Ledger ($1,000); Jim Detjen, Poughkeepsie (N.Y.) Journal ($1,000); William Braun, St. Petersburg Times ($750); David A. Milne, UPI ($750); Nash Herndon, Winston-Salem Sentinel ($750).

Missouri Awards for Distinguished Service, by the Univ. of Missouri: Sylvia Porter, Edwin Newman, Robert Hyland, St. Louis Post-Dispatch, Marsteller Inc., Sports Illustrated, Newspaper Enterprise Association.

National Magazine Awards, by Columbia Univ. Graduate School of Journalism: The New Yorker, reporting excellence; Consumer Reports, public service; Country Journal and National Lampoon, visual excellence; Redbook, fiction; Esquire; Medical Economics.

Overseas Press Club of America Awards, for distinguished service in foreign journalism: Robert G. Kaiser. Washington Post; W. Eugene Smith, freelance; Lou Cioffi, ABC radio news; John Palmer. Tom Streithorst, Phil Brady, and Liz Trotta. NBC news; Ovie Carter, Chicago Tribune; Phillip W. Whitcomb. Christian Science Monitor; Frances FitzGerald. Harper's; Robert Shaplen, New Yorker; Donald L. Bartlett, James B. Steele. Philadelphia Inquirer; Eddie Adams, Time Magazine; John Chancellor. NBC radio news; ABC radio news. Team Effort.

George Polk Memorial Awards, by Long Island Univ. for achievement in journalism: Foreign Reporting, Donald Kirk, Chicago Tribune; National Reporting, Seymour M. Hersh. N.Y. Times; Metropolitan Reporting, Richard Severo, N.Y. Times; Community Service, William E. Anderson, Harley R. Bierce, Richard E. Cady, Indianapolis Star; Magazine Reporting. Edward M. Brecher, Robert H. Harris, Consumer Reports; Television Documentary, NBC News; News Photography, Werner Baum, German Press Agency; Book, Mary Adelaide Mendelson, *Tender Loving Greed.*

Ernie Pyle Memorial Award, by the Scripps-Howard Foundation to the newspaperman most nearly exemplifying the style and craftsmanship of Ernie Pyle, $1,000: William D. Montalbano. Miami Herald; Special award, $500: Dick Feagler. Cleveland Press.

Science-in-Society Awards ($1,000 each): by the National Association of Science Writers: John Failka, Washington Star; Peter Stoler, Time.

Sigma Delta Chi Awards, for distinguished service in journalism. Newspapers: General reporting, Frank Sutherland, Nashville Tennessean; Editorial writing, Michael Pakenham, Philadelphia Inquirer; Washington correspondence, Seth Kantor, Detroit News; Foreign correspondence, Donald L. Bartlett, James B. Steele, Philadelphia Inquirer; News photography, Werner Baum, German Press Agency; Editorial cartoons. Mike Peters, Dayton Daily News; Public service, Indianapolis Star; Distinguished teaching in journalism, John Hohenberg, Columbia University.

Silurian Awards, by the Silurians, a society of present and former N.Y. newspapermen: Spot News, staff of Daily Item, Port Chester, N.Y.; Feature News,

John Pascal, Newsday; News Analysis, Barbara Yuncker, Post; Public Service, John L. Hess, Times; Spot Photo, Charles Frattini, News; Feature Photo, Ron Frehm, AP; Editorial, James Ahearn, N.J. Sunday Record; Story by reporter in profession less than five years, Leslie Maitland, Times.

Walker Stone Award, by the Scripps-Howard Foundation for editorial writing, $1000: John R. Harrison, Lakeland (Fla.) Ledger; Second prize: $500, Oliver Starr, St. Louis Globe-Democrat.

Broadcasting and Theater Awards

Emmy Awards, by the Academy of Television Arts and Sciences. Actors: special, Laurence Olivier, Love Among the Ruins; drama series, Robert Blake, Baretta; comedy series, Tony Randall, The Odd Couple; limited series, Peter Falk, Columbo. Actresses: special, Katharine Hepburn, Love Among the Ruins; drama series, Jean Marsh, Upstairs, Downstairs; comedy series, Valerie Harper, Rhoda; limited series, Jessica Walter, Amy Prentiss. Best special: The Law, NBC; limited series: Benjamin Franklin, CBS; comedy, variety, or music special: An Evening with John Denver, ABC; comedy series: Mary Tyler Moore Show CBS; drama series: Upstairs, Downstairs, PBS; variety series: The Carol Burnett Show.

James K. Hackett Medal for achievement in the theater: Ira Gershwin, lyricist.

Margo Jones Award, for significant contribution to the theater: Hartford Stage Company, and its producing director, Paul Weidner.

New York Drama Critics Circle Awards, 1974-75 season: best play: Equus; best American play, The Taking of Miss Janie; best musical: A Chorus Line.

George Foster Peabody Broadcasting Awards, Radio: KTW, Seattle, The Hit and Run Players; CBS, The CBS Radio Mystery Theater; NBC, Second Sunday; KFAC, Los Angeles. Through the Looking Glass; WSB, Atlanta, dealing with community problems;

WMAL, Washington, D. C., Battles Just Begun; WNBC, Pledge a Job. Television: WCKT, Miami, investigative reports; NBC, dramatic programs; CBS, Benjamin Franklin series; PBS, Theater in America; WGBH, Boston, Nova; ABC, Free to Be . . . You and Me; NBC, Go; KING, Seattle, How Come?; WCCO, Minneapolis, From Belfast With Love; ABC, Sadat: Action Biography; NBC, Tornado! 4:40 P.M., Xenia, Oh.; National Public Affairs Center for Television, outstanding overall effort; KPRC, Houston, The Right Man.

Antoinette Perry Awards (Tonys), by the League of New York Theaters, 1974-75 season. Musical: actress Angela Lansbury, Gypsy; actor, John Cullum, Shenandoah; supporting actress, Dee Dee Bridgewater, The Wiz; supporting actor, Ted Ross, The Wiz; best musical, The Wiz; director, Geoffrey Holder, The Wiz; book, James Lee Barrett, Shenandoah; costume design, Geoffrey Holder, The Wiz; choreography George Faison, The Wiz; score, Charlie Smalls, The Wiz. Drama: actress, Ellen Burstyn, Same Time Next Year; actor, John Kani and Winston Ntshona, Sizwe Banzi Is Dead; supporting actress Rita Moreno, The Ritz; supporting actor, Frank Langella, Seascape; best play, Equus; director, John Dexter, Equus; scenic design, Carl Toms, Sherlock Holmes. Special award: over-all contribution to the theater, Neil Simon.

Miscellaneous Awards

Florence E. Allen Award, by N.Y. Women's Bar Association: Rep. Martha W. Griffiths.

Ralph Bunche Institute Awards: Gunnar and Alva Myrdal, sociologists.

Avery Fisher Prizes ($5,000 each plus N.Y. Philharmonic solo engagement): Lynn Harrell, Murray Perahia.

Society of Four Arts Sculpture Contest, First Prize ($25,000): Robert Morris; Second Prize ($10,000): Isamu Noguchi; Third Prize ($5,000): Richard Stankiewicz.

Freedoms Foundation Awards, given annually by the Freedoms Foundation at Valley Forge for contribution toward a better understanding and greater appreciation of the American way of life. Special National Freedom Awards: Hugh O'Brian, O'Brian Foundation; Dr. Kenneth McFarland, Topeka, Kan.; Frank E. Harris, Denver, Col.; Dr. George S. Benson, Searcy, Ark., Martin DeVries, Long Beach, Cal.

Sidney Hillman Awards for achievement in mass communication: Seymour M. Hersh, N.Y. Times; CBS, The Autobiography of Miss Jane Pittman; Noel Mostert, Supership; Boston Globe, integration coverage; Richard Barnet and Ronald Muller, Global Reach; WNET-TV, N.Y., outstanding programming.

Humanist of the Year, by American Humanist Association: Dr. Henry Morgenthaler, abortionist, and Betty Friedan, writer.

Human Rights Award, by International League for the Rights of Man: Mstislav Rostropovich, Galina Vishnevskaya.

Albert Lasker Medical Research Awards (awarded Nov. 1974). Clinical ($10,000): John Charnley; Basic ($5,000 each): Ludwik Gross, Howard Earle Skipper, Sol Spiegelman, Howard M. Temin.

John Muir Award by Sierra Club: Justice William O. Douglas.

National Institute of Arts and Letters, Award for Distinguished Service to the Arts: George Balanchine; **Gold Medal** for Painting: Willem de Kooning; **Arnold W. Brunner Prize** in Architecture, $1,000: Lewis Davis and Samuel Brody; Art Awards, $3,000 each: Barbara Falk, Claus Hoie, Leonid and Seymour Pearlstein, Calvin Albert, Harry Bertoia, William Talbot; Music Awards, $3,000 each: Marc-Antonio Consoli, Charles Dodge, Daniel Perlongo, Christian Wolff; **Richard and Hinda Rosenthal Award** in Painting, $2,500: Richard Merkin; **Marjorie Peabody Waite Award** in Composing, $1,500: Leo Ornstein; **Charles E. Ives Scholarships,** $5,000 each: Chester Biscardi, Stephen Chatman, David Koblitz.

Rita V. Tishman Human Relation Award by Anti-Defamation League: Betty Ford.

Westinghouse Science Talent Search: Paul Andrew Zeitz, Brooklyn, N.Y. $10,000; Alan Stuart Geller, Ridgewood, N.J. and Daniel Robert Marshak, La Jolla, Cal., $8,000 each; Byron Bong Siu, Bronx, N.Y., Richard James Foch, Titusville, Fla., and Robert Mark Claudson, Richland, Wash., $6,000 each; Charlene Gail Sanders, Narberth, Pa., Lorraine Alice Pillus, Cocoa, Fla., Craig Franklin Miller, Whitestone, N.Y. and H. Britton Sanderford, Metairie, La., $4,000 each.

Society of Women Geographers Gold Medal: Dr. Eugenie Clark, Marion I. Sterling, Dr. Mary Douglas Leakey.

Women of the Year, by Ladies Home Journal: communications: Helen Thomas; creative arts: Lillian Hellman; education: Joan Ganz Cooney; humanitarian and community service: Larue Diaforli; government and diplomacy: Maj. Gen. Jeanne Holm; quality of life: Lady Bird Johnson; political life: Barbara Jordan; business and economics: Sylvia Porter.

Motion Picture Academy Awards
(Oscars)

1927-28
Actor: Emil Jannings, The Way of All Flesh.
Actress: Janet Gaynor, Seventh Heaven.
Picture: Wings, Paramount.

1928-29
Actor: Warner Baxter, In Old Arizona.
Actress: Mary Pickford, Coquette.
Picture: Broadway Melody, MGM.

1929-30
Actor: George Arliss, Disraeli.
Actress: Norma Shearer, The Divorcee.
Picture: All Quiet on the Western Front, Univ.

1930-31
Actor: Lionel Barrymore, Free Soul.
Actress: Marie Dressler, Min and Bill.
Picture: Cimarron, RKO.

1931-32
Actor: Fredric March, Dr. Jekyll and Mr. Hyde.
Actress: Helen Hayes, Sin of Madelon Claudet.
Picture: Grand Hotel, MGM.
Special: Walt Disney, Mickey Mouse.

1932-33
Actor: Charles Laughton, Private Life of Henry VIII.
Actress: Katharine Hepburn, Morning Glory.
Picture: Cavalcade, Fox.

1934
Actor: Clark Gable, It Happened One Night.
Actress: Claudette Colbert, same.
Picture: It Happened One Night, Columbia.

1935
Actor: Victor McLaglen, The Informer
Actress: Bette Davis, Dangerous.
Picture: Mutiny on the Bounty, MGM.

1936
Actor: Paul Muni, Story of Louis Pasteur.
Actress: Luise Rainer, The Great Ziegfeld.
Picture: The Great Ziegfeld, MGM.

1937
Actor: Spencer Tracy, Captains Courageous.
Actress: Luise Rainer, The Good Earth.
Picture: Life of Emile Zola, Warner.

1938
Actor: Spencer Tracy, Boys Town.
Actress: Bette Davis, Jezebel.
Picture: You Can't Take It With You, Columbia.

1939
Actor: Robert Donat, Goodbye Mr. Chips.
Actress: Vivien Leigh, Gone With the Wind.
Picture: Gone With the Wind, Selznick International.

1940
Actor: James Stewart, The Philadelphia Story.
Actress: Ginger Rogers, Kitty Foyle.
Picture: Rebecca, Selznick International.

1941
Actor: Gary Cooper, Sergeant York.
Actress: Joan Fontaine, Suspicion.
Picture: How Green Was My Valley, 20th Cent.-Fox.

1942
Actor: James Cagney, Yankee Doodle Dandy.
Actress: Greer Garson, Mrs. Miniver.
Picture: Mrs. Miniver, MGM.

1943
Actor: Paul Lukas, Watch on the Rhine.
Actress: Jennifer Jones, The Song of Bernadette.
Picture: Casablanca, Warner.

1944
Actor: Bing Crosby, Going My Way.
Actress: Ingrid Bergman, Gaslight.
Picture: Going My Way, Paramount.

1945
Actor: Ray Milland, The Lost Weekend.
Actress: Joan Crawford, Mildred Pierce.
Picture: The Lost Weekend, Paramount.

1946
Actor: Fredric March, Best Years of Our Lives.
Actress: Olivia de Havilland, To Each His Own.
Picture: The Best Years of Our Lives, Goldwyn, RKO.

1947
Actor: Ronald Colman, A Double Life.
Actress: Loretta Young, The Farmer's Daughter.
Picture: Gentleman's Agreement, 20th Cent.-Fox.

1948
Actor: Laurence Olivier, Hamlet.
Actress: Jane Wyman, Johnny Belinda.
Picture: Hamlet, Two Cities Film, Universal International.

1949
Actor: Broderick Crawford, All the Kings Men.
Actress: Olivia de Havilland, The Heiress.
Picture: All the King's Men, Columbia.

1950
Actor: Jose Ferrer, Cyrano de Bergerac.
Actress: Judy Holliday, Born Yesterday.
Picture: All About Eve, 20th Century-Fox.

1951
Actor: Humphrey Bogart, The African Queen.
Actress: Vivien Leigh, A Streetcar Named Desire.
Picture: An American in Paris, MGM.

1952
Actor: Gary Cooper, High Noon.
Actress: Shirley Booth, Come Back, Little Sheba.
Picture: Greatest Show on Earth, Cecil B. DeMille, Paramount.

1953
Actor: William Holden, Stalag 17.
Actress: Audrey Hepburn, Roman Holiday.
Picture: From Here to Eternity, Columbia.

1954
Actor: Marlon Brando, On the Waterfront.
Actress: Grace Kelly, The Country Girl.
Picture: On The Waterfront, Horizon-American Corp., Columbia.

1955
Actor: Ernest Borgnine, Marty.
Actress: Anna Magnani, The Rose Tattoo.
Picture: Marty, Hecht and Lancaster's Steven Productions, U.A.

1956
Actor: Yul Brynner, The King and I.
Actress: Ingrid Bergman, Anastasia.
Picture: Around the World in 80 Days, Michael Todd Co., U.A.

1957
Actor: Alec Guinness, The Bridge on the River Kwai.
Actress: Joanne Woodward, The Three Faces of Eve.
Picture: The Bridge on the River Kwai, Columbia.

1958
Actor: David Niven, Separate Tables.
Actress: Susan Hayward, I Want to Live.
Picture: Gigi, Arthur Freed Production, MGM.

1959
Actor: Charlton Heston, Ben-Hur.
Actress: Simone Signoret, Room at the Top.
Picture: Ben-Hur, MGM.

1960
Actor: Burt Lancaster, Elmer Gantry.
Actress: Elizabeth Taylor, Butterfield 8.
Picture: The Apartment, Mirisch Co., U.A.

1961
Actor: Maximilian Schell, Judgment at Nuremberg.
Actress: Sophia Loren, Two Women.
Picture: West Side Story, United Artists.

1962
Actor: Gregory Peck, To Kill a Mockingbird.
Actress: Anne Bancroft, The Miracle Worker.
Picture: Lawrence of Arabia, Columbia.

1963
Actor: Sidney Poitier, Lilies of the Field.
Actress: Patricia Neal, Hud.
Picture: Tom Jones, Woodfall Prod., UA-Lopert Pictures.

1964
Actor: Rex Harrison, My Fair Lady.
Actress: Julie Andrews, Mary Poppins.
Picture: My Fair Lady, Warner Bros.

1965
Actor: Lee Marvin, Cat Ballou.
Actress: Julie Christie, Darling.
Picture: The Sound of Music, 20th Century-Fox.

1966
Actor: Paul Scofield, A Man for All Seasons.
Actress: Elizabeth Taylor, Who's Afraid of Virginia Woolf?
Picture: A Man for All Seasons, Columbia.

1967
Actor: Rod Steiger, In the Heat of the Night.
Actress: Katharine Hepburn, Guess Who's Coming to Dinner.
Picture: In the Heat of the Night.

1968
Actor: Cliff Robertson, Charly.
Actress: Katharine Hepburn, The Lion in Winter, Barbra Streisand, Funny Girl (tie).
Picture: Oliver.

1969
Actor: John Wayne, True Grit.
Actress: Maggie Smith, The Prime of Miss Jean Brodie.
Picture: Midnight Cowboy.

1970
Actor: George C. Scott, Patton (refused).
Actress: Glenda Jackson, Women in Love.
Picture: Patton.

1971
Actor: Gene Hackman, The French Connection.
Actress: Jane Fonda, Klute.
Picture: The French Connection.

1972
Actor: Marlon Brando, The Godfather (refused).
Actress: Liza Minnelli, Cabaret.
Picture: The Godfather.

1973
Actor: Jack Lemmon, Save the Tiger.
Actress: Glenda Jackson, A Touch of Class.
Picture: The Sting.

1974
Actor: Art Carney, Harry and Tonto.
Actress: Ellen Burstyn, Alice Doesn't Live Here Anymore.
Picture: The Godfather, Part II.
Supporting Actor: Robert De Niro, The Godfather, Part II.
Supporting Actress: Ingrid Bergman, Murder on the Orient Express.

Director: Francis Ford Coppola, The Godfather, Part II.
Foreign Language Film: Amarcord.
Documentary (feature): Peter Davis, Bert Schneider, Hearts and Minds; (short): Robin Lehman, Don't.
Short Subject (animated): Will Vinton, Bob Gardiner, Closed Mondays; (live): Paul Clauden, Edmond Sechan, One-Eyed Men are Kings.
Sound: Ronald Pierce, Melvin Metcalfe Sr., Earthquake.
Editing: Harold F. Kress, Carl Kress, The Towering Inferno.
Costume Design: Theoni V. Aldredge, The Great Gatsby.
Cinematography: Fred Koenekamp, Joseph Biroc, The Towering Inferno.
Art Direction: Dean Tavoularis, Angelo Graham, The Godfather, Part II.
Set Decoration: George R. Nelson, The Godfather, Part II.
Screenplay (original): Robert Towne, Chinatown; (adapted): Mario Puzo, Frances Ford Coppola, The Godfather, Part II.
Original Score: Nino Rota, Carmine Coppola, The Godfather, Part II.
Scoring: Nelson Riddle, The Great Gatsby.
Song: Al Kasha, Joel Hirshhorn, We May Never Love Like This Again.
Jean Hersholt Humanitarian Award: Arthur B. Krim.
Visual Effects: Earthquake.
Special Awards: Jean Renoir, Howard Hawks.

Canadian Film Awards

Source: Canadian Film Institute

1968
Actor: Gerard Parkes, Isabel
Actress: Genevieve Bujold, Isabel
Picture: A Place to Stand

1969
Actor: Chris Wiggins, The Best Damn Fiddler from Calabogie to Kaladar
Actress: Jackie Burroughs, Dulcima
Picture: The Best Damn Fiddler from Calabogie to Kaladar

1970
Actor: Doug McGrath and Paul Bradley (tied), Goin' Down the Road
Actress: Genevieve Bujold, Act of the Heart
Picture: Psychocratie

1971
Actor: Jean Duceppe, Mon oncle Antoine
Actress: Ann Knox, The Only Thing You Know
Picture: Mon oncle Antoine

1972
Actor: Gordon Pinsent, The Rowdyman
Actress: Micheline Lanctot, Vrai nature de Bernadette
Picture: Wedding in White

1973
Actor: Jacques Godin, O.K. Laliberte
Actress: Genevieve Bujold, Kamouraska
Picture: Slipstream

1974
No Awards Made

National Teacher of the Year Award

Awarded by the Ladies' Home Journal magazine for distinguished service in elementary and secondary schools.

1952—Geraldine Jomes, first grade, Hope Public School, Santa Barbara, Calif.
1953—Dorothy Hamilton, social studies, Milford H.S., Milford, Conn.
1954—Willard Widerberg, seventh grade, DeKalb Junior H.S., DeKalb, Ill.
1955—Margaret Perry Teufel, fourth grade, Monmouth Elementary, Monmouth, Ore.
1956—Richard Nelson, science, Flathead County H.S., Kalispell, Montana.
1957—(tie) Eugene Guy Bizzell, speech, English & debate; A.N. McCallum H.S., Austin, Texas; and Mary Field Scharz, third grade, Bristol Elementary, Kansas City, Mo.
1958—Jean Listebarger Humphrey, second grade, Edwards Elementary, Ames, Iowa.
1959—Edna Donley, mathematics and speech, Alva H.S., Alva, Okla.
1960—Hazel Bragg Davenport, first grade, Central Elementary, Beckley, W. Va.
1961—Helen Adams, kindergarten, Cumberland Public School, Cumberland, Wisc.
1962—Marjorie French, mathematics, Topeka H.S., Topeka, Kansas.
1963—Elmon Ousley, speech, American government & world problems, Bellevue Senior H.S., Bellevue, Wash.
1964—Lawana Trout, English, Charles Page H.S., Sand Springs, Okla.
1965—Richard E. Klinck, sixth grade, Reed Street Elementary, Wheat Ridge, Colo.
1966—Mona Dayton, first grade, Walter Douglas Elementary, Tucson, Ariz.
1967—Roger Tenney, music, Owatonna Junior-Senior H.S., Owatonna, Minn.
1968—David E. Graf, vocational education & industrial arts, Sandwich Comm. H.S., Sandwich, Ill.
1969—Barbara Goleman, language arts, Miami Jackson H.S., Miami, Fla.
1970—Johnnie T. Dennis, physics, math analysis, Walla Walla H.S., Walla Walla, Wash.
1971—Martha Marion Stringfellow, first grade, Lewisville Elementary, Chester Co., S.C.
1972—James Marshall Rogers, American history & Black studies, Durham H.S., Raleigh, N.C.
1973—John A. Ensworth, sixth grade, Kenwood school, Bend, Ore.
1974—Vivian Tom, social studies, Lincoln High, Yonkers, N.Y.
1975—Robert G. Heyer, science, Johanna Junior H.S., St. Paul, Minn.

The Spingarn Medal

The Spingarn Medal has been awarded annually since 1914 by the National Association for the Advancement of Colored People for the highest achievement by an American Negro.

1945—Thurgood Marshall
1946—Dr. Percy L. Julian
1947—Channing H. Tobias
1948—Ralph J. Bunche
1949—Charles Hamilton Houston
1950—Mabel Keaton Staupers
1951—Harry T. Moore
1952—Paul R. Williams
1953—Theodore K. Lawless
1954—Carl Murphy

1955—Jack Roosevelt Robinson
1956—Martin Luther King, Jr.
1957—Mrs. Daisy Bates and the Little Rock Nine
1958—Edward Kennedy (Duke) Ellington
1959—Langston Hughes
1960—Kenneth B. Clark
1961—Robert C. Weaver
1962—Medgar Wiley Evers
1963—Roy Wilkins

1964—Leontyne Price
1965—John H. Johnson
1966—Edward W. Brooke
1967—Sammy Davis, Jr.
1968—Clarence M. Mitchell, Jr.
1969—Jacob Lawrence
1970—Leon Howard Sullivan
1971—Gordon Parks
1972—Wilson C. Riles
1973—Damon Keith
1974—Henry (Hank) Aaron

Notable New York Openings, 1974-75 Season

A Doll's House, new version of the Ibsen classic; with Liv Ullmann and Sam Waterson.

Absurd Person Singular, comedy by Alan Ayckbourn about 3 couples on 3 different Christmas eves; with Richard Kiley, Larry Blydon, Sandy Dennis, Geraldine Page, Tony Roberts, and Carole Shelley.

All Over Town, comedy written by Murray Schisgal and directed by Dustin Hoffman; with Cleavon Little.

Cat on a Hot Tin Roof, revival of the Tennessee Williams drama of a wealthy southern family; with Elizabeth Ashley and Keir Dullea.

Chicago, musical directed by Bob Fosse; with Gwen Verdon, Chita Rivera, and Jerry Orbach.

A Chorus Line, Michael Bennett production of a Marvin Hamlisch musical; with Robert LuPone, Sammy Williams, Carole Bishop, Donna McKechnie, Pricilla Lopez.

Clams On the Half Shell Revue, musical starring Bette Midler.

Dance With Me, musical comedy by Greg Antonacci; with Mr. Antonacci and Annie Abbott.

Death of a Salesman, revival of the Arthur Miller play; with George C. Scott, Teresa Wright, James Farentino, and Harvey Keitel.

Equus, psychological inquiry into a crime; written by Peter Shaffer; with Anthony Hopkins and Peter Firch.

God's Favorite, comedy by Neil Simon based on the story of Job; with Vincent Gardenia, Maria Karnilova, and Charles Nelson Reilly.

Good News, revival of De Sylva and Henderson musical; with Alice Faye and Gene Nelson.

Goodtime Charley, musical about Joan of Arc and the Dauphin; with Joel Grey and Ann Reinking.

Gypsy, revival of Jule Styne and Stephen Sondheim musical about the life of Gypsy Rose Lee; with Angela Lansbury.

In Praise of Love, Terence Rattigan drama about a husband and wife; with Rex Harrison and Julie Harris.

Mack and Mabel, Jerry Herman musical about the silent film era; with Robert Preston and Bernadette Peters.

Of Mice and Men, revival of the John Steinbeck classic; with James Earl Jones and Kevin Conway.

Same Time, Next Year, comedy about a happily married man's yearly rendevous with a married woman; with Ellen Burstyn and Charles Grodin.

Saturday Sunday Monday, comedy about an Italian family; with Walter Abel and Sada Thompson.

Seascape, drama by Edward Albee about a man and wife discussing life with a pair of man-sized lizards; with Deborah Kerr, Barry Nelson, Frank Langella, and Maureen Anderman.

Shenandoah, civil war musical; with John Cullum and Penelope Milford.

Sherlock Holmes, comedy-drama about the famous sleuth; with John Wood and Nicholas Selby.

Sizwe Banzi is Dead, drama about the treatment of blacks in South Africa; written by Athol Furard, John Kani and Winston Ntshona.

The Island, drama about prison life in South Africa; written by Athol Fugard, John Kani and Winston Ntshona.

The Night That Made America Famous, musical by Harry Chapin; with Mr. Chapin, Kelly Garrett, and Delores Hall.

Rubbers, and Yanks 3 Detroit O Top of the Seventh, a pair of comedies by Jonathan Reynolds; with Tony Lo Bianco.

The Ritz, Terrence McNally comedy that takes place in a steam bath; with Rita Moreno, Jerry Stiller, and Jack Weston.

The Rules of the Game, drama by Pirandello; with John McMartin and Joan Van Ark.

The Wiz, musical by Charlie Smalls based on "The Wonderful Wizard of Oz"; with Stephanie Mills.

Who's Who in Hell, comedy by Peter Ustinov; with Beau Bridges and George S. Irving.

Record Long Run Broadway Plays *Still Running July 1, 1975

Fiddler on the Roof	3,242	
Life With Father	3,213	
Tobacco Road	3,182	
Hello Dolly	2,844	
My Fair Lady	2,717	
Man of La Mancha	2,328	
Abie's Irish Rose	2,327	
Oklahoma!	2,246	
South Pacific	1,925	
Harvey	1,775	
Hair	1,750	
Born Yesterday	1,643	
Mary, Mary	1,572	
Voice of the Turtle	1,558	
Barefoot in the Park	1,532	
Mame	1,508	
Arsenic and Old Lace	1,444	
The Sound of Music	1,442	
How to Succeed in Business Without Really Trying	1,416	
*Grease	1,407	
Hellzapoppin	1,404	
The Music Man	1,376	
Funny Girl	1,348	
Oh! Calcutta!	1,314	
Angel Street	1,295	
Lightnin'	1,291	
Promises, Promises	1,281	
The King and I	1,246	
Cactus Flower	1,234	
Sleuth	1,222	
"1776"	1,217	
Guys and Dolls	1,200	
Cabaret	1,166	
Mister Roberts	1,157	
Annie Get Your Gun	1,147	
Butterflies Are Free	1,128	
*Pippin	1,121	
Pins and Needles	1,108	
Plaza Suite	1,098	

Plays in London
Running Aug. 19, 1975. Date listed is opening.

Absent Friends, 7/23/75.
Absurd Person, 7/4/73.
Alphabetical Order, 4/8/75.
Billy, 5/1/74.
Black Mikado, 4/24/75.
Case in Question, 3/10/75.
Clarence Darrow, 7/16/75.
Entertaining Sloane, 4/17/75.
Family and Fortune, 4/10/75.
Godspell, 6/10/75.
Hair, 6/7/75.

Hans Anderson, 12/17/74.
Harvey, 4/9/75.
Hinge Bracket, 7/31/75.
Jesus Christ Superstar, 8/9/72.
Kwa Zulu, 7/24/75.
Let My People Come, 8/29/74.
Let's Get Laid, 9/2/74.
Little Night Music, 4/15/75.
Mousetrap, 11/25/52.
Murder Vicarage, 7/23/75.
No Man's Land, 7/15/75.

No Sex Please, 7/3/72.
Norman Conquests, 8/1/74.
Oh, Calcutta, 9/30/70.
Otherwise Engaged, 7/30/75.
Rosencrantz and Guildenstern Are Dead 8/4/75.
Sleuth, 2/12/70.
Tarantara, 7/22/75.
Touch of Spring, 5/13/75.
Travesties, 8/13/75.

Symphony Orchestras of the United States and Canada

(As of Aug. 10, 1975)
Source: American Symphony Orchestra League, Inc.
Classifications are based on annual budgets of orchestras.

Major Symphony Orchestras

		Conductors
Atlanta Symphony	1280 Peachtree St., N.E., Atlanta, GA. 30309	Robert Shaw
Baltimore Symphony	120 West Mount Royal Ave., Baltimore, MD. 21201	Sergiu Comissiona
Boston Symphony	Symphony Hall, Boston, MA. 02115	Seiji Ozawa
Buffalo Philharmonic	26 Richmond Ave., Buffalow, N.Y. 14222	Michael Thomas
Chicago Symphony	220 S. Michigan Ave., Chicago, IL. 60604	Sir Georg Solti
Cincinnati Symphony	1241 Elm St., Cincinnati, OH. 45210	Thomas Schippers
Cleveland Orchestra	11001 Euclid Ave., Cleveland, OH. 44106	Lorin Maazel
Dallas Symphony	P.O. Box 26207, Dallas, TX 75226	Louis Lane
Denver Symphony	1615 California St., Denver, CO. 80202	Brian Priestman
Detroit Symphony	20 Auditorium Dr., Detroit, MI. 48226	Aldo Ceccato
Honolulu Symphony	1000 Bishop St., Honolulu, HA 96813	Robert LaMarchina
Houston Symphony	615 Louisiana, Houston, TX. 77002	Lawrence Foster
Indianapolis Symphony	4600 Sunset Ave., Indianapolis, IN. 46208	Izler Solomon
Kansas City Philharmonic	210 W. 10th St., Kansas City, MO 64105	Maurice Press
Los Angeles Philharmonic	135 North Grand, Los Angeles, CA. 90012	Zubin Mehta
Milwaukee Symphony	929 N. Water St., Milwaukee, WI 53202	Kenneth Schermerhorn
Minnesota Orchestra	1111 Nicollet Mall, Minneapolis, MN 55403	S. Skrowaczewski
Montreal Symphony	Place des Arts, Montreal, Que., Can., H2X 1Y1	Franz-Paul Decker
National Symphony	JFK Center for the Performing Arts, Wash., DC 20566	Antal Dorati
New Jersey Symphony	150 Halsey St., Newark, NJ 07102	Henry Lewis
New Orleans Philharmonic	203 Carondelet St. New Orleans, LA 70130	W. Torkanowsky
New York Philharmonic	Broadway at 65th St., New York, NY 10023	Pierre Boulez
Philadelphia Orchestra	230 S. 15th St., Philadelphia, PA 19102	Eugene Ormandy
Pittsburgh Symphony	600 Penn Ave., Pittsburgh, PA 15222	William Steinberg
Rochester Philharmonic	60 Gibbs St., Rochester, NY 14604	David Zinman
St. Louis Symphony	718 N. Grand Blvd., St. Louis, MO 63103	George Semkow
San Antonio Symphony	109 Lexington Ave., San Antonio, TX 78205	Victor Alessandro
San Francisco Symphony	War Memorial Veterans' Bldg., San Fran., CA 94102	Seiji Ozawa
Seattle Symphony	305 Harrison St., Seattle, WA 98109	Milton Katims
Toronto Symphony	215 Victoria St., Toronto, Ontario, Can. M5B 1V1	Andrew Davis
Utah Symphony	55 W. 1st So. St., Salt Lake City, UT 84101	Maurice Abravanel

Metropolitan Orchestras

		Conductors
Akron Symphony	Thomas Hall, Hill & Center Sts., Akron, OH 44303	Louis Lane
Albany Symphony	19 Clinton Ave., Albany, NY 12207	Julius Hegyi
Albuquerque Symphony	120 Madeira N.E., Albuquerque, NM 87108	Yoshimi Takeda
Amarillo Symphony	P.O. Box 2552, Amarillo, TX 79105	Michael Paul Matesky
Arkansas Orchestra Society	Robinson Aud., Markham & Broadway, Little Rock, AR 72201	Kurt Klippstatter
Austin Symphony	701 West 15th St., Austin, TX 78701	Akiro Endo
Birmingham Symphony	City Hall, Birmingham, AL 35203	Amerigo Marino
Brooklyn Philharmonia	30 Lafayette Ave., Brooklyn, NY 11217	Lukas Foss
Calgary Philharmonic	830 Ninth Ave., S.W., Calgary, Alberta, Can. T2P 1L7	Maurice Handford
Canton Symphony	1001 Market Ave. N.., Canton, OH 44702	Robert Marcellus
Cedar Rapids Symphony	605 Dows Bldg., Cedar Rapids, IA 52401	Richard D. Williams
Charlotte Symphony	511 E. Morehead St., Charlotte, NC 28202	Jacques Brourman
Chattanooga Symphony	730 Cherry St., Chattanooga, TN 37402	Richard Cormier
Chautauqua Symphony	Chatauqua Institution, Chautauqua, NY 14722	Guest Conductors
Clarion Music Society	415 Lexington Ave., New York, NY 10017	Newell Jenkins
Colorado Springs Symphony	P.O. Box 1692, Colorado Springs, CO 80901	Charles Ansbacher
Columbus Symphony	101 East Town St., Columbus, OH 43215	Evan Whallon
Corpus Christi Symphony	P.O. Box 495, Corpus Christi, TX 78403	Cornelius Eberhardt
Dayton Philharmonic	15 East First St., Dayton, OH 45402	Paul Katz
Des Moines Symphony	318 Securities Bldg., Des Moines, IA 50309	Yuri Krasnapalsky
Duluth-Superior Symphony	506 W. Michigan St., Duluth, MN 55802	Joseph Hawthorne
Eastern Music Festival	712 Summit Ave., Greensboro, NC 27405	Sheldon Morgenstern
Edmonton Symphony	P.O. Box 4232, Edmonton, Alberta, Can. T6E 4T2	Pierre Hetu
El Paso Philharmonic	P.O. Box 180, El Paso, TX 79942	Abraham Chavez Jr.
Erie Philharmonic	720 G. Daniel Baldwin Bldg., Erie, PA 16501	Harold Bauer
Evansville Philharmonic	P.O. Box 84, Evansville, IN 44701	Minas Christian
Flint Symphony	1025 E. Kearsley St., Flint, MI 48502	Guest Conductors
Florida Gulf Coast Symphony	P.O. Box 569, St. Petersburg, FL 33731	Irwin Hoffman
Florida Symphony	P.O. Box 782, Orlando, FL 32802	Pavle Despalj
Florida West Coast Symphony	P.O. Box 1107, Sarasota, FL 33578	Paul C. Wolfe
Fort Lauderdale Symphony	450 E. Las Olas Blvd., Fort Lauderdale, FL 33301	Emerson Buckley
Fort Wayne Philharmonic	927 S. Harrison, Fort Wayne, IN 4682	Thomas Briccetti
Fort Worth Symphony	4401 Trail Lake Dr., Ft. Worth, TX 76109	John Giordano
Fresno Philharmonic	1362 N. Fresno St., Fresno, CA 93703	Guy Taylor
Glendale Symphony	121 W. Lexington Dr., Glendale, CA 91203	Carmen Dragon
Grand Rapids Symphony	Exhibitors Bldg., Grand Rapids, MI 49502	Theo Alcantara
Hamilton Philharmonic	50 Main St. W. Hamilton, Ont. Can. L8N 3H8	Boris Brott
Hartford Symphony	15 Lewis St., Hartford, CT 06103	Arthur Winograd
Hudson Valley Philharmonic	30 Garfield Pl., Poughkeepsie, NY 12602	Claude Monteux
Jackson Symphony	P.O. Box 4584 Jackson, MS 39216	Lewis Daivit
Jacksonville Symphony	46 W. Duval St., Jacksonville, FL 32202	Willis Page
Kalamazoo Symphony	426 S. Park St., Kalamazoo, MI 49007	Yoshimi Takeda
Knoxville Symphony	618 Gay St., Knoxville, TN 37902	Arpod Joo
Lexington Philharmonic	P.O. Box 838, Lexington, KY 40501	George Zack
London Symphony	202-195 Dundas St., London, Ont., Can. 1G5	Clifford Evens
Long Beach Symphony	121 Linden Ave., Long Beach, CA 90802	George Zack
Louisville Orchestra	333 W. Broadway, Louisville, KY 40202	Jorge Mester
Madison Symphony	211 N. Carroll St., Madison, WI 53703	Roland Johnson

(Continued)

Memphis Symphony	1503 Monroe,Memphis, TN 38104	Vincent DeFrank
Miami Beach Symphony	420 Lincoln Rd. Mall, Miami Beach, FL 33139	Barnett Breeskin
Miami Philharmonic	1200 Anastasia Ave., Coral Gables, FL 33134	(To be announced)
Midland Odessa Sym. & Chorale	P.O. 6266, Air Terminal Sta., Midland, TX 79701	Thomas Hohstadt
Monterey County Symphony	P.O. Box 3965, Carmel, CA 93921	Haymo Taeuber
Nashville Symphony	1805 West End Ave., Nashville, TN 37203	John Nelson
New Haven Symphony	33 Whitney Ave., New Haven, CT 06511	Erich Kunzel
New World, Symphony of the	2504 W. 57th St., New York NY 10019	Everett Lee
Norfolk Symphony	P.O. Box 26, Norfolk, VA 23501	Russell Stanger
North Carolina Symphony	P.O. Box 28026, Raleigh, NC 27611	John Gosling
Northeastern Penna., Philharmonic Soc. of	P.O. Box 71, Avoca, PA 18641	Thomas Michalak
Oakland Symphony	2025 Broadway, Oakland, CA 94612	Harold Farberman
Oklahoma City Symphony	Civic Center Music Hall, Oklahoma City, OK 73102	Ainslee Cox
Omaha Symphony	P.O. Box 897, Omaha, NE 68101	Yuri Krasnapolsky
Orchestra Da Camera	200 Emory Rd., Mineola, NY 11501	Herbert Grossman
Oregon Symphony	1119 S.W. Park, Portland, OR 97205	Lawrence Smith
Pasadena Symphony	300 E. Green St., Pasadena, CA 91101	Daniel Lewis
Peoria Symphony	1508 W. Moss Ave., Peoria, IL 61606	Robert Kreis
Phoenix Symphony	6328 N. 7th St., Phoenix, AZ 85014	Eduardo Mata
Portland Symphony	30 Myrtle St., Portland, ME 04111	Paul Vermel
Puerto Rico Symphony	GPO Box 2350, San Juan, Puerto Rico 00936	Victor Tevah
Quebec Symphony	745 Rue St. Cyrille Ouest, Que., Can. G1R 3B2	Pierre Dervaux
Rhode Island Philharmonic	39 The Arcade, Providence, RI 02903	Francis Madeira
Richmond Symphony	112 E. Franklin St., Richmond, VA 23219	Jacques Houtmann
Sacramento Symphony	451 Parkfair Dr., Sacramento, CA 95825	Harry Newstone
Saginaw Symphony	P.O. Box 889, Saginaw, MI 48606	Gideon Graw
San Diego Symphony	P.O. Box 3175, San Diego, CA 92103	Peter Eros
San Jose Symphony	St. Claire Hotel, San Jose, CA 95113	George Cleve
Santa Barbara Symphony	210 E. Figueroa, Santa Barbara, CA 93101	Ronald Ondrejka
Savannah Symphony	P.O. Box 9505, Savannah, GA 31402	Michael Charry
Shreveport Symphony	P.O. Box 4057, Shreveport, LA 71104	John Shenaut
Spokane Symphony	W. 245 Spokane Falls Blvd., Spokane, WA 99201	Donald Thulean
Springfield Symphony	49 Chestnut St., Springfield, MA 01103	Robert Gutter
Syracuse Symphony	113 E. Onondaga St., Syracuse, NY 13202	Frederik Prausnitz
Toledo Orchestra	One Stranahan Sq., Toledo, OH 43604	Serge Fournier
Tri-City Symphony	P.O. Box 67, Davenport, IA 52801	James Dixon
Tucson Symphony	8 Paseo Redondo, Tucson, AZ 85705	Gregory Millar
Tulsa Philharmonic	2210 S. Main, Tulsa, OK 74114	Thomas Lewis
Utica Symphony	255 Genesee St., Utica, NY 13501	Fritz Maraffi
Vancouver Symphony	873 Beatty St., Vancouver, B.C., Can. V6B 2M6	Kazuyoshi Akiyama
Vermont Symphony	P.O. Box 548, Middlebury, VT 05753	Efrain Guigui
Victoria Symphony	748 Johnson St., Victoria, B.C., Can. V8W 1N1	Lazlo Gati
Wheeling Symphony	51 16th St., Wheeling, WV 23006	Jeff Holland Cook
Wichita Symphony	225 W. Douglas, Wichita, KS 67202	Francois Huybrechts
Winnipeg Symphony	555 Main St. Winnipeg, Manitoba, Can. R2G 2B3	Piero Gamba
Winston-Salem Symphony	610 Coliseum Dr., Winston-Salem, NC 27106	John Iuele
Youngstown Symphony	260 West Federal St., Youngstown, OH 44503	Franz Bibo

Chamber Orchestras

Los Angeles Chamber Orch.	1017 N. LaCienega Blvd., Los Angeles, CA 90069	Neville Marriner
St. Paul Chamber Orch.	75 W. 5th St., St. Paul, MN 55102	Dennis Davies

Recordings

Disc and Tape Sales Go Down, Revenues Go Up

Revenues from sales of phonograph records and pre-recorded tapes went up by 9% in 1974 although unit sales were down 3%, it was reported by the Recording Industry Association of America.

The revenue increase resulted from higher prices charged by the U.S. recording industry to counteract rising costs of recording and materials, the RIAA said.

Revenues reached a record high of $2.2 billion for the year, compared to $2.017 in 1973. Unit sales were 594 million in 1974, 616 million in 1973.

Most of the loss was in sales of single records, down from 228 million in 1973 to 204 million, a loss of 10.5 percent. Long-playing album sales dropped from 280 million to 276 million, a decrease of 1.4%. Sales of tapes rose from 108 million in 1973 to 114 million in 1974, revenues rising from $581 million to $650 million.

In 1974, a new high of 195 Gold Record Award certifications was issued by RIAA.

A change in requirements for Gold Record Awards was effected by RIAA starting Jan. 1, 1975. While the awards would continue to be made for singles selling one million copies each, new criteria were set for play albums and their tape equivalents: a minimum sale of 500,000 units, provided sales volume is not less than $1 million, based on one-third of the list price of the album or tape. Also, a multi-record or tape package would be considered as one unit.

Gold Record Awards during late 1974-75 follow:

Artists and Recording Titles
(A) Album. (S) Single.
September 1974
Golden Earring: Moontan. (A).
Lynrd Skynyrd: Second Helping. (A).

Eagles: Desperado. (A).
Souther-Hillman Furay Band: The Souther-Hillman Furay Band. (A).
Mac Davis: Stop and Smell the Roses. (A).
Neil Young: On the Beach. (A).

October 1974

Santana: Santana's Greatest Hits. (A).
Andy Kim: Rock Me Gently. (S).
The Beach Boys: The Beach Boys in Concert. (A).
Dionne Warwicke & The Spinners: Then Came You. (S).
Black Oak Arkansas: Black Oak Arkansas. (A).
Olivia Newton-John: I Honestly Love You. (S).
Quincy Jones: Body Heat. (A).
Cheech & Chong: Cheech & Chong's Wedding Album. (A).
Bachman-Turner Overdrive: Bachman-Turner Overdrive. (A).
Olivia Newton-John: Let Me Be There. (A).
Alice Cooper: Alice Cooper's Greatest Hits. (A).
Billy Preston: Nothing from Nothing. (S).
Carole King: Wrap Around Joy. (A).
Jim Croce: Photographs and Memories. His Greatest Hits. (A).
John Lennon: Walls and Bridges. (A).
Charlie Rich: There Won't Be Anymore. (A).
Ohio Players: Skin Tight. (S).
Neil Diamond: Serenade. (A).
America: Holiday. (A).
The Rolling Stones: It's Only Rock 'n' Roll. (A).

November 1974

The Isley Brothers: Live It Up. (A).
Traffic: When the Eagle Flies. (A).
David Bowie: David Live. (A).
Sly & The Family Stone: Small Talk. (A).
Jethro Tull: War Child. (A).
Elton John: Greatest Hits. (A).
Gladys Knight & The Pips: I Feel a Song. (A).
Paul Anka: Anka. (A).
B.T. Express: Do It ('Til You're Satisfied). (S).
Loggins & Messina: Mother Lode. (A).
Joni Mitchell: Miles of Aisles. (A).
Helen Reddy: I Don't Know How to Love Him. (A).
Carl Douglas: Kung Fu Fighting. (S).

December 1974

Billy Swan: I Can Help. (S).
Moody Blues: This Is the Moody Blues. (A).
Various Artists: Here's Johnny . . . Magic Moments from the Tonight Show. (A).
Bobby Vinton: Melodies of Love. (A).
Bobby Vinton: My Melody of Love. (S).
The Who: Odds and Sods. (A).
Ringo Starr: Goodnight Vienna. (A).
The Three Degrees: When Will I See You Again. (S).
Bachman-Turner Overdrive: You Ain't Seen Nothing Yet. (S).
Ohio Players: Fire. (A).
George Harrison: Dark Horse. (A).
Harry Chapin: Verities and Balderdash. (A).
Kris Kristofferson: Me and Bobby McGee. (A).
Edgar Winter: Roadwork. (A).
The Spinners: New and Improved. (A).
Yes: Relayer. (A).
Barry White: You're the First, the Last, My Everything. (S).
Helen Reddy: Free and Easy. (A).
Grand Funk Railroad: All the Girls in the World Beware!!! (A).
Lynyrd Skynyrd: Pronounced Leh-nerd Skin-nerd. (A).
Jackson Browne: Late for the Sky. (A).
Bread: The Best of Bread: Vol. II. (A).
Rufus: Rufusized. (A).
Harry Chapin: Cat's in the Cradle. (S).

January 1975

John Denver: Back Home Again. (S).
Barbra Streisand: Butterfly. (A).
Elvis Presley: Elvis, A Legendary Performer, Vol I. (A).

Charley Pride: Did You Think to Pray. (A).
Charley Pride: (Country) Charley Pride. (A).
Deep Purple: Stormbringer. (A).
Al Green: Al Green Explores Your Mind. (A).
Helen Reddy: Angie Baby. (S).
Average White Band: Average White Band. (A).
Three Dog Night: Joy to the World—Their Greatest Hits. (A).
Joe Walsh: So What. (A).
Millie Jackson: Caught Up. (A).
Al Green: Sha-La-La (Makes Me Happy). (S).
Ohio Players: Fire. (S).
Elton John: Lucy in the Sky with Diamonds. (S).
Barry Manilow: Mandy. (S).
Linda Ronstadt: Heart Like a Wheel. (A).
Dawn: Dawn's New Ragtime Follies. (A).

February 1975

Carpenters: Please Mr. Postman. (S).
Bob Dylan: Blood on the Tracks. (A).
John Denver: An Evening with John Denver. (A).
Jefferson Starship: Dragon Fly. (A).
Marie & Donny Esmond: I'm Leaving It All up to You. (A).
Olivia Newton-John: Have You Never Been Mellow. (A).
Todd Rundgren: Something/Anything? (A).
Foghat: Energized. (A).
Bobby Bland-B.B. King: Together for the First Time. (A).

March 1975

Olivia Newton-John: Have You Never Been Mellow. (S).
Average White Band: Pick up the Pieces. (S).
Led Zeppelin: Physical Graffiti. (A).
B.T. Express: Do It ('Til You're Satisfied). (A).
Johnny Rivers: A Touch of Gold. Vol. II. (A).
Johnny Rivers: Johnny Rivers' Golden Hits. (A).
Soundtrack Recording: Tommy. (A).
Minnie Riperton: Perfect Angel. (A).
LaBelle: Lady Marmalade. (S).
Chicago: Chicago VIII. (A).

April 1975

Tony Orlando & Dawn: Tuneweaving. (A).
Frankie Valli: My Eyes Adored You. (S).
Minnie Riperton: Lovin' You. (S).
Love Unlimited Orchestra: White Gold. (A).
Barry White: Just Another Way to Say I Love You. (A).
Earth, Wind & Fire: That's the Way of the World. (A).
Phoebe Snow: Phoebe Snow. (A).
The Doobie Bros.: Black Water. (S).
Aerowsmith: Get Your Wings. (A).
The Elton John Band: Philadelphia Freedom. (S).
The Beach Boys: Spirit of America. (A).

May 1975

Styx: Styx II. (A).
Sammy Johns: Chevy Van. (S).
The Electric Light Orchestra: Eldorado. (A).
LaBelle: Nightbirds. (A).
Bad Company: Straight Shooter. (A).
Steely Dan: Katy Lied. (A).
Ramsey Lewis: Sun Goddess. (A).
Elton John: Captain Fantastic and the Brown Dirt Cowboy. (A).
Freddy Fender: Before the Next Teardrop Falls. (S).
B.J. Thomas: (Hey Won't You Play) Another Somebody Done Somebody Wrong Song. (S).
Bachman-Turner Overdrive: Four Wheel Drive. (A).
The Doobie Bros.: Stampede. (A).
Alice Cooper: Welcome to My Nightmare. (A).

June 1975

Wings: Venus & Mars. (A).
Tony Orlando & Dawn: He Don't Love You (Like I Love You). (S).
The O'Jays: Survival. (A).
Janis Joplin: Janis Joplin's Greatest Hits. (A).
America: Hearts. (A).
Carpenters: Horizon. (A).
Earth, Wind & Fire: Shining Star. (S)
The O'Jays: Live in London. (A).
Major Harris: Love Won't Let Me Wait. (S).
John Denver: Thank God I'm a Country Boy. (S).
Van McCoy & The Soul City Symphony: The Hustle. (S).
Z.Z. Top: Fandango. (A).
Lynyrd Skynyrd: Nuthin' Fancy. (A).

Eagles: One of these Nights. (A).
The Isley Bros.: The Heat Is on Featuring Fight the Power. (A).
Harold Melvin & The Blue Notes, with Theodore Pendergrass. (A).

July 1975

Captain & Tennille: Love Will Keep Us Together. (S).
David Bowie: Young Americans. (A).
Isaac Hayes: Chocolate Chip. (A).
Barry Manilow: Barry Manilow II: (A).
Michael Murphy: Wildfire. (S).
Average White Band: Cut the Cake. (A).
War: Why Can't We Be Friends. (A).
Charlie Daniels: Fire on the Mountain. (A).

Best-Selling Books of 1974-1975

Listed According to frequency of citation on best seller reports for Sept. 1974 through July 1975.

Numbers in parantheses show rank on final list for calendar year 1974 according to Publishers Weekly.

Fiction

1. Centennial; James A. Michener. (1)
2. The Seven-Per-Cent Solution; Dr. John H. Watson. (9)
3. Something Happened; Joseph Heller. (5)
4. The Moneychangers; Arthur Hailey.
5. Tinker, Tailor, Soldier, Spy; John le Carre. (4)
6. The Dreadful Lemon Sky; John D. MacDonald.
7. The Dogs of War; Frederick Forsyth. (6)
8. Lady; Thomas Tryon.
9. The Promise of Joy; Allen Drury.
10. The Ebony Tower; John Fowles.
11. The Pirate; Harold Robbins. (7)
12. Shardik; Richard Adams.
13. Looking for Mr. Goodbar; Judith Rossner.
14. Harlequin; Morris West.
15. Jaws; Peter Benchley. (3)
16. Watership Down; Richard Adams. (2)
17. A Month of Sundays; John Updike.
18. Black Sunday; Thomas Harris.
19. The War Between the Tates; Alison Lurie.
20. Ragtime; E.L. Doctorow.
21. The Massacre at Fall Creek; Jessamyn West.
22. The Great Train Robbery; Michael Crichton.
23. Spindrift; Phyllis A. Whitney.
24. Shogun; James Clavell.
25. The Rhinemann Exchange; Robert Ludlum.

General

1. The Bermuda Triangle; Charles Berlitz with J. Manson Valentine. (9)
2. All Things Bright and Beautiful; James Herriot. (8)
3. The Ascent of Man; Jacob Bronowski.
4. Helter Skelter; Vincent Bugliosi with Curt Gentry.
5. The Palace Guard; Dan Rather with Gary Paul Gates.
6. Strictly Speaking; Edwin Newman.
7. Breach of Faith; Theodore H. White.
8. Here at the New Yorker; Brendan Gill.
9. The Woman He Loved; Ralph G. Martin.
10. The Memory Book; Harry Lotayne with Jerry Lucas. (10)
11. All the President's Men; Carl Bernstein and Bob Woodward. (2)
12. A Bridge Too Far; Cornelius Ryan.
13. Total Fitness in 30 Minutes a Week; Laurence E. Morehouse and Leonard Gross.
14. Tales of Power; Carlos A. Castaneda.
15. How the Good Guys Finally Won; Jimmy Breslin.
16. The Bankers; Martin Mayer.
17. T.M.: Discovering Energy and Overcoming Stress; Harold H. Bloomfield.
18. Conversations with Kennedy; Benjamin Bradlee.
19. The Pleasure Bond; William H. Masters and Virginia E. Johnson.
20. The Total Woman; Marabel Morgan. (1)
21. More Joy; edited by Alex Comfort.
22. The Ultra Secret; Frederick Winterbotham.
23. Sylvia Porter's Money Book; Sylvia Porter.
24. The Lives of a Cell; Lewis Thomas.
25. Alive; Piers Paul Read.

Miss America Winners

For the winners of 1921 through 1958 see the 1972 issue of the World Almanac

		Height	Bust	Waist	Hips	Wgt.-	Age	Hair	Eyes
1959	Mary Ann Mobley, Brandon, Miss.	5-5	34½	22	35	114	21	Brown	Brown
1960	Lynda Lee Mead, Natchez, Miss.	5-7	36	24	36	120	20	Brown	Green
1961	Nancy Fleming, Montague, Michigan.	5-6	35	22	35	116	18	Brown	Green
1962	Maria Fletcher, Asheville, N.C.	5-5½	35	24	35	118	19	Brown	Hazel
1963	Jacquelyn Mayer, Sandusky, Ohio.	5-5	36	22	36	115	20	Brown	Hazel
1964	Donna Axum, El Dorado, Arkansas.	5-6½	35	23	35	124	21	Brown	Brown
1965	Vonda Kay Van Dyke, Phoenix, Ariz.	5-6	36	24	36	124	21	Brown	Brown
1966	Deborah Irene Bryant, Overland Park, Kansas.	5-7	36	23	36	115	19	Brown	Blue
1967	Jane Anne Jayroe, Laverne, Oklahoma.	5-6	36	24	35	116	19	Brown	Green
1968	Debra Dene Barnes, Moran, Kansas.	5-9	36½	24	36½	135	20	Brown	Blue
1969	Judith Anne Ford, Belvidere, Ill.	5-7	36	24½	36	125	18	Blonde	Blue
1970	Pamela Anne Eldred, Birmingham, Mich.	5-5½	34	21½	34	110	21	Blonde	Green
1971	Phyllis Ann George, Denton, Texas.	5-8	36	23	36	121	21	Brown	Brown
1972	Laurie Lea Schaefer, Columbus, Ohio.	5-7	36	24	34	118	22	Auburn	Green
1973	Terry Anne Meeuwsen, DePere, Wisconsin.	5-8	36	25	36	120	23	Brown	Brown
1974	Rebecca Ann King, Denver, Colorado.	5-9	36	24	36	125	23	Blonde	Blue
1975	Shirley Cothran, Fort Worth, Texas.	5-8	36	24	36	119	21	Brown	Hazel

Leading U. S. Advertisers, 1974

(Reprinted by permission of Advertising Age. Aug. 18, 1975
Copyright ⊕ Crain Communications Inc. 1975)

Rank	Company	Ad Costs (000)	Sales (000)	Ads as % Sales	Rank	Company	Ad Costs (000)	Sales (000)	Ads as % Sales
	Cars					**Liquor**			
2	General Motors Corp.	$247,000	$26,500,000	0.9	13	Heublein Inc.	95,600	1,497,785	6.4
8	Ford Motor Co.	132,000	23,620,600	0.6	29	The Seagram Co. Ltd.	72,368	1,840,986	3.9
15	Chrysler Corp.	86,200	7,570,270	1.1		**Tires**			
50	Volkswagen of America	44,400	7,069,308	0.6	27	Goodyear Tire & Rubber	73,690	5,256,247	1.4
	Food				37	Firestone Tire & Rubber	61,000	3,674,890	1.7
4	General Foods Corp.	189,000	2,745,200	6.9		**Soft drinks**			
23	Norton Simon Inc.	75,000	1,386,511	5.4	25	Coca-Cola Co.	74,450	2,522,149	3.0
26	Kraftco Corp.	74,400	3,788,964	2.0	38	PepsiCo Inc.	60,000	1,831,068	3.3
28	General Mills Inc.	72,700	2,309,000	3.1		**Appliances, tv, radio**			
33	Nabisco Inc.	68,100	1,200,000	5.7	18	RCA Corp.	84,000	4,626,900	1.8
34	Ralston Purina Co.	66,000	3,073,210	2.1	21	General Electric Co.	80,000	13,413,000	0.6
39	McDonald's Corp.	58,870	1,943,000	3.0	36	Westinghouse Electric Corp.	62,000	5,798,513	1.1
44	Beatrice Foods Co.	54,000	3,296,308	1.6		**Retail chains**			
45	Kellogg Co.	49,950	1,009,818	4.9	3	Sears, Roebuck & Co.	220,000	13,101,210	1.7†
47	Pillsbury Co.	48,800	1,197,426	4.1	32	J. C. Penney Co.	69,000	6,935,700	1.0
	Soaps, cleansers (and allied)					**Chemicals**			
1	Procter & Gamble Co.	325,000	4,425,000*	7.3	22	American Cyanamid	76,000	1,779,872	4.3
9	Colgate-Palmolive Co.	118,000	1,100,000	10.7	43	Du Pont	54,176	6,910,000	0.8
16	Lever Bros.	85,000	669,200	12.7		**Photographic equipment**			
	Tobacco				42	Eastman Kodak Co.	54,600	4,583,629	1.2
11	R. J. Reynolds Industries, Inc.	102,000	4,500,000	2.3		**Telephone service, equipment**			
20	Philip Morris Inc.	81,000	3,010,961	2.7	12	American Telephone & Telegraph Co.	96,500	26,174,412	0.4
30	American Brands	70,000	3,570,426	2.0	14	International Telephone & Telegraph Corp.	92,221	5,000,000	1.8
31	Brown & Williamson Tobacco Co.	69,400	959,284*	7.2		**Miscellaneous**			
	Drugs and cosmetics				10	U.S. Government	110,800	—	—
5	Warner-Lambert Co.	156,000	1,090,221	14.3	35	Rapid-American Corp.	62,500	2,571,817	2.4
6	Bristol-Myers Co.	150,000	1,590,949	9.4	46	CBS Inc.	49,331	1,751,341	2.8
7	American Home Products	135,000	1,528,991	8.8	48	Loews Corp.	48,763	793,341	6.1
16	Sterling Drug Inc.	85,000	564,437	15.1	49	Greyhound Corp.	45,000	3,469,281	1.3
19	Richardson-Merrell	83,561	576,441	14.5					
23	Gillette Co.	75,000	1,246,422	6.0					
40	Schering-Plough Corp.	57,500	392,300	14.7					
41	Johnson & Johnson	56,500	1,138,126	5.0					

Domestic sales estimated by AA. †Percentage shown would be two and a half times more if Sears' $275,000,000 in local advertising
were added to the $220,000,000 national total. The other retail chain (J.C. Penney) ad total also does not include local advertising.
Note: All ad totals are domestic. Whenever possible, AA reported the company's domestic sales figure in this table, although for some
companies only a worldwide sales total was available. Covers total 1974 ad expenditures, including measured and unmeasured
media.

Commercial Broadcast Stations on the Air
Source: Federal Communications Commission (1974)

State	Total	AM	FM	TV	State	Total	AM	FM	TV
Total	7,526	4,357	2,448	721	Nebraska	84	48	21	15
United States	7,426	4,305	2,413	708	Nevada	39	21	11	7
Alabama	213	136	60	17	New Hampshire	46	27	15	4
Alaska	28	18	3	7	New Jersey	68	37	27	4
Arizona	84	54	19	11	New Mexico	84	57	19	8
Arkansas	142	87	47	8	New York	303	161	113	29
California	441	226	162	53	North Carolina	299	203	78	18
Colorado	110	67	32	11	North Dakota	47	26	9	12
Connecticut	64	38	21	5	Ohio	268	121	120	27
Delaware	16	10	6	—	Oklahoma	115	67	39	9
Dist. of Columbia	20	7	7	6	Oregon	117	80	24	13
Florida	317	194	96	27	Pennsylvania	314	173	118	23
Georgia	268	173	77	18	Rhode Island	24	15	7	2
Hawaii	39	25	4	10	South Carolina	163	104	47	12
Idaho	59	43	10	6	South Dakota	54	30	14	10
Illinois	265	123	118	24	Tennessee	237	154	66	17
Indiana	187	86	84	17	Texas	481	284	140	57
Iowa	141	74	54	13	Utah	47	32	12	3
Kansas	104	60	32	12	Vermont	26	18	6	2
Kentucky	198	110	76	12	Virginia	207	128	64	15
Louisiana	154	92	45	17	Washington	148	93	40	15
Maine	61	36	18	7	West Virginia	96	60	27	9
Maryland	91	51	33	7	Wisconsin	200	99	83	18
Massachusetts	112	64	38	10	Wyoming	35	29	3	3
Michigan	237	124	92	21					
Minnesota	153	89	53	11	Other areas	100	52	35	13
Mississippi	166	102	53	11	Puerto Rico	89	48	31	10
Missouri	188	108	57	23	Guam	3	1	1	1
Montana	66	41	13	12	Virgin Islands	8	3	3	2

Global Communication
Source: UNESCO; data for 1971-72

Nation	No. of daily newspapers	Copies per 1,000 pop.	No. of radio transmitters	Radios per 1,000 pop.	No. of TV transmitters[1]	TV sets per 1,000 pop.	No. of film theaters	Theater seats per 1,000 pop.	Avg. visits per year pop.
Algeria	4	18	25	46	13	10	640	14	6
Argentina	180	180	147	424	59	191	1,637	31	2
Australia	58	321	212	220	199	234	1,100	64	3
Austria	31	328	366	287	322	226	835	37	4
Bahrain	3[2]	29	3	341	0	59	9	45	6
Bangladesh	25	N/A	16	N/A	-1	N/A	(est.100)	N/A	N/A
Belgium	55	N/A	29	366	17	235	740	41	3
Bolivia[3]	16	33	133	260	1	2	120	13	0.6
Brazil	261	35	994	58	50	66	3,194	19	2
Bulgaria	13	206	26	268	118	150	3,106	82	13
Canada	121	234	729	821	534	334	1,156	30	4
Chile	46	N/A	229	156	25	56	360	27	5
China (P.R.)	N/A	N/A	N/A	19	(est. 20)[4]	0.7	N/A	N/A	N/A
Colombia	36	105	131	130	18	53	378	13	3
Cuba	16	107	110	154	19	66	428	N/A	N/A
Czechoslovakia	27	280	119	266	680	228	3,469	68	7
Denmark	53	364	31	329	25	284	350	28	4
Ecuador	22	43	336	261	14	23	164	18	3
Egypt	14	20	43	144	28	15	246	6	2
Ethiopia	3	2	9	20	6	1	30	1	0.4
Finland	60	425	97	409	70	255	318	21	2
France	106	233	294	312	1,961	244	4,237	39	3
Germany, E.	40	425	106	355	455	283	1,197	21	5
Germany, W.	1,093	330	313	340	958	455	3,171	21	2
Ghana	3	30	23	85	4	2	13	2	0.1
Greece	104	N/A	50	313	17	58	1,034	N/A	15
Guinea	1	1	5	21	—	(no TV)	28	2	N/A
Hungary	27	216	29	244	12	193	3,755	57	7
Iceland	5	439	29	303	59	206	25	44	7
India	821	N/A	137	21	2	0.1	4,716	5	6
Indonesia	120	10	140	114	12	33	490	N/A	N/A
Iran	39	25	38	230	70	33	437	9	0.9
Iraq	7	N/A	21	169	5	25	24	N/A	0.8
Ireland	7	233	12	209	20	168	N/A	N/A	7
Israel	24	183	47	220	21	119	252	59	11
Italy	78	142	1,874	230	1,193	201	10,719	N/A	10
Jamaica	2	69	14	408	11	55	42	21	3
Japan	172	529	889	441	4,991	229	2,673	12	2
Kenya	3	10	18	64	4	2	32	2	0.6
Korea, S.	42	138	123	128	39	28	793	15	4
Kuwait	6	44	14	439	7	165	7	13	4
Lebanon	52	N/A	6	210	8	113	170	30	17
Liberia	1	5	16	255	3	4	8	N/A	0.5
Libya	7	17	12	41	2	0.5	28	9	2
Malaysia	40	77	61	162	18	24	550	31	7
Mexico	200	N/A	590	266	78	57	1,765	28	5
Morocco	6	N/A	35	95	14	14	260	9	1
Netherlands	95	307	34	303	16	245	321	14	2
New Zealand	40	367	58	704	7	249	239	49	N/A
Nigeria	11	N/A	37	23	7	1	183	0.7	1
Norway	79	391	248	313	525	227	450	37	5
Pakistan	98	N/A	22	18	7	2	578	5	0.3
Panama	7	86	114	329	13	82	23	19	3
Paraguay	4	30	37	71	1	20	61+	N/A	N/A
Peru	56	N/A	304	138	19	28	276	N/A	N/A
Philippines	19	17	327	42	15	11	951	N/A	N/A
Poland	44	231	51	177	52	159	2,465	18	3
Portugal	33	N/A	95	146	23	40	485	28	3
Rhodesia	4	15	22	38	3	20	90	9	N/A
Romania	57	173	52	152	111	83	6,244	N/A	9
Saudi Arabia	5	7	11	31	6	19	(no public movies)		
Senegal	1	5	12	67	1	0.4	87	13	1
Singapore	10	193	16	130	2	95	75	29	17
S. Africa	21	47	177	102	N/A	N/A	685	22	N/A
Spain	115	99	463	205	641	169	6,064	129	8
Sri Lanka	17	48	29	66	—	(no TV)	303	10	8
Sweden	108	515	292	367	299	333	1,334	N/A	3
Switzerland	98	390	200	310	446	243	554	32	5
Syria	5	9	11	375	7	22	70	N/A	N/A
Tanzania	7	4	9	11	—	—	36	1	0.4
Thailand	35	24	144	85	30	10	392	12	N/A
Tunisia	4	21	6	49	11	16	104	9	2
Turkey	432	N/A	19	132	7	5	700	N/A	N/A
USSR	639	333	3,034	430	1,466	185	147,200	N/A	19
UK	109	437	396	699	314	299	1,482	25	3
U.S.A.	1,761	314	6,719	1,695	3,695	472	14,300	48	5
Uruguay	29	269	99	507	17	101	180	42	N/A
Venezuela	42	91	235	182	37	89	429	49	3
Vietnam, S.[5]	56	5	22	319	4	26	143	5	1
Yugoslavia	25	89	463	241	348	120	1,393	23	4
Zaire	6	N/A	27	0.9	2	0.3	57	0.8	0.05
Zambia	2	13	20	55	3	4	29	3	N/A

[1]No. of TV transmitters indicates breadth of coverage; mountainous countries require more transmitters. [2]Bahrain, non dailies. [3]Bolivia, data 1963, 64, 68. [4]Originating stations. [5]Vietnam, S., pre-PRG. N/A-not available.

Estimated Advertising Expenditures in the United States

Source: Advertising Age; prepared by
Robert J. Coen of McCann-Erickson, Inc.

MEDIUM	1972 Dollars-millions	1972 Per cent of total	1973 Dollars-millions	1973 Per cent of total	1974 Dollars-millions	1974 Per cent of total	% Change '74 vs. '73
Newspapers							
Total	7,008	30.1	7,595	30.2	8,001	29.8	+ 5.1
National	1,103	4.7	1,111	4.4	1,194	4.5	+ 7.5
Local	5,905	25.4	6,484	25.8	6,807	25.4	+ 5.0
Magazines							
Total	1,440	6.2	1,448	5.8	1,504	5.6	+ 3.9
Weeklies	610	2.6	583	2.3	630	2.3	+ 8.1
Women's	368	1.6	362	1.5	372	1.4	+ 2.8
Monthlies	462	2.0	503	2.0	502	1.9	− 0.2
Farm Publications	59	0.3	65	0.3	72	0.3	+10.8
Television							
Total	4,091	17.6	4,493	17.9	4,950	18.5	+11.0
Network	1,804	7.7	1,968	7.8	2,185	8.1	+11.0
Spot	1,318	5.7	1,450	5.8	1,515	5.6	+10.0
Local	969	4.2	1,075	4.3	1,250	4.7	+12.1
Radio							
Total	1,612	6.9	1,690	6.7	1,835	6.8	+ 6.5
Network	74	0.3	70	0.3	72	0.3	+ 5.9
Spot	402	1.7	380	1.5	408	1.5	+ 2.0
Local	1,136	4.9	1,240	4.9	1,355	5.1	+ 8.0
Direct Mail	3,420	14.7	3,698	14.7	3,920	14.6	+ 6.0
Business Papers	781	3.3	865	3.4	900	3.4	+ 4.0
Outdoor							
Total	292	1.2	308	1.2	345	1.3	+12.0
National	192	0.8	200	0.8	225	0.8	+12.5
Local	100	0.4	108	0.4	120	0.4	+11.1
Miscellaneous							
Total	4,597	19.7	4,958	19.7	5,293	19.7	+ 6.8
National	2,437	10.4	2,590	10.3	2,760	10.3	+ 7.2
Local	2,160	9.3	2,368	9.4	2,533	9.4	+ 6.3
Total							
National	13,030	55.9	13,845	55.1	14,755	55.0	+ 7.1
Local	10,270	44.1	11,275	44.9	12,065	45.0	+ 6.3
Grand Total	23,300	100.0	25,120	100.0	26,820	100.0	+ 6.8
Inflation Adjustment (1967 Dollars)	18,617	—	18,890	—	18,157	—	− 3.9

U.S. Television Sets and Stations

Set Ownership
(Nielsen Est. as of Sept. 1974)

Total TV Homes (Est. 9/1/75)	68,500,000 (70,100,000)	100%
Homes with:		
Color TV Sets	46,850,000	68%
B&W only	21,650,000	32
2 or more Sets	28,360,999	41
One Set	40,140,000	59
CATV	8,619,000	13
UHF	61,197,000	89

Station Facilities
(FCC as of April 1, 1975)

Commercial TV	698
VHF	507
UHF	191
Educational TV	221
VHF	89
UHF	132
Total TV	919

Network TV Program Ratings

Source: A.C. Nielsen, November 1974

Program Type	TV Households Rating	TV Households No. (000)	Men 18-34	Men 25-54	Men 55+	Women 18-34	Women 25-54	Women 55+	Women Working	Teens 12-17	Children 6-11
Today (7:30-8:00)	6.2	4,250	1.3	1.4	4.9	2.6	4.7	6.3	3.0	.8	.3
CBS News (7:00-8:00)	2.1	1,440	.4	.8	2.3	.8	1.0	3.3	1.3	*	.6
Daytime:											
Drama	8.3	5,690	1.2	1.0	2.3	6.9	7.6	8.2	2.9	1.3	.8
Quiz & Aud. Part.	7.0	4,770	1.5	1.4	3.6	3.9	4.9	7.3	2.5	1.5	1.6
All 10:00-4:30	7.5	5,120	1.4	1.2	3.0	5.2	5.9	7.6	2.6	1.5	1.3
Evening News	13.7	9,360	5.3	7.4	16.1	6.3	8.5	17.0	8.7	3.5	3.7
Evening:											
General Drama	18.2	12,490	9.5	10.5	12.8	15.0	14.6	17.1	13.6	10.2	11.3
Susp. & Myst.	18.7	12,810	11.6	13.6	15.0	14.4	15.0	15.4	13.9	8.8	8.3
Situation Comedy	22.9	15,720	11.7	14.3	19.1	16.6	18.3	22.3	18.3	14.0	16.3
Western Drama	19.3	13,210	10.1	11.2	17.6	12.4	13.8	20.8	12.4	9.9	16.0
Feature Film	20.3	13,930	15.3	15.8	13.0	17.6	17.2	12.6	14.6	10.2	10.5
All 7:30-11:00	19.4	13,290	12.1	13.7	14.7	14.8	15.2	15.5	13.9	10.8	11.1

*Less than 0.2 rating.

Movies of the Year (Oct. 1, 1974 to Sept. 1, 1975)

Selected and Rated by the New York Daily News Film Critics

Listed below alphabetically, are films rated by the New York Daily News star system: ★★★★ is for excellent. ★★★¹/₂ very good. ★★★ good. ★★¹/₂ fair. ★★ mediocre. ★¹/₂ poor. ★ very poor. 0★ not worth rating.

Kathleen Carroll, N.Y. Daily News Movie Editor and Critic

Movie	Star Rating	Stars	Director
Abdication, The	★★¹/₂	Peter Finch, Liv Ullmann	Anthony Harvey
Airport 1975	★★¹/₂	Charlton Heston, Karen Black	Jack Smight
Alice Doesn't Live Here Anymore	★★★¹/₂	Ellen Burstyn, Kris Kristofferson	Martin Scorsese
Amarcord	★★★¹/₂		Federico Fellini
And Now My Love	★★★¹/₂	Andre Dussollier, Marthe Keller	Claude Lelouche
Arthur Rubinstein-Love of Life	★★★¹/₂	Documentary	Francois Reichenbach
At Long Last Love	★★	Cybill Shepard, Burt Reynolds	Peter Bogdanovich
Benji	★★★	Peter Breck, Cynthia Smith	Joe Camp
Bite The Bullet	★★★¹/₂	Gene Hackman, Candice Bergen	Richard Brooks
Breakout	★★¹/₂	Charles Bronson, Jill Ireland	Tom Gries
Brief Vacation, A	★★★¹/₂	Florinda Bolkan, Rinato Salvatori	Vittorio de Sica
Cooley High	★★★	Glynn Turmann Cynthia Davis	Michael Schultz
Day of The Locust	★★★¹/₂	Donald Sutherland, Karen Black	John Schlesinger
Dove, The	★★¹/₂	Joseph Bottoms, Deborah Raffin	Charles Jarrott
Drowning Pool, The	★★¹/₂	Paul Newman, Joanne Woodward	Stuart Rosenberg
Earthquake	★★★	Charlton Heston, Ava Gardner	Mark Robson
Eiger Sanction, The	★★¹/₂	Clint Eastwood, Vonetta McGee	Clint Eastwood
Farewell, My Lovely	★★★¹/₂	Robert Mitchum, Sylvia Miles	Dick Richards
Fortune, The	★★¹/₂	Warren Beatty, Stockard Channing	Mike Nichols
Four Musketeers, The	★★★	Michael York, Raquel Welch	Richard Lester
French Connection II, The	★★★★	Gene Hackman, Fernando Rey	John Frankenheimer
Front Page, The	★★★¹/₂	Jack Lemon, Walter Matthau	Billy Wilder
Funny Lady	★★★★	Barbra Streisand, James Caan	Herbert Ross
Gambler, The	★★★¹/₂	James Caan, Paul Sorvino	Karel Reisz
Godfather, Part II, The	★★★★	Al Pacino, Robert DuVall	Francis Ford Coppola
Gold	★★★¹/₂	Roger Moore, Susannah York	Peter Hunt
Great Waldo Pepper, The	★★★	Robert Redford, Bo Swenson	George Roy Hill
Happy Hooker, The	★	Lynn Redgrave, Jean-Pierre Aumont	Nicholas Sgarro
Hearts and Minds	★★★¹/₂	Documentary	Peter Davis
Hennessy	★★¹/₂	Rod Steiger, Lee Remick	Don Sharp
In Celebration	★★¹/₂	Bill Owen, Constance Chapman	Lindsay Anderson
Janis	★★★¹/₂	Documentary	Howard Alk, Seaton Findlay
Jaws	★★★¹/₂	Roy Scheider, Robert Shaw	Steven Spielberg
Klansman, The	★★	Lee Marvin, Richard Burton	Terrence Young
Lacombe, Lucien	★★★¹/₂	Pierre Blaise, Aurore Clement	Louis Malle
Lancelot of The Lake	★★★¹/₂	Luc Simon, Laura Condominas	Robert Bresson
Law and Disorder	★★★¹/₂	Carroll O'Connor, Ernest Borgnine	Ivan Passer
Lenny	★★★¹/₂	Dustin Hoffman, Valerie Perrine	Bob Fosse
Les Violons duBal	★★★¹/₂	Marie-Josee Nat, Jean-Louis Trintignant	Michael Drach
Love and Death	★★★¹/₂	Woody Allen, Diane Keaton	Woody Allen
Macon County Line	★	Alan Vint, Cheryl Waters	Richard Compton
Mandingo	★★¹/₂	James Mason, Susan George	Richard Fleischer
Murder on the Orient Express	★★★¹/₂	Albert Finney, Lauren Bacall	Sidney Lumet
Nashville	★★★★	Karen Black, Henry Gibson	Robert Altman
Night Moves	★★¹/₂	Gene Hackman, Susan Clark	Arthur Penn
Night Porter	★★¹/₂	Dirk Bogarde, Charlotte Rampling	Liliana Cavani
Once Is Not Enough	★★	Kirk Douglas, Alexis Smith	Guy Green
Posse	★★¹/₂	Kirk Douglas, Bruce Dern	Kirk Douglas
Passenger, The	★★★¹/₂	Jack Nicholson, Maria Schneider	Michelangelo Antonioni
Prisoner of Second Avenue	★★★¹/₂	Jack Lemon, Anne Bancroft	Melvin Frank
Rafferty and The Gold Dust Twins	★★★	Alan Arkin, Sally Kellerman	Dick Richards
Report to The Commissioner	★★★¹/₂	Michael Moriarity, Susan Blakley	Milton Katselas
Return of The Pink Panther	★★★★	Peter Sellers, Cathrine Schell	Blake Edwards
Rollerball	★★¹/₂	James Caan, Maude Adams	Norman Jewison
Rosebud	★★	Peter O'Toole, Claude Dauphine	Otto Preminger
Savage Is Loose, The	★★	George C. Scott, Trish Van Devere	George C. Scott
Scenes From A Marriage	★★★★	Liv Ullmann, Erland Josephson	Ingmar Bergman
Shampoo	★★¹/₂	Warren Beatty, Julie Christe	Hal Ashby
Shelia Levine Is Dead and Living in New York	★★	Jeannie Berlin, Roy Scheider	Sidney J. Furie
Stavisky	★★★	Jean-Paul Belmondo, Anny Duperey	Alain Resnais
Stepford Wives	★★	Kathrine Ross, Paula Prentiss	Bryan Forbes
Taking of The Pelham One, Two, Three, The	★★★¹/₂	Walter Matthau, Robert Shaw	Joseph Sargent
Tommy	★★¹/₂	Roger Daltrey, Ann-Margret	Ken Russell
Towering Inferno, The	★★★¹/₂	Steve McQueen, Paul Newman	John Guillermen, Irwin Allen
Trial of Billy Jack, The	★★★	Tom Loughlin, Delores Taylor	Frank Loughlin
White Line Fever	★★¹/₂	Jan-Michael Vincent, Kay Lenz	Jonathan Kaplan
Wind and The Lion, The	★★★	Sean Connery, Candice Bergen	John Milius
Woman Under The Influence, A	★★★★	Peter Falk, Gena Rowlands	John Cassavetes
Young Frankenstein	★★★¹/₂	Gene Wilder, Marty Feldman	Mel Brooks

Famous Paintings and Where You Can See Them

These paintings are listed because of their fame, not necessarily their artistic merit, and because they are in public collections. They are listed chronologically.

Giotto: Pieta, 1305; Arena Chapel, Padua.

Fra Filippo Lippi: Adoration of the Child, c. 1435; Staatliches Museum, Berlin.

Piero Della Francesca: Duke of Urbino, 1465; Uffizi Gallery, Florence.

Giovanni Bellini: Pieta, c. 1466; Brera, Milan.

Botticelli: The Birth of Venus, c. 1480; Uffizi.

Hieronymus Bosch: Christ Crowned with Thorns, c. 1500; National Gallery, London.

Leonardo da Vinci: Mona Lisa (La Gioconda), c. 1505; Louvre, Paris.

Michelangelo: Creation of Adam, 1508-12; Sistine Chapel, Vatican, Rome.

Giorgione: Sleeping Venus, c. 1508, Gemaldegalerie, Dresden.

Raphael: The Sistine Madonna, 1515-19; Gemaldegalerie, Dresden.

Titian: The Tribute Money, 1516; Gemaldegalerie.

Durer: The Four Apostles, 1523-26; Alte Pinakothek, Munich.

Holbein: Henry VIII, 1540; National Gallery, Rome.

Pieter Brueghel the Elder: Massacre of the Innocents, 1566; Kunsthistorisches Museum, Vienna.

El Greco: The Burial of Count Orgaz, 1586; Santo Tome, Toledo, Spain.

Rubens: Venus and Adonis, c. 1620; Met., N. Y.

Frans Hals: Laughing Cavalier, 1624; Wallace Collection, London.

Van Dyck: Charles I of England, c. 1635; Louvre.

Ribera: The Martyrdom of St. Bartholomew, 1630-39; Prado, Madrid.

Rembrandt: The Night Watch, 1642; Rijksmuseum, Amsterdam.

Velasquez: Maids of Honor, 1656; Prado, Madrid.

Vermeer: Young Woman with a Water Jug, c. 1658-64; Met., N.Y.

Ruisdael: View of Haarlem, c. 1670; Rijksmuseum.

Murillo: Virgin and Child, c. 1672; Met., N. Y.

Watteau: The Embarkation for Cythera, c. 1712; Louvre.

Hogarth: The Orgy (Rake's Progress), 1734; Soane's Museum, London.

Fragonard: The Love Letter, c. 1769; Met., N. Y.

Gainsborough: The Blue Boy, c. 1770; Huntington Gallery, San Marino, Cal.

John Singleton Copley: Watson and the Shark, 1778; Museum of Fine Arts, Boston.

Joshua Reynolds: Mrs. Siddons as the Tragic Muse, 1784; Huntington Gallery, San Marino, Cal.

John Trumbull: The Declaration of Independence, 1786-94; Capitol, Washington, D. C.

Gilbert Stuart: George Washington, c. 1795; Museum of Fine Arts, Boston. (Others in Met., N. Y., etc.)

David: The Rape of the Sabines, 1799; Louvre.

Goya: The Naked Maja, 1799; Prado, Madrid.

Ingres: Odalisque, 1814; Louvre.

John Constable: The Hay Wain, 1821; National Gallery, London.

Thomas Lawrence: Calmady Children, 1823; Met., N.Y.

John James Audubon: Birds of America (433 of the original 435 paintings), early 19th Century; New York Historical Society.

Joseph M. W. Turner: The Grand Canal, Venice, early 19th Century; Met., N. Y.

George Caleb Bingham: Fur Traders Descending the Missouri, 1845; Met., N. Y.

Emanuel Leutze: Washington Crossing the Delaware, 1851; Washington Crossing State Park, Pa.

Rosa Bonheur: The Horse Fair, 1855; Met., N.Y.

Jean-Baptiste Corot: Le Lac de Terni, 1861; Corcoran Gallery, Washington.

Honore Daumier: The Third-Class Carriage, c. 1862; Met., N. Y.

Jean-Francois Millet: Man with the Hoe, 1863; San Francisco Museum.

James McNeil Whistler: Arrangement in Grey and Black—The Artist's Mother, c. 1872; Louvre.

Thomas Eakins: The Gross Clinic, 1875; Jefferson Medical College, Philadelphia.

A. M. Willard: Spirit of '76, 1876; (3 versions): Cleveland City Hall; Western Reserve Historical Society, Cleveland; Abbot Hall, Marblehead, Mass.

Edgar Degas: La Danseuse au Bouquet, 1878; Rhode Island School of Design, Providence.

Edouard Manet: In a Boat, 1879; Met., N. Y.

Pierre Auguste Renoir: Luncheon of the Boating Party, 1881; Phillips Collection, Washington.

Georges Seurat: Sunday Afternoon on the Grande Jatte, 1884-86; Art Institute of Chicago.

Paul Cezanne: Mont Sainte-Victoire, 1885-87; Met., N.Y.

Vincent Van Gogh: Wheat Field and Cypress Trees, 1889; National Gallery, London.

Albert Pinkham Ryder: Toilers of the Sea, c. 1890; Addison Gallery, Andover, Mass.

Paul Gauguin: Ia Orana Maria (Hail Mary), 1891; Met., N. Y.

Henri De Toulouse-Lautrec: At the Moulin Rouge, 1892; Art Institute of Chicago.

Claude Monet: Rouen Cathedral, 1894; Met., N. Y.

Winslow Homer: Gulf Stream, 1899; Art Institute of Chicago.

John Singer Sargent: Wyndham Sisters, 1900; Met., N.Y.

Frederic Remington: Cavalry Charge on the Southern Plains, 1907; Met., N. Y.

Georges Braque: Head of a Woman, 1909; Musee d'Art Moderne, Paris.

Henri Rousseau: The Dream, 1910; Modern Art, N. Y.

Marc Chagall: I and the Village, 1911; Modern Art, N. Y.

Marcel Duchamp: Nude Descending a Staircase, 1912; Philadelphia Museum of Art.

Paul Chabas: September Morn, 1912; Met., N. Y.

Amadeo Modigliani: Portrait of Madame Zboroski, 1917-18; Rhode Island School of Design, Providence.

Piet Mondrian: Composition, 1921; Kunstmuseum, Basel, Switzerland.

Paul Klee: Twittering Machine, 1922; Modern Art, N. Y.

George Bellows: The Dempsey-Firpo Fight, 1924; Whitney Museum of American Art, N. Y.

Vasily Kandinsky: Several Circles, 1926; Guggenheim Museum, N. Y.

Henri Matisse: Odalisque, 1928; Musee d'Art Moderne, Paris.

Grant Wood: American Gothic, 1930; Art Institute of Chicago.

Joan Miro: Man, Woman and Child, 1931; Philadelphia Museum of Art.

Jose Clemente Orozco: Zapatistas, 1931; Modern Art, N. Y.

Maurice Utrillo: Sacred-Heart and Montmartre Square, 1932; Musee d'Art et d'Histoire, Geneva.

William Gropper: The Senate, 1935; Modern Art, N. Y.

Pablo Picasso: Guernica, 1937; Modern Art, N. Y.

Georges Rouault: The Old King, 1937; Carnegie Institute Museum, Pittsburgh.

Thomas Hart Benton: Threshing Wheat, 1939; Swope Gallery, Terre Haute, Ind.

John Steuart Curry: John Brown, 1939; Met., N. Y.

Anna (Grandma) Moses: The Thanksgiving Turkey, 1943; Met., N. Y.

Andrew Wyeth: Christina's World, 1948; Modern Art, N. Y.

Jackson Pollock: Autumn Rhythm, 1950; Met., N. Y.

Salvador Dali: Crucifixion, 1954; Met., N. Y.

Raphael Soyer: Hugo Kastor, 1957; Met., N. Y.

Famous Sculptures and Where You Can See Them

The statues, monuments, and other sculptures in the following list have been chosen because of the fame they have won, independent of their artistic merit, and because they are on public view. They are listed chronologically, except for the group titled Non-Western. Some of the works are representative of a famed artist, many of whose works are equally well-known. The creators of some of the earliest works are unknown.

Ancient Egypt

The Great Sphinx, c. 2900 B.C., limestone and masonry; Giza, Egypt.

Queen Nefertiti, c. 1365 B.C., painted limestone; State Museum, West Berlin.

Colossi of Ramses II, c. 1230 B.C., sandstone; Abu Simbel, Egypt.

Ancient Greece

Charioteer of Delphi, c. 470 B.C., bronze; Delphi, Greece, Museum.

Myron: Discobolus (Discus Thrower), marble Roman copy of Myron's bronze original of c. 450 B.C.; Terme Museum, Rome.

Phidias: Parthenon Sculptures, c. 438 B.C., marble (by or under direction of Phidias); British Museum, London.

Polyclitus: Doryphorus (Spear Bearer), marble Roman copy of Polyclitus original of late 5th Century B.C.; National Museum, Naples.

Praxiteles: Hermes with the Infant Dionysus, c. 350 B.C., Museum, Olympia; **Aphrodite of Cnidus,** marble Roman copy of Praxiteles' original of 330 B.C.; Vatican, Rome.

Scopas: Head from the Temple at Tegea, c. 350 B.C.; National Museum, Athens.

Lysippus: Apoxyomenos (athlete cleansing himself with a scraper), marble Roman copy of Lysippus' bronze original of 330 B.C.; Vatican, Rome.

Nike of Samothrace (Winged Victory), c. 300 B.C., marble; Louvre, Paris.

Aphrodite of Melos (Venus de Milo), 2d Century B.C., marble; Louvre, Paris.

Laocoon, 2d Century B.C., marble, by Agesander, Athenodorus, and Polydorus of Rhodes; Vatican, Rome.

Ancient Rome

Augustus, c. 20 B.C., marble; Vatican, Rome.

Caracalla, 211-217 A.D., marble; National Museum, Naples.

Gothic

Virgin of Paris, early 14th Century, stone; Notre Dame Cathedral, Paris.

Claus Sluter: Moses, c. 1400, stone; Champmol Monastery, near Dijon.

Tomb of Philippe Pot, c. 1480, painted stone; Louvre, Paris.

Renaissance

Donatello: St. George, c. 1415, marble; National Museum, Florence; **Gattamelata,** 1445-50, bronze; Piazza del Santo, Padua.

Andrea del Verrocchio: Colleoni, c. 1485, bronze; Campo SS. Giovani e Paolo, Venice.

Michelangelo Buonarroti: David, 1501-04, marble; Academy, Florence; **Pieta,** 1498-99, marble; St. Peter's, Rome.

Benvenuto Cellini: Perseus with the Head of Medusa, 16th Century, marble; Loggia dei Lanzi, Florence.

Gianlorenzo Bernini: Ecstasy of St. Theresa, 1645-52, marble; Santa Maria della Vittoria Church, Rome.

Non-Western

Buddha Vairocana, 8th Century A.D., bronze; Nara, Japan.

Thaloc (Toltec Rain God), 900 A.D. or earlier, stone; Anthropology Museum, Mexico City.

Amida Buddha, 1252, bronze; Kamakura, Japan.

Aztec Calendar Stone, 1427-29, painted volcanic rock; Anthropology Museum, Mexico City.

Stone Heads, 17th Century or earlier, Easter Island.

Mask with Horns, 19th Century, wood, from southeast Congo (Baluba); Royal Museum of Central Africa, Tervuren, Belgium.

Buddha, 1960, concrete; Changhua, Taiwan.

18th-19th Centuries

Jean Antoine Houdon: George Washington, 1788-92, marble; State Capitol, Richmond, Va.

Thomas Crawford: Statue of Freedom, bronze, 1863; atop the Capitol dome, Washington, D. C.

Frederic Auguste Bartholdi: Liberty Enlightening the World, 1886, copper on steel frame; Liberty Is., N.Y.

Auguste Rodin: The Thinker, 1879-89, bronze; Metropolitan Museum of Art, N. Y.

Augustus St. Gaudens: Abraham Lincoln, 1887, bronze; Lincoln Park, Chicago.

John Quincy Adams Ward: Henry Ward Beecher, bronze, 1891; Cadman Plaza, Brooklyn, N. Y.

20th Century

Aristide Maillol: The Mediterranean, 1902-05, bronze; Museum of Modern Art, N. Y.

Mateo Alonso: Christ of the Andes, 1904, bronze; Uspallata Pass, Chile-Argentina border.

Ivan Mestrovic: My Mother, 1908, marble; State Museum, Belgrade.

Constantin Brancusi: The Kiss, 1908, stone; Philadelphia Museum of Art; **Bird in Space,** 1927, bronze; Museum of Modern Art, N. Y.

Wilhelm Lehmbruck: Kneeling Woman, 1911, cast stone; Museum of Modern Art, N. Y.

Edvard Erichsen: The Little Mermaid, 1913, bronze, Copenhagen harbor.

Daniel Chester French: Abraham Lincoln, 1922, marble; Lincoln Memorial, Washington, D. C.

William Zorach: Child with Cat, 1926, marble; Museum of Modern Art, N. Y.

Gaston Lachaise: Standing Woman, 1912-27, bronze; Albright Art Gallery, Buffalo.

Ernst Barlach: Hovering Angel, 1927, bronze; Antoniter Church, Cologne.

Jacob Epstein: Madonna and Child, 1927, bronze; Riverside Church, N. Y.

Heitor da Silva Costa and Paul Landowski: Christ the Redeemer, 1931, reinforced concrete; Corcavado Mtn., Rio de Janeiro.

Vernon March: Canadian War Memorial, 1926-32 (dedicated 1939), bronze; Confederation Sq., Ottawa.

Paul Manship: Prometheus, 1934, bronze and goldleaf; Rockefeller Center, N. Y.

Alexander Calder: Lobster Trap and Fish Tail, 1939, steel wire, aluminum; Museum of Modern Art, N. Y.

Carl Milles: Meeting of the Waters Fountain, 1940; Aloe Plaza, St. Louis; **Millesgarden Sculptures,** Stockholm.

Gutzon Borglum: Mt. Rushmore Natl. Memorial, 1927-41, granite; near Keystone, S.D.

Gustav Vigeland: Sculpture Park, 1906-43, stone and bronze, Oslo.

Pablo Picasso: She-Goat, bronze, 1950; Museum of Modern Art, N.Y.

Felix de Weldon: Marine Corps War Memorial (Iwo Jima Flag-Raising), 1954, bronze; near Arlington National Cemetery, Va.

Jose de Creeft: Alice in Wonderland, 1959, bronze; Conservatory Lake, Central Park, N. Y.

Henry Moore: Reclining Figure, 1963-65, bronze; Lincoln Center, N. Y.

Selected U.S. Daily Newspapers' Circulation

Source: Audit Bureau of Circulations' FAS-FAX Report. Average paid circulation for 6 months to Mar. 31, 1975. †3 months to Mar. 31, 1975. °6 months to Sept. 30, 1974. On Sept. 30, 1974, there were 1,713 English language dailies in the U.S. (334 morning, 1,363 evening, 16 all day). Audited circulation was 62,419,760. Sunday papers numbered 615, with audited circulation of 50,636,808. (m) morning; (e) evening; *Mon.-Fri. average. Brackets indicate joint publication.

Newspaper	Daily	Sunday
Albany, N.Y. Times-Union (m)	{76,009	133,032
Albany, N.Y. Knickerbocker	}	
News-Union Star (e)	{63,257	
Akron Beacon Journal (e)	170,714	213,225
Allentown Call-Chronicle (m&e)	*123,700	151,512
Atlanta Constitution (m)	}214,294	
Atlanta Journal (e)	{244,222	539,403
Baltimore News-American (e)	*202,895	275,679
Baltimore Sun (m&e)	*363,244	340,441
Birmingham News (e)	{*181,153	219,220
Birmingham Post-Herald (m)	{ *73,943	
Boston Globe (m&e)	*475,346	583,787
Boston Herald American (m) &		
Sunday Advertiser	*338,786	496,312
Buffalo Courier-Express (m)	121,279	271,087
Buffalo News (e)	*279,753	
Charlotte News (e)	{ 58,654	
Charlotte Observer (m)	{164,943	215,475
Chicago News (e)	{*425,220	
Chicago Sun-Times (m)	{*567,780	700,918
Chicago Tribune	*806,083	1,112,638
Christian Science Monitor (m)	*202,065	
Cincinnati Enquirer (m)	188,791	283,712
Cincinnati Post (e)	216,713	
Cleveland Plain Dealer (m)	378,388	462,458
Cleveland Press (e)	357,147	
Columbia, S.C. State (m)	{103,004	121,249
Columbia, S.C. Record (e)	{ 31,915	
Columbus, Ga. Enquirer (m)	{*31,361	61,450
Columbus, Ga. Ledger (e)	{*30,371	
Columbus, O. Citizen-Journal (m)	111,324	
Columbus, O. Dispatch (e)	202,407	326,956
Dallas News (m)	259,276	314,588
Dallas Times Herald (e)	*223,821	301,144
Dayton Journal Herald (m)	102,651	
Dayton News (e)	150,516	219,032
Denver Post (e)	*251,282	343,136
Denver: Rocky Mountain News (m)	219,341	244,428
Des Moines Register (m)	{237,336	455,901
Des Moines Tribune (e)	{ 99,256	
Detroit Free Press (m)	*615,774	737,461
Detroit News (e)	*635,669	819,920
Ft. Worth Star-Telegram (m&e)	219,570	219,459
Fresno Bee (e)	114,396	140,772
Grand Rapids Press (e)	126,640	135,651
Hackensack Record (e)	**151,010	†191,298
Hartford Courant (m)	177,293	237,323
Hartford Times (e)	*83,642	81,205
Honolulu Advertiser (m)	{ 75,022	
Honolulu Star-Bulletin (e)	{118,199	183,039
Houston Chronicle (e)	*298,991	369,288
Houston Post (m)	*294,556	349,068
Indianapolis News (e)	{*161,751	
Indianapolis Star (m)	{†217,901	†357,834
Jacksonville Journal (e)	{ 57,966	
Jacksonville: Fla. Times Union (m)	{147,769	179,351
Kansas City Star (e)	{293,365	389,021
Kansas City Times (m)	{315,497	
Knoxville News-Sentinel (e)	105,550	162,434
Little Rock: Ark. Democrat (e)	*63,369	95,844
Little Rock: Ark. Gazette (m)	*121,135	143,635
Long Beach Independent (m)	{*57,226	141,291
Long Beach Press-Telegram (e)	{*96,448	
Los Angeles Herald-Examiner (e)	*394,910	389,374
Los Angeles Times (m)	1,024,040	1,230,468
Louisville Courier-Journal (m)	{220,469	354,186
Louisville Times (e)	{165,880	
Memphis Commercial Appeal (m)	{210,447	289,090
Memphis Press Scimitar (e)	{115,652	
Miami Herald (m)	{420,348	527,537
Miami News (e)	{*81,501	
Milwaukee Journal (e)	{347,364	537,612
Milwaukee Sentinel (m)	{168,407	
Minneapolis Star (e)	{250,238	
Minneapolis Tribune (m)	{229,549	615,169
Nashville Banner (e)	88,068	
Nashville Tennessean (m)	128,633	225,127
New Haven Register (e)	{*103,363	128,944
New Haven Journal-Courier (m)	{ *30,893	
New Orleans Times-Picayune (m)	{206,960	†309,288
New Orleans States-Item (e)	{**121,220	
New York: Long Island Press (e)	312,675	297,170
New York: Newsday (e)	450,923	394,375
New York News (m)	*1,967,116	2,827,760
New York Post (e)	*583,892	
New York Times (m)	*870,510	1,459,318
Newark Star-Ledger (m)	*364,697	559,394
Norfolk Ledger-Star (e)	{ †95,834	
Norfolk Virginian-Pilot (m)	{†125,641	†184,390
Oakland Tribune (e)	*164,442	194,325
Oklahoma City Oklahoman (m)	{*176,941	292,267
Oklahoma City Times (e)	{ *95,236	
Omaha World-Herald (m&e)	*238,181	275,752
Orlando Sentinel-Star (m&e)	*181,914	213,043
Philadelphia Bulletin (e)	*574,346	669,430
Philadelphia Inquirer (m)	°*427,251	°824,023
Philadelphia News (e)	*237,995	
Phoenix Republic (m)	{†217,700	†323,104
Phoenix Gazette (e)	{†108,880	
Pittsburgh Post Gazette (m)	*196,709	
Pittsburgh Press (e)	*283,017	676,136
Portland, Me. Press-Herald (m)	{53,483	
Portland, Me. Express (e) & Maine	}	
Sunday.Telegram	{29,590	107,838
Portland Oregonian (m)	226,524	393,072
Portland: Oregon Journal (e)	*109,935	
Providence Journal (m)	*67,085	209,620
Providence Bulletin (e)	*145,180	
Raleigh News & Observer (m)	{129,438	157,248
Raleigh Times (e)	{ 32,534	
Richmond News Leader (e)	{113,669	
Richmond Times Dispatch (m)	{132,367	196,510
Rochester Democrat-Chronicle (m)	{131,332	221,238
Rochester Times-Union (e)	{137,071	
Sacramento Bee (e)	*170,025	200,370
Sacramento Union (e)	*95,834	90,794
St. Louis Globe-Democrat (m)	*270,516	271,136
St. Louis Post-Dispatch (e)	*279,015	472,468
St. Paul Dispatch (e)	{122,430	
St. Paul Pioneer Press (m)	{104,070	238,321
St. Petersburg Independent (e)	{ 33,734	
St. Petersburg Times (m)	{198,532	245,824
Salt Lake Tribune (m)	{99,918	170,276
Salt Lake City Deseret News (e)	{71,613	
San Antonio Express (m)	{*80,839	158,236
San Antonio News (e)	{*72,612	
San Antonio Light (e)	*128,258	175,492
San Diego Union (m)	†180,417	†290,231
San Diego Tribune (e)	*128,089	
San Francisco Examiner (e)	{*163,391	
San Francisco Chronicle (m)	{*457,310	642,194
San Jose Mercury (m)	{133,543	226,489
San Jose News (e)	{ 67,422	
Santa Ana Register (m&e)	*193,595	218,144
Seattle Post-Intelligencer (m)	*195,970	250,978
Seattle Times (e)	*226,773	299,721
South Bend Tribune (e)	115,327	124,621
Spokane Chronicle (e)	{64,051	
Spokane Spokesman-Review (m)	{78,912	125,318
Springfield, Ill. State Journal-		
Register (m&e)	73,163	71,801
Springfield, Mass. Union (m)	{75,719	
Springfield, Mass. News (e) &	}	
Sunday Republican	{82,513	137,810
Syracuse Herald-Journal (e) &		
Sun. Herald-American	{122,870	240,287
Syracuse Post-Standard (m)	{*80,855	
Tampa Tribune (m)	{175,416	210,461
Tampa Times (e)	{ 22,602	
Toledo Blade (e)	170,954	207,739
Tulsa Tribune (e)	} †79,262	
Tulsa World (m)	{†116,333	†200,764
Wall St. Journal (m) (total)	*1,463,641	
Washington, D.C. Post (m)	*536,350	725,241
Washington, D.C. Star (e)	*369,626	350,836
West Palm Beach Post (m)	{*73,610	109,263
West Palm Beach Times (e)	{*31,258	
Wichita Eagle (m)	{120,851	178,213
Wichita Beacon (e)	{ 51,376	
Winston-Salem Journal (m)	{66,798	89,688
Winston-Salem Sentinel (e)	{39,381	
Youngstown Vindicator (e)	†99,439	†155,328

Circulation of Leading U.S. Magazines

Source: Audit Bureau of Circulations' FAS-FAX Report

General magazines, exclusive of groups and comics. Based on total average paid circulation during the 6 months prior to Dec. 31, 1974. *Indicates circulation for the 6 months prior to Dec. 31, 1973.

TV Guide	19,382,471	Seventeen	1,500,635	American Girl	690,868
Reader's Digest	18,000,607	Today's Education	1,485,014	Modern Romances	688,226
Natl. Geographic	8,868,656	Playgirl	1,421,809	New Ingenue	680,070
Family Circle	8,326,379	Sport	1,350,134	Motor Trend	679,533
Woman's Day	8,112,263	Oui	1,339,106	TV Radio Mirror	676,598
Better Homes &		Sports Afield	1,317,402	Popular Photo'y	675,238
Gardens	7,895,879	Sunset	1,280,331	Lion Magazine	672,743
McCall's	7,511,034	Ebony	1,271,359	Smithsonian	664,480
Ladies' Home Jour	7,064,190	Esquire	1,238,412	Decorating & Craft	650,921
Playboy	6,125,330	Grit	1,226,812	Vogue & Vanity Fair	641,174
Good Housekeeping	5,458,448	Scouting	1,224,827	Forbes	627,487
Redbook	4,754,981	Southern Living	1,147,312	Flower & Garden	627,162
Time	4,307,638	Photoplay	1,109,990	Jet	626,262
Penthouse	4,000,147	True	1,096,444	Sat'day Evening Post	625,779*
National Equirer	3,806,252	House & Garden	1,095,009	Sphere Magazine	616,811*
Sr. Scholastic Unit	2,953,067	People	1,060,345	Fortune	598,984
Newsweek	2,933,158	Jr. Scholastic	1,055,129	Scientific American	597,054
American Legion	2,640,748	Psychology Today	975,996	Viva	577,105
American Home	2,600,022	Argosy	967,404	Gourmet	556,542
Sports Illustrated	2,277,801	Nation's Business	932,951	Golf	553,281
Workbasket	2,093,462	Midnight	928,832	Weight Watchers	551,814
Boy's Life	2,059,423	Family Health	914,819	Money	530,721
U.S. News & World		Co-ed	887,844	Saturday Rev/World	524,055
Report	2,039,448	National Lampoon	886,597	Catholic Digest	520,979*
True Story	1,933,165	House Beautiful	871,379	Harper's Bazaar	504,045
Cosmopolitan	1,932,134	Hot Rod	853,509	National Observer	503,089
Field & Stream	1,924,758	Mademoiselle	832,427	Modern Photo'y	495,844
Parent's Magazine	1,923,933	'Teen	826,318	New Yorker	487,206
Outdoor Life	1,901,536	Modern Screen	769,817	Apartment Life	482,182
Popular Science	1,768,672	Family Handyman	750,423*	Holiday	463,850
Popular Mechanics	1,750,486	Business Week	748,572	Skiing	456,822
V.F.W. Magazine	1,743,684	Signature	731,524*	Rotarian	451,085
Glamour	1,684,657	Car & Driver	700,440	Capper's Weekly	450,282
Elks Magazine	1,568,815	Simplicity Home Cat	697,060*	Cycle	438,716
Mechanix Illus	1,549,319	Golf Digest	695,998	Westways	437,297

Sunday Magazines Weekly Circulation

Family Weekly 10,700,000   Parade 19,072,000

Canadian Daily Newspapers of Large Circulation

Source: Audit Bureau of Circulations' FAS-FAX Report of average paid circulation for 6 months ending Mar. 31, 1975. (†) Indicates 3 month circulation average.

As of Sept. 30, 1974, there were 102 English language and 12 French language daily newspapers in Canada (23 morning; 91 evening) with a combined circulation of 4,827,337. Sunday newspapers numbered 9 with a total circulation of 883,501.

(m) Morning; (e) Evening; *Based on Monday to Friday average. Brackets indicate joint publication.

Newspaper	Daily	Sunday	Newspaper	Daily	Sunday
Calgary Albertan (m)	*34,441		Regina Leader Post (e)	66,336	
Calgary Herald (e)	116,974		St. Catharines Standard (e)	†39,379	
Edmonton Journal (e)	167,754		St. John's Telegram (e)	*30,765	
Halifax Chronicle-Herald (m)	{ 68,571		Saint John Telegraph-Journal (m)	{ 33,368	
Halifax Mail-Star (e)	{ 50,331		Saint John Times Globe (e)	{ 28,940	
Hamilton Spectator (e)	†137,226		Saskatoon Star-Phoenix (e)	49,189	
Kitchener-Waterloo Record (e)	†63,667		Sherbrooke: La Tribune (e)	38,858	
London Free Press (m & e)	125,817		Sudbury Star (e)	34,263	
Moncton Times (m)	{ 17,902		Toronto Globe and Mail (m)	254,050	
Moncton Transcript (e)	{ 22,325		Toronto Star (e)	540,354	
Montreal Gazette (m)	120,437		Toronto Sun (m)	*105,508	161,305
Montreal: La Presse (e)	195,632		Trois Rivieres Nouvelliste (e)	50,148	
Montreal: Le Devoir (m)	30,627		Vancouver Province (m)	127,467	
Montreal: Le Journal de Montreal (m)	*147,346	148,150	Vancouver Sun (e)	245,971	
Montreal-Matin (m)	*125,667	102,378	Victoria Colonist (m)'	{ 37,771	43,454
Montreal Star (e)	177,540		Victoria Times (e)	{ 28,434	
Ottawa Citizen (e)	93,215		Windsor Star (e)	84,013	
Ottawa Journal (e)	80,737		Winnipeg Free Press (e)	136,663	
Ottawa: Le Droit (e)	43,191		Winnipeg Tribune (e)	70,167	
Quebec: Le Soleil (e)	136,434		(1) Excludes Monday		

Circulation of Leading Canadian Magazines

Source: Audit Bureau of Circulations' FAS-FAX Report.

General magazines, exclusive of groups and comics. Statistics based on average paid circulation during the 6 months prior to Dec. 31, 1974.

Magazine	Circulation	Magazine	Circulation	Magazine	Circulation
Reader's Digest		Maclean's Magazine		Chatelaine (French)	263,212
(English-French)	1,496,657	(English-French)	879,904	T.V. Hebdo	243,788
Chatelaine (English-French)	1,250,307	Maclean's Magazine (English)	731,015	Miss Chatelaine	154,238
		Time Canada	549,785	La Maclean	148,889
Reader's Digest (English)	1,230,308	Legion Magazine	392,643	Actualite	139,551
Chatelaine (English)	987,095	Selection du Reader's Digest	266,349	Canadian Motorist	122,511

WORLD FACTS
Early Explorers of the Western Hemisphere

The first men to discover the New World or Western Hemisphere are believed to have walked across a "land bridge" from Siberia to Alaska, an isthmus since broken by the Bering Strait. From Alaska, these ancestors of the Indians spread through North, Central, and South America. Anthropologists have placed these crossings at between 18,000 and 14,000 B.C.; but evidence found in 1967 near Puebla, Mex., indicates mankind reached there as early as 35,000-40,-000 years ago.

At first, these people were hunters using flint weapons and tools. In Mexico, about 7000-6000 B.C., they founded farming cultures, developing corn, squash, etc. Eventually, they created complex civilizations — Olmec, Toltec, Aztec, and Maya and, in South America, Inca. Carbon-14 tests show men lived about 8000 B.C. near what are now Front Royal, Va., Kanawha, W. Va., and Dutchess Quarry, N.Y. The Hopewell Culture, based on farming, flourished about 1000 B.C.; remains of it are seen today in large mounds in Ohio and other states.

Norsemen (Norwegian Vikings sailing out of Iceland and Greenland) are credited by most scholars with being the first Europeans to discover America, with at least five voyages around 1000 A.D. to areas they called Helluland, Markland, and Vinland—possibly Labrador, Nova Scotia or Newfoundland, and New England.

The remains of a settlement at L'Anse-aux-Meadows, near the northern tip of Newfoundland, were uncovered by Dr. and Mrs. Helge Ingstad, Norwegian archeologists, 1960-63, with the aid of a grant from the National Geographic Society. They identified the settlement as Norse. Carbon-14 tests from hearths and the remains of a smithy indicated the site was occupied about 900 A.D. and during several hundred years before and after.

Christopher Columbus, most famous of the explorers, was born at Genoa, Italy, but made his discoveries sailing for the Spanish rulers Ferdinand and Isabella. Dates of his voyages, places he discovered, and other information follow:

1492—First voyage. Left Palos, Spain, Aug. 3 with 88 men (est.). Discovered San Salvador (Guanahani or Watling Is., Bahamas) Oct. 12. Also Cuba, Hispaniola (Haiti-Dominican Republic); built Fort La Navidad on latter.

1493—Second voyage, first part, Sept. 25, with 17 ships, 1,500 men. Dominica (Lesser Antilles) Nov. 3; Guadaloupe, Montserrat, Antigua, San Martin, Santa Cruz, Puerto Rico, Virgin Islands. Settled Isabela on Hispaniola. **Second part** (Columbus having remained in Western Hemisphere). Jamaica, Isle of Pines, La Mona Is.

1498—Third voyage. Left Spain May 30, 1498, 6 ships. Discovered Trinidad. Saw South American continent Aug. 1, 1498, but called it Isla Sancta (Holy Island). Entered Gulf of Paria and landed, first time on continental soil. At mouth of Orinoco Aug. 14 he decided this was mainland.

1502—Fourth voyage, 4 caravels, 150 men. St. Lucia, Guanaja off Honduras; Cape Gracias a Dios, Honduras; San Juan River, Costa Rica; Almirante, Portobelo, and Laguna de Chiriqui, Panama.

A.D.	Explorer	Nationality and Employer	Discovery or Exploration
1497	John Cabot	Italian-English	Newfoundland or Nova Scotia
1498	John and Sebastian Cabot	Italian-English	Labrador to Hatteras
1499	Alonso de Ojeda	Spanish	South American coast, Venezuela
1500, Feb.	Vicente y Pinzon	Spanish	South American coast, Amazon River
1500, Apr.	Pedro Alvarez Cabral	Portuguese	Brazil (for Portugal)
1500-02	Gaspar Corte-Real	Portuguese	Labrador
1501	Rodrigo de Bastidas	Spanish	Central America
1513	Vasco Nunez de Balboa	Spanish	Pacific Ocean
1513	Juan Ponce de Leon	Spanish	Florida
1515	Juan de Solis	Spanish	Rio de la Plata
1519	Alonso de Pineda	Spanish	Mouth of Mississippi River
1519	Hernando Cortes	Spanish	Mexico
1520	Ferdinand Magellan	Portuguese-Spanish	Straits of Magellan, Tierra del Fuego
1524	Giovanni da Verrazano	Italian-French	Atlantic Coast-New York harbor
1531	Alfonso de Souza	Portuguese	Rio de Janeiro
1532	Francisco Pizarro	Spanish	Peru
1534	Jacques Cartier	French	Canada, Gulf of St. Lawrence
1536	Pedro de Mendoza	Spanish	Buenos Aires
1536	A. N. Cabeza de Vaca	Spanish	Texas coast and interior
1539	Francisco de Ulloa	Spanish	California coast
1539-41	Hernando de Soto	Italian-Spanish	Mississippi River near Memphis
1539	Marcos de Niza	Spanish	Southwest (now U.S.)
1540	Francisco V. de Coronado	Spanish	Southwest (now U.S.)
1540	Hernando Alarcon	Spanish	Colorado River
1540	Garcia de L. Cardenas	Spanish	Grand Canyon of the Colorado
1541	Francisco de Orellana	Spanish	Amazon River
1542	Juan Rodriquez Cabrillo	Portuguese-Spanish	San Diego harbor
1565	Pedro Menendez	Spanish	St. Augustine
1573	Pedro Marquez	Spanish	Chesapeake Bay
1576	Martin Frobisher	English	Frobisher's Bay, Canada
1577-80	Francis Drake	English	California coast
1582	Antonio de Espejo	Spanish	Southwest (named New Mexico)
1584	Amadas & Barlow (for Raleigh)	English	Virginia
1585-87	Sir Walter Raleigh's men	English	Roanoke Is., N.C.
1595	Sir Walter Raleigh	English	Orinoco River
1602	Bartholomew Gosnold	English	Martha's Vineyard and Massachusetts
1603-09	Samuel de Champlain	French	Canadian interior, Lake Champlain
1604	Samuel de Champlain	French	Mt. Desert Island
1607	Capt. John Smith	English	Atlantic coast
1609-10	Henry Hudson	English-Dutch	Hudson River, Hudson Bay
1634	Jean Nicolet	French	Lake Michigan; Wisconsin
1673	Jacques Marquette, Louis Jolliet	French	Mississippi S to Arkansas

Continued
1682 . . . . Sieur de la Salle . . . . French . . . . Mississippi S to Gulf of Mexico
1789 . . . . Alexander Mackenzie . . . . Canadian . . . . Canadian Northwest

Arctic Exploration

Early Explorers

1587 — John Davis (England). Davis Strait to Sanderson's Hope, 72° 12′ N.

1596 — Willem Barents and Jacob van Heemskerck (Holland). Discovered Bear Island, touched northwest tip of Spitsbergen, 79°49′ N, rounded Novaya Zemlya, wintered at Ice Haven.

1607 — Henry Hudson (England). North along Greenland's east coast to Cape Hold-with-Hope, 73° 30′, then north of Spitsbergen to 80° 23′. Returning he discovered Hudson's Touches (Jan Mayen).

1616 — William Baffin and Robert Bylot (England). Baffin Bay to Smith Sound.

1728 — Vitus Bering (Russia). Proved Asia and America were separate by sailing through strait.

1733-40 — Great Northern Expedition (Russia). Surveyed Siberian Arctic coast.

1741 — Vitus Bering (Russia). Sighted Alaska from sea, named Mount St. Elias. His lieutenant, Chirikof, discovered coast.

1771 — Samuel Hearne (Hudson's Bay Co.). Overland from Prince of Wales Fort (Churchill) on Hudson Bay to mouth of Coppermine River.

1778 — James Cook (Britain). Through Bering Strait to Icy Cape, Alaska, and North Cape, Siberia.

1789 — Alexander Mackenzie (North West Co., Britain). Montreal to mouth of Mackenzie River.

1806 — William Scoresby (Britain). North of Spitsbergen to 81° 30′.

1820-3 — Ferdinand von Wrangel (Russia). Completed a survey of Siberian Arctic coast. His exploration joined that of James Cook at North Cape, confirming separation of the continents.

1845 — Sir John Franklin (Britain) was one of many to seek the Northwest Passage — an ocean route connecting the Atlantic and Pacific via the Arctic. His two ships (the Erebus and Terror) were last seen entering Lancaster Sound Jul. 26.

1888 — Fridtjof Nansen (Norway) crossed Greenland's icecap, 1893-96 — Nansen in Fram drifted from New Siberian Is. to Spitsbergen; tried polar dash in 1895, reached Franz Josef Land.

1896 — Salomon A. Andree (Sweden) and companion, in June, made first attempt to reach North Pole by balloon; failed and returned in August. On Jul. 11, 1897, Andree and 2 others started in balloon from Danes Is., Spitsbergen, to drift across pole to America, and disappeared. Over 33 years later, Aug. 6, 1930, Dr. Gunnar Horn (Norway) found their frozen bodies on White Is., 82° 57′ N. 29° 52′ E.

1903-06 — Roald Amundsen (Norway) first sailed Northwest Passage.

Discovery of North Pole

Robert E. Peary began exploring in 1886 on Greenland, when he was 30. With his hq. at McCormick Bay he explored Greenland's coast 1891-92, tried for North Pole 1893, returned with large meteorites. In 1900 he reached northern limit of Greenland and 83° 50′ N; in 1902 he reached 84° 06′N; in 1906 he went from Ellesmere Is. to 87° 06′N. He sailed in the Roosevelt, Jul., 1908, to winter off Cape Sheridan, Grant Land. The dash for the North Pole began Mar. 1 from

Cape Columbia, Ellesmere Land. Peary reached the pole, 90° N, Apr. 6, 1909.

Peary had several supporting groups carrying supplies until the last group, under Capt. Robt. A. Bartlett, turned back at 87° 47′N. Peary, Matthew Henson, and 4 Eskimos proceeded with dog teams and sleds. They crossed the pole several times, finally built an igloo at 90°, remained 36 hours. Started south Apr. 7 at 4 p.m. for Cape Columbia. Eskimos were Coqueeh, Ootah, Eginwah, and Seegloo. Adm. Peary died Feb. 20, 1920. Henson, a Negro, born Aug. 8, 1866, died in New York, N.Y., Mar. 9, 1955, aged 88. Ootah, the last survivor, died near Thule, Greenland, May, 1955, aged 80.

1914 — Donald Macmillan (U.S.). Northwest, 200 miles, from Axel Hieberg Island to seek Peary's Crocker Land.

1915-17 — Vihjalmur Stefansson (Canada) discovered Borden, Brock, Meighen, and Lougheed Islands.

1918-20 — Amundsen sailed Northeast Passage.

1926 — Richard E. Byrd and Floyd Bennett (U.S.) reached 87° 44′N. in attempt to fly to North Pole from Spitsbergen.

1926 — Richard E. Byrd and Floyd Bennett (U.S.) first over North Pole by air, May 9.

1926 — Amundsen, Ellsworth, and Umberto Nobile (Italy) flew from Spitsbergen over North Pole May 12, to Teller, Alaska, in dirigible Norge.

1928 — Nobile crossed North Pole in airship Italia May 24, crashed May 25. Amundsen lost while trying to effect rescue by plane.

1928 — Sir Hubert Wilkins and Eielson flew from Point Barrow to Spitsbergen, 84° N.

Submarine Records

On Aug. 3, 1958, the Nautilus, under Comdr. William R. Anderson, became the first ship to cross the North Pole beneath the Arctic ice.

On Aug. 12, 1958, the nuclear submarine Skate, Comdr. James F. Calvert, became the second ship to make an underwater crossing of the North Pole.

In March, 1959, the Skate returned to the Arctic and, on its third attempt, broke through at the North Pole, the first time any ship had been on the surface at 90° N.

The nuclear-powered U. S. submarine Seadragon, Comdr. George P. Steele 2d, made the first east-west underwater transit through the Northwest Passage during August, 1960. It sailed from Portsmouth, N.H., headed between Greenland and Labrador through Baffin Bay, then west through Lancaster Sound and McClure Strait to the Beaufort Sea. Traveling submerged for the most part, the submarine made 850 miles from Baffin Bay to the Beaufort Sea in six days. The vessel made a 300-foot dive to sail under an iceberg in Baffin Bay.

In February, 1960, the nuclear submarine Sargo traveled under the Arctic ice pack to and around the North Pole. The Sargo departed from and returned to Honolulu, and spent 31 days and 4 hours under the ice. The submarine successfully smashed its way through ice three feet thick.

Antarctic Exploration

Early History

Antarctica has been approached since 1773-75, when Capt. Jas. Cook (Britain) reached 71°10′S. Many sea and landmarks bear names of early explorers. Bellingshausen (Russia) discovered Peter I and Alexander I Islands, 1819-21. Nathaniel Palmer (U.S.) discovered Palmer Peninsula, 60°W, 1820, without realizing that this was a continent. Jas. Weddell (Britain) found Weddell Sea, 74°15′S, 1823.

First to announce existence of the continent of Antarctic was Charles Wilkes (U.S.), who followed

the coast for 1,500 mi., 1840. Adelie Coast, 140° E. was found by Dumont d'Urville (France), 1840. Ross Ice Shelf was found by Jas. Clark Ross (Britain), 1841-42.

1895 — Leonard Kristensen, Norwegian whaling captain, landed a party on the coast of Victoria Land in Jan. 1895. They were the first ashore on the main continental mass. C. E. Borchgrevink, a member of that party, returned in 1899 with a British expedition, first to winter on Antarctica.

1902-04 — Robert F. Scott (Britain) discovered Edward VII Peninsula. In 1902 he reached 82°17′S. 146°33′E from McMurdo Sound.

1908-09 — Ernest Shackleton, in 1908, introduced the use of Manchurian ponies in Antarctic sledging. In 1909 he reached 88°23'S, discovering a route on to the plateau by way of the Beardmore Glacier and pioneering the way to the Pole.

Discovery of South Pole

1911 — Roald Amundsen (Norway) with four men and dog teams reached the Pole Dec. 14, 1911.

1912 — Capt. Scott reached the Pole from Ross Island Jan. 18, 1912, with four companions (Dr. E. A. Wilson, Lt. Bowers, Capt. Oates, and Petty Officer Edgar Evans), where they found Amundsen's tent. Of Scott's party, Oates and Evans died first; Scott, Wilson, and Boers died in a tent around March 29. They were found Nov. 12, 1912.

1928 — First man to use an airplane over Antarctica was Hubert Wilkins (Britain).

1929 — Richard E. Byrd (U.S.) established Little America on Bay of Whales. On 1600-mi. airplane flight begun Nov. 28 he crossed South Pole Nov. 29 with pilot Bernt Balchen, a radio operator, and a photographer. Dropped U. S. flag over Pole, temp. 16° below zero.

1934-35 — Richard E. Byrd (U.S.) led second expedition to Little America, which explored 450,000 sq. mi. Byrd wintered alone at an advance weather station in 80°08'S.

1934-37 — John Rymill led British Graham Land expedition of 1934-37; discovered that Palmer Peninsula is part of Antarctic mainland.

1935 — Lincoln Ellsworth (U.S.) flew south along Palmer Peninsula's east coast, then crossed continent to Little America, making four landings on unprepared terrain in bad weather, a new feat.

1939-41 — U. S. Antarctic Service built West Base on Ross Ice Shelf under Paul Siple, and East Base on Palmer Peninsula under Richard Black. U. S. Navy plane flights discovered about 150,000 sq. miles of new land.

1940 — Richard E. Byrd (U.S.) charted most of coast between Ross Sea and Palmer Peninsula.

1946-47 — U. S. Navy undertook Operation Highjump under Rear Admiral Byrd. Ships were commanded by Rear Admiral Richard H. Cruzen. Expedition included 13 ships and 4,000 men. Twenty-nine land-based flights from Little America and 35 by seaplanes from tenders photomapped coastline and penetrated beyond Pole.

1946-48 — Ronne Antarctic Research Expedition, Comdr. Finn Ronne, USNR, determined the Antarctic to be only one continent with no strait between Weddell Sea and Ross Sea; discovered 250,000 sq. miles of land by flights to 79°S Lat., and made 14,000 aerial photographs over 450,000 sq. miles of land. Mrs. Ronne and Mrs. H. Darlington, who accompanied their husbands, were the first women to winter on Antarctica.

1955-57 — U. S. Navy's Operation Deep Freeze led by Adm. Richard E. Byrd. Supporting U. S. scientific efforts for the International Geophysical Year, the operation was commanded by Rear Adm. George Dufek. It established five coastal stations fronting the Indian, Pacific, and Atlantic Oceans and also three interior stations; explored more than 1,000,000 sq. miles in Wilkes Land. Seven Navy men under Adm. Dufek landed by plane at the Pole Oct. 31, 1956, and landed radar reflectors.

1957-58 — During the International Geophysical year, Jul., 1957, through Dec., 1958, scientists from 12 countries conducted ambitious programs of Antarctic research. A network of some 60 stations on the continent and sub-Arctic islands studied oceanography, glaciology, meteorology, seismology, geomagnetism, the ionosphere, cosmic rays, aurora, and airglow. A party from Ellsworth IGY station (U.S.) south of Weddell Sea under the direction of Captain Finn Ronne explored beyond 1947 flight and delineated Berkner Island imbedded in the Filchner Ice Shelf. Pensacola Mountains, first sighted by Argentines in Oct., 1955, and seen by U. S. Navy in Jan., 1956, were accurately located. New mountain ranges about 11,609 ft. high were discovered in Edith Ronne Land.

Dr. V. E. Fuchs led a 12-man Trans-Antarctic Expedition on the first land crossing of Antarctica. Starting from the Weddell Sea, they reached Scott Station Mar. 2, 1958, after traveling 2,158 miles in 98 days.

1958 — A group of 5 U. S. scientists led by Edward C. Thiel, seismologist, moving by tractor from Ellsworth Station on Weddell Sea, identified a huge mountain range, 5,000 ft. above the ice sheet and 9,000 ft. above sea level. The range, originally seen by a Navy plane, was named the Dufek Massif, for Rear Adm. George Dufek.

1959 — Twelve nations — Argentina, Australia, Belgium, Chile, France, Japan, New Zealand, Norway, South Africa, the Soviet Union, the United Kingdom, and the U. S. — signed a treaty suspending any territorial claims for 30 years and reserving the continent for research.

1960-61 — Scientists at Cape Adare found a wooden building erected in 1899 by the first men (led by C. E. Borchgrevink) to winter on the continent.

1961-62 — Scientists discovered a trough, the Bentley Trench, running from Ross Ice Shelf, Pacific, into Marie Byrd Land, around the end of the Ellsworth Mtns., toward the Weddell Sea, which may be the long-suspected link between the Atlantic and Pacific Oceans.

1962 — First nuclear power plant began operation at McMurdo Sound.

1963 — On Feb. 22 a U. S. plane made the longest nonstop flight ever made in the S. Pole area, covering 3,600 miles in 10 hours. The flight was from McMurdo Station south past the geographical S. Pole to Shackleton Mtns., southeast to the "Area of Inaccessibility" and back to McMurdo Station.

1963 — Three turbine-powered helicopters made the first copter landings on the S. Pole.

1964 — A British survey team was landed by helicopter on Cook Island, the first recorded visit since its discovery in 1775.

1964 — New Zealanders completed one of the last and most important surveys when they mapped the mountain area from Cape Adare west some 400 miles to Pennell Glacier.

1966-67 — Fifteen Antarctic areas set aside as Specially Protected Areas for the conservation of flora and fauna.

Exploring Pre-History

Excavation in Ethiopia Yields Dramatic Finds

The discovery of fossilized human remains believed to be as much as 4 million years old in Ethiopia's Hadar River Basin, virtually a paleontologist's paradise, is revolutionizing thinking on the origins of man.

Last October, Alemeyu Asfew, of the Ethiopian Antiquities Commission and member of the French-American Afar Research Expedition, spotted some jaw bone fragments lying on the surface of a volcanic deposit on the Hadar, a tributary of the Awash River in north-central Ethiopia. The fossils, all with teeth, lay in a stratigraphic layer 150 feet below and, consequently, probably older than a volcanic layer dated at 3.01 to 3.25 million years ago. As further substantiation of the fossils' age, animal remains found in the same stratum compared favorably with samples from other sites in the East African Rift Valley System which have been reliably dated at 4 million years old.

The expedition, headed by Dr. Donald C. Johanson of Case Western Reserve University and Maurice

Taieb of the French National Center for Scientific Research, released the following statement: "These specimens clearly exhibit traits which must be considered as indicative of the genus Homo. Taken together they represent the most complete remains of this genus from anywhere in the world at a very ancient time. All previous theories of the origin of the lineage which lead to modern man must now be totally revised. We must throw out many existing theories and consider the possibility that man's origins go back well over four million years."

In addition, the small size of the teeth, Johanson speculated, may show genus Homo was "walking, eating meat, and probably using tools, perhaps bones, to kill animals" earlier than previously thought.

If the age and identification of the specimens — 3 believed to be from the genus Homo and one from the genus Australopithecus — is confirmed, the find would support the theory that the precursors of modern man, the genus Homo, lived contemporaneously with one or more "near men" of the genus Australopithecus, some ½ million years earlier than previously believed. Richard Leakey's discovery of the "1470" skull in Kenya 3 years before had put the age for Homo at 2,500,000 years.

Further excavation in the Hadar River basin has yielded strong support for the co-existence theory.

Dr. Johanson, last February, at a news conference in Cleveland, Oh., displayed "Lucy," a 40-bone fossil skeleton, believed to have been a female who lived 3 million years ago. The skeleton, which Johanson described as the most nearly complete reconstruction to date of an early manlike creature, is not believed to be a direct ancestor of modern man, but rather a creature of closely linked lineage who lived contemporaneously with early humans.

The find of 40 bones, all from a 20-square-yard area, was also significant in that it is unusual to find even a half dozen bones from a single individual from so early a period. That the bones were all from one creature was evident from the fact they were all found very close together and that many adjoining bones fitted together perfectly.

"You just don't expect to find this much of a single individual, just bits and pieces," said Johanson. "We were just astounded when we realized what we were finding."

New Light on Early Man Vs. Woman

A new body of evidence collected by anthropologist Richard Borshay Lee of the University of Toronto seriously questions the age-old assumption that early woman was dependent on early man.

His study of hunter-gatherers, based on field work with the Kung bushmen in Botswana, indicates that men and women shared power. While the man did the hunting, the women gathered plant food and fish. As a result, the women were neither economically nor politically dependent on the men. Because the culture of the bushmen and other like groups, such as the Australian Aborigine and some Eskimos, is similar to that of man throughout the ages, many anthropologists use them as models to search for clues about early social forms.

As further evidence, Lee noted that the bushmen often marry outside of their own groups and, according to tradition, join the bride's group as outsiders without influence based on blood kinship. This phenomenon, Lee concludes, points to several influences rather than a single male dominance in male-female relationships.

Although Lee grants that his reconstruction of prehistoric society may be inexact, he believes "hunter-gatherer data should make us view with suspicion any theory that seeks to 'prove' that the male dominance in our present social order is part of our evolutionary heritage."

Huge Flying Reptile Fossils Found

Did prehistoric flying reptiles actually flap their featherless, leathery wings like birds or did they mount high perches and leap into air currents to soar like gliders? A recent discovery in Texas is rekindling this half-century-old debate.

During 3 years of exploration in Big Bend National Park in Brewster County, Tex., Douglas A. Lawson, a graduate student at the University of California at Berkeley, found the fossils of a pterosaur, the largest known creature to have ever flown. The extinct reptile which lived more than 60 million years ago had an estimated wingspan of 51 feet — larger than a F-4 jet-fighter and twice as large as that of a pteranodon, the largest previously known pterodactyl or winged reptile.

Dr. Wann Langston Jr., director of the University of Texas's Vertebrate Paleontology Laboratory, said, "The thing that's so extraordinary about the thing is its tremendous size." It is the creature's large size that leads many scientists to believe the reptile could not have risen into the air on wing power alone. And, unfortunately, since no reliable estimate exists of how much such creatures weighed, it is virtually impossible to calculate their aerodynamic properties.

The discovery of the fossils in nonmarine sediments, suggesting they lived away from the ocean, has raised additional questions. Previously, pterosaurs had been considered fish eaters who glided over the waters to scoop up their prey. Lawson believes the Texas pterosaurs may have been carrioneaters who fed on dead dinosaurs. His assumption is based on the reptile's unusually long neck, a feature common to carrion-eating birds which enables the creature to reach deeply within a dead body to feed.

Neanderthal Man's Demise

Neanderthal man, the beetle-browed member of genus Homo, co-existed with other subspecies during the Wurm glacial period, 100,000 to 45,000 years ago in what is now Europe.

Whether Neanderthal man died out, evolved, or interbred has long been debated by anthropologists. Now Brown University linguist Philip Lieberman and Yale Medical School anatomist Edmund Crelin offer a new controversial hypothesis. He died out, they argue, because of a selective physiological disadvantage — the internal shape of his throat made Neanderthal man incapable of talking a sophisticated language. In the long run, he could not compete with contemporaries whose capacity for rapidly spoken complex communications inevitably led to a more intricate society.

Lieberman and Crelin theorized on the basis of a model of the Neanderthal voice tract which they constructed by comparing Neanderthal skulls with those of modern human adults and newborns as well as modern chimpanzees and apes. They discovered that the Neanderthal voice tract could not articulate sounds, expecially vowels, found in every known human language.

Oldest North American Fossils?

Imprints of large marine worms in slabs of hardened mud, found recently in North Carolina, may be the oldest fossils in the United States and possibly in North America.

A team of geologists from Virginia Polytechnic Institute discovered the imprints in volcanic deposits in North Carolina's Piedmont region. The fossils have been dated to the Pre-Cambrian period, more than 620 million years ago, long before vertebrates had evolved and before the North American and African continents first separated. Since then the 2 continents have come together again and drifted apart once again to form the present Atlantic.

VPI geology professor Dr. Lynn Glover, who found the fossils, contends. "The worms probably lived in burrows on beaches along volcanic islands that once existed in this part of North Carolina." Then, judging from the geological content of the fossils, the mud was loosened by earthquake activity and slid into deeper water where it was buried and preserved in volcanic ash. Further geological activity — faulting, uplifting, and compression of colliding continents —

placed the fossils in their present location.

The North Carolina worm imprints are similar to fossils discovered in Newfoundland, England, and Australia. Although the Newfoundland specimens have to date been considered the oldest in North America, the North Carolina worm fossils may prove to be older.

The slab with fossil imprints has been shipped to the U. S. Geological Survey headquarters in Reston, Va., for display during the American Bicentennial.

Fossil Bonanza in Baja

Many square miles of land covered with fossils and fossil beds thousands of feet thick are earning Baja California a reputation as "the last great frontier" in paleontology.

Recently at a meeting of the Vertebrate Paleontological Society of America in Flagstaff, Ariz., Shelton Applegate and William Morris from the Natural History Museum of Los Angeles County reported a find of some 18 fossil sites on the Baja peninsula in a region stretching from Santa Rosalia to Cabo San Lucas.

Most significant among the sites are yet unexplored deposits of marine and terrestrial fossils which may prove to be the largest in North America. The deposits have been dated back 60 million years.

The scientists have also found chips of flint and obsidian which they contend may be human artifacts. Since the seabeds may be as old as 50,000 years, the artifacts may prove to be the earliest evidence of man's presence in North America. Previously, most widely accepted evidence of man's presence in North America is dated at 25,000 to 40,000 years old.

Also exciting, according to Applegate, was a find of marine fossils dating to the Oligocene period, 37 to 26 million years ago, a rare find in fossil beds. Discovery of shark teeth previously known from Mississippi deposits suggests a water link between the Gulf of Mexico and the Pacific Ocean. The find supports geological evidence that North and South America were once separated by a seaway, possibly where the Isthmus of Panama lies today.

How To Slay a Mammoth

How, some 11,000 years ago, the first primitive hunters in North America were able to slay the huge mammoth has long remained a mystery. The enormous extinct elephant with 10-foot spiraling tusks stood 12 feet high at the shoulder.

Archeologists Larry Lahren of the University of Calgary and Robson Bonnischen of the University of Maine have discovered bone foreshafts — the foreward part of an arrow or shaft to which the head is attached—at a burial site near Wilsal, Mon., which may help clear up the mystery. Included in the find were beveled and cross-hatched pieces of bone and fluted projectile points.

By constructing wooden replicas, they discovered that 2 beveled foreshaft pieces, when lashed to a projectile point and a wooden lance, gave the weapon stability. The foreshaft pieces, they said, "act like pliers grasping the projectile point" and prevent slippage. They deduced that the early hunters, after stabbing a mammoth, could have pulled the lance out while leaving the detachable point unit buried deep in the wound. Then, seconds later, they could have replaced the projectile point and struck again. If the primitive hunters had been aware of vulnerable nerve centers, they could have successfully slain the giant beast.

New Evidence on Early Life in America

Recently uncovered evidence is destroying the popular misconception that early Indians living in the Central Mississippi River Valley in 6500 B. C. were primitive savages struggling to survive.

Excavation by Northwestern University archeologists and scientists at the Koster site near Kampsville in West Central Illinois indicates that a comparatively sophisticated people lived as families in substantial wooden huts, ate well on the abundant wildlife, and lived harmoniously with their neighbors.

Digging at the site, which now resembles an open-pit quarry, is currently in the 11th horizon or stratum which has been positively dated to 6500 B. C. Test squares dug into the 12th horizon, according to Dr. Stuart Struever, head of the dig team, yielded well preserved human and animal remains which may date to 7,000 years B.C. and earlier. Struever believes levels below the 12th could yield materials back to 8,000 and 10,000 years B. C.

Materials from the 11th horizon indicate that around 6500 B. C., some 50 people lived as families at the site in permanent structures on half-acre plots. Evidence of flint and bone tools indicates the families worked and wore leather. Dog bones show the early inhabitants domesticated dogs and kept them as pets. A plethora of animal and fish bones indicate that food was abundant. The excavations also found no signs of fortifications or death by violence.

Field Trip Makes Exciting Find

An expedition that began as a student field trip on how to set up an archeological dig may have unearthed the oldest existing site of human habitation in North America east of the Mississippi River.

A group of students led by James Adovasio of the University of Pittsburgh found numerous articles, including a burned bark basket which may be 4,000 years old, at Meadowcroft Village, a restored community of early 19th century homes and buildings in Arella, Pa.

Charcoal samples from firepits at the excavation site were radiocarbon-dated by the Smithsonian Institution at 14,000 and 15,000 years old. Although similar dates have been established from human habitation in the western United States and Alaska, the find was the first so dated in the eastern U.S. The discovery leads to speculation that Ice Age peoples did not confine their travels to the west, but migrated across the entire continent.

One of Earliest Chinese Cities Unearthed

Excavation at the site of one of China's earliest cities has unearthed the foundations of a palace built at least 3,400 years ago. The discovery was made at the remains of the ancient city of Panlung, near Wuhan in central China's Hupei province. A rotten coffin bearing the oldest wood carvings extant in China was also found.

According to Hsinhua, the official Chinese news agency, the discovery shows that the Shang dynasty (18th to 12th century B.C.) culture had spread south from its origins in the Yellow River region to the Yangtze early in its development.

The palace, which covered an area 125 feet by 36 feet, consisted of 4 chambers leading off an outer corridor and used at least 43 columns to support the roof.

Relics Back Chinese Claim to Paracels

Chinese archeologists have unearthed ancient relics which may back up Peking's claim that the Paracel Islands have been China's territory since ancient times. The Paracels, in dispute between China and South Vietnam, have recently gained importance with the discovery of oil reserves in the South China Sea and their suitability as a base for military operations.

According to Kwangming Jih Pao, a Chinese newspaper devoted to cultural affairs, the relics, including 95 pieces of porcelain, nearly half a ton of copper coins, religious artifacts, and stone tablets, date back to the Tang Dynasty which lasted from the 7th to 10th century. The porcelain, the newspaper article asserted, is characteristic of that produced in South China during that period.

Volcanoes of the World

Source: National Geographic Society, Washington, D.C.

(E) Eruption year in parentheses **(R)** Rumbling **(St.)** Steaming **(D)** Dormant

Mt. Vesuvius, dominating the Bay of Naples, is the most famous of volcanoes. In Aug., 79 A.D., it buried Pompeii (c. 20,000 pop.) under hot ash and Herculaneum and Stabiae under mud flows. Three-fifths of Pompeii has been excavated; also part of Herculaneum, most of which lies under Resina. Stabiae lies under Castellammare. There was a big eruption in 1139, and a major one in Dec., 1631, when 5 towns were destroyed and 4,000 people killed. Minor eruptions have occurred in 1779, 1793, 1872, 1906, and 1944.

Krakatau, on an island in the Sunda Strait between Sumatra and Java, exploded Aug. 27, 1883, creating a depth of 1,000 ft. in the ocean. The explosion was heard 2,500 mi. away, and tidal waves killed 35,000. In 1927 Krakatau formed the island of Anak Krakatau, which exploded, 1929, depositing an island in the hole caused in 1883.

Mont Pelee, Martinique, destroyed St. Pierre and more than 30,000 people May 8, 1902. Eruptions slightly less powerful occurred May 20 and Aug. 30, 1902. A major eruption began Sept. 16, 1929, and lasted 3 years.

Mt. Agung, 10,308 ft., on the island of Bali, erupted in January, March, and May, 1963; the last two eruptions claimed a total of more than 1,500 lives and a third of Bali's farm land, and left 85,000 homeless. Bali's **Mt. Batur**, 5,636 ft., erupted in Sept., 1963, forcing 1,200 persons to leave their homes at its base; rumblings and explosions could be heard for 50 miles.

In Alaska's Valley of 10,000 Smokes, the lowest of **Mt. Trident's** 3 peaks erupted Apr. 1, 1963; the cloud of smoke and dust was visible 100 miles away.

Name	Location	Ht. Ft.
Africa		
Kilimanjaro (D)	Tanzania	19,340
Cameroon Mt. (E-1959)	Cameroon	13,350
Teide (D)	Canary Is.	12,198
Nyiragongo (E-1972)	Zaire	11,400
Nyamlagira (E-1971)	Zaire	10,028
Fogo (E-1951)	Cape Verde Is	9,281
Tristan da Cunha (E-1961)	Atlantic Ocean	6,760
Erta Ale (E-1973)	Ethiopia	1,650
Antarctica		
Erebus (E-1974)		12,450
Melbourne (St.)		8,500
Deception Island (E-1970)		1,890
Asia — Oceania		
Klyuchevskaya (R)	USSR	15,584
Kerintji (St.)	Sumatra	12,467
Fuji (D)	Japan	12,388
Rindjani (E-1964)	Indonesia	12,224
Tolbachik (E-1941)	USSR	12,080
Semeru (E-1963)	Java	12,060
Ichinskaya	USSR	11,880
Kronotskaya (D)	USSR	11,575
Koryakskaya (E-1957)	USSR	11,339
Slamet (E-1953)	Java	11,247
Raung (St.)	Java	10,932
Shiveluch (E-1964)	USSR	10,771
Dempo (St.)	Sumatra	10,364
Welirang (D)	Java	10,354
Agung (E-1964)	Bali	10,308
Sundoro (D)	Java	10,285
Tjareme (E-1938)	Java	10,098
Ontake (E-1970)	Japan	10,049
Gede (E-1949)	Java	9,705
Merapi (E-1969)	Java	9,551
Bezymyannaya (E-1961)	USSR	9,514
Marapi (D)	Sumatra	9,485
Apo (D)	Philippines	9,369
Tambora (D)	Indonesia	9,353
Ruapehu (E-1974)	New Zealand	9,175
Peuetsagoe (D)	Sumatra	9,121
Bromo (St.)	Java	9,088
Avachinskaya (St.)	USSR	9,026
Big Ben (E-1950)	Heard Island	9,007
Balbi (D)	Solomons	9,000
Papandajan (St.)	Java	8,602
Guereudong (E-1924)	Sumatra	8,497
Asama (E-1973)	Japan	8,340
Sumbing (E-1926)	Sumatra	8,225
Tandikat (E-1924)	Sumatra	8,166
Mayon (E-1968)	Philippines	8,077
Yake Dake (E-1963)	Japan	8,064
Sinabung (St.)	Sumatra	8,041
Idjen (D)	Java	7,828
Alaid (E-1972)	Kuril Is.	7,662
Ulawan (E-1973)	New Britain	7,532
Ngauruhoe (E-1975)	New Zealand	7,515
Guntur (D)	Java	7,379
Bamus (D)	New Britain	7,338

Name	Location	Ht. Ft.
Galunggung (E-1920)	Java	7,113
Amburombu (E-1924)	Indonesia	7,051
Sorikmarapi (E-1917)	Sumatra	7,037
Petarangan (E-1939)	Java	7,005
Sibajak (St.)	Sumatra	6,870
Tokachi (E-1962)	Japan	6,813
Tangkubanperahu (R)	Java	6,637
Bagana (E-1966)	Solomons	6,560
Tongariro (E-1950)	New Zealand	6,458
Zheltovskaya (E-1972)	USSR	6,407
Sangeang (E-1953)	Indonesia	6,394
Kaba (E-1941)	Sumatra	6,358
Awu (E-1966)	Indonesia	6,102
Tiatia (E-1973)	Kuril Islands	6,013
Manam (E-1974)	Bismarck Arch.	6,000
Soputan (E-1947)	Celebes	5,994
Piton de la Fournaise (E-1973)	Reunion Is.	5,981
Siau (E-1974)	Indonesia	5,853
Kelud (E-1966)	Java	5,679
Batur (E-1963)	Bali	5,636
Belerang (St.)	Sumatra	5,636
Ternate (E-1938)	Indonesia	5,627
Hibok Hibok (E-1960)	Philippines	5,619
Lewotobi Perampuan (E-1935)	Indonesia	5,591
Kirishima (St.)	Japan	5,577
Karymskaya (E-1970)	USSR	5,560
Mutu (D)	Indonesia	5,545
Lamongna (St.)	Java	5,482
Boleng (E-1950)	Indonesia	5,443
Gamkonora (E-1949)	Indonesia	5,364
Aso (E-1970)	Japan	5,223
Lewotobi Lakilaki (E-1940)	Indonesia	5,217
Lokon (E-1970)	Celebes	5,184
Bulusan (E-1966)	Philippines	5,115
Sarycheva (E-1960)	Kuril Is.	4,960
Meakan (E-1959)	Japan	4,931
Ibu (D)	Indonesia	4,921
Lewotolo (D)	Indonesia	4,757
Lopevi (E-1960)	New Hebrides	4,755
Ambrim (E-1951)	New Hebrides	4,376
Mahawu (D)	Celebes	4,367
Long Island (E-1953)	Bismarck Arch.	4,278
Mt. Langila (E-1973)	New Britain	3,924
Tongkoko (D)	Celebes	3,770
Komaga Dake (E-1971)	Japan	3,740
Werung (E-1948)	Indonesia	3,678
Sakurajima (E-1974)	Japan	3,668
Langla (E-1965)	New Britain	3,586
Dukono (E-1950)	Indonesia	3,566
Lamington (E-1951)	New Guinea	3,500
Minami (E-1971)	Japan	3,478
Yasur (R)	New Hebrides	3,420
Lolobau (D)	Bismarck Arch.	3,058
Asuncion (St.)	Marianas	2,923
Paloe (E-1973)	Indonesia	2,871
Sirung (E-1947)	Indonesia	2,828

Name	Location	Ht.Ft.
O Yama (E-1962)	Japan	2,674
Krakatau (E-1953)	Indonesia	2,667
Bam Island (D)	Bismarck Arch.	2,625
Nila (E-1932)	Indonesia	2,562
Batu Tara (St.)	Indonesia	2,454
Alamagan (E-1945)	Marianas	2,441
Ruang (E-1949)	Indonesia	2,379
Bango (D)	New Britain	2,375
Tinakula (E-1971)	Santa Cruz Is.	2,200
Ija (E-1969)	Indonesia	2,162
Banda (D)	Indonesia	2,152
Teun (D)	Indonesia	2,149
Serua (D)	Indonesia	2,103
Mihara (E-1964)	Japan	2,028
Pagan (E)	Marianas	1,870
Tofua (D)	Tonga Islands	1,660
Unauna (E-1960)	Indonesia	1,640
Farallon de Pajaros (E-1952)	Marianas	1,096
White Island (E-1971)	New Zealand	1,075
Taal (E-1971)	Philippines	984
Didicas (E-1952)	Philippines	900
Niuafo'ou (E-1946)	Tonga	853
Tavurvur (E-1941)	New Britain	741
Fonualei (E-1939)	Tonga	600
Anak Krakatau (E-1960)	Indonesia	510

Central America—Caribbean

Name	Location	Ht.Ft.
Tajumulco (R)	Guatemala	13,845
Tacana (R)	Guatemala	13,428
Acatenango (R)	Guatemala	12,992
Fuego (E-1974)	Guatemala	12,582
Santa Maria (E-1973)	Guatemala	12,362
Atitlan (R)	Guatemala	11,565
Irazu (E-1964)	Costa Rica	11,260
San Pedro (R)	Guatemala	9,921
Poas (St.)	Costa Rica	8,930
Pacaya (E-1972)	Guatemala	8,346
Izalco (E-1967)	El Salvador	7,749
San Miguel (E-1970)	El Salvador	6,988
Rincon de la Vieja (E-1970)	Costa Rica	6,234
El Viejo (E-1971)	Nicaragua	5,840
Ometepe (Concepcion) (E-1957)	Nicaragua	5,106
Arenal (E-1970)	Costa Rica	5,092
Pelee (D)	Martinique	4,583
Momotombo (E-1952)	Nicaragua	4,199
Conchagua (E-1947)	El Salvador	4,100
Soufriere (E-1972)	St. Vincent	4,048
Telica (E-1971)	Nicaragua	3,409
Negro (E-1971)	Nicaragua	3,204
Santiago (St.)	Nicaragua	1,969

South America

Name	Location	Ht.Ft.
Guallatiri (E-1959)	Chile	19,882
Lascar (E-1951)	Chile	19,652
Cotopaxi (St.)	Ecuador	19,347
Misti (D)	Peru	19,098
Cayambe (D)	Ecuador	18,996
Tupungatito (E-1959)	Chile	18,504
Sangay (E-1946)	Ecuador	17,159
Tungurahua (R)	Ecuador	16,512
Cotacachi (E-1955)	Ecuador	16,204
Pichincha (D)	Ecuador	15,696
Purace (E-1950)	Colombia	15,604
Lautaro (St.)	Chile	11,090
Llaima (E-1955)	Chile	10,239
Villarrica (E-1972)	Chile	9,318
Hudson (E-1973)	Chile	8,580

Name	Location	Ht. Ft.
Shoshuenco (E-1960)	Chile	7,743
Ventisquero (E-1971)	Chile	7,546
Puyehue (E-1972)	Chile	7,349
Calbuco (E-1961)	Chile	6,611
Casablanca (E-1960)	Chile	6,529
Cauye (E-1960)	Chile	4,692
Alcedo (E-1970)	Galapagos Is.	3,599

Mid-Pacific

Name	Location	Ht. Ft.
Mauna Kea (D)	Hawaii	13,796
Mauna Loa (E-1975)	Hawaii	13,680
Kilauea (E-1973)	Hawaii	4,077

Europe

Name	Location	Ht. Ft.
Etna (E-1974)	Sicily, Italy	10,902
Beeren Berg (E-1971)	Norway	7,470
Askja (E-1961)	Iceland	4,954
Hekla (E-1970)	Iceland	4,892
Vesuvius (St.)	Italy	4,190
Katla (E-1918)	Iceland	3,182
Stromboli (E-1971)	Italy	3,038
Thera (E-1956)	Greece	1,824
Vulcano (D)	Italy	1,637
Kirkjufell (E-1973)	Iceland	725
Surtsey (E-1965)	Iceland	568
Ilha Nova (E-1958)	Azores	200

North America

Name	Location	Ht. Ft.
Citlaltepec (D)	Mexico	18,700
Popocatepetl (St.)	Mexico	17,887
Wrangell (St.)	Alaska	14,163
Colima (St.)	Mexico	14,003
Torbert (E-1953)	Alaska	11,413
Spurr (E-1953)	Alaska	11,069
Baker (St.)	Washington	10,778
Lassen (D)	California	10,457
Redoubt (E-1966)	Alaska	10,197
Iliamna (St.)	Alaska	10,016
Shishaldin (St.)	Aleutians	9,387
Pavlof (E-1973)	Alaska	8,261
Veniaminof (D)	Alaska	8,225
Griggs (St.)	Alaska	7,600
Paricutin (D)	Mexico	7,451
Mageik (St.)	Alaska	7,250
Douglas (St.)	Alaska	7,064
Chiginagak (D)	Alaska	6,900
Katmai (E-1962)	Alaska	6,715
Kukak (St.)	Alaska	6,700
Makushin (D)	Aleutians	6,680
Pogromni (E-1964)	Aleutians	6,568
Martin (E-1960)	Alaska	6,050
Trident (E-1963)	Alaska	6,010
Tanaga (D)	Aleutians	5,925
Great Sitkin (E-1974)	Aleutians	5,710
Cleveland (E-1944)	Aleutians	5,675
Gareloi (D)	Aleutians	5,334
Korovin (D)	Aleutians	4,852
Kanaga (D)	Aleutians	4,416
Aniakchak (D)	Alaska	4,400
Akutan (E-1974)	Aleutians	4,275
Kiska (1962)	Aleutians	4,004
Augustine (E-1935)	Alaska	3,927
Little Sitkin (St.)	Aleutians	3,897
Okmok (E-1958)	Aleutians	3,519
Seguam (D)	Aleutians	3,458
Yunaska (D)	Aleutians	3,133
Kagamil (D)	Aleutians	2,930
Novarupta (St.)	Alaska	2,760
Cerberus (D)	Alaska	2,541

Eruptions 1974 — 1975

Guatemala's Fuego, 12,582 ft., erupted in Oct. 1974, ejecting voluminous hot ash flows which destroyed crops and grazing lands in surrounding areas, forced thousands of persons to abandon their homes, and disrupted communications and roads.

Kilauea, 4,077 ft., on the island of Hawaii, erupted Dec. 31, 1974, following 3 months of continuous activity, and sent out lava flows up to 7 miles in length. Quiet since 1950, Mauna Loa erupted July 5, 1975.

Persistent activity since Oct. 1974 on the northeast summit of Sicily's Mt. Etna, 10,902 ft., shifted, in Feb. 1975, to a moderate lava outpouring from the volcano's north rift zone.

New Zealand's Ngauruhoe, 7,515 ft., in Feb. 1975, started its most voluminous pyroclastic eruption since the 1954 lava flows.

The crater lake of New Zealand's Ruapehu, 9,175 ft., erupted in Apr. 1975, ejecting large amounts of water and damaging some surrounding bridges and recreation facilities and poisoning fish in several streams and rivers.

Highest and Lowest Continental Altitudes

Source: National Geographic Society, Washington, D.C.

(In feet)

Continent	Highest Point	Elevation	Lowest Point	Below Sea Level
Asia	Mount Everest, Nepal-Tibet	29,028	Dead Sea, Israel-Jordan	1,302
South America	Mount Aconcagua, Argentina	22,834	Peninsula Valdes, Argentina	131
North America	Mount McKinley, Alaska	20,320	Death Valley, California	282
Africa	Kibo (Kilimanjaro), Tanzania	19,340	Lake Assal, Afars & Issas Terr.	512
Europe	Mount El'brus USSR Caucasus Mts.	18,510	Caspian Sea, USSR	92
Antarctica	Vinson Massif	16,860	Unknown	. . .
Australia	Mount Kosciusko, New South Wales	7,310	Lake Eyre, South Australia	52

Height of Mount Everest

Mt. Everest was considered to be 29,002 ft. tall when Edmund Hillary and Tenzing Norkay scaled it in 1953. This triangulation figure had been accepted since 1850. In 1954 the Surveyor General of the Republic of India set the height at 29,028 ft. plus or minus 10 ft. because of snow. The National Geographic Society accepts the new figure, but many mountaineering groups still use 29,002 ft.

High Peaks in United States, Canada, Mexico

Name	Place	Feet
McKinley	Alas	20,320
Logan	Can	19,850
Citlaltepec (Orizaba)	Mexico	18,700
St. Elias	Alas-Can	18,008
Popocatepetl	Mexico	17,887
Foraker	Alas	17,400
Iztaccihuatl	Mexico	17,343
Lucania	Can	17,147
King	Can	16,971
Steele	Can	16,644
Bona	Alas	16,550
Blackburn	Alas	16,523
Kennedy	Alas	16,286
Sanford	Alas	16,237
South Buttress	Alas	15,885
Wood	Can	15,885
Vancouver	Alas-Can	15,700
Churchill	Alas	15,638
Fairweather	Alas-Can	15,300
Zinantecatl (Toluca)	Mexico	15,016
Hubbard	Alas-Can	15,015
Bear	Alas	14,831
Walsh	Can	14,780
East Buttress	Alas	14,730
Matlalcueyetl	Mexico	14,636
Hunter	Alas	14,573
Alverstone	Alas-Can	14,565
Browne Tower	Alas	14,530
Whitney	Cal	14,494
Elbert	Col	14,433
Massive	Col	14,421
Harvard	Col	14,420
Rainier	Wash	14,410
Williamson	Cal	14,375
Blanca	Col	14,345
La Plata	Col	14,336
Uncompahgre	Col	14,309

Name	Place	Feet
Crestone	Col	14,294
Lincoln	Col	14,286
Grays	Col	14,270
Antero	Col	14,269
Torreys	Col	14,267
Castle	Col	14,265
Quandary	Col	14,265
Evans	Col	14,264
Longs	Col	14,255
McArthur	Can	14,253
Mt. Wilson	Col	14,246
White	Cal	14,242
North Palisade	Cal	14,242
Shavano	Col	14,229
Belford	Col	14,197
Princeton	Col	14,197
Crestone Needle	Col	14,197
Yale	Col	14,196
Bross	Col	14,172
Kit Carson	Col	14,165
Wrangell	Alaska	14,163
Shasta	Cal	14,162
Sill	Cal	14,162
El Diente	Col	14,159
Maroon	Col	14,156
Tabeguache	Col	14,155
Oxford	Col	14,153
Sneffels	Col	14,150
Point Success	Wash	14,150
Democrat	Col	14,148
Liberty Cap	Wash	14,133
Capitol	Col	14,130
Pikes Peak	Col	14,110
Snowmass	Col	14,092
Windom	Col	14,087
Russell	Cal	14,086
Eolus	Col	14,084

Name	Place	Feet
Columbia	Col	14,073
Augusta	Alas-Can	14,070
Missouri	Col	14,067
Humboldt	Col	14,064
Bierstadt	Col	14,060
Sunlight	Col	14,059
Split	Cal	14,058
Nauhcampatepetl (Cofre de Perote)	Mexico	14,049
Handies	Col	14,048
Culebra	Col	14,047
Lindsey	Col	14,042
Middle Palisade	Cal	14,040
Little Bear	Col	14,037
Sherman	Col	14,036
Redcloud	Col	14,034
Langley	Cal	14,028
Conundrum	Col	14,022
Tyndall	Cal	14,018
Pyramid	Col	14,018
Wilson Peak	Col	14,017
Muir	Cal	14,015
Wetterhorn	Col	14,015
North Maroon	Col	14,014
San Luis	Col	14,014
Huron	Col	14,005
Holy Cross	Col	14,005
Colima	Mexico	14,003
Sunshine	Col	14,001
Grizzly	Col	14,000
Barnard	Cal	13,990
Stewart	Col	13,980
Keith	Cal	13,977
Le Conte	Cal	13,960
Meeker	Col	13,911
Kennedy	Can	13,905

South America

Peak	Country	Feet
Aconcagua, Argentina		22,834
Bonete, Argentina		22,546
Ojos del Salado, Arg.-Chile		22,539
Tupungato, Argentina-Chile		22,310
Pissis, Argentina		22,241
Mercedario, Argentina		22,211
Huascaran, Peru		22,205
Llullaillaco, Argentina-Chile		22,057
El Libertador, Argentina		22,047
Cachi, Argentina		22,047
Yerupaja, Peru		21,765
Galan, Argentina		21,654
El Muerto, Argentina-Chile		21,457
Sajama, Bolivia		21,391
Nacimiento, Argentina		21,302
Illimani, Bolivia		21,201
Coropuna, Peru		21,079

Peak	Country	Feet
Laudo, Argentina		20,997
Ancohuma, Bolivia		20,958
Ausangate, Peru		20,945
Toro, Argentina-Chile		20,932
Illampu, Bolivia		20,873
Tres Cruces, Argentina-Chile		20,853
Huandoy, Peru		20,852
Parinacota, Bolivia-Chile		20,768
Tortolas, Argentina-Chile		20,745
Ampato, Peru		20,702
Condor, Argentina		20,669
Salcantay, Peru		20,574
Chimborazo, Ecuador		20,561
Huancarhuas, Peru		20,531
Cen. Manuel Belgrano, Arg		20,505
Pumasillo, Peru		20,492

Peak	Country	Feet
Solo, Argentina		20,492
Polleras, Argentina		20,456
Pular, Chile		20,423
Chani, Argentina		20,341
Aucanquilcha, Chile		20,295
Juncal, Argentina		20,276
Negro, Argentina		20,184
Quela, Argentina		20,128
Condoriri, Bolivia		20,095
Palermo, Argentina		20,079
Solimana, Peru		20,068
San Juan, Argentina-Chile		20,049
Sierra Nevada, Arg.-Chile		20,023
Antofalla, Argentina		20,013
Marmolejo, Argentina-Chile		20,013
Licancabur, Argentina-Chile		19,425

The highest point in the West Indies is in the Dominican Republic, Pico Duarte (10,417 ft.)

Africa, Australia and Oceania

Mountain and Country	Feet	Mountain and Country	Feet	Mountain and Country	Feet
Kibo (Kilimanjaro), Tanzania	19,340	Mandala, New Guinea	15,420	Toubkal Morocco	13,665
Kenya, Kenya	17,058	Ras Dashan, Ethiopia	15,158	Kinabalu, Malaysia	13,455
Margherita Pk., Uganda-Zaire	16,763	Meru, Tanzania	14,979	Lesatima, Kenya	13,104
Djaja, New Guinea	16,500	Wilhelm, New Guinea	14,793	Kerintji, Sumatra	12,467
Pilmsit, New Guinea	15,748	Karisimbi, Zaire-Rwanda	14,787	Cook, New Zealand	12,349
Trikora, New Guinea	15,585	Elgon, Kenya-Uganda	14,178	Teide, Canary Islands	12,198
		Batu, Ethiopia	14,131	Kosciusko, Australia	7,310
		Gughe, Ethiopia	13,780		

Europe

Peak	Feet	Peak	Feet	Peak	Feet	Peak	Feet
Alps		Hohberghorn	13,842	Fiescherhorn	13,283	**Pyrenees**	
Mont Blanc	15,771	Alphubel	13,799	Grunhorn	13,266	Aneto	11,168
Monte Rosa (highest peak of group)	15,203	Rimpfischhorn	13,776	Lauteraarhorn	13,261	Posets	11,073
Dom	14,911	Aletschorn	13,763	Durrenhorn	13,238	Perdido	11,007
Liskamm	14,852	Strahlhorn	13,747	Allalinhorn	13,213	Maladeta	10,866
Weisshorn	14,780	Dent d'Herens	13,686	Weissmies	13,199	Vignemale	10,820
Taschhorn	14,733	Breithorn	13,665	Lagginhorn	13,156	Long	10,479
Matterhorn	14,690	Bishorn	13,645	Zupo	13,120	Estats	10,304
Dent Blanche	14,293	Jungfrau	13,642	Fletschhorn	13,110	Montcalm	10,105
Nadelhorn	14,196	Ecrins	13,461	Adlerhorn	13,081	**Caucasus (Europe-Asia)**	
Grand Combin	14,154	Monch	13,448	Gletscherhorn	13,068	El'brus	18,510
Lenzpitze	14,088	Pollux	13,422	Schalihorn	13,040	Shkara	17,064
Finsteraarhorn	14,022	Schreckhorn	13,379	Scerscen	13,028	Dykh Tau	17,054
Castor	13,865	Ober Gabelhorn	13,330	Eiger	13,025	Kashtan Tau	16,877
Zinalrothorn	13,849	Gran Paradiso	13,323	Jagerhorn	13,024	Kazbek	16,558
		Bernina	13,284	Rottalhorn	13,022	Dzhangi Tau	16,565

Asia

Peak	Country	Feet	Peak	Country	Feet
Everest	Nepal-Tibet	29,028	Istoro Nal	Pakistan	24,240
K2 (Godwin Austen)	Kashmir	28,250	Tent Peak	Nepal-Sikkim	24,165
Kanchenjunga	Nepal-Sikkim	28,208	Chomo Lhari	Tibet-Bhutan	24,040
Lhotse I (Everest)	Nepal-Tibet	27,923	Chamlang	Nepal	24,012
Makalu I	Nepal-Tibet	27,824	Kabru	Nepal-Sikkim	24,002
Lhotse II (Everest)	Nepal-Tibet	27,560	Alung Gangri	Tibet	24,000
Dhaulagiri	Nepal	26,810	Baltoro Kangri	Kashmir	23,990
Manaslu I	Nepal	26,760	Mussu Shan	Sinkiang	23,890
Cho Oyu	Nepal-Tibet	26,750	Mana	India	23,860
Nanga Parbat	Kashmir	26,660	Baruntse	Nepal	23,688
Anaprna	Nepal	26,504	Nepal Peak	Nepal-Sikkim	23,500
Gasherbrum	Kashmir	26,470	Amne Machin	China	23,490
Broad	Kashmir	26,400	Gauri Sankar	Nepal-Tibet	23,440
Gasainthan	Tibet	26,287	Badrinath	India	23,420
Annapurna II	Nepal	26,041	Nunkun	Kashmir	23,410
Gyachung Kang	Nepal-Tibet	25,910	Lenina Peak	USSR	23,405
Disteghil Sar	Kashmir	25,868	Api	Nepal	23,399
Himalchuli	Nepal	25,801	Pauhunri	Sikkim-Tibet	23,385
Nuptse (Everest)	Nepal-Tibet	25,726	Trisul	India	23,360
Masherbrum	Kashmir	25,660	Kangto	India-Tibet	23,260
Nanda Devi	India	25,645	Nyenchhen Thanglha	Tibet	23,255
Chomo Lonzo	Nepal-Tibet	25,640	Tirsuli	India	23,210
Rakaposhi	Kashmir	25,550	Pumori	Nepal-Tibet	23,190
Kamet	India-Tibet	25,447	Dunagiri	India	23,184
Namcha Barwa	Tibet	25,445	Lombo Kangra	Tibet	23,165
Gurla Mandhata	Tibet	25,355	Saipal	Nepal	23,100
Ulugh Muz Tagh	Tibet-Sinkiang	25,340	Macha Pucchare	Nepal	22,958
Kungur	Sinkiang	25,325	Numbar	Nepal	22,817
Tirich Mir	Pakistan	25,230	Kanjiroba	Nepal	22,580
Makalu II	Nepal-Tibet	25,120	Pyramid	Nepal-Sikkim	22,430
Minya Konka	China	24,900	Ama Dablam	Nepal	22,350
Kula Gangri	Tibet-Bhutan	24,784	Cho Polu	Nepal	22,093
Changtse (Everest)	Nepal-Tibet	24,780	Lingtren	Nepal-Tibet	21,972
Muz Tagh Ata	Sinkiang	24,757	Khumbutse	Nepal-Tibet	21,785
Skyang Kangri	Kashmir	24,750	Hlako Gangri	Tibet	21,266
Communism Peak	USSR	24,590	Mt. Grosvenor	China	21,190
Jongsong Peak	Nepal-Sikkim	24,472	Thagchhab Gangri	Tibet	20,970
Pobedy Peak	Sinkiang-USSR	24,406	Damavand	Iran	18,934
Sia Kangri	Kashmir	24,350	Ararat	Turkey	16,946
Haramosh Peak	Pakistan	24,270			

Antarctica

Peak	Feet	Peak	Feet	Peak	Feet
Vinson Massif	16,860	Miller	13,650	Falla	12,549
Tyree	16,290	Long Gables	13,620	Rucker	12,520
Shinn	15,750	Dickerson	13,517	Goldthwait	12,510
Gardner	15,375	Giovinetto	13,412	Morris	12,500
Epperly	15,100	Wade	13,400	Erebus	12,450
Kirkpatrick	14,855	Fisher	13,386	Campbell	12,434
Elizabeth	14,698	Fridtjof Nansen	13,350	Don Pedro Christophersen	12,355
Markham	14,290	Wexler	13,202	Lysaght	12,326
Bell	14,117	Lister	13,200	Huggins	12,247
Mackellar	14,098	Shear	13,100	Sabine	12,200
Anderson	13,957	Odishaw	13,008	Astor	12,175
Bentley	13,934	Donaldson	12,894	Mohl	12,172
Kaplan	13,878	Ray	12,808	Frakes	12,064
Andrew Jackson	13,750	Sellery	12,779	Jones	12,040
Sidley	13,720	Waterman	12,730	Gjelsvik	12,008
Ostenso	13,710	Anne	12,703	Coman	12,000
Minto	13,668	Press	12,566		

How Deep Is the Ocean?

Principal Ocean Depths. **Source:** Defense Mapping agency Hydrographic Center

Name of Area	Location	Depth Meters	Depth Fathoms	Feet	Ship and/or Country	Year
Pacific Ocean						
Mariana Trench......	11°21′N, 142°12′E........	11,034	6,033	36,198	Vityaz (USSR).................	1957
	11°19′N, 142°15′E........	10,863	5,939	35,631	HMS Challenger..............	1951
	11°20′N, 142°16′E........	10,815	5,910	35,460	" " (UK)	1951
	11°18.5′N, 142°15.5′E........	10,910	5,967	35,800	Bathyscaph Trieste...........	1960
Tonga Trench........	23°15.3′S, 174°44.7′W......	10,882	5,950	35,702	Vityaz (USSR).................	1957
	24°00′S, 175°00′W......	10,850	5,933	35,598	Nat'l Geographic.............	1965
	23°16′S, 174°46′W......	10,633	5,814	34,884	R/V Horizon (U.S.)...........	1953
Kuril Trench.........	44°15.2′N, 150°34.2′E......	10,542	5,764	34,587	Vityaz (USSR).................	1954
	44°18′N, 150°30′E........	10,382	5,677	34,062	Vityaz (USSR).................	1953
Philippine Trench....	10°24′N, 126°40′E........	10,539	5,763	34,578	Galathea(Danish)............	1951
(Mindanao)	10°27′N, 126°39.5′E........	10,497	5,740	34,440	USS Cape Johnson...........	1945
Izu Trench...........	30°32′N, 142°31′E........	10,374	5,673	34,033	USS Ramapo.................	1932
	30°30′N, 142°30′E........	9,985	5,459	32,751	Bathymetric Map (USSR).......	1964
	31°54′N, 142°00′E........	9,915	5,420	32,521	Bathymetric Map (USSR).......	1964
	30°49′N, 142°18′E........	9,441	5,159	30,954	Mansyu (Japan).............	1924
Kermadec Trench....	31°52.8′S, 177°20.6′W......	10,047	5,494	32,964	Vityaz (USSR).................	1957
	31°51′S, 177°02′W......	9,994	5,465	32,790	Galathea (Danish)...........	1952
Bonin Trench........	24°30′N, 143°24′E........	9,156	5,005	30,032	Vityaz (USSR).................	1964
	24°17′N, 143°23′E........	9,150	5,002	30,012	USS Salt Lake City..........	1945
New Britain Trench..	06°34′S, 153°55′E........	9,140	4,998	29,988	Planet(German).............	1910
	06°18′S, 153°48′E........	9,103	4,976	29,858	Bathmetric Map (USSR).......	1964
	06°18′S, 153°43′E........	8,936	4,886	29,316	SS Blackfin.................	1959
Yap Trench.........	08°33′N, 138°02′E........	8,527	4,662	27,976	Vityaz (USSR).................	1958
	08°08′N, 137°49′E........	8,028	4,390	26,340	USCGG Kukui.............	1965
	07°55′N, 137°39′E........	8,028	4,390	26,340	SS Greenfish...............	1965
Japan Trench........	36°08′N, 142°43′E........	8,412	4,597	27,591	Bathymetric Map (USSR).......	1964
Palau Trench........	07°40′N, 135°04′E........	8,138	4,449	26,693	Stefan (Germany)...........	1905
	07°31′N, 134°56′E........	7,324	4,005	24,030	USCGG Ironwood...........	1966
Aleutian Trench......	50°53′N, 176°23′E........	8,100	4,429	26,574	USCGC Bering Strait.........	1953
	51°13′N, 174°48′E........	7,882	4,276	25,656	USCGC CChelan............	1936
	50°51′N, 172°16′E........	7,679	4,199	25,194	Coast & Geodetic...........	1936
	50°41′N, 177°11′E........	7,666	4,192	25,152	Coast & Geodetic...........	1966
Peru Chile Trench....	23°18′S, 71°41′W......	8,064	4,409	26,454	R/VSpencerF.Baird.........	1957
(Atacama Trench)	23°27′S, 71°21′W......	8,064	4,409	26,454	IGY..................	
	21°00′S, 71°15′W......	7,920	4,330	25,980	R/V Atlantis................	1955
New Hebrides Trench..	20°36′S, 168°37′E........	7,570	4,138	24,830	Planet(Germany)............	1910
Ryukyu Trench.......	25°15′N, 128°32′E........	7,507	4,105	24,629	Mansyu (Japan).............	1925
	24°00′N, 126°48′E........	7,181	3,926	23,554	Bathymetric Map (USSR).......	1964
Mid. America Trench...	14°02′N, 93°39′W........	6,669	3,642	21,852	USS Epce.................	1965
Atlantic Ocean						
Puerto Rico Trench....	19°35′N, 68°17′W..........	8,648	4,729	28,374	SS Archerfish.............	1961
	19°45′N, 67°49′W..........	8,528	4,663	27,978	USS Rehoboth...............	1955
	19°44′N, 67°22′W..........	8,497	4,646	27,876	USS San Pablo, USS Rehoboth..	1955
	19°53′N, 66°55′W..........	8,476	4,635	27,810	USS San Pablo..............	1955
	19°41′N, 67°17′W..........	8,416	4,602	27,612	USS San Pablo..............	1955
	19°45.5′N, 67°09.7′W..........	8,604	4,589	27,534	USNS Wyman...............	1972
	19°42′N, 67°05′W..........	8,381	4,583	27,498	R/V Vema (U.S.)..............	1954
Cayman Trench......	19°12′N, 80°00′W..........	7,535	4,120	24,720	R/V Vema (U.S.)..............	1960
	18°59′N, 80°12′W..........	7,211	3,943	23,658	(British Admiralty)...........	1955
	18°59′N, 80°23′W..........	7,191	3,932	23,592	" "	1955
	19°03′N, 80°22′W..........	7,491	4,096	24,576	(Germany).................	1937
So. Sandwich Trench..	55°14′S, 26°29′W..........	8,252	4,512	27,072	USS Eltanin...............	1963
	55°08′S, 26°04′W..........	8,246	4,509	27,054	USS Eltanin...............	1963
	55°08′S, 26°05′W..........	8,219	4,494	26,964	USS Eltanin...............	1963
	55°07′S, 26°46′W..........	8,264	4,518	27,113	Meteor (Germany)..........	1926
Romanche Gap.......	00°16′S, 18°35′W..........	7,864	4,300	25,800	R/V Vema (U.S.).............	1957
	00°13′S, 18°26′W..........	7,729	4,226	25,356	USS Albatross..............	1948
Brazil Basin..........	09°10′S, 23°02′W..........	5,119	3,346	20,076	R/V Vema (U.S.).............	1956
Indian Ocean						
Java Trench.........	10°15′S, 109°E′(approx.)....	7,725	4,224	25,344	Nat'l Geographic............	1967
	10°20′S, 110°10′E........	7,450	4,073	24,442	(British Admiralty)...........	1928
	10°19′S, 108°50′E........	7,457	3,977	23,862	Australian Navy Hydrographer..	1962
Ob Trench............	(no position)...............	6,874	3,759	22,553	Nat'l Geographic............	1967
Vema Trench.........	(no position)...............	6,402	3,501	21,004	Nat'l Geographic............	1967
Agulhas Basin........	(no position)...............	,6,195	3,388	20,325	Nat'l Geographic............	1967
Diamantina Trench...	35°00′S, 105°35′E........	6,062	3,315	19,800	Nat'l Geographic............	1967
Arctic Ocean						
Eurasia Basin.........	82°23′N, 19°31′E........	5,450	2,980	17,880	Fidor Lithke (USSR)..........	1955
Mediterranean Sea						
Ionian Basin..........	36°32′N, 21°06′E........	5,150	2,816	16,896	USS Tanner.................	1955
	35°51′N, 22°18′E........	5,005	2,737	16,420	Calypso (French).............	1955
	36°34′N, 21°08′E........	5,093	2,717	16,302	R/V Chain.................	1959

Ocean Area and Average Depth

Four major bodies of water are recognized by geographers and mapmakers. They are: the Pacific, Atlantic, Indian and Arctic Oceans. The Atlantic and Pacific Oceans are considered divided at the equator into the No. and So. Atlantic; the No. and So. Pacific. The Arctic Ocean is the name for waters north of the continental land masses in the region of the Arctic Circle.

	Sq. Miles	Avg. Depth		Sq. Miles	Avg. Depth
Pacific Ocean	64,186,300	13,739	Hudson Bay	281,900	305
Atlantic Ocean	33,420,000	12,257	East China Sea	256,600	620
Indian Ocean	28,350,500	12,704	Andaman Sea	218,100	3,667
Arctic Ocean	5,105,700	4,362	Black Sea	196,100	3,906
South China Sea	1,148,500	4,802	Red Sea	174,900	1,764
Caribbean Sea	971,400	8,448	North Sea	164,900	308
Mediterranean Sea	969,100	4,926	Baltic Sea	147,500	180
Bering Sea	873,000	4,893	Yellow Sea	113,500	121
Gulf of Mexico	582,100	5,297	Persian Gulf	88,800	328
Sea of Okhotsk	537,500	3,192	Gulf of California	59,100	2,375
Sea of Japan	391,100	5,468			

The Malayan Sea is not considered a geographical entity but a term used for convenience for waters between the South Pacific and the Indian Ocean.

Principal World Rivers

Source: National Geographic Society, Washington, D.C. (Length in miles)

River	Outflow	Lgth	River	Outflow	Lgth	River	Outflow	Lgth
Albany	James Bay	610	Japura	Amazon River	1,750	Rio de la Plata	Atlantic Ocean	150
Amazon	Atlantic Ocean	4,000	Jordan	Dead Sea	200	Rio Grande	Gulf of Mexico	1,885
Amu	Aral Sea	1,578	Kootenay	Columbia River	485	Rio Roosevelt	Aripuana	400
Amur	Tatar Strait	2,700	Lenea	Laptev Sea	2,680	Saguenay	St. Lawrence R.	434
Angara	Yenisey River	1,151	Loire	Bay of Biscay	634	St. John	Bay of Fundy	418
Arkansas	Mississippi	1,450	Mackenzie	Arctic Ocean	2,635	St. Lawrence	Gulf of St. Law.	800
Back	Arctic Ocean	605	Madeira	Amazon River	2,013	St. Maurice	St. Lawrence R.	350
Brahmaputra	Bay of Bengal	1,800	Magdalena	Caribbean Sea	956	Salween	Andaman Sea	1,500
Bug, Southern	Dnieper River	532	Marne	Seine River	326	Sao Francisco	Atlantic Ocean	1,988
Bug, Western	Wisla River	481	Mekong	S. China Sea	2,600	Saskatchewan	Lake Winnipeg	1,205
Canadian	Arkansas River	906	Meuse	North Sea	580	Seine	English Chan.	482
Churchill, Man.	Hudson Bay	1,000	Mississippi	Gulf of Mexico	2,348	Shannon	Atlantic Ocean	230
Churchill, Que.	Atlantic Ocean	532	Missouri	Mississippi	2,533	Snake	Columbia Riv.	1,038
Colorado	Gulf of Calif.	1,450	Murray-Darling	Indian Ocean	2,310	Sungari	Amur River	1,150
Columbia	Pacific Ocean	1,243	Negro	Amazon	1,400	Syr	Aral Sea	1,370
Congo	Atlantic Ocean	2,718	Nelson	Hudson Bay	1,600	Tajo, Tagus	Atlantic Ocean	626
Danube	Black Sea	1,776	Niger	Gulf of Guinea	2,600	Tennessee	Ohio River	652
Dnieper	Black Sea	1,420	Nile	Mediterranean	4,145	Thames	North Sea	215
Dniester	Black Sea	877	Ob-Irtysh	Gulf of Ob	3,460	Tiber	Tyrrhenian Sea	252
Don	Sea of Azov	1,224	Oder	Baltic Sea	567	Tigris	Euphrates	1,180
Drava	Danube River	447	Ohio	Mississippi	1,306	Tisza	Danube River	600
Dvina, North	White Sea	824	Orange	Atlantic Ocean	1,300	Tocantins	Para River	1,677
Dvina, West.	Gulf of Riga	634	Orinoco	Atlantic Ocean	1,281	Ural	Caspian Sea	1,575
Ebro	Mediterranean	565	Ottawa	St. Lawrence R.	790	Uruguay	Rio de la Plata	1,000
Elbe	North Sea	724	Paraguay	Parana River	1,584	Usumacinta	Gulf of Mexico	270
Euphrates	Persian Gulf	2,235	Parana	Rio de la Plata	2,500	Volga	Caspian Sea	2,290
Fraser	Str. of Georgia	850	Peace	Slave River	1,195	Weser	North Sea	454
Gambia	Atlantic Ocean	700	Pilcomayo	Paraguay River	1,000	Wisla	Bay of Danzig	675
Ganges	Bay of Bengal	1,560	Po	Adriatic Sea	405	Yangtze	E. China Sea	3,400
Garonne	Bay of Biscay	357	Purus	Amazon River	2,100	Yellow (See Huang)		
Hsi	S. China Sea	1,200	Red	Mississippi	1,270	Yenisey	Kara Sea	2,566
Huang	Yellow Sea	3,000	Red River of N.	Lake Winnipeg	545	Yukon	Bering Sea	1,979
Indus	Arabian Sea	1,800	Rhine	North Sea	820	Zambezi	Indian Ocean	1,700
Irrawaddy	Bay of Bengal	1,300	Rhone	Gulf of Lions	505			

Continental Statistics

Source: National Geographic Society, Washington, D.C.

Continents	Area (sq. mi.)	% of Earth	Population (est.)	% World Total	Highest Point (in feet)	Lowest Point
Asia	16,988,000	29.5	2,316,312,000	58.4	Everest, 29,028	Dead Sea, 1,302
Africa	11,506,000	20.0	401,000,000	10.1	Kilimanjaro, 19,340	Lake Assal, −512
North America	9,390,000	16.3	342,700,000	8.6	McKinley, 20,320	Death Valley, −282
South America	6,795,000	11.8	219,000,000	5.5	Aconcagua, 22,834	Valdes Penin., −131
Europe	3,745,000	6.5	660,313,000	16.6	El'brus, 18,510	Caspian Sea, −92
Australia	2,968,000	5.2	13,800,000	0.3	Kosciusko, 7,310	Lake Eyre, −52
Antarctica	5,500,000	9.6	—	—	Vinson Massif, 16,860	Not Known
Total			**3,953,125,000**			

Important Islands and Their Areas

Source: National Geographic Society, Washington, D.C.

Figure in parentheses shows rank among the world's 10 largest islands, some islands have not been surveyed accurately; in such cases estimated areas are shown. *See footnotes.

Location-Ownership
Area in Square Miles

Arctic Ocean
Canadian Islands

Axel Heiberg	16,671
Baffin (5)	195,928
Banks	27,038
Bathurst	6,194
Devon	21,331
Ellesmere (10)	75,767
Melville	16,274
Prince of Wales	12,872
Somerset	9,570
Southampton	15,913
Victoria (9)	83,896

USSR Islands

Franz Josef Land	6,400
Novaya Zemlya (two is.)	31,900
Wrangel	2,800

Norwegian Islands

Svalbard	23,957
Nordaust Landet	5,610
Spitsbergen	15,075

Atlantic Ocean

Anticosti, Canada	3,066
Ascension, UK	34
Azores, Portugal	888
Faial	66
Sao Miguel	299
Bahama Is.	5,380
Bermuda Is., UK	20
Block, Rhode Island	11
Canary Is., Spain	2,808
Fuerteventura	670
Gran Canaria	592
Tenerife	919
Cape Breton, Canada	3,981
Cape Verde, Portugal	1,557
Faeroe Is., Denmark	540
Falkland Is., UK	4,618
Fernando de Noronha (Archipelago), Brazil	7
Fernando Poo, Equatorial Guinea	785

British Isles

Great Britain, mainland (8)	84,186
Channel Islands	75
Guernsey	24
Jersey	45
Sark	2
Hebrides	2,662
Ireland	32,598
Irish Republic	27,136
Northern Ireland	5,462
Man	227
Orkney Is.	375
Scilly	6
Shetland Is.	549
Skye	670
Wight	147

Greenland, Denmark (1)	840,000
Iceland	39,768
Long Island, N. Y.	1,723
Madeira Is., Portugal	308
Marajo, Brazil	15,528
Martha's Vineyard, Mass.	109
Mount Desert, Me.	105
Nantucket, Mass.	57
Newfoundland, Canada	42,031
Prince Edward, Canada	2,184

Location-Ownership
Area in Square Miles

St. Helena, UK	47
South Georgia, UK	1,450
Tierra del Fuego, Chile and Argentina	18,800
Tristan da Cunha, UK	40

Baltic Sea

Aland, Finland	572
Bornholm, Denmark	227
Gotland, Sweden	1,212

Caribbean Sea

Antigua, UK	170
Aruba, Netherlands	74
Barbados	166
Cuba	44,218
Isle of Pines	1,180
Curacao, Netherlands	182
Dominica, UK	290
Guadeloupe, France	687
Hispaniola (Haiti and Dominican Republic)	29,530
Jamaica	4,232
Martinique, France	425
Puerto Rico, U. S.	3,435
Tobago	116
Trinidad	1,864
Virgin Is., U.S.	133

Indian Ocean

Andamans, India	2,500
Ceylon	25,332
Madagascar (Malagasy Republic) (4)	226,657
Mauritius	720
Pemba, Tanzania	380
Reunion, France	969
Seychelles, UK	145
Zanzibar, Tanzania	640

Persian Gulf

Bahrain	231

Mediterranean Sea

Balearic Is., Spain	1,936
Corfu, Greece	246
Corsica, France	3,367
Crete, Greece	3,207
Cyprus	3,572
Elba, Italy	86
Euboea, Greece	1,508
Malta	122
Rhodes, Greece	545
Sardinia, Italy	9,194
Sicily, Italy	9,817

Pacific Ocean

Aleutian Is., U. S.	6,821
Adak	289
Amchitka	114
Attu	318
Kanaga	135
Kiska	110
Tanaga	185
Umnak	675
Unalaska	1,064
Unimak	1,600
Canton, U. S., UK*	4
Caroline Is., U. S. trust terr.	463
Christmas, U. S., UK*	94
Diomede, Big USSR	11.3
Diomede, Little, U.S.	2.4

Location-Ownership
Area in Square Miles

Easter, Chile	64
Formosa (Taiwan)	13,885
Funafuti, U.K., U.S.*	2
Galapagos Is., Ecuador	3,028
Guadalcanal, UK	1,130
Hainan, China	13,000
Hawaiian, U. S.	6,450
Hawaii	4,038
Oahu	608
Hong Kong, UK	29
Japan	143,750
Hokkaido	30,313
Honshu (7)	89,008
Iwo Jima	8
Kyushu	16,204
Okinawa	454
Shikoku	7,245
Kodiak, U.S.	3,670
Mariana Is., U.S. trust terr. excluding Guam	184
Guam, U. S.	212
Marquesas Is., France	492
Marshall Is., U.S. trust terr.	70
Bikini*	3
Nauru	8
New Caledonia, France	6,530
New Guinea (2)	305,577
New Hebrides, UK-Fr.	5,700
New Zealand	103,747
Chatham	372
North	44,190
South	58,192
Stewart	674
Philippines	115,830
Leyte	3,090
Luzon	41,845
Mindanao	36,381
Mindoro	3,995
Negros	5,278
Palawan	5,751
Panay	4,749
Samar	5,184
Quemoy, Formosa	50
Sakhalin, USSR	29,498
Samoa Islands	1,173
American Samoa	76
Tutuila	53
Western Samoa	1,097
Savaii	662
Upolu	433
Santa Catalina, U.S.	72
Tahiti, France	402
Tasmania, Australia	26,383
Tonga Is.	270
Vancouver, Canada	12,079
Vanua Levi (Fiji)	2,137
Viti Levu (Fiji)	4,010

East Indies

Bali, Indonesia	2,269
Borneo, Indonesia-Malaysia, UK (3)	280,107
Celebes, Indonesia	72,987
Java, Indonesia	48,763
Madura, Indonesia	2,113
Moluccas, Indonesia	28,767
New Britain, Aust.	14,600
New Ireland, Aust.	3,340
Sumatra, Indonesia (6)	182,860
Timor	13,094
Indonesian Timor	5,800
Portuguese Timor	5,763

Australia, often called an island, is a continent. Its mainland area is 2,941,526 sq. mi.

Islands in minor waters: Manhattan (31 sq. mi.) Staten (64 sq. mi.) and Governors (173 acres), all in New York Harbor, U.S.; Isle Royale (210 sq. mi.). Lake Superior, U.S.; Manitoulin (1,068 sq. mi.). Lake Huron, Canada; Penang (110 sq. mi.), Strait of Malacca, Malaysia; Singapore (224 sq. mi.), Singapore Strait, Singapore.

Atolls: Bikini (lagoon area, 280 sq. mi., land area 3 sq. mi.). U.S. Trust Territory of the Pacific Islands; Canton (lagoon 20 sq. mi., land 4 sq. mi.). U.S. and UK; Christmas (lagoon 140 sq. mi., land 94 sq. mi.). U.S. and UK; Funafuti (lagoon 84 sq. mi., land 2 sq. mi.). U.S. and UK.

Major Rivers in North America

Source: U.S. Geological Survey

River	Source or Upper Limit of Length	Outflow	Miles
Alabama	Gilmer County, Ga.	Mobile River	735
Albany	Lake St. Joseph	James Bay	320
Allegheny	Potter County, Pa.	Ohio River	325
Altamaha-Ocmulgee	Junction of Yellow and South Rivers, Newton County, Ga.	Atlantic Ocean	392
Apalachicola-Chattahoochee	Towns County, Ga.	Gulf of Mexico, Fla.	524
Assiniboine	Eastern Saskatchewan	Red River	450
Arkansas	Lake County, Col.	Mississippi River, Ark.	1,459
Atchafalaya	Red River, La.	Grand Lake, La.	135
Attawapiskat	Attawapiskat	James Bay	465
Black (N.W.T)	Contwoyto Lake	Chantrey Inlet	600
Big Black (Miss.)	Webster County, Miss.	Mississippi River	330
Big Horn	Junction of Wind and Popo Agie Rivers, Fremont County, Wy.	Yellowstone River, Mon.	336
Black (Mo.-Ark.)	Junction Middle and West Forks, Reynolds County, Mo.	White River	280
Bow	Rocky Mountains	South Saskatchewan River	315
Brazos	Junction of Salt and Double Mountain Forks, Stonewall County, Tex.	Gulf of Mexico	870
Canadian	Las Animas County, Col.	Arkansas River, Okla.	906
Cape Fear	Junction of Haw and Deep Rivers, Chatham County, N.C.	Alantic Ocean	202
Cedar (Iowa)	Dodge County, Minn.	Iowa River, Ia.	329
Cheyenne	Junction of Antelope Creek and Dry Fork, Converse County, Wy.	Missouri River	290
Churchill	Methy Lake	Hudson Bay	1,000
Cimarron	Colfax County, N. M.	Arkansas River, Okla.	600
Clark Fork-Pend Oreille	Silver Bow County, Mon.	Columbia River, B.C.	505
Colorado (Ariz.)	Rocky Mountain National Park, Col. (90 miles in Mexico)	Gulf of Cal., Mexico	1,450
Colorado (Texas)	West Texas	Matagorda Bay	840
Columbia	Columbia Lake, British Columbia	Pacific Ocean, bet. Ore. and Wash.	1,243
Columbia, Upper	Columbia Lake, British Columbia	To mouth of Snake River	890
Colville	Brooks Range	Beaufort Sea	350
Connecticut	Third Connecticut Lake, N.H.	L.I. Sound, Conn.	407
Coosa	Junction of Etowah and Oostanaula River, Floyd County, Ga.	Alabama River	286
Copper	Alaska Range	Gulf of Alaska	280
Coppermine (N.W.T.)	Lac de Gras	Coronation Gulf (Atlantic Ocean)	525
Cumberland	Letcher County, Ky.	Ohio River	720
Delaware	Schoharie County, N.Y.	Liston Point, Delaware Bay	390
Deschutes	Lava Lake, Deschutes County, Ore.	Columbia River	250
Des Moines	Junction of East and West Forks, Humboldt County, Ia.	Mississippi River	327
Dolores	Dolores County, Col.	Colorado River	230
Flint	Hapeville, Fulton County, Ga.	Apalachicola River	265
Fraser	Near Mount Robson (on Continental Divide)	Strait of Georgia	850
French Broad	Junction of North and West Forks, Transylvania County, N.C.	Tennessee River	210
Gila	Catron County, N.M.	Colorado River, Ariz.	630
Grand (Mich.)	Jackson County, Mich.	Lake Michigan	260
Great Whale (Que.)	Lake Bienville	Hudson Bay	230
Green (Ky.)	Lincoln County, Ky.	Ohio River, Ky.	360
Green (Ut.-Wy.)	Junction of Wells and Trail Creeks, Sublette County, Wy.	Colorado River, Ut.	730
Hamilton (Lab.)	Lake Ashuanipi	Atlantic Ocean	600
Hudson	Henderson Lake, Essex County, N.Y.	Upper N.Y. Bay, N.Y.-N.J.	306
Humboldt	Wells, Nev.	Humboldt Lake	390
Illinois	St. Joseph County, Ind.	Mississippi River	420
Iowa	Hancock County, Ia.	Mississippi River	291
James (N.D.-S.D.)	Wells County, N.D.	Missouri River, S.D.	710
James (Va.)	Junction of Jackson and Cowpasture Rivers, Botetourt County, Va.	Hampton Roads	340
Jefferson-Beaverhead-Red Rock	Source of Red Rock River in Beaverhead County, Mon.	Missouri River	217
John Day	Blue Mountains, Grant County, Ore.	Columbia River	281
Kanawha-New	Junction of North and South Forks of New River, N.C.	Ohio River	352
Kentucky	Junction of North and Middle Forks, Lee County, Ky.	Ohio River	259
Klamath	Lake Ewauna, Klamath Falls, Ore.	Pacific Ocean	250
Koyukuk	Endicott Mountains, Alaska	Yukon River	470
Kuskokwim	Alaska Range	Kuskokwim Bay	680
Liard	Southern Yukon	Mackenzie River	570
Licking	Magoffi County, Ky.	Ohio River	350
Little Colorado	Latitude 34°, Apache County, Ariz.	Colorado River	300
Little Missouri	Crook County, Wy.	Missouri River	560
Mackenzie	Great Slave Lake	Arctic Ocean	900
Milk	Junction of North and South Forks, Alberta Province	Missouri River, Mon.	625
Minnesota	Big Stone Lake, Minn.	Mississippi River, St. Paul, Minn.	332
Mississippi	Lake Itasca, Minn.	Mouth of Southwest Pass	2,348

River	Source or Upper Limit of Length	Outflow	Miles
Mississippi, Upper	Lake Itasca, Minn.	To mouth of Missouri R.	1,171
Mississippi-Missouri-Red Rock	Source of Red Rock River, Mon.	Mouth of Southwest Pass	3,710
Missouri	Junction of Jefferson, Madison, and Gallatin Rivers, Madison County, Mon.	Mississippi River	2,315
Missouri-Red Rock	Source of Red Rock River, Mon.	Mississippi River	2,533
Mobile-Alabama-Coosa	Gilmer County, Ga.	Mobile Bay	780
Neches	Van Zandt County, Tex.	Sabine Lake	280
Nelson (Manitoba)	Lake Winnipeg	Hudson Bay	410
Neosho	Morris County, Kan.	Arkansas River, Okla.	460
Neuse	Junction of Eno, Little, and Flat Rivers, Durham County, N.C.	Pamlico Sound	260
New	Junction of North and South Forks, Ashe County, N.C.	Kanawha River	255
Niobrara	Niobrara County, Wy.	Missouri River, Neb.	431
Noatak	Brooks Range, Alas.	Kotzebue Sound	350
North Canadian	Union County, N.M.	Canadian River, Okla.	760
North Platte	Junction of Grizzly and Little Grizzly Creeks, Jackson County, Col.	Platte River, Neb.	618
Nueces	Edwards County, Tex.	Nueces Bay	338
Ohio	Junction of Allegheny and Monogahela Rivers, Pittsburgh, Pa.	Mississippi River, Ill.-Ky.	981
Ohio-Allegheny	Potter County, Pa.	Mississippi River	1,306
Osage	East-central Kansas	Missouri River, Mo.	500
Ottawa	Lake Capimitchigama	St. Lawrence	696
Ouachita	Polk County, Ark.	Red River, La.	605
Owyhee	Elko County, Nev.	Snake River	250
Pearl	Neshoba County, Miss.	Gulf of Mexico, Miss.-La.	411
Peace	Stikine Mountains	Slave River	1,054
Pecos	Mora County, N.M.	Rio Grande, Tex.	735
Pee Dee	Junction of Yadkin and Uwharrie Rivers, Montgomery County, N.C.	Winyah Bay	233
Pee Dee-Yadkin	Watauga County, N.C.	Winyah Bay, S.C.	435
Pend Oreille	Near Butte, Mon.	Columbia River	490
Platte	Junction of North and South Platte Rivers, Neb.	Missouri River, Neb.	310
Porcupine	Ogilvie Mountains, Alaska	Yukon River, Alaska	460
Potomac	Garrett County, Md.	Chesapeake Bay	383
Powder	Junction of South and Middle Forks, Wy.	Yellowstone River, Mon.	375
Red (Okla.-Tex.-La.)	Curry County, N.M.	Mississippi River	1,270
Red River of the North	Junction of Otter Tail and Boise de Sioux Rivers, Wilkin County, Minn.	Lake Winnipeg, Manitoba	545
Republican	Junction of North Fork and Arikaree River, Neb.	Kansas River, Kan.	445
Rio Grande	San Juan County, Col.	Gulf of Mexico	1,885
Roanoke	Junction of North and South Forks, Montgomery County, Va.	Albemarle Sound, N.C.	380
Rock (Ill.-Wis.)	Dodge County, Wis.	Mississippi River, Ill.	300
Sabine	Junction of South and Caddo Forks, Hunt County, Tex.	Sabine Lake, Tex.-La.	380
Sacramento	Siskiyou County, Cal.	Suisun Bay	377
St. Francis	Iron County, Mo.	Mississippi River, Ark.	425
St. Johns (Fla.)	Lake Washington, Brevard County, Fla.	Atlantic Ocean	276
St. Joseph	Hillsdale County, Mich.	Lake Michigan	210
St. Lawrence	Lake Ontario	Gulf of St. Lawrence (Atlantic Ocean)	800
Salmon (Idaho)	Custer County, Ida.	Snake River, Ida.	420
San Joaquin	Junction of South and Middle Forks, Madera County, Cal.	Suisun Bay	350
San Juan	Silver Lake, Archuleta County, Col.	Colorado River, Ut.	360
Santee-Wateree-Catawba	McDowell County, N.C.	Atlantic Ocean, S.C.	538
Saskatchewan, North	Rocky Mountains	Lake Winnipeg	1,100
Saskatchewan, South	Rocky Mountains	Lake Winnipeg	1,205
Savannah	Junction of Seneca and Tugaloo Rivers, Anderson County, S.C.	Atlantic Ocean, Ga.-S.C.	314
Scioto	Auglaize County, O.	Ohio River	237
Severn (Ontario)	Sandy Lake	Hudson Bay	610
Skeena (B.C.)	Skeena Mountains	Pacific Ocean	360
Smoky Hill	Cheyenne County, Col.	Kansas River, Kan.	540
Snake	Teton County, Wy.	Columbia River, Wash.	1,038
South Platte	Junction of South and Middle Forks, Park County, Col.	Platte River, Neb.	424
Stikine	Stikine Range, B.C.	Pacific Ocean	310
Susitna	Alaska Range	Cook Inlet	300
Susquehanna	Otsego Lake, Otsego County, N.Y.	Chesapeake Bay, Md.	444
Tallahatchie	Tippah County, Miss.	Yazoo River, Miss.	301
Tallapoosa	Near Embry in Paulding County, Ga.	Alabama River	268
Tanana	Wrangell Mountains	Yukon River, Alaska	620
Tar-Pamlico	Person County, N.C.	Pamlico Bay	215
Tennessee	Junction of French Broad and Holston Rivers	Ohio River, Ky.	652
Tennessee-French Broad	Bland County, Va.	Ohio River	900
Tombigbee	Prentiss County, Miss.	Mobile River, Ala.	525
Tongue	Junction of North and South Forks, Sheridan County, Wy.	Yellowstone River	246
Trinity	North of Dallas, Tex.	Galveston Bay, Tex.	360
Wabash	Darke County, O.	Ohio River, Ill.-Ind.	529
Washita	Hemphill County, Tex.	Red River, Okla.	500
White (Ark.-Mo.)	Madison County, Ark.	Mississippi River	720
Willamette	Douglas County, Ore.	Columbia River	270
Wisconsin	LeVieux Desert, Vilas County, Wis.	Mississippi River	430
Yellowstone	Park County, Wy.	Missouri River, N.D.	671
Yukon	Junction of Lewes and Pelly Rivers, Yukon	Bering Sea, Alaska	1,770

Flows of Largest Rivers in the United States

(Ranked according to average discharge in cubic feet per second (cfs) at mouth)
Source: U.S. Geological Survey (Average discharges for the period 1941-70)

Rank	River	Average Discharge	Length[a] (miles)	Drainage Area	Most Distant Source	Maximum Discharge at Gaging Station Farthest Downstream	(date)
1	Mississippi	[b]640,000	[c]3,710	[d]1,247,300	Beaverhead Co., Mont.	2,080,000	2-17-37
2	Columbia	262,000	1,243	258,000	Columbia Lake, B.C.	1,240,000	Jun. 1894
3	Ohio	258,000	1,306	203,900	Potter Co., Pa.	1,850,000	2-1-37
4	St. Lawrence	[e]243,000	—	[e]302,000	——	[f]314,000	May 1870
5	Yukon	[g]240,000	1,770	327,600	Coast Mountains, B.C.	1,030,000	6-22-64
6	[h]Atchafalaya	183,000	135	95,105	Curry Co., N. Mex.	——	
7	Missouri	76,300	2,533	529,400	Beaverhead Co., Mont.	- 892,000	Jun. 1844
8	Tennessee	64,000	900	40,910	Bland Co., Va.	500,000	2-17-48
9	Red	[i]62,300	1,270	93,244	Curry Co., N. Mex.	233,000	4-17-45
10	Kuskokwim	62,000	680	49,000	Alaska Range, Alaska	392,000	6-5-64
11	Mobile	61,400	780	43,800	Gilmer, Co., Ga.	——	
12	Snake	50,000	1,038	109,000	Teton Co., Wyo.	409,000	Jun. 1894
13	Arkansas	45,100	1,459	160,600	Lake Co., Col.	536,000	5-27-43
14	Copper	[j]43,000	280	24,000	Alaska Range, Alaska	[k]280,000	7-15-71
15	Tanana	[l]41,000	620	44,000	Wrangell Mtn., Alaska	186,000	8-18-67
16	Susitna	[m]40,000	300	20,000	Alaska Range, Alaska	90,700	6-7-64
17	Susquehanna	37,190	444	27,570	Otsego Co., N.Y.	1,080,000	6-23-72
18	Willamette	35,660	270	11,200	Douglas Co., Ore.	500,000	12-4-1861
19	Alabama	32,400	735	22,600	Gilmer Co., Ga.	267,000	3-7-61
20	White	32,100	720	28,000	Madison Co., Ark.	343,000	4-17-45
21	Wabash	30,400	529	33,150	Darke Co., Oh.	428,000	3-30-13
22	Pend Oreille	29,900	490	25,820	Near Butte, Mont.	171,300	6-13-48
23	Tombigbee	27,300	525	20,100	Prentiss Co., Miss.	280,000	1874 and 1900
24	Cumberland	[n]26,900	720	18,080	Letcher Co., Ky.	201,000	2-18-50
25	Stikine	[o]26,000	310	20,000	Stikine Range, B.C.	120,000	6-26-55
26	Sacramento	——	377	27,100	Siskiyou Co., Cal.	[p]332,000	12-25-64
27	Apalachicola	24,700	524	19,600	Towns Co., Ga.	293,000	3-20-29
28	Illinois	22,800	420	27,900	St. Joseph Co., Ind.	123,000	May 1943
29	Koyukuk	[q]22,000	470	32,400	Endicott Mtns., Alaska	266,000	6-6-64
30	Porcupine	[r]20,000	460	45,000	Ogilvie Mtns., Alaska	289,000	5-25-71
31	Hudson	19,500	306	13,370	Essex Co., N.Y.	215,000	3-19-36
32	Allegheny	19,290	325	11,700	Potter Co., Pa.	365,000	3-18-36
33	Delaware	[s]17,200	390	11,440	Schoharie Co., N.Y.	329,000	8-20-55

(a)-Because river lengths and methods of measurement may change from time to time, the length figures given are subject to revision; (b)-about 25 percent of flow occurs in the Atchafalaya River; (c)-the length from mouth to source of the Mississippi River in Minnesota is 2,348 miles; (d)-at Baptiste Collete Bayou, Louisiana; (e)-at international boundary lat. 45°; (f)maximum monthly discharge; (g)-period 1957-70; (h)-continuation of Red River; (i)-flow of Quachita River added; (j)-period 1956-69; (k)-provisional; (l)-period 1962-69; (m)-based on records of Chulitna, Talkeetna, and Yetna Rivers; (n)-period 1931-60; (o)-period 1954-63, summer records only; (p)-discharge of American River not included; (q)-period 1960-69; (r)-period 1964-69; (s)-at Liston Point on Delaware Bay.

Large Rivers in Canada

Source: "Facts from Canadian Maps" Published by Canada Department of Energy Mines and Resources
(Ranked according to mean discharge in cubic feet per second (cfs))

Rank	River	Mean Discharge	Length (miles)	Drainage Area (sq. mi.)
1	St. Lawrence River	348,000	1,900	396,000[1]
2	Mackenzie (to head of Finlay)	343,000	2,635	697,000
3	Fraser	125,000	850	84,800
4	Columbia (International Boundary to head of Columbia Lake)	98,700	498	59,700[2]
5	Nelson (to head of Bow)	83,600	1,600	414,000[3]
6	Yukon (International Boundary to head of Nisutlin)	82,000	714	114,800[4]
7	Ottawa	69,000	790	56,500
8	Churchill (to head of Ashuanipi)	55,700	532	30,800
9	Churchill (to head of Churchill Lake)	42,400	1,000	108,600
10	Saskatchewan (to head of Bow)	24,800	1,205	130,000

(1) Including 195,000 sq. mi. in U.S.A. (2) Including 20,000 sq. mi. in U.S.A. (3) Including 69,500 sq. mi. in U.S.A. (4) Including 9,000 sq. mi. in U.S.A.

The Largest Lake in Each Province of Canada

Source: Standard Encyclopedia of the World's Rivers and Lakes. 1965 & The Canada Yearbook. 1970-1971

Province	Largest within:	Largest partly in:	Shared with	Origin	Area sq. miles	Ft. above sea level
Alta.	Claire			Natural	545	699
		Athabasca	Sask.	Natural	940	699
B.C.	Kootenay			Natural	168	1,745
Man.	Winnipeg			Natural	9,465	713
Nfld.	Melville			Natural	1,133	S.L.
N.B.	Grand			Natural	65	Tidal
N.W.T.	Great Bear			Natural	12,275	511
N.S.	Bras d'Or			Natural	360	Tidal
Ont.	Nipigon			Natural	1,870	855
P.E.I.		Huron	U.S.A.	Natural	15,353	580
Que.	Mistassini			Natural	840	1,220
Sask.	Wollaston			Natural	796	1,300
		Athabasca	Alta.	Natural	2,180	699

The Largest Lake in Each State of the United States

Source: National Geographic Society, Washington, D.C.

*indicates reservoir

State	Largest entirely within state	Largest partly in another state	Shared with	Origin	Total Area in square miles	Feet above sea level	Maximum depth feet	Shoreline length miles
Ala.	Wheeler			Man-made	104.8	556	58	1,063
		Guntersville	Tenn.	Man-made	108	595	60	962
Alaska.	Iliamna			Natural	1,010	44	980	297
Ariz.	Painted Rock*			Man-made	83	661	181	—
		Powell	Ut.	Man-made	252	3,700	580	1,800
Ark.	Ouachita			Man-made	57	571	190	640
		Bull Shoals	Mo.	Man-made	71	654	203	740
Cal.	Salton Sea			Natural	360	-235	48	—
		Tahoe	Nev.	Natural	192	6,229	1,644	71
Col.	Blue Mesa*			Man-made	14.3	7,519	333	96
		Navajo*	N.M.	Man-made	24.3	6,102	382	157
Conn.	Candlewood			Man-made	8.5	429	85	65
Del.	Lum's Pond			Man-made	.31	50	10	6
Fla.	Okeechobee			Natural	700	14	20	117
Ga.	Sidney Lanier			Man-made	59.4	1,070	156	540
		Clark Hill	S.C.	Man-made	109.4	330	150	1,200
Ha.	Waita*			Man-made	.66	233	23	3
Ida.	Pend Oreille			Natural	146.9	2,064	1,400	120
Ill.	Carlyle			Man-made	40	445	40	83
		Michigan	Wis., Ind., Mich.	Natural	22,300	579	923	1,660
Ind.	Monroe			Man-made	16.8	538	45	142
		Michigan	Wis., Ill., Mich.	Natural	22,300	579	923	1,660
Ia.	Rathbun*			Man-made	32.8	926	71	180
Kan.	Milford*			Man-made	25.3	1,144	78	163
Ky.	Cumberland			Man-made	78.5	723	183	1,085
		Kentucky	Tenn.	Man-made	247.3	359	60	2,025
La.	Pontchartrain			Natural	621	sea lev.	15	117
Me.	Moosehead			Natural	117	1,058	246	—
Md.	Deep Creek			Man-made	7.0	2,462	60	55
		Conowingo*	Pa.	Man-made	13.4	109	110	38
Mass.	Quabbin*			Man-made	39.4	524	150	104
Mich.	Houghton			Natural	30.6	1,138	20	32
		Superior	Wis., Minn., Ont.	Natural	31,700	600	1,333	2,980
Minn.	Red			Natural	451.2	1,175	35	127
		Superior	Wis., Mich., Ont.	Natural	31,700	600	1,333	2,980
Miss.	Ross Barnett*			Man-made	51.5	297	50	150
Mo.	Lake of the Ozarks			Man-made	91.5	660	120	1,150
Mon.	Fort Peck			Man-made	385.9	2,234	220	1,520
Neb.	McConaughty			Man-made	54.7	3,270	142	105
Nev.	Pyramid			Natural	168.7	3,789	330	66
		Mead	Ariz.	Man-made	247	1,221	432	550
N.H.	Winnipesaukee			Natural	69.6	504	169	240
N.J.	Hopatcong			Natural	4.2	915	60	22
N.M.	Elephant Butte*			Man-made	58.9	4,450	193	250
N.Y.	Oneida			Natural	80	369	55	55
		Erie	Mich., Pa., Ont., Oh.	Natural	9,910	570	210	856
N.C.	Norman			Man-made	50.8	760	100	520
		John H. Kerr*	Va.	Man-made	76.4	320	120	800
N.D.	Sakakawea			Man-made	609	1,850	180	1,605
		Oahe*	S.D.	Man-made	579.7	1,620	200	2,250
Oh.	Grand			Man-made	20	869	10	60
		Erie	Mich., Pa., N.Y., Ont.	Natural	9,910	570	210	856
Okla.	Eufaula			Man-made	160.1	585	87	600
Ore.	Klamath			Natural	145.3	4,143	45	165
		Goose Lake	Cal.	Natural	193.7	4,716	24	90
Pa.	Wallenpaupack			Man-made	9	1,182	50	45
		Erie	Mich., Pa., N.Y., Oh., Ont.	Natural	9,910	570	210	856
R.I.	Scituate*			Man-made	5.68	284	80	38
S.C.	Marion			Man-made	157	75	35	299
S.D.	Francis Case			Man-made	159.4	1,375	140	540
		Oahe*	N.D.	Man-made	579.7	1,620	200	2,250
Tenn.	Watts Bar*			Man-made	60.3	741	105	783
		Kentucky	Ky.	Man-made	250.5	359	88	2,380
Tex.	Sam Rayburn			Man-made	178.9	173	84	560
		Toledo Bend*	La.	Man-made	308.8	175	—	1,200
Ut.	Great Salt Lake			Natural	1,650	4,200	30	—
Vt.	Bornoseen			Natural	3.7	411	55	19
		Champlain	N.Y., Que.	Natural	490	95	399	—
Va.	Smith Mountain			Man-made	32.2	795	217	500
		John H. Kerr*	N.C.	Man-made	76.4	320	120	800
Wash.	F.D. Roosevelt			Man-made	123.4	1,288	375	660
W. Va.	Tygart			Man-made	5.44	1,010	—	106
Wis.	Winnebago			Natural	215.26	747	21.6	92
		Superior	Minn., Mich., Ont.	Natural	31,700	600	1,333	2,980
Wyo.	Yellowstone			Natural	139	7,733	309	110
		Flaming Gorge*	Utah	Man-made	65.7	6,040	437	400

Famous Waterfalls

Source: National Geographic Society, Washington, D. C.

Height=total drop in one or more leaps. †=falls of more than one leap; *= falls that diminish greatly seasonally; **=falls that reduce to a trickle or are dry for part of each year. If river names not shown, they are same as the falls. R.=river; L.=lake; (C)=cascade-type. See notes following list.

Name and Location	Ft.
Africa	
Angola	
Duque de Braganca,	
Lucala R.	344
Ruacana, Cunene R.	406
Ethiopia	
Baratieri, Ganale	
Dorya R.	459
Dal Verme, Ganale	
Dorya R.	98
Fincha *	508
*Tesissat, Blue Nile R.	140
Lesotho	
Maletsunyane	630
Rhodesia-Zambia	
*Victoria, Zambezi R.	355
South Africa	
*Aughrabies, Orange R.	480
Howick, Umgeni R.	311
† Tugela (5 falls)	3,110
Highest fall	1,350
Tanzania-Zambia	
*Kalambo	726
Uganda	
Kabalega (Murchison) Victoria	
Nile R.	140
Zambia	
Chirombo, Leisa R.	880
Asia	
India—**Cauvery	330
† **Gersoppa (Jog),	
Sharavati R.	830
Japan	
**Kegon, L. Chuzenji.	330
Yudaki, L. Yuno	335
Australasia	
Australia	
New South Wales	
† Wentworth	518
Highest fall	360
Wollomombi	1,100
Queensland.	
Coomera	210
Tully.	450
New Zealand	
*Bowen (from Glaciers)	540
Helena.	890
Stirling	505
† Sutherland, Arthur R.	1,904
Europe	
Austria—†Gastein, Ache R.	373
Highest Fall	271
† Golling, Schwarzbach R.	200
‡ Krimmi (Glacier)	1,250
France—† Gavarnie (C)	1,385
Great Britain—Wales	
Pistyll Cain.	150
Pistyll Rhaiadr	240
Scotland	
Glomach	370
Iceland—Detti, Jokul R.	144
Gull, Hvita R.	101

Name and Location	Ft.
Italy—Toce (C)	470
Norway—	
† Eastern Mardal	1,696
Highest fall.	974
Western Mardal	1,535
(Both on L. Eikesdal)	
Skjeggedal	525
Skykkje, Skykkjua R	820
†Vetti, Morkedola R.	1,214
Highest Fall	889
Voring, Bjoreia R	597
Sweden	
† Handol, Handol Cr	345
† *Stora Sjofallet, Lule R.	130
Tannforsen, Are R	120
Switzerland	
† Diesbach	394
† Giessbach	1,312
† Gietroz (Glacier) (C)	1,640
Handegg, Aare R.	151
Iffigen	394
Pissevache, La Salanfe R	213
† Reichenbach	656
Rhine	65
† Simmen, Simme R.	459
Stauber, Brunnibach R.	590
Staubbach	984
† Trummelbach	1,312
North America	
Canada	
British Columbia	
†Takakkaw (Daly Glacier)	1,650
Highest fall	1,200
Della Falls	1,443
Panther, Nigel Cr	600
Labrador	
Churchill Falls,	245
Mackenzie District	
Virginia, S. Nahanni R	315
Quebec	
Montmorency	274
Canada—United States	
Niagara: American	193
Horseshoe	186
United States	
California	
Feather, Fall R	640
Yosemite National Park	
Bridalveil	620
Illilouette	370
Nevada	594
**Ribbon	1,612
Silver Strand	1,170
Vernal	317
†Yosemite	2,425
*Yosemite (upper)	1,430
*Yosemite (lower)	320
*Yosemite (middle)	675
Colorado	
Seven	266
Georgia	
† Tallulah	251
Hawaii	
Akaka	442

Name and Location	Ft.
Idaho	
**Shoshone, Snake R	212
**Twin, Snake R	125
Kentucky	
Cumberland.	68
Maryland	
Great, Potomac R. (C)	90
Minnesota	
**Minnehaha.	54
Montana	
Missouri	75
New Jersey	
**Passaic	70
New York	
Taughannock	215
Oregon	
† Multnomah	620
Highest fall	542
Tennessee	
Fall Creek	256
Rock House Creek	125
Washington	
Fairy Falls	700
Mt. Rainier Natl. Park.	
Narada, Paradise R.	168
Sluiskin, Paradise R.	300
Palouse	198
Snoqualmie	270
Wisconsin	
Manitou, Black R.	165
Wyoming	
Yellowstone Pk. Tower	132
Yellowstone (upper)	109
Yellowstone (lower)	308
Mexico—El Salto	218
**Juanacatian, Santiago R.	72
South America	
Argentina—Brazil	
† Iguazu	237
Brazil	
Glass	1,325
Herval	400
Patos-Maribondo, Rio Grande.	115
Paulo Afonso, Sao Francisco R.	275
Urubupunga, Alto Parana R.	40
Brazil-Paraguay	
Sete Quedas, or Guaira	
Alto Parana R.	130
Colombia	
Tequendama, Bogota R	427
Catarata de Candelas,	
Cusiana R	984
Ecuador	
Agoyan, Pastaza R.	200
Guyana	
Kaieteur, Potaro R	741
King George VI, Utshi R	1,600
† Marina, Ipobe R	500
Highest Fall	300
Peru	
Sewerd, Cutibirene R	877
Venezuela—† Angel	3,212
Highest fall	2,648
Cuquenan	2,000

The earth has thousands of waterfalls, some of considerable magnitude. Their importance is determined not only by height but volume of flow, steadiness of flow, crest width, whether the water drops sheerly or over a sloping surface, and one leap or a succession of leaps. A series of low falls flowing over a considerable distance is known as a cascade.

Sete Quedas or Guaira is the world's greatest waterfall when its mean annual flow (estimated at 470,000 cusecs, cubic feet per second) is combined with height. A greater volume of water passes over Stanley Falls, though not one of its seven cataracts, spread over nearly 60 miles of the Congo River, exceeds 10 feet.

Estimated mean annual flow, in cusecs, of other major waterfalls are: Niagara, 212,200; Paulo Afonso, 100,000; Urubupunga, 97,000; Iguazu, 61,600; Patos-Maribondo, 53,000; Victoria, 38,400; Churchill, Labrador, 40,000; and Kaieteur, 23,400.

Notable Bridges in North America

Source: State Highway Engineers; Canadian Civil Engineering — ASCE

Asterisk (*) designates Railroad Bridge. Span of a bridge is distance (in feet) between its supports.

Year	Bridge	Location	Longest Span
	Suspension		
1964	Verrazano-Narrows	New York, N.Y.	4,260
1937	Golden Gate	San Fran. Bay, Cal.	4,200
1957	Mackinac	Sts. of Mackinac	3,800
1931	Geo. Washington	Hudson River.	3,500
1952	Tacoma	Washington	2,800
1936	¹Transbay	San Fran. Bay, Cal.	2,310
1939	Bronx-Whitestone	East R., N.Y.C.	2,300
1970	Quebec Road.	Quebec.	2,190
1951	Del. Memorial.	Wilmington, Del.	2,150
1968	Del. Mem. (new).	Wilmington, Del.	2,150
1957	Walt Whitman	Phila., Pa.	2,000
1929	Ambassador	Detroit-Canada.	1,850
1961	Throgs Neck	Long Is. Sound	1,800
1926	Benjamin Franklin	Philadelphia.	1,750
1924	Bear Mt., N.Y.	Hudson River.	1,632
1952	²Wm. Preston Lane Mem.	Sandy Point, Md.	1,600
1903	Williamsburg	East R., N.Y.C.	1,600
1969	Newport	Narragansett Bay, R.I.	1,600
1883	Brooklyn	East R., N.Y.C.	1,595
1930	Mid-Hudson, N.Y.	Poughkeepsie	1,500
1964	Vincent Thomas	Los Angeles Harbor	1,500
1909	Manhattan.	East R., N.Y.C.	1,470
1936	Triborough	East R., N.Y.C.	1,380
1931	St. Johns	Portland, Ore.	1,207
1929	Mount Hope	Rhode Island	1,200
1939	Deer Isle	Maine	1,080
1931	Maysville (Ky.)	Ohio River	1,060
1867	Cincinnati.	Ohio River	1,057
1900	Miampimi.	Mexico.	1,030
1849	Wheeling, W. Va.	Ohio River	1,010
1929	Royal Gorge.	Colorado.	880
1938	Thousand Islands	St. Lawrence R.	800
1933	Anthony Wayne	Ohio.	782
1915	Belpre, O.-W. Va.	Ohio River	775
1904	E. Liv'p'l, O.-W. Va.	Ohio River	750
1933	South 10th St.	Pittsburgh, Pa.	750
1932	Waldo-Hancock	Maine	750
1935	Memorial Twin (Ill.).	Mississippi R.	710
	Cantilever		
1917	*Quebec (Railway)	Quebec.	1,800
1970	Chester, Pa.	Delaware River	1,644
1958	New Orleans, La.	Mississippi R.	1,575
1936	Transbay.	San Fran. Bay.	1,400
1968	Baton Rouge, La.	Mississippi R.	1,235
1955	Nyack-Tarrytown	Hudson River.	1,212
1930	Longview	Columbia River.	1,200
1909	Queensboro.	East R., N.Y.C.	1,182
1892	Muscatine, Ia.	Mississippi River.	1,164
1932	Savanna-Sabvia, Ill.	Mississippi River.	1,160
1927	Carquinez Strait.	California	1,100
1958	Parallel Span		1,100
1968	Isaiah D. Hare.	Jacksonville, Fla.	1,088
1957	³Richmond	San Fran. Bay, Cal.	1,070
1929	Grace Memorial	Charleston, S.C.	1,050
1918	MacArthur, Ill.-Mo.	Mississippi River.	1,000
1963	Newburgh-Beacon.	Hudson R., N.Y.	1,000
1975	Caruthersville, Mo.	Mississippi R.	920
1969	Ohio River.	Pt. Pleasant, W.Va.	900
1940	Natchez	Mississippi R.	875
1938	Blue Water.	Pt. Huron, Mich.	871
1972	Vicksburg.	Mississippi River.	870
1954	St. Petersburg, Fla.	Tampa Bay.	864
1940	*Baton Rouge.	Mississippi R.	848
1899	*Cornwall.	St. Lawrence R.	843
1940	Greenville	Mississippi R.	840
1961	Helena, Ark.	Mississippi R.	840
1963	Brent Spence	Covington, Ky.	831
1963	Cincinnati, Oh.	Ohio River	830
1956	Earl C. Clements.	Ohio R., Ill.-Ky.	825⁴
1930	*Vicksburg.	Mississippi R.	825
1929	Louisville.	Ohio River	820
1943	Jeff'rson Barr'ks., Mo.	Mississippi R.	804
1950	Maurice J. Tobin.	Boston, Mass.	800
1935	Rip Van Winkle	Catskill, N.Y.	800
1938	Cairo, Ill.	Ohio River	800
1940	Ludlow Ferry.	Potomac R.	800
1932	Washington Mem.	Seattle, Wash.	800

Year	Bridge	Location	Longest Span
1930	Cairo, Ill.	Mississippi R.	800
1936	North Bend, Ore.	Coos Bay.	793
1936	McCullough.	Coos Bay, Ore.	793
1935	⁴Huey P. Long.	New Orleans.	790
1916	*Memphis (Harahan).	Mississippi R.	790
1892	*Memphis.	Mississippi R.	790
1949	Memphis-Arkansas.	Mississippi R.	790
1904	*Mingo Jct., W. Va.	Ohio River	769
1910	*Beaver, Pa.	Ohio River	767
1966	⁵S.N. Pearman.	Charleston, S.C.	760
1940	Owensboro.	Ohio River	750
1911	Sewickley, Pa.	Ohio River	750
1928	Outerbridge, N.Y.-N.J.	Arthur Kill.	750
1964	Sunshine, Don'ville.	Mississippi R., La.	750
1964	Ohio River.	Henderson, Ky.	720
1956	Talmadge Memorial.	Savannah, Ga.	710
1940	Bridge of the Gods.	Oregon.	705
1927	Bellaire, Oh.	Ohio River	700
1955	Belpre, Oh.-W. Va.	Ohio River	700
1927	Rim to Rim.	Twin Falls, Ida.	700
1928	Goethals, N.Y.-N.J.	Arthur Kill.	672
1905	*Thebes, Ill.	Mississippi R.	671
1942	Chester, Ill.	Mississippi R.	670
1957	Rappahannock	White Stone, Va.	648
1959	Corpus Christi.	Nueces Co., Tex.	620
1968	Reedy Point.	Ches. & Del. Can.	600
1960	Summit.	Ches. & Del. Can.	600
1959	Castleton.	Hudson R., N.Y.	600
1943	Gold Star.	New London, Conn.	540
1934	Gastineau Channel.	Juneau, Alaska.	516
1960	West River.	Brattleboro, Vt.	440
1953	Luck Peak Reservoir.	nr. Boise, Ida.	432
1965	Jeremiah Morrow.	Warren Co., Oh.	427
1952	Mormon Pioneer.	Omaha.	420
1930	Plattsmouth, Neb.	Missouri River.	403
	Simple Truss		
1917	*Metropolis.	Ohio River.	720
1929	Paducah, Ky.	Ohio River.	716
1922	*Tanana River.	Nenana, Alaska.	700
1911	MacArthur.	St. Louis.	668
1933	*Henderson.	Ohio River.	665
1967	I-77, Ohio River.	Marietta, Oh.	650
1919	Louisville.	Ohio River.	644
1933	Atchafalaya.	Morgan City, La.	608
1924	*Castleton.	Hudson River.	598
1906	Elizabethtown.	Great Miami R., Oh.	586
1929	*Louisville.	Ohio River.	546
1889	*Cincinnati.	Ohio River.	542
1951	Allegheny River.	Allegheny Co., Pa.	533
1914	Pittsburgh.	Allegheny R.	531
1930	*Martinez.	California.	528
1967	Tanana River.	Alaska.	500
1963	216 Nenana River.	Rex, Alaska.	406
	Steel Truss		
1940	Gov. Nice Mem.	Potomac River, Md.	800
1937	US-60, Ky.	Ohio River.	800
1938	US-62, Ky.	Green River.	700
1952	US-62, Ky.	Cumberland River.	700
1940	Jamestown.	Jamestown, R.I.	640
1940	Greenville.	Mississippi R., Ark.	640
1949	Memphis.	Mississippi R., Ark.	621
1938	US-421.	Ohio River, Ky.	600
1960	Summit.	Chespeak-Del. Canal.	600
1938	US-22.	Delaware River, N.J.	540
1972	Mississippi River.	Muscatine, Ia.	512
1896	Newport.	Ohio River, Ky.	511
1897	Missouri River.	Sioux City, Neb.-Ia.	504
1931	US-60.	Cumberland R., Ky.	500
1958	Lake Oahe.	Mobridge, S.D.	500
1958	Lake Oahe.	Gettysburg, S.D.	500
1874	McKinley, St. Louis.	Mississippi River.	500
1963	Millard E. Tydings.	Susquehanna R., Md.	490
1930	Lake Champlain.	Lake Champlain, N.Y.	434
1952	Bellevue (GAR).	Missouri R., Neb.	420
1947	Mayo.	Blountstown, Fla.	420
1929	Clarendon.	White River, Ark.	400
1931	US-60.	Tennessee R., Ky.	400
1965	Moyie Springs.	Moyie River, Ida.	378
1944	US-68.	Tennessee R., Ky.	368

Year	Bridge	Location	Length
929	Augusta	White River, Ark.	360
932	US-62	Kentucky River	360
951	SR-80	Fishing Creek, Ky.	360
953	Lake Francis Case	Chamberlain, S.D.	336
876	High Bridge, Ky.	Kentucky River	332
963	US-68	Cumberland R., Ky.	321
939	US-431	Green & Rough R., Ky.	320
940	Deep Creek Lake	Deep Creek Lake, Md.	300
953	Montague Twp.	Delaware River, N.J.	300
958	Little Colorado	Cameron, Ariz.	296
950	Somerset	Cumberland R., Ky.	280
927	US-27	Kentucky River, Ky.	275
951	Comm. Isaac Hull	Housatonic R., Conn.	254

Continuous Truss

Year	Bridge	Location	Length
959	Rocheport, Mo.	Missouri River	2,500⁹
939	Lyons-Fulton	Mississippi R., Ill.	1,340
966	Astoria, Ore.	Columbia R.	1,232
966	Marquam	Willamette R., Ore.	1,044
IC	(1975) Miss. R.	Dyersburg, Tenn.	900
969	Irondequoit Bay	Rochester, N.Y.	891
943	Dubuque, Ia.	Mississippi R.	845
953	John E. Mathews	Jacksonville, Fla.	810
957	Kingston-Rhinecliff	Hudson R., N.Y.	800
961	Sherman Minton	New Albany, Ind.	800
918	*Sciotoville	Ohio River	775
929	Madison-Milton	Ohio River	727
973	1275, Boone Co., Ky.	Ohio River	720
964	John F. Kennedy	Louisville, Ky.	700
966	Matthew E. Welsh	Mauckport, Ind.	707⁶
929	Chain of Rocks	Mississippi R.	699
966	Braga	Taunton R., Mass.	682
938	Port Arthur-Orange	Texas	680
929	*Cincinnati	Ohio River	675
932	Mt. Carmel, Ill.	Wabash River	675
928	Cape Girardeau, Mo.	Mississippi R.	672
946	Chester, Ill.	Mississippi R.	670
930	Quincy, Ill.	Mississippi R.	628
934	Bourne	Cape Cod Canal	616
935	Sagamore	Cape Cod Canal	616
965	Clarion River	Clarion Co., Pa.	612
965	Rio Grande Gorge	Taos, N.M.	600
941	Columbia River	Kettle Falls, Wash.	600
962	W. Br. Feather River	Oroville, Cal.	576
936	Meredosia	Illinois River	567
936	Mark Twain Mem.	Hannibal, Mo.	562
937	Homestead	Pittsburgh	553
961	Ship Canal	Seattle, Wash.	552
932	Pulaski Skyway	Passaic R., N.J.	550
927	Ross Island	Portland, Ore.	535
936	South Omaha	Mo. R., Neb.-Ia.	525
962	Columbia River	Beebe, Wash.	520
970	Snake River	Central Ferry, Wash.	520
954	Columbia River	Pasco, Wash.	520
962	Columbia River	Vantage, Wash.	520
958	Stevenson, Ala.	Tennessee R.	500
922	Memorial	Missouri River, N.D.	475
962	Martinez, Cal.	Carquinex Strait	475
967	Mississippi River	Minneapolis, Minn.	456
963	175 Ky. (Twin)	Kentucky R.	448
956	Decatur, Neb.	Missouri R.	420
939	Florence, Ala.	Tennessee R.	420

Continuous Box and Plate Girder

Year	Bridge	Location	Length
953	Neches River	Orange County, Tex.	850
967	San Mateo-Hayward No. 2	San Fran. Bay, Cal.	750
969	San Diego-Coronado	San Diego Bay, Cal.	660⁷
972	Ship Channel	Houston, Tex.	630
967	Poplar St.	St. Louis, Mo.	600
967	Lake Koocanusa	Lincoln Co., Mon.	500
967	LaCrosse	Mississippi R., Wis.	450
967	Mississippi R.	LaCrescent, Minn.	450
972	Sitka Harbor	Sitka, Alaska	450
974	I-430	Arkansas R.	430
972	Kansas City	Missouri R., Kan-Mo.	425
967	Chattanooga	Tennessee R., Tenn.	420
941	Susquehanna	Susquehanna R., Md.	400
963	Lake Charles B'Pass.	Louisiana	399
971	St. Croix River	Hudson, Minn.	390
957	Conn. Turnpike	Quinnipiac R.	387
960	Route 34	New Haven, Conn.	379
971	S.H. No. 1	Pendleton, Ark.	377
960	Tennessee River	Chattanooga, Tenn.	375
966	LeClaire	LeClaire, Ia.	370
971	Sacramento R.	Bryte, Cal.	370
966	Benton-Humphrey	Tennessee R., Tenn.	366
967	San Mateo Creek	Hillsborough, Cal.	360
...	Gunnison River	Gunnison, Col.	360

Year	Bridge	Location	Length
1950	US-62	Tennessee R., Ky.	350
1961	Whiskey Creek	Trinity Co., Cal.	350
1972	Franklin Falls	Snoq'lmie Pass, Wash.	350
1971	Don Pedro Reserv.	Tuolumne Co., Cal.	350
1970	Columbia River	Brewster, Wash.	343
1968	Darmouth	Minneapolis	340
1967	Lexington Ave.	St. Paul	340
1971	Cumberland River	Nashville, Tenn.	330
1969	Buffalo Creek	Armstrong Co., Pa.	325
1970	Arkansas R.	Dardanelle, Ark.	325
1969	Arkansas R.	Morrilton, Ark.	322
1963	Western Ky. Pkwy.	Green River, Ky.	320
1965	Blue Grass Pkwy.	Kentucky River, Ky.	320
1964	Cumberland River	Nashville, Tenn.	320
1967	Carroll County	Kentucky R., Ky.	320
1936	Kentucky River	Frankfort, Ky.	315
1966	Washington Ave.	Minneapolis	315
1959	William H. Putnam	Conn. River, Conn.	311
1971	Copper River	Chitina, Alaska	310
1973	Main Street	Little Rock, Ark.	303
1967	Rouge River	Detroit, Mich.	300
1972	Mission Valley	San Diego, Cal.	300
1953	Carrollton	Kentucky R., Ky.	300
1950	Guthrie	Guthrie, Ariz.	300
1942	Charter Oak	Hartford, Conn.	300
1970	Sacramento River	Elkhorn, Cal.	285
1964	West Camas Slough	Camas, Wash.	284
1950	US-231	Green River, Ky.	276
1964	Duwamish R. (Twins)	Seattle	275
1940	Lakefront	Cleveland, Oh.	271
1951	SR-61	Green River, Ky.	260
1954	Wenatchee River	Wenatchee, Wash.	260
1971	Lake Bomoseen	Castleton, Vt.	260
1973	East 148 St.	Seattle, Wash.	258
1966	Hansen	Hansen, Ida.	258
1965	Susitna River	Alaska	250
1940	Thomas A. Edison	Raritan River	250
1965	Barren River	165, Kentucky	250
1962	Snohomish River	Monroe, Wash.	255
1954	Garden State Pkwy	Raritan River, N.J.	250
1958	P't Wash'gt'n Narr.	Bremerton, Wash.	250
1966	Lake Francis Case	Platte, S.D.	250
1973	Swinomish Slough	Mt. Vernon, Wash.	246
1972	Arkansas River	Pine Bluff, Ark.	243
1948	Baldwin	Connecticut R.	240
1968	Sharon	Sharon, Vt.	239
1962	Lake Sharpe	Pierre, S.D.	235
1959	Mulholland Dr.	Los Angeles, Cal.	235
1968	11th (Twins)	Anacostia R., Wash., D.C.	234
1967	White River	Hartford, Vt.	233
1968	Royalton	Royalton, Vt.	225
1964	Theodore Roosevelt	Potomac R., Wash., D.C.	222
1961	W'r'w Wilson Mem.	Potomac River	222
1969	Snohomish R.	Monroe, Wash.	222
1973	Chattahoochee R.	Ft. Gaines, Ga.	220
1940	Tallulah River	Tallulah Gorge, Ga.	220
1970	Chulitna River	Alaska	220

Continuous Plate

Year	Bridge	Location	Length
1965	New Chain of Rocks	Mississippi R., Ill.	2,755⁹
1973	Great Congress Gty.	Schenectady, N.Y.	1,870
1971	Congress St.	Troy, N.Y.	1,420
1965	Rock Island	Mississippi R., Ill.	1,136
1955	Four Bears	Missouri R., N.D.	475
1966	I-480	Missouri R., Ia.-Neb.	425
1972	I-80	Missouri R., Ia.-Neb.	425
1970	Green River	Hendersonville, N.C.	350
1969	Fort Smith	Arkansas River	340
1957	Snake River	Alpine Jct., Wy.	264
1973	Lewis & Clark	Williston, N.D.	235
1971	Washburn	Missouri R., N.D.	235
1965	Grant-Marsh	Missouri R., N.D.	235
1964	Galveston Bay	Galveston Co., Tex.	215

I-Beam Girder

Year	Bridge	Location	Length
1941	US-31E	Rolling Fork R., Ky.	340
1948	US-27	Licking River, Ky.	316
1947	US-31E	Green River, Ky.	316
1941	US-62	Rolling Fork, Ky.	240
1942	Licking River	Owingsville, Ky.	240
1954	Fuller Warren	Jacksonville, Fla.	224
1957	Freeway	Arkansas River	210

Steel Arch

Year	Bridge	Location	Length
1931	Bayonne, N.J.	Kill Van Kull	1,652
1972	Fremont	Portland, Ore.	1,255

1964	Port Mann	British Columbia	1,200
1959	Glen Canyon	Colorado River	1,028
1967	Trois-Rivieres	St. Lawrence R., P.Q.	1,100
1962	Lewiston-Queenston	Niagara River, Ont.	1,000
1917	*Hell Gate	East R., N.Y.C.	977
1941	Rainbow	Niagara Falls	950
1970	Lake Quinsigamond	Worcester, Mass.	849
1966	Charles Braga	Somerset, Mass.	840
1967	Lincoln Trail	Ohio R., Ind.-Ky.	825
1966	Lincoln Trail	Cannelton, Ind.	806
1961	Sherman Minton	Louisville, Ky.	800
1936	Henry Hudson	Harlem River	800
1936	French King	Conn. R. (Rt. 2, Mass.)	782
1931	West End	Pittsburgh	778
1972	Piscataqua R	I-95, N.H.-Me.	756
1963	Cold Spring Canyon	Santa Barbara, Cal.	700
1964	John Kennedy	Ohio River, Ind.-Ky.	700
1973	I-24, Paducah, Ky.	Ohio River	700
1955	Pa.-N.J. Turnpike	Delaware River	682
1964	Burro Creek	(Wikieup) Ariz.	680
1954	Newark-Bayonne	Newark Bay, N.J.	670
1924	*Michigan Central	Niagara Falls	640
1955	Missouri River	Jefferson City, Mo.	640
1929	Navajo	Colorado River, Ariz.	616
1961	Duluth Harbor	Lake Superior	600
1961	St. Louis Bay	Superior, Wis.	600
1938	Middletown	Connecticut	600
1936	Yaquina Bay	Oregon	600
1954	Gt. S. Bay	West Islip, N.Y.	600
1963	Fire Is. Inlet	Fire Is., N.Y.	600
1916	Colorado River	Ariz.-Cal.	592
1917	Cuyahoga River	Cleveland, Oh.	591
1929	Palmyra Boro	Delaware R., N.J.	550
1949	Chesapeake City	Ches. & Del. Can.	540
1941	St. Georges	Ches. & Del. Can.	540
1940	Centennial	Miss. R., Ill.-Ia.	539
1967	Gerald Desmond	Long Bea. H'b'r, Cal.	527
1874	Eads, St. Louis	Mississippi R.	520
1951	Hastings, Minn.	Mississippi R.	514
1888	Washington, N.Y.C.	Harlem River	509
1962	Alex'der Hamilton	Harlem R., N.Y.	505
1848	High Bridge, N.Y.C.	Harlem River	496
1956	Wabash Memorial	Wabash River, Ind.	441

Concrete Arch

1934	New River	Ripplemead, Va.	1,321[9]
1932	Clark Memorial	Wabash River	1,033[9]
1971	Selah Creek (twin)	Selah, Wash.	549
1968	Cowlitz River	Mossyrock, Wash.	520
1931	Westinghouse	Pittsburgh	425
1923	Cappelen	Minneapolis	400
1930	Jack's Run	Pittsburgh	400
1973	Elwha River	Port Angeles, Wash.	380
1931	Bixby Creek	Monterey Coast, Cal.	330
1953	Arroyo Seco	Pasadena, Cal.	320
1927	Mendota	Ft. Snelling, Minn.	304
1915	Rocky River	Cleveland, Oh.	280
1929	10th Ave.	Minneapolis	266
1918	Third Ave.	Minneapolis	211
1929	Chisholm Pk.	Rumford, Me.	210
1934	Waldport	Alsea Bay, Ore.	210
1925	Key	Potomac R.,Wash.D.C.	208
1930	Cornwall, Conn.	Housatonic R.	184

Twin Concrete Trestle

1963	Slidell, La.	L. Pontchartrain	28,547[9]

Concrete Slab Dam

1927	Conowingo Dam	Maryland	4,611
1952	John H. Kerr Dam	Roanoke River, Va.	2,785
1936	Hoover Dam	Boulder City, Nev.	1,324

Drawbridges
Vertical Lift

1959	*Arthur Kill	N.Y.-N.J.	558
1935	*Cape Cod Canal	Massachusetts	544
1960	*Delair, N.J.	Delaware River	542
1937	Marine Parkway	New York City	540
1931	Burlington, N.J.	Delaware R.	534
1912	*A-S-B Fratt.	Kansas City	428
1945	*Harry S. Truman.	Kansas City	427
1932	*M-K-T R.R.	Missouri R.	414
1969	Wilm'gtn Mem.	Wilmington, N.C.	408
1930	Duluth	Minnesota.	386
1941	St. Johns River	Jack'ville, Fla.	386
1941	Doremus	Passaic River, N.J.	366
1922	*Cincinnati	Ohio River	365
1967	Benj. Harrison Mem	James River, Va.	363
1961	Corpus Christi, Tex.,	Port Aransas-	
	RR.-Highway	Corpus Christi	344
1933	Troy-Menands	Hudson River.	341
1962	Sand Island Aess.	Oahu, Hawaii.	340
1929	Carlton	Bath-Woolwich, Me.	328
1930	*Martinez	California.	328
1960	West Bay	Panama City, Fla.	327
1929	*Penn-Lehigh	Newark Bay.	322
1920	*Chattanooga	Tennessee R.	310
1936	Triboro, N.Y.C.	Harlem River	310
1936	Hardin	Illinois River.	309
1960	Sacramento River.	Rio Vista, Cal.	306
1957	Claiborne Ave.	New Orleans.	305
1927	Cochrane	Mobile, Ala.	300
1928	James River	Newport News	300
1929	San Mateo	California.	300
1926	*Missouri Pacific	Kragen, Ark.	300
1956	Sidney Lanier	Brunswick, Ga.	295
1960	Interstate	Columbia River,	
		Ore.-Wash.	279
1928	Jordan	Norfolk, Va.	277
1959	Houghton-Hancock	Michigan.	268
1955	Hackensack, N.J.	Hackensack River	222
1949	Newark, N.J.	Passaic River	222

Bascule

1926	*AT&SFRR (Ia.-Ill.)	Mississippi R.	525
1969	Pearl River	Slidell, La.	482
1916	Keokui Municipal.	Mississippi R., Ia.	377
1940	Lorain, Ohio.	Black River.	295
1969	Elizabeth River.	Chesapeake, Va.	281
1957	Craig Memorial	I-280, Toledo, Oh.	271
1952	Downtown	Norfolk, Va.	230

Swing Bridges

1950	Douglass Memorial	Anac'tia R., Wash. D.C.	386
1945	Lord Delaware	Mattaponi River, Va.	252
1957	Eltham	Pamunkey River, Va.	237
1939	Chickahominy River.	Route 5, Va.	222
1930	Nansemond River.	Route 125, Va.	200

Swing Span

1927	*Fort Madison	Mississippi R.	525
1908	*Willamette R.	Portland, Ore.	521
1903	*East Omaha	Missouri R.	519
1952	Yorktown	York River, Va.	500
1897	*Duluth, Minn.	St. Louis Bay	486
1899	*C.M.&N.R.R.	Chicago	474
1895	Sioux City, Ia.	Missouri R.	470
1914	*Coos Bay	Oregon	458

Floating Pontoon

1963	Evergreen Pt.	Seattle, Wash.	7,518
1940	Lacey V. Murrow	Seattle.	6,561
1961	Hood Canal.	Pt. Gamble, Wash.	6,471

(1) The Transbay Bridge has 2 spans of 2,310 ft. each. (2) A second bridge in parallel will be completed. (3) The Richmond Bridge has twin spans 1,070 ft. each. (4) Railroad and vehicular bridge. (5) Two spans each 760 ft. (6) Two spans each 707 ft. (7) Two spans each 660 ft. (8) Two spans each 825 ft. (9) Total length of bridge. (10) Dumbarton has 7 spans each 225 ft. long.

Construction Details of Large and Unusual Bridges

Verrazano-Narrows Bridge, between Staten Island and Brooklyn, N.Y., has a suspension span of 4,260 ft., longest in the world and exceeding the Golden Gate Bridge, San Francisco, by 60 ft. One level in use Nov., 1964, second opened Jun. 28, 1969. The name is a compromise; it spans the Narrows and commemorates a visit to New York Harbor in Apr., 1524, deduced from certain notes left by Giovanni da Verrazano, Italian navigator sailing for Francis I of France.

Allegheny River Bridge (Interstate 80) near Emlenton, Pa., 270 ft. above the water, tallest in eastern U.S., a continuous truss, 688 ft. long, 1968.

Angostura, suspension type, span 2,336 feet, 1967 at Ciudad Bolivar, Venezuela. Total length, 5,507.

Charles Braga Bridge over Taunton River between Fall River and Somerset, Mass. It is 5,780 feet long.

Bendorf Bridge on the Rhine River, 5 mi. n. of Coblenz, completed 1965, is a 3-span cement girder bridge, 3,378 ft. overall length, 101 ft. wide, with the main span 682 ft.

Burro Creek Bridge with 4 spans over Burro Creek on highway 93 near Kingman, Ariz. Main span steel truss 680 ft. Others plate girder, 110 and 2 of 85 ft. 1966.

Champlain Bridge at Montreal crossing the St. Lawrence River was opened 1962. It is 4 miles long. Three others connect Montreal with the South Bank, the Jacques Cartier, Victoria, and Mercier bridges.

Corpus Christi, Tex., has a high level port entrance bridge. It is a cantilever truss with anchor spans 310 ft. and main span 620 ft., total length approx. 5,862 ft.

Cross Bay Parkway Bridge (N.Y.), 3,000 feet long with 6 traffic lanes, 11 eight foot wide precast, prestressed concrete T girders to support spans 130 feet long each with main span 275 feet.

Delaware Memorial Bridge over Delaware River near Wilmington. A twin suspension bridge paralleling the original 250 ft. upstream has a 2,150-ft. main span suspended from 440-ft. towers.

Eads Bridge across the Mississippi R. between St. Louis and E. St. Louis, built in 1874 has 4 main spans 1,520 ft., 2,502 ft., and 1,118 ft. crossing Miss. R., a railroad and a road.

Evergreen Point Bridge in Wash. consists of 33 floating concrete pontoons weighing 4,700 tons each, held in place by 77 ton crete anchors. Pontoon structure is 6,561 ft. long, with approaches bridge is 12,596 ft. long.

Fremont Bridge. Part of Stadium Freeway, Portland, Ore., crossing Williamette R. 1,255 ft. steel arch span with two 452 ft. flanking steel arch spans. 1971.

Frontenac Bridge, Quebec, suspension, span 2,190 ft., open 1970.

Gladesville Bridge at Sydney, Australia, has the longest concrete arch in the world (1,000 ft. span).

George Washington Bridge, New York City, 4th longest suspension bridge in the world, spans the Hudson River between W. 178th St., Manhattan, and Ft. Lee, N.J.; 4,760 ft. between anchorages, two levels, 14 traffic lanes. Triborough Bridge connects Manhattan, the Bronx, and Queens; project comprises a suspension bridge, a vertical lift bridge, and a fixed bridge, all connected by long viaducts. The famous Brooklyn Bridge over the East River, connecting Manhattan and Brooklyn, was completed in 1883, breaking all previous records by spanning 1,595 ft.

Golden Gate Bridge, crossing San Francisco Bay, has the second longest single span, 4,200 ft.

Hampton Roads Bridge-Tunnel, Va. crossing completed in 1957 consisting of 2 man-made islands, 2 concrete trestle bridges, and one tunnel, under Hampton Roads with a length of 7,479 ft. A parallel facility is under construction with estimated completion date in 1974.

Hood Canal Floating Bridge, Wash., 23 floating concrete pontoons 4,980 tons each. Roadway is supported on crete T-beam sections mounted on pontoons 20 feet above canal. Floating section is 6,471 ft. long, overall 7,866 ft.

International Bridge, a series of 8 arch and truss bridges crossing St. Mary's and the Soo Locks between Mich. and Ontario. Two-mile toll completed 1962.

Lacy V. Murrow Floating Bridge, Wash., 25 floating pontoons of 4,558 tons each. Bridge with approaches is 8,583 ft.

Lake Pontchartrain Twin Causeway, a twin-span crete trestle bridge and 24-mile link within metropolitan New Orleans that connects the north and south shore. First span opened 1956, second 1969.

Lavaca Bay Causeway, Tex., 2.2 miles long, consisting of one 260 ft. continuous plate girder unit and 194 precast, prestressed concrete spans of 60 ft. length. 1961.

Newport Bridge between Newport and Jamestown, R. I. Total length 11,248 ft., a main suspension span of 1,600 feet, 2 side spans each 688 feet long. It has U.S.A.'s first prefabricated wire strands.

New York City bridges, see *Verrazano-Narrows Bridge* and *George Washington Bridge* above.

Ogdensburg-Prescott Internat'l Bridge across the St. Lawrence River from Ogdensburg, N.Y., to Johnston, Ont., opened 1970, is 13,510 ft. long with approaches and 7,260 ft. between abutments.

Oland Island Bridge under construction in Sweden will be completed in 1972. It will be 19,882 feet long when completed and will be Europe's longest.

Oosterscheldebrug, opened Dec. 15, 1965, is a 3.125-mile causeway for automobiles over a sea arm in Zeeland, the Netherlands. It completes a direct connection between Flushing and Rotterdam.

Poplar St. Bridge over the Mississippi at St. Louis, a 5-span continuous orthotropic deck plate girder bridge, longest span 600 ft. Eight lane 2,165 ft. long.

Quebec Road, suspension, span 2,190 feet, 1969, Quebec, Canada.

Rio-Niteroi, Guanabara Bay, Brazil, under construction, will be world's longest continuous box and plate girder bridge, 8 miles, 3,363 feet long, with a center span of 984 feet and a span on each side of 656 feet.

Robert Opie Norris Bridge, Rappahannock R. between Greys Pt. and White Stone, Va. 9,989 ft. long. Main spans are two 144 foot cantilever truss spans with a 360 foot truss span suspended between them.

Rockville Bridge, world's longest 4-track stone arch bridge, 3,810 ft., with 48 arches. Part of the Penn-Central RR system west of Harrisburg, Pa. It contains 440,000,000 lbs. of stone, 100,000 cubic yds. of masonry and crosses the Susquehanna Riv. to Rockville, Pa.

Royal Gorge Bridge, 1,053 ft. above the Arkansas River in Colorado, is the highest bridge above water. Opened Dec. 8, 1929, it is 1,260 ft. long with a main span of 880 ft., width 18 ft.

San Mateo-Hayward Bridge across San Francisco Bay is first major orthotropic bridge in U.S. It is 6.7 miles long, 4.9 mile low-level concrete trestle and 1.8 miles high-level steel bridge.

Seven Mile Bridge is the longest of an expanse of bridges connecting the Florida Keys. It was built by the Florida East Coast Railway between 1904 and 1916, now a state highway.

Shenandoah River Bridges, one spans the south fork, 1,924 ft. long, the other the north fork 1,090 ft. long, Warren County Va.

Straits of Mackinac Bridge, completed in 1957, is the longest suspension bridge between anchorages and with approaches extends nearly 5 mi. between Mackinaw City and St. Ignace, Mich.

Sunshine Skyway, a 15-mile-long bridge-causeway with twin roadbeds that crosses Tampa Bay at St. Petersburg, Fla., a system of twin bridges 864 feet long and 4 smaller bridges with 6 causeways.

Tagus River Bridge near Lisbon, Portugal, longest suspension bridge outside the United States, has a 3,323-ft. main span. Opened Aug. 6, 1966, it was named Salazar Bridge for the former premier.

Thomas A. Edison Memorial Bridge (causeway) across Sandusky Bay between Martin Point and Danbury, Oh., is 2.67 miles long. The main bridge is 2,044 feet long.

Thousand Island Bridge, St. Lawrence River. American span 800 ft.; Canadian 750 ft.

Union St. Bridge in Woodstock, Vt., a Timber Lattice Truss with a span of 122 feet built in 1969 using old time procedure of hand drilled holes and wooden pegs.

Vancouver Bridge, Canada's longest railway lift span connecting Vancouver and North Vancouver over Burrard Inlet. It is in 3 sections, the longest 493 ft. Spans are part of a project that includes a 2-mile tunnel under Vancouver Hts.

Woodrow Wilson Memorial Bridge across the Potomac River at Alexandria, Va., is over a mile long.

Zoo Bridge across the Rhine at Cologne, with steel box girders, has a main span of 850 ft.

The Interstate Highway 610 crossing of the Houston Ship Channel in Texas is 6,300 feet in length and consists of various lengths of prestressed concrete beam and slab approach spans and a 1,233 foot main unit of two 471'6" plate girder units and one 290 ft. simple span.

Underwater Vehicular Tunnels in North America
Over 3,000 feet in length

Name	Location	Waterway	Lgth. Ft.
Bart Trans-Bay Tube (Rapid Transit)....	San Francisco, Cal........	S.F. Bay................................	3.6 miles
Brooklyn-Battery.....................	New York, N.Y..........	East River..............	9,117
Holland Tunnel.......................	New York, N.Y..........	Hudson River	8,557
Lincoln Tunnel.......................	New York, N.Y..........	Hudson River	8,216
Baltimore Harbor Tunnel	Baltimore, Md...........	Patapsco River...........	7,650
Hampton Roads......................	Norfolk, Va............	Hampton Roads	7,479
Queens Midtown......................	New York, N.Y..........	East River............	6,414
Thimble Shoal Channel	Cape Henry, Va.........	Chesapeake Bay.......	5,738
Sumner Tunnel.......................	Boston, Mass..........	Boston Harbor	5,650
Chesapeake Channel	Cape Charles, Va.......	Chesapeake Bay.......	5,450
Louis-Hippolyte Lafontaine Tunnel	Montreal, Que...........	St. Lawrence River.......	5,280
Detroit-Windsor	Detroit, Mich...........	Detroit River...........	5,135
Callahan Tunnel	Boston, Mass...........	Boston Harbor	5,046
Midtown Tunnel......................	Norfolk, Va............	Elizabeth River.........	4,194
Baytown Tunnel	Baytown, Tex...........	Houston Ship Channel......	4,111
Posey Tube..........................	Oakland, Cal...........	Oakland Estuary..........	3,500
Downtown Tunnel	Norfolk, Va............	Elizabeth River.........	3,350
Webster St..........................	Alameda, Cal...........	Oakland Estuary..........	3,350
Bankhead Tunnel	Mobile, Ala............	Mobile River...........	3,109
I-10 Twin Tunnel	Mobile, Ala............	Mobile River...........	3,000

Land Vehicular Tunnels in United States (Over 1,000 feet long)

Name	Location	Lgth. Ft.	Name	Location	Lgth. Ft.
Eisenhower Memorial ..	Route 70, Col...........	8,941	Battery Park.........	New York City........	2,300
Copperfield............	Copperfield, Ut.........	6,989	Battery St...........	Seattle, Wash........	2,140
Allegheny (Twin).....	Penna. Turnpike.......	6,070	Big Oak Flat........	Yosemite Natl. Park ...	2,083
Liberty Tubes.........	Pittsburgh, Pa..........	5,920	Prudential..........	Boston, Mass........	1,980
Zion Natl. Park........	Rte. 1, Utah...........	5,766	Internatl. Underpass....	Los Angeles, Cal......	1,910
East River Mt. (Twin) .	Interstate 77, W.Va.-Va.	5,661	Street-Car..........	Providence, R.I........	1,793
Tuscarora (Twin).....	Penna. Turnpike.......	5,326	Broadway.........	San Francisco, Cal......	1,616
Kittatinny (Twin)......	Penna. Turnpike.......	4,727	9th Street Expy........	Washington, D.C........	1,610
Lehigh...............	Penna. Turnpike.......	4,379	F.D. Roosevelt Dr.......	42-48 Sts. NYC.......	1,600
Blue Mountain (Twin) .	Penna. Turnpike.......	4,339	Lowry Hill..........	Minneapolis........	1,496
Wawona..............	Yosemite Natl. Park....	4,233	Wheeling..........	Interstate 70, W. Va....	1,490
Squirrel Hill..........	Pittsburgh, Pa.........	4,225	Mt. Baker Ridge (3)....	Seattle, Wash........	1,466
Big Walker Mt........	Route I-77, Va.........	4,200	Knowls Creek........	Lane County, Ore.......	1,430
Fort Pitt.............	Pittsburgh, Pa.........	3,560	Mule Pass...........	Near Bisbee, Ariz.......	1,400
Mall Tunnel..........	Dist. of Columbia.......	3,400	Arch Cape...........	Oregon Coast Hwy. 9....	1,228
Caldecott............	Oakland, Cal..........	3,371	Queen Creek........	Superior, Ariz........	1,200
Kalihi...............	Honolulu, Ha..........	2,780	West Rock..........	New Haven, Conn......	1,200
Memorial............	W. Va. Tpke. (I-77).....	2,669	Green River.........	Route I-80, Wyo........	1,135
Cross-Town..........	178 St. N.Y.C.........	2,414	Nouanu Pali........	Koolau Mt. Oahu, Ha....	1,080
F.D. Roosevelt Dr......	81-89 Sts. NYC........	2,400	Elk Creek...........	Umpqua Hwy 45, Ore...	1,080
Dewey Sq............	Boston, Mass.........	2,400	Golden............	Clear Cr'k Canyon, Col..	1,068

World's Longest Railway Tunnels
Source: Railway Directory & Year Book. Tunnels over 4 miles in length.

Tunnel	Date	Miles	Yds	Operating Railway	Country
Simplon No. I and II	1922	12	559	Swiss Fed. & Italian St............	Switz.-Italy
Apennine.............	1934	11	892	Italian State.............	Italy
Cotthard.............	1882	9	562	Swiss Federal..............	Switzerland
Lotsberg.............	1913	9	140	Bern-Lotschberg-Simplon.....	Switzerland
Hokuriku.............	1962	8	1,089	Japanese National................	Japan
Mont Cenis (Frejus).....	1871	8	855	Italian State..........	France-Italy
Cascade.............	1929	7	1,397	Great Northern..........	United States
Flathead Tunnel, Mont.....	1970	6	1,758	Great Northern...........	United States
Arlberg..............	1884	6	650	Austrian Federal............	Austria
Moffat...............	1928	6	373	Denver & Rio Grande...........	United States
Shimizu.............	1931	6	50	Japanese National..........	Japan
Kvineshei............	1943	5	1,112	Norwegian State............	Norway
Rimutaka............	1955	5	821	New Zealand Gov...........	New Zealand
Ricken...............	1910	5	608	Swiss Federal............	Switzerland
Grenchenberg.........	1915	5	581	Swiss Federal............	Switzerland
Otira................	1923	5	564	New Zealand Gov...........	New Zealand
Tauern...............	1909	5	551	Austrian Federal...........	Austria
Haegebostad.........	1943	5	467	Norwegian State...........	Norway
Ronco...............	1889	5	277	Italian State.............	–Italy
Hauenstein (Lower)....	1916	5	95	Swiss Federal.............	Switzerland
Connaught...........	1916	5	39	Canadian Pacific...........	Canada
Karawanken.........	1906	4	1,683	Austrian Federal...........	Austria-Yugo
New Tanna...........	1964	4	1,663	Japanese National.........	Japan
Somport.............	1928	4	1,572	French National............	France-Spain
Tanna...............	1934	4	1,493	Japanese National..........	Japan
Ulrikken.............	1964	4	1,338	Norwegian State..........	Norway
Hoosac..............	1875	4	1,230	Boston & Maine............	United States
Monte Orso..........	1927	4	1,230	Italian State............	Italy
Lupacino............	1958	4	1,178	Italian State............	Italy
Vivola..............	1927	4	1,004	Italian State............	Italy
Monte Adone.........	1934	4	760	Italian State............	Italy
Jungfrau.............	1912	4	750	Jungfrau.............	Switzerland
Borgallo.............	1884	4	700	Italian State............	Italy
Severn..............	1886	4	628	Western Region...........	Great Britain
Lusse (Vosges)........	1937	4	474	French National............	France

Dams and Reservoirs; Water Conservation

Source: Bureau of Reclamation

The Bureau of Reclamation, an agency of the Department of the Interior, administers a multiple-purpose water resources program that develops projects for municipal, industrial and irrigation water supply, hydroelectric power generation, flood control, water quality improvement, fish and wildlife enhancement, outdoor recreation, and maintenance of a satisfactory natural environment. To these ends it builds dams, reservoirs, hydropower plants, canals, and tunnels in the 17 contiguous western states, and conducts a many-faceted water resources research program to develop new sources of water supply and also water and land conservation techniques.

Projects with major construction programs underway in 1974 included the Columbia Basin Project, Washington; Lower Teton Division, Teton Basin Project, Idaho; Auburn-Folsom South Unit, Central Valley Project, California; Central Arizona Project, Arizona; Curecanti Unit, Colorado; Navajo Indian Irrigation Project, New Mexico; Garrison Diversion Unit, North Dakota; and the Fryingpan-Arkansas Project, Colorado.

In the Pacific Northwest Region, a $3.8 million contract for completion of Teton Power and Pumping Plant was awarded in November 1974. The project is about 50 percent complete with initial power generation and water deliveries scheduled for early 1976.

Construction of the Columbia Basin Project Third Powerplant at Grand Coulee Dam on the Columbia River with a generating capacity of 3,900,000 kilowatts reached the 70 percent completion mark. The first of the three 600,000 kilowatt units is scheduled for power generation in 1975.

Water storage was initiated in Henry Hagg Lake being formed by Scoggins Dam on the Tualatin Project in Oregon, with completion of the dam in 1975. Work continues on pumping plants and lateral systems. The project will provide water for irrigation of 17,000 acres of land and will provide some 14,000 acre-feet of water annually for municipal and industrial needs. Additional benefits are fish and wildlife, recreation, flood control and water quality control.

On the Central Arizona Project, the construction tempo picked up with the award of a $10 million contract for a reach of the Granite Reef Aqueduct including construction of the Paradise Valley Flood Detention Dike. Early completion of the dike will help reduce major flooding north of Phoenix, Scottsdale and North Tempe, Arizona. Designs were completed and a contract was awarded for construction of the $58 million Buckskin Mountain Tunnel which will convey water from Lake Havasu to the Granite Reef Aqueduct.

On the Colorado River Storage Project, a $18.3 million construction contract was awarded in July 1974 for Currant Creek Dam and Reservoir, a principal storage feature on the Bonneville Unit, Central Utah Project. Also, major equipment contracts were awarded for the Crystal Powerplant on the Curecanti Unit in Colorado.

Construction continued on the Navajo Indian Irrigation Project in New Mexico which is being constructed for the Bureau of Indian Affairs. Work is underway on some $40 million of contracts and a contract was awarded in April 1974 for construction of laterals and drains for Block I lands. The first lands are scheduled for irrigation in the spring of 1976. Water stored in Navajo Reservoir will eventually irrigate 110,000 acres of Navajo Indian lands.

Construction of the Mountain Park Project located in Jackson and Kiowa Counties in Oklahoma, including Mountain Park Dam and Reservoir, is over 50 percent complete. A $7.6 million contract for construction of the Altus Aqueduct and Pumping Plant was awarded in April 1974. In addition to recreation, fish and wildlife, and flood control benefits, the project will provide 16,000 acre-feet of water annually for municipal and industrial use.

A $5.1 million contract was awarded in June 1974 for the construction of Nambe Falls Dam on the San Juan-Chama Project in New Mexico. The structure, consisting of a thin-arch, double curvature dam 140 feet high and 320 feet long and an earth and rockfill embankment, will be located on the Rio Nambe about 25 miles north of Santa Fe, on the Nambe Indian reservation. The new reservoir will provide an assured supply of supplemental irrigation water to 2,768 acres of Indian and non-Indian lands served by the Pojaaque Irrigation District.

Work was initiated on the Oahe Unit, Pick-Sloan Missouri Basin Program, with award of a $10 million contract in April 1974 for construction of the Oahe Pumping Plant. The new plant will pump water from the existing Lake Oahe on the Missouri River for delivery to central and northeastern South Dakota. A municipal and industrial water supply will be provided from the canal system for 17 municipalities. The project plant also provides for the irrigation of 190,000 acres of land adjacent to the James River in Spink and Brown Counties.

On the Garrison Diversion Unit, North Dakota, construction of the Snake Creek Pumping Plant is complete with work continuing on construction of the 74-mile McClusky Canal. The multipurpose project will provide a full supply of water for the irrigation of 250,000 acres, presently dry-farmed.

Construction on the Fryingpan-Arkansas Project, Colorado, is now 40 percent complete with water storage in three reservoirs, Ruedi, Turquoise Lake, and Pueblo.

Alaska Power Administration, located in Juneau, Alaska, is the agency of the Department of the Interior given charge of promoting development and use of the water, power and related resources of Alaska. The hydro power resources of Alaska are practically untouched. Of the 32 million kilowatts of hydroelectric power potential, the 30,000-kilowatt Eklutna Project is the only major operating project. When completed, the Snettisham Project will add 70,000 kilowatts of capacity to the APA system.

Southeastern Power Administration (Dept. of the Interior) with headquarters at Elberton, Ga., markets power produced at projects controlled by the Corps of Engineers in Va., W. Va., N.C., S.C., Ga., Fla., Ky., Ala., Miss., and Tenn.

Southwestern Power Administration, with hq. in Tulsa, Okla., is the agency of the Dept. of the Interior designated to market surplus hydroelectric power and energy generated at federal multiple purpose reservoirs in a 6 state area of the southwest. Of 23 hydro-electric plants 19 are in commercial operation, and 4 are under construction.

Tennessee Valley Authority

TVA is a corporate agency of the federal government, established by Congress in 1933 to develop the Tennessee River system and to aid in the development of other resources of the Tennessee Valley region. This includes resource development work in flood control, navigation, electric power, recreation, agriculture, forestry, and water quality.

TVA has built or acquired 27 major dams on the Tennessee and its tributary rivers, and by agreement with Alcoa controls water releases at 6 of its major dams. These structures make the main stream of the Tennessee navigable over its 650-mile length from Knoxville to the Ohio River, regulate flood waters, and generate hydroelectric power.

TVA is a wholesale power supplier to 160 local electric systems serving 2 million customers in parts of 7 states, and sells power directly to several large atomic, military, and industrial installations

The TVA Power System is financially self-supporting and self-liquidating.

Major World Dams

Source: Bureau of Reclamation, Dept. of the Interior, Revised May 1975. *Replaces existing dam.

Volume in cubic yards. Capacity (Gross) in acre feet. Year of completion. U.C. under construction.
Type: A—Arch. B—Buttress. E—Earthfill. G—Gravity. R—Rockfill. MA—Multi-arch.

Name of Dam	Type	Year	River and Basin	Country	Height Feet	Crest Length Feet	Volume (1,000 C.Y.)	Res. Cap. (1,000 A.F.)
Akosombo-Main	R	1965	Volta	Ghana	463	2,100	10,400	120,000
Almendra	A	UC	Tormes-Douro	Spain	649	13,438	3,267	2,025
Alpe Gera	G	1965	Comor-Adda-Po	Italy	584	1,710	2,265	53
Amir Kabir*	A	1962	Karadj-Caspian Sea	Iran	591	1,280	821	166
Auburn	MA	UC	N. F. American-Sacramento	U.S.A.	695	4,000	6,000	2,300
Balimela	E	UC	Sileru	India	230	15,200	29,600	3,100
Beas	E	UC	Beas-Indus	India	436	6,401	42,261	6,600
W.A.C. Bennett*	E	1967	Peace-Mackenzie	Canada	600	6,700	57,203	57,006
Bhakra	G	1963	Sutlent-Indus	India	742	1,700	5,400	8,000
Bhumiphol (Yanhee)	GA	1964	Ping-Chao Phraya	Thailand	505	1,594	1,307	9,891
Bratsk	GE	1964	Angara	USSR	410	17,105	22,219	137,214
Bukhtarma	G	1960	Irtish	USSR	295	1,247	1,530	42,970
Cabora Basa	A	UC	Zambezi	Mozambique	550	994	589	129,389
Canelles	A	1960	Noguera Ribagorzana-Ebro	Spain	492	689	436	549
Castaic	E	1971	Castaic Cr.-Santa Clara	U.S.A.	340	5,200	44,000	350
Charvak	E	1970	Chirchik-Sir Darya	USSR	551	2,499	24,975	1,620
Chirkey	UC		Sulak-Caspian Sea	USSR	764	1,109	1,602	2,252
Cochiti	A	UC	Rio Grande	U.S.A.	251	28,200	41,100	602
Contra	A	1965	Verzasca-Ticino-Po	Switz	754	1,246	863	70
Curnera	A	1967	Rein de Curnera-Rhine	Switz	499	1,115	735	32.4
Dneprodzerzhinsk	GE	1964	Dnieper	USSR	115	119,038	35,857	1,985
Don Pedro*	ER	1970	Tuoume-San Joaquin	U.S.A.	585	1,900	16,760	2,030
Dworshak	G	UC	N. F. Clearwater Columbia	U.S.A.	717	3,287	6,500	3,453
Elephant Butte	G	1916	Rio Grande	U.S.A.	301	1,674	630	2,201
Emosson	A	UC	Barberine	Switz	590	1,736	1,400	182
Esmeralda	E	UC	Bota	Colombia	754	919	14,126	661
Flaming Gorge	GA	1964	Green-Colorado	U.S.A.	502	1,285	987	3,789
Fort Peck	E	1940	Missouri	U.S.A.	250	21,026	125,600	19,400
Fort Randall	E	1956	Missouri	U.S.A.	165	10,700	50,200	6,100
Gardiner*	E	1968	South Saskatchewan	Canada	223	16,700	85,739	8,000
Garrison	E	1956	Missouri	U.S.A.	210	11,300	66,500	24,500
Gatum	E	1912	Chagres	Panama	115	7,700	22,958	4,413
Gepatsch	A	1964	Faggenbach-Inn	Austria	500	2,070	9,250	114
Glen Canyon	A	1964	Colorado	U.S.A.	710	1,560	4,901	27,000
Gokcekaya	A	UC	Sakarya	Turkey	518	1,529	850	737
Gorky	EG	1955	Volga-Caspian S.	USSR	105	42,340	57,969	7,055
Goschenalp	E	1960	Goschenerreuss-Rhine	Switz	508	1,771	12,230	61
Grand Coulee	G	1942	Columbia	U.S.A.	550	4,173	10,585	9,724
Grande Dixence	G	1962	Dixence-Rhone	Switz	932	2,296	7,792	324
Gran Suarna	MA	UC	Navia	Spain	499	1,150	882	567
Guri	GER	1968	Caroni-Orinoco	Venezuela	348	2,264	4,917	14,349
High Aswan (Saad-El-Aali)	ER	1971	Nile	UAR	364	12,565	55,747	133,000
Hirakud	GE	1956	Mahanadi	India	202	15,748	25,100	6,600
Hoover	A	1936	Colorado	U.S.A.	726	1,244	4,400	29,755
Hungry Horse	AG	1953	S.F. Flathead-Columbia	U.S.A.	564	2,115	3,086	3,468
Idikki	MA	UC	Periyar	India	561	1,201	609	1,182
Ihla Solteria	EG	UC	Parana Rio de la Plata	Brazil	291	20,300	35,741	17,172
Inguri	A	UC	Inguri	USSR	892	2,513	4,967	891
Irkutsk	GE	1956	Angara	USSR	144	8,989	16,220	37,290
Iroquois	G	1958	St. Lawrence	Canada	76	2,665		24,288
Ivankovo	EG	1937	Volga-Caspian S.	USSR	98	31,398	20,207	908
Jari	E	1967	Jari	Pakistan	234	5,700	42,400	400
Jaya Kwadi	E	UC	Godavari	India	120	32,493	15,409	2,110
Daniel Johnson*	MA	1968	Manicougan-St. Lawrence	Canada	703	4,311	2,950	115,000
Kakhovka	EG	1955	Dnieper	USSR	121	5,380	46,617	14,755
Kanev	E	UC	Dnieper	USSR	82	52,950	49,520	2,125
Kapchagay	E	1970	Ili	USSR	164	1,542	5,078	22,813
Kariba	G	1959	Zambezi	Rhodesia-Zambia	420	2,025	1,350	130,000
Keban	RG	UC	First (Euphrates)	Turkey	679	3,598	19,600	25,110
Kiev	E	1964	Dnieper	USSR	72	177,448	57,552	3,021
King Paul (Kremasta)	ER	1965	Acheloos	Greece	541	1,510	10,686	3,850
Krasnoyarsk	G	UC	Yenisei	USSR	407	3,493	5,685	59,425
Kremenchug	EG	1961	Dnieper	USSR	98	35,727	36,282	10,945
Kurobegawa No. 4	A	1964	Kurobe	Japan	610	1,603	1,782	162
Las Portas	A	UC	Camba	Spain	498	1,587	977	609
Luzzone	A	1963	Brenno di Luzzone-Ticino	Switz	682	1,738	1,776	70
Mangla	E	1967	Jhelum	Pakistan	380	11,000	85,872	5,150
Marimbondo	E	UC	Grande	Brazil	295	11,970	24,328	5,184
Mauvoisin	A	1958	Drance de Bagnes-Rhone	Switz	777	1,706	2,655	146
Mica	R	UC	Columbia	Canada	794	2,600	42,000	20,000
Mohamed Re Chah Pahlavi	A	1963	Dez-Karun	Iran	66	696	608	2,717
Mingechaur	E	1953	Kura	USSR	262	5,085	20,400	12,970
Monteynard	A	1962	Drac-Isere-Rhone	France	509	705	595	195
Mossyrock	MA	1968	Cowlitz-Columbia	U.S.A.	605	1,750	1,240	1,300
Mratinje	A	UC	Piva-Drina-Danube	Yugo.	722	853	1,019	749
Nagawado	A	UC	Azua-Shinano	Japan	508	1,200	865	100
New Bullards Bar	A	1968	North Yuba-Sacramento	U.S.A.	635	2,200	2,700	930
New Melones	R	UC	Stanislaus-San Joaquin	U.S.A.	625	1,600	15,970	2,400
Nurek	E	1972	Vakhsh	USSR	1,040	2,390	75,864	8,424
Oahe	E	1963	Missouri	U.S.A.	245	9,300	92,000	23,600
Okutadami	G	1961	Tadami	Japan	515	1,575	2,145	487
Oroville	E	1968	Feather-Sacramento	U.S.A.	770	6,920	78,008	3,538
Owen Falls	G	1954	Lake Victoria-Nile	Uganda	100	2,725		166,000
Place Moulin	AG	1965	Buthier-Dora Baltea	Italy	502	2,181	1,962	81

Name of Dam	Type	Year	River and Basin	Country	Height	Length	Vol.	Cap.
Reza Shah Kabir	A	UC	Karoun	Iran	656	1,247	1,570	2,351
Roselend	AB	1961	Doronde Beaufort-Rhone	France	492	2,644	1,236	152
Ross	A	1949	Skagit	U.S.A.	540	1,300	909	1,405
Rybinsk	GE	1941	Volga-Caspian S.	USSR	98	2,060	3,329	20,590
Sakuma	G	1956	Tenryu	Japan	510	963	1,465	265
Sanmen Hsia	G	1962	Hwang Ho-Yellow	China	351	2,752		52,700
San Luis	E	1967	San Luis-San Joaquin	U.S.A.	382	18,600	77,670	2,110
Santa Giustina	A	1950	Noce-Adige	Italy	500	407	148	148
Saratov	E	UC	Volga-Caspian S.	USSR	131	4,130	34,531	10,458
Sayansk	A	UC	Yenisei	USSR	774	3,503	11,916	25,353
Shasta	G	1945	Sacramento	U.S.A.	602	3,460	8,711	4,500
Speccheri	A	1957	Leno Di Vallarsa-Adige	Italy	514	631	153	8
Swift	E	1958	Lewis-Columbia	U.S.A.	512	2,100	15,431	756
Tachien	A	UC	Tachia	Taiwan	656	853	940	235
Talbingo	R	1971	Tumut	Australia	530	2,300	18,500	747
Tankiangkow	G	1962	Tan & Han	China	427			41,833
Tarbela	ER	UC	Indus	Pakistan	470	9,000	186,000	11,100
Tignes	A	1952	Isere-Rhone	France	592	1,411	830	186
Toktogul	A	UC	Naryn-Syr Darya	USSR	705	1,352	3,480	15,800
Trinity	E	1962	Trinity-Klamath	U.S.A.	537	2,600	29,251	2,500
Tsimlyansk	EG	1952	Don	USSR	128	43,411	44,323	17,715
Tuttle Creek	ER	1962	Big Blue-Missouri	U.S.A.	157	7,500	21,000	2,367
Twin Buttes	E	1963	Concho-Colorado Texas	U.S.A.	134	42,460	21,442	641
Ust-Ilim	GE	UC	Angara	USSR	344	11,695	11,382	48,100
Vajont	MA	1961	Vaoiont-Piave	Italy	858	624	460	137
Verkhne-Svirskaya	EG	1952	Svir	USSR	105	1,775	1,988	14,190
Vidraru	A	1965	Arges-Danube	Romania	544	1,000	653	377
Volga-22d congress USSR	ERG	1958	Volga-Caspians	USSR	144	13,038	33,020	27,160
Volga-V. I. Lenin	EG	1955	Volga-Caspian S.	USSR	148	12,405	44,298	47,020
Yellowtail	A	1966	Bighorn-Missouri	U.S.A.	525	1,480	1,456	1,375
Zervreila	A	1957	Valserrhein-Rhine	Switz	495	1,753	819	81
Zeuzier	A	1957	Lienne-Rhone	Switz	512	918	392	41
Zeya	G	UC	Zeya	USSR	371	2,312	10,456	55,080

Major Public and Private Dams and Reservoirs in U.S.

Source: Corps of Engineers, U.S. Army

Heights over 280 feet, volume over 1,000,000 cubic yards.

Where reservoir name is different it is shown in italics

Height—Difference in elevation in feet, between lowest point in foundation and top of dam, exclusive of parapet or other projections.
Length—Overall length of barrier in feet; main dam and its integral features as located between natural abutments.
Volume—Total volume in cubic yards of all material in main dam and its appurtenant works.
Year—Date structure was originally completed for use. (UC) Under construction subject to revision.
River—Mainstream.
Purpose—Irr or I—Irrigation; FC—Flood Control; P—Power Production; N—navigation; WS—Water Supply; RR—River Regulation; DC—Debris Control.
Parentheses after name indicate type of dam as follows: (C)—Concrete; (E) Earth; (G)—Gravity; (M)—Masonry; (R)—Rock Fill.
*Replacing existing dam.

Name of dam	State	River	Ht.	Lgth.	Vol. (1,000)	Purpose	Yr.
Oroville (RE)	Cal.	Feather River	742	6800	78000	I R	1968
Hoover (VA)	Nev.	Colorado River	726	1242	4400	IHCO	1936
Dworshak (PG)	Ida.	North Fork of Clearwater	717	3287	6500	HCR	1972
Glen Canyon (VA)	Ariz.	Colorado River	710	1560	4901	HCSR	1964
Auburn (PG)	Cal.	N.F. American	680	3500	6000	ISCH	UC
New Bullards Bar (VA)	Cal.	North Yuba River	635	2200	2600	S D	1970
New Melones (ER)	Cal.	Stanislaus River	625	1600	15970	IH	UC
Swift Dam (RE)	Wash.	North Fork Lewis River	610	2100	15800	HR	1958
Mossyrock Dam (VA)	Wash.	Cowlitz River	605	1300	1231	HCR	1968
Shasta (PG)	Cal.	Sacramento River	602	3460	8711	ISHN	1945
Kopperston No. 3 Refuse Bank (DT)	W.Va.	Jones Br of Toney Cr.	580	1100		O	1963
Don Pedro (RE)	Cal.	Tuolumne River	568	1800	16000	H I	1971
Hungry Horse (VA)	Mon.	South Fork of Flathead River	564	2115	3086	IHCN	1953
Grand Coulee (PG)	Wash.	Columbia River	550	4173	10585	IHCN	1942
Ross Dam (VA)	Wash.	Skagit River	540	1235	905	HR	1949
Trinity (RE)	Cal.	Trinity River	537	2600	29410	IHCR	1962
Yellowtail (VA)	Mon.	Bighorn River	525	1480	1546	ICHR	1966
Cougar (ER)	Ore.	South Fork McKenzie River	519	1600	13000	HCIR	1964
Flaming Gorge (VA)	Ut.	Green River	502	1285	987	HCSR	1964
Fontana Dam (PG)	N.C.	Little Tennessee River	480	2365	3576	H	1944
New Exchequer (ER)	Cal.	Merced River	479	1240	5169	H I	1926
Morrow Point (VA)	Col.	Gunnison River	468	741	365	HCRO	1968
Carters Main Dam (ER,RE)	Ga.	Coosawattee River	464	1950	15000	CHR	1974
Detroit (PG)	Ore.	North Santiam River	463	1580	1500	HCRI	1953
Anderson Ranch (RE)	Ida.	South Fork Boise River	456	1350	9653	IHCR	1950
Union Valley (RE)	Cal.	Silver Cr.	453	1800	10000	S H	1963
Elmore Mine Refuse Dump (OT)	W.Va.	Tr-Guyandotte River	447	1975		O	1973
Round Butte Dam (RE,ER)	Ore.	Deschutes River	440	1450	9600	HR	1964
Pine Flat Lake (PG)	Cal.	Kings River	440	1840	2400	CIRH	1954
Kopperston No. 4 Dam (OT)	W.Va.	Crane Fk of Clear Fk.	435	1100		O	1963
Jocassee (ER)	S.C.	Keowee River	435	1800	11600	H	1973
Mud Mountain Dam (ER)	Wash.	White River	425	700	2300	C	1948
Libby Dam (PG)	Mon.	Kootenai River	420	3055	13760	HC	1973
Owyhee Dam (VA)	Ore.	Owyhee River	417	833	538	ICR	1932
Lower Hell Hole (ER)	Cal.	Rubicon River	410	1550	8315	S D	1966
Mammoth Pool (RE)	Cal.	San Joaquin River	406	820	5355	H S	1960
Navajo (RE)	N.M.	San Juan River	402	3648	26840	IR	1963
Stirrat No. 15 Embankment (OT)	W.Va.	Rockhouse Br. of Island Cr.	400	1200		O	1973
Toxaway Lake (RE)	S.C.	Jocassee River	400	1000		H	1972
Diablo Dam (VA)	Wash.	Skagit River	400	1142	350	HR	1930
Trout Lake Dam (RE)	Col.	Lake Fork San Miguel River	395	870		H	1906
Brownlee Dam (ER)	Ida.	Snake River	395	1380	6700	H	1959
Summersville Dam (ER)	W.Va.	Cauley River	393	2280	13565	CRSO	1965
Blue Mesa (RE)	Col.	Gunnison River	390	785	3093	HCRO	1966
Pyramid (ER)	Cal.	Piru Creek	386	1080	6952	I R	1973
Boundary Dam (VA)	Wash.	Pend Oreille River	385	740	240	H	1967
San Luis (RE)	Cal.	San Luis Creek	382	1860	77664	ISHR	1967
Green Peter (PG)	Ore.	Middle Santiam River	378	1517	1142	CHRI	1967

Name of dam	State	River	Ht.	Lgth.	Vol. (1,000)	Purpose	Yr.
Pacoima (VA)	Cal.	Pacoima Creek	365	640	226	C	1929
Yale Dam (RE)	Wash.	Lewis River	357	1600	4200	HR	1952
Abiquiu Dam (RE)	N.M.	Rio Chama	354	1540	11793	C DD	1963
Arrowrock (VA)	Ida.	Boise River	350	1150	636	IC	1915
Pardee (PG)	Cal.	Mokelumne River	345	1337	615	S	1929
Hills Creek (RE)	Ore.	Middle Fork Willamette River	341	2306	10800	CHIS	1962
Folsom (PG)	Cal.	American River	340	10200	8980	ISHC	1956
Whitman Cr. Embankment (OT)	W.Va.	Whitman Cr. of Coopers Fk.	340	625		O	1952
Reservoir No. 22 (VA)	Col.	Boulder Creek	340	1090		S	1953
Gross Dam (PG)	Col.	South Boulder Creek	340	1050	592	S	1955
Castaic (RE)	Cal.	Castaic Cr.	340	5200	44000	I R	1973
Casitas (RE)	Cal.	Coyote Creek	334	2000	9112	ISC	1959
Smith Dam (RE)	Ore.	Smith River	333	1150	2500	H	1962
Upper Baker Dam (PG)	Wash.	Baker River	332	1220	628	HR	1961
Joe Branch (Itman No. 2) (OT)	W.Va.	Joe Br. of Guyandotte River	330	500		O	1973
Hell's Canyon (PG)	Ida.	Snake River	330	910	640	H	1967
Copper Cities Tailings Dam 2 (RE)	Ariz.	Tinhorn Wash	325	7600	30000	O	1973
Buffalo Bill VA)	Wy.	Shoshone River	325	200	83	ICHR	1910
Ruedi (RE)	Col.	Fryingpan River	322	1042	3745	IRC	1968
San Gabriel No. 1 (ER)	Cal.	San Gabriel River	320	1520	10600	C	1938
Parker (VA)	Ariz.	Colorado River	320	856	380	HRO	1938
Grapevine Br. (OT)	W.Va.	Grapevine Br. of Tug Fork	320	1250		O	1973
Alder Dam (VA)	Wash.	Nisqually River	320	1600	425	HR	1945
Tieton (RE)	Wash.	Tieton River	319	920	2049	ICR	1925
Friant (PG)	Cal.	San Joaquin River	319	3488	2135	ISCR	1942
Ariel Dam (VA)	Wash.	Lewis River	319	1250	238	HR	1932
Watauga (ER,RE)	Tenn.	Watauga River	318	900	3478	CHNR	1948
Lucky Peak (RE)	Ida.	Boise River	316	1700	6300	CR	1955
Salt Springs (ER)	Cal.	N. Fk. Mokelumne River	315	1300	3000	H	1931
Cherry Valley (ER)	Cal.	Cherry Creek	315	2630	7000	H S	1956
O'Shaughnessy (PG)	Cal.	Tuolumne River	312	900	663	H S	1923
Blue River (RE)	Ore.	Blue River	312	1250	4873	CR	1968
Courtright (ER)	Cal.	Helms Creek	311	862	1560	H	1958
Green Mountain (RE)	Col.	Blue River	309	1150	4360	IHR	1943
Kensico (PG)	N.Y.	Bronx River	307	1843	2975	S	1913
Hiwassee Dam (PG)	N.C.	Hiwassee River	307	1376	769	H C	1940
Lewis Smith (RE,ER)	Ala.	Sipsey Fork	305	2200	5140	HCR	1961
Horse Mesa (VA)	Ariz.	Salt River	305	600	162	IHR	1937
Monticello (VA)	Cal.	Putah Creek	304	1023	339	ISR	1957
Elephant Butte (VA)	N.M.	Rio Grande River	301	1674	630	IHCR	1916
New Croton Reservoir Dam (PG)	N.Y.	Croton	300	1000	1100	S	1905
Monclo Impoundment (OT)	W.Va.	Pigeon Roost Br. of Beech Cr.	300	1500	5800	O	1915
Keystone Refuse No. 1 (OT)	W.Va.	Clarks Br. of Elkhorn Cr.	300	500		O	1973
Granby (RE)	Col.	Colorado River	298	861	2974	IR	1950
Copper Cities Tailings Dam 8 (RE)	Ariz.	Miami Wash Offstream	297	1100	7140	O	1973
Bloomington (OT)	Md.	N. Branch of Potomac R.	296	2130	10000	CSOR	1973
Seminoe (VA)	Wyo.	North Platte River	295	530	210	IHR	1939
Donnells (VA)	Cal.	Mid Fk. Stanislaus River	291	714	200	H I	1958
Baker Dam (VA)	Wash.	Baker River	290	570	115	HR	1925
Six Dam (ER)	Ky.	Dix River	287	1700		H S	1925
Bartlett (MV)	Ariz.	Verde River	287	800	1820	IR	1939
South Holston (ER,RE)	Tenn.	South Fork Holston River	285	1600	5884	CHNR	1950
Gorge Dam (VA,PG)	Wash.	Skagit River	285	670	284	HR	1961
Lemon (RE)	Col.	Florida River	284	1360	3042	I	1963
Alamo Reservoir (RE)	Ariz.	Bill Williams River	283	975	3045	C	1968
Whiskeytown (RE)	Cal.	Clear Creek	282	4070	4535	IHCR	1963
Laurel (ER)	Ky.	Laurel	282	1420	3000	CHR	1972
Theodore Roosevelt (VA)	Ariz.	Salt River	280	723	356	IHR	1911
Quabbin Winsor (RE,PG)	Me.	Swift River	280	2600	4000	S	1938
La Grande Dam (PG)	Wash.	Nisqually River	280	680	87	HR	1945
Harry L. Englebright Lake (VA)	Cal.	Yuba River	280	1142	365	DHR	1941
Eastern Coal-McAndrews Refuse Dam (OT)	Ky.	Pond Creek-offstream	280	800		O	1973
Cushman Dam No. 1 (VA,RE)	Wash.	North Fork Skokomish River	280	980	79	HR	1926
Mansfield Dam (RE,PG) Marshall Ford	Tex.	Colorado River	278	7098	33890	HCSR	1942
McDonald Fork (Coal Mountain) (OT)	W.Va.	McDonald Fk. of Big Club Cr.	260	620		O	1965
East Canyon (VA)	Ut.	East Canyon Creek	260	436	36	ISCO	1966

World's Largest Dams

Source: Bureau of Reclamation, Dept. of the Interior

Based on total volume of structure. All dams listed are predominantly earthfill or rockfill and may contain concrete sections. UC—Under Construction.

Name of Dam	Cubic Yards	Completed	Name of Dam	Cubic Yards	Completed
Tarbela, Pakistan	186,000,000	UC	W.A.C. Bennett, Canada[2]	57,203,000	1968
Fort Peck, U.S.A.	125,612,000	1940	High Aswan Saad-El-Aili, Egypt	55,747,000	1970
Oahe, U.S.A.	92,008,000	1963	Fort Randall, U.S.A.	50,205,000	1956
Mangla, Pakistan	85,872,000	1967	Kanev, USSR	49,520,000	UC
Gardiner, Canada[1]	85,743,000	1968	Kakhovka, USSR	46,617,000	1955
Oroville, U.S.A.	78,008,000	1968	Volga, V.I. Lenin, USSR	44,298,000	1955
San Luis, U.S.A.	77,666,000	1967	Castaic, U.S.A.	44,000,000	1971
Nurek, USSR	75,864,000	UC	Jari, Pakistan	42,400,000	1967
Nagarjuna Sagar, India	73,575,000	UC	Beas, India	42,261,000	UC
Garrison, U.S.A.	66,506,000	1956	Mica, Canada	42,001,000	UC
Cochiti, U.S.A.	61,005,000	UC	Kremenchug, USSR	41,192,000	1961
Gorky, USSR	57,967,000	1955	[1]Formerly South Saskatchewan		
Kiev, USSR	57,552,000	1964	[2]Formerly Portage Mt.		

NATIONS OF THE WORLD

The nations of the world are listed in alphabetical order, except for Canada and the United States (see Index for listings). Initials in the following articles include UN (United Nations), OAS (Organization of American States), NATO (North Atlantic Treaty Org.), EC (European Communities or Common Market), OAU (Org. of African Unity), CENTO (Central Treaty Org. of the Middle East), SEATO (Southeast Asia Treaty Org.). Areas based upon U.S. State Department figures.

See special color section for maps and flags of all nations.

Afghanistan

Area: 253,861 sq. mi. Population (UN est. 1974): 18,800,000. Capital: Kabul. Monetary unit: Afghani.

Afghanistan is a landlocked republic occupying a mountainous area much of which is 4,000 ft. and more above sea level. It is slightly smaller than Texas. Its neighbors are Iran, Pakistan, and the USSR. The northeast tip of the country just touches China's Sinkiang Province; both India and Pakistan claim Kashmir, which borders on Afghanistan.

The Hindu Kush mountains tower 16,000 ft. above the capital of Kabul and reach a height of more than 25,000 ft. some 200 miles to the E. Trade with Pakistan flows through the 35-mile long Khyber Pass from Kabul to Peshawar. The climate is dry, with extreme temperatures.

Resources and Industries. About 90% of the country's exports ($90 million in 1972) are agricultural products. Chief items: natural gas, cotton, wool, karakul pelts, hides, oilseeds, and fruit. Hand-woven carpets, cotton, wool, fruits and nuts, and sheepskin coats are exported. Some 4 million head of broadtail karakul sheep are raised, as well as goats and camels. The sheep provide the principal meat, and the tightly curled, glossy black coats of the newborn lambs are a valuable fur. Minerals include copper, lead, gas, coal, zinc, iron, silver, asbestos, and oil. The country has received considerable economic aid from the U.S., USSR and China. The USSR is Afghanistan's largest trading partner.

Textile mills, cement factories, highways and irrigation projects are among recent developments.

Famine, following a drought, brought death to thousands in 1972. The U.S. led other nations in gifts of relief wheat.

History and Government. Afghanistan was so named in about the middle of the 18th Century. In ancient times it was known as Aryana, in the Middle Ages as Khorasan. Pukhtuns (Pushtuns) comprise 53.5% of the population; Tajiks 36.7%; Uzbeks 6%; Hazaras 3%.

In 1964 a Grand Assembly approved a new constitution providing for an elected Lower House, partly-elected Upper House, an independent judiciary, a prime minister chosen by the king. The last king was Mohammed Zahir Shah, who ascended the throne Nov. 8, 1933, on the assassination of his father, Mohammad Nadir Shah. Leading a July 17, 1973, coup, Gen. Mohammad Daud, the king's brother-in-law, proclaimed Afghanistan a republic with himself as president and premier.

Bordering on both Russia and China, Afghanistan has been traditionally neutral. Armed forces: over 80,000.

Education and Religion. Education is free and, where facilities are available, compulsory. The University of Kabul was established in 1932. Principal languages are Pushtu and Persian. English is taught. Islam is the predominant religion.

Albania

Area: 11,100 sq. mi. Population (1974 est.): 2,420,-000. Capital: Tirana. Monetary unit: Lek.

Albania, a Balkan communist republic, is a narrow mountainous land, slightly larger than Maryland, extending for 225 mi. along the E coast of the Adriatic. Yugoslavia and Greece are its neighbors. Mt. Korab, 9,066 ft., is the tallest peak.

Resources and Industries. Still a preponderantly agricultural nation, Albania in the 1960s and 1970s pressed programs of industrialization and agricultural modernization with the aid of communist China.

New industrial installations included chemical fertilizer, textile, electric cable, and electric power plants.

Principal exports include petroleum, bitumen, chrome, iron, and copper; cotton textiles, wood products, and tobacco. More than half of Albania's foreign trade is with communist China.

History and Government. Albania has been overrun by warring armies for over 2,000 years. It declared its independence from the Turks in 1912; this was backed by a conference of European powers which placed Prince William of Wied on the throne in 1914. He fled within months because of uprisings. During World War I several nations occupied the land by turns. In 1920, a republic was set up. In 1925, Ahmed Zogu seized the presidency; in 1928 he proclaimed himself king, assuming the title Zog I.

King Zog fled in 1939 when Italy invaded and annexed Albania. When Italy surrendered to the Allies in 1943, German troops took over; they left in 1944 and communist partisans seized power. Gen. Enver Hoxha was named provisional president; a communist front won a 1945 election; in 1946 a new constitution, modeled on that of the USSR, was adopted under Hoxha's leadership.

The U.S. and Britain voted against Albanian admission to the UN in 1946; it finally won admission in 1955 with Britain voting "yes" and the U. S. abstaining. In 1955 it was admitted to the Warsaw Pact. Its policies have been strongly pro-Stalinist, anti-Khrushchev, pro-China and hostile to Tito's Yugoslav regime. The USSR broke relations with Albania in Dec. 1961 and in 1962 barred it from Warsaw Pact meetings. Albania withdrew from the pact in 1968.

In 1970 China and Albania signed a new treaty providing for expanded trade and additional Chinese financial credits for Albania. In 1971, after years of mistrust, Albania resumed diplomatic relations with Yugoslavia and Greece.

Education and Religion. Historically, the largest segment of the population was Moslem, followed by Orthodox Christians and Roman Catholics. Primary education nominally is compulsory and free under the constitution. In 1969 there were 14,000 university and college students.

Ethnically the Albanians are mainly Ghegs in the north and Tosks in the south.

Defense. Military strength totals 38,000.

Algeria

Area: 919,951 sq. mi. Population (Govt. est. 1974): 16,280,000. Capital: Algiers. Monetary unit: Dinar.

Algeria, an independent republic more than 3 times the size of Texas, is located in northern Africa extending for 640 mi. along the Mediterranean Sea between Tunisia and Morocco. The southern Saharan Departments extend into the Sahara Desert and border on Niger, Mali, and Mauritania. The Tell, located on the coast, comprises fertile plains from 50 to 100 mi. wide. Several chains of the Atlas Mtns., running roughly E-W and reaching altitudes of 7,000 ft., separate the coast regions from inland plateaus and the Sahara, and its vast mineral deposits. Algiers, the capital, is the largest city.

Resources and Industries. Agricultural products include wheat, barley, oats, corn, potatoes, artichokes, flax, tobacco, wine, and olive oil. Dates, pomegranates and figs grow abundantly. Cattle raising is important. There are large deposits of oil, iron, zinc, lead, mercury, coal, copper.

Exports consist of wines, fruits, iron and zinc ores, phosphate rock, cork, tobacco products, vegetables, liquefied natural gas and petroleum. Algeria is the world's 14th largest oil-producing nation. Oil is exported to pay for necessary food imports. Imports in 1973 totalled $2,125 million, exports $1,775 million.

In 1967-71 most foreign oil distribution and producing companies were nationalized. Industrialization has progressed with an oil refinery, natural gas liquefication, iron, steel, fertilizer, plastics, and textile factories, financed with oil revenues.

History and Government. The fertile Tell plains have attracted a succession of conquerors to Algeria from before the time of Christ. Once ruled by Carthage, the country after 146 B.C. came under control of the Romans. But it was the Arabs, who arrived in the 7th Century, who were to have the most lasting influence on the country. In 1518 Algiers and the coastal area came under Turkish domination. France took control in 1830, annexed it in 1842 and began to develop the land.

From 1954-62 growing Arab nationalism led to warfare between the French and the Algerians. The political impasse was not broken until French president Charles de Gaulle negotiated with the Front de Liberation Nationale (FLN). Algeria in a referendum July, 1962, voted overwhelmingly for independence; de Gaulle proclaimed it independent July 3.

Internal strife continued, however, between opposing Algerian factions, and Ahmed Ben Bella, with Army support, assumed control in Aug. 1962.

A constitution was approved Sept. 8, 1963, and Premier Ben Bella, sole candidate, was elected president for a 5-year term Sept. 15. Nationalization of lands and industries proceeded rapidly. Algeria received a $100 million long-term industrial loan from the USSR in 1963; French aid continued.

Ben Bella was arrested and deposed June 19, 1965, in a bloodless, army-backed coup d'etat led by Col. Houari Boumediene (born Mohammed Boukharouba), defense minister. Col. Boumediene, on July 11, announced a new cabinet with himself as president.

Algeria is a member of the UN, OAU, and Arab League.

Education and Religion. The population before independence included approx. 1 million Europeans, 80% of them Algerian-born, since reduced to about 80,000. Most Algerians are Arabs and Berbers, of Moslem faith. There are 3 universities and 21 technical institutes.

Defense. Armed forces, modernized with USSR aid, total 63,000.

Andorra

Area: 179 sq. mi. Population (1973 Census): 25,000. Capital: Andorra la Vella. Monetary units: Franc, Peseta.

Andorra is a tiny principality of valleys and mountains set high in the Pyrenees on the border of France and Spain. It has two co-princes, the president of France and the Spanish Catholic bishop of Urgel, whose representatives are charged with the administration of justice, but the country has enjoyed practical sovereignty since 1278. It pays an annual tribute of 960 francs to France and 460 pesetas to the bishop of Urgel.

Actual government is in the hands of a Council-General of 24 members elected by universal suffrage, who enact laws and elect a syndic general, the top administrator. Women won voting rights in 1970.

The main industry is tourism (215 hotels), followed by sheep-raising. Andorra has considerable iron, lead, alum, stone, and timber. Skiing, trout fishing, and chamois hunting are among tourist attractions.

The official language is Catalan; Spanish and French are spoken; principal religion is Roman Catholicism.

Angola

Area: 481,351. Population (Govt. est. 1972): 5,800,-000. Capital: Luanda.

Angola stretches 1,000 mi. along the Atlantic in SW Africa, bordering Namibia (South-West Africa), Zambia, and Zaire. Cabinda, an enclave separated from the rest of the country by the short Atlantic coast of Zaire, borders on the Congo Republic.

Most of Angola, which is twice the size of Texas, consists of a plateau elevated 3,000 to 5,000 feet above sea level, rising sharply from a narrow coastal strip. There is also a temperate highland area in the west-central region, a desert in the south, and a tropical rain forest covering Cabinda.

Resources and Industries. Angola produces 5% of world's coffee. Other products are corn, sugar, palm oil, cotton, wheat, tobacco, cacao, sisal, wax, fish, and fishmeal. Livestock totaled 4.4 million head in 1971. Angola is an important exporter of iron and diamonds. Copper, manganese, sulphur, and phosphates are also found. Exploitation of large oil fields in Cabinda is growing. Manufactures include alcohol, cotton goods, paper, footwear, soap, and sugar.

History and Government. Portuguese settlers arrived in the Congo region in 1491, and founded Luanda, 1575. Angola became a major slaving center, with about 3 million slaves sent to the New World until the middle of the nineteenth century. Portugal increased its colonization efforts in the 20th Century. The white population rose to about 340,000, with the rest divided among four major and many minor Bantu tribal groups.

A 1961 insurrection against Portuguese rule continued until 1974, when the new regime in Portugal offered independence. By then, the independence movement was divided into three groups, the National Front, based in Zaire, the Soviet-backed Popular Movement, and the moderate National Union. Each group's power was in part tribally based. Despite agreements for joint rule, fighting broke out in 1975 between followers of the National Front and Popular Movement; over 3,000 were killed in Luanda. With independence scheduled for November, 1975, the capital was controlled by the Popular Movement, and the northern area by the National Front. The fighting had halved economic output, helped drive most of the whites from the country, and stimulated a secession movement in Cabinda.

Education and Religion. About 550,000 students attended school under the Portuguese, but illiteracy was 85%. Portuguese was the only nation-wide language. About 2.2 million Angolans are Roman Catholic. The rest adhere to local cults, excepting some Protestants.

Argentina

Area: 1,072,067 sq. mi. Population (Govt. est. 1974): 25,050,000. Capital: Buenos Aires. Monetary unit: Peso.

Argentina, 4 times the size of Texas, extends from Bolivia 2,300 miles to Tierra del Fuego and from the Andes to the South Atlantic, and is the 2d largest and 2d most populous country in South America.

The mountains are grouped into 4 isolated systems: the Andean, Central, Misiones, and Southern. Aconcagua is the highest peak in the Western Hemisphere, altitude 22,834 ft.

East of the Andes are great plains, heavily wooded and called the Gran Chaco in the north, and the fertile, treeless Pampas, given over to wheat and cattle raising, in the central region. Patagonia, in the south, is bleak and arid; petroleum and sheep are its main products.

Rio de la Plata is the estuary of one of the world's great drainage systems. It is a wide gulf of mostly fresh water, 170 mi. long, 140 mi. wide at its mouth. On its banks are 3 important cities, Buenos Aires and La Plata in Argentina, and Montevideo in Uruguay.

Emptying into it are the Parana River, 2,500 mi. long, and the Uruguay, 1,000, both starting far to the north in Brazil. Further south, other large rivers flow from the Andes, in the west, to the Atlantic, including the Colorado and Negro.

Resources and Industries. The mountains of Argentina contain deposits of coal, lead, zinc, iron, sulphur, silver, copper, and gold. Petroleum is important.

Cotton, wheat, barley, rye, linseed, oats, alfalfa are important. Sugar, wine, cotton, fruit, corn, sorghum, tobacco, and peanuts are produced. Sheep, cattle, horses, goats, and pigs form the chief wealth of the ranches. In 1975 there were 58 million cattle and 39 million sheep, both high in world rankings. Meat processing is the chief industry. Flour milling is 2d. Argentina is the world's 4th largest meat exporter.

Railroads are state-owned.

Also important in the country's growing industrialization are chemicals, textiles, sugar-refining, and machinery. But successive governments were unable to control inflation, which reached a 200% annual rate in 1975, and balance of payment problems.

Foreign trade, in thousands of U. S. Dollars:

	Imports	Exports
1972	$1,905,000	$1,941,000
1973	$2,235,000	$3,266,000

History and Government. Discovered 1515-16 by Spanish explorers headed by Juan Diaz de Solis, Argentina remained under Spanish domination until the provinces, in a revolt, established an independent republic, May 25, 1810. In 1853 a liberal constitution was adopted. The present constitution, proclaimed May 1, 1956, is essentially that of 1853.

There are 22 provinces which elect their own governors and legislatures, and a Federal District, Buenos Aires (area 72 sq. mi.), whose mayor is appointed by the president.

The president and vice president must be Roman Catholic and Argentine by birth. They are elected for 4-year terms by direct popular vote. Congress consists of a Senate of 69 and a House of Deputies. Voting is compulsory for both men and women.

After the election of Juan D. Peron, an army officer, as president in 1946, Argentine democracy was replaced by dictatorship. By concessions to labor Peron built a following; he then suppressed freedom of speech and press and religious schools and ran the country deeply into debt. Civilians, clericals and part of the armed forces unseated Peron Sept. 16, 1955, and he went into exile. A provisional government was replaced November, 1955, by a military junta, which restored civil liberties, dissolved the Peronist party and returned expropriated property.

In the first free elections in 12 years, Feb. 22, 1958, Dr. Arturo Frondizi was elected president. Dissension among military leaders, democratic parties and the Peronist unions which had supported Dr. Frondizi resulted in a bloodless military coup Mar. 29, 1962. Another election and another military coup followed. In March 1971, Lt. Gen. Alejandro A. Lanusse took over as president; he ordered a return to civilian government.

In March 1973 elections, Hector J. Campora, a follower of Peron, was elected president. On July 13, 1973, Campora resigned and Peron, 77, returned and was elected president Sept. 23, taking office Oct. 12. His 3d wife, Maria Estela, was elected vice president.

Peron died July 1, 1974, and Mrs. Peron, 43, succeeded, becoming the first woman president in the Western Hemisphere. Her influence was curbed by violent struggle between left and right Peronists.

Terrorist violence increased in the 1970's with hundreds of political slayings and lucrative kidnapings netting tens of millions of dollars.

Argentina is a member of the UN and OAS.

Education and Religion. The population is about 92% Roman Catholic, the constitutional religion since 1810. There are 600,000 Jews. Primary education is free, secular, and compulsory. There are national universities in Cordoba (founded in 1613), Buenos Aires and 9 other cities, and numerous private uni-

versities. The language is Spanish. The people are of Spanish and Italian descent, with Basques, Swiss, Germans and British.

Defense. The 3 services total over 135,000 plus several hundred thousand reserves.

Australia

Area: 2,967,909 sq. mi. (7,678,700 sq. km.). Population (Govt. est. 1975): 13,542,100. Capital: Canberra. Monetary unit: Australian dollar.

The continent of Australia, an island almost the size of the 48 conterminous U. S. states, is SE of Asia and below Indonesia. The Indian O. is W and S, the Pacific E; they meet N of Australia in the Timor and Arafura Seas. The Great Barrier Reef is along the NE coast. About 150 mi. S of the state of Victoria lies the island state Tasmania. Branches of the Pacific are the Coral Sea, NE, and the Tasman Sea, SE.

The Tropic of Capricorn bisects Australia. The Great Dividing Range along the E coast has Mt. Kosciusko, 7,316 ft., in New South Wales. The W plateau rises to 2,000 ft., with arid areas in the Great Sandy and Great Victoria Deserts. The NW part of Western Australia and Northern Territory are arid and torrid; Arnhem Land, in the latter, is a rugged wooded area reserved for aborigines. The NE has heavy rainfall and Cape York Peninsula has jungles. The Murray River rises in New South Wales, flows 1,600 mi. to the Indian Ocean and fuels power plants.

States and territories of Australia with their areas in sq. mi. and 1973 est. populations were:

	Area	Population
New South Wales	309,433	4,738,100
Victoria	87,884	3,615,800
Queensland	667,000	1,946,500
South Australia	380,070	1,211,100
Western Australia	975,920	1,084,400
Tasmania	26,383	399,100
Northern Territory	520,280	98,100
Australian Capital Terr.	939	175,400
Totals	2,967,909	13,268,500

The capitals are: NSW, Sydney; Vict., Melbourne; Queens., Brisbane; South Aust. Adelaide; West. Aust., Perth; Tasm., Hobart; North. Terr., Darwin; Capital Terr., Canberra.

Home of the kangaroo, Australia also is the habitat of other strange flora and fauna: the koala, or living teddy bear; the platypus, wombat, dingo, Tasmanian devil, a blind mole, and barking and frilled lizards.

By 1973, Australia had added almost 3 million population from immigration since World War II. About one-half was British. Australia's aborigines are mostly detribalized. Government policy aims at self-determination.

The Melbourne Cup horse race is the biggest annual sports event; cricket, tennis, and football are played extensively. Excellent beaches are numerous.

Resources and Industries. Almost from earliest days of settlement a primary producing country, Australia has become highly industrialized. More than 25% of the total labor force of approx. 5,550,000 work in factories; about 15% are engaged in rural occupations.

Wool and meat are important products. With an annual clip of more than 1.9 billion lbs., Australia produces 30% of the world's wool, 50% of its merino wool and is the largest exporter of beef and second in lamb. It is also one of the largest wheat producers, with 10.5 million tons in 1974. Over one-half is exported. Other important products are sugar, wine, fruit, vegetables, meat, grains, minerals, including uranium, gold, coal, copper, iron, silver, lead, tin, bauxite, rutile and petroleum products.

Discovery of vast iron ore deposits in Western Australia brought a mining boom to desolate areas in 1965. New oil and gas was discovered 1965-1968, nickel in 1969, uranium in 1972 and 1974.

Principal manufactures include iron and steel, textiles, electrical and radio equipment, drugs, chemicals, paints, machinery, metal work, clothing, motor cars and engines, aircraft and ships. Unemployment rose to 4.8% of the work force. Gross domestic product in 1973-74 was $A49,754 million ($US68.2 billion).

In recent years exports of mineral and industrial products have increased considerably. Foreign aid takes 0.55% of gross national product, fifth highest rate in the world.

Australia changed its currency from pounds-shillings-pence to dollars and cents Feb. 14, 1966, with its dollar worth half the old Australian pound. It will complete adoption of metric weights and measures by 1980.

Foreign trade, in thousands of U.S. dollars:

	Imports	Exports
1973	$6,802,000	$9,389,000
1974	$11,078,000	$10,785,000

Tourism is rapidly expanding. In 1973 Australia had 472,124 overseas visitors.

History and Government. Australia has been settled by Europeans since 1788. The Commonwealth, proclaimed Jan. 1, 1901, is a self-governing federation of 6 states and 2 territories. Parliament consists of the Crown (represented by the governor-general), the Senate and House of Representatives. In Dec. 1972 elections, the Labor party ended 23 years of rule by the Liberal and Country parties coalition. In May 1974 elections, Labor won 66 House seats; the Liberal and Country parties won 61. Each group won 29 Senate seats.

Gough Whitlam, Labor prime minister, ended restrictions on non-white immigrants, ended the draft and military aid to South Vietnam and recognized China and North Vietnam.

Pension acts provide for payments of war, old age and invalid pensions; also cover the blind, the ill and the unemployed. The National Health Scheme provides free drugs and subsidizes hospital and medical expenses.

A maternity act provides for the payment of a maternity allowance for every child born in Australia. Social security for children includes child endowment payments for children under 16.

Education and Religion. Education is free and compulsory. There are 15 universities and 3 university colleges. The Church of England claims 37.7% of the population, the remainder being Roman Catholic, 23.3%; Presbyterian, 9.7%; Methodist, 10.8%.

Defense. Armed forces total 68,450.

Australian Territories

Norfolk Island was taken over by Australia, 1914. It has an area of 13.5 sq. mi. and a population (est. 1973) of 1,380. The soil is very fertile and is suitable for citrus fruits, bananas, and coffee. Many of the inhabitants are descendants of the Bounty mutineers; some moved to Norfolk in 1856 from Pitcairn Is.

Coral Sea Islands Territory, 1 sq. mi., is administered from Norfolk Is.

Territory of Ashmore and Cartier Islands, area 2 sq. mi., in the Indian Ocean came under the authority of Australia May 1934 and are administered as part of Northern Territory. **Heard and McDonald Islands** are governed by the Department of Science.

Cocos (Keeling) Islands, 27 small coral islands in the Indian Ocean 1,300 miles NW of Australia. Pop. (est. 1972): 618; area: 5 sq. mi.

Christmas Island, 52 sq. mi., pop. 3,361 (est. 1970), 230 mi. S. of Java, was transferred by Britain in 1958. It has phosphate deposits.

Australian Antarctic Territory was claimed by Australia in 1933, including 2,472,000 sq. mi. of territory S of 60th parallel S. Lat. and between 160th-45th meridians E. Long.

Austria

Area: 32,374 sq. mi. Population (Govt. est. 1974): 7,530,000. Capital: Vienna. Monetary unit: Schilling.

Austria is a republic in the mountainous region of central Europe, 360 mi. long, 160 mi. wide — slightly smaller than Maine. Mountain passes cross frontiers; the Brenner, below the Stubai Alps, has been a major route to Italy since ancient times.

Principal river, the Danube, flows from Bavaria in NW to Czechoslovakia, E. Others are the Enns, Inn, Drau, Ill, Mur, and Salzach, some furnishing hydroelectric power. There are numerous lakes and popular spas, such as Bad Gastein and Bad Ischl.

Resources and Industries. Austria produces iron ore, oil, timber, magnesite, aluminum, coal, lignite, cement, and copper. It is an important source of high-grade graphite. Hydroelectric power has been widely developed. Manufactures include steel, machinery, vehicles, electrical and optical instruments, glassware, sporting goods, paper, yarns, textiles, fertilizers, chemicals, and artistic leather goods.

Although farmland is limited, Austria produces about 85% of its foodstuffs. It grows wheat, rye, barley, oats, corn, potatoes, sugar beets. Vineyards flourish in Lower Austria and in Burgenland.

Over 11 million tourists visit annually. The Salzburg Festival, the Vienna State Opera, skiing and spas are among attractions.

Principal exports are iron, steel, paper, textiles, machinery, chemicals, metal products, vehicles, aluminum, electric power. Trade is heavy with West Germany, Italy, and the U.S.

Foreign trade in thousands of U.S. dollars:

	Imports	Exports
1973	$7,121,000	$5,289,000
1974	$9,020,000	$7,161,000

History and Government. Austria, the East Mark (Ost Mark) of Charlemagne (788 A.D.) came under the Hapsburgs in 1278. Tyrol was added 1363, Bohemia (Czech) and Hungary, 1526. The Turks were twice turned back at Vienna, 1529 and 1683. Austrian dominance of German lands was challenged in the 18th Century and Empress Maria Theresa (ruled 1740-1780) lost Silesia to Frederick II (the Great) of Prussia. Austria took slices of Poland in the partitions of 1772, 1793 and 1795. Austria was the scene of major Napoleonic battles and helped defeat him. The Congress of Vienna, 1815, awarded it Istria, Illyria, and the Italian provinces of Lombardy and Venetia. Austria lost Lombardy to Italy 1859 and Venetia 1866, after Prussia defeated Austria.

Under the Dual Monarchy of Austria-Hungary, established 1867 to recognize the aspirations of the Magyars, Francis Joseph was Emperor of Austria and King of Hungary. The nation had an area of 261,259 sq. mi., population c. 51 million. It contained Austria, Hungary, Bohemia, Transylvania, Polish Galicia, Trentino, Slavonia, Croatia, Bosnia, Herzegovina, Banat. After Archduke Francis Ferdinand, heir to the Austrian throne, and his consort were assassinated in Sarajevo, Bosnia, June 28, 1914, Austria declared war on Serbia, which helped precipitate World War I. It was dismembered after that war; became a republic composed of 9 small states in 1918.

Between the 2 world wars Austria had a turbulent political history. Socialists introduced some socio-economic changes. These were checked by Chancellor Engelbert Dollfuss, 1934. Dollfuss was murdered by Nazi conspirators July 25, 1934. Germany, under Hitler, occupied Austria Mar. 13, 1938, and proclaimed its union with Germany. It was reestablished as a republic in 1945.

Dr. Karl Renner was president of the provisional government after liberation by the Allies, 1945. After 17 years of occupation, delayed by tactics of the Soviet Union, a 1955 treaty restored the frontiers of Jan. 1, 1938, prohibited union with Germany, required support of democratic institutions. Austria formally regained sovereignty July 27, 1955. It declared perpetual neutrality.

The president is elected by secret ballot for a 6-year term. He appoints the chancellor; Parliamentary elections Oct. 10, 1971, gave the Socialist party a majority of seats; Socialists were elected president in each postwar election.

Austria belongs to UN and EFTA. In 1972 Austria and 5 other EFTA members joined with EC (Common Market) members in pacts for abolition of industrial tariffs.

Education and Religion. The predominant religion is Roman Catholicism. Elementary education is free and compulsory between the ages of 6 and 15. There are universities in Vienna, Graz, Innsbruck, and Salzburg. The language is German.

Defense. Armed forces total 52,000.

The Bahamas

Area: 4,404 sq. mi. Population (Govt. est. 1974): 200,000. Capital: Nassau. Monetary unit: Bahamian dollar.

The Commonwealth of the Bahamas achieved full independence from Great Britain on July 10, 1973. The Bahamas comprise nearly 700 islands (30 inhabited) and over 2,000 islets in the western Atlantic. They extend 760 mi. NW to SE from a point 50 mi. off Florida to about 70 mi. from Haiti.

Christopher Columbus first set foot in the New World on the island of San Salvador (also called Watling Is.) on the eastern fringe of the Bahamas in 1492. British settlement started in 1647; the islands became a British colony in 1783. Internal self-government was granted by Britain in 1964. Elections to the Assembly in 1967 led to the selection of the first black prime minister, Lynden O. Pindling.

The prime minister leads the majority part of the 38-member, elected Assembly. The 16-member Senate is appointed by the governor-general (nominally representing the British queen) on the advice of the prime minister and the opposition leader. The Bahamas belong to the UN and Commonwealth.

Tourism is the main industry; second is international banking and investment management. Fruit and vegetables are grown mostly for local use. There are cement and pharmaceutical plants. Exports are salt, lobster, tomatoes, cucumbers, handicrafts.

English is the official language; Anglican is the predominant religion. Elementary schools are free and compulsory except on a few of the "Out Islands." About 85% of the population is of African descent.

Bahrain

Area: 231 sq. mi. Population: (Govt. est. 1974): 240,000. Capital: Manama. Monetary unit: Dinar.

Bahrain, long a British Protected State, declared its complete independence Aug. 14, 1971. It includes the main island, Bahrain, and several smaller islands midway along the Persian (also called Arabian) Gulf, about 20 mi. off the Arabian Peninsula's NE coast.

Pearls, shrimp, fruit, and vegetables were the mainstays of the economy until oil was discovered in 1932. By the 1970's, oil reserves showed signs of depletion. Contributions were made to the economy by a large refinery handling oil pumped undersea from Saudi Arabia as well as local oil, by a large aluminum smelter using local natural gas, and by increased use of Bahrain as a trans-shipment center. Bahrain took part in the 1973-74 Arab oil embargo against the U. S. and other nations. The government bought controlling interest in the oil industry in 1975.

Long ruled by the Khalifa family, Bahrain signed a treaty in 1861 giving Great Britain responsibility for defense and foreign relations. When Britain announced it would remove its military forces from the Persian Gulf area by the end of 1971, Bahrain sought to form a federation with the 7 Trucial Sheikhdoms (now the United Arab Emirates) and Qatar, which were also British Protected States. The attempt failed and Bahrain declared itself independent. It is ruled by an Emir, a Prime Minister, and a Council of Ministers (cabinet). In 1973 a constitution created the first parliament, the National Assembly; 30 members are elected by male citizens 18 or over; 14 Cabinet members also sit in the Assembly.

Most Bahrainis are of north Arabian descent, half of them Sunni Moslems, half of them Shi'ites. Arabic is the official language; Persian and English are also spoken. Education and health care are free.

The future of a 1971 agreement for a small U. S. Navy base remained in doubt in 1975.

Bangladesh

Area: 55,126 sq. mi. Population (1974 census): 71,316,517. Capital: Dacca. Monetary unit: Taka.

East Pakistan, the smaller but more populous of the 2 sections of Pakistan, achieved independence as Bangladesh (Bengal Nation) during the Dec. 3-16, 1971, India-Pakistan war. Separated from West Pakistan by 1,000 mi. of India, it is mostly a low plain cut by the Ganges and Brahmaputra Rivers and is bounded by India, Burma, and the Bay of Bengal. It is subject to heavy monsoon rains. A Nov. 13, 1970, cyclone killed at least 300,000 persons in coastal areas.

Resources and Industries. Bangladesh is primarily agricultural, with small, fertile farms. The area normally produces most of the world's jute, used in twine and sacks, and has large rice crops. Resources include rivers for irrigation and hydroelectric power, and natural gas. Small industries include cement and fertilizer plants. Food shipments and other aid were provided by India, the U.S., USSR, and others. In Mar., 1972, Bangladesh announced nationalization of banks and some industries. Offshore oil deposits have been found, some in areas disputed by India, but 1974 floods and high world oil prices caused famine deaths to soar.

History and Government. British rule in the Indian sub-continent, dating from the 18th Century, ended in Aug. 1947 when India and Pakistan became independent. Pakistan's government power was centered in W. Pakistan, while E. Pakistan, with about 56% of the population, demanded greater economic benefits and political reforms. There were riots in 1968-69.

In Dec. 1970 elections, the Awami League, which demanded greater autonomy for E. Pakistan, won a majority in the National Assembly. But Pakistan Pres. A. M. Yahya Khan postponed the Assembly sessions. A general strike and riots swept E. Pakistan and on Mar. 25, 1971, W. Pakistani troops launched attacks on rebellious Bengalis. Awami League leaders declared independence the next day. Months of fighting followed in which it was estimated a million or more died as, it was charged, W. Pakistani troops conducted repressive attacks on the populace and guerrilla forces. Some 10 million fled to India, which supported their cause.

India and Pakistan each declared on Dec. 3, 1971, that the other had launched war. Pakistani troops surrendered Dec. 15 in the East; the Pakistan government accepted India's offer of a cease-fire on both east and west fronts Dec. 16. India had recognized Bangladesh as independent Dec. 6. The U. S., which had earlier indicated sympathy with Pakistan, recognized Bangladesh Apr. 4, 1972.

Sheik Mujibur Rahman, Awami League leader arrested in Mar. 1971, was freed by Pakistan and became Bangladesh prime minister Jan. 12, 1972.

Bangladesh joined the Commonwealth in 1972 and the UN in 1974.

A constitution took effect Dec. 16, 1972. In 1973 elections, Sheik Mujib's Awami League party won 305 of 313 seats. The government assumed emergency powers in 1974 to curb widespread violence. In 1975 a presidential form of government went into effect.

In Aug. 1973 India and Pakistan agreed to exchange war prisoners, leading to release of Bangladesh and Pakistani nationals stranded in each other's country. By 1974 most prisoners were returned to Pakistan which then accepted more than 100,000 Biharis, 500,-

000 of whom sought to leave Bangladesh.

Most of the Bangladesh people are Moslem Bengalis. The official language is Bengali.

Barbados

Area: 166 sq. mi. Population (UN est. 1974): 240,000. Capital: Bridgetown. Monetary unit: East Caribbean dollar.

Barbados achieved full independence from Great Britain Nov. 30, 1966. Furthest east of the West Indies, the island is about 2½ times the size of the District of Columbia; it lies alone in the Atlantic almost completely surrounded by coral reefs. Its highest point is Mt. Hillaby, 1,115 ft. The name Barbados (bearded) was believed given it by Portuguese or Spanish sailors, referring to bearded fig trees.

An English ship visited in 1605; English settlers arrived in 1627. Slaves were imported, but freed in 1834. Most of the islanders are Negroes; the language is English and the religion of most is Anglican.

A charter of 1652 provided for a governor-general, council and assembly. Self-rule was achieved gradually; universal suffrage was granted in 1950, cabinet government in 1958, full internal self-government in 1961. It has a parliament and prime minister and, as a member of the Commonwealth, a governor-general.

Sugar, molasses, rum, cotton, and building lime are the main products; there is a lively flying fish industry and, thanks mainly to the attractions of excellent beaches, the tourist business has boomed. But unemployment is high. In 1973 Barbados joined other West Indies states in the Caribbean Common Market.

With over 1,400 persons per sq. mi., the population density is one of the world's highest. Barbados has a high literacy rate.

Belgium

Area: 11,779 sq. mi. Population (Govt. est. 1974): 9,757,000. Capital: Brussels. Monetary unit: Franc.

Belgium's seacoast of 40 mi. borders on the North Sea at the Strait of Dover. Slightly larger than Maryland, the country shares borders with the Netherlands, Germany, Luxembourg, and France. The Meuse (Maas) River crosses the country from France to the Netherlands. The Scheldt (Escaut Schelde) makes Antwerp an ocean port via the Netherlands.

Brussels, Bruges, Ghent, and Antwerp are noted for art and architecture; Liege and Charleroi are important industrially. Antwerp is the world's 3d largest port.

Resources and Industries. Coal is the nation's only important mineral. Although Belgium is essentially a manufacturing country, agriculture and forestry are profitable industries. The principal crops are oats, rye, wheat, potatoes, barley, and sugar beets.

Important industries are mining, steel manufacture, glassware, diamond cutting, food and beverages, fishing, textiles, and chemicals. Beurs voor Diamant in Antwerp is the world's largest diamond trading center.

Belgium lives by its foreign trade; about 40% of its entire production is sold abroad (75% of steel and glass). The Belgium-Luxembourg Economic Union is one of the world's foremost exporters of steel.

Foreign trade of Belgium-Luxembourg, in thousands of U. S. dollars:

	Imports	Exports
1973	$21,925,000	$22,399,000
1974	$29,704,000	$28,263,000

History and Government. Belgium, land of the Belgae conquerd by Julius Caesar, was for 1800 years ruled by conquerors, including the Romans, Franks, Burgundy, Spain, Austria, and France. After the fall of Napoleon, 1815, Belgium was made a part of the Netherlands. Belgium became an independent constitutional monarchy in 1830 and chose Prince Leopold of Saxe-Coburg king, as Leopold I.

By the treaty of London, Apr. 19, 1839, Austria, France, Great Britain, Netherlands, Prussia, and Russia guaranteed the inviolability of Belgium; this was the "scrap of paper" repudiated by Germany when its troops entered Belgium, Aug. 2, 1914. After World War I Belgium was awarded 382 sq. mi. of territory formerly held by Germany, including Malmedy.

During World War II, Leopold III surrendered to Germany, May 28, 1940, to avoid bloodshed. His cabinet maintained a government-in-exile in London. Nevertheless, Belgium suffered heavily. Ancient churches, houses, and records were ruined at Nivelles, Mons, Tournai. Liege, Louvain; the University Library at Louvain, burned in both World Wars, was each time restored with U. S. aid. About 50,000 Belgians died, some in Nazi prison camps.

In 1950 Belgians voted 57% in favor of recalling Leopold III (who had been in Switzerland since being freed from German internment), but Socialists forced the king to abdicate and his son became King Baudouin I July 17, 1951. Born Sept. 7, 1930, he was the son of Leopold's first wife, Princess Astrid of Sweden. Baudouin married (Dec. 15, 1960) Dona Fabiola de Mora y Aragon of Spain.

Universal suffrage is in force and those who fail to vote are fined. Women have voted since 1949.

Parliament consists of a Senate with members elected for 4 years, partly directly and partly indirectly; the number elected directly is equal to half the number of members of the House of Representatives. The representatives are directly elected, for 4 years, by proportional representation (one for every 40,000 population).

The Flemings of northern Belgium speak Dutch while French is the language of the Walloons in the south. The language difference has been a perennial source of controversy, particularly as it affects education, with Flemish parents unwilling to have their children taught in French.

Disagreement between the 2 groups became embittered in 1968 elections in which minority extremist parties increased their strength. In 1971 and 1974 Belgium sought to solve the problem through creation of decentralized administrative and cultural communities.

Belgium is a member of the UN, NATO, EC, and the Benelux economic union.

Education and Religion. Roman Catholicism is the religion of the great majority. Part of the income of the ministers of the Catholic, Jewish, Church of England, and Protestant Evangelical religions is paid by the government. There are universities in Ghent, Liege, Brussels, Mons, Antwerp, and Louvain and agricultural, technical, art, and music schools.

Defense: Armed forces total 89,000.

Bhutan

Area: 19,305 sq. mi. Population (Govt. est. 1974): 1,034,774. Capital: Thimphu. Monetary unit: Ngultrum.

The tiny kingdom of Bhutan or Druk-Yul (Dragon-Nation) is a constitutional monarchy in the eastern Himalayas, adjoining Tibet and India. It is 190 mi. long from east to west and 90 mi. across, with both mountains and jungles. Over half the people are Bhotias of Tibetan origin and are Buddhists; a minority are Hindus of Nepalese descent, with indigenous Buddhists in the east.

Agriculture is the chief industry. The principal products are rice, corn, wheat, oranges, cardamom, yak butter, lac, wax, cloth, elephants, ponies, and timber.

The ruler of the kingdom is the "Dragon King," Jigme Singye Wangchuk (born 1955), who inherited the throne July 24, 1972, and was crowned June 2, 1974. Bhutan joined the UN in 1971.

Modernization has begun, including the country's first road network usable by automobiles, linking central Bhutan and India. There is also airline service from India. Dzongs (castle-monasteries) and game sanctuaries are among attractions.

Bolivia

Area: 424,162 sq. mi. Population (Govt. est. 1974): 5,470,000. Capital: Sucre. Seat of govt.: La Paz. Monetary unit: Peso.

Bolivia is a landlocked nation, over 8 times the size of N.Y. State. It lies across the Andes. The great central plateau, at an altitude of 12,000 ft., over 500 mi. long, lies between two great cordilleras having 3 of the highest peaks in South America. More than 65% of the population are Indians; 10% are white, and 25% are mixed (cholo).

Lake Titicaca, on the Peruvian-Bolivian border, is the highest lake in the world on which steamboats ply (12,506 ft.), and is the 2d largest lake in South America (est. 3,200 sq. mi.).

The legal capital is Sucre, but La Paz, a city more accessible, is the actual seat of government. La Paz lies in the heart of a gigantic canyon about 3 mi. wide, 10 mi. long and 1,500 ft. deep, at an altitude of about 11,800 ft., and framed with high Andean peaks. Its huge cathedral seating 12,000 was dedicated 1933.

Resources and Industries. Agriculture claims 50% of the work force. Products include potatoes, sugar, coffee, barley, cocoa, highland rice, corn, bananas, citrus, rubber, and cinchona bark.

The most important industry is mining. There are large deposits of tin, silver, copper, lead, zinc, petroleum, antimony, bismuth, wolfram, gold, iron, cadmium, borate of lime, and natural gas. More than 12% of the world's output of tin is produced in Bolivia, running to 28,000 tons or more annually. The 3 largest tin producers were nationalized in 1952. The oilfields and plants of a U.S. company were nationalized in Oct. 1969. High world tin and oil prices yielded a $140 million 1974 trade surplus.

Bolivian miners' attempts to negotiate better working conditions with the government-owned mining corp. were led in 1967-68 by a group of priests. An agreement was reached in 1968 in which the corporation agreed to permit union activities and provide better conditions, more housing, and hospitals.

Bolivia receives aid from the U. S., the Inter-American Development Bank, the World Bank and the International Monetary Fund. It is a member of the UN and OAS. In May 1969 Bolivia joined Chile, Colombia, Ecuador and Peru in an Andean Common Market.

History and Government. Once part of the ancient Inca empire, Bolivia was under Spanish domination for centuries before it gained independence Aug. 6, 1825, naming itself after Simon Bolivar, famed liberator.

Bolivia's 16th constitution, adopted in 1967, provides for strong executive power, nationalization of mines, and agrarian reform. The Congress it provided for was dissolved in Sept. 1969.

Dr. Victor Paz Estenssoro, elected to a 3d term as President May 31, 1964, was ousted Nov. 4 and the government was taken over in one of a series of military coups. Military and civilian anti-Communist forces under Col. Hugo Banzer Suarez took over the government in a brief conflict, Aug. 19-22, 1971. In 1973 the government pressed school-building and oil-exploration programs. In 1974 Brazil contracted to build steel, cement and petrochemical plants in Bolivia and a pipeline to carry Bolivian natural gas 1,000 mi. to Sao Paulo, Brazil.

Unrest continued as peasants and miners staged protests; in 1974 Banzer dismissed civilian members of his cabinet, banned political parties and labor unions and postponed elections until 1980.

Education and Religion. Primary education is free and compulsory. Adult illiteracy at 58% is being lowered. There are 7 universities. Roman Catholi-

cism is predominant; Spanish is the official language. **Defense.** Bolivia's armed forces total over 21,000.

Botswana

Area: 219,815 sq. mi. Population (Govt. est. 1974): 660,000. Capital: Gaborone. Monetary unit: South African rand.

The former British Protectorate of Bechuanaland received full independence Sept. 30, 1966, and joined the UN Oct. 17, 1966.

In the center of Southern Africa and populated predominantly by blacks, Botswana shares borders with the Republic of South Africa, South-West Africa (Namibia), and Rhodesia. It also claims to border on Zambia, its nearest black-ruled neighbor. It is slightly smaller than Texas.

The Kalahari Desert, supporting only nomadic Bushmen and a few wild animals, spreads over the southwestern areas of Botswana; there are swamplands and farming areas in the north, and rolling plains in the east where livestock are grazed.

Cattle raising is the largest industry. Large copper, coal, and nickel deposits were discovered in 1967 and diamonds in 1969. Corn, sorghum, beans, and peanuts are raised in the north. Tourism is flourishing; black-maned lions and swamp antelopes are hunted.

Many workers have become migrant laborers in South Africa and much of the country's chief export, meat, goes to that country.

In 1885, Bechuanaland was made a British protectorate after local chiefs appealed to Great Britain for aid to halt encroachment on their territories by Boers of South Africa's Transvaal.

It is a republic with a president, a House of Chiefs (which handles questions of tradition) and a National Assembly.

Brazil

Area: 3,286,470 sq. mi. Population (Govt. est. 1975): 107,661,000. Capital: Brasilia. Monetary unit: Cruzeiro.

Brazil is the largest nation in South America in area and population. Larger in area than the 48 states in conterminous U.S., it is smaller than the 50 states. It has a coastline on the Atlantic Ocean of 4,603 mi., and extends 2,689 from N to S and 2,684 from E to W. The northern part is the great, heavily-wooded basin of the Amazon (1,465,637 sq. mi. in Brazil) which rises in the Peruvian Andes and empties into the Atlantic.

The Amazon basin has a network of rivers which are navigable for 15,814 mi. The Amazon River by itself flows 2,093 mi. through Brazil, and is navigable for 2,300 mi., to the Peruvian riverport of Iquitos.

The majestic falls of the Iguazu, 230 ft. high but extremely wide, are on the Brazil-Argentina border; Glass Falls, in Bahia west of Salvador, are 1,325 ft. high. Tallest mountain is Pico da Neblina, 10,046 ft., on the Venezuela border.

The south central region, favored by climate, resources and communications, has 45% of the population and produces 75% of agricultural goods and 80% of industrial output.

Brasilia, the capital city, was inaugurated Apr. 21, 1960, superseding Rio de Janeiro. Fast-growing Sao Paulo is the largest city in South America.

Resources and Industries: Brazil has vast mineral wealth and exploitation is being spurred. It leads the world in output of quartz crystal and beryl; it is 2d in sheet mica; 3d in manganese, columbium and tantalum; 4th in iron ore. It has large deposits of iron (one-third of the world's reserves) and monazite, a source of thorium, alternate to uranium as a supplier of fissionable material. Gold output is about 142,000 troy oz. annually. Also important are nickel, chrome, diamonds, coal, tungsten, tin, bauxite, various gem stones. New oil finds have raised hopes for self-sufficiency.

Cotton weaving is among important manufacturing industries, occupying 20% of workers. Brazil produces 7.5 million tons of steel annually, 30% in the Volta Redonda national mills. Automotive, aluminum, petrochemical, cement, pharmaceutical, plastics, food and beverage, electrical appliances, shipbuilding, ceramics, shoe, tire, paper, glass, and heavy machinery industries are growing.

Brazil, world's greatest coffee grower, supplies about 30% of the coffee consumed in the U.S. Cotton, soybeans, sugar, cocoa, iron ore, and industrial products are also important exports. There are large crops of bananas, manioc, oranges, pineapples, rice, and corn.

Brahman (zebu) cattle of India thrive in Brazil, which is 5th among world leaders with 91 million cattle. It also has 35 million hogs and 27 million sheep.

Brazil's economy boomed in the 1970s; the gross national product was up 10% in 1974. Exports also showed strong gains. But inflation, though slowed, remained a problem. In 1974 Brazil completed its 3,150-mi. Trans-Amazon Highway, stretching from the Atlantic coast to Peru.

West Germany agreed in 1975 to supply Brazil with the technology for a complete nuclear energy industry, in exchange for uranium.

Foreign trade in thousands of U.S. dollars:

	Imports	Exports
1973	$ 7,170,000	$6,199,000
1974	$12,555,000	$7,968,000

History and Government. Pedro Alvares Cabral, a Portuguese navigator, is generally credited as the first European to reach Brazil, 1500.

Brazil was developed as a colony of Portugal until the royal house of Braganca, fleeing from Lisbon before Napoleon's army in 1807, transferred the seat of government to Rio de Janeiro, March, 1808. Brazil thereupon became a kingdom under Dom Joao VI. After his return to Portugal, his son Pedro I, proclaimed the independence of the country, Sept. 7, 1822, and was acclaimed emperor. The second emperor, Dom Pedro II, was driven from the throne Nov. 15, 1889, by a revolution which established a republic, the United States of Brazil. In Jan. 1967 a new constitution changed the name to Federative Republic of Brazil.

There are 21 states, with limited autonomy, a federal district and 4 territories: Roraima, Rondonia, Amapa and Fernando de Noronha Is.

Brazil is a member of both the UN and OAS.

A military junta took control in 1930. Getulio Vargas became provisional president until 1933, when he was elected president under a new constitution. Out in 1945, he was reelected in 1950, but in 1954 the army forced him to retire.

In 1964, after a succession of presidents, economic and social problems brought the ouster of Pres. Joao Goulart, in a part-military, part-civilian coup. Gen. Humberto Castelo Branco was named president. A new constitution, adopted in 1967, strengthened the powers of the presidency, reducing those of Congress. Both Pres. Castelo Branco and his successor, Pres. Arthur da Costa e Silva, an army marshal elected by Congress in 1966, at times ruled by decree.

Pres. Costa e Silva died in 1969. Military leaders named Gen. Emilio G. Medici to succeed him. He said certain curbs on civil liberties would be continued. He named Gen. Ernesto Geisel to succeed him, and on Jan. 15, 1974, an electoral college consisting of representatives of Congress and of the state legislatures, elected Geisel president. In 1974 elections, the democratic opposition took control of the Chamber of Deputies; but cases of torture by police elements were still being reported.

Education and Religion. Roman Catholicism is the predominant religion.

There are 65 universities in Brazil as well as other institutions of higher education. Primary, 5-year schools number more than 167,000 and there are more than 24,000 median level schools. Primary and secondary schools are free. A national program promotes adult literacy. The language is Portuguese.

Armed forces total over 200,000.

Bulgaria

Area: 42,829 sq. mi. Population (Govt. est. 1974): 8,706,000. Capital: Sofia. Monetary unit: Lev.

The People's Republic of Bulgaria, fronting on the Black Sea, is about the size of Ohio. It is bounded by Romania, Turkey, Greece and Yugoslavia. The Balkan Mtns. stretch across the center of the country with the Danubian Plain in the north and the Rhodope Mts. and Thracian Plain in the south.

Resources and Industries. Under communism after World War II, farms were collectivized, resources nationalized and foreign trade made a government monopoly. The principal crops are wheat, fruit, rye, barley, oats, corn, potatoes and tobacco. The country has been industrialized under a nationalized planned economy which emphasizes electric power, chemicals, coal, machinery, metals, textiles, building materials, fur, leather goods and oil. About 70% of the work force is non-agricultural.

In 1971 productive enterprises were centralized into some 60 state economic amalgamations. The index of industrial production (1970 = 100) reached 142 in 1974. Tourism is promoted and nearly 4 million tourists visit Bulgaria annually.

About 73% of trade is with nations of the communist bloc. Exports include machinery, industrial and agricultural vehicles, chemicals, vegetables, tobacco, rose attar, lead, zinc, cement, and wine.

Foreign trade, in thousands of U.S. dollars:

	Imports	Exports
1972	$2,548,000	$2,603,000
1973	$3,266,000	$3,301,000

History and Government. The Bulgars settled Bulgaria in the 7th cent., became Christians in the 9th, and set up a powerful empire in the 10th-12th. The Turks conquered in 1396. A revolt in 1876 led to autonomy in 1878 and an independent kingdom in 1908. It expanded after the first Balkan war but lost its Aegean coastline in World War I, when it sided with Germany.

Under the influence of King Boris III, Bulgaria joined the Axis in World War II, occupying considerable Balkan territory. In 1944 Bulgaria withdrew from the war, but the USSR refused to recognize its neutrality and declared war Sept. 5. Four days later, an anti-fascist government seized power and declared war on Germany. In a plebiscite Sept. 8, 1946, the monarchy was abolished and a republic voted. Georgi Dimitrov, Communist party leader, became the first premier.

The 1971 constitution provides that the National Assembly, elected for 5 years, is the supreme organ of government. The Assembly chooses a premier and a State Council whose president is the head of state. Only one slate is permitted, dominated by the Communist Party.

Bulgaria belongs to the UN and the Warsaw Pact.

Education and Religion. Bulgarian is a Slavic language, the earliest to be written. Elementary education is obligatory from 7 to 14 years of age. There are 27 higher educational establishments, with over 100,-000 students. The main religion is Eastern Orthodox. There are several hundred thousand Moslems. Religious observance is discouraged.

Defense. Armed forces total over 150,000.

Burma

Area: 261,789 sq. mi. Population (est. 1973): 29,560,000. Capital: Rangoon. Monetary unit: Kyat.

The Union of Burma, slightly smaller than Texas, is

a republic in the western part of the former Indochinese peninsula. It is bounded by China, Laos, Thailand, India, Bangladesh, and the Bay of Bengal. Rivers flowing from the rugged mountains in the north provide habitable valleys down the peninsula. The largest is the Irrawaddy which is navigable for 900 mi.

The Burma Road, from Lashio to Kunming in Yunnan province, China, was the principal military supply line from Burma into China 1938-1942.

Rangoon, on the Gulf of Martaban, is the chief port. Mingaladon airport, near Rangoon, handles international traffic.

Resources and Industries. Mineral wealth is great; included are petroleum, lead, silver, tin, tungsten, zinc, rubies, sapphires, and jade. Principal products are rice, cotton, maize, teakwood, tobacco, tin, silver, rubber, and petroleum. In value of exports, rice accounts for 40%. However, production in some industries declined in the 1960's.

History and Government. Burma was a Buddhist monarchy in the Middle Ages. Britain, through 3 wars, gained Lower Burma in 1824 and Upper Burma in 1884 and administered them as part of India until 1937, when Burma became a self-governing unit of the British Commonwealth. It was overrun by Japan in World War II. Burma became independent outside the Commonwealth by treaty effective Jan. 4, 1948, and a member of the UN in 1948.

The constitution which went into effect in 1948 created a parliamentary democracy and provided for nationalization of certain industries. In a 1958 political crisis, Gen. Ne Win took over the government from Premier U Nu. Elections were held in 1960 and the Union party, headed by U Nu, won a large majority; he again became premier in April, 1960.

Political and economic problems continued and the government was again taken over by Gen. Ne Win, Mar. 2, 1962; he set up a Revolutionary Council with himself as chief of state, setting aside the constitution. In 1972 he became premier.

The Ne Win government pursued a socialist program and nationalized nearly all of industry and trade, which had been controlled by Indian and Chinese minorities. It continued a neutralist foreign policy, and isolated the nation from most foreign contacts. On Jan. 4, 1974, a new constitution, aimed at making Burma a "socialist republic" under one-party rule, was adopted. Ne Win continued as premier.

Recurrent problems facing the government have been the need to stimulate production, rebellions staged by Chinese-backed Communist forces, and pressures from extremist groups seeking greater autonomy for local ethnic groups. The government claimed to have crushed Communist guerrillas in 1975.

Education and Religion. The Burmans are the main ethnic group; others are Karens, Shans, Kachins, Chins, etc. Burmese or one of its variants is spoken by nearly three-fourths of the population. Higher education is provided at the Universities of Rangoon, Mandalay and 5 smaller cities. A state-controlled system of schools was introduced after 1948.

The chief religion is Buddhism (about 90%).

Defense. Armed forces total about 150,000.

Burundi

Area: 10,739 sq. mi. Population (UN est. 1974): 3,680,000. Capital: Bujumbura. Monetary unit: Franc.

Burundi, a country the size of Maryland in east central Africa, became independent July 1, 1962. Formerly part of the Belgian UN Trusteeship of Ruanda-Urundi, it is bordered by Rwanda, Tanzania, Lake Tanganyika and Zaire. Much of the country is grasslands and mountains.

For 3 centuries in the present Burundi and Rwanda area, the Tutsi, a minority tribe, were overlords and political masters of the Hutu. (The Tutsi tend to be extremely tall; the Hutu, the vast majority, are of average height; a 3d tribe, the Twa, are pygmies.) Under German control in the late 19th century, the area was taken over by Belgium in World War I; the League of Nations in 1923 gave the king of Belgium a mandate over the combined Ruanda-Urundi territory; Belgium received a UN Trusteeship in 1946.

Burundi became an independent constitutional monarchy in 1962 with Mwami Mwambutsa IV as king; there were a premier and cabinet, an Assembly elected by universal suffrage and a senate. The government was mainly supported by the Uprena party, a coalition of moderate Tutsi and Hutu. Two premiers were slain by extremists and in Oct. 1965 a 3d, Leopold Biha, was severely wounded. Hutu extremists opposed the power of the minority Tutsi in the government; Tutsi extremists, accused of receiving Communist Chinese aid, opposed the government as too moderate.

In July 1966 the king's son, Prince Charles, 19, deposed him, appointing Michael Micombero premier. Extremist Tutsi returned to power; on Sept. 1 Prince Charles was proclaimed King Mwami Ntare V. But in a coup d'etat Nov. 28, he was overthrown by Micombero, who declared himself president and Burundi a republic. Ntare was killed in April 1972, supposedly during an attempt to seize power.

A Hutu revolt, starting Apr. 29, 1972, was put down; it was estimated 10,000 Tutsi were slain by rebels and 100,000 Hutu by government troops. In 1973 renewed fighting was reported and thousands of Hutu fled to Tanzania and Zaire.

The economy is agricultural, with 90% of the people farmers or livestock raisers. Coffee is the main crop and export. Much of the land is over-grazed and eroded. The nation receives aid from Belgium and the UN. It is a member of the UN and OAU.

Cotton production has become increasingly important. With outside technical aid, tea plantations have been established.

Over half the population is Christian, mostly Roman Catholic. Many others believe in a supreme deity, Imana, called the Principle of Good. Kirundi, a Bantu tongue, and French are the official languages; Swahili is also widely used. (See also Rwanda.)

Cambodia

Area: 69,898 sq. mi. Population (UN est. 1974): 7,890,000. Capital: Phnom Penh. Monetary unit: Riel.

Cambodia, or Khmer, is in southeast Asia and, with Vietnam and Laos, comprised the former associated states of French Indochina. It is slightly larger than N.D. It is bordered by Laos, Thailand, the Gulf of Siam and South Vietnam. Three-fourths is forested; the central part is level, forming a basin for the Mekong River. The climate is tropical.

Resources and Industries. The country is largely undeveloped; 50% of the land is virgin forest. Main industries are forestry, fishing, and agriculture, rice occupying about 80% of the land usage. Other products are rubber, maize, pepper, kapok, palm-sugar, tobacco, cotton, silk, oil seeds, beans. Cattle flourish; the forests have valuable hardwoods. Some iron, copper, manganese and gold exist. Industry includes textiles, paper, plywood. An oil refinery opened in 1968.

Continuing warfare created a rice shortage; until 1970 Cambodia was an exporter of rice, but now imports.

History and Government. Early kingdoms dating from that of Founan in the 1st century A.D. culminated in the great Khmer civilization which flourished from the 9th century to the 13th. The Khmer "God-Kings" built a series of monumental cities, distinguished for their temple tower architecture and striking wall sculptures. Most famous temple is that of Angkor Wat.

Cambodia came under French protection in 1863. A national constitution promulgated May 6, 1947, replaced the former absolutism. It became an associated state within the French Union by a treaty of Nov. 8, 1949, but declared its independence from France Nov. 9, 1953. It is a UN member.

Prince Norodom Sihanouk was king, 1941-55; he abdicated in favor of his father, Norodom Suramarit, who died Apr. 3, 1960. On June 13, 1960, Sihanouk, refusing to become king again, was named chief of state. Sihanouk broke off relations with the U.S. in 1965 after an attack by S. Vietnamese planes on Vietcong forces fleeing into Cambodia. In 1968 Sihanouk said Viet communists were arming Cambodian insurgents. In July 1969 relations with the U.S. were restored. In 1969-70 the U.S. bombed N. Viet forces in Cambodia but did not announce that until 1973.

In Mar. 1970, while Sihanouk was in Europe, the Cambodian government demanded, without result, that N. Vietnam and the Vietcong withdraw their troops, estimated at 40,000, from Cambodia. On Mar. 18, 1970, Sihanouk's premier, Lt. Gen. Lon Nol, took power. Sihanouk later announced in Peking formation of a government-in-exile.

In Oct. 1970 the monarchy was abolished and Cambodia's name was changed to the Khmer Republic. Lon Nol was voted president in June 1972.

The Lon Nol government charged increasing attacks on its troops by the communist forces and appealed for arms from other nations. The U.S. provided heavy military and economic aid.

On Apr. 30, 1970, U.S. President Nixon announced that U.S. troops were moving into Cambodia to drive communist forces from S. Vietnam border area sanctuaries. More than 30,000 U.S. troops and over 40,000 S. Vietnamese took part in the operations. On June 30 Nixon announced the end of the U.S. incursion.

Khmer Rouge forces completed their takeover April 17, 1975, after 5 years of war in which over 100,000 died. Sihanouk was named chief of state for life April 25, but Red commander Khieu Samphan emerged as the leading figure.

The new government immediately evacuated all cities and towns, sending virtually the entire population to clear jungle, forest and scrub for rice cultivation, reportedly with no tools. Refugees in Thailand reported arbitrary killings and massive hardship deaths.

The government claimed international neutrality and expelled all diplomats, including Soviet personnel, though Chinese advisors were reported present. Border clashes with Thailand occurred. At least 15 U.S. troops were killed in the May 14, 1975, recovery of the merchant ship Mayaguez, seized by Cambodia two days earlier.

Education and Religion. The national language is Cambodian, or Khmer; French is widely spoken and English is taught. In 1965 there were over 4,000 schools and 37 faculties of higher learning. Buddhism is the majority religion.

Cameroon

Area: 183,568 sq. mi. Population (govt. est. 1974): 6,400,000. Capital: Yaounde. Monetary unit: CFA franc.

Cameroon, which became a republic in 1960, lies on the western coast of Africa, bounded N and NW by Nigeria, NE by Chad, E by Central African Republic, S by People's Republic of Congo, Gabon and Equatorial Guinea, W by Gulf of Guinea. It is larger than California.

Cameroon was composed of 2 states: East Cameroon, formerly the republic of Cameroon, previously a French mandate and trusteeship; and West Cameroon, formerly British Southern Cameroons. A united republic was declared May 20, 1972. Douala has the principal seaport and one of 9 airports.

The population comprises some 200 tribes, including Bantus, Semitic and Sudanese peoples, Kirdis, Foulbes and Bamilekes. There are about 600,000 Christians and 600,000 Moslems; others are animists.

Resources and Industries. Mainly agricultural, Cameroon exports cocoa, coffee, palm products, leather, timber, rubber, peanut oil, tea, bananas, cotton, and tobacco.

Aluminum processing is the most important manufacturing industry. Trade is heavy with France and United Kingdom. Import and export totals are each over $350 million annually. New railroad and power dam construction and agricultural modernization were pressed in the 1970s.

History and Government. Cameroon embraces the larger part of the former German protectorate of Kamerun which was occupied by France and Britain in 1916, and placed under trusteeship, 1919. France passed a statute Dec. 31, 1958, conferring internal autonomy on the French trusteeship as a step toward complete independence which took effect Jan. 1, 1960.

Following a referendum by the UN in former British Cameroons, the southern section joined the republic to form the Federal Republic of Cameroon Oct. 1, 1961. (The northern section of British Cameroons voted to become part of Nigeria.) Cameroon belongs to the UN and OAU.

The president and the 120-member national assembly are elected for 5-year terms by direct universal suffrage.

Canada

See Index

Cape Verde Islands

Area: 1,557 sq. mi. Population (UN est. 1974): 290,000. Capital: Praia.

The Cape Verde Islands, 15 in number, lie in the North Atlantic Ocean, 280 miles west of Dakar, Africa. Principal products are coffee, which is exported, fruits, salt, tuna, hides, and grain. An 8-year drought continued in 1975, with Portugal and the UN supplying nearly all the country's food.

The uninhabited Cape Verde Islands were discovered by the Portuguese in 1460. The first Portuguese colonists landed in 1462; African slaves were brought soon after. Most Cape Verdeans descend from both groups. Many Cape Verdeans, who have a relatively high educational level, served as officials in Portuguese African colonies, and also led the independence movement in Guinea-Bissau.

After over 500 years of Portuguese rule, the Cape Verdes became independent July 5, 1975. All 56 members of the new national assembly belonged to the Party for the Independence of Guinea-Bissau and the Cape Verde Islands, though the party's resistance activities had been confined to Guinea-Bissau. The party favored unification of the 2 former colonies.

Most of the population speaks only Portuguese. Roman Catholicism is practiced by 98%.

Central African Republic

Area: 241,313 sq. mi. Population (UN est. 1974): 1,720,000. Capital: Bangui. Monetary unit: CFA franc.

The Central African Republic in equatorial Africa is 350 mi. NE of the Gulf of Guinea and is bounded by Chad, Sudan, Congo, Zaire and Cameroon. Slightly N of the equator, it is mostly rolling plateau, average alt. about 2,000 ft., with rivers draining S to the Congo and N to Lake Chad. Landlocked, it is slightly smaller than Texas.

As the French terriory of Ubangi-Shari, it achieved partial self-government in 1958. Complete independence was proclaimed Aug. 13, 1960. The republic is a UN member.

A few months after his election in 1960, Pres. David Dacko dissolved all political parties. He was re-elected Jan. 1965, running as the sole candidate. The country became a center for Communist Chinese activities.

On Jan. 1, 1966, Col. Jean Bedel Bokassa deposed Dacko; a few days later Pres. Bokassa broke off diplomatic relations with Peking. He was named president-for-life Mar. 8, 1972. Elizabeth Domitien became premier in 1975, the first woman to assume such a post in Africa.

French is the official language; Sangho is a lingua franca of the 4 ethnic groups: Banda, M'Baka, Zande, Mandjia-Baya.

Diamonds are the main export. Export earnings amount to about $40 million annually. Uranium, iron and copper have been found. Cotton, coffee and peanuts are the chief cash crops; production was increased in the late 1960s. There are large herds of cattle and sheep; lumber exports have increased. About 90% of the population is agricultural.

Small factories for textiles, food processing, soap and beer and for assembling motorbikes and radios have been given impetus.

Republic of Chad

Area: 495,752 sq. mi. Population (Govt. est. 1974): 3,950,000. Capital: N'Djamena. Monetary unit: CFA franc.

A former French Overseas Territory in Equatorial Africa, 500 mi. NE of the Gulf of Guinea, 550 mi. S of the Mediterranean, Chad is bounded N by Libya, E by Sudan, S by Central African Republic, W by Cameroon, Nigeria, Niger. It is four-fifths the size of Alaska.

Sudanic Moslem groups predominate in the north, and Bantu animists and Christians in the south. Chad has a southern wooded savannah, a steppe, and a desert, part of the Sahara, in the N. On the W. is Lake Chad.

Chad proclaimed complete independence Aug. 11, 1960, and joined the UN Sept. 20. There is a president and a National Assembly elected by universal adult suffrage. Chad is a member of the OAU and UN. French is the official language; but in 1974 the nation began replacing French names with African ones. The capital, Fort-Lamy, became N'Djamena.

Cotton is the main export; others are refrigerated meat, leather, dried fish and sodium carbonate. Uranium has been found.

In 1969-71, with the aid of French troops, government forces fought many skirmishes with rebellious Arab nomads in the northeast. French troops began leaving in 1972. Chad had accused Libya of aiding the rebels. In 1973 Chad broke off diplomatic relations with Israel, and Libya reportedly responded by halting aid to the rebels.

Years of drought which began in 1969 afflicted Chad and 5 other nations in the Sahel, the sub-Sahara region of West Africa. U.S. gifts of food were increased in 1972 and other Western nations aided in 1973; the U.S. provided over 40% of food shipments, over twice as much as any other nation.

President Ngarta Tombalbaye, who had ruled since independence, was killed in a military coup in April, 1975.

Chile

Area: 286,396 sq. mi. Population (Govt. est. 1974): 10,410,000. Capital: Santiago. Monetary unit: Escudo.

The Republic of Chile lies along the southern half of the west coast of South America, a narrow strip of land 2,620 mi. long between the towering Andes and the South Pacific. It is slightly larger than Texas.

Most of Chile lies in the temperate zone, but the Atacama Desert in the north is one of the world's driest regions, with little or no rainfall. The Christ of the Andes, a heroic-size statue in Uspallata Pass, symbolizes peace between Chile and Argentina.

Tierra del Fuego is the largest (18,800 sq. mi.) island in the archipelago of the same name at the southern tip of South America, an area of majestic mountains, tortuous channels and high winds. It was discovered 1520 by Magellan; he named the island Land of Fire because of its many Indian bonfires. Part of the island is in Chile, part in Argentina. Punta Arenas, on a mainland peninsula in Chile, is a center of sheep-raising and the world's southernmost city (pop. over 64,000); Puerto Williams, pop. 949, at a Chilean naval base on Navarino Is., is the southernmost settlement. Beagle Channel, between Navarino and the main island, and Mt. Darwin were named for Charles Darwin's visit to the area aboard the ship Beagle.

Possessions in Pacific: Sala y Gomez and **Easter Is. (Rapa Nui)**, with huge stone statues, both over 2,000 mi. to the W, **San Ambrosio** and **San Felix**, 600 mi. W, and **Juan Fernandez Islands**, 450 mi. W, the place where Alexander Selkirk, who reputedly was the inspiration for Defoe's Robinson Crusoe, lived for 4 years.

Resources and Industries. The arid deserts of northern Chile contain incalculable mineral wealth. Mining industries account for more than 70% of Chile's exports. Nitrate production is about 100,000 metric tons a month. About 47% of the world's supply of iodine is a by-product of Chilean nitrate works. Chile produces about 12% of world copper output.

The provinces of Atacama and Coquimbo have enormous iron deposits estimated at a billion tons. Coal reserves are estimated at 2 billion tons. Oil wells, mostly in Tierra del Fuego, partly supply Chile's needs and natural gas offers an export potential. Other minerals are gold, silver, molybdenum, cobalt, zinc, manganese, borate, mica, mercury, iodine, salt, sulphur, marble, onyx. Chile has abundant waterpower. Patagonia, the sparsely-populated southern third of the nation, is undergoing extensive industrial development.

There are many large dairy farms. Wheat, rice, barley, oats, beans, lentils, apples, melons, peaches, plums, nectarines, peas, and potatoes are grown in abundance. Sugar beet, automotive, and textile industries are being developed. Vineyards cover 250,000 acres and much wine is exported. Forests have large reserves of hard and soft woods. Coastal waters have shellfish, lobster, tuna, swordfish, sardines. Chile ranks 10th in weight of its fish catch.

Besides minerals the exports are mainly fishmeal, barley, oats, wine, onions, garlic, leather, lentils, fruits, fish, sea-food, cellulose, newsprint, wood.

Chile is served by 15 international airlines. The Pan American Highway runs 2,000 mi. from Arica in the N to Puerto Montt.

In the late 1960s the government pressed a wide program of social and economic reforms.

In 1970 Dr. Salvador Allende Gossens, a Marxist, was elected president and in July 1971 a constitutional amendment provided for full nationalization of copper mines owned by 3 U.S. companies, with compensation to be negotiated. A policy of nationalizing large industries and banks and expropriating large farms was launched. In 1972 middle class groups staged street demonstrations protesting food shortages and socialist policies. Strikes and riots increased in 1973. Food shortages and inflation continued.

A U.S. Senate Foreign Relations subcommittee in 1973 accused the International Telephone & Telegraph Corp. and the U.S. Central Intelligence Agency of discussing, but not carrying out, plans to prevent Allende's election in 1970. The Allende government nationalized ITT phone systems in Chile, without compensation.

In an attack on the Presidential Palace, Sept. 11, 1973, a military junta seized power and said Allende killed himself. A few thousand were killed in street fighting and junta reprisals. The junta named Gen. Augusto Pinochet Ugarte president, swore in a mostly-military cabinet and broke off diplomatic relations with Cuba, which Allende had resumed. Pinochet announced the junta would "exterminate Marxism."

A year after the coup, some 5,000 Allende sympathizers were reported still in prison camps, some reportedly subjected to torture; at least 80 had been executed, and more than 1,000, mostly foreigners, had been allowed to leave the country. Inflation, which had raged under the Allende administration, reached 400% in 1974. The Pinochet government agreed to pay U.S. companies for property expropriated under Allende.

History and Government. Diego de Almagro entered Chile for Pizarro 1536 and Valdivia completed Spanish conquest 1540.

Independence was gained 1810-18, under Jose de San Martin and Bernardo O'Higgins; the latter as supreme director, 1817-1823, sought social and economic reforms until deposed. Chile defeated Peru and Bolivia in 1836-39 and 1879-84, taking Tacna and Arica provinces from Peru, returned Tacna, 1929. Arica (town) and Antofagasta are now free ports for landlocked Bolivia.

Under the suspended constitution the president is elected for 6 years, the 50 senators for 8 and 150 deputies for 4, all by direct popular vote. Voting age was lowered from 21 to 18 in 1970. Chile is a member of the UN and OAS.

About two-thirds of the Chileans are of mixed Spanish and Indian descent; about one-fourth of Spanish only; a small percentage are Indian only; there are some of German and other European descent.

Education and Religion. Education is free and compulsory between 7 and 15. There are 9 universities. The Roman Catholic religion is dominant. The language is Spanish.

People's Republic of China

Area: 3,691,502 sq. mi. Population (Chinese Govt. est. 1974): "Almost 800 million." Capital: Peking. Monetary unit: Yuan.

China, with about one-fifth of the world's population, occupies a territory in the eastern part of Asia slightly larger than the United States.

The mainland is of rolling topography, rising to high elevations in the N in the Khinghan Mtns., separating Manchuria and Mongolia; the Tarabagata Mtns. in Sinkiang; the Himalayan and Kunlun Mtns., in the SW in Tibet. Its length from N to S is 1,860 mi. and its breadth from E to W more than 2,000 mi.

The eastern half of China is one of the best-watered lands in the world. Three great river systems, the Yangtze, the Hwang (Yellow) and the Si (Si Kiang) provide water for vast farmlands.

China comprises 22 provinces, including Taiwan, which it claims; 5 autonomous regions (Inner Mongolia, Sinkiang-Uighur, Kwangsi-Chuang, Ningsia-Hui, Tibet-Chamdo) and 3 municipalities — Peking, Tientsin, and Shanghai. The government pressed birth control programs.

History. One of the oldest of monarchies, with a history reaching back to 2205 B.C., China became a republic Jan. 1, 1912, following the Wuchang Uprising inspired by Dr. Sun Yat-sen, begun Oct. 10, 1911.

For a period of 50 years after the Sino-Japanese War, 1894-95, China was involved in conflicts with Japan. On Sept. 18, 1931, Japan seized the Northeastern Provinces (Manchuria) and set up a puppet state called Manchukuo. The border province of Jehol was cut off as a buffer state in 1933. Japan invaded China in the vicinity of Peking July 7, 1937, precipitating war. After its defeat in World War II Japan returned all seized land.

After the war with Japan ended, Aug. 15, 1945, internal disturbances arose involving the Kuomintang, Communists, and other factions. Manchuria was lost by the Nationalist regime in 1948, and China proper came under domination of Chinese Communist armies during 1949-1950. The Nationalist government moved to Taipei, Taiwan (Formosa), 90 mi. off the mainland, Dec. 8, 1949.

The People's Republic of China was proclaimed in Peking (Peiping) Sept. 21, 1949, by the Chinese People's Political Consultative Conference under Mao Tse-tung, communist leader. Chou En-lai was named premier and foreign minister Oct. 1, 1949.

The communist regime and the USSR signed a 30-year treaty of "friendship, alliance and mutual assistance," Feb. 15, 1950, repudiating the 1945 treaty between the Soviet Union and nationalist China authorized by the Yalta Agreement. Great Britain recognized the People's Republic in 1950 and France did so in 1964. By 1975, over 100 nations had recognized the regime.

The U.S. refused recognition, and after its consular officers met with abuse, withdrew them. On Nov. 26, 1950, the People's Republic sent armies of "volunteers" into Korea against U.S. troops and forced a stalemate.

By the 1960s, relations with the USSR deteriorated, with disagreements on borders, ideology and leadership of world communism. The USSR cancelled aid accords, and China, with Albania, launched anti-Soviet propaganda drives.

On Mar. 2, 1969, Chinese and Russian soldiers fought one of a series of clashes on an island in the Ussuri River on the border between the two nations in the Far East. The island, called Chenpao by Chinese and Damansky by Russians, was claimed by both nations. Both sides reported dead and wounded. There were later clashes and reports of skirmishes to the west on the Sinkiang-USSR border. In 1970, ambassadors were exchanged for the first time since 1966. In 1974 China seized a Soviet helicopter on spy charges. Border talks through 1975 were unsuccessful.

China has sought to promote revolutionary movements in Africa, Asia and South America. The program suffered serious setbacks, 1965-66. By the 1970s, China was reported sending military and economic aid to several established governments.

In April 1971, after the U.S. relaxed restrictions on visits by its citizens, a U.S. table tennis team was invited to the People's Republic.

On Oct. 25, 1971, the UN General Assembly ousted nationalist China from the UN and seated communist China in its place. The U.S. had supported the mainland's admission but opposed Taiwan's expulsion.

U.S. President Nixon visited China Feb. 21-28, 1972, on invitation from Premier Chou En-lai, ending years of antipathy between the 2 nations. They agreed to continue progress toward normalization of relations. In April, U.S. businessmen made purchases at the Canton export fair. China and the U.S. moved close to formal diplomatic relations by opening liaison offices in each other's capitals, May-June 1973.

In 1973, because of food shortages, China ordered 6 million tons of grain from the U.S., Australia and other countries. In 1974, 2-way trade with the U.S. neared $1 billion.

Government. On Feb. 27, 1957, Mao Tse-tung, then chief of state, condemned the Stalinist terror but admitted an est. 800,000 anti-communist Chinese were executed 1949-54. Leniency for political criticism, proposed by Mao Tse-tung, led to anti-communist disturbances among students and a quick return to repressive measures. In 1958, the regime announced all "rights" in government service had been removed.

Early in 1966, a long, widespread purge of "anti-party intellectuals" was launched; it was viewed as a possible symptom of a struggle for power and the succession to the aging Mao. Premier Chou En-lai called the purge a "cultural revolution." Ousted from office and denounced were the chief of the Army's General Staff, minister of culture, the party propaganda chief, 3 university presidents, newspaper editors and writers, opera producers, youth officials, economists, Peking's mayor, etc. Education, industrial production and foreign relations were disrupted.

By late 1968-69 the long disruption had tapered off; much power was taken from the students and given to Revolutionary Committees and the military, and some purge victims were restored to office. In 1974 a new ideological campaign was launched; it was aimed at the teachings of the ancient sage, Confucius, but its purpose was obscure. Once again, production suffered.

In August 1966, Defense Minister Lin Piao emerged as top deputy and heir apparent to Mao. But in 1972 China said Lin died in a 1971 plane crash trying to flee to the USSR after attempting a coup.

Resources and Industry. Until communism prevailed, China was chiefly agricultural. Wheat, barley, corn, koaliang, and millet and other cereals, peas and soy beans are produced in the north; rice, sugar and indigo in the south. Rice is the staple food of the Chinese and mainland China is the world's largest producer. Fiber crops include abutilon, hemp, jute, ramie and flax. Cotton is produced mostly in the Yangtze and Yellow River valleys. Tea is cultivated principally in the west and south. One of the most important industries is silk production which has flourished for 4,000 years. Livestock is raised in large numbers. Food shortages remain but improved distribution has reduced the incidence of famine. Most of the work force is agricultural.

China is the world's 3d largest coal producer. Other minerals are iron ore, tin, antimony, tungsten, molybdenum, salt. Petroleum production reached 1.5 million barrels per day in 1975, much of it sold to Japan.

Application of radical theories to industry and agriculture resulted in erratic economic development. Serious food shortages existed beginning in 1959 after floods, drought and failure of the "Great Leap Forward" 5-year plan. The regime was forced to obtain grain from Argentina, Mexico, Canada and Australia. Light industries dependent on agriculture for their raw materials also were affected — cotton textiles, knitted goods, vegetable oils, sugar and cigarets. The "people's commune" system of agriculture in effect since 1958 was drastically modified in 1960-61 to increase individual incentives to stimulate production, but collectivization was renewed in 1963-64. Thousands fled to overcrowded Hong Kong.

Education has been radically revised since the cultural revolution; university enrollment has fallen. Millions of urban dwellers and non-manual workers were moved to rural areas.

In 1969-1972, after the "cultural revolution" eased off, industry and agriculture showed production gains.

China leads all nations in numbr of hogs, is 3d in sheep, 4th in cattle. Its fish catch is 2d in value to Japan's.

Defense. Regular forces total 3,000,000. There is a growing stockpile of nuclear weapons and intermediate range missiles. Military spending declined 25% 1971-75.

On Oct. 16, 1964, China exploded a low-yield atomic bomb in Sinkiang Province, becoming the 5th nation to possess such power. An explosion of a hydrogen bomb was announced June 17, 1967. The nation's first orbiting space satellite was launched Apr. 24, 1970.

Religion. Buddhism had the largest following. Confucianism, which reveres God but stresses ethical and philosophical principles rather than divine revelation, had wide acceptance. Taoism (after Lao Tze, b. 604 B.C.) is more metaphysical and looks to immortality. Islam, at one time, had 50 million followers; there were 3,280,000 Roman Catholics and 700,000 Protestants. On the mainland foreign missionaries and church schools are no longer tolerated.

Manchuria, 404,428 sq. mi., is divided into three provinces. Seized by Japan in 1931, it was renamed Manchukuo, a puppet "independent" nation, Mar. 1,

1932. In 1945 it was returned to China.

Kuantung is the southern part of the Liaotung peninsula, the southernmost portion of Manchuria. Russia in 1898 forced China to lease it Kuantung and constructed the fortified city of Port Arthur (Lushun) and the nearby ice-free port of Dairen (Luta).

Japan seized Port Arthur in 1905, and at the close of the Russo-Japanese War took over the lease in the Treaty of Portsmouth. It was restored to the USSR by the Yalta Agreement, Feb. 11, 1945, which also internationalized Dairen. Following the 1950 Soviet-Chinese treaty the USSR returned the Changchun railroad, Port Arthur and Dairen to Communist China.

Inner Mongolia was organized by the People's Republic as an Autonomous Region on May 12, 1947. Its boundaries have undergone frequent changes. In 1950 it comprised northern Chahar and parts of former Manchuria. Suiyan province was incorporated June 1954, and parts of Jehol in Aug. 1955. Population is about 6,200,000 of which less than 20% are Mongol. Capital: Huhehot (Kweisui).

Outer Mongolia: *For People's Republic of Mongolia, see Mongolia in Index.*

Sinkiang Uigur Autonomous Region, in Central Asia, comprising Chinese Turkestan, Kulia and Kashgaria, is 633,802 sq. mi.; pop. (est. 1958), 6 million, of whom 75% are Uigurs, a Turkic Moslem group, with a heavy Chinese increase in recent years. Urumchi is the capital. It is China's richest region in strategic materials, including tungsten, wolfram, molybdenum, copper, zinc, coal, uranium and oil.

Tibet, 470,000 sq. mi., is a thinly populated region of high plateaus and massive mountains. The Himalayas ring it on the S, the Kunluns on the N. Lofty passes link it with India and Nepal to the S; roads lead into China proper. The capital is Lhasa. The average altitude is 15,000 ft. Jiachan, 15,870 ft., is believed to be the highest inhabited town on earth. Agricultural methods are primitive. Cereals are the main crops. The religion is Lamaism, a form of Buddhism. Pop. (1964 est.) 1,300,000.

With only token resistance, Tibet accepted suzerainty of Communist China under a pact signed May 23, 1951. A communist Tibetan Autonomous Government was announced Dec. 20, 1953, revising the quasi-religious administration of the Dalai and Panchen Lamas.

A revolt against the communists occurred in 1959, when the latter attempted to arrest the Dalai Lama. The Tibetan cabinet denounced the 1951 treaty. The communists crushed the revolt and placed the Panchen Lama on the Tibetan throne. The Dalai Lama fled to India. The Panchen Lama was demoted Dec. 1964. A new ruler was sponsored by Peking Sept. 9, 1965, when it announced election of Ngapo Ngawang Jigme as chairman of the newly-established Tibet Autonomous Region. Revolts continued in 1965 and 1966.

A reform program, including land redistribution and abolition of serfdom (assertedly practiced in some monasteries) was announced July 3, 1959.

The International Commission of Jurists at Geneva in 1961 charged the Communist regime with genocide in Tibet. About 20,000 Tibetans have fled to India since the Chinese takeover.

Republic of China

Area: 13,592. Population (Govt. est. 1974): 15,902,071. Capital: Taipei. Monetary unit: Taiwan dollar.

The Kuomintang government of China, after its defeat in 1949, moved to the island of Taiwan, where it still governs. Both the Taipei and Peking governments assert that Taiwan is an integral part of China.

· Taiwan lies 110 mi. E. of the mainland, but the term Taiwan is used by the Nationalist government to include 14 other islands nearby and 64 others comprising the Penghu group.

Taiwan was ceded by China to Japan in 1895, after the Sino-Japanese War and was returned to China as a province, 1945, after World War II.

A range of mountains forms the backbone of the island. The eastern half is exceedingly steep and craggy but the western slope is flat, fertile and well cultivated, yielding 2 rice crops a year. The principal crops, besides rice, are tea, sugar, sweet potatoes, ramie, jute, turmeric and camphor. Minerals include gold, silver, copper and coal.

The **Penghus** (Pescadores), 50 sq. mi., pop. (1964) 108,800, lie between Taiwan and the coast of China.

The islands of **Quemoy** and **Matsu** are within a few miles of the mainland.

The 1947 constitution is still formally in effect. The National Assembly is the supreme organ. Members are elected on the basis of territorial and professional representation. The Assembly elects the president and vice president, who serve 6-year terms. An elected Yuan (Council), serves as the legislature. The cabinet, appointed by the president, is responsible to the Yuan. Most Yuan members have remained in office since 1948, representing areas of mainland China. A Provincial Assembly is elected every four years.

Generalissimo Chiang Kai-shek, except for a period of semi-retirement, was virtual ruler since 1927. Upon his death in 1975, his son, Premier Chiang Ching-Kuo, became the effective ruler. The government was a founding member of the UN. On Oct. 25, 1971, the UN General Assembly expelled Nationalist China from the UN and admitted Communist China in its place. By July 1975 only 26 nations, including the U.S., still recognized the Taipei regime, but informal commercial relations continued with many others.

Although agriculture remains a vital and growing part of the economy, industrial production has grown much more rapidly. Important industries include textiles, clothing, electrical and electronic equipment, TV sets, processed foods, chemicals, glass, metals and machinery.

Foreign trade, with 1974 imports at $US 6.9 billion and exports at $US 5.6 billion, has also shown strong and steady growth. Gross national product was $US 14.12 billion in 1974, though inflation soared.

U.S. economic aid, begun in 1951 and totaling $1.5 billion, essentially terminated June 30, 1965. Military aid, which totaled $2.5 billion, continued, but at a reduced scale. The republic has extended technical assistance to some 30 countries in Asia, Africa and Latin America.

Defense. Armed forces total 500,000. The government signed a mutual defense treaty with the U.S., in force Mar. 3, 1955. It provides for consultation on threats of attack and promises that if Taiwan is subject to unprovoked attack the U.S. will act according to its constitutional procedures. About 2,800 U.S. troops are stationed on Taiwan.

Colombia

Area: 455,335 sq. mi. Population (Gov't. est. 1974): 23,950,000. Capital: Bogota, Monetary unit: Peso.

The Republic of Colombia, in the extreme northwest of South America, extends up the Isthmus of Panama to the Republic of Panama. It has a coastline of 913 mi. on the Pacific, and 1,094 mi. on the Caribbean Sea. It borders Venezuela and Brazil on the E, and Ecuador and Peru on the S. Its area is greater than those of Texas and California combined.

Three great ranges of the Andes, the Western, Central and Eastern Cordilleras, run through the country from N to S. The eastern range consists mostly of high table lands, cool and healthful, and densely populated. The Magdalena River, in the NE, rises in the high Andes and flows N into the Caribbean Sea near Bar-

ranquilla. It is navigable for over 800 mi. The Magdalena Valley is a plain of rich alluvial land.

Snow-crested mountains standing almost directly over the Equator are one of many examples of scenic splendor. Tourists are also attracted by Tequendama Falls near Bogota, 427 ft. high.

Bogota, the capital, founded in 1538, is in the Andes, 8,660 ft. above sea level.

Resources and Industries. Colombia is second to Brazil in exports of coffee, accounting for 40% of its export trade. Rice, tobacco and cotton are cultivated, besides cocoa, maize, potatoes, sugar and bananas. Dye-woods, rubber, balsam and copaiba trees are important.

The country is rich in minerals. It has become a producer of petroleum. Seventy-five miles from Bogota are the Muzo emerald mines which have been in operation for 4 centuries. Colombia produces 95% of the world's gem emeralds. Other minerals are gold, silver, copper, lead, mercury, cinnabar, manganese, platinum, coal, iron, nickel, salt. Colombia is accelerating expansion of its hydro-electric power which has est. potential of 85 million kw. Food processing is the leading manufacturing industry; other products are textiles, hides, rubber goods, steel, and chemicals. Textiles have become a major export.

Loans from international agencies have helped expand industry and modernize agriculture. An oil pipeline from the Orito field in the SE, crosses the Andes to the Pacific; it was finished in 1969.

The government has sought to reduce vast land holdings and increase the size of small farms. From 1961 to 1970 the Institute for Land Reform acquired or developed 9,800,000 acres; more than 95,000 families were given title to farm plots.

History and Government. The country, conquered and ruled for 300 years by Spain, won its freedom in the revolt of the Spanish-American colonies 1810-1824. The liberator, Simon Bolivar, established the Republic of Greater Colombia in 1819; Venezuela and Ecuador withdrew in 1829-1830. From the remainder of the confederation evolved the Republic of Colombia under a constitution dated Aug. 5, 1886. Panama withdrew Nov. 3, 1903, becoming a separate republic. Colombia is a member of the UN and OAS.

The Congress consists of a Senate of 118 members and a House of Representatives with 210 members, elected directly by the people for 4-year terms. The president is elected by direct vote for 4 years and is ineligible for re-election. Political violence and banditry have resulted in repeated states of emergency since the 1950s.

Education and Religion. Most of the people are of mixed Indian and white descent; the next largest group is white; the smallest groups are Indians and Negroes. Education is free but not compulsory. National Univ., founded 1572, is in Bogota. Roman Catholicism prevails. Spanish is the language.

Defense. Armed forces total 63,000.

Comoro Islands

Area: 838 sq. mi. Population: (UN est. 1974): 300,000. Capital: Moroni. Monetary unit: CFA franc.

The Comoro Islands are a volcanic archipelago in the Mozambique Channel between NW Madagascar and SE Africa. An active volcano is on Grand Comoro. Leading crops are vanilla, copra, perfume plants, and tropical fruits. Perfume is distilled and exported.

The islands were controlled by Moslem sultans until the French acquired them 1841-1909. They were ruled as part of Madagascar 1912-1947, and became an autonomous French Overseas Territory in 1961. A 1974 referendum overwhelmingly favored independence, with only the non-Moslem island of Mayotte preferring association with France. The French National Assembly decided in June, 1975 to allow each of the islands to decide its own fate. The Comoro Chamber of Deputies unilaterally declared the country's independence July 6, 1975, to forestall a Mayotte separatist move.

The inhabitants are predominantly Moslem, deriving from Arab, African, and East Indian ancestors.

People's Republic of Congo

Area: 132,046 sq. mi. Population (UN est. 1974): 1,031,000. Capital: Brazzaville. Monetary unit: CFA franc.

Formerly the French Middle Congo Overseas Territory, the People's Republic of the Congo straddles the Equator. It is bounded on the E and S by Zaire; on the W by Cabinda (an Angolan enclave), the Atlantic and Gabon; on the N by Cameroon and Central African Republic. It is twice the size of Missouri.

Complete independence was proclaimed Aug. 15, 1960, and the republic joined the UN Sept. 20. Fulbert Youlou was elected president Nov. 21, 1959, and resigned in Aug. 1963 in a coup sparked by trade unions. Under his successor, President Alphonse Massamba-Debat, the country came under Communist China's influence and announced a "scientific Socialist state" with one-party control.

In Aug. 1965 the U. S. withdrew its embassy staff, a step short of breaking off relations, charging harassment of American officials. Massamba-Debat was ousted in a military coup, Sept. 4, 1968. Maj. Marien Ngouabi became president Jan. 1, 1969.

In Jan. 1970, the earlier name, Republic of the Congo-Brazzaville, was changed to People's Republic of the Congo. The government advocates socialism.

The nation has received aid from both France and Communist China.

Forests are a prime resource, covering 54 million acres, and wood products form a major export. Chief commercial agricultural products are palm oil and kernels, cocoa, bananas, and peanuts. Industrialization has progressed and its output now accounts for 11% of the total national product. Potash reserves are extensive.

Costa Rica

Area: 19,653 sq. mi. Population (Govt. est. 1974): 1,920,000. Capital: San Jose. Monetary unit: Colon.

Costa Rica, in Central America, borders Nicaragua on the N and Panama on the S. The lowlands by the Caribbean are tropical. The interior plateau, with an altitude of about 4,000 ft., is temperate.

San Jose, the capital, situated inland (103 mi. by rail from Puerto Limon on the Atlantic, 93 by rail from Puntarenas on the Pacific) is the country's industrial and cultural center. Limon and Puntarenas are the principal ports. The crater atop Poas Volcano is the largest in the world. Puerto Limon occupies one of the sites where Columbus landed on his fourth and last visit to America.

Resources and industries. A 1962 law giving new industries a tax holiday of up to 10 years brought in a wide variety of factories. The Irazu volcano near San Jose erupted from Mar. 1963 to Dec. 1964, dropping millions of tons of ash which severely damaged coffee, vegetable and dairy crops. Coffee of a high quality is the chief crop and export, followed by bananas, sugar, cocoa, beef, cotton, fish and hemp.

Despite growing, small-scale industrialization, agriculture remains the mainstay of the economy, employing half the work force. New industries include fiberglass products, aluminum processing, textiles, fertilizer, roofing and cement.

The forests are extensive, and the lumber industry is important. Gold and silver are mined on the Pacific slope. Other minerals are quartz, alabaster, granite, oil, alum, slate, onyx, mercury, sulphur, copper.

Chief imports are flour, industrial machinery,

gasoline, leather, hardware and tools. Nearly half of the foreign trade is with the U. S.

The nation has a comparatively high standard of living and of social services.

History and Government. Once a part of the Confederation of Central America, 1824-1829, Costa Rica has been independent since 1821.

An unusual constitution was adopted Nov. 8, 1949. It abolishes the army as a permanent institution. The legislative power is vested in a chamber of deputies, 57 in number, with 4-year terms, under universal suffrage. The president, elected for 4 years, appoints a cabinet of 12. Deputies may not serve successive terms but may be reelected after an intervening 4 years. A president may not be reelected. There is a fine for not voting.

In Feb. 1974 a liberal, Daniel Oduber Quiros, was elected president.

Religion and Education. Primary education is compulsory. Higher education is free. There are universities in Cartago, Heredia, San Jose and Turrialba. The language is Spanish; English is taught in the public schools. Roman Catholicism is predominant.

Defense. Order within the country is kept by a civil guard and police forces. Costa Rica is a member of the UN and OAS.

Cuba

Area: 44,218 sq. mi. Population (Govt. est. 1974): 9,090,000. Capital: Havana. Monetary unit: Peso.

Cuba, "Pearl of the Antilles," is an island, the largest in the West Indies, and a nation about the size of Pennsylvania. The Straits of Florida lie to the N, the Gulf of Mexico to the W, the Caribbean to the S.

Key West, Fla., is about 90 mi. N. The Windward Passage, 50 mi. wide, separates Cuba from Haiti to the E, and Jamaica lies 90 mi. to the S. Cuba's length is 730 mi.; its breadth averages 50 mi. The coastline, including the larger keys, is about 2,500 mi. It has numerous harbors, notably that of Havana, one of the finest in the world.

The Isle of Pines, off the SW coast, is 1,180 sq. mi. in area. Mountains rise in Pinar del Rio Province in the W, and in Oriente in the E, with Pico Turquino, 6,467 ft., the highest.

Havana, pop. over 1,500,000, is the busiest port. Santiago de Cuba, in the SE, is the next largest port.

Resources and Industries. Chief barometer of the nation's economy is the sugar industry which represents about 80% of exports. American-owned sugar mills, seized by the revolutionary regime in 1960, represented an investment of about $275 million, producing about 40% of Cuba's output.

Tobacco, cigars and cigarettes rank 2d. Other products are molasses, coffee, pineapples, bananas, citrus fruit and coconuts. Textiles, cabinet woods (mahogany and cedar), dye-woods, fibers, gums, resins and oils are important. Iron, copper, manganese, nickel and salt are some of the minerals. Industries include rayon, cement, chemicals.

Poor sugar crops and food shortages resulted in collectivization of farms and stringent labor controls under the revolutionary government. Rationing of food, shoes, clothing, gasoline, was ordered. Some rationing and economic difficulties continued in the 1970s, despite massive aid from the USSR and assistance from other Communist countries. Health and education services were improved.

History. Cuba was discovered by Christopher Columbus in Oct. 1492. Its name derives from the Indian Cubanacan. Except for British occupation of Havana, 1762-63, Cuba remained Spanish until 1898.

Under Spanish governors Cubans were denied citizenship, slavery was retained until 1886, and patriots who revolted were executed. On Oct. 10, 1868, Carlos Manuel de Cespedes led Cubans in a proclamation of independence. Their 10-years' war ended in 1878 with guarantees of rights by Spain, which Spain failed to carry out. A full-scale movement began Feb. 24, 1895, under Jose Marti, with the military under the command of Maximo Gomez, Antonio Maceo and Calixto Garcia. The Spanish governor, Valeriano Weyler, destroyed sugar plantations, banned export of tobacco and held patriots in "reconcentration camps." A U. S. offer to mediate was rejected by Spain.

The movement to help Cuba gain its independence was speeded by the sinking of the U.S.S. Maine in Havana harbor. The U. S. declared war on Spain Apr. 25, 1898, and defeated it in the short Spanish-American War. In the Treaty of Paris, Dec. 10, 1898, Spain gave up all claims to Cuba. The U. S. formally withdrew May 20, 1902, when Tomas Estrada Palma was inaugurated first president of the republic.

Under 1903 and 1934 agreements, the U. S. leases a site for its naval base at Guantanamo Bay, in the SE.

In 1952 Fulgencio Batista seized control of the government and imposed a dictatorship. Opposition to the corrupt Batista regime became vigorous in 1956 under leadership of Fidel Castro, born 1927, lawyer and former leader of student opposition. The rebels in 1958 carried on intensified guerrilla warfare. Batista quit Jan. 1, 1959. He died in Spain Aug. 6, 1973.

Castro proclaimed Dr. Manuel Urrutia Lleo provisional president. Urrutia dissolved the Cuban Congress. Jan. 6, 1959. Castro became premier Feb. 16.

Pres. Urrutia resigned after accusing communists of plotting treason. The government, quickly dominated by left-wing extremists, began a program of sweeping economic and social changes, led by an agrarian reform law in May 1959. It executed hundreds of dissidents, and ousted moderates.

The National Institute of Agrarian Reform nationalized cattle and tobacco lands and instituted a system of cooperatives. All private enterprise was brought under control by a Central Planning Board created Feb. 20, 1960. By the end of 1960 all Cuban banks and industrial companies had been nationalized, including an est. $1 billion worth of U. S.-owned properties.

Soviet, Communist Chinese and Czechoslovakian economic penetration was extended by trade and credit agreements, including sugar purchases and USSR credits for construction of factories, etc.

Citing the open hostility of the regime, the U. S. cut back Cuba's remaining 1960 sugar quota by 700,000 tons. On Oct. 19 the U. S. imposed an extensive embargo on exports to Cuba and, Feb. 4, 1962, President Kennedy ordered a total embargo.

On Apr. 17, 1961 about 1,400 Cuban exiles, who had trained in the U.S. and Guatemala, landed at the Bahia de Cochinos (Bay of Pigs) on Cuba's southern coast. They were overwhelmed by Castro forces and killed or imprisoned. The attempt created severe criticism in Congress of activities of the U.S Central Intelligence Agency. President Kennedy previously had declared there would be no intervention by the U. S. On Dec. 21, 1962, Castro agreed to release 1,113 prisoners in exchange for medical supplies worth a reputed $53 million. American drug concerns and religious groups raised the supply.

In the fall, 1962, the U.S. ascertained that the Soviet Union was delivering nuclear missiles and other weapons to Cuba and building bases. On Oct 22 President Kennedy warned that any missile launched from Cuba would be regarded as an attack by the Soviet Union and would call for full retaliation. He asked Premier Khrushchev to halt this "clandestine, reckless and provocative threat to world peace." Khrushchev removed the missiles.

The OAS nations voted July 26, 1964, 15-4, a resolution for mandatory sanctions against Cuba and for strengthening defenses against Cuban subversion efforts. The sanctions were lifted in 1975, with the tacit support of the U.S.

Cuba complained of numerous raids by infiltrators, 1964-70.

In Feb. 1973, Cuba and the U.S. signed an agreement providing for extradition or punishment of hijackers of planes or vessels, and for each nation to bar activity from its territory against the other.

In 1974, U.S. President Ford said relations with Cuba could be improved, adding that the U. S. would act in concert with the other OAS nations.

In 1975, France expelled three Cuban diplomats in connection with a probe of a world-wide terrorist network.

More than 650,000 Cubans have gone into exile since the Castro takeover, most of them to the U.S.

Cuba is a member of the UN and Comecon.

Education and Religion. Education is compulsory between the ages of 6 and 14. Among the institutions of higher learning is the University of Havana, founded in 1721. The Roman Catholic religion is dominant. The language is Spanish with English widely understood. Education was nationalized June 7, 1961, and many Catholic schools were seized. Many Catholic priests of Spanish origin were deported.

Defense. Armed forces total 108,000.

Cyprus

Area: 3,572 sq. mi. Population (Govt. est. 1973): 660,000. Capital: Nicosia. Monetary unit: Pound.

Cyprus, former British Crown Colony, became a republic Aug. 16, 1960, and joined the Commonwealth, UN and Council of Europe. It is the third largest island in the Mediterranean Sea, 40 mi. S. of Turkey, 60 mi. W of Syria, and 350 mi. E of Crete. Two mountain ranges run E-W, separated by a wide, fertile plain. It is smaller than Connecticut.

Four-fifths of the inhabitants are Greek Orthodox Christians, nearly all the rest are Turkish Moslems. Greek and Turkish are official languages; English is widely spoken.

Resources and Industries. Cyprus is mainly agricultural, with cereals, grapes, wine, carobs, citrus fruits, potatoes and olives as principal crops. Agricultural products account for about 60% of the island's exports. Minerals are important but declining — copper, iron pyrites, asbestos, gypsum, chrome and umber. Manufacturing is limited mainly to light industries. Exports include shoes and clothing. Cement and oil refining industries are under development. The economy was disrupted by the 1974-75 political crisis.

The nation suffers an unfavorable balance of trade, offset by tourism.

History and Government. Cyprus was inhabited as early as the New Stone Age in the 4th millennium B.C. Achaeans from Greece traded with the early Cypriots from 1600 B.C., set up colonies after the end of the Trojan War (c. 1184 B.C.). From the middle of the 8th Century B.C., Cyprus was dominated successively by Phoenicians, Assyrians, Egyptians, Persians, Alexander and the Ptolemies, Romans, Byzantines, Moslems, Crusaders, Venetians and Turks. Great Britain took over administration in 1878 under an agreement with Turkey, annexed the island in 1914, made it a Crown Colony in 1925.

Agitation for enosis (union) with Greece resulted in the British abolishing the legislative council in 1931. Demands for enosis were renewed after World War II; the Turkish minority was opposed. Widespread violence in 1955-56, led by EOKA, an underground organization, brought harsh disciplinary measures, including the temporary exiling of Archbishop Makarios III, head of the Independent Orthodox Church in Cyprus and leader of the enosis movement.

In 1959, conflict was brought to a temporary halt by an agreement signed by British, Greek, Turkish and Cypriot leaders. Cyprus would become a republic, with a president elected from and by the ethnic Greek community, and a vice president from and by the Turkish community. A 70-30% proportion of the Greek and Turkish communities was to be represented in the House of Representatives. Greek and Turkish Communal Chambers dealt with religious, educational and other communal affairs. Britain retained 2 military enclaves, Akrotiri and Dhekelia.

Archbishop Makarios was elected president for a 5-year term and Dr. Fazil Kutchuk, a Turkish Cypriot, vice president, Dec. 14, 1959. The constitution was approved April 6, 1960; independence became final Aug. 16, 1960, and Pres. Makarios took office.

Communal strife again broke out in December, 1963, following proposals by Makarios to make changes in the constitution which the Turkish minority felt would reduce their rights.

The UN Security Council approved Mar. 4, 1964, a resolution providing for an international peace-keeping force and UN troops took stations Mar. 27.

Tension worsened after Turkey charged that Turkish Cypriots had been massacred. Turkey bombed and strafed Greek areas Aug. 7-10, 1964. Both sides accepted a cease-fire.

War between Greece and Turkey over Cyprus appeared imminent in Nov. 1967 but was averted mainly because of mediation work by Cyrus R. Vance, special envoy of U.S. President Johnson.

Archbishop Makarios, whose term as president had been twice extended by Parliament, was re-elected Feb. 25, 1968, by an overwhelming popular vote, and again on Feb. 8, 1973.

The Cypriot National Guard, led by officers from the Army of Greece, seized the government July 15, 1974, and named Nikos Sampson, an advocate of union with Greece, president. Makarios fled the country. On July 20, Turkey invaded the island; Greece mobilized its forces but did not intervene. A cease-fire was arranged July 22. On the 23d, Sampson turned over the presidency to Glafkos Clerides (on the same day, Greece's military junta resigned). A peace conference collapsed Aug. 14; fighting resumed. Greek Cypriots and Turks charged each other with massacres and atrocities. By Aug. 16 Turkish forces had occupied the NE third of the island, despite the presence of UN peace forces. On Aug. 19 the U.S. ambassador to Cyprus was slain by a bullet during a riot in Nicosia. Makarios resumed the presidency in December.

Turkish Cypriots voted overwhelmingly June 8, 1975 to form a separate Turkish Cypriot federated state. Some 200,000 refugees had left the Turkish-controlled area.

Czechoslovakia

Area: 49,371 sq. mi. Population (Govt. est. 1974): 14,690,000. Capital: Prague. Monetary unit: Koruna.

Czechoslovakia is a central European socialist republic about 600 mi. long and 50 to 100 mi. wide — about the area of New York State. It is bounded by West Germany (Bavaria), East Germany (Saxony), Poland, the Soviet Union, Austria and Hungary.

The Vltava (Moldau) and Labe (Elbe) flow from Bohemia to Germany; the Danube separates Slovakia from Hungary. The Carpathian Mtns. are in the E and NE; tallest are the Tatras, with Gerlachovka peak 8,737 ft.

Resources and Industries. Czechoslovakia has considerable natural resources, developed by farming, mining and industry. The nation is highly industrialized but agriculture is important; chief crops are wheat, sugar beets, potatoes, rye, hops.

Coal and iron are mined; oil, imported mainly from the USSR, is refined at Bratislava. Jachymov has Europe's richest deposits of pitchblende (for uranium and radium). Czechoslovakia is a major exporter of arms and machinery. Ostrava and Kosice are important steel centers. There is a large glass and china industry; other products include chemicals, beer, aircraft, wood pulp, textiles, shoes.

Imports for 1974 were valued at $7.5 billion, exports at $7.3 billion.

History and Government. In Feb. 1948

Czechoslovakia became a unitary socialist republic composed of 2 Slav nations—the Czechs and the Slovaks—with a socialist constitution, nationalized industry and one-slate elections. The Czechs make up 65% of the population and Slovaks about 30%. In addition, there are some 450,000 Hungarians, 200,000 Germans, 200,000 gypsies, 100,000 Ruthenian-Ukrainians and 100,000 Poles. Large numbers of Hungarians were moved out of Slovakia and many Slovaks were moved from Hungary to Slovakia in 1945-46. An estimated 3 million Sudeten Germans were transferred to Germany under the Potsdam Agreement.

Bohemia, Moravia and Slovakia were part of the Great Moravian Empire when overrun by the Magyars 906 A.D. Bohemia and Moravia later became part of the Holy Roman Empire. Under the kings of Bohemia, Prague in the 14th Century was the cultural center of Central Europe. In 1526 Ferdinand, brother of Holy Roman Emperor Charles V, became king of Bohemia and Hungary. Later the lands became part of Austria-Hungary.

In 1914-1918 Thomas G. Masaryk and Eduard Benes formed a provisional government with the support of Slovak leaders, of whom Milan Stefanik organized freedom fighters in foreign countries. When Austria fell, Oct. 28, 1918, they proclaimed the Republic of Czechoslovakia Oct. 30. Masaryk became president, Benes foreign minister and Stefanik minister of war. Benes succeeded Masaryk in 1935.

By 1938 Adolf Hitler of Nazi Germany had worked up disaffection among German-speaking citizens in Sudetenland and demanded its cession. To avoid war, Prime Minister Neville Chamberlain of Great Britain, with the acquiescence of France, signed an agreement with Hitler at Munich, Sept. 30, 1938, agreeing to the cession, with a guarantee of peace by Hitler and Mussolini. Nazi Germany occupied Sudetenland Oct. 1-2. President Benes resigned Oct. 5.

Hitler on Mar. 15, 1939, dissolved Czechoslovakia, made protectorates of Bohemia and Moravia, and supported the autonomy of Slovakia, which was proclaimed independent Mar. 14, 1939, with Jozef Tiso president.

Soviet troops with some Czechoslovak contingents entered eastern Czechoslovakia in 1944 and reached Prague in May 1945; Benes returned as president. In May 1946 elections, the Communist Party won 38% of the votes, largest for a single party, and Benes accepted Klement Gottwald, a communist, as prime minister. Tiso was executed in 1947.

In Feb. 1948 a crisis resulted in the resignation of 12 anti-Communist ministers and Benes accepted a new Gottwald Cabinet Feb. 25. Jan Masaryk, son of Thomas Masaryk, had not resigned as foreign minister. He was found dead March 10, apparently a suicide, but there was widespread speculation he was murdered.

In May 1948 a new constitution was approved; Benes refused to sign it. On May 30 the voters were offered a one-slate ballot and the communists won full control. Benes resigned June 7, Gottwald became president and Benes died Sept. 3.

In Jan. 1968 a liberalization movement spread explosively through Czechoslovakia. Antonin Novotny, long the communist boss of the nation, was deposed as party leader and succeeded by Alexander Dubcek, a Slovak, who declared he intended to make communism democratic. On Mar. 22 Novotny resigned as president and was succeeded by Gen. Ludvik Svoboda. On Apr. 6, Premier Joseph Lenart resigned and was succeeded by Oldrich Cernik, whose new cabinet was pledged to carry out democratization and economic reforms.

In July 1968 the USSR and 4 hard-core Warsaw Pact nations demanded an end to liberalization. On Aug. 20, Russian, Polish, East German, Hungarian and Bulgarian military forces invaded Czechoslovakia.

Some Soviet troops remained and Soviet pressure brought agreements from officials that the liberal policies would be "normalized." Despite demonstrations and riots by students and workers, press censorship was imposed, many liberal leaders were ousted from office and promises of loyalty to Soviet policies were made by some old-line Communist party leaders.

On Apr. 17, 1969, Dubcek resigned as leader of the Communist party and was succeeded by Gustav Husak. In Jan. 1970, Premier Cernik was ousted. Censorship was tightened and the Communist Party expelled a third of its members. In 1972, more than 40 liberals were jailed on subversion charges. In 1973, amnesty was offered to some of the 40,000 who fled the country after the 1968 invasion.

On Jan. 2, 1969, Czechoslovakia became a federal state. In addition to a federal president, premier and Assembly for the Czechoslovak Socialist Republic, there were separate governments, a Czech Socialist Republic and a Slovak Socialist Republic, each with a National Council, a premier and Cabinet. The central government retained control over foreign affairs, defense and finance. In the Federal Assembly, a House of People was chosen by electoral districts; a House of Nations had 75 Czech and 75 Slovak members.

West Germany and Czechoslovakia resumed diplomatic relations in 1973 and declared the 1938 Munich pact void.

Education and Religion. An estimated 75% of the population is Roman Catholic, the rest are Protestant (Hussite), Greek Orthodox, etc.

Institutions of higher learning are Charles University in Prague, founded in 1348; the Universities of Brno, Bratislava, Kosice, Hradec Kralove, Plzen; also technical universities. Czech and Slovak are official languages.

Defense. Military forces total 190,000.

Dahomey

Area: 43,483 sq. mi. Population (Govt. est. 1974): 3,030,000. Capitals: Porto-Novo, Cotonou. Monetary unit: CFA franc.

The Republic of Dahomey, former Overseas Territory in French West Africa, is a narrow strip 415 mi. long and 77 mi. wide, bounded by the Republics of the Niger and Upper Volta, Nigeria, Gulf of Guinea and the Republic of Togo. It is about as large as Tennessee.

In accordance with the 1958 French constitution, Dahomey became fully independent Aug. 1, 1960, and became a member of the UN Sept. 20. Dahomey signed agreements Apr. 24, 1961, providing for close ties with France.

Under the constitution the president and National Assembly are elected for 5-year terms. Pres. Hubert Maga, elected Dec. 11, 1960, was deposed Oct. 28, 1963, and replaced by a provisional government headed by Gen. Christophe Soglo. The constitution of the second republic was adopted Dec. 19, 1963; Sourou Migan Apithy was elected president Jan. 24, 1964; several coups followed. In Oct. 1972 Maj. Mathieu Kerekou became president in a military coup.

Principal products: palm oil, kernels and nuts; peanuts, cotton, kapok, coffee, tobacco.

Small industries were constructed in the late 1960s, including a bicycle plant, cotton mill and peanut-oil plant. Oil was discovered offshore in 1969. France gives the nation an annual subsidy.

French is the official language. About 65% of the people are animists; 15%, in the S, are Christians; 13%, in the N, are Moslems.

Denmark

Area: 17,028 sq. mi. Population including Faeroe Islands and Greenland (Govt. est. 1974): 5,130,000. Capital: Copenhagen. Monetary unit: Krone.

Denmark occupies the peninsula of Jutland, thrusting out to the N from Germany, which is its only land neighbor, between the North Sea and the Baltic Sea, and adjacent islands. The Skagerrak separates it from Norway; the Kattegat and Oresund from Sweden. The country consists of low undulating plains. It is about the size of New Hampshire and Massachusetts combined.

The **Faeroe Islands** in the North Atlantic, about 300 mi. NE of the Shetlands, and 850 mi. from Denmark proper, 18 inhabited, have an area of 540 sq. mi. and pop. (est. 1975) of 40,000. They are self-governing in most matters.

Resources and Industries. About 7.5% of the population lives by agriculture on more than 70% of the usable land. Denmark exports much butter, cheese, poultry, eggs, bacon and beef. Its fishing industry ranks 11th in the world. Tourist trade accounts for 10% of foreign exchange. Denmark exports machinery, ships, textiles, furniture, iron and steel goods. Most raw materials and fuels have to be imported, but manufactures have increased; industrial exports surpass agricultural.

Denmark is the world's largest exporter of pork and 3rd largest of meat in general.

The first cooperative consumers' society was established 1866; the system currently has about 1,650 affiliated societies and includes 863,000 households, about 51%.

More than a million tourists visit Denmark annually. Many leave their children in Danish camps while visiting other countries.

Foreign trade in thousands of U.S. dollars:

	Imports	Exports
1973	$7,802,000	$6,249,000
1974	$10,076,000	$7,819,000

History and Government. The origin of Copenhagen dates back to ancient times, when the fishing and trading place named Havn (port) grew up on a cluster of islets, but Bishop Absalon (1128-1201) is regarded as the actual founder of the city. On one of the islets he built a stronghold against the pirating Wends and the remnants of this still exist underground in front of Christiansborg. Elsinore (Helsingor) contains the reputed grave of Hamlet, the Danish prince immortalized by Shakespeare.

Denmark is a constitutional monarchy with a Queen. A new constitution, signed June 5, 1953, substituted a unicameral parliament, the Folketing, of 179 members for the former two-chamber Rigsdag. A cabinet of ministers, which must have the support of a majority in the Folketing, conducts the government.

The Queen of Denmark is Margrethe II (born Apr. 16, 1940) who succeeded to the throne Jan. 14, 1972, after the death of her father, King Frederik IX. She was married June 10, 1967, to Count Henri Marie Andre Laborde de Monpezat of France who became Prince Henrik of Denmark. They had 2 sons: Prince Frederik (born May 26, 1968), heir to the throne, and Prince Joachim (born June 7, 1969). Queen Margrethe had 2 sisters: Princess Benedikte (born Apr. 29, 1944), married to German Prince Richard Casimir of Sayn-Wittgenstein, and Princess Anne-Marie (born Aug. 30, 1946)–who married King Constantine of Greece and became Queen of Greece.

Denmark has public assistance, health insurance, disability and old-age pensions, workmen's compensation and unemployment insurance. Pensions are paid to men aged 67, women aged 62.

Denmark is a member of the UN and NATO, and joined the EC Jan. 1, 1973.

Education and Religion. Evangelical Lutheranism is the established religion, but there is complete religious freedom. Education is compulsory and includes vocational courses. The University of Copenhagen was founded in 1479.

Defense. Military forces total 45,000.

Greenland

Greenland, a huge island between the North Atlantic and the Polar Sea, is separated from the North American continent by Davis Strait and Baffin Bay

Its total area is 840,000 sq. mi., 705,234 of which are ice-capped. Most of the island is a lofty plateau 9,000 to 10,000 ft. in altitude. The average thickness of the ice cap is 1,000 ft. The population (est. 1975) is 50,000. The capital is Godthaab. Under the 1953 Danish constitution the colony became an integral part of the realm with representatives in the Folketing. Fish and fur are exported.

Dominican Republic

Area: 18,704 sq. mi. Population (Govt. est. 1974): 4,560,000. Capital: Santo Domingo. Monetary unit: Peso.

The Dominican Republic occupies the eastern two-thirds of the Island of Hispaniola (discovered by Columbus in 1492), second largest of the Greater Antilles, lying between Cuba on the W and Puerto Rico on the E. The boundary between it and the Republic of Haiti, which occupies the western part of the island, is 241 mi. long. It has a coastline of 979 mi. It is twice the size of New Hampshire. Climate is generally sub-tropical.

The city of Santo Domingo, founded 1496, is the oldest settlement by Europeans in the hemisphere and has the supposed ashes of Columbus in an elaborate tomb in its ancient cathedral.

Resources and Industries. The land is fertile. Chief products are sugar, cocoa, coffee, tobacco, corn, peanuts, bananas and livestock products.

The country has nickel, gold, copper, iron, salt, chalk, bauxite, marble, amber, kaolin.

Chief manufactures are sugar, molasses, rum, alcohol, cement, peanut oil, chocolate, tobacco products, cordage, textiles, apparel, lumber, furniture. The U. S. buys more than 50% of its exports, mostly sugar, cocoa and coffee, and supplies about 50% of imports.

Agricultural products, including sugar, showed strong gains in the early 1970's. A large nickel refining plant opened in 1972.

History and Government. Spain ceded Santo Domingo to France, 1795. Toussaint L'Ouverture, Haitian leader, seized it, 1801. Spain returned intermittently 1803-1821, and several native republics came and went. From 1822 to 1844 Haiti governed it. The republic was formed 1844. Spain occupied it 1861-63.

The country was occupied by U.S. Marines from 1916 until 1924, when a constitutionally elected government was installed.

In 1930, Gen. Rafael Leonidas Trujillo Molina was elected president. Trujillo remained in power, ruling the nation with an iron hand (though turning the presidency over to his brother, Hector, in 1952 and to Joaquin Balaguer in 1960) until his assassination May 30, 1961.

Balaguer resigned under pressure Jan. 17, 1962. Pending general elections, the country was governed by a 7-member Council of State headed by Rafael F. Bonnelly who was named president Jan. 18, 1962. He was succeeded by Juan Bosch, elected president Dec. 20, 1962, in first free elections in 38 years. Bosch was overthrown Sept. 25, 1963, and his regime replaced by an army-backed civilian triumvirate led by Donald Reid Cabral.

On April 24, 1965, a revolt was launched by followers of Bosch and others, including communists, and led by Col. Francisco Caamano Deno. The Reid Cabral government was ousted, but the rebel regime was replaced Apr. 28 by a 3-man counter-revolutionary junta led by Gen. Elias Wessin y Wessin; on May 7 it was succeeded by a 5-man regime headed by Gen. Antonio Imbert Barreras, another anti-Bosch leader; fighting continued in Santo Domingo.

A force of 405 U. S. Marines landed by helicopter April 28, primarily, according to U. S. President Johnson, to save American and other lives; U. S. forces were expanded to a high of 24,000.

At U. S. urging, the Organization of American States sent an Inter-American Peace Force to Santo Domingo May 23, under a Brazilian commander with the head of U. S. forces as deputy commander. Some U. S. forces were withdrawn and the Inter-American Force consisted of 11,200 men, including 9,400 U.S. troops, 1,100 Brazilians, and units from Honduras, Nicaragua, Paraguay and Costa Rica.

On Sept. 3, Hector Garcia-Godoy became provisional president under sponsorship of the OAS with agreement by all major local groups.

An election was held June 1, 1966; Balaguer defeated Bosch, 754,409 votes to 517,783. The Balaguer Reformist party won control of Congress. The new president was inaugurated July 1. The Inter-American Peace Force completed their departure Sept. 20. Balaguer was reelected, 1970 and 1974, the latter time without real opposition.

In 1971, scores of leftists were reported killed by rightist terrorists.

Education and Religion. The population is mostly mixed white and Negro, plus about 15% whites and a slightly larger percentage of blacks. Roman Catholicism is the state religion. Education is free and compulsory. The language is Spanish. The University of Santo Domingo was established 1538.

Defense. Armed forces total over 15,000. The nation is a member of the UN and OAS.

Ecuador

Area: 105,685 sq. mi. Population (Census, 1974): 6,500,845. Capital: Quito. Monetary unit: Sucre.

On the NW coast of South America, Ecuador (Sp. for Equator) extends 100 mi. into the Northern Hemisphere, 400 into the Southern. It is bounded by Colombia, Peru and the Pacific. Two ranges of the Andes run N and S, splitting the country into 3 zones: hot, humid lowlands on the coast; temperate highlands between the ranges, and rainy, tropical lowlands to the E. There are 22 peaks over 14,000 ft.; highest is Chimborazo, 20,561 ft.; many are snowcapped; some volcanoes have erupted in recent years. Ecuador is larger than Arizona.

The **Galapagos Islands,** 600 mi. to the W, are the home of huge tortoises and other unusual animals. Charles Darwin visited the islands aboard the Beagle in 1835; his studies of wildlife there provided most of the facts for his theory of evolution.

Ecuador has sought revision of its Amazon valley boundary with Peru. It claims jurisdiction over Pacific waters 200 mi. out from its coast. It has seized and fined U.S. fishing boats within that limit. In Jan. 1971 the U.S. in reply temporarily suspended military sales to Ecuador. But other U.S. aid continued.

Guayaquil, Ecuador's largest city, is the chief seaport and, together with Quito, is served by major airlines. Rail lines link Quito with Guayaquil and San Lorenzo on the coast. Quito is famed for its 17th Century churches.

Resources and Industries. The country is rich in minerals with large deposits of copper, iron, lead, coal and sulphur. In 1972 Ecuador became an important exporter of oil, brought by pipeline from eastern Ecuador to the Pacific. Modern farm methods have helped make Ecuador the world's largest exporter of bananas. Other products are rice, cereals, potatoes, fruits, cocoa, coffee, kapok, rubber, mangrove bark.

Industry now contributes 20% to national income, with production increases in cement, edible oils, textiles, sugar, chemicals. Ecuador is the chief source of light but strong balsa wood, and was the original home of the Cinchona tree, source of quinine.

History and Government. Spain conquered the region, which was the northern Inca empire, in the 16th Century. Liberation forces defeated the Spanish May 24, 1822, near Quito. Ecuador became part of the Great Columbia Republic but seceded, May 13, 1830.

In June 1968 elections, Dr. Jose Maria Velasco Ibarra, who had been elected president 4 times but had been ousted 3 times by coups, was again chosen by the voters. In June 1970, he assumed dictatorial powers. On Feb. 15, 1972, he was ousted by a military junta which named Gen. Guillermo Rodriguez Lara president.

Education and Religion. Roman Catholicism is the chief religion. Primary education is compulsory. The language is Spanish. The population is over one-third Indian and one-third mixed; whites, mostly of Spanish descent, and Negroes are minority groups.

Defense. Armed forces total about 22,000.

Egypt

Area (1966): 386,872 sq. mi. Population (Govt. est. 1974): 36,420,000. Capital: Cairo. Monetary unit: Egyptian pound.

The Arab Republic of Egypt occupies the NE corner of Africa on the Mediterranean. On the E lie Israel and the Red Sea which separates Egypt from Saudi Arabia. Libya is to the W and Sudan to the S. The Gulf of Suez and the Suez Canal (linking the gulf to the Mediterranean) separate Egypt's main area in Africa from its Sinai Peninsula, in Asia.

Alexandria, founded 332 B.C., is the chief port. Cairo, largest city, is rich in archeological treasures, cafes, bazaars. Tourist attractions include the pyramids, Sphinx, temple ruins at Karnak and Luxor, and other ancient monuments.

Resources and Industries. Productive acreage lies in the Valley of the Nile and in its delta, or Lower Egypt, north of Cairo. The Nile flows through 960 mi. in Egypt, and covers 2,850 sq. mi. with waters and marshes. Irrigated lands produce cotton, cereals, vegetables and sugar cane. Fruit is plentiful and includes grapes, dates, figs, pomegranates, peaches, apricots, oranges, lemons, bananas and olives. Egypt is the world's 7th largest producer of cotton.

The billion-dollar Aswan High Dam project, begun 1960, completed 1971, provided irrigation for more than a million acres of land and a potential of 10 billion kwh of electricity per year. Artesian wells, drilled in the Western Desert, reclaimed 43,000 acres, 1960-66.

A variety of minerals is found in Egypt; petroleum is most important, with fields in the Red Sea and the Western Desert. Other minerals are phosphate rock, salt, iron, manganese, cement, gold, gypsum, kaolin, titanium.

A series of decrees in July, 1961, nationalized about 90% of industry and reduced land holdings to 52 acres per family. In 1974 an economic liberalization was begun, with more emphasis on private domestic and foreign investment. Workers demonstrated against high prices.

Egypt has textile plants, chemical, steel, cement and fertilizer factories, and a film industry supplying the Middle East, Africa and Asia. Principal exports are cotton, rice, petroleum, textiles, refrigerators, tires, cement, electrical instruments.

History and Government. Archeological records of ancient empires in Egypt go back to 4000 B.C. A high civilization of rulers and priests dominated the lowly serfs. Hyksos, Assyrians, Persians, Greeks (Alexander of Macedon), Romans, Saracens, Turks, French (Napoleon) and British invaded Egypt. Under Turkish sultans the khedive as hereditary viceroy had wide authority but repeated insolvency led to regulation by European powers. Britain, which supervised the administration after 1882, made Egypt a protectorate 1914-1922. Britain then recognized Egypt as a sovereign state but reserved defense, security of British communications, and the Sudan.

The sultan became King Fouad I in 1922 and a constitution was adopted in 1923. King Fouad I died in 1936 and was succeeded by his son, Farouk, who abdicated in 1952 and left the country. His son was named nominal ruler under a regency council, Aug. 5, 1952, but the crown was abolished when Egypt was declared a republic, June 18, 1953.

In 1936 an Anglo-Egyptian treaty of alliance revised the conditions of association. Britain agreed to a condominium over the Sudan, with British and Egyptian troops cooperating, obtained the right to retain 10,000 soldiers and 400 airmen to defend the Suez Canal for 20 years until Egypt would take over, and also held naval bases in Alexandria and Port Said.

Egypt became a charter member of the UN and in 1944 led in organizing the Arab League. In 1947 Egypt brought before the UN Security Council a demand for unification of Egypt and Sudan and evacuation of all British troops from the Suez. In Oct. 1951 Egypt abrogated its 1936 treaty with Britain. The Sudan, with UN support, became independent in 1956.

Delays in reforms, corruption in public office and royal extravagance led to an uprising July 23, 1952, led by the Society of Free Officers which named Maj. Gen. Mohammed Naguib commander in chief and forced Farouk to abdicate. Naguib became premier Sept. 7, 1952. When the republic was proclaimed June 18, 1953, Naguib became its first president and premier. Lt. Col. Gamal Abdel Nasser, the principal influence behind the revolt, removed Naguib and succeeded him as premier on Apr. 18, 1954. On June 23, 1956, voters elected Nasser president. Nasser died in 1970 and was replaced as president by Vice President Anwar Sadat.

A new constitution, guaranteeing individual rights, was approved Sept. 11, 1971. At the same time, Egypt adopted the name Arab Republic of Egypt, dropping the name United Arab Republic, which it had used since its brief union with Syria, 1958-1961. Egypt has a president, premier and National Assembly all of whose 350 members must be members of the only legal party, the Arab Socialist Union.

In July, 1956, the United States and Great Britain withdrew support for loans to start the Aswan High Dam. President Nasser nationalized the Suez Canal and seized control of the assets of the canal company. Later he obtained credits and technicians from the USSR to build the dam.

When the state of Israel was proclaimed in 1948, Egypt joined other Arab nations invading Israel and was defeated. No peace treaties were made and Egypt later denied Israeli shipping the use of the Suez Canal.

Border hostilities with Israel heightened and on Oct. 29, 1956, Israeli forces invaded Egypt's Sinai Peninsula. Egypt rejected a cease-fire demand by Britain and France; on Oct. 31 the 2 nations dropped bombs and on Nov. 5-6 landed forces. Egypt and Israel accepted a UN cease-fire, followed by Britain and France; fighting ended Nov. 7.

A UN Emergency Force guarded the 117-mile long border between Egypt and Israel until May 19, 1967, when it was withdrawn at Nasser's demand. Egyptian troops took over the Gaza Strip and the heights at Sharm el Sheikh and 3 days later closed the Strait of Tiran leading into the Gulf of Aqaba to all Israeli shipping. Full-scale war broke out June 5 and before it ended under a UN cease-fire June 10, Israel had captured Gaza and the Sinai Peninsula, controlled the east bank of the Suez Canal and reopened the gulf.

Sporadic fighting with Israel broke out late in 1968. In 1969-70 there were almost daily artillery duels across the Suez Canal, ground forays and air raids in which Israeli planes penetrated deep into Egypt. Military and economic aid was received from the USSR and it was est. in 1971 there were 19,000 or more Soviet military personnel in Egypt. Israel and Egypt agreed, Aug. 7, 1970, to a cease-fire and peace negotiations proposed by the U.S. Negotiations, pressed by the UN and U.S., failed to achieve results, but the cease-fire continued into 1973.

In July 1972 Sadat ordered most of the 20,000 Soviet military advisers and personnel to leave Egypt. They complied, leaving behind bases and equipment they had installed for the Egyptians.

In a surprise attack Oct. 6, 1973 (Yom Kippur, most sacred day on the Jewish calendar), Egyptian forces crossed the Suez Canal into the Sinai, attacked Israeli forces and established 2 bridgeheads along the E side of the canal. (At the same time, Syrian forces attacked Israelis on the Golan Heights.) Egypt was supplied by a USSR military airlift; the U.S. responded with an airlift to Israel. Israel counter-attacked, crossed the canal between the Egyptian bridgeheads, surrounded Suez City and trapped the Egyptian 3d Army in its Sinai bridgehead. A UN cease-fire took effect Oct. 24; a UN peace-keeping force went to the area.

A disengagement agreement was signed Jan. 18, 1974, mainly through the efforts of U.S. Secretary of State Henry Kissinger. Under it, Israeli forces withdrew from the canal's W bank; limited numbers of Egyptians forces occupied a strip, 6 to 7.5 mi. wide, along the E bank from the Mediterranean to the Gulf of Suez. UN forces took over a buffer zone, 3.5 to 5 mi. wide, E of the Egyptians; Israelis, further E, could have only limited forces adjoining the UN zone. Withdrawals to the new lines were completed Mar. 4. Negotiations on further peace moves occurred in 1975.

The U.S. and Egypt resumed, in Feb. 1974, diplomatic relations, severed by Egypt after the 1967 war. In June, U. S. President Nixon announced during an Egyptian visit he would provide Egypt nuclear technology for peaceful purposes, but the plan faltered. Major arms deals with Britain and France were set in 1975.

Sadat charged in Aug. that Libyan leader Muammar el-Quaddafi had backed a plot to overthrow the Egyptian government. Iran, Saudi Arabia, and Kuwait provided low interest loans in 1975.

Education and Religion. There are 3 ethnic elements: the Fellahin, basic Egyptian group; the Bedouin, nomadic Arabs; Nubians, a mixed group. Moslems form 92% of the population and Coptic Christians about 7%.

Education is compulsory for all children beginning at age 7 and free through high school. There is a famous seat of Moslem learning in the University of Al-Azhar in Cairo, founded about 968 A.D. Four modern universities are Cairo, Alexandria, Ein-Shams and Assiut. Arabic is the official language.

Defense. Military forces total 280,000 with reserves of about 500,000.

The Suez Canal

The Suez Canal, 103 mi. long, links the Mediterranean and the Red Sea. It was begun April 25, 1859, by a French corporation under Ferdinand de Lesseps and opened Nov. 17, 1869. Benjamin Disraeli, British prime minister, obtained control for Britain Nov. 24, 1875, by buying 176,752 shares from the Khedive Ismail of Egypt for about $20 million.

The British ended a 74-year military occupation of the canal area June 13, 1956, withdrawing all troops. On July 26, Egypt proclaimed nationalization of the canal, seizing it from its French and British stockholders. It had barred Israeli ships and cargoes destined for Israel since 1948.

A final agreement between Egypt and the Universal Suez Canal Co., signed July 13, 1958, called for payments to stockholders of $64,400,000. Final payments were made Jan. 1, 1963.

After nationalization, Egypt widened and deepened the canal, improving its capacity. The canal was closed to all shipping by Cairo at the height of the Israeli-Arab War in June 1967. Subsidies to replace lost canal revenues were paid the UAR by Saudi Arabia, Kuwait and Libya. In 1974, operations to clear the canal of war debris began, with aid from the U.S. and others. The canal was reopened June 5, 1975.

El Salvador

Area: 8,260 sq. mi. Population (Govt. est. 1974): 3,980,000. Capital: San Salvador. Monetary unit: Colon.

El Salvador, smallest of the 6 Central American republics and the only one without an Atlantic seacoast, is bounded by Guatemala, Honduras and a Pacific coastline of about 160 mi. A country of mountains, including many volcanoes, and upland plains, it is entirely within the tropics, but tropic heat is modified by the elevation. It is about the size of Massachusetts.

The 3 racial types are white, 5%; mixed white and Indian descent, 85%; Indian, 10%.

Resources and Industries. Mountain slope plantations make El Salvador the world's 8th largest producer and a large exporter of coffee. Cotton production has made large strides; coffee represents 44% of the value of exports, cotton 8%. Primarily agricultural, the country is becoming industrialized; it produces cement, refined sugar and textiles.

Economic development has been helped by U.S. aid.

History and Government. El Salvador became independent of Spain in 1821; member of the Central American Federation until 1839. The constitution provides for a unicameral legislative system, the National Assembly of Deputies, elected by popular vote. Voting is compulsory for all over 18 years of age. Executive power is vested in the president who is elected for a 5-year term by direct, popular vote and is ineligible for immediate reelection.

In July 1969, a dispute over the presence of 300,000 Salvadorean workers and settlers in Honduras broke into open warfare between the two nations; 2,000 people were killed. After 5 days, the OAS arranged a truce. In 1970, after new clashes, a demilitarized zone was agreed on. Clashes continued in 1974.

Education and Religion. Education is free but illiteracy rate is 50%. The language is Spanish. The dominant religion is Roman Catholicism.

Defense. Military forces number about 5,500. El Salvador is a member of the UN and OAS.

Equatorial Guinea

Area: 10,832 sq. mi. Population (UN est. 1974): 310,-000. Capital: Malabo. Monetary uni: Peseta Guineana.

The Republic of Equatorial Guinea, which received its independence from Spain on Oct. 12, 1968, consists of the Province of Macias Nguema Biyogo, including Macias Nguema Is., in the Gulf of Guinea off the W. coast of Africa, and Pagalu Is., 370 mi. SW., and the Province of Rio Muni, on the mainland facing the gulf. Malabo, the capital, is on Macias Nguema Is., which has an area of 780 sq. mi. and population (est. 1972) of 90,000.

Self-government and independence were achieved in steps, with local elections in 1960 and increased autonomy in 1964. A 1973 constitution provided for a president, a 60-member Assembly and two Provincial Councils, all elected by universal adult suffrage. Francisco Macias Nguema was elected the first president. In 1971 he assumed complete control of the government and in 1972 was named president for life.

Important exports are cocoa and timber for plywood. Other exports are coffee, bananas and palm oil.

Most of the population is nominally Roman Catholic. Spanish is the official language; numerous African languages are also spoken. Macias Nguema natives were mostly Bubis; by the late 1960s Nigerian workers and settlers numbered almost half the island population. In Rio Muni, the Fangs were the largest group. Before a 1969 confrontation, there were about 7,000 Europeans, mostly Spanish, but many left during the dispute.

The nation is a member of the UN and OAU.

Ethiopia

Area: 457,142 sq. mi. Population (Govt. est. 1974): 27,240,000. Capital: Addis Ababa. Monetary unit: Ethiopian dollar.

Ethiopia is a ruggedly mountainous, independent state in NE Africa. It faces on the Red Sea, but its main rivers are important tributaries of the Nile: the Abbai or Blue Nile, one of the 2 main branches of that mighty river, has its source in Ethiopia's Lake Tana. The country is as large as Texas, Oklahoma and New Mexico combined.

Resources and Industries. Economy is some 70% agricultural but industrial resources are potentially great, including vast hydroelectric power. Industries include food processing, cement, shoes, textiles.

Fertile soil and abundant rainfall produce 2 crops annually. Coffee, wheat, barley, millet, tobacco, and sugar are principal crops. Coffee of extremely high quality from Kaffa, in SW Ethiopia, reputed birthplace of the coffee plant, accounts for half of the country's foreign exchange. Over 185,000 tons are exported annually. Value of exports in 1973 rose to $237 million; imports totaled $213 million.

Cattle, sheep, mules and goats are raised. Hides and skins, oilseeds and vegetables also are exported. Mineral resources include platinum, gold, silver, manganese, tin, copper, asbestos, potash, sulphur, mica, cement and salt. There are known deposits of coal and iron.

Ethiopia has used large credits from the World Bank and other agencies for road building (there are over 4,000 mi. of all-weather roads). Aid and investment funds are received from the U. S. and other western nations and from communist countries. Ethiopia is a member of the UN and Addis Ababa is hq. for the Organization of African Unity.

History and Government. The Ethiopian monarchy derived from a number of earlier kingdoms, descendants of ancient Hamite and Semite tribes. Italy invaded the country in 1880 and acquired a sphere of influence and later organized its colony of Eritrea. In 1936 Italy invaded Ethiopia without declaring war. The League of Nations applied sanctions against Italy, which proved ineffective. Mussolini added Ethiopia to Italy. British forces freed Ethiopia in 1941.

The last emperor, Haile Selassie I, 225th consecutive Solomonic ruler, was born July 23, 1892, crowned Nov. 2, 1930. He established a parliament and judiciary system, 1931, and promulgated a new constitution 1955, but barred all political parties.

A 1973 famine killed over 100,000 people, causing unrest. An army mutiny, strikes and student demonstrations led to the dethronement of Selassie Sept. 12, 1974, and the execution of 60 former officials in November. The ruling junta pledged to form a one-party socialist state. The influence of the Coptic Church was curbed. The monarchy was abolished March 21, 1975. A famine in the east killed thousands in 1975.

Education and Religion. Ethiopian culture has been influenced by Greece and Egypt. Christianity was for centuries the predominant religion, embraced in 330 A.D.; the Coptic, Monophysite branch is practiced. Until 1952 the Egyptian Coptic patriarch was the head of the church, but the archbishop has since been an Ethiopian. The population is largely composed of a mixture of Hamites, Semites and Negroes. The largest religious groups are Coptic Christians and Moslems; others practice tribal religions.

There are 2 universities and a number of colleges. The official language is Amharic; English is widely taught.

Eritrea, which had been an Italian colony since 1890, was administered after World War II by Great Britain; the UN General Assembly voted to return it to Ethiopia and the action became effective Sept. 11, 1952. In 1970-75 secessionist guerrillas were active in Eritrea, receiving military and political support from Arab and Moslem states.

Fiji

Area: 7,055 sq. mi. Population (Govt. est. 1974): 560,000. Capital: Suva. Monetary unit: Fiji dollar.

The Fiji Islands lie in the South Pacific, E of Australia and N of New Zealand. There are about 840 islands (106 inhabited), many of them mountainous, with tropical forests and large fertile areas. The capital, Suva, is on Viti Levu, the largest island (4,011 sq. mi.).

Descendants of the native Fijians (Melanesians and Polynesians) form about 43% of the population but have been protected by law in ownership of 83% of the land. Descendants of Indian contract laborers, brought to the islands in the late 19th Century, make up slightly over 51%. Most of the others are of Chinese or European descent. English is the official language. Most of the Fijians are Christians; the Indians are about 80% Hindu, 15% Moslem. Literacy is about 85%.

A British colony since 1874, Fiji received gradual measures of self-government in the 1960s. On Oct. 10, 1970, Fiji became a fully independent parliamentary democracy, with a Senate, a House of Representatives, a prime minister and, as a member of the Commonwealth, a governor-general representing the British Queen. It is a member of the UN.

Sugar is the main export, along with molasses, cement, coconut products, timber, ginger and gold. Tourism is important. A cement factory, shipyards and small manufacturing plants have been built.

Finland

Area: 130,119 sq. mi. Population (Govt. est. 1974): 4,680,000. Capital: Helsinki. Monetary unit: Markka.

Finland is a republic in northern Europe, with Sweden, Norway and the USSR for neighbors. South and central Finland are mostly flat areas with low hills; there are mountainous areas, 3,000-4,000 ft., in the N. It is half the size of Texas.

About 70% of the land is forested. Lakes and canal waterways are navigable for 3,000 mi. Rail and air transport is well developed.

Aland, constituting an autonomous department, is a group of small islands, 572 sq. mi., in the Gulf of Bothnia, 25 mi. from Sweden, 16 mi. from Finland. They are demilitarized. Mariehamn is the principal port.

Resources and Industries. Rapid industrialization has taken place with 25% of output exported. Forest products (paper, etc.) are 55% of exports, metals 25%, foods 5%. Principal crops are oats, barley, wheat, rye, potatoes, hay. There are machinery, metal, shipbuilding, textiles, leather and chemicals industries. In 1972, 2 million tourists visited Finland.

Foreign trade, in thousands of U. S. dollars:

	Imports	Exports
1973	$4,347,000	$3,827,000
1974	$7,232,000	$5,827,000

History and Government. The early Finns probably migrated from the Ural area at about the beginning of the Christian era. Swedish settlers brought the country into the kingdom of Sweden, 1154 to 1809, when Finland became an autonomous grand duchy of the Russian Empire. Russian exactions created a strong national spirit; on Dec. 6, 1917, Finland declared its independence and on July 17, 1919, became a republic. On Nov. 30, 1939, the Soviet Union invaded Finland, and although the Finns took heavy toll, in March, 1940, they were forced to cede 16,173 sq. mi., including the Karelian Isthmus, Viipuri, and an area on Lake Ladoga. When Germany attacked the USSR June 22, 1941, Finland again was involved. An armistice was signed Sept. 19, 1944, and the USSR took the former cessions, plus Petsamo in the N. and a lease for 50 years on Porkkala, near Helsinki, for a military base. The treaty of Feb. 10, 1947, also exacted $300 million in goods in term payments. In April, 1948, Finland signed a treaty of mutual assistance and friendship with the USSR; in Jan. 1956 Russia returned Porkkala.

The president is chosen for a term of six years by an electoral college of 300 named by direct vote; he appoints the cabinet. There is a single legislative chamber, the Eduskunta, numbering 200, elected to 4-year terms. Voting is by proportional representation. The prime minister and cabinet normally represent a coalition of parties in the Eduskunta.

Education and Religion. The Evangelical Lutheran Church is the leading religion, and both Finnish and Swedish are official languages. There is no illiteracy. There are 6 major universities (the oldest founded 1640) and 6 colleges of university level.

Defense. Military strength for 1972-73 was 39,500, including 34,000 in the Army, 3,000 in the Air Force and 2,500 in the Navy.

Finland is a member of the UN, Nordic Council and EFTA, and has a trade agreement with the EC and a cooperation accord with the Council for Mutual Economic Assistance.

France

Area: 212,973 sq. mi. Population (Govt. est. 1974): 52,510,000. Capital: Paris. Monetary unit: Franc.

France has coastlines on the Atlantic and Mediterranean and is about four-fifths the size of Texas. It shares borders with Belgium, Luxembourg, Germany, Switzerland, Italy, Andorra and Spain. It is separated from England by the English Channel and the Strait of Dover. The Rhine River is on the German boundary, the Jura Mts. form the Swiss boundary and the Pyrenees Mtns. rise along the borders of Andorra and Spain.

Mont Blanc, on the Franco-Italian border, is the tallest W of the Caucasus, 15,771 ft. A highway tunnel, 7.25 mi., under Mont Blanc, was opened in 1965, linking France and Italy.

There are 4 important rivers, the Seine, the Loire, the Garonne and the Rhone. There are some 5,005 mi. of navigable rivers and canals.

The island of Corsica, in the Mediterranean W of Italy and N of Sardinia, is an integral part of France. It has an area of 3,369 sq. mi. and a population of 269,-831 (1968 census). The capital is Ajaccio, birthplace of Napoleon.

Resources and Industries. Agriculturally, France is a country of small diversified farms involving 45,800,000 acres and 12% of the employed, making France the biggest food producer in Western Europe. Agricultural exports are valued at more than $1.7 billion annually. Leading crops are wheat, barley, corn, oats, rice, and a wide variety of fruits and vegetables. Cattle, poultry, forestry and fishing are large-scale. France is the world's 4th ranking producer of beef and of pork. Approx. 1,500,000 farmers belong to cooperative unions.

The country is rich in minerals, and the basins of Pas de Calais and Lorraine are noted for their huge coal deposits, iron ore, bauxite, pyrites, mineral oils, auriferous ore, asphalt, rock salt and potash salts. The iron ore deposits in eastern France and the bauxite deposits in central France are among the richest in the world. Power stations produced about 174 million kwh in 1973.

France tested atomic bombs in the Sahara beginning in 1960 and, beginning in 1966 exploded nuclear devices at Mururoa, an atoll 750 mi. SE of Tahiti, continuing the tests through 1974. (France was not a signer of the 1963 treaty banning such tests.) Australia and New Zealand protested the tests and in 1973 the International Court of Justice asked France to suspend the tests.

Manufacturing includes chemicals, silk and cotton textiles, perfumes, automobiles, aircraft, ships, instruments, plastics, electronic equipment. Index of industrial production (1970 = 100) was 123 in 1974.

France leads the world in wine-making, producing over 1.5 billion gallons a year.

Foreign trade in thousands of U.S. dollars

	Imports	Exports
1973	$36,987,000	$35,565,000
1974	$49,296,000	$46,377,000

History and Government. The monarchial system was overthrown by the French Revolution (1789-1793) and succeeded by the First Republic; thereafter successively followed by the First Empire under Napoleon (1804-1814), a monarchy (1814-1848), the Second Republic (1848-1852), the Second Empire (1852-1870), the Third Republic (1871-1946), the Fourth Republic (1946-1958), Fifth Republic (1958).

France suffered severe losses in manpower and wealth in the first World War, 1914-1918, when it was invaded by Germany. By the Treaty of Versailles, France exacted return of Alsace and Lorraine, French provinces seized by Germany in 1871. Germany invaded France again in May, 1940, occupied Paris June 14, 1940, and signed an armistice with a government that made its hq. in Vichy. Marshal Philippe Petain became chief of state. After France was liberated by the Allies Sept., 1944, Gen. Charles De Gaulle became premier of the provisional government, serving from Nov. 1944 to Jan. 1946.

De Gaulle again became premier June 1, 1958. His proposed constitution for the Fifth Republic and new French Community was approved by the voters by an overwhelming margin. De Gaulle was elected first president of the Fifth Republic Dec. 21, 1958; inaugurated Jan. 8, 1959. De Gaulle ran for reelection Dec. 5, 1965; he failed to win a majority of the votes. In a runoff, Dec. 19, De Gaulle won with about 55%.

The constitution provides for a strong executive branch headed by the president, and a legislature composed of a National Assembly and a Senate.

A constitutional amendment adopted by referendum Oct. 28, 1962, provided that future presidents be elected by popular vote rather than by an electoral college. The president, elected for 7 years, appoints the premier (formerly invested by the Assembly), and may dissolve the Assembly and call for new elections; he may call for referendums on specific issues and may assume full powers in a national emergency.

Women, who had less than equal rights under provisions of the 1804 Code Napoleon, won the right to take jobs, open checking accounts and own their own businesses by a 1966 law.

In May 1968 rebellious students at the Sorbonne and elsewhere rioted, battled police and were joined by some 10 million workers who launched nationwide strikes and took over many factories. The government awarded pay increases to the strikers May 26; on May 30 De Gaulle dissolved the Assembly. A threat of civil war was eased as Army tank units, loyal to the government, maneuvered in Paris outskirts. By early June, normalcy was returned. In elections to the Assembly in late June 1968, De Gaulle's backers won a landslide victory.

In Nov. 1968 De Gaulle weathered an economic storm, refusing to devalue the franc. But on Apr. 28, 1969, he resigned from office after losing a nationwide referendum on his proposals for constitutional reform.

A nationwide election for a successor, June 1, resulted in a runoff election June 15 in which the winner was Georges Pompidou, who had been De Gaulle's premier from 1962 until July 1968. Pompidou died Apr. 2, 1974. Valery Giscard d'Estaing, a conservative, was elected president, May 19, 1974, with 50.81% of the vote, defeating Socialist Francois Mitterrand.

Education and Religion. Primary, secondary and higher education are free and instruction is compulsory between the ages of 6 and 16.

The country is predominantly Roman Catholic, with 800,000 Protestants and 550,000 Jews. The state recognizes no religion and tolerates all.

Both employers and employes contribute to the old-age pension fund. There is provision for family allowances and compulsory social insurance for illness, maternity, disability and death. A profit-sharing agreement was signed Jan. 7, 1959.

Defense. Military forces total over 500,000; reserves number over 600,000.

France is a member of the UN, SEATO and EC but

announced in 1973 it would stop paying dues to SEATO after 1974.

In 1966, France withdrew all its troops from the integrated military command of NATO. NATO headquarters and bases were removed from France. But France continued to attend political meetings of NATO.

Afars and Issas Territory

The French Territory of the Afars and the Issas, formerly French Somaliland, borders Ethiopia and Somalia and is separated by the Straits of Bab-el-Mandeb from Yemen.

The area is 8,800 sq. mi. and population (est. 1974), 150,000; the capital is Djibouti. France took control of the area in gradual steps, beginning in 1862.

The territory has few industries, except fishing and livestock. Salt is its most valuable product. Half of Ethiopia's foreign commerce passes along the rail line from Addis Ababa and through the port of Djibouti.

In a referendum Mar. 19, 1967, the territory elected to remain French. It sends a deputy and a senator to the French Parliament. There were clashes between Afar and Issa tribes in 1975.

Reunion

Reunion, Overseas Department, is an island in the Indian Ocean, about 420 miles east of Madagascar, and has belonged to France since 1665. The area is 969 sq. mi.; the population (est. 1974) 490,000, is 30% of French extraction. Capital: Saint-Denis. The chief products are sugar, rum, corn, perfume essences, vanilla and spices. It elects 3 deputies, 2 senators to the French Parliament.

Guadeloupe

Guadeloupe, Overseas Department in the West Indies' Leeward Islands, consists of 2 large islands, Basse-Terre and Grande-Terre, separated by the Salt River, plus Marie Galante and the Saintes group to the S and, to the N, Desirade, St. Barthelemy, and over half of St. Martin (the Netherlands portion is St. Maarten). A French possession since 1635, the department is represented in the French Parliament by 2 senators and 3 deputies; administration consists of a prefect (governor) and an elected General Council.

Area of the islands is 687 sq. mi.; population (est. 1974) 350,000, mainly descendants of slaves; capital is Basse-Terre on Basse-Terre Is. The land is fertile; sugar, rum and bananas are exported; tourism is an important industry.

Martinique

Martinique, one of the Windward Islands, in the West Indies, has been a possession since 1635, and a Department since March, 1946. It is represented in the French Parliament by 2 senators and 3 deputies. Martinique's famous volcano, Mt. Pelee, erupted May 8, 1902, destroying the city of St. Pierre with more than 30,000 inhabitants. The island was the birthplace of Napoleon's Empress Josephine.

Martinique has an area of 426 sq. mi. and population (est. 1974) 360,000 mostly descendants of slaves. The capital is Fort-de-France. It is a popular tourist stop.

The chief exports are sugar, rum, bananas, pineapples and cocoa. Trade is mainly with France and the U.S.

St. Pierre and Miquelon

St. Pierre and Miquelon, an Overseas Territory, are 2 groups of rocky barren islands close to the SW coast of Newfoundland, inhabited by fishermen. A governor, assisted by a Council, rules the islands. The exports are chiefly cod, dried and fresh, and other fish products.

The St. Pierre group has an area of 10 sq mi.; Miquelon, 83 sq. mi. Total population (est. 1974), 5,450. The capital is St. Pierre. A deputy and a senator are elected to the French Parliament.

French Guiana

French Guiana, an Overseas Department, is on the NE coast of South America with Surinam on the W and Brazil on the E and S. Its area is 37,740 sq. mi.; population (est. 1974), 60,000. Guiana sends one senator and one deputy to the French Parliament. Guiana has a prefect and a Council General of 15 elected members; capital is Cayenne.

In 1944 France closed the famous penal colony, Devil's Island, and repatriated 2,800 inmates.

Immense forests of rich timber cover 90% of the land. Very little of the land is cultivated. The principal crops are rice, corn, manioc, cacao, bananas, and sugar cane. Placer gold mining is the most important industry. Exports comprise cocoa, bananas, various woods, gold, fish glue, rum, rosewood essence, shrimp and hides.

Pacific Islands

French Polynesia, Overseas Territory, comprises 130 islands widely scattered among 5 archipelagos in the South Pacific; administered by a governor, Territorial Assembly and a Council with headquarters at Papeete, Tahiti, one of the Society Islands. A deputy and a senator are elected to the French Parliament.

Other groups are the Marquesas Islands, the Tuamotu Archipelago, the Gambier Islands, and the Austral Islands.

Total area of the islands administered from Tahiti is 1,544 sq. mi.; pop. (est. 1974), 130,000, more than half on Tahiti. Tahiti is picturesque and mountainous with a productive coastline bearing coconut, bananas and orange trees, sugar cane and vanilla.

Tahiti was visited by Capt. James Cook in 1769 and by Capt. Bligh in the Bounty, 1788-89. Its beauty impressed Herman Melville, Paul Gauguin, Charles Darwin and Robert Louis Stevenson who called Tahitians "God's sweetest works."

New Caledonia and its dependencies, an Overseas Territory, are a group of islands in the Pacifc Ocean about 1,115 mi. E of Australia and approx. the same distace NW of New Zealand. Dependencies are the Loyalty Islands, the Isle of Pines, Huon Islands and the Chesterfield Islands.

New Caledonia, the largest, has 6,530 sq. mi. Total area of the territory is 8,548 sq. mi.; population (est. 1974) 130,000. The group was acquired by France in 1853.

The territory is administered by a governor and government council. There is a popularly elected Territorial Assembly. A deputy and a senator are elected to the French Parliament. Capital: Noumea.

Mining is the chief industry. New Caledonia is the world's third largest nickel producer. Other minerals found are chrome, cobalt, manganese, antimony, mercury, cinnebar, silver, gold, lead and copper. Agricultural products include coffee, copra, cotton, manioc (cassava), corn, tobacco, bananas and pineapples.

Wallis and Futuna Islands, 2 archipelagos raised to status of Overseas Territory July 29, 1961, are in the SW Pacific S of the Equator between Fiji and Samoa. The islands have a total area of 106 sq. mi. and population (est. 1972) of 7,500. Alofi, attached to Futuna, is uninhabited. Capital: Mata-Utu. Chief products are copra, yams, taro roots, bananas. A senator and a deputy are elected to the French Parliament.

New Hebrides, a condominium administered since 1906 by France and Great Britain, is a group of 11 main islands and about 69 islets 250 mi. NE of New Caledonia and 500 mi. W of Fiji. It has 5,790 sq. mi. and population (est. 1974) of 90,000, mostly Melanesian. It has 2 administrations—French and British. Chief products are copra, frozen fish, cocoa and coffee.

French Antarctica

French Southern and Antarctic Lands, Overseas Territory, comprises **Adelie Land,** on Antarctica, and 4 island groups in the Indian Ocean. Adelie, discov. 1840, has 2 research bases, a coastline of 185 mi. and tapers 1,240 mi. inland to the South Pole. Heights rise to 8,200 ft. There are 2 huge glaciers, Ninnis, 22 mi. wide, 99 mi. long, and Mentz, 11 mi. wide, 140 mi. long. Climate varies from -36° F. to 40° F. The Indian Ocean groups are:

Kerguelen Archipelago, discovered 1772, has 300 islands. The chief is 87 mi. long, 74 mi. wide, and has Mt. Ross, 6,429 ft. tall. Principal research station is Port-aux-Francais. Seals often weigh 2 tons; there are blue whales, coal, peat, semi-precious stones. **Crozet Archipelago** (discov. 1772), covers 195 sq. mi. Eastern Island rises to 6,560 ft. **Saint Paul,** in southern Indian Ocean, has warm springs and tropical climate, with earth at places heating to 120° to 390° F. **New Amsterdam,** nearby, has temperate climate, produces cod and rock lobster.

Gabon Republic

Area: 102,317 sq. mi. Population (UN est. 1974): 520,000. Capital: Libreville. Monetary unit: CFA franc.

A former French Overseas Territory, Gabon is on the west coast of Equatorial Africa, straddling the Equator and bounded by Cameroon, Equatorial Guinea, People's Republic of Congo and the Atlantic. Heavily forested, the country consists of coastal lowlands, plateaus in N, E and S, mountains in N, SE and center. It is about the size of Colorado.

Gabon's economy is thriving; exports far exceed imports in value. Valuable timber, plywood and veneers were the main export until the late 1960s when manganese, crude oil and uranium topped them, in value. There are also huge iron ore deposits. New rail lines will aid resource exploitation. Foreign private investment has been welcomed.

Agriculture, roads, port facilities and hydroelectric power are being developed. Main crops are cocoa, coffee, rice, peanuts, palm products, cassava, bananas, but some food is imported.

Gabon proclaimed independence Aug. 17, 1960; it became a UN member Sept. 20. It is a republic, with an elected president and unicameral National Assembly. The first president, Leon M'ba, died in 1967; he was succeeded Dec. 1 by vice president Albert Bongo, who declared a one-party state.

Dr. Albert Schweitzer, Nobel Peace Prize winner, founded a hospital for lepers and others in 1913 at Lambarene. He died Sept. 4, 1965.

The Gambia

Area: 4,003 sq. mi. Population (Govt. est. 1974): 510,000. Captial: Banjul. Monetary unit: Dalasi.

Gambia is a former British colony and protectorate in western Africa. It includes the island of Banjul at the mouth of the Gambia River and a 10-mile wide strip of territory on each side of the river. Except for its Atlantic coastline, Gambia is surrounded by Senegal.

Gambia attained internal self-government Oct. 4, 1963. Its legislature comprises a speaker and 32 elected members. Britain granted complete independence to the colony Feb. 18, 1965.

In April 1970, after a referendum, Gambia became a republic within the Commonwealth. Former Prime Minister Dawda K. Jawara became the first president.

Peanuts are the main export. Rice and other foods are also grown. Tourism has become important. Britain provides development aid.

English is the official language. Islam and animism are the main religions.

Germany

Now comprises 2 nations: Federal Republic of Germany (West Germany), German Democratic Republic (East Germany).

Germany, prior to World War II, was a central European nation composed of numerous states which had a common language and traditions and which had been united in one country since 1871; since World War II it has been split in 2 parts (see below).

The climate and terrain are varied, with fertile lowlands in the N, rolling farmlands and forests in the center, and mountainous areas in the S.

Resources and Industries. Some of more important crops are wheat, rye, barley, oats, potatoes, sugar beets and hay. Other commercial products are fruit, tobacco, hops, nuts.

Principal minerals are coal, lignite, iron, zinc, lead, copper, salt, potash and petroleum. Bulk of mining is in North Rhine-Westphalia, Central Germany, the Harz, and Westerwald. Oil comes chiefly from Emsland near the Netherlands border, and Lower Saxony. Iron and steel production is greatest in the Ruhr and Saar.

History and Government. Germanic tribes were defeated by Julius Caesar, 55 and 53 B. C. but Roman expansion N of the Rhine was stopped with the wiping out of 3 legions under Varus in 9 A.D. Charlemagne, ruler of the Franks, consolidated Saxon, Bavarian, Rhenish, Frankish and other lands; after him the eastern part became the German Empire. The Thirty Years' War, 1618-1648, split Germany into small principalities and kingdoms. After Napoleon, Austria contended with Prussia for dominance, but lost the Seven Weeks' War to Prussia, 1866. Otto von Bismarck, Prussian chancellor, formed the North German Confederation, 1867.

In 1870 Bismarck maneuvered Napoleon III into declaring war. After the quick defeat of France Bismarck formed the **German Empire** and on Jan. 18, 1871, in Versailles, proclaimed King Wilhelm I of Prussia German emperor (Deutscher kaiser).

The German Empire reached its peak before World War I in 1914, with 208,780 sq. mi., plus a colonial empire. After that war Germany ceded Alsace-Lorraine to France; Eupen and Malmedy to Belgium; parts of Silesia to Poland and Czechoslovakia; part of Schleswig to Denmark; lost all of its colonies as well as the ports of Memel and Danzig.

Republic of Germany, 1919-1933, adopted the Weimar constitution; met reparation payments and elected Friedrich Ebert and Gen. Paul von Hindenburg presidents.

Third Reich, 1933-1945. Adolf Hitler, born in Austria, 1889, led the National Socialist German Workers' (Nazi) party after World War I. In 1923 he attempted to unseat the Bavarian government in the "Beer Hall putsch," and was imprisoned. He wrote Mein Kampf while in prison. President von Hindenburg named Hitler chancellor Jan. 30, 1933; on Aug. 3, 1934, the day after Hindenburg's death, the cabinet joined the offices of president and chancellor and made Hitler fuehrer (leader). Hitler abolished freedom of speech and assembly, and began a long series of persecutions climaxed by the mass extermination of Jews and opponents.

Hitler repudiated the Versailles treaty and reparations agreements. He remilitarized the Rhineland 1936 and annexed Austria (Anschluss, 1938). At Munich he made an agreement with Neville Chamberlain, British prime minister, enabling him to annex Czechoslovakia's Sudetenland. He signed a non-aggression treaty with the Soviet Union, 1939. He declared war on Poland Sept. 1, 1939, precipitating World War II.

With total defeat near, Hitler committed suicide in Berlin Apr. 30, 1945. The victorious Allies voided all acts and annexations of Hitler's Reich.

Postwar changes — The zones of occupation administered by the Allied Powers and later relinquished gave the Soviet Union Saxony, Saxony-Anhalt, Thuringia, and Mecklenburg, and the former Prussian provinces of Saxony and Brandenburg. The U.S. administered territory included parts of Bavaria, Wurtemberg, Baden, Hesse and Hesse-Nassau, and the city state of Bremen.

The territory E of the Oder-Neisse line within 1937 boundaries comprising the provinces of Silesia, Pomerania, West Prussia and the southern part of East Prussia, totaling about 41,220 sq. mi., population (1939) 9,600,000, was taken by Poland. Northern East Prussia was taken by the Soviet Union.

The Western Allies ended the state of war with Germany in 1951. The USSR did so in 1955.

There was also created the area of Greater Berlin, within but not part of the Soviet zone, administered by the 4 occupying powers under the Allied Command. In 1948 the Soviet Union withdrew and established its single command in East Berlin. The Communists cut off supplies, whereupon the Allies utilized a gigantic airlift to bring food to West Berlin during 1948-1949. In Aug. 1961 the East Germans built a wall dividing Berlin.

West Germany

Area (including West Berlin): 95,815 sq. mi. Population (Govt. est. 1974): 62,040,000. Capital: Bonn. Monetary unit: Deutsche Mark.

The Federal Republic of Germany was proclaimed May 23, 1949, in Bonn, after a constitution had been drawn up by a consultative assembly formed by representatives of the 11 laender (states) in the French, British and American zones. Later reorganized into 9 units, the laender numbered 10 with the addition of the Saar Jan. 1, 1957: Schleswig-Holstein, Hamburg, Lower Saxony, Bremen, North Rhine-Westphalia, Hesse, Rhineland-Palatinate, Baden-Wuerttemberg, Bavaria, Saarland. Berlin also was granted land (state) status, but the 1945 occupation agreements placed restrictions on it.

The occupying powers, the U.S., Britain and France, restored the civil status, Sept. 21, 1949. The U. S. resumed diplomatic relations July 2, 1951. The powers lifted controls and the republic became fully independent May 5, 1955.

Parliament has 2 chambers, serving 4-year terms. The Bundestag, lower house, is elected. It has 496 voting members from the republic and 22 nonvoting observers from West Berlin. The Bundesrat, upper house, represents the states; it has 41 delegates from the laender and 4 non-voting members from West Berlin. The Bundesrat president serves one year and acts as deputy to the federal president.

The federal president is elected for a 5-yr. term by the Federal Assembly, convened for this purpose only and made up of deputies of the Bundestag and an equal number of delegates from the land parliaments. Re-election is possible only once. The president concludes treaties with foreign states, and signs laws, which must be countersigned by the chancellor and the minister in charge. The chancellor is elected for a four-year term by the Bundestag.

Dr. Konrad Adenauer, Christian Democrat, was made chancellor Sept. 15, 1949, re-elected 1953, 1957, 1961. Dr. Ludwig Erhard, Christian Democrat, was elected 1963. Kurt Georg Kiesinger was elected chancellor Dec. 1, 1966, heading a coalition government of Christian Democrats and Social Democrats. Willy Brandt, heading a coalition of Social Democrats and Free Democrats, became chancellor Oct. 21, 1969.

In 1970 Brandt signed friendship treaties with the USSR and Poland. In 1971, the U.S., Britain, France and the USSR signed an agreement on Western access to West Berlin. In 1972 the Bundestag approved the USSR and Polish treaties and East and West Germany signed their first formal treaty, implementing the agreement easing access to West Berlin. In 1973 a West Germany-Czechoslovakia pact normalized relations and nullified the 1938 "Munich Agree-

ment." In 1974 Bonn agreed to extend $350 million yearly in long-term credits to East Germany until 1981.

In May 1974 Brandt resigned, saying he took full responsibility for "negligence" for allowing an East German spy to become a member of his staff. Helmut Schmidt, Brandt's finance minister, succeeded him.

West Germany is a member of NATO, EC, European Coal and Steel Community and Council of Europe. Both West and East Germany gained full membership in the UN in Sept. 1973.

Resources and Industries. West Germany has experienced tremendous economic growth since 1950. It is one of the world's top industrial nations. The index of industrial production (1970=100) was 112 for 1974.

West Germany leads Western Europe as a steel producer. Shipyards annually produce more than 1 million gross registered tons of shipping, more than half of it for export. The oil industry has a refining capacity of more than 133 million tons annually. Some of the 2.5 million foreigners working in West Germany left during a 1974-75 economic slowdown.

Germany lost most of its merchant marine during World War II. However, the merchant fleet recovered rapidly and on Jan. 1, 1974, comprised 702 vessels over 1,000 gross tons each.

Frankfurt Rhine-Main airport, 3d largest in Europe, handles annually about 5 million passengers and is 2d largest in freight shipments.

Foreign trade, in thousands of U.S. dollars:

	Imports	Exports
1973	$55,499,000	$68,571,000
1974	$69,381,000	$88,979,000

Education and Religion. The Federal Republic and West Berlin have 33 universities, 9 technical universities and over 100 musical, theological and other institutions of higher education. School attendance is compulsory, ages 6 to 15.

Complete religious freedom is guaranteed by the constitution. The country is 49% Protestant, 44.6% Roman Catholic. The Evangelical Church in Germany (EKD) was formed by the Lutheran, United and Reformed churches after World War II, supplanting an earlier group.

Defense. Armed Forces, 1974, total 480,000. About 200,000 U.S. and 50,000 British troops are stationed in West Germany.

Helgoland, an island of 130 acres in the North Sea, was taken from Denmark by a British Naval Force in 1807 and later ceded to Germany to become a part of Schleswig-Holstein province in return for rights in East Africa. The heavily fortified island was surrendered to Great Britain, May 23, 1945, demilitarized in 1947 and returned to West Germany, Mar. 1, 1952. It is a free port.

The Saar (Fr. Sarre), 10th land (state) of the Federal Republic, is an industrial and mining area N of Lorraine, originally 738 sq. mi., now extended to about 991 and population (1973) of 1.1 million. Capital: Saarbrucken. After World War II it had semi-autonomy and economic links to France until it became a German state again Jan. 1, 1957.

East Germany

Area: 40,646 sq. mi. Population (UN est. 1974): 17,170,000. Capital: East Berlin. Monetary unit: DDR Mark.

The German Democratic Republic was proclaimed in the Soviet sector of Berlin Oct. 7, 1949. Wilhelm Pieck was named president, reelected 1953, and 1957 (died Sept. 7, 1960); Willi Stoph, prime minister; Walter Ulbricht, Communist party secretary. The unicameral legislature is called the Volkskammer or People's Chamber. A ministry of state security, the SSD, and a militarized People's Police were organized.

The Soviet Union proclaimed East Germany a sovereign republic Mar. 25, 1954, but kept Soviet troops there on grounds of security and the 4-power Potsdam agreement.

The Volkskammer approved a constitutional amendment Sept. 12, 1960, that abolished the presidency, replacing it with a new Council of State designated as East Germany's highest governing body, with Walter Ulbricht as chairman.

Ulbricht negotiated a treaty with Poland placing Poland's boundary at the line formed by the Oder and Neisse Rivers. The U.S. registered its disapproval, declaring that it violated the Potsdam agreement and that no boundaries could be settled "unilaterally or bilaterally" outside a peace treaty. The Republic also ratified an agreement with Czechoslovakia, accepting the expulsion of over 2 million Germans from Sudetenland as "permanent and just." Its industry was integrated with other communist nations.

The Volkskammer abolished, 1952, the 5 traditional provinces of East Germany as administrative units in favor of 14 districts of 217 counties. Brandenburg, Mecklenburg, Saxony and Thuringia were divided into 3 districts each, Saxony-Anhalt into 2.

Coincident with the entrance of West Germany into the European Defense Community, May 27 1952, the East German government decreed a prohibited zone 3 mi. deep along its 600-mile border with West Germany and cut Berlin's telephone system into 2 sections. Berlin was further divided by erection of a fortified wall, 1961, but the exodus of refugees from East Germany into West sectors continued though on a much smaller scale. By 1974 37 000 had crossed to the west since 1961.

The regime signed a 20-year treaty of friendship and co-operation with the USSR June 12, 1964.

East Germany suffered severe economic problems until the mid-1960s. A "new economic system" was introduced, easing the former central planning controls and allowing factories to make "profits" provided they were reinvested in operations or distributed to workers as bonuses. By the early 1970s, the economy was highly industrialized, and was the world's ninth greatest industrial power. In May 1972, the few remaining private firms were ordered sold to the government. The nation was credited with the highest standard of living among communist countries. Exports in 1973 totaled $7.521 million, with imports of $7,854,000.

On Apr. 8, 1968, a new constitution, announced as approved by 94.49% of voters, went into effect. It reaffirmed Communist party control and close ties with the USSR. A 1974 amendment removed all mention of reunification.

In May 1971 Ulbricht resigned as leader of the Communist party and was replaced by Erich Honecker, but retained his post as chairman of the Council of State. Ulbricht died Aug. 1, 1973.

Travel restrictions between the 2 Germanies were eased slightly in the first formal treaty signed by the 2, in May 1972. The GDR gained admission to the UN in Sept. 1973.

The U.S. and East Germany established diplomatic relations Sept. 4, 1974. East Germany agreed to negotiate claims of U.S. citizens for properties seized under the Nazis.

Regular armed forces total 145,000. An est. 533,000 Soviet troops are stationed in East Germany.

Ghana

Area: 92,100 sq. mi. Population (Govt. est. 1974): 9,610,000. Capital: Accra. Monetary unit: Cedi.

The Republic of Ghana, a member of the UN and the Commonwealth, is composed of the former British Gold Coast colony including Ashanti and Northern Territories, and British Togoland, former UN trusteeship. Slightly smaller than Oregon, it faces the Gulf of Guinea in Western Africa, bounded N by Upper Volta, E by Togo and W by the Ivory Coast.

Resources and Industries. Ghana is rich in mineral wealth. It ranks among world leaders in production of diamonds (mostly industrial type), manganese, gold, and bauxite.

Ghana is the world's leading cocoa producer; it exports over 350,000 tons annually, about 30% of world output. Timber is 2d in value, including mahogany and rare woods.

The huge Akosombo hydroelectric project on the Volta River, partly financed by U.S., was completed in 1965 and began serving Ghana's 1st giant industry, an aluminum reduction plant near the port of Tema, built by U.S. companies. In 1972-73 the government pressed a program of both small and large farms, "Operation Feed-Yourself," to cut costly food imports.

History and Government. Named after an earlier African state along the Niger River, 800-1076 A.D., Ghana has long been settled by the Ashanti, Akwamu, Ga and other tribes, and was ruled by Great Britain for 113 years. Its independence was gained by rapid steps after 1951 when Britain granted the colony a new constitution and its chief spokesman, Kwame Nkrumah, was elected prime minister. The UN General Assembly on Dec. 13, 1956, approved termination of the British Togoland trusteeship and merger of the territory with the new state following a 1956 plebiscite.

Full independence within the Commonwealth, with a British governor-general, was effective Mar. 6, 1957. It became a republic July 1, 1960, but remained within the Commonwealth. Kwame Nkrumah became president.

In 1964 a referendum gave Nkrumah dictatorial powers and made Ghana a one-party Socialist state.

Nkrumah built hospitals and schools, raised the literacy rate, created a state-owned airline and ship line, but ran the country into debt, jailed hundreds of political dissenters and was accused of corruption.

On Feb. 24, 1966, a National Liberation Council of Army and police officers took over the government. The Council expelled Communist Chinese and East German teachers and technicians. It promised a "balanced neutrality" and slashed expenditures.

Elections were held in Aug. 1969 and Ghana returned to civilian rule, with an elected National Assembly, a prime minister and a president.

On Jan. 13, 1972, a National Redemption Council, headed by Army Col. Ignatius K. Acheampong, took over the government in a bloodless coup. His government has sought national self-reliance.

Greece

Área: 50,547 sq. mi. Population (UN est. 1974): 8,960,000. Capital: Athens. Monetary unit: Drachma.

Greece occupies the southern part of the Balkan peninsula, reaching into the Mediterranean Sea with the Ionian Sea on the W and the Aegean Sea on the E. Its neighbors are Albania, Yugoslavia, Bulgaria and Turkey. The Pindus Mtns. run through the country N to S. Total length of the heavily indented coastline is 9,385 mi. Hundreds of islands account for 8,918 sq. mi. of the total land area, which is approx. that of Alabama; 166 islands are inhabited, among them Crete, Rhodes, Milos, Kerkira (Corfu), Chios, Lesbos, Samos. Principal seaport is Piraeus, near Athens.

Resources and Industries. Greece is still largely agricultural. Only one-fourth of the total area is arable; 13,350,000 of the total of 16,074,000 acres are covered by mountains, lakes and rivers. Four-fifths of the forests are state-owned. Chief agricultural products are wheat, rye, barley, oats, corn, rice, cotton, tobacco, olives, citrus fruits, raisins and figs. Sheep are the most important livestock.

Heavily damaged in World War II, Greece's industrial and agricultural output has far surpassed prewar levels thanks to economic development programs helped in part by U.S. aid. Hydroelectric development is remedying the lack of coal. Principal industries are textiles, food-processing, wine, cement, chemicals, aluminum.

Greek-owned merchant marine tonnage is among world leaders, but much of it is registered under other flags.

Exports are mainly agricultural — tobacco, cotton, citrus fruits, raisins, vegetables. Ores, esp. bauxite, are also important. Aiding the economy is the tourist industry, which produces over $300 million annually.

Foreign trade, in thousands of U.S. dollars:

	Imports	Exports
1973	$3,473,000	$1,454,000
1974	$4,331,000	$2,040,000

History and Government. The achievements of Ancient Greece in art, architecture, science, mathematics, philosophy, drama, literature and democracy became legacies for succeeding ages. Greece reached the height of its glory and power, particularly in the Athenian city-state, in the 5th Century B.C.

Greece fell under Roman rule in the 2d and 1st Centuries B.C. In the 4th Century A.D. it became part of the Byzantine Empire and, after the fall of Constantinople to the Turks in 1453, part of the Ottoman Empire.

Greece won its war of independence from Turkey 1821-1829, and became a kingdom under guarantee of Britain, France and Russia, 1830. A republic was established 1925; the monarchy was restored, 1935, and George II, King of the Hellenes, resumed the throne. In Oct., 1940, Greece rejected an ultimatum from Italy and, when attacked, Greece drove the Italians back into Albania. Nazi support resulted in the defeat and occupation of Greece by Germans, Italians and Bulgarians. By the end of 1944 the invaders withdrew. Communist resistance forces were defeated by Royalist and British troops.

A plebiscite recalled King George II. He died Apr. 1, 1947, and was succeeded by his brother, Paul I.

Communists waged guerrilla war 1947-49 against the government but were defeated with the aid of the U.S. (acting under the Truman Doctrine).

A period of reconstruction and rapid development followed, mainly with conservative governments under Premier Constantine Karamanlis. The Center Union led by George Papandreou won elections in 1963 and 1964. King Constantine, who succeeded his father March 6, 1964, forced Papandreou to resign. A period of political maneuvers ended in the military takeover of April 21, 1967, by Col. George Papadopoulos. King Constantine tried to reverse the consolidation of the harsh dictatorship Dec. 13, 1967, but failed and fled to Italy. Papadopoulos was ousted Nov. 25, 1973, in a coup led by rightist Brig. Demetrius Ioannides.

·Greek army officers serving in the National Guard of Cyprus staged a coup on the island July 15, 1974. Turkey invaded Cyprus a week later, precipitating the collapse of the Greek junta, which was implicated in the Cyprus coup.

The military turned the government over to former Premier Karamanlis, called back from exile. Karamanlis named a civilian cabinet, including anti-junta elements, freed political prisoners, and sought to settle the Cyprus crisis. Karamanlis held elections Nov. 17, 1974, which gave his party a large parliamentary majority, though local elections in 1975 showed leftist gains. A referendum held Dec. 8, 1974, resulted in the proclamation of a parliamentary republic.

Education and Religion. Greek Orthodox is the official church. Nine years of education is compulsory. There are 6 schools of university rank in Athens, and others in Thessaloniki, Patras and Ioannina.

Defense. Military strength totaled 160,000.

Greece is a member of the UN and an associate member of EC. It withdrew its forces from NATO during the 1974 crisis with Turkey over Cyprus.

Dodecanese and Crete

The **Dodecanese** are a group of 13 islands in the southeastern Aegean Sea. They were occupied by Italy during the Balkan War of 1912 against Turkey and though claimed by Greece were retained by Italy. Rhodes is the capital.

After World War II the islands were ceded to Greece at the Paris Conference of Foreign Ministers, June 27, 1946, and annexed Mar. 7, 1948.

Crete, largest Greek island and 5th largest in Mediterranean, original site of Minoan civilization, lies south of the Peloponnesus peninsula and is 160 mi. long, 35 mi. wide, with area of 3,207 sq. mi. Principal towns: Heraklion (Candia) and Khania (Canea).

Grenada

Area: 133 sq. mi. Population: (census 1970) 110,000. Capital: St. George's. Monetary unit: East Caribbean dollar.

Southernmost in the long arc of the Windward Islands, Grenada (pronounced gren-ay-dah) lies in the SE Caribbean, 90 mi. N of the Venezuelan coast. The main island is mountainous and roughly 21 mi. by 12; the nation's territory includes Carriacou and Petit Martinique, 13 sq. mi. together.

Formerly a British Associated State with limited self-government, Grenada became fully independent Feb. 7, 1974 during a general strike. It is the smallest independent nation in the Western Hemisphere. It is a member of the Commonwealth group of nations and the UN.

First European visitor was Christopher Columbus, 1498. First European settlers were French, 1650. The island was held alternately by France and England until final British occupation, 1784. Beginning in 1925, self-government was gradually increased.

Over 50% of the population is of African descent; over 40% of mixed descent, including descendants of indentured laborers from India; there are a few Carib Indians, descendants of the original inhabitants, and a few whites. About 60% are Roman Catholics; others include Anglicans and Methodists. The language is English; a French-African patois is also spoken.

The economy is agricultural; main products are nutmegs, bananas, cocoa, sugar, rum, and mace.

Guatemala

Area: 42,042 sq. mi. Population (UN est. 1973): 5,540,000. Capital: Guatemala City. Monetary unit: Quetzal.

Guatemala lies between Mexico on the N and El Salvador and Honduras on the S. To the east is Belize (British Honduras) which Guatemala claims. It is about the size of Ohio. It faces on both the Caribbean and the Pacific. There are numerous volcanoes in the south, more than a half dozen over 11,000 ft. About 50% of the population is pure Indian and most of the remainder is of mixed Spanish and Indian descent.

There are famous Mayan ruins in Uaxatcun, Tikal and other sites in the north. Other Mayan ruins of temples and monoliths are at Zaculeu in the west and at Quirigua, about 140 mi. from Guatemala City.

Santo Tomas and Puerto Barrios, main ports on the Atlantic, are connected by rail and road with Guatemala City in the highlands and ports on the Pacific.

Resources and Industries. Agriculture is the most important industry, the Guatemalan soil being exceedingly fertile. Coffee accounts for a third of the exports. Other important export crops are sugar, meat, bananas, cotton, chicle gum. Rare woods and cattle are important. Silver, gold, copper, iron, lead, zinc, and nickel are found. A search for oil is being pressed in the north, where natural gas has been found. Shoes and textiles are manufactured.

History and Government. The old Mayan Indian empire flourished in what is today Guatemala for over 1,000 years before the Spanish conquest.

Guatemala was a Spanish colony 1524-1821; briefly a part of Mexico and then of the U.S. of Central America; the republic was established in 1839.

Since 1945 when a liberal government was elected to replace the long-term dictatorship of Jorge Ubico, the country has seen a swing toward socialism, an armed revolt, renewed attempts at social reform and a military coup. Assassinations and political violence from left and right plagued the country. Leftist guerrillas killed a U. S. ambassador in 1968 and a West German ambassador in 1970.

In Mar. 1974 Gen. Kjell Laugerud Garcia was elected president, amidst charges of voting fraud.

Education and Religion. Roman Catholicism is the dominant religion. Education is compulsory. There are 5 universities in Guatemala City, with divisions in Quezaltenango. The language is Spanish.

Guatemala is a member of the UN and OAS.

Guinea

Area: 94,925 sq. mi. Population (UN est. 1974): 4,310,000. Capital: Conakry. Monetary unit: Syli.

Guinea, a former French Overseas Territory, is in western Africa with the Atlantic on the W, Guinea-Bissau, Senegal and Mali on the N, Ivory Coast on the E and Liberia and Sierra Leone on the S. Chief tribes are the Fullah, Malinke, and Soussou. Guinea is about the size of Oregon.

Guinea has a variety of climates, from the humid coastal tropics (Conakry, the capital has an average annual rainfall of 169") to cooler plateaus and uplands. Wildlife is varied and abundant, including elephant, hippopotamus, buffalo, antelope, lion, leopard, chimpanzee.

Resources and Industries. Although Guinea is still primarily an agricultural country, the importance of minerals to its economy is growing. Bauxite, iron and diamonds (both gem and industrial) are the principal minerals. Bauxite mines have been developed by both private Western and Soviet programs.

Economic progress has been aided by large grants from both communist and non-communist countries. Acceleration of agricultural output is a government goal. Chief agricultural exports are bananas and pineapples. Production of rice, the staple food of the population, has been expanded. Other crops include corn, palm nuts, coffee and honey.

History and Government. With France's acquiescence, Guinea proclaimed itself an independent republic Oct. 2, 1958. Premier Sekou Toure became first president. The nation's first constitution was adopted Nov. 12, 1958. It provided for rule by a president with a term of 7 years and a National Assembly elected by universal suffrage. The Political Bureau of the single legal party, the Parti Democratique de Guinee, exercises great power in making governmental decisions. Guinea is a member of the UN and OAU. French is the official language.

It has agreements with Czechoslovakia, East Germany, Poland, USSR and Communist China, and has criticized U. S. "colonial" attitudes in Africa, but continues to avow a neutral course.

Guinea-Bissau

Area: 13,948 sq. mi. Population (UN est. 1974): 520,000. Capital: Bissau.

Portuguese Guinea, a colonial possession of Portugal, achieved independence as Guinea-Bissau, a republic, Sept. 10, 1974. Almost twice the size of New Jersey, it is in West Africa, facing the Atlantic to the W. with Senegal to the N and Guinea to the E and S. The land is mostly level and low, with forests, swamps and numerous offshore islands.

Portuguese mariners explored the area in the mid-15th Century; the slave trade flourished in the 17th and 18th Centuries, but in the 19th colonization began. In the early 20th Century, Portuguese troops put down uprisings in the interior.

Beginning in the 1960s, the African Party for the Independence of Guinea-Bissau and the Cape Verde Islands conducted guerrilla warfare against Portuguese troops and formed a government in the interior with an elected National Assembly. The party's founder, Dr. Amilcar Cabral was slain in nearby Guinea in 1973 and his brother Luiz became Guinea-Bissau's first president.

The Cape Verde Islands, once linked with Portuguese Guinea, lie in the Atlantic some 300 mi. NW of Bissau. The islands, independent in 1975, were expected to merge with Guinea-Bissau.

Most of the Guinea-Bissau population is black with about 2,200 white and 10,000 of mixed descent. Most follow tribal religions; a large minority are Moslems.

There is little industry. Chief products are peanuts, palm oil and hides. In 1972 a large deposit of bauxite and traces of oil were discovered. The country belongs to the UN and OAU.

Guyana

Area: 83,000 sq. mi. Population (UN est. 1974): 770,000. Capital: Georgetown. Monetary unit: Guyana dollar.

British Guiana, a British colony for 152 years, became the independent nation of Guyana on May 26, 1966. It was the first South American nation to become independent since Venezuela in 1830.

Fronting on the Atlantic in northern South America, Guyana borders on Venezuela, Brazil and Surinam. It is about the size of Kansas. The population is about 50% of East Indian (from India) descent, 31.5% of African descent, 12% of mixed descent, 4.6% American Indian descent, and small numbers of Chinese or European descent. Ethnic tensions have influenced political life.

Dense tropical forests cover much of the land, although a flat coastal area about 50 mi. wide, where 90% of the population lives, provides space for agriculture.

Sugar and rice are the main cash crops and account for almost half the total exports. Other products are coconuts, coffee, cocoa, citrus fruits, timber and livestock.

The main industry is the mining of bauxite ore; Guyana is the 5th largest producer of the mineral, supplying over 6% of the world's needs; the industry has been nationalized. Also exported are gold and diamonds. Deposits of a wide range of other minerals have been found but not yet exploited.

Manufacturing has shown an average 5% annual growth; products include cigarettes, rum, clothing, furniture, drugs and insecticides.

Guyana was visited in 1499 by Spanish sailors. The country became a British possession in 1814. African slaves and indentured servants from India were brought in to work on plantations. The Indians soon outnumbered the Negro population and still do. Venezuela has claimed ownership of the western half of Guyana. In 1970 an agreement suspended the claim for 12 years. The Surinam border is also disputed.

A parliamentary democracy with a British governor-general since 1966, Guyana became a republic, with a president, prime minister and National Assembly on Feb. 23, 1970. It is a UN and Commonwealth member.

Haiti

Area: 10,714 sq. mi. Population (Govt. est. 1974): 4,510,000. Capital: Port-Au-Prince. Monetary unit: Gourde.

Haiti occupies the western third of the island known as Hispaniola, the second largest of the Greater Antilles, lying between Cuba on the W and Puerto Rico on the E. The boundary which separates Haiti from the Dominican Republic to the E is 241 mi. long. Haiti is a little larger in area than Maryland.

Blacks comprise over 90% of the population, the remainder being mixed descendants of both slaves and French settlers.

Resources and Industries. Major mineral exports are bauxite and copper. Other minerals are gold, silver and cement.

Coffee is the chief product, along with sisal, cotton, sugar, bananas, cocoa, tobacco and rice. Molasses and rum are produced; valuable woods are exported.

Haiti encourages tourism and is served by several major airlines, with an international jet airport at Port-au-Prince. However, tourist spending and private foreign investment in Haiti dwindled under the regime of President Francois Duvalier. They revived in 1971 after his death. Economic improvement was reported, 1972-74, but drought and famine struck in 1975.

History and Government. Haiti, visited by Columbus, 1492, and a French colony from 1677, attained its independence, 1804, following the rebellion begun by Toussaint L'Ouverture. There were Republican constitutions in 1806 and 1816. In 1811 Henri Christophe proclaimed himself king in the north; the south continued to be a republic, with a president. Henri died in 1820 and President Jean Pierre Boyer reunited the nation. Following a period of political violence, 1910-1915, the U. S. occupied the country. The occupation terminated Aug. 14, 1934.

Five regimes failed between 1950-1957. In Sept., 1957, Dr. Duvalier was elected president for a 6-year term. In June 1964 a new constitution made Dr. Duvalier president-for-life. There were unsuccessful outbreaks against his rule in 1963 and 1970. He died Apr. 21, 1971, and was succeeded by his son, Jean-Claude Duvalier, 19, as president-for-life.

Haiti is a member of the UN and OAS.

Education and Religion. Roman Catholicism and Voodoo are the main religions. Education is compulsory, but illiteracy rate is est. at 90%. French is the official language of the country, but French Creole, a dialect, is spoken by the majority.

Honduras

Area: (Govt. est.): 43,277 sq. mi. Population (UN est. 1974): 2,930,000. Capital: Tegucigalpa. Monetary unit: Lempira.

Honduras is a republic in Central or Middle America, bounded on the N by the Caribbean; E and S by Nicaragua; S by Pacific Ocean and El Salvador; W by Guatemala. It is about the size of Pennsylvania.

The Caribbean coast is 500 mi. long. On the Pacific side the coast, on the Gulf of Fonseca, is 40 mi. long. There are ports on both coasts. The country is mountainous, very fertile, with rich forests. The inhabitants are mostly of Spanish and Indian descent.

At Copan, near the western border, are the imposing remains of a large Mayan city which flourished around the 4th Century A.D.; it had declined by the time Spaniards arrived in 1576.

Resources and Industries. Minerals are abundant but undeveloped and include gold, silver, copper, lead, zinc, iron, antimony and coal. The chief export is bananas. Coffee, timber, cotton, sugar, tobacco and cattle raising are important.

Manufacturing industries are small but growing;

they include clothing, textiles, cement, chemicals, food products. In 1974 the government said it would nationalize the lumber industry; lumber export is controlled by the government.

History and Government. Honduras became independent after freeing itself from Spain, Sept. 15, 1821, and from the Fed. of Central America, 1838.

Pres. Ramon Villeda Morales, elected Nov. 15, 1957, was overthrown in a military coup Oct. 3, 1963, and replaced by a military regime headed by Oswaldo Lopez Arellano. The country returned to constitutional government and Lopez was inaugurated president June 6, 1965.

The 1965 constitution provided for a president and Congress, both elected for 6 years. In free elections, Mar. 28, 1971, Ramon Ernesto Cruz was chosen president. In Dec. 1972 Lopez seized the presidency again; he was ousted by the army in 1975 over charges of pervasive bribery by United Brands Co. of the U.S.

Honduras and El Salvador fought a 5-day war in July 1969 over the presence in Honduras of 300,000 Salvadorean workers and settlers. After new clashes in 1970, a demilitarized zone was agreed on.

Honduras is a member of the UN and OAS.

Education and Religion. Education is secular and free. The literacy rate is about 50%. Roman Catholicism is the prevailing religion. The language is Spanish.

Hungary

Area: 35,919 sq. mi. Population (Govt. est. 1974): 10,460,000. Capital: Budapest. Monetary unit: Forint.

The Hungarian People's Republic, in central Europe, is bounded by Czechoslovakia, the USSR, Romania, Yugoslavia and Austria. It is about the size of Indiana.

The Danube forms the Czech border in the NW, then swings S to bisect the country. The eastern half of Hungary is mainly a great fertile plain, the Alfold; the west and north are hilly.

Resources and Industries. Before World War II, Hungary was primarily agricultural, but industry has surpassed it in value. The index of industrial production (1970 = 100) was 129 for 1974. Most means of production have been socialized.

Major economic reforms were launched early in 1968, switching from a central planning system to one where market forces and a profit principle control much of production. Productivity was reportedly increased.

About 70% of foreign trade is with Eastern bloc countries. Value of imports reached $5.576 million in 1974, with exports at $5.130 million.

In addition to a wide range of grains and vegetable crops, fruit production has expanded. Near Tokay, in the northeast, the best-known Hungarian wines are vinted.

Industries include iron and steel, machines, machine tools, chemicals, vehicles, railways and communications equipment, milling and distilling. Hungary has become an important supplier of industrial products to communist bloc countries. Hungary produces large amounts of bauxite. Also important is natural gas.

History and Government. Earliest settlers, chiefly Slav and Germanic, were overrun by Huns and Magyars from the east. Stephen I (997-1038) was made king by Pope Silvester II in 1001 A.D. The country suffered repeated Turkish invasions in the 15th-17th centuries. After the defeats of the Turks, 1686-1697, Austria dominated, but Hungary obtained concessions until it regained internal independence in 1867, with the emperor of Austria as king of Hungary in a dual monarchy with a single diplomatic service. Defeated with the Central Powers in 1918, Hungary lost Transylavania to Romania, Croatia and Bacska to Yugoslavia, Slovakia and Carpatho-Ruthenia to

Czechoslovakia. A republic under Michael Karoly and a bolshevist revolt under Bela Kun were followed by a vote for a monarchy in 1920 with Admiral Nicholas Horthy as regent.

Hungary joined Germany in World War II; Horthy was removed and Nazi supporters put in power, 1944. Russian troops captured most of the country, 1945. By terms of an armistice with the Allied powers Hungary agreed to give up territory acquired by the 1938 dismemberment of Czechoslovakia and to return to its borders of 1937.

Hungary declared for a republic Feb. 1, 1946, and elected Zoltan Tildy president. In 1947 the communists forced Tildy out. A Soviet-type constitution was adopted Aug. 18, 1949, which vests formal power in a Presidential Council and a National Assembly of 349 members elected for 4-year-terms. Hungary is a member of the UN and Warsaw Pact.

Premier Imre Nagy, in office since mid-1953, was ousted for his moderate policy of favoring agriculture and consumer production, April 18, 1955.

In 1956, popular demands for the ousting of Erno Gero, Communist party secretary, and for formation of a government by Nagy, resulted in the latter's appointment Oct. 23; demonstrations against communist rule developed into open revolt when police fired on demonstrators. Gero called in Soviet forces. The insurrection appeared halted by Oct. 18 when Nagy said the Soviet Union had agreed to withdraw its troops. However, by Nov. 1 Soviet forces again surrounded Budapest and launched a massive attack against the city Nov. 4 with 200,000 troops, 2,500 tanks and armored cars.

The bid for free government was crushed. Estimates varied from 6,500 to 32,000 dead. Many rebels were reported executed and thousands deported. Between 170,000 and 196,000 persons fled the country. The U.S. received 38,248 under a refugee emergency program. In the spring of 1963 the regime freed many anti-communists and captives from the revolution in a sweeping amnesty.

Nagy was executed by the Russians. Janos Kadar, sponsored by the USSR, became first secretary of the Hungarian Workers (Communist) party. By the 1970's, Hungary led the communist nations in tolerance for cultural freedoms and small private enterprise.

In 1973 Hungary agreed to pay the U.S. $18,900,000 for nationalized U.S. properties in Hungary.

Education and Religion. There is no state religion, and all are tolerated. About two-thirds of the population were Roman Catholics; most of the remainder, Calvinists.

Public school education is compulsory and free for 8 years. Most church schools were nationalized in 1948. There are 91 insititutes of higher learning. The language is Hungarian (Magyar).

Jozsef Cardinal Mindszenty, Roman Catholic primate, was jailed in 1949. He was freed by the 1956 insurgents and granted refuge in the U. S. Embassy. In 1971 he went into exile in Vienna. In 1975 he was removed as primate by Pope Paul VI.

Defense. Military forces totaled 103,000. About 40,000 USSR troops are stationed in Hungary.

Iceland

Area: 39,702 sq. mi. Population (Govt. est. 1974): 220,000. Capital: Reykjavik. Monetary unit: Krona.

The Republic of Iceland is an island of volcanic origin, close to the Arctic Circle in the North Atlantic. There are geysers and hot springs and the climate is modified by the Gulf Stream. Iceland is about the size of Virginia.

Natural hot water from volcanic springs is piped into towns and provides heat for office buildings, homes and hot houses. In Jan. 1973 a volcanic erup-

tion on Heimaey forced evacuation of 5,500 residents of the small island off the SE coast of Iceland.

Resources and Industries. Agriculture engages about 13% of the population; industry and services 70%; fisheries 14%. About six-sevenths of the land is unproductive and only about 65,000 acres are under cultivation, producing potatoes, turnips and hay. The fishing industry is most important. It includes herring, cod and haddock. Fish products, in salted, smoked, canned or frozen form, account for 78% of exports.

Iceland's largest industrial plants include an ammonium nitrate factory, an aluminum smelter, a cement factory and a diatomite plant and hydroelectric power is being developed.

History and Government. Iceland was an independent republic, 930-1262; then it joined with Norway. The two came under Danish rule in 1380. Denmark acknowledged Iceland as a sovereign state, 1918, united with Denmark only in that the Danish King Christian X, was also king of Iceland. In 1941 the Althing (Parliament) voted to dissolve all ties with Denmark, and adopt the constitution of a republic. The republic, with a president and prime minister was proclaimed June 17, 1944.

Iceland celebrated the 1,000th anniversary of the Althing, the oldest parliamentary assembly in the world, in 1930. The prime minister and his cabinet are responsible to the Althing. There is universal suffrage for men and women at age 20.

In 1972 Iceland barred foreign ships from fishing within 50 mi. of its coast. British trawlers defied the ban and in 1973 were fired on by Icelandic gunboats. British frigates were sent to the disputed waters. In Nov. 1973 the dispute was settled; Britain agreed to limit its catch.

A conservative coalition won power in June 1974 and stopped plans to oust U. S. NATO Air Force and Navy personnel, which totalled 2,900 in 1975.

Education and Religion. The Icelandic language has maintained its purity, as in Eddas and Sagas, for 1,000 years. Danish and English also are taught. Eight years of elementary education is compulsory. There is no illiteracy. There are 5 colleges and a university. The national church is Evangelical Lutheran, but there is complete religious freedom.

Defense: Iceland has no Army, Navy, Air Force or forts. It is a charter member of NATO. It is also a member of the UN, Council of Europe and Nordic Council.

India

Area: 1,229,919 sq. mi. Population (Govt. est. 1974): 586,270,000. Capital: New Delhi. Monetary unit: Rupee.

An independent republic since 1950 and a member of the Commonwealth, India occupies most of the subcontinent of India. It is a third the size of the U.S.

India's climate varies from tropical heat in the south to the nearly Arctic cold of the Himalayas. Approximately 22.3% of the area is forested.

The population is 80% rural, 20% urban. The annual increase rate, 2½%, causes food and housing shortages. In 1967 the government supplemented its birth control programs with monetary inducements to men to volunteer for sterilization. In 1974 the government reported 14 million persons had undergone operations.

Sikkim, bordered by Tibet, Bhutan, Nepal and India, formerly British protected, became a protectorate of India in 1950. Area, 2,818 sq. mi.; population 1974, 210,000; capital, Gangtok. In Apr. 1973 the chogyal, the hereditary ruler, asked Indian troops to help suppress demonstrations against his rule. In May he and India signed an agreement providing for a legislative assembly. In Sept. 1974 India's Parliament voted to make Sikkim an associate Indian state, absorbing it into India. The monarchy was abolished in an April, 1975 referendum.

Kashmir, a predominantly Moslem region in the northwest, has been in dispute between India and Pakistan since 1947 when British rule was ending and Indian and Pakistani troops entered the area. A cease-fire was negotiated by the UN, Jan. 1, 1949; it gave Pakistan control of one-third of the area, in the west and northwest, and India the remaining two-thirds, the Indian state of Jammu and Kashmir. In late Aug. 1965, clashes broke out along the line and soon involved the armed forces of the 2 nations in a spreading war.

On Sept. 20, 1965, the UN Security Council demanded a cease-fire; both sides agreed. The USSR invited India and Pakistan to a conference at Tash-kent, USSR, and on Jan. 10, 1966, the 2 signed the "Tashkent Declaration," pledging to withdraw their forces to behind the old cease-fire line. A new truce line, slightly altering the old cease-fire line, was agreed on in Dec. 1972, accommodating changes made during Dec. 1971 fighting.

There were also clashes in April 1965 along the Assam-East Pakistan border and in the **Rann** (swamp) **of Cutch** area along the West Pakistan-Gujarat border near the Arabian Sea. An international arbitration commission on Feb. 19, 1968, awarded 90% of the Rann to India, 10% to Pakistan.

France, 1952-54, peacefully yielded to India its 5 colonies on the Bay of Bengal, former French India, comprising Pondicherry, Kirkal, Mahe, Yanaon and Chandernagor, totalling 196 sq. mi. and 346,000 pop.

Goa, 1,426 sq. mi., pop., 1962, 626,978, which had been ruled by Portugal since 1505 A.D., was taken by India by military action Dec. 18, 1961, together with 2 other Portuguese enclaves, Damao and Diu, located about 250 mi. S of Bombay.

India is a union of 22 states and 9 centrally administered union territories.

Resources and Industries. Agriculture occupies 70% of the workers. Principal food products are rice, corn, millet, wheat, barley, coffee, sugar cane, spices, tea, cashew nuts. Other important products include cotton, copra, coir, jute, linseed, rubber, lumber.

Severe droughts in northern areas have repeatedly threatened mass starvation and brought large shipments of grain from the U.S. In July 1967 plentiful rains broke the drought; there were bumper crops, 1968-72; the drought and food shortages returned in 1972-75.

Indian agriculture has made progress with high-yield seeds, fertilizers, irrigation and limited mechanization.

For many years India has had large textile industries with a wide variety of cotton, woolen and silk products. In the 1960s, other industries, including steel, processed foods, cement, machinery, chemicals and fertilizers came into prominence, along with many finished products such as sewing machines, typewriters, bicycles, telephones and transportation equipment.

India's 1st nuclear power plant, built with U.S. help, was dedicated in 1970 near Bombay; Canada helped India build 2 reactors. In May 1974 India exploded a nuclear device underground, assertedly for peaceful development. Canada halted shipments of nuclear equipment and material to India and the U.S. announced a halt in its shipments. An Indian space satellite was launched by the USSR April 19, 1975.

The 1972 index of industrial production (1963=100) was 154; the 1973 index rose only to 155. Much industrial production, distribution, and prices are regulated by law. Railroads, airlines, banks, insurance and coal industries are state-owned, as are some steel plants.

India is a leading producer of coal, mica and manganese; also important are salt, iron ore, bauxite and gypsum. Exports include tea, sugar, raw and processed jute, cotton fabrics and other textiles, tanned hides and skins, manganese ore, pepper, tobacco. Largest trade is with the U.S. There are indications of offshore oil in the Bay of Bengal.

Foreign trade, in thousands of U.S. dollars:

	Imports	Exports
1973	$3,066,000	$2,940,000
1974	$4,775,000	$3,904,000

History and Government. India has one of the oldest civilizations in the world. Excavations trace the Indus Valley civilization back for at least 5,000 years. Paintings in the mountain caves of Ajanta in South India, richly carved temples, the Taj Mahal in Agra and the Kutab Minar in Delhi are among relics of the past.

Vasco da Gama established Portuguese trading posts 1498-1503. The Dutch followed. The British East India Co. sent Capt. William Hawkins, 1609, to get concessions from the Mogul emperor for spices and textiles. Operating as the East India Co. the British gained control of most of India. The British parliament assumed political direction; under Lord Bentinck, 1828-35, rule by rajahs was curbed, infanticide stopped, suttee (suicide of a widow on her husband's funeral pyre) made illegal. After the Sepoy troops mutinied, 1857-58, the British supported the native rulers.

Nationalism grew rapidly after World War I. The National Congress and the Moslem League demanded constitutional reform. A leader emerged in Mohandas K. Gandhi (called Mahatma, or Great Soul), born Oct. 2, 1869, assassinated Jan. 30, 1948. A Hindu, trained in law in England, he began advocating self-rule, non-violence, pursuit of native handicrafts, removal of untouchability (which forced millions of poor to remain menials by heredity) in 1919. In 1930 he launched "civil disobedience," including boycott of British goods and rejection of taxes without representation.

In 1935 Britain gave India a constitution providing a bicameral federal congress. Suffrage was granted about 30 million. Mohammed Ali Jinnah, head of the Moslem League, sought creation of a Moslem nation, Pakistan.

Following more than 40 years' active struggle for freedom by both Hindus and Moslems, the British government announced Feb. 20, 1947, its intention to partition India into 2 dominions and set June, 1948, for British withdrawal from India. Aug. 15, 1947, was designated Indian Independence Day. India became a self-governing member of the Commonwealth and a member of the UN. The dominion became a democratic republic, Jan. 26, 1950.

It was estimated that more than 11 million refugees (Hindus and Moslems) crossed the India-Pakistan borders in a mass transferral of some of the two peoples during 1947; about 200,000 were killed in communal fighting.

The constitution provides for a president, elected for a 5-year term by an electoral college consisting of members of both houses of Parliament (Council of States and House of the People), and elected members of the lower houses of the federating states. A Council of Ministers (cabinet) is headed by a prime minister who is the practical head of the government. The federating states have governors, appointed by the president, at the head of state organizations similar to the federal system.

Prime Minister Mrs. Indira Gandhi, named Jan. 19, 1966, succeeded Lal Bahadur Shastri, who on June 2, 1964, succeeded India's first prime minister, Jawaharlal Nehru. Mrs. Gandhi, Nehru's daughter, was no relation to Mahatma Gandhi. Nehru, prime minister from the beginning of India's independence in 1947, died May 27, 1964.

Long the dominant power in India's politics, the Congress party lost some of its near monopoly by 1967. The party split into New and Old Congress parties in 1969. Mrs. Gandhi's New Congress party won control of the House.

Threatened with adverse court rulings in a voting law case, an opposition protest campaign and strikes, Gandhi invoked emergency provisions of the constitution June, 1975. Thousands of opponents were arrested and press censorship imposed. Measures to control prices, protect small farmers and improve productivity were adopted.

After Pakistan troops began attacks on Bengali separatists in East Pakistan, Mar. 25, 1971, some 10 million refugees fled into India. On Aug. 9, India and the USSR signed a 20-year friendship pact while U.S.-India relations soured. India and Pakistan went to war Dec. 3, 1971, on both the East and West fronts. Pakistan troops in the East surrendered Dec. 16; Pakistan agreed to a cease-fire in the West Dec. 17.

India and Pakistan signed a pact agreeing to withdraw troops from their borders and seek peaceful solutions, July 3, 1972. In Aug. 1973 India agreed to release 93,000 Pakistanis held prisoner since 1971; the return was completed in Apr. 1974.

Education and Religion. The constitution provides for free, compulsory education through age 14. There are now 90 universities, 1,946 colleges, and 27 research institutes.

There are 14 language groups, 12 originating from Sanskrit, and over 1,600 "mother tongues." Hindi is spoken by nearly 50%, with Urdu, the principal Moslem language, spoken by 10%. Hindi became the official language in Jan. 1965 with English the associate official language. Much government work and instruction at universities is done in English.

The religion of 83% of the people is Hinduism. The constitution guarantees freedom of worship. Moslems are the largest minority, 61,417,934 in the 1971 census; there were 14,223,382 Christians, 10,378,797 Sikhs, 3,812,325 Buddhists, 2,604,646 Jains. Hindus totaled 453,292,086.

Defense. Military forces total 978,000.

Indonesia

Area: 735,268 sq. mi. Population (1973 est.): 127,-590. Capital: Jakarta. Monetary unit: Rupiah.

Indonesia, world's largest archipelago, lies along the Equator SE of Asia, N and NW of Australia. Indonesia comprises about 13,000 islands, including Java (one of the most densely populated areas in the world with 1,500 persons to the sq. mi.), Sumatra, Kalimantan (most of Borneo), Sulawesi (Celebes) and West Irian (Irian Jaya, the west half of New Guinea). Among others are Bangka, Billiton, Madura, Bali, Lombok, Sumbawa, part of Timor. The land area is 6 times that of New Mexico.

Many races are included, the principal ones being Achinese, Bataks, Menangkabaus, Javanese, Sundanese, Madurese, Balinese, Sasaks, Menadonese, Buginese, Dayaks and Papuans.

The capital, called Batavia by the Dutch, is Jakarta, on the island of Java.

Resources and Industries. Indonesia is one of the richest countries in natural resources. There are vast supplies of tin, oil and coal, and sizable deposits of bauxite, manganese, copper, nickel, gold and silver.

Agriculture occupies 80% of the population. Products include rice, maize, casava, peanuts, soybeans, tobacco, coffee, rubber, cinchona, pepper, kapok coconuts, palm oil, tea, sugar and indigo.

Inflation spiraled during the 1960's, but by 1969 comparative stability was achieved and a 5-year development plan was undertaken. Oil accounts for more than half of export income, followed by rubber and timber. Indonesia is the world's 12th largest oil producer. There are food processing, textile and other small factories.

History and Government. Until March, 1942, Indonesia was a Netherlands overseas territory. Following Japanese military occupation, 1942-1945, nationalists, led by Dr. Sukarno and Dr. Hatta, proclaimed a republic Aug. 17, 1945. Four years of intermittent warfare between Netherlands and Indonesian forces ended with agreements signed Nov. 2, 1949, transferring sovereignty over all Indonesia

except Netherlands New Guinea (West Irian) to a new interim government effective Dec. 27, 1949. Dr. Sukarno was elected president, Dec. 16, 1949. On July 20, 1950, the member states agreed to form a strongly centralized government; a unitarian state with an amended constitution was proclaimed Aug. 15 and its name formally changed to Republic of Indonesia. It joined the UN 1950.

After the Dutch in Nov. 1957 rejected proposals for new negotiations over West Irian, Indonesia's government stepped up the seizure of Dutch property. A U.S. mediator's plan was adopted in 1962, providing that West Irian be turned over temporarily to the UN, then to Indonesia. Under the agreement Indonesia pledged to hold a plebiscite allowing the people of West Irian the choice of staying with Indonesia or separating from it. The UN turned the area over to Indonesia May 1, 1963. In 1969, voting by tribal chiefs and other representatives favored staying with Indonesia.

President Sukarno suspended the original elected 257-member Parliament Mar. 5, 1960, and announced a new 261-member appointed group, Mar. 27, and swept aside anti-leftist criticism. He was named president-for-life May 18, 1963.

The USSR announced in 1964 plans to step up its contributions of modern arms to Indonesia to aid in attempting to "crush" the new nation. Malaysia, formation of which Indonesia opposed. In 1964 and 1965 Indonesia staged numerous guerrilla raids into Malaysia.

Indonesia withdrew from the UN in Jan. 1965. Many anti-American demonstrations were staged at U.S. consulates, including stonings, during the year.

Indonesia's large, pro-Peking Communist party tried to seize complete control Sept. 30, 1965, taking strategic points and murdering 6 high generals. The army smashed the coup and later intimated that Sukarno had played a role in it. In Central and East Java, Reds seized control of several districts and fighting continued. It was later reported that at least 100,000 communists were executed.

Gen. Suharto was named head of the Army; on Mar. 11, 1966, Sukarno turned over all government powers to him but continued as president, apparently in name only. Gen. Suharto was officially named president for a 5-year term by the Consultative Assembly Mar. 27, 1968. He was reelected in Mar. 1973.

On Aug. 11, 1966, Indonesia and Malaysia signed an agreement ending the Sukarno policy of hostility to Malaysia. On Sept. 28 Indonesia resumed membership in the UN. The U. S. resumed economic aid.

In July 1971, in the first popular vote in 16 years, a coalition party backing the Suharto government won a strong majority in the House of Representatives.

Education and Religion. 90% of the inhabitants are Moslems, the remainder Christians, Hindus and Buddhists. There is compulsory primary education for children 6 to 12, plus optional secondary training and higher education. There are 7 institutions of higher education. Many languages are spoken; the official one is Bahasa Indonesia, derived from Malay.

Iran

Area: 636,363 sq. mi. Population (UN est. 1974): 31,960,000. Capital: Tehran. Monetary unit: Riai.

A constitutional monarchy, Iran is a mountainous land, much of it a high plateau region, in SW Asia. Slightly larger than Alaska, it has coastlines on the Caspian Sea, Persian Gulf and Gulf of Oman. For neighbors it has the USSR, Afghanistan, Pakistan, Iraq and Turkey. Large salt deserts comprise 25% of the land but there are many oases and forest areas.

Tehran, Isfahan, Shiraz and Abadan have jet airports. Shiraz is noted for ancient ruins of Persepolis.

Resources and Industries. Iran is the world's 4th-largest oil producer and 2d largest exporter; petroleum provides most of its foreign exchange and government income. Iran refused to join the 1973-74 Arab oil embargo, but did join in raising oil prices.

In 1974 Iran invested some of its oil wealth in a multi-billion dollar trade pact with France including nuclear energy facilities; a 25% interest in West Germany's Krupp enterprises, and a $1.2 billion loan to Britain. In 1975, Iran signed an 8-year agreement to facilitate $25 billion in purchases in the U.S., to further Iran's five-year development plan, including 8 large nuclear power plants.

Other mineral wealth includes chromite, copper, iron, lead, manganese, zinc, barite, sulphur and coal. Also mined are emeralds and turquoise.

Foreign trade, in thousands of U. S. dollars:

	Imports	Exports
1973	$3,370,000	$ 6,939,000
1974	$5,974,000	$26,110,000

The first Iranian steel mill, near Isfahan, was built by the Soviet Union and paid for by natural gas piped to the USSR. Iran has contracted with the French for development of a petrochemical industry. There are cement, vehicle assembly and sugar refining plants.

Agriculture is a prime industry; wheat, barley, corn, rice, fruits, gums, wool, tobacco, raw silk, sugar beets and cotton are the chief products. Some wines are famous, as are Persian carpets. Sturgeon fishing in Caspian Sea is important, especially for caviar. Major dams built in the 1960s provide hydroelectric power and aid irrigation.

Under Shah Mohammed Reza Pahlavi's leadership, Iran has undergone an economic and social revolution. Improvements included land reform, the spread of literacy and wide gains in women's rights.

History and Government. Iran (related to Aryan) is the proper name to the country long referred to as Persia. The Iranians, who came from the E during the 2d millenium B.C., were an Indo-European people related to the Aryans of India, and included Medes, Persians and other groups. Use of the name Iran became widespread in the 1920s and 1930s.

In 549 B.C. Cyrus the Great united the Medes and Persians in the Persian Empire, conquered Babylonia, 538 B.C., restored Jerusalem to the Jews. Darius I began the invasion of Greece, was defeated at Salamis, 480 B.C. and Plataea, 479 B.C. Alexander the Great of Macedon defeated Darius III 333 B.C.

Subsequently Persia was ruled by the Seleucids; the Parthians beginning c. 250 B.C.; the Sassanians, c. 226 A.D. Arabs brought Islam to Persia in the 7th Century and for many years the religious-political Caliphate ruled the land. Omar Khayyam (c. 1050-c. 1123) wrote his famous Rubaiyat and created a calendar renowned for its accuracy.

Mongols invaded the country in 1250 and again under Tamerlane c. 1370. After the downfall of the Mongols in 1502 Persia became a monarchy under a shah.

In 1906 a constitution was enacted. It provided for an executive with power vested in a cabinet and government officials who act in the name of the shah. The legislature has a national assembly (Majlis) elected for 4 years and a senate of 60, 30 elected and 30 nominated by the shah. Women voted and were elected to the legislature for the first time in 1963. Only one party is tolerated.

The shah is Mohammed Reza Pahlavi (born Oct. 26, 1919), ascended in 1941. After divorcing his first two wives for failing to bear a male heir, the shah married Farah Diba Dec. 21, 1959; Crown Prince Reza Pahlavi was born Oct. 31, 1960.

British and Russian forces entered Iran Aug. 25, 1941, withdrawing later. Britain and the USSR signed an agreement Jan. 29, 1942, to respect Iran's integrity and give economic aid. In 1946 a Soviet attempt to take over the Azerbijan region in the NW was defeated when a puppet regime was ousted by force.

In 1951 the Majlis nationalized the oil industry, the Anglo-Iranian Oil Co. closed its refinery.

The shah in 1954 signed an agreement with a consortium of British, U.S., Dutch and French companies. In 1973 a new agreement gave the National Iranian Oil Co. control over all operations.

In 1969-74 Iran and Iraq were involved in a dispute over Iran's right to use the Shatt al Arab, a border river estuary, for shipping. Border clashes, reflecting rivalry for power in the Persian Gulf area, continued in 1974. Iraq acceeded to Iran's border claims in a June 13, 1975 pact. In late 1971, Iran occupied 3 islands at the mouth of the gulf, claimed by states of the United Arab Emirates. Iran in the 1970's modernized its military forces, aided by multi-billion dollar purchases from the U.S. Economic aid to Egypt, and military aid against leftist Oman rebels advanced Iran's regional status in the 1970s.

Education and Religion. The Shiah branch of Islam predominates. Education is free and nominally compulsory. There are 7 universities. A Literacy Corps of high school and college graduates teaches in rural areas in lieu of military service. A Health Corps is patterned after the Literacy Corps. The language is Farsi (Persian), written in Arabic script.

Defense. Military strength totals over 250,000.

Iran is a member of the UN and CENTO.

Iraq

Area: 167,567 sq. mi. Population (Govt. est. 1974): 10,770,000. Capital: Baghdad. Monetary unit: Dinar.

Iraq is the modern name for Mesopotamia, the area around the Euphrates and Tigris Rivers, about twice the size of Utah. It is bounded by Turkey, Iran, the Persian (also called Arabian) Gulf, Kuwait, Saudi Arabia, Jordan and Syria.

The country is mostly alluvial plain. The temperature varies widely: 120°F in the shade is common, contrasted with severe frosts in the winter.

Resources and Industries. Wheat, barley, rice, dates, millet and cotton are the chief crops, with tobacco in the Kurdish hills. Sheep are raised in the north and wool and skins are exported; textiles are produced.

Iraq is the world's 8th largest oil producer. About 70% of its national income is from oil. New fields were developed with USSR aid, 1970-72. In June 1972 Iraq nationalized the Western-controlled Iraq Petroleum Co., and nationalized other U.S. oil interests in Oct. 1973. Exports, 1974, were $7.551 billion.

History and Government. The Tigris-Euphrates valley was the site of the ancient cities of Eridu, Ur, Nineveh and Babylon. The Sumerian culture of 3000 B.C. influenced Crete, Egypt and Greece.

Iraq, then known as Mesopotamia, was taken from Turkey in World War I. The League of Nations gave a mandate to Britain, which ended 1932 when Iraq was recognized as a sovereign state.

Emir Faisal, then king of the Hejaz, was chosen ruler by a referendum in 1921; a constitutional monarchy was created in 1924. On his death, 1933, he was succeeded by his son Ghazi, who died, 1939; succeeded by his son, Faisal II.

King Faisal was assassinated July 14, 1958, when the Free Officers, led by Brig. Gen. Abdul Karim Kassem revolted and proclaimed Iraq "part of the Arab nation." Gen. Kassem became premier of a republic. Iraq received Soviet arms aid. It withdrew from the Baghdad pact and 3 U.S. arms agreements.

After several coups, the government was taken over by a group headed by Gen. Ahmed Hassan al-Bakr, a member of the international Baath Socialist Party, July 17, 1968.

On June 7, 1967, Iraq broke diplomatic relations with the U. S. following Egyptian charges that America was aiding Israel in the 6-day, 1967 war, but U.S. exports grew in the 1970s.

In 1969, in a series of trials, Iraq condemned and executed more than a score of citizens as spies for Israel, Iran and the U.S. It had border clashes for several years with Iran in a dispute over navigation rights on the Shatt al Arab, a border river estuary, till a 1975 pact conceded Iranian claims. Iraq reportedly maintained 12,000 troops in Jordan as part of the Arab confrontation with Israel. It withdrew them in 1971. In April 1972 Iraq and the USSR signed a friendship pact. Soviet military aid was increased; several thousand Soviet advisers were sent. In Mar. 1973 Kuwait charged Iraqi troops entered its territory in a border dispute. In the 1973 "Yom Kippur" war, Iraq sent forces to aid Syria, but disputes with Syria persisted over sharing of river waters.

Years of battling with the Kurds, a minority in the northeast area, led to a 1970 recognition by the government of partial Kurdish autonomy. Renewed fighting resulted in total defeat for the Kurds in 1975, when Iran withdrew support.

Education and Religion. Elementary and secondary education is free and compulsory. Arabic is the language of the majority. The people are preponderantly Moslems, divided between the Sunni and Shiah sects. Christians number 150,000.

Defense. Military strength for 1973-74 was 101,800.

Ireland

Area 26,600 sq. mi. Population (Govt. est. 1974): 3,090,000. Capital: Dublin. Monetary unit: Irish pound.

Ireland, or Eire, an island in the Atlantic near the European mainland, is a republic about the size of W. Va. It is separated from Great Britain on the E by the Irish Sea and the North Channel and on the SE by St. George's Channel. The northern one-sixth of the island is part of the United Kingdom.

Ireland consists mainly of a central plateau surrounded by isolated groups of hills and mountains. Ireland's coastline is much indented by the sea, affording many inlets and coves. The mean annual temperature ranges from 48°F, in the N to 52°F, in the S. There are numerous lakes (called loughs); the best known are those of Killarney. The most important river is the Shannon, about 250 mi. long. Tallest mountains are in SW; Carrantuohill, 3,414 ft. in Kerry; Brandon Hill on the coast, 3,127 ft.

Tourist attractions include the scenery, historic houses, cultural and folk festivals and medieval banquets. The famous Blarney stone is in an old castle in the village of Blarney, 4 mi. NW of Cork.

Emigration had been high and for years the population remained static. Since 1961, however, it has annually increased and emigration has recently decreased.

Resources and Industries. About 28% of the work force is employed in agriculture, forestry and fishing. The nearness of the Gulf Stream causes considerable rainfall; lush pastures of the "Emerald Isle" support an extensive cattle and dairy industry. Important crops are potatoes, wheat, oats, barley, sugar beets, fruits and vegetables. Food and animals comprise 43% of the exports.

Industrialization increased, 1962-74, with over 750 new factories, many with foreign participation. Major industries are tobacco, food processing, vehicle assembly, metals, textiles, chemicals and brewing. Gains have been recorded in electrical and nonelectrical machinery, fertilizers and computers.

A mining boom, following discovery of zinc, lead and silver deposits, brought new strength to the economy. The index for general industrial production rose (1970=100) to 124 in 1974. Natural gas was discovered off the SE coast in May 1974.

Tourism normally provides Ireland with earnings of over $250 million annually.

Foreign trade, in thousands of U. S. dollars:

	Imports	Exports
1973	$2,793,000	$2,131,000
1974	$3,813,000	$2,626,000

A switch to decimal currency was made in 1971.

History and Government. Celtic tribes invaded the islands about the 4th Century B. C.; their Gaelic culture and literature flourished and spread to Scotland and elsewhere in the 5th Century A. D., the same century in which St. Patrick converted the Irish to Christianity. Invasions by Norsemen began in the 8th Century, but were ended with defeat of the Danes by the Irish King Brian Boru in 1014. English invasions started in the 12th Century; for over 700 years the Anglo-Irish struggle continued with bitter rebellions and savage repressions.

The Easter Monday Rebellion (1916) failed but was followed by guerrilla warfare and harsh reprisals by British troops, the "Black and Tans." The Dail Eireann, or Irish parliament, reaffirmed independence in Jan. 1919. The British offered dominion status to Ulster (6 counties) and southern Ireland (26 counties) Dec. 1921. The constitution of the Irish Free State, a British dominion, was adopted Dec. 11, 1922. By treaty with Britain Northern Ireland could vote itself out, which it did, Dec. 12, 1922.

A new constitution adopted by plebiscite came into operation Dec. 29, 1937. It declared the name of the state Eire in the Irish language and Ireland in the English and declared it a sovereign democratic state.

On Dec. 21, 1948, an Irish law declared the country a republic rather than a dominion and withdrew it from the Commonwealth. In 1949 the British Parliament recognized both actions, but re-asserted its claim to incorporate the 6 northeastern counties in the United Kingdom. This claim has not been recognized by Ireland. See United Kingdom — Northern Ireland.

First president was William T. Cosgrove, 1922-32. Eamon de Valera, hero of the rebellion, was president 1932-38, 1959-66, 1966-73. He was prime minister 1937-48, 1951-54, 1957-59. Erskine Childers, a Protestant, was elected president in 1973.

Following Feb. 28, 1973, elections the Fianna Fail party was ousted from power after 16 years, although it won 69 seats, by a coalition of Fine Gael, 54 seats, and Labor, 19. Independents won 2. Liam Cosgrave became president.

The parliament is composed of a house, Dail Eireann, of 144 elected members, and a senate, Seanad Eireann, of 60, 11 of them nominated by the prime minister, 6 by the universities and the rest elected from 5 panels of candidates representing public interests.

Irish governments have favored peaceful unification of all Ireland. Ireland cooperated with England against terrorist groups. In 1974 Ireland and Britain agreed to create a Council of Ireland, a body with limited functions of which both the Republic and Northern Ireland would be represented.

Education and Religion. Roman Catholicism is the prevailing religion, claiming more than 90% of the population. In a 1972 referendum voters repealed a Constitutional provision giving the Roman Catholic Church a "special position."

Elementary education is free and compulsory. The Irish language is a required study, though English is the native tongue of most.

Defense. Armed forces total 10,500.

Ireland is a member of the UN, Council of Europe and the EC.

Israel

Area: (pre-1967) 8,017 sq. mi.; (post 1967) over 30,-000 sq. mi. Population (Govt. est. 1974, pre-1967 territory): 3,330,000. Capital: Jerusalem. Monetary unit: Israeli pound.

The state of Israel was re-established, as a republic, in 1948. It occupies part of the ancient land first called Canaan,.then Israel, then Palestine. About the size of New Jersey, it faces the Mediterranean to the W, Lebanon to the N, Syria and Jordan to the E, and Egypt to the SW.

The coastal plain on the W is 120 mi. long, 15 wide, fertile and well watered. In the center is the plateau of Judea. A triangular-shaped semi-desert region, the Negev, extends from south of Beersheba to an apex at the head of the Gulf of Aqaba. The eastern border drops sharply into the depressed valley of the River Jordan and the Dead Sea which is 46 mi. long, with an average width of 8 mi., 1,296 ft. below sea level, lowest point on the earth's surface.

Israel's area, as defined by armistices with the Arab nations, includes all the land assigned to it under the 1947 partition resolution of the UN General Assembly, as well as Western Galilee and a corridor to Jerusalem. By the terms of the armistice with Syria, July 20, 1949, last of the Arab states to end military action after the creation of modern Israel,' demilitarized zones were set up on the eastern edge of Lake Huleh and the southeastern shore of the Sea of Galilee, site of Israel's Ein Gev settlement.

In Israel-Arab war of June 1967 Israel occupied the Sinai Peninsula, the west bank of the Jordan and a small area of Syria. Parts of Sinai were surrendered in 1974 and 1975 accords.

Non-Jewish population (1973): Moslem, 374,000; Christian, 82,300; Druse and others, 40,000.

The chief ports are Haifa, Elath and Ashdod.

Resources and Industries. Citrus fruit is the most valuable agricultural product. Other principal crops include wheat, barley, durra, olives, melons, grapes, figs, tomatoes, bananas. cotton. Since 1955 total cultivated area has been increased from 412,500 to more than 1,058,000 acres, of which 448,000 acres are under irrigation. Wine making is extensive.

Israel has deposits of limestone, sandstone, gypsum, copper, iron, phosphates, magnesium, manganese, ceramic clays. The valley of Jordan and the Dead Sea yield rock salt, sulphur and potash.

Israel's over-all economy and industrialization have both grown rapidly. The economy has been aided by German reparations payments. U. S. aid, international loans and contributions. West Germany completed payment of $860 million in reparations (cash and goods) in 1965. The 2 countries also set up full diplomatic relations.

The index of industrial production (1970=100) was 135.

The Negev region in the south is Israel's primary development area, receiving nearly half of the immigrants. It has large phosphate deposits, copper, oil, natural gas and potash.

A 150-mi. pipeline, major link in Israel's national water plan, was completed in June 1964 and began carrying water from Lake Kinneret (Sea of Galilee) to the Negev. Desalination plants have been built.

In 1970 Israel completed construction of a 160-mi., 42-inch, oil pipeline from Elath on the Gulf of Aqaba to Ashkelon on the Mediterranean.

Israel's first atomic reactor at Nahal Rubin began operations in July, 1960. The nation launched its first successful solid-fuel rocket 50 mi. into the atmosphere July 5. 1961, for meteorological study.

Israel's main exports are citrus fruits, polished diamonds, chemicals, textiles and fashion goods, machinery, plastics, tires and pharmaceutical products. In 1975, Israel signed agreements with the U.S. to facilitate investments in Israel, and with the Common Market allowing free trade.

Tourism is second only to citrus products in earnings, over $150 million annually.

Foreign trade in thousands of U. S. dollars:

	Imports	Exports
1973	$2,987,000	$1,449,000
1974	$4,198,000	$1,717,000
	(9 mos.)	

History and Government. The Jewish people lived in Israel from before 1200 B.C.; many were driven from the land by various conquerors. The Judaic moral and ethical code and the Bible originated here. The modern Zionist movement for a homeland in Palestine, led by Dr. Chaim Weizmann caused the cabinet of Great Britain to give its support in the Balfour Declaration, Nov. 2, 1917. Under the Palestine Mandate, about four-fifths of historic Palestine was detached in 1922 to form Trans-Jordan, now the Kingdom of Jordan. When the Nazi persecutions began in Germany great numbers of Jews set out for Palestine. The UN General Assembly voted Nov. 29,. 1947, to partition Palestine into two independent states by Oct. 1, 1948. A separate enclave of Jerusalem, area 289 sq. mi., was to be administered by a UN official. Britain gave up its mandate May 15, 1948.

A new state, the Republic of Israel, was proclaimed May 14, 1948. A few hours later, the armies of Egypt, Jordan, Syria, Lebanon and Iraq, with Saudi Arabian contingents, crossed the frontiers at several points. They were defeated.

Separate armistices with the Arab nations were signed in 1949, but no general peace settlement was obtained. The Arab nations continued policies of economic boycott, blockade in the Suez Canal, political warfare and local incitement.

Saying an Arab attack was imminent, Israel invaded Egypt's Sinai, Oct. 29, 1956, aided briefly by British and French forces. A UN ceasefire was arranged Nov. 6.

An uneasy truce between Israel and the Arab countries, supervised by a UN Emergency Force, prevailed until May 19, 1967, when the UN force withdrew at the demand of Egypt's President Gamal Abdel Nasser. Egyptian forces rapidly reoccupied the Gaza Strip and closed the Gulf of Aqaba to Israeli shipping. In a full-scale 6-day war that started June 5, the Israelis took the Gaza strip, occupied the Sinai Peninsula to the Suez Canal, and captured Old Jerusalem. Syria's Golan Heights and Jordan's West Bank. The fighting was halted June 10 by UN-arranged cease-fire agreements.

By 1969-70 there were almost daily Egyptian-Israeli artillery duels across the Suez Canal as well as ground forays and air raids with Israeli planes penetrating deep into Egypt. Palestinian guerrilla raids and Israeli reprisals continued across the Jordanian. Syrian. and Lebanese frontiers; there were also encounters with Syrian and Jordanian forces.

It was est. in 1970 there were 10,000 or more Soviet military men in Egypt, and increasing supplies of Soviet planes and anti-aircraft missiles, some of which Israel charged were manned by Russians. In July 1972 most of the Russians, then est. at 20,000, were sent home by Egypt.

In June 1970 the U.S. proposed a 3-month, standstill cease-fire and peace negotiations. Israel, Egypt and Jordan agreed. Palestinian guerrilla groups said they would continue attacks.

The cease-fire was formally ended by Egypt Mar. 7, 1971. but continued unofficially. Guerrilla terrorist attacks continued in 1972-73 and Israel made reprisal raids against guerrilla groups in Lebanon and Syria.

Egypt and Syria launched a surprise war on Israel, Oct. 6, 1973 (Yom Kippur, most solemn day on the Jewish calendar). Egyptian forces crossed the Suez Canal and established 2 bridgeheads along the E side of the canal. Syrian forces drove into the Israeli-held Golan Heights. Egypt and Syria were supplied by massive USSR military airlifts; the U.S. responded with an airlift to Israel. Israel counter-attacked, driving the Syrians back, but halting 20 mi. short of Damascus. Then the Israelis crossed the Suez Canal between the Egyptian bridgeheads, surrounded Suez City and trapped the Egyptian 3d Army in its Sinai salient.

Israel and Egypt agreed to a UN cease-fire which took effect Oct. 24; a UN peace-keeping force went to the area. A disengagement agreement was signed Jan. 18. 1974, following negotiations by U.S. Secretary of State Henry Kissinger. Israel withdrew from the canal's W bank; limited numbers of Egyptians occupied a strip. 5 to 7.5 mi. wide along the canal's E bank; UN forces took over a buffer zone between them and an Israeli limited-forces zone futher E. The withdrawals were completed Mar. 4.

Israel and Syria agreed to disengage June 1; Israel completed withdrawing from its salient (and a small part of the land taken in the 1967 war) June 25.

In the wake of the war, Golda Meir, long Israel's premier resigned; severe inflation gripped the nation. Palestinian guerillas staged massacres, killing scores of civilians 1974-75. Israel conducted preventive attacks on guerrilla areas in Lebanon through 1975. By mid-1974 the USSR had replenished arms and equipment lost by Syria in 1973.

Israel is a parliamentary democracy. The first constituent assembly (Knesset), was formed Feb. 14, 1949, with 120 members, including 8 Arabs. The assembly elected Dr. Chaim Weizmann first president of Israel Feb. 17, 1949. He died Nov. 9, 1952. Israel's first premier was David Ben-Gurion.

The Knesset (Parliament) members are elected by universal suffrage for 4-year terms by all citizens over 18, under proportional representation.

Israel had diplomatic relations with 100 nations. Specialists in many fields shared their knowledge with those in less developed nations in Africa and elsewhere. But nearly all European Communist and black African nations broke off relations with Israel in 1972-74, the latter reportedly at the urging of Libya.

Education. Israel has compulsory education from 5 years of age to 16. Total enrollment in 6,360 schools in 1974 was 984,869. Of these, 140,719 were enrolled in Arab schools.

Over 53,000 students attend 7 universities and other specialized institutes.

Defense. Military service is compulsory for men and, between ages 18-26, unmarried women. Military forces total 145,000 which can be raised to 400,000 by mobilization of reservists.

Israel became a member of the UN in 1949.

Italy

Area: 116,303 sq. mi. Population (Govt. est. 1974): 55,586,000. Capital: Rome. Monetary unit: Lira.

The Republic of Italy occupies a long peninsula shaped like a boot, extending SE from the Alps into the Mediterranean, with the island of Sicily separated from the mainland by the 2-mi. Strait of Messina at the toe of the boot. The country is about 700 mi. long and not over 220 mi. wide. Its area is about the same as Arizona's. Lying directly W of mid-Italy is the major island of Sardinia, slightly smaller than Sicily.

Sicily, 9,927 sq. mi., pop. (1971) 2,985,678, is an island 180 by 120 mi., seat of a region that embraces the island of **Pantelleria,** 32 sq. mi., and the **Lipari** group, 44 sq. mi., pop. 14,000, including 2 active volcanoes: **Vulcano,** 1,637 ft. and **Stromboli,** 3,038 ft. From prehistoric times Sicily has been settled by various peoples; a Greek state had its capital at Syracuse. Rome took Sicily from Carthage 215 B.C. **Mt. Etna,** 10,705 ft. active volcano, is tallest peak. Sicily leads in citrus fruits, also produces wheat, grapes, wine, sulphur, salt, olives. Cattle and sheep are raised.

Sardinia, 9,283 sq. mi., pop. (1971) 1,106,345, lies in the Mediterranean, 115 mi. W. of Italy and 7½ mi. S of Corsica. Like Sicily, it is under a regional administration. It is 160 mi. long, 68 mi. wide, mountainous, with mining of coal, zinc, lead, copper; it raises grapes, olives, tobacco, also cattle and sheep. In 1720 Sardinia was added to the possessions of the Dukes of Savoy in Piedmont and Savoy to form the Kingdom of Sardinia. Giuseppe Garibaldi is buried on the nearby isle of Caprera. Capital: Cagliari.

Elba, 87 sq. mi., pop. 30,000, lies 6 mi. west of Tuscany. Industries include fishing, iron mining, wine making. Napoleon I lived in exile on Elba 1814-1815.

Capri, 4 sq. mi., pop. c. 9,000, 20 mi. SW of Naples, is famous for its beauty and equable climate.

The allure of historical monuments, great museums of painting and sculpture, imposing churches, as well as good living attracts about 28 million tourists a year.

The 3.4-mi. Great St. Bernard tunnel, between Italy and Switzerland, first auto tunnel in the Alps, was opened Mar. 19, 1964. The Mont Blanc tunnel, 7.25 mi. linking Italy and France, was opened July 16, 1965.

Resources and Industries. Italy has enjoyed an extraordinary industrial growth since World War II. But in 1973-74, a fourfold increase in international oil prices helped disrupt the economy. Taxes were boosted in July 1974; in Aug. West Germany gave Italy a $2 billion loan to ease the financial crisis, and stabilization was achieved in 1975.

Grapes, olives, citrus fruits, vegetables, wheat, rice and cattle are the major agricultural products, but rural declines have necessitated increasing food imports. The wines of Italy have great variety. Chianti from Tuscany is popular, as are Asti Spumante, Orvieto, Capri.

White marble is quarried at Carrara, Volterra and Pisa; colored marble at Verona, Siena and Vicenza. Alabaster comes chiefly from Volterra.

Natural gas is found in the valley of the Po, the Marches, Abruzzi, Apulia, Basilicata and Sicily.

In 1973 electric plants produced about 140 billion kwh. There were nuclear power plants. The electrical industry was nationalized in 1962.

Steel production was 21 million metric tons in 1973. Italy is a heavy producer of industrial and electrical machinery, automobiles, steel products, typewriters, shoes, textiles, synthetic fabrics, machine tools. Its chemical industry has expanded rapidly.

The index of industrial production (1970=100) was 119 for 1974.

Italy's merchant marine ranks high. It has over 635 ships of more than 1,000 gross tons.

Tourism brings in $1.5 billion a year.

Foreign trade, in thousands of U.S. dollars:

	Imports	Exports
1973	$27,797,000	$22,224,000
1974	$40,931,000	$30,242,000

History and Government. Divided and dismembered since the fall of the Roman Empire, Italy began to reunite after the war of 1859 when Lombardy came under the crown of King Victor Emmanuel II of Sardinia. By plebiscite in 1860, Parma, Modena, Romagna and Tuscany joined, followed by Sicily and Naples, and by the Marches and Umbria. The first Italian parliament declared Victor Emmanuel king of Italy Mar. 17, 1861. Mantua and Venetia were added in 1866 as an outcome of the Austro-Prussian war. The Papal States were taken by Italian troops Sept. 20, 1870, on the withdrawal of the French garrison. The states were annexed to the kingdom by plebiscite. Italy recognized the State of Vatican City as independent Feb. 11, 1929.

Fascism appeared in Italy Mar. 23, 1919, when the original Fascisti organized an association against communism and socialism under the guidance of Benito Mussolini. They took over the government at the invitation of the king Oct. 28, 1922. Mussolini acquired dictatorial powers and was called duce (leader). He made war on Ethiopia and proclaimed Victor Emmanuel III emperor, defied the sanctions of the League of Nations, joined the Berlin-Tokyo axis, sent troops to fight for Franco against the Republic of Spain and joined Germany in World War II.

After Fascism was overthrown in 1943, Italy declared war on Germany and Japan and contributed to the Allied victory. It surrendered conquered lands and lost its colonies. Mussolini was killed by partisans Apr. 28, 1945.

Victor Emmanuel III abdicated May 9, 1946; his son Humbert II was king until June 10, when Italy became a republic after a referendum, June 2-3.

The senate has 315 members elected for 5-year terms, plus 5 whom the president may appoint for life. Ex-presidents are eligible for life membership. The chamber of deputies has 630 members elected for 5 years. Titles of nobility are no longer recognized. Reorganization of the Fascist party is forbidden. The cabinet normally represents a coalition of the Christian Democrats, largest of Italy's many parties, and one or 2 other parties Voting age was lowered to 18 in 1975.

Twenty regional governments now perform functions previously belonging to central and local governments. Four were governed by the Communist Party or Communist-led coalitions in 1975.

Trieste. Following prolonged negotiations an agreement was signed Oct. 5, 1954, by Italy and Yugoslavia which gave Italy provisional administration over the northern section and the seaport of Trieste, with 90 sq. mi. and about 300,000 pop., and Yugoslavia the part of Istrian peninsula it had occupied, 200 sq. mi. and 73,500 pop., and provision for emergency access to the port. The 2 areas are treated as parts of Italy and Yugoslavia.

Italy is a member of NATO, EC and Council of Europe; admitted to the UN Dec. 14, 1955.

Education and Religion. Roman Catholicism is the state religion. In 1974 Italians voted by a 3-to-2 margin to retain a 3-year-old law permitting divorce which was opposed by the church.

Italy has 34 state universities, including Bologna (founded 1088), and 24 other institutes of higher education. Education is compulsory between 6 and 14.

Defense. Military forces total 421,000. A large proportion are committed to NATO.

Ivory Coast

Area: 124,503 sq. mi. Population (UN est. 1974): 4,770,000. Capital: Abidjan. Monetary unit: CFA franc.

The Republic of Ivory Coast, a former French Overseas Territory in West Africa, is on the coast of the Gulf of Guinea. Roughly oblong in shape and about the area of New Mexico, it is bounded by Liberia, Guinea, Mali, Upper Volta and Ghana and has 340 mi. of coastline on the Atlantic. Abidjan, the capital, is the chief port. A new port, San Pedro, opened in 1971.

Under the 1958 constitution of France, Ivory Coast became fully independent Aug. 7, 1960. Its present constitution was adopted Oct. 31, 1960. It signed an agreement, 1961, retaining close ties with France. Ivory Coast is a member of the West African economic community, formed in 1972, with Dahomey, Mali, Mauritania, Niger, Senegal and Upper Volta.

Agriculture, forestry, stock raising and fishing occupy 90% of the population. Chief export crops are coffee, cocoa, tropical woods and bananas; cotton, rice, oil palms also are raised. Electric power, lumbering and industrialization are being expanded.

The Ivory Coast has been the most prosperous of tropical African nations. It has a favorable balance of trade. Exports grew and continued to exceed imports in 1974. The number of small factories also increased.

About 18% of the people are Catholics or Protestants; 20% are Moslems and the rest animists. French is the official language.

Jamaica

Area: 4,411 sq. mi. Population (UN est. 1974): 2,000,000. Capital: Kingston. Monetary unit: Jamaican dollar.

Jamaica is a mountainous island in the Caribbean Sea, 90 mi. S of Cuba. Its area is 12% less than that of Connecticut.

Temperatures range from 80 to 86 on the coast and down to 40 in the Blue Mtns. Montego Bay and Ocho Rios are among popular resort areas; most of about 500,000 annual tourists are American.

Jamaica was visited by Columbus, 1494, and ruled by Spanish (under whom native Arawak Indians died out) until seized by the English, 1655. The island figures largely in the history of the buccaneers of the West Indies around the time of Sir Henry Morgan, once its governor. Port Royal, old haunt of the pirate, was largely destroyed by earthquake, 1692.

Jamaica won independence from Britain Aug. 6, 1962. There is a governor-general representing the British crown, an elected house of representatives and an appointed senate; executive power lies with a prime minister and cabinet.

Principal exports are bauxite (world's largest production) and alumina. Other products include sugar cane, coffee, bananas, rum, coconuts, ginger, molasses, cocoa, pimento, fruits, cigars and petroleum products.

Value of imports exceeds that of exports but earnings from tourism help offset this. Manufacturing plants have grown in number, aided by government-sponsored incentives. In 1974 Jamaica sought a large increase in taxes paid by U.S. and Canadian companies which mine bauxite on the island. The socialist government has moved to take control of the industry from U.S. and Canadian firms.

Japan

The World Almanac is sponsored in Japan by the Mainichi Newspapers, 1-1 Hitotsubashi, Chiyoda-ku, Tokyo 100; phone 03-212-0321. Mainichi founded 1876, Osaka, Japan; circulation 4,883,095 (m), 2,915,-364 (e). (Mainichi Daily News, English language 45,-412); president Mitsuharu Yamamoto; vice president, executive editor Toshio Sumimoto.

Area: 143,574 sq. mi. Population (Govt. est. 1974): 109,670,000. Capital: Tokyo. Monetary unit: Yen.

Japan consists of 4 main islands: Honshu ("mainland"), 88,952 sq. mi.; Hokkaido, 30,304; Kyushu, 16,191; and Shikoku, 7,240. Total area is about twice that of Missouri. The islands lie in the North Pacific separated from the Soviet Union and Korea by the Sea of Japan and from China by the East China Sea.

The Japanese coast is deeply indented, measuring 16,654 mi. The northern islands are a continuation of the Sakhalin mountain chain running through Hokkaido and the main island. The continuation of the Kunlun mountain range of China appears in the southern islands, the ranges meeting in the Japanese Alps. In the vast transverse fissure crossing the main island from the Sea of Japan to the Pacific rises a group of volcanoes, mostly extinct or dormant, with Fuji-San (Fujiyama), 60 mi. SW of Tokyo, lifting its white cone 12,388 ft.

Most important ports are Kobe, the world's 3d busiest, Nagoya, Yokohama, and Osaka. Tokyo, the capital, is one of the 3 largest cities of the world. It has a modern business section centering about the Ginza, a major avenue. The Imperial Palace, surrounded by a moat on a 250-acre site, and the white-marble Diet building, erected in 1936, are also in Tokyo. Its International Airport is Asia's busiest. Tokyo Tower is a 1,089-ft. steel structure built for radio-TV broadcasting and sightseeing.

At Kamakura, 30 mi. SW of Tokyo, is the Great Buddha or Daibutsu, a bronze figure 42 ft. 6 in. tall with base, cast in 1252. The Hakone hot spring area is noted for the reflection in Lake Ashino of Fuji-San. Also famous is the Toshogu Shrine at Nikko, where a national park of 347,000 acres preserves the natural beauty of Japanese flora. Kyoto, for 1,000 years a capital city, with massive temples and colorful shrines, is a cultural center.

The 2.34-mi. Kanmon undersea highway tunnel connecting Honshu and Kyushu is the world's first double-deck tunnel, with one level for vehicles and one for pedestrians.

Resources and Industries. More than half the arable land is used for growing rice, the chief food. Wheat, barley, potatoes, tobacco, tea, beans, peaches, pears, apples, grapes, persimmons and mandarins are also produced. Minerals include some amounts of gold, silver, copper, lead, zinc, chromite, white arsenic, coal, sulphur, salt and petroleum, but most minerals have to be imported.

The principal industries are iron and steel products, transportation equipment, machinery, electronics, shipbuilding, precision instruments, chemicals, fertilizers, textiles (cotton, wool, silks, synthetics), ceramics, wood products, fisheries. The 1972 fish catch, valued at $3.4 billion, led all nations.

Japan is 2d to the U.S. in motor vehicle production; 6,624,000 autos, trucks and buses were produced in 1974. It is also 2d to the U.S. in number of telephones in use. The index of industrial production (1970=100) was 126 in 1974.

Japan's shipyards lead the world, especially in construction of super tankers and bulk carriers of over 300,000 tons. Japan's own merchant fleet included 2,145 ships of 1,000 or more gross tons in 1974, 3d among nations.

Electric power production was about 460 billion kwh in 1974, close to half from hydroelectric plants. An atomic power station at Tokai, near Tokyo, began commercial distribution of electricity in 1966.

Major exports are steel and related products, clothing, chemicals, motor vehicles, optical goods, ships, radio and TV sets, toys.

Tourism is an increasingly important source of foreign exchange; in 1972, 723,744 visitors spent over $210 million.

The U.S. is Japan's biggest customer, taking about one-third of all its exports. In 1973, value of imports topped that of exports for the first time in many years.

Foreign trade in thousands of U.S. dollars:

	Imports	Exports
1973	$38,314,000	$36,930,000
1974	$62,061,000	$55,580,000

History and Government. According to Japanese legend, the empire was founded by Emperor Jimmu, 660 B.C. Political power was held by successive families of shoguns (military dictators), 1192-1867, until recovered by the Emperor Meiji in 1868. The Portuguese and Dutch had minor trade with Japan in the 16th and 17th Centuries. U.S. Commodore Matthew C. Perry opened it to U.S. trade in a treaty ratified 1854. Japan fought China, 1894-95, gaining Taiwan. In war with Russia, 1904-05, Russia's fleet was wiped out at Tsushima; Russia ceded S half of Sakhalin and gave concessions in China. Japan annexed Korea 1910. In World War I Japan ousted Germany from Shantung, took over German Pacific islands as mandates from the League of Nations. Japan took Manchuria 1931, started war with China 1932. Japan launched war against the U.S. by attack on Pearl Harbor Dec. 7, 1941. Japan surrendered Aug. 14, 1945, and Gen. Douglas MacArthur headed occupation of Japan as supreme commander for the Allied Powers.

In a new constitution adopted May 3, 1947, Japan renounced the right to wage war; the emperor was acknowledged as hereditary symbol of the nation, but gave up claims to divinity; the Diet became the sole law-making authority. The House of Councilors has 252 members elected for 6 yr. terms and the House of Representatives 491 members, elected for 4 yrs., both by popular vote. The constitution separates church and state. Japan has granted suffrage to women and lowered the voting age to 20.

The emperor is Hirohito, the 124th of his line, born April 29, 1901, succeeded to the throne Dec. 25, 1926. The crown prince is Akihito Tsugu No Miya, born Dec. 23, 1933.

The U.S. and 48 other non-communist nations signed a peace treaty and the U.S. a bilateral defense agreement with Japan, in San Francisco Sept. 8, 1951, restoring Japan's sovereignty as of April 28, 1952. Under the treaty, Japan was reduced territorially to the 4 main islands, but it was to have an opportunity eventually to regain the Ryukyu and Bonin Islands. Japan signed separate treaties with Nationalist China, 1952; India, 1952; a declaration with USSR ending a technical state of war, 1956. In Dec. 1965 Japan and South Korea agreed to resume diplomatic relations.

On June 26, 1968, the U.S. returned to Japanese control the Bonin Islands, the Volcano Islands (including Iwo Jima) and Marcus Island. On May 15, 1972, Okinawa, the other Ryukyu Islands and the Daito Islands were returned to Japan by the U.S., but it was agreed the U.S. would continue to maintain large military bases on Okinawa.

On Sept. 29, 1972, Japan and mainland China agreed to resume diplomatic relations; Japan and Taiwan severed relations.

Education and Religion. The principal forms of religion are Buddhism, with 12 sects, and Shintoism with 13. There are over 100,000 Shinto shrines, 106,-634 Buddhist temples and several thousand Christian churches.

Nine years of education is compulsory, consisting of 6 years of elementary and 3 years of lower secondary education. There were 397 colleges and universities and 491 junior colleges in 1972. English is required study in lower secondary schools.

Defense. Legislation effective July 1, 1954, established new Self-Defense Forces. Military strength is 233,000.

During 1969 the U.S. began turning over 50 military installation sites, a third of its facilities in Japan, to the Japanese. The U.S. reduced its forces in Japan in 1971.

Jordan

Area: 37,297 sq. mi. (including West Bank). **Population (Govt. est. 1974):** 2,620,000. **Capital:** Amman. **Monetary unit:** Dinar.

Jordan is a constitutional monarchy in SW Asia. The country's former name, Transjordan, was dropped Apr. 26, 1949, after it occupied the West Bank lands, W of the Jordan River, in favor of the constitutional name, Hashemite Kingdom of Jordan.

About 12% of the land is fertile; the rest is arid. In the extreme south is its only port, Aqaba, on the Gulf of Aqaba. It shares the Dead Sea (1,296 ft. below sea level) with Israel. Jordan is slightly larger than Indiana.

Resources and Industries. The fertile western portions have a high agricultural potential. Principal crops are tomatoes, vegetables, wheat, barley, olives, grapes, citrus fruits and bananas.

Industries include tobacco, flour milling, distilling, building materials, olive oil, soap, mother-of-pearl, textiles, plastics, cement, steel, batteries, leather.

Potash from the Dead Sea and phosphate rock are the main minerals. Phosphate is 30% of value of exports.

History and Government. The area was part of the

Ottoman Empire from the 16th century until World War I. It was set up within the Palestine Mandate Sept. 1, 1922, and gained independence as Transjordan in 1946. Abdullah Ibn Al Husein, born 1882, was proclaimed king May 25, 1946; he was assassinated by an Arab extremist, 1951. His eldest son became King Talal I. Parliament removed Talal on medical advice, installing his son King Hussein I (born 1935) May 11, 1952. His marriage to Sherifa Deena (a daughter was born 1956) was dissolved 1958. He married (May 25, 1961) Antoinette Avril Gardiner, of England, entitled Princess Muna. They had 2 sons and 2 daughters. But in 1965 Hussein designated a younger brother, Hassan, to be heir to the throne. In Dec. 1972 Hussein divorced Muna and married Alia Toukan, a West Bank Arab.

Legislature has a senate of 30 named by the king and a lower house of 60 elected by manhood suffrage. Jordan is a member of the UN and Arab League.

After creation of Israel May 14, 1948, Jordan joined in the Arab attack on Israel and seized areas of central Palestine including the West Bank and the old city of Jerusalem. Several hundred thousand Palestinian refugees fled into Jordan. But Jordan lost all the territories to Israel in the June 1967 war.

In 1968-70 Palestinian guerrillas based in Jordan continued raids on Israel, including artillery attacks. Israel staged reprisal raids against commando bases inside Jordan.

Fighting between Jordanian troops and Palestinian commandos in 1970 included a 10-day civil war in Sept. In renewed fighting in July 1971 Jordanian troops dispersed thousands of commandos from their bases. Syria, Algeria and Libya suspended relations with Jordan, and Iraq closed its border. Syria reopened its border in 1972.

In the Oct. 1973 Arab war on Israel, Jordan sent troops to aid Syria, but the Israel-Jordan border remained peaceful.

In Oct. 1974 an Arab summit meeting designated the Palestine Liberation Organization as sole representative of Arabs on the West Bank. Jordan accepted the move. Arab oil states agreed to pay Jordan a $300 million annual subsidy. Jordan and Syria entered a military cooperation pact in 1975.

Education and Religion. The population is chiefly Arab, of whom the majority are Moslems; there are 250,000 Christians and 10,000 Moslem Circassians. The language is Arabic. Public school education is growing. The Jordanian Univ. was established in 1962.

Defense. Military forces total 75,000. The U.S. has provided military aid.

Kenya

Area: 224,960 sq. mi. Population (Govt. est. 1974): 12,910,000. Capital: Nairobi. Monetary unit: Kenya shilling.

Kenya, former British Colony and Protectorate which became independent in 1963, extends from its Indian Ocean coast NE to Somalia, N to Ethiopia, W to Uganda, and S to Tanzania. It has twice the area of New Mexico.

The northern three-fifths is arid. Most economic production is centered in the south, a low coastal area and a plateau varying from 3,000 to 10,000 ft. The main products are coffee, tea, cereals, cotton, sisal, dairy products, hides, bark extract, timber and minerals. Kenya is the largest producer of tea in Africa.

In 1953 Kenya became the scene of terroristic activities of the Mau Mau, an oath-bound unit of some of the Kikuyu, Meru, Embu and other tribes which killed Africans and whites during an 8-year rebellion.

Kenya won independence Dec. 12, 1963. Jomo Kenyatta, once imprisoned as a Mau Mau leader, became its first prime minister. It became a republic within the Commonwealth Dec. 12, 1964, and Kenyatta became its first president. The National Assembly is a unicameral legislature.

Since independence, Kenya's economy has continued to grow, including both agriculture and manufacturing. Tourism has boomed. Schools and health centers have increased. Drought caused setbacks in 1971 and 1973.

In Jan. 1968 Kenya and Somalia resumed diplomatic relations as efforts were made to end 4 years of skirmishes caused by "invasions" of nomadic Somali herders seeking grass and water.

From 1968 through 1973 thousands of Asians holding old British passports were ordered evicted from Kenya. In 1973 it was announced Swahili would become the national language, with English still used for international communications.

Years of political stability ended in 1974-75, with opposition charges of corruption and repression.

Republic of Korea

Area: 38,031 sq. mi. Population (Govt. est. 1974): 33,460,000. Capital: Seoul. Monetary unit: Won.

Korea, Land of the Morning Calm, is a mountainous peninsula in NE Asia between the Yellow Sea and the Sea of Japan. South Korea is about the about the size of Indiana.

Resources and Industries. Once chiefly an agricultural country, South Korea has a cultivated area of about 5,095,655 acres. Main crops are rice, barley, wheat, tobacco and beans, but the mountainous terrain, poor soil and cold winters limit yields. Population growth has been sharply curbed.

Division of Korea in 1945 left the South with only light industry and about 10% of power generating capacity. Large infusions of foreign aid helped build an industrial base especially in mining of tungsten (supplies 6% of world's needs), coal, iron ore, bismuth, fluorspar, graphite and cement. The fishing, timber, rubber, glass, shipbuilding, electronics and silk industries have expanded rapidly; chemical and fertilizer plants and oil refineries have been built. Growth was at record highs, 1971-73, but oil price increases caused soaring inflation in 1974-75.

U.S. support in South Korea has been military, financial, technical and educational. Since 1954 it has totaled more than $2.2 billion. Index of industrial production (1970=100) was 230 for 1974.

Foreign trade in thousands of U.S. dollars:

	Imports	Exports
1973	$4,218,000	$3,221,000
1974	$6,814,000	$4,713,000

History and Government. Korea, once called the Hermit Kingdom, has a recorded history since the 1st century B.C. It was united in a kingdom under the Silla Dynasty, 668 A.D. It was at times associated with the Chinese empire; the treaty that concluded the Sino-Japanese war of 1894-95 recognized Korea's complete independence. In 1910 Japan forcibly annexed Korea as Chosun.

At the Potsdam conference, July, 1945, the 38th parallel was designated as the line dividing the Soviet and the American occupation. Russian troops entered Korea Aug. 10, 1945, U.S. troops entered Sept. 8, 1945. The Soviet military organized socialists and communists and blocked efforts to let the Koreans unite their country. A UN commission to supervise elections in Korea in 1948 was denied admission to North Korea. *(See Index for Korean War.)*

The South Koreans formed the Republic of Korea in May 1948 with Seoul as the capital. Dr. Syngman Rhee was chosen president July 20 and the republic was formally proclaimed Aug. 15, 1948. President Rhee was reelected to a 4th term Mar. 15, 1960, when 85 years old. A movement spearheaded by college students forced his resignation Apr. 26, amid charges of corruption and election fraud.

A constitutional amendment passed June 15, 1960, replaced an autocratic presidential system with a cabinet system. But in an army coup May 16, 1961, Gen. Park Chung Hee became chairman of the ruling junta. He was formally elected president Oct. 15, 1963; a referendum Nov. 22, 1972, provided more presidential powers and allowed him to be reelected for 6-year terms unlimited times. In 1974 scores of political dissidents were jailed in a long series of trials. Eight accused of subversion were executed in 1975. An assassin, firing at Park, fatally wounded Mrs. Park.

North Korean raids across the border tapered off in 1971, but 2 South Korean soldiers were killed in 1973; in 1974, 2 South Korean boats were sunk and North Koreans fired on a U.S. helicopter south of the neutral zone. In July 1972 South and North Korea agreed on a common goal of reunifying the 2 nations by peaceful means. Red Cross delegates from both nations met to find ways to aid divided families.

Education and Religion. Christianity, Confucianism, Buddhism and Chondogyo are principal religions.

Primary education is compulsory. In 1973 there were 6,269 primary schools, 1,916 junior high schools, 1,015 high schools, 248 universities and colleges.

Defense. Military strength is over 625,000. By Mar. 1973 South Korea withdrew the last of 50,000 troops that had been aiding the South Vietnam government.

During 1970-71 U.S. forces authorized in South Korea were reduced; in 1974 there were 38,000. South Korean troops replaced U.S. forces on the armistice border.

North Korea

Area: 46,768 sq. mi. Population (UN est. 1974): 15,440,000. Capital: Pyongyang. Monetary unit: Won.

The Democratic People's Republic of Korea was formed May 1, 1948. The U.S. did not recognize it.

North Korea has good mineral resources that are fairly well developed. The country ranks among the first 5 in the world in the output of tungsten, graphite and magnesite. Other products of significance include lead, zinc, pyrite, cement, iron ore, copper, gold, phosphate, salt and fluorspar. A well-developed hydroelectric system and sizeable reserves of coal provide power needs for industry. Agriculture is collectivized and industry nationalized.

North Korea is slightly larger than N. Y. State.

The import and export trade is largely with Communist countries, particularly China and Russia.

The USSR signed a military aid treaty with North Korea July 6, 1961, pledging defense protection and financial help. A similar treaty was signed with Communist China. *(See Index for Korean War.)*

Soviet prestige declined in the early 1960s as North Korea sided with the Chinese in the Sino-Soviet dispute. By 1974 North Korea apparently had good relations with both Communist super-powers.

North Korean patrol boats seized the U.S. Navy intelligence ship Pueblo on Jan. 23, 1968, charged it had entered North Korean territorial waters and held its crew captive. The 82 surviving crew members were freed Dec. 23 (Korean time).

North Korean planes shot down a U.S. Navy intelligence plane over the Sea of Japan Apr. 15, 1969 (Korean time). No survivors were found.

In July 1972 North and South Korea agreed they would seek reunification of the two nations by peaceful means, but little progress was made by 1975.

North Korea's armed forces totaled 467,000, including a large air force.

Kuwait

Area: 7,780 sq. mi. Population (Govt. est. 1974): 930,000. Capital: Kuwait City. Monetary unit: Kuwaiti dinar.

Kuwait, a small Arab state formerly under British protection, became fully independent June 19, 1961. It extends along the NW coast of the Persian (also called Arabian) Gulf, bordered by Iraq and Saudi Arabia. Kuwait City is a principal Gulf port. In area, Kuwait is slightly larger than Connecticut.

Resources and Industries. Oil, first exported in 1946, is Kuwait's economic mainstay; the tiny nation has become the world's 6th largest producer. Reserves are about 10 billion tons, 15% of the world's total.

Crude oil production in 1974 was 850 million barrels. Annual payments to the Kuwait government in royalties and taxes are about $8 billion. Per capita income was estimated at more than $10,000 in 1974.

Revenues from oil from a former Kuwait-Saudi neutral zone are split 50-50 with Saudi Arabia.

History and Government. Kuwait is governed by members of the Al-Sabah dynasty founded in 1756. Under a treaty of 1899 Great Britain administered foreign relations and guaranteed territorial integrity until Kuwait became fully independent, 1961, by mutual agreement. It joined the Arab League 1961, the UN 1963. The nation's first constitution was proclaimed in Jan. 1963, when the first elections for a 50-member national assembly were held. The majority of the population are non-Kuwaiti (including many Palestinians) and do not have voting rights.

The Emir Sabah Al-Salim Al-Sabah became ruler Nov. 27, 1965, after the death of his older brother.

Iraqi troops crossed the Kuwait border in Mar. 1973 but soon withdrew; Iraq demanded possession of 2 islands claimed by Kuwait. Kuwait has ordered 20 Mirage F1 fighters from France, and other advanced weapons from the U.S.

Education and Religion. The government has utilized its enormous national income to create a welfare state with free medical care, education and social security. A $600 million fund aids other Arab nations. There are no taxes except customs duties. Educational facilities are being rapidly expanded. There were, in 1973, 225 schools of all types, with 150,000 students and over 9,000 teachers. The University of Kuwait was opened in Oct. 1966. Islam is the official religion.

Laos

Area: 91,428 sq. mi. Population (Govt. est. 1974): 3,260,000. Capitals: Vientiane, Luang Prabang. Monetary unit: Kip.

Laos is a constitutional monarchy in SE Asia, one of the 3 former French Indo-Chinese states. It is bounded by China, North and South Vietnam, Cambodia, Thailand and Burma. It is landlocked, smaller than Oregon, largely jungle and mountains.

Laos became a French protectorate in 1893 and a member of the Indo-Chinese Union in 1899. Nationalist aims grew in the 1940s, and the king promulgated a constitution May 11, 1947, providing for a constitutional monarchy under the Luang Prabang dynasty, and a parliamentary government. Laos became independent by a treaty with France July 19, 1949.

The king is Sri Savang Vatthana, acceded Oct. 30,

1959, on the death of his father, King Sisavang Vong. The national assembly is elected for 5 years.

Conflicts among neutralist, communist and conservative factions created a chaotic political situation despite 1954 agreements. Although Laos was intended to be neutral, rivalry between the communist Pathet Lao movement in the northern third of the country, led by Prince Souphanouvong, and rightwing and neutralist factions prevented integration of the Pathet Lao into the royalist army. Armed conflict increased after 1960 with the arrival of Russian arms and North Vietnamese troops.

The 3 factions formed a coalition government in June 1962, with neutralist Prince Souvanna Phouma as premier. A 14-nation conference in Geneva signed agreements July 23, 1962, guaranteeing neutrality and independence of Laos.

By 1964 the Pathet Lao had withdrawn from the coalition, and, with aid from N. Vietnamese troops, renewed sporadic attacks on government positions. Both Laos and U.S. planes bombed the Ho Chi Minh trail, supply line from N. Vietnam to communist forces in northern Laos and S. Vietnam.

In 1970 communist forces seized more territory in central and southeast Laos. On March 6 U.S. President Nixon confirmed that the U.S. had stepped up air support and military aid to Laos government forces. There were an est. 67,000 North Vietnamese troops in Laos, and some 15,000 Thai "irregulars" financed by the U.S. Laotian and North Vietnamese forces continued fighting in 1972.

Following a Feb. 21, 1973, ceasefire, the neutralists and Pathet Lao signed an agreement Sept. 14 for a coalition government and withdrawal of foreign troops. The coalition, with Souvanna Phouma as premier and Souphanouvong as president of a National Political Council, took office in Apr. 1974.

After Pathet Lao military gains, Souvanna Phouma in May 1975 ordered government troops to cease fighting, and Pathet Lao troops took effective control of the country. The formal coalition remained in effect. The U. S. withdrew its huge aid mission.

Chief products are tin, rice, maize, tobacco, cotton, opium, citrus fruits, benzoin, shellac, teakwood and coffee. The population comprises peoples of Thai, Indonesian and Chinese origin. Lao and French are the most important languages. Buddhism is the state religion.

Lebanon

Area: 4,015 sq. mi. Population (UN est. 1974): 2,780,000. Capital: Beirut. Monetary unit: Lebanese pound.

The Republic of Lebanon, in SW Asia, occupies a strip along the Mediterranean coast about 120 mi. long and 30 to 35 mi. wide, extending from the Israeli frontier on the S to Syria on the E and N. It is smaller than Connecticut. There is a narrow coastal strip and 2 main mountain ranges running N and S with fertile land between. Beirut, with one-third of the country's population, is the chief sea and airport.

Resources and Industries. Trade provides two-thirds of national income. Agriculture employs half the workers; chief crops are apples, citrus fruit, olives, tobacco, grapes, vegetables, cereals. Manufacturing is growing rapidly; important are food products, textiles, leather goods, cement, oil refining. Tripoli and Sidon are terminals of oil pipelines from Iraq and Saudi Arabia. Large hydroelectric and irrigation projects are being developed. Beirut is an Arab publishing center.

Lebanon has a free enterprise economy and banking secrecy. Private capital from other Arab states has poured into the country. Tourism is important.

History and Government. Lebanon was formed from 5 former Turkish Empire districts and became, along with Syria, an independent state Sept. 1, 1920, administered under French Mandate 1920-1941. In 1944 France yielded its powers. French troops withdrew in 1946.

Attempts to undermine the pro-western administration led to a revolt in May 1958. The U.S. sent Marines in reply to a government call for help. The revolt dwindled and American forces withdrew in Oct. 1958.

On Dec. 28, 1968, an Israeli helicopter raid on Beirut Airport destroyed 13 Lebanese airliners; Israel had accused Lebanon of aiding Arab terrorists. Lebanon's efforts to restrict Palestinian commandos caused armed clashes in 1969. Continued commando raids against Israeli civilians, 1970-75, brought Israeli reprisal and preventive raids against guerrilla camps and Lebanese villages.

Several hundred people were killed and massive damage inflicted in 1975 communal fighting. Palestinian units and leftist Lebanese Moslems fought against the Maronite militia, the Phalange. Foreign Arab governments helped impose a truce.

The republic's constitution instituted a democratic parliamentary regime. There is a unicameral legislature (Chamber of Deputies) of 99, elected every 4 years. The president is elected for a 6-year term. Traditionally he is a Christian, the premier a Moslem. All public positions are divided among the various religious communities according to the provisions of the 1943 National Covenant. Lebanon is a member of the UN and Arab League.

Education and Religion. Christians (mostly Maronites) number nearly half the population; Moslems most of the remainder, divided into Sunni and Shi'ite sects. There are 8 universities and institutions of higher learning in Beirut. Arabic is the official language; French and English are widely spoken.

Lesotho

Area: 11,716 sq. mi. Population (Govt. est. 1974): 1,020,000. Capital: Maseru. Monetary unit: S. Afr. Rand.

The former British dependency, Basutoland, became independent as the Kingdom of Lesotho Oct. 4, 1966. An African state without white settlers or landowners, it is about the size of Maryland and completely surrounded by the Republic of South Africa.

The land is mountainous, altitudes ranging from 5,000 to 11,000 ft. There are air, rail and road links with South Africa. Agriculture has been advanced with U.S. and UN technical aid. Maize, sorghum, barley, beans and peas are grown. The main industry is livestock raising which produces wool and mohair, the chief exports. There are small industries including diamond polishing. About 110,000 men work in South African mines. Up to 70% of males work abroad. Tourism is being promoted.

In 1868, Lesotho became a British protectorate upon the request of Moshesh, the paramount chieftain, who sought protection against the Boers of South Africa. The British granted a constitution for the area in 1959 providing for a universally elected Legislative Council. The government consists of a king, an elected National Assembly of 60, a Senate, Cabinet and prime minister. In 1970, elections were suspended by Prime Minister Leabua Jonathan.

Liberia

Area: 43,000 sq. mi. Population (UN est. 1974): 1,670,000. Capital: Monrovia. Monetary unit: U. S. dollar, also Liberian silver and copper coinage.

The Republic of Liberia is in West Africa adjacent to Sierra Leone, Guinea and Ivory Coast, and has an Atlantic coast of about 350 mi. Much of the country is forest. It is slightly larger than Ohio.

Liberia has no natural harbors. The Free Port of Monrovia, built 1945-48 with U.S. funds was turned over to the Liberian government in 1964, with payments to be concluded by 1999. The country is served by several international airlines.

Resources and Industries. Iron ore and rubber are the main products; loans from the U. S. and other Western nations helped increase production in the 1960s. In 1970 a U. S. company began developing the nation's timber resources.

Diamonds and gold are mined; other products are fibers, palm kernels, rice, cassava, coffee, cocoa and sugar. U. S. aid is promoting schools, hospitals, and food production.

History and Government. Liberia was founded in 1822 when a settlement was made at Monrovia by black freedmen from the U. S. with the assistance of American colonization societies. It was declared a republic July 26, 1847. Its constitution is modeled on that of the U. S. Only persons of African descent may acquire citizenship and only citizens may own real estate.

There is a president elected for one 8-year term (thereafter for 4-year terms); a Senate of 18 elected for 6 years and a House of Representatives of 52, elected for 4 years. William V. S. Tubman, president since 1943, died July 23, 1971, and was succeeded by the vice president, William R. Tolbert. Descendants of freedman dominate politics.

Education and Religion. About 7% are Christian, 3% Moslem, the rest nativists. There are nearly 4,000 schools, one university and two colleges. English is the official language, but African languages are spoken by the majority.

Libya

Area: 679,536 sq. mi. Population (UN est. 1974): 2,350,000. Capital: Tripoli. Monetary unit: Libyan Dinar.

Libya is an Arab republic comprising 10 provinces in the former states of Tripolitania, Cyrenaica and Fezzan. Larger than Alaska, it is on the North African coast, bounded by the Mediterranean, Egypt, Sudan, Chad, Niger, Algeria and Tunisia.

Resources and Industries. Discovery of major oil fields in the northern part of the country beginning in 1957 brought prosperity and an improved standard of living to the country. Production was cut drastically after 1970, but price hikes kept income high.

In 1973 Libya expropriated 51% of several U.S. oil firms' assets. In 1974 it took over complete ownership. It joined the 1973-74 Arab oil embargo against Western nations. Libya was the world's ninth largest petroleum producer in 1974.

In the 1960s-70s, several hundred schools were built, boosting enrollment from 40,000 to over 365,-000. Homes, hospitals, roads and power stations were constructed. Per capita gross national product rose from $145 in 1959 to $2,262 in 1972. Education and health services are provided free.

Libya had been basically agricultural, producing dates, olives, lemons, almonds, figs, grapes and tobacco. Carpets, leather goods and embroidered fabrics are also produced. Food processing and other factories have been built.

In 1973 "people's committees" took over many factories, firms, radio and TV stations, hospitals and farms, with government approval.

History and Government. Libya has come under the domination successively of Carthage, Rome, the Vandals, the Ottoman Empire and Italy. After World War II Tripoli and Cyrenaica were placed under British administration, the Fezzan under French.

Emir Mohammed Idris El Senussi (born 1890), ruler of the Senussi tribesmen, was recognized by Great Britain as emir of Cyrenaica, June, 1949. He promulgated a constitution and set up an interim government over internal affairs, Sept. 18, 1949. Libya, as a sovereign state, was approved by the UN, 1949, effective Jan. 2, 1952. A constituent assembly approved a constitutional monarchy and named the

emir as king of Libya, Dec. 3, 1950. A hereditary monarchy was proclaimed by King Idris I, Dec. 24, 1951.

On Sept. 1, 1969, a Revolutionary Command Council headed by Col. Muammar el-Qaddafi overthrew the government and announced formation of the Arab Republic of Libya.

On Sept. 1, 1971, Libya joined Egypt and Syria in a Federation of Arab Republics. In Aug. 1972 Libya and Egypt agreed to prepare unification of the 2 nations by Sept. 1, 1973. But Egypt put off the union and in Aug. 1974 charged that Qaddafi conspired in the bombing of an Egyptian presidential palace. Qaddafi and Tunisia's president, Habib Bourguiba, announced in Jan. 1974 their nations would unite, but Bourgiba soon dropped the plan.

Education and Religion. Libya's population is mostly Arab Moslems and Islam is the state religion. Schools were taken over by the "people's committees" in 1973. There are 2 universities.

Defense. In 1970, Libya arranged to buy jet planes from France and received tanks and other arms from the USSR; the U.S. turned over its Wheelus Air Force Base to Libya. The USSR sold over $1 billion in advanced arms in 1975; 1,000 Soviet advisers were present. Armed forces total 32,000.

Liechtenstein

Area: 62 sq. mi. Population (Govt. est. 1974): 23,700. Capital: Vaduz. Monetary unit: Swiss franc.

Liechtenstein is a principality on the Upper Rhine between Austria and Switzerland. It is slightly smaller than the District of Columbia. It received independence in 1866 when the German Confederation dissolved and was in an economic union with Austria from 1852 to 1918. By treaty with Switzerland (1920-23) that country administers its posts and telegraphs, customs and foreign interests. There is no army, only a police force of 40 with 25 auxiliaries.

The country is highly industrialized. Industries are machines and tools, cotton spinning and weaving, precision instruments, false teeth, pharmaceuticals, ceramics and canned food. Finely engraved postage stamps are sold around the world. Exports from 1974 were valued at $206 million. Thousands of foreign workers are employed in Liechtenstein and constitute about 36% of the resident population.

Liechtenstein is a constitutional monarchy. Under the constitution, granted in 1921, legislative powers rest in a Diet of 15 members, elected for four years by direct vote, on a basis of male suffrage and proportional representation. The reigning prince is Franz Joseph II. He succeeded his uncle, Prince Franz I, on the latter's abdication March 30, 1938. Taxes are very low and consequently many international corporations have made their headquarters there.

The country is predominantly Catholic. German is the language.

Luxembourg

Area: 999 sq. mi. Population (UN est. 1974): 340,-000. Capital: Luxembourg. Monetary unit: Luxembourg franc.

Luxembourg is a European Grand Duchy, bounded by Germany, Belgium and France. It measures only 55 mi. long by 34 mi. wide, smaller than Rhode Island.

Resources and Industries. About 9,500 farmers cultivate 336,000 acres. The principal crops are oats, wheat, rye, barley and potatoes.

Luxembourg's iron ore deposits, in the south, are the basis for an important steel industry. It employs 17% of the labor force, and accounts for 45% of total industrial production, and 65% of the value of exports. The country also produces chemicals, beer, tires, tobacco and metal products, cement, roses and dairy products.

History and Government. Luxembourg, founded

about 963, passed under the domination of Burgundy, Spain, Austria and France from 1443 to 1815; regained autonomy under the Treaty of Vienna, 1815. It left the Germanic Confederation in 1866, its integrity and neutrality guaranteed by the Treaty of London, 1867. Overrun by Germany in 2 World Wars, Luxembourg abolished its unarmed neutrality in 1948. Customs union with Netherlands and Belgium was adopted 1948, expanded to the Benelux Economic Union, 1958. Luxembourg is a member of the UN, NATO, OECD, Council of Europe, Western European Union and the EC.

As a Grand Duchy, Luxembourg is a constitutional monarchy, governed under the constitution of 1868, with modifications. Legislative power rests with a Council of State of 21, chosen for life, and a 59-member Chamber of Deputies elected by universal suffrage with executive power delegated to a minister of state and a Cabinet. Grand Duke Jean (b. Jan. 5, 1921) became chief of state Nov. 12, 1964, when his mother, Grand Duchess Charlotte, abdicated in his favor.

The population is almost entirely Roman Catholic. Education is compulsory. Official languages are French and German; national language is Luxembourgeois.

Madagascar

Area: 203,035 sq. mi. Population (Govt. est. 1973): 7,655,134. Capital: Tananarive. Monetary unit: Ariary.

Formerly a French Overseas Territory, Madagascar is a large island off the SE coast of Africa, from which it is separated by the 240-mi. wide Mozambique Channel. It is about 980 mi. long and 360 mi. wide at its greatest breadth. It is a little smaller than Texas. There is a humid coastal strip on the E, fertile valleys in the mountainous center plateau region, and a wider coastal strip on the W.

The name of the nation and the island is Madagascar; the government is officially the Malagasy Republic.

The people consist of many ethnic groups from succeeding waves of immigration, including those of SE Asian, Arab and African descent. They speak Malagasy, a language of Malayan origin; but coastal tribes have distinct dialects, and have charged dominance by the highland Merinas. Over 3 million are animists; 3 million are Christians, about equally divided between Catholics and Protestants.

Madagascar became a French protectorate, 1885, and a French colony 1896. It proclaimed itself autonomous 1958. Independence came June 26, 1960.

Discontent with inflation and French domination of the university led to student demonstrations, followed by a coup in May 1972. President Philibert Tsiranana was ousted. In Oct. a referendum approved a new government with Gen. Gabriel Ramanantsoa as head of government, a Superior Council and a National Popular Council.

Most of the population is engaged in agriculture. Chief crops are coffee, cloves, vanilla (producing 80% of the world's supply), rice, livestock, sugar, sisal, tobacco, peanuts, etc. Small factories have been established.

Malawi

Area: 45,747 sq. mi. Population (Govt. est. 1974): 4,900,000. Capital: Lilongwe. Monetary unit: Kwacha.

Malawi, in SE Africa, stretches 560 mi. north and south along Lake Malawi (Lake Nyasa), most of which belongs to Malawi. High mountains, dense forests and broad plains make it a scenic country. It is about the size of Pennsylvania.

Visited by Dr. David Livingstone in 1859, it became a British protectorate, Nyasaland, in 1891. From 1953 to 1963 it was a member of the Federation of Rhodesia and Nyasaland. On Feb. 1, 1963, it became internally self-governing and, on July 6, 1964, achieved full independence from Britain, taking the name Malawi. It became a republic July 6, 1966.

Malawi is almost entirely an agricultural country with only a few light industries. Four crops—tea, tobacco, peanuts and cotton— account for 90% of the exports. Other important products are sugar, rubber, soybeans and coffee.

Since 1967, factories have been buil for textiles, shoes, sugar, farm implements, and other products formerly imported.

Main trading partners are the United Kingdom, South Africa and the U.S. Malawi is dependent on Mozambique for her rail trade routes to the sea. Construction continued in 1974 on a new capital at Lilongwe.

The Univ. of Malawi, which has 3 colleges, was built partly with U.S. aid; the first class graduated in July 1969. Population is mostly African; there are about 12,000 Indians and 8,000 of European descent.

Malaysia

Area: 128,328 sq. mi. Population (Govt. est. 1974): 11,700,000. Capital: Kuala Lumpur. Monetary unit: Malaysian dollar.

Occupying the southern part of the Malay Peninsula in SE Asia and the northern part of the island of Borneo, Malaysia produces about 40% of the world's output of both rubber and tin. Total area is larger than Arizona.

Malaysia was created Sept. 16, 1963. It included the old Federation of Malaya (11 Malayan states which had become an independent constitutional monarchy and member of the Commonwealth Aug. 31, 1957), plus the formerly-British Singapore (an island and city off the southern tip of the Malay Peninsula), Sabah (former British North Borneo) and Sarawak (former British Colony in NW Borneo.).

Indonesia harassed the new nation with guerrilla action 1963-65. After Indonesian President Sukarno lost power, Malaysia and Indonesia agreed Aug. 11, 1966, to restore normal relations; full relations were restored Aug. 31, 1967.

On Aug. 9, 1965, the separation of Singapore from Malaysia was announced under an agreement by Malaysia and Singapore officials that this was the best way to end tensions between the ethnic Chinese, largest group in Singapore, and the Malays, who were in control of the Malaysia government.

With Singapore's departure, the Malays numbered 44% of Malaysian's population and ethnic Chinese 36%.

Forming East Malaysia are Sabah (capital, Kota Kinabalu) and Sarawak (capital, Kuching). They lie on the N Coast of the island of Borneo and have a total pop. of 1,900,000 (1974). area of 77.638 mi.

A monarch, known as the yang dipertuan agong (supreme head of Malaysia) is elected by a council of hereditary rulers of the Malayan states every 5 years. There is a Senate, House of Representatives, prime minister and Cabinet. The ruling National Front dominates political life.

In May 1969 at least 180 persons died in riots between ethnic Chinese and Malays in Kuala Lumpur. Communist guerrillas renewed activities in 1971 and 1972.

Resources and industries: Rubber, tin, timber, iron ore, palm oil and copra are the main products. Rubber, much of it produced by new high-yield trees, accounts for 41% of exports; tin amounts to 13% of exports. A million tourists visited in 1974.

Other agricultural products are rice, coconuts, tapioca, sugar, pepper, camphor. Small-scale industry includes rubber goods, pottery, cement, pewterware, furniture, bricks, tiles, soap, fertilizers, processing plants.

Religion and Language. The Malays and some others are Moslems; other religions are Buddhism, Christianity and Hinduism. Malay is the official language in W. Malaysia; Malay and English are official in E. Malaysia.

Defense. After 1971 Malaysia increased its armed forces to 66,200 to compensate for reduction of British Southeast Asia forces. Britain, Australia and New Zealand maintain small forces in Malaysia to aid its defense.

Republic of Maldives

Capital: Male. Area: 115 sq. mi. Population (Govt. census 1973): 122,673. Monetary unit: Rupee.

The Maldive Islands are a group of 19 atolls containing 1,087 islands, 210 of which are inhabited. Totaling about twice the area of the District of Columbia, they are in the Indian Ocean 300 mi. SW of the southern tip of India. The country obtained full independence from Great Britain on July 26, 1965, in an agreement under which Britain retained its RAF base on Gan Is. in Addu Atoll in the southern Maldives. The Maldives became a member of the UN, 1965.

The island had been a British-protected state since 1887, with Britain responsible for their defense and foreign relations until the 1965 agreement. Long a sultanate, the islands became briefly a republic in 1953 and a sultanate again in 1954. After a referendum, the country became a republic once more, Nov. 11, 1968, with a popularly elected president and legislature (Mallis).

The people are Moslems and seafarers. Coconuts, fruit and millet are grown; chief occupation is fishing; production of processed fish, marketed in Ceylon, is the main industry. Also exported are coir, copra and shells.

Mali

Area: 464,873 sq. mi. Population (UN est. 1974): 5,560,000. Capital: Bamako. Monetary unit: Mali franc.

The Republic of Mali, a one-time French Overseas Territory in West Africa, is a landlocked nation larger than Texas but smaller than Alaska. It is a vast plain in the upper basins of the Senegal and Niger Rivers, extending N into the Sahara.

From the 11th to 15th Centuries the area was part of the great Mali Empire which stretched from the western Sudan to the Atlantic; Timbuktu was a renowned center of Islamic learning.

Under provisions of the 1958 French constitution French Sudan became the Sudanese Republic, an autonomous republic, and formed with neighboring Senegal Jan. 17, 1959, the Mali Federation. Complete independence was proclaimed June 20, 1960. Senegal withdrew from the federation Aug. 20, 1960, and Sudan took the name Republic of Mali Sept. 22. It signed economic and cultural agreements with France. On June 8, 1963, Mali and Senegal reached customs, trade and railway traffic agreements, with use of Senegalese harbors by Mali.

On Nov. 19, 1968, a coup ended the socialist regime of President Modibo Keita; Lt. Moussa Traore became president Dec. 6, 1968.

The country is mainly agricultural and pastoral. Millet, rice and peanuts are the chief crops. Cotton, rubber and river fishing are also important. Livestock raising is a major prop of the economy. Famine, following a long drought, struck Mali and other sub-Saharan nations in 1973-74. Aid was sent by many nations, 40% of it from the U. S., but loss of livestock and dislocation of 700,000 Tuareg nomads remained problems.

The people are mostly Moslem, with a minority of Christians. French is the official language.

Malta

Area: 122 sq. mi. Population (Govt. est. 1974): 315,-756. Capital: Valetta. Monetary unit: Pound.

Malta lies in the Mediterranean 58 mi. S of Sicily and 180 mi. from Africa. The island of Malta itself is 95 sq. mi.; the other islands in the group are Gozo, 26 sq. mi., and Comino, one sq. mi.

For 35 centuries Malta was under successive rule by Phoenicians, Carthaginians, Romans, Arabs, Normans, the Knights of Malta, France and Britain (which annexed Malta in 1814). It withstood Axis air attacks for 3 years in WWII. It achieved limited self-government in 1887; home rule, 1961. On Sept. 21, 1964, it became independent, with the British monarch as head of state, and agreed to permit British forces to maintain a base for 10 years. Malta became a republic Dec. 13, 1974. It is a member of the Commonwealth, Council of Europe and UN. A House of Representatives with 65 members is elected by universal suffrage; the prime minister and Cabinet derive authority from the House.

Population density is high; there is continuous emigration, much of it to Australia, the United Kingdom and Canada.

A Labor party victory in June 1971 elections led to the ouster of NATO naval hq. In 1972 Malta agreed to Britain's use of its military bases for 7 years in return for greatly increased payments; USSR forces would be barred. Malta is non-aligned.

Leading industries are ship repairing, food and beverages, textiles and tourism. Visiting tourists rose from 23,000 in 1962 to 280,000 in 1974. Historic sites, a casino and village fetes are among attractions. Maltese is an Arab dialect written in Latin characters. Nearly all inhabitants are Roman Catholic.

Mauritania

Area: 419,229 sq. mi. Population (Govt. est. 1974): 1,290,000. Capital: Nouakchott. Monetary unit: Ouguiya.

The Islamic Republic of Mauritania, former French Overseas Territory in West Africa, is bounded by the Atlantic Ocean, Spanish Sahara, Algeria, Mali and Senegal. Population is 80% Morrish. Mauritania is about four-fifths the size of Alaska.

The economy has been agricultural and pastoral. Products include dates, grain, meat, fish. There are large herds of cattle, camels, sheep and goats and large deposits of iron and copper.

A large new iron mine was opened in 1963 to add to the nation's annual production of 12 million tons of iron ore; fishing, which produced 270,000 tons of fish in 1970, was being expanded; a copper mine opened in 1971, with annual yield of 30,000 metric tons; a new cattle slaughterhouse and freezing plant was opened. It has received aid from France and China. Drought and famine struck in 1973-74; aid was sent by Western nations, 40% of it from the U. S.

Mauritania became fully independent Nov. 28, 1960. Prime Minister Mokhtar Ould Daddah, appointed June 26, 1959, became president by popular vote in Aug. 1962.

Mauritius

Area: 787 sq. mi. Population (Govt. est. 1974): 875,-000. Capital: Port Louis. Monetary unit: Rupee.

Mauritius, an island in the Indian Ocean 550 mi. E of Madagascar, became an independent nation within the Commonwealth on Mar. 12, 1968, after 158 years of British rule. It has a parliamentary government.

Mauritius has one of the world's most complex racial, religious and political mixtures as well as one of the world's highest population densities. There are 4 main groups: over 408,000 Hindus; 224,000 of mixed European and African descent and whites; 130,000 Moslems and 25,000 Chinese. Although the official language is English, French is spoken by many persons, and Creole, a French patois, is the lingua franca. Chinese and Indian languages are also spoken.

The country had a nearly one-crop economy, sugar. However, a flourishing tea industry has been developed and tourism is growing. Commonwealth subsidies support sugar prices and aid the economy. Unemployment was about 19% in 1973; the literacy rate is very high.

Mauritius was uninhabited until 1638 when the Dutch settled there, introduced sugar cane and gave the island its present name in honor of Prince Maurice of Nassau. The French took over in 1721 and imported African slaves. The British, who seized the island in 1810, brought Hindus and Moslems from India to work the sugar plantations.

Mexico

Area: 761,601 sq. mi. Population (Govt. est. 1974): 58,120,000. Capital: Mexico City. Monetary unit: Peso.

Second most populous nation in Latin America and 3d largest in area, Mexico compiled an enviable record for progress, social improvement and fiscal responsibility in the middle decades of the 20th century.

With housing, health, farm and industrial programs, the nation lifted itself and its people into the mainstream of the modern world; life expectancy, for example, was raised from 39 years in 1940 to 61 years in 1972.

Ever-growing streams of foreign visitors (958,000 in 1962; 2,234,682 in 1972) find spectacular scenery, striking art and architecture, remains of Indian civilizations, cosmopolitan and colonial cities and luxurious resorts.

The Sierra Madre Occidental Mtns. run NW-SE near the west coast. The Sierra Madre Oriental Mtns., a continuation of the Rockies, run near the Gulf of Mexico coast nearly as far S as Veracruz.

Between the 2 ranges lies the central plateau of Mexico, altitude from 5,000 to 8,000 ft. with a pleasant climate and with the vegetation and products of the temperate zone. The lowlands along the coast are tropical, rising to subtropical in the foothills, with a heavy rainfall on the Gulf side. Along the Pacific slope and in the interior irrigation is needed. Mexico is nearly 3 times the size of Texas.

Tampico and Veracruz, on the Gulf, are the busiest of Mexico's 49 ocean ports.

Mexico's population is composed of descendants of the Toltecs, Aztecs, Mayas and the Spaniards who conquered and colonized the country.

Resources and Industries. Mexico is rich in minerals and timber. It is one of the top 5 producers of silver; also important are gold, copper, lead, zinc, antimony, mercury, arsenic, amorphous graphite, molybenum, sulphur, coal and opal. Mexico is the world's 14th largest petroleum producer and is self-sufficient in oil; vast new reserves have been uncovered in Yucatan. The industry is nationalized. Natural gas is sold to the U. S. Electric power generated in 1973 rose to 37 billion kwh.

Farming, stock raising and fishing are important. The land is rich, but the rugged topography and lack of sufficient rainfall are major obstacles. Crops and farm prices are controlled, as are export and import. Large estates have been expropriated; since 1915 the government has distributed about 160 million acres to small farmers through landholding communities (ejidos). Major irrigation projects in Sonora and Sinaloa have increased production of cotton and wheat.

Principal export crops are cotton, coffee, cane sugar, tomatoes, cattle, fruit fresh and frozen meats.

Mexico is the 5th largest coffee producer; other major crops are corn, rice, tobacco, garbanzos, cocoa, sisal, bananas. About 50% of the world supply of sisal comes from Yucatan, in southern Mexico.

Mexican industry is producing products formerly imported, especially in iron and steel, chemicals, electric goods. Other products are cotton, wool and synthetic textiles, flour, beverages, soap, cigarettes and cigars, rubber, paper, rubber products, cement, shoes, glass, furniture and tiles. Mexico is famous for industrial and native handicraft in silver, pottery, leather, wood, fibers and textiles. The U.S. buys a large portion of Mexico's exports.

Index of industrial production (1970 = 100) was 123 in 1973.

Foreign trade, in thousands of U.S. dollars:

	Imports	Exports
1973	$4,146,000	$2,452,000
1974	$6,519,000	$3,420,000

History and Government. Mexico was the site of advanced Indian civilizations before the Spanish conquest. The Mayas, an agricultural people, moved up from Yucatan and built immense stone pyramids and invented a calendar. The Toltecs were overcome by the Aztecs, who founded Tenochtitlan 1325 A.D., now Mexico City. Hernando Cortes, Spanish conquistador, destroyed the Aztec empire, 1519-1521.

After 3 centuries of misrule the people rose, under Fr. Miguel Hidalgo y Costilla (a priest), 1810, Fr. Morelos y Payon (another priest), 1812, and Gen. Agustin Iturbide, who made independence effectual Sept. 27, 1821, but made himself emperor as Agustin I. A republic was chosen in 1823.

Mexican territory extended into the present American Southwest and California until Texas revolted and established a republic in 1836; the Mexican legislature refused recognition but was unable to enforce its authority there. After numerous clashes, the U.S.-Mexican War, 1846-48, resulted in the loss by Mexico of the lands north of the Rio Grande, about half its total area.

French arms supported an Austrian archduke on the throne of Mexico as Maximilian I, 1864-67, but pressure from the U.S. forced France to withdraw troops, causing Maximilian's defeat by Mexicans under Benito Juarez, and subsequent execution. A dictatorial rule by Porfirio Diaz, president 1877-80, 1884-1911, led to fighting by rival forces until the new constitution of Feb. 5, 1917 provided social reform. Since then Mexico has developed large-scale programs of social security, labor protection and school improvement. A constitutional provision requires management to share profits with labor.

Mexico is a federal democratic republic of 29 states, with president, legislature and judiciary elected by universal suffrage; 2 territories (Baja California Sur and Quintana Roo) with governors appointed by the president, and a federal district (Distrito Federal) containing Mexico City. The president is elected for 6 years and thereafter ineligible; 60 senators for 6 years and deputies for 3 years, ineligible for reelection until one term has intervened.

The Institutional Revolutionary party has been dominant in politics since 1929. In 1970 the legal voting age was lowered from 21 to 18.

Education and Religion. Education is secular, with primary education free and compulsory up to 15 years of age. Vocational instruction particularly in agriculture is promoted and there are many technical schools. The National University of Mexico continues an educational foundation of 1551 A.D. Spanish is the language.

Most of the people are Roman Catholics. All church real estate is vested in the nation, but care of church buildings is the responsibility of the clergy.

Defense. The armed forces total 82,000 regulars, 250,000 conscripts. Mexico is a member of the UN and OAS.

(See also Index for Mexico City.)

Monaco

Area: 453 acres. Population (est. 1973): 30,000. Capital: Monaco. Monetary unit: French franc.

Monaco is a small principality on the Mediterranean surrounded on all but the sea side by France. It is noted for its mild climate and magnificent scenery. There is a local police force of 200.

Resources and Industries. Monaco's fame as a tourist resort and international conference city is widespread. Its revenues derive from indirect taxation, a tobacco monopoly, postage and the gambling tables of the Monte Carlo Casino.

History and Government. An independent principality for over 300 years, Monaco has belonged to the House of Grimaldi except during the French Revolution. It was placed under the protectorate of Sardinia in 1815, and under that of France, 1861. The Prince of Monaco was an absolute ruler until a constitution was promulgated in 1911.

A new constitution, proclaimed Dec. 17, 1962, provided for female suffrage and abolition of capital punishment, and established a court to guarantee liberties. The legislature (National Council) consists of 18 members elected for 5 years.

The ruler of Monaco is Prince Rainier III who succeeded his grandfather, Prince Louis II, who died May 9, 1949. He married Grace Kelly, American motion picture actress, Apr. 18, 1956. A daughter, Princess Caroline Louise Marguerite, was born Jan. 23, 1957. The heir apparent, Prince Albert Alexander Louis Pierre, was born Mar. 14, 1958. Princess Stephanie Marie Elizabeth was born Feb. 1, 1965.

In 1967 the government purchased for $8 million the holdings of Aristotle Onassis in the Societe des Bains de Mer, owner of the Casino and other interests. The prince launched a program of reclaiming land from the sea and developing new tourist facilities.

Mongolia

Area: 604,247 sq. mi. Population (Govt. est. 1974): 1,400,000. Capital: Ulan Bator. Monetary unit: Tughrik.

The Mongolian People's Republic comprises Outer Mongolia in northeastern Asia. It is bounded on the N by the Siberian provinces of USSR, and on 3 other sides by Mainland China. It is larger than Alaska. Much of Mongolia is a high plateau with vast grasslands; arid lands in the south are part of the Gobi Desert.

Resources and Industries. In the early 1970s Mongolia was changing from a nomadic culture to one of settled agriculture and growing industries with aid from the USSR and East European nations. Irrigation and scientific farming methods were pressed to increase grain crops and fodder for the large livestock herds which long were the mainstay of the economy. Food processing, textile, chemical, brick and cement factories were established in growing cities in the north. Electric power plants were built, running on coal; Mongolia has large coal deposits as well as tungsten, copper, molybdenum, gold, tin.

History and Government. One of the world's oldest countries, Mongolia reached the zenith of its power in the 13th Century when Genghis Khan and his successors conquered all of China and extended their influence as far W as Hungary and Poland. In later centuries, the empire dissolved and Mongolia came under the suzerainty of China.

With the advent of the 1911 Chinese revolution, Mongolia, with Russian backing, declared its independence. A Mongolian Communist regime was established July 11, 1921.

The constitution vests power in the elected Great People's Khural from which is drawn a 7-member Presidium and a Council of Ministers. Actual power is in the hands of the Communist party and its 9-man Politburo.

Mongolia has sided with the Russians in the Sino-Soviet dispute. A Mongolian-Soviet mutual assistance pact was signed Jan. 15, 1966, and thousands of Soviet troops are based in the country. Mongolia is a UN member.

Education and Religion. There are primary, secondary and technical schools, and 7 higher educational institutes. Buddhist Lamaism is the leading religion. Khalka Mongol is the main language, written since 1941 in the Cyrillic alphabet.

Morocco

Area: 171,953 sq. mi. Population (Govt. est. 1974): 16,880,000. Capital: Rabat. Monetary unit: Dirham.

The monarchy of Morocco lies on the NW tip of Africa separated from Europe by the 8-mile-wide Strait of Gibraltar. It is bounded by Algeria, Spanish Sahara (which Morocco claims), the Mediterranean and the Atlantic.

It consists of 5 natural regions: A series of mountain ranges (Riff, facing Gibraltar; Middle Atlas, extending NW of Marrakesh; Upper Atlas, and Anti-Atlas); a series of rich plains in the W; the alluvial plains of Haouz in the SW; the "mesata," a well-cultivated series of plateaus in the center; a pre-Saharan zone extending from S to E.

The inhabitants largely are a mixture of Arabs and the original Berbers.

Resources and Industries. Morocco is primarily agricultural and pastoral. Cereals rank first among agricultural products, including barley, wheat and corn. Fruit and vineyards are abundant and dates a staple crop. Carpets, leather goods, clothing and textiles are among the manufactures.

Morocco ranks 3d in world production of phosphate rock and is first in phosphate exports. It produces 5% of the world's cobalt. Other minerals are antimony manganese, zinc, lead, oil and coal.

In the late 1960s, a number of dams were constructed for irrigation, including a large project built with U.S. aid. Foreign-owned agricultural lands were nationalized in 1973.

Tourism attracts 1,000,000 visitors annually to see Morocco's casbahs, Roman ruins, old fortresses and oases.

History and Government. Morocco is a remnant of an early empire founded by the Arabs at the close of the 7th Century which encompassed all NW Africa and most of the Iberian Peninsula.

Part of Morocco came under Spanish rule in the 19th Century; in the early 20th France took control of the rest. A general uprising of tribes in 1910 led to the dispatch of a French expeditionary force that occupied Fez in 1911. Uprisings continued for 2 decades until the exile of Abdelkarim el Khattabi in 1926 and the surrender of Sidi Ali Hociene in 1933.

Morocco became independent Mar. 2, 1956, after agreement by France to end its protectorate. Spain signed similar agreements.

Tangier, a seaport which had been internationalized, was turned over to Moroccan control in 1956. Ifni, a small Spanish enclave on the Atlantic coast, was turned over to Morocco June 30, 1969.

Mohammed V, Sultan since 1927 (with the title of king since 1957), died Feb. 26, 1961. His eldest son became King Hassan II.

Under a constitution approved by referendum Dec. 7, 1962, Morocco became a constitutional monarchy. The first Parliament was elected May 17, 1963.

The king suspended Parliament in June 1965. A new constitution was approved by voters in July 1970, providing for a unicameral, elected Chamber of Deputies. An attempted army revolt failed in July 1971. Air force pilots tried unsuccessfully to assassinate the king in Aug. 1972.

Morocco accepted U.S. and USSR military and economic aid on a basis of non-interference in its internal affairs. It has agreements with France on economic, technical and cultural cooperation. It is a member of the UN, OAU and Arab League.

Education and Religion. Trade schools and agricultural training centers have been developed, in addition to regular schools. The main university is in Rabat. Arabic is the official language. The population is Sunni Moslem.

Defense. Armed forces total 56,000.

Mozambique

Area: 303,373 sq. mi. Population (UN est. 1974): 9,030,000. Capital: Lourenco Marques.

The Peoples' Republic of Mozambique faces the Indian Ocean and Mozambique Channel in SW Africa, and borders on Tanzania, Malawi, Zambia, Rhodesia, South Africa, and Swaziland. It is somewhat larger than Texas.

Coastal lowlands comprise 44% of the country, with plateaus rising in steps to the mountains along the western border.

Resources and Industries. Agriculture dominates the economy, and cashews, cotton, sugar, copra, sisal, and tea are exported. Fishing is important. Coal is the leading mineral currently produced, but tantalite, copper, iron, bauxite, and gold have been found. Manufactures include cement, alcohol, food products, and textiles. A vast hydro-power complex is being built at Cabora Bassa on the Zambezi River, which bisects the country.

History and Government. The first Portuguese post on the Mozambique coast was established in 1505, on the trade route to the East. Mozambique became independent June 25, 1975, after a ten-year war against Portuguese colonial domination. The 1974 revolution in Portugal paved the way for the orderly transfer of power to Frelimo (Front for the Liberation of Mozambique), which had earlier gained complete control of the independence movement. Frelimo took over local administration Sept. 20, 1974, over the opposition, in part violent, of some blacks and whites. The new government, led by Maoist Pres. Samora Machel, promised a gradual transition to a communist system, beginning with indoctrination to combat "individualism" and capitalist or traditionalist values. All private schools were closed. Rural collective farms were called for in a July 27, 1975, directive. Immediate economic problems included the emigration of most of the country's 160,000 whites, a politically untenable dependence on white-ruled regimes in Rhodesia and South Africa, and an external debt of $640 million.

The population is divided into various Bantu tribes, with those in the south more influenced by Portuguese culture and language. Catholicism and Islam have made many converts, and Protestant missions are present. The majority of the population is as yet illiterate, though schools in 1970 enrolled over one-half million students.

Nauru

Area: 8 sq. mi. Population (census 1972): 6,817. Capital: Uaboe District. Monetary unit: Australian dollar.

Nauru, one of the world's smallest nations, became an independent republic Jan. 31, 1968, after 80 years of foreign rule. In the western Pacific 26 mi. S of the Equator and 1,300 mi. NE of Australia, Nauru is comfortably affluent because of its high-grade phosphate deposits.

Phosphate exports provide one of the world's highest per capita revenues for the 3,500 native Nauruans (883 Chinese, 627 Europeans and 1,787 Pacific Islanders also live in Nauru, many working in the phosphate industry). The deposits are expected to be nearly exhausted by 1990.

The island was discovered in 1798 by the British but was formally annexed to the German Empire in 1888. After World War I, Nauru became a League of Nations mandate administered by Australia. During World War II the Japanese occupied the island and shipped 1,200 Nauruans to the fortress island of Truk as slave laborers.

In 1947 Nauru was made a UN trust territory, administered by Australia on behalf of the 3 trust powers: Australia, Great Britain and New Zealand. Because of its small size Nauru has not sought UN membership.

An elected Parliament has 18 members.

Nepal

Area: 54,362 sq. mi. Population (Govt. est. 1974): 12,320,000. Capital: Katmandu. Monetary unit: Nepalese rupee.

Nepal is a monarchy in the Himalayas, bounded on the N by China (Tibet) and E, S and W by India. It is about the size of Arkansas.

There are many fertile valleys lying in the slopes of the lofty mountains, including Mt. Everest, on the Tibet border. The capital is in the valley of Katmandu, 15 mi. long and 20 wide, which is noted for its many, lavishly decorated shrines.

Virtually closed to the outside world for centuries, Nepal is now linked to India and Pakistan by modern roads and air service and to Tibet by road.

Nepal has established a 500 sq. mi. game preserve for elephants, tigers, rhinoceroses, leopards, boars, crocodiles and over 500 species of birds.

Resources and Industries. Nepal has rich forests and quartz deposits. The country exports jute, rice, grain, cattle, hides, wheat and drugs. Trade is 90% with India. Tourism provides vital funds.

U.S technical aid has made possible settlement of the fertile but once inaccessible Rapti Valley with a 53-mi. $500,000 highway. Nepal also receives financial aid from India, China and others. Its 4th 5-year plan stresses hydroelectric power and roads.

History and Government. Nepal was originally a group of petty principalities, the inhabitants of one of which, the Gurkhas, became dominant about 1769. In 1951 King Tribhubana Bir Bikram, member of the Shah family, ended the system of rule by hereditary premiers of the Ranas family, who had kept the kings virtual prisoners. He established a cabinet system of government Feb. 18, 1951.

King Tribhubana died Mar. 13, 1955, and was succeeded by his son, Mahendra Bir Bikram Shah Dev, who died Jan. 31, 1972, and was succeeded by his son, Birendra Bir Bikram Shah Dev. King Mahendra promulgated a new constitution Dec. 16, 1962, providing for a three-tier system of indirectly elected councils topped by a National Assembly or National Panchayat.

Education and Religion. There are more than 2,400 English schools in addition to Sanskrit and Nepali schools and other institutions of learning. Buddha was born at Lumbini in South-Central Nepal. Hinduism and Buddhism are the main religions. Polygamy, child marriage and the caste system were officially abolished in 1963.

The Netherlands

Area (land): 14,192 sq. mi. Population (Census 1975): 13,597,616. Capital: Amsterdam. Monetary unit: Guilder.

The Kingdom of the Netherlands a constitutional monarchy in NW Europe, is bounded by Germany, Belgium, and the North Sea. Its surface is flat, with an average height above sea level of 37 ft., with much land below sea level, reclaimed and protected by dikes, of which there are 1,500 mi. The country is about twice the area of New Jersey.

Since 1927 the government has been draining the IJsselmeer, formerly the Zuider Zee, and converting the reclaimed land into farms. The total will add over 550,000 acres. By 1972, 410,000 acres had been reclaimed. Work is also progressing on damming the southwest estuaries.

The Hague is the seat of government, but Amsterdam is the sole capital of the kingdom and the inaugurations of sovereigns are held there.

Rotterdam, located along the principal mouth of the Rhine, handles the most cargo of any ocean port in the world.

Resources and Industries. About 43% of total land area is given to pasture, farming takes 22%, heath, dunes and forest 7%, horticulture 3.4%. Of the arable land 80% is in holdings of fewer than 50 acres and about 25% of fewer than 10 acres. Cereals, potatoes, sugar beets, vegetables and fruits are raised. Agriculture and fishing engage about 6% of the workers. Dairy products are a major export. In pork exports the nation ranks 2d to Denmark. Flowers, bulbs, seeds and trees are grown commercially.

The most important industries are metals and machinery, food, chemicals, textiles, oil refining. Amsterdam is famous for diamond cutting; Delft for pottery. Eindhoven has electrical and radio factories. Natural gas reserves are large. Index of industrial production (1970 - 100) was 121 for 1974.

Canals, of which there are 3,478 mi., are important in transportation. The Rhine, Meuse and Schelde reach the sea through the Netherlands and carry enormous traffic.

The 1973-74 Arab oil embargo against Western nations was not lifted from the Netherlands until July 1974; the Dutch had refused Arab demands to condemn Israel.

Foreign trade in thousands of U.S. dollars:

	Imports	Exports
1973	$23,835,000	$23,910,000
1974	$33,816,000	$33,568,000

History and Government. After the empire of Charlemagne (d. 814) fell apart, the Netherlands (Holland, Belgium, Flanders), split among counts, dukes and bishops, passed to Burgundy and thence to Charles V of Spain. His son, Philip II, tried to check the Dutch drive toward political freedom and Protestantism (1568-1573). William the Silent, prince of Orange, led a confederation of the northern provinces, called Estates, in the Union of Utrecht, 1579. The Estates retained individual sovereignty, but were represented jointly in the States-General, a body that had control of foreign affairs and defense. In 1581 they repudiated allegiance to Spain. The rise of the Dutch republic to naval, economic and artistic eminence came in the 17th Century.

The United Dutch Republic ended 1795 when the French formed the Batavian Republic. Napoleon made his brother Louis king of Holland, 1806; Louis abdicated 1810 when Napoleon annexed Holland. In 1813 the French were expelled. In 1815 the Congress of Vienna formed a kingdom of the Netherlands, including Belgium, under William I. In 1830, the Belgians seceded and formed a separate kingdom.

The constitution, promulgated 1814, and subsequently revised, assures a hereditary constitutional monarchy. Executive power rests in the crown (the queen and ministers). Legislative powers are exercised jointly by the crown and Parliament (States-General) of 2 chambers: First Chamber, 75, members, elected for 6 years (one half every 3d year) by the provincial legislatures, and the Second Chamber, 150 deputies, elected for 4 years directly. Universal suffrage for all citizens over 18 and proportional representation are in force. The sovereign exercises the executive authority through a Council of Ministers, the president thereof corresponding to a prime minister. There is a State Council named by the sovereign, of which she is president, to be consulted on all legislative and some executive matters.

The reigning sovereign since Sept. 6, 1948, is Queen Juliana Louise Emma Marie Wilhelmina, born April 30, 1909. Queen Juliana on Jan. 7, 1937, married Prince Bernard of Lippe-Biesterfeld, the Prince of the Netherlands. They have 4 daughters. Princess Beatrix Wilhelmina Armgard, born Jan. 31, 1938, heir presumptive, married Claus von Ambsberg, West German diplomat, Mar. 10, 1966. On Apr. 27, 1967, Princess Beatrix gave birth to the first of three sons Willem-Alexander, Prince of Orange, first male heir to the throne in 3 generations.

Education and Religion. There is complete liberty of worship. The royal family belongs to the Netherlands Reformed Church. The population is 39.5% Roman Catholic; 30% Protestant; others 8%; nonchurch members 22.5%. Education is obligatory from ages 6 through 15. Instruction is free in both public and denominational schools and teachers are paid by the state. There are 13 universities.

Defense. Military forces total 113,900.

The Netherlands is a member of the UN, NATO, EEC, Council of Europe and Benelux.

Netherlands Antilles

A revision of the Netherlands charter, promulgated Dec. 15, 1954, raised Surinam and the Netherlands Antilles to equality with the Netherlands homeland in the Kingdom of the Netherlands, with complete internal autonomy and a voice in government of the kingdom. Surinam was slated for independence in 1975 (see separate article).

The Netherlands Antilles consist of 2 groups of islands in the West Indies. Curacao, Aruba and Bonaire are near the South American coast; St. Eustatius, Saba and the southern part of St. Maarten are SE of Puerto Rico. Northern two-thirds of St. Maarten belong to French Guadeloupe; the French call the island St. Martin. Total area of the 2 groups is 395 sq. mi., including:Aruba 70, Bonaire 112, Curacao 180, St. Eustatius 12, Saba 5, St. Maarten (Dutch part) 16.

The Netherlands Antilles population (est. 1974) was 240,000. Willemstad is the capital. Chief products are corn, pulse, salt and phosphate; principal industry is the refining of crude oil from Venezuela. Tourism is an important industry, as are electronics and shipbuilding.

New Zealand

Area: 103,736 sq. mi. (268,676 sq. km.). Population (Govt. est. 1975): 3,106,000. Capital: Wellington. Monetary unit: New Zealand dollar.

The main islands of New Zealand lie in the South Pacific about 1,300 mi. E of Australia; total area is about that of Colorado. Including remote islands to the N and the Ross Dependency to the S, the reach of New Zealand is from the tropics to Antarctica.

Snow-topped mountains, smoking volcanoes, deep fjords, boiling geysers, golden beaches and the glowworm caves of Waitomo are among attractions.

New Zealand comprises North Island, 44,281 sq. mi.; South Island, 58,093 sq. mi.; Stewart Island, 670 sq. mi.; Chatham Islands, 372 sq. mi. Both the North and South Islands slightly exceed 500 mi. in length. Cook Strait, separating the two, is only 16 mi. wide at its narrowest.

In 1965, the Cook Islands (pop. 1974, 19,522; area 93 sq. mi.) became self-governing although New Zealand retains responsibility for defense and foreign affairs.

Niue, New Zealand territory, lies 400 mi. to W (pop. 1971, 4,992; area 100 sq. mi.). Tokelau Is., (pop. 1971, 2,000; area 4 sq. mi.) are 300 mi. N of Samoa.

Wellington and Auckland, on North Is., are the chief ports. South Is. has the picturesque Southern Alps and Tasman, Fox and Franz Josef Glaciers. There are 15 named peaks over 10,000 ft., the highest being Mt. Cook, 12,349 ft. Christchurch and Dunedin are the main cities of South Is.

Resources and Industries. New Zealand is largely dependent on agricultural products for export income; wool, meat and dairy products account for 80% of the total value. Next to Australia, New Zealand is the world's largest exporter of meat (mostly lamb).

Imports totaled $3.65 billion (in U.S. dollars) in 1974; exports were $2.44 billion.

Agriculture engages 12% of the population, manufacturing industries 35%. Private enterprise is basic in the economy, but state ownership or regulation affects many industries. Railroads are largely state-owned.

Food processing is the largest industry.

The pulp and paper industry on North Is. is partly powered by natural steam from volcanic areas. The first iron and steel plant commenced production in 1968. Natural gas was discovered at Kapuni, North Is., 1967, and is piped to several towns. A large hydroelectric plant at Lake Manapouri, South Is., began providing power for an aluminum smelter in 1971.

About 200,000 tourists visit New Zealand annually, over 50,000 of them from the U.S.

History and Government. New Zealand was discovered in 1642 by Abel Janszoon Tasman, a Dutch navigator, and its coasts were explored by British Capt. James Cook, 1769-1770. British sovereignty was proclaimed in 1840, with organized settlement commencing in the same year. Representative institutions were granted in 1853. The Colony became a Dominion in 1907 and is an independent member of the Commonwealth.

The native Maoris are Polynesians. Early in the 19th Century they numbered an est. 200,000; violence and European diseases cut them to 40,000 by the end of the century. Recently they have increased at 3% annually and totaled 246,200 in 1974.

Government consists of a governor-general, representing the British Crown; a House of Representatives whose members are elected by universal suffrage for 3-year terms; a prime minister and Cabinet who are members of the House and accountable to it. In Nov. 1972 elections the Labor party returned to power after 12 years of National (conservative) party rule.

In July 1973, to protest France's testing of nuclear devices above Mururoa Atoll, a New Zealand Navy frigate cruised just outside the French South Pacific island's 12-mi. limit but within the test area.

New Zealand is a member of the UN, Commonwealth, SEATO and ANZUS.

New Zealand's tax rates reach a maximum of 50 cents per dollar at the $16,000 income level. "Cradle-to-grave" social security includes maternity, school, medical, hospital, medicine, pension and other benefits.

Education and Religion. Education is free and compulsory between the ages of 6 and 15. There are 6 universities. The Anglican and Presbyterian Churches have the largest followings.

Defense. Military forces total 12,800. New Zealand had a force of 265 in Vietnam in 1971; it was withdrawn at the end of that year.

Ross Dependency, administered by New Zealand since 1923, comprises 160,000 sq. mi. of Antarctic territory.

Nicaragua

Area: 57,143 sq. mi. Population (Govt. est. 1974): 2,080,000. Capital: Managua. Monetary unit: Cordoba.

Nicaragua, largest of the Central or Middle American States, lies between the Caribbean and the Pacific with more than 200 mi. of coastline on each. The country is bordered by Honduras on the N and Costa Rica on the S. The Cordillera range of mountains, including many volcanic peaks, runs NW-SE through the middle of the country. Between this range and a range of volcanic peaks to the W lie Lake Managua, 38 Mi. by 15, and Lake Nicaragua, 100 mi. by 45, of great importance to the transport system. The government-owned Pacific Railroad, Corinto to Leon and Managua to Granada, 171 mi., is the principal rail line.

Resources and Industries. The nation has valuable forests, some gold is mined. It is essentially an agricultural country, but industrialization, including oil refining, is growing. On the broad tropical plains of the east coast, bananas, cotton, fruit and yucca are cultivated. Products of the western half include coffee, sugar, corn, beans, cocoa, rice, tobacco and wheat.

Cotton, coffee and sugar account for 70% of the value of exports.

A severe earthquake, Dec. 23, 1972, destroyed much of Managua; about 10,000 died and 200,000 were left homeless. The nation was also hit by severe drought, lasting into 1973.

History and Government. After gaining independence from Spain, 1821, Nicaragua was united for a short period with Mexico then with the United Provinces of Central America, finally becoming an independent republic, 1838.

The constitution, revised in 1960, provided for a Congress of 2 chambers, A House of Deputies of 45 members and a Senate of 18 members, all elected by popular vote. Ex-presidents also serve in the Senate and are appointed for life. The president is elected for 5 years and may not succeed himself.

Gen. Anastasio Somoza Debayle was elected president 1967. He resigned 1972 and was succeeded by a 3-man National Junta. He was elected president again Sept. 1, 1974. The Somozas, richest Nicaraguan family, have dominated politics for four decades.

Education and Religion. Roman Catholicism is the prevailing religion. There are 3 universities. Spanish is the official language Nicaragua is a UN and OAS member.

Niger

Area: 489,206 sq. mi. Population (Govt. est. 1974): 4,480,000. Capital: Niamey. Monetary unit: CFA franc.

The Republic of the Niger, a former French Overseas Territory in the heart of West Africa, is bounded by Libya, Algeria, Chad, Upper Volta, Dahomey,- Nigeria and Mali. Chief access to the country, a vast plateau almost twice the size of Texas, is by air. The Niger River flows through the western corner.

Niger became fully independent Aug. 3, 1960. It signed a bilateral agreement Apr. 24, 1961, retaining close ties with France. The republic has a president and National Assembly, elected for 5-year terms. Hamani Diori, president since independence, was overthrown in a military coup, Apr. 15, 1974.

Niger is an agricultural and pastoral land. Peanuts are the principal cash crop; livestock (cattle, sheep, camels donkeys, goats) are second in importance. Cotton is being promoted. Drought and famine struck in 1973-74; aid was sent by several nations, half of it by the U.S. Half the country's livestock died during the drought.

Uranium mines began production in 1971.

The people are predominantly Moslems. French is the official language.

Nigeria

The World Almanac is sponsored in Nigeria by the Daily and Sunday Times, 3 Kakawa St., Lagos, Nigeria; founded 1925; circulation 210,000 daily, 320,000 Sunday; published by The Daily Times of Nigeria, Ltd.

Area: 356,669 sq. mi. Population (1973 census): 79,758,969. Capital: Lagos. Monetary unit: Naira.

The Federal Republic of Nigeria, Africa's most populous country, became independent of Britain in 1960. Larger than Texas and Oklahoma combined, it lies on the southern side of the West African bulge, between Dahomey and Cameroon, with Niger to the N and Chad NE. It comprises nearly 250 tribal and linguistic groups, including the Hausas in the N, Ibos in the E. Yorubas in the W.

The northern desert region gives way to savannah and open woodland; tropical rain forests are in the south, with mangrove swamps along the coast.

Nigeria's rich natural resources include oil, coal, iron, limestone and natural gas. It produces much of the world's columbium ore (for steel alloys).

By 1975, Nigeria became the world's 6th largest petroleum producer; oil accounted for 80% of export value with cocoa 2d. Other exports are tobacco, tin, palm oil, palm kernels, cotton lint, hides and skins, lumber, rubber and peanuts. Under an "indigenization" program, 55 categories of businesses were to be run by blacks only by 1974.

Foreign trade in thousands of U.S. dollars:

	Imports	Exports
1973	1,877,000	3,462,000
1974	2,734,000	9,559,000

Nigeria became a sovereign country Oct. 1, 1960, and a republic Oct. 1, 1963. It is a member of the UN and Commonwealth. Its first constitution provided for 4 regions with local autonomy, and a federal Parliament and prime minister.

In 1966 there were 2 military coups and periods of inter-tribal strife ending a long period of coalition governments of the majority Northern Region and other regions. On Jan. 15, junior Army officers seized control; Gen. Johnson Aguyi-Ironsi, an easterner, made himself head of state, Prime Minister Abubakar Tafawa Balewa was assassinated. On Aug. 1, Col. Yakubu Gowon, a northerner, became head of state; Gen. Ironsi was assassinated.

On May 27,1967, the military government created 12 new states, replacing the 4 regions. On May 30, the Eastern Region seceded, proclaiming itself the Republic of Biafra. The move plunged the country into civil war.

Casualties in the war were estimated at over 1 million, including many "Biafrans" (mostly Ibos) who died of starvation despite international efforts to provide relief. The secessionists, after steadily losing ground, capitulated Jan. 12, 1970; Gen Odumegwu Ojukwu, rebel leader, fled to the Ivory Coast. Gen. Gowon announced a general amnesty. In July 1975; Gowon himself was ousted in a military coup.

Nigeria led in the formation of the West African Economic Community, linking 15 French, English, and Portuguese-speaking countries.

The northern parts of the nation are predominantly Moslem; there are many animists, Christians and Moslems in the south.

Norway

Area: 125,181 sq. mi. Population (Govt. est. 1975): 4,000,000. Capital: Oslo. Monetary unit: Krone.

Norway occupies the W part of the Scandinavian Penisula in NW Europe. It shares borders with Sweden, Finland and the USSR. The rocky W coast is deeply cut by fjords of scenic grandeur. Norway's area is about that of New Mexico.

The country's greatest length is 1,100 mi.; its width varies from 270 to only 4 mi. at the narrowest point. The coastline, including the fjords and largest of the 150,000 islands, is 17,000 mi. long. The climate is mild and moist on the W coast, but fairly cold and dry in the E.

The midnight sun is a phenomenon of the northern area where the sun does not set from the middle of May until the end of July, and does not rise above the horizon from approximately Nov. 20 to Jan. 24.

Resources and Industries. Only 3% of the land, 4,300 sq. mi., is cultivated; rivers and lakes occupy 5,000; forests 29,455.

Forests supply a sizable wood and paper industry. Large quantities of cod, herring, mackerel and salmon are caught. Norway has the world's 5th largest fish catch. Mines yield copper, pyrites, nickel, iron, zinc, lead. North Sea oil production began in 1971. Norway was to become a net oil exporter by 1976, with pipes

to Germany and the UK. Norway has harnessed its waterfalls to provide power. Important industries by rank, are engineering (including shipbuilding), metallurgical, food, beverages, chemical, paper and pulp, mining. Farm products include oats, rye, potatoes, dairy products and fruits. Industry employs 30% of workers, services 40%, agriculture and fisheries 10.5%.

Norway's merchant marine fleet is the world's 4th largest. It earnings help offset the unfavorable balance of trade. Foreign trade in thousands of U.S. dollars:

	Imports	Exports
1973	$6,240,000	$4,688,000
1974	$8,414,000	$6,274,000

History and Government. The first supreme ruler of Norway was Harald the Fairhaired who came to power in 872 A.D. Between 800 and 1000, Norway's Vikings raided and occupied parts of Europe. Christianity was introduced 1030.

The country was united with Denmark 1381-1814, with Sweden 1814-1905. Germany attacked Norway Apr. 9, 1940, and held it until liberation May 8, 1945.

Norway is a constitutional monarchy . The king is Olav V (born July 2, 1903); he became king Sept. 21, 1957. The heir to the throne, Crown Prince Harald, was born Feb. 21, 1937.

Legislative power is vested in the Storting, whose 155 members are elected for 4 years. Executive power is held by a prime minister and his cabinet.

Social security includes health and unemployment insurance and pensions.

Education and Religion. The Evangelical Lutheran religion is endowed by the state. All religions enjoy complete freedom of worship. Education is free at all levels and compulsory from ages 7 to 16. Universities are subsidized by the state.

Defense. Armed forces total 41,000, plus a Home Guard of 80,000.

Norway is a member of UN, NATO, EFTA, Nordic Council and Council of Europe. A trade agreement was reached with the EC in 1973. Norwegians rejected EC membership in a 1972 referendum.

Svalbard

Svalbard is a group of mountainous islands in the Arctic Ocean, c. 23,957 sq. mi., pop. varying seasonally from 1,500 to 3,000. The largest, West Spitsbergen, c. 15,000 sq. mi., seat of governor, is about 370 mi. N of Norway. By a treaty signed in Paris, 1920, major European powers recognized the sovereignty of Norway, which incorporated it 1925. Both Norway and the U.S.S.R. mine rich coal deposits. Mt. Newton (West Spitsbergen) is 5,633 ft. tall.

Oman

Area: 82,000 sq. mi. Population (UN est. 1974): 750,-000. Capital: Muscat. Monetary unit: Riyal Omani.

The Sultanate of Oman (formerly Muscat and Oman) is an independent monarchy occupying the SE corner of the Arabian Peninsula and including the tip of a nearby peninsula, Ruus-al-Jebal, to the N. The Sultanate has a coastline of 1,000 mi. along the Gulf of Oman to the NE and the Arabian Sea to the SE. Climate is generally hot and dry.

There is a narrow coastal plain up to 10 mi. wide, a range of barren mountains with Jebal Akhdar, the highest, reaching c. 9,900 ft., and a wide, stony, mostly waterless plateau averaging 1,000 ft. in altitude. The Sultanate is the size of Utah.

Exports are mainly oil, dates and some dried fish, limes and pomegranates. Cultivated areas also produce bananas, grapes, wheat, vegetables, coconuts and frankincense. Goats and sheep are raised.

Oil was discovered in 1964 and production began in 1967. By 1975 Oman was the world's 18th largest producer.

The people are predominantly Arab, but there are

also Indians, Baluchi, Negroes and others. The language is Arabic, but Hindi, Urdu, Baluchi and others are also spoken. The religion is mainly Islam of the Ibadhi sect.

A long history of rule by other lands ended with ouster of the Persians in 1744. On July 23, 1970, Sultan Said bin Taimur was overthrown by his son, who became Sultan Qabus bin Said. The new sultan changed the nation's name to Sultanate of Oman. He launched a domestic development program and battled leftist rebels in the southern Dhofar area. The government received arms aid and over 2,000 advisors from Iran; the guerrillas reportedly got arms from the U.S.S.R., Iraq, and Southern Yemen.

Pakistan

Area: 342,750 sq. mi. Population (Gov. est. 1974): 68,210,000. Capital: Islamabad. Monetary unit: Rupee.

Pakistan became a sovereign nation Aug. 14, 1947, when what had been the British Empire of India achieved independence and was partitioned into 2 countries, Pakistan and India. At first a dominion, Pakistan declared itself a republic on Mar. 23, 1956. Pakistan was divided into 2 sections, West Pakistan and East Pakistan. The 2 areas were nearly 1,000 mi. apart on opposite sides of India.

East Pakistan became the separate, independent nation of Bangladesh as a result of its 1971 rebellion and the Dec. 3-17, 1971, Pakistan-India war.

Pakistan (the former West Pakistan) adjoins Iran, Afghanistan, India and the Arabian Sea. In the NE is Kashmir, ownership long disputed with India.

Pakistan is a land of rugged mountains and river valleys, where irrigation aids agriculture, the occupation of 80% of the people. The Indus flows for c.1,-000 mi. from the base of the Himalayas to the Arabian Sea and with its tributaries supplies reservoirs, canals and hydroelectric plants. In the W are the Hindu Kush Mts., with Tirich Mir 25,230 ft. In the N is Mt. K2 (Godwin Austen), 28,250 ft., 2d highest in the world. The climate is mostly dry with little rainfall and summer temperatures up to 120°F.

Resources and Industries. Rice, wheat, cotton, oilseeds, tobacco, sugar, flour, wool and fish are important products. Minerals include sulphur, gypsum, salt, chromite, cement, petroleum, gas, coal, asbestos, antimony, magnesite and silica.

Pakistan manufactures cotton textiles (its largest industry), wool, silk, rayon, cement, card and paper board, sugar, chemicals, dyes, synthetic fertilizers.

Foreign trade in thousands of U.S. dollars:

	Imports	Exports
1973	$981,000	$958,000
1974	$1,738,000	$1,105,000

History and Government. The land now called Pakistan shares the 5,000-year history of the India-Pakistan sub-continent. At the present day sites of Harappa and Mohenjo Daro, the Indus Valley Civilization, with large cities and elaborate irrigation systems, flourished c. 4000-2500 B.C.

A lasting influence on Pakistan was the arrival of Islam with the first Arab invasion of 711 A.D.

After World War I the Moslems of British India began agitation for minority rights in elections.

Mohammad Ali Jinnah (1876-1948) was the principal architect of Pakistan. A lawyer who studied in England, he was a leader of the Moslem League from 1916, and worked for dominion status for India. From 1940 he advocated a separate Moslem state.

When the British withdrew Aug. 14, 1947, the Islamic majority areas of India acquired self-government as Pakistan, with dominion status in the Commonwealth. Jinnah became the first governor-general (1947-1948). He died in 1948.

Pakistan became a republic in 1956. In Oct. 1958, Gen. Mohammad Ayub Khan took power in a coup. He was elected president in 1960 and reelected in 1965. Pakistan had a National Assembly (legislature)

with equal membership from East and West Pakistan, and 2 Provincial Assemblies.

Ayub resigned Mar. 25, 1969, after several months of violent rioting and unrest, most of it in East Pakistan. There were demands for a parliamentary form of government, for direct elections and economic reforms. In East Pakistan, which had about 56% of the population, there were demands for autonomy.

The government was turned over to Gen. Agha Mohammad Yahya Khan and martial law was declared; Yahya assumed the presidency.

The Awami League, which sought regional autonomy for East Pakistan, won a majority in Dec. 1970 elections to a National Assembly which was to write a new constitution. In March 1971 Yahya postponed the Assembly. Rioting and strikes broke out in the East.

On Mar. 25, 1971, government troops launched attacks in the East, allegedly to forestall an Awami League rebellion. The Easterners proclaimed the independent nation of Bangladesh. In months of widespread fighting, countless thousands were killed. Some 10 million Easterners fled into India.

Pakistan and India went to war Dec. 3, 1971, on both the East and West fronts. Pakistan troops in the East surrendered Dec. 16; Pakistan agreed to a cease-fire in the West Dec. 17. India recognized Bangladesh as a separate nation Dec. 6.

Zulfikar Ali Bhutto, leader of the Pakistan People's party, which had won the most West Pakistan votes in the Dec. 1970 elections, became president Dec. 20. In 1972 he announced new land reforms and said the government would control management of major industries.

On July 3, 1972, Pakistan and India signed a pact agreeing to withdraw troops from their borders and seek peaceful solutions to all problems.

In Aug. 1973 India agreed to release 93,000 Pakistani prisoners held since 1971. The return was completed in April 1974. Pakistan agreed to repatriate 200,000 Bengali nationals stranded in Pakistan, and agreed to accept some Biharis (non-Bengalis) unwanted in Bangladesh.

A new constitution adopted Apr. 10, 1973, made Pakistan a federal Islamic republic, with a 2-chamber Parliament and a president, but with executive power given to the prime minister. Bhutto became prime minister Aug. 15.

(See article on India for disputes over Kashmir, Rann of Cutch, etc.).

Education and Religion. Most of the population is Moslem. Education is free through the tenth grade. Urdu is the national language.

Defense. Armed forces total 392,000.

Pakistan is a member of the UN and CENTO. Following clashes between India and China in 1962, Pakistan made commercial and aid agreements with Communist China. U.S. aid to both Pakistan and India was suspended during the 1966 war over Kashmir but both economic aid and "nonlethal" military aid were resumed in 1966. Military aid was suspended again in 1975. The embargo was modified in 1973 and lifted in 1975.

Panama

Area: 28,753 sq. mi. Population (Govt. est. 1974): 1,630,000. Capital: Panama. Monetary unit: Balboa.

The Republic of Panama occupies the isthmus of Panama, connecting Central and South America. Smaller than South Carolina, it has a shoreline of 477 mi. on the Caribbean and 767 mi. on the Pacific. Its width varies from about 37 to 110 mi. It is bounded by Colombia and Costa Rica, and is bisected by the 10-mi. wide U.S. Canal Zone.

Resources and Industries. Panama has extensive forests, and exports mahogany. Only half the rich arable land is cultivated. Sufficient cement, clay and salt are produced for domestic needs. Bananas are the largest export, rivaled by products of a large petroleum refinery (which imports crude oil). Also exported are pineapples, cocoa, coconuts, sugar, shrimp.

Due to easy Panama ship regulations and strictures in the U.S., merchant tonnage registered in Panama since World War II ranks high in size. Registered number of ships more than 1,000 gross tons each is over 1,100.

History and Government. The coast of Panama was sighted by Rodrigo de Bastidas, sailing with Columbus for Spain in 1501, and was visited by Columbus in 1502. Vasco Nunez de Balboa crossed the isthmus and "discovered" the Pacific Ocean Sept. 13, 1513. Spanish colonies were ravaged by Francis Drake, 1572-95, and Henry Morgan, 1668-71. Morgan destroyed the old city of Panama which had been founded in 1519. Freed from Spain, Panama joined Colombia in 1821. Separatist forces in Panama sought to gain independence from Colombia several times.

Panama declared its independence from Colombia Nov. 3, 1903, with U.S. recognition. U.S. Naval forces deterred action by Colombia. On Nov. 18, 1903, Panama granted use, occupation and control of the Canal Zone to the U.S. by treaty, ratified Feb. 26, 1904. (See also Canal Zone and Panama Canal.)

Rioting began Jan. 9, 1964, in a dispute over the flying of the U.S. and Panamanian flags and terms of the 1903 treaty. At least 21 Panamanians and 3 U.S. soldiers died in the rioting.

In 1967 new treaties were proposed, but in 1970 Panama said the proposed treaties were unacceptable. New negotiations started in 1971. In Feb. 1974 the U.S. and Panama agreed to negotiate a new treaty which would give the U.S. the right to operate and protect the canal for a certain period, with Panama sharing in the revenues, and would also set a date for final transfer of jurisdiction to Panama. Opposition by U.S. Senators stalled the talks.

Panama adopted its 4th constitution in 1972, providing for a president, Legislative Council and an elected Assembly. The Assembly gave Gen. Omar Torrijos powers as head of government.

Education and Religion. Most Panamanians are Roman Catholics. Education is compulsory, ages 7-15. Two universities are in Panama Ciy. Spanish is the official language; English is widely spoken.

Papua New Guinea

Area: 178,260 sq. mi. Population (UN est. 1974): 2,600,000. Capital: Port Moresby. Monetary unit: Kina.

Papua New Guinea occupies the eastern half of the island of New Guinea, second largest in the world. It lies N of Australia and just S of the Equator, and borders on West Irian, controlled by Indonesia. Thickly forested mountains cover much of the center of the country, with lowlands along the coasts. Included in the country are the nearby islands of the Bismarck and Solomon groups, including the **Admiralty Is., New Ireland, New Britain** and **Bougainville;** the latter two enjoy some autonomy. Papua New Guinea is somewhat larger than California.

Commercial crops include coconuts, cocoa, coffee and rubber. Livestock raising is being developed. Timber and prawns are exported. Copper, gold, and silver are produced, and natural gas has been found.

The southern half of the country was first claimed by Britain in 1884, and transferred to Australia in 1905. The northern half was claimed by Germany in 1884, but captured in the first World War by Australia, which was granted a League of Nations mandate and then a UN trusteeship over the area. The two territories were administered jointly after 1949, were given self-government Dec. 1, 1973, and were scheduled for complete independence Sept. 16, 1975. Australia promised $US750 million in aid for the first three years of independence, and pledged assistance in defence and foreign affairs.

Apart from 40,000 Australians, Europeans, and Chinese, the population descends from a huge number of indigenous Melanesian tribes, many living in almost complete isolation. More than 600 mutually unintelligible languages are spoken, with pidgin English the medium of communication. Over 250,000 students attend school. The University of Papua New Guinea opened in 1966.

Paraguay

Area: 157,047 sq. mi. Population (UN est. 1974): 2,570,000. Capital: Asuncion. Monetary unit: Guarani.

The Republic of Paraguay, one of the 2 landlocked countries of South America, is bounded by Bolivia (also landlocked), Brazil and Argentina. Extensive plains are excellent for pastures and farms, and the mountain slopes are covered with luxuriant forests. Paraguay is about the size of California. The Paraguay River, the most important waterway, is 1,800 mi. long.

Resources and Industries. Timber resources are large. Most of the population is agricultural and pastoral, with cattle breeding the principal industry. Most important agricultural crops are corn, wheat, cotton, beans, peanuts, tobacco and citrus fruits.

Chief exports are beef and other food products: cotton, wood products, hides, tobacco, yerba mate (tea), vegetable oils.

The first stages of a large hydroelectric project were completed in 1968-70; a highway to Brazil to aid trade shipments for the landlocked nation was completed.

In 1974 Paraguay and Brazil announced partnership plans to build a 10-million-kilowatt hydroelectric plant, largest in the world, at Itaipu on the Parana River, the border between the 2 nations.

History and Government. Visited by Sebastian Cabot in 1527 and settled as a Spanish possession in 1535, Paraguay gained its independence from Spain in 1811. After fighting Brazil, Argentina and Uruguay (War of the Triple Alliance 1865-1870) it adopted in 1870 a democratic constitution.

A new constitution, adopted in Aug. 1967, provided for a president, a Senate of 30 members, and a House of representatives of 60.

In elections held Feb. 11, 1973, Gen. Alfredo Stroessner, who had ruled Paraguay since 1954, was reelected president for a 5-year term.

Education and Religion. Roman Catholicism is the established religion but others are guaranteed freedom. Primary education is compulsory, ages 7-14. Spanish is the official language; but Spanish and Guarani, an Indian tongue spoken exclusively by half the population, are designated national languages.

Peru

Area: 496,222 sq. mi. Population (Govt. est. 1974): 15,380,000. Capital: Lima. Monetary unit: Sol.

Peru, on the Pacific coast of South America, is bounded by Ecuador, Colombia, Brazil, Bolivia, Chile and the Pacific. It has a Pacific coastline of 1,410 mi. and an extreme width, from western coast to eastern jungle, of about 800 mi. It is about the size of Arizona, New Mexico and Texas combined.

The Andes reach 22,205 ft. (Mt. Huascaran); 7 peaks tower above 19,000 ft. The uplands of western slopes of the Andes are well watered as are the eastern slopes and lowlands reaching the Amazon basin, where the port of Iquitos loads ocean-going vessels for a 2,300-mi. trip down the Amazon through Brazil.

The coastal area on the west is almost rainless, but the soil is fertile, and irrigation, using rivers pouring down from the Andes, has made the area highly productive.

Lima, the capital, is in the coastal region and is also the nation's commercial center. Callao, the chief seaport, is 7 mi. west of Lima.

Inca and earlier Chimu ruins make Peru a mecca for archeologists, notably at Cuzco, Chan Chan and the Andean city of Machu Picchu.

A severe earthquake hit northern Peru May 31, 1970, destroying many towns and killing an est. 50,000.

Resources and Industries. Agriculture and stock raising occupy half the population.

The leading agricultural product is cotton. Wool, hides, skins, sugar, coffee, rice, potatoes, beans, barley and tobacco also are produced. Corn, native to Peru, is a staple food.

Peru is normally the world's top fishing nation; it takes about a sixth of total world tonnage, mostly anchovies from the plankton-rich waters of the coastal Peru current. Most of the take is ground into fish meal for poultry and livestock feed. But in 1972 the industry was crippled by a disappearance of anchovies from offshore waters. In 1973 the government nationalized the crippled industry. In 1974, a shift in the ocean currents brought the anchovies back.

The mountains are rich in minerals. The Toquepala copper mine in the southern Andes is one of the world's largest. The steel industry has expanded. The first petroleum shipments from rich eastern fields went down the Amazon in 1974. Oil self-sufficiency is expected in 1976.

Fishmeal is the leading export with copper 2d. Other exports are cotton, sugar, iron ore, lead.

In 1968-74, the military government converted large farmlands into cooperatives, expropriated several large U.S. companies/with compensation, forced foreign mining companies to expand investments and ordered local industries to turn over 50% of ownership to their workers.

A $620 million copper mining project was begun in 1975.

History and Government. The powerful Inca empire had its seat at Cuzco in the Andes (alt. 11,000 ft.) when Francisco Pizarro, Spanish conquistador, began raiding Peru for its wealth, 1532. In 1533 he had the ruling Inca, Atahualpa, fill a room with gold, then executed him and enslaved the natives.

Lima was the seat of Spanish viceroys until the Argentine liberator, Jose de San Martin, captured it in 1821; Spain was defeated by Simon Bolivar and Antonio J. de Sucre and recognized Peruvian independence, 1824. Chile defeated Peru and Bolivia, 1879-84, and took Tarapaca, Tacna and Arica; returned Tacna, 1929.

The constitution provided for a president and a bicameral legislature, all elected for 6-year terms. On Oct. 3, 1968, a military coup ousted Pres. Fernando Belaunde Terry and Gen. Juan Velasco Alvarado assumed the presidency.

Education and Religion. Roman Catholicism is the state religion.

About 47% of the population is Indian; most of the remainder are of Spanish descent, or mestizos (mixed), with small percentages of Negroes, Chinese and Japanese.

Education is free and compulsory, ages 7-14. There are 33 universities. Spanish and Quechua are the official languages; Aymara is also spoken. About 5 million Indians do not speak Spanish. The government has tried to preserve the Indian heritages. Peru is a member of the UN and OAS.

Philippines

Area: 115,707 sq. mi. Population (Govt. est. 1974): 41,500,000. Capital: Quezon City. Monetary unit: Piso.

The Republic of the Philippines occupies an archipelago in the western Pacific, 500 mi. from the SE coast of Asia. Over 7,100 islands extend 1,150 mi. N to S, 682 E to W.

Eleven of the islands comprise the bulk of the area. The country is about the size of Arizona.

The archipelago has a coastline of 10,850 mi. Manila Bay, with an area of 770 sq. mi., and a circumfer-ence of 120 mi., is the finest harbor in the Far East.

Resources and Industries. Agriculture, manufacturing, mining, lumbering and fishing are the main activities. Forests, which cover 42% of the area, provide a variety of products from lumber and resins to medicinal plants. In 1972 the nation had the world's 5th most valuable fish catch.

The islands are rich in mineral resources. Gold, silver, lead, zinc, nickel, copper, iron, coal, chromite, asbestos and manganese are mined.

Chief agricultural products are manila hemp, copra, sugar, rice, pineapple and tobacco.

In the late 1960s, self-sufficiency in rice production was achieved after introduction of "miracle" high-yield varieties.

In 1972 and 1974, severe floods destroyed crops in central Luzon. In 1974, the first in a series of flood-control dams, built with U.S. aid, was dedicated.

Manufacturing showed steady gains, mostly in processing or assembly of food, clothing, pharmaceuticals, paper products, appliances. Tourists number over 200,000 annually, providing further income.

History and Government. The archipelago was visited by Magellan 1521. The Spanish founded Manila 1571. The islands, named for King Philip II of Spain, were ceded by Spain to the U.S. in the Treaty of Paris, Dec. 10, 1898, following the Spanish-American War. The U.S. paid Spain $20 million for the territory.

Japan attacked the Philippines Dec. 8, 1941 (Far Eastern time). Gen. Douglas MacArthur was put in command of the U.S.-Filipino forces (15,000 Americans, 40,000 in Filipino Army, 100,000 Filipino reservists). Japan conquered the islands in May, 1942. It was ousted by Sept. 1945.

On July 4, 1946, independence was proclaimed in accordance with an act passed by the U.S. Congress in 1934, providing for Philippine independence in 1946.

A republic, with a president, Senate and House, was established.

All natural resources of the Philippines belong to the state and their exploitation is limited to citizens of the Philippines or corporations and associations of which 60% of the capital is owned by citizens. In 1946 the right to develop natural resources and to own and operate public utilities until 1974 was extended to U.S. citizens.

President Ferdinand E. Marcos in 1966 concluded a pact reducing U.S. base leases from 99 to 25 years. There were riots by radical youth groups and terrorism by leftist guerrillas and outlaws, increasing from 1970. On Sept. 21, 1972, Marcos declared martial law to combat terrorists. Ruling by decree, he ordered land reform, cut crime and stabilized prices. On Jan. 17, 1973, he proclaimed a new constitution, established a parliamentary government with himself as both president and premier. Marcos offered amnesty to terrorists in 1974. In 1975, diplomatic and trade ties were set with China.

Government troops battled Moslem secessionists in 1973-74 in southern Mindanao; in 1975, autonomy was offered to the Moros (Moslems).

Education and Religion. Primary and secondary education is free, instruction is in English. There are several universities.

The official national language is Filipino, based on Tagalog. English and Spanish, also official, are commonly used in government and commerce.

About 83% of the inhabitants are Roman Catholics and about 10% belong to the Philippine Independent Church, organized by a Filipino priest, Fr. Gregorio Aglipay. Other Christians, Moslems, Buddhists are among minorities.

Defense. The Philippines and U. S. have treaties for U. S. military and naval bases and a 1951 Mutual Defense Treaty. President Marcos sought renegotiation of U.S. defense arrangements in 1975. Military forces total 55,000. The republic is a member of the UN and SEATO. A battalion of 2,200 construction troops served with the U.S. in Vietnam, 1966-69.

Poland

Area: 120,359 sq. mi. Population (Govt. est. 1974): 33,690,000. Capital: Warsaw. Monetary unit: Zloty.

The Polish People's Republic, in Central Europe, is bounded by the Baltic Sea, USSR, Czechoslovakia and East Germany. It is about the size of New Mexico.

Its terrain consists largely of lowlands, often forested; there are mountains in the south. Gdynia, Gdansk (once Danzig), Szczecin, Swinoujscie and Kolobrzeg are the principal ports.

Resources and Industries. About 22% of the population was still engaged in agriculture in the early 1970s. Chief crops are rye, wheat, barley, oats, potatoes, sugar beets, tobacco, flax. Coal mining, shipbuilding, textiles, chemicals, woodworking and metal industries are important. Products include automobiles, tractors, heavy machinery, aircraft. Key industries are nationalized and operate under a planned economy. About 85% of the farms and some businesses are privately operated. The index of industrial production (1970 = 100) was 149 in 1974; Poland has become the world's 10th largest industrial power.

Poland produces 7% of world bituminous and lignite coal output and much zinc. Other minerals are sulphur, cement, salt, cadmium, iron, and copper. Imported raw materials supply aluminum plants and oil refineries. Foreign trade in thousands of U.S. dollars:

	Imports	Exports
1973	$ 7,814,000	$6,374,000
1974	$10,482,000	$8,315,000

History and Government. Poland was a great power from the 14th to the 17th centuries. In 3 partitions (1772, 1793, 1795) it was apportioned among Prussia, Russia and Austria. Overrun by the Austro-German armies in World War I, its independence, self-declared on Nov. 11, 1918, was recognized by the Treaty of Versailles June 28, 1919.

Nazi Germany and the Soviet Union invaded Poland Sept. 1-27, 1939, and divided the country. With Germany's defeat, a Polish government-in-exile in London was recognized by the U.S., but the Soviet Union pressed the claims of a rival group. The U.S. and Britain compromised with Stalin when he agreed to free elections. However, he rejected international supervision and the election of 1947 was completely dominated by the communists.

In compensation for 69,860 sq. mi. ceded to the USSR, 1945, Poland received approx. 40,000 sq. mi. of German territory east of the Oder-Neisse line comprising Silesia, Pomerania, West Prussia and part of East Prussia.

The 1952 constitution describes Poland as a people's republic with a Sejm (parliament) elected for 4-year terms by direct ballot. The Sejm elects a Council of State and a Council of Ministers (cabinet). Policy is decreed by the Communist party Politburo.

During 12 years of rule by Stalinist extremists large estates were abolished, industry was nationalized, schools secularized and some Roman Catholic prelates jailed. Farm production fell off. Harsh working conditions caused a riot by workmen in Poznan June 28-29, 1956.

A new Politburo, committed to development of a more independent Polish Communism, was named Oct. 1956, with Wladyslaw Gomulka as first secretary of the Communist party. Collectivization of farms was ended and many collectives were abolished.

In 1970, Poland and West Germany signed a treaty to normalize relations.

In Dec. 1970 workers in port cities rioted because of price rises and new incentive wage rules. On Dec. 20 Gomulka resigned as party leader; he was succeeded by Edward Gierek; the incentive rules were dropped, price rises were revoked. In June 1971 a new 5-year plan was announced, placing more stress on housing and consumer goods production.

Poland was the first Communist state to get most-favored nation trade terms from the U.S. A 10-year W. Germany cooperation pact was signed in 1974.

Education and Religion. Education is free and compulsory. There are 75 institutions of higher learning. Roman Catholicism is the predominant religion. A law promulgated Feb. 13, 1953, required government consent to high church appointments. In 1956 Gomulka released Stefan Cardinal Wyszynski from prison and agreed to permit religious liberty in public institutions and religious publications, provided the church kept out of politics. But in 1961 religious studies in public schools were halted. Government relations with the Church improved in the 1970s.

Defense. Military forces total 303,000. Poland is a UN and Warsaw Pact member.

Portugal

Area: 35,340 sq. mi. Population (UN est. 1974): 8,740,000. Capital: Lisbon. Monetary unit: Escudo.

Portugal occupies the SW part of the Iberian Peninsula and is bordered by Spain and the Atlantic. It is about the size of Indiana. The **Azores Islands**, in the Atlantic, 740 mi. W. of Portugal, have an area of 904 sq. mi. and population (1970) of 291,028. The **Madeira Islands**, 360 mi. off the NW coast of Africa, have an area of 307 sq. mi. and a population (1970) of 253,220.

Portugal is mountainous, but about two-thirds of the land is cultivated.

Resources and Industries. Wheat, corn, oats, barley, rye and rice are important crops. Wines, olive oil, sardines, anchovies, resins and fruits are major industries. Forests of pine, oak and chestnut cover 19% of the country, and the nation leads the world in cork production. Among main industries are textiles, pottery, shipbuilding, petrochemical products, paper and glassware. Tourism is important, as well as remittances from Portuguese workers abroad. A trade agreement was signed with the EC in 1973.

History and Government. Portugal, an independent state since the 12th Century, was a kingdom until a revolution in 1910 drove out King Manoel II and a republic was proclaimed.

From 1932 a strong, repressive government was headed by Premier Antonio de Oliveira Salazar. Illness forced his retirement in Sept. 1968; he was succeeded by Marcello Caetano. Portugal was the last European nation to hold an extensive empire in Africa, maintaining over 140,000 troops there to battle various independence movements.

On Apr. 25, 1974, the government was seized by a military junta. Gen. Antonio de Spinola, who had led Portuguese troops in Africa, was named president May 15 and installed a government dedicated to establishing democracy in Portugal and Africa.

The new government reached agreements providing independence for Guinea-Bissau, Mozambique, Cape Verde Islands, Angola, and Sao Tome and Principe. Spinola resigned Sept. 30, 1974, in face of increasing pressure from leftist officers. Despite a 64% victory for democratic parties in April 1975, the Soviet-supported Communist Party increased its influence. Banks, insurance companies, transport and other industries were nationalized.

Education and Religion. The dominant religion is Roman Catholicism; there is freedom of worship. Primary education is compulsory. There are 9 universities, 3 university schools, 4 colleges of music, 43 lyceums, a number of technical and art schools.

Defense. Military forces total 200,000. A 1951 agreement gave the U.S. rights to use defense facilities in the Azores. In the 1973 Middle East war Portugal allowed U.S. airlift-to-Israel planes to refuel there. Portugal is a member of NATO and the U.N.

Portuguese Overseas Provinces

(For former colonies, see Angola, Cape Verde, Guinea-Bissau, Mozambique, Sao Tome)

Macao, with an area of 6 sq. mi., is an enclave, a peninsula and 2 small islands, at the mouth of the Canton River in China. Population (UN est. 1974): 270,000.

Portuguese Timor occupies the E part of the island of Timor N of Australia in the Timor Sea. Indonesia owns the W part. The area is 7,332 sq. mi. and the population (UN est. 1974): 660,000. Exports are coffee, sandlewood, sandal root, copra and wax. Capital, Dili.

Qatar

Area: 4,000 sq. mi. Population: (UN est. 1974): 90,-000. Capital: Doha. Monetary unit: Riyal.

Qatar, formerly a British Protected State, declared its complete independence Sept. 1, 1971. It occupies a peninsula extending into the Persian (also called Arabian) Gulf from the coast of Arabia.

A mainly arid land, slightly larger than Connecticut. Qatar was the world's 15th largest petroleum producer in 1974. Production started in 1949 and provides an income of several hundred million dollars. Doha has become a modern town with seawater desalting plants. Commercial fishing, government-aided agriculture and herds of camels, sheep and goats are also important.

Qatar was under Turkish control from 1872 to 1915. In a treaty signed in 1916 Qatar gave Great Britain responsibility for its defense and foreign relations. After Britain announced it would remove its military forces from the Persian Gulf area by the end of 1971, Qatar sought a federation with other British Protected States in the area; this failed and Qatar declared itself independent. It is a monarchy, ruled by an emir aided by a prime minister, Council of Ministers and Advisory Council. Its first ruler under independence, Emir Ahmed bin Ali al-Thani, was replaced by his cousin, Khalifa bin Hamad al-Thani, Feb. 22, 1972, in a bloodless coup. Qatar is a member of the UN and Arab League.

Most Qataris are Arabs of the Sunni branch of Islam. Arabic is the official language. Education is free and compulsory, ages 6-16.

Rhodesia

Area: 150,333 sq. mi. Population (Govt. est. 1974): 6,100,000. Capital: Salisbury. Monetary unit: Rhodesian dollar.

Rhodesia is mostly high plateau country, bordered by the Zambezi River and Zambia to the N, Mozambique to the E, the Republic of South Africa to the S and Botswana to the W. It is almost the size of California.

Victoria Falls on the Zambezi, partly in Zambia, are 355 ft. high, 5,580 ft. wide.

The vast majority of the people are Africans (mostly Bantus); there are about 270,000 whites and small minorities of Asians and mixed descent. English is the official language but the majority speak Bantu languages.

Rich farmlands and mineral deposits are the mainstays of the economy. Tobacco is normally the leading export, followed by asbestos, meat, sugar, copper, clothing, iron, chemical products, cotton, coal and chrome.

Britain took over the area as Southern Rhodesia in 1923 from the British South Africa Co. and granted internal self-government. Under a 1961 constitution, there was a governor representing the British Crown, a prime minister and Legislative Assembly with voting restricted to maintain whites in power. On Nov. 11, 1965, Prime Minister Ian D. Smith announced his country's unilateral declaration of independence. Britain termed the act illegal, and demanded Rhodesia broaden voting rights to provide for eventual rule by the majority Africans.

Urged by Britain, the UN imposed sanctions, including embargoes on oil shipments to Rhodesia, which were backed by most nations including the U.S. Some oil and gasoline reached Rhodesia, however, from South Africa and Mozambique, before the latter became independent in 1975. Some African nations denounced Britain for refusing to use force against the Rhodesian government. In May 1968, the UN Security Council ordered a trade embargo.

Rhodesia claimed the sanctions were ineffective. A new constitution came into effect Mar. 2, 1970, providing for a republic with a president and prime minister; a Senate of 23 members, and a House of Assembly elected by separate white and black voter rolls, eventually to have 50 representatives each (but effectively delaying full black representation through income tax requirements).

A proposed British-Rhodesian settlement was dropped in May 1972 when a British commission reported most Rhodesian blacks opposed it. In 1973-74 there were small clashes between black nationalist guerrillas and Rhodesian security forces. A Dec. 1974 ceasefire was followed by preliminary negotiations between the government and black leaders.

In 1974 U.S. President Ford sought repeal of a U.S. law allowing U.S. import of Rhodesian chrome.

Romania

Area: 91,699 sq. mi. Population (Govt. est. 1974): 21,030,000. Capital: Bucharest. Monetary unit: Leu.

The Socialist Republic of Romania, a Balkan state in SE Europe is almost the size of Oregon. It is bounded by the USSR, the Black Sea, Bulgaria, Yugoslavia and Hungary. The Danube flows along the southern border and through eastern Romania into the Black Sea. The Carpathian Mtns. enclose the north-central Transylvanian plateau. There are wide plains S and E of the mountains.

Resources and Industries. Romania has become industrialized, industry accounting for more than half the total national product by the late 1960s. Industrial growth rate for 1974 was 15%. But 40% of labor was still agricultural.

Main industries are iron-steel, other metallurgy, machinery, oil and chemicals, building materials, timber, textiles, footwear, food processing.

There is considerable mineral wealth: oil, natural gas, coal, salt, bauxite, manganese, lead, zinc, gold, silver. In 1974 14.49 million tons of crude oil were produced, while 8 million tons of steel were scheduled; both figures were increases over previous years.

Farms and forests contribute 29% of the national product. State farms and cooperatives own 96.4% of arable land. Romania is the world's 6th largest corn producer; also important are wheat, sugar beets, grapes and fruits. In 1974, 3.9 million foreigners visited Black Sea and other Romanian resorts.

In 1974, Romania had 14 million sheep, 9 million hogs, 6 million cattle.

Imports in 1973 were valued at $3.47 billion, exports at $3.70 billion.

History and Government. Romania's earliest known people were merged with invading Proto-Thracians, preceding by centuries the Dacians. The Dacian kingdom was occupied by Rome 106 A.D.-271 A.D.; the people and language were Romanized. The principalities of Wallachia and Moldavia, dominated by Turkey, were united in 1859; became Romania in 1861. In 1877 Romania proclaimed independence from Turkey, became an independent state by the Treaty of Berlin, 1878, and kingdom, 1881, under Carol I. In 1886 Romania became a constitutional monarchy with a bicameral legislature.

Romania helped Russia against Turkey, 1877-78. After World War I it acquired Bessarabia, Bukovina, Transylvania and Banat. In 1940 it ceded Bessarabia and Northern Bukovina to the USSR and part of Southern Dobrudja to Bulgaria.

Marshal Ion Antonescu, leader of a militarist movement, came to power and forced Romania to join Germany against the USSR in World War II in 1941. In 1944 Antonescu was overthrown by King Michael with Soviet help and Romania joined the Allies.

With occupation by Soviet troops the National Democratic Front, headed by the Communist party, displaced the National Peasant party. A People's Republic was proclaimed, Dec. 30, 1947, and Michael was forced to abdicate. Land owners were dispossessed and most banks, factories and transportation units were nationalized. A new constitution on the Soviet model was voted Sept. 24, 1952. A modification, March 1961, replaced the Presidium with the State Council, elected by the Grand National Assembly from its own membership. A Council of Ministers is the administrative body. The Assembly has 465 deputies, elected for 5-year terms.

On Aug. 22, 1965, a new constitution proclaimed Romania a Socialist, rather than People's Republic. Since 1966, Romania has adopted an increasingly independent attitude toward the USSR, a stand pointed up by the visit of U.S. President Nixon in Aug. 1969. Romanian President Nicolae Ceausescu visited the U.S. in 1970 and 1973. The U.S. granted most-favored-nation tariff treatment in 1975. Since 1959, USSR troops have not been permitted to enter Romania. In 1974, Ceausescu declared Russia was Romania's top ally.

Education and Religion. Education is compulsory for 10 years, all education is free. There are universities in Bucharest, Jassy, Cluj, Craiova, Timisoara, Brasov. The language has a Latin base, with traces of French, Greek, Slav and Turkish influences.

Romanian Orthodox clergy are paid by the state, other clergy receive subsidies but church and state are called separated. Roman Catholic orders have been abolished and the Greek Catholic Church has been absorbed by the Romanian Orthodox.

Defense. Military forces total 171,000. Romania is a member of the UN and Warsaw Pact.

Rwanda

Area: 10,169 sq. mi. Population (Govt. est. 1974): 4,120,000. Capital: Kigali. Monetary unit: Rwanda franc.

The Republic of Rwanda, which became independent July 1, 1962, had been part of the former Belgian UN Trusteeship of Ruanda-Urundi. Rwanda lies in East Central Africa, bounded N by Uganda, E by Tanzania, W by Zaire and S by Burundi.

The source of the Nile River, long sought by explorers and geographers, has been located in the headwaters of the Kagera River, SW of Kigali.

About the size of Maryland, Rwanda is one of the most densely populated nations in Africa. The population includes the Hutu (90% of population), the Tutsi (Watusi, 8%) and the Twa (2%). For centuries the Tutsi (an extremely tall race) subjugated the Hutu (average height) and the Twa (pygmies). A civil war broke out in 1960 and Tutsi power was ended. *(See Index for Burundi.)*

The majority of Rwandans are Christians. French and Kinyarwanda are the official languages.

A Legislative Council, organized in Oct. 1960, declared Rwanda a republic Jan. 28, 1961, and a referendum, Sept. 25, abolished the monarchic system. The new government was dominated by the Hutu. A president and National Assembly are elected for 4-year terms. The government was overthrown in a 1973 military coup. Rwanda is a member of the UN and OAU.

Coffee is the principal crop; cotton, tea, pyrethrum, tobacco, cattle and hides also are produced. Minerals include tin, gold, wolframite.

Kagera National Park, in the northeast, covers a tenth of the country; here the ecology of East Central Africa is preserved. Lake Kivu, on the nation's western border with Zaire, is 4,788 ft. above sea level and considered one of Africa's most beautiful.

San Marino

Capital: San Marino. Area: 23.5 sq. mi. Population (Govt. est. 1974): 19,502. Monetary unit: Italian and San Marino lira.

San Marino, one of the world's smallest nations, lies on the slopes of Mt. Titano in the Apennines near the Adriatic, in north central Italy. It is one-third the size of the District of Columbia.

Principal industries are printing postage stamps, tourism, woolen goods, paper, cement, industrial ceramics. Cradle-to-grave social security is provided. A ceremonial army of 180 men is maintained.

History and Government. The republic claims to be the oldest state in Europe and to have been founded in the 4th century. It has had a treaty of friendship with Italy since 1862. It is a member of the International Court of Justice.

San Marino is governed by a Grand Council of 60 members elected by popular vote, 2 of whom are chosen to exercise executive power for a term of 6 months. Women were allowed to vote for the first time Sept. 13, 1964. A Sept. 1973 law gave them the right to hold public office and make legal contracts. Three women were elected to the Council in 1974.

Sao Tome and Principe

Area: 372 sq. mi. Population (UN est. 1974): 80,000. Capital: Sao Tome.

The Democratic Republic of Sao Tome and Principe became independent July 12, 1975. The nation is comprised of the islands of Sao Tome and Principe, which lie in the Gulf of Guinea about 125 miles off West Central Africa. Each of the two islands is made up of northeast and southwest lowlands with volcanic hills in the center.

Cocoa is the principal product, followed by coffee and coconut palm products. Low cocoa prices, the emigration of most of the 1,000 whites, and the repatriation of Cape Verdean plantation foremen stymied the economy at independence.

The islands were uninhabited when discovered in 1471 by the Portuguese, who brought the first settlers — convicts and exiled Jews. Sugar planting was replaced by the slave trade as the chief economic activity until coffee and cocoa were introduced in the nineteenth century.

Portugal agreed in 1974 to turn the colony over to the Gabon-based Movement for the Liberation of Sao Tome and Principe, which proclaimed as the first president its East-German-trained leader Manuel Pinto da Costa.

Nearly all the population is black, with many laborers imported in recent years from Angola and Mozambique.

Saudi Arabia

Area: 873,000 sq. mi. Population (est. 1973): 8,100,-000. Capital: Riyadh. Monetary unit: Riyal.

Saudi Arabia occupies four-fifths of the Arabian Peninsula, with the Red Sea on most of its W coast and the Persian Gulf (also called Arabian Gulf) on the E. The highlands of the W, up to 9,000 ft., slope as an arid, barren desert to the Persian Gulf. Its neighbors are Jordan, Iraq, Kuwait, Bahrain, Qatar, United Arab Emirates, Oman and the 2 Yemens. It is more than 3 times the size of Texas.

Saudi Arabia comprises 4 provinces: the former sultanate of **Nejd,** the old kingdom of **Hejaz, Asir** and **El Hasa** (now known as the Eastern Province).

The Hejaz contains the holy cities of Islam — Medina where the Mosque of the Prophet enshrines the tomb of Mohammed, who died in the city June 7, 632, and Mecca, his birthplace, containing a great mosque sheltering the sacred shrine, the Kaaba. More than 400,000 Moslems from 60 nations pilgrimage to Mecca annually.

Two major airports, Dhahran and Jidda, handle the bulk of international traffic. Jidda, on the Red Sea, is the main seaport.

Resources and Industries. Saudi Arabia possesses the world's largest oil reserves and is the 3d largest producer, accounting for 14.6% of world total. Production centers along the Persian gulf. Refineries and piers for tankers are at Ras Tanura, and a pipeline runs to the Lebanese coast. Operations are mostly in the hands of the Arabian American Oil Co. (Aramco), formerly owned by several American companies. Most of the oil is shipped to Western Europe. Government income from oil, 1974, was $30 billion much of it invested or banked in the U.S. and Britain. In 1973, the Saudi government acquired 25% ownership of Aramco's operations, and in 1974 increased that to 60%.

A five-year $140 billion development plan was approved in 1975, calling for the importation of 500,000 workers.

An agricultural country except for oil and recently discovered gold, silver and rich iron ore, Saudi Arabia's products are dates, wheat, barley, fruit, hides, wool. Camels, horses, donkeys and sheep are raised. Some hides, wool and gum are exported. It receives UN technical assistance. A steel mill and fertilizer plant have been built.

History and Government: Nejd, long an independent state and center of the Wahhabi sect, fell under Turkish rule in the 18th century, but in 1913 Ibn Saud, founder of the Saudi dynasty, overthrew the Turks and captured the Turkish province of Hasa; took the Hejaz in 1925 and by 1926 most of Asir.

The form of government is a hereditary monarchy. Crown Prince Khalid was proclaimed king on Mar. 25, 1975, after the assassination of King Faisal. There is no constitution and no parliament. The king exercises authority together with a Council of Ministers, in accordance with the Moslem Koran.

Education and Religion. Elementary, secondary and higher education are free, but not compulsory.

Development of education is extensive, taking more than 10% of the government budget. But illiteracy was still high in 1974. Population is almost entirely Moslem.

Defense. Military forces total 42,000. Saudi Arabia is a member of the UN and Arab League. Billions of dollars in arms purchases have been from Britain, France and the U.S.

Saudi Arabia and Egypt opposed each other during the 1960s civil war in Yemen, Egyptian troops aiding the republicans and Saudi Arabia providing supplies to the royalists, who lost. But, beginning with the 1967 Arab-Israeli war, Saudi Arabia provided large annual financial gifts to Egypt; aid was later extended to Syria, Jordan, Palestinian guerrilla groups, as well as to other Moslem countries.

Faisal played a leading role in the 1973-74 Arab oil embargo against the U.S. and other nations in an attempt to force them to adopt an anti-Israel policy.

Senegal

Area: 76,124 sq. mi. Population (UN est. 1974): 4,320,000. Capital: Dakar, Monetary unit: CFA franc.

A former French Overseas Territory on the Atlantic coast of western Africa, Senegal borders Mauritania, Mali, Guinea, and Guinea-Bissau and surrounds Gambia on 3 sides. It is the size of South Dakota.

Senegal became an autonomous state in 1958 and with the Sudanese Republic formed the Mali Federation, Jan. 17, 1959. The federation became completely independent June 20, 1960, but after political conflict arose Senegal withdrew from the federation Aug. 20, 1960. The Sudanese Republic assumed the name Mali. The president and National Assembly are elected by adult suffrage.

About 70% of the population is engaged in agriculture and stock raising; peanuts are the mainstay of the economy. Dakar is an important seaport, handling 4,000 ships annually. Phosphates are an important export, along with peanut oil and canned fish. Developing industries include food processing, chemicals, cement. A long drought brought famine in 1972-73. Food supplies were sent to Senegal and its neighbors; 40% was from the U.S.

French is the official language, but the majority speak various tribal languages. About 80% of the population is Moslem.

Seychelles

Area: 107 sq. mi. Population (UN est. 1974): 60,000. Capital: Victoria. Monetary unit: Seychelles rupee.

The Seychelles are a group of 86 islands and islets in the Indian Ocean 700 miles N of Madagascar. Largest island is Mahe, 57 sq. mi., on which lies Victoria, the capital, which has a port and coaling station.

Most of the working population is engaged in agriculture or fishing. Coconut products are the chief exports, followed by cinnamon, guano, shark fins, and tortoise shell. Vanilla, tea, and patchouli are also grown. An international airport was opened in 1972 to serve the growing tourist industry.

The islands were occupied by France in 1768, and seized by Britain in 1794. Ruled as part of Mauritius from 1814, the Seychelles became a separate colony in 1903. Several island groups were detached in 1965. The ruling party had opposed independence as impractical, but pressure from the OAU and the UN Committee on Colonialism became irresistible, and independence was scheduled for the end of 1975.

The population descends almost entirely from early French settlers and African slaves. Most of the people speak Creole, a French patois; 5% speak French. English is also used. Literacy is fairly high, with over 11,000 students in school. Over 98% of the population profess Christianity.

Sierra Leone

Area: 27,925 sq. mi. Population (Govt. est. 1974): 2,710,000. Capital: Freetown. Monetary unit: Leone.

Sierra Leone, former British Colony and Protectorate, became an independent state within the Commonwealth Apr. 27, 1961. It is in the SW corner of the West African bulge. The coastline on the Atlantic is about 210 mi.; the country extends inland about 180 mi., between Guinea and Liberia. It is a bit smaller than South Carolina. Its name, meaning Mountain of the Lion, was applied by an early Portuguese mariner because of thunderstorms around its coastal peaks.

Freetown, the capital, was founded in 1787 by the British government as a home for destitute freed slaves. Their descendants, known as Creoles, number more than 50,000.

Principal exports are industrial diamonds, iron ore, bauxite, cocoa, coffee, palm kernels, kola nuts, ginger, piassava (palm fiber). More than 80% are employed in agriculture.

Successive steps toward independence followed introduction of the first constitution in 1951. The Sierra Leone People's party was dominant until a military junta took over in March 1967.

Col. A. T. Juxon-Smith, who headed the coup, was himself ousted in another coup, Apr. 8, 1968, led by non-commissioned officers. The nation was returned to civilian rule with swearing-in of Siaka Stevens as prime minister, Apr. 26. Sierra Leone became a republic Apr. 19, 1971, and Stevens was named president.

English is the official language but the majority speaks Krio (pidgin English) or tribal languages. Most of the people are animists; there are over 700,000 Moslems and over 100,000 Christians.

Singapore

Area: 226 sq. mi. Population (Govt. est. 1974): 2,236,000. Capital: Singapore. Monetary unit: Singapore dollar.

Singapore is an island republic 25 mi. long and 14 mi. wide at the southern tip of the Malay Peninsula in SE Asia. About 3 times the size of the District of Columbia, the main island is linked to the mainland by a three-quarter-mile-long causeway. The narrow Straits of Singapore separate it from its isles to the south.

Singapore, the capital, is the world's 4th largest port and the largest in SE Asia.

Founded in 1819 by Sir Thomas Stamford Raffles,

Singapore was a British colony until 1959 when it became autonomous within the Commonwealth. On Sept. 16, 1963, it joined with Malaya, Sarawak and Sabah to form the Federation of Malaysia.

Tensions between Malayans, dominant in the federation, and ethnic Chinese, dominant in Singapore, led to an agreement under which Singapore became a separate nation, Aug. 9, 1965. It has a one-house Parliament, elected by compulsory suffrage; a president elected by Parliament, and a prime minister. Most British and Australian troops were removed in 1975.

Singapore's population is 76% Chinese, 15% Malay and 9% Indians, Pakistanis, Ceylonese, Eurasians, etc. Administration is in English. Industries include shipbuilding, oil refining, banking, textiles, and food, rubber, and lumber processing. Manufacturing has replaced shipping as the basis of the economy, pushing per capita income to second place in Asia, following Japan.

Tourism is an important source of income; there were over a million visitors in 1973.

Primary education for 6 years is free but not compulsory. There are 2 universities, 2 technical colleges, and an institute of education. Literacy exceeds 75%.

Armed forces total 20,000. Singapore is a member of the Commonwealth and UN.

Somalia

Area: 246,155 sq. mi. Population (UN est. 1974): 3,090,000. Capital: Mogadishu. Monetary unit: Somali shilling.

The Somali Democratic Republic is composed of the former protectorate of British Somaliland and the former Italian UN trusteeship of Somalia in eastern Africa. It is bordered by the Gulf of Aden, Indian Ocean, Kenya, Ethiopia, and the French Territory of Afars and Issas. It is about the size of Texas. The population is predominantly Moslem.

Resources and Industries. Somalia has a weak economy and long depended on outside aid, part of it from the U.S., Italy, Great Britain, and the USSR. Principal occupations are livestock-raising and agriculture. Products include incense, sugar, bananas, sorghum, corn, gum, hides, kapok.

Its mineral resources, largely undeveloped, include iron, tin, gypsum, sandstone, bauxite, meerschaum, titanium, and others. In 1968 the government announced discovery of large uranium deposits.

History and Government. Many of the Somali peoples are nomadic and include large numbers in Kenya and Ethiopia. The Italian Protectorate of Somalia, 194,000 sq. mi., extended along the Indian Ocean from the Gulf of Aden to the Juba River. It was proclaimed a protectorate by Italy, 1889. The UN General Assembly in 1949 approved eventual creation of Somalia as a sovereign state and on April 1, 1950, Italy took over the trusteeship held by Great Britain since World War II.

British Somaliland, formed in the 19th Century in the northwest, had 68,000 sq. mi. Britain gave it independence June 26, 1960, and on July 1 it joined with the former Italian part to create the independent Somali Republic.

On Oct. 21, 1969, a Supreme Revolutionary Council seized power in a bloodless army and police coup, named a mainly civilian cabinet to aid it, and abolished the Assembly. It made Somali the official language, a Hamitic tongue written in Latin script. In May, 1970, several foreign companies were nationalized.

A severe drought in 1975 killed tens of thousands, and spurred efforts to resettle nomads on collective farms. The U.S. charged that Soviet naval facilities at Berbera included a missile storage site.

Republic of South Africa

Area: 471,819 sq. mi. Population (Govt. est. 1974): 24,920,000. Capitals: Pretoria and Cape Town. Monetary unit: Rand.

The Republic of South Africa occupies the southern portion of the continent and includes the former colonies of the Cape of Good Hope, Natal, the Transvaal and the Orange Free State, which became provinces. It is close to twice the size of Texas.

Cape Town, seat of Parliament, is the legislative capital and Pretoria the administrative capital. Largest cities are Johannesburg, Cape Town and Durban.

Population of government-designated racial groups in 1970 census was: Bantu, 15,057,952; white, 3,751,-328; Colored (mixed) 2,018,453; Asians, 620,436. Among Bantu, the census reported the largest groups to be: Zulu, 4,026,058; Xhosa 3,930,087; Tswana, 1,719,367; Sotho, 3,471,000.

Kruger National Park, an 8,000-sq.-mi. wild game preserve; Cape Peninsula, and the Drakensberg Mtns. are among numerous tourist attractions.

Resources and Industries. Corn, wool, wheat, tobacco, sugar, fruit, peanuts, wine, karacul, butter and cheese are major agricultural products. Industry products include steel, tires, electric motors, textiles, furniture, plastics.

South Africa leads the world in production of gold, gem diamonds and antimony; it is among top producers of platinum, chrome, copper, uranium, vanadium, vermiculite, manganese and asbestos. Coal, iron, lead and zinc resources are large. Annual production of more than 50 minerals is est. at over $6 billion.

South Africa has enjoyed an industrial boom. Index numbers of industrial production (1970 = 100) was 122 in 1974 for manufacturing. An advanced nuclear energy industry has developed.

Foreign trade (in thousands of U.S. dollars), excluding gold:

	Imports	Exports
1973	$5,020,000	$3,435,000
1974	$7,222,000	$4,988,000

History and Government. The Cape of Good Hope area was settled by Dutch, beginning in the 17th century. Britain seized the Cape in 1806. Many Dutch trekked north and founded 2 republics, the Transvaal and the Orange Free State. Diamonds were discovered, 1867, and gold, 1886. The Dutch (Boers) resented encroachments by the British and others; the Anglo-Boer War followed, 1899-1902. Britain won and, effective May 31, 1910, created the Union of South Africa, incorporating the British colonies of the Cape and Natal, the Transvaal and the Orange Free State.

It was a dominion within the British Commonwealth until it became, after a referendum, the Republic of South Africa, May 31, 1961, and withdrew from the Commonwealth.

With the election victory of Daniel Malan's National party in 1948, the policy of separate development of the races, or apartheid, already existing unofficially, became official. This called for separate development, separate residential areas and ultimate political independence for the whites, Bantus, Asians and Coloreds. In 1959 the government passed acts providing the eventual creation of 9 Bantu nations or Bantustans on 13% of the country's land area. In 1963, the Transkei, an area in the SE, became the first of these partially self-governing territories or "Homelands." By 1974 there were 8: Transkei, Ciskei, Lebowa, Bophuthatswana, KwaZulu, Basotho-Qwaqwa, Gazankulu and Venda.

The white-operated government includes a president chosen for a 7-year term by the Senate and Assembly, and a prime minister who holds the actual executive power. Members of the partly appointed, partly indirectly-elected Senate, and of the elected Assembly, are chosen for 5-year terms; all members must be white. There is a separate, advisory Indian Council, partly elected, partly appointed, to represent those of Asian Indian descent. In 1969, a Colored People's Representative Council was created. There is an elected Provincial Council in each of the 4 provinces.

Education and Religion. There are 16 universities, 11 of them for white students; enrollment exceeds

88,000. Primary education is free to all citizens.

Dutch Protestant churches predominate, with Anglicans and Methodists next. The majority of Bantus are Christian. Hindus, Moslems, and Jews are present. English and Afrikaans are official languages.

Defense. Military forces total 110,000.

South-West Africa or Namibia

South-West Africa, a sparsely populated land twice the size of California, became the object of international dispute in 1966. Made a German protectorate in 1884, it was surrendered to South Africa in 1915 and was administered by that country under an old League of Nations mandate. South Africa refused to accept UN authority under the trusteeship system.

Other African nations charged South Africa imposed apartheid, built military bases and exploited S-W Africa; 36 African states called on the UN to take over the mandate. The UN General Assembly in May 1968 created an 11-nation council to take over administration of S-W Africa and lead it to independence. In April 1968 the council charged that South Africa had blocked its effort to visit S-W Africa.

In 1968 the UN General Assembly gave the area the name Namibia. In Jan. 1970 the UN Security Council condemned South Africa for "illegal" control of the area. In an advisory opinion in June 1971 the International Court of Justice declared South Africa was occupying the area illegally. In 1973, a South Africa-style "homeland," Ovamboland, in the northern area, was given limited self-government.

Most of S-W Africa is a plateau, 3,600 ft. high, with plains in the N, Kalahari Desert to the E, Orange River on the S, the Atlantic on the W. Area is 318,261 sq. mo.; population (UN est. 1974) 690,000 including over 96,000 whites; capital, Windhoek. There is a South African administrator; voters choose 18 members of a Legislative Assembly and send 6 members to the South African Assembly; 4 are appointed to the South Africa Senate.

Products include cattle, sheep, diamonds, lead, zinc, vanadium, fish. People include Namas (Hottentots), Ovambos (Bantus), Bushmen and others.

Spain

Area: 194,883 sq. mi. Population (Govt. est. 1974): 35,220,000. Capital: Madrid. Monetary unit: Peseta.

Spain, a nominal monarchy, occupies the entire Iberian peninsula in Western Europe, except for Portugal. It is separated from France by the Pyrenees.

The interior is a high arid plateau traversed E and W by mountain ranges. Spain is twice the size of Wyoming.

The **Balearic Islands** in the western Mediterranean, 1,935 sq. mi., are a province of Spain; they include **Majorca** (Mallorca), with the capital, Palma; **Minorca, Cabrera, Ibiza** and **Formentera.** The **Canary Islands,** 2,807 sq. mi., in the Atlantic W of Morocco, form 2 provinces, including the islands of **Tenerife, Palma, Gomera, Hierro, Grand Canary, Fuerteventura** and **Lanzarote** with Las Palmas and Santa Cruz thriving ports. **Ceuta** and **Melilla,** small enclaves on Morocco's Mediterranean coast, are part of Metropolitan Spain.

Spanish Sahara is an overseas province on the W coast of Africa, S of Morocco; area 102,703 sq. mi., population (1970 census) 76,425. It is claimed by both Morocco and Mauritania, but Spain has offered self-determination. It has world's greatest phosphate deposits.

Spain has sought return of Gibraltar, in British control since 1704. (See Index.)

Resources and Industries. Only about 40% of the land is cultivable, the remainder is arid or mountainous. Farm mechanization and irrigation are increasing.

Principal agricultural products are wheat, barley, oats, rye, olives, grapes, lemons, oranges and other fruit, onions, almonds, esparto, flax, hemp, pulse and cork. Tobacco, cotton, and rice are also grown. Wine making is a large industry. Spain has abundant minerals, including lead, iron, copper, zinc, coal, cobalt, mercury, silver, sulphur and phosphates.

Between 1960 and 1974 Spain changed from an agricultural nation into one of the world's top industrial powers. Manufacturing includes machinery, cotton and woolen goods, shoes, paper, automobiles, cork and cement. Spain's fish catch is the world's 4th largest, by value. Coal production is more than 13 million metric tons annually. Foreign trade in thousands of U.S. dollars:

	Imports	Exports
1973	$9,538,000	$5,162,000
1974	$15,298,000	$7,036,000

The index of general industrial production (1970=100) was 153 in 1974. A trade pact with the USSR was signed in 1972. Spain recognized Communist China in 1973. More than 30 million tourists spend $2.5 billion a year in Spain.

History and Government. Spain was settled by Iberians, Basques and Celts, partly overrun by Carthaginians, conquered by Rome c. 200 B.C. The Visigoths, in power by the 5th Century A.D., adopted Christianity but by 711 A.D. lost to the Islamic invasion from Africa. Christian reconquest from the N led to a Spanish nationalism. In 1469 the kingdoms of Aragon and Castile were united by the marriage of Ferdinand II and Isabella I, and the last Moorish power broken by the fall of the kingdom of Granada, 1492. Spain became a bulwark of Roman Catholicism.

Spain obtained a colonial empire with the discovery of America by Columbus, 1492, the conquest of Mexico by Cortes and Peru by Pizarro. It also controlled the Netherlands and parts of Italy and Germany. Spain lost Mexico, Peru and other American colonies in the 1820s. It lost Cuba, the Philippines and Puerto Rico during the Spanish-American War, 1898.

Primo de Rivera became dictator in 1923. King Alfonso XII revoked the dictatorship, 1930, but was forced to leave the country 1931. A republic was proclaimed which disestablished the church, curtailed its privileges and secularized education. A conservative reaction occurred 1933 but was followed by a Popular Front (1936-1939) composed of socialists, communists, republicans, and anarchists.

Army officers headed a revolt against the government, 1936, under Francisco Franco (b. Dec. 14, 1892). In a destructive 3-yr. war, in which one million were said to have died, Franco received help from Italy and Germany, while the Soviet Union, France and Mexico went active on behalf of the republic. War ended Mar. 28, 1939. Franco was named caudillo, or leader of the nation.

Spain was neutral in World War II but its relations with facist countries caused its exclusion from the UN in 1946. It was admitted in 1955.

Dec. 14, 1966, a new constitution, was approved by the people in a plebiscite. The new law implied a liberalization of government policy, but enforcement was limited.

In July 1969, Franco and the Cortes designated Prince Juan Carlos, then 31, as the future king and chief of state, to assume office in the event of the death or incapacitation of Gen. Franco, who was then 76. Juan Carlos was the son of the pretender to the throne, Don Juan of Bourbon.

Education and Religion. Franco reestablished Catholicism as the state religion. Primary education is compulsory and free. There are 13 universities. More than two-thirds speak Castilian; Basque is spoken in the N; Galician in the NW, and Catalan in the NE. Non-Castilians have protested cultural and political repression.

Defense. Military forces total 284,000. Under a 1953 agreement with the U.S., renewed in 1970, Spain received military aid and the U.S. was granted use of bases; renewal talks were held in 1975.

Sri Lanka

Area: 25,332 sq. mi. Population (UN est. 1974): 13,680,000. Capital: Colombo. Monetary unit: Rupee.

Sri Lanka, formerly Ceylon, is an island republic in the Indian Ocean 20 mi. off the southern tip of India. Its greatest length from N to S is 270 mi., and its greatest width, 140 mi. The coastal area is flat, but the central part is mountainous with the highest peak, Pidurutalagala, 8,281 ft. The climate is hot, with high relative humidity. There are many mountain streams, navigable only by small river craft. Colombo is served by world airlines.

Resources and Industries. Minerals and metals include graphite, limestone, iron, precious and semiprecious stones, ilmenite, monazite, zircon, quartz. Manufactures include plywood, paper, glassware, ceramics, cement, chemicals, textiles, fertilizers and vegetable oil products.

Principal agricultural products are tea, rubber, coconuts, rice, cacao, cinnamon, citronella, tobacco. Accounting for 90% of exports are tea, rubber and coconuts.

A major source of precious stones, the island produces about 20 varieties including sapphires, rubies, alexandrites, topaz, tourmalines and cat's-eyes. Most are mined at pits in Ratnapura.

History and Government. The island was known to the ancient world as Taprobane (Greek for coppercolored) and later as Serendip (from Arabic). Colonists from northern India subdued the indigenous Veddahs about 543 B.C.; their descendants, the Sinhalese, still form most of the population. Descendants of Tamil immigrants from southern India account for one-fifth of the population. Parts of the maritime areas were occupied in turn by the Portuguese in 1505 and by the Dutch in 1658. The British seized the island in 1796 and it became a Crown colony in 1802. Universal suffrage was granted in 1931 and a new constitution on the British model in 1946.

As Ceylon it became an independent member of the Commonwealth in 1948. It is a member of the UN.

Prime Minister W. R. D. Bandaranaike, appointed Apr. 12, 1956, was assassinated Sept. 25, 1959. In new elections, the Freedom party was victorious. Its leader, Mrs. Sirimavo Bandaranaike, widow of the former prime minister, was sworn in to the office.

Her regime pledged itself to a neutralist policy and nationalized a number of industries. In April, 1962, the government expropriated service and terminal facilities of one British and 2 U.S. oil companies. In March 1965 elections, the conservative, pro-Western United National party won the largest number of seats and its leader, Dudley Senanayake, became prime minister.

In Dec. 1965, the new government agreed to pay compensation for the seized oil companies. The U.S. in Feb. 1966, agreed to resume economic aid, which had been cut off when the oil companies were expropriated.

After May 1970 elections, Mrs. Bandaranaike became prime minister again. In 1971 the nation suffered economic problems and terrorist activities by ultra-leftists, thousands of whom were executed. Unemployment among graduates and food shortages plagued the nation in 1973 and 1974.

On May 22, 1972, Ceylon became the Republic of Sri Lanka with a president, prime minister and a unicameral National Assembly.

Education and Religion. All education is free in government schools from kindergarten to university. The majority of the population, Sinhalese, belongs to the Buddhist faith. The Tamils, mostly Hindu, are est. at about 2 million. Sinhalese became the official language in 1961, but laws must also be written in Tamil. Literacy is 81%.

Defense. Armed forces total 12,000.

Sudan

Area: 967,491 sq. mi. Population (Govt. est. 1974): 17,324,000. Capital: Khartoum. Monetary unit: Pound.

Sudan proclaimed itself a republic Jan. 1, 1956. It is bounded by Egypt, the Red Sea, Ethiopia, Uganda, Kenya, Zaire, the Central African Republic, Chad and Libya. It is about the size of Texas, Alaska and New Mexico combined.

The northern zone consists of the Libyan Desert, in the W, and the mountainous Nubian Desert, extending to the Red Sea on the E, separated by the narrow valley of the Nile; the central zone contains large fertile areas, including the rainlands of Kassala and Tokar, the Gezira Plain and the pastures and gum forests of Kordofan; in the southern equatorial belt the soil is richest and watered by tropical rains.

The White Nile flows N through the center of the country; the Blue Nile, flowing from the mountains of Ethiopia, joins the White at Khartoum; the combined river flows N in a huge S curve to enter Egypt N of Wadi Halfa.

Resources and Industries. The Sudan is the world's principal source of gum arabic. Chief grain crop is durra (sorghum), the country's staple food. Cotton is the principal export; American and extra-long staple cottons are grown in the fertile Gezira, between the White and Blue Niles. Other important products are sesame, peanuts, rice, coffee, sugarcane, tobacco, wheat, dates, hides, mahogany, chrome. Live camels and sheep are exported to Egypt. There are textile and food-processing factories.

History and Government. In the 1820s Egypt took over the Sudan, defeating the last of earlier empires, including the Fung. In the 1880s a revolution was led by Mohammed Ahmed who called himself the Mahdi (leader of the faithful) and his followers, the dervishes. British Gen. Charles Gordon (Chinese Gordon), who had earlier put down the slave trade in the Sudan, was sent by Egypt to evacuate its troops; he was besieged and slain at Khartoum, 1885.

In 1898 Horatio Kitchener led an Anglo-Egyptian force which crushed the Mahdi's successors.

In Oct. 1951 the Egyptian Parliament abrogated its 1899 and 1936 treaties with Great Britain, and amended the constitution, Oct. 16, to provide for a separate Sudanese constitution.

Sudan voted for complete independence effective Jan. 1, 1956. A 5-member Supreme Commission (Council of State) and a Cabinet were sworn in.

A parliamentary government was set up but in 1958 Gen. Ibrahim Abboud took power; he resigned under pressure in 1964; a Constituent Assembly was elected in 1965 which approved a coalition government.

In May 1969, in a second military coup, a Revolutionary Council took power, but a civilian premier and cabinet were appointed and the new government announced it would create a socialist state. It also announced plans to negotiate an end to guerrilla warfare, which had beset the southern third of the nation for years. The northern 5 provinces are predominantly Arab-Moslem and have been dominant in the central government. The 3 southern provinces, in which there was a strong separatist movement, are Negro and predominantly pagan, with small Christian and Moslem minorities. A peace agreement, giving the South regional autonomy, was reached in 1972. Renewed flare-ups occurred in 1975.

The government nationalized a number of businesses in May 1970. An attempted communist coup in July 1971 failed, leading to a temporary diplomatic break with the U.S.S.R.

Diplomatic relations with the U.S., broken by Sudan during the 1967 Arab-Israeli war, were restored in 1972; locally-owned firms were denationalized and foreign firms compensated.

On Mar. 2, 1973, the U. S. ambassador and the charge d'affaires and a Belgian diplomat were tortured and slain in Khartoum by 8 Palestinian terrorists. The 8 were convicted of murder by a Sudanese court in June 1974 but were promptly freed and turned over to a Palestinian liberation group in Egypt. The U. S. recalled its ambassador.

Education and Religion. Sudanese inhabitants are Arabs, Negroes, and Nubians (of mixed Arab and Negro blood); the Arabs and Nubians are Mohammedans. Higher education is available at Khartoum Univ. Arabic is the national language; many tribal languages are spoken in the South.

Surinam

Area: 63,251. Population: (UN est. 1974): 410,000. Capital: Paramaribo. Monetary unit: Surinam florin.

Surinam is on the N coast of South America, between the Atlantic Ocean and Brazil; to the E is French Guiana, to the W is Guyana, both of which have disputed parts of their Surinam borders. Surinam is about the size of Washington State.

Most of the population is concentrated along the coast, where dikes permit agriculture. Farther inland is a forest belt; to the south, largely unexplored hills cover three-fourths of the country.

Minerals abound, especially bauxite, which is the major export, in raw or refined form. Hydroelectric power and lumbering are being developed. Oil has been discovered. Rice is the major crop; sugar cane, bananas, citrus fruits, and shrimp are also important.

The Netherlands acquired Surinam in 1667 from Britain, in exchange for New Netherlands (New York). The 1954 Dutch constitution raised the colony to a level of equality with the Netherlands and the Netherlands Antilles. In the 1970s the Dutch government pressured for Surinam independence, which was scheduled for late 1975, despite objections from East Indians and some Bush Negroes. A Legislative Council (Staten) is elected by universal suffrage for four-year terms; a Council of Ministers is responsible to the Staten.

The population is extremely diverse; East Indians make up over 35%, Creoles (racially mixed descendants of freed African slaves) 30%, Javanese 15%, Bush Negroes (forest-dwelling descendants of runaway slaves) 10%; the remainder is composed of European, Chinese, and Amerindian groups. About 90,000 have emigrated to the Netherlands. Dutch is the official language, but the Creole tongue Sranan Tongo is universally understood. Nearly all major world religions are represented.

Primary education is free and compulsory; 150,000 attend schools. There are four teacher-training colleges and a university.

Swaziland

Area: 6,705 sq. mi. Population (Govt. est. 1974): 480,000. Capital: Mbabane. Monetary unit: Lilangeni.

The Kingdom of Swaziland is in SE Africa, almost completely surrounded by the Republic of South Africa except for part of the E border which adjoins Mozambique. The Swazis came under British protection in 1903.

The example of neighboring former British territories Bechuanaland and Basutoland, which became the independent nations of Botswana and Lesotho in 1966, encouraged the drive for Swazi independence; Swaziland was economically the most healthy of the 3. On Apr. 25, 1967, it achieved full internal self-government under a constitution and on Sept. 6, 1968, it became completely independent and a member of the Commonwealth.

The constitution provided for a partly-elected, partly-appointed Assembly and Senate, and a prime minister; the former paramount chief, Sobhuza II, became King Sobhuza, a constitutional head of state. The royal house of Swaziland traces back 400 years, and remains one of Africa's last ruling dynasties. In

April 1973 the king repealed the constitution and assumed full powers.

Polygamy has been the common marital status, but women have the right to vote.

About 97% of the residents are Swazi, a Bantu group. South African whites constitute a small minority; English and Siswati are the official languages.

The country is rich in mineral resources, including one of the world's largest asbestos mines, the Havelock Mine, and iron ore resources estimated at some 47 million tons. In addition, there are gold, tin, coal, mica and other minerals. Tourism has grown.

In recent years Swaziland developed a multimillion-dollar timber and pulp industry, a railway link out of the landlocked country to ports in Mozambique, hydro-electric power and tarred roads. The major export items are asbestos, iron ore, wood pulp, citrus fruits and sugar. The land is fertile and has abundant water, producing such other crops as corn, cotton, rice, pineapples, and cattle. About 8,000 Swazis hold jobs in South Africa.

Sweden

Area: 173,665 sq. mi. Population (Census 1974): 8,176,691. Capital: Stockholm. Monetary unit: Krona.

Sweden occupies the eastern and larger part of the Scandinavian peninsula in NW Europe. Its greatest N-S length is 977 mi.; greatest width 311 mi. The country is 10% larger than California. Sweden is separated from Norway on the W by the Kjolen Mtns., and from Finland on the E by the Baltic Sea except in the N where the 2 meet along the Tornea River.

Stockholm and Goteborg are the largest ports.

Resources and Industries. Although half of the country is forested, Sweden contains much productive land on which the Swedes have attained high efficiency in agriculture. Of the total land area, 9.9% is cultivated, 2.5% pasture. Chief agricultural products are dairy products, beef, pork, grains, potatoes, sugar beets, and vegetable oils.

Main natural resources are forests, iron ore and water power. Coal and oil have to be imported. Industry employs 37% of the work-population, agriculture 7%. Swedish steel is of especial value for toolmaking. Other metals produced are lead, copper, zinc, gold and silver. In 1974, 74.2 billion kwh were produced; the Stornorrforsen hydroelectric plant on the Ume River is the largest in Western Europe.

Although over 95% of the economy is in private hands, the government holds a large interest in water power production and the railroads are operated by a public agency.

Consumer cooperatives are in extensive operation, with 1,700,000 member households served by about 2,650 stores. Cooperatives also are important in agriculture and housing.

Shipping is privately operated. The merchant fleet included (1974) about 650 units totaling about 10 million tons d.w.

Sweden is one of the leading exporters of iron ore and cellulose. About one-fourth of the exports come from pulp, lumber, paper and other forestry products. Other important products are machinery, instruments, autos, iron and steel, ships.

Foreign trade in thousands of U. S. dollars:

	Imports	Exports
1973	$10,628,000	$12,198,000
1974	$17,197,000	$17,295,000

History and Government. Sweden is a parliamentary democracy with a king as head of state and a prime minister as chief executive. The Riksdag (Parliament) has 349 members; all citizens 18 and over may vote.

King Gustaf VI Adolf died at the age of 90, Sept. 15, 1973. He was succeeded by his grandson, Carl XVI Gustaf, 27. Under a constitutional change effective

Jan. 1, 1975, only symbolic powers are left to the king.

In elections Sept. 16, 1973, the Social Democrats, in power 41 years, and the non-Socialist parties each won 175 of the seats, then numbering 350.

About 20% of the national income is redistributed through the social welfare system which includes compulsory health insurance, pensions, unemployment and industrial injuries insurance, family and educational allowances. Unemployment during 1974 averaged 1.5%.

Sweden provided haven to 450 U.S. Vietnam War deserters and draft resisters. The U.S. and Sweden in 1974 ended a 15-month diplomatic "freeze" and exchanged ambassadors.

Sweden is a member of the Nordic Council, UN, EFTA, and Council of Europe and has a free-trade agreement with EC.

Education and Religion. The population is homogeneous, except for 650,000 foreign workers. About 95% of the people are Lutheran, which is the state religion. Education is compulsory and illiteracy is non-existent. There are 5 state universities with several branches.

Defense. Full mobilizable strength exceeds 750,-000. Military service is compulsory for men. The air force is among the largest in Europe.

Switzerland

Area: 15,941 sq. mi. Population (UN est. 1974); 6,480,000. Capital: Bern. Monetary unit: Franc.

Switzerland, a federal republic in Central Europe, is bounded by France, Germany, Austria, Liechtenstein and Italy. It is twice the size of New Jersey.

Switzerland is the most mountainous of all European countries. The Alps cover 60% of land area, the Jura 10%; running between them NE to SW are the midlands, about 30%. Swiss lakes are famous for their beauty. The Rhine, Rhone and feeders of the Danube and Po originate in Switzerland.

Resources and Industries. Switzerland's abundant streams power 431 major hydroelectric plants, but 80% of energy comes from imported fuels. Most important industries, in descending order: machinery, instruments, watches (40% of world production), textiles, foodstuffs (cheese, chocolate, etc.). Steel, chemicals, and pharmaceuticals are also important. Machine making employs 26% of all factory workers and accounts for 34% of exports. Included are textile machinery, machine tools, dynamo-electric plants, transformers and diesels. About 20% of workers are foreign residents.

Foreign trade in thousands of U.S. dollars:

	Imports	Exports
1973	$11,626,000	$9,472,000
1974	$14,421,000	$11,788,000

Switzerland is one of the world's great banking centers. Stability of its currency brings funds from many quarters. Nearly 7 million tourists visit annually.

History and Government. Switzerland, the Helvetia of ancient times, is a federation of 22 cantons (19 full cantons and 6 half cantons), 3 of which in 1291 created a defensive league and later were joined by other districts. (Voters in the French-speaking Jura approved a breakaway canton in 1974.) In 1648 the Swiss Confederation obtained its independence from the Holy Roman Empire. The cantons were joined under a federal constitution in 1848, with large powers of local control retained by each canton. Legislative authority vests in a parliament of 2 chambers, a Standerat or State Council to which each canton sends 2 members; and a lower house, Nationalrat or National Council.

Executive power is vested in the 7-member Bundesrat (Federal Council). The president is selected from members of the Federal Council, serves for a year and customarily is succeeded by the vice president. Women won the right to vote in federal

elections in 1971; some were elected to parliament.

Switzerland enters into no military alliance and is not a member of UN or NATO. It is however a member of UN agencies such as the ILO, WHO, UNESCO, FAO. In 1972 it signed an agreement with the EC for gradual abolition of industrial tariffs.

Geneva is the seat of a number of UN agencies, International Committee of the Red Cross, League of Red Cross Societies, Int'l. Union for Telecommunications. The Universal Postal Union is in Bern.

Education and Religion. Primary education has been free and compulsory since 1874. There are 9 universities. Swiss German dialects are spoken by a majority of the people in 16 of the cantons; other languages are French, Italian, and Romansch.

There is complete freedom of worship; 47.8% of the people are Protestants, 49.4% Roman Catholics.

Defense. Service in the national militia is compulsory. Its easily mobilized divisions comprise more than 600,000 men. The air force has about 300 combat craft.

Syria

Area: 71,498 sq. mi. Population (Govt. est. 1974): 7,120,000. Capital: Damascus. Monetary unit: Syrian pound.

The Syrian Arab Republic has a short coastline on the eastern shore of the Mediterranean, then stretches E and S with fertile valleys and plains alternating with mountains and desert. Main rivers are Euphrates and Orontes. Chief seaport is Latakia. Syria is about the size of South Dakota.

Resources and Industries. Syria is primarily an agricultural and stock-raising nation. Cotton, barley, wheat, fruits, vegetables, meat, textiles and wool are the main exports. Growing industries include flour milling, oil refining, textiles, cement, tobacco, glassware, sugar and brassware. In 1965 the Socialist regime nationalized most industries. Oil production is growing. Royalties are collected from Iraqi and Saudi Arabian pipelines crossing to Mediterranean ports. In 1973 a $300 million power and irrigation dam was completed on the upper Euphrates, leading to a dispute with Iraq over water use.

History and Government. One of the world's ancient inhabited lands, the state of Syria was formed from former Turkish Empire Sanjaks (districts). Syria was made a separate entity by the Treaty of Sevres 1920 and divided into the states of Syria and Greater Lebanon. Both were administered under a French League of Nations mandate 1920-1941.

Syria was proclaimed a republic by the occupying French Sept. 16, 1941, and exercised full independence effective Jan. 1, 1944. French troops left in 1946.

Syria joined with Egypt in Feb. 1958 in the United Arab Republic but seceded Sept. 30, 1961. The Socialist Baath party and military leaders seized power in Mar. 1963. The Baath, a pan-Arab organization, became the only legal party. In Mar. 1973 voters approved, by 97%, a new constitution providing for a 186-member People's Council but giving most powers to the president.

In the Israeli-Arab war of June 1967, Israel seized and occupied the Golan Heights area inside Syria, from which Israeli settlements had for years been shelled by Syria.

Syria aided Palestinian guerrillas fighting Jordanian forces in Sept. 1970, and, after a renewal of that fighting in July 1971, broke off relations with Jordan. But by 1975 the 2 countries had entered a military coordination pact.

Syria received large shipments of arms from the USSR in 1972-73 and on Oct. 6, 1973, Syria joined Egypt in an attack on Israel. (For details, see article on Israel.) Arab oil states agreed in 1974 to give Syria $1 billion a year to aid anti-Israel moves. Military supplies used or lost in the 1973 war were replaced by the USSR in 1974.

It is member of the UN.

Education and Religion. The population is composed mainly of Sunni Moslems but there are many Christians. Arabic is the official language. Syria has universities in Damascus, Aleppo and Latakia. Education is free through the university level.

Tanzania

Area: 363,708 sq. mi. Population (Govt. est. 1974): 14,760,000. Capital: Dar es Salaam. Monetary unit: Tanzanian shilling.

The Republic of Tanganyika in E. Africa and the Republic of Zanzibar, an island in the Indian Ocean off the coast of Tanganyika, joined in a single nation, the United Republic of Tanzania, Apr. 26, 1964. The new central government at Dar es Salaam (Haven of Peace), an important port and capital of Tanganyika, was given jurisdiction over defense, foreign affairs and public services.

Julius K. Nyerere, Tanganyika's president, became president of the new nation; Zanzibar's president became first vice president.

In 1967 the government nationalized all banks, including some in which U.S. banks held a part interest, and many industries; some of the latter were taken over completely, in others the government took a part interest. The government also ordered that Swahili, not English, be used in all official business.

Tanzania is a member of the UN and Commonwealth. In 1974 a road to Zambia was completed with U.S. aid and a railroad to Zambia was finished with aid from the People's Republic of China.

Tanganyika

Tanganyika stretches from the Indian Ocean on the E to 3 of Africa's Great Lakes: Victoria, Tanganyika and Nyasa (now also called Malawi). Its area is 362,-688 sq. mi., larger than Texas and Oklahoma combined; pop. is over 14 million. Most of the people are Bantus and speak Swahili.

Snow-capped Mt. Kilimanjaro, tallest in Africa, rises 19,340 ft. in the N. Nearby are the famed Serengeti Plains, teeming with vast herds of wild animals, protected in one of Tanzania's several large national park game preserves. Safaris, sport fishing and mountain climbing are among attractions.

Principal products are sisal, cotton, coffee, tea, tobacco and hides. Both gem and industrial diamonds are mined, as are gold, salt, tin and mica. Diamonds accounted for 91% of the mineral income in 1973.

Factories include food processing, clothing.

Arab colonization began in the 8th century A.D.; Portuguese sailors explored the coast by about 1500. Other Europeans followed.

In 1885 Germany established German East Africa of which Tanganyika formed the bulk. After World War I it was taken by Britain as a League of Nations mandate and after 1946 as a UN trust territory.

Constitutional changes gave it internal autonomy in Sept. 1960. It became fully independent Dec. 9, 1961, and was proclaimed a republic within the Commonwealth a year later.

Zanzibar

Zanzibar, the Isle of Cloves, lies 23 mi. off the coast of Tanganyika; its area is 640 sq. mi. The island of Pemba, 25 mi. to the NE, area 380 sq. mi., is included in the administration. The population is mainly Africans and Arabs. The total area of the 2 islands is about that of Rhode Island; population (Govt. est. 1967): 354,360.

Chief industry is the production of cloves and clove oil, of which Zanzibar and Pemba produce the bulk of the world's supply.

Portugal ruled Zanzibar for 2 centuries until ousted by Arabs around 1700. Zanzibar became an independent Sultanate in 1856 and a British Protectorate in 1890. Independence came Dec. 10, 1963. Revolutionary forces overthrew the Sultan Jan. 12, 1964. The new government ousted American and British diplomats and newsmen and nationalized farms. Union with Tanganyika followed, 1964.

Thailand

Area: 198,455 sq. mi. Population (Govt. est. 1974): 41,020,000. Capital: Bangkok. Monetary unit: Baht.

Thailand is a constitutional monarchy in SE Asia bordered by Burma, Laos, Cambodia, the Gulf of Thailand (or Siam) and Malaysia. It is about twice the size of Colorado with large areas under irrigation.

Bangkok, the capital, is a modern city. Its Don Muang airfield is one of the largest and most modern in SE Asia, served by 24 international airlines. It is also an important port. There is an extensive inland waterway system and network of roads.

Resources and Industries. There are large forests, teakwood being an important article of export. Agriculture occupies 80% of the population.

Thailand is the world's 4th largest producer of tin ore; other minerals are iron, manganese, tungsten, antimony. Offshore natural gas was discovered, 1974.

The chief crop is rice, the staple food of the people and heavily exported, accounting for about 19% of foreign exchange earnings. Other important exports are tin, rubber, corn, teak, tapioca, and tungsten. Coconuts, tobacco, pepper, peanuts, beans, and cotton are produced.

Foreign investment in industry is encouraged — auto assembly plants, pharmaceuticals, textiles, electrical goods. Tourism is important.

History and Government. Thailand, an ancient monarchy, noted for picturesque architecture and pageantry, is the only country in SE Asia never taken over by a colonial power, thanks to King Mongkut and his son King Chulalongkorn who ruled from 1851 to 1910, modernized the country and signed trade treaties with both Britain and France.

Thailand underwent a bloodless revolution in 1932. King Prajadhipok, a liberal, signed a new constitution, establishing a limited monarchy, but he refused to sign a measure abdicating the royal power of life and death and resigned. He was succeeded by his nephew, Prince Ananda, who was found dead of a bullet wound, June 9, 1946, and the legislature named his brother, Prince Phumiphol Aduldet (Bhumibol Adulyadej) (born 1927), to succeed him. The new king formally took the throne May 5, 1950, as Rama IX.

A military-civilian junta, headed by Gen. Thanom Kittikachorn, took over the government in Nov. 1971. Civilians, led by students, overwhelmed police, Oct. 1973, and forced Thanom to resign as premier. A civilian cabinet was named. After free elections in January 1975, a coalition government was sworn in.

There was sporadic terrorism in the NE and far S, 1965-74, by communists and ethnic minorities.

Education and Religion. Education is compulsory between 7 and 14. There are 9 universities, 31 training colleges and many vocational schools. The language is Thai, derived from Pali and Sanskrit. English is widely used. About 94% of the people are Buddhists; others are 1.5 million Moslems, some Christians, etc.

Defense. Military strength for 1972-73 was 195,500. Thailand is a member of the UN.

U.S. forces in Thailand, mostly airmen, totaled 45,-000 in 1973; during the year, U.S. Southeast Asia military hq. was moved from Saigon to Nakhon Phanom in Thailand. The U.S. withdrew most of its forces from Thailand during 1973 and 1974. The new Thai government obtained U.S. agreement to withdraw all troops by March 1976.

The last of 11,000 Thai troops were withdrawn from South Vietnam in 1972. About 15,000 Thai "irregular" forces, financed by the U.S., returned from Laos in 1974.

Togo

Area: 21,853 sq. mi. Population (Govt. est. 1974): 2,170,000. Capital: Lome. Monetary unit: CFA franc.

The republic of Togo is composed of part of the one-time German colony of Togoland, surrendered in 1914, and administered by France as a UN trusteeship, 1946-1960.

Togo is a thin sliver of land on the southern edge of the West African bulge. It is bounded by Upper Volta, Dahomey, the Atlantic and Ghana.

In 1958 France received UN approval to end its trusteeship and the republic was proclaimed Apr. 27, 1960. Official language is French.

A draft constitution on the U.S. model was published Mar. 20, 1961. It provided for a president and a 46-member unicameral parliament. First president, Sylvanus Olympio, elected Apr. 9, 1961, was assassinated by a military junta, Jan. 13, 1963. His successor was Nicolas Grunitzky, elected May 5, 1963. Grunitzky resigned Jan. 13, 1967, and was replaced by Gnassingbe Eyadema, head of the armed forces.

Togo has received aid from France, the U.S. and West Germany. Tourism is a growing industry.

Principal products: phosphates, coffee, cocoa, palm kernels, copra, cotton, kapok and peanuts. There are textile and shoe factories. Togo has led efforts toward West African economic unity.

Ewe and Cabrai are official languages.

Tonga

Area: 269 sq. mi. Population (UN est. 1974): 100,-000. Capital: Nukualofa. Monetary unit: Pa'anga.

The Kingdom of Tonga, a constitutional monarchy, comprises 150 volcanic and coral islands (45 inhabited) in the South Pacific, NE of New Zealand and S of Samoa. The capital, Nukualofa, is on the main island, Tongatapu.

The islands were first visited by the Dutch in the early 17th Century. A series of civil wars ended in 1845 with establishment of the Tupou dynasty. In 1900 Tonga became a British protectorate. On June 4, 1970, Tonga became completely independent and a member of the Commonwealth.

Government consists of a king, a prime minister and a partly elected Legislative Assembly.

Agriculture and fishing are the mainstays of the economy. Chief exports are coconut products and bananas. Tourism is being encouraged.

The Tongans are Polynesians; languages are Tongan and English. Education is free and compulsory, ages 6-14; medical care is free.

Trinidad and Tobago

Area: 1,979 sq. mi. Population (UN est. 1973): 1,060,000. Capital: Port of Spain. Monetary unit: Trinidad and Tobago Dollar.

Trinidad, area 1,864 sq. mi., is the most southerly of the West Indies, lying off the NE coast of South America approx. 7 mi. from Venezuela. It was discovered by Columbus in 1498. Tobago, 116 sq. mi. lies 20 mi. to the NE of Trinidad.

Second largest of the old British West Indies and a British possession since 1802, Trinidad and Tobago won independence Aug. 31, 1962. A governor-general represents the British crown. A prime minister is the actual executive. Parliament consists of a 24-member Senate, appointed by the prime minister and the opposition, and a 36-member House of Representatives, elected by universal suffrage. The country is a member of the UN, Commonwealth and OAS.

Import trade is heaviest with England, export trade with the U. S. Exports are mostly petroleum, sugar, asphalt, rum, cocoa, coffee, citrus, bananas, cement, bitters. Oil production has increased with offshore finds.

The nation is one of the most prosperous in the West Indies, but unemployment averages 13%.

Trinidad claims to have originated the steel band, calypso songs and the limbo dance. Tourism is an important source of revenue.

The population is mixed: Black 43%, East Indian

(descended from immigrants from India) 36%; Lebanese, Syrians, Europeans and Chinese comprise the rest. Religions include Roman Catholic 36%, Protestant 34%, Hindu 23%, Moslem 6%.

Public primary and secondary education is free to age 18. Some units of the Univ. of West Indies are in Trinidad, some in Jamaica. There are 2 technical institutes.

Tunisia

Area: 63,378 sq. mi. Population (Govt. est. 1974): 5,564,000. Capital: Tunis. Monetary unit: Dinar.

Tunisia is a former French protectorate which became independent Mar. 20, 1956. It is on the Mediterranean coast of Africa wedged between Algeria and Libya. It is about the size of Florida. The people are mostly Arabs and Berbers.

Resources and Industries. The chief pursuit is agriculture; an abundance of grains, dates, olives, citrus fruits, almonds, figs, vegetables, alfa grass is produced. Livestock is extensively raised. Phosphates, iron, oil, lead and zinc are leading minerals.

Industries include food processing, textiles, clothing, leather, oil refining, construction materials. Principal exports are olive oil, wine, iron ore, lead, phosphate, fruits, oil and grains. A farm collectivization program was dropped in 1970. Private local and foreign investment is encouraged, and the economy has prospered.

Tourism is growing and attractions include numerous well-preserved Roman ruins, excellent beaches, and resorts on Djerba Is., reputed home of the Lotus Eaters of the Odyssey.

The tourist industry earns over $100 million a year. New industries include steel and auto-assembly plants, a paper mill and sugar refinery.

History and Government. Site of ancient Carthage, and a former Barbary state under the suzerainty of Turkey, Tunisia became a protectorate of France under a treaty signed May 12, 1881. After receiving increasing measures of self-government since 1947, a constituent assembly, elected Mar. 25, 1956, chose a government headed by Habib Bourguiba, named premier Apr. 10. The basic law, adopted by the assembly, Apr. 13, vested sovereignty in the people, ignoring the titular ruler, Mohammed el Amim, bey of Tunis. The assembly unanimously voted, July 25, 1957, to end the monarchy. It proclaimed a republic; Bourguiba became president; he was re-elected three times. Bourguiba was named president for life of the single legal party in 1974; a new constitutional provision assured the party chief of the national presidency.

Although Tunisia is a member of the Arab League, Bourguiba in the 1960s urged negotiations to end Arab-Israeli disputes and was denounced by other members. In 1966 he broke relations with Egypt but resumed them after the 1967 Israeli-Arab war. He again urged negotiations with Israel in June 1973.

Tunisia and Libya announced in Jan. 1974 that the 2 nations would merge, but Bourguiba soon dropped the plan.

Education and Religion. The majority of the population is Moslem. Europeans number fewer than 100,-000. Arabic is the national and official language. From 1956-1970 Tunisia raised the number of primary school students from 200,000 to 964,000, secondary from 15,500 to 184,000, and higher education from 1,350 to 14,000.

Defense. The armed forces total over 24,000.

Turkey

Area: 301,380 sq. mi. Population (Govt. est. 1974): 36,270,000. Capital: Ankara. Monetary unit: Lira.

About 90% of Turkey's population lives in the Asian portion of the country on the Anotolian Peninsula — an area of 292,184 sq. mi. The remainder live in the

European part which is bordered by Bulgaria and Greece. A republic since 1923, Turkey is a little larger than Texas and has extensive coastlines on the Black Sea, the Mediterranean and the Aegean. Its Asian neighbors are the USSR, Iran, Iraq and Syria.

Central Turkey has wide plateaus, with hot dry summers and cold winters with snow remaining until May. High mountains ring the interior on all but the W side. More than 20 peaks top 10,000 ft.

The world's 4th longest suspension bridge, linking Europe and Asia across the Bosporus, opened in 1973.

Resources and Industries. About 60% of the labor force is engaged in agriculture, the products including tobacco (it is the world's 6th largest producer), cereals, cotton, olive oil, wool, mohair, silk, figs, nuts, fruits, sugar, opium, and gums. About 45 million acres are in forests.

In June 1971 Turkey agreed to stop all opium poppy production, in return for $37.5 million in economic aid from the U.S. In 1974 it announced it would resume opium production, for medical use only.

There are large deposits of antimony, borate, copper and chrome (of which Turkey is one of the world's largest producers). Other minerals include manganese, lead, zinc, coal, iron, oil, silver, mercury, sulphur, molybdenum, magnesite and asbestos.

Turkey manufactures silk, cotton and woolen yarn and cloth, steel, foundry products, sugar, footwear, office furniture, cement, paper, glassware and appliances. About 12% of trade is with the U.S.

Foreign trade, in thousands of U.S. dollars:

	Imports	Exports
1973	$2,049,000	$1,317,000
1974	$3,720,000	$1,532,000

History and Government. Just before World War I, Turkey, or the Ottoman Empire, ruled Syria, Lebanon, Iraq, Jordan, Palestine, Arabia, Yemen and islands in the Aegean Sea.

Turkey joined Germany and Austria in World War I and its defeat resulted in loss of much territory and fall of the sultanate. A republic was declared Oct. 29, 1923, with Mustafa Kemal Ataturk first president. The Caliphate (spiritual leadership of Islam) was renounced 1924. Turkey was permitted (1936) to refortify the Dardanelles and Bosporus, to close them if threatened, but to permit free passage of merchant vessels in peace or war. The USSR proposed joint control of the straits but Turkey refused.

In 1968 Turkey and the USSR agreed on a $200 million loan from the Soviet Union to build factories in Turkey which would be paid for in Turkish products.

The present constitution, adopted July 9, 1961, provides for a bicameral legislature composed of a Senate of 150 and a National Assembly of 450 deputies. The president is elected by Parliament to a 7-year term and is ineligible for reelection. A premier is chosen from a leading party.

Turkey is a member of the UN, CENTO, NATO, Council of Europe and an associate in EC. Communism is outlawed, and many leftist terrorists have been jailed. Martial law, imposed in 1971, was ended in 1973.

Long embroiled with Greece over Cyprus, off Turkey's south coast, Turkey invaded the island July 20, 1974, after Greek officers seized the Cypriot government as a step toward unification with Greece. Turkey sought a new government for Cyprus, with Greek Cypriot and Turkish Cypriot zones. In reaction to Turkey's moves, the U.S. Congress cut off military aid in 1975. Turkey, in turn, suspended the use of most U.S. bases.

Education and Religion. About 98% of the population is Moslem. Public elementary education is free and compulsory; higher public education is free.

Defense. Armed forces total 453,000. Most of the forces were assigned to NATO.

Uganda

Area: 91,134 sq. mi. Population (Govt. est. 1974):
11,170,000. Capital: Kampala. Monetary unit: Uganda shilling.

The Republic of Uganda, a former British protectorate, is in east-central Africa with Kenya to the E, Lake Victoria and Tanzania to the S, Lakes Albert and Edward (also called Lakes Sese Seko and Idi Amin) and Zaire to the W, Sudan to the N. It is about the size of Oregon. On the border with Zaire, the Rewenzori Range rises 16,000 ft. In the SW there are several volcanoes over 11,000 ft. high.

Uganda is the world's 6th largest coffee producer. Cotton, tea, maize, peanuts, sisal, oil seeds, tobacco, sugar, are also produced. Copper and tin are important mineral exports. Textile, steel and chemical plants have been built. The expulsion of Asians and Europeans threw the economy into chaos in the 1970's.

Uganda became independent Oct. 9, 1962; a republic Oct. 9, 1963. It is a member of the UN, OAU and Commonwealth.

A long-standing political feud erupted Feb. 22, 1966, when Milton Obote, then prime minister, seized full power and on Mar. 2 ousted President Edward Mutesa (who earlier had been king).

Gen. Idi Amin seized control Jan. 25, 1971, and was named president.

In 1972 Amin expelled all Asians holding British passports (Indians and Pakistanis). There were reportedly over 25,000, many of them business and professional men. Britain, the U.S. and some other nations accepted the deportees. In 1973 the U.S., Canada and Norway ended economic aid programs; Amin seized all British firms.

Nearly half the population is Christian (mostly Roman Catholics). English, Luganda, and Luo are the main languages. Idi Amin and others are Moslems.

At Owen Falls on the Victoria Nile, outlet of Lake Victoria, a major dam and hydroelectric project has been constructed.

Union of Soviet Socialist Republics

Area: 8,647,250 sq. mi. Population (Govt. est. 1974): 250,900,000. Capital: Moscow. Monetary unit: Ruble.

The Union of Soviet Socialist Republics—in area the largest country in the world—stretches across 2 continents from the North Pacific to the Baltic Sea. It occupies the northern part of Asia and the eastern half of Europe. Its western borders brush against Norway, Finland, the Baltic, Poland, Czechoslovakia, Hungary and Romania. To the S are the Black Sea, Turkey, Iran, Afghanistan, China, Mongolian Peoples Republic and North Korea. In the far NE, Bering Strait separates it from Alaska.

The vast territory of the USSR, one-sixth of the earth's land surface, contains every phase of climate, except the distinctly tropical, and a varied topography. The European portion is a vast low plain with the Ural Mtns. on its eastern edge, the Caucasus Mtns. and others on the S. The Urals, separating the European from the Asiatic portions of the country, stretch N-S for 2,500 mi. The Asiatic portion also consists largely of an immense plain, with mountain ranges on the S and in the E.

There are some 150,000 rivers and 250,000 lakes. The larger European rivers include the Dnieper, flowing into the Black Sea, the Volga and the Ural into the Caspian Sea, the Don into the Sea of Azov, the Western Dvina into the Baltic and the Northern Dvina into the White Sea. The Asiatic section is drained by the Ob, the Yenisei and the Lena, each over 2,000 mi. long, flowing into the Arctic Ocean, and the Amur, flowing into the Pacific.

*The Caspian Sea, with its S end in Iran, is the world's largest lake in surface area (143,550 sq. mi.). Other lakes are the Aral Sea (25,300 sq. mi.), Lake Baykal (11,780 sq. mi.), Lake Balkhash (6,720 sq. mi.), Lake Ladoga (6,835 sq. mi.).

In Moscow, the Kremlin, ancient citadel of the Czars, forms the nerve center of the federated republics. Leningrad (formerly St. Petersburg and Petrograd), in the delta of the Neva River, is the 2d largest city. Kiev, the 1,000-year-old capital of the Ukrainian SSR, is the industrial center of the south. The Crimea and the eastern shore of the Black Sea, beneath the towering Caucasus Mtns., are resort areas.

Beginning in 1939 the USSR by means of military action and negotiation overran contiguous territory and independent republics, including all or part of Lithuania, Latvia, Estonia, Poland, Czechoslovakia, Romania, Germany, Tannu Tuva, and Japan.

Political Organization

The USSR is a federation consisting of 15 union republics, within certain of which are further subdivisions. Four of the union republics contain 20 autonomous soviet socialist republics and 8 autonomous regions; the largest union republic, the Russian Soviet Federal Socialist Republic, has also 10 national districts. Nationalist agitation has occasionally been reported in several of the republics. The Union Republics are:

Republic	Area, sq. miles	Pop. (Census 1970)
Russian SFSR	6,593,391	130,090,000
Ukrainian SSR	232,046	47,136,000
Kazakh SSR	1,064,092	12,850,000
Uzbek SSR	158,069	11,963,000
Byelorussian SSR	80,154	9,003,000
Azerbaijan SSR	33,436	5,111,000
Georgian SSR	26,911	4,688,000
Moldavian SSR	13,012	3,572,000
Lithuanian SSR	26,173	3,129,000
Kirghiz SSR	76,642	2,933,000
Tadzhik SSR	54,019	2,900,000
Armenian SSR	11,306	2,493,000
Latvian SSR	24,695	2,365,000
Turkmen SSR	188,417	2,158,000
Estonian SSR	17,413	1,357,000

The Russian Soviet Federal Socialist Republic, contains over 50% of the population of the Soviet Union and includes 76% of its territory. Its territories stretch from the old Estonian, Latvian and Finnish borders and the Byelorussian and Ukrainian lines on the W, to the shores of the Pacific, and from the Arctic on the N to the Black and Caspian Seas and the borders of Kazakh SSR, Mongolia and Manchuria on the S. Siberia, divided into a number of administrative units, encompasses a large part of the RSFSR area. Capital: Moscow.

Parts of Eastern and Western Siberia have been transformed by steel mills, huge dams, oil and gas industries, electric railroads and highways.

Ukrainian SSR is the most densely populated of the constituent republics. It borders on the Black Sea, with Poland, Czechoslovakia, Hungary and Romania on the W and SW. The population is 80% Ukrainian. Capital: Kiev.

The Ukraine contains the arable black soil belt, the chief wheat-producing section of the Soviet Union. Sugar beets, potatoes and livestock are important.

The Donets Basin has large deposits of coal, iron and other metals. There are chemical and machine industries and salt mines.

Byelorussian SSR (White Russia), bordering on Poland, suffered greatly under the Czars from periodical pogroms and from inter-ethnic struggles. In the World Wars it was a field for military operations. Capital: Minsk. Chief industries include machinery, tools, appliances, tractors, clocks, cameras, steel, cement, textiles, paper, leather, glass. Main crops are grain, flax, potatoes.

Azerbaijan SSR boasts near Baku, the capital, important oil fields. Its natural wealth includes deposits of iron ore, cobalt, etc. Irrigation has boosted cotton production. A high-yield winter wheat also is grown, as are fruits. It produces iron, steel, cement,

fertilizers, synthetic rubber, electrical and chemical equipment. It borders on Iran and Turkey.

Georgian SSR, which lies in the western part of Transcaucasia, contains the largest manganese mines in the world. There are rich timber resources and coal mines. Basic industries are food, textiles, iron, steel. Grain, tea, tobacco, fruits, grapes are grown. Capital: Tbilisi (Tiflis).

Armenian SSR is mountainous, sub-tropical, extensively irrigated. Copper, zinc, aluminum, molybdenum, and marble are mined. Instrument making is important. Capital: Erevan.

Uzbek SSR, most important economically of the Central Asia republics, produces 68% of USSR cotton, 33% of silk, 34% of astrakhan, 85% of hemp. Industries include iron, steel, cars, tractors, TV and radio sets, textiles, food. Mineral wealth includes coal, sulphur, copper and oil. Capital: Tashkent.

Turkmen SSR in Central Asia, produces cotton, maize, carpets, chemicals. Minerals: oil, coal, sulphur, barite, lime, salt, gypsum. The Kara Kum desert occupies four-fifths of the area. Capital: Ashkhabad.

Tadzhik SSR (Tadzhikistan), formed from the former regions of Bokhara and Turkestan, was admitted as a constituent republic Dec. 5, 1929. Over half the population are Tadzhiks, mostly Moslems, speaking an Iranian dialect. Chief occupations are farming and cattle breeding. Cotton, grain, rice and a variety of fruits are grown. Heavy industry, based on rich mineral deposits, coal and hydroelectric power, has replaced handicrafts. Capital: Dushanbe.

Kazakh SSR extends from the lower reaches of the Volga in Europe to the Altai Mtns. on the Chinese border. It has vast deposits of coal, oil, iron, tin, copper, etc. Fish for its canning industry are caught in Lake Balkhash and the Caspian and Aral Seas. Manufacturing, grains and cattle are important. The capital is Alma-Ata.

Kirghiz SSR is in the eastern part of Soviet Central Asia, on the frontier of Sinkiang (western China). The people, once nomadic, breed cattle and horses and grow tobacco, cotton, rice, sugar beets. New industries include machine and instrument making, chemicals. Capital: Frunze.

Moldavian SSR in the SW part of the USSR, is a fertile black earth plain bordering Romania, and includes Bessarabia. It is an agricultural region that grows grains, fruits, vegetables and tobacco. Textiles, wine, food and electrical equipment industries have been developed. Capital: Kishinev.

Lithuanian SSR, on the Baltic, produces cattle, hogs, electric motors and appliances. The capital is Vilnius (Vilna). The Latvian SSR on the Baltic and the Gulf of Riga, has timber and peat resources estimated at 3 billion tons. In addition to agricultural products it produces rubber goods, dyes, fertilizers, glassware, telephone apparatus, TV and radio sets, railroad cars. The capital is Riga. The Estonian SSR also on the Baltic, has textiles, shipbuilding, timber, roadmaking and mining equipment industries and a shale oil refining industry. Tallinn is the capital. The 3 Baltic states were provinces of imperial Russia before World War I, were independent nations between World Wars I and II, and became SSRs, within the USSR, in 1940. They were occupied by Germany 1941-44. The U.S. has never formally recognized the incorporation of Lithuania, Latvia and Estonia into the USSR.

Economics and Production

The economic foundation of the USSR is the socialist ownership of the instruments and means of production. Socialist property exists in 2 forms: (1) State property; (2) Cooperative and collective farm property. State property includes the land, minerals, waters, forests, mills, factories, mines, rail, water and air transport, banks, communications, large agricultural enterprises and the bulk of dwellings.

The common enterprises of collective farms and cooperative organizations, their output and common buildings constitute their socialized property. Members may use small plots of land attached to their dwellings.

"Backyard" farms, from which farmers may sell produce and keep the profit, swelled in size and number in the 1960s.

Cultivated land in 1972 was about 518.7 million acres. There were 32,100 collective farms and 15,744 state farms. In 1974 there were 109 million cattle (topped by India and the U. S.), 72 million hogs (2d to China) and 145 million sheep (2d to Australia). The fish catch is 2d only to Japan's.

In poor crop years, the USSR has been forced to make huge purchases of grain from Canada and other countries. About $1.1 billion worth was ordered from the U. S. in 1972, with additional amounts for 1973 and 1974. Further huge orders were made in 1975 from the U. S. and Canada, to compensate for drought shortfalls.

The USSR is incalculably rich in natural resources. It claims to possess 57% of the world's coal deposits, about half of its oil, 41% of iron ore, 88% of manganese, 54% of potassium salts, 30% of phosphates, and 25% of all timber land.

In 1973, the USSR produced 26% of world iron ore output, 19.5% of steel, 22% of coal, 16% of gold. Oil production and steel production in 1974 led the world. The index of industrial production (1970 = 100) was 134 for 1974.

In 1966 many major factories were put on an incentive profit-sharing system, while bonuses to farms and farm workers (called "Socialist competition") were introduced to spur food production. In 1973 steps were taken to group factories into "production associations" partly resembling large U.S. corporations.

In 1971 a proposed new 5-year plan set goals of a 37-40% rise in national income. Premier Kosygin stressed growth in consumer goods, but subsequent adjustments restored priority to heavy industry, and reduced overall goals.

Foreign Trade

Exports include petroleum and its products, iron and steel, rolled non-ferrous metals, industrial plant equipment, arms, lumber, cotton, asbestos, gold, manganese and others. Most of its trade is with Socialist nations, but trade with the West is increasing, aided by some long-term credits.

Foreign trade, in thousands of U.S. dollars:

	Imports	Exports
1973	$21,108,000	$21,463,000
1974	$24,877,000	$27,381,000

Early History

The first Russian state centered on Kiev in the 9th Century. In the 13th Century the Mongols overran the country. It recovered under the grand dukes and princes of Muscovy, or Moscow, and by 1480 freed itself from the Mongols. Ivan the Terrible was the first to be formally proclaimed Czar (1547). Peter the Great (1682-1725), extended the domain and in 1721 founded the Russian Empire.

Revolution of 1917

The abortive Revolution of 1905 demonstrated the insecurity of the czarist regime and led to mild concessions. The 1917 Revolution began in March with a series of sporadic strikes for higher wages by factory workers. A provisional democratic government under Prince Georgi Lvov was established but was quickly followed in May by the second provisional government, led by Alexander Kerensky. The Kerensky government and the freely-elected Constituent Assembly were overthrown in a communist coup led by Vladimir Ilyich Lenin Nov. 7.

Lenin's death Jan. 21, 1924, resulted in an internal power struggle from which Joseph Stalin eventually emerged the absolute ruler of Russia. Stalin secured his position at first by exiling opponents such as Leon Trotsky. But from the 1930s to 1953 he resorted to a series of "purge" trials, mass executions and mass exiles in work camps. In 1974 it was estimated there still were 10,000 political prisoners, mostly in labor camps.

Khrushchev, Brezhnev

After Stalin died, Mar. 5, 1953, Nikita Khrushchev was elected first secretary of the Central Committee. In 1956 he condemned Stalin and his tyrannical methods before the Soviet Communist Party Congress in Moscow, said Stalin cultivated a "cult of personality" and subverted communist aims. Khrushchev lifted some restrictions, extended barter and trade policies. The names of Stalin, Molotov, Malenkov and other supporters of Stalin were eliminated from regions, cities and other sites in 1961-62 after Stalin's body was removed from the Lenin-Stalin tomb in Moscow.

Khrushchev was elected premier by the Supreme Soviet, Mar. 27, 1958, succeeding Marshal Bulganin.

Under Khrushchev the open antagonism of Poles and Hungarians toward domination by Moscow was brutally suppressed in 1956. He advocated peaceful co-existence with the capitalist countries, but continued arming the USSR with nuclear weapons, promised aid to all "suppressed peoples" and to so-called wars of liberation. He aided the Cuban revolution under Fidel Castro but withdrew Soviet missiles from Cuba during confrontation by U.S. President Kennedy, Sept.-Oct. 1962.

The USSR, the U. S. and Great Britain initialed a joint treaty July 25, 1963, banning above-ground nuclear tests.

The co-existence policy alienated the leaders of Albania and Communist China. The latter continued to preach world revolution and denounced the Khrushchev methods as deviating from true Communism.

Khrushchev was suddenly deposed, Oct. 14-15, 1964, and replaced as party first secretary by Leonid I. Brezhnev, 57, and as premier by Aleksei N. Kosygin, 60. Brezhnev's title was changed in 1966 to general secretary. Internal controls were tightened.

Communist China's Premier Chou En-lai visited the new USSR chiefs in Nov. 1964 but the visit failed to heal the growing rift between the 2 communist powers.

In 1968, the U. S. and USSR joined 59 other nations in signing a treaty to bar spread of nuclear weapons.

In Aug. 1968 Russian, Polish, East German, Hungarian and Bulgarian military forces invaded Czechoslovakia to put a curb on liberalization policies of the Czech government. The USSR declared it had a duty to intervene in nations where socialism was "imperiled," the "Brezhnev Doctrine."

In March 1969 troops of the USSR and Communist China fought the first of a series of clashes on a disputed island in the Ussuri River on the border between the 2 nations in the Far East, north of Vladivostok. In 1970 ambassadors were exchanged, after a lapse; but both nations increased their border forces. In the 1970s the USSR forged close ties with India and Bangladesh.

The USSR in 1971 continued heavy arms shipments to Egypt. In July 1972 Egypt ordered most of the 20,000 Soviet military personnel in that country to leave. The USSR then increased arms shipments to Syria. A large Soviet fleet was maintained in the Mediterranean, about 55 ships in 1973, plus fleets in other seas.

When Egypt and Syria attacked Israel in Oct. 1973, the USSR launched huge arms airlifts to the 2 Arab nations. In 1974, the Soviet replenished the arms used or lost by the Syrians in the 1973 war, and continued some shipments to Egypt.

'Detente'

During the May 1972 visit of U.S. President Nixon, the U. S. and USSR reached temporary agreements to freeze intercontinental missiles at their current levels, to limit defensive missiles to 200 each, to cooperate on health and environment problems, to stage a joint space flight and to set up commissions for trade and scientific cooperation.

In the June 1973 visit of Brezhnev to the U.S., agreements were signed to seek ways to promote trade, peace and cultural and scientific exchanges. Meanwhile, under Brezhnev, dissident intellectuals were repressed and purge-type trials resumed. Andrei Sakharov, creator of the USSR hydrogen bomb, and other Soviet dissidents, warned Western nations that aid given Russia would be used against them.

On Aug. 1, 1975, 35 countries of Europe and North America signed a European security declaration tacitly approving current boundaries and urging freer movement of people and ideas.

Government

The first Soviet constitution was adopted in 1918 for the RSFSR. The USSR was formed in Dec. 1922 and the first Union constitution adopted 1923. The current constitution was adopted 1936. Voting age is 18; candidates for election must have reached 23. Each Union republic is organized similarly to the central government.

The mainly nominal legislative authority is the Supreme Soviet consisting of 2 chambers, the Soviet of the Union and the Soviet of Nationalities. The first house is elected on the basis of population, the second has deputies from each major national homeland. The Supreme Soviet normally meets briefly twice a year, serves for a 4-year term. It elects a 37-member Presidium which serves between sessions.

Titular chief of state, chairman of the Presidium of the Supreme Soviet, Nikolai V. Podgorny, was chosen Dec. 9, 1965.

Elections for the Supreme Soviet are by universal suffrage but from single slates of candidates approved by the party; voters are offered a choice only to strike out names.

The highest judicial organ is the Supreme Court, whose members are elected by the Supreme Soviet for 5-year terms. Other courts are elected within the constituent republics.

The highest executive and administrative organ of state power is the Council of Ministers (premier and deputies) appointed by and theoretically responsible to the Supreme Soviet.

The Communist party of the USSR is the only legal party. Its highest organ is the Party Congress of about 1,500 representatives meeting once every 4 years. It elects a Central Committee, the party's directive body, and other committees. The Central Committee elects from its number a Politburo which makes party policy between Central Committee meetings; and a Secretariat, the party's chief executive body. The Politburo normally consists of 15 full members and 6 candidate members.

Membership in the Communist party in 1973 was reported at about 14,800,000.

Education

Education is free. It is compulsory from ages 7 to 15/16. In 1972 there were 49.3 million students in primary, secondary, and technical schools, and 4.6 million in universities, institutes, and other places of higher education, half of them in correspondence or evening courses. There were 7.2 million children 3-7 years old in kindergartens.

Social Benefits

All workers are entitled to free public health services, paid vacations, sickness insurance, pensions for men at 60 and women at 55. There are lower pension requirements for those in hazardous or difficult occupations. State payments are made to mothers on the birth of the 3d and successive children. In 1968 there were 35 million receiving pensions.

Religion

Separation of church and state was effected in 1918. Nine branches of Christianity are represented,

led by the Orthodox Church, which in 1956 had 22,-000 congregations. Islam has the second largest following. Jewish and Buddhist faiths are also present.

Since 1970 many Jews have sought to leave the USSR. About 100,000 left in 1970-74. Emigration was sharply curtailed in 1975, after the U. S. Congress limited export credits and linked tariff cuts to further emigration.

Defense

Armed forces on active duty are est. to total 3,525,-000. The Army had about 1.8 million men, organized in 167 divisions. There were 31 divisions stationed in satellite nations (20 of them in East Germany); 63 divisions in European Russia; 23 in the Caucasus, 5 in central Asia; 45 in the Far East. The Army was equipped with tactical missiles, including nuclear warheads. Several thousand military aid personnel were stationed in Syria, Iraq, Egypt, Somalia, and other countries.

Navy personnel totaled 475,000. The main power of the Soviet fleet was its 245 submarines, some 70 of which were nuclear-powered. Some were equipped with ballistic nuclear missiles. The Russian fleet in 1974 had over 1,000 ships.

Air Force personnel totaled 400,000; there was a total of about 8,000 combat aircraft including intercontinental bombers. Air Defense service has 500,-000 men, border and security troops number 310,000.

In 1974 the USSR reportedly had 1,587 intercontinental nuclear missiles in place, the U. S. 1,054. The USSR reportedly had 720 submarine-borne missiles, the U. S. 656. The USSR was advancing development of multiple warhead (MIRV) missiles, and of more accurate and more powerful missiles.

The USSR is a member of the UN and Warsaw Pact.

United Arab Emirates

Area: 32,278 sq. mi. Population (UN est. 1974): 220,-000. Capital: Abu Dhabi. Monetary unit: Dirham.

The United Arab Emirates, formerly known as the Trucial States or Trucial Sheikdoms, were British Protected States until they became an independent nation Dec. 2, 1971. The UAE stretches 400 mi. along the Persian (also called Arabian) Gulf and the Gulf of Oman. It borders on Saudi Arabia, Quatar and Oman.

The 7 sheikdoms signed treaties with Britain in the 19th century giving Britain control of defense and foreign relations. When Britain announced it would let the treaties lapse by the end of 1971, the 7 sought to form a federation with Bahrain and Qatar. The attempt failed. The UAE was formed by 6 of the 7, Abu Dhabi, Dubai, Sharja, Ajman, Fujaira and Umm al Quaiwan. The 7th, Ras al Khaima, joined shortly after. The city of Abu Dhabi became the capital and the Abu Dhabi ruler became president. There is a prime minister, a Supreme Council of Rulers and a National Council or legislature.

Abu Dhabi, Dubai and Sharja have large and increasing oil production, totaling the 10th largest in the world. Fujaira and Ras al Khaima have substantial food production. In Sept. 1974 Abu Dhabi acquired a 60% interest in the Abu Dhabi Petroleum Co.; full nationalization came in 1975.

A 1968 census gave Dubai 59,000 inhabitants; Abu Dhabi, 49,000; Sharja, 31,500; Ras al Khaima, 24,500; Fujaira, 9,700; Ajman, 4,200; Umm al Quaiwan, 3,700. They are predominantly Arab, plus some Iranians, Indians and Baluchis.

United Kingdom

Area: 94,209 sq. mi. Population (UN est. 1973): 55,930,000. Capital: London. Monetary Unit: Pound.

The United Kingdom of Great Britain and Northern Ireland comprises England, Wales, Scotland and Northern Ireland.

The British Isles lie off the W. coast of Europe, with the North Atlantic on the N and W. Separating Britain from the mainland are the North Sea on the E, the Strait of Dover on the SE and the English Channel on the S. The Thames, 210 mi. from its source to the North Sea, is England's longest river.

England has an area of 50,331 sq. mi. and Wales has 8,016 sq. mi.; combined population (est. 1972), 49,029,000; Scotland, 30,411 sq. mi., 5,210,000; Northern Ireland, 5,451 sq. mi., 1,549,000.

The climate of the British Isles is mild and somewhat warmer than that of the continent because of the Gulf Stream modifying the temperature, which has a mean of 48°. Rainfall averages 41 inches a year.

Queen and Royal Family. The ruling sovereign is Elizabeth II of the House of Windsor, born Apr. 21, 1926, eldest daughter of King George VI. She succeeded to the throne Feb. 6, 1952, and was crowned June 2, 1953. As Princess Elizabeth, she was married Nov. 20, 1947 to Lt. Philip Mountbatten, born June 10, 1921, former Prince of Greece. He was created Duke of Edinburgh Nov. 19, 1947, H.R.H. Prince Philip Nov. 20, 1947, and given the title Prince of the United Kingdom Feb. 22, 1957. They have 4 children. Prince Charles Philip Arthur George, born Nov. 14, 1948, is the prince of Wales and heir apparent.

Parliament is the legislative governing body for the United Kingdom, with certain powers over dependent units. It consists of 2 Houses. The **House of Lords** includes hereditary and life peers and peeresses, legal advisers, archbishops and bishops. Total membership is over 1,000 but actual attendance is approximately 200. Women became eligible to sit in the House of Lords for the first time in 1958. The **House of Commons** has 635 members, who are elected by direct ballot and divided as follows: England 516; Wales and Monmouth 36; Scotland 71; Northern Ireland 12.

Clergymen of the Church of England, ministers of the Church in Scotland and Roman Catholic clergymen are disqualified from sitting as members, as are certain government officers and sheriffs. Women have had the right to vote since 1918.

A two-tier system of local government controls a large variety of social and economic activity. Reforms occurred in 1974-75

Resources and Industries. Great Britain's major occupations are manufacturing and trade. Metals and metal-using industries contribute more than 50% of the exports. Agriculture provides wheat, barley, oats, sugar beets, rye, livestock products and garden truck. Of about 60 million acres of land in England, Wales and Scotland, 49 million are farmed, of which 18 million are arable, the rest pastures.

Large oil and gas fields have been found in the North Sea, and oil self-sufficiency is expected by 1980, with projected output of two million barrels a day. There are large deposits of coal; annual output averages 125 million tons. Limestone, igneous rock and iron ore are valuable products. Other important minerals are salt, clay, chalk, gypsum, lead ore, tin ore and silica.

There are 150 civil and 50 service airports in Great Britain. The railroads, nationalized since 1948, have been reduced in total length, with a basic network of 11,326 mi. designated for modernization and development.

There are about 17.6 million telephones. Broadcast receiving licenses in 1974 totaled 11,042,000 for black-and-white TV, 6,418,000 for color.

The government in 1967 took ownership of 14 steel companies which comprised 90% of the nation's steelmaking industry, paying shareholders over $1.4 billion. Further industry takeovers and intervention were foreseen in 1974 government proposals.

The Labor government raised taxes, 1966-69; devalued the pound to $2.40 in 1967 and took various measures to improve exports and cut imports. The

Conservative government put a freeze on prices, wages and rents in 1972 to combat inflation. In 1973 it substituted "restraints." A Labor government, elected in 1974, failed to control inflation, and the pound dropped further in value.

Britons backed continued EC membership by a 67% vote in a referendum June 5, 1975.

On Feb. 15, 1971, Britain completed a changeover to decimal currency. By 1975 it had converted to the metric system as well.

Tourism ranks high in earnings. Visitors from abroad totaled more than 6 million in 1974, of whom 1.3 million were from the U. S. Index of industrial production (1970 = 100) was 106.6 in 1974. The merchant marine totaled 32,153,000 gross registered tons in Jan. 1975, comprising over 10% of active world shipping. British shipyards have an estimated annual capacity of 1,259,000 tons.

The world's first power station using atomic energy to create electricity for civilian use began operation Oct. 17, 1956, at Calder Hall in Cumberland.

Britain's aid to less developed countries has more than doubled since 1956, totaling over $3 billion and amounting to several hundred million dollars a year.

The United Kingdom is a member of the UN, Commonwealth, NATO, SEATO, CENTO, Council of Europe and, since Jan. 1, 1973, EC.

Britain imports all of its cotton, rubber, sulphur, four-fifths of its wool, half of its food and iron ore, also certain amounts of paper, tobacco, chemicals. Manufactured goods made from these basic materials have been exported since the industrial age began.

Main exports are machinery, chemicals, woolen and synthetic textiles, autos and trucks, iron and steel, locomotives, jet aircraft, farm machinery, drugs, radio, TV, radar and navigation equipment, arms, whisky.

Foreign trade in thousands of U.S. dollars:

	Imports	Exports
1973	$38,846,000	$30,535,000
1974	$54,142,000	$38,639,000

Religion and Churches. The Church of England is Protestant Episcopal. The queen is supreme governor, with rights of appointment to archbishoprics, bishoprics and other offices. There are 2 provinces, Canterbury and York, each headed by an archbishop. The Church of England has an est. 27,600,000 members. In 1970 there were 14,260 parishes. Most famous church is Westminster Abbey (1050-1760), site of coronations; tombs of Elizabeth I, Mary of Scots, kings, poets and of the Unknown Warrior.

Roman Catholic Church membership in the United Kingdom was about 5,500,000 in 1974. There were about 14,000 Methodist churches and 601,000 full members in 1974.

Others: There are an est. 410,000 Jews in Great Britain; 80% of them are Orthodox and more than half live in the London area. There are 191,000 Baptists and 192,410 members of the United Reformed Church (Congregational and Presbyterian). The Calvinistic Methodist (Presbyterian) Church of Wales has 102,000 communicants. The Unitarians have 330 chapels. The Society of Friends has 21,000 members. There are 72,000 Mormons. The Church of Christ Scientist has 302 branches in Great Britain and Ireland. The Presbyterian Church in Ireland has a membership in Northern Ireland of about 140,000. The number of Hindus and Moslems has been growing steadily with immigration.

The Church of Scotland is Presbyterian. It is presided over by a moderator chosen annually. Members numbered 1,100,000 in 1974.

Education. Education is free and compulsory from 5 to 16. The most celebrated British universities are Oxford and Cambridge, each dating to the 13th century. There are 40 other universities.

Social Welfare. National Insurance provides for virtually universal compulsory insurance covering sickness, maternity, unemployment and industrial accidents, and death benefits and pensions for widows, orphans and the aged. The National Health Service provides free medical and nursing care, small dental fees and minimum charges for certain appliances and prescriptions. Under the Family Allowance Act the government pays 90 pence a week for each child of compulsory school age, after the first, and one pound each for the third or more. Supplementary benefits provide for those not fully protected by National Insurance. Contributions vary according to sex and classification (employed, self-employed, non-employed). In the case of employed, the employer pays slightly over half.

Defense: Armed forces total 342,500 (1975). Britain exploded its 1st atomic bomb in 1952 and has a stockpile of these weapons. A 10-year program to cut forces 10% and almost eliminate Britain's non-European presence was announced in 1974.

Wales

The Principality of Wales and Monmouthshire in western Britain has an area of 7,969 sq. mi. and a population (est. 1971) of 2,723,596.

England and Wales are administered as a unit. More than one-fourth the population speak both English and Welsh; under 50,000 speak Welsh solely. Welsh nationalism is advocated by a segment. The UK government favors creation of an elected Wales Assembly.

Early Anglo-Saxon invaders drove Celtic peoples into the mountains of Wales, terming them Waelise (Welsh, or foreign). There they developed a distinct nationality. Members of the ruling house of Gwynedd in the 13th century fought England but were crushed, 1283. Edward of Caernarvon, son of Edward I of England, was created Prince of Wales, 1301.

Scotland

Scotland, a kingdom now united with England and Wales in Great Britain, occupies the northern 37% of the main British island, and the Hebrides, Orkney, Shetland and smaller islands. Length, 275 mi., breadth approx. 150 mi., area, 30,411 sq. mi., population (est. 1972) 5,210,000.

The Lowlands, a belt of land approximately 60 miles wide from the Firth of Clyde to the Firth of Forth, divide the farming region of the Southern Uplands from the granite Highlands of the north. Only one-tenth of the land area, the Lowlands contain three-quarters of the population and most of the industry. The Highlands, famous for hunting and fishing, have been opened to industry by many hydroelectric power stations.

Edinburgh, pop. (1972) 449,632, is the capital. It lies on the Firth of Forth in Midlothian County and has notable memorials of its royal and cultural history. Glasgow, pop. (1972) 861,898, is the largest city, 3d largest in Britain, and Britain's greatest industrial center. It is a shipbuilding complex on the Clyde and an ocean port. Aberdeen, pop. (1972) 181,548, NE of Edinburgh, is a major North Sea port, center of granite industry and fish processing. Dundee, pop. (1972) 182,842, NE of Edinburgh, is an industrial and fish processing center.

History. Scotland was called Caledonia by the Romans who battled early Picts and Celtic tribes and occupied southern areas from the 1st to the 4th centuries. The Scots were an Irish tribe from Scotia (an early name for Ireland). Missionaries from Britain introduced Christianity in the 4th century; St. Columba, an Irish monk, converted most of Scotland in the 6th century.

The Kingdom of Scotland was founded in 1018. William Wallace, patriot leader, defeated an English army, 1297, and Robert Bruce defeated another, 1314. John Knox led the Scottish Reformation in the 16th century.

In 1603 James VI of Scotland, son of Mary, Queen of Scots, succeeded to the throne of England as James I, and effected the Union of the Crowns. In 1707 Scotland received representation in the British Parliament, resulting from the union of former separate Parliaments. Its executive in the British cabinet is the Secretary of State for Scotland. The growing Scottish Nationalist party urges independence. The UK government has proposed creation of an elected Scotland Assembly.

There are 8 universities. Memorials of Robert Burns, Sir Walter Scott, John Knox, Mary, Queen of Scots draw many tourists, as do the beauties of the Trossachs, Loch Katrine, Loch Lomond and abbey ruins.

Industries. Engineering products are the most important industry, with growing emphasis on lighter products such as office machinery, autos, electronics and other consumer goods and less dependence on locomotives, ships, boilers, pumps, valves and other industrial machinery. Oil has been discovered off-shore in the North Sea, stimulating on-shore support industries.

Scotland produces fine woolens, worsteds, tweeds; silks, fine linens and jute. It is known for its special breeds of cattle and sheep, Shetland ponies and Clydesdale draft horses. Fisheries have large hauls of herring, cod, whiting. Whisky is the biggest export.

Atomic projects produce plutonium and electrical energy at Dounreay, Chapelcross, Hunterston.

The Hebrides are a group of c. 500 islands, 100 inhabited, off the W coast. The Inner Hebrides include **Skye, Mull** and **Iona**, the last famous for the arrival of St. Columba, 563 AD. The Outer Hebrides include **St. Kilda** and **Harris.** Industries include sheep raising and weaving. **The Orkney Islands,** c. 90, are to the NE. The capital is Kirkwall, on Pomona Is. Fish curing, sheep raising and weaving are occupations. NE of the Orkneys are the 200 **Shetland Islands,** 24 inhabited, home of Shetland pony.

Northern Ireland

Six of the 9 counties of Ulster, the NE corner of Ireland, constitute Northern Ireland, with the parliamentary boroughs of Belfast and Londonderry. The country has an area of 5,451 sq. mi. and a population (1971 census prelim.) 1,528,000. Belfast is the capital and chief industrial center.

Industries. Shipbuilding, including large tankers, has long been an important industry, centered in Belfast, the largest port. Linen manufacture is also important, along with apparel and rope and twine. Growing diversification has added engineering products, synthetic fibers and electronics. There are large numbers of cattle, hogs and sheep; potatoes, poultry and dairy foods are also produced. There is an agricultural surplus, mostly shipped to England.

Government. An act of the British Parliament, 1920, divided Northern from Southern Ireland, each with a parliament and government. When Ireland became a dominion, 1921, and later a republic, Northern Ireland chose to remain a part of the United Kingdom. It elects 12 members to the British House of Commons.

During 1968-69, large demonstrations were conducted by Roman Catholics who charged they were discriminated against in voting rights, housing and employment. The Catholics, a minority comprising about a third of the population, demanded abolition of property qualifications for voting in local elections and institution of "one man, one vote." Violence and terrorism intensified, involving branches of the Irish Republican Army (outlawed in the Irish Republic), Protestant groups, police and up to 15,000 British troops.

A succession of Northern Ireland prime ministers pressed reform programs but failed to satisfy extremists on both sides. About 1,100 were killed in 6 years of bombings and shootings, some in England itself. Britain suspended the Northern Ireland parliment Mar. 30, 1972, and imposed direct British rule. A coalition government was formed in 1973 when moderates won election to a new one-house Assembly. But a Protestant general strike overthrew the government in 1974. A cease-fire was in effect in 1975.

Education and Religion. Northern Ireland is ²/₃ Protestant, ¹/₃ Roman Catholic. Elementary education is compulsory through age 15. There are 2 universities and 24 technical colleges.

Channel Islands

The Channel Islands, area 75 sq. mi., est. pop. 1974 130,000, off the NW coast of France, the only parts of the one-time Dukedom of Normandy belonging to England, are **Jersey, Guernsey** and the dependencies of Guernsey — **Alderney, Brechou, Great Sark, Little Sark, Herm, Jethou and Lihou.** Jersey and Guernsey have separate legal existences and lieutenant governors named by the Crown. The islands were the only British soil occupied by German troops in World War II.

Isle of Man

The Isle of Man, area 227 sq. mi., est. 1974 pop. 60,000, is in the Irish Sea, 20 mi. from Scotland, 30 mi. from Cumberland. It is rich in lead and iron. The island has its own laws and a lt. gov. appointed by the Crown. The Tynwald (legislature) consists of the Legislative Council, partly elected, and House of Keys, elected. Capital: Douglas. Farming, tourism, fishing (kippers, scallops) are chief occupations. Man is famous for the Manx tailless cat.

Gibraltar

Gibraltar, a colony southeast of Spain, guards the entrance to the Mediterranean. The width of the strait dividing Europe from Africa varies from 7.75 mi. at the narrowest part to 23.75 at the widest. The Rock has been in British possession since 1704. There is a large harbor and a naval base. The Rock is 2.75 mi. long. ³/₄ of a mi. wide and 1,396 ft. in height; a narrow isthmus connects it with the mainland. Est. pop. 1974: 30,000.

In 1966 Spain called on Britain to give "substantial sovereignty" of Gibraltar to Spain and imposed a partial blockade. In 1967, residents voted 12,138 for remaining under Britain, 44 for returning to Spain. A new constitution, May 30, 1969, gave an elected House of Assembly more control in domestic affairs. A UN General Assembly resolution requested Britain to end Gibraltar's colonial status by Oct. 1, 1969. Britain did not do so.

British West Indies

Swinging in a vast arc from the coast of Venezuela NE, then N and NW toward Puerto Rico are the Windward and Leeward Islands, forming a coral and volcanic barrier sheltering the Caribbean from the open Atlantic. Many of the islands are self-governing British possessions. Universal suffrage was instituted 1951-54; ministerial systems were set up 1956-1960.

Moving northward from the southern end of the arc lie the British **Windward Islands: St. Vincent,** (1973 pop. 100,000, area 150 sq. mi., capital Kingstown), **St. Lucia** (1974 pop. 110,000, area 238 sq. mi., capital Castries) and **Dominica** (1974 pop. 70,000, area 290 sq. mi., capital Roseau).

Further north, in the **Leeward Islands,** are Montserrat (1970 pop. 12,300, area 33 sq. mi., capital Plymouth), **Antigua** (1974 pop. 70,000, area 171 sq. mi., capital St. John's) and **St. Christopher-Nevis-Anguilla,** also referred to as **St. Kitts** (1974 pop. 70,000, area 138 sq. mi., capital Basseterre

on St. Christopher). Nearby are the small **British Virgin Islands.**

Britain granted self-government to 5 of these islands and island groups in 1967-1969; each became an Associated State, with Britain controlling foreign affairs and defense. These were Antigua, Dominica, St. Lucia, the St. Christopher-Nevis-Anguilla Federation, and St. Vincent.

Anguilla declared its independence June 16, 1967, but accepted appointment of a British administrator. In March 1969 British troops were landed. They left in Sept. A commission administers Anguilla, still legally part of the Federation. Area is 35 sq. mi., pop. 5,000.

Sugar is the major crop of Antigua and St. Kitts; bananas are the main product of the Windwards; Dominica produces cocoa; Antigua, Montserrat, St. Kitts, and St. Vincent have Sea Island cotton; St. Vincent has arrowroot; Dominica grows citrus fruits. Imports include foods, clothing, machinery. Tourism is growing. Dominica tried in 1975 to suppress leftist terrorists.

The three **Cayman Islands,** a colony, lie S of Cuba, NW of Jamaica. Population is 10,423 (1970), most of it on Grand Cayman. It is a free port; in the 1970s Grand Cayman became a tax-free refuge for foreign funds and branches of many Western banks were opened there in the 1970s. Total area: 93 sq. mi. Capital: Georgetown.

The **Turks and Caicos Islands,** at the SE end of the Bahama Islands, are a separate British possession. There are about 30 islands, only 6 inhabited, pop. est. 6,000, area 166 sq. mi., capital Grand Turk. Salt, crayfish and conch shells are the main exports.

Bermuda

Bermuda is a British dependency governed by a royal governor and an Assembly, the oldest legislative body among British dependencies. Capital is Hamilton.

It is a group of 360 small islands of coral formation, 20 inhabited, comprising 21 sq. mi. in the western Atlantic, 580 mi. E. of North Carolina. Population, 1974, was 60,000 (about 63% of African descent). Density is high.

The Assembly dated from 1620. In elections May 22, 1968, the first on the basis of universal adult suffrage, the predominantly white United Bermuda party won 30 of the 40 Assembly seats; 16 of the 40 elected were blacks. A black, Sir Edward Richards, became prime minister in 1971. The Assembly runs local affairs. Bermuda adopted a dollar-decimal currency in 1970.

Gov. Richard Sharples and an aide were slain by gunmen in 1973. The police commissioner was shot to death in 1972.

The U.S. has air and naval bases under long-term lease, and a NASA tracking station.

Bermuda boasts many resort hotels, serving over 280,000 visitors a year. The government raises most revenue from import duties. Exports: lilies, drugs, cosmetics.

Belize

Belize (formerly called British Honduras) is in Central America facing the Caribbean to the E, with Mexico on the N and Guatemala on the W. Population (UN est. 1974) 140,000, area 8,866 sq. mi., capital Belmopan.

Internal self-government was granted by Britain in 1964.

The area has long been claimed by Guatemala, but also was promised independence by Britain. In Apr. 1968, a mediator proposed that British Honduras be made independent but have close association with Guatemala. The proposal was rejected by Belize.

Main export is sugar, along with citrus fruits, mahogany and other hardwoods, chicle, seafood.

South Atlantic Dependencies

Falkland Islands and Dependencies, a British Colony, lies 300 mi. E of the Strait of Magellan at the southern end of South America.

The Falklands or Islas Malvinas include about 200 islands with an area of 4,618 sq. mi. and pop. (1970) of 2,045. Sheep-grazing is the main industry; wool is the principal export. There are indications of large oil and gas deposits. The islands are also claimed by Argentina. **South Georgia,** area 1,450 sq. mi., and pop. 439, and the uninhabited **South Sandwich Islands** are dependencies of the Falklands.

British Antarctic Territory, south of 60° S lat., was made a separate colony in 1962 and comprises mainly the **South Shetland Islands,** the **South Orkneys and Graham's Land.** A chain of meteorological stations is maintained.

St. Helena, an island 1,200 mi. off the W. coast of Africa and 1,800 E of South America, has 47 sq. mi. and est. pop., 1970 of 4,952. Flax, lace and rope making are the chief industries. After Napoleon Bonaparte was defeated at Waterloo the British exiled him to St. Helena, where he lived from Oct. 16, 1815, to his death, May 5, 1821. His remains were transferred to Paris in 1840. Capital is Jamestown.

Tristan da Cunha is the principal of a group of islands of volcanic origin, total area 40 sq. mi., half way between the Cape of Good Hope and South America. The other islands are inaccessible, Gough (or Diego Alvarez) and the 3 Nightingale Is. A volcanic peak 6,760 ft. high erupted in 1961. The 262 inhabitants were removed to England, but most returned in 1963. The islands are dependencies of St. Helena.

Ascension is an island of volcanic origin, 34 sq. mi. in area, 700 mi. NW of St. Helena, through which it is administered. It is a communications relay center for Britain, and has a U. S. satellite tracking center. Est. pop., 1971, was 1,232, half of them communications workers. The island is noted for sea turtles.

Asian and Indian Ocean Dependencies

Brunei has been since 1888 a protected sultanate on the N side of the Island of Borneo, between the Malaysian states of Sarawak and Sabah. Its area is 2,226 sq. mi., the size of Delaware, with population (1974 UN est.), 140,000, two-thirds Malay and indigenous races, one-third of Chinese descent.

A 1959 constitution was amended, 1965, to provide for general elections to the Legislative Council, some members of which are appointed. There is a sultan and a British high commissioner. A 1971 agreement gave Brunei full internal self-government.

Brunei's rich Seria oilfield provides tax revenues well in excess of expenditures. Rubber is also exported. Some of the surplus has been spent on a growing program of schools and social services.

Hong Kong is a Crown Colony at the mouth of the Canton River in China, 90 mi. south of Canton. Its nucleus is Hong Kong Island, 35¹/₂ sq. mi., acquired from China 1841, on which is located Victoria, the capital. Opposite is Kowloon Peninsula, 3 sq. mi. and Stonecutters Island, ¹/₄ sq. mi., added, 1860. An additional 355 sq. mi. known as the New Territories, comprised of a mainland area and islands, were leased from China, 1898, for 99 years. Total area of the colony is 391 sq. mi., with a population, 1974 UN est., of 4,250,000 including fewer than 20,000 British. From 1949 to 1962 Hong Kong absorbed more than a million refugees from the mainland. The flow of refugees continued, on a lesser scale, into the 1970's.

Hong Kong harbor was long an important British naval station and one of the world's great trans-shipment ports. Britain planned in 1974 to reduce the garrison.

Principal industries are shipbuilding and textiles; also iron and steel, apparel, fishing, cement, and small manufactures. American tourists spend an est. $29 million yearly.

Spinning mills, among the best in the world, and low wages compete with textiles elsewhere and have resulted in protective measures in some countries. Hong Kong also has a booming electronics industry. The U. S. is the largest market for Hong Kong products.

During 1967 Communist China launched a campaign against British authority in Hong Kong, including demonstrations, strikes, riots, bombings, border incidents and slowdowns in supplying food. The campaign later subsided.

(For Seychelles, see separate article.)

British Indian Ocean Territory was formed Nov. 1965, embracing islands formerly dependencies of Mauritius or Seychelles: the Chagos Archipelago (including Diego Garcia), Aldabra, Farquhar and Des Roches. Population, 558. In 1973 the U. S. Navy established a communications station on Diego Garcia and in 1975 began constructing a naval base. The USSR and Asian nations opposed the step.

Pacific Ocean Dependencies

Pitcairn Island is in the Pacific, halfway between South America and Australia. The island was discovered in 1767 by Carteret but was not inhabited until 23 years later when the mutineers of the Bounty landed there. The area is 18 sq. mi. and population, 1974, was 78. It is a British colony and is administered by a British Representative in New Zealand and a local Council. The uninhabited islands of **Henderson, Ducie** and **Oeno** are in the Pitcairn group.

The **British Solomon Islands,** a protectorate, number 10 large islands and 4 groups of small islands with a total area of 11,500 sq. mi. and population, est. 1974, of 180,000, mostly Melanesians. The Solomons lie E of New Guinea. The chief islands in the group are **Guadalcanal, Malaita, San Cristobal, New Georgia, Santa Isabel, Choiseul, Shortland, Mono or Treasury, Vella Lavella, Ganongga, Gizo, Rendova, Russell, Florida** and **Rennel.** Among the groups of islands are the **Lord Howe, Santa Cruz, Tucopia, Mitre, Duff or Wilson** and **Reef.** Self-government was set for 1975 and independence for 1977. Exports: copra, timber, nuts, and trochus shell.

The **Gilbert and Ellice Islands** were proclaimed a protectorate in 1892. Self-government was granted in 1971. The colony includes the **Gilbert Islands** (16), **Ellice Islands** (9), **Phoenix Islands, Ocean Island, Line Islands,** composed of **Fanning, Washington** and **Christmas Islands,** the last the largest atoll in the Pacific (also claimed by the U. S.). The total area is 369 sq. mi. and the population, 1974 est., 60,000. Exports: chiefly copra and phosphates.

New Hebrides, a condominium jointly administered since 1906, by Great Britain and France, is a group of 11 main islands and about 69 islets lying 500 mi. W of Fiji, with an aggregate area of 5,790 sq. mi. Population, 1974 UN est. 90,000, mostly Melanesian. Chief products are copra, cotton, cocoa, fish and coffee. British and French resident commissioners are joint heads of the administration; representative bodies were elected in 1975. **Banks** (309 sq. mi.) and **Torres** (40 sq. mi.) **Islands,** with pop. of 2,640, are attached to the New Hebrides for administration.

United States

(See Index for listings)

Upper Volta

Area: 105,869 sq. mi. Population (UN est. 1974):

5,900,000. Capital: Ouagadougou. Monetary unit: CFA franc.

The Republic of Upper Volta, one-time French Overseas Territory, is an inland plateau region in west Africa, bounded by Mali, Niger, the Ivory Coast, Ghana, Togo and Dahomey. It is the size of Colorado.

More than 90% of the people are subsistence farmers. Greatest wealth is in livestock, mostly cattle and sheep, accounting for 55% of exports. Principal market crops are cotton, rice, peanuts and karite. Climate is extremely dry but irrigation efforts, using water from the Black Volta, White Volta and pumped from underground, have been started with aid from the UN Special Fund. There are rich manganese deposits. A long drought brought famine in 1973-74; the U. S. provided 40% of the aid sent to the area.

Upper Volta became an autonomous state in 1958. It became fully independent Aug. 5, 1960 and a member of the UN. It signed a bilateral agreement, 1961, maintaining close ties with France.

A constitution, adopted 1960, provided for a presidential form of government and a unicameral National Assembly. In 1966 the army chief of staff, Gen. Sangoule Lamizana, took over the presidency during demonstrations against austerity measures. A new constitution, providing for a premier, was adopted 1970. In Feb. 1974 Lamizana dissolved the Assembly, suspended the constitution, and named a mostly military cabinet. A border dispute with Mali was resolved, July 1975.

Uruguay

Area: 68,548 sq. mi. Population (Govt. est. 1974): 3,030,000. Capital: Montevideo. Monetary unit: Peso.

Uruguay is one of the smallest republics in South America. Slightly larger than Missouri, it is a country of rich, rolling, grassy plains on the South Atlantic coast. Brazil and Argentina are its neighbors, with the Uruguay River forming the boundary line with Argentina.

Resources and Industries. Some 85% of Uruguay's area is devoted to stock raising; 9.6% to agriculture; 3.5% woods and forest; 1.8% is unproductive. The chief products are meat, wool, hides, corn, wheat, citrus fruits, rice, oats and linseed. Meat-packing, metallurgical, textile and wine-making industries are large.

More than a third of the population lives in one city, Montevideo. More than a third of the workers are employed by the government. The state owns the power, telephone, railroad, cement, oil-refining and other industries.

Uruguay's standard of living was one of the highest in South America. Inflation, plus floods, drought and a cold wave in 1967 and a general strike in 1968 brought attempts by the government to strengthen the economy through a series of devaluations of the peso and wage and price controls. But inflation continued. The cost of living rose 97.2% in 1973 and 71.4% in 1974.

History and Government. Once a part of the Spanish Viceroyalty of Rio de la Plata and later a province of Brazil, Uruguay declared its independence, Aug. 25, 1825. The constitution provides for a president, a Chamber of Deputies and a Senate elected for 5-year terms. Suffrage is universal.

Uruguay has one of the world's most extensive social welfare programs with old age pensions, child welfare.

Leftist guerrillas, drawn from the upper classes and called Tupamaros, increased terrorist actions in 1970; a U. S. police adviser was slain in Aug. In 1971 the guerrillas kidnaped and, after 8 months, freed the British ambassador. Violence continued and in Feb. 1973 President Juan Maria Bordaberry agreed to military control of his administration. In June he abolished Congress and set up a Council of State in its place. By 1974 the military had apparently defeated

the Tupamaros, using severe repressive measures, but the economic decline continued.

Education and Religion. Church and state are separate and there is complete religious tolerance. Preponderant religion is Roman Catholic. Education, including college, is free; primary education is compulsory. The language is Spanish.

Defense. Armed forces total 21,000, all paid volunteers. Uruguay is a member of the UN and OAS.

State of Vatican City

Area: 108.7 acres. Population: about 700.

The popes for many centuries, with brief interruptions, held temporal sovereignty over mid-Italy (the so-called Papal States), comprising an area of some 16,000 sq. mi., with a population in the 19th Century of more than 3 million. This territory was incorporated in the new Kingdom of Italy, the sovereignty of the pope being confined to the palaces of the Vatican and the Lateran in Rome and the villa of Castel Gandolfo, by an Italian law, May 13, 1871. This law also guaranteed to the pope and his successors a yearly indemnity of over $620,000. This allowance, however, remained unclaimed.

A Treaty of Conciliation, a Concordat and a financial convention were signed Feb. 11, 1929, by Cardinal Gasparri and Premier Mussolini. The documents established the independent state of Vatican City, and gave the Catholic religion special status in Italy. The treaty (Lateran Agreement) was made part of the Constitution of Italy (Article 7) in 1947.

Vatican City includes St. Peter's, the Vatican Palace and Museum covering over 13 acres, the Vatican gardens, and neighboring buildings between Viale Vaticano and the Church. Thirteen buildings in Rome, outside the boundaries, enjoy extra-territorial rights; these buildings house congregations or officers necessary for the administration of the Holy See.

The legal system is based on the code of canon law, the apostolic constitutions and the laws especially promulgated for the Vatican City by the pope. In cases not covered the Italian law of Rome applies. The Secretariat of State represents the Holy See in its diplomatic relations. By the Treaty of Conciliation the pope is pledged to a perpetual neutrality unless his mediation is specifically requested. This, however, does not prevent the defense of the Church whenever it is persecuted. A total of 70 nations maintain diplomatic representatives in Vatican City. The U.S. does not have an official ambassador, but in June 1970 President Nixon named Henry Cabot Lodge to be his personal envoy.

The present sovereign of the State of Vatican City is the Supreme Pontiff Paul VI, Giovanni Battista Montini, born in Concesio, Italy, Sept. 26, 1897, elected June 21, 1963, in succession to Angelo Giuseppe Roncali, John XXIII, who died June 3, 1963.

Venezuela

Area: 352,143 sq. mi. Population (Gov. est. 1974): 11,630,000. Capital: Caracas. Monetary unit: Bolivar.

Venezuela, a land of wide plains and lofty mountains, lies within the torrid zone in northern South America, with a 1,750-mi. coast on the Caribbean and Atlantic. Its neighbors are Guyana, Brazil and Colombia. It includes 72 islands totaling 14,650 sq. mi., the largest being Margarita, 40 mi. by 20, which is one of Venezuela's 20 states and an important pearl center. Venezuela is more than twice the size of California.

The Orinoco River with its tributaries drains about four-fifths of the country. About 1,700 mi. in length and 13.5 mi. across at its widest point, it is the 2d largest river system in South America, and is navigable for about 700 mi.

Caracas, the capital, is 12 mi. inland from its port, La Guaira. It is noted for its modern architecture. In its Pantheon are enshrined the ashes of Simon Bolivar, South American liberator (1783-1830.).

Resources and Industries. Mining, agriculture, fishing and manufacturing are the chief industries. Venezuela in 1974 was the world's 5th largest oil producer. Lake Maracaibo is the largest oil field in South America. Venezuela helped found the Organization of Petroleum Exporting States. In 1975 the government announced plans to nationalize the oil industry with compensation. The same year, development began of the Orinoco tar belt, believed to contain the world's largest oil reserves. Iron ore production was nationalized Jan. 1, 1975.

Other minerals are iron, gold, copper, coal, salt, nickel, manganese, asbestos, diamonds and mica. Iron ore production was 26 million tons in 1974 and is the 2d most important export, next to oil.

Coffee is the major agricultural product. Exports also include cocoa, canned fish, fruit, sugar, steel products, rice. Industries include steel, petrochemicals, textiles, containers, tobacco products, paper, tires, shoes. Tourists increased from 95,000 in 1965 to 453,331 in 1973.

Construction is booming, including a new $3.8 billion city, Ciudad Guyana, 300 mi. SE of Caracas; and a 4,175-ft. bridge across the Orinoco opened in 1967.

Oil profits help finance the extensive industrial development. The gross national product rose from $8.9 billion in 1966 to over $20 billion in 1974. Government efforts at income redistribution were thwarted by inflation in 1974-5.

History and Government. Columbus first set foot on the South American continent on the peninsula of Paria, Aug. 1498. Alonso de Ojeda, 1499, found Lake Maracaibo, called the land Venezuela, or Little Venice, because natives had houses on stilts. Venezuela was under Spanish domination until 1821. The republic was formed after secession from the Colombian Federation in 1830.

The 1961 constitution provided for a strong central government; a president, Senate and Chamber of Deputies elected for 5 years by direct universal vote, and a Supreme Court appointed by the Congress. Member: UN, OAS.

Education and Religion. The language is Spanish and Roman Catholic is the religion of the majority. All education, including college, is free. Primary education is compulsory.

Defense. Armed forces total 39,500.

Vietnam

Total area: 126,436 sq. mi. Total population (UN est. 1973): 42,650,000. Vietnam is split between 2 governments.

Vietnam occupies the eastern half of the Indo-Chinese peninsula, bounded on the N. by China, on the E and S by the South China Sea, and on the W. by Cambodia and Laos. It consists of the historic regions Tonkin, Annam, and Cochin China. Principal cities are Saigon, Hanoi, Haiphong, Hue and Danang.

Resources and industries. Chief products are rice, principal food staple; rubber; and coal. Peacetime exports included rubber, rice, fish, coal, lumber, pepper, cattle and hides, corn, zinc and tin. Tea, coffee, and quinine are grown in the South. Coal is a chief product in the North; also coffee, tea, maize, sweet potatoes, tobacco, sugar cane and shellac.

History and Government. Vietnam's recorded history began in Tonkin before the Christian era. Settled by Viets from central China, Vietnam was held by China, 111 B.C.-939 A.D., and was a vassal state during subsequent periods. Vietnam defeated the armies of Kublai Khan, 1288. Conquest by France began in 1858 and ended in 1884 with protectorate status.

In 1940 Vietnam was occupied by Japan; during the occupation nationalist aims gathered force. A number of groups formed the Vietminh (Independence) League, headed by Ho Chi Minh, communist guerrilla leader. In Aug. 1945 the Vietminh forced out Bao Dai, former emperor of Annam, head of a regime sponsored by Japan. France, seeking to reestablish colonial control, battled communist and nationalist forces, 1946-1954, and was finally defeated at Dienbienphu, May 8, 1954. Meanwhile, on July 1, 1949, Bao Dai had formed a State of Vietnam, with himself as chief of state, with French approval. Communist China backed Ho Chi Minh.

A cease-fire accord signed in Geneva July 21, 1954, divided Vietnam along the Ben Hai River. It provided for a buffer zone, withdrawal of French troops from the north and elections to determine the country's future. Under the agreement the communists gained control of territory north of the 17th parallel, 22 provinces with area of 62,000 sq. mi. and 13 million pop., with its capital at Hanoi and Ho Chi Minh as president. South Vietnam was to comprise the 39 southern provinces with approx. area of 65,000 sq. mi. and pop. of 12 million. Some 900,000 North Vietnamese fled to South Vietnam. Neither South Vietnam nor the U.S. signed the agreement.

South Vietnam

Area: 66,280 sq. mi. Population (UN est. 1973): 19,370,000. Capital: Saigon. Monetary unit: Piastre.

On Oct. 26, 1955, Ngo Dinh Diem, premier of the interim government of South Vietnam, proclaimed the Republic of Vietnam and became its first president, following a referendum Oct. 23.

Fighting persisted from 1956, with the communist Vietcong, aided by North Vietnam, pressing war in the south and South Vietnam receiving U.S. aid and, by June 1965, active U.S. combat participation.

A serious political conflict arose in 1963 when Buddhists denounced authoritarianism and brutality. This paved the way for a military coup Nov. 1-2, 1963, which overthrew Diem.

Several military coups followed. In elections Sept. 3, 1967, Chief of State Nguyen Van Thieu was chosen president. A 60-member Senate was also elected Sept. 3 and a 137-member House on Sept. 22. Thieu was reelected in a one-candidate election, Oct. 3, 1971.

In 1964, the U.S. began air strikes against North Vietnam. Beginning in 1965, the raids were stepped up and U.S. troops became combatants. U.S. troop strength in Vietnam, which reached a high of 543,400 in Apr. 1969, was ordered reduced by U.S. President Nixon in a series of withdrawals, beginning in June 1969.

A ceasefire agreement which President Nixon said would bring "peace with honor" was signed in Paris Jan. 27, 1973 (EST), by the U.S., North and South Vietnam, and the Vietcong, to take effect the same day (Jan. 28 in Vietnam). It provided for withdrawal of U.S. troops (about 23,000 were still in Vietnam) and return of U.S. prisoners (590), both within 90 days, an International Commission to supervise the ceasefire, and for the U.S. and North Vietnam to respect the South Vietnamese people's right to self-determination. U.S. aid was curbed in 1974 by the U.S. Congress.

Massive numbers of North Vietnamese troops, aided by tanks, launched attacks against remaining government outposts in the Central Highlands in the first months of 1975. Government retreats turned into a rout, and the Saigon regime surrendered April 30. Conquest of the country was effectively completed within days.

A Provisional Revolutionary Government assumed control, aided by officials and technicians from Hanoi, and first steps were taken to transform society along communist lines. Ultimate reunification of the two Vietnams was called for, though both countries applied for UN membership.

The U.S. accepted over 130,000 Vietnamese fleeing the new regime, while some thousands more sought refuge in other countries.

The war's toll included — Combat deaths: U.S. 46,-079; South Vietnam over 200,000; other allied forces 5,225. Civilian casualties were over a million. Displaced war refugees in South Vietnam totaled over 6,500,000.

(See also Vietnam in Index).

Most Vietnamese practice parts of several religions or mixtures of Confucianism, Taoism, Buddhism, ancestor worship and animism. About 20% practice Buddhism and about 12% Roman Catholicism. New indigenous religions include Cao Dai (1919) and Hoa Hao (1939). There are 7 universities.

Democratic Republic of Vietnam

Area: 60,156 sq.mi. Population (UN est. 1973): 23,930,000. Capital: Hanoi. Monetary unit: Dong.

The Democratic Republic of Vietnam adopted a constitution Dec. 31, 1959, based on communist principles and calling for reunification of all Vietnam. It provides for a president elected by Parliament and a prime minister appointed by the president. President Ho Chi Minh, reelected July 15, 1960, by unanimous vote of the National Assembly, had held office since 1945. He died Sept. 3, 1969, and was succeeded as president by Ton Duc Thang.

North Vietnam sought to take over South Vietnam beginning in 1954. Aid to Vietcong guerrillas was intensified in 1959 and with large-scale troop infiltration in 1964. In that year U.S. began bombing of military targets in North Vietnam; the bombings were ended in 1968 but renewed 1972-73. North Vietnam had large forces in Laos and Cambodia. After the fall of the South Vietnam government April 30, 1975, Hanoi sent officials and technicians to aid in communist transformation of the south. Both North and South Vietnam applied for UN membership in 1975. Industry and agriculture were stymied during years of war.

(See also Republic of Vietnam, above.)

Western Samoa

Area: 1,133 sq. mi. Population (Govt. est. 1974): 160,000. Capital: Apia. Monetary unit: Tala.

Western Samoa, which became an independent nation Jan. 1, 1962, comprises 4 inhabited islands of a group in the South Pacific lying about 2,613 mi. SW of Hawaii. Largest of the islands are **Savaii** and **Upolu**. Eastern Samoa, the smaller portion of the group with its capital at Pago Pago, is a dependency of the U.S.

Western Samoa was a German colony, 1899 to 1914, when New Zealand landed troops and took over. It became a New Zealand mandate under the League of Nations and, in 1945, a New Zealand UN Trusteeship.

An elected local government took office in Oct. 1959 and the country became fully independent in 1962. New Zealand has continued economic aid and educational assistance. Western Samoa changed from pounds to decimal currency July 10, 1967.

The population is composed almost solely of Polynesians. The islands are fertile. Chief products are tropical hardwoods, fish, cocoa, coconuts, bananas, taro, coffee, bark cloth (tapa), mats.

Robert Louis Stevenson's grave is on a hill near Apia.

Arab Republic of Yemen

Area: 75,289 sq. mi. Population (UN est. 1974): 6,480,000. Capital: Sana. Monetary unit: Rial.

Yemen is an ancient, mountainous country, near the southern tip of the Arabian Peninsula on the Red Sea. Its neighbors are the People's Democratic Republic of Yemen (formerly Southern Yemen) and Saudi Arabia. It is about the size of Nebraska.

Hodeida, Mocha and Loheiya are major ports. Marib and Sana are archeological sites.

Resources and Industries. On the plateau of El Jebel, the most fertile section of Arabia, coffee, barley and grain are grown. Mocha coffee, hides, dates, cotton, sesame, herbs, fruits and precious stones are exported. There are periodic droughts.

History and Government. Yemen's territory once was part of the ancient kingdom of Sheba, or Saba, a prosperous link in trade between Africa and India. A Biblical reference speaks of its gold, spices and precious stones as gifts borne by the Queen of Sheba to King Solomon. Imam Ahmed ruled 1948-1962. The king was reported assassinated Sept. 26, 1962, and a revolutionary group headed by Brig. Gen. Abdullah al-Salal declared the country to be the Yemen Arab Republic. He became president.

The Imam Ahmed's heir, the Imam Mohamad al-Badr, fled to the mountains where tribesmen joined royalist forces; internal warfare between them and the republican forces continued. Egyptian president Nasser sent 70,000 troops to aid the republicans; Saudi Arabia supported the royalists with military aid.

After Egypt's defeat in the June 1967 Israeli-Arab war, Egypt announced it would withdraw its troops from Yemen; the last of them left Nov. 29, 1967, and Saudi Arabia said it would stop aiding the royalists.

This was accompanied by a bloodless coup Nov. 5, 1967. Leadership was taken over by a Presidential Council headed by Abdul Rahman al-Iryani, who later became president.

Fighting continued between the republican and royalist forces. Saudi Arabia announced in Feb. 1968 it was renewing its aid to the royalists, charging that both Russia and Syria, as well as Southern Yemen, were aiding the republicans.

In April 1970 hostilities ended with an agreement between Yemen and Saudi Arabia and appointment of several royalists to the Yemen government.

There were border skirmishes with forces of the People's Democratic Republic of Yemen in 1972-73. The U.S. and Yemen in 1972 resumed diplomatic relations, broken by Yemen after the 1967 Arab-Israeli war.

On June 13, 1974, an Army group, led by Col. Ibrahim al-Hamidi, seized the government.

Yemen is a member of the UN and Arab League.

People's Democratic Republic of Yemen

Area: 112,000 sq. mi. Population (Govt. est. 1974): 1,630,000. Capitals: Aden and Medina as-Shaab. Monetary unit: Dinar.

This nation became independent as the People's

Republic of Southern Yemen Nov. 30, 1967, after 129 years of British rule. It changed its name to People's Democratic Republic of Yemen on Nov. 30, 1970. It consists of the port city of Aden, 17 states of the former South Arabian Federation, 3 small sheikdoms, 3 larger sultanates, Quaiti, Kathiri and Mahri, which made up the Eastern Aden Protectorate, and Socotra, the largest island in the Arabian Sea.

Aden, mentioned in the Bible, has been a port for trade in incense, spices and silk between the East and West for 2,000 years. British rule began in 1839. Aden provided Britain with a controlling position at the southern entrance to the Red Sea.

With only 1% of the land fertile and few mineral deposits, the Port of Aden has been the area's most valuable natural resource. The port is 10 mi. across, well-sheltered and deep. In 1966 more than 6,000 ships put in at Aden for refueling, servicing and transshipment of goods, bringing over 227,000 visitors. Cotton and grains are grown.

But, with the closing of the Suez Canal after the Israeli-Arab War in June 1967, the port lost much of its business. Local products exported are cotton, fish, coffee, hides. The canal was reopened in 1967.

A war for independence began in 1963. The National Liberation Front (NLF) and the Egypt-supported Front for the Liberation of Occupied South Yemen, waged a guerrilla war against the British and local dynastic rulers. The 2 groups vied with each other for control. The NLF won out, but in a 1969 coup the left wing of the NLF seized power.

The new government broke off relations with the U.S. and nationalized some foreign firms. Aid has been furnished by the USSR and Communist China.

In 1972-73 there were border skirmishes with forces of the Yemen Arab Republic. South Yemen aided leftist guerrillas in neighboring Oman.

In 1974 South Yemen agreed to grant to the Arab League a 99-year lease on Perim Island, at the southern end of the Red Sea.

Yugoslavia

Area: 98,766 sq. mi. Population (Govt. est. 1974): 21,160,000. Capital: Belgrade. Monetary unit: Dinar.

The Socialist Federal Republic of Yugoslavia is a rugged mountainous land, densely forested, which rises from the eastern shore of the Adriatic Sea. Its neighbors are Italy, Austria, Hungary, Romania, Bulgaria, Greece and Albania. It is about the size of Wyoming.

The federation comprises 6 republics: Serbia, Croatia, Slovenia, Montenegro, Bosnia-Herzegovina and Macedonia, and 2 autonomous provinces: Kosovo and Voyvodina.

Resources and Industries. Chief crops are maize, wheat, barley, rye, tobacco, oats, hops and fruits. Principal minerals are coal, iron, copper, chrome, antimony, manganese, lead, mercury, salt and bauxite.

Most industry is socialized and private enterprise is restricted to small-scale production. Since 1952 workers are guaranteed a basic wage and a share in cooperative profits.

Management of industrial enterprises is handled by workers' councils. Farmland is 85% privately owned but farms are restricted to 25 acres.

Yugoslavia has conducted several large-scale programs to improve its economy. Beginning in the late 1950s, successful efforts were made to strengthen agriculture by improving fertilizers, grain varieties and livestock.

Tourism was promoted, particularly along the country's colorful Adriatic coast. Large numbers of visitors from nations of the West provided an important source of foreign income.

Beginning in 1965, reforms designed to decentralize the administration of economic development and to force industries to produce more efficiently in competition with foreign producers were introduced.

Yugoslavia has developed considerable trade with Western Europe as well as with the USSR and Eastern European countries and elsewhere. While its import-export balance has continued to show deficits, money earned by Yugoslavs working temporarily in Western Europe, and money brought in by tourists come close to making these up. In 1970 a trade treaty was signed with the EC. Unemployment and inflation became serious in 1975.

The index for industrial production (1970 = 100) was 140 for 1974.

Foreign trade in thousands of U.S. dollars:

	Imports	Exports
1973	$4,775,000	$3,024,000
1974	$8,071,000	$4,071,000

History and Government. Serbia, which had since 1389 been a vassal principality of Turkey, was established as an independent kingdom by the Treaty of Berlin, 1878. After the Balkan wars its boundaries were enlarged by the annexation of Old Serbia and Macedonia, 1913. When the Austrian Archduke Francis Ferdinand and wife were assassinated at Sarajevo June 28, 1914, the Austrian government forced war on Serbia, the onset of World War I, 1914-1918.

When the Austro-Hungarian empire collapsed, the Kingdom of the Serbs, Croats, and Slovenes was formed from the former provinces of Croatia, Dalmatia, Bosnia, Herzegovina, Slovenia, Voyvodina and the independent state of Montenegro, with Peter I of Serbia as king. The name was later changed to Yugoslavia. Peter (d. 1921) was succeeded by his son Alexander I, assassinated in 1934. Prince Paul, regent, was overthrown in Mar. 1941 and Crown Prince Peter became king. Germany invaded April, 1941, and King Peter II fled to London.

Many Yugoslav troops continued to fight the Nazis. Among these guerrillas were the Chetniks led by Draja Mikhailovich, who fought other partisans led by Josip Broz, known as Marshal Tito. Tito, backed by the USSR and Britain, was in control by the time the Germans had been driven from Yugoslavia in 1944. Mikhailovich was executed July 17, 1946, by the Tito regime, accused of collaboration with the Nazis.

A constituent assembly proclaimed Yugoslavia a republic Nov. 29, 1945. It became a federated republic Jan. 31, 1946, and Marshal Tito, a communist, became head of the government. By terms of a treaty with Italy the greater part of Venezia-Giulia, Zara, Pelagosa and adjacent islands were ceded to Yugoslavia.

The Stalin policy of dictating to all communist nations was rejected by Tito. He accepted economic aid and military equipment from the U. S. and received aid in foreign trade also from France and Great Britain.

Yugoslavia is governed by the president, as chairman of a 9-man collective presidency (created in 1971), a premier, and a parliament (Federal Assembly), from which cabinet members are drawn.

A new constitution, approved by the Assembly in Feb. 1974, provided that representatives in the Assembly be chosen by subordinate assemblies consisting of delegates from labor organizations. Tito was elected president-for-life in Feb. 1974.

Tito supported the liberalization government of Czechoslovakia in 1968 before the Russian invasion, but he paid a friendship visit to Moscow in 1972.

A separatist movement among Croatians, 2d to the Serbs in numbers, brought arrests and a change of leaders in the Croatian Republic in Jan. 1972.

Education and Religion. Education is free, and compulsory to age 14. There are 9 universities. Main languages are Slovene, Macedonian, Serbo-Croat. All religions are recognized. Serbo-Orthodox comprises 42%. Roman Catholic 32%. Moslem 12%. Serbian uses Cyrillic, Croatian uses Latin letters.

Complete social security is in force, including unemployment, medical, maternity benefits.

Defense. Military forces total 230,000.

Zaire

Area: 905,063 sq. mi. Population (Govt. est. 1974): 24,220,000. Capital; Kinshasa. Monetary unit: Zaire.

The Democratic Republic of Congo changed its name to Republic of Zaire on Oct. 27, 1971; the Congo River was changed to Zaire (its traditional name) and in 1972 Zairians with Christian names were ordered to change them to African names.

Zaire lies in Equatorial Africa, entirely inland except for 25 mi. on the Atlantic Ocean, N of the mouth of the Zaire River. It is larger than Texas and Alaska combined.

Along the eastern border lie several of Africa's Great Lakes, North of the Equator on the Uganda border, stand the Ruwenzori Mtns., believed to be the "Mountains of the Moon" of ancient legend. Mt. Margherita is 16,763 ft.

The Zaire River, one of the world's longest, rises near the Zambian border in the SE and flows 2,718 mi. N, then W and finally SW, emptying into the South Atlantic.

Wildlife is abundant and includes most of the species Africa is famous for: elephant, lion, gorilla, hippopotamus, crocodile, python, etc.

Resources and Industry. There are extensive mineral depostits in the Katanga, Ituri and Kivu highlands. Zaire in 1973 produced 7% of the world's copper, 67% of its cobalt and a third of its industrial diamonds. Also produced are cadmium, gold, silver, tin, germanium, zinc, iron, tungsten, manganese, uranium, zinc, and radium.

Tropical rain forests cover much of the land; trees often are 150 to 200 ft. tall. They include mahogany, ebony, teak, copal, palms, cedars and gum and resin trees. Bananas, coffee, rubber, mangoes, plantain, manioc, rice, sugar cane, and coconuts are grown. Chief agricultural exports are fats and oil, timber, coffee, cotton, rubber, tea, cocoa, bananas.

History and Government. Leopold II, king of the Belgians, formed an international group to exploit the Congo in 1876. In 1877 Henry M. Stanley explored the Congo and in 1878 the king's group sent him back to organize the region and win over the native chiefs. The Conference of Berlin, 1884-85, organized the Congo Free State with Leopold as king and chief owner. Exploitation of native laborers on the rubber plantations caused international criticism and led to granting of a colonial charter, 1908.

Belgian and Congolese leaders agreed Jan. 27, 1960, that the Congo would become independent June 30. In the first general elections, May 31, the National Congolese movement of Patrice Lumumba won 35 of 137 seats in the National Assembly, lower House of Parliament. He was appointed premier June 21, and formed a coalition cabinet.

Widespread violence caused Europeans and others to flee. Pres. Moise Tshombe of Katanga seceded from the republic July 11, but ended the secession in 1963. Katanga was the seat of the famous copper-mines. The UN Security Council Aug. 9, 1960, called on Belgium to withdraw its troops and sent a UN contingent to guard against civil war. President Kasavubu removed Lumumba as premier. Lumumba fought for control backed by Ghana, Guinea and India. On Feb. 12, 1961, Lumumba was murdered.

The last UN troops left the Congo June 30, 1964, and Tshombe became president.

On Sept. 7, 1964, leftist rebels set up a "People's Republic" in Stanleyville. Tshombe hired foreign mercenaries and sought to rebuild the Congolese Army. In Nov. and Dec. 1964 rebels slew scores of white hostages and thousands of Congolese; Belgian paratroops, dropped from U.S. transport planes, rescued hundreds. By July 1965 the rebels had lost their effectiveness.

In 1965 Gen. Joseph D. Mobutu was named president. He later changed his name to Mobutu Sese Seko. In March 1966 Mobutu took over from Parliament all of its legislative powers. On July 1 he renamed Leopoldville Kinshasa; Stanleyville, Kisangani; and Elisabethville, Lubumbashi.

In 1969-74, political stability under Mobutu was reflected in improved economic conditions. In 1970, he was elected to a 7-year term as president. In 1974 most foreign-owned businesses were ordered sold to Zaire citizens.

Education and Religion. The population is principally Bantu. More than 200 tribes are represented. Swahili, Lingala, Tshiluba and Kikongo are widely spoken; French is the official language. There are an estimated 9 million African Christians, predominantly Roman Catholic. There are 3 universities.

Zambia

Area: 290,724 sq. mi. Population (UN est. 1974): 4,750,000. Capital: Lusaka. Monetary unit: Kwacha.

The Republic of Zambia is a land-locked country in South Central Africa, bordering Zaire, Tanzania, Malawi, Mozambique, Rhodesia, Botswana, Southwest Africa (Namibia) and Angola. It is slightly larger than Texas.

The terrain is mostly high plateau covered with thick forest and suitable for both farming and grazing. The country is rich in minerals, including copper (10% of world production), zinc, cobalt, gold, vanadium, manganese, and coal.

Victoria Falls on the Zambezi River, the border with Rhodesia, is 3 times the width and more than twice the height of Niagara.

As Northern Rhodesia, the country was under the administration of the South Africa Company, 1889 until 1924 when the office of governor was established, and, subsequently, a legislature.

A new constitution, announced in 1963, granted self-government effective Jan. 22, 1964. The United National Independence party won the first elections Jan. 21 and its leader, Kenneth D. Kaunda, became prime minister. He was elected president and, on Oct. 24, 1964, Zambia became an independent republic within the Commonwealth. It has a National Assembly of 125 elected members and 10 nominated by the president. In 1973 a new constitution provided for a one-party system.

After the white government of Rhodesia declared its independence from Britain Nov. 11, 1965, relations between Zambia and Rhodesia became strained and use of their jointly owned railroad was disputed.

Britain gave Zambia an extra $12 million aid in 1966 after imposing an oil embargo on Rhodesia, and Zambia set up a temporary airlift to carry copper out from its mines and gasoline in. In Aug. 1968 a 1,058-mi. pipeline was completed, bringing oil from Tanzania. In 1973 a truck road to carry copper to Tanzania's port of Dar es Salaam was completed with U.S. aid. A railroad, built with Chinese aid across Tanzania, reached the Zambian border in 1974.

As part of a program of government participation in major industries, a government corporation in 1970 took over 51% of the ownership of 2 foreign-owned copper mining companies, paying with bonds. Privately-held land and other enterprises were nationalized in 1975, as were all newspapers.

United Nations

History, Membership, Organization and Purpose

The 30th regular session of the United Nations General Assembly opened Sept. 16, 1975. *See Chronology for developments at UN sessions during 1975.*

Foundations of the United Nations were laid at the Dumbarton Oaks Conference in Washington between the United States, the United Kingdom and the Soviet Union, Aug. 21-Sept. 28, 1944, and between the United States, the United Kingdom and the Republic of China (Nationalist) Sept. 29-Oct. 7, 1944. Proposals to establish an organization of nations for maintenance of world peace led to the United Nations Conference on International Organization at San Francisco, Apr. 25-June 26, 1945, where the charter of the United Nations was drawn up. It was signed June 26 by 50 nations, and by Poland, one of the original 51, on Oct. 15, 1945. The charter came into effect Oct. 25, 1945, when the requisite ratification by the 5 permanent members of the Security Council, China,

France, Soviet Union, United Kingdom and United States, and a majority of other signatories had been completed.

United Nations headquarters are located in New York, N.Y., between First Ave. and Roosevelt Drive and E. 42nd St. and E. 48th St. The General Assembly Bldg. (opened 1952). Secretariat, Conference and Library bldgs. are interconnected. The Dag Hammarskjold Library, built by a $6,200,000 grant from the Ford Foundation, was dedicated Nov. 16, 1961. It has room for 400,000 vols. To build the headquarters the U.S. Government advanced an interest-free loan of $65,000,000, payable in annual installments until 1982. John D. Rockefeller, Jr., contributed $8,000,000 for land and the City of New York contributed an est. $26,500,000 for adapting the site. United Nations has a post office originating its own stamps. *See Postal Information.*

Roster of the United Nations

(As of mid-1975)

The 141 Members of the United Nations, with the dates on which they became Members.

Member	Date	Member	Date	Member	Date
Afghanistan.....	Nov. 19, 1946	Gabon.........	Sept. 20, 1960	Mexico........	Nov. 7, 1945
Albania.........	Dec. 14, 1955	Gambia........	Sept. 21, 1965	Mongolia.......	Oct. 27, 1961
Algeria........	Oct. 8, 1962	Germany, East..	Sept. 18, 1973	Morocco.......	Nov. 12, 1956
Argentina......	Oct. 24, 1945	Germany, West..	Sept. 18, 1973	Mozambique.....	Sept. 16, 1975
Australia......	Nov. 1, 1945	Ghana.........	Mar. 8, 1957		
Austria..../....	Dec. 14, 1955	Greece........	Oct. 25, 1945	Nepal.........	Dec. 14, 1955
		Grenada........	Sept. 17, 1974	Netherlands....	Dec. 10, 1945
Bahamas........	Sept. 18, 1973	Guatemala......	Nov. 21, 1945	New Zealand....	Oct. 24, 1945
Bahrain........	Sept. 21, 1971	Guinea........	Dec. 12, 1958	Nicaragua......	Oct. 24, 1945
Bangladesh......	Sept. 17, 1974	Guinea-Bissau...	Sept. 17, 1974	Niger..........	Sept. 20, 1960
Barbados.......	Dec. 9, 1966	Guyana........	Sept. 20, 1966	Nigeria........	Oct. 7, 1960
Belgium........	Dec. 27, 1945			Norway........	Nov. 27, 1945
Bhutan........	Sept. 21, 1971	Haiti..........	Oct. 24, 1945		
Bolivia.........	Nov. 14, 1945	Honduras.......	Dec. 17, 1945	Oman..........	Oct. 7, 1971
Botswana.......	Oct. 17, 1966	Hungary........	Dec. 14, 1955		
Brazil.........	Oct. 24, 1945			Pakistan........	Sept. 30, 1947
Bulgaria........	Dec. 14, 1955	Iceland........	Nov. 19, 1946	Panama.........	Nov. 13, 1945
Burma..........	Apr. 19, 1948	India..........	Oct. 30, 1945	Paraguay.......	Oct. 24, 1945
Burundi........	Sept. 18, 1962	Indonesia......	Sept. 28, 1950	Peru...........	Oct. 31, 1945
Byelorussian SSR.	Oct. 24, 1945	Iran..........	Oct. 24, 1945	Philippines......	Oct. 24, 1945
		Iraq..........	Dec. 21, 1945	Poland..........	Oct. 24, 1945
Cambodia.....	Dec. 14, 1955	Ireland........	Dec. 14, 1955	Portugal........	Dec. 14, 1955
Cameroon.......	Sept. 20, 1960	Israel..........	May 11, 1949		
Canada........	Nov. 9, 1945	Italy..........	Dec. 14, 1955	Qatar.........	Sept. 21, 1971
Cape Verde.....	Sept. 16, 1975	Ivory Coast.....	Sept. 20, 1960		
Central African R.	Sept. 20, 1960			Romania........	Dec. 14, 1955
Chad..........	Sept. 20, 1960	Jamaica........	Sept. 18, 1962	Rwanda........	Sept. 18, 1962
Chile..........	Oct. 24, 1945	Japan..........	Dec. 18, 1956		
China⁴........	Oct. 24, 1945	Jordan........	Dec. 14, 1955	Sao Tome Principe	Sept. 16, 1975
Colombia.......	Nov. 5, 1945			Saudi Arabia....	Oct. 24, 1945
Congo.........	Sept. 20, 1960	Kenya.........	Dec. 16, 1963	Senegal........	Sept. 28, 1960
Costa Rica......	Nov. 2, 1945	Kuwait........	May 14, 1963	Sierra Leone	Sept. 27, 1961
Cuba..........	Oct. 24, 1945			Singapore......	Sept. 21, 1965
Cyprus........	Sept. 20, 1960	Laos..........	Dec. 14, 1955.	Somalia........	Sept. 20, 1960
Czechoslovakia..	Oct. 24, 1945	Lebanon........	Oct. 24, 1945	South Africa⁵....	Nov. 7, 1945
		Lesotho........	Oct. 17, 1966	Spain..........	Dec. 14, 1955
Dahomey.......	Sept. 20, 1960	Liberia.........	Nov. 2, 1945	Sri Lanka......	Dec. 14, 1955
Denmark.......	Oct. 24, 1945	Libya..........	Dec. 14, 1955	Sudan..........	Nov. 24, 1956
Dominican Rep...	Oct. 24, 1945	Luxembourg....	Oct. 24, 1945	Swaziland.......	Sept. 24, 1968
				Sweden........	Nov. 19, 1946
Ecuador........	Dec. 21, 1945	Malagasy Rep....	Sept. 20, 1960	Syria².........	Oct. 24, 1945
Egypt²²........	Oct. 24, 1945	Malawi........	Dec. 1, 1964		
El Salvador......	Oct. 24, 1945	Malaysia¹¹.......	Sept. 17, 1957	Thailand........	Dec. 16, 1946
Equatorial Guinea	Nov. 12, 1968	Maldives.......	Sept. 21, 1965	Togo..........	Sept. 20, 1960
Ethiopia........	Nov. 13, 1945	Mali..........	Sept. 28, 1960	Trinidad & Tob...	Sept. 18, 1962
		Malta..........	Dec. 1, 1964	Tunisia........	Nov. 12, 1956
Fiji..........	Oct. 13, 1970	Mauritania.....	Oct. 27, 1961	Turkey........	Oct. 24, 1945
Finland........	Dec. 14, 1955	Mauritius......	Apr. 24, 1968		
France.........	Oct. 24, 1945			Uganda........	Oct. 25, 1962

Member	Date	Member	Date	Member	Date
Ukrainian SSR . . .	Oct. 24, 1945	United States	Oct. 24, 1945	Yemen	Sept. 30, 1947
Union of Soviet		United Rep. of . . .		Yemen, South. . . .	Dec. 14, 1967
Soc. Repub's. . .	Oct. 24, 1945	Tanzania³.	Dec. 14, 1961	Yugoslavia.	Oct. 24, 1945
United Arab		Upper Volta	Sept. 20, 1960		
Emirates.	Dec. 9, 1971	Uruguay.	Dec. 18, 1945	Zaire	Sept. 20, 1960
United Kingdom .	Oct. 24, 1945	Venezuela.	Nov. 15, 1945	Zambia.	Dec. 1, 1964

(1.) The Federation of Malaya joined the UN on Sept. 17, 1957. On Sept. 16, 1963, changed its name to Malaysia following the admission to the new federation of Singapore. Sabah (North Borneo) and Sarawak. Singapore became an independent State Aug. 9, 1965 and a member of the UN Sept. 21.

(2.) Egypt and Syria were original members of the United Nations from Oct. 24, 1945. Following a plebiscite held on Feb. 21, 1958, the United Arab Republic was established by a union of Egypt and Syria and continued as a single Member of the United Nations. On Oct. 13 1961, Syria resumed its separate membership.

(3.) Tanganyika was a member of the United Nations from Dec. 14, 1961, and Zanzibar was a member from Dec. 16, 1963. Following the ratification on Apr. 26 1964, of Articles of Union between Tanganyika and Zanzibar, the United Republic of Tanganyika and Zanzibar continued as a single Member of the United Nations, later changing its name to United Republic of Tanzania.

(4.) The General Assembly voted Oct. 25 1971 to expel the Chinese National government of Taiwan and admit the Peking government in its place.

(5.) The General Assembly rejected the credentials of the South African government delegates Sept. 30, 1974, and suspended the country from the Assembly Nov. 12.

Operations of the United Nations Under Its Charter

The following article describes both the powers of the United Nations and its present organization. It is based on the provisions of the charter of the United Nations, and on an official report furnished by the Secretariat. The text of the Charter may be obtained from the Office of Public Information, United Nations, N. Y.

General Assembly

Pres. of 29th Session — Abdelaziz Bouteflika, Algeria.

The General Assembly is composed of representatives of all the member nations. Each nation may send not more than five representatives to each session. Each nation is entitled to one vote.

The General Assembly meets in regular annual sessions and in special session when necessary. Special sessions are convoked by the Secretary General at the request of the Security Council or of a majority of the members of the UN.

Any matter within the scope of the charter may be brought before the General Assembly, which may make recommendations on all except issues on the agenda of the Security Council. However, the General Assembly in November, 1950, decided that if the Security Council, because of lack of unanimity of the permanent members, fails to exercise its primary responsibility for the maintenance of international peace and security, in any case where there appears to be a threat to the peace, breach of the peace or act of aggression, the Assembly may consider it and recommend collective measures including, in the case of a breach of peace or act of aggression, the use of armed forces to maintain or restore peace. In such cases, the General Assembly may be convened within 24 hours in an emergency special session.

On important questions a two-thirds majority of members present and voting is required; on other questions a simple majority is sufficient. Questions that require a two-thirds majority include: recommendations on maintenance of international peace and security, election of non-permanent members of the Security Council, election of members of the Economic and Social Council, election of members of the UN that are to designate the members of the Trusteeship Council, admission of members to the UN, suspension and expulsion of members, trusteeship questions and budgetary matters.

The General Assembly must approve the budget and apportion expenses among members. A member in arrears will have no vote if the amount of arrears equals or exceeds the amount of the contributions due for the preceding two full years. The General Assembly may permit such a member to vote if it is satisfied that the failure is due to conditions beyond control.

A general or steering committee co-ordinates the proceedings of the Assembly and is composed of 26 members—the president of the Assembly, the 18 vice-presidents, and the chairmen of the seven main committees.

Security Council

The Security Council consists of 15 members, 5 with permanent seats. The remaining 10 are elected for 2-year terms by the General Assembly; they are not eligible for immediate re-election.

Non-permanent members in 1975 were Byelorussia, Cameroon, Costa Rica, Guyana, Iraq, Italy, Japan, Mauritania, Sweden, Tanzania.

Permanent members of the Council: China, France, USSR, United Kingdom, United States.

The Presidency of the Council is held monthly in turn by the member states in English alphabetical order.

The Security Council has the primary responsibility for maintaining international peace and security and members agree to carry out its decisions. The Council may investigate any dispute that threatens international peace and security. When the Security Council is handling a dispute or situation the General Assembly makes no recommendation unless the Council requests it.

The Security Council functions continuously, each member being represented at all times. It may change its place of meeting. Any member of UN at UN headquarters may participate in its discussions and a nation not a member of UN may appear if it is a party to a dispute.

Decisions on procedural questions are made by an affirmative vote of 9 members. On all other matters the affirmative vote of 9 members must include the concurring votes of all permanent members; it is this clause which gives rise to the so-called "veto." A party to a dispute must refrain from voting.

The Security Council may decide to enforce its decisions without the use of arms. Such measures include interruption of economic relations, break in transportation and communications, and severance of diplomatic relations. If such measures fail the Council may call on UN members to furnish armed forces, assistance and facilities, based on agreements made by the Council with the states and subject to ratification by the members of the UN "in accordance with their constitutional processes."

The right of individual or collective self-defense is not prohibited by membership in the UN, and if a member nation is attacked it may do what is necessary, reporting this to the Security Council, which may take independent action. However, the Council encourages regional arrangements or agencies by means of which local disputes can be settled without getting as far as the Council, after the Council has approved this method.

In the event of a conflict between the obligations of members to the UN and to other international bodies of which they may be members, then obligations to the UN are paramount.

Economic and Social Council

The Economic and Social Council consists of 54 members elected by the General Assembly for 3-year terms of office. The council is responsible under the General Assembly for carrying out the functions of the United Nations with regard to international economic, social, cultural, educational, health and related matters. The council meets usually twice a year.

The Economic and Social Council had the following commissions in 1974:

Functional Commissions

Statistical; Population; Social Development; Narcotic Drugs; Human Rights (and its Sub-Commission on the Prevention of Discrimination and the Protection of Minorities); Status of Women.

Regional Economic Commissions

Economic Commission for Europe.
Economic Commission for Asia and the Far East.
Economic Commission for Latin America.
Economic Commission for Africa.
Economic Commission for Western Asia.

Trusteeship Council

The administration of Trust territories is subject to the supervision of the United Nations. Administering authorities are required to render an account of their stewardship to the Trusteeship Council. The Council may entertain petitions from private persons or organizations regarding conditions in the Trust territories and may dispatch missions to study conditions there.

The membership of the Council is made up of (1) countries which administer trust territories (Australia and the United States); (2) countries which are permanent members of the Security Council but which do not administer trust territories (China, France, the United Kingdom, USSR); and (3) as many other countries as may be necessary to ensure equal representation in the Council between administering and non-administering members. Those in the last named category are elected by the General Assembly for 3-year terms and are eligible for immediate reelection.

With the scheduled 1975 independence of Papua New Guinea, part of which had been an Australian trust territory, the only remaining trust territory was the Pacific Islands, administered by the U.S.

Non-Self-Governing Territories

Members of the United Nations responsible for the administration of non-self-governing territories not under trusteeships recognize the principle that the interests of the inhabitants are paramount and promote their welfare. They are bound by the charter to transmit to the Secretary-General technical information concerning economic, social and educational conditions in the territories. This information is summarized, analyzed and classified by the Secretariat. Since 1961 a Special Committee on Colonial Countries has been studying the implementation of the 1960 General Assembly declaration on the granting of independence to colonial countries and peoples. This committee also receives the reports on non self-governing territories.

International Court of Justice

The International Court of Justice is the principal judicial organ of the United Nations. All members are *ipso facto* parties to the statute of the Court. Other states may become parties to the Court's statute on conditions determined in each case by the General Assembly on the recommendation of the Security Council.

The jurisdiction of the Court comprises cases which the parties submit to it and matters especially provided for in the charter or in treaties. The Court gives advisory opinions and renders judgments. Its decisions, which are final, are only binding between the parties concerned and in respect to a particular dispute. If any party to a case fails to heed a judgment of the Court, the other party may have recourse to the Security Council, which may decide what is to be done.

The Court consists of 15 judges elected for 9-year terms by the General Assembly and the Security Council voting independently. No two of the judges may be nationals of the same state. Retiring judges are eligible for re-election. The Court remains permanently in session, except during the judicial vacations. A quorum of 9 judges suffices to constitute the Court. All questions are decided by majority. In the event of a tie, the President of the Court or the judge who acts in his place casts the deciding vote.

Judges

Nine year term in office ending 1982:
Isaac Forster, Senegal.
Andre Gros, France.
Jose Maria Ruda, Argentina.
Nagendra Singh, India.
Sir Humphrey Waldock, Britain.

Nine year term in office ending 1979:
Hardy C. Dillard, U.S.
Louis Ignacio-Pinto, Dahomey,
Federico de Castro, Spain.
Platon D. Morozov, USSR.
Eduardo Jimenez de Arechaga, Uruguay.

Nine-year term of office ending 1976:
Sture Petran, Sweden
Cesar Bengzon, Philippines
Fouad Ammoun, Lebanon
Manfred Lachs, Poland
Charles D. Onyeama, Nigeria

The president until 1976 is Manfred Lachs, Poland, and the vice president is Fouad Ammoun, Lebanon.

Agencies Related to the United Nations

Working in partnership with the United Nations in various economic, social, scientific and technical fields is a group of intergovernmental organizations related to the United Nations by special agreements. Among these agencies (with their headquarters) are:

International Atomic Energy Agency (IAEA) aims to promote the peaceful uses of atomic energy. (Vienna)

International Labor Org. (ILO) aims to promote social justice; improve labor conditions and living standards; and promote economic stability. (Geneva)

Food & Agriculture Org. (FAO) aims to increase

production from farms, forests and fisheries; improve distribution, marketing and nutrition. (Rome)

United Nations Educational, Scientific & Cultural Org. (UNESCO) aims to promote collaboration among nations through education, science and culture. (Paris)

World Health Org. (WHO) aims to aid the attainment of the highest possible level of health. (Geneva)

International Bank for Reconstruction & Development (World Bank) aims to help in the economic development of members by facilitating investment of capital; promote foreign investment and supplement private investment by providing loans for productive purposes out of its capital funds raised by it and its other resources; and to promote growth of international trade and equilibrium in balance of payments. (Washington, D. C.)

International Development Assn. (IDA) aims to further economic development of members by financing on terms bearing less heavily on balance of payments than those of conventional loans. (Washington, D. C.)

International Finance Corp. (IFC) aims to further economic development in member countries by encouraging private enterprise, particularly in less developed areas. It is empowered to invest in private enterprises in association with private investors, and without government guarantee of repayment in cases where sufficient private capital is not available on reasonable terms; and to bring together private capital and management. (Washington, D. C.)

International Monetary Fund (IMF) aims to promote international monetary co-operation and currency stabilization. Sells currency to help members meet temporary foreign payments difficulties. (Washington, D. C.)

International Civil Aviation Org. (ICAO) promotes international civil aviation standards and regulations. (Montreal)

Universal Postal Union (UPU) aims to perfect postal services and promote international collaboration. To this end, members agree to handle other members mail by the best means used for its own mail. (Berne)

International Telecommunication Union (ITU) sets up international regulations of radio, telegraph, telephone and space radio-communications. Allocates radio frequencies. (Geneva)

World Meteorological Org. (WMO) aims to co-ordinate, standardize and improve world meteorological work and weather data exchange. (Geneva)

Intergovernmental Maritime Consultative Org. (IMCO) aims to promote co-operation on technical matters affecting international shipping. (London)

General Agreement on Tariffs and Trade (GATT) was drafted in 1946. It establishes and administers code for orderly conduct of international trade. Aids export promotion in developing countries. (Geneva)

United Nation's Children's Fund (UNICEF) helps requesting countries meet the urgent needs of their children. Supported entirely by voluntary contributions from governments and individuals. (New York)

United Nations Industrial Development Organization (UNIDO). Acts as a conduit for development funds and promotes industrialization.

Secretariat

The Secretariat is composed of a Secretary General appointed by the General Assembly upon the recommendation of the Security Council and such staff as the organization may require.

The Secretary General is the chief administrative officer of the UN. He may bring to the attention of the Security Council any matter that threatens international peace. He reports to the General Assembly.

Kurt Waldheim (Austria), Secretary General, was chosen to succeed U Thant by the UN Security Council and General Assembly for a 5-year term begining Jan. 1, 1972.

United Nations Budget

The General Assembly voted a gross budget of $540,473,000 for 1974-75. It also approved estimates of income totalling $92,646,000 for 1974-75 bringing the net budget for 1974-75 to $447,827,000.

Sources of Information

Public Inquiries Unit, Office of Public Information, United Nations, N. Y. Provides pamphlets, study guides, speakers, films; arranges group visits, provides information on UN activities: (212) 754-1234.

UN Publications: UN Bookshop, United Nations, N.Y.

United Nations Assn. of the United States of America Inc., 345 E. 46th St., New York, N.Y.

Major International Organizations

(See also United Nations)

COMMONWEALTH OF NATIONS, originally called the British Commonwealth of Nations, is an association of nations and dependencies loosely joined by a common interest based on having been parts of the old British Empire. The British monarch is the symbolic head of the Commonwealth.

There are 33 self-governing independent nations which are full members of the Commonwealth, plus various colonies and protectorates. As of August, 1975, the members were the United Kingdom of Great Britain and Northern Ireland and ten other nations recognizing the British monarch, represented by a governor-general, as their head of state: Australia, Bahamas, Barbados, Canada, Fiji, Grenada, Jamaica, Mauritius, New Zealand, Trinidad and Tobago; and 22 countries with their own heads of state: Bangladesh, Botswana, Cyprus, Gambia, Ghana, Guyana, India, Kenya, Lesotho, Malawi, Malaysia, Malta, Nigeria, Sierra Leone, Singapore, Sri Lanka (Ceylon), Swaziland, Tanzania, Tonga, Uganda, Western Samoa, Zambia. In addition, Nauru and various Caribbean islands take part in certain Commonwealth activities.

The Commonwealth facilitates consultation among member states through meetings of prime ministers and finance ministers, and through a permanent

Secretariat established in 1949. Members consult on economic, scientific, educational, financial, legal, and military matters, and try to coordinate policies. Population (est. 1975) was close to 900 million in the member nations; total area was over ten million sq. mi.

EUROPEAN COMMUNITIES (EC) is the collective designation of three organizations with common membership: the European Economic Community (Common Market), the European Coal and Steel Community, and the European Atomic Energy Community. The nine full members are: Belgium, Denmark, France, West Germany, Ireland, Italy, Luxembourg, Netherlands, United Kingdom. The Common Market also includes as associate members Greece, Turkey, Cyprus, Malta and 24 African countries, and has trade agreements with other countries.

A coordinated structure for the communities went into effect July 1, 1967, though the component organizations date back to 1951 and 1957. A Council of Ministers, an expert Commission, a European Parliament and a Court of Justice comprise the permanent structure. The communities aim to integrate their economies, coordinate social developments, and ultimately, bring about political union of the democratic states of Europe.

EUROPEAN FREE TRADE ASSOCIATION (EFTA), consisting in 1975 of Austria, Iceland, Norway, Portugal, Sweden, Switzerland and associate member Finland, was created by treaty Jan. 4, 1960, effective May 3, to gradually reduce customs duties and quantitative restrictions between members on industrial products. By Dec. 31, 1966, tariffs and restrictions had been eliminated. The United Kingdom and Denmark withdrew to become members of EEC Jan. 1, 1973, Other EFTA members joined in an industrial tariff elimination pact with EEC in 1972.

NORTH ATLANTIC TREATY ORG. (NATO) was created April 4, 1949, in a treaty signed in Washington, effective Aug. 24, by Belgium, Canada, Denmark, France, Iceland, Italy, Luxembourg, the Netherlands, Norway, Portugal, the United Kingdom, and the U.S. Greece, Turkey, and West Germany have joined since. The members agreed to settle disputes by peaceful means; to develop their individual and collective capacity to resist armed attack; to regard an attack on one as an attack on all, and to take necessary action to repel an attack under Article 51 of the United Nations Charter.

Parallel military and civilian institutions comprise NATO's permanent structure. The civilian side includes the North Atlantic Council, a Defense Planning Committee, an international Secretariat, and specialized committees. A Military Committee includes professional military representatives from all member nations except France and Iceland. North Atlantic Council meetings may consist of heads of government, cabinet ministers, or permanent NATO representatives, who hold ambassadorial rank. The Military Committee may include Chiefs of Staff of the member nations.

Armed forces of NATO members include forces assigned to NATO commands, forces earmarked for NATO commands, and forces under national command. The NATO military command has five branches: Allied Command Europe, Allied Command Atlantic, Allied Command Channel, Canada-U.S. Regional Planning Group, and Allied Air Force, Central Europe.

Following announcement in 1966 of nearly total French withdrawal from the military affairs of NATO, the organization moved its headquarters in 1967 from Paris to Brussels. In August, 1974, Greece announced a total withdrawal of armed forces from NATO, in response to Turkish intervention in Cyprus.

ORGANIZATION OF AFRICAN UNITY (OAU), formed May 25, 1963 by 30 African countries (42 in 1975) to coordinate cultural, political, scientific and economic policies; to end colonialism in Africa; to promote a common defense of members' independence. It holds annual conferences of heads of government, has a council of foreign ministers meeting at least twice a year, a secretary-general and a mediation-arbitration commission. Hq. is in Addis Ababa, Ethiopia.

ORGANIZATION OF AMERICAN STATES (OAS) was formed in Bogota, Colombia, in 1948. Hq. are in Washington, D.C. It has a Permanent Council, Inter-American Economic and Social Council, and Inter-American Council for Education, Science and Culture. The Permanent Council can call meetings of foreign ministers, to deal with urgent security matters. A General Assembly meets annually. A Secretary General and Assistant are elected for 5-year terms. There are 25 members, each with one vote in the various organizations: Argentina, Barbados, Bolivia, Brazil, Chile, Colombia, Costa Rica, Cuba, Dominican Republic, Ecuador, El Salvador, Grenada, Guatemala, Haiti, Honduras, Jamaica, Mexico, Nicaragua, Panama, Paraguay, Peru, Trinidad-Tobago, U.S., Uruguay, Venezuela. In 1962, the OAS excluded Cuba from OAS activities but not from membership.

ORGANIZATION FOR ECONOMIC COOPERATION AND DEVELOPMENT (OECD) was established in 1960 to promote stable economic growth in member countries and the world at large, and to help expand free trade. Nearly all the industrialized "free market" countries belong, with Yugoslavia as an associate member. OECD is active in collecting and disseminating economic and environmental information, and in channeling resources to developing countries. Members in 1975 were: Australia, Austria, Belgium, Canada, Denmark, Finland, France, West Germany, Greece, Iceland, Ireland, Italy, Japan, Luxembourg, Netherlands, New Zealand, Norway, Portugal, Spain, Sweden, Switzerland, Turkey, United Kingdom, United States.

ORGANIZATION OF PETROLEUM EXPORTING COUNTRIES (OPEC) was created in 1960 at Venezuelan initiative. The group has successfully maintained high oil prices, and has tried to advance members' interests in trade and development dealings with industrialized oil-consuming nations. Members in 1975 were Algeria, Ecuador, Gabon, Indonesia, Iran, Iraq, Kuwait, Libya, Nigeria, Qatar, Saudi Arabia, United Arab Emirates, Venezuela.

LEAGUE OF ARAB STATES (THE ARAB LEAGUE) was created March 22, 1945, by Egypt, Iraq, Jordan, Lebanon, Saudi Arabia, Syria and Yemen. Joining later were Algeria, Bahrain, Kuwait, Libya, Mauritania, Morocco, Oman, Qatar, Somalia, Southern Yemen, Sudan, Tunisia and United Arab Emirates. Cairo is headquarters for the Secretary-General. The League mediates disputes between Arab states, represents Arab states in certain international negotiations, and coordinates the military, economic, and diplomatic offensive against Israel. The League fosters cultural and communications ties among the Arab states.

WARSAW TREATY ORGANIZATION (WARSAW PACT) was created May 14, 1955, as a mutual defense alliance by Albania, Bulgaria, Czechoslovakia, East Germany, Hungary, Poland, Romania and the USSR. It provides for a unified military command with headquarters in Moscow; if one member is attacked, the others will aid it with all necessary steps including armed force; joint maneuvers are held; there is a Political Consultative Committee and economic cooperation is advanced. Albania was barred from meetings in 1962, withdrew in 1968.

Heads of States and Prime Ministers

Data to July, 1975

Country	Head of State, Title	Born	Acceded or Elected	Premier or Prime Minister
Afghanistan	Mohammed Daud, pres.		July 19, 1973	Mohammed Daud
Albania	Maj.-Gen. Haxhi Lleshi, pres.	1913	July 1953	Maj. Gen. Mehmet Shehu
Algeria	Houari Boumediene, pres.	1925	June 19, 1965	
Andorra	Pres. of France & Spanish bishop of Urgel.			
Argentina	Maria Estela M. de Peron, pres.	Feb. 6, 1931	July 1, 1974	
Australia (C)	Sir John R. Kerr, gov.-gen.(*).	Sept. 24, 1914	July 11, 1974	Edward Gough Whitlam
Austria	Rudolf Kirchschlaeger, pres.	Mar. 20, 1915	June 23, 1974	Dr. Bruno Kreisky
Bahamas (C)	Milo B. Butler, gov.-gen.(*).	Aug. 11, 1906	Aug. 1, 1973	Lynden O. Pindling

Continued

Country	Head of State	Born	In office	Other
Bahrain	Isa bin Sulman al-Khalifa, sheik	July 3, 1933	Dec. 16,1961	Khalifa bin Sulman al-Khalifa
Bangladesh(C)	Khondakar Mushtaque Ahmed		Aug. 15, 1975	
Barbados(C)	Sir A.W. Scott, gov.-gen.(*)	Mar. 17, 1900	May 18, 1967	Errol W. Barrow
Belgium	Baudouin I, king	Sept. 7, 1930	July 17, 1951	Leo Tindemans
Bhutan	Jigme Singye Wangchuk, king	Nov. 11, 1955	July 24, 1972	
Bolivia	Gen. Hugo Banzer Suarez, pres	May 10, 1926	Aug. 21, 1971	
Botswana(C)	Sir Seretse Khama, pres	July 1, 1921	Sept. 10, 1966	
Brazil	Gen. Ernesto Geisel, pres	Aug. 3, 1907	Jan. 15, 1974	
Bulgaria	Todor Zhivkov, pres	Sept. 7, 1911	July 7, 1971	Stanko Todorov
Burma	Ne Win	1911	Mar. 2, 1962	Sein Win
Burundi	Michel Micombero, pres	1939	Nov. 28, 1966	
Cambodia (Khmer Rep.)	Norodom Sihanouk, prince	Oct. 31, 1932	April 25, 1975	Penn Nouth
Cameroon	Ahmadou Ahidjo, pres	Aug. 24, 1924	Jan. 1, 1960	
Canada(C)	Jules Leger, gov.-gen.(*)	Apr. 4, 1913	Jan. 14, 1974	Pierre E. Trudeau
Cape Verde	Aristedes Pereira, pres		July 5, 1975	Pedro Pires
Central African Rep.	Gen. Jean-Bedel Bokassa, pres	Feb. 22, 1920	Jan. 1, 1966	Elisabeth Donitien
Chad Rep.	Felix Malloum	Sept. 10, 1932	April 16, 1975	
Chile	Augusto Pinochet Ugarte, pres.	Nov. 25, 1915	June 27, 1974	
China, People's Republic				Chou En-lai
China (Taiwan)	Yen Chia-kan		Apr. 6, 1975	Chiang Ching-kuo
Colombia	Alfonso Lopez Michelsen, pres	June 30, 1913	Aug. 7, 1974	
Comoro Is.	Ali Soilih		Aug. 3, 1975	
Congo, People's Rep.	Maj. Marien Ngouabi, pres	1937	Jan. 1, 1969	Henri Lopes
Costa Rica	Daniel Oduber Quiros, pres	Aug. 25, 1921	May 8, 1974	
Cuba	Osvaldo Dorticos Torrado, pres	1919	July 17, 1959	Fidel Castro
Cyprus(C)	Archbishop Makarios	Aug. 13, 1913	Dec. 14, 1959	
Czechoslovakia	Gustav Husek	1913	May 29, 1975	Lubomir Strougal
Dahomey Rep.	Maj. Mathieu Kerekou, pres	1933	Oct. 28, 1972	
Denmark	Margrethe II, queen	Apr. 16, 1940	Jan. 14, 1972	Anker Joergensen
Dominican Rep.	Dr. Joaquin Balaguer, pres	1908	July 1, 1966	
Ecuador	Guillermo Rodriguez Lara, pres	Nov. 4, 1923	Feb. 15, 1972	
Egypt	Anwar Sadat, pres	Dec. 25, 1918	Oct. 17, 1970	Mamdouh Salem
El Salvador	Arturo Armando Molina, pres	Aug. 6, 1927	July 1, 1972	
Equatorial Guinea	Francisco Macias Nguema, pres	Jan. 1, 1924	Oct. 12, 1968	
Ethiopia	Tafari Banti, chmn., Mil. Cncl.		Nov. 28, 1974	
Fiji(C)	Sir George Cakobau, gov.-gen.(*)	Nov. 6, 1912	Jan. 13, 1973	Sir Kamisese Mara
Finland	Dr. Urho Kekkonen, pres	Sept. 3, 1900	Feb. 15, 1956	Kalevi Sorsa
France	Giscard d'Estaing, pres	Feb. 2, 1926	May 27, 1974	Jacques Chirac
Gabon Rep.	Omar Bongo, pres	Dec. 30, 1935	Dec. 1, 1967	
Gambia(C)	Sir Dawda Kairaba Jawara, pres	May 16, 1924	Apr. 24, 1970	
Germany, Fed. Rep.	Walter Scheel, pres	July 8, 1919	May 15, 1974	Helmut Schmidt
Germany, East	Willi Stoph, chmn. council of state	July 9, 1914	Aug. 1973	Horst Sindermann
Ghana(C)	Col. Ignatius K. Acheampong	Sept. 23, 1931	Jan. 13, 1972	
Greece	Michael Stassinopoulos	1903	Dec. 18, 1974	Constantine Caramanlis
Grenada(C)	Leo deGale, gov.-gen.(*)		Feb. 7, 1975	Eric Matthew Gairy
Guatemala	Gen. Kjell Laugerud-Garcia, pres	Jan. 24, 1930	July 1, 1974	
Guinea	Sekou Toure, pres	Jan. 19, 1922	Oct. 2, 1958	Lansana Beavogui
Guinea-Bissau	Luis Cabral, pres	1931	Sept. 24, 1973	
Guyana(C)	Arthur Chung, pres	Jan. 10, 1918	Feb. 23, 1970	Linden Forbes Burnham
Haiti	Jean-Claude Duvalier, pres	July 3, 1951	Apr. 21, 1971	
Honduras	Col. Juan Alberto Melgar Castro		Apr. 22, 1975	
Hungary	Pal Losonczi, pres	1919	Apr. 14, 1967	Gyorgy Lazar
Iceland	Kristjan Eldjarn, pres	Dec. 16, 1916	Aug. 1, 1968	Geir Hallgrimsson
India(C)	Fakhruddin Ali Ahmed, pres	May 13, 1905	Aug. 24, 1974	Indira Nehru Gandhi
Indonesia	Suharto, pres	June 8, 1921	Mar. 11, 1967	
Iran	Mohammed Reza Pahlavi, shah	Oct. 26, 1919	Sept. 18, 1941	Amir Abbas Hoveyda
Iraq	Ahmed Hassan al-Bakr, pres	1912	July 17, 1968	
Ireland	Cearbhall O Dalaigh	1910	Dec. 19, 1974	Liam Cosgrave
Israel	Ephraim Katzir, pres	May 16, 1916	Apr. 10, 1973	Yitzhak Rabin
Italy	Giovanni Leone, pres	Nov. 3, 1908	Dec. 24, 1971	Aldo Moro
Ivory Coast	Felix Houphouet-Boigny, pres	Oct. 18, 1905	Nov. 27, 1960	
Jamaica(C)	Florizel A. Glasspole, gov.-gen.(*)	Sept. 25, 1909	June 27, 1973	Michael Manley
Japan	Hirohito, emperor	Apr. 29, 1901	Dec. 25, 1926	Takeo Miki
Jordan	Hussein I, king	Nov. 14, 1935	May 2, 1952	Zaid al-Rifai
Kenya(C)	Jomo Kenyatta, pres	1890	Dec. 12, 1964	
Korea, Republic	Park Chung Hee, pres	Sept. 30, 1917	Nov. 26, 1963	Kim Jong Pil
Korea, People's Dem Rep.	Kim Il-sung, pres	1912		Kim Il-Sung
Kuwait	Sabah al-Salim al-Sabah, emir	1915	Nov. 24, 1965	Jaber al-Ahmed al-Jaber
Laos	Sri Savang Vatthana, king	Nov. 13, 1907	Oct. 30, 1959	Souvanna Phouma
Lebanon	Suleiman Franjieh, pres	June 14, 1910	Sept. 23, 1970	Rashid Karami
Lesotho(C)	Motlotlehi Moshoeshoe II, king	1898	Oct. 4, 1969	Chief Leabua Jonathan
Liberia	William R. Tolbert, Jr. pres	May 13, 1913	July 23, 1971	
Libya	Muammar el-Qaddafi, chmn., revolutionary cncl.	1942	Sept.1, 1969	Abdel Salam Jalloud
Liechtenstein	Franz Joseph II, prince	Aug. 16, 1906	July 26, 1938	Dr. Walter Keiber
Luxembourg	Jean, grand duke	Jan. 5, 1921	Nov. 12, 1964	Gaston Thorn
Madagascar	Didier Ratsiraka, pres		Feb. 12, 1975	
Malawi(C)	Dr. H. Kamuzu Banda, pres	1902	July 6, 1966	
Malaysia (C)	Abdul Halim Muadzam, king	Nov. 28, 1927	Sept. 21, 1970	Abdul Razak
Maldives, Rep. of	Amir Ibrahim Nasir, pres	Sept. 2, 1926	Nov. 11, 1968	
Mali	Moussa Traore, pres	Sept. 25, 1936	Nov. 19, 1968	

Continued

Nation	Head of State	Born	Date	Other
Malta (C)	Sir Anthony Mamo, pres.	Jan. 9, 1909	Dec. 13, 1974	Dom Mintoff
Mauritania	Moktar O. Daddah, pres.	Apr. 25, 1924	Nov., 1958	Moktar O. Daddah
Mauritius (C)	Sir Raman Osman gov.-gen.(*)	Aug., 1902	Dec. 27, 1972	Sir Seewoosagur Ramgoolan
Mexico	Luis Echeverria Alvarez	Jan. 17, 1922	July 5, 1970	
Monaco	! Rainier III, prince	May 31, 1923	May 9, 1949	
Mongolia	Y. Tsendenbal, presidium chmn.	Sept. 17, 1916	June 11, 1974	Jambyn Batmunkh
Morocco	Hassan II, king	July 11, 1929	Mar. 3, 1961	Ahmed Osman
Mozambique	Samora Machel, pres.	1934	June 25, 1975	
Nauru (C)	Hammer DeRoburt, pres.	Sept. 25, 1922	Jan. 31, 1968	
Nepal	Birendra Bir Bikram, king.	Dec. 28, 1945	Jan. 31, 1972	Nagendra Prashah Rijal
Netherlands	Juliana, queen	Apr. 30, 1909	Sept. 6, 1948	Joop M. den Uyl
New Zealand (C)	Sir Denis Blundell, gov.-gen.(*)	May 29, 1907	Sept. 27, 1972	Wallace E. Rowling
Nicaragua	Gen. Anastasio Somoza Debalye, pres.		Dec. 1, 1974	
Niger	Seyni Kountche, chief of state		Apr. 17, 1974	
Nigeria (C)	Gen. Muritala Rufei Mohammed		Aug. 5, 1975	
Norway	Olav V, king	July 2, 1903	Sept. 21, 1957	Trygve M. Bratelli
Oman	Qabus bin Said, sultan	Nov. 18, 1940	July 23, 1970	
Pakistan	Chaudhri Fazal Elahi, pres.	1904	Aug. 14, 1973	Zulfikar Ali Bhutto
Panama	Demetrio B. Lakas, pres.	Aug. 29, 1925	Mar., 1972	Gen. Omar Torrijos Herrera
Papua New Guinea (C)				Michael Somare
Paraguay	Gen. Alfredo Stroessner, pres.	Nov. 3, 1912	Aug. 15, 1954	
Peru	Gen. Juan Velasco Alvarado, pres.	1910	Oct. 3, 1968	Gen. Francisco Morales Bermudez
Philippines	Ferdinand Marcos, pres.	Sept. 11, 1917	Dec. 30, 1965	Ferdinand Marcos
Poland	Henryk Jablonski, chmn. council of state		Mar. 28, 1972	Piotr Jaroszewicz
Portugal	Francisco da Costa Gomez, pres.	June 30, 1914	Nov. 30, 1974	Vasco dos Santos Goncalves
Qatar	Khalifa bin Hamad Al-Thani.	Feb., 1929	Feb. 22, 1972	Khalifa bin Haman Al-Thani
Rhodesia	Clifford W. Dupont, pres.	Dec. 6, 1905	Mar. 2, 1970	Ian Smith
Romania	Nicolae Ceausescu, state council pres.	Jan. 26, 1918	Dec. 7, 1967	Manea Manescu
Rwanda	Maj. Gen. Habyalimana Juvenal, pres.		July 5, 1973	
San Marino	Co-regents			
Sao Tome & Principe	Manuel Pinto da Costa, pres.		July 12, 1975	
Saudi Arabia	Khalid Bin Abdul Aziz, king	1913	Mar. 25, 1975	Khalid Bin Abdul Aziz
Senegal Rep.	Leopold S. Senghor, pres.	Oct. 9, 1906	Sept., 1960	Abdou Diouf
Sierra Leone (C)	Siaka Stevens, pres.	1906	Apr. 28, 1971	S. Ibrahim Koroma
Singapore (C)	Benjamin H. Sheares, pres.	Aug. 12, 1907	Jan. 2, 1971	Lee Kuan Yew
Somali, Dem. Rep.	Mohamed Siad Barre, council pres.	1912	Oct. 15, 1969	
South Africa	Nicolaas Diederichs	Nov. 11, 1903	Apr. 19, 1975	B. John Vorster
Spain	Gen. Francisco Franco Bahamonde, chief of state	Dec. 4, 1892	Aug. 9, 1939	Carlos Arias Navarro
Sri Lanka (Ceylon) (C)	William Gopallawa, pres.	Sept. 16, 1897	May 22, 1972	Mrs. Sirimavo Bandaranaike
Sudan	Gaafar al-Nimeiry, pres.	1929	May 25, 1969	
Swaziland (C)	Sobhuza II, king	July 22, 1899	Apr. 25, 1967	Prince Makhosini Damini
Sweden	Carl XVI Gustaf, king	Apr. 30, 1946	Sept. 15, 1973	Olof Palme
Switzerland (1)	Pierre Graber, pres.	Mar. 10, 1914	Jan. 1, 1975	Rudolf Gnagi, vice pres.
Syria	Hafez al-Assad, chief of state	Mar., 1930	Mar. 14, 1971	Mahmoud Al-Ayoubi
Tanzania (C)	Julius K. Nyerere, pres.	1922	Apr. 26, 1964	Rashid M. Kawawa
Thailand	Bhumibol Adulyadej, king	Dec. 5, 1927	June 9, 1946	Kukrit Pramoj
Togo	Gen. Gnassingbe Eyadema, pres.	1932	Jan. 13, 1967	
Tonga	Taufa'ahau Tupou IV, king	July 4, 1918	July 5, 1967	Prince Tu'Pelehake
Trinidad-Tobago (C)	Sir Ellis E. I. Clarke, gov.-gen.(*)	Dec. 28, 1917	Feb., 1973	Eric E. Williams
Tunisia	Habib Bourguiba, pres.	Aug. 3, 1903	July 25, 1957	Hedi Nouira
Turkey	Fahri Koruturk, pres.	1903	Apr. 6, 1973	Suleyman Demirel
Uganda (C)	Field Marshall Idi Amin, pres.	1925	Jan. 25, 1971	
USSR	Nikolai V. Podgorny, presidium pres.	Feb. 18, 1903	Dec. 9, 1965	Aleksei N. Kosygin
United Arab Emirates	Zayed bin Sultan al-Nahayan, pres.	1923	Dec. 2, 1972	
United Kingdom (C)	Elizabeth II, queen	Apr. 21, 1926	Feb. 6, 1952	Harold Wilson
United States	Gerald R. Ford, pres.	July 14, 1913	Aug. 9, 1974	
Upper Volta	Gen. Sangoule Lamizana, pres.	1921	Jan. 3, 1966	
Uruguay	Juan M. Bordaberry, pres.	1928	Mar. 1, 1972	
Vatican City	Giovanni Battista Montini, Pope Paul VI.	Sept. 26, 1897	June 21, 1963	
Venezuela	Carlos Andres Perez, pres.	Oct. 27, 1922	Mar. 12, 1974	
Vietnam, Dem. Republic of	Ton Duc Thang	1888	Sept. 23, 1969	Pham Van Dong
Vietnam, South				
Western Samoa (C)	Malietoa Tanumafili II, king	Jan. 4, 1913	Jan. 1, 1962	
Yemen, People's Dem. Rep. of	Salem Robaye Ali, council pres.	1934	June 23, 1969	Ali Nasser Hassani
Yemen Arab Rep.	Lt. Col. Ibrahim Al-Hamdy, pres.	1944	June 13, 1974	Abdulaziz Abdul Ghani
Yugoslavia	Josip Broz Tito, pres.	May 25, 1892	Jan. 31, 1946	Dzemal Bijedic
Zaire	Mobutu Sese Seko, pres.	Oct. 14, 1930	Nov. 24, 1965	
Zambia (C)	Kenneth Kaunda, pres.	Apr. 28, 1924	Oct. 24, 1964	M. Mainza Chona

(1) President serves one-year term, the vice president customarily succeeds him.
(C) Member of the Commonwealth of Nations.
(*) gov.-gen. acts as representative of the British monarch, who is recognized as head of state.

Ambassadors and Envoys

As of mid-1975
The address of foreign embassies to the United States is Washington, D.C.

Countries	Envoys from United States	Envoys to United States
Afghanistan	Theodore L. Eliot Jr., Amb.	Abdullah Malikyar, Amb.
Algeria	Richard B. Parker,Amb.	Abdelkader Maadini, Charge
Argentina	Robert C. Hill, Amb.	Alejandro Orfila, Amb.
Australia	Vacant.	Sir Patrick Shaw, Amb.
Austria	Wiley T. Buchanan, Amb.	Arno Halusa, Amb.
Bahamas	Seymour Weiss, Amb.	Livingston B. Johnson, Amb.
Bahrain	Joseph W. Twinam, Amb.	
Bangladesh	Davis E. Boster, Amb.	M. Hossain Ali, Amb.
Barbados	Theodore R. Britton, Amb.	Cecil B. Williams. Amb.
Belgium	Leonard K. Firestone, Amb.	Willy Van Cauwenberg, Amb.
Bolivia	William P. Stedman Jr., Amb.	Roberto Capriles, Amb.
Botswana	David B. Bolen, Amb.	Amos M. Dambe, Amb.
Brazil	John Hugh Crimmins, Amb.	Joao Augusto de Araujo Castro, Amb.
Bulgaria	Martin F. Herz, Amb.	Lubomir D. Popov, Amb.
Burma	David L. Osborn, Amb.	U Lwin, Amb.
Burundi	David E. Mark, Amb.	Joseph Ndabaniwe, Amb.
Cambodia (Khmer)[1]		Francois-Xavier Tchoungui, Amb.
Cameroon	C. Robert Moore, Amb.	Marcel Cadieux, Amb.
Canada	William J. Porter, Amb.	David Nguindo, Charge
Centr. African Rep.	William N. Dale, Amb.	Bawoyeu Alingue, Amb.
Chad	Edward S. Little, Amb.	Manuel Trucca, Amb.
Chile	David H. Popper, Amb.	James C. H. Shen, Amb.
China (Taiwan)	Leonard Unger, Amb.	Huang Chen
China, People's Rep.[2]	George H. Bush	Julio Cesar Turbay-Ayala, Amb.
Colombia	Viron P. Vaky, Amb.	
Congo (Brazzaville)[3]		
Costa Rica	Terence A. Todman, Amb.	Rodolfo Silva Vargas, Amb.
Cuba[4]		Nicos G. Dimitriou, Amb.
Cyprus	William R. Crawford Jr. Amb.	Vincent Buzek, Charge
Czechoslovakia	Albert W. Sherer Jr., Amb.	Tiamiou Adjibade, Amb.
Dahomey	James B. Engle, Amb.	Eyvind Bartels, Amb.
Denmark	Philip K. Crowe, Amb.	Horacio Vicioso-Soto, Amb.
Dominican Republic	Robert A. Hurwitch, Amb.	Jose C. Cardenas, Amb.
Ecuador	Robert C. Brewster, Amb.	Ashraf A. Ghorbal, Amb.
Egypt	Hermann F. Eilts, Amb.	Francisco Bertrand Galindo, Amb.
El Salvador	James F. Campbell, Amb.	Vacant
Equatorial Guinea	C. Robert Moore, Amb.	Ernst Jaakson, Consul General
Estonia[5]		Ghebeyehou Mekbib, Charge
Ethiopia	Arthur W. Hummel Jr., Amb.	S. K. Sikivou, Amb.
Fiji	Armistead I. Selden Jr., Amb.	Leo Tuominen, Amb.
Finland	Mark Austad, Amb.	Jacques Kosciusko-Morizet, Amb.
France	Kenneth Rush, Amb.	Vincent Mavoungou, Amb.
Gabon	John A. McKesson 3d, Amb.	Vacant
Gambia	O. Rudolph Aggrey, Amb.	Berndt von Staden, Amb.
Germany, West	Martin J. Hillenbrand, Amb.	Rolf Sieber, Amb.
Germany, East	John Sherman Cooper, Amb.	Samuel Ernest Quarm, Amb.
Ghana	Shirley Temple Black, Amb.	Menelas D. Alexandrakis, Amb.
Greece	Jack B. Kubisch, Amb.	Marie J. McIntyre, Amb.
Grenada		Julio Asensio-Wunderlich, Amb.
Guatemala	Francis E. Meloy Jr., Amb.	Habib Bah, Amb.
Guinea	Vacant.	Frederick Hillborn Talbot, Amb.
Guyana	Max V. Krebs, Amb.	Georges Salomon, Amb.
Haiti	Heyward Isham, Amb.	Roberto Lazarus, Amb.
Honduras	Phillip V. Sanchez, Amb.	Karoly Kovacs, Charge
Hungary	Richard F. Pedersen, Amb.	Haraldur Kroyer, Amb.
Iceland	Frederick Irving, Amb.	Triloki Nath Kaul, Amb.
India	William B. Saxbe, Amb.	Rusmin Nurjadin, Amb.
Indonesia	David D. Newsom, Amb.	Ardeshir Zahedi, Amb.
Iran	Richard Helms, Amb.	
Iraq	Arthur Lowrie, principal officer.	Vacant
Ireland	Walter Curley, Amb.	John G. Molloy, Amb.
Israel	Malcolm Toon, Amb.	Simcha Dinitz, Amb.
Italy	John A. Volpe, Amb.	Egidio Ortona, Amb.
Ivory Coast	Robert S. Smith, Amb.	Timothee N'Guetta Ahoua, Amb.
Jamaica	Sumner Gerard, Amb.	Kenneth G. A. Hill, Charge
Japan	James D. Hodgson, Amb.	Takeshi Yasukawa, Amb.
Jordan	Thomas R. Pickering, Amb.	Abdullah Salah, Amb.
Kenya	Anthony D. Marshall, Amb.	Bernard Adundo, Charge
Korea, South	Richard L. Sneider, Amb.	Pyong-choon Hahm, Amb.
Kuwait	William A. Stoltzfus Jr., Amb.	Jamil Al-Hassani
Laos	Galen L. Stone, Amb.	Khamphan Panya
Latvia[5]		Dr. Anatole Dinbergs, Charge
Lebanon	G. McMurtrie Godley, Amb.	Najati Kabbani, Amb.
Lesotho	David B. Bolen, Amb.	Ephraim Tsepa Manare, Amb.
Liberia	Melvin L. Manfull, Amb.	S. Edward Peal, Amb.
Libya	Vacant.	Ali A. El-Gayed, Charge
Lithuania[5]		Joseph Kajeckas, Charge
Luxembourg	Dr. Ruth Lewis Farkas, Amb.	Adrien Meisch, Amb.
Madagascar	Joseph A. Mendenhall, Amb.	Henri Raharijaona, Amb.
Malawi	Robert A. Stevenson, Amb.	Robert B. Mbaya, Amb.

Countries	Envoys from United States	Envoys to United States
Malaysia	Francis T. Underhill Jr., Amb.	Mohamed Khir Johari, Amb.
Maldives, Rep.	Christopher Van Hollen, Amb.	*Vacant*
Mali	Ralph J. McGuire, Amb.	Alpha Amadou Diaw, Charge
Malta	Robert P. Smith, Amb.	Joseph Attard-Kingswell, Amb.
Mauritania	Holsey G. Handyside, Amb.	Ahmedou Ould Abdallah, Amb.
Mauritius	Philip W. Manhard, Amb.	Pierre Guy Girald Balancy, Amb.
Mexico	Joseph J. Jová, Amb.	Dr. Jose Juan de Olloqui, Amb.
Morocco	Robert G. Neumann, Amb.	Abdelhadi Boutaleb, Amb.
Nauru	*Vacant*	*Vacant*
Nepal	William I. Cargo, Amb.	Yadu Nath Khanal, Amb.
Netherlands	Kingdon Gould Jr., Amb.	Age R. Tammenoms Bakker, Amb.
New Zealand	Armistead I. Selden Jr., Amb.	Lloyd White, Amb.
Nicaragua	James D. Theberge, Amb.	Dr. Guillermo Sevilla-Sacasa, Amb.
Niger	L. Douglas Heck, Amb.	Illa Salifou, Amb.
Nigeria	John E. Reinhardt, Amb.	John M. Garba, Amb.
Norway	Thomas R. Byrne, Amb.	Soren Christian Sommerfelt, Amb.
Oman	William D. Wolle, Amb.	Ahmed Macki, Amb.
Pakistan	Henry A. Byroade, Amb.	Sahabzada Yaqub-Khan, Amb.
Panama	William J. Jorden, Amb.	Nicolas Gonzalez-Revilla, Amb.
Paraguay	George W. Landau, Amb.	Miguel Solano-Lopez, Amb.
Peru	Robert W. Dean, Amb.	Jose Arce, Amb.
Philippines	William H. Sullivan, Amb.	Eduardo Z. Romualdez, Amb.
Poland	Richard T. Davies, Amb.	Witold Trampczynski, Amb.
Portugal	Frank C. Carlucci, Amb.	Joao Hall Themido, Amb.
Qatar	Robert P. Paganelli, Amb.	Abdullah Saleh Al-Mana, Amb.
Romania	Harry G. Barnes Jr., Amb.	Corneliu Bogdan, Amb.
Rwanda	Robert E. Fritts, Amb.	Joseph Nizeyimana, Amb.
Saudi Arabia	James E. Akins, Amb.	Ibrahim Al-Sowayel, Amb.
Senegal	O. Rudolph Aggrey, Amb.	Andre Coulbary, Amb.
Sierra Leone	Michael A. Samuels, Amb.	Philip J. Palmer, Amb.
Singapore	John H. Holdridge, Amb.	Dr. Ernest Steven Monteiro, Amb.
Somali, Democratic Rep.	*Vacant*	Dr. Abdullahi Ahmed Abbou, Amb.
South Africa	William G. Bowdler, Amb.	Johan S. F. Botha, Amb.
Spain	Wells Stabler, Amb.	Jaime Alba, Amb.
Sri Lanka (Ceylon)	Christopher Van Hollen, Amb.	Neville Kanakaratne, Amb.
Sudan	William D. Brewer, Amb.	Francis M. Deng, Amb.
Swaziland	David B. Bolen, Amb.	J.L.F. Simelane, Amb.
Sweden	Robert Strauszhupe, Amb.	Count Wilhelm Wachtmeister, Amb.
Switzerland	Peter Dominic, Amb.	Felix Schnyder, Amb.
Syrian Arab Rep.	Richard W. Murphy, Amb.	Sabah Kabbani, Amb.
Tanzania	W. Beverly Carter Jr., Amb.	Paul Bomani, Amb.
Thailand	Charles S. Whitehouse, Amb.	Anand Panyarachun, Amb.
Togo	Nancy V. Rawls, Amb.	Messanvi Kokou Kekeh, Amb.
Tonga	Armistead I. Selden Jr., Amb.	*Vacant*
Trinidad and Tobago	Lloyd I. Miller, Amb.	Victor C. McIntyre, Amb.
Tunisia	Talcott W. Seelye, Amb.	Ali Hedda, Amb.
Turkey	William B. Macomber Jr., Amb.	Melih Esenbel, Amb.
Uganda[7]	*Vacant*	S.M. Nsubuga, Charge
USSR	Walter J. Stoessel Jr., Amb.	Anatoliy F. Dobrynin, Amb.
United Arab Emirates	Michael Sterner, Amb.	Saeed Ahmad Ghobash, Amb.
United Kingdom	Elliot L. Richardson, Amb.	Sir Peter Ramsbotham, Amb.
Upper Volta	Pierre R. Graham, Amb.	Telesphore Yaguibou, Amb.
Uruguay	Ernest V. Siracusa, Amb.	Jose Perez Caldas, Amb.
Venezuela	Harry W. Shlaudeman, Amb.	Miguel Angel Burelli, Amb.
Vietnam[1]		
Western Samoa	Armistead I. Selden Jr., Amb.	*Vacant*
Yemen South		
Yemen Arab Rep.	Thomas J. Scotes, Amb.	Hassan M. Makki, Amb.
Yugoslavia	*Vacant*	Toma Granfil, Amb.
Zaire	*Vacant*	Mbeka Makosso, Amb.
Zambia	Jean M. Wilkowski, Amb.	Siteke Gibson Mwale, Amb.

(1) U.S. embassy closed in 1975 during Communist takeover; (2) no formal relations; liaison offices; (3) U.S. embassy closed in 1965; West Germany acts as protective power; (4) relations severed in 1961; Switzerland protects U.S. interests; (5) U.S. does not officially recognize 1940 annexation by USSR; (6) relations severed in 1967, limited staff returned in 1972; Belgium protects U.S. interests; (7) U.S. embassy closed in 1973; West Germany protects U.S. interests; (8) U.S. embassy closed in 1969; UK serves as protective power.

Special Missions

U.S. Mission to North Atlantic Treaty Organization, Brussels—David K. Bruce.
U.S. Mission to the European Communities, Brussels—Joseph A. Greenwald.
U.S. Mission to the International Atomic Energy Agency, Vienna—Gerald F. Tape.
U.S. Mission to the United Nations, New York—Daniel P. Moynihan.
U.S. Mission to the European Office of the UN & Other Internatl. Organizations, Geneva—Francis L. Dale.
U.S. Mission to the Organization for Economic Cooperation and Development, Paris—William C. Turner.
U.S. Mission to the International Civil Aviation Organization Montreal—Mrs. Betty Crites Dillon.
U.S. Mission to the Organization of American States—William S. Maillard.

U.S. Aid to Foreign Countries

Source: Bureau of Economic Analysis, U.S. Department of Commerce

Data shown by country includes the military supplies and services furnished under the Foreign Assistance Act and direct Defense Department appropriations. This aid is principally to the Southeast Asia countries. Data shown include credits which have been extended to private entities in the country specified.

Grants are largely outright gifts for which no payment is expected or which at most involve an obligation on the part of the receiver to extend aid to the U.S. or other countries to achieve a common objective.

Net grants and credits take into account all known returns to the U.S. government, including reverse grants, returns of grants and payments of principal. A minus sign indicates that the total of these returns to the U.S. is greater than the total of grants or credits.

Other assistance represents the transfer of U.S. farm products in exchange for foreign currencies, less the government's disbursements of the currencies as grants, credits, or for purchases. The net acquisitions of currencies represents net transfers of resources to foreign currencies in addition to those classified as grants or credits.

Amounts do not include investments in international financial institutions in 1974 as follows: Asian Development Bank, $2,011,000; Inter-American Development Bank, $191,550,000; International Development Assn., $343,881,000.

In millions of dollars or equivalent (*Less than $500,000)

Calendar Year 1974	Total	Net grants	Net credits	Net other
TOTAL	6,768	7,360	-343	-249
Military grants	2,836	2,836	—	—
Other grants, credits, ass't.	3,932	4,524	-343	-249
Western Europe	132	8	125	-1
Austria	-2	—	-2	—
Belgium-Luxembourg	15	—	15	—
Denmark	10	—	10	—
Finland	*	—	*	—
France	-11	—	-11	—
Germany, West	46	—	46	*
Iceland	-3	—	-3	*
Ireland	-15	—	-15	—
Italy	-8	—	-8	—
Netherlands	34	—	34	—
Norway	95	—	95	—
Portugal	7	—	7	—
Spain	91	3	89	*
Sweden	6	—	6	—
United Kingdom	-162	—	-162	*
Yugoslavia	-27	*	-27	*
Atomic EC	-5	—	-5	—
Coal-Steel EC	-5	—	-5	—
Other & unspecified	67	5	62	*
Eastern Europe	-102	1	-82	-21
Hungary	-1	—	-1	—
Poland	-24	1	-4	-21
Romania	27	—	27	—
Soviet Union	-104	—	-104	—
Near East & South Asia	622	2,513	-1,685	-206
Afghanistan	9	6	4	*
Bangladesh	105	64	41	*
Cyprus	1	1	*	*
Egypt	26	41	-8	-7
Greece	65	*	65	*
India	-178	2,138	-2,114	-202
Iran	37	1	36	*
Iraq	-2	—	-2	—
Israel	199	98	101	*
Jordan	57	45	12	*
Kuwait	-10	—	-10	—
Lebanon	21	16	5	—
Nepal	6	6	*	*
Pakistan	122	24	95	4
Saudi Arabia	-21	*	-21	—
Sri Lanka (Ceylon)	2	5	-3	*
Syria	*	—	*	—
Turkey	121	6	114	*
Yemen (Sana)	8	8	—	—
Other & unspecified	54	54	—	—
East Asia & Pacific	1,370	946	441	-18
Australia	-62	—	-62	—
Brunei	*	—	*	—
Burma	*	*	-1	1
Cambodia	288	156	133	-1
China-Taiwan	119	*	119	*
Hong Kong	13	*	13	—
Indonesia	125	26	99	*
Japan	2	-2	5	—
Korea (So.)	63	14	50	-1
Laos	36	36	—	—
Malaysia	19	4	15	—
New Zealand	16	—	16	—
Papua New Guinea	*	*	—	—
Philippines	43	38	5	*
Thailand	19	12	7	*
Trust Terr. Pacific	73	73	—	—
Vietnam (So.)	585	585	16	-16
Other & unspecified	29	3	25	*
Africa	458	224	235	-2
Algeria	115	1	114	—
Cameroon	1	1	*	—
Chad	7	7	—	—
Dahomey	3	1	2	—
Ethiopia	26	18	8	*
Ghana	1	5	-4	*
Guinea	6	2	6	-2
Ivory Coast	3	2	1	*
Kenya	9	4	6	—
Lesotho	5	5	—	—
Liberia	-3	4	-7	—
Madagascar	1	*	*	—
Malawi	4	*	4	—
Mali	20	20	*	—
Morocco	29	27	4	-2
Niger	25	25	*	—
Nigeria	10	8	2	—
Senegal	7	6	2	*
Sierra Leone	3	3	*	*
Somalia	*	*	*	*
Sudan	7	3	5	*
Tanzania	11	9	2	—
Togo	3	2	2	—
Tunisia	17	10	4	3
Uganda	1	1	*	—
Upper Volta	10	10	—	—
Zaire	63	4	60	*
Zambia	9	*	9	—
Other & unspecified	59	45	14	*
Western Hemisphere	802	176	627	-1
Argentina	-4	*	-4	*
Bahamas	-1	—	-1	—
Bermuda	-2	—	-2	—
Bolivia	26	7	20	*
Brazil	265	16	250	-1
Canada	87	—	87	—
Cayman Islands	10	—	10	—
Chile	87	6	81	*
Colombia	45	18	27	*
Costa Rica	9	4	5	—
Dominican Republic	10	7	2	*
Ecuador	7	8	-1	*
El Salvador	4	3	1	—
Guatemala	17	6	11	*
Guyana	5	1	4	*
Haiti	3	5	-2	—
Honduras	13	6	7	—
Jamaica	22	3	19	—
Mexico	95	5	90	—
Nicaragua	18	4	14	*
Panama	27	7	20	—
Paraguay	7	2	5	*
Peru	-19	8	-28	*
Trinidad-Tobago	6	*	6	—
Uruguay	1	1	*	*
Venezuela	-13	1	-14	—
Other & unspecified	77	58	19	—
International organizations & unspecified areas	651	656	-5	—

National Population Density, Growth Rate, Life Expectancy

Source: United Nations Demographic Yearbook 1974

Country	Density[1]	Growth Rate[2]	Life Expectancy[3]	Country	Density[1]	Growth Rate[2]	Life Expectancy[3]
Afghanistan	28	2.3	37.5*	Lebanon	294	3.1	N.A.
Algeria	7	3.2	50.7*	Liberia	15	2.9	45.8
Argentina	9	1.5	64.06	Libya	1	3.7	52.1*
Australia	2	1.6	67.92	Mali	4	2.1	37.2*
Bangladesh	497	N.A.	N.A.	Malawi	40	2.6	38.5*
Belgium	320	0.4	67.73	Mexico	28	3.5	61.03
Bolivia	5	2.6	49.71	Morocco	37	N.A.	50.5*
Brazil	12	2.8	60.7*	Mozambique	11	N.A.	41.0*
Bulgaria	78	0.5	68.81	Netherlands	329	1.0	70.8
Burma	44	2.3	47.5*	Niger	3	2.3	41.0*
Thailand	77	3.2	53.6	Nigeria	65	2.7	37.2
Cameroon	13	1.9	41.0*	Norway	12	0.7	71.24
Canada	2	1.2	68.75	Pakistan	83	3.6	53.72
Chad	3	2.0	29.0	Panama	20	3.1	57.62
Chile	14	1.7	60.48	Paraguay	7	3.9	59.4*
China	85	1.7	50.0*	Peru	12	3.2	52.59
Colombia	20	3.2	44.18	Philippines	134	3.0	48.81
Costa Rica	37	2.7	61.87	Poland	107	0.9	66.83
Cuba	78	1.7	66.8*	Portugal	93	−0.4	65.30
Czechoslovakia	114	0.5	66.23	Puerto Rico	332	2.8	68.92
Denmark	117	0.6	70.7	Rhodesia	15	3.6	51.4*
Ecuador	24	3.4	51.04	Romania	88	0.9	66.27
Egypt	36	2.2	51.6	Rwanda	151	2.7	41.0*
Ethiopia	21	1.9	38.5*	Saudi Arabia	4	2.9	42.3*
Finland	14	0.4	65.88	Senegal	20	2.5	41.0*
France	95	0.9	68.5	Singapore	3,761	1.7	65.1
Germany, East	157	−0.2	68.85	Somalia	5	2.5	38.5*
Germany, West	249	0.7	67.41	Spain	69	1.1	69.69
Ghana	39	2.7	46.0*	Sudan	7	2.5	47.6*
Greece	68	0.7	67.46	Sri Lanka (Ceylon)	202	1.9	64.8
Guatemala	51	2.8	48.29	Sweden	18	0.4	71.97
Guinea	17	2.4	26.0	Switzerland	156	1.3	69.21
Haiti	160	1.6	44.5*	Syria	37	3.3	52.8*
Honduras	25	3.5	49.0*	Tanzania	15	2.7	41.0*
Hong Kong	3,980	1.7	66.74	Thailand	77	3.2	53.6
Hungary	112	0.3	66.87	Togo	38	2.4	31.6
Iceland	2	1.3	70.7	Tunisia	34	2.4	51.7*
India	175	2.1	41.89	Turkey	49	2.5	53.7*
Indonesia	84	N.A.	47.5	Uganda	46	3.3	47.5*
Iran	19	3.0	50.0*	USSR	11	1.0	65.0
Ireland	43	0.9	68.58	United Kingdom	229	0.3	67.81
Israel	154	3.0	70.14	United States	22	0.9	67.4
Italy	182	0.8	67.87	Upper Volta	21	2.1	32.1
Ivory Coast	14	2.4	41.0*	Uruguay	17	1.2	65.51
Jamaica	180	1.9	62.65	Venezuela	12	2.8	63.8*
Japan	291	1.3	70.49	Vietnam, North	142	2.0	50.0*
Kenya	21	3.6	46.9	Vietnam, South	111	1.8	50.0*
Korea, North	125	2.8	57.7*	Yugoslavia	82	1.0	65.59
Korea, South	334	1.7	59.74	Zaire	10	2.8	37.64
Kuwait	50	5.8	66.14	Zambia	6	3.5	43.5*

(1) persons per sq. kilometer; (2) percent annual rate of increase, 1970-73; (3) for males at birth, except(*)both sexes; life expectancy figures are for a variety of years after 1950, and may not reflect recent changes; (N.A.) not available.

Gross National Product Estimates
For Calendar Year 1974 in Current Market Prices—U.S. $
Compiled by Agency for International Development

Nation	GNP Total $ Millions	GNP Per Capita	Nation	GNP Total $ Millions	GNP Per Capita	Nation	GNP Total $ Millions	GNP Per Capita
Afghanistan	1,466	81	Congo	425	423	Iceland	1,025	4,835
Algeria	7,730	504	Costa Rica	1,461	775	India	71,000	117
Angola	2,980	492	Cyprus	963	1,459	Indonesia	15,370	115
Argentina	81,385	1,246	Dahomey	348	122	Iran	25,598	762
Australia	52,160	3,998	Denmark	27,350	5,342	Iraq	6,680	645
Austria	27,900	3,710	Dominican Republic	2,378	509	Ireland	6,560	2,165
Bahrain	216	935	Ecuador	2,496	371	Israel	8,950	2,732
Bangladesh	7,730	100	Egypt	9,100	259	Italy	138,270	2,520
Belgium	45,740	4,686	El Salvador	1,335	344	Ivory Coast	2,393	511
Bolivia	1,014	202	Ethiopia	2,240	83	Jamaica	1,714	868
Brazil	77,220	750	Fiji	367	640	Japan	413,070	3,812
Burma	2,416	82	Finland	17,060	3,661	Jordan	575	286
Burundi	284	74	France	255,060	4,851	Kenya	2,249	172
Cambodia	627	81	Gabon	634	1,248	Korea, South	12,380	376
Cameroon	1,418	232	Germany, West	348,170	5,618	Kuwait	7,165	8,449
Canada	118,900	5,372	Ghana	2,857	287	Laos	320	100
Central African Rep.	302	176	Greece	16,290	1,780	Lebanon	2,841	874
Chad	350	88	Guatemala	2,545	454	Lesotho	97	99
Chile	7,640	777	Guinea	575	137	Liberia	417	248
China (Taiwan)	10,226	663	Guinea-Bissau	158	275	Libya	6,230	2,984
Colombia	9,968	413	Guyana	294	380	Luxembourg	1,829	5,226
			Haiti	694	143	Madagascar	1,258	174
			Honduras	869	291	Malawi	535	112
			Hong Kong	5,998	1,435	Malaysia	6,565	554
						Mali	397	73

Malta	353	1,096	Peru	9,080	617	Syria	2,379	345
Mauritania	245	196	Philippines	10,330	246	Tanzania	1,834	127
Mexico	48,650	870	Portugal	11,200	1,308	Thailand	9,180	232
Morocco	5,012	286	Rhodesia	2,493	406	Togo	393	185
Mozambique	2,905	334	Qatar	511	5,938	Tunisia	2,515	459
Nepal	1,078	90	Rwanda	280	71	Turkey	22,036	576
Netherlands	59,670	4,440	Saudi Arabia	7,520	1,299	Uganda	1,715	161
New Zealand	11,710	3,930	Senegal	1,014	252	United Arab		
Nicaragua	1,065	503	Sierra Leone	455	162	Emirates	1,425	6,736
Niger	525	125	Singapore	4,283	1,929	United Kingdom	174,800	3,120
Nigeria	14,802	250	Somalia	236	79	United States	1,294,900	6,155
Norway	18,750	4,735	South Africa	26,125	1,077	Upper Volta	450	79
Oman	355	492	Spain	60,230	1,728	Uruguay	2,585	865
Pakistan	8,340	126	Sri Lanka	2,612	198	Venezuela	16,120	1,357
Panama	1,418	904	Sudan	2,300	135	Yemen, South	175	110
Papua New			Swaziland	140	310	Yemen, North	500	80
Guinea	945	365	Sweden	50,100	6,155	Zaire	3,129	147
Paraguay	979	402	Switzerland	40,870	6,346	Zambia	2,425	503

Cost of Living in Various Cities of the World

This comparison of the cost of living in various cities was drawn up in 1975 by the UN Statistical Office, based on prices for goods, services and housing for international officials stationed in these cities. Figures show relative costs, based on about 120 items. New York City was assigned the index figure 100. Thus, while expenditure for certain items might be $1,000 in New York, it would be $1,170 for them in Paris and $910 in Rio de Janeiro. Figures with an asterisk (*) omit cost of housing (rent, utilities and domestic service) in cities where they are furnished at nominal cost by governments.

Index	City	Index	City	Index	City
*123	Abidjan, Ivory Coast	123	The Hague, Netherlands	113	Ouagadougou, Upper Volta
*104	Accra, Ghana	89	Havana, Cuba	88	Panama City, Panama
97	Addis Ababa, Ethiopia	71	Islamabad, Pakistan	117	Paris, France
87	Aden, Yemen (Dem.)	98	Jakarta, Indonesia	94	Port-au-Prince, Haiti
*106	Algiers, Algeria	86	Kabul, Afghanistan	69	Port Louis, Mauritius
94	Amman, Jordan	*110	Kampala, Uganda	79	Port-of-Spain, Trinidad
73	Ankara, Turkey	80	Katmandu, Nepal	82	Quito, Ecuador
*97	Apia, Western Samoa	*112	Kigali, Rwanda	91	Rabat, Morocco
75	Asuncion, Paraguay	95	Kingston, Jamaica	88	Rangoon, Burma
94	Athens, Greece	109	Kinshasa, Zaire	91	Rio de Janeiro, Brazil
77	Baghdad, Iraq	94	Kuala Lumpur, Malaysia	93	Rome, Italy
110	Bamako, Mali	90	Kuwait, Kuwait	*108	Saigon, Vietnam
84	Bangkok, Thailand	*111	Lagos, Nigeria	87	Sana, Yemen (Rep.)
*133	Banqui, Cen. African Rep.	83	LaPaz, Bolivia	91	San Jose, Costa Rica
100	Beirut, Lebanon	*124	Libreville, Gabon	86	San Salvador, El Salvador
90	Belgrade, Yugoslavia	84	Lima, Peru	68	Santiago, Chile
67	Bogota, Colombia	88	London, United Kingdom	94	Seoul, South Korea
123	Bonn, West Germany	*116	Lusaka, Zambia	100	Singapore, Singapore
*125	Brazzaville, Congo	93	Managua, Nicaragua	78	Suva, Fiji
94	Bridgetown, Barbados	90	Manila, Philippines	95	Sydney, Australia
84	Buenos Aires, Argentina	79	Mbabane, Swaziland	101	Tananarive, Malagasy
77	Cairo, Egypt	90	Mexico City, Mexico	87	Tegucigalpa, Honduras
88	Caracas, Venezuela	88	Mogadishu, Somalia	88	Tehran, Iran
72	Colombo, Sri Lanka	*90	Monrovia, Liberia	*106	Tokyo, Japan
133	Conakry, Guinea	69	Montevideo, Uruguay	*123	Tripoli, Libya
124	Copenhagen, Denmark	83	Montreal, Canada	91	Tunis, Tunisia
104	Cotonou, Dahomey	86	Nairobi, Kenya	*100	Ulan Bator, Mongolia
76	Damascus, Syria	77	New Delhi, India	64	Valetta, Malta
110	N'Djamena, Chad	100	New York, U.S.	113	Vienna, Austria
*105	Freetown, Sierra Leone	*113	Niamey, Niger	77	Vientiane, Laos
133	Geneva, Switzerland	79	Nicosia, Cyprus	92	Washington, D.C., U.S.
65	Georgetown, Guyana	*124	Nouakchott, Mauretania	101	Yaounde, Cameroon

Population of World's Largest Urban Areas

City populations often cannot be used to compare urban areas because city limits may fall short of or exceed the built-up or urban area. The problem of comparison is compounded by the difficulty in obtaining reliable population data for a common year. The ranking of urban areas below represents one attempt at comparing the world's largest urban areas, taking into account, where necessary and within the limits of available data, urban development extending outward from the principal city named in the table. Thus, the Tokyo area included Tokyo plus neighboring smaller cities, towns and villages. (Some computations include Yokohama as part of Tokyo's urban population.) New York's urban area in 1970 included part or all the population of 10 New Jersey and 5 New York counties in addition to the 5 boroughs of New York city.

New York, N.Y. (census 1970)	16,206,841	Seoul, Rep. of Korea (census 1970)	5,536,377
Tokyo, Japan (census 1973)	11,324,417	Essen (Ruhr-Gebiet), W. Ger. (est. 1971)	5,425,000
Shanghai, China (est. 1970)	10,820,000	Cairo, Egypt (est. 1970)	4,961,000
Paris, France (est. 1970)	9,250,647	Philadelphia, Pa. (census 1970)	4,817,914
Mexico City, Mexico (census 1970)	8,589,630	Rio de Janeiro, Brazil (est. 1973)	4,658,000
Buenos Aires, Argentina (census 1970)	8,352,900	Jakarta, Indonesia (census 1971)	4,576,009
Osaka, Japan (census 1973)	7,838,722	Detroit, Mich. (census 1970)	4,431,390
Sao Paulo, Brazil (est. 1973)	7,693,000	Tientsin, China (est. 1970)	4,280,000
Peking, China (est. 1970)	7,570,000	Victoria-Hong Kong (est. 1970)	4,250,000
London, England (est. 1971)	7,418,020	Leningrad, USSR (est. 1972)	4,066,000
Moscow, USSR (est. 1972)	7,300,000	Delhi-New Delhi, India (census 1971)	4,065,698
Los Angeles-Long Beach, Calif. (census 1970)	7,032,075	Teheran, Iran (est. 1973)	3,800,000
Calcutta, India (census 1971)	7,031,382	Karachi, Pakistan (est. 1972)	3,650,000
Chicago, Ill. (census 1970)	6,978,947	Berlin, E. & W. Germany (est. 1970)	3,218,028
Bombay, India (census 1971)	5,970,575	Madras, India (census 1971)	3,169,930

Madrid, Spain (census 1970)	3,146,071
San Francisco-Oakland, Calif. (census 1970)	3,109,519
Bangkok, Thailand (census 1970)	3,051,000
Manila, Philippines (census 1973)	3,000,000
Washington, D.C.-Md.-Va. (census 1970)	2,908,801
Boston, Mass. (census 1970)	2,899,101
Bogota, Colombia (est. 1972)	2,818,300
Shenyang (Mukden), China (est. 1970)	2,800,000
Rome, Italy	2,799,836
Montreal, Canada (census 1971)	2,743,210
Sydney, Australia (census 1971)	2,725,064
Santiago, Chile (census 1970)	2,661,920
Toronto, Canada (census 1971)	2,628,043
Wuhan, China (est. 1970)	2,560,000
Lima, Peru (est. 1970)	2,541,300
Athens, Greece (census 1971)	2,540,000
St. Louis, Mo. (census 1970)	2,410,163
Pittsburgh, Pa. (census 1970)	2,401,245
Manchester, England (census 1971)	2,386,774
Dallas-Ft. Worth, Tex. (census 1970)	2,377,979*
Birmingham, England (census 1971)	2,369,205
Melbourne, Australia (census 1971)	2,342,000
Yokohama, Japan (est. 1971)	2,342,000
Chungking, China (est. 1970)	2,300,000
Istanbul, Turkey (census 1970)	2,247,630
Singapore (est. 1974)	2,220,000
Canton, China (est. 1970)	2,200,000
Caracas, Venezuela (est. 1970)	2,175,400
Lahore, Pakistan (est. 1972)	2,073,000
Baltimore, Md. (census 1970)	2,070,670
Cleveland, O. (census 1970)	2,064,194
Rangoon, Burma (est. 1973)	2,056,118
Newark, N.J. (census 1970)	2,054,928
Nagoya, Japan (est. 1971)	2,052,000
Alexandria, Egypt (est. 1970)	2,032,000
Budapest, Hungary (est. 1971)	2,027,300
Taipei, China (est. 1974)	2,000,409
Pusan, Rep. of Korea (census 1970)	1,880,710
Vienna, Austria (census 1971)	1,858,700
Hamburg, W. Germany (est. 1970)	1,818,600
Saigon, Rep. of Vietnam (est. 1971)	1,804,880
Hyderabad, India (census 1971)	1,796,339

Population of Important World Cities

Source: Latest census reports and latest official estimates; *(asterisk) denotes capital;
Gr. denotes Greater, or metropolitan area   See index for U.S. and Canadian cities

Afghanistan
*Kabul, Gr...... 498,800
Kandahar...... 133,799
Albania
*Tirana.......... 171,300
Algeria
*Algiers, Gr..... 1,116,493
Constantine..... 243,558
Oran........... 327,493
Angola
Luanda, Gr...... 475,328
Argentina
*Buenos Aires... 2,972,453
*Buenos Aires, Gr.
.... 8,352,900
Cordoba, Gr.... 825,000
La Plata, Gr.... 510,000
Mendoza, Gr.... 400,000
Rosario, Gr..... 875,000
Australia
Adelaide, Gr.... 842,693
Brisbane, Gr.... 867,784
*Canberra, Gr.... 158,594
Melbourne, Gr.. 2,503,450
Newcastle, Gr... 351,010
Perth, Gr....... 703,199
Sydney, Gr..... 2,807,828
Austria
Graz........... 249,211
Linz........... 204,627
*Vienna, Gr..... 1,940,000
Bahamas
*Nassau, Gr..... 101,503
Bahrain
*Manama, Gr..... 145,000
Bangladesh
Chittagong...... 416,733
*Dacca, Gr..... 1,629,402
Khulna........ 436,000
Barbados
*Bridgetown, Gr... 115,000
Belgium
Antwerp, Gr.... 1,155,000
*Brussels, Gr.... 2,000,000
Ghent, Gr....... 320,000
Liege, Gr....... 880,000
Belize (Br. Honduras)
*Belize, Gr....... 48,421
Bermuda
*Hamilton, Gr.... 18,000
Bolivia
*La Paz........ 700,000
Santa Cruz..... 200,000
*Sucre.......... 53,000
Botswana
*Gaborone........ 17,718
Brazil
Belem.......... 762,000
Belo Horizonte.. 1,542,000
*Brasilia, Gr...... 600,000
Porto Alegre... 1,105,000
Recife........ 1,352,000
Rio de Janeiro.. 4,658,000

Salvador...... 1,311,000
Santos......... 262,048
Sao Paulo, Gr... 7,693,000
Bulgaria
Plovdiv....... 305,091
*Sofia.......... 1,055,100
Burma
Mandalay....... 393,000
*Rangoon...... 2,056,118
Burundi
*Bujumbura, Gr.... 78,810
Cambodia (Khmer Rep.)
*Phnom-Penh.... 393,995
Cameroon
Douala, Gr...... 350,000
*Yaounde....... 200,000
Central African Rep.
*Bangui, Gr....... 187,000
Chad
*N'Djamena, Gr.... 179,000
Chile
Concepcion...... 196,317
*Santiago, Gr.... 2,661,920
Valparaiso...... 292,847
China
Anshan....... 1,050,000
Canton....... 2,200,000
Changchun.... 1,200,000
Chungking.... 2,300,000
Fushun....... 1,080,000
Harbin....... 1,670,000
Kunming..... 1,100,000
Lanchow..... 1,450,000
Nanking..... 1,750,000
*Peking...... 7,570,000
Port Arthur,
Dairen..... 1,650,000
Shanghai... 10,820,000
Shenyang.... 2,800,000
Sian........ 1,500,000
Taiyuan..... 1,350,000
Tientsin..... 4,280,000
Tsinan...... 1,100,000
Tsingtao.... 1,300,000
Wuhan....... 2,560,000
China (Taiwan)
*Taipei...... 2,000,149
Colombia
Barranquilla.... 816,706
*Bogota, Gr.... 2,818,300
Bucaramanga... 324,400
Cali......... 1,100,000
Cartagena..... 315,200
Medellin..... 1,091,600
Congo, People's Rep.
*Brazzaville, Gr.... 175,000
Costa Rica
*San Jose, Gr..... 418,000
Cuba
Camaguey...... 196,900
*Havana, Gr.... 1,755,000
Santa Clara..... 131,500
Santiago de Cuba. 276,000

Cyprus
*Nicosia, Gr.... 115,000
Czechoslovakia
Bratislava...... 293,333
Brno.......... 338,985
*Prague...... 1,101,257
Dahomey
Cotonou....... 111,100
*Porto Novo.... 74,500
Denmark
Arhus......... 233,162
*Copenhagen, Gr. 1,383,073
Dominican Republic
*Santo Domingo.. 671,402
Ecuador
Guayaquil...... 795,477
*Quito......... 597,133
Egypt
Alexandria.... 2,032,000
*Cairo....... 4,961,000
Giza.......... 711,900
Port Said...... 313,000
Suez.......... 315,000
El Salvador
*San Salvador, Gr.. 600,000
Ethiopia
*Addis Ababa.... 881,400
Asmara....... 240,700
Fiji
*Suva.......... 60,000
Finland
*Helsinki...... 532,182
France
Bordeaux...... 270,996
Le Havre...... 200,940
Lyon.......... 535,000
Marseille...... 893,771
Nantes....... 265,009
Nice......... 325,400
*Paris........ 2,607,625
*Paris, Gr..... 9,250,647
St. Etienne..... 216,020
Strasbourg..... 254,038
Toulouse...... 380,340
Gabon
*Libreville, Gr..... 73,000
Gambia
*Banjul, Gr....... 52,640
Germany (West)
Berlin (West).. 2,134,300
Bochum....... 346,900
*Bonn......... 299,400
Bremen....... 607,200
Brunswick..... 225,200
Cologne...... 866,300
Dortmund..... 648,900
Duesseldorf.... 680,000
Duisburg..... 457,900
Essen....... 704,800
Frankfurt..... 660,400
Gelsenkirchen... 348,600
Hamburg..... 1,817,100
Hannover..... 517,800

Kassel......... 213,500
Kiel.......... 276,600
Krefeld...... 228,700
Mannheim..... 330,900
Munich...... 1,326,300
Nuremberg.... 477,100
Oberhausen.... 249,000
Stuttgart...... 628,400
Wiesbaden..... 260,600
Wuppertal..... 414,700
Germany (East)
*Berlin (East).... 1,086,374
Dresden...... 502,432
Halle........ 257,261
Karl Marx Stadt
(Chemnitz).... 299,411
Leipzig...... 583,885
Magdeburg.... 272,237
Ghana
*Accra, Gr..... 736,718
Greece
*Athens-Piraeus. 2,540,000
Thessaloniki
(Salonika)...... 345,799
Guatemala
*Guatemala City.. 730,991
Guinea
*Conakry, Gr..... 197,267
Guyana
*Georgetown, Gr.. 167,078
Haiti
*Port-au-Prince, Gr.
.... 493,932
Honduras
*Tegucigalpa...... 270,650
Hong Kong
Victoria, Gr..... 4,250,000
Hungary
*Budapest..... 2,027,300
Iceland
*Reykjavik, Gr.... 110,000
India
Agra......... 594,858
Ahmedabad... 1,588,378
Allahabad..... 491,702
Amritsar...... 432,663
Bangalore..... 1,540,741
Bombay..... 5,970,575
Calcutta..... 3,148,746
Calcutta, Gr... 7,031,382
Delhi-
*New Delhi..... 4,065,698
Howrah...... 737,877
Hyderabad... 1,612,276
Kanpur..... 1,154,388
Lucknow..... 750,512
Madras, Gr... 3,169,930
Madurai..... 549,114
Nagpur..... 866,144
Patna....... 474,349
Poona...... 856,105
Varanasi (Benares)
.... 583,856

Indonesia
Bandung...... 1,201,730
*Jakarta........ 4,576,009
Jogjakarta....... 342,267
Makassar........ 434,766
Malang.......... 422,428
Medan.......... 635,562
Palembang...... 532,961
Semarang...... 646,590
Surabaja...... 1,556,255
Iran
Abadan........ 300,000
Isfahan........ 546,200
Mashhad....... 530,500
Shiraz........ 335,700
Tabriz........ 475,600
*Tehran....... 3,800,000
Iraq
*Baghdad, Gr.... 2,183,800
Basra.......... 370,900
Mosul......... 293,100
Ireland
Cork......... 128,235
*Dublin......... 568,772
Israel
Haifa......... 217,100
*Jerusalem...... 315,000
Tel Aviv-Jaffa, Gr.
.... 1,150,000
Italy
Bari........... 356,733
Bologna....... 491,873
Catania........ 413,670
Florence....... 461,602
Genoa......... 841,978
Messina....... 273,526
Milan......... 1,724,173
Naples....... 1,277,438
Palermo....... 661,477
*Rome........ 2,799,836
Trieste........ 277,752
Turin......... 1,183,864
Venice........ 363,062
Ivory Coast
*Abidjan, Gr.... 510,000
Jamaica
*Kingston, Gr..... 475,548
Japan
Amagasaki..... 553,696
Fukuoka...... 853,270
Hiroshima...... 541,998
Kawasaki...... 973,486
Kitakyushu.... 1,042,321
Kobe.......... 1,288,937
Kyoto....... 1,419,165
Nagasaki...... 421,114
Nagoya...... 2,052,000
Osaka........ 2,980,487
Sapporo...... 1,010,023
Sendai......... 545,065
*Tokyo, Gr.... 11,454,000
Yokohama..... 2,342,000
Jordan
*Amman........ 520,700
Kenya
Mombasa, Gr.... 255,400
*Nairobi, Gr...... 535,200
Korea, Dem. People's Rep. of
*Pyong Yang...... 840,000
Korea, Republic of
Inchon.......... 646,013
Pusan........ 1,880,710
*Seoul........ 5,536,377
Taegu....... 1,082,750
Kuwait
*Kuwait, Gr...... 560,000
Laos
*Vientiane....... 145,000
Lebanon
*Beirut, Gr........ 893,00
Lesotho
*Maseru, Gr....... 29,000
Liberia
*Monrovia......... 96,226
Libya
*Bengazi........ 170,000
*Tripoli.......... 264,000
Luxembourg
*Luxembourg.... 78,032

Macau
*Macau.......... 241,413
Madagascar
*Tananarive, Gr... 347,466
Malawi
Blantyre-Limbe,
Gr............. 169,000
*Zomba, Gr...... 19,666
Malaysia
*Kuala Lumpur... 500,000
Maldives, Rep. of
*Male............ 15,740
Mali
Bamako, Gr...... 196,800
Malta
*Valletta.......... 15,401
Mauritania
*Nouakchott..... 120,000
Mauritius
*Port Louis, Gr.... 370,000
Mexico
Chihuahua, Gr... 363,850
Guadalajara, Gr. 1,196,218
Juarez, Gr....... 436,054
Mexicali, Gr..... 390,411
*Mexico......... 7,005,855
*Mexico, D.F.... 8,589,630
Monterrey, Gr.. 1,177,361
Puebla, Gr...... 521,885
Tijuana, Gr...... 335,125
Mongolian Rep.
*Ulan Bator....... 310,000
Morocco
Casablanca..... 1,506,373
Fez........... 325,327
Marrakech..... 332,741
Meknes........ 248,369
*Rabat—Sale.... 530,366
Tangier........ 187,994
Mozambique
*Lourenco Marques,
Gr............. 354,700
Namibia
*Windhoek........ 61,260
Nepal
*Katmandu, Gr.... 210,000
Netherlands
*Amsterdam, Gr. 1,055,157
Eindhoven..... 193,711
Groningen..... 170,275
The Hague..... 482,879
Haarlem...... 170,667
Rotterdam, Gr.. 1,018,641
New Zealand
Auckland, Gr.... 747,339
Christchurch, Gr. 313,210
*Wellington, Gr... 337,680
Nicaragua
*Managua...... 398,514
Niger
*Niamey........ 78,991
Nigeria
Ibadan......... 758,332
Kano........... 357,098
*Lagos, Gr..... 1,250,000
Ogbomosho.... 386,650
Norway
Bergen......... 214,000
*Oslo, Gr........ 720,000
Oman
*Muscat.......... 6,000
Pakistan
Hyderabad, Gr... 834,000
*Islamabad...... 50,000
Karachi, Gr.... 3,650,000
Lahore, Gr.... 2,073,000
Lyalpur, Gr.... 1,109,000
Panama
*Panama........ 418,013
Papua
*Port Moresby.... 66,244
Paraguay
Asuncion, Gr.... 550,000
Peru
Arequipa........ 304,653
Cuzco......... 108,900
*Lima, Gr....... 2,541,300
Philippines
Cebu.......... 372,146
Davao......... 438,769

Manila, Gr...... 3,000,000
*Quezon City..... 348,788
Poland
Gdansk (Danzig).. 370,800
Krakow....... 595,100
Lodz........... 765,400
Poznan........ 476,300
*Warsaw, Gr.... 1,775,000
Wroclaw (Breslau) 531,100
Portugal
*Lisbon, Gr..... 1,640,000
Porto........... 310,437
Qatar
*Doha.......... 95,000
Rhodesia
*Salisbury, Gr..... 477,000
Romania
*Bucharest...... 1,488,328
Saudi Arabia
Jidda.......... 194,000
Mecca......... 185,000
*Riyadh......... 225,000
Senegal
*Dakar, Gr....... 581,000
Sierra Leone
*Freetown....... 200,000
Singapore
*Singapore..... 2,220,000
Somalia
*Mogadishu...... 230,000
South Africa
*Cape Town, Gr.. 1,125,000
Durban, Gr..... 1,040,000
Johannesburg, Gr.
.... 2,550,000
*Pretoria, Gr..... 575,000
Spain
Barcelona, Gr.. 3,165,000
Bilbao......... 410,490
Cordoba....... 235,632
*Madrid....... 3,580,000
Seville......... 548,072
Valencia....... 653,690
Zaragoza....... 479,845
Sri Lanka (Ceylon)
*Colombo, Gr.... 2,700,000
Sudan
*Khartoum, Gr.... 675,000
Omdurman..... 258,532
Surinam
*Paramaribo..... 110,867
Sweden
Goteborg...... 445,482
Malmo........ 246,622
*Stockholm...... 671,453
*Stockholm, Gr.. 1,352,359
Switzerland
Basel.......... 212,857
*Berne........ 162,405
Geneva........ 173,618
Zurich........ 422,640
Syria
Aleppo........ 639,361
*Damascus...... 836,668
Tanzania
*Dar es Salaam.... 343,911
Thailand
*Bangkok, Gr.... 3,051,000
Togo Rep.
*Lome.......... 192,745
Trinidad and Tobago
*Port of Spain, Gr.. 310,000
Tunisia
*Tunis, Gr........ 685,000
Turkey
*Ankara....... 1,208,791
Istanbul....... 2,247,630
Izmir......... 520,686
Uganda
*Kampala...... 331,889
USSR
Alma-Ata...... 776,000
Baku.......... 884,000
Barnaul....... 459,000
Chelyabinsk.... 910,000
Dniepropetrovsk.. 903,000
Donetsk....... 905,000
Erevan........ 818,000
Frunze........ 452,000
Gorky....... 1,213,000

Irkutsk........ 473,000
Ivanovo........ 434,000
Karaganda :.... 541,000
Kazan......... 904,000
Khabarovsk.... 462,000
Kharkov...... 1,280,000
Kiev......... 1,764,000
Krasnodar..... 491,000
Krasnoyarsk.... 698,000
Krivoy Rog..... 600,000
Kuibyshev.... 1,094,000
Leningrad, Gr.. 4,066,000
Lvov......... 579,000
Makeyevka..... 396,000
Minsk........ 996,000
*Moscow, Gr.... 7,300,000
Novokuznetsk.. 508,000
Novosibirsk.... 1,199,000
Odessa........ 941,000
Omsk......... 876,000
Perm......... 881,000
Riga.......... 755,000
Rostov........ 823,000
Saratov....... 790,000
Sverdlovsk.... 1,073,000
Tashkent..... 1,461,000
Tbilisi........ 927,000
Ufa.......... 821,000
Vladivostok.... 472,000
Volgograd..... 852,000
Voronezh...... 693,000
Yaroslavl...... 538,000
Zaporozh'ye.... 697,000
United Arab Emirates
Dubai........ 57,500
United Kingdom
England
Birmingham... 1,013,366
Bristol....... 426,170
Coventry...... 334,839
Leeds........ 501,080
Leicester..... 283,549
Liverpool..... 606,834
*London, Gr.... 7,418,020
Manchester.... 542,430
Newcastle..... 222,153
Nottingham.... 299,758
Sheffield...... 519,703
Wales
*Cardiff....... 278,221
Scotland
Aberdeen...... 186,006
Dundee....... 182,084
*Edinburgh..... 453,422
Glasgow...... 896,958
Northern Ireland
*Belfast....... 360,150
Londonderry.... 53,744
Upper Volta
*Ougadougou.... 110,000
Uruguay
*Montevideo.... 1,202,757
Venezuela
*Caracas, Gr.... 2,500,000
Maracaibo..... 650,002
Valencia...... 366,154
Vietnam, Dem. Republic
Haiphong...... 182,490
*Hanoi........ 414,620
Vietnam, South
Danang........ 437,668
Hue.......... 199,893
*Saigon....... 1,804,880
Western Samoa
*Apia, Gr....... 30,593
Yemen
*Sana......... 120,000
Yemen, Southern
Aden......... 250,000
Yugoslavia
Belgrade...... 800,000
Sarajevo...... 244,000
Skopje....... 313,000
Zagreb....... 566,000
Zaire
*Kinshasa, Gr.... 1,623,760
Lubumbash.... 357,369
Luluabourg.... 428,960
Zambia
*Lusaka, Gr..... 381,000

AFGHANISTAN

ALBANIA

ALGERIA

ANDORRA

ARGENTINA

AUSTRALIA

AUSTRIA

BAHAMAS

BAHRAIN

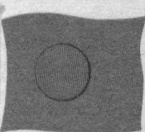
BANGLADESH

BARBADOS

BELGIUM

BHUTAN

BOLIVIA

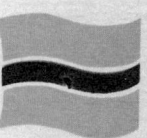
BOTSWANA

BRAZIL

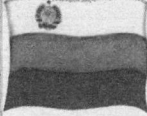
BULGARIA

BURMA

BURUNDI

CAMBODIA

CAMEROON

CANADA

CENTRAL AFRICAN
REPUBLIC

CHAD

CHILE

CHINA (MAINLAND)

CHINA (TAIWAN)

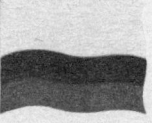
COLOMBIA

CONGO

COSTA RICA

CUBA

CYPRUS

CZECHOSLOVAKIA

DAHOMEY

DENMARK

DOMINICAN REPUBLIC

ECUADOR

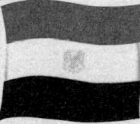
EGYPT

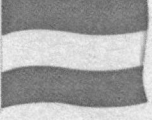
EL SALVADOR

EQUATORIAL GUINEA

Flags shown are *national* flags in common use and vary slightly from official *state* flags, most particularly by omitting coats of arms in some cases.

ETHIOPIA	 FIJI	 FINLAND	 FRANCE	 GABON
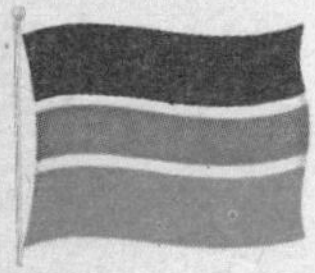 GAMBIA	 GERMAN DEM. REP.	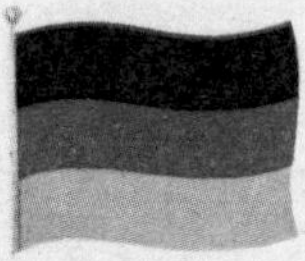 GERMANY, FED. REP. OF	 GHANA	 GREECE
 GRENADA	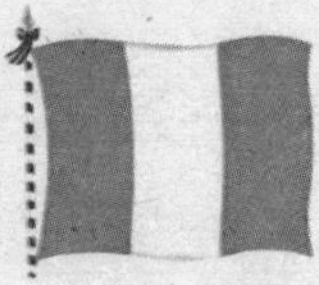 GUATEMALA	 GUINEA	 GUYANA	 HAITI
 HONDURAS	 HUNGARY	 ICELAND	 INDIA	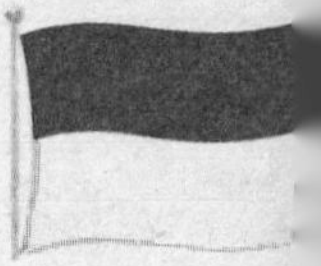 INDONESIA
 IRAN	 IRAQ	 IRELAND	 ISRAEL	 ITALY
 IVORY COAST	 JAMAICA	JAPAN	 JORDAN	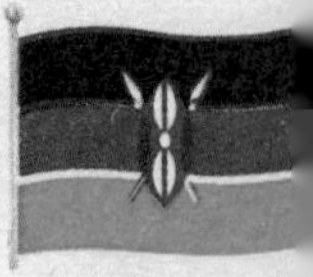 KENYA
 KOREA, NORTH	 KOREA, SOUTH	 KUWAIT	 LAOS	 LEBANON
 LESOTHO	 LIBERIA	 LIBYA	 LIECHTENSTEIN	 LUXEMBOURG

Though Angola, Cape Verde Islands, Comoro Islands, Netherlands Antilles, Sao Tome & Principe, and Surinam became independent last year, the precise design or colors of their national flags were not available at press time.

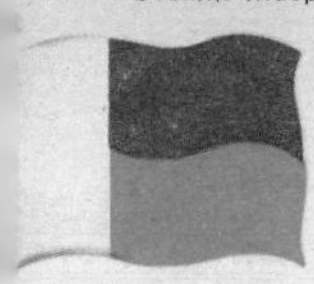

MADAGASCAR

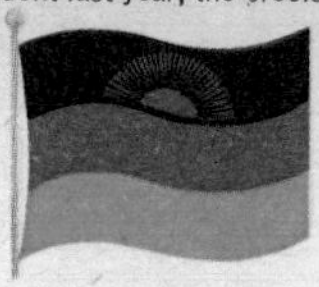

MALAWI

MALAYSIA

MALDIVES

MALI

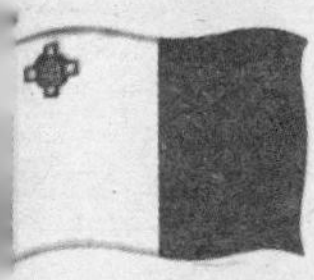

MALTA

MAURITANIA

MAURITIUS

MEXICO

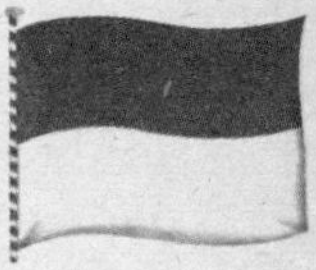

MONACO

MONGOLIA

MOROCCO

MOZAMBIQUE

NAURU

NEPAL

NETHERLANDS

NEW ZEALAND

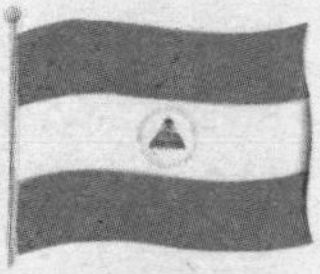

NICARAGUA

NIGER

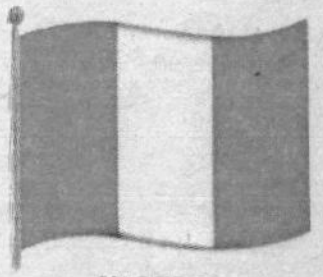

NIGERIA

NORWAY

OMAN

PAKISTAN

PANAMA

PAPUA NEW GUINEA

PARAGUAY

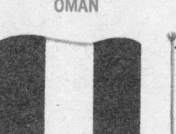

PERU

PHILIPPINES

POLAND

PORTUGAL

QATAR

RHODESIA

ROMANIA

RWANDA

SAN MARINO

SAUDI ARABIA

SENEGAL

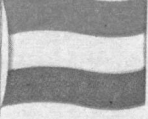

SIERRA LEONE

SINGAPORE

SOMALIA

SOUTH AFRICA

SPAIN

SRI LANKA

SUDAN

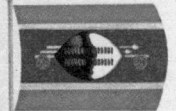

SWAZILAND

SWEDEN

SWITZERLAND

SYRIA

TANZANIA

THAILAND

TOGO

TONGA

TRINIDAD & TOBAGO

TUNISIA

TURKEY

UGANDA

U.S.S.R.

UNITED ARAB EMIRATES

UNITED KINGDOM

UNITED STATES

UPPER VOLTA

URUGUAY

VATICAN CITY

VENEZUELA

VIETNAM, NORTH

VIETNAM, SOUTH

WESTERN SAMOA

YEMEN

YEMEN, P.D.R. OF

YUGOSLAVIA

ZAIRE

ZAMBIA

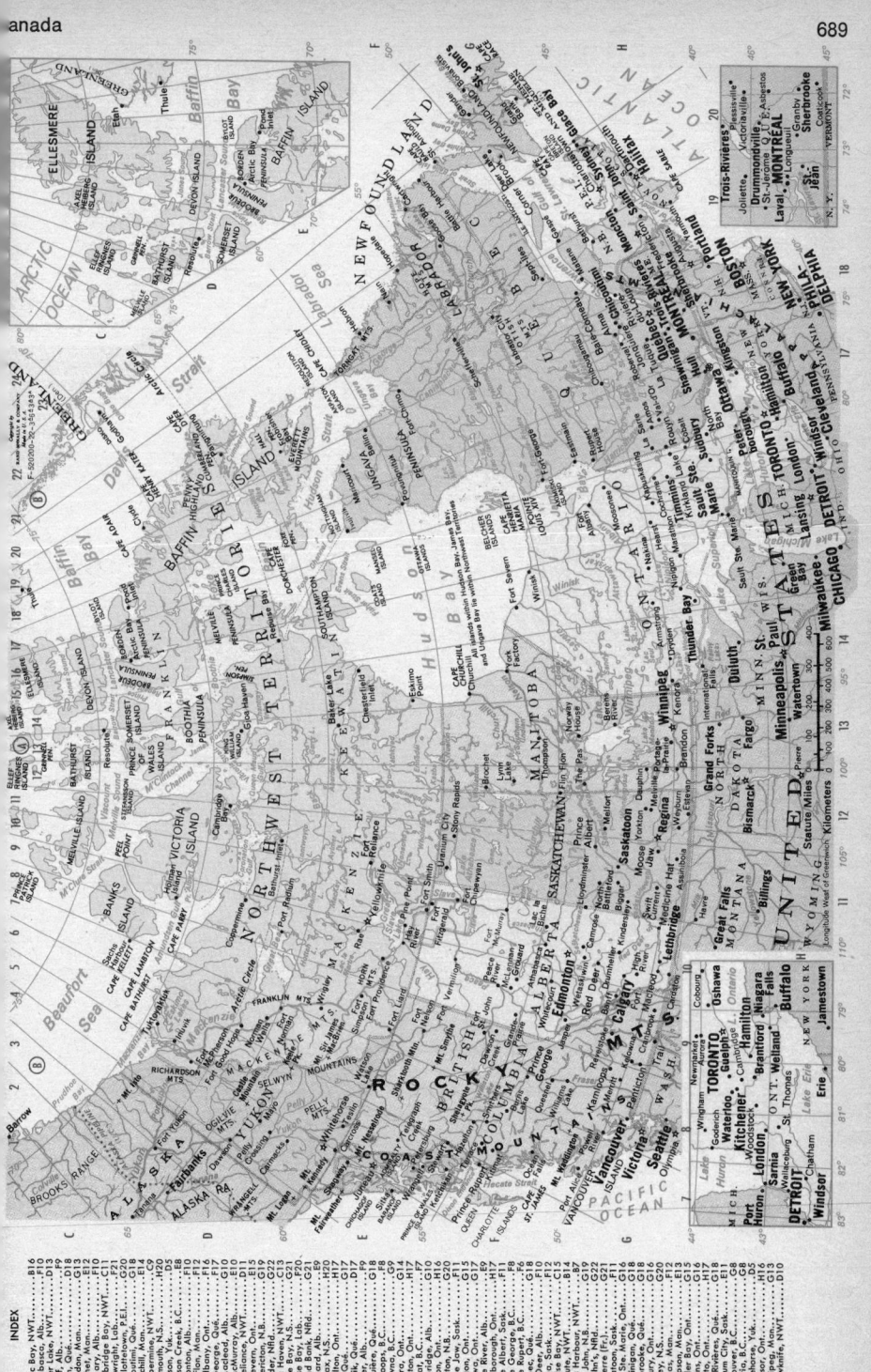

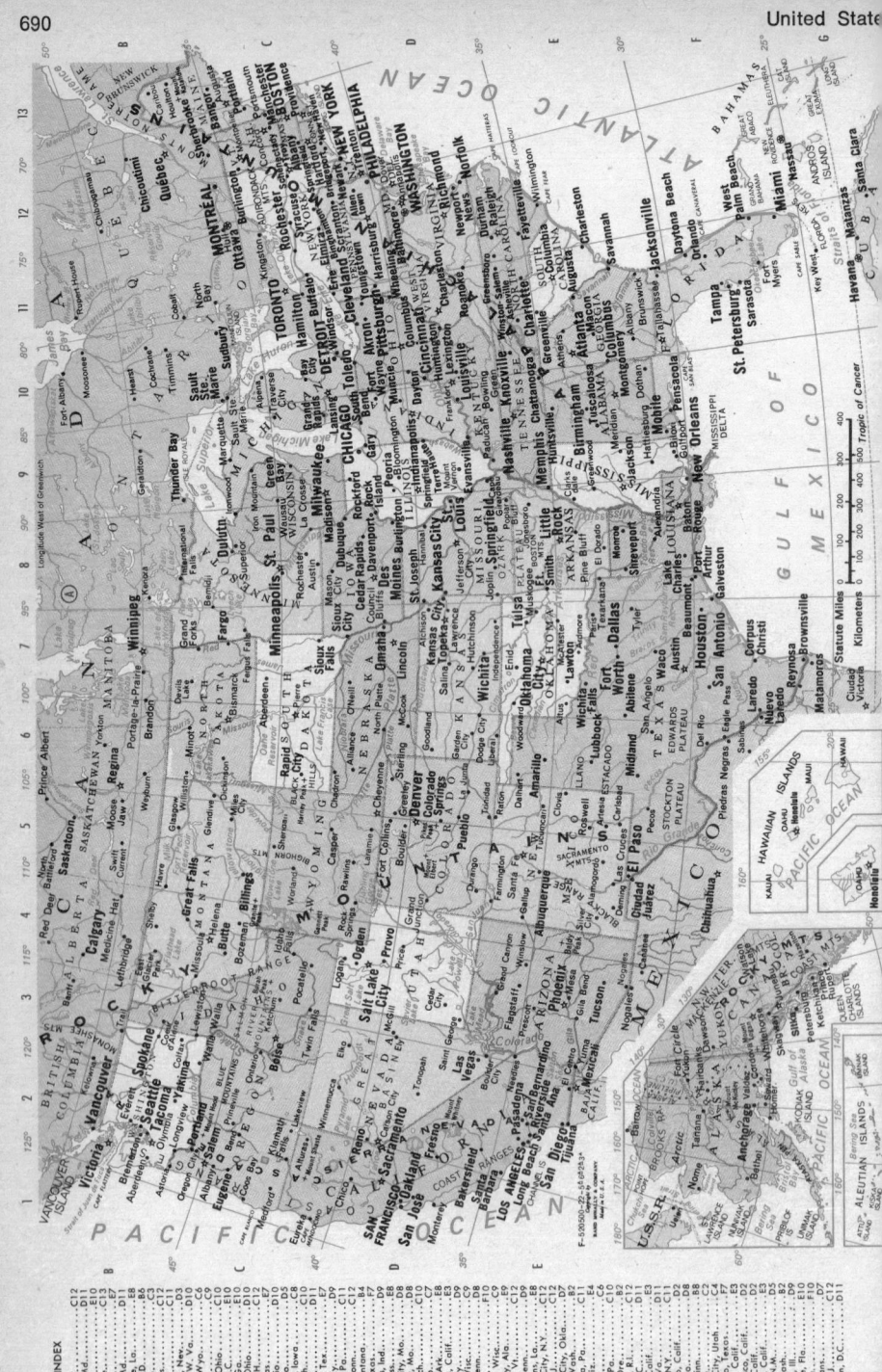

INDEX

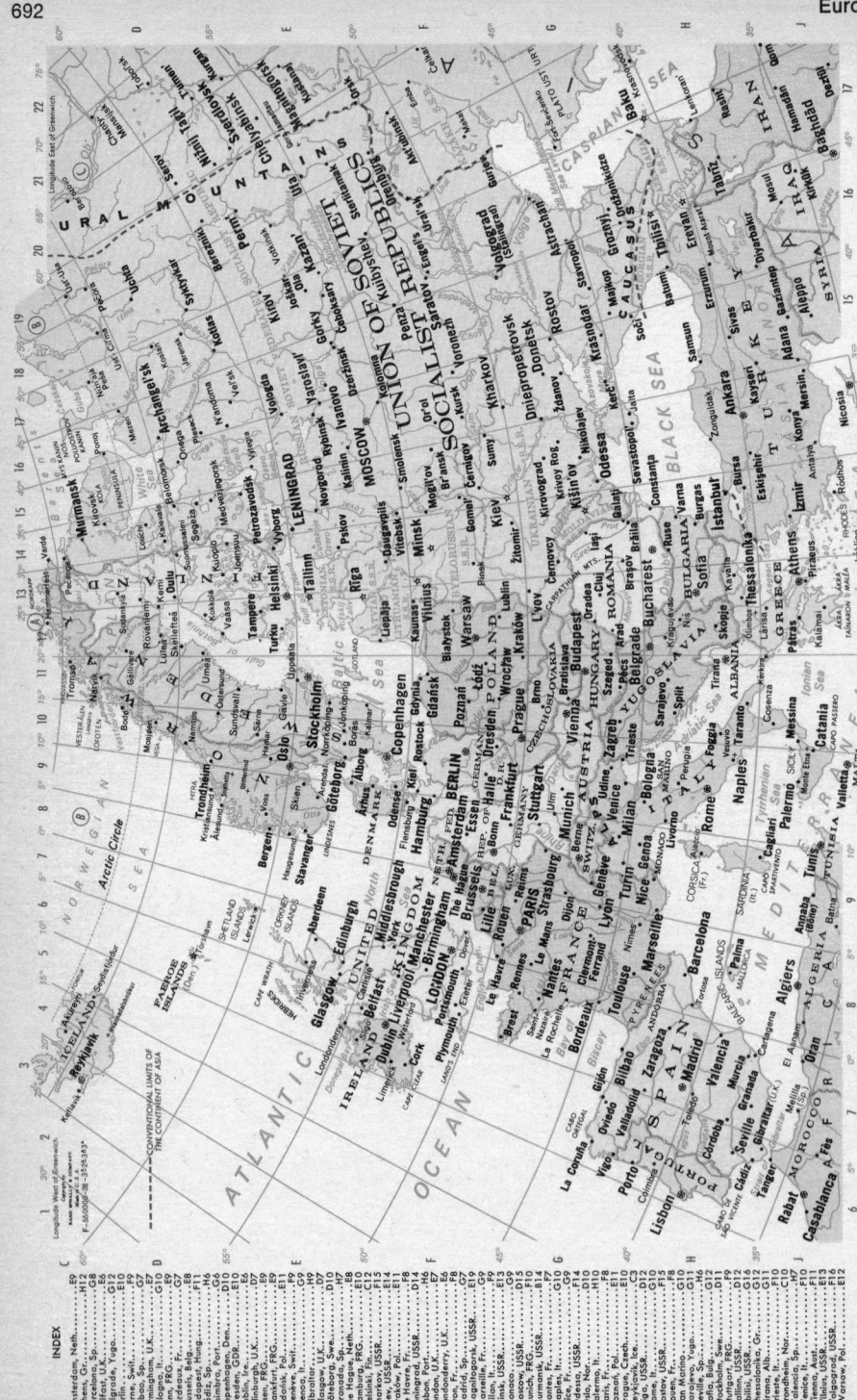

Map of Africa (and surrounding regions including Europe, the Middle East, and the Atlantic and Indian Oceans). Principal labels as shown:

Oceans and seas: ATLANTIC OCEAN, INDIAN OCEAN, North Sea, Bay of Biscay, Black Sea, Mediterranean Sea, Red Sea, Gulf of Aden, Gulf of Guinea, Strait of Gibraltar, Aral Sea.

Europe and USSR: SHETLAND ISLANDS (U.K.), Stockholm, LENINGRAD, Glasgow, Riga, Kirov, Perm', URAL MTS., Chelyabinsk, Belfast, Copenhagen, MOSCOW, Gorky, Ufa, Omsk, Dublin, UNITED KINGDOM, DENMARK, Vilnius, Minsk, UNION OF SOVIET SOCIALIST REPUBLICS, IRELAND, LONDON, NETH., GER., BERLIN, Warsaw, Saratov, Orenburg, Plymouth, BEL., LUX., Bonn, Prague, EUROPE, Kiev, Kharkov, VOLGOGRAD, PARIS, VIENNA, CZECHOSLOVAKIA, BUDAPEST, ODESSA, Rostov, Novokazalinsk, FRANCE, SWITZ., AUST., HUNG., ROMANIA, Bucharest, PLATO UST-URT, Lyon, MILAN, YUGOSLAVIA, Belgrade, BULGARIA, Sofia, ISTANBUL, TBILISI, BAKU, Marseille, Bilbao, PYRENEES, CORSICA, ITALY, ALB., GREECE, Ankara, CAUCASUS, Porto, MADRID, BARCELONA, ROME, SARDINIA, Athens, İzmir, TURKEY, Tabrīz, Lisbon, SPAIN, Palermo, SICILY, CRETE, CYPRUS, Aleppo, SYRIA, Baghdād, TEHERAN, AÇORES (Port.), Rabat, Oran, Algiers, Tunis, Beirut, Damascus, IRAQ, IRAN, Işfahān, ISLAS CANARIAS / CANARY ISLANDS (Sp.), Casablanca, Fès, TUNISIA, Tripoli, ISRAEL, JERUSALEM, JORDAN, KUWAIT, Ābādān, Shīrāz, Santa Cruz, Las Palmas, Marrakech, ATLAS MTS., Béchar, Touggourt, Benghazi, Alexandria, CAIRO, AN-NAFŪD, BAHRAIN, QATAR, U.A.E.

Africa: El Aaiún, Tindouf, ALGERIA, LIBYA, EGYPT, Asyūt, Aswān, NAFŪD, Jidda, Mecca, Riyadh, SAUDI ARABIA, SPANISH SAHARA, SAHARA, FAZZAN, Marzūq, Tropic of Cancer, AS-SAHRA AL-LIBIYAH, NUBIAN DESERT, AR-RUB'AL-KHĀLĪ, OMAN, Villa Cisneros, Nouadhibou, CAP BLANC, Atar, MAURITANIA, TIBESTI, Bûr Sudân, 'Atbarah, P.D.R. OF YEMEN, SUQUTRA, Nouakchott, MALI, NIGER, CHAD, SUDAN, Khartoum, Asmara, YEMEN, Aden, Berbera, CAPE VERDE ISLANDS, SENEGAL, Dakar, Tombouctou, Gao, Agadez, Zinder, Abéché, Al-Fāshir, El-Ubayyid, Gonder, AFARS AND ISSAS, Djibouti, GAMBIA, GUINEA-BISSAU, Bamako, Kankan, Niamey, Ouagadougou, UPPER VOLTA, Kano, Maiduguri, N'Djamena, CENTRAL AFRICAN REPUBLIC, Sarh, Addis Ababa, Dire Dawa, Hargeysa, ETHIOPIA, Conakry, SIERRA LEONE, Monrovia, LIBERIA, IVORY COAST, GHANA, DAHOMEY, Kaduna, NIGERIA, Ibadan, Enugu, Bangui, SOMALIA, Abidjan, Accra, Lomé, Lagos, Porto-Novo, Yaoundé, CAMEROON, UGANDA, KENYA, Mogadishu, CAPE PALMAS, SAO TOME AND PRINCIPE, EQUAT. GUI., GABON, Libreville, CONGO BASIN, ZAIRE, Kisangani, Kampala, Nairobi, Equator, Brazzaville, RWANDA, BURUNDI, Bujumbura, Kilimanjaro, Mombasa, Pointe-Noire, CABINDA (Angola), Kinshasa, Matadi, TANZANIA, Zanzibar, Dar-es-Salaam, Luanda, COMORO ISLANDS, CAP D'AMBRE, Lobito, ANGOLA, Lubumbashi, Diego-Suarez, Nova Lisboa, Ndola, Lilongwe, MALAWI, MOÇAMBIQUE, Moçâmedes, ZAMBIA, Lusaka, Salisbury, RHODESIA, Beira, Tamatave, SAINT HELENA (U.K.), ASCENSION (St. Helena), Tropic of Capricorn, Walvisbaai (S. Afr.), Windhoek, BOTSWANA, KALAHARI DESERT, Bulawayo, MADAGASCAR, Tuléar, Tananarive, SOUTH WEST AFRICA (S. Afr. Admin.), Gaborone, Pretoria, Lourenço Marques, Mbabane, SWAZILAND, GREAT NAMALAND, JOHANNESBURG, Maseru, LESOTHO, Durban, CAP SAINTE-MARIE, SOUTH AFRICA, Cape Town, CAPE OF GOOD HOPE, CAPE AGULHAS, GREAT KARROO, East London, Port Elizabeth.

Scale: Statute Miles 0 300 600 900 1200 · Kilometers 0 300 600 900 1200 1500 1800 · Longitude West of Greenwich · Longitude East of Greenwich

F-580000-21-9588344

Copyright by RAND McNALLY & COMPANY — Made in U.S.A.

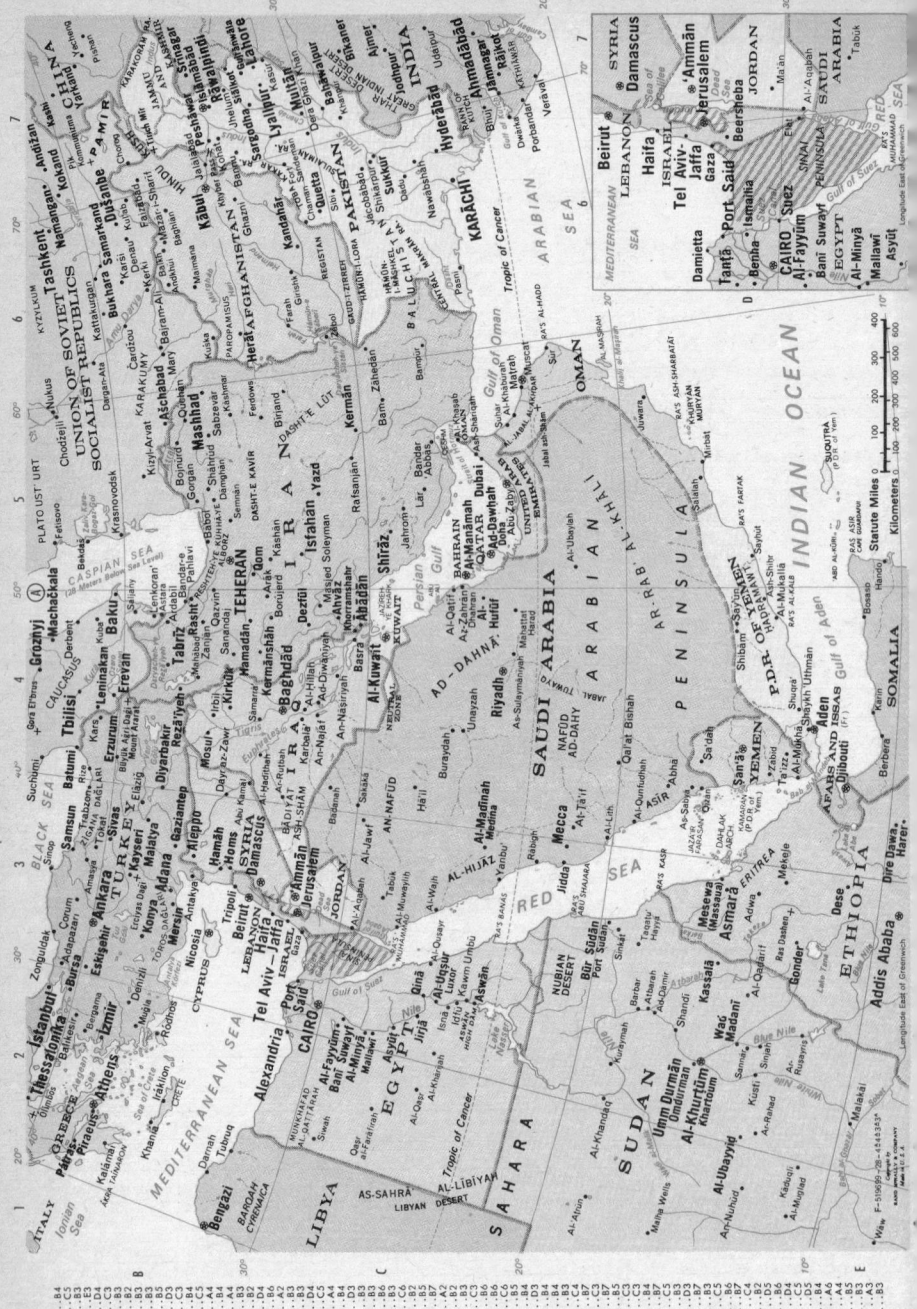

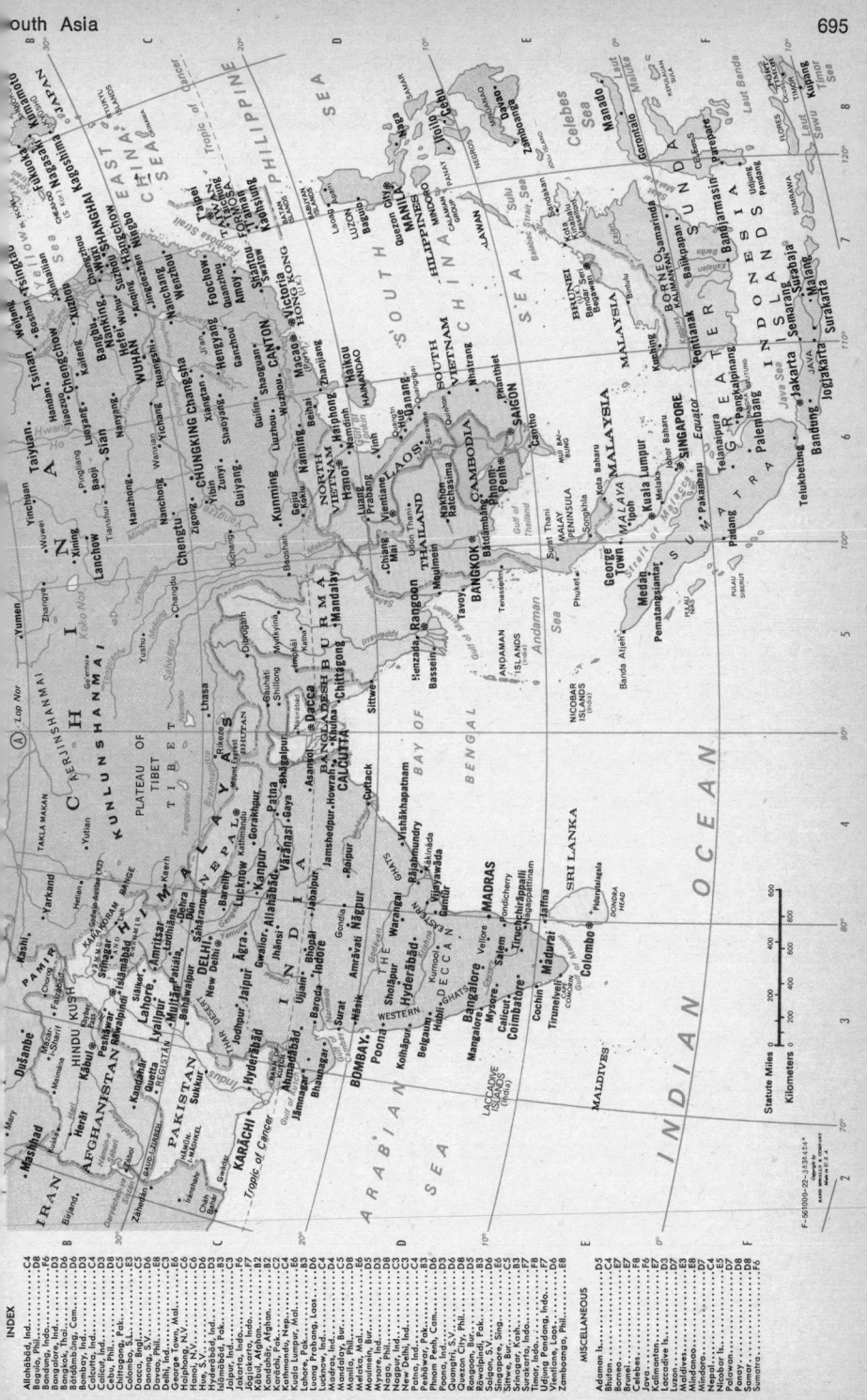

CANADA

Capital: Ottawa. Area: 3,851,809 sq. mi. Population (Govt. est., Jan. 1975): 22,659,000. Monetary unit: Canadian dollar.

Government and Politics

The Canadian political spectrum has embraced a plethora of political parties. Since the year of Confederation, 1867, there have been over 45 different party labels in official existence and contesting elections. Most of these parties have never attained any national prominence; indeed, the majority disappeared into oblivion without electing a single candidate.

Political power in Canada has been completely dominated by the 2 major parties — the Progressive Conservatives and the Liberals. Since 1867 these 2 parties have alternated in forming the government and in monopolizing political power. In the 30 federal elections conducted in Canada, the Conservatives have won 12, holding power for 47 years; the Liberals have gained office in 18 elections, governing the country for 61 years. A noteworthy feature of these 2 parties' political rule has been the tendency for one or the other to remain entrenched in office for a considerable length of time.

Although the Conservatives and the Liberals have been the only 2 parties to form the government of Canada and have clearly dominated Canadian political life, the role of 3d parties in Canadian politics has been significant. Since 1961, 2 minority parties, the New Democratic Party and Social Credit have exerted some measure of influence on political outcomes. The NDP, Canada's most persistent 3d party, has been the more important of the 2. Pressure from the NDP on the left has pushed the 2 major parties to a position close to the center stream of the political spectrum. Minority party success at the polls has not been particularly spectacular. At best the NDP has succeeded in obtaining 31 seats or 12% with 18% of the popular vote.

In contrast to the NDP, the Social Credit Party is to the extreme right. The SC came into national prominence in the 1962 election following a sudden sweep in the Province of Quebec when the party succeeded in winning 26 of the 75 seats in that province. This victory increased to party's federal strength to 30 seats (12%), the highest it has ever been. In the 1974 election the party received only 11 seats of the total 264 and captured a mere 5% of the popular vote.

Foreign Relations

Prime Minister Trudeau visited the Soviet Union in 1971, Peking in 1973 and Japan in 1974. The steady development of more fruitful relations between Japan and Canada reflects the fact that, since 1973, Japan has replaced the United Kingdom as Canada's 2d largest trading partner.

While Canada's new forays abroad have proved newsworthy and show signs of a broadening of Canada's commitment to closer cooperation with other nations not previously within its ambit, the year 1975 has seen a reawakening of Canada's traditional role in Europe and the United States. Prime Minister Trudeau's visit to Europe in Mar. 1975 is a recognition of the importance of the European community. Canada's European ties include over 25 years of contribution to NATO. Despite his criticism of NATO, the Prime Minister has pledged continued Canadian support to the defense of Europe.

The most thorny area of Canada's foreign policy has been relations with the United States. Canada's excessive vulnerability to the impact of United States culture and economy means that Canada-American relations must take high priority. Canada's forays in Europe and the Far East are best seen as an attempt to supplement and strengthen Canada's connections abroad without supplanting or weakening Canada's long-standing relations with the U.S.

The Economy

The 1975 economic outlook for Canada is expected to compare unfavorably with 1974, although the latest forecast suggests a real growth in the gross national product of 5%, a marked improvement over previous forecasts calling for 1 to 3% growth.

Canada's gross national product in 1974 was $139.5 billion, 17.3% higher than in 1973. The economy's growth in real terms was only 3.7%, compared to a real growth rate of 6.8% in 1973.

Prices continued to escalate rapidly. The implicit price index for gross national expenditure rose by 13.1% after an increase of 7.6% in 1973. The 1974 increase is the largest on record, out-ranking that of 1948 when prices rose by 12.2%.

Employment increased by an above-average 4.3% in 1974, after the record-breaking increase of 5.2% in 1973. Labor force participation rate was 58.3%. In 1974 unemployment reached 5.4%. In Mar. 1975 the over-all unemployment rate was 8.6%, up from 6.4% for the same month in 1974. Labor income increased by 16.8% in 1974, the largest annual rate of growth since 1951.

Corporate profits increased slightly. The annual increase of 28.4% in corporation profits was down from the 35.7% increase shown in 1973.

An all-time high was reached for production of Canadian minerals during 1974. The total value was expected to exceed $11.6 billion. Over-all metals accounted for a value of $4.9 billion which was an increase of 27.8% over the previous year. Mineral or fossil fuels recorded a 60.2% increase in value to reach a new peak of $5.2 billion.

In the agricultural sector, total cash receipts from farming operations for 1974 were estimated at $8.4 billion compared to a level of $6.7 billion for the corresponding period in 1973.

Total expenditures of all levels of government combined, excluding inter-governmental transfers, rose by 22% in 1974. Total revenues of all levels of government combined increased by 25%. Reflecting the rise in personal income, revenue from personal direct taxes rose by 22%. Almost half of the total increase resulted from revenues collected under the oil export tax.

As a result of revenues rising more sharply than expenditures, the surplus, on a national account basis, of the government sector as a whole increased from $612 million in 1973 to $1.7 billion in 1974.

The Land

Canada is the world's 2d largest country in land size, extending south from the North Pole to the U.S. border and including all the islands of the Arctic from near Greenland to near the Alaskan border. Its seacoast, one of the longest in the world, includes 17,-860 miles of mainland and 41,810 miles of islands.

A great sweep of the nation, stretching across the northern territories and prairies through northern Ontario and Quebec down to the Atlantic provinces, is known as the Canadian Shield, where past ice ages scraped most soil and vegetation off the land. This is the world's oldest surface rock, and it is here that most Canadian mineral discoveries have been made.

Canada's continental climate, while generally temperate, can run to freezing cold and blistering heat. The range is well beyond 100 degrees Fahrenheit.

History

French explorer Jacques Cartier is generally regarded as the founder of Canada. But his 1534 exploration of the Gulf of St. Lawrence followed by 37 years the sighting of Newfoundland in 1497 by English seaman John Cabot. Centuries prior to that, increasing evidence shows, Vikings had reached Newfoundland and Canada's Atlantic coast.

France pioneered Canadian settlement and the French have multiplied to become about 27% of the Canadian population today. Quebec was settled as early as 1608, Montreal in 1642; New France was declared a colony in 1663.

Britain and France clashed in Canada as a result of European rivalries and British expansion in America. Britain acquired Acadia (later Nova Scotia) in 1713, and captured Quebec in 1759, obtaining control of the rest of New France in 1763. The Quebec Act in 1774 gave the French rights to their own language, religion, and civil law. This was one reason why the French-Canadian settlers did not join American colonists in the War of Independence.

During the American Revolution, many former colonials moved north to settle in Canada, proudly calling themselves United Empire Loyalists.

The fur trade and exploration opened up the western plains and led Canadians across the continent to the Pacific. Alexander Mackenzie scrawled on a rock by the Pacific "From Canada, by land, 1793."

In Upper and Lower Canada (later called Ontario and Quebec) and in the Maritimes, legislative assemblies appeared in the 18th century and reformers called for responsible government. But the War of 1812 with the U.S. intervened. The war ended in a stalemate that was symbolic of the end to armed conflict between Canada and the U.S.

In 1837 political agitation for more democratic government culminated in rebellions in Upper and Lower Canada. The British sent Lord Durham to investigate and, in a famous report, he recommended union of the two parts into one colony called Canada. The union lasted until Confederation brought 2 additional colonies, Nova Scotia and New Brunswick, to join the new country in 1867. During the period 1840 to 1867, the Canadian colonies won the right to internal self-government.

The Dominion of Canada was launched on July 1, 1867, by the proclamation of the British North America Act, which became the country's written constitution, establishing a federal system of government on the model of a British parliament and cabinet structure under the crown. Canada was proclaimed a self-governing Dominion within the British Empire in 1931. Empire has now given way to Commonwealth, and Canada remains an independent member.

World War I had much to do with the development of Canadian nationhood. The pride it engendered and the industrial base it created in Canada led to the demand for full sovereignty.

But the achievement of nationhood was dulled by the blight of the Great Depression in the 1930s. It took World War II and Canada's accomplishments in it to revive the country's pride and sense of direction. It also fired the furnaces of industry, converting the country into an urban, industrial state.

Industrial Boom

On the Pacific coast a chain of rivers and lakes was reversed to flow backwards through the mountains to power electric generators for the huge aluminum smelters at Kitimat. The Columbia and Kootenay Rivers and Arrow Lakes were dammed to provide electricity. Oil wells and mineral strikes led to an El Dorado. Immense iron ore resources were discovered and developed in the wilds of Labrador. Uranium was unearthed in northern Ontario and turned into nuclear power.

Canada joined with the U.S. to build the St. Lawrence River Seaway, and Ottawa shared costs with the provinces to complete the Trans-Canada Highway, the longest in the world. Two million immigrants arrived in Canada in the 2 decades after World War II and the country imported a billion dollars a year of foreign capital to finance a new industrial boom.

Economic System

The Canadian economy is a blend of private and public ownership. Despite a long historical tradition of state aid which has been necessary because of Canada's harsh climate and sparse population, private enterprise has flourished. But like Sweden, with which it vies for the 2d highest standard of living in the world, Canada accepts the idea of state capitalism and collectivism.

Most hydroelectric and many transportation and communication facilities are owned by either federal, provincial, or municipal governments. Air Canada, one of the largest airlines in the world, is a federal crown corporation, while the competing Canadian Pacific airline is privately owned. Canadian National Railways is another crown corporation. Its chief rival is the Canadian Pacific company. The Canadian Broadcasting Corp. is publicly owned, although independently managed. There are also private radio chains and private television networks.

Social Security

Under the British North America Act (1867), the provinces are responsible for welfare programs to benefit their citizens. The federal government helps the provinces bear the cost of welfare programs. Federal payments reimburse up to 50% of the cost of welfare assistance provided by the provinces. Ottawa has also used its fiscal strength to launch the social security system and help bring about a certain uniformity in the existing programs, ensuring a high level of equity in programs among the provinces.

In the mid-1960s the federal government conceived of a universal and compulsory medicare and hospitalization system. Strenuous provincial opposition to the federal government's proposals delayed implementation of a revised plan until 1968.

The Social Security system in Canada covers several schemes: Family Allowances, Shared Cost Welfare Programs of the Federal and Provincial Governments; Old Age Security; Guaranteed Income Supplement; The Canada Pension Plan; and Veterans Benefits. Payments under almost all of these schemes are adjusted to the cost of living index.

The Political Parties

Canadian parties, from whatever point in the political spectrum they begin, tend to move to the middle of the road where most of the votes lie. They all take much of the same kind of moderate line.

Conservatives—The oldest party, they have adopted the prefix "Progressive" and moved to the left, advocating farm support programs and endorsing an extension of social welfare. Their support comes from older voters, Protestants, and English-speaking rural residents.

Liberals—Originally the Canadian equivalent of the American Jacksonian Democrats, favoring strict representation by population and the rural pioneer against the urban elite, they now get most of their electoral support from the middle and upper classes in cities, from ethnic voters, and among French-speaking Canadians. Liberals are cautious about extending the welfare state.

New Democratic Party—Successor to the Cooperative Commonwealth Federation, which combined the agrarian protest movement in western Canada with a democratic socialism of the British Labor party variety, the N.D.P. was founded in 1961. It now attempts to attract the vote of middle-class Canadians and fuse it with the party's labor support.

Social Credit — Adopting the unorthodox monetary theories of its English founder, Major C. H. Douglas, Social Credit has appealed to the have-nots, especially now in rural Quebec.

Canada: Party Representation by Regions, 1949-1974

	1949	1953	1957	1958	1962	1963	1965	1968	1972	1974
Canada[1]										
Liberal	193	171	105	49	100	129	131	155	109	141
Conservative	41	51	112	208	116	95	97	72	107	95
New Dem.	13	23	25	8	19	17	21	22	31	16
Soc. Cred.	10	15	19	—	30	24	14	14	15	11
Other	5	5	4	—	—	—	2	1	2	1
Ontario										
Liberal	56	51	21	15	44	52	51	64	36	55
Conservative	25	33	61	67	35	27	25	17	40	25
New Dem.	1	1	3	3	6	6	9	6	11	8
Quebec										
Liberal	68	66	62	25	35	47	56	56	56	60
Conservative	2	4	9	50	14	8	8	4	2	3
Soc. Cred.	—	—	—	—	26	20	9	14	15	11
Atlantic										
Liberal	26	27	12	8	14	20	15	7	10	13
Conservative	7	5	21	25	18	13	18	25	22	17
New Dem.	1	1	—	—	1	—	—	—	—	1
Western										
Liberal	43	27	10	1	7	10	9	27	7	13
Conservative	7	9	21	66	49	47	46	25	42	49
New Dem.	11	21	22	5	12	11	12	16	19	6
Soc. Cred.	10	15	19	—	4	4	5	—	—	—

[1]Total seats in 1968, 1972 and 1974 elections include one each for Yukon and North West Territories.

Provinces of Canada

Alberta

CAPITAL: Edmonton. AREA: 255,285 sq. mi., rank 4th. POPULATION: 1,747,000 (est. Jan. 1975). FLOWER: The Wild Rose. ENTERED CONFEDERATION: 1905.

The vast area of Alberta was controlled by the Hudson's Bay Co. until 1870 at which time it was transferred to the North West Territories.

Along with Saskatchewan, Alberta is nicknamed the "sunshine" province because of its good weather. The weather is strongly affected by the "Chinook," a warm wind blowing eastward over the Rockies. The Rocky Mountains provide such famous tourist attractions as Banff and Jasper parks, Lake Louise, and the Columbian ice fields.

Wheat and cattle gave Alberta its start but the economy was transformed by the discovery of huge petroleum and natural gas supplies at Leduc near Edmonton in 1947. Since then the province has become the 3d wealthiest in Canada in terms of per capita income which was $3,756 in 1972.

Alberta ranked highest among the provinces in mineral production, and accounted for 38% of Canada's total. Crude petroleum and natural gas and their by-products make up 95% of the province's mineral production.

The government's budget early in 1975 gave Albertans a $140 average annual cut in income taxes. Albertans don't have a sales tax.

Conservative Premier Peter Lougheed captured 69 of the 75 seats in the provincial parliament in the election of March 1975. Premier Lougheed's first victory in 1971 ended 36 years of Social Credit rule.

British Columbia

CAPITAL: Victoria. AREA: 366,255 sq. mi., rank 3d. POPULATION: 2,441,000 (est. Jan. 1975).

FLOWER: The Dogwood. ENTERED CONFEDERA-
TION: 1871.

Canada's most westerly province, British Columbia, on the Pacific coast, has mild winters and
moderate summer temperatures which give the
province the warmest climate in Canada and makes
it a haven for tourists and retired people. The interi-
or is a series of rugged mountain ranges.

In 1849 the territory of the province became a British colony. The first significant settlement of the area
took place in 1858 with the Fraser River gold rush.
The full emergence of British Columbia as a distinct
province came about by the union of the two former
British colonies of Victoria and British Columbia.

In 1974, B.C.'s total lumber production was down
15.1% compared to 1973. B.C. is the leading producer
of copper. Copper, crude oil and coal accounted for
two-thirds of the total value of minerals produced in
the province.

Unemployment in the province reached 6.0% in
1974, a figure well above the country's average of
5.4%. The province continues to lead Canada in average weekly wages; they climbed to $178.22 in 1973.

The New Democratic Party, headed by Premier
David Barrett, elected in 1972, controls the government of British Columbia.

Manitoba

CAPITAL: Winnipeg. AREA: 251,000 sq. mi., rank
6th. POPULATION: 1,014,000 (est. Jan. 1975).
FLOWER: The Prairie Crocus. ENTERED CONFED-
ERATION: 1870.

Most easterly of the Prairie provinces, Manitoba is
called the "keystone" province because it links the
eastern and western halves of the country.

Previously called the Red River Colony, and controlled by the Hudson's Bay Co., the area was purchased by the Dominion of Canada in 1870. The Red
River Colony is of great historical importance because it was the site of the Riel rebellion that occured
in 1869. The execution of Riel in 1885 had a dramatic
impact on the course of Canadian history..

Manitoba's cheerful economic outlook in 1974
showed the extent to which the province managed to
escape the economic slowdown that hit other provinces due to decline in business activity with the U.S.

Total value of cash receipts from farming operations in 1974 amounted to $819,981,000, an increase
of 32% over 1973. Total value of wheat production
was up 84%; barley increased 56%; flaxseed rose
57%; and rapeseed jumped by 59%.

The province had the 3d lowest unemployment rate
in Canada. The annual average unemployed for 1974
was 3.1%, a drop from the 3.9% rate in 1973. The
average weekly wage was $144.76 in 1973, 6th in
Canada.

Edward Schreyer is the first New Democratic
Party Premier.

New Brunswick

CAPITAL: Fredericton. AREA: 27,835 sq. mi., rank
8th. POPULATION: 670,000 (est. Jan. 1975).
FLOWER: The Purple Violet. ENTERED CONFED-
ERATION: 1867.

The rectangular Atlantic province has an extensive
seacoast and the world's highest tides on the Bay of
Fundy.

Total value of mineral production reached
$218,733,000 in 1974, an increase of 34% over 1973.
The provincial total was 2% of Canada's total. Mineral production is concentrated chiefly in zinc, silver,
lead, and copper, which altogether make up 85% of
the total value.

Farm cash receipts reached $102,930,000 in 1974, a

gain of 7.7% over 1973.

In 1974 the unemployment rate was 9.2%, the 2d
highest in Canada. The average weekly wage in 1973
was $133.97, 2d lowest in Canada.

The province is governed by a Progressive Conservative government under Premier Richard
Hatfield.

Newfoundland

CAPITAL: St. John's. AREA: 156,185 sq. mi., rank
7th. POPULATION: 546,000 (est. Jan. 1975).
FLOWER: The Pitcher-Plant. ENTERED CONFED-
ERATION: 1949.

Newfoundland consists of two parts: an Atlantic island of 43,359 sq. mi. and the 112,826 sq. mi. of
Labrador. Both sections are hilly, rugged, and generally barren.

Newfoundland's key fishery industry experienced
another severe setback in 1974, closely related to the
decline in the frozen fish market in the northeastern
United States. During 1974, the estimated value of
fish landings was off 24% to 512.5 million pounds.
Value of landings dropped to an estimated $42.8 mil-
lion from $47.3 million.

Total value of mineral production in the province
made up about 4% of Canada's total. Iron ore mining
alone accounted for more than 80% of the province's
total value.

The province had the highest unemployment rate
in Canada in 1974, 15.7%. In 1973, the average weekly
wage was $149.09.

The Progressive Conservative party under Premier
Frank Moores has governed the province since 1972.

Nova Scotia

CAPITAL: Halifax. AREA: 21,425 sq. mi., rank 9th.
POPULATION: 818,000 (est. Jan. 1975). FLOWER:
The Trailing Arbutus. ENTERED CONFEDERA-
TION: 1867.

Nova Scotia is called "The Wharf of North America" because of its many excellent harbors, of which
Halifax, the capital, is the most extensive and
famous.

Of the Canadian provinces, Nova Scotia has the
longest history, beginning with John Cabot's visit to
Cape Breton in 1497. The province gained its name in
1621 with the establishment of New Scotland.

Once considered the wealthiest of the British
North American colonies, the province has long been
looked upon as a "have not" province, because its
economy has not kept pace with rapid industrialization.

Tourism is a major industry in Nova Scotia. Revenue from tourism in 1974 is expected to total about
$125 million.

Total value of farm cash receipts in 1974 reached
$101.2 million, an increase of 7% over 1973.

Unemployment in Nova Scotia for 1974 was 6.7%.
The average weekly wage was $134.44 in 1973.

The Liberal party, headed by Premier Gerald
Regan, was re-elected in 1974.

Ontario

CAPITAL: Toronto. AREA: 412,582 sq. mi., rank
2d. POPULATION: 8,171,000 (est. Jan. 1975).
FLOWER: The White Trillium. ENTERED CONFED-
ERATION: 1867.

The first big wave of settlers in Ontario consisted of
Loyalists forced to flee from the rebelling American
colonies. At the time, the area was part of Quebec.
Conflict between the English-speaking settlers and
the French-speaking inhabitants led to the division of

the province. Upper Canada later became Ontario. The vast industrialization of the region following World War II led to the arrival of millions of immigrants. Between 1946 and 1972, Ontario alone received over 50% of all immigrants into Canada, a fact which has drastically altered the ethnic and racial composition of the province.

Ontario occupies the heartland of Canada, stretching from the Great Lakes to Hudson and James Bays in the north.

Total value of mineral production reached $2,422,312,000 in 1974 which made up 21% of Canada's total. The province is the leading metal producer.

Manufacturing is the largest industry of Ontario. The province produces over one-half of all Canada's manufactured goods. Economic prosperity in Ontario is highly dependent on sales to American markets.

The province's cash receipts from farming operations reached $2,313,998,000 in 1974, an increase of 19% over 1973.

The Conservatives have ruled Ontario for 32 years. Premier William Davis now heads the government and was first elected in 1971.

Prince Edward Island

CAPITAL: Charlottetown. AREA: 2,184 sq. mi., rank 10th. POPULATION: 118,000 (est. Jan. 1975). FLOWER: Lady's Slipper. ENTERED CONFEDERATION: 1873.

Prince Edward Island in the Gulf of St. Lawrence is the smallest province of Canada both in area and population. It is often called "The Garden of the Gulf".

P.E.I.'s revenue from tourism rose to $31.7 million in 1974 from $25.4 million in 1973. Agriculture is P.E.I.'s primary industry. Total value of farm cash receipts amounted to $83,286,000 in 1974, an increase of 16% over 1973.

The province has the lowest average weekly wage in Canada, $111.17 in 1973.

The Liberal party led by Premier Alexander Campbell governs the province.

Quebec

CAPITAL: Quebec City. AREA: 594,860 sq. mi., rank 1st. POPULATION: 6,165,000 (est. Jan. 1975). FLOWER: The White Garden Lily. ENTERED CONFEDERATION: 1867.

Quebec was founded by Champlain in 1608 as a French colony and continues to struggle today to maintain its French heritage and culture. Quebec City, the provincial capital, dates to about 1625. The commercial and industrial center of the province is located in Montreal, Canada's largest city. Scene of Expo '67, Montreal will be the site of the 1976 Olympic Games.

The rocky and barren Canadian shield spreads over the largest part of the province north of the St. Lawrence River. South of the river, the Appalachian Mountains run east and south to the U.S.A. A fertile agricultural band called the St. Lawrence Lowlands surrounds the western end of the river. Quebec experiences the most severe climatic conditions in Canada. In the north and northwest the winters are long and harsh, the summers short and hot. The upper St. Lawrence Valley has a more moderate climate, but in the lower reaches of the river from Quebec to Gaspe winter arrives early and is followed by a late spring and hot summer.

Quebec, along with Ontario forms the industrial backbone of Canada. The pulp and paper industry is the mainstay of Quebec, followed by tourism. The province is the leading producer of asbestos, and in 1974 ranked 2d in the production of iron ore.

Farm cash receipts in the province totalled $1,107,380,000 in 1974, up 15% from the year before. Quebec's unemployment rate climbed in 1974 to 7.3%. The average weekly wage was $134.30 in 1973.

The Liberal party, headed by Premier Robert Bourassa controls the government of the province.

Saskatchewan

CAPITAL: Regina. AREA: 251,700 sq. mi., rank 5th. POPULATION: 912,000 (est. Jan. 1975). FLOWER: The Prairie Lily. ENTERED CONFEDERATION: 1905.

Formerly part of the Northwest Territories, Saskatchewan became a province in 1905. The southern portion is an arable plain devoted to the production of wheat.

Mineral resources include gold (which has dropped off in production since 1942), coal, copper, and zinc.

Farm cash receipts form the most important single indicator of the economic prosperity of Saskatchewan. Farm cash receipts amounted to $1,941,776,000 in 1974, a 32% increase over the previous year. But the production of all three of the large volume grain crops—wheat, barley, and oats—was down in 1974.

Saskatchewan elected the first democratic socialist government in North America in 1944. Defeated by the Liberals in 1964, the socialists regained office under the New Democratic Party label in 1971. Premier of the province is Allan Blakeney

Superlative Canadian Statistics

Area	Total: Land 3,560,238 sq. mi.; Water 291,571 sq. mi.	3,851,809 sq. mi.
Largest city in area	Whitehorse	162 sq. mi.
Smallest city in area (east)	Thetford Mines, Que.	7 sq. mi.
Smallest city in area (west)	Prince George, B.C.	17 sq. mi.
Northernmost point	Cape Columbia, N.W.T.	83°07′N.
Northernmost town	Inuvik, N.W.T.	68°21′N.
Southernmost point	Middle Island (Lake Erie), Ont.	42°41′N.
Southernmost town	Kingsville, Ont.	42°02′N.
Westernmost point	Mount St. Elias, Yukon	141°W.
Westernmost town	Dawson, Yukon	139°25′W.
Easternmost point	Cape Spear, Nfld.	52°37′W.
Easternmost town	St. John's, Nfld.	52°43′W.
Highest city	Rossland, B.C. at R.R. Stn. (49°05′ 117°47′)	3,465 ft.
Highest town	Lake Louise, Alta.	5,051 ft.
Highest waterfall	Takakkaw Falls, B.C. (51°30′ 116°29′)	1,248 ft.
Longest river	Mackenzie (from head of Finlay R.)	2,635 mi.
Highest mountain	Mt. Logan	19,850 ft.
Rainiest spot	Henderson Lake, Vancouver Is. yrly avg. rainfall	262.0 inches
Highest lake	Chilco Lake (51°20′ 124°05′) 75.1 sq. mi.	3,842 ft.

The Government of Canada

Canada is a constitutional monarchy with a parliamentary system of government. It is also a federal state. The head of state is Queen Elizabeth, represented in Canada, a self-governing member of the Commonwealth of Nations, by a resident Governor-General, appointed by Her Majesty on the advice of the federal cabinet.

The cabinet is drawn from members of the party holding the largest number of seats in the House of Commons. Its members are appointed by the Governor-General on the advice of the prime minister, the leader of the party. The prime minister is the head of the executive branch of government which is composed of the cabinet and the Governor-General, the formal title of the body being "the governor-in-council", also known constitutionally as the Privy Council.

Canada has a bicameral Parliament. The House of Commons, the more important chamber, is composed of 264 members elected at least every 5 years. The prime minister chooses the date within this period.

The upper house is the senate, comprised of 102 Senators who now are appointed to serve until 75. Prime ministers are free to choose appointees, the tradition being that they are party patronage nominations. The British North America Act requires that 30 members come from the Atlantic provinces, 24 from Quebec, 24 from Ontario, and 24 from the 4 western provinces.

Legislation becomes law by receiving 3 "readings" in the Commons, passing in the Senate and obtaining assent from the Governor-General. Financial bills can be introduced only in the Commons.

Each province has a modified version of the Ottawa pattern. Each province has a unicameral legislature. The executive head in the province is referred to usually as the Premier.

Head of State

Queen Elizabeth, succeeded to the throne in 1952, is represented by Governor-General Rt. Hon. Jules Leger, appointed 1974.

The Cabinet

(listed according to precedence) (June 1975)

Prime Minister — Pierre Elliott Trudeau
President of the Queen's Privy Council — Mitchell Sharp
Secretary of State for External Affairs — Allan J. MacEachen
Science and Technology and Public Works (Minister) — C. M. Drury
Transport — Jean Marchand
Finance — John Napier Turner
President of Treasury Board — Jean Chretien
Postmaster General — Bryce S. Mackasey
Energy, Mines and Resources — Donald S. Macdonald
Labour (Minister) — John Carr Munro
Communications (Minister) — Gerard Pelletier
National Revenue (Minister) — S. Ronald Basford
Regional Economic Expansion (Minister) — Donald C. Jamieson
Manpower and Immigration (Minister) — Robert K. Andras
National Defence (Minister) — James A. Richardson
Justice and Attorney General of Canada (Minister) —
Otto E. Lang
Supply and Services (Minister) — Jean-Pierre Goyer
Industry, Trade and Commerce (Minister) — Alastair W. Gillespie
Agriculture (Minister) — Eugene F. Whelan
Solicitor General of Canada — Warren Allmand
Secretary of State of Canada — J. Hugh Faulkner
Consumer and Corporate Affairs (Minister) — Andre Ouellet
Veterans Affairs (Minister) — Daniel J. MacDonald
National Health and Welfare (Minister) — Marc Lalonde
Environment and Fisheries (Minister) — Jeanne Sauve
Leader of the Government in the Senate — Raymond J. Perrault
Minister of State for Urban Affairs — Barnett J. Danson
Indian Affairs and Northern Development (Minister) — J. Judd Buchanan
Minister of State (Fisheries) — Romeo LeBlanc

Governors-General of Canada Since Confederation, 1867

Name	Term
The Viscount Monck of Ballytrammon	1867-1868
The Baron Lisgar of Lisgar and Bailieborough	1869-1872
The Earl of Dufferin	1872-1878
The Marquis of Lorne	1878-1883
The Marquis of Lansdowne	1883-1888
The Baron Stanley of Preston	1888-1893
The Earl of Aberdeen	1893-1898
The Earl of Minto	1898-1904
The Earl Grey	1904-1911
Field Marshal H.R.H. The Duke of Connaught	1911-1916
The Duke of Devonshire	1916-1921

Name	Term
General The Baron Byng of Vimy	1921-1926
The Viscount Willingdon of Ratton	1926-1931
The Earl of Bessborough	1931-1935
The Baron Tweedsmuir of Elsfield	1935-1940
Major General The Earl of Athlone	1940-1946
Field Marshal The Viscount Alexander of Tunis	1946-1952
The Right Hon. Vincent Massey	1952-1959
General The Right Hon. Georges P. Vanier	1959-1967
The Right Hon. Roland Michener	1967-1974
The Right Hon. Jules Leger	1974-

Prime Ministers of Canada

Name	Party	Term
Sir John A. Macdonald	Conservative	1867-1873
		1878-1891
Alexander Mackenzie	Liberal	1873-1878
Sir John J. C. Abbott	Conservative	1891-1892
Sir John S. D. Thompson	Conservative	1892-1894
Sir Mackenzie Bowell	Conservative	1894-1896
Sir Charles Tupper	Conservative	1896
Sir Wilfrid Laurier	Liberal	1896-1911
Sir Robert L. Borden	Conservative Unionist	1911-1920

Name	Party	Term
Arthur Meighen	Conservative	1920-1921
	Unionist	1926
W. L. M. King	Liberal	1921-1926
		1926-1930
		1935-1948
R. B. Bennett	Conservative	1930-1935
Louis St. Laurent	Liberal	1948-1957
John G. Diefenbaker	Prog. Cons.	1957-1963
Lester B. Pearson	Liberal	1963-1968
Pierre Elliott Trudeau	Liberal	1968-

Canadian Armed Forces

In Feb. 1968, Canada carried out the unification of its traditionally separate services: the Royal Canadian Navy, the Canadian Army, and the Royal Canadian Air Force. The first step towards a unified force was taken in 1964 when the 3 services were brought together under one control with common logistics and supply and training systems, but retaining their separate legal entities. The positions of Chairman of the Chiefs of Staff and Chiefs of the Navy, Army, and Air Force were abolished and replaced by the Chief of Defence Staff. On Feb. 1, 1968, the 3 services ceased to exist. They were unified into the Canadian Armed Forces in which all officers, men, and women are managed within a single body, with a common uniform.

Chief of the Defence Staff: General J. A. Dextraze

Vice Chief of the Defence Staff: Vice Admiral R. H. Falls

Air Defence Command	— Maj. Gen. W. M. Garton	Canadian Forces Europe	— Maj. Gen. J. W. Quinn
Air Transport Command	— Maj. Gen. K. E. Lewis	Maritime Command	— Vice Admiral D. S. Boyle
Communication Command	— Col. L. H. Wylie	Mobile Command	— Lieut. Gen. S. C. Waters
Training Command	— Rear Admiral R. S. Stephens		

Regular Forces Strength

March 31	Navy	Army	Air Force	Total	March 31	Navy	Army	Air Force	Total
1940	6,135	76,678	9,483	92,296	1968	17,439	40,192	44,045	101,676
1945	92,529	494,258	174,254	761,041	1969	......	......	......	98,340
1950	9,259	20,652	17,274	47,185	1971	......	......	......	89,563
1955	19,207	49,409	49,461	118,077	1972	......	......	......	84,933
1960	20,675	47,185	51,737	119,597	1973	......	......	......	82,402
1965	19,756	46,264	48,144	114,164	1974	......	......	......	81,243

Canadian Military Participation in Major Conflicts

Northwest Rebellion (1885)[1]
Participants—3,323
Killed—38
Last veteran died at the age of 104 in 1971.
South African War (1899-1902)
Participants—7,368[2]
Killed—89
Living Veterans—less than 50
First World War (1914-1918)
Participants—626,636[3]

Killed—61,332[4]
Living Veterans—96,900
Second World War (1939-1945)
Participants—1,086,343 (inc. 45,423 women)
Killed—37,714 (inc. 8 women)
Living Veterans—801,000
Korean War (1950-1953)
Participants—25,583
Killed—314
Living Veterans—25,000

[1]First battle in history to be fought entirely by Canada troops. [2]Includes Canadians in the South African constabulary and 8 nursing sisters. [3]Includes 2,854 nursing sisters. [4]Includes 21 nursing sisters and 1,563 airmen serving with the British air forces.

Canadian Peacekeeping Operations

Canada has provided either policing or observer troops for every peacekeeping operation since World War II.

Nearly 900 Canadian soldiers served in the Gaza Strip following the Israeli-Egyptian crisis of 1956 until the force was disbanded in 1967.

In the Congo, a 300-man signals unit provided communications for the UN Force from 1960 to 1964.

Canadian participation in the International Commission for Control and Supervision in Vietnam and Laos began in 1954 and at the high point of participation in 1973, following the US military withdrawal from Vietnam, there were 245 Canadian Forces personnel involved in the supervision of the ceasefire. The Canadian Vietnam supervisory contingent was withdrawn in July 1973 and the Laos mission was withdrawn in the spring of 1974.

Canada's largest peacekeeping commitment at the present time (mid-1975) is in the Middle East where approximately 1,100 Canadian Forces personnel are serving with the United Nations Emergency Force.

The UN Force in Cyprus is another of Canada's large military commitments. Since 1964 Canadian participation included provision of a reduced Infantry Battalion and a Canadian element in the UN Headquarters—a total of approximately 580 officers and men. However, in July 1974, following the troubles in Cyprus, Canada, at the request of the UN, augmented the Cyprus contingent by an additional force of approximately 480 officers and men and some additional military equipment.

Other Canadian peacekeeping operations in 1975 are as follows:

— 11 Canadian Forces personnel with the UN Military Observer Group, India-Pakistan.

— 20 Canadian officers with the UN Truce Supervisory Organization, Israel.

— 2 Canadian Forces personnel in Korea with the UN Military Armistice Commission.

In view of the easing of tension in Cyprus, the Canadian contingent was reduced to approximately 500 by mid-1975.

Canadian Winners of the Victoria Cross

The Victoria Cross is Britain's highest military honor. It has been accorded to 94 Canadians since its inception in 1856. The cross was originally cast from metal of a Russian cannon captured during the Crimean War. Canadian winners in World War II:

Name	Unit	Theater of War & Date
Sgt. Mjr. J. R. Osborn	Winnipeg Grenadiers	Hong Kong, Dec. 19, 1941
Lt. Col. C. E. Merritt	S. Sask. Regiment	Dieppe, Aug. 19, 1942
Capt. J. W. Foote	Royal Hamilton Light Infantry	Dieppe, Aug. 19, 1942
Capt. F. T. Peters	Royal Navy	Oran, North Africa, Nov. 8, 1942
Capt. Paul Triquet	Royal 22d Regiment	Casa Berardi, Dec. 14, 1943
Maj. C. F. Hoey	Lincolnshire Regiment	Burma, Feb. 16, 1944
Maj. John K. Mahoney	Westminster Regiment	Melfa River, May 24, 1944
P.O.A.C. Mynarksi	RCAF	Camria, France, June 12, 1944
Flt. Lieut. D. E. Hornell	RCAF	"Northern waters", June 25, 1944
Sqd. Ldr. Ian Bazalgette	RAF	Trossy St. Maximin, Aug. 4, 1944
Maj. D. V. Currie	South Alberta Regiment	Normandy, Aug. 20, 1944
Pvt. E. A. Smith	Seaforth Highlanders	Savio River, Italy, Oct. 22, 1944
Sgt. Aubrey Cosens	Queen's Own Rifles	Holland, Feb. 26, 1945
Maj. F. A. Tilston	Essex Scottish	Hochwald Forest, Mar. 1, 1945
Cpl. F. G. Topham	1st Canadian Parachute Battalion	Germany, Mar. 24, 1945
Lt. R. H. Gray	Royal Canadian Navy	Pacific, Aug. 9, 1945

Canadian Shipping Traffic

Source: Canadian Statistical Review, Apr. 1975 (thousand short tons)

Year and Month	Halifax	Saint John	Quebec	Montreal	Toronto	Vancouver	All Ports	Coastwise
1971	10,999	7,438	10,811	21,690	4,710	30,813	286,606	122,536
1972	11,355	10,263	14,901	20,431	4,534	29,894	298,076	122,403
1973	13,703	12,181	15,946	21,177	4,170	39,126	320,498	122,436
1974 Jan.	1,156	635	673	336	24	2,766	11,400	3,505
Feb.	796	857	612	381	28	2,505	11,587	3,696
Mar.	1,127	647	364	257	8	3,499	11,660	3,638

Personal Expenditure on Consumer Goods and Services in Current Dollars

(millions of dollars)
Source: Statistics Canada

	1965	1967	1968	1969	1970	1971	1972	1973
Food, Beverage, and Tobacco	8,097	9,240	9,739	10,411	11,235	12,021	13,462	15,670
Clothing and Footwear	2,855	3,354	3,617	3,908	4,034	4,381	4,871	5,670
Gross Rent, Fuel and Power	6,064	7,247	7,960	8,742	9,623	10,351	11,273	12,610
Furniture, Furnishings, Household Equipment and Operation	3,426	4,024	4,322	4,658	4,785	5,227	5,974	6,915
Medical Care and Health Services	1,516	1,789	1,902	1,912	1,758	1,571	1,715	1,944
Transportation and Communication	5,114	5,940	6,458	6,863	6,945	7,733	8,671	10,116
Recreation, Entertainment, Education and Cultural Services	2,400	3,334	3,682	4,104	4,467	5,023	5,775	6,353
Personal Goods and Services	4,460	5,497	6,034	6,683	7,106	7,582	8,410	9,642
Net Expenditure Abroad	15	-463	-10	151	133	100	126	—
Total	33,947	39,972	43,704	47,492	50,084	53,989	60,277	69,094
Durable Goods	5,085	5,915	6,494	6,975	6,798	7,776	9,030	10,718
Semi-Durable Goods	4,671	5,539	5,953	6,426	6,645	7,224	8,113	9,497
Non-Durable Goods	11,526	13,219	14,019	15,073	16,205	17,376	19,414	22,528
Services	12,665	15,299	17,238	19,018	20,438	21,613	23,720	26,351

Canadian Time Zones

There are seven time zones in Canada. In terms of the number of hours behind the Universal Time established on the zero meridian at Greenwich these are, from east to west:

Newfoundland Standard Time	3½ hours	Mountain Standard Time	7 hours
Atlantic Standard Time	4 hours	Pacific Standard Time	8 hours
Eastern Standard Time	5 hours	Yukon Standard Time	9 hours
Central Standard Time	6 hours		

The location of the time zone boundaries in Canada, together with other regulations governing time, is a matter of provincial jurisdiction. The adoption or rejection of Daylight Saving Time, therefore, is decided by provincial legislation except in those cases where the province leaves the decision to the municipalities.

Canadian Postal Code

The Canadian Postal Code consists of 6 alphanumeric characters with 2 components separated by a single space. The Area Code is a combination of letter-number-letter. The Local Code is a combination of number-letter-number.

The Postal Code precisely describes the location of the point of delivery for each item of mail. The Area Code makes it possible to sort mail into geographic areas, or forward sortation areas. The Local Code makes it possible to sort mail for post offices in rural areas, for letter carrier routes, large volume points of delivery, or forms of delivery service in urban areas.

As a matter of interest, only 18 letters are used in the first position, whereas 20 letters are used in 3d and 5th position. There are a total of 7,200,000 possible codes, i.e., (18 x 10 x 20) (10 x 20 x 10) but only about 10% will be used initially.

Canadian Government Budget
(in millions of dollars)
Source: Canadian Statistical Review, Apr. 1975

Expenditures

Fiscal Year or Month	National Defense	Health and Welfare	Agriculture	Post Office	Public Works	Transport	Veterans Affairs	Payments to Provinces	Total Expenditures
1971-72...	1,895.2	2,706.1	286.1	413.3	336.8	512.4	423.3	1,425.5	14,840.9
1972-73...	1,932.2	2,916.0	322.3	496.5	374.1	598.9	452.3	1,501.4	16,120.7
1973-74...	2,232.0	3,759.3	426.4	591.2	469.7	827.5	538.3	1,874.0	20,039.2
Apr......	120.4	151.8	9.2	27.4	10.7	46.6	35.8	112.4	1,934.8
July......	175.0	258.2	17.9	44.4	35.7	79.0	44.1	115.0	1,459.1
Dec......	181.5	286.0	48.5	48.4	30.1	73.9	44.8	127.2	1,445.7
1974-75									
Apr......	131.2	242.6	19.7	47.2	16.9	58.2	46.9	141.9	2,201.9
July......	190.5	420.0	31.3	57.5	35.4	45.7	48.1	166.7	1,872.7
Dec......	202.9	283.0	22.4	66.6	48.7	214.4	47.6	216.4	2,108.4

Revenues[1]

Fiscal Year or Month	Personal Income Tax	Corporation Income Tax	Sales Tax	Other Excise Tax[2]	Excise Duties	Customs Duties	Estate Taxes	Post Office	Total Budgetary Revenues
1971-72...	5,582.0	2,183.1	1,984.7	388.4	606.6	988.6	132.4	403.8	14,226.6
1972-73...	7,172.8	2,653.5	2,288.7	400.4	638.0	1,181.8	61.4	470.1	16,601.6
1973-74...	7,925.8	3,411.0	2,692.9	694.6	685.9	1,384.6	14.7	480.0	19,366.8
Apr......	506.9	510.7	154.1	21.9	44.0	91.2	1.2	34.0	1,475.0
July......	741.5	317.0	232.9	38.6	50.2	114.6	0.7	36.4	1,694.7
Dec......	740.8	217.4	230.6	37.2	57.9	96.8	0.7	50.1	1,727.7
1974-75									
Apr......	442.2	644.9	72.0	54.6	56.0	92.3	2.5	38.3	1,578.7
July......	896.1	394.4	320.1	161.5	58.3	180.1	—	29.2	2,205.3
Dec......	904.6	276.5	261.7	164.1	72.9	136.4	0.4	45.3	2,199.2

(1) This statement includes only receipts relating to budgetary revenue. Excluded are non-budgetary revenues such as Old Age Security Fund taxes. Prairie Farm Assistance Act levies, employer and employee contributions to government-held funds.
(2) Beginning in Dec. 1973, this category includes oil export tax.

Canadian Consumer Price Index
Source: Canadian Statistical Review, July 1974 (1961:100)

	All Items	Food	Shelter	Clothing	Transportation	Health Personal	Recreation, Education	Tobacco, Alcohol	Total Services
1972.....	139.8	141.4	157.9	132.0	133.3	149.2	139.4	132.1	157.9
1973.....	150.4	162.0	168.7	138.6	136.8	156.4	145.2	136.3	167.6
1974									
Jan...	157.6	174.0	173.8	114.8	143.5	161.8	149.0	136.9	173.4
Apr...	161.9	180.8	176.8	149.5	145.9	166.8	152.9	141.5	177.0
July..	168.0	190.2	181.1	152.5	152.4	169.9	160.4	143.9	181.8
Oct...	172.2	196.3	185.7	156.3	153.4	175.4	164.3	147.8	186.2
1975									
Jan...	176.6	202.3	187.5	157.8	158.7	179.3	166.7	155.1	190.0
Feb..	178.0	204.0	188.7	157.9	160.2	182.0	168.3	156.3	192.4

Assets and Deposits of Chartered Banks in Canada
(in thousands)
Source: Supplement to the Canada Gazette (July 6, 1974)

Bank	Assets	Deposits
Royal Bank of Canada..	22,765,626	20,595,956
Canadian Imperial Bank of Commerce.........................	20,172,959	18,308,332
Bank of Montreal..	18,551,916	18,971,525
Bank of Nova Scotia.......................................	14,771,534	13,224,479
Toronto-Dominion Bank.....................................	12,914,475	11,664,902
Banque Canadienne Nationale...............................	4,442,483	4,088,812
Banque Provinciale du Canada..............................	2,767,410	2,639,602
Mercantile Bank of Canada.................................	777,562	681,873
Bank of British Columbia..................................	511,523	468,919
Unity Bank of Canada......................................	164,078	138,676

Canadian Foreign Trade
Source: Canadian Statistical Review (July, 1974)
(in millions of dollars)

Year and Month	Exports including re-exports				Imports			
	All Countries	U.S.	U.K.	All other countries	All countries	U.S.	U.K.	All other countries
1969...............	14,931	10,614	1,113	3,204	14,130	10,243	791	3,096
1970...............	16,820	10,917	1,485	4,404	13,951	9,917	738	3,296
1971...............	17,744	12,006	1,361	4,377	15,607	10,941	837	3,827
1972...............	20,140	13,932	1,358	4,780	18,678	12,878	950	4,844
1973...............	25,325	17,070	1,598	6,632	23,302	16,483	1,005	5,813
1974...............	32,052	21,262	1,894	8,894	31,578	21,250	1,126	9,202
1975 Jan...........	2,683.5	1,649.7	178.6	885.3	2,813.1	1,725.7	107.5	979.8
Feb. (Preliminary)	2,424.2	1,668.1	166.3	589.8	2,616.0	1,729.8	98.8	787.4

Population and Area of Canada by Provinces
Source: Statistics Canada

| Province, territory | Capital | Area in square miles | | | 1966 Census | 1971 Census | Jan. 1975 Estimate |
		Land	Fresh Water	Total			
Newfoundland	St. John's	143,045	13,140	156,185	493,396	522,105	546,000
Prince Edward Island	Charlottetown	2,184	...	2,184	108,645	111,645	118,000
Nova Scotia	Halifax	20,402	1,023	21,425	756,039	788,960	818,000
New Brunswick	Fredericton	27,385	519	28,354	616,788	634,555	670,000
Quebec	Quebec	523,860	71,000	594,860	5,780,845	6,027,765	6,165,000
Ontario	Toronto	344,092	68,490	412,582	6,960,870	7,703,110	8,171,000
Manitoba	Winnipeg	211,775	39,225	251,000	963,066	988,245	1,014,000
Saskatchewan	Regina	220,182	31,518	251,700	955,344	926,245	912,000
Alberta	Edmonton	248,800	6,485	255,285	1,463,203	1,627,870	1,747,000
British Columbia	Victoria	359,279	6,976	366,255	1,873,674	2,184,620	2,441,000
Northwest Territories	Yellowknife	1,253,438	51,465	1,304,903	28,738	34,805	37,000
Yukon Territory	Whitehorse	205,345	1,730	207,076	1,382	18,390	20,000
Total		**3,560,238**	**291,571**	**3,851,809**	**20,014,880**	**21,568,315**	**22,659,000**

Population by Mother Tongue, for Canada and Provinces, 1971
Source: Statistics Canada

Province	English	French	German	Indian, Eskimo	Italian	Dutch	Polish	Ukrain- ian	Other
Newfoundland	514,520	3,635	515	1,620	175	120	45	50	1,430
Prince Edward Island	103,105	7,360	140	145	35	280	40	30	510
Nova Scotia	733,560	39,330	2,000	2,710	1,495	1,850	555	435	7,020
New Brunswick	410,400	215,730	1,110	2,725	755	665	155	110	2,905
Quebec	789,185	4,867,250	31,025	21,050	135,455	4,660	15,480	11,385	152,265
Ontario	5,971,520	482,045	184,880	28,590	344,285	77,475	73,985	80,230	460,050
Manitoba	662,720	60,550	82,720	31,665	7,265	10,385	15,900	72,925	44,130
Saskatchewan	685,920	31,605	75,885	26,020	2,045	4,695	7,675	53,385	39,025
Alberta	1,263,935	46,500	92,800	29,920	15,570	20,670	13,730	70,895	73,855
British Columbia	1,807,250	38,035	89,020	18,550	31,030	23,955	7,100	20,055	149,620
Yukon	15,345	450	565	1,030	75	100	55	150	620
Northwest Territories	16,305	1,160	425	15,800	175	80	60	205	595
Total	12,973,810	5,793,650	561,085	179,825	538,360	144,920	134,780	309,855	932,020

Canadian Cities with Metropolitan Populations Over 100,000
Source: Statistics Canada

	Metro Area*	City		Metro Area*	City
Montreal, Que	2,743,208	1,214,352	Kitchener, Ont	226,846	111,804
Toronto, Ont	2,628,043	712,786	Halifax, N.S	222,637	122,035
Vancouver, B.C.	1,082,352	426,256	Victoria, B.C.	195,800	61,761
Ottawa, Ont	602,510	302,341	Sudbury, Ont	155,424	90,535
Winnipeg, Man	540,262	246,246	Regina, Sask	140,734	139,469
Hamilton, Ont	498,523	309,173	Chicoutimi, Que	133,703	33,893
Edmonton, Alta	495,702	438,152	St. John's, Nfld	131,814	88,102
Quebec, Que	480,502	186,088	Saskatoon, Sask	126,449	126,449
Calgary, Alta	403,319	403,319	Oshawa, Ont	120,318	91,587
St. Catharines, Ont	303,429	109,722	Thunder Bay, Ont	112,093	108,411
London, Ont	286,011	223,222	Saint John, N.B.	106,744	89,039
Windsor, Ont	258,643	203,300			

*1971 Census Metropolitan Area

Immigration to Canada, by Province of Intended Destination
Source: Canadian Statistical Review (July, 1975)

Year	Canada	Nfld.	P.E.I.	N.S.	N.B.	Que.	Ont.	Man.	Sask.	Alta.	B.C.	Yukon N.W.T.
1972	122,006	686	175	1,872	1,301	18,592	63,805	5,262	1,511	8,390	20,107	305
1973	184,200	984	273	2,548	1,729	26,871	103,187	6,621	1,866	11,904	27,949	268
1974	218,465	1,036	311	2,601	2,207	33,458	120,115	7,423	2,244	14,289	34,481	300

Immigration to Canada, by Country of Last Permanent Residence
Source: Canadian Statistical Review (July, 1975)

Year	Total	U.K. and Ireland	France	Germany	Nether- lands	Greece	Italy
1972	122,006	18,317	2,742	2,025	1,471	4,016	4,608
1973	184,200	28,102	3,586	2,564	1,898	5,833	5,468
1974	218,465	39,748	4,232	3,621	2,103	5,632	5,226

Year	Portugal	Other Europe	Asia	Austra- lasia	United States	West Indies	All Other
1972	8,737	8,871	23,831	2,148	22,618	8,214	14,408
1973	13,483	10,949	43,193	2,671	25,242	19,281	21,930
1974	16,333	11,799	50,566	2,594	26,541	23,670	26,400

Births and Deaths in Canada by Province

Source: Statistics Canada

Province	Births 1974	1973	Deaths 1974	1973	Province	Births 1974	1973	Deaths 1974	1973
Nfld.	11,267	11,895	2,972	3,163	Manitoba.	17,609	17,268	8,562	8,491
P.E.I.	1,937	1,875	993	911	Sask.	15,213	14,713	7,765	7,574
N.S.	12,955	13,448	6,919	7,042	Alberta.	29,645	29,416	11,687	10,784
N.B.	11,699	11,697	5,359	5,138	B.C.	35,321	34,142	19,775	17,962
Quebec.	84,564	87,627	41,957	42,816	Total.	346,168	347,261	167,631	164,307
Ontario.	125,958	125,180	61,642	60,426					

Suicide Deaths—Canada, 1973

Source: Statistics Canada

Province	Number	Rate*	Province	Number	Rate*
Total.	2,773	12.6	Manitoba.	135	13.5
Newfoundland	26	48	Saskatchewan.	118	13.0
Prince Edward Island.	12	10.4	Alberta.	216	12.8
Nova Scotia.	89	11.1	British Columbia.	428	18.5
New Brunswick.	58	8.9	Yukon.	6	30.5
Quebec.	693	11.4	Northwest Terr.	8	21.2
Ontario.	984	12.4	*Rate per 100,000 population		

Marriages, Divorces, and Rates in Canada

(Rates per 1,000 population)

Year	Marriages No.	Rate	Divorces No.	Rate	Year	Marriages No.	Rate	Divorces No.	Rate
1936	82,941	7.4	1,570	0.14	1967	165,879	8.1	11,165	0.54
1940	125,799	10.8	2,416	0.21	1968	171,766	8.3	11,343	0.54
1945	111,376	9.0	5,101	0.42	1969	182,183	8.7	26,079	1.23
1950	125,083	9.1	5,386	0.39	1970	188,428	8.8	29,775	1.37
1955	128,029	8.2	6,053	0.38	1971	191,324	8.9	29,626	1.39
1960	130,338	7.3	6,980	0.39	1972	200,470	9.2	32,364*	1.48
1965	145,519	7.4	8,974	0.45	1973	199,064	9.0	36,704	1.66
*Preliminary.									

Marriages and Divorces in Canada by Province, 1973

Source: Statistics Canada

Province	Marriages	Divorces	Province	Marriages	Divorces
Newfoundland.	5,048	224	Saskatchewan.	7,847	887
Prince Edward Island.	1,014	54	Alberta.	16,280	4,435
Nova Scotia.	7,273	1,249	British Columbia.	21,303	5,687
New Brunswick.	6,357	574	Northwest Territories.	226	42
Quebec.	51,943	8,091	Yukon.	206	60
Ontario.	72,371	13,781	Total.	199,064	36,704
Manitoba.	9,196	1,620			

Divorces and Rates — Canada and Provinces, 1961-1973

	Canada	Nfld.	P.E.I.	N.S.	N.B.	Que.	Ont.	Man.	Sask.	Alta.	B.C.	Yukon	N.W.T.
1961	6,563	6	8	245	194	348	2,739	312	251	1,039	1,397	24	—
1962	6,768	—	5	229	181	—	3,140	339	281	1,084	1,490	14	5
1963	7,686	8	8	271	172	491	3,237	369	331	1,268	1,516	13	2
1964	8,623	7	5	315	210	834	3,508	418	315	1,389	1,596	24	2
1965	8,974	3	16	323	237	226	4,087	443	312	1,348	1,961	12	6
1966	10,239	11	18	406	155	988	4,101	524	321	1,567	2,124	21	3
1967	11,165	11	18	394	292	727	4,350	477	399	1,736	2,734	21	6
1968	11,343	15	20	497	143	606	5,036	465	384	1,916	2,220	30	11
1969*	26,093	103	102	791	347	2,947	11,845	1,334	882	3,446	4,224	42	30
1970*	29,775	140	65	823	386	4,865	12,451	1,234	871	3,771	5,111	41	17
1971*	29,685	150	61	721	483	5,203	12,211	1,384	816	3,656	4,928	47	25
1972	32,389	177	65	927	466	6,426	13,190	1,415	827	3,772	5,041	47	36
1973	36,704	224	54	1,249	574	8,091	13,781	1,620	887	4,435	5,687	60	42
					Rate per 100,000 population								
1961	36.0	1.3	7.6	33.2	32.4	6.6	43.9	33.9	27.1	78.0	85.8	164.1	—
1962	36.4	—	4.7	30.7	29.9	—	49.4	36.2	30.2	79.2	89.8	93.3	20.0
1963	40.6	1.7	7.4	36.1	28.2	9.0	49.9	38.9	35.5	90.4	89.2	86.7	7.7
1964	44.7	1.4	4.6	41.7	34.4	14.9	52.9	43.6	33.4	97.1	91.5	160.0	7.4
1965	45.7	0.6	14.7	42.7	38.5	4.0	60.2	45.9	32.8	93.0	109.1	85.7	22.2
1966	51.2	2.2	16.6	53.7	25.1	17.1	58.9	54.4	33.6	107.1	113.4	146.0	10.4
1967	54.8	2.2	16.5	51.8	47.1	12.4	61.0	49.5	41.7	116.5	140.6	140.0	20.7
1968*	54.8	3.0	18.2	64.8	22.9	10.2	69.3	47.9	40.0	125.7	110.8	200.0	36.7
1969*	124.2	20.0	91.9	102.1	55.3	49.2	160.4	136.3	92.1	221.0	205.0	262.5	96.8
1970*	139.8	27.1	59.1	105.2	61.6	80.9	164.9	125.5	92.6	236.4	240.2	241.2	51.5
1971*	137.6	28.7	54.5	91.4	76.1	86.3	158.5	140.1	88.1	225.6	225.6	266.1	71.4
1972	148.4	33.3	57.5	116.6	72.5	106.2	168.6	142.6	90.3	228.1	224.3	247.4	100.0
1973	166.1	41.4	47.0	155.2	88.0	133.1	173.6	162.3	97.7	263.5	245.7	300.0	110.5

*These include divorces granted under old as well as new legislation of July 2, 1968; hence these totals differ from the subsequent tables in which only those divorces filed under new legislation are considered.

Number of Canadian Households with Television Sets[1]

Source: Statistics Canada (April 1974)

Province	Number Households	Black & White			Color		
		One Set	Two Sets or More	No Sets	One Set	Two Sets or More	No Sets
Newfoundland.	118	87	10	20	28	*	89
Prince Edward Island.	29	20	*	7	7	*	22
Nova Scotia.	219	144	21	54	77	*	138
New Brunswick.	165	108	15	41	58	*	105
Quebec.	1,721	1,084	293	344	667	30	1,024
Ontario.	2,453	1,499	286	667	1,086	51	1,316
Manitoba.	306	192	30	84	124	7	175
Saskatchewan.	264	154	23	87	125	4	135
Alberta.	497	291	36	170	247	12	238
British Columbia.	722	404	55	263	351	11	360
Total.	6,493	3,984	772	1,736	2,770	122	3,601

(1) Estimates in thousands. *Less than 4,000.

Value of Canadian Fishery Products and By-products[1]

Source: Statistics Canada ($1,000)

Province	1969	1970	1971	1972	1973
Total[3].	408,802	450,631	463,013	545,587	·722,086
Newfoundland.	72,302	85,104	94,943	100,599	144,780
Prince Edward Island.	12,701	18,375	16,143	19,964	22,322
Nova Scotia.	123,492	105,939	127,215	142,102	175,685
New Brunswick.	64,820	67,404	68,629	86,380	89,988
Quebec.	19,026	24,130	26,022	25,938	35,478
Ontario.	14,778	13,070	13,896	16,238	20,752
Manitoba.	6,700	—	—	—	—
Saskatchewan.	4,587	13,276	12,674	15,449	16,590
Alberta.	1,563	—	—	—	—
Northwest Territories.	946	—	—	—	—
British Columbia[2].	87,852	123,333	120,167	159,132	285,052
Yukon.	35	—	42	46	—

(1) Final sales for the provinces by fish processors, handlers and fishermen.
(2) Includes halibut landed in United States ports.
(3) The sum of the provincial totals differ from the Canada total as duplications (intershipments between provinces) have been removed from the Atlantic Coast totals.

Canadian Sea Fish Catch and Exports[1]

(in millions of pounds)
Source: Canadian Statistical Review-April, 1975

Year and month	Total[2] Value ($1,000)	Landings of Sea Fish							Exports to[3]		Exports By Type	
		Total Quantity	Nfld	P.E.I.	N.S.	N.B.	Que.	B.C.	Total	United States	Other	Salmon	Lobster
1971.	192,993	2,466.1	871.6	97.5	658.1	370.1	240.2	228.7	607.6	438.3	169.3	58.5	22.5
1972.	219,829	2,215.1	649.3	59.9	654.0	394.5	182.1	336.7	642.0	443.6	169.3	77.6	19.8
1973.	296,288	2,190.4	675.9	62.9	615.4	286.1	161.3	388.8	752.6	491.6	211.1	93.1	20.1
1974.	245,870	1,644.1	345.9	35.6	620.3	248.4	114.8	279.0	551.4	394.6	155.0	78.5	18.2
1975 Jan.	3,597	60.5	7.9	0.1	47.3	00.6	1.7	2.9	46.1	31.0	15.1	4.4	2.2

[1] Monthly totals for current years are not equivalent to annual data due to receipt of additional statistics which cannot be allocated months.
[2] Includes also seaweeds and other species such as whales, worms, etc.
[3] Exports include sea and freshwater fish and shellfish products but exclude bait, meal, oils, offal, livers, fish roe, n.e.s. and fishery foods and feeds n.e.s.

Approximate Land and Freshwater Areas

Source: Canada Year Book

Province or Territory	Land sq. miles	Freshwater sq. miles	Total sq. miles	Percentage of Total Area
Newfoundland.	143,045	13,140	156,185	4.1
Island of Newfoundland.	41,164	2,195	43,359	1.1
Labrador.	101,881	10,945	112,826	3.0
Prince Edward Island.	2,184	—	2,184	0.1
Nova Scotia.	20,402	1,023	21,425	0.6
New Brunswick.	27,835	519	28,354	0.7
Quebec.	523,860	71,000	594,860	15.4
Ontario.	344,092	68,490	412,582	10.7
Manitoba.	211,775	39,225	251,000	6.5
Saskatchewan.	220,182	31,518	251,700	6.5
Alberta.	248,800	6,485	255,285	6.6
British Columbia.	359,279	6,976	366,255	9.5
Yukon Territory.	205,346	1,730	207,076	5.4
Northwest Territories.	1,253,438	51,465	1,304,903	33.9
Franklin.	541,753	7,500	549,253	14.3
Keewatin.	218,460	9,700	228,160	5.9
Mackenzie.	493,225	34,265	527,490	13.7
Canada.	3,560,238	291,571	3,851,809	100.0

MEMORABLE DATES

Consult also Chronology, Aviation Records, Polar Explorations, Fast Ocean Passages, Train Records, Marine Disasters, Political Assassinations, Earthquakes, Fires, Tornadoes, Amendments to the Constitution, Noted Personalities, Astronomical Data, Space Exploration, Sports, and other classifications.

B.C. or B.C.E.
Before Christ or Before Common Era

3000
Indus Valley Civilization sites at Mohenjo-Daro and Harappa in West Pakistan. Civilization had complex form of government, elaborate irrigation and drainage system, writing, well planned streets, houses of several stories. Ended about **1500 B. C.**

Pyramids begun by kings of Egypt at Sakkara. Cheops built great pyramid at Giza. Sphinx built about **2900 B.C.**

c. 1792-1750
Hammurabi ruled Semitic kingdom of Babylon; wrote extensive code of laws. Ruled Canaan in days of Abraham.

c. 1450 or c. 1275
Moses led the Israelites out of Egypt.

1360
Ikhnaton introduced monotheistic worship of Aton, or sun, in Egypt. A successor, Tutankhamen, revived polytheistic orthodoxy **1350 B. C.** Tutankhamen buried at Thebes **1344 B. C.**, tomb opened by Howard Carter and Lord Carnarvon **1923-24 A. D.**

1184
Troy (Ilium) fell to Greeks after 10-year siege, according to Homer's Iliad. Excavations show numerous battles were waged on site, NW corner of Asia Minor, 3 mi. from Hellespont (Dardanelles).

In **1871 A. D.** Heinrich Schliemann, German archeologist, excavated site of Troy on hill of Hissarlik and found layered remains of 7 cities. Dorpfeld found 2 more. Schliemann identified 2d city with Homer's Troy, but objects found in 6th city correspond better with Greek remains of **1200 to 1100 B. C.** found at Agamemnon's Mycenae in Greece.

1000
On death of King Saul **c. 1000 B. C.** David became king of Israel, but for 7½ years ruled only the southern kingdom of Judah. Thereafter he ruled all Israel, made Jerusalem capital. Solomon, son of David and Bathsheba, ruled **c. 973-933 B. C.**

753
Romulus founded Rome, according to legend.

612
Babylonians destroyed Nineveh, Assyrian capital. Nebuchadnezzar's Babylonians defeated Egyptians at Carchemish **605 B.C.** Built famed hanging gardens. Destroyed Solomon's temple **589 B. C.**

563
Gautama (Sakyamuni) Buddha, "the Enlightened," born near Himalayas; died **483 B. C.**, aged 80. Taught that pain in life is caused by desire; if desire is overcome, pain ends.

551
Confucius (Latinized form of K'ung-fu-tze) Chinese social philosopher, born; died **478 B.C.**

490
King Darius' Persian army landed at Marathon to march on Athens. Athenian infantry (10,000) routed 30,000 Persians.

484-480
Persian King Xerxes assembled a large army at Sardis to invade Greece. His Phoenicians and Egyptians built 2 ship bridges across Hellespont from Abydos (Nagara) to Sestos, 2,000 yds. long. One bridge of planks and dirt rested on 360 ships; the other on 314. Herodotus reported army crossing took 7 days and 7 nights.

At Thermopylae Pass, 480 B.C., Leonidas and 300 Spartans, supported by 700 Thespians and 400 Thebans, held off Persians until overcome. Persians took Athens and Attica. Athenians under Themistocles destroyed Persian fleet at Salamis under eyes of Xerxes, won land battle. Rallying about 70,000 from Greek states, they routed Persians at Plataea **479 B. C.**

438
Parthenon completed at Athens, 101'4'' by 228'2''; Doric columns 33' tall, roof height 60'. Ictinus and Callicrates, designers; Phidias, chief sculptor.

431
Peloponnesian Wars began between Athens and Sparta. Wars ended **404 B.C.** with Sparta victorious.

399
Socrates, Greek Philosopher, condemned by Athenian state, drank poison hemlock. Plato, his student, recorded 35 dialogues, famed philosophical work. Xenophon, another student, recorded memorabilia.

356
Alexander "The Great" of Macedon born. Ruthless and energetic military leader, defeated Persians at Granicus, Issus, Arbela; conquered Asia Minor and Egypt, burned Persian capital, Persepolis, carried war to the Punjab in India. Founded Alexandria in Egypt. Died of fever at Babylon **323 B. C.**

300
Invention of Mayan calendar in Yucatan (approximate date) giving solar year 365.24 days and lunar month 29.52 days. Considered more exact than older calendars of Babylon, Assyria, Egypt, Greece.

264
Rome began first Punic War against Carthage, rich commercial seaport on Bay of Tunis. In **241 B. C.** Carthage ceded Sicily and Lipari Islands; in **239 B. C.** Rome annexed Sardinia and Corsica.

218-146
Hannibal, Carthaginian General, in a campaign against Rome during 2d Punic War, crossed from Spain to Italy via the Alps with 20,000 infantry, 6,000 cavalry, and about 40 elephants. Defeated Romans at Lake Trasimene **217 B. C.** and Cannae **216 B. C.** Victories nullified by Fabius, "the delayer," hence "Fabian retreat." War closed with defeat of Carthage in Africa by Publius Scipio **202 B. C.** Hannibal, after career in Asia Minor, committed suicide in Bithynia upon betrayal to Romans, c. **183 B.C.**

Third Punic War 149-146 B. C., ended with total destruction of Carthage. Later, Roman colony built there; eventually destroyed by Saracens **698 A. D.**

60-27
Julius Caesar formed political triumvirate with Pompey and Crassus **60 B.C.**; defeated Helvetia, Belgae, **58-57 B. C.**; entered Britain **55** and **54 B. C.** Crossed Rubicon River into Italy, despite Senate orders, defeated Pompey at Pharsalus **48 B. C.** Defeated Pharnaces at Zela, Asia Minor, **47 B.C.** Lived with Cleopatra, queen of Egypt, in Rome **46-44 B. C.** Was dictator but refused crown.

Caesar assassinated in Roman Senate by group led by Cassius and Brutus **44 B. C.** Caesar's will made his grand-nephew, Gaius Octavius, successor; he formed new triumvirate, Octavius ruling West, Mark Antony East and Lepidus Africa. At Philippi **42 B. C.** Antony defeated Cassius and Brutus, both committed suicide. Antony joined Cleopatra in Alexandria; they had 3 sons. Octavius defeated their fleet at Actium **31 B. C.**; they committed suicide. Octavius received title of Augustus (venerated) **27 B. C.**, called first Roman emperor. Roman advance into northern Europe ended **9 A. D.** when Germans under Arminius defeated Varus. Augustus died **14 A. D.**

4
Birth of Jesus Christ in Bethlehem.

1 B. C. and 1 A. D.
*The year 1 B. C. is the first year before the begin-
ning of the Christian era. The year 1 A. D. is the first
year of the Christian era. Jan. 1, 1 B. C. is just one
year before Jan. 1, 1 A. D. The elapsed number of
years between a date B. C. and the same date A. D. is
one less than the sum of the years. The Christian era
was calculated by the monk Dionysius Exiguus in the
6th century after Christ. He placed Jesus' birth on
Dec. 25 in the year 753 of Rome and decided 754
should be the first year of the Christian era. Biblical
scholars find his calculations in error and place the
birth of Jesus in the Roman year 750 (4 B. C.) or
earlier.*

A.D.
The Christian or Common Era
29
Crucifixion of Jesus in reign of Roman emperor
Tiberius; Pontius Pilate procurator in Judea. The
Roman Catholic church gives the date of the crucifix-
ion as **April 7, 30 A. D.**

43
Roman Emperor Claudius subdued Britons; occupation of 300 years begun.

64
Persecution of Christians by Nero; burning of
Rome. Apostles Paul and Peter martyred c. **67.**

70
Jerusalem destroyed by Titus. Christians persecuted, worship in catacombs of Rome.

79
Pompeii, Herculanéum and Stabii destroyed by
eruption of Mt. Vesuvius.

180
Death of Marcus Aurelius; onset of Roman decline.

311
Emperor Galerius, on deathbed, agreed to tolerance of Christians, Emperor Constantine **313** promulgated Edict of Milan, made Christianity legal.

325
Council of Nicaea called by Constantine in Bithynia, Asia Minor, to get churchmen to define orthodox
Christian belief. Divinity of Christ and Holy Trinity
endorsed; minority view of Arius rejected.

330
Constantine dedicated Byzantium capital of Eastern Empire, henceforth called Constantinople, now
Istanbul. Baptized a Christian on his deathbed by Eu-
sebius **337.**

380
Theodosius, Roman emperor, made Christianity
based on Nicene creed official religion, banned worship of old pagan gods.

410
Rome sacked by Alaric, the Goth; by Genseric, the
Vandal, **455.**

432
Bishop (later Saint) Patrick, was missionary to Ireland; labored 30 years, converting inhabitants to
Christianity. In **563** Irish Missionary (later Saint)
Columba founded church on Iona, Scottish Island. In
597 (Saint) Augustine founded church at Canterbury
in England.

449
Anglo-Saxon migrations from continent to Britain.

483
Justinian I, Byzantine emperor, born; died **565.**
During reign had Tribonian prepare Justinian Code
(Corpus Juris Civilis) which became basic Roman law
used later as a model by many modern European
states.

570
Mohammed born in Mecca; Hegira, flight from
Mecca to Medina, July 16, 622 is beginning of Moslem
calendar. Saracens crossed to Spain **711**, established
Moorish kingdom, lasted until **1492.**

731
Great period of Mayan empire began; ended **987.**

732
Charles Martel, Frankish ruler, defeated 90,000
Moors at Tours, France; height of Moslem invasion of
Western Europe.

800
Charlemagne, king of Franks, proclaimed Holy
Roman Emperor by Pope Leo III on Christmas Day in
St. Peter's. Charlemagne fought Saxons, Lombards,
Saracens 30 years to Christianize them; extended
empire from Atlantic to eastern boundaries of Hun-
gary. Died 814, aged 72, was buried in his cathedral at
Aix.

1000
Leif Ericsson's Norsemen reach Vinland (land of
grape vines). Variously identified as Labrador, New
England coast and Martha's Vineyard.

1014
Brian Boru, Irish king, defeated Danes at Clontarf.

1027
Second Maya empire in Yucatan. Disintegrated
1480. Destruction of Tayasal, Guatemala, Itza capital,
by Spanish governor of Yucatan in **1697** ended Mayan
millennium.

1054
Final break between Eastern (Orthodox) and Western (Roman) church came when Pope Leo IX excommunicated Michael Cerularius and his followers.
Eastern Orthodox Church became established religion of Russia under the Czars. Russian patriarchate
formed **1589.**

1066
William of Normandy conquered England at Hastings Oct. 14; Harold, last Saxon king of England,
slain.

1096
First crusade, preached by Peter of Amiens, sup-
ported by Pope Urban II, raised 100,000 men. Cap-
tured Jerusalem 1099, Acre, 1104. Second, 1146, lost
Jerusalem to Saladin, a Kurd. Third, 1189, Richard I
of England took Jaffa. Fourth, 1200, besieged Con-
stantinople 1204. Fifth, 1216, achieved 10-year truce.
Sixth, 1238, lost ground. Seventh, 1245, led by Louis
IX (St. Louis) of France who was captured 1250.
Eighth, 1270, led by Louis, who died near Tunis 1270.
Children's crusade, 1212, 50,000 children (est.); most
died of disease and hunger or were sold as slaves in
North Africa.

1162
Genghis Khan, Mongol chief, born; died 1227. Captured Peking 1215, defeated Russians 1223, conquered most of Central Asia and massacred population of
Herat, Afghanistan. By 1241 Mongols under Batu had
burned Moscow and Kiev and invaded Poland, Hungary and the Danube Valley.

1215
Magna Carta, the great charter of England, signed
by King John at Runnymede at insistence of 2,000
English barons who refused to fight on foreign soil
and demanded end of illegal levies by king. Charter
guaranteed privileges of nobility, church free from
secular interference, right of freemen to legal
protection. Freemen were privileged class; common
people were villein farmers, practically serfs. But
400 years later Edward Coke and Puritans demanded
protection for the common people under these rights
of freemen. Also invoked Clause 39, out of which trial
by jury developed. It reads: *No freeman shall be
taken or imprisoned, or dispossessed, or outlawed, or
banished, or in any way destroyed, nor will we go
upon him, nor send upon him, except by the legal
judgment of his peers or by the law of the land.*

1271
Marco Polo started with father and uncle for
Cathay (China), Mongol kingdom of Kublai Khan.
Served under Khan, returned to Venice 1295. Wrote
Travels.

1274
Thomas Aquinas, Italian, renowned scholastic philosopher, died.

1300
Dante and Giotto flourished; dawn of Renaissance.

1309
Clement V, French pope, made Avignon seat of church; Urban V returned to Rome 1367, warfare caused him to return to Avignon, 1370. Gregory XI finally reentered St. Peter's 1377. During the Great Schism, 1378-1417, French and Italian factions chose popes for Avignon and Rome; breach healed by Martin V 1417.

1346
Battle of Crecy, France, Aug. 26. Edward III of England defeated larger French force of Philip VI; first use of English longbow in continental warfare.

1348
Black Death (bubonic plague) reached Venice, rapidly spreading to rest of Europe by 1349. An estimated one-fourth of European population killed.

1382
John Wycliffe, English forerunner of Reformation, directed translation of Vulgate Bible into English vernacular. Supported bill in parliament declaring it sinful for clergy to hold property. By elevating Scriptures above church authority he anticipated Lutheran doctrine by 150 years.

1415
John Huss, Bohemian preacher, follower of Wycliffe, agitator of ecclesiastic reforms, burned at stake in Konstanz, Germany, July 6 for heresy after German Emperor Sigismund revoked his safe-conduct.

1429
Joan of Arc, Maid of Orleans, obeying "voices" of saints, rallied French against English, raised siege of Orleans, effected coronation of Charles VII at Rheims. Through carelessness or treachery she was captured by Burgundians May 24, 1430, and sold to English for 10,000 livres. Placed on trial before bishop of Beauvais at Rouen for magic, disobeying parents, wearing male attire, and heresy, she made a retraction (which she later revoked), but was given life imprisonment. Tricked to resume male attire, she was condemned to death by a French court and burned at Rouen by the English May 30, 1431. Sentence revoked 25 years later.

1453
Constantinople captured by Ottoman Turks.
End of 100-years' war between England and France, begun 1338. England lost all except Calais which the French captured 1558.

1456
Johann Gutenberg completed first Bible printed from movable type; 2 vols., 42 lines 2 columns to page. Printing took 5 years. Date established by note in Mazarin copy.

1457
Johann Fust and Peter Schoeffler produced a psalter, the first book printed in colors, and having printers' name, date and place.

1475
William Caxton printed first book in English, translation of a French history of Troy, at Bruges. He moved to Westminster, London, where he printed the first dated book in England 1477.

1492
Christopher Columbus, Genoese navigator, gained support of Spain's Queen Isabella for westward voyage. Left Palos de la Frontera Aug. 3 with Santa Maria, 100 tons, 52 men; Pinta 50 tons, 18 men; Nina, 40 tons, 18 men. On Oct. 12 at 2 a.m., Rodrigo de Triana on Pinta discovered land. Columbus landed on Guanahani (Watling Is.), Bahamas, called it San Salvador. Discovered Cuba and Hispaniola (Haiti or San Domingo); built first fort, La Navidad, there.

1497
John Cabot, Venetian employed by English, reached Canada. His son Sebastian joined 2d voyage 1498. English claim to Canada was based on their discoveries.
Amerigo Vespucci, Italian-born Spanish navigator, asserted he reached American mainland (New World) a year before Columbus. Martin Waldseemuller of St. Die in map and book 1507 called New World America "because Americus discovered it."

1498
Savonarola, preached against luxury and power of clergy, burned as heretic in Florence May 23.
Vasco da Gama, Portuguese navigator, reached India, discovering all-sea, around-Africa route from W. Europe.

1506
Pope Julius II (della Rovere) started new St. Peter's; employed Michelangelo, Bramante, Raphael.

1509
Henry VIII became king of England. Defeated Scots at Flodden Field 1513. Named Defender of the Faith by Pope Leo X for attacking Luther 1521. When pope refused to annul his marriage to Catherine of Aragon for lack of male issue, Henry divorced Catherine, married Anne Boleyn 1533. Act of Supremacy abrogated pope's authority, made king head of church in England 1534. He ordered monasteries closed 1536.
Queen Anne Boleyn was tried for adultery on order of Henry VIII in 1536 and beheaded. Henry married Jane Seymour, who died 1537, after giving birth to son who became Edward VI in 1547. Henry married Anne of Cleves, divorced her 1540. Married Catherine Howard, beheaded her 1542, then married Catherine Parr 1543 who survived him.

1513
Juan Ponce de Leon, veteran of one Columbus voyage, discovered and named Florida.
Vasco Nunez de Balboa crossed the Isthmus of Panama, discovered South Sea, later called Pacific by Magellan.

1517
Martin Luther, Augustinian monk, preached faith over works, attacked abuse of selling papal indulgences, posted 95 theses (propositions) on Wittenberg church door Oct. 31. Diet of Worms, under Charles V Jan. 1521 ordered recantation. Luther, backed by German princes, refused; put Scriptures above papal authority. Translated Greek New Testament into German 1522. Became head of German evangelical movement, broke with Rome, married a former nun. Augsburg Confession, basic Lutheran creed, presented to Diet there by Melanchthon 1530.

1519
Hernando Cortes began conquest of Mexico.

1520
Fernando Magellan discovered Strait of Magellan; killed in Philippines 1521. His crew completed first circumnavigation of the world arriving in Spain Sept. 6, 1522. Voyage proved the world round, showed large proportion of water to land, and revealed the Americas to be a "New World."

1524
Giovanni da Verrazzano, Italian, explored New England coast for French, probably New York Bay.

1526
William Tyndale produced in Cologne first printed version of New Testament in English, suppressed in England. Tyndale executed for heresy Oct. 6, 1536, at Vilvarde, near Brussels.

1529
Turks failed in siege of Vienna; 2d siege 1683, was broken by Polish King John Sobieski's landmark victory.

1531-35
Francisco Pizarro conquered Peru for Spain.

1534
John Calvin, French-born religious reformer, published his Institutes of the Christian Religion, influential Protestant doctrine. Rejected Lutheran doctrine of consubstantiation; believed in religious base of citizenship, original sin, infant damnation. Influence extended to Scottish Presbyterians, English and New England Puritans.
Jacques Cartier, sent by Francis I of France, in 2 voyages 1534-36 discovered St. Lawrence River, reached site of Montreal. Basis of French claims to Canada.

1535

Miles Coverdale published first complete Bible in English. Also worked on first authorized Bible, "The Great Bible," completed **1539.** Other editions: Whittingham's New Testament, with Calvin's introduction **1557;** Geneva Bible **1560;** Bishop's Bible **1568.**

1540

Francisco Coronado, searching for gold and "Seven Cities of Cibola," explored Southwest north of Rio Grande with 70 horse and 30 foot soldiers. Hernando de Alarcon discovered Colorado River. Don Garcia Lopez de Cardenas discovered Grand Canyon.

1541

Hernando de Soto discovered Mississippi River.

1545

Council of Trent, in Austrian Tyrol, urged on Pope Paul III by Emperor Charles V, to define Catholic dogma and remedy ecclesiastical abuses, opened **Dec. 13;** continued intermittently until **1563;** reiterated supreme papal authority, outlined Roman Catholic faith.

1555

Bishops Ridley and Latimer burned at Oxford **Oct. 16;** Archbishop Cranmer of Canterbury burned **Mar. 21, 1556;** 277 other religious leaders burned in attempt of Queen Mary Tudor (Bloody Mary) to restore Catholic authority. Elizabeth I became queen **1558,** made Anglican communion official church.

1560

Some 1,200 Huguenots hanged at Amboise. Catherine de Medici, regent of France for son, Charles IX, by **Edict of Jan. 1562,** granted Huguenots right to worship outside walled towns. Infraction of edict led to massacre of Huguenots at Vassy **Mar. 1, 1562,** beginning of 8 religious wars. Massacre of St. Bartholomew **Aug. 24, 1572,** encouraged by Charles IX on marriage of sister, Marguerite de Valois to Henry of Navarre (non-Catholic). Henry III, who caused assassination of Catholic leaders Duc de Guise and Cardinal of Lorraine, was himself murdered **Aug. 1, 1589.** Henry IV (of Navarre) first Bourbon king, promulgated **Edict of Nantes Apr. 13, 1598,** giving Huguenots and Catholics equality before law. Henry converted to Catholicism; assassinated **May 14, 1610.** Revocation of edict by Louis XIV **Oct. 23, 1685,** led to large Huguenot emigration to England and America.

1564

William Shakespeare born; traditional date **Apr. 23;** Baptismal record **Apr. 26.**

1565

St. Augustine, Fla. founded by Pedro Menendez, Spaniard. Razed by Francis Drake **1586.**

1579

Francis Drake claimed California for Britain. Left metal plate found in Marin Co. **1936.**

1582

First Catholic New Testament in English issued at Rheims; Old Testament translated at Douai **1609.**

1587

Mary, Queen of Scots, executed on charge of treason against Elizabeth I.

Virginia Dare, first child born of English parents in the New World, on Roanoke Is., N.C., **Aug. 18,** 7 days after **Sir Walter Raleigh's** 2d expedition with 117 persons landed. (First, **1585,** returned to England **1586.**) By **1590** all trace of settlement had vanished except for a tree inscribed enigmatically "Croatoan."

1588

Spanish Armada, 132 ships, 33,000 soldiers, sent by Philip II of Spain against England, destroyed by Drake's attacks and storms **July 21-29.** Only 50 ships returned to Spain. Fading of Spanish power; flourishing of Elizabethan England.

1590

Edmund Spenser began The Faerie Queen. First Shakespeare poem, Venus and Adonis, registered **1593.** First play to appear in quarto, Titus Andronicus registered **1594.** Romeo and Juliet performed **1597.**

1600

Shakespeare's most productive decade opened. He retired to Stratford-on-Avon **1610;** died **Apr. 23, 1616,** the same date **Cervantes** died. First folio of 36 plays published **1623;** 2d, **1632;** 3d. **1663;** 4th, **1675.**

1605

Gunpowder Plot of Guy Fawkes to blow up King James I and parliament foiled when 36 barrels of gunpowder were found in Parliament's cellar **Nov. 4.**

1607

Capt. John Smith and 105 cavaliers in 3 ships landed on Virginia coast and started first permanent English settlement in New World at Jamestown **May 13.**

1609

Henry Hudson, English explorer of Northwest Passage, employed by Dutch East India Co.; sailed sloop Half Moon into New York harbor **Sept.** and up river to Albany. In **1610,** in English ship Discovery, 55 tons, explored Hudson Bay.

Spaniards settled Santa Fe, N.M., erected presidio.

1611

King James version of English Bible published; ordered by James I in **1604** it reconciled earlier versions and became basic Protestant Bible.

1618

Thirty Years' War began in Bohemia between Catholic and Protestant armies; ended **1648** with Peace of Westphalia, Alsace given to France. Holland and Switzerland received independence.

1619

House of Burgesses, first representative assembly in New World, elected by popular vote **July 30** at Jamestown, Va., establishing principle of self-government for royal colony.

First Negro laborers—indentured servants—in English N. American colonies, landed by Dutch at Jamestown, **Aug.**

1620

Plymouth Pilgrims, Puritan separatists from Church of England, some living in Leyden, Holland, since **1609,** left Plymouth, England, **Sept. 16** in Mayflower, 101 passengers, 48 crew. Original destination Virginia, they reached Cape Cod **Nov. 9-19,** explored coast, landed **Dec. 21** (Dec. 11, Old Style) at Plymouth, so named for Plymouth, England, Co. on map made **1614** by Capt. John Smith. Mayflower Compact, signed on shipboard, was agreement to form a local government and abide by its laws; elected own first Governor, John Carver. Started first house **Dec. 25.** Half of colony perished during hard winter.

1624

Dutch left 8 men from ship, New Netherland, on Manhattan **May.** Rest proceeded to Albany.

1626

Peter Minuit bought Manhattan from Man-a-hat-a Indians **May 6** for trinkets valued at $24.

1636

Harvard College founded **Oct. 28.**

1642

Great Rebellion of the Puritan Parliament against the civil and religious policies of Charles I of England began **July** after Charles rejected parliament's demands for control of militia and church affairs and for right to appoint and dismiss the king's ministers.

Oliver Cromwell led army of Roundheads for parliament, defeated Charles' Cavaliers at **Marston Moor 1644** and Naseby **1645.** Charles was delivered to parliament by the Scots **1648.** Beheaded **1649.**

Galileo died, **Newton** was born (100 years after **Copernicus** published heliocentric theory.) Galileo defended theory: "Holy Spirit intended to teach us in the Bible how to go to Heaven, not how the heavens go." But in **1616** the Inquisition at Rome declared the assertion of earth's motion to be heretical and placed works of Copernicus, Kepler, and Galileo on the Index of Forbidden Books until **1822.**

1648

Taj Mahal outside Agra, India, completed by Mogul Emperor Shah Jehan in memory of his favorite wife Mumtaz Mahal. Begun in **1630.**

1649

Charles I condemned by House of Commons sitting as high court; beheaded, **Jan. 30.**

Commonwealth ruled by Commons and Council of State (John Milton, Latin secretary) with Cromwell at head. Cromwell made protector for life (actually dictator), 1653.

Cromwell died 1658. His son Richard resigned rule. Puritan government collapsed and parliament called Charles II to rule the nation.

1660

Restoration under Charles II, "Merry Monarch." Charles' Cavalier parliament restored Anglican church and refused freedom of worship to "dissenters."

1664

King Charles II ordered Col. Nicolls and 300 men to seize New Netherland (Manhattan and environs) from Dutch, granted territory to his brother James, Duke of York. Peter Stuyvesant, Dutch director-general, yielded peacefully; province of New Netherland and city of New Amsterdam became New York. The Dutch recaptured both Aug. 9, 1673, but ceded all. by treaty to Britain Nov. 10, 1674.

1665

Great Plague in London killed 68,000. In 1666 great fire destroyed 13,200 houses, 89 churches.

1676

Nathaniel Bacon led planters, oppressed by taxes, against Gov. Berkeley at Jamestown, burned town, Bacon died suddenly; 23 followers executed.

Bloody Indian war in New England ended Aug. 12. King Philip', Wampanog chief, and many Narragansett Indians killed.

1682

Robert Cavelier, Sieur de la Salle, claimed lower Mississippi River country for Louis XIV, called it Louisiana Apr. 9. Had built French outposts in Illinois, established fort at Lavaca, Tex. 1684 with 400 men, killed by his own men in a mutiny on Trinity River, Tex., Mar. 19, 1687.

1683

William Penn signed treaty with Indians.

1689

King William's War, British in America vs. French and Indians, began; ended 1697.

1692

Witchcraft delusion at Salem (now Danvers, Mass.), inspired by preaching; 19 persons hanged, 1 man crushed to death. Executions in Europe of women for witchcraft between 1484 and 1782 believed to have reached 300,000. Last in England 1716, in Scotland 1722.

1696

Capt. William Kidd, American, hired by British king and nobles to fight pirates and take booty, became pirate. Returned to New York with treasure 1698, buried it on Gardiner's Island. Arrested and sent to England for trial. He was hanged 1701.

1704

Indians attacked Deerfield, Mass., Feb. 28-29, killed 40, carried off 100.

Gibraltar taken by Britain from Spain July 24; formally ceded by Spain in Treaty of Utrecht 1713.

Boston News Letter, first regular newspaper, started by John Campbell, postmaster. (Publick Occurences was suppressed after one issue 1690.)

1709

British-Colonial troops captured French fort, Port Royal, Nova Scotia, in Queen Anne's War 1701-13. France yielded Nova Scotia by treaty 1713.

1712

Slaves revolted in New York Apr. 6. Six committed suicide, 21 were executed. Second rising, 1741; 13 slaves hanged, 13 burned, 71 deported.

1720

"Mississippi Bubble." John Law, a Scot, comptroller of finance in France, issued paper currency without security to back trading scheme. On basis of wild stories of gold in Louisiana, shares reached $4,000 value before collapse; provoked large immigration to Louisiana.

1728

Pennsylvania Gazette founded by Samuel Keimer in Philadelphia. Benjamin Franklin bought interest 1729.

1735

Freedom of the press recognized in New York by acquittal of John Peter Zenger, editor Weekly Journal, on charge of libeling British Gov. Cosby by criticizing his conduct in office.

1740-1741

Capt. Vitus Bering, Dane employed by Russians, discovered Alaska.

1743

King George's War. British and colonials vs. French. Siege of Louisbourg, Cape Breton Is. was led by Gov. William Shirley of Massachusetts. Surrendered June 17, 1745. Returned to France by Treaty of Aix la Chapelle 1748.

1746

English defeated Scots at Culloden Moor, near Inverness, Apr. 16, routing Stuart pretender, Prince Charles. The last battle fought on British soil, it terminated attempts of Stuarts to recover the English throne.

1751

Publication of the Encyclopedie, great popularizer of the Enlightenment, began in France

1752

Benjamin Franklin, flying kite in thunderstorm, proved lightning is electricity June 15.

Gregorian calendar adopted by Great Britain and American colonies, dropping 11 days after Sept. 2; next day Sept. 14.

1754

French and Indian War (in Europe called 7 Years War, started 1756) started after French occupied uncompleted British post, called it Ft. Duquesne (site of Pittsburgh). Col. George Washington with Virginia troops clashed with French at Great Meadows, dug in at Ft. Necessity; capitulated and withdrew July 3, 1754. Boston's 3,000 provincial troops took French forts in Nova Scotia June 16, 1755. French and Indians ambushed Gen. Edward Braddock's expedition 10 mi. from Ft. Duquesne (now Braddock, Pa.) July 9; Braddock fatally wounded, 714 killed. Gen. Sir William Johnson defeated French and Indians under Baron Dieskau at Lake George Sept. 8. British moved Acadian French from Nova Scotia to Louisiana Nov. Britain formally declared war May 18, 1756. Surrendered Ft. William Henry (Lake George) to Montcalm. Montcalm at Ft. Ticonderoga, N.Y., repulsed 17,000 British July 8, 1758. French gave up Louisburg, Ft. Frontenac, Ft. Duquesne in 1758; Niagara, Ticonderoga, Crown Point in 1759. British captured Quebec Sept. 18, 1759 in battles in which Montcalm and Gen. James Wolfe (Br.) died. Peace signed Feb. 10, 1763. French lost Canada and American Midwest.

1755

Great earthquake in Lisbon, Portugal, Nov. 1, 60,-000 died; 12,000 in Fez, Morocco; half of Madeira leveled.

Samuel Johnson published his English Dictionary.

Black Hole of Calcutta. Nawab of Bengal, attacking British East India Co., threw 146 British prisoners into room less than 20 ft. square June 20; only 23 survived overnight. Lord Robert Clive with 3,000 British troops defeated the Nawab's force of 50,000 June 1757.

1769

Napoleon Bonaparte born Aug. 15 in Ajaccio, Corsica; died at Longwood, St. Helena, May 5, 1821.

1772

First Partition of Poland by Austria, Prussia, and Russia. Second and third partitions of 1793 and 1795 erased Poland from map of Europe, not to re-emerge until after World War I.

For American Revolution:
Origins, Battles, Results (1764-1783)
See Index

1781

Bank of North America incorporated in Philadelphia May 26. First chartered bank, Bank of Pennsylvania Mar. 1, 1780 operated 1782-1784.

1783

Massachusetts Supreme Court outlawed slavery, noting the words in the state Bill of Rights "all men are born free and equal."

1784

First successful daily newspaper, Pennsylvania Packet & General Advertiser, published Sept. 21.

1785

First steamboat experiment by John Fitch. Fitch demonstrated 3 mph steamboat with 12 mechanical oars on Delaware River Aug. 22, 1787. He operated steamboat between Trenton and Philadelphia 1790. He died 1798.

1786

Delegates from 5 states at Annapolis asked Congress to call convention in Philadelphia to write practical constitution for the 13 states.

1787

Shays' rebellion in Massachusetts, led by Capt. Daniel Shays; the attempt to seize U. S. Arsenal in Springfield failed Jan. 25.

Northwest Ordinance adopted July 13 by Continental Congress made effective Ordinance of 1784 drafted by Jefferson. Determined government of Northwest Territory north of Ohio River, west of New York; 5,000 male voters could establish legislature: 60,000 inhabitants could get statehood. Guaranteed freedom of religion, support for schools, no slavery.

James Rumsey, encouraged by George Washington, ran steamboat with power pump on Potomac Dec. 3 and 11. Patented 1791. He died 1792.

Constitutional convention opened at Philadelphia May 14 with George Washington presiding. Constitution adopted by delegates Sept. 17; ratification by 9th state, New Hampshire, June 21, 1788, meant adoption; declared in effect Mar. 4, 1789.

1788

First British settlement in Australia, a penal colony at Port Jackson, now Sydney.

1789

George Washington chosen president by all electors voting (73 eligible, 69 voting, 4 absent); John Adams, vice president, 34 votes, Feb. First U. S. Congress called Mar. 4, at Federal Hall, New York; regular sessions began Apr. 6. Washington inaugurated there Apr. 30. Supreme Court created by Federal Judiciary Act Sept. 24.

The French Revolution began June 20 when the delegates to the Third Estate (Commons) met on a tennis court and took an oath not to disband until the king had granted France a constitution; Paris mob stormed the Bastille July 14 to capture ammunition; released 7 non-political prisoners. France was declared a limited monarchy under Louis XVI; the king and family were arrested June 21, 1791; Revolutionary Tribunal set up on Aug. 19, 1792; National Convention opened Sept. 17, 1792, a republic was established on Sept. 22. Louis was beheaded Jan. 21, 1793; the Reign of Terror began May 31, 1793; Charlotte Corday killed Marat July 13, 1793; Queen Marie Antoinette was beheaded Oct. 16, 1793; Danton Apr. 5, 1794; Robespierre July 28, 1794. Revolutionary Tribunal abolished Dec. 15, 1794. Moderate Directory of 5 men established to rule France 1795.

Mutiny on the British ship Bounty Apr. 28; Capt. William Bligh and 18 sailors set adrift in a launch. They rowed 3,618 mi., to Timor, near Java. The Bounty, in command of Fletcher Christian, rebel mate, sailed to Tahiti. Some of the crew and 18 Polynesians, including 12 women, went on to Pitcairn Is., arriving in 1790.

1791

Continued attacks on settlements north of Ohio River by Indians armed by British, led Washington to send Gen. Arthur St. Clair and Gen. Wilkinson to area with 1,400 men. St. Clair was surprised near Wabash River in Ohio Nov. 4, lost 630 killed.

1792-94

Gen. Anthony Wayne made commander, took 2 years to train American Legion; established string of forts. Routed Indians (Ottawas, Shawnees, Miamis, Iroquois) at Fallen Timers on Maumee River Aug. 20, 1794, checked British at Ft. Miami.

Whiskey Rebellion, west Pennsylvania farmers protesting "discriminatory" liquor tax of 1791, was suppressed by 15,000 militiamen Sept. 1794. Alexander Hamilton used incident to establish authority of the new federal government in enforcing its laws.

1795

Gen. Wayne built Ft. Wayne; signed peace with Indians at Fort Greeneville.

Triple Alliance formed by Great Britain, Russia and Austria, Sept. 28.

U. S. bought peace from Algiers and Tunis by paying $800,000, supplying a frigate and annual tribute of $25,000 Nov. 28. (See 1801.)

1796

Washington's Farewell Address as President delivered Sept. 19. Gave strong warnings against permanent alliances with foreign powers, partiality toward favorite nations, big public debt, large military establishment and devices of "small artful, enterprising minority" to control or change government; praised reciprocal checks of Constitution; stressed need for enlightened public opinion; declared "religion and morality lead to political prosperity."

Vaccination discovered by Edward Jenner May 14; laid foundation for modern immunology.

1797

U. S. frigate United States launched at Philadelphia July 10; Constellation at Baltimore Sept. 7; Constitution (Old Ironsides) at Boston Sept. 20.

France ordered capture of all neutral ships carrying British cargoes.

1798

War with France threatened over French raids on U. S. shipping and rejection of U. S. diplomats. Congress voided all treaties with France, ordered Navy to capture French armed ships. Navy (45 ships) and 365 privateers captured 84 French ships. U. S. Constellation took French warship Insurgente 1799. Napoleon stopped French raids after becoming First Consul.

Napoleon invaded Egypt and won Battle of the Pyramids July 1798; British Adm. Nelson destroyed French fleet Aug. 1-2 in Aboukir Bay. Rosetta stone, found in Egypt by one of Napoleon's officers 1799, contained 3 identical inscriptions in ancient Egyptian hieroglyphics, demotic (common) Greek, and classical Greek. Jean Champollion, a young French scholar, compared these writings and deciphered ancient Egypt's hieroglyphics. Napoleon fled secretly to France 1799, became First Consul Nov. 9-10, 1799, after coup d'etat.

1801

Tripoli declared war June 10 against U. S., which refused added tribute to commerce-raiding Arab corsairs. U. S. frigate Philadelphia captured in Tripoli harbor Oct. 1803 burned by Stephen Decatur Feb. 16, 1804. Expedition under William Eaton forced Tripoli to conclude peace June 4, 1805.

1803

Robert Emmet convicted of treason by British in Ireland; executed in Dublin Sept. 19.

Louisiana Purchase. President Jefferson sent James Monroe to Paris to join Robert R. Livingston, U. S. minister, in offering up to $10 million for the Isle of Orleans (New Orleans) and West Florida. Napoleon, who had recovered Louisiana from Spain by secret treaty, offered all of Louisiana for $11,250,-000 in bonds, plus $3,750,000 indemnities to American citizens with claims against France. U. S. took title Dec. 20.

1804

Lewis and Clark expedition ordered by President Jefferson to explore what is now northwest U. S. Started from St. Louis May 14; ended Sept. 23, 1806.

An Indian woman named Sacajawea served as guide and interpreter.

Alexander Hamilton (ex-Secretary of the Treasury) and Vice President Aaron Burr, after years of bitter political rivalry, fought a duel **July 11** on the Hudson Palisades, Weehawken, N.J. Hamilton was mortally wounded, died **July 12**.

Code Napoleon systematized French law under the auspices of Napoleon Bonaparte. It became a model for many countries.

John Stevens, of Hoboken, N.J., operated experimental steamboat with twin-screw propellers for 9 mi.

1805

Napoleon, emperor since **May 18, 1804,** defeated Austrians at Ulm **Oct. 17;** Russo-Austrians at Austerlitz, "masterpiece of battles," **Dec. 2.** Dissolved Holy Roman Empire. Made brothers Joseph, king of Naples, Louis, king of Holland.

Lord Nelson defeated French-Spanish fleet at Cape Trafalgar **Oct. 21;** lost his own life.

1806

Napoleon defeated Prussians at Jena **Oct. 14.** In 1807 he defeated Russians at Eylau; signed peace of Tilsit with Czar Alexander I. Made brother Jerome king of Westphalia; allotted Finland to Russia.

1807

Robert Fulton made first practical steamboat trip on Clermont (open boat, 140 by 13 ft., 7 ft. draft, side paddle wheels). Left New York **Aug. 17,** reached Albany, 150 mi., in 32 hrs.

Aaron Burr was tried for treason in Richmond, Va., **May 22.** Charged with "assembling an armed force . . . to seize the city of New Orleans . . . and to separate the western from the Atlantic states," he was acquitted **Sept. 1.** Chief Justice John Marshall sitting as U.S. Circuit Court judge ruled that treason must be attested to by 2 witnesses. After trial Burr went to Europe to avoid prosecution on Hamilton murder charge.

War of 1812 Between United States and Great Britain.

The War of 1812, coming only 30 years after the end of the Revolution, had 3 major causes: (1) Britain, blockading France, seized American ships trading with France; (2) Britain, refusing to recognize naturalized American sailors, seized 4,000 by 1810 and impressed two-thirds into British service; (3) Britain armed Indians who raided western border. Under President Jefferson U.S., **1807** and **1809,** stopped trade with Europe which ruined American shippers. Under President Madison **1810** trade with Britain only was stopped.

War might have been averted. The British raised the blockade for American ships **June 16, 1812,** but the news did not reach U. S. by **June 18** when Congress by a small majority voted a declaration of war. Congress voted to raise army from 11,744 to 44,500 and to use militia. The navy had 20 major ships of 500 guns. The West favored war; New England opposed it. The British were handicapped by war with France.

War on Land

Americans made many blunders due to poor leadership and refusal of regulars to work with militia. Brig. Gen. William Hull surrendered Detroit **Aug. 16, 1812,** Maj. Gen. Stephen Van Rensselaer with 2,300 took Queenston Heights, Canada, **Oct. 13,** but retired when regulars did not support. Brig. Gen. William H. Harrison had 1,000 casualties near Ft. Malden. Brig. Gen. Zebulon M. Pike took York (Toronto) **Apr. 27, 1813,** died in explosion. Gen. Henry Dearborn **May 27** took Ft. George and Queenston Heights aided by amphibious assault led by Col. Winfield Scott and Master Commandant Oliver Hazard Perry. British defeated 2,000 Americans a few days later.

Battle of the Thames, Ontario, Can., **Oct. 5, 1813.** Harrison with 3,500 men took Ft. Malden, pursued British 85 mi. Cavalry charge by Kentucky riflemen routed British and Indians, killing Shawnee chief, Tecumseh. Detroit frontier was safe for U. S. Both Brig. Gen. Wade Hampton with 4,000 and Maj. Gen. James Wilkinson with 6,000 mismanaged attempts to invade Canada. British recaptured Fts. George and Niagara, burned Buffalo; Americans burned Newark and Queenston.

Battle of Lundy's Lane. Brig. Gen. Winfield Scott led fighting of Brown's army at Lundy's Lane, on road to Burlington **July 25, 1814;** result a draw with heavy losses, Scott was wounded.

Burning of Washington. in **August** British landed 4,000 men under Adm. Sir George Cockburn and Maj. Gen. Robert Ross. At Bladensburg, Md., **Aug. 24, 1814,** Ross routed 5,000 hastily assembled U. S. troops, then burned Capitol and White House; Maryland militia stopped British **Sept. 12** from reaching Baltimore; Ross was killed.

Battle of New Orleans. Maj. Gen. Andrew Jackson, who had defeated the Creek Indians at Horseshoe Bend on the Tallapoosa **Mar. 27, 1814,** and captured British base at Pensacola, Fla., in Nov.; on **Dec. 23** engaged 2,000 British east of New Orleans. **Jan. 8, 1815,** 5,300 British under Maj. Gen. Sir Edward Pakenham attacked American entrenchments at Chalmette. Jackson had 3,500, a reserve of 1,000, 20 guns and an armed schooner. British had over 2,000 casualties. Pakenham was killed; Americans lost 71. British withdrew and left by sea **Jan. 18.** On **Feb. 8** they took Mobile. News came **Feb. 14** that a treaty of peace had been signed at Ghent **Dec. 24, 1814.** U.S. ratified it **Feb. 17, 1815.**

War at Sea

Brilliant American gunnery brought naval victories. USS Essex captured Alert **Aug. 13, 1812.** USS Constitution, 44 guns, Capt. Isaac Hull, destroyed Guerriere **Aug. 19;** thereafter nicknamed **Old Ironsides.** USS Wasp took Frolic **Oct. 18.** USS United States, Capt. Stephen Decatur, defeated Macedonian off Azores **Oct. 25.** Constitution beat Java **Dec. 29, 1812.** USS Chesapeake captured by Shannon **June 1, 1813;** Capt. James Lawrence, dying, called out: "Don't give up the ship!" USS Enterprise took Boxer **Sept. 5.**

Battle of Lake Erie. Commodore Oliver H. Perry defeated British fleet near Put-in-Bay **Sept. 10, 1813.** Perry sent message to Harrison: "We have met the enemy and they are ours: 2 ships, 2 brigs, 1 schooner, 1 sloop."

USS Essex, Capt. David Porter, first U. S. warship to sail around South America, was defeated off Valparaiso, Chile, **Mar. 28, 1814.**

Bombardment of Ft. McHenry, Baltimore, for 25 hours, **Sept. 13-14, 1814,** by British fleet failed. Francis Scott Key wrote words to Star Spangled Banner.

Battle of Lake Champlain. Commodore Thomas Macdonough defeated fleet of Sir George Prevost near Plattsburg **Sept. 11, 1814** while Brig. Gen. Thomas Macomb held 4,500 ready to oppose 11,000. British withdrew to Canada.

U. S. frigate President was captured **Jan. 1815.** Constitution captured Cyane and Levant **Feb. 20, 1815.** Hornet captured Penguin **Mar. 23.**

The War of 1812 gave recognition to westerners, made Andrew Jackson a political power.

1808-09

French occupied Madrid in March; Rome in April; Napoleon made brother Joseph king of Spain in Peninsular War begun by British 1808, continued until 1814. Napoleon defeated Austrians at Wagram July 6, 1809; annexed Papal States.

Phoenix, world's first ocean-going steamboat, built by John Stevens, left New York for Philadelphia June 8, 1809.

1810

Napoleon annulled marriage with the Empress Josephine; married Austrian Archduchess Marie Louise in March.

1811

William Henry Harrison, governor of Indiana Territory, defeated Indians under the Prophet, brother of Tecumseh, in battle of Tippecanoe Nov. 7.

1812

Napoleon invaded Russia June 22 with first modern conscript army of 500,000 men; Russian army, outnumbered 3 to 1, retreated and used "scorched earth" policy. Napoleon's army defeated Russians at Borodino Sept. 7; took Moscow Sept. 14. Moscow destroyed by fire; lacking shelter and supplies, Napoleon ordered retreat Oct. 19. Army suffered from cold, starvation and Cossack attacks; only 30,000 survived.

1813

Napoleon with 180,000 French decisively defeated at Leipzig by 200,000 allied Prussians, Austrians, Russians, under Austrian Gen. Schwartzenberg in Battle of the Nations Oct. 16-19.

1814

Allies entered Paris Mar. 21; Napoleon abdicated Apr. 11; Louis XVIII restored to throne, May 3; Congress of Vienna opened Nov. 3. Napoleon exiled to Elba.

1815

Napoleon re-entered France Mar. 1, assumed command for the famed "Hundred Days," Mar. 20-June 22. Defeated at Waterloo, Belgium, June 18, by Duke of Wellington (British), Count von Blucher (Prussian) and allies. Deported to St. Helena; died there May 5, 1821.

Holy Alliance, formed by Russia, Austria and Prussia; signed in Paris Sept. 26; promulgated in Frankfort Feb. 2, 1816 and acceded to, 1818, by the rulers of Great Britain and France.

1817

Rush-Bagot treaty signed Apr. 28-29 limited U. S., Canadian naval armaments on the Great Lakes.

1820

Henry Clay's Missouri Compromise bill passed by Congress Mar. 3. Slavery was allowed in Missouri, but not elsewhere west of the Mississippi River north of 36° 30′ latitude (the southern line of Missouri). Repealed 1854.

1822

Brazil proclaimed independence from Portugal Sept. 7. Dom Pedro, son of Portugal's King John VI, was crowned emperor Dec. 1; abdicated 1831; succeeded by his son. A republic proclaimed 1888.

Mexico separated from Spain, made Iturbide emperor May; formed republic Oct. 1823.

1823

Monroe Doctrine declared Dec. 2.

Mississippi River first ascended by steamboat, the Virginia, as far as Fort Snelling, Minn., Apr. 21-May 10, 729 mi.

Gas vacuum (internal combustion) engine operated successfully by Samuel Brown in London.

1824

Simon Bolivar liberator of Venezuela, Colombia, Ecuador, Peru broke Spanish power in South America.

1825

Great Britain repeals laws against trade unions.

First railroad to use steam locomotive (on level grade only), Stockton & Darlington RR, opened in England Sept. 27 with Stephenson's engine "Locomotion." First public railroad to use steam exclusively for passenger and freight traffic, Liverpool & Manchester, opened Sept. 15, 1830.

Erie Canal opened, first boat left Buffalo Oct. 26, reached N.Y. City Nov. 4. Canal cost $7 million but cut travel time by one-third, shipping costs one-tenth; opened Great Lakes area, made N. Y. City chief Atlantic port.

First iron steamboat built in America, the Codorus, at York, Pa., by John Elgar.

1827

Slavery in New York State abolished July 4.

Steamship Curacao, first European-built oceanic vessel to use steam power only, crossed the Atlantic April from Antwerp to Paramaribo, Dutch Guiana. The Royal William launched in Montreal Apr. 29, 1831, left there Aug. 18, 1833, crossed to Europe in 25 days using only steam.

1828

First passenger railroad in U.S., Baltimore & Ohio, was begun July 4: first 14 mi. opened to horsedrawn railcar traffic May 24, 1830.

1830

Mormon church organized by Joseph Smith in Fayette, N. Y., Apr. 6.

Revolution in France. Charles X abdicated Aug. 2 and was succeeded by the duke of Orleans as Louis Philippe I. There were revolts in Brunswick, Saxony and Belgium. Belgium became independent kingdom.

First regularly scheduled passenger train service in United States using steam power opened at Charleston on South Carolina Railroad Dec. 25 with 3½-ton U. S.-built locomotive, Best Friend of Charleston.

1831

Nat Turner, a Negro slave from Virginia, led a band of men in a slave rebellion, killed 57 whites, in August. Army called in, Turner captured, tried and hanged.

1832

Black Hawk War (Ill.-Wis.) Apr. - Sept. pushed Sac & Fox Indians west across Mississippi.

South Carolina convention passed **Ordinance of Nullification** Nov. 1832 against permanent tariff protection policy, declaring that if the federal government attempted to enforce the tariff the state would consider itself no longer a member of the Union. Congress Feb. 1833 passed a compromise tariff act, whereupon South Carolina repealed act.

British Reform Bill: middle class enfranchised; step toward political democracy Mar. 23.

1833

Slavery in British Empire outlawed Aug. 28 as of Aug. 1, 1834. About 700,000 were liberated at cost of £20 million. (Slavery was abolished in Britain June 22, 1772. Slave trade was suppressed 1807.)

Oberlin College, first in U. S. to adopt coeducation. Oberlin refused to bar students on account of race 1835.

1835

Texas proclaimed independence from Mexico in convention Nov. 1, provisional government formed. Stephen Austin and Sam Houston leaders.

Fire in New York City Dec. 16-17 destroyed 674 buildings.

Gold discovered on Cherokee land in Georgia. Indians forced to cede lands Dec. 20 and to cross Mississippi.

1836

Texans besieged in Alamo (San Antonio) by Mexicans under Santa Anna Feb. 23-Mar. 6; garrison including William Travis, Jim Bowie and David Crockett died defending the fort. At San Jacinto Apr. 21 Sam Houston and 800 Texans defeated 3,000 Mexicans. Santa Anna signed treaties ending hostilities, promised to recognize Texan independence but Mexican Congress repudiated treaties.

Marcus Whitman, H. H. Spaulding and wives reached Fort Walla Walla on Columbia River, Oregon. First white women to cross plains.

Seminole Indians in Florida under Osceola began attacks **Nov. 1, 1836**, protesting forced removal. The unpopular 8-year war ended **Aug. 14, 1842**; Indians sent to Oklahoma. War was the most costly Indian war; 1,500 soldiers died, $30 million spent.

1837
Victoria, 18, niece of William IV, became queen of England. Married her first cousin, German Prince Albert of Saxe-Coburg, **1840**. He died **1861.**

1838
The Great Western, a steamship 236 ft. long, 450 horsepower, 1,340 gross tons, left Bristol, England, **Apr. 8,** arrived in N. Y. City **Apr. 23.** The Sirius, 178 ft. long, 703 tons, left Liverpool **Mar. 28** and Queenstown **Apr. 4,** reached N. Y. City **Apr. 22,** using only steam power.

1839
Belgium and the Kingdom of the Netherlands were separated by treaties signed by those 2 countries and by Great Britain, France, Austria, Prussia and Russia at London **Apr. 19.** To the treaties was annexed a document declaring Belgium independent and perpetually neutral (called "scrap of paper" by Germany in World War I when it invaded Belgium.)
Opium War broke out between China and Britain. China tried to prohibit opium trade in Canton. British resisted and took Canton. War ended with Treaty of Nanking **Aug. 1842.**

1840
Antarctic was found to be a continent by Comdr. Charles Wilkes of first U. S. exploring expedition; named Wilkes Land **Jan.-Feb.**

1841
First emigrant wagon train for California, 47 persons, left Independence, Mo., **May 1,** reached Stanislaus River, **Nov. 4.**
First passenger train on Erie R.R. **June 30.**

1842
First use of anaesthetic (sulphuric ether gas) by Dr. Crawford W. Long in Jefferson, Ga. Dr. William T. G. Morton, dentist, used ether for painless extraction of tooth **Sept. 30, 1846;** administered ether in tumor operation **Oct. 16, 1846,** at Massachusetts General Hospital, Boston.

1844
First message over first telegraph line sent from U.S. Supreme Court room **May 24** to Baltimore by inventor **Samuel F. B. Morse:** "What hath God wrought!"
Joseph Smith, founder of Mormons, and brother Hyrum killed in Carthage, Ill. jail by mob **June 27.**

1845
Texas voted for annexation to U. S. **July 4.** Congress admitted Texas as 28th state **Dec. 29.**

1846
Mexican War. President James K. Polk ordered **Gen. Zachary Taylor** to seize disputed Texan land settled by Mexicans. After border clash, U. S. declared war **May 13;** Mexico **May 23.**
Bear flag of Republic of California raised by American settlers at Sonoma **June 14.** Gen. John C. Fremont took charge **July 5.** Commodore J. S. Sloat took Monterey **July 7,** declared California annexed to U. S. Commodore Robert Stockton succeeded Sloat, was ordered to recognize Gen. Kearny as governor and commander-in-chief in California. Kearny was defeated by Mexicans **Dec. 6,** retreated to San Diego.
Gen. Taylor defeated Mexicans at Buena Vista **Feb. 23, 1847.** Gen. Winfield Scott with 12,000 troops (est.) took Vera Cruz **Mar. 27;** Mexico City **Sept. 14,** captured dictator Santa Anna. By treaty, **Feb. 1848,** Mexico ceded claims to Texas, California, Arizona, New Mexico, Nevada, Utah, part of Colorado. U. S. assumed $3 million American claims and paid Mexico $15 million.
Treaty with Great Britain June 15, set boundary in Oregon Territory at 49th parallel (extension of existing line). Water boundary settled 1873. Expansionists in U. S. seeking boundary farther North used slogan "54° 40' or fight!"
Mormons, after violent clashes with settlers over polygamy, left Nauvoo, Ill., for West under Brigham Young, settled **July 1847** at Salt Lake City, Utah.

1847
First adhesive U. S. postage stamps on sale **July 1;** Benjamin Franklin 5c, Washington 10c.

1848
Gold discovered Jan. 24 by James W. Marshall, who was erecting sawmill in partnership with Capt. John A. Sutter on American River, branch of the Sacramento, near Coloma, Cal. Small finds of gold were reported 45 mi. northwest of Los Angeles 1841-44.
Louis Philippe dethroned in France; Second Republic set up **Feb. 26.**
In Austria **Ferdinand I** abdicated **Dec. 2** in favor of his nephew Franz Josef. In Hungary, freedom was briefly declared under Louis Kossuth; revolts in Ireland, Lombardy, Venice, Denmark and Schleswig-Holstein.
Communist Manifesto written by Karl Marx (1818-1883) and Friedrich Engels (1820-1895); still the basic doctrine of communism.

1850
Senator Henry Clay's Compromise of 1850 passed; admitted California as 31st state **Sept. 9,** slavery forbidden; made Utah and New Mexico territories without decision on slavery; amended Fugitive Slave Law punishing those who aided fugitives and abolished jury trial for fugitives, ended slave trade in Dist. of Columbia.
Jenny Lind's first American concert at Castle Garden, New York City, **Sept. 11;** P. T. Barnum was manager.
Taiping Rebellion, led by Hung Hsiu-ch'uan, began in Kwangsi province, China. One of the largest civil wars in history, it resulted in the death of an estimated 20 to 40 million people, devastated entire provinces and nearly toppled the Manchu dynasty. The Taiping movement, aimed at foreign exploitation, was finally suppressed **1864** by Tseng Kuo-fan with the help of the "Ever Victorious Army" of Gen. Charles G. (Chinese) Gordon.

1851
New York & Hudson River R.R., New York to Albany, opened **Oct.**

1852
Louis Napoleon crowned emperor of the French.
Uncle Tom's Cabin, by Harriet Beecher Stowe, published.

1853
Commodore Matthew C. Perry, U.S.N., received by Lord of Toda, Japan, **July 14;** negotiated treaty to open Japan to U.S. ships. Ratified **Mar. 8, 1854.**
Crimean War. A dispute between Greek Orthodox and Roman monks over holy places held by Turkey in Palestine led Russian Czar Nicholas I to extend protection to Greeks. Russia occupied Turkish-held Moldavia and Wallachia. Turkey declared war **Oct. 4, 1853.** Britain and France, fearing Russian expansion declared war on Russia **May 28, 1854.** Fighting concentrated in the Crimea and included famous **Charge of the Light Brigade** at Balaklava **Oct. 25, 1854;** 400 of 607 killed; Russian defeat at Inkerman **Nov. 5, 1854;** fall of Sebastopol **Sept. 11, 1855.** Sardinia sent 15,000 troops to Allies; Prussia and Sweden cooperated. **Florence Nightingale** established first dressing stations. By Treaty of Paris **Mar. 30, 1856,** Russia ceded part of Bessarabia to Moldavia, freed Danube for navigation. Black Sea closed to warships (later repudiated).

1854
Republican party started at Ripon, Wis., **Feb. 28;** first state organization, Jackson, Mich., **July 6.** Opposed Kansas-Nebraska Act (became law **May 30**) which left issue of slavery in Kansas and Nebraska to vote of settlers.
Henry D. Thoreau wrote Walden.

1855
Walt Whitman published Leaves of Grass; Henry W. Longfellow wrote Song of Hiawatha.

1856

First railroad train crossed Mississippi River on the river's first bridge at **Rock Island, Ill.-Davenport, Ia., Apr. 21.**

Republican party's first nominee for president, John C. Fremont **June-Nov.**, defeated by James Buchanan. Abraham Lincoln made 50 speeches for Fremont.

Lawrence, Kan., **sacked May 21** by slavery party; abolitionist John Brown led anti-slavery men against Missourians at Osawatomie, Kan., **Aug. 30.**

1857

Dred Scott decision of U. S. Supreme Court, 6-3, that a Negro slave did not become free when taken into a free state and had no rights as a citizen. Abraham Lincoln denounced decision. Minnesota outlawed slavery.

Great Mutiny in India (Sepoy Rebellion) began in Merrut **May 10** when Indian soldiers revolted against British officers; crushed 1858. British East India Co. abolished and India placed under crown rule as a result of mutiny.

John D. Lee, a Mormon, led raid against wagon train at Mountain Meadows **Sept. 11**, killed 120, spared only 17 children under 7. U. S. Army supplies burned. Government sent 6,000 troops to suppress "rebellion." Mormon Church unjustly accused.

Major Events of Civil War, 1861-1865

For origins of the Civil War see Index for Confederate States and Secession.

South Carolina, Georgia, Alabama, Mississippi, Louisiana, and Florida formed the Confederate States of America **Feb. 8**, chose Jefferson Davis provisional president; were joined later by Texas, North Carolina, Arkansas, Virginia, and Tennessee.

First Year of War — 1861

Gen. Pierre Beauregard demanded surrender of Ft. Sumter in Charleston, S.C., harbor **Apr. 11.** Maj. Robert Anderson, USA, refused. Bombardment started at 4:30 a.m. **April 12.** Anderson surrendered **Apr. 14.**

President Lincoln called for 75,000 militia from states by quotas **April 15.**

Battle of Bull Run or Manassas. Brig. Gen. Irvin McDowell attacked Beauregard's forces on the Warrenton Road **July 21**, pushed them back to Henry House hill. Gen. Joseph E. Johnston's army from Winchester, including forces commanded by Brig. Gen. Thomas J. Jackson and Gen. E. Kirby Smith reinforced Confederates, and with help of Gen. Jubal Early's brigade routed Federals. Brig. Gen. B. E. Bee, CSA, said:"Look, there is Jackson standing like a stone wall!" McDowell had 28,455 troops, 18,500 engaged, 2,708 casualties; Confederates had 32,072 available, 18,000 engaged, 1,967 casualties. Congress **July 22** authorized an army of 500,000.

Events of 1862

Forts Henry and Donelson — Brig. Gen. U.S. Grant with 17,000 attacked **Ft. Henry** on Tennessee River; it fell **Feb. 6.** Grant rushed troops across 10 mi. of bogs to **Ft. Donelson** on the Cumberland, sent his "unconditional surrender" message to Brig. Gen. Simon B. Buckner, CSA, who gave up with 11,500 **Feb. 16.**

Shiloh—Gen. Albert S. Johnston, CSA, with 40,000 men surprised Grant at **Shiloh Church** near **Pittsburg Landing**, Tenn. **Apr. 6**; Johnston was killed. Gen. Beauregard retreated **Apr. 7** after Brig. Gen. Don Carlos Buell reinforced Grant with about 20,000 men. U.S. had 44,895 engaged, with 1,734 killed of 13,047 total casualties; CSA, 1,728 killed of 10,699 casualties.

Fighting ships and gunboats under Flag Officer David G. Farragut, Commodore D. D. Porter, on the Mississippi silenced **Chalmette** batteries; with Gen. Benjamin F. Butler, took forts: **New Orleans** surrendered **Apr. 25.** Farragut made rear admiral.

Monitor and Merrimack — Confederates rebuilt scuttled US frigate Merrimack into ironclad Virginia. Sank Cumberland, USN, destroyed Congress, USN, at Hampton Roads, Va., **Mar. 8.** Three other U.S. ships ran aground including Minnesota. Monitor, flat-decked ironclad, 900 tons, 172 ft. long with revolving turret and 2 11-in. guns, built by John Ericsson at $275,000 cost; Lt. John L. Worden commander, crew of 58, badly damaged Virginia **Mar. 9.** After Union took Virginia's base, Confederates scuttled ship **May 11.**

Peninsular Campaign — McClellan moved Army of the Potomac by sea to Fort Monroe, Va., 70 mi. from Richmond. Confederates sent Stonewall Jackson up Shenandoah Valley to divert U.S. troops; Jackson lost at **Kernstown, Va.**, but routed U.S. troops at **McDowell, Front Royal, Winchester, Cross Keys, Port Republic Mar. 23-June 9.** McClellan's advance troops clashed with Maj. Gen. James Longstreet at **Willimasburg May 5.** On May 25, 2 U.S. corps crossed to south side of Chickahominy leaving 3 on north side. Gen. Joseph E. Johnston attacked south side **May 30. Battle of Fair Oaks or Seven Pines**, was repulsed. Johnston was wounded and Lee took over Army of Northern Virginia.

Gen. Lee started **Seven Days' Battles** at Mechanicsville **Va. June 26.** McClellan withdrew to **Gaines Mill** (1st Cold Harbor) where Lee with 57,000 assaulted Brig. Gen. Fitz John Porter's 34,000 **June 27.** McClellan held off Lee at Savage Station **June 29, Frayser's Farm** or Glendale **June 30**; stopped Stonewall Jackson at **White Oak Swamp June 30.** At Malvern Hill July 1 Confederates had 5,500 casualties, mostly from U.S. artillery; Union casualties were 2,000. Despite this success McClellan withdrew army to Harrison's Landing. With over 115,000 men available against Confederates' 95,000, McClellan from June 25-July 1 had 1,734 killed, 8,062 wounded, 6,053 missing; CSA had 3,478 killed, 16,261 wounded, 875 missing. McClellan's army was sent to join Gen. John Pope's in northern Virginia.

Second Bull Run (Manassas). Stonewall Jackson and Maj. Gen. A. P. Hill, CSA, attacked Maj. Gen. Nathaniel P. Banks (part of Pope's Army of Virginia) at Cedar Mountain, Va. **Aug. 9.** Jackson destroyed Pope's supplies at Manassas **Aug. 26.** Major battle was fought **Aug. 30.** Pope was checked by Jackson and Longstreet, withdrew; was relieved.

Antietam (Sharpsburg). Lee with 50,000 crossed Potomac **Sept. 4** to Frederick, Md., moved across South Mountain to Hagerstown, Md. McClellan, fought Longstreet and D. H. Hill at **South Mountain Sept. 14**, Lee dropped back to Antietam creek near Sharpsburg, Md., **Sept. 15**; Jackson took **Harpers Ferry** where only 1,300 cavalry of 12,000 USA escaped. McClellan attacked **Sept. 17**; stopped Lee, but failed to use reserve and let Lee withdraw across Potomac. U.S. had 70,000 engaged, 13,000 casualties; CSA had 50,000 engaged, 13,000 casualties.

Fredericksburg, Va. Lincoln relieved McClellan, gave Army of the Potomac to Maj. Gen. Ambrose E. Burnside. Burnside crossed Rappahannock, made frontal attacks on Marye's Heights above Fredericksburg **Dec. 13.** Lee, Longstreet and Jackson with 75,000 repulsed him. USA lost 12,653; CSA 5,377.

Preliminary proclamation, **Sept. 22**, by President Lincoln announced that **Jan. 1, 1863**, slaves would be declared free in territory then in rebellion.

Events of 1863

Lincoln's Emancipation Proclamation Jan. 1 declared free forever the slaves in Arkansas, Texas, Louisiana (certain parishes already occupied excepted); Mississippi, Alabama, Florida, Georgia, South Carolina, North Carolina, Tennessee, and Virginia (West Virginia and other portions excepted). About 3 million slaves were thus declared free.

1858

First Atlantic cable completed by Cyrus W. Field **Aug. 5.** Queen Victoria and President Buchanan exchanged greetings, but cable failed **Sept. 1.** Field tried again in 1865, succeeded in 1866.

Lincoln-Douglas debates in Illinois **Aug. 21-Oct. 15.**

1859

Dixie, composed by Daniel D. Emmett; was first performed by him with Bryant's Minstrels at Mechanics Hall, N. Y. City **Apr. 4.**

First commercially productive oil well, drilled near Titusville, Pa., by Edwin L. Drake **Aug. 27**, started boom.

Abolitionist John Brown with 21 men seized U.S. Armory at Harpers Ferry (then Va.) **Oct. 16.** U.S. Marines under Lt. Col. Robert E. Lee captured raiders, killing 11. One Marine and 5 civilians also killed. Brown was hanged for treason by Virginia **Dec. 2** as were 5 of his band, at Charlestown (now Charles Town, W. Va.).

Darwin's Origin of Species published.

1860

Abraham Lincoln, Republican, elected president by 1,866,452 popular and 180 electoral votes; Stephen A. Douglas had 1,375,157 and 12; John C. Breckinridge, 847,953 and 72; John Bell 590,631 and 39. Lincoln took office **Mar. 4, 1861.**

Emancipation and Lincoln's Assassination

Chancellorsville, Va. —Maj. Gen. Joseph E. Hooker succeeded Burnside and with 90,000 available, attempted to envelop Lee **May 2**. Jackson led 32,000 around US Army, drove in right of Maj. Gen. O. O. Howard. Jackson wounded by own troops **May 2** died **May 10**; succeeded by Maj. Gen. J. E. B. Stuart. Maj. Gen. John Sedgwick forced Confederates out of Marye's Heights; was pushed back **May 4**. Hooker overruled his advisers and withdrew across Rappahannock. U.S. casualties 17,197; CSA 13,000. Lincoln called for 100,000 men for 6 months **June 15**.

Gettysburg — Lee with 76,224 and 272 guns, invaded Penn. Army of the Potomac had 115,256, about 90,000 effective, 362 guns. Lincoln gave Maj. Gen. George G. Meade top command **June 28**. 1st U.S. Cavalry under Gen. John Buford pushed back at Gettysburg by Lt. Gen. A. P. Hill, CSA, **July 1**. Lt. Gen. Richard S. Ewell, CSA, forced U.S. back to Cemetery Hill; U.S. took Culp's Hill, extended line to Round Top. Lee's attacks checked **July 2**. On **July 3** Maj. Gen. George E. Pickett, Maj. Gen. Isaac Trimble, and Brig. Gen. James J. Pettigrew with 15,000 made assault on foot from Seminary Ridge vs. U.S. center held by Gen. W. S. Hancock; were repulsed with 4,500 casualties. Lee retreated into Virginia; Meade did not pursue. Losses: U.S. 3,155 killed, 14,529 wounded, 5,365 missing; CSA, 3,903 killed, 12,709 wounded, 5,425 missing. Many of the missing were prisoners. Total casualties estimated at 23,049 USA, 20,451 CSA.

Vicksburg — Gen. William T. Sherman took Jackson, Miss., **May 14**. Lt. Gen. John C. Pemberton, CSA, commanding 30,000 men, was defeated at **Champion's Hill** and **Black River Bridge**, and besieged in Vicksburg by Grant. He surrendered **July 4**; Grant paroled prisoners. Gen. Nathaniel Banks with 15,000 captured **Port Hudson July 8**, giving U.S. control of Mississippi River.

Tennessee — Maj. Gen. William S. Rosecrans, USA took **Chattanooga Sept. 9**. Braxton Bragg CSA, drove him back to **Chickamauga** but Maj. Gen. George H. Thomas checked Bragg **Sept. 18-20**; was called "Rock of Chickamauga." Hooker took Lookout Mt., fought "Battle Above the Clouds" **Nov. 24**. Sherman and Thomas dislodged Bragg at **Missionary Ridge Nov. 25**. Bragg retreated to Georgia.

Events of 1864

Grant made general in chief Mar. 12. Sherman succeeded him in West. Draft for 500,000 men to serve 3 yrs. or duration begun **Mar. 10**; 200,000 more **Mar. 14**.

Rear Adm. David G. Farragut won naval battle of **Mobile Bay Aug. 5**.

Wilderness, Spotsylvania — Bloody battles followed when Grant crossed the Rapidan and was attacked by Lee in the "Wilderness," tangled woods west of Fredericksburg, **May 5**. Grant attacked Lee at Spotsylvania Court House May 10 (2d Wilderness). Maj. Gen. Francis C. Barlow USA took Spotsylvania salient, including **Bloody Angle May 12** (3d Wilderness). U.S. killed and wounded May 5-12 est. 26,813, missing 4,183. Maj. Gen. Philip H. Sheridan's cavalry defeated Maj. Gen. J.E.B. Stuart at Yellow Tavern, Va., **May 11**; Stuart was fatally wounded, died **May 12** in Richmond.

Cold Harbor — Lee took strong position near the Chickahominy. Grant made frontal attacks **June 3**, lost 7,000 casualties in 30 minutes, 11,000 **June 1-3**.

USS Kearsarge — Capt. John A. Winslow defeated CSS Alabama, Capt. Raphael Semmes, off Cherbourg, France, **June 19**; Alabama surrendered and sank.

Early vs. Sheridan — Lee sent Maj. Gen. Jubal A. Early to hold Shenandoah Valley. Sheridan defeated Early at **Winchester** Sept. 19, **Fisher's Hill** Sept. 22. Early surprised Gen. Horatio Wright at **Cedar Creek** Oct. 19; Sheridan's famous ride from Winchester rallied troops, brought victory.

Sherman's Campaign for Atlanta — Sherman defeated J. E. Johnston at **Resaca**, Ga., May 14-15. Johnston repulsed Sherman at **Kenesaw Mtn.** June 27 (U.S. casualties 3,000, CSA 600), but told Jefferson Davis he could not annihilate Sherman's large forces, was superseded by Gen. J. B. Hood, CSA, **July 17**. Lt. Gen. William J. Hardee, CSA, defeated at **Peach Tree Creek** July 20. Hardee defeated in battle of **Atlanta** July 22 by Gen. J. B. McPherson who was killed. Sherman occupied Atlanta **Sept. 2**, burned it **Nov. 15**, started **March to the Sea**, reached Savannah Dec. 21. Thomas defeated Hood at **Nashville**, Tenn.

Events of 1865

Confederates evacuated Columbia, S.C., and **Charleston**, S.C., Feb. 17, lost Cape Fear River forts Feb. 20-21. Brig. Gen. George A. Custer defeated Early at **Waynesboro**, Va., Mar. 2. Confederates evacuated **Petersburg** and **Richmond** Apr. 2-3. Lee surrendered 27,805 to Grant at **Appomattox Court House**, Va., **Apr. 9**. J. E. Johnston surrendered 31,243 to Sherman at **Durham Station**, N.C., **Apr. 18**.

Murder of Lincoln

Lincoln was shot by John Wilkes Booth, an actor, in Ford's Theatre, in Washington, D.C., **April 14**, died **April 15**. Booth died of a bullet wound **April 26**, in burning barn, on a farm near Bowling Green, Va. Hanged for complicity in Lincoln's assassination were Mrs. Mary E. Surratt, David E. Herold, George A. Atzerodt, and Lewis Payne (Powell) **July 7**. Also convicted of conspiracy were Dr. Samuel A. Mudd, who set Booth's broken ankle, Samuel Arnold, Michael O'Laughlin, and Edward Spangler. All were sentenced to life imprisonment except Spangler, who received a 6-year sentence. They were sent to Dry Tortugas prison, off Key West, where O'Laughlin died during an 1867 outbreak of yellow fever. Dr. Mudd's unselfish services as a physician during the outbreak won him a pardon; Arnold and Spangler were freed with Dr. Mudd in 1869. John H. Surratt, son of Mary E., fled to Europe, was brought back, tried and freed. Booth's body was buried under the stone floor of a naval prison in Washington, D. C., later reburied in the Booth family plot in Baltimore.

Slavery was abolished by adoption of the 13th amendment to the U. S. Constitution **Dec. 18**.

First Pony Express between Sacramento, Cal., and St. Joseph, Mo., 1,980 mi. apart, started from each place at 5 p.m., Apr. 3; 80 men each rode 75 mi. on 429 horses, changed every 10 mi. There were 190 relay stations. The service ended Oct. 24, 1861, when first transcontinental telegraph line was completed.

Giuseppe Garibaldi led 1,000 volunteers to Sicily in May to unify Italy by force; deposed Francis II of Naples; named Victor Emmanuel king of Italy.

**1861-65—Civil War.
See Article Pages 718-719**

1861

Emancipation of Russian serfs by Czar Alexander II. Paved the way for later reforms by Alexander.

1863

Draft riots in N.Y. City killed an estimated 1,000, including Negroes who were hung by mobs July 13-16; protested provision allowing money payment in place of military service. Property loss about $1.5 million. Payment in place of service ended 1864.

1864

Sand Creek massacre of Cheyenne and Arapaho Indians by Col. John M. Chivington Nov. 29 in a raid by 900 cavalrymen who killed between 150-500 men, women and children; 9 soldiers died. The tribes were awaiting surrender terms when attacked.

1866

Ku Klux Klan formed secretly in South to terrorize Negroes who voted. Disbanded 1869-1871. A 2d Ku Klux Klan was organized 1915.

First post of the Grand Army of the Republic formed at Decatur, Ill., Apr. 6. First national encampment met. Nov. 2 in Indianapolis. For years this Union veterans organization was a political force in the nation. Last encampment held Aug. 31, 1949, in Indianapolis; 6 of the 16 surviving veterans attended.

1867

Alaska sold to U.S. by Russia for $7.2 million (2 cents an acre) Mar. 30 through efforts of Secretary of State William H. Seward and Sen. Charles Sumner.

Emperor Maximillian of Mexico executed by Juarez supporters June 19. He was an Austrian archduke placed on throne Apr. 10, 1864, by French.

Dominion of Canada established July 1.

Abolition of the Shogunate and restoration of the Mikado marked beginning of Meiji reforms that industrialized and modernized Japan; feudalism abolished 1871; Constitution promulgated 1889.

1868

The World Almanac, a publication of the New York World newspaper, appeared for the first time.

Thomas D'Arcy McGee, a "Father of Confederation," shot in first Canadian political assassination.

President Andrew Johnson, blocked by Senate in attempt to remove Edwin M. Stanton, secretary of war, for opposing his policies, was impeached for violation of Tenure of Office Act by House; tried by Senate and acquitted March-May. Stanton resigned.

1869

Financial "Black Friday" in New York Sept. 24; caused by gold corner attempt.

Transcontinental railroad completed; golden spike driven at Promontory, Utah May 10 marking the junction of Central Pacific and Union Pacific.

Woman's suffrage law passed in Territory of Wyoming Dec. 10.

1870

Franco-Prussian War. Napoleon III, French emperor, tricked into declaring war on Prussia by Bismarck, Prussian chancellor, over Spanish succession issue; surrendered with large army at Sedan Sept. 4. Nationalists declared republic Sept. 4.

The troops of Victor Emmanuel II, under Gen. Cadorna, took possession of Rome Sept. 20 in the name of the kingdom of Italy. Rome and the rest of the Papal States then were annexed after a plebiscite taken Oct. 2.

1871

Court of Arbitration awarded United States damages of $15.5 million in gold against Britain because British equipped Alabama and 12 other Confederate raiders. After sinking 6 U.S. ships, Alabama was destroyed by U.S.S. Kearsarge off Cherbourg 1864.

William I of Hohenzollern proclaimed German emperor (kaiser) at Versailles Jan. 18. Paris "Red Republicans" organized commune Mar. 18-May 29; burned Hotel de Ville, Tuileries palace, executed 67 hostages. Communards overcome by French army; deaths est. 20,000.

Treaty of Frankfort ended Franco-Prussian War May 23. France ceded Alsace, most of Lorraine, paid 5 billion francs indemnity.

The Law of Guarantees, passed by the Italian Parliament May 13, granted the pope and his successors possession of the Vatican, the Lateran and the villa of Castel Gandolfo and a yearly 3,225,000 lire, or about $645,000. The money was not claimed.

Great fire destroyed Chicago Oct. 8-11; loss est. at $196 million. Supposedly started in Mrs. O'Leary's barn, 558 DeKoven St., by cow upsetting lantern.

Henry M. Stanley sent by James Gordon Bennett, owner of New York Herald, to find David Livingstone, missionary, greeted him Nov. 10 at Ujiji in Central Africa, now Tanzania, with "Dr. Livingstone, I presume?"

1872

Amnesty Act restored civil rights to citizens of the South May 22 except 500 Confederate leaders.

1873

Panic in New York City began with bank failures Sept. 20.

First U. S. postal card issued May 1.

1874

"Boss" William Tweed of N.Y. City convicted of fraud Nov. 19 and sentenced to 12 years in prison; the court released him from Blackwells Island prison June 1875 on a technicality; he was committed to Ludlow St. jail in a civil suit, escaped Dec. 4, 1875, and went to Cuba, then to Spain; brought back to N.Y. City Nov. 1876; died in jail Apr. 12, 1878.

1875

Congress passed first Civil Rights Act. Mar. 1 which guaranteed equal rights to Negroes in public accommodations and jury duty. Act invalidated in 1883 by Supreme Court ruling that the federal government can protect only political, not social, rights.

First Kentucky Derby held in May at Churchill Downs at Louisville, Ky.

Mary Baker Eddy published "Science and Health."

1876

Samuel J. Tilden, Democrat, received majority of 250,000 popular votes for president over Rutherford B. Hayes, Republican, and had 184 electoral votes against 163, with returns from South Carolina, Florida, Louisiana and Oregon, 22 electoral votes, in dispute. Bitter contest for delegates with charges of corruption; issue left to Congress, which appointed electoral commission, 8 Republicans, 7 Democrats; Hayes given presidency by strict party vote.

Col. George A. Custer and 264 soldiers of the 7th Cavalry killed June 25 in "last stand," Battle of the Little Big Horn, Mont., in Sioux Indian War, by Indian tribes united by Sitting Bull; fighting led by Chiefs Gall and Crazy Horse.

James Butler (Wild Bill) Hickok, shot dead from behind by Jack McCall, a desperado, in Deadwood, S. D., Aug. 2. A vigilance committee acquitted McCall but the U.S. Court in Yankton, S.D., found him guilty and he was hanged.

1877

Molly Maguires, Irish terrorist society in Scranton, Pa., mining areas, broken up by hanging of 11 leaders for murders of mine officials and police.

1878

First commercial telephone exchange opened, New Haven, Conn., Jan. 28, 1878. First private exchange, used by physicians, reported in use July 1877 at Hartford, Conn.

1879

F. W. Woolworth opened his first five-and-ten store in Utica, N. Y., Feb. 22.

Henry George published Progress & Poverty, advocating single tax on land.

1881

President James A. Garfield shot in Washington, D.C., July 2; died in Elberon, N. J., Sept. 19.

Federation of Organized Trades and Labor Unions formed Aug. 2 at Terre Haute, Ind.; later joined with 25 independent unions to form the American Federation of Labor at Columbus, Ohio, Dec. 1886.

1882

Prof. Robert Koch announced, in Berlin, discovery of the tuberculosis bacillus Mar. 24.

1883

Brooklyn Bridge opened May 24; panic on it May 30, 12 trampled to death.

1884

Financial panic in New York May 5-7.

1885

Gen. Charles G. (Chinese) Gordon, British governor of the Sudan, sent there to aid Egyptian troops, was slain Jan. 26 by a Moslem soldier, at Khartoum. Several thousand whites were massacred by troops of the Mahdi, Sudanese leader. Gen. Kitchener defeated the Mahdi's army Sept. 2, 1898.

First electric street railway in U.S. opened in Baltimore by Leo Daft Aug. 10.

Canadian rebel Louis Riel hanged for treason at Regina, following crushing of Northwest Rebellion.

Last spike driven Nov. 7 in Canadian Pacific Railway at Craigellachie, British Columbia, completed Canadian transcontinental railway.

1886

Haymarket riot, evening of May 4, followed bitter labor battles for 8-hour day in Chicago, attacks on strike-breakers, police violence and attempts of anarchists to incite workers. A bomb killed 7 police and wounded 66. Eight anarchists found guilty. Gov. John P. Altgeld denounced trial as unfair.

Geronimo, Apache Indian, surrendered Mar. 27 to U.S. Gen. George Crook in Sonora, Mex., but fled the next day and finally surrendered Sept. 4 to U. S. Gen. Nelson A. Miles in Arizona.

Dr. Arthur Conan Doyle created famous detective Sherlock Holmes, in story, A Study in Scarlet.

1887

Flood in Hwang-ho River, China; 900,000 persons perished.

Opera Comique in Paris burned May 25; 200 dead.

1888

Great blizzard in eastern U. S. Mar. 11-14; 400 deaths.

1889

Crown Prince Rudolf of Austria and Baroness Maria Vetsera found slain in his hunting lodge, Mayerling, near Vienna Jan. 29.

Johnstown, Pa., flood May 31; 2,200 lives lost.

Universal Exhibition in Paris May 6-Nov. 6. Eiffel Tower (984.25 ft.) opened. First automobile exhibited, a Benz.

Dom Pedro II, emperor of Brazil, forced off throne by planters after he freed slaves. Died in Paris 1891; last emperor on American soil.

1890

First execution by electrocution; William Kemmler Aug. 6 at Auburn Prison, Auburn, N. Y., for murder.

Battle of Wounded Knee, S. D., Dec. 29, the last major conflict between Indians and U. S. troops,

---

Spanish-American War of 1898; United States Becomes Naval Power

Spanish misrule in Cuba led to repeated attempts by Cuban patriots to gain rights of citizenship, abolition of slavery, and finally independence. When South America broke from Europe in the 1820s proslavery influence in the U.S. blocked movements to free Cuba and Puerto Rico. But in 1852, President Fillmore refused to join Great Britain and France in guaranteeing Spanish authority in Cuba. In 1854, the Ostend Manifesto, written largely by James Buchanan, urged the U.S. to buy Cuba or seize it to abolish oppression. Grant's administration offered to buy Cuba, but Spain rejected the offer.

In Cuba revolts led by Narciso Lopez and Joaquin de Aguero, 1848-1851, were suppressed and the leaders executed. In 1868, a major revolt was led by Carlos de Cespedes and Manuel de Quesada; it lasted 10 years. In 1873, the Virginius expedition, flying the American flag, was seized by the Spaniards, and Americans and Cubans aboard were shot. This did not stop supplying of arms from the U.S. In 1895, the insurrection had spread so widely under Generals Calixto Garcia, Maximo Gomez, and Antonio Macea that Spain landed 150,000 troops, but by 1896 over half of the island was in the hands of the patriots. The U.S. offered to mediate but was repulsed. The country was laid waste by Spanish troops and the accounts of suffering increased sentiment in the U.S. in favor of a free Cuba.

The U.S. battleship Maine, under Capt. Charles D. Sigsbee, sent to Havana in January on goodwill tour, was blown up Feb. 15, 1898; 264 men, 2 officers killed. U.S. inquiry, Capt. William T. Sampson, board president, blamed external explosion Mar. 2. Spanish inquiry Mar. 28 blamed internal explosion. Congress Mar. 9 voted $50 million for defense. President McKinley Mar. 27 demanded Spain grant armistice

for negotiation with Cuba via U.S., end relocation of noncombatants in special military enclaves. Spain Mar. 31 offered to arbitrate Maine charges, end relocation, but wanted Cubans to ask for armistice. After appeal by foreign ministers Spain granted armistice Apr. 9. McKinley Apr. 11 asked Congress for authority to intervene in Cuba. Congress Apr. 20-25 debated joint resolution recognizing independence of Cuba, asked Spain to withdraw and empowered president to enforce it; adopted it with statement war existed since Apr. 21. Spain declared war Apr. 24.

Commodore George Dewey, with 6 warships destroyed the Spanish fleet (10 ships) in Manila Bay May 1, occupied Cavite. Spain, 167 dead; U.S., 7 wounded. Marines landed at Guantanamo May 11. Maj. Gen. William R. Shafter landed 10,000 men at Daiquiri and Siboney, including 1st U.S. Volunteer Cavalry (Rough Riders) recruited by Lt. Col. Theodore Roosevelt, commanded by Col. Leonard Wood. Brig. Gen. H. W. Lawton, Brig. Gen. Adna R. Chaffee with 6,654 men attacked El Caney, defended by 500 Spaniards July 1. Maj. Gen. Joseph Wheeler, Brig. Gen. J. F. Kent carried San Juan Hill with 8,336, same day.

Admiral Cervera's fleet left Santiago harbor July 3, was destroyed by ships of acting Rear Adm. Sampson and Commodore Winfield S. Schley; 353 Spaniards killed, 151 wounded; 1 American killed. Santiago surrendered July 17. Maj. Gen. Nelson A. Miles took Puerto Rico July 25-28. Armistice signed Aug. 12. Peace treaty signed in Paris Dec. 10 eliminated Spain from lands discovered by Columbus. U. S. acquired Puerto Rico, Guam and Philippines, paying $20 million for all Spanish claims in latter; guaranteed Cuban independence (ratified Feb. 6, 1899.) U.S. had treaty rights in Cuba until 1934; granted Philippines independence July 4, 1946.

occurred when a band of Sioux were captured and brought to Wounded Knee Creek where Col. J. W. Forsyth ordered them disarmed. Some Indians resisted, sparking the battle which killed about 200 Indian men, women, and children; 29 soldiers died, 33 wounded.

Castle Garden closed as immigration depot and Ellis Island opened Dec. 31; closed 1954.

1892

Homestead, Pa., strike at Carnegie steel mills, near Pittsburgh; conflict between 300 Pinkerton guards and strikers; 7 guards and 11 strikers and spectators shot to death, many wounded **July 6.**

1893

Ford's Theater building, Washington, D. C., where Lincoln was shot, used by Pension Bureau, collapsed **June 9** killing 22.

1894

Chinese-Japanese War began **July 25; Battle of** Yalu **Sept. 17;** Treaty of Shimonoseki **April 17, 1895** gave Japan the Liaotung Peninsula, Formosa (Taiwan) and the Pescadores.

Jacob S. Coxey led 500 unemployed from the Midwest into Washington, D. C., **Apr. 29.** Coxey was arrested for trespassing on the Capitol grounds.

Strike of employees of Pullman Co., South Chicago, Ill., June, led Eugene V. Debs to call sympathetic strike of American Railway Union. President Cleveland called out Federal troops over protest of Gov. Altgeld (Ill.). Debs and 3 others were imprisoned 6 months for contempt of court. Strike ended **Aug. 7.**

Thomas A. Edison's kinetoscope (invented 1887) given first public showing at 1155 Broadway, N.Y. City **Apr. 14,** was patented **1891** for U. S. only.

Capt. Alfred Dreyfus found guilty of betraying French army secrets **Dec. 22** in sensational frame-up; real culprit, Major Esterhazy, acquitted; Dreyfus condemned to Devil's Island, off French Guiana. Recalled for second trial by efforts of Emile Zola and Georges Clemenceau; again condemned **Sept. 9, 1899.** Public clamor led to pardon **Sept. 19.** Further proofs of innocence led to complete exoneration, **1906.** He served as a lieutenant colonel in World War I.

1895

Cuban Revolution resumed Feb. 20; Gen. Antonio Maceo, leader of the insurrection, was killed in action **Dec. 7, 1896.**

X-rays discovered by Wilhelm Konrad Roentgen, a German physicist; Nobel prize winner **1901.**

1896

President Cleveland intervened in boundary dispute between Venezuela and British Guiana on basis of Monroe Doctrine; appointed arbitration commission which settled it **Feb. 2, 1897.**

Guglielmo Marconi received first wireless (radio) patent from Britain **June 2.**

William Jennings Bryan delivered "Cross of Gold" speech at Democratic National Convention in Chicago **July 8.** Bryan nominated for president but defeated by Republican William McKinley.

1897

Eugene V. Debs formed Social Democratic party.

1898

Radium discovered by Pierre Curie, his wife, Marie, and G. Bemont in Paris.

1898—Spanish-American War
See Article Page 721

1899

South African (Boer) War began **Oct. 11;** Ladysmith relieved Feb. 28, 1900; Pretoria fell June 5, 1900; war ended May 31, 1902 with loss of independence of Boer republics. Transvaal and Orange Free State, now in Republic of South Africa. British losses: 5,773 killed; 16,171 dead of wounds or disease; 22,829 wounded. Boers engaged est. 65,000; losses unknown.

Filipino insurgents (est. 12,000 under arms) unable to get recognition of independence from U. S. started guerrilla war **Feb. 4.** Crushed with capture **Mar. 23,**

1901 of leader, Emilio Aguinaldo, by Brig. Gen. Frederick Funston.

Open-Door Policy of U. S. Secy. of State John Hay supported by 6 nations. Policy was to make China an open market for international commerce and to preserve its integrity as a nation.

Boxer anti-foreign uprising started in China: Westerners and Westernized Chinese murdered.

1900

Carry Nation, Kansas anti-saloon agitator, began raiding with hatchet.

Boxers in China killed German minister **June 20.** Foreigners besieged in Peking legations. Relief expedition of 18,000 American, British, French, Japanese, and Russian troops took Tientsin **July 13;** Peking **Aug. 14.** U. S. had 2,500 men under Maj. Gen. A. R. Chaffee. Germans arrived and Field Marshal Count Alfred von Waldersee led army of occupation. Russia refused to yield parts of Manchuria. Dowager empress of China accepted allied terms **Sept. 1901.** All except U. S. exacted large concessions and indemnity of $333 million payable in 39 years. U.S. used half its $25 million share to provide Chinese students scholarships.

Campaign to wipe out yellow fever in Cuba begun June 26 by Drs. Walter Reed, Aristides Agramonte, Jesse Lazear, and James Carroll.

Galveston hurricane and tidal wave **Sept. 8.** An est. 5,000 lives lost.

1901

President William McKinley was shot at the Pan-American Exposition in Buffalo, N. Y., **Sept. 6** by Leon Czolgosz, anarchist; died **Sept. 14.** Theodore Roosevelt, 42, became youngest U. S. president.

Marconi signalled letter "S" by wireless telegraph across Atlantic from Cornwall, England, to Newfoundland **Dec. 12.**

1902

Anglo-Japanese alliance formed **Jan. 30** to protect Japan against encroaching Russians.

Cuban Republic inaugurated. American occupation under Gen. Leonard Wood ended **May 20.**

First International Arbitration Court opened in The Hague, Holland, **October.**

1903

First automobile trip across U. S. from San Francisco to New York **May 23-Aug. 1.**

Henry Ford, having withdrawn from the Detroit Automobile Co. in **1901,** organized Ford Motor Co.

Treaty between U. S. and Colombia to have U. S. dig Panama Canal signed **Jan. 22, 1903,** rejected by Colombia. Panama declared independence **Nov. 3;** recognized by President Theodore Roosevelt **Nov. 6.**

First successful flight in heavier-than-air mechanically propelled airplane by Orville Wright (1871-1948) **Dec. 17, 1903,** rising from base of Kill Devil Hill, 4 miles south of Kitty Hawk, N. C., 120 ft. in 12 sec. Fourth flight same day by Wilbur Wright (1867-1912), 852 ft., in 59 sec. Plane patented **May 22, 1906.**

1904

Russo-Japanese War began **Feb. 6.** Port Arthur surrendered to Japanese **Jan. 2, 1905.** Peace treaty signed in Portsmouth, N. H., **Sept. 5, 1905.**

New York subway opened **Oct. 27.**

1905

Russian revolution crushed by Czar Nicholas II. Resulted in creation of Duma (parliament) to placate liberals. First meeting **May 10;** dissolved **July.**

Norway dissolved union with Sweden.

1906

San Francisco earthquake and fire **Apr. 18-19.** Dead: 452. Loss: $350 million.

Harry K. Thaw, Pittsburgh millionaire, shot and killed architect Stanford White on roof of Madison Square Garden, N.Y. (26th and Madison) **June 25** on ground of avenging honor of wife Evelyn Nesbit.

1907

Financial panic in the U.S.

Standard Oil of Indiana fined $29,240,000 by Judge K. M. Landis in U. S. Court, Chicago, for accepting freight rebates **Apr. 3.** Set aside **July 22, 1908.** Railroads found guilty of giving rebates.

First round-world cruise of U.S. "Great White Fleet"; 16 battleships, 12,000 men; exhibited U.S. naval strength.

1908

Chelsea, Mass., destroyed by fire; loss more than $6 million, Apr. 12.

1909

Admiral Robert E. Peary reached North Pole Apr. 6 on 6th attempt, accompanied by Matthew Henson, a black, and 4 Eskimos.

Louis Bleriot flew across the English Channel from Calais to Dover, 31 mi. in 37 min., July 25.

Budget in Britain: "Soak the rich" taxation financed social security measures.

1910

Boy Scouts of America founded Feb. 8.

Glenn H. Curtiss won $10,000 offered by the New York World for first continuous flight, Albany to N.Y. City, 137 mi., 152 min., May 29.

Dynamite explosion at Los Angeles Times Oct. 1 caused fire killing 21 in labor dispute.

1911

Italian-Turkish war began Sept. 29. Italians made first combat use of aircraft in warfare; Libya acquired by Italy.

First transcontinental airplane flight (with numerous stops) by C. P. Rodgers, New York to Pasadena, Sept. 17-Nov. 5; time in air 82 hr., 4 min.

Capt. Roald Amundsen, Norwegian explorer, reached South Pole Dec. 14.

Mexican Revolution. Porfirio Diaz, president of Mexico since 1877 (except 1880-84, resigned May 25 after successful revolt by Francisco L. Madero who succeeded him. People living in poverty wanted restoration of communal lands (ejidos), better conditions. In 1912 Madero, supported by Gen. Huerta, put down revolts. In Feb. 1913 Huerta helped depose Madero; Madero, his brother and Vice President Suarez were murdered. President Wilson refused recognition to Huerta and "government by assassination." Venustiano Carranza, rallying Maderos, was opposed by Gen. Francisco (Pancho) Villa in north. When American sailors were arrested at Tampico Apr. 9, 1914, the U.S. sent Atlantic fleet to Veracruz. Huerta resigned July 14, 1914, Carranza occupied Mexico City Aug. 20. Villa, supported by Zapata, warred on Carranza. U.S. recognized Carranza Oct. 19, 1915, placed embargo on arms to other generals. Villa raided Santa Isabel, Mexico Jan. 10, 1916, killed several Americans; raided Columbus, N. M., Mar. 9, 1916, killed 17. Gen. John J. Pershing with 12,000 sent into Mexico Mar. 15. Fight at Parral and Chihuahua Apr. 12. Carranza's troops attacked June 21. U. S. troops withdrawn Feb. 4, 1917. Carranza called constitutional convention, Feb. 15, 1917, became legal president May 1, 1917. He restored some of the land, nationalized coal and oil, expropriated some foreign holdings. Discontent caused new uprising and he was ambushed and killed. Obregon became president Dec. 1, 1920. Villa was killed in ambush at Parral July 20, 1923.

Chinese Revolution led by Sun Yat-sen overthrew Manchu dynasty. Republic formed Feb. 12, 1912; Yuan shih-K'ai elected president Feb. 15.

Parliament Act of 1911 reduced the power of British House of Lords to a suspensory veto which could delay but not kill bills.

1912

Capt. Robert F. Scott and 4 companions reached South Pole Jan. 17; all 5 died on return journey.

White Star liner Titanic wrecked on maiden trip, from Southampton to N.Y. City; hit iceberg off Newfoundland Apr. 14-15; U. S. reported 1,517 lost; British Board of Trade reported 1,503 lost. There were 2,307 persons aboard. The ship was 882 1/2 ft. long, cost $7.5 million.

War in Balkans against Turkey by Montenegro, Bulgaria, Serbia, and Greece Oct. 8-Dec. 3. Turks driven from Europe except for Constantinople (Istanbul) area.

1913

Sixteenth Amendment effective Feb. 25 empowered Congress to levy and collect income taxes.

1914-1918 World War I
See Article pages 724-725

1914

Ford Motor Co. raised basic wage rates from $2.40 for 9-hr. day to $5 for 8-hr. day, Jan. 5.

First ship passed through Panama Canal Aug. 15.

Second International: Brussels meeting of International Socialist Bureau July. Members included 5 men later heads of governments: Lenin (Russia); Ebert (German Republic); Stauning (Denmark); Branting (Sweden); MacDonald (Britain).

1915

First telephone talk, New York to San Francisco, Jan. 25 by Alexander Graham Bell and Thomas A. Watson.

First successful wireless from moving Lackawanna train to station, Feb. 7.

Twenty-one Demands presented by Japan to China; called for almost complete control of China.

1916

Gregory Rasputin, confessor to czarina, killed in Petrograd (Leningrad) December.

Bomb exploded during San Francisco Preparedness Day Parade July 22, killed 10, wounded 40. Thomas J. Mooney, 33, labor organizer; Mrs. Mooney; Warren K. Billings, shoe worker; Israel Weinberg, and Edward D. Nolan were charged with murder. Mooney was sentenced to death, Billings to life imprisonment; others went free. President Wilson interceded for Mooney, who got life imprisonment 1918. Mooney was pardoned by Gov. C. L. Olson Jan. 7, 1939; Billings freed Oct. 16, 1939.

Black Tom explosion at munitions docks in Jersey City, N. J., July 30; 2 killed, $40 million damages; traced to German saboteurs.

1917

The 18th (Prohibition) Amendment to the Constitution was submitted to the states by Congress Dec. 18. On Jan. 16, 1919, the 36th state (Nebraska) ratified it, whereupon, by proclamation of the Secretary of State it became effective Jan. 16, 1920. It was not ratified by Connecticut and Rhode Island. The Volstead (Prohibition Enforcement) Act was passed by Congress Oct. 1919, was vetoed by President Wilson, passed over his veto Jan. 17, 1920. New York, Montana and Wisconsin canceled their enforcement acts by 1929; Franklin D. Roosevelt, as 1932 presidential candidate, endorsed repeal; 21st Amendment repealed 18th; ratification completed Dec. 5, 1933.

Balfour Declaration Nov. 2 favored establishment of a national homeland in Palestine for Jewish people.

1918

Romanovs killed. Czar Nicholas II of Russia, the Empress Alexandra; their daughters, Olga, Tatiana, Marie, Anastasia; their son, Alexis, and aides were shot by Bolshevist orders in Ekaterinburg July 16; in Perm July 12 the Bolshevists assassinated the Czar's brother, Grand Duke Michael.

Influenza epidemic killed estimated 20 million throughout world, 548,000 in U.S.

1919

Rosa Luxemburg and Karl Liebknecht, leading German communists and founders of the Spartacus party, shot and killed Jan. by soldiers who were taking them to prison.

Peace conference opened in Paris Jan. 18; treaty, including President Wilson's proposed League of Nations, signed in palace at Versailles June 28 between German representatives and Allied powers and U.S. President Wilson submitted treaty to Senate July 10. Ratified by Germany July 10, Britain July 26, Italy Oct. 7, France Oct. 13, Japan Oct. 27. Not signed by China. Rejected by U.S. Senate Nov. 19 which considered American sovereignty not properly safeguarded in League of Nations. Never ratified by U.S. *(See 1921.)*

First Transatlantic Flight. U.S. Navy seaplane NC-4, commanded by Lt. Com. Albert Cushing Read, left Rockaway, N.Y., **May 8**; stopped at Trepassey, Newfoundland; left **May 16**, reached Azores **May 17**; Lisbon **May 27**; Plymouth, England, **May 31**; covered 4,500 mi. **John Alcock** and **A. W. Brown** made **June 14-15**, a non-stop air flight from Newfoundland to Ireland. A British dirigible, R-34, left Scotland **July 2** and descended in Mineola, N. Y., **July 6**. It left for England **July 10** and arrived there **July 13**. A roundtrip transcontinental air race, New York to San Francisco, was won by **Lt. W.B. Maynard** and **Lt. Alex Pearson** Oct. 8-18.

1920

League of Nations held first meeting at Geneva, Switzerland, **Jan. 10**; was dissolved **Jan. 10, 1946.**

The 19th (Woman Suffrage) Amendment, having been adopted by Congress, 1918-1919, and ratified by Tennessee (36th state to do so) **Aug. 18, 1920**, was proclaimed adopted **Aug. 26** by the Secretary of State. It had been first introduced in Congress in 1878; by 1918, women had won the vote under laws of 15 states, mostly in the West and Midwest, but including New York. The amendment gave women full, nationwide voting rights.

Nicola Sacco, 29, shoe factory employee and radical agitator, and **Bartolomeo Vanzetti**, 32, fish peddler and anarchist, accused of killing 2 men in payroll holdup at South Braintree, Mass., **Apr. 15**. Found guilty 1921 they became objects of 6-year campaign for release on grounds of want of conclusive evidence and prejudice of court. Appeals failing, they were executed at Charlestown, Mass., prison **Aug. 22, 1927.** Trial sharply criticized by Wickersham Commission on law procedure.

Wall St., N.Y. City, bomb explosion killed 30, injured 100: did $2 million damage **Sept. 16.**

1921

Joint Congressional resolution declaring peace with Germany and Austria signed **July 2** by President Harding. Treaty signed **Aug. 25**, ratified by Senate **Oct. 18.**

Limitation of Armaments Conference met in Washington **Nov. 12, 1921—Feb. 6, 1922.** U.S., Britain, France, Italy, Japan agreed to curtail naval construc-

---

Principal Events of World War I, 1914-1918:

Origins. Since the defeat of France by Prussia in 1870-71 major powers of Europe had kept peace by diplomatic negotiations and a balance of power. Triple Alliance, of Germany, Austria, and Italy was defensive, with reservations; Triple Entente was an understanding between Britian, France, and Russia. Nationalist aspirations in the Balkans had resulted in several wars and Italy had fought with Turkey and Ethiopia. Austria annexed Bosnia, Herzegovina, former Turkish Balkan provinces, in 1908. Russia backed Serbia's efforts to get a port on the Adriatic. Germany's industrial expansion led to building of powerful navy, which Britain matched 2 for one. Germany's universal military service led France to adopt 3-year training.

On **June 28, 1914**, Archduke Francis Ferdinand, heir to Austrian throne, was assassinated, with his wife, by Gavrilo Princip, Bosnian Serb terrorist, in Sarajevo, Bosnia. Austria-Hungary, through Count Berchthold, foreign minister, made 10 demands on Serbia for suppression of anti-Austrian agitation. Serbia conceded all but 2, which called for Austrian enforcement police inside Serbia. It asked reference to The Hague peace tribunal. Austria demanded all or nothing.

Russia, fearing Austrian action was aimed at Russia, supported Serbia. Germany backed Austria. Britain, France, Italy proposed mediation, Sir Edward Grey, British foreign minister, **July 26** proposed conference of 4 major powers; Germany refused to join.

Austria declared war on Serbia **July 28**. Germany, citing Russian mobilization, declared war on Russia **Aug. 1**; on France **Aug. 3**. Germans entered Belgium in violation of treaty, of which Britian was cosigner. Britain asked Germany to guarantee neutrality of Belgium by midnight **Aug. 4**; Germany refused; British declared war **Aug. 4**. Italy, declaring German aggression made Triple Alliance inoperative, proclaimed neutrality. Japan declared war on Germany **Aug. 23** because of Anglo-Japanese treaty on Far East. Turkey joined Central Powers **Nov. 23.**

Lord Kitchener became British secy. for war. Belgian forts at Liege stopped Germans until **Aug. 7**, delayed German schedule. Germans entered Brussels **Aug. 20**; pushed back British Expeditionary Force (Sir John French) at Mons **Aug. 23-24**; burned most of Louvain **Aug. 25**. Von Hindenburg and Ludendorff defeated Russians at Tannenberg, East Prussia, **Aug. 26-31**; at Masurian Lakes **Sept. 5-10.**

In first Battle of the Marne, **Sept. 5-10**, French under Joseph Jottre, Ferdinand Foch and Joseph Gallieni, stopped German advance of Von Kluck and Von Bülow toward Paris; forced them back to Aisne where trench warfare began. British repulsed Germans at Ypres **Oct. 16-Nov. 24**. Belgians lost Antwerp **Oct. 9**. Russians forced Austrians back in Galicia. Austrians took and lost Belgrade **Dec. 2-15.**

British bombarded Dardanelles forts **Nov. 3**; declared war on Turkey, annexed Cyprus **Nov. 5**. Japan took German-leased Tsingtao **Nov. 6.**

1915—Submarine War Begins

In 1915 the war became a desperate battle of attrition on land and sea. British sank Ger. cruiser Bluecher **Jan. 24**. Germany ordered submarine blockade of Britain to start **Feb. 18**. U. S. held Germany to "strict accountability" for American losses. Germans used liquid fire in Vosges **Mar. 3**. Roving German cruiser Dresden sunk in Pacific **Mar. 15**. Three Br.-Fr. battleships sunk at Dardanelles **Mar. 18**. Germans sank Falaba **Mar. 28**, one American lost. Turks sank British battleship Lord Nelson **Apr. 6**. Germans introduced poison gas at Ypres **Apr. 22**, Canadians saved the line. Allies landed at Gallipoli **Apr. 25**. Germans torpedoed Gulflight, U.S. tanker, **Apr. 30**, 2 Americans lost.

German sub sank Cunard liner **Lusitania** off Old Head of Kinsale, Ireland, **May 7**; of 1,959 aboard, including 702 crew, 1,198, including 124 Americans, died. This started a series of protests by U.S. to Germany. Secy. of State William J. Bryan resigned **June 8**; considered Wilson's Lusitania note too severe. After sinking Arabic **Aug. 19** Germans agreed not to sink liners without warning, but U.S. considered promises inadequate. U.S. dismissed Austrian Ambassador Dumba and Germans Boy-Ed and Von Papen for illegal activities.

South Africans under Gen. Botha captured German S. W. Africa. Italy declared war on Austria-Hungary May 23, on Turkey **Aug. 20**, on Germany **Aug. 27**. Bulgaria declared war on Serbia **Oct. 14**; Allies against Bulgaria **Oct. 15-19**. Germans occupied Russian Baltic ports, took Vilna; Austrians occupied Serbia. Allies landed at Salonika **Oct. 5**. Sir John French replaced by Sir Douglas Haig on British front **Dec. 15**. Allies began evacuation of Gallipoli (Dardanelles) **Dec. 19.**

1916—Great Battles

Germany announced Feb. 10 that armed merchant ships would be considered warships and sunk without warning. U.S. retorted **Feb. 15** international law permitted self-defense of commercial ships. Germans

tion. Nine powers outlawed poison gas and restricted submarine attack on merchantmen. U.S., Britain, France, Japan agreed on integrity of China. Ratified **Aug. 5, 1925.**

1922

Roof of Knickerbocker (movie) Theatre collapsed in Washington, D. C., **Jan. 28; 98 dead.**

Violence during coal-mine strike at Herrin, Ill., June 22-23 cost 36 lives, 21 of them non-union miners.

Fascist march on Rome Oct 30; Mussolini's power in Italy began.

1923

Occupation of Ruhr by French and Belgian troops to enforce reparations began **Jan. 11.**

First sound-on-film moving picture "Phonofilm" was shown by Lee de Forest at Rivoli Theatre, N.Y. City, beginning **Apr.**

Beer Hall Putsch in Munich led by Gen. Ludendorff and Adolf Hitler **Nov. 8-9.** Several supporters killed in street clashes. Ludendorff was arrested and paroled; Hitler was wounded. He was arrested **Nov. 12** and imprisoned at Landsberg where he wrote Mein Kampf (served 9 months of 5-year sentence).

1924

Dawes Reparation Plan accepted by Allies and Germany in London **Aug. 16:** Owen D. Young put in charge. French troops began evacuation of the Ruhr **Aug. 18.**

Nellie Taylor Ross elected governor of Wyoming **Nov. 9** after death of her husband **Oct. 2;** installed **Jan. 5, 1925,** as first woman governor. Miriam (Ma) Ferguson was elected governor of Texas **Nov. 9;** installed **Jan. 20, 1925.**

1925

Floyd Collins unable to find way out of Sand Cave, near Cave City, Ky., died within 300 ft. of entrance **Feb.**

John T. Scopes was found guilty of having taught evolution in Dayton, Tenn., high school and was fined $100 and costs **July 24.** William Jennings Bryan, chief counsel for prosecution, died in Dayton **July 26.** Clarence Darrow, chief defense counsel, died **Mar. 13, 1938.** Scopes died **Oct. 21, 1970.** The last law prohibiting teaching evolution in U. S. public schools was ruled unconstitutional by the Mississippi Supreme Court **Dec. 2. 1970.**

Why United States Intervened

made huge effort vs. Verdun **Feb. 21,** took Ft. Douaumont **Feb. 8.** Germany declared war on Portugal **Mar. 8.** Russians invaded Persia **Mar. 10.** Wilson threatened **Apr. 18-19** to break relations unless Germany revised sub warfare; Germany met most of U.S. demands.

Uprising in Ireland Apr. 24-May 1. Patrick Pearse et al, executed; Sir Roger Casement hanged **Aug. 3.** Britain adopted conscription **May 24. Jutland** naval battle **May 31-June 1:** British Admirals Jellicoe and Beatty lost 5 major cruisers, 8 destroyers, 6,091 men; German Admirals Scheer and von Hipper lost 2 major ships, also cruisers, destroyers, 2,545 men. **Battle of Ypres June 2.** Lord Kitchener drowned when Hampshire sunk off Orkneys June 5. **Battle of the Somme July 1-10;** second battle **July 11-Aug. 3.** Romania joined Allies **Aug. 16,** was defeated by January, 1917. U.S. **Nov. 29,** protested deportation of Belgian workers into Germany.

Germany and its allies called for peace negotiations **Dec. 12, 1916** to halt bloodshed. Germany told the Vatican it was fighting for the integrity of its frontiers and development in peaceful competition. On **Dec. 18, 1916,** President Wilson asked the belligerents to state their aims and terms; in order to end rival alliances he asked formation of a League of Nations and protection of "weak peoples." The Allies called the German offer "empty and insincere." They also told President Wilson they wanted "restorations, reparations, indemnities."

1917—U. S. Enters War

When **Germany began unrestricted submarine war,** the U.S. **Feb. 3** broke relations, refused negotiations until order was rescinded. Wilson **Feb. 26** asked Congress to order arming of merchant ships; when Senate refused Wilson armed them by executive order **Mar. 12.** Intercepted note of German Foreign Sec. **Zimmerman to** German minister in Mexico suggested Mexico be asked to enter war to recover U.S. Southwest **Feb. 28.** U.S. declared war on Germany **Apr. 6,** adopted selective conscription **May 18,** registered men aged 21-30 **June 5.** First of American Expeditionary Force (AEF) landed in France **June 26;** Gen. John J. Pershing, commander-in-chief. Adm. William S. Sims, chief Naval Operations, Europe. U.S. declared war on Austria-Hungary **Dec. 7.**

Collapse of Russian Empire. When navy and army revolted **Mar. 11-15** Czar Nicholas II abdicated. Provisional govt. made **Kerensky** premier **July 20.** Offensive in Galicia failed. In **April** Germans moved **Lenin**

and associates from Switzerland to Russia via Sweden to disrupt war. Bolshevists overthrew Kerensky **Nov. 7,** formed socialist republic of workers and peasants with Lenin president of Council of Commissars; made peace with Germany, Austria-Hungary, Bulgaria and Turkey at **Brest-Litovsk Mar. 3, 1918.** Russians withdrew from Lithuania, Estonia, Latvia, Ukraine, Poland, Finland, Aland Is., Erivan, Kars, Batum.

Other Fronts. Huge losses by Allies at Vimy, Arras, Cambrai, Passchendaele, Verdun. Petain succeeded Nivelle as French commander-in-chief. British took Jaffa, Baghdad, Jerusalem. Germans forced Italians back to Piave River.

1918—Victory for U. S. & Allies

German submarine war, Feb. 1, 1917-Feb. 1, 1918, cost U. S. 69 ships (171,061 tons); U. S. seized 686,494 German-Austrian tonnage. British lost 1,169 ships. Allies & neutrals lost 6,617,000 tons.

President Wilson presented his **14 points** for peace to Congress **Jan. 8.** Asked open diplomacy; freedom of seas; restoration of Alsace-Lorraine to France; independence for Poland and Austrian minorities; "a general association of nations" to guarantee political and economic independence.

Collapse of Russian front released German troops for powerful thrusts on West front. **Battle of the Somme, Mar. 21-Apr. 6.** Gen. Foch made supreme commander **Mar. 26. Battle of the Aisne May 27-June 5;** AEF took Cantigny **May 28.** Germans reached Marne, AEF fought at Chateau Thierry, Belleau Woods. German retreat began **July 19.** AEF took St. Mihiel salient **Sept. 12-20,** fought at **Meuse-Argonne Sept. 20-Nov. 11.** British broke Hindenburg line **Sept. 27.**

Bulgaria gave up **Sept. 30;** Czar Ferdinand abdicated. Turkish armistice **Oct. 30.** Italians defeated Austrians at **Vittorio Veneto,** Austria and Hungary formed separate republics **Nov. 1,** Austria surrendered **Nov. 4.**

Germans accepted President Wilson's **terms** and recalled submarines **Oct. 20;** U. S. troops reached Sedan **Nov. 7;** revolution in Kiel and Hamburg **Nov. 7;** Bavaria proclaimed a republic **Nov. 8;** Kaiser abdicated **Nov. 9.** fled to Holland. Armistice signed in Marshal Foch's railway coach, near Compiegne, France, took effect **Nov. 11;** bugles sounded "cease firing" at 11 a.m. German fleet surrendered to British **Nov. 21;** AEF entered Mainz **Dec. 6;** crossed Rhine **Dec. 13.**

Pickwick Club, Boston, collapsed July 4; 44 died.

By Treaty of Locarno Oct. 16 Germany agreed to demilitarization of Rhineland and security of Franco-German and Belgo-German frontiers.

1926

Dr. Robert H. Goddard demonstrated the practicality of rockets Mar. 16 at Auburn, Mass., with the first liquid fuel rocket flight; the rocket traveled 184 ft. in 2.5 secs.

General strike paralyzed Britain May 3-12. Parliament passed act making general strike criminal conspiracy against nation.

Germany admitted to the League of Nations Sept. 8. Locarno treaties with Germany (1925) went into effect Sept. 14.

1927

About 1,000 U.S. Marines landed in China Mar. 5 to protect property in civil war. U.S. and British consulates looted by nationalists Mar. 24.

Albert Snyder, art editor, killed Mar. 20 by his wife, Ruth Brown Snyder, and Henry Judd Gray, corset salesman. Both confessed and were executed at Sing Sing Jan. 12, 1928.

Capt. Charles A. Lindbergh, U.S. air mail pilot, left Roosevelt Field, N. Y., at 7:52 a.m., May 20 alone in monoplane, Spirit of St. Louis, competing for Raymond Orteig's offer of $25,000 for first New York-Paris non-stop flight. Reached Le Bourget airfield, Paris, 5:21 p.m. (10:21 p.m. Paris time) May 21, 3,610 mi. in 33 hrs. 29 min., 30 sec. Returned on U.S. cruiser Memphis with plane; welcomed by President Coolidge in Washington June 11, given rank of colonel. Tremendous ticker tape parade, N. Y. City June 13.

The Jazz Singer, with Al Jolson, demonstrated part-talking pictures in N.Y. City Oct. 6.

1928

The St. Francis water-supply dam, 40 mi. north of Los Angeles, Cal., collapsed; 450 lives lost, 700 houses swept away Mar. 13.

First all-talking picture, Lights of New York, presented at Strand, N.Y. City, July 6.

Times Square subway wreck, N.Y. City (IRT line) Aug. 24, killed 18, injured 97.

Kellogg-Briand Peace Pact signed Aug. 27 by 62 nations. Condemned the use of war as an instrument of national policy.

Dirigible Graf Zeppelin, Capt. Hugo Eckener, with 20 passengers and 38 crew, flew from Friedrichshafen, Germany to Lakehurst, N.J., Oct. 11-15; returned Oct. 29-31. Made round-the-world trip from Friedrichshafen with 20 passengers Aug. 14-Sept. 4, 1929, via Tokyo, Los Angeles, Lakehurst, N.J.

Stalin issued first 5-year plan: rapid, ruthless industrialization of Russian economy.

1929

"St. Valentine's Day massacre" in Chicago Feb. 14; gangsters killed 7 rivals.

The Papal State, extinct since 1870, revived as State of Vatican City, at Rome June 7.

U.S. paper money one-third smaller in size went into circulation July 10.

Albert B. Fall, former secretary of the interior was convicted of accepting a bribe of $100,000 from Edward L. Doheny in the leasing of the Elk Hills (Teapot Dome) naval oil reserve. He was sentenced Nov. 1 to $100,000 fine and a year in prison.

Stock Market crash Oct. 29 marked end of postwar prosperity as stock prices plummeted. Decline in value estimated at $15 billion by end of 1929; stock losses for 1929-1931 estimated at $50 billion; worst American depression began.

1930

London Naval Reduction Treaty signed by U.S., Britain, Italy, France, and Japan Apr. 22; in effect Jan. 1, 1931. Set proportional reductions of the navies of each country. Its terms expired Dec. 31, 1936.

Joseph F. Crater, a justice of the state Supreme Court in N.Y. City, vanished Aug. 6.

1931

British Parliament gave legal status to declaration of Imperial Conference of 1926 proclaiming Britain and the dominions, including Canada, completely equal and "in no way subordinate one to another."

Mukden Incident occurred Sept. 18 when Japanese troops attacked Mukden garrison and then overran Manchuria. China protested to League of Nations.

1932

Japan sends troops into China Jan. 27 following murder of Japanese Buddhist priest in Shanghai Jan. 15.

Manchuria became Manchukuo (Japanese puppet state) Feb. 18; Henry Pu Yi, Manchu emperor who abdicated in 1912, installed as ruler Mar. 9.

Charles Lindbergh Jr. kidnaped Mar. 1, found dead, May 12.

Bonus March on Washington May 29 by World War I veterans demanding Congress pay their bonus in full. Army, under Gen. Douglas MacArthur, disbanded the marchers on President Hoover's orders.

1933

Adolf Hitler became German Chancellor Jan. 30.

German Reichstag building in Berlin was destroyed Feb. 27 by fire believed set by Nazis, although Marinus van der Lubbe, Dutch communist, was found guilty; beheaded Jan. 10, 1934.

All banks in the U.S. were ordered closed by President Roosevelt Mar. 6.

Gold standard dropped by U.S.; announced by President Roosevelt on Apr. 19 and ratified by Congress June 5.

Spain, by parliamentary edict, May 17 disestablished the Roman Catholic church.

Germany quit the League of Nations Oct. 14 and withdrew from disarmament conference.

President Roosevelt accorded diplomatic recognition to the Soviet Union Nov. 16.

Prohibition ended in the U.S. as Utah, 36th state, ratified 21st Amendment to Constitution Dec. 5, repealing 18th (Prohibition) Amendment.

1934

The Dionne sisters, first quintuplets to survive beyond infancy, were born May 28 in Callender, Ont., Canada; to Mr. and Mrs. Oliva Dionne.

President von Hindenburg of Germany died Aug. 2. Adolf Hitler consolidated offices of president and chancellor, became "fuehrer."

Long March by Chinese Communists started Oct. Mao Tse-tung led 100,000 in 6,000-mi. trek from south to north China; only 20,000 completed journey and reached Yenan Oct. 1935.

Italy refused to arbitrate disputes on Italian Somaliland border between Italian and Ethiopian troops, demanded reparations, apology Dec. 19.

1935

Hitler renounced Versailles Treaty, ordered conscription in Germany Mar. 10.

Will Rogers, 56, comedian, and Wiley Post, 36, aviator, were killed Aug. 15 when Post's plane crashed in a fog near Point Barrow, Alaska.

Social Security Act passed by Congress Aug. 14.

Ethiopia appealed to League of Nations against Italy. Italy invaded Ethiopia Oct. 2-4.

Economic sanctions against Italy went into effect Nov. 18 supported by 52 nation-members of the League of Nations, and by one non-member, Egypt. The sanctions ended July 15, 1936.

1936

King George V, 70, died Jan. 20 on his estate at Sandringham, England, and was succeeded by his eldest son, Prince of Wales, 42, who took the title of King Edward VIII. He abdicated Dec. 11, 1936, and was succeeded by his brother, the Duke of York, who became King George VI. The ex-ruler was created Duke of Windsor with the title of "His Royal Highness" which was not extended to his wife. He gave up the throne, he said, because he could not marry "the woman I love," Mrs. Wallis Warfield of Baltimore, Md., who obtained a divorce Oct. 27 in Ipswich, England, from Ernest A. Simpson, an insurance agent. The decree became absolute May 3, 1937. The couple was married **June 3, 1937,** in Monts, France.

Reoccupation of demilitarized Rhineland zone, in violation of the Locarno pact, begun by German troops **May. 7.**

Emperor Haile Selassie of Ethiopia escaped Italian 'advance by boarding British cruiser for Palestine **May 1.** Premier Mussolini of Italy announced end of war **May 5,** proclaimed annexation of Ethiopia with King Victor Emmanuel emperor. Haile Selassie restored 1941; deposed Sept. 12, 1974.

Revolt against Spain's Republican government began **July 17** in Morocco and spread to Spain, included much of the army and air force and half of the navy; Jose Giral became Loyalist premier; **July 18** Loyalists defeated insurgents in Madrid and **July 19** insurgents gained control in Cadiz, Huelva, Seville, Cordoba and Granada; insurgents set up own government **July 24;** insurgents began aerial bombing of Madrid **Aug. 24;** took San Sebastian and Toledo **Sept. 12;** Gen. Francisco Franco proclaimed head of the nationalist (insurgent) government **Oct. 1;** seige of Madrid begun by insurgents **Oct. 21;** Loyalist government moved from Madrid to Valencia, **Nov. 6.**

Japan and Germany signed an anti-Comintern pact **Nov. 25.** Italy joined **Nov. 6, 1937.**

1937

Spanish insurgents took Malaga **Feb. 8.** Warships of Great Britain, France, Italy, and Germany **March 13** began to police the coasts of Spain under the 27-nation neutrality agreement. Gen. Franco **Apr. 19** set up a one-party state, dissolving the Falange and Carlist organizations. New Loyalist government formed **May 17** under Premier Juan Negrin; Loyalists shifted government to Barcelona **Oct. 28;** insurgents proclaimed blockade of all Loyalist ports **Nov. 28.**

Fighting in China, west of Peking, was renewed by Japanese **July;** Tungchow was attacked **July 27;** the Japanese **July 29** bombed Tientsin destroying Nankai University; **Aug. 9** they took formal possession of Peking; **Aug. 11** they landed marines at Shanghai and shelled Nankow; Nanking, Canton, and other eastern cities were attacked by Japanese planes **Oct. 23;** Suiyuan Province declared independence from China, Chinese forces abandoned Shanghai and Japanese took control **Nov. 8.** Premier Chiang Kai-shek moved to Hankow **Dec. 12.**

Japanese bombs sank the U. S. gunboat Panay **Dec. 12** with loss of 2 lives; and several American oil carriers (the captain of one died) on the Yangtze River above Nanking. The Japanese apologized and paid indemnity.

Hitler repudiated war guilt clause of Versailles Treaty **Jan. 30.** Treaty blamed Germany for World War I. Hitler stated that Germany was free from obligations imposed upon her by the treaty.

Amelia Earhart Putnam, aviator, and co-pilot Fred Noonan lost **July 2** near Howland Is. in the Pacific.

Italy gave notice Dec. 11 of withdrawal from the League of Nations.

1938

Spanish insurgent planes from Majorca began daily bombing of Barcelona **Jan. 16.** Insurgent ship Baleares sunk off Cartagena **Mar. 6** by Loyalist forces. Insurgent air raids killed 1,000 in Barcelona **Mar. 7;** insurgents took Lerida, cutting Loyalist Spain in half **Apr. 15.** Italy began token withdrawal of 10,000 troops **Oct. 10.** Insurgents began final campaign **Dec. 23** against Barcelona which fell **Jan. 26, 1939.**

Hitler invaded Austria Mar. 11. After resignation of Chancellor Kurt von Schuschnigg and President Wilhelm Miklas **Mar. 13** the new chancellor, Arthur Seyss-Inquart, proclaimed the union of Germany and Austria. This was ratified by a popular vote, excluding Jews, in Austria **Apr. 10.** The Italian Grand Council, headed by Mussolini, voted approval.

Douglas G. Corrigan of Los Angeles, flew from Brooklyn to Dublin **July 17-18.** Having no permit or passport, he jokingly said he flew the "wrong way."

. At a conference in **Munich,** Britain and France yielded **Sept. 30** to Nazi demands for the cession of the Sudetenland to Germany to Czechoslovakia, thus ending a 15-day international crisis during which British Prime Minister Neville Chamberlain made 2 flying visits to Hitler. Mussolini backed Hitler's territorial demands. Hitler signed a "peace declaration" with Britain **Sept. 30,** occupied Sudetenland **Oct. 1-10.** Eduard Benes, president of Czechoslovakia, resigned **Oct. 5.**

About 4,000 sq. mi. of Czech land was awarded to Hungary **Nov. 2** by German-Italian arbitrators. The area was populated by Hungarians. Cessions to Poland were agreed on between Prague and Warsaw.

1939

Uranium atom was first measured in U. S. at Columbia Univ. **Jan. 25.** In 1940, uranium 235, a rare isotope, proved to be prime fissionable form.

The Loyalist Spanish government surrendered Barcelona to the insurgents **Jan. 26.** Madrid surrendered **Mar. 24;** war ended **Mar. 29** with Franco victor.

The Republic of Czechoslovakia was dissolved **Mar. 14;** Hungarian troops seized Carpatho-Ukraine **Mar. 14;** Nazis occupied Bohemia and Moravia which became German protectorates **Mar. 16.**

Japanese troops in Manchukuo and Soviet and Mongol troops near Lake Bor began 6-month border fight **May 11;** 20,000 killed.

Germany and Italy signed military pact **May 22.**

Germany and Soviet Union signed a non-aggression treaty **Aug. 24,** invaded Poland in **Sept.**

N. Y. World's Fair opened **Apr. 30,** closed **Oct. 31;** reopened **May 11, 1940** and finally closed **Oct. 21.**

President Roosevelt proclaimed a limited national emergency **Sept. 8,** an unlimited emergency **May 27, 1941.** Both ended by President Truman **Apr. 28, 1952.**

Russia invaded Finland Nov. 30.

1939-1945 World War II
See Article Pages 728-729

1940

Finnish-Russian peace signed in Moscow **Mar. 12.**

Estonia, Latvia, and Lithuania annexed by Soviet Russia **July 14.**

1941

The Four Freedoms termed essential by President Roosevelt in a speech to Congress **Jan. 6:** freedom of speech and expression, freedom of worship, freedom from want, and freedom from fear.

U.S. Marines occupied Iceland **July 7** on invitation from that country.

The Atlantic Charter, an 8-point joint U.S.-British declaration of principles, issued by President Roosevelt and Prime Minister Churchill **Aug. 14** after conference aboard battleship off Newfoundland.

President Roosevelt and Secretary of State Hull Nov. 17 received special Japanese envoys, Saburo Kurusu and Admiral Nomura, for conference on the Far East.

Japan attacked U.S. fleet at Pearl Harbor **Dec. 7** as first act of war. *(See World War II.)*

Hitler ordered policy of genocide as the "final solution" to the Jewish "problem." By end of war an estimated 6 million Jews had been killed in Nazi concentration camps. Other religious, ethnic, and political groups were also persecuted and some 4 to 6 million members were murdered by Nazis.

1942

Fire swept through Cocoanut Grove, a Boston night club, **Nov. 28,** killing 491 and injuring scores.

First nuclear chain reaction (fission of uranium isotope, U-235) at Univ. of Chicago, under physicists Arthur Compton, Enrico Fermi, et al., **Dec. 2.**

1943

President Roosevelt signed June 10 the pay-as-you-go income tax bill. Starting **July 1** wage and salary earners were subject to a paycheck withholding tax.

Race riot in Detroit June 21; 34 dead, 700 injured. Riot in Harlem section of N.Y. City; 6 Negroes killed.

1944

Ringling Brothers and Barnum & Bailey Circus fire in Hartford, Conn., caused a stampede in the main tent; 168 killed, 487 injured **July 6.**

1945

Yalta Conference met in the Crimea, USSR, **Feb. 3-11.** Roosevelt, Churchill and Stalin agreed Russia would enter war against Japan.

President Roosevelt, 63, died of cerebral hemorrhage in Warm Springs, Ga. **Apr. 12.**

Mussolini caught by partisans near Dongo while trying to flee to Switzerland; executed **Apr. 28.**

Hitler committed suicide in ruined chancellery, Berlin, **Apr. 30,** with wife Eva Braun. Goebbels and wife poisoned children, committed suicide.

United Nations Conference on International Organization of 46 nations, San Francisco, opened **Apr. 25;** closed **June 26** with address by President Truman and adoption of UN charter.

Potsdam, Germany, conference of Truman, Stalin and Churchill **July 17-Aug. 2.** After **July 25** Clement Atlee, new prime minister, replaced Churchill.

First atomic bomb, produced at Los Alamos, N. M., exploded at Alamogordo, N. M., **July 16.** Bomb dropped on Hiroshima **Aug. 6,** on Nagasaki **Aug. 9.**

U.S. forces entered Korea south of 38th parallel to

Principal Events of World War II, 1939-1945

Major Belligerents — German army invaded Poland **Sept. 1, 1939;** Norway and Denmark **April 9, 1940;** the Netherlands, Belgium, and Luxemburg **May 10, 1940; invaded France, reaching Paris June 14.** Occupied France (Vichy) signed an armistice with Germany **June 22, 1940.** Germany invaded Russia **June 22, 1941,** unoccupied France and Italy Nov. 11, 1942. Surrendered unconditionally May 7, 1945 (May 6 EST). War with Germany formally declared ended by Britain, France, Australia, New Zealand on July 9, 1951; by U. S. Oct. 19, 1951.

Great Britain declared war on Germany Sept. 3, 1939, as did Australia and New Zealand. Union of South Africa declared war Sept. 6; Canada Sept. 10. Britain declared war on Italy June 11, 1940; on Finland, Hungary, and Romania, Dec. 7, 1941; on Japan Dec. 8, 1941; on Bulgaria Dec. 13, 1941; on Thailand Jan. 25, 1942.

France declared war on Germany Sept. 3, 1939; on Italy June 11, 1940. Free French (De Gaulle) declared war on Japan Dec. 8, 1941.

Italy (under Benito Mussolini) declared war on Great Britain and France June 10, 1940; on the U.S. Dec. 11, 1941. Surrendered unconditionally Sept. 8, 1943. Declared war against Germany Oct. 13, 1943, against Japan **July 14, 1945.** Signed treaty of peace **Feb. 10, 1947,** in Paris, with Britain, France, U.S. and USSR.

Japan invaded French Indochina **Sept. 22, 1940;** attacked Pearl Harbor naval station and the Philippines by air **Dec. 7, 1941** and declared war on the U.S., Great Britain, Australia, Canada, New Zealand and the Union of South Africa **Dec. 7, 1941;** on the Netherlands Jan. 11, 1942. Japan accepted the Allied terms unconditionally Aug. 14, 1945; signed surrender terms **Sept. 1, 1945** (Sept. 2, Tokyo time) on board USS Missouri; signed treaty of peace with all big powers (except USSR) and a total of 49 nations at San Francisco Sept. 8, 1951.

Union of Soviet Socialist Republics (Russia) signed non-aggression pact with Germany Aug., 1939; invaded Poland, Sept. 17, 1939, and Finland, Nov. 30, 1939. Signed peace with Finland Mar. 12, 1940. Russia was invaded by Germany and Romania June 22, 1941. Finland declared war on Russia June 25, 1941. Armistice with Finland Sept. 19, 1944, peace treaty Feb. 10, 1947. Declared war on Japan Aug. 8, 1945, effective Aug. 9. Signed treaties of peace with Italy, Hungary, Romania, Bulgaria and Finland Feb. 10, 1947

U.S. declared war on Japan Dec. 8, 1941. Germany and Italy declared war on U.S. **Dec. 11, 1941.** A few hours later U.S. declared war on Germany and Italy; also Bulgaria, Hungary and Romania June 5, 1942; signed peace treaties with Italy, Bulgaria, Hungary and Romania **Feb. 10, 1947;** with Japan **Sept. 8, 1951.**

The German Blitzkrieg forces outflanked the Maginot Line May 13, 1940, and quickly occupied northern France.

Retreat from Dunkirk by British Expeditionary Force took place May 26-June 4, 1940, when 900 vessels took 338,226 troops across the English Channel, 26,175 of them French.

Nazi bombing of Britain began July 10, 1940, and reached its height Sept. 7, Oct. 15, and Dec. 29.

Coventry was destroyed **Nov. 14;** Birmingham was hit **Nov.19-22.** Many London churches were burned **Dec. 29.** Desperate attacks on German aircraft by RAF stopped threat of invasion. Of this defense Prime Minister Churchill said: "Never in the field of human conflict was so much owed by so many to so few."

Pearl Harbor. Over 100 Japanese planes attacked Hickam Field and U.S. Pacific fleet (86 ships) anchored at Pearl Harbor, Hawaii on **Dec. 7, 1941.** (7:55 a.m. Hawaiian time; 1:25 p.m. EST.) Totally destroyed: battleship Arizona. Severely damaged: battleships Oklahoma, Nevada, California, West Virginia, 3 destroyers, 1 target ship, 1 minelayer. Damaged and repaired: battleships Pennsylvania, Maryland, Tennessee; cruisers Helena, Honolulu, Raleigh. Casualties: navy, 2,117 officers and men killed, 960 missing, 876 wounded; army, 226 officers and men killed, 396 wounded.

Planes over Tokyo. Lt. Col. James H. Doolittle, with 16 B-25s and 79 pilots and crewmen, took off **Apr. 18, 1942,** from carrier Hornet, 688 mi. from Tokyo; dropped 500-lb. bombs on Tokyo, 2 on Nagoya, Kobe. Eight airmen were captured off China coast; 3 were shot, others imprisoned. Total dead, 9. One plane landed near Vladivostok and was interned by Russians; the crew escaped to Iran.

Loss and recapture of Philippines. Manila and Cavite taken by Japan **Jan. 2, 1942.** U.S. forces in Bataan were attacked by 200,000 Japanese **Jan. 10.** Gen. Douglas MacArthur ordered to leave Philippines, reached Australia **Mar. 17,** vowed, "I shall return," Maj. Gen. Jonathan M. Wainwright defended Bataan until **Apr. 8, 1942.** Japan took 35,000 U.S. and Filipino troops prisoner, including 5,000 Marines, forced them into prison via the "Death March" of Bataan. Wainwright surrendered **Corregidor May 6** with 11,-574 troops. Gen. MacArthur returned to the Philippines near Palo on Leyte, **Oct. 20, 1944.** U.S. entered Luzon via Lingayen Gulf Jan. 9, 1945. Manila was taken Feb. 3; Corregidor reoccupied Feb. 16-Mar.1.

Germany attacked the Soviet Union June 22, 1941; took Minsk, Smolensk, Kiev, Kharkov, Orel; besieged Leningrad, fought a long battle in the ruins of Stalingrad **August 1942** and extended the German lines to the Caucasus Mts.; tide turned in **Nov. 1942;** the Russians encircled Stalingrad and the Nazi army there surrendered **Jan. 31, 1943.** Russian army reached the Oder River Feb. 1945.

North African Campaign began **Aug. 6, 1941,** when Marshal Graziani led Italian forces against the British with some success. The first counteroffensive in December relieved Tobruk, where British had held out 8 months. The British pushed the Germans under Rommel back to El Agheila but Rommel regained the lost ground. He captured Tobruk with its garrison of 25,000 British **June 21, 1942,** and pushed the British back to within 70 mi. of Alexandria. On Oct. 23, the British, heavily reinforced and under Lt. Gen. Bernard L. Montgomery, attacked Rommel at El Alamein, Egypt, and inflicted heavy losses on the Germans and Italians, driving them back over 1,000 mi. to Tunisia.

displace Japanese **Sept. 8.**
•Gen. Douglas MacArthur took over supervision of Japan **Sept. 9.**
Vidkun Quisling, pro-Nazi premier of Norway, executed by a firing squad in Oslo **Oct. 23.**

1946
William Joyce, "Lord Haw Haw," broadcaster for Nazis, hanged in London for treason **Jan. 3.**
The first **General Assembly** of the **United Nations** opened in London **Jan. 10.**
League of Nations in Geneva, Switzerland, trans-

fered physical assets to the United Nations **Apr. 18.**
Philippines given independence by U.S. **July 4;** Manuel Roxas elected first president of new republic.
Twenty-two Nazi leaders convicted of war crimes **Sept. 30** by International Tribunal in Nuremberg. Eleven Nazis were sentenced to death by hanging **Oct. 1.** Hermann Goering committed suicide by poison in Nuremberg Prison, 2 hours before he was scheduled to be hanged **Oct. 15.** The 10 other top Nazis were hanged individually. They were: Hans Frank, Wilhelm Frick, Col. Gen. Alfred Jodl, Gestapo

Summary of Aerial, Naval and Military Actions

North African Invasion by U.S. and Britain landed 150,000 American and 140,000 British troops in French Algeria **Nov. 8, 1942** (Nov. 7 EST), with Lt. Gen. Dwight D. Eisenhower in command; Axis forces were driven from Africa by May 12, 1943. U.S. 7th Army under Maj. Gen. George S. Patton Jr. and British-Canadian 8th Army landed on Sicily **July 10.** Mussolini was forced to resign July 25 and escaped to German lines Sept. 12. The Italian mainland was invaded and Italy surrendered **Sept. 8, 1943,** but heavy fighting with Germans followed and they were not dislodged until spring of 1945.
Battle of the Coral Sea on **May 7-8, 1942,** took heavy toll of ships and planes on both sides, was first battle fought by naval planes from ships that had neither sight nor range of enemy. U.S. lost carrier (Lexington), 66 planes, 543 men; Japan lost 80 planes, 900 men. **Battle of Midway** June 3-6, 1942, U. S. lost 1 carrier (Yorktown), 1 destroyer, 150 planes, 307 men; Japan lost 4 carriers, 253 planes, 3,500 men. The Japanese navy halted its advance toward Australia and withdrew northward.
Guadalcanal, in the southern Solomon Islands, assaulted by U. S. Marines **Aug. 7, 1942,** in one of the most costly Allied Pacific campaigns, finally won by the Allies in January 1943.
U.S. Return to Philippines: battle for Leyte Gulf, biggest naval action ever fought, **Oct. 22-27, 1944,** in 3 engagements destroying Japanese naval power. Battles were fought in Surigao Strait, off Samar and off Cape Engano. Ships engaged: U.S. 166, Japanese 65. Airplanes, U.S. 1,280; Japanese 716. Losses for Philippine campaign — Japan: 3 large carriers, 3 light carriers, one escort carrier, 4 battleships, 14 cruisers, 32 destroyers, 11 submarines, total 68. U. S.: one light carrier, 3 escort carriers, 6 destroyers, 3 destroyer escorts, one high-speed transport, 7 submarines, total 21. U.S. lost one ship to a kamikaze (suicide) plane at Leyte and 5 in subsequent actions. Total plane losses for Philippine campaign from Oct., 1944-Jan. 1945: Japan (est.) 7,000, including 722 kamikaze; U. S. 967.
D-Day: Invasion of France — Invasion of France by Allies **June 6, 1944.** About 1,000 planes and gliders dropped paratroopers on Cotentin Peninsula near Normandy, 5 a.m. London time. About 1,000 R.A.F., 1,400 U.S. bombers attacked installations. First assault troops landed 6:30 a.m. on beaches along line Carentan-Bayeux-Caen; U.S. on west, British-Canadians on east. Total Allied strength available 2,876,439, including 17 British divisions of which 3 Canadian; 20 U. S. divisions, one French, one Polish.
Gen. Dwight D. Eisenhower was Supreme Commander of Allied Expeditionary Forces.
British took Bayeux June 7; Carentan fell June 13; U.S. took Cherbourg June 27; British-Canadians took Caen July 9 after desperate fighting Lt. Gen. George S. Patton Jr. with 3d U.S. Army attacked south and west of St. Lo Aug. 1. Canadians took Falaise Aug. 16. German army routed **Aug. 23** in the Argentan-Falaise gap by U.S.-Canadian armies and Allied aircraft. Allies were then free to overrun northern France and liberate Paris **Aug. 25.**

Allies invaded Southern France Aug. 14-15, 1944, east of the Rhine River with 1,000 ships (641 U.S., 316 British).
The Ardennes Bulge was a violent counter-attack by 15 German divisions (Gen. von Rundstedt commander-in-chief) launched **Dec. 16, 1944.** By Dec. 19, the 1st U.S. Army was pushed out of Germany and the Germans penetrated 60 mi. west of Celles, Belgium. Patton's 3d U.S. Army rescued besieged Americans at Bastogne, Belgium, **Dec. 21** and Nazi drive was stopped by **Dec. 25.** Allies wiped out the Bulge by **Jan. 31, 1945.** Near Malmedy, Belgium, Germans shot captured American soldiers with machine guns and left them dead on the field. U. S. losses estimated at 40,000; Germans lost 220,000 dead and prisoners.
Rhine Crossing — On **Mar. 7, 1945,** the 9th Armored Div., 3d Corps, First Army, found Lundendorff Bridge at Remagen on the Rhine intact; Gen. Eisenhower ordered Gen. Omar N. Bradley to put 5 divisions across; on 5th day army ceased using bridge, used Treadway floating bridge, built in 10 hr. 11 min.; Remagen bridge collapsed Mar. 17.
Iwo Jima assaulted by U. S. joint expeditionary force **Feb. 19, 1945,** with land action by U. S. Marines; invasion used 800 ships, including 17 aircraft carriers and 1,170 planes. U. S. troops engaged, 111,308 of which 75,144 were assault troops. Island was conquered by Mar. 16. U. S. lost 4,590 killed; Japanese deaths est. over 20,000.
Okinawa, principal Japanese base in the Ryukyu group, was invaded **Apr. 1, 1945,** in the final land campaign in the Far East. The troops used 1,300 vessels, including airplane carriers. After 83 days of fighting the end was marked by the formal suicide of the 2 Japanese generals. U. S. men engaged up to June 30, 1945, reached 176,491 army, 88,500 marines, 18,000 navy. Japanese strength at start was 77,199. U.S. losses were 49,151 of which 12,520 were killed or missing, 36,631 wounded. The Japanese lost 110,071 killed, wounded and 7,400 prisoners.
U. S. lost 763 aircraft; Japan lost 7,830 of which 1,020 were destroyed on the ground. U. S. lost 36 ships sunk, 369 damaged; Japan lost 16 sunk. The Yamato, world's largest battleship, full load displacement 72,809 tons, 861 ft. long, 3,333 personnel, was sunk by 10 aerial torpedoes; 300 survived.
V-E Day — German armies began surrendering May 4, 1945. Unconditional surrender signed **May 7** at 2:41 a.m., French time, in Rheims Hq., designating cessation of operations May 9 at 12:01 a.m., London time (May 8, 6:01 p.m., Eastern U. S. War Time). Surrender also signed in Berlin. **May 8** celebrated as V-E Day.
Atomic bombs — First atomic bomb ever used in war was dropped by U. S. plane **Aug. 6, 1945,** on Hiroshima, Japan (pop. 343,969). Second U. S. bomb dropped on Nagasaki (pop. 252,630) **Aug. 9, 1945.** Estimates of dead from bombs and radiation exposure vary: Hiroshima, 80,000 to over 200,000; Nagasaki, 39,000 to 74,000. Japan surrendered **Aug. 14.** Formal surrender aboard USS Missouri **Sept. 2, 1945,** Far Eastern Time, celebrated as V-J Day.

Consult Index for additional listings under World War II.

Chief Ernst Kaltenbrunner, Field Marshal Wilhelm Keitel, Alfred Rosenberg, Fritz Sauckel, Arthur Seyss-Inquart, Julius Streicher, Foreign Minister Joachim von Ribbentrop.

Others sentenced for war crimes: Gen. Anton Dostler, Nazi, hanged in Rome Dec. 1, 1945, for shooting 15 U.S. soldiers without trial; Joseph Kramer, "Beast of Belsen" and 10 others hanged Dec. 14, by British for atrocities at Belsen and Auschwitz concentration camps; Gen. Yamashita, Japanese commander in Philippines, hanged Feb. 23, 1946; Lt. Gen. Homma, who ordered Bataan death march, shot near Manila Apr. 3, 1946; Marshal Ion Antonescu, dictator of Romania, hanged June 1, 1946; Karl Hermann Frank, Nazi ruler in Czechoslovakia, hanged in Prague May 22 for ordering massacre at Lidice; 48 Nazi officers and guards hanged by the U.S. Army at Landsberg, Germany, May, 1947, for mass murders at Mauthausen camp.

President Truman proclaimed the cessation of hostilities of World War II Dec. 31.

1947

British Labor government took ownership of coal mines, cables and wireless communications Jan. 1.

Peace treaties for Hitler's European satellites, imposing $1.33 billion in reparations, signed Feb. 10.

Truman Doctrine. President Truman asked Congress to appropriate $400 million for aid to Greece and Turkey to combat communism, Mar. 12. Approved May 15.

The United Nations Security Council voted unanimously Apr. 2 to place under U. S. trusteeship the Pacific islands formerly mandated to Japan.

Taft-Hartley Labor Act approved by U.S. Senate May 13. The House concurred June 4. The measure was vetoed by President Truman June 20, but Congress overrode the veto.

Proposals known later as the Marshall Plan, under which the U.S. would extend financial aid to all European countries "willing to assist in the task of recovery," were made by Sec. of State George C. Marshall June 5. Congress authorized the spending in the next 3½ years of some $12 billion on Marshall Plan aid, which was credited with restoring economic health to free Europe and halting the march of communism in those countries cooperating.

Hindu India and Moslem Pakistan, formerly parts of British India, gained independence Aug. 15.

1948

British Labor Government nationalized railways Jan. 1.

Mohandas K. Gandhi, Hindu spiritual leader and champion of freedom for India, was shot and killed by a Hindu fanatic in New Delhi Jan. 30.

Czechoslovakia joined the communist block in Eastern Europe after President Benes yielded Feb. 25 to an ultimatum to install a pro-Soviet cabinet. He resigned June 7; succeeded by Klement Gottwald, communist. Benes died Sept. 3. Communists reported Jan Masaryk, foreign minister, committed suicide Mar. 10.

A land blockade of Berlin's Allied sectors was started Apr. 1 by the Soviet military, which refused to permit U.S. and British supply trains to pass through the Soviet zone of Germany. This blockade and a Western counter-blockade were lifted Sept. 30, 1949, after British and U.S. planes had airlifted 2,343,315 tons of food and coal into West Berlin.

Charter of the Organization of American States signed Apr. 30 at 9th International Conference of American States at Bogota, Colombia.

The Free State of Israel was proclaimed in Tel Aviv May 14 as the British evacuated Palestine. First de facto recognition came from the U.S. May 14. Soviet Russia granted recognition May 17. Chaim Weizmann elected president by the Constituent Assembly Feb. 14, 1949.

The Cominform (Communist Information Bureau) at a Prague meeting June 28, denounced Marshal Tito and other leaders of the Yugoslav Communist party

as deserters from the Marxist-Leninist doctrine.

Alger Hiss, former State Department official, was indicted Dec. 15 on 2 perjury charges after he had denied passing secret documents to Whittaker Chambers, a former magazine editor, for transmission to a communist spy ring. A jury failed to reach an agreement July 8, 1949. His second trial Nov. 17, 1949-Jan. 21, 1950 ended with conviction on 2 counts and a sentence of 5 years in federal prison. Appeals to higher courts were rejected and Hiss began his sentence Mar. 22, 1951. He was released Nov. 27, 1954, his term shortened for good conduct.

Former Premier Hideki Tojo and 6 other Japanese war leaders were hanged Dec. 23 as war criminals.

Joseph Cardinal Mindszenty, Roman Catholic primate of Hungary, arrested by Communist government in Budapest on charges of treason Dec. 27. Convicted, given life imprisonment Feb. 8, 1949. All persons taking part in the cardinal's prosecution were excommunicated by Pope Pius XII. Mindszenty freed Oct. 31, 1956. After 15 years in U.S. Embassy in Budapest the cardinal left Hungary Sept. 28, 1971, for West Europe.

1949

Mildred E. (Axis Sally) Gillars was convicted by a federal jury in N.Y. City Mar. 10 of treason in broadcasting Nazi propaganda during war. She received 10 to 30 years in prison. Freed 1961.

North Atlantic Treaty adopted Mar. 18 by U.S., Canada and 10 Western European nations, agreeing that "an armed attack against one or more of them in Europe and North America shall be considered an attack against all."

Ireland severed last ties with Britain by leaving Commonwealth Apr. 18.

End of American A-bomb monopoly revealed by President Truman's announcement Sept. 23 that an atomic explosion had occurred in the USSR.

Mrs. I. Toguri D'Aquino, (Tokyo Rose) of Japanese wartime broadcasts, was sentenced in San Francisco Oct. 7 to 10 years in prison for treason. Paroled 1956.

Eleven leaders of U.S. Communist party convicted Oct. 14, after 9-month trial in N.Y. City, of advocating violent overthrow of U.S. Government. Federal Judge Harold R. Medina Oct. 21 sentenced 10 defendants to 5 years in prison each and the 11th, a war veteran, to 3 years. Supreme Court upheld the convictions June 4, 1951. Seven surrendered July 2, 1951; of the other 4, hunted as fugitives, one, Gus Hall, was captured Oct. 8, 1951, and given 3 additional years. Robert G. Thompson was captured Aug. 27, 1953. Five defense lawyers, cited for contempt during the trial, received sentences ranging from one to 6 months Apr. 24, 1952.

Nationalist China's government fled to Formosa Dec. 7. Chinese Communists took Yunnan and Kunming as Nationalists deserted.

1950

Great Britain recognized Communist China Jan. 6 one day after breaking diplomatic relations with Chiang Kai-shek's nationalist Chinese regime.

U.S. Jan. 14 recalled all consular officials from Communist China after the latter seized the American consulate general in Peking.

Masked bandits robbed Brink's Inc., Boston express office, Jan. 17 of $2,775,395.12, of which $1,218,211.29 was in cash. Case solved 1956 by FBI; 8 men sentenced to life.

President Truman authorized AEC to produce the hydrogen bomb (H-bomb), Jan. 31.

Dr. Klaus J. E. Fuchs, German-born atomic research physicist at Harwell, England, pleaded guilty Mar. 1 to violating the Official Secrets Act and received 14 years in prison. He had communicated atomic information to Russian agents since 1942. Released June 23, 1959, went to E. Germany.

The Army seized all railroads Aug. 27, on orders of President Truman to prevent a general strike after unions had rejected terms of an 18-cents-an-hour raise for yardmen but none for trainmen. Roads returned to owners May 23, 1952 after new contract.

In an attempt to kill President Truman, 2 members of a Puerto Rican nationalist movement attacked Blair House in Washington, Nov. 1. *(See Assassinations.)*

U. S. Dec. 8 banned shipments to Communist China and to Asiatic ports trading with it.

1951

Ilse Koch was sentenced to life imprisonment by a German court in Frankfurt Jan. 15 for inciting the murder of a Buchenwald prisoner.

With Sen. Estes Kefauver (D. Tenn.) as chairman, the Senate Committee to Investigate Organized Crime in Interstate Commerce exposed nationwide criminal organizations that reaped huge illegal profits, used these funds to enter legitimate businesses, influenced politicians and bought protection. Preliminary report Feb. 28 said gambling take was over $20 billion a year.

Julius Rosenberg, his wife, Ethel, and Morton Sobell, all U.S. citizens, were found guilty Mar. 29 of conspiracy to commit wartime espionage. Rosenbergs sentenced to death, Sobell to 30 years; appeals denied. David Greenglass, brother of Mrs. Rosenberg and a state witness, received 15 years in prison. Rosenbergs executed at Sing Sing prison, Ossining, N.Y., June 19, 1953. Sobell released Jan. 14, 1969.

President Truman relieved Gen. Douglas MacArthur of his command in the Far East Apr. 11. *(See Korean War).*

European Coal and Steel Plan proposed by French Foreign Minister Robert Schuman May 9. France, West Germany, Italy, Belgium, Netherlands, and Luxembourg agreed to conference. Treaty ratified June 16, 1952.

UN General Assembly voted arms embargo against Communist China May 18.

Tariff concessions by the U.S. to the Soviet Union, Communist China; and all communist-dominated lands were suspended Aug. 1.

Transcontinental television inaugurated Sept. 4 with President Truman's address at the Japanese Peace Treaty Conference in San Francisco.

Japanese Peace Treaty signed in San Francisco Sept. 8 by U.S. and 48 other nations.

War between Germany and the U.S. formally ended Oct. 19. Great Britain and France ended war with Germany July 9.

1952

Queen Elizabeth II proclaimed queen of United Kingdom and Canada Feb. 6, marking first time monarch was specifically enthroned in name of Canada.

U.S. seizure of nation's steel mills was ordered by President Truman Apr. 8 to avert a strike by 600,000 CIO United Steelworkers. Seizure was ruled illegal by the Supreme Court June 2. Strike followed June 3, was settled July 24.

First jetliner passenger service opened May 2, British DeHavilland Comet, London to Johannesburg.

Peace contract between West Germany, U.S., Great Britain, and France was signed in Bonn May 26. Allied high commissions abolished.

Puerto Rico became an "associated free state" or commonwealth of the U.S. July 25 after President Truman gave approval to a new constitution.

West Germany agreed Sept. 10 to pay Israel and Jews $822 million over 12 to 14 years as indemnity for damages inflicted by Nazis.

Britain successfully completed its first atomic test off northwest Australia Oct. 3 detonating a bomb aboard a naval vessel.

First hydrogen device explosion Nov. 1 at AEC Eniwetok proving grounds in Pacific reported by wit-

---

Korean War and United States Intervention

Republic of Korea was invaded June 25, 1950 (June 24 EST) by over 60,000 North Korean troops spearheaded by over 100 Russian-built tanks. UN Security Council demanded cessation of hostilities and withdrawal to 38th parallel (Russia not present, having staged "walkout" from Council.) On June 27, Council asked UN members to help carry out its demand. President Truman June 27, ordered Gen. of the Army Douglas MacArthur to aid South Korea, and the U.S. 7th Fleet to protect Formosa against possible aggression and keep the Chinese Nationalist forces from attacking the mainland. Requested by the UN to name a commander, the president designated Gen. MacArthur July 8, 1950.

North Korean forces took Seoul, South Korean capital June 29. U.S. ground forces entered the conflict June 30. Truman termed the intervention a "police action."

The war had 3 phases:

(1) The North Korean drive as checked by U.S. and allied troops, with help of a brilliant landing by U.S. Marines at Inchon Sept. 15. Pyongyang, North Korean capital, was taken Oct. 20. U.S. 7th Div. reached Manchurian border Nov. 20.

(2) Counter-attack by 200,000 Chinese Communist "volunteers," who crossed Yalu River Nov. 26, forced evacuation of 105,000 UN troops and 91,000 Korean civilians at Hungnam Dec. 24. The Chinese pushed across 38th parallel, drove 70 mi. into South Korea. The UN General Assembly Feb. 1, 1951, named Communist China the aggressor in Korea. UN troops pushed Chinese back across parallel Apr. 3, stopped offensive by 600,000 Chinese Apr. 22-30.

(3) Removal of Gen. MacArthur from command Apr. 11, 1951, and start of negotiations for truce along 38th parallel July 10, 1951.

President Truman removed Gen. MacArthur from all Far East commands and replaced him with Gen. Matthew B. Ridgway, commander of 8th Army. MacArthur had wished to pursue Chinese across Yalu River to their air depots in Manchuria and on Mar. 25

had threatened Communist China with air and naval attack. He had been warned to clear all announcements of policy through Washington. The president opposed his views. Senate inquiry May 3-June 27, 1951, found that MacArthur was not charged with insubordination, but had disregarded the president's order to clear policy statements through the Defense Department.

Cease-fire and armistice talks began July 1951 and dragged on with numerous breakdowns until July 27, 1953 (July 26, EST) when armistice was signed; fighting ended 12 hrs. later. A military armistice commission supervised truce; 10 joint UN-Communist teams policed demilitarized zone; Neutral Nations Supervisory Commission watched military movements in ports; voluntary repatriation of prisoners was provided and Communists won privilege of interviewing prisoners refusing repatriation.

Prisoner repatriation began Aug. 6, 1953, at Panmunjom, ended Sept. 6, 1953. UN turned over 75,790 prisoners (70,150 North Koreans and 5,640 Chinese). Communists released 12,760, including 7,850 South Koreans, 3,597 Americans, 945 Britons, 228 Turks.

The Supervisory Commission, made up of members from Czechoslovakia, Poland, Sweden, and Switzerland, was reduced one-half in Sept. 1955 on repeated complaints that the communist members were spying in South Korea. Repeated reports indicated that the North Koreans had violated many terms of the armistice, built numerous airfields and received naval vessels. The UN Command expelled the commission from South Korea in June 1956, on grounds that its Czech and Polish members and the North Korean government had frustrated the operation of the armistice agreement. The UN Command announced in June 1957, that it could no longer be bound by armistice provisions controlling importation of military equipment into Korea, but would modernize UN forces "to restore the relative balance of military strength that the armistice was intended to preserve."

nesses but not officially confirmed for more than a year. President Eisenhower told Congress Feb. 2, 1954, that the 1952 test was "the first full-scale thermonuclear explosion in history."

Alan Nunn May, British scientist who gave atom secrets to the USSR, was released from prison Dec. 29, after serving 6 yr. 8 mo. of his 10-yr. term.

1953

Joseph Stalin died Mar. 5. By 1955, Nikita Khrushchev emerged as dominant political leader of USSR.

Mau Mau or "Hidden Ones" of Kenya's Kikuyu tribe, formed to force whites from Kenya and to regain ancestral lands from government, climaxed sporadic violence Mar. 26, by murdering 71 and wounding 100 fellow Kikuyus who remained loyal to colonial government. Jomo Kenyatta, tribal leader, found guilty Apr. 8 of organizing Mau Mau, sentenced to 7 years on Dec. 12, 1963. Kenya became independent and Jomo Kenyatta became prime minister and president Dec. 12, 1964.

Mount Everest was conquered May 29 by Edmund P. Hillary of New Zealand and Tensing Norkay, a Nepalese living in India.

Demonstration by workers in East Berlin against increased work quotas June 16 erupted into an anticommunist riot by 20,000 to 50,000 persons June 17. Soviet troops quelled disturbances, killed 16.

Lavrenti P. Beria, chief of Soviet secret police, was dismissed July 10 as an enemy of the people. He was executed Dec. 23 along with 6 of his aides.

First USSR announcement of H-bomb explosion Aug. 20; AEC reported explosion occurred Aug. 12.

1954

Nautilus, first atomic-powered submarine, was launched at Groton, Conn., Jan. 21.

Five members of Congress were wounded in the House Mar. 1 by 4 Puerto Ricans, one a woman, who fired pistols at random from a spectators' gallery, shouting for Puerto Rican independence. The wounded recovered; the attackers were imprisoned.

Dien Bien Phu, French military outpost in NW Vietnam, fell to the Vietminh army of Ho Chi Minh May 7.

Geneva Conference on Far Eastern Affairs was held Apr. 26-July 21 by 19 nations, including Communist China. Free elections in Korea foundered on communist objections to UN supervision. Armistice, effective Aug. 11, ended 7½ years of war in Indochina with French withdrawal; Vietminh received 62,000 sq. mi. and 13 million people in North Vietnam, Cambodia and Laos became independent.

Racial segregation in public schools was unanimously ruled unconstitutional by the Supreme Court May 17.

Southeast Asia Treaty Organization (SEATO) formed by collective defense pact signed in Manila Sept. 8 by the U. S., Britain, France, Australia, New Zealand, Philippines, Pakistan, and Thailand.

Agreement signed in Paris Oct. 23 provided for West German sovereignty, rearmament and entrance into NATO and the Western European Union.

Condemnation of Sen. Joseph R. McCarthy (R. Wis.) voted by Senate, 67-22, Dec. 2 for contempt of a Senate elections subcommittee, for abuse of its members and for insults to the Senate during investigation Apr. 22-June 17 of charges brought by the Dept. of the Army against him growing out of his investigation of alleged subversive activities.

1955

Afro-Asian conference of 29 nations met in Bandung, Indonesia, Apr. Conference gave expression to the new nationalism of developing nations.

Federal Republic of West Germany became a soverign state May 5. President Eisenhower signed an order ending U. S. occupation but troops remained on a contractual basis.

The Warsaw Pact, a 20-yr. mutual defense treaty, was signed at Warsaw May 14 by USSR, Albania, Bulgaria, Czechoslovakia, Hungary, Poland, Romania, and East Germany. Albania was barred from meetings 1963; withdrew from pact 1968.

A meeting of heads of state "at the summit" proposed by U. S., Great Britain and France, to the USSR, took place July 18-23 in Geneva, Switzerland, with President Eisenhower representing the U.S.

Juan D. Peron, president and dictator of Argentina, was deposed Sept. 19 after a revolt begun June 16 by naval and marine corps units. Maj. Gen. Eduardo Lonardi became provisional president Sept. 23, was displaced Nov. 13 by a military junta which chose Maj. Gen. Pedro Aramburu provisional president.

Rosa Parks refused Dec. 1 to give her seat to a white man on a bus in Montgomery, Ala. Bus segregation ordinance declared unconstitutional by a federal court following boycott and NAACP protest.

Merger of America's 2 largest labor organizations was effected Dec. 5 under the name American Federation of Labor and Congress of Industrial Organizations. George Meany became president, Walter Reuther became vice president in charge of the industrial department. The merged AFL-CIO had a membership estimated at 15 million.

1956

At 20th Congress of Soviet Communist party in Moscow Feb. 14-25 party chief Nikita S. Khrushchev and other leaders denounced Joseph Stalin, repudiated cruelties of Stalinism, and proclaimed a policy of peaceful coexistence with the West. New party line helped to alienate Chinese communists and hasten Sino-Soviet split.

Workers in Poznan, Poland, revolted June 28; uprising crushed with 44 killed, many wounded.

Principles of Organization of American States outlined in Panama Declaration signed in Panama City July 22 by President Eisenhower and heads of 18 other Western Hemisphere states.

Egypt seized Suez Canal July 26 under nationalization decree after President Gamal Abdel Nasser denounced Western withdrawal of proposed Aswan dam financing.

Polish Communist leaders Oct. 19-21 defied Kremlin leadership and elected Wladyslaw Gomulka to head more independent government.

Hungarian revolt against Soviet-dominated regime began Oct. 23, was crushed Nov. 4 by Soviet.

Israel invaded Egypt's Sinai Peninsula Oct. 29, saying an Arab attack was imminent. France and Britain landed forces Nov. 5-6. U.S. condemned attack, supported cease-fire demand by UN. Egypt and Israel accepted cease-fire. Britain and France followed, fighting stopped Nov. 7.

UN established first international police force Nov. 5 to supervise truce in Middle East.

1957

Britain set off its first hydrogen bomb in Pacific test May 15.

Soviet Union announced Aug. 26 that it had successfully tested an intercontinental ballistic missile.

Sen. Strom Thurmond (D. S.C.) held Senate floor for 24 hrs., 18 min., Aug. 28-29, eclipsing record by Sen. Wayne Morse (D. Ore.) in 1953.

First underground nuclear explosion set off by Atomic Energy Commission in Nevada Sept. 19.

A federal-state controversy over admission of Negroes to the previously all-white Central High School in Little Rock, Ark., reached a showdown Sept. 4 when National Guardsmen ordered out by Gov. Orval Faubus (D.) barred 9 Negro students from entering the school. A conference between Faubus and President Eisenhower brought no result but Faubus complied Sept. 21 with a federal court order to remove the National Guardsmen. The Negroes entered school Sept. 23 but were ordered to withdraw by local authorities because of fear of mob violence. President Eisenhower sent federal troops to Little Rock Sept. 24 to enforce the court's order and the school began operation on an integrated basis.

First man-made satellite, Sputnik I, was launched by Soviet scientists Oct. 4. The 184-lb. sphere circled the earth about every 1½ hours in an elliptical orbit at altitudes ranging from some 140 to 560 mi. above earth. The Russians Nov. 3 launched Sputnik II, weighing 1,120 lbs., carrying a live dog, Laika, as the world's first space passenger and orbiting the earth about every 103.7 minutes at altitudes ranging from some 160 mi. to about 1,062 mi. Soviet authorities announced the dog's death Nov. 10.

1958

First U. S. earth satellite to go into orbit, Explorer I, launched by Army Jan. 31 at Cape Canaveral, Fla.

Gen. Charles de Gaulle became French premier June 1 averting threatened civil war; De Gaulle constitution, increasing power of executive, overwhelmingly adopted Sept. 28. De Gaulle elected Dec. 21 as first president of 5th Republic.

Arab nationalist rebels seized Iraqi government July 14, killed King Faisal II, proclaimed republic. President Eisenhower sent U.S. marines to Lebanon July 15 to forestall alleged effort by Soviet Union and United Arab Republic (Egypt and Syria) to engineer overthrow of Lebanon regime. Withdrawal of U. S. troops began Aug. 12.

Jet airliner passenger service across Atlantic was opened Oct. 4 by British Overseas Airways Corp.

First domestic jet airline passenger service in U.S. opened by National Airlines Dec. 10 between New York and Miami.

1959

Fidel Castro assumed power in Cuba following collapse of Fulgencio Batista's government Jan. 1.

St. Lawrence Seaway opened Apr. 25.

The George Washington, first U.S. ballistic-missile submarine, launched at Groton, Conn., June 9.

N.S. Savannah, world's first atomic-powered merchant ship. launched July 21 at Camden, N. J.

Soviet Premier Khrushchev paid unprecedented visit to U.S. Sept. 15-27, made transcontinental tour.

1960

A wave of sit-ins began Feb. 1 when 4 Negro college students in Greensboro, N. C., refused to move from a Woolworth lunch counter when they were denied service. By Sept. 1961 more than 70,000 students, whites and blacks, had participated in sit-ins.

First French nuclear test explosion set off Feb. 13 in Sahara Desert.

Caryl Chessman, who had won 8 stays of execution since his 1948 conviction on robbery, kidnaping and attempted rape charges, was put to death May 2 in the gas chamber at San Quentin prison, Cal.

A U-2 reconnaissance plane of the U.S., piloted by Francis Gary Powers, was shot down in the Soviet Union May 1. Soviet Premier Khrushchev refused to participate in the Paris summit conference scheduled for May 16 unless President Eisenhower apologized for U-2 flights over the USSR; the Big Four leaders went to Paris but the conference did not take place. Powers was freed Feb. 10, 1962, in exchange for convicted Soviet spy Rudolf Abel, who was serving a 30-year term imposed by U. S. in 1957.

Adolf Eichmann's capture in Argentina by Israeli agents announced May 22; former Nazi SS general accused of playing a major role in killing of millions of Jews. After 4-month trial in Jerusalem, sentenced by Israeli court Dec. 15, 1961, hanged for crimes against humanity May 31, 1962.

1961

The U. S. severed diplomatic and consular relations with Cuba Jan. 3.

Maj. Yuri Gagarin of the Soviet Union became Apr. 12 the first human orbital traveler; he was launched into orbit from Siberia in a spacecraft called Vostok I and returned to earth after one circuit of the globe.

Invasion of Cuba "Bay of Pigs" Apr. 17 by Cuban exiles attempting to overthrow the regime of Premier Fidel Castro was repulsed.

Commander Alan B. Shepard Jr. was rocketed from Cape Canaveral, Fla., 116.5 mi. above the earth in a Mercury capsule May 5 in the first U. S. manned sub-orbital space flight; he landed safely in the Atlantic 302 mi. away.

East Germany closed the border between East and West Berlin Aug. 12-13 to stop the exodus of East Germans to the West; the East Germans built a wall

dividing the city.

Dag Hammarskjold, Sec. General of the UN, was killed in a plane crash near Ndola, Northern Rhodesia Sept. 18. U Thant of Burma was elected acting Sec. General Nov. 3.

Nuclear blasts of 25 megatons and over 50 megatons, largest man-made explosions to date, were set off by the Soviet Union Oct. 23 and Oct. 30, respectively, despite world protests.

1962

Lt. Col. John H. Glenn Jr. became the first American in orbit Feb. 20 when he circled the earth 3 times in the Mercury capsule Friendship 7.

A truce agreement Mar. 18 ended the 7-yr. Moslem revolt against French rule in Algeria. Algerians cast an overwhelming vote for independence in a referendum July 1 and French President Charles de Gaulle declared the country independent July 3.

The 3d Soviet astronaut was sent into orbit Aug. 11 and the 4th followed him into a nearly identical orbit Aug. 12, both descended Aug. 15. They were Maj. Andrian G. Nikolayev, who made a record 64 orbits of the earth, and Lt. Col. Pavel R. Popovich, who made 48 orbits.

The largest cash robbery to date in U. S. history occurred Aug. 14 when a gang held up a U. S. mail truck near Plymouth, Mass., and stole $1,551,277.

A Soviet offensive buildup in Cuba was revealed to the American people Oct. 22 by President Kennedy, who ordered a naval and air quarantine on shipment of offensive military equipment to the island. President Kennedy and Soviet Premier Khrushchev reached agreement Oct. 28 on a formula to end the crisis. Kennedy announced Nov. 2 that Soviet missile bases in Cuba were being dismantled.

1963

The first woman space traveler, Soviet Jr. Lt. Valentina V. Tereshkova, was launched into orbit in Vostok VI June 16; landed June 19 after 48 orbits.

U.S. Supreme Court ruled, 8-1, June 17 that state and local laws requiring recitation of the Lord's Prayer or Bible verses in public schools were unconstitutional.

A limited nuclear test-ban treaty was agreed upon July 25 by the U. S., the Soviet Union, and Britain, barring all nuclear tests except those conducted underground. It became effective Oct. 10.

The biggest robbery to date occurred Aug. 8 when an armed holdup gang stole more than $7 million (£2.5 million) in currency from a mail train near Cheddington, England. Some of the money was recovered and a dozen men were sentenced to prison.

Washington demonstration by 200,000 persons Aug. 28 in support of Negro demands for equal rights. Highlight was speech in which Dr. Martin Luther King said: "I have a dream that this nation will rise up and live out the true meaning of its creed, 'We hold these truths to be self evident: that all men are created equal'."

The South Vietnamese government of President Ngo Dinh Diem was overthrown Nov. 1-2 in a coup by the armed forces. Diem and his brother, secret police chief Ngo Dinh Nhu, were captured and killed.

President John F. Kennedy was shot and fatally wounded by an assassin Nov. 22 as he rode in a motorcade through downtown Dallas, Tex. Gov. John B. Connally Jr. of Texas, riding in the same car, was also shot but not fatally injured. Vice President Lyndon B. Johnson was inaugurated president shortly afterward in Dallas. Lee Harvey Oswald was arrested and charged with the murder of the president. Oswald was shot and fatally wounded Nov. 24 by Jack Ruby, 52, a Dallas nightclub owner, who was convicted of murder Mar. 14, 1964, and was sentenced to death. The murder conviction was reversed by the Texas Court of Criminal Appeals. Ruby died of natural causes Jan. 3, 1967 while awaiting re-trial.

1964

Pope Paul VI toured the Holy Land Jan. 4-6, the first pope to visit there since Christianity began, the first to travel by air, and, the first to leave Italy in over 150 years.

Three civil rights workers were reported missing in Mississippi June 22. The bodies of Michael Schwerner, Andrew Goodman and James E. Chaney were found buried near Philadelphia, Miss., Aug. 4. Twenty-one white men were arrested. On Oct. 20, 1967, an all-white federal jury convicted 7 of conspiracy in the slayings.

The Warren Commission released Sept. 27 a report

Vietnam War and United States Intervention

American combat involvement in Vietnam for about 12 years made the Vietnam War the longest in U.S. history. U.S. interest in the area began when President Harry S. Truman June 27, 1950, sent a 35-man military advisory team to aid the French in their fight against communist forces in North Vietnam.

After the French stronghold of Dien Bien Phu fell to communist forces May 8, 1954, France and North Vietnam agreed at the Geneva Conference on Indochina, May 8 to July 21, to partition Vietnam pending reunification elections. President Eisenhower offered South Vietnam economic aid Oct. 24, 1954, and agreed to help train the South Vietnamese army Feb. 12, 1955. In July, the South Vietnamese government refused a North Vietnamese request to prepare for reunification elections on grounds that free elections would be impossible in North Vietnam.

North Vietnam announced Dec. 1960 the formation of the National Liberation Front (Vietcong) of South Vietnam; terrorism in the South increased. The number of U.S. military advisers in South Vietnam rose from about 2,000 in Dec. 1961 to over 15,000 by the end of 1963.

Ngo Dinh Diem, South Vietnam president since 1955, was assassinated during a military coup Nov. 1, 1963. Stable government did not return to South Vietnam until June, 1965, when Gen. Nguyen Van Thieu assumed command of a military government.

The major American commitment in Vietnam began after the U.S. destroyers Maddox and C. Turner Joy were reportedly attacked Aug. 2, 1964, by North Vietnamese torpedo boats in the Gulf of Tonkin. The U.S. Congress Aug. 7 passed the Gulf of Tonkin Resolution giving the president power to "take all necessary measures to repel any armed attack against the forces of the U.S. and to prevent further aggression." In Feb. 1965, President Johnson ordered continuous bombing raids over North Vietnam below the 20th parallel.

U.S. commanders were authorized to commit 23,-000 advisers to combat June 8, 1965. U.S. army, navy, air and marine forces committed to Vietnam reached 184,300 men by year's end. The U.S. began bombing strikes in the Hanoi-Haiphong area June 29, 1966. By Dec. 31, 1966, U.S. forces in Vietnam reached 385,300 men, not including some 60,000 men in the U.S. fleet and some 33,000 men stationed in Thailand.

The unconventional conflict in South Vietnam required the use of new ground warfare tactics. "Search and destroy" missions and "free-fire zones" for artillery were the most publicized of these new tactics because of their potential hazard to non-combatants. Armed helicopters were used extensively because of their mobility.

As the fighting and American casualties escalated, large-scale protests against the war erupted in the U.S. Thousands of war protesters marched Oct. 21-22, 1967, in Washington, D.C., and hundreds were arrested when they stormed the Pentagon. Nevertheless, American troop strength climbed to 474,300 men in Dec., 1,500 more than peak U.S. strength in Korea during the Korean War.

In the "Tet offensive" Jan. 30, 1968, the Vietcong and North Vietnamese attacked 30 provincial capitals in South Vietnam. The city of Hue was held by the Vietcong for 25 days, with bitter street fighting ending Feb. 24. Saigon was heavily attacked and the U.S. Embassy was occupied for 6 hrs. Record casualties were suffered on both sides. President Johnson Mar. 31 announced a bombing halt over 90% of North Vietnam and asked Hanoi for a peaceful response.

While the fighting continued, preliminary peace talks between the U.S. and North Vietnam opened in Paris May 10. In Chicago, police and troops clashed with 10,000-15,000 anti-war demonstrators during the Democratic National Convention Aug. 26-29.

Expanded peace talks, including representatives from South Vietnam and the Vietcong, opened in Paris Jan. 18, 1969. American forces in South Vietnam reached a final peak of 543,400 men in Apr. 1969. U.S. battle deaths Apr. 3 totaled 33,641 men, surpassing by 12 those killed in the Korean War. Withdrawal of U.S. combat troops began July 8, 1969, and on Nov. 3 President Nixon announced a Vietnamization policy which would transfer the fighting to South Vietnamese forces.

Protests in the U.S. continued, however, as hundreds of thousands of Americans demonstrated opposition to the Vietnam War Oct. 15 in a nationwide "moratorium." Some 250,000 demonstrators gathered in Washington, D.C., Nov. 15 in the largest anti-war protest in U.S. history.

As the Paris talks continued, U.S. and South Vietnamese forces invaded neutral Cambodia Apr. 30, 1970, to destroy communist supply bases in border area sanctuaries. On May 4 at Kent State Univ. in Ohio, 4 students were slain and 9 wounded when National Guardsmen opened fire during a demonstration against the Cambodian incursion; 100 U.S. colleges were closed down to protest the Cambodian invasion and Kent State killings. A year later, during massive anti-war protests in Washington, D.C., between May 3-5, police arrested some 12,614 people, at least 7,000 of them on the first day — a record high for arrests in a civil disturbance in U.S. history.

President Nixon revealed Jan. 25, 1972, that secret peace negotiations had been conducted since the previous June by presidential adviser Henry A. Kissinger. In the biggest communist attack since 1968, North Vietnamese forces Mar. 30 launched an offensive in force against South Vietnam through the demilitarized zone (DMZ) between the 2 Vietnams. Bombing of North Vietnam resumed Apr. 15, the first intensive bombing of North since 1968. Quang Tri, capital city of South Vietnam's northernmost province, fell to Hanoi troops May 1. The mining of Haiphong and other North Vietnamese ports was ordered by President Nixon May 8. After initial setbacks, South Vietnamese troops brought the invasion to a halt.

The last U.S. combat troops left Vietnam Aug. 11. Hanoi announced Oct. 26 that secret talks had achieved a tentative agreement. But the peace talks broke down and, on Dec. 18 President Nixon ordered the heaviest bombing of the war against North Vietnam. B-52 bombers were used for the first time against targets in Hanoi; some 15 were shot down by Hanoi's surface-to-air missiles.

Peace talks resumed Jan. 8, 1973, and President Nixon ordered a halt to all offensive military operations against North Vietnam Jan. 15. Peace pacts were formally signed in Paris Jan. 27 by the U.S., North and South Vietnam, and the Vietcong. A ceasefire began in Vietnam on Jan. 28. Between Feb. 12 and Apr. 1, 590 American POWs were released by North Vietnam. Some 1,359 Americans were reported missing in Indochina. The last American troops left Vietnam Mar. 29, officially ending any direct U.S. military role. U.S. combat deaths were counted at 46,079 as of Aug. 25, 1973. Total dead were estimated at some 2 million.

concluding that Lee Harvey Oswald was solely responsible for the Kennedy assassination.

Soviet Premier Khrushchev was ousted as premier and Soviet Communist party chief **Oct. 14-15.** Aleksei N. Kosygin replaced him as premier and Leonid I. Brezhnev took over the party leadership.

Communist China conducted a successful test explosion of its first atomic bomb **Oct. 16.**

1965

A Selma to Montgomery, Ala., civil rights march was led by Dr. Martin Luther King Jr., **Mar. 21-25.** The march started with 3,200 and swelled to 25,000. They were guarded along the way by 4,000 troops dispatched by President Johnson.

U.S. armed forces sent to Dominican Republic to protect U.S. citizens and prevent a revolution **Apr. 28.** The Organization of American States **May 23** set up a peace-keeping force to maintain order.

Los Angeles riot by discontented blacks living in Watts area resulted in death of 35 persons and property damage est. at $200 million **Aug. 11-16.**

Pope Paul VI visited N.Y. City **Oct. 4** and delivered a personal appeal for peace to the UN. It was the first time a pope had come to America.

Massive electric power failure blacked out most of northeastern U.S., parts of 2 Canadian provinces the night of **Nov. 9-10.** Approximately 80,000 sq. mi. with a population of 30 million were affected. In N.Y. City over 800,000 were trapped in the subways for hours.

Independence proclaimed in Rhodesia by minority white regime **Nov. 11.**

1966

Kwame Nkrumah, president of Ghana since independence in 1957, was overthrown **Feb. 24.**

France withdrew all its armed forces from the integrated NATO military alliance **July 1.**

Medicare, government program to pay part of the medical expenses of citizens over 65, began **July 1.**

A sniper atop the Univ. of Texas tower in Austin, Tex., shot 44 persons **Aug. 1,** killing 14. Shot to death by police, the sniper was identified as Charles J. Whitman, 25, an honor student at the university. Police later found the bodies of his wife and his mother.

Edward Brooke (R. Mass.) elected **Nov. 8** as first Negro U.S. Senator in 85 years.

1967

Rep. Adam Clayton Powell (D. N.Y.) was denied **Mar. 1** his seat in 90th Congress because House of Representatives charged him with misuse of government funds and nepotism. Re-elected in 1968, he was seated by the 91st Congress but was fined $25,000 and stripped of his 22 years' congressional seniority.

In 6-day Israeli-Arab war June 5-10, Israel smashed armed forces of United Arab Republic (Egypt), Syria and Jordan; Israel captured territory 4 times its own area. A U.S. communications ship, the U.S.S. **Liberty,** was attacked by Israeli planes and torpedo boats **June 8** in international waters off the Sinai Peninsula. Thirty-four U.S. crewmen were killed and 75 wounded. Israel apologized for the attack, which it called accidental.

Pres. Johnson and Soviet Premier Aleksei Kosygin met **June 23 and 25** at Glassboro State College in N.J.; agreed not to let any crisis push them into nuclear war.

Black riots in Newark, N.J., July 12-17 killed some 26, injured 1,500; over 1,000 arrested. In Detroit, Mich., **July 23-30** at least 40 died, 2,000 injured, and 5,000 left homeless by rioting, looting, burning in city's black ghetto. Quelled by 4,700 federal paratroopers and 8,000 National Guardsmen.

Thurgood Marshall sworn in **Oct. 2** as first black U.S. Supreme Court Justice. **Carl B. Stokes** (D. Cleveland) and **Richard G. Hatcher** (D. Gary, Ind.), elected first black mayors of major U.S. cities **Nov. 7.**

Dr. Christiaan Barnard, Capetown, South Africa, performed first successful human heart transplant **Dec. 3** on Louis Washkansky, who lived for 18 days.

1968

U.S.S. Pueblo and 83-man crew seized in Sea of Japan **Jan. 23** by North Koreans; 82 men released **Dec. 22.**

White racism cited as chief cause of black violence in Kerner Commission report on civil disorders **Feb. 29.**

President Johnson said Mar. 31 he would not seek or accept the Democratic nomination for president.

The Rev. Dr. Martin Luther King Jr., 39, assassinated **Apr. 4** in Memphis, Tenn. Riots in Washington, D.C., caused President Johnson to call out troops. By **Apr. 14** racial violence erupted in 125 cities in 29 states. James Earl Ray, an escaped convict, pleaded guilty to the slaying, was sentenced to 99 years.

Six New Left students' protest at Univ. of Nanterre, France, **May 2** grew into nearly a month of civil violence and by **May 24** 10 million strikers paralyzed country. De Gaulle saved regime with broad reforms.

Sen. Robert F. Kennedy, 42 (D. N.Y.) shot **June 5** in Hotel Ambassador, Los Angeles, after celebrating Cal. and S.D. presidential primary victories. Died **June 6.** Sirhan Bishara Sirhan, a Jordanian Arab living in Los Angeles, convicted of murder.

Soviet Union and other Warsaw Pact nations invaded Czechoslovakia **Aug. 20-21** to crush Alexander Dubcek's liberal regime.

1969

Dwight D. Eisenhower, 78, 34th president of the U.S. and Supreme Allied Commander in Europe during World War II, died of heart disease. **Mar. 28.**

Unarmed U.S. reconnaissance plane, with 31 aboard, shot down by North Korean jets **Apr. 15** in the Sea of Japan about 100 mi. from the mainland.

Charles de Gaulle resigned as president of France **Apr. 28** after narrowly losing a referendum.

Supreme Court Justice Abe Fortas resigned **May 14,** the first judge in the tribunal's history to do so because of public pressure.

A car driven by Sen. **Edward M. Kennedy** (D. Mass.) plunged off a bridge into a tidal pool on Chappaquiddick Is., Martha's Vineyard, Mass., **July 18.** The body of Mary Jo Kopechne, a 28-year-old secretary, was found drowned, in the car.

U.S. astronaut Neil A. Armstrong, 38, commander of the Apollo 11 mission, became the first man to set foot on the moon **July 20.** After stepping onto the moon Armstrong said: "That's one small step for a man, one giant leap for mankind." Air Force Col. **Edwin E. Aldrin Jr.** accompanied Armstrong.

1970

The 31-month Nigerian civil war ended with the surrender **Jan. 12** of secessionist Biafra after a loss of about 2 million lives.

A federal jury Feb. 18 found the defendants in the turbulent 21-week trial of the "Chicago 7" innocent of conspiring to incite riots during the 1968 Democratic National Convention. However, 5 were convicted of crossing state lines with intent to incite riots.

The U.S. cast its first veto in the UN Security Council **Mar. 17** when it joined Britain in rejecting a resolution calling on UN members to cut all communications with Rhodesia.

More than 6,000 N.Y. City postmen, angry over Congressional delays in granting pay raises, walked off the job **Mar. 18** and began the first large-scale strike in the postal service's 195-year history.

Millions of Americans participated in anti-pollution demonstrations **Apr. 22** to mark the first Earth Day.

The first women generals in American history were named by President Nixon **May 15** when he promoted Col. Elizabeth P. Hoisington, director of the Women's Army Corps, and Col. Anna Mae Hays, chief of the Army Nurse Corps, to the rank of brigadier general.

The Norwegian explorer Thor Heyerdahl and a multi-national crew of 7 set sail from Morocco **May 17** in a frail papyrus boat, the Ra II, in an attempt to prove that ancient Egyptians could have reached the new world. The craft sailed into Bridgetown Harbor, Barbados, **July 12.**

An earthquake in Peru May 31 wiped out scores of cities and villages and left more than 50,000 dead, 20,000 missing and 150,000 to 200,000 injured. U.S. Geological Survey experts termed the disaster "the most destructive historic earthquake in the Western hemisphere."

A postal reform measure was signed by President Nixon Aug. 12, creating an independent U.S. Postal Service, thus relinquishing governmental control of the U.S. mails after almost 2 centuries. Began operating July 1, 1971.

Egypt's Pres. Gamal Abdel Nasser, 52, the most powerful leader in the Arab world, died in Cairo Sept. 28.

Salvador Allende Gossens, 62, first democratically elected Marxist head of government in the world, was sworn in as Chile's president Nov. 3.

Charles De Gaulle, 79, died of a heart attack in Colombey-les-Deux Eglises Nov. 9.

A cyclone and giant waves devastated a 2,338-square-mi. area of Pakistan's Bay of Bengal coast Nov. 13 in one of the worst disasters of modern times. An estimated 300,000 persons were killed.

1971

Charles Manson, 36, and 3 of his followers were found guilty Jan. 26 of first-degree murder in the brutal slaying in 1969 of actress Sharon Tate and 6 others.

A treaty prohibiting installation of nuclear weapons on the seabed beyond any nation's 12-mi. coastal zone was signed by 63 nations Feb. 11.

A Constitutional Amendment lowering the voting age to 18 in all elections was approved in the Senate by a vote of 94-0 Mar. 10. The proposed 26th Amendment received House approval by a 400-19 vote Mar. 23; Ohio ratified it on June 30 making it law.

Civil war between East and West Pakistan beginning Mar. 25 brought death from war and starvation to hundreds of thousands and caused 9 million refugees to pour into India.

A court-martial Jury of 6 officers Mar. 29 after 13 days deliberation, convicted Lt. William L. Calley Jr., of premeditated murder of 22 South Vietnamese men, women and children at My Lai on Mar. 16, 1968. He was sentenced to life imprisonment Mar. 31. Sentence reduced to 20 years Aug. 20, 1971, by Lt. Gen. Albert O. Conner.

Haiti's Francois (Papa Doc) Duvalier, 64, died Apr. 21. His son Claude, 19, succeeded him Apr. 22.

Amtrak, the nation's new rail passenger system, went into operation May 1 with the goal to "get people back on trains."

Publication of classified Pentagon papers on the U.S. involvement in Vietnam was begun June 13 by the New York Times. In a 6-3 vote, the U.S. Supreme Court June 30 upheld the right of the Times and the Washington Post to publish the documents under the protection of the First Amendment. Daniel Ellsberg, admitted leaker of the 47-volume Pentagon analysis, was arraigned June 28 on charges of unauthorized possession of secret documents.

President Nixon began a sweeping new economic program Aug. 15 calling for a 90-day wage, price and rent freeze, to be effective immediately. He also freed the dollar for devaluation against other currencies by cutting its tie with gold, and halted the conversion of foreign held dollars into gold.

More than 1,000 N.Y. State troopers and police stormed the Attica State Correctional Facility where 1,200 inmates held 38 guards hostage Sept. 13, ending a 4-day rebellion in the maximum-security prison. Nine hostages and 28 convicts were shot to death in the assault.

Chile virtually expropriated the Anaconda and Kennecott copper mines Sept. 28 when President Allende subtracted $774 million from proposed compensation for the U.S. owners. He claimed the deduction was for "excess profits" harvested by the U.S. firms over 16 years.

Communist China was granted UN membership when the General Assembly by a vote of 76 to 35, with

17 abstentions, adopted an Albanian resolution Oct. 25 to seat Mao Tse-tung's communists and oust Chiang Kai-shek's nationalists.

India invaded Pakistan Dec. 3 in defense of splinter nation of Bangladesh, formerly East Pakistan. Following India's victory in the 14-day war, Shiek Mujibur Rahman, the father of the secessionist rebellion, became the prime minister of Bangladesh Jan. 12.

President Nixon announced Dec. 18 an 8.57% devaluation of the U.S. dollar to allow American goods to be more competitive in the world market, while raising the price of certain imports; the devaluation was accomplished by a $3 increase in the price of gold, from $35 an ounce to $38.

1972

President Nixon arrived in Peking Feb. 21 for an 8-day visit to China, which he called a "journey for peace." The unprecedented visit ended with a joint communique pledging that both powers would work for "a normalization of relations".

Author Clifford Irving and his wife admitted Mar. 13 that his purported interviews with multi-millionaire Howard Hughes and his subsequent biography of Hughes were hoaxes.

By a vote of 84 to 8, the Senate approved Mar. 22 a Constitutional Amendment banning legal discrimination against women because of their sex and sent the measure to the states for ratification.

Britain imposed direct rule over North Ireland Mar. 30, ending 51 years of semi-autonomous rule by the North Ireland government.

J. Edgar Hoover, 77, director of the Federal Bureau of Investigation (FBI) for all of its 48 years, serving under 8 presidents, died May 2.

Alabama Gov. George C. Wallace, campaigning at a Laurel, Md., shopping center May 15, was shot and seriously wounded as he greeted a large, enthusiastic crowd. Arthur H. Bremer, 21, was sentenced Aug. 4 to 63 years in prison for the shooting of Wallace and 3 bystanders.

In the first visit of a U.S. president to Moscow, President Nixon arrived May 22 for a week of summit talks with Kremlin leaders which culminated in a landmark arms pact aimed at a standoff between the missile forces of the 2 nuclear giants.

The Environmental Protection Agency announced June 14 a near-total ban on agricultural and other uses of the pesticide DDT, to become effective Dec. 31.

Five men were arrested June 17 for breaking into the offices of the Democratic National Committee in the Watergate office complex in Washington, D.C.

Hurricane Agnes hit Florida June 19 and went on a 10-day rampage up 250-mi. of eastern seaboard with winds and rains which unleashed "the most extensive" floods in the country's history, causing 118 deaths and more than $3 billion in property damage.

Atty. Gen. John N. Mitchell, confidant and campaign manager of President Nixon, quit July 1 as chairman of the Committee to Re-elect the President.

The White House announced July 8 that the U.S. would sell the Soviet Union at least $750 million of American wheat, corn and other grains over a period of 3 years.

Less than 2 weeks after Sen. Thomas F. Eagleton received the Democrats' nomination for vice-president, he confirmed July 25 reports that he had undergone electroshock treatment on 2 occasions in the 1960s. Eagleton withdrew as nominee July 31. R. Sargent Shriver was named as vice presidential candidate Aug. 8.

By a vote of 88 to 2, the Senate Aug. 3 ratified the strategic arms treaty limiting the U.S. and Russia to 2 antiballistic missile sites each. In White House ceremonies Oct. 3 President Nixon and Soviet Foreign Min. Andrei Gromyko signed and exchanged the final documents implementing the accords, which also limited the 2 powers' land-based and submarine-borne nuclear missile forces.

Eight Arab guerrillas, members of the Black September terrorist group, invaded the Israeli dormitory in the Olympics village in Munich early **Sept. 5** killing 2 members of the Israeli squad. Twenty-three hours later, after tense negotiations, 5 of the terrorists and 9 hostages were killed.

Japan's Prime Min. Kakuei Tanaka and China's premier Chou En-lai terminated more than 40 years of enmity **Sept. 29** when they signed an accord to end the technical state of war existing between the 2 Asian powers since 1937, and renewed diplomatic relations.

Life ended publication with its **Dec. 29** issue after 36 years as the leading weekly pictorial magazine.

1973

Great Britain, Ireland, and Denmark formally entered the European Common Market **Jan. 1.**

All mandatory wage and price controls were ended by President Nixon **Jan. 11,** some 17 months after their establishment under the Economic Stabilization Act. **All state laws that limited** a woman's right to an abortion during the first 3 months of pregnancy were overturned **Jan. 22** by the U.S. Supreme Court in a 7-2 decision.

The end of the military draft was announced **Jan. 27** by Defense Secretary Melvin R. Laird.

U. S. Secy. of the Treasury George P. Shultz announced **Feb. 12** a 10% devaluation of the U.S. dollar against nearly all major world currencies.

Some 200-300 members of the militant American Indian Movement **Feb. 27** seized the trading post and church at historic Wounded Knee on the Oglala Sioux Reservation in South Dakota. The insurgents demanded that the U.S. Senate Foreign Relations Committee hold hearings on treaties made with Indians, and that the Senate start a "full-scale investigation" of government treatment of Indians. After numerous negotiation failures both sides signed an agreement **May 5** stipulating removal of government armored personnel carriers and concurrent surrender of weapons by the insurgent Indians. The hamlet was evacuated **May 8.**

Palestinian terrorists invaded a reception **Mar. 1** at the Saudi Arabian embassy in Khartoum, Sudan, and held 6 diplomats hostage. After a breakdown of negotiations between the gunmen and Sudanese government officials, the 8 Palestinians **Mar. 2** tortured and executed 2 U.S. envoys and a Belgian charge d'affaires.

James W. McCord, a key figure in the Watergate conspiracy, said **Mar. 23** in a letter to the court that he and others had been under "political pressure" to plead guilty and remain silent. He said there were others involved who had escaped indictment.

President Nixon responded to the Watergate crisis in an address over radio and television **Apr. 30.** Although he himself had not played a role in the Watergate case, he said, he accepted, as "top man in the organization," full responsibility for those "people whose zeal exceeded their judgment." Earlier the same day 3 of his top aides resigned: chief of staff H. R. Haldeman, domestic affairs assistant John D. Ehrlichman and presidential counsel John W. Dean 3d. Atty. Gen. Richard G. Kleindienst also resigned.

The West German Bundestag ratified a treaty **May 11** establishing formal relations with the German Democratic Republic in East Germany.

Presiding Judge William M. Byrne dismissed **May 11** all government charges of espionage, theft, and conspiracy against Daniel Ellsberg and Anthony J. Russo Jr., the defendants in the 89-day Pentagon Papers trial. The decision precluded a retrial, but did not vindicate the defendants nor resolve the major constitutional issues in the controversial case. The crucial revelation leading to dismissal of the case came **Apr. 27** when Judge Byrne released a Justice Dept. memorandum stating that 2 of the convicted Watergate defendants, E. Howard Hunt and G. Gordon Liddy, had broken into the office of Ellsberg's psychiatrist with the intention of stealing Ellsberg's medical records. Byrne released E. Howard Hunt's grand jury testimony **May 14** in which Hunt stated

that the White House had conceived the plot and supervised and paid for the break-in.

Hearings by the Senate Select Committee on Presidential Campaign Activities into the Watergate scandal opened in Washington, D.C., **May 17** chaired by Sam J. Ervin (D.,N.C.) assisted by Howard H. Baker (R.,Tenn.).

President Nixon released a statement **May 22** in which he asserted that he made legitimate efforts to restrict investigation into some matters related to the Watergate affair because they impinged on national security. The president further stated that his concern over foreign policy leaks and the publication of the Pentagon Papers led to the establishment in 1971 of a small White House investigative unit, the "plumbers," supervised by John D. Ehrlichman.

Premier George Papadopoulos announced **June 1** that the military-led Greek government had abolished the monarchy and proclaimed a republic.

President Nixon set a freeze June 13 on retail prices. The freeze included prepared-food prices but excluded rents, interest, dividends, and raw agricultural products.

The U.S. and USSR signed 9 agreements during Soviet Communist party General Secretary Leonid I. Brezhnev's **June 16-25** visit to the U. S. One agreement obliged the 2 nations to enter into immediate consultations if relations between them or between one of them and some other country "appear to involve risk of nuclear conflict."

John Dean, former presidential counsel, **June 25** testified to a widespread cover-up of the Watergate conspiracy. He said the cover-up had spread from the White House staff and the Committee to Re-elect the President to the Justice Dept. and to the "Oval Office" of the president.

Former President Juan D. Peron returned June 20 to Argentina after almost 20 years of exile. He was re-elected president of Argentina **Sept. 23,** but died 9 months later, July 1, 1974.

The Federal Trade Commission July 9 charged 8 of the largest U.S. oil companies with conspiracy to monopolize the refining of petroleum products. The commission said the 23-year conspiracy had led to shortages of gasoline, forcing "substantially higher prices" on American consumers, and caused some independent petroleum marketers to close down.

The Senate Armed Services Committee July 16 began a probe into allegations that the U.S. Air Force had made secret B-52 bombing raids into Cambodia in 1969 and 1970. Defense Secretary James R. Schlesinger verified the secret raids **July 16** describing them as "fully authorized" and necessary for the protection of U.S. servicemen.

Herbert Kalmbach, formerly attorney and fund raiser for President Nixon, told the Senate Watergate Committee **July 16** that he had raised $220,000 for the 7 defendants in the Watergate trial, believing the money was intended for legal fees and support of the defendant's families.

White House tape recording of all conversation in the president's offices since Mar. 1971 was revealed by Alexander P. Butterfield, former presidential deputy assistant, in a surprise appearance before the Senate Watergate Committee **July 16.** On July 23 citing separation of powers and executive privilege, President Nixon refused to release any tapes to Senate investigators.

Afghanistan was proclaimed a republic **July 17** following a coup d'etat by junior officers led by Lt. Mohammad Daud Khan, King Mohammad Zahir Shah's brother-in-law and cousin.

The U. S. officially ceased bombing in Cambodia at midnight **Aug. 14** in accord with a June Congressional action. The bombing halt was preceded by several days of intensive bombing around Phnom Penh.

Forty-six years of civilian rule in Chile ended **Sept. 11** when a 4-man military junta overthrew President Salvador Allende Gossens in a violent military coup. Allende's Popular Unity Coalition was the world's first freely-elected Marxist government.

Henry A. Kissinger's nomination as Sec. of State was confirmed **Sept. 21.**

President Nixon's 1972 campaign finance aides revealed **Sept. 28** that campaign fund raisers had collected a record $60.2 million.

The 4th and biggest Arab-Israeli War in 25 years erupted **Oct. 6** along the 103-mile-long Suez Canal and on the Golan Heights. The war began on the afternoon of Yom Kippur, the Jewish Holy Day of Atonement, and was marked by heavy troop and materiel losses on both sides. UN observers in the Middle East reported that Egyptian forces had crossed the Suez Canal at 5 points and that Syrian forces had attacked at 2 points on the Golan Heights. By **Oct. 11** the Egyptian army had established a bridgehead of about 60,000 men in the Sinai. The Egyptian army's advance was greatly aided by use of new Russian SAM-6 missiles which stymied the Israeli air offensive against the bridgehead.

After losing ground on both fronts, Israel counterattacked. Israel claimed **Oct. 12** that its forces had pushed to within 18 mi. of Damascus, despite the arrival of Iraqi and Jordanian forces on the Syrian front. Israel **Oct. 16** said it had sent a task force across the Suez Canal to attack Egyptian tanks, artillery and missile sites on the west bank. By **Oct. 24,** this Israeli force had isolated the city of Suez and the Egyptian 3d Army in Sinai.

The UN Security Council **Oct. 22** passed, 14-0, a U.S.-USSR sponsored resolution calling for a ceasefire in place. Fighting continued until a 2d cease-fire went into effect **Oct. 24** with UN supervision.

A total ban on oil exports to the U.S. was imposed by Arab oil-producing nations **Oct. 19-21.** The ban was lifted Mar. 18, 1974.

The U. S. **Oct. 25** suddenly placed its military forces on a world-wide "precautionary alert." The crisis ended when the USSR and U.S. joined in a Security Council vote barring the superpowers from participation in a Middle East peace-keeping force. A 7,000-man UN peace-keeping force was approved **Oct. 27** for an initial period of 6 months.

Vice President Spiro T. Agnew Oct. 10 resigned and pleaded "nolo contendere" (no contest) to charges of tax evasion on payments made to him by Maryland contractors. Agnew was sentenced to 3-years probation and fined $10,000.

Violent student demonstrations, culminating in bloody clashes with troops **Oct. 14** forced the resignation of Thailand's Premier Thanom Kittikachorn.

Atty. Gen. Elliott Richardson resigned, and his deputy William D. Ruckelshaus and Watergate Special Prosecutor Archibald Cox were fired by President Nixon **Oct. 20** when Cox threatened to secure a judicial ruling that President Nixon was violating a court order to turn tapes over to Judge John Sirica.

A massive expression of public outrage was followed **Oct. 23** by an agreement among Congressional leaders that the House Judiciary Committee should inquire into the possible impeachment of President Nixon.

Leon Jaworski, conservative Texas Democrat, was named **Nov. 1** by the Nixon administration to be special prosecutor to succeed Archibald Cox, with the understanding Jaworski would have "complete freedom" to investigate administrative wrongdoing.

Congress overrode Nov. 7 President Nixon's veto of the war powers bill which curbed the president's power to commit armed forces to hostilities abroad without Congressional approval.

The U.S. and Egypt announced Nov. 7 they would renew diplomatic relations.

Sentencing 6 Watergate break-in defendants **Nov. 9,** Federal Judge John J. Sirica dealt E. Howard Hunt 2½-8 years and a $10,000 fine; James W. McCord Jr. 1-5 years; Frank A. Sturgis, Eugenio R. Martinez, and Virgilio R. Gonzalez 1-4 years; Bernard L. Barker 18 months to 6 years. The 7th defendant, G. Gordon Liddy, had already been sentenced to 20 years, reflecting his refusal to cooperate with the prosecution.

Watergate Special Prosecutor Archibald Cox's firing, Oct. 20, was ruled illegal by Washington, D.C., Federal Court **Nov. 14.**

Alaska pipeline bill, permitting construction of 789-mi. pipe from Alaska's North Shore oilfield to port of Valdez, signed by President Nixon **Nov. 16.**

Greek President George Papadopoulos was deposed **Nov. 25** in bloodless military coup after student-worker riots.

Egil Krogh Jr., former head of the "plumbers," White House investigative unit, pleaded guilty **Nov. 30** to violating civil rights of Daniel Ellsberg's psychiatrist, Dr. Lewis J. Fielding, in burglary of Fielding's office. Krogh was sentenced Jan. 24, 1974, to 6 months.

Gerald Rudolph Ford was sworn in **Dec. 6** as 40th vice president under XXVth Amendment procedures.

President Nixon disclosed his financial records **Dec. 8,** showing large income tax deductions based on gift of his vice presidential papers to the National Archives. He said he would let a joint Congressional committee decide if he owed more taxes.

Allocations for fuel oil and gasoline were announced by energy chief William Simon **Dec. 12,** giving priorities to essential services.

Nelson A. Rockefeller resigned as governor of New York **Dec. 18,** after 15 years.

A 3-day work week was ordered by British government **Dec. 13** because of Arab oil embargo and coal miners' slowdown.

Spanish Premier Louis Carrero Blanco was assassinated **Dec. 20** in Madrid. Basque terrorists claimed credit.

Arab nations doubled oil prices and said they would increase oil flow to some nations by 10%, but would continue embargo against U.S., the Netherlands and Denmark, after meetings **Dec. 23-25.**

1974

U.S. oil companies reported huge profits for the 4th quarter of 1973, during the Arab oil embargo, in their **Jan. 1974** reports. Exxon profits were up 59% over the same period of 1972; Mobil, 68%; Texaco, 70%; Ashland, 52%.

In Northern Ireland Brian Faulkner quit as head of the Unionists, a Protestant party, **Jan. 7** but continued as head of the Protestant-Catholic coalition which assumed power Jan. 1. Militant Protestants disrupted the new Assembly, **Jan. 23.**

A disengagement agreement was reached by Israel and Egypt **Jan. 17** with U.S. aid. Egyptian forces occupied a narrow strip on the east side of the Suez Canal; a UN-patrolled buffer zone separated them from Israeli forces further east; Israelis withdrew from west of the canal. Troops and equipment in forward zones were limited.

Impeachment proceedings against President Nixon began as the House voted its Judiciary Committee full inquiry powers **Feb. 6.**

The Skylab 3 astronauts splashed down in the Pacific **Feb. 8,** completing longest space flight: 84 days, 1 hr., 17 mins.

Alexander Solzhenitsyn, Nobel Prize-winning author, was deported by Soviet Russia to West Germany **Feb. 13.** He had exposed the Soviet prison camp system in Gulag Archipelago, book published in Paris. His family was also allowed to leave Russia.

Herbert W. Kalmbach, President Nixon's personal lawyer and fundraiser, pleaded guilty **Feb. 25** to running an illegal campaign committee in, 1970 and promising a contributor an ambassadorship for a $100,000 contribution. Sentenced **June 17,** he got 6 to 8 months and a $10,000 fine.

Seven former White House and campaign aides of President Nixon were indicted **Mar. 1** for taking part in the cover-up of the Watergate scandals. The 7 were former chief of staff H. R. Haldeman, former Attorney General and campaign director John N. Mitchell, Presidential Domestic Assistant John D. Ehrlichman, former Special Counsel Charles W. Colson, former campaign aide Robert C. Mardian, former campaign committee attorney Kenneth W. Parkinson, former Haldeman aide Gordon C. Strachan.

Japanese World War II survivor Lt. Hiroo Onoda, 52, missing in Philippines since war's end, was found **Mar. 10.** He was enthusiastically welcomed home Mar. 12.

Arab nations ended their oil embargo against the U.S. **Mar. 18** but continued it against Denmark and the Netherlands, designating them "unfriendly" states.

President Nixon said Apr. 3 he would pay $432,787.13 in back taxes plus interest for 1969 through 1972, after Joint Congressional Committee, acting on request from Nixon, found him liable.

Lt. Gov. Ed Reinecke of California was indicted **Apr. 3** for lying to the Senate Judiciary Committee. Convicted **July 27,** he resigned and received an 18-month suspended sentence.

Israeli Premier Golda Meir resigned Apr. 10 in dispute over blame for Israel's unpreparedness in the Oct. 1973 war. Itzhak Rabin was named premier **Apr. 23.**

W. A. Boyle, deposed United Mine Workers president, was convicted **Apr. 11** of murder for ordering the slayings of union rival Joseph A. Yablonski and Yablonski's wife and daughter. The conviction carried a mandatory life sentence.

Arab guerrillas killed 18, mostly women and children, in attack on Qiryat Shemona, Israel, **Apr. 11.** Israelis raided guerrilla sanctuaries in southern Lebanon in reprisal **Apr. 12.**

Charging Soviet Russia was trying to influence Egyptian actions by putting off requests for more arms, President Anwar Sadat said **Apr. 18.** Egypt would end its reliance on Soviet arms aid.

Portugal's Premier Marcello Caetano was ousted **Apr. 25** by a military group pledging democracy and peace for Portugal's African territories. Gen. Antonio de Spinola headed the new government.

Former Attorney General John N. Mitchell and former Commerce Sec. Maurice H. Stans were acquitted **Apr. 28** in N.Y. City Federal Court of attempting to impede a Securities and Exchange Commission probe of financier Robert L. Vesco in return for a $200,000 cash donation to the 1972 Nixon re-election campaign.

West German Chancellor Willy Brandt resigned **May 6,** taking responsibility for "negligence" that allowed an East German spy on his staff. Helmut Schmidt succeeded him.

Canadian Prime Minister Pierre Elliott Trudeau's government lost a vote of confidence in the House of Commons **May 8** but, in elections **July 8,** won a clear majority in the House.

Impeachment hearings were opened **May 9** against President Nixon by the House Judiciary Committee.

Arab terrorists seized 90 students in the Israeli town of Maalot **May 15** after murdering a family of 3. Israeli troops freed the hostages, but 21 students, one Israeli soldier, and the 3 terrorists died.

Ex-Attorney General Richard G. Kleindienst pleaded guilty **May 16** to a misdemeanor charge that he did not testify accurately and fully before a Congressional committee probing handling of an ITT anti-trust settlement. He received 30 days and a $100 fine, both suspended, **June 7.**

India exploded a nuclear device May 18, becoming the 6th nation with nuclear bomb capability.

Jeb Stuart Magruder, former deputy director of the Committee to Re-elect the President, was sentenced **May 21** to 10 months to 4 years for his role in the Watergate break-in and cover-up.

Sen. J. W. Fulbright, longtime Foreign Relations Committee chairman, was beaten almost 2 to 1 in the Arkansas Democratic primary **May 28** by Dale Bumpers, who also won the November election to the Senate.

Northern Ireland's Protestant-Catholic coalition government collapsed after a strike; the British government took over direct rule of Ulster **May 29.**

Israel and Syria signed a disengagement agreement **May 31.** Israel gave up some of the Golan Heights territory she had taken in 1967 and 1973; forces on both sides were limited in strips separated by a UN-patrolled buffer zone.

Charles W. Colson, ex-counsel to the president, pleaded guilty **June 3** to attempting to obstruct justice; he was sentenced **June 21** to 1 to 3 years and fined $5,000.

President Nixon visited the Middle East, **June 12-19;** in Cairo he agreed to provide Egypt nuclear technology for peaceful purposes; in Israel he assured that nation long-term military and economic aid.

Mrs. Alberta Williams King, 69, mother of slain civil rights leader Dr. Martin Luther King Jr., was shot and killed **June 30,** along with a church deacon, in Atlanta's Ebenezer Baptist Church. Marcus Wayne Chenault, 23, of Dayton, Oh., was convicted **Sept. 12** and sentenced to die.

President Juan Domingo Peron of Argentina, 78, died **July 1;** he was succeeded by his vice president and wife, Isabel Martinez de Peron.

Turkey announced July 1 it would again allow the growth and sale of opium, but under strict control; in 1971 Turkey had promised the U.S. to outlaw the trade; the U.S. had agreed to give Turkey $35.7 million over 4 years.

John D. Ehrlichman and 3 White House "plumbers" were found guilty **July 12** of conspiring to violate the civil rights of Dr. Lewis Fielding, formerly psychiatrist to Daniel Ellsberg, by breaking into his Beverly Hills, Cal., office. On **July 31,** Ehrlichman, Nixon domestic aide, drew 20 mos. to 5 yrs.; G. Gordon Liddy got 1 to 3 years.; Bernard L. Barker and Eugenio Martinez won suspended sentences.

Turkey invaded Cyprus July 20. Earlier, 650 Greek officers, **July 15,** led the Cypriot National Guard in a violent coup, overthrowing President Makarios, who fled to London. Negotiations brought a promise from Greece to replace gradually the 650 Greek officers but she refused to recall them immediately. The Turkish invasion followed, ostensibly to protect the Turkish minority, 18% of the Cyprus population. An uneasy UN-sponsored cease-fire was reached between Turkey and the Greek Cypriots **July 22.**

Greece's military government resigned **July 23:** former Premier Constantine Karamanlis returned from exile to become chief of state. On Cyprus, fighting continued until Turkey, in possession of the NE third of the island, declared a new cease-fire **Aug. 16.**

The U.S. Supreme Court ruled, 8-0, **July 24** that President Nixon had to turn over 64 tapes of White House conversations sought by Watergate Special Prosecutor Leon Jaworski.

The House Judiciary Committee, in televised hearings **July 24-30,** recommended 3 articles of impeachment against President Nixon. The first, voted 27-11, **July 27,** charged Nixon with taking part in a criminal conspiracy to obstruct justice in the Watergate cover-up. The second, voted 28-10, **July 29,** charged he "repeatedly" failed to carry out his constitutional oath in a series of alleged abuses of power. The third, voted 21-17, **July 30,** accused him of unconstitutional defiance of committee subpoenas. The House of Representatives **Aug. 20,** without debate, voted 412-3 to accept the committee report, which included the recommended impeachment articles.

The U.S. Supreme Court held, 5-4, that busing pupils across school district lines between a black inner city (Detroit) and white suburbs was improper, **July 25.**

Ex-presidential counsel John W. Dean 3d was sentenced **Aug. 2** to 1 to 3 years. on his plea of guilty to conspiracy to obstruct justice.

President Richard M. Nixon resigned and Vice President Gerald R. Ford was sworn in as president **Aug. 9.** Nixon's support in the Watergate struggle began eroding **Aug. 5** when Nixon released 3 tapes, admitting he originated plans to have the FBI stop its probe of the Watergate break-in for political as well as national security reasons. Supporters in both

House and Senate said, **Aug. 6-7**, they would vote for his impeachment.

Former N.Y. Gov. Nelson A. Rockefeller was nominated to be vice president by President Ford **Aug. 20.**

Portugal began dissolving its African empire **Aug. 26**, signing an agreement to free Portuguese Guinea **Sept. 10**; the new nation became Guinea-Bissau.

George M. Steinbrenner, Cleveland industrialist and principal owner of the N.Y. Yankees, was fined $15,000 **Aug. 30** after pleading guilty to making illegal corporate contributions to campaigns of Richard Nixon and several Democratic congressmen. His American Shipbuilding Co. was fined $20,000.

The U.S. and East Germany established diplomatic relations **Sept.** 4.

An unconditional pardon to ex-President Nixon for all federal crimes that he "committed or may have committed" while president was issued by President Gerald Ford **Sept. 8**, one month after Nixon resigned. Ford's press secretary, J. F. terHorst resigned in protest. The administration also announced a **Sept. 6** agreement under which the ex-president's papers and tapes would be held for 3 years; after that Nixon could destroy the tapes.

Ethiopian Emperor Haile Selassie, 82, was peacefully deposed **Sept. 12** by armed forces leaders who had been strengthening their power since February.

Conditional amnesty to Vietnam era draft evaders and deserters who would be willing to work up to 2 years in public service jobs was proposed by President Ford **Sept. 16**. Organized groups of exiles condemned the program and few took advantage of it.

Charges against Wounded Knee defendants Dennis J. Banks and Russell C. Means, Indian leaders, were dismissed **Sept. 16** by Federal Judge Fred J. Nichol in the 1973 takeover of the South Dakota village. Nichol said that during the trial the FBI had been shown to lie and suborn perjury.

Ex-President Nixon entered a Long Beach, Cal., hospital **Sept. 23** for care of a flare-up of the phlebitis he suffered in his left leg during his June Middle East trip.

The court martial conviction of Lt. William L. Calley Jr. in the 1968 massacre of civilians in Mylai, South Vietnam, was overturned **Sept. 25** by Federal Court Judge J. Robert Elliott in Columbus, Ga.

The provisional president of Portugal, Gen. Antonio de Spinola, resigned **Sept. 30** with several associates, accused of a right-wing plot; the government was left chiefly in the hands of leftist officers and civilians.

A temporary restraining order, barring the Ford administration from carrying out its Sept. 6 agreement on returning Nixon's tapes, was issued **Oct. 21** by Federal Judge Charles Richey.

Leaders of 20 Arab nations declared Palestine Liberation Organization leader Yasir Arafat the "sole legitimate representative" of Palestinian Arabs **Oct. 28**. The UN General Assembly had voted **Oct. 14** to give the PLO a voice at its meetings.

Ex-president Nixon underwent surgery for a blood clot **Oct. 29**, suffered internal bleeding and shock, but recovered; in Long Beach, Cal. hospital.

For events of 1975 and late 1974, see Chronology.

---

100 Years Ago in the Almanac

Exposure of illegal activities in the liquor and mining industries and ensuing indictments made major headlines in the United States in 1875.

The *St. Louis Democrat*, in May, exposed the "Whisky Ring," a large-scale St. Louis-based conspiracy of distillery owners and federal revenue officials to withhold liquor taxes from the government.

Sixteen distilleries in St. Louis, Milwaukee, and Chicago were seized and 238 persons indicted in connection with the fraud which, over a 10-month period, had cheated the government of an estimated $1,650,000 in internal revenue taxes. A subsequent investigation, ordered by the Secretary of the Treasury, revealed that O.E. Babcock, Pres. Ulysses S. Grant's private secretary and personal friend, had been a chief organizer of the conspiracy.

The 1875 murder of Thomas Sanger, a young English mine official, instigated investigation of the "Molly Maguires," a secret miners' union in Pennsylvania. Through the undercover work of Pinkerton detective James McParlan, who infiltrated the secret organization, numerous members of the "Molly Maguires" were indicted and convicted of murder. By 1880, 19 had been hanged and many more imprisoned.

The discovery of gold in the Deadwood and Whitewood gulches of South Dakota brought a flood of some 15,000 would-be millionaires into the Black Hills Indian reservation area. The influx of gold-seekers along with corruption among Indian affairs officials and expansion of the Northern Pacific Railway led to the beginning of the Second Sioux War.

The Balkans Ignite

Discontent with Turkish rule led to insurrection in Bosnia and Herzegovina, igniting a 3-year period of acute tension in the Near East. Serbia immediately supported the insurrection, hoping to gain the 2 provinces for itself. Russia, partly out of compassion for her Slavic brothers and partly out of ambitions to destroy the Turkish empire, supported the Bosnia-Herzegovinan cause.

In late 1875, Egypt went to war with Ethiopia. In surprise defeats, the Egyptian Khedive's troops were massacred at Kherad Iska and fled from Gonda Gondii. However, by early 1876, the Egyptians won a crushing victory leading to defeat of Ethiopia.

The year 1875 marked the beginning of British penetration into the Suez. The Egyptian Khedive, perpetually in financial difficulties, in a transaction masterfully negotiated by Benjamin Disraeli, sold his 49% of Suez Canal shares to the British government.

A Year of Firsts

1875 was a year of significant firsts. The first Kentucky Derby, then a mile-and-a-half course, was run at Churchill Downs at Louisville, Ky., on May 17. Aristides, ridden by O. Lewis, took home the $2,850 purse.

Equipped with "richly upholstered" adjustable chairs that revolved on swivels, the "Maritana," the first railroad parlor car, built by George Mortimer Pullman, went into operation.

Consecrated as Bishop of Portland, Bishop James Augustine Healey became the U.S.'s first black Catholic bishop. In another first for the Catholic church, John McCloskey, archbishop of New York, was elected the first American cardinal.

The collaboration of numerous printers, notably Andrew Campbell and Stephen D. Tucker, both Americans, produced the rotary perfecting press. The press made possible printing on both sides of a sheet at once and delivery of cut and folded newspapers in one operation.

Also in 1875, Madame Blavatsky founded the Theosophical Society, Georges Bizet wrote *Carmen*, Mark Twain published the *Adventures of Tom Sawyer*, and Mary Baker Eddy's *Science and Health* appeared.

Some Notable Marine Disasters Since 1865

(Figures Indicate Estimated Lives Lost)

1865, Apr. 27—Sultana; a Mississippi River steamer blew up; 1,400.

1868, Mar. 18—Magnolia; steamboat blew up on Ohio River; 80.

1868, Apr. 9—Sea Bird; steamer burned on Lake Michigan; 100.

1868, Dec. 4—United States and America; steamboats collided, burned, on Ohio River near Warsaw, Ky.; 72.

1869, Oct. 27—Stonewall; steamer burned on Mississippi River below Cairo, Ill.; 200.

1870, Jan. 24—Oneida; American ship sank in collision off Yokohama; 115.

1870, Jan. 28—City of Boston; American steamer of Inman Line vanished between New York and Liverpool; 191.

1871, July 30—Westfield; Staten Island ferryboat exploded in New York Harbor; 100.

1872, Nov. 7—Mary Celeste; American half-brig sailed from New York for Genoa; found abandoned in Atlantic 4 weeks later in mystery of sea; crew never heard from; loss of life unknown.

1873, Jan. 22—Northfleet; British steamer foundered off Dungeness, England; 300.

1873, Apr. 1—Atlantic; British (White Star) steamer wrecked off Nova Scotia; 547.

1873, Nov. 23—Ville de Havre; French steamer, New York to Havre, sank after collision with Loch Earn; 230.

1875, Nov. 7—Schiller; German mail steamer wrecked off Scilly Islands; 200.

1875, Nov. 4—Pacific; American steamer sank after collision off Cape Flattery; 236.

1875, Dec. 6—Deutschland; German steamer, Bremen to New York, wrecked at mouth of Thames; 157.

1877, Nov. 24—Huron; U. S. warship wrecked off North Carolina; 100.

1878, Jan. 31—Metropolis; American steamer wrecked off North Carolina; 100.

1878, Sept. 3—Princess Alice; British steamer sank after collision in Thames; 700.

1878, Dec. 18—Byzantin; French steamer sank after Dardanelles collision; 210.

1880, Nov. 24—Uncle Joseph; French steamer sank in collision off Spezzia, Greece; 250.

1881, May 24—Victoria; steamer capsized in Thames River, Canada; 200.

1883, Jan. 19—Cambria; German steamer hit iceberg in North Sea; 389.

1884, Jan. 18—City of Columbus; American steamer wrecked off Gay Head Light, Mass.; 103.

1887, Nov. 15—Wah Yeung; British steamer burned at sea; 400.

1887, Nov. 19—W. A. Scholten; Dutch steamer sank in English Channel collision; 134.

1890, Feb. 17—Duburg; British steamer wrecked, China Sea; 400.

1890, Mar. 1—Quetta; British steamer wrecked off Cape York, Australia; 124.

1890, Sept. 19—Ertogrul; Turkish frigate foundered off Japan; 540.

1891, Mar. 17—Utopia; British steamer sank in collision off Gibraltar; 574.

1892, Oct. 28—Roumania; British steamer wrecked off Portugal; 113.

1893, Feb. 8—Trinacria; British steamer wrecked off Spain; 115.

1895, Jan. 30—Elbe; German steamer sank in collision with British steamer Crathie in North Sea; 335.

1895, Mar. 11—Reina Regenta; Spanish cruiser foundered near Gibraltar; 400.

1898, Feb. 15—Maine; U.S. battleship blown up in Havana Harbor; 266.

1898, July 4—La Bourgogne, Cromartyshire; French steamer and British sailing ship collided off Nova Scotia; 560.

1898, Nov. 26—Portland; American steamer wrecked off Cape Cod; 157.

1900, June 30—Main, Bremen and Saale; German steamers destroyed in $10 million dock fire at Hoboken, N.J.; 145.

1901, Feb. 22—Rio de Janeiro; American mail steamer wrecked in San Francisco Harbor; 128.

1903, June 7—Libau; French steamer sank in collision near Marseilles; 150.

1904, June 15—General Slocum; excursion steamer burned in East River, New York City; 1,030.

1904, June 28—Norge; steamer wrecked on Rockall Reef off Scotland; 590.

1906, Jan. 22—Valencia; American steamer lost off Vancouver Island; 129.

1906, Aug. 4—Sirio; Italian steamer wrecked off Cape Palos, Spain; 350.

1907, Feb. 12—Larchmont; American steamer sank in Long Island Sound; 131.

1907, July 20—Columbia and San Petro; American steamers collided off California coast; 100.

1908, Mar. 23—Matsu Maru; Japanese steamer sank in collision near Hakodate, Japan; 300.

1909, Aug. 1—Waratah; British steamer, Sydney to London, vanished; 300.

1910, Feb. 9—General Chanzy; French steamer wrecked off Minorca, Spain; 200.

1911, Sept. 25—Liberte; French battleship exploded at Toulon; 285.

1912, Mar. 5—Principe de Asturias; Spanish steamer wrecked off Spanish coast; 500.

1912, Apr. 14-15—Titanic; British (White Star) liner hit iceberg in North Atlantic; 1,517.

1912, Sept. 28—Kichemaru; Japanese steamer sank off Japanese coast; 1,000.

1913, Mar. 1—Calvados; British steamer lost in Sea of Marmora, Turkey; 200.

1914, May 29—Empress of Ireland; Canadian steamer sank after collision with collier in St. Lawrence River; 1,024.

1915, May 7—Lusitania; British (Cunard Line) steamer torpedoed by German submarine, sank off Ireland; 1,198.

1915, July 24—Eastland; excursion steamer capsized in Chicago River; 812.

1916, Feb. 26—Provence; French cruiser sank in Mediterranean; 3,100.

1916, Aug. 29—Hsin Yu; Chinese steamer sank off Chinese coast; 1,000.

1917, Dec. 6—Mont Blanc, Imo; French ammunition ship and Belgian steamer collided in Halifax Harbor; 1,600.

1918, Apr. 25—Kiang-Kwan Chinese steamer sank in collision off Hankow; 500.

1918, July 6—Columbia; steamer sank in Illinois River at Wesley City; 87.

1918, July 12—Kawachi; Japanese battleship blew up in Tokayama Bay; 500.

1918, Oct. 25—Princess Sophia; Canadian steamer sank off Alaskan coast; 398.

1919, Jan. 17—Chaonia; French steamer lost in Straits of Messina, Italy; 460.

1919, Sept. 9—Valbanera; Spanish steamer lost off Florida coast; 500.

1921, Mar. 18—Hong Kong; steamer wrecked in South China Sea; 1,000.

1922, Aug. 26—Niitaka; Japanese cruiser sank in storm off Kamchatka, USSR; 300.

1923, Apr. 23—Mossamedes; Portuguese mail steamer went aground at Cape Frio, Africa; 220.

1924, Jan. 10—L-24; British submarine in collision off Portland, England; 48.

1924, Mar. 19—No. 43; Japanese submarine in collision off Sasebo, Japan; 49.

1925, Sept. 25—S-51; American submarine in collision with steamer City of Rome off Block Island, R. I.; 34.

1925, Nov. 11—M-1; British submarine in English Channel collision; 69.

1927, Oct. 25—Principessa Mafalda; Italian steamer blew up, sank off Porto Seguro, Brazil; 314.

1927, Dec. 17—S-4; American submarine in collision off Provincetown, Mass.; 40.

1928, Nov. 12—Vestris; British steamer sank in gale off Virginia coast; 113.

1934, Sept. 8—Morro Castle; American steamer, Havana to New York, burned off Asbury Park, N. J.; 125.

1939, May 23—Squalus; American submarine sank off Portsmouth, N. H.; 26.

1941, June 16—O-9; American submarine lost in test dive off Maine; 33.

1942, Feb. 18—Truxton and Pollux; American destroyer and cargo ship ran aground, sank off Newfoundland; 204.

1942, Oct. 2—Curacao; British cruiser sank after collision with liner Queen Mary; 335.

1947, Jan. 19—Himera; Greek steamer hit a mine off Athens; 392.

1947, Apr. 16—Grandcamp; French freighter exploded in Texas City, Tex., Harbor, starting fires; 510.
1949, Sept. 17—Noronic; Canadian Great Lakes steamer burned at Toronto; 119.
1950, Jan. 12—Truculent; British submarine in Thames collision; 65.
1951, Apr. 16—Affray; British submarine lost in English Channel; 75.
1952, Apr. 26—Hobson and Wasp; American destroyer and aircraft carrier collided in Atlantic; 176.
1952, Sept. 24—La Sibylle; French submarine lost off Toulon; 48.
1953, Oct. 16—Leyte; U.S. aircraft carrier damaged by explosion below decks in Boston; 37.
1954, May 26—Bennington; U.S. aircraft carrier damaged by explosions, fire, off Quonset Point, R. I.; 103.
1954, Sept. 26—Toya Maru; Japanese ferry sank in Tsugaru Strait, Japan; 1,172.
1956, July 26—Andrea Doria and Stockholm; Italian liner and Swedish liner collided off Nantucket; 51.
1957, July 14—Eshghabad; Soviet ship ran aground in Caspian Sea; 270.
1959, Jan. 30—Hans Hedtoft; Danish passenger-freighter hit iceberg, Greenland; 95.
1960, Dec. 19—Constellation; U.S. aircraft carrier burned in Brooklyn Navy Yard; 50.
1961, Apr. 8—Dara; British liner burned in Persian Gulf; 212.
1961, July 8—Save; Portuguese ship ran aground off Mozambique; 259.
1963, Feb. 3—Marine Sulphur Queen; American tanker vanished in Gulf of Mexico; 39.
1963, Apr. 10—Thresher; U.S. Navy atomic submarine sank in North Atlantic; 129.
1964, Feb. 10—Voyager, Melbourne; Australian destroyer sank after collision with Australian aircraft carrier Mel-

bourne off New South Wales; 82.
1965, Nov. 13—Yarmouth Castle; Panamanian registered cruise ship burned, sank off Nassau; 89.
1966, Oct. 26—Oriskany; U.S. aircraft carrier caught fire, Gulf of Tonkin; 43.
1967, July 29—Forrestal; U.S. aircraft carrier caught fire off North Vietnam; 134.
'1968, Jan. 25—Dakar; Israeli submarine vanished in Mediterranean; 69.
1968, Jan. 27—Minerve; French submarine vanished in Mediterranean; 52.
1968, May 21—Scorpion; U.S. nuclear submarine sank in Atlantic near Azores; 99.
1969, Jan. 14—Enterprise; U.S. aircraft carrier suffered fires and explosions off Hawaii; 27.
1969, June 2—Evans; U.S. destroyer cut in half by Australian carrier Melbourne, S. China Sea; 74.
1970, Mar. 4—Eurydice; French submarine sank in Mediterranean near Toulon; 57.
1970, Dec. 15—Namyong-Ho; South Korean ferry sank in Korea Strait; 308.
1972, Nov. 15—Merlin; Greek troopship sank after colliding with tanker near Piraeus, Greece; 46.
1973, May 5— Three river boats collided near Dacca, Bangladesh; c. 250.
1973, Dec. 24— Ferry capsized off coast of Ecuador; nearly 200.
1974, Feb. 22— Ferry capsized off Chungmu, So. Korea; 157.
1974, May 1— Motor launch capsized off Bangladesh coast; 250.
1974, Sept. 26— Soviet destroyer burned and sank in Black Sea; est. 200.
1974, Oct. 25— Ferry capsized off Bangladesh coast; over 200.

(See also Chronology)

Floods, Tidal Waves

Date; Location, Number of Deaths—*See also Chronology*

1887	. . . .	Hwang-ho Riv., China.	900,000
1889	May 31	Johnstown, Pa.	2,200
1900	Sept. 8	Galveston, Tex.	5,000
1903	June 15	Heppner, Ore.	325
1911	. . . .	Yangtze River, China.	100,000
1913	Mar. 25-27	Ohio, Indiana.	732
1915	Aug. 17	Galveston, Tex.	275
1927	. . . .	Mississippi River Valley. . . .	214
1928	Mar. 13	Collapse of St. Francis Dam, Santa Paula, Cal. . . .	450
1928	Sept. 13	Lake Okeechobee, Fla.	2,000
1937	Jan. 22	Ohio, Miss. Valleys.	250
1939	. . . .	Northern China.	200,000
1947	. . . .	Honshu Island, Japan.	1,900
1951	Aug.	Manchuria	1,800
1953	Jan. 31	Western Europe.	2,000
1954	Aug. 17	Farahzad, Iran.	2,000
1955	Oct. 7-12	India, Pakistan.	1,700
1959	Nov. 1	Western Mexico.	2,000
1959	Dec. 2	Frejus, France.	412
1960	Oct. 10	East Pakistan.	6,000
1960	Oct. 31	East Pakistan.	4,000
1962	Feb. 17	German North Sea coast. . .	343
1962	Sept. 27	Barcelona, Spain.	445
1963	Oct. 9	Dam collapse, Vaiont, Italy.	1,800
1965	June 11	Sanderson, Tex.	10
1966	Nov. 4-6	Florence, Venice, Italy.	113
1967	Jan. 18-24	Eastern Brazil.	894
1967	Mar. 19	Rio de Janeiro, Brazil.	436
1968	Aug. 7-14	Gujarat state, India.	1,000
1968	Oct. 7	Northeastern India.	780
1969	Jan. 18-26	Southern California.	91
1969	Mar. 17	Mundau Valley, Alagoas, Braz.	218
1969	July 4	Northern Ohio.	41
1969	Oct. 1-8	Tunisia.	500
1969	Aug. 25	Western Virginia.	189
1969	Sept. 15	South Europe.	250
1970	May 20	Central Romania.	160
1970	July 22	Himalayans, India.	500
1971	Feb. 26	Rio de Janeiro, Brazil.	130
1972	June 9	Rapid City, S.D.	236
1972	Aug. 7	Luzon Is., Philippines	454
1974	Mar. 29	Tubaro, Brazil.	1,000
1974	Aug. 12	Bangladesh, Monty-Long. . .	2,500

Major Earthquakes

Date, Location, Number of Deaths—*See also Chronology*

Year		Place	Deaths	Year		Place	Deaths
1057	. . . . . .	China, Chihli	25,000	1875	May 16	Venezuela, Colombia.	16,000
1268	. . . . . .	Asia Minor, Silicia.	60,000	1896	June 15	Japan, sea wave	22,000
1290	Sept. 27	China, Chihli	100,000	1906	Apr. 18-19	Cal., San Francisco	452
1293	May 20	Japan, Kamakura	30,000	1906	Aug. 16	Chile, Valparaiso	1,500
1531	Jan. 26	Portugal, Lisbon.	30,000	1908	Dec. 28	Italy, Messina	75,000
1556	Jan. 24	China, Shensi.	830,000'	1915	Jan. 13	Italy, Avezzano	29,970
1667	Nov.	Caucasia, Shemaka.	80,000	1920	Dec. 16	China, Kansu	180,000
1693	Jan. 11	Italy, Catania.	60,000	1923	Sept. 1	Japan, Tokyo	143,000
1737	Oct. 11	India, Calcutta.	300,000	1932	Dec. 26	China, Kansu	70,000
1755	June 7	Northern Persia.	40,000	1933	Mar. 10	Cal., Long Beach.	115
1755	Nov. 1	Portugal, Lisbon.	60,000	1935	May 31	India, Quetta.	60,000
1783	Feb. 4	Italy, Calabria.	50,000	1939	Jan. 24	Chile, Chillan	30,000
1797	Feb. 4	Ecuador, Quito.	41,000	1939	Dec. 27	Turkey, Erzincan	23,000
1811	Dec. 16	U.S. New Madrid, Mo.		1946	May 31	Eastern Turkey.	1,300
1822	Sept. 5	Asia Minor, Aleppo.	22,000	1946	Dec. 21	Japan, Honshu.	2,000
1828	Dec. 28	Japan, Echigo.	30,000	1948	June 28	Japan, Fukui.	5,131
1868	Aug. 13-15	Peru and Ecuador.	25,000	1949	Aug. 5	Ecuador, Pelileo.	6,000

1950	Aug. 15	India, Assam	1,500
1953	Mar. 18	Northwestern Turkey	1,200
1954	Sept. 9-12	Northern Algeria	1,657
1956	June 10-17	Northern Afghanistan	2,000
1957	July 2	Northern Iran	2,500
1957	Dec. 13	Western Iran	2,000
1960	Feb. 29	Morocco, Agadir	12,000
1960	May 21-30	Southern Chile	5,700
1962	Sept. 1	Northwestern Iran	10,000
1963	July 26	Yugoslavia, Skopje	1,100
1964	Mar. 27	Alaska	131
1966	Aug. 19	Eastern Turkey	2,529
1968	Aug. 31	Northeastern Iran	11,588
1970	Mar. 28	Western Turkey	1,086
1970	May 31	Northern Peru	66,794
1971	Feb. 9	Southern California	65
1972	Apr. 10	Southern Iran	5,057
1972	Dec. 23	Nicaragua	6,000
1974	Dec. 28	Pakistan (9 towns)	5,200

Fires

Date, Location and Number of Persons Killed—See also Chronology

1871	Oct. 8	Chicago, $196,000,000 loss	250
1871	Oct. 9	Peshtigo, Wis., forest fire	1,182
1876	Dec. 5	Brooklyn (N. Y.) Theater	295
1877	June 20	St. John, N. B., Canada	100
1881	Dec. 8	Ring Theater, Vienna	850
1887	May 25	Opera Comique, Paris	200
1887	Sept. 4	Exeter, England, theater	200
1894	Sept. 1	Hinckley, Minn., forest fire	413
1897	May 4	Charity bazaar, Paris	150
1900	June 30	Hoboken, N. J., docks	326
1902	Sept. 20	Church, Birmingham, Ala.	115
1903	Dec. 30	Iroquois Theater, Chicago	602
1904	Feb. 7	Baltimore, Md.	0
1908	Jan. 13	Rhoads Thea., Boyertown, Pa.	170
1908	Mar. 4	School, Collinwood, Ohio	176
1911	Mar. 25	Triangle factory, N. Y. City	145
1914	June 26	1,000 bldgs., Salem, Mass.	0
1918	Apr. 13	Norman, Okla., state hospital	38
1918	Oct. 12	Cloquet, Minn., forest fire	400
1919	June 20	Mayaguez Theater, San Juan	150
1923	May 17	School, Camden, S. C.	76
1924	Dec. 24	School, Hobart, Okla.	35
1929	May 15	Clinic, Cleveland, Ohio	125
1930	Apr. 21	Penitentiary, Columbus, Ohio	320
1931	July 24	Pittsburgh, Pa., home for aged	48
1938	May 16	Atlanta, Ga., Terminal Hotel	35
1940	Apr. 23	Dance hall, Natchez, Miss.	198
1942	Nov. 28	Cocoanut Grove, Boston	491
1943	Sept. 7	Gulf Hotel, Houston	55
1944	July 6	Ringling Circus, Hartford	168
1946	June 5	LaSalle Hotel, Chicago	61
1946	Dec. 7	Winecoff Hotel, Atlanta	119
1946	Dec. 12	New York, ice plant, tenement	37
1949	Apr. 5	Hospital, Effingham, Ill.	77
1950	Jan. 7	Davenport, Ia., Mercy Hospital	41
1953	Mar. 29	Largo, Fla., nursing home	35
1953	Apr. 16	Chicago, metalworking plant	35
1957	Feb. 17	Home for aged, Warrenton, Mo.	72
1957	Nov. 16	Niagara Falls, N. Y., tenement	18
1958	Mar. 19	New York City loft building	24
1958	Nov. 8	Tenement, Montreal, Can.	21
1958	Dec. 1	Parochial school, Chicago	95
1958	Dec. 16	Store, Bogota, Colombia	83
1959	Mar. 5	School near Little Rock, Ark.	24
1959	June 23	Resort hotel, Stalheim, Norway	34
1960	Mar. 12	Pusan, Korea, chemical plant	68
1960	June 11	Liverpool, England, store	22
1960	July 14	Mental hospital, Guatemala City	225
1960	Nov. 13	Movie theater, Amude, Syria	152
1961	Jan. 6	Thomas Hotel, San Francisco	20
1961	May 15	Tenement, Hong Kong	25
1961	Dec. 8	Hospital, Hartford, Conn.	16
1961	Dec. 17	Circus, Niteroi, Brazil	323
1963	May 4	Theater, Diourbel, Senegal	64
1963	Nov. 18	Surfside Hotel, Atlantic City, N.J.	25
1963	Nov. 23	Rest home, Fitchville, Ohio	63
1963	Dec. 29	Roosevelt Hotel, Jacksonville, Fla.	22
1964	May 8	Apartment building, Manila	30
1964	Dec. 18	Nursing Home, Fountaintown, Ind.	20
1965	Mar. 1	Apartment, LaSalle, Canada	28
1965	Dec. 20	Jewish center, Yonkers, N. Y.	12
1966	Mar. 11	Numata, Jap., 2 ski resorts	31
1966	Aug. 13	Melbourne, Austr., hotel	29
1966	Sept. 12	Anchorage, Alaska, hotel	14
1966	Oct. 17	N. Y. City bldg. (firemen)	12
1966	Dec. 7	Erzurum, Turkey, barracks	68
1967	Feb. 7	Restaurant, Montgomery, Ala.	25
1967	May 22	Store, Brussels, Belgium	322
1967	July 16	State prison, Jay, Fla.	37
1968	Jan. 9	Brooklyn, N. Y., tenement	13
1968	Feb. 16	Moberly, Mo., tavern	12
1968	Feb. 26	Shrewsbury, England, hospital	22
1968	May 11	Vijayawada, Ind., wedding hall	58
1968	Nov. 18	Glasgow, Scotland, factory	24
1969	Jan. 26	Victoria Hotel, Dunnville, Ont.	13
1969	Dec. 2	Nursing home, Notre Dame, Can.	54
1970	Jan. 9	Nursing home, Marietta, Ohio.	27
1970	Mar. 20	Hotel, Seattle, Wash.	19
1970	Nov. 1	Dance hall, Grenoble, France	145
1970	Nov. 5	Nursing home, Pointes-aux-Trembles, Que.	17
1970	Dec. 20	Hotel, Tucson, Arizona.	28
1971	Mar. 6	Psychiatric clinic, Burghoezli, Switz.	28
1971	Apr. 20	Hotel, Bangkok, Thailand	24
1971	Oct. 19	Nursing home, Honesdale, Pa.	15
1972	July 5	Sherborne, England, hospital	30
1973	Feb. 6	Paris, France, school	21
1973	Nov. 6	Fukui, Japan, train	28
1973	Nov. 29	Kumamoto, Japan, department store	107
1973	Dec. 2	Seoul, Korea, theater	50
1974	Feb. 1	Sao Paulo, Brazil, bank building	189
1974	June 30	Port Chester, N.Y., discotheque	24
1974	Nov. 3	Seoul, So. Korea, hotel discotheque	88

Major Railroad Wrecks in the U.S.

Source: Federal Railroad Admin., Office of Safety
Date, Location and Number of Persons Killed. See also Chronology

1876	Dec. 29	Ashtabula, Ohio	92
1880	Aug. 11	Mays Landing, N. J.	40
1887	Aug. 10	Chatsworth, Ill.	81
1888	Oct. 10	Mud Run, Pa.	55
1896	July 30	Atlantic City, N. J.	60
1903	Dec. 23	Laurel Run, Pa.	53
1904	Aug. 7	Eden, Col.	96
1904	Sept. 24	New Market, Tenn.	56
1906	Mar. 16	Florence, Col.	35
1906	Oct. 28	Atlantic City, N.J.	40
1906	Dec. 30	Washington, D. C.	53
1907	Jan. 2	Volland, Kans.	33
1907	Jan. 19	Fowler, Ind.	29
1907	Feb. 16	New York City	22
1907	Feb. 23	Colton, Cal.	26
1907	July 20	Salem, Mich.	33
1907	Sept. 15	Canaan, N. H.	24
1910	Mar. 1	Wellington, Wash.	96
1910	Mar. 21	Green Mountain, Ia.	55
1911	Aug. 25	Manchester, N. Y.	29
1912	July 4	East Corning, N. Y.	39
1912	July 5	Ligonier, Pa.	23
1913	Sept. 2	North Haven, Conn.	21
1914	Aug. 5	Tipton Ford, Mo.	43
1914	Sept. 15	Lebanon, Mo.	28
1916	Mar. 29	Amherst, Ohio	27
1917	Feb. 27	Mount Union, Pa.	20
1917	Sept. 28	Kellyville, Okla.	23
1917	Dec. 20	Shepherdsville, Ky.	46
1918	June 22	Ivanhoe, Ind.	68
1918	July 9	Nashville, Tenn.	101
1918	Nov. 2	Brooklyn, N.Y., Malbone St. Tunnel	97
1919	Jan. 12	South Byron, N. Y.	22
1919	July 1	Dunkirk, N. Y.	12
1919	Dec. 20	Onawa, Maine	23
1921	Feb. 27	Porter, Ind.	37
1921	Dec. 5	Woodmont, Pa.	27
1922	Aug. 5	Sulphur Spring, Mo.	34

1922	Dec. 13	Humble, Tex.	22
1923	Sept. 27	Lockett, Wyo.	31
1925	June 16	Hackettstown, N. J.	50
1925	Oct. 27	Victoria, Miss.	21
1926	Sept. 5	Waco, Col.	30
1928	Aug. 24	I.R.T subway, N.Y., Times Sq.	18
1938	June 19	Saugus, Mont.	47
1939	Aug. 12	Harney, Nev.	24
1940	Apr. 19	Little Falls, N. Y.	31
1940	July 31	Cuyahoga Falls, Ohio.	43
1943	Aug. 29	Wayland, N. Y.	27
1943	Sept. 6	Frankford Junction, Philadelphia	79
1943	Dec. 16	Between Rennert and Buie, N.C.	72
1944	July 6	High Bluff, Tenn.	35
1944	Aug. 4	Near Stockton, Ga.	47
1944	Sept. 14	Dewey, Ind.	29
1944	Dec. 31	Bagley, Utah.	50
1945	Aug. 9	Michigan, N. D.	34
1946	Apr. 25	Naperville, Ill.	45

1947	Feb. 18	Gallitzin, Pa.	24
1950	Feb. 17	Rockville Centre, N. Y.	31
1950	Sept. 11	Coshocton, Ohio.	33
1950	Nov. 22	Richmond Hill, N. Y.	79
1951	Feb. 6	Woodbridge, N. J.	84
1951	Nov. 12	Wyuta, Wyo.	17
1951	Nov. 25	Woodstock, Ala.	17
1953	Mar. 27	Conneaut, Ohio	21
1956	Jan. 22	Los Angeles, Cal.	30
1956	Feb. 28	Swampscott, Mass.	13
1956	Sept. 5	Springer, N. M.	20
1957	June 11	Vroman, Col.	12
1958	Sept. 15	Elizabethport, N. J.	48
1960	Mar. 14	Bakersfield, Cal.	14
1962	July 28	Steelton, Pa.	19
1966	Dec. 28	Everett, Mass.	13
1971	June 10	Salem, Ill.	11
1972	Oct. 30	Chicago, Ill.	45

World's worst wreck occurred Dec. 12, 1917, Modane, France, passenger train derailed, 543 killed.

Historic Assassinations Since 1865

1865—Apr. 14. U. S. President Abraham Lincoln, shot in Washington, D. C.; died Apr. 15.

1881—Mar. 13. Alexander II, of Russia—July 2. James A. Garfield, president of the United States, in Washington; died Sept. 19.

1900—July 29. Humbert I, king of Italy.

1901—Sept. 6. U. S. President William McKinley in Buffalo, N.Y., died Sept. 14. Leon Czolgosz executed for the crime Oct. 29.

1913—Feb. 23. Francisco. I. Madero, president of Mexico and José Pino Suarez, the vice-president.—Mar. 18. George, king of Greece.

1914—June 28. Archduke Francis Ferdinand of Austria-Hungary and his wife in Sarajevo, Bosnia (later part of Yugoslavia), by Gavrillo Princip.

1916—Dec. 30. Grigori Rasputin, politically powerful Russian monk.

1918—July 12. Grand Duke Michael of Russia, at Perm.—July 16. Nicholas II, abdicated as czar of Russia; his wife, the Czarina Alexandra; their son, Czarevitch Alexis, and their daughters, Grand Duchesses Olga, Tatiana, Marie, Anastasia, and 4 members of their household were murdered by Bolsheviks at Ekaterinburg.

1920—May 20. Gen. Venustiano Carranza, president of Mexico, in Tiaxcaltenago.

1922—Aug. 22. Michael Collins, Irish revolutionary.

1923—July 20. Gen. Francisco "Pancho" Villa, ex-rebel leader, in Parral, Mexico.

1928—July 17. Gen. Alvaro Obregon, president-elect of Mexico, in San Angel, Mexico.

1933—Feb. 15. In Miami, Fla., Joseph Zangara, anarchist, shot at President-elect Franklin D. Roosevelt, but a woman seized his arm, and the bullet fatally wounded Mayor Anton J. Cermak, of Chicago, who died Mar. 6. Zangara was electrocuted on Mar. 20, 1933.

1934—July 25. In Vienna, Engelbert Dollfuss, Chancellor of Austria, by Nazi, in the chancellery. Otto Planetta convicted and hanged.

1935—Sept. 8. U. S. Senator Huey P. Long, shot in Baton Rouge, La., by Dr. Carl Austin Weiss, who was slain by Long's bodyguards.

1940—Aug. 20. Leon Trotsky (Lev Bronstein), 63, exiled Russian war minister, near Mexico City. Killer, identified as Ramon Mercador del Rio, a Spaniard, served 20 years in Mexican prison.

1948—Jan. 30. Mohanda K. Gandhi, 78, shot in New Delhi, India, by Nathuran Vinayak Godse, 36—Sept. 17. Count Folke Bernadotte, UN mediator for Palestine, ambushed in Jerusalem.

1951—July 20. King Abdul ibn Hussein of Jordan.

1956—Sept. 21. Anastasio Somoza, president of Nicaragua, in Leon; died Sept. 29.

1957—July 26. President Carlos Castillo Armas of Guatemala, in Guatemala City by one of his own guards, who then committed suicide.

1958—July 14. King Faisal of Iraq; his uncle, Crown Prince Abdul Illah, and July 15, Premier Nuri as-Said, by rebels in Baghdad.

1959—Sept. 25. Prime Minister S.W.R.D. Bandaranaike of Ceylon, by Buddhist monk in Colombo.

1961—Jan. 17. Ex-Premier Patrice Lumumba of the Congo, in Katanga Province—May 30. Dominican dictator Rafael Leonidas Trujillo Molina shot to death by assassins near Ciudad Trujillo.

1963—Jan. 13. President Sylvanus Olympio of Togo, by ex-soldiers at Lome.—June 12. Medgar W. Evers, NAACP's Mississippi field secretary, in Jackson, Miss.—Nov. 12. President Ngo Dinh Diem of the Republic of Vietnam and his brother, Ngo Dinh Nhu, in a military coup.—Nov. 22. U. S. President John F. Kennedy fatally shot in Dallas, Tex.; accused Lee Harvey Oswald murdered while awaiting trial.

1965—Jan. 21. Irani Premier Hassan Ali Mansour fatally wounded by assassin in Teheran; 4 executed. —Feb. 21. Malcolm X, Negro nationalist, fatally shot in N. Y. City; 3 sentenced to life.

1966—Sept. 6. Prime Minister Hendrik F. Verwoerd of South Africa stabbed to death in parliament at Capetown by drifter later ruled insane.

1968—Apr. 4. Rev. Dr. Martin Luther King Jr. fatally shot in Memphis, Tenn.; James Earl Ray sentenced to 99 years.—June 5. Sen. Robert F. Kennedy (D-N.Y.) fatally shot in Los Angeles; Sirhan Sirhan, resident alien, sentenced to death.

1969—July 5. Tom Mboya, Kenya's minister of economic planning and development, in Nairobi.—Oct. 17. A. A. Shermarke, president of Somalia, at Las Anos, Somalia.

1971—Nov. 28. Jordan Prime Minister Wasfi Tal, in Cairo, by Palestinian guerrillas.

1973—Mar. 2. U. S. Ambassador Cleo A. Noel Jr., U. S. Charge d'Affaires George C. Moore and Belgian Charge d'Affaires Guy Eid tortured and killed by Palestinian guerrillas in Khartoum.

1974—Aug. 15. Mrs. Park Chung Hee, wife of president of South Korea, hit by bullet meant for her husband. Police said plot was organized in No. Korea.— Aug. 19. U. S. Ambassador to Cyprus Rodger P. Davies, killed by sniper's bullet in Nicosia.

1975—Feb. 11. President Richard Ratsimandrava, 43, of Madagascar, machine-gunned in Tananarive.— Mar. 25. King Faisal of Saudi Arabia shot by nephew Prince Musad Abdel Aziz, 31, in royal palace, Riyadh.

Assassination Attempts

1910—Aug. 6. N. Y. City Mayor Wm. J. Gaynor shot and seriously wounded by discharged city employee.

1912—Oct. 14. Former U. S. President Theodore Roosevelt shot and seriously wounded by demented man in Milwaukee.

1950—Nov. 1. In an attempt to assassinate President Truman, 2 men identified as members of a Puerto Rican nationalist movement — Griselio Torresola and Oscar Collazo — tried to shoot their way into Blair House. Torresola was killed, and a guard, Pvt. Leslie Coffelt was fatally shot. Collazo, wounded, recovered and was tried and convicted Mar. 7, 1951 for the murder of Coffelt. His death sentence was commuted to life imprisonment by President Truman.

1970—Nov. 27. Pope Paul VI unharmed by knife-wielding assailant dressed as priest who attempted to attack him in Manila airport. Benjamin Mendoza, Bolivian, charged with attempted murder.

1972—May 15. Alabama Gov. George Wallace shot in Laurel, Md.; seriously crippled.

1972—Dec. 7. Mrs. Ferdinand E. Marcos, wife of the Philippine president, was stabbed and seriously injured in Pasay City, Philippines.

See also Chronology and Memorable Dates.

Major Kidnapings

Edward A. Cudahy Jr., 16, in Omaha, Neb., **Dec. 18, 1900.** Returned Dec. 20 after $25,000 paid. Pat Crowe confessed.

Robert Franks, 13, in Chicago, **May 22, 1924**, by two youths, Loeb and Leopold, who killed boy. Demand for $10,000 ignored. Loeb died in prison, Leopold paroled 1958, freed 1963.

Charles A. Lindbergh Jr., 20 mos. old, in Hopewell, N.J., **Mar. 1, 1932**; found dead May 12. Ransom of $50,000 was paid to man identified as Bruno Richard Hauptmann, 35, paroled German convict who entered U.S. illegally. Hauptmann passed ransom bill and $14,000 marked money was found in his garage. He was convicted after spectacular trial at Flemington, and electrocuted in Trenton, N.J., prison, Apr. 3, 1936.

William A. Hamm Jr., 39, in St. Paul, **June 15, 1933.** $100,000 paid. Alvin Karpis given life, paroled in 1969.

Charles F. Urschel, in Oklahoma City, **July 22, 1933.** Released July 31 after $200,000 paid. George (Machine Gun) Kelly and 5 others given life.

George Weyerhaeuser, 9, in Tacoma, Wash., **May 24, 1935.** Returned home June 1 after $200,000 paid. Kidnapers given 20 to 60 years.

Charles Mattson, 10, in Tacoma, Wash., **Dec. 27, 1936.** Found dead Jan. 11, 1937. Kidnaper asked $28,000, failed to contact.

Arthur Fried, in White Plains, N. Y., **Dec. 4, 1937.** Body not found. Two kidnapers executed.

Peter Levine, 12, in New Rochelle, N. Y., **Feb. 24, 1938.** Dismembered body found May 29.

Robert C. Greenlease, 6, son of a Kansas City, Mo., motor car dealer, taken from school **Sept. 28, 1953**, and held for $600,000. Body found Oct. 7, when Mrs. Bonnie Brown Heady and Carl A. Hall were arrested. They pleaded guilty and were executed Dec. 18.

Peter Weinberger, 32 days old, Westbury, N.Y., **July 4, 1956**, for $2,000 ransom, not paid. Child found dead. Angelo John LaMarca, 31, convicted, executed.

Cynthia Ruotolo, 6 wks. old, taken from carriage in front of Hamden, Conn. store **Sept. 1, 1956.** Body found in lake.

Lee Crary, 8, in Everett, Wash., **Sept. 22, 1957**, for $10,-000 ransom, not paid. Escaped after 3 days, led police to George E. Collins, convicted.

Eric Peugeot, 4, taken from playground at St. Cloud golf course, Paris, **Apr. 12, 1960.** Released unharmed 3 days later after payment of undisclosed sum to kidnaper who had demanded $100,000. Two sentenced to prison.

Frank Sinatra Jr., 19, from hotel room in Lake Tahoe, Cal., **Dec. 8, 1963.** Released Dec. 11 after his father paid $240,000 ransom. John W. Irwin, Barry W. Keenan and Joseph C. Amsler sentenced to prison; most of ransom recovered.

Barbara Jane Mackle, 20, abducted **Dec. 17, 1968**, from Atlanta, Ga., motel, was found unharmed 3 days later, buried in a coffin-like wooden box 18 inches underground, after her father had paid $500,000 ransom; Gary Steven Krist sentenced to life, Ruth Eisenmann-Schier to 7 years; most of ransom recovered.

Anne Katherine Jenkins, 22, abducted **May 10, 1969**, from her Baltimore apartment, freed 3 days later after her father paid $10,000 ransom; Edward Lee Dull and Marie Calvert charged with crime.

Mrs. Roy Fuchs, 35, and 3 children held hostage 2 hours **May 14, 1969**, in Long Island, N.Y., released after her husband, a bank manager, paid kidnapers $129,000 in bank funds; 4 men arrested, ransom recovered.

C. Burke Elbrick, U.S. ambassador to Brazil, kidnaped by Brazilian revolutionaries in Rio de Janeiro **Sept. 4, 1969**; released 3 days later after Brazil yielded to kidnapers' demands by publishing manifesto and releasing 15 political prisoners.

Patrick Dolan, 18, found shot to death near Sao Paulo, Brazil, **Nov. 5, 1969**, after he was kidnaped and $12,500 paid.

Sean M. Holly, U.S. diplomat, in Guatemala **Mar. 6, 1970**; freed 2 days later upon release of 3 terrorists from prison.

Lt. Col. Donald J. Crowley, U.S. air attache, in Dominican Republic **Mar. 24, 1970**; released after government allowed 20 prisoners to leave the country.

Count Karl von Spreti, W. German ambassador to Guatemala, **Mar. 31, 1970**; slain after Guatemala refused demands for $700,000 and release of 22 prisoners.

Rudy W. Martinez, Guatemalan coffee exporter, by terrorists **Apr. 23, 1970**; released on payment of large ransom.

Pedro Eugenio Arambaru, former Argentine president, by terrorists **May 29, 1970**; body found July 17.

Ehrenfried von Holleben, W. German ambassador to Brazil, by terrorists **June 11, 1970**; freed after release of 40 prisoners.

Daniel A. Mitrione, U.S. diplomat, **July 31, 1970**, by terrorists in Montevideo, Uruguay; body found Aug. 10 after government rejected demands for release of all political prisoners.

Aloysio Dias Gomide, Brazilian vice consul, in Montevideo, **July 31, 1970**; released Feb. 21, 1971, after wife paid ransom estimated at over $250,000.

Claude L. Fly, U.S. agronomist, by terrorists in Montevideo **Aug. 7, 1970**; released Mar. 2, 1971, after suffering illness.

James R. Cross, British trade commissioner, **Oct. 5, 1970**, by French Canadian separatists in Quebec; freed Dec. 3 after 3 kidnapers and relatives flown to Cuba by government.

Pierre Laporte, Quebec Labor Minister, by separatists **Oct. 10, 1970**; body found Oct. 18.

Eugen Beihl, W. German businessman, by Basque separatists, in San Sebastian, Spain, **Dec. 1, 1970**; released Dec. 25 unharmed.

Giovanni E. Bucher, Swiss ambassador **Dec. 7, 1970**, by revolutionaries in Rio de Janeiro; freed Jan. 16, 1971, after Brazil released 70 political prisoners.

Geoffrey Jackson, British ambassador, in Montevideo, **Jan. 8, 1971** by Tupamaro terrorists. Held as ransom for release of imprisoned terrorists, he was released Sept. 9, after the prisoners escaped.

Four U.S. airmen, in Ankara, by Turkish leftist terrorists on **Mar. 4, 1971.** $400,000 ransom was not paid, but they were released unharmed Mar. 8.

Ephraim Elrom, Israel consul general in Istanbul, **May 17, 1971.** Held as ransom for imprisoned terrorists, he was found dead May 23.

Mrs. Virginia Piper, 49, abducted **July 27, 1972**, from her home in suburban Minneapolis; found unharmed near Duluth 2 days later after her husband paid $1 million ransom to the kidnapers.

Victor E. Samuelson, Exxon executive, **Dec. 6, 1973**, in Campana, Argentina, by Marxist guerrillas, freed Apr. 29, 1974, after payment of record $14.2 million ransom.

J. Paul Getty 3d, 17, grandson of the Texas oil mogul, released by kidnapers **Dec. 15, 1973**, in southern Italy after family paid $2.8 million ransom. Kidnapers had severed his right ear, sent it with ransom demand.

Patricia (Patty) Hearst, 19, taken from her Berkeley, Cal., apartment **Feb. 4, 1974**. Symbionese Liberation Army demanded her father, Randolph A. Hearst, publisher, give millions to poor. Hearst offered $2 million in food; the Hearst Corp. offered $4 million worth. Kidnapers objected to way food was distributed. Patricia, in message, said she had joined SLA; she was identified by FBI as taking part in a San Francisco bank holdup, **Apr. 15**; she claimed, in message, she had been coerced. Again identified by FBI in a store holdup, **May 16**, she was classified by FBI as "an armed, dangerous fugitive."

J. Reginald Murphy, 40, an editor of Atlanta (Ga.) Constitution, kidnaped **Feb. 20, 1974**, freed **Feb. 22** after payment of $700,000 ransom by the newspaper. Police arrested William A. H. Williams, a contractor; most of the money was recovered.

J. Guadalupe Zuno Hernandez, 83, father-in-law of Mexican President Luis Echeverria Alvarez, seized by 4 terrorists **Aug. 28, 1974**; government refused to negotiate;

he was released Sept. 8.

E. B. Reville, Hepzibah, Ga., banker and wife Jean kidnaped Sept. 30, 1974. Ransom of $30,000 paid. He was found alive; Mrs. Reville was found dead of carbon monoxide fumes in car trunk Oct. 2.

Jack Teich, Kings Point, N.Y., steel executive, seized Nov. 12, 1974; released Nov. 19 after payment of $750,000.

See also Chronology.

Some Major Tornadoes Since 1925

Source: National Climatic Center, NOAA, Dept. of Commerce

Date	Place	Dead	Date	Place	Dead
1925 Mar. 18	Mo., Ill., Ind.	689	1952 Mar. 21	Ark., Mo., Tenn. (series)	208
1926 Nov. 25	Belleville to Portland, Ark.	53	1953 May 11	Waco, Tex.	114
1927 Apr. 12	Rock Springs, Tex.	74	1953 June 8	Flint to Lakeport, Mich.	116
1927 May 9	Arkansas, Poplar Bluff, Mo.	92	1953 June 9	Worcester and vicinity, Mass.	90
1927 Sept. 29	St. Louis, Mo.	72	1953 Dec. 5	Vicksburg, Miss.	38
1929 Apr. 25	S.E.-Central Ga.	40	1955 May 25	Udall, Kan.	80
1930 May 6	Hill & Ellis Co., Tex.	41	1957 May 20	Williamsburg, Kan. to Ruskin Heights, Mo.	48
1932 Mar. 21	Ala. (series of tornadoes)	200	1958 June 4	Northwestern Wisconsin	30
1936 Apr. 5	Tupelo, Miss.	216	1959 Feb. 10	St. Louis, Mo.	21
1936 Apr. 6	Gainesville, Ga.	203	1960 May 5,6	S. E. Oklahoma, Arkansas	30
1938 Sept. 29	Charleston, S. C.	32	1965 Apr. 11	Ind., Ill., Mich., Wis.	271
1942 Mar. 16	Central to N.E. Miss.	75	1966 Mar. 3	Jackson, Miss.	57
1942 Apr. 27	Rogers & Mayes Co., Okla.	52	1966 Mar. 3	Mississippi, Alabama	61
1944 June 23	Ohio, Pa., W. Va., Md.	150	1967 April 21	Illinois.	33
1945 Apr. 12	Okla.-Ark.	102	1968 May 15	Arkansas	34
1946 Jan. 4	N. E. Texas	30	1969 Jan. 23	Mississippi	32
1947 Apr. 9	Texas, Okla. & Kans.	169	1970 Apr. 18	Texas Panhandle (series)	25
1948 Mar. 19	Bunker Hill & Gillespie, Ill.	33	1970 May 11	Lubbock, Tex.	26
1949 Jan. 3	La. & Ark.	58	1971 Feb. 21	Miss. delta	110

Number of Tornadoes in U.S. Since 1924, Deaths

Year	No.	Deaths	Year	No.	Deaths	Year	No.	Deaths	Year	No.	Deaths
1924	130	376	1937	147	29	1950	199	70	1963	461	31
1925	119	794	1938	213	183	1951	272	34	1964	713	73
1926	111	144	1939	152	87	1952	236	230	1965	899	298
1927	163	540	1940	124	65	1953	437	516	1966	570	99
1928	203	92	1941	118	53	1954	549	35	1967	912	116
1929	197	274	1942	167	384	1955	593	125	1968	661	131
1930	192	179	1943	152	58	1956	532	83	1969	604	66
1931	94	36	1944	169	275	1957	864	191	1970	649	73
1932	151	394	1945	121	210	1958	565	66	1971	888	156
1933	258	362	1946	106	78	1959	589	58	1972	84	27*
1934	147	47	1947	165	313	1960	618	47	1973	1109†	87
1935	180	70	1948	183	140	1961	682	51	1974	945	361
1936	151	552	1949	249	212	1962	658	28	Total	20,886	10,943

*Record low; †Record high.   Average.....:.409   214

Hurricanes, Typhoons, Blizzards, Other Storms

Date, Locations, Number of Deaths—*See also Chronology*—Names of hurricanes and typhoons in italics

Date	Location	Deaths	Date	Location	Deaths
1888 Mar. 11-14	Blizzard, East U. S.	400	1964 Sept. 5	*T. Ruby*, Hong Kong and China	735
1900 Sept. 8	Hurricane, Galveston, Tex.	6,000	1964 Sept. 14	Flooding, Central S. Korea	563
1926 Sept. 16-22	Hurricane, Fla., Ala.	372	1964 Nov. 12	Flooding, S. Vietnam.	7,000
1926 Oct. 20	Hurricane, Cuba.	600	1965 May 11-12	Windstorm, E. Pakistan	17,000
1928 Sept. 12-17	Hurricane, W. Indies, Fla.	4,000	1965 June 1-2	Windstorm, E. Pakistan	30,000
1930 Sept. 3	Hurricane, San Domingo.	2,000	1965 Sept. 7-10	*H. Betsy*, Fla., Miss., La.	74
1938 Sept. 21	Hurricane, New England.	600	1965 Dec. 15	Windstorm, E. Pakistan.	10,000
1942 Oct. 15-16	Hurricane, Bengal, India	11,000	1966 June 4-10	*H. Alma*, Honduras, s.e. U. S.	51
1944 Sept. 12-16	Hurricane, N.C. to New Eng.	389	1966 Sept. 24-30	*H. Inez*, Carib., Fla., Mex.	293
1953 Sept. 25-27	Typhoon, Vietnam, Japan.	1,300	1967 July 9	*T. Billie*, Japan.	347
1954 Aug. 30	*H. Carol*, northeast U. S.	68	1967 Sept. 5-23	*H. Beulah*, Carib., Mex., Tex.	54
1954 Sept. 11	*H. Edna*, n.e. US., Canada	23	1967 Dec. 20	Blizzard, southwest U. S.	51
1954 Oct. 12-16	*H. Hazel*, east U.S., Haiti.	347	1968 Nov. 18-28	*T. Nina*, Philippines.	63
1955 Aug. 12-13	*H. Connie*, Carolinas, Va., Md.	43	1969 Aug. 17-18	*H. Camille*, Miss., La.	258
1955 Aug. 18-19	*H. Diane*, eastern U. S.	400	1969 July 4-5	Flooding, Wind and electrical storms, N. Ohio.	41
1955 Sept. 19	*H. Hilda*, Mexico	200			
1955 Sept. 22-28	*H. Janet*, Caribbean	500	1970 July 30-Aug 5	*H. Celia*, Cuba, Fla., Tex.	31
1956 Feb. 1-29	Blizzard, western Europe	1,000	1970 Aug. 20-21	*H. Dorothy*, Martinique.	42
1957 June 27-30	*H. Audrey*, La., Tex.	430	1970 Sept. 15	*T. Georgia*, Philippines	300
1958 Feb. 15-16	Blizzard, n.e. U. S.	171	1970 Oct. 14	*T. Sening*, Philippines	583
1959 Sept. 17-19	*T. Sarah*, Far East.	2,000	1970 Oct. 15	*T. Titang*, Philippines.	526
1959 Sept. 26-27	*T. Vera*, Honshu, Japan.	4,466	1970 Nov. 13	Cyclone, East Pakistan est.	300,000
1960 Sept. 4-12	*H. Donna*, Caribbean, e. U. S.	148	1971 Aug. 1	*T. Rose*, Hong Kong.	130
1962 Feb. 17	Flooding, German North Sea Coast.	343	1972 June 19-29	*H. Agnes*, Fla. to N. Y.	118
			1972 Dec. 3	*T. Theresa*, Philippines.	169
1962 Sept. 27	Flooding, Barcelona, Spain.	445	1973 June-Aug.	Monsoon rains in India.	1,217
1963 May 28-29	Windstorm, E. Pakistan	22,000	1974 June 11	Storm *Dinah*, Luzon Is., Philip.	71
1963 Oct. 4-8	*H. Flora*, Cuba, Haiti.	6,000	1974 July 11	*T. Gilda*, Japan, So. Korea.	108
1964 Oct. 4-7	*H. Hilda*, La., Miss., Ga.	38	1974 Sept. 19-20	*H. Fifi*, Honduras.	2,000
1964 June 30	*T. Winnie*, N. Philippines.	107	1974 Dec. 25	Cyclone leveled Darwin, Aus.	50

Explosions

Date, Location, Number of Deaths—*See also Marine Disasters, Fires and Chronology*

Date	Location	Deaths	Date	Location	Deaths
1910 Oct. 1	Los Angeles Times Bldg.	21	1917 Dec. 6	Halifax Harbor, Canada.	1,654
1913 Mar. 7	Dynamite, Baltimore harbor.	55	1918 July 2	Explosives, Split Rock, N. Y.	50
1915 Sept. 27	Gasoline tank car, Ardmore, Okla.	47	1918 Oct. 4	Shell plant, Morgan Station, N.J.	64
1917 Apr 10	Munitions plant, Eddystone, Pa.	133	1919 May 22	Food plant, Cedar Rapids, Ia.	44

1920 Sept. 16	Wall Street, New York, bomb....		30
1924 Jan. 3	Food plant, Pekin, Ill............		42
1937 Mar. 18	New London, Tex., school.......		294
1940 Sept. 11	Hercules Powder, Kenvil, N. J....		51
1942 June 5	Ordnance plant, Elwood, Ill.......		49
1944 Apr. 14	Bombay, India, harbor..........		700
1944 July 17	Port Chicago, Calif., pier........		322
1944 Oct. 21	Liquid gas tank, Cleveland.......		135
1947 Apr. 16	Texas City, Tex., pier		561
1948 July 28	Farben works, Ludwigshafen, Ger.		184
1950 May 19	Munition barges, S. Amboy, N. J..		30
1956 Aug. 7	Dynamite trucks, Cali, Colombia..		1,100
1958 Apr. 18	Sunken munitions ship, Okinawa..		40
1958 May 22	Nike missiles, Leonardo, N. J....		10
1959 Apr. 10	World War II bomb, Philippines..		38
1959 June 2	Gas truck, Penn. Turnpike.......		10
1959 June 28	Rail tank cars, Meldrin, Ga.......		25
1959 Aug. 7	Dynamite truck, Roseburg, Ore...		13
1959 Nov. 2	Jamuri Bazar, India, explosives...		46
1959 Dec. 13	Dortmund, Ger., 2 apt. bldgs......		26
1960 Mar. 4	Belgian munition ship, Havana...		100
1960 Oct. 25	Gas, Windsor, Ont., store........		11
1962 Jan. 16	Gas pipeline, Alberta, Canada....		19
1962 Mar. 3	Gasoline truck, Syria............		31
1962 Oct. 3	Telephone Co. office, N. Y. City...		23
1963 Jan. 2	Packing plant, Terre Haute, Ind...		16
1963 Mar. 9	Dynamite plant, So. Africa.......		45
1963 Mar. 9	Steel plant, Belecke, W. Germany.		19
1963 Aug. 13	Explosives dump, Gauhiti, India..		32
1963 Oct. 31	State Fair Coliseum, Indianapolis.		73
1964 July 23	Bone, Algeria, harbor munitions..		100
1965 Mar. 4	Gas pipeline Natchitoches, La.....		17
1965 Aug. 9	Missile silo, Searcy, Ark.........		53
1965 Oct. 21	Bridge, Tila Bund, Pakistan......		80
1965 Oct. 30	Marketplace, Cartagena, Col......		48
1965 Nov. 24	Armory, Keokuk, Iowa...........		20
1966 Oct. 13	Chemical plant, La Salle, Que.....		11
1967 Feb. 17	Chemical plant, Hawthorne, N.J...		11
1967 Dec. 25	Apartment bldg., Moscow.........		20
1968 Apr. 6	Sports store, Richmond, Ind.......		43
1970 Apr. 8	Subway construction, Osaka, Japan...................		73
1970 Nov. 11	Oil well, Tulsa, Okla.............		9
1970 Dec. 11	Tavern building, N. Y. City.......		9
1971 June 24	Tunnel, Sylmar, Calif............		17
1971 June 28	School, fireworks, Pueblo, Mex....		13
1971 Oct. 21	Shopping center, Glasgow, Scot....		20
1973 Feb. 10	Liquified gas tank, Staten Is., N.Y..		40

Principal Mine Disasters in the U. S.
Source: Bureau of Mines

Note: Prior to 1968, only disasters with losses of 50 or more lives are listed; for 1968-72, all disasters in which 5 or more men are killed are listed. Only fatalities to mining company employees are included. All Bituminous-coal mines unless otherwise specified.

Date	Location	Killed	Date	Location	Killed
1855 Mar.	Coalfield, Va..................	55	1915 Mar. 2	Layland, W. Va..............	112
1867 Apr. 3	Winterpock, Va...............	69	1917 Apr. 27	Hastings, Col...............	121
1869[1] Sept. 6	Plymouth, Pa.................	110	1917[2] Jun. 8	Butte, Mont.................	163
1883 Feb. 16	Braidwood, Ill................	69	1917 Aug. 4	Clay, Ky....................	62
1884 Jan. 24	Crested Butte, Col............	59	1919[1] Jun. 5	Wilkes-Barre, Pa............	92
1884 Mar. 13	Pocahontas, Va...............	112	1922 Nov. 6	Spangler, Pa................	77
1891 Jan. 27	Mount Pleasant, Pa...........	109	1922 Nov. 22	Dolomite, Ala...............	90
1892 Jan. 7	Krebs, Okla..................	100	1923 Feb. 8	Dawson, N.M................	120
1895 Mar. 20	Red Canyon, Wyo.............	60	1923 Aug. 14	Kemmerer, Wyo.............	99
1896[1] June 28	Pittston, Pa..................	58	1924 Mar. 8	Castle Gate, Utah............	171
1900 Jan. 1	Scofield, Utah................	200	1924 Apr. 28	Benwood, W. Va.............	119
1902 May 19	Coal Creek, Tenn.............	184	1925 Feb. 20	Sullivan, Ind................	52
1902 Jul. 10	Johnstown, Pa................	112	1925 May 27	Coal Glen, N.C..............	53
1903 Jun. 30	Hanna, Wyo..................	169	1925 Dec. 10	Acmar, Ala..................	53
1904 Jan. 25	Cheswick, Pa.................	179	1926 Jan. 13	Wilburton, Okla..............	91
1905 Feb. 20	Virginia City, Ala............	112	1926[2] Nov. 3	Ishpeming, Mich.............	51
1907 Jan. 29	Stuart W. Va.................	84	1927 Apr. 30	Everettville, W. Va...........	97
1907 Dec. 6	Monongah, W. Va.............	361	1928 May 19	Mather, Pa..................	195
1907 Dec. 16	Yolande, Ala.................	57	1929 Dec. 17	McAlester, Okla.............	61
1907 Dec. 19	Jacobs Creek, Pa.............	239	1930 Nov. 5	Millfield, Ohio..............	79
1908 Mar. 28	Hanna, Wyo..................	59	1932 Dec. 23	Moweaqua, Ill...............	54
1908 Nov. 28	Marianna, Pa.................	154	1940 Jan. 10	Bartley, W. Va..............	91
1908 Dec. 29	Switchback, W. Va............	50	1940 Mar. 16	St. Clairsville, Ohio..........	72
1909 Jan. 12	Switchback, W. Va............	67	1940 Jul. 15	Portage, Pa.................	63
1909 Nov. 13	Cherry, Ill...................	259	1942 May 12	Osage, W. Va................	56
1910 Jan. 31	Primero, Col.................	75	1943 Feb. 27	Washoe, Mont...............	74
1910 May 5	Palos, Ala...................	90	1944 Jul. 5	Belmont, Ohio...............	66
1910 Oct. 8	Starkville, Col...............	56	1947 Mar. 25	Centralia, Ill................	111
1910 Nov. 8	Delagua, Col.................	79	1951 Dec. 21	West Frankfort, Ill...........	119
1911 Apr. 7	Throop, Pa...................	72	1968[3] Mar. 6	Calumet, La.................	21
1911 Apr. 8	Littleton, Ala................	128	1968 Aug. 7	Greenville, Ky..............	9
1911 Dec. 9	Briceville, Tenn..............	84	1968 Nov. 20	Farmington, W. Va...........	78
1912 Mar. 20	McCurtain, Okla..............	73	1970 Dec. 30	Hyden, Ky..................	38
1912 Mar. 26	Jed, W. Va...................	83	1971[2] Apr. 12	Rosiclare, Ill................	7
1913 Apr. 23	Finleyville, Pa...............	96	1972[2] May 2	Kellogg, Idaho..............	91
1913 Oct. 22	Dawson, N.M.................	263	1972 Jul. 22	Blacksville, W. Va...........	9
1914 Apr. 28	Eccles, W. Va................	181	1972 Dec. 16	Itmann, W. Va...............	5
1914 Oct. 27	Royalton, Ill.................	52			

World's worst mine disaster killed 1,549 workers in Honkeiko Colliery in Manchuria Apr. 25, 1942.

(1) Anthracite mine. (2) Metal mine. (3) Nonmetal mine.

Some Notable Aircraft Disasters Since 1937

Date	Aircraft	Site of Accident	Deaths
1937 May 6	German zeppelin Hindenburg........	Burned at mooring, Lakehurst, N. J.....................	36
1944 Aug. 23	U.S. Air Force B-24..............	Hit school, Freckelton, England...................	76[1]
1945 July 28	U.S. Army B-25.................	Hit Empire State bldg., N.Y.C....................	14[1]
1949 Nov. 1	Eastern Air Lines DC-4............	Rammed by Bolivian P-38, Wash., D.C...........	55
1952 Dec. 20	U. S. Air Force C-124.............	Fell, burned, Moses Lake, Wash..................	87
1953 Mar. 3	Canadian Pacific Comet Jet.........	Karachi, Pakistan...................	11[2]
1953 June 18	U. S. Air Force C-124.............	Crashed, burned near Tokyo...................	129
1955 Nov. 1	United Air Lines DC-6B...........	Exploded, crashed near Longmont, Col...........	44[3]
1956 June 20	Venezuelan Super-Constellation....	Crashed in Atlantic off Asbury Park, N. J...........	74
1956 June 30	TWA Super-Const., United DC-7....	Collided over Grand Canyon, Arizona.............	128
1957 Aug. 11	Maritime, Central Airways DC-4....	Crashed in swamp near Quebec...................	79

1960 July 27	Sikorsky S-58 helicopter	Crashed in Chicago suburbs	13[4]
1960 Dec. 16	United DC-8 jet, TWA Super-Constellation	Collided over New York City	134[5]
1961 Sept. 10	President Airlines DC-6	Crashed at Shannon, Ireland	83
1961 Nov. 8	Imperial Airlines Constellation	Crashed near Richmond, Va	77[6]
1962 Mar. 1	Amer. Airlines Boeing 707 jet	Crashed after takeoff, New York City	95
1962 Mar. 4	Br. Caledonian Airlines DC-7C	Crashed near Douala, Cameroun	111
1962 Mar. 16	Flying Tiger Super-Const	Vanished in western Pacific	107
1962 June 3	AirFrance Boeing 707 jet	Crashed on takeoff from Paris	130
1962 June 22	Air France Boeing 707 jet	Crashed in storm, Guadeloupe, W. I	113
1963 June 3	Chartered Northw. Airlines DC-7	Crashed in Pacific off British Columbia	101
1963 Nov. 29	Trans-Canada Airlines DC-8F	Crashed after takeoff from Montreal	118
1963 Dec. 8	Pan American Boeing 707	Crashed near Elkton, Md	82
1964 Feb. 29	Br. Eagle Bristol Britannia	Crashed near Innsbruck, Austria	83
1964 Mar. 1	Paradise Airline Constellation	Crashed in snow storm, Lake Tahoe, Cal	85
1965 Feb. 8	Eastern Air Lines DC-7B	Plunged into Atlantic after takeoff, New York	84
1965 May 20	Pakistani Boeing 720-B	Crashed at Cairo, Egypt, airport	121
1966 Jan. 24	Air India Boeing 707 jetliner	Crashed on Mont Blanc, France-Italy	117
1966 Feb. 4	All-Nippon Boeing 727	Plunged into Tokyo Bay	133
1966 Mar. 5	BOAC Boeing 707 jetliner	Crashed on Japan's Mount Fuji	124
1966 Apr. 22	Military-chartered Electra	Crashed in storm near Ardmore, Okla	82
1966 Dec. 24	U. S. military-chartered, CL-44	Crashed into village in South Vietnam	129[1]
1967 Mar. 9	TWA DC-9, Beechcraft	Collided in air at Urbana, Ohio	26
1967 Apr. 20	Swiss Britannia turboprop	Crashed at Nicosia, Cyprus	126
1967 July 19	Piedmont Boeing 727, Cessna 310	Collided in air, Hendersonville, N. C	82
1968 Apr. 20	S. African Airways Boeing 707	Crashed on takeoff, Windhoek, S. W. Africa	122
1968 May 3	Braniff International Electra	Crashed in storm near Dawson, Tex	85
1968 Sept. 11	Air France Caravelle	Caught fire, crashed off Nice, France	95
1969 Mar. 16	Venzuelan DC-9	Crashed after takeoff from Maracaibo, Venezuela	155[7]
1969 Mar. 20	United Arab Ilyushin-18	Crashed at Aswan airport	87
1969 June 4	Mexican Boeing 727	Rammed into mountain near Monterrey, Mexico	79
1969 Sept. 9	Allegheny DC-9	Collided with student pilot's plane, Shelbyville, Ind	83
1969 Nov. 20	Nigerian VC-10	Crashed near Iju, Nigeria	87
1969 Dec. 8	Olympia Airways DC-6B	Crashed near Athens in storm	93
1970 Feb. 15	Dominican DC-9	Crashed into sea on takeoff from Santo Domingo	102
1970 July 3	British chartered jetliner	Crashed near Barcelona, Spain	112
1970 July 5	Air Canada DC-8	Crashed near Toronto International Airport	108
1970 Aug. 9	Peruvian turbojet	Crashed after takeoff from Cuzco, Peru	101[1]
1970 Oct. 2	Chartered Martin 404	Crashed in Rocky Mts. near Silver Plume, Col	30[8]
1970 Nov. 14	Southern Airways DC-9	Crashed in mountains near Huntington, W. Va	75[9]
1970 Dec. 31	Soviet Aeroflot Ilyushin 18	Crashed on takeoff, Leningrad	90
1971 July 30	All-Nippon Boeing 727, Japanese Air Force F-86	Collided over Morioka, Japan	162[7]
1971 Aug.	Soviet Aeroflot Tupolev-104	Crashed at Irkutsk airport, USSR	97
1971 Sept. 4	Alaska Airlines Boeing 727	Crashed into mountain near Juneau, Alaska	111
1972 Mar. 14	Danish Airliner	Crashed near Dubai, U. of A. Emirates	112
1972 Aug. 14	E. German Ilyushin-62	Crashed on take-off East Berlin	156
1972 Oct. 13	Aeroflot Ilyushin-62	E. German airline crashed near Moscow	176
1972 Dec. 4	Chartered Spanish airliner	Crashed on take-off, Canary Islands	155
1972 Dec. 29	Eastern Airlines Lockheed Tristar	Crashed on approach to Miami Int'l. Airport	100
1973 Jan. 22	Chartered Boeing 707	Burst into flames during landing, Kano Airport, Nigeria	176
1973 Apr. 10	British Vanguard turboprop	Crashed during snowstorm at Basel, Switzerland	104
1973 June 3	Soviet Supersonic TU-144	Exploded in air near Goussainville, Franc	14[11]
1973 July 11	Brazilian Boeing 707	Crashed on approach to Orly airport Paris	122
1973 July 31	Delta Airlines jetliner	Crashed on landing in heavy fog at Logan Int'l. Airport, Boston	89
1973 Aug. 13	Spanish Caravelle jet	Exploded and crashed near La Coruna, Spain	85
1973 Dec. 23	French Caravelle jet	Crashed in Morocco	106
1974 Jan. 31	Pan American Boeing 707 jet	Crashed in Pago Pago, American Samoa	96
1974 Mar. 3	Turkish DC-10 jet	Crashed at Ermenonville near Paris	345
1974 Apr. 23	Pan American 707 jet	Crashed in Bali, Indonesia	107
1974 Sept. 8	TWA 707 jet	Crashed in Ionian Sea off Greece, after bomb explosion; Arab guerrilla group claimed responsibility	80
1975 Apr. 4	Air Force Galaxy C-58	Crashed near Saigon, So. Vietnam, after takeoff with load of orphans	172
1975 June 24	Eastern Airlines 727 jet	Crashed short of landing strip in storm, JFK Airport, N.Y.	112

(1) Including those on the ground and in buildings. (2) First fatal crash of commercial jet plane. (3) Caused by bomb planted by John G. Graham in insurance plot to kill his mother, a passenger. (4) First crash of commercial helicopter. (5) Including all 128 aboard the planes and 6 on ground. (6) Including 74 Army recruits. (7) Killed 84 on plane and 71 on ground. (8) Including 13 members of Wichita State U. football team. (9) Including 43 Marshall U. football player and coaches. (10) Airline-fighter crash, pilot of fighter parachuted to safety, was arrested for negligence. (11) First supersonic plane crash killed 6 crewmen and 8 on the ground; there were no passengers.

Record Oil Spills, 1967-1971

Source: U. S. Geological Survey, Conservation Division

Name and Place	Date		Cause of Spill	Barrels
Tanker, Torrey Canyon, England	Mar. 18,	1967	Grounding	700,000
Tanker, World Glory, South Africa	June 13,	1968	Hull failure	322,000
Tanker, Atlantic Ocean	Mar. 27,	1971	Sinking	220,000
Tanker, Keo, Massachusetts	Nov. 5,	1969	Hull failure	210,000
Storage tank, Sewaren, N. J.	Nov.	1969	Tank failure	200,000
Pipeline, West Delta area, La.	Oct. 15,	1967	Anchor dragging	160,000
Tanker, Japan	Nov. 30,	1971	Tanker broke in half	149,080
Tanker, R. C. Stoner, Wake Island	Sept. 6,	1967	Grounding	143,300
Tanker, Andron, West African coast	May 5,	1968	Sinking	117,000

ASTRONOMY AND CALENDAR

Edited by Dr. Kenneth L. Franklin, Astronomer
American Museum-Hayden Planetarium

Celestial Events Highlights, 1976
(All Times are Greenwich Mean Time)

A rare event will be observable over most of North America on the evening of April 8th; Mars will occult the star Epsilon Geminorum. Mars is then about magnitude +1.2 and the star is +3.2. Although Mars is a little over 4,000 miles in diameter, at its distance this night of 137.58 million miles it appears as a disk 6.3 seconds of arc across. The geometric shadow of Mars in the light of the star is a cylinder also about 4,000 miles in diameter, but the atmosphere of the planet may cause a slight taper so that at the earth the diameter may be smaller. Astronomers can use this event to study the atmosphere of Mars and to improve the mathematics of motions in the solar system.

The moon occults several planets and Spica this year, in addition to occulting many faint stars. Only the occultations of Neptune on March 21 and May 4, and of Spica August 28, can be seen from parts of North America. Other occultations noted below refer to close approaches of the moon to the object. These close approaches may have esthetic and photographic appeal.

The two lunar eclipses are rather uninteresting and do not involve North America. The solar eclipses are not visible here, but they may be worth traveling to see them. The April eclipse is annular and seldom observed by professionals, but the experience may be rewarding if the eclipse is short enough. The October eclipse is total and visible from land only in the southeastern tip of Australia where totality will last about 3 minutes.

The planets are not spectacular this year, Saturn being in opposition in January and Jupiter in November. Venus will serve as a holiday star being bright in the western sky this winter and appearing with the crescent moon on December 24.

January

Mercury is 7° south of a beautiful thin crescent moon (only 39 hours past New Moon) on the 3d; at greatest eastern elongation (19° east of the sun) the brightest stellar object in western Capricornus on the 7th; stationary on the 13th and at inferior conjunction on the 23d, 61.8 million miles from earth, when it becomes a morning star.

Venus is the brilliant Morning Star just 7° north of red Antares at dawn of the 8th. An opportunity to find **Neptune** occurs at dawn on the 12th, when it will be about 0° .5 south and west of Venus. Use binoculars to find 8th magnitude Neptune in Ophiuchus about halfway between Antares and Eta Ophiuchi. Neptune is 2.9 billion miles from Earth at this time. Venus is 2° south of the waning crescent moon on the 28th.

Mars is in Taurus near Elnath (Beta Tauri) and in retrograde motion after having been at opposition 1975 December 15th. About magnitude —1.4 at the first of the month, it drops to about —0.2 at the end. It is 5° north of the gibbous moon on the 14th. It is stationary on the 20th, and resumes its direct motion thereafter.

Jupiter is 4° south of the First Quarter Moon on the 9th. It is about —2 magnitude all month, outshining any star in Pisces by over 250 times.

Saturn is in opposition 752 million miles away on the 20th, after appearing a star of magnitude zero in Cancer, 5° north of the moon on the 17th. This is the best time to observe this beautiful planet. After opposition, it is an evening star.

Moon passes Mercury on the 3rd, Jupiter on the 9th, occults Ceres on the 13th, passes Mars on the 14th, Saturn on the 17th, occults Spica on the 23d and Neptune on the 26th, and passes Venus on the 28th. New Moon, 1st; First Quarter, 9th; Full Moon, 17th; Last Quarter, 23d. Apogee, 8th (251,300 miles); perigee, 20th (228,000 miles).

Jan. 4 — Earth at perihelion, 91.45 million miles from the sun. Quadrantid meteor shower may peak tonight; the moon sets early.

Jan. 19 — Sun enters Capricornus.

Jan. 20 — Saturn in opposition in Cancer.

Jan. 23 — Mercury in inferior conjunction.

February

Mercury is stationary on the 3d, and at greatest western elongation (26° from the sun) on the 16th in western Capricornus, south of its position on the 3d of January.

Venus is approaching the sun and is becoming lost in the brightening dawn twilight. It is 6° south of the thin crescent moon on the 27th.

Mars is about zero magnitude all month in Taurus, and is 5° north of the gibbous moon on the 10th.

Jupiter is still bright in Pisces, 4° south of the thick crescent moon on the 6th.

Saturn, in retrograde motion in Cancer, is 5° north of the gibbous moon on the 13th.

Moon passes Jupiter on the 6th, Mars on the 10th, Saturn on the 13th, occults Juno on the 16th, Spica on the 19th, and Neptune on the 23d, passes Venus on the 27th and Mercury on the 28th. First Quarter, 8th; Full Moon, 15th; Last Quarter, 22d; New Moon on Leap Day, 29th. Apogee, 5th (251,700 miles); perigee, 17th (224,500 miles).

Feb. 16 — Sun enters Aquarius.

March

Mercury is uninteresting this month.

Venus is lost in the morning glare of the sun. It is 6° south of the moon on the 29th.

Mars is 6° north of the First Quarter Moon on the 9th and crosses into Gemini in mid-month.

Jupiter is 3° south of the moon on the 4th in Pisces, and by month's end is lost in the bright evening twilight.

Saturn is 5° north of the moon on the 12th and resumes its direct motion on the 27th when it is stationary in Gemini.

Moon passes Jupiter on the 4th, Mars on the 9th, Saturn on the 12th, occults Spica on the 17th, Uranus on the 18th and Neptune on the 21st, and passes Venus on the 29th. First apogee, 4th (252,300 miles), perigee, 16th (222,200 miles), second apogee, 31st (252,600 miles).

Mar. 11 — Sun enters Pisces.

Mar. 20 — Spring begins in the Northern Hemisphere at 11:50 AM, Greenwich Time (6:50 AM, EST). At that time the sun is overhead at the equator in the Gulf of Guinea almost due south of Lagos, Nigeria. The sun will remain north of the equator for 186 days 9 hours 58 minutes.

Mar. 21 — The Moon occults Neptune about 10 AM GMT (5 AM EST, 2 AM PST). This occultation is visible for anyone in most of North America who has good binoculars or telescopes. Neptune appears as an 8th magnitude star in southern Ophiuchus, northeast of Antares.

Mar. 27 — Saturn is stationary in Gemini.

Mar. 30 — Pluto is in opposition in Virgo just north of Epsilon Virginis. It is 2.76 billion miles away from Earth, and resembles a star of magnitude 14.

April

Mercury is in superior conjunction, becoming an evening star on the 1st, 125 million miles away. It passes 1° .9 north of Jupiter on the 12th and is at greatest eastern elongation on the 28th, 21° east of the sun. This is a good chance to find zero magnitude Mercury in the western sky. It will set a little more than 2 hours after the sun.

Venus, lost in the sun's glare, is 3° south of the moon on the 28th.

Mars is 7° north of the moon on the 7th, in Gemini, now fainter than 1st magnitude, and occults Epsilon Geminorum on the 8th.

Jupiter is 2° south of the moon on the 1st, 1° .9 south of Mercury on the 12th, and in conjunction with the sun on the 27th, 556 million miles away, when it becomes a morning star.

Saturn is 6° north of the moon on the 8th.

Moon passes Jupiter on the 1st, Mars on the 7th, Saturn on the 8th, occults Spica on the 14th, Uranus on the 15th, Neptune on the 17th, passes Venus on the 28th, and provides us with an annular eclipse of the sun of the 29th. First Quarter, 7th; Full Moon, 14th; Last Quarter, 21st; New Moon, 29th. Perigee, 14th (221,800 miles); apogee, 27 (252,500 miles). Perigee precedes Full Moon by about 5 hours. Tidal range may be extreme on this day, with exceptional highs and lows.

Apr. 1 — Mercury in superior conjunction.

Apr. 8 — Occultation of Epsilon Geminorum by Mars.

Apr. 18 — Sun enters Aries.

Apr. 25 — Uranus at opposition, 1.63 billion miles from earth.

Apr. 27 — Jupiter in conjunction.

Apr. 29 — Annular eclipse of the sun.

May

Mercury is 4° north of the Moon on the 1st, stationary on the 9th in Taurus, and at inferior conjunction on the 20th, 51.3 million miles away, when it becomes a morning star.

Venus, too near the Sun to be seen easily in the morning sky, is 0° .2 south of Jupiter on the 11th, and about 1° north of the moon on the 28th.

Mars, nearly as faint as a 2d magnitude star in Gemini, is 5° south of Pollux and 7° north of the Moon on the 5th, passes into Cancer on the 11th, and is 1° .3 north of Saturn on the 12th.

Jupiter, in Aries, is occulted by the moon on the 27th.

Saturn is 6° north of the moon on the 5th, 1° .3 south of Mars on the 12th.

Moon passes Mercury on the 1st, Mars and Saturn on the 5th, occults Spica on the 11th and Uranus on the 12th, is partially eclipsed on the 13th, occults 8th magnitude Neptune for some North American viewers on the 15th, and occults Jupiter on the 27th. First Quarter, 7th; Full Moon, 15th; Last Quarter, 29th; New Moon, 29th. Perigee, 12th (223,200 miles); apogee, 25th (252,000 miles).

May 11 — Venus 0° .2 south of Jupiter. Binoculars are necessary because of the bright morning twilight.

May 13 — Partial eclipse of the moon. Sun moves into Taurus.

May 15 — Occultation of Neptune.

June

Mercury is stationary in Taurus and resumes direct motion on the 1st. At greatest western elongation (23° from the sun) on the 15th, it is 3° north of Aldebaran on the 22d, and is occulted by the moon on the 25th.

Venus is in superior conjunction on the 18th, 161 million miles away, and becomes an evening star, although still lost in the sun's glare.

Mars is 7° north of the moon on the 3d, and, looking like a 2d magnitude star, moves into Leo on the 15th.

Jupiter is occulted by the moon on the 23d.

Saturn in Cancer, is 6° north of the moon on the 2d and again on the 29th.

Moon passes Saturn on the 2d, Mars on the 3d, occults Spica on the 8th, Neptune on the 11th, Jupiter on the 23d, Vesta and Mercury on the 25th, and passes Saturn again on the 29th. First Quarter, 5th; Full Moon, 12th; Last Quarter, 19th; New Moon, 27th. Perigee, 9th (225,900 miles); apogee, 21st (251,400 miles).

June 3 — Neptune at opposition in Ophiuchus, 2.72 billion miles away.

June 15 — Mercury at greatest western elongation (23° from the sun).

June 18 — Venus in superior conjunction.

June 20 — Sun enters Gemini.

June 21 — Summer begins in the Northern Hemisphere at 6:24 AM GMT (1:24 AM EST; 10:24 PM PST on the 20th), when the sun is directly overhead where the Tropic of Cancer crosses the Irrawaddy River north of Mandalay, Burma.

July

Mercury is in superior conjunction and becomes an evening star on the 15th, nearly 124 million miles away. It is 0° .4 north of Venus on the 24th.

Venus is 0° .4 south of Mercury on the 24th and 6° north of the moon on the 28th.

Mars is 6° north of the crescent moon on the 1st, 0° .7 north of Regulus on the 5th, and 5° north of the moon on the 30th.

Jupiter is occulted by the moon on the 21st.

. **Saturn** is in conjunction with the sun on the 29th, 941 million miles away, and becomes a morning star.

Moon passes Mars on the 1st, occults Spica on the 5th, Uranus on the 6th, Neptune on the 8th, Jupiter on the 21st. and Vesta on the 24th, and passes Mars on the 30th. First Quarter, 4th; Full Moon, 11th; Last Quarter. 19th; New Moon, 27th. Perigee, 7th (228,900 miles); apogee, 19th (251.100 miles).

July 3 — Earth at aphelion. 94.6 million miles away from the sun.

July 15 — Mercury in superior conjunction.

July 20 — Sun enters Cancer.

July 29 — Saturn is in conjunction with the sun.

August

Mercury is 0° .7 north of Regulus on the 3d, at greatest eastern elongation, 27° east of the sun in Virgo on the 26th, and occulted by the moon on the 27th.

. **Venus** is 1° .1 north of Regulus on the 7th and 5° north of the moon on the 27th.

Mars is 4° north of the moon on the 27th.

Jupiter is occulted by the moon on the 18th.

Saturn is 6° north of the moon on the 23d, but still too near the sun to be seen in the morning twilight.

Moon occults Spica on the 1st, Uranus on the 2d, Jupiter on the 18th, passes Saturn on the 23d and Venus on the 27th and occults Mercury 15 hours later, passes Mars on the 27th, and occults Spica at about 11 PM GMT (6 PM EST) on the 28th and Uranus on the 29th. First Quarter, 2d; Full Moon, 10th; Last Quarter, 18th; New Moon, 25th. Perigee, 1st (229,300 miles); apogee, 16th (251,200 miles); perigee, 28th (226,500 miles).

Aug. 10 — Sun enters Leo.

Aug. 10-14 — Perseid meteor shower peaks in this period, but the bright gibbous moon will limit visibility to the brightest meteors.

Aug. 27 — Telescopes and binoculars will be necessary to watch this month's occultation of Spica in the bright western sky. Find Spica about 5 PM EST, and watch the thin crescent moon move in from the west.

September

Mercury is 5° south of Venus on the 6th; stationary on the 8th in Virgo; in inferior conjunction, over 60 million miles away. on the 22d when it becomes a morning star; and stationary again on the eastern edge of Leo on the 30th, when it resumes its direct motion.

Venus is 0° .4 north of Mars on the 10th, 3° north of Spica on the 20th, occulted by the moon on the 25th, and 0° .5 south of Uranus on the 30th.

Mars is 0° .4 south of Venus on the 10th, 2° north of the moon on the 25th, and 3° north of Spica on the 27th.

Jupiter is 1° north of the moon on the 14th, and stationary on the 19th in Taurus when it begins retrograde motion.

Saturn is 6° north of the moon on the 20th, barely visible in the morning twilight.

Moon passes Jupiter on the 14th, Saturn on the 20th, Mars on the 25th, occults Spica and Venus 11 hours later on the 25th, and occults Uranus on the 26th. First Quarter on the 1st; Full Moon, 8th; Last Quarter, 16th; New Moon, 23d; First Quarter, 30th. Apogee, 12th (251,800 miles); perigee, 25th (223,600 miles).

Sept. 16 — Sun enters Virgo.

Sept. 22 — At 1 hour past midnight, GMT, Mercury is in inferior conjunction; at 9:48 PM GMT (4;48 PM EST), Autumn begins. At this moment the sun passes the equator into the southern hemisphere to remain for 178 days 19 hours 55 minutes.

October

Mercury is at greatest elongation, 18° west of the sun in Virgo on the 7th.

Venus is 4° south of the thin crescent moon on the 25th, and 3° north of Antares on the 28th, and is getting more prominent in the evening twilight.

Mars is 0.4° south of Uranus on the 18th.

Jupiter is 1° north of the moon on the 12th.

Saturn is 6° north of the moon on the 18th.

Moon passes.Jupiter on the 12th, Saturn on the 18th, totally eclipses the sun on the 23d, and passes Venus on the 25th. Full Moon, 8th; Last Quarter, 16th; New Moon, 23d; First Quarter, 29th. Apogee, 10th (252,400 miles); perigee, 23d (221,900 miles).

Oct. 4 — Pluto in conjunction with the sun, 2.932 billion miles away.

Oct. 7 — Mercury at greatest western elongation.

Oct. 21 — Orionid meteor shower is in the dark of the moon. May be good.

Oct. 23 — Total solar eclipse.

Oct. 30 — Sun enters Libra.

November

Mercury is in superior conjunction on the 7th, 133.8 million miles away, and becomes an evening star.

Venus is 7° south of the crescent moon on the 24th.

Mars is in conjunction with the sun on the 25th, 233 million miles away, and becomes a morning star.

Jupiter is occulted by the moon on the 8th, and is at opposition in Taurus on the 18th, 374 million miles away, when it becomes an evening star.

Saturn is 6° north of the moon on the 14th and stationary on the 28th in Cancer, beginning retrograde motion.

Moon is in penumbral eclipse on the 6th, occults Jupiter on the 8th, passes Saturn on the 14th, occults Spica on the 19th and Uranus on the 20th, and passes Venus on the 24th. Full Moon, 6th; Last Quarter, 14th; New Moon, 21st; First Quarter, 28th. Apogee, 6th (252,500 miles); perigee, 21st (222,100 miles).

Nov. 6 — Penumbral eclipse of the moon.

Nov. 7 — Mercury in superior conjunction.

Nov. 22 — Sun enter Scorpius.

Nov. 25 — Mars is in conjunction with the sun.

Nov. 29 — Sun enters Ophiuchus.

December

Mercury is at greatest elongation on the 20th, 20° east of the sun. It is 6° south of the moon on the 22d, and stationary in Sagittarius on the 27th.

Venus is our holiday star this year, bright in the western evening twilight all month, 7° south of the crescent moon on the 24th.

Mars is invisible in the glare of the sun.

Jupiter is occulted by the moon on the 5th.

Saturn is 6° north of the moon on the 11th and continues to brighten throughout the month.

Moon occults Jupiter on the 5th, passes Saturn on the 11th, occults Spica on the 16th, and Uranus on the 17th, passes Mercury on the 22d, and Venus on the 24th. Full Moon, 6th; Last Quarter, 14th; New Moon, 21st; First Quarter, 28th. Apogee, 3d (252,200 miles); perigee, 19th (224,300 miles); apogee, 31st (251,700 miles).

Dec. 5 — Neptune in conjunction with the sun, 2.909 billion miles away.

Dec. 14 — Try for the Geminid meteor shower, in spite of the moon. It usually produces some bright fireballs.

Dec. 16 — Sun enters Sagittarius.

Dec. 21 — At 5:36 PM GMT (12:36 PM EST), the sun reaches its most southerly point in the sky over the Tropic of Capricorn. Winter begins in the north, summer in the south.

Planets and the Sun

The planets of the solar system, in order of their distance from the sun are Mercury, Venus, Earth, Mars, Jupiter, Saturn, Uranus, Neptune and Pluto. Uranus, Neptune and Pluto are not included in the celestial list because they are too faint to be seen without optical aid. Both Uranus and Neptune are visible through good field glasses, but Pluto is so distant and so small that only large telescopes or long exposure photographs can make it visible.

Since Mercury and Venus are nearer to the sun than is the earth, their motions about the sun are seen from the earth as wide swings first to one side of the sun and then to the other, although they are both passing continuously around the sun in orbits that are almost circular. When their passage takes them either between the earth and the sun, or beyond the sun as seen from the earth, they are invisible to us. Because of the laws which govern the motions of planets about the sun, both Mercury and Venus require much less time to pass between the earth and the sun than around the far side of the sun, so their periods of invisibility are unequal.

The planets that lie farther from the sun than does the earth may be seen for longer periods of time and are invisible only when they are so located in our sky that they rise and set about the same time as the sun when, of course, they are overwhelmed by the sun's great brilliance. None of the planets has any light or exterior heat of its own but each shines only by reflecting sunlight from its surface. Mercury and Venus, because they are between the earth and the sun, show phases very much as the moon does. The planets farther from the sun are always seen as full, although Mars does occasionally present a slightly gibbous phase — like the moon when not quite full.

The planets move rapidly among the stars because they are very much nearer to us than the stars are. The stars are also in motion, some of them at tremendous speeds, but they are so far away that their motion does not change their apparent positions in the heavens sufficiently for anyone to perceive that change in a single lifetime. The very nearest star is about 7,000 times as far away as the most distant planet.

Visible Planets of the Solar System
Mercury, Venus, Mars, Jupiter and Saturn

Mercury

Mercury, nearest planet to the sun, is also the smallest of the nine planets known to be orbiting the sun. Its diameter is 3,100 miles and its mean distance from the sun is 36,000,000 miles.

Mercury moves with great speed in its journey about the sun, averaging about 30 miles a second to complete its circuit in 88 of our days. Mercury rotates upon its axis over a period of nearly 59 days, thus exposing all of its surface periodically to the sun. It is believed that the surface passing before the sun may have a temperature of about 800° F., while the temperature on the side turned temporarily away from the sun does not fall as low as might be expected. This night temperature has been described by Russian astronomers as "room temperature" — possibly about 70°. This would contradict the former belief that Mercury did not possess an atmosphere, for some sort of atmosphere would be needed to retain some of the fierce solar radiation that must strike Mercury at its small distance from the sun. A shallow but dense layer of carbon dioxide would produce the "greenhouse" effect in which heat accumulated during exposure to the sun, would not completely escape at night. The actual presence of a carbon dioxide atmosphere is in dispute.

This uncertainty about conditions upon Mercury and its motion arise from its short angular distance from the sun as seen from the earth, for Mercury is always too much in line with the sun to be observed against a dark sky, but is always seen during either morning or evening twilight.

Mariner 10 made three passes by Mercury in 1974 and 1975. A large fraction of the surface was photographed from varying distances, revealing a degree of cratering similar to that of the moon. An atmosphere of hydrogen and helium may be made up of gases of the solar wind temporarily concentrated by the disturbing presence of Mercury. The discovery of a weak but permanent magnetic field was a surprise. It has been held that both a fluid core and rapid rotation (such as that of earth) were necessary for the generation of a planetary magnetic field. Mercury may demonstrate these conditions to be unnecessary, or the field may reveal something about the history of Mercury.

Venus

Venus is slightly smaller than the earth. Its diameter is about 200 miles less than the earth's diameter. Venus moves about the sun at a mean distance of 67,000,000 miles in 225 of our days. Its synodical revolution — its return to the same relationship with the earth and the sun, which is a result of the combination of its own motion and that of the earth — is 584 days. Venus will, then, be nearer to the earth every 19 months than any of the other planets of the solar system. We have never been able to see the surface of Venus because the planet is covered with a dense, white cloudy atmosphere that conceals whatever is below it. This same cloud reflects sunlight efficiently so that when Venus is favorably situated, it is the third brightest object in the sky, exceeded only by the sun and the moon.

Ordinary telescopic observation has been unable to reveal much about the nature of the surface of Venus, not even its periods of axial rotation. Spectral analysis of sunlight reflected from Venus' cloud tops has shown features that can best be explained by identifying the material of the clouds as sulphuric acid (oil of vitriol). Infrared spectroscopy from a balloonborne telescope nearly 20 miles above the earth's surface gave indications of a small amount of water vapor present in the same region of the atmosphere of Venus. In 1956, a breakthrough in our knowledge came from radio astronomers at the Naval Research Laboratories in Washington, D. C. Their observations indicated a temperature for Venus of about 600 degrees Fahrenheit, in marked contrast to minus 125 degrees Fahrenheit, previously found at the cloud tops. Subsequent radio work confirmed a high temperature and produced evidence for this temperature to be associated with the solid body of Venus. With this peculiarity in mind, space scientists devised experiments for the U.S. space probe Mariner 2 to perform when it flew by in 1962. Mariner 2 confirmed the high temperature and the fact that it pertained to the ground rather than to some special activity of the atmosphere. In addition, Mariner 2 was unable to detect any radiation belts similar to the earth's so-called Van Allen belts. Nor was it able to detect the existence of a magnetic field even as weak as 1/100,-000 of that of the earth.

An international scientific drama occurred in 1966 when a Russian space probe, Venus 4, and the American Mariner 5 arrived at Venus within a few hours of each other. Venus 4 was unique in that it was designed to allow an instrument package to land gently on the planet's surface via parachute. It ceased transmission of information after 75 minutes when the temperature it read went above 500 degrees Fahrenheit. After considerable controversy, it was agreed that it still had 20 miles to go to reach the surface. The U.S. probe, Mariner 5, went around the dark side of Venus at a distance of about 6,000 miles. Again, it detected no significant magnetic field, but its radio signals passed to earth through Venus' atmosphere twice — once on the night side and once on the day side. The results are startling. Venus' atmosphere is nearly all carbon dioxide and must exert a pressure at the planet's surface of up to 100 times the earth's normal sea-level pressure of one atmosphere. Since the earth and Venus are about the same size, and were presumably formed at the same time by the same general process from the same mixture of chemical elements, one is faced with the question: which is the planet with the unusual history — earth or Venus?

In the last several years, astronomers using radar techniques involving powerful transmitters as well as sensitive receivers and computers have succeeded in determining the rotation period of Venus. It turns out to be 243 days clockwise — in other words, contrary to the spin of most of the other planets and to its own motion around the sun. If it were exactly 243.16 days, Venus would always present the same face toward the earth at every inferior conjunction. This rate and sense of rotation allows a "day" on Venus of 117.4 earth days. Any part of Venus will receive sunlight on its clouds for over 58 days and will be in darkness for 58 days.

Mariner 10 passed Venus before traveling on to Mercury. The carbon dioxide molecule found in such abundance in the atmosphere is rather opaque to certain ultraviolet wavelengths, enabling sensitive television cameras to take 3-dimensional pictures of the Venusian cloud cover. Photos radioed to earth show a spiral pattern in the clouds from equator to the poles. Long-lived features in the clouds have been detected moving at speeds of the order of a hundred miles per hour or more. If this is typical of the wind speed over the ground of Venus, it can account for the transfer of heat to the night side in spite of the low rotation rate of the planet.

Recent radar observations have shown surface features below the clouds. Large craters have been identified. Before the end of 1976, we should have radar-derived pictures of Venus that are as revealing as ordinary telescopic views of our moon taken by earth-based telescopes.

Mars

Mars is the first planet beyond the earth, away from the sun. Mars' diameter is about 4,200 miles, although a determination of the radius and mass of Mars by the space-probe, Mariner 4, which flew by Mars on July 14, 1965, at a distance of less than 6,000 miles, indicated that these dimensions were slightly larger than had been previously estimated. While Mars' orbit is also nearly circular, it is somewhat more eccentric than the orbits of many of the other planets, and Mars is more than 30 million miles farther from the sun in some parts of its year than it is at others. Mars takes 687 of our days to make one circuit

of the sun, traveling at about 15 miles a second. Mars rotates upon its axis in almost the same period of time that the earth does — 24 hours and 37 minutes. Mars' mean distance from the sun is 141 million miles, so that the temperature on Mars would be lower than that on the earth even if Mars' atmosphere were about the same as ours. The atmosphere is not, however, for Mariner 4 reported that atmospheric pressure on Mars is between 1% and 2% of the earth's atmospheric pressure. This thin atmosphere appears to be largely carbon dioxide. No evidence of free water was found.

There appears to be no magnetic field about Mars. This would eliminate the previous conception of a dangerous radiation belt around Mars similar to the Van Allen Belt around the earth. The same lack of a magnetic field would expose the surface of Mars to an influx of cosmic radiation about 100 times as intense as that on earth.

Deductions from years of telescopic observation indicate that 5/8ths of the surface of Mars is a desert of reddish rock, sand and soil. The rest of Mars is covered by irregular patches that appear generally green in hues that change through the Martian year. These were formerly held to be some sort of primitive vegetation, but with the findings of Mariner 4 of a complete lack of water and oxygen, such growth does not appear possible. The nature of the green areas is now unknown. They may be regions covered with volcanic salts whose color changes with changing temperatures and atmospheric conditions, or they may be gray, rather than green. Optical experiments show that when large gray areas are placed beside large red areas, the gray areas will appear green to the eye.

Mars' axis of rotation is inclined from a vertical to the plane of its orbit about the sun by about 25° and therefore has seasons as does the earth, except that the Martian seasons are longer because Mars' year is longer. White caps form about the winter pole of Mars, growing through the winter and shrinking in summer. These polar caps were thought to be frozen water which, when it melted, nourished the green areas. In view of the negative findings of Mariner 4, however, the caps are thought to be carbon dioxide.

The canals of Mars have become more of a mystery than they were before the voyage of Mariner 4. Markings forming a network of fine lines crossing much of the surface of Mars have been seen there by men who have devoted much of their professional time to the study of the planet, but no canals have shown clearly enough upon previous photographs to be universally accepted. A few of the 21 photographs sent back to earth by Mariner 4 covered areas crossed by canals. The pictures show faint, ill-defined, broad, dark markings, but no positive identification of the nature of the markings.

Mariners 6 & 7 in 1969 sent back many more photographs of higher quality than those of the pioneering Mariner 4. These pictures showed cratering similar to the earlier views, but in addition showed two other types of terrain. Some regions seemed featureless for many square miles, but others were chaotic, showing high relief without apparent organization into mountain chains or craters.

Mariner 9, the first artificial body to be placed in an orbit about Mars, has transmitted over 10,000 photographs covering 100% of the planet's surface. Preliminary study of these photos and other data shows that Mars resembles no other planet we know. Using terrestrial terms, however, scientists describe features that seem to be clearly of volcanic origin. One of these features is Nix Olympica, apparently a caldera whose outer slopes are over 300 miles in diameter. Some features may have been produced by cracking (faulting) of the surface and the sliding of one region over or past another. Many craters seem to have been produced by impacting bodies such as may have come from the nearby asteroid belt. Features near the south pole may have been produced by glaciers that are no longer present. Flowing water, non-existent on Mars at the present time, probably carved canyons, one 10 times longer and 3 times deeper than the Grand Canyon.

Although the Russians landed a probe on the Martian surface, it transmitted for only 20 seconds. The U.S., in its Viking program, expects to land two very sophisticated craft on Mars in mid-1976 in an attempt to detect, among other things, if life exists or has ever existed on the planet.

Mars' position in its orbit and its speed around that orbit in relation to the earth's position and speed bring Mars fairly close to the earth on occasions about two years apart and then move Mars and the earth too far apart for accurate observation and photography. Every 15-17 years, the close approaches are especially favorable for an all-out astronomical attack on Mars.

Mars has two satellites. They are small, estimated to be about 5 and 10 miles in diameter if their surfaces have properties similar to that of our moon. They were discovered in 1877 by Asaph Hall. The outer satellite is named Deimos and it revolves around Mars in about 31 hours. The inner satellite, Phobos, whips around Mars in a little more than 7 hours, making three trips around the planet each Martian day.

The Mariner flights of 1969 produced a photograph accidentally taken showing Phobos, silhouetted against the planet. An analysis of the image gives dimensions of Phobos as about 14 miles by 8 miles, proportions resembling those of a potato. The ability of Phobos to reflect light appears to be even less than that of the earth's moon. Mariner 9 has confirmed those results and added information that Phobos and Deimos are pitted with large craters and are of irregular shape, suggesting a history of fragmentation.

Jupiter

Jupiter is the largest of the planets. Its equatorial diameter is 88,000 miles, 11 times the diameter of the earth. Its polar diameter is about 6,000 miles shorter. This is caused by the almost fluid condition of its atmosphere and its extremely rapid rate of rotation. Jupiter's day is just under 10 hours long. For a planet of this size, this rotational speed is amazing, and it carries a point on Jupiter's equator along at a speed of 22,000 miles an hour, as compared with 1,000 miles an hour for a point on the earth's equator. Jupiter is at an average distance of 480 million miles from the sun and takes almost 12 of our years to make one complete circuit of the sun.

The only directly observable chemical constituents of Jupiter's atmosphere are methane (CH_4) and ammonia (NH_3), but it is reasonable to assume the same mixture of elements available to make Jupiter as to make the sun. This would mean a large fraction of hydrogen and helium must be present also, as well as water, H_2O. The temperature at the tops of the clouds may be about minus 260 degrees Fahrenheit. The clouds are probably ammonia ice crystals, becoming ammonia droplets lower down. There may be a space before water ice crystals show up as clouds; in turn, these become water droplets near the bottom of the entire cloud layer. The total atmosphere may be only a few hundred miles in depth, pulled down by the surface gravity (= 2.64 times earth's) to a relatively thin layer. Of course, the gases become denser with depth until they may turn into a slush or a slurry. Perhaps there is no solid surface—no real interface between solid and gas. Its temperature may approach 1,000 degrees Fahrenheit. Long before the center is reached, hydrogen and helium become a fluid metal and perhaps a solid metal near the center. Jupiter's cloudy atmosphere is a fairly good reflector of sunlight and makes it far brighter than any of the stars among which it wanders.

Jupiter has 13 satellites. Four of these are large and bright, rivaling our own moon and the planet Mercury in diameter, and may be seen through a field glass. They move rapidly around Jupiter and their change of position from night to night is extremely interesting to watch. The 9 additional satellites are much smaller and in all but one instance much farther from Jupiter and cannot be seen except through powerful telescopes. The 4 outermost satellites are revolving around Jupiter clockwise as seen from the north, contrary to the motions of the great majority of the satellites in the solar system and to the direction of revolution of the planets around the sun. The reason for this retrograde motion is not known, but one theory is that Jupiter's tremendous gravitational power may have captured 4 of the minor planets or asteroids that move about the sun between Mars and Jupiter, and that these 4 may be running backwards. Jupiter's mass is more than twice the mass of all the other planets put together, and accounts for Jupiter's tremendous gravitational field and so, probably, for its numerous satellites and its dense atmosphere.

In December, 1973, Pioneer 10 passed about 80,000 miles from the equator of Jupiter and was whipped into a path taking it out of our solar system in about 50 years. In December, 1974, Pioneer 11 passed within 30,000 miles of Jupiter, moving roughly from south to north, over the poles. Photographs from both encounters reveal much detail in the clouds, including what appear to be cyclonic storms. The Great Red Spot shows a spiral nature suggesting it is a long lived hurricane-like feature. The magnetic field is eccentric and tilted. It is stronger than was thought and of the opposite sign to that of the earth. The action of the trapped particles — the Jovian Van Allen Belts — is too violent to let man pass through in present spacecraft without serious radiation injury. Analysis of the paths of the Pioneers and of other facts about Jupiter indicate the planet may be almost entirely fluid, with a gaseous atmosphere and liquid ball, except for, perhaps, an earth-size core that is solid.

Both Pioneers contain a pictorial message that has been included for the benefit of extra-solar system finders of the derelicts. Before Pioneer 11 leaves the solar system, it will make a visit to Saturn in September, 1979.

Saturn

Saturn, last of the planets visible to the unaided eye, is almost twice as far from the sun as Jupiter, almost 900 million miles. It is second in size to Jupiter but its mass is much smaller. Saturn's specific gravity is less than that of water. Its diameter is about 71,000 miles at the equator; its rotational speed spins it completely around in a little more than 10 hours, and its atmosphere is much like that of Jupiter, except that its temperature at the top of its cloud layer is at least 100° colder. At about 300° F. below zero, the ammonia would be frozen out of Saturn's clouds. The theoretical construction of Saturn resembles that of Jupiter; it is either all gas, or it has a small dense center surrounded by a layer of liquid and a deep atmosphere.

Saturn has ten satellites, the 10th having been discovered by the French astronomer Audouin Dollfus in December, 1966. The newly found satellite is a few thousand miles outside of the edge of Saturn's ring system. Its discovery was made possible by an edge-on presentation of the rings.

Saturn's ring system begins about 7,000 miles above the visible disk of Saturn, lying above its equator and extending about 35,000 miles into space. The diameter of the ring system, including Saturn itself, is about 170,000 miles; the rings are estimated to be no thicker than 10 miles. In 1973, radar observation showed the ring particles to be large chunks of material averaging a meter on a side.

The rings cannot be seen except in a telescope of at least 3-inch aperture. Because of Saturn's inclination, as stated above, there are two periods during Saturn's journey around the sun when the rings are presented to us edge-on. At these times, the rings disappear. Nothing that is only 10 miles wide can be seen from a distance of nearly 900 million miles. The rings are receding from a favorable position to be seen. They were edge-on in 1966 and reached maximum visibility again in 1973.

Planetary Configurations, 1976

Greenwich Mean Time

(0 designates midnight; 12 designates noon)

Mo.	d.	h.	m.	
Jan.	3	06	—☌☿☽	☿ 7° S
	4	11	—	⊕ at perihelion
	7	05	—	☿ gr. elong. E (19°)
	8	12	—☌♀*	♀ 7° N of Antares
	9	12	—☌♃☽	♃ 4° S
	14	03	—☌♂☽	♂ 5° N
	17	13	—☌♄☽	♄ 5° N
	20	11	—☍♄☉	
	23	06	—☌☿☉	Inferior
	28	08	—☌♀☽	♀ 2° S
Feb.	6	03	—☌♃☽	♃ 4° S
	10	16	—☌♂☽	♂ 5° N
	13	19	—☌♄☽	♄ 5° N
	16	15	—	☿ gr. elong. W (26°)
	27	14	—☌♀☽	♀ 6° S
	28	00	—☌☿☽	☿ 7° S
Mar.	4	20	—☌♃☽	♃ 3° S
	9	19	—☌♂☽	♂ 6° N
	12	03	—☌♄☽	♄ 5° N
	20	11	50	☉ enters ♈ spring begins
	29	00	—☌♀☽	♀ 6° S
Apr.	1	14	—☌♃☽	♃ 2° S
	1	18	—☌☿☉	superior
	7	03	—☌♂☽	♂ 7° N
	8	12	—☌♄☽	♄ 6° N
	12	18	—☌☿♃	☿ 1°.9 N
	27	20	—☌♃☉	
	28	02	—	☿ gr. elong. E (21°)
	29	10	33☌☽☉	☉ annular eclipse
May	1	04	—☌☿☽	☿ 4° N
	5	04	—☌♂*	♂ 5° S of Pollux
	5	14	—☌♂☽	♂ 7° N
	5	20	—☌♄☽	♄ 6° N
	11	14	—☌♃♀	♃ 0°.2 N
	12	02	—☌♂♄	♂ 1°.3 N
	13	19	39☍☽☉	☽ partial eclipse
	20	12	—☌☿☉	inferior
	27	04	—☌♃☽	♃ 0°.8 S conjunction
June	2	06	—☌♄☽	♄ 6° N
	3	02	—☌♂☽	♂ 7° N
	15	09	—	☿ gr. elong. W (23°)
	18	04	—☌♀☉	superior
	21	06	24	☉ enters ♋ summer begins
	22	17	—☌☿*	☿ 3° N of Aldebaran
	23	23	—☌♃☽	♃ 0°.1 S occultation
	25	22	—☌☿☽	☿ 1° N occultation
	29	18	—☌♄☽	♄ 6° N
July	1	14	—☌♂☽	♂ 6° N
	3	04	—	⊕ at aphelion
	5	18	—☌♂*	♂ 0°.7 N of Regulus
	15	15	—☌☿☉	superior
	21	17	—☌♃☽	♃ 0°.5 N occultation
	24	14	—☌☿♀	☿ 0°.4 N
	29	14	—☌♄☉	
	30	02	—☌♂☽	♂ 5° N
Aug.	3	06	—☌☿*	☿ 0°.7 N of Regulus
	7	16	—☌♀*	♀ 1°.1 N of Regulus
	18	09	—☌♃☽	♃ 1° N occultation
	23	23	—☌♄☽	♄ 6° N
	26	10	—	☿ gr. elong. E (27°)
	27	00	—☌♀☽	♀ 5° N
	27	11	—☌☿☽	☿ 0°.5 N occultation
	27	15	—☌♂☽	♂ 4° N
Sep.	6	04	—☌☿♀	☿ 5° S
	10	22	—☌♂♀	♂ 0°.4 S
	14	19	—☌♃☽	♃ 1° N
	20	15	—☌♄☽	♄ 6° N
	22	01	—☌☿☉	inferior
	22	21	48	☉ enters ♎ autumn begins
	25	05	—☌♂☽	♂ 2° N
	25	18	—☌♀☽	♀ 0°.7 N occultation
	27	19	—☌♂*	♂ 3° N of Spica
Oct.	7	16	—	☿ gr. elong. W (18°)
	12	01	—☌♃☽	♃ 1° N
	18	05	—☌♄☽	♄ 6° N
	23	06	22☌☽☉	☉ total eclipse
	25	13	—☌♀☽	♀ 4° S
	28	01	—☌♀*	♀ 3° N of Antares
Nov.	6	22	34☍☽☉	☽ penumbral eclipse
	7	09	—☌☿☉	superior
	8	01	—☌♃☽	♃ 1° N occultation
	14	15	—☌♄☽	♄ 6° N
	18	08	—☍♃☉	
	25	01	—☌♂☉	
Dec.	5	00	—☌♃☽	♃ 0°.8 N occultation
	11	21	—☌♄☽	♄ 6° N
	20	10	—	☿ gr. elong. E (20°)
	21	17	36	☉ enters ♑ winter begins
	22	15	—☌☿☽	☿ 6° S
	24	15	—☌♀☽	♀ 7° S

Planetary Configurations, 1977

As a service to those who wish to consult the planetary configurations for early 1977 in the preceding fall, THE WORLD ALMANAC publishes the configurations for January, February, March and April, 1977.

Mo.	d.	h.	m.	
Jan.	3	10	—	⊕ at perihelion
	6	08	—☌☿☉	inferior
	12	12	—☌☿♂	☿ 4° N
	24	12	—	♀ gr. elong. E (47°)
	29	00	—	☿ gr. elong. W (25°)
Feb.	2	10	—☍♄☉	
	12	19	—☌☿♂	☿ 0°.1 S
Mar.	1	02	—	☿ gr. brilliancy
	16	05	—☌☿☉	superior
	20	17	43	☉ enters ♈ spring begins
	27	19	—☌☿♀	☿ 8° S
Apr.	6	06	—☌♀☉	inferior
	10	16	—	☿ gr. elong. E (19°)
	30	17	—☌☿☉	inferior

Moon's Perigee and Apogee, 1976

Perigee

Day		Hour GMT	Hour EST
Jan.	20	13	08
Feb.	17	10	05
Mar.	16	19	14
Apr.	14	07	02
May	12	17	12
June	9	19	14
July	7	02	21*
Aug.	1	04	23*
Aug.	28	02	21*
Sept.	25	03	22*
Oct.	23	13	08
Nov.	21	01	20*
Dec.	19	12	07

*Previous date.

Apogee

Day		Hour GMT	Hour EST
Jan.	8	17	12
Feb.	5	13	08
Mar.	4	04	23*
Mar.	31	10	05
Apr.	27	12	07
May	25	00	19*
June	21	17	12
July	19	11	06
Aug.	16	06	01
Sept.	12	23	18
Oct.	10	12	07
Nov.	6	15	10
Dec.	3	18	13
Dec.	31	09	04

Rising and Setting of Planets, 1976

Greenwich Mean Time (0 designates midnight)

Date	20° N. Latitude Rise	Set	30° N. Latitude Rise	Set	40° N. Latitude Rise	Set	50° N. Latitude Rise	Set	60° N. Latitude Rise	Set
Venus, 1976										
Jan. 1	3:36	14:47	3:52	14:31	4:11	14:11	4:38	13:44	5:22	13:00
15	3:56	14:57	4:15	14:38	4:39	14:14	5:12	13:41	6:07	12:46
Feb. 1	4:21	15:17	4:41	14:57	5:06	14:32	5:42	13:56	6:43	12:55
15	4:37	15:38	4:56	15:19	5:19	14:56	5:52	14:23	6:48	13:27
Mar. 1	4:49	16:02	5:04	15:46	5:23	15:28	5:49	15:02	6:31	14:20
15	4:54	16:23	5:04	16:12	5:17	15:59	5:35	15:42	6:02	15:15
Apr. 1	4:55	16:46	4:59	16:42	5:03	16:38	5:09	16:32	5:19	16:22
15	4:53	17:04	4:51	17:06	4:49	17:09	4:45	17:12	4:40	17:18
May 1	4:52	17:25	4:44	17:34	4:33	17:45	4:18	17:59	3:55	18:22
15	4:54	17:46	4:40	18:00	4:23	18:17	3:58	18:41	3:19	19:21
Jun. 1	5:03	18:13	4:44	18:32	4:19	18:57	3:45	19:31	2:45	20:31
15	5:17	18:35	4:55	18:57	4:28	19:25	3:47	20:05	2:34	21:19
Jul. 1	5:40	18:58	5:18	19:20	4:50	19:48	4:10	20:29	2:56	21:42
15	6:03	19:13	5:43	19:32	5:19	19:57	4:44	20:32	3:43	21:33
Aug. 1	6:30	19:22	6:16	19:36	5:58	19:54	5:34	20:18	4:54	20:58
15	6:50	19:24	6:41	19:32	6:31	19:43	6:17	19:57	5:54	20:20
Sept. 1	7:13	19:21	7:12	19:22	7:10	19:24	7:07	19:26	7:04	19:29
15	7:31	19:18	7:36	19:13	7:42	19:07	7:50	18:59	8:02	18:47
Oct. 1	7:53	19:17	8:04	19:05	8:19	18:50	8:39	18:31	9:10	18:00
15	8:14	19:20	8:31	19:03	8:52	18:42	9:22	18:12	10:11	17:23
Nov. 1	8:42	19:32	9:04	19:10	9:31	18:43	10:11	18:03	11:21	16:53
15	9:03	19:49	9:27	19:25	9:57	18:56	10:40	18:13	11:59	16:53
Dec. 1	9:22	20:13	9:44	19:51	10:12	19:23	10:52	18:43	12:03	17:32
15	9:31	20:33	9:50	20:15	10:12	19:52	10:45	19:20	11:38	18:26
Mars, 1976										
Jan. 1	15:36	5:03	15:11	5:27	14:39	5:59	13:53	6:46	12:20	8:18
15	14:31	3:57	14:07	4:22	13:35	4:53	12:49	5:39	11:19	7:10
Feb. 1	13:28	2:53	13:03	3:18	12:32	3:49	11:46	4:35	10:18	6:04
15	12:45	2:11	12:21	2:36	11:49	3:07	11:03	3:53	9:33	5:24
Mar. 1	12:07	1:34	11:42	1:58	11:11	2:30	10:25	3:16	8:53	4:48
15	11:37	1:03	11:12	1:27	10:41	1:59	9:54	2:46	8:23	4:17
Apr. 1	11:05	0:30	10:41	0:54	10:10	1:25	9:24	2:10	7:57	3:38
15	10:41	0:04	10:18	0:27	9:48	0:57	9:05	1:40	7:43	3:03
May 1	10:17	23:35	9:55	23:57	9:27	0:25	8:47	1:05	7:34	2:18
15	9:57	23:10	9:37	23:30	9:11	23:56	8:35	0:32	7:31	1:36
Jun. 1	9:34	22:38	9:17	22:56	8:54	23:18	8:23	23:49	7:30	0:42
15	9:16	22:12	9:00	22:27	8:41	22:46	8:15	23:13	7:31	23:56
Jul. 1	8:55	21:41	8:43	21:53	8:27	22:08	8:06	22:29	7:33	23:03
15	8:37	21:13	8:27	21:22	8:16	21:34	8:00	21:50	7:35	22:15
Aug. 1	8:15	20:38	8:09	20:44	8:02	20:51	7:52	21:01	7:37	21:16
15	7:57	20:10	7:54	20:13	7:51	20:16	7:47	20:21	7:39	20:28
Sept. 1	7:36	19:36	7:37	19:35	7:39	19:34	7:40	19:32	7:43	19:30
15	7:20	19:09	7:24	19:05	7:30	19:00	7:36	18:53	7:47	18:42
Oct. 1	7:02	18:40	7:10	18:32	7:20	18:22	7:33	18:09	7:53	17:49
15	6:48	18:15	7:00	18:04	7:13	17:51	7:31	17:32	8:00	17:03
Nov. 1	6:33	17:48	6:48	17:33	7:06	17:15	7:31	16:51	8:11	16:11
15	6:22	17:28	6:40	17:11	7:01	16:50	7:31	16:20	8:20	15:31
Dec. 1	6:11	17:09	6:31	16:49	6:56	16:25	7:30	15:50	8:30	14:50
15	6:02	16:55	6:23	16:34	6:50	16:07	7:28	15:29	8:35	14:23
Jupiter, 1976										
Jan. 1	12:21	0:12	12:25	0:08	11:57	0:36	11:49	0:44	11:37	0:56
15	11:16	23:37	11:11	23:42	11:05	23:48	12:56	23:56	10:43	0:09
Feb. 1	10:16	22:40	10:40	22:46	10:03	22:53	9:53	23:03	9:38	23:18
15	9:28	21:55	9:22	22:02	9:14	22:10	9:02	22:21	8:45	22:38
Mar. 1	8:39	21:09	8:31	21:16	8:22	21:26	8:09	21:38	7:49	21:59
15	7:53	20:26	7:45	20:35	7:34	20:46	7:19	21:00	6:57	21:23
Apr. 1	6:59	19:36	6:49	19:46	6:37	19:58	6:20	20:15	5:54	20:41
15	6:15	18:56	6:04	19:06	5:50	19:20	5:32	19:38	5:02	20:08
May 1	5:25	18:09	5:13	18:21	4:58	18:36	4:37	18:57	4:04	19:30
15	4:41	17:29	4:28	17:42	4:12	17:58	3:50	18:20	3:14	18:56
Jun. 1	3:48	16:39	3:34	16:54	3:16	17:11	2:52	17:35	2:12	18:15
15	3:03	15:58	2:49	16:13	2:30	16:32	2:04	16:56	1:22	17:40
Jul. 1	2:12	15:10	1:57	15:26	1:37	15:45	1:10	16:13	0:24	16:58
15	1:27	14:26	1:11	14:43	0:50	15:03	0:21	15:32	23:34	16:19
Aug. 1	0:30	13:32	0:13	13:48	13:55	14:10	23:22	14:40	22:32	15:29
15	23:42	12:44	23:24	13:02	23:03	13:23	22:32	13:54	21:41	14:45
Sep. 1	22:40	11:44	22:23	12:01	22:01	12:24	21:30	12:55	20:37	13:47
15	21:47	10:51	21:30	11:09	21:08	11:31	20:36	12:02	19:44	12:55
Oct. 1	20:44	9:47	20:26	10:05	20:04	10:27	19:33	10:58	18:41	11:51
15	19:46	8:49	19:28	9:06	19:06	9:28	18:36	9:59	17:44	10:50
Nov. 1	18:32	7:34	18:15	7:51	17:54	8:12	17:24	8:42	16:34	9:32
15	17:30	6:31	17:14	6:47	16:53	7:08	16:24	7:37	15:35	8:26
Dec. 1	16:15	5:14	15:59	5:30	15:39	5:50	15:11	6:18	14:24	7:05
15	15:14	4:12	14:58	4:28	21:43	4:47	14:11	5:15	13:25	6:01

Saturn, 1976

Date	20° N. Latitude Rise	Set	30° N. Latitude Rise	Set	40° N. Latitude Rise	Set	50° N. Latitude Rise	Set	60° N. Latitude Rise	Set
Jan. 1	19:04	8:11	18:46	8:29	18:22	8:52	17:49	9:25	16:53	10:22
15	18:00	7:07	17:41	7:26	17:17	7:50	16:44	8:23	15:46	9:21
Feb. 1	16:42	5:51	16:23	6:10	15:59	6:34	15:25	7:08	14:26	8:08
15	15:43	4:52	15:23	5:12	14:59	5:36	14:24	6:11	13:24	7:11
Mar. 1	14:40	3:50	14:20	4:10	13:56	4:34	13:21	5:09	12:20	6:10
15	13:43	2:53	13:23	3:13	12:58	3:38	12:23	4:13	11:22	5:14
Apr. 1	12:35	1:46	12:16	2:06	11:51	2:30	11:15	3:06	10:14	4:08
15	11:42	0:52	11:22	1:12	10:57	1:37	10:22	2:12	9:21	3:13
May 1	10:44	23:50	10:25	0:09	10:02	0:32	9:29	1:05	8:33	2:01
15	9:52	23:01	9:32	23:20	9:08	23:45	9:08	23:45	7:33	1:19
Jun. 1	8:52	22:00	8:33	22:19	8:09	22:43	7:35	23:17	6:36	0:15
15	8:03	21:11	7:45	21:29	7:21	21:53	6:48	22:26	5:51	23:23
Jul. 1	7:09	20:15	6:51	20:33	6:28	20:56	5:55	21:29	5:00	22:24
15	6:22	19:26	6:04	19:44	5:41	20:07	5:10	20:38	4:15	21:32
Aug. 1	5:25	18:28	5:07	18:45	4:46	19:07	4:15	19:37	3:23	20:29
15	4:38	17:39	4:21	17:56	4:00	18:17	3:30	18:47	3:00	19:37
Sep. 1	3:40	16:40	3:24	16:56	3:03	17:17	2:35	17:46	1:47	18:34
15	2:52	15:51	2:36	16:07	2:16	16:27	1:48	16:55	1:02	17:41
Oct. 1	1:57	14:54	1:41	15:09	1:22	15:29	0:54	15:56	0:10	16:41
15	1:07	14:03	0:52	14:18	0:32	14:37	0:06	15:09	23:22	15:47
Nov. 1	0:05	13:00	23:50	13:15	22:31	13:33	23:05	14:00	22:22	14:42
15	23:12	12:06	22:57	12:21	22:38	12:40	22:12	13:06	21:30	13:48
Dec. 1	22:09	11:04	21:55	11:19	21:36	11:38	21:10	12:04	20:27	12:46
15	21:13	10:08	20:58	10:23	20:39	10:42	20:13	11:08	19:30	11:51

The Planets and the Solar System

Name of Planet	Mean Daily Motion ″	Orbital Velocity Miles Per Sec.	Sidereal Revolution Days	Synodical Revolution Days	Dist. from Sun in Millions of Miles Max.	Min.	Approx. miles from Earth in Millions Max.	Min.	Light at Peri-helion	Aphe-lion
Mercury	14732.420	29.75	87.9693	115.9	43.403	28.597	136	50	10.58	4.59
Venus	5767.668	21.76	224.7009	583.9	67.726	66.813	161	25	1.94	1.89
Earth	3548.329	18.51	365.2564	——	94.555	91.445	——	——	1.03	0.97
Mars	1886.519	14.99	686.9796	779.9	154.936	128.471	248	35	0.524	0.360
Jupiter	299.176	8.12	4332.0466	398.9	507.046	460.595	600	368	0.0408	0.0336
Saturn	120.138	5.99	10775.056	378.1	937.541	838.425	1031	745	0.01230	0.00984
Uranus	42.400	4.23	30572.21	369.7	1859.748	1699.331	1953	1606	0.00300	0.00250
Neptune	21.616	3.38	60050.04	367.5	2821.686	2760.386	2915	2667	0.00114	0.00109
Pluto	14.401	2.95	89952.8	366.7	4551.386	2756.427	4644	2663	0.00114	0.00042

Light at Perihelion and Aphelion is solar illumination in units of mean illumination at Earth.

Name of Planet	Mean Longitude of:* Ascending Node °	′	″	Perhelion °	′	″	Inclination* of Orbit to Ecliptic °	′	″	Mean Distance*	Eccentricity* of Orbit	Mean Longitude at the Epoch* °	′	″
Mercury	48	02	51	77	04	59	7	00	15	0.387099	0.205630	29	22	34
Venus	76	27	5	131	14	03	3	23	40	0.723332	0.006784	80	34	50
Earth	—	—	—	102	31	43	—	—	—	1.000000	0.016719	18	56	38
Mars	49	22	22	335	37	06	1	50	59	1.523691	0.093383	117	05	18
Jupiter	100	11	50	13	58	55	1	18	20	5.202252	0.0479819	13	34	06
Saturn	113	28	31	92	12	56	2	29	17	9.555627	0.0564725	24	31	27
Uranus	73	56	05	168	08	42	0	46	21	19.13233	0.0453321	42	09	14
Neptune	131	35	30	46	23	24	1	46	15	29.97991	0.0116945	205	59	22
Pluto	109	56	42	223	57	33	17	08	26	39.30105	0.2456137	339	47	53

*Values are consistent at Epoch = 1976 Jan. 23.0.

Sun and Planets	Semi-Diameter At Unit Distance ″	At Mean Least Dist. ″	In Miles Mean S.D.)	Volume ⊕=1.	Mass. ⊕=1.	Density ⊕=1.	Axial Rotation d.	h.	m.	s.	Gravity at Surface ⊕=1.	Reflecting Power Pct.	Probable Temperature F.
Sun	15 59.63	___	432000	1300000.	332000.	0.26	24	16	48		27.9	___	+10,000
Mercury	3.34	5.45	1505	0.056	0.0543	0.68	59				0.38	0.07	+ 600
Venus	8.41	30.40	3805	0.910	0.8136	0.94	243	(R)			0.88	0.76	+ 100
Earth	___	___	3959	1.000	1.000	1.00		23	56	4	1.00	0.39	+ 50
Moon	2.44	932.58	1080	0.020	0.0120	0.60	27	7	43	12	0.16	0.07	+ 215
Mars	4.68	8.94	2070	0.150	0.1069	0.71		24	37	23	0.39	0.15	+ 0
Jupiter	1 35.19	22.60	43450	1312.	318.35	0.24		9	50		2.65	0.51	- 150
Saturn	1 18.95	9.24	35750	763.	95.3	0.12		10	14		1.17	0.50	- 250
Uranus	34.28	1.88	14750	53.	14.54	0.28		10	45	(R)	1.05	0.66	- 350
Neptune	36.56	1.26	15750	65.	17.2.	0.26		15	48		1.23	0.62	400

The planet Pluto was located by C. W. Tombaugh of Lowell Observatory Mar. 13, 1930. Its mass is about 0.18 of the mass of the Earth. It rotates on its axis in 6 days 9 hours. Its average distance from the sun is 3,664,000,000 miles. On Mar. 30 at 22 hours, GMT, it is in opposition in Virgo at right ascension 13 hrs. 4 mins. 21 secs. and declination, North 12 degrees 6 minutes 41 seconds, northeast of Epsilon Virginis, Pluto will have a magnitude of about 14. (R) Venus and Uranus are in retrograde motion, rotating in opposite direction from other planets.

Four Eclipses in 1976
Greenwich Mean Time

First Eclipse

An annular eclipse of the sun, April 29. Partial phases will be visible over all of Europe, North and West Africa, the Near East and Western Siberia. Nowhere on the earth will the moon totally eclipse the sun, because it will appear smaller than the sun. The path of annularity begins in the Atlantic Ocean, enters the African continent at Dakar, passes over western Crete, runs the length of Turkey, crosses the southern half of the Caspian Sea, ending in western China. Maximum duration of annularity: 6 minutes 36 seconds.

Circumstances of the Eclipse

Eclipse begins.........	April 29, 07:22.3
Central Eclipse begins..	29, 08:32.0
Central eclipse at local noon...............	29, 10:32.6
Central eclipse ends....	29, 12:14.8
Eclipse ends..........	29, 13:24.6

Second Eclipse

A partial eclipse of the moon, May 13. Only 13% of the moon's diameter will be covered by the earth's shadow in this eclipse. Beginning of the umbral phase generally visible in Australia, Asia—except the northeastern part, the eastern part of Europe, Africa —except the northwestern part, Antarctica, part of New Zealand, the Indian Ocean, and the eastern part of the South Atlantic Ocean. The end is visible in Australia except the eastern part, Africa, Antarctica, the Indian Ocean, Europe except the northwestern part, Asia except the northeastern part, the extreme northeastern part of South America, and the South Atlantic Ocean.

Circumstances of the Eclipse

Moon enters penumbra.	May 13, 17:46.6
Moon enters umbra....	13, 19:15.7
Middle of eclipse.......	13, 19:54.3
Moon leaves umbra....	13, 20:32.9
Moon leaves penumbra.	13, 22:02.0

Third Eclipse

A total eclipse of the sun, October 23. Partial phases visible throughout most of the Indian Ocean, including Madagascar, Ceylon, Java, Australia, and part of Antarctica. The path of totality begins south of Lake Victoria, Uganda, passes north of Madagascar and encounters land at the southeastern tip of Australia, north of Melbourne. Maximum duration of totality is 4 minutes 46 seconds. In Australia, it is about 3 minutes.

Circumstances of the Eclipse

Eclipse begins.........	Oct. 23, 02:38.5
Central eclipse begins..	23, 03:35.6
Central eclipse at local noon.............:....	23, 05:21.9
Central eclipse ends....	23, 06:50.1
Eclipse ends..........	23, 07:47.3

Fourth Eclipse

A penumbral eclipse of the moon, November 6-7. Technically, this is an eclipse, but practically it is an invisible phenomenon. From no part of the moon will the sun be entirely hidden by the earth. From any part of the moon an observer would see a partial eclipse of the sun. A slight darkening of the moon, deeper in that part closer to the earth's umbra, may be detectable by instruments or alert observers located in western Australia, Asia except the extreme eastern part, the arctic regions, Africa, Greenland, the extreme northwestern part of North America, the extreme northeastern part of South America, most of the Atlantic Ocean, and the Indian Ocean. The end is visible in Africa, South America, western Asia, Europe, Greenland, North America except the northwestern part, the arctic regions, Atlantic Ocean and the eastern part of the South Pacific Ocean. Magnitude of the eclipse is 0.86.

Circumstances of the Eclipse

Moon enters penumbra.	Nov. 6, 20:45.6
Middle of eclipse.......	6, 23:01.1
Moon leaves penumbra.	7, 01:16.5

Morning and Evening Stars, 1976
(Greenwich Mean Time)

	Morning	Evening		Morning	Evening
Jan.	Mercury (Jan. 23)	Mercury (Jan. 23)	July	Mercury (July 15)	Mercury (July 15)
	Venus	Mars		Jupiter	Venus
	Saturn (Jan. 20)	Jupiter		Saturn (July 29)	Mars
		Saturn (Jan. 20)			Saturn (July 29)
Feb.	Mercury	Mars	Aug.	Jupiter	Mercury
	Venus	Jupiter		Saturn	Venus
		Saturn			Mars
Mar.	Mercury	Mars	Sept.	Mercury (Sept. 22)	Mercury (Sept. 22)
	Venus	Jupiter		Jupiter	Venus
		Saturn		Saturn	Mars
Apr.	Mercury (Apr. 1)	Mercury (Apr. 1)	Oct.	Mercury	Venus
	Venus	Mars		Jupiter	Mars
	Jupiter (Apr. 27)	Jupiter (Apr. 27)		Saturn	
		Saturn	Nov.	Mercury (Nov. 7)	Mercury (Nov. 7)
May	Mercury (May 20)	Mercury (May 20)		Mars (Nov. 25)	Venus
	Venus	Mars		Jupiter (Nov. 28)	Mars (Nov. 25)
	Jupiter	Saturn		Saturn	Jupiter (Nov. 28)
June	Mercury	Venus (June 18)	Dec.	Mercury	Venus
	Venus (June 18)	Mars		Mars	Jupiter
	Jupiter	Saturn		Saturn	

Right Ascension of Mean Sun, 1976
0ʰ Greenwich Mean Time

Date	h	m	Date	h	m	Date	h	m	Date	h	m	Date	h	m
Jan. 1	18	38.9	Mar. 1	22	35.6	May 10	3	11.7	July 9	7	08.2	Sept. 7	11	05.0	Nov. 6	15	01.3
11	19	18.4	11	23	15.3	20	3	51.1	19	7	47.6	17	11	44.4	16	15	40.7
21	19	57.9	21	23	54.7	30	4	30.4	25	8	27.1	27	12	23.8	26	16	20.0
31	20	37.4	31	0	34.1	June 9	5	09.9	Aug. 8	9	06.6	Oct. 7	13	08.7	Dec. 6	16	59.4
Feb. 10	21	16.9	Apr. 10	1	13.5	19	5	49.3	18	9	46.0	17	13	42.6	16	17	38.8
20	21	56.3	20	1	52.9	29	6	28.7	28	10	25.5	27	14	22.0	26	18	18.2
			30	2	32.3												

Largest Telescopes are in Northern Hemisphere

· Most of the world's major astronomical installations are in the northern hemisphere, while many of astronomy's major problems have been found in the southern sky. This imbalance has long been recognized and is being remedied at this time. For several years, large telescopes have been under construction in South America and Australia. Many of these will soon be in use.

In the northern hemisphere the very large reflectors include 3 in California: at Palomar Mtn., 200 inches; at Lick Observatory, Mt. Hamilton, 120 inches; and at Mt. Wilson Observatory, 100 inches. Also in the U.S. are a 158 inch reflector at Kitt Peak, Arizona, dedicated in June 1973, and a 107 inch telescope at the McDonald Observatory on Mt. Locke in Texas. A telescope at the Crimean Astrophysical observatory in the Soviet Union has a 104-inch mirror, and the USSR is building one with a mirror 236 inches in diameter which will be placed in operation soon.

Placed in service in 1975 were three large reflectors for the southern hemisphere. Associated Universities for Research in Astronomy (AURA), the operating organization of Kitt Peak National Observatory, dedicated the 158 inch reflector (twin of the telescope on Kitt Peak) at Cerro Tololo International Observatory, Chile; the European Southern Observatory began using its 150 inch reflector at La Silla, Chile; and the Anglo-Australian telescope, 140 inches in diameter, opened at Siding Spring Observatory in Australia.

Tremendous advances in the study of the central region of the Milky Way and of the Magellanic Clouds, as well as more detailed studies of many other regions hitherto unavailable to giant telescopes, will be made through the use of these new instruments.

Optical Telescopes

Optical astronomical telescopes are of two kinds, refracting and reflecting. In the first, light passes through a lens which brings the light rays into focus, where the image may be examined after being magnified by a second lens, the eye-piece, or directly photographed.

The reflector consists of a concave parabolic mirror, generally of Pyrex or now of a relatively heat insensitive material, cervit, coated with silver or aluminum, which reflects the light rays back toward the upper end of the telescope, where they are either magnified and observed by the eye-piece or, as in the case of the refractors, photographed. In most reflecting telescopes, the light is reflected again by a secondary mirror and comes to a focus after passing through a hole in the side of the telescope, where the eye-piece or camera is located, or after passing through a hole in the center of the primary mirror.

World's Largest Refractors
Location and diameter in inches

Yerkes Obs., Williams Bay, Wis.	40
Lick Obs., Mt. Hamilton, Cal.	36
Astrophys. Obs., Potsdam, E. Germany	32
Paris Observatory, Meudon, France	32
Allegheny Obs., Pittsburgh, Pa.	30
Univ. of Paris, Nice, France	30
Royal Greenwich Obs., Herstmonceux, England	28
Union Obs., Johannesburg, South Africa	26.5
Universitats-Sternwarte, Vienna, Austria	26.5
University of Virginia	26
Obs., Academy of Sciences, Pulkova, USSR	26
Astronomical Obs., Belgrade, Yugoslavia	26
Leander McCormick Obs., Charlottesville, Va.	26

Obs. Mitaka, Tokyo-to, Japan	26
US Naval Obs., Washington, D.C.	26
Mt. Stromlo Obs., Canberra, Australia	26

The Schmidt Telescopes are strictly cameras and cannot be used for visual observation. Light enters the upper end of the telescope tube, is refracted slightly by a correcting lens and is then reflected from a spherical mirror with a short focus. A camera placed inside the telescope at the focus of the mirror can photograph large areas of the sky without distortion at the edges of the photograph. The diameters of Schmidt telescopes are given in two figures; first, the diameter of the correcting lens, followed by the diameter of the mirror.

The lists are partial lists including refractors from 26 inches and reflectors of 40-inches aperture or larger.

World's Largest Reflectors

Hale Obs., Palomar Mtn., Cal.	200
Kitt Peak National Obs., Tucson, Ariz.	158
Cerro Tololo, Chile	158
La Silla, Chile	150
Siding Spring, Australia	140
Lick Obs., Mt. Hamilton, Cal.	120
McDonald Obs., Fort Davis, Tex.	107
Crimean Astrophys. Obs., Nauchny, USSR	104
Hale Obs., Mount Wilson, Cal.	100
Royal Greenwich Obs., Herstmonceux, England	98
Mauna Kea Obs., Univ. of Hawaii, Hawaii	88
Kitt Peak National Obs., Tucson, Ariz.	84
McDonald Obs., Fort Davis, Tex.	82
Saint Michel l'Observatoire, (Basses Alpes), Fr.	77
Tokyo Obs., Japan	74
David Dunlap Obs., Ontario, Canada	74
Helwan Obs., Helwan, Egypt	74
Astrophys. Obs., Kamogata, Okayama-ken, Japan	74
Radcliffe Obs., Pretoria, South Africa	74
Dominion Astrophys. Obs., Victoria, B.C.	73
Perkins Obs., Flagstaff, Ariz.	72
Agassiz Station Harvard Obs., Cambridge, Mass.	61
National Obs., Bosque Alegre Sta., Argentina	61
Arizona Univ. Obs., Tucson, Ariz.	60
Boyden Obs., Bloemfontein, South Africa	60
Mt. Wilson Obs., Pasadena, Cal.	60
Observatorium der Deutschen Tautenberg, Germany	(Schmidt) 54-80
Mt. Stromlo Obs., Canberra, Australia	50
Observatorio Astronomico, Merate, Como, Italy	50
Sternberg Astronomical Inst., Crimea, USSR	50
Berlin-Babelsberg, Obs., Germany	49
Obs. Padua Univ., Asiago, Italy	48
Melbourne, Australia	48
Astrophys, Obs., Nauchny, Crimea, USSR	48
Dominion Astrophys. Obs., Victoria, B.C.	48
Saint Michel l'Observatoire, (Basses Alpes), Fr.	48
Nizamiah Obs., Osmania Univ., Hyderabad, India	48
Palomar Obs., Mt. Palomar, Cal.	(Schmidt) 48-72
Paris Obs., St. Michel, France	47
Lowell Obs., Flagstaff, Ariz.	42
Hamburg-Bergedorf Sternwarte, Germany	40
Kvistaberg Obs., Uppsala U., Swe.	(Schmidt) 40-54
Observatoire Geneva, Switzerland	40
Observatorio Merate, Como, Italy	40
Royal Obs., Cape of Good Hope, S. Africa	40
Stockholm Obs., Saltsjobaden, Sweden	40
US Naval Obs., Flagstaff, Ariz.	40
Pulkovo Obs., Russia	40
Mt. Stromlo, Canberra Australia.	40
Uccle Obs., Belgium	(Schmidt) 33-46

Major Planetariums in the United States

A planetarium projector is perhaps the most complicated instructional device ever made. The first modern planetarium projector was designed and built in 1923 by Walter Bauersfeld of the Zeiss Optical Company. Other instruments had been attempted with only fair success before this time and modern projectors have developed from this beginning. There are now several manufacturers who make elaborate planetarium projectors frequently employing computers and industrial electronic circuitry.

A typical projector for a large auditorium can project the images of nearly 9,000 stars against the reflective surface of a hemispherical dome. In addition, the Milky Way, star clusters, nebulae, and other objects sufficiently bright to be seen under ideal conditions by the unaided eye are shown.

Planetarium projectors are usually in the form of two globes, one at either end of a latticed cylinder. The globes contain projectors for the stars, one for the northern hemisphere and the other for the southern. In the latticed cylinder are projectors for the sun, the moon, and the five planets visible to the eye. The motions of all of these objects are duplicated by the projector with amazing fidelity. First of all, the projector can be set in latitude so that it will produce the sky as it might be seen from any location on earth. The daily motion of the earth, which appears to move the sky throughout the day and night, is the most obvious effect produced. Then there is annual motion, the progress of the sun, moon, and planets through the year, including the phasing of the moon. Finally, the precession of the equinoxes, the slow swing of the poles of the earth which is accomplished in 25,800 years and which slowly changes our view of the sky, is also built into the mechanism of these instruments.

The effects of the projector itself are usually supplemented by auxiliary projectors mounted around the edges of the auditorium to produce the color effects of sunrise and sunset, the aurora, clouds, rainbows, eclipses, and many other phenomena. Most of the functions of the projector are controlled by the lecturer, who produces them from an array of switches and rheostats mounted in a control console usually situated near the north side of the auditorium.

There are literally hundreds of small planetarium projectors in schools and museums in the United States and several planetariums whose auditoriums will seat hundreds. Some of the major planetariums in the United States are listed below:

Academy Planetarium, U. S. Air Force Academy.
Adler Planetarium, Chicago, Ill.
American Museum-Hayden Planetarium, N. Y. C.
Buhl Planetarium, Pittsburgh, Pa.
Charles Hayden Planetarium, Boston, Mass.
Fels Planetarium, Philadelphia, Pa.
Fernback Science Center Planetarium, Atlanta, Ga.
Griffith Planetarium, Los Angeles, Cal.
La. Arts and Science Planetarium, Baton Rouge, La.
McDonnell Planetarium, St. Louis, Mo.
Morehead Planetarium, Chapel Hill, N.C.
Morrison Planetarium, San Francisco, Cal.
Robert T. Longway Planetarium, Flint, Mich.
Straslenbrugh Planetarium, Rochester, N. Y.

Comet Table 1976-1986

Name	Year of Disc.	Due to Return		Period in Years	Peri-helion Dist.	Aphe-lion Dist.	Inclina-tion to Ecliptic Degree	Long. of Ascend. Node Degree	From Asc. Node to Perihelion Degree
Gunn	1970*	Feb.	1976	6.80	2.44	4.74	10	68	197
Wolf	1884	Feb.	1976	8.43	2.51	5.78	27	204	161
Churyumou-Gerasimenko	1969*	Mar.	1976	6.55	1.28	5.72	7	50	11
Harrington-Abell	1955	July	1976	7.19	1.77	5.68	17	146	338
Schaumasse	1911	Aug.	1976	8.18	1.20	6.92	12	86	52
Klemola	1965*	Aug.	1976	11.0	1.76	8.1	11	182	148
d'Arrest	1851	Aug.	1976	6.23	1.17	5.61	17	141	179
Pons-Winnecke	1819	Nov.	1976	6.34	1.25	5.61	22	93	172
Kojima	1970*	Dec.	1976	6.19	1.63	5.11	4	291	198
Johnson	1949	Jan.	1977	6.77	2.20	4.96	14	118	206
Dutoit-Neujmin	1941	Feb.	1977	6.31	1.68	5.15	3	188	116
Van Houten	1961	Feb.	1977	15.75	3.94	8.03	7	23	15
Kopff	1906	Mar.	1977	6.42	1.57	5.34	5	120	163
Faye	1843	Mar.	1977	7.39	1.62	5.98	9	199	204
Grigg-Skjellerup	1902	Apr.	1977	5.12	1.00	4.94	21	213	359
Encke	1786	Aug.	1977	3.30	0.39	4.10	12	334	186
Temple I	1867	Jan.	1978	5.50	1.50	4.73	10	68	179
Arend-Rigaux	1951	Feb.	1978	6.84	1.44	5.76	18	122	329
Temple II	1873	Feb.	1978	5.26	1.36	4.68	12	119	191
Wolf-Harrington	1924	Mar.	1978	6.55	1.62	5.38	18	254	187
Whipple	1933	Mar.	1978	7.47	2.48	5.16	10	188	190
Tsuchinshan I	1965	May	1978	6.64	1.50	5.57	10	96	23
Comas-Sola	1926	May	1978	8.55	1.77	6.60	13	63	40
Daniel	1909	June	1978	7.09	1.66	5.72	20	68	11
Ashbrook-Jackson	1948	Aug.	1978	7.43	2.28	5.33	12	2	349
Tsuchinshan II	1965	Sept.	1978	6.80	1.78	5.40	7	288	203
Jackson-Neujmin	1936	Dec.	1978	8.39	1.43	6.83	14	163	196
VanBiesbroeck	1954	Dec.	1978	12.41	2.41	8.31	7	149	134
Halley	240BC	May	1986	76.1	0.59	35.3	162	58	112

*One appearance only.

Notes on the Comet Table

Most of the comets in the table will not be seen except by professional astronomers or by well-equipped amateurs. At any given time, these observers may be able to follow about a half dozen comets of which the public is unaware. An easily seen comet is rare, one or two every ten to fifteen years.

Comets are named for their discoverers, up to three independent observers being so honored. If a comet becomes unusual, it may be well-known by these names. Usually, however, a preliminary designation is used. This is the year followed by a letter of the alphabet assigned in the order of discovery during that year. About two years later, after any likely late discoveries, comets are given their permanent designation which states the year of their perihelion passage and a Roman numeral giving the order of passage during that year. Well-known periodic comets will receive these designations at each appearance, but the literature and the Comet Table will continue to identify them by their discoverers' names.

Astronomical Constants; Speed of Light

The following astronomical constants were adopted in 1968, in accordance with the resolutions and recommendations of the International Astronomical Union (Hamburg 1964): Velocity of light, 299,792.5 kilometers per second, or about 186,282 statute miles per second; solar parallax, 8".794; constant of nutation, 9".210; and constant of aberration, 20".496.

The Sun

The sun, the controlling body of our solar system, is a star whose dimensions cause it to be classified among stars as average in size, temperature, and brightness. Its proximity to the earth makes it appear to us as tremendously large and bright. A series of thermo-nuclear reactions involving the atoms of the elements of which it is composed produces the heat and light that make life possible on the earth.

The sun has a diameter of 864,000 miles and is distant, on the average, 92,900,000 miles from the earth. It is 1.41 times as dense as water. The light of the sun reaches the earth in 499.02 seconds or slightly more than 8 minutes. The average solar surface temperature has been measured by several indirect methods which agree closely on a value of 6,000° Kelvin or about 10,000° Fahrenheit. The interior temperature of the sun is about 35,000,000° Fahrenheit.

When sunlight is analyzed with a spectroscope, it is found to consist of a continuous spectrum composed of all the colors of the rainbow in order, crossed by many dark lines. The "absorption lines" are produced by gaseous materials in the atmosphere of the sun. More than 60 of the natural terrestrial elements have been identified in the sun, all in gaseous form because of the intense heat of the sun.

Spheres and Corona

The radiating surface of the sun is called the **photosphere**, and just above it is the **chromosphere**. The chromosphere is visible to the naked eye only at times of total solar eclipses, appearing then to be a pinkish-violet layer with occasional great prominences projecting above its general level. With proper instruments the chromosphere can be seen or photographed whenever the sun is visible without waiting for a total eclipse. Above the chromosphere is the **corona**, also visible to the naked eye only at times of total eclipse. Instruments also permit the brighter portions of the corona to be studied whenever conditions are favorable. The pearly light of the corona surges millions of miles from the sun. Iron, nickel, and calcium are believed to be principal contributors to the composition of the corona, all in a state of extreme attenuation and high ionization that indicates temperatures on the order of a million degrees Fahrenheit.

Sunspots

There is an intimate connection between sunspots and the corona. At times of low sunspot activity, the fine streamers of the corona will be much longer above the sun's equator than over the polar regions of the sun, while during high sunspot activity, the corona extends fairly evenly outward from all regions of the sun, but to a much greater distance in space. Sunspots are dark, irregularly-shaped regions whose diameters may reach tens of thousands of miles. The average life of a sunspot group is from two to three weeks, but there have been groups that have lasted for more than a year, being carried repeatedly around as the sun rotated upon its axis. The record for the duration of a sunspot is 18 months. Sunspots reach a low point every 11.3 years, with a peak of activity occurring irregularly between two successive minima.

The sun is 400,000 times as bright as the full moon and gives the earth 6 million times as much light as do all the other stars put together. Actually, most of the stars that can be easily seen on any clear night are brighter than the sun.

The Moon

The moon completes a circuit around the earth in a period whose mean or average duration is 27 days 7 hours 43.2 minutes. This is the moon's sidereal period. Because of the motion of the moon in common with the earth around the sun, the mean duration of the lunar month — the period from one new moon to the next new moon — is 29 days 12 hours 44.05 minutes. This is the moon's synodical period.

The mean distance of the moon from the earth according to the American Ephemeris is 238,857 miles. Because the orbit of the moon about the earth is not circular but elliptical, however, the maximum distance from the earth that the moon may reach is 252,710 miles and the least distance is 221,463 miles. All distances are from the center of one object to the center of the other.

The moon's diameter is 2,160 miles. If we deduct the radius of the moon, 1,080 miles, and the radius of the earth, 3,963 miles from the minimum distance or perigee, given above, we shall have for the nearest approach of the bodies' surfaces 216,420 miles.

The moon rotates on its axis in a period of time exactly equal to its sidereal revolution about the earth — 27.321666 days. The moon's revolution about the earth is irregular because of its elliptical orbit. The moon's rotation, however, is regular and this, together with the irregular revolution, produces what is called "libration in longitude" which permits us to see first farther around the east side and then farther around the west side of the moon. The moon's variation north or south of the ecliptic permits us to see farther over first one pole and then the other of the moon and this is "libration in latitude." These two libration effects permit us to see a total of about 60% of the moon's surface over a period of time. The hidden side of the moon was photographed in 1959 by the Soviet space vehicle Lunik III. Since then many excellent pictures of nearly all of the moon's surface have been transmitted to earth by Lunar Orbiters launched by the U.S.

The tides are caused mainly by the moon, because of its proximity to the earth. The ratio of the tide-raising power of the moon to that of the sun is 11 to 5.

The Zodiac

The sun's apparent yearly path among the stars is known as the **ecliptic**. The zone 16° wide, 8° on each side of the ecliptic, is known as the **zodiac**. Inside of this zone are the apparent paths of the sun, moon, earth, and major planets. Beginning at the point on the ecliptic which marks the position of the sun at the vernal equinox, and thence proceeding eastward, the zodiac is divided into twelve signs of 30° each, as shown herewith.

These signs are named from the twelve constellations of the zodiac with which the signs coincided in the time of the astronomer Hipparchus, about 2,000 years ago. Owing to the precession of the equinoxes, that is to say, to the retrograde motion of the equinoxes along the ecliptic, each sign in the zodiac has, in the course of 2,000 years, moved backward 30° into the constellation west of it; so that the sign Aries is now in the constellation Pisces, and so on. The vernal equinox will move from Pisces into Aquarius about the middle of the 26th Century. The signs of the zodiac with their Latin and English names are as follows:

Spring	1. ♈Aries.	The Ram.		5. ♌Leo.	The Lion.		9. ♐Sagittarius.	The Archer.
	2. ♉Taurus.	The Bull.		6. ♍Virgo.	The Virgin.	Winter	10. ♑Capricorn.	The Goat.
	3. ♊Gemini.	The Twins.	Autumn	7. ♎Libra.	The Balance.		11. ♒Aquarius.	The Water Bearer.
Summer	4. ♋Cancer.	The Crab.		8. ♏Scorpio.	The Scorpion.		12. ♓Pisces	The Fish.

The Earth: Size, Computation of Time, Seasons

Size and Dimensions

The earth is the fifth largest planet and the third from the sun. Its mass is 6 sextillion, 588 quintillion short tons. Using the parameters of an ellipsoid adopted by the International Astronomical Union in 1964 and recognized by the International Union of Geodesy and Geophysics in 1967, the length of the equator is 24,901.55 miles, the length of a meridian is 24,859.82 miles, the equatorial diameter is 7,926.41 miles, and the area of this reference ellipsoid is approximately 196,938,800 square miles.

The earth is considered a solid, rigid mass with a dense core of magnetic, probably metallic material. The outer part of the core is probably liquid. Around the core is a thick shell or mantle of heavy crystalline rock which in turn is covered by a thin crust forming the solid granite and basalt base of the continents and ocean basins. Over broad areas of the earth's surface the crust has a thin cover of sedimentary rock such as sandstone, shale, and limestone formed by weathering of the earth's surface and deposition of sands, clays, and plant and animal remains.

The temperature in the earth increases about 1°F. with every 100 to 200 feet in depth, in the upper 100 kilometers of the earth, and the temperature near the core is believed to be near the melting point of the core materials under the conditions at that depth. The heat of the earth is believed to be derived from radioactivity in the rocks, pressures developed within the earth, and original heat (if the earth in fact was formed at high temperature).

Atmosphere of the Earth

The earth's atmosphere is a blanket composed of gases and some water vapor. The principal gases are nitrogen, oxygen and argon, in amounts of about 78,21, and 1% by volume. Also present in minute quantities are carbon dioxide, hydrogen, neon, helium, krypton and xenon.

Water vapor displaces other gases and varies from nearly zero to about 4% by volume. The height of the ozone layer varies from approximately 12 to 21 miles above the earth. Traces exist as low as 6 miles and as high as 35 miles. Traces of methane have been found.

The atmosphere rests on the earth's surface with the weight equivalent to a layer of water 34 ft. deep. For about 300,000 ft. upward the gases remain in the proportions stated. Gravity holds the gases to the earth. The weight of the air compresses it at the bottom, so that the greatest density is at the earth's surface. Pressure, as well as density, decreases as height increases because the weight pressing upon any layer is always less than that pressing upon the layers below.

The temperature of the air drops with increased height, until the **tropopause** is reached. This may vary from 25,000 to 60,000 ft. The atmosphere below the tropopause is the **troposphere**; the atmosphere for about twenty miles above the tropopause is the **stratosphere**, where the temperature generally increases with height except at high latitudes in winter. A temperature maximum near the 30-mile level is called the **stratopause**. Above this boundary is the **mesosphere** where the temperature decreases with height to a minimum, the **mesopause**, at a height of 50 miles. Extending above the mesosphere to the outer fringes of the atmosphere is the **thermosphere**, a region where temperature increases with height to a value measured in thousands of degrees Fahrenheit. The lower portion of this region, extending from 50 to about 400 miles in altitude, is characterized by a high ion density, and is thus called the **ionosphere**. The outer region is called **exosphere**; this is the region where gas molecules traveling at high speed may escape into outer space, above 600 miles.

Latitude, Longitude

Position on the globe is measured by means of meridians and parallels. Meridians, which are imaginary lines drawn around the earth through the poles, determine **longitude**. The meridian running through Greenwich, England, is the **prime meridian of longitude**, and all others are either east or west. Parallels, which are imaginary circles parallel with the equator, determine **latitude**. The length of a degree of longitude varies as the cosine of the latitude. At the equator a degree is 69.171 statute miles; this is gradually reduced toward the poles. Value of a longitude degree at the poles is zero.

Latitude is reckoned by the number of degrees north or south of the equator, an imaginary circle on the earth's surface everywhere equidistant between the two poles. According to the IAU Ellipsoid of 1964, the length of a degree of latitude is 68.708 statute miles at the equator and varies slightly north and south because of the oblate form of the globe; at the poles it is 69.403 statute miles.

Computation of Time

The earth rotates on its axis and follows an elliptical orbit around the sun. The rotation makes the sun appear to move across the sky from East to West. It determines day and night and the complete rotation, in relation to the sun, is called the **apparent** or **true solar day**. This varies but an average determines the **mean solar day** of 24 hours.

The mean solar day is in universal use for civil purposes. It may be obtained from apparent solar time by correcting observations of the sun for the equation of time, but when high precision is required, the mean solar time is calculated from its relation to sidereal time. These relations are extremely complicated, but for most practical uses, they may be considered as follows:

Sidereal time is the measure of time defined by the diurnal motion of the vernal equinox, and is determined from observation of the meridian transits of stars. One complete rotation of the earth relative to the equinox is called the **sidereal day**. The **mean sidereal day** is 23 hours, 56 minutes, 4.091 seconds of mean solar time.

The **Calendar Year** begins at 12 o'clock precisely local clock time, on the night of Dec. 31-Jan. 1. The day and the calendar month also begin at midnight by the clock. The interval required for the earth to make one absolute revolution around the sun is a **sidereal year**; it consisted of 365 days, 6 hours, 9 minutes, and 9.5 seconds of mean solar time (approximately 24 hours per day) in 1900, and is increasing at the rate of 0.0001-second annually.

The **Tropical Year**, on which the return of the seasons depends, is the interval between two consecutive returns of the sun to the vernal equinox. The tropical year consisted of 365 days, 5 hours, 48 minutes, and 46 seconds. It is decreasing at the rate of 0.530 seconds per century.

In 1956 the unit of time interval was defined to be identical with the second of **Ephemeris Time**, 1/31,556,925.9747 of the tropical year for 1900 January 0d 12th hour E.T. A physical definition of the second based on a quantum transition of cesium (atomic second) was adopted in 1964. The atomic second is equal to 9,192,631,770 cycles of the emitted radiation. In 1967 this atomic second was adopted as the unit of time interval for the Intern'l System of Units.

The Zones and Seasons

The five zones of the earth's surface are the Torrid, lying between the Tropics of Cancer and Capricorn; North Temperate, between Cancer and the Arctic Circle; South Temperate, between Capricorn and the

Antarctic Circle; the Frigid Zones, between the polar Circles and the Poles.

The inclination or tilt of the earth's axis with respect to the sun determines the seasons. These are commonly marked in the North Temperate Zone, where spring begins at the vernal equinox, summer at the summer solstice, autumn at the autumnal equinox and winter at the winter solstice.

In the South Temperate Zone, the seasons are reversed. Spring begins at the autumnal equinox, summer at the winter solstice, etc.

If the earth's axis were perpendicular to the plane of the earth's orbit around the sun there would be no change of seasons. Day and night would be of nearly constant length and there would be equable conditions of temperature. But the axis is tilted 23° 27' away from a perpendicular to the orbit and only in March and September is the axis at right angles to the sun.

The points at which the sun crosses the equator are the equinoxes, when day and night are most nearly equal. The points at which the sun is at a maximum distance from the equator are the solstices. Days and nights are then most unequal.

In June the North Pole is tilted 23° 27' toward the sun and the days in the northern hemisphere are longer than the nights, while the days in the southern hemisphere are shorter than the nights. In December the North Pole is tilted 23° 27' away from the sun and the situation is reversed.

The Seasons in 1976

In 1976 the 4 seasons will begin as follows: add one hour to EST for Atlantic Time; subtract one hour for Central, two hours for Mountain, 3 hours for Pacific, 4 hours for Yukon, 5 hours for Alaska-Hawaii and six hours for Bering Time. Also shown in Greenwich Mean Time.

		Date	GMT	EST
Vernal Equinox	Spring	Mar. 20	11:50	6:50 am
Summer Solstice	Summer	June 21	06:24	1:24 am
Autumnal Equinox	Autumn	Sept 22	21:48	4:48 pm
Winter Solstice	Winter	Dec. 21	17:36	12:36 pm

Poles and Rotation of the Earth

Poles of The Earth

Source: National Oceanic and Atmospheric Admn.

The geographic (rotation) poles, or points where the earth's axis of rotation cuts the surface, are not absolutely fixed in the body of the earth. The pole of rotation describes an irregular curve about its mean position.

Two periods have been detected in this motion: (1) an annual period due to seasonal changes in barometric pressure, load of ice and snow on the surface and to other phenomena of seasonal character; (2) a period of about 14 months due to the shape and constitution of the Earth.

In addition there are small but as yet unpredictable irregularities. The whole motion is so small that the actual pole at any time remains within a circle of 30 or 40 feet in radius centered at the mean position of the pole.

The pole of rotation for the time being is of course the pole having a latitude of 90° and an indeterminate longitude.

Magnetic Poles

The **north magnetic pole** of the earth is that region where the magnetic force is vertically downward and the **south magnetic pole** that region where the magnetic force is vertically upward. A compass placed at the magnetic poles experiences no directive force.

There are slow changes in the distribution of the earth's magnetic field. These changes were at one time attributed in part to a periodic movement of the magnetic poles around the geographical poles, but later evidence refutes this theory and points, rather, to a slow migration of "disturbance" foci over the earth.

There appear shifts in position of the magnetic poles due to the changes in the earth's magnetic field. The center of the area designated as the north magnetic pole was estimated to be in about latitude 70.5° N and longitude 96° W in 1905; from recent nearby measurements and studies of the secular changes, the position in 1970 is estimated as latitude 76.2° N and longitude 101° W. Improved data rather than actual motion account for at least part of the change.

The position of the south magnetic pole in 1912 was near 71° S and longitude 150° E; the position in 1970 is estimated at latitude 66° S and longitude 139.1° E.

The direction of the horizontal components of the magnetic field at any point is known as magnetic north at that point, and the angle by which it deviates east or west of true north is known as the magnetic declination, or in the mariner's terminology the **variation of the compass.**

A compass without error points in the direction of magnetic north. (In general this is *not* the direction of the magnetic north pole.) If one follows the direction indicated by the north end of the compass, he will travel along a rather irregular curve which eventually reaches the north magnetic pole (though not usually by a great-circle route). However, the action of the compass should not be thought of as due to any influence of the distant pole, but simply as an indication of the distribution of the earth's magnetism at the place of observation.

Rotation of The Earth

Source: U.S. Naval Observatory

The speed of rotation of the earth about its axis has been found to be slightly variable. The variations may be classified as:

(A) **Secular.** Tidal friction acts as a brake on the rotation and causes a slow secular increase in the length of the day, about 1 millisecond per century.

(B) **Irregular.** The speed of rotation may increase for a number of years, about 5 to 10, and then start decreasing. The maximum difference from the mean in the length of the day during a century is about 5 milliseconds. The accumulated difference in time has amounted to approximately 44 seconds since 1900. The cause is probably motion in the interior of the earth.

(C) **Periodic.** Seasonal variations exist with periods of one year and six months. The cumulative effect is such that each year the earth is late about 30 milliseconds near June 1 and is ahead about 30 milliseconds near Oct. 1. The maximum seasonal variation in the length of the day is about 0.5 millisecond. It is believed that the principal cause of the annual variation is the seasonal change in the wind patterns of the Northern and Southern Hemispheres. The semi-annual variation is due chiefly to tidal action of the sun, which distorts the shape of the earth slightly.

The secular and irregular variations were discovered by comparing time based on the rotation of the earth with time based on the orbital motion of the moon about the earth and of the planets about the sun. The periodic variation was determined largely with the aid of quartz-crystal clocks. The introduction of the cesium-beam atomic clock in 1955 made it possible to determine in greater detail than before the nature of the irregular and periodic variations.

Twilight

Date 1976	20° Begin	20° End	30° Begin	30° End	40° Begin	40° End	50° Begin	50° End	60° Begin	60° End
	h m	h m	h m	h m	h m	h m	h m	h m	h m	h m
Jan. 1	5 16	6 50	5 30	6 35	5 45	6 21	6 00	6 07	6 18	5 49
11	5 19	6 56	5 33	6 43	5 46	6 30	6 00	6 17	6 15	6 01
21	5 21	7 01	5 32	6 51	5 43	6 40	5 55	6 30	6 06	6 18
Feb. 1	5 21	7 07	5 29	6 58	5 38	6 51	5 45	6 44	5 51	6 38
11	5 18	7 11	5 24	7 05	5 29	7 01	5 32	6 59	5 32	7 01
21	5 13	7 15	5 17	7 12	5 17	7 12	5 16	7 14	5 09	7 23
Mar. 1	5 08	7 18	5 08	7 19	5 06	7 21	4 59	7 29	4 44	7 45
11	5 00	7 21	4 58	7 24	4 50	7 32	4 38	7 46	4 12	8 12
21	4 52	7 24	4 45	7 32	4 33	7 44	4 14	8 04	3 37	8 43
Apr. 1	4 42	7 28	4 31	7 39	4 14	7 57	3 47	8 25	2 53	9 21
11	4 32	7 32	4 18	7 47	3 56	8 09	3 20	8 47	2 03	10 10
21	4 23	7 36	4 04	7 54	3 37	8 23	2 52	9 11	0 37	11 47
May 1	4 14	7 41	3 52	8 04	3 19	8 37	2 22	9 39		
11	4 08	7 46	3 41	8 13	3 03	8 53	1 49	10 09		
21	4 02	7 52	3 32	8 22	2 48	9 07	1 13	10 46		
June 1	3 58	7 58	3 26	8 30	2 36	9 20	0 21	11 52		
11	3 56	8 03	3 22	8 36	2 29	9 30				
21	3 57	8 06	3 22	8 40	2 28	9 35				
July 1	3 59	8 07	3 25	8 41	2 30	9 35				
11	4 03	8 06	3 30	8 39	2 40	9 30				
21	4 08	8 03	3 39	8 33	2 52	9 18	1 12	11 23		
Aug. 1	4 15	7 56	3 48	8 23	3 09	9 01	1 49	10 20		
11	4 20	7 50	3 56	8 13	3 22	8 46	2 21	9 46		
21	4 24	7 41	4 05	8 01	3 34	8 27	2 47	9 15		
Sept. 1	4 29	7 31	4 14	7 46	3 51	8 08	3 13	8 43	1 40	10 02
11	4 32	7 20	4 20	7 33	4 02	7 50	3 33	8 16	2 36	9 12
21	4 35	7 11	4 26	7 19	4 14	7 31	3 52	7 52	3 11	8 31
Oct. 1	4 38	7 02	4 33	7 05	4 25	7 13	4 10	7 28	3 41	7 54
11	4 40	6 53	4 40	6 53	4 35	6 58	4 26	7 05	4 07	7 23
21	4 43	6 47	4 45	6 44	4 45	6 43	4 41	6 46	4 32	6 55
Nov. 1	4 46	6 41	4 52	6 34	4 56	6 30	5 08	6 27	4 56	6 27
11	4 50	6 38	4 59	6 28	5 06	6 21	5 13	6 14	5 17	6 08
21	4 55	6 36	5 06	6 25	5 16	6 15	5 26	6 04	5 37	5 52
Dec. 1	5 00	6 37	5 13	6 24	5 25	6 11	5 38	5 58	5 53	5 42
11	5 06	6 40	5 20	6 26	5 34	6 12	5 48	5 57	6 06	5 38
21	5 11	6 45	5 25	6 30	5 39	6 16	5 55	6 00	6 15	5 40
31	5 15	6 50	5 30	6 35	5 44	6 21	6 00	6 06	6 18	5 48

Harvest Moon and Hunter's Moon

The Harvest Moon, the full moon nearest the Autumnal Equinox, ushers in a period of several successive days when the moon rises soon after sunset. This phenomenon gives farmers in temperate latitudes extra hours of light in which to harvest their crops before frost and winter come. The 1976 Harvest Moon falls on Sept. 8. Harvest moon in the south temperate latitudes falls on Mar. 16.

The next full moon after Harvest Moon is called the Hunter's Moon, accompanied by a similar phenomenon but less marked; — Oct. 8, northern hemisphere, Apr. 14, southern hemisphere.

Aurora Borealis and Aurora Australis

The Aurora Borealis, also called the Northern Lights, is a broad display of rather faint light in the northern skies at night. The Aurora Australis, a similar phenomenon, appears at the same time in southern skies. The aurora appears in a wide variety of forms. Sometimes it is seen as a quiet glow, almost foglike in character; sometimes as vertical streamers in which there may be considerable motion; sometimes as a series of luminous expanding arcs. There are many colors, with white, yellow, and red predominating.

The auroras are most vivid and most frequently seen at about 20 degrees from the magnetic poles, along the northern coast of the North American continent and the eastern part of the northern coast of Europe. They have been seen as far south as Key West and as far north as Australia and New Zealand, but such occasions are rare.

While the cause of the auroras is not known beyond question, there does seem to be a definite correlation between

auroral displays and the sun-spot activity. It is thought that atomic particles expelled from the sun by the forces that cause solar flares speed through space at velocities of 400 to 600 miles per second. These particles are entrapped by the earth's magnetic field, forming what are termed the Van Allen belts. The encounter of these clouds of the solar wind with the earth's magnetic field weakens the field so that previously trapped particles are allowed to impact the upper atmosphere. The collisions between solar and terrestrial atoms result in the glow in the upper atmosphere called the aurora. The glow may be vivid where the lines of magnetic force converge near the magnetic poles.

The auroral displays appear at heights ranging from 50 to about 600 miles and have given us a means of estimating the extent of the earth's atmosphere.

The auroras are often accompanied by magnetic storms whose forces, also guided by the lines of force of the earth's magnetic field, disrupt electrical communication.

Latitude, Longitude and Altitude of North American Cities

Source: National Ocean Survey (NOAA) for geographic position.
Source for Canadian Cities: Geodetic Survey of Canada, Dept. of Energy, Mines and Resources.
Altitudes U.S. Geological Survey and various sources. °Approx. altitude at downtown business area U.S.; in Canada at tower of major airport.

City	Lat. N ° ' "	Long. W ° ' "	Alt.* Feet	City	Lat. N ° ' "	Long. W ° ' "	Alt.* Feet
Abilene, Texas........	32 27 54	99 42 48	1710	Edmonton, Alta.:......	53 32 45	113 29 15	2,373
Akron, Ohio..........	41 05 00	81 30 44	874	El Paso, Tex..........	31 45 36	106 29 11	3,695
Albany, N.Y..........	42 39 01	73 45 01	20	Elizabeth, N.J........	40 39 43	74 12 59	21
Albuquerque, N.M.....	35 05 01	106 39 05	4,945	Enid, Okla...........	36 23 42	97 52 30	1,240
Allentown, Pa........	40 36 11	75 28 06	255	Erie, Pa.............	42 07 15	80 04 57	685
Alert, N.W.T.........	82 29 50	62 21 15	95	Eugene, Ore..........	44 03 16	123 05 30	422
Altoona, Pa..........	40 30 55	78 24 03	1,180	Eureka, Cal..........	40 46 54	124 09 24	45
Amarillo, Tex........	35 12 27	101 50 04	3,685	Evansville, Ind.......	37 58 20	87 34 21	385
Anchorage, Alaska....	61 10 00	149 59 00	118				
Ann Arbor, Mich......	42 16 59	83 44 52	880	Fairbanks, Alaska.....	64 48 00	147 51 00	448
Asheville, N.C........	35 35 42	82 33 26	1,985	Fall River, Mass......	41 42 06	71 09 18	40
Ashland, Ky..........	38 28 36	82 38 23	536	Fargo, N.D...........	46 52 30	96 47 18	900
Atlanta, Ga..........	33 45 10	84 23 37	1,050	Flagstaff, Ariz.......	35 11 36	111 39 06	6,900
Atlantic City, N.J.....	39 21 32	74 25 53	10	Flint, Mich..........	43 01 18	83 41 00	750
Augusta, Ga..........	33 28 20	81 58 00	143	Ft. Smith, Ariz.......	35 23 06	94 25 06	440
Augusta, Me..........	44 18 53	69 46 29	45	Fort Wayne, Ind......	41 04 21	85 08 26	790
Austin, Tex..........	30 16 09	97 44 37	505	Fort Worth, Tex......	32 44 55	97 19 44	670
				Fredericton, N.B......	45 57 40	66 38 30	67
Bakersfield, Cal......	35 22 30	119 01 18	400	Fresno, Cal..........	36 44 12	119 47 11	285
Baltimore, Md........	39 17 26	76 36 45	20				
Bangor, Me..........	44 48 13	68 46 18	20	Gadsden, Ala.........	34 00 57	86 00 41	555
Baton Rouge, La......	30 26 58	91 11 00	57	Gainesville, Fla.......	29 39 36	82 19 48	175
Battle Creek, Mich....	42 18 58	85 10 48	820	Gallup, N.M..........	35 31 30	108 44 30	6,540
Bay City, Mich.......	43 36 04	83 53 15	595	Galveston, Tex.......	29 18 10	94 47 43	5
Beaumont, Tex.......	30 05 20	94 06 09	20	Gary, Ind...........	41 36 12	87 20 19	590
Belleville, Ont.......	44 09 30	77 22 30	280	Grand Junction, Conn.	39 04 06	108 33 06	4,590
Bellingham, Wash.....	48 45 02	122 28 36	60	Grand Rapids, Mich....	42 58 03	85 40 13	610
Berkeley, Cal........	37 52 10	122 16 17	40	Great Falls, Mont.....	47 30 06	111 17 06	3,340
Bethlehem, Pa........	40 37 16	75 22 34	235	Green Bay, Wis.......	44 30 48	88 00 50	590
Billings, Mont........	45 47 00	108 30 04	3,120	Greensboro, N.C......	36 04 17	79 47 25	839
Biloxi, Miss..........	30 23 48	88 53 00	20	Greenville, S.C.......	34 50 50	82 24 01	966
Binghamton, N.Y.....	42 06 03	75 54 47	865	Guelph, Ont..........	43 32 30	80 15 30	1,075
Birmingham, Ala......	33 31 01	86 48 36	600	Gulfport, Miss........	30 22 04	89 05 36	20
Bismarck, N.D........	46 48 23	100 47 17	1,674				
Bloomington, Ill......	40 28 54	88 59 36	800	Halifax, N.S.........	44 38 39	63 34 34	476
Boise, Idaho.........	43 37 07	116 11 58	2,704	Hamilton, Ont........	43 15 17	79 52 28	776
Boston, Mass.........	42 21 24	71 03 25	21	Hamilton, Ohio.......	39 23 59	84 33 47	600
Bowling Green, Ky....	36 59 18	86 27 03	510	Harrisburg, Pa.......	40 15 43	76 52 59	365
Brattleboro, Vt......	42 51 06	72 33 48	300	Hartford, Conn.......	41 46 12	72 40 49	40
Brandon, Man........	49 51 00	99 57 00	1,265	Helena, Mont........	46 35 33	112 02 24	4,155
Brantford, Ont.......	43 07 30	80 15 30	705	Hilo, Hawaii.........	19 43 30	155 05 24	40
Bridgeport, Conn.....	41 10 49	73 11 22	10	Holyoke, Mass........	42 12 29	72 36 36	115
Brockton, Mass.......	42 05 02	71 01 25	130	Honolulu, Hawaii.....	21 18 22	157 51 35	21
Brownsville, Tex......	25 54 07	97 29 58	35	Houston, Tex.........	29 45 26	95 21 37	40
Buffalo, N.Y.........	42 52 52	78 52 21	585	Hull, Que............	45 26 00	75 44 00	225
Burlington, Ont.......	43 18 30	79 46 30	875	Huntington, W.Va.....	38 25 12	82 26 33	565
Burlington, Vt........	44 28 34	73 12 46	110	Huntsville, Ala.......	34 43 54	86 35 12	640
Butte, Mont.........	46 01 06	112 32 11	5,765	Indianapolis, Ind.....	39 46 07	86 09 46	710
				Iowa City, Iowa.......	41 39 37	91 31 53	685
Calgary, Alta........	51 02 46	114 03 24	3,557				
Cambridge, Mass......	42 22 01	71 06 22	20	Jackson, Mich........	42 14 43	84 24 22	940
Camden, N.J.........	39 56 41	75 07 14	30	Jackson, Miss........	32 17 56	90 11 06	298
Canton, Ohio........	40 47 50	81 22 37	1,030	Jacksonville, Fla......	30 19 44	81 39 42	20
Carson City, Nev......	39 10 00	119 46 00	4,680	Jersey City, N.J......	40 43 50	74 03 56	20
Cedar Rapids, Iowa....	41 58 01	91 39 53	730	Johnstown, Pa........	40 19 35	78 55 03	1,185
Central Islip, N.Y.....	40 47 24	73 12 00	80	Joplin, Mo...........	37 05 36	94 30 42	990
Champaign, Ill........	40 07 05	88 14 48	740	Juneau, Alaska.......	58 18 12	134 24 30	50
Charleston, S.C.......	32 46 35	79 55 53	9				
Charleston, W.Va.....	38 21 01	81 37 52	601	Kalamazoo, Mich......	42 17 29	85 35 14	755
Charlotte, N.C........	35 13 44	80 50 45	720	Kansas City, Kan.....	39 07 04	94 38 24	750
Charlottetown, P.E.I...	46 14 00	63 07 45	181	Kansas City, Mo......	39 04 56	94 35 20	750
Chattanooga, Tenn....	35 02 41	85 18 32	675	Kenosha, Wis.	42 35 33	87 50 11	610
Cheyenne, Wyo.......	41 08 09	104 49 07	6,100	Key West, Fla........	24 33 30	81 48 12	5
Chicago, Ill..........	41 52 28	87 38 22	595	Kingston, Ont........	44 13 30	76 30 00	310
Churchill, Man.......	58 45 15	94 10 00	94	Kitchener, Ont.......	43 26 59	80 29 17	1,031
Cincinnati, Ohio......	39 06 07	84 30 35	550	Knoxville, Tenn.......	35 57 39	83 55 07	890
Cleveland, Ohio......	41 29 51	81 41 50	660				
Colorado Springs......	38 50 07	104 49 16	5,980	Lafayette, Ind........	40 25 11	86 53 39	550
Columbia, Mo........	38 57 03	92 19 46	730	Lancaster, Pa........	40 02 25	76 18 29	355
Columbia, S.C........	34 00 02	81 02 00	190	Lansing, Mich........	42 44 01	84 33 15	830
Columbus, Ga........	32 28 07	84 59 24	265	Laredo, Tex..........	27 30 22	99 30 30	440
Columbus, Ohio......	39 57 47	83 00 17	780	La Salle, Que.........	45 25 30	73 38 30	100
Concord, N.H.........	43 12 22	71 32 25	290	Las Vegas, Nev.......	36 10 20	115 08 37	2,030
Corpus Christi, Tex...	27 47 51	97 23 45	35	Laval, Que...........	45 35 30	73 45 30	100
				Lawrence, Mass.......	42 42 16	71 10 08	65
Dallas, Tex..........	32 47 09	96 47 37	435	Lethbridge, Alta......	49 41 30	112 49 00	2,990
Dartmouth, N.S.......	44 38 39	63 34 34	476	Lexington, Ky........	38 02 50	84 29 46	955
Davenport, Iowa......	41 31 19	90 34 33	590	Lihue, Hawaii........	21 58 48	159 22 30	210
Dawson, Yukon.......	64 03 30	139 26 00	1,211	Lima, Ohio..........	40 44 35	84 06 20	865
Dayton, Ohio........	39 45 32	84 11 43	574	Lincoln, Nebr........	40 48 59	96 42 15	1,150
Daytona Beach, Fla...	29 12 44	81 01 10	7	Little Rock, Ark......	34 44 42	92 16 37	286
Decatur, Ill.........	39 50 42	88 56 47	682	London, Ont.........	42 59 00	81 15 00	912
Denver, Colo........	39 44 58	104 59 22	5,280	Long Beach, Cal......	33 46 14	118 11 18	35
Des Moines, Iowa.....	41 35 14	93 37 00	805	Lorain, Ohio.........	41 28 05	82 10 49	610
Detroit, Mich........	42 19 48	83 02 57	585	Los Angeles, Cal......	34 03 15	118 14 28	340
Dodge City, Kans.....	37 45 17	100 01 09	2,480	Louisville, Ky........	38 14 47	85 45 49	450
Dubuque, Iowa.......	42 30 12	90 40 30	620	Lowell, Mass.........	42 38 25	71 19 14	100
Duluth, Minn.........	46 46 56	92 06 24	610	Lubbock, Tex.........	33 35 05	101 50 33	3,195
Durham, N.C.........	36 00 00	78 54 45	405				
				Macon, Ga...........	32 50 12	83 37 36	335
Eau Claire, Wis........	44 48 48	91 29 42	790	Madison, Wis.........	43 04 23	89 22 55	860

City	Lat. N ° ′ ″	Long. W ° ′ ″	Alt.* Feet
Manchester, N.H.	42 59 28	71 27 41	175
Marshall, Texas	32 33 00	94 23 00	410
Memphis, Tenn.	35 08 46	90 03 13	275
Meriden, Conn.	41 32 06	72 47 30	190
Mexico City, Mexico	19 25 45	99 07 00	7,347
Miami, Fla.	25 46 37	80 11 32	10
Milwaukee, Wis.	43 02 19	87 54 15	635
Minneapolis, Minn.	44 58 57	93 15 43	815
Minot, N.D.	48 14 18	101 17 48	1,550
Mississauga, Ont.	43 33 00	79 35 00	260
Mobile, Ala.	30 41 36	88 02 33	5
Moline, Ill.	41 30 31	90 30 49	585
Moncton, N.B.	46 05 30	64 47 30	75
Montgomery, Ala.	32 22 33	86 18 31	160
Montpelier, Vt.	44 15 36	72 34 41	485
Montreal, Que.	45 30 30	73 33 20	117
Moose Jaw, Sask.	50 23 30	105 32 30	1,810
Muncie, Ind.	40 11 28	85 23 16	950
Nashville, Tenn.	36 09 33	86 46 55	450
Natchez, Miss.	31 33 48	91 23 30	210
Newark, N.J.	40 44 14	74 10 19	55
New Bedford, Mass.	41 38 13	70 55 41	15
New Britain, Conn.	41 40 08	72 46 59	200
New Haven, Conn.	41 18 25	72 55 30	40
New Orleans, La.	29 56 53	90 04 10	5
New York, N.Y.	40 45 06	73 59 39	55
Niagara Falls, N.Y.	43 05 34	79 03 26	570
Niagara Falls, Ont.	43 05 30	79 03 30	585
Nome, Alaska	64 30 00	165 25 00	25
Norfolk, Va.	36 51 10	76 17 21	10
North Bay, Ont.	46 18 30	79 27 30	925
Oakland, Cal.	37 48 03	122 15 54	25
Ogden, Utah.	41 13 31	111 58 21	4,295
Oklahoma City.	35 28 26	97 31 04	1,195
Omaha, Nebr.	41 15 42	95 56 14	1,040
Orlando, Fla.	28 32 42	81 22 38	70
Oshawa, Ont.	43 54 00	78 52 00	350
Ottawa, Ont.	45 25 40	75 42 45	374
Paducah, Ky.	37 05 13	88 35 56	345
Pasadena, Cal.	34 08 44	118 08 41	830
Paterson, N.J.	40 55 01	74 10 21	100
Pensacola, Fla.	30 24 51	87 12 56	15
Peoria, Ill.	40 41 42	89 35 33	470
Peterborough, Ont.	44 18 00	78 19 30	685
Philadelphia, Pa.	39 56 58	75 09 21	100
Phoenix, Ariz.	33 27 12	112 04 28	1,090
Pierre, S.D.	44 22 18	100 20 54	1,480
Pittsburgh, Pa.	40 26 19	80 00 00	745
Pittsfield, Mass.	42 26 53	73 15 14	1,015
Pocatello, Idaho.	42 52 24	112 27 00	4,460
Port Arthur, Texas.	29 52 30	93 56 15	10
Portland, Me.	43 39 33	70 15 19	25
Portland, Ore.	45 31 06	122 40 35	77
Portsmouth, N.H.	43 04 30	70 45 24	20
Portsmouth, Va.	36 50 07	76 18 14	10
Prince Rupert, B.C.	54 19 00	130 19 00	125
Providence, R.I.	41 49 32	71 24 41	80
Provo, Utah.	40 14 06	111 39 24	4,550
Pueblo, Col.	38 16 17	104 36 33	4,690
Quebec City, Que.	46 48 46	71 12 20	239
Racine, Wis.	42 43 49	87 47 12	630
Rapid City, S.D.	44 04 48	103 13 42	3,230
Raleigh, N.C.	35 46 38	78 38 21	365
Reading, Pa.	40 20 09	75 55 40	265
Regina, Sask.	50 27 02	104 36 30	1,894
Reno, Nev.	39 31 27	119 48 40	4,490
Richmond, Va.	37 32 15	77 26 09	160
Roanoke, Va.	37 16 13	79 56 44	905
Rochester, Minn.	44 01 21	92 28 03	990
Rochester, N.Y.	43 09 41	77 36 21	515
Rockford, Ill.	42 16 07	89 05 48	715
Sacramento, Cal.	38 34 57	121 29 41	30
Saginaw, Mich.	43 25 52	83 56 05	595
St. Catharines, Ont.	43 09 30	79 14 30	362
Saint John, N.B.	45 16 00	66 04 30	80
St. Cloud, Minn.	45 34 00	94 10 24	1,040
St. John's, Nfld.	47 34 00	52 43 30	200
St. Joseph, Mo.	39 45 57	94 51 02	850
St. Louis, Mo.	38 37 45	90 12 22	455
St. Paul, Minn.	44 57 19	93 06 07	780
St. Petersburg, Fla.	27 46 18	82 38 19	20
Salem, Ore.	44 56 24	123 02 00	155

City	Lat. N ° ′ ″	Long. W ° ′ ″	Alt.* Feet
Salina, Kan.	38 50 06	97 36 30	1,229
Salt Lake City, Utah	40 45 23	111 53 26	4,390
San Angelo, Tex.	31 27 39	100 26 03	1,845
San Antonio, Tex.	29 25 37	98 29 06	650
San Bernardino, Cal.	34 06 30	117 17 28	1,080
San Diego, Cal.	32 42 53	117 09 21	20
San Francisco, Cal.	37 46 39	122 24 40	65
San Jose, Cal.	37 20 16	121 53 24	90
San Juan, P.R.	18 27 00	66 04 15	35
Santa Barbara, Cal.	34 25 18	119 41 55	100
Santa Cruz, Cal.	36 58 18	122 01 18	20
Santa Fe, N.M.	35 41 11	105 56 10	6,950
Sarasota, Fla.	27 20 12	82 31 54	20
Saskatoon, Sask.	52 07 50	106 39 41	1,653
Sault Ste. Marie, Ont.	46 31 30	84 20 00	650
Savannah, Ga.	32 04 42	81 05 37	20
Schenectady, N.Y.	42 48 42	73 55 42	245
Scranton, Pa.	41 24 32	75 39 46	725
Seattle, Wash.	47 36 32	122 20 12	10
Sheboygan, Wis.	43 45 35	87 44 54	630
Sherbrooke, Que.	45 24 00	71 53 30	625
Sheridan, Wyo.	44 47 48	106 57 42	3,740
Shreveport, La.	32 30 46	93 44 58	204
Sioux City, Iowa	42 29 46	96 24 30	1,110
Sioux Falls, S.D.	43 32 35	96 43 35	1,395
Somerville, Mass.	42 23 15	71 06 07	13
South Bend, Ind.	41 40 33	86 15 01	710
Spartanburg, S.C.	34 57 03	81 56 06	875
Spokane, Wash.	47 39 32	117 25 33	1,890
Springfield, Ill.	39 47 58	89 38 51	610
Springfield, Mass.	42 06 21	72 35 32	85
Springfield, Mo.	37 13 03	93 17 32	1,300
Springfield, Ohio.	39 55 38	83 48 29	980
Stamford, Conn.	41 03 09	73 32 24	35
Steubenville, Ohio.	40 21 42	80 36 53	660
Stockton, Cal.	37 57 30	121 17 16	20
Sudbury, Ont.	46 28 30	80 58 30	917
Superior, Wis.	46 43 14	92 06 07	630
Sydney, N.S.	46 08 30	60 11 00	50
Syracuse, N.Y.	43 03 04	76 09 14	400
Tacoma, Wash.	47 14 59	122 26 15	110
Tallahassee, Fla.	30 26 42	84 16 54	150
Tampa, Fla.	27 56 58	82 27 25	15
Terre Haute, Ind.	39 28 03	87 24 26	496
Texarkana, Texas.	33 25 48	94 02 30	324
Thunder Bay, Ont.	48 25 00	89 14 00	650
Toledo, Ohio.	41 39 14	83 32 39	585
Topeka, Kan.	39 03 16	95 40 23	930
Toronto, Ont.	43 39 12	79 23 00	532
Trenton, N.J.	40 13 14	74 46 13	35
Trois-Rivieres, Que.	46 21 00	72 33 00	115
Troy, N.Y.	42 43 45	73 40 58	35
Tucson, Ariz.	32 13 15	110 58 08	2,390
Tulsa, Okla.	36 09 12	95 59 34	804
Urbana, Ill.	40 06 42	88 12 06	
Utica, N.Y.	43 06 12	75 13 33	415
Vancouver, B.C.	49 16 30	123 07 30	388
Victoria, B.C.	48 25 40	123 21 45	....
Waco, Tex.	31 33 12	97 08 00	405
Walla Walla, Wash.	46 04 08	118 20 24	936
Washington, D.C.	38 53 51	77 00 33	25
Waterbury, Conn.	41 33 13	73 02 31	260
Waterloo, Iowa	42 29 40	92 20 20	850
West Palm Beach, Fla.	26 43 00	80 03 12	15
Wheeling W. Va.	40 04 03	80 43 20	650
Whitehorse, Yukon	60 43 15	135 03 15	2,305
White Plains, N.Y.	41 02 00	73 45 48	220
Wichita, Kan.	37 41 30	97 20 16	1,290
Wichita Falls, Tex.	33 54 34	98 29 28	945
Wilkes-Barre, Pa.	41 14 32	75 53 17	640
Wilmington, Del.	39 44 46	75 32 51	135
Wilmington, N.C.	34 14 12	77 55 24	35
Windsor, Ont.	42 19 50	83 03 00	590
Winnipeg, Man.	49 53 56	97 08 20	765
Winston-Salem, N.C.	36 05 52	80 14 42	860
Worcester, Mass.	42 15 37	71 48 17	475
Yakima, Wash.	46 35 42	120 30 48	1,060
Yellowknife, N.W.T.	62 28 15	114 22 00	674
Yonkers, N.Y.	40 55 55	73 53 54	10
York, Pa.	39 57 35	76 43 36	370
Youngstown, Ohio.	41 05 57	80 39 02	840
Yuma, Ariz.	32 42 54	114 37 24	160
Zanesville, Ohio.	39 56 18	82 00 30	720

World Cities

City	Lat. N	Long. W	Alt.* Feet
London, UK (Greenwich)	51 30 00N	0 0 0	245
Paris, France	48 50 14N	2 20 14E	300
Berlin, Germany	52 32 00N	13 25 00E	110
Rome, Italy.	41 53 00N	12 30 00E	95
Warsaw, Poland.	52 15 00N	21 00 00E	360
Moscow, U.S.S.R.	55 45 00N	37 42 00E	394
Athens, Greece.	37 58 00N	23 44 00E	300
Jerusalem, Israel.	31 47 00N	35 13 00E	2,500
Johannesburg, So. Afr.	26 10 00S	28 02 00E	5,740
New Delhi, India.	28 38 00N	77 12 00E	770
Peking, China	39 54 00N	116 28 00E	600
Rio de Janeiro, Brazil.	22 53 43S	43 13 22W	30
Tokyo, Japan.	35 45 00N	139 45 00E	30
Sydney, Australia.	33 52 00S	151 12 00E	25

Calendar Adjustment Tables

The tables below will allow you to determine the approximate time of the rise or set of the sun and moon at your specific location. Rise and set times of the moon for your location can be more than one-half hour later than the times given on the following pages.

First find your latitude and longitude or that of a nearby city in the tables on pages 765-766. On the calendar tables look for the time given for the nearest latitude to your south. Compare that time with the time given for the next latitude to your north.

On Table A below, find the difference between the two latitudes in the top row. Run your finger down the column until you reach the row that indicates how far north you are of the southern latitude. Adjust the time given for the southern latitude by the number of minutes shown in Table A.

Now compare the time given for the southern latitude on the day you're seeking and for the next day. Using Table B, find the time difference between the two days. Run your finger down the column until you reach the row that belongs to the longitude nearest you. Add the minutes given there to your previous figure.

Finally, to adjust for local time, you must determine how many degrees of longitude you are from your time zone meridian: Atlantic — 60°, Eastern — 75°, Central — 90°, Mountain — 105°, Pacific — 120° and Alaska-Hawaii — 150°. For every degree of longitude west of the meridian you must add 4 minutes of time; for every degree of longitude east, subtract 4 minutes.

Example: Find the moonrise time for Superior, Wisconsin for March 7, 1975. Superior is at 92° 06′ longitude and 46° 43′ latitude.
Calendar time given for 40° — 3:05
Calendar time given for 50° — 3:37
Difference — 32 minutes
Table A at 30 min. and 6° 40′ — 20 minutes
First adjusted time — 3:25
Time for 40° on March 3 — 3:43
Difference between Mar. 7 and Mar. 8 — 38 minutes
Table B at 40 min. and 90° 00′ — 10 minutes
Second adjusted time — 3:35
Local time adjustment 2° x 4 min. — 8 minutes
Moonrise on March 7 — about 3:43 a.m.

Table A: Latitude Adjustment

Diff. in Min. Lat.	10	20	30	40	50	60	70	80	90	100	110	120
0°20	0	1	1	1	2	2	2	3	3	3	4	4
40	1	1	2	3	3	4	5	5	6	7	7	8
1 00	1	2	3	4	5	6	7	8	9	10	11	12
20	1	3	4	5	7	8	9	11	12	13	15	16
40	2	3	5	7	8	10	12	13	15	17	18	20
2 00	2	4	6	8	10	12	14	16	18	20	22	24
20	2	5	7	9	12	14	16	19	21	23	26	28
40	3	5	8	11	13	16	19	21	24	27	29	32
3 00	3	6	9	12	15	18	21	24	27	30	33	36
20	3	7	10	13	17	20	23	27	30	33	37	40
40	4	7	11	15	18	22	26	29	33	37	40	44
4 00	4	8	12	16	20	24	28	32	36	40	44	48
20	4	9	13	17	22	26	30	35	39	43	48	52
40	5	9	14	19	23	28	33	37	42	47	51	56
5 00	5	10	15	20	25	30	35	40	45	50	55	60
20	5	11	16	21	27	32	37	43	48	53	59	64
40	6	11	17	23	28	34	40	45	51	57	62	68
6 00	6	12	18	24	30	36	42	48	54	60	66	72
20	6	13	19	25	32	38	44	51	57	63	70	76
40	7	13	20	27	33	40	47	53	60	67	73	80
7 00	7	14	21	28	35	42	49	56	63	70	77	84
20	7	15	22	29	37	44	51	59	66	73	81	88
40	8	15	23	31	38	46	54	61	69	77	84	92
8 00	8	16	24	32	40	48	56	64	72	80	88	96
20	8	17	25	33	42	50	58	67	75	83	92	100
40	9	17	26	35	43	52	61	69	78	87	95	104
9 00	9	18	27	36	45	54	63	72	81	90	39	108
20	9	19	28	37	47	56	65	75	84	93	103	112
40	10	19	29	39	48	58	68	77	87	97	106	116

Table B: Longitude Adjustment

Diff. in Min. Long.	10	20	30	40	50	60	70	80	90	100	110	120
50°	1	3	4	6	7	8	10	11	12	14	15	17
55	2	3	5	6	8	9	11	12	14	15	17	18
60	2	3	5	7	8	10	12	13	15	17	18	20
65	2	4	5	7	9	11	13	14	16	18	20	22
70	2	4	6	8	10	12	14	16	18	19	21	23
75	2	4	6	8	10	12	15	17	19	21	23	25
80	2	4	7	9	11	13	16	18	20	22	24	27
85	2	5	7	9	12	14	16	19	21	24	26	28
90	2	5	8	10	12	15	18	20	22	25	28	30
95	3	5	8	11	13	16	18	21	24	26	29	32
100	3	6	8	11	14	17	19	22	25	28	31	33
105	3	6	9	12	15	18	20	23	26	29	32	35
110	3	6	9	12	15	18	21	24	28	31	34	37
115	3	6	10	13	16	19	22	26	29	32	35	38
120	3	7	10	13	17	20	23	27	30	33	37	40
125	4	7	10	14	17	21	24	28	31	35	38	42
130	4	7	11	14	18	22	25	29	32	36	40	43
135	4	8	11	15	19	22	26	30	34	38	41	45
140	4	8	12	16	19	23	27	31	35	39	43	47
145	4	8	12	16	20	24	28	32	36	40	44	48
150	4	8	12	17	21	25	29	33	38	42	46	50
155	4	9	13	17	22	26	30	34	39	43	47	52
160	4	9	13	18	22	27	31	36	40	44	49	53
165	5	9	14	18	23	28	32	37	41	46	50	55
170	5	9	14	19	24	28	33	38	42	47	52	57

1st Month   January, 1976   31 Days

Greenwich Mean Time

NOTE: Light figures indicate Sun. **Dark** figures indicate **Moon.** *Degrees are North Latitude.*
CAUTION: Must be converted to local time. For instruction see page 767.

Day of month / week / year	Sun on meridian / Moon phase (h m s)	20° Rise Sun/Moon (h m)	20° Set Sun/Moon (h m)	30° Rise Sun/Moon (h m)	30° Set Sun/Moon (h m)	40° Rise Sun/Moon (h m)	40° Set Sun/Moon (h m)	50° Rise Sun/Moon (h m)	50° Set Sun/Moon (h m)	60° Rise Sun/Moon (h m)	60° Set Sun/Moon (h m)
1Th	12 02 29	6 35	17 32	6 55	17 11	7 22	16 45	7 59	16 08	9 03	15 04
1	14 40 ●	6 14	17 39	6 33	17 21	6 56	16 59	7 28	16 28	8 22	15 35
2Fr	12 02 58	6 35	17 32	6 56	17 12	7 22	16 46	7 59	16 09	9 02	15 06
2		7 04	18 36	7 21	18 21	7 41	18 01	8 09	17 35	8 55	16 51
3Sa	12 03 26	6 35	17 33	6 56	17 12	7 22	16 46	7 58	16 10	9 02	15 07
3		7 50	19 30	8 04	19 18	8 20	19 03	8 43	18 43	9 19	18 10
4Su	12 03 53	6 36	17 33	6 57	17 13	7 22	16 47	7 58	16 11	9 01	15 09
4		8 32	20 23	8 42	20 15	8 40	20 04	9 11	19 50	9 37	19 27
5Mo	12 04 21	6 36	17 34	6 57	17 14	7 22	16 48	7 58	16 12	9 01	15 10
5		9 11	21 14	9 17	21 09	9 25	21 03	9 36	20 56	9 52	20 43
6Tu	12 04 48	6 36	17 35	6 57	17 15	7 22	16 49	7 58	16 13	9 00	15 12
6		9 48	22 03	9 51	22 02	9 54	22 01	9 58	22 00	10 05	21 58
7We	12 05 14	6 36	17 35	6 57	17 16	7 22	16 50	7 57	16 14	8 59	15 14
7		10 24	22 51	10 22	22 54	10 21	22 58	10 19	23 03	10 16	23 11
8Th	12 05 40	6 37	17 36	6 57	17 16	7 22	16 51	7 57	16 16	8 58	15 15
8		10 59	23 39	10 54	23 46	10 48	23 54	10 41		10 26	
9Fr	12 06 05	6 37	17 36	6 57	17 17	7 22	16 52	7 56	16 17	8 57	15 17
9	12 40 ☽	11 35		11 27		11 17		11 03	0 06	10 42	0 24
10Sa	12 06 30	6 37	17 37	6 57	17 18	7 22	16 53	7 56	16 18	8 56	15 19
10		12 14	0 28	12 02	0 38	11 47	0 51	11 28	1 09	10 57	1 36
11Su	12 06 55	6 37	17 38	6 57	17 19	7 22	16 54	7 55	16 19	8 55	15 21
11		12 54	1 18	12 40	1 32	12 22	1 48	11 57	2 12	11 17	2 49
12Mo	12 07 18	6 37	17 39	6 57	17 20	7 21	16 55	7 55	16 21	8 53	15 23
12		13 39	2 10	13 21	2 26	13 00	2 46	12 31	3 14	11 43	4 01
13Tu	12 07 42	6 38	17 39	6 57	17 20	7 21	16 56	7 54	16 22	8 52	15 26
13		14 27	3 02	14 08	3 21	13 45	3 43	13 12	4 15	12 18	5 09
14We	12 08 04	6 38	17 40	6 57	17 51	7 20	16 57	7 54	16 36	8 50	15 28
14		15 19	3 56	15 00	4 15	14 36	4 39	14 02	5 13	13 05	6 10
15Th	12 09 26	6 38	17 41	6 57	17 22	7 20	16 58	7 53	16 25	8 49	15 30
15		16 16	4 50	15 57	5 09	15 34	5 33	15 02	6 06	14 07	7 01
16Fr	12 08 47	6 38	17 42	6 57	17 23	7 20	16 59	7 52	16 27	8 47	15 32
16		17 15	5 43	16 58	6 00	16 38	6 22	16 09	6 52	15 22	7 41
17Sa	12 09 07	6 38	17 42	6 57	17 24	7 19	17 00	7 51	16 28	8 46	15 34
17	04 47 ◷	18 15	6 34	18 02	6 48	17 45	7 06	17 22	7 31	16 46	8 11
18Su	12 09 27	6 38	17 43	6 56	17 24	7 19	17 02	7 51	16 30	8 44	15 37
18		19 16	7 22	19 06	7 33	18 55	7 47	18 39	8 05	18 14	8 34
19Mo	12 09 46	6 38	17 43	6 56	17 25	7 18	17 03	7 50	16 31	8 43	15 39
19		20 16	8 09	20 11	8 16	20 05	8 24	19 57	8 35	19 45	8 53
20Tu	12 10 04	6 38	17 44	6 56	17 26	7 18	17 04	7 49	16 33	8 41	15 41
20		21 16	8 54	21 16	8 56	21 16	8 59	21 16	9 03	21 15	9 09
21We	12 10 22	6 38	17 44	6 56	17 27	7 17	17 05	7 48	16 35	8 39	15 44
21		22 16	9 38	22 21	9 36	22 26	9 33	22 34	9 30	22 46	9 24
22Th	12 10 39	6 38	17 45	6 55	17 28	7 17	17 06	7 47	16 36	8 37	15 46
22		23 16	10 22	23 25	10 16	23 36	10 03	23 51	9 57		9 40
23Fr	12 10 55	6 37	17 46	6 55	17 28	7 16	17 08	7 46	16 38	8 35	15 49
23	23 04 ◔		11 08		10 57		10 44		10 26	0 15	9 58
24Sa	12 11 11	6 37	17 46	6 54	17 29	7 16	17 09	7 45	16 39	8 33	15 51
24		0 16	11 56	0 29	11 41	0 45	11 24	1 07	10 59	1 43	10 20
25Su	12 11 25	6 37	17 47	6 54	17 30	7 15	17 10	7 44	16 41	8 31	15 54
25		1 16	12 46	1 32	12 29	1 52	12 08	2 20	11 38	3 07	10 49
26Mo	12 11 39	6 37	17 48	6 54	17 31	7 14	17 11	7 43	16 43	8 29	15 57
26		2 15	13 39	2 33	13 20	2 56	12 56	3 29	12 23	4 23	11 28
27Tu	12 11 52	6 37	17 48	6 53	17 32	7 13	17 12	7 42	16 44	8 27	15 59
27		3 12	14 34	3 31	14 15	3 56	13 50	4 30	13 16	5 28	12 18
28We	12 12 04	6 37	17 49	6 52	17 33	7 12	17 14	7 40	16 46	8 25	16 02
28		4 07	15 30	4 25	15 11	4 49	14 48	5 22	14 16	6 18	13 21
29Th	12 12 16	6 37	17 49	6 52	17 34	7 12	17 15	7 39	16 47	8 23	16 04
29		4 57	16 26	5 15	16 09	5 36	15 49	6 06	15 20	6 55	14 33
30Fr	12 12 26	6 37	17 50	6 52	17 35	7 11	17 16	7 38	16 49	8 21	16 07
30		5 44	17 20	5 59	17 07	6 17	16 50	6 42	16 27	7 22	15 49
31Sa	12 12 36	6 37	17 51	6 51	17 36	7 10	17 17	7 37	16 51	8 19	16 10
31	06 20 ●	6 28	18 14	6 39	18 03	6 53	17 51	7 13	17 34	7 43	17 07

2nd Month   February, 1976   29 Days

Greenwich Mean Time

NOTE: Light figures indicate Sun. **Dark** figures indicate **Moon**. *Degrees are North Latitude.*

CAUTION: Must be converted to local time. For instruction see page 767.

Day of month / week / year	Sun on meridian Moon phase	20° Rise Sun/Moon	20° Set Sun/Moon	30° Rise Sun/Moon	30° Set Sun/Moon	40° Rise Sun/Moon	40° Set Sun/Moon	50° Rise Sun/Moon	50° Set Sun/Moon	60° Rise Sun/Moon	60° Set Sun/Moon
		h m	h m	h m	h m	h m	h m	h m	h m	h m	h m
1 Su	12 12 45	6 36	17 51	6 51	17 37	7 09	17 18	7 35	16 53	8 16	16 12
32		7 08	19 05	7 16	18 56	7 25	18 51	7 39	18 40	7 59	18 23
2 Mo	12 12 53	6 36	17 52	6 50	17 37	7 09	17 20	7 34	16 54	8 14	16 15
33		7 46	19 55	7 50	19 52	7 55	19 49	8 02	19 45	8 13	19 39
3 Tu	12 13 01	6 35	17 52	6 50	17 38	7 08	17 21	7 32	16 56	8 11	16 17
34		8 22	20 44	8 22	20 45	8 23	20 47	8 24	20 49	8 25	20 52
4 We	12 13 07	6 35	17 53	6 49	17 39	7 07	17 22	7 31	16 58	8 09	16 20
35		8 58	21 32	8 54	21 37	8 51	21 43	8 45	21 52	8 38	22 05
5 Th	12 13 13	6 35	17 54	6 48	17 40	7 06	17 23	7 29	17 00	8 07	16 23
36		9 34	22 21	9 27	22 29	9 19	22 40	9 08	22 55	8 51	23 18
6 Fr	12 13 18	6 34	17 54	6 48	17 41	7 05	17 24	7 28	17 01	8 04	16 25
37		10 11	23 10	10 01	23 22	9 48	23 36	9 31	23 57	9 05	
7 Sa	12 13 22	6 34	17 55	6 47	17 41	7 03	17 24	7 26	17 03	8 02	16 28
38		10 50		10 37		10 20		9 58		9 23	0 30
8 Su	12 13 25	6 33	17 55	6 47	17 42	7 02	17 27	7 25	17 04	7 59	16 30
39	10 05 ☽	11 32	0 00	11 16	0 15	10 56	0 33	10 29	0 59	9 45	1 41
9 Mo	12 13 28	6 33	17 56	6 46	17 43	7 01	17 28	7 23	17 06	7 57	16 33
40		12 17	0 51	11 59	1 08	11 37	1 30	11 06	1 59	10 15	2 49
10 Tu	12 13 29	6 32	17 56	6 45	17 44	7 00	17 29	7 21	17 08	7 54	16 36
41		13 07	1 43	12 48	2 02	12 24	2 25	11 51	2 58	10 55	3 53
11 We	12 13 30	6 32	17 57	6 44	17 45	6 59	17 30	7 19	17 10	7 52	16 38
42		14 00	2 36	13 41	2 55	13 18	3 19	12 45	3 52	11 49	4 48
12 Th	12 13 30	6 31	17 57	6 44	17 45	6 58	17 32	7 18	17 11	7 49	16 41
43		14 57	3 28	14 39	3 47	14 17	4 09	13 47	4 41	12 56	5 33
13 Fr	12 13 30	6 31	17 58	6 43	17 46	6 57	17 33	7 16	17 13	7 47	16 43
44		15 56	4 20	15 41	4 36	15 23	4 56	14 57	5 23	14 15	6 08
14 Sa	12 13 28	6 30	17 58	6 42	17 47	6 56	17 34	7 14	17 15	7 44	16 46
45		16 57	5 10	16 46	5 23	16 32	5 39	16 13	6 00	15 42	6 34
15 Su	12 13 26	6 29	17 59	6 41	17 48	6 55	17 35	7 12	17 17	7 41	16 49
46	16 43 ☉	17 59	5 58	17 52	6 07	17 44	6 18	17 32	6 33	17 13	6 56
16 Mo	12 13 23	6 29	17 59	6 40	17 49	6 53	17 36	7 10	17 19	7 38	16 51
47		19 01	6 45	18 59	6 50	18 56	6 55	18 52	7 03	18 46	7 14
17 Tu	12 13 19	6 28	18 00	6 39	17 49	6 52	17 37	7 09	17 20	7 36	16 54
48		20 04	7 31	20 06	7 31	20 09	7 31	20 13	7 31	20 20	7 31
18 We	12 13 15	6 28	18 00	6 38	17 50	6 50	17 38	7 07	17 22	7 33	16 56
49		21 06	8 17	21 13	8 13	21 22	8 07	21 34	7 59	21 53	7 48
19 Th	12 13 10	6 27	18 01	6 37	17 51	6 49	17 39	7 05	17 24	7 30	16 59
50		22 08	9 04	22 19	8 55	22 33	8 44	22 53	8 29	23 24	8 06
20 Fr	12 13 04	6 26	18 01	6 36	17 52	6 48	17 40	7 03	17 26	7 27	17 02
51		23 09	9 53	23 24	9 40	23 43	9 24		9 02		8 27
21 Sa	12 12 58	6 26	18 02	6 35	17 53	6 46	17 41	7 01	17 27	7 24	17 04
52			10 43		10 27		10 07	0 09	9 40	0 52	8 55
22 Su	12 12 51	6 25	18 02	6 34	17 53	6 45	17 43	7 00	17 29	7 22	17 07
53	08 16 ☾	0 10	11 36	0 27	11 18	0 49	10 55	1 20	10 23	2 12	9 30
23 Mo	12 12 43	6 25	18 03	6 33	17 54	6 43	17 44	6 58	17 30	7 19	17 09
54		1 08	12 30	1 27	12 11	1 50	11 48	2 24	11 14	3 20	10 17
24 Tu	12 12 35	6 24	18 03	6 32	17 55	6 42	17 45	6 56	17 32	7 16	17 12
55		2 03	13 26	2 22	13 07	2 45	12 44	3 18	12 11	4 14	11 16
25 We	12 12 26	6 23	18 03	6 31	17 56	6 41	17 46	6 54	17 34	7 13	17 15
56		2 54	14 21	3 12	14 04	3 34	13 43	4 05	13 13	4 55	12 24
26 Th	12 12 17	6 23	18 04	6 30	17 56	6 39	17 47	6 52	17 36	7 10	17 17
57		3 42	15 15	3 57	15 01	4 16	14 43	4 43	14 18	5 25	13 37
27 Fr	12 12 07	6 22	18 04	6 29	17 57	6 38	17 49	6 50	17 37	7 07	17 20
58		4 25	16 08	4 38	15 57	4 54	15 43	5 15	15 24	5 48	14 53
28 Sa	12 11 56	6 22	18 05	6 28	17 57	6 36	17 50	6 48	17 39	7 04	17 22
59		5 06	16 59	5 15	16 51	5 27	16 42	5 42	16 29	6 06	16 09
29 Su	12 11 45	6 21	18 05	6 22	17 58	6 35	17 51	6 46	17 41	7 01	17 25
60	23 25 ●	5 44	17 49	5 50	17 45	5 57	17 40	6 06	17 34	6 21	17 23

3rd Month   March, 1976   31 Days

Greenwich Mean Time

NOTE: Light figures indicate Sun. **Dark** figures indicate **Moon.** *Degrees are North Latitude.*

CAUTION: Must be converted to local time. For instruction see page 767.

Day of month / week / year	Sun on meridian / Moon phase (h m s)	20° Rise Sun/Moon	20° Set Sun/Moon	30° Rise	30° Set	40° Rise	40° Set	50° Rise	50° Set	60° Rise	60° Set
1 Mo	12 11 34	6 20	18 05	6 26	17 59	6 33	17 52	6 44	17 43	6 58	17 28
01		6 21	18 38	6 23	18 38	6 26	18 38	6 29	18 38	6 34	18 37
2 Tu	12 11 22	6 19	18 06	6 25	18 00	6 32	17 53	6 42	17 44	6 55	17 00
62		6 57	19 27	6 55	19 30	6 53	19 35	6 51	19 41	6 47	19 50
3 We	12 11 09	6 19	18 06	6 24	18 00	6 30	17 54	6 39	17 46	6 53	17 33
63		7 33	20 15	7 28	20 22	7 21	20 31	7 13	20 43	6 59	21 02
4 Th	12 10 56	6 18	18 07	6 23	18 01	6 29	17 55	6 37	17 47	6 50	17 35
64		8 10	21 04	8 01	21 14	7 50	21 28	7 36	21 46	7 14	22 14
5 Fr	12 10 43	6 17	18 07	6 22	18 02	6 27	17 56	6 35	17 49	6 47	17 38
65		8 48	21 53	8 36	22 07	8 22	22 24	8 02	22 47	7 30	23 25
6 Sa	12 10 29	6 16	18 07	6 21	18 03	6 26	17 57	6 33	17 51	6 44	17 40
66		9 29	22 43	9 14	22 59	8 56	23 20	8 31	23 48	7 51	
7 Su	12 10 14	6 15	18 07	6 20	18 03	6 24	17 58	6 31	17 52	6 41	17 43
67		10 12	23 34	9 55	23 52	9 34		9 05		8 17	0 34
8 Mo	12 10 00	6 15	18 08	6 18	18 04	6 23	18 00	6 29	17 54	6 38	17 45
68		10 59		10 40		10 18	0 14	9 46	0 46	8 53	1 38
9 Tu	12 09 45 / 04 38 ☽	6 14	18 08	6 17	18 04	6 21	18 01	6 27	17 55	6 35	17 48
69		11 49	0 25	11 30	0 44	11 07	1 07	10 34	1 40	9 39	2 35
10 We	12 09 29	6 13	18 08	6 16	18 05	6 20	18 02	6 25	17 57	6 32	17 50
70		12 42	1 17	12 24	1 35	12 02	1 58	11 31	2 30	10 38	3 24
11 Th	12 09 13	6 12	18 08	6 15	18 06	6 18	18 03	6 23	17 59	6 29	17 52
71		13 39	2 07	13 23	2 24	13 03	2 45	12 35	3 14	11 49	4 02
12 Fr	12 08 57	6 11	18 09	6 14	18 06	6 17	18 04	6 21	18 00	6 26	17 55
72		14 38	2 56	14 25	3 11	14 08	3 29	13 46	3 53	13 10	4 32
13 Sa	12 08 41	6 11	18 09	6 12	18 07	6 15	18 05	6 18	18 02	6 23	17 57
73		15 38	3 45	15 29	3 56	15 17	4 09	15 02	4 28	14 37	4 56
14 Su	12 08 24	6 10	18 10	6 11	18 07	6 14	18 06	6 16	18 03	6 20	18 00
74		16 40	4 32	16 35	4 39	16 29	4 47	16 21	4 59	16 08	5 16
15 Mo	12 08 07	6 09	18 10	6 10	18 08	6 12	18 07	6 14	18 05	6 17	18 02
75		17 43	5 19	17 43	5 21	17 43	5 24	17 42	5 28	17 42	5 34
16 Tu	12 07 50 / 02 53 🌕	6 08	18 10	6 09	18 09	6 10	18 08	6 12	18 07	6 14	18 05
76		18 46	6 05	18 51	6 03	18 57	6 00	19 05	5 57	19 17	5 51
17 We	12 07 33	6 07	18 10	6 08	18 09	6 09	18 09	6 10	18 08	6 11	18 07
77		19 51	6 53	20 00	6 47	20 11	6 38	20 27	6 27	20 53	6 09
18 Th	12 07 15	6 06	18 11	6 06	18 10	6 07	18 10	6 07	18 10	6 08	18 10
78		20 55	7 43	21 08	7 32	21 25	7 18	21 48	7 00	22 25	6 30
19 Fr	12 06 57	6 05	18 11	6 05	18 10	6 06	18 11	6 05	18 11	6 -05	18 12
79		21 58	8 35	22 15	8 20	22 35	8 02	23 04	7 37	23 52	6 56
20 Sa	12 06 40	6 04	18 11	6 04	18 11	6 04	18 12	6 03	18 13	6 02	18 15
80		22 59	9 29	23 18	9 12	23 41	8 50		8 20		7 30
21 Su	12 06 22	6 03	18 11	6 03	18 12	6 02	18 13	6 02	18 13	5 59	18 17
81		23 57	10 24		10 06		9 42	0 13	9 10	1 07	8 15
22 Mo	12 06 04 / 18 54 ☾	6 02	18 11	6 02	18 13	6 01	18 14	5 59	18 16	5 56	18 20
82			11 21	0 16	11 02	0 39	10 39	1 12	10 06	2 08	9 11
23 Tu	12 05 46	6 02	18 12	6 00	18 13	5 59	18 15	5 56	18 18	5 53	18 22
83		0 51	12 17	1 09	11 59	1 31	11 38	2 02	11 07	2 54	10 17
24 We	12 05 27	6 01	18 12	5 59	18 14	5 58	18 16	5 54	18 19	5 50	18 25
84		1 40	13 11	1 56	12 56	2 16	12 38	2 43	12 12	3 28	11 29
25 Th	12 05 09	6 00	18 12	5 58	18 15	5 56	18 17	5 52	18 21	5 47	18 27
85		2 25	14 04	2 38	13 52	2 55	13 37	3 17	13 17	3 53	12 43
26 Fr	12 04 51	5 59	18 12	5 57	18 16	5 54	18 18	5 50	18 23	5 44	18 29
86		3 06	14 56	3 16	14 47	3 29	14 36	3 46	14 22	4 12	13 58
27 Sa	12 04 33	5 58	18 13	5 56	18 16	5 52	18 19	5 48	18 24	5 41	18 32
87		3 45	15 46	3 52	15 41	4 00	15 34	4 11	15 26	4 28	15 12
28 Su	12 04 15	5 57	18 13	5 54	18 17	5 51	18 20	5 45	18 26	5 37	18 34
88		4 22	16 35	4 25	16 33	4 29	16 32	4 34	16 29	4 42	16 26
29 Mo	12 03 57	5 56	18 14	5 53	18 17	5 49	18 21	5 43	18 27	5 34	18 37
89		4 58	17 23	4 57	17 25	4 57	17 28	4 56	17 32	4 55	17 38
30 Tu	12 03 39 / 17 08 ●	5 55	18 14	5 52	18 18	5 47	18 22	5 41	18 29	5 31	18 39
90		5 34	18 11	5 30	18 17	5 25	18 25	5 18	18 35	4 08	18 50
31 We	12 03 21	5 54	18 14	5 51	18 19	5 45	18 23	5 39	18 31	5 28	18 41
91		6 10	19 00	6 03	19 09	5 53	19 21	5 41	19 37	5 22	20 02

4th Month   April, 1976   30 Days

Greenwich Mean Time

NOTE: Light figures indicate Sun. **Dark** figures indicate **Moon.** *Degrees are North Latitude.*
CAUTION: Must be converted to local time. For instruction see page 767

Day of month / week / year	Sun on meridian / Moon phase (h m s)	20° Rise Sun/Moon	20° Set Sun/Moon	30° Rise Sun/Moon	30° Set Sun/Moon	40° Rise Sun/Moon	40° Set Sun/Moon	50° Rise Sun/Moon	50° Set Sun/Moon	60° Rise Sun/Moon	60° Set Sun/Moon
1 Th	12 03 03	5 53	18 14	5 50	18 19	5 44	18 24	5 37	18 32	5 25	18 44
92		6 48	19 49	6 37	20 02	6 24	20 17	6 06	20 39	5 38	21 13
2 Fr	12 02 45	5 53	18 14	5 48	18 20	5 42	18 25	5 34	18 34	5 22	18 46
93		7 28	20 39	7 14	20 54	6 57	21 13	6 34	21 39	5 57	22 23
3 Sa	12 02 28	5 52	18 15	5 47	18 20	5 41	18 26	5 32	18 35	5 19	18 49
94		8 10	21 29	7 54	21 47	7 34	22 08	7 06	22 38	6 22	23 28
4 Su	12 02 10	5 51	18 15	5 46	18 21	5 39	18 27	5 30	18 37	5 16	18 51
95		8 55	22 20	8 38	22 38	8 15	23 01	7 45	23 33	6 54	
5 Mo	12 01 53	5 50	18 15	5 45	18 22	5 38	18 28	5 28	18 38	5 13	18 53
96		9 44	23 10	9 25	23 29	9 02	23 52	8 30		7 35	0 23
6 Tu	12 01 36	5 49	18 16	5 44	18 22	5 36	18 29	5 26	18 40	5 10	18 56
97		10 35		10 17		9 54		9 22	0 32	8 28	1 18
7 We	12 01 19 / 19 02 ☽	5 49	18 16	5 42	18 23	5 35	18 30	5 24	18 41	5 07	18 58
98		11 28	0 00	11 12	0 17	10 51	0 39	10 22	1 09	9 33	1 59
8 Th	12 01 02	5 48	18 17	5 41	18 23	5 33	18 31	5 22	18 43	5 04	19 01
99		12 24	0 48	12 10	1 03	11 52	1 22	11 27	1 49	10 47	2 31
9 Fr	12 00 45	5 47	18 17	5 40	18 24	5 32	18 32	5 20	18 44	5 01	19 03
100		13 22	1 35	13 11	1 47	12 57	2 03	12 39	2 24	12 09	2 57
10 Sa	12 00 29	5 46	18 17	5 39	18 25	5 30	18 33	5 18	18 46	4 58	19 06
101		14 21	2 21	14 14	2 30	14 05	2 41	13 54	2 55	13 35	3 18
11 Su	12 00 13	5 45	18 17	5 38	18 25	5 29	18 34	5 16	18 47	4 55	19 08
102		15 22	3 06	15 19	3 11	15 16	3 17	15 12	3 24	15 05	3 36
12 Mo	11 59 57	5 45	18 18	5 36	18 26	5 27	18 35	5 13	18 49	4 52	19 11
103		16 24	3 52	16 26	3 52	16 29	3 53	16 32	3 53	16 38	3 53
13 Tu	11 59 42	5 44	18 18	5 35	18 26	5 26	18 36	5 11	18 50	4 49	19 13
104		17 27	4 39	17 34	4 35	17 43	4 29	17 54	4 22	18 13	4 11
14 We	11 59 27 / 11 49 ☻	5 43	18 18	5 34	18 27	5 24	18 37	5 09	18 52	4 46	19 16
105		18 32	5 28	18 44	5 19	18 58	5 08	19 17	4 53	19 48	4 31
15 Th	11 59 12	5 42	18 18	5 33	18 28	5 22	18 38	5 07	18 54	4 43	19 18
106		19 38	6 19	19 53	6 06	20 12	5 50	20 38	5 29	21 20	4 54
16 Fr	11 58 58	5 41	18 19	5 32	18 28	5 21	18 39	5 05	18 55	4 40	19 21
107		20 42	7 14	21 00	6 58	21 22	6 38	21 53	6 10	22 44	5 25
17 Sa	11 58 44	5 41	18 19	5 31	18 29	5 19	18 40	5 03	18 57	4 38	19 23
108		21 44	8 11	22 03	7 53	22 26	7 30	22 59	6 58	23 55	6 06
18 Su	11 58 30	5 40	18 20	5 30	18 29	5 18	18 41	5 01	18 58	4 35	19 26
109		22 42	9 09	23 00	8 51	23 23	8 27	23 55	7 54		6 59
19 Mo	11 58 17	5 39	18 20	5 29	18 30	5 16	18 42	4 59	19 00	4 32	19 28
110		23 39	10 07	23 51	9 50		9 27		8 56	0 49	8 03
20 Tu	11 58 04	5 38		5 28	18 31	5 15	18 43	4 57	19 02	4 29	19 31
111			11 04		10 49	0 12	10 29	0 41	10 01	1 28	9 16
21 We	11 57 52 / 07 14 ☽	5 37	18 20	5 27	18 31	5 13	18 44	4 55	19 03	4 26	19 33
112		0 22	11 59	0 36	11 46	0 54	11 30	1 18	11 08	1 56	10 31
22 Th	11 57 40	5 37	18 21	5 26	18 32	5 12	18 46	4 53	19 05	4 23	19 36
113		1 05	12 52	1 16	12 42	1 30	12 30	1 49	12 13	2 18	11 47
23 Fr	11 57 29	5 36	18 21	5 25	18 32	5 10	18 47	4 51	19 06	4 20	19 38
114		1 45	13 42	1 53	13 36	2 02	13 29	2 15	13 18	2 35	13 02
24 Sa	11 57 18	5 35	18 21	5 24	18 33	5 09	18 48	4 49	19 08	4 17	19 41
115		2 22	14 32	2 27	14 29	2 32	14 26	2 39	14 22	2 49	14 15
25 Su	11 57 07	5 34	18 21	5 23	18 34	5 08	18 49	4 47	19 10	4 14	19 43
116		2 59	15 20	2 59	15 21	3 00	15 23	3 01	15 25	3 03	15 28
26 Mo	11 56 58	5 34	18 22	5 22	18 34	5 07	18 50	4 45	19 11	4 11	19 46
117		3 34	16 08	3 31	16 13	3 28	16 19	3 23	16 27	3 16	16 40
27 Tu	11 56 48	5 33	18 22	5 21	18 35	5 05	18 51	4 44	19 13	4 09	19 48
118		4 11	16 56	4 04	17 05	3 56	17 15	3 46	17 29	3 29	17 51
28 We	11 56 39	5 33	18 23	5 20	18 35	5 04	18 52	4 42	19 14	4 06	19 51
119		4 48	17 45	4 38	17 57	4 26	18 11	4 10	18 31	3 45	19 03
29 Th	11 56 31 / 10 20 ●	5 32	18 23	5 19	18 36	5 03	18 53	4 40	19 16	4 03	19 53
120		5 27	18 35	5 14	18 50	4 58	19 08	4 37	19 32	4 03	20 13
30 Fr	11 56 23	5 31	18 23	5 18	18 37	5 02	18 54	4 38	19 17	4 00	19 55
121		6 09	19 26	5 53	19 42	5 34	20 03	5 08	20 32	4 26	21 20

5th Month   May, 1976   31 Days

Greenwich Mean Time

NOTE: Light figures indicate Sun. **Dark** figures indicate **Moon.** *Degrees are North Latitude.*

CAUTION: Must be converted to local time. For instruction see page 767.

Day of month / week / year	Sun on meridian / Moon phase	20° Rise	20° Set	30° Rise	30° Set	40° Rise	40° Set	50° Rise	50° Set	60° Rise	60° Set
		Sun / **Moon**	Sun / **Moon**	Sun / **Moon**	Sun / **Moon**	Sun / **Moon**	Sun / **Moon**	Sun / **Moon**	Sun / **Moon**	Sun / **Moon**	Sun / **Moon**
		h m	h m	h m	h m	h m	h m	h m	h m	h m	h m
1 Sa	11 56 16	5 31	18 24	5 17	18 37	5 01	18 55	4 36	19 14	3 58	19 58
122		**6 53**	**20 17**	**6 36**	**20 35**	**6 14**	**20 57**	**5 45**	**21 29**	**4 55**	**22 22**
2 Su	11 56 09	5 30	18 24	5 17	18 38	4 59	18 50	4 35	19 12	3 55	20 00
123		**7 41**	**21 07**	**7 22**	**21 26**	**7 00**	**21 49**	**6 28**	**22 21**	**5 34**	**23 15**
3 Mo	11 56 03	5 30	18 25	5 16	18 38	4 58	18 57	4 33	19 11	3 53	20 03
124		**8 31**	**21 57**	**8 13**	**22 14**	**7 50**	**22 37**	**7 18**	**23 08**	**6 24**	**23 59**
4 Tu	11 55 57	5 29	18 25	5 15	18 39	4 57	18 58	4 31	19 23	3 50	20 05
125		**9 24**	**22 45**	**9 06**	**23 01**	**8 45**	**23 21**	**8 14**	**23 49**	**7 24**	
5 We	11 55 52 05 17)	5 29	18 25	5 14	18 40	4 56	18 59	4 29	19 25	3 47	20 08
126		**10 18**	**23 31**	**10 03**	**23 45**	**9 44**		**9 17**		**8 34**	**0 33**
6 Th	11 55 47	5 28	18 26	5 13	18 40	4 55	19 00	4 28	19 26	3 45	20 10
127		**11 13**		**11 01**		**10 46**	**0 01**	**10 25**	**0 24**	**9 51**	**1 00**
7 Fr	11 55 43	5 28	18 26	5 13	18 41	4 53	19 01	4 26	19 28	3 42	20 13
128		**12 10**	**0 16**	**12 02**	**0 26**	**11 51**	**0 39**	**11 36**	**0 56**	**11 13**	**1 22**
8 Sa	11 55 40	5 27	18 27	5 12	18 41	4 52	19 02	4 25	19 29	3 40	20 15
129		**13 08**	**1 00**	**13 03**	**1 06**	**12 58**	**1 14**	**12 50**	**1 25**	**12 39**	**1 41**
9 Su	11 55 37	5 27	18 27	5 11	18 42	4 51	19 03	4 23	19 31	3 37	20 18
130		**14 07**	**1 44**	**14 07**	**1 46**	**14 07**	**1 49**	**14 07**	**1 52**	**14 07**	**1 58**
10 Mo	11 55 34	5 26	18 27	5 10	18 43	4 50	19 04	4 22	19 32	3 35	20 20
131		**15 08**	**2 28**	**15 12**	**2 26**	**15 18**	**2 23**	**15 26**	**2 20**	**15 38**	**2 14**
11 Tu	11 55 33	5 26	18 28	5 09	18 44	4 49	19 05	4 20	19 34	3 32	20 23
132		**16 11**	**3 15**	**16 20**	**3 08**	**16 31**	**3 00**	**16 46**	**2 49**	**17 11**	**2 32**
12 We	11 55 31	5 25	18 28	5 09	18 44	4 48	19 05	4 19	19 35	3 30	20 25
133		**17 15**	**4 04**	**17 28**	**3 53**	**17 44**	**3 39**	**18 07**	**3 21**	**18 44**	**2 53**
13 Th	11 55 30 20 04 ○	5 25	18 29	5 08	18 45	4 47	19 06	4 17	19 37	3 27	20 28
134		**18 20**	**4 56**	**18 36**	**4 42**	**18 57**	**4 24**	**19 26**	**3 59**	**20 13**	**3 19**
14 Fr	11 55 30	5 24	18 29	5 07	18 46	4 46	19 07	4 16	19 38	3 25	20 30
135		**19 24**	**5 52**	**19 43**	**5 35**	**20 06**	**5 14**	**20 38**	**4 44**	**21 32**	**3 54**
15 Sa	11 55 31	5 24	18 29	5 06	18 47	4 45	19 08	4 15	19 39	3 23	20 32
136		**20 26**	**6 51**	**20 44**	**6 33**	**21 08**	**6 09**	**21 40**	**5 37**	**22 36**	**4 42**
16 Su	11 55 32	5 24	18 30	5 06	18 47	4 44	19 09	4 13	19 41	3 20	20 34
137		**21 22**	**7 51**	**21 40**	**7 33**	**22 02**	**7 10**	**22 33**	**6 37**	**23 23**	**5 42**
17 Mo	11 55 33	5 23	18 30	5 05	18 48	4 43	19 10	4 12	19 42	3 18	20 37
138		**22 14**	**8 51**	**22 29**	**8 34**	**22 48**	**8 13**	**23 15**	**7 43**	**23 57**	**6 54**
18 Tu	11 55 35	5 23	18 31	5 05	18 48	4 42	19 11	4 10	19 44	3 15	20 39
139		**23 00**	**9 48**	**23 13**	**9 34**	**23 28**	**9 16**	**23 49**	**8 51**		**8 11**
19 We	11 55 38	5 23	18 31	5 04	18 49	4 41	19 12	4 09	19 45	3 13	20 41
140		**23 42**	**10 44**	**23 51**	**10 32**		**10 19**		**10 00**	**0 22**	**9 29**
20 Th	11 55 41 21 22 (	5 23	18 31	5 04	18 50	4 40	19 13	4 08	19 46	3 11	20 43
141			**11 36**		**11 29**	**0 03**	**11 19**	**0 18**	**11 06**	**0 41**	**10 46**
21 Fr	11 55 45	5 22	18 32	5 03	18 50	4 40	19 14	4 07	19 47	3 09	20 45
142		**0 21**	**12 27**	**0 27**	**12 23**	**0 34**	**12 18**	**0 43**	**12 12**	**0 57**	**12 01**
22 Sa	11 55 49	5 22	18 32	5 03	18 51	4 39	19 14	4 05	19 49	3 07	20 48
143		**0 58**	**13 16**	**1 00**	**13 15**	**1 03**	**13 15**	**1 06**	**13 15**	**1 11**	**13 15**
23 Su	11 55 54	5 21	18 33	5 02	18 51	4 39	19 15	4 04	19 50	3 05	20 50
144		**1 35**	**14 04**	**1 33**	**14 07**	**1 31**	**14 12**	**1 28**	**14 18**	**1 24**	**14 27**
24 Mo	11 56 00	5 21	18 33	5 02	18 52	4 38	19 16	4 03	19 51	3 03	20 52
145		**2 10**	**14 52**	**2 05**	**14 59**	**1 59**	**15 08**	**1 50**	**15 20**	**1 37**	**15 39**
25 Tu	11 56 06	5 21	18 33	5 02	18 53	4 37	19 17	4 02	19 52	3 01	20 54
146		**2 47**	**15 41**	**2 39**	**15 51**	**2 28**	**16 04**	**2 14**	**16 22**	**1 52**	**16 50**
26 We	11 56 12	5 21	18 34	5 01	18 53	4 37	19 18	4 01	19 53	2 59	20 56
147		**3 26**	**16 31**	**3 14**	**16 44**	**2 59**	**17 01**	**2 40**	**17 24**	**2 09**	**18 01**
27 Th	11 56 19	5 20	18 34	5 01	18 54	4 36	19 18	4 00	19 55	2 58	20 58
148		**4 07**	**17 21**	**3 52**	**17 37**	**3 34**	**17 57**	**3 09**	**18 25**	**2 30**	**19 10**
28 Fr	11 56 26	5 20	18 35	5 00	18 54	4 36	19 19	3 59	19 56	2 56	21 00
149		**4 50**	**18 12**	**4 34**	**18 30**	**4 13**	**18 52**	**3 44**	**19 23**	**2 57**	**20 15**
29 Sa	11 56 34 01 47 ●	5 20	18 35	5 00	18 55	4 35	19 20	3 58	19 57	2 54	21 02
150		**5 37**	**19 03**	**5 19**	**19 22**	**4 57**	**19 45**	**4 25**	**20 17**	**3 32**	**21 12**
30 Su	11 56 43	5 20	18 35	5 00	18 56	4 34	19 21	3 57	19 58	2 52	21 04
151		**6 27**	**19 54**	**6 09**	**20 12**	**5 46**	**20 35**	**5 13**	**21 06**	**4 19**	**21 59**
31 Mo	11 56 51	5 20	18 36	5 00	18 56	4 34	19 22	3 56	19 59	2 51	21 06
152		**7 20**	**20 43**	**7 02**	**21 00**	**6 40**	**21 21**	**6 08**	**21 50**	**5 16**	**22 37**

6th Month   June, 1976   30 Days

Greenwich Mean Time

NOTE: Light figures indicate Sun. **Dark** figures indicate **Moon.** *Degrees are North Latitude.*

CAUTION: Must be converted to local time. For instruction see page 767.

Day of month / week / year	Sun on meridian Moon phase (h m s)	20° Rise Sun/Moon (h m)	20° Set Sun/Moon (h m)	30° Rise Sun/Moon	30° Set Sun/Moon	40° Rise Sun/Moon	40° Set Sun/Moon	50° Rise Sun/Moon	50° Set Sun/Moon	60° Rise Sun/Moon	60° Set Sun/Moon
1 Tu 153	11 57 00	5 20	18 36	4 59	18 57	4 33	19 22	3 56	20 00	2 49	21 07
		8 14	21 30	7 58	21 45	7 38	22 02	7 10	22 27	6 24	23 06
2 We 154	11 57 10	5 20	18 37	4 59	18 57	4 33	19 23	3 55	20 01	2 48	21 09
		9 09	22 15	8 56	22 27	8 39	22 41	8 16	23 00	7 40	23 29
3 Th 155	11 57 20	5 20	18 37	4 59	18 58	4 32	19 24	3 54	20 02	2 46	21 11
		10 05	22 59	9 55	23 07	9 43	23 16	9 26	23 29	9 00	23 49
4 Fr 156	11 57 30	5 20	18 37	4 49	18 58	4 32	19 25	3 54	20 03	2 45	21 12
		11 02	23 42	10 56	23 46	10 48	23 50	10 38	23 56	10 23	
5 Sa 157	11 57 40 12 20)	5 20	18 37	4 49	18 59	4 32	19 25	3 53	20 04	2 44	21 14
		11 59		11 57		11 55		11 52		11 48	0 05
6 Su 158	11 57 51	5 20	18 38	4 58	18 59	4 31	19 26	3 53	20 05	2 43	21 15
		12 57	0 25	13 00	0 24	13 03	0 24	13 08	0 23	13 15	0 21
7 Mo 159	11 58 02	5 20	18 38	4 58	19 00	4 31	19 26	3 52	20 06	2 42	21 17
		13 57	1 09	14 04	1 04	14 13	0 58	14 25	0 50	14 44	0 38
8 Tu 160	11 58 14	5 20	18 38	4 58	19 00	4 31	19 27	3 52	20 07	2 41	21 18
		14 58	1 55	15 09	1 46	15 24	1 35	15 43	1 20	16 14	0 56
9 We 161	11 58 25	5 20	18 38	4 58	19 00	4 31	19 28	3 52	20 08	2 41	21 19
		16 01	2 44	16 16	2 31	16 35	2 15	17 01	1 53	17 43	1 19
10 Th 162	11 58 37	5 20	18 39	4 58	19 01	4 31	19 28	3 51	20 08	2 40	21 20
		17 05	3 37	17 22	3 21	17 44	3 01	18 15	2 33	19 06	1 48
11 Fr 163	11 58 49	5 20	18 39	4 58	19 01	4 30	19 29	3 51	20 09	2 39	21 22
		18 07	4 33	18 26	4 15	18 49	3 53	19 22	3 21	20 18	2 28
12 Sa 164	11 59 01 04 15 ☺	5 20	18 40	4 58	19 02	4 30	19 29	3 50	20 09	2 38	21 23
		19 06	5 33	19 25	5 14	19 48	4 51	20 20	4 17	21 14	3 22
13 Su 165	11 59 14	5 20	18 40	4 58	19 02	4 30	19 30	3 50	20 10	2 37	21 24
		20 01	6 33	20 18	6 15	20 39	5 53	21 08	5 21	21 55	4 28
14 Mo 166	11 59 26	5 20	18 40	4 58	19 02	4 30	19 30	3 50	20 10	2 37	21 25
		20 51	7 33	21 05	7 17	21 23	6 57	21 46	6 30	22 24	5 45
15 Tu 167	11 59 39	5 20	18 40	4 58	19 02	4 30	19 31	3 50	20 11	2 36	21 26
		21 36	8 30	21 47	8 18	22 00	8 02	22 18	7 40	22 46	7 04
16 We 168	11 59 52	5 21	18 41	4 59	19 03	4 31	19 31	3 50	20 11	2 36	21 26
		22 18	9 25	22 25	9 16	22 34	9 05	22 46	8 49	23 04	8 24
17 Th 169	12 00 05	5 21	18 41	4 59	19 03	4 31	19 31	3 50	20 12	2 35	21 26
		22 56	10 18	23 00	10 12	23 04	10 06	23 10	9 56	23 19	9 42
18 Fr 170	12 00 18	5 21	18 41	4 59	19 03	4 31	19 31	3 50	20 12	2 35	21 27
		23 33	11 08	23 33	11 07	23 33	11 05	23 33	11 02	23 32	10 57
19 Sa 171	12 00 31 06 29 ☾	5 21	18 41	4 59	19 03	4 31	19 31	3 50	20 12	2 35	21 27
			11 58		12 00		12 02	23 55	12 06	23 45	12 11
20 Su 172	12 00 44	5 21	18 41	4 59	19 03	4 31	19 32	3 50	20 12	2 35	21 27
		0 09	12 46	0 06	12 52	0 01	12 59		13 09	23 59	13 23
21 Mo 173	12 00 57	5 22	18 42	5 00	19 04	4 32	19 32	3 51	20 13	2 36	21 28
		0 46	13 35	0 39	13 44	0 30	13 55	0 18	14 11		14 35
22 Tu 174	12 01 10	5 22	18 42	5 00	19 04	4 32	19 33	3 51	20 13	2 36	21 28
		1 24	14 24	1 13	14 36	1 00	14 52	0 43	15 13	0 15	15 46
23 We 175	12 01 23	5 22	18 42	5 00	19 04	4 32	19 33	3 51	20 13	2 36	21 28
		2 04	15 14	1 50	15 29	1 33	15 48	1 11	16 14	0 35	16 56
24 Th 176	12 01 36	5 22	18 42	5 00	19 04	4 32	19 33	3 51	20 13	2 37	21 28
		2 46	16 05	2 30	16 22	2 10	16 44	1 43	17 13	0 59	18 03
25 Fr 177	12 01 49	5 22	18 42	5 00	19 04	4 32	19 33	3 52	20 13	2 37	21 28
		3 32	16 57	3 14	17 15	2 52	17 38	2 21	18 10	1 31	19 04
26 Sa 178	12 02 01	5 23	18 43	5 01	19 05	4 33	19 33	3 52	20 13	2 38	21 27
		4 21	17 48	4 02	18 06	3 39	18 30	3 07	19 02	2 13	19 56
27 Su 179	12 02 14 01 39 ●	5 23	18 43	5 01	19 05	4 32	19 33	3 53	20 13	2 38	21 27
		5 13	18 38	4 55	18 56	4 32	19 18	4 00	19 48	3 06	20 38
28 Mo 180	12 02 26	5 23	18 43	5 01	19 05	4 33	19 33	3 53	20 13	2 39	21 27
		6 07	19 27	5 51	19 43	5 30	20 02	5 00	20 28	4 12	21 11
29 Tu 181	12 02 38	5 23	18 43	5 01	19 05	4 34	19 33	3 54	20 13	2 40	21 26
		7 03	20 14	6 49	20 26	6 31	20 42	6 06	21 03	5 26	21 36
30 We 182	12 02 50	5 24	18 43	5 02	19 05	4 34	19 33	3 54	20 13	2 41	21 25
		8 00	20 59	7 49	21 08	7 35	21 19	7 16	21 34	6 46	21 57

7th Month   July, 1976   31 Days

Greenwich Mean Time

NOTE: Light figures indicate Sun. **Dark** figures indicate **Moon**. *Degrees are North Latitude.*

CAUTION: Must be converted to local time. For instruction see page 767.

In each day the upper line is **Sun**, the lower line is **Moon**. Times are h m.

Day / week / year	Sun on meridian / Moon phase	20° Rise	20° Set	30° Rise	30° Set	40° Rise	40° Set	50° Rise	50° Set	60° Rise	60° Set
1 Th	12 03 02	5 24	18 44	5 02	19 05	4 35	19 32	3 55	20 12	2 42	21 25
183		8 57	21 42	8 50	21 47	8 41	21 54	8 28	22 02	8 09	22 15
2 Fr	12 03 13	5 25	18 44	5 03	19 05	4 35	19 32	3 55	20 12	2 40	21 24
184		9 54	22 25	9 51	22 26	9 47	22 27	9 42	22 29	9 34	22 31
3 Sa	12 03 25	5 25	18 44	5 03	19 05	4 36	19 32	3 56	20 12	2 44	21 23
185		10 52	23 08	10 53	23 05	10 55	23 01	10 57	22 55	11 00	22 47
4 Su	12 03 35	5 25	18 44	5 03	19 05	4 37	19 32	3 57	20 11	2 45	21 22
186	17 28)	11 50	23 53	11 56	23 45	12 03	23 36	12 12	23 23	12 27	23 04
5 Mo	12 03 46	5 25	18 44	5 04	19 05	4 37	19 33	3 58	20 11	2 47	21 21
187		12 50		12 59		13 12		13 28	23 54	13 55	23 24
6 Tu	12 03 56	5 26	18 43	5 04	19 04	4 38	19 31	3 58	20 10	2 48	21 20
188		13 50	0 39	14 04	0 28	14 21	0 14	14 44		15 22	23 50
7 We	12 04 06	5 26	18 43	5 05	19 04	4 38	19 31	3 59	20 10	2 50	21 19
189		14 52	1 29	15 08	1 14	15 29	0 56	15 58	0 31	16 46	
8 Th	12 04 15	5 26	18 43	5 05	19 04	4 39	19 31	4 00	20 09	2 51	21 18
190		15 53	2 23	16 11	2 05	16 34	1 44	17 06	1 14	18 01	0 24
9 Fr	12 04 24	5 26	18 43	5 06	19 04	4 40	19 31	4 01	20 08	2 53	21 16
191		16 52	3 19	17 11	3 01	17 35	2 37	18 07	2 05	19 03	1 10
10 Sa	12 04 32	5 27	18 43	5 06	19 04	4 40	19 30	4 02	20 08	2 55	21 15
192		17 49	4 18	18 06	3 59	18 28	3 36	18 59	3 04	19 50	2 09
11 Su	12 04 40	5 27	18 43	5 07	19 03	4 41	19 30	4 03	20 07	2 56	21 13
193	13 09 ○	18 41	5 17	18 56	5 00	19 15	4 39	19 42	4 10	20 24	3 20
12 Mo	12 04 48	5 28	18 43	5 07	19 03	4 41	19 29	4 04	20 07	2 58	21 12
194		19 28	6 16	19 41	6 02	19 56	5 44	20 17	5 19	20 50	4 38
13 Tu	12 04 55	5 28	18 43	5 08	19 03	4 42	19 29	4 05	20 06	3 00	21 10
195		20 12	7 12	20 21	7 01	20 32	6 48	20 47	6 29	21 10	5 59
14 We	12 05 01	5 28	18 43	5 09	19 03	4 43	19 28	4 06	20 05	3 02	21 08
196		20 52	8 07	20 57	7 59	21 04	7 50	21 13	7 38	21 26	7 18
15 Th	12 05 07	5 29	18 43	5 09	19 02	4 44	19 28	4 07	20 04	3 04	21 07
197		21 30	8 59	21 32	8 55	21 34	8 51	21 36	8 45	21 40	8 36
16 Fr	12 05 13	5 29	18 42	5 10	19 02	4 44	19 27	4 09	20 03	3 05	21 05
198		22 07	9 49	22 05	9 50	22 03	9 50	21 59	9 50	21 54	9 51
17 Sa	12 05 18	5 30	18 42	5 10	19 01	4 45	19 27	4 10	20 02	3 07	21 04
199		22 44	10 39	22 38	10 43	22 31	10 48	22 22	10 54	22 08	11 05
18 Su	12 05 23	5 30	18 42	5 11	19 01	4 46	19 26	4 11	20 01	3 09	21 02
200		23 21	11 28	23 12	11 35	23 01	11 45	22 46	11 57	22 23	12 17
19 Mo	12 05 27	5 30	18 42	5 11	19 01	4 47	19 25	4 12	20 00	3 11	21 00
201	06 29 (		12 17	23 48	12 27	23 23	12 41	23 13	12 59	22 41	13 29
20 Tu	12 05 31	5 31	18 42	5 12	19 00	4 48	19 24	4 13	19 59	3 13	20 58
202		0 00	13 06		13 37	23 43	14 01	23 02	14 39		
21 We	12 05 34	5 31	18 41	5 12	19 00	4 48	19 24	4 15	19 57	3 16	20 55
203		0 41	13 56	0 26	14 13	0 08	14 33		15 01	23 31	15 47
22 Th	12 05 36	5 32	18 41	5 13	18 59	4 49	19 23	4 16	19 56	3 18	20 53
204		1 25	14 47	1 08	15 05	0 47	15 27	0 18	15 58		16 50
23 Fr	12 05 38	5 32	18 41	5 13	18 58	4 50	19 22	4 17	19 55	3 20	20 51
205		2 13	15 39	1 54	15 57	1 32	16 20	1 00	16 52	0 08	17 46
24 Sa	12 05 39	5 32	18 41	5 14	18 58	4 51	19 21	4 18	19 54	3 22	20 49
206		3 03	16 30	2 45	16 48	2 22	17 10	1 50	17 41	0 56	18 33
25 Su	12 05 40	5 33	18 40	5 14	18 58	4 52	19 20	4 20	19 52	3 24	20 47
207		3 57	17 20	3 40	17 36	3 18	17 50	2 47	18 25	1 56	19 10
26 Mo	12 05 40	5 33	18 40	5 15	18 57	4 52	19 20	4 21	19 51	3 27	20 44
208		4 53	18 08	4 38	18 22	4 18	18 39	3 51	19 02	3 07	19 39
27 Tu	12 05 40	5 34	18 39	5 15	18 57	4 53	19 19	4 23	19 49	3 29	20 42
209	01 39 ●	5 50	18 55	5 38	19 05	5 22	19 18	5 01	19 36	4 26	20 03
28 We	12 05 39	5 34	18 39	5 16	18 56	4 54	19 18	4 24	19 48	3 31	20 40
210		6 49	19 40	6 40	19 46	6 29	19 55	6 14	20 06	5 50	20 22
29 Th	12 05 37	5 34	18 38	5 17	18 55	4 55	19 17	4 25	19 47	3 33	20 38
211		7 47	20 24	7 42	20 26	7 37	20 29	7 29	20 33	7 17	20 39
30 Fr	12 05 35	5 35	18 38	5 17	18 55	4 56	19 16	4 26	19 45	3 36	20 35
212		8 46	21 08	8 46	21 06	8 45	21 04	8 45	21 01	8 44	20 56
31 Sa	12 05 32	5 35	18 37	5 18	18 54	4 57	19 15	4 28	19 44	3 38	20 33
213		9 45	21 52	9 49	21 46	9 54	21 39	10 01	21 29	10 12	21 13

8th Month

August, 1976

31 Days

Greenwich Mean Time

NOTE: Light figures indicate Sun. **Dark** figures indicate **Moon.** *Degrees are North Latitude.*
CAUTION: Must be converted to local time. For instruction see page 767.

Day of month week year	Sun on meridian Moon phase h m s	20° Rise Sun Moon h m	20° Set Sun Moon h m	30° Rise Sun Moon h m	30° Set Sun Moon h m	40° Rise Sun Moon h m	40° Set Sun Moon h m	50° Rise Sun Moon h m	50° Set Sun Moon h m	60° Rise Sun Moon h m	60° Set Sun Moon h m
1 Su 214	12 05 28	5 36 10 44	18 37 22 38	5 18 10 53	18 54 22 28	4 58 11 03	19 14 22 16	4 29 11 17	19 42 21 59	3 41 11 40	20 30 21 33
2 Mo 215	12 05 24 22 07 ☽	5 36 11 45	18 36 23 27	5 19 11 57	18 53 23 13	4 59 12 12	19 13 22 56	4 30 12 33	19 41 22 33	3 43 13 07	20 28 21 57
3 Tu 216	12 05 19	5 36 12 45	18 36	5 20 13 01	18 52	4 59 13 20	19 12 23 41	4 32 13 47	19 39 23 13	3 45 14 31	20 25 22 27
4 We 217	12 05 14	5 36 13 45	18 35 0 18	5 20 14 03	18 51 0 02	5 01 14 25	19 11	4 33 14 56	19 38	3 48 15 48	20 23 23 07
5 Th 218	12 05 08	5 37 14 44	18 35 1 13	5 21 15 03	18 50 0 54	5 02 15 26	19 09 0 32	4 35 15 58	19 36 0 00	3 50 16 58	20 20
6 Fr 219	12 05 02	5 37 15 40	18 34 2 09	5 21 15 58	18 49 1 51	5 03 16 21	19 08 1 28	4 36 16 52	19 35 0 55	3 53 17 45	20 18 0 00
7 Sa 220	12 04 54	5 37 16 33	18 34 3 07	5 22 16 49	18 48 2 49	5 04 17 09	19 07 2 27	4 38 17 38	19 33 1 57	3 55 18 24	20 15 1 05
8 Su 221	12 04 47	5 37 17 21	18 33 4 05	5 23 17 35	18 47 3 49	5 05 17 52	19 06 3 30	4 39 18 15	19 31 3 03	3 57 18 52	20 12 2 19
9 Mo 222	12 04 38 23 44 ☉	5 38 18 06	18 33 5 01	5 23 18 17	18 46 4 49	5 06 18 30	19 05 4 33	4 41 18 47	19 29 4 12	4 00 19 15	20 09 3 37
10 Tu 223	12 04 29	5 38 18 48	18 32 5 56	5 24 18 55	18 46 5 47	5 06 19 03	19 03 5 36	4 42 19 15	19 28 5 21	4 02 19 32	20 07 4 57
11 We 224	12 04 19	5 39 19 27	18 32 6 49	5 24 19 30	18 45 6 44	5 07 19 34	19 02 6 37	4 44 19 40	19 26 6 29	4 05 19 48	20 04 6 15
12 Th 225	12 05 09	5 39 20 05	18 31 7 40	5 25 20 04	18 44 7 39	5 08 20 04	19 01 7 37	4 45 20 03	19 24 7 35	4 07 20 02	20 01 7 31
13 Fr 226	12 03 59	5 39 20 42	18 30 8 31	5 26 20 38	18 43 8 33	5 09 20 33	19 00 8 36	4 46 20 26	19 22 8 40	4 09 20 16	19 58 8 46
14 Sa 227	12 03 48	5 39 21 19	18 29 9 20	5 26 21 11	18 42 9 26	5 10 21 02	18 58 9 33	4 48 20 50	19 20 9 43	4 12 20 31	19 55 9 59
15 Su 228	12 03 36	5 40 21 57	18 29 10 19	5 27 21 47	18 41 10 18	5 11 21 33	18 57 10 30	4 49 21 15	19 19 10 46	4 14 20 47	19 53 11 11
16 Mo 229	12 03 24	5 40 22 37	18 28 10 58	5 27 22 24	18 40 11 11	5 12 22 07	18 55 11 26	4 51 21 44	19 17 11 47	4 16 21 08	19 50 12 21
17 Tu 230	12 03 11	5 40 23 20	18 27 11 48	5 28 23 04	18 39 12 03	5 13 22 44	18 54 12 22	4 52 22 17	19 15 12 48	4 19 21 33	19 47 13 30
18 We 231	12 02 58 00 13 ☾	5 40	18 26 12 38	5 29 23 47	18 38 12 55	5 14 23 26	18 53 13 16	4 54 22 55	19 13 13 46	4 21 22 05	19 44 14 35
19 Th 232	12 02 44	5 41 0 05	18 26 13 29	5 29	18 37 13 47	5 15	18 51 14 09	4 55 23 41	19 11 14 41	4 24 22 48	19 41 15 33
20 Fr 233	12 02 30	5 41 0 53	18 25 14 19	5 30 0 35	18 36 14 37	5 16 0 12	18 50 15 00	4 57	19 09 15 31	4 26 23 42	19 39 16 24
21 Sa 234	12 02 15	5 42 1 45	18 25 15 09	5 30 1 27	18 35 15 26	5 17 1 05	18 48 15 47	4 58 0 34	19 07 16 17	4 29	19 36 17 05
22 Su 235	12 02 00	5 42 2 39	18 24 15 58	5 31 2 23	18 34 16 13	5 18 2 03	18 47 16 32	5 00 1 34	19 05 16 57	4 31 0 47	19 33 17 38
23 Mo 236	12 01 45	5 42 3 36	18 23 16 46	5 32 3 22	18 33 16 58	5 19 3 25	18 45 17 13	5 01 2 41	19 03 17 33	4 33 2 02	19 30 18 04
24 Tu 237	12 01 29	5 42 4 34	18 22 17 32	5 32 4 24	18 32 17 40	5 20 4 11	18 44 17 51	5 03 3 53	19 01 18 05	4 36 3 24	19 27 18 26
25 We 238	12 01 12 11 01 ●	5 43 5 34	18 21 18 18	5 33 5 27	18 30 18 22	5 21 5 19	18 42 18 27	5 04 5 08	18 58 18 34	4 38 4 51	19 24 18 45
26 Th 239	12 00 56	5 43 6 34	18 20 19 03	5 33 6 31	18 29 19 03	5 22 6 29	18 41 19 03	5 06 6 25	18 56 19 03	4 41 6 19	19 21 19 03
27 Fr 240	12 00 39	5 43 7 34	18 19 19 48	5 34 7 37	18 28 19 44	5 23 7 39	18 39 19 39	5 07 7 43	18 54 19 31	4 43 7 49	19 18 19 20
28 Sa 241	12 00 21	5 43 8 36	18 18 20 35	5 35 8 42	18 27 20 27	5 24 8 51	18 38 20 16	5 09 9 02	18 52 20 02	4 45 9 20	19 15 19 40
29 Su 242	12 00 03	5 43 9 37	18 17 21 24	5 35 9 48	18 26 21 12	5 25 10 01	18 36 20 57	5 10 10 20	18 50 20 36	4 48 10 50	19 12 20 03
30 Mo 243	11 59 45	5 44 10 39	18 17 22 16	5 36 10 53	18 25 22 00	5 26 11 11	18 35 21 41	5 12 11 36	18 48 21 14	4 50 12 16	19 10 20 32
31 Tu 244	11 59 26	5 44 11 40	18 16 23 09	5 36 11 57	18 24 22 52	5 27 12 18	18 33 22 30	5 13 12 47	18 46 22 00	4 53 13 36	19 07 21 09

9th Month   September, 1976   30 Days

Greenwich Mean Time

NOTE: Light figures indicate Sun. **Dark** figures indicate **Moon**. *Degrees are North Latitude.*
CAUTION: Must be converted to local time. For instruction see page 767.

Day of month / week / year	Sun on meridian / Moon phase (h m s)	20° Rise Sun/Moon	20° Set Sun/Moon	30° Rise Sun/Moon	30° Set Sun/Moon	40° Rise Sun/Moon	40° Set Sun/Moon	50° Rise Sun/Moon	50° Set Sun/Moon	60° Rise Sun/Moon	60° Set Sun/Moon
1 We 245	11 59 07	5 44	18 15	5 37	18 23	5 28	18 32	5 15	18 44	4 55	19 04
	3 35 ☽	12 39		12 57	23 47	13 20	23 24	13 52	22 52	14 45	21 58
2 Th 246	11 58 48	5 44	18 14	5 38	18 22	5 29	18 30	5 16	18 42	4 57	19 01
		13 36	0 05	13 54		14 16		14 48	23 51	15 41	22 58
3 Fr 247	11 58 29	5 44	18 13	5 38	18 21	5 30	18 29	5 18	18 40	5 00	18 58
		14 29	1 02	14 45	0 44	15 06	0 22	15 36		16 23	
4 Sa 248	11 58 09	5 45	18 13	5 39	18 19	5 30	18 27	5 19	18 37	5 02	18 55
		15 18	1 59	15 32	1 43	15 50	1 23	16 15	0 55	16 55	0 08
5 Su 249	11 57 49	5 45	18 12	5 39	18 18	5 31	18 26	5 21	18 35	5 05	18 52
		16 03	2 55	16 15	2 41	16 29	2 24	16 48	2 01	17 19	1 24
6 Mo 250	11 57 29	5 45	18 11	5 40	18 17	5 32	18 24	5 22	18 33	5 07	18 49
		16 45	3 49	16 53	3 39	17 03	3 26	17 17	3 09	17 38	2 41
7 Tu 251	11 57 08	5 45	18 10	5 40	18 16	5 33	18 22	5 24	18 31	5 09	18 46
		17 25	4 42	17 29	4 35	17 35	4 27	17 43	4 16	17 55	3 58
8 We 252	11 56 48	5 45	18 09	5 41	18 14	5 34	18 20	5 25	18 29	5 11	18 43
	12 52 ☉	18 03	5 33	18 04	5 30	18 05	5 27	18 07	5 22	18 09	5 14
9 Th 253	11 56 27	5 46	18 08	5 41	18 13	5 35	18 19	5 27	18 26	5 14	18 39
		18 40	6 24	18 37	6 24	18 34	6 26	18 30	6 27	18 24	6 29
10 Fr 254	11 56 06	5 46	18 07	5 42	18 11	5 36	18 17	5 28	18 24	5 16	18 36
		19 17	7 13	19 11	7 18	19 04	7 23	18 54	7 31	18 38	7 42
11 Sa 255	11 55 45	5 46	18 06	5 42	18 10	5 37	18 15	5 30	18 22	5 18	18 33
		19 55	8 02	19 46	8 10	19 34	8 20	19 19	8 34	18 54	8 55
12 Su 256	11 55 24	5 46	18 05	5 43	18 09	5 38	18 13	5 31	18 20	5 20	18 30
		20 35	8 52	20 22	9 03	20 07	9 17	19 46	9 36	19 13	10 06
13 Mo 257	11 55 02	5 47	18 04	5 43	18 08	5 39	18 12	5 33	18 18	5 23	18 27
		21 16	9 41	21 01	9 55	20 42	10 12	20 17	10 36	19 37	11 15
14 Tu 258	11 54 41	5 47	18 04	5 44	18 06	5 40	18 10	5 34	18 15	5 25	18 24
		21 59	10 31	21 43	10 47	21 22	11 07	20 53	11 35	20 06	12 20
15 We 259	11 54 20	5 48	18 03	5 44	18 05	5 41	18 09	5 36	18 13	5 28	18 21
		22 46	11 20	22 28	11 38	22 06	12 00	21 35	12 30	20 44	13 21
16 Th 260	11 53 58	5 48	18 02	5 45	18 04	5 42	18 08	5 37	18 11	5 30	18 18
	17 20 ☾	23 35	12 10	23 17	12 28	22 55	12 50	22 24	13 22	21 31	14 14
17 Fr 261	11 53 37	5 48	18 01	5 46	18 03	5 43	18 05	5 39	18 09	5 32	18 15
			12 59		13 16	23 49	13 38	23 19	14 08	22 30	14 58
18 Sa 262	11 53 16	5 48	18 00	5 46	18 02	5 44	18 04	5 40	18 07	5 35	18 12
		0 27	13 47	0 10	14 03		14 23		14 50	23 39	15 34
19 Su 263	11 52 54	5 49	17 59	5 47	18 00	5 44	18 02	5 42	18 04	5 37	18 09
		1 21	14 35	1 06	14 48	0 48	15 05	0 22	15 27		16 03
20 Mo 264	11 52 33	5 49	17 58	5 47	17 59	5 45	18 01	5 43	18 02	5 40	18 06
		2 18	15 21	2 06	15 31	1 51	15 44	1 30	16 01	0 47	16 27
21 Tu 265	11 52 12	5 49	17 57	5 48	17 58	5 46	17 59	5 45	18 00	5 42	18 03
		3 16	16 07	3 07	16 13	2 57	16 21	2 42	16 31	2 20	16 47
22 We 266	11 51 51	5 49	17 56	5 48	17 57	5 47	17 57	5 46	17 57	5 44	18 00
		4 16	16 52	4 11	16 54	4 06	16 57	3 58	17 00	3 47	17 06
23 Th 267	11 51 30	5 49	17 55	5 49	17 56	5 48	17 56	5 48	17 56	5 47	17 57
	19 55 ●	5 16	17 38	5 16	17 36	5 17	17 33	5 17	17 29	5 17	17 24
24 Fr 268	11 51 09	5 50	17 55	5 49	17 54	5 49	17 54	5 49	17 53	5 49	17 54
		6 19	18 26	6 23	18 19	6 29	18 11	6 37	18 00	6 49	17 43
25 Sa 269	11 50 49	5 40	17 54	5 50	17 53	5 50	17 53	5 51	17 51	5 51	17 51
		7 22	19 16	7 31	19 05	7 42	18 52	7 58	18 34	8 22	18 06
26 Su 270	11 50 28	5 50	17 53	5 50	17 52	5 51	17 51	5 52	17 49	5 53	17 48
		8 26	20 08	8 39	19 54	8 55	19 36	9 17	19 12	9 53	18 33
27 Mo 271	11 50 08	5 50	17 52	5 51	17 51	5 52	17 49	5 54	17 47	5 55	17 45
		9 30	21 03	9 45	20 46	10 05	20 25	10 33	19 56	11 19	19 09
28 Tu 272	11 49 48	5 50	17 51	5 51	17 50	5 53	17 47	5 55	17 45	5 58	17 42
		10 31	21 59	10 49	21 41	11 11	21 19	11 42	20 47	12 34	19 55
29 We 273	11 49 28	5 51	17 50	5 52	17 48	5 54	17 46	5 57	17 42	6 00	17 39
		11 30	22 57	11 48	22 39	12 11	22 17	12 43	21 45	13 36	20 53
30 Th 274	11 49 08	5 51	17 49	5 52	17 47	5 55	17 44	5 58	17 40	6 02	17 36
	11 12 ☽	12 25	23 54	12 42	23 38	13 04	23 17	13 34	22 48	14 23	22 00

10th Month   October, 1976   31 Days

Greenwich Mean Time

NOTE: Light figures indicate Sun. **Dark** figures indicate **Moon.** *Degrees are North Latitude.*

CAUTION: Must be converted to local time. For instruction see page 767.

Day of month week year	Sun on meridian Moon phase h m s	20° Rise Sun Moon h m	20° Set Sun Moon h m	30° Rise Sun Moon h m	30° Set Sun Moon h m	40° Rise Sun Moon h m	40° Set Sun Moon h m	50° Rise Sun Moon h m	50° Set Sun Moon h m	60° Rise Sun Moon h m	60° Set Sun Moon h m
1 Fr 275	11 48 49	5 51 13 16	17 48	5 53 13 31	17 46	5 56 13 50	17 42	6 00 14 16	17 38 23 54	6 05 14 58	17 33 23 14
2 Sa 276	11 48 30	5 51 14 02	17 47 0 51	5 54 14 14	17 45 0 36	5 57 14 30	17 40 0 19	6 02 14 51	17 36	6 07 15 24	17 30
3 Su 277	11 48 11	5 51 14 44	17 46 1 45	5 54 14 54	17 44 1 34	5 58 15 05	17 39 1 20	6 03 15 20	17 34 1 01	6 10 15 44	17 27 0 31
4 Mo 278	11 47 53	5 52 15 24	17 46 2 38	5 55 15 30	17 42 2 30	5 59 15 37	17 37 2 21	6 05 15 47	17 32 2 07	6 12 16 01	17 24 1 47
5 Tu 279	11 47 35	5 52 16 03	17 45 3 29	5 55 16 05	17 41 3 25	6 00 16 07	17 36 3 20	6 06 16 11	17 30 3 13	6 15 16 17	17 21 3 02
6 We 280	11 47 17	5 52 16 40	17 44 4 19	5 56 16 38	17 40 4 19	6 01 16 37	17 34 4 18	6 08 16 34	17 28 4 17	6 17 16 31	17 18 4 16
7 Th 281	11 46 59	5 52 17 17	17 43 5 08	5 57 17 12	17 39 5 12	6 02 17 06	17 33 5 16	6 09 16 58	17 26 5 21	6 19 16 46	17 15 5 29
8 Fr 282	11 46 43 04 55 ☉	5 52 17 54	17 42 5 58	5 57 17 46	17 38 6 04	6 03 17 36	17 31 6 13	6 11 17 22	17 24 6 24	6 22 17 01	17 12 6 42
9 Sa 283	11 46 26	5 53 18 33	17 42 6 47	5 58 18 22	17 36 6 57	6 04 18 08	17 30 7 09	6 12 17 49	16 21 7 26	6 24 17 19	17 09 7 53
10 Su 284	11 46·10	5 53 19 14	17 41 7 36	5 58 19 00	17 35 7 49	6 05 18 42	17 28 8 05	6 14 18 19	17 19 8 27	6 27 17 41	17 06 9 03
11 Mo 285	11 45 54	5 53 19 56	17 40 8 25	5 59 19 40	17 34 8 41	6 06 19 20	17 27 9 00	6 15 18 53	17 17 9 26	6 29 18 08	17 03 10 10
12 Tu 286	11 45 39	5 53 20 42	17 39 9 15	6 00 20 24	17 33 9 32	6 07 20 02	17 25 9 53	6 17 19 32	17 15 10 23	6 32 18 43	17 00 11 12
13 We 287	11 45 25	5 54 21 29	17 38 10 04	6 00 21 11	17 32 10 22	6 08 20 49	17 24 10 44	6 18 20 18	17 13 11 15	6 34 19 26	16 57 12 07
14 Th 288	11 45 11	5 54 22 19	17 38 10 53	6 01 22 02	17 30 11 10	6 09 21 40	17 22 11 32	6 20 21 10	17 11 12 03	6 37 20 20	16 54 12 54
15 Fr 289	11 44 57	5 55 23 11	17 37 11 40	6 01 22 55	17 29 11 57	6 10 22 36	17 21 12 17	6 21 22 08	17 09 12 46	6 39 21 23	16 51 13 32
16 Sa 290	11 44 45 08 59 ☾	5 55	17 36 12 27	6 02 23 52	17 28 12 41	6 11 23 35	17 19 12 59	6 23 23 12	17 07 13 24	6 42 22 35	16 48 14 03
17 Su 291	11 44 32	5 55 0 05	17 35 13 12	6 03	17 27 13 23	6 12	17 18 13 38	6 25	17 05 13 57	6 44 23 53	16 45 14 28
18 Mo 292	11 44 21	5 56 1 01	17 34 13 56	6 04 0 50	17 26 14 04	6 13 0 38	17 16 14 15	6 26 0 20	17 03 14 28	6 47	16 42 14 49
19 Tu 293	11 44 10	5 56 1 58	17 34 14 41	6 04 1 51	17 25 14 45	6 15 1 43	17 15 14 50	6 28 1 32	17 01 14 57	6 49 1 15	16 40 15 08
20 We 294	11 43 59	5 57 2 56	17 33 15 25	6 05 2 54	17 24 15 26	6 16 2 51	17 13 15 26	6 29 2 48	16 59 15 26	6 52 2 42	16 37 15 26
21 Th 295	11 43 50	5 57 3 57	17 32 16 12	6 06 3 59	17 23 16 08	6 17 4 02	17 12 16 02	6 31 4 06	16 57 15 55	6 54 4 12	16 34 15 44
22 Fr 296	11 43 41	5 57 5 00	17 31 17 01	6 07 5 07	17 22 16 52	6 18 5 15	17 11 16 41	6 33 5 26	16 27	6 57 5 44	16 31 16 05
23 Sa 297	11 43 32 05 10 ●	6 04 5 58	17 53 17 31	6 15 6 07	17 40 17 21	6 29 6 19	17 25 17 09	6 48 6 35	17 03 16 53	7 18 6 59	16 30 16 28
24 Su 298	11 43 25	5 58 7 10	17 30 18 48	6 08 7 24	17 20 18 32	6 20 7 43	17 06 18 13	6 36 8 08	16 52 17 46	7 02 8 49	16 26 17 02
25 Mo 299	11 43 18	5 59 8 15	17 30 19 46	6 08 8 32	17 19 19 28	6 21 8 53	17 06 19 06	6 38 9 23	16 50 18 36	7 04 10 13	16 23 17 45
26 Tu 300	11 43 12	5 59 9 18	17 29 20 46	6 09 9 36	17 18 20 28	6 22 9 58	17 05 20 05	6 40 10 30	16 48 19 33	7 07 11 23	16 20 18 40
27 We 301	11 43 06	5 59 10 17	17 28 21 45	6 10 10 34	17 17 21 28	6 23 10 56	17 04 21 07	6 42 11 27	16 46 20 37	7 10 12 18	16 17 19 47
28 Th 302	11 43 01	6 00 11 10	17 28 22 44	6 11 11 26	17 16 22 29	6 24 11 46	17 03 22 10	6 43 12 14	16 43 21 44	7 12 12 58	16 15 21 01
29 Fr 303	11 42 57 22 05 ☽	6 00 11 59	17 27 23 40	6 11 12 13	17 16 23 28	6 26 12 29	17 01 23 13	6 45 12 52	16 41 22 52	7 15 13 28	16 12 22 18
30 Sa 304	11 42 54	6 01 12 44	17 27	6 12 12 54	17 15	6 27 13 07	17 00	6 46 13 24	16 38 23 59	7 17 13 50	16 10 23 36
31 Su 305	11 42 51	6 01 13 25	17 26 0 34	6 13 13 31	17 14 0 25	6 28 13 40	16 59 0 14	6 48 13 51	16 36	7 20 14 09	16 07

11th Month   November, 1976   30 Days

Greenwich Mean Time

NOTE: Light figures indicate Sun. **Dark** figures indicate **Moon.** *Degrees are North Latitude.*

CAUTION: Must be converted to local time. For instruction see page 767.

Day of month / week / year	Sun on meridian Moon phase (h m s)	20° Rise Sun/Moon	20° Set Sun/Moon	30° Rise Sun/Moon	30° Set Sun/Moon	40° Rise Sun/Moon	40° Set Sun/Moon	50° Rise Sun/Moon	50° Set Sun/Moon	60° Rise Sun/Moon	60° Set Sun/Moon
1 Mo	11 42 50	6 01	17 26	6 14	17 13	6 29	16 58	6 50	16 35	7 22	16 04
306		14 03	1 26	14 07	1 21	14 11	1 14	14 16	1 05	14 24	0 52
2 Tu	11 42 49	6 02	17 25	6 15	17 12	6 30	16 57	6 51	16 34	7 25	16 02
307		14 40	2 16	14 40	2 14	14 40	2 13	14 39	2 10	14 39	2 06
3 We	11 42 49	6 02	17 25	6 15	17 12	6 32	16 55	6 53	16 32	7 27	15 59
308		15 17	3 05	15 13	3 07	15 09	3 10	15 03	3 13	14 53	3 19
4 Th	11 42 49	6 03	17 24	6 16	17 11	6 33	16 54	6 54	16 31	7 33	15 57
309		15 54	3 54	15 47	4 00	15 38	4 07	15 26	4 16	15 08	4 31
5 Fr	11 42 51	6 03	17 24	6 17	17 10	6 34	16 53	6 56	16 30	7 32	15 54
310		16 33	4 43	16 22	4 52	16 09	5 03	15 52	5 18	15 25	5 42
6 Sa	11 42 53	6 04	17 24	6 18	17 09	6 35	16 52	6 58	16 29	7 35	15 52
311	23 15 ☽	17 12	5 32	16 59	5 44	16 43	5 59	16 21	6 19	15 46	6 52
7 Su	11 42 56	6 04	17 23	6 19	17 09	6 36	16 51	7 00	16 27	7 37	15 49
312		17 55	6 22	17 39	6 36	17 20	6 54	16 54	7 19	16 11	8 00
8 Mo	11 43 00	6 05	17 23	6 19	17 08	6 37	16 50	7 01	16 26	7 40	15 47
313		18 39	7 11	18 22	7 28	18 01	7 48	17 31	8 17	16 43	9 05
9 Tu	11 43 05	6 05	17 22	6 20	17 08	6 38	16 49	7 03	16 24	7 42	15 44
314		19 26	8 01	19 08	8 18	18 46	8 40	18 15	9 11	17 23	10 02
10 We	11 43 11	6 06	17 22	6 21	17 07	6 39	16 48	7 05	16 23	7 45	15 42
315		20 15	8 50	19 57	9 07	19 35	9 30	19 05	10 01	18 14	10 52
11 Th	11 43 17	6 07	17 22	6 22	17 06	6 40	16 47	7 07	16 22	7 48	15 40
316		21 06	9 37	20 50	9 54	20 29	10 15	20 00	10 45	19 13	11 33
12 Fr	11 43 25	6 07	17 21	6 23	17 06	6 41	16 46	7 08	16 20	7 50	15 37
317		21 58	10 23	2 44	10 39	21 26	10 58	21 01	11 24	20 21	12 06
13 Sa	11 43 23	6 08	17 21	6 23	17 05	6 43	16 46	7 10	16 19	7 53	15 35
318		22 52	11 08	22 40	11 21	22 26	11 37	22 06	11 58	21 35	12 32
14 Su	11 43 32	6 08	17 20	6 24	17 05	6 44	16 45	7 11	16 17	7 55	15 32
319	22 39 ☾	23 46	11 51	23 38	12 01	23 28	12 13	23 15	12 29	22 53	12 54
15 Mo	11 43 52	6 09	17 20	6 25	17 04	6 45	16 44	7 13	16 16	7 58	15 30
320			12 34		12 40		12 47		12 57		13 12
16 Tu	11 44 03	6 10	17 20	6 26	17 04	6 46	16 43	7 15	16 15	8 00	15 28
321		0 42	13 17	0 38	13 19	0 33	13 21	0 26	13 25	0 15	13 30
17 We	11 44 15	6 10	17 20	6 27	17 03	6 47	16 42	7 16	16 14	8 03	15 26
322		1 40	14 01	1 40	13 59	1 40	13 56	1 40	13 52	1 40	13 47
18 Th	11 44 28	6 11	17 19	6 27	17 03	6 49	16 42	7 18	16 12	8 05	15 24
323		2 39	14 47	2 44	14 40	2 49	14 32	2 57	14 22	3 08	14 06
19 Fr	11 44 31	6 11	17 19	6 28	17 02	6 50	16 41	7 19	16 11	8 08	15 22
324		3 41	15 36	3 50	15 25	4 01	15 12	4 16	14 55	4 39	14 28
20 Sa	11 44 55	6 12	17 19	6 29	17 02	6 51	16 40	7 21	16 10	8 10	15 20
325		4 46	16 29	4 58	16 15	5 14	15 57	5 36	15 33	6 11	14 55
21 Su	11 45 10	6 13	17 19	6 30	17 02	6 52	16 40	7 22	16 09	8 12	15 18
326	15 11 ●	5 51	17 26	6 07	17 09	6 27	16 48	6 54	16 19	7 40	15 32
22 Mo	11 45 26	6 13	17 19	6 31	17 02	6 53	16 39	7 24	16 08	8 15	15 16
327		6 57	18 26	7 14	18 08	7 36	17 45	8 08	17 14	9 00	16 21
23 Tu	11 45 43	6 14	17 19	6 31	17 01	6 54	16 39	7 25	16 07	8 17	15 15
328		7 59	19 28	8 17	19 10	8 40	18 48	9 12	18 16	10 05	17 24
24 We	11 46 00	6 14	17 19	6 32	17 01	6 55	16 38	7 27	16 06	8 20	15 13
329		8 58	20 29	9 15	20 13	9 36	19 53	10 05	19 24	10 53	18 38
25 Th	11 46 18	6 15	17 19	6 33	17 01	6 56	16 38	7 28	16 05	8 22	15 11
330		9 51	21 29	10 05	21 15	10 24	20 58	10 49	20 35	11 29	19 57
26 Fr	11 46 37	6 16	17 19	6 34	17 01	6 57	16 38	7 30	16 04	8 24	15 10
331		10 39	22 26	10 50	22 15	11 05	22 03	11 24	21 45	11 55	21 17
27 Sa	11 46 57	6 16	17 19	6 35	17 01	6 58	16 37	7 31	16 04	8 26	15 08
332		11 22	23 20	11 30	23 13	11 41	23 05	11 54	22 54	12 15	22 36
28 Su	11 47 17	6 17	17 19	6 36	17 00	7 00	16 37	7 33	16 03	8 29	15 07
333	12 59 ☽	12 02		12 07		12 13		12 20		12 32	23 52
29 Mo	11 47 38	6 17	17 19	6 37	17 00	7 01	16 36	7 34	16 03	8 31	15 05
334		12 41	0 11	12 42	0 08	12 43	0 05	12 45	0 00	12 47	
30 Tu	11 48 00	6 18	17 19	6 38	17 00	7 02	16 36	7 36	16 02	8 33	15 04
335		13 18	1 01	13 15	1 02	13 12	1 03	13 08	1 04	13 01	1 06

12th Month   December, 1976   31 Days

Greenwich Mean Time

NOTE: Light figures indicate Sun. **Dark** figures indicate **Moon.** *Degrees are North Latitude.*

CAUTION: Must be converted to local time. For instruction see page 767.

Day of month week year	Sun on meridian Moon phase	20° Rise Sun Moon	20° Set Sun Moon	30° Rise Sun Moon	30° Set Sun Moon	40° Rise Sun Moon	40° Set Sun Moon	50° Rise Sun Moon	50° Set Sun Moon	60° Rise Sun Moon	60° Set Sun Moon
	h m s	h m	h m	h m	h m	h m	h m	h m	h m	h m	h m
1 We 336	11 48 22	6 19 / 13 55	17 19 / 1 50	6 39 / 13 49	17 00 / 1 55	7 03 / 13 41	16 36 / 2 00	7 37 / 13 31	16 01 / 2 08	8 35 / 13 16	15 03 / 2 19
2 Th 337	11 48 45	6 19 / 14 32	17 19 / 2 39	6 39 / 14 23	17 00 / 2 47	7 04 / 14 12	16 36 / 2 57	7 38 / 13 56	16 01 / 3 10	8 37 / 13 32	15 02 / 3 30
3 Fr 338	11 49 08	6 20 / 15 11	17 20 / 3 28	6 40 / 14 59	17 00 / 3 39	7 05 / 14 44	16 35 / 3 53	7 40 / 14 24	16 00 / 4 11	8 39 / 13 51	15 00 / 4 41
4 Sa 339	11 49 32	6 20 / 15 53	17 20 / 4 17	6 40 / 15 38	17 00 / 4 31	7 06 / 15 20	16 35 / 4 48	7 41 / 14 55	17 00 / 5 12	8 41 / 14 14	14 59 / 5 50
5 Su 340	11 49 57	6 21 / 16 36	17 20 / 5 07	6 41 / 16 20	17 00 / 5 23	7 07 / 15 59	16 35 / 5 43	7 42 / 15 30	15 59 / 6 10	8 43 / 14 44	14 58 / 6 56
6 Mo 341	11 50 22 / 18 15 ☺	6 22 / 17 23	17 20 / 5 57	6 42 / 17 05	17 00 / 6 14	7 08 / 16 43	16 35 / 6 36	7 43 / 16 12	15 59 / 7 06	8 45 / 15 21	14 57 / 7 57
7 Tu 342	11 50 48	6 22 / 18 11	17 20 / 6 46	6 43 / 17 54	17 00 / 7 04	7 09 / 17 31	16 35 / 7 27	7 44 / 17 00	15 59 / 7 58	8 46 / 16 08	14 57 / 8 50
8 We 343	11 51 14	6 23 / 19 02	17 21 / 7 35	6 43 / 18 45	17 01 / 7 52	7 09 / 18 24	16 35 / 8 14	7 45 / 17 54	15 58 / 8 44	8 48 / 17 05	14 56 / 9 34
9 Th 344	11 51 41	6 23 / 19 55	17 21 / 8 22	6 44 / 19 39	17 01 / 8 38	7 10 / 19 20	16 35 / 8 58	7 46 / 18 54	15 58 / 9 25	8 49 / 18 11	14 56 / 10 10
10 Fr 345	11 52 08	6 24 / 20 48	17 21 / 9 07	6 45 / 20 35	17 01 / 9 21	7 11 / 20 20	16 35 / 9 38	7 47 / 19 58	15 58 / 10 01	8 51 / 19 23	14 55 / 10 38
11 Sa 346	11 52 35	6 25 / 21 42	17 21 / 9 51	6 46 / 21 32	17 01 / 10 02	7 12 / 21 21	16 35 / 10 15	7 48 / 21 05	15 58 / 10 33	8 52 / 20 40	14 55 / 11 01
12 Su 347	11 53 03	6 25 / 22 36	17 22 / 10 33	6 46 / 22 30	17 01 / 10 41	7 13 / 22 23	16 35 / 10 50	7 49 / 22 14	15 58 / 11 02	8 53 / 21 59	14 54 / 11 20
13 Mo 348	11 53 32	6 26 / 23 31	17 22 / 11 15	6 47 / 23 30	17 02 / 11 19	7 13 / 23 27	16 36 / 11 23	7 50 / 23 25	15 58 / 11 29	8 55 / 23 20	14 54 / 11 38
14 Tu 349	11 54 00 / 10 14 ☾	6 26 / —	17 23 / 11 57	6 47 / —	17 02 / 11 56	7 14 / —	16 36 / 11 56	7 51 / —	15 58 / 11 55	8 56 / —	14 53 / 11 54
15 We 350	11 54 29	6 27 / 0 28	17 23 / 12 40	6 48 / 0 30	17 02 / 12 36	7 15 / 0 33	16 36 / 12 30	7 52 / 0 38	15 58 / 12 23	8 57 / 0 44	14 53 / 12 11
16 Th 351	11 54 58	6 28 / 1 26	17 23 / 13 26	6 49 / 1 33	17 02 / 13 17	7 16 / 1 41	16 36 / 13 07	7 53 / 1 53	15 58 / 12 52	8 58 / 2 11	14 53 / 12 31
17 Fr 352	11 55 28	6 28 / 2 27	17 24 / 14 15	6 49 / 2 38	17 03 / 14 02	7 16 / 2 51	16 37 / 13 47	7 53 / 3 09	15 59 / 13 26	8 59 / 3 39	14 53 / 12 54
18 Sa 353	11 55 57	6 29 / 3 30	17 24 / 15 08	6 50 / 3 44	17 03 / 14 52	7 17 / 4 02	16 37 / 14 33	7 54 / 4 27	15 59 / 14 07	8 59 / 5 07	14 54 / 13 24
19 Su 354	11 56 27	6 29 / 4 34	17 25 / 16 05	6 50 / 4 51	17 04 / 15 48	7 17 / 5 12	16 38 / 15 26	7 54 / 5 41	16 00 / 14 55	9 00 / 6 30	14 54 / 14 05
20 Mo 355	11 56 57	6 30 / 5 38	17 25 / 17 06	6 51 / 5 56	17 04 / 16 48	7 18 / 6 18	16 38 / 16 25	7 55 / 6 50	16 00 / 15 53	9 01 / 7 43	14 54 / 15 00
21 Tu 356	11 57 27 / 02 08 ●	6 30 / 6 39	17 26 / 18 08	6 52 / 6 56	17 05 / 17 51	7 18 / 7 19	16 38 / 17 29	7 56 / 7 50	16 01 / 16 59	9 02 / 8 42	14 55 / 16 08
22 We 357	11 57 57	6 31 / 7 36	17 26 / 19 10	6 52 / 7 52	17 05 / 18 55	7 19 / 8 12	16 39 / 18 36	7 56 / 8 40	16 01 / 18 10	9 02 / 9 25	14 55 / 17 26
23 Th 358	11 58 27	6 31 / 8 26	17 27 / 20 10	6 53 / 8 41	17 06 / 19 58	7 19 / 8 58	16 39 / 19 43	7 57 / 9 20	16 02 / 19 22	9 03 / 9 56	14 56 / 18 49
24 Fr 359	11 58 57	6 32 / 9 15	17 27 / 21 07	6 53 / 9 25	17 06 / 20 59	7 20 / 9 37	16 40 / 20 48	7 57 / 9 54	16 02 / 20 34	9 03 / 10 20	14 56 / 20 11
25 Sa 360	11 59 27	6 32 / 9 58	17 28 / 22 02	6 54 / 10 04	17 07 / 21 57	7 20 / 10 12	16 40 / 21 51	7 58 / 10 23	16 03 / 21 43	9 04 / 10 39	14 57 / 21 31
26 Su 361	11 59 56	6 32 / 10 38	17 29 / 22 54	6 54 / 10 41	17 08 / 22 53	7 20 / 10 44	16 41 / 22 52	7 58 / 10 48	16 04 / 22 50	9 04 / 10 55	14 58 / 22 48
27 Mo 362	12 00 26	6 33 / 11 16	17 29 / 23 44	6 54 / 11 15	17 08 / 23 47	7 21 / 11 14	16 42 / 23 50	7 58 / 11 12	16 05 / 23 55	9 04 / 11 10	14 59 / —
28 Tu 363	12 00 55 / 07 48 ☽	6 33 / 11 54	17 30 / —	6 55 / 11 49	17 09 / —	7 21 / 11 43	16 42 / —	7 59 / 11 36	16 05 / —	9 03 / 11 25	15 00 / 0 02
29 We 364	12 01 25	6 34 / 12 31	17 30 / 0 33	6 55 / 12 23	17 09 / 0 40	7 22 / 12 13	16 43 / 0 48	7 59 / 12 00	16 06 / 0 58	9 03 / 11 40	15 01 / 1 15
30 Th 365	12 01 54	6 34 / 13 10	17 31 / 1 22	6 55 / 12 59	17 10 / 1 32	7 22 / 12 45	16 44 / 1 44	7 59 / 12 27	16 07 / 2 00	9 03 / 11 58	15 02 / 2 26
31 Fr 366	12 02 22	6 34 / 13 50	17 32 / 2 11	6 55 / 13 36	17 11 / 2 24	7 22 / 13 19	16 45 / 2 40	7 59 / 12 56	16 08 / 3 01	9 03 / 12 19	15 03 / 3 36

The Julian Period

How many days have you lived? To determine this, you must multiply your age by 365, add the number of days since your last birthday until today, and account for all the leap years. Chances are your answer would be wrong. Astronomers, however, find it convenient to express dates and long time intervals in days rather than in years, months and days. This is done by placing events within the Julian period.

The Julian period was devised in 1582 by Joseph Scaliger and named after his father Julius (not after the Julian calendar). Scaliger had Julian Day (JD) #1 begin at noon, Jan. 1, 4713 B. C., the most recent time that three major chronological cycles began on the same day — 1) the 28-year solar cycle, after which

dates in the Julian calendar (e.g., Feb. 11) return to the same days of the week (e.g., Monday); 2) the 19-year lunar cycle, after which the phases of the moon return to the same dates of the year; and 3) the 15-year indiction cycle, used in ancient Rome to regulate taxes. It will take 7980 years to complete the period, the product of 28, 19 and 15.

Noon of Dec. 31, 1975, marks the beginning of JD 2,442,778; that many days will have passed since the start of the Julian period. The JD at noon of any date in 1976 may be found by adding to this figure the day of the year for that date, which is given in the left hand column in the chart below. Simple JD conversion tables are used by astronomers.

Days Between Two Dates

Table covers period of two ordinary years. Example—Days between Feb. 10, 1973 and Dec. 15, 1974; subtract 41 from 714; answer is 673 days. For leap year, such as 1976, one day must be added after Feb. 28.

Date	Jan.	Feb.	Mar.	April	May	June	July	Aug.	Sept.	Oct.	Nov.	Dec.	Date	Jan.	Feb.	Mar.	April	May	June	July	Aug.	Sept.	Oct.	Nov.	Dec.
1	1	32	60	91	121	152	182	213	244	274	305	335	1	366	397	425	456	486	517	547	578	609	639	670	700
2	2	33	61	92	122	153	183	214	245	275	306	336	2	367	398	426	457	487	518	548	579	610	640	671	701
3	3	34	62	93	123	154	184	215	246	276	307	337	3	368	399	427	458	488	519	549	580	611	641	672	702
4	4	35	63	94	124	155	185	216	247	277	308	338	4	369	400	428	459	489	520	550	581	612	642	673	703
5	5	36	64	95	125	156	186	217	248	278	309	339	5	370	401	429	460	490	521	551	582	613	643	674	704
6	6	37	65	96	126	157	187	218	249	279	310	340	6	371	402	430	461	491	522	552	583	614	644	675	705
7	7	38	66	97	127	158	188	219	250	280	311	341	7	372	403	431	462	492	523	553	584	615	645	676	706
8	8	39	67	98	128	159	189	220	251	281	312	342	8	373	404	432	463	493	524	554	585	616	646	677	707
9	9	40	68	99	129	160	190	221	252	282	313	343	9	374	405	433	464	494	525	555	586	617	647	678	708
10	10	41	69	100	130	161	191	222	253	283	314	344	10	375	406	434	465	495	526	556	587	618	648	679	709
11	11	42	70	101	131	162	192	223	254	284	315	345	11	376	407	435	466	496	527	557	588	619	649	680	710
12	12	43	71	102	132	163	193	224	255	285	316	346	12	377	408	436	467	497	528	558	589	620	650	681	711
13	13	44	72	103	133	164	194	225	256	286	317	347	13	378	409	437	468	498	529	559	590	621	651	682	712
14	14	45	73	104	134	165	195	226	257	287	318	348	14	379	410	438	469	499	530	560	591	622	652	683	713
15	15	46	74	105	135	166	196	227	258	288	319	349	15	380	411	439	470	500	531	561	592	623	653	684	714
16	16	47	75	106	136	167	197	228	259	289	320	350	16	381	412	440	471	501	532	562	593	624	654	685	715
17	17	48	76	107	137	168	198	229	260	290	321	351	17	382	413	441	472	502	533	563	594	625	655	686	716
18	18	49	77	108	138	169	199	230	261	291	322	352	18	383	414	442	473	503	534	564	595	626	656	687	717
19	19	50	78	109	139	170	200	231	262	292	323	353	19	384	415	443	474	504	535	565	596	627	657	688	718
20	20	51	79	110	140	171	201	232	263	293	324	354	20	385	416	444	475	505	536	566	597	628	658	689	719
21	21	52	80	111	141	172	202	233	264	294	325	355	21	386	417	445	476	506	537	567	598	629	659	690	720
22	22	53	81	112	142	173	203	234	265	295	326	356	22	387	418	446	477	507	538	568	599	630	660	691	721
23	23	54	82	113	143	174	204	235	266	296	327	357	23	388	419	447	478	508	539	569	600	631	661	692	722
24	24	55	83	114	144	175	205	236	267	297	328	358	24	389	420	448	479	509	540	570	601	632	662	693	723
25	25	56	84	115	145	176	206	237	268	298	329	359	25	390	421	449	480	510	541	571	602	633	663	694	724
26	26	57	85	116	146	177	207	238	269	299	330	360	26	391	422	450	481	511	542	572	603	634	664	695	725
27	27	58	86	117	147	178	208	239	270	300	331	361	27	392	423	451	482	512	543	573	604	635	665	696	726
28	28	59	87	118	148	179	209	240	271	301	332	362	28	393	424	452	483	513	544	574	605	636	666	697	727
29	29	—	88	119	149	180	210	241	272	302	333	363	29	394	—	453	484	514	545	575	606	637	667	698	728
30	30	—	89	120	150	181	211	242	273	303	334	364	30	395	—	454	485	515	546	576	607	638	668	699	729
31	31	—	90	—	151	—	212	243	—	304	—	365	31	396	—	455	—	516	—	577	608	—	669	—	730

Lunar Calendar, Chinese New Years, Vietnamese Tet

The ancient Chinese lunar calendar is divided into 12 months of either 29 or 30 days (compensating for the fact that the mean duration of the lunar month is 29 days, 12 hours, 44.05 minutes). The calendar is synchronized with the solar year by the addition of extra months at fixed intervals.

The Chinese calendar runs on a sexagenary cycle, i.e., 60 years. The cycles 1861-1923 and 1924-1983, with the years grouped under their twelve animal designations, are printed below. The year 1976 is found in the fifth column, under Dragon, and is known as a "Year of the Dragon." Readers can find the animal name for the year of their birth, marriage, etc. in the same chart. (Note: the first 3-7 weeks of each of the western years belong to the previous Chinese year and animal designation.)

Both the western (Gregorian) and traditional lunar calendars are used publicly in China, and two New Year's celebrations are held. On Taiwan, in overseas Chinese communities and in Vietnam, the lunar calendar has been used only to set the dates for traditional festivals, with the Gregorian system in general use.

The four-day Chinese New Year, Hsin Nien, and the three-day Vietnamese New Year festival, Tet, begin at the first new moon after the sun enters Aquarius. The day may fall, therefore, between Jan. 21 and Feb. 19 of the Gregorian calendar. Jan. 31, 1976, marks the start of the new Chinese year. The date is fixed according to the date of the new moon in the Far East. Since this is west of the International Date Line the date may be one day later than that of the new moon in the United States.

Rat	Ox	Tiger	Hare (Rabbit)	Dragon	Snake	Horse	Sheep (Goat)	Monkey	Rooster	Dog	Pig
1864	1865	1866	1867	1868	1869	1870	1871	1872	1873	1874	1875
1876	1877	1878	1879	1880	1881	1882	1883	1884	1885	1886	1887
1888	1889	1890	1891	1892	1893	1894	1895	1896	1897	1898	1899
1900	1901	1902	1903	1904	1905	1906	1907	1908	1909	1910	1911
1912	1913	1914	1915	1916	1917	1918	1919	1920	1921	1922	1923
1924	1925	1926	1927	1928	1929	1930	1931	1932	1933	1934	1935
1936	1937	1938	1939	1940	1941	1942	1943	1944	1945	1946	1947
1948	1949	1950	1951	1952	1953	1954	1955	1956	1957	1958	1959
1960	1961	1962	1963	1964	1965	1966	1967	1968	1969	1970	1971
1972	1973	1974	1975	1976	1977	1978	1979	1980	1981	1982	1983

Julian and Gregorian Calendars; Leap Year

Calendars based on the movements of sun and moon have been used since ancient times, but none has been perfect. The Julian calendar, under which western nations measured time until 1582 A. D., was authorized by Julius Caesar in 46 B.C., the year 709 of Rome. His expert was a Greek, Sosigenes. The Julian calendar, on the assumption that the true year was 365¼ days long, gave every fourth year 366 days. The Venerable Bede, an Anglo-Saxon monk, announced in 730 A.D. that the 365¼-day Julian year was 11 min., 14 sec. too long, making a cumulative error of about a day every 128 years, but nothing was done about it for over 800 years.

By 1582 the accumulated error was estimated to have amounted to 10 days. In that year Pope Gregory XIII decreed that the day following Oct. 4, 1582, should be called Oct. 15, thus dropping 10 days.

However, with common years 365 days and a 366-day leap year every fourth year, the error in the length of the year would have recurred at the rate of a little more than 3 days every 400 years. So 3 of every 4 centesimal years (ending in 00) were made common years, not leap years. Thus, 1600 was a leap year; 1700, 1800 and 1900 were not, but 2000 will be. Leap years are those divisible by 4 except centesimal years, which are common unless divisible by 400.

The Gregorian calendar was adopted at once by France, Italy, Spain, Portugal and Luxembourg. Within two years most German Catholic states, Belgium and parts of Switzerland and the Netherlands were brought under the new calendar, and Hungary followed in 1587. The rest of the Netherlands, along with Denmark and the German Protestant states made the change in 1699-1700 (though the German Protestants retained the old reckoning of Easter until 1776).

The British Government imposed the Gregorian calendar on all its possessions, including the American colonies, in 1752. The British decreed that the day following Sept. 2, 1752, should be called Sept. 14, a loss of 11 days. All dates preceding were marked O.S., for Old Style. In addition, New Year's Day was moved to Jan. 1 from Mar. 25. (E.g., under the old reckoning, Mar. 24, 1700, had been followed by Mar. 25, 1701.) George Washington's birth date, which was Feb. 11, 1731, O.S., became Feb. 22, 1732, N.S. In 1753 Sweden too went Gregorian, retaining the old Easter rules until 1844.

In 1793 the French Revolutionary Government adopted a calendar of 12 months of 30 days each with 5 extra days in September of each common year and a 6th extra day every 4th year. Napoleon reinstated the Gregorian calendar in 1806.

The Gregorian system later spread to non-European regions, first in the European colonies, then in the independent countries, replacing traditional calendars at least for official purposes. Japan in 1873, Egypt in 1875, China in 1912 and Turkey in 1917 made the change, usually in conjunction with political upheavals. In China, the republican government began reckoning years from its 1911 founding — e.g., 1948 was designated the year 37. After 1949, the Communists adopted the Common, or Christian Era year count, even for the traditional lunar calendar.

In 1918 the revolutionary government in Russia decreed that the day after Jan. 31, 1918, Old Style, would become Feb. 13, 1918, New Style. Greece followed in 1923. (In Russia the Orthodox Church has retained the Julian calendar, as have various Middle Eastern Christian sects.) For the first time in history, all major cultures have been brought under one calendar.

To change from the Julian to the Gregorian calendar, add 10 days to dates Oct. 5, 1582, through Feb. 28, 1700; after that date add 11 days through Feb. 28, 1800, 12 days through Feb. 28, 1900, and 13 days through Feb. 28, 2100.

Gregorian Calendar

Pick desired year from table below or on next page. The number shown with each year shows which calendar to use for that year, as shown on the next two pages. (The Gregorian calendar was inaugurated Oct. 15, 1582. From that date to Dec. 31, 1582, use calendar 6.)

1583-1799

1583... 7	1603... 4	1623... 1	1643... 5	1663... 6	1683... 6	1703...2	1723... 6	1743... 3	1763... 7	1783... 5
1584... 8	1604... 12	1624... 9	1644... 13	1664... 10	1684... 14	1704...10	1724... 14	1744...11	1764... 8	1784... 12
1585... 3	1605... 7	1625... 4	1645... 1	1665... 5	1685... 2	1705...5	1725... 2	1745... 6	1765... 3	1785... 7
1586... 4	1606... 1	1626... 5	1646... 2	1666... 6	1686... 3	1706...6	1726... 3	1746... 7	1766... 4	1786... 1
1587... 5	1607... 2	1627... 6	1647... 3	1667... 7	1687... 4	1707...7	1727... 4	1747... 1	1767... 5	1787... 2
1588... 13	1608... 10	1628... 14	1648... 11	1668... 8	1688... 12	1708...8	1728... 12	1748... 9	1768... 13	1788... 10
1589... 1	1609... 5	1629... 2	1649... 6	1669... 3	1689... 7	1709...3	1729... 7	1749... 4	1769... 1	1789... 5
1590... 2	1610... 6	1630... 3	1650... 7	1670... 4	1690... 1	1710...4	1730... 1	1750... 5	1770... 2	1790... 6
1591... 4	1611... 7	1631... 4	1651... 1	1671... 5	1691... 2	1711...5	1731... 2	1751... 6	1771... 3	1791... 7
1592... 11	1612... 8	1632... 12	1652... 9	1672... 13	1692... 10	1712...13	1732... 10	1752... 14	1772... 11	1792... 8
1593... 6	1613... 3	1633... 7	1653... 4	1673... 1	1693... 5	1713...1	1733... 5	1753... 2	1773... 6	1793... 3
1594... 7	1614... 4	1634... 1	1654... 5	1674... 2	1694... 6	1714...2	1734... 6	1754... 3	1774... 7	1794... 4
1595... 1	1615... 5	1635... 2	1655... 6	1675... 3	1695... 7	1715...3	1735... 7	1755... 4	1775... 1	1795... 5
1596... 9	1616... 13	1636... 10	1656... 14	1676... 11	1696... 8	1716...11	1736... 8	1756... 12	1776... 9	1796... 13
1597... 4	1617... 1	1637... 5	1657... 2	1677... 6	1697... 3	1717...6	1737... 3	1757... 7	1777... 4	1797... 1
1598... 5	1618... 2	1638... 6	1658... 3	1678... 7	1698... 4	1718...7	1738... 4	1758... 1	1778... 5	1798... 2
1599... 6	1619... 3	1639... 7	1659... 4	1679... 1	1699... 5	1719...1	1739... 5	1759... 2	1779... 6	1799... 3
1600... 14	1620... 11	1640... 8	1660... 12	1680... 9	1700... 6	1720...9	1740... 13	1760... 10	1780... 14	....
1601... 2	1621... 6	1641... 3	1661... 7	1681... 4	1701... 7	1721...4	1741...1	1761... 5	1781... 2	....
1602... 3	1622... 7	1642... 4	1662... 1	1682... 5	1702... 1	1722...5	1742... 2	1762... 6	1782... 3	....

Julian Calendar

To find which of the 14 calendars printed on the next two pages applies to any year under the Julian system, find the century for the desired year in the three left-hand columns below; read across. Then find the year in the four top rows; read down. The number in the intersection is the calendar designation for that year.

			Year (last two figures of desired year)						
			01 02 03 04	05 06 07 08	09 10 11 12	13 14 15 16	17 18 19 20	21 22 23 24	25 26 27 28
			29 30 31 32	33 34 35 36	37 38 39 40	41 42 43 44	45 46 47 48	49 50 51 52	53 54 55 56
			57 58 59 60	61 62 63 64	65 66 67 68	69 70 71 72	73 74 75 76	77 78 79 80	81 82 83 84
Century		00	85 86 87 88	89 90 91 92	93 94 95 96	97 98 99			
0	700	1400	12	7 1 2 10	5 6 7 8	3 4 5 13	1 2 3 11	6 7 1 9	4 5 6 14	2 3 4 12
100	800	1500	11	6 7 1 9	4 5 6 14	2 3 4 12	7 1 2 10	5 6 7 8	3 4 5 13	1 2 3 11
200	900	1600	10	5 6 7 8	3 4 5 13	1 2 3 11	6 7 1 9	4 5 6 14	2 3 4 12	7 1 2 10
300	1000	1700	9	4 5 6 14	2 3 4 12	7 1 2 10	5 6 7 8	3 4 5 13	1 2 3 11	6 7 1 9
400	1100	1800	8	3 4 5 13	1 2 3 11	6 7 1 9	4 5 6 14	2 3 4 12	7 1 2 10	5 6 7 8
500	1200	1900	14	2 3 4 12	7 1 2 10	5 6 7 8	3 4 5 13	1 2 3 11	6 7 1 9	4 5 6 14
600	1300	2000	13	1 2 3 11	6 7 1 9	4 5 6 14	2 3 4 12	7 1 2 10	5 6 7 8	3 4 5 13

PERPETUAL CALENDAR

1975

DIRECTIONS: Pick desired year from box at top left. The number shown with each year indicates the calendar to use for that year.

Standard Time Differences — North American Cities

At 12 o'clock noon, Eastern Standard Time, the standard time in N.A. cities is as follows:

Akron, Ohio	12.00	NOON	Fort Worth, Texas	11.00	A.M.	Philadelphia, Pa.	12.00	NOON
Albuquerque, N.M.	10.00	A.M.	Frankfort, Ky.	12.00	NOON	*Phoenix, Ariz.	10.00	A.M.
Atlanta, Ga.	12.00	NOON	Galveston, Tex.	11.00	A.M.	Pierre, S. Dak.	11.00	A.M.
Austin, Tex.	11.00	A.M.	Grand Rapids, Mich.	12.00	NOON	Pittsburgh, Pa.	12.00	NOON
Baltimore, Md.	12.00	NOON	Halifax, N.S.	1.00	P.M.	Portland, Me.	12.00	NOON
Birmingham, Ala.	11.00	A.M.	Hartford, Conn.	12.00	NOON	Portland, Oreg.	9.00	A.M.
Bismarck, N. Dak.	11.00	A.M.	Helena, Mont.	10.00	A.M.	Providence, R.I.	12.00	NOON
Boise, Idaho	10.00	A.M.	*Honolulu, Hawaii	7.00	A.M.	*Regina, Sask.	11.00	A.M.
Boston, Mass.	12.00	NOON	Houston, Tex.	11.00	A.M.	Reno, Nev.	9.00	A.M.
Buffalo, N.Y.	12.00	NOON	*Indianapolis, Ind.	12.00	NOON	Richmond, Va.	12.00	NOON
Butte, Mont.	10.00	A.M.	Jacksonville, Fla.	12.00	NOON	Rochester, N.Y.	12.00	NOON
Calgary, Alta.	10.00	A.M.	Juneau, Alaska	9.00	A.M.	Sacramento, Calif.	9.00	A.M.
Charleston, S.C.	12.00	NOON	Kansas City, Mo.	11.00	A.M.	St. John's, Nfld.	1.30	P.M.
Charleston, W. Va.	12.00	NOON	Knoxville, Tenn.	12.00	NOON	St. Louis, Mo.	11.00	A.M.
Charlotte, N.C.	12.00	NOON	Lexington, Ky.	12.00	NOON	St. Paul, Minn.	11.00	A.M.
Charlottetown, P.E.I.	1.00	P.M.	Lincoln, Nebr.	11.00	A.M.	Salt Lake City, Utah.	10.00	A.M.
Chattanooga, Tenn.	12.00	NOON	Little Rock, Ark.	11.00	A.M.	San Antonio, Tex.	11.00	A.M.
Cheyenne, Wyo.	10.00	A.M.	Los Angeles, Calif.	9.00	A.M.	San Diego, Calif.	9.00	A.M.
Chicago, Ill.	11.00	A.M.	Louisville, Ky.	12.00	NOON	San Francisco, Calif.	9.00	A.M.
Cleveland, Ohio	12.00	NOON	*Mexico City	11.00	A.M.	Santa Fe, N.M.	10.00	A.M.
Colorado Spr., Colo.	10.00	A.M.	Memphis, Tenn.	11.00	A.M.	Savannah, Ga.	12.00	NOON
Columbus, Ohio.	12.00	NOON	Miami, Fla.	12.00	NOON	Seattle, Wash.	9.00	A.M.
Dallas, Tex.	11.00	A.M.	Milwaukee, Wis.	11.00	A.M.	Shreveport, La.	11.00	A.M.
*Dawson, Yuk.	8.00	A.M.	Minneapolis, Minn.	11.00	A.M.	Sioux Falls, S. Dak.	11.00	A.M.
Dayton, Ohio	12.00	NOON	Mobile, Ala.	11.00	A.M.	Spokane, Wash.	9.00	A.M.
Denver, Colo.	10.00	A.M.	Montreal, Que.	12.00	NOON	Tampa, Fla.	12.00	NOON
Des Moines, Iowa.	11.00	A.M.	Nashville, Tenn.	11.00	A.M.	Toledo, Ohio	12.00	NOON
Detroit, Mich.	12.00	NOON	New Haven, Conn.	12.00	NOON	Topeka, Kan.	11.00	A.M.
Duluth, Minn.	11.00	A.M.	New Orleans, La.	11.00	A.M.	*Tucson, Ariz.	10.00	A.M.
El Paso, Tex.	10.00	A.M.	New York, N.Y.	12.00	NOON	Tulsa, Okla.	11.00	A.M.
Erie, Pa.	12.00	NOON	Nome, Alaska	6.00	A.M.	Vancouver, B.C.	9.00	A.M.
Evansville, Ind.	11.00	A.M.	Norfolk, Va.	12.00	NOON	Washington, D.C.	12.00	NOON
Fairbanks, Alaska	7.00	A.M.	Okla. City, Okla.	11.00	A.M.	Wichita, Kan.	11.00	A.M.
Flint, Mich.	12.00	NOON	Omaha, Nebr.	11.00	A.M.	Wilmington, Del.	12.00	NOON'
*Fort Wayne, Ind.	12.00	NOON	Peoria, Ill.	11.00	A.M.	Winnipeg, Man.	11.00	A.M.

*Cities with an asterisk do not observe daylight savings time. During much of the year, it is necessary to add one hour to the cities which do observe daylight savings time to get the proper time relation.

Standard Time Differences — World Cities

The time indicated in the table is fixed by law and is called the legal time, or, more generally, Standard Time. *Indicates morning of the following day. At 12 o'clock noon, Eastern Standard Time, the standard time in foreign cities is as follows:

Alexandria	7:00 P.M.	Copenhagen	6:00 P.M.	Liverpool	5:00 P.M.	Seoul	2:00 A.M.*
Amsterdam	6:00 P.M.	Dacca	11:00 P.M.	London	5:00 P.M.	Shanghai	1:00 A.M.*
Athens	7:00 P.M.	Delhi	10:30 P.M.	Madrid	6:00 P.M.	Singapore	12:30 A.M.*
Auckland	5:00 A.M.*	Djakarta	12:00 MID.	Manila	1:00 A.M.*	Stockholm	6:00 P.M.
Baghdad	8:00 P.M.	Dublin	5:00 P.M.	Melbourne	3:00 A.M.*	Sydney	
Bangkok	12:00 MID.	Gdansk	6:00 P.M.	Montevideo	2:00 P.M.	(Australia)	3:00 A.M.*
Belfast	5:00 P.M.	Geneva	6:00 P.M.	Moscow	8:00 P.M.	Tashkent	11:00 P.M.
Berlin	6:00 P.M.	Havana	12:00 NOON	Nagasaki	2:00 A.M.*	Teheran	8:30 P.M.
Bogota	12:00 NOON	Helsinki	7:00 P.M.	Oslo	6:00 P.M.	Tel Aviv	7:00 P.M.
Bombay	10:30 P.M.	Hong Kong	1:00 A.M.*	Paris	6:00 P.M.	Tokyo	2:00 A.M.*
Bremen	6:00 P.M.	Istanbul	7:00 P.M.	Peking	1:00 A.M.*	Valparaiso	1:00 P.M.
Brussels	6:00 P.M.	Jerusalem	7:00 P.M.	Prague	6:00 P.M.	Vladivostok	3:00 A.M.*
Bucharest	7:00 P.M.	Johannesburg	7:00 P.M.	Rangoon	11:30 P.M.	Vienna	6:00 P.M.
Budapest	6:00 P.M.	Karachi	10:00 P.M.	Rio de Janeiro	2:00 P.M.	Warsaw	6:00 P.M.
Buenos Aires	2:00 P.M.	Le Havre	6:00 P.M.	Rome	6:00 P.M.	Wellington	
Calcutta	10:30 P.M.	Leningrad	8:00 P.M.	Saigon	1:00 A.M.*	(N.Z.)	5:00 A.M.*
Cape Town	7:00 P.M.	Lima	12:00 NOON	Santiago		Yokohama	2:00 A.M.*
Caracas	1:00 P.M.	Lisbon	6:00 P.M.	(Chile)	1:00 P.M.	Zurich	6:00 P.M.

Chronological Eras, 1976

The year 1976 of the Christian Era comprises the latter part of the 200th and the beginning of the 201st year of the independence of the United States of America.

Era	Year	Begins in 1976	Era	Year	Begins in 1976
Byzantine	7485	Sept. 14	Japanese	2636	Jan. 1
Jewish	5737	Sept. 24 (sunset)	Grecian (Seleucidae)	2288	Sept. 14 or Oct. 14
Olympiads	2752	July 1	Indian (Saka)	1898	Mar. 21
(Fourth year of Olympiad 688)			Diocletian	1693	Sept. 11
Roman (Ab Urbe Condita)	2729	Jan. 14	Mohammedan (Hegira)	1396	Jan. 2
Nabonassar (Babylonian)	2725	Apr. 29			(sunset)

Chronological Cycles, 1976

Dominical Letter	DC	Golden Number (Lunar Cycle)	1	Roman Indiction	14
Epact	29	Solar Cycle	25	Julian Period (year in)	6689

Standard Time, Daylight Saving Time and Others

Source: Defense Mapping Agency Hydrographic Center; Department of Transportation; National Bureau of Standards and U.S. Naval Observatory

Standard Time

Standard time is reckoned from Greenwich, England, recognized as the Prime Meridian of Longitude. The world is divided in 24 zones, each 15° of arc, or one hour in time apart. The Greenwich meridian (0°) extends through the center of the initial zone, and the zones to the east are numbered from 1 to 12 with the prefix "minus" indicating the number of hours to be subtracted to obtain Greenwich Time.

Westward zones are similarly numbered, but prefixed "plus" showing the number of hours that must be added to get Greenwich Time. While these zones apply generally to sea areas, it should be noted that the Standard Time maintained in many countries does not coincide with zone time. A graphical representation of the zones is shown on the Standard Time Zone Chart of the World published by the Defense Mapping Agency Hydrographic Center, Washington, D.C. 20390.

The United States and possessions are divided into eight Standard Time zones, as set forth by the Uniform Time Act of 1966, which also provides for the use of Daylight Saving Time therein. Each zone is approximately 15° of longitude in width. All places in each zone use, instead of their own local time, the time counted from the transit of the "mean sun" across the Standard Time meridian which passes near the middle of that zone.

These time zones are designated as Atlantic, Eastern, Central, Mountain, Pacific, Yukon, Alaska-Hawaii, and Bering, and the time in these zones is basically reckoned from the 60th, 75th, 90th, 105th, 120th, 135th, 150th, 165th meridians west of Greenwich. The line wanders to conform to local geographical regions. The time in the various zones is earlier than Greenwich Time by 4, 5, 6, 7, 8, 9, 10, and 11 hours respectively.

High Precision Time and Frequency are broadcast by U.S. Navy Stations which are maintained on frequency with the aid of Atomic Clocks (cesium beam and atomic hydrogen masers). The stations are as follows: NBA: NSS: NLK: NAA: NPM: NWC: NPN: NPG: NDT: Omega.

Loran-C Navigational Transmissions at 100 KHz of the East Coast, Central Pacific, Mediterranean, Northwest Pacific and the Norwegian sea chains may be used for time and frequency comparisons.

Standard Frequency Stations

The National Bureau of Standards (NBS) radio stations WWV at Fort Collins, Colorado, and WWVH on the island of Kauai, Hawaii, broadcast a number of technical services continuously night and day. These services are: 1. standard radio frequencies, 2.5, 5, 10, 15, 20 and 25 MHz (WWV) and 2.5, 5, 10, 15 and 20 MHz (WWVH); 2. standard time voice announcements (WWV—male, 7.5 seconds before the minute; WWVH —female, 15 seconds before the minute); 3. standard time intervals of one second and one minute; 4. corrections to adjust atomic time to astronomical time; 5. standard audio frequencies of 500 and 600 Hz on alternate minutes and a 440 Hz tone (the musical pitch A above middle C) once each hour; 6. a slow time code at 100 Hz giving the day, hour and minute in binary coded decimal form; 7. hourly radio propagation forecasts; 8. geophysical alerts on events in process and summaries of solar and geophysical events of the last 24 hours; and 9. storm warnings. The NBS also broadcasts time and frequency signals from its low frequency station (60kHz). WWVB, also located at Fort Collins, Colorado.

Each hour there are periods with no tone modulation during which the carrier, seconds ticks, minute time announcements, and 100 Hz time code continue. They occur during the 16th through the 20th minute on WWVH and the 46th through the 50th minute on WWV.

The National Research council of Canada continually transmits precision time signals from Ottawa over station CHU on 3 frequencies, 3330, 7335, and 14670 kHz.

Storm warnings cover the waters of the Atlantic and Eastern Pacific from WWV and the Pacific from WWVH and are given at the 8th, 9th and 10th minute of each hour from WWV and at the 48th, 49th and 50th minute of each hour from WWVH. Times of issue are 0500, 1100, 1600, and 2300 UT from WWV, and 0000, 0600, 1200, and 1800 UT from WWVH.

The time and frequency broadcasts are controlled by the NBS atomic frequency standards, which realize the internationally defined cesium resonance frequency with an accuracy of 1 part in 10^{13}. (The cesium atom invariably resonates at a little over 9 billion oscillations per second.)

The atomic time scale is uniform and does not reflect the variable rotational speed of the earth. The time signals are adjusted by introducing a leap second about once a year (at the end of June or December) so that the broadcast time never departs more than eight-tenths of a second from mean solar time, determined by the rotational position of the earth.

Special Publication 236 describes in detail the standard frequency and time service of the National Bureau of Standards. Single copies may be obtained upon request from the National Bureau of Standards, Boulder, Colorado, 80302. Quantities may be obtained from the Superintendent of Documents, U.S. Gov. Printing Office, Wash., D.C. 20402, at 25c per copy.

Daylight Saving Time

Daylight Saving Time is achieved by advancing the clock one hour. Under the Uniform Time Act, which became effective in 1967, all states, the District of Columbia and U. S. possessions were to observe Daylight Saving Time beginning at 2 a.m. on the last Sunday in April and ending at 2 a.m. on the last Sunday in October. Any state could, by law, exempt itself; a 1972 amendment to the act authorized states split by time zones to take that into consideration in exempting themselves. Arizona, Hawaii, Puerto Rico, the Virgin Islands, and parts of Michigan, Indiana, and Ohio are now exempt. Some local zone boundaries in Kansas, Texas, Florida, and Michigan have been modified in the last several years by the Dept. of Transportation, which oversees the act. To conserve energy Congress put most of the nation on year-round Daylight Saving Time for two years effective January 6, 1974 through April 27, 1975; but a further bill, signed in October, 1974, restored Standard Time from the last Sunday in that month to the last Sunday in February, 1975.

24-Hour Time

24-hour time is widely used in scientific work throughout the world. In the United States it is used also in operations of the Armed Forces. In Europe it is used in preference to the 12-hour a.m. and p.m. system. With the 24-hour system the day begins at midnight and hours are numbered 0 through 23.

International Date Line

The Date Line is a zig-zag line that approximately coincides with the 180th meridian, and it is where each calendar day begins. The date must be advanced one day when crossing in a westerly direction and set back one day when crossing in an easterly direction. The line is deflected between north latitude 48° and 75°, so that all Asia lies to the west of it.

Tides and Their Causes
Source: National Ocean Survey (NOAA)

The tides are a natural phenomenon involving the alternating rise and fall in the large fluid bodies of the earth caused by the combined gravitational attraction of the sun and moon. The combination of these two variable force influences, as modified by certain factors such as depth of the water, configuration of the shoreline, and geographic location produce the complex recurrent cycle of the tides. Tides may occur in both oceans and seas, to a limited extent in large lakes, the atmosphere, and, to a very minute degree, in the earth itself. The period between succeeding tides varies as the result of many factors and force influences.

The tide-generating force represents the difference between (1) the centrifugal force produced by the revolution of the earth around the common center-of-gravity of the earth-moon system and (2) the gravitational attraction of the moon acting upon the earth's overlying waters. Similar tide-producing forces exist in the earth-sun system. Since, on the average, the moon is only 238,857 miles from the earth compared with the sun's much greater distance of 93,000,000 miles, this closer distance outranks the much smaller mass of the moon compared with that of the sun, and the moon's tide-raising force is, accordingly, 2^1/s times that of the sun.

The effect of the tide-generating forces of the moon and sun acting tangentially to the earth's surface (the so-called "tractive force"), tends to cause a maximum accumulation of the waters of the oceans at two diametrically opposite positions on the surface of the earth and to withdraw compensating amounts of water from all points 90° removed from the positions of these tidal bulges. The presence of the continents, as well as other factors, prevent the total free movement of water. However, as the earth rotates beneath the maxima and minima of these tide-generating forces, a sequence of two high tides, separated by two low tides, ideally is produced each day.

Twice in each lunar month, when the sun, moon, and earth are directly aligned, with the moon between the earth and the sun (at new moon) or on the opposite side of the earth from the sun (at full moon),

the sun and the moon exert their gravitational force in a mutual or additive fashion. Higher high tides and lower low tides are produced. These are called spring tides. At two positions 90° in between, the gravitational forces of the moon and sun — imposed at right angles—tend to counteract each other to the greatest extent, and the range between high and low tides is reduced. These are called neap tides. This semi-monthly variation between the spring and neap tides is called the phase inequality.

The inclination of the moon's orbit to the equator also produces a difference in the height of succeeding high tides and in the extent of depression of succeeding low tides which is known as the diurnal inequality. In extreme cases, this phenomenon can result in only one high tide and one low tide each day. The changing distance of the moon from the earth in each lunar month due to the elliptical orbit of the moon, produces a difference in the height of the tides known as the lunar parallactic inequality. The changing distance of the earth from the sun during the earth's annual revolution around the sun similarly introduces the solar parallactic inequality.

The actual amount of the uplift of the waters in the deep ocean may amount to only one or two feet. However, as this tide approaches shoal waters and its effects are augmented the tidal range may be greatly increased. In Nova Scotia along the narrow channel of the Bay of Fundy, the range of tides or difference between high and low waters, may reach 43^1/2 feet or more (under spring tide conditions) due to resonant amplification.

At New Orleans, the periodic rise and fall of the tide varies with the state of the Mississippi, being about 10 inches at low stage and zero at high. The Canadian Tide Tables for 1972 gave a maximum range of nearly 50 feet at Leaf Basin, Ungava Bay.

In every case, actual high or low tide can vary considerably from the average due to weather conditions such as strong winds, abrupt barometric pressure changes, or prolonged periods of extreme high or low pressure.

The Average Rise and Fall of Tides
Source: National Ocean Survey (NOAA)

Places	Ft.	In.	Places	Ft.	In.	Places	Ft.	In.
Baltimore	1	1	Mobile, Ala.	1	6	San Diego, Calif.	4	1
Boston, Mass.	9	6	New London, Conn.	2	7	Sahdy Hook, N.J.	4	7
Charleston, S.C.	5	2	Newport, R.I.	3	6	San Francisco, Calif.	4	0
Colon, Panama	1	1	New York, N.Y.	4	6	Savannah, Ga.	7	5
Eastport, Me.	18	2	Old Pt. Comfort, Va.	2	6	Seattle, Wash.	7	7
Galveston, Tex.	1	5	Philadelphia, Pa.	5	11	Tampa, Fla.	2	10
Halifax, N.S.	4	5	Portland, Me.	9	0	Vancouver, B.C.	10	6
Key West, Fla.	1	4	St. John's, Nfld.	2	7	Washington, D.C.	2	11

Wind Chill Table
Source: National Oceanic and Atmospheric Administration

Both temperature and wind cause heat loss from body surfaces. A combination of cold and wind makes a body feel colder than the actual temperature. The table shows, for example, that a temperature of 20 degrees Fahrenheit, plus a wind of 20 miles per hour, causes a body heat loss equal to that in minus 9 degrees with no wind. In other words, the wind makes 20 degrees feel like minus 9.

Top line of figures shows actual temperatures. Column at left shows wind speeds.

MPH	35	30	25	20	15	10	5	0	−5	−10	−15	−20	−25	−30	−35	−40	−45
5	33	27	21	16	12	7	1	−6	−11	−15	−20	−26	−31	−35	−41	−47	−52
10	21	16	8	2	−2	−9	−15	−22	−27	−34	−40	−45	−52	−58	−64	−70	−77
15	16	9	1	−6	−11	−18	−25	−31	−38	−45	−51	−58	−65	−72	−78	−85	−92
20	12	3	−4	−9	−17	−24	−32	−40	−46	−52	−60	−68	−74	−81	−88	−96	−103
25	7	0	−7	−15	−22	−29	−37	−45	−52	−58	−67	−75	−81	−89	−96	−104	−110
30	5	−2	−11	−18	−26	−33	−41	−49	−56	−63	−70	−78	−87	−94	−101	−109	−117
35	4	−4	−12	−20	−27	−35	−43	−52	−58	−67	−74	−83	−90	−98	−105	−113	−121
40	3	−4	−13	−21	−29	−36	−45	−54	−60	−69	−76	−84	−92	−101	−107	−116	−124
45	2	−6	−15	−23	−31	−38	−46	−54	−63	−70	−78	−85	−94	−101	−108	−118	−126
50	1	−7	−15	−23	−31	−38	−47	−56	−63	−70	−79	−87	−96	−103	−112	−120	−128

(Wind speeds greater than 50 mph have little additional chilling effect.)

National Weather Service Watches and Warnings

Source: National Weather Service, NOAA, Dept. of Commerce

National Weather Service forecasters issue a Tornado Watch for a specific area where it is reasonably possible that tornadoes may occur during the valid time of the watch. A Watch is to alert people to watch for tornado activity and listen for a Tornado Warning. A Tornado Warning means that a tornado has been sighted or indicated by radar, and that safety precautions should be taken at once. A Hurricane Watch means that an existing hurricane poses a threat to coastal and inland communities in the area specified by the Watch. A Hurricane Warning means hurricane force winds and/or dangerously high water and exceptionally high waves are expected in a specified coastal area within 24 hours.

Definitions

Tornado—a violent rotating column of air pendant from a thundercloud, usually recognized as a funnel-shaped vortex accompanied by a loud roar. With rotating winds est. up to 300 mph., it is the most destructive storm. Tornado paths have varied in length from a few feet to nearly 300 miles (avg. 5 mi.); diameter from a few feet to over a mile (average 220 yards); average forward speed, 25-40 mph.

Cyclone—An atmospheric circulation of winds rotating counterclockwise in the northern hemisphere and clockwise in the southern hemisphere. Tornadoes, hurricanes, and the Lows shown on weather maps are all examples of cyclones having various sizes and intensities. Cyclones are usually accompanied by precipitation or stormy weather.

Hurricane—A severe cyclone originating over tropical ocean waters and having winds 74 miles an hour or higher. (In the western Pacific, such storms are known as typhoons.) The area of strong winds takes the form of a circle or an oval, sometimes as much as 500 miles in diameter. In the lower latitudes hurricanes usually move toward the west or northwest at 10 to 15 mph. When the center approaches 25° to 30° North Latitude, direction of motion often changes to northeast, with increased forward speed.

Blizzard—A severe weather condition characterized by low temperatures and by strong winds bearing a great amount of snow (mostly fine, dry snow picked up from the ground). The National Weather Service specifies, for blizzard, a wind of 35 miles an hour or higher, temperatures 20°F. or lower, and sufficient falling and/or blowing snow to reduce visibility to less than 1/4 of a mile. For "severe blizzard" wind speeds of 45 mph or more, temperature near or below 10°F., and visibility reduced by snow to near zero.

Monsoon—A name for seasonal winds (derived from Arabic "mausim," a season). It was first applied to the winds over the Arabian Sea which blow for six months from northeast and six months from southwest, but it has been extended to similar winds in other parts of the world. The monsoons are strongest on the southern and eastern sides of Asia.

Flood—The condition that occurs when water overflows the natural or artificial confines of a stream or other body of water, or accumulates by drainage over low-lying areas.

National Weather Service Marine Warnings and Advisories

Source: National Weather Service, NOAA, Dept. of Commerce

Small Craft Advisory: A Small Craft Advisory alerts mariners to sustained (exceeding two hours) weather and/or sea conditions either present or forecast, potentially hazardous to small boats. Hazardous conditions may include winds of 18 to 33 knots and/or dangerous wave or inlet conditions. It is the responsibility of the mariner, based on his experience and size or type of boat, to determine if the conditions are hazardous. When a mariner becomes aware of a Small Craft Advisory, he should immediately obtain the latest marine forecast to determine the reason for the Advisory. The visual signal is a red pennant by day, a red over white light at night.

Gale Warning: Two red pennants displayed by day and a white light above a red light at night to indicate that winds within the range 34 to 47 knots are forecast for the area.

Storm Warning: A single square red flag with a black center displayed during daytime and two red lights at night to indicate that winds 48 knots and above, no matter how high the speed, are forecast for the area. However, if the winds are associated with a tropical cyclone (hurricane), the storm warning display indicates that winds within the range 48 to 63 knots are forecast.

Hurricane Warning: Displayed only in connection with a hurricane or typhoon. Two square red flags with black centers displayed by day and a white light between two red lights at night to indicate that winds 64 knots and above are forecast for the area.

Primary sources of dissemination are commercial radio, TV, U.S. Coast Guard Radio stations, and NOAA VHF-FM broadcasts. These broadcasts on 162.40 and 162.55 MHz can usually be received 20-40 miles from the transmitting antenna site, depending on terrain and quality of the receiver used. Where transmitting antennas are on high ground, the range is somewhat greater, reaching 60 miles or more.

The frequencies 162.55 and 162.40 MHz require narrow band FM receivers of +5 kilohertz deviation. In selecting a suitable receiver, special attention should be paid to the manufacturer's rating of the receiver's sensitivity. Generally speaking, a receiver with a sensitivity of one microvolt or less should pick up a broadcast at a distance of about 40-50 miles depending upon antenna height and terrain.

Dissemination is also made by means of visual displays (flags, pennants, and lights). These are indicated under each warning and advisory category.

Hurricane Names in 1976

The National Weather Service has used girls' names to identify hurricanes in the Atlantic, Caribbean, and Gulf of Mexico since 1953. A semi-permanent list of 10 sets of names in alphabetical order was established in 1971. Hurricane season begins June 1 and ends Nov. 30.

Names assigned to hurricanes: 1976 — Anna, Belle, Candice, Dottie, Emmy, Frances, Gloria, Holly, Inga, Jill, Kay, Lilias, Maria, Nola, Orpha, Pamela, Ruth, Shirley, Trixie, Vilda, and Wynne.

Hurricanes and typhoons in the Eastern North Pacific are also identified by girls' names: 1976 — Annette, Bonny, Celeste, Diana, Estelle, Fernanda, Gwen, Hyacinth, Iva, Joanne, Kathleen, Liza, Madeline, Naomi, Orla, Pauline, Rebecca, Simone, Tara, Valerie, Willa.

Monthly Normal Temperature and Precipitation

Source: National Climatic Center, NOAA, Dept. of Commerce

These normals are based on records for the thirty-year period 1941 to 1970 inclusive. See explanation on page 791. For stations that did not have continuous records from the same instrument site for the entire 30 years, the means have been adjusted to the record at the present site.

AP indicates airport station; those not so marked are city office stations.

T, Temperature in Fahrenheit; P, precipitation in inches; L, less than .05 inch.

Stations	Jan. T.	Jan. P.	Feb. T.	Feb. P.	Mar. T.	Mar. P.	Apr. T.	Apr. P.	May T.	May P.	June T.	June P.	July T.	July P.	Aug. T.	Aug. P.	Sept. T.	Sept. P.	Oct. T.	Oct. P.	Nov. T.	Nov. P.	Dec. T.	Dec. P.
Albany, N. Y. (AP)	22	2.2	24	2.1	33	2.6	47	2.7	58	3.3	68	3.0	72	3.1	70	2.9	62	3.1	51	2.6	40	2.8	26	2.9
Albuquerque, N. M. (AP)	35	0.3	40	0.4	46	0.5	56	0.5	65	0.5	75	0.5	79	1.4	77	1.3	70	0.8	58	0.8	45	0.3	36	0.5
Anchorage, Alaska (AP)	12	0.8	18	0.8	24	0.6	35	0.6	46	0.6	55	1.1	58	2.1	56	2.3	48	2.4	35	1.4	21	1.0	13	1.1
Asheville, N. C. (AP)	38	3.4	39	3.6	46	4.7	56	3.5	64	3.3	71	4.0	74	4.9	73	4.5	67	3.6	57	3.3	46	2.9	39	3.6
Atlanta, Ga. (AP)	42	4.3	45	4.4	51	5.8	61	4.6	69	3.7	76	3.7	78	4.9	78	3.5	72	3.2	62	2.5	51	3.4	44	4.2
Baltimore, Md. (AP)	42	2.9	44	2.8	53	3.7	65	3.1	75	3.6	83	3.8	87	4.1	85	4.2	79	3.1	68	2.8	56	3.1	44	3.3
Barrow, Alaska (AP)	-15	0.2	-19	0.2	-15	0.2	-1	0.2	19	0.2	33	0.4	39	0.9	38	1.0	30	0.6	15	0.6	-1	0.3	-12	0.2
Birmingham, Ala. (AP)	44	4.8	47	5.3	53	6.2	63	4.6	71	3.6	77	4.0	80	5.2	79	4.3	74	3.6	63	2.6	52	3.7	45	5.2
Bismarck, N. D. (AP)	8	0.5	14	0.4	25	0.7	43	1.4	54	2.2	64	3.6	71	2.2	69	2.0	58	1.3	47	0.8	29	0.6	16	0.5
Boise, Ida. (AP)	29	1.5	36	1.2	41	1.0	49	1.1	57	1.3	65	1.1	75	0.2	72	0.3	63	0.4	52	0.8	40	1.3	32	1.4
Boston, Mass. (AP)	29	3.7	30	3.5	38	4.0	49	3.5	59	3.5	68	3.2	73	2.7	71	3.5	65	3.2	55	3.0	45	4.5	33	4.2
Buffalo, N. Y. (AP)	24	2.9	24	2.6	32	2.9	45	3.2	55	3.0	66	2.2	70	2.9	68	3.5	62	3.3	52	3.0	40	3.7	28	3.0
Burlington, Vt. (AP)	17	1.7	19	1.7	29	1.9	43	2.6	55	3.0	65	3.5	70	3.5	67	3.7	59	3.1	49	2.7	37	2.9	23	2.2
Caribou, Me. (AP)	11	2.0	13	2.1	24	2.2	37	2.4	50	3.0	60	3.4	65	4.0	62	3.8	54	3.5	44	3.3	31	3.5	16	2.6
Charleston, S. C. (AP)	49	2.9	51	3.3	57	4.8	65	3.0	72	3.8	78	6.3	80	8.2	80	6.4	75	5.2	66	3.1	56	2.1	49	3.1
Chicago, Ill. (AP)	24	1.9	27	1.6	37	2.7	50	3.8	60	3.4	71	4.0	75	4.1	74	3.1	66	3.0	55	2.6	40	2.2	29	2.1
Cincinnati, Oh.	32	3.4	34	3.0	43	4.1	55	3.9	64	4.0	73	3.9	76	4.0	75	3.0	68	2.7	58	2.2	45	3.1	34	2.9
Cleveland, Oh. (AP)	27	2.6	28	2.2	36	3.1	48	3.5	58	3.5	68	3.3	71	3.5	70	3.0	64	2.8	54	2.6	42	2.8	30	2.4
Columbus, Oh. (AP)	28	2.9	30	2.3	39	3.4	51	3.7	61	4.1	70	4.1	74	4.2	72	2.9	65	2.4	54	1.9	42	2.7	31	2.4
Dallas, Tex. (AP)	45	2.0	49	2.6	56	3.0	66	4.7	74	4.9	82	3.3	86	1.8	86	2.4	78	3.3	68	3.2	56	2.6	48	2.3
Denver, Col. (AP)	30	0.6	33	0.7	37	1.2	48	1.9	57	2.6	66	1.9	73	1.8	72	1.3	63	1.1	52	1.1	39	0.8	33	0.4
Des Moines, Iowa (AP)	19	1.1	24	1.1	34	2.3	50	2.9	61	4.2	71	4.9	75	3.3	73	3.3	64	3.1	54	2.1	38	1.4	25	1.1
Detroit, Mich. (AP)	26	1.9	27	1.8	35	2.3	48	3.1	58	3.4	69	3.0	73	3.0	72	3.0	65	2.3	54	2.5	41	2.3	30	2.2
Dodge City, Kan. (AP)	31	0.5	35	0.6	41	1.1	54	1.7	64	3.1	74	3.3	79	3.1	78	2.6	69	1.7	58	1.7	43	0.6	33	8.5
Duluth, Minn. (AP)	9	1.2	12	0.9	24	1.8	39	2.6	49	3.4	59	4.4	66	3.7	64	3.8	54	3.1	45	2.3	28	1.7	14	1.4
Eureka, Cal.	47	7.4	48	5.2	48	4.8	50	3.0	53	2.1	55	0.7	56	0.1	57	0.3	57	0.7	54	3.2	52	5.8	49	6.6
Fairbanks, Alaska (AP)	-12	0.6	-3	0.5	10	0.5	29	0.3	47	0.7	59	1.4	61	1.9	55	2.2	44	1.1	25	0.7	3	0.7	-10	0.7
Ft. Worth, Tex. (AP)	45	1.8	49	2.4	55	2.5	65	4.3	73	4.5	81	3.1	85	1.8	85	2.3	78	3.2	68	2.7	56	2.0	48	1.8
Fresno, Cal. (AP)	45	1.8	50	1.7	54	1.6	60	1.2	67	0.3	74	0.1	81	L	78	L	74	0.1	64	0.4	54	1.2	46	1.7
Galveston, Tex.	54	3.0	56	2.7	61	2.6	69	2.6	76	3.2	81	4.1	83	4.4	83	4.4	80	5.6	73	2.8	64	3.2	57	3.7
Grand Junction, Col. (AP)	27	0.6	34	0.6	41	0.8	52	0.8	62	0.6	71	0.6	79	0.5	75	1.1	67	0.8	55	0.9	40	0.6	30	0.6
Gr. Rapids, Mich. (AP)	23	1.9	25	1.5	33	2.5	47	3.4	57	3.2	67	3.4	72	3.1	70	2.5	62	3.3	52	2.6	39	2.8	27	2.2
Helena, Mon. (AP)	18	0.6	25	0.4	31	0.7	43	0.9	52	1.8	59	2.4	68	1.0	66	1.0	56	1.0	45	0.6	32	0.6	23	0.6
Honolulu, Ha. (AP)	72	4.4	72	2.5	73	3.2	75	1.4	77	1.0	79	0.3	80	0.6	81	0.8	80	0.7	79	1.5	77	3.0	74	3.7
Houston, Tex. (AP)	52	3.6	55	3.5	61	2.7	69	3.5	76	5.1	81	4.5	83	4.1	83	4.4	79	4.7	71	4.1	61	4.0	55	4.0
Huron, S. D. (AP)	13	0.4	18	0.8	29	1.1	46	2.0	57	2.8	67	3.8	74	2.2	72	2.0	61	1.8	50	1.5	32	0.7	19	0.5
Indianapolis, Ind. (AP)	28	2.9	31	2.4	40	3.8	52	3.9	62	4.1	72	4.2	75	3.7	73	2.8	66	2.9	56	2.5	42	3.1	31	2.7
Jacksonville, Fla. (AP)	55	2.8	56	3.6	61	3.6	68	3.1	74	3.2	79	6.3	81	7.4	81	7.9	78	7.8	71	4.5	61	1.8	55	2.6
Juneau, Alaska (AP)	24	3.9	28	3.4	32	3.6	39	3.8	47	3.3	53	2.9	56	4.7	54	5.0	49	6.9	42	7.9	33	5.5	27	4.5
Kansas City, Mo. (AP)	28	1.3	33	1.3	41	2.6	55	3.5	65	4.3	74	5.6	79	4.4	77	3.8	69	4.2	59	3.2	44	1.5	32	1.5
Knoxville, Tenn. (AP)	41	4.7	43	4.7	50	4.9	60	3.6	68	3.3	76	3.6	78	4.7	77	3.2	72	2.8	61	2.7	49	3.6	42	4.5
Lander, Wy. (AP)	20	0.5	26	0.7	31	1.2	43	2.4	53	2.6	61	1.9	71	0.6	69	0.4	58	1.1	47	1.2	32	0.9	23	0.5
Little Rock, Ark. (AP)	40	4.2	43	4.4	50	4.9	62	5.3	70	5.3	78	3.5	81	3.4	81	3.0	73	3.6	62	3.0	50	3.9	42	4.1
Los Angeles, Cal.	57	3.0	48	2.8	59	2.2	62	1.3	65	0.1	68	L	73	L	74	L	73	0.2	68	0.3	63	2.0	58	2.2
Louisville, Ky. (AP)	33	3.5	36	3.5	44	5.1	56	4.1	65	4.2	73	4.1	77	3.8	76	3.0	69	2.9	58	2.4	45	3.3	36	3.3
Marquette, Mich.	18	1.5	20	1.5	27	1.9	40	2.6	50	2.9	60	3.4	66	3.1	66	3.0	57	3.5	49	2.4	34	3.0	24	2.0
Memphis, Tenn. (AP)	41	4.9	44	4.7	51	5.1	63	5.4	71	4.4	79	3.5	82	3.5	80	3.3	74	3.0	63	2.6	51	3.9	43	4.7
Miami, Fla. (AP)	67	2.2	68	2.0	71	2.1	75	3.6	78	6.1	81	9.0	82	6.9	83	6.7	82	8.7	78	8.2	72	2.7	68	1.6
Milwaukee, Wis. (AP)	19	1.6	23	1.1	31	2.2	45	2.8	54	2.9	65	3.6	70	3.4	69	2.7	61	3.0	51	2.0	37	2.0	24	1.8
Minneapolis, Minn. (AP)	12	0.7	17	0.8	28	1.7	45	2.0	57	3.4	67	3.9	72	3.7	70	3.1	60	2.7	50	1.8	32	1.2	19	0.9
Mobile, Ala. (AP)	51	4.7	54	4.8	59	7.1	68	5.6	75	4.5	80	6.1	82	8.9	82	6.9	78	6.6	69	2.6	59	3.4	53	5.9
Moline, Ill. (AP)	22	1.7	26	1.3	36	2.6	51	3.8	61	3.9	71	4.4	75	4.6	73	3.4	65	3.8	54	2.7	39	1.9	27	1.8
Nashville, Tenn. (AP)	38	4.8	41	4.4	49	5.0	60	4.1	69	4.1	77	3.4	80	3.8	79	3.2	72	3.1	61	2.2	48	3.5	40	4.5
Newark, N. J. (AP)	31	2.9	33	3.0	41	3.9	52	3.4	62	3.6	71	3.0	76	4.0	75	4.3	68	3.4	58	2.8	46	3.6	35	3.5
New Haven, Conn. (AP)	29	3.2	30	3.1	37	4.0	48	3.7	57	3.7	67	2.7	72	3.1	71	3.8	65	3.1	55	3.1	44	4.3	32	4.1
New Orleans, La. (AP)	53	4.5	56	4.8	61	5.5	69	4.2	75	4.2	80	4.7	82	6.7	82	5.3	78	5.6	70	2.3	60	3.9	55	5.1
New York City, N. Y.	32	2.9	33	3.1	41	4.0	52	3.6	62	3.4	72	2.9	77	3.9	75	4.5	68	3.2	58	3.0	47	3.8	35	3.6
Nome, Alaska (AP)	6	0.9	5	0.8	7	0.8	19	0.7	35	0.7	46	1.0	50	2.4	49	3.6	42	2.4	29	1.4	16	1.0	4	0.7
Norfolk, Va. (AP)	41	3.4	41	3.3	48	3.4	58	2.7	67	3.3	75	3.6	78	5.7	77	5.9	72	4.2	62	3.1	52	2.9	42	3.1
Okla. City, Okla. (AP)	37	1.1	41	1.3	48	2.1	60	3.5	68	5.2	77	4.2	82	2.7	81	2.6	73	3.6	62	2.6	49	1.4	40	1.3
Omaha, Neb. (AP)	23	0.8	28	1.0	37	1.6	52	3.0	63	4.1	72	4.9	77	3.7	76	4.0	66	3.3	56	1.9	40	1.1	28	0.8
Parkersburg, W.Va.	33	3.1	35	2.8	43	3.8	55	3.5	64	3.6	72	4.0	75	4.3	74	3.3	67	2.8	57	2.1	45	2.5	35	2.8
Philadelphia, Pa. (AP)	34	3.9	34	3.0	47	3.5	53	6.7	60	4.1	75	7.9	78	2.4	79	2.0	71	3.4	59	2.2	48	0.6	39	6.3
Phoenix, Ariz. (AP)	51	0.1	58	1.4	57	1.7	67	0.1	81	0.1	88	L	94	1.3	93	L	85	L	74	L	61	1.4	55	L
Pittsburgh, Pa. (AP)	30	2.0	29	1.8	48	3.9	49	4.7	56	5.9	71	3.1	73	2.2	73	3.4	67	3.6	56	4.5	44	2.7	33	2.2
Portland, Me. (AP)	23	2.6	23	2.6	38	2.6	46	9.9	51	6.3	64	4.9	71	1.7	71	3.5	58	2.2	49	3.4	38	2.4	34	9.6
Portland, Ore. (AP)	39	3.7	45	1.9	48	2.5	52	1.3	59	1.4	64	1.5	70	0.1	66	1.4	64	3.3	54	3.1	44	11.6	45	10.0
Providence, R. I. (AP)	28	3.5	29	3.5	37	4.0	47	3.7	57	3.5	66	2.7	72	2.9	70	3.9	63	3.3	54	3.3	43	4.5	32	4.1
Raleigh, N. C. (AP)	41	3.2	42	3.3	49	3.4	60	3.1	67	3.3	74	3.7	78	5.1	77	4.9	71	3.8	60	2.8	50	2.8	41	3.1
Rapid City, S. D. (AP)	22	0.5	26	0.6	31	1.0	45	2.1	55	2.8	64	3.7	73	2.1	72	1.5	61	1.2	50	0.9	35	0.5	27	0.4
Reno, Nev. (AP)	32	1.2	37	0.9	40	0.7	47	0.5	55	0.7	62	0.4	69	0.3	67	0.2	60	0.2	50	0.4	40	0.7	33	1.1
Richmond, Va. (AP)	38	2.9	39	3.0	47	3.4	58	2.8	67	3.4	74	3.5	78	5.6	76	5.1	70	3.6	59	2.9	49	3.2	39	3.2
St. Louis, Mo. (AP)	31	1.9	35	2.1	43	3.0	57	3.9	66	3.9	75	4.4	79	3.7	77	2.9	70	2.9	59	2.8	45	2.5	35	2.0
Salt Lake City, Ut. (AP)	20	1.5	32	0.9	42	2.7	48	1.6	62	1.7	70	0.2	77	1.1	77	1.2	62	4.1	54	0.7	41	2.5	33	2.3
San Antonio, Tex. (AP)	51	1.7	55	2.1	61	1.5	70	2.5	76	3.1	82	2.8	84	1.7	85	2.4	79	3.7	71	2.8	60	1.8	53	1.5
San Diego, Cal. (AP)	56	1.7	60	1.6	58	2.3	62	0.1	63	L	68	L	69	L	71	L	69	L	67	L	61	1.6	58	0.2
San Francisco, Cal. (AP)	48	4.4	51	3.0	53	2.5	55	1.6	58	0.4	62	0.1	63	L	63	0.0	64	0.2	61	1.0	55	2.3	50	4.0
San Juan, P. R. (AP)	75	3.7	75	2.5	76	2.0	78	3.4	79	6.5	81	5.6	81	6.4	81	7.0	81	6.1	81	5.6	79	5.5	77	4.7
Sault Ste. Marie, Mich.	14	1.9	15	1.5	24	1.7	38	2.2	49	3.0	59	3.3	64	2.6	63	3.1	55	3.9	46	2.9	33	3.3	20	2.4
Savannah, Ga. (AP)	50	2.9	52	2.9	58	4.4	66	2.9	73	4.2	79	5.9	81	7.9	81	6.5	76	5.6	67	2.8	57	1.9	50	3.3
Sea.-Tac. Wash. (AP)	38	5.8	42	4.2	44	3.6	49	2.5	55	1.7	60	1.5	65	0.7	64	1.1	60	2.0	52	3.9	45	5.9	41	5.9
Spokane, Wash. (AP)	25	2.5	32	1.7	38	1.5	46	1.1	55	1.5	62	1.4	70	0.4	68	0.6	60	0.8	48	1.4	36	2.2	29	2.4
Springfield, Mo. (AP)	33	1.7	37	2.2	44	3.0	57	4.3	65	4.9	74	4.7	78	3.6	77	2.9	69	4.1	59	3.4	46	2.3	36	2.5
Syracuse, N. Y. (AP)	24	2.7	25	2.8	33	3.0	47	3.1	57	3.0	67	3.1	72	3.1	70	3.5	63	2.7	53	3.1	41	3.3	28	3.1
Tampa, Fla. (AP)	60	2.3	62	2.9	66	3.9	72	2.1	77	2.4	81	6.5	82	8.4	82	8.0	81	6.4	75	2.5	67	1.8	62	2.2
Trenton, N.J.	32	2.8	33	2.7	41	3.8	52	3.2	62	3.4	71	3.2	76	4.7	74	4.2	67	3.2	57	2.5	46	3.3	35	3.3
Vicksburg, Miss.	48	4.9	51	5.3	57	.5	66	5.4	73	4.2	79	3.3	82	3.6	81	3.0	76	2.8	67	2.3	56	4.1	50	5.5
Washington, D. C. (AP)	36	2.6	37	2.5	45	3.3	56	2.9	66	3.7	75	3.5	79	4.1	77	4.7	71	3.1	60	2.7	48	2.9	37	3.0
Wilmington, Del. (AP)	32	2.9	34	2.8	42	3.7	52	3.2	62	3.4	71	3.2	76	4.3	74	4.0	68	3.4	57	2.6	46	3.5	35	3.3

Annual Climatological Data

Source: National Oceanic & Atmospheric Administration, National Climatic Center

1974

Station	Elev. ft	Highest	Date	Lowest	Date	Total (in.)	Greatest 24 hrs	Date	Total (in.)	Greatest 24 hrs	Date	MPH	Date	Clear*	Cloudy*	Prec. .01 in. or more	Snow, sleet 1 in. or more
Albany, N.Y.	275	92	7/4	-14	1/18	38.47	2.01	7/29-30	54.0	10.7	4/8-9	47	3/10	56	209	148	13
Albuquerque, N.M.	5311	105	6/28	3	12/28	9.83	1.15	9/20-21	16.8	4.5	1/2	54	7/4	159	98	73	4
Anchorage, Alaska	114	78	7/1	-18	1/20	13.42	0.60	10/13-14	75.9	6.4	12/30-31	39	1/12	44	241	116	26
Asheville, N.C.	2140	90	6/22	13	2/27	48.44	2.89	4/3-4	7.5	5.3	11/30-12/1	40	11/21	101	163	134	3
Atlanta, Ga.	1010	92	7/19	17	2/26	47.30	1.62	4/3-4	T	T	12/17	48	3/21	105	161	123	0
Baltimore, Md.	148	96	7/9	9	2/10	37.76	2.11	3/29-30	9.2	6.3	2/8	43	12/1	91	165	121	3
Barrow, Alaska	31	66	7/29	-51	12/31	3.06	0.35	7/27-28	17.7	2.1	9/29-30	41	11/11	92	150	75	4
Birmingham, Ala.	620	95	7/3	18	2/26	56.00	2.98	12/23-24	0.4	0.4	12/1	45	2/21	93	171	130	0
Bismarck, N.D.	1647	100	7/7	-42	1/12	10.66	1.17	8/14	20.4	5.7	12/22	45	5/1	93	160	89	6
Boise, Ida.	2838	105	6/17	-5	1/9	9.46	0.66	10/20-21	19.6	5.1	3/7-8	50	2/26	136	141	79	7
Boston, Mass.	15	95	7/4	-3	1/18	40.24	2.65	10/15-16	42.5	11.1	2/2	61	1/31	88	177	132	11
Buffalo, N.Y.	705	90	7/4	0	2/8	36.31	1.29	6/21	108.3	12.6	11/14-15	51	4/15	36	240	186	32
Burlington, Vt.	332	93	6/10	-24	1/18	34.69	2.15	6/24-25	97.3	13.0	4/9	46	7/9	48	227	181	27
Charleston, S.C.	40	97	6/1	23	2/27	54.61	4.69	8/16	0.0	0.0	. . .	52	5/26	104	160	114	0
Charleston, W. Va.	939	92	5/14	11	12/10	43.46	2.48	5/11-12	27.0	6.3	2/8	43	4/1	47	212	157	9
Chicago, Ill.	607	99	7/14	-9	1/12	37.53	2.08	7/1-2	53.7	7.0	12/20-21	41	7/14	84	187	142	15
Cincinnati, Oh.	869	91	7/9	7	2/26	46.76	3.45	6/22-23	19.4	6.0	11/30-12/1	37	4/14	64	195	137	6
Cleveland, Oh.	777	95	7/14	0	1/13	39.88	2.06	12/1-2	72.4	12.2	12/1-2	50	5/11	64	213	186	22
Columbus, Oh.	812	93	7/19	4	1/13	36.99	2.31	3/29-30	19.8	4.4	3/23-24	52	4/14	61	200	145	7
Concord, N.H.	342	93	7/4	-22	1/18	34.45	2.27	3/16-17	54.0	7.0	12/25	49	3/10	88	189	132	15
Dallas, Tex.	551	106	7/22	17	1/1	39.63	2.57	5/5	T	T	12/26	39	8/1	128	124	78	0
Denver, Col.	5283	96	6/28	-17	1/5	14.03	1.82	6/7-8	65.9	8.5	4/13	43	6/13	132	102	83	22
Des Moines, Ia.	938	104	7/21	-23	1/12	35.67	3.80	4/28	38.2	6.0	2/21-22	40	6/14	112	171	110	12
Detroit, Mich.	633	97	7/14	-8	1/12	31.88	2.83	8/16-17	75.3	19.2	12/1-2	50	1/27	68	189	146	24
Dodge City, Kan.	2582	107	6/29	-10	1/5	19.83	3.18	8/8-9	7.6	2.1	12/30-31	55	7/24	135	124	72	3
Duluth, Minn.	1428	92	7/13	-31	1/8	25.50	3.40	7/21	74.7	7.2	12/15	50	10/31	69	188	141	22
Fairbanks, Alaska	436	83	8/30	-49	12/29	7.72	0.47	6/29	85.1	10.4	10/16-17	40	6/27	83	184	95	30
Fresno, Cal.	328	107	7/25	25	12/24	9.31	1.04	10/27-28	T	T	10/28	31	12/3	210	101	41	0
Galveston, Tex.	7	94	7/14	33	1/4	43.26	3.41	5/1	0.0	0.0	. . .	34	5/31	NA	NA	99	0
Grand Rapids, Mich.	784	93	7/14	-12	2/8	36.82	2.32	6/8	69.8	6.2	2/1-2	50	3/22	59	214	152	23
Helena, Mont.	3828	96	7/14	-30	1/6	10.45	1.86	8/19-20	24.7	5.0	1/30	43	12/21	76	187	76	7
Honolulu, Ha.	7	92	9/23	58	3/24	24.02	3.34	4/19-20	0.0	0.0	. . .	34	12/17	75	95	118	0
Houston, Tex.	96	98	7/28	26	2/26	49.29	3.55	10/31-11/1	0.0	0.0	. . .	40	7/2	100	158	114	0
Huron, S.D.	1281	106	7/13	-30	1/1	13.03	1.65	6/9	18.7	4.4	2/1-2	70	7/2	109	144	79	8
Indianapolis, Ind.	792	93	7/18	-4	1/12	41.31	1.93	6/22-23	26.5	6.4	2/24	44	1/26	57	201	140	10
Jackson, Miss.	310	96	7/22	19	2/26	60.21	4.40	4/12	T	T	11/14	39	2/21	117	138	116	0
Jacksonville, Fla.	26	93	8/19	23	2/26	48.52	3.83	8/16	0.0	0.0	. . .	44	7/30	92	136	102	0
Juneau, Alaska	12	78	8/15	-12	3/7	63.85	2.62	8/23-24	106.3	16.0	2/3-4	43	12/31	34	285	224	30
Kansas City, Mo.	1014	107	7/21	-13	1/12	36.12	4.26	5/17-18	8.5	2.6	1/9-10	42	5/13	126	160	100	2
Lander, Wy.	5563	97	7/13	-21	1/11	10.08	0.68	10/21-22	83.9	10.7	2/5	70	1/30	124	110	71	19
Little Rock, Ark.	257	105	7/20	15	1/1	57.96	7.96	4/21-22	.03	0.3	1/3	56	6/8	99	168	121	0
Los Angeles, Cal.	97	100	10/16	35	12/25	12.78	2.28	12/3-4	T	T	1/6	46	10/28	143	103	32	0
Louisville, Ky.	477	91	7/3	15	1/2	42.93	2.15	8/11	6.9	2.8	3/23-24	54	4/3	63	193	138	3
Marquette, Mich.	677	97	7/8	-11	1/2	29.09	1.85	8/3-4	86.2	6.1	2/21-22	50	7/2	57	211	160	27
Memphis, Tenn.	258	98	7/19	17	1/1	64.57	4.08	5/31	1.6	0.9	1/2-3	32	8/17	104	164	128	0
Miami, Fla.	7	93	7/11	44	2/11	49.00	4.67	6/3-4	0.0	0.0	. . .	31	10/4	61	89	141	0
Milford, Ut.	5028	100	6/15	-17	1/3	6.43	0.60	1/20-21	35.7	10.4	1/20-21	52	4/24	170	86	59	11
Milwaukee, Wis.	672	94	7/13	-11	1/12	34.88	1.91	4/13-14	74.7	12.6	2/5-6	50	8/11	74	210	139	15
Minneapolis, Minn.	834	101	7/8	-30	1/1	19.11	1.59	6/6	40.5	7.2	4/3-4	49	6/20	78	167	101	15
Mobile, Ala.	211	96	8/12	25	2/26	61.55	6.82	9/7-8	0.0	0.0	. . .	35	4/2	94	148	117	0
Moline, Ill.	582	98	7/14	-26	1/12	46.83	2.69	6/22	48.1	8.2	11/29-30	57	6/20	91	176	129	15
Nashville, Tenn.	590	95	7/19	12	2/26	60.70	3.67	1/10-11	2.4	1.6	12/1-2	37	3/29	88	175	147	1
New Orleans, La.	4	96	7/12	24	2/27	72.79	4.64	3/26-27	0.0	0.0	. . .	35	5/11	99	153	115	0
New York, N.Y.	13	97	7/9	10	1/8	37.10	2.46	12/16	21.5	6.3	2/8	46	12/2	95	149	110	7
Nome, Alaska	13	76	8/5	-38	12/30	10.66	1.25	7/26-27	33.9	5.0	11/9-10	46	11/11	137	158	80	13
Norfolk, Va.	24	97	7/15	23	2/27	47.96	3.81	7/26	8.4	7.5	3/25	37	2/22	105	160	118	1
Oklahoma City, Okla.	1285	107	7/22	5	1/12	39.45	3.41	9/1-2	5.2	2.0	12/11	44	9/1	143	112	71	3
Omaha, Neb.	977	110	7/21	-22	1/12	20.21	2.88	9/11-12	32.4	4.6	12/14-15	44	8/16	113	156	97	11
Philadelphia, Pa.	5	95	7/9	8	2/9	37.78	1.93	10/15-16	17.0	6.0	2/8	40	5/12	87	160	116	3
Phoenix, Ariz.	1117	116	6/27	26	12/24	8.18	1.13	8/4-5	T	T	12/25	54	8/14	229	59	38	0
Pittsburgh, Pa.	1137	92	7/3	7	1/8	41.83	2.13	5/11-12	34.8	12.5	12/1-2	46	4/14	58	210	161	9
Portland, Me.	43	88	8/4	-16	1/18	43.55	2.91	6/16-17	45.2	6.7	4/9-10	43	1/31	89	196	139	14
Portland, Ore.	21	96	9/24	12	1/9	40.28	2.61	1/14-15	T	T	12/29	50	3/1	81	221	150	0
Providence, R.I.	51	94	7/4	2	1/18	44.06	2.19	10/15-16	30.3	6.0	1/3-4	37	2/23	73	180	132	10
Raleigh, N.C.	434	93	7/15	18	2/27	40.74	1.57	1/28	2.9	2.9	3/25	34	6/23	99	167	115	1
Rapid City, S.D.	3162	105	6/26	-20	1/1	9.12	1.01	4/10-11	15.3	3.7	4/11	49	2/8	114	129	78	4
Reno, Nev.	4404	98	7/28	-5	12/29	5.38	0.80	1/16-17	22.8	4.6	3/2	60	2/28	178	96	46	9
Richmond, Va.	164	98	7/15	14	11/27	35.70	3.25	8/6-7	5.0	4.9	2/8	35	3/16	86	178	106	1
Rochester, N.Y.	547	94	7/14	-3	2/5	36.60	3.85	5/16-17	102.9	10.5	3/17-18	45	1/27	51	227	164	34
St. Louis, Mo.	535	99	7/19	-10	1/1	36.83	2.94	5/30-31	18.8	6.5	3/23	50	6/9	94	178	121	5
Salt Lake City, Ut.	4220	102	6/15	-8	1/11	14.46	2.37	4/9-10	79.2	16.2	4/9-10	45	3/2	149	131	76	20
San Antonio, Tex.	788	99	7/26	22	2/26	37.00	4.33	11/23-24	T	T	12/10	35	7/3	113	154	88	0
San Diego, Cal.	13	92	10/16	36	12/25	8.13	1.43	12/4	0.0	0.0	. . .	33	3/8	138	118	29	0
San Francisco, Cal.	8	90	9/24	32	12/25	15.60	1.43	1/3-4	0.0	0.0	. . .	39	2/28	168	107	58	0
San Juan, P.R.	13	96	8/23	68	3/13	41.68	3.75	10/24-25	0.0	0.0	. . .	36	9/14	71	67	186	0
Sault Ste. Marie, Mich.	721	90	7/13	-21	2/5	39.44	5.92	8/3	95.6	8.8	12/7	47	1/31	56	213	168	34
Savannah, Ga.	46	95	7/30	21	2/27	41.93	3.39	5/11-12	0.0	0.0	. . .	39	3/21	100	156	116	0
Seattle, Wash.	400	91	9/2	16	1/9	37.87	2.51	12/26-27	13.5	9.8	12/26-27	37	4/11	58	228	152	3
Sioux City, Ida.	1095	103	7/19	-24	1/12	17.96	1.70	7/31-8/1	22.2	3.7	12/14-15	40	6/22	105	148	91	8
Spokane, Wash.	2356	97	7/30	-12	1/9	16.04	0.77	1/14-15	39.6	8.2	1/30-31	42	12/21	83	189	106	16
Springfield, Mo.	1268	102	7/22	-5	1/1	49.87	4.09	3/9-10	18.5	7.5	11/29	42	8/17	118	161	119	4
Syracuse, N.Y.	410	94	6/10	-5	1/18	50.23	4.07	7/2-3	112.0	9.6	3/30-31	60	1/27	47	217	170	31
Tampa, Fla.	19	94	9/20	30	2/27	33.90	5.53	6/26-27	0.0	0.0	. . .	26	6/14	100	125	79	0
Trenton, N.J.	56	95	7/9	10	1/18	42.52	2.42	12/16	21.6	6.0	2/25	52	12/2	88	161	114	6
Washington, D.C.	10	96	7/9	18	2/10	35.96	2.11	3/29-30	5.8	4.0	2/8	42	12/1	80	157	114	2
Williston, N.D.	1899	101	7/17	-36	1/11	13.51	1.55	5/12-13	26.5	4.5	3/14	54	2/27	80	173	95	10
Wilmington, Del.	74	95	7/9	9	2/10	39.61	1.77	10/15-16	13.9	6.4	2/8	35	12/1	82	173	113	3

*To get partly cloudy days deduct the total of clear and cloudy days from 365 (1 yr.). T—trace. (1) Date shown is the starting date of the storm (in some cases it lasted more than one day).

Normal Temperatures, Highs, Lows, Precipitation

Source: National Climatic Center, NOAA, Dept. of Commerce

These normals are based on records for the thirty-year period 1941-1970. (See explanation on page 791.) The extreme temperatures (thru 1974) are listed for the stations shown and may not agree with the state's records shown on page 789.

AP indicates airport station; those not so marked are city office stations. The minus (—) sign indicates temperatures below zero. Fahrenheit thermometer registration.

State	Station	Normal temperature January Max.	Min.	July Max.	Min.	Extreme temperature Highest	Lowest	Normal annual precipitation (inches)
Alabama	Mobile (AP)	61	41	91	73	102	8	66.98
Alabama	Montgomery (AP)	59	38	92	72	102	5	50.69
Alaska	Juneau (AP)	29	18	64	48	86	—22	54.67
Arizona	Phoenix (AP)	65	38	105	78	116	19	7.05
Arkansas	Little Rock (AP)	50	29	93	70	108	—4	48.52
California	Los Angeles	67	47	83	64	110	28	14.05
California	San Francisco (AP)	55	41	71	54	106	24	19.53
Colorado	Denver (AP)	44	16	87	59	103	—25	15.51
Connecticut	*New Haven (AP)	37	22	81	63	100	—8	46.02
Delaware	Wilmington (AP)	40	24	86	66	102	—4	40.25
Dist. of Col	Washington (AP)	44	28	88	69	101	3	38.89
Florida	Jacksonville (AP)	65	45	90	72	105	12	54.47
Florida	Key West (AP)	74	65	87	79	95	46	39.99
Florida	Miami (AP)	76	59	89	76	96	34	59.80
Georgia	Atlanta (AP)	51	33	87	69	98	—3	48.34
Hawaii	Honolulu (AP)	79	65	87	73	92	53	22.90
Idaho	Boise (AP)	36	21	91	59	111	—23	11.50
Illinois	Chicago (AP) Midway	32	17	84	65	101	—16	34.44
Indiana	Indianapolis (AP)	36	20	85	65	99	—20	38.74
Iowa	Des Moines (AP)	28	11	85	65	104	—24	30.85
Iowa	Dubuque (AP)	27	11	84	62	97	—28	35.71
Kansas	Wichita (AP)	42	22	92	69	113	—12	28.41
Kentucky	Louisville (AP)	42	25	87	66	101	—20	43.11
Louisiana	New Orleans (AP)	62	44	90	73	100	14	56.77
Maine	Portland (AP)	31	12	79	57	100	—39	40.80
Maryland	Baltimore (AP)	42	25	87	66	102	—7	40.46
Massachusetts	Boston (AP)	36	23	81	65	99	—4	42.52
Michigan	Detroit (AP) City	32	19	83	63	105	—16	30.96
Michigan	Sault Ste. Marie	22	6	75	53	98	—28	31.70
Minnesota	Minn.-St. Paul (AP)	21	3	82	61	101	—34	25.94
Mississippi	**Vicksburg	57	41	90	73	101	2	49.50
Missouri	St. Louis (AP)	40	23	88	69	106	—11	35.89
Montana	Helena (AP)	28	8	84	52	105	—38	11.38
Nebraska	Omaha (AP)	33	12	89	66	110	—22	30.18
Nevada	Winnemucca (AP)	40	15	92	50	106	—34	8.63
New Hampshire	Concord (AP)	31	10	83	57	102	—29	36.17
New Jersey	Atlantic City (AP)	43	27	84	66	106	—8	42.36
New Mexico	Albuquerque (AP)	47	24	92	65	105	—17	7.77
New Mexico	Roswell (AP)	55	21	95	62	110	—8	11.62
New York	Albany (AP)	30	13	84	60	98	—28	33.36
New York	New York (AP) La Guardia	38	26	84	69	107	—2	41.61
No. Carolina	Charlotte (AP)	51	34	89	70	100	2	43.38
No. Carolina	Raleigh (AP)	51	30	88	67	98	0	42.54
No. Dakota	Bismarck (AP)	19	—3	84	57	109	—43	16.16
Ohio	Cincinnati (AP) Abbe	40	24	87	66	109	—17	40.03
Ohio	Cleveland (AP)	33	20	82	61	98	—19	34.99
Oklahoma	Oklahoma City (AP)	48	26	93	70	108	—1	31.37
Oregon	Portland	44	33	79	55	107	—3	37.61
Pennsylvania	Harrisburg (AP)	39	24	87	65	107	—8	37.65
Pennsylvania	Philadelphia (AP)	40	24	87	67	104	—5	39.93
Rhode Island	Block Island (AP)	38	26	76	63	91	—4	40.45
So. Carolina	Charleston (AP)	60	37	89	71	103	8	52.12
So. Dakota	Huron (AP)	23	2	87	61	112	—39	19.44
So. Dakota	Rapid City (AP)	34	10	86	59	110	—27	17.12
Tennessee	Nashville (AP)	48	29	90	69	103	—6	46.00
Texas	Amarillo (AP)	50	24	94	67	104	—9	19.67
Texas	Galveston	59	48	87	79	101	8	42.20
Texas	Houston (AP)	63	42	94	73	101	19	48.19
Utah	Salt Lake City (AP)	37	18	93	61	107	—18	15.17
Vermont	Burlington (AP)	26	8	81	59	98	—27	32.54
Virginia	Norfolk (AP)	49	32	87	70	103	8	44.68
Washington	Seattle-Tacoma (AP)	43	33	75	54	99	6	38.79
Washington	Spokane (AP)	31	20	84	55	108	—25	17.42
West Virginia	Parkersburg	41	24	86	65	106	—27	38.44
Wisconsin	Madison (AP)	26	9	82	60	98	—30	30.16
Wisconsin	Milwaukee (AP)	27	11	80	59	99	—24	29.07
Wyoming	Cheyenne (AP)	37	14	85	55	98	—27	15.06
Puerto Rico	San Juan (AP)	81	67	87	74	96	60	64.21

*Closed June 14,1969.　　**Closed December 1966.

Mean Annual Snowfall (inches) based on record thru 1972: Boston, Mass. 42.8, Sault Ste. Marie, Mich., 108.2, Albany, N.Y., 67.3, Rochester, N.Y., 86.3, Burlington, Vt., 79, Cheyenne, Wyo., 51.7, Juneau, Alaska, 106.3.

Wettest Spot: Mount Waialeale, Hawaii, on the island of Kauai, is the rainiest place in the world, according to the National Geographic Society, with an average annual rainfall of 460 inches.

Highest Temperature: A temperature of 136° F. observed at Azizia, Tripolitania in Northern Africa on Sept. 13, 1922, is generally accepted as the world's highest temperature recorded under standard conditions.

The record high in the United States was 134° in Death Valley, Calif., July 10, 1913.

Lowest Temperature: A record low temperature of —126.9° F. (—88.3° C.) was recorded at the Soviet Antarctic station Vostok on Aug. 24, 1960.

The record low in the United States was —80° at Prospect Creek, Alaska, Jan. 23, 1971.

The lowest official temperature on the North American continent was recorded at 81 degrees below zero in February, 1947, at a lonely airport in the Yukon called Snag.

These are the meteorological champions—the official temperature extremes—but there are plenty of other claimants to thermometer fame. However, sun readings are unofficial records, since meteorological data to qualify officially must be taken on instruments in a sheltered and ventilated location.

Temp. Records of National Weather Service Thru 1974

State	Lowest °F	Highest	Latest Date			Place	Approximate Elevation
Alabama	-27		Jan.	30, 1966		New Market	725
		112	Sept.	5, 1925		Centerville	345
Alaska	-79.8		Jan.	23, 1971		Prospect Creek Camp	1,100
		100	Jun.	27, 1915		Fort Yukon	*419
Arizona	-40		Jan.	7, 1971		Hawley Lake	8,180
		127	Jul.	7, 1905		Parker	345
Arkansas	-29		Feb.	13, 1905		Pond	1,250
		120	Aug.	10, 1936		Ozark	396
California	-45		Jan.	20, 1937		Boca	5,532
		134	Jul.	10, 1913		Greenland Ranch	-178
Colorado	-60		Feb.	1, 1951		Taylor Park	9,206
		118	Jul.	11, 1888		Bennett	5,484
Connecticut	-32		Jan.	22, 1961		Coventry	480
		105	Jul.	22, 1926		Waterbury	409
Delaware	-17		Jan.	17, 1893		Millsboro	535
		110	Jul.	21, 1930		Millsboro	20
Dist. of Col.	-15		Feb.	11, 1899		Washington	112
		106	Jul.	20, 1930		Washington	112
Florida	-2		Feb.	13, 1899		Tallahassee	193
		109	Jun.	29, 1931		Monticello	207
Georgia	-17		Jan.	27, 1940		CCC Camp F-16	1,000
		112	Jul.	24, 1952		Louisville	337
Hawaii	18		Feb.	20, 1962		Mauna Loa Slope Obs.	11,146
		100	Apr.	27, 1931		Pahala	850
Idaho	-60		Jan.	18, 1943		Island Park Dam	6,285
		118	Jul.	28, 1934		Orofino	1,027
Illinois	-35		Jan.	22, 1930		Mount Carroll	817
		117	Jul.	14, 1954		E. St. Louis	410
Indiana	-35		Feb.	2, 1951		Greensburg	954
		116	Jul.	14, 1936		Collegeville	672
Iowa	-47		Jan.	12, 1912		Washta	1,157
		118	Jul.	20, 1934		Keokuk	614
Kansas	-40		Feb.	13, 1905		Lebanon	1,812
		121	Jul.	24, 1936		Alton (near)	1,651
Kentucky	-34		Jan.	24, 1963		Bonnieville (closed Oct. 1966)	730
	-34		Jan.	28, 1963		Cynthiana	719
		114	Jul.	28, 1930		Greensburg	581
Louisiana	-16		Feb.	13, 1899		Minden	194
		114	Aug.	10, 1936		Plain Dealing	268
Maine	-48		Jan.	19, 1925		Van Buren	510
		105	Jul.	10, 1911		North Bridgton	450
Maryland	-40		Jan.	13, 1912		Oakland	2,461
		109	Jul.	10, 1936		Cumberland and Frederick	623-325
Massachusetts	-34		Jan.	18, 1957		Birch Hill Dam	840
		106	Jul.	4, 1911		Lawrence	51
Michigan	-51		Feb.	9, 1934		Vanderbilt	785
		112	Jul.	13, 1936		Mio	963
Minnesota	-59		Feb.	16, 1903		Pokegama Dam	1,280
		114	Jul.	6, 1936		Moorhead	940
Mississippi	-19		Jan.	30, 1966		Corinth	420
		115	Jul.	29, 1930		Holly Springs	600
Missouri	-40		Feb.	13, 1905		Warsaw	700
		118	Jul.	14, 1954		Warsaw	687
Montana	-70		Jan.	20, 1954		Rogers Pass	5,470
		117	Jul.	5, 1937		Medicine Lake	1,950
Nebraska	-47		Feb.	12, 1899		Camp Clarke	3,700
		118	Jul.	24, 1936		Minden	2,169
Nevada	-50		Jan.	8, 1937		San Jacinto	5,200
		122	Jun.	23, 1954		Overton	1,240
New Hampshire	-46		Jan.	8, 1968		Mt. Washington	6,262
		106	Jul.	4, 1911		Nashua	125
New Jersey	-34		Jan.	5, 1904		River Vale	70
		110	Jul.	10, 1936		Runyon	18
New Mexico	-50		Feb.	1, 1951		Gavilan	7,350
		116	Jul.	14, 1934		Orogrande	4,171
New York	-52		Feb.	9, 1934		Stillwater Reservoir	1,670
		108	Jul.	22, 1926		Troy	35
North Carolina	-29		Jan.	30, 1966		Mt. Mitchell	6,525
		109	Sept.	7, 1954		Weldon	81
North Dakota	-60		Feb.	15, 1936		Parshall	1,929
		121	Jul.	6, 1936		Steele	1,857
Ohio	-39		Feb.	10, 1899		Milligan	800
		113	Jul.	21, 1934		Gallipolis (near)	673
Oklahoma	-27		Jan.	18, 1930		Watts	958
		120	Jul.	26, 1943		Tishomingo	670
Oregon	-54		Feb.	10, 1933		Seneca	4,700
		119	Aug.	10, 1898		Pendleton	1,074
Pennsylvania	-42		Jan.	5, 1904		Smethport	1,469
		111	Jul.	10, 1936		Phoenixville	100
Rhode Island	-23		Jan.	11, 1942		Kingston	100
		102	Jul.	30, 1949		Greenville	420
South Carolina	-13		Jan.	26, 1940		Longcreek (near)	1,631
		111	Jun.	28, 1954		Camden	170
South Dakota	-58		Feb.	17, 1936		McIntosh	2,277
		120	Jul.	5, 1936		Gannvalley	1,750
Tennessee	-32		Dec.	30, 1917		Mountain City	2,471
		113	Aug.	9, 1930		Perryville	377

State	Lowest °F	Highest	Latest Dates			Station	Approximate Elevation
Texas	—23		Feb.	8,	1933	Seminole	3,275
		120	Aug.	12,	1936	Seymour	1,291
Utah	—50		Jan.	5,	1913	Strawberry Tunnel	7,650
		116	June	28,	1892	Saint George	2,880
Vermont	—50		Dec.	30,	1933	Bloomfield	915
		105	July	4,	1911	Vernon	310
Virginia	—29		Feb.	10,	1899	Monterey	3,008
		110	July	15,	1954	Balcony Falls	725
Washington	—48		Dec.	30,	1968	Mazama	2,120
	—48		Dec.	30,	1968	Winthrop	1,755
		118	Aug.	5,	1961	Ice Harbor Dam	475
West Virginia	—37		Dec.	30,	1917	Lewisburg	2,200
		112	July	10,	1936	Martinsburg	435
Wisconsin	—54		Jan.	24,	1922	Danbury	908
		114	July	13,	1936	Wisconsin Dells	900
Wyoming	—63		Feb.	9,	1933	Moran	6,770
		114	July	12,	1900	Basin	3,500

Low and High Temp. Records Through 1967

Source: Atmospheric Environment Service. Dept. of Environment

Province	Lowest °F	Highest	Latest Dates			Station	Approximate Elevation
Alberta	—78		Jan.	11,	1911	Fort Vermilion	915
		108	Jul.	12,	1886	Medicine Hat	2,365
British Columbia	—74		Jan.	31,	1947	Smith River	2,208
		112	Jul.	17,	1941	Chinook Cove	1324
		112	Jul.	17,	1941	Lillooet	950
		112	Jul.	17,	1941	Lytton	600
Manitoba	—63		Jan.	9,	1899	Norway House	720
		112	Jul.	12,	1936	Emerson	792
		112	Jul.	11,	1936	St. Albans	1,180
Newfoundland	—56		Mar.	7,	1968	Twin Falls	1,499
		107	Aug.	11,	1914	Northwest River	200
New Brunswick	—53		Feb.	1,	1955	Sisson Dam	915
		103	Aug.	18,	1935	Nespisquit Falls	350
		103	Aug.	18,	1935	Woodstock	150
		103	Aug.	19,	1935	Rexton	20
Nova Scotia	—42		Jan.	31,	1920	Upper Stewiacke	75
		101	Aug.	19,	1935	Collegeville	250
Ontario	—73		Jan.	23,	1935	Iroquois Falls	800
		108	Jul.	20,	1919	Biscotasing	1,300
		108	Jul.	11,	1936	Atikokan	1,289
		108	Jul.	13,	1936	Fort Frances	1,160
Prince Edward Island	—35		Jan.	26,	1884	Kilmahumaig	20
		98	Aug.	19,	1935	Charlottetown	74
Quebec	—66		Feb.	5,	1923	Doucet	1,236
		104	Jul.	6,	1921	Barrage Temiscaminigue	595
		104	Aug.	15,	1928	Bark Lake	1,195
Saskatchewan	—70		Feb.	1,	1893	Prince Albert	1,432
		113	Jul.	5,	1937	Midale	1,908
		113	Jul.	5,	1937	Yellow Grass	1,899
North West Territories	—71		Dec.	26,	1917	Fort Smith	665
		103	Jul.	18,	1941	Fort Smith	680
Yukon Territory	—81		Feb.	3,	1947	Snag	1,925
		95	Jun.	18,	1950	Mayo	1,625

Canadian Normal Temperatures, Highs, Lows, Precipitation

Source: Atmospheric Environment Service. Dept. of Environment

These normals are based on varying periods of record over the thirty-year period 1941 to 1970 inclusive. Extreme temperatures are based on varying periods of record for each station thru 1970. AP indicates airport station; those not so marked are city office stations. The minus (—) sign indicates temperatures below zero. Fahrenheit thermometer registration.

Province	Station	Normal January Max.	Normal January Min.	Normal July Max.	Normal July Min.	Extreme Highest	Extreme Lowest	Precipitation Normal Annual (inches)
Alberta	Calgary (AP)	23	2	74	49	97	—49	17.21
Alberta	Edmonton (Industrial AP)	14	3	74	53	94	—55	17.58
British Columbia	Prince George (AP)	19	2	72	46	94	—58	24.43
British Columbia	Victoria (AP)	43	32	71	52	97	4	33.72
British Columbia	Vancouver (AP)	41	31	72	55	92	0	42.05
Manitoba	Churchill (AP)	—11	—25	63	45	91	—49	15.61
Manitoba	Winnipeg (AP)	8	—10	79	56	105	—49	21.06
Newfoundland	Gander (AP)	28	14	71	52	96	—17	42.45
Newfoundland	St. John's (AP)	31	19	68	51	87	—10	59.50
New Brunswick	Fredericton (AP)	25	7	78	55	98	—35	41.74
New Brunswick	Moncton (AP)	26	9	76	55	99	—26	43.27
New Brunswick	Saint John (AP)	28	9	72	53	91	—34	55.13
Nova Scotia	Halifax (AP)	29	14	74	55	93	—14	54.94
Nova Scotia	Sidney (AP)	31	17	74	55	95	—13	52.78
Ontario	Ottawa (AP)	21	4	80	59	100	—33	33.50
Ontario	Sudbury (AP)	17	—1	77	55	97	—36	32.87
Ontario	Toronto (AP)	28	13	81	58	101	—24	29.61
Ontario	Windsor (AP)	31	18	82	62	101	—15	32.91
Prince Edward Island	Charlottetown (AP)	27	13	75	58	98	—23	41.69
Quebec	Montreal (AP)	22	6	79	61	96	—36	37.05
Quebec	Quebec City (AP)	19	3	77	56	96	—33	42.85
Quebec	Val-d'Or (AP)	12	—9	74	52	94	—47	35.52
Saskatchewan	Prince Albert (AP)	5	—17	77	51	100	—58	15.31
Saskatchewan	Regina (AP)	10	—9	79	53	110	—58	15.66
North West Territories	Alert	—19	—33	44	34	68	—57	6.15
North West Territories	Yellowknife (AP)	—12	—27	69	53	90	—60	9.84
Yukon Territory	Dawson	—13	—26	72	48	95	—73	12.81
Yukon Territory	Whitehorse	6	—9	68	47	94	—62	10.24

Canadian Monthly Normal Temperature and Precipitation

Source: Atmospheric Environment Service, Dept. of Environment

Normal refers to the mean daily temperature and total monthly precipitation based on varying periods of record over the thirty-year period 1941 to 1970 inclusive. In most cases no adjustment factor was used.

AP indicates airport station; Those not so marked are city office stations.

T, Temperature in Fahrenheit; P, Precipitation in inches; L, less than .05 inch.

Stations	Jan. T. P.	Feb. T. P.	Mar. T. P.	Apr. T. P.	May T. P.	Jun. T. P.	Jul. T. P.	Aug. T. P.	Sept. T. P.	Oct. T. P.	Nov. T. P.	Dec. T. P.
Calgary, Alta. (AP)	12 0.7	19 0.8	24 0.8	38 1.2	49 2.0	56 3.6	62 2.7	59 2.2	51 1.4	42 0.7	27 0.6	18 0.6
Charlottetown, P.E.I. (AP)	20 3.8	20 3.2	27 3.0	37 2.9	49 3.1	58 3.1	66 2.9	65 3.5	58 3.6	48 3.9	39 4.5	26 3.9
Churchill, Man. (AP)	-17 0.6	-16 0.5	- 5 0.7	12 0.9	28 1.1	43 1.6	54 1.9	53 2.3	42 2.0	30 1.6	10 1.6	- 7 0.8
Dawson, Yukon	-20 0.8	- 9 0.6	7 0.5	29 0.4	46 0.9	57 1.5	60 2.1	55 2.0	44 1.1	26 1.1	2 1.0	-14 1.0
Edmonton, Alta. (Indus. AP)	6 1.0	13 0.8	22 0.7	39 0.9	52 1.4	58 2.9	63 3.2	61 2.8	52 1.4	42 0.7	24 0.7	13 0.8
Fredericton, N.B.(AP)	16 3.7	17 3.6	28 2.7	39 2.9	51 3.2	61 3.1	67 3.4	64 3.4	56 3.2	46 3.4	35 4.3	21 4.4
Frobisher Bay, N.W.T. (AP)	-15 0.9	-13 1.1	- 8 0.8	7 0.8	26 0.9	38 1.4	46 2.0	44 2.2	36 1.7	23 1.6	9 1.4	- 5 1.0
Halifax, N.S. (AP)	21 5.3	20 5.0	28 4.0	37 4.2	48 3.8	58 3.1	64 3.1	64 4.2	57 3.7	48 4.6	39 6.4	27 7.0
Hamilton, Ont.	25 2.2	26 2.3	33 2.7	45 2.7	56 3.0	67 2.3	72 2.9	71 2.9	62 2.4	52 2.5	40 2.3	29 2.3
Kitchener, Ont.	20 2.3	21 2.1	30 2.8	44 2.7	54 3.2	65 3.2	69 3.5	68 3.0	60 2.8	49 2.8	37 3.0	25 2.9
London, Ont. (AP)	21 3.0	22 2.5	31 2.8	44 3.0	54 2.9	65 3.1	69 3.2	67 2.8	60 3.1	50 2.9	38 3.2	26 3.4
Moncton, N.B. (AP)	18 4.2	18 3.9	27 3.6	38 3.3	49 3.1	59 3.5	65 3.1	64 3.1	56 2.8	46 3.5	36 4.4	22 4.2
Montreal, Que. (AP)	14 2.9	16 2.7	28 2.7	43 2.9	55 2.6	65 3.2	70 3.3	68 3.4	59 3.1	49 2.9	36 3.4	20 3.3
Ottawa, Ont. (AP)	12 2.3	15 2.2	26 2.4	42 2.6	54 2.7	65 2.8	69 3.2	67 3.2	58 3.1	48 2.6	34 3.0	18 3.0
Quebec City, Que. (AP)	11 3.3	13 3.0	24 2.7	38 2.9	51 3.1	61 4.0	67 4.2	64 4.0	56 4.1	45 3.2	32 3.9	17 3.9
Regina, Sask. (AP)	1 0.7	6 0.6	17 0.7	38 0.9	51 1.6	59 3.2	66 2.2	64 1.9	53 1.4	41 0.7	23 0.7	9 0.6
Saint John, N.B. (AP)	19 5.7	18 5.1	27 4.1	37 4.4	48 4.0	56 3.7	63 3.8	54 4.0	46 4.3	37 6.0	24 6.1	
St. John's, Nfld. (AP)	25 5.7	24 6.1	28 5.2	34 4.4	42 3.9	51 3.4	59 3.2	60 4.5	54 4.4	45 5.4	38 6.3	30 6.6
Saskatoon, Sask. (AP)	- 2 0.7	5 0.7	16 0.6	38 0.8	51 1.3	60 2.2	66 2.0	63 1.7	52 1.3	41 0.7	22 0.7	7 0.7
Sault Ste. Marie, Ont. (AP)	13 3.2	11 2.1	23 2.2	38 2.2	48 3.3	58 3.4	64 2.8	62 2.6	56 3.7	47 3.1	34 4.1	20 3.7
Toronto, Ont. (AP)	21 2.1	22 1.9	30 2.3	43 2.5	54 2.8	65 2.4	69 2.9	68 2.8	60 2.4	50 2.3	38 2.4	26 2.2
Vancouver, B.C. (AP)	36 5.8	40 4.5	42 3.6	48 2.4	54 1.8	59 1.7	63 1.1	63 1.4	58 2.4	50 4.8	43 5.5	39 6.5
Victoria, B.C. (AP)	37 5.7	40 3.8	42 2.7	47 1.7	53 1.2	58 1.1	61 0.7	61 0.9	57 1.4	50 3.4	43 5.0	40 5.7
Whitehorse, Yukon (AP)	- 2 0.7	8 0.5	18 0.5	32 0.4	45 0.5	54 1.1	57 1.3	54 1.4	46 1.1	33 0.7	16 0.8	- 4 0.7
Windsor, Ont. (AP)	24 2.1	26 2.0	34 2.6	47 3.2	57 3.2	68 3.7	73 3.2	70 3.2	63 2.3	53 2.4	40 2.4	28 2.5
Winnipeg, Man. (AP)	- 1 0.9	4 0.7	17 1.0	38 1.4	51 2.2	62 3.1	67 3.1	66 2.9	55 2.0	44 1.3	24 1.0	7 0.9
Yellowknife, N.W.T. (AP)	-19 0.5	-14 0.4	- 1 0.4	18 0.4	39 0.5	54 0.6	61 1.3	57 1.4	44 1.1	30 1.2	6 0.9	-11 0.7

Canadian Annual Climatological Data

Source: Atmospheric Environment Service, Dept. of Environment

Station	Elev. ft.	Temperature				Precipitation			Snow or Sleet			Wind Fastest		No. of days	
1974		Highest	Date D./Mo.	Lowest	Date D./Mo.	Total (in.)	Greatest in 24 hrs.	Date D./Mo.	Total (in.)	Greatest in 24 hrs.	Date D./Mo.	MPH	Date D./Mo.	Prec. .01 in. or more	Snow, sleet 1 in. or more
Calgary	3540	90	5/8	-26	31/1	13.63	1.16	26/4	49.5	4.3	29/1	55	26/4	111	63
Charlottetown	186	87	12/8	-16	17/1	45.91	2.06	26/11	119.7	13.6	5/2	40	20/10	142	73
Churchill	115	88	24/6	-47	1/2	12.06	0.65	10/8	49.3	3.7	9/11	42	24/10	135	81
Dawson	1062	84	17/7	-56	31/1	13.12	0.62	22/8	86.0	4.5	22/8	32	15/2	132	79
Edmonton	2358	88	23/6	-31	31/1	20.76	3.15	26/6	67.4	5.4	21/12	34	1/1	135	61
Frederickton	74	91	9/6	-19	14/1	41.18	1.28	21/9	106.1	14.2	26/11	35	21/11	163	63
Frobisher Bay	68	72	6/7	-44	26/1	13.66	0.86	7/6	62.4	4.3	1/10	33	25/3	115	75
Halifax	461	84	9/6	-9	17/1	50.38	1.58	10/7	93.6	13.0	20/10	38	15/1	172	46
Hamilton	808	94	9/7	-5	8/2	31.79	1.50	12/8	45.8	5.5	6/2	38	27/1	148	56
Waterloo-Wellington	1125	91	9/7	-12	8/2	33.26	1.75	20/11	55.1	3.4	6/2	38	27/1	172	68
London	912	91	9/7	-11	8/2	33.93	1.24	20/11	62.5	3.2	6/2	42	27/1	180	75
Moncton	248	89	22/8	-20	17/1	49.24	1.44	5/2	148.0	11.5	5/2	57	18/2	179	74
Montreal	98	87	10/6	-18	17/1	35.28	1.50	8/12	75.0	9.6	16/12	44	23/2	153	60
Ottawa	413	90	8/7	-17	18/1	33.26	1.37	12/5	97.0	9.8	16/12	32	1/5	163	62
Quebec City	245	86	14/7	-26	18/1	50.25	2.36	30/7	110.7	6.6	17/12	36	21/11	187	71
Regina	1884	96	25/6	-42	10/1	16.30	1.48	20/5	52.7	7.5	27/2	40	26/9	116	61
Saint John	352	87	9/6	-17	17/1	52.60	3.35	9/12	81.1	7.8	20/10	47	14/1	158	53
Saint John's	463	82	30/6	0	3/3	61.08	2.85	16/10	159.9	18.0	11/3	60	12/3	219	93
Saskatoon	1645	94	19/7	-40	12/1	17.11	1.70	26/5	46.3	4.3	2/3	43	26/11	134	71
Sault Ste. Marie	620	89	13/7	-31	5/2	33.59	1.78	9/6	88.8	8.1	7/12	48	31/12	175	78
Thunder Bay	644	95	13/7	-34	1/1	29.17	1.48	29/6	87.1	5.4	1/4	36	14/1	155	67
Toronto	578	96	9/7	-1	5/2	31.08	2.31	16/5	40.3	6.5	8/1	40	27/1	140	36
Vancouver	16	81	2/9	17	7/1	49.12	1.94	9/3	16.0	6.1	12/1	40	26/9	157	8
Victoria	67	84	2/9	25	6/1	25.85	2.04	2/2	5.1	2.8	12/1	53	13/3	135	7
Whitehorse	2289	81	31/8	-53	16/1	14.43	1.12	5/8	60.8	4.6	30/9	30	31/12	136	73
Windsor	637	96	9/7	-3	13/1	32.29	1.96	10/7	71.5	12.7	1/12	40	27/1	151	53
Winnipeg	786	96	28/6	-43	1/1	20.06	2.14	19/5	43.6	4.5	25/1	36	29/9	123	67
Yellowknife	682	84	4/8	-54	31/1	15.93	0.86	1/7	81.7	5.4	3/10	38	1/1	145	92

Explanation of Normal Temperatures

Normal temperatures listed in the tables on pages 786 and 788 are based on records of the National Weather Service for the 30-year period from 1941—1970 inclusive.

To obtain the average maximum temperature for any month, the daily maximum temperatures are added; the total is then divided by the number of days in that month. The average minimum temperature for the month is obtained by adding the daily minimum temperatures during that month and dividing by the number of days in that month.

The normal maximum temperature for January, for example, is obtained by adding the average maximums for January, 1941, January, 1942, etc., through January, 1970. The total is then divided by 30. The normal minimum temperature is obtained in a similar manner by adding the average minimums for each January in the 30-year period and dividing by 30. The normal temperature for January is one-half of the sum for the normal maximum and minimum temperatures for that month.

The mean temperature for any one day is one-half the total of the maximum and minimum temperatures for that day.

Speed of Winds in Canada

Source: Atmospheric Environment Service. Dept. of Environment

Miles per hour-average in most cases is for the period of record 1955 to 1972. High is based on varying periods of record dependent on the origin of the station thru 1972.

Stations	Avg.	High	Stations	Avg.	High	Stations	Avg.	High
Calgary	13.3	65	London	10.2	63	Sault Ste. Marie	9.5	55
Charlottetown	12.0	64	Moncton	11.6	62	Thunder Bay	8.8	50
Churchill	14.7	78	Montreal	9.8	51	Toronto	10.7	56
Dawson	4.2	32	Ottawa	9.4	54	Vancouver	7.5	55
Edmonton	9.2	44	Quebec City	10.4	68	Victoria	11.0	68
Fredericton	8.8	50	Regina	13.4	60	Whitehorse	9.4	50
Frobisher Bay	10.3	80	Saint John	11.8	60	Windsor	10.6	57
Halifax	11.4	60	Saint John's	15.1	85	Winnipeg	12.0	56
Hamilton	7.9	41	Saskatoon	11.2	65	Yellowknife	10.0	45

Speed of Winds in the United States

Miles per hour — average thru 1973. High thru 1974. Wind velocities in true values.
Source: National Climatic Center, NOAA, Dept. of Commerce

Stations	Avg.	High	Stations	Avg.	High	Stations	Avg.	High
Albany, N. Y.	8.8	71	Helena, Mont.	7.9	73	Pensacola, Fla.	8.2	(b)59
Albuquerque, N. M.	8.9	90	Jacksonville, Fla.	8.7	82	Philadelphia, Pa.	9.6	73
Atlanta, Ga.	9.1	70	Key West, Fla.	11.3	122	Pittsburgh, Pa.	9.4	58
Bismarck, N.D.	10.7	72	Knoxville, Tenn.	7.3	73	Portland, Ore.	7.7	88
Boston, Mass.	12.7	61	Little Rock, Ark.	8.2	65	Rochester, N.Y.	9.6	73
Buffalo, N. Y.	12.3	91	Louisville, Ky.	8.4	61	St. Louis, Mo.	9.5	(b)91
Cape Hatteras, N. C.	11.8	(b)110	Memphis, Tenn.	9.2	57	Salt Lake City, Utah.	8.7	71
Chattanooga, Tenn.	6.3	82	Miami, Fla.	9.0	(a)74	San Diego, Calif.	6.7	51
Chicago, Ill.	10.4	60	Minneapolis, Minn.	10.6	92	San Francisco, Calif.	10.5	56
Cincinnati, Ohio	7.1	49	Mobile, Ala.	9.4	(b)63	Savannah, Ga.	8.3	66
Cleveland, Ohio	10.8	74	Montgomery, Ala.	6.8	60	Spokane, Wash.	8.6	59
Denver, Colo.	9.0	56	Nashville, Tenn.	7.9	73	Toledo, Ohio	9.5	72
Detroit, Mich.	10.2	46	New Orleans, La.	8.4	(b)98	Washington, D. C.	9.3	78
Fort Smith, Ark.	7.7	58	New York, N. Y.(c)	9.5	70	Mt. Wash'ton, N. H.	35.2	231
Galveston, Texas	11.0	(d)100	Omaha, Nebr.	10.9	109			

(a) Highest velocity ever recorded in Miami area was 132 mph, at former station in Miami Beach in September, 1926. (b) Previous location. (c) Data for Central Park. Battery Place data through 1960, avg. 14.5, high 113. (d) Recorded before anemometer blew away. Estimated high 120.

Wind Guide

The National Weather Service classifies winds according to their strength, measured in miles per hour, with official descriptive names or designations, shown in the table below. A similar classification is the Beaufort Scale, in which winds are designated as Force 1, Force 2, etc.

Name	MPH Beau.	Name	MPH Beau.	Name	MPH Beau.	Name	MPH Beau.
Calm	less than 1 0	Moderate breeze	13-18 4	Near gale	32-38 7	Storm	55-63 10
Light air	1-3 1	Fresh breeze	19-24 5	Gale	39-46 8	Violent storm	64-73 11
Light breeze	4-7 2	Strong breeze	25-31 6	Strong gale	47-54 9	Hurricane	74 and up 12
Gentle breeze	8-12 3						

The Beaufort Scale further classifies 74-82 mph as Force 12; 83-92, Force 13; 93-103, Force 14; 104-114, Force 15; 115-124, Force 16; 125-136, Force 17.

Temperature-Humidity (Discomfort) Index

The temperature-humidity index, THI, is a measure of summertime human discomfort resulting from the combined effects of temperature and humidity. (The THI may be calculated by adding wet-bulb and dry-bulb temperatures, multiplying the sum by 0.4 and adding 15.)

The following chart shows the combinations of temperature degrees and humidity percentages which produce discomfort for most persons (the equivalent of a THI value of 75) and those which produce acute discomfort for almost everyone (equivalent to a THI of 80).

Discomfort Temp.-Humid.	Acute Discomfort Temp.-Humid.	Discomfort Temp.-Humid.	Acute Discomfort Temp.-Humid.	Discomfort Temp.-Humid.	Acute Discomfort Temp.-Humid.
75°—100%	81°—100%	82°—49%	88°—54%	90°—14%	96°—20%
76°— 91%	82°— 93%	83°—43%	89°—49%	91°—10%	97°—16%
77°— 82%	83°— 86%	84°—38%	90°—43%	92°— 7%	98°—13%
78°— 75%	84°— 78%	85°—33%	91°—38%	93°— 5%	99°—11%
79°— 68%	85°— 71%	86°—29%	92°—34%	94°— 3%	100°— 8%
80°— 61%	86°— 65%	87°—25%	93°—30%	95°— 1%	101°— 6%
81°— 55%	87°— 59%	88°—20%	94°—26%	96°— 1%	102°— 3%
		89°—17%	95°—23%	97°— 1%	103°— 1%

From 95 degrees up there is discomfort at any humidity. When the temperature is over 102 degrees there is acute discomfort at any humidity.

The Meaning of "One Inch of Rain"

An acre of ground contains 43,560 square feet. Consequently, a rainfall of 1 inch over 1 acre of ground would mean a total of 6,272,640 cubic inches of water. This is equivalent of 3,630 cubic feet.

As a cubic foot of pure water weighs about 62.4 pounds, the exact amount varying with the density, it follows that the weight of a uniform coating of 1 inch of rain over 1 acre of surface would be 226,512 pounds, or 113 1/4 short tons. The weight of 1 U.S. gallon of pure water is about 8.345 pounds. Consequently a rainfall of 1 inch over 1 acre of ground would mean 27,154 gallons of water.

Major Holidays, Events, and Anniversaries — 1976

a. denotes anniversary

Jan. 1 (Thurs.)	—New Year's Day.
Jan. 2 (Fri.)	—Moslem New Year's Day.
Jan. 4, 1896	—Utah enters Union; 80th a.
Jan. 15 (Thurs.)	—Martin Luther King Day.
Jan. 18 (Sun.)	—Superbowl.
Jan. 20, 1801	—John Marshall named to Sup. Ct.; 175th a.
Jan. 22, 1901	—Queen Victoria dies; 75th a.
Jan. 27, 1756	—Wolfgang A. Mozart born; 220th a.
Jan. 28, 1916	—Louis Brandeis named to Sup. Ct.; 60th a.
Jan. 31 (Sat.)	—Chinese New Year's Day, Tet.
Feb. 2, 1876	—Baseball National League formed. 100th a.
Feb. 2 (Mon.)	—Groundhog Day.
Feb. 4 (Wed.)	—Winter Olympics begin.
Feb. 5 (Thurs.)	—Mexico Constitution Day.
Feb. 12 (Thurs.)	—Lincoln's Birthday.
Feb. 14 (Sat.)	—Valentine's Day.
Feb. 16 (Mon.)	—Washington's Birthday observed.
Feb. 24, 1956	—Khrushchev denounces Stalin; 20th a.
Feb. 29 (Sun.)	—Leap Year Day.
Mar. 2 (Tues.)	—Mardi Gras (Shrove Tuesday).
Mar. 3 (Wed.)	—Ash Wednesday.
Mar. 3, 1901	—Natl. Bureau of Standards founded; 75th a.
Mar. 6, 1836	—Alamo falls; 140th a.
Mar. 9, 1916	—Pancho Villa invades U.S.; 60th a.
Mar. 10, 1876	—Bell demonstrates telephone; 100th a.
Mar. 15, 44 B.C.	—Julius Caesar assassinated; 2020th a.
Mar. 16, 1751	—James Madison born; 225th a.
Mar. 17 (Wed.)	—St. Patrick's Day.
Mar. 19 (Fri.)	—Swallows back at Capistrano.
Mar. 20 (Sat.)	—Spring begins, 11:50 A.M.
Apr. 1 (Thurs.)	—April Fool's Day.
Apr. 5, 1856	—Booker T. Washington born; 120th a.
Apr. 11 (Sun.)	—Palm Sunday.
Apr. 12, 1961	—First man in space; 15th a.
Apr. 14 (Wed.)	—Pan-American Day.
Apr. 15 (Thurs.)	—Passover, first day.
Apr. 16 (Fri.)	—Good Friday.
Apr. 18 (Sun.)	—Easter.
Apr. 22 (Thurs.)	—Earth Day.
Apr. 25 (Sun.)	—Eastern Orthodox Easter.
Apr. 30 (Fri.)	—Arbor Day.
May 1 (Sat.)	—Kentucky Derby; May Day.
May 3, 1911	—First workmen's compensation law; 65th a.
May 4, 1886	—Haymarket riot; 90th a.
May 6, 1626	—Dutch buy Manhattan; 350th a.
May 6, 1856	—Sigmund Freud born; 120th a.
May 9 (Sun.)	—Mother's Day.
May 10, 1676	—Bacon's Rebellion in Virginia; 300th a.
May 14, 1796	—Smallpox vaccination discovered; 180th a.
May 15 (Sat.)	—Armed Forces Day.
May 19, 1536	—Ann Boleyn beheaded; 440th a.
May 22 (Sat.)	—National Maritime Day.
May 25, 1926	—Mammoth Cave Natl. Park established; 50th a.
May 29, 1876	—Final U.S.-Canada border demarcation; 100th a.
May 30 (Sun.)	—Indianapolis 500.
May 31 (Mon.)	—Memorial Day.
June 1, 1926	—Marilyn Monroe born; 50th an.
June 11 (Fri.)	—Kamehameha Day (in Hawaii).
June 14 (Mon.)	—Flag Day.
June 15, 1836	—Arkansas enters Union; 140th a.
June 19, 1846	—First organized baseball; 130th a.
June 20 (Sun.)	—Father's Day.
June 21 (Mon.)	—Summer begins, 6:24 AM.
June 25, 1876	—Custer's Last Stand; 100th a.
July 1 (Thurs.)	—Dominion Day in Canada.
July 4 (Sun.)	—Bicentennial Independence Day.
July 14 (Wed.)	—Bastille Day in France.
July 15, 1606	—Rembrandt van Rijn born; 370th a.
July 17 (Sat.)	—Summer Olympics begin.
July 25 (Sun.)	—Commonwealth Day (in Puerto Rico).
Aug. 1, 1876	—Colorado enters Union; 100th a.
Aug. 4, 1916	—U.S. gets Virgin Is.; 60th a.
Aug. 6, 1926	—Gertrude Ederle swims Eng. Channel; 50th a.
Aug. 19 (Thurs.)	—Aviation Day.
Sept. 1, 1916	—U.S. curbs child labor; 60th a.
Sept. 2, 1666	—Great fire of London; 310th a.
Sept. 6 (Mon.)	—Labor Day.
Sept. 8, 1951	—U.S.-Japan peace treaty; 25th a.
Sept. 10, 1846	—Sewing machine patented; 130th a.
Sept. 14, 1901	—McKinley assassinated; 75th a.
Sept. 22 (Wed.)	—Autumn begins, 9:48 AM.
Sept. 24 (Fri.)	—American Indian Day.
Sept. 25 (Sat.)	—Jewish New Year's Day.
Sept. 25, 1926	—Henry Ford sets 40-hour week; 50th a.
Oct. 4 (Mon.)	—Yom Kippur.
Oct. 6, 1876	—Amer. Library Assoc. begun; 100th a.
Oct. 10, 1911	—Chinese Republic founded; 65th a.
Oct. 11 (Mon.)	—Columbus Day.
Oct. 12, 1876	—First cantilever bridge begun (Kentucky R.); 100th a.
Oct. 14, 1066	—Normans defeat English at Battle of Hastings; 910th a.
Oct. 15 (Fri.)	—Poetry Day.
Oct. 25 (Mon.)	—Veterans Day (federal).
Oct. 31 (Sun.)	—Halloween.
Nov. 1 (Mon.)	—All Saint's Day.
Nov. 2 (Tues.)	—Election Day.
Nov. 11 (Thurs.)	—Veteran's Day. (most states)
Nov. 14, 1851	—Melville's Moby Dick published; 125th a.
Nov. 15, 1806	—Pike sights Pike's Peak; 170th a.
Nov. 25 (Thurs.)	—Thanksgiving Day.
Nov. 27, 1826	—First overland trip to California; 150th a.
Dec. 7, 1941	—Japanese attack Pearl Harbor; 35th a.
Dec. 8, 1886	—Amer. Federation of Labor formed; 90th a.
Dec. 11, 1901	—First trans-Atlantic radio transmission; 75th a.
Dec. 21 (Tues.)	—Winter begins, 5:36 PM.
Dec. 22, 1951	—First electricity from nuclear energy; 25th a.
Dec. 25 (Sat.)	—Christmas.
Dec. 28, 1846	—Iowa enters Union; 130th a.
Dec. 31 (Fri.)	—New Year's Eve.

Weights and Measures

Source: National Bureau of Standards, Department of Commerce

U.S. Moving, Inch by 25.4 mm, to Metric System

The U.S. is the only industrial country in the world which is not on the metric system and is not yet involved in an official changeover program. Sen. Claiborne Pell (D.-R.I.) has estimated that the U.S. loses $10 billion to $25 billion a year because U.S. measurements are not compatible with world standards.

On Jul. 2, 1971, following the report of a metric conversion study committee, Commerce Secy. Maurice H. Stans recommended a gradual U.S. changeover during a 10-year period at the end of which the U.S. would be predominantly, but not exclusively, on the metric system. Proposals to that effect are now pending in Congress.

The International System (Metric)

Two systems of weights and measures exist side by side in the United States today, with roughly equal but separate legislative sanction: the U.S. Customary System and the International (Metric) System. Throughout U.S. history, the Customary System (inherited from, but now different from, the British Imperial System) has been, as its name implies, customarily used; a plethora of federal and state legislation has given it, through implication, standing as our primary weights and measures system. However, the Metric System (incorporated in the scientists' new SI or Systeme International d'Unites) is the only system that has ever received specific legislative sanction by Congress. The "Law of 1866" reads:

It shall be lawful throughout the United States of America to employ the weights and measures of the metric system; and no contract or dealing, or pleading in any court, shall be deemed invalid or liable to objection because the weights or measures expressed or referred to therein are weights or measures of the metric system.

Over the last 100 years, the Metric System has seen slow, steadily increasing use in the United States and, today, is of importance nearly equal to the Customary System.

On Feb. 10, 1964, the National Bureau of Standards issued the following bulletin:

Henceforth it shall be the policy of the National Bureau of Standards to use the units of the International System (SI), as adopted by the 11th General Conference on Weights and Measures (October 1960), except when the use of these units would obviously impair communication or reduce the usefulness of a report.

What had been the Metric System became the International System (SI), a more complete scientific system.

Seven units have been adopted to serve as the base for the International System as follows: **Length**—meter; **Mass**—kilogram; **Time**—second; **Electric Current**—ampere; **Thermodynamic Temperature**—kelvin; **Amount of Substance**—Mole; and **Light Intensity**—Candela.

Prefixes

The following prefixes, in combination with the basic unit names, provide the multiples and submultiples in the International System. For example, the unit name "meter," with the prefix "kilo" added, produces "kilometer," meaning "1,000 meters."

Prefix	Symbol	Multiples and Submultiples	Equivalent	Prefix	Symbol	Multiples and Submultiples	Equivalent
tera	T	10^{12}	trillionfold	centi	c	10^{-2}	hundredth part
giga	G	10^{9}	billionfold	milli	m	10^{-3}	thousandth part
mega	M	10^{6}	millionfold	micro	u	10^{-6}	millionth part
kilo	k	10^{3}	thousandfold	nano	n	10^{-9}	billionth part
hecto	h	10^{2}	hundredfold	pico	p	10^{-12}	trillionth part
deka	da	10	tenfold	femto	f	10^{-15}	quadrillionth part
deci	d	10^{-1}	tenth part	atto	a	10^{-18}	quintillionth part

Tables of Metric Weights and Measures

Linear Measure

10 millimeters (mm)	= 1 centimeter (cm)
10 centimeters	= 1 decimeter (dm) = 100 millimeters
10 decimeters	= 1 meter (m) = 1,000 millimeters
10 meters	= 1 dekameter (dam)
10 dekameters	= 1 hectometer (hm) = 100 meters
10 hectometers	= 1 kilometer (km) = 1,000 meters

Area Measure

100 square millimeters (mm²)	= 1 square centimeter (cm²)
10,000 square centimeters	= 1 square meter (m²) = 1,000,000 square millimeters
100 square meters	= 1 are (a)
100 ares	= 1 hectare (ha) = 10,000 square meters
100 hectares	= 1 square kilometer (km²) = 1,000,000 square meters

Volume Measure

10 milliliters (ml)	= 1 centiliter (cl)
10 centiliters	= 1 deciliter (dl) = 100 milliliters

10 deciliters	= 1 liter (l) = 1,000 milliliters
10 liters	= 1 dekaliter (dal)
10 dekaliters	= 1 hectoliter (hl) = 100 liters
10 hectoliters	= 1 kiloliter (kl) = 1,000 liters

Cubic Measure

1,000 cubic millimeters (mm³)	= 1 cubic centimeter (cm³)
1,000 cubic centimeters	= 1 cubic decimeter (dm³) = 1,000,000 cubic millimeters
1,000 cubic decimeters	= 1 cubic meter (m³) = 1 stere = 1,000 cubic decimeters = 1,000,000 cubic meters = 1,000,000,000 cubic millimeters

Weight

10 milligrams (mg)	= 1 centigram (cg)
10 centigrams	= 1 decigram (dg) = 100 milligrams
10 decigrams	= 1 gram (g) = 1,000 milligrams
10 grams	= 1 dekagram (dag)
10 dekagrams	= 1 hectogram (hg) = 100 grams
10 hectograms	= 1 kilogram (kg) = 1,000 grams
1,000 kilograms	= 1 metric ton (t)

Table of United States Customary Weights and Measures

Linear Measure

12 inches (in)	= 1 foot (ft)
3 feet	= 1 yard (yd)
5½ yards	= 1 rod (rd), pole, or perch (16½ feet)
40 rods	= 1 furlong (fur) = 220 yards = 660 feet
8 furlongs	= 1 statute mile (mi) = 1,760 yards = 5,280 feet
3 miles	= 1 league = 5,280 yards = 15,840 feet
6076.11549 feet	= 1 International Nautical Mile

Liquid Measure

When necessary to distinguish the liquid pint or quart from the dry pint or quart, the word "liquid" or the abbreviation "liq" should be used in combination with the name or abbreviation of the liquid unit.

4 gills	= 1 pint (pt) = 28.875 cubic inches
2 pints	= 1 quart (qt) = 57.75 cubic inches
4 quarts	= 1 gallon (gal) = 231 cubic inches = 8 pints = 32 gills

Area Measure

Squares and cubes of units are sometimes abbreviated by using "superior" figures. For example, ft² means square foot, and ft³ means cubic foot.

144 square inches	= 1 square foot (ft²)
9 square feet	= 1 square yard (yd²)=1,296 square inches
30¹/₄ square yards	= 1 square rod (rd²)=272¹/₄ square feet
160 square rods	= 1 acre=4,840 square yards= 43,560 square feet
640 acres	= 1 square mile (mi²)
1 mile square	= 1 section (of land)
6 miles square	= 1 township=36 sections=36 square miles

Cubic Measure

1,728 cubic inches (in³)	= 1 cubic foot (ft³)
27 cubic feet	= 1 cubic yard (yd³)

Gunter's or Surveyors' Chain Measure

7.92 inches (in)	= 1 link
100 links	= 1 chain (ch)=4 rods=66 feet
80 chains	= 1 statute mile (mi)=320 rods =5,280 feet.

Troy Weight

24 grains	= 1 pennyweight (dwt)
20 pennyweights	= 1 ounce troy (oz t)=480 grains
12 ounces troy	= 1 pound troy (lb t)=240 pennyweights=5,760 grains

Dry Measure

When necessary to distinguish the dry pint or quart from the liquid pint or quart, the word "dry" should be used in combination with the name or abbreviation of the dry unit.

2 pints (pt)	= 1 quart (qt)(=67.2006 cubic inches)
8 quarts	= 1 peck (pk)(=537.605 cubic inches) 16 pints
4 pecks	= 1 bushel (bu) (=2,150.42 cubic inches)=32 quarts

Avoirdupois Weight

When necessary to distinguish the avoirdupois ounce or pound from the troy ounce or pound, the word "avoirdupois" or the abbreviation "avdp" should be used in combination with the name or abbreviation of the avoirdupois unit.

(The "grain" is the same in avoirdupois and troy weight.)

27 11/32 grains	= 1 dram (dr)
16 drams	= 1 ounce (oz)=437¹/₂ grains
16 ounces	= 1 pound (lb)=256 drams 7,000 grains
100 pounds	= 1 hundredweight (cwt)°
20 hundredweights	= 1 ton=2,000 pounds°

In "gross" or "long" measure, the following values are recognized:

112 pounds	= 1 gross or long hundredweight°
20 gross or long hundredweights	= 1 gross or long ton=2,240 pounds°

°When the terms "hundredweight" and "ton" are used unmodified, they are commonly understood to mean the 100-pound hundredweight and the 2,000-pound ton, respectively: these units may be designated "net" or "short" when necessary to distinguish them from the corresponding units in gross or long measure.

Tables of Equivalents

When the name of a unit is enclosed in brackets thus, [71 hand], this indicates (1) that the unit is not in general current use in the United States, or (2) that the unit is believed to be based on "custom and usage" rather than on formal definition. **See above about superior figures in Area Measure.**

Equivalents involving decimals are, in most instances, rounded off to the third decimal place except where they are exact, in which cases these exact equivalents are so designated.

Lengths

Angstrom (A)	0.1 nanometer (exactly) 0.000 1 micron (exactly) 0.000 000 1 millimeter (exactly) 0.000 000 004 inch
1 cable's length	120 fathoms 720 feet 219.456 meters (exactly)
1 centimeter (cm)	0.3937 inch
1 chain (ch) (Gunter's or surveyors)	66 feet 20.1168 meters (exactly)
1 chain (engineers)	100 feet 30.48 meters (exactly)
1 decimeter (dm)	3.937 inches
1 dekameter (dam)	32.808 feet
1 fathom	6 feet 1.8288 meters (exactly)
1 foot (ft)	0.3048 meters (exactly)
1 furlong (fur)	10 chains (surveyors) 660 feet 220 yards ¹/₈ statute mile 201.168 meters
[1 hand]	4 inches
1 inch (in)	2.54 centimeters (exactly)
1 kilometer (km)	0.621 mile 3,280.8 feet
1 league (land)	3 statute miles 4.828 kilometers
1 link (Gunter's or surveyors)	7.92 inches 0.201 meter
1 link (engineers)	1 foot 0.305 meter
1 meter (m)	39.37 inches 1.094 yards
1 micron (μ) [the Greek letter mu]	0.001 millimeter (exactly) 0.000 039 37 inch
1 mil	0.001 inch (exactly) 0.025 4 millimeter (exactly)

1 mile (mi) (statute or land)	5,280 feet 1.609 kilometers
1 International Nautical Mile (INM)	1,852 kilometers (exactly) 1.150779 statute miles 6,076.11549 feet
1 millimeter (mm)	0.039 37 inch
1 nanometer (nm)	0.001 micron (exactly) 0.000 000 039 37 inch (exactly)
1 point (typography)	0.013 837 inch (exactly) 0.351 millimeter
1 rod (rd), pole, or perch	16¹/₂ feet 5¹/₂ yards 5.029 meters
1 yard (yd)	0.9144 meter (exactly)

Areas or Surfaces

1 acre	43,560 square feet 4,840 square yards 0.405 hectare
1 are (a)	119.599 square yards 0.025 acre
1 hectare (ha)	2.171 acres
[1 square (building)]	100 square feet
1 square centimeter (cm²)	0.155 square inch
1 square decimeter (dm²)	15.500 square inches
1 square foot (ft²)	929.030 square centimeters
1 square inch (in²)	6.452 square centimeters
1 square kilometer (km²)	247.105 acres 0.386 square mile
1 square meter (m²)	1,196 square yards 10.764 square feet
1 square mile (mi²)	258.999 hectares
1 square millimeter (mm²)	0.002 square inch
1 square rod (rd²)sq. pole, or sq. perch	25.293 square meters
1 square yard (yd²)	0.836 square meter

Capacities or Volumes

1 barrel (bbl) liquid	31 to 42 gallons°

°There are a variety of "barrels," established by law or usage. For example: federal taxes on fermented liquors are based on a barrel of 31 gallons: many state laws fix the "barrel for liquids" as 31¹/₂ gallons; one state fixes a 36-gallon barrel for cistern measurement; federal law recognizes a 40-gallon barrel for "proof spirits"; by custom, 42 gallons comprise a barrel of crude oil or petroleum products for statistical purposes, and this equivalent is recognized "for liquids" by four states.

1 barrel (bbl), standard, for fruits, vegetables, and other dry commodities except dry cranberries	7,056 cubic inches 105 dry quarts 3.281 bushels, struck measure
1 barrel (bbl), standard, cranberry	5,826 cubic inches 86⁴⁶/₆₄ dry quarts 2.709 bushels, struck measure
1 bushel (bu) (U.S.) (struck measure)	2,150.42 cubic inches (exactly) 35.238 liters 2,747.715 cubic inches
[1 bushel, heaped (U.S.)]	1.278 bushels, struck measure°

°Frequently recognized as 1¼ bushels, struck measure.

[1 bushel (bu) (British Imperial) (struck measure)]	1.032 U.S. bushels, struck measure 2,219.36 cubic inches
1 cord (cd) (firewood)	128 cubic feet
1 cubic centimeter (cm³)	0.061 cubic inch
1 cubic decimeter (dm³)	61.024 cubic inches
1 cubic inch (in³)	0.554 fluid ounce 4.433 fluid drams 16.387 cubic centimeters
1 cubic foot (ft³)	7.481 gallons 28.317 cubic decimeters
1 cubic meter (m³)	1.308 cubic yards
1 cubic yard (yd³)	0.765 cubic meter
1 cup, measuring	8 fluid ounces ½ liquid pint
[1 dram, fluid (fl dr) (British)]	0.961 U.S. fluid dram 0.217 cubic inch 3.552 milliliters
1 dekaliter (dal)	2.642 gallons 1.135 pecks
1 gallon (gal) (U.S.)	231 cubic inches 3.785 liters 0.833 British gallon 128 U.S. fluid ounces
[1 gallon (gal) British Imperial]	277.42 cubic inches 1.201 U.S. gallons 4.546 liters 160 British fluid ounces
1 gill	7.219 cubic inches 4 fluid ounces 0.118 liter
1 hectoliter (hl)	26.417 gallons 2.838 bushels
1 liter	1.057 liquid quarts 0.908 dry quart 61.024 cubic inches
1 milliliter (ml)	0.271 fluid dram 16.231 minims 0.061 cubic inch
1 ounce, liquid (U.S.)	1.805 cubic inches 29.573 milliliters 1.041 British fluid ounces
[1 ounce, fluid (fl oz) (British)]	0.961 U.S. fluid ounce 1.734 cubic inches 28.412 milliliters

1 peck (pk)	8.810 liters
1 pint (pt), dry	33.600 cubic inches 0.551 liter
1 pint (pt) liquid	28.875 cubic inches (exactly) 0.473 liter
1 quart (qt) dry (U.S.)	67.201 cubic inches 1.101 liters 0.969 British quart
1 quart (qt) liquid (U.S.)	57.75 cubic in (exactly) 0.946 liter 0.833 British quart
[1 quart (qt) (British)]	69.354 cubic inches 1.032 U.S. dry quarts 1.201 U.S. liquid quarts
1 tablespoon	3 teaspoons° 4 fluid drams ½ fluid ounce
1 teaspoon	⅓ tablespoon° 1⅓ fluid drams°

°The equivalent "1 teaspoon — 1⅓ fluid drams" has been found by the bureau to correspond more closely with the actual capacities of "measuring" and silver teaspoons than the equivalent "1 teaspoon — 1 fluid dram" which is given by many dictionaries.

Weights or Masses

1 assay ton∞ (AT)	29.167 grams

∞Used in assaying. The assay ton bears the same relation to the milligram that a ton of 2,000 pounds avoirdupois bears to the ounce troy; hence the weight in milligrams of precious metal obtained from one assay ton of ore gives directly the number of troy ounces to the net ton.

1 carat (c)	200 milligrams 3.086 grains
1 dram avoirdupois (dr avdp) gamma, see microgram	27¹¹/₃₂ (=27.344) grains 1.772 grams
1 grain	64.799 milligrams
1 gram	15.432 grains 0.035 ounce, avoirdupois
1 hundredweight, gross or long∞ (gross cwt)	112 pounds 50.802 kilograms
1 hundredweight, net or short (cwt. or net cwt.)	100 pounds 45.359 kilograms
1 kilogram (kg)	2.205 pounds
1 microgram (γ[the Greek letter gamma)	0.000001 gram (exactly)
1 milligram (mg)	0.015 grain
1 ounce, avoirdupois (oz avdp)	437.5 grains (exactly) 0.911 troy ounce 28.350 grams
1 ounce troy (oz t)	480 grains 1.097 avoirdupois ounces 31.103 grams
1 pennyweight (dwt)	1.555 grams
1 pound, avoirdupois (lb avdp)	7,000 grains 1.215 troy pounds 453.592 37 grams (exactly)
1 pound, troy (lb t)	5,760 grains 0.823 avoirdupois pound 373.242 grams
1 ton, gross or long ∞∞∞ (gross tn)	2,240 pounds° 1.12 net tons (exactly) 1.016 metric tons

∞∞∞The gross or long ton and hundredweight are used commercially in the United States to only a limited extent, usually in restricted industrial fields. These units are the same as British "ton" and "hundredweight."

1 ton, metric (t)	2,204.623 pounds 0.984 gross ton 1.102 net tons
1 ton, net or short (sh ton)	2,000 pounds 0.893 gross ton 0.907 metric ton

Density of Gases and Vapors

Source: National Bureau of Standards (Grams per liter)

Gas	Wt.	Gas	Wt.	Gas	Wt.
Acetylene	1.171	Ethylene	1.260	Methyl fluoride	1.545
Air	1.293	Fluorine	1.696	Mono methylamine	1.38
Ammonia	.759	Helium	.178	Neon	.900
Argon	1.784	Hydrogen	.090	Nitric oxide	1.341
Arsene	3.48	Hydrogen bromide	3.50	Nitrogen	1.250
Butane-iso	2.60	Hydrogen chloride	1.639	Nitrosyl chloride	2.99
Butane-n	2.519	Hydrogen iodide	5.724	Nitrous oxide	1.997
Carbon dioxide	1.977	Hydrogen selenide	3.66	Oxygen	1.429
Carbon monoxide	1.250	Hydrogen sulfide	1.539	Phosphine	1.48
Carbon oxysulfide	2.72	Krypton	3.745	Propane	2.020
Chlorine	3.214	Methane	.717	Silicon tetrafluoride	4.67
Chlorine monoxide	3.89	Methyl chloride	2.25	Sulfur dioxide	2.927
Ethane	1.356	Methyl ether	2.091	Xenon	5.897

Tables of Interrelation of Units of Measurement

Bold face type indicates exact values

Units of Length

Units	Inches	Links	Feet	Yards	Rods	Chains	Miles	Cm	Meters
1 inch=	1	0.126 263	0.083 333	0.027 778	0.005 051	0.001 263	0.000 016	2.54	0.025 4
1 link=	7.92	1	0.66	0.22	0.04	0.01	0.000 125	20.117	0.201 168
1 foot=	12	1.515 152	1	0.333 333	0.060 606	0.015 152	0.000 189	30.48	0.304 8
1 yard=	36	4.545 45	3	1	0.181 818	0.045 455	0.000 568	91.44	0.914 4
1 rod=	198	25	16.5	5.5	1	0.25	0.003 125	502.92	5.029 2
1 chain=	792	100	66	22	4	1	0.012 5	2011.68	20.116 8
1 mile=	63.360	8000	5280	1760	320	80	1	160 934.4	1609.344
1 cm=	0.3937	0.049 710	0.032 808	0.010 936	0.001 988	0.000 497	0.000 006	1	0.01
1 meter=	39.37	4.970 970	3.280 840	1.093 613	0.198 839	0.049 710	0.000 621	100	1

Units of Area

Units	Sq. inches	Sq. links	Sq. feet	Sq. yards	Sq. rods	Sq. chains
1 sq. inch=	1	.015 942 3	0.006 944	0.000 771 605	0.000 025 5	0.000 001 594
1 sq. link=	62.726 4	1	0.435 6	0.0484	0.0016	0.000 1
1 sq. foot=	144	2.295 684	1	0.111 111 1	0.003 673 09	0.000 229 568
1 sq. yard=	1296	20.661 16	9	1	0.033 057 85	0.002 066 12
1 sq. rod=	39 204	625	272.25	30.25	1	0.062 5
1 sq. chain=	627 264	10 000	4356	484	16	1
1 acre=	6 272 640	100 000	43 560	4 840	160	10
1 sq. mile=	4 014 489 600	64 000 000	27 878 400	3 097 600	102 400	6400
1 sq. cm=	0.155 000 3	0.002 471 05	0.001 076	0.000 119 599	0.000 003 954	0.000 000 247
1 sq. meter=	1550.003	24.710 54	10.763 91	1.195 990	0.039 536 86	0.002 471 054
1 hectare=	15 500 031	247.105	107 639.1	11 959.90	395.368 6	24.710 54

Units	Acres	Sq. miles	Sq. cm	Sq. meters	Hectares
1 sq. inch=	0.000 000 159 423	0.000 000 000 249 10	6.451 6	0.000 645 16	0.000 000 065
1 sq. link=	0.000 01	0.000 000 015 625	404.685 642 24	0.040 468 56	0.000 004 047
1 sq. foot=	0.000 022 956 84	0.000 000 035 870 06	929.030 4	0.092 903 04	0.000 009 290
1 sq. yard=	0.000 206 611 6	0.000 000 322 830 6	8 361.273 6	0.836 127 36	0.000 083 613
1 sq. rod=	0.006 25	0.000 009 765 625	252 928.526 4	25.292 852 64	0.002 529 285
1 sq. chain=	0.1	0.000 156 25	4 046 856	404.685 642 24	0.040 468 564
1 acre=	1	0.001 562 5	40 468 564	4046.856 422 4	0.404 685 642
1 sq. mile=	640	1	25 899 881 103	2 589 988.11	258.998 811 034
1 sq. cm=	0.000 000 024 711	0.000 000 000 038 610	1	0.000 1	0.000 000 01
1 sq. meter=	0.000 247 105 4	0.000 000 386 102 2	10 000	1	0.0001
1 hectare=	2.471 054	0.003 861 022	100 000 000	10 000	1

Units of Mass Not Greater Than Pounds and Kilograms

Units	Grains	Pennyweights	Avdp drams	Avdp ounces
1 grain=	1	0.041 666 67	0.036 571 43	0.002 285 71
1 pennyweight=	24	1	0.877 714 3	0.054 857 14
1 dram avdp=	27.343 75	1,139 323	1	0.062 5
1 ounce avdp=	437.5	18.229 17	16	1
1 ounce troy=	480	20	17.554 29	1.097 143
1 pound troy=	5760	240	210.651 4	13.165 71
1 pound avdp=	7000	291.666 7	256	16
1 milligram=	0.015 432	0.000 643 015	0.000 564 383	0.000 035 274
1 gram=	15.432 36	0.643 014 9	0.564 383 4	0.035 273 96
1 kilogram=	15 432.36	643.014 9	564.383 4	35.273 96

Units	Troy ounces	Troy pounds	Avdp pounds	Milligrams	Grams	Kilograms
1 grain=	0.002 083 33	0.000 173 611	0.000 142 857	64.798 91	0.064 798 91	0.000 064 799
1 pennyw't.=	0.05	0.004 166 667	0.003 428 571	1555.173 84	1.555 173 84	0.001 555 174
1 dram avdp=	0.056 966 15	0.004 747 179	0.003 906 25	1771.845 195	1.771 845 195	0.001 771 845
1 oz avdp=	0.911 458 3	0.075 954 86	0.062 5	28 349.523 125	28.349 523 125	0.028 349 52
1 oz troy=	1	0.083 333 333	0.068 571 43	31 103.476 8	31.103 476 8	0.031 103 48
1 lb troy=	12	1	0.822 857 1	373 241.721 6	373.241 721 6	0.373 241 722
1 lb avdp=	14.583 33	1.215 278	1	453 592.37	453.592 37	0.453 592 37
1 milligram=	0.000 032 151	0.000 002 679	0.000 002 205	1	0.001	0.000 001
1 gram=	0.032 150 75	0.002 679 229	0.002 204 623	1000	1	0.001
1 kilogram=	32.150 75	2.679 229	2.204 623	1000 000	1000	1

Units of Mass Not Less Than Avoirdupois Ounces

Units	Avdp oz	Avdp lb	Short cwt	Short tons	Long tons	Kilograms	Metric tons
1 oz av=	1	0.0625	0.000 625	0.000 031 25	0.000 027 902	0.028 349 523	0.000 028 350
1 lb av=	16	1	0.01	0.000 5	0.000 446 429	0.453 592 37	0.000 453 592
1 sh cwt=	1 600	100	1	0.05	0.044 642 86	45.359 237	0.045 359 237
1 sh ton=	32 000	2000	20	1	0.892 857 1	907.184 74	0.907 184 74
1 long ton=	35 840	2240	22.4	1.12	1	1016.046 908 8	1.016 046 909
1 kg=	35.273 96	2.204 623	0.022 046 23	0.001 102 311	0.000 094 207	1	0.001
1 metric ton=	35 273.96	2204.623	22.046 23	1.102 311	0.984 206 5	1000	1

Continued on next page

Continued from previous page

Units of Volume

Units	Cubic inches	Cubic feet	Cubic yards	Cubic cm	Cubic dm	Cubic meters
1 cubic inch=	1	0.000 578 704	0.000 021 433	16.387 064	0.016 387	0.000 016 387
1 cubic foot=	1728	1	0.037 037 04	28 316.846 592	28.316 847	0.028 316 847
1 cubic yard=	46 656	27	1	764 554.857 984	764.554 858	0.764 554 858
1 cubic cm=	0.061 023 74	0.000 035 315	0.000 001 308	1	0.001	0.000 000 001
1 cubic dm=	61.023 74	0.035 314 67	0.000 001 307 951	1 000	1	0.001
1 cubic meter	61 023.74	35.314 67	1.307 951	1 000 000	1000	1

Units of Capacity (Liquid Measure)

Units	Minims	Fluid drams	Fluid ounces	Gills	Liquid pt
1 minim=	1	0.016 666 7	0.002 083 33	0.000 520 833	0.000 130 208
1 liquid dram=	60	1	0.125	0.031 25	0.007 812 5
1 liquid ounce=	480	8	1	0.25	0.062 5
1 gill=	1920	32	4	1	0.25
1 liquid pint=	7680	128	16	4	1
1 liquid quart=	15 360	256	32	8	2
1 gallon=	61 440	1024	128	32	8
1 cubic inch=	265.974	4.432 900	0.554 112 6	0.138 528 1	0.034 632 03
1 cubic foot=	459 603.1	7660.052	957.506 5	239.376 6	59.844 16
1 milliliter=	16.230 73	0.270 512 18	0.033 814 02	0.008 453 506	.002 113 376
1 liter=	16 230.73	270.512 18	33.814 02	8.453 506	2.113 376

Units	Liquid quarts	Gallons	Cubic inches	Cubic feet	Liters
1 minim=	0.000 065 104 17	0.000 016 276 04	0.003 759 766	0.000 002 175 790	0.000 061 611 52
1 liq. dram=	0.003 906 25	0.000 976 562 5	0.225 585 9	0.000 130 547 4	0.03 696 691
1 liquid oz=	0.031 25	0.007 812 5	1.804 687 5	0.001 044 379	0.029 573 53
1 gill=	0.125	0.031 25	7.218 75	0.004 177 517	0.118 294 118 25
1 liquid pt=	0.5	0.125	28.875	0.016 710 07	0.473 176 473
1 liquid qt=	1	0.25	57.75	0.033 420 14	0.946 352 946
1 gallon=	4	1	231	0.133 680 6	3.785 411 784
1 cubic in.=	0.017 316 02	0.004 329 004	1	0.000 578 703 7	0.016 387 064
1 cubic foot=	29.922 08	7.480 519	1728	1	28.316 846 592
1 liter=	1.056 688	0.264 172 05	61.023 74	0.035 314 67	1

Units of Capacity (Dry Measure)

Units	Dry pints	Dry quarts	Pecks	Bushels	Cubic in.	Liters
1 dry pint=	1	0.5	0.062 5	0.015 625	33.600 312 5	0.550 610 47
1 dry quart=	2	1	0.125	0.031 25	67.200 625	1.101 220 9
1 peck=	16	8	1	0.25	537.605	8.809 767 5
1 bushel=	64	32	4	1	2150.42	35.239 07
1 cubic inch=	0.029 761 6	0.014 880 8	0.001 860 10	0.000 465 025	1	0.016 387 064
1 liter=	1.816 166	0.908 083	0.113 510 37	0.028 377 59	61.023 74	1

Weight of Water

1	cubic inch............ .0360	pound	1	imperial gallon....... 10.0	pounds
12	cubic inches.......... .433	pound	11.2	imperial gallons...... 112.0	pounds
1	cubic foot............ 62.4	pounds	224	imperial gallons...... 2240.0	pounds
1	cubic foot............ 7.48052	U.S. gal	1	U. S. gallon........... 8.33	pounds
1.8	cubic feet............ 112.0	pounds	13.45	U.S. gallons.......... 112.0	pounds
35.96	cubic feet............ 2240.0	pounds	269.0	U. S. gallons.......... 2240.0	pounds

Temperature Conversion Table

The numbers in **bold face type** refer to the temperature either in degrees Celsius or Fahrenheit which are to be converted. If converting from degrees Fahrenheit to Celsius, the equivalent will be found in the column on the left, while if converting from degrees Celsius to Fahrenheit the answer will be found in the column on the right.

For temperatures not shown. To convert Fahrenheit to Celsius subtract 32 degrees and multiply by 5, divide by 9; to convert Celsius to Fahrenheit, multiply by 9, divide by 5 and add 32 degrees.

Celsius		Fahrenheit	Celsius		Fahrenheit	Celsius		Fahrenheit
—273.2	—459.7	....	— 17.8	0	32	35.0	95	203
—184	—300	....	— 12.2	10	50	36.7	98	208.4
—169	—273	—459.4	— 6.67	20	68	37.8	100	212
—157	—250	—418	— 1.11	30	86	43	110	230
—129	—200	—328	4.44	40	104	49	120	248
—101	—150	—238	10.0	50	122	54	130	266
— 73.3	—100	—148	15.6	60	140	60	140	284
— 45.6	— 50	— 58	21.1	70	158	66	150	302
— 40.0	— 40	— 40	23.9	75	167	93	200	392
— 34.4	— 30	— 22	26.7	80	176	121	250	482
— 28.9	— 20	— 4	29.4	85	185	149	300	572
— 23.3	— 10	14	32.2	90	194			

Water boils at 212° Fahrenheit at sea level. For every 550 feet above sea level, boiling point of water is lower by about 1° Fahrenheit. Methyl alcohol boils at 148° Fahrenheit. Average human oral temperature, 98.6° Fahrenheit. Water freezes at 32° Fahrenheit. Although "Centigrade" is still frequently used, the International Committee on Weights and Measures and the National Bureau of Standards have recommended since 1948 that this scale be called "Celsius."

Squares, Square Roots, Cubes and Cube Roots of Nos. 1 to 100

No.	Sq.	Cube	Sq. Root	Cube Root	No.	Sq.	Cube	Sq. Root	Cube Root	No.	Sq.	Cube	Sq. Root	Cube Root
1	1.000	1.000	1.000	1.000	35	1225	42875	5.916	3.271	68	4624	314432	8.246	4.081
2	4	8	1.414	1.259	36	1296	46656	6.000	3.301	69	4761	328509	8.306	4.101
3	9	27	1.732	1.442	37	1369	50653	6.082	3.332	70	4900	343000	8.366	4.121
4	16	64	2.000	1.587	38	1444	54872	6.164	3.362	71	5041	357911	8.426	4.140
5	25	125	2.236	1.710	39	1521	59319	6.245	3.391	72	5184	373248	8.485	4.160
6	36	216	2.449	1.817	40	1600	64000	6.324	3.420	73	5329	389017	8.544	4.179
7	49	343	2.645	1.913	41	1681	68921	6.403	3.448	74	5476	405224	8.602	4.198
8	64	512	2.828	2.000	42	1764	74088	6.480	3.476	75	5625	421875	8.660	4.217
9	81	729	3.000	2.080	43	1849	79507	6.557	3.503	76	5776	438976	8.717	4.235
10	100	1000	3.162	2.154	44	1936	85184	6.633	3.530	77	5929	456533	8.775	4.254
11	121	1331	3.316	2.224	45	2025	91125	6.708	3.556	78	6084	474552	8.831	4.272
12	144	1728	3.464	2.289	46	2116	97336	6.782	3.583	79	6241	493039	8.888	4.290
13	169	2197	3.605	2.351	47	2209	103823	6.855	3.608	80	6400	512000	8.944	4.308
14	196	2744	3.741	2.410	48	2304	110592	6.928	3.634	81	6561	531441	9.000	4.326
15	225	3375	3.873	2.466	49	2401	117649	7.000	3.659	82	6724	551368	9.055	4.344
16	256	4096	4.000	2.519	50	2500	125000	7.071	3.684	83	6889	571787	9.110	4.362
17	289	4913	4.123	2.571	51	2601	132651	7.141	3.708	84	7056	592704	9.165	4.379
18	324	5832	4.242	2.620	52	2704	140608	7.211	3.732	85	7225	614125	9.219	4.396
19	361	6859	4.358	2.668	53	2809	148877	7.280	3.756	86	7396	636056	9.273	4.414
20	400	8000	4.472	2.714	54	2916	157464	7.348	3.779	87	7569	658503	9.327	4.431
21	441	9261	4.582	2.758	55	3025	166375	7.416	3.803	88	7744	681472	9.380	4.448
22	484	10648	4.690	2.802	56	3136	175616	7.483	3.825	89	7921	704969	9.434	4.464
23	529	12167	4.795	2.843	57	3249	185193	7.549	3.848	90	8100	729000	9.486	4.481
24	576	13824	4.899	2.884	58	3364	195112	7.615	3.870	91	8281	753571	9.539	4.497
25	625	15625	5.000	2.924	59	3481	205379	7.681	3.893	92	8464	778688	9.591	4.514
26	676	17576	5.099	2.962	60	3600	216000	7.746	3.914	93	8649	804357	9.643	4.530
27	729	19683	5.196	3.000	61	3721	226981	7.810	3.936	94	8836	830584	9.695	4.546
28	784	21952	5.291	3.036	62	3844	238328	7.874	3.957	95	9025	857375	9.746	4.562
29	841	24389	5.385	3.072	63	3969	250047	7.937	3.979	96	9216	884736	9.798	4.578
30	900	27000	5.477	3.107	64	4096	262144	8.000	4.000	97	9409	912673	9.848	4.594
31	961	29791	5.567	3.141	65	4225	274625	8.062	4.020	98	9604	941192	9.899	4.610
32	1024	32768	5.656	3.174	66	4356	287496	8.124	4.041	99	9801	970299	9.949	4.626
33	1089	35937	5.744	3.207	67	4489	300763	8.185	4.061	100	10000	1000000	10.000	4.641
34	1156	39304	5.831	3.239										

Square Roots and Cube Roots, 1000 to 2000

No.	Square Root	Cube Root	No.	Square Root	Cube Root	No.	Square Root	Cube Root	No.	Square Root	Cube Root
1000	31.62	10.00	1255	35.43	10.79	1510	38.86	11.47	1765	42.01	12.09
1005	31.70	10.02	1260	35.50	10.80	1515	38.92	11.49	1770	42.07	12.10
1010	31.78	10.03	1265	35.57	10.82	1520	38.99	11.50	1775	42.13	12.11
1020	31.94	10.07	1275	35.71	10.84	1530	39.12	11.52	1785	42.25	12.13
1025	32.02	10.08	1280	35.78	10.86	1535	39.18	11.54	1790	42.31	12.14
1030	32.09	10.10	1285	35.85	10.87	1540	39.24	11.55	1795	42.37	12.15
1035	32.17	10.12	1290	35.92	10.89	1545	39.31	11.56	1800	42.43	12.16
1045	32.33	10.15	1300	36.06	10.91	1555	39.43	11.59	1810	42.54	12.19
1050	32.40	10.16	1305	36.12	10.93	1560	39.50	11.60	1815	42.60	12.20
1060	32.56	10.20	1315	36.26	10.96	1570	39.62	11.62	1825	42.72	12.22
1065	32.63	10.21	1320	36.33	10.97	1575	39.69	11.63	1830	42.78	12.23
1075	32.79	10.24	1330	36.47	11.00	1585	39.81	11.66	1840	42.90	12.25
1080	32.86	10.26	1335	36.54	11.01	1590	39.87	11.67	1845	42.95	12.26
1085	32.94	10.28	1340	36.61	11.02	1595	39.94	11.68	1850	43.01	12.28
1090	33.02	10.29	1345	36.67	11.04	1600	40.00	11.70	1855	43.07	12.29
1095	33.09	10.31	1350	36.74	11.05	1605	40.06	11.71	1860	43.13	12.30
1100	33.17	10.32	1355	36.81	11.07	1610	40.12	11.72	1865	43.19	12.31
1105	33.24	10.34	1360	36.88	11.08	1615	40.19	11.73	1870	43.24	12.32
1110	33.32	10.35	1365	36.95	11.09	1620	40.25	11.74	1875	43.30	12.33
1115	33.39	10.37	1370	37.01	11.11	1625	40.31	11.76	1880	43.36	12.34
1120	33.47	10.38	1375	37.08	11.12	1630	40.37	11.77	1885	43.42	12.35
1125	33.54	10.40	1380	37.15	11.13	1635	40.44	11.78	1890	43.47	12.36
1130	33.62	10.42	1385	37.22	11.15	1640	40.50	11.79	1895	43.53	12.37
1135	33.69	10.43	1390	37.28	11.16	1645	40.56	11.80	1900	43.59	12.39
1140	33.76	10.45	1395	37.35	11.17	1650	40.62	11.82	1905	43.65	12.40
1145	33.84	10.46	1400	37.42	11.19	1655	40.68	11.83	1910	43.70	12.41
1150	33.91	10.48	1405	37.48	11.20	1660	40.74	11.84	1915	43.76	12.42
1155	33.99	10.49	1410	37.55	11.21	1665	40.80	11.85	1920	43.82	12.43
1160	34.06	10.51	1415	37.62	11.23	1670	40.87	11.86	1925	43.87	12.44
1165	34.13	10.52	1420	37.68	11.24	1675	40.93	11.88	1930	43.93	12.45
1170	34.21	10.54	1425	37.75	11.25	1680	40.99	11.89	1935	43.99	12.46
1175	34.28	10.55	1430	37.82	11.27	1685	41.05	11.90	1940	44.05	12.47
1180	34.35	10.57	1435	37.88	11.28	1690	41.11	11.91	1945	44.10	12.48
1185	34.42	10.58	1440	37.95	11.29	1695	41.17	11.92	1950	44.16	12.49
1190	34.50	10.60	1445	38.01	11.31	1700	41.23	11.93	1955	44.22	12.50
1195	34.57	10.61	1450	38.08	11.32	1705	41.29	11.95	1960	44.27	12.51
1200	34.64	10.63	1455	38.14	11.33	1710	41.35	11.96	1965	44.33	12.53
1205	34.71	10.64	1460	38.21	11.34	1715	41.41	11.97	1970	44.38	12.54
1210	34.79	10.66	1465	38.28	11.36	1720	41.47	11.98	1975	44.44	12.55
1215	34.86	10.67	1470	38.34	11.37	1725	41.53	11.99	1980	44.50	12.56
1220	34.93	10.69	1475	38.41	11.38	1730	41.59	12.00	1985	44.55	12.57
1225	35.00	10.70	1480	38.47	11.40	1735	41.65	12.02	1990	44.61	12.58
1235	35.14	10.73	1490	38.60	11.42	1745	41.77	12.04	1995	44.67	12.59
1245	35.28	10.76	1500	38.73	11.45	1755	41.89	12.06	2000	44.72	12.60

Electrical Units

The watt is the unit of power (electrical, mechanical, thermal, etc.). Electrical power is given by the product of the voltage and the current.

Energy is sold by the joule, but in common practice the billing of electrical energy is expressed in terms of the kilowatt-hour, which is 3,600,000 joules or 3.6 megajoules.

The horsepower is a non-metric unit sometimes used in mechanics. It is equal to 746 watts.

The ohm is the unit of electrical resistance and represents the physical property of a conductor which offers a resistance to the flow of electricity, permitting just 1 ampere to flow at 1 volt of pressure.

Mathematical Formulas

To find the CIRCUMFERENCE of a:

Circle — Multiply the diameter by 3.14159265 (usually 3.1416).—

To find the AREA of a:

Circle—Multiply the square of the diameter by .785398 (usually .7854).

Rectangle—Multiply the length of the base by the height.

Sphere (surface)—Multiply the square of the radius by 3.1416 and multiply by 4.

Square—Square the length of one side.

Trapezoid—add the two parallel sides, multiply by the height and divide by 2.

Triangle—Multiply the base by the height and divide by 2.

To find the VOLUME of a:

Cone—Multiply the square of the radius of the base by 3.1416, multiply by the height, and divide by 3.

Cube—Cube the length of one edge.

Cylinder—Multiply the square of the radius of the base by 3.1416 and multiply by the height.

Pyramid—Multiply the area of the base by the height and divide by 3.

Rectangular Prism—Multiply the length by the width by the height.

Sphere—Multiply the cube of the radius by 3.1416, multiply by 4 and divide by 3.

Multiplication and Division Table

A number in the top line (19) multiplied by a number in the last column on the left (18) produces the number where the top line and the side line meet (342), and so on throughout the table.

A number in the table (342) divided by the number at the top of that column (19) results in the number (18) at the extreme left; also, a number in the table (342) divided by the number (18) at the extreme left gives the number (19) at the top of the column, and so throughout the table.

1	2	3	4	5	6	7	8	9	10	11	12	13	14	15	16	17	18	19	20	21	22	23	24	25	1
2	4	6	8	10	12	14	16	18	20	22	24	26	28	30	32	34	36	38	40	42	44	46	48	50	2
3	6	9	12	15	18	21	24	27	30	33	36	39	42	45	48	51	54	57	60	63	66	69	72	75	3
4	8	12	16	20	24	28	32	36	40	44	48	52	56	60	64	68	72	76	80	84	88	92	96	100	4
5	10	15	20	25	30	35	40	45	50	55	60	65	70	75	80	85	90	95	100	105	110	115	120	125	5
6	12	18	24	30	36	42	48	54	60	66	72	78	84	90	96	102	108	114	120	126	132	138	144	150	6
7	14	21	28	35	42	49	56	63	70	77	84	91	98	105	112	119	126	133	140	147	154	161	168	175	7
8	16	24	32	40	48	56	64	72	80	88	96	104	112	120	128	136	144	152	160	168	176	184	192	200	8
9	18	27	36	45	54	63	72	81	90	99	108	117	126	135	144	153	162	171	180	189	198	207	216	225	9
10	20	30	40	50	60	70	80	90	100	110	120	130	140	150	160	170	180	190	200	210	220	230	240	250	10
11	22	33	44	55	66	77	88	99	110	121	132	143	154	165	176	187	198	209	220	231	242	253	264	275	11
12	24	36	48	60	72	84	96	108	120	132	144	156	168	180	192	204	216	228	240	252	264	276	288	300	12
13	26	39	52	65	78	91	104	117	130	143	156	169	182	195	208	221	234	247	260	273	286	299	312	325	13
14	28	42	56	70	84	98	112	126	140	154	168	182	196	210	224	238	252	266	280	294	308	322	336	350	14
15	30	45	60	75	90	105	120	135	150	165	180	195	210	225	240	255	270	285	300	315	330	345	360	375	15
16	32	48	64	80	96	112	128	144	160	176	192	208	224	240	256	272	288	304	320	336	352	368	384	400	16
17	34	51	68	85	102	119	136	153	170	187	204	221	238	255	272	289	306	323	340	357	374	391	408	425	17
18	36	54	72	90	108	126	144	162	180	198	216	234	252	270	288	306	324	342	360	378	396	414	432	450	18
19	38	57	76	95	114	133	152	171	190	209	228	247	266	285	304	323	342	361	380	399	418	437	456	475	19
20	40	60	80	100	120	140	160	180	200	220	240	260	280	300	320	340	360	380	400	420	440	460	480	500	20
21	42	63	84	105	126	147	168	189	210	231	252	273	294	315	336	357	378	399	420	441	462	483	504	525	21
22	44	66	88	110	132	154	176	198	220	242	264	286	308	330	352	374	396	418	440	462	484	506	528	550	22
23	46	69	92	115	138	161	184	207	230	253	276	299	322	345	368	391	414	437	460	483	506	529	552	575	23
24	48	72	96	120	144	168	192	216	240	264	288	312	336	360	384	408	432	456	480	504	528	552	576	600	24
25	50	75	100	125	150	175	200	225	250	275	300	325	350	375	400	425	450	475	500	525	550	575	600	625	25
	2	3	4	5	6	7	8	9	10	11	12	13	14	15	16	17	18	19	20	21	22	23	24	25	

Common Fractions Reduced to Decimals

8ths	16ths	32ds	64ths		8ths	16ths	32ds	64ths		8ths	16ths	32ds	64ths	
			1	.015625				23	.359375				45	.703125
		1	2	.03125	3	6	12	24	.375				46	.71875
			3	.046875				25	.390625				47	.734375
	1	2	4	.0625			13	26	.40625	6	12	24	48	.75
			5	.078125				27	.421875				49	.765625
		3	6	.09375		7	14	28	.4375			25	50	.78125
			7	.109375				29	.453125				51	.796875
1	2	4	8	.125			15	30	.46875		13	26	52	.8125
			9	.140625				31	.484375				53	.828125
		5	10	.15625	4	8	16	32	.5			27	54	.84375
			11	.171875				33	.515625				55	.859375
	3	6	12	.1875			17	34	.53125	7	14	28	56	.875
			13	.203125				35	.546875				57	.890625
		7	14	.21875		9	18	36	.5625			29	58	.90625
			15	.234375				37	.578125				59	.921875
2	4	8	16	.25			19	38	.59375		15	30	60	.9375
			17	.265625				39	.609375				61	.953125
		9	18	.28125	5	10	20	40	.625			31	62	.96875
			19	.296875				41	.646625				63	.984375
	5	10	20	.3125			21	42	.65625	8	16	32	64	1.
			21	.328125				43	.671875					
		11	22	.34375		11	22	44	.6875					

World Weights and Measures

Source: National Bureau of Standards, Department of Commerce

Denominations	Where Used	Amer. Equiv.
Almude	Portugal	4.423 gal
Ardeb	Egypt	5.6189 bu
Arratel (Libra)	Portugal	1.012 lb
Arroba	Argentina	25.32 lb
"	Brazil	32.38 lb
"	Cuba	25.36 lb
"	Paraguay	25.32 lb
"	Venezuela	25.40 lb
" (liquid)	Cuba, Spain and Venezuela	4.263 gal
Arshine	USSR	28 in
" (sq)	"	5.44 sq ft
Artel	Morocco	1.12 lb
Baril	Argentina and Mexico	20.077 gal / 20.0787 gal
Barile (wine)	Malta	11.2 gal
Berkovets	USSR	361.128 lb
Bongkal	Malaysia	832 grains
Bouw	Sumatra	7,096.5 sq meter
Bu	Japan	0.12 inch
Bushel	British	1.03205 U.S. bu
Caballeria	Cuba	33.162 acres
Caban (cavan)	Philippines	2.13 bu / 19.8 gal
Caffiso	Malta	5.40 gal
Candy	Bombay	560 lb
"	India (Madras)	500 lb
Cantaro	Malta	175 lb
Carat (metric)	World	3.086 grains
Catty	China	1.333¹/₃ lb
" (see Kin)	Japan	
"	Java, Malacca	1.36 lb
"	Thailand	2²/₃ lb
" (stand)	Thailand	1.32 lb
"	Sumatra	2.12 lb
Centaro	Central America	4.2631 gal
Centner	Brunswick	117.5 lb
"	Bremen	127.5 lb
"	Denmark, Norway	110.23 lb
"	Germany	113.44 lb
"	Sweden	93.7 lb
Chetvert	USSR	5.957 bu
Ch'ih	China	12.60 in
" (metric)	China	39.37 in=1 meter
Cho	Japan	2.451 acres
Coomb	England	4.1282 bu
Coyan	Thailand	2,645.5 lb.
Cuadra	Argentina	4.2 acres
"	Paraguay	94.71 yd
" (sq)	Paraguay	1.85 acres
"	Uruguay	1.82 acres
Cwt. (hund. weight)	British	112 lb
Dessiatine	USSR	2.6997 acres
Drachma	Greece	49.38 grains
Dunam	Israel	0.22239 acre
Fanega (dry)	Ecuador, Salvador	1.5745 bu
"	Chile	2.75268 bu
" (dry)	Guatemala, Spain	1.57744 bu
"	Mexico	2.57716 bu
" (dry)	Spain	1.57501 bu
" (liquid)	Spain	16 gal
" (dry)	Trinidad & Tobago	110 lb
" (double)	Uruguay	7.776 bu
" (single)	Uruguay	3.888 bu
"	Venezuela	3.334 bu
Feddan	Egypt	1.04 acres
Frail (raisins)	Spain	50 lb
Frasco	Argentina	2.51 liq qt
Frasila	Zanzibar	35 lb
Fuder	Luxemburg	264.18 gal
Funt	USSR	0.9028 lb
Gallon	British	1.20094 U.S. gal
Garniec	Poland	1.0567 gal
Jerib	Iran	2.471 acres
Joch	Austria	1.422 acres
"	Hungary	1.067 acres
Kantar	Egypt	99.05 lb
"	Morocco	112 lb
"	Turkey	124.45 lb
Ken	Japan	5.97 feet
Kin	Japan	1.32 lb

Denominations	Where Used	Amer. Equiv.
Klafter	Austria	2.074 yd
Klafter	Germany	1.90 yd
Koku	Japan	5.119 bu
Kwan	Japan	8.2673 lb
Last	Belgium, Holland	85.134 bu
"	England	82.56 bu
"	Germany	2 metric tons
"	Prussia	112.29 bu
League (land)	Paraguay	4.633 acres
Li	China	1890 ft
"	China	0.01260 in = (1/1000 ch'ih)
Libra (lb)	Argentina	1.0128 lb
"	C. America, Chile	1.014 lb
"	Cuba	1.0143 lb
"	Mexico	1.01467 lb
"	Peru, Venezuela	1.0143 lb
"	Uruguay	1.0127 lb
Load, timber	England	50 cu ft
Manzana	Nicaragua	1.742 acres
"	Costa Rica	1.727 acres
"	Salvador	1.727 acres
Marco	Bolivia	0.507 lb
Maund	Bengal	82²/₇ lb
Mil	Denmark	4.68 miles
Milla	Nicaragua	1.1594 miles
"	Honduras	1.1493 miles
Mina	Greece	0.95 lb
Morgen	Germany	0.63 acre
Oka (Oke)	Greece	2.82 lb
Oke	(Egypt)	2.7514 lb
"	Turkey	2.826 lb
Pic	Egypt	22.83 inches
Picul	Borneo—Celebes	135.64 lb
"	China	133¹/₃ lb
"	Java	136.16 lb
"	Philippines	139.44 lb
Pie	Argentina	0.9471 ft
"	Spain	0.91416 ft
Pik	Turkey	27.9 inches
Pood	Russia	36.113 lb
Pund (lb)	Denmark	1.102 lb
Quart	British	1.20094 liq qt
"	"	1.03205 dry qt
Quarter	"	8.256 bu
Quintal	Argentina	101.3 lb
"	Brazil	129.54 lb
"	Castile, Peru, Chile	101.43 lb
"	Mexico	101.47 lb
Rotl	Israel	6.35 lb
Sagene	USSR	7 feet
Salm	Malta	8.26 bu
Se	Japan	0.02451 acre
Seer	India	2 2/35 lb
Shaku	Japan	11.9303 in
Sho	"	1.91 liq qt
Skalpund	Sweden	0.937 lb
Stone	British	14 lb
Sun	Japan	1.193 inches
Tael (Kuping)	China	575.64 grs (troy)
Tan	Japan	0.25 acre
To	Japan	2.05 pecks
Tonde (cereal)	Denmark	3.9480 bu
Tonde (land)	Denmark	1.36 acres
Tonne	France	2204.62 lb
Tsubo	Japan	35.58 sq ft
Ts'un	China	1.26 inches
Tunna (wheat)	Sweden	4.16 bu
Tunnland	"	1.22 acres
Vara	Argentina	34.0944 inches
"	Costa Rica, Salva	32.913 inches
"	Guatemala	32.909 inches
"	Honduras	32.874 inches
"	Nicaragua	33.057 inches
"	Chile and Peru	32.913 inches
"	Cuba	33.386 inches
"	Mexico	32.992 inches
Vedro	USSR	3.249 gal
Verst	"	0.663 mile
Vloka	Poland	41.50 acres
Wey	Scotland, Ireland	40 bu

The metric carat of 200 milligrams is now very generally in use. The word carat also is used to denote the proportion of alloy in a metal. Thus, pure gold is 24 carats fine.

Chemical Elements, Discoverers, Atomic Weights

Atomic weights, based on the exact number 12 as the assigned atomic mass of the principal isotope of carbon, carbon 12, are provided through the courtesy of the International Union of Pure and Applied Chemistry and Butterworth Scientific Publications.

For the radioactive elements with the exception of uranium and thorium, the mass number of either the isotope of longest half-life (marked with a star) or the better known isotope (marked with two stars) is given.

Chemical element	Symbol	Atomic number	Atomic weight	Year discov.	Discoverer
Actinium	Ac	89	227*	1899	Debierne
Aluminum	Al	13	26.9815	1825	Oersted
Americium	Am	95	243*	1944	Seaborg, et al.
Antimony	Sb	51	121.75	1450	Valentine
Argon	Ar	18	39.948	1894	Rayleigh, Ramsay
Arsenic	As	33	74.9216	13th C.	Magnus
Astatine	At	85	210*	1940	Corson, et al.
Barium	Ba	56	137.34	1808	Davy
Berkelium	Bk	97	247*	1949	Thompson, Ghiorso, Seaborg
Beryllium	Be	4	9.0122	1798	Vanquelin
Bismuth	Bi	83	208.980	15th C.	Valentine
Boron	B	5	10.811a	1808	Davy
Bromine	Br	35	79.904b	1826	Balard
Cadmium	Cd	48	112.40	1817	Stromeyer
Calcium	Ca	20	40.08	1808	Davy
Californium	Cf	98	249**	1950	Thompson, et al.
Carbon	C	6	12.01115a	B.C.	
Cerium	Ce	58	140.12	1803	Klaproth
Cesium	Cs	55	132.905	1861	Bunsen, Kirchoff
Chlorine	Cl	17	35.453b	1774	Scheele
Chromium	Cr	24	51.996b	1797	Vanquelin
Cobalt	Co	27	58.9332	1735	Brandt
Copper	Cu	29	63.546b	B.C.	
Curium	Cm	96	247*	1944	Seaborg, et al.
Dysprosium	Dy	66	162.50	1886	Boisbaudran
Einsteinium	Es	99	254*	1952	Ghiorso, et al.
Erbium	Er	68	167.26	1843	Mosander
Europium	Eu	63	151.96	1901	Demarcay
Fermium	Fm	100	257*	1953	Ghiorso, et al.
Fluorine	F	9	18.9984	1771	Scheele
Francium	Fr	87	223*	1939	Perey
Gadolinium	Gd	64	157.25	1886	Marignac
Gallium	Ga	31	69.72	1875	Boisbaudran
Germanium	Ge	32	72.59	1886	Winkler
Gold	Au	79	196.967	B.C.	
Hafnium	Hf	72	178.49	1923	Coster, Hevesy
Hahnium	Ha	105	262*	1970	Ghiorso, et al.
Helium	He	2	4.0026	1895	Ramsay
Holmium	Ho	67	164.930	1879	Cleve
Hydrogen	H	1	1.00797a	1766	Cavendish
Indium	In	49	114.82	1863	Reich, Richter
Iodine	I	53	126.9044	1811	Courtois
Iridium	Ir	77	192.2	1804	Tennant
Iron	Fe	26	55.847b	B.C.	
Krypton	Kr	36	83.80	1898	Ramsay, Travers
Lanthanum	La	57	138.91	1839	Mosander
Lawrencium	Lr	103	260*	1961	Ghiorso, T. Sikkeland, A.E. Larsh, and R. M. Latimer
Lead	Pb	82	207.19	B.C.	
Lithium	Li	3	6.939	1817	Arfvedson
Lutetium	Lu	71	174.97	1907	Welsbach, Urbain
Magnesium	Mg	12	24.312	1830	Liebig, Bussy
Manganese	Mn	25	54.9380	1774	Gahn
Mendelevium	Md	101	258*	1955	Ghiorso, et al.
Mercury	Hg	80	200.59	B.C.	
Molybdenum	Mo	42	95.94	1782	Hjelm
Neodymium	Nd	60	144.24	1885	Welsbach
Neon	Ne	10	20.183	1898	Ramsay, Travers
Neptunium	Np	93	237*	1940	McMillan, Abelson
Nickel	Ni	28	58.71	1751	Cronstedt
Niobium(Form. Columbium)	Nb	41	92.906	1801	Hatchett
Nitrogen	N	7	14.0067	1772	Rutherford
Nobelium	No	102	259*	1958	Ghiorso, et al.
Osmium	Os	76	190.2	1804	Tennant
Oxygen	O	8	15.9994a	1774	Priestly, Scheele
Palladium	Pd	46	106.4	1803	Wollaston
Phosphorus	P	15	30.9738	1669	Brandt
Platinum	Pt	78	195.09	1735	Ulloa
Plutonium	Pu	94	242**	1940	Seaborg, et al.
Polonium	Po	84	210**	1898	P. and M. Curie
Potassium	K	19	39.102	1807	Davy
Praseodymium	Pr	59	140.907	1885	Welsbach
Promethium	Pm	61	147**	1945	Glendenin, Marinsky
Protactinium	Pa	91	231*	1917	Hahn, Meltner
Radium	Ra	88	226*	1898	P. & M. Curie, Bemont
Radon	Rn	86	222*	1900	Dorn
Rhenium	Re	75	186.2	1925	Noddack, Tacke
Rhodium	Rh	45	102.905	1803	Wollaston
Rubidium	Rb	37	85.47	1861	Bunsen, Kirchoff
Ruthenium	Ru	44	101.07	1845	Claus

Chemical element	Symbol	Atomic number	Atomic weight	Year discov.	Discoverer
Rutherfordium	Rf.	104	261*	1969	Ghiorso, et al.
Samarium	Sm.	62	150.35	1879	Boisbaudran
Scandium	Sc.	21	44.956	1879	Nilson
Selenium	Se.	34	78.96	1817	Berzelius
Silicon	Si.	14	28.086a	1823	Berzelius
Silver	Ag.	47	107.868b	B.C.	
Sodium	Na.	11	22.9898	1807	Davy
Strontium	Sr.	38	87.62	1790	Crawford
Sulfur	S.	16	32.064a	B.C.	
Tantalum	Ta	73	180.948	1802	Eckeberg
Technetium	Tc.	43	99**	1937	Perrier and Segre
Tellurium	Te	52	127.60	1782	Von Reichenstein
Terbium	Tb	65	158.924	1843	Mosander
Thallium	Tl	81	204.37	1861	Crookes
Thorium	Th.	90	232.038	1828	Berzelius
Thulium	Tm.	69	168.934	1879	Cleve
Tin	Sn	50	118.69	B.C.	
Titanium	Ti	22	47.90	1789	Gregor
Tungsten (Alternate Wolfram)	W	74	183.85	1783	d'Elhujar
Uranium	U.	92	238.03	1789	Klaproth
Vanadium	V.	23	50.942	1830	Sefstrom
Xenon	Xe.	54	131.30	1898	Ramsay, Travers
Ytterbium	Yb.	70	173.04	1878	Marignac
Yttrium	Y.	39	88.905	1794	Gadolin
Zinc	Zn.	30	65.37	B.C.	
Zirconium	Zr.	40	91.22	1789	Klaproth

a. Atomic weights so designated are known to be variable because of natural variations in isotopic composition. The observed ranges are: hydrogen±0.0001; boron±0.003; carbon±0.0005; oxygen±0.0001; silicon±0.001; sulfur±0.003.

b. Atomic weights so designated are believed to have the following experimental uncertainties: chlorine±0.001; chromium±0.001; iron±0.003; bromine±0.001; silver±0.001; copper±0.001.

Medical Signs and Abbreviations

Source: American Medical Association

℞ (Lat. Recipe)	take	a.c.	before meals	gr.	grain
Ʒ	drachm	ad	to, up to	gtt.	drops
f Ʒ	fluid drachm	ad libitum	at pleasure	h.s.	at bedtime
℥	ounce	agit.	shake	inject	injection
f ℥	fluid ounce	aqua	water	lb.	pound
℥ ss	half an ounce	b.i.d.	twice daily	m.	mix
℥ i	one ounce	cap.	capsule	mg.	milligram
℥ iss	one ounce and a half	cum, or c	with	ml.	milliliter
℥ ii	two ounces	e.m.p.	as directed	non. rep. or n.r.	
m.	minim, or drop	fiant (ft)	make		do not repeat
o	pint	gargarisma	a gargle	p.c.	after meals
aa	of each	Gm.	gram	p.r.n.	as circumstances may require

pulvis	powder
q. 3 h	every three hours
q.i.d.	four times daily
q.s.	as much as is sufficient
sig.	sign, write
solutio.	a solution
ss	one-half
stat	at once
tab.	tablet
t.i.d.	three times daily
ung.	ointment
ut dict	as directed

Bell Time on Shipboard

Source: Maritime Administration

Time, A.M.		Time, A.M.		Time, A.M.		Time, P.M.		Time, P.M.		Time, P.M.	
1 Bell	12:30	1 Bell	4:30	1 Bell	8:30	1 Bell	12:30	1 Bell	4:30	1 Bell	8:30
2 Bells	1:00	2 Bells	5:00	2 Bells	9:00	2 Bells	1:00	2 Bells	5:00	2 Bells	9:00
3 "	1:30	3 "	5:30	3 "	9:30	3 "	1:30	3 "	5:30	3 "	9:30
4 "	2:00	4 "	6:00	4 "	10:00	4 "	2:00	4 "	6:00	4 "	10:00
5 "	2:30	5 "	6:30	5 "	10:30	5 "	2:30	5 "	6:30	5 "	10:30
6 "	3:00	6 "	7:00	6 "	11:00	6 "	3:00	6. "	7:00	6 "	11:00
7 "	3:30	7 "	7:30	7 "	11:30	7 "	3:30	7 "	7:30	7 "	11:30
8 "	4:00	8 "	8:00	8 "	Noon	8 "	4:00	8 "	8:00	8 "	Midnight

Breaking the Sound Barrier; Speed of Sound

The prefix Mach is used to describe supersonic speed. It derives from Ernst Mach, a Czech-born German physicist, who contributed to the study of sound. When a plane moves at the speed of sound it is Mach 1. When twice the speed of sound it is Mach 2. When it is near but below the speed of sound its speed can be designated at less than Mach 1, for example, Mach .0. Mach is defined as "in jet propulsion, the ratio of the velocity of a rocket or a jet to the velocity of sound in the medium being considered."

When a plane passes the sound barrier—flying faster than sound travels—listeners in the area hear thunderclaps, but pilots do not hear them.

Sound is produced by vibrations of an object and is transmitted by alternate increase and decrease in pressures that radiate outward through a material media of molecules-somewhat like waves spreading out on a pond after a rock has been tossed.

The frequency of sound is determined by the number of times the vibrating waves undulate per second, and is measured in cycles per second. The slower the cycle of waves, the lower the sound. As frequencies increase, the sound is higher.

Sound is audible to human beings only if the frequency falls within a certain range. The human ear is usually not sensitive to frequencies of less than 20 vibrations per second, or more than about 20,000 vibrations per second-although this range varies among individuals. Anything at a pitch higher than the human ear can hear is termed ultrasonic.

Intensity or loudness is the strength of the pressure of these radiating waves, and is measured in decibels. The human ear responds to intensity in a range from zero to 120 decibels. Any sound with pressure over 120 decibels is painful.

The speed of sound is generally placed at 1088 ft. per second at sea level at 32°F. It varies in other temperatures and in different media. Sound travels faster in water than in air, and even faster in iron and steel. If in air it travels a mile in 5 seconds, it does a mile under water in 1 second, and through iron in ⅓ of a second. It travels through ice cold vapor at approximately 4,708 ft. per sec., ice-cold water, 4,938; granite, 12,960; hardwood, 12,620; brick, 11,-960; glass, 16,410 to 19,690; silver, 8,658; gold, 5,717.

Great Inventions and Scientific Discoveries

Invention	Date	Inventor	Nation
Adding machine	1642	Pascal	French
Adding machine	1885	Burroughs	U.S.
Addressograph	1892	Duncan	U.S.
Aerosol spray	1941	Goodhue	U.S.
Air brake	1868	Westinghouse	U.S.
Air conditioning	1911	Carrier	U.S.
Air pump	1650	Guericke	German
Airplane, automatic pilot	1929	Green	U.S.
Airplane, experimental	1896	Langley	U.S.
Airplane jet engine	1939	Ohain	German
Airplane with motor	1903	Orville and Wilbur Wright	U.S.
Airplane, hydro	1911	Curtiss	U.S.
Airship	1852	Giffard	French
Airship, rigid dirigible	1900	Zeppelin	German
Arc tube	1923	Alexanderson	U.S.
Autogyro	1920	de la Cierva	Spanish
Automobile, differential gear	1885	Benz	German
Automobile, electric	1892	Morrison	U.S.
Automobile, exp'mtl	1875	Marcus	Austrian
Automobile, gasoline	1887	Daimler	German
Automobile, gasoline	1892	Duryea, C. E.	U.S.
Automobile, magneto	1897	Bosch, R.	German
Automobile muffler	. .	Maxim, H.P.	U.S.
Automobile self-starter	1911	Kettering	U.S.
Automobile, steam	1889	Roper	U.S.
Babbitt metal	1839	Babbitt	U.S.
Bakelite	1907	Baekeland	Belg., U.S.
Balloon	1783	Montgolfier	French
Barometer	1643	Torricelli	Italian
Bicycle, modern	1884	Starley	English
Bifocal lens	1780	Franklin	U.S.
Block signals, railway	1867	Hall	U.S.
Bomb, depth	1916	Tait	U.S.
Bottle machine	1903	Owens	U.S.
Braille printing	1829	Braille	French
Burner, gas	1855	Bunsen	German
Calculating machine	1823	Babbage	English
Camera, Polaroid Land	1948	Land	U.S.
Car coupler	1873	Janney	U.S.
Carburetor, gasoline	1876	Daimler	German
Card time recorder	1894	Cooper	U.S.
Carding machine	1797	Whittemore	U.S.
Carpet sweeper	1876	Bissell	U.S.
Cash register	1879	Ritty	U.S.
Cathode ray tube	1878	Crookes	English
Cellophane	1911	Brandenberger	Swiss
Celluloid	1870	Hyatt	U.S.
Cement, Portland	1845	Aspdin	English
Chronometer	1735	Harrison	English
Circuit breaker	1925	Hilliard	U.S.
Clock, pendulum	1657	Huygens	Dutch
Coaxial cable system	1929	Affel, Espensched	U.S.
Coke oven	1893	Hoffman	Austrian
Compressed air rock drill	1871	Ingersoll	U.S.
Comptometer	1887	Felt	U.S.
Computer, automatic sequence	1939	Aiken et al.	U.S.
Condenser microphone (telephone)	1920	Wente	U.S.
Cotton gin	1793	Whitney	U.S.
Cream separator	1880	DeLaval	Swedish
Cultivator, disc	1878	Mallon	U.S.
Cystoscope	1877	Nitze	German
Dental plate, rubber	1855	Goodyear	U.S.
Diesel engine	1895	Diesel	German
Dynamite	1866	Nobel	Swedish
Dynamo, continuous current	1860	Picinotti	Italian
Dynamo, hydrogen cooled	1915	Schuler	U.S.
Electric battery	1800	Volta	Italian
Electric fan	1882	Wheeler	U.S.
Electrocardiograph	1903	Einthoven	Dutch
Electroencephalograph	1929	Berger	German
Electromagnet	1824	Sturgeon	English
Electron spectrometer	1944	Deutsch, Elliott, Evans	U.S.
Electron tube multigrid	1913	Langmuir	U.S.
Electroplating	1805	Brugnatelli	Italian
Electrostatic generator	1929	Van de Graff	U.S.
Elevator brake	1852	Otis	U.S.
Elevator, push button	1922	Larson	U.S.
Engine, automobile	1879	Benz	German
Engine, coal-gas 4-cycle	1877	Otto	German
Engine, compression ignition	1883	Daimler	German
Engine, electric ignition	1880	Benz	German
Engine, gas, compound	1926	Eickemeyer	U.S.
Engine, gasoline	1872	Brayton, Geo.	U.S.
Engine, gasoline	1886	Daimler	German
Engine, steam, piston	1705	Newcomen	English
Engine, steam, piston	1769	Watt	Scottish
Engraving, half-tone	1893	Ives	U.S.
Filament, tungsten	1915	Langmuir	U.S.
Flanged rail	1831	Stevens	U.S.
Flatiron, electric	1882	Seeley	U.S.
Furnace (for steel)	1861	Siemens	German
Galvanometer	1820	Sweigger	German
Gas discharge tube	1922	Hull	U.S.
Gas lighting	1792	Murdoch	Scottish
Gas mantle	1885	Welsbach	Austrian
Gasoline (lead ethyl)	1922	Midgely	U.S.
Gasoline, cracked	1913	Burton, W.M.	U.S.
Gasoline, high octane	1930	Ipatieff	Russian
Geiger counter	1913	Geiger	German
Glass, laminated safety	1909	Benedictus	French
Glider	1853	Cayley	English
Gun, breechloader	1811	Thornton	U.S.
Gun, Browning	1916	Browning	U.S.
Gun, magazine	1875	Hotchkiss	U.S.
Gun, silencer	1909	Maxim, H. P.	U.S.
Guncotton	1846	Schoenbein	German
Gyrocompass	1911	Sperry	U.S.
Gyroscope	1852	Foucault	French
Harvester	1836	Moore	U.S.
Harvester-thresher	1888	Matteson	U.S.
Helicopter	1939	Sikorsky	U.S.
Hydrometer	1768	Baume	French
Ice-making machine	1851	Gorrie	U.S.
Iron lung	1928	Drinker, Slaw.	U.S.
Kaleidoscope	1817	Brewster	English
Kinetoscope	1887	Edison	U.S.
Kodak	1888	Eastman, Walker	U.S.
Lacquer, nitrocellulose	1921	Flaherty	U.S.
Lamp, arc	1879	Brush	U.S.
Lamp, incandescent	1879	Edison	U.S.
Lamp, incand., frosted	1924	Pipkin	U.S.
Lamp, incand., gas	1916	Langmuir	U.S.
Lamp, Klieg	1911	Kliegl, A.&J.	U.S.
Lamp, mercury vapor	1912	Hewitt	U.S.
Lamp, miner's safety	1816	Davy	English
Lamp, neon	1915	Claude	French
Lathe, turret	1845	Fitch	U.S.
Launderette	1934	Cantrell	U.S.
Lens, achromatic	1758	Dollond	English
Lens, fused bifocal	1908	Borsch	U.S.
Leydenjar (condenser)	1745	von Kleist	German
Lightning rod	1752	Franklin	U.S.
Linoleum	1860	Walton	English
Linotype	1885	Mergenthaler	U.S.
Lock, cylinder	1865	Yale	U.S.
Locomotive, electric	1851	Vail	U.S.
Locomotive, exp'mtl	1801	Trevithick	English
Locomotive, exp'mtl	1812	Fenton et al	English
Locomotive, exp'mtl	1813	Hedley	English
Locomotive, exp'mtl	1814	Stephenson	English
Locomotive practical	1829	Stephenson	English
Locomotive, 1st U.S.	1830	Cooper, P.	U.S.
Loom, power	1785	Cartwright	English
Loudspeaker, dynamic	1924	Rice, Kellogg	U.S.
Machine gun	1861	Gatling	U.S.
Machine gun, improved	1872	Hotchkiss	U.S.
Machine gun (Maxim)	1883	Maxim, H.S.	U.S.,-Eng.
Magnet, electro	1828	Henry	U.S.
Mantle, gas	1885	Welsbach	Austrian
Mason jar	1858	Mason, J.	U.S.
Match, friction	1827	John Walker	English
Mercerized textiles	1843	Mercer, J.	English
Meter, induction	1888	Shallenberger	U.S.

Invention	Date	Inventor	Nation
Meter, parking	1935	Magee	U.S.
Metronome	1816	Malzel	Austrian
Micrometer	1636	Gascoigne	English
Microphone	1877	Berliner	U.S.
Microscope, compound	1590	Janssen	Dutch
Microscope, electronic	1931	Knoll, Ruska	German
Monitor, warship	1861	Ericsson	U.S.
Monotype	1887	Lanston	U.S.
Motor, AC	1892	Tesla	U.S.
Motor, induction	1887	Tesla	U. S.
Motorcycle	1885	Daimler	German
Movie machine	1894	Jenkins	U.S.
Movie, panoramic	1952	Waller	U. S.
Movie, talking	1927	Warner Bros.	U.S.
Mower, lawn	1868	Hills	U. S.
Mowing machine	1831	Manning	U. S.
Neoprene	1930	Carothers	U. S.
Nylon synthetic	1930	Carothers	U. S.
Nylon	1937	Du Pont lab.	U. S.
Oil cracking furnace	1891	Gavrilov	Russian
Oil filled power cable	1921	Emanueli	Italian
Oleomargarine	1868	Mege-Mouries	French
Ophthalmoscope	1851	Helmholtz	German
Paper machine	1809	Dickinson	U. S.
Parachute	1785	Blanchard	French
Pen, ballpoint	1888	Loud	U. S.
Pen, fountain	1884	Waterman	U. S.
Pen, steel	1780	Harrison	English
Pendulum	1581	Galileo	Italian
Percussion cap	1814	Shaw	U.S.
Phonograph	1877	Edison	U. S.
Photo, color	1892	Ives	U.S.
Photo film, celluloid	1887	Goodwin	U. S.
Photo film transparent	1878	Eastman, Goodwin	U.S.
Photoelectric cell	1895	Elster	German
Photographic paper	1898	Baekeland	U.S.
Photography	1835	Fox-Talbot	English
Photography	1837	Daguerre	French
Photography	1839	Niepce	French
Photophone	1880	Bell	U.S.
Phototelegraphy	1925	Bell lab	U.S.
Piano	1709	Cristofori	Italian
Piano, player	1863	Fourneaux	French
Pin, safety	1849	Hunt	U.S.
Pistol (revolver)	1835	Colt	U. S.
Plow, cast iron	1797	Newbold	U.S.
Plow, disc	1896	Hardy	U.S.
Pneumatic hammer	1890	King	U.S.
Powder, smokeless	1863	Schultze	German
Printing press, rotary	1846	Hoe	U.S.
Printing press, web	1865	Bullock	U.S.
Propeller, screw	1804	Stevens	U.S.
Propeller, screw	1837	Ericsson	Swedish
Punch card accounting	1884	Hollerith	U.S.
Radar	1922	Taylor, Young	U.S.
Radio amplifier	1907	De Forest	U.S.
Radio beacon	1928	Donovan	U. S.
Radio crystal oscillator	1918	Nicolson	U. S.
Radio receiver, cascade tuning	1913	Alexanderson	U.S.
Radio receiver, heterodyne	1913	Fessenden	U. S.
Radio transmitter triode modulation	1914	Alexanderson	U. S.
Radio tube-diode	1905	Fleming	English
Radio tube oscillator	1915	De Forest	U. S.
Radio tube triode	1907	De Forest	U.S.
Radio, signals	1895	Marconi	Italian
Radio, magnetic detector	1902	Marconi	Italian
Radio FM 2-path	1929	Armstrong	U. S.
Rayon	1883	Swan	English
Razor, electric	1931	Schick	U.S.
Razor, safety	1895	Gillette	U.S.
Reaper	1834	McCormick	U. S.
Record, cylinder	1887	Bell, Tainter	U.S.
Record, disc	1887	Berliner	U.S.
Record, long playing	1948	Goldmark	U.S.
Record, wax cylinder	1888	Edison	U.S.

Invention	Date	Inventor	Nation
Refrigerants, low-boiling. fluorine compound	1930	Midgely and co-workers	U.S.
Refrigerator car	1868	David	U. S.
Resin, synthetic	1931	Hill	English
Rifle, repeating	1860	Spencer	U. S.
Rocket engine	1929	Goddard, R.H.	U. S.
Rubber, vulcanized	1839	Goodyear	U. S.
Saw, band	1808	Newberry	English
Saw, circular	1777	Miller	English
Searchlight, arc	1915	Sperry	U. S.
Sewing machine	1846	Howe	U. S.
Shoe-sewing machine	1860	McKay	U. S.
Shrapnel shell	1784	Shrapnel	English
Shuttle, flying	1733	Kay	English
Sleeping-car	1858	Pullman	U. S.
Slide rule	1620	Oughtred	English
Soap, hardware	1928	Bertsch	German
Spectroscope	1859	Kirchoff, Bunsen	German.
Spectroscope (mass)	1918	Dempster	U. S.
Spinning jenny	1767	Hargreaves	English
Spinning mule	1779	Crompton	English
Steamboat, exp'mtl.	1783	Jouffroy	French
Steamboat, exp'mtl.	1785	Fitch	U.S.
Steamboat, exp'mtl.	1787	Rumsey	U. S.
Steamboat, exp'mtl.	1788	Miller	Scottish
Steamboat, exp'mtl.	1803	Fulton	U. S.
Steamboat, exp'mtl.	1804	Stevens	U. S.
Steamboat, practical	1802	Symington	Scottish
Steamboat, practical	1807	Fulton	U. S.
Steam car	1770	Cugnot	French
Steam turbine	1884	Parsons	English
Steel	1856	Bessemer	English
Steel alloy	1891	Harvey	U. S.
Steel alloy, high-speed	1901	Taylor, White	U. S.
Steel, electric	1900	Heroult	French
Steel, manganese	1884	Hadfield	English
Steel, stainless	1916	Brearley	English
Stereoscope	1838	Wheatstone	English
Stethoscope	1819	Laennec	French
Stethoscope, binaural	1840	Cammann	U. S.
Stock ticker	1870	Edison	U. S.
Storage battery, electric	1812	Ritter	German
Stove, electric	1896	Hadaway	U. S.
Submarine	1891	Holland	U. S.
Submarine, even keel	1894	Lake	U. S.
Submarine, torpedo	1776	Bushnell	U. S.
Tank, military	1914	Swinton	English
Tape recorder, magnetic	1899	Poulsen	Danish
Telegraph, magnetic	1837	Morse	U.S.
Telegraph, quadruplex	1874	Edison	U. S.
Telegraph, railroad	—	Woods	U. S.
Telegraph, wireless, high frequency	1896	Marconi	Italian
Telephone	1876	Bell	U. S.
Telephone amplifier	1912	De Forest	U. S.
Telephone, automatic	1891	Stowger	U.S.
Telephone, radio	1902	Poulsen, Fessender	U. S.
Telephone, radio	1906	De Forest	U. S.
Telephone, radio, l. d	1915	AT&T	U. S.
Telephone, recording	1898	Poulson	Danish
Telephone, wireless	1899	Collins	U. S.
Telescope	1608	Lippershey	Neth.
Telescope	1609	Galileo	Italian
Telescope, astronomical	1611	Kepler	German
Teletype	1928	Morkrum. Kleinschmidt	U. S.
Television, iconoscope	1923	Zworykin, V.	U. S.
Television, electronic	1927	Farnsworth, P.	U. S.
Television, (mech. scanner)	1926	Baird	Scottish
Thermometer	1593	Galileo	Italian
Thermometer	1710	Reaumur	French
Thermometer, mercury	1714	Fahregheit	German
Time recorder	1890	Bundy	U. S.
Time, self-regulator	1918	Bryce	U. S.
Tire, double-tube	1845	Thompson	English
Tire, pneumatic	1888	Dunlop	Irish
Toaster, automatic	1918	Strite	U. S.
Tool, pneumatic	1865	Law	English
Torpedo, marine	1804	Fulton	U.S.
Tractor, crawler	1900	Holt	U. S.
Transformer A.C.	1885	Stanley	U. S.

Invention	Date	Inventor	Nation	Invention	Date	Inventor	Nation
Transistor	1947	Shockley, Brattain, Bardeen	U. S.	Vacuum cleaner, electric	1907	Spangler	U. S.
Trolley car, electric	1884 -87	Van Depoel & Sprague	U. S.	Washer, electric	1907	Hurley Co.	U. S.
				Welding, atomic hydrogen	1924	Langmuir- Palmer	U. S.
Tungsten, ductile	1912	Coolidge	U. S.	Welding, electric	1877	Thomson	U. S.
Turbine, gas	1899	Curtis, C.G.	U. S.	Wind tunnel	1923	Munk	U. S.
Turbine, hydraulic	1849	Francis	U. S.	Wire, barbed	1874	Glidden	U. S.
Turbine, steam	1896	Curtis, C.G.	U. S.	Wire, barbed	1875	Haisn	U. S.
Type, movable	1450	Gutenberg	German	X-ray tube	1913	Coolidge	U. S.
Typewriter	1868	Soule, Glidden	U. S.	Zipper	1891	Judson	U. S.

Discoveries and Innovations: Chemistry, Physics, Biology, Medicine

Product	Date	Discoverer	Nation
Acetylene gas	1892	Wilson	U.S.
ACTH	1949	Armour & Co.	U.S.
Adrenalin	1901	Takamine	Japan
Aluminum, electrolytic process	1886	Hall	U.S.
Aluminum, isolated	1825	Oersted	Danish
Analine dye	1856	Perkin	English
Anesthesia, ether	1842	Long	U.S.
Anesthesia, local	1885	Koller	Austria
Anesthesia, spinal	1898	Bier	German
Anti-rabies	1885	Pasteur	French
Antitoxin, diphtheria	1891	Von Behring	German
Antiseptic surgery	1867	Lister	English
Argyrol	...	Barnes	U.S.
Arsphenamine	1910	Ehrlich	German
Aspirin	1889	Dresser	German
Atomic numbers	1913	Moseley	English
Atomic theory	1803	Dalton	English
Atomic time clock	1947	Libby	U.S.
Atom-smashing theory	1919	Rutherford	English
Atabrine	...	Mietzsch, et al	German
Aureomycin	1948	Duggar	U.S.
Bacitracin	1945	Johnson et al.	U.S.
Bacteria (described)	1676	Leeuwenhoek	Dutch
Barbital	1903	Fischer	German
Bleaching powder	1798	Tennant	English
Blood, circulation	1628	Harvey	English
Bordeaux mixture	1885	Millardet	French
Bromine from sea	1924	Edgar-Kramer	U.S.
Calcium carbide	1888	Wilson	U.S.
Calculus	1670	Newton	English
Carbon oxides	1925	Fisher	German
Carbomycin	1952	Tanner	U.S.
Camphor synthetic	1896	Haller	French
Canning (food)	1804	Appert	French
Chlorine	1810	Davy	English
Chloroform	1831	Guthrie, S.	U.S.
Chloromycetin	1947	Burkholder	U.S.
Classification of plants and animals	1735	Linnaeus	Swedish
Cocaine	1860	Niermann	German
Combustion explained	1777	Lavoisier	French
Conditioned reflex	1914	Pavlov	Russian
Conteben	1950	Belmisch, Mietzsch, Domagn	German
Cortisone	1936	Kendall	U.S.
Cortisone, synthesis	1946	Sarett	U.S.
Cosmic rays	1910	Gockel	Swiss
Cyanimide	1905	Frank-Caro	German
Cyclotron	1930	Lawrence	U.S.
DDT	1874	Zeidler	German
(Not applied as insecticide until 1939)			
Deuterium (heavy hydrogen)	1932	Urey, Brick-Wedde Murphy	U.S.
DNA (structure)	1951	Crick	English
		Watson	U.S.
		Wilkins	English
Electric resistance (law)	1827	Ohm	German
Electric waves	1888	Hertz	German
Electrolysis	1852	Faraday	English
Electromagnetism	1819	Oersted	Danish
Electron	1897	Thomson, J.	English
Electron diffraction	1936	Thomson, G.	English
		Davisson	U.S.
Electroshock treatment	1938	Cerletti, Bini	Italy
Erythromycin	1952	McGuire	U.S.

Product	Date	Discoverer	Nation
Evolution, natural selection	1858	Darwin	English
Falling bodies, law	1590	Galileo	Italian
Gases, law of combining volumes	1808	Gay-Lussac	French
Geometry, analytic	1619	Descartes	French
Gold (cyanide process for extraction)	1887	MacArthur-Forest	British
Gravitation, law	1687	Newton	English
Holograph	1948	Gabor	British
Human heart transplant	1967	Barnard	S. Africa
Indigo, synthesis of	1880	Baeyer	German
Induction, electric	1830	Henry	U.S.
Insulin	1922	Banting, Best, MacLeod	Canada
Intelligence testing	1905	Binet and Simon	French
Isniazid	1952	Hoffman-La Roche	U.S.
		Domagh	German
Isotopes, theory	1912	Soddy	English
Laser (light amplification by stimulated emission of radiation)	1958	Townes, Schawlow	U.S.
Light, velocity	1675	Roemer	Danish
Light, wave theory	1690	Huygens	Dutch
Lithography	1796	Senefelder	Bohemia
Lobotomy	1935	Egas Oniz	Portugal
LSD-25	1943	Hoffman	Swiss
Mendelian laws	1866	Mendel	Austrian
Mercator's projection (map)	1568	Mercator (Kremer)	Flemish
Methanol	1925	Patard	French
Milk condensation	1853	Borden	U.S.
Molecular hypothesis	1811	Avogadro	Italian
Motion, laws of	1687	Newton	English
Neomycin	1949	Waksman & Lechevalier	U.S.
Neutron	1932	Chadwick	English
Nitric acid	1648	Glauber	German
Nitric oxide	1772	Priestley	English
Nitroglycerin	1846	Sobrero	Italian
Ohm's law	1827	Ohm, Georg	German
Oil cracking process	1891	Dewar	U.S.
Oxygen	1774	Priestley	English
Ozone	1840	Schonbein	German
Paper, from wood pulp, sulfate process	1884	Dahl	German
Paper, sulfite process	1867	Tilghman	U.S.
Penicillin	1929	Alex. Fleming	English
Practical use	1941	Florev- Chain	English
Periodic law and table of elements	1869	Mendelejeff	Russian
Planetary motion, laws	1609	Kepler	German
Plutonium fission	1940	Kennedy, J.W.	U.S.
		Wahl, A. C.	U.S.
		Seaborg, G. T.	U.S.
		Segre, Emilio	U.S.
Polymixin	1947	Ainsworth	English
Positron	1932	Anderson	U.S.
Proton	1919	Rutherford	English
Psychoanalysis	1900	Freud	Austrian
Quantum theory	1900	Planck	German
Quasars	1963	Matthews & Sandage	U.S.
Quinine-synthetic	1918	Rabe	German
Radioactivity	1896	Becquerel	French
Radium	1898	Curie, Pierre	French
		Curie, Marie	Polish
Relativity theory	1905	Einstein	German

Product	Date	Discoverer	Nation
Reserpine	1949	Jal Vaikl	India
Salvarsan (606)	1910	Ehrlich	German
Schick test, diphtheria	1913	Schick	U.S.
Silicon	1823	Berzelius	Swedish
Streptomycin	1945	Waksman	U.S.
Sulfanilamide theory	1908	Gelmo	German
Sulfanilamide	1934	Domag	German
Sulfadiazine	1940	Roblin	U.S.
Sulfapyridine	1938	Ewins Phelps	English
Sulfathiazole	. . .	Fosbinder, Walter	U.S.
Sulfuric acid	1831	Phillips	English
Sulfuric acid, lead	1746	Roebuck	English
Terramycin	1950	Finlay, et al	U.S.
Tuberculin	1890	Koch	German
Uranium fission (theory)	1939	Hahn, Strassmann	German
		Borr	Danish
		Einstein	U.S.
		Fermi	Italian
		Pegram	U.S.
		Wheeler	U.S.

Product	Date	Discoverer	Nation
Uranium fission, atomic reactor	1942	Enrico Fermi	Italian
		Leo Szilard	U.S.
Vaccine, measles	1954	Enders, John	U.S.
		Peebles, T.	U.S.
Vaccine, polio	1955	Sabin, Alb. E.	U.S.
Vaccine, polio	1953	Salk, Jonas E.	U.S.
Vaccine, rabies	1885	Pasteur	French
Vaccine, smallpox	1796	Jenner, Edw.	English
Vaccine, typhus	1909	Nicolle, J.	French
Van Allen belts, radiation	1958	Van Allen	U.S.
Vitamin A	1913	McCollum, Davis	U.S.
Vitamin B	1916	McCollum	U.S.
Vitamin C	1912	Holst, Froelich	Norway
Vitamin D	1922	McCollum	U.S.
Wassermann test, syphilis	1906	Wassermann	German
Xerography	1938	Carlson	U.S.
X-ray	1895	Roentgen	German

Playing Cards and Dice Chances

Poker Hands (Four-Suit)

Hand	Number Possible	Odds Against
Royal Flush	4	649,739 to 1
Other Straight Flush	36	72,192 to 1
Four of a kind	624	4,164 to 1
Full House	3,744	693 to 1
Flush	5,108	508 to 1
Straight	10,200	254 to 1
Three of a kind	54,912	46 to 1
Two Pairs	123,552	20 to 1
One Pair	1,098,240	4 to 3 (1.37 to 1)
Nothing	1,302,540	1 to 1
Total	**2,598,960**	

Dice
Probabilities of Consecutive Winning Plays

No. Consecutive Wins	By 7, 11, or Point	No. Consecutive Wins	By 7, 11, or Point
1	244 in 495	6	1 in 70
2	24 in 100	7	1 in 141
3	3 in 25	8	1 in 287
4	1 in 17	9	1 in 582
5	1 in 34		

Dice
Totals Probabilities on Two Dice

Total	Odds Against (Single toss)	Total	Odds Against (Single toss)
2	35 to 1	8	31 to 5
3	17 to 1	9	8 to 1
4	11 to 1	10	11 to 1
5	8 to 1	11	17 to 1
6	31 to 5	12	35 to 1
7	5 to 1		

Pinochle Auction
Odds Against Finding in "Widow" of Three Cards

Open Places	Odds Against	Open Places	Odds Against
1	5 to 1	4	3 to 2 for
2	2 to 1	5	2 to 1 for
3	Even		

Bridge

The odds—Against suit distribution in a hand of 4-4-3-2 are about 4 to 1, against 5-4-2-2 about 8 to 1, against 6-4-2-1 about 20 to 1, against 7-4-1-1 about 254 to 1, against 8-4-1-0 about 2.211 to 1, and against 13-0-0-0 about 158,753,389,899 to 1.

Simple Interest Table

	Time	4%	5%	6%	7%	8%
$1.00	1 month	$.003	$.004	$.005	$.005	$.006
,,	2 months	.007	.008	.010	.011	.013
,,	3	.010	.013	.015	.017	.020
,,	6	.020	.025	.030	.035	.040
,,	12	.040	.050	.060	.070	.080
$100.00	1 day	.011	.013	.016	.019	.022
,,	2 days	.022	.027	.032	.038	.044
,,	3	.034	.041	.050	.058	.067

	Time	4%	5%	6%	7%	8%
$100.00	4 days	$.045	$.053	$.066	$.077	$.889
,,	5	.056	.069	.082	.097	.111
,,	6	.067	.083	.100	.116	.133
,,	1 month	.334	.416	.500	.583	.667
,,	2 months	.667	.832	1.000	1.166	1.333
,,	3	1.000	1.250	1.500	1.750	2.000
,,	6	2.000	2.500	3.000	3.500	4.000
,,	12	4.000	5.000	6.000	7.000	8.000

Colors of the Spectrum

Color, an electromagnetic wave phenomenon, is a sensation produced through the excitation of the retina of the eye by rays of light. The colors of the spectrum may be produced by viewing a light beam refracted by passage through a prism, which breaks the light into its wave lengths.

Customarily, the primary colors of the spectrum are thought of as those 6 monochromatic colors which occupy relatively large areas of the spectrum: red, orange, yellow, green, blue and violet. However, Sir Isaac Newton named a 7th, indigo, situated between blue and violet on the spectrum. Aubert estimated (1865) the solar spectrum to contain approximately 1,000 distinguishable hues of which according to Rood (1881) 2 million tints and shades can be distinguished; Luckiesh stated (1915) that 55 distinctly different hues have been seen in a single spectrum.

By many physicists only 3 primary colors are recognized: red, yellow and blue (Mayer, 1775); red, green and violet (Thomas Young, 1801); red, green and blue (Clerk Maxwell, 1860).

The color sensation of black is due to complete lack of stimulation of the retina, that of white to complete stimulation. The infra-red and ultra-violet rays, below the red (long) end of the spectrum and the violet end (short end) respectively, are invisible. Heat is the principal effect of the infra-red rays and chemical action that of the ultra-violet rays.

Copyright Law of the United States

Source: Copyright Office, Library of Congress

An author, or other owner who derives his rights from the author, may obtain protection for a literary, musical, or artistic work by complying with the provisions of the copyright law (Title 17 of the United States Code). The law gives the copyright owner the exclusive right to print, reprint, publish, copy and sell the copyrighted work; to revise or adapt it; and, with certain limitations, to perform and record it. Applications for registration of claims to copyright are filed with the Copyright Office, Library of Congress, Washington, D.C. 20559. Application forms and information circulars covering various subjects are furnished by the Copyright Office free upon request.

Categories of Works

The copyright law provides that the application for registration of any work shall specify to which of the following classes the work in which copyright is claimed belongs:

(A) Books, including composite and cyclopedic works, directories, gazetteers and other compilations; (B) periodicals, including newspapers; (C) lectures, sermons and addresses prepared for oral delivery; (D) dramatic or dramatico-musical compositions; (E) musical compositions; (F) maps; (G) works of art, models or designs for works of art; (H) reproductions of a work of art; (I) drawings or sculptural works of a scientific or technical character; (J) photographs; (K) prints and pictorial illustrations including prints or labels used for articles of merchandise; (L) motion-picture photoplays; (M) motion pictures other than photoplays; and (N) sound recordings.

How Copyright is Secured

Between the time a work is created and the time statutory copyright is secured, it is protected, while unpublished, by the common law against unauthorized copying or other use, without any action being required by the Copyright Office.

Copyright in a published work is secured by publishing the work with the required notice of copyright, and it is important that all copies published bear the notice. The law provides that the notice shall consist of either the word "Copyright," or the abbreviation "Copr.," or the symbol ©, accompanied by the name of the copyright owner. If the work is a printed literary, musical or dramatic work, the notice shall include also the year in which the copyright was secured by publication. For example: © John Doe 1975. In the case, however, of copies of works specified in classes F through K above, the notice may consist of the symbol © accompanied by the initials, monogram, mark, or symbol of the owner, provided that his name appears on some accessible part of the copies. The notice required to secure copyright for sound recordings fixed and first published on or after Feb. 15, 1972 is the symbol ℗, the year date of first publication of the sound recording, and the name of the copyright owner. For example: ℗ 1975 Doe Records, Inc. NOTE: Copyright for a sound recording protects against unauthorized reproduction of the same series of sounds; it is not a substitute for registration of the musical or literary work recorded.

Promptly after publication, there should be sent to the Copyright Office, Library of Congress, Washington, D.C. 20559, two copies of the best edition of the work, together with an application for registration and a $6 fee.

Manufacturing Requirements

For books and periodicals to be copyrightable, if they are by American authors, or by foreign authors who are domiciled in the U.S. at the time of first publication, the typesetting, printing, and binding of the copies used for first publication must have been done in the U.S. The only general exception to this rule is that a book or periodical in the English language manufactured and first published abroad may secure a 5-year ad interim copyright, provided that registra-

tion is made within 6 months of the date of first publication abroad. If ad interim copyright is secured, the importation of 1,500 copies is permitted. Books by American authors manufactured abroad may generally not be imported while they are under U.S. copyright protection, unless an Import Statement issued by the Copyright Office at the time of the ad interim registration is presented to U.S. Customs at the port of entry. Further information may be obtained from the Copyright Office.

Copyright for Unpublished Works

Statutory copyright may be had for certain classes of unpublished works by depositing in the Copyright Office one copy of the work, together with an application for registration and the $6 fee. Works for which registration may be made in unpublished form include those in classes C, D, E, G, I, J, L and M, above. There are special provisions concerning what should be deposited in the case of 3-dimensional works of art and motion pictures; information about them is obtainable from the Copyright Office. NOTE: Certain kinds of material are not registrable in unpublished form. These include "book material" such as fiction, nonfiction, poetry, directories and catalogs, as well as manuscripts of articles, stories and other works that are to be first published as contributions to periodicals. Such works are, as mentioned above, protected by the common law against unauthorized use while unpublished.

Duration of Copyright

The original term of copyright endures for 28 years, measured from the exact date of first publication of the work; or in the case of works registered in unpublished form, from the date of registration. During the last (the 28th) year of the first term, the copyright may be renewed by filing in the Copyright Office an application for renewal and a fee of $4. If they are not received by the Copyright Office before the original term has expired the work falls into the public domain and the copyright cannot be restored.

Fees

All copyright fees are established by law. Remittances should be in the form of checks or money orders made payable to the Register of Copyrights. The schedule of fees follows:

Registration of copyright claims (including a certificate bearing the Copyright Office seal) all classes of works, $6.

For registration of a claim to renewal, $4.

Each additional certificate, $2.

Other certifications, including certifications of photocopies of Copyright Office records, $3.

For recording each assignment, agreement or other document of 6 pages or fewer, listing no more than one title, $5. For each page over 6 and each title over one, 50c.

Searches: for each hour spent by the Copyright Office staff in searching the official records, $5.

International Protection

The U.S. has copyright relations with some 60 countries, under which works of American authors are protected in those countries, and the works of their authors are protected in the U.S. The basic feature of this protection is "national treatment," under which the alien author is treated by a country in the same manner that it treats its own authors. Relations exist by virtue of bilateral agreements or through the Buenos Aires Convention or the Universal Copyright Convention. Legislation implementing the latter convention, which became effective Sept. 16, 1955, gives the works of foreign authors the benefit of exemptions from the manufacturing requirements of the U.S. copyright law, provided the works are first published abroad with a copyright notice including the symbol©, the name of the copyright owner and the year date of first publication, and that the work either is by an author who is a citizen of a foreign country which belongs to the Convention or is first published in a foreign member country. Conversely, works of U.S., authors are exempt from certain burdensome requirements in particular foreign member countries.

Trademarks: How to Obtain and Protect Them

U. S. Govt. Bureaus have adopted trademark as a single word compounded from the former trade mark.

A trademark, as defined by Act of Congress, "includes any word, name, symbol, or device, or any combination thereof, adopted and used by a manufacturer or merchant to identify his goods and distinguish them from those manufactured or sold by others." Rights in trademarks are acquired by use, which must continue if those rights are to be preserved. In order to be eligible for registration a mark must be in use in commerce which may be lawfully regulated by Congress.

Trademarks are registered on the Principal Register and the Supplemental Register of the U.S. Patent and Trademark Office. "Coined, arbitrary, fanciful or suggestive marks, usually called technical marks, if otherwise qualified," may be registered on the Principal Register. A trademark that is merely descriptive of goods, or their regional origin, or is primarily a surname, is placed on the Supplemental Register.

The Trademark Act of 1946 provides that "For the purposes of registration on the supplemental register, a mark may consist of any trademark, symbol, label package, configuration of goods, name, word, slogan, phrase, surname, geographical name, numeral, or device, or any combination of any of the foregoing, but such mark must be capable of distinguishing the applicant's goods or services."

A trademark cannot be registered if it comprises immoral, deceptive or scandalous matter, or matter that may disparage or falsely suggest a connection with persons living or dead, institutions, beliefs, or national symbols. It cannot use the flag or coat of arms or other insignia of the United States, any state, municipality or foreign nation. It cannot use a portrait, signature or name of a living individual without his consent, or those of a deceased President of the United States without consent of his widow.

An application for registration must be filed in the name of the owner of the mark, who may submit his case or be represented by an attorney at law, or other person authorized to practice in trademark matters. A complete application comprises a written application, a drawing of the mark, five specimens or facsimiles and the filing fee.

The Patent and Trademark Office publishes a pamphlet, General Information Concerning Trademarks, which describes the way applications and drawings are to be prepared and gives sample forms for applications. The Patent and Trademark Office, upon request, will supply forms for the registration of a trademark in the name of (1) an individual, (2) a firm, and (3) a corporation. If facilities permit, the Office will make drawings from the applicant's direction and at his expense. If the application is allowed, the trademark will be published in the Trademark Official Gazette so that anyone who considers that he will be damaged by the new mark may file his opposition in 30 days.

The Trademark Act of 1946 also provides for the registration of service marks, certification marks and collective marks. A service mark is a title, symbol or name used in sale or advertising of services to identify them. A certification mark is used by others than the owner to certify origin or quality, such as work by a union. A collective mark is used by members of a cooperative, an association or other group and indicates membership in a union or other organization. A digest of registered trademarks may be inspected at the Patent and Trademark Office.

A trademark is registered for 20 years and may be renewed for periods of 20 years if still in use in commerce regulated by Congress, or if nonuse is due to special circumstances which excuse nonuse and is not due to any intention to abandon the mark. The fee for the original application is $35, and for the renewal is $25, with lesser fees for corrections, amendments, abstracts of title and other services.

The pamphlet, General Information Concerning Trademarks, is a general guide. The Trademark Rules of Practice of the Patent Office with Forms and Statutes is also published. The Trademark Official Gazette, issued weekly, contains information concerning trademarks published for opposition, registered, and renewed. For these and other trademark publications inquiries may be addressed to the Supt. of Documents, Government Printing Office, Washington, D.C. 20402.

Patents and How to Apply for Them

A patent for an invention is granted by the United States Patent and Trademark Office to the inventor of any new and useful process, machine, manufacture, or composition of matter, or any new and useful improvements in these categories. The grant to the patentee is of "the right to exclude others from making, using or selling the invention throughout the United States" for the term of 17 years. A patent is also granted for certain distinct and new varieties of plants, also for 17 years.

Patents for new, original and ornamental designs for articles of manufacture may be obtained for 3½, 7 and 14 years, as requested by the inventor. The filing fee on each design application is $20; the issue fee is $10 for a 3½-yr. term, $20 for 7 years and $30 for 14 years.

Except in special circumstances, an application must be made by the inventor; if two are associated in the invention both must apply; if the inventor is mentally ill or dead, application may be made by the guardian or administrator of the estate. The specification must include a written description of the invention and of the manner and process of making and using it, and is required to be in such full, clear, concise, and exact terms as to enable any person skilled in the art to which the invention pertains, or with which it is most nearly connected, to make and use the same. The claims are full descriptions of the subject matter of the invention. A drawing is required by the statute in all cases which admit of drawings. The filing fee is $65, with $2 additional for each claim in excess of 10, and $10 additional for each claim in independent form in excess of one.

The Patent and Trademark Office examines the application to determine whether the invention is new and useful and whether the application otherwise complies with the law. If the application is allowed, a notice is sent the applicant and the final fee of $100, plus $10 for each page or portion thereof of specification as printed and $2 for each sheet of drawing, is due within 3 months. The terms "patent applied for" and "patent pending" have no legal significance but falsely using this marking is punishable by a fine.

If the Patent and Trademark Office rejects an application, the applicant may ask for reconsideration, giving reason; if rejected again he may appeal to the Board of Appeals of the Patent and Trademark Office, and if rejected there, may go to the Court of Customs and Patent Appeals or file a civil action in the U.S. District Court for the District of Columbia.

Under certain conditions a license must be obtained before an application for a patent can be filed in a foreign country. The Commissioner of Patents and Trademarks may order an invention kept secret if publication would hurt the national safety or defense. Copies of the Patent Laws, (37 Code of Federal Regulations) and General Information Concerning Patents, can be obtained from the Superintendent of Documents, Government Printing Office, Washington, D.C. 20402.

Delegates from over 40 nations took part in Washington May 25-June 19, 1970, in a diplomatic conference on a Patent Cooperation Treaty. It was unanimously approved and was signed by representatives of 20 governments, including the United States, Great Britain, Germany, Canada and Japan, with many others expected to sign later. The treaty will simplify the filing of patent applications on the same invention in different countries by means of centralized filing procedures and standardized formalities.

Lincoln's Address at Gettysburg, 1863

Fourscore and seven years ago our fathers brought forth on this continent a new nation, conceived in liberty and dedicated to the proposition that all men are created equal.

Now we are engaged in a great civil war, testing whether that nation or any nation so conceived and so dedicated can long endure. We are met on a great battle field of that war. We have come to dedicate a portion of that field, as a final resting-place for those who here gave their lives that that nation might live. It is altogether fitting and proper that we should do this.

But, in a larger sense, we can not dedicate — we can not consecrate — we can not hallow — this ground. The brave men, living and dead, who struggled here, have consecrated it, far above our poor power to add or detract. The world will little note, nor long remember, what we say here, but it can never forget what they did here. It is for us the living, rather, to be dedicated here to the unfinished work which they who fought here have thus far so nobly advanced. It is rather for us to be here dedicated to the great task remaining before us — that from these honored dead we take increased devotion to that cause for which they gave the last full measure of devotion — that we here highly resolve that these dead shall not have died in vain — that this nation, under God, shall have a new birth of freedom — and that government of the people, by the people, for the people, shall not perish from the earth.

History of the Address

President Lincoln delivered his address at the dedication of the military cemetery at Gettysburg, Pa., Nov. 19, 1863. The battle had been fought July 1-3, 1863. He was preceded by Edward Everett, former president of Harvard, secretary of state and senator from Massachusetts, then 69 and one of the nation's great orators. Everett gave a full resume of the battle, Lincoln's speech was so short that the photographer did not get his camera adjusted in time. The report that newspapers ignored Lincoln's address is not entirely accurate; Everett's address swamped their columns, but the greatness of Lincoln's speech was immediately recognized. Everett wrote him: "I should be glad if I could flatter myself that I came as near the central idea of the occasion in two hours as you did in two minutes."

Five copies of the Gettysburg address in Lincoln's hand are extant. The first and 2d drafts, prepared in Washington and Gettysburg just before delivery, are in the Library of Congress. The 3d draft, written at the request of Everett to be sold at a fair in New York for the benefit of soldiers, was given the Illinois State Historical Library by popular subscription.

The 4th copy was written out by Lincoln for George Bancroft, the historian, and remained in custody of the Bancroft family until 1929, when it was acquired by Mrs. Nicholas H. Noyes, of Indianapolis, Ind. In 1949 Mrs. Noyes presented this copy to the Cornell University Library, Ithaca, N.Y. The 5th copy, usually described as the clearest and best, was also written by Lincoln for George Bancroft, for facsimile reproduction in a volume to be sold for the benefit of soldiers and sailors in Baltimore, where Bancroft lived. It is the 2d Bancroft copy. It passed to Bancroft's stepchildren, named Bliss, and was sold for $54,000 by the estate of Dr. William J. A. Bliss in New York Apr. 27, 1949, to Oscar B. Cintas, former Cuban ambassador to the United States. He died in May 1957 and willed it to the Lincoln Room of the White House, where it was placed in Mar. 1959. Lincoln's spelling of battle field and can not as separated words in that version is reproduced above.

Sen. John Sherman Cooper (R. Ky.), president of the Lincoln Sesquicentennial Commission, on June 17, 1959, presented a Latin translation of Lincoln's Gettysburg Address to the Apostolic Delegation of the Roman Catholic Church, in Washington, D. C. It was engrossed on vellum and was to be sent to Pope John XXIII for deposit in the Vatican Library. The presentation took place in the presence of government officials and members of the diplomatic corps. The translation was made by the Rt. Rev. Edwin Ryan of White Plains, N. Y. The Latin version was ordered printed in the Congressional Record.

Washington's Letter on Bigotry and Persecution

During a tour of various New England states in 1790, then President George Washington was greeted by various leaders in Newport, R. I. Among the clergy was Moses Seixas, the warden of the Hebrew congregation, who greeted Washington and praised the new government for its opposition to bigotry. Washington acknowledged the greeting in a letter to the congregation:

Gentlemen:

While I received with much satisfaction, your address replete with expressions of affection and esteem; I rejoice in the opportunity of assuring you, that I shall always retain a grateful remembrance of the cordial welcome I experienced in my visit to Newport from all classes of Citizens.

The reflection on the days of difficulty and danger which are past is rendered the more sweet, from a consciousness that they are succeeded by days of uncommon prosperity and security. If we have wisdom to make the best use of the advantages with which we are now favored, we cannot fail, under the just administration of a good Government, to become a great and happy people.

The Citizens of the United States of America have a right to applaud themselves for having given to mankind examples of an enlarged and liberal policy; a policy worthy of imitation. All possess alike liberty of conscience and immunities of citizenship. It is now no more that toleration is spoken of, as if it was by the indulgence of one class of people, that another enjoyed the exercise of their inherent natural rights. For happily the Government of the United States, which gives to bigotry no sanction, to persecution no assistance, requires only that they who live under its protection, should demean themselves as good citizens, in giving it on all occasions their effectual support.

It would be inconsistent with the frankness of my character not to avow that I am pleased with your favorable opinion of my administration, and fervent wishes for my felicity. May the Children of the Stock of Abraham, who dwell in this land, continue to merit and enjoy the good will of the other Inhabitants; while everyone shall sit in safety under his own vine and fig tree, and there shall be none to make him afraid. May the father of all mercies scatter light and not darkness in our paths, and make us all in our several vocations useful here, and in his own due time and way everlastingly happy.

Go. Washington

U. S. Passport, Visa and Health Requirements

Source: Passport Office, U.S. Dept. of State and U.S. Public Health Service

Passports are issued by the United States Department of State to citizens and nationals of the United States for the purpose of documenting them for their foreign travel and to identify them as Americans. Some countries require a visa, or stamp of approval, to be affixed to the passport by the consulate of the country to be visited, while others waive this formality. Also some countries, which do not require visas, require tourist cards from visitors making a short stay.

Unless specifically endorsed, passports may not be used for travel into or through Cuba, North Korea or North Vietnam, or for travel into or through other countries or areas as determined to be in the national interest by the Secretary of State.

How to Obtain a Passport

An applicant for a passport who has never been previously issued a passport in his own name, must execute an application in person before (1) a Passport Agent; (2) a clerk of any Federal court; (3) a clerk of any State court of record or a judge or clerk of any probate court; (4) a postal employee designated by the Postmaster at a Post Office which has been selected to accept passport applications; or (5) a diplomatic or consular officer of the U.S. abroad. A wife/husband who is to be included in the passport must appear with the applicant and execute the application. Passport Agencies are located at Boston (John F. Kennedy Bldg., Government Center), Chicago (Federal Office Bldg., 230 S. Dearborn); Honolulu (Fed. Bldg.); Los Angeles (Hawthorne Fed. Bldg., 15000 Aviation Blvd., Rm. 2W16, Lawndale, Calif.); Miami (51 S.W. First Ave.); New Orleans (International Trade Mart, 2 Canal Street); New York (630 Fifth Ave.); Philadelphia, (Federal Bldg., 600 Arch Street); San Francisco (Fed. Bldg., 450 Golden Gate Ave.); Seattle (Federal Bldg., 915 Second Ave.); Washington D.C. (Passport Office, 1425 K St., N.W.)

A passport previously issued to, or one in which the applicant was included, will be accepted as proof of citizenship in lieu of the following documents. A person born in the United States shall present his birth certificate. To be acceptable, the certificate must show the given name and surname, the date and place of birth and that the birth record was filed shortly after birth. The certificate must also be certified with the registrar's signature and the raised, impressed, embossed, or multi-colored seal of his office. Uncertified copies of birth certificates are not acceptable. A delayed birth certificate (a record filed more than one year after the date of birth) is acceptable provided that it shows that the report of birth was supported by acceptable secondary evidence of birth as described below.

If such primary evidence is not obtainable, a notice from the registrar shall be submitted stating that no birth record exists. The notice shall be accompanied by the best obtainable secondary evidence such as a baptismal certificate, a certificate of circumcision, a hospital birth record, affidavits of persons having personal knowledge of the facts of the birth or other documentary evidence such as early census, school or family bible records, newspaper files and insurance papers. Secondary evidence should be created as close to the time of birth as possible.

A person in the U.S. who has been issued a passport in his own name within the last eight years may obtain a new passport by filling out, signing and mailing a passport by mail application together with his previous passport, two identical signed photographs taken within the last 6 months and the established fee to the nearest Passport Agency or to the Passport Office in Wash., D.C. If, however, an applicant is applying for a passport for the first time, if his prior passport was issued before his 18th birthday, if he wishes to include a person other than himself in the passport, or if he is applying for an official, diplomatic, or other no-fee passport, he must execute a passport application in person before a Passport Agent; a clerk of any Federal court, a clerk of any State court of record or a judge or clerk of any probate court, a postal employee designated by the Postmaster at a Post Office which has been selected to accept passport applications; or a diplomatic or consular officer of the U.S. abroad.

A naturalized citizen should present his naturalization certificate. A person born abroad claiming citizenship through either a native-born or naturalized citizen must submit a certificate of citizenship issued by the Immigration and Naturalization Service; or a Consular Report of Birth or Certification of Birth issued by the Dept. of State. If one of the above documents has not been obtained, he must submit evidence of citizenship of the parent(s) through whom citizenship is claimed and evidence which would establish the parent/child relationship. Additionally, if through birth to one American and one alien parent, an affidavit from parent(s) showing periods and places of residence in the United States and abroad, specifying periods spent abroad in the employment of the U.S. Government, including the Armed Forces, or with certain international organizations; if through naturalization of parents, evidence of admission to the United States for permanent residence.

A married woman must submit evidence of citizenship and, under certain conditions, marriage. Special laws govern women married prior to Sept. 22, 1922; should be discussed with the person executing the application.

The applicant shall establish his identity to the satisfaction of the person executing the application. Proof of identity may be established through a personal knowledge of the applicant by the Clerk or Agent or by an item which contains the signature and either a physical description or photograph of the applicant. The following items of identification are acceptable; previous United States Passport; certificate of naturalization; driver's license (not temporary or learner's license); a governmental (Federal, State, Municipal) identification card or pass.

If the applicant is not able to establish his identity by personal knowledge or by presentation of one of the above acceptable documents, he should be accompanied by an identifying witness who has known him for at least 2 years, and who is a U.S. citizen or a permanent resident alien of the United States. The witness shall be required to establish his own identity to the satisfaction of the person executing the application by one of the above means.

The identifying witness shall sign an affidavit in the presence of the same person who executes the passport application. The affidavit shall show:

The witness resides at a specific address:

The witness knows or has reason to believe that the applicant is a citizen of the United States:

The basis of the witness' knowledge concerning the applicant;

The information set forth in the affidavit is true to the best of his knowledge and belief.

A person included in the passport of another may not use the passport for travel unless he is accompanied by the bearer.

Aliens — An alien leaving the U.S. must request passport facilities from his home government. He must have a permit from his local Collector of Internal Revenue, and if he wishes to return he should request a re-entry permit from the Immigration and Naturalization Service if it is required.

Contract Employees — Persons traveling because of a contract with the Government must submit with their applications letters from their employer stating position, destination and purpose of travel and Armed Forces contract number when pertinent.

Photographs and Fees

Photographs — Identical photographs taken within six months, both signed by the applicant and which are a good likeness, must accompany the passport application. A group photograph is preferred if more than one person is included in the passport. Photographs may be in color or in black and white. They must be full face, printed on a thin, nonglossy paper base on a light background and must be no smaller than $2^1/_2$ x $2^1/_2$ inches nor larger than 3 x 3 inches in size. They must also be capable of withstanding a mounting temperature of over 200°F.

Fees — The passport fee is $10. A fee of $3 shall be charged for execution of the application. No execution fee is payable where a passport is applied for by mail. All applicants must pay the passport fee and, where applicable, the execution fee unless specifically exempted by law. If applying in person, service will be expedited by presenting exact fees. An emergency service fee of $10 is charged in addition to all other fees where work must be performed after hours. The only other fees are for special postage. A passport is valid for five years. Upon expiration, passports may no longer be renewed. New passports must be obtained for travel.

During the calendar year 1974 the Passport Office, Dept. of State, issued 2,415,003 passports to American citizens.

The loss of a valid passport is a serious matter and should be reported in writing immediately to the Passport Office, Dept. of State, Wash., D.C. 20524, or to the nearest consular office of the U.S. when abroad.

Foreign Regulations

A visa is an endorsement or a notation, usually rubber stamped in a passport by a representative of the country to be visited. It certifies that the bearer of the passport is to be permitted to enter that country for a certain purpose and length of time. With the exception of the Iron Curtain countries, no visas are required for brief tourist travel to Western European countries. Authoritative visa information can be obtained by writing directly to foreign consular officials. The locations of foreign consular offices in the U.S. may be obtained by consulting the Congressional Directory available in most libraries. (Check appropriate city telephone directories for complete address.)

Health Information

Smallpox — Smallpox vaccination is required for travel to most countries of the world except Europe. However, in the event of an outbreak of smallpox in any country in Europe, most countries remaining on the itinerary following a visit to the infected country will require a Vaccination Certificate. A Certificate is not required for travel from the United States directly to and from Europe, Canada, Mexico, Australia, and New Zealand. For travel to more than one island in the Caribbean, a Certificate will probably be required. The United States requires a Certificate upon the traveler's return only if, in the preceding 14 days, he has visited a country reporting smallpox.

Yellow Fever — A few African countries require a Vaccination Certificate of all travelers. A number of countries require vaccination if travelers arrive from infected or endemic areas. Vaccination is recommended for travel to infected areas, currently parts of Africa and South America. The United States has no vaccination requirement.

Cholera — A few countries require vaccination if travelers arrive from infected areas. The United States has no vaccination requirement.

Plague — Vaccination is not required by any country as a condition of entry. Selective immunization is advisable for travelers to Vietnam, Khmer Republic, and Laos.

Vaccination Information — Yellow fever vaccine must be obtained at an officially designated Yellow Fever Vaccination Center, and the Certificate, valid for 10 years, must be stamped by the Center. Other vaccinations may be obtained from licensed physicians, and sometimes from local health departments. The Smallpox Certificate, valid for 3 years, and the Cholera Certificate, valid for 6 months, must be stamped by the State or local health department.

Vaccinations must be recorded on an approved version of PHS-731, International Certificates of Vaccination, which are available from State and local health departments, passport offices, travel agencies, and the Superintendent of Documents, U.S. Printing Office, Washington, D.C. 20402.

Travelers are advised to contact their local health department 2 weeks prior to departure to obtain the most current information on countries to be visited.

Customs Exemptions and Advice to Travelers

United States residents returning after a stay abroad of at least 48 hours are, generally speaking, granted customs exemptions of $100 each. Each returning resident may bring home free of duty articles totaling $100 in fair retail value in the country of acquisition, subject to limitations on liquors and cigars. These articles must accompany the traveler at the time of his return, must be for his personal or household use, must have been acquired as an incident of his trip, and must be properly declared to Customs. Not more than one quart of alcoholic beverages may be included in the $100 exemption.

If a U. S. resident arrives directly or indirectly from American Samoa, Guam, or the Virgin Islands of the United States, his purchase may be valued up to $200 fair retail value, but not more than $100 of the exemption may be applied to the value of articles acquired elsewhere than in such insular possessions, and one gallon of alcoholic beverages may be included in his exemption, but not more than 1 quart of such beverages may have been acquired elsewhere than in the designated islands.

The exemption for articles acquired in the Virgin Islands of the United States and in Mexico is not conditional upon the 48-hour absence requirement.

In either case, the exemption for alcoholic beverages is accorded only when the returning resident has attained 21 years of age at the time of his arrival. One hundred cigars may be included (except Cuban products) in either exemption.

The $100 or $200 exemption may be granted only if the exemption, or any part of it, has not been used within the preceding 30-day period.

Bona fide gifts costing no more than $10 fair retail value or $20 from American Samoa, Guam, or Virgin Islands, may be mailed to friends at home duty-free; addressee cannot receive in a single day gifts exceeding the $10 limit.

Air Travel

On a first-class trans-Atlantic flight a passenger may carry 66 lbs. of luggage free; a tourist class passenger, 44 lbs. free. A charge is made for extra weight.

Precautions for Travel

In some cases naturalized United States citizens desiring to visit the countries of their birth, and sometimes their American-born children traveling to those countries, may be subject to military service and other regulations there. The United States Department of State advises such travelers to get specific information from the consulates of the countries concerned before departure.

Service in Foreign Armed Forces

Voluntary service in the armed forces of a foreign state engaged in hostilities against the U. S. is highly persuasive evidence of an intention to relinquish citizenship and will normally result in loss of U. S. citizenship. Voluntary service in the armed forces of a foreign state not engaged in hostilities against the U. S. does not result in loss of U. S. citizenship unless there is persuasive evidence of an intent to transfer or abandon allegiance by reason of such military service.

United States Immigration Law

The national origins quota system disappeared from United States immigration procedures July 1, 1968, as provided by the Act. of Oct. 3, 1965, which amended the Immigration and Nationality Act.

The Immigration and Nationality Act, as amended, provides for numerical limitations on immigration from the Eastern and Western Hemispheres. Not subject to any numerical limitations, however, are immigrants who are spouses or children of U.S. citizens, or parents of citizens who are 21 years of age or older; returning residents; certain former U.S. citizens; ministers of religion; and certain long-term U. S. Government employees.

The Act of Oct. 3, 1965, established new controls to protect the American labor market from an influx of skilled and unskilled foreign labor. The primary responsibility was placed on the would-be immigrant to obtain the Secretary of Labor's clearance, prior to the issuance of a visa, establishing that there are not sufficient workers in the U. S. at the alien's destination who are able, willing and qualified to perform the skilled or unskilled labor; and that the employment of the alien will not adversely affect wages and working conditions of workers in the U. S. similarly employed.

Eastern Hemisphere Immigrants

Persons born in countries of the Eastern Hemisphere and dependent areas thereof are subject to an annual limitation of 170,000. Within this numerical limitation there is an annual limitation of 20,000 for each country and 200 for each dependent area. Applicants are classified as either preference or nonpreference.

The preference visa categories are based on certain relationships to persons in the U. S.; i.e., unmarried sons and daughters of United States citizens, spouses and unmarried sons and daughters of resident aliens, married sons and daughters of U.S. citizens, and brothers and sisters of U. S. citizens (first, second, fourth, and fifth preference, respectively); Certain professions and skills (third preference); and certain categories of workers which are in short supply in the U. S. (6th preference); refugees (7th preference). Spouses and children of preference applicants are entitled to the same preference if accompanying or following to join such persons.

Except for refugee status, preference status is based upon approved petitions, filed with the Immigration and Naturalization Service, by the appropriate relative or employer (or in the 3rd preference by the alien himself). Visa numbers for qualified preference applicants are made available in the order of the preference classes and, within such classes, in the order of the filing dates of the petitions.

Immigrants not entitled to classification within one of the above-mentioned preference groups are nonpreference applicants and receive only those visa numbers not needed by preference applicants.

A prerequisite for nonpreference classification is a labor certification under Section 212(a) (14) of the Immigration and Nationality Act, or satisfactory evidence that the provisions of that section do not apply to the alien's case. The availability of nonpreference visa numbers is contingent on the level of preference demand and cannot therefore be predicted with real accuracy. However, in some countries and dependent areas the higher preference categories may utilize the entire numerical limitation which will prevent any visa numbers from becoming available for persons from such countries or areas in the nonpreference category.

Western Hemisphere Immigrants

The Act establishes an annual ceiling of 120,000 on immigration by persons born in independent countries of the Western Hemisphere (Canada, Mexico, Central and South America and the Caribbean Area). Within this over-all ceiling there is no numerical limitation set for individual countries, and no preference classes have been established for such applicants. Visas within the 120,000 limitation will be made available to qualified applicants in the chronological order of the priority dates. An applicant's date is the date a labor certification for the applicant is accepted for processing by the Dept. of Labor or the date proof is received by a consular officer that a labor certification is not required.

Excludable Aliens

Aliens who are excludable on medical grounds are those who are mentally retarded, insane, psychopathic, mentally defective, sexual deviates, chronic alcoholics, narcotic addicts, and those who are afflicted with any dangerous contagious disease or who have a physical defect impairing the ability to earn a living. Also excludable are paupers, beggars, illiterates, stowaways, prostitutes, persons engaged in commercial vice, narcotics traffickers, persons convicted of crimes involving moral turpitude, persons who obtain or try to obtain a visa by fraud, or who left the U. S. to avoid military service. Those excludable on security grounds include persons who are anarchists, members or affiliates of certain proscribed organizations, and those who teach or advocate overthrow of the U. S. Government by force or violence.

For more detailed information consult the nearest office of the U. S. Immigration & Naturalization Service, or any U. S. Consul abroad.

Naturalization: How to Become an American Citizen

Source: The Federal Statutes

A person who desires to be naturalized as a citizen of the United States may obtain the necessary application form as well as detailed information from the nearest office of the Immigration and Naturalization Service or from the clerk of a court handling naturalization cases.

There are no racial bars to naturalization. Women have the same right as men to become naturalized.

An applicant must be at least 18 years old. He must have been a lawful resident of the United States continuously for 5 years. For husbands and wives of U.S. citizens the period is 3 years in most instances. Special provisions apply to certain veterans of the Armed Forces.

An applicant must have been physically present in this country for at least half of the required 5 years' residence.

Every applicant for naturalization must:

(1) sign the petition in his own handwriting, if physically able to write.

(2) demonstrate an understanding of the English language, including an ability to read, write, and speak words in ordinary usage in the English language (persons physically unable to do so, and per-

sons who were on December 24, 1952 over 50 years of age and had been residing in the United States for 20 years are excepted).

(3) have been a person of good moral character, attached to the principles of the Constitution, and well disposed to the good order and happiness of the United States for five years just before filing the petition or for whatever other period of residence is required in his case and continue to be such a person until admitted to citizenship; and

(4) demonstrate a knowledge and understanding of the fundamentals of the history, and the principles and form of government, of the U.S.

The petitioner also is obliged to have two credible citizen witnesses. These witnesses must have personal knowledge of the applicant.

A person not of good moral character includes a habitual drunkard, an adulterer, a polygamist, a violator of criminal law, a gambler, one who gave false testimony to obtain a benefit under the immigration law, one in prison for 180 days or more, one convicted of murder.

Naturalization is denied to any person who, within 10 years, has been subversive, including communists and others who favor totalitarian government, and who were members of a proscribed organization, unless the petitioner was under 16 or joined under duress.

A law approved Aug. 20, 1958, provides for the expeditious naturalization of alien spouses and adopted children of U.S. citizens who are missionaries or performing religious duties and are stationed abroad.

When the applicant files his petition he pays the court clerk $25. At the preliminary hearing he may be represented by a lawyer or social service agency. There is a 30-day wait. If action is favorable, there is a final hearing before a judge, who administers the following oath of allegiance:

Oath of Allegiance

I hereby declare, on oath, that I absolutely and entirely renounce and abjure all allegiance and fidelity to any foreign prince, potentate, state or sovereignty, to whom or which I have heretofore been a subject or citizen; that I will support and defend the Consititution and laws of the United States of America against all enemies, foreign and domestic; that I will bear true faith and allegiance to the same; that I will bear arms on behalf of the United States when required by the law; that I will perform noncombatant service in the armed forces of the United States when required by the law; that I will perform work of national importance under civilian direction when required by the law; and that I take this obligation freely without any mental reservation or purpose of evasion; so help me God.

Immigrants Admitted From All Countries

Source: Immigration and Naturalization Service, U.S. Dept. of Justice

Year	Number	Year	Number	Year	Number	Year	Number
1820	8,385	1881-1890	5,246,613	1951-1960	2,515,479	1969	358,579
1821-1830	143,439	1891-1900	3,687,564	1962	283,763	1970	373,326
1831-1840	599,125	1901-1910	8,795,386	1963	306,360	1971	370,478
1841-1850	1,713,251	1911-1920	5,735,811	1964	292,248	1972	384,685
1851-1860	2,598,214	1921-1930	4,107,209	1965	296,697	1973	400,063
1861-1870	2,314,824	1931-1940	528,431	1966	323,040	1974	394,861
1871-1880	2,812,191	1941-1950	1,035,039	1968	454,448	1820-1974	46,712,725

Passports Issued and Renewed

Source: Passport Office, Dept. of State

Passports are actual count; other data based on sample.

Item	1960	1965	1969[5]	1970	1971	1972	1973	1974
New and renewed passports	853,087	1,330,290	1,820,192	2,219,159	2,398,968	2,728,021	2,729,104	2,415,003
Object of Travel.[1]								
Government	115,910	119,130	167,562	146,169	98,938	136,901	146,494	206,343
Nongovernment	737,177	1,139,160	1,652,630	2,072,990	2,300,030	2,591,120	2,582,610	2,208,660
Personal reasons[2]	321,590	487,470	1,475,630	1,791,330	2,156,640	2,042,560	1,245,780	384,930
Pleasure[3]	350,897	535,150	130,670	216,700	109,210	441,010	1,077,240	1,382,100
Business[4]	24,540	76,210	25,180	39,940	15,570	68,700	154,820	267,980
Education	31,240	31,120	15,490	20,230	16,040	33,290	95,240	153,210
Religion	6,780	6,780	2,180	3,350	1,380	3,980	7,930	16,510
Health	1,460	500	220	640	130	800	1,140	1,860
Other	670	1,930	3,260	800	1,060	780	460	2,070
First area destination:								
Africa	8,440	19,580	19,760	18,790	14,820	29,750	26,420	32,110
Australia and Oceania	35,220	50,750	68,190	51,210	48,350	78,580	80,670	101,250
Europe	669,662	992,800	1,460,212	1,910,169	2,139,508	2,244,161	2,181,114	1,714,613
Far East	55,960	111,320	125,100	116,730	73,250	135,230	139,740	162,130
North Central and South America	58,935	99,620	91,850	72,410	68,630	135,720	189,280	287,260
Middle-East	24,670	56,070	54,990	48,890	54,380	103,870	111,000	117,110
World Tour	200	150	90	960	30	710	880	530
Mode of Travel — departure:[6]								
Ship	226,245	39,340	2,766	....	....	....	....	....
Air	626,842	1,290,950	1,817,426	....	....	....	....	....
Sex of Passport Recipients:								
Male	419,615	700,080	945,520	1,123,620	1,266,770	1,358,530	1,321,050	1,154,940
Female	433,472	630,210	874,672	1,095,539	1,132,198	1,369,491	1,408,054	1,260,063
Citizenship of Passport Recipients:								
Native	710,172	1,236,797	1,702,320	2,072,560	2,270,610	2,553,750	2,511,266	2,154,920
Naturalized	142,915	93,493	117,872	146,599	128,358	174,271	217,838	260,083

(1). Data not entirely comparable because of changes in classifications in 1961.
(2). Includes "Personal business," "Join husband," "Accompany husband," "Business and pleasure," "Visit family."
(3). Includes "Sightsee," "Vacation," "Visit," and "Tourist."
(4). Includes applicants formerly listed under "Employment" and "Commercial business."
(5). Legislation effective Aug. 26, 1968, eliminated passport renewals.
(6) Data eliminated. Over 99% of passport recipients indicate departure by air.

Forms of Address for Persons of Rank and Public Office

In these examples John Smith is used as a representative American name. The salutation Dear Sir is always permissible when addressing a person not known to the writer.

President of the United States

Address: The President, The White House, Washington, D.C. 20500. Also, The President and Mrs. ——.
Salutation: Dear Sir or Mr. President or Dear Mr. President. More intimately: My dear Mr. President. Also: Dear Mr. President and Mrs. ——
The vice president takes the same forms.

Cabinet Officers

Address: Mr. John Smith, Secretary of State, Washington, D.C. or The Hon. John Smith. Similar addresses for other members of the cabinet. Also: Secretary and Mrs. John Smith.
Salutation: Dear Sir, or Dear Mr. Secretary. Also: Dear Mr. and Mrs. Smith.

The Bench

Address: The Hon. John Smith, Chief Justice of the United States. The Hon. John Smith, Associate Justice of the Supreme Court of the United States. The Hon. John Smith, Associate Judge, U. S. District Court.
Salutations: Dear Sir or Dear Mr. Chief Justice. Dear Mr. Justice. Dear Judge Smith.

Members of Congress

Address: The Hon. John Smith, United States Senate, Washington, D.C. 20510, or Sen. John Smith, etc. Also The Hon. John Smith, House of Representatives, Washington, D.C. 20515, or Rep. John Smith, etc.
Salutation: Dear Mr. Senator or Dear Mr. Smith; for Representative, Dear Mr. Smith.

Officers of Armed Forces

Address: Careful attention should be given to the precise rank, thus: General of the Army John Smith, Fleet Admiral John Smith. The rules for Air Force are same as Army.
Salutation: Dear Sir, or Dear General. All general officers, whatever rank, are entitled to be addressed as generals. Likewise a lieutenant colonel is addressed as colonel and first and second lieutenants are addressed as lieutenant.
Warrant officers and flight officers are addressed as Mister. Chaplains are addressed as Chaplain. A Catholic chaplain may be addressed as Father. Cadets of the United States Military Academy and Air Force Academy are addressed as Cadet. Noncommissioned officers are addressed by their titles. In the U. S. Navy all men from midshipman at Annapolis up to and including lieutenant commander are addressed as Mister.

Ambassador, Governor, Mayor

Address: The Hon. John Smith, followed by his title. He can be addressed either at his embassy, or at the Department of State, Washington, D.C. A foreign ambassador is His Excellency.
Salutation: Dear Mr. Ambassador. A foreign ambassador is Your Excellency.
Governors and mayors are often addressed as The Hon. John Smith, Governor of ——, or The Hon. John Smith, Mayor of ——; also Governor John Smith, State House, Albany, N.Y., or Mayor John Smith, City Hall, Erie, Pa.

The Clergy

Address: His Holiness, the Pope, or His Holiness Pope (name), State of Vatican City, Italy.
Salutation: Your Holiness or Most Holy Father.
Also: His Eminence, John, Cardinal Smith; salutation: Your Eminence. An archbishop or a bishop is addressed The Most Reverend, and the salutation is Your Excellency. A monsignor who is a papal chamberlain is The Very Reverend Monsignor and the salutation is Dear Sir or Very Reverend Monsignor; a monsignor who is a domestic prelate is The Right Reverend Monsignor and salutation is Right Reverend Monsignor. A priest is addressed Reverend John Smith. A brother of an order is addressed Brother ——. A sister takes the same form.
A bishop of the Protestant Episcopal Church is The Right Reverend John Smith; salutation is Right Reverend Sir, or Dear Bishop Smith. If a clergyman is a doctor of divinity, he is addressed: The Reverend John Smith, D.D., and the salutation is Reverend Sir, or Dear Dr. Smith. When a clergyman does not have the degree the salutation is Dear Mr. Smith.
A bishop of the Methodist Church is addressed Bishop John Smith with titles following.

Royalty and Nobility

An emperor is to be addressed in a letter as Sir, or Your Imperial Majesty.
A king or queen is addressed as His Majesty (Name), King of (Name), or Her Majesty (Name), Queen of (Name). Salutation: Sir, ðr Madam, or May it please Your Majesty.
Princes and princesses and other persons of royal blood are addressed as His (or Her) Royal Highness, and saluted with May it please Your Royal Highness.
A duke or marquis is My Lord Duke (or Marquis), a duke is His (or Your) Grace.

Famous Fairs and Expositions

1851	Great Exhibition opened, Crystal Palace, Hyde Park, London.
1853 July 14	New York World's Fair opened, Crystal Palace, N. Y. C.
1867 Apr. 1	International Exhibition, Paris.
1873 May 1	International Exhibition, Vienna.
1876 May-Nov.	Centennial Expos., Philadelphia.
1889 May 6-Nov. 6.	Universal Exposition, Paris.
1893 May 1-Oct. 30.	World's Columbian Exposition, Chicago.
1898 June 1-Oct. 31	Trans-Mississippi International Exposition, Omaha.
1900 Apr. 15	International Exposition, Paris.
1901 May 1-Nov. 2.	Pan-American Expo: Buffalo.
1904 Apr. 20-Dec. 1	Louisiana Purchase Exposition, St. Louis.
1905 June 1	Lewis and Clark Centennial Exposition opened, Portland, Ore.
1907 Apr. 26	Jamestown, Va., Tercentenary Exposition, opened.
1909 June 1-Oct. 16	Alaska-Yukon-Pacific Exposition, Seattle.
1909 Sept. 25-Oct. 2.	Hudson-Fulton Celebration, N.Y.
1910 Apr. 23	International Exhibition, Brussels.
1913 Apr. 26	International Exposition opened, Ghent, Belgium.
1915 Feb. 20-Dec. 4.	Panama-Pacific International Exposition, San Francisco.
1915	Panama-California Exposition, San Diego.
1922-23	Brazilian Expos., Rio de Janeiro.
1924-25	British Empire Expo. Wembley.
1926 May 31-Nov. 30.	Sesquicentennial Exposition, Phila.
1931	International Colonial and Overseas Exposition, Paris.
1933 May 27-Nov. 12.	Century of Progress, Chicago.
1934 May 26-Oct. 31.	Century of Progress, Chicago.
1936	Texas Centennial Expos., Dallas.
1936-1937	Great Lakes Expos., Cleveland.
1939 Feb. 18-Oct. 29	Golden Gate International Exposition, San Francisco.
1939 Apr. 20-Oct. 31.	New York World's Fair.
1940 May 11-Oct. 21.	New York World's Fair.
1957 Apr. 26-Oct. 30.	Jamestown, Va., 350th Anniv.
1958 Apr. 17-Oct. 19.	World's Fair, Brussels.
1962 Apr. 21-Oct. 21.	Century 21 Exposition, Seattle.
1964 Apr. 22-Oct. 18.	New York World's Fair.
1965 Apr. 21-Oct. 17.	New York World's Fair.
1967 Apr. 28-Oct. 27.	Universal and International Exhibition (Expo 67), Montreal.
1968 Apr. 6-Oct. 6.	HemisFair 1968, San Antonio.
1970 Mar. 15-Sept. 13.	Expo '70 (Japan World Exposition), Osaka, Japan.
1974 May 4-Nov. 3.	Expo 74, Spokane, Wash.

Memorable Manned Space Flights

Sources: National Aeronautics and Space Administration and The World Almanac.

Crew, Date	Mission Name	Orbits[1]	Duration	Remarks
Yuri A. Gagarin (4/12/61)............	Vostok 1	1	1h 48m	First manned orbital flight.
Alan Z. Shepard Jr. (5/5/61).............	Mercury-Redstone 3	(2)	15m 22s	First American in space.
Virgil I. Grissom (7/21/61)............	Mercury-Redstone 4	(2)	15m 37s	Spacecraft sank, Grissom rescued.
Gherman S. Titov (8/6-7/61)............	Vostok 2	16	25h 18m	First space flight of more than 24 hrs.
John H. Glenn Jr. (2/20/62).............	Mercury-Atlas 6	3	4h 55m 23s	First American in orbit.
M. Scott Carpenter (5/24/62)............	Mercury-Atlas 7	3	4h 56m 05s	Manual retrofire error caused 250 mi. landing overshoot.
Andrian G. Nikolayev (8/11-15/62).........	Vostok 3	64	94h 22m	Vostok 3 and 4 made first group flight.
Pavel R. Popovich (8/12-15/62).........	Vostok 4	48	70h 57m	On first orbit it came within 3 miles of Vostok 3.
Walter M. Schirra, Jr. (10/3/62).........	Mercury-Atlas 8	6	9h 13m 11s	Closest splashdown to target to date (4.5 mi.).
L. Gordon Cooper (5/15-16/63).........	Mercury-Atlas 9	22	34h 19m 49s	First U.S. evaluation of effects on man of one day in space.
Valery F. Bykovsky (6/14-6/19/63).......	Vostok 5	81	119h 06m	Vostok 5 and 6 made 2d group flight.
Valentina V. Tereshkova (6/16-19/63).........	Vostok 6	48	70h 50m	First woman in space.
Vladimir M. Komarov, Konstantin P. Feoktistov, Boris B. Yegorov (10/12/64)............	Voskhod 1	16	24h 17m	First 3-man orbital flight; first without space suits.
Pavel I. Belyayev, Aleksei A. Leonov (3/18/65).............	Voskhod 2	17	26h 02m	Leonov made first "space walk" (10 min.).
Virgil I. Grissom, John W. Young (3/23/65)............	Gemini-Titan 3	3	4h 53m 00s	First manned spacecraft to change its orbital path.
James A. McDivitt, Edward H. White 2d, (6/3-7/65)............	Gemini-Titan 4	62	97h 56m 11s	White was first American to "walk in space" (20 min.).
L. Gordon Cooper Jr., Charles Conrad Jr. (8/21-29/65).........	Gemini-Titan 5	120	190h 55m 14s	First use of fuel cells for electric power; evaluated guidance and navigation system.
Frank Borman, James A. Lovell Jr. (12/4-18/65).........	Gemini-Titan 7	206	330h 35m 31s	Longest duration Gemini flight.
Walter M. Schirra Jr., Thomas P. Stafford (12/15-16/65)........	Gemini-Titan 6-A	16	25h 51m 24s	Completed world's first space rendezvous with Gemini 7.
Neil A. Armstrong, David R. Scott (3/16-17/66).........	Gemini-Titan 8	6.5	10h 41m 26s	First docking of one space vehicle with another; mission aborted, control malfunction.
Thomas P. Stafford, Eugene A. Cernan (6/3-6/66)............	Gemini-Titan 9-A	44	72h 21m 00s	Made rendezvous, but didn't dock due to malfunction; landed 0.38 mi. from target.
John W. Young, Michael Collins (7/18-21/66).........	Gemini-Titan 10	43	70h 46m 39s	First use of Agena target vehicle's propulsion systems; rendezvoused with Gemini 8.
Charles Conrad Jr., Richard F. Gordon Jr. (9/12-15/66).........	Gemini-Titan 11	44	71h 17m 08s	Docked, made 2 revolutions of earth tethered; set Gemini altitude record (739.2 mi.).
James A. Lovell Jr., Edwin E. Aldrin Jr. (11/11-15/66)........	Gemini-Titan 12	59	94h 34m 31s	Final Gemini mission; record 5½ hrs. of extravehicular activity.
Vladimir M. Komarov (4/23/67)............	Soyuz 1	17	26h 40m	Crashed after re-entry killing Komarov.
Walter M. Schirra Jr., Donn F. Eisele, R. Walter Cunningham (10/11-22/68)........	Apollo-Saturn 7	163	260h 09m 03s	First manned flight of Apollo spacecraft command-service module only.
Georgi T. Beregovoi (10/26-30/68)........	Soyuz 3	64	94h 51m	Made rendezvous with unmanned Soyuz 2.
Frank Borman, James A. Lovell Jr., William A. Anders (12/21-27/68).........	Apollo-Saturn 8	10[3]	147h 00m 42s	First flight to moon (command-service module only); views of lunar surface televised to earth.
Vladimir A. Shatalov (1/14-17/69).........	Soyuz 4	45	71h 14m	Docked with Soyuz 5.

Crew (date)	Spacecraft	Orbits	Duration	Remarks
Boris V. Volyanov, Aleksei S. Yeliseyev, Yevgeny V. Khrunov (1/15-18/69)	Soyuz 5	46	72h 46m	Docked with Soyuz 4; Yeliseyev and Khrunov transferred to Soyuz 4.
James A. McDivitt, David R. Scott, Russell L. Schweickart (3/3-13/69)	Apollo-Saturn 9	151	241h 00m 54s	First manned flight of lunar module.
Thomas P. Stafford, Eugene A. Cernan, John W. Young (5/18-26/69)	Apollo-Saturn 10	31[4]	192h 03m 23s	First lunar module orbit of moon.
Neil A. Armstrong, Edwin E. Aldrin Jr., Michael Collins (7/16-24/69)	Apollo-Saturn 11	30[3]	195h 18m 35s	First lunar landing made by Armstrong and Aldrin; collected 48.5 lbs. of soil, rock samples; lunar stay time 21 h, 36 m, 21 s.
Georgi S. Shonin, Valery N. Kubasov (10/11-16/69)	Soyuz 6	79	118h 42m	First welding of metals in space.
Anatoly V. Filipchenko, Vladislav N. Volkov, Viktor V. Gorbatko (10/12-17/69)	Soyuz 7	79	118h 41m	Space lab construction tests made; Soyuz 6, 7 and 8 — first time 3 spacecraft 7 crew orbited earth at once.
Vladimir A. Shatalov, Aleksei S. Yeliseyev (10/13-18/69)	Soyuz 8	79	118h 41m	Orbiting space laboratory construction tests were made.
Charles Conrad Jr., Richard F. Gordon, Alan L. Bean (11/14-24/69)	Apollo-Saturn 12	45[3]	244h 36m 25s	Conrad and Bean made 2d moon landing; collected 74.7 lbs. of samples, lunar stay time 31 h, 31 m.
James A. Lovell Jr., Fred W. Haise Jr., John L. Swigart Jr. (4/11-17/70)	Apollo-Saturn 13	. .	142h 54m 41s	Aborted after service module oxygen tank ruptured; crew returned safely using lunar module oxygen and power.
Adrian G. Nikolayev, Vitaly I. Sevastyanov (6/17/70)	Soyuz 9	287	424h 59m	Studied man's physical reactions to long periods of weightlessness during space travel.
Alan B. Shepard Jr., Stuart A. Roosa, Edgar D. Mitchell (1/31-2/9/71)	Apollo-Saturn 14	34[3]	216h 01m 57s	Shepard and Mitchell made 3d moon landing, collected 96 lbs. of lunar samples; lunar stay 33 h, 31 m.
Vladimir A. Shatalov, Aleksei S. Yeliseyev, Nikolai Rukavishnikov (4/22-24/71)	Soyuz 10	32	47h 46m	Docked with prototype Salyut orbiting space station for 5 1/2 hrs, then mission was aborted.
Georgi T. Dobrovolsky, Vladislav N. Volkov, Viktor I. Patsayev (6/6-30/71)	Soyuz 11	360	569h 40m	Docked with Salyut space station; and orbited in Salyut for 23 days; crew died during re-entry from loss of pressurization.
David R. Scott, Alfred M. Worden, James B. Irwin (7/26-8/7/71)	Apollo-Saturn 15	74[3]	295h 11m 53s	Scott and Irwin made 4th moon landing; first lunar rover use; first deep space walk; 170 lbs. of samples; 66 h, 55 m, stay.
Charles M. Duke Jr., Thomas K. Mattingly, John W. Young (4/16-27/72)	Apollo-Saturn 16	64[3]	265h 51m 05s	Young and Duke made 5th moon landing; collected 213 lbs. of lunar samples; lunar stay time 71 h, 2 m.
Eugene A. Cernan, Ronald E. Evans, Harrison H. Schmitt (12/7-19/72)	Apollo-Saturn 17	75[3]	301h 51m 59s	Cernan and Schmitt made 6th manned lunar landing; collected 243 lbs. of samples; record lunar stay of 75 h.
Charles Conrad Jr., Joseph P. Kerwin, Paul J. Weitz (5/25-6/22/73)	Skylab 2	. .	672h 49m 49s	First American manned orbiting space station; made long-flights tests, crew repaired damage caused during boost.
Alan L. Bean, Jack R. Lousma, Owen K. Garriott (7/28-9/25/73)	Skylab 3	. .	1,427h 09m 04s	Crew systems and operational tests, exceeded pre-mission plans for scientific activities; space walk total 13 h, 44 m.
Gerald P. Carr, Edward G. Gibson, William Pogue (11/16/73-2/8/74)	Skylab 4	. .	2,017h 16m 30s	Final Skylab mission; record space walk of 7 h, 1 m., record space walks total for a mission 22 h, 21 m.

U.S.-Soviet joint mission, *see Chronology.*

(1) The Americans measure orbital flights in revolutions while the Soviets use "orbits." (2) suborbital. (3) Moon orbits in command module. (4) Moon orbits.

Fire aboard spacecraft Apollo I on the ground at Cape Kennedy, Fla. killed Virgil I. Grissom, Edward H. White and Roger B. Chaffee on Jan. 27, 1967. They were the only U.S. astronauts killed in space tests.

Notable Ocean and Intercontinental Flights

Pilot, Plane	From	To	Miles	Time	Date
Dirigible Balloons					
British R-34 (1)	East Fortune, Scot	Mineola, N.Y.	....	108 hrs.	Jul. 2-6, 1919
	Mineola, N.Y.	Pulham, Eng.	....	75 hrs.	Jul. 9-13, 1919
Amundsen-Ellsworth-Nobile expedition	Spitsbergen	Teller, Alaska	....	80 hrs.	May 11-14, 1926
Graf Zeppelin	Friedrichshafen	Lakehurst, N.J.	6,630	4d 15h 46m	Oct. 11-15, 1928
Hindenburg Zeppelin	Germany	Lakehurst, N.J.	....	51h 17m	Jun. 30-Jul. 2, 1936
	Lakehurst, N.J.	Frankfort, Ger.	....	42h 53m	Aug. 9-11, 1936
USN ZPG-2 Blimp	S. Weymouth, Mass.	Africa	....		
	Africa	Key West, Fla.	7,000	275h	Mar. 4-16, 1957
Airplanes					
USN NC-4	Rockaway, N.Y.	Lisbon, Port	....	....	May 8-27, 1919
John Alcock-A. W. Brown (2)	St. John's, Nfld.	Clifden, Ireland	1,960	16h 12m	Jun. 14-15, 1919
Richard E. Byrd(3)	Spitsbergen	North Pole	1,545	15h 30m	May 9, 1926
Charles Lindbergh (4)	Mineola, N.Y.	Paris	3,610	33h 29m 30s	May 20-21, 1927
C. Levin C. Chamberlin (5)	Roosevelt Field, Mineola, N.Y.	Isleben, Germany	3,911	42h 31m	Jun. 4-6, 1927
Baron G. von Huenefeld, crew (6)	Dublin	Greenly Isl., Lab	....	37 hrs.	Apr. 12-13, 1928
Sir Hubert Wilkins (9)	Point Barrow, Alaska	Spitsbergen	....		Apr. 16, 1928
Sir Chas. Kingsford-Smith, crew (7)	Oakland, Cal	Brisbane, Aust	....		May 31-Jun. 8, 1928
Amelia Earhart Putnam, W. Stultz, L. Gordon	Trepassy, Nfld	Burry Port, Wales	....	20h 40m	Jun. 17-18, 1928
Richard E. Byrd (8)	Bay of Wales	South Pole	....		Nov. 28-29, 1929
D. Coste-M. Bellonte	Paris	Valley Stream, N.Y.	4,100	37h 18m 30s	Sept. 1-2, 1930
Wiley Post-Harold Gatty	Harbor Grace, Nfld.	England	2,200	16h 17m	Jun. 23-24, 1931
Clyde Pangborn-Hugh Herndon Jr. (10)	Tokyo	Wenatchee, Wash	4,458	41h 34m	Oct. 3-5, 1931
Amelia Earhart Putnam (11)	Harbor Grace, Nfld	Ireland	2,026	14h 56m	May 20-21, 1932
James A. Mollison (12)	Portmarnock, Ire	Pennfield, N.B.	....	....	Aug. 18, 1932
China Clipper (Pan Am. Airways) (13)	San Francisco	Manila, P.I.	.....	.....	Nov. 22-28, 1935
	Manila, P.I.	San Francisco	.....	.....	Dec. 1-6, 1935
Gromoff, Yumasheff, Danilin (USSR)	Moscow, USSR	San Jacinto, Cal	6,262	62h 02m	Jul. 12-14, 1937
Douglas C. Corrigan	New York	Dublin, Ire	....	28h 13m	Jul. 17-18, 1938
B-29 (C.J. Miller)	Honolulu	Washington, D.C.	4,640	17h 21m	Sept. 1, 1945
C-54 (Maj. G.E. Cain)	Tokyo	Washington, D.C.	....	31h 24m	Sept. 3, 1945
Col. David C. Schilling, USAF (14)	England	Limestone, Me	3,300	10h 01m	Sept. 22, 1950
Chas. F. Blair Jr.	New York	London	3,500	7h 48m	Jan. 31, 1951
Chas. F. Blair Jr. (15)	Bardufoss, Norway	Fairbanks, Alaska	3,300	10h 29m	May 29, 1951
Chas. F. Blair, Jr.	Fairbanks, Alaska	New York	3,450	9h 31m	May 30, 1951
Canberra Bomber	England	Australia	....	20h 20m	Mar. 16, 1952
Two U. S. S-55 Helicopters (16)	Westover AFB, Mass.	Prestwick, Scotland	3,410	42h 30m	Jul. 15-31, 1952
Canberra Bomber (17)	Aldergrove, N.Ire.	Gander, Nfld	2,073	4h 34m	Aug. 26, 1952
	Gander, Nfld	Aldergrove, N.Ire.	2,073	3h 25m	Aug. 26, 1952
British Comet	London-Tokyo	Tokyo-London	20,400	74h 52m	Apr. 3-7, 1953
British Comet	London	Rio de Janeiro	6,000	12h 30m	Sept. 13-14, 1953
Max Conrad (solo)	New York	Paris	....	22h 23m	Nov. 7, 1954
Canberra Bomber	London (round trip)	New York	6,920	14h 21m 45.4s	Aug. 23, 1955
Capt. William F. Judd	New York	Paris	....	24h 11m	Jan. 29-30, 1956
Three USAF F-100Cs	London	Los Angeles, Cal	6,710	14h 5m	May 13, 1957
Spirit of St. Louis II (USAF F-100F jet)	McGuire AFB, N.J.	Le Bourget, Paris	....	6h 38m	May 21, 1957
USAF KC-135	Tokyo	Lajes AFB, Azores	10,230	18h 48m	Apr. 7-8, 1958
Max Conrad (solo)	New York	Palermo, Sicily	4,440	32h 55m	Jun. 22-23, 1958
Capt. Marion Boling	Manila, P.I.	Pendleton, Ore	6,979	45h 42m	Jul. 31-Aug. 1, 1958
USAF KC-135	Yokota AB, Japan	Washington, D.C.	7,100	12h 28m	Sept. 12, 1958
Max Conrad (solo)	Chicago	Rome	5,000	34 3m	Mar. 5-6, 1959
Max Conrad (solo)	Casablanca, Africa	Los Angeles	7,700	58h 36m	Jun. 2-4, 1959
USSR TU-114 (18)	Moscow	New York	5,092	11h 6m	Jun. 28, 1959
Boeing 707 airliner	San Francisco	Sydney, Australia	7,630	16h 10m	Jul. 2, 1959
Boeing 707-320	New York	Moscow	c. 5,090	8h 54m	Jul. 23, 1959
Max Conrad (solo)	Casablanca, Mor	El Paso, Tex	6,911	56h 26m	Nov. 22-26, 1959
Col. J.B. Swindal	Washington, D.C.	Moscow	5,004	8h 39m 02.2s	May 19, 1963
Mrs. Jerrie Mock (19)	Columbus, Oh.	Columbus, Oh.	23,206	29d 11h 59m	Mar. 19-Apr. 18, 1964
Joan Merriam (20)	Oakland, Cal	Oakland, Cal	27,750	56d	Mar. 17-May 12, 1964
Elgen Long (solo) (21)	San Francisco	San Francisco	38,896	28d 00h 43m	Nov. 5-Dec. 3, 1971

Notable first flights: 1, Atlantic aerial round trip. 2, Non-stop transatlantic flight. 3, Polar flight. 4, Solo transatlantic flight in the Ryan monoplane the "Spirit of St. Louis." 5, Transatlantic passenger flight. 6, East-West flight. 7, U.S. to Australia flight. 8, South Pole flight. 9, Trans-Arctic flight. 10, Non-stop Pacific flight. 11, Woman's transoceanic solo flight. 12, Westbound transatlantic solo flight. 13, Pacific airmail and U.S. to Philippines crossing. 14, Non-stop jet transatlantic flight. 15, Solo across North Pole. 16, Transatlantic helicopter flight. 17, Transatlantic round trip on same day. 18, Non-stop between Moscow and New York. 19, First woman pilot to circle globe; first woman to fly both North Atlantic and Pacific. 20, Followed route Amelia Earhart partly completed in 1937. 21, Speed record around the world over both the earth's poles.

International Aeronautical Records

Source: The National Aeronautic Association, 806 15th St., N.W.,Washington, D.C. 20005, representative in the United States of the Federation Aeronautique Internationale, certifying agency for world aviation and space records. The International Aeronautical Federation was formed in 1905 by representatives from Belgium, France, Germany, Great Britain, Spain, Italy, Switzerland, and the United States, with headquarters in Paris. Regulations for the control of official records were signed Oct. 14, 1905. World records are defined as maximum performance, regardless of class or type of aircraft used. Records to June, 1975.

World Air Records—Maximum Performance in any Class

Speed over a straight course—3,331,507 kmph. (2,070.101 mph) — Col. R. L. Stephens, USAF, Lockheed YF-12; Edwards Air Force Base, Calif., May 1, 1965.

Speed over a closed circuit—2,981.5 kmph. (1,850.61 mph)—Mikhail Komarov, USSR; E-266 jet; Oct. 5, 1967.

Distance in a straight line—20,168.75 kms (12,532.28 mi.)—Maj. Clyde P. Evely, USAF, Boeing B52-H; Kadena, Okinawa, to Madrid, Spain, Jan. 11, 1962.

Distance over a closed circuit—18,245.5 kms (11,336.92 mi.)—Capt. William Stevenson, USAF, Boeing B52h; Seymour-Johnson, N.C., June 6-7, 1962.

Altitude — 95,935.99 meters (314,750 feet)—Maj. Robert M. White, USAF, North American X-15-1; Edwards AFB, Cal., July 17, 1962.

Altitude in horizontal flight—24,462,596 meters (80,257.86 ft.)—Col. R. L. Stephens, USAF, Lockheed F1-2A; Eards Air Force Base, Cal., May 1, 1965.

Manned Space Craft

Duration — 84 days 1 hr. 15 min. 32 sec.—Gerald P. Carr, Edward G. Gibson, William R. Pogue, U.S.; Skylab 3 Nov. 16, 1973-Feb. 8, 1974.

Altitude — 377,668.0 kms (234,672.5 mi.) — Frank Borman, James A. Lovell Jr., William Anders, Spacecraft Apollo 8; Dec. 21-27, 1968.

Greatest mass lifted—127,980 kgs. (282,197 lbs.)—Frank Borman, James S. Lovell Jr., William Anders, Spacecraft Apollo 8; Dec. 21-27,1968.

Distance — 55,560,000 kms. (34,523,000 mi.)—Gerald P. Carr, Edward G. Gibson, William R. Pogue, U.S.; Skylab 3; Nov. 16, 1973-Feb. 8, 1974.

World "Class" Records

All other records, international in scope, are termed World "Class" records and are divided into classes; airships, free balloons, airplanes, seaplanes, amphibians, gliders, and rotorplanes. Airplanes (Class C) are sub-divided into four groups: Group I—piston engine aircraft, Group II—turbo-prop aircraft, Group III—jet aircraft, Group IV—rocket powered aircraft. A partial listing of world records follows:

Airplanes (Class C, Group 1—Piston Engine)

Distance, closed circuit—14,441.26 kms (8,974 mi.)—James R. Bede, United States: BD-2, 1 Continental 360-C engine, Columbus, Ohio to Kansas City course, Nov. 7-9, 1969.

Distance, airline (international) — 18,081.990 kms. (11,235.6 miles) — Cmdr. Thomas D. Davies, USN; Cmdr. Eugene P. Rankin, USN; Cmdr. Walter S. Reid, USN, and Lt. Comdr. Ray A. Tabeling,.USN; Lockheed P2V-1; from Pearce Field, Perth, Australia, to Port Columbus, Ohio, Sept. 29-Oct. 1, 1946.

Maximum speed over 3-kilometer measured course (international)—776.449 kmph. (482.462 mph)—Darryl Greenamyer, United States, Grumman F8F Bearcat, Edwards AFB, Cal., Aug. 16, 1969. (United States)—663.054 kmph. (412.002 mph.) Jacqueline Cochran, United States; North American F-51, Thermal, Cal., Dec. 17, 1947.

Speed for 100 kilometers (62.137 miles) without payload (international)—755.668 kmph (469.549 mph.)—Jacqueline Cochran, United States; North American P-51; Coachella Valley, Cal., Dec. 10, 1947.

Speed for 1,000 kilometers (621.369 miles) without payload (international)—693.78 kmph. (431.09 mph.)—Jacqueline Cochran, United States; North American P-51; Santa Rosasummit, Cal. — Flagstaff, Arizona course, May 24, 1948.

Speed for 5,000 kilometers (3,106.849) without payload — 544.59 kmph. (338.39 mph.)—Capt. James Bauer, USAF, Boeing B-29; Dayton, Ohio, June 28, 1946.

Speed around the world — 318.28 kmph. (197.77 mph.)—Trevor K. Brougham, Australia; Beechcraft Baron C-55, 2 Rolls-Royce Continental 10-470-L engines; Darwin, Australia, Aug. 5-10, 1971. Time: 5 days 5 hrs. 57 min.

Light Airplanes—Class C-1.d

Distance airline (international) — 12,341.26 kms. (7,668.48 miles)—Max Conrad, United States; Piper Comanche 250, Lycoming 0540-A1A5 250 hp.; Casablanca, Morocco to Los Angeles, June 2-4, 1959.

Speed for 100 kilometers — (62.137 miles) in a closed circuit (international) —519.480 kmph. (322.789 mph.)—Miss R. M Sharpe, Great Britain; Vickers Supermarine Spitfire 5-B; Wolverhampton, June 17, 1950.

Gliders (Class D—Single-place)

Distance, straight line—1,460.8 kms. (907.7 miles)—Hans Werner Grosse, West Germany; ASK12 sailplane;Luebeck to Biarritz, Apr. 25, 1972.

Altitude above sea level — 14,102 meters (46,267 feet)—Paul F. Bikle, United States; Sailplane Schweizer SGS 123E; Mojave, Lancaster, Cal., Feb. 25, 1961.

Helicopters (Class E-1)

Distance in a straight line—3,561.55 kms. (2,213.04 miles)—Robert G. Ferry, United States; Hughes YOH-6A helicopter; Culver City, Cal., to Daytona, Fla., Apr. 6-7, 1966.

Speed over 3-km. course — 348.971 kmph. (216.839 mph.)—Byron Graham, United States; Sikorsky S-67 helicopter; Windsor Locks, Conn., Dec. 14, 1970.

Airplanes (Class C, Group II—Turbo-prop)

Distance in a straight line — 14,052.95 kms. (8,732.09 miles) — Lt. Col. Edgar L. Allison Jr., U. S. Lockheed HC-130 Hercules aircraft; Feb. 20, 1972.

Speed over a 15-25 km. course — Cmdr. D. H. Lilienthal,USN, Lockheed P3C Orion aircraft; 806 kmph. (501 mph.); Jan. 27,1971.

Altitude —15,549 meters (51,014 ft.) — Donald R. Wilson, Greenville, Tex., LTV L450F aircraft; Mar. 27, 1972.

Speed for 1,000 kilometers (621.369 miles) without payload (international) — 871.38 kmph. (541.449 mph.) — Ivan Souk-homline, Boris Timochok, and crew, USSR; TU-114 swept wing monoplane, 4 turbo-prop TB-12 engines; Sternberg Course, Mar. 24, 1960.

Speed for 5.000 kilometers (3,106.849 miles) without payload (international) — 877.212 kmph. (545.072 mph.) — Ivan

Soukhomline, K. Sapielkine, and crew, USSR; TU-114 swept wing monoplane, 4 turbo-prop TB-12 engines; Sternberg-Svierdlovsk-Sebastopol-Sternberg, Apr. 9, 1960.

Airplanes (Class C, Group III—Jet-powered)

Distance in a straight line — 20,168.78 kms. (12,532.28 mi.) — Maj. Clyde P. Evely, USAF, Boeing B52-H,8 Pratt & Whitney TF-33P-3 engines; Kadena, Okinawa, to Madrid, Spain, Jan. 10-11,1962.

Distance in a closed circuit —18,245.05 kms. (11,326.92 miles) — Capt. William Stevenson, USAF, Boeing B52h, 8 Pratt & Whitney TF-33P-3 engines; terminal: Seymour-Johnson, N. C., June 6-7, 1962.

Altitude — 34,714 meters (113,890.848 feet) — Gueorgui Mossolov, USSR; E-66A jet monoplane, triangular wing, T.R.D. and G.R.D. engines; Podmoskovnoe, USSR, Apr. 28, 1961.

Speed over a 3-kilometer course — 1,452.777 kmph (902,769 mph) — Lt. Hunt Hardisty, USN, McDonnell F4H Phantom, 2 GE J-79 jet engines; White Sands, N. M., Aug. 29, 1961.

Speed for 100 kilometers — 2,600 kmph. (1,615 mph.) — Alexander Fedotov, USSR; E-266 airplane, 2 RD jet engines, Apr. 8, 1973.

Speed for 500 kilometers in a closed circuit — 2,981.5 kmph. (1,852.61 mph.) — Mikhail Komarov, USSR; E-266 airplane, 2 RD jet engines, Oct. 5, 1967.

Speed for 1,000 kilometers in a closed circuit — 2,920.67 kmph. (1,814.81 mph.) — Pyotr Ostapenko, USSR; E-266 airplane, 2 RD jet engines, Oct. 27, 1967.

Speed for 2,000 kilometers in closed circuit — 1,708.817 kmph. (1,061.808 mph.) — Maj. H. J. Deutchendorf Jr., USAF, Convair B-58 Hustler Bomber; Desert, Stoval, Boundary, Morris, Desert, Edwards AFB, Cal. course, Jan. 12, 1961.

Sustained altitude —24,462.596 meters (80,257.86 Feet) — Col. R. L. Stephens, USAF; Lockheed YF-12A, 2 Pratt & Whitney J 58 engines; Edwards AFB, Cal., May 1, 1965.

Free Balloons (Tenth category, 4001 cu. meters or more)

Altitude — 34,668 meters (113,739.9 feet) — Cmdr. Malcolm D. Ross, USNR, United States; Lee Lewis Memorial Winzen Research Balloon; Gulf of Mexico, May 4, 1961.

F.A.I. Course Records

Los Angeles to New York —1,954.79 kmph (1,214.65 mph)—Capt. Robert G. Sowers, USAF; Convair B58 Hustler, 4 GE-J-79-5B engines; Elapsed time: 2 hrs. 58.71 sec., Mar. 5, 1962.

New York to Los Angeles —1,741 kmph (1,081.80 mph)—Capt. Robert G. Sowers, USAF; Convair B58 Hustler; Elapsed time: 2 hrs. 15 min. 50.08 sec., Mar. 5, 1962.

Los Angeles-New York-Los Angeles — 1,681.71 kmph (1,044.46 mph)—Capt. Robert G. Sowers, USAF; Convair B58 Hustler; elapsed time: 4 hrs. 41 min. 14.98 sec., Mar. 5, 1962.

New York to Paris — 1,753.068 kmph (1,089.36 mph)—Maj. W. R. Payne, United States; Convair B58 Hustler; Elapsed time: 3 hrs. 10 min. 58 sec., May 26, 1961.

London to New York (international) — 945.423 kmph (587.457 mph)—Maj. Burl B. Davenport, Lt. James J. Jones and crew USAF; Boeing KC-135 Stratotanker; London International Airport to Idlewild International Airport, New York, June 27, 1958. Elapsed time: 5 hours 29 minutes 14.64 seconds.

Baltimore to Moscow, USSR — 906.64 kmph (563.36 mph)—Col. James B. Swindal, USAF; Boeing VC-137 (707), May 19, 1963. Elapsed time: 8 hours 33 minutes 45.4 seconds.

Moscow to Washington, D.C. — 788.67 kmph (490.06 mph)—Col. James B. Swindal, USAF; Boeing VC-137 (707). Elapsed tm: 9 hrs. 54 min. 48.5 sec. May 20-21, 1963.

Belfast to Gander, Newfoundland (international) — 774.255 kmph (481.099 mph) — Wing Commander R. P. Beamont and crew, Great Britain; Camberra bomber, two Rolls-Royce turbo-jet engines, Aug. 31, 1951. Elapsed time: 4 hours 18 min. 24.4 sec.

New York to London (international) — 2,914.3 kmph (1,810.9 mph)—Maj. James V. Sullivan, USAF; Lockheed SR-71; Elapsed time 1 hr. 55 min. 32 sec., Sept. 1, 1974.

London to Los Angeles (international) — 2,394.39 kmph (1,487.81 mph)—Capt. Harold B. Adams, USAF; Lockheed SR-71; Elapsed time: 3 hrs. 47 min. 39 sec., Sept. 13, 1974.

Aviation Hall of Fame

The Aviation Hall of Fame at Dayton, Oh., is dedicated to honoring aviation's outstanding pioneers. It operates as a non-profit privately supported organization under a charter granted in 1964 by the Congress of the U. S.

1962
Orville Wright
Wilbur Wright

1963
Octave Chanute
Samuel Pierpont Langley
Frank Purdy Lahm
Benjamin Delahauf Foulois

1964
Thomas Scott Baldwin
Theodore Gordon Ellyson
Henry W. Walden
Glenn Hammond Curtiss
Calbraith Perry Rodgers
John Joseph Montgomery

1965
Alexander Graham Bell
Alfred Austell Cunningham
Albert Cushing Read

Eugene Burton Ely
A. Roy Knabenshue
Thomas Etholen Selfridge
Charles Edward Taylor
Edward Vernon Rickenbacker

1966
Lincoln Beachey
William Edward Boeing
Robert Hutchings Goddard
Glenn Luther Martin
William "Billy" Mitchell
John Henry Towers

1967
Henry Harley "Hap" Arnold
James Harold Doolittle
Charles Augustus Lindbergh
Carl Andrew Spaatz

1968
Richard Evelyn Byrd

Amelia Earhart Putnam
John Arthur MacReady
Igor Ivan Sikorsky

1969
Donald Wills Douglas
Grover Cleveland Loening
Wiley Hardeman Post
Juan Terry Trippe

1970
Alexander P. deSeversky
Ira Clarence Eaker
Robert Ellsworth Gross

1971
William McPherson Allen
Jacqueline Cochran (Odlum)
Harry Frank Guggenheim
George Churchill Kenney

1972
Claire Lee Chennault

Leroy Randle Grumman
J.H. "Dutch" Kindelberger
Curtis Emerson LeMay

1973
Bernt Balchen
Howard Robard Hughes
Elmer Ambrose Sperry Sr.
Charles Elwood Yeager

1974
C.L. "Kelly" Johnson
John K. Northrop
Cyrus R. Smith
T. Claude Ryan
Leigh Wade

1975
Reuben H. Fleet
Frank Luke Jr.
Robert C. Reeve
Roscoe Turner

Consolidated Airline Traffic

Source: Civil Aeronautics Board Air Carrier Traffic Statistics, Calendar year, 1974.

	1972	1973	1974
Passenger Traffic			
Revenue passengers enplaned	195,305,000	202,208,000	207,449,000
Revenue passenger miles	164,015,261,000	161,957,307,000	162,917,241,000
Available seat miles	297,966,766,000	310,597,107,000	297,004,332,000
Cargo Traffic (ton miles)	6,388,595,000	6,494,432	6,483,147,000
Freight	5,110,974,000	5,182,735,000	5,251,470,000
Express	87,424,000	100,497,000	80,845,000
Priority U.S. Mail	581,705,000	608,491,000	727,578,000
Overall Traffic and Service			
Nonscheduled traffic-total	2,058,659,000	1,685,764,000	1,474,969,000
Total revenue ton miles	22,805,047,000	22,241,875,000	22,425,070,000
Total available ton miles	48,682,429,000	49,019,300,000	46,848,027,000

Fastest Trips Around the World

Fast circuits of the earth have been a subject of wide interest since Jules Verne, French novelist, described an imaginary trip by Phileas Fogg in Around the World in 80 Days, assertedly occurring Oct. 2 to Dec. 20, 1872. Notable actual such events follow:

Craft, pilot	Terminal	Miles	Time	Date
Nellie Bly	New York, N.Y.		72d 06h 11m	1889
George Francis Train	New York, N.Y.		67d 12h 03m	1890
Charles Fitzmorris	Chicago		60d 13h 29m	1901
J. W. Willis Sayre	Seattle		54d 09h 42m	1903
Henry Frederick			54d 07h 02m	1903
Col. Burnlay-Campbell			40d 19h 30m	1907
Andre Jaeger-Schmidt			39d 19h 42m 38s	1911
John Henry Mears			35d 21h 36m	1913
Two U.S. Army airplanes	Seattle (57 hops, 21 countries)	26,103	35d 1h 11m	1924
Edward S. Evans and Linton Wells (New York World) (1)	New York	18,400	28d 14h 36m 05s	June 16-July 14, 1926
John H. Mears and Capt. C. B. D. Collyer	New York		23d 15h 21m 03s	June 29-July 22, 1928
Graf Zeppelin	Friedrichshafen, Ger. via Tokyo, Los Angeles, Lakehurst, N.J.	21,700	20d 04h	Aug. 14-Sept. 4, 1929
Wiley Post and Harold Gatty (Monoplane Winnie Mae)	Roosevelt Field, via Arctic Circle	15,474	08d 15h 51m	June 23-July 1, 1931
Wiley Post (Monoplane Winnie Mae) (2)	Floyd Bennett Field, via Arctic Circle	15,596	115h 36m 30s	July 15-22, 1933
H. R. Ekins (Scripps-Howard Newspapers in race) (Zeppelin Hindenburg to Germany, airplanes from Frankfurt)	Lakehurst, N.J., via Frankfurt, Germany	25,654	18d 11h 14m 33s	Sept. 30-Oct. 19, 1936
Howard Hughes and 4 assistants	New York, Paris, Moscow, Siberia, Fairbanks, Alaska	14,824	03d 19h 08m 10s	July 10-13, 1938
Mrs. Clara Adams (Pan American Clipper)	Port Washington, N.Y., return Newark, N.J.		16d 19h 04m	June 28-July 15, 1939
Globester, U.S. Air Transport Command	Washington, D.C.	23,279	149h 44m	Sept. 28-Oct. 4, 1945
Capt. William P. Odom (A-26 Reynolds Bombshell)	New York, via Paris, Cairo, Tokyo, Alaska	20,000	78h 55m 12s	Apr. 12-16, 1947
America, Pan American 4-engine Lockheed Constellation (3)	New York, eastward	22,219	101h 32m	June 17-30, 1947
Col. Edward P. F. Eagan	New York	20,559	147h 15m	Dec. 13, 1948
USAF B-50 Lucky Lady II (Capt. James Gallagher) (4)	Fort Worth, Texas	23,452	94h 01m	Feb. 26-Mar. 2, 1949
Jean-Marie Audibert	Paris		04d 19h 38m	Dec. 11-15, 1952
Pamela Martin	Midway Airport, Chicago		90h 59m	Dec. 5-8, 1953
Three USAF B-52 Stratofortresses (5)	Merced, Cal., via Nfld., Morocco, Saudi Arabia, India, Ceylon, P.I., Guam	24,325	45h 19m	Jan. 15-18, 1957
Joseph Cavoli	Cleveland, Ohio		89h 13m 37s	Jan. 31-Feb. 4, 1958
Peter Gluckmann (solo)	San Francisco	22,800	29d	Aug. 22-Sept. 20, 1959
Milton Reynolds	San Francisco		51h 45m 22s	Jan. 12-14, 1960
Sue Snyder	Chicago	21,219	62h 59m	June 22-24, 1960
Max Conrad (solo)	Miami, Fla.	25,946	08d 18h 35m 57s	Feb. 28-Mar. 8, 1961
Sam Miller & Louis Fodor	New York		46h 28m	Aug. 3-4, 1963
Henry G. Beaird	Wichita, Kan.	22,992	65h 38m 49s	May 23-26, 1966
Robert & Joan Wallick (6)	Manila, Philippines	23,129	05d 6h 17m 10s	June 2-7, 1966
Arthur Godfrey, Richard Merrill Fred Austin, Karl Keller	New York	23,333	86h 9m 1s	June 4-7, 1966
Trevor K. Brougham	Darwin, Australia	24,800	05d 05h 57m	Aug. 5-10, 1972

1. Mileage by train and auto, 4,110; by plane, 6,300; by steamship, 8,000. 2. First to fly solo around northern circumference of the world, also first to fly twice around the world. 3. Inception of regular commercial global air service. 4 First non-stop round-the-world flight, refueled 4 times in flight. 5. First non-stop global flight by jet planes; refueled in flight by KC-97 aerial tankers; average speed approx. 525 mph. 6. Official world record for light planes.

The Busiest Airports, 1974

(Total take-offs and landings)

United States

Source: Dept. of Transportation

O'Hare (Chicago)	665,331	(1)
Santa Ana, Cal.	605,530	
Van Nuys, Cal.	586,680	
Long Beach, Cal.	544,923	
Atlanta	484,562	(2)
Los Angeles	460,713	(3)
Opalocka, Fla.	421,822	
Torrance, Cal.	421,091	
Phoenix, Ariz.	417,998	
San Jose, Cal.	415,083	
John F. Kennedy (New York City)		(4)
Dallas-Fort Worth, Tex.		(5)

Canada

Source: Ministry of Transport

Pitt Meadows, B.C.	242,679	
Toronto International, Ont.	241,735	(1)
St. Hubert (Montreal) P.Q.	237,727	
Edmonton Industrial, Alta.	236,778	
Buttonville, Ont.	214,261	
Vancouver International, B.C.	196,521	(3)
Montreal International, P.Q.	192,958	(2)
Hamilton City, Ont.	184,532	
Ottawa International, Ont.	183,186	
Springbank, Alta.	183,069	
St. Andrews	174,257	
Langley	173,740	

Numbers in parentheses indicate top 5 in air carrier operations only.

Air Line Distances Between Selected Cities of the World

Source: Defense Mapping Agency Aerospace Center (Statute Miles)

Point-to-point measurements are usually from City Hall

	Bangkok	Berlin	Cairo	Capetown	Caracas	Chicago	Hong Kong	Honolulu	Lima	London
Bangkok	....	5,352	4,523	6,300	10,555	8,570	1,077	6,609	12,244	5,933
Berlin	5,352	....	1,797	5,961	5,238	4,414	5,443	7,320	6,896	583
Cairo	4,523	1,797	....	4,480	6,342	6,141	5,066	8,848	7,726	2,185
Capetown	6,300	5,961	4,480	....	6,366	8,491	7,376	11,535	6,072	5,989
Caracas	10,555	5,238	6,342	6,366	....	2,495	10,165	6,021	1,707	4,655
Chicago	8,570	4,414	6,141	8,491	2,495	....	7,797	4,256	3,775	3,958
Hong Kong	1,077	5,443	5,066	7,376	10,165	7,797	....	5,556	11,418	5,990
Honolulu	6,609	7,320	8,848	11,535	6,021	4,256	5,556	....	5,947	7,240
London	5,933	583	2,185	5,989	4,655	3,958	5,990	7,240	6,316	....
Madrid	6,337	1,165	2,087	5,308	4,346	4,189	6,558	7,872	5,907	785
Melbourne	4,568	9,918	8,675	6,425	9,717	9,673	4,595	5,505	8,059	10,500
Mexico City	9,793	6,056	7,700	8,519	2,234	1,690	8,788	3,789	2,639	5,558
Montreal	8,338	3,740	5,427	7,922	2,438	745	7,736	4,918	3,970	3,254
Moscow	4,389	1,006	1,803	6,279	6,177	4,987	4,437	7,047	7,862	1,564
New Delhi	1,813	3,598	2,758	5,769	8,833	7,486	2,339	7,412	10,432	4,181
New York	8,669	3,979	5,619	7,803	2,120	714	8,060	4,969	3,639	3,469
Paris	5,877	548	1,998	5,786	4,732	4,143	5,990	7,449	6,370	214
Peking	2,046	4,584	4,698	8,044	8,950	6,604	1,217	5,077	10,349	5,074
Rio de Janeiro	9,994	6,209	6,143	3,781	2,804	5,282	11,009	8,288	2,342	5,750
Rome	5,494	737	1,326	5,231	5,195	4,824	5,774	8,040	6,750	895
San Francisco	7,931	5,672	7,466	10,248	3,902	1,859	6,905	2,398	4,518	5,367
Singapore	883	6,164	5,137	6,008	11,402	9,372	1,605	6,726	11,689	6,747
Stockholm	5,089	528	2,096	6,423	5,471	4,331	5,063	6,875	7,166	942
Tokyo	2,865	5,557	5,958	9,154	8,808	6,314	1,791	3,859	9,631	5,959
Warsaw	5,033	322	1,619	5,935	5,559	4,679	5,147	7,366	7,215	905
Washington	8,807	4,181	5,822	7,895	2,047	596	8,155	4,838	3,509	3,674

	Madrid	Melbourne	Mexico City	Montreal	Moscow	Nairobi	New Delhi	New York	Paris	Peking
Bangkok	6,337	4,568	9,793	8,338	4,389	4,483	1,813	8,669	5,877	2,046
Berlin	1,165	9,918	6,056	3,740	1,006	3,949	3,598	3,979	548	4,584
Cairo	2,087	8,675	7,700	5,427	1,803	2,186	2,758	5,619	1,998	4,698
Capetown	5,308	6,425	8,519	7,922	6,279	2,542	5,769	7,803	5,786	8,044
Caracas	4,346	9,717	2,234	2,438	6,177	7,178	8,833	2,120	4,732	8,950
Chicago	4,189	9,673	1,690	745	4,987	8,011	7,486	714	4,143	6,604
Hong Kong	6,558	4,595	8,788	7,736	4,437	5,449	2,339	8,060	5,990	1,217
Honolulu	7,872	5,505	3,789	4,918	7,047	10,741	7,412	4,969	7,449	5,077
London	785	10,500	5,558	3,254	1,564	4,231	4,181	3,469	214	5,074
Madrid	....	10,758	5,643	3,448	2,147	3,841	4,530	3,593	655	5,745
Melbourne	10,758	....	8,426	10,395	8,950	7,153	6,329	10,359	10,430	5,643
Mexico City	5,643	8,426	....	2,317	6,676	9,219	9,120	2,090	5,725	7,753
Montreal	3,448	10,395	2,317	....	4,401	7,267	7,012	331	3,432	6,519
Moscow	2,147	8,950	6,676	4,401	....	3,930	2,698	4,683	1,554	3,607
New Delhi	4,530	6,329	9,120	7,012	2,698	3,374	....	7,318	4,102	2,353
New York	3,593	10,359	2,090	331	4,683	7,364	7,318	....	3,636	6,844
Paris	655	10,430	5,725	3,432	1,554	4,022	4,102	3,636	....	5,120
Peking	5,745	5,643	7,753	6,519	3,607	5,727	2,353	6,844	5,120	....
Rio de Janeiro	5,045	8,226	4,764	5,078	7,170	5,560	8,753	4,801	5,684	10,768
Rome	851	9,929	6,377	4,104	1,483	3,339	3,684	4,293	690	5,063
San Francisco	5,803	7,856	1,887	2,543	5,885	9,597	7,691	2,572	5,577	5,918
Singapore	7,080	3,759	10,327	9,203	5,228	4,638	2,571	9,534	6,673	2,771
Stockholm	1,653	9,630	6,012	3,714	716	4,281	3,414	3,986	1,003	4,133
Tokyo	6,706	5,062	7,035	6,471	4,660	6,999	3,638	6,757	6,053	1,307
Warsaw	1,427	9,598	6,337	4,022	721	3,801	3,277	4,270	852	4,325
Washington	3,792	10,180	1,885	489	4,876	7,551	7,500	205	3,840	6,942

	Rio de Janiero	Rome	San Francisco	Singapore	Stockholm	Teheran	Tokyo	Vienna	Warsaw	Wash. D.C.
Bangkok	9,994	5,494	7,931	883	5,089	3,391	2,865	5,252	5,033	8,807
Berlin	6,209	737	5,672	6,164	528	2,185	5,557	326	322	4,181
Cairo	6,143	1,326	7,466	5,137	2,096	1,234	5,958	1,481	1,619	5,822
Capetown	3,781	5,231	10,248	6,008	6,423	5,241	9,154	5,656	5,935	7,895
Caracas	2,804	5,195	3,902	11,402	5,471	7,320	8,808	5,372	5,559	2,047
Chicago	5,282	4,824	1,859	9,372	4,331	6,502	6,314	4,698	4,679	596
Hong Kong	11,009	5,774	6,905	1,605	5,063	3,843	1,791	5,431	5,147	8,155
Honolulu	8,288	8,040	2,398	6,726	6,875	8,070	3,859	7,632	7,366	4,838
London	5,750	895	5,367	6,747	942	2,743	5,959	771	905	3,674
Madrid	5,045	851	5,803	7,080	1,653	2,978	6,706	1,128	1,427	3,792
Melbourne	8,226	9,929	7,856	3,759	9,630	7,826	5,062	9,790	9,598	10,180
Mexico City	4,764	6,377	1,887	10,327	6,012	8,184	7,035	6,320	6,337	1,885
Montreal	5,078	4,104	2,543	9,203	3,714	5,880	6,471	4,009	4,022	489
Moscow	7,170	1,483	5,885	5,228	716	1,532	4,660	1,043	721	4,876
New Delhi	8,753	3,684	7,691	2,571	3,414	1,583	3,638	3,465	3,277	7,500
New York	4,801	4,293	2,572	9,534	3,986	6,141	6,757	4,234	4,270	205
Paris	5,684	690	5,577	6,673	1,003	2,625	6,053	645	852	3,840
Peking	10,768	5,063	5,918	2,771	4,133	3,490	1,307	4,648	4,325	6,942
Rio de Janeiro	....	5,707	6,613	9,785	6,683	7,374	11,532	6,127	6,455	4,779
Rome	5,707	....	6,259	6,229	1,245	2,127	6,142	477	820	4,497
San Francisco	6,613	6,259	....	8,448	5,399	7,362	5,150	5,994	5,854	2,441
Singapore	9,785	6,229	8,448	....	5,936	4,103	3,300	6,035	5,843	9,662
Stockholm	6,683	1,245	5,399	5,936	....	2,173	5,053	780	494	4,183
Tokyo	11,532	6,142	5,150	3,300	5,053	4,775	....	5,689	5,347	6,791
Warsaw	6,455	820	5,854	5,843	494	1,879	5,689	347	....	4,472
Washington	4,779	4,497	2,441	9,662	4,183	6,341	6,791	4,438	4,472	....

SPORTS OF 1975

Olympic Games Records

The modern Olympic Games, first held in Athens, Greece, in 1896, were the result of efforts by Baron Pierre de Coubertin, a French educator, to promote interest in education and culture, also to foster better international understanding through the universal medium of youth's love of athletics.

His source of inspiration for the Olympic Games was the ancient Greek Olympic Games, most notable of the four Panhellenic celebrations. The games were combined patriotic, religious, and athletic festivals held every four years. The first such recorded festival was that held in 776 B.C., the date from which the Greeks began to keep their calendar by "Olympiads," or four-year spans between the games.

The first Olympiad is said to have consisted merely of a 200-yard foot race near the small city of Olympia, but the games gained in scope and became demonstrations of national pride. Only Greek citizens — amateurs — were permitted to participate. Winners received laurel, wild olive, and palm wreaths and were accorded many special privileges. Under the Roman emperors, the games deteriorated into professional carnivals and circuses. Emperor Theodosius banned them in 394 A.D.

Baron de Coubertin enlisted 9 nations to send athletes to the first modern Olympics in 1896; now more than 100 nations compete. Winter Olympic Games were started in 1924.

Sites and Unofficial Winners of Games

1896 Athens (U.S.)	**1912** Stockholm (U.S.)	**1936** Berlin (Germany)	**1964** Tokyo (U.S.)
1900 Paris (U.S.)	**1920** Antwerp (U.S.)	**1948** London (U.S.)	**1968** Mexico City (U.S.)
1904 St. Louis (U.S.)	**1924** Paris (U.S.)	**1952** Helsinki (U.S.)	**1972** Munich (USSR)
1906 Athens (U.S.)*	**1928** Amsterdam (U.S.)	**1956** Melbourne (USSR)	**1976** Montreal (July 17-
1908 London (U.S.)	**1932** Los Angeles (U.S.)	**1960** Rome (USSR)	Aug. 1)

*Games not recognized by International Olympic Committee.

Olympic Games Champions 1896—1972

(*Indicates Olympic Record)

Track and Field—Men

60 Meter Run

1900	Alvin Kraenzlein, United States	7s*
1904	Archie Hahn, United States	7s*

100 Meter Run

1896	Thomas Burke, United States	12s
1900	Francis W. Jarvis, United States	10.8s
1904	Archie Hahn, United States	11s
1906	Archie Hahn, United States	11.2s
1908	Reginald Walker, South Africa	10.8s
1912	Ralph Craig, United States	10.8s
1920	Charles Paddock, United States	10.8s
1924	Harold Abrahams, Great Britain	10.6s
1928	Percy Williams, Canada	10.8s
1932	Eddie Tolan, United States	10.3s
1936	Jesse Owens, United States	10.3s
1948	Harrison Dillard, United States	10.3s
1952	Lindy Remigino, United States	10.4s
1956	Bobby Morrow, United States	10.5s
1960	Armin Hary, Germany	10.2s
1964	Bob Hayes, United States	10.0s
1968	Jim Hines, United States	9.9s*
1972	Valeri Borzov, USSR.	10.1s

200 Meter Run

1900	J. W. B. Tewksbury, United States	22.2s
1904	Archie Hahn, United States	21.6s
1908	Robert Kerr, Canada	22.4s
1912	Ralph Craig, United States	21.7s
1920	Allan Woodring, United States	22s
1924	Jackson Scholz, United States	21.6s
1928	Percy Williams, Canada	21.8s
1932	Eddie Tolan, United States	21.2s
1936	Jesse Owens, United States	20.7s
1948	Mel Patton, United States	21.1s
1952	Andrew Stanfield, United States	20.7s
1956	Bobby Morrow, United States	20.6s
1960	Livio Berruti, Italy	20.5s
1964	Henry Carr, United States	20.3s
1968	Tommie Smith, United States	19.8s*
1972	Valeri Borzov, USSR.	20s

400 Meter Run

1896	Thomas Burke, United States	54.2s
1900	Maxey Long, United States	49.4s
1904	Harry Hillman, United States	49.2s
1906	Paul Pilgrim, United States	53.2s
1908	Wyndham Halswelle, Great Britain, walkover	50s
1912	Charles Reidpath, United States	48.2s
1920	Bevil Rudd, South Africa	49.6s
1924	Eric Liddell, Great Britain	47.6s
1928	Ray Barbuti, United States	47.8s
1932	William Carr, United States	46.2s
1936	Archie Williams, United States	46.5s
1948	Arthur Wint, Jamaica, B.W.I.	46.2s

1952	George Rhoden, Jamaica, B.W.I.	45.9s
1956	Charles Jenkins, United States	46.7s
1960	Otis Davis, United States	44.9s
1964	Michael Larrabee, United States	45.1s
1968	Lee Evans, United States	43.8s*
1972	Vincent Matthews, United States	44.7s

800 Meter Run

1896	Edwin Flack, Great Britain	2m. 11s
1900	Alfred Tysoe, Great Britain	2m. 1.4s
1904	James Lightbody, United States	1m. 56s
1906	Paul Pilgrim, United States	2m. 1.2s
1908	Mel Sheppard, United States	1m. 52.8s
1912	James Meredith, United States	1m. 51.9s
1920	Albert Hill, Great Britain	1m. 53.4s
1924	Douglas Lowe, Great Britain	1m. 52.4s
1928	Douglas Lowe, Great Britain	1m. 51.8s
1932	Thomas Hampson, Great Britain	1m. 49.8s
1936	John Woodruff, United States	1m. 52.9s
1948	Mal Whitfield, United States	1m .49.2s
1952	Mal Whitfield, United States	1m. 49.2s
1956	Thomas Courtney, United States	1m. 47.7s
1960	Peter Snell, New Zealand	1m. 46.3s
1964	Peter Snell, New Zealand	1m. 45.1s
1968	Ralph Doubell, Australia	1m. 44.3s*
1972	Dave Wottle, United States	1m .45.9s

1,500 Meter Run

1896	Edwin Flack, Great Britain	4m. 33.2s
1900	Charles Bennett, Great Britain	4m. 6s
1904	James Lightbody, United States	4m. 5.4s
1906	James Lightbody, United States	4m. 12s
1908	Mel Sheppard, United States	4m. 3.4s
1912	Arnold Jackson, Great Britain	3m. 56.8s
1920	Albert Hill, Great Britain	4m. 1.8s
1924	Paavo Nurmi, Finland	3m. 53.6s
1928	Harry Larva, Finland	3m.53.2s
1932	Luigi Beccali, Italy	3m. 51.2s
1936	Jack Lovelock, New Zealand	3m. 47.8s
1948	Henri Eriksson, Sweden	3m. 49.8s
1952	Joseph Barthel, Luxemburg	3m. 45.2s
1956	Ron Delany, Ireland	3m. 41.2s
1960	Herb Elliott, Australia	3m. 35.6s
1964	Peter Snell, New Zealand	3m. 38.1s
1968	Kipchoge Keino, Kenya	3m. 34.9s*
1972	Pekka Vasala, Finland	3m. 36.3s

3,000 Meter Steeplechase

1920	Percy Hodge, Great Britain	10m. 2.4s
1924	Willie Ritola, Finland	9m. 33.6s
1928	Toivo Loukola, Finland	9m. 21.8s
1932	Volnari Iso-Hollo, Finland	10m. 33.4s
	(About 3450 mtrs. extra lap by error)	
1936	Volnari Iso-Hollo, Finland	9m. 3.8s

1948	Thure Sjoestrand, Sweden.	9m. 4.6s
1952	Horace Ashenfelter, United States	8m. 45.4s
1956	Chris Brasher, Great Britain	8m. 42.2s
1960	Zdzislaw Krzyszkowiak, Poland	8m. 34.2s
1964	Gaston Roelants, Belgium	8m. 30.8s
1968	Amos Biwott, Kenya	8m. 51s
1972	Kipchoge Keino, Kenya	8m. 23.6s*

5,000 Meter Run

1912	Hannes Kolehmainen, Finland	14m. 36.6s
1920	Joseph Guillemot, France	14m. 55.6s
1924	Paavo Nurmi, Finland.	14m. 31.2s
1928	Willie Ritola, Finland.	14m. 38s
1932	Lauri Lehtinen, Finland.	14m. 30s
1936	Gunnar Hockert, Finland.	14m. 22.2s
1948	Gaston Reiff, Belgium.	14m. 17.6s
1952	Emil Zatopek, Czechoslovakia.	14m. 6.0s
1956	Vladimir Kuts, USSR.	13m. 39.6s
1960	Murray Halberg, New Zealand	13m. 43.4s
1964	Bob Schul, United States	13m. 48.8s
1968	Mohamed Gammoudi, Tunisia	14m. 05.0s
1972	Lasse Viren, Finland	13m. 26.4s*

Cross-Country

1912	Hannes Kolehmainen, Finland	45m. 11.6s

5 Mile Run

1906	H. Hawtrey, Great Britain	26m. 26.2s
1908	Emil Voigt, Great Britain.	25m. 11.2s*

10,000 Meter Run

1912	Hannes Kolehmainen, Finland	31m. 20.8s
1920	Paavo Nurmi, Finland.	31m. 45.8s
1924	Willie Ritola, Finland.	30m. 23.2s
1928	Paavo Nurmi, Finland.	30m. 18.8s
1932	Janusz Kusocinski, Poland	30m. 11.4s
1936	Ilmari Salminen, Finland.	30m. 15.4s
1948	Emil Zatopek, Czechoslovakia.	29m. 59.6s
1952	Emil Zatopek, Czechoslovakia.	29m. 17.0s
1956	Vladimir Kuts, USSR.	28m. 45.6s
1960	Pytor Bolotnikov, USSR.	28m. 32.2s
1964	Billy Mills, United States.	28m. 24.4s
1968	Naftali Temu, Kenya.	29m. 27.4s
1972	Lasse Viren, Finland	27m. 38.4s*

Marathon

1896	Spyros Loues, Greece	2h. 55m. 20s
1900	Michael Teato, France	2h. 59m. 45s
1904	Thomas Hicks, United States	3h. 28m. 53s
1906	W. J. Sherring, Canada.	2h. 51m. 23.6s
1908	John J. Hayes, United States	2h. 55m. 18.4s
1912	Kenneth McArthur, South Africa	2h. 36. 54.8s
1920	Hannes Kolehmainen, Finland.	2h. 32m. 35.8s
1924	Albin Stenroos, Finland.	2h. 41m. 22.6s
1928	El Ouafl, France	2h. 32m. 57s
1932	Juan Zabala, Argentina.	2h. 31m. 36s
1936	Kitei Son, Japan.	2h. 29m. 19.2s
1948	Delfo Cabera, Argentina.	2h. 34m. 51.6s
1952	Emil Zatopek, Czechoslovakia.	2h. 23m. 03.2s
1956	Alain Mimoun, France	2h. 25m.
1960	Abebe Bikila, Ethiopia.	2h. 15m. 15.2s
1964	Abebe Bikila, Ethiopia.	2h. 12m. 11.2s*
1968	Mamo Wolde, Ethiopia.	2h. 20m. 26.4s
1972	Frank Shorter, United States.	2h. 12m. 19.8s

10,000 Meter Cross-Country

1920	Paavo Nurmi, Finland.	27m. 15s*
1924	Paavo Nurmi, Finland.	32m. 54.8s

1,500 Meter Walk

1906	George V. Bonhag, United States	7m. 12.6s

3,000 Meter Walk

1920	Ugo Frigerio, Italy.	13m. 14.2

3,500 Meter Walk

1908	George Larner, Great Britain.	14m. 55s

10,000 Meter Walk

1912	George Goulding, Canada	46m. 28.4s
1920	Ugo Frigerio, Italy.	48m. 6.2s
1924	Ugo Frigerio, Italy.	47m. 49s
1948	John Mikaelsson, Sweden	45m. 13.2s
1952	John Mikaelsson, Sweden	45m. 02.8s*

20,000 Meter Walk

1956	Leonid Spirine, USSR.	1h. 31m. 27.4s
1960	Vladimir Golubnickiy, USSR.	1h. 34m. 7.2s

1964	Kenneth Mathews, Great Britain	1h. 29m. 34.0s
1968	Vladimir Golubnichiy, USSR.	1h. 35m. 58.4s
1972	Peter Frenkel, E. Germany.	1h. 26m. 42.4s*

50,000 Meter Walk

1932	Thomas W. Green, Great Britain	4h. 50m. 10s
1936	Harold Whitlock Great Britain.	4h. 30m. 41.4s
1948	John Lundgren, Sweden.	4h. 41m. 52s
1952	Giuseppe Bordoni, Italy.	4h. 28m. 07.8s
1956	Norman Read, New Zealand.	4h. 30m. 42.8s
1960	Donald Thompson, Great Britain.	4h. 25m. 30s
1964	Abdon Pamich, Italy.	4h. 11m. 11.2s
1968	Christoph Hohne, E. Germany.	4h. 20m. 13.6s
1972	Bern Kannenberg, W. Germany.	3h. 56m. 11.6s*

110 Meter Hurdles

1896	Thomas Curtis, United States	17.6s
1900	Alvin Kraenzlein, United States.	15.4s
1904	Frederick Schule, United States.	16s
1906	R. G. Leavitt, United States.	16.2s
1908	Forrest Smithson, United States	15.0s
1912	Frederick Kelly, United States.	15.1s
1920	Earl Thomson, Canada.	14.8s
1924	Daniel Kinsey, United States	15s
1928	Sydney Atkinson, South Africa.	14.8s
1932	George Saling, United States.	14.6s
1936	Forrest Towns, United States.	14.2s
1948	William Porter, United States.	13.9s
1952	Harrison Dillard, United States.	13.7s
1956	Lee Calhoun, United States	13.5s
1960	Lee Calhoun, United States.	13.8s
1964	Hayes Jones, United States.	13.6s
1968	Willie Davenport, United States.	13.3s
1972	Rod Milburn, United States.	13.2s*

200 Meter Hurdles

1900	Alvin Kraenzlein, United States.	25.4s
1904	Harry Hillman, United States.	24.6s*

400 Meter Hurdles

1900	J. W. B. Tewksbury, United States	57.6s
1904	Harry Hillman, United States.	53s
1908	Charles Bacon, United States.	55s
1920	Frank Loomis, United States.	54s
1924	F. Morgan Taylor, United States.	52.6s
1928	Lord Burghley, Great Britain.	53.4s
1932	Robert Tisdall, Ireland.	51.8s
1936	Glenn Hardin, United States.	52.4s
1948	Roy Cochran, United States.	51.1s
1952	Charles Moore, United States.	50.8s
1956	Glenn Davis, United States.	50.1s
1960	Glenn Davis, United States.	49.3s
1964	Rex Cawley, United States.	49.6s
1968	Dave Hemery, Great Britain.	48.1s
1972	John Akii-Bua, Uganda.	47.8s*

Standing High Jump

1900	Ray Ewry, United States.	5ft. 5 in.
1904	Ray Ewry, United States.	4ft. 11 in.
1906	Ray Ewry, United States.	5ft. 1 5-8 in.
1908	Ray Ewry, United States.	5ft. 2 in.
1912	Platt Adams, United States.	5ft. 4 1-4 in.*

Running High Jump

1896	Ellery Clark, United States	5ft. 11 1-4 in.
1900	Irving Baxter, United States.	6ft. 2 4-5 in.
1904	Samuel Jones, United States	5ft. 11 in.
1906	Con Leahy, Ireland.	5ft. 9 7-8 in.
1908	Harry Porter, United States	6ft. 3 in.
1912	Almer W. Richards, United States.	6ft. 4 in.
1920	Richard Landon, United States	6ft. 4 3-8 in.
1924	Harold Osborn, United States.	6ft. 6 in.
1928	Robert W. King, United States.	6ft. 4 3-8 in.
1932	Duncan McNaughton, Canada.	6ft. 5 5-8 in.
1936	Cornelius Johnson, United States	6ft, 7 15-16 in.
1948	John L. Winter, Australia.	6ft. 6 in.
1952	Walter Davis, United States	6ft. 8.32 in.
1956	Charles Dumas, United States	6ft. 11 1-4 in.
1960	Robert Shavlakadze, USSR.	7ft. 1in.
1964	Valery Brumel, USSR.	7ft. 1 7-8 in.
1968	Dick Fosbury, United States.	7ft. 4 1-4 in.*
1972	Yuri Tarmak, USSR.	7ft. 3 3-4 in.

Standing Broad Jump

1900	Ray Ewry, United States	10ft. 6 2-5 in.
1904	Ray Ewry, United States	11ft. 4 7-8 in.*
1906	Ray Ewry, United States	10ft. 10 in.
1908	Ray Ewry, United States	10ft. 11 1-4 in.
1912	Constantin Tsicilitras, Greece	11ft. 3-4 in.

Long Jump

1896	Ellery Clark, United States	20ft. 9 3-4 in.
1900	Alvin Kraenzlein, United States	23ft. 6 7-8 in.
1904	Myer Prinstein, United States	24ft. 1in.
1906	Myer Prinstein, United States	23ft. 7 1-2 in.
1908	Frank Irons, United States	24ft. 6 1-2 in.
1912	Albert Gutterson, United States	24ft. 11 1-4 in.
1920	Wm. Petterssen, Sweden	23ft. 5 1-2 in.
1924	DeHart Hubbard, United States	24ft. 5 1-8 in.
1928	Edward B. Hamm, United States	25ft. 4 3-4 in.
1932	Edward Gordon, United States	25ft. 3-4 in.
1936	Jesse Owens, United States	26ft. 5 5-16 in.
1948	William Steele, United States	25ft. 8 in.
1952	Jerome Biffle, United States	24ft. 10.03 in.
1956	Gregory Bell, United States	25ft. 8 1-4 in.
1960	Ralph Boston, United States	26ft. 7 3-4 in.
1964	Lynn Davies, Great Britain	26ft. 5 3-4 in.
1968	Bob Beamon, United States	29ft. 2 1-2 in.*
1972	Randy Williams, United States	27ft. 1-2 in.

400 Meter Relay

1912	Great Britain	42.4s
1920	United States	42.2s
1924	United States	41s
1928	United States	41s
1932	United States	40s
1936	United States	39.8s
1948	United States	40.3s
1952	United States	40.1s
1956	United States	39.5s
1960	Germany (U.S. disqualified)	39.5s
1964	United States	39.0s
1968	United States	38.2s*
1972	United States	38.2s*

1,600 Meter Relay

1908	United States	3m. 27.2s
1912	United States	3m. 16.6s
1920	Great Britain	3m. 22.2s
1924	United States	3m. 16s
1928	United States	3m. 14.2s
1932	United States	3m. 8.2s
1936	Great Britain	3m. 9s
1948	United States	3m. 10.4s
1952	Jamaica, B.W.I.	3m. 03.9s
1956	United States	3m. 04.8s
1960	United States	3m. 02.2s
1964	United States	3m. 00.7s
1968	United States	2m. 56.1s*
1972	Kenya	2m. 59.8s

Pole Vault

1896	William Hoyt, United States	10ft. 9 3-4 in.
1900	Irving Baxter, United States	10ft. 9.9 in.
1904	Charles Dvorak, United States	11ft. 6 in.
1906	Fernand Gauder, France	11ft. 6 in.
1908	A. C. Gilbert, United States	
	Edward Cook Jr., United States	12ft. 2 in.
1912	Harry Babcock, United States	12ft. 11 1-2 in.
1920	Frank Foss, United States	13ft. 5 in.
1924	Lee Barnes, United States	12ft. 11 1-2 in.
1928	Sabin W. Carr, United States	13ft. 9 1-2 in.
1932	William Miller, United States	14ft. 1 7-8 in.
1936	Earle Meadows, United States	14ft. 3 1-4 in.
1948	Guinn Smith, United States	14ft. 1 1-4 in.
1952	Robert Richards, United States	14ft. 11 1-4 in.
1956	Robert Richards, United States	14ft. 11 1-2 in.
1960	Don Bragg, United States	15ft. 5 1-8 in.
1964	Fred Hansen, United States	16ft. 8 1-2 in.
1968	Bob Seagren, United States	17ft. 8 1-2 in.
1972	Wolfgang Nordwig, E. Germany	18ft. 1-2 in.*

16-Lb. Hammer Throw

1900	John Flannagan, United States	167ft. 4 in.
1904	John Flannagan, United States	168ft. 1 in.
1908	John Flannagan, United States	170ft. 4 1-4 in.
1912	Matt McGrath, United States	179ft. 7 1-8 in.
1920	Pat Ryan, United States	172ft. 5 5-8 in.
1924	Fred Tootell, United States	174ft. 10 1-8 in.
1928	Patrick O'Callaghan, Ireland	168ft. 7 3-8 in.
1932	Patrick O'Callaghan, Ireland	176ft. 11 1-8 in.
1936	Karl Hein, Germany	185ft. 4 3-16 in.
1948	Imre Nemeth, Hungary	183ft. 11 1-2 in.
1952	Jozsef Csermak, Hungary	197ft. 11.67 in.
1956	Harold Connolly, United States	207ft. 3 1-4 in.
1960	Vasily Rudenkov, USSR	220ft. 2 in.
1964	Romuald Klim, USSR	228ft. 9 1-2 in.
1968	Gyula Zsivotsky, Hungary	240ft. 8 in.
1972	Anatoli Bondarchuk, USSR	248ft. 8 in.*

Discus Throw

1896	Robert Garrett, United States	95ft. 7 1-2 in.
1900	Rudolf Bauer, Hungary	118ft. 2.9-10in.
1904	Martin Sheridan, United States	128ft. 10 1-2 in.
1906	Martin Sheridan, United States	136ft. 1-3 in.
1908	Martin Sheridan, United States	134ft. 2 in.
1912	Armas Taipale, Finland	148ft. 4 in.
	Both hands—Armas Taipale, Finland	271ft. 10 1-4 in.
1920	Elmer Niklander, Finland	146ft. 7 1-4 in.
1924	Clarence Houser, United States	151ft. 5 1-8 in.
1928	Clarence Houser, United States	155ft. 3 in.
1932	John Anderson, United States	162ft. 4 7-8 in.
1936	Ken Carpenter, United States	165ft. 7 3-8 in.
1948	Adolfo Consolini, Italy	173ft. 2 in.
1952	Sim Iness, United States	180ft. 6.85 in.
1956	Al Oerter, United States	184ft. 11 in.
1960	Al Oerter, United States	194ft. 2 in.
1964	Al Oerter, United States	200ft. 1 1-2 in.
1968	Al Oerter, United States	212ft. 6 1-2 in.*
1972	Ludik Danek, Czechoslovakia	211ft. 3 in.

Standing Hop, Step, and Jump

1900	Ray Ewry, United States	34ft. 8 1-2 in.*
1904	Ray Ewry, United States	34ft. 7 1-4 in.

Triple Jump

1896	James Connolly, United States	45 ft.
1900	Myer Prinstein, United States	47ft. 4 1-4 in.
1904	Myer Prinstein, United States	47 ft.
1906	P. G. O'Connor, Ireland	46ft. 2 in.
1908	Timothy Ahearne, Great Britain	48ft. 11 1-4 in.
1912	Gustaf Lindblom, Sweden	48ft. 5 1-8 in.
1920	Vilho Tuulos, Finland	47ft. 7 in.
1924	Archie Winter, Australia	50ft. 11 1-4in.
1928	Mikio Oda, Japan	49ft. 11 in.
1932	Chuhei Nambu, Japan	51ft. 7 in.
1936	Naoto Tajima, Japan	52ft. 5 7-8 in.
1948	Arne Ahman, Sweden	50ft. 6 1-4 in.
1952	Adhemar de Silva, Brazil	53ft. 2.59 in.
1956	Adhemar de Silva, Brazil	53ft. 7 1-2 in.
1960	Jozef Schmidt, Poland	55ft. 1 3-4 in.
1964	Jozef Schmidt, Poland	55ft. 3 1-2 in.
1968	Viktor Saneev, USSR	57ft. 3-4 in.*
1972	Viktor Saneev, USSR	56ft. 11 in.

16-Lb. Shot Put

1896	Robert Garrett, United States	36ft. 2 in.
1900	Robert Sheldon, United States	46ft. 3 1-8 in.
1904	Ralph Rose, United States	48ft. 7 in.
1906	Martin Sheridan, United States	40ft. 4.8 in.
1908	Ralph Rose, United States	46ft. 7 1-2 in.
1912	Pat McDonald, United States	50ft. 4 in.
	Both hands—Ralph Rose,	
	United States	90ft. 5 1-2 in.
1920	Ville Porhola, Finland	48ft. 7 1-8 in.
1924	Clarence Houser, United States	49ft. 2 3-8 in.
1928	John Kuck, United States	52ft. 3-4 in.
1932	Leo Sexton, United States	52ft. 6 3-16 in.
1936	Hans Woelke, Germany	53ft. 1 13-16 in.
1948	Wilbur Thompson, United States	56ft. 2 in.
1952	Parry O'Brien, United States	57ft. 1.43 in.
1956	Parry O'Brien, United States	60ft. 11 in.
1960	William Nieder, United States	64ft. 6 3-4 in.
1964	Dallas Long, United States	66ft. 8 1-2 in.
1968	Randy Matson, United States	67ft. 4 3-4 in.
1972	Wladyslaw Komar, Poland	69ft. 6 in.*

Discus Throw—Greek Style

1906	Werner Jaevinen, Finland	115ft. 4 in.
1908	Martin Sheridan, United States	124ft. 8 in.*

Javelin Throw

1906	Erik Lemming, Sweden	175ft. 6 in.
1908	Erik Lemming, Sweden	178ft. 7 1-2 in.
	Held in middle—Erik Lemming,	
	Sweden	179ft. 10 1-2 in.
1912	Erik Lemming, Sweden	198ft. 11 1-4 in.
	Both hands, Julius Saaristo,	
	Finland	358ft. 11 7-8 in.
1920	Jonni Myrra, Finland	215ft. 9 3-4 in.
1924	Jonni Myrra, Finland	206ft. 6 3-4 in.
1928	Eric Lundquist, Sweden	218ft. 6 1-8 in.
1932	Matti Jarvinen, Finland	238ft. 7 in.
1936	Gerhard Stoeck, Germany	235ft. 8 5-16 in.
1948	Kaj T. Rautavaara, Finland	228ft. 10 1-2 in.
1952	Cy Young, United States	242ft. 0.79 in.
1956	Egil Danielsen, Norway	281ft. 2 1-4 in.
1960	Viktor Tsibulenko, USSR	277ft. 8 3-8 in.
1964	Pauli Nevala, Finland	271ft. 2 1-2 in.

| 1968 | Yanis Lusis, USSR | 295ft. 7 1-4 in. |
| 1972 | Klaus Wolferman, W. Germany | 296ft. 10 in.* |

Modern Pentathlon

1952	Lars Hall, Sweden	32 pts.
1956	Lars Hall, Sweden	4,833 pts.
1960	Ferenc Nemeth, Hungary	5,024 pts.
1964	Ferenc Torok, Hungary	5,116 pts.
1968	Bjoern Ferm, Sweden	4,964 pts.
1972	Andras Balczo, Hungary	5,412 pts.*

Decathlon

1912	Hugo Wieslander, Sweden	7,724.49 pts.
1920	Helge Loveland, Norway	6,804.35 pts.
1924	Harold Osborn, United States	7,710.775 pts.
1928	Paavo Yrjola, Finland	8,056.20 pts.
1932	James Bausch, United States	8,462.23 pts.
1936	Glenn Morris, United States	7,900 pts.
1948	Robert Mathias, United States	7,139 pts.
1952	Robert Mathias, United States	7,887 pts.
1956	Milton Campbell, United States	7,937 pts.
1960	Rafer Johnson, United States	8,392 pts.
1964	Willi Holdorf, Germany	7,887 pts.
1968	Bill Toomey, United States	8,193 pts.
1972	Nikola Avilov, USSR	8,454 pts.*

former point system, 1936-1960

Track and Field—Women

100 Meter Run

1928	Elizabeth Robinson, United States	12.2s
1932	Stella Walsh, Poland	11.9s
1936	Helen Stephens, United States	11.5s
1948	Francina Blankers-Koen, Netherlands	11.9s
1952	Marjorie Jackson, Australia	11.5s
1956	Betty Cuthbert, Australia	11.5s
1960	Wilma Rudolph, United States	11.0s*
1964	Wyomia Tyus, United States	11.4s
1968	Wyomia Tyus, United States	11.0s*
1972	Renate Stecher, E. Germany	11.1s

200 Meter Run

1948	Francina Blankers-Koen, Netherlands	24.4s
1952	Marjorie Jackson, Australia	23.7s
1956	Betty Cuthbert, Australia	23.4s
1960	Wilma Rudolph, United States	24.0s
1964	Edith McGuire, United States	23.0s
1968	Irene Szewinska, Poland	22.5s
1972	Renate Stecher, E. Germany	22.4s*

400 Meter Run

1964	Betty Cuthbert, Australia	52s
1968	Colette Besson, France	52s
1972	Monika Zehrt, E. Germany	51s*

800 Meter Run

1928	Linda Radke, Germany	2m. 16.8s
1960	Ludmila Shevcova, USSR	2m. 4.3s
1964	Ann Packer, Great Britain	2m. 1.1s'
1968	Madeline Manning, United States	2m. 0.9s
1972	Hildegard Falck, W. Germany	1m. 58.6s*

1500 Meter Run

| 1972 | Ludmila Bragina, USSR | 4m. 1.4s* |

400 Meter Relay

1928	Canada	48.4s
1932	United States	47.0s
1936	United States	46.9s
1948	Netherlands	47.5s
1952	United States	45.9s
1956	Australia	44.5s
1960	United States	44.5s
1964	Poland	43.6s
1968	United States	42.8s*
1972	West Germany	42.8s*

100 Meter Freestyle

1896	Alfred Hajos, Hungary	1:22.2
1904	Zoltan de Halmay, Hungary (100 yards)	1:02.8
1906	Charles Daniels, U.S.	1:13.0
1908	Charles Daniels, U.S.	1:05.6
1912	Duke P. Kahanamoku, U.S.	1:03.4
1920	Duke P. Kahanamoku, U.S.	1:01.4
1924	John Weissmuller, U.S.	59.0
1928	John Weissmuller, U.S.	58.6

1600 Meter Relay

| 1972 | East Germany | 3m. 23s* |

80 Meter Hurdles

1932	Mildred Didrikson, United States	11.7s
1936	Trebisonda Villa, Italy	11.7s
1948	Francina Blankers-Koen, Netherlands	11.2s
1952	Shirley Strickland de la Hunty, Australia	10.9s
1956	Shirley Strickland de la Hunty, Australia	10.7s
1960	Irina Press, USSR	10.8s
1964	Karen Balzer, Germany	10.5s
1968	Maureen Caird, Australia	10.3s*

100 Meter Hurdles

| 1972 | Annelie Ehrhardt, E. Germany | 12.6* |

High Jump

1928	Ethel Catherwood, Canada	5ft. 3 in.
1932	Jean Shiley, United States	5ft. 5 1-4 in.
1936	Ibolya Csak, Hungary	5ft. 3 in.
1948	Alice Coachman, United States	5ft. 6 1-8 in.
1952	Esther Brand, South Africa	5ft. 5 3-4 in.
1956	Mildred L. McDaniel, United States	5ft. 9 1-4 in.
1960	Iolanda Balas, Romania	6ft. 1-4 in.
1964	Iolanda Balas, Romania	6ft. 2 7-8 in.*
1968	Miloslava Reskova, Czechoslovakia	5 ft. 11 3-4 in.
1972	Ulrike Meyfarth, W. Germany	6ft. 3 1-4 in.

Discus Throw

1928	Helena Konopacka, Poland	129ft. 11 7-8 in.
1932	Lillian Copeland, United States	133ft. 2 in.
1936	Gisela Mauermayer, Germany	156ft. 3 3-16 in.
1948	Micheline Ostermeyer, France	137ft. 6 1-2 in.
1952	Nina Romaschkova, USSR	168ft. 8 1-2 in.
1956	Olga Fikotova, Czechoslovakia	176ft. 1 1-2 in.
1960	Nina Ponomareva, USSR	180ft. 8 1-4 in.
1964	Tamara Press, USSR	187ft. 10 1-2 in.
1968	Lia Manolin, Romania	191ft. 2 1-2 in.
1972	Faina Melnik, USSR	218ft. 7 in.*

Javelin Throw

1932	Mildred Didrikson, United States	143ft. 4 in.
1936	Tilly Fleischer, Germany	148ft. 2 3-4 in.
1948	Herma Bauma, Austria	149ft. 6 in.
1952	Dana Zatopekova, Czechoslovakia	165ft. 7 in.
1956	Inessa Janzeme, USSR	176ft. 8 in.
1960	Elvira Ozolina, USSR	183ft. 8 in.
1964	Mihaela Penes, Romania	198ft. 7 1-2 in.
1968	Angela Nemeth, Hungary	198ft. 1-2 in.
1972	Ruth Fuchs, E. Germany	209ft. 7 in.*

Shot Put

1948	Micheline Ostermeyer, France	45ft. 1 1-2 in.
1952	Galina Zybina, USSR	50ft. 1 1-2 in.
1956	Tamara Tishkyevich, USSR	54ft. 5 in.
1960	Tamara Press, USSR	56ft. 9 7-8 in.
1964	Tamara Press, USSR	59ft. 6 1-4 in.
1968	Margitta Gummel, E. Germany	64ft. 4 in.
1972	Nadezwda Chizova, USSR	69ft.*

Long Jump

1948	Olga Gyarmati, Hungary	18ft. 8 1-4 in.
1952	Yvette Williams, New Zealand	20ft. 5 3-4 in.
1956	E. Krzeskinska, Poland	20ft. 9 3-4 in.
1960	Vyera Krepina, USSR	20ft. 10 3-4 in.
1964	Mary Rand, Great Britain	22ft. 2 1-4 in.
1968	V. Viscopoleanu, Romania	22ft. 4 1-2 in.*
1972	Heidemarie Rosendahl, W. Germany	22ft. 3 in.

Pentathlon

1964	Irina Press, USSR	5,246 pts.
1968	Ingred Becker, W. Germany	5,098 pts.
1972	Mary Peters, England	4,801 pts.*

Former point system, 1964-1968

Swimming-Men

1932	Yasuji Miyazaki, Japan	58.2
1936	Ferenc Csik, Hungary	57.6
1948	Wally Ris, U.S.	57.3
1952	Clark Scholes, U.S.	57.4
1956	Jon Henricks, Australia	55.4
1960	John Devitt, Australia	55.2
1964	Don Schollander, U.S.	53.4
1968	Mike Wenden, Australia	52.2
1972	Mark Spitz, U.S.	51.2*

200 Meter Freestyle

1968	Mike Wenden, Australia	1:55.2
1972	Mark Spitz, U.S.	1:52.8*

400 Meter Freestyle

1904	C. M. Daniels, U.S. (440 yards)	6:16.2
1906	Otto Sheff, Austria	6:23.8
1908	Henry Taylor, Great Britain	5:36.8
1912	George Hodgson, Canada	5:24.4
1920	Norman Ross, U.S.	5:26.8
1924	John Weissmuller, U.S.	5:04.2
1928	Albert Zorilla, Argentina	5:01.6
1932	Clarence Crabbe, U.S.	4:48.4
1936	Jack Medica, U.S.	4:44.5
1948	William Smith, U.S.	4:41.0
1952	Jean Boiteux, France	4:30.7
1956	Murray Rose, Australia	4:27.3
1960	Murray Rose, Australia	4:18.3
1964	Don Schollander, U.S.	4:12.2
1968	Mike Burton, U.S.	4:09.0
1972	Brad Cooper, Australia	4:00.3*

1,500 Meter Freestyle

1908	Henry Taylor, Great Britain	22:48.4
1912	George Hodgson, Canada	22:00.0
1920	Norman Ross, U.S.	22:23.2
1924	Andrew Charlton, Australia	20:06.6
1928	Arne Borg, Sweden	19:51.8
1932	Kasuo Kitamura, Japan	19:12.4
1936	Noboru Terada, Japan	19:13.7
1948	James P. McClane, U.S.	19:18.5
1952	Ford Konno, U.S.	18:30.0
1956	Murray Rose, Australia	17:58.9
1960	Jon Konrads, Australia	17:19.6
1964	Robert Windle, Australia	17:01.7
1968	Mike Burton, U.S.	16:38.9
1972	Mike Burton, U.S.	15:52.6*

400 Meter Medley Relay

1960	United States	4:05.4
1964	United States	3:58.4
1968	United States	3:54.9
1972	United States	3:48.2*

400 Meter Freestyle Relay

1964	United States	3:33.2
1968	United States	3:31.7
1972	United States	3:26.4*

800 Meter Freestyle Relay

1908	Great Britain	10:55.6
1912	Australia	10:11.6
1920	United States	10:04.4
1924	United States	9:53.4
1928	United States	9:36.2
1932	Japan	8:58.4
1936	Japan	8:51.5
1948	United States	8:46.0
1952	United States	8:31.1
1956	Australia	8:23.6
1960	United States	8:10.2
1964	United States	7:52.1
1968	United States	7:52.3
1972	United States	7:38.8*

100 Meter Backstroke

1904	Walter Brack, Germany (100 yds.)	1:16.8
1908	Arno Bieberstein, Germany	1:24.6
1912	Harry Hebner, U.S.	1:21.2
1920	Warren Kealoha, U.S.	1:15.2
1924	Warren Kealoha, U.S.	1:13.2
1928	George Kojac, U.S.	1:08.2
1932	Masaji Kiyokawa, Japan	1:08.6
1936	Adolph Kiefer, U.S.	1:05.9
1948	Allen Stack, U.S.	1:06.4
1952	Yoshi Oyokawa, U.S.	1:05.4
1956	David Thiele, Australia	1:02.2
1960	David Thiele, Australia	1:01.9
1968	Roland Matthes, E. Germany	58.7
1972	Roland Matthes, E. Germany	56.6*

200 Meter Backstroke

1964	Jed Graef, U.S.	2:10.3
1968	Roland Matthes, E. Germany	2:09.6
1972	Roland Matthes, E. Germany	2:02.8*

100 Meter Breaststroke

1968	Don McKenzie, U.S.	1:07.7
1972	Nobutaka Taguchi, Japan	1:04.9*

200 Meter Breaststroke

1908	Frederick Holman, Great Britain	3:09.2
1912	Walter Bathe, Germany	3:01.8
1920	Haken Malmroth, Sweden	3:04.4
1924	Robert Skelton, U.S.	2:56.6
1928	Yoshiyuki Tsuruta, Japan	2:48.8
1932	Yoshiyuki Tsuruta, Japan	2:45.4
1936	Tetsuo Hamuro, Japan	2:42.5
1948	Joseph Verdeur, U.S.	2:39.3
1952	John Davies, Australia	2:34.4
1956	Masura Furukawa, Japan	2:34.7
1960	William Mulliken, U.S.	2:37.4
1964	Ian O'Brien, Australia	2:27.8
1968	Felipe Munoz, Mexico	2:28.7
1972	John Hencken, U.S.	2:21.5*

100 Meter Butterfly

1968	Doug Russell, U.S.	55.9
1972	Mark Spitz, U.S.	54.3*

200 Meter Butterfly

1956	William Yorzyk, U.S.	2:18.6
1960	Michael Troy, U.S.	2:12.8
1964	Kevin J. Berry, Australia	2:06.6
1968	Carl Robie, U.S.	2:08.7
1972	Mark Spitz, U.S.	2:00.7*

200 Meter Individual Medley

1968	Charles Hickcox, U.S.	2:12.0
1972	Gunnar Larsson, Sweden	2:07.2*

400 Meter Individual Medley

1964	Dick Roth, U.S.	4:45.4
1968	Charles Hickcox, U.S.	4:48.4
1972	Gunnar Larsson, Sweden	4.32*

Springboard Diving

		Points
1904	Dr. G. E. Sheldon, U.S.	12 2-3
1906	Gottlob Walz, Germany	
1908	Albert Zuerner, Germany	85.5
1912	Paul Guenther, Germany	6
1920	Louis Kuehn, U.S.	6
1924	Albert White, U.S.	7
1928	Pete Desjardins, U.S.	185.04
1932	Michael Gallitzen, U.S.	161.38
1936	Richard Degener, U.S.	161.57
1948	Bruce Harlan, U.S.	163.64
1952	David Browning, U.S.	205.29
1956	Robert Clothworthy, U.S.	159.56
1960	Gary Tobian, U.S.	170.00
1964	Kenneth Sitzberger, U.S.	159.90
1968	Bernie Wrightson, U.S.	170.15
1972	Vladimir Vasin, USSR	594.09

Platform Diving

1928	Pete Desjardins, U.S.	98.74
1932	Harold Smith, U.S.	124.80
1936	Marshall Wayne, U.S.	113.58
1948	Sammy Lee, U.S.	130.05
1952	Sammy Lee, U.S.	156.28
1956	Joaquin Capilla, Mexico	152.44
1960	Robert Webster, U.S.	165.56
1964	Robert Webster, U.S.	148.58
1968	Klaus Dibiasi, Italy	164.18
1972	Klaus Dibiasi, Italy	504.12

Water Polo

1900	Great Britain	1936	Hungary
1904	United States	1948	Italy
1908	Great Britain	1952	Hungary
1912	Great Britain	1956	Hungary
1920	Great Britain	1960	Italy
1924	France	1964	Hungary
1928	Germany	1968	Yugoslavia
1932	Hungary	1972	USSR

Swimming—Women

100 Meter Freestyle

1912	Fanny Durack, Australia	1:22.2
1920	Ethelda Bleibtrey, U.S.	1:13.6
1924	Ethel Lackie, U.S.	1:12.4
1928	Albina Osipowich, U.S.	1:11.0
1932	Helene Madison, U.S.	1:06.8
1936	Hendrika Mastenbroek, Holland	1:05.9
1948	Greta Anderson, Denmark	1:06.3
1952	Katalin Szoke, Hungary	1:06.3
1956	Dawn Fraser, Australia	1:02.0

1960	Dawn Fraser, Australia	1:01.2
1964	Dawn Fraser, Australia	59.5
1968	Jan Henne, U.S.	1:00.0
1972	Sandra Neilson, U.S.	58.6*

200 Meter Freestyle

| 1968 | Debbie Meyer, U.S. | 2:10.5 |
| 1972 | Shane Gould, Australia | 2:03.6* |

400 Meter Freestyle

1924	Martha Norelius, U.S.	6:02.2
1928	Martha Norelius, U.S.	5:42.8
1932	Helene Madison, U.S.	5:28.5
1936	Hendrika Mastenbroek, Netherlands	5:26.4
1948	Ann Curtis, U.S.	5:17.8
1952	Valerie Gyenge, Hungary	5:12.1
1956	Lorraine Crapp, Australia	4:54.6
1960	Susan Chris von Saltza, U.S.	4:50.6
1964	Virginia Duenkel, U.S.	4:43.3
1968	Debbie Meyer, U.S.	4:31.8
1972	Shane Gould, Australia	4:19.0*

800 Meter Freestyle

| 1968 | Debbie Meyer, U.S. | 9:24.0 |
| 1972 | Keena Rothhammer, U.S. | 8:53.7* |

400 Meter Medley Relay

1960	United States	4:41.1
1964	United States	4:33.9
1968	United States	4:28.3
1972	United States	4:20.7*

400 Meter Freestyle Relay

1912	Great Britain	5:52.8
1920	United States	5:11.6
1924	United States	4:58.8
1928	United States	4:47.6
1932	United States	4:38.0
1936	Netherlands	4:36.0
1948	United States	4:29.2
1952	Hungary	4:24.4
1956	Australia	4:17.1
1960	United States	4:08.9
1964	United States	4:03.8
1968	United States	4:02.5
1972	United States	3:55.2*

100 Meter Backstroke

1924	Sybil Bauer, U.S.	1:23.3
1928	Marie Braun, Netherlands	1:22.0
1932	Eleanor Holm, U.S.	1:19.4
1936	Dina Senff, Netherlands	1:18.9
1948	Karen Harup, Denmark	1:14.4
1952	Joan Harrison, South Africa	1:14.3
1956	Judy Grinham, Great Britain	1:12.9
1960	Lynn Burke, U.S.	1:09.3
1964	Cathy Ferguson, U.S.	1:07.7
1968	Kaye Hall, U.S.	1:06.2
1972	Melissa Belote, U.S.	1:05.8*

200 Meter Backstroke

| 1968 | Pokey Watson, U.S. | 2:24.8 |
| 1972 | Melissa Belote, U.S. | 2:19.2* |

100 Meter Breaststroke

| 1968 | Djurdjica Bjedov, Yugoslavia | 1:15.8 |
| 1972 | Cathy Carr, U.S. | 1:13.6* |

200 Meter Breaststroke

1924	Lucy Morton, Great Britain	3:32.2
1928	Hilde Schrader, Germany	3:12.6
1932	Clare Dennis, Australia	3:06.3
1936	Hideko Maehata, Japan	3:03.6
1948	Nelly Van Vliet, Netherlands	2:57.2
1952	Eva Szekely, Hungary	2:51.7
1956	Ursula Happe, Germany	2:53.1
1960	Anita Lonsbrough, Great Britain	2:49.5
1964	Galina Prozumenschikova, USSR	2:46.4
1968	Sharon Wichman, U.S.	2:44.4
1972	Beverly Whitfield, Australia	2:41.7*

200 Meter Medley

| 1968 | Claudia Kolb, U.S. | 2:24.7 |
| 1972 | Shane Gould, Australia | 2:23.1* |

400 Meter Medley

1964	Donna de Varona, U.S.	5:18.7
1968	Claudia Kolb, U.S.	5:08.5
1972	Gail Neall, Australia	5:03.0*

100 Meter Butterfly

1956	Shelley Mann, U.S.	1:11.0
1960	Carolyn Schuler, U.S.	1:09.5
1964	Sharon Stouder, U.S.	1:04.7
1968	Lynn McClements, Australia	1:05.5
1972	Mayumi Aoki, Japan	1:03.3*

200 Meter Butterfly

| 1968 | Ada Kok, Netherlands | 2:24.7 |
| 1972 | Karen Moe, U.S. | 2:15.6* |

Springboard Diving — Points

1920	Aileen Riggin, U.S.	9
1924	Elizabeth Becker, U.S.	8
1928	Helen Meany, U.S.	78.62
1932	Georgia Coleman, U.S.	87.52
1936	Marjorie Gestring, U.S.	89.27
1948	Victoria M. Draves, U.S.	108.74
1952	Patricia McCormick, U.S.	147.30
1956	Patricia McCormick, U.S.	142.36
1960	Ingrid Kramer, Germany	155.81
1964	Ingrid Engel-Kramer, Germany	145.00
1968	Sue Gossick, U.S.	150.77
1972	Micki King, U.S.	450.03

Platform Diving — Points

1928	Elizabeth B. Pinkston, U.S.	31.60
1932	Dorothy Poynton, U.S.	40.26
1936	Dorothy Poynton Hill, U.S.	33.93
1948	Victoria M. Draves, U.S.	68.87
1952	Patricia McCormick, U.S.	79.37
1956	Patricia McCormick, U.S.	84.85
1960	Ingrid Kramer, Germany	91.28
1964	Lesley Bush, U.S.	99.80
1968	Milena Duchkova, Czech	109.59
1972	Ulrika Knape, Sweden	390.00

Leading Olympic Game Medal Winners, 1896-1972

Nation	Gold	Silver	Bronze	Total
United States	583	412(a)	373	1368
Soviet Union	211	182	170	563
Great Britain	143	194	157	494
Sweden	123	124	156	403
Germany(b)	108	150	135	393
France	121	124	129	374
Italy	116	98	98	312
Hungary	102	90	105	297
Finland	83	70	97	250
Japan	65	60	51	176
Australia	63	52	61	176
Switzerland	37	53	48	138
The Netherlands	41	44	47	132
Denmark	28	48	48	124
Poland	30	33	60	123
Czechoslovakia	38	41	32	111
Canada	23	39	49	111

Nation	Gold	Silver	Bronze	Total
Norway	39	29	30	98
Greece	21	40	33	94
East Germany(b)	29	32	30	91
Belgium	20	37	30	87
Romania	18	22	32	72
Austria	15	23	30	68
West Germany(b)	18	21	26	65
South Africa	16	15	22	53
Bulgaria	13	25	15	53
Argentina	13	19	13	45
Turkey	23	12	7	42
Yugoslavia	12	15	9	36
Cuba	9	11	7	27
Iran	4	10	13	27
Mexico	6	9	10	25
New Zealand	12	2	10	24

(a) Refused Basketball Medal in 1972. (b) East and West began competing separately in 1968.

Winter Olympic Games Champions, 1924-1972

Sites and Unofficial Winners of Games

1924—Chamonix, France (Norway)
1928—St. Moritz, Switzerland (Norway)
1932—Lake Placid, N.Y. (U.S.)
1936—Garmisch-Partenkirchen (Norway)

1948—St. Moritz (Sweden)
1952—Olso, Norway (Norway)
1956—Cortina d'Ampezzo, Italy (USSR)
1960—Squaw Valley, Cal. (USSR)

1964—Innsbruck, Austria (USSR)
1968—Grenoble, France (Norway)
1972—Sapporo, Japan (USSR)
1976—Innsbruck, Austria, Feb. 4-15

Biathlon

	Time
1960—Klas Lestander, Sweden	1:33:21.6
1964—Vladimir Melanin, USSR	1:20:26.8
1968—Magnar Solberg, Norway	1:13:45.9
1972—Magnar Solberg, Norway	1:15:55.5

Biathlon Relay

	Time
1968—USSR, Norway, Sweden	2:13.02
1972—USSR, Finland, E. Germany	1:51.44

Bobsledding
4-Man Bob

(Driver in parentheses)	Time
1924—Switzerland (Edward Scherrer)	5:45.54
*1928—United States (William Fiske)	3:20.5
1932—United States (William Fiske)	7:53.68
1936—Switzerland (Pierre Musy)	5:19.85
1948—United States (Edward Rimkus)	5:20.1
1952—Germany (Andreas Ostler)	5:07.84
1956—Switzerland (Frank Kapus)	5:10.44
1964—Canada (Victor Emery)	4:14.46
1968—Italy (Eugenio Monti)	2:17.39
1972—Switzerland (Jean Wicki)	4:43.07

*Five-man bobsled

2-Man Bob

	Time
1932—U.S.A. (Hubert Stevens)	8:14.74
1936—U.S.A. (Ivan Brown)	5:29.29
1948—Switzerland (F. Endrich)	5:29.2
1952—Germany (Andreas Ostler)	5:24.54
1956—Italy (Dalla Costa)	5:30.14
1964—Great Britain (Antony Nash)	4:21.90
1968—Italy (Eugenio Monti)	4:41.54
1972—W. Germany (Wolfgang Zimmerer)	4:47.07

Figure Skating
Men's Singles

1908	Ulrich Sachow, Sweden
1920	Gillis Grafstrom, Sweden
1924	Gillis Grafstrom, Sweden
1928	Gillis Grafstrom, Sweden
1932	Karl Schaefer, Austria
1936	Karl Schaefer, Austria
1948	Richard T. Button, U.S.
1952	Richard T. Button, U.S.
1956	Hayes Alan Jenkins, U.S.
1960	David W. Jenkins, U.S.
1964	Manfred Schnelldorfer, Germany
1968	Wolfgang Schwartz, Austria
1972	Ondrej Nepela, Czechoslovakia

Women's Singles

1908	Madge Syers, Great Britain
1920	Magda Julin-Mauroy, Sweden
1924	Mrs. Heima von Szabo-Planck, Austria
1928	Sonja Henie, Norway
1932	Sonja Henie, Norway
1936	Sonja Henie, Norway
1948	Barbara Ann Scott, Canada
1952	Jeanette Altwegg, Great Britain
1956	Tenley Albright, U.S.
1960	Carol Heiss, U.S.
1964	Sjoukje Dijkstra, Netherlands
1968	Peggy Fleming, U.S.
1972	Beatrix Schuba, Austria

Pairs

1908	Anna Hubler & Heinrich Burger, Germany
1920	Ludovika & Walter Jakobsson, Finland
1924	Helene Engelman & Alfred Berger, Austria
1928	Andree Joly & Pierre Brunet, France
1932	Andree Joly & Pierre Brunet, France
1936	Maxie Herber & Ernest Baier, Germany
1948	Micheline Lannoy & Pierre Baugniet, Belgium
1952	Ria and Paul Falk, Germany
1956	Elisabeth Schwarz & Kurt Oppelt, Austria
1960	Barbara Wagner & Robert Paul, Canada
1964	Ludmila Beloussova & Oleg Protopopov, USSR
1968	Ludmila Beloussova & Oleg Protopopov, USSR
1972	Irina Rodnina & Alexei Ulanov, USSR

Alpine Skiing
Men's Downhill

	Time
1948—Henri Oreiller, France	2:55.0
1952—Zeno Colo, Italy	2:30.8
1956—Anton Sailer, Austria	2:52.2
1960—Jean Vuarnet, France	2:06.0
1964—Egon Zimmermann, Austria	2:18.16
1968—Jean Claude Killy, France	1:59.85
1972—Bernhard Russi, Switzerland	1:51.43

Men's Giant Slalom

	Time
1952—Stein Eriksen, Norway	2:25.0
1956—Anton Sailer, Austria	3:00.1
1960—Roger Staub, Switzerland	1:48.3
1964—Francois Bonlieu, France	1:46.7
1968—Jean Claude Killy, France	3:29.28
1972—Gustavo Thoeni, Italy	3:09.62

Men's Slalom

	Time
1948—Edi Reinalter, Switzerland	2:10.3
1952—Othmar Schneider, Austria	2:00.0
1956—Anton Sailer, Austria	194.7 pts.
1960—Ernst Hinterseer, Austria	2:08.9
1964—Josef Stiegler, Austria	2:11.13
1968—Jean Claude Killy, France	1:39.73
1972—Francisco Fernandez Ochoa, Spain	1:09.27

Women's Downhill

	Time
1948—Hedi Schlunegger, Switzerland	2:28.3
1952—Trude Jochum-Beiser, Austria	1:47.1
1956—Madeline Bethod, Switzerland	1:40.7
1960—Heidi Biebl, Germany	1:37.6
1964—Christl Haas, Austria	1:55.3
1968—Olga Pall, Austria	1:40.87
1972—Marie Therese Nadig, Switzerland	1:36.68

Women's Giant Slalom

	Time
1952—Andrea Mead Lawrence, U.S.	2:06.8
1956—Ossi Reichert, Germany	1:56.5
1960—Yvonne Ruegg, Switzerland	1:39.9
1964—Marielle Goitschel, France	1:52.2
1968—Nancy Greene, Canada	1:51.97
1972—Marie Therese Nadig, Switzerland	1:29.90

Women's Slalom

	Time
1948—Gretchen Fraser, U.S.	1:57.2
1952—Andrea Mead Lawrence, U.S.	2:10.6
1956—Renee Colliard, Switzerland	112.3 pts.
1960—Anne Heggtveigt, Canada	1:49.6
1964—Christine Goitschel, France	1:35.11
1968—Marielle Goitschel, France	1:25.86
1972—Barbara Cochran, U.S.	1:31.24

Nordic Skiing
Men's Cross-Country Events
15 Kilometers (9.3 miles) or Equivalent

	Time
1924—Thorleif Haug, Norway	1:14:31
1928—Johan Grottumsbraaten, Norway	1:37:01
1932—Sven Utterstrom, Sweden	1:23:07
1936—Erik-August Larsson, Sweden	1:14:38
1948—Martin Lundstrom, Sweden	1:13:50
1952—Hallgeir Brenden, Norway	1:01:34
1956—Hallgeir Brenden, Norway	49:39.0
1960—Haakon Brusveen, Norway	51:55.0
1964—Eero Mantyranta, Finland	50:54.1
1968—Harald Groenningen, Norway	47:54.2
1972—Sven-Ake Lundback, Sweden	45:28.2

(Note: Approx. 18-kilometer course 1924-1952)

30 Kilometers (18.6 miles)

	Time
1956—Veikko Hakulinen, Finland	1:44:06.0
1960—Sixten Jernberg, Sweden	1:51:03.9
1964—Eero Mantyranta, Finland	1:30:50.7
1968—Franco Nones, Italy	1:35:39.2
1972—Vyacheslav Vedenin, USSR	1:36:31.1

50 Kilometers (31 miles)

	Time
1924—Thorleif Haug, Norway	3:44:32.0
1928—Per Erik Hedlund, Sweden	4:52:03.0

1932—Veli Saarinen, Finland	4:28:00.0
1936—Elis Viklund, Sweden	3:30:11.0
1948—Nils Karlsson, Sweden	3:47:48.0
1952—Veikko Hakulinen, Finland	3:33:33.0
1956—Sixten Jernberg, Sweden	2:50:27.0
1960—Kalevi Hamalainen, Finland	2:59:06.3
1964—Sixten Jernberg, Sweden	2:43:52.6
1968—Ole Ellefsaeter, Norway	2:28:45.8
1972—Paal Tyldum, Norway	2:43:14.7

40 Kilometer Cross-Country Relay

	Time
1936—Finland, Norway, Sweden	2:41:33.0
1948—Sweden, Finland, Norway	2:32:08.0
1952—Finland, Norway, Sweden	2:20:16.0
1956—USSR, Finland, Sweden	2:15:30.0
1960—Finland, Norway, USSR	2:18:45.6
1964—Sweden, Finland, USSR	2:18:34.6
1968—Norway, Sweden, Finland	2:08:33.5
1972—USSR, Norway, Switzerland	2:04:47.9

15 Km. Cross-Country & Jumping

	Points
1924—Thorleif Haug, Norway	453.800
1928—Johan Grottumsbraaten, Norway	427.800
1932—Johan Grottumsbraaten, Norway	446.200
1936—Oddbjorn Hagen, Norway	430.300
1948—Heikki Hasu, Finland	448.800
1952—Simon Slattvik, Norway	451.621
1956—Sverre Stenersen, Norway	455.000
1960—Georg Thoma, Germany	457.952
1964—Tormod Knutsen, Norway	469.280
1968—Franz Keller, W. Germany	449.040
1972—Ulrich Wehling, E. Germany	413.340

Ski Jumping (90 Meters)

	Points
1924—Jacob T. Thams, Norway	227.5
1928—Alfred Andersen, Norway	230.5
1932—Birger Ruud, Norway	228.0
1936—Birger Ruud, Norway	232.0
1948—Petter Hugsted, Norway	228.1
1952—A. Bergmann, Norway	226.0
1956—Antti Hyvarinen, Finland	227.0
1960—Helmut Recknagel, Germany	227.2
1964—Toralf Engan, Norway	230.7
1968—Vladimir Beloussov, USSR	231.3
1972—Wojiech Fortuna, Poland	219.9

Ski Jumping (70 Meters)

	Points
1964—Veikko Kankkonen, Finland	229.9
1968—Jiri Raska, Czechoslovakia	216.5
1972—Yukio Kasaya, Japan	244.2

Women's Events
5 Kilometers (approx. 3.1 miles)

	Time
1964—Claudia Boyarskikh, USSR	17:50.5
1968—Toini Gustafsson, Sweden	16:45.2
1972—Galina Koulacova, USSR	17:00.5

10 Kilometers (6.2 miles)

	Time
1952—Lydia Wideman, Finland	41:40.0
1956—Lyubov Kosyreva, USSR	38:11.0
1960—Maria Gusakova, USSR	39:46.6
1964—Claudia Boyarskikh, USSR	40:24.3
1968—Toini Gustafsson, Sweden	36:46.5
1972—Galina Koulacova, USSR	34:17.8

15 Kilometer Cross-Country Relay

	Time
1956—Finland, USSR, Sweden	1:09:01.0
1960—Sweden, USSR, Finland	1:04:21.4
1964—USSR, Sweden, Finland	59:20.2
1968—Norway, Sweden, USSR	57:30.0
1972—USSR, Finland, Norway	48:46.1

Ice Hockey
(Three medal winners, in order)

1920	Canada, U.S., Czechoslovakia
1924	Canada, U.S., Great Britain
1928	Canada, Sweden, Switzerland
1932	Canada, U.S., Germany
1936	Great Britain, Canada, U.S.
1948	Canada, Czechoslovakia, Switzerland
1952	Canada, U.S., Sweden
1956	USSR, U.S., Canada
1960	U.S., Canada, USSR
1964	USSR, Sweden, Czechoslovakia
1968	USSR, Czechoslovakia, Canada
1972	USSR, U.S., Czechoslovakia

Luge
Men's Singles

	Time
1964—Thomas Kohler, Germany	3:26.77
1968—Manfred Schmid, Austria	2:52.48
1972—Wolfgang Scheidel, E. Germany	3:27.58

Men's Doubles

	Time
1964—Austria	1:41.62
1968—East Germany	1:35.85
1972—Italy, E. Germany (tie)	1:28.35

Women's Singles

	Time
1964—Ortun Enderlein, Germany	3:24.67
1968—Erica Lechner, Italy	2:28.66
1972—Anna M. Muller, E. Germany	2:59.18

Speed Skating
Men's Events
500 Meters

	Time
1924—Charles Jewtraw, U.S.	0:44.0
1928—Clas Thunberg, Finland & Bernt Evensen, Norway (tie)	0:43.4
1932—John A. Shea, U.S.	0:43.4
1936—Ivar Ballangrud, Norway	0:43.4
1948—Finn Helgesen, Norway	0:43.1
1952—Kenneth Henry, U.S.	0:43.2
1956—Evgeniy Grishin, USSR	0:40.2
1960—Evgeniy Grishin, USSR	0:40.2
1964—R. Terrence McDermott, U.S.	0:40.1
1968—Erhard Keller, W. Germany	0:40.3
1972—Erhard Keller, W. Germany	0:39.4

1,500 Meters

	Time
1924—Clas Thunberg, Finland	2:20.8
1928—Clas Thunberg, Finland	2:21.1
1932—John A. Shea, U.S.	2:57.2
1936—Charles Mathiesen, Norway	2:19.2
1948—Sverre Farstad, Norway	2:17.6
1952—Hjalmar Anderson, Norway	2:20.4
1956—Evgeniy Grishin, USSR	2:08.6
1960—Roald Edgar Aas, Norway & Evgeniy Grishin, USSR (tie)	2:10.4
1964—Ants Anston, USSR	2:10.3
1968—Cornelis Verkerk, Netherlands	2:03.4
1972—Ard Schenk, Netherlands	2:02.9

5,000 Meters

	Time
1924—Clas Thunberg, Finland	8:39.0
1928—Ivar Ballangrud, Norway	8:50.5
1932—Irving Jaffee, U.S.	9:40.8
1936—Ivar Ballangrud, Norway	8:19.6
1948—Reidar Liakleb, Norway	8:29.4
1952—Hjalmar Anderson, Norway	8:10.6
1956—Boris Shilkov, USSR	7:48.7
1960—Viktor Kosichkin, USSR	7:51.3
1964—Knut Johannesen, Norway	7:38.4
1968—F. Anton Maier, Norway	7:22.4
1972—Ard Schenk, Netherlands	7:23.6

10,000 Meters

	Time
1924—Julius Skutnabb, Finland	18:04.8
1928—Event not held, thawing of ice	
1932—Irving Jaffee, U.S.	19:13.6
1936—Ivar Ballangrud, Norway	17:24.3
1948—Ake Seyffarth, Norway	17:26.3
1952—Hjalmar Anderson, Norway	16:45.8
1956—Sigvard Ericsson, Sweden	16:35.9
1960—Knut Johannesen, Norway	15:46.6
1964—Jonny Nilsson, Sweden	15:50.1
1968—Jonny Hoeglin, Sweden	15:23.6
1972—Ard Schenk, Netherlands	15:01.3

Women's Events
500 Meters

	Time
1960—Helga Haase, Germany	0:45.9
1964—Lydia Skoblikova, USSR	0:45.0
1968—Ludmila Titova, USSR	0:46.1
1972—Anne Henning, U.S.	0:43.3

1,000 Meters

	Time
1960—Klara Guseva, USSR	1:34.1
1964—Lydia Skoblikova, USSR	1:33.2
1968—Carolina Geijssen, Netherlands	1:32.6
1972—Monika Pflug, W. Germany	1:31.4

1,500 Meters

	Time
1960—Lydia Skoblikova, USSR	2:52.2
1964—Lydia Skoblikova, USSR	2:22.6
1968—Kaija Mustonen, Finland	2:22.4
1972—Dianne Holum, U.S.	2:20.8

3,000 Meters

	Time
1960—Lydia Skoblikova, USSR	5:14.3
1964—Lydia Skoblikova, USSR	5:14.9
1968—Johanna Schut, Netherlands	4:56.2
1972—Stien Baas-Kaiser, Netherlands	4:52.1

Olympic Information

Olympic Symbol: Five rings or circles, linked together to represent the sporting friendship of all peoples. The rings also symbolize the 5 continents — Europe, Asia, Africa, Australia, and America. Each ring is a different color — blue, yellow, black, green, and red.

Olympic Flag: The symbol of the 5 rings on a plain white background.

Olympic Motto: "Citius, Altius, Fortius," Latin meaning "faster, higher, braver", or the modern interpretation "swifter, higher, stronger". The motto was coined by Father Didon, a French educator, in 1895.

Olympic Creed: "The most important thing in the Olympic Games is not to win but to take part, just as the most important thing in life is not the triumph but the struggle. The essential thing is not to have

conquered but to have fought well."

Olympic Oath: An athlete of the host country recites the following at the opening ceremony. "In the name of all competitors I promise that we will take part in these Olympic Games, respecting and abiding by the rules which govern them, in the true spirit of sportsmanship for the glory of sport and the honor of our teams." Both the oath and the creed were composed by Pierre de Coubertin, the founder of the modern Games.

Olympic Flame: Symbolizes the continuity between the ancient and modern Games. The modern version of the flame was adopted in 1936. The torch used to kindle the flame is first lit by the sun's rays at Olympia, Greece, and then carried to the site of the Games by relays of runners. Ships and planes are used when necessary.

Speed Ice-Skating Championships in 1975

National Outdoor Championship
Lake Como, Minn., Jan. 25-26, 1975

Senior Men

440 Yds. —Bill Heinkel.**Time—0:35.92.**
880 Yds. —Rich Wurster.**Time—1:12.85.**
³/₄ Mile —B. Levy.**Time—2:23.86.**
One Mile —Ed Jacquin.**Time—2:55.35.**
2 Miles —B. Levy.**Time—6:02.72.**
5 Miles —Mike Passarella.**Time—13.40.68.**
Champion —Rich Wurster.

Senior Women

440 Yds. —Nancy Class.**Time—0:41.10.**
³/₄ Mile —Nancy Swider.**Time—2:27.31.**
880 Yds. —Nancy Swider.**Time—1:23.86.**
One Mile —Nancy Swider.**Time—3:06.66.**
Champion —Nancy Swider.

National Indoor Championship
Champaign, Ill., March 8-9, 1975

Senior Men

400 Yds. —Bud Campbell.**Time—0:37.38.**
880 Yds. —Alan Rattray.**Time—1:15.97.**
³/₄ Mile —Bud Campbell.**Time—1:59.39.**
One Mile —Bill Lanigan.**Time—2:41.67.**
2 Miles —Bill Lanigan.**Time—5:49.99.**
Champion —Bud Campbell

Senior Women

440 Yds. —Peggy Hartrich.**Time—0:42.11.**
880 Yds. —Michele Conroy.**Time—1:25.20.**
³/₄ Mile —Michele Conroy.**Time—2:14.97.**
One Mile —Michele Conroy.**Time—3:11.09.**
Champion —Michele Conroy.

North American Indoor Championship
Lake Placid, N.Y., March 22-23, 1975

Senior Men

400 Meters —J. Lynch.**Time—0:40.45.**
800 Meters —J. Jayner.**Time—1:25.09.**
1,000 Meters —J. Lynch.**Time—1:45.73.**
1,500 Meters —J. Lynch.**Time—2:42.00.**
3,000 Meters —R. Scholefield.
Champion —J. Lynch.

Senior Women

400 Meters —Peggy Hartrich.
800 Meters —C. Moore.
1,000 Meters —Peggy Hartrich.
1,500 Meters —Peggy Hartrich.
Champion —Peggy Hartrich.

The America's Cup

Competition for the America's Cup grew out of the first contest to establish a world yachting championship, one of the carnival features of the London Exposition of 1851. The race, open to all classes of yachts from all over the world, covered a 60-mile course around the Isle of Wight, the prize was a cup worth about $500, donated by the Royal Yacht Squadron of England, known as the "America's Cup" because it was first won by the United States yacht America. Successive efforts of British and Australian yachtsmen have failed to win the famous trophy, which remains in the United States.

On Sept. 17, 1974, the 66-foot 12-Meter yacht Courageous won a fourth straight victory over the Australian challenger, Southern Cross, to keep the symbol of world sailing supremacy in the United States. In four races, Southern Cross lost to Courageous by a total of 18 minutes 51 seconds. The U.S. yacht was designed by Olin Stephens and skippered by Ted Hood.

Winners of the America's Cup

1851	America
1870	Magic defeated Cambria, England, (1-0)
1871	Columbia (first three races) and Sappho (last two races) defeated Livonia, England, (4-1)
1876	Madeline defeated Countess of Dufferin, Canada, (2-0)
1881	Mischief defeated Atalanta, Canada, (2-0)
1885	Puritan defeated Genesta, England, (2-0)
1886	Mayflower defeated Galatea, England, (2-0)
1887	Volunteer defeated Thistle, Scotland, (2-0)
1893	Vigilant defeated Valkyrie II, England, (3-0)
1895	Defender defeated Valkyrie III, England, (3-0)
1899	Columbia defeated Shamrock, England, (3-0)

1901	Columbia defeated Shamrock II, England, (3-0)
1903	Reliance defeated Shamrock III, England, (3-0)
1920	Resolute defeated Shamrock IV, England, (3-2)
1930	Enterprise defeated Shamrock V, England, (4-0)
1934	Rainbow defeated Endeavour, England, (4-2)
1937	Ranger defeated Endeavour II, England, (4-0)
1958	Columbia defeated Sceptre, England, (4-0)
1962	Weatherly defeated Gretel, Australia, (4-1)
1964	Constellation defeated Sovereign, England, (4-0)
1967	Intrepid defeated Dame Pattie, Australia, (4-0)
1970	Intrepid defeated Gretel II, Australia, (4-1)
1974	Courageous defeated Southern Cross, (4-0)

Figure Skating Champions

	National Champions		World Champions	
Year	**Men**	**Women**	**Men**	**Women**
1951	Richard Button	Sonya Klopfer	Richard Button, US.	Jeannette Altwegg, Eng.
1952	Richard Button	Tenley Albright	Richard Button, U.S.	Jacqueline du Bief, France
1953	Hayes Jenkins	Tenley Albright	Hayes Jenkins, U.S.	Tenley Albright, U.S.
1954	Hayes Jenkins	Tenley Albright	Hayes Jenkins, U.S.	Gundi Busch, W. Germany
1955	Hayes Jenkins	Tenley Albright	Hayes Jenkins, U.S.	Tenley Albright, U.S.
1956	Hayes Jenkins	Tenley Albright	Hayes Jenkins, U.S.	Carol Heiss, U.S.
1957	Dave Jenkins	Carol Heiss	Dave Jenkins, U.S.	Carol Heiss, U.S.
1958	Dave Jenkins	Carol Heiss	Dave Jenkins, U.S.	Carol Heiss, U.S.
1959	Dave Jenkins	Carol Heiss	Dave Jenkins, U.S.	Carol Heiss, U.S.
1960	Dave Jenkins	Carol Heiss	Alain Giletti, France	Carol Heiss, U.S.
1961	Bradley Lord	Laurence Owen	none	none
1962	Monty Hoyt	Barbara Roles Pursley	Don Jackson, Canada	Sjoukje Dijkstra, Neth.
1963	Tommy Litz	Lorraine Hanlon	Don McPherson, Canada	Sjoukje Dijkstra, Neth.
1964	Scott Allen	Peggy Fleming	Manfred Schnelldorfer, W. Germany	Sjoukje Dijkstra, Neth.
1965	Gary Visconti	Peggy Fleming	Alain Calmat, France	Petra Burka, Canada
1966	Scott Allen	Peggy Fleming	Emmerich Danzer, Austria	Peggy Fleming, U. S.
1967	Gary Visconti	Peggy Fleming	Emmerich Danzer, Austria	Peggy Fleming, U.S.
1968	Tim Wood	Peggy Fleming	Emmerich Danzer, Austria	Peggy Fleming, U.S.
1969	Tim Wood	Janet Lynn	Tim Wood, U.S.	Gabriele Seyfert, E. Ger.
1970	Tim Wood	Janet Lynn	Tim Wood, U.S.	Gabriele Seyfert, E. Ger.
1971	John Misha Petkevich	Janet Lynn	Ondrej Nepela, Czech.	Beatrix Schuba, Austria
1972	Ken Shelley	Janet Lynn	Ondrej Nepela, Czech.	Beatrix Schuba, Austria
1973	Gordon McKellen Jr.	Janet Lynn	Ondrej Nepela, Czech.	Karen Magnussen, Canada
1974	Gordon McKellen Jr.	Dorothy Hamill	Jan Hoffman, E. Germany	Christine Errath, E. Germany
1975	Gordon McKellen Jr.	Dorothy Hamill	Sergei Volkov, USSR	Dianne de Leeuw, Neth.-U.S.

Canadian National Figure Skating Champions

Year	**Men**	**Women**	**Year**	**Men**	**Women**
1958	Charles Snelling	Marg. Crosland	1967	Donald Knight	Valerie Jones
1959	Donald Jackson	Marg. Crosland	1968	Jay Humphrey	Karen Magnussen
1960	Donald Jackson	Wendy Griner	1969	Jay Humphrey	Linda Carbonetto
1961	Donald Jackson	Wendy Griner	1970	David McGillivray	Karen Magnussen
1962	Donald Jackson	Wendy Griner	1971	Toller Cranston	Karen Magnussen
1963	Donald McPherson	Wendy Griner	1972	Toller Cranston	Karen Magnussen
1964	Charles Snelling	Petra Burka	1973	Toller Cranston	Karen Magnussen
1965	Donald Knight	Petra Burka	1974	Toller Cranston	Lynn Nightingale
1966	Donald Knight	Petra Burka	1975	Toller Cranston	Lynn Nightingale

Westminster Kennel Club

Year	**Best-in-show**	**Breed**	**Owner**
1965	Ch. Charmichael's Fanfare	Scottish terrier	Mr. and Mrs. Charles C. Stalter
1966	Ch. Zeloy Mooremaides Magic	Wire Fox terrier	Marion G. Bunker
1967	Ch. Bardene Bingo	Scottish terrier	E. H. Stuart
1968	Ch. Stingray of Derryabah	Lakeland terrier	Mr. and Mrs. James A. Farrell Jr.
1969	Ch. Glamoor Good News	Skye terrier	Walter & Mrs. Adele F. Goodman
1970	Ch. Arriba's Prima Donna	Boxer	Dr. & Mrs. P. J. Pagano & Dr. Theodore S. Fickles
1971	Ch. Chinoe's Adamant James	English springer spaniel	Dr. Milton Prickett
1972	Ch. Chinoe's Adamant James	English springer spaniel	Dr. Milton Prickett
1973	Ch. Acadia Command Performance	Poodle	Mrs. Jo Ann Sering & Edward B. Jenner
1974	Ch. Gretchenhof Columbia River	German pointer	Dr. Richard Smith
1975	Ch. Sir Lancelot of Barvan	Old English sheepdog	Mr. and Mrs. Ronald Vanword

Leonard Brumby, Sr. Memorial Trophy

Junior Winner at Westminster Kennel Club

1964—Clare Hodge, Byrn Mawr, Pa. **Breed**—Whippet.
1965—Jennifer Sheldon, Massapequa, N. Y. **Breed**—Afghan.
1966—Laura Swyler, Commack, N.Y. **Breed**—Dox.
1967—David L. Brumbaugh, Perry, Ga. **Breed**—Min. Schnauzer.
1968—Cheryl Baker, Kennesaw, Ga. **Breed**—Beagle.
1969—Charles Garvin, Columbus, Ohio. **Breed**—Dalmatian.
1970—Pat Hardy, Cincinnati, Ohio. **Breed**—Golden Retriever.

1971—Heidi Shellenbarger, Costa Mesa, Cal. **Breed**—Whippet.
1972—Deborah Dagny Von Aherns, Edison Township, N. J. **Breed**—Afghan.
1973—Teresa Nail, Ft. Worth, Texas. **Breed**—Doberman Pinscher.
1974—Leslie Church, St. Louis, Mo. **Breed**—Min. Schnauzer.
1975—Virginia Westfield, Huntington, N.Y. **Breed**—Bulldog.
1975—Virginia Westfield, Huntington, N.Y. **Breed**—Bulldog.

National Duckpin Bowling Champions, 1975

Men's Singles—Jeffrey Ferrand, Salisbury, Md., 469.
Women's Singles—Delina Rock, Glastonbury, Conn., 437.
Men's Doubles—George Teague-Bernie Ruzin Sr., Baltimore, Md., 867.
Women's Doubles—Dotti Warren-Norma Gallagher, Hyattsville, Md., 804.
Men's Team—Fair Lanes Westview, Baltimore, Md.. 2008.

Women's Team—Eastwood Trophies, Baltimore, Md., 1904.
Men's All Events—Bob Wilson, Baltimore, Md., 1310.
Women's All Events—Wilda Guerrette, Glastonbury, Conn., 1209.
Mixed Doubles—Medora Kaltenbach-Wayne Krauss, Towson-Baltimore, Md., 890.

National Basketball Association, 1974-75
Final Standings
Eastern Conference

Atlantic Division					Central Division				
Club	W.	L.	Pct.	G.B.	Club	W.	L.	Pct.	G.B.
Boston Celtics	60	22	.732	—	Washington Bullets	60	22	.732	—
Buffalo Braves	49	33	.598	11	Houston Rockets	41	41	.500	19
New York Knickerbockers	40	42	.488	20	Cleveland Cavaliers	40	42	.488	20
Philadelphia 76ers	34	48	.415	26	Atlanta Hawks	31	51	.378	29
					New Orleans Jazz	23	59	.280	37

Western Conference

Midwest Division					Pacific Division				
Club	W.	L.	Pct.	G.B.	Club	W.	L.	Pct.	G.B.
Chicago Bulls	47	35	.573	—	Golden State Warriors	48	34	.585	—
K.C.-Omaha Kings	44	38	.537	3	Seattle SuperSonics	43	39	.524	5
Detroit Pistons	40	42	.488	7	Portland Trail Blazers	38	44	.463	10
Milwaukee Bucks	37	44	.463	9	Phoenix Suns	32	50	.390	16
					Los Angeles Lakers	30	52	.366	18

NBA Playoff Results

Houston defeated New York 2 games to 1.
Seattle defeated Detroit 2 games to 1.
Boston defeated Houston 4 games to 1.
Washington defeated Buffalo 4 games to 3.
Golden State defeated Seattle 4 games to 2.

Chicago defeated K.C.-Omaha 4 games to 2.
Washington defeated Boston 4 games to 2.
Golden State defeated Chicago 4 games to 3.
Golden State defeated Washington 4 games to 0.

Final Statistics

Individual Scoring Leaders
(Minimum 70 Games Played or 1400 Points)

	G.	FG	FT	Pts.	Avg.
McAdoo, Buffalo	82	1095	641	2831	34.5
Barry, Golden St.	80	1028	394	2450	30.6
Abdul-Jabbar, Milwaukee	65	812	325	1949	30.0
Archibald, K.C.-Omaha	82	759	652	2170	26.5
Scott, Phoenix	69	703	274	1680	24.3
Lanier, Detroit	76	731	361	1823	24.0
Hayes, Washington	82	739	409	1887	23.0
Goodrich, L.A.	72	656	318	1630	22.6
Haywood, Seattle	68	608	309	1525	22.4
Carter, Phila.	77	715	256	1686	21.9
Chenier, Washington	77	690	311	1681	21.8
Wicks, Portland	82	692	394	1778	21.7
Maravich, N.O.	79	655	390	1700	21.5
Frazier, New York	78	672	331	1675	21.5
F. Brown, Seattle	81	737	226	1700	21.0
Monroe, New York	78	668	297	1633	20.9
Tomjanovich, Houston	81	694	289	1677	20.7
Dandridge, Milwaukee	80	691	211	1593	19.9
Cunningham, Phila.	80	609	345	1563	19.5
Ch. Walker, Chicago	76	524	413	1461	19.2

Field Goal Leaders
(Minimum 300 Made)

	FGM	FGA	Pct.
D. Nelson, Boston	423	785	.539
Beard, Golden State	408	773	.528
Tomjanovich, Houston	694	1323	.525
Abdul-Jabbar, Milwaukee	812	1584	.513
McAdoo, Buffalo	1095	2138	.512
Kunnert, Houston	346	676	.512
Westphal, Boston	342	670	.510
Lanier, Detroit	731	1433	.510
Snyder, Cleveland	498	988	.504
McMillian, Buffalo	347	695	.499

Free Throw Leaders
(Minimum 125 Made)

	ETM	FTA	Pct.
Barry, Golden State	.394	436	.904
Murphy, Houston	.341	386	.883
Bradley, New York	.144	165	.873
Archibald, K.C.-Omaha	.652	748	.872
Price, Milwaukee	.169	194	.871
Havlicek, Boston	.289	332	.870
Marin, Buffalo	.193	222	.869
Newlin, Houston	.265	305	.869
Chet Walker, Chicago	.413	480	.860
J. Walker, K.C.-Omaha	.247	289	.855

Assists Leaders
(Minimum 70 Games or 400 Assists)

	G	No.	Avg.
K. Porter, Washington	81	650	8.0
Bing, Detroit	79	610	7.7
Archibald, K.C.-Omaha	82	557	6.8
R. Smith, Buffalo	82	534	6.5
Maravich, New Orleans	79	488	6.2
Barry, Golden State	80	492	6.2
Watts, Seattle	82	499	6.1
Frazier, New York	78	474	6.1
Goodrich, Los Angeles	72	420	5.8
Van Lier, Chicago	70	403	5.8

Rebound Leaders
(Minimum 70 Games or 800 Rebounds)

	G	Off.	def.	Tot.	Avg.
Unseld, Washington	73	318	759	1077	14.8
Cowens, Boston	65	229	729	958	14.7
Lacey, K.C.-Omaha	81	228	921	1149	14.2
McAdoo, Buffalo	82	307	848	1155	14.1
Abdul-Jabbar, Milwaukee	65	194	718	912	14.0
Hairston, Los Angeles	74	304	642	946	12.8
Silas, Boston	82	348	677	1025	12.5
Hayes, Washington	82	221	783	1004	12.2
Lanier, Detroit	76	225	689	914	12.0
Perry, Phoenix	79	347	593	940	11.9

Blocked Shots Leaders
(Minimum 70 Games or 100 Blocked Shots)

	G	No.	Avg.
Abdul-Jabbar, Milwaukee	65	212	3.26
E. Smith, Los Angeles	74	216	2.92
Thurmond, Chicago	80	195	2.44
Hayes, Washington	82	187	2.28
Lanier, Detroit	76	172	2.26
McAdoo, Buffalo	82	174	2.12
Lacey, K.C.-Omaha	81	168	2.07
Burleson, Seattle	82	153	1.87
Heard, Buffalo	67	120	1.79
Chones, Cleveland	72	120	1.67

Steals Leaders
(Minimum 70 Games or 125 Steals)

	G	No.	Avg.
Barry, Golden State	80	228	2.85
Frazier, New York	78	190	2.44
Steele, Portland	76	183	2.41
Watts, Seattle	82	190	2.32
F. Brown, Seattle	81	187	2.31
Chenier, Washington	77	176	2.29
Sloan, Chicago	78	171	2.19
Allen, Los Angeles	66	136	2.06

NBA Champions 1947-1975

Year	Regular Season Eastern Conference	Western Conference	Playoffs Winner	Runner-Up
1947	Washington	Chicago	Philadelphia	Chicago
1948	Philadelphia	St. Louis	Baltimore	Philadelphia
1949	Washington	Rochester	Minneapolis	Washington
1950	Syracuse	Minneapolis	Minneapolis	Syracuse
1951	Philadelphia	Minneapolis	Rochester	New York
1952	Syracuse	Rochester	Minneapolis	New York
1953	New York	Minneapolis	Minneapolis	New York
1954	New York	Minneapolis	Minneapolis	Syracuse
1955	Syracuse	Ft. Wayne	Syracuse	Ft. Wayne
1956	Philadelphia	Ft. Wayne	Philadelphia	Ft. Wayne
1957	Boston	St. Louis	Boston	St. Louis
1958	Boston	St. Louis	St. Louis	Boston
1959	Boston	St. Louis	Boston	Minneapolis
1960	Boston	St. Louis	Boston	St. Louis
1961	Boston	St. Louis	Boston	St. Louis
1962	Boston	Los Angeles	Boston	Los Angeles
1963	Boston	Los Angeles	Boston	Los Angeles
1964	Boston	San Francisco	Boston	San Francisco
1965	Boston	Los Angeles	Boston	Los Angeles
1966	Philadelphia	Los Angeles	Boston	Los Angeles
1967	Philadelphia	San Francisco	Philadelphia	San Francisco
1968	Philadelphia	St. Louis	Boston	Los Angeles
1969	Baltimore	Los Angeles	Boston	Los Angeles
1970	New York	Atlanta	New York	Los Angeles

Year	Atlantic	Central	Midwest	Pacific		Winner	Runner-Up
1971	New York	Baltimore	Milwaukee	Los Angeles	Milwaukee		Baltimore
1972	Boston	Baltimore	Milwaukee	Los Angeles	Los Angeles		New York
1973	Boston	Baltimore	Milwaukee	Los Angeles	New York		Los Angeles
1974	Boston	Capital	Milwaukee	Los Angeles	Boston		Milwaukee
1975	Boston	Washington	Chicago	Golden State	Golden State		Washington

NBA Scoring Leaders

Year	Scoring Champion	Pts.	Avg.	Year	Scoring Champion	Pts.	Avg.
1947	Joe Fulks, Philadelphia	1,389	23.2	1962	Wilt Chamberlain, Philadelphia	4,029	50.4
1948	Max Zaslofsky, Chicago	1,007	21.0	1963	Wilt Chamberlain, San Francisco	3,586	44.8
1949	George Mikan, Minneapolis	1,698	28.3	1964	Wilt Chamberlain, San Francisco	2,948	36.5
1950	George Mikan, Minneapolis	1,865	27.4	1965	Wilt Chamberlain, San Fran., Phila.	2,534	34.7
1951	George Mikan, Minneapolis	1,932	28.4	1966	Wilt Chamberlain, Philadelphia	2,649	33.5
1952	Paul Arizin, Philadelphia	1,674	25.4	1967	Rick Barry, San Francisco	2,775	35.6
1953	Neil Johnston, Philadelphia	1,564	22.3	1968	Dave Bing, Detroit	2,142	27.1
1954	Neil Johnston, Philadelphia	1,759	24.4	1969	Elvin Hayes, San Diego	2,327	28.4
1955	Neil Johnston, Philadelphia	1,631	22.7	1970	Jerry West, Los Angeles	2,309	31.2
1956	Bob Pettit, St. Louis	1,849	25.7	1971	Lew Alcindor, Milwaukee	2,596	31.7
1957	Paul Arizin, Philadelphia	1,817	25.6	1972	Kareem Abdul-Jabbar (Alcindor),		
1958	George Yardley, Detroit	2,001	27.8		Milwaukee	2,822	34.8
1959	Bob Pettit, St. Louis	2,105	29.2	1973	Nate Archibald, Kansas City-Omaha	2,719	34.0
1960	Wilt Chamberlain, Philadelphia	2,707	37.9	1974	Bob McAdoo, Buffalo	2,261	30.6
1961	Wilt Chamberlain, Philadelphia	3,033	38.4	1975	Bob McAdoo, Buffalo	2,831	34.5

NBA All-Star Team, 1975

Position	First Team	Second Team
Forward	Rick Barry, Golden State	John Havlicek, Boston
Forward	Elvin Hayes, Washington	Spencer Haywood, Seattle
Center	Bob McAdoo, Buffalo	Dave Cowens, Boston
Guard	Walt Frazier, New York	Phil Chenier, Washington
Guard	Nate Archibald, K.C.-Omaha	Jo Jo White, Boston

NBA All-Defensive Team, 1975

Position	First Team	Second Team
Forward	John Havlicek, Boston	Elvin Hayes, Washington
Forward	Paul Silas, Boston	Bob Love, Chicago
Center	Kareem Abdul-Jabbar, Milwaukee	Dave Cowens, Boston
Guard	Jerry Sloan, Chicago	Don Chaney, Boston
Guard	Walt Frazier, New York	Norm Van Lier, Chicago

1975 NBA Player Draft

The following are the first round picks of the National Basketball Assn.

Atlanta	David Thompson, N.C. State
Los Angeles	David Meyers, UCLA
Atlanta	Marvin Webster, Morgan State
Phoenix	Alvan Adams, Oklahoma
Philadelphia	Darryl Dawkins, Maynard Evans H.S.
Portland	Lionel Hollins, Arizona State
New Orleans	Rich Kelley, Stanford
Los Angeles	Junior Bridgeman, Louisville
New York	Gene Short, Jackson State
Kansas City	Bill Robinzine, De Paul
Houston	Joe Meriweather, Southern Illinois
Seattle	Frank Oleynick, Seattle
Kansas City	Bob Bigelow, Penn.
Golden State	Joe Bryant, La Salle
Cleveland	John Lambert, USC
Phoenix	Ricky Sobers, Nevada-Las Vegas
Boston	Tom Boswell, South Carolina
Washington	Kevin Grevey, Kentucky

Podoloff Cup Winners

Bob McAdoo of the Buffalo Braves was selected as the winner of the Maurice Podoloff Cup (named after the former league commissioner) for Most Valuable Player in the NBA for the 1974-75 season.

1956—Bob Pettit, St. Louis
1957—Bob Cousy, Boston
1958—Bill Russell, Boston
1959—Bob Pettit, St. Louis
1960—Wilt Chamberlain, Philadelphia
1961—Bill Russell, Boston
1962—Bill Russell, Boston
1963—Bill Russell, Boston
1964—Oscar Robertson, Cincinnati
1965—Bill Russell, Boston

1966—Wilt Chamberlain, Philadelphia
1967—Wilt Chamberlain, Philadelphia
1968—Wilt Chamberlain, Philadelphia
1969—Wes Unseld, Baltimore
1970—Willis Reed, New York
1971—Lew Alcindor, Milwaukee
1972—Kareem Abdul-Jabbar (Alcindor), Milwaukee
1973—Dave Cowens, Boston
1974—Kareem Abdul-Jabbar, Milwaukee
1975—Bob McAdoo, Buffalo

NBA Rookie of the Year Awards

1954—Don Meineke, Ft. Wayne
1955—Ray Felix, Baltimore
1956—Maurice Stokes, Rochester
1957—Tom Heinsohn, Boston
1958—Woody Sauldsberry, Phil.
1959—Elgin Baylor, Minnesota
1960—Wilt Chamberlain, Philadelphia
1961—Oscar Robertson, Cincinnati

1962—Walt Bellamy, Chicago
1963—Terry Dischinger, Chicago
1964—Jerry Lucas, Cincinnati
1965—Willis Reed, New York
1966—Rick Barry, San Francisco
1967—Dave Bing, Detroit
1968—Earl Monroe, Baltimore
1969—Wes Unseld, Baltimore

1970—Lew Alcindor, Milwaukee
1971—Dave Cowens, Boston;
         Geoff Petrie, Portland (Tie)
1972—Sidney Wicks, Portland
1973—Bob McAdoo, Buffalo
1974—Ernie DiGregorio, Buffalo
1975—Keith Wilkes, Golden State

Sports Arenas

The seating capacity of sports arenas can vary depending on the event being presented. The figures below are the normal seating capacity for basketball. (*) indicates hockey seating capacity.

Name and location		Name and location	
Ak-Sar-Ben Coliseum, Omaha, Neb.	*6,000	Mid-South Coliseum, Memphis	11,065
Alexander Memorial Coliseum, Atlanta.	6,996	Midwest Coliseum, Richfield Township, Ohio.	*18,500
Allen County Mem., Ft. Wayne	*8,025	Milwaukee Arena	10,938
Amarillo Civic Center, Texas	5,001	Mobile Municipal Auditorium	13,100
Astrodome, Houston	19,000	Monroe Civic Center, Monroe, La.	8,000
Astrohall, Houston	10,000	Montreal Forum	*18,350
Atlantic City Audit., Atlantic City, N.J.	40,000	Moody Coliseum, Dallas	9,500
Baltimore Civic Center	13,043-*11,329	Municipal Auditorium, Kansas City	9,929
Bismarck Coliseum, N. Dakota	7,000	Municipal Auditorium, New Orleans	7,853
Boston Arena	*6,000	Nashville Municipal Auditorium	8,000
Boston Garden	15,314-*15,003	Nassau Veterans Memorial Coliseum, Uniondale, N.Y.	
Buffalo Memorial Auditorium	17,300-*15,845		16,000-*14,865
Capital Center, Landover, Md.	17,500-*16,926	New Orleans Municipal Auditorium.	9,100
Charlotte Coliseum.	11,666-*9,575	Norfolk Scope, Va.	10,600-*9,364
Chicago Stadium	17,374-*18,000	Oakland Alemeda County Coliseum	12,961-*12,500
Cincinnati Gardens	11,650-*10,606	Oakland Auditorium.	6,500
Cleveland Arena	11,000-*9,300	Oklahoma City Myriad	*13,400
Cobo Arena, Detroit.	11,055-*10,500	Olympia, Detroit.	*14,200
Convention Center, San Antonio	10,146	Olympic Auditorium, Los Angeles	10,500
Convention Hall, Philadelphia.	9,200-*9,500	Omaha Civic Auditorium	9,144
Cow Palace, San Francisco	14,500	The Omni, Atlanta.	16,818-*15,278
Dallas Memorial Auditorium.	8,088	Onondaga County Audit., Syracuse	*6,300
Dallas State Fair Coliseum.	*7,490	Ottawa Civic Center	*9,355
Denver Auditorium Arena.	7,000	Pacific Coliseum, Vancouver.	*15,569
Denver Coliseum.	*9,038	Penn Palestra, Philadelphia.	9,200
Dorton Arena, Raleigh, N.C.	8,058	Philadelphia Civic Center.	*9,100
Duluth Arena Auditorium.	6,919	Pittsburgh Civic Arena.	*13,402
Eastern States Coliseum, Springfield, Mass.	*5,934	Providence Civic Center	11,619-*10,108
Edmonton Coliseum, Alberta	*15,000	Portland Memorial Coliseum.	11,781-*10,500
Edmonton Gardens, Alberta	*5,800	Quebec Coliseum	*10,000
Fairgrounds Coliseum, Indianapolis.	9,479	Reynolds Coliseum, Raleigh, N.C.	12,400
Freedom Hall, Louisville, Ky.	16,613	Rhode Island Auditorium, Providence	*5,175
Greensboro Coliseum	15,500-*13,280	Richmond Coliseum, Virginia.	10,700-*9,674
Halifax Forum, Nova Scotia.	*5,206	Riverfront Coliseum, Cincinnati	*16,500
Hampton Roads Coliseum, Virginia.	10,000-*7,771	Roanoke Civic Center, Virginia	10,100
Hara Arena, Dayton.	*5,600	Rochester (N.Y.) Memorial Auditorium	*7,010
Hartford Civic Center	*10,346	St. Louis Arena.	*18,006
HemisFair Arena, San Antonio	10,146	St. Paul Civic Center, Minn.	*16,180
Hershey (Pa.) Sports Arena.	*7,259	Salt Palace, Salt Lake City	12,201-*12,000
Hobart Arena, Troy, Ohio.	6,000	Sam Houston Coliseum, Houston	8,925-*9,300
Hofheinz Pavilion, Houston.	10,218	San Diego Intl. Sports Arena.	14,000-*13,600
International Amphitheatre, Chicago	9,000	San Francisco Civic Auditorium.	7,500
Jacksonville Coliseum	*7,900	Seattle Center Coliseum	14,065-*12,300
Kemper Memorial Arena, Kansas City	16,659-*16,500	Spectrum, Philadelphia.	17,156-*17,000
Kiel Auditorium, St. Louis	10,574	Spokane Coliseum.	6,300
Kitchener Memorial Auditorium, Ontario.	*6,250	Springfield Civic Center, Mass.	*7,466
Las Vegas Convention Center.	9,000	Tarrant County Convention Center, Ft. Worth.	13,500
Long Beach Arena, Cal.	11,168	Tingley Coliseum, Albuquerque.	*12,000
Los Angeles Forum.	17,505-*16,005	Toledo Sports Arena.	*6,200
Los Angeles Sports Arena.	15,333-*11,325	Tulsa Civic Center.	*6,923
Lubbock Municipal Coliseum, Texas	10,400	Uline Arena, Washington, D.C.	11,000
Macon Coliseum	*8,000	Varsity Arena, Toronto.	*9,300
Madison Square Garden, New York	19,694-*17,500	Veterans Memorial Audit., Des Moines	15,000
Maple Leaf Gardens, Toronto.	17,000-*16,316	Veterans Memorial Coliseum, New Haven.	*8,808
Market Square Arena, Indianapolis.	17,500-*15,872	Veterans Memorial Coliseum, Phoenix.	12,834-*12,800
McElroy Auditorium, Waterloo, I.	7,200	Will Rogers Coliseum, Ft. Worth, Tex.	*6,800
Met. Sports Center, Bloomington, Minn.	*15,184	Winnipeg Arena.	*11,000
		Winston-Salem Coliseum	9,020

American Basketball Association, 1974-75

Eastern Division

Club	W.	L.	Pct.	G.B.
Kentucky Colonels(a)	58	26	.690	—
New York Nets	58	26	.690	—
Spirits of St. Louis	32	52	.381	26
Memphis Sounds	27	57	.321	31
Virginia Squires	15	69	.179	43

(a) Won playoff with New York for first place.

Western Division

Club	W.	L.	Pct.	G.B.
Denver Nuggets	65	19	.774	—
San Antonio Spurs	51	33	.607	14
Indiana Pacers	45	39	.536	20
Utah Stars	38	46	.452	27
San Diego Conquistadors	31	53	.369	34

ABA Playoff Results

Kentucky defeated Memphis 4 games to 0.
Indiana defeated San Antonio 4 games to 2.
St. Louis defeated New York 4 games to 1.
Denver defeated Utah 4 games to 2.

Kentucky defeated St. Louis 4 games to 1.
Indiana defeated Denver 4 games to 3.
Kentucky defeated Indiana 4 games to 1.

Final Statistics

Individual Scoring
(Minimum of 1,000 points)

	G	FG	FT	Pts.	Avg.
McGinnis, Indiana	79	811	545	2353	29.7
Erving, New York	84	885	486	2343	27.8
Boone, Utah	84	862	363	2117	25.2
Grant, San Diego	53	575	182	1335	25.1
Barnes, St. Louis	77	777	295	1849	24.0
Gilmore, Kentucky	84	783	412	1981	23.5
Gervin, San Antonio	84	767	380	1965	23.3
Lewis, St. Louis	69	561	355	1531	22.1
Lamar, San Diego	77	642	247	1606	20.8
Simpson, Denver	82	693	303	1692	20.6
C. Jones, San Diego	75	597	264	1467	19.5
Calvin, Denver	74	480	475	1444	19.5
Silas, San Antonio	82	578	430	1586	19.3
R. Jones, San Antonio	83	636	287	1598	19.2
Malone, Utah	83	591	375	1557	18.7
Kenon, New York	84	675	217	1570	18.6
Carter, Memphis	82	580	318	1508	18.3
Issel, Kentucky	83	614	237	1465	17.6
Johnson, Memphis	82	630	63	1443	17.6
Green, Denver	81	593	225	1411	17.4
Knight, Indiana	80	576	207	1371	17.1
Dampier, Kentucky	83	560	161	1395	16.8
Paultz, New York	80	524	214	1262	15.7
Gerard, St. Louis	84	553	206	1315	15.6

Three-point field goals—McGinnis 62, Erving 29, Boone 10, Grant 1, Gilmore 1, Gervin 17, Lewis 18, Lamar 25, Simpson 1, C. Jones 3, Calvin 3, R. Jones 13, Kenon 1, Carter 10, Johnson 40, Knight 4, Dampier 38, Gerard 1.

Two-point Percentage
(Minimum of 250 made)

	FGM	FGA	Pct.
R. Jones, Denver	529	875	.605
Gilmore, Kentucky	783	1349	.580
Malone, Utah	591	1034	.572
Twardzik, Virginia	358	651	.550
Grant, San Diego	575	1056	.545
Green, Denver	593	1091	.544
Nater, San Antonio	495	913	.542
Irvine, Virginia	298	552	.540
Knight, Indiana	576	1071	.538

Three-point Percentage
(Minimum of 27 made)

	FGM	FGA	Pct.
Shepherd, Memphis	60	143	.420
Dampier, Kentucky	38	96	.396
Smith, Utah	34	94	.362
McGinnis, Indiana	62	175	.354
Brown, Indiana	35	100	.350
Erving, New York	29	87	.333
Keller, Indiana	80	240	.333
Jabali, San Diego	62	193	.321
Buse, Indiana	38	123	.309

Free Throws
(Minimum of 200 Made)

	FTM	FTA	Pct.
Calvin, Denver	475	530	.896
Silas, San Antonio	430	486	.885
Robisch, Denver	304	346	.879
Boone, Utah	363	422	.860

(Free Throws Con't.)

	FTM	FTA	Pct.
Lewis, St. Louis	355	421	.843
Eakins, Utah	291	348	.836
Gervin, San Antonio	380	458	.830
Twardzik, Virginia	317	384	.826
Freeman, San Antonio	289	352	.821
C. Williams, Memphis	212	260	.815

Rebounds
(Minimum of 600 Rebounds)

	G.	Off.	Def.	Tot.	Avg.
Nater, San Antonio	78	369	910	1279	16.4
Gilmore, Kentucky	84	427	934	1361	16.2
Barnes, St. Louis	77	419	783	1202	15.6
Malone, Utah	83	455	754	1209	14.5
McGinnis, Indiana	79	396	730	1126	14.2
C. Jones, San Diego	75	306	754	1060	14.1
Owens, Memphis	82	296	609	905	11.0
Erving, New York	84	284	630	914	10.7
Vaughn, Virginia	83	276	618	894	10.7
Kenon, New York	84	279	621	900	10.7
Lucas, St. Louis	80	282	534	816	10.2
Paultz, New York	80	174	598	772	9.6

Assists
(Minimum of 250)

	G.	No.	Avg.
Calvin, Denver	74	570	7.7
C. Williams, Memphis	81	576	7.1
McGinnis, Indiana	79	495	6.2
Jabali, San Diego	62	358	5.7
Lamar, San Diego	77	427	5.5
O'Brien, San Diego	79	439	5.5
Erving, New York	84	462	5.5
Dampier, Kentucky	83	449	5.4
Simpson, Denver	82	442	5.3
Lewis, St. Louis	69	367	5.3

Blocked Shots
(Minimum of 100)

	G.	No.	Avg.
C. Jones, San Diego	75	246	3.2
Gilmore, Kentucky	84	258	3.0
Green, Denver	81	174	2.1
Erving, New York	84	157	1.8
B. Jones, Denver	84	153	1.8
Barnes, St. Louis	77	137	1.7
Paultz, New York	80	137	1.7
Gervin, San Antonio	84	138	1.6
Hillman, Indiana	81	132	1.6
Malone, Utah	83	128	1.5

Steals
(Minimum of 100)

	G.	No.	Avg.
B. Taylor, New York	79	221	2.8
McGinnis, Indiana	79	206	2.6
R. Taylor, Denver	76	172	2.2
Erving, New York	84	186	2.2
Lewis, St. Louis	69	147	2.1
Buse, Indiana	80	166	2.0
Simpson, Denver	82	166	2.0

ABA Champions

	Regular Season		Playoffs	
Year	Eastern Division	Western Division	Winner	Runner-Up
1968	Pittsburgh	New Orleans	Pittsburgh	New Orleans
1969	Indiana	Oakland	Oakland	Indiana
1970	Indiana	Denver	Indiana	Los Angeles
1971	Virginia	Indiana	Utah	Kentucky
1972	Kentucky	Utah	Indiana	New York
1973	Carolina	Utah	Indiana	Kentucky
1974	New York	Utah	New York	Utah
1975	Kentucky	Denver	Kentucky	Indiana

ABA Most Valuable Player & Rookie of Year

Year	MVP	Rookie
1968	Connie Hawkins, Pittsburgh	Mel Daniels, Indiana
1969	Mel Daniels, Indiana	Warren Armstrong, Oakland
1970	Spencer Haywood, Denver	Spencer Haywood, Denver
1971	Mel Daniels, Indiana	Dan Issel, Kentucky; Charlie Scott, Virginia (tie)
1972	Artis Gilmore, Kentucky	Artis Gilmore, Kentucky
1973	Billy Cunningham, Carolina	Brian Taylor, New York
1974	Julius Erving, New York	Swen Nater, San Antonio
1975	Julius Erving, New York;	Marvin Barnes, St. Louis
	George McGinnis, Indiana (tie)	

ABA Scoring Leaders

Year	Scoring Champion	Pts.	Avg.	Year	Scoring Champion	Pts.	Avg.
1968	Connie Hawkins, Pittsburgh	1,875	26.7	1972	Charlie Scott, Virginia	2,524	34.5
1969	Rick Barry, Oakland	1,190	34.0	1973	Julius Erving, Virginia	2,268	31.9
1970	Spencer Haywood, Denver	2,519	29.9	1974	Julius Erving, New York	2,299	27.3
1971	Dan Issel, Kentucky	2,480	29.8	1975	George McGinnis, Indiana	2,353	29.7

ABA All-Star Team, 1975

Position	First Team	Second Team
Forward	Julius Erving, New York	Marvin Barnes, St. Louis
Forward	George McGinnis, Indiana	George Gervin, San Antonio
Center	Artis Gilmore, Kentucky	Swen Nater, San Antonio
Guard	Ron Boone, Utah	Brian Taylor, New York
Guard	Mack Calvin, Carolina	James Silas, San Antonio

Basketball Hall of Fame

Springfield, Mass.

The Naismith Memorial Basketball Hall of Fame was incorporated in 1959 to serve as a memorial to James Naismith, who invented the game of basketball for students of the School for Christian Workers (now Springfield College) in December, 1891, at Springfield, Mass. The following persons have been enshrined in the Basketball Hall of Fame for outstanding contributions to basketball:

Players

Beckman, John
Borgmann, Bennie
Brennan Joseph
Cousy, Robert J.
Davies, Robert
DeBernardi, Forrest
Dehnert, Henry G.
Endacott, Paul
Foster, Harold
Friedman, Max
Gruenig, Robert
Hanson, Victor
Holman, Nat
Hyatt, Charles
Kurland, Robert
Lapchick, Joe
Luisetti, Angelo
McCracken, Branch
McCracken, Jack
Macauley, C. Edward
Mikan, George L.
Murphy, Charles
Page, H. O. "Pat"
Pettit, Robert L.
Phillip, Andy
Roosma, Col. John S.

Russell, John
Russell, Bill
Schayes, Dolph
Schmidt, Ernie
Schommer, John J.
Sedran, Barney
Steinmetz, Christian
Thompson, John A.
Vandivier, Robert
Wachter, Edward A.
Wooden, John R.

Coaches

Auerbach, Arnold J.
Blood, Ernest A.
Cann, Howard G.
Carlson, Dr. H. Clifford
Carnevale, Ben
Dean, Everett S.
Diddle, Edgar A.
Drake, Bruce
Gill, Amory T.
Hobson, Howard A.
Iba, Henry P.
Julian, Alvin F.
Keaney, Frank W.
Keogan, George E.

Lambert, Ward L.
Loeffler, Kenneth D.
Lonborg, Arthur
Meanwell, Dr. Walter E.
Rupp, Adolph F.
Sachs, Leonard D.
Wooden, John R.

Contributors

Allen, Dr. Forrest C.
Bee, Clair F.
Brown, Walter A.
Bunn, John W.
Douglas, Robert L.
Fisher, Harry
Gootlieb, Edward
Gulick, Dr. Luther H.
Hickox, Edward J.
Hinkle, Paul D.
Irish, Ned
Jones, R. William
Liston, Emil S.
Mokray, William G.
Morgan, Ralph
Morgenweck, Frank
Naismith, Dr. James
O'Brien, John J.

Olsen, Harold G.
Podoloff, Maurice
Porter, H. V.
Ripley, Elmer
St. John, Lynn W.
Saperstein, Abe
Schabinger, Arthur A.
Stagg, Amos Alonzo
Taylor, Charles H.
Tower, Oswald
Trester, Arthur L.
Wells, W. R. Clifford

Referees

Kepbron, George T.
Hoyt, George
Kennedy, Matthew P.
Quigley, Ernest C.
Tobey, David
Walsh, David H.

Teams

First Team
Original Celtics
Buffalo Germans
Renaissance

U.S. National Squash Racquets Champions

Year	Champion	Year	Champion	Year	Champion
1965	Stephen Vehslage, N.Y., N.Y.	1969	Anil Nayar, Boston, Mass.	1973	Vic Niederhoffer, N.Y., N.Y.
1966	Vic Niederhoffer, N.Y., N.Y.	1970	Anil Nayar, Boston, Mass.	1974	Vic Niederhoffer, N.Y., N.Y.
1967	Samuel Howe 3d, Phila., Pa.	1971	Colin Adair, Canada	1975	Vic Niederhoffer, N.Y., N.Y.
1968	Colin Adair, Canada	1972	Vic Niederhoffer, N.Y., N.Y.		

Lacrosse Championships in 1975

Source: Jack Kelly, U.S. Lacrosse Information

NCAA University Champions—Univ. of Maryland
NCAA College Champions—Cortland State Univ. of N.Y.
National Club Lacrosse Champion—Mt. Washington Club of Baltimore
U.S. Intercollegiate Lacrosse Association Champions—Univ. of Maryland
Ivy League Champion—Cornell Univ.
South Atlantic Division Champion—Univ. of North Carolina
New England Intercollegiate Champion—Brown Univ.
East Coast Lacrosse League Champion—Univ. of Delaware
Middle Atlantic Division—Franklin & Marshall
Mason-Dixon Division—UMBC
Colonial Division (New England)—Boston State
Knickerbocker Division—Kean College
Independent Division—Ithaca College
Florida Open Champion—Pensacola Naval Air Station

NCAA University Championship
at Homewood, Baltimore, Md., May 31; Maryland 20, Navy 13.

NCAA Semi-finals
Maryland 15, Washington & Lee 5; Navy 15, Cornell 12.

NCAA Quarter-finals
Maryland 19, Hofstra 11; Wash. & Lee 11, Johns Hopkins 7; Cornell 18, Rutgers 5; Navy 17, Pennsylvania 6.

All-Star College Game
Ithaca, N.Y.-June 14; North 25, South 24 (o.t.).

U.S. Club Lacrosse Association Championship
at Baltimore, Md.-June 21; Mt. Washington 18, Long Island A.C. 9.

NCAA College Division Championship
at C.W. Post College, Greenvale, N.Y.-May 24; Cortland 12, Hobart 11.

Junior College Championship
at Catonsville, Md., May 10; Nassau C.C. 17, Farmingdale 10.

USILA University All America Team, 1975

Position	Player	College
Goalie	Rodney Rullman	Virginia
Defense	John Lawlor	Navy
Defense	Mike Farrell	Maryland
Defense	Rob Lindsay	Washington & Lee
Midfield	Frank Urso	Maryland
Midfield	Doug Radebaugh	Maryland
Midfield	Bob Desimone	Navy
Midfield	Dale Kohler	Johns Hopkins
Attack	Eamon McEneaney	Cornell
Attack	Franz Wittelsberger	Johns Hopkins
Attack	Mike French	Cornell

Note—4 midfield players selected for the 3 midfield positions.

USILA University Top Ten Teams, 1975

Rank	University	Rank	University
1	Maryland	6	Hofstra
2	Navy	*7	Pennsylvania
3	Johns Hopkins	*7	Virginia
4	Cornell	9	Rutgers
5	Washington & Lee	10	Princeton

*Tie—seventh rank

USILA College Division Top Ten Teams, 1975

Rank	College	Rank	College
1	Cortland State of N.Y.	7	Roanoke (Va.)
2	Hobart	8	Adelphi (N.Y.)
3	Towson State (Md.)	9	Ohio Wesleyan
4	UMBC	*10	Baltimore
5	Washington (Md.)	*10	Morgan State
6	Salisbury State (Md.)		* Tie

Rodeo Championship Standings 1974

Source: Rodeo Cowboys Assn., Inc.

Event	Winner	Money Won	Event	Winner	Money Won
All Around	Tom Ferguson, Miami, Oklahoma	$66,929	Calf Roping	Tom Ferguson, Miami, Oklahoma	$40,839
Saddle Bronc	John McBeth, Burden, Kansas	36,730	Steer Wrestling	Tommy Puryear, Norman, Oklahoma	26,253
Bareback Bronc	Joe Alexander, Cora, Wyoming	36,073	Team Roping	H.P. Evetts, Hanford, California	23,018
Bull Riding	Don Gay, Mesquite, Texas	32,917			

Rodeo Cowboy All Around Champions

Year	Winner	Money Won	Year	Winner	Money Won
1960	Harry Tompkins, Dublin, Texas	$32,522	1968	Larry Mahan, Salem, Oregon	$49,129
1961	Benny Reynolds, Melrose, Mont.	31,309	1969	Larry Mahan, Brooks, Oregon	57,726
1962	Tom Nesmith, Bethel, Okla.	32,611	1970	Larry Mahan, Brooks, Oregon	41,493
1963	Dean Oliver, Boise, Idaho.	31,329	1971	Phil Lyne, George West, Texas	49,245
1964	Dean Oliver, Boise, Idaho.	31,150	1972	Phil Lyne, George West, Texas	60,852
1965	Dean Oliver, Boise, Idaho.	33,163	1973	Larry Mahan, Dallas, Texas.	64,447
1966	Larry Mahan, Brooks, Oregon	40,358	1974	Tom Ferguson, Miami, Oklahoma	66,929
1967	Larry Mahan, Brooks, Oregon	51,996			

Canadian Intercollegiate Athletic Union Champions

Basketball

1968	Waterloo Lutheran
1969	Windsor
1970	British Columbia
1971	Acadia
1972	British Columbia
1973	St. Mary's
1974	Guelph
1975	Waterloo

Football

1967	Alberta
1968	Manitoba
1969	Manitoba
1970	Western Ontario
1971	Western Ontario
1972	Alberta
1973	St. Mary's
1974	Western Ontario

Soccer

1972	Alberta
1973	Loyola
1974	British Columbia

Swimming and Diving

1968	Toronto
1969	Toronto
1970	Toronto
1971	Toronto
1972	McGill
1973	Toronto
1974	Toronto
1975	Toronto

Wrestling

1970	Alberta
1971	Alberta
1972	Alberta
1973	Assoc. Champion
1974	Assoc. Champion
1975	Ontario Assoc. Champion

Hockey

1964	Alberta
1965	Manitoba
1966	Toronto
1967	Toronto
1968	Alberta
1969	Toronto
1970	Toronto
1971	Toronto
1972	Toronto
1973	Toronto
1974	Waterloo
1975	Alberta

Volleyball

1969	Winnipeg
1970	Montreal
1971	Winnipeg
1972	Winnipeg
1973	Winnipeg
1974	Winnipeg
1975	Alberta

Badminton Championships in 1975
U.S. National Championship
Waukesha, Wis., April 2-5, 1975

Men's Singles—Mike Adams, Flint, Mich. def. Gary Higgins, Alhambra, Cal., 15-9, 15-4.
Women's Singles—Judianne Kelly, Norwalk, Cal. def. Cindy Baker, Salt Lake City, 11-6, 11-8.
Men's Doubles—Don Paup, Washington, D.C. and Jim Poole, Westminster, Cal. def. Dave Ogata, Los Angeles and Mike Walker, Manhattan Beach, Cal., 18-13, 15-12.
Women's Doubles—Diane Hales, Claremont, Cal. and Carlene Starky, La Mesa, Cal. def. Judianne Kelly and Rosine Lemon, New York, N.Y., 15-8, 15-10.
Mixed Doubles—Mike Walker and Judianne Kelly def. Don Paup and Rosine Lemon, 18-13, 15-10.
Senior Men's Singles—Jim Poole def. Tom Heden, Millwood, N.Y., 15-0, 15-0.
Senior Men's Doubles—Bob Carpenter, New York, N.Y., and

Bill Goodman, Wellesley Hills, Mass., def. Red Thomas, Natchitoches, La. and Dick Witte, St. Louis, Mo., 15-8, 15-3.
Senior Women's Doubles—Ethel Marshall and Bea Massman, Buffalo, N.Y. def. Ket Hoffman, Rochester, Minn. and Jean Safford, Royal Oak, Minn., 15-5, 15-10.
Senior Mixed Doubles—Jim Poole and Helen Tibbetts, Alhambra, Cal. def. Tom Heden and Ket Hoffman, 15-2, 15-3.
Master Men's Singles—Ed Phillips, Warwick, R.I. def. Red Thomas, 15-5, 17-15.
Master Men's Doubles—Larry Calvert, Pacific Palisades, Cal. and Ed Phillips def. Harold Clark, Dallas and Red Thomas, 18-13, 15-10.
Master Mixed Doubles—Scott Garman, Lititz, Pa. and Ethel Marshall def. Larry Calvert and Helen Tibbetts, 15-10, 15-7.

All-England Championships
Wembley, England, March 19-22, 1975

Men's Singles—Svend Pri, Denmark def. Rudy Hartono, Indonesia, 15-11, 17-14.
Women's Singles—Hiroe Yuki, Japan def. Fillian Gilks, England, 11-5, 11-9.
Men's Doubles—Tjun Tjun and J. Wahjudi, Indonesia def.

Christian and Ade Chandra, Indonesia, 15-11, 15-5.
Women's Doubles—M. Aizawa and E. Takenaka def. T. Widiastuti and I. Wigoeno, Indonesia, 12-15, 15-12, 15-9.
Mixed Doubles—Elliott Stuart and Nora Gardner, England def. R. Maywald and B. Steden, 15-9, 15-3.

Canadian Open Championships
Montreal, Que., Apr. 10-13, 1975

Men's Singles—Ray Stevens, England def. Tom Kihlstrom, Denmark, 1-15, 15-5, 15-10.
Women's Singles—Margaret Beck, England def. Joke Van Beusekom, Holland, 11-4, 11-3.
Men's Doubles—Mike Tredgett and Ray Stevens, England def.

Nobutaka Ikeda and Shoichi Toganoo, Japan, 17-16, 12-15, 15-12.
Women's Doubles—Margaret Beck and Joke Van Beusekom def. Jane Youngberg and Barbara Welch, Canada, 15-12, 11-15, 15-4.

U.S. National Junior Championships
Philadelphia, Pa., March 26-29, 1975

Boy's Singles—Matt Fogarty, Duxbury, Ma. def. Peter Cornell, Philadelphia, 8-15, 15-5, 15-9.
Girl's Singles—Carrie Morrison, Port Angeles, Wash. def. Madalene Steinbroner, Manhattan Beach, Cal., 10-12, 11-8, 11-1.
Boy's Doubles—Pat Tryon, Wilmington, Del. and Matt Fogarty

def. Peter Cornell and Mike Kelly, Manhattan Beach, Cal., 15-10, 2-15, 15-4.
Girl's Doubles—Carrie Morrison and Madalene Steinbroner def. Monica Czarnecki and Barbara Taft, Flint, Mich., 15-4, 15-1.
Mixed Doubles—Matt Fogarty and Monica Czarnecki def. Mike Kelly and Madalene Steinbroner, 18-13, 15-10.

Table Tennis Championships in 1975
45th U.S. National Open Championship
Houston, Texas, May 22-25, 1975

Men's Singles—Kjell Johansson, Sweden.
Women's Singles—Onung Hyun Sook, South Korea.
Mixed Doubles—Choi Sung Kuk & Sung Nak So, South Korea.
Women's Doubles—Ann-Christin Hellman & Eva Stroemvall, Sweden.
Men's Doubles—Dragutin Surbek & Anton Stipancic, Yugoslavia.

Boys Under 17—Dror Polak, Israel.
Boys Under 17 Doubles—Peter Joe & Ed Lo, Vancouver.
Girls under 17—Eva Stroemvall, Sweden.
Girls Under 17 Doubles—Mariann Domonkos & Biruta Plucas, Canada.
Men's Team—Sweden.
Women's Team—South Korea.

33rd World's Table Tennis Championships
Calcutta, India, Feb. 6-16, 1975

Men's Singles—Istvan Jonyer, Hungary.
Women's Singles—Yung Sun Kim, Korea DPR.
Mixed Doubles—Stanislav Gomozkov & Tatjana Ferdman, USSR.
Women's Doubles—Maria Alexandru & Shoko Takahashi,

Rumania & Japan.
Men's Doubles—Istvan Johyer & Gabor Gergely, Hungary.
Jubilee Cup—Karl Noeller, Luxemburg.
Swaythling Cup for Men's Team—China.
Corbillon Cup for Women's Team—China.

79th Annual Boston Marathon

Will Rodgers covered the traditional distance of 26 miles 285 yards in 2 hours 9 minutes 55 seconds to win the 1975 Boston Marathon. Aided by a 20-mile-an-hour tailwind, Rodger's time was the fastest ever run by an American. The leading finishers and their times follow:

1—William H. Rodgers, Boston	2:09.55	12—Tony Brien, Marymount College	2:17.20
2—Steve Hoag, Minneapolis	2:11.54	13—Art-Pekka Gylling, Finland	2:17.32
3—Tom Fleming, N.Y. Athletic Club	2:12.05	14—Herb Lorenz, Penn. A.C.	2:17.43
4—Thomas Howard, Vancouver, B.C.	2:13.23	15—Don Kennedy, Ft. Worth	2:18.31
5—Ron Hill, England	2:13.28		
6—James Stanley, Summit A.C.	2:14.54	**Leading Women**	
7—Russell Pate, Columbia Track Club	2:15.22	1—Liane Winter, West Germany	2:42.24
8—Peter Fredriksson, San Diego	2:15.38	2—Kathy Switzer, New York	2:51.27
9—Mario Cuevas, Mexico	2:16.03	3—Gayle Barron, Atlanta	2:54.11
10—Andrew Boychuk, Canada	2:16.13	4—Marilyn Revans, Baltimore	2:55.52
11—Leed Fidler, Atlanta	2:16.51	5—Merry Cushing, Amherst, Mass	2:54.57

Hockey in 1974-75

National Hockey League
Final Standings
Clarence Campbell Conference

Lester Patrick Division	W.	L.	T.	Pts.	GF	GA	Conn Smythe Division	W.	L.	T.	Pts.	GF	GA
Philadelphia	51	18	11	113	293	181	Vancouver	38	32	10	86	271	254
N.Y. Rangers	37	29	14	88	319	276	St. Louis	35	31	14	84	269	266
N.Y. Islanders	33	25	22	88	264	221	Chicago	37	35	8	82	268	241
Atlanta	34	31	15	83	243	233	Minnesota	23	50	7	53	221	341
							Kansas City	15	54	11	41	184	328

Prince of Wales Conference

Charles F. Adams Division	W.	L.	T.	Pts.	GF	GA	James Norris Division	W.	L.	T.	Pts.	GF	GA
Buffalo	49	16	15	113	354	240	Montreal	47	14	19	113	374	225
Boston	40	26	14	94	345	245	Los Angeles	42	17	21	105	269	185
Toronto	31	33	16	78	280	309	Pittsburgh	37	28	15	89	326	289
California	19	48	13	51	212	316	Detroit	23	45	12	58	259	335
							Washington	8	67	5	19	181	446

Stanley Cup Playoff Results

Pittsburgh defeated St. Louis 2 games to 0.
Chicago defeated Boston 2 games to 1.
N.Y. Islanders defeated N.Y. Rangers 2 games to 1.
Toronto defeated Los Angeles 2 games to 1.
Philadelphia defeated Toronto 4 games to 0.
N.Y. Islanders defeated Pittsburgh 4 games to 3.

Buffalo defeated Chicago 4 games to 1.
Montreal defeated Vancouver 4 games to 1.
Buffalo defeated Montreal 4 games to 2.
Philadelphia defeated N.Y. Islanders 4 games to 3.
Philadelphia defeated Buffalo 4 games to 2.

Leading Scorers

Player—Club	G.	Goals	Asts.	Pts.	Player—Club	G.	Goals	Asts.	Pts.
Orr, Boston	80	46	89	135	Lemaire, Montreal	80	36	56	92
Esposito, Boston	79	61	66	127	Ratelle, Rangers	79	36	55	61
Dionne, Detroit	80	47	74	121	Vickers, Rangers	80	41	48	89
Lafleur, Montreal	70	53	66	119	Grant, Detroit	80	50	36	86
Mahovlich, Montreal	80	35	82	117	Mikita, Chicago	79	36	50	86
Clarke, Philadelphia	80	27	89	116	Schock, Pittsburgh	80	23	63	86
Robert, Buffalo	74	40	60	100	Bucyk, Boston	78	29	52	81
Gilbert, Rangers	76	36	61	97	Sittler, Toronto	72	36	44	80
Perreault, Buffalo	68	39	57	96	Unger, St. Louis	80	36	44	80
Martin, Buffalo	68	52	43	95	MacLeish, Philadelphia	80	38	41	79

Leading Goalies

Goalie—Club	G.	GA.	ShO.	Avg.	Goalie—Club	G.	GA.	ShO.	Avg.
Parent, Philadelphia	68	137	12	2.03	Myre, Atlanta	40	114	5	2.85
Vachon, Los Angeles	54	121	6	2.24	Larocque, Montreal	25	74	3	3.00
Edwards, Los Angeles	27	61	3	2.34	Smith, Vancouver	72	197	6	3.09
Resch, Islanders	25	59	3	2.47	Inness, Pittsburgh	57	161	2	3.09
Dryden, Montreal	56	149	4	2.69	Bromley, Buffalo	50	144	4	3.10
Esposito, Chicago	71	193	6	2.74	Johnston, St. Louis	30	93	2	3.10
Bouchard, Atlanta	40	111	3	2.77	Gilbert, Boston	53	158	3	3.13
Smith, Islanders	58	156	3	2.78					

Club Scoring Leaders

Atlanta Player	G.	Goals	Asts.	Pts.	Chicago Player	G.	Goals	Asts.	Pts.
Tom Lysiak	77	25	52	77	Stan Mikita	79	36	50	86
Curt Bennett	80	31	33	64	Ivan Boldirev	80	24	43	67
Eric Vail	72	39	21	60	Jim Pappin	71	36	27	63
Buster Harvey	79	17	27	44	Cliff Koroll	80	27	32	59
Gerry Meehan	74	14	26	40	Dick Redmond	80	14	43	57

Boston Player	G.	Goals	Asts.	Pts.	Detroit Player	G.	Goals	Asts.	Pts.
Bobby Orr	80	46	89	135	Marcel Dionne	80	47	74	121
Phil Esposito	79	61	66	127	Danny Grant	80	50	36	86
John Bucyk	78	29	52	81	Nick Libett	80	23	27	50
Gregg Sheppard	76	30	48	78	Phil Robert	53	13	29	42
Carol Vadnais	80	18	56	74	Bill Hogaboam	60	14	26	40

Buffalo Player	G.	Goals	Asts.	Pts.	Kansas City Player	G.	Goals	Asts.	Pts.
Rene Robert	74	40	60	100	Simon Nolet	72	26	32	58
Gilbert Perreault	68	39	57	96	Guy Charron	77	14	39	53
Rick Martin	68	52	43	95	Dave Hudson	70	9	32	41
Don Luce	80	33	42	75	Wilf Paiement	78	26	13	39
Rick Dudley	78	31	39	70	Eddie Gilbert	80	16	22	38

California Player	G.	Goals	Asts.	Pts.	Los Angeles Player	G.	Goals	Asts.	Pts.
Larry Patey	79	25	20	45	Bob Nevin	80	31	41	72
Stan Weir	80	18	27	45	Mike Murphy	80	30	38	68
Dave Hrechkosy	72	29	14	43	Dan Maloney	80	27	39	66
Al MacAdam	80	18	25	43	Whitey Widing	80	26	34	60
John Stewart	76	19	19	38	Butch Goring	60	27	32	59

Minnesota

Player	G.	Goals	Asts.	Pts.
Dennis Hextall	80	17	56	73
Bill Goldsworthy	71	37	35	72
Ernie Hicke	62	17	19	36
Norm Gratton	59	17	18	35
Murray Oliver	80	19	15	34

Montreal

Player	G.	Goals	Asts.	Pts.
Guy Lafleur	70	53	66	119
Pete Mahovlich	80	35	82	117
Jacques Lemaire	80	36	56	92
Guy Lapointe	80	28	47	75
Yvan Cournoyer	76	29	45	74

N.Y. Islanders

Player	G.	Goals	Asts.	Pts.
Denis Potvin	79	21	55	76
Billy Harris	80	25	37	62
Bob Nystrom	76	27	28	55
J. P. Parise	79	23	32	55
Eddie Westfall	73	22	33	55

N.Y. Rangers

Player	G.	Goals	Asts.	Pts.
Rod Gilbert	76	36	61	97
Jean Ratelle	79	36	55	91
Steve Vickers	80	41	48	89
Bill Fairbairn	80	24	36	60
Pete Stemkowski	77	24	35	59

Philadelphia

Player	G.	Goals	Asts.	Pts.
Bobby Clarke	80	27	89	116
Rick MacLeish	80	38	41	79
Reg Leach	80	45	33	78
Bill Barber	79	34	37	71
Ross Lonsberry	80	24	25	49

Pittsburgh

Player	G.	Goals	Asts.	Pts.
Ron Schock	80	23	63	86
Syl Apps	79	24	55	79
Jean Pronovost	78	43	32	75
Vic Hadfield	78	31	41	72
Pierre Larouche	79	31	37	68

St. Louis

Player	G.	Goals	Asts.	Pts.
Garry Unger	80	36	44	80
Pierre Plante	80	34	32	66
Wayne Merrick	76	28	37	65
Chuck Lefley	75	24	28	52
Denis Dupere	75	23	21	44

Toronto

Player	G.	Goals	Asts.	Pts.
Darryl Sittler	72	36	44	80
Ron Ellis	79	32	29	61
Dave Keon	78	16	43	59
George Ferguson	69	19	30	49
Lanny McDonald	64	17	27	44

Vancouver

Player	G.	Goals	Asts.	Pts.
Andre Boudrias	77	16	62	78
Don Lever	80	38	30	68
John Gould	78	34	31	65
Dennis Ververgaert	57	19	32	51
Chris Oddleifson	60	16	35	51

Washington

Player	G.	Goals	Asts.	Pts.
Tommy Williams	73	22	36	58
Ace Bailey	71	19	39	58
Ron Lalonde	74	14	17	29
Mike Marson	76	16	12	28
Yvon Labre	76	4	23	27

Conn Smythe Trophy (MVP in Playoffs)

1965—Jean Beliveau, Montreal
1966—Roger Crozier, Detroit
1967—Dave Keon, Toronto
1968—Glenn Hall, St. Louis
1969—Serge Sevard, Montreal
1970—Bobby Orr, Boston
1971—Ken Dryden, Montreal
1972—Bobby Orr, Boston
1973—Yvan Cournoyer, Montreal
1974—Bernie Parent, Philadelphia
1975—Bernie Parent, Philadelphia

Stanley Cup Champions

1928—New York
1929—Boston
1930—Montreal
1931—Montreal
1932—Toronto
1933—New York
1934—Chicago
1935—Montreal Maroons
1936—Detroit
1937—Detroit
1938—Chicago
1939—Boston
1940—New York
1941—Boston
1942—Toronto
1943—Detroit
1944—Montreal
1945—Toronto
1946—Montreal
1947—Toronto
1948—Toronto
1949—Toronto
1950—Detroit
1951—Toronto
1952—Detroit
1953—Montreal
1954—Detroit
1955—Detroit
1956—Montreal
1957—Montreal
1958—Montreal
1959—Montreal
1960—Montreal
1961—Chicago
1962—Toronto
1963—Toronto
1964—Toronto
1965—Montreal
1966—Montreal
1967—Toronto
1968—Montreal
1969—Montreal
1970—Boston
1971—Montreal
1972—Boston
1973—Montreal
1974—Philadelphia
1975—Philadelphia

NHL All Star Team, 1975

	First Team	Second Team
Goal	Bernie Parent, Philadelphia	Rogatien Vachon, Los Angeles
Defense	Bobby Orr, Boston	Guy Lapointe, Montreal
Defense	Denis Potvin, N.Y. Islanders	Bjore Salming, Toronto
Center	Bobby Clarke, Philadelphia	Phil Esposito, Boston
Right Wing	Guy Lafleur, Montreal	Rene Robert, Buffalo
Left Wing	Rick Martin, Buffalo	Steve Vickers, N.Y. Rangers

NHL Amateur Draft

First Round Selections

Team	Player	Position	1974-75 Team
1-Philadelphia	Mel Bridgman	Center	Victoria
2-Kansas City	Barry Dean	Left Wing	Medicine Hat
3-California	Ralph Klassen	Center	Saskatoon
4-Minnesota	Bryan Maxwell	Defense	Medicine Hat
5-Detroit	Rick Lapointe	Defense	Victoria
6-Toronto	Don Ashby	Center	Calgary
7-Chicago	Greg Vaydik	Center	Medicine Hat
8-Atlanta	Richard Mulhern	Defense	Sherbrooke
9-Montreal	Robin Sadler	Defense	Edmonton
10-Vancouver	Rick Blight	Right Wing	Brandon
11-Islanders	Pat Price	Defense	Calgary
12-Rangers	Wayne Dillon	Center	Toronto
13-Pittsburgh	Gord Laxton	Goal	New Westminster
14-Boston	Doug Halward	Defense	Peterborough
15-Montreal	Pierre Mondou	Center	Montreal
16-Los Angeles	Tim Young	Center	Ottawa
17-Buffalo	Robert Sauve	Goal	Laval
18-Washington	Alex Forsyth	Center	Kingston

Hockey Trophy Winners

Ross Trophy Leading Scorer	Norris Trophy Best Defenseman	Calder Trophy Best Rookie
1975—Bobby Orr, Boston	Bobby Orr, Boston	Eric Vail, Atlanta
1974—Phil Esposito, Boston	Bobby Orr, Boston	Denis Potvin, N.Y. Islanders
1973—Phil Esposito, Boston	Bobby Orr, Boston	Steve Vickers, N.Y. Rangers
1972—Phil Esposito, Boston	Bobby Orr, Boston	Ken Dryden, Montreal
1971—Phil Esposito, Boston	Bobby Orr, Boston	Gil Perreault, Buffalo
1970—Bobby Orr, Boston	Bobby Orr, Boston	Tony Esposito, Chicago
1969—Phil Esposito, Boston	Bobby Orr, Boston	Danny Grant, Minn.
1968—Stan Mikita, Chicago	Bobby Orr, Boston	Derek Sanderson, Boston
1967—Stan Mikita, Chicago	Harry Howell, N.Y. Rangers	Bobby Orr, Boston
1966—Bobby Hull, Chicago	Jacques Laperriere, Montreal	Brit Selby, Toronto
1965—Stan Mikita, Chicago	Pierre Pilote, Chicago	Roger Crozier, Detroit
1964—Stan Mikita, Chicago	Pierre Pilote, Chicago	Jacques Laperriere, Montreal

Hart Trophy M.V.P.	Vezina Trophy Leading Goalie	Lady Byng Trophy Sportsmanship
1975—Bobby Clarke, Philadelphia	Bernie Parent, Philadelphia	Marcel Dionne, Detroit
1974—Phil Esposito, Boston	Tony Esposito, Chicago	John Bucyk, Boston
	Bernie Parent, Philadelphia	
1973—Bobby Clarke, Philadelphia	Ken Dryden, Montreal	Gilbert Perreault, Buffalo
1972—Bobby Orr, Boston	Esposito, Smith, Chicago	Jean Ratelle, N.Y. Rangers
1971—Bobby Orr, Boston	Giacomin, Villemure, New York	John Bucyk, Boston
1970—Bobby Orr, Boston	Tony Esposito, Chicago	Phil Goyette, St. Louis
1969—Phil Esposito, Boston	Hall, Plante, St. Louis	Alex Devecchio, Detroit
1968—Stan Mikita, Chicago	Worsley, Vachon, Montreal	Stan Mikita, Chicago
1967—Stan Mikita, Chicago	Hall, De Jordy, Chicago	Stan Mikita, Chicago
1966—Bobby Hull, Chicago	Hodge, Worsley, Montreal	Alex Devecchio, Detroit
1965—Bobby Hull, Chicago	Sawchuck, Bower, Toronto	Bobby Hull, Chicago
1964—Jean Beliveau, Montreal	Charlie Hodge, Montreal	Ken Wharram, Chicago

Players in the Hockey Hall of Fame
Canadian National Exhibition Park, Toronto, Ont.

Sid Abel
John J. (Jack) Adams
C. J. S. (Syl) Apps
George Armstrong
Ace Bailey
Donald Bain
Hobart (Hobey) Baker
Martin (Marty) Barry
Jean Beliveau
Clint (Benny) Benedict
Douglas (Doug) Bentley
Max Bentley
Hector (Toe) Blake
Richard (Dickie) Boon
Emile (Butch) Bouchard
Frank Boucher
George (Buck) Boucher
Russell Bowie
Frank Brimsek
H. L. (Punch) Broadbent, M.M.
Walter (Turk) Broda
Billy Burch
H. H. (Harry) Cameron
Francis (King) Clancy
Aubrey (Dit) Clapper
Sprague Cleghorn
Neil Colville
Charles Conacher
Alex Connell
William (Bill) Cook
Art Coulter
W. M. (Bill) Cowley
Samuel R. (Rusty) Crawford
John P. (Jack) Darragh
Allan (Scotty) Davidson
Clarence (Hap) Day
Cyril (Cy) Denney

Gordon Drillon
Charles G. Drinkwater
Tommy Dunderdale
William (Bill) Durnan
Mervyn (Red) Dutton
Cecil H. (Babe) Dye
Arthur Farrell
Frank Foyston
Frank Fredrickson
W. A. (Bill) Gadsby
Charles (Chuck) Gardiner
Herbert Gardiner
James H. (Jimmy) Gardner
Bernard (Boom Boom) Geoffrion
Edward (Eddie) Gerard
H. L. (Billy) Gilmour
E. R. (Ebbie) Goodfellow
F.X. (Moose) Goheen
Michael (Mike) Grant
Wilfred (Shorty) Green
Silas (Si) Griffis
George Hainsworth
Glenn Hall
Joseph (Joe) Hall
Doug Harvey
George Hay
W.M. (Riley) Hern
Bryan Hextall
Harry (Hap) Holmes
Thomas (Tom) Hooper
G. R. (Red) Horner
Gordon Howe
Sydney (Syd) Howe
John B. (Bouse) Hutton
Harry Hyland
James Dickenson Irvin
H. (Busher) Jackson

Ernest (Moose) Johnson
I. W. (Ching) Johnson
T. C. (Tom) Johnson
Aurel Joliat
Gordon (Duke) Keats
Leonard (Red) Kelly
Theodore (Teeder) Kennedy
Elmer Lach
Edouard (Newsy) Lalonde
J. B. (Jack) Laviolette
Hugh Lehman
Percy LeSueur
Ted Lindsay
Duncan (Mickey) MacKay
Sylvio Mantha
Joseph Malone
John (Jack) Marshall
Fred (Steamer) Maxwell
Frank McGee
W. G. (Billy) McGimsie
George McNamara
Dickie Moore
Patrick (Paddy) Moran
H. W. (Howie) Morenz
Bill Mosienko
Frank Nighbor
Reginald Noble
Harold (Harry) Oliver
Lester Patrick
Thomas (Tom) Phillips
Pierre Pilote
Didier (Pit) Pitre
Walter (Babe) Pratt
Joseph (Joe) Primeau
Harvey Pulford
Frank Rankin
Chuck Rayner

Kenneth (Ken) Reardon
Maurice (The Rocket) Richard
George Richardson
Gordon Roberts
Arthur H. Ross
Blair Russell
Ernie Russell
J. D. (Jack) Ruttan
T. G. (Terry) Sawchuk
Fred Scanlan
Milt Schmidt
David (Sweeney) Schriner
Earl Walter Seibert
Oliver Seibert
Edward William Shore
Albert (Babe) Siebert
H. J. (Bullet Joe) Simpson, M.M.
Alfred (Alf) Smith
Reginald (Hooley) Smith
Tommy Smith
Russell (Barney) Stanley
John (Black Jack) Stewart
Nelson Stewart
Bruce Stuart
Horace (Hod) Stuart
Fred (Cyclone) Taylor, OBE
Harry J. Trihey
Cecil (Tiny) Thompson
Georges Vezina
Martin Walsh
John (Jack) Walker
Harry Watson
Harry Westwick
R. C. (Cooney) Weiland
Fred Whitcroft
Gordon (Phat) Wilson
Roy Worters

1975 Final Standings
American League

North Division

	P.	W.	L.	T.	GF	GA	Pts.
Providence	76	43	21	12	317	263	98
Rochester	76	42	25	9	318	243	93
Nova Scotia	75	40	26	9	270	227	89
Springfield	75	33	30	12	299	256	78
New Haven	76	30	35	11	283	302	71

*—suspended operations

South Division

	P.	W.	L.	T.	GF	GA	Pts.
Virginia	75	31	31	13	254	250	75
Richmond	75	29	39	7	261	293	65
Hershey	75	27	38	10	259	303	64
Syracuse	75	21	43	11	252	332	53
*Baltimore	46	14	22	10	136	180	38

Central League

North Division	P.	W.	L.	T.	GF	GA	Pts.
Salt Lake	78	43	24	11	317	245	97
Denver	78	36	29	13	285	263	85
Omaha	78	34	33	11	254	268	79
Seattle	78	29	38	11	258	296	69

South Division	P.	W.	L.	T.	GF	GA	Pts.
Dallas	78	40	30	8	302	259	88
Oklahoma	78	33	33	12	267	267	78
Tulsa	78	27	41	10	262	289	64
Fort Worth	78	26	40	12	264	322	64

Ontario Major League

	P.	W.	L.	T.	GF	GA	Pts.
Toronto	70	48	13	9	458	303	105
Peterborough	70	37	20	13	311	254	57
Hamilton	70	37	24	9	337	271	83
Ottawa	70	33	30	7	379	382	73
Sudbury	70	31	29	10	324	289	72
St. Catharines	70	30	33	7	284	300	67

	P.	W.	L.	T.	GF	GA	Pts.
Oshawa	70	28	33	9	288	306	65
Kingston	70	25	35	10	297	345	60
London	70	26	37	7	295	368	59
Sault	70	25	36	9	312	367	59
Kitchener	70	17	47	6	239	351	40

Western Canada League

Eastern Division	P.	W.	L.	T.	GF	GA	Pts.
Saskatoon	70	38	22	10	344	244	88
Lethbridge	70	28	32	10	302	315	66
Regina	70	29	36	5	260	288	63
Brandon	70	24	35	11	276	320	59
Winnipeg	70	23	35	12	265	366	58
Flin Flon	70	19	42	9	262	389	47

Western Division	P.	W.	L.	T.	GF	GA	Pts.
Victoria	70	47	18	5	416	257	99
Medicine Hat	70	40	22	8	380	291	88
New Westminster	70	37	22	11	319	260	85
Kamloops	70	38	24	8	329	279	84
Edmonton	70	34	29	7	340	321	75
Calgary	70	11	51	8	236	399	30

World Hockey Association

Final Standings

East Division						
Club	W.	L.	T.	Pts.	GF	GA
New England	43	30	5	91	274	279
Cleveland	35	40	3	73	236	258
Chicago	30	47	1	61	261	312
Indianapolis	18	57	3	39	216	338

*Formerly the Michigan Stags.

West Division						
Club	W.	L.	T.	Pts.	GF	GA
Houston	53	25	0	106	369	247
San Diego	43	31	4	90	326	268
Minnesota	42	33	3	87	308	279
Phoenix	39	31	8	86	300	265
*Baltimore	21	53	4	46	205	341

Canadian Division

Club	W.	L.	T.	Pts.	GF	GA
Quebec	46	32	0	92	331	299
Toronto	43	33	2	88	349	304
Winnipeg	38	35	5	81	322	293

Club	W.	L.	T.	Pts.	GF	GA
Vancouver	37	39	2	76	256	270
Edmonton	36	38	4	76	279	279

WHA Playoff Results

Houston defeated Cleveland 4 games to 1.
Quebec defeated Phoenix 4 games to 1.
Minnesota defeated New England 4 games to 2.
San Diego defeated Toronto 4 games to 2.

Quebec defeated Minnesota 4 games to 2.
Houston defeated San Diego 4 games to 0.
Houston defeated Quebec 4 games to 0.

Leading Scorers

Player—Club	G.	Goals	Asts.	Pts.
Lacroix, San Diego	78	41	106	147
Hull, Winnipeg	78	77	65	142
Bernier, Quebec	76	54	68	122
Nilsson, Winnipeg	78	26	94	120
Lund, Houston	78	33	75	108
Rivers, San Diego	78	54	53	107
Hedberg, Winnipeg	65	53	47	100
G. Howe, Houston	75	34	65	99
Dillon, Toronto	77	29	66	95
Walton, Minnesota	75	48	45	93
Houle, Quebec	64	40	52	92
Tardif, Quebec	76	50	39	89
Hinse, Houston	75	39	47	86

Player—Club	G.	Goals	Asts.	Pts.
Sentes, San Diego	74	44	41	85
Rogers, Edmonton	78	35	48	83
Mahovlich, Toronto	73	38	44	82
Nedomansky, Toronto	78	41	40	81
Morrison, San Diego	78	20	61	81
Simpson, Toronto	70	52	28	80
Peacosh, San Diego	78	43	36	79
MacGregor, Chicago	78	44	34	78
Harris, Vancouver	79	33	44	77
Sobchuk, Phoenix	78	32	45	77
Mark Howe, Houston	74	36	40	76
Lawson, Vancouver	78	33	43	76

Leading Goalies

Goalie—Club	G.	GA	ShO.	Avg.
Grahame, Houston	43	131	4	3.03
Rutledge, Houston	35	113	2	3.24
Wakely, San Diego	41	131	3	3.25
Cheevers, Cleveland	52	167	4	3.26
Norris, Phoenix	33	107	1	3.27

Goalie—Club	G.	GA	ShO.	Avg.
Garrett, Minnesota	58	180	2	3.28
Kurt, Phoenix	47	156	2	3.29
McLeod, Vancouver	71	230	1	3.35
Smith, New England	59	202	2	3.47
Daley, Winnipeg	51	175	1	3.62

WHA All-Star Team, 1975

Position	First Team	Second Team
Goal	Ron Grahame, Houston	Gerry Cheevers, Cleveland
Defense	J.C. Tremblay, Quebec	Poul Popeil, Houston
Defense	Kevin Morrison, San Diego	Barry Long, Edmonton
Center	Andre Lacroix, San Diego	Serge Bernier, Quebec
Right Wing	Gordie Howe, Houston	Wayne Rivers, San Diego
Left Wing	Bobby Hull, Winnipeg	Marc Tardiff, Quebec

Stadiums

For stadiums that house a major league baseball team and college stadiums see index.

Name and location	Capacity	Name and location	Capacity
Joseph Albi Memorial Stadium, Spokane	31,820	Long Beach (Cal.) Veterans Memorial	15,000
American Legion Memorial, Charlotte, N.C.	22,315	Los Angeles Memorial Coliseum	90,000
Arrowhead Stadium, Kansas City, Mo.	78,034	Louisiana Superdome, New Orleans	74,726
Balboa Stadium, San Diego, Calif.	34,500	Memphis Memorial Stadium	50,000
Bowman Grey Stad., Winston-Salem, N.C.	16,841	Mile High Stadium, Denver	51,706
Buffalo War Memorial Stadium	46,206	Mississippi Memorial Stadium, Jackson	46,000
Columbus (Ga.) Memorial Stadium	35,000	Orange Bowl, Miami, Fla.	80,045
Cotton Bowl, Dallas, Texas	72,000	Ottawa Stadium, Ottawa, Canada	27,872
Downing Stadium, New York, N.Y.	27,000	Pontiac Metropolitan Stadium, Mich.	80,399
Empire Stadium, Vancouver	32,759	Portland Civic Stadium	33,000
Exhibition Stadium, Toronto.	39,485	Rich Stadium, Buffalo, N.Y.	80,020
Franklin Field, Philadelphia	60,658	Richmond (Va.) City Stadium	22,009
Gator Bowl, Jacksonville, Fla.	70,000	Roanoke (Va.) Victory Stadium.	30,000
Halawa Stadium, Hawaii	50,000	Roosevelt Stadium, Jersey City	25,000
Honolulu Stadium	25,000	Rose Bowl, Pasadena, Cal.	106,721
John F. Kennedy Stadium, Philadelphia	105,000	Rubber Bowl, Akron, Ohio	35,007
Robert F. Kennedy Memorial Stadium, Wash., D.C.	53,041	Schaefer Stadium, Foxboro, Mass.	61,279
Kentucky Exposition Stadium, Louisville	21,000	Sicks Stadium, Seattle.	24,420
Kezar Stadium, San Francisco	59,636	Soldier Field, Chicago.	55,701
King County Domed Stadium, Seattle.	65,000	Sugar Bowl, New Orleans, La.	80,982
Ladd Memorial Stadium, Mobile, Ala.	40,605	Sun Bowl, El Paso, Texas.	30,000
Lambeau Field, Green Bay, Wis.	56,267	Tampa Stadium, Tampa, Fla.	45,005
Las Vegas Stadium.	16,000	Texas Stadium, Dallas.	65,111
Legion Field, Birmingham, Ala.	72,000		

Intercollegiate Rowing Association Regatta

Onondaga Lake, Syracuse, N. Y. (Three miles)

Year	Winner	Time	Year	Winner	Time	Year	Winner	Time
1956	Cornell	16:22.4	1963	Cornell	17:24.0	1970	Washington (A)	—
1957	Cornell	15:26.6	1964	California (A)	6:31.1	1971	Cornell (A)	6:06.0
1958	Cornell	17:12.1	1965	Navy	16:51.3	1972	Penn (A)	6:22.6
1959	Wisconsin	18:01.7	1966	Wisconsin	16:03.4	1973	Wisconsin (A)	6:21.0
1960	California	15:57.0	1967	Penn	16:15.9	1974	Wisconsin (A)	6:33.0
1961	California	16:49.2	1968	Penn (A)	6:15.6	1975	Wisconsin (A)	6:08.2
1962	Cornell	17:02.9	1969	Penn (A)	6:30.4	(A) Race at 2,000 meters.		

99th National Rowing Championships, 1975

Cooper River, N.J., July 27, 1975

Elite Quarter-Mile Singles—Jim Dietz, New York AC.
Senior Singles—Guy Iverson, Undine BC.
Senior Doubles—Mexico.
Senior Fours With Coxswain—Detroit BC.
Elite Fours—Vesper BC.
Senior Pairs—Fairmount RA.
Elite Lightweight Fours—Potomac BC.

Elite Lightweight Pairs—New York AC.
Senior Eights—Detroit BC.
Elite Eights—U.S. National Team.
Elite Doubles—New York AC.
Elite Pairs With Coxswain—Vesper BC.
Elite Lightweight Doubles—New York AC.

Curling Champions

World Champions

Year	Country & Skip	Year	Country & Skip	Year	Country & Skip
1964	Canada (Lyall Dagg)	1968	Canada (Ron Northcott)	1972	Canada (Orest Melesnuk)
1965	United States (Bud Somerville)	1969	Canada (Ron Northcott)	1973	Sweden (Kjell Oscarius)
1966	Canada (Ron Northcott)	1970	Canada (Don Duguid)	1974	United States (Bud Somerville)
1967	Scotland (Chuck Hay)	1971	Canada (Don Duguid)	1975	Switzerland

U. S. National Champions

Year	State & Skip	Year	State & Skip	Year	State & Skip
1965	Wisconsin (Bud Somerville)	1969	Wisconsin (Bud Sommerville)	1973	Massachusetts (Barry Blanchard)
1966	North Dakota (Joe Zbacnik)	1970	North Dakota (Art Tallackson)	1974	Wisconsin (Bud Somerville)
1967	Washington (Bruce Roberts)	1971	North Dakota (Dale Dalziel)	1975	Washington (Ed Risling)
1968	Wisconsin (Bud Somerville)	1972	North Dakota (Bob LaBonte)		

National AAU Judo Championships in 1975

Los Angeles, Cal., Mar. 14-15, 1975

Men
139 Lbs.—K. Nakasone, Pacific Assn.
154 Lbs.—P. Maruyama, U.S. Air Force.
176 Lbs.—S. Cohen, Central.
205 Lbs.—T. Martin, Pacific.
Heavyweight—A. Coage, New Jersey.
Open—D. Davis, Central.
Grand Champion—Tommy Martin, Pacific.

Women
Under 110 Lbs.—L. Lewis, New England.
110-120 Lbs.—D. Pierce, Minnesota.
120-130 Lbs.—F. Tomlinson, Potomac Valley.
130-142 Lbs.—D. Nelson, Pacific.
142-154 Lbs.—B. Korte, Ozark.
154-166 Lbs.—R. McCalmont, Pacific Southwest.
Over 166 Lbs.—D. Fisher, Pacific.
Open—M. Braziel, Metropolitan.
Grand Champion—Bonnie Korte, Ozark.

Sports on Television
Source: A. C. Nielsen

	Average Audiences			Ages of Men Viewers		
	Percent House-holds	Percent Men	Percent Women	18-34	35-49	50+
Football						
NFL Superbowl	41.6%	61%	39%	36%	28%	35%
ABC-NFL	21.2	63	37	38	31	31
CBS-NFL	14.1	66	34	35	29	36
NBC-NFL	13.4	66	34	36	27	37
College Bowl & All Star	21.6	60	40	32	27	41
NCAA Reg. Season	12.2	63	37	36	25	39
Baseball						
World Series	30.7	54	46	29	27	44
All Star Game	23.8	60	40	35	22	43
Regular Season	9.0	59	41	28	20	52
Horse Racing						
Kentucky Derby	16.5	45	55	20	24	56
Preakness	14.9	56	44	39	18	43
Other Racing	5.2	46	54	19	29	52
Hockey						
Regular Season	4.9	—	—	—	—	—
Stanley Cup	6.0	—	—	—	—	—
Basketball						
NBA Regular Season	9.3	67	33	47	25	28
NBA Playoffs	13.5	61	39	41	26	33
NBA All Star Game	12.6	60	40	52	22	26
ABA Playoffs	4.3	57	43	36	37	27
Bowling						
Pro Bowl Tour	9.0	51	49	31	26	43
Brunswick Open	6.0	40	60	43	11	46
Auto Racing	7.7	54	46	37	26	37
Golf						
CBS Golf Classic	4.1	57	43	26	26	48
Tournaments	8.6	55	45	28	22	50
Tennis						
CBS Tennis Classic	4.5	54	54	36	26	38
Alan King Tennis	3.6	52	48	22	40	38
Family Circle Tennis	4.1	54	54	33	19	48
World Champ Tennis	4.7	59	41	38	26	36
Wimbledon	4.5	49	51	35	21	44
Boxing						
Madison Sq. Garden	5.1	65	35	35	16	49
Multi-Sports Series						
American Sportsman	9.4	61	39	40	24	36
ABC WW Sports	11.6	59	41	40	25	35
CBS Sports Spectacular	6.4	54	46	35	25	40

Chess

Chess dates back to antiquity. Its exact origin is unknown. The strongest players of their time, and therefore regarded by later generations as world champions, were Francois Philidor, France; Alexandre Deschappelles, France; Louis de la Bourdonnais, France; Howard Staunton, England; Adolph Anderssen, Germany and Paul Morphy, United States. In 1866 Wilhelm Steinitz of Austria defeated Adolph Anderssen and claimed the title of World Champion. The official world champions, since the title was first used follow:

1866-1894	Wilhelm Steinitz, Vienna	1937-1946	Dr. Alexander A. Alekhine, Paris	1961-1963	Mikhail Botvinnik, USSR
1894-1921	Dr. Emanuel Lasker, Berlin			1963-1969	Tigran Petrosian, USSR
1921-1927	Jose R. Capablanca, Havana	1948-1957	Mikhail Botvinnik, USSR	1969-1972	Boris Spassky, USSR
1927-1935	Dr. Alexander A. Alekhine, Paris	1957-1958	Vassily Smyslov, USSR	1972-1975	Bobby Fisher, U.S.(A)
		1958-1959	Mikhail Botvinnik, USSR	1975	Anatoly Karpov, USSR
1935-1937	Dr. Max Euwe, Holland	1960-1961	Mikhail Tal, USSR		

(A) Stripped of championship after refusal to accept International Chess Federation rules for a championship match, April 1975.

United States Champions

1852-1862	Paul Morphy	1897-1906	Harry Nelson Pillsbury	1946	Samuel Reshevsky	1963-1967	Bobby Fischer
1871-1887	George Mackenzie			1948	Herman Steiner	1968	Larry Evans
1887-1892	Max Judd	1906-1909	Jackson Showalter	1951-1953	Larry Evans	1969-1971	Samuel Reschevsky
1892-1894	Simon Lipschultz	1909-1936	Frank J. Marshall	1954	Arthur B. Bisguier	1973	Robert Byrne
1894	Jackson Showalter	1936-1944	Samuel Reshevsky	1958-1961	Bobby Fischer	1974	Walter Browne
1894	Albert B. Hodges	1944-1946	Arnold S. Denker	1962	Larry Evans	1975	Walter Browne
1894-1897	Jackson Showalter						

AAU Freestyle Wrestling Championships in 1975
Bloomington, Ind., March 20-22, 1975

105.5 Lbs. — David Range, Cleveland, Ohio
114.5 Lbs. — John Morley, Long Island, N.Y.
125.5 Lbs. — Mark Massery, Savannah, Ill.
136.5 Lbs. — Doug Moses, Waterloo, Iowa.
149.5 Lbs. — Gene Davis, Long Beach, Cal.
163 Lbs. — Carl Adams, Iowa State

180.5 Lbs. — John Peterson, Lancaster, Pa.
198 Lbs. — Russ Hellickson, Madison, Wis.
220 Lbs. — Greg Wojciechowski, Toledo WC.
Heavyweight — Mike McCready, Dubuque, Iowa.
Team Champion — Athletes-In-Action.

Contract Bridge Championships in 1974-75

Winners of Major Events at 3 ACBL Championship Tournaments
Fall 1974 — Spring and Summer 1975 and World Championships
Source: American Contract Bridge League. Memphis. Tenn.

Fall Championships
San Antonio, Tex., Nov. 29-Dec. 8, 1974; attendance, 8,419 tables

Reisinger Board-a-Match Teams — Ira Rubin, Paramus, N.J.; Fred Hamilton, Taylor, Mich.; Erik Paulsen, Culver City, Cal.; Hugh Ross, Oakland, Cal.
Blue Ribbon Pairs — Norman Kay, Narberth, Pa. and Edgar Kaplan, New York, N.Y.
Life Master Men's Pairs — Gerald Michaud, Wichita, Kan. and G. Robert Nail, Houston, Tex.

Life Master Women's Pairs — Bernice Larson, Greenfield, Wis. and Joan Stein, Milwaukee, Wis.
Mixed Pairs — Helen Utegaard, Gaithersburg, Md. and Gerald Caravelli, Des Plaines, Ill.
Most Master Points for the Tournament — Fred Hamilton, Taylor, Mich., 202 Master Points.

Spring Championships
Honolulu, Ha., March 14-23, 1975; attendance, 10,234 tables

Vanderbilt Knockout Teams — Dr. Jorge Rosenkranz, Mexico City; Roger Bates, Dr. Richard Katz, Larry Cohen, John Mohan, all of Los Angeles, Cal.
Men's Teams — George Rapee, William Grieve, Matt Granovetter, Ronald Rubin, all of New York, N.Y.
Women's Teams — Emma Jean Hawes, Fort Worth, Tex.; Dorothy Truscott, Jacqui Mitchell, Gail Moss, all of New York, N.Y.; Marilyn Johnson, Houston, Tex.; Mary Jane Farell, Beverly Hills, Cal.

Men's Pairs — Harlow Lewis, Wynnewood, Pa.; and Art Waldmann, New Preston, Conn.
Women's Pairs — Jacqui Mitchell and Gail Moss, New York, N.Y.
Open Pairs — Daniel Hyland, Arlington Heights, Ill. and Gary Hayden, Tucson, Ariz.
Most Master Points for the Tournament — Roger Bates, Los Angeles, Cal. 213 Master Points.

Summer Championships
Miami Beach, Fla., Aug. 1-10, 1975; attendance, 10,368 tables

Spingold Knockout Teams — John Fejervary, Palo Alto, Cal.; Ron Von der Porten - Grant Baze, San Francisco; Piyush Vakil, Fremont, Cal.; Lew Stansby, Oakland, Cal.
Grand National Teams —Bobby Wolff, Bob Hamman, Dr. John Fisher, Jim Hooker, Charles Gabriel and Charles Weed, all of Dallas, Tex.
Master Mixed Teams — Nancy Gruver, Ellicott City, Md.; Gerald Caravelli, Des Plaines, Ill.; Helen Utegaard, Gaithersburg,

Md.; Jim Linhart, Englewood Cliffs, N.J.
Life Master Pairs — Eugene O'Neill, Reston, Va.; Roy Fox, Alexandria, Va.
Senior and Advanced Senior Master Pairs — Robert Schachter, W. Hempstead, N.Y.; Kitty Munson, Cambridge, Mass.
Most Master Points for Tournament — Grant Baze, San Francisco, Cal. 176 Master Points.

1975 World Championship
Southampton, Bermuda. Jan. 24-Feb. 1, 1975

World Team Champion — Italy — Sergio Zucchelli, Arturo Franco, Giorgio Belladonna, Vito Pittala, Benito Garozzo, Gianfranco Facchini. (Sandro Salvetti, non-playing captain).

National Skeet Shooting Association World Championships, 1975

All-Around Championship — 550 Targets
Champion — Robert Paxton, San Antonio, Tex., 549.
Woman — Jackie Ramsey, Dallas, Tex., 540.
Junior Woman — Catherine Forbush, Hamburg, N. Y., 358x-400.
Junior Boy — Steven Pyles, Temple Hill, Md., 538.
Veteran — Tom Sanfilipo, Fairfield, Cal., 533.
Sub Senior — R. A. Rowden, San Antonio, Tex., 542.
Senior — M. E. Kidd, Monroe, La., 536.
Collegiate — Robert Paxton, San Antonio, Tex., 549.

12 Gauge — 250 Targets
Champion — Ken Barnes, Bakersfield, Cal., 250.
Woman — Karla Roberts, Bridgeton, Mo., 249.
Junior Woman — Stanica Petrovich, Roselle, Ill., 95.
Junior Boy — Ed Simmons, Houston, Tex., 249.
Veteran — Tom Sanfilipo, Fairfield, Cal., 246.
Sub-Senior — R. A. Rowden, San Antonio, Tex., 249.
Senior — Angel Marchand, Santurce, Puerto Rico, 249.
Collegiate — Robert Hutter, Quincy, Ill., 250.

20 Gauge — 100 Targets
Champion — Doug Burdett, Belleville, Ont., 100.
Woman — Jackie Ramsey, Dallas, Tex., 100.
Junior Woman — Catherine Forbush, Hamburg, N. Y., 93.

Junior Boy — Dana Hersom, San Jose, Cal., 100.
Veteran — Tom Sanfilipo, Fairfield, Cal., 100.
Sub-Senior — James Dozier, Sr., Crowville, La., 100.
Senior — Chet Crites, Detroit, Mich., 100.
Collegiate — Peter Stocks, La Habra, Cal., 100.

28 Gauge — 100 Targets
Champion — Martin F. Wood, Dallas, Tex., 100.
Woman — Jackie Ramsey, Dallas, Tex., 99.
Junior Woman — Catherine Forbush, Hamburg, N. Y., 89.
Junior Boy — Alan Clark, Delmar, Cal., 99.
Veteran — Tom Sanfilipo, Fairfield, Cal., 99.
Sub-Senior — S. C. Haynes, Houston, Tex., 100.
Senior — M. E. Kidd, Monroe, La., 98.
Collegiate — Pat Bartel, San Antonio, Tex., 100.

410 Gauge — 100 Targets
Champion — Al Mullins, APO, N. Y., 100.
Woman — Elaine Ralph, Diamond Bar, Cal., 96.
Junior Woman — Catherine Forbush, Hamburg, N. Y., 89.
Junior Boy — Steve Andrew, Gadsden, Ala., 96.
Veteran — Henry Alcus, New Orleans, La., 95.
Sub-Senior — Clarence Johnson, Valley Station, Va., 97.
Senior — Frank Laudano, Port Arthur, Tex., 97.
Collegiate — Robert Paxton, San Antonio, Tex., 100.

National Skeet Shooting Association International Championships

Champion — J. H. Sheffield, Scarboro, Ont., 196.
Woman — Ila Hill, Troy, Mich., 184.

Junior — John Haynes III, Vivian, La., 179.
Senior — Cy Witham, Santa Barbara, Cal., 169.

Shuffleboard Championships in 1975

National Singles Championship, St. Petersburg, Fla., Mar. 3-5—Men's Open, William Folberth; Men's Closed, Lefty Krapp; Women's Open, Mary Eldridge; Women's Closed, Maude Mitchell.
National Doubles Championship, Jan. 13-15—Men, Merritt Gordon and Jason Baade; Women, Marie Sutton and Mary Eldridge.
Summer National Championships, Lakeside, Ohio, July 21-26—Men's Open, Art Davis; Men's Closed, Dr. H. A. Rutschow; Ladies Open, Betty Stone; Ladies Closed, Elsie Hodges; Men's Doubles, Bill Crowe and Denver Donelson; Ladies Division, Kay Smock and Elsie Hawkins.

World Record Fish Caught by Rod and Reel

Source: Salt-Water: International Game Fish Association. Fresh-Water: Field & Stream Magazine.
Records confirmed to July, 1975

Salt Water Fish

The International Game Fish Assn. revised its standards for world records, effective July 1, 1970. Line samples and line tests are now required in order for a world record application to be recognized. Records listed below are based on the new standards.

Species	Weight	Length	Girth	Where caught	Date	Angler
Albacore	74 lbs. 13 oz.	4'2"	34³/₄"	Arguineguin, Canary Islands	Oct. 28, 1973	Olof Idegren
Amberjack	149 lbs.	5'11"	41³/₄"	Bermuda	June 21, 1964	Peter Simons
Barracuda, Great	83 lbs.	6''/₄'	29"	Lagos, Nigeria	Jan. 13, 1952	K. J. W. Hackett
Bass, Black Sea	8 lbs.	1'10"	19"	Nantucket Sound, Mass.	May 13, 1951	H. R. Rider
Bass, Giant Sea	563 lbs. 8 oz.	7'5"	72"	Anacapa Island, California	Aug. 20, 1968	James D. McAdam, Jr.
Bass, Sea	8 lbs.	1'10"	19"	Nantucket Sound, Mass.	May 13, 1951	H.R. Rider
Bass, Striped	72 lbs.	4'6¹/₂"	31"	Cuttyhunk, Mass.	Oct. 10, 1969	Edward J. Kirker
Blackfish (or Tautog)	21 lbs. 6 oz.	2'7¹/₂'	23¹/₂"	Cape May, N.J.	June 12, 1954	R. N. Sheafer
Bluefish	31 lbs. 12 oz.	3'11"	23"	Hatteras Inlet, North Carolina	Jan. 30, 1972	James M. Hussey
Bonefish	19 lbs.	3'3⁵/₈"	17"	Zululand, S. Africa	May 26, 1962	Brian W. Batchelor
Bonito, Oceanic	39 lbs. 15 oz.	3'3"	28"	Walker Cay, Bahamas	Jan. 21, 1952	F. Drowley
(Skipjack Tuna)	40 lbs.	3'2²/₄"	27¹/₂"	Baie du Tambeau, Mauritius	Apr. 19, 1971	Joseph R. P. Caboche, Jr.
Cobia	110 lbs. 5 oz.	5'3"	34"	Mombasa, Kenya	Sept. 8, 1964	Eric Tinworth
Cod	98 lbs. 12 oz.	5'3"	41"	Isle of Shoals, Mass.	June 8, 1969	Alphonse Bielevich
Dolphin	85 lbs.	5'9"	37¹/₂"	Spanish Wells, Bahamas	May 29, 1968	Richard Seymour
Drum, Black	111 lbs.	4'5¹/₂"	45³/₄"	Cape Charles, Va.	May 20, 1973	Betty Hall
	111 lbs.	4'8"	45"	Cape Charles, Va.	May 3, 1974	G. L. Hopkins
Drum, Red	90 lbs.	4'7¹/₂"	38¹/₄"	Rodanthe, N.C.	Nov. 7, 1973	Elvin Hooper
Flounder	30 lbs. 12 oz.	3'2¹/₂'	30¹/₂"	Vina del Mar, Chile	Nov. 1, 1971	Augusto Nunez Moreno
Jewfish	680 lbs.	7'1¹/₂'	66"	Fernandina Beach, Fla.	May 20, 1961	Lynn Joyner
Marlin, King	78 lbs. 12 oz.	5'5¹/₂'	30"	La Romana, Dominican Republic	Nov. 26, 1971	Fernando Viyella
Marlin, Black	1,560 lbs.	14'6"	81"	Cabo Blanco, Peru	Aug. 4, 1953	A. C. Glassell, Jr.
Marlin, Atlantic Blue	1,142 lbs.	13'9"	80"	Nags Head, N.C.	July 26, 1974	Jack Herrington
Marlin, Pacific Blue	1,153 lbs.	14'8"	73"	Guam	Aug. 21, 1969	Greg Perez
Marlin, Striped	415 lbs.	11'	52"	Cape Brett, N.Z.	Mar. 31, 1964	B. C. Bain
Marlin, White	159 lbs. 8 oz.	9'	36"	Pompano Beach, Fla.	Apr. 25, 1953	W. E. Johnson
Permit	50 lbs. 8 oz.	3'8³/₄'	33³/₄"	Key West, Fla.	Mar. 15, 1971	Marshall Earnest
Pollock	43 lbs. 12 oz.	4'2"	29³/₄"	Nantucket Is., Mass.	Sept. 9, 1974	Donald Bedford
Runner, Rainbow	30 lbs. 15 oz.	3'11"	22"	Kauai, Hawaii	Apr. 27, 1963	Holbrook Goodale
Roosterfish	114 lbs.	5'4''	33''	La Paz, Mex.	June 1, 1960	Abe Sackheim
Sailfish, Atlantic	128 lbs. 1 oz.	8'10¹/₄'	34¹/₄"	Luanda Angola	Mar. 27, 1974	Harm Steyn
Sailfish, Pacific	221 lbs.	10'9''	....	Santa Cruz Is.	Feb. 12, 1947	C. W. Stewart
Seabass, White	83 lbs. 12 oz.	5'5¹/₂'	34"	San Felipe, Mexico	Mar. 31, 1953	L. C. Baumgardner
Seatrout, Spotted	15 lbs. 6 oz.	2'11"	23³/₄"	Jensen Beach, Fla.	May 4, 1969	Michael J. Foremny
Shark, Blue	410 lbs.	11'6"	52"	Rockport, Mass.	Sept. 1, 1960	R. C. Webster
	410 lbs.	11'2''	52¹/₂''	Rockport, Mass.	Aug. 17, 1967	Martha Webster
Shark, Hammerhead	406 lbs.	8'4"	54"	Lottin Point, N.Z.	Feb. 26, 1974	Mrs. H. M. Wood
Shark, Mako	1,061 lbs.	12'2''	79¹/₂''	Mayor Island, N.Z.	Feb. 17, 1970	James Penwarden
Shark, Man-Eater or White	2,664 lbs.	16'10''	9'6''	Cedunea, So. Australia	Apr. 21, 1959	Alfred Dean
Shark, Porbeagle	430 lbs.	8'	63''	Channel Island, Eng.	June 29, 1969	Desmond Bougourd
Shark, Thresher	739 lbs.	8'10"	68"	Tutukaka, N.Z.	Feb. 17, 1975	Brian Galvin
Shark, Tiger	1,780 lbs.	13'10¹/₂'	103"	Cherry Grove, S.C.	June 14, 1964	Walter Maxwell
Snook	52 lbs. 6 oz.	4'1¹/₂'	26"	La Paz, Mexico	Jan. 9, 1963	Jane Haywood
Swordfish	1,182 lbs.	14'11¹/₂'	78''	Iquique, Chile	May 7, 1953	L. Marron
Tanguigue	81 lbs.	5'11¹/₂"	29¹/₄"	Karachi, Pakistan	Aug. 27, 1960	George E. Rusinak

Species	Weight	Length	Girth	Where caught	Date	Angler
Tarpon	283 lbs.	7'2¹/₂"	....	L. Maracaibo, Venezuela	Mar. 19, 1956	M. Salazar
Tuna, Allison (Yellowfin)	308 lbs.	7'	57"	San Benedicto Isl., Mexico	Jan. 18, 1973	Harold J. Tolson
Tuna, Atlantic Bigeye	321 lbs. 12 oz.	7'4¹/₄"	58¹/₄"	Hudson Canyon, N.J.	Aug. 19, 1972	Vito LoCaputo
Tuna, Pacific Bigeye	435 lbs.	7'9"	63¹/₂"	Cabo Blanco, Peru	Apr. 17, 1957	Dr. Russel Lee
Tuna, Blackfin	38 lbs.	3'3¹/₄"	28³/₄"	Bermuda	June 26, 1970	Archie L. Dickens
	38 lbs.	3'5"	28"	Islamorada, Fla.	May 21, 1973	Elizabeth Jean Wade
Tuna, Bluefin	1,120 lbs.	12'2"	85¹/₂"	P.E.I., Canada	Oct. 19, 1973	Lee Coffin
Tunny, Little	20 lbs. 2 oz.	3¹/₂"	20⁵/₈"	Charleston, S.C.	May 19, 1974	Mrs. Alberta Herring
Wahoo	149 lbs.	6'7³/₄"	37¹/₂"	Cat Cay, Bahamas	June 15, 1962	John Pirovano
Weakfish	19 lbs. 8 oz.	3'1"	23³/₄"	Trinidad, W. Indies	Apr. 13, 1962	Dennis Hall
Yellowtail	111 lbs.	5'2"	38"	Bay of Islands, New Zealand	June 11, 1961	A. F. Plim

Freshwater Fish

Species	Weight	Length	Girth	Where caught	Date	Angler
Bass, Largemouth	22 lbs. 4 oz.	32¹/₂"	28¹/₂"	Montgomery Lake, Ga.	June 2, 1932	George W. Perry
Bass, Redeye	6 lbs. ¹/₂ oz.	20¹/₂"	15⁴/₅"	Hallawakee Creek, Ala.	Mar. 24, 1967	Thomas Sharpe
Bass, Rock	3 lbs.	13¹/₂"	10³/₄"	York River, Ont.	Aug. 1, 1974	Peter Gulgin
Bass, Smallmouth	11 lbs. 15 oz.	27"	21²/₃"	Dale Hollow Lake, Ky.	July 9, 1955	David L. Hayes
Bass, Spotted	8 lbs. 10¹/₂ oz.	23¹/₂"	19⁷/₈"	Smith Lake, Ala.	Feb. 25, 1972	Billy Henderson
Bass, White	5 lbs. 5 oz.	19¹/₂"	17"	Ferguson Lake, Calif.	March 8, 1972	Norman W. Mize
Bass, Yellow	2 lbs. 2 oz.	14"	13"	Lake Monona, Wis.	Jan. 18, 1972	James Thrun
Black Bullhead	8 lbs.	24"	17³/₄"	Lake Waccabuc, N.Y.	Aug. 1, 1951	Kani Evans
Bluegill	4 lbs. 12 oz.	15"	18¹/₄"	Ketona Lake, Ala.	Apr. 9, 1950	T. S. Hudson
Bowfin	19 lbs. 12 oz.	39"		Lake Marion, S.C.	Nov. 5, 1972	M. R. Webster
Buffalo, Bigmouth	43 lbs. 6 oz.	40"	38"	West Okoboji Lake, Iowa	Apr. 30, 1974	James D. Grim
Buffalo, Smallmouth	22 lbs. ¹/₂ oz.	33¹/₂"	22¹/₂"	Barbwell Creek, Wis.	May 25, 1973	Greg Hougelin
Carp	55 lbs. 5 oz.	42"	31"	Clearwater Lake, Minn.	July 10, 1952	Frank J. Ledwein
Catfish, Blue	97 lbs.	57"	37"	Missouri River, S.D.	Sept. 16, 1959	E. B. Elliott
Catfish, Channel	58 lbs.	47¹/₂"	29¹/₈"	Santee-Cooper Res., S.C.	July 7, 1964	W. B. Whaley
Catfish, Flathead	79 lbs. 8 oz.	44"	27"	White River, Ind.	Aug. 13, 1955	Glenn T. Simpson
Char, Arctic	29 lbs. 11 oz.	39³/₄"	26"	Arctic River, N.W.T.	Aug. 21, 1968	Jeanne P. Branson
Crappie, Black	5 lbs.	19¹/₄"	18⁵/₈"	Santee-Cooper Res., S.C.	Mar. 15, 1957	Paul E. Foust
Crappie, White	5 lbs. 3 oz.	21"	19"	Enid Dam, Miss.	July 31, 1957	Fred L. Bright
Dolly Varden	32 lbs.	40¹/₂"	29³/₄"	L. Pend Oreille, Idaho	Oct. 27, 1949	N. L. Higgins
Drum, Freshwater	54 lbs. 8 oz.	31¹/₂"	29"	Nickajack Lake, Tenn.	Apr. 20, 1972	Benny E. Hull
Gar, Alligator	279 lbs.	93"	....	Rio Grande R., Texas	Dec. 2, 1951	Bill Valverde
Gar, Longnose	50 lbs. 5 oz.	72¹/₄"	22¹/₄"	Trinity River, Texas	July 30, 1954	Townsend Miller
Grayling, American	5 lbs. 15 oz.	29¹/₄"	15¹/₄"	Katseyedie River, N.W.T.	Aug. 16, 1967	Jeanne P. Branson
Kokanee	5 lbs.	24¹/₂"	13"	Priest Lake, Idaho	June 9, 1974	Melissa Stevens
Muskellunge	69 lbs. 15 oz.	64¹/₂"	31³/₄"	St. Lawrence River, N.Y.	Sept. 22, 1957	Arthur Lawton
Perch, White	4 lbs. 12 oz.	19¹/₂"	13"	Messalonskee Lake, Maine	June 4, 1949	Mrs. Earl Small
Perch, Yellow	4 lbs. 3¹/₂ oz.	....	....	Bordentown, N.J.	May, 1865	Dr. C. C. Abbot
Pickerel, Chain	9 lbs. 6 oz.	31"	14"	Homerville, Ga.	Feb. 17, 1961	Baxley McQuaig, Jr.
Pike, Northern	46 lbs. 2 oz.	52¹/₂"	25"	Sacandaga Res., N.Y.	Sept. 15, 1940	Peter Dubuc
Redhorse, Silver	4 lbs. 2 oz.	20¹/₂"	14"	Gasconade River, Mo.	Oct. 5, 1974	C. Larry McKinney
Salmon, Atlantic	79 lbs. 2 oz.	....	....	Tana River, Norway	1928	Henrik Henriksen
Salmon, Chinook	92 lbs.	58¹/₂"	36"	Skeena River, B.C.	July 19, 1959	Heinz Wichmann
Salmon, Chum	24 lbs. 4 oz.	40¹/₂"	22⁷/₈"	Margarita Bay, Alaska	Aug. 19, 1974	Richard Coleman
Salmon, Landlocked	22 lbs. 8 oz.	36"	est.20"	Sebago Lake, Maine	Aug. 1, 1907	Edward Blakely

Species	Weight	Length	Girth	Where caught	Date	Angler
Salmon, Silver	31 lbs.	....	....	Cowichan Bay, B. C.	Oct. 11, 1947	Mrs. Lee Hallberg
Sauger	8 lbs. 12 oz.	28''	15''	Lake Sakakawea, N. D.	Oct. 6, 1971	Mike Fischer
Shad, American	9 lbs. 2 oz.	25''	17$^1/_2$''	Enfield, Conn.	Apr. 28, 1973	Edward P. Nelson
Sturgeon, White	360 lbs.	111''	86''	Snake River, Idaho	April 24, 1956	Willard Cravens
Sunfish, Green	2 lbs. 2 oz.	14$^3/_4$''	14''	Stockton Lake, Mo.	June 18, 1971	Paul M. Dilley
Sunfish, Redear	4 lbs. 8 oz.	16$^1/_4$''	17$^3/_4$''	Chase City, Va.	June 19, 1970	Maurice E. Ball
Trout, Brook	14$^1/_2$ lbs.	31$^1/_2$''	11$^1/_2$''	Nipigon River, Ontario	July, 1916	Dr. W. J. Cook
Trout, Brown	39$^1/_2$ lbs.	....	....	Lock Awe, Scotland	1866	W. Muir
Trout, Cutthroat	41 lbs.	39''	....	Pyramid Lake, Nev.	Dec., 1925	J. Skimmerhorn
Trout, Golden	11 lbs.	28''	16''	Cook's Lake, Wyo.	Aug. 5, 1948	Charles S. Reed
Trout, Lake	65 lbs.	52"	38"	Great Bear Lake, N.W.T.	Aug. 8, 1970	Larry Daunis
Trout, Rainbow or Kamloops	42 lbs. 2 oz.	43''	23$^1/_2$''	Bell Island, Alaska	June 22, 1970	David Robert White
Trout, Sunapee	11 lbs. 8 oz.	33''	17$^1/_4$''	Lake Sunapee, N. H.	Aug. 1, 1954	Ernest Theoharis
Trout, Tiger	10 lbs.	27"	16$^3/_4$"	Deerskin River, Wis.	May 23, 1974	Charles J. Mattek
Walleye	25 lbs.	41''	29''	Old Hickory Lake, Tenn.	Aug. 1, 1960	Mabry Harper
Warmouth	2 lbs.	12"	12$^1/_2$"	Sylvania, Ga.	May 4, 1974	Carlton Robbins
Whitefish, Lake	13 lbs.	32$^1/_4$"	19"	Great Bear Lake, N.W.T.	July 14, 1974	Robert L. Stintsman
Whitefish, Mountain	5 lbs.	19''	14''	Athabasca R., Alberta	June 3, 1963	Orville Welch

James E. Sullivan Memorial Trophy Winners

The James E. Sullivan Memorial Trophy, named after the former president of the AAU and inaugurated in 1930, is awarded annually by the AAU to the athlete who "by his or her performance, example and influence as an amateur, has done the most during the year to advance the cause of sportsmanship."

Year	Winner	Sport
1930	Bobby Jones	Golf
1931	Barney Berlinger	Track
1932	Jim Bausch	Track
1933	Glenn Cunningham	Track
1934	Bill Bonthron	Track
1935	Lawson Little	Golf
1936	Glenn Morris	Track
1937	Don Budge	Tennis
1938	Don Lash	Track
1939	Joe Burk	Rowing
1940	Greg Rice	Track
1941	Leslie Mac Mitchell	Track
1942	Cornelius Warmerdam	Track
1943	Gilbert Dodds	Track
1944	Ann Curtis	Swimming
1945	Doc Blanchard	Football
1946	Arnold Tucker	Football
1947	John Kelly Jr.	Rowing
1948	Robert Mathias	Track
1949	Dick Button	Skating
1950	Fred Wilt	Track
1951	Rev. Robert Richards	Track
1952	Horace Ashenfelter	Track
1953	Dr. Sammy Lee	Diving
1954	Mal Whitfield	Track
1955	Harrison Dillard	Track
1956	Patricia McCormick	Diving
1957	Bobby Joe Morrow	Track
1958	Glenn Davis	Track
1959	Parry O'Brien	Track
1960	Rafer Johnson	Track
1961	Wilma Rudolph Ward	Track
1962	James Beatty	Track
1963	John Pennel	Track
1964	Don Schollander	Swimming
1965	Bill Bradley	Basketball
1966	Jim Ryun	Track
1967	Randy Matson	Track
1968	Debbie Meyer	Swimming
1969	Bill Toomey	Track
1970	John Kinsella	Swimming
1971	Mark Spitz	Swimming
1972	Frank Shorter	Track
1973	Bill Walton	Basketball
1974	Rick Wohlhutter	Track

National Amateur Bicycle Championships in 1975

Milwaukee, Wis. (Road); North Brook, Ill. (Track)

Road

Senior Men—John Howard, Texas
Junior Men—Larry Shields, Cal.
Senior Women—Linda Stein, Cal.
Intermediate Boys—Chris Springer, Cal.
Midget Boys—Troy Stetina, Ind.
Veterans—Nikola Farac-Ban, Cal.

Senior Men 10 Mile—Leroy Gatto, Cal.
Senior Men 1000 Meter—Steve Woznick.
Senior Women Sprints—Sue Novara, Mich.
Senior Women 3000 Meter Pursuit—Mary Jane Reoch, Pa.
Junior Men—Kurtis Miller, Cal.
Intermediate Boys—Chris Springer, Cal.
Intermediate Girls—Connie Paraskevin, Mich.
Midget Boys—Kevin Johnson, Mich.
Midget Girls—Jacque Bradley, Iowa
4000 Meter Team Pursuit—Ralph Therrio, Ron Skarin, Chris Haley, Rene Averseng, Cal.

Track

Senior Men Sprints—Steve Woznick, N.J.
Senior Men 4000 Meter Pursuit—Ron Skarin, Cal.

National AAU Gymnastics Championship in 1975

Cedar Rapids, Iowa

Men
Vaulting—Shinsuke Shoji, Memphis, Tenn.
Parallel Bars—Shinsuke Shoji.
Rings—Pete Studenski, Nebraska.
Pommel Horse—Russell Hoffman, West Chicago, Ill.
Floor Exercise—Ron Galimore, Tallahassee, Fla.
Horizontal Bar—Tim Shaw, California.

Women
Floor Exercise—Ann Carr, Philadelphia, Pa.
Uneven Bars—Ann Carr.
Vaulting—Ann Carr.
Balance Beam—Roxanne Pierce, Philadelphia, Pa.

Annual Results of Major Bowl Games

Rose Bowl, Pasadena

1902—Michigan 49, Stanford 0
1916—Wash. State 14, Brown 0
1917—Oregon 14, Pennsylvania 0
1918-19—Service Teams
1920—Harvard 7, Oregon 6
1921—California 28, Ohio State 0
1922—Wash. & Jeff. 0, California 0
1923—So. California 14, Penn State 3
1924—Navy 14, Washington 14
1925—Notre Dame 27, Stanford 10
1926—Alabama 20, Washington 19
1927—Alabama 7, Stanford 7
1928—Stanford 7, Pittsburgh 6
1929—Georgia Tech 8, California 7
1930—So. California 47, Pittsburgh 14
1931—Alabama 24, Wash. State 0
1932—So. California 21, Tulane 12
1933—So. California 35, Pittsburgh 0
1934—Columbia 7, Stanford 0
1935—Alabama 29, Stanford 13
1936—Stanford 7, So. Methodist 0

1937—Pittsburgh 21, Washington 0
1938—California 13, Alabama 0
1939—So. California 7, Duke 3
1940—So. California 14, Tennessee 0
1941—Stanford 21, Nebraska 13
1942—Oregon St. 20, Duke 16
    (at Durham)
1943—Georgia 9, UCLA 0
1944—So. California 29, Washington 0
1945—So. California 25, Tennessee 0
1946—Alabama 34, So. California 14
1947—Illinois 45, UCLA 14
1948—Michigan 49, So. California 0
1949—Northwestern 20, California 14
1950—Ohio State 17, California 14
1951—Michigan 14, California 6
1952—Illinois 40, Stanford 7
1953—So. California 7, Wisconsin 0
1954—Mich. State 28, UCLA 20
1955—Ohio State 20, So. California 7

1956—Mich. State 17, UCLA 14
1957—Iowa 35, Oregon St. 19
1958—Ohio State 10, Oregon 7
1959—Iowa 38, California 12
1960—Washington 44, Wisconsin 8
1961—Washington 17, Minnesota 7
1962—Minnesota 21, UCLA 3
1963—So. California 42, Wisconsin 37
1964—Illinois 17, Washington 7
1965—Michigan 34, Oregon St. 7
1966—UCLA 14, Mich. State 12
1967—Purdue 14, So. California 13
1968—Southern Cal. 14, Indiana 3
1969—Ohio State 27, Southern Cal 16
1970—Southern Cal 10, Michigan 3
1971—Stanford 27, Ohio State 17
1972—Stanford 13, Michigan 12
1973—So. California 42, Ohio State 17
1974—Ohio State 42, So. California 21
1975—So. California 18, Ohio State 17

Orange Bowl, Miami

1933—Miami (Fla.) 7, Manhattan 0
1934—Duquesne 33, Miami (Fla.) 7
1935—Bucknell 26, Miami (Fla.) 0
1936—Catholic U. 20, Mississippi 19
1937—Duquesne 13, Miss. State 12
1938—Auburn 6, Mich. State 0
1939—Tennessee 17, Oklahoma 0
1940—Georgia Tech 21, Missouri 7
1941—Miss. State 14, Georgetown 7
1942—Georgia 40, TCU 26
1943—Alabama 37, Boston Col. 21
1944—LSU 19, Texas A&M 14
1945—Tulsa 26, Georgia Tech 12
1946—Miami (Fla.) 13, Holy Cross 6
1947—Rice 8, Tennessee 0

1948—Georgia Tech 20, Kansas 14
1949—Texas 41, Georgia 28
1950—Santa Clara 21, Kentucky 13
1951—Clemson 15, Miami (Fla.) 14
1952—Georgia Tech 17, Baylor 14
1953—Alabama 61, Syracuse 6
1954—Oklahoma 7, Maryland 0
1955—Duke 34, Nebraska 7
1956—Oklahoma 20, Maryland 6
1957—Colorado 27, Clemson 21
1958—Oklahoma 48, Duke 21
1959—Oklahoma 21, Syracuse 6
1960—Georgia 14, Missouri 0
1961—Missouri 21, Navy 14

1962—LSU 25, Colorado 7
1963—Alabama 17, Oklahoma 0
1964—Nebraska 13, Auburn 7
1965—Texas 21, Alabama 17
1966—Alabama 39, Nebraska 28
1967—Florida 27, Georgia Tech 12
1968—Oklahoma 26, Tennessee 24
1969—Penn State 15, Kansas 14
1970—Penn State 10, Missouri 3
1971—Nebraska 17, Louisiana St. 12
1972—Nebraska 38, Alabama 6
1973—Nebraska 40, Notre Dame 6
1974—Penn State 16, Louisiana St. 9
1975—Notre Dame 13, Alabama 11

Sugar Bowl, New Orleans

1935—Tulane 20, Temple 14
1936—TCU 3, LSU 2
1937—Santa Clara 21, LSU 14
1938—Santa Clara 6, LSU 0
1939—TCU 15, Carnegie Tech 7
1940—Texas A&M 14, Tulane 13
1941—Boston Col. 19, Tennessee 13
1942—Fordham 2, Missouri 0
1943—Tennessee 14, Tulsa 7
1944—Georgia Tech 20, Tulsa 18
1945—Duke 29, Alabama 26
1946—Oklahoma A&M 33, St. Mary's 13
1947—Georgia 20, No. Carolina 10
1948—Texas 27, Alabama 7

1949—Oklahoma 14, No. Carolina 6
1950—Oklahoma 35, LSU 0
1951—Kentucky 13, Oklahoma 7
1952—Maryland 28, Tennessee 13
1953—Georgia Tech. 24, Mississippi 7
1954—Georgia Tech 42, West Virginia 19
1955—Navy 21, Mississippi 0
1956—Georgia Tech 7, Pittsburgh 0
1957—Baylor 13, Tennessee 7
1958—Mississippi 39, Texas 7
1959—LSU 7, Clemson 0
1960—Mississippi 21, LSU 0
1961—Mississippi 14, Rice 6
1962—Alabama 10, Arkansas 3

1963—Mississippi 17, Arkansas 13
1964—Alabama 12, Mississippi 7
1965—LSU 13, Syracuse 10
1966—Missouri 20, Florida 18
1967—Alabama 34, Nebraska 7
1968—LSU 20, Wyoming 13
1969—Arkansas 16, Georgia 2
1970—Mississippi 27, Arkansas 22
1971—Tennessee 34, Air Force 13
1972—Oklahoma 40, Auburn 22
*1972 (Dec.)—Oklahoma 14, Penn State 0
1973—Notre Dame 24, Alabama 23
1974—Nebraska 13, Florida 10
  *Penn St. awarded game by forfeit

Cotton Bowl, Dallas

1937—TCU 16, Marquette 6
1938—Rice 28, Colorado 14
1939—St. Mary's 20, Texas Tech 13
1940—Clemson 6, Boston Col. 3
1941—Texas A&M 13, Fordham 12
1942—Alabama 29, Texas A&M 21
1943—Texas 14, Georgia Tech 7
1944—Randolph Field 7, Texas 7
1945—Oklahoma A&M 34, TCU 0
1946—Texas 40, Missouri 27
1947—Arkansas 0, LSU 0
1948—So. Methodist 13, Penn State 13
1949—So. Methodist 21, Oregon 13

1950—Rice 27, No. Carolina 13
1951—Tennessee 20, Texas 14
1952—Kentucky 20, TCU 7
1953—Texas 16, Tennessee 0
1954—Rice 28, Alabama 6
1955—Georgia Tech 14, Arkansas 6
1956—Mississippi 14, TCU 13
1957—TCU 28, Syracuse 27
1958—Navy 20, Rice 7
1959—TCU 0, Air Force 0
1960—Syracuse 23, Texas 14
1961—Duke 7, Arkansas 6
1962—Texas 12, Mississippi 7

1963—LSU 13, Texas 0
1964—Texas 28, Navy 6
1965—Arkansas 10, Nebraska 7
1966—LSU 14, Arkansas 7
1967—Georgia 24, So. Methodist 9
1968—Texas A&M 20, Alabama 16
1969—Texas 36, Tennessee 13
1970—Texas 21, Notre Dame 17
1971—Notre Dame 24, Texas 11
1972—Penn State 30, Texas 6
1973—Texas 17, Alabama 13
1974—Nebraska 19, Texas 3
1975—Penn State 41, Baylor 20

Liberty Bowl, Memphis

1959—Penn State 7, Alabama 0
1960—Penn State 41, Oregon 12
1961—Syracuse 15, Miami 14
1962—Oregon 6, Villanova 0
1963—Miss. State 16, N. C. State 12
1964—Utah 32, West Virginia 6

1965—Mississippi 13, Auburn 7
1966—Miami (Fla.) 14, Va. Tech 7
1967—N. C. State 14, Georgia 7
1968—Mississippi 34, Va. Tech 17
1969—Colorado 47, Alabama 33

1970—Tulane 17, Colorado 3
1971—Tennessee 14, Arkansas 13
1972—Georgia Tech 31, Iowa State 30
1973—No. Carolina St. 31, Kansas 18
1974—Tennessee 7, Maryland 3

Fiesta Bowl, Phoenix

1971—Arizona St. 45, Florida St. 38
1972—Arizona St. 49, Missouri 35

1973—Arizona St. 28, Pittsburgh 7

1974—Okla. St. 16, Brigham Young 6

Sun Bowl, El Paso

936—Hardin Simmons 14, New Mex. St. 14
937—Hardin-Simmons 34, Texas Mines 6
938—West Virginia 7, Texas Tech 6
939—Utah 26, New Mexico 0
940—Catholic U. 0, Arizona St. 0
941—Western Reserve 26, Arizona St. 13
942—Tulsa 6, Texas Tech 0
943—Second Air Force 13, Hardin-Simmons 7
944—Southwestern (Tex.) 7, New Mexico 0
945—Southwestern (Tex.) 35, U. of Mex. 0
946—New Mexico 34, Denver 24
947—Cincinnati 38, Virginia Tech 6

1948—Miami (O.) 13, Texas Tech 12
1949—West Virginia 21, Texas Mines 12
1950—Texas Western 33, Georgetown 20
1951—West Texas St. 14, Cincinnati 13
1952—Texas Tech 25, Col. Pacific 14
1953—Col. Pacific 26, Miss. Southern 7
1954—Texas Western 37, Miss. Southern 14
1955—Texas Western 47, Florida St. 20
1956—Wyoming 21, Texas Tech 14
1957—Geo. Washington 13, Tex. Western 0
1958—Louisville 34, Drake 20
1959—Wyoming 14, Hardin-Simmons 6
1960—New Mexico St. 28, No. Texas St. 8
1961—New Mexico St. 20, Utah State 13

1962—Villanova 17, Wichita 9
1963—West Texas St. 15, Ohio U. 14
1964—Oregon 21, So. Methodist 14
1965—Georgia 7, Texas Tech 0
1966—Texas Western 13, TCU 12
1967—Wyoming 28, Florida St. 20
1968—UTex El Paso 14, Mississippi 7
1969—Auburn 34, Arizona 10
1969—(Dec. 20) Nebraska 45, Georgia 6
1970—Georgia Tech. 17, Texas Tech. 9
1971—LSU 33, Iowa State 15
1972—North Carolina 32, Texas Tech 28
1973—Missouri 34, Auburn 17
1974—Mississippi St. 26, North Carolina 24

Gator Bowl, Jacksonville

946—Wake Forest 26, So. Car. 14
947—Oklahoma 34, N.C. State 13
948—Maryland 20, Georgia 20
949—Clemson 24, Missouri 23
950—Maryland 20, Missouri 7
951—Wyoming 20, Wash. & Lee 7
952—Miami (Fla.) 14, Clemson 0
953—Florida 14, Tulsa 13
954—Texas Tech 35, Auburn 13
955—Auburn 33, Baylor 13

1956—Vanderbilt 25, Auburn 13
1957—Georgia Tech 21, Pittsburgh 14
1958—Tennessee 3, Texas A&M 0
1959—Mississippi 7, Florida 3
1960—Arkansas 14, Georgia Tech 7
1961—Florida 13, Baylor 12
1962—Penn State 30, Georgia Tech 15
1963—Florida 17, Penn State 7
1964—No. Carolina 35, Air Force 0
1965—Florida St. 36, Oklahoma 19

1966—Georgia Tech 31, Texas Tech 21
1967—Tennessee 18, Syracuse 12
1968—Penn State 17, Florida St. 17
1969—Missouri 35, Alabama 10
1969—(Dec. 27) Florida 14, Tenn. 13
1971—Auburn 35, Mississippi 28
1972—Georgia 7, N. Carolina 3
1973—Auburn 24, Colorado 3
1973—(Dec.) Tex. Tech. 28, Tenn. 19
1974—Auburn 27, Texas 3

Peach Bowl, Atlanta

968—LSU 31, Florida St. 27
969—West Virginia 14, S. Carolina 3
970—Arizona St. 48, N. Carolina 26

1971—Mississippi 41, Georgia Tech. 18
1972—N. Carolina St. 49, W. Va. 13

1973—Georgia 17, Maryland 16
1974—Vanderbilt 6, Texas Tech. 6

Bluebonnet Bowl, Houston

959—Clemson 23, TCU 7
960—Texas 3, Alabama 3
961—Kansas 33, Rice 7
962—Missouri 14, Georgia Tech 10
963—Baylor 14, LSU 7
964—Tulsa 14, Mississippi 7

1965—Tennessee 27, Tulsa 6
1966—Texas 19, Mississippi 0
1967—Colorado 31, Miami (Fla.) 21
1968—SMU 28, Oklahoma 27
1969—Houston 36, Auburn 7

1970—Oklahoma 24, Alabama 24
1971—Colorado 29, Houston 17
1972—Tennessee 24, Louisiana St. 17
1973—Houston 47, Tulane 7
1974—N. Carolina St. 31, Houston 31

College Football Conference Champions

Atlantic Coast

961—Duke
962—Duke
963—No. Carolina St., No. Carolina
964—No. Carolina St.
965—Duke
966—Clemson
967—Clemson
968—No. Carolina St.
969—So. Carolina
970—Wake Forest
971—North Carolina
972—North Carolina
973—No. Carolina St.
974—Maryland

Ivy League

1961—Columbia, Harvard
1962—Dartmouth
1963—Dartmouth, Princeton
1964—Princeton
1965—Dartmouth
1966—Dartmouth, Harvard, Princeton
1967—Yale
1968—Yale, Harvard
1969—Princeton, Dartmouth, Yale
1970—Dartmouth
1971—Dartmouth, Cornell
1972—Dartmouth
1973—Dartmouth
1974—Yale, Harvard

Big Eight

1961—Colorado
1962—Oklahoma
1963—Nebraska
1964—Nebraska
1965—Nebraska
1966—Nebraska
1967—Oklahoma
1968—Kansas, Oklahoma
1969—Missouri, Nebraska
1970—Nebraska
1971—Nebraska
1972—Nebraska
1973—Oklahoma
1974—Oklahoma

Big Ten

1961—Ohio State
1962—Wisconsin
1963—Illinois
1964—Michigan
1965—Michigan St.
1966—Michigan St.
1967—Indiana, Purdue, Minn.
1968—Ohio State
1969—Michigan, Ohio State
1970—Ohio State
1971—Michigan
1972—Ohio State, Michigan
1973—Ohio State, Michigan
1974—Ohio State, Michigan

Mid-America

961—Bowling Green
962—Bowling Green
963—Ohio Univ.
964—Bowling Green
965—Bowling Green, Miami
966—Miami, Western Mich.
967—Toledo, Ohio Univ.
968—Ohio Univ.
969—Toledo
970—Toledo
971—Toledo
972—Kent State
973—Miami
974—Miami

Missouri Valley

1961—Wichita
1962—Tulsa
1963—Cincinnati, Wichita
1964—Cincinnati
1965—Tulsa
1966—No. Texas, Tulsa
1967—North Texas
1968—Memphis State
1969—Memphis State
1970—Louisville
1971—Memphis State
1972—Louisville, W. Texas, Drake
1973—No. Texas St., Tulsa
1974—Tulsa

Southeastern

1961—Alabama, Louisiana St.
1962—Mississippi
1963—Mississippi
1964—Alabama
1965—Alabama
1966—Alabama, Georgia
1967—Tennessee
1968—Georgia
1969—Tennessee
1970—Louisiana State
1971—Alabama
1972—Alabama
1973—Alabama
1974—Florida

Southwest

1961—Texas, Arkansas
1962—Texas
1963—Texas
1964—Arkansas
1965—Arkansas
1966—Southern Methodist
1967—Texas A & M
1968—Texas, Arkansas
1969—Texas
1970—Texas
1971—Texas
1972—Texas
1973—Texas
1974—Baylor

Pacific Eight

961—UCLA
962—USC
963—Washington
964—Oregon St., USC
965—UCLA
966—USC
967—USC

1968—USC
1969—USC
1970—Stanford
1971—Stanford
1972—USC
1973—USC
1974—USC

Southern

1962—VMI
1963—Virginia Tech
1964—West Virginia
1965—West Virginia
1966—E. Carolina, William & Mary
1967—West Virginia

1968—Richmond
1969—Richmond, Davidson
1970—William & Mary
1971—Richmond
1972—East Carolina
1973—East Carolina
1974—VMI

College Football

University Division

Team	Nickname	Team Colors	Conference	Coach	1974 Record (W-L-T)
Air Force	Falcons	Blue & Silver	Independent	Ben Martin	2-9-0
Alabama	Crimson Tide	Crimson & White	Southeastern	Paul Bryant	11-1-0
Appalachian State	Mountaineers	Black & Gold	Southern	Jim Brakefield	6-5-0
Arizona State	Sun Devils	Maroon & Gold	Western Athletic	Frank Kush	7-5-0
Arizona	Wildcats	Red & Blue	Western Athletic	Jim Young	9-2-0
Arkansas	Razorbacks	Cardinal & White	Southwest	Frank Broyles	6-4-1
Arkansas State	Indians	Scarlet & Black	Southland	Bill Davidson	7-3-0
Army	Cadets	Black, Gold, Gray	Independent	Homer Smith	3-8-0
Auburn	Tigers	Orange & Blue	Southeastern	Ralph Jordan	10-2-0
Ball State	Cardinals	Cardinal & White	Mid-American	Dave McClain	6-4-0
Baylor	Bears	Green & Gold	Southwest	Grant Teaff	8-4-0
Boston College	Eagles	Maroon & Gold	Independent	Joseph Yukica	8-3-0
Bowling Green	Falcons	Orange & Brown	Mid-American	Don Nehlen	6-4-1
Brigham Young	Cougars	Royal Blue & White	Western Athletic	LaVell Edwards	7-4-1
Brown	Bruins	Brown & Cardinal	Ivy	John Anderson	5-4-0
California	Golden Bears	Blue & Gold	Pacific-8	Mike White	7-3-1
Central Michigan	Chippewas	Maroon & Gold	Mid-American	Roy Kramer	12-1-0
Cincinnati	Bearcats	Red & Black	Independent	Tommy Mason	7-4-0
Citadel	Bulldogs	Blue & White	Southern	Bobby Ross	4-7-0
Clemson	Tigers	Purple & Orange	Atlantic Coast	Jim Parker	7-4-0
Colgate	Red Raiders	Maroon	Independent	Neil Wheelwright	4-6-0
Colorado State	Rams	Green & Gold	Western Athletic	Sarkis Arslanian	4-6-1
Colorado	Buffaloes	Silver & Gold	Big Eight	Bill Mallory	5-6-0
Columbia	Lions	Blue & White	Ivy	Bill Campbell	1-8-0
Cornell	Big Red	Carnelian & White	Ivy	George Seifert	3-5-1
Dartmouth	Big Green	Dartmouth Green	Ivy	Jake Crouthamel	3-6-0
Davidson	Wildcats	Red & Black	Southern	Ed Farrell	2-7-0
Dayton	Flyers	Red & Blue	Independent	Ron Marciniak	3-8-0
Drake	Bulldogs	Blue & White	Missouri Valley	Jack Wallace	3-7-1
Duke	Blue Devils	Blue & White	Atlantic Coast	Mike McGee	6-5-0
East Carolina	Pirates	Purple & Gold	Southern	Pat Dye	7-4-0
Florida State	Seminoles	Garnet & Gold	Independent	Darrell Mudra	1-10-0
Florida	Gators	Orange & Blue	Southeastern	Doug Dickey	8-4-0
Fresno State	Bulldogs	Cardinal & Blue	Pacific Coast	J.R. Boone	5-7-0
Furman	Paladins	Purple & White	Southern	Art Baker	5-6-0
Georgia Tech	Yellow Jackets	Old Gold & White	Independent	Pepper Rodgers	6-5-0
Georgia	Bulldogs	Red & Black	Southeastern	Vince Dooley	6-6-0
Harvard	Crimson	Crimson	Ivy	Joe Restic	7-2-0
Hawaii	Rainbow Warriors	Green & White	Independent	Larry Price	6-5-0
Holy Cross	Crusaders	Royal Purple	Independent	Ed Doherty	5-5-1
Houston	Cougars	Scarlet & White	Southwest	Bill Yeoman	8-3-1
Idaho	Vandals	Silver & Gold	Big Sky	Ed Troxel	2-8-1
Illinois	Fighting Illini	Orange & Blue	Big Ten	Bob Blackman	6-4-1
Indiana	Fightin' Hoosiers	Cream & Crimson	Big Ten	Lee Corso	1-10-0
Iowa State	Cyclones	Cardinal & Gold	Big Eight	Earle Bruce	4-7-0
Iowa	Hawkeyes	Old Gold & Black	Big Ten	Bo Commings	3-8-0
Kansas State	Wildcats	Purple & White	Big Eight	Ellis Rainsberger	4-7-0
Kansas	Jayhawks	Crimson & Blue	Big Eight	Bud Moore	4-7-0
Kent State	Golden Flashes	Blue & Gold	Mid-American	Dennis Fitzgerald	7-4-0
Kentucky	Wildcats	Blue & White	Southeastern	Fran Curci	6-5-0
Lamar	Cardinals	Red & White	Southland	Vernon Glass	8-2-0
Long Beach State	Forty Niners	Brown & Gold	Pacific Coast	Wayne Howard	6-5-0
Louisiana State	Fighting Tigers	Purple & Gold	Southeastern	Charles McClendon	5-5-1
Louisiana Tech	Bulldogs	Red & Blue	Southland	Maxie Lambright	11-1-0
Louisville	Cardinals	Red, Black, White	Missouri Valley	Vince Gibson	4-7-0
Marshall	Thundering Herd	Green & White	Independent	Frank Ellwood	1-10-0
Maryland	Terps	Red & White	Atlantic Coast	Jerry Claiborne	8-4-0
McNeese State	Cowboys	Blue & Gold	Southland	Jack Doland	6-4-1
Memphis State	Tigers	Blue & Gray	Independent	Richard Williamson	7-4-0
Miami (Fla.)	Hurricanes	Orange, Green, White	Independent	Carl Selmer	6-5-0
Miami (Ohio)	Redskins	Red & White	Mid-American	Dick Crum	10-0-1
Michigan State	Spartans	Green & White	Big Ten	Denny Stolz	7-3-1
Michigan	Wolverines	Maize & Blue	Big Ten	Bo Schembechler	10-1-0
Minnesota	Golden Gophers	Maroon & Gold	Big Ten	Cal Stoll	4-7-0
Mississippi State	Bulldogs	Maroon & White	Southeastern	Bob Tyler	9-3-0
Mississippi	Rebels	Red & Blue	Southeastern	Ken Cooper	3-8-0
Missouri	Tigers	Old Gold & Black	Big Eight	Al Onofrio	7-4-0
Navy	Midshipmen	Navy Blue & Gold	Independent	George Welsh	4-7-0
Nebraska	Cornhuskers	Scarlet & Cream	Big Eight	Tom Osborne	9-3-0
New Mexico State	Aggies	Crimson & White	Missouri Valley	Jim Bradley	5-6-0
New Mexico	Lobos	Cherry & Silver	Western Athletic	Bill Mondt	4-6-1
North Carolina	Tar Heels	Blue & White	Atlantic Coast	Bill Dooley	7-5-0
North Carolina State	Wolfpack	Red & White	Atlantic Coast	Lou Holtz	9-2-1
North Texas State	Mean Green	Green & White	Independent	Hayden Fry	2-7-2
Northern Illinois	Huskies	Cardinal & Black	Mid-American	Jerry Ippoliti	4-7-0
Northeast Louisiana	Indians	Maroon & Gold	Independent	Ollie Keller	4-6-0
Northwestern	Wildcats	Purple & White	Big Ten	John Pont	3-8-0
Notre Dame	Fighting Irish	Gold & Blue	Independent	Dan Devine	10-2-0
Ohio State	Buckeyes	Scarlet & Gray	Big Ten	Woody Hayes	10-2-0
Ohio Univ.	Bobcats	Green & White	Mid-American	Bill Hess	6-5-0
Oklahoma State	Cowboys	Orange & Black	Big Eight	Jim Stanley	7-5-0
Oklahoma	Sooners	Crimson & Cream	Big Eight	Barry Switzer	11-0-0

?am	Nickname	Team Colors	Conference	Coach	1974 Record (W-L-T)
?egon State	Beavers	Orange & Black	Pacific-8	Dee Andros	3-8-0
?egon	Ducks	Green & Yellow	Pacific-8	Don Read	2-9-0
?cific	Tigers	Orange & Black	Pacific Coast	Chester Caddas	6-5-0
?nn State	Nittany Lions	Blue & White	Independent	Joe Paterno	10-2-0
?nnsylvania	Red & Blue	Red & Blue	Ivy	Harry Gamble	6-2-1
?tsburgh	Panthers	Old Gold & Navy Blue	Independent	John Majors	7-4-0
?inceton	Tigers	Orange & Black	Ivy	Bob Casciola	4-4-1
?rdue	Boilermakers	Old Gold & Black	Big Ten	Alex Agase	4-6-1
?ce	Owls	Blue & Gray	Southwest	Al Conover	2-8-1
?chmond	Spiders	Red & Blue	Southern	Jim Tait	5-5-0
?tgers	Scarlet Knights	Scarlet	Independent	Frank Burns	7-3-1
?n Diego State	Aztecs	Scarlet & Black	Pacific Coast	Claude Gilbert	8-2-1
?n Jose State	Spartans	Gold & White	Pacific Coast	Darryl Rogers	8-3-1
?uth Carolina	Fighting Gamecocks	Garnet & Black	Independent	Jim Carlen	4-7-0
?uthern California	Trojans	Cardinal & Gold	Pacific-8	John McKay	10-1-1
?uthern Illinois	Salukis	Maroon & White	Independent	Doug Weaver	2-9-0
?uthern Methodist	Mustangs	Red & Blue	Southwest	Dave Smith	6-4-1
?uthern Mississippi	Golden Eagles	Black & Gold	Independent	Bobby Collins	6-5-0
?uthwestern La.	Ragin' Cajuns	Vermilion & White	Southland	Augie Tamariello	2-9-0
?anford	Cardinals	Cardinal & White	Pacific-8	Jack Christiansen	5-4-2
?racuse	Orangemen	Orange	Independent	Frank Maloney	2-9-0
?mple	Owls	Cherry & White	Independent	Wayne Hardin	8-2-0
?nnessee	Volunteers	Orange & White	Southeastern	Bill Battle	7-3-2
?xas A & M.	Aggies	Maroon & White	Southwest	Emory Bellard	8-3-0
?xas Christian	Horned Frogs	Purple & White	Southwest	Jim Shofner	1-10-0
?xas Tech	Red Raiders	Scarlet & Black	Southwest	Steve Sloan	6-4-2
?xas	Longhorns	Orange & White	Southwest	Darrell Royal	8-4-0
?ledo	Rockets	Blue & Gold	Mid-American	Jack Murphy	6-5-0
?lane	Green Wave	Olive Green & Sky Blue	Independent	Bennie Ellender	5-6-0
?lsa	Golden Hurricane	Blue, Crimson, Gold	Missouri Valley	F. A. Dry	8-3-0
?CLA	Bruins	Navy Blue & Gold	Pacific-8	Dick Vermeil	6-3-2
?ah State	Aggies	Navy Blue & White	Independent	Phil Krueger	8-3-0
?ah	Utes	Crimson & White	Western Athletic	Tom Lovat	1-10-0
Texas Arlington	Mavericks	Royal Blue & White	Southland	Bud Elliott	1-10-0
Texas El Paso	Miners	Orange & White	Western Athletic	Gil Bartosh	4-7-0
?anderbilt	Commodores	Black & Gold	Southeastern	Fred Pancoast	7-3-2
?llanova	Wildcats	Blue & White	Independent	Dick Bedesem	3-8-0
?MI	Keydets	Red, White, Yellow	Southern	Bob Thalman	7-4-0
?rginia Polytech Inst.	Gobblers	Orange & Maroon	Independent	Jimmy Sharpe	4-7-0
?rginia	Cavaliers	Orange & Blue	Atlantic Coast	Sonny Randle	4-7-0
?ake Forest	Demon Deacons	Old Gold & Black	Atlantic Coast	Chuck Mills	1-10-0
?ashington State	Cougars	Crimson & Gray	Pacific-8	Jim Sweeney	2-9-0
?ashington	Huskies	Purple & Gold	Pacific-8	Don James	5-6-0
?estern Michigan	Broncos	Brown & Gold	Mid-American	Elliot Uzelac	3-8-0
?est Texas State	Buffaloes	Maroon & White	Missouri Valley	Gene Mayfield	6-5-0
?est Virginia	Mountaineers	Old Gold & Blue	Independent	Bobby Bowden	4-7-0
?ichita State	Shockers	Gold & Black	Missouri Valley	Jim Wright	1-9-1
?illiam & Mary	Indians	Green, Gold, Silver	Southern	Jim Root	4-7-0
?isconsin	Badgers	Cardinal & White	Big Ten	John Jardine	7-4-0
?yoming	Cowboys	Brown & Yellow	Western Athletic	Fred Akers	2-9-0
?ale	Bulldogs	Yale Blue	Ivy	Carmen Cozza	8-1-0

Selected College Division Teams

?kron	Zips	Blue & Gold	Independent	Jim Dennison	5-5-0
?abama A & M	Bulldogs	Maroon & White	Southern IAC	Louis Crews	4-7-0
?corn State	Braves	Purple & Gold	Southwestern	Marino Casem	9-2-0
?ma	Scots	Maroon & Cream	Michigan	Phil Brooks	4-5-0
?ustin Peay	Governors	Scarlet & White	Ohio Valley	Jack Bushofsky	3-7-1
?aldwin-Wallace	Yellow Jackets	Brown & Gold	Ohio	Lee J. Tressel	8-2-0
?ise State	Broncos	Orange & Blue	Big Sky	Tony Knap	10-2-0
?oston Univ.	Terriers	Scarlet & White	Yankee	Paul Kemp	5-4-1
?utler	Bulldogs	Blue & White	Indiana	Bill Sylvester	8-2-0
?arleton	Carls	Maize & Blue	Midwest	Dale Quist	4-5-0
?ase Reserve	Spartans	Blue & Gray	Presidents Athletic	Flory Mauriocourt	2-7-0
?hico State	Wildcats	Cardinal & White	Far Western	Dick Trimmer	4-7-0
?oast Guard	Cadets	Blue & White	Independent	Otto Graham	4-6-0
?oe	Kohawks	Crimson & Gold	Midwest	Wayne Phillips	8-1-0
?olorado Western	Mountaineers	Crimson & Slate	Rocky Mountain	William Noxon	6-3-0
?onnecticut	Huskies	Blue & White	Yankee	Larry Naviaux	4-6-0
?.W. Post	Pioneers	Green & Gold	Metropolitan	Dom Anile	6-4-0
?efiance	Yellow Jackets	Purple & Gold	Hoosier-Buckeye	Mike Snyder	5-5-0
?elaware	Fightin' Blue Hens	Blue & Gold	Independent	Harold Raymond	12-2-0
?enison	Big Red	Red & White	Ohio	Keith Piper	3-5-1
?e Pauw	Tigers	Old Gold & Black	Indiana	Tom Mont	7-3-0
?oane	Tigers	Orange & Black	Nebraska Inter.	Ray Best	6-3-0
?astern Michigan	Hurons	Green & White	Mid-American	George Mans	4-6-1
?mory & Henry	Wasps	Blue & Gold	Independent	Jimmy Hughes	3-8-0
?vansville	Purple Aces	Purple & White	Indiana	James Byers	8-2-0
?orida A & M	Rattlers	Orange & Green	Southern IAC	Rudy Hubbard	6-5-0
?aho State	Bengals	Orange & Black	Big Sky	Bob Griffin	5-5-0
?inois State	Redbirds	Red & White	Independent	Gerry Hart	6-5-0
?ohn Carroll	Blue Streaks	Blue & Gold	Presidents	Jerry Schweickert	7-2-0
?alamazoo	Hornets	Orange & Black	Michigan	Ed Baker	2-6-0
?enyon	Lords	Purple & White	Ohio	Philip Morse	2-6-1
?nox	Siwash	Purple & Gold	Midwest	Albert Reilly	1-8-0

Team	Nickname	Team Colors	Conference	Coach	1974 Record (W-L-T)
Lafayette	Leopards	Maroon & White	Independent	Neil Putnam	3-7
Lawrence	Vikings	Navy & White	Midwest	Ron Roberts	7-2
Lehigh	Engineers	Brown & White	Independent	Fred Dunlap	7-3
Los Angeles State	Diablos	Black & Gold	Cal. Collegiate	Jim Williams	5-4
Maine	Black Bears	Blue & White	Yankee	Walt Abbott	4-6
Massachusetts	Minutemen	Maroon & White	Yankee	Richard MacPherson	5-6
Michigan Tech	Huskies	Silver & Gold	Northern	Jim Kapp	9-0
Middlebury	Panthers	Blue & White	Independent	Mickey Heinecken	5-3
Middle Tenn	Blue Raiders	Blue & White	Ohio Valley	Ben Hurt	3-8
Montana State	Bobcats	Blue & Gold	Big Sky	Sonny Holland	7-3
Montana	Grizzlies	Copper, Silver, Gold	Big Sky	Jack Swarthout	3-6
Moorhead State	Dragons	Scarlet & White	Northern	Ross Fortier	4-5
Morgan State	Bears	Blue & Orange	Mid-Eastern	Nathaniel Taylor	5-5
Mt. Union	Purple Raiders	Purple & White	Ohio	Ken Wable	7-2
Muhlenberg	Mules	Cardinal & Gray	Middle Atlantic	Frank Marino	2-7
New Hampshire	Wildcats	Blue & White	Yankee	William Bowes	5-4
Norfolk State	Spartans	Green & Gold	Central	Dick Price	8-3
North Dakota State	Bison	Yellow & Green	North Central	Ev Kjelbertson	7-4
North Dakota	Sioux	Green & White	North Central	Jerry Olson	6-4
Northern Arizona	Lumberjacks	Blue & Gold	Big Sky	Joe Salem	3-6
Northern Michigan	Wildcats	Old Gold & Green	Independent	Gil Krueger	0-10
Ohio Northern	Polar Bears	Burnt Orange, Black	Ohio	A. Wallace Hood	2-7
Ohio Wesleyan	Battling Bishops	Red & Black	Ohio	Jack Fouts	4-5
Olivet	Comets	Cardinal & White	Michigan	Douglas Kay	7-2
Portland State	Vikings	Green & White	Independent	Darrel Davis	5-6
Puget Sound	Loggers	Green, Gold, Blue	Independent	Paul Wallrof	4-5
Redlands	Bulldogs	Maroon & Gray	So. Cal	Frank Serrao	7-2
Rhode Island	Rams	Blue & White	Yankee	Jack Gregory	5-5
Ripon	Redmen	Crimson & White	Midwest	William Connor	7-2
Rochester	Yellow Jackets	Yellow, Blue	Independent	Peter Stark	3-6
St. Cloud State	Huskies	Red & Black	Northern	Mike Simpson	5-5
St. Lawrence	Saints	Scarlet & Brown	ICAC	Ted Stratford	7-2
St. Norbert	Knights	Green & Gold	Independent	Howie Kolstad	8-2
St. Olaf	Lions	Black & Gold	Minn. IAC	Tom Porter	3-6
Santa Clara	Broncos	Cardinal & White	Independent	Pat Malley	7-3
Slippery Rock	Rockets	Green & White	Pennsylvania	Bob Di Spirito	8-1
So. Carolina State	Bulldogs	Garnet & Blue	Mid-Eastern	Willie Jeffries	8-4
South Dakota	Coyotes	Vermilion & White	North Central	Bernard Cooper	8-3
So. Dakota State	Jackrabbits	Yellow & Blue	North Central	John Gregory	6-5
Southern Oregon	Red Raiders	Red & Black	Evergreen	Scott Johnson	6-4
Swarthmore	Little Quakers	Garnet	Middle Atlantic	Lewis Elverson	0-7
Tennessee Tech	Golden Eagles	Purple & Gold	Ohio Valley	Don Wade	6-5
Texas Southern	Tigers	Maroon & Grey	Southwestern	Roderick Paige	6-4
Thiel	Tomcats	Blue & Gold	President's Athletic	James McCullough	4-4
Trenton State	Lions	Blue & Gold	New Jersey State	Dick Curl	5-4
Tufts	Jumbos	Blue & Brown	Independent	Paul Pawlak	3-5
Tuskegee	Golden Tigers	Gold, Crimson	Southern IAC	Haywood Scissum	11-1
Upsala	Vikings	Blue & Gray	Middle Atlantic	John Hooper	0-8
Valparaiso	Crusaders	Brown & Gold	Indiana	Norm Amundsen	3-6
Wash. & Jeff	Presidents	Red & Black	Presidents Athletic	Pat Mondock	1-7
Wash. & Lee	Generals	Royal Blue, White	Independent	William McHenry	1-8
Wayne State	Tartars	Green & Gold	Independent	Dick Lowry	7-3
Weber State	Wildcats	Purple & White	Big Sky	Dick Gwinn	4-7
Wesleyan	Cardinals	Red & Black	Little Three	Bill Macdermott	2-6
Western Carolina	Catamounts	Purple & Gold	Independent	Bob Waters	9-2
Western Illinois	Leathernecks	Purple & Gold	Independent	Brodie Westen	7-3
Western Kentucky	Hilltoppers	Red & White	Ohio Valley	Jimmy Feix	7-3
Wilkes	Colonels	Navy & Gold	Middle Atlantic	Roland Schmidt	7-2
Williams	Ephmen	Purple	Little Three	Robert Odell	7-1
Wittenberg	Tigers	Red & White	Ohio	Dave Maurer	7-1
Wooster	Fighting Scots	Black, Gold	Ohio	Don Hunsinger	2-6
Youngstown State	Penguins	Red & White	Independent	Bill Narduzzi	8-2

Heisman Trophy Winners

The Heisman Trophy is named after John Heisman, football coach and athletic director of the New York Downtown Athletic Club. Awarded annually to the nation's outstanding college football player.

Year	Player, College, Pos.	Year	Player, College, Pos.	Year	Player, College, Pos.
1935	Jay Berwanger, Chicago, HB	1949	Leon Hart, Notre Dame, E	1962	Terry Baker, Oregon State, QB
1936	Larry Kelley, Yale, E	1950	Vic Janowicz, Ohio State, NB	1963	Roger Staubach, Navy, QB
1937	Clinton Frank, Yale, QB	1951	Richard Kazmaier, Princeton, HB	1964	John Huarte, Notre Dame, QB
1938	David O'Brien, Tex. Christian, QB	1952	Billy Vessels, Oklahoma, HB	1965	Mike Garrett, USC, HB
1939	Nile Kinnick, Iowa, QB	1953	John Lattner, Notre Dame, NB	1966	Steve Spurrier, Florida, QB
1940	Tom Harmon, Michigan, HB	1954	Alan Ameche, Wisconsin, FB	1967	Gary Beban, UCLA, QB
1941	Bruce Smith, Minnesota, HB	1955	Howard Cassady, Ohio St., NB	1968	O. J. Simpson, USC, RB
1942	Frank Sinkwich, Georgia, HB	1956	Paul Hornung, Notre Dame, QB	1969	Steve Owens, Oklahoma, RB
1943	Angelo Bertelli, Notre Dame, QB	1957	John Crow, Texas A & M, HB	1970	Jim Plunkett, Stanford, QB
1944	Leslie Horvath, Ohio State, QB	1958	Pete Dawkins, Army, HB	1971	Pat Sullivan, Auburn, QB
1945	Felix Blanchard, Army, FB	1959	Billy Cannon, LSU, HB	1972	Johnny Rodgers, Nebraska, RB-P
1946	Glenn Davis, Army, HB	1960	Joe Bellino, Navy, HB	1973	John Cappelletti, Penn State, RB
1947	John Lujack, Notre Dame, QB	1961	Ernest Davis, Syracuse, HB	1974	Archie Griffin, Ohio State, RB
1948	Doak Walker, SMU, HB				

College Football Stadiums

School	Capacity	School	Capacity
Alabama Univ. of (Denny Stad.) University, Ala.	59,000	North Texas St. Univ. (Fouts Field), Denton	20,200
Arizona State Univ. (Sun Devil), Tempe	51,000	Northern Illinois Univ. (Huskie Stad.) DeKalb	20,257
Arizona, Univ. of (Arizona Stad.) Tucson	40,000	Northwestern Univ. (Dyche Stad.), Evanston, Ill.	55,000
Arkansas, Univ. of (Razorback Stad.) Fayetteville	43,500	Notre Dame Stad., South Bend, Ind.	59,075
Auburn Univ. (Jordan Hare Stad.), Auburn, Ala.	62,291	Ohio State Univ. (Ohio Stad.), Columbus	83,080
Baylor Univ. Stad., Waco, Texas.	48,000	Ohio Univ. (Don Peden Stad.), Athens	17,550
Boston Coll. (Alumni Stad.) Boston, Mass.	32,000	Oklahoma State (Lewis Stad.), Stillwater.	51,000
Bowling Green State Univ. (Doyt Perry Field).	23,272	Oklahoma, Univ. of (Owen Field), Norman	61,826
Brigham Young Univ. Utah.	30,000	Old Dominion Univ. (Foreman Field), Norfolk	32,000
Brown Stad., Providence, R. I.	20,000	Oregon St. Univ. (Parker Stad.), Corvallis.	41,000
Butler Univ. (Butler Bowl), Indianapolis, Ind.	19,500	Oregon, Univ. of (Autzen Stad.), Eugene	41,097
Cal., Univ. of (Memorial Stad.), Berkeley.	77,000	Pacific, Univ. of the (Pacific Memorial), Calif.	35,975
Central Mich. Univ. (Shorts Stad.), Mt. Pleasant	20,000	Penn. State Univ. (Beaver Stad.)	57,723
Cincinnati, Univ. of (Nippert), Ohio.	25,692	Penn., Univ. of (Franklin Field), Phila.	60,546
Citadel (Johnson Hagood Stadium), Charleston	22,500	Pittsburgh, Univ. of (Pitt. Stad.), Pa.	56,500
Clemson Univ. (Memorial Stad.), S.C.	43,451	Princeton, (Palmer Stad.), Princeton, N.J.	45,725
Colorado St. Univ. (Hughes Stad.), Ft. Collins	30,000	Purdue, (Ross-Ade Stad.), Lafayette, Ind.	69,250
Colorado, Univ. of (Folsom Field), Boulder.	50,126	Rice Stad., Houston, Texas.	70,000
Columbia Univ. (Baker Field), N.Y., N.Y.	32,000	Rutgers Stad., New Brunswick, N.J.	23,000
Cornell (Schoellkopf Crescent), Ithaca, N.Y.	30,000	San Jose St. Univ. (Spartan Stad.)	18,155
Dartmouth Coll. (Memorial), Hanover, N.H.	20,816	So. Carolina, Univ. of (Williams-Brice), Columbia	54,564
Delaware, Univ. of (Delaware Stad.), Newark.	21,919	So. Illinois Univ. (McAndrew), Carbondale	17,500
Drake Stad., Des Moines, Iowa.	18,000	Southwestern La., (Cajun Field), Lafayette, La.	27,000
Duke Univ., (Wade Stad.), Durham, N.C.	44,000	Stanford Stad., Stanford, Cal.	86,352
East Carolina Univ. (Ficklen Stad.), Greenville	20,000	Syracuse Univ. (Archbold Stad.).	26,388
Eastern Kentucky (Hanger Stadium), Richmond	20,000	Tampa, Univ. of (Tampa Stad.), Fla.	47,000
Florida State, (Campbell Stad.), Tallahassee	40,500	Temple Stad., Phil.	20,547
Florida, Univ. of (Florida Field), Gainesville	62,000	Tenn., Univ. of (Neyland Stad.), Knoxville	70,650
Georgia Inst. of Tech. (Grant Field), Atlanta.	58,121	Texas A. & M. Univ. (Kyle Field).	48,000
Georgia, Univ. of (Sanford Stad.), Athens.	59,200	Texas Christian Univ. (Carter Stad.), Ft. Worth	46,000
Harvard Stad., Boston, Mass.	37,289	Texas Tech. Univ. (Jones Stad.), Lubbock	47,000
Hawaii, Univ. of (Aloha Stad.).	50,000	Texas, Univ. of (Memorial), Austin.	80,000
Holy Cross (Fitton Field), Worcester, Mass.	25,000	Toledo, Univ. of (Glass Bowl), Ohio.	18,210
Idaho Stad., Univ. of, Moscow.	18,000	Trinity Univ. (Alamo Stad.), San Antonio, Tex.	22,500
Illinois, Univ. of (Memorial Stad.), Urbana.	71,229	Tulane Stad. (Sugar Bowl), New Orleans, La.	80,997
Indiana St. (Memorial Stad.), Terre Haute.	20,500	Tulsa, Univ. of (Skelly), Tulsa, Okla.	40,235
Indiana Univ. Stad., Bloomington	52,354	U. S. Air Force Acad. (Falcon Stad.), Col.	49,068
Iowa State Univ. (Clyde Williams Field).	35,000	U. S. Military Academy (Michie Stad.).	41,428
Iowa, Univ. of Stad., Iowa City.	60,200	U. S. Naval Academy (Navy-Marine Corps Mem. Stad.),	
Kansas State Univ. Stad., Manhattan	42,000	Annapolis, Md.	28,000
Kansas, Univ. of (Memorial Stad.), Lawrence	51,500	Utah State Univ. (Romney Stad.), Logan	20,000
Kent State Univ. (Dix Stad.), Kent.	28,415	Utah, Univ. of (Robert Rice Stad.), Salt Lake City	30,000
Kentucky, Univ. of (Commonwealth), Lexington	58,000	Vanderbilt, (Dudley Stad.), Nashville.	34,000
La. State Univ. (Tiger), Baton Rouge.	67,720	Va. Poly Inst. (Lane Stad.), Blacksburg.	38,000
Louisiana Tech. Univ. (Joe Aillet Stad.), Ruston.	23,318	Virginia, Univ. of (Scott Stad.), Charlottesville	25,000
Maryland, Univ. of (Byrd), College Park.	35,000	Wake Forest (Groves Stad.), Winston-Salem, N.C.	31,000
Memphis State (Memphis Memorial).	50,164	Washington State Univ. (Clarence D. Martin).	28,000
Michigan State Univ. (Spartan Stadium).	76,000	Washington, Univ. of (Husky Stad.), Seattle.	58,946
Michigan, Univ. of (Mich. Stad.), Ann Arbor.	101,701	West Texas State Univ. (Kimbrough), Canyon.	20,000
Minnesota, Univ. of (Memorial Stad.).	56,725	West Virginia Univ. (Mountaineer Field)	37,000
Mississippi St. Univ. (Scott Field)	35,000	Western Illinois Univ. (Hanson Field), Macomb	18,000
Mississippi, Univ. of (Hemingway Stad.).	37,500	Western Kentucky Univ. (L. T. Smith Stad.).	19,250
Missouri, Univ. of (Faurot Field) Columbia.	55,000	Western Mich. Univ. (Waldo Stad.), Kalamazoo.	24,500
Nebraska, Univ. of (Memorial Stad.), Lincoln.	76,400	Wichita State Univ. (Cessna Stadium).	30,500
New Mexico, Univ. Stad., Albuquerque.	30,000	Wisconsin, Univ. of (Camp Randall).	77,280
North Carolina St. U. (Carter Stad.), Raleigh.	41,000	Wyoming, Univ. of (Memorial), Laramie.	27,000
North Carolina, Univ. of (Kenan Stad.).	47,000	Yale Bowl, New Haven, Conn.	70,874

National College Football Champions

The NCAA recognizes as unofficial national champion the team selected each year by the AP (poll of writers) and the UPI (poll of coaches). When the polls disagree both teams are listed. The AP poll originated in 1936 and the UPI poll in 1950.

1936 Minnesota	1946 Notre Dame	1955 Oklahoma	1965 Alabama, Mich. State
1937 Pittsburgh	1947 Notre Dame	1956 Oklahoma	1966 Notre Dame
1938 Texas Christian	1948 Michigan	1957 Auburn, Ohio State	1967 Southern Cal.
1939 Texas A&M	1949 Notre Dame	1958 Louisiana State	1968 Ohio State
1940 Minnesota	1950 Oklahoma	1959 Syracuse	1969 Texas
1941 Minnesota	1951 Tennessee	1960 Minnesota	1970 Nebraska, Texas
1942 Ohio State	1952 Michigan State	1961 Alabama	1971 Nebraska
1943 Notre Dame	1953 Maryland	1962 Southern Cal.	1972 Southern Cal.
1944 Army	1954 Ohio State, UCLA	1963 Texas	1973 Notre Dame, Alabama
1945 Army		1964 Alabama	1974 Oklahoma, So. Cal.

Outland Awards

Honoring the outstanding interior lineman selected by the Football Writers' Association of America.

Year	Player, College, Pos.	Year	Player, College, Pos.	Year	Player, College, Pos.
1946	George Connor, Notre Dame, T	1956	Jim Parker, Ohio State, G	1966	Loyd Phillips, Arkansas, T
1947	Joe Steffy, Army, G	1957	Alex Karras, Iowa, T	1967	Ron Yary, Southern Cal, T
1948	Bill Fischer, Notre Dame, G	1958	Zeke Smith, Auburn, G	1968	Bill Stanfill, Georgia, T
1949	Ed Bagdon, Michigan St., G	1959	Mike McGee, Duke, T	1969	Mike Reid, Penn State, DT
1950	Bob Gain, Kentucky, T	1960	Tom Brown, Minnesota, G	1970	Jim Stillwagon, Ohio State, LB
1951	Jim Weatherall, Oklahoma, T	1961	Merlin Olsen, Utah State, T	1971	Larry Jacobson, Nebraska, DT
1952	Dick Modzelewski, Maryland, T	1962	Bobby Bell, Minnesota, T	1972	Rich Glover, Nebraska, MG
1953	J. D. Roberts, Oklahoma, G	1963	Scott Appleton, Texas, T	1973	John Hicks, Ohio State, G
1954	Bill Brooks, Arkansas, G	1964	Steve Delong, Tennessee, T	1974	Randy White, Maryland, DE
1955	Calvin Jones, Iowa, G	1965	Tommy Nobis, Texas, G		

Professional Sports Directory
Baseball

Commissioner's Office
75 Rockefeller Plaza
New York, N.Y. 10019

National League

National League Office
Mills Bldg.
220 Montgomery St.
San Francisco, Cal. 94104

Atlanta Braves
PO Box 4064
Atlanta, Ga. 30302

Chicago Cubs
Wrigley Field
Chicago, Ill. 60613

Cincinnati Reds
100 Riverfront Stadium
Cincinnati, Ohio 45202

Houston Astros
Astrodome
Houston, Texas 77001

Los Angeles Dodgers
Dodger Stadium
1000 Elysian Park Ave.
Los Angeles, Cal. 90012

Montreal Expos
PO Box 500, Station R
Montreal, Quebec

New York Mets
William A. Shea Stadium
Roosevelt Ave. & 126th St.
Flushing, N.Y. 11368

Philadelphia Phillies
Philadelphia Veterans Stadium
Broad St. & Pattison Ave.
Philadelphia, Pa. 19148

Pittsburgh Pirates
600 Stadium Circle
Pittsburgh, Pa. 15212

St. Louis Cardinals
Busch Memorial Stadium
250 Stadium Plaza
St. Louis, Mo. 63102

San Diego Padres
PO Box 2000
San Diego, Cal. 92120

San Francisco Giants
Candlestick Park
San Francisco, Cal. 94124

American League

American League Office
280 Park Ave.
New York, N.Y. 10017

Baltimore Orioles
Memorial Stadium
Baltimore, Md. 21218

Boston Red Sox
24 Jersey St.
Boston, Mass. 02215

California Angels
Anaheim Stadium
2000 State College Blvd.
Anaheim, Cal. 92806

Chicago White Sox
White Sox Park
Dan Ryan & 35th St.
Chicago, Ill. 60616

Cleveland Indians
Municipal Stadium
Cleveland, Ohio 44114

Detroit Tigers
Tiger Stadium
Detroit, Mich. 48216

Kansas City Royals
Harry S. Truman Sports Compl
PO Box 1969
Kansas City, Mo. 64141

Milwaukee Brewers
Milwaukee County Stadium
Milwaukee, Wis. 53246

Minnesota Twins
Metropolitan Stadium
8001 Cedar Ave.
Bloomington, Minn. 55420

New York Yankees
Parks Administration Bldg.
Flushing, N.Y. 11368

Oakland A's
Oakland-Alameda County
Coliseum
Oakland, Cal. 94621

Texas Rangers
Arlington Stadium
PO Box 1111
Arlington, Texas 76010

Basketball

National Basketball Assn.

League Office
2 Pennsylvania Plaza
Suite 2010
New York, N.Y. 10001

Atlanta Hawks
100 Techwood Drive
Atlanta, Ga. 30303

Boston Celtics
North Station
Boston, Mass. 02114

Buffalo Braves
Memorial Auditorium
Buffalo, N.Y. 14202

Chicago Bulls
333 North Michigan Ave.
Chicago, Ill. 60611

Cleveland Cavaliers
The Coliseum
2923 Streetsboro Rd.
Richfield Township, Ohio 44286

Detroit Pistons
Cobo Arena
Detroit, Mich. 48226

Golden State Warriors
556 Golden Gate Ave.
San Francisco, Cal. 94102

Houston Rockets
3930 Kirby Drive
Houston, Texas 77006

Kansas City-Omaha Kings
106 W. 12th St.
Kansas City, Mo. 64105
1804 Capitol Ave.
Omaha, Neb. 68102

Los Angeles Lakers
The Forum
3900 W. Manchester Blvd.
or PO Box 10
Inglewood, Cal. 90306

Milwaukee Bucks
901 North 4th St.
Milwaukee, Wis. 53203

New Orleans Jazz
Braniff Place Hotel
1500 Canal St.
New Orleans, La. 70140

New York Knickerbockers
Madison Square Garden Center
4 Pennsylvania Plaza
New York, N.Y. 10001

Philadelphia 76ers
The Spectrum
Philadelphia, Pa. 19148

Phoenix Suns
PO Box 1369
Phoenix, Ariz. 85001

Portland Trail Blazers
Lloyd Bldg.
700 NE Multnomah St.
Portland, Ore. 97232

Seattle SuperSonics
221 West Harrison St.
Seattle, Wash. 98119

Washington Bullets
Capital Centre
Landover, Md. 20786

American Basketball Assn.

League Office
1700 Broadway
New York, N.Y. 10019

Baltimore Claws
Baltimore Civic Center
201 Baltimore St.
Baltimore, Md. 21201

Denver Nuggets
1108 15th St.
Denver, Col. 80202

Indiana Pacers
Market Square Center
Indianapolis, Ind. 46204

Kentucky Colonels
Executive Inn
Louisville, Ky. 40213

New York Nets
One Old Country Rd.
Carle Place, N.Y. 11514

Spirits of St. Louis
5050 Oakland Ave.
St. Louis, Mo. 63110

San Antonio Spurs
603 Navarro
San Antonio, Texas 78205

San Diego Sails
3500 Sports Arena Blvd.
San Diego, Cal. 92110

Utah Stars
Salt Palace
Salt Lake City, Utah 84101

Virginia Squires
Norfolk Scope
Norfolk, Va. 23510

Hockey

National Hockey League

League Office
920 Sun Life Bldg.
Montreal, Quebec

Atlanta Flames
100 Techwood Dr., NW
Atlanta, Ga. 30303

Boston Bruins
150 Causeway St.
Boston, Mass. 02114

Buffalo Sabres
Memorial Auditorium
Buffalo. N.Y. 14202

California Golden Seals
Oakland-Alameda County
Coliseum
303 Hegenberger Rd.
Oakland, Cal. 94621

Chicago Black Hawks
1800 W. Madison St.
Chicago, Ill. 60612

Detroit Red Wings
5920 Grand River
Detroit, Mich. 48208

Kansas City Scouts
Crosby Kemper Memorial Arena
Genesee St.
Kansas City, Mo. 64102

Los Angeles Kings
PO Box 10
Inglewood, Cal. 90306

Minnesota North Stars
7901 Cedar Ave.
Bloomington, Minn. 55420

Montreal Canadiens
2313 St. Catherine St., West
Montreal, Quebec

New York Islanders
155 Conklin St.
Farmingdale, N.Y. 11735

New York Rangers
Madison Square Garden
4 Pennsylvania Plaza
New York, N.Y. 10001

Philadelphia Flyers
The Spectrum
Pattison Place
Philadelphia, Pa. 19148

Pittsburgh Penguins
Civic Arena
Pittsburgh, Pa. 15219

St. Louis Blues
5700 Oakland Ave.
St. Louis, Mo. 63110

Toronto Maple Leafs
60 Carlton St.
Toronto, Ont.

Vancouver Canucks
Pacific Coliseum
100 North Renfrew St.
Vancouver, B.C.

Washington Capitals
Capital Center
Landover, Md. 20786

World Hockey Assn.

League Office
415 Yonge St.
Toronto, Ont.

Calgary Cowboys
1418 McLedd Trail
Calgary, Alta.

Cincinnati Stingers
3610 Carew Tower
Cincinnati, Ohio 45202

Cleveland Crusaders
2923 Streetsboro Rd.
Richfield Township, Ohio 44286

Denver Spurs
3601 So. Monaco Pkwy.
Denver, Col. 80237

Edmonton Oilers
MacDonald Hotel
Edmonton, Alberta

Houston Aeros
810 Bagby St.
Houston, Texas 77002

Indianapolis Racers
Market Square Arena
Indianapolis, Ind. 46204

Minnesota Fighting Saints
143 W. 4th St.
St. Paul, Minn. 55102

New England Whalers
1 Civic Center Plaza
Hartford, Conn. 06103

Phoenix Roadrunners
1826 W. McDowell Rd.
Phoenix, Ariz. 85007

Quebec Nordiques
2025 Ave. Du Colisee
Quebec, Quebec.

San Diego Mariners
3500 Sports Arena Blvd.
San Diego, Cal. 92138

Toronto Toros
14 Carlton St.
Toronto, Ont.

Winnipeg Jets
15-1430 Maroons Rd.
Winnipeg, Man.

Football

National Football League

NFL League Office
410 Park Avenue
New York, N.Y. 10022

Atlanta Falcons
521 Capitol Ave. SW
Atlanta, Ga. 30312

Baltimore Colts
Executive Plaza
Hunt Valley, Md. 21031

Buffalo Bills
1 Bills Drive
Orchard Park, N.Y. 14127

Chicago Bears
173 W. Madison St.
Chicago, Ill. 60602

Cincinnati Bengals
200 Riverfront Stadium
Cincinnati, Ohio 45202

Cleveland Browns
Cleveland Stadium
Cleveland, Ohio 44114

Dallas Cowboys
6116 North Central Expressway
Dallas, Texas 75206

Denver Broncos
5700 Logan St.
Denver, Col. 80216

Detroit Lions
1401 Michigan Ave.
Detroit, Mich. 48216

Green Bay Packers
1265 Lombardi Ave.
Green Bay, Wis. 54303

Houston Oilers
6910 Fannin
Houston, Texas 77025

Kansas City Chiefs
1 Arrowhead Drive
Kansas City, Mo. 64129

Los Angeles Rams
10271.W. Pico Blvd.
Los Angeles, Cal. 90064

Miami Dolphins
330 Biscayne Blvd.
Miami, Fla. 33132

Minnesota Vikings
7110 France Ave. So.
Edina, Minn. 55435

New England Patriots
Schaefer Stadium
Foxboro, Mass. 02035

New Orleans Saints
944 St. Charles Ave.
New Orleans, La. 70130

New York Giants
10 Columbus Circle
New York, N.Y. 10019

New York Jets
598 Madison Ave.
New York, N.Y. 10022

Oakland Raiders
7811 Oakport St.
Oakland, Cal. 94621

Philadelphia Eagles
Veterans Stadium
Philadelphia, Pa. 19148

Pittsburgh Steelers
Three Rivers Stadium
Pittsburgh, Pa. 15212

St. Louis Cardinals
200 Stadium Plaza
St. Louis, Mo. 63102

San Diego Chargers
San Diego Stadium
San Diego, Cal. 92120

San Francisco 49ers
1255 Post St.
San Francisco, Cal. 94109

Washington Redskins
PO Box 17247
Dulles Intl. Airport
Washington, D.C. 20041

National Football League
Final 1974 Standings

National Conference

Eastern Division

	W.	L.	T.	Pct.	PF	PA
St. Louis.......	10	4	0	.714	285	218
Washington.....	10	4	0	.714	320	196
Dallas.........	8	6	0	.571	297	235
Philadelphia....	7	7	0	.500	242	217
New York Giants.	2	12	0	.143	195	299

Central Division

	W.	L.	T.	Pct.	PF	PA
Minnesota......	10	4	0	.714	310	195
Detroit........	7	7	0	.500	256	270
Green Bay......	6	8	0	.429	210	206
Chicago.......	4	10	0	.286	152	279

Western Division

	W.	L.	T.	Pct.	PF	PA
Los Angeles....	10	4	0	.714	263	181
San Francisco...	6	8	0	.429	226	236
New Orleans...	5	9	0	.357	166	263
Atlanta........	3	11	0	.214	111	271

American Conference

Eastern Division

	W.	L.	T.	Pct.	PF	PA
Miami.........	11	3	0	.786	327	216
Buffalo........	9	5	0	.643	264	244
New York Jets...	7	7	0	.500	279	300
New England...	7	7	0	.500	348	289
Baltimore......	2	12	0	.143	190	329

Central Division

	W.	L.	T.	Pct.	PF	PA
Pittsburgh......	10	3	1	.750	305	189
Cincinnati......	7	7	0	.500	283	259
Houston........	7	7	0	.500	236	282
Cleveland......	4	10	0	.286	251	344

Western Division

	W.	L.	T.	Pct.	PF	PA
Oakland.......	12	2	0	.857	355	228
Denver........	7	6	1	.536	302	294
Kansas City....	5	9	0	.357	233	293
San Diego.....	5	9	0	.357	212	285

NFC Playoffs — Minnesota 30, St. Louis 14; Los Angeles 19, Washington 10; Minnesota 14, Los Angeles 10.
AFC Playoffs — Oakland 28, Miami 26; Pittsburgh 32, Buffalo 14; Pittsburgh 24, Oakland 13.
Championship Game — Pittsburgh 16, Minnesota 6.

Pittsburgh Defeats Minnesota in Super Bowl

The Pittsburgh Steelers defeated the Minnesota Vikings 16-6 to win the 1975 Super Bowl game. The game was played at Tulane Stadium in New Orleans on January 12 before a crowd of over 80,000 plus an estimated 60 million television viewers.

Score by Quarters

Pittsburgh....................	0	2	7	7	16
Minnesota....................	0	0	0	6	6

Scoring

Pittsburgh—Safety, Tarkenton tackled in end zone.
Pittsburgh—Harris 9 run (Gerela kick).
Minnesota—T. Brown recovered blocked punt in end zone (kick failed).
Pittsburgh—L. Brown 4 pass from Bradshaw (Gerela kick).

Team Statistics

	Pittsburgh	Minnesota
First downs.....................	17	9
Rushing yardage.................	57-249	20-17
Passing yardage.................	84	102
Return yardage..................	114	62
Passes........................	9-14-0	11-27-3
Punts.........................	7-34.7	6-37.2
Fumbles-Lost...................	4-2	3-2
Penalties-Yardage...............	7-107	3-18
Attendance—80,997.		

Individual Statistics

Pittsburgh Rushing—Bleier, 17 for 65 yards; Harris, 34 for 158; Bradshaw, 5 for 33; Swan, 1 for minus 7.
Minnesota rushing—Osborn, 8 for minus 1 yard; Foreman, 12 for 18.
Pittsburgh passing—Bradshaw, 9 of 14 for 96 yards (0 interceptions).

Minnesota passing—Tarkenton, 11 of 27 for 102 yards (3 interceptions).
Pittsburgh pass receiving—Lewis, 1 for 12 yards; L. Brown, 3 for 49; Stallworth, 3 for 24; Bleier, 2 for 11.
Minnesota pass receiving—Gilliam, 1 for 16 yards; Osborn, 2 for 7; Foreman 5 for 50; Voigt, 2 for 31; Reed 1 for minus 2.

Super Bowl

Year	Winner	Loser	Site
1967...	Green Bay Packers, 35	Kansas City Chiefs, 10	Los Angeles Coliseum
1968...	Green Bay Packers, 33	Oakland Raiders, 14	Orange Bowl, Miami
1969...	New York Jets, 16	Baltimore Colts, 7	Orange Bowl, Miami
1970...	Kansas City Chiefs, 23	Minnesota Vikings, 7	Tulane Stadium, New Orleans
1971...	Baltimore Colts, 16	Dallas Cowboys, 13	Orange Bowl, Miami
1972...	Dallas Cowboys, 24	Miami Dolphins, 3	Tulane Stadium, New Orleans
1973...	Miami Dolphins, 14	Washington Redskins, 7	Los Angeles Coliseum
1974...	Miami Dolphins, 24	Minnesota Vikings, 7	Rice Stadium, Houston
1975...	Pittsburgh Steelers, 16	Minnesota Vikings, 6	Tulane Stadium, New Orleans

Jim Thorpe Trophy Winners

The winner of the Jim Thorpe Trophy, named after the athletic great, is picked by Murray Olderman of Newspaper Enterprise Assn in a poll of players from the 26 NFL teams. It goes to the most valuable NFL player and is the oldest and highest professional football award.

Year	Player and Team
1955	Harlon Hill, Chicago Bears
1956	Frank Gifford, N. Y. Giants
1957	John Unitas, Baltimore Colts
1958	Jim Brown, Cleveland Browns
1959	Charley Conerly, N. Y. Giants
1960	Norm Van Brocklin, Philadelphia Eagles
1961	Y. A. Tittle, N. Y. Giants
1962	Jim Taylor, Green Bay Packers
1963	(tie) Jim Brown, Cleveland Browns and Y. A. Tittle, N. Y. Giants

Year	Player and Team
1964	Lenny Moore, Baltimore Colts
1965	Jim Brown, Cleveland Browns
1966	Bart Starr, Green Bay Packers
1967	John Unitas, Baltimore Colts
1968	Earl Morrall, Baltimore Colts
1969	Roman Gabriel, Los Angeles Rams
1970	John Brodie, San Francisco
1971	Bob Griese, Miami
1972	Larry Brown, Washington
1973	O. J. Simpson, Buffalo
1974	Ken Stabler, Oakland

National Football League

Year	Winners (W-L-T) (East)	Winners (W-L-T) (West)	Playoff
1933	New York Giants (11-3-0)	Chicago Bears (10-2-1)	Chicago Bears 23, New York 21
1934	New York Giants (8-5-0)	Chicago Bears (13-0-0)	New York 30, Chicago Bears 13
1935	New York Giants (9-3-0)	Detroit Lions (7-3-2)	Detroit 26, New York 7
1936	Boston Redskins (7-5-0)	Green Bay Packers (10-1-1)	Green Bay 21, Boston 6
1937	Washington Redskins (8-3-0)	Chicago Bears (9-1-1)	Wash. 28, Chicago Bears 21
1938	New York Giants (8-2-1)	Green Bay Packers (8-3-0)	New York 23, Green Bay 17
1939	New York Giants (9-1-1)	Green Bay Packers (9-2-0)	Green Bay 27, New York 0
1940	Washington Redskins (9-2-0)	Chicago Bears (8-3-0)	Chicago Bears 73, Wash. 0
1941	New York Giants (8-3-0)	Chicago Bears (10-1-1) (A)	Chicago Bears 37, New York 9
1942	Wash. Redskins (10-1-1)	Chicago Bears (11-0-0)	Wash. 14, Chicago Bears 6
1943	Wash. Redskins (6-3-1) (A)	Chicago Bears (8-1-1)	Chicago Bears 41, Wash. 21
1944	New York Giants (8-1-1)	Green Bay Packers (8-2-0)	Green Bay 14, New York 7
1945	Wash. Redskins (8-2-0)	Cleveland Rams (9-1-0)	Cleveland 15, Washington 14
1946	New York Giants (7-3-1)	Chicago Bears (8-2-1)	Chicago Bears 24, New York 14
1947	Philadelphia Eagles (8-4-0) (A)	Chicago Cardinals (9-3-0)	Chicago Cardinals 28, Phila. 21
1948	Philadelphia Eagles (9-2-1)	Chicago Cardinals (11-1-0)	Phila. 7, Chicago Cardinals 0
1949	Philadelphia Eagles (11-1-0)	Los Angeles Rams (8-2-2)	Philadelphia 14, Los Angeles 0
1950	Cleveland Browns (10-2-0) (A)	Los Angeles Rams (9-3-0) (A)	Cleveland 30, Los Angeles 28
1951	Cleveland Browns (11-1-0)	Los Angeles Rams (8-4-0)	Los Angeles 24, Cleveland 17
1952	Cleveland Browns (8-4-0)	Detroit Lions (9-3-0) (A)	Detroit 17, Cleveland 7
1953	Cleveland Browns (11-1-0)	Detroit Lions (10-2-0)	Detroit 17, Cleveland 16
1954	Cleveland Browns (9-3-0)	Detroit Lions (9-2-1)	Cleveland 56, Detroit 10
1955	Cleveland Browns (9-2-1)	Los Angeles Rams (8-3-1)	Cleveland 38, Los Angeles 14
1956	New York Giants (8-3-1)	Chicago Bears (9-2-1)	New York 47, Chicago Bears 7
1957	Cleveland Browns (9-2-1)	Detroit Lions (8-4-0) (A)	Detroit 59, Cleveland 14
1958	New York Giants (9-3-0) (A)	Baltimore Colts (9-3-0)	Baltimore 23, New York 17 (B)
1959	New York Giants (10-2-0)	Baltimore Colts (9-3-0)	Baltimore 31, New York 16
1960	Philadelphia Eagles (10-2-0)	Green Bay Packers (8-4-0)	Philadelphia 17, Green Bay 13
1961	New York Giants (10-3-1)	Green Bay Packers (11-3-0)	Green Bay 37, New York 0
1962	New York Giants (12-2-0)	Green Bay Packers (13-1-0)	Green Bay 16, New York 7
1963	New York Giants (11-3-0)	Chicago Bears (11-1-2)	Chicago 14, New York 10
1964	Cleveland Browns (10-3-1)	Baltimore Colts (12-2-0)	Cleveland 27, Baltimore 0
1965	Cleveland Browns (11-3-0)	Green Bay Packers (10-3-1) (A)	Green Bay 23, Cleveland 12
1966	Dallas Cowboys (10-3-1)	Green Bay Packers (12-2-0)	Green Bay 34, Dallas 27

(A) Won divisional playoff. (B) Won at 8:15 sudden death overtime period.

Year	Conference	Division	Winners (W-L-T)	Playoffs
1967	East	Century	Cleveland (9-5-0)	Dallas 52, Cleveland 14
		Capitol	Dallas (9-5-0)	
	West	Central	Green Bay (9-4-1)	Green Bay 28, L. A. 7
		Coastal	Los Angeles (11-1-2) (A)	Green Bay 21, Dallas 17
1968	East	Century	Cleveland (10-4-0)	Cleveland 31, Dallas 20
		Capitol	Dallas (12-2-0)	
	West	Central	Minnesota (8-6-0)	Baltimore 24, Minnesota 14
		Coastal	Baltimore (13-1-0)	Baltimore 34, Cleveland 0
1969	East	Century	Cleveland (10-3-1)	Cleveland 38, Dallas 14
		Capitol	Dallas (11-2-1)	
	West	Central	Minnesota (12-2-0)	Minnesota 23, Los Angeles 20
		Coastal	Los Angeles (11-3-0)	Minnesota 27, Cleveland 7
1970	American	Eastern	Baltimore (11-2-1)	Baltimore 17, Cincinnati 0
		Central	Cincinnati (8-6-0)	Oakland 21, Miami 14
		Western	Oakland (8-4-2)	Baltimore 27, Oakland 17
	National	Eastern	Dallas (10-4-0)	Dallas 5, Detroit 0
		Central	Minnesota (12-2-0)	San Francisco 17, Minnesota 14
		Western	San Francisco (10-3-1)	Dallas 17, San Francisco 10
1971	American	Eastern	Miami (10-3-1)	Miami 27, Kansas City 24
		Central	Cleveland (9-5-0)	Baltimore 20, Cleveland 3
		Western	Kansas City (10-3-1)	Miami 21, Baltimore 0
	National	Eastern	Dallas (11-3-0)	Dallas 20, Minnesota 12
		Central	Minnesota (11-3-0)	San Francisco 24, Washington 20
		Western	San Francisco (9-5-0)	Dallas 14, San Francisco 3
1972	American	Eastern	Miami (14-0-0)	Miami 20, Cleveland 14
		Central	Pittsburgh (11-3-0)	Pittsburgh 13, Oakland 7
		Western	Oakland (10-3-1)	Miami 21, Pittsburgh 17
	National	Eastern	Washington (11-3-0)	Washington 16, Green Bay 3
		Central	Green Bay (10-4-0)	Dallas 30, San Francisco 28
		Western	San Francisco (8-5-1)	Washington 26, Dallas 3
1973	American	Eastern	Miami (12-2-0)	Miami 34, Cincinnati 16
		Central	Cincinnati (10-4-0)	Oakland 33, Pittsburgh 14
		Western	Oakland (9-4-1)	Miami 27, Oakland 10
	National	Eastern	Dallas (10-4-0)	Dallas 27, Los Angeles 16
		Central	Minnesota (12-2-0)	Minnesota 27, Washington 20
		Western	Los Angeles (12-2-0)	Minnesota 27, Dallas 10
1974	American	Eastern	Miami (11-3-0)	Oakland 28, Miami 26
		Central	Pittsburgh (10-3-1)	Pittsburgh 32, Buffalo 14
		Western	Oakland (12-2-0)	Pittsburgh 24, Oakland 13
	National	Eastern	St. Louis (10-4-0)	Minnesota 30, St. Louis 14
		Central	Minnesota (10-4-0)	Los Angeles 19, Washington 10
		Western	Los Angeles (10-4-0)	Minnesota 14, Los Angeles 10

George Halas Trophy Winners

The Halas Trophy, named after football coach George Halas, is awarded annually to the outstanding defensive player in football in a poll conducted by Murray Olderman of Newspaper Enterprise Assn.

1966—Larry Wilson, St. Louis
1967—Deacon Jones, Los Angeles
1968—Deacon Jones, Los Angeles
1969—Dick Butkus, Chicago
1970—Dick Butkus, Chicago
1971—Carl Eller, Minnesota
1972—Joe Greene, Pittsburgh
1973—Alan Page, Minnesota
1974—Joe Greene, Pittsburgh

American Football League

Year	Eastern Division	Western Division	Playoff
1960	Houston Oilers (10-4-0)	L. A. Chargers (10-4-0)	Houston 24, Los Angeles 16
1961	Houston Oilers (10-3-1)	San Diego Chargers (12-2-0)	Houston 10, San Diego 3
1962	Houston Oilers (11-3-0)	Dallas Texans (11-3-0)	Dallas 20, Houston 17 (b)
1963	Boston Patriots (8-6-1) (a)	San Diego Chargers (11-3-0)	San Diego 51, Boston 10
1964	Buffalo Bills (12-2-0)	San Diego Chargers (8-5-1)	Buffalo 20, San Diego 7
1965	Buffalo Bills (10-3-1)	San Diego Chargers (9-2-3)	Buffalo 23, San Diego 0
1966	Buffalo Bills (9-4-1)	Kansas City Chiefs (11-2-1)	Kansas City 31, Buffalo 7
1967	Houston Oilers (9-4-1)	Oakland Raiders (13-1-0)	Oakland 40, Houston 7
1968	New York Jets (11-3-0)	Oakland Raiders (12-2-0) (a)	New York 27, Oakland 23
1969	New York Jets (10-4-0)	Oakland Raiders (12-1-1)	Kansas City 17, Oakland 7 (c)

(a) won divisional playoff (b) won at 2:45 of second overtime. (c) K. C. def. Jets to make playoffs.

National Football Conference Leaders

(National Football League, 1962-1969)

Passing

Year	Player	Atts.	Com.	YG	TD
1962	Bart Starr, Green Bay	285	178	2,438	9
1963	Y. A. Tittle, N. Y. Giants	367	221	3,145	14
1964	Bart Starr, Green Bay	272	163	2,144	4
1965	Rudy Bukich, Chicago	312	176	2,641	9
1966	Bart Starr, Green Bay	251	156	2,257	3
1967	Sonny Jurgensen, Washington	508	288	3,747	16
1968	Earl Morrall, Baltimore	317	182	2,909	17
1969	Sonny Jurgensen, Washington	422	274	3,102	15
1970	John Brodie, San Francisco	378	223	2,941	24
1971	Roger Staubach, Dallas	211	126	1,882	15
1972	Norm Snead, N. Y. Giants	325	196	2,307	17
1973	Roger Staubach, Dallas	286	179	2,428	23
1974	Sonny Jurgensen, Washington	167	107	1,185	11

Pass-Receiving

Year	Player	Ct.	YG	TD
1962	Bobby Mitchell, Washington	72	1,384	11
1963	Bobby Conrad, Cards, St. Louis	73	967	10
1964	Johnny Morris, Chicago	93	1,200	10
1965	Dave Parks, San Francisco	80	1,344	12
1966	Charlie Taylor, Washington	72	1,119	12
1967	Charlie Taylor, Washington	70	990	9
1968	Clifton McNeil, San Francisco	71	944	7
1969	Dan Abramowicz, New Orleans	73	1,015	7
1970	Dick Gordon, Chicago	71	1,026	13
1971	Bob Tucker, Giants	59	791	4
1972	Harold Jackson, Philadelphia	62	1,048	4
1973	Harold Carmichael, Philadelphia	67	1,116	9
1974	Charles Young, Philadelphia	63	696	3

Scoring

Year	Player	TDs	PAT	FG	Pts.
1962	Jim Taylor, Green Bay	19	0	0	114
1963	Don Chandler, New York	0	52	18	106
1964	Lenny Moore, Baltimore	20	0	0	120
1965	Gale Sayers, Chicago	22	0	0	132
1966	Bruce Gossett, Los Angeles	0	29	28	113
1967	Jim Bakken, St. Louis	0	36	27	117
1968	Leroy Kelly, Cleveland	20	0	0	120
1969	Fred Cox, Minnesota	0	43	26	121
1970	Fred Cox, Minnesota	0	35	30	125
1971	Curt Knight, Washington	0	27	29	114
1972	Chester Marcol, Green Bay	0	29	33	128
1973	David Ray, Los Angeles	0	40	30	130
1974	Chester Marcol, Green Bay	0	19	25	94

Rushing

Year	Player	YG	Atts.	TD
1962	Jim Taylor, Green Bay	1,474	272	19
1963	Jimmy Brown, Cleveland	1,863	291	12
1964	Jimmy Brown, Cleveland	1,446	280	7
1965	Jimmy Brown, Cleveland	1,544	289	17
1966	Gale Sayers, Chicago	1,231	229	8
1967	Leroy Kelly, Cleveland	1,205	235	11
1968	Leroy Kelly, Cleveland	1,239	248	16
1969	Gale Sayers, Chicago	1,032	236	8
1970	Larry Brown, Washington	1,125	237	5
1971	John Brockington, Green Bay	1,105	216	4
1972	Larry Brown, Washington	1,216	285	8
1973	John Brockington, Green Bay	1,144	265	3
1974	Larry McCutcheon, Los Angeles	1,109	236	3

American Football Conference Leaders

(American Football League, 1962-1969)

Passing

Year	Player	Atts.	Com.	YG	TD
1962	Len Dawson, Dallas	310	189	2,749	17
1963	Tobin Rote, San Diego	287	170	2,510	17
1964	Len Dawson, Kansas City	354	199	2,879	18
1965	Jack Hadl, San Diego	348	174	2,798	21
1966	Len Dawson, Kansas City	284	159	2,527	10
1967	Daryle Lamonica, Oakland	425	220	3,228	20
1968	Len Dawson, Kansas City	224	131	2,109	9
1969	Greg Cook, Cincinnati	197	106	1,845	11
1970	Daryle Lamonica, Oakland	356	179	2,516	22
1971	Bob Griese, Miami	263	145	2,089	19
1972	Earl Morrall, Miami	150	83	1,360	11
1973	Ken Stabler, Oakland	260	163	1,997	14
1974	Ken Anderson, Cincinnati	328	213	2,667	18

Pass-Receiving

Year	Player	Ct.	YG	TD
1962	Lionel Taylor, Denver	77	908	4
1963	Lionel Taylor, Denver	78	1,101	10
1964	Charlie Hennigan, Houston	101	1,561	8
1965	Lionel Taylor, Denver	85	1,131	6
1966	Lance Alworth, San Diego	73	1,383	13
1967	George Sauer, N. Y. Jets	75	1,189	6
1968	Lance Alworth, San Diego	68	1,312	10
1969	Lance Alworth, San Diego	64	1,003	4
1970	Marlin Briscoe, Buffalo	57	1,036	8
1971	Fred Biletnikoff, Oakland	61	929	9
1972	Fred Biletnikoff, Oakland	58	802	7
1973	Fred Willis, Houston	57	371	1
1974	Lydell Mitchell, Baltimore	72	544	2

Scoring

Year	Player	TD	PAT	FG	Pts.
1962	Gene Mingo, Denver	4	32	27	137
1963	Gino Cappelletti, Boston	2	35	22	113
1964	Gino Cappelletti, Boston	7	36	25	155
1965	Gino Cappelletti, Boston	9	27	17	132
1966	Gino Cappelletti, Boston	6	35	16	119
1967	George Blanda, Oakland	0	56	20	116
1968	Jim Turner, N. Y. Jets	0	43	34	145
1969	Jim Turner, N. Y. Jets	0	33	32	129
1970	Jan Stenerud, Kansas City	0	26	30	116
1971	Garo Yepremian, Miami	0	33	28	117
1972	Bobby Howfield, N. Y. Jets	0	40	27	121
1973	Roy Gerela, Pittsburgh	0	36	29	123
1974	Roy Gerela, Pittsburgh	0	33	20	93

Rushing

Year	Player	YG	Atts.	TD
1962	Cookie Gilchrist, Buffalo	1,096	214	13
1963	Clem Daniels, Oakland	1,098	214	3
1964	Cookie Gilchrist, Buffalo	981	230	6
1965	Paul Lowe, San Diego	1,121	222	7
1966	Jim Nance, Boston	1,458	299	11
1967	Jim Nance, Boston	1,216	269	7
1968	Paul Robinson, Cincinnati	1,023	238	8
1969	Dick Post, San Diego	873	182	6
1970	Floyd Little, Denver	901	209	3
1971	Floyd Little, Denver	1,133	284	6
1972	O. J. Simpson, Buffalo	1,251	292	6
1973	O. J. Simpson, Buffalo	2,003	332	12
1974	Otis Armstrong, Denver	1,407	263	9

1974 NFL Individual Leaders

National Conference

Passing*

	Att.	Comp.	Pct. Comp.	Yards Gained	TD. Pass	Int.	Avg. Yd. Gained	Rating
Jurgensen, Washington	167	107	64.1	1185	11	5	7.10	94.6
Harris, Los Angeles	198	106	53.5	1544	11	6	7.80	85.3
Kilmer, Washington	234	137	58.5	1632	10	6	6.97	83.4
Tarkenton, Minnesota	351	199	56.7	2598	17	12	7.40	82.0
Hart, St. Louis	388	200	51.5	2411	20	8	6.21	79.5
Munson, Detroit	292	166	56.8	1874	8	7	6.42	75.2
Staubach, Dallas	360	190	52.8	2552	11	15	7.09	68.5
Snead, San Francisco	159	97	61.0	983	5	8	6.18	68.2
Gabriel, Philadelphia	338	193	57.1	1867	9	12	5.52	66.7
Morton, New York	239	124	51.9	1522	9	13	6.37	62.1
Owen, San Francisco	184	88	47.8	1327	10	15	7.21	55.0
Hadl, Green Bay	299	142	47.5	1752	8	14	5.86	55.5
Huff, Chicago	283	142	50.2	1663	6	17	5.88	50.4
Manning, New Orleans	261	134	51.3	1429	6	16	5.48	49.9
Tagge, Green Bay	146	70	47.9	709	1	10	4.86	36.3
Lee, Atlanta	172	78	45.3	852	3	14	4.95	32.4

Kickers

	XP—XPA	FG—FGA	Pts.
Marcol, Green Bay	19—19	25—39	94
Mann, Detroit	23—26	23—32	92
Moseley, Washington	27—29	18—30	81
Bakken, St. Louis	30—36	13—22	69
Cox, Minnesota	32—39	12—20	68
Gossett, San Francisco	25—27	11—24	58
Herrera, Dallas	33—33	8—13	57
Dempsey, Philadelphia	26—30	10—16	56
Ray, Los Angeles	25—31	9—16	52
Gogolak, New York	21—23	10—19	51

Rushing

	Att.	Yds.	Avg.	TDs.
McCutcheon, Los Angeles	236	1109	4.7	3
Brockington, Green Bay	266	883	3.3	5
Hill, Dallas	185	844	4.6	7
Foreman, Minnesota	199	777	3.9	9
Sullivan, Philadelphia	244	760	3.1	11
Metcalf, St. Louis	152	718	4.7	6
Maxson, New Orleans	165	714	4.3	2
Jackson, San Francisco	174	705	4.1	0
Otis, St. Louis	158	664	4.2	1
Schreiber, San Francisco	174	634	3.6	3

Pass Receiving

	No.	Yds.	Avg.	TDs.
Young, Philadelphia	63	696	11.0	3
Pearson, Dallas	62	1087	17.5	2
Carmichael, Philadelphia	56	649	11.6	8
Jessie, Detroit	54	761	14.1	3
Taylor, Washington	54	738	13.7	5
Foreman, Minnesota	53	586	11.1	6
Metcalf, St. Louis	50	377	7.5	1
Dawkins, New York	46	332	7.2	3
J. Smith, Washington	44	554	12.6	3
Jefferson, Washington	43	654	15.2	4

Touchdowns

	Tot.	Rush.	Pass.	Ret.	Pts.
Foreman, Minnesota	15	9	6	0	90
Sullivan, Philadelphia	12	11	1	0	72
Metcalf, St. Louis	8	6	1	1	48
Carmichael, Philadelphia	8	0	8	0	48
Hill, Dallas	7	7	0	0	42
Brown, Washington	7	3	4	0	42

American Conference

Passing*

	Att.	Comp.	Pct. Comp.	Yards Gained	TD. Pass	Int.	Avg.Yd. Gained	Rating
Anderson, Cincinnati	328	213	64.9	2667	18	10	8.13	95.9
Stabler, Oakland	310	178	57.4	2469	26	12	7.96	94.8
Johnson, Denver	244	136	55.7	1969	13	9	8.07	84.4
Griese, Miami	253	152	60.1	1968	16	15	7.78	81.0
Pastorini, Houston	247	140	56.7	1571	10	10	6.36	72.5
Namath, New York	361	191	52.9	2616	20	22	7.25	69.3
Ferguson, Buffalo	232	119	51.3	1588	12	12	6.84	69.0
Dawson, Kansas City	235	138	58.7	1573	7	13	6.69	66.0
Plunkett, New England	352	173	49.1	2457	19	22	6.98	63.8
Jones, Baltimore	270	143	53.0	1610	8	12	5.96	62.8
Gilliam, Pittsburgh	212	96	45.3	1274	4	8	6.01	55.4
Fouts, San Diego	237	115	48.5	1732	8	13	7.31	61.4
Bradshaw, Pittsburgh	148	67	45.3	785	7	8	5.30	55.1
Phipps, Cleveland	256	117	45.7	1384	9	17	5.41	46.9
Livingston, Kansas City	141	66	46.8	732	4	10	5.19	42.5
Domres, Baltimore	153	77	50.3	803	0	12	5.25	33.4

Kickers

	XP—XPA	FG—FGA	Pts.
Gerela, Pittsburgh	33—35	20—29	93
J. Smith, New England	42—43	16—22	90
Leypoldt, Buffalo	25—29	19—33	82
Blanda, Oakland	44—46	11—17	77
Stenerud, Kansas City	24—26	17—24	75
Cockroft, Cleveland	29—30	14—16	71
Turner, Denver	35—38	11—21	68
Yepremian, Miami	43—43	8—15	67
Muhlmann, Cincinnati	32—35	11—18	65

Pass Receiving

	No.	Yds.	Avg.	TDs.
Mitchell, Baltimore	72	544	7.6	2
Branch, Oakland	60	1092	18.2	13
Podolak, Kansas City	43	306	7.1	1
Odoms, Denver	42	639	15.2	6
Biletnikoff, Oakland	42	593	14.1	7
Garrison, San Diego	41	785	19.1	5
Barkum, New York	41	524	12.8	3
Knight, New York	40	579	14.5	4
Caster, New York	38	745	19.6	7
Herron, New England	38	474	12.5	5

*At least 140 attempted passes needed to qualify. Leader based on percentage of completions — touchdown passes — intercepions — and average yards.

American Conference (Con't)

Rushing	Att.	Yds.	Avg.	TDs.
Armstrong, Denver	263	1407	5.3	9
Woods, San Diego	227	1162	5.1	7
Simpson, Buffalo	270	1125	4.2	3
Harris, Pittsburgh	208	1006	4.8	5
Hubbard, Oakland	188	865	4.6	4
Herron, New England	231	824	3.6	7
Cunningham, New England	166	811	4.9	9
Mitchell, Baltimore	214	757	3.5	5

Touchdowns	Tot.	Rush.	Pass.	Ret.	Pts.
Branch, Oakland	13	0	13	0	78
Armstrong, Denver	12	9	3	0	72
Herron, New England	12	7	5	0	72
Cunningham, New England	11	9	2	0	66
Keyworth, Denver	10	10	0	0	60
Woods, San Diego	10	7	3	0	60
Curtis, Cincinnati	10	0	10	0	60
Csonka, Miami	9	9	0	0	54

1974 NEA All-NFL Team

Offense	First Team	Second Team
Wide Receiver	Cliff Branch, Oakland	Drew Pearson, Dallas
Wide Receiver	Mel Gray, St. Louis	Ike Curtis, Cincinnati
Tight End	Riley Odoms, Denver	Charles Young, Philadelphia
Right Tackle	Ron Yary, Minnesota	Russ Washington, San Diego
Left Tackle	Art Shell, Oakland	Dan Dierdorf, St. Louis
Right Guard	Ed White, Minnesota	Joe DeLamielleure, Buffalo
Left Guard	Gale Gillingham, Green Bay	Gene Upshaw, Oakland
Center	Jim Langer, Miami	Jack Rudnay, Kansas City
Quarterback	Ken Stabler, Oakland	Jim Hart, St. Louis
Running Back	O.J. Simpson, Buffalo	Chuck Foreman, Minnesota
Running Back	Lawrence McCutcheon, L.A.	Otis Armstrong, Denver
Placekicker	Jan Stenerud, Kansas City	Roy Gerela, Pittsburgh

Defense	First Team	Second Team
Left End	Claude Humphrey, Atlanta	L.C. Greenwood, Pittsburgh
Right End	Fred Dryer, Los Angeles	Bill Stanfill, Miami
Left Tackle	Joe Greene, Pittsburgh	Larry Brooks, Los Angeles
Right Tackle	Alan Page, Minnesota	Ernie Holmes, Pittsburgh
Middle Linebacker	Willie Lanier, Kansas City	Bill Bergey, Philadelphia
Outside Linebacker	Ted Hendricks, Green Bay	Isiah Robertson, Los Angeles
Outside Linebacker	Jack Ham, Pittsburgh	Chris Hanberger, Washington
Corner Back	Roger Wehrli, St. Louis	Emmitt Thomas, Kansas City
Corner Back	Robert James, Buffalo	Lemar Parrish, Cincinnati
Strong Safety	Dick Anderson, Miami	Ken Houston, Washington
Free Safety	Tony Greene, Buffalo	Cliff Harris, Dallas
Punter	Ray Guy, Oakland	Jerrel Wilson, Kansas City

1975 NFL Player Draft

The following are the first round picks of the National Football League

Team	Player	Pos.	College	Team	Player	Pos.	College
1—Atlanta	Steve Bartkowski	QB	California	14—Cincinnati	Glenn Cameron	LB	Florida
2—Dallas	Randy White	DE	Maryland	15—Houston	Don Hardeman	RB	Texas A&I
3—Baltimore	Ken Huff	G	North Carolina	16—New England	Russ Francis	TE	Oregon State
4—Chicago	Walter Payton	RB	Jackson State	17—Denver	Louie Wright	DB	San Jose State
5—Cleveland	Mack Mitchell	DE	Houston	18—Dallas	Tom Henderson	LB	Langston, Okla.
6—Houston	Robert Brazile	LB	Jackson State	19—Buffalo	Tom Rudd	LB	Nebraska
7—New Orleans	Larry Burton	WR	Purdue	20—Los Angeles	Doug France	T	Ohio State
8—San Diego	Gary Johnson	DT	Grambling	21—St. Louis	Tim Gray	DB	Texas A&M
9—Los Angeles	Mike Fanning	DT	Notre Dame	22—San Diego	Mike Williams	DB	Louisiana State
10—San Francisco	Jimmy Webb	DE	Mississippi State	23—Miami	Darryl Carlton	T	Tampa
11—Los Angeles	Dennis Harrah	G	Miami	24—Oakland	Neal Colzie	DB	Ohio State
12—New Orleans	Kurt Schumacher	T	Ohio State	25—Minnesota	Mark Mullaney	DT	Colorado State
13—Detroit	Lynn Boden	G	So. Dakota State	26—Pittsburgh	Dave Brown	DB	Michigan

Pro Football's Hall Of Fame

Canton, Ohio

Cliff Battles	Bill George	Bobby Layne	Jim Parker
Sammy Baugh	Otto Graham	Vince Lombardi	Joe Perry
Chuck Bednarik	Red Grange	Sid Luckman	Pete Pihos
Bert Bell	Lou Groza	Link Lyman	Hugh (Shorty) Ray
Raymond Berry	Joe Guyon	Tim Mara	Dan Reeves
Charles Bidwell	George Halas	Gino Marchetti	Andy Robustelli
Jim Brown	Ed Healey	George Marshall	Art Rooney
Paul Brown	Mel Hein	Ollie Matson	Joe Schmidt
Roosevelt Brown	Pete Henry	George McAfee	Ernie Stautner
Tony Canadeo	Arnold Herber	Hugh McElhenny	Ken Strong
Joe Carr	Bill Hewitt	John (Blood) McNally	Joe Stydahar
Guy Chamberlin	Clarke Hinkle	Mike Michalske	Jim Thorpe
Jack Christiansen	Elroy Hirsch	Wayne Millner	Y. A. Tittle
Dutch Clark	Cal Hubbard	Lenny Moore	George Trafton
George Connor	Lamar Hunt	Marion Motley	Charlie Trippi
Jim Conzelman	Don Hutson	Bronko Nagurski	Emlen Tunnell
Art Donovan	Walt Kiesling	Greasy Neale	Clyde (Bulldog) Turner
Paddy Driscoll	Frank (Bruiser) Kinard	Ernie Nevers	Norm Van Brocklin
Bill Dudley	Curly Lambeau	Leo Nomellini	Steve Van Buren
Turk Edwards	Dick (Night Train) Lane	Steve Owen	Bob Waterfield
Tom Fears	Dante Lavelli	Clarence (Ace) Parker	Alex Wojciechowicz
Dr. Daniel Fortmann			

All-Time Pro Football Records
(NFL, AFL, and AAFC—All-American Football Conference)
Leading Lifetime Rushers (As of Sept. 20, 1975)

Player	League	Yrs.	Att.	Yards	Avg.	Player	League	Yrs.	Att.	Yards	Avg.
Jim Brown	NFL	9	2,359	12,312	5.2	Steve Van Buren	NFL	8	1,320	5,860	4.3
Joe Perry	AAFC-NFL	16	1,929	9,723	5.0	Bill Brown	NFL	14	1,649	5,838	3.4
Jim Taylor	NFL	10	1,941	8,597	4.4	Rick Casares	NFL-AFL	12	1,431	5,797	4.1
Leroy Kelly	NFL	10	1,727	7,274	4.2	Mike Garrett	AFL-NFL	9	1,308	5,481	4.2
John Henry Johnson	NFL-AFL	13	1,571	6,803	4.3	Larry Brown	NFL	6	1,413	5,467	3.9
O. J. Simpson	AFL-NFL	6	1,378	6,306	4.6	Dick Bass	NFL	10	1,218	5,417	4.4
Don Perkins	NFL	8	1,500	6,217	4.1	Jim Nance	NFL-AFL	8	1,341	5,401	4.0
Ken Willard	NFL	10	1,622	6,105	3.8	Hugh McElhenny	NFL	13	1,124	5,231	4.7
Larry Csonka	AFL-NFL	7	1,286	5,900	4.6	Lenny Moore	NFL	12	1,069	5,174	4.8
Floyd Little	AFL-NFL	8	1,516	5,878	3.9	Ollie Matson	NFL	14	1,170	5,173	4.4

Most Yards Gained, Season — 2,003, O.J. Simpson, Buffalo Bills, 1973.
Most Yards Gained, Game — 250, Orban (Spec) Sanders, New York Yankees vs. Chicago Rockets, Oct. 24, 1947; O. J. Simpson, Buffalo vs. New England, Sept. 16, 1973.
Most games, 100 Yards or more, Season — 11, O.J. Simpson, Buffalo Bills, 1973.
Most Games, 100 Yards or more, Career — 58, Jim Brown, Cleveland Browns, 1957-1965.
Most Touchdowns Rushing, Career — 106, Jim Brown, Cleveland Browns, 1957-1965.
Most Touchdowns Rushing, Season — 19, Jim Taylor, Green Bay Packers, 1962.
Most Touchdowns Rushing, Game — 6, Ernie Nevers, Chicago Cardinals vs. Chicago Bears, Nov. 8, 1929.
Most Rushing Attempts, Season — 332, O.J. Simpson, Buffalo Bills, 1973.
Most Rushing Attempts, Game — 40, Lydell Mitchell, Baltimore vs. N. Y. Jets, Oct. 4, 1974.
Longest run from Scrimmage — 97 yds., Andy Uram, Green Bay vs. Chicago Cardinals, Oct. 8, 1939; Bob Gage, Pittsburgh vs. Chicago Bears, Dec. 4, 1949. (Both scored touchdown.)

Leading Lifetime Passers (Minimum 1500 attempts)

Player	League	Yrs.	Att.	Comp.	Yds.	Pts.*	Player	League	Yrs.	Att.	Comp.	Yds.	Pts.*
Otto Graham	AAFC-NFL	10	2,626	1,464	23,584	86.8	Don Meredith	NFL	9	2,308	1,170	17,199	74.7
Sonny Jurgensen	NFL	18	4,262	2,433	32,224	82.8	Y.A. Tittle	AAFC-NFL	17	4,395	2,427	33,070	74.4
Len Dawson	NFL-AFL	18	3,601	2,043	27,616	82.1	Earl Morrall	NFL	19	2,620	1,343	20,388	74.3
Fran Tarkenton	NFL	14	4,800	2,658	35,846	80.6	Bob Griese	AFL-NFL	8	2,014	1,081	14,309	74.1
Bart Starr	NFL	16	3,149	1,808	24,718	80.3	Frank Albert	AAFC-NFL	7	1,564	831	10,795	73.5
Johnny Unitas	NFL	18	5,186	2,830	40,239	78.2	Craig Morton	NFL	10	1,545	807	11,789	73.4
Frank Ryan	NFL	13	2,133	1,090	16,042	77.7	Daryle Lamonica	AFL-NFL	12	2,601	1,288	19,154	72.9
Norm Van Brocklin	NFL	12	2,895	1,553	23,611	75.3	John Brodie	NFL	17	4,491	2,469	31,548	72.3
Sid Luckman	NFL	12	1,744	904	14,686	75.3	Billy Wade	NFL	13	2,523	1,370	18,530	72.2
Roman Gabriel	NFL	13	4,111	2,168	27,309	74.9	Sammy Baugh	NFL	16	2,995	1,693	21,886	72.0

*Rating points based on performances in the following categories: Percentage of completions, percentage of touchdown passes, percentage of interceptions and average gain per pass attempt.

Most Yards Gained, Season — 4,007, Joe Namath, New York Jets, 1967.
Most Yards Gained, Game — 554, Norm Van Brocklin, Los Angeles Rams vs. New York Yankees, Sept. 18, 1951 (27 completions in 41 attempts).
Most Touchdowns Passing, Career — 290, John Unitas, Baltimore Colts, 1956-1972, San Diego Chargers, 1973.
Most Touchdowns Passing, Season — 36, George Blanda, Houston Oilers, 1961 and Y. A. Tittle, N.Y. Giants, 1963.
Most Touchdowns Passing, Game — 7, Sid Luckman, Chicago Bears vs. New York Giants, Nov. 14, 1943; Adrian Burk, Philadelphia Eagles vs. Washington Redskins Oct. 17, 1954; George Blanda, Houston Oilers vs. New York Titans, Nov. 19, 1961; Y. A. Tittle, New York Giants vs. Washington Redskins, Oct. 28, 1962; Joe Kapp, Minnesota Vikings vs. Baltimore Colts, Sept. 28, 1969.
Most Passing Attempts, Season — 508, Sonny Jurgensen, Washington Redskins, 1967 (288 completions).
Most Passing Attempts, Game — 68, George Blanda, Houston Oilers vs. Buffalo Bills, Nov. 1, 1964 (37 completions).
Most Passes Completed, Season — 288, Sonny Jurgensen, Washington Redskins, 1967 (508 attempts).
Most Passes Completed, Game — 37, George Blanda, Houston Oilers vs. Buffalo Bills, Nov. 1, 1964 (68 attempts).
Most Consecutive Passes Completed — 17, Bert Jones, Baltimore Colts vs. N.Y. Jets, Dec. 15, 1974.

Leading Lifetime Receivers

Player	League	Yrs.	No.	Yds.	Avg.	Player	League	Yrs.	No.	Yds.	Avg.
Don Maynard	AFL-NFL	15	633	11,834	18.7	Boyd Dowler	NFL	12	474	7,270	15.4
Ray Berry	NFL	13	631	9,275	14.7	Jackie Smith	NFL	12	459	7,601	16.6
Charlie Taylor	NFL	11	582	8,208	14.0	Pete Retzlaff	NFL	11	452	7,412	16.4
Lionel Taylor	AFL	9	567	7,195	12.7	Fred Biletnikoff	AFL-NFL	10	450	7,105	15.8
Lance Alworth	AFL-NFL	11	542	10,266	18.9	Carroll Dale	NFL	14	438	8,271	18.9
Bobby Mitchell	NFL	11	521	7,954	15.3	Mike Ditka	NFL	12	427	5,812	13.6
Billy Howton	NFL	12	503	8,459	16.8	Bobby Joe Conrad	NFL	12	422	5,902	14.0
Tom McDonald	NFL	12	495	8,410	17.0	Charley Hennigan	AFL	7	410	6,823	16.6
Don Hutson	NFL	11	488	7,991	16.4	Otis Taylor	AFL-NFL	11	410	7,306	17.8
Art Powell	AFL-NFL	10	479	8,046	16.8	Roy Jefferson	NFL	10	409	6,920	16.9

Most Yards Gained, Season — 1,746, Charley Hennigan, Houston Oilers, 1961.
Most Yards Gained, Game — 303, Jim Benton, Cleveland Rams vs. Detroit Lions, Nov. 22, 1945 (10 receptions).
Most Pass Receptions, Season — 101, Charley Hennigan, Houston Oilers, 1964.
Most Pass Receptions, Game — 18, Tom Fears, Los Angeles Rams vs. Green Bay Packers, Dec. 3, 1950 (189 yards).
Most Consecutive Games, Pass Receptions — 105, Dan Abramowicz, New Orleans Saints, 1967-1973; San Francisco 49ers, 1973-1974.
Most Touchdown Passes, Career — 99, Don Hutson, Green Bay Packers, 1935-1945.
Most Touchdown Passes, Season — 17, Don Hutson, Greeyn Bay Packers, 1942; Elroy Hirsch, Los Angeles Rams, 1951; Bill Groman, Houston Oilers, 1961.
Most Touchdown Passes, Game — 5, Bob Shaw, Chicago Cardinals vs. Baltimore Colts, Oct. 2, 1950.
Most Consecutive Games, Touchdown Passes — 11, Elroy Hirsch, Los Angeles Rams, 1950-1951; Buddy Dial, Pittsburgh, 1959-60.

Leading Lifetime Scorers

Player	League	Yrs.	TD	PAT	FG	Total	Player	League	Yrs.	TD	PAT	FG	Total
George Blanda	NFL-AFL	25	9	899	322	1,919	Pete Gogolak	AFL-NFL	10	0	344	173	863
Lou Groza	AAFC-NFL	21	1	810	264	1,608	Jan Stenerud	AFL-NFL	8	0	257	196	845
Fred Cox	NFL	12	0	416	242	1,142	Don Hutson	NFL	11	105	172	7	823
Gino Cappelletti	AFL	11	42	350	176	1,130	Paul Hornung	NFL	9	62	190	66	760
Jim Bakken	NFL	13	0	399	225	1,074	Jim Brown	NFL	9	126	0	0	756
Jim Turner	AFL-NFL	11	0	368	231	1,061	Tom Davis	NFL	11	0	348	130	738
Bruce Gossett	NFL	11	0	374	219	1,031	Mike Clark	NFL	10	0	325	133	724
Sam Baker	NFL	15	2	428	179	977	Lenny Moore	NFL	12	113	0	0	678
Lou Michaels	NFL	13	1	386	187	955*	Ben Agajanian	AAFC-NFL					
Bobby Walston	NFL	12	46	365	80	881		AFL	13	0	343	104	655
*Includes safety.							Gordy Soltau	NFL	9	25	284	70	644

Most Points, Season — 176, Paul Hornung, Green Bay Packers, 1960 (15 TD's, 41 PAT's, 15 FG's).

Most Points, Game — 40, Ernie Nevers, Chicago Cardinals vs. Chicago Bears, Nov. 28, 1929 (6 TD's, 4 PAT's).

Most Touchdowns, Season — 22, Gale Sayers, Chicago Bears, 1965 (14 rushing, 6 pass receptions, 1 punt return, 1 kickoff return).

Most Touchdowns, Game — 6, Ernie Nevers, Chicago Cardinals vs. Chicago Bears Nov. 28, 1929 (6 rushing); Dub Jones, Cleveland Browns vs. Chicago Bears, Nov. 25, 1951 (4 rushing, 2 pass receptions); Gale Sayers, Chicago Bears vs. San Francisco 49ers, Dec. 12, 1965 (4 rushing, 1 pass reception, 1 punt return).

Most Points After Touchdown, Season — 64, George Blanda, Houston Oilers, 1961 (65 attempts).

Most Consecutive Points After Touchdown — 234, Tommy Davis, San Francisco 49ers, 1959-1965.

Most Field Goals, Game — 7, Jim Bakken, St. Louis Cardinals vs. Pittsburgh Steelers, Sept. 24, 1967.

Most Field Goals, Season — 34, Jim Turner, New York Jets, 1968 and 1969.

Most Field Goals Attempted, Season — 49, Bruce Gossett, Los Angeles Rams, 1966; Curt Knight, Washington Redskins, 1971.

Most Field Goals Attempted, Game — 9, Jim Bakken, St. Louis Cardinals vs. Pittsburgh Steelers, Sept. 24, 1967 (7 successful).

Most Consecutive Field Goals — 16, Jan Stenerud, Kansas City Chiefs, Nov. 2, 1969-Dec. 7, 1969.

Most Consecutive Games, Field Goal — 31, Fred Cox, Minnesota Vikings, 1968-1970.

Longest Field Goal — 63 yds., Tom Dempsey, New Orleans Saints vs. Detroit Lions, Nov. 8, 1970.

Highest Field Goal Percentage, Career (400 attempts) — 66.4, Jan Stenerud, Kansas City Chiefs, 1967-1974 (196 FG's in 295 attempts).

Highest Field Goal Completion Percentage, Season (20 attempts) — 88.5, Lou Groza, Cleveland Browns, 1953 (23 FG's in 26 attempts).

Pass Interceptions

Most Passes Had Intercepted, Game — 8, Jim Hardy, Chicago Cardinals vs. Philadelphia Eagles, Sept. 24, 1950 (39 atts).

Most Passes Had Intercepted, Season — 42, George Blanda, Houston Oilers, 1962 (418 attempts).

Most Passes Had Intercepted, Career — 276. George Blanda, Chicago Bears, 1949-1958; Houston Oilers, 1960-1966; Oakland Raiders, 1967-1974 (4,000 Attempts).

Most Consecutive Passes Attempted Without Interception — 294, Bart Starr, Green Bay Packers, 1964-1965.

Most Interceptions By, Season — 14, Dick Lane, Los Angeles Rams, 1952.

Most Interceptions By, Career — 79, Emlen Tunnell, New York Giants, 1948-1958; Green Bay Packers, 1959-1961.

Most Consecutive Games, Passes Intercepted By — 8, Tom Morrow, Oakland Raiders, 1962 (4), 1963 (4).

Most Touchdowns Scored via Pass Interceptions, Lifetime — 9, Ken Houston, Houston Oilers, 1967 (2); 1968 (2); 1969; 71 (4).

Punting

Highest Punting Average, Career (300 Punts) — 45.10, Sam Baugh, Washington Redskins, 1937-1952 (338 Punts).

Highest Punting Average, Season (20 Punts) — 51.3, Sam Baugh, Washington Redskins, 1940 (35 Punts).

Highest Punting Average, Game (4 Punts) — 59.4 Sam Baugh, Washington Redskins vs. Detroit Lions, Oct. 27, 1940 (5 punts).

Longest Punt — 98 yds., Steve O'Neal, New York Jets vs. Denver Broncos, Sept. 21, 1969.

Kickoff Returns

Most Yardage Returning Kickoffs, Career — 6,922 Ron Smith, Chicago Bears, 1965; Atlanta Falcons, 1966-67; Los Angeles Rams, 1968-69; Chicago Bears, 1970-72, San Diego Chargers, 1973; Oakland Raiders, 1974.

Most Yardage Returning Kickoffs, Season — 1,317, Bobby Jancik, Houston Oilers, 1963.

Most Yardage Returning Kickoffs, Game — 294, Wally Triplett, Detroit Lions vs. Los Angeles Rams, Oct. 29, 1950 (4 returns).

Most Touchdowns Scored via Kickoff Returns, Career — 6, Ollie Matson, Chicago Cardinals, 1952 (2), 1954, 1956, 1958 (2); Gale Sayers, Chicago Bears, 1965, 1966 (2), 1967 (3); Travis Williams, Green Bay Packers, 1967 (4), 1969; Los Angeles Rams, 1971.

Most Touchdowns Scored via Kickoff Returns, Season — 4, Travis Williams, Green Bay Packers, 1967; Cecil Turner, Chicago Bears, 1970.

Most Touchdowns Scored via Kickoff Returns, Game — 2, Tim Brown, Philadelphia Eagles vs. Dallas Cowboys, Nov. 6, 1966; Travis Williams, Green Bay Packers vs. Cleveland Browns, Nov. 12, 1967.

Most Kickoff Returns, Career — 275, Ron Smith, Chicago Bears, 1965; Atlanta Falcons, 1966-67; Los Angeles Rams, 1968-69; Chicago Bears, 1970-72, San Diego Chargers, 1973; Oakland Raiders, 1974.

Most Kickoff Returns, Season — 47, Odell Barry, Denver Broncos, 1964.

Longest Kickoff Return — 106 yds., Al Carmichael, Green Bay Packers vs. Chicago Bers, October 7, 1956 (scored touchdown); Noland Smith, Kansas City vs. Denver, Dec. 17, 1967 (scored touchdown).

Punt Returns

Most Yardage Returning Punts, Career — 2,209, Emlen Tunnell, New York Giants, 1948-1958; Green Bay Packers, 1959-1961.

Most Yardage Returning Punts, Season — 612, Rodger Bird, Oakland Raiders, 1967.

Most Yardage Returning Punts, Game — 205, George Atkinson, Oakland Raiders vs. Buffalo Bills, Sept. 15, 1968.

Most Touchdowns Scored via Punt Returns, Career — 8, Jack Christiansen, Detroit Lions, 1951 (4), 1952 (2), 1954, 1956.

Most Punt Returns, Career — 258, Emlen Tunnell, New York Giants, 1948-1958; Green Bay Packers, 1959-1961.

Most Punt Returns, Season — 53, Alvin Haymond, L. A. Rams, 1970.

Most Punt Returns, Game — 9, Rodger Bird, Oakland Raiders vs. Denver Broncos, Sept. 10, 1967.

Longest Punt Return — 98, Gil LeFebvre, Cincinnati Reds vs. Brooklyn Dodgers, Dec. 3, 1933 (scored touchdown); Charles West, Minnesota Vikings vs. Washington Redskins, Nov. 3, 1968 (scored touchdown); Dennis Morgan, Dallas Cowboys vs. St. Louis Cardinals, Oct. 13, 1974 (scored touchdown).

Miscellaneous Records

Most Fumbles, Season — 16, Don Meredith, Dallas Cowboys, 1964.
Most Fumbles, Game — 7, Len Dawson, Kansas City Chiefs vs. San Diego Chargers, Nov. 15, 1964.
Longest Run with Recovered Fumble — 104 yds., Jack Tatum, Oakland Raiders vs. Green Bay Packers, Sept. 24, 1972.
Longest Winning Streak (Regular Season) — 17 games, Chicago Bears, 1933-1934.
Longest Undefeated Streak (Includes Tie Games) — 29 games, Cleveland Browns, 1947-1949 (Won 27, Tied 2).
Most Seasons, Active Player — 25, George Blanda, Chicago Bears, 1949-1958; Houston Oilers, 1960-1966 and Oakland, 67-74.

NFL Attendance

The National Football League drew 10,236,332 fans for the 182 regular season games in 1974, a decline of 4.6% from the previous year.

Federal legislation requires clubs to make available for local television any game sold out 72 hours prior to kickoff. During the 1974 regular season, 11% of tickets sold were not used. In 1972, when local games were blacked out, 5.98% of the tickets sold were not used.

World Football League
1974 Final Standings

Eastern Division

	W	L	T	Pct.	PF	PA
Florida	14	6	0	.700	419	280
Charlotte	10	10	0	.500	467	350
Philadelphia	8	11	0	.421	491	413
*Jacksonville	4	10	0	.286	258	358

Central Division

	W	L	T	Pct.	PF	PA
Memphis	17	3	0	.850	629	365
Birmingham	15	5	0	.750	500	394
*Chicago	7	12	0	.368	446	600
*Detroit	1	13	0	.071	209	358

Western Division

	W	L	T	Pct.	PF	PA
So. California	13	7	0	.650	486	341
Hawaii	9	11	0	.450	413	422
Portland	7	12	1	.375	264	426
Shreveport	7	12	1	.375	240	415

*Disbanded during season. Charlotte began season in New York; Shreveport began season in Houston. Championship (World Bowl) — Birmingham 22, Florida 21.

Canadian Football League
1974 final standings

EASTERN CONFERENCE

	W.	L.	T.	PF	PA	Pts.
Montreal	9	5	2	339	271	20
Ottawa	7	9	0	261	271	14
Hamilton	7	9	0	279	313	14
Toronto	6	9	1	281	314	13

WESTERN CONFERENCE

	W.	L.	T.	PF	PA	Pts.
Edmonton	10	5	1	345	247	21
Saskatchewan	9	7	0	305	289	18
British Columbia	8	8	0	306	299	16
Winnipeg	8	8	0	258	350	16
Calgary	6	10	0	285	305	12

East semifinal—Ottawa 21, Hamilton 19
West semifinal—Saskatchewan 24, British Columbia 14
East final—Montreal 14, Ottawa 4
West final—Edmonton 31, Saskatchewan 27
Championship (Grey Cup)—Montreal 20, Edmonton 7

Canadian Football League (Grey Cup)

Winners of Eastern divisions meet in championship game for Grey Cup (donated by Governor-General Earl Grey in 1909). Canadian football features 3 downs, 110-yard field, and each team can have 12 players on field at one time.

1948—Calgary Stampeders 12, Ottawa Rough Riders 7
1949—Montreal Alouettes 28, Calgary Stampeders 15
1950—Toronto Argonauts 13, Winnipeg Blue Bombers 0
1951—Ottawa Rough Riders 21, Saskatchewan Roughriders 14
1952—Toronto Argonauts 21, Edmonton Eskimos 11
1953—Hamilton Tiger-Cats 12, Winnipeg Blue Bombers 6
1954—Edmonton Eskimos 26, Montreal Alouettes 25
1955—Edmonton Eskimos 34, Montreal Alouettes 19
1956—Edmonton Eskimos 50, Montreal Alouettes 27
1957—Hamilton Tiger-Cats 32, Winnipeg Blue Bombers 7
1958—Winnipeg Blue Bombers 35, Hamilton Tiger-Cats 28
1959—Winnipeg Blue Bombers 21, Hamilton Tiger-Cats 7
1960—Ottawa Rough Riders 16, Edmonton Eskimos 6
1961—Winnipeg Blue Bombers 21, Hamilton Tiger-Cats 14

1962—Winnipeg Blue Bombers 28, Hamilton Tiger-Cats 27
1963—Hamilton Tiger-Cats 21, British Columbia Lions 10
1964—British Columbia Lions 34, Hamilton Tiger-Cats 24
1965—Hamilton Tiger-Cats 22, Winnipeg Blue Bombers 16
1966—Saskatchewan Roughriders 29, Ottawa Rough Riders 14
1967—Hamilton Tiger-Cats 24, Saskatchewan Roughriders 1
1968—Ottawa Rough Riders 24, Calgary Stampeders 21
1969—Ottawa Rough Riders 29, Saskatchewan Roughriders 11
1970—Montreal Alouettes 23, Calgary Stampeders 10
1971—Calgary Stampeders 14, Toronto Argonauts 11
1972—Hamilton Tiger-Cats 13, Saskatchewan Rough Riders 10
1973—Ottawa Rough Riders 22, Edmonton Eskimos 18
1974—Montreal Alouettes 20, Edmonton Eskimos 7

World Horseshoe Pitching Champions

Year	Champion	W.	L.	Ringer %	Year	Champion	W.	L.	Ringer %
1964	Harold Reno, Sabina, Oh.	32	3	84.1	1970	Dan Kuchcinski, Erie, Pa.	34	1	84.9
1965	Elmer Hohl, Wellesley, Ont.	32	3	84.6	1971	Curt Day, Frankfort, Ind.	35	0	85.0
1966	Curt Day, Frankfort, Ind.	26	2	86.6	1972	Elmer Hohl, Wellesley, Ont.	33	2	86.0
1967	Dan Kuchcinski, Erie, Pa.	34	1	84.4	1973	Elmer Hohl, Wellesley, Ont.	32	3	83.5
1968	Elmer Hohl, Wellesley, Ont.	35	0	88.5	1974	Curt Day, Frankfort, Ind.	32	3	81.8
1969	Dan Kuchcinski, Erie, Pa.	35	0	84.7	1975	Elmer Hohl, Wellesley, Ont.	33	2	84.5

Year	Ladies Champion	Ringer %	Junior Champion	Ringer %
1968	Lorraine Thomas, Lockport, N.Y.	74.6	Farron Eisemann, Riverton, Wy.	78.5
1969	Vicki Winston, Lamonte, Mo.	79.6	Mark Seibold, Huntington, Ind.	83.7
1970	Ruth Hangen, Buffalo, N.Y.	72.0	Bill Holland, Indianapolis, Ind.	79.2
1971	Ruth Hangen, Buffalo, N.Y.	73.4	Walter Ray Williams, Eureka, Cal.	86.7
1972	Ruth Hangen, Buffalo, N.Y.	76.6	Walter Ray Williams, Eureka, Cal.	89.2
1973	Ruth Hangen, Getzville, N.Y.	79.6	Jeffrey Williams, Eureka, Cal.	85.5
1974	Lorraine Thomas, Lockport, N.Y.	80.2	Doug Kienia, Kittery, Me.	81.2
1975	Vicki Winston, Lamonte, Mo.	73.5	Walter Ray Williams, Auburn, Cal.	86.6

American Bowling Congress Championships, 1975

Dayton, Ohio

Regular Division

Individual

1. Jim Setser, Dayton, Oh. 219, 279, 258 — 756.
2. Bob Ruhland, Madison, Wis. 248, 258, 213 — 719.
3. Gary Fukuda, Berkley, Mich. 210, 276, 232 — 718.

Runners-up — Mike Fiedler, Lockport, N.Y. 717; Carl Alsip, Cincinnati, Oh. and Gil Wojciechowski, Milwaukee, Wis. 716; Bart Miller, Pawtucket, R.I. 715; William Diedrich, Bloomingdale, Mich. and Mac Lowry, Seattle, Wash. 712; Asa Morris, St. Louis, Mo. 711.

All-Events

1. Bobby Meadows, Dallas, Tex. 636, 701, 696 — 2033.
2. Rich Black, Kansas City, Kan. 673, 695, 651 — 2019.
3. Tie-Asa Morris, St. Louis, Mo. 596, 679, 711 — 1986. Gary Brooks, Lancaster, Pa. 628, 675, 683 — 1986.

Runners-up — William Foster, Marion, Ind. 1978; Tom Jankowski, Milwaukee, Wis. 1977; Frank Paul, Grand Rapids, Mich. 1970; Mike White, Lincoln, Neb. and Tim Menge, Cleveland Oh. 1962; Rick Musialowski, Buffalo, N.Y. 1961.

Doubles

1. Bob Metz, Dayton, Oh. 253, 258, 225 — 746; Steve Partlow, Dayton, Oh. 180, 223, 211 — 614. Aggregate — 1360.
2. Jim Turner, Cincinnati, Oh. 210, 247, 234 — 691; Mike Kuhn, Cincinnati, Oh. 189,194, 277 — 660. Aggregate — 1351.
3. Don Parsons Jr., Oakland, Md. 199, 257, 213 — 669; Allen Wheeler Jr., Johnstown, Pa. 211, 224, 246 — 681. Aggregate — 1350.

Runners-up — Craig Bishop-Paul Thistlewaite, Sheridan, Ind. 1336; Mark Perrin-Bob Altfillisch, Des Moines, Iowa 1335; Chuck Radick-Nich Renchkovsky, Albany, N.Y. 1334; Al Mathes-Charles Boike, Center Line, Mich. and Tom and Art Krueger, Ft. Worth, Tex. 1326; Bob Meadows and Jim Hensley, Dallas, Bill Baume Jr. and Tom Lamb Augusta, Ga. and Frank Clay and Leo, Gorowski Chicago 1317.

Teams

1. Black Chrysler, Cleveland, Ohio — Dan Toronski Sr. 277, 212, 225 — 714; Howie Niederding 214, 204, 182 — 600; Rich Mersek 184, 238, 236 — 658; Mike Rossie 233, 200, 205 — 638; Ron Barney 211, 199, 214 — 624. Aggregate — 3234.
2. M & M Bowling Supply, Endwell, N.Y. — Ray Kenney 182, 194, 197 — 573; Donald Karn 225, 256, 196 — 677; David Lewis 212, 215, 201 — 628; Robert Gensler 236, 193, 202 — 631; Mike Randesi Jr. 183, 209, 225 — 617. Aggregate — 3126.

Classic Division

Individual

1. Les Zikes, Chicago, Ill. 224, 217, 269 — 710.
2. Bill Beach, Sharon, Pa. 242, 237, 227 — 706.
3. Jack Winters, Philadelphia, Pa. 268, 189, 246 — 703.

Runners-up — Andy Rogoznica, Chicago, Ill. 702; Kike Totsky, Detroit, Mich. 695; Rick Goergen, Sioux City, Iowa 687; Bill Karach, Kenosha, Wis. 686; Jim Godman, Vero Beach, Fla. 684; Gus Lampo, Endicott, N.Y. 681; Ron Hoffman, Denver, Col. 679.

All-Events

1. Bill Beach, Sharon, Pa. 607,685, 706 — 1993.
2. Marty Piraino, Syracuse, N.Y. 546, 772, 671 — 1989.
3. Les Schissler, Denver, Col. 690, 615, 668 — 1973.

Runners-up — Curt Schmidt, Ft. Wayne, Ind. 1967; LeRoy Langager, Minneapolis, Minn. 1943; Ron Hoffman, Denver, Col. 1942; Rick Goergen, Sioux City, Iowa 1939; Jim Godman, Vero Beach, Fla. 1934; Greg Baderdeen, Ontario, Cal. 1931; Paul Colwell, Tucson, Ariz. 1925.

Doubles

1. Marty Piraino, Syracuse, N.Y. 241, 300, 231 — 772; Bill Bunetta, Fresno, Cal. 175, 235, 210 — 620. Aggregate — 1392.
2. Floyd Christensen, Cheney, Wash. 196, 246, 248 — 690; David Deken, Plattsburgh, N.Y. 223, 222, 201 — 646. Aggregate — 1336.
3. Gus Lampo, Endicott, N.Y. 202, 194, 234 — 630; Mike Orlovsky, Endicott, N.Y. 225, 258, 212 — 695. Aggregate 1325.

Runners-up — Dave McCarty-LeRoy Lanager, Minneapolis, Minn. 1320; Harry Golden-John Coder, Akron, Ohio 1319; Edward Davis Jr.-Joe Ciufo, Aberdeen, Md. 1303; Don Carter, Miami, Fla.-Jim Godman, Vero Beach, Fla. 1296; Ron Hoffman-Earle Faulkner, Denver, Col. 1294; Charles Faino, Philadelphia, Pa.-Curt Schmidt Ft. Wayne, Ind. and John Petraglia, Brooklyn, N.Y.-Butch Gearhart Houston Tex. 1293.

Teams

1. Munsingwear No. 2, Minneapolis, Minn. — Roy Buckley 199, 269, 193 — 661; Norm Meyers 195, 237, 161 — 593; Barry Asher 179, 192, 161 — 532; Bud Horn 161, 235, 181 — 577; Nelson Burton Jr. 176, 213, 228 — 617. Aggregate — 2980.
2. Stroh's Beer, Detroit, Mich. — Bob Hart 236, 224, 214 — 674; Fred Vitali 182, 149, 199 — 530; Bill Spargo 225, 191, 182 — 598; Harry Campbell 182, 206, 179; Mike Totsky 221, 206, 179 — 606. Aggregate — 2975.

Other Bowling Championships in 1975

5th U.S. Open — Grand Prairie, Tex., Mar. 23-29 — Steve Neff, Sarasota, Fla. Average 232, prize $10,000. Women — Toledo, Ohio, May 17-22 — Paul Sperber, Miami, Fla. Average 207, prize $6,000.

National Intercollegiate Championships — Dayton, Ohio. April 6. Doubles — Craig Elkins, Santa Clara and Bob Pfeil, California, Davis; Singles — Vic Martin, Armstrong State; all events

— Nick Romaniello, S. Conn. State.

Invitational Bowling Tournament of the Americas — Miami, Fla.-July 13-19. Men's Doubles — Gary Brooks-Tom Kelley, U.S.; Singles — Gary Brooks, U.S.; All-Events — Gary Brooks, U.S. Women's Doubles — Adela de Cardoze-Lizzie Phillips, Panama; Singles — Tere Mejia, Mexico; All-Events — Ivonne Mayorca, Venezuela.

Masters Bowling Tournament Champions

Year	Winner	Runner-up	W.L.	Avg.
1963	Harry Smith, St. Louis, Mo.	Bobby Meadows, Dallas, Tex.	7-0	219-3
1964	Billy Welu, St. Louis, Mo.	Harry Smith, Baltimore, Md.	7-0	227
1965	Billy Welu, St. Louis, Mo.	Don Ellis, Houston, Tex.	9-1	202-12
1966	Bob Strampe, Detroit, Mich.	Al Thompson, Cleveland, Ohio.	7-0	219-8
1967	Lou Scalia, Miami, Fla.	Bill Johnson, New Orleans, La.	7-0	216-9
1968	Pete Tountas, Tucson, Ariz.	Buzz Fazio, Detroit, Mich.	9-1	220-15
1969	Jim Chestney, Denver, Col.	Barry Asher, Costa Mesa, Cal.	10-1	223-2
1970	Don Glover, Bakersfield, Cal.	Bob Strampe, Detroit, Mich.	9-1	215-10
1971	Jim Godman, Lorain, Ohio.	Don Johnson, Akron, Ohio.	9-1	229-8
1972	Bill Beach, Sharon, Pa.	Jim Godman, Lorain, Ohio	8-1	220-27
1973	Dave Soutar, Gilroy, Cal.	Dick Ritger, Hartford, Wis.	7-0	218-61
1974	Paul Colwell, Tucson, Ariz.	Steve Neff, Sarasota, Fla.	7-0	234-17
1975	Ed Ressler Jr., Allentown, Pa.	Sam Flanagan, Parkersburg, W. Va.	9-1	213-57

All-Time Records for League and Tournament Play

Type of record	Holder of record	Year	Score	Competition
High team total	Budweiser Beer, St. Louis	1958	3,858	League
High team game	Hook Grip Five, Lodi, N.J.	1950	1,342	League
High doubles total	Nelson Burton Jr., Billy Walden, St. Louis.	1970	1,614	Tournament
High doubles game	Tom Dern-Ron Spohn, Columbus, Ohio.	1965	587	League
High individual total	Albert Brandt, Lockport, N.Y.	1939	886	League
High all events score	Frank Benkovic, Milwaukee, Wis.	1932	2,259	Tournament

Record Averages for Consecutive Tournaments

No. in row	Name of record holder	Span	Games	Average
Two	Jim Goodman, Vero Beach, Fla.	1974-75	18	228.78
Three	Steve Nagy, Cleveland, Ohio	1951-53	27	221.02
Four	Bob Strampe, Detroit, Mich.	1964-67	48	215.40
Five	Bob Strampe, Detroit, Mich.	1964-68	57	215.28
Ten	Bob Strampe, Detroit, Mich.	1961-70	111	211.10

Official Records of Annual ABC Tournaments

Type of record	Holder of record	Year	Score
High team total	Ace Mitchell Shur-Hooks, Akron, Ohio	1966	3,357
High team game	Falstaff Beer, San Antonio, Texas	1958	1,226
High doubles score	John Klares-Steve Nagy, Cleveland, Ohio	1952	1,453
High doubles game	John Gworek-Henry Kmidowski, Buffalo, N.Y.	1946	544
High singles total	Lee Jouglard, Detroit, Mich.	1951	775
High all events score	Jim Godman, Vero Beach, Fla.	1974	2,184
High team all events	Falstaff Beer, St. Louis, Mo.	1958	9,608
High life-time pin total	Bill Doehrman, Ft. Wayne, Ind.	1908 to 1975	105,471

Bowlers With Six or More Sanctioned 300 Games

Elvin Mesger, Sullivan, Mo. 26	Tom Hennessey, St. Louis. 9	Salvatore Bivona, Paterson, N.J. 6
George Billick, Old Forge, Pa. 17	Howard Holmes, Los Angeles 8	Lou Campi, Dumont, N.J. 6
Dick Weber, St. Louis 16	Casey Jones, Plymouth, Wis. 8	Ed Davis, Milford, N.J. 6
Al Faragalli, Wayne, N.J. 14	Russell Field, San Jose, Cal. 8	Don Dubro, St. Louis 6
Dave Soutar, Gilroy, Cal. 14	Roger Fink, Lodi, Cal. 8	*Bill Flynn, Cleveland 6
Don Carter, Miami, Fla. 13	George Pappas, Charlotte, N.C. 8	Sam Garofalo, St. Louis. 6
Ray Bluth, St. Louis 12	Dennis Wright, Milwaukee 8	Joe Joseph, Lansing, Mich. 6
Ron Graham, Louisville 12	Ray Eklund, Milwaukee 8	Pete Kozloski, Plains, Pa. 6
Walter Ward, Cleveland. 12	Walter King, Detroit, Mich. 8	Vince Lucci, Trenton, N.J. 6
*Hank Marino, Milwaukee 11	Junie McMahon, Lodi, N.J. 8	Steve Nagy, Cleveland 6
Frank Clause, Old Forge, Pa. 11	Joe Donato, Schenectady, N.Y. 7	Frank Poliak, Pittsburgh 6
Ed Lubanski, Detroit. 11	Eddie Botten, Union City, N.J. 7	Robert Pinkalla, Milwaukee 6
Pat Patterson, St. Louis. 11	Dick Hoover, Akron. 7	Harold Schaeffer, St. Louis. 6
Dennis Soper, Tustin, Cal. 11	Ken McKenzie, Dallas 7	Harry Smith, Rochester, N.Y. 6
Don Johnson, Las Vegas. 10	Ray Schanen, Milwaukee 7	Bob Strampe, Detroit, Mich. 6
Mike Durbin, Lorain, Ohio. 10	Wayne Pinkalla, Milwaukee 7	Jerry Tharp, St. Louis 6
Boss Bosco, Akron, O. 9	George Pappas, Charlotte 7	George Tomek, Plymouth, Pa. 6
Al Savas, Milwaukee 9	Bob Ramirez, Los Angeles 7	Stephen Tomek, Plymouth, Pa. 6
Lou Foxie, Paterson, N.J. 9	Don McCune, Munster, Ind. 7	William Capleton, Prospect Park, N.J. 6
Jerry Woji, Stockton, Cal. 9	Bud Horn, Los Angeles. 7	Mark Sutter, St. Louis. 6
Norm Meyers, St. Louis 9	Don Glover, Bakersfield, Cal. 7	

*Bowled two 300 games in official 3-game-series.

PBA Winter Tour, 1975

Date	Event	Winner	Winner's Share
Dec. 30-Jan. 4	ARC Alameda Open, Alameda, Cal.	Barry Asher	$7,000
Jan. 7-11	Los Angeles Open	Earl Anthony	7,000
Jan. 14-18	Showboat Invitational, Las Vegas	Carmen Salvino	14,000
Jan. 21-25	Denver Open	Larry Laub	7,000
Jan. 28-Feb. 1	King Louie Open, Kansas City, Mo.	Mark Roth	7,000
Feb. 4-8	Copenhagen Open, Cleveland	Paul Colwell	10,000
Feb. 11-15	Fair Lanes Open, Springfield, Va.	Gary Dickinson	7,500
Feb. 18-22	Long Island Open, Garden City, N.Y.	Earl Anthony	7,000
Feb. 25-Mar. 1	Midas Open, Hartford, Conn.	Nelson Burton Jr.	14,000
Mar. 4-8	Ebonite Don Carter Classic, Miami	Dick Ritger	7,500
Mar. 11-15	Lincoln-Mercury Open, St. Louis.	Ed Ressler	8,000
Mar. 18-22	Monroe Max-Air Open, New Orleans	Don Helling	10,000
Mar. 23-29	BPAA U.S. Open, Dallas	Steve Neff	10,000
Apr. 1-5	Miller High Life Open, Milwaukee	Dave Davis	10,000
Apr. 8-12	Ebonite Open, Toledo, Ohio.	Louie Moore	10,000
Apr. 15-19	Firestone Tournament of Champions, Akron	Dave Davis	25,000

Leading PBA Averages in 1974

	Name, City	Tournaments	Games	Pinfall	Average
1.	Earl Anthony, Tacoma, Wash.	28	981	215,229	219.394
2	Johnny Petraglia, Staten Island, N.Y.	21	683	147,106	215.382
3.	Mark Roth, New York, N.Y.	21	662	142,459	215.195
4	Larry Laub, San Francisco, Cal.	30	963	207,084	214.838
5.	Gary Mage, Seattle, Wash.	19	602	128,668	213.734
6.	Dick Weber, St. Louis, Mo.	20	730	155,717	213.311
7.	Dave Davis, Atlanta, Ga.	24	770	164,066	213.073
8.	Butch Soper, Tustin, Cal.	14	399	84,913	212.815
9.	Roy Buckley, Columbus, Oh.	27	485	173,571	212.040
10.	Nelson Burton, St. Louis, Mo.	28	841	178,598	211.770
11.	Dick Ritger, Hartford, Conn.	24	773	164,069	211.581
12.	Jay Robinson, Los Angeles, Cal.	31	969	204,787	211.422
13.	Jim Stefanich, Joliet, Ill.	27	771	162,734	210.942
14.	Butch Gearhart, Houston, Tex.	19	583	122,976	210.937
15.	Carmen Salvino, Chicago, Ill.	31	935	197,142	210.817
16.	Johnny Guenther, Seattle, Wash.	14	426	89,732	210.638
17.	Gary Dickinson, Ft. Worth, Tex.	31	803	169,359	210.622
18.	Don McCune, Munster, Ind.	31	913	192,868	210.193
19.	Don Johnson, Akron, Oh.	25	661	138,688	209.815
20.	Craig Mueller, Union, N.J.	15	373	78,159	209.542

Firestone Tournament of Champions

This is professional bowling's richest tournament and has been held each year since its inception in 1965, in Akron, Oh., the home of the Professional Bowlers Association. First prize is $25.000.

Year	Winner	Year	Winner	Year	Winner	Year	Winner
1965....	Billy Hardwick	1968....	Dave Davis	1971....	Johnny Petraglia	1974....	Earl Anthony
1966....	Wayne Zahn	1969....	Jim Godman	1972....	Mike Durbin	1975....	Dave Davis
1967....	Jim Stefanich	1970....	Don Johnson	1973....	Jim Godman		

Leading PBA Averages by Years

Year	Player	Tour- naments	Average	Year	Player	Tour- naments	Average
1962 — Don Carter, St. Louis, Mo.....		25	212.844	1969 — Bill Hardwick, Louisville, Ky...		33	212.957
1963 — Billy Hardwick, Louisville, Ky..		26	210.346	1970 — Nelson Burton, Jr., St. Louis, Mo.		32	214,908
1964 — Ray Bluth, St. Louis, Mo......		27	210.512	1971 — Don Johnson, Akron, Oh.....		31	213.977
1965 — Dick Weber, St. Louis, Mo....		19	211.895	1972 — Don Johnson, Akron, Oh.....		30	215.290
1966 — Wayne Zahn, Atlanta, Ga.....		27	208.663	1973 — Earl Anthony, Tacoma, Wash..		29	215.799
1967 — Wayne Zahn, Atlanta, Ga.....		29	212.342	1974 — Earl Anthony, Tacoma, Wash..		28	219.394
1968 — Jim Stefanich, Joliet, Ill.......		33	211.895				

PBA Leading Money Winners

Total winnings are from PBA, ABC Masters, and BPAA All-Star tournaments only, and do not include numerous other tournaments nor earnings from special television shows and matches.

Year	Player	Total	Year	Player	Total	Year	Player	Total
1959	Dick Weber.........	$ 7,672	1965	Dick Weber.........	47,674	1970	Mike McGrath.......	52,049
1960	Don Carter.........	22,525	1966	Wayne Zahn........	54,720	1971	Johnny Petraglia....	85,065
1961	Dick Weber.........	26,280	1967	Dave Davis........	54,165	1972	Don Johnson........	56,648
1962	Don Carter.........	49,972	1968	Jim Stefanich......	67,377	1973	Don McCune........	69,000
1963	Dick Weber.........	46,333	1969	Billy Hardwick......	64,160	1974	Earl Anthony........	99,585
1964	Bob Strampe........	33,592						

Women's International Bowling Congress Champions

Year	Individual	All Events	Two- Woman Teams	Five- Woman Teams
1969	Joan Bender, Arvada, Col....... **690**	Helen Duval, Berkeley, Cal... **1,927**	Gloria Bouvia, Portland, Ore.- Judy Cook, Grandview, Mo... **1,315**	Fitzpatrick Chevrolet, Concord, Cal..... **2,986**
1970	Dorothy Fothergill, N. Attleboro, Mass.. **695**	Dorothy Fothergill.. **1,984**	Gloria Bouvia, Portland, Ore.- Judy Cook, Kansas City, Mo... **1,256**	Parker-Fothergill Pro Shop, Cranston, R.I............ **3,034**
1971	Mary Scruggs, Richmond, Va..... **698**	Lorrie Koch, Carpentersville, Ill............. **1,840**	Dorothy Fothergill, N. Attleboro, Mass.- Mildred Martorella, Rochester, N.Y.... **1,263**	Koenig & Strey Real Estate, Wilmette, Ill..... **2,891**
1972	D. D. Jacobson, Playa Del Rey, Cal.. **737**	Mildred Martorella, Rochester, N.Y... **1,877**	Judy Roberts- Betty Remmick, Denver, Lakewood, Col............ **1,247**	Angeltown Creations, Placentia, Cal..... **2,838**
1973	Bobbie Buffaloe, Costa Mesa, Cal..... **706**	Toni Calvery, Midwest City, Okla............ **1,910**	Dorothy Fothergill, N. Attleboro, Mass.- Mildred Martorella, Rochester, N.Y.... **1,238**	Fitzpatrick Chevrolet, Concord, Cal..... **2,897**
1974	Shirley Garms, Lake Island, Ill..... **702**	Judy Cook Soutar, Kansas City, Mo... **1,944**	Jane Leszczynski, Milwaukee-Carol Miller, Waukesha, Wis............ **1,313**	Kalicak International Construction, Kansas City, Mo... **2,973**
1975	Barbara Leicht, Albany, N.Y. ... **689**	Virginia Park, Whittier, Cal..... **1,821**	Jennette James, Oyster Bay, N.Y., and Dawn Raddatz, E. Northport, N.Y. **1,234**	Atlanta Bowling Center (Ga.) Buffalo, N.Y...... **2,836**

Records of 300 Games in WIBC Sanctioned Play

1973-74—Irene Arslan, Sunnyvale, Cal.; Nancy Bassett, Salina, Kan.; Leemoi Bekey, San Rafael, Cal.; Josephine Borges, Oakland, Cal.; Lydia Brewer, LaMirada, Cal.; Judith Chapman, Littleton, Col.; Ferrie Crawford, Philadelphia, Pa.; Ethel Dezell, Staples, Minn.; Mary Ickes, Woodville, Ohio; Barbara Kaufold, Butler, Pa.; Nell Kleinschmidt, Mt. Carmel, Ill.; Betty Morris, Stockton, Cal.; Lou Lane, Austin, Texas; Patsy Lynn, Spokane, Wash.; Lupe McCabe, Fresno, Cal.; Cindy Pearl, Louisville, Ky.; Roslyn Stewart, Detroit, Mich.; Mel Williams, Fayetteville, N.C.; Jacqueline Wissler, Reading, Pa.

1972-73—Betty Geisler, San Antonio, Texas; Helen Gilkerson, Lexington, Ky.; Connie Graham, Victorville, Cal.; Rita Justice, Wilmington, Del.; Barbara Keicher, Depew, N.Y.; Cindy Kimbirauskas, Lansing, Mich.; Joan Lilly, Covington, Ky.; Paula Martin, Houston, Texas; Phyllis Max, Toledo, Ohio; Nancy Mazzier, Weed, Cal.; Dorothy McMullen, Madison, Ill.; Jean Nash, Toledo, Ohio; Marge Pacanovski, Westfield, N.Y.; Ann Pcisguy, Oregon, Ohio; Joan Ray, Yuma, Ariz.; Barbara

Skokan, Perth Amboy, N.J.; Gaylene Suedbeck, Slayton, Minn.; Katherine Thompkins, Seattle, Wash.; Val Tridico, Mansfield, Ohio; Bonnie Triptow, Taylorsville, Utah; Geneva Tucker, Nashville, Tenn.; Jeannine Williams, Fremont, Cal.; Kenda Williams, Amarillo, Texas; Susan Zaluk, Garwood, N.J.

1974-75—Mary Altmeyer, St. Louis, Mo. (2); Dianne Bonney, New London, Ohio; Ann Carroll, Fort Worth, Texas; Linda Clayton, Alexandria, La.; Virginia Copeland, Cypress, Cal.; Shirley Davis, Asheville, N.C.; Charlene Grossman, Rothbury, Mich.; Linda Harris, Minot, N.D.; Linda Huffman, Topeka, Kan.; Barbara Leicht, Albany, N.Y.; Joan McCord, Cedar Rapids, Iowa; Myrtie Minster, Irving, Texas; Sharon Pippitt, Liberal, Kan.; Judy Soutar, Grandview, Mo.; Cecilia Straley, Omaha, Neb.; Barbara Urban, St. Paul, Minn.; Barbara Waling, Northville, Mich.; Claudine Walker, Chicago, Ill.; Jean Worthy, Norwalk, Cal.; Patricia Paulson, Mt. Prospect, Ill.; Barbara Cunningham, Waco, Texas.

Rifle and Pistol Individual Championships in 1975
Source: National Rifle Association of America

National Rifle & Pistol Championships (Outdoor, Conventional)

Pistol—SFC Bonnie D. Harmon, USA, Ft. Benning, Ga., 2615-95X.

Civilian Pistol — Dr. Darius R. Young, Winterburn, Alberta 2584-91X.

Woman Pistol—SFC. Barbara J. Hile, UDA, Ft. Benning, Ga., 2522-56X.

Senior Pistol—Gil Hebard, Knoxville, Ill., 2555-79X.

Police Pistol—Elwyn M. Burnett, Romeo, Mich., 2593-75X.

Smallbore Rifle Prone—Maj. Lones W. Wigger, Jr., USA, Columbus, Ga., 6399-556X.

Woman Smallbore Rifle Prone—Schuyler Helbing, Ft. Worth, Texas, 6390-523X.

Senior Smallbore Rifle Prone—George J. Stidworthy, Jr., Prescott, Ariz., 6388-503X.

Civilian Smallbore Rifle Prone—David P. Weaver, Oil City, Pa., 6396-519X.

Smallbore Rifle Position—Lt. Robert A. Gustin, Jr., San Dimas, Cal., 1557-71X.

Senior Smallbore Rifle Position—Robert A. Makielski, Mishawaka, Ind., 1527-55X.

Junior Smallbore Rifle Position—Sherri A. Lewellen, Canoga Park, Cal., 1548-61X.

High Power Rifle—Gary L. Anderson, Axtell, Neb., 1580-71X.

Match Rifle Regular Service—TSGT Grantland D. Gruver, USAF, Council Bluffs, Iowa, 1566-57X.

Match Rifle Senior—Creighton O. Audette, Springfield, Vt., 1550-51X.

Match Rifle Woman—Betty J. Swarthout, Westland, Mich., 1506-30X.

Match Rifle Junior—Randy S. Ciavarelli, Plymouth, Iowa, 1537-39X.

Match Rifle Collegiate—G. David Tubb, Canadian, Texas, 1576-55X.

Service Rifle Champion—SFC Earl L. Waterman, USA, Ft. Benning, Ga., 1579-70X.

Service Rifle Civilian—Thomas W. Matpack, Painesville, Ohio, 1510-36X.

Service Rifle Woman—PO3 Mary B. Feeney, USN, San Diego, Cal., 1499-42X.

Service Rifle Junior—Stephen Florich, Ft. Meade, Md., 1479-25X.

Service Rifle Senior—MSG Gerritt H. Stekeur, NGUS, Latham, N.Y., 1563-48X.

Service Rifle Collegiate—Lee Deneke, Nashville, Tenn., 1505-25X.

U. S. NRA International Shooting Championships

English Match—Capt. Margaret Murdock, USAR, Topeka, Kan., 1779.

Smallbore 3-Position—Maj. Lones W. Wigger, Jr., USA, Columbus, Ga., 3468.

Air Rifle—Capt. David Cramer, Aliquippa, Pa., 380.

Junior Air Rifle—Gloria Parmentier, Alexandria, Va., 379.

Ladies Air Rifle—Marie Alire, Mesa, Ariz., 375.

Free Rifle, 300 Meter—Capt. Lanny Bassham, USA, Columbus, Ga., 3346.

Running Boar—Lt. Louis Theimer, USA. Columbus, Ga., 1659.

Running Boar, Mixed Speed—Lt. Louis Theimer, USA, Columbus, Ga., 372.

Rapid Fire Pistol—SP4 Terry Anderson, NGUS, Gulfport, Miss., 1761.

Air Pistol—CW2 Pasquale Melaragno, USAR, Providence, R. I., 386.

Ladies Air Pistol—PFC Ruby Fox, USAR, Parker, Ariz., 368.

Junior Air Pistol—Brian J. Hopkins, Omaha, Neb., 363.

Center Fire Pistol—SFC Hershel L. Anderson, USA, Columbus, Ga., 1779.

Ladies Smallbore Pistol—SFC Barbara J. Hile, USA, Columbus, Ga., 1731.

Standard Pistol—SGT Jimmy Dorsey, USMC., Spokane, Wash., 1725.

Free Pistol—SFC Hershel L. Anderson, USA, Columbus, Ga., 1670.

Ladies Standard Rifle Prone—PFC Sue Sandusky, USAR, Ft. Worth, Texas, 1745.

Junior Standard Rifle Prone—Matthew Stark, Alexandria, Va., 1757.

Junior Standard Rifle 3-Position—Timothy Rennie, Wilmington, Del., 1669.

Ladies Standard Rifle 3-Position—Capt. Margaret Murdock, USAR, Topeka, Kan., 1727.

Standard Rifle 3-Position—Carl Guenther, Los Angeles, Cal., 1719.

Clay Pigeon—SP5 Donald Haldeman, USAR, Souderton, Pa., 297.

Ladies Clay Pigeon—Audrey Grosch, Minneapolis, Minn., 284.

Junior Clay Pigeon—Guy Avedisian, Hindale, Ill., 280.

Int'l. Skeet—SP4 John Satterwhite, USAR, Kirkland, Wash., 292.

Ladies Int'l. Skeet—Connie Hoyle, Poway, Cal., 276.

Junior Int'l. Skeet—Dean Clark, Garrettsville, Ohio, 275.

Big Bore Standard Rifle—Lt. Edward F. Etzel, USA, Columbus, Ga., 1131.

National Indoor Rifle & Pistol Championships

Conventional Rifle—Capt. John H. Writer, USAR, Clarendon Hills, Ill., 799.

Conventional Rifle Woman—Karen E. Monex, San Leandro, Cal., 797.

International Rifle—Capt. Lanny R. Bassham, USA, Ft. Benning, Ga., 579.

International Rifle Woman—Lt. Diana T. Zimmerman, USA, Ft. Benning, Ga., 579.

NRA 3-Position Rifle—Capt. Lanny R. Bassham, 591.

NRS 3-Position Rifle Woman—Lt. Diana T. Zimmerman, 575.

Conventional Pistol—James R. Lenardson, Lambertville, Mich., 890.

Conventional Pistol Woman—SFC Barbara J. Hile, USA, Ft. Benning, Ga., 860.

International Pistol—SSgt. Marvin D. Black, USA, Ft. Benning, Ga., 569.

International Pistol Woman—Capt. Sharon Best, USA, Ft. Benning, Ga., 535.

National Intercollegiate Rifle & Pistol Championships

NRA 3-Position Rifle—L. Lynn Howell, E. Tenn. State, 290.

NRA 3-Position Rifle Woman—L. Lynn Howell, 290.

NRA 3-Position Rifle ROTC—Robert G. Lott, Tenn. Tech, 290.

International Rifle—Wanda R. Oliver, E. Wash. State, 581.

International Rifle Woman—Wanda R. Oliver, 581.

International Rifle ROTC—Wanda R. Oliver, 581.

Conventional Pistol—Stanley P. Siefke, USAF Academy, 862.

Conventional Pistol Woman—Lynn C. Buchan, Ohio State, 788.

Conventional Pistol ROTC—Joseph Evans, SW Oklahoma State, 844.

International Pistol—Stephan C. Goldstein, MIT, 818.

International Pistol Woman—Annmarie E. Condon, Boston State, 658.

International Pistol ROTC—Brian J. Peter, USMMA, 784.

AAU Karate Championships, 1975
Cleveland, Ohio, July 19-20

Men

Advanced Sparring—Billy Blanks, Erie, Pa.

Intermediate Sparring—Jeff Hodges, N. Canton, Oh.

Novice Sparring—James Hopkins, Boston, Mass.

Advanced Forms—Will Haynie, Virginia Beach, Va.

Intermediate Forms—Carlton Francis, Boston, Mass.

Novice Forms—Gary Yano, Parma, Oh.

Weapons—Brother Wayne Welling, Toledo, Oh.

Women

Advanced Sparring—Sandra Wather, Detroit, Mich.

Intermediate Sparring—Gail Kleinschmidt, Manchester, Conn.

Novice Sparring—Hazel Provis, Greensville, Miss.

Advanced Forms—S. Anne Small, Maumee, Oh.

Intermediate Forms—Jane Beer, E. Berlin, Conn.

Novice Forms—Betsy Uhlman, Bowling Green, Oh.

Weapons—Karen Tolczyk, New Britain, Conn.

World Swimming Records

As of Sept. 1, 1975

Effective June 1, 1969, FINA will recognize only records made over a 50-meter course.

Men's Freestyle

Distance	Time	Holder	Country	Where made	Date
100 Meters	0:50.59	Jim Montgomery	U.S.A.	Kansas City, Kan.	Aug. 23, 1975
200 Meters	1:50.32	Bruce Furniss	U.S.A.	Long Beach, Cal.	June 18, 1975
400 Meters	3:53.31	Tim Shaw	U.S.A.	Long Beach, Cal.	June 19, 1975
800 Meters	8:15.88	Stephen Holland	Australia	Christchurch	Jan. 31, 1974
1,500 Meters	15:20.91	Tim Shaw	U.S.A.	Long Beach, Cal.	June 20, 1975

Men's Breaststroke

100 Meters	1:03.88	John Hencken	U.S.A.	Concord, Cal.	Aug. 31, 1974
200 Meters	2:18.21	John Hencken	U.S.A.	Concord, Cal.	Sept. 1, 1974

Men's Butterfly

100 Meters	0.54.27	Mark Spitz	U.S.A.	Munich	Aug. 31, 1972
200 Meters	2:00.07	Mark Spitz	U.S.A.	Munich	Aug. 28, 1972

Men's Backstroke

100 Meters	0:56.30	Roland Matthes	E. Germany	Munich	Sept. 4, 1972
200 Meters	2:01.87	Roland Matthes	E. Germany	Belgrade	Sept. 6, 1973

Men's Individual Medley

200 Meters	2:06.32	David Wilkie	Scotland	Vienna	Aug. 24, 1974
		Steve Furniss	U.S.A.	Concord, Cal.	Sept. 1, 1974
400 Meters	4:28.89	Andras Hargitay	Hungary	Vienna	Aug. 20, 1974

Men's Freestyle Relays

400 M. (4x100)	3:24.85	Nat'l Team (B. Furniss, Coan, Montgomery, Murphy)	U.S.A.	Cali, Colombia	July 23, 1975
800 M. (4x200)	7:30.54	Long Beach (Cal.) (Favero, Shaw, S. Furniss, B. Furniss)	U.S.A.	Kansas City, Kan.	Aug. 22, 1975

Men's Medley Relays

400 M. (4x100)	3:48.16	Nat'l Team (Stamm, Bruce, Spitz, Heidenreich)	U.S.A.	Munich, W. Germany	Sept. 4, 1972

Women's Freestyle

100 Meters	0:56.96	Kornelia Ender	E. Germany	Vienna	Aug. 19, 1974
200 Meters	2:02.27	Kornelia Ender	E. Germany	Dresden	Mar., 1975
400 Meters	4:14.76	Shirley Babashoff	U.S.A.	Long Beach, Cal.	June 20, 1975
800 Meters	8:43.48	Jenny Turrall	Australia	London	Mar. 31, 1975
1,500 Meters	16:33.94	Jenny Turrall	Australia	Concord, Cal.	Aug. 25, 1974

Women's Breaststroke

100 Meters	1:12.28	Renate Vogel	E. Germany	Concord, Cal.	Sept. 1, 1974
200 Meters	2:34.99	Carla Linke	E. Germany	Vienna	Aug. 19, 1974

Women's Butterfly

100 Meters	1:01.24	Kornelia Ender	E. Germany	Cali, Colombia	July 24, 1975
200 Meters	2:13.76	Rosemarie Kother	E. Germany	Belgrade	Sept. 8, 1973

Women's Backstroke

100 Meters	1:02.98	Ulrike Richter	E. Germany	Concord, Cal.	Sept. 1, 1974
200 Meters	2:15.46	Brigit Treiber	E. Germany	Cali, Colombia	July 25, 1975

Women's Individual Medley

200 Meters	2:18.83	Ulrike Tauber	E. Germany	Wittenberg, E. Ger.	June, 1975
400 Meters	4:52.2	Ulrike Tauber	E. Germany	Wittenberg, E. Ger.	June, 1975

Women's Freestyle Relays

400 M. (4x100)	3:51.99	Nat'l Team (Heddy, Marshall, Peyton, Babashoff)	U.S.A.	Concord, Cal.	Aug. 8, 1974

Women's Medley Relays

400 M. (4x100)	4:13.78	Nat'l Team (Richter, Vogel, Kother, Ender)	E. Germany	Vienna	Aug. 24, 1974

National AAU Indoor Diving Championships in 1975

Cleveland, Ohio, Apr. 2-5, 1975

Men

One-Meter Springboard — Tim Moore, Columbus, Ohio, 553.-68 pts.

Three-Meter Springboard — Phil Boggs, USAF, 596.82 pts.

Ten-Meter Platform — Tim Moore, 522.99 pts.

Women

One-Meter Springboard — Jenni Chandler, Lincoln, Ala., 446.-49 pts.

Three-Meter Springboard — Carrie Irish, New Canaan, Conn., 511.41 pts.

Ten-Meter Platform — Carrie Irish, 346.83 pts.

Swimming Events in 1975
National AAU Short Course Championship
Cincinnati, Ohio, Apr. 9-12, 1975

Men

100 Yd. Freestyle—Andy Coan. **Time—0:44.501.**
200 Yd. Freestyle—Tim Shaw. **Time—1:38.357.**
500 Yd. Freestyle—Tim Shaw. **Time—4:22.570.**
1,650 Yd. Freestyle—John Naber. **Time—15:09.510.**
100 Yd. Backstroke—John Naber. **Time—0:50.368.**
200 Yd. Backstroke—John Naber. **Time—1:48.135.**
100 Yd. Breaststroke—John Hencken. **Time—0:56.166.**
200 Yd. Breaststroke—John Hencken. **Time—2:00.894.**
100 Yd. Butterfly—Gary Hall. **Time—0:48.863.**
200 Yd. Butterfly—Greg Jagenburg. **Time—1:47.283.**
200 Yd. Individual Medley—Lee Engstrand. **Time—1:50.317.**
400 Yd. Individual Medley—Andras Hargitay. **Time—3:54.916.**
400 Yd. Medley Relay—Southern California. **Time—3:19.722.**
400 Yd. Freestyle Relay—Indiana. **Time—2:59.340.**
800 Yd. Freestyle Relay—Southern California. **Time—6:35.613.**
Team Champion—Southern California.

Women

100 Yd. Freestyle—Shirley Babashoff. **Time—0:50.974.**
200 Yd. Freestyle—Shirley Babashoff. **Time—1:49.528.**
500 Yd. Freestyle—Shirley Babashoff. **Time—4:50.950.**
1,650 Yd. Freestyle—Jo Harshbarger. **Time—16:27.114.**
100 Yd. Backstroke—Tauna Vandeweghe. **Time—0:58.128.**
200 Yd. Backstroke—Nancy Garapick. **Time—2:02.843.**
100 Yd. Breaststroke—Kim Dunson. **Time—1:05.254.**
200 Yd. Breaststroke—Marcia Morey. **Time—2:18.775.**
100 Yd. Butterfly—Deena Deardurff. **Time—0:55.708.**
200 Yd. Butterfly—Valerie Lee. **Time—2:00.702.**
200 Yd. Individual Medley—Jenni Franks. **Time—2:04.747.**
400 Yd. Medley Relay—Santa Clara SC. **Time—3:53.709.**
400 Yd. Freestyle Relay—Mission Viejo. **Time—3:27.249.**
800 Yd. Freestyle Relay—Mission Viejo. **Time—7:28.779.**
Team Champion—Mission Viejo.

World Swimming Championships, 1975
Cali, Colombia, July 18-27, 1975

Men

100 Meter Freestyle—Andy Coan, U.S. **Time—0:51.25.**
200 Meter Freestyle—Tim Shaw, U.S. **Time—1:51.04**
400 Meter Freestyle—Tim Shaw. **Time—3:54.88.**
1,500 Meter Freestyle—Tim Shaw. **Time—15:28.92.**
100 Meter Backstroke—Roland Matthes, E. Germany. **Time—0:58.15.**
200 Meter Backstroke—Zoltan Verraszto, Hungary. **Time—2:05.05.**
100 Meter Breaststroke—David Wilkie, Great Britain. **Time—1:04.26.**
200 Meter Breaststroke—David Wilkie. **Time—2:18.23.**
100 Meter Butterfly—Greg Jagenburg, U.S. **Time—0:55.63.**
200 Meter Butterfly—Bill Forrester, U.S. **Time—2:01.95.**
200 Meter Individual Medley—Andra Hargitay, Hungary. **Time—2:07.72.**
400 Meter Individual Medley—Andra Hargitay. **Time—4:32.57.**
400 Meter Medley Relay—United States. **Time—3:49.00.**
400 Meter Freestyle Relay—United States. **Time—3:24.85.**
800 Meter Freestyle Relay—West Germany. **Time—7:39.44.** (U.S. disqualified).
Springboard Diving—Phil Boggs, U.S. **597.12 pts.**
Platform Diving—Klaus Dibiasi Italy. **547.98 pts.**

Women

100 Meter Freestyle—Kornelia Ender, E. Germany. **Time—0:56.50.**
200 Meter Freestyle—Shirley Babashoff, U.S. **Time—2:02.50.**
400 Meter Freestyle—Shirley Babashoff. **Time—4:16.87.**
800 Meter Freestyle—Jenny Turrall, Australia. **Time—8:44.75.**
100 Meter Backstroke—Ulrike Richter, E. Germany. **Time—1:03.30.**
200 Meter Backstroke—Brigit Treiber, E. Germany. **Time—2:15.46.**
100 Meter Breaststroke—Hannelore Anke, E. Germany. **Time—1:12.72.**
200 Meter Breaststroke—Hannelore Anke. **Time—2:37.25.**
100 Meter Butterfly—Kornelia Ender, E. Germany. **Time—1:01.24.**
200 Meter Butterfly—Rosemarie Kother, E. Germany. **Time—2:13.82.**
200 Meter Individual Medley—Kathy Heddy, U.S. **Time—2:19.80.**
400 Meter Individual Medley—Ulrike Tauber, E. Germany. **Time—4:52.76.**
400 Meter Medley Relay—E. Germany. **Time—4:14.74.**
400 Meter Freestyle Relay—E. Germany. **Time—3:49.37.**
Springboard Diving—Irinna Kalina, USSR. **489.81 pts.**
Platform Diving—Janet Ely, U.S. **403.89 pts.**

North American Soccer League, 1975
Final Standings

Northern Division	Won	Lost	GF	GA	Bonus Points	Total Points	Central Division	Won	Lost	GF	GA	Bonus Points	Total Points
Boston	13	9	41	29	38	116	St. Louis	13	9	38	34	37	115
Toronto	13	9	39	36	36	114	Chicago	12	10	39	33	34	106
New York	10	12	39	38	31	91	Denver	9	13	37	42	31	85
Rochester	6	16	29	49	28	64	Dallas	9	13	33	38	29	83
Hartford	6	16	27	51	25	61	San Antonio	6	16	24	46	23	59
Eastern Division							**Western Division**						
Tampa Bay	16	6	46	27	39	135	Portland	16	6	43	27	42	138
Miami	14	8	47	30	39	123	Seattle	15	7	42	28	39	129
Washington	12	10	42	47	40	112	Los Angeles	12	10	42	33	35	107
Philadelphia	10	12	33	42	30	90	Vancouver	11	11	38	28	33	99
Baltimore	9	13	34	52	33	87	San Jose	8	14	37	48	35	83

Total points: Win-6 pts., Loss-0 pts. Bonus Points-one point is awarded for each goal scored up to a maximum of three per team per game. Playoff winner — Tampa Bay.

Top Scorers

Player (Team)	Goals	Assists	Pts.	Player (Team)	Goals	Assists	Pts.
Steven David (Miami)	23	6	52	Ade Coker (Boston)	10	6	26
Gordon Hill (Chicago)	16	7	39	Partick Netsolenque (Denver)	10	5	25
Derek Smethurst (Tampa Bay)	18	3	39	John Rowlands (Seattle)	10	5	25
Peter Withe (Portland)	16	6	38	John Coyne (Toronto)	7	11	25
Uri Banhoffer (Los Angeles)	14	9	37	Chris Bahr (Philadelphia)	11	2	24
Tommy Ord (Rochester/N.Y.)	16	3	35	Mike Flater (Denver)	10	4	24
Ilija Mitic (San Jose)	15	3	33	John Hawley (St. Louis)	11	2	24

Top Goalkeepers

Goalkeeper (Team)	Minutes	Goals	Avg.	Goalkeeper (Team)	Minutes	Goals	Avg.
Shep Messing (Boston)	1639.32	17	0.93	Graham Brown (Portland)	1948.55	26	1.20
Barry Watling (Seattle)	2032.52	26	1.15	Zeljko Bilecki (Toronto)	1949.40	27	1.25

World Track and Field Records

As of Sept., 1975
*Indicates pending record; a number of new records await confirmation

Men   Running

Event	Record	Holder	Country	Date	Where made
100 yds.	9.0 s.	Ivory Crockett	U.S.A.	May 11, 1974	Knoxville, Tenn.
220 yds.	19.5 s.	Tommie Smith	U.S.A.	May 7, 1966	San Jose, Cal.
220 yds.	*19.9 s (Turn)	Don Quarrie	Jamaica	June, 1975	Eugene, Ore.
		Steve Williams	U.S.A.	June, 1975	Eugene, Ore.
440 yds.	44.5	John Smith	U.S.A.	June 26, 1972	Eugene, Ore.
880 yds.	*1 m., 43.9 s.	Rick Wohlhuter	U.S.A.	June, 1974	Los Angeles
1 mile	3 m., 49.4 s.	John Walker	New Zealand	Aug. 12, 1975	Goteborg, Sweden
2 miles	8 m., 13.8 s.	Brendon Foster	Gt. Britain	Aug. 27, 1973	London
3 miles	12 m., 47.8 s.	Emiel Puttemans	Belgium	Sept. 20, 1972	Brussels
6 miles	26 m., 47.0 s.	Ron Clarke	Australia	July 14, 1965	Oslo
10 miles	46 m., 04.2 s.	Willy Polleunis	Belgium	Sept. 20, 1972	Brussels
15 miles	1 hr., 12 min., 22.6 s.	Seppo Nikkari	Finland	Oct. 14, 1973	Jyvdskyld

Running — Metric Distances

100 meters	9.9 s.	Jim Hines	U.S.A.	June 20, 1968	Sacramento
		Charlie Greene	U.S.A.	June 20, 1968	Sacramento
		Ronnie Smith	U.S.A.	June 20, 1968	Sacramento
		Jim Hines	U.S.A.	Oct. 14, 1968	Mexico City
		Eddie Hart	U.S.A.	July 1, 1972	Eugene, Ore.
		Reynaud Robinson	U.S.A.	July 1, 1972	Eugene, Ore.
		Steve Williams	U.S.A.	June 21, 1974	Los Angeles
		Reggie Jones	U.S.A.	July, 1975	Boston
200 meters	19.5 s.	Tommie Smith	U.S.A.	May 7, 1966	San Jose, Cal.
200 meters	19.8 s. (Turn)	Tommie Smith	U.S.A.	Oct. 16, 1968	Mexico City
		Donald Quarrie	Jamaica	Aug. 3, 1971	Cali, Colombia
400 meters	43.8 s.	Lee Evans	U.S.A.	Oct. 18, 1968	Mexico City
800 meters	1 m., 43.7 s.	Marcello Fiasconaro	Italy	June 27, 1973	Milan, Italy
1,000 meters	2 m., 13.9 s.	Rick Wohlhuter	U.S.A.	July 30, 1974	Oslo
1,500 meters	3 m., 32.2 s.	Filbert Bayi	Tanzania	Feb. 2, 1974	Christchurch, N.Z.
2,000 meters	4 m., 56.2 s.	Michel Jazy	France	Oct. 12, 1966	Saint Maur, France
3,000 meters	7 m., 35.2 s.	Brendon Foster	Gt. Britain	Aug. 3, 1974	Gateshead, Eng.
5,000 meters	13 m., 13 s.	Emiel Puttemans	Belgium	Sept. 20, 1972	Brussels
10,000 meters	27 m., 30.8 s.	Dave Bedford	Gr. Britain	July 13, 1973	London
20,000 meters	57 m., 44.4 s.	Gaston Roelants	Belgium	Sept. 20, 1972	Brussels
25,000 meters	1 hr., 14 m., 55.6 s.	Seppo Nikkari	Finland	Oct. 14, 1971	Jyvdskyld
30,000 meters	1 hr., 31 m., 30.4 s.	Jim Alder	Gr. Britain	Sept. 5, 1970	London
3,000 meter stpl.	*8 m, 09.8 s.	Anders Gaerderud	Sweden	June, 1975	Stockholm

Hurdles

120 yards	13.0 s.	Rod Milburn	U.S.A.	June 25, 1971	Eugene, Ore.
		Rod Milburn	U.S.A.	June 20, 1973	Eugene, Ore.
220 yards	21.9 s.	Don Styron	U.S.A.	Apr. 2, 1960	Baton Rouge
440 yards	48.7 s.	Jim Bolding	U.S.A.	July 24, 1974	Turin, Italy
110 meters	*13.0 s	Guy Drut	France	Aug., 1975	W. Berlin
200 meters	21.9 s.	Don Styron	U.S.A.	Apr. 2, 1960	Baton Rouge
200 meters	22.5 s..(Turn)	Martin Lauer	W.Germany	July 7, 1959	Zurich
		Glenn Davis	U.S.A.	Aug. 20, 1960	Berne
400 meters	47.8 s.	John Akii-Bua	Uganda	Sept. 2, 1972	Munich

Relay Races

440 yds. (4x110) (2 Turns)	38.6 s.	USC (McCullough, Kuller, Simpson, Miller)	U.S.A.	June 17, 1967	Provo, Utah
880 yds. (4x220)	1 m., 21.7 s.	Texas A&M. (Rogers, Woods, M. Mills, C. Mills)	U.S.A.	Apr. 24, 1970	Des Moines
1 mile (4x440)	*3 m., 02.4 s.	National Team (Ray, Taylor, Peoples, Vinson)	U.S.A.	July, 1975	Durham, N.C.
2 miles (4x880)	7 mi., 10.4 s.	Chicago TC (Bach, Sparks, Paul, Wohlhuter)	U.S.A.	May 12, 1973	Durham, N.C.
4 miles (4x1 mile)	16 m., 02.8 s.	New Zealand Nat'l. Team	New Zealand	Feb. 3, 1972	Auckland, N.Z.

Relay Races—Metric Distances

400 mtrs.	38.2 s.	Nat'l. Team (Greene, Pender, R. Smith, Hines)	U.S.A.	Oct. 20, 1968	Mexico City
		Nat'l. Team (Black, Taylor, Tinker, Hart)	U.S.A.	Sept. 10, 1972	Munich
800 mtrs. (4x200)	1 m.,21.5s	Nat'l. Team. (Ossola, Obeti, Benedetti, Mennea)	Italy	July 21, 1972	Barletta
1,600 mtrs. (4x400)	2 m., 56.1 s.	Nat'l. Team (Matthews, Freeman, James, Evans)	U.S.A.	Oct. 20, 1968	Mexico City
3,200 mtrs. (4x800)	7 m., 08.6 s.	Nat'l. Team (Kinder, Adams, Bogatzki, Kemper)	W. Germany	Aug. 13, 1966	Wiesbaden

Field Events

High Jump	7 ft., 6½ in.	Dwight Stones	U.S.A.	June 11, 1973	Munich
Long Jump	29 ft., 2½ in.	Bob Beamon	U.S.A.	Oct. 18, 1968	Mexico City
Triple Jump	57 ft., 2¾ in.	Victor Saneyev	USSR	Oct. 17, 1972	Sukhumi, USSR
Pole Vault	*18 ft., 6½ in.	Dave Roberts	U.S.A.	Mar. 28, 1975	Gainesville, Fla.
16 lb. shot put	74 ft., 7 in.	Al Feuerbach	U.S.A.	May 5, 1975	San Jose, Cal.
Discus throw	*226 ft., 8 in.	John Powell	U.S.A.	May 4, 1975	Long Beach, Cal.
Javelin throw	308 ft., 8 in.	Klaus Wolfermann	W. Germany	May 5, 1973	W. Germany
16 lb. hammer throw	*260 ft., 2 in.	Walter Schmidt	W. Germany	Aug., 1975	Frankfurt
Decathlon	*8,524 pts.	Bruce Jenner	U.S.A.	Aug. 11, 1975	Eugene, Ore.

Walking

20 miles	2 h., 31 m., 33.0 s.	Anatoliy Vedjakov	USSR	Aug. 23, 1958	Moscow
30 miles	3 h., 51 m., 48.6 s.	Gerhard Weidner	W. Germany	Apr. 8, 1973	
2 hours	26,911 meters	Karl-Heinz Stadtmuller	E. Germany	Apr. 16, 1972	Berlin
30 km	2 h., 14 m., 45.6 s.	Karl-Heinz Stadtmuller	E. Germany	Apr. 16, 1972	Berlin
50 km	4 h., 00 m., 27.2 s.	Gerhard Weidner	W. Germany	Apr. 8, 1973	

Women   Running

100 yards	10.0 s.	Chi Cheng	Taiwan	June 13, 1970	Portland, Ore.
220 yards	22.6 s.	Chi Cheng	Taiwan	July 3, 1970	Los Angeles
440 yards	52.2 s.	Kathy Hammond	U.S.A.	Aug. 12, 1972	Urbana, Ill.
		Debra Sapenter	U.S.A.	June 29, 1974	Bakersfield, Cal.
880 yards	2 m., 02.0 s.	Judy Pollock	Australia	July 5, 1967	Sweden
		Dixie Willis	Australia	Mar. 3, 1962	Perth, Aust.
1 mile	4 m., 28.5 s.	Francie Larrieu	U.S.A.	Mar., 1975	Richmond, Va.
60 meters	7.2 s.	Betty Cuthbert	Australia	Feb. 27, 1960	Australia
		Irina Bochkaryova	USSR	Aug. 28, 1960	Moscow
100 meters	10.8 s.	Renate Stecher	E. Germany	July 20, 1973	Dresden
200 meters	*22 s.	Irena Szewinska	Poland	June 13, 1974	Potsdam
400 meters	49.9 s.	Irena Szewinska	Poland	June 22, 1974	Warsaw
800 meters	1m., 57.5 s.	Svetla Zlateva	Bulgaria	Aug. 24, 1973	Athens
1500 meters	4 m, 01.4 s.	Ludmila Bragina	USSR	Sept. 9, 1972	Munich
3000 meters	*8 m., 46.6 s	Grete Andersen	Norway	June, 1975	Oslo

Hurdles

100 meters	12.3 s.	Annelie Ehrhardt	E. Germany	July 22, 1973	Dresden
200 meters	25.7 s.	Pamela Ryan	Australia	Nov. 25, 1971	Melbourne
400 meters	57.3 s.	Maria Sykora	Austria	June, 1973	Frankfurt

Field Events

High jump	6 ft., 5 in.	Rosemarie Witschas	E. Germany	Sept. 8, 1974	Rome
Shot put	*70 ft., 10½ in.	Marianne Adam	E. Germany	Aug., 1975	E. Berlin
Long jump	22 ft., 5¼ in.	Heide Rosendahl	W. Germany	Sept. 3, 1970	Turin, Italy
Discus throw	*230 ft., 4 in.	Faina Melnik	USSR	Aug. 20, 1975	Zurich
Javelin	220 ft., 6 in.	Ruth Fuchs	E. Germany	Sept. 3, 1974	Rome
Pentathlon	4,932 pts.	Burglinde Pollak	E. Germany	Sept 22, 1973	Bonn

Relay Races

400 mtrs. (4x100)	*42.5 s.	National Team	E. Germany	Sept.8, 1974	Rome
800 mtrs. (4x200)	1 m., 33.8 s.	Nat'l. Team (Tranter, James, Simpson, Peal)	Gt. Britain	Aug. 24, 1968	London
880 yds. (4x220)	1 m., 35.8 s.	(Hoffman, Boyle, Kilborn, Lamy)	Australia	Nov. 9, 1969	Brisbane, Aust.
1,600 mtrs. (4x400)	3 m., 23.0 s.	Nat'l. Team	E. Germany	Sept. 10, 1972	Munich
1 mile (4x440)	*3 m., 30.3 s.	National Team (Krause, Jost, Weinstein, Barth)	W. Germany	July, 1975	Durham, N.C.

Evolution of the World Record for the One Mile Run

The table below shows how the world record for the one-mile has been lowered in the past 111 years.

Time	Individual	Year	Time	Individual	Year
4:56	Charles Lawes, Britain	1864	4:06.8	Glen Cunningham, U. S.	1934
4:36.5	Richard Webster, Britain	1865	4:06.4	Sydney Wooderson, Britain	1937
4:29	William Chinnery, Britain	1868	4:06.2	Gunder Haegg, Sweden	1942
4:28.8	W. C. Gibbs, Britain	1868	4:06.2	Arne Andersson, Sweden	1942
4:26	Walter Slade, Britain	1874	4:04.6	Gunder Haegg, Sweden	1942
4:24.5	Walter Slade, Britain	1875	4:02.6	Arne Andersson, Sweden	1943
4:23.2	Walter George, Britain	1880	4:01.6	Arne Andersson, Sweden	1944
4:21.4	Walter George, Britain	1882	4:01.4	Gunder Haegg, Sweden	1945
4:19.4	Walter George, Britain	1882	3:59.4	Roger Bannister, Britain	1954
4:18.4	Walter George, Britain	1884	3:58	John Landy, Australia	1954
4:18.2	Fred Bacon, Scotland	1894	3:57.2	Derek Ibbotson, Britain	1957
4:17	Fred Bacon, Scotland	1895	3:54.5	Herb Elliott, Australia	1958
4:15.6	Thomas Conneff, U. S.	1895	3:54.4	Peter Snell, New Zealand	1962
4:15.4	John Paul Jones, U. S.	1911	3:54.1	Peter Snell, New Zealand	1964
4:14.6	John Paul Jones, U. S.	1913	3:53.6	Michel Jazy, France	1965
4:12.6	Norman Taber, U. S.	1915	3:51.3	Jim Ryun, U. S.	1966
4:10.4	Paavo Nurmi, Finland	1923	3:51.1	Jim Ryun, U. S.	1967
4:09.2	Jules Ladoumegue, France	1931	3:51	Filbert Bayi, Tanzania	1975
4:07.6	Jack Lovelock, New Zealand	1933	3:49.4	John Walker, New Zealand	1975

Track and Field Events, 1975

68th Annual Millrose Games
New York, N.Y., Jan. 24, 1975

60 Yds.—Hasley Crawford, Eastern Mich. **Time—0:06.1.**
60 Yd. High Hurdles—Charles Foster, No. Carolina Central, **Time—0:07.**
500 Yds.—Claver Kamanya, Tanzania. **Time—0:57.5.**
600 Yds.—Stan Vinson, Eastern Mich. **Time—1:10.3.**
Half Mile—Rick Wohlhuter, Chicago TC. **Time—1:51.**
1,000 Yds.—Keith Francis, Boston College. **Time—2:08.4.**
One Mile—Filbert Bayi, Tanzania. **Time—3:59.3.**

Shot Put—Al Feuerbach, Pacific Coast Club. **68 ft. 11½ in.**
Pole Vault—Vic Dias, Beverly Hills Striders. **16 ft. 10 in.**
High Jump—Mel Embree, Harvard. **7 ft. 2 in.**
Women's 60 Yds.—Alice Annum, Sports Intl. **Time—0:06.7.**
Women's 600 Yds.—(tie) Robin Campbell, Sports Intl. and Pat Helms, Padukies. **Time—1:22.7.**
Women's 1,000 Yds.—Francie Larrieu, Pacific Coast Club. **Time—2:26.8.**

Toronto Star-Maple Leaf Indoor Games
Toronto, Ont., Feb. 14, 1975

Men

50 Yds.—Steve Williams, San Diego. **Time—0:05.1.**
50 Yd. High Hurdles—Danny Smith, Florida State. **Time—0:05.8.**
600 Yds.—Jim Bolding, Pacific Coast Club. **Time—1:11.6.**
1,000 Yds.—Mark Winzenreid, Beverly Hills Striders. **Time—2:08.7.**
One Mile—John Walker, New Zealand. **Time—3:58.0.**
3 Miles—Miruts Yifter, Ethiopia. **Time—13:07.8.**
Shot Put—Al Feuerbach, Pacific Coast Club. **67 ft. 11¼ in.**
Pole Vault—Wojciech Buciarski, Poland. **17 ft. 6¾ in.**

Women

50 Yds.—Alice Annum, Sports Intl. **Time—0:05.6.**
50 Yd. Hurdles—Annelle Ehrhardt, E. Germany. **Time—0:06.2.**
600 Yds.—Yvonne Saunders, Guelph Legion TC. **Time—1:19.5.**
880 Yds.—Maureen Crowley, British Columbia Intl. **Time—2:08.4.**
1,500 Meters—Francie Larrieu, Pacific Coast Club. **Time—4:10.4.**

7th U.S. Olympic Invitation Track Meet
New York, N.Y., Feb. 23, 1975

Men

50 Meters—Cliff Outlin, Auburn. **Time—0:05.6.**
50 Meter Hurdles—Charles Foster, No. Carolina Central. **Time—0:07.2.**
400 Meters—Clyde McPherson, N.Y. Pioneers. **Time—0:49.3.**
500 Meters—Fred Sowerby, Sports Intl. **Time—1:04.6.**
800 Meters—Mark Belger, Villanova. **Time—1:52.5.**
1,000 Meters—Rick Wohlhuter, Chicago TC. **Time—2:22.2.**
1,500 Meters—Filbert Bayi, Tanzania. **Time—3:41.2.**

3,000 Meters—Suleiman Nyambui, Tanzania. **Time—8:01.6.**
High Jump—Dwight Stones, Pacific Coast Club. **7 ft. 5¾ in.**
Pole Vault—Don Baird, Australia. **17 ft. 9 in.**

Women

50 Meters—Alice Annum Sports Intl. **Time—0:06.3.**
400 Meters—Robin Campbell, Sports Intl. **Time—0:55.0.**
800 Meters—Cheryl Toussaint, Atoms TC. **Time—2:07.1.**
1,500 Meters—Francie Larrieu, Pacific Coast Club. **Time—4:17.4.**

11th Annual NCAA Indoor Track and Field Championships
Detroit, Mich., March 15, 1975. Sponsored by the Detroit News

60 Yds.—Hasely Crawford, Eastern Mich. **Time—0:06.0.**
60 Yd. High Hurdles—Danny Smith, Florida St. **Time—0:07.0.**
440 Yds.—Mike Sands, Penn State. **Time—0:48.5.**
600 Yds.—Stan Vinson, Eastern Mich. **Time—1:10.2.**
880 Yds.—Mark Enyeart, Utah State. **Time—1:52.4.**
1,000 Yds.—Keith Francis, Boston College. **Time—2:08.4.**
One Mile—Eamonn Coghlan, Villanova. **Time—4:02.0.**
2 Miles—Nick Rose, Western Kentucky. **Time—8:44.0.**
3 Miles—John Ngeno, Washington State. **Time—13:14.4.**

Distance Medley Relay—Kansas State. **Time—9:48.2.**
One Mile Relay—Florida. **Time—3:15.8.**
2 Mile Relay—Princeton. **Time—7:35.0.**
Pole Vault—Earl Bell, Arkansas State. **17 ft. 2 in.**
High Jump—Greg Joy, Texas, El Paso. **7 ft. 2 in.**
Triple Jump—Arnold Grimes, Texas, El Paso. **55 ft. 4 in.**
Shot Put—Hans Hoglund, Texas, El Paso. **67 ft. 9¾ in.**
Team Champion—Texas, El Paso.

AAU Indoor Track and Field Championships
New York, N.Y., Feb. 28, 1975

Men

60 Yds.— Hasely Crawford, Eastern Mich. **Time — 0:06.0.**
600 yds.— Wes Williams, Mickey's Missiles. **Time — 1:11.2.**
1,000 Yds.— Rick Wohlhuter, Chicago TC. **Time — 2:06.4.**
One Mile— Filbert Bayi, Tanzania. **Time — 4:02.1.**
3 Miles— Miruts Yifter, Ethiopia. **Time — 13:07.6.**
2 Mile Walk— Ron Daniel, NYAC. **Time — 13:36.8.**
High Hurdles— Charles Foster, No. Carolina Central. **Time — 0:07.1.**
High Jump— Dwight Stones, Pacific Coast Club. **7 ft. 3 in.**
Long Jump— Arnie Robinson, Mickey's Missiles. **26 ft. 3½ in.**
Triple Jump— Tommy Haynes, U.S. Army. **53 ft. 8¾ in.**
Pole Vault— Roland Carter, Gulf Coast TC. **17 ft. 6 in.**
Shot Put— Al Feuerbach, Pacific Coast Club. **67 ft. 10 in.**
35 lb. Weight Throw— George Frenn, Hawaiian Gardens. **69 ft. 4 in.**
One Mile Relay— Seton Hall. **Time — 3:15.1.**
2 Mile Relay— Chicago TC. **Time — 7:31.2.**
Sprint Medley Relay— Penn State. **Time — 2:04.9.**
Team Champion— New York AC.

Women

60 Yds.— Alice Annum, Sports Intl. **Time — 0:06.6.**
220 Yds.— Rosalyn Bryant, Mayor Daley Youth Fdn. **Time — 0:23.6.**
440 Yds.— Robin Campbell, Sports Int. **Time — 0:55.1.**
880 Yds.— Kathy Weston, Will's Spikettes. **Time — 2:07.6.**
One Mile— Francie Larrieu, Pacific Coast Club. **Time — 4:42.8.**
2 Miles— Brenda Webb, Kettering Striders. **Time — 10:22.0.**
High Hurdles— Modupe Oshikoya, Sports Intl. **Time — 0:07.6**
One Mile Walk— Susan Brodock, Rialto Road Runners. **Time — 7:22.5.**
High Jump— Joni Huntley, Oregon TC. **6 ft.**
Long Jump— Martha Watson, Lakewood Intl. **21 ft. 2 in.**
4 Kilo Shot Put— Faina Melnik, USSR **55 ft. 7 in.**
640 Yd. Relay— Sports Intl. **Time — 1:10.4.**
880 Yd. Medley Relay— Atoms TC. **Time — 1:43.2.**
One Mile Relay— Atoms TC. **Time — 3:51.2.**
Team Champion— Sports International.

National AAU Outdoor Track and Field Championships
Eugene, Ore., June 20-21, 1975

100 Meters—Don Quarrie, Beverly Hills Striders. Time—0:10.16.
200 Meters—Don Quarrie. Time—0:20.12.
400 Meters—David Jenkins, Gateshead Harriers. Time—0:44.93.
800 Meters—Mark Enyeart, Utah State. Time—1:44.87.
1,500 Meters—Len Hilton, Pacific Coast Club. Time—3:38.26.
110 Meter High Hurdles—Gerald Wilson, Beverly Hills Striders. Time—0:13.38.
400 Meter Intermediate Hurdles—Ralph Mann, Beverly Hills Striders. Time—0:48.74.
5,000 Meters—Marty Liquori, New York AC. Time—13:29.00.
10,000 Meters—Frank Shorter, Florida TC. Time—28:02.17.

3,000 Meter Steeplechase—Randall Smith, Wichita State. Time—8:28.16.
5,000 Meter Walk—Ron Laird, New York AC. Time—22:08.6.
High Jump—Tom Woods, Pacific Coast Club. 7 ft. 5¹/₂ in.
Long Jump—Arnie Robinson. 26 ft. 5 in.
Triple Jump—Antony Terry, West Valley TC. 54 ft. 9 ³/₄ in.
Pole Vault—Don Baird, Maccabi TC. 17 ft. 6 in.
Shot Put—Al Feuerbach, Pacific Coast Club. 68 ft. 10³/₄ in.
Discus—John Powell, Pacific Coast Club. 208 ft. 10 in.
Javelin—Richard George, BYU. 272 ft. 11 in.
Hammer Throw—Boris Djerassi, New York AC. 222 ft. 10 in.
Team Champion—Beverly Hills Striders.

National AAU Women's Track and Field Championships
White Plains, N.Y., June 27-28, 1975

100 Meters—Rosalyn Bryant, Chicago, Ill. Time—0:11.6.
200 Meters—Debra Armstrong, Washington, D.C. Time—0:23.0.
400 Meters—Debra Sapenter, Prairie View, Tex. Time—0:51.6.
800 Meters—Madeline Manning Jackson, Cleveland, Oh. Time —2:00.5.
1,500 Meters—Julie Brown, Los Angeles, Cal. Time—4:13.5.
3,000 Meters—Lynn Bjorklund, Albuquerque, N.M. Time—9:10.6.
110 Meter Hurdles—Jane Frederick, Los Angeles, Cal. Time—0:13.8.
400 Meter Hurdles—Debbie Esser, Ainsworth, Neb. Time—0:57.3.

400 Meter Relay—Tenn State TC. Time—0:45.8.
800 Yd. Sprint Medley Relay—Sports International. Time—1:40.0.
One Mile Relay—Atoms TC, Brooklyn, N.Y. Time—3:37.9.
2 Mile Relay—Blue Ribbon, Wyckliff, Oh. Time—8:46.4.
1,500 Meter Walk—Lisa Metheny, Rialto, Cal. Time—6:46.6.
High Jump—Joni Huntley, Oregon TC. 6 ft.
Long Jump—Martha Watson, Lakewood, Cal. 21 ft. 3 in.
Shot Put—Maren Seidler, Chicago, Ill. 53 ft. 2¹/₂ in.
Javelin—Kathy Schmidt, Los Angeles, Cal. 209 ft. 7 in.
Discus—Jean Roberts, Newark, Del. 159 ft. 7 in.
Team Champion—Los Angeles TC.

National Interscholastic Outdoor Track and Field Records
Source: National Federation of State High School Associations. Records approved to June, 1975.

Event	Record	Holder	School	Site and year
100 yds.	0:09.0	Houston McTear	Baker H.S.	
			Baker, Fla.	Winter Park, Fla., 1975
220 yds. (straightaway)	0:20.2	Forrest Beaty	Herbert Hoover H.S.	
			Glendale, Cal.	Chaffey, Cal., 1961
220 yds. (full curve)	0:20.6	Melvin Clipper	Muir H.S.	
			Pasadena, Cal.	El Monte, Cal., 1958
440 yds.	0:45.8	Ronald E. Ray	Ferguson H.S., Newport News, Va.	Charlottesville, Va., 1972
880 yds.	1:48.8	Richard J. Joyce	Sierra H.S., Whittier, Cal.	Bakersfield, Cal., 1965
1 mile	3:58.3	James Ryun	Wichita East H.S., Wichita, Kan.	Wichita, Kan., 1965
2 mile	8:41.5	Steve Prefontaine	Marshfield High School, Coos Bay, Ore.	Corvallis, Ore., 1969
120 yd. high hurdles	0:13.2	Michael Robertson	Winter Pk. H.S. Winter Pk., Fla.	Winter Pk., Fla., 1975
		Dedy Cooper	Ells H.S. Richmond, Cal.	San Diego, Cal., 1975
180 yd. low hurdles	0:18.1	Donald Castronovo	Oceanside H.S. Oceanside, N.Y.	Ithaca, N.Y., 1964
		Earl McCullouch	Polytechnic H.S., Long Beach, Cal.	Norwalk, Cal., 1964
High jump	7 ft. 1³/₄ in.	Mark Wilson	Monte Vista H.S., Danville, Cal.	Fresno, Cal., 1974
Long jump	25 ft. 9¹/₂ in.	Gerald Hardeman	Edison H.S. Fresno, Cal.	Porterville, Cal., 1972
Pole vault	16 ft. 7 in.	Casey Carringan	Orting High School, Orting, Wash.	Bellingham, Wash., 1969
		Robert Pullard	Los Angeles H.S. Los Angeles, Cal.	Los Angeles, Cal., 1969
Triple jump	52 ft. 6¹/₄ in.	David Tucker	San Joaquin Mem. H.S., Fresno, Cal.	Bakersfield, Cal., 1970
Shot put (12 lbs.)	72 ft. 3¹/₄ in.	Sam Walker	W. W. Samuell H.S., Dallas, Tex.	Corpus Christi, Tex., 1968
Discus	201 ft. 3 in.	Christopher James Adams.	Los Altos H.S. Los Altos, Cal.	Berkeley, Cal., 1970
Javelin	254 ft. 11 in.	Russell Francis	Pleasant Hill H.S. Pleasant Hill, Ore.	Pleasant Hill, Ore., 1971
440 yd. relay	0:40.2	Delley, G. Pouncy, J. Pouncy, Shaw	Lincoln High School, Dallas, Texas	Austin, Texas, 1970
880 yd. relay	1:25.4	Jackson, James, Reed, Hill.	White Plains (N.Y.) H.S.	Jamaica, N.Y., 1966
1 mile relay	3:11.8	Bouche, Bradley, Brents, Morton	Memorial H.S., Houston, Texas.	Baytown, Texas, 1967
		Anderson, Black, Thompkins, Thompson	Killian High School, Miami, Fla.	Gainesville, Fla., 1969
2 mile relay	7:41.9	Mentz, Jakosa, Bowman, Grant.	Proviso West H.S., Hillside, Ill.	Glen Ellyn, Ill., 1965
Sprint Medley Relay (1 mile)	3:23.3	Corson, Brake, Brents, Morton	Memorial H.S., Houston, Texas.	Houston, Texas, 1967

USTA National Champions

Men's Singles

Year	Champion	Final Opponent	Year	Champion	Final Opponent
1920	Bill Tilden	William Johnston	1948	Pancho Gonzales	Eric Sturgess
1921	Bill Tilden	Wallace Johnston	1949	Pancho Gonzales	F. R. Schroeder Jr.
1922	Bill Tilden	William Johnston	1950	Arthur Larsen	Herbert Flam
1923	Bill Tilden	William Johnston	1951	Frank Sedgman	E. Victor Seixas Jr.
1924	Bill Tilden	William Johnston	1952	Frank Sedgman	Gardnar Mulloy
1925	Bill Tilden	William Johnston	1953	Tony Trabert	E. Victor Seixas Jr.
1926	Rene Lacoste	Jean Borotra	1954	E. Victor Seixas, Jr.	Rex Hartwig
1927	Rene Lacoste	Bill Tilden	1955	Tony Trabert	Ken Rosewall
1928	Henri Cochet	Francis Hunter	1956	Kenneth Rosewall	Lewis Hoad
1929	Bill Tilden	Francis Hunter	1957	Malcolm Anderson	Ashley Cooper
1930	John Doeg	Francis Shields	1958	Ashley Cooper	Malcolm Anderson
1931	H. Ellsworth Vines	George Lott	1959	Neale A. Fraser	Alejandro Olmedo
1932	H. Ellsworth Vines	Henri Cochet	1960	Neale A. Fraser	Rod Laver
1933	Fred Perry	John Crawford	1961	Roy Emerson	Rod Laver
1934	Fred Perry	Wilmer Allison	1962	Rod Laver	Roy Emerson
1935	Wilmer Allison	Sidney Wood	1963	Rafael Osuna	F. A. Froehling 3d
1936	Fred Perry	Don Budge	1964	Roy Emerson	Fred Stolle
1937	Don Budge	Baron G. von Cramm	1965	Manuel Santana	Cliff Drysdale
1938	Don Budge	C. Gene Mako	1966	Fred Stolle	John Newcombe
1939	Robert Riggs	S. Welby Van Horn	1967	John Newcombe	Clark Graebner
1940	Don McNeill	Robert Riggs	1968	Arthur Ashe	Tom Okker
1941	Robert Riggs	F. L. Kovacs	1969	Rod Laver	Tony Roche
1942	F. R. Schroeder Jr.	Frank Parker	1970	Ken Rosewall	Tony Roche
1943	Joseph Hunt	Jack Kramer	1971	Stan Smith	Jan Kodes
1944	Frank Parker	William Talbert	1972	Ilie Nastase	Arthur Ashe
1945	Frank Parker	William Talbert	1973	John Newcombe	Jan Kodes
1946	Jack Kramer	Thomas Brown Jr.	1974	Jimmy Connors	Ken Rosewall
1947	Jack Kramer	Frank Parker	1975	Manuel Orantes	Jimmy Connors

Men's Doubles

Year	Doubles Champions	Year	Doubles Champions
1920	William Johnston and Clarence Griffin	1948	Gardnar Mulloy and William Talbert
1921	Bill Tilden and Vincent Richards	1949	John Bromwich and William Sidwell
1922	Bill Tilden and Vincent Richards	1950	John Bromwich and Frank Sedgman
1923	Bill Tilden and Brian Norton	1951	Frank Sedgman and Kenneth McGregor
1924	Howard Kinsey and Robert Kinsey	1952	Mervyn Rose and E. Victor Seixas Jr.
1925	R. Norris Williams and Vincent Richards	1953	Rex Hartwig and Mervyn Rose
1926	R. Norris Williams and Vincent Richards	1954	E. Victor Seixas, Jr. and Tony Trabert
1927	Bill Tilden and Francis Hunter	1955	Kosei Kamo and Atsushi Miyagi
1928	George Lott and John Hennessey	1956	Lewis Hoad and Kenneth Rosewall
1929	George Lott and John Doeg	1957	Ashley Cooper and Neale Fraser
1930	George Lott and John Doeg	1958	Hamilton Richardson and Alejandro Olmedo
1931	Wilmer Allison and John Van Ryn	1959	Neale A. Fraser and Roy Emerson
1932	H. Ellsworth Vines and Keith Gledhill	1960	Neale A. Fraser and Roy Emerson
1933	George Lott and Lester Stoefen	1961	Dennis Ralston and Chuck McKinley
1934	George Lott and Lester Stoefen	1962	Rafael Osuna and Antonio Palafox
1935	Wilmer Allison and John Van Ryn	1963	Dennis Ralston and Chuck McKinley
1936	Don Budge and C. Gene Mako	1964	Dennis Ralston and Chuck McKinley
1937	Baron G. von Cramm and Henner Henkel	1965	Roy Emerson and Fred Stolle
1938	Don Budge and C. Gene Mako	1966	Roy Emerson and Fred Stolle
1939	Adrian Quist and John Bromwich	1967	John Newcombe and Tony Roche
1940	Jack Kramer and Frederick Schroeder Jr.	1968	Robert Lutz and Stan Smith
1941	Jack Kramer and Frederick Schroeder Jr.	1969	Fred Stolle and Ken Rosewall
1942	Gardnar Mulloy and William Talbert	1970	Pierre Barthes and Nicki Pilic
1943	Jack Kramer and Frank Parker	1971	John Newcombe and Roger Taylor
1944	Don McNeill and Robert Falkenburg	1972	Cliff Drysdale and Roger Taylor
1945	Gardnar Mulloy and William Talbert	1973	John Newcombe and Owen Davidson
1946	Gardnar Mulloy and William Talbert	1974	Bob Lutz and Stan Smith
1947	Jack Kramer and Frederick Schroeder Jr.	1975	Jimmy Connors and Ilie Nastase

Men's Indoor Champions

Year	Singles	Doubles	Year	Singles	Doubles
1962	Chas. McKinley	R. Laver-C. McKinley	1969	Stan Smith	Stan Smith-Robert Lutz
1963	Dennis Ralston	D. Ralston-C. McKinley	1970	Ilie Nastase	Stan Smith-Arthur Ashe
1964	Chas. McKinley	M. Santana-J. L. Arilla	1971	Clark Graebner	Juan Gisbert-Manuel Orantes
1965	Jan Erik Lundquist	D. Ralston-C. McKinley	1972	Stan Smith	Andres Gimeno-Manuel Orantes
1966	Charles Pasarell	Robert Lutz-Stan Smith	1973	Jimmy Connors	Juan Gisbert-Jurgen Fassbender
1967	Charles Pasarell	Arthur Ashe-Charles Pasarell	1974	Jimmy Connors	None
1968	Cliff Richey	Thomas Koch-Tom Okker	1975	Jimmy Connors	Jimmy Connors-Ilie Nastase

Women's Indoor Champions

Year	Champion	Doubles Champions	Year	Champion	Doubles Champions
1963	Carol Hanks	Carol Hanks & Mary Ann Eisel	1969	Mary Ann E. Curtis	Mary Ann Eisel & Valerie Ziegenfuss
1964	Mary Ann Eisel	Mary Ann Eisel & Katharine Hubbell	1970	Mary Ann E. Curtis	Peaches Bartkowicz & Nancy Richey
1965	Nancy Richey	Carol Hanks Aucamp & Mary Ann Eisel	1971	Billie Jean King	Billie Jean King & Rosemary Casals
1966	Billie Jean King	Billlie Jean King & Rosemary Casals	1972	Virginia Wade	Rosemary Casals & Virginia Wade
1967	Billie Jean King	Carol Hanks Aucamp & Mary Ann Eisel	1973	Evonne Goolagong	Olga Morozova & Marina Kroskina
1968	Billie Jean King	Billie Jean King & Rosemary Casals	1974	Billie Jean King	None
			1975	Martina Nauratilova	Billie Jean King & Rosemary Casals

Women's Singles, Doubles, Mixed Doubles

Year	Singles Champions	Doubles Champions	Mixed Doubles Champions
'35	Helen Jacobs............	Helen Jacobs & Mrs.Sarah P. Fabyan......	Mrs. Sarah P. Fabyan & Enrique Maier
'36	Alice Marble.............	Mrs. M. G. Van Ryn & Carolin Babcock.....	Alice Marble & C. Gene Mako
'37	Anita Lizana.............	Mrs. Sarah P. Fabyan & Alice Marble.......	Mrs. Sarah P. Fabyan & Don Budge
'38	Alice Marble.............	Alice Marble & Mrs. Sarah P. Fabyan......	Alice Marble & Don Budge
'39	Alice Marble.............	Alice Marble & Mrs. Sarah P. Fabyan.......	Alice Marble & Harry Hopman
'40	Alice Marble.............	Alice Marble & Mrs. Sarah P. Fabyan.......	Alice Marble & Robert Riggs
'41	Mrs. Sarah P. Cooke	Mrs. S. P. Cooke & Margaret Osborne.......	Mrs. Sarah P. Cooke & Jack Kramer
'42	Pauline Betz.............	A. Louise Brough & Margaret Osborne.......	A. Louise Brough & Frederick Schroeder
'43	Pauline Betz.............	A. Louise Brough & Margaret Osborne.......	Margaret Osborne & William Talbert
'44	Pauline Betz.............	A. Louise Brough & Margaret Osborne.......	Margaret Osborne & William Talbert
'45	Sarah P. Cooke	A. Louise Brough & Margaret Osborne.......	Margaret Osborne & William Talbert
'46	Pauline Betz.............	A. Louise Brough & Margaret Osborne.......	Margaret Osborne & William Talbert
'47	A. Louise Brough..........	A. Louise Brough & Margaret Osborne.......	A. Louise Brough & John Bromwich
'48	Mrs. Margaret O. du Pont	A. Louise Brough & Mrs. M. O. du Pont......	A. Louise Brough & Thomas Brown, Jr.
'49	Mrs. Margaret O. du Pont	A. Louise Brough & Mrs. M. O. du Pont......	A. Louise Brough & Eric Sturgess
'50	Mrs. Margaret O. du Pont	A. Louise Brough & Mrs. M. Q. du Pont......	Mrs. M. O. du Pont & Kenneth MacGregor
'51	Maureen Connolly	Doris Hart & Shirley Fry...............	Doris Hart & Frank Sedgman
'52	Maureen Connolly	Doris Hart & Shirley Fry...............	Doris Hart & Frank Sedgman
'53	Maureen Connolly	Doris Hart & Shirley Fry...............	Doris Hart & E. Victor Seixas, Jr.
'54	Doris Hart................	Doris Hart & Shirley Fry...............	Doris Hart & E. Victor Seixas, Jr.
'55	Doris Hart...............	A. Louise Brough & Mrs. M. O. du Pont......	Doris Hart & E. Victor Seixas, Jr.
'56	Shirley J. Fry.............	A. Louise Brough & Mrs. M. O. du Pont......	Mrs. M. O. du Pont & Kenneth Rosewall
'57	Althea Gibson............	A. Louise Brough & Mrs. M. O. du Pont......	Althea Gibson and Kurt Nielsen
'58	Althea Gibson............	Darlene Hard & Jeanne Arth............	Mrs. M. O. du Pont & Neale Fraser
'59	Maria Bueno.............	Darlene Hard & Jeanne Arth............	Mrs. M. O. du Pont & Neale Fraser
'60	Darlene Hard.............	Darlene Hard & Maria Bueno...........	Mrs. M. O. du Pont & Neale Fraser
'61	Darlene Hard.............	Darlene Hard & Lesley Turner...........	Margaret Smith & Robert Mark
'62	Margaret Smith...........	Maria Bueno & Darlene Hard............	Margaret Smith & Fred Stolle
'63	Maria Bueno.............	Margaret Smith & Robyn Ebbern........	Margaret Smith & Kenneth Fletcher
'64	Maria Bueno.............	Billie Jean Moffit & Karen Susman	Margaret Smith & John Newcombe
'65	Margaret Smith...........	Carole C. Graebner & Nancy Richey.......	Margaret Smith & Fred Stolle
'66	Maria Bueno.............	Maria Bueno & Nancy Richey............	Donna Floyd Fales & Owen Davidson
'67	Billie Jean King...........	Rosemary Casals & Billie Jean King........	Billie Jean King & Owen Davidson
'68	Virginia Wade............	Maria Bueno & Margaret S. Court..........	Mary Ann Eisel & Peter Curtis
'69	Margaret Smith Court.......	Francoise Durr & Darlene Hard...........	Margaret S. Court & Marty Riessen
'70	Margaret Smith Court.......	M. S. Court & Judy Tegart Dalton..........	Margaret S. Court & Marty Riessen
'71	Billie Jean King...........	Rosemary Casals & Judy Tegart Dalton......	Billie Jean King & Owen Davidson
'72	Billie Jean King...........	Francoise Durr & Betty Stove............	Margaret S. Court & Marty Riessen
'73	Margaret Smith Court.......	Margaret S. Court & Virginia Wade	Billie Jean King & Owen Davidson
'74	Billie Jean King...........	Billie Jean King & Rosemary Casals	Pam Teeguarden & Geoff Masters
'75	Chris Evert...............	Margaret Court & Virginia Wade..........	Rosemary Casals & Dick Stockton

NCAA Tennis Champions

Year	Singles	College	Doubles	College
'65	Arthur Ashe..............	UCLA	Arthur Ashe & Ian Crookenden...................	UCLA
'66	Charles Pasarell...........	UCLA	Charles Pasarell & Ian Crookenden	UCLA
'67	Bob Lutz.................	USC	Stan Smith & Bob Lutz.........................	USC
'68	Stan Smith...............	USC	Stan Smith & Bob Lutz.........................	USC
'69	Joaquin Loyo Mayo	USC	Joaquin Loyo Mayo & Marcelo Lara	USC
'70	Jeff Borowiak.............	UCLA	Pat Cramer & Luis Garcia.......................	Miami (Fla.)
'71	Jimmy Connors...........	UCLA	Jeff Borowiak & Haroon Rahim...................	UCLA
'72	Dick Stockton	Trinity (Tex.)	Sandy Mayer & Roscoe Tanner..................	Stanford
'73	Sandy Mayer	Stanford	Sandy Mayer & Jim Delaney....................	Stanford
'74	John Whitlinger...........	Stanford	John Whitlinger & Jim Delaney..................	Stanford
'75	Billie Martin..............	UCLA	Butch Walts & Bruce Manson...................	USC

Clay Court Champions

Year	Champion	Year	Champion	Year	Champion	Year	Champion
'52	Arthur Larsen	1958	Bernard Bartzen	1964	Dennis Ralston	1970	Cliff Richey
'53	E. Vic Seixas, Jr.	1959	Bernard Bartzen	1965	Dennis Ralston	1971	Zeljko Franulovic
'54	Bernard Bartzen	1960	Barry MacKay	1966	Cliff Richey	1972	Bob Hewitt
'55	Tony Trabert	1961	Bernard Bartzen	1967	Arthur Ashe	1973	Manuel Orantes
'56	Herbert Flam	1962	Chuck McKinley	1968	Clark Graebner	1974	Jimmy Connors
'57	E. Victor Seixas, Jr.	1963	Chuck McKinley	1969	Zeljko Franulovic	1975	Manuel Orantes

British (Wimbledon) Champions
Inaugurated 1877

Year	Men's Singles	Women's Singles	Year	Men's Singles	Women's Singles
'46 ...	Yvon Petra	Pauline Betz	1961 ...	Rod Laver	Angela Mortimer
'47 ...	Jack Kramer	Margaret Osborne	1962 ...	Rod Laver	Karen Hantze Susman
'48 ...	Bob Falkenburg	A. Louise Brough	1963 ...	Chuck McKinley	Margaret Smith
'49 ...	Fred R. Schroeder	A. Louise Brough	1964 ...	Roy Emerson	Maria Bueno
'50 ...	Budge Patty	A. Louise Brough	1965 ...	Roy Emerson	Margaret Smith
'51 ...	Dick Savitt	Doris Hart	1966 ...	Manuel Santana	Billie Jean King
'52 ...	Frank Sedgman	Maureen Connolly	1967 ...	John Newcombe	Billie Jean King
'53 ...	Victor Seixas	Maureen Connolly	1968 ...	Rod Laver	Billie Jean King
'54 ...	Jaroslav Drobny	Maureen Connolly	1969 ...	Rod Laver	Ann Jones
'55 ...	Tony Trabert	A. Louise Brough	1970 ...	John Newcombe	Margaret S. Court
'56 ...	Lewis Hoad	Shirley Fry	1971 ...	John Newcombe	Evonne Goolagong
'57 ...	Lewis Hoad	Althea Gibson	1972 ...	Stan Smith	Billie Jean King
'58 ...	Ashley Cooper	Althea Gibson	1973 ...	Jan Kodes	Billie Jean King
'59 ...	Alex Olmedo	Maria Bueno	1974 ...	Jimmy Connors	Chris Evert
'60 ...	Neale Fraser	Maria Bueno	1975 ...	Arthur Ashe	Billie Jean King

Davis Cup International Tennis—Challenge Round

Year	Winner	Loser	Score	Year	Winner	Loser	Score	Year	Winner	Loser	Score
1900	U.S.	Brit. Isles	3-0	1927	France	U.S.	3-2	1953	Australia	U.S.	3-2
1902	U.S.	Brit. Isles	3-2	1928	France	U.S.	4-1	1954	U.S.	Australia	3-2
1903	British	U.S.	4-1	1929	France	U.S.	3-2	1955	Australia	U.S.	5-0
1904	British	Belgium	5-0	1930	France	U.S.	4-1	1956	Australia	U.S.	5-0
1905	British	U.S.	5-0	1931	France	Gt. Britain	3-2	1957	Australia	U.S.	3-2
1906	British	U.S.	5-0	1932	France	U.S.	3-2	1958	U.S.	Australia	3-2
1907	Australasia	British	3-2	1933	Gt. Britain	France	3-2	1959	Australia	U.S.	3-2
1908	Australasia	U.S.	3-2	1934	Gt. Britain	U.S.	4-1	1960	Australia	Italy	4-1
1909	Australasia	U.S.	5-0	1935	Gt. Britain	U.S.	5-0	1961	Australia	Italy	5-0
1911	Australasia	U.S.	5-0	1936	Gt. Britain	Australia	3-2	1962	Australia	Mexico	5-0
1912	British	Australasia	3-2	1937	U.S.	Gt. Britain	4-1	1963	U.S.	Australia	3-2
1913	U.S.	British	3-2	1938	U.S.	Australia	3-2	1964	Australia	U.S.	3-2
1914	Australasia	U.S.	3-2	1939	Australia	U.S.	3-2	1965	Australia	Spain	4-1
1919	Australasia	British	4-1	1940-1945	(Not played)			1966	Australia	India	4-1
1920	U.S.	Australasia	5-0	1946	U.S.	Australia	5-0	1967	Australia	Spain	4-1
1921	U.S.	Japan	5-0	1947	U.S.	Australia	4-1	1968	U.S.	Australia	4-1
1922	U.S.	Australasia	4-1	1948	U.S.	Australia	5-0	1969	U.S.	Romania	5-0
1923	U.S.	Australasia	4-1	1949	U.S.	Australia	4-1	1970	U.S.	W. Germany	5-0
1924	U.S.	Australasia	5-0	1950	Australia	U.S.	4-1	1971	U.S.	Romania	3-2
1925	U.S.	France	5-0	1951	Australia	U.S.	3-2	1972	U.S.	Romania	3-2
1926	U.S.	France	4-1	1952	Australia	U.S.	4-1	1973	Australia	U.S.	5-0
								1974	S. Africa	India	(default)

National Junior Tennis Champions

Boys' 18 Singles
- 1969 Eric Van Dillen
- 1970 Brian Gottfried
- 1971 Raul Ramirez
- 1972 Patrick DuPre
- 1973 Billy Martin
- 1974 Ferd Taygan
- 1975 Howard Schoenfield

Girls' 18 Singles
- 1969 Sharon Walsh
- 1970 Sharon Walsh
- 1971 Chris Evert
- 1972 Ann Kiyomura
- 1973 Carrie Fleming
- 1974 Rayni Fox
- 1975 Beth Norton

Boys' 18 Doubles
- 1969 Richard Stockton and Eric Van Dillen
- 1970 Brian Gottfried and Alex Mayer, Jr.
- 1971 Jim Delaney and Chip Fisher
- 1972 Steve Mott and Brian Teachar
- 1973 Billy Martin and Trey Waitke
- 1974 Francisco Gonzalez and Rocky Maguire
- 1975 Larry Gottfried and John McEnroe

Girls' 18 Doubles
- 1969 Gail Hansen and Patty Ann Reese
- 1970 Kristien Kemmer and Nancy Ornstein
- 1971 Janet Newberry and Eliza Pande
- 1972 Marita Redondo and Laurie Tenney
- 1973 Susan Boyle and Kathy May
- 1974 Anne Bruning and Barbara Hallquist
- 1975 Lea Antonoplis and Berta McCallum

Boys' 16 Singles
- 1969 James Hagey
- 1970 Freddy DeJesus
- 1971 Billy Martin
- 1972 Bill Maze
- 1973 Ben McKnown
- 1974 Walter Redondo
- 1975 Larry Gottfried

Girls' 16 Singles
- 1969 Eliza Pande
- 1970 Chris Evert
- 1971 Carrie Fleming
- 1972 Marita Redondo
- 1973 Betsy Nagelson
- 1974 Zenda Leiss
- 1975 Lea Antonoplis

Boys' 16 Doubles
- 1969 James E. Delaney and Chip Fisher
- 1970 Freddy DeJesus and John Whitinger
- 1971 Billy Martin and Trey Waitke
- 1972 Bruce Manson and Perry Wright
- 1973 Nial Brash and Matt Mitchell
- 1974 Jeff Robbins and Van Winitsky
- 1975 Tony Giammalua and Billy Scanlon

Girls' 16 Doubles
- 1969 Chris Evert and Susan Epstein
- 1970 Barbara Downs and Ann Kiyomura
- 1971 Ann Kiyomura and Marita Redondo
- 1972 Jeanne Evert and Kathy Kendall
- 1973 Susan Mehmedbasich and Robin Tenney
- 1974 Sherry Acker and Anne Smith
- 1975 Lea Antonoplis and Berta McCallum

Tennis Championships in 1975

Australian Open (Melbourne) — Men's Singles: John Newcombe d. Jimmy Connors 7-5, 3-6, 6-4, 7-6; Men's Doubles: Alexander-Dent d. Stone-Carmichael 6-3, 7-6; Women's Singles: Evonne Goolagong d. Martina Navratilova 6-3, 6-2; Women's Doubles: Goolagong-Michel d. Court-Morozova 7-6, 7-6.

Italian Open (Rome) — Men's Singles: Raul Ramirez d. Manuel Orantes 7-6, 7-5, 7-5; Men's Doubles: Gottfried-Ramirez d. Nastase-Connors 6-4, 7-6, 2-6, 6-1; Women's Singles: Chris Evert d. Martina Navratilova 6-1, 6-0; Women's Doubles: Evert-Navratilova d. Barker-Coles 6-1, 6-2.

French Open (Paris) — Men's Singles: Bjorn Borg d. Guillermo Vilas 6-2, 6-3, 6-4; Men's Doubles: Gottfried-Ramirez d. Alexander-Dent 6-4, 2-6, 6-2, 6-4; Women's Singles: Chris Evert d. Martina Navratilova 2-6, 6-2, 6-1; Women's Doubles: Evert-Navratilova d. Morozova-Anthony 6-3, 6-2.

Women's Collegiates — Singles: Stephanie Tolleson (Trinity); Doubles: JoAnne Russell-Donna Stockton (Trinity).

Federation Cup — Women's teams of all nations — final round — Czechoslovakia defeated Australia 2-1.

Leading Tennis Money Winners, 1974

Men		Women	
1. Jimmy Connors, United States	$281,309	1. Chris Evert, United States	$261,46
2. Guillermo Vilas, Argentina	274,327	2. Billie Jean King, United States	173,32
3. John Newcombe, Australia	273,299	3. Evonne Goolagong, Australia	102,50
4. Bjorn Borg, Sweden	215,229	4. Virginia Wade, Great Britain	85,38
5. Ilie Nastase, Romania	190,752	5. Rosemary Casals, United States	72,83
6. Stan Smith, United States	163,326	6. Julie Heldman, United States	60,51
7. Arthur Ashe, United States	146,424	7. Kerry Melville, Australia	56,02
8. Rod Laver, Australia	134,600	8. Francoise Durr, France	41,22
9. Manuel Orantes, Spain	129,090	9. Olga Morozova, USSR	40,87
10. Tom Okker, Netherlands	114,649	10. Betty Stove, Netherlands	40,24

World Championship Tennis, 1975

ate	Event—City	Singles Winner	Doubles
an. 20-26	U.S. Pro Indoor Championships (all groups), Philadelphia	Marty Riessen	Brian Gottfried-Raul Ramirez

Red Group

eb. 10-16	Rothmans International, Toronto	Harold Solomon	Dick Stockton-Erik van Dillen
eb. 17-23	Robintech Tennis Classic, Forth Worth	John Alexander	Bob Lutz-Stan Smith
eb. 23-Mar. 2	San Antonio Tennis Classic, San Antonio	Dick Stockton	John Alexander-Phil Dent
ar. 10-16	Xerox Tennis Classic, Washington, D.C.	Mark Cox	Mike Estep-Jeff Simpson
lar. 17-23	Memphis Tennis Classic, Memphis	Harold Solomon	Dick Stockton-Erik van Dillen
ar. 24-30	First National Bank-WCT Classic, Atlanta	Mark Cox	Anand Amritraj-Vijay Amritraj
or. 14-20	WCT-Kawasaki Classic, Tokyo	Bob Lutz	Bob Lutz-Stan Smith
or. 21-17	River Oaks-American General, Houston	Ken Rosewall	Bob Lutz-Stan Smith

Blue Group

eb. 3-9	Havatampa-Raymond, James Classic, St. Petersburg	Raul Ramirez	Brian Gottfried-Raul Ramirez
eb. 17-23	Michelob Pro-Celebrity, La Costa	Rod Laver	Brian Gottfried-Raul Ramirez
lar. 10-16	WCT-Copersucar, Sao Paulo	Rod Laver	Ross Case-Geoff Masters
lar. 17-23	20th Altamira Tennis Club International, Caracas	Rod Laver	Ross Case-Geoff Masters
lar. 24-30	The Classic, Orlando	Rod Laver	Brian Gottfried-Raul Ramirez
or. 7-13	St. Louis Tennis Classic, St. Louis	Vitas Gerulaitis	Colin Dibley-Ray Ruffels
or. 14-20	United Bank Tennis Classic, Denver	Jimmy Connors	Roy Emerson-Rod Laver
or. 21-27	NCNB Classic, Charlotte	Raul Ramirez	Patricio Cornejo-Jaime Fillol

Green Group

an. 27-Feb. 2	WCT-Richmond International, Richmond	Bjorn Borg	Hans Kary-Fred McNair
eb. 6-12	WCT International-Bologna, Bologna	Bjorn Borg	Paolo Bertolucci-Adriano Panatta
eb. 17-23	Catalana Bank Classic, Barcelona	Arthur Ashe	Arthur Ashe-Tom Okker
eb. 24-Mar. 2	Algemene Bank Nederland-World Tennis, Rotterdam	Arthur Ashe	Bob Hewitt-Frew McMillan
lar. 10-16	WCT-Munich International, Munich	Arthur Ashe	Bob Hewitt-Frew McMillan
lar. 24-30	Marlboro Classic, Monte Carlo	Manuel Orantes	Bob Hewitt-Frew McMillan
\pr. 11-19	Clows Classic, Johannesburg	Buster Mottram	Arthur Ashe-Tom Okker
\pr. 21-27	Opel International Cup, Stockholm	Arthur Ashe	Arthur Ashe-Tom Okker

WCT Final Championship Summaries

Singles Quarterfinals

.she defeated Cox 1-6, 6-4, 6-4, 7-6
Jexander defeated Tanner 6-3, 6-2, 6-3
3org defeated Ramirez 7-6, 7-6, 6-0
aver defeated Solomon 4-6, 6-0, 6-2, 3-6, 6-3

Old Spice Doubles Quarterfinals

Gottfried-Ramirez def. Amritraj-Amritraj 6-3, 6-2, 7-6
Ashe-Okker def. Alexander-Dent 4-6, 6-3, 7-6, 6-3
Case-Masters def. Stockton-van Dillen 2-6, 6-4, 6-2, 6-4
Cox-Drysdale def. Lutz-Smith 7-6, 6-7, 7-6

Semifinals

\she defeated Alexander 3-6, 6-1, 6-3, 6-4
3org defeated Laver 7-6, 3-6, 5-7, 7-6, 6-2

Old Spice Doubles Semifinals

Gottfried-Ramirez def. Ashe-Okker 7-6, 7-6, 7-6
Cox-Drysdale def. Case-Masters 6-4, 6-7, 6-1, 3-6, 7-6

Third Place

.aver defeated Alexander 6-4, 6-2

Old Spice Doubles Finals

Gottfried-Ramirez def. Cox-Drysdale 7-6, 6-7, 6-2, 7-6

Finals

\she defeated Borg 3-6, 6-4, 6-4, 6-0

World Doubles Championship

Gottfried-Ramirez def. Hewitt-McMillan 7-5, 6-3, 4-6, 2-6, 7-5

World Team Tennis

Final Standings

Eastern Division

	W.	L.	Pct.
ittsburgh	36	8	.818
ew York	34	10	.773
oston	20	26	.435
diana	18	26	.409
leveland	16	28	.364

Western Division

	W.	L.	Pct.
Golden Gate	29	15	.659
Phoenix	22	22	.500
Los Angeles	20	24	.455
Hawaii	14	32	.304
San Diego	14	32	.304

.ayoff Winner — Pittsburgh

American Casting Assn. Combined Championships in 1975

San Francisco, Cal., Aug. 4-9, 1975

(Distance plugs includes the 3 longest casts in 3 separate events — 3/8 oz. plug, 5/8 oz. plug, and 1 ounce plug. The 9 casts
are added to determine the champion.

Men

3rand All Around — Steve Rajeff, San Francisco, Cal.
\nglers All Around — Steve Rajeff
\ll Accuracy — Steve Rajeff, 592 pts.
\)istance Plugs — Steve Rajeff, 3,622 ft.
\)istance Flies — Steve Rajeff, 1,588 ft.
\ccuracy Plugs — Steve Rajeff, 295 pts.
\ccuracy Flies — Steve Rajeff, 297 pts.

Women

\ll Accuracy — Pauline Cathcart, La Canada, Cal., 517 pts.

Accuracy Plugs — Barbara Rohrer, Santa Ana, Cal., 244 pts.
Accuracy Flies — Pauline Cathcart, 264 pts.

Intermediates

All Accuracy — Vince Rodgers, Santa Ana, Cal., 552 pts.
Accuracy Plugs — Keith Pryor, Oakland, Cal., 275 pts.
Accuracy Flies — Vince Rodgers, 286 pts.

Juniors

Accuracy Plugs — Baker Burke, Jackson, Ky., 263 pts.

Golf Records

United States Amateur

Year	Winner	Year	Winner	Year	Winner	Year	Winner
1900	Walter Travis	1919	Davidson Herron	1937	John Goodman	1958	Charles Coe
1901	Walter Travis	1920	Chick Evans Jr.	1938	Willie Turnesa	1959	Jack Nicklaus
1902	Louis James	1921	Jesse Guilford	1939	Bud Ward	1960	Deane Beman
1903	Walter Travis	1922	Jess Sweetser	1940	Dick Chapman	1961	Jack Nicklaus
1904	Chandler Egan	1923	Max Marston	1941	Bud Ward	1962	Labron Harris Jr.
1905	Chandler Egan	1924	Bob Jones	1942-45	(Not Played)	1963	Deane Beman
1906	Eben Byers	1925	Bob Jones	1946	Ted Bishop	1964	Bill Campbell
1907	Jerome Travers	1926	George Von Elm	1947	Skee Riegel	1965	Robert Murphy Jr.
1908	Jerome Travers	1927	Bob Jones	1948	Willie Turnesa	1966	Gary Cowan
1909	Robert Gardner	1928	Bob Jones	1949	Charles Coe	1967	Bob Dickson
1910	William Fownes Jr.	1929	Harrison Johnston	1950	Sam Urzetta	1968	Bruce Fleisher
1911	Harold Hilton	1930	Bob Jones	1951	Billy Maxwell	1969	Steve Melnyk
1912	Jerome Travers	1931	Francis Ouimet	1952	Jack Westland	1970	Lanny Wadkins
1913	Jerome Travers	1932	Ross Somerville	1953	Gene Littler	1971	Gary Cowan
1914	Francis Ouimet	1933	George Dunlap Jr.	1954	Arnold Palmer	1972	Vinnie Giles
1915	Robert Gardner	1934	Lawson Little	1955	Harvie Ward	1973	Craig Stadler
1916	Chick Evans, Jr.	1935	Lawson Little	1956	Harvie Ward	1974	Jerry Pate
1917-18	(Not Played)	1936	John Fischer	1957	Hillman Robbins	1975	Fred Ridley

Women's United States Amateur

Year	Winner	Year	Winner	Year	Winner	Year	Winner
1903	Bessie Anthony	1921	Marion Hollins	1938	Patty Berg	1958	Anne Quast
1904	Georgiana Bishop	1922	Glenna Collett	1939	Betty Jameson	1959	Barbara McIntire
1905	Pauline Mackay	1923	Edith Cummings	1940	Betty Jameson	1960	JoAnne Gunderson
1906	Harriot Curtis	1924	Mrs. D. C. Hurd	1941	Mrs. Frank New	1961	Anne Q. Decker
1907	Margaret Curtis	1925	Glenna Collett	1942-45	(Not Played)	1962	JoAnne Gunderson.
1908	Kate Harley	1926	Mrs. G. Stetson	1946	Babe Zaharias	1963	Anne Q. Welts
1909	Dorothy Campbell	1927	Mrs. M. Horn	1947	Louise Suggs	1964	Barbara McIntire
1910	Dorothy Campbell	1928	Glenna Collett	1948	Grace Lenczyk	1965	Jean Ashley
1911	Margaret Curtis	1929	Glenna Collett	1949	Dorothy Porter	1966	JoAnne Carner
1912	Margaret Curtis	1930	Glenna Collett	1950	Beverly Hanson	1967	Lou Dill
1913	Gladys Raven Scroft	1931	Helen Hicks	1951	Dorothy Kirby	1968	JoAnne Carner
1914	Mrs. H. A. Jackson	1932	Virginia Van Wie	1952	Jackie Pung	1969	Catherine Lacoste
1915	Mrs. C. H. Vanderbeck	1933	Virginia Van Wie	1953	Mary Faulk	1970	Martha Wilkinson
1916	Alexa Stirling	1934	Virginia Van Wie	1954	Barbara Romack	1971	Laura Baugh
1917-18	(Not Played)	1935	Glenna C. Vare	1955	Pat Lesser	1972	Mary Budke
1919	Alexa Stirling	1936	Pamela Barton	1956	Marlene Stewart	1973	Carol Semple
1920	Alexa Stirling	1937	Mrs. J. A. Page	1957	JoAnne Gunderson	1974	Cynthia Hill
						1975	Beth Daniel

United States Open

Year	Winner	Year	Winner	Year	Winner	Year	Winner
1896	James Foulis	1915	Jerome Travers*	1935	Sam Parks, Jr.	1957	Dick Mayer
1897	Joe Lloyd	1916	Chick Evans*	1936	Tony Manero	1958	Tommy Bolt
1898	Fred Herd	1917-18	(Not played)	1937	Ralph Guldahl	1959	Billy Casper
1899	Willie Smith	1919	Walter Hagen	1938	Ralph Guldahl	1960	Arnold Palmer
1900	Harry Vardon	1920	Edward Ray	1939	Byron Nelson	1961	Gene Littler
1901	Willie Anderson	1921	Jim Barnes	1940	Lawson Little	1962	Jack Nicklaus
1902	L. Auchterlonie	1922	Gene Sarazen	1941	Craig Wood	1963	Julius Boros
1903	Willie Anderson	1923	Bob Jones*	1942-45	(Not played)	1964	Ken Venturi
1904	Willie Anderson	1924	Cyril Walker	1946	Lloyd Mangrum	1965	Gary Player
1905	Willie Anderson	1925	Willie MacFarlane	1947	L. Worsham	1966	Billy Casper
1906	Alex Smith	1926	Bob Jones*	1948	Ben Hogan	1967	Jack Nicklaus
1907	Alex Ross	1927	Tommy Armour	1949	Cary Middlecoff	1968	Lee Trevino
1908	Fred McLeod	1928	John Farrell	1950	Ben Hogan	1969	Orville Moody
1909	George Sargent	1929	Bob Jones*	1951	Ben Hogan	1970	Tony Jacklin
1910	Alex Smith	1930	Bob Jones*	1952	Julius Boros	1971	Lee Trevino
1911	John McDermott	1931	Wm. Burke	1953	Ben Hogan	1972	Jack Nicklaus
1912	John McDermott	1932	Gene Sarazen	1954	Ed Furgol	1973	Johnny Miller
1913	Francis Ouimet*	1933	John Goodman*	1955	Jack Fleck	1974	Hale Irwin
1914	Walter Hagen	1934	Olin Dutra	1956	Cary Middlecoff	1975	Lou Graham

U. S. Women's Open Golf Champions

Year	Winner	Year	Winner	Year	Winner	Year	Winner
1948	Mrs. M. D. Zaharias	1955	Fay Crocker	1962	Murie Lindstrom	1969	Donna Caponi
1949	Louise Suggs	1956	Mrs. K. Cornelius	1963	Mary Mills	1970	Donna Caponi
1950	Mrs. M. D. Zaharias	1957	Betsy Rawls	1964	Mickey Wright	1971	JoAnne Gunderson
1951	Betsy Rawls	1958	Mickey Wright	1965	Carol Mann		Carner
1952	Louise Suggs	1959	Mickey Wright	1966	Sandra Spuzich	1972	Susie Maxwell Bernir
1953	Betsy Rawls	1960	Betsy Rawls	1967	Catherine Lacoste (a)	1973	Susie Maxwell Bernir
1954	Mrs. M. D. Zaharias	1961	Mickey Wright	1968	Susie Maxwell Berning	1974	Sandra Haynie
						1975	Sandra Palmer

(a) Amateur

Canadian Open Golf Champions

Year	Winner	Year	Winner	Year	Winner	Year	Winner
1947	Bobby Locke	1955	Arnold Palmer	1961	Jacky Cupit	1968	Bob Charles
1948	C.W. Congdon	1956	Doug Sanders	1962	Ted Kroll	1969	Tommy Aaron
1949	E.J. Harrison	1957	George Bayer	1963	Doug Ford	1970	Kermit Zarley
1950	Jim Ferrier	1958	Wes Ellis, Jr.	1964	Kel Nagle	1971	Lee Trevino
1951	Jim Ferrier	1959	Doug Ford	1965	Gene Littler	1972	Gay Brewer
1952	John Palmer	1960	Art Wall, Jr.	1966	Don Massengale	1973	Tom Weiskopf
1953	Dave Douglas			1967	Billy Casper	1974	Bobby Nichols
1954	Pat Fletcher					1975	Tom Weiskopf

Professional Golf Tournaments in 1975

Date	Event	Winner	Score	Prize
Jan. 12	Phoenix Open	Johnny Miller	260	$30,000
Jan. 19	Dean Martin-Tucson Open	Johnny Miller	263	40,000
Jan. 26	Bing Crosby National Pro-Amateur, Pebble Beach, Cal.	Gene Littler	280	37,000
Feb. 3	Hawaiian Open, Honolulu	Gary Groh	274	44,000
Feb. 9	Bob Hope Desert Classic, Palm Springs, Cal.	Johnny Miller	339	32,000
Feb. 16	Andy Williams—San Diego Open	J. C. Snead	*279	34,000
Feb. 23	Glen Campbell—Los Angeles Open	Pat FitzSomons	275	30,000
Mar. 2	Jackie Gleason-Inverrary Classic, Lauder Hill, Fla.	Bob Murphy	273	52,000
Mar. 9	Florida Citrus Open, Orlando, Fla.	Lee Trevino	276	40,000
Mar. 16	Doral-Eastern Open, Miami	Jack Nicklaus	276	30,000
Mar. 23	Greater Jacksonville Open	Larry Ziegler	276	30,000
Mar. 30	Heritage Golf Classic, Hilton Head Island, S.C.	Jack Nicklaus	271	40,000
Apr. 6	Greater Greensboro Open	Tom Weiskopf	275	45,000
Apr. 13	Masters Tournament, Augusta, Ga.	Jack Nicklaus	276	35,000
Apr. 20	Pensacola (Fla.) Open	Jerry McGee	271	25,000
Apr. 27	Tournament of Champions, Carlsbad, Cal.	Al Geiberger	*277	40,000
Apr. 27	Tallahassee (Fla.) Open	Rik Massengale	274	12,000
May 4	Houston Open	Bruce Crampton	273	30,000
May 12	Bryon Nelson Golf Classic, Dallas	Tom Watson	269	35,000
May 18	New Orleans Open	Billy Casper	271	30,000
May 25	Danny Thomas—Memphis Classic	Gene Littler	270	35,000
June 1	Atlanta Classic, Atlanta, Ga.	Hale Irwin	271	45,000
June 8	Kemper Open, Charlotte, N.C.	Ray Floyd	278	50,000
June 16	IVB Classic, Whitemarsh, Pa.	Tom Jenkins	275	30,000
June 23	U.S. Open, Medinah, Ill.	Lou Graham	*287	40,000
June 29	Western Open, Oak Brook, Ill.	Hale Irwin	283	40,000
July 5	Greater Milwaukee Open	Art Wall	271	26,000
July 13	Quad Cities Open, Moline, Ill.	Roger Maltbie	275	15,000
July 20	Pleasant Valley Tournament, Sutton, Mass.	Roger Maltbie	276	40,000
July 27	Canadian Open, Ile Bizard, Que.	Tom Weiskopf	274	40,000
Aug. 3	Westchester Classic, Harrison, N.Y.	Gene Littler	*271	50,000
Aug. 10	PGA Championship, Akron, Ohio	Jack Nicklaus	276	45,000
Aug. 17	Greater Hartford Open	Don Bies	*267	40,000
Aug. 24	Tournament of Champions, Ft. Worth, Tex.	Al Geiberger	270	50,000
Sept. 1	B.C. Open, Endicott, N.Y.	Don Iverson	274	35,000
Sept. 7	World Series of Golf, Akron, Ohio	Tom Watson	142	50,000
Sept. 7	Southern Open, Columbus, Ga.	Hubert Green	264	20,000
Sept. 14	World Open, Pinehurst, N.C.	Jack Nicklaus	*280	40,000
Sept. 28	Saraha Invitational Tournament, Las Vegas	Dave Hill	*270	27,000

Women

Date	Event	Winner	Score	Prize
Jan. 19	Triple Crown Tournament, Miami	Kathy Whitworth	144	$15,000
Feb. 9	Naples Lely Tournament, Naples, Fla.	Sandra Haynie	211	5,700
Feb. 23	Orange Blossom Classic, St. Petersburg, Fla.	Amy Alcott	207	5,000
Mar. 23	Bing Crosby San Isidro Tournament, Guadalajara	Sue Roberts	214	6,400
Mar. 29	LPGA Classic, Scottsdale, Ariz.	Jane Blalock	209	10,000
Apr. 20	Colgate-Dinah Shore Tournament, Palm Springs, Cal.	Sandra Palmer	283	32,000
Apr. 27	Charity Tournament, Ft. Worth, Tex.	Sandra Haynie	*212	6,400
May 11	Lady Tara Tournament, Atlanta	Donna Young	214	5,700
May 25	Raleigh (N.C.) Tournament	JoAnne Carner	*206	5,700
June 1	LPGA Championship, Baltimore	Kathy Whitworth	288	8,000
June 8	Girl Talk Classic, Pine Plains, N.Y.	JoAnne Carner	213	7,000
June 15	Medina (Ohio) Open	Carol Mann	217	7,000
June 22	Hoosier Classic, Plymouth, Ind.	Betsy Cullen	211	5,700
June 29	Peter Jackson Classic, Toronto	JoAnne Carner	*214	12,000
July 6	Wheeling (W. Va.) Classic	Susie McAllister	212	5,700
July 20	U.S. Women's Open, Northfield, N.J.	Sandra Palmer	295	8,044
July 27	George Washington Classic, Horsham, Pa.	Carol Mann	206	5,700
Aug. 3	Lady Keystone Open, Harrisburg, Pa.	Susie Berning	142	4,000
Aug. 17	Patty Berg Classic, St. Paul, Minn.	Joanne Washam	206	6,400
Aug. 24	National Jewish Hospital Open, Littleton, Col.	Judy Rankin	207	5,700
Sept. 7	Dallas Civitan Women's Open, Dallas	Carol Mann	208	6,200
Sept. 14	Southgate Open, Kansas City	Kathy Whitworth	213	5,700
Sept. 21	Portland (Ore.) Classic	Joanne Washam	215	5,700

* Won playoff

British Open Golf Champions

Year	Winner	Year	Winner	Year	Winner	Year	Winner
1906	James Braid	1926	Bob Jones	1946	Sam Snead	1961	Arnold Palmer
1907	Arnaud Massy	1927	Bob Jones	1947	Fred Daly	1962	Arnold Palmer
1908	James Braid	1928	Walter Hagen	1948	Henry Cotton	1963	Bob Charles
1909	J. H. Taylor	1929	Walter Hagen	1949	Bobby Locke	1964	Tony Lema
1910	James Braid	1930	Bob Jones	1950	Bobby Locke	1965	Peter Thomson
1911	Harry Vardon	1931	Tommy Armour	1951	Max Faulkner	1966	Jack Nicklaus
1912	Ted Ray	1932	Gene Sarazen	1952	Bobby Locke	1967	Roberto de Vicenzo
1913	J. H. Taylor	1933	Denny Shute	1953	Ben Hogan	1968	Gary Player
1914	Harry Vardon	1934	Henry Cotton	1954	Peter Thomson	1969	Tony Jacklin
1915-19	(Not played)	1935	Alf Perry	1955	Peter Thomson	1970	Jack Nicklaus
1920	George Duncan	1936	Alf Padgham	1956	Peter Thomson	1971	Lee Trevino
1921	Jock Hutchison	1937	T. H. Cotton	1957	Bobby Locke	1972	Lee Trevino
1922	Walter Hagen	1938	R. A. Whitcombe	1958	Peter Thomson	1973	Tom Weiskopf
1923	Arthur Havers	1939	Richard Burton	1959	Gary Player	1974	Gary Player
1924	Walter Hagen	1940-45	(Not played)	1960	Ken Nagle	1975	Tom Watson
1925	Jim Barnes						

Masters Golf Tournament Champions

Year	Winner	Year	Winner	Year	Winner	Year	Winner
1934	Horton Smith	1946	Herman Keiser	1956	Jack Burke	1966	Jack Nicklaus
1935	Gene Sarazen	1947	Jimmy Demaret	1957	Doug Ford	1967	Gay Brewer, Jr.
1936	Horton Smith	1948	Claude Harmon	1958	Arnold Palmer	1968	Bob Goalby
1937	Byron Nelson	1949	Sam Snead	1959	Art Wall, Jr.	1969	George Archer
1938	Henry Picard	1950	Jimmy Demaret	1960	Arnold Palmer	1970	Billy Casper
1939	Ralph Guldahl	1951	Ben Hogan	1961	Gary Player	1971	Charles Coody
1940	Jimmy Demaret	1952	Sam Snead	1962	Arnold Palmer	1972	Jack Nicklaus
1941	Craig Wood	1953	Ben Hogan	1963	Jack Nicklaus	1973	Tommy Aaron
1942	Byron Nelson	1954	Sam Snead	1964	Arnold Palmer	1974	Gary Player
1943-1945 (Not played)		1955	Cary Middlecoff	1965	Jack Nicklaus	1975	Jack Nicklaus

Professional Golfers' Association Championships

Year	Winner	Year	Winner	Year	Winner	Year	Winner
1916	Jim Barnes	1933	Gene Sarazen	1948	Ben Hogan	1962	Gary Player
1919	Jim Barnes	1934	Paul Runyan	1949	Sam Snead	1963	Jack Nicklaus
1920	Jock Hutchison	1935	Johnny Revolta	1950	Chandler Harper	1964	Bob Nichols
1921	Walter Hagen	1936	Denny Shute	1951	Sam Snead	1965	Dave Marr
1922	Gene Sarazen	1937	Denny Shute	1952	James Turnesa	1966	Al Geiberger
1923	Gene Sarazen	1938	Paul Runyan	1953	Walter Burkemo	1967	Don January
1924	Walter Hagen	1939	Henry Picard	1954	Melvin Harbert	1968	Julius Boros
1925	Walter Hagen	1940	Byron Nelson	1955	Doug Ford	1969	Ray Floyd
1926	Walter Hagen	1941	Victor Ghezzi	1956	Jack Burke	1970	Dave Stockton
1927	Walter Hagen	1942	Sam Snead	1957	Lionel Hebert	1971	Jack Nicklaus
1928	Leo Diegel	1944	Bob Hamilton	1958	Dow Finsterwald	1972	Gary Player
1929	Leo Diegel	1945	Byron Nelson	1959	Bob Rosburg	1973	Jack Nicklaus
1930	Tommy Armour	1946	Ben Hogan	1960	Jay Hebert	1974	Lee Trevino
1931	Tom Creavy	1947	Jim Ferrier	1961	Jerry Barber	1975	Jack Nicklaus
1932	Olin Dutra						

British Amateur Golf Champions

Year	Winner	Year	Winner	Year	Winner	Year	Winner
1930	Bobby Jones (U.S.)	1946	James Bruen	1956	John Beharrell	1966	Bobby Cole
1931	E. Martin-Smith	1947	Willie Turnesa	1957	Reid Jack	1967	Bob Dickson (U.S.)
1932	J. De Forest	1948	Frank Stranahan (U.S.)	1958	Joseph Carr	1968	Mike Bonallack
1933	Michael Scott	1949	Sam McCready	1959	Deane Beman (U.S.)	1969	Mike Bonallack
1934	Lawson Little (U.S.)	1950	Frank Stranahan (U.S.)	1960	Joseph Carr	1970	Mike Bonallack
1935	Lawson Little (U.S.)	1951	Dick Chapman (U.S.)	1961	Michael Bonallack	1971	Steve Melnyk (U.S.)
1936	H. Thompson	1952	Harvie Ward (U.S.)	1962	Richard Davies (U.S.)	1972	Trevor Homer
1937	Robert Sweeny	1953	Joseph Carr	1963	Michael Lunt	1973	Dick Siderowe (U.S.)
1938	C. Yates (U.S.)	1954	Doug Bachli	1964	Gordon Clark	1974	Trevor Homer
1939	Alex Kyle	1955	Joseph Conrad (U.S.)	1965	Mike Bonallack	1975	Vinny Giles (U.S.)
1940-45 (Not played)							

PGA Hall of Fame

Established in 1940 to honor those who have made outstanding contributions to the game by their lifetime playing ability.

Anderson, Willie
Armour, Tommy
Barnes, Jim
Boros, Julius
Brady, Mike
Burke, Billy
Cooper, Harry
Cruickshank, Bobby
Demaret, Jimmy
Diegel, Leo
Dudley, Edward
Dutra, Olin
Evans, Chick
Farrell, Johnny
Ghezzi, Vic
Guldahl, Ralph
Hagen, Walter
Harbert, M. R. (Chick)
Harper, Chandler
Harrison, E. J.
Hogan, Ben
Hutchison, Jock, Sr.
Jones, Bob
Little, W. Lawson
Mangrum, Lloyd
McDermott, John
McLeod, Fred
Middlecoff, Cary
Nelson, Byron
Ouimet, Francis
Picard, Henry
Revolta, Johnny
Runyan, Paul
Sarazen, Gene
Shute, Denny
Smith, Alex
Smith, Horton
Smith, MacDonald
Snead, Sam
Travers, Jerry
Travis, Walter
Wood, Craig

PGA Leading Money Winners

Year	Player	Dollars	Year	Player	Dollars	Year	Player	Dollars
1945	Byron Nelson	52,511	1955	Julius Boros	65,121	1965	Jack Nicklaus	140,752
1946	Ben Hogan	42,556	1956	Ted Kroll	72,835	1966	Billy Casper	121,944
1947	Jimmy Demaret	27,936	1957	Dick Mayer	65,835	1967	Jack Nicklaus	188,998
1948	Ben Hogan	36,812	1958	Arnold Palmer	42,407	1968	Billy Casper	205,168
1949	Sam Snead	31,593	1959	Art Wall, Jr.	53,167	1969	Frank Beard	175,223
1950	Sam Snead	35,758	1960	Arnold Palmer	75,262	1970	Lee Trevino	157,037
1951	Lloyd Mangrum	26,088	1961	Gary Player	64,540	1971	Jack Nicklaus	244,490
1952	Julius Boros	37,032	1962	Arnold Palmer	81,448	1972	Jack Nicklaus	320,542
1953	Lew Worsham	34,002	1963	Arnold Palmer	128,230	1973	Jack Nicklaus	308,362
1954	Bob Toski	65,819	1964	Jack Nicklaus	113,284	1974	Johnny Miller	353,201

LPGA Leading Money Winners

Year	Winner	Dollars	Year	Winner	Dollars	Year	Winner	Dollars
1952	Betsy Rawls	14,505	1960	Louise Suggs	16,892	1968	Kathy Whitworth	48,379
1953	Louise Suggs	19,816	1961	Mickey Wright	22,236	1969	Carol Mann	49,152
1954	Patty Berg	16,011	1962	Mickey Wright	21,641	1970	Kathy Whitworth	30,235
1955	Patty Berg	16,492	1963	Mickey Wright	31,269	1971	Kathy Whitworth	41,181
1956	Marlene Hagge	20,235	1964	Mickey Wright	29,800	1972	Kathy Whitworth	65,063
1957	Patty Berg	16,272	1965	Kathy Whitworth	28,658	1973	Kathy Whitworth	82,854
1958	Beverly Hanson	12,629	1966	Kathy Whitworth	33,517	1974	JoAnne Carner	87,094
1959	Betsy Rawls	26,774	1967	Kathy Whitworth	32,937			

PGA Career Money Winners
(as of January 1, 1975)

Player	Dollars	Player	Dollars	Player	Dollars
Jack Nicklaus	2,243,623	Julius Boros	957,445	Dave Stockton	741,598
Arnold Palmer	1,664,096	Frank Beard	929,163	Johnny Miller	721,034
Billy Casper	1,479,330	Miller Barber	912,875	Tommy Aaron	716,095
Lee Trevino	1,264,445	Bobby Nichols	856,441	Gay Brewer	668,589
Bruce Crampton	1,190,867	Dave Hill	841,700	Bert Yancey	656,834
Gary Player	1,089,210	George Archer	800,243	Chi Chi Rodriguez	637,014
Gene Littler	1,020,658	Doug Sanders	760,003	Bruce Devlin	633,827
Tom Weiskopf	1,005,714	Dan Sikes	751,381	Bob Goalby	620,418

Ryder Cup Matches
United States vs. Great Britain Professional (biennial)
Series Standing, United States 17, Great Britain 3, 1 Tie

Series Record	Series Record
1953 United States 6¹/₂; Great Britain 5¹/₂	1965 United States 19¹/₂; Great Britain 12¹/₂
1955 United States 8; Great Britain 4	1967 United States 23¹/₂; Great Briain 8¹/₂
1957 Great Britain 7; United States 4	1969 United States 16; Great Britain 16
1959 United States 8¹/₂; Great Britain 3¹/₂	1971 United States 18¹/₂; Great Britain 13¹/₂
1961 United States 14¹/₂; Great Britain 9¹/₂	1973 United States 10; Great Britain 13
1963 United States 23; Great Britain 9	1975 United States 21; Great Britain 11

International Walker Cup Golf Match
United States vs. Great Britain — Men's Amateur (Biennial)
Series Standing — United States 22, Great Britain 2, 1 Tie

Series Record	Series Record
1953 United States 9; Great Britain 3	1965 United States 11; Great Britain 11
1955 United States 10; Great Britain 2	1967 United States 13; Great Britain 7
1957 United States 8; Great Britain 3	1969 United States 10; Great Britain 8
1959 United States 9; Great Britain 3	1971 Great Britain 13; United States 11
1961 United States 11; Great Britain 1	1973 United States 14; Great Britain 10
1963 United States 9; Great Britain 3	1975 United States 15¹/₂; Great Britain 8¹/₂

International Curtis Cup Golf Match
United States vs. Great Britain — Women's Amateur (Biennial)
Series Standing — United States 14, Great Britain 2, 2 Ties

Series Record	Series Record
1952 Great Britain 5; United States 4	1964 United States 10¹/₂; Great Britain 7¹/₂;
1954 United States 6; Great Britain 3	1966 United States 13; Great Britain 5
1956 Great Britain 5; United States 4	1968 United States 10¹/₂; Great Britain 7¹/₂
1958 Great Britain 4¹/₂; United States 4¹/₂	1970 United States 11¹/₂; Great Britain 6¹/₂
1960 United States 6¹/₂; Great Britain 2¹/₂	1972 United States 10; Great Britain 8
1962 United States 8; Great Britain 1	1974 United States 13; Great Britain 5

Polo Records

National Open Tournament
1965—Oak Brook 11, Bunn Tyco Chicago 5.
1966—Tulsa 10, Fountain Grove 5.
1967—Bunntyco-Oakbrook 8, Milwaukee 2.
1968—Midland 9, Milwaukee 0.
1969—Tulsa Green Hill 11, Milwaukee 10.
1970—Tulsa Green Hill 9, Oak Brook 5.
1971—Oak Brook 8, Green Hill Farm 7.
1972—Milwaukee 9, Tulsa 5.
1973—Oak Brook 9, Willow Bend 4.
1974—Milwaukee 7, Houston 6.

Intercollegiate Championship
1965—Yale 12, Cornell 3
1966—Cornell 12, Yale 10
1967—Yale 12, Cornell 11
1968—Yale 17, Cornell 13
1969—Yale 17, Cornell 16
1970—Yale 22, Cornell 10
1971—Yale 12, Virginia 11
1972—Univ. of Conn. 17, Univ of Virginia 15
1973—Univ. of Conn. 19, Univ. of Virginia 10
1974—Univ. of Conn. 18, Cornell 16
1975—Univ. of Cal.-Davis 15, Yale 12

Silver Cup
1965—Santa Barbara-Oak Brook 7, Milwaukee 2.
1966—Sunny Climes 9, Oak Brook 7.
1967—Milwaukee 11, Keswick-Blue Ridge 7.
1968—Oak Brook 12, Keswick Sunny Climes 9.
1969—Oak Brook 7, Milwaukee 6.
1970—Oak Brook 9, Tulsa Green Hill 7.
1971—Green Hill Farm 8, Milwaukee 6.
1972—Red Doors Farm 10, Sun Ranch 6.
1973—Houston 6, Willow Bend 4.

Other Tournaments, 1975
Delegate's Cup—Los Gouchos 7, Fairfield 6.
America Cup—Tulsa 9, Milwaukee 6.
Butler Handicap—Good Hope 11, Tulsa-Dallas 10.
Continental Cup—Milwaukee 10, Good Hope 9.
Gold Cup—Tulsa-Dallas 9, Milwaukee 8.
U.S. Open—Milwaukee 14, Tulsa-Dallas 6.
National President's Cup—Broad Acres 11, Queen City 6.

The World Cup

The World Cup, emblematic of international soccer supremacy, was won by West Germany on July 7, 1974, with a 2-1 victory over the Netherlands. By winning the championship, West Germany became the fourth host country to emerge as champion since the trophy was put up in 1930. The next World Cup will be held in 1978 in Argentina. Winners and sites of previous World Cup play follow:

Year	Winner	Site	Year	Winner	Site
1930	Uruguay	Uruguay	1958	Brazil	Sweden
1934	Italy	Italy	1962	Brazil	Chile
1938	Italy	France	1966	England	England
1950	Uruguay	Brazil	1970	Brazil	Mexico City
1954	W. Germany	Switzerland	1974	W. Germany	W. Germany

Water Ski Champions in 1975
33rd Annual National Water Ski Championships
Tomahawk, Wis., Aug. 20-24, 1975

Men's Overall — Ricky McCormick, Hialeah, Fla., 2335 points.
Men's Slalom — Kris LaPoint, Castro Valley, Cal., 56 buoys.
Men's Tricks — Tony Krupa, Jackson, Mich. 4880 points.
Men's Jumping — Wayne Grimditch, Hillsboro Beach, Fla., 164 feet.
Women's Overall — Liz Allan Shetter, Groveland, Fla., 2647 points.
Women's Slalom — Cindy Todd, Pierson, Fla., 56 buoys.
Women's Tricks — Liz Allan Shetter, 3520 points.
Women's Jumping — Liz Allan Shetter, 117 feet.
Senior Men's Overall — Ken White, Honolulu, Hawaii, 2779 points.
Senior Men's Slalom — Ken White, 47 buoys.
Senior Men's Tricks — Jerry Hosner, Fenton, Mich., 3870 points.
Senior Men's Jumping — Ken White, 118 feet.
Senior Women's Overall — Barbara Cleveland, Hawthorne, Fla., 3332 points.
Senior Women's Slalom — Barbara Cleveland, 44.5 buoys.
Senior Women's Tricks — Thelma Salmas, Novato, Cal., 3200 points.

Senior Women's Jumping — Thelma Salmas, 97 feet.
Boys' Overall — Wayne Reece, Winter Park, Fla., 2491 points.
Boys' Slalom — Joe Cornell, Bethel Island, Cal., 40 buoys.
Boys' Tricks — Tony Cecil, Louisville, Ky., 4130 points.
Boys' Jumping — Wayne Reece, 128 feet.
Girls' Overall — Camille Duvall, Greenville, S. C., 3418 points.
Girls' Slalom — Camille Duvall, 48 buoys.
Girls' Tricks — Camille Duvall, 3510 points.
Girls' Jumping — Deena Brush, Sacramento, Cal., 110 feet.
Junior Boys' Overall — Michael Morgan, Norfolk, Va., 3975 points.
Junior Boys' Slalom — Michael Morgan, 45 buoys.
Junior Boys' Tricks — Craig Pickos, Kenosha, Wis., 5260 points.
Junior Boys' Jumping — Sammy Duvall, Greenville, S. C., 115 feet.
Junior Girls' Overall — Karin Roberge, San Diego, Cal., 2931 points.
Junior Girls' Slalom — Terri Olson, Globes, Mich,, 41 buoys.
Junior Girls' Tricks — Kris Golden, Syracuse, Ind., 2380 points.
Junior Girls' Jumping — Ann Weikert, Souci, Iowa, 89 feet.

17th Annual Masters Tournament
Callaway Gardens, Ga., July 12-13, 1975

Men's Overall — Ricky McCormick, Hialeah, Fla., 2732.1 points.
Men's Slalom — Bob LaPoint, Castro Valley, Calif., 52.5 buoys.
Men's Tricks — Ricky McCormick, 4640 points.
Men's Jumping — Wayne Grimditch, Hillsboro Beach, Fla., 180 feet.
Women's Overall — Liz Allan Shetter, Groveland, Fla., 2537.3 points.

Women's Slalom — Liz Allan Shetter, 51 buoys.
Women's Tricks — Maria Victoria Carrasco, Caracas, Venezuela, 4950 points.
Women's Jumping — Liz Allan Shetter, 119 feet.

14th World Water Ski Championships
Thorpe Water Park, Surrey, England, Sept. 3-6, 1975

Men's Overall — Carlos Suarez, Venezuela, 3669 points.
Men's Slalom — Roby Zucchi, Italy, (2 rounds) 60.25 buoys.
Men's Tricks — Carlos Suarez, (2 rounds) 11,420 points.
Men's Jumping — Wayne Grimditch, U.S., (2 rounds) 101.70 meters.
Women's Overall — Liz Allan Shetter, U.S., 4296 points.
Women's Slalom — Liz Allan Shetter, (2 rounds) 46 buoys.

Women's Tricks — Maria Victoria Carrasco, Venezuela, (2 rounds) 10,610 points.
Women's Jumping — Liz Allan Shetter, (2 rounds) 71.55 meters.
Team Results — 1. U.S., 12,226 pts.; 2. Australia, 9608 pts.; 3. Venezuela, 9184 pts.

U.S. Amateur Roller Skating Championship, 1975
Lincoln, Nebraska, July 28-Aug. 9

Artistic

American Senior Dance — John LaBriola - Debra Coyne, Whittier, Cal.
American Esquire Dance — David Spitz - Eleanor Burke, Norwood, Ma.
American Free Dance — Edward Nilson - Fleurette Arseneault, Waltham, Ma.
International Senior Dance — Kerry Cavazzi - Jane Puracchio, East Meadow, N.Y.
International Junior Dance — Larry Chopp - Judy Landau, Livonia, Mich.
American Senior Men's Figures — Kim Rouse, Akron, Ohio.
American Senior Ladies' Figures — Kathleen O'Brien, Edgewater Park, N.J.
American Junior Men's Figures — Chris Morante, East Meadow, N.Y.
American Junior Ladies' Figures — Jean O'Loughlin, Waltham, Ma.
International Senior Men's Skating — Keith King, East Meadow, N.Y.
International Senior Ladies' Skating — Debbie Palm, East Meadow, N.Y.

American Senior Men's Singles — Michael Glatz, San Diego, Cal.
American Senior Ladies' Singles — Moana Brigham, San Diego, Cal.
American Junior Men's Singles — James Bray, Orange, Cal.
American Junior Ladies' Singles — Janet Kerner, Toledo, Ohio.
Senior Mixed Pairs — Ron Sabo & Darlene Waters, Columbus, Ohio.
Junior Mixed Pairs — Brian Barrett & Mari Barrett, Brook Park, Ohio.

Speed

Senior Men's Speed — Tim Small, Ft. Lauderdale, Fla.
Senior Ladies' Speed — Marcia Yager, Cincinnati, Ohio.
Junior Men's Speed — Curtis Cook, Kennewick, Wash.
Junior Ladies' Speed — Diane Merrell, Santa Ana, Cal.
Senior Four Man Relay — Peter Deibele, Tim Small, Tom Small, John Garrett; Ft. Lauderdale, Fla.
Senior Four Lady Relay — Patty Lipscombe, Brenda Haggard, Marcia Yager, Linda Dorso, Cincinnati, Ohio.

Leading Money-Winning Horses
(As of Aug., 1975.)

Horse, Year Foaled	Sts.	1st	2d	3d	Dollars
Kelso, 1957	63	39	12	2	1,977,896
Round Table, 1954	66	43	8	5	1,749,869
Buckpasser, 1963	31	25	4	1	1,462,014
Secretariat, 1970	21	16	3	1	1,316,808
Nashua, 1952	30	22	4	1	1,288,565
Carry Back, 1958	62	21	11	11	1,241,165
Dahlia, 1970	29	12	2	5	1,216,705
Damascus, 1964	32	21	7	3	1,176,781
Cougar, 2nd, 1966	50	20	7	17	1,162,725
Riva Ridge, 1969	30	17	3	1	1,111,497
Fort Marcy, 1964	75	21	18	14	1,109,791
Citation, 1945	45	32	10	2	1,085,760
Susan's Girl, 1969	56	25	14	8	1,040,886
Forego, 1970	37	22	5	6	1,036,676
Native Diver, 1959	81	37	7	12	1,026,500
Dr. Fager, 1964	22	18	2	1	1,002,642

Kentucky Derby, 3 Year Olds

Churchill Downs, Louisville, Ky.

Inaugurated 1875, Distance 1¼ miles; 1½ miles until 1896

Year	Winner	Jockey	Wt.	Second	Winner's Share	Time
1902	Alan-a-Dale	J. Winkfield	117	Inventor	$4,850	2:08.3-4
1903	Judge Himes	H. Booker	117	Early	4,850	2:09
1904	Elwood	F. Prior	117	Ed Tierney	4,850	2:08.1-5
1905	Agile	J. Martin	122	Ram's Horn	4,850	2:10.3-4
1906	Sir Huon	R. Troxer	117	Lady Navarre	4,850	2:08.4-5
1907	Pink Star	A. Minder	117	Zal	4,850	2:12.3-5
1908	Stone Street	A. Pickens	117	Sir Cleges	4,850	2:15.1-5
1909	Wintergreen	V. Powers	117	Miami	4,850	2:08.1-5
1910	Donau	F. Herbert	117	Joe Morris	4,850	2:06.2-5
1911	Meridian	G. Archibald	117	Governor Gray	4,850	2:05
1912	Worth	C. H. Shilling	117	Duval	4,850	2:09.2-5
1913	Donerail	R. Goose	117	Ten Point	5,475	2:04.4-5
1914	Old Rosebud	J. McCabe	114	Hodge	9,125	2:03.2-5
1915	Regret*	J. Notter	112	Pebbles	11,450	2:05.2-5
1916	George Smith	J. Loftus	117	Star Hawk	16,600	2:04.3-5
1917	Omar Khayyam	C. Borel	117	Ticket	9,750	2:04
1918	Exterminator	W. Knapp	114	Escoba	14,700	2:10.4-5
1919	Sir Barton	J. Loftus	112	Billy Kelly	20,825	2:09.4-5
1920	Paul Jones	T. Rice	126	Upset	30,375	2:09
1921	Behave Yourself	C. Thompson	126	Black Servant	38,450	2:04.1-5
1922	Morvich	A. Johnson	126	Bet Mosie	46,775	2:04.3-5
1923	Zev	E. Sande	126	Martingale	53,600	2:05.2-5
1924	Black Gold	J. D. Mooney	126	Chilhowee	52,775	2:05.1-5
1925	Flying Ebony	E. Sande	126	Captain Hal	52,950	2:07.3-5
1926	Bubbling Over	A. Johnson	126	Bagenbaggage	50,075	2:03.4-5
1927	Whiskery	L. McAtee	126	Osmand	51,000	2:06
1928	Reigh Count	C. Lang	126	Misstep	55,375	2:10.2-5
1929	Clyde Van Dusen	L. McAtee	126	Naishapur	53,950	2:10.4-5
1930	Gallant Fox	E. Sande	126	Gallant Knight	50,725	2:07.3-5
1931	Twenty Grand	C. Kurtsinger	126	Sweep All	48,725	2:01.4-5
1932	Burgoo King	E. James	126	Economic	52,350	2:05.1-5
1933	Brokers Tip	D. Meade	126	Head Play	48,925	2:06.4-5
1934	Cavalcade	M. Garner	126	Discovery	28,175	2:04
1935	Omaha	W. Saunders	126	Roman Soldier	39,525	2:05
1936	Bold Venture	I. Hanford	126	Brevity	37,725	2:03.3-5
1937	War Admiral	C. Kurtsinger	126	Pompoon	52,050	2:03.1-5
1938	Lawrin	E. Arcaro	126	Dauber	47,050	2:04.4-5
1939	Johnstown	J. Stout	126	Challedon	46,350	2:03.2-5
1940	Gallahadion	C. Bierman	126	Bimelech	60,150	2:05
1941	Whirlaway	E. Arcaro	126	Staretor	61,275	2:01.2-5
1942	Shut Out	W. D. Wright	126	Alsab	64,225	2:04.2-5
1943	Count Fleet	J. Longden	126	Blue Swords	60,275	2:04
1944	Pensive	C. McCreary	126	Broadcloth	64,675	2:04.1-5
1945	Hoop, Jr.	E. Arcaro	126	Pot o' Luck	64,850	2:07
1946	Assault	W. Mehrtens	126	Spy Song	96,400	2:06.3-5
1947	Jet Pilot	E. Guerin	126	Phalanx	92,160	2:06.3-5
1948	Citation	E. Arcaro	126	Coaltown	83,400	2:05.2-5
1949	Ponder	S. Brooks	126	Capot	91,600	2:04.1-5
1950	Middleground	W. Boland	126	Hill Prince	92,650	2:01.3-5
1951	Count Turf	C. McCreary	126	Royal Mustang	98,050	2:02.3-5
1952	Hill Gail	E. Arcaro	126	Sub Fleet	96,300	2:01.3-5
1953	Dark Star	H. Moreno	126	Native Dancer	90,050	2:02
1954	Determine	R. York	126	Hasty Road	102,050	2:03
1955	Swaps	W. Shoemaker	126	Nashua	108,400	2:01.4-5
1956	Needles	D. Erb	126	Fabius	123,450	2:03.2-5
1957	Iron Liege	W. Hartack	126	Gallant Man	107,950	2:02.1-5
1958	Tim Tam	I. Valenzuela	126	Lincoln Road	116,400	2:05
1959	Tomy Lee	W. Shoemaker	126	Sword Dancer	119,650	2:02.1-5
1960	Venetian Way	W. Hartack	126	Bally Ache	114,850	2:02.2-5
1961	Carry Back	J. Sellers	126	Crozier	120,500	2:04
1962	Decidedly	W. Hartack	126	Roman Line	119,650	2:00.2-5
1963	Chateaugay	B. Baeza	126	Never Bend	108,900	2:01.4-5
1964	Northern Dancer	W. Hartack	126	Hill Rise	114,300	2:00
1965	Lucky Debonair	W. Shoemaker	126	Dapper Dan	112,000	2:01.1-5
1966	Kauai King	D. Brumfield	126	Advocator	120,500	2:02
1967	Proud Clarion	R. Ussery	126	Barbs Delight	119,700	2:00.3-5
1968	Dancer's Image (A)	R. Ussery	126	Forward Pass	122,600	2:02.1-5
1969	Majestic Prince	W. Hartack	126	Arts and Letters	113,200	2:01.4-5
1970	Dust Commander	M. Manganello	126	My Dad George	127,800	2:03.2-5
1971	Canonero II	G. Avila	126	Jim French	145,500	2:03.1-5
1972	Riva Ridge	R. Turcotte	126	No Le Hace	140,300	2:01.4-5
1973	Secretariat	R. Turcotte	126	Sham	155,050	1:59.2-5
1974	Cannonade	A. Cordero	126	Hudson County	274,000	2:04
1975	Foolish Pleasure	J. Vasquez	126	Avatar	209,611	2:02

(A) Dancer's Image was disqualified from purse money by order of the Churchill Downs stewards after tests disclosed that he had run with a pain-killing drug, phenylbutazone, in his system. All wagers were paid on Dancer's Image. Forward Pass was awarded first place money.

The Kentucky Derby has been won five times by two jockeys, Eddie Arcaro, 1938, 1941, 1945, 1948 and 1952; and Bill Hartack, 1957, 1960, 1962, 1964 and 1969; and three times by each of three jockeys, Isaac Murphy, 1884, 1890 and 1891; Earle Sande, 1923, 1925 and 1930, and Willie Shoemaker, 1955, 1959, 1965.

Regret only filly ever to win the Derby.

Belmont Stakes
Elmont, N.Y. Inaugurated 1867; 1½ Miles, 3 year olds

Year	Winner	Jockey	Wt.	Second	Winning Share	Time
1936	Granville	J. Stout	126	Mr. Bones	$29,800	2:30
1937	War Admiral	C. Kurtsinger	126	Sceneshifter	38,020	2:28.3-
1938	Pasteurized	J. Stout	126	Dauber	34,530	2:29.2-
1939	Johnstown	J. Stout	126	Belay	37,020	2:29.3-
1940	Bimelech	F. A. Smith	126	Your Chance	35,030	2:29.3-
1941	Whirlaway	E. Arcaro	126	Robert Morris	39,770	2:31
1942	Shut Out	E. Arcaro	126	Alsab	44,520	2:29.1-
1943	Count Fleet	J. Longden	126	Fairy Manhurst	35,340	2:28.1-
1944	Bounding Home	G. L. Smith	126	Pensive	55,000	2:32.1-
1945	Pavot	E. Arcaro	126	Wildlife	52,675	2:30.1-
1946	Assault	W. Mehrtens	126	Natchez	75,400	2:30.4-
1947	Phalanx	R. Donoso	126	Tide Rips	78,900	2:29.2-
1948	Citation	E. Arcaro	126	Better Self	77,700	2:28.1-
1949	Capot	T. Atkinson	126	Ponder	60,900	2:30.1-
1950	Middleground	W. Boland	126	Lights Up	61,350	2:28.3-
1951	Counterpoint	D. Gorman	125	Battlefield	82,000	2:29
1952	One Count	E. Arcaro	126	Blue Man	82,400	2:30.1-
1953	Native Dancer	E. Guerin	126	Jamie K.	82,500	2:28.3-
1954	High Gun	E. Guerin	126	Fisherman	89,000	2:30.4-
1955	Nashua	E. Arcaro	126	Blazing Count	83,700	2:29
1956	Needles	D. Erb	126	Career Boy	83,600	2:29.4-
1957	Gallant Man	W. Shoemaker	126	Inside Tract	77,300	2:26.3-
1958	Cavan	P. Anderson	126	Tim Tam	73,440	2:30.1-
1959	Sword Dancer	W. Shoemaker	126	Bagdad	98,525	2:28.2-
1960	Celtic Ash	W. Hartack	126	Venetian Way	96,785	2:29.3-
1961	Sherluck	B. Baeza	126	Globemaster	104,900	2:29.1-
1962	Jaipur	W. Shoemaker	126	Admiral's Voyage	109,550	2:28.4-
1963	Chateaugay	B. Baeza	126	Candy Spots	101,700	2:30.1-
1964	Quadrangle	M. Ycaza	126	Roman Brother	110,850	2:28.2-
1965	Hail to All	J. Sellers	126	Tom Rolfe	104,150	2:28.2-
1966	Amberoid	W. Boland	126	Buffle	117,700	2:29.3-
1967	Damascus	W. Shoemaker	126	Cool Reception	104,950	2:28.4-
1968	Stage Door Johnny	H. Gustines	126	Forward Pass	117,700	2:27.1-
1969	Arts and Letters	B. Baeza	126	Majestic Prince	104,050	2:28.4-
1970	High Echelon	J. L. Rotz	126	Needles N Pens	115,000	2:34
1971	Pass Catcher	W. Blum	126	Jim French	97,710	2:30.2-
1972	Riva Ridge	R. Turcotte	126	Ruritania	93,950	2:28
1973	Secretariat	R. Turcotte	126	Twice A Prince	90,120	2:24
1974	Little Current	M. Rivera	126	Jolly Johu	101,970	2:29.1-
1975	Avatar	W. Shoemaker	126	Foolish Pleasure	116,160	2:28.1-

Preakness
Pimlico, Baltimore, Md.; inaugurated 1773; 1 3-16 miles, 3 year olds

Year	Winner	Jockey	Wt.	Second	Winning Share	Time
1936	Bold Venture	G. Woolf	126	Granville	$27,325	1:59
1937	War Admiral	C. Kurtsinger	126	Pompoon	45,600	1:58.2
1938	Dauber	M. Peters	126	Cravat	51,875	1:59.4-
1939	Challedon	G. Seabo	126	Gilded Knight	53,710	1:59.4-
1940	Bimelech	F. A. Smith	126	Mioland	53,230	1:58.3-
1941	Whirlaway	E. Arcaro	126	King Cole	49,365	1:58.4-
1942	Alsab	B. James	126	Requested. Sun Again	58,175	1:57
1943	Count Fleet	J. Longden	126	Blue Swords	43,190	1:57.2-
1944	Pensive	C. McCreary	126	Platter	60,075	1:59.1-
1945	Polynesian	W. D. Wright	126	Hoop Jr.	66,170	1:58.4-
1946	Assault	W. Mehrtens	125	Lord Boswell	96,620	2:01.2-
1947	Faultless	D. Dodson	126	On Trust	98,005	1:59
1948	Citation	E. Arcaro	126	Vulcan's Forge	91,870	2:02.2-
1949	Capot	T. Atkinson	126	Palestinian	79,985	1:56
1950	Hill Prince	E. Arcaro	126	Middleground	56,115	1:59.1-
1951	Bold	E. Arcaro	126	Counterpoint	83,110	1:56.2-
1952	Blue Man	C. McCreary	126	Jampol	86,135	1:57.2-
1953	Native Dancer	E. Guerin	126	Jamie K.	65,200	1:57.4-
1954	Hasty Road	J. Adams	126	Correlation	91,600	1:57.2-
1955	Nashua	E. Arcaro	126	Saratoga	67,550	1:54.3-
1956	Fabius	W. Hartack	126	Needles	84,250	1:58.2-
1957	Bold Ruler	E. Arcaro	126	Iron Liege	65,250	1:56.1-
1958	Tim Tam	I. Valenzuela	126	Lincoln Road	97,900	1:57.1-
1959	Royal Orbit	W. Harmatz	126	Sword Dancer	136,200	1:57
1960	Bally Ache	R. Ussery	126	Victoria Park	121,000	1:57.3-
1961	Carry Back	J. Sellers	126	Globemaster	126,200	1:57.3-
1962	Greek Money	J. L. Rotz	126	Ridan	135,800	1:56.1-
1963	Candy Spots	W. Shoemaker	126	Chateaugay	127,500	1:56.1-
1964	Northern Dancer	W. Hartack	126	The Scoundrel	124,200	1:56.4-
1965	Tom Rolfe	R. Turcotte	126	Dapper Dan	128,100	1:56.1-
1966	Kauai King	D. Brumfield	126	Stupendous	129,000	1:55.2-
1967	Damascus	W. Shoemaker	126	In Reality	141,500	1:55.1-
1968	Forward Pass	I. Valenzuela	126	Out of the Way	142,700	1:56.4-
1969	Majestic Prince	W. Hartack	126	Arts and Letters	129,500	1:55.3-
1970	Personality	E. Belmonte	126	My Dad George	151,300	1:56.1-
1971	Canonero II	G. Avila	126	Eastern Fleet	137,400	1:54
1972	Bee Bee Bee	E. Nelson	126	No Le Hace	135,300	1:55.3-
1973	Secretariat	R. Turcotte	126	Sham	129,900	1:54.2-
1974	Little Current	M. Rivera	126	Neopolitan Way	156,000	1:56.3-
1975	Master Derby	D. McHargue	126	Foolish Pleasure	158,100	1:56.25

American Thoroughbred Records

Dirt Course

Distance Furlongs	Horse, Age, Weight	Track, State	Date	Time
3	El Macho	Gulfstream, Fla.	Feb. 26, 1974	0:32 1-5
3½	Deep Sun, 7, 120	Shenandoah Downs, W. Va.	July 11, 1959	0:39
	Crying For More, 7, 128	Shenandoah Downs, W. Va.	Mar. 18, 1972	0:39
4 (½ mile)	Tamran's Jet, 2, 118	Sunland Park, N.M.	Mar. 22, 1968	0:44 4-5
	Crimson Saint, 2, 119	Oaklawn Park, Ark.	Apr. 1, 1971	0:44 4-5
	Mighty Mr. A., 3, 116	Sportsman Park, Ill.	Nov. 1, 1971	0:44 4-5
	Thief of Bagdad, 5, 114	Sportsman Park, Ill.	Nov. 5, 1971	0:44 4-5
	Argus Ruler, 5, 114	Cahokia Downs, Ill.	Apr. 25, 1973	0:44 4-5
4½	Kathryn's Doll, 2, 111	Turf Paradise, Ariz.	Apr. 9, 1967	0:50 2-5
	Bold Liz, 2, 118	Sunland Park, N.M.	Mar. 19, 1972	0:50 2-5
	Dear Ethel, 2, 114	Miles Park, Ky.	July 4, 1967	0:50 2-5
5	Zip Pocket, 3, 122	Turf Paradise, Ariz.	Apr. 22, 1967	0:55 2-5
5½	Zip Pocket, 3, 129	Turf Paradise, Ariz.	Nov. 19, 1967	1:01 2-5
6 (¾ mile)	Grey Papa, 6, 116	Longacres, Wash.	Sept. 4, 1972	1:07 1-5
6½	Best Hitter, 4, 114	Longacres, Wash.	Aug. 24, 1973	1:13 4-5
7	Triple Bend, 4, 123	Hollywood, Cal.	May 6, 1972	1:19 4-5
7½	Aurecolt, 3, 122	Churchill Downs, Ky.	Nov. 12, 1957	1:29
8 (1 mile)	Dr. Fager, 4, 134	Arlington, Ill.	Aug. 24, 1968	1:32 1-5
8½	Swaps, 4, 130	Hollywood, Cal.	June 23, 1956	1:39
9	Secretariat, 3, 124	Belmont, N.Y.	Sept. 15 1973	1:45 2-5
9½	Riva Ridge, 4, 127	Aqueduct, N.Y.	July 4, 1973	1:52 2-5
10	Noor, 5, 127	Golden Gate, Cal.	June 24, 1950	1:58 1-5
	Quack, 3, 115	Hollywood, Cal.	July 15, 1972	1:58 1-5
10½	Tempted, 4, 128	Aqueduct, N.Y.	Oct. 12, 1959	2:09
11	Man o' War, 3, 126	Belmont, N.Y.	June 12, 1920	2:14 1-5
11½	Theoretic, 6, 111	Sportsman Park, Ill.	Oct. 15, 1973	2:24 1-5
12 (1½ miles)	Secretariat, 3, 126	Belmont, N.Y.	June 9, 1973	2:24
13	Swaps, 4, 130	Hollywood, Cal.	July 25, 1956	2:38 1-5
14	Noor, 5, 117	Santa Anita, Cal.	Mar. 4, 1950	2:52 4-5
15	Pharawell, 5, 119	Gulfstream, Fla.	Apr. 8, 1947	3:13 4-5
16 (2 miles)	Kelso, 7, 124	Aqueduct, N.Y.	Oct. 31, 1964	3:19 1-5
18	Fenelon, 4, 119	Belmont, N.Y.	Oct. 4, 1941	3:47
20	Miss Grillo, 6, 118	Pimlico, Md.	Nov. 12, 1948	4:14 3-5

Annual Leading Jockey—Money Won

Year	Jockey	Dollars	Year	Jockey	Dollars	Year	Jockey	Dollars
1942	Arcaro, E.	481,949	1953	Shoemaker, W.	1,784,187	1964	Shoemaker, W.	2,649,553
1943	Longden, J.	573,276	1954	Shoemaker, W.	1,876,760	1965	Baeza, B.	2,582,702
1944	Atkinson, T.	899,101	1955	Arcaro, E.	1,864,796	1966	Baeza, B.	2,951,022
1945	Longden, J.	981,977	1956	Hartack, W.	2,343,955	1967	Baeza, B.	3,088,888
1946	Atkinson, T.	1,036,825	1957	Hartack, W.	3,060,501	1968	Baeza, B.	2,835,108
1947	Dodson, D.	1,429,949	1958	Shoemaker, W.	2,961,693	1969	Velasquez, J.	2,542,315
1948	Arcaro, E.	1,686,230	1959	Shoemaker, W.	2,843,133	1970	Pincay, L. Jr.	2,626,526
1949	Brooks, S.	1,316,817	1960	Shoemaker, W.	2,123,961	1971	Pincay, L. Jr.	3,784,377
1950	Arcaro, E.	1,410,160	1961	Shoemaker, W.	2,690,819	1972	Pincay, L. Jr.	3,225,827
1951	Shoemaker, W.	1,329,890	1962	Shoemaker, W.	2,916,844	1973	Pincay, L. Jr.	4,093,492
1952	Arcaro, E.	1,859,591	1963	Shoemaker, W.	2,526,925	1974	Pincay, L. Jr.	4,251,060

Annual Leading Money-Winning Horses

Year	Horse	Dollars	Year	Horse	Dollars	Year	Horse	Dollars
1942	Shut Out	238,872	1953	Native Dancer	513,425	1964	Gun Bow	580,100
1943	Count Fleet	174,055	1954	Determine	328,700	1965	Buckpasser	568,096
1944	Pavot	179,040	1955	Nashua	752,550	1966	Buckpasser	669,078
1945	Busher	273,735	1956	Needles	440,850	1967	Damascus	817,941
1946	Assault	424,195	1957	Round Table	600,383	1968	Forward Pass	546,674
1947	Armed	376,325	1958	Round Table	662,780	1969	Arts and Letters	555,604
1948	Citation	709,470	1959	Sword Dancer	537,004	1970	Personality	444,049
1949	Ponder	321,825	1960	Bally Ache	455,045	1971	Riva Ridge	503,263
1950	Noor	346,940	1961	Carry Back	565,349	1972	Droll Roll	471,633
1951	Counterpoint	250,525	1962	Never Bend	402,969	1973	Secretariat	860,404
1952	Crafty Admiral	277,255	1963	Candy Spots	604,481	1974	Chris Evert	551,063

Triple Crown Turf Winners, Owners and Jockeys

(Kentucky Derby, Preakness and Belmont Stakes)

Year	Horse	Owner	Jockey	Year	Horse	Owner	Jockey
1919	Sir Barton	J. K. L. Ross	J. Loftus	1943	Count Fleet	Mrs. J. D. Hertz	J. Longden
1930	Gallant Fox	W. Woodward	E. Sande	1946	Assault	R. J. Kleberg	W. Mehrtens
1935	Omaha	W. Woodward	W. Sanders	1948	Citation	Warren Wright	E. Arcaro
1937	War Admiral	S. D. Riddle	C. Kurtsinger	1973	Secretariat	Meadow Stable	R. Turcotte
1941	Whirlaway	Warren Wright	E. Arcaro				

Ruffian Destroyed

Ruffian, the unbeaten 3-year-old filly, was put to death July 7, after an operation to repair shattered sesamoid bones in her right leg. The injury occurred the previous day in a match race against Foolish Pleasure at Belmont Park, N.Y.

Major Stakes Races, 1975

Event	Track	Added Value	Winner	Dist. Fur.	Time Seconds in Fifths	Jockey
3 Year Olds and Up						
Arlington Hdcp.	Arlington	100,000	Royal Glint	8¹/₂	1:55.4	J. Tejeira
Bowling Green Hdcp.	Belmont	50,000	Barcas	12	2:32.1	M. Castaneda
Brooklyn Hdcp.	Aqueduct	100,000	Forego	10	1:59.4	H. Gustines
Campbell Hdcp.	Bowie	100,000	Jolly Johu	10	2:05.1	B. Feliciano
Carter Hdcp.	Belmont	50,000	Forego	7	1:21.3	H. Gustines
Cornhusker Hdcp.	Ak-Sar-Ben	100,000	Stonewalk	9	1:48.2	R. Turcotte
Excelsior Hdcp.	Aqueduct	50,000	Step Nicely	9	1:48.2	A. Cordero
Governor Stakes	Belmont	100,000	Wajima	9	1:47.1	B. Baeza
Grey Lag Hdcp.	Aqueduct	75,000	Gold and Myrrh	10	2:01.3	W. Blum
Gulfstream Hdcp.	Gulfstream	100,000	Gold and Myrrh	10	2:01.4	W. Blum
Haskell Hdcp.	Monmouth	100,000	Royal Glint	10	2:00.3	C. Perret
Hialeah Turf Cup.	Hialeah	100,000	Outdoors	12	2:27.2	D. Montoya
Marlboro Cup	Belmont	350,000	Wajima	10	2:00	B. Baeza
Massachusetts Hdcp.	Suffolk Downs	100,000	Stonewalk	9	1:48.3	R. Turcotte
Metropolitan Hdcp.	Aqueduct	100,000	Gold and Myrrh	8	1:33.3	W. Blum
New Orleans Hdcp.	Fair Grounds	100,000	Lord Rebeau	9	1:50.3	C. H. Marquez
Pan American Hdcp.	Gulfstream	125,000	Buffalo Lark	12	2:27.3	L. Snyder
San Juan Capistrano Hdcp.	Santa Anita	125,000	La Zanzara	14	2:52.1	D. Pierce
Santa Anita Hdcp.	Santa Anita	150,000	Stardust Mel	10	2:06.2	W. Shoemaker
Sheepshead Bay Hdcp.	Belmont	50,000	Gems and Roses	9	2:01.3	M. Venezia
Surburban Hdcp.	Belmont	100,000	Forego	12	2:27.4	H. Gustines
Whitney Stakes	Saratoga	75,000	Ancient Title	9	1:48.1	S. Hawley
Woodward Stakes	Belmont	100,000	Forego	12	2:27.1	H. Gustines
3 Year Olds and Up, Fillies and Mares						
Beldame Stakes	Belmont	100,000	Susan's Girl	9	1:48.2	B. Baeza
Black Helen Hdcp.	Hialeah	50,000	Garland of Roses	9	1:49	A. Cordero
Delaware Hdcp.	Delaware	100,000	Susan's Girl	10	2:01.4	R. Broussard
Matchmaker Stakes	Atlantic City	150,000	Susan's Girl	9¹/₂	1:55.1	R. Broussard
Molly Pitcher Hdcp.	Monmouth	50,000	Honky Star	8¹/₂	1:43	J. Tejeira
Muskett Hdcp.	Belmont	75,000	Let Me Linger	8	1:35.1	L. Pincay
Santa Margarita Hdcp.	Santa Anita	100,000	Tinza	9	1:48.3	D. Pierce
Vagrancy Hdcp.	Aqueduct	50,000	Honorable Miss	7	1:22.1	J. Vasquez
3 Year Olds						
Belmont Stakes	Belmont	150,000	Avatar	12	2:28.1	W. Shoemaker
California Derby	Golden Gate	100,000	Diabolo	9	1:46.3	L. Pincay
Flamingo	Hialeah	100,000	Foolish Pleasure	9	1:48.2	J. Vasquez
Florida Derby	Gulfstream	125,000	Prince Thou Art	9	1:50.2	B. Baeza
Illinois Derby	Sportsman's Park	100,000	Colonel Power	9	1:50.1	P. Rubbicco
Jersey Derby	Garden State	100,000	Singh	9	1:50.4	A. Cordero
Kentucky Derby	Churchill Downs	125,000	Foolish Pleasure	10	2:02	J. Vasquez
Louisiana Derby	Fair Grounds	100,000	Master Derby	9	1:49.3	D. McHargue
Preakness	Pimlico	150,000	Master Derby	9¹/₂	1:56.2	D. McHargue
Santa Anita Derby	Santa Anita	100,000	Avatar	9	1:47.3	J. Tejeira
Travers Stakes	Saratoga	100,000	Wajima	10	2:02	B. Baeza
Wood Memorial	Aqueduct	100,000	Foolish Pleasure	9	1:48.4	J. Vasquez
3-Year-Old Fillies						
Acorn	Aqueduct	50,000	Ruffian	8	1:34.2	J. Vasquez
Alabama Stakes	Saratoga	75,000	Spout	10	2:04	J. Cruguet
Coaching Club American Oaks	Belmont	100,000	Ruffian	12	2:27.4	J. Vasquez
Gazelle Hdcp.	Belmont	50,000	Land Girl	9	1:49.2	J. Vasquez
Mother Goose Stakes	Aqueduct	75,000	Ruffian	9	1:47.4	J. Vasquez
2 Year Olds						
Arlington-Wash. Futurity	Arlington	150,000	Honest Pleasure	6¹/₂	1:18.1	D. McHargue
Del Mar Futurity	Del Mar	100,000	Telly's Pop	8	1:36	F. Mena
Futurity	Belmont	100,000	Soy Numero Uno	6¹/₂	1:17.4	J. Vasquez
Sapling	Monmouth	100,000	Full Out	6	1:11.3	B. Thornburg
2-Year-Old Fillies						
Arlington Lassie Stakes	Arlington	100,000	Dearly Precious	6	1:11.1	M. Hole
Lassie Stakes	Hollywood	100,000	Walk in the Sun	6	1:10.3	F. Olivares
Sorority Stakes	Monmouth	100,000	Dearly Precious	6	1:10.2	M. Hole

Queen's Plate

The Queen's Plate (known as the King's Plate during reign of male), Canada's most famous thoroughbred race, is the oldest continuously run stakes race in North America. Originated in 1860 over 1¹/₈ miles (now 1¹/₄ miles) for 3-year-olds. Canadian-foaled, race is staged under Royal tutelage for trophy and 50 gold sovereigns plus purse. Trophy is not a plate but a foot-high gold cup valued at $5,000. However, race is identified as a plate race because of 17th century English tradition of awarding plates.

Year	Winner, Jockey	Time	Dollars	Year	Winner, Jockey	Time	Dollars
1962	Flaming Page, J. Fitzsimmons	2:04.3-5	51,225	1969	Jumping Joseph, A. Gomez	2:04.1-5	55,022
1963	Canebora, M. Ycaza	2:04	54,850	1970	Almoner, S. Hawley	2:04.4-5	57,395
1964	Northern Dancer, W. Hartack	2:02.1-5	49,234	1971	Kennedy Road, S. Hawley	2:03	54,388
1965	Whistling Sea, T. Inouye	2:03.4-5	47,852	1972	Victoria Song, R. Platts	2:02	56,143
1966	Titled Hero, A. Gomez	2:03.3-5	52,173	1973	Royal Chocolate, T. Colangelo	2:08	80,697
1967	Jammed Lovely, J. Fitzsimmons	2:03	51,821	1974	Amber Herod, R. Platts	2:09.1-5	96,541
1968	Merger, W. Harris	2:05.2-5	53,641	1975	L'Enjoleur, S. Hawley	2:02.3-5	95,351

College Basketball

Final Standings in 1974-75 Season. *Won Playoff. †Did Not Compete for League Title.

Ivy

	Conference Games W. L.		All Games W. L.	
Pennsylvania	13	1	23	5
Princeton	12	2	22	8
Brown	9	5	14	12
Harvard	9	5	12	13
Dartmouth	5	9	8	18
Cornell	4	10	7	18
Columbia	2	12	4	22
Yale	2	12	3	20

East Coast

Eastern Section

American U.	5	1	16	10
LaSalle	5	1	22	7
Temple	4	2	7	19
Hofstra	3	3	11	13
St. Joseph's	3	3	8	17
West Chester	1	5	8	17
Drexel	0	6	12	11

Western Section

Lafayette	7	1	22	6
Rider	5	3	16	11
Bucknell	4	4	14	12
Delaware	4	4	12	13
Lehigh	0	8	1	23

Yankee

Massachusetts	10	2	18	8
Connecticut	9	3	18	10
Vermont	8	4	16	10
Boston U.	7	4	12	13
Rhode Island	3	7	5	20
New Hampshire	2	10	6	18
Maine	1	10	11	14

Atlantic Coast

Maryland	10	2	24	5
N.C. State	8	4	22	6
North Carolina	8	4	23	8
Clemson	8	4	17	11
Virginia	4	8	12	13
Duke	2	10	13	13
Wake Forest	2	10	13	13

Southeastern

Kentucky	15	3	26	5
Alabama	15	3	22	5
Auburn	12	6	18	8
Tennessee	12	6	18	8
Vanderbilt	10	8	15	11
Florida	8	10	12	16
Louisiana St.	6	12	10	16
Miss. State	5	13	9	17
Mississippi	4	14	8	18
Georgia	3	15	8	17

Southern

Furman	13	0	22	7
East Carolina	12	3	19	9
William & Mary	7	5	16	12
VMI	6	6	13	13
Richmond	7	8	10	16
Davidson	4	7	7	19
Citadel	2	11	5	15
Appalachian	1	12	3	23

Ohio Valley

Middle Tenn.	12	2	23	5
Western Ky.	11	3	16	8
Austin Peay	10	4	17	10
Tenn. Tech	7	7	13	13
Morehead St.	5	9	13	13
East Tenn.	5	9	9	14
Murray St.	3	11	10	15
Eastern Ky.	3	11	7	18

Mid-Eastern

N.C. A&T.	10	2	18	7
Morgan St.(a)	8	4	19	10
Delaware St.	7	5	17	9
S.C. State	7	5	15	11
Howard U.	6	6	13	13
N.C. Central.	4	8	10	16
UMd., E. Shore	0	2	2	24

(a) Forfeited games to S.C. State and Delaware St.

Big Ten

Indiana	18	0	31	1
Michigan	12	6	19	8
Purdue	11	7	17	11
Minnesota	11	7	18	8
Mich. State	10	8	17	9
Ohio State	8	10	14	14
Iowa	7	11	10	16
Wisconsin	5	13	8	18
Illinois	4	14	8	18
Northwestern	4	14	6	20

Mid-American

Central Mich.	10	4	22	6
Bowling Green	9	5	18	10
Toledo	9	5	17	9
Miami (O.)	8	5	19	7
Western Mich	8	6	16	10
Eastern Mich	4	9	12	14
Ohio U.	4	10	12	14
Kent State	3	11	6	20
†Ball State	—	—	10	15
†Northern Ill.	—	—	8	15

Ohio

Marietta	11	2	19	4
Wittenberg	10	3	20	8
Capital	9	4	19	6
Denison	8	4	16	6
Muskingum	7	5	14	9
Heidelberg	7	6	13	10
Kenyon	7	6	14	11
Mount Union	6	6	13	10
Otterbein	6	7	10	11
Ohio Northern	4	8	13	14
Wooster	4	8	10	13
Oberlin	3	8	13	11
Baldwin-Wallace	3	10	5	19
Ohio Wesleyan	2	10	4	17

Indiana

St. Joseph's	10	2	21	7
Ind. Central	8	4	14	10
Valparaiso	8	4	14	11
Evansville	6	6	13	13
Butler	6	6	10	16
DePauw	2	10	6	19
Wabash	2	10	4	22

Big Eight

Kansas	11	3	19	8
Kansas St.	10	4	20	9
Missouri	9	5	18	9
Nebraska	7	7	14	12
Oklahoma	6	8	13	13
Okla. State	5	9	10	16
Iowa State	4	10	10	16
Colorado	4	10	7	19

Southland

McNeese St.	6	2	16	8
Louisiana Tech	5	3	12	13
Lamar	4	4	7	16
Arkansas St.	3	5	13	12
UTex. Arlington	2	6	6	20

Missouri Valley

Louisville	12	2	28	3
New Mexico St.	11	3	20	7
Drake	9	5	19	10
Bradley	7	7	15	11
Wichita St.	6	8	13	13
Tulsa	5	9	15	14
West Texas St.	3	11	9	17
North Texas St.	3	11	6	20
†Southern Ill.	—	—	18	9

Southwest

Texas A&M.	12	2	20	7
Arkansas	11	3	17	9
Texas Tech.	11	3	18	8
Texas	6	8	10	15
Baylor	6	8	10	16
Texas Christian	4	10	9	16
So. Methodist	4	10	8	18
Rice	2	12	5	21
†Houston	—	—	16	10

Southwestern

Jackson	11	1	25	4
Alcorn St.	8	4	25	10
Southern U.	7	5	19	8
Prairie View	6	6	16	10
Grambling	5	7	16	12
Miss. Valley	4	8	15	14
Texas Southern	1	11	8	16

Western

Arizona St.	12	2	25	4
UTex. El Paso	10	4	20	6
Arizona	9	5	22	7
Utah	7	7	17	9
Col. State	6	8	14	12
Brigham Young	5	9	12	14
New Mexico	4	10	13	13
Wyoming	3	11	10	16

Big Sky

Montana	13	1	21	8
Idaho St.	9	5	16	10
Boise St.	7	7	13	13
Gonzaga	7	7	13	13
Weber St.	6	8	11	15
Northern Ariz.	5	9	9	17
Montana St.	5	9	11	15
Idaho	4	10	10	16

Pacific—8

UCLA	12	2	28	3
Oregon St.	10	4	19	12
Southern Cal.	8	6	18	8
California	7	7	17	9
Oregon	6	8	21	9
Washington	6	8	16	10
Stanford	6	8	12	14
Wash. State	1	13	10	16

West Coast

UN Las Vegas	13	1	24	5
San Francisco	9	5	19	7
Pepperdine	8	6	17	8
St. Mary's	7	7	14	12
Loyola, Cal.	7	7	14	12
Seattle	6	8	8	18
Santa Clara	4	10	10	16
UN Reno	2	12	10	16

Pacific Coast

Long Beach St.	8	2	19	7
San Diego St.	6	4	14	13
Fresno St.	5	5	16	10
San Jose St.	4	6	16	13
Fullerton St.	4	6	13	11
Pacific	3	7	12	14

Major Basketball Independents, 1975

East	W.	L.		W.	L.		W.	L.		W.
Rutgers	22	7	St. Francis, Pa.	11	14	Samford	9	17	Oklahoma City	12
Syracuse	23	9	Villanova	9	18	Georgia St.	8	18	St. Louis	12
Holy Cross	20	8	Colgate	8	16	Georgia Southern	8	18		
Boston College	21	9	Buffalo	8	17	Baptist, S.C.	4	20		
St. John's, N.Y.	21	10	Iona	4	19				**Southwest**	
Providence	20	11	Army	3	22	**Midwest**			Pan American	22
Georgetown	18	10				Marquette	23	4	Houston Baptist	9
George Washington	17	10	**South**			Cincinnati	23	6	Hardin-Simmons	5
Pittsburgh	18	11				Notre Dame	19	10		
Canisius	15	10	UNC Charlotte	23	3	Detroit	17	9		
Seton Hall	16	11	Stetson	22	4	Illinois St.	16	10	**Rocky Mountain**	
Duquesne	14	11	Memphis St.	20	7	DePaul	15	10	Utah State	21
St. Peter's	15	12	South Alabama	19	7	Cleveland St.	13	11	Air Force	13
Manhattan	14	12	Florida St.	18	8	Marshall	13	13	Colorado Coll.	7
Long Island U.	13	12	Va. Commonwealth	17	8	Indiana St.	12	14	Denver	9
West Virginia	14	13	South Carolina	19	9	Xavier	11	15	Metropolitan St.	7
St. Bonaventure	14	13	Tulane	16	10	Loyola, Ill.	10	15		
Navy	12	12	Virginia Tech	16	10	Dayton	10	16		
Northeastern	12	12	NE Louisiana	15	10	UW Milwaukee	8	18	**Pacific Coast**	
Niagara	13	14	South Florida	15	10				Portland St.	18
Fairfield	13	14	Jacksonville	15	11	**Missouri Valley**			UC Santa Barbara	18
Fordham	12	13	Georgia Tech	11	15				Hawaii	14
Penn State	11	12	Southern Miss.	11	15	Creighton	20	7	L.A. State	13
Fairleigh Dickinson	11	13	Mercer	9	17	Oral Roberts	20	8	Portland	13

NCAA Individual Statistics, 1974-75

Scoring

	G.	FG	FT	Pts.	Avg.
McCurdy, Richmond	26	321	213	855	32.9
Dantley, Notre Dame	29	315	253	883	30.4
Thompson, N.C. State	28	347	144	838	29.9
Burden, Utah	26	295	157	747	29.7
Ivy, Iowa State	26	315	107	737	28.3
Coleman, So. Miss.	20	233	98	564	28.2
Oleynick, Seattle	26	287	135	709	27.3
Scaife, Arkansas St.	25	289	100	678	27.1
Rogers, Pan American	22	248	92	588	26.7
Adams, Oklahoma	26	279	133	691	26.6
King, Tennessee	25	273	115	661	26.4
Dorsey, Georgia	25	267	112	646	25.8
Luckett, Ohio U.	26	257	143	657	25.3
Fogle, Canisius	19	198	78	474	24.9
Birdsong, Houston	26	268	104	646	24.6
Jackson, UNC Charlotte	24	248	94	590	24.6
Dunbar, Houston	26	260	113	633	24.3
Grunfield, Tennessee	20	184	107	475	23.8
Bass, Iona	23	211	123	545	23.7
Grevey, Kentucky	31	303	124	730	23.5
Elliott, Arizona	29	273	131	677	23.3
Jones, Tenn. Tech	25	244	94	582	23.3
McKeever, Citadel	20	185	89	459	23.0
Hicks, Tulane	26	251	89	591	22.7
Sellers, Rutgers	29	254	149	657	22.7
Brown, Wake Forest	26	250	89	589	22.7
Pickett, NE Louisiana	25	221	120	562	22.5
Smith, Missouri	27	249	106	604	22.4

	G.	FG	FGA	P
Andreas, Ohio State	27	210	347	.60
Kupchak, North Carolina	31	239	397	.60
Tampa, East Tenn. St.	23	117	195	.60
Cutter, Western Mich.	26	134	224	.59
Brown, Brown	26	194	327	.59
Winton, Army	24	201	343	.58

Free Throw Percentage
(Minimum three free throws per game)

	G.	FT	FTA	Pc
Oleynick, Seattle	26	135	152	.88
Caldwell, Florida	28	102	115	.88
Brookins, Creighton	27	98	111	.88
Johnson, Auburn	24	102	116	.87
Kraft, Air Force	25	83	95	.87
Lee, Syracuse	32	98	114	.86
Hays, Montana	29	91	106	.85
Johnson, Morehead St.	25	91	106	.85
Krueger, Texas	21	102	119	.85
Rose, NE Louisiana	25	83	97	.85
Zumbro, Denver	25	88	103	.85
Ramsay, Seton Hall	27	82	96	.85

Rebounds

	G.	No.	Avg
Irving, Hofstra	21	323	15.
Warner, Maine	25	352	14.
Roane, UMd. Eastern Shore	26	356	13.
Mayes, Furman	29	394	13.
Robinzine, DePaul	25	338	13.
Barnett, Samford	26	350	13.
Sorrell, Middle Tenn.	28	373	13.
King, Pan American	22	293	13.
Adams, Oklahoma	26	346	13.
Hayes, Idaho St.	26	346	13.
Coleman, Houston Bapt.	26	344	13.
Winton, Army	24	315	13.

Field Goal Percentage
(Minimum five field goals per game)

	G.	FG	FGA	Pct.
King, Tennessee	25	273	439	.622
Fleischer, Duke	26	178	287	.620
Meriweather, So. Ill.	27	229	370	.619
Roundfield, Central Mich.	28	216	353	.612
Glenn, Southern Ill.	27	196	321	.611
Allison, Arkansas	26	172	282	.610

College Basketball Coach of the Year

(United Press International)

Year Winner, College	Year Winner, College	Year Winner, College
1952—Dudley Moore, LaSalle	1960—Pete Newell, California	1968—Guy Lewis, Houston
1953—Branch McCracken, Indiana	1961—Fred Taylor, Ohio State	1969—John Wooden, UCLA
1954—Dudley Moore, LaSalle	1962—Fred Taylor, Ohio State	1970—John Wooden, UCLA
1955—Phil Woolpert, San Francisco	1963—Ed Jucker, Cincinnati	1971—Al McGuire, Marquette
1956—Phil Woolpert, San Francisco	1964—John Wooden, UCLA	1972—John Wooden, UCLA
1957—Frank McGuire, North Carolina	1965—Dave Strack, Michigan	1973—John Wooden, UCLA
1958—Tex Winter, Kansas State	1966—Adolph Rupp, Kentucky	1974—Digger Phelps, Notre Dame
1959—Adolph Rupp, Kentucky	1967—John Wooden, UCLA	1975—Bobby Knight, Indiana

Major-College Records

(Restricted to games between four-year colleges.)

Career Scoring Averages

Player, Team	Last Year	Games	FG	FT	Pts.	Avg.
Pete Maravich, LSU	1970	83	1,387	893	3,667	44.2
Austin Carr, Notre Dame	1971	74	1,017	526	2,560	34.6
Oscar Robertson, Cincinnati	1960	88	1,052	869	2,973	33.8
Calvin Murphy, Niagara	1970	77	947	654	2,548	33.1
Frank Selvy, Furman	1954	78	922	694	2,538	32.5
Rick Mount, Purdue	1970	72	910	503	2,323	32.3
Darrell Floyd, Furman	1956	71	868	545	2,281	32.1
Nick Werkman, Seton Hall	1964	71	812	649	2,273	32.0
Willie Humes, Idaho St.	1971	48	565	380	1,510	31.5
Elgin Baylor, Col. Idaho-Seattle	1958	80	956	588	2,500	31.3
William Averitt, Pepperdine	1973	49	615	311	1,541	31.4
Dwight Lamar, SW Louisiana	1973	112	1,445	603	3,493	31.2
Elvin Hayes, Houston	1968	93	1,215	454	2,884	31.0
Bill Bradley, Princeton	1965	83	856	791	2,503	30.2

Season Averages

Player, Team	Year	Games	FG	FT	Pts.	Avg.
Pete Maravich, LSU	1970	31	522	337	1,381	44.5
Pete Maravich, LSU	1969	26	433	282	1,148	44.2
Pete Maravich, LSU	1968	26	432	274	1,138	43.8
Frank Selvy, Furman	1954	29	427	355	1,209	41.7
Johnny Neumann, Mississippi	1971	23	366	191	923	40.1
Billy McGill, Utah	1962	26	394	221	1,009	38.8
Calvin Murphy, Niagara	1968	24	337	242	916	38.2
Austin Carr, Notre Dame	1970	29	444	218	1,106	38.1
Austin Carr, Notre Dame	1971	29	430	241	1,101	38.0
Rick Barry, Miami (Fla.)	1965	26	340	293	973	37.4
Elvin Hayes, Houston	1968	33	519	176	1,214	36.8
Howard Komives, Bowling Green	1964	23	292	260	844	36.7

Single-Game Scoring

Player, Team (Opponent)	Year	Pts.	Player, Team (Opponent)	Year	Pts.
Selvy, Furman (Newberry)	1954	100	Floyd, Furman (Morehead St.)	1955	67
Bilkvy, Temple (Wilkes)	1951	73	Maravich, LSU (Tulane)	1969	66
Maravich, LSU (Alabama)	1970	69	Handlan, W. & Lee (Furman)	1951	66
Murphy, Niagara (Syracuse)	1969	68	Zawoluk, St. John's (St. Peter's)	1950	65

Individual Records, Season

Field Goal Percentage	Alcindor, UCLA, 1967	.667	Rebounds Per Game	Slack, Marshall, 1955	25.6
	Martens, Ab. Christian, 1972	.667	Rebounds	Dukes, Seton Hall, 1953	734
	Fleming, Arizona, 1974	.667	Field Goals Attempted	Maravich, LSU, 1970	1,168
Free Throw Percentage	Boyer, Arkansas, 1962	.933	Free Throws Attempted	Selvy, Furman, 1954	444

National Invitation Tournament Champions

Year	Champion	Year	Champion	Year	Champion	Year	Champion
1938	Temple	1948	St. Louis	1958	Xavier (Ohio)	1967	Southern Illinois
1939	Long Island Univ.	1949	San Francisco	1959	St. John's	1968	Dayton
1940	Colorado	1950	CCNY	1960	Bradley	1969	Temple
1941	Long Island Univ.	1951	Brigham Young	1961	Providence	1970	Marquette
1942	West Virginia	1952	LaSalle	1962	Dayton	1971	North Carolina
1943	St. John's	1953	Seton Hall	1963	Providence	1972	Maryland
1944	St. John's	1954	Holy Cross	1964	Bradley	1973	Virginia Tech
1945	DePaul	1955	Duquesne	1965	St. John's	1974	Purdue
1946	Kentucky	1956	Louisville	1966	Brigham Young	1975	Princeton
1947	Utah	1957	Bradley				

NCAA Basketball Champions

Year	Champion	Year	Champion	Year	Champion	Year	Champion
1939	Oregon	1949	Kentucky	1958	Kentucky	1967	UCLA
1940	Indiana	1950	CCNY	1959	California	1968	UCLA
1941	Wisconsin	1951	Kentucky	1960	Ohio State	1969	UCLA
1942	Stanford	1952	Kansas	1961	Cincinnati	1970	UCLA
1943	Wyoming	1953	Indiana	1962	Cincinnati	1971	UCLA
1944	Utah	1954	La Salle	1963	Loyola (Chi.)	1972	UCLA
1945	Oklahoma A&M	1955	San Francisco	1964	UCLA	1973	UCLA
1946	Oklahoma A&M	1956	San Francisco	1965	UCLA	1974	No. Carolina State
1947	Holy Cross	1957	North Carolina	1966	Texas Western	1975	UCLA
1948	Kentucky						

NCAA College Division Basketball Champions

Year	Champion	Year	Champion	Year	Champion	Year	Champion
1957	Wheaton	1962	Mt. St. Mary's	1967	Winston-Salem	1972	Roanoke
1958	South Dakota	1963	South Dakota St.	1968	Kentucky Wesleyan	1973	Kentucky Wesleyan
1959	Evansville	1964	Evansville	1969	Kentucky Wesleyan	1974	Morgan State
1960	Evansville	1965	Evansville	1970	Philadelphia Textile	1975	Old Dominion
1961	Wittenberg	1966	Kentucky Wesleyan	1971	Evansville		

Auto Racing
Indianapolis 500 Winners

Year	Winner	Chassis	Engine	MPH	Gross	Runner up
1940	Wilbur Shaw	Maserati	Maserati	114.277	$85,525	Rex Mays
1941	Floyd Davis, Mauri Rose	Wetteroth	Offenhauser	115.117	90,925	Rex Mays
1946	George Robson	Adams	Sparks	114.820	115,450	Jimmy Jackson
1947	Mauri Rose	Deidt	Offenhauser	116.338	137,425	Bill Holland
1948	Mauri Rose	Deidt	Offenhauser	119.814	171,075	Bill Holland
1949	Bill Holland	Deidt	Offenhauser	121.327	179,050	Johnnie Parsons
1950	Johnnie Parsons	Kurtis Kraft	Offenhauser	124.002(a)	201,135	Bill Holland
1951	Lee Wallard	Kurtis Kraft	Offenhauser	126.244	207,650	Mike Nazaruk
1952	Troy Ruttman	Kuzma	Offenhauser	128.922	230,100	Jim Rathmann
1953	Bill Vukovich	Kurtis Kraft 500A	Offenhauser	128.740	246,300	Art Cross
1954	Bill Vukovich	Kurtis Kraft 500A	Offenhauser	130.840	269,375	Jim Bryan
1955	Bob Sweikert	Kurtis Kraft 500C	Offenhauser	128.209	270,400	Tony Bettenhausen
1956	Pat Flaherty	Watson	Offenhauser	128.490	282,052	Sam Hanks
1957	Sam Hanks	Epperly	Offenhauser	135.601	300,252	Jim Rathmann
1958	Jimmy Bryan	Epperly	Offenhauser	133.791	305,217	George Amick
1959	Rodger Ward	Watson	Offenhauser	135.857	338,100	Jim Rathmann
1960	Jim Rathmann	Watson	Offenhauser	138.767	369,150	Rodger Ward
1961	A. J. Foyt	Watson	Offenhauser	139.130	400,000	Eddie Sachs
1962	Rodger Ward	Watson	Offenhauser	140.293	426,152	Len Sutton
1963	Parnelli Jones	Watson	Offenhauser	143.137	494,031	Jim Clark
1964	A. J. Foyt	Watson	Offenhauser	147.350	506,625	Rodger Ward
1965	Jim Clark	Lotus	Ford	151.388	628,399	Parnelli Jones
1966	Graham Hill	Lola	Ford	144.317	691,809	Jim Clark
1967	A. J. Foyt	Coyote	Ford	151.207	737,109	Al Unser
1968	Bobby Unser	Eagle	Offenhauser	152.882	809,627	Dan Gurney
1969	Mario Andretti	Hawk	Ford	156.867	805,127	Dan Gurney
1970	Al Unser	P. J. Colt	Ford	155.749	1,000,002	Mark Donohue
1971	Al Unser	P. J. Colt	Ford	157.735	1,001,604	Peter Revson
1972	Mark Donohue	McLaren	Offenhauser	163.465	1,011,846	Al Unser
1973	Gordon Johncock	Eagle	Offenhauser	163.465	1,011,846	Billy Vukovich
1974	Johnny Rutherford	McLaren	Offenhauser	158.589	1,015,686	Bobby Unser
1975	Bobby Unser	Eagle	Offenhauser	149.213(c)	1,101,322	Johnny Rutherford

(a) 345 miles. (b) 332.5 miles. (c) 435 miles. Race Record—163.465 MPH, Mark Donohue, 1972.

1975 Indianapolis 500 Standings

Driver	Money Won	Driver	Money Won
1—Bobby Unser, Albuquerque, N.M.	$214,031	7—Bill Puterbaugh, Indianapolis	28,78
2—Johnny Rutherford, Fort Worth, Tex.	97,886	8—George Snider, Bakersfield, Cal.	24,68
3—A. J. Foyt, Houston, Tex.	74,677	9—Wally Dalenbach, Basalt, Col.	42,71
4—Duane Carter, Brownsburg, Ind.	33,424	10—Bob Harkey, Indianapolis	
5—Roger McCluskey, Tucson, Ariz.	31,002	(Salf Walther, Dayton, relief driver)	22,89
6—Bill Vukovich, Fresno, Cal.	28,473		

World's Land Speed Records—Evolution of the Mile Record

Date	Driver	Car	MPH	Date	Driver	Car	MPH
12/18/98	Chasseloup-Laubat	Jeantaud	39.24	4/22/28	Keech	White Triplex	207.552
4/29/99	Jenatzy	Jamais Contente		3/11/29	Seagrave	Irving-Napier	231.446
	Jenatzy		65.79	2/ 5/31	Campbell	Napier-Campbell	246.086
11/17/02	Augieres	Mars	77.13	2/24/32	Campbell	Napier-Campbell	253.96
11/ 5/03	Duray	Gabron-Brillie	84.73	2/22/33	Campbell	Napier-Campbell	272.109
12/30/04	Barras	Darracq	109.65	9/ 3/35	Campbell	Bluebird Spl.	301.13
1/25/05	Bowden	Mercedes	109.75	11/19/37	Eyston	Thunderbolt 1	311.42
1/26/06	Marriott	Stanley (Steam)	127.659	9/16/38	Eyston	Thunderbolt 1	357.5
3/16/10	Oldfield	Benz	131.724	8/23/39	Cobb	Railton	368.9
4/23/11	Burman	Benz	141.732	9/16/47	Cobb	Railton-Mobil	394.2
2/12/19	DePalma	Packard	149.875	8/ 5/63	Breedlove	Spirit of America	407.45
4/27/20	Milton	Dusenberg	155.046	10/27/64	Arfons	Green Monster	536.71
4/28/26	Parry-Thomas	Thomas Spl.	170.624	11/15/65	Breedlove	Spirit of America	600.601
3/29/27	Seagrave	Sunbeam	203.790	10/23/70	Gary Gabelich	Blue Flame	622.407

World Grand Prix Champions

Year	Driver	Year	Driver	Year	Driver
1950	Nino Farina, Italy	1959	Jack Brabham, Australia	1967	Denis Hulme, New Zealan
1951	Juan Fangio, Argentina	1960	Jack Brabham, Australia	1968	Graham Hill, England
1952	Alberto Ascari, Italy	1961	Phil Hill, United States	1969	Jackie Stewart, Scotland
1953	Alberto Ascari, Italy	1962	Graham Hill, England	1970	Jochen Rindt, Austria
1954	Juan Fangio, Argentina	1963	Jim Clark, Scotland	1971	Jackie Stewart, Scotland
1955	Juan Fangio, Argentina	1964	John Surtees, England	1972	Emerson Fittipaldi, Brazil
1956	Juan Fangio, Argentina	1965	Jim Clark, Scotland	1973	Jackie Stewart, Scotland
1957	Juan Fangio, Argentina	1966	Jack Brabham, Australia	1974	Emerson Fittipaldi, Brazil
1958	Mike Hawthorne, England			1975	Nicki Lauda, Austria

U.S. Auto Club National Champions

Year	Driver	Year	Driver	Year	Driver	Year	Driver
1950	Henry Banks	1957	Jimmy Bryan	1963	A. J. Foyt	1969	Mario Andretti
1951	Tony Bettenhausen	1958	Tony Bettenhausen	1964	A. J. Foyt	1970	Al Unser
1952	Chuck Stevenson	1959	Rodger Ward	1965	Mario Andretti	1971	Joe Leonard
1953	Sam Hawks	1960	A. J. Foyt	1966	Mario Andretti	1972	Joe Leonard
1954	Jimmy Bryan	1961	A. J. Foyt	1967	A. J. Foyt	1973	Roger McCluskey
1955	Bob Sweikert	1962	Rodger Ward	1968	Bobby Unser	1974	Bobby Unser
1956	Jimmy Bryan						

Grand Prix for Formula 1 Cars, 1975

Grand Prix	Winner, Car
gentine	Emerson Fittipaldi, McLaren
ustrian	Vittorio Brambilla, March
elgian	Niki Lauda, Ferrari
ritish	Emerson Fittipaldi, McLaren
azilian	Carlos Pace, Brabham
utch	James Hunt, Hesketh
ench	Niki Lauda, Ferrari
alian	Clay Regazzoni, Ferrari

Grand Prix	Winner, Car
Monte Carlo	Niki Lauda, Ferrari
South African	Jody Scheckter, Tyrrell-Ford
Spanish	Jochen Mass, Texaco-McLaren
Swedish	Niki Lauda, Ferrari
Swiss	Clay Regazzoni, Ferrari
United States	Niki Lauda, Ferrari
West German	Carlos Reutemann, Brabham

NASCAR Racing in 1975
Winston Cup Grand National Races

ate	Race & Site	Winner	Car	Money Won
an. 19	Winston Western 500, Riverside, Cal.	Bobby Allison	Matador	$12,035
eb. 16	Daytona 500, Daytona Beach, Fla.	Benny Parsons	Chevrolet	40,900
eb. 23	Richmond 500, Richmond, Va.	Richard Petty	Dodge	6,265
lar. 2	Carolina 500, Rockingham, N.C.	Cale Yarborough	Chevrolet	14,200
lar. 16	Southeastern 500, Bristol, Tenn.	Richard Petty	Dodge	5,350
lar. 23	Atlanta 500, Atlanta, Ga.	Richard Petty	Dodge	16,500
pr. 6	Gwyn Staley 400, N. Wilkesboro, N.C.	Richard Petty	Dodge	6,675
pr. 13	Rebel 500, Darlington, S.C.	Bobby Allison	Matador	15,080
pr. 27	Virginia 500, Martinsville, Va.	Richard Petty	Dodge	18,000
lay 4	Winston 500, Talladega, Ala.	Buddy Baker	Ford	25,725
lay 10	Music City USA 420, Nashville, Tenn.	Darrell Waltrip	Chevrolet	6,500
lay 19	Mason-Dixon 500, Dover, Del.	David Pearson	Mercury	14,925
lay 25	World 600, Charlotte, N.C.	Richard Petty	Dodge	27,290
une 8	Tuborg 400, Riverside, Cal.	Richard Petty	Dodge	15,135
une 15	Motor State 400, Brooklyn, Mich.	David Pearson	Mercury	14,405
uly 4	Firecracker 400, Daytona Beach, Fla.	Richard Petty	Dodge	16,935
uly 20	Nashville 420, Nashville, Tenn.	Cale Yarborough	Chevrolet	5,735
ug. 3	Purolator 500, Mt. Pocono, Pa.	David Pearson	Mercury	15,225
ug. 17	Talladega 500, Talladega, Ala.	Buddy Baker	Ford	23,390
ug. 24	Champion Spark Plug 400, Brooklyn, Mich.	Richard Petty	Dodge	15,140
ept. 1	Southern 500, Darlington, S.C.	Bobby Allison	Matador	20,870
ept. 14	Delaware 500, Dover, Del.	Richard Petty	Dodge	15,250
ept. 21	Wilkes 400, N. Wilkesboro, N.C.	Richard Petty	Dodge	7,960
ept. 28	Old Dominion 500, Martinsville, Va.	Dave Marcis	Dodge	12,500
ct. 5	National 500, Charlotte, N.C.	Richard Petty	Dodge	27,970

Daytona 500 Winners

Year	Driver (Car)	Avg. MPH
1959	L. Petty (Oldsmobile)	135.521
1960	J. Johnson (Chevrolet)	124.740
1961	M. Panch (Pontiac)	149.601
1962	F. Roberts (Pontiac)	152.529
1963	T. Lund (Ford)	151.566
1964	R. Petty (Plymouth)	154.334
a) 1965	F. Lorenzen (Ford)	141.539
b) 1966	R. Petty (Plymouth)	160.627
1967	M. Andretti (Ford)	146.926

Year	Driver (Car)	Avg. MPH
1968	C. Yarborough (Mercury)	143.251
1969	L. Yarbrough (Ford)	160.875
1970	P. Hamilton (Plymouth)	149.601
1971	R. Petty (Plymouth)	144.456
1972	A. J. Foyt (Mercury)	161.550
1973	R. Petty (Dodge)	157.205
(c) 1974	R. Petty (Dodge)	140.894
1975	B. Parsons (Chevrolet)	153.649

a)322.5 miles because of rain.   (b)495 miles because of rain.   (c)450 miles.

1975 Leading Daytona 500 Finishers

Driver, Car	Laps	Purse
1—Benny Parsons, Chevrolet	200	$40,900
2—Bobby Allison, Matador	199	25,100
3—Cale Yarborough, Chevrolet	198	17,900
4—David Pearson, Mercury	198	13,450
5—Ramo Stott, Chevrolet	197	11,350

Driver, Car	Laps	Purse
6—Dave Marcis, Dodge	197	$10,000
7—Richard Petty, Dodge	192	9,100
8—Richie Panch, Dodge	191	7,850
9—G. C. Spencer, Dodge	191	7,150
10—James Hylton, Chevrolet	189	6,450

Grand National Champions (NASCAR)

ear	Driver
949	Red Byron
950	Bill Rexford
951	Herb Thomas
952	Tim Flock
953	Herb Thomas
954	Lee Petty

Year	Driver
1955	Tim Flock
1956	Buck Baker
1957	Buck Baker
1958	Lee Petty
1959	Lee Petty
1960	Rex White

Year	Driver
1961	Ned Jarrett
1962	Joe Weatherly
1963	Joe Weatherly
1964	Richard Petty
1965	Ned Jarrett
1966	David Pearson
1967	Richard Petty

Year	Driver
1968	David Pearson
1969	David Pearson
1970	Bobby Isaac
1971	Richard Petty
1972	Richard Petty
1973	Benny Parsons
1974	Richard Petty

Motorcycle Racing
Grand National Champion

ear	Champion
951	Bobby Hill
952	Bobby Hill
953	Bill Tuman
954	Joe Leonard
955	Brad Andres
956	Joe Leonard

Year	Champion
1957	Joe Leonard
1958	Carroll Resweber
1959	Carroll Resweber
1960	Carroll Resweber
1961	Carroll Resweber
1962	Bart Markel

Year	Champion
1963	Dick Mann
1964	Roger Reiman
1965	Bart Markel
1966	Bart Markel
1967	Gary Nixon
1968	Gary Nixon

Year	Champion
1969	Mert Lawwill
1970	Gene Romero
1971	Dick Mann
1972	Mark Brelsford
1973	Ken Roberts
1974	Ken Roberts

Major League Pennant Winners, 1901-1975

National League

Year	Winner	Won	Lost	Pct.	Manager
1901	Pittsburgh	90	49	.647	Clarke
1902	Pittsburgh	103	36	.741	Clarke
1903	Pittsburgh	91	49	.650	Clarke
1904	New York	106	47	.693	McGraw
1905	New York	105	48	.686	McGraw
1906	Chicago	116	36	.763	Chance
1907	Chicago	107	45	.704	Chance
1908	Chicago	99	55	.643	Chance
1909	Pittsburgh	110	42	.724	Clarke
1910	Chicago	104	50	.675	Chance
1911	New York	99	54	.647	McGraw
1912	New York	103	48	.682	McGraw
1913	New York	101	51	.664	McGraw
1914	Boston	94	59	.614	Stallings
1915	Philadelphia	90	62	.592	Moran
1916	Brooklyn	94	60	.610	Robinson
1917	New York	98	56	.636	McGraw
1918	Chicago	84	45	.651	Mitchell
1919	Cincinnati	96	44	.686	Moran
1920	Brooklyn	93	60	.604	Robinson
1921	New York	94	56	.614	McGraw
1922	New York	93	61	.604	McGraw
1923	New York	95	58	.621	McGraw
1924	New York	93	60	.608	McGraw
1925	Pittsburgh	95	58	.621	McKechnie
1926	St. Louis	89	65	.578	Hornsby
1927	Pittsburgh	94	60	.610	Bush
1928	St. Louis	95	59	.617	McKechnie
1929	Chicago	98	54	.645	McCarthy
1930	St. Louis	92	62	.597	Street
1931	St. Louis	101	53	.656	Street
1932	Chicago	90	64	.584	Grimm
1933	New York	91	61	.599	Terry
1934	St. Louis	95	58	.621	Frisch
1935	Chicago	100	54	.649	Grimm
1936	New York	91	62	.597	Terry
1937	New York	95	57	.625	Terry
1938	Chicago	89	63	.586	Hartnett
1939	Cincinnati	97	57	.630	McKechnie
1940	Cincinnati	100	53	.654	McKechnie
1941	Brooklyn	100	54	.649	Durocher
1942	St. Louis	106	48	.688	Southworth
1943	St. Louis	105	49	.682	Southworth
1944	St. Louis	105	49	.682	Southworth
1945	Chicago	98	56	.636	Grimm
1946	St. Louis	98	58	.628	Dyer
1947	Brooklyn	94	60	.610	Shotton
1948	Boston	91	62	.595	Southworth
1949	Brooklyn	97	57	.630	Shotton
1950	Philadelphia	91	63	.591	Sawyer
1951	New York	98	59	.624	Durocher
1952	Brooklyn	96	57	.627	Dressen
1953	Brooklyn	105	49	.682	Dressen
1954	New York	97	57	.630	Durocher
1955	Brooklyn	98	55	.641	Alston
1956	Brooklyn	93	61	.604	Alston
1957	Milwaukee	95	59	.617	Haney
1958	Milwaukee	92	62	.597	Haney
1959	Los Angeles	88	68	.564	Alston
1960	Pittsburgh	95	59	.617	Murtaugh
1961	Cincinnati	93	61	.604	Hutchinson
1962	San Francisco	103	62	.624	Dark
1963	Los Angeles	99	63	.611	Alston
1964	St. Louis	93	69	.574	Keane
1965	Los Angeles	97	65	.599	Alston
1966	Los Angeles	95	67	.586	Alston
1967	St. Louis	101	60	.627	Schoendienst
1968	St. Louis	97	65	.599	Schoendienst

American League

Year	Winner	Won	Lost	Pct.	Manager
1901	Chicago	83	53	.610	Griffith
1902	Philadelphia	83	53	.610	Mack
1903	Boston	91	47	.659	Collins
1904	Boston	95	59	.617	Collins
1905	Philadelphia	92	56	.622	Mack
1906	Chicago	93	58	.616	Jones
1907	Detroit	92	58	.613	Jennings
1908	Detroit	90	63	.588	Jennings
1909	Detroit	98	54	.645	Jennings
1910	Philadelphia	102	48	.680	Mack
1911	Philadelphia	101	50	.669	Mack
1912	Boston	105	47	.691	Stahl
1913	Philadelphia	96	57	.627	Mack
1914	Philadelphia	99	53	.651	Mack
1915	Boston	101	50	.669	Carrigan
1916	Boston	91	63	.591	Carrigan
1917	Chicago	100	54	.649	Rowland
1918	Boston	75	51	.595	Barrow
1919	Chicago	88	52	.629	Gleason
1920	Cleveland	98	56	.636	Speaker
1921	New York	98	55	.641	Huggins
1922	New York	94	60	.610	Huggins
1923	New York	98	54	.645	Huggins
1924	Washington	92	62	.597	Harris
1925	Washington	96	55	.636	Harris
1926	New York	91	63	.591	Huggins
1927	New York	110	44	.714	Huggins
1928	New York	101	53	.656	Huggins
1929	Philadelphia	104	46	.693	Mack
1930	Philadelphia	102	52	.622	Mack
1931	Philadelphia	107	45	.704	Mack
1932	New York	107	47	.695	McCarthy
1933	Washington	99	53	.651	Cronin
1934	Detroit	101	53	.656	Cochrane
1935	Detroit	93	58	.616	Cochrane
1936	New York	102	51	.667	McCarthy
1937	New York	102	52	.662	McCarthy
1938	New York	99	53	.651	McCarthy
1939	New York	106	45	.702	McCarthy
1940	Detroit	90	64	.584	Baker
1941	New York	101	53	.656	McCarthy
1942	New York	103	51	.669	McCarthy
1943	New York	98	56	.636	McCarthy
1944	St. Louis	89	65	.578	Sewell
1945	Detroit	88	65	.575	O'Neill
1946	Boston	104	50	.675	Cronin
1947	New York	97	57	.630	Harris
1948	Cleveland	97	58	.626	Boudreau
1949	New York	97	57	.630	Stengel
1950	New York	98	56	.636	Stengel
1951	New York	98	56	.636	Stengel
1952	New York	95	59	.617	Stengel
1953	New York	99	52	.656	Stengel
1954	Cleveland	111	43	.721	Lopez
1955	New York	96	58	.623	Stengel
1956	New York	97	57	.630	Stengel
1957	New York	98	56	.636	Stengel
1958	New York	92	62	.597	Stengel
1959	Chicago	94	60	.610	Lopez
1960	New York	97	57	.630	Stengel
1961	New York	109	53	.673	Houk
1962	New York	96	66	.593	Houk
1963	New York	104	57	.646	Houk
1964	New York	99	63	.611	Berra
1965	Minnesota	102	60	.630	Mele
1966	Baltimore	97	63	.606	Bauer
1967	Boston	92	70	.568	Williams
1968	Detroit	103	59	.636	Smith

National League

	East					West				Playoff
Year	Winner	W.	L.	Pct.	Manager	Winner	W.	L.	Pct.	Manager	Winner
1969	N.Y. Mets	100	62	.617	Hodges	Atlanta	93	69	.574	Harris	New York
1970	Pittsburgh	89	73	.549	Murtaugh	Cincinnati	102	60	.630	Anderson	Cincinnati
1971	Pittsburgh	97	65	.599	Murtaugh	San Francisco	90	72	.556	Fox	Pittsburgh
1972	Pittsburgh	96	59	.619	Virdon	Cincinnati	95	59	.617	Anderson	Cincinnati
1973	N.Y. Mets	82	79	.509	Berra	Cincinnati	99	63	.611	Anderson	New York
1974	Pittsburgh	88	82	.543	Murtaugh	Los Angeles	102	60	.630	Alston	Los Angeles
1975	Pittsburgh	92	69	.571	Murtaugh	Cincinnati	108	54	.667	Anderson	Cincinnati

American League

| | East | | | | West | | | | | Playoff |
Year	Winner	W.	L.	Pct.	Manager	Winner	W.	L.	Pct.	Manager	Winner
1969	Baltimore	109	53	.673	Weaver	Minnesota	97	65	.599	Martin	Baltimore
1970	Baltimore	108	54	.677	Weaver	Minnesota	98	64	.605	Rigney	Baltimore
1971	Baltimore	101	57	.639	Weaver	Oakland	101	60	.627	Williams	Baltimore
1972	Detroit	86	70	.551	Martin	Oakland	93	72	.600	Williams	Oakland
1973	Baltimore	97	65	.599	Weaver	Oakland	94	68	.580	Williams	Oakland
1974	Baltimore	91	71	.562	Weaver	Oakland	90	72	.556	Dark	Oakland
1975	Boston	95	65	.594	Johnson	Oakland	98	64	.605	Dark	Boston

All-Star Baseball Games, 1933-1975

Year	Winner	Score	Location	Year	Winner	Score	Location
1933	American	4-2	Chicago	1957	American	6-5	St. Louis
1934	American	9-7	New York	1958	American	4-3	Baltimore
1935	American	4-1	Cleveland	1959	National	5-4	Pittsburgh
1936	National	4-3	Boston	1959	American	5-3	Los Angeles
1937	American	8-3	Washington	1960	National	5-3	Kansas City
1938	National	4-1	Cincinnati	1960	National	6-0	New York
1939	American	3-1	New York	1961	National(3)	5-4	San Francisco
1940	National	4-0	St. Louis	1961	Called-Rain	1-1	Boston
1941	American	7-5	Detroit	1962	National(3)	3-1	Washington
1942	American	3-1	New York	1962	American	9-4	Chicago
1943*	American	5-3	Philadelphia	1963	National	5-3	Cleveland
1944*	National	7-1	Pittsburgh	1964	National	7-4	New York
1945	(not played)			1965	National	6-5	Minnesota
1946	American	12-0	Boston	1966	National(3)	2-1	St. Louis
1947	American	2-1	Chicago	1967	National(4)	2-1	Anaheim
1948	American	5-2	St. Louis	1968*	National	1-0	Houston
1949	American	11-7	New York	1969	National	9-3	Washington
1950	National (1)	4-3	Chicago	1970*	National(2)	5-4	Cincinnati
1951	National	8-3	Detroit	1971*	American	6-4	Detroit
1952	National	3-2	Philadelphia	1972*	National	4-3	Atlanta
1953	National	5-1	Cincinnati	1973*	National	7-1	Kansas City
1954	American	11-9	Cleveland	1974*	National	7-2	Pittsburgh
1955	National(2)	6-5	Milwaukee	1975*	National	6-3	Milwaukee
1956	National	7-3	Washington				

(1.) 14 innings. (2.) 12 innings. (3.) 10 innings. (4.) 15 innings. *Night game.

Cy Young Award Winners

Year	Player, Club	Year	Player, Club	Year	Player, Club
1956	Don Newcombe, Dodgers	1967	(NL) Mike McCormick, Giants	1971	(NL) Ferguson Jenkins, Cubs
1957	Warren Spahn, Braves		(AL) Jim Lonborg, Red Sox		(AL) Vida Blue, A's
1958	Bob Turley, Yankees	1968	(NL) Bob Gibson, Cardinals	1972	(NL) Steve Carlton, Phillies
1959	Early Wynn, White Sox		(AL) Dennis McLain, Tigers		(AL) Gaylord Perry, Indians
1960	Vernon Law, Pirates	1969	(NL) Tom Seaver, Mets	1973	(NL) Tom Seaver, Mets
1961	Whitey Ford, Yankees		(AL) (tie) Dennis McLain, Tigers		(AL) Jim Palmer, Orioles
1962	Don Drysdale, Dodgers		Mike Cuellar, Orioles	1974	(NL) Mike Marshall, Dodgers
1963	Sandy Koufax, Dodgers	1970	(NL) Bob Gibson, Cardinals		(AL) Jim (Catfish) Hunter, A's
1964	Dean Chance, Angels		(AL) Jim Perry, Twins		
1965	Sandy Koufax, Dodgers				
1966	Sandy Koufax, Dodgers				

Baseball Stadiums

National League

| | | Home Run Distances (in ft.) | | | Seating |
Team	Stadium	LF	Center	RF	Capacity
Atlanta Braves	Atlanta-Fulton County Stadium	330	402	330	52,870
Chicago Cubs	Wrigley Field	355	400	353	37,741
Cincinnati Reds	Riverfront Stadium	330	404	330	51,786
Houston Astros	Astrodome	330	400	330	45,000
Los Angeles Dodgers	Dodger Stadium	330	395	330	56,000
Montreal Expos	Jarry Park	340	420	340	28,000
New York Mets	Shea Stadium	341	410	341	55,300
Philadelphia Phillies	Veterans Stadium	330	408	330	56,581
Pittsburgh Pirates	Three Rivers Stadium	335	400	335	50,235
St. Louis Cardinals	Busch Memorial Stadium	330	404	330	50,126
San Diego Padres	San Diego Stadium	330	410	330	47,634
San Francisco Giants	Candlestick Park	335	410	335	58,000

American League

		LF	Center	RF	Capacity
Baltimore Orioles	Memorial Stadium	309	410	309	52,137
Boston Red Sox	Fenway Park	315	420	302	33,379
California Angels	Anaheim Stadium	333	404	333	43,200
Chicago White Sox	White Sox Park	352	400	352	44,492
Cleveland Indians	Municipal Stadium	320	400	320	76,977
Detroit Tigers	Tiger Stadium	340	440	325	54,220
Kansas City Royals	Royals Stadium	330	410	330	40,762
Milwaukee Brewers	Milwaukee County Stadium	320	402	315	47,500
Minnesota Twins	Metropolitan Stadium	330	410	330	45,919
New York Yankees	Yankee Stadium	301	461	296	65,010
Oakland A's	Oakland-Alameda County Coliseum	330	400	330	50,000
Texas Rangers	Arlington Stadium	330	400	330	35,698

Yankee's played at Shea Stadium in 1974 and 1975.

Home Run Leaders

Year	National League	HR.	Year	American League	HR
1919	Gavvy Cravath, Philadelphia	12	1919	Babe Ruth, Boston	29
1920	Cy Williams, Philadelphia	15	1920	Babe Ruth, New York	54
1921	George Kelly, New York	23	1921	Babe Ruth, New York	59
1922	Rogers Hornsby, St. Louis	42	1922	Ken Williams, St. Louis	39
1923	Cy Williams, Philadelphia	41	1923	Babe Ruth, New York	41
1924	Jacques Fournier, Brooklyn	27	1924	Babe Ruth, New York	46
1925	Rogers Hornsby, St. Louis	39	1925	Bob Meusel, New York	33
1926	Hack Wilson, Chicago	21	1926	Babe Ruth, New York	47
1927	Hack Wilson, Chi; Cy Williams, Phil.	30	1927	Babe Ruth, New York	60
1928	Hack Wilson, Chi.; Jim Bottomley, S.L.	31	1928	Babe Ruth, New York	54
1929	Charles Klein, Philadelphia	43	1929	Babe Ruth, New York	46
1930	Hack Wilson, Chicago	56	1930	Babe Ruth, New York	49
1931	Charles Klein, Philadelphia	31	1931	Babe Ruth, Lou Gehrig, New York	46
1932	Charles Klein, Philadelphia, Mel Ott, N.Y.	38	1932	Jimmy Foxx, Philadelphia	58
1933	Charles Klein, Philadelphia	28	1933	Jimmy Foxx, Philadelphia	48
1934	Collins, S.L.; Mel Ott, N.Y.	35	1934	Lou Gehrig, New York	49
1935	Walter Berger, Boston	34	1935	Jimmy Foxx, Phil., Hank Greenberg, Det.	36
1936	Mel Ott, New York	33	1936	Lou Gehrig, New York	49
1937	Mel Ott, N.Y.; Joe Medwick, S.L.	31	1937	Joe DiMaggio, New York	46
1938	Mel Ott, New York	36	1938	Hank Greenberg, Detroit	58
1939	John Mize, St. Louis	28	1939	Jimmy Foxx, Boston	35
1940	John Mize, St. Louis	43	1940	Hank Greenberg, Detroit	41
1941	Dolph Camilli, Brooklyn	34	1941	Ted Williams, Boston	37
1942	Mel Ott, New York	30	1942	Ted Williams, Boston	36
1943	Bill Nicholson, Chicago	29	1943	Rudy York, Detroit	34
1944	Bill Nicholson, Chicago	33	1944	Nick Etten, New York	22
1945	Tommy Holmes, Boston	28	1945	Vern Stephens, St. Louis	24
1946	Ralph Kiner, Pittsburgh	23	1946	Hank Greenberg, Detroit	44
1947	Ralph Kiner, Pitts.; John Mize, N.Y.	51	1947	Ted Williams, Boston	32
1948	Ralph Kiner, Pitts.; John Mize, N.Y.	40	1948	Joe DiMaggio, New York	39
1949	Ralph Kiner, Pittsburgh	54	1949	Ted Williams, Boston	43
1950	Ralph Kiner, Pittsburgh	47	1950	Al Rosen, Cleveland	37
1951	Ralph Kiner, Pittsburgh	42	1951	Gus Zernial, Chicago-Philadelphia	33
1952	Ralph Kiner, Pittsburgh; Hank Sauer, Chicago	37	1952	Larry Doby, Cleveland	32
1953	Ed Mathews, Milwaukee	47	1953	Al Rosen, Cleveland	43
1954	Ted Kluszewski, Cincinnati	49	1954	Larry Doby, Cleveland	32
1955	Willie Mays, New York	51	1955	Mickey Mantle, New York	37
1956	Duke Snider, Brooklyn	43	1956	Mickey Mantle, New York	52
1957	Hank Aaron, Milwaukee	44	1957	Roy Sievers, Washington	42
1958	Ernie Banks, Chicago	47	1958	Mickey Mantle, New York	42
1959	Ed Mathews, Milwaukee	46	1959	Rocky Colavito, Cleveland, Harmon Killebrew, Washington	42
1960	Ernie Banks, Chicago	41	1960	Mickey Mantle, New York	40
1961	Orlando Cepeda, San Francisco	46	1961	Roger Maris, New York	61
1962	Willie Mays, San Francisco	49	1962	Harmon Killebrew, Minnesota	48
1963	Hank Aaron, Milwaukee; Willie McCovey, San Francisco	44	1963	Harmon Killebrew, Minnesota	45
1964	Willie Mays, San Francisco	47	1964	Harmon Killebrew, Minnesota	49
1965	Willie Mays, San Francisco	52	1965	Tony Conigliaro, Boston	32
1966	Hank Aaron, Atlanta; Willie McCovey, San Francisco	44 44	1966	Frank Robinson, Baltimore	49
1967	Hank Aaron, Atlanta	39	1967	Carl Yastrzemski, Boston; Harmon Killebrew, Minnesota	44
1968	Willie McCovey, San Francisco	36	1968	Frank Howard, Washington	44
1969	Willie McCovey, San Francisco	45	1969	Harmon Killebrew, Minnesota	49
1970	Johnny Bench, Cincinnati	45	1970	Frank Howard, Washington	44
1971	Willie Stargell, Pittsburgh	48	1971	Bill Melton, Chicago	33
1972	Johnny Bench, Cincinnati	40	1972	Dick Allen, Chicago	37
1973	Willie Stargell, Pittsburgh	44	1973	Reggie Jackson, Oakland	32
1974	Mike Schmidt, Philadelphia	36	1974	Dick Allen, Chicago	32
1975	Mike Schmidt, Philadelphia	38	1975	George Scott, Milwaukee; Reggie Jackson, Oak.	36

All-time Major League Record (154-game Season)—60—Babe Ruth, New York Yankees (A), 1927. **(162-game Season)—61**—Roger Maris, New York Yankees, 1961. Prior to the 1931 season a batted ball that bounced into the stands was a home run (now a ground-rule double). None of Babe Ruth's record 60 homers bounced into the stands.

Runs Batted In Leaders

Year	National League	RBI	Year	American League	RBI
1938	Joe Medwick, St. Louis	122	1938	Jimmy Foxx, Boston	175
1939	Frank McCormick, Cinn.	128	1939	Ted Williams, Boston	145
1940	John Mize, St. Louis	137	1940	Hank Greenberg, Detroit	150
1941	Dolph Camilli, Brooklyn	120	1941	Joe DiMaggio, New York	125
1942	John Mize, New York	137	1942	Ted Williams, Boston	137
1943	Bill Nicholson, Chi.	128	1943	Rudy York, Detroit	118
1944	Bill Nicholson, Chi.	122	1944	Vern Stephens, St. Louis	109
1945	Dixie Walker, Brooklyn	124	1945	Nick Etten, New York	111
1946	Enos Slaughter, St. Louis	130	1946	Hank Greenberg, Detroit	127
1947	John Mize, New York	138	1947	Ted Williams, Boston	114
1948	Stan Musial, St. Louis	131	1948	Joe DiMaggio, New York	155
1949	Ralph Kiner, Pittsburgh	127	1949	Ted Williams, Vern Stephens, Boston	159
1950	Del Ennis, Philadelphia	126	1950	Walt Dropo, Vern Stephens, Boston	144
1951	Monte Irvin, New York	121	1951	Gus Zernial, Chi.-Phila.	129
1952	Hank Sauer, Chicago	121	1952	Al Rosen, Cleveland	105
1953	Roy Campanella, Brooklyn	142	1953	Al Rosen, Cleveland	145
1954	Ted Kluszewski, Cincinnati	141	1954	Larry Doby, Cleveland	126
1955	Duke Snider, Brooklyn	136	1955	Ray Boone, Detroit, Jack Jensen, Boston	116
1956	Stan Musial, St. Louis	109	1956	Mickey Mantle, New York	130
1957	Hank Aaron, Milwaukee	132	1957	Roy Sievers, Washington	114

Year	Player	RBI	Year	Player	RBI
58	Ernie Banks, Chicago	129	1958	Jack Jensen, Boston	122
59	Ernie Banks, Chicago	143	1959	Jack Jensen, Boston	112
60	Hank Aaron, Milwaukee	126	1960	Roger Maris, New York	112
61	Orlando Cepeda, San Francisco	142	1961	Roger Maris, New York	142
62	Tommy Davis, Los Angeles	153	1962	Harmon Killebrew, Minn.	126
63	Hank Aaron, Milwaukee	130	1963	Dick Stuart, Boston	118
64	Ken Boyer, St. Louis	119	1964	Brooks Robinson, Baltimore	118
65	Deron Johnson, Cincinnati	130	1965	Rocky Colavito, Cleveland	108
66	Hank Aaron, Atlanta	127	1966	Frank Robinson, Baltimore	122
67	Orlando Cepeda, St. Louis	111	1967	Carl Yastrzemski, Boston	121
68	Willie McCovey, San Francisco	105	1968	Ken Harrelson, Boston	109
69	Willie McCovey, San Francisco	126	1969	Harmon Killebrew, Minn.	140
70	Johnny Bench, Cincinnati	148	1970	Frank Howard, Wash.	126
71	Joe Torre, St. Louis	137	1971	Harmon Killebrew, Minn.	119
72	Johnny Bench, Cincinnati	125	1972	Dick Allen, Chicago	113
73	Willie Stargell, Pittsburgh	119	1973	Reggie Jackson, Oakland	117
74	Johnny Bench, Cincinnati	129	1974	Jeff Burroughs, Texas	118
75	Greg Luzinski, Philadelphia	120	1975	George Scott, Milwaukee	109

Batting Champions

	National League				American League		
Year	Player	Club	Pct.	Year	Player	Club	Pct.
09	Honus Wagner	Pittsburgh	.339	1909	Ty Cobb	Detroit	.377
10	Sherwood Magee	Philadelphia	.331	1910	Ty Cobb	Detroit	.385
11	Honus Wagner	Pittsburgh	.334	1911	Ty Cobb	Detroit	.420
12	Henry Zimmerman	Chicago	.372	1912	Ty Cobb	Detroit	.410
13	Jacob Daubert	Brooklyn	.350	1913	Ty Cobb	Detroit	.390
14	Jacob Daubert	Brooklyn	.329	1914	Ty Cobb	Detroit	.368
15	Larry Doyle	New York	.320	1915	Ty Cobb	Detroit	.369
16	Hal Chase	Cincinnati	.339	1916	Tris Speaker	Cleveland	.386
17	Edd Roush	Cincinnati	.341	1917	Ty Cobb	Detroit	.383
18	Zack Wheat	Brooklyn	.335	1918	Ty Cobb	Detroit	.382
19	Edd Roush	Cincinnati	.321	1919	Ty Cobb	Detroit	.384
20	Rogers Hornsby	St. Louis	.370	1920	George Sisler	St. Louis	.407
21	Rogers Hornsby	St. Louis	.397	1921	Harry Heilmann	Detroit	.394
22	Rogers Hornsby	St. Louis	.401	1922	George Sisler	St. Louis	.420
23	Rogers Hornsby	St. Louis	.384	1923	Harry Heilmann	Detroit	.403
24	Rogers Hornsby	St. Louis	.424	1924	Babe Ruth	New York	.378
25	Rogers Hornsby	St. Louis	.403	1925	Harry Heilmann	Detroit	.393
26	Eugene Hargrave	Cincinnati	.353	1926	Henry Manush	Detroit	.378
27	Paul Waner	Pittsburgh	.380	1927	Harry Heilmann	Detroit	.398
28	Rogers Hornsby	Boston	.387	1928	Goose Goslin	Washington	.379
29	Lefty O'Doul	Philadelphia	.398	1929	Lew Fonseca	Cleveland	.369
30	Bill Terry	New York	.401	1930	Al Simmons	Philadelphia	.381
31	Chick Hafey	St. Louis	.349	1931	Al Simmons	Philadelphia	.390
32	Lefty O'Doul	Brooklyn	.368	1932	Dale Alexander	Det.-Bos.	.367
33	Charles Klein	Philadelphia	.368	1933	Jimmy Foxx	Philadelphia	.356
34	Paul Waner	Pittsburgh	.362	1934	Lou Gehrig	New York	.363
35	Arky Vaughan	Pittsburgh	.385	1935	Buddy Myer	Washington	.349
36	Paul Waner	Pittsburgh	.373	1936	Luke Appling	Chicago	.388
37	Joe Medwick	St. Louis	.374	1937	Charlie Gehringer	Detroit	.371
38	Ernie Lombardi	Cincinnati	.342	1938	Jimmy Foxx	Boston	.349
39	John Mize	St. Louis	.349	1939	Joe DiMaggio	New York	.381
40	Debs Garms	Pittsburgh	.355	1940	Joe DiMaggio	New York	.352
41	Pete Reiser	Brooklyn	.343	1941	Ted Williams	Boston	.406
42	Ernie Lombardi	Boston	.330	1942	Ted Williams	Boston	.356
43	Stan Musial	St. Louis	.357	1943	Luke Appling	Chicago	.328
44	Dixie Walker	Brooklyn	.357	1944	Lou Boudreau	Cleveland	.327
45	Phil Cavarretta	Chicago	.355	1945	George Stirnweiss	New York	.309
46	Stan Musial	St. Louis	.365	1946	Mickey Vernon	Washington	.353
47	Harry Walker	Philadelphia	.363	1947	Ted Williams	Boston	.343
48	Stan Musial	St. Louis	.376	1948	Ted Williams	Boston	.369
49	Jackie Robinson	Brooklyn	.342	1949	George Kell	Detroit	.343
50	Stan Musial	St. Louis	.346	1950	Billy Goodman	Boston	.354
51	Stan Musial	St. Louis	.355	1951	Ferris Fain	Philadelphia	.344
52	Stan Musial	St. Louis	.336	1952	Ferris Fain	Philadelphia	.327
53	Carl Furillo	Brooklyn	.344	1953	Mickey Vernon	Washington	.337
54	Willie Mays	New York	.345	1954	Roberto Avila	Cleveland	.341
55	Richie Ashburn	Philadelphia	.338	1955	Al Kaline	Detroit	.340
56	Hank Aaron	Milwaukee	.328	1956	Mickey Mantle	New York	.353
57	Stan Musial	St. Louis	.351	1957	Ted Williams	Boston	.388
58	Richie Ashburn	Philadelphia	.350	1958	Ted Williams	Boston	.328
59	Hank Aaron	Milwaukee	.355	1959	Harvey Kuenn	Detroit	.353
60	Dick Groat	Pittsburgh	.325	1960	Pete Runnels	Boston	.320
61	Roberto Clemente	Pittsburgh	.351	1961	Norm Cash	Detroit	.361
62	Tommy Davis	Los Angeles	.346	1962	Pete Runnels	Boston	.326
63	Tommy Davis	Los Angeles	.326	1963	Carl Yastrzemski	Boston	.321
64	Roberto Clemente	Pittsburgh	.339	1964	Tony Oliva	Minnesota	.323
65	Roberto Clemente	Pittsburgh	.329	1965	Tony Oliva	Minnesota	.321
66	Matty Alou	Pittsburgh	.342	1966	Frank Robinson	Baltimore	.316
67	Roberto Clemente	Pittsburgh	.357	1967	Carl Yastrzemski	Boston	.326
68	Pete Rose	Cincinnati	.335	1968	Carl Yastrzemski	Boston	.301
69	Pete Rose	Cincinnati	.348	1969	Rod Carew	Minnesota	.332
70	Rico Carty	Atlanta	.366	1970	Alex Johnson	California	.328
71	Joe Torre	St. Louis	.363	1971	Tony Oliva	Minnesota	.337
72	Billy Williams	Chicago	.333	1972	Rod Carew	Minnesota	.318
73	Pete Rose	Cincinnati	.338	1973	Rod Carew	Minnesota	.350
74	Ralph Garr	Atlanta	.353	1974	Rod Carew	Minnesota	.364
75	Bill Madlock	Chicago	.354	1975	Rod Carew	Minnesota	.359

Most Valuable Player Awards

Source: Baseball Writers' Association

National League

Year	Player	Club
1931	Frank Frisch	St. Louis
1932	Charles Klein	Philadelphia
1933	Carl Hubbell	New York
1934	Dizzy Dean	St. Louis
1935	Gabby Hartnett	Chicago
1936	Carl Hubbell	New York
1937	Joe Medwick	St. Louis
1938	Ernie Lombardi	Cincinnati
1939	Bucky Walters	Cincinnati
1940	Frank McCormick	Cincinnati
1941	Dolph Camilli	Brooklyn
1942	Mort Cooper	St. Louis
1943	Stan Musial	St. Louis
1944	Martin Marion	St. Louis
1945	Phil Cavarretta	Chicago
1946	Stan Musial	St. Louis
1947	Bob Elliott	Boston
1948	Stan Musial	St. Louis
1949	Jackie Robinson	Brooklyn
1950	Jim Konstanty	Philadelphia
1951	Roy Campanella	Brooklyn
1952	Hank Sauer	Chicago
1953	Roy Campanella	Brooklyn
1954	Willie Mays	New York
1955	Roy Campanella	Brooklyn
1956	Don Newcombe	Brooklyn
1957	Henry Aaron	Milwaukee
1958	Ernie Banks	Chicago
1959	Ernie Banks	Chicago
1960	Dick Groat	Pittsburgh
1961	Frank Robinson	Cincinnati
1962	Maury Wills	Los Angeles
1963	Sandy Koufax	Los Angeles
1964	Ken Boyer	St. Louis
1965	Willie Mays	San Francisco
1966	Roberto Clemente	Pittsburgh
1967	Orlando Cepeda	St. Louis
1968	Bob Gibson	St. Louis
1969	Willie McCovey	San Francisco
1970	Johnny Bench	Cincinnagi
1971	Joe Torre	St. Louis
1972	Johnny Bench	Cincinnati
1973	Pete Rose	Cincinnati
1974	Steve Garvey	Los Angeles

American League

Year	Player	Club
1931	Lefty Grove	Philadelphia
1932	Jimmy Foxx	Philadelphia
1933	Jimmy Foxx	Philadelphia
1934	Mickey Cochrane	Detroit
1935	Henry Greenberg	Detroit
1936	Lou Gehrig	New York
1937	Charley Gehringer	Detroit
1938	Jimmy Foxx	Boston
1939	Joe DiMaggio	New York
1940	Hank Greenberg	Detroit
1941	Joe DiMaggio	New York
1942	Joe Gordon	New York
1943	Spurgeon Chandler	New York
1944	Hal Newhouser	Detroit
1945	Hal Newhouser	Detroit
1946	Ted Williams	Boston
1947	Joe DiMaggio	New York
1948	Lou Boudreau	Cleveland
1949	Ted Williams	Boston
1950	Phil Rizzuto	New York
1951	Yogi Berra	New York
1952	Bobby Shantz	Philadelphia
1953	Al Rosen	Cleveland
1954	Yogi Berra	New York
1955	Yogi Berra	New York
1956	Mickey Mantle	New York
1957	Mickey Mantle	New York
1958	Jackie Jensen	Boston
1959	Nellie Fox	Chicago
1960	Roger Maris	New York
1961	Roger Maris	New York
1962	Mickey Mantle	New York
1963	Elston Howard	New York
1964	Brooks Robinson	Baltimore
1965	Zoilo Versalles	Minnesota
1966	Frank Robinson	Baltimore
1967	Carl Yastrzemski	Boston
1968	Denny McLain	Detroit
1969	Harmon Killebrew	Minnesota
1970	John (Boog) Powell	Baltimore
1971	Vida Blue	Oakland
1972	Dick Allen	Chicago
1973	Reggie Jackson	Oakland
1974	Jeff Burroughs	Texas

Rookie of the Year Award (Baseball Writers Assn.)

1947—Combined Selection—Jackie Robinson, Brooklyn, 1b
1948—Combined Selection—Alvin Dark, Boston, N. L. ss

National League

Year	Winner	Year	Winner	Year	Winner
1949	Don Newcombe, Brooklyn, p	1958	Orlando Cepeda, S. F., 1b	1966	Tommy Helms, Cinn., 2b
1950	Sam Jethroe, Boston, of	1959	Willie McCovey, S. F., 1b	1967	Tom Seaver, N. Y., p
1951	Willie Mays, N. Y., of	1960	Frank Howard, Los Angeles, of	1968	Johnny Bench, Cinn., c
1952	Joe Black, Brooklyn, p	1961	Billy Williams, Chicago, of	1969	Ted Sizemore, L. A., 2b
1953	Jim Gilliam, Brooklyn, 2b	1962	Ken Hubbs, Chicago, 2b	1970	Carl Morton, Mont., p
1954	Wally Moon, St. Louis, of	1963	Pete Rose, Cinn., 2b	1971	Earl Williams, Atl., c
1955	Bill Virdon, St. Louis, of	1964	Richie Allen, Phil., 3b	1972	Jon Matlack, N. Y., p
1956	Frank Robinson, Cinn., of	1965	Jim Lefebvre, L. A., 2b	1973	Gary Matthews, S. F., of
1957	Jack Sanford, Phil., p			1974	Bake McBride, S. L., of

American League

Year	Winner	Year	Winner	Year	Winner
1949	Roy Sievers, St. Louis, of	1958	Albie Pearson, Wash., of	1966	Tommie Agee, Chicago, of
1950	Walt Dropo, Boston, 1b	1959	Bob Allison, Wash., of	1967	Rod Carew, Minn., 2b
1951	Gil McDougald, N. Y., 3b	1960	Ron Hansen, Balt., ss	1968	Stan Bahnsen, N. Y., p
1952	Harry Byrd, Phil., p	1961	Don Schwall, Boston, p	1969	Lou Piniella, K. C., of
1953	Harvey Kuenn, Detroit, ss	1962	Tom Tresh, N. Y., if-of	1970	Thurman Munson, N. Y., c
1954	Bob Grim, N. Y., p	1963	Gary Peters, Chicago, p	1971	Chris Chambliss, Cleve., 1b
1955	Herb Score, Cleveland, p	1964	Tony Oliva, Minn., of	1972	Carlton Fisk, Bos., c
1956	Luis Aparicio, Chicago, ss	1965	Curt Blefary, Balt., of	1973	Al Bumbry, Balt., of
1957	Tony Kubek, N. Y., if-of			1974	Mike Hargrove, Texas, 1b

1975 Little League World Series

Lakewood Township of Ocean County, N.J., won the 1975 United States Little League Championship by defeating a Tampa, Fla. all-star team 4-3 on Aug. 23 at Williamsport, Pa. The Little League board of directors had assured a victory by a United States team by barring foreign teams from this year's tournament. Taiwan had won the Little League championship the last 4 years.

National League Records, 1975

Final Standings

Eastern Division

	W.	L.	Pct.	G.B.
Pittsburgh	92	69	.571	—
Philadelphia	86	76	.531	6½
New York	82	80	.506	10½
St. Louis	82	80	.506	10½
Chicago	75	87	.463	17½
Montreal	75	87	.463	17½

Western Division

	W.	L.	Pct.	G.B.
Cincinnati	108	54	.667	—
Los Angeles	88	74	.543	20
San Francisco	80	81	.497	27½
San Diego	71	91	.438	37
Atlanta	67	94	.416	40½
Houston	64	97	.398	43½

National League Playoffs

Oct. 4—Cincinnati 8, Pittsburgh 3.
Oct. 5—Cincinnati 6, Pittsburgh 1.

Oct. 7—Cincinnati 5, Pittsburgh 3.

Club Batting

Club	Pct.	AB	R.	H.	HR	SB
St. Louis	.273	5597	662	1527	81	116
Cincinnati	.271	5581	840	1515	124	168
Philadelphia	.269	5592	735	1506	125	126
Pittsburgh	.263	5489	712	1444	138	49
Chicago	.259	5470	712	1419	95	67
San Francisco	.259	5447	659	1412	84	99
New York	.256	5587	646	1430	101	32
Houston	.254	5515	664	1401	84	133
Los Angeles	.248	5453	648	1355	118	138
Montreal	.244	5518	601	1346	98	108
Atlanta	.244	5424	583	1323	107	55
San Diego	.244	5429	552	1324	78	85

Club Pitching

Club	ERA	CG	IP	H.	R.	BB	SO
Los Angeles	2.92	51	1470	1215	534	448	894
Pittsburgh	3.01	43	1437	1302	565	551	768
Cincinnati	3.37	22	1459	1422	586	487	663
New York	3.39	40	1466	1344	625	580	989
San Diego	3.48	40	1463	1494	683	521	713
St. Louis	3.57	33	1455	1452	689	571	824
Montreal	3.72	30	1480	1448	690	665	831
San Francisco	3.74	37	1443	1406	671	612	856
Philadelphia	3.82	33	1455	1353	694	546	897
Atlanta	3.91	32	1430	1543	739	519	669
Houston	4.03	39	1458	1436	711	679	839
Chicago	4.49	27	1444	1587	827	551	850

Individual Batting

Leaders—450 or More At Bats

Player—Club	Pct.	AB	R.	H.	HR	RBI	SB
Madlock, Chicago	.354	514	77	182	7	64	9
Simmons, St. Louis‡	.332	581	80	193	18	100	1
Sanguillen, Pittsburgh	.328	481	60	158	9	58	5
Morgan, Cincinnati	.327	498	107	163	17	94	67
Watson, Houston	.324	485	67	157	18	85	3
Garvey, Los Angeles	.319	659	85	210	18	95	11
Joshua, San Francisco†	.318	507	75	161	7	43	20
Rose, Cincinnati	.317	662	112	210	7	74	0
Cardenal, Chicago	.317	574	85	182	9	69	34
Brock, St. Louis†	.309	528	78	163	3	47	56

Individual Pitching

Leaders—162 or More Innings

Pitcher—Club	W.	L.	ERA	G.	IP	H.	BB	SO
Jones, San Diego†	20	12	2.24	37	285	242	56	103
Messersmith, L.A.	19	14	2.29	42	322	244	96	213
Seaver, New York	22	9	2.38	36	280	217	88	243
Reuss, Pittsburgh†	18	11	2.54	32	237	224	78	131
Forsch, St. Louis	15	10	2.86	34	230	213	70	108
Sutton, Los Angeles	16	13	2.87	35	254	202	62	175
*Montefusco, S.F.	15	9	2.88	35	244	210	86	215
Rooker, Pittsburgh†	13	11	2.97	28	197	177	76	102
Barr, San Francisco	13	14	3.06	35	244	244	58	77
Hooton, Los Angeles	18	9	3.06	34	235	190	68	153

*Rookie　†Bats—Pitches Lefthanded　‡Switch Hitter

Individual Batting (over 100 at-bats) Individual Pitching (over 50 innings)

Atlanta Braves

BATTING	Pct.	G.	AB	R.	H.	HR	RBI	SB
Office†	.290	126	355	30	103	3	30	2
Garr†	.278	151	625	74	174	6	31	14
May†	.276	82	203	28	56	12	40	1
Perez	.275	120	461	50	127	2	34	2
Baker	.261	142	494	63	129	19	72	12
*Pocoroba‡	.255	67	188	15	48	1	22	0
Evans†	.243	156	567	82	138	22	73	12
*Gilbreath	.243	90	202	24	49	2	16	5
Gaston	.241	64	141	17	34	6	15	1
Williams	.240	111	383	42	92	11	50	0
Blanks	.234	141	471	49	110	3	38	4
Lum†	.228	124	364	32	83	8	36	2
*Belloir	.219	43	105	11	23	0	9	0
Correll	.215	103	325	37	70	11	39	0
Goodson†	.208	86	197	15	41	2	16	0

PITCHING	W.	L.	ERA	G.	IP	H.	BB	SO
House†	7	7	3.19	58	79	79	36	36
Niekro	15	15	3.20	39	276	285	72	144
*Beard†	4	0	3.21	34	70	71	28	27
Dal Canton	2	7	3.36	26	67	63	24	38
Morton	17	16	3.50	39	278	302	82	78
Sadecki†	3	3	4.09	33	77	86	28	32
Leon	2	1	4.13	50	85	90	33	53
Capra	4	7	4.27	12	78	77	28	35
Sosa	2	5	4.30	57	90	92	43	46
Thompson	0	6	4.67	16	52	60	32	42
Harrison	3	4	4.75	15	55	58	19	22
*Easterly†	2	9	4.96	21	69	73	42	34
Odom	1	7	7.07	15	56	78	28	30

Chicago Cubs

BATTING	Pct.	G.	AB	R.	H.	HR	RBI	SB
Madlock	.354	130	514	77	182	7	64	9
Cardenal	.317	154	574	85	182	9	69	34
Thornton	.293	120	372	70	109	18	60	3
Morales	.270	153	578	62	156	12	91	3
Monday†	.267	136	491	89	131	17	60	8
Hosley	.255	62	141	22	36	6	20	1
*Trillo	.248	154	545	55	135	7	70	1
Kessinger‡	.243	154	601	77	146	0	46	4
LaCock*	.229	106	249	30	57	6	30	0
Mitterwald	.220	84	200	19	44	5	26	0
Swisher	.213	93	254	20	54	1	22	1
*Sperring	.208	65	144	25	30	1	9	0

PITCHING	W.	L.	ERA	G.	IP	H.	BB	SO
R. Reuschel	11	17	3.73	38	234	244	67	155
Stone	12	8	3.95	33	214	198	80	139
Burris	15	10	4.12	36	238	259	73	108
Zahn†	2	8	4.62	18	66	69	31	22
Bonham	13	15	4.72	38	229	254	109	165
Zamora	5	2	5.07	52	71	84	15	28
Dettore	5	4	5.40	36	85	88	31	46
Frailing†	2	5	5.43	41	53	61	26	39
Knowles†	6	5	5.83	58	88	107	36	63

Cincinnati Reds

BATTING	Pct.	G.	AB	R.	H.	HR	RBI	SB
Morgan†	.327	146	498	107	163	17	94	67
Rose‡	.317	162	662	112	210	7	74	0
Griffey†	.305	132	463	95	141	4	46	16
Foster	.300	134	463	71	139	23	78	2
Bench	.283	142	530	83	150	28	110	11
Perez	.282	137	511	74	144	20	109	1
Driessen†	.281	88	210	38	59	7	38	10
Concepcion	.274	140	507	62	139	5	49	33
*Flynn	.268	88	127	17	34	1	20	3
Geronimo†	.257	148	501	69	129	6	53	13
Rettenmund	.239	93	188	24	45	2	19	5
Chaney†	.219	71	160	18	35	2	26	3
Plummer	.182	65	159	17	29	1	19	1

PITCHING	W.	L.	ERA	G.	IP	H.	BB	SO
Gullett†	15	4	2.42	22	160	127	56	98
McEnaney†	5	2	2.47	70	91	92	23	48
*Eastwick	5	3	2.60	58	90	77	25	61
C. Carroll	7	5	2.63	56	96	93	32	44
Borbon	9	5	2.95	67	125	145	21	29
Nolan	15	9	3.16	32	211	202	29	74
*Darcy	11	5	3.57	27	131	134	59	46
Norman‡	12	4	3.73	34	188	163	84	119
Billingham	15	10	4.11	33	208	222	76	79
Kirby	10	6	4.70	26	111	113	54	48

Houston Astros

BATTING	Pct.	G.	AB	R.	H.	HR	RBI	SB
Watson	.324	132	485	67	157	18	85	3
Gross†	.294	132	483	67	142	0	41	2
Cedeno	.288	131	500	93	144	13	63	50
Howard‡	.283	121	392	62	111	0	21	32
Johnson	.276	122	340	52	94	20	65	1
Cabell	.264	117	348	43	92	2	43	12
Cruz†	.257	120	315	44	81	9	49	6
Boswell†	.242	86	178	16	43	0	21	0
May†	.241	111	386	29	93	4	52	1
*Andrews	.238	103	277	29	66	0	19	12
Metzger‡	.227	127	450	54	102	2	26	4
Rader	.223	129	448	41	100	12	48	5
Milbourne	.212	73	151	17	32	1	9	1
Helms	.207	64	135	7	28	0	14	0

PITCHING	W.	L.	ERA	G.	IP	H.	BB	SO
Cosgrove‡	1	2	3.04	32	71	62	37	32
Niekro	6	4	3.07	40	88	79	39	54
Forsch	4	8	3.22	34	109	114	30	54
Crawford†	3	5	3.62	44	87	92	37	37
Granger	2	5	3.65	55	74	76	23	30
Dierker	14	16	4.00	34	232	225	91	127
Roberts†	8	14	4.27	32	198	182	73	101
Richard	12	10	4.34	33	203	178	138	176
Konieczny	6	13	4.47	32	171	184	87	89
Griffin	3	5	5.35	17	79	89	46	56

Los Angeles Dodgers.

BATTING	Pct.	G.	AB	R.	H.	HR	RBI	SB
Garvey	.319	160	659	85	210	18	95	11
Lacy	.314	101	306	44	96	7	40	5
Cey	.283	158	566	72	160	25	101	5
Crawford†	.263	124	373	46	98	9	46	5
Lopes	.262	155	618	108	162	8	41	77
Wynn	.248	130	412	80	102	18	58	7
Buckner†	.243	92	288	30	70	6	31	8
Yeager	.228	135	452	34	103	12	54	2
Auerbach	.224	85	170	18	38	0	12	3
*Hale†	.211	71	204	20	43	6	22	1
Ferguson	.208	66	202	15	42	5	23	2
Russell	.206	84	252	24	52	0	14	5
Paciorek	.193	62	145	14	28	1	5	4

PITCHING	W.	L.	ERA	G.	IP	H.	BB	SO
Messersmith	19	14	2.29	42	322	244	96	213
Sutton	16	13	2.87	35	254	202	62	175
Downing†	2	1	2.88	22	75	59	28	39
Hough	3	7	2.95	38	61	43	34	34
Hooton	18	9	3.06	34	235	190	68	153
*Rhoden	3	3	3.09	26	99	94	32	40
Rau†	15	9	3.10	38	258	227	61	151
Marshall	9	14	3.30	57	109	98	39	64

Montreal Expos

BATTING	Pct.	G.	AB	R.	H.	HR	RBI	SB
Bittner†	.315	121	346	34	109	3	28	2
Morales	.301	93	163	18	49	2	25	0
*Parrish	.274	145	532	50	146	10	65	4
Bailey	.273	106	227	23	62	5	30	4
Dwyer†	.272	81	206	26	56	3	21	4
*Carter	.270	144	503	58	136	17	68	5
Jorgensen†	.261	144	445	58	116	18	67	3
Mangual	.245	140	514	84	126	9	45	33
Foli	.238	152	572	64	136	1	29	13
*Mackanin	.225	130	448	59	101	12	44	11
Foote	.194	118	387	25	75	7	30	0
*Scanlon†	.183	60	109	5	20	2	15	0
*Scott‡	.182	92	143	19	26	0	11	·5

PITCHING	W.	L.	ERA	G.	IP	H.	BB	SO
*Warthen†	8	6	3.11	40	168	130	87	128
Rogers	11	12	3.29	35	252	248	88	137
Carrithers	5	3	3.30	19	101	90	38	37
Fryman†	9	12	3.32	38	157	141	68	118
Taylor	2	2	3.53	54	74	72	24	28
Blair	8	15	3.81	30	163	150	106	82
Scherman†	4	4	3.87	50	93	105	45	57
Murray	15	8	4.05	63	111	134	39	43
Renko	6	12	4.08	31	170	175	76	99
DeMola	4	7	4.13	60	98	92	42	63
McNally†	3	6	5.26	12	77	88	36	36

New York Mets

BATTING	Pct.	G.	AB	R.	H.	HR	RBI	SB
Kranepool†	.323	106	325	42	105	4	43	1
*Vail	.302	38	162	17	49	3	17	0
Grote	.295	119	386	28	114	2	39	0
Unser†	.294	147	531	65	156	10	53	4
Millan	.283	162	676	81	191	1	56	1
Staub†	.282	155	574	93	162	19	105	2
Garrett†	.266	107	274	49	73	6	34	3
Alou	.265	62	102	8	27	0	11	0
Phillips†	.251	126	414	34	104	1	29	4
Torre	.247	114	361	33	89	6	35	0
Kingman	.231	134	502	65	116	36	88	7
Clines	.227	82	203	25	46	0	10	4
Heidemann	.214	61	145	12	31	1	16	1
Milner†	.191	91	220	24	42	7	29	1
*Stearns	.189	59	169	25	32	3	10	4

PITCHING	W.	L.	ERA	G.	IP	H.	BB	SO
Apodaca	3	4	1.48	46	85	66	28	45
Seaver	22	9	2.38	36	280	217	88	243
*Baldwin	3	5	3.34	54	97	97	34	54.
Koosman†	14	13	3.41	36	240	234	98	173
Matlack†	16	12	3.42	33	229	224	58	154
*Webb	7	6	4.07	29	115	102	62	38
*Tate	5	13	4.43	26	138	121	86	99
Hall†	4	3	4.57	36	63	60	33	51
Stone†	3	3	5.05	13	57	75	21	41

Philadelphia Phillies

BATTING	Pct.	G.	AB	R.	H.	HR	RBI	SB
Johnstone†	.329	122	350	50	115	7	54	7
Bowa‡	.305	136	583	79	178	2	38	24
Cash	.305	162	699	111	213	4	57	13
Brown	.303	84	145	19	44	6	26	1
Luzinski	.300	161	596	85	179	34	120	3
Oates†	.282	98	287	28	81	1	25	1
Maddox	.272	116	426	54	116	5	50	25
Anderson	.259	115	247	24	64	4	28	1
Schmidt	.249	158	562	93	140	38	95	29
Hutton†	.248	113	165	24	41	3	24	2
Boone	.246	97	289	28	71	2	20	1
Taylor	.243	79	103	13	25	1	17	3
Allen	.233	119	416	54	97	12	62	11
*Martin	.212	57	113	15	24	2	11	2

PITCHING	W.	L.	ERA	G.	IP	H.	BB	SO
Hilgendorf‡	7	3	2.13	53	97	82	38	52
McGraw†	9	6	2.97	56	103	84	36	55
Carlton†	15	14	3.56	37	255	217	104	192
Garber	10	12	3.60	71	110	103	27	69
Christenson	11	6	3.66	29	172	149	45	88
Lonborg	8	6	4.13	27	159	161	45	72
*Underwood†	14	13	4.15	35	219	221	84	123
Twitchell	5	10	4.43	36	134	132	78	101
Schueler	4	4	5.23	46	93	88	40	69

Pittsburgh Pirates

BATTING	Pct.	G.	AB	R.	H.	HR	RBI	SB
Sanguillen.....	.328	133	481	60	158	9	58	5
Parker†.......	.308	148	558	75	172	25	101	8
Stargell‡......	.295	124	461	71	136	22	90	0
Zisk........	.290	147	504	69	146	20	75	0
Stennett......	.286	148	616	89	176	7	62	5
Oliver†.......	.280	155	628	90	176	18	84	4
Robinson.....	.280	92	200	26	56	6	33	3
Robertson.....	.274	75	124	17	34	6	18	0
Hebner†......	.246	128	472	65	116	15	57	0
Kirkpatrick†....	.236	89	144	15	34	5	16	1
Dyer........	.227	48	132	8	30	3	16	0
Taveras......	.212	134	378	44	80	0	23	17
Howe........	.171	63	146	13	25	1	10	1

PITCHING	W.	L.	ERA	G.	IP	H.	BB	SO
*Tekulve......	1	2	2.25	34	56	43	23	28
Reuss†.......	18	11	2.54	32	237	224	78	131
*Candelaria†..	8	6	2.75	18	121	95	36	95
Demery.......	7	5	2.90	45	115	95	43	59
Giusti.......	5	4	2.93	61	92	79	42	38
Hernandez†....	7	2	2.95	46	64	62	28	43
Rooker†......	13	11	2.97	28	197	177	76	102
Kison.......	12	11	3.23	33	192	160	92	89
Brett††......	9	5	3.36	23	118	110	43	47
Moose.......	2	5	3.71	23	68	63	25	34
Ellis........	8	9	3.79	27	140	163	43	69

St. Louis Cardinals

BATTING	Pct.	G.	AB	R.	H.	HR	RBI	SB
Simmons‡.....	.332	157	581	80	193	18	100	1
Brock†.......	.309	136	528	78	163	3	47	56
Smith†.......	.302	135	477	67	144	19	76	9
Fairly†.......	.301	107	229	32	69	7	37	0
McBride†.....	.300	116	413	70	124	5	36	26
Davis†.......	.291	98	350	41	102	6	50	10
Reitz.......	.269	161	592	43	159	5	63	1
Tyson.......	.266	122	368	45	98	2	37	5
Melendez.....	.265	110	291	33	77	2	27	3
*Hernandez†..	.250	64	188	20	47	3	20	0
Sizemore.....	.240	153	562	56	135	3	49	1
Guerrero.....	.239	64	184	17	44	0	11	0
Lintz‡.......	.207	73	150	24	31	0	4	21

PITCHING	W.	L.	ERA	G.	IP	H.	BB	SO
Hrabosky†....	13	3	1.67	65	97	72	33	82
Garman......	3	8	2.39	66	79	73	48	48
Forsch.......	15	10	2.86	34	230	213	70	108
Curtis†......	8	9	3.43	39	147	151	65	67
Reed........	13	13	3.53	34	250	274	53	139
*Rasmussen..	5	5	3.78	14	81	86	20	59
McGlothen....	15	13	3.92	35	239	231	97	146
*Denny......	10	7	3.97	25	136	149	51	72
Gibson.......	3	10	5.04	22	109	120	62	60
Parker.......	2	4	5.09	32	53	58	29	35

San Diego Padres

BATTING	Pct.	G.	AB	R.	H.	HR	RBI	SB
Locklear†.....	.321	100	237	31	76	5	27	4
Roberts......	.283	33	113	7	32	2	12	3
Fuentes‡......	.280	146	565	57	158	4	43	8
Grubb†.......	.269	144	553	72	149	4	38	2
Winfield.......	.267	143	509	74	136	'15	76	23
Torres.......	.259	112	352	31	91	5	26	2
Tolan†.......	.255	147	506	58	129	5	43	11
McCovey†.....	.252	122	413	43	104	23	68	1
*Ivie........	.249	111	377	36	94	8	46	4
*Davis.......	.234	43	128	6	30	0	7	0
Kubiak‡......	.224	87	196	13	44	0	14	3
Hernandez....	.218	116	344	37	75	0	19	20
Hundley......	.206	74	180	7	37	2	14	0
Kendall......	.199	103	286	16	57	0	24	0
Sharon.......	.194	91	160	14	31	4	20	0

PITCHING	W.	L.	ERA	G.	IP	H.	BB	SO
Jones†.......	20	12	2.24	37	285	242	56	103
Strom†.......	8	8	2.55	18	120	103	33	56
Frisella......	1	6	3.12	65	98	86	51	67
Tomlin†......	4	2	3.25	67	83	87	31	48
*McIntosh....	8	15	3.69	37	183	195	60	71
Greif.......	4	6	3.88	59	72	74	38	43
Folkers†.....	6	11	4.18	45	142	155	39	87
Spillner.....	5	13	4.26	37	167	194	63	104
Freisleben....	5	14	4.28	36	181	206	82	77
Johnson......	3	1	5.17	21	54	60	31	18

San Francisco Giants

BATTING	Pct.	G.	AB	R.	H.	HR	RBI	SB
Joshua†......	.318	129	507	75	161	7	43	20
Montanez†....	.302	156	602	61	182	10	101	6
Murcer†......	.298	147	526	80	157	11	91	9
Rader†.......	.291	98	292	39	85	5	31	1
Ontiveros‡....	.289	108	325	21	94	3	31	2
Matthews.....	.280	116	425	67	119	12	58	13
Thomas‡......	.276	144	540	99	149	6	48	28
Speier.......	.271	141	487	60	132	10	69	4
Miller.......	.239	99	309	21	74	1	31	0
Sadek.......	.236	42	106	14	25	0	9	1
Thomasson†...	.227	114	326	44	74	7	32	9
*Hill........	.214	72	182	14	39	5	23	0

PITCHING	W.	L.	ERA	G.	IP	H.	BB	SO
*Heaverlo....	3	1	2.39	42	64	62	31	35
*Montefusco..	15	9	2.88	35	244	210	86	215
*Lavelle†.....	6	3	2.96	65	82	80	48	51
Barr........	13	14	3.06	35	244	244	58	77
Halicki......	9	13	3.49	24	160	143	59	153
Williams.....	5	3	3.49	55	98	94	66	45
Moffitt......	4	5	3.89	55	74	73	32	39
*Falcone†....	12	11	4.17	34	190	171	111	131
Caldwell†.....	7	13	4.80	38	163	194	48	57

Major League Baseball Attendance

National League

Club	1975	1974	Increase Decrease
Atlanta.........	534,672	981,085	− 446,413
Chicago........	1,034,819	1,015,378	+ 19,441
Cincinnati.......	2,315,603	2,164,307	+ 151,296
Houston........	858,004	1,090,728	− 232,724
Los Angeles.....	2,539,349	2,632,474	− 93,125
Montreal.......	908,292	1,019,134	− 110,842
New York.......	1,730,566	1,722,209	+ 8,357
Philadelphia.....	1,909,236	1,808,648	+ 100,588
Pittsburgh......	1,270,023	1,110,552	+ 159,471
St. Louis.......	1,695,394	1,838,413	− 143,019
San Diego......	1,281,747	1,075,399	+ 206,348
San Francisco...	522,925	519,987	+ 2,938
**Totals....... **	**16,600,630**	**16,978,314**	**− 377,684**

American League

Club	1975	1974	Increase Decrease
Baltimore.......	1,002,157	962,572	+ 39,585
Boston.........	1,748,443	1,556,411	+ 192,032
California.......	1,058,163	917,269	+ 140,894
Chicago........	770,800	1,149,596	− 378,796
Cleveland......	977,195	1,114,262	− 137,067
Detroit........	1,058,836	1,243,080	− 184,244
Kansas City.....	1,151,836	1,173,292	− 21,456
Milwaukee.....	1,213,357	955,741	+ 257,616
Minnesota......	737,156	662,401	+ 74,755
New York.......	1,288,045	1,273,075	+ 14,970
Oakland.......	1,077,684	845,693	+ 231,991
Texas.........	1,127,933	1,193,902	− 65,969
**Totals....... **	**13,211,605**	**13,047,294**	**+ 164,311**

Major League Attendance Records

All-time Season Records, Both Leagues—30,122,191 in 1973
All-time Season Record, One Club—2,755,184—Los Angeles Dodgers, 1962.
Record Attendance, World Series—420,784—1959 Series between Los Angeles Dodgers and Chicago White Sox.
Record Attendance, World Series Game—92,706—fifth game, 1959 Series, Los Angeles, Oct. 6.
Record Attendance, Regular Season Game—84,587—Municipal Stadium, Cleveland, Sept. 12, 1954, in doubleheader between the Indians and Yankees (Not including pass list of 1,976.)
Attendance, Regular-Season Single Game—78,672—Los Angeles Memorial Coliseum, April 18, 1958, in opening game between Los Angeles Dodgers and San Francisco Giants.

American League Records, 1975

Final Standings

Eastern Division

	W.	L.	Pct.	G.B.
Boston	95	65	.594	—
Baltimore	90	69	.566	4½
New York	83	77	.519	12
Cleveland	79	80	.497	15½
Milwaukee	68	94	.420	28
Detroit	57	102	.358	37½

Western Division

	W.	L.	Pct.	G.B.
Oakland	98	64	.605	—
Kansas City	91	71	.562	7
Texas	79	83	.488	19
Minnesota	76	83	.478	20½
Chicago	75	86	.466	22½
California	72	89	.447	25½

American League Playoffs

Oct. 4 — Boston 7, Oakland 1.
Oct. 5 — Boston 6, Oakland 3

Oct. 7 — Boston 5, Oakland 3.

Club Batting

Club	Pct.	AB	R.	H.	HR	SB
Boston	.275	5448	796	1500	134	66
Minnesota	.271	5514	724	1497	121	81
New York	.264	5415	681	1430	110	102
Cleveland	.261	5404	688	1409	153	106
Kansas City	.261	5491	710	1431	118	155
Texas	.256	5599	714	1431	134	102
Chicago	.255	5490	655	1400	94	101
Oakland	.254	5415	758	1376	151	183
Baltimore	.252	5474	682	1382	124	104
Milwaukee	.250	5377	675	1342	146	65
Detroit	.249	5366	570	1338	125	63
California	.246	5376	628	1324	55	220

Club Pitching

Club	ERA	CG	IP	H.	R.	BB	SO
Baltimore	3.17	70	1451	1285	553	500	717
Oakland	3.28	36	1448	1267	606	523	784
New York	3.29	70	1424	1325	588	502	809
Kansas City	3.47	52	1457	1422	649	498	815
Cleveland	3.84	37	1435	1395	703	599	800
Texas	3.86	60	1466	1456	733	518	792
California	3.89	59	1453	1385	723	613	975
Chicago	3.93	34	1452	1489	703	655	799
Boston	3.98	62	1437	1463	709	490	720
Minnesota	4.05	57	1423	1381	736	617	846
Detroit	4.27	52	1396	1496	786	533	787
Milwaukee	4.34	36	1432	1496	792	624	643

Individual Batting
Leaders — 450 or More At Bats

Player—Club	Pct.	AB	RR.	RH.	HR	RBI	SB
Carew, Minnesota‡	.359	535	89	192	14	80	35
*Lynn, Boston†	.331	528	103	175	21	105	10
Munson, New York	.318	597	83	190	12	102	3
*Rice, Boston	.309	564	92	174	22	102	10
C. Washington, Oak†	.308	590	86	182	10	77	40
Brett, Kansas City†	.308	634	84	195	11	89	13
McRae, Kansas City	.306	480	58	147	5	71	11
Orta, Chicago†	.304	542	64	165	11	83	16
Chambliss, New York†	.304	562	66	171	9	72	0
Hargrove, Texas†	.303	519	82	157	11	62	4

Individual Pitching
Leaders — 162 or More Innings

Pitcher—Club	W.	L.	ERA	G.	IP	H.	BB	SO
Palmer, Baltimore	23	11	2.09	39	323	253	80	193
Hunter, New York	23	14	2.58	39	328	248	83	177
*Eckersley, Cleveland	13	7	2.60	34	187	147	90	152
Tanana, California†	16	9	2.63	34	257	211	73	269
Figueroa, California	16	13	2.90	33	245	213	84	139
Blyleven, Minnesota	15	10	3.00	35	276	219	84	233
Blue, Oakland†	22	11	3.01	39	278	243	99	189
Torrez, Baltimore	20	9	3.06	36	271	238	133	119
May, New York†	14	12	3.06	32	212	179	99	145
Busby, Kansas City	18	12	3.08	34	260	233	81	160

*Rookie　†Bats — Pitches Lefthanded　‡Switch Hitter

Individual Batting (over 100 at-bats) Individual Pitching (over 50 innings)

Baltimore Orioles

BATTING	Pct.	G.	AB	R.	H.	HR	RBI	SB
Singleton‡	.300	155	586	88	176	15	55	3
Davis	.283	116	460	43	130	6	57	2
Baylor	.282	145	524	79	148	25	76	32
Muser†	.275	123	193	22	53	0	17	2
Northrup†	.273	84	194	27	53	5	29	0
Bumbry†	.269	114	349	47	94	2	32	16
May	.262	146	580	67	152	20	99	1
Grich	.260	150	524	81	136	13	57	14
*DeCinces	.251	61	167	20	42	4	23	0
Belanger	.226	152	442	44	100	3	27	16
Blair	.218	140	440	51	96	5	31	17
Hendricks†	.215	85	223	32	48	8	38	0
Duncan	.205	96	307	30	63	12	41	0
Robinson	.201	144	482	50	97	6	53	0

PITCHING	W.	L.	ERA	G.	IP	H.	BB	SO
Palmer	23	11	2.09	39	323	253	80	193
Alexander	8	8	3.05	32	133	127	47	46
Torrez	20	9	3.06	36	271	238	133	119
*Mitchell	3	0	3.63	11	57	41	19	31
Cuellar†	14	12	3.66	36	256	229	84	105
Garland	2	5	3.72	29	87	80	31	46
Grimsley†	10	13	4.07	35	197	210	47	89

Boston Red Sox

BATTING	Pct.	G.	AB	R.	H.	HR	RBI	SB
*Lynn†	.331	145	528	103	175	21	105	10
Fisk	.331	79	263	47	87	10	52	4
Cooper†	.311	106	305	49	95	14	44	1
*Rice	.309	144	564	92	174	22	102	10
Doyle†	.298	97	325	50	97	4	36	5
Beniquez	.291	78	254	43	74	2	17	7
Evans	.274	128	412	61	113	13	56	3
Yastrzemski†	.269	149	543	91	146	14	60	8
Carbo†	.257	107	319	64	82	15	50	2
Burleson	.252	158	580	66	146	6	62	8
Griffin	.240	100	287	21	69	1	29	2
D. Johnson	.239	151	565	68	135	19	75	0
Petrocelli	.239	115	402	31	96	7	59	0
Montgomery	.226	62	195	16	44	2	26	1
Heise	.214	63	126	12	27	0	21	0
Blackwell‡	.197	59	132	15	26	0	6	0
Miller†	.194	77	108	21	21	0	15	3

PITCHING	W.	L.	ERA	G.	IP	H.	BB	SO
*Burton†	1	2	2.89	29	53	58	19	39
Moret†	14	3	3.60	36	145	132	76	80
Drago	2	2	3.82	40	73	69	31	43
Lee†	17	9	3.95	41	260	274	69	78
Wise	19	12	3.95	35	255	262	72	141
Tiant	18	14	4.02	35	260	262	72	142
Pole	4	6	4.40	18	90	102	32	42
Cleveland	13	9	4.42	31	171	173	52	78
Segui	2	5	4.82	33	71	71	43	45

California Angels

BATTING	Pct.	G.	AB	R.	H.	HR	RBI	SB
Bochte†	.285	107	375	41	107	3	48	3
Rivers†	.285	155	615	70	175	1	53	70
Chalk	.273	149	513	59	140	3	56	6
Etchebarren	.267	39	120	10	32	3	20	1
*Collins‡	.266	93	319	41	85	3	29	24
Garrett†	.262	37	107	17	28	6	18	3
Stanton	.261	137	440	67	115	14	82	18
*Remy†	.258	147	569	82	147	1	46	34
*Balaz	.242	45	120	10	29	1	10	0
*Ramirez	.240	44	100	10	24	0	4	9
Rodriguez	.235	90	226	20	53	3	27	2
Nettles†	.231	112	294	50	68	0	23	22.
Meoli†	.214	70	126	12	27	0	6	3
Lahoud†	.214	76	192	21	41	6	33	2
*Smith‡	.203	59	143	10	29	0	14	1
Llenas	.186	56	113	6	21	0	11	0
*Miley	.174	70	224	17	39	4	26	0

PITCHING	W.	L.	ERA	G.	IP	H.	BB	SO
Tanana†	16	9	2.63	34	257	211	73	269
Figueroa	16	13	2.90	33	245	213	84	139
*Kirkwood	6	5	3.11	44	84	85	28	49
Scott‡	4	2	3.31	50	68	59	18	31
Ryan	14	12	3.45	28	198	151	132	186
Singer	7	15	4.98	29	179	171	81	78
Lange	4	6	5.21	30	102	119	53	45
Hassler†	3	12	5.95	30	133	158	53	82

Chicago White Sox

BATTING	Pct.	G.	AB	R.	H.	HR	RBI	SB
Orta	.304	140	542	64	165	11	83	16
Hairston‡	.283	69	219	26	62	0	23	1
Kelly†	.274	133	471	73	129	9	45	18
*Varney	.271	36	107	12	29	2	8	2
May†	.271	128	454	55	123	8	53	12
Stein	.270	76	226	23	61	3	21	2
Dent	.264	157	602	52	159	3	58	2
Henderson‡	.251	140	513	65	129	9	53	5
Downing	.240	138	420	58	101	7	41	13
Melton	.240	149	512	62	123	15	70	5
*Nyman†	.226	106	327	36	74	2	28	10
Coluccio	.202	83	223	30	45	5	18	5

PITCHING	W.	L.	ERA	G.	IP	H.	BB	SO
Gossage	9	8	1.84	62	142	99	70	130
Kaat†	20	14	3.11	43	304	321	77	142
Hamilton†	7	7	3.26	41	105	105	47	71
Wood†	16	20	4.11	43	291	309	92	140
Osteen†	7	16	4.37	37	204	237	92	63
*Osborn	3	0	4.50	24	58	57	37	38
Jefferson	5	11	4.93	26	115	105	102	71
Gogolewski	0	0	5.24	19	55	61	28	37

Cleveland Indians

BATTING	Pct.	G.	AB	R.	H.	HR	RBI	SB
Carty	.308	118	383	57	118	18	64	2
Powell†	.297	134	435	64	129	27	86	1
*Kuiper†	.292	90	346	42	101	0	25	19
*Manning†	.285	120	480	69	137	3	35	19
Bell	.271	153	553	66	150	10	59	6
Gamble†	.261	121	348	60	91	15	45	11
Hendrick	.258	145	561	64	145	24	86	6
Brohamer†	.244	69	217	15	53	6	16	2
Duffy	.243	146	482	44	117	1	47	10
Lowenstein†	.242	91	265	37	64	12	33	15
Robinson	.237	49	118	19	28	9	24	0
Crosby†	.234	61	128	12	30	0	7	0
Ellis	.230	92	296	22	68	7	32	0
Spikes	.229	111	345	41	79	11	33	7
*Ashby‡	.224	90	254	30	57	5	32	3

PITCHING	W.	L.	ERA	G.	IP	H.	BB	SO
LaRoche†	5	3	2.20	61	82	61	57	94
Buskey	5	3	2.57	50	77	69	29	29
*Eckersley	13	7	2.60	34	187	147	90	152
*Waits†	6	2	2.96	16	70	57	25	34
Kern	1	2	3.75	13	72	60	45	55
Bibby	7	15	3.88	36	181	172	78	93
Peterson†	14	8	3.95	25	146	154	40	47
Brown	6	7	4.24	42	140	142	64	76
Hood†	6	10	4.40	29	135	136	57	51
Harrison	7	7	4.79	19	126	137	46	52
Reynolds	0	5	5.22	33	50	62	18	32
*Raich	7	8	5.52	18	93	118	31	34

Detroit Tigers

BATTING	Pct.	G.	AB	R.	H.	HR	RBI	SB
Oglivie†	.286	100	332	45	95	9	36	11
Horton	.275	159	615	62	169	25	92	1
Sutherland	.258	129	503	51	130	6	39	0
LeFlore	.258	136	550	66	142	8	37	28
*Roberts	.257	129	447	51	115	10	38	3
Stanley	.256	52	164	26	42	3	19	1
*Veryzer	.252	128	404	37	102	5	48	2
Freehan	.246	120	427	42	105	14	47	2
Rodriquez	.245	151	507	47	124	13	60	1
*Meyer†	.236	122	470	56	111	8	47	8
*Pierce†	.235	53	170	19	40	8	22	0
*Wockenfuss	.229	35	118	15	27	4	13	0
Michael‡	.214	56	145	15	31	3	13	0
Colbert	.147	45	156	16	23	4	18	0

PITCHING	W.	L.	ERA	G.	IP	H.	BB	SO
Hiller†	2	3	2.15	36	71	52	36	87
Lolich†	12	18	3.77	32	241	260	64	139
*Ruhle	11	12	4.03	32	190	199	65	67
LaGrow	7	14	4.39	32	164	183	66	75
Lemanczyk	2	7	4.46	26	109	120	46	67
Walker	3	8	4.46	36	115	116	40	60
Bare	8	13	4.47	29	151	174	47	71
*Arroyo	2	1	4.58	14	53	56	22	25
Coleman	10	18	5.55	31	201	234	85	125

Kansas City Royals

BATTING	Pct.	G.	AB	R.	H.	HR	RBI	SB
Brett	.308	159	634	84	195	11	89	13
McRae	.306	126	480	58	147	5	71	11
Mayberry†	.291	156	554	95	161	34	106	5
Cowens	.277	120	328	44	91	4	42	12
Stinson‡	.265	63	147	18	39	1	9	1
Solaita†	.260	93	231	35	60	16	44	0
Healy	.255	56	188	16	48	2	18	4
Wohlford	.255	116	353	45	90	0	30	12
Rojas	.254	120	406	34	103	2	37	4
White	.250	111	304	43	76	7	36	11
Otis	.247	132	470	87	116	9	46	39
Patek	.228	136	483	58	110	5	45	32
Martinez	.226	80	226	15	51	3	23	1
Pinson†	.223	103	319	38	71	4	22	5
Killebrew	.199	106	312	25	62	14	44	1

PITCHING	W.	L.	ERA	G.	IP	H.	BB	SO
Mingori†	0	3	2.52	36	50	42	20	25
Busby	18	12	3.08	34	260	233	81	160
Splittorff†	9	10	3.17	35	159	156	56	76
Pattin	10	10	3.25	44	177	173	45	89
Bird	9	6	3.26	51	105	100	40	81
Fitzmorris	16	12	3.57	35	242	239	76	78
*Leonard	15	7	3.78	32	212	212	90	146
McDaniel	5	1	4.15	40	78	81	24	40
Briles	6	6	4.26	24	112	127	25	73

Milwaukee Brewers

BATTING	Pct.	G.	AB	R.	H.	HR	RBI	SB
Moore	.290	73	241	26	70	1	29	1
*Sheldon†	.287	53	181	17	52	0	14	0
Scott	.285	158	617	86	176	36	109	6
Money	.277	109	405	58	112	15	43	7
Yount	.267	147	558	67	149	8	52	12
Hegan†	.251	93	203	19	51	5	22	1
Sharp†	.250	143	408	38	102	1	38	0
Mitchell	.249	93	229	39	57	9	41	3
*Lezcano	.247	134	429	55	106	11	43	5
Darwin	.234	103	355	45	83	13	41	6
Aaron	.234	137	465	45	109	12	60	0
Porter†	.232	130	409	66	95	18	60	2
Bevacqua	.229	104	258	30	59	2	24	3
Garcia	.223	98	301	40	67	6	38	12
Thomas	.179	121	240	34	43	10	28	4

PITCHING	W.	L.	ERA	G.	IP	H.	BB	SO
*Castro	3	2	2.52	18	75	78	17	25
Rodriguez	7	0	3.48	43	88	77	44	65
*Hausman	3	6	4.10	29	112	110	47	46
Broberg	14	16	4.13	38	220	219	106	100
Colborn	11	13	4.28	36	206	215	65	79
Travers†	6	11	4.30	28	136	130	60	57
Slaton	11	18	4.52	37	217	238	90	119
Murphy	1	9	4.63	52	72	85	27	32
Sprague	1	7	4.70	18	67	81	40	21
Champion	6	6	5.89	27	110	125	55	40

Minnesota Twins

BATTING	Pct.	G.	AB	R.	H.	HR	RBI	SB
Carew†	.359	143	535	89	192	14	80	35
Hisle	.314	80	255	37	80	11	51	17
Braun†	.302	136	453	70	137	11	45	0
Roof	.302	63	126	18	38	7	21	0
Soderholm	.286	117	419	62	120	11	58	3
Terrell‡	.286	108	385	48	110	1	36	4
*Bostock†	.282	98	369	52	104	0	29	2
*Ford	.280	130	440	72	123	15	59	6
Thompson	.270	112	355	25	96	5	37	0
Oliva†	.270	131	455	46	123	13	58	0
*McKay	.256	33	125	8	32	2	16	1
Brye	.252	86	246	41	62	9	34	2
Briggs†	.246	115	338	56	83	10	44	6
Kusick	.237	57	156	14	37	6	27	0
Borgmann	.207	125	352	34	73	2	33	0
*Kelly†	.181	49	127	11	23	1	11	0

PITCHING	W.	L.	ERA	G.	IP	H.	BB	SO
Blyleven	15	10	3.00	35	276	219	84	133
Burgmeier†	5	8	3.08	46	76	76	23	41
Goltz	14	14	3.67	32	243	235	72	128
Campbell	4	6	3.79	47	121	119	46	76
*Hughes	16	14	3.82	37	250	241	127	130
Albury†	6	7	4.53	32	135	115	97	72
Corbin	5	7	5.10	18	90	105	38	49
Butler†	5	4	5.93	23	82	100	35	55

New York Yankees

BATTING	Pct.	G.	AB	R.	H.	HR	RBI	SB
Munson	.318	157	597	83	190	12	102	3
Maddox	.307	55	218	36	67	1	23	9
Chambliss†	.304	150	562	66	171	9	72	0
White‡	.290	148	556	81	161	12	59	16
Williams	.281	82	185	27	52	5	16	0
Bonds	.270	145	529	93	143	32	85	30
Nettles*	.267	157	581	71	155	21	91	1
Dempsey	.262	71	145	18	38	1	11	0
Johnson	.261	52	119	15	31	1	15	2
Herrmann†	.255	80	200	16	51	6	30	0
Blomberg*	.255	34	106	18	27	4	17	0
Alomar‡	.239	151	489	61	117	2	39	28
Coggins‡	.224	51	107	7	24	1	6	3
Stanley	.222	117	252	34	56	0	15	3
*Bladt	.222	52	117	13	26	1	11	6
Piniella	.196	74	199	7	39	0	22	0
Mason†	.152	94	223	17	34	2	16	0

PITCHING	W.	L.	ERA	G.	IP	H.	BB	SO
Hunter	23	14	2.58	39	328	248	83	177
May†	14	12	3.06	32	212	179	99	145
Tidrow	6	3	3.13	37	69	65	31	38
Lyle†	5	7	3.13	49	89	94	36	65
Medich	16	16	3.51	38	272	271	72	132
Gura†	7	8	3.52	26	151	173	41	65
Dobson	11	14	4.07	33	208	205	83	129

Oakland A's

BATTING	Pct.	G.	AB	R.	H.	HR	RBI	SB
C. Washington†	.308	148	590	86	182	10	77	40
Rudi	.278	126	468	66	130	21	75	2
North‡	.273	140	524	74	143	1	43	30
Campaneris	.265	137	509	69	135	4	46	24
Tovar	.256	121	453	58	116	3	31	20
Tenace	.255	158	498	83	127	29	87	7
Harper	.254	123	354	51	90	5	38	26
Jackson†	.253	157	593	91	150	36	104	17
*Garner	.246	160	488	46	120	6	54	4
Williams†	.244	155	520	68	127	23	81	0
Bando	.230	160	562	64	129	15	78	7
Mangual	.220	62	109	13	24	1	6	0
Holt†	.220	102	123	7	27	2	16	0
Fosse	.140	82	136	14	19	0	12	0

PITCHING	W.	L.	ERA	G.	IP	H.	BB	SO
Todd	8	3	2.36	58	122	104	33	50
Linblad†	9	1	2.73	68	122	105	43	58
Fingers	10	6	2.98	75	127	95	33	115
Blue†	22	11	3.01	39	278	243	99	189
Holtzman†	18	14	3.15	39	266	217	108	122
Bosman	11	6	3.64	28	151	145	32	53
Siebert	4	4	3.69	17	61	60	31	44
Abbott	5	4	4.26	30	114	109	50	51
Bahnsen	10	13	4.37	33	167	166	77	80
J. Perry	4	10	5.40	23	105	107	44	44

Texas Rangers

BATTING	Pct.	G.	AB	R.	H.	HR	RBI	SB
Hargrove†	.303	145	519	82	157	11	62	4
Harrah	.293	151	522	81	153	20	93	23
Grieve	.276	118	369	46	102	14	61	0
Randle‡	.276	156	601	85	166	4	57	16
*Moates†	.274	54	175	21	48	3	14	9
Spencer†	.266	132	403	50	107	11	47	0
Fregosi	.262	77	191	25	50	7	33	0
*Howell†	.251	125	383	43	96	10	51	2
Davis†	.249	42	169	16	42	5	17	13
Cardenas	.235	55	102	15	24	1	5	0
*Smalley†	.228	78	250	22	57	3	33	4
Burroughs	.226	152	585	81	132	29	94	4
*Cubbage†	.224	58	143	12	32	4	21	0
Lovitto†	.208	50	106	17	22	1	8	2
Sundberg	.199	155	472	45	94	6	36	3

PITCHING	W.	L.	ERA	G.	IP	H.	BB	SO
Perzanowski	3	3	3.00	12	66	59	25	26
*Thomas	4	4	3.11	46	81	72	34	46
G. Perry	18	17	3.24	37	306	277	70	233
Hargan	9	10	3.81	33	189	203	62	93
Jenkins	17	18	3.93	37	270	261	56	157
Hands	6	7	4.01	18	110	118	28	67
Foucault	8	4	4.12	59	107	96	55	56
*Umbarger†	8	7	4.12	56	131	134	59	50
Wright†	4	6	4.45	25	93	105	47	32

Leading Pitchers. Earned-Run Average

Based on 154 innings until A.L. expanded in '61, N.L. in '62, then 162 innings.

National League

Year	Pitcher, Club	G	IP	ERA
1956	Lew Burdette, Milwaukee	39	256	2.71
1957	Johnny Podres, Brooklyn	31	196	2.66
1958	Stu Miller, San Francisco	41	182	2.47
1959	Sam Jones, San Francisco	50	271	2.82
1960	Mike McCormick, San Fran	40	253	2.70
1961	Warren Spahn, Milwaukee	38	263	3.01
1962	Sandy Koufax, Los Angeles	28	184	2.54
1963	Sandy Koufax, Los Angeles	40	311	1.88
1964	Sandy Koufax, Los Angeles	29	223	1.74
1965	Sandy Koufax, Los Angeles	43	336	2.04
1966	Sandy Koufax, Los Angeles	41	323	1.73
1967	Phil Niekro, Atlanta	46	207	1.87
1968	Bob Gibson, St. Louis	34	305	1.12
1969	Juan Marichal, San Francisco	37	300	2.10
1970	Tom Seaver, New York	37	291	2.81
1971	Tom Seaver, New York	36	286	1.76
1972	Steve Carlton, Philadelphia	41	346	1.98
1973	Tom Seaver, New York	36	290	2.07
1974	Buzz Capra, Atlanta	39	217	2.28
1975	Randy Jones, San Diego	37	285	2.24

American League

Year	Pitcher, Club	G	IP	ERA
1956	Whitey Ford, New York	31	226	2.47
1957	Bobby Shantz, New York	30	173	2.01
1958	Whitey Ford, New York	30	219	2.01
1959	Hoyt Wilhelm, Baltimore	32	226	2.19
1960	Frank Baumann, Chicago	47	185	2.68
1961	Dick Donovan, Washington	23	169	2.40
1962	Hank Aguirre, Detroit	42	216	2.21
1963	Gary Peters, Chicago	41	243	2.33
1964	Dean Chance, Los Angeles	46	278	1.56
1965	Sam McDowell, Cleveland	42	274	2.17
1966	Gary Peters, Chicago	29	204	2.03
1967	Joe Horlen, Chicago	35	258	2.06
1968	Luis Tiant, Cleveland	34	258	1.60
1969	Dick Bosman, Washington	31	193	2.19
1970	Diego Segui, Oakland	47	162	2.56
1971	Vida Blue, Oakland	39	312	1.82
1972	Luis Tiant, Boston	43	179	1.91
1973	Jim Palmer, Baltimore	38	296	2.40
1974	Catfish Hunter, Oakland	41	318	2.49
1975	Jim Palmer, Baltimore	39	323	2.09

ERA is computed by multiplying the number of earned runs allowed by 9, then dividing by the number of innings pitched.

World Series, 1975
Composite Box Scores
Cincinnati Reds

	G.	AB	R.	H.	2B	3B	HR	RBI	SO	BB	BA	PO	A.	E.	FA
Pete Rose, 3b	7	27	3	10	1	1	0	2	1	5	.370	7	8	0	1.000
Joe Morgan, 2b	7	27	4	7	1	0	0	3	1	5	.259	17	28	0	1.000
Johnny Bench, c	7	29	5	6	2	0	1	4	4	2	.207	44	6	0	1.000
Tony Perez, 1b	7	28	4	5	0	0	3	7	9	3	.179	66	5	1	.986
George Foster, lf	7	29	1	8	1	0	0	2	1	1	.276	13	1	0	1.000
Dave Concepcion, ss	7	28	3	5	1	0	1	4	1	0	.179	12	23	1	.972
Ken Griffey, rf	7	26	4	7	3	1	0	4	2	4	.269	10	1	0	1.000
Cesar Geronimo, cf	7	25	3	7	0	1	2	3	5	3	.280	23	1	0	1.000
Don Gullett, p	3	7	1	2	0	0	0	0	2	0	.286	0	0	0	.000
Clay Carroll, p	5	0	0	0	0	0	0	0	0	0	.000	2	0	0	1.000
Will McEnaney, p	5	1	0	1	0	0	0	0	0	0	1.000	0	0	0	.000
Jack Billingham, p	3	2	0	0	0	0	0	0	0	0	.000	0	2	0	1.000
Pedro Borbon, p	3	1	0	0	0	0	0	0	0	0	.000	0	0	0	.000
Merv Rettenmund, ph	3	3	0	0	0	0	0	0	1	0	.000	0	0	0	.000
Rawly Eastwick, p	5	1	0	0	0	0	0	0	0	0	.000	0	0	0	.000
Gary Nolan, p	2	1	0	0	0	0	0	0	0	0	.000	1	0	0	1.000
Pat Darcy, p	2	1	0	0	0	0	0	0	1	0	.000	0	1	0	1.000
Ed Armbrister, ph	4	1	1	0	0	0	0	0	0	2	.000	0	0	0	.000
Fred Norman, p	2	1	0	0	0	0	0	0	0	0	.000	0	0	0	.000
Terry Crowley, ph	2	2	0	1	0	0	0	0	1	0	.500	0	0	0	.000
Darrel Chaney, ph	2	2	0	0	0	0	0	0	1	0	.000	0	0	0	.000
Dan Driessen, ph	2	2	0	0	0	0	0	0	0	0	.000	0	0	0	.000
Total	7	244	29	59	9	3	7	29	30	25	.242	195	76	2	.993

Boston Red Sox

	G.	AB	R.	H.	2B	3B	HR	RBI	SO	BB	BA	PO	A.	E.	FA
Dwight Evans, rf	7	24	3	7	1	1	1	5	4	3	.292	23	1	0	1.000
Denny Doyle, 2b	7	30	3	8	1	1	0	4	1	2	.267	12	23	3	.921
Carl Yastrzemski, lf-1b	7	29	7	9	0	0	0	4	1	4	.310	36	1	0	1.000
Carlton Fisk, c	7	25	5	6	0	0	2	4	7	7	.240	37	3	2	.952
Fred Lynn, cf	7	25	3	7	1	0	1	5	5	3	.280	23	1	0	1.000
Rico Petrocelli, 3b	7	26	3	8	1	0	0	4	6	3	.308	7	15	0	1.000
Rick Burleson, ss	7	24	1	7	1	0	0	2	2	4	.292	9	19	1	.966
Cecil Cooper, 1b-ph	5	19	0	1	1	0	0	1	3	0	.053	40	1	0	1.000
Luis Tiant, p	3	8	2	2	0	0	0	0	4	2	.250	0	4	0	1.000
Bill Lee, p	2	6	0	1	0	0	0	0	3	0	.167	1	0	0	1.000
Dick Drago, p	2	0	0	0	0	0	0	0	0	0	.000	0	1	0	1.000
Bernie Carbo, ph-lf	4	7	3	3	1	0	2	4	1	1	.429	1	1	0	1.000
Rick Wise, p	2	2	0	0	0	0	0	0	0	0	.000	0	0	0	.000
Jim Burton, p	2	0	0	0	0	0	0	0	0	0	.000	0	0	0	.000
Reggie Cleveland, p	3	2	0	0	0	0	0	0	2	0	.000	0	0	0	.000
Jim Willoughby, p	3	0	0	0	0	0	0	0	0	0	.000	1	0	0	1.000
Roger Moret, p	3	0	0	0	0	0	0	0	0	0	.000	0	1	0	1.000
Juan Beniquez, lf-ph	3	8	0	1	0	0	0	1	1	1	.125	6	1	0	1.000
Rick Miller, lf	3	2	0	0	0	0	0	0	0	0	.000	1	0	0	1.000
Doug Griffin, ph	1	1	0	0	0	0	0	0	0	0	.000	0	0	0	.000
Dick Pole, p	1	0	0	0	0	0	0	0	0	0	.000	0	0	0	.000
Diego Segui, p	1	0	0	0	0	0	0	0	0	0	.000	0	0	0	.000
Bob Montgomery, ph	1	1	0	0	0	0	0	0	0	0	.000	0	0	0	.000
Total	7	239	30	60	7	2	6	30	40	30	.251	196	72	6	.978

Pitching Summary
Cincinnati

	G.	CG	IP	H.	R	BB	SO	HB	WP	W.	L.	Pct.	ER	ERA
Don Gullett	3	0	18²/₃	19	9	10	15	0	1	1	1	.500	9	4.34
Clay Carroll	5	0	5²/₃	4	2	2	3	0	0	1	0	1.000	2	3.18
Will McEnaney	5	0	6²/₃	3	2	2	5	0	0	0	0	.000	2	2.70
Jack Billingham	3	0	9	8	2	5	7	1	0	0	0	.000	1	1.00
Pedro Borbon	3	0	3	3	3	2	1	0	0	0	0	.000	2	6.00
Rawly Eastwick	5	0	8	6	2	3	4	0	0	2	0	1.000	2	2.25
Gary Nolan	2	0	6	6	4	1	2	0	0	0	0	.000	4	6.00
Pat Darcy	2	0	4	3	2	2	1	0	1	0	1	.000	2	4.50
Fred Norman	2	0	4	8	4	3	2	0	1	0	1	.000	4	9.00
Total	7	0	65	60	30	30	40	1	3	4	3	.571	28	3.88

Boston

	G.	CG	IP	H.	R	BB	SO	HB	WP	W.	L.	Pct.	ER	ERA
Luis Tiant	3	2	25	25	10	8	12	0	0	2	0	1.000	10	3.60
Bill Lee	2	0	14¹/₃	12	5	3	7	0	0	0	0	.000	5	3.14
Dick Drago	2	0	4	3	1	1	1	1	0	0	1	.000	1	2.25
Rick Wise	2	0	5¹/₃	6	5	2	2	0	0	1	0	1.000	5	8.44
Jim Burton	2	0	1	1	1	3	0	0	0	0	1	.000	1	9.00
Reggie Cleveland	3	0	6²/₃	7	5	3	5	0	0	0	1	.000	5	6.75
Jim Willoughby	3	0	6¹/₃	3	1	0	2	1	0	0	0	.000	0	0.00
Roger Moret	3	0	1²/₃	2	0	3	1	0	0	0	0	.000	0	0.00
Dick Pole	1	0	0	0	1	2	0	0	0	0	0	.000	1	...
Diego Segui	1	0	1	0	0	0	0	0	0	0	0	.000	0	0.00
Total	7	2	65¹/₃	59	29	25	30	2	0	3	4	.429	28	3.86

Composite Score By Innings

Cincinnati	2	0	0	6	7	5	3	2	3	1	0	0—29
Boston	5	1	3	5	0	2	7	3	3	0	0	1—30

1975 World Series Box Scores

First Game
Fenway Park, Boston, Oct. 11, 1975

Cincinnati	ab	r	h	bi	Boston	ab	r	h	bi
Rose, 3b	4	0	0	0	Evans, rf	4	1	1	0
Morgan, 2b	4	0	2	0	Doyle, 2b	3	1	2	0
Bench, c	4	0	0	0	Yastrzemski, lf	4	1	1	1
Perez, 1b	4	0	0	0	Fisk, c	3	1	0	1
Foster, lf	4	0	2	0	Lynn, cf	4	0	2	0
Concepcion, ss	4	0	0	0	Petrocelli, 3b	3	1	2	2
Griffey, rf	3	0	1	0	Burleson, ss	3	0	3	1
Geronimo, cf	1	0	0	0	Cooper, 1b	3	0	0	1
Gullett, p	3	0	0	0	Tiant, p	3	1	1	0
C. Carroll, p	0	0	0	0					
McEnaney, p	0	0	0	0					
Total	**31**	**0**	**5**	**0**	**Total**	**30**	**6**	**12**	**6**

Cincinnati . . . . 0 0 0   0 0 0   0 0 0—0
Boston . . . . 0 0 0   0 0 0   6 0 x—6

Double plays—Cincinnati 2. Left on base—Cincinnati 6, Boston 9. Two-base hits—Petrocelli, Griffey. Sacrifices—Doyle, Evans. Sacrifice fly—Cooper.

	ip	h	r	er	bb	so
Gullett (L, 0-1)	6	10	4	4	4	3
C. Carroll	0	0	1	1	1	0
McEnaney	2	2	1	1	1	1
Tiant (W, 1-0)	9	5	0	0	2	3

Balk—Tiant. Time of game—2:27.
Attendance—35,205.

How runs were scored—Six in Red Sox seventh: Tiant singled. Evans bunted, Tiant beat the throw to second, Evans reaching first. Doyle singled, loading the bases. Yastrzemski singled, scoring Tiant. Fisk walked, scoring Evans. Petrocelli singled, scoring Doyle and Yastrzemski. Burleson singled, scoring Fisk. Cooper hit a sacrifice fly, scoring Petrocelli.

Second Game
Fenway Park, Boston, Oct. 12

Cincinnati	ab	r	h	bi	Boston	ab	r	h	bi
Rose, 3b	4	0	2	0	Cooper, 1b	5	0	1	0
Morgan, 2b	3	1	0	0	Doyle, 2b	4	0	1	0
Bench, c	4	1	2	0	Yastrzemski, lf	3	2	1	0
Perez, 1b	3	0	0	1	Fisk, c	3	0	1	1
Foster, lf	4	0	1	0	Lynn, cf	4	0	0	0
Concepcion, ss	4	1	1	1	Petrocelli, 3b	4	0	2	1
Griffey, rf	4	0	1	1	Evans, rf	2	0	0	0
Geronimo, cf	3	0	0	0	Burleson, ss	4	0	1	0
Billingham, p	2	0	0	0	Lee, p	3	0	0	0
Borbon, p	0	0	0	0	Carbo, ph	1	0	0	0
McEnaney, p	0	0	0	0	Drago, p	0	0	0	0
Rettenmund, ph	1	0	0	0	**Total**	**33**	**2**	**7**	**2**
Eastwick, p	1	0	0	0					
Total	**33**	**3**	**7**	**3**					

Cincinnati . . . . 0 0 0   1 0 0   0 0 2—3
Boston . . . . 1 0 0   0 0 1   0 0 0—2

Error—Concepcion. Double plays—Cincinnati 1. Left on base—Cincinnati 6, Boston 8. Two-base hits—Cooper, Bench, Griffey. Stolen base—Concepcion.

	ip	h	r	er	bb	so
Billingham	5²/₃	6	2	1	2	5
Borbon	¹/₃	0	0	0	0	0
McEnaney	1	0	0	0	0	2
Eastwick (W, 1-0)	2	1	0	0	1	1
Lee	8	5	2	2	2	5
Drago (L, 0-1)	1	2	1	1	1	0

Hit by pitch—by Billingham (Evans). Time of game—2:38.
Attendance—35,205.

How runs were scored—One in Red Sox first: Cooper doubled. Doyle singled. Yastrzemski's grounder forced Doyle at second, Cooper was tagged out trying to score, Yastrzemski going to second. Fisk singled, scoring Yastrzemski.
One in Reds fourth: Morgan walked. Bench singled. Perez grounded out, advancing Morgan.
One in Red Sox sixth: Yastrzemski singled. Fisk was safe on an error. Petrocelli singled, scoring Yastrzemski.
Two in Reds ninth: Bench doubled. Concepcion singled, scoring Bench. Concepcion stole second. Griffey doubled, scoring Concepcion.

Third Game
Riverfront Stadium, Cincinnati, Oct. 14

Boston	ab	r	h	bi	Cincinnati	ab	r	h	bi
Cooper, 1b	5	0	0	0	Rose, 3b	4	1	1	0
Doyle, 2b	5	0	1	0	Griffey, rf	3	0	0	0
Yastrzemski, lf	4	1	0	0	Rettenmund, ph	1	0	0	0
Fisk, c	3	1	1	1	Morgan, 2b	4	0	1	2
Lynn, cf	3	0	1	0	Perez, 1b	3	1	0	0
Petrocelli, 3b	4	1	2	2	Bench, c	4	1	1	2
Evans, rf	4	1	2	2	Foster, lf	3	0	0	0
Burleson, ss	4	0	2	0	Concepcion, ss	4	1	1	1
Wise, p	2	0	0	0	Geronimo, cf	4	2	2	1
Burton, p	0	0	0	0	Nolan, p	1	0	0	0
Cleveland, p	0	0	0	0	Darcy, p	1	0	0	0
Carbo, ph	1	1	1	1	Carroll, p	0	0	0	0
Willoughby, p	0	0	0	0	McEnaney, p	1	0	1	0
Moret, p	0	0	0	0	Eastwick, p	0	0	0	0
					Armbrister, ph	1	0	0	0
Total	**35**	**5**	**10**	**5**	**Total**	**34**	**6**	**7**	**6**

Boston . . . . 0 1 0   0 0 1   1 0 2—5
Cincinnati . . . . 0 0 0   2 3 0   0 0 1—6

Errors—Fisk, 2. Left on base—Boston 5, Cincinnati 5. Three-base hits—Rose. Home runs—Fisk, Carbo, Evans, Bench, Concepcion, Geronimo. Stolen bases—Foster, Perez. Sacrifices—Willoughby. Sacrifice fly—Morgan, Lynn. Double plays—Boston, Cincinnati, 2.

	ip	h	r	er	bb	so
Wise	4¹/₃	4	5	5	2	1
Burton	¹/₃	0	0	0	1	0
Cleveland	1¹/₃	4	0	0	0	2
Willoughby (L, 0-1)	3	2	1	0	0	1
Moret	¹/₃	1	0	0	1	1
Nolan	4	3	1	1	1	0
Darcy	2	2	1	1	2	0
Carroll	²/₃	1	1	1	0	1
McEnaney	1²/₃	1	1	1	0	2
Eastwick (W, 1-0)	1²/₃	3	1	1	1	0

Wild pitch—Darcy. Time of game—3:03.
Attendance—55,392.

How runs were scored—One in Red Sox second: Fisk hit a home run.
Two in Reds fourth: Perez walked. Bench hit a home run.
Three in Reds fifth: Concepcion hit a home run. Geronimo hit a home run. Rose tripled. Morgan hit a sacrifice fly, scoring Rose.
One in Red Sox sixth: Yastrzemski and Fisk walked and each advanced a base on a wild pitch. Lynn hit a sacrifice fly, scoring Yastrzemski.
One in Red Sox seventh: Carbo hit a home run.
Two in Red Sox ninth: Petrocelli singled. Evans hit a home run.
One in Reds tenth: Geronimo singled. Fisk threw Armbrister's sacrifice bunt into center field, Geronimo going to third, Armbrister to second. The Red Sox claimed Armbrister had interfered with Fisk as he was fielding the ball. Rose walked. Morgan singled, scoring Geronimo.

Fourth Game
Riverfront Stadium, Cincinnati, Nov. 15

Boston	ab	r	h	bi	Cincinnati	ab	r	h	bi
Beniquez, lf	4	0	1	1	Rose, 3b	3	1	1	0
Miller, lf	1	0	0	0	Griffey, rf	5	0	1	1
Doyle, 2b	5	0	1	0	Morgan, 2b	3	1	0	0
	4	0	2	1	Perez, 1b	4	0	0	0
Fisk, c	5	1	1	0	Bench, c	4	0	1	1
Lynn, cf	4	1	1	0	G. Foster, lf	4	1	2	2
Petrocelli, 3b	4	0	1	0	Concepcion, ss	4	1	1	1
Evans, rf	4	1	2	2	Geronimo, cf	4	0	3	1
Burleson, ss	4	1	1	1	Norman, p	1	0	0	0
Tiant, p	3	1	1	0	Borbon, p	0	0	0	0
					Crowley, ph	1	0	0	0
					C. Carroll, p	0	0	0	0
					Chaney, ph	1	0	0	0
					Eastwick, p	0	0	0	0
					Armbrister, ph	0	0	0	0
Total	**38**	**5**	**11**	**5**	**Total**	**34**	**4**	**9**	**4**

Boston . . . . 0 0 0   5 0 0   0 0 0—5
Cincinnati . . . . 2 0 0   2 0 0   0 0 0—4

Errors—Perez, Doyle. Double plays—Cincinnati 1. Left on base—Boston 8, Cincinnati 8. Two base hits—Griffey, Bench, Burleson, Concepcion. Three base hits—Evans, Geronimo. Sacrifice—Armbrister.

(Fourth game continued)

	ip	h	r	er	bb	so
Tiant (W, 2-0)	9	9	4	4	4	4
Norman (L, 0-1)	3¹/₃	7	4	4	1	2
Borbon	²/₃	2	1	0	0	0
C. Carroll	2	2	0	0	0	2
Eastwick	3	0	0	0	1	0

Wild pitch—Norman. Time of game—2:52. Attendance—55,392.

How runs were scored—Two in Reds first: Rose singled. Griffey doubled, scoring Rose. Griffey was out trying for third. Morgan walked. Bench doubled, scoring Morgan.

Five in Red Sox fourth: Fisk and Lynn singled. The runners advanced on a wild pitch. Evans tripled, scoring Fisk and Lynn. Burleson doubled, scoring Evans. Tiant singled. Burleson scored on an infield error. Yastrzemski singled, scoring Tiant.

Two in Reds fourth: Foster had an infield hit and went to second on an error. Concepcion doubled, scoring Foster. Geronimo tripled, scoring Concepcion.

Fifth Game

Riverfront Stadium, Cincinnati, Oct. 16

Boston	ab	r	h	bi
Beniquez, lf	3	0	0	0
Doyle, 2b	4	1	1	0
Yastrzemski, 1b	3	1	1	1
Fisk, c	4	0	1	0
Lynn, cf	4	0	1	1
Petrocelli, 3b	4	0	0	0
Evans, rf	3	0	1	0
Burleson, ss	3	0	0	0
Cleveland, p	2	0	0	0
Willoughby, p	0	0	0	0
Griffin, ph	1	0	0	0
Pole, p	0	0	0	0
Segui, p	0	0	0	0
Total	**31**	**2**	**5**	**2**

Cincinnati	ab	r	h	bi
Rose, 3b	3	0	2	1
Griffey, rf	4	0	1	0
Morgan, 2b	3	1	1	0
Bench, c	3	2	1	0
Perez, 1b	3	2	2	4
Foster, lf	4	0	0	0
Concepcion, ss	2	0	0	1
Geronimo, cf	4	0	0	0
Gullett, p	3	1	1	0
Eastwick, p	0	0	0	0
Total	**29**	**6**	**8**	**6**

Boston ....1 0 0 0 0 0 0 0 1—2
Cincinnati ....0 0 0 1 1 3 0 1 x—6

Double play—Boston 2. Left on base—Boston 4, Cincinnati 5. Two base hits—Rose, Lynn. Three base hits—Doyle. Home runs Perez 2(2). Stolen bases—Morgan, Concepcion. Sacrifice fly — Yastrzemski, Concepcion.

	ip	h	r	er	bb	so
Cleveland (L, 0-1)	5	7	5	5	2	3
Willoughby	2	1	0	0	0	1
Pole	0	0	1	1	2	0
Segui	1	0	0	0	0	0
Gullett (W, 1-1)	8²/₃	5	2	2	1	7
Eastwick	¹/₃	0	0	0	0	1

Save—Eastwick (1). Hit by pitch—by Willoughby (Concepcion). Time of game—2:23. Attendance—56,393.

How runs were scored—One in Red Sox first: Doyle tripled. Yastrzemski hit a sacrifice fly, scoring Doyle.

One in Reds fourth: Perez hit a home run.

One in Reds fifth: Gullett singled. Rose doubled, scoring Gullett.

Three in Reds sixth: Morgan walked. Bench singled. Perez hit a home run.

One in Reds eighth: Bench and Perez walked. Bench went to third on an outfield fly. Concepcion hit a sacrifice fly, scoring Bench.

One in Red Sox ninth: Yastrzemski and Fisk singled. Lynn doubled, scoring Yastrzemski.

Sixth Game

Fenway Park, Boston, Oct. 21

Cincinnati	ab	r	h	bi
Rose, 3b	5	1	2	0
Griffey, rf	5	2	2	2
Morgan, 2b	6	1	1	0
Bench, c	6	0	1	1
Perez, 1b	6	0	2	0
Foster, lf	6	0	2	2
Concepcion, ss	6	0	1	0
Geronimo, cf	6	1	2	1
Nolan, p	0	0	0	0
Chaney, ph	1	0	0	0
Norman, p	0	0	0	0
Billingham, p	0	0	0	0
Armbrister, ph	0	1	0	0
C. Carroll, p	0	0	0	0
Crowley, ph	1	0	1	0
Borbon, p	1	0	0	0
Eastwick, p	0	0	0	0

(Sixth game continued)

Cincinnati	ab	r	h	bi
McEnaney, p	0	0	0	0
Driessen, ph	1	0	0	0
Darcy, p	0	0	0	0
Total	**50**	**6**	**14**	**6**

Boston	ab	r	h	bi
Cooper, 1b	5	0	0	0
Drago, p	0	0	0	0
Miller, ph	1	0	0	0
Wise, p	0	0	0	0
Doyle, 2b	5	0	1	0
Yastrzemski, lf	6	1	3	0
Fisk, c	4	2	2	1
Lynn, cf	4	2	2	3
Petrocelli, 3b	4	1	0	0
Evans, rf	5	0	1	0
Burleson, ss	3	0	0	0
Tiant, p	2	0	0	0
Moret, p	0	0	0	0
Carbo, lf	2	1	1	3
Total	**41**	**7**	**10**	**7**

Cincinnati.............0 0 0 0 3 0 2 1 0 0 0 0—6
Boston...............3 0 0 0 0 0 0 3 0 0 0 1—7

E—Burleson. DP—Cincinnati 1, Boston 1. LOB—Cincinnati 11, Boston 9. 2B—Doyle, Evans, Foster. 3B—Griffey. HR—Lynn (1), Geronimo (2), Carbo (2), Fisk (2). SB—Concepcion. S—Tiant.

	ip	h	r	er	bb	so
Nolan	2	3	3	3	0	2
Norman	²/₃	1	0	0	2	0
Billingham	1¹/₃	1	0	0	1	1
C. Carroll	1	1	0	0	0	0
Borbon	2	1	2	2	2	1
Eastwick	1¹/₃	2	1	1	1	2
McEnaney	²/₃	0	0	0	1	0
Darcy (L, 0-1)	2	1	1	1	0	1
Tiant	7	11	6	6	2	5
Moret	1	0	0	0	0	0
Drago	3	1	0	0	0	1
Wise (W, 1-0)	1	2	0	0	0	1

HBP—by Drago (Rose). T—4:01. A—35,205.

How runs were scored — Three in Red Sox first: Yastrzemski and Fisk singled. Lynn hit a home run.

Three in Reds fifth: Armbrister walked. Rose singled. Griffey tripled, scoring Armbrister and Rose. Bench singled, scoring Griffey.

Two in Reds seventh: Griffey and Morgan singled. Foster doubled, scoring Griffey and Morgan.

One in Reds eighth: Geronimo hit a home run.

Three in Red Sox eighth: Lynn singled. Petrocelli walked. Carbo hit a home run.

One in Red Sox twelfth: Fisk hit a home run.

Seventh Game

Fenway Park, Boston, Oct. 22

Cincinnati	ab	r	h	bi
Rose, 3b	4	0	2	1
Morgan, 2b	4	0	2	1
Bench, c	4	1	0	0
Perez, 1b	5	1	1	2
Foster, lf	4	0	1	0
Concepcion, ss	4	0	1	0
Griffey, rf	2	2	1	0
Geronimo, cf	3	0	0	0
Gullett, p	1	0	1	0
Rettenmund, ph	1	0	0	0
Billingham, p	0	0	0	0
Armbrister, ph	0	0	0	0
C. Carroll, p	0	0	0	0
Driessen, ph	1	0	0	0
McEnaney, p	0	0	0	0
Total	**33**	**4**	**9**	**4**

Boston	ab	r	h	bi
Carbo, lf	3	1	1	0
Miller, lf	0	0	0	0
Beniquez, ph	1	0	0	0
Doyle, 2b	4	1	1	0
Montgomery, ph	1	0	0	0
Yastrzemski, 1b	5	1	1	1
Fisk, c	3	0	0	0
Lynn, cf	2	0	0	0
Petrocelli, 3b	3	0	1	1
Evans, rf	2	0	0	1
Burleson, ss	3	0	0	0
Lee, p	3	0	1	0
Moret, p	0	0	0	0
Willoughby, p	0	0	0	0
Cooper, ph	1	0	0	0
Burton, p	0	0	0	0
Cleveland, p	0	0	0	0
Total	**31**	**3**	**5**	**3**

Cincinnati.....................0 0 0 0 0 2 1 0 1—4
Boston.........................0 0 3 0 0 0 0 0 0—3

E—Doyle 2. DP—Cincinnati 1, Boston 2. LOB—Cincinnati 9, Boston 9. 2B—Carbo. HR—Perez (3). SB—Morgan, Griffey. S—Geronimo.

	ip	h	r	er	bb	so
Gullett	4	4	3	3	5	5
Billingham	2	1	0	0	2	1
C.Carroll (W,1-0)	2	0	0	0	1	1
McEnaney	1	0	0	0	0	0
Lee	6¹/₃	7	3	3	1	2
Moret	¹/₃	1	0	0	2	0
Willoughby	1¹/₃	0	0	0	0	0
Burton (L,0-1)	²/₃	1	1	1	2	0
Cleveland	¹/₃	0	0	0	1	0

Save—McEnaney (1). WP—Gullett. T—2:52. A—35,205.

How runs were scored — Three in Red Sox third: Carbo walked. Doyle singled. Yastrzemski singled, scoring Carbo. Fisk walked. Petrocelli walked, scoring Doyle. Evans walked, scoring Yastrzemski.

Two in Reds sixth: Rose singled. Bench forced Rose at second. Perez hit a home run.

One in Reds seventh: Griffey walked. Armbrister walked. Rose singled, scoring Griffey.

One in Reds ninth: Griffey walked. Geronimo sacrificed Griffey to second. Rose walked. Morgan singled, scoring Griffey.

World Series Results, 1903-1975

1903 Boston AL 5, Pittsburgh NL 3
1904 No Series
1905 New York NL 4, Philadelphia AL 1
1906 Chicago AL 4, Chicago NL 2
1907 Chicago NL 4, Detroit AL 0, 1 tie
1908 Chicago NL 4, Detroit AL 1
1909 Pittsburgh NL 4, Detroit AL 3
1910 Philadelphia AL 4, Chicago NL 1
1911 Philadelphia AL 4, New York NL 2
1912 Boston AL 4, New York NL 3, 1 tie
1913 Philadelphia AL 4, New York NL 1
1914 Boston NL 4, Philadelphia AL 0
1915 Boston AL 4, Philadelphia NL 1
1916 Boston AL 4, Brooklyn NL 1
1917 Chicago AL 4, New York NL 2
1918 Boston AL 4, Chicago NL 2
1919 Cincinnati NL 5, Chicago AL 3
1920 Cleveland AL 5, Brooklyn NL 2
1921 New York NL 5, New York AL 3
1922 New York NL 4, New York AL 0, 1 tie
1923 New York AL 4, New York NL 2
1924 Washington AL 4, New York NL 3
1925 Pittsburgh NL 4, Washington AL 3
1926 St. Louis NL 4, New York AL 3
1927 New York AL 4, Pittsburgh NL 0

1928 New York AL 4, St. Louis NL 0
1929 Philadelphia AL 4, Chicago NL 1
1930 Philadelphia AL 4, St. Louis NL 2
1931 St. Louis NL 4, Philadelphia AL 3
1932 New York AL 4, Chicago NL 0
1933 New York NL 4, Washington AL 1
1934 St. Louis NL 4, Detroit AL 3
1935 Detroit AL 4, Chicago NL 2
1936 New York AL 4, New York NL 2
1937 New York AL 4, New York NL 1
1938 New York AL 4, Chicago NL 0
1939 New York AL 4, Cincinnati NL 0
1940 Cincinnati NL 4, Detroit AL 3
1941 New York AL 4, Brooklyn NL 1
1942 St. Louis NL 4, New York AL 1
1943 New York AL 4, St. Louis NL 1
1944 St. Louis NL 4, St. Louis AL 2
1945 Detroit AL 4, Chicago NL 3
1946 St. Louis NL 4, Boston AL 3
1947 New York AL 4, Brooklyn NL 3
1948 Cleveland AL 4, Boston NL 2
1949 New York AL 4, Brooklyn NL 1
1950 New York AL 4, Philadelphia NL 0
1951 New York AL 4, New York NL 2

1952 New York AL 4, Brooklyn NL 3
1953 New York AL 4, Brooklyn NL 2
1954 New York NL 4, Cleveland AL 0
1955 Brooklyn NL 4, New York AL 3
1956 New York AL 4, Brooklyn NL 3
1957 Milwaukee NL 4, New York AL 3
1958 New York AL 4, Milwaukee NL 3
1959 Los Angeles NL 4, Chicago AL 2
1960 Pittsburgh NL 4, New York AL 3
1961 New York AL 4, Cincinnati NL 1
1962 New York AL 4, San Francisco NL 3
1963 Los Angeles NL 4, New York AL 0
1964 St. Louis NL 4, New York AL 3
1965 Los Angeles NL 4, Minnesota AL 3
1966 Baltimore AL 4, Los Angeles NL 0
1967 St. Louis NL 4, Boston AL 3
1968 Detroit AL 4, St. Louis NL 3
1969 New York NL 4, Baltimore AL 1
1970 Baltimore AL 4, Cincinnati NL 1
1971 Pittsburgh NL 4, Baltimore AL 3
1972 Oakland AL 4, Cincinnati NL 3
1973 Oakland AL 4, New York NL 3
1974 Oakland AL 4, Los Angeles NL 1
1975 Cincinnati NL 4, Boston AL 3

All-Time Home Run Leaders

Player	HR	Player	HR	Player	HR	Player	HR
Hank Aaron	745	Al Kaline	399	Roy Sievers	318	Brooks Robinson	264
Babe Ruth	714	Frank Howard	382	Carl Yastrzemski	317	Tony Perez	258
Willie Mays	660	Orlando Cepeda	379	Al Simmons	307	Bob Allison	256
Frank Robinson	583	Norm Cash	377	Rogers Hornsby	302	Vada Pinson	256
Harmon Killebrew	573	Rocco Colavito	374	Chuck Klein	300	Reggie Jackson	254
Mickey Mantle	536	Gil Hodges	370	Robert Johnson	288	Joe Gordon	253
Jimmy Foxx	534	Ralph Kiner	369	Hank Sauer	288	Larry Doby	253
Ted Williams	521	Willie Stargell	368	Del Ennis	288	Fred (Cy) Williams	251
Ed Mathews	512	Joe DiMaggio	361	Frank Thomas	286	Leon Goslin	248
Ernie Banks	512	John Mize	359	Ken Boyer	282	Willie Horton	248
Mel Ott	511	Yogi Berra	358	Ted Kluszewski	279	Lee May	248
Lou Gehrig	493	Ron Santo	342	Rudy York	277	Vernon Stephens	247
Stan Musial	475	Joe Adcock	336	Roger Maris	275	Joe Torre	246
Willie McCovey	458	Dick Allen	331	Jim Wynn	273	Deron Johnson	245
Billy Williams	415	Hank Greenberg	331	Vic Wertz	266	Hack Wilson	244
Duke Snider	407	John (Boog) Powell	330	Bobby Thomson	264		

Members of National Baseball Hall of Fame and Museum

The shrine of organized baseball, dedicated June 12, 1939, is located in Cooperstown, N.Y.

Alexander, Grover Cleveland
Anson, Cap
Averill, Earl
Appling, Luke
Baker, Home Run
Bancroft, Dave
Barrow, Edward G.
Beckley, Jake
Bell, Cool Papa
Bender, Chief
Berra, Yogi
Bottomley, Jim
Boudreau, Lou
Bresnahan, Roger
Brouthers, Dan
Brown (Three Finger), Mordecai
Bulkeley, Morgan C.
Burkett, Jesse C.
Campanella, Roy
Carey, Max
Cartwright, Alexander
Chadwick, Henry
Chance, Frank
Chesbro, John
Clarke, Fred
Clarkson, John
Clemente, Roberto
Cobb, Ty
Cochrane, Mickey
Collins, Edward T.
Collins, James

Combs, Earle
Comiskey, Charles A.
Conlan, Jocko
Connolly, Thomas H.
Coveleski, Stan
Crawford, Sam
Cronin, Joe
Cummings, Candy
Cuyler, Kiki
Dean, Dizzy
Delahanty, Ed
Dickey, Bill
DiMaggio, Joe
Duffy, Hugh
Evans, Billy
Evers, John
Ewing, Buck
Faber, Urban
Feller, Bob
Flick, Elmer H.
Ford, Whitey
Foxx, James E.
Frick, Ford
Frisch, Frank
Galvin, Pud
Gehrig, Lou
Gehringer, Charles
Gibson, Josh
Gomez, Lefty
Goslin, Goose

Greenberg, Hank
Griffith, Clark
Grimes, Burleigh
Grove, Lefty
Hafey, Chick
Haines, Jessee
Hamilton, Bill
Harridge, Will
Harris, Bucky
Hartnett, Gabby
Heilmann, Harry
Herman, Billy
Hooper, Harry
Hornsby, Rogers
Hoyt, Waite
Hubbell, Carl
Huggins, Miller
Irvin, Monte
Jennings, Hugh
Johnson, Byron
Johnson, William (Judy)
Johnson, Walter
Keefe, Timothy
Keeler, William
Kelley, Joe
Kelly, George
Kelly, King
Kiner, Ralph
Klem, Bill
Koufax, Sandy

Lajoie, Napoleon
Landis, Kenesaw M.
Leonard, Buck
Lyons, Ted
Mack, Connie
Mantle, Mickey
Manush, Henry
Maranville, Rabbit
Marquard, Rube
Mathewson, Christy
McCarthy, Joe
McCarthy, Thomas
McGinnity, Joe
McGraw, John
McKechnie, Bill
Medwick, Joe
Musial, Stan
Nichols Kid
O'Rourke, James
Ott, Mel
Paige, Satchel
Pennock, Herb
Plank, Ed
Radbourne, Charlie
Rice, Sam
Rickey, Branch
Rixey, Eppa
Robinson, Jackie
Robinson, Wilbert
Roush, Edd

Ruffing, Red
Ruth, Babe
Schalk, Ray
Simmons, Al
Sisler, George
Spahn, Warren
Spalding, Albert
Speaker, Tris
Stengel, Casey
Terry, Bill
Thompson, Sam
Tinker, Joe
Traynor (Pie), Harold J.
Vance, Dazzy
Waddell, Rube
Wagner, Honus
Wallace, Roderick
Walsh, Ed
Waner, Lloyd
Waner, Paul
Ward, John
Weiss, George
Welch, Mickey
Wheat, Zach
Williams, Ted
Wright, George
Wright, Harry
Wynn, Early
Young, Cy
Youngs, Ross

Ryan's Fastball Clocked

Nolan Ryan of the California Angels twice threw a ball 100.9 mph in a game against the Tigers on Aug. 20, 1974. The entire game was clocked by infra-red radar. Ryan broke Bob Feller's 28 year-old record of 98.6 mph.

Major League Perfect Games

Year	Player	Clubs	Score	Year	Player	Clubs	Score
1904	Cy Young	Boston vs. Phil. (AL)	3-0	1956	Don Larson (b)	N.Y. Yankees vs. Brooklyn	2-0
1908	Addie Joss	Cleveland vs. Chicago (AL)	1-0	1964	Jim Bunning	Phil. vs. N.Y. Mets (NL)	6-0
1917	Ernie Shore (a)	Boston vs. Wash. (AL)	4-0	1965	Sandy Koufax	Los Angeles vs. Chic. (NL)	1-0
1922	Charles Robertson	Chicago vs. Detroit (AL)	2-0	1968	Jim Hunter	Oakland vs. Minn. (AL)	4-0

(a) Babe Ruth, the starting pitcher, was ejected from the game after walking the first batter. Shore replaced him, and the base-runner was out stealing. Shore retired the next 26 batters. (b) World Series.

Amateur Softball Association Champions in 1975

Division	National Champion
Men's Slow Pitch	Pyramid Cafe, Lakewood, Ohio
Women's Slow Pitch	Mark's Bros. Dots, N. Miami, Fla.
Men's Fast Pitch	Rising Sun Hotel, Reading, Pa.
Women's Fast Pitch	Stratford, Conn.
Industrial Slow Pitch	Nassau County Police Dept., Mineola, N.Y.
Modified Pitch	Silverstri's, Staten Island, N.Y.
Church Tournament	Hickory Hammock, Milton, Fla.

Trapshooting Championship in 1975

Source: Trap & Field Magazine

76th Grand American Tournament
Vandalia, Ohio, Aug. 18-23, 1975

Grand American Handicap
Men—Wayne Hegwood, Jackson, Miss.
Women—Ann Kisner, Muscatine, Ia.
Juniors—David Keefe, Tiptonville, Tenn.
Sub-Juniors—Kelli Wiseman, St. Petersburg, Fla.
Veterans—Walter Swogger, Walcottville, Ind.
Industry—Bob Oxsen, Livermore, Cal.
Past Trophy Winner—Herman Welch, Downers Grove, Ill.
Jimmy Robinson Trophy to High Canadian—Robert Myslik, Guelph, Ont.

Clay Target Championship
Men—Steve Carmichel, Kansas City, Mo.
Women—Barbara Chesser, London, Ohio
Juniors—Greg Oldsen, DeWitt, Ia.
Sub-Juniors—Mack Morrison, Goldsmith, Tex.
Veterans—Vic Reinders, Waukesha, Wis.
Industry—Bob Oxsen, Livermore, Cal.

Champion of Champions
Men—Billy Joe White, Tazwell, Tenn.
Women—Susan Nattrass, Calgary, Alta.
Junior—Mark Morrisey, Blair, Neb.

High-Over-All
Men—Don Bonillas, Los Banos, Cal.
Women—Kathleen Sedlecky, Butler, Pa.
Juniors—Joe Loitz, Peotone, Ill.
Sub-Juniors—David Craite, Grosse Point Farms, Mich.
Veterans—Andy Long, Shamokin, Pa.
Industry—Bob Oxsen, Livermore, Cal.

All-Around Championship
Men—Steve Carmichael, Kansas City, Mo.
Women—Laura Christopher, Brunswick, Ohio.
Junior—Lee Bannerman, Brighton, Mich.
Sub-Juniors—David Craite, Grosse Point Farms, Mich.
Veteran—Vic Reinders, Waukesha, Wis.
Industry—Bob Oxsen, Livermore, Cal.

Black Athletes Hall of Fame

(Chosen by Black Sports Journal)

Baseball	Track & Field	Basketball	Football	Boxing
Henry Aaron	Alice Coachman	Elgin Baylor	Jim Brown	Muhammad Ali
Roy Campanella	Harrison Dillard	Chuck Cooper	Hank McDonald	Henry Armstrong
Roberto Clemente	De Hart Hubbard	Bob Douglas	Fritz Pollard	Joe Frazier
Josh Gibson	Rafer Johnson	Bill Russell	Gale Sayers	Jack Johnson
Monte Irvin	Herb McKenley	Abe Saperstein	Buddy Young	Joe Louis
John Henry (Pop) Lloyd	Ralph Metcalfe	Maurice Stokes	**Soccer**	Ray Robinson
Willie Mays	Jesse Owens	Jack Twyman	Lindy Delapenha	**Golf**
Satchel Paige	Eulace Peacock	**Cricket**	Pele	Charlie Sifford
Branch Rickey	Wilma Rudolph	Leary Constantine	**Tennis**	**Historians**
Jackie Robinson	Willye Whyte	George Headly	Arthur Ashe	Dr. E. B. Henderson
	Arthur Wint	Garfield Sobers	Althea Gibson	Morris Levitt
	Joe Yancey	Frank Worrell		

U.S. National Fencing Champions in 1975

Men's Foil—Edward Ballinger, Salle Santelli, N.Y.
Men's Epee—Scott Bozek, Tanner City Fencers Club.
Men's Sabre—Peter Westbrook, N.Y. Fencers Club.
Women's Foil—Nikki Tomlinson, Liberty Fencers Club.

Men's Foil Team—N.Y. Fencers Club.
Men's Epee Team—N.Y. Athletic Club.
Men's Sabre Team—N.Y. Fencers Club.
Women's Foil Team—Halberstadt Fencers Club, Cal.

Pan-American Games Final Medal Standings

Mexico City, Mexico, Oct. 12-27, 1975

	Gold	Silver	Bronze	Total		Gold	Silver	Bronze	Total
United States	116	82	46	244	Panama	0	2	4	6
Cuba	55	45	30	130	Puerto Rico	0	2	7	9
Canada	18	34	39	91	Jamaica	0	1	4	5
Mexico	9	34	39	82	Venezuela	0	1	11	12
Brazil	8	13	23	44	Bahamas	0	1	1	2
Argentina	3	5	8	16	Neth. Antilles	0	1	0	1
Colombia	2	3	4	9	Trinidad	0	1	0	1
Ecuador	1	1	1	3	Dominican Rep.	0	1	8	9
Guyana	1	1	0	2	Uruguay	0	0	2	2
Peru	1	1	0	2	Chile	0	0	2	2

Quarter Horse Racing

The richest horse race in the world, the All American Futurity is run each Labor Day at Ruidoso Downs, New Mexico. It is open to 2-year-old Quarter Horses. The distance of the event was 400 yards through 1972; 440 yards starting in 1973.

Year	Winner	Weight	Time	Value to Winner	Jockey	Owner
1960	Tonto Bars Hank	119	20.2	$65,122	C. Pemer	Milo and C. G. Whitcomb
1961	Pokey Bar	119	20.1	101,212	K. Chapman	Hugh Huntley
1962	Hustling Man	119	20.3	96,425	C. Detiege	J.B. Ferguson
1963	Goetta	116	20.40	127,500	C. Smith	Hugh Huntley
1964	Decketta	119	20.30	134,030	B. Morris	W. W. Wilson
1965	Savannah Jr.	120	20.30	192,730	J. Wallace	J. R. and R. E. Cates
1966	Go Dick Go	119	20.27	198,300	B. Nesmith	Joe V. Leitner
1967	Laico Bird	119	20.11	228,300	B. Harmon	F. H. Jones Jr.
1968	Three Oh's	119	20.06	160,372	J. Nicodemus	Donald G. Strole
1969	Easy Jet	119	20.46	159,840	W. Lovell	Walter Merrick
1970	Rocket Wrangler	119	20.09	178,488	J. Nicodemus	John R. Adams
1971	Mr. Kid Charge	120	19.65	200,841	J. Cox	Will F. Whitehead
1972	Possumjet	119	20.04	336,629	P. Herrera	Jack Byers
1973	Time To Thinkrich	120	21.58	330,000	J. Watson	Vessels Stallion Farm
1974	Easy Date	120	21.60	330,000	D. Knight	Walter Merrick
1975	Bugs Alive in 75	119	21.98	330,000	J. Burgess	Ralph W. Shebester

World Pocket Billiards Champions

1931—Ralph Greenleaf
1932—Ralph Greenleaf
1933—Erwin Rudolph
1934—Erwin Rudolph
1935—Andrew Ponzi
1936—James Caras
1937—Ralph Greenleaf
1938—James Caras
1939—James Caras
1940—Andrew Ponzi
1941—Willie Mosconi, Erwin Rudolph
1942—Irving Crane
1943—Andrew Ponzi

1944—Willie Mosconi
1945—Willie Mosconi
1946—Irving Crane
1947—Willie Mosconi
1948—Willie Mosconi
1949—James Caras
1950—Willie Mosconi
1951—Willie Mosconi
1952—Willie Mosconi
1953—Willie Mosconi
1954—none
1955—Irving Crane, Willie Mosconi
1956-62—none

1963—Luther Lassiter
1964—Luther Lassiter, Arthur Cranfield
1965—Joe Balsis
1966—Luther Lassiter
1967—Luther Lassiter
1968—Irving Crane
1969—Ed Kelly
1970—Irving Crane
1971—Ray Martin
1972—Irving Crane
1973—Lou Butera
1974—Ray Martin
1975—none

Skiing in 1975
U.S. National Cross-Country Championship
Putney, Vt.

Men

10 km—Bill Koch, Guilford, Vt.
15 km—Bill Koch.
30 km—Tim Caldwell, Putney, Vt.
50 km—Tim Caldwell.

Women

5 km—Martha Rockwell, West Lebanon, N.H.
10 km—Martha Rockwell.
20 km—Martha Rockwell.

The World Cup Winners

Men

1967—Jean Claude Killy, France
1968—Jean Claude Killy, France
1969—Karl Schranz, Austria
1970—Karl Schranz, Austria
1971—Gustavo Thoeni, Italy
1972—Gustavo Thoeni, Italy
1973—Gustavo Thoeni, Italy
1974—Piero Gros, Italy
1975—Gustavo Thoeni, Italy

Women

1967—Nancy Greene, Canada
1968—Nancy Greene, Canada
1969—Gertrud Gabl, Austria
1970—Michele Jacot, France
1971—Annemarie Proell, Austria
1972—Annemarie Proell, Austria
1973—Annemarie Proell, Austria
1974—Annemarie Proell, Austria
1975—Annemarie Proell, Austria

Power Boat Racing Champions
APBA Gold Cup Race

Year	Boat	Owner	Driver	Winner's fastest Heat	Site
1961	Miss Century 21	Willard Rhodes	Bill Muncey	102.399	Reno, Nev.
1962	Miss Century 21	Willard Rhodes	Bill Muncey	101.446	Seattle, Wash.
1963	Miss Bardahl	Ole Bardahl	Ron Musson	114.650	Detroit, Mich.
1964	Miss Bardahl	Ole Bardahl	Ron Musson	108.104	Detroit, Mich.
1965	Miss Bardahl	Ole Bardahl	Ron Musson	110.655	Seattle, Wash.
1966	Tahoe Miss	Harrah's	Mira Slovak	97.861	Detroit, Mich.
1967	Miss Bardahl	Ole Bardahl	Bill Schumacher	104.691	Seattle, Wash.
1968	Miss Bardahl	Ole Bardahl	Bill Schumacher		Detroit, Mich.
1969	Miss Budweiser	Bernard Little & Tom Friedkin	Bill Sterett	103.587	San Diego, Cal.
1970	Miss Budweiser	Hydroplanes, Inc.	Dean Chenoweth	101.848	San Diego, Cal.
1971	Miss Madison	Miss Madison, Inc.	Jim McCormick	101.522	Madison, Ind.
1972	Atlas Van Lines	Atlas Van Lines	Bill Muncey	103.547	Detroit, Mich.
1973	Miss Budweiser	Hydroplanes, Inc.	Dean Chenoweth	104.046	Tri-Cities, Wash.
1974	Pay'N Pak	David J. Heerensperger	George Henley	112.056	Seattle, Wash.
1975	Pay 'N Pak	David J. Heerensperger	George Henley	113.350	Tri-Cities, Wash.

Trotting and Pacing Records

Source: Philip Pikelny, United States Trotting Association. Records to Oct., 1975

Trotting Records

Asterisk (*) denotes record was made in a race. Times—seconds in fifths.

One Mile Records (Mile Track)

All-age — 1:54.4 — Nevele Pride, Indianapolis, Ind., Aug. 31, 1969.

Two-year-old — *1:58.2 — Nevele Pride, Lexington, Ky., Oct. 4, 1967.

Three-year-old — *1:56.2 — Super Bowl, Du Quoin, Ill., Aug. 30, 1972.

(Half-Mile Track)

All-age — *1:56.4 — Nevele Pride, Saratoga Springs, N.Y., Sept. 6, 1969.

Two-year-old — *2:00.1 — Ayres, Delaware, Ohio, 1963.

Three-year-old Colt — *1:58.3 — Songcan, Delaware, Ohio, 1972.

Odd Distances

1-1/16 Miles — *2:05.3 — Senator Frost, Inglewood, Cal., Oct. 17, 1959.

1-1/16 Miles, Half-mile Track — *2:07.2 — Nevele Pride, Westbury, N.Y., 1969.

1-3/16 Miles — *2:22.4 — Scotch Victor, Inglewood, Cal., Nov. 6, 1954.

1¼ Miles — *2:30.3 — Pronto Don, Inglewood, Cal., Nov. 24, 1951.

1¼ Miles, Half-mile Track — *2:31.2 — Speedy Scot, Westbury, N.Y., 1964; Noble Victory, Westbury, N.Y., 1966.

1½ Miles — 3:02.1 — Greyhound, Indianapolis, Ind., Sept. 14, 1937.

1½ Miles, Half-mile Track — *3:05.2 — Snow Speed, Yonkers, N.Y., 1969.

2 Miles — 4:06 — Greyhound, Indianapolis, Ind., Sept. 19, 1939.

2 Miles, Half-mile Track — *4:10.4 — Pronto Don, Westbury, N.Y., Sept. 13, 1951.

Fastest Two Heats — *1:57.2; *1:56.2 — Super Bowl, Du Quoin, Ill., Aug. 29, 1972.

Fastest Two Heats, Half-Mile Track — *1:58.4, *2:00.3 — Speedy Rodney, Goshen, N.Y., 1966. and ***2:00.4; *1:58.3**, Songcan, Delaware, Ohio, 1972.

Pacing Records

One Mile Records (Mile Track)

All-age — 1:52 — Steady Star, Lexington, Ky., Oct. 1, 1971.

Two-year-old — *1:54.4 — Alert Bret, Lexington, Ky., 1974.

Three-year-old — 1:54 — Steady Star, Lexington, Ky., Oct. 7, 1970

(Half-Mile Track)

All-age — 1:55.3 — Adios Butler, Delaware, Ohio, Sept. 21, 1961; Albatross, Delaware, Ohio, 1972.

Two-year-old — *1:58.4 — Columbia George, Yonkers, N.Y., Nov. 8, 1969; J. R. Skipper, Delaware, Ohio, 1972.

Three-year-old — 1:56.3 — Strike Out, Delaware, Ohio, 1972.

Odd Distances

1¼ Miles — *2:30.2 — Dr. Stanton, Arcadia, Cal., May 15, 1948.

1¼ Miles, Half-mile Track — *2:29.3 — Irvin Paul, Westbury, N.Y., Sept. 1, 1962.

1-1/16 Miles — *2:03.1 — Adios Vic, Inglewood, Cal., Oct. 23, 1965.

1-1/16 Miles, Half-mile Track — *2:06 — Albatross, Westbury, N.Y., 1972.

1⅛ miles — *2:09.1 — True Duane, Hollywood Park, 1966.

1½ Miles — *3:05.2 — Right Time, Inglewood, Cal., 1961: and K. D. Senator, E. Boston, Mass., 1963.

1½ Miles, Half-mile Track — *3:02.3 — Overcall, Westbury, N.Y., June 5, 1969.

2 Miles — 4:17 — Dan Patch, Macon, Ga., 1903.

2 Miles, Half-mile Track — *4:08.4 — Irvin Paul, Yonkers, N.Y., June 28, 1962.

Fastest Two Heats — *1:54.4, 1:54.4 — Albatross, Lexington, Ky., Oct. 2, 1971.

The Hambletonian (3-year-old trotters) Du Quoin, Ill.

Year	Winner	Best Time	Purse
1940	Spencer Scott	2:02	$43,658
1941	Bill Gallon	2:05	38,729
1942	The Ambassador	2:04	38,954
1943	Volo Song	2:02 1-2	42,298
1944	Yankee Maid	2:04	33,577
1945	Titan Hanover	2:04	50,190
1946	Chestertown	2:02 1-2	50,905
1947	Hoot Mon	2:00	46,267
1948	Demon Hanover	2:02	59,941
1949	Miss Tilly	2:01 2-5	69,791
1950	Lusty Song	2:02	75,209
1951	Mainliner	2:02 3-5	95,263
1952	Sharp Note	2:02 3-5	87,637
1953	Helicopter	2:01 3-5	117,118
1954	Newport Dream	2:02 3-5	106,830
1955	Scott Frost	2:00 3-5	86,863
1956	The Intruder	2:01 3-5	98,591
1957	Hickory Smoke	2:00 1-5	111,126
1958	Emily's Pride	1:59 4-5	$106,719
1959	Diller Hanover	2:01 1-5	125,284
1960	Blaze Hanover	1:59 3-5	144,590
1961	Harlan Dean	1:58 2-5	131,573
1962	A.C.'s Viking	1:59 3-5	116,312
1963	Speedy Scot	1:58	115,549
1964	Ayres	1:56 4-5	115,281
1965	Egyptain Candor	2:04 3-5	122,245
1966	Kerry Way	1:58 1-5	122,540
1967	Speedy Streak	2:00	122,650
1968	Nevele Pride	1:59 2-5	116,190
1969	Lindy's Pride	1:57 3-5	124,910
1970	Timothy T	2:00 1-5	143,630
1971	Speedy Crown	1:57 2-5	128,770
1972	Super Bowl	1:56 2-5	119,090
1973	Flirth	1:57 1-5	144,710
1974	Christopher T	1:58 3-5	160,150
1975	Bonefish	1:59	150,924

Little Brown Jug (3-Year-Old Pacers)

Year	Winner	Winning Driver	Purse
1953	Keystoner	Frank Ervin	$54,972
1954	Adios Harry	Morris MacDonald	69,332
1955	Quick Chief	Billy Haughton	66,608
1956	Noble Adios	John Simpson, Sr.	52,666
1957	Torpid	John Simpson Sr.	73,528
1958	Shadow Wave	Joe O'Brien	65,252
1959	Adios Butler	Clint Hodgins	76,582
1960	Bullet Hanover	John Simpson, Sr.	66,510
1961	Henry T. Adios	Stanley Dancer	70,069
1962	Lehigh Hanover	Stanley Dancer	75,038
1963	Overtrick	John Patterson, Sr.	68,294
1964	Vicar Hanover	Billy Haughton	66,590
1965	Bret Hanover	Frank Ervin	$71,447
1966	Romeo Hanover	George Sholty	74,616
1967	Best of All	James Hackett	84,778
1968	Rum Customer	Billy Haughton	104,226
1969	Laverne Hanover	Billy Haughton	109,731
1970	Most Happy Fella	Stanley Dancer	100,110
1971	Nansemond	Herve Filion	102,944
1972	Strike Out	Keith Waples	104,916
1973	Melvin's Woe	Joe O'Brien	120,000
1974	Ambro Omaha	Billy Haughton	132,630
1975	Seatrain	Ben Webster	147,816

"Parked Out" Computations

Harness Racing mathematicians have compiled these figures on the added distance in each mile that a horse travels when "parked out" (racing outside another horse, five feet out from the point at which the track is measured).

½ mile track (4 turns to mile) .... 62.832 feet
⅝ mile track (3 turns to mile) .... 47.124 feet
¾ mile track with chute, and mile track (2 turns to mile) .... 31.416 feet

Major Harness Races Of 1975

Purse	Event	Winner	Time
$232,192	Hambletonian (3-year-old trot)	Bonefish	1:59
230,521	Monticello-N.Y.C.OTB Classic (3-year-old pace)	Silk Stockings	1:57.3h
200,000	Yonkers Trot (3-year-old trot)	Surefire Hanover	2:03h
200,000	Cane (3-year-old pace)	Nero	1:58.4h
200,000	International trot (1 1/4m-world inv.)	Savoir	2:32.1h
160,000	U.S. Pacing Championship (FFA)	Sir Dalrae	1:57.3
147,813	Little Brown Jug (3-year-old pace)	Seatrain	1:56.4h
140,000	Prix d'Ete (3-year-old pace)	Albert's Star	1:58f
122,970	Colonial (3-year-old trot)	Meadow Bright	2:02f
118,525	Dexter Cup (3-year-old trot)	Songflori	2:02.2h
111,752	American-National (4-year-old pace)	Title Holder	1:56.2f
111,646	Adios (3-year-old pace)	Nero	1:57.2f
111,000	Empire State Trot (3-year-old trot)	Bonefish	1:58.1
101,550	Realization (1 1/16m-4-year-old trot)	Hero Almahurst	2:11h
101,550	Realization (1 1/16m-4-year-old pace)	Timmy Lobell	2:07.4h
100,000	Fox Stake (2-year-old pace)	Bit O Fun	1:57.4
100,000	Kentucky Futurity (3-year-old trot)	Noble Rogue	1:59.3
100,000	Yonkers International (1 1/4m-world inv.)	Handle With Care	2:30.1h
94,900(div)	Maple Leaf Trot (FFA)	Savoir	2:01.4f
		Delmonica Hanover	2:02.2f
92,300(div)	Canadian Pacing Derby (3-year-old & up)	Rambling Willie	1:58.4f
		Pickwick Baron	1:58.4f
81,500	Thomas P. Gaines Mem. (3-year-old pace)	Nero	1:56.3
80,550(div)	Erwin F. Dygert Mem. (FFA trot)	Quick Work	2:01.4
		McElwyn's Danger	2:02
75,000	Old Glory Pace (1 1/2m-inv.)	Nickawampus Leroy	3:05.2h
70,200	American National (4-year-old trot)	Golden Sovereign	1:59.4f
68,000	Founder's Gold Cup (3-year-old trot)	Bonefish	1:59
60,000	Canadian-American Series Final (3&4-year-old pace)	Right Tie	1:59.2f
59,567	Hambletonian Filly Stake (3-year-old trot)	Keystone Pioneer	1:59
52,500	Cane Prep (3-year-old pace)	Nero	1:59h
50,000	Challenge Cup Trot (1 1/4m-inv.)	Savoir	2:33.1h
50,000	Charles Coon Memorial (4-year-old trot)	Golden Viking	2:09.3h
50,000	Charles Coon Memorial (4-year-old pace)	Dancing Knox	2:02.1h

(h) denotes half-mile track; (f) five-eighths mile track; no designation refers to mile track.

Leading Drivers

Year	Races Won		Grand Circuit		Money Won	
1957	Bill Haughton	156	John Simpson	$367,670	Bill Haughton	$586,950
1958	Bill Haughton	176	Joe O'Brien	267,342	Bill Haughton	816,659
1959	William Gilmour	165	Joe O'Brien	263,636	Bill Haughton	711,435
1960	Del Insko	156	Del Miller	338,594	Del Miller	567,282
1961	Bob Farrington	201	Jimmy Arthur	248,211	Stanley Dancer	674,723
1962	Bob Farrington	203	Stanley Dancer	306,454	Stanley Dancer	760,343
1963	Donald Busse	201	Ralph Baldwin	299,899	Bill Haughton	790,086
1964	Bob Farrington	312	Stanley Dancer	269,080	Stanley Dancer	1,051,538
1965	Bob Farrington	310	Joe O'Brien	304,791	Bill Haughton	889,943
1966	Bob Farrington	283	George Sholty	293,531	Stanley Dancer	1,218,403
1967	Bob Farrington	277	Bill Haughton	448,294	Bill Haughton	1,305,773
1968	Herve Filion	407	Bill Haughton	448,040	Bill Haughton	1,654,172
1969	Herve Filion	394	Bill Haughton	489,495	Del Insko	1,635,463
1970	Herve Filion	486	Stanley Dancer	439,019	Herve Filion	1,647,837
1971	Herve Filion	543	Stanley Dancer	462,694	Herve Filion	1,915,945
1972	Herve Filion	605	Billl Haughton	416,626	Herve Filion	2,473,265
1973	Herve Filion	445	Bill Haughton	456,192	Herve Filion	2,233,302

Harness Horse of the Year

1947 — Victory Song
1948 — Rodney
1949 — Good Time
1950 — Proximity
1951 — Pronto Don
1952 — Good Time
1953 — Hi Lo's Forbes
1954 — Stenographer
1955 — Scott Frost
1956 — Scott Frost
1957 — Torpid
1958 — Emily's Pride
1959 — Bye Bye Byrd
1960 — Adios Butler
1961 — Adios Butler
1962 — Su Mac Lad
1963 — Speedy Scot
1964 — Bret Hanover
1965 — Bret Hanover
1966 — Bret Hanover
1967 — Nevele Pride
1968 — Nevele Pride
1969 — Nevele Pride
1970 — Fresh Yankee
1971 — Albatross
1972 — Albatross
1973 — Sir Dalrae
1974 — Delmonica Hanover

30th Annual National Field Archery Championships

Jay, Vermont, July 21-25, 1975

Freestyle

Senior men—Cal Hedden, Ill.
Senior Women—Erma Nelson, Utah.
Professional Men—Gale Cavallin, Costa Mesa, Cal.
Open Men—Terry Ragsdale, White Oak, Tex.
Professional Women—Eva Troncoso, Cal.
Open Women—Barbara Morris, Frankfort, Ky.
Amateur Women—Michelle Sanderson, Hastings, Minn.
Amateur Men—John Ashburn Jr., Barrington, Ill.

Freestyle — Limited

Professional Men—David Grimsley, Brownwood, Tex.
Open Men—Richard Phillips, Bristol, R.I.
Amateur Men—Luke Wood, Arden, N.C.
Professional Women—Marita Gilmer, Minneapolis, Minn.
Open Women—Lois Potter, Painted Post, N.Y.
Amateur Women—Barbara Brown, Rochester, N.Y.

Barebow

Open Men—Al R. Tuller, Missouri.
Amateur Men—Don Morehead, Weaton, Illinois.
Open Women—Gloria M. Shelley, Connecticut.
Amateur Women—Eunice Schewe, Illinois.

Bowhunter

Professional Men—Bob Jensen, Orange, Cal.
Open Men—Cal Vogt, Canoga Park, Cal.
Open Women—Jeanne Owen, Las Vegas, Nev.
Amateur Men—Charles Maloney, Bolingbrook, Ill.
Amateur Women—Deborah Halfpenny, Hawaii.

Boxing Champions by Classes
Recognized by Ring Magazine as of Sept. 15, 1975

Heavyweight . . . . Muhammad Ali, Chicago, Ill.	Lightweight (135 lbs.) . . . . Roberto Duran, Panama
Light-Heavyweight (175 lbs.) . . vacant	Junior Lightweight (130 lbs.) . . . Ben Villaflor, Philippines
Middleweights (160 lbs.) . . . . Carlos Monzon, Argentina	Featherweight (126 lbs.) . . . . . . Alexis Arguello, Nicaragua
Jr. Middleweight (154 lbs.) . . . . Jae Do Yuh, S. Korea	Bantamweight (118 lbs.) . . . . . . Alfonso Zamora, Mexico
Welterweight (147 lbs.) . . . . Jose Napoles, Mexico	Flyweight (112 lbs.) . . . . Miguel Canto, Mexico
Jr. Welterweight (140 lbs.) . . . . Antonio Cervantes, Colombia	

As of Aug. 15, 1975, the only universally accepted title holder was in the heavyweight division. The following are the recognized champions of the World Boxing Assn. and the World Boxing Council.

	WBA	WBC
Heavyweight	Muhammad Ali, Chicago, Ill.	Muhammad Ali
Light Heavyweight	Victor Galindez, Argentina	John Conteh, England
Middleweights	Rodrigo Valdez, Colombia	Carlos Monzon, Argentina
Jr. Middleweight	Miguel de Oliviera, Brazil	Jae Do Yuh, S. Korea
Welterweight	Angel Espada, Puerto Rico	Jose Napoles, Mexico
Jr. Welterweight	Antonio Cervantes, Columbia	Shengsak Muangsurin, Thailand
Lightweight	Roberto Duran, Panama	Ishimatsu Suzuki, Japan
Jr. Lightweight	Ben Villaflor, Philippines	Alfredo Escalera, Puerto Rico
Featherweight	Alexis Arguello, Nicaragua	Ruben Olivares, Mexico
Bantamweight	Alfonso Zamora, Mexico	Rodolfo Martinez, Mexico
Flyweight	Erbito Salvarria, Philippines	Miguel Canto, Mexico

Ring Champions by Years
*Abandoned title

Heavyweights

1882-1892	John L. Sullivan (A)
1892-1897	James J. Corbett (B)
1897-1899	Robert Fitzsimmons
1899-1905	James J. Jeffries (C)
1905-1906	Marvin Hart
1906-1908	Tommy Burns
1908-1915	Jack Johnson
1915-1919	Jess Willard
1919-1926	Jack Dempsey
1926-1928	Gene Tunney*
1928-1930	Vacant
1930-1932	Max Schmeling
1932	Jack Sharkey
1933	Primo Carnera
1934	Max Baer
1935-1937	James J. Braddock
1937-1949	Joe Louis*
1949-1951	Ezzard Charles
1951-1952	Joe Walcott
1952-1956	Rocky Marciano*
1956-1959	Floyd Patterson
1959	Ingemar Johansson
1960-1962	Floyd Patterson
1962-1964	Sonny Liston
1964-1967	Cassius Clay* (Muhammad Ali) (D)
1970-1973	Joe Frazier
1973-1974	George Foreman
1974	Muhammad Ali

(A) London Prize Ring (bare knuckle champion).

(B) First Marquis of Queensberry Champion.

(C) Jeffries abandoned the title (1905) and designated Marvin Hart and Jack Root as logical contenders and agreed to referee a fight between them, the winner to be declared champion. Hart defeated Root in 12 rounds (1905) and in turn was defeated by Tommy Burns (1906) who immediately laid claim to the title. Jack Johnson defeated Burns (1908) and was recognized as champion. He clinched the title by defeating Jeffries in an attempted comeback (1910).

(D) Title declared vacant by the World Boxing Assn. and other groups in 1967 after Clay's refusal to fulfill his military obligation.

Light Heavyweights

1903	Jack Root, George Gardner
1903-1905	Bob Fitzsimmons
1905-1912	Philadelphia Jack O'Brien*
1912-1916	Jack Dillon
1916-1920	Battling Levinsky
1920-1922	Georges Carpentier
1922-1923	Battling Siki
1923-1925	Mike McTigue
1925	Paul Berlenbach
1926-1927	Jack Delaney*
1927-1929	Tommy Loughran*
1930-1934	Maxey Rosenbloom
1934-1935	Bob Olin
1935-1939	John Henry Lewis*

1939	Melio Bettina
1939-1941	Billy Conn*
1941	Anton Christoforidis (won NBA title)
1941-1948	Gus Lesnevich, Freddie Mills
1948-1950	Freddie Mills
1950-1952	Joey Maxim
1952-1960	Archie Moore
1961-1962	Vacant
1962-1963	Harold Johnson
1963-1965	Willie Pastrano
1965-1966	Jose Torres
1966-1968	Dick Tiger
1968-1974	Bob Foster*

Middleweights

1884-1891	Jack "Nonpareil" Dempsey
1891-1897	Bob Fitzsimmons*
1897-1907	Tommy Ryan*
1907-1908	Stanley Ketchel, Billy Papke
1908-1910	Stanley Ketchel
1911-1913	Vacant
1913	Frank Klaus, George Chip
1914-1917	Al McCoy
1917-1920	Mike O'Dowd
1920-1923	Johnny Wilson
1923-1926	Harry Greb
1926-1931	Tiger Flowers, Mickey Walker
1931-1932	Gorilla Jones (NBA)
1932-1937	Marcel Thil
1938	Al Hostak (NBA), Solly Krieger (NBA)
1939-1940	Al Hostak (NBA)
1941	Tony Zale (NBA)
1942-1947	Tony Zale
1947-1948	Rocky Graziano
1948	Tony Zale, Marcel Cerdan
1949	Marcel Cerdan, Jake LaMotta
1950	Jake LaMotta
1951	Ray Robinson, Randy Turpin, Ray Robinson*
1953-1955	Carl (Bobo) Olson
1955-1957	Ray Robinson
1957	Gene Fullmer, Ray Robinson, Carmen Basilio
1958	Carmen Basilio, Ray Robinson
1959	Gene Fullmer (NBA); Ray Robinson (N.Y.)
1960	Gene Fullmer (NBA); Paul Pender (New York and Mass.)
1961	Gene Fullmer (NBA); Terry Downes (New York, Mass., Europe)
1962	Gene Fullmer, Dick Tiger (NBA); Paul Pender (New York and Mass.)*
1963	Dick Tiger (universal).
1963-1965	Joey Giardello
1965-1966	Dick Tiger
1966-1967	Emile Griffith
1967	Nino Benvenuti
1967-1968	Emile Griffith
1968-1970	Nino Benvenuti
1970	Carlos Monzon

Welterweights

1892-1894	Mysterious Billy Smith
1894-1896	Tommy Ryan
1896	Kid McCoy (outgrew class)
1900	Rube Ferns, Matty Matthews
1901	Matty Matthews, Rube Ferns
1901-1904	Joe Walcott
1904-1906	Dixie Kid, Joe Walcott, Honey Mellody
1907-1911	Mike Sullivan
1911-1915	Vacant
1915-1919	Ted Lewis, Jack Britton
1919-1922	Jack Britton
1922-1926	Mickey Walker
1926	Pete Latzo
1927-1929	Joe Dundee
1929	Jackie Fields
1930	Jackie Fields, Jack Thompson, Tommy Freeman
1931	Freeman, Thompson, Lou Brouillard
1932	Jackie Fields
1933	Young Corbett, Jimmy McLarnin
1934	Barney Ross, Jimmy McLarnin
1935-1938	Barney Ross
1938-1940	Henry Armstrong
1940	Fritzie Zivic
1941-1946	Fred Cochrane
1946-1946	Marty Servo*; Ray Robinson (A)
1946-1950	Ray Robinson*
1951	Johnny Bratton (NBA): Kid Gavilan
1951-1954	Kid Gavilan
1954-1955	Johnny Saxton
1955	Tony De Marco, Carmen Basilio
1956	Carmen Basilio, Johnny Saxton, Carmen Basilio
1957	Carmen Basilio*
1958-1960	Virgil Akins, Don Jordan
1960	Benny Paret
1961	Emile Griffith, Benny Paret
1962	Benny Paret, Emile Griffith
1963	Luis Rodriguez, Emile Griffith
1964-1966	Emile Griffith*
1966-1969	Curtis Cokes
1969-1970	Jose Napoles, Billy Backus
1971	Jose Napoles

(A) Robinson gained the title by defeating Tommy Bell in an elimination agreed to by the NY Commission and the N.B.A. Both claimed Robinson waived his title when he won the middleweight crown from LaMotta in 1951. Gavilan defeated Bratton in an elimination to find a successor.

Lightweights

1896-1899	Kid Lavigne
1899-1902	Frank Erne
1902-1908	Joe Gans
1908-1910	Battling Nelson
1910-1912	Ad Wolgast
1912-1914	Willie Ritchie
1914-1917	Freddie Welsh
1917-1925	Benny Leonard*
1925	Jimmy Goodrich, Rocky Kansas
1926-1930	Sammy Mandell
1930	Al Singer, Tony Canzoneri
1930-1933	Tony Canzoneri
1933-1935	Barney Ross*
1935-1936	Tony Canzoneri
1936-1938	Lou Ambers
1938	Henry Armstrong
1939	Lou Ambers
1940	Lew Jenkins
1941-1943	Sammy Angott
1944	S. Angott (NBA), J. Zurita (NBA)
1945-1951	Ike Williams (NBA: later universal)
1951-1952	James Carter
1952	Lauro Salas, James Carter
1953-1954	James Carter
1954	Paddy De Marco; James Carter
1955	James Carter; Bud Smith
1956	Bud Smith, Joe Brown
1956-1962	Joe Brown
1962-1965	Carlos Ortiz
1965	Ismael Laguna
1965-1968	Carlos Ortiz
1968-1969	Teo Cruz
1969-1970	Mando Ramos
1970	Ismael Laguna
1970-1972	Ken Buchanan
1972	Roberto Duran

Featherweights

1892-1900	George Dixon (disputed)
1900-1901	Terry McGovern, Young Corbett*
1901-1912	Abe Attell
1912-1923	Johnny Kilbane
1923	Eugene Criqui, Johnny Dundee
1923-1925	Johnny Dundee*
1925-1927	Kid Kaplan*
1927-1928	Benny Bass, Tony Canzoneri
1928-1929	Andre Routis
1929-1932	Battling Battalino*
1932-1934	Tommy Paul (NBA)
1933-1936	Freddie Miller
1936-1937	Petey Sarron
1937-1938	Henry Armstrong*
1938-1940	Joey Archibald (B)
1942-1948	Willie Pep
1948-1949	Sandy Saddler
1949-1950	Willie Pep
1950-1957	Sandy Saddler*
1957-1959	Hogan (Kid) Bassey
1959-1963	Davey Moore
1963-1964	Sugar Ramos
1964-1969	Vicente Saldivar*
1969	John Famechon
1970	Vicente Saldivar
1970-1972	Kuniaki Shibata
1972	Clemente Sanchez*
1974	Ruben Olivares
1975	Alexis Arguello

(B) After Petey Scalzo knocked out Archibald (Dec. 5, 1938) in an overweight match and was refused a title bout, the NBA named Scalzo champion. The NBA title succession was: Petey Scalzo, 1938-1941: Richard Lemos, 1941: Jackie Wilson, 1941-1943: Jackie Callura, 1943: Phil Terranova, 1943-1944: Sal Bartolo, 1944-1946.

Bantamweights

1890-1892	George Dixon*
1892-1894	Vacant
1894-1899	Jimmy Barry*
1899-1900	Terry McGovern*
1901-1902	Harry Harris*
1902-1903	Harry Forbes
1903-1904	Frankie Neil
1904	Joe Bowker*,
1905-1907	Jimmy Walsh*
1907-1910	Vacant
1910-1914	Johnny Coulon
1914-1917	Kid Williams
1917-1920	Pete Herman
1920-1921	Joe Lynch
1921	Pete Herman, Johnny Buff
1922	Johnny Buff, Joe Lynch
1922-1924	Joe Lynch
1924	Abe Goldstein, Eddie Martin
1925	Eddie Martin, Charley (Phil) Rosenberg
1925-1926	Charley (Phil) Rosenberg
1927-1928	Bud Taylor* (NBA only)
1929-1935	Al Brown
1935-1936	Baltazar Sangchili
1936	Tony Marino, Sixto Escobar
1937	Sixto Escobar, Harry Jeffra
1938-1940	Sixto Escobar*
1941-1942	Lou Salica
1942-1947	Manuel Ortiz
1947	Harold Dade, Manuel Ortiz
1948-1950	Manuel Ortiz
1950-1952	Vic Toweel
1952-1954	Jimmy Carruthers*
1954-1956	Robert Cohen
1956-1957	Mario D'Agata
1957-1959	Alphonse Halimi
1959-1960	Jose Becerra*
1961-1965	Eder Jofre
1965-1968	Fighting Harada
1968-1969	Lionel Rose
1969-1970	Ruben Olivares
1970-1971	Chuchu Castillo
1971-1972	Ruben Olivares
1972	Rafael Herrera
1972-1973	Enrique Pinder
1973	Romero Anaya, Arnold Taylor
1974-1975	Soo Hawn Hong
1975	Alfonso Zamora

History of Heavyweight Championship Bouts
*Title Changed Hands

1889—July 8—John L. Sullivan beat Jake Kilrain, 75 rounds, Richburg, Miss. (Last championship bare knuckles bout.)

*1892**—Sept. 7—James J. Corbett defeated John L. Sullivan, 21 rounds, New Orleans. (Used big gloves for first time.)

1894—Jan. 25—James J. Corbett ko'd Charley Mitchell, 3 rounds, Jacksonville, Fla.

*1897**—March 17—Bob Fitzsimmons defeated James J. Corbett, 14 rounds, Carson City, Nev.

*1899**—June 9—James J. Jeffries beat Bob Fitzsimmons, 11 rounds, Coney Island, N.Y.

1899—Nov. 3—James J. Jeffries beat Tom Sharkey, 25 rounds, Coney Island, N.Y.

1900—May 11—James J. Jeffries knocked out James J. Corbett, 23 rounds, Coney Island, N.Y.

1901—Nov. 15—James J. Jeffries, ko'd Gus Ruhlin, 5 rounds, San Francisco.

1902—July 25—James J. Jeffries knocked out Bob Fitzsimmons, 8 rounds, San Francisco.

1903—Aug. 14—James J. Jeffries knocked out James J. Corbett, 10 rounds, San Francisco.

1904—Aug. 26—James J. Jeffries knocked out Jack Monroe, 2 rounds, San Francisco.

*1905**—James J. Jeffries retired, July 3—Marvin Hart knocked out Jack Root, 12 rounds, Reno. Jeffries refereed and presented the title to the victor. Jack O'Brien also claimed the title.

*1906**—Feb. 23—Tommy Burns defeated Marvin Hart, 20 rounds, Los Angeles.

1906—Nov. 28—Philadelphia Jack O'Brien and Tommy Burns, 20 rounds, draw, Los Angeles.

1907—May 8—Tommy Burns defeated Jack O'Brien, 20 rounds, Los Angeles.

1907—July 4—Tommy Burns knocked out Bill Squires, 1 round, Colma, Cal.

1907—Dec. 2—Tommy Burns knocked out Gunner Moir, 10 rounds, London.

1908—Feb. 10—Tommy Burns knocked out Jack Palmer, 4 rounds, London.

1908—March 17—Tommy Burns knocked out Jem Roche, 1 round, Dublin.

1908—April 18—Tommy Burns knocked out Jewey Smith, 5 rounds, Paris.

1908—June 13—Tommy Burns knocked out Bill Squires, 8 rounds, Paris.

1908—Aug. 24—Tommy Burns knocked out Bill Squires, 13 rounds, Sydney, New South Wales.

1908—Sept. 2—Tommy Burns knocked out Bill Lang, 2 rounds, Melbourne, Australia.

*1908**—Dec. 26—Jack Johnson stopped Tommy Burns, 14 rounds, Sydney, Australia. Police halted contest.

1909—May 19—Jack Johnson and Jack O'Brien, 6 rounds, draw, Philadelphia.

1909—June 30—Jack Johnson and Tony Ross, 6 rounds, draw, Pittsburgh, Pa.

1909—Sept. 9—Jack Johnson and Al Kaufman, 10 rounds, no decision, San Francisco.

1909—Oct. 16—Jack Johnson knocked out Stanley Ketchel, 12 rounds, Colma, Cal.

1910—July 4—Jack Johnson knocked out Jim Jeffries, 15 rounds, Reno, Nev. (Jeffries came back from retirement.)

1912—July 4—Jack Johnson won on points from Jim Flynn, 9 rounds, Las Vegas, N.M. (contest stopped by police)

1913—Nov. 28—Jack Johnson knocked out Andre Spaul, 2 rounds, Paris.

1913—Dec. 9—Jack Johnson and Jim Johnson, 10 rounds, draw, Paris. (Bout called a draw when Jack Johnson declared he had broken his arm.)

1914—June 27—Jack Johnson won from Frank Moran, 20 rounds, Paris.

*1915**—April 5—Jess Willard knocked out Jack Johnson, 26 rounds, Havana, Cuba.

1916—March 25—Jess Willard and Frank Moran, 10 rounds (no decision), New York City.

*1919**—July 4—Jack Dempsey knocked out Jess Willard, Toledo, Oh. (Willard failed to answer bell for fourth round.)

1920—Sept. 6—Jack Dempsey knocked out Billy Miske, 3 rounds, Benton Harbor, Mich.

1920—Dec. 14—Jack Dempsey knocked out Bill Brennan, 12 rounds, New York City.

1921—July 2—Jack Dempsey knocked out George Carpentier, 4 rounds, Boyle's Thirty Acres, Jersey City, N.J. (Carpentier had held the so-called white heavyweight title since July 16,-1914, in a series established in 1913, after Jack Johnson's exile in Europe late in 1912.)

1923—July 4—Jack Dempsey won on points from Tom Gibbons, 15 rounds, Shelby, Mont.

1923—Sept. 14—Jack Dempsey knocked out Luis Firpo, 2 rounds, New York City.

*1926**—Sept. 23—Gene Tunney beat Jack Dempsey, 10 rounds, decision, Philadelphia.

1927—Sept. 22—Gene Tunney beat Jack Dempsey, 10 rounds, decision, Chicago.

1928—July 26—Gene Tunney knocked out Tom Heeney, 11 rounds, Yankee Stadium, New York; soon afterward he announced his retirement.

*1930**—June 12—Max Schmeling of Germany defeated Jack Sharkey in 4th round when Sharkey fouled Schmeling in a bout which was generally considered to have resulted in the election of a successor to Gene Tunney, New York.

1931—July 3—Max Schmeling knocked out Young Stribling, 15 rounds, Cleveland.

*1932**—June 21—Jack Sharkey defeated Max Schmeling, 15 rounds, decision, New York City.

*1933**—June 29—Primo Carnera knocked out Jack Sharkey, 6th round, New York City.

1933—Oct. 22—Primo Carnera defeated Paulino Uzcudun, 15 rounds, Rome.

1934—March 1—Primo Carnera defeated Tommy Loughran in 15 rounds, Miami.

*1934**—June 14—Max Baer knocked out Primo Carnera, 11 rounds, New York City.

*1935**—June 13—James J. Braddock defeated Max Baer, 15 rounds, New York City.

*1937**—June 22—Joe Louis knocked out James J. Braddock, 8 rounds, Chicago.

1937—Aug. 30—Joe Louis defeated Tommy Farr, 15 rounds, decision, New York City.

1938—Feb. 23—Joe Louis knocked out Nathan Mann, 3 rounds, New York City.

1938—April 1—Joe Louis knocked out Harry Thomas, 5 rounds, New York City.

1938—June 22—Joe Louis knocked out Max Schmeling, one round, New York City.

1939—Jan. 25—Joe Louis knocked out John H. Lewis, 1 round, New York City.

1939—April 17—Joe Louis knocked out Jack Roper, 1 round, Los Angeles.

1939—June 28—Joe Louis knocked out Tony Galento, 4 rounds, New York City.

1939—Sept. 20—Joe Louis knocked out Bob Pastor, 11 rounds, Detroit, Mich.

1940—February 9—Joe Louis defeated Arturo Godoy, 15 rounds, decision, New York City.

1940—March 29—Joe Louis knocked out Johnny Paychek, 2 rounds, New York City.

1940—June 20—Joe Louis knocked out Arturo Godoy, 8 rounds, New York City.

1940—Dec. 16—Joe Louis knocked out Al McCoy, 6 rounds, Boston.

1941—Jan. 31—Joe Louis knocked out Red Burman, 5 rounds, New York City.

1941—Feb. 17—Joe Louis knocked out Gus Dorzaio, 2 rounds, Philadelphia.

1941—March 21—Joe Louis knocked out Abe Simon, 13 rounds, Detroit, Mich.

1941—April 8—Joe Louis knocked out Tony Musto, 9 rounds, St. Louis, Mo.

1941—May 23—Joe Louis beat Buddy Baer, 7 rounds, Washington, D. C., on a disqualification.

1941—June 18—Joe Louis knocked out Billy Conn, 13 rounds, New York City.

1941—Sept. 29—Joe Louis knocked out Lou Nova, 6 rounds, New York City.

1942—Jan. 9—Joe Louis knocked out Buddy Baer, 1 round, New York City.

1942—March 27—Joe Louis knocked out Abe Simon, 6 rounds, New York City.

1946—June 19—Joe Louis knocked out Billy Conn, 8 rounds, New York City.

1946—Sept. 18—Joe Louis knocked out Tami Mauriello, 1 round, New York City.

1947—Dec. 5—Joe Louis defeated Joe Walcott in a 15-round bout by a split decision, New York City.

1948—June 25—Joe Louis knocked out Joe Walcott, 11 rounds, New York City.

*1949**—June 22—Following Joe Louis' retirement Ezzard Charles defeated Joe Walcott by a unanimous decision, 15 rounds, Chicago, Ill. (N.B.A. recognition only).

1949—Aug. 10—Ezzard Charles knocked out Gus Lesnevich, 7 rounds. New York City.

1949—Oct. 14—Ezzard Charles knocked out Pat Valentino, 8 rounds, San Francisco (clinched American title).

1950—Aug. 15—Ezzard Charles knocked out Freddy Beshore, 14 rounds, Buffalo, N.Y.

1950—Sept. 27—Ezzard Charles defeated Joe Louis in latter's attempted comeback, 15 rounds. New York City (universal recognition).
1950—Dec. 5—Ezzard Charles knocked out Nick Barone, 11th round, Cincinnati, Ohio.
1951—Jan. 12—Ezzard Charles knocked out Lee Oma, 10th round, New York, N.Y.
1951—March 7—Ezzard Charles outpointed Joe Walcott, 15 rounds, Detroit, Mich.
1951—May 30—Ezzard Charles outpointed Joey Maxim, light heavyweight champion, 15 rounds, Chicago.
*1951—July 18—Joe Walcott knocked out Ezzard Charles, 7th round, Pittsburgh, Pa.
1952—June 5—Joe Walcott outpointed Ezzard Charles, 15 rounds, Philadelphia, Pa.
*1952—Sept. 23—Rocky Marciano knocked out Joe Walcott, 13th round, Philadelphia, Pa.
1953—May 15—Rocky Marciano knocked out Joe Walcott, first round, Chicago, Ill.
1953—Sept. 24—Rocky Marciano knocked out Roland LaStarza, 11th round, Polo Grounds, New York, N.Y.
1954—June 17—Rocky Marciano outpointed Ezzard Charles, 15 rounds, Yankee Stadium, New York, N.Y.
1954—Sept. 17—Rocky Marciano knocked out Ezzard Charles, 8th round, Yankee Stadium, New York, N.Y.
1955—May 16—Rocky Marciano knocked out Don Cockell, 9th round, Kezar Stadium, San Francisco.
1955—Sept. 21—Rocky Marciano knocked out Archie Moore, 9th round, Yankee Stadium, N.Y. Marciano retired undefeated, Apr. 27, 1956.
*1956—Nov. 30—Floyd Patterson knocked out Archie Moore, 5th round, Chicago, Ill.
1957—July 29—Floyd Patterson knocked out Hurricane Jackson, 10th round, Polo Grounds, New York, N.Y.
1957—Aug. 22—Floyd Patterson knocked out Pete Rademacher, 6th round, Seattle, Wash.
1958—Aug. 18—Floyd Patterson knocked out Roy Harris, 12th round, Los Angeles.
1959—May 1—Floyd Patterson knocked out Brian London, 11th round, Indianapolis, Ind.
*1959—June 26—Ingemar Johansson, Sweden, knocked out Floyd Patterson, 3rd round, Yankee Stadium, New York City.
*1960—June 20—Floyd Patterson knocked out Ingemar Johansson, 5th round, Polo Grounds, New York, N.Y. (First heavyweight in boxing history to regain title.)
1961—Mar. 13—Floyd Patterson knocked out Ingemar Johansson, 6th round, Convention Hall, Miami Beach, Fla.
1961—Dec. 4—Floyd Patterson knocked out Tom McNeeley, 4th round, Toronto, Ont. Canada.
*1962—Sept. 25—Sonny Liston knocked out Floyd Patterson, first round, Comiskey Park, Chicago, Ill.

1963—July. 22—Sonny Liston knocked out Floyd Patterson, first round, Las Vegas, Nevada.
*1964—Feb. 25—Cassius Clay knocked out Sonny Liston, 7th round, Miami Beach, Fla.
1965—May 25—Cassius Clay knocked out Sonny Liston, first round, Lewiston, Maine.
1965—Nov. 11—Cassius Clay knocked out Floyd Patterson, 12th round, Las Vegas, Nev.
1966—Mar. 29—Cassius Clay outpointed George Chuvalo, 15 rounds, Toronto, Ont.
1966—May 21—Cassius Clay knocked out Henry Cooper, 6th round, London, Eng.
1966—Aug. 6—Cassius Clay knocked out Brian London, 3rd round, London, Eng.
1966—Sept. 10—Cassius Clay knocked out Karl Mildenberger, 12th round, Frankfurt, Germany.
1966—Nov. 14—Cassius Clay knocked out Cleveland Williams, 3rd round, Houston, Tex.
1967—Feb. 6—Cassius Clay outpointed Ernie Terrell, 15 rounds, Houston, Tex.
1967—Mar. 22—Cassius Clay knocked out Zora Folley, 7th round, New York. Clay was stripped of his title by the WBA and others for refusing military service.
*1970—Feb. 16—Joe Frazier knocked out Jimmy Ellis, 5th round, New York.
1970—Nov. 18—Joe Frazier knocked out Bob Foster, 2nd round, Detroit.
1971—Mar. 8—Joe Frazier outpointed Cassius Clay (Muhammad Ali), 15 rounds, New York, N.Y.
1972—Jan. 15—Joe Frazier knocked out Terry Daniels, fourth round, New Orleans.
1972—May 25—Joe Frazier knocked out Ron Stander, fifth round, Omaha.
*1973—Jan. 22—George Foreman knocked out Joe Frazier, 2nd round, Kingston, Jamaica.
1973—Sept. 1—George Foreman knocked out Joe Roman, first round, Tokyo.
1974—Mar. 3—George Foreman knocked out Ken Norton, 2nd round, Caracas.
*1974—Oct. 30—Muhammad Ali knocked out George Foreman, 8th round, Zaire.
1975—Mar. 24.—Muhammad Ali knocked out Chuck Wepner, 15th round, Cleveland.
1975—May 16—Muhammad Ali knocked out Ron Lyle, 11th round, Las Vegas.
1975—June 30—Muhammad Ali outpointed Joe Bugner, 15 rounds, Malaysia.
1975—Oct. 1—Muhammad Ali knocked out Joe Frazier, 14th round, Manila.

Other Notable Professional Boxing Bouts
Oct., 1974 — Sept., 1975
1974

Date	Winner	Loser	Result	Site
Nov. 12	Oscar Bonavena	Mani Vaka	KO-5	Honolulu
Nov. 22	Vito Aufuofermo	Emile Griffith	D-10	New York
Nov. 28	Guts Ishimatsu	Rodolfo Gonzalez	KO-12	Osaka, Japan
Nov. 30	Rodrigo Valdes	Gratien Tonna	KQ-11	Paris
Dec. 28	Soo Hwan Hong	Fernando Cabanela	D-15	Seoul, S. Korea

1975

Date	Winner	Loser	Result	Site
Jan. 7	Jose Duran	Franz Csandl	D-15	Vienna
Jan. 8	Miguel Canto	Shoji Oguma	D-15	Japan
Jan. 13	Bunny Johnson	Danny McAlinden	KO-9	London
Feb. 11	Jimmy Young	Ron Lyle	D-10	Honolulu
Feb. 27	Guts Ishimatsu	Ken Buchanan	D-15	Tokyo
Mar. 2	Joe Frazier	Jimmy Ellis	KO-9	Melbourne
Mar. 2	Roberto Duran	Ray Lampkin	KO-14	Panama City
Mar. 11	John Conteh	Lonnie Bennett	KO-15	London
Mar. 15	Alfonso Zamora	Soo Hwan Hong	KO-4	Inglewood, Cal.
Mar. 24	Ken Norton	Jerry Quarry	KO-5	New York
Mar. 27	Kuniaki Shibata	Ould Makhloufi	D-15	Japan
Apri. 1	Erbito Salavarria	Susumu Hanagata	D-15	Japan
Apr. 7	Victor Galindez	Pierre Fourie	D-15	South Africa
May 7	Miguel de Oliviera	Jose Duran	D-15	Monte Carlo
May 17	Antonio Cervantes	Esteban de Jesus	D-15	Panama City
May 26	Miguel Canto	Betulio Gonzalez	D-15	Mexico
June 1	Rodolfo Martinez	Baba Jimenez	KO-7	Colombia
June 21	Ruben Olivares	Bobby Chacon	KO-2	Inglewood, Cal.
June 30	Victor Galindez	Jorge Ahumada	D-15	New York
June 30	Carlos Monzon	Tony Licata	KO-10	New York
July 5	Alfredo Escalera	Kuniaki Shibata	KO-2	Japan
July 25	Ken Buchanan	Giancarlo Usia	KO-12	Sardinia
July 25	Pedro Soto	Mike Quarry	D-10	Las Vegas
Aug. 11	John Conteh	Willie Taylor	D-10	Scranton, Pa.
Aug. 31	Alfonso Zamora	Thanomjit Sukhothai	KO-4	Anaheim, Cal.
Sept. 13	Victor Galindez	Pierre Fourie	D-15	So. Africa

CHRONOLOGY OF YEAR'S EVENTS

Reported Month By Month in 3 Categories: National, International, and General

—Nov. 1, 1974, to Nov. 1, 1975

NOVEMBER 1974
National

Economy Declines, Ford Faces Recession — Economic indicators continued to paint a bleak picture in November. Department of Labor statistics, released Nov. 1, revealed unemployment had risen to 6% of the work force, the highest level in 3 years. The Federal Reserve Board reported, Nov. 15, industrial output had declined 0.6%. Pres. Gerald R. Ford, who had reserved top priority for fighting inflation, in a turnabout, Nov. 28, said concern about recession required the same top priority.

"Bombshell" Document Revealed at Watergate Trial — James F. Neal, the chief prosecutor in the Watergate cover-up trial, Nov. 4, disclosed the existence of a November 1972 memorandum written by E Howard Hunt to remind Nixon White House officials and re-election campaign managers of their commitments of money and pardons to the defendants in the Watergate break-in case in return for their silence. In testimony on Oct. 29, Hunt had asserted he had prepared the document for his attorney William O. Bittman to turn over to Kenneth W. Parkinson, an attorney for the re-election committee. Bittman, who had originally denied the memo existed, then recanted and turned a copy over to the prosecution. In other developments, the prosecution, Nov. 18-20, played a series of White House tapes backing their contention that the 5 defendants, former Pres. Richard M. Nixon, and others tried to conceal the facts of the break-in through various means including offers of clemency and hush money. On a January 1973 tape of a Nixon conversation with Charles W. Colson, played Nov. 18, the jury heard Nixon assent to a plan to give clemency to E. Howard Hunt. On Nov. 19, the jurors heard Nixon, via an April 1973 tape, tell his aides he would give full pardons to various Watergate participants before he left the presidency. In another April 1973 tape, played Nov. 20, Nixon directed former aide John D. Ehrlichman to have aides put out a line stating they had in fact raised funds for the 7 original defendants, but with the purpose of keeping them from talking to the press rather than to withhold the truth from authorities. Following 29 days of testimony, including 28 witnesses, 29 White House tapes and 2 other tapes, the prosecution, Nov. 25, rested its case. On Nov. 26, former Attorney General John N. Mitchell took the stand in his own defense and consistently denied any connection with the decision to pay hush money to the original 7 Watergate defendants.

Calley Released — Army Secretary Howard H. Callaway, Nov. 8, announced former Lt. William L. Calley Jr. would be paroled Nov. 19 after serving one-third of his 10-year prison term. Calley had been convicted of murdering 22 South Vietnamese civilians at Mylai in 1968. The announcement came a few hours after a U.S. Court of Appeals decision in New Orleans, La., that Calley should be freed promptly on bail. On Nov. 9, in Columbus, Ga., U.S. District Court Judge J. Robert Elliott, who earlier had overturned Calley's original conviction, ordered Calley freed immediately on a personal recognizance bond of $1,000. The army said it would continue to appeal the decision overturning Calley's original conviction.

Ex-Nixon Attorney Pleads Guilty — Former White House attorney Edward L. Morgan pleaded guilty, Nov. 8, in Washington, D.C., to participating in a criminal conspiracy to create a $576,000 tax deduction for former Pres. Richard M. Nixon. Morgan admitted that he had knowingly backdated documents confirming the gift of Nixon's pre-presidential papers to the government. The false dates made it appear that the papers had been given before Congress repealed the law granting deductions for such gifts.

Gibson Out, Zarb In — Pres. Gerald R. Ford, Nov. 12, withdrew his nomination of Andrew E. Gibson as Federal Energy Administrator after learning that Gibson had a 10-year employment separation contract with a petroleum-industry company. On Nov. 25, Ford named Frank G. Zarb, a 39-year-old Wall Street management expert, to the post. Already shaping energy policy for the administration, Zarb would remain executive director of the Energy Resources Council. The Senate, Dec. 11, confirmed the nomination.

Rockefeller Hearings Continue — Facing television cameras and the Senate Rules Committee, Nelson A. Rockefeller, Nov. 13, in hearings on his nomination as vice president, called his involvement with a derogatory biography of Arthur J. Goldberg the most embarrassing episode of his political career but denied the involvement was comparable to the "dirty tricks" associated with the Watergate scandals. Rockefeller also insisted the prevailing motives behind his generous financial gifts to friends and associates were affection, respect, and their compelling needs. Rockefeller, Nov. 14, pledged he would make no gifts or loans to federal employees if he were confirmed as vice president with the exception of nominal birthday or wedding gifts or "in the event of medical hardships of a compelling human character." On Nov. 18, New York and New Jersey Port Authority Chairman Dr. William J. Ronan told the Senate committee there had been no "sinister purpose" behind the $625,000 in gifts he had received from Rockefeller. The rules committee, Nov. 22, voted, 9-0, to recommend confirmation of Rockefeller to the full Senate. In other developments, facing questioning by the House Judiciary Committee, Rockefeller, Nov. 21, said he would place all his financial holdings in a blind trust if confirmed as vice president.

U.S. Sues AT&T — The U.S. government, Nov. 20, in U.S. District Court in Washington, D.C., filed an anti-trust suit against the American Telephone and Telegraph Company charging the world's largest privately-owned company with illegally monopolizing the telecommunications business. The government contended that AT&T, along with the Western Electric Co., Bell Laboratories, and 23 Bell System companies conspired to prevent other telecommunications businesses from interconnecting with the Bell System. The government's suit sought to force AT&T to divest itself of the Western Electric Co., a wholly-owned subsidiary which manufactures telecommunications equipment for the Bell System. Western Electric would be divided into 2 or more competing firms, if necessary, to assure competition in the manufacture and sale of telecommunications equipment. The suit also sought to require AT&T either to get out of most of its long-distance business or divest itself of some of its 23 local companies. "Astonished" at the suit, AT&T chairman John D. deButts said the divestitures "could lead to fragmentation of responsibility for the nation's telephone network." "If that happens," deButts said, "telephone service would deteriorate and cost much, much more."

Udall Enters '76 Race — Rep. Morris K. Udall (D. Ariz.), 52, Nov. 23, announced, in Manchester, N.H., that he would enter the 1976 presidential primaries in New Hampshire and Vermont. With the announcement, coming 2 days after Sen. Walter F. Mondale (D. Minn.) had withdrawn from the race, Udall became the first Democrat to announce officially his candidacy. "The three E's — environment, economy, energy," Udall said, would dominate his campaign.

Panel Reports on Nixon's Health — A panel of 3 doctors appointed at the request of U.S. District Court Judge John J. Sirica reported, Nov. 29, that former Pres. Richard M. Nixon would not be physically able to testify before the Watergate cover-up trial or give a written deposition from his home until Jan. 6 or later. Following a 3-week hospitalization during which he underwent surgery for a phlebitis condition and passed through a critical condition from vascular shock, Nixon, Nov. 14, left Memorial Medical Center in Long Beach, Cal., in a wheelchair.

International

Violence in Angola, Coalition Delayed — Rioting and shooting in Luanda, Angola, and surrounding suburbs, Nov. 5-10, left as many as 100 persons dead and 200 injured. Much of the violence, centered in the vast African slum suburbs of the city, was believed to be sparked by a faction of the Popular Movement for the Liberation of Angola (MPLA). Calm was restored by the evening of Nov. 11, as police, soldiers and armed members of the National Front for the Liberation of Angola (FNLA), the largest of the 3 liberation movements in Angola, patrolled the streets. It was announced, Nov. 12, that Portuguese negotiators had temporarily shelved a plan for an interim coalition government which would include the former guerrillas. The decision was blamed on the refusal of the MPLA to participate unless allotted 60-70% of the government posts. Instead of the proposed coalition, the negotiators decided to set up a commission of liberation groups which would advise the Portuguese government and the present colonial administration in Angola.

World Food Conference Meets — The World Food Conference, which had convened in Rome, Italy, Nov. 5, adjourned Nov. 16, having approved a general program to "end the scourge of hunger and malnutrition." The body's negotiating group, representing 130 nations, approved, Nov. 16, the establishment of a new United Nations agency to be called the World Food Council which would supervise programs to give the world, particularly the less developed nations, more and better food. The conference, however, did not take direct action to provide immediate food aid to the world's millions facing starvation. Nevertheless, the chief U.S. delegate, Edwin M. Martin, praised the results of the conference which, he said, "was not called to get food to people tomorrow but to lay a plan of action to prevent the crisis that we now have from recurring." The conference also approved several programs for the proposed council to oversee, including an agricultural development fund, a fertilizer-aid program, a nutrition-aid program, and an irrigation, drainage and flood control program to aid developing countries. In earlier develop-

ments, the conference promised to create an internationally-coordinated system of nationally held grain reserves, a 10-million-ton-per-year food aid program, and an early-warning data dissemination system for information crucial to the world food supply.

UN Suspends South Africa — In an unprecedented move, the United Nations General Assembly, Nov. 12, voted, 91-22 with 19 abstentions including the United States and United Kingdom, to suspend South Africa from the current Assembly session. The move did not exclude South Africa from actual membership in the UN, but would deprive the South African delegation of its right to take its seats, speak, make proposals or vote. The South African government, Nov. 13, recalled its chief delegate, Roelf F. Both, for consultations.

Arafat Addresses UN, PLO Granted Observer Status — Palestine Liberation Organization leader Yasir Arafat, Nov. 13, addressed the United Nations General Assembly and called for "one democratic state where Christian, Jew, and Moslem live in justice, equality, and fraternity" in the Middle East. In his speech opening the General Assembly debate on the Palestine question, Arafat concluded, "I have come bearing an olive branch and a freedom fighter's gun. Do not let the olive branch fall from my hands." In rebuttal, Israeli delegate Yosef Tekoah vowed his country would continue implacably to fight the terroristic, murderous Palestinian guerrillas. Arafat was the first person not representing a government to address the General Assembly since Pope Paul V. in 1965. At the end of the 9-day debate in which each member nation was limited to one major speech, the General Assembly adopted 2 resolutions supporting the Palestinian cause. The body, Nov. 22, voted, 89-8 with 37 abstentions including the U.S. and Israel, that the Palestinian people are entitled to self-determination and to national independence and sovereignty. The resolution also affirmed the "inalienable right of the Palestinians to return to their homes from which they have been displaced and uprooted." In a 2d resolution, the General Assembly granted, 95-17 with 19 abstentions, permanent observer status in the assembly to the PLO. Tekoah stated that by its action the UN "has plunged itself into an abyss from which there is no exit" and decried the Palestinian debate as "a Sodom and Gomorrah of ideals and values."

War Scare Tenses Middle East — Israel mobilized part of its armed forces reserves, Nov. 14, and shifted troops to the Syrian and Lebanese borders, creating a threat of renewed war in the Middle East. Israeli Foreign Minister Shimon Peres, Nov. 16, attributed the partial mobilization to "unexplained movements" by Syrian forces near the Golan Heights. The war scare subsided, Nov. 17, after the U.S. delivered to Israel assurances that Syria had no intention of attacking Israel.

Caramanlis Overwhelms Greek Elections — Premier Constantine Caramanlis and his New Democracy Party, Nov. 17, swept the first free election held in Greece since 1964. Final results showed the New Democracy Party won 54.37% of the popular vote and 220 of the 300 total seats in the parliament. During the campaign, Caramanlis had appealed to Greek voters to give his party a clear mandate to complete the "mission" it had started 4 months previously. On Nov. 18, Caramanlis said he would focus on the "extremely crucial" problems of the future of Cyprus and reforming the Greek political system. Former Foreign Minister George Mavros' Center Union-New Political Forces party was 2d in the vote

with the 20.42% and 60 seats in the parliament. Andreas Papandreous' Pan-Hellenic Socialist Movement
showed a poor 3d with 13.58% of the vote and 12 seats
in parliament.

Arab Guerrillas Kill 4 Israelis — In a predawn raid,
3 Arab terrorists, **Nov. 19**, attacked an apartment
block in Beit Shean, Israel, and killed 4 Israelis before being shot in a gunfight with Israeli soldiers.
Another 19 Israelis were injured in the attack. Following the gunfight, a mob of angry Israelis, scream-
ing "Burn Arafat! Burn Arafat!", seized the bodies of
the dead terrorists and threw them on a bonfire. By
mistake the mob also burned the body of one of the
slain Israelis. A Palestinian guerrilla official in
Damascus, Syria, claimed his organization, the Popular Democratic Front for the Liberation of Palestine,
was responsible for the raid and asserted such raids
would continue until Israel agreed to negotiate with
the PLO. The communique tied the raid to demonstrations, **Nov. 16-19**, staged on the West Bank of the
Jordan to mark "the great Palestinian victory at the
UN."

Arms Pact Highlights Ford's Asian Trip — Meeting
at a health spa on the outskirts of Vladivostok, USSR,
U.S. Pres. Gerald R. Ford and Soviet Communist
Party leader Leonid I. Brezhnev, **Nov. 24**, reached a
tentative agreement, subject to negotiation on technical questions in 1975 at Geneva, to limit the numbers of all offensive strategic and delivery vehicles
through 1985. The actual figures were not disclosed
officially until a **Dec. 2** news conference at which
Ford announced the tentative agreement put a ceiling of 2,400 on the total number of ICBMs,
submarine-launched missiles and bombers for each
country. According to the agreement, only 1,320
could be armed with multiple warheads (MIRVs). Before meeting in Vladivostok with Brezhnev, Ford,
Nov. 18-22, visited Japan for what was largely a goodwill ceremonial visit. Ford next stopped for a one-day
visit in Seoul, South Korea, to affirm American-South
Korean "friendship and to give it new life and meaning." Opponents of South Korean Pres. Park Chung
Hee criticized the visit as a sign of American approval of Park's allegedly dictatorial and repressive
policies.

British Plane Hijacked — Four Palestinian guerrillas who hijacked a British Airways jetliner in Dubai,
Nov. 22, finally surrendered, **Nov. 25**, in Tunis, Tunisia, after receiving a promise of asylum from the
Tunisian government. However, after the surrender,
Tunisian Foreign Minister Habib Chatti denied any
binding agreement, stating his government had ver-
bally agreed to the hijackers' demand that they not
be turned over to the PLO. After the hijacking, the
gunmen, members of a Palestinian splinter group
opposing PLO leader Yasir Arafat, had forced the
plane, with 47 persons aboard, to fly to Tunis. They
threatened to kill the hostages unless the Egyptian
government freed 13 Palestinian terrorists imprisoned in Cairo, 8 convicted of the Mar. 1973 slayings
of 3 diplomats in Sudan and 5 charged with the Dec.
1973 attack on the Rome airport. After initial refusal,
Egypt, **Nov. 23**, agreed to release the 5 terrorists involved in the Rome airport attack. Two Palestinian
guerrillas held in the Netherlands, who had been
added to the terrorists' list, were also released. The
guerrillas, **Nov. 23**, released some of the hostages
and, **Nov. 25**, released the remainder, but threatened
to blow up the plane, themselves, the 3 crewmem-
bers, and the 7 released terrorists unless they were
granted asylum by the Tunisian government.

Japanese Premier Resigns — Japanese Premier
Kakuei Tanaka, **Nov. 26**, officially told leaders of his
Liberal-Democratic party that he would resign, but
would remain in office until the party had picked a
successor. The resignation came in the wake of allegations Tanaka had used his political office to enlarge
his personal fortune and after Tanaka made the poor-
est showing of any postwar premier in popularity
polls. "As a public figure," Tanaka stated, "I am solely to blame for the fact that my personal affairs
invited the people's misunderstanding, and I feel
pain that I cannot bear." Since Tanaka had taken office in 1972 with promises of decision and action,
Japan had faced a succession of economic problems
from inflation, recession, and layoffs to declining
profits.

IRA Outlawed — The British House of Commons,
Nov. 29, approved a government bill for 6-month
emergency legislation to outlaw the IRA and to give
the police sweeping powers of arrest and detention
and stricter control over travel between England and
Ireland. British Home Secretary Roy Jenkins had
outlined the provisions, **Nov. 25**, following bombings
at 2 bars in Birmingham that killed 21 persons and injured some 200 others. Under the new legislation,
which Jenkins called "unprecedented in peacetime,"
the government would also have the power to declare
other terrorist organizations illegal and could jail for
up to 5 years or longer all members and supporters,
"financial and otherwise," of such organizations.
Under the new law, police would be able to arrest
suspected terrorists without warrant and hold them
without charge for up to 7 days.

General

Kent State Guardsmen Acquitted — U.S. District
Court Judge Frank J. Battisti, **Nov. 8**, in Cleveland,
Oh., acquitted 8 former Ohio National Guardsmen of
charges arising from the 1970 Kent State University
slayings of 4 students. In response to a defense motion for dismissal on basis of insufficient evidence,
Battisti ruled the prosecution had not proved "beyond a reasonable doubt" that the guardsmen had
willfully deprived the students of their civil rights.
He added, however, "It is vital that state and National Guard officials not regard this decision as authorizing or approving the use of force against
demonstrators, whatever the occasion or the issue
involved."

Alpert Surrenders — Ending 4 years in hiding,
Jane L. Alpert, **Nov. 14**, surrendered to federal authorities in New York City. In 1970, after pleading
guilty to a series of 1969 bombings in New York City,
Alpert had jumped bail and disappeared before sentencing. Alpert was sentenced, **Jan. 13, 1975**, to 27
months in prison for her part in the 1969 terrorist
bombings.

Barnard Implants 2d Heart — In a 5-hour operation at Groote-Schuur Hospital in Capetown, S. Africa, Dr. Christiaan Barnard, **Nov. 25**, placed a 2d heart
into the chest of 58-year-old Ivan Taylor to ease the
burden on the patient's diseased heart. The new
heart, used in the first implant without the removal
of the original heart, came from a 10-year-old killed
in an accident **Nov. 24**. Barnard, after removing one-
third of the diseased left ventricle, attached the new
heart at the left ventricle. He then cut holes slightly
larger than a silver dollar into the heart tissue and attached the atria and aorta of both hearts at those
points. On **Jan. 1, 1975**, another implantation of a 2d
heart by Dr. Barnard was reported. Both Taylor and
the 2d recipient, Leonard Goss, 47, were reported in
good condition **Jan. 3**. However, on **Apr. 13**, Taylor
died. No reason for the death was given.

Disasters — A fire laid to a careless smoker, **Nov. 3,** destroyed the 6th floor of a downtown Seoul, S. Korea, hotel, killing 88 persons, most of them inside the hotel's discotheque . . . Some 80 persons were feared dead following the **Nov. 3** collision between 2 passenger trains about 43 miles west of Cotonou, Dahomey . . . A West German jumbo jet crashed and burned shortly after take-off, **Nov. 20,** from Nairobi, Kenya, killing 59 persons . . . The Nepal Foreign Ministry, **Nov. 26,** reported 142 persons feared drowned following the collapse of a suspension bridge on the India-Nepal border.

DECEMBER 1974

National

House Dems Push Reforms, Mills Resigns — Over a period of 4 days, Democrats in the House of Representatives, **Dec. 2-5,** enacted major reforms in the system of committee assignments. The House Democratic caucus, **Dec. 2,** divested the Democrats on the Ways and Means Committee and its chairman Wilbur D. Mills of authority to name representatives to other committees. The secret caucus voted to turn over the responsibility for assignments to the Steering and Policy Committee. That power, held by the Ways and Means Committee since 1911, had been the major source of Mills' extraordinary influence in the House. Mills, the sudden subject of derision because of his relationship with strip tease dancer Fanne Fox, **Dec. 3,** entered Bethesda Naval Medical Center, pleading exhaustion. Earlier in the day, House Democrats had voted to increase from 25 to 37 the number of seats on the Ways and Means Committee and begun steps to remove Mills from its chairmanship. The committee leadership was temporarily placed in the hands of its 2d-ranking Democrat, Oregon Rep. Al Ullman. In further action, the Democratic caucus voted, **Dec. 4,** to bar chairmen of major committees from serving simultaneously as chairmen of other major committees including standing, select, and joint House-Senate committees. On **Dec. 10,** Mills resigned his leadership of the Ways and Means Committee. On **Dec. 30,** Mills publicly attributed his recent erratic behavior to alcoholism and pledged total abstinence. Mills said he would retain his seat in the House.

New Coal Pact Reached — Following its ratification by 56% of union members, United Mine Workers Pres. Arnold R. Miller, **Dec. 5,** signed a 3-year labor contract with the coal industry. The signing officially ended a 24-day strike by mine workers. The contract, the first subject to rank-and-file ratification, provided for a basic wage increase totaling 18% by the end of 3 years, as well as a complicated cost-of-living escalator provision. Also included were gains in pensions and medical benefits and new mine safety strictures.

Democrats Approve Charter — In the first non-presidential party convention in U.S. history, some 2,000 Democrats met, **Dec. 6-8,** in Kansas City, Mo., and **Dec. 7,** adopted a charter, the first in American political history. Unanimous approval of the charter, which will go into effect in 1980, followed a compromise to avert a walkout by minority delegates. In the compromise, the charter was amended to require affirmative action "in all party affairs" to involve women, blacks, Indians, and young voters "as indicated by their presence in the Democratic electorate." On **Dec. 6,** the convention approved a program of "economic recovery" as an alternative to the "callous economic nonsense" offered by the Ford administration. The Democrats' program called for an across-the-board system of economic controls, a jobs program, tax reform, and mandatory energy conservation measures.

Economy Falls Further — Pres. Gerald R. Ford, **Dec. 11,** speaking at the Business Council in New York City, conceded the U.S. "economy is in difficult straits" and said the administration would shift its focus from fighting inflation to deal with the new threat of recession. Ford, however, said he did not intend to introduce any "quick fixes," such as wage and price controls. Ford maintained that due to rapidly changing economic conditions, economic policies would have to be flexible to deal with new developments. To help ease pressure on the nation's 6 million unemployed, the Congress, **Dec. 18,** passed legislation appropriating $1 billion for new jobs in 1975. The measure was part of a $5-billion appropriations bill which also allocated $2 billion plus for increased unemployment compensation, and $875 million for states and communities to create public service jobs for the unemployed.

Carter Seeks Presidency — Georgia Gov. Jimmy Carter, a Democrat, **Dec. 12,** announced that he would seek the presidency in 1976. Carter said he would enter all state primaries and seek delegates in nonprimary states.

Administration in Transition — Attorney General William B. Saxbe, **Dec. 13,** resigned to take the post of U.S. ambassador to India, replacing Daniel P. Moynihan. Office of Management and Budget Director Roy L. Ash, **Dec. 17,** said he would leave his office in early 1975 after he completed work on the budget. A 3d Nixon administration appointee, Transportation Secretary Claude S. Brinegar, **Dec. 18,** , tendered his resignation effective Feb. 1, 1975.

U.S. Steel Cuts Back Price Hike — One day after the U.S. Steel Corporation announced price rises ranging from 8 to 10% for 2/3's of its product line, Pres. Ford, **Dec. 17,** ordered the corporation to justify the increases immediately to the Council on Wage and Price Stability. In a surprise move, U.S. Steel, **Dec. 23,** reduced price hikes approximately 20%, bringing increases down to 7 to 8%.

Rockefeller Assumes Vice Presidency — Nelson Aldrich Rockefeller, **Dec. 19,** was sworn in as the 41st vice president of the United States, becoming the 2d man to assume the office without a public vote. Rockefeller was sworn in on a family Bible by Chief Justice Warren E. Burger shortly after the House of Representatives approved his nomination, 287-128. The Senate, **Dec. 10,** had approved the nomination in a 90-7 vote. The ceremony culminated 4 months of intensive hearings by the Senate Rules Committee and House Judiciary Committee on Rockefeller's past political record and substantial family wealth. In remarks following the swearing-in, Rockefeller said, "I feel a great sense of gratitude for the privilege of serving the country I love." He ended on an optimistic note, stating that although the U.S. faced "tremendous difficulties and unprecedented problems both at home and abroad, there is nothing wrong with America that Americans cannot right." White House spokesman Ron Nessen, **Dec. 22,** announced that Pres. Ford had appointed the new vice president to serve as vice chairman of the Domestic Council and that he expected Rockefeller to play a major role in "explaining" the president's domestic and foreign programs "throughout the country." Rockefeller, Nessen added, would also serve as vice chairman of the National Security Council, serve on the Murphy Commission which analyzes American foreign policy, and play a role in planning the 1976 bicentennial.

Trade Bill Passed — The Senate, 72-4, and the House of Representatives, 323-36, **Dec. 20,** approved comprehensive foreign trade bill. Passage came despite disavowal by Tass, the official Soviet press agency, **Dec. 18,** of specific assurances that conditions or emigration of Soviet citizens would be eased in exchange for U.S. trade concessions and credits, a provision attached to the trade bill. The compromise on concessions had been set forth in a series of letters revealed in October by Sen. Henry M. Jackson. Tass Director Leonid M. Zamyatin, **Dec. 28,** charged that the U.S. had violated a 1972 trade agreement linking trade concessions to freer emigration and warned the USSR might re-examine its economic obligations toward the U.S.

CIA Abuse Alleged — The New York Times reported, **Dec. 21,** that, according to well-placed overnment sources, the Central Intelligence Agency had operated in violation of its charter under the Nixon administration by conducting massive, illegal domestic operations aimed at the anti-war movement and other dissident groups. According to the Times, a special CIA unit had kept files on at least 10,000 American citizens and had reported directly to then CIA director Richard Helms, now serving as ambassador to Iran. The Times further revealed that a check ordered by James Schlesinger, then CIA direc-

tor, in 1973 had found evidence that beginning in the 1950s the CIA had conducted illegal break-ins, wire-tapping, and surreptitious inspection of mail as part of operations focused at suspected foreign intelligence agents operating in the U.S. Pres. Gerald R. Ford, **Dec. 22,** announced that he had told the CIA he would not tolerate activity violating the agency's charter. He added that William E. Colby, currently director of the CIA, had assured him no comparable activity was now underway. Sen. William Proxmire (D-Wis.) demanded that Helms resign and said he would demand that the Justice Department investigate allegations of illegal spying by the CIA. Congressional committees which oversee the CIA, **Dec. 23,** said they would hold hearings on the allegations when the new Congress convened in January. On **Dec. 24,** CIA Counterintelligence Chief James Angleton, who had publicly been linked to the alleged spying, announced his resignation and said some of the allegations published by the New York Times were true. However, on **Dec. 24,** Helms denied that the CIA had conducted illegal spying under his leadership. On **Dec. 29,** 3 other high-ranking CIA officials announced that they would resign at the end of the year. The New York Times, **Dec. 30,** reported that Watergate burglar E. Howard Hunt had told Senate investigators in Dec. 1973 that he had served as the first head of the CIA's Domestic Operations Division

Mitchell, Haldeman, Ehrlichman, and Mardian
Guilty of All Charges in Watergate Cover-up

After 15 hours of deliberation, a jury of 9 women and 3 men, in U.S. District Court in Washington, D.C., **Jan. 1,** found John N. Mitchell, H.R. Haldeman, John D. Ehrlichman, and Robert C. Mardian guilty of all charges in connection with the cover-up of the June 17, 1972 break-in at the Democratic National Committee Headquarters in the Watergate complex. A fifth defendant, Kenneth W. Parkinson, was acquitted.

The verdict of guilty was read 14 times in the quiet, tense courtroom: former Attorney General John N. Mitchell, guilty of conspiracy, obstruction of justice, and 3 counts of perjury; former presidential adviser H.R. Haldeman, guilty of conspiracy, obstruction of justice, and 3 counts of perjury; former presidential domestic adviser John D. Ehrlichman, guilty of conspiracy, obstruction of justice, and 2 counts of perjury; Robert C. Mardian, an attorney for the Nixon reelection committee, guilty of conspiracy to obstruct justice. All 4 stated they would appeal the verdict.

Parkinson, who had been hired by the reelection committee to represent it in a civil suit brought by the Democrats over the original break-in, was found not guilty of conspiracy to obstruct justice. Parkinson, who called the decision a "new lease on life," had contended that he had been deceived by Mitchell and had never met some of the defendants until the trial started.

Former Pres. Richard M. Nixon, named as an unindicted co-conspirator in the cover-up indictment and a central figure in the 64-day trial, never appeared in the courtroom nor was he required to give written testimony. Judge John J. Sirica, **Dec. 5,** had ruled that for reasons of health Nixon need not testify either on the stand or through a deposition. Sirica had also questioned the value of such testimony considering Nixon was an unindicted co-conspirator in the case. However, through the testimony of others and White House tapes played during the trial, Nixon dominated the proceedings. The tapes established Nixon had played a major role in the cover-up and had approved

clemency for the Watergate burglars in return for silence.

All of the defendants took the stand in their own defense and each attempted to establish their noninvolvement in the cover-up.

Mitchell, taking the stand **Nov. 26, 27 and 29,** maintained that on 3 occasions he had rejected G. Gordon Liddy's break-in schemes. Mitchell argued that when he had learned of the break-in, he had withheld information from the FBI and grand jury because of his paramount concern not to injure Nixon's reelection chances.

Haldeman, in his testimony **Nov. 29, Dec. 2-5,** argued that much of the discussion on White House tapes was open to different interpretations. He maintained that when he had been told at a White House meeting that E. Howard Hunt had been taken care of, he had not understood what the statement meant. On cross-examination, **Dec. 4,** assistant special prosecutor Richard Ben-Veniste introduced 2 previously undisclosed transcripts of Apr. 1973 White House conversations which he contended showed Nixon had offered Haldeman and Ehrlichman $300,000 and $200,000, respectively, in the "context" that the 3 men "all understood they were protecting each other." Haldeman responded that both he and Ehrlichman had rejected the offer which had actually been made to meet their impending legal fees.

Ehrlichman, in often tearful testimony **Dec. 9-12,** argued that he had known "pitifully little about Watergate" until 9 months after the cover-up began. He pleaded that he had been manipulated and deceived by Nixon "in at least four major instances."

Mardian took the stand **Dec. 13, 16,** and **17** and argued his involvement in the affair was the result of his job as attorney for the reelection committee to deal with Watergate-related matters. However, Mardian maintained he had no part in fabricating the cover-up or paying of hush money.

At the trial's end, Judge Sirica released the 4 convicted defendants on personal bond pending sentencing.

when it was established in 1962. The Times further reported, **Dec. 31**, that Colby had confirmed allegations of illegal CIA spying in a report to Pres. Ford.

Strip Mining Bill Vetoed — Pres. Gerald R. Ford, **Dec. 30**, exercised a pocket veto on the strip mining bill, asserting that it would hurt domestic coal production "when the nation can ill afford significant losses from this critical energy source." The product of many months of debate on Capital Hill, the bill basically would have curbed the most flagrant abuses of strip mining and could have forced strip miners to restore stripped land to its "approximate original contour." In connection with the bill, a flurry had arisen, **Dec. 18**, when it was learned that Pres. Ford had decided to trade ski houses in Vail, Col., with Richard D. Bass, an oil millionaire and ski resort developer, who holds a 20,700-acre federal coal lease in Wyoming. If the bill had been signed Bass would have had to pay the government the cost of reclaiming previously stripped land, possibly up to $100 million. Bass maintained the house swap had nothing to do with politics.

International

Japan Picks New Premier — Japan's Liberal-Democratic Party, **Dec. 2**, chose Takeo Miki to succeed Kakuei Tanaka as premier. A compromise candidate, Miki had previously served in the cabinet as foreign minister and deputy premier. Miki, **Dec. 14**, in his first major policy address, told the Japanese people that they faced "unprecedented trials from within and without the country" and warned that they must prepare for sacrifices.

Scali Assails UN tyranny — Chief U.S. delegate to the UN John A. Scali, **Dec. 6**, warned the General Assembly that support for the United Nations was eroding in Congress and among the American people. Referring to the recent trend toward domination of the UN by a coalition of developing countries, Scali threatened that when majority rule became "the tyranny of the majority, the minority will cease to respect or obey it." He reminded the General Assembly that its resolutions were often adopted by majorities that represent only a small fraction of the world's population. Whereas, Scali continued, the minority may, in fact, be a practical majority "in terms of its capacity to support this organization and implement its decisions." Many delegates appeared stunned by Scali's words. Arab delegates, **Dec. 11**, charged the U.S. and its allies with "duplicity, double standards and self-righteous statements" and accused them of resorting to "blackmail and intimidation."

Makarios Returns to Cyprus — Greeted by cheering throngs of Greek Cypriots, Cyprian President Archbishop Makarios, **Dec. 7**, returned to Cyprus for the first time since he fled for his life after a coup the previous summer. Makarios vowed that "on no account" would he "recognize and accept accomplished facts" created by the Turkish invasion. He said he would not accept partition of the island between ethnic Greeks and Turks, but would accept a settlement giving self-government to the Turkish Cypriot minority. In a conciliatory move, Makarios offered amnesty to those Greek Cypriots who had ousted him in the coup last July. Rauf Dentkash, vice president and leader of the Turkish Cypriot community, **Dec. 8**, stated that Makarios' speech offered "very, very slight hope" for a settlement on Cyprus. Without Greek Cypriot acceptance of 2 geographic zones administered separately within a federation, Dentkash asserted, attempts at a settlement stood at an impasse. Before returning to Cyprus, Makarios, at a

meeting in Athens **Dec. 1**, reached an agreement with Greek Premier Constantine Caramanlis and acting Cyprian Pres. Glafkos Clerides that Greece and Greek Cypriots would take a "common line in negotiations on the future of Cyprus.

Greeks Reject Monarchy — By a more than 2-to-1 margin, the Greek people, **Dec. 8**, rejected the nation's 142-year-old monarchy and chose to remain a parliamentary republic. Premier Constantine Caramanlis warned deposed King Constantine, who had expressed a desire to return no matter the result of the referendum, that it "would not be very wise" to return "before some time goes by." On **Dec. 9**, the newly-elected Greek parliament met for the first time in 7 years.

Rhodesian Cease-fire Reached — Rhodesian Prime Minister Ian D. Smith, **Dec. 11**, announced that his white minority government and black nationalists had agreed on an immediate cease-fire to halt fighting on the country's northern border. He said all detained black nationalist leaders and followers would be released immediately and a conference would be held to fix a role for the black majority in the government. Earlier, in Lusaka, Zambia, the 3 banned Rhodesian black liberation movements, **Dec. 8**, overcame previous division and agreed to unite and prepare with Smith's minority government for "any conference for the transfer of power to the majority."

U.S., France to Coordinate Energy Policies — Ending a 2-day summit on Martinique, U.S. Pres. Gerald R. Ford and French Pres. Valery Giscard d'Estaing, **Dec. 16**, reached a compromise agreement to coordinate their nations' energy policies. The U.S. agreed to take part in a French-proposed conference of oil-producing and oil-importing nations to be held as soon as possible and to be preceded in Mar. 1975 by a preparatory conference of producers and consumers to work out procedural matters. The French, in turn, conceded to intensive consultations among the consumer countries to prepare a united position. In the final communique, both leaders "stressed the importance of solidarity among oil-importing nations" on energy conservation and "the setting up of a new mechanism of financial solidarity." The 2 leaders also agreed that any nation that so wished could adopt current market prices of gold as the basis of valuation for its gold. Prior to the summit, d'Estaing, on a stopover at Pointe-a-Pitre, Gaudeloupe, **Dec. 12**, had been assailed by angry demonstrators protesting metropolitan France's neglect for its overseas departments.

Leading Nicaraguans Seized — A band of 8 armed guerrillas representing the Sandista National Liberation Front, **Dec. 28**, seized about 30 hostages, including 3 leading Nicaraguan diplomats, at a party for the U.S. ambassador in Managua, Nicaragua. With the aid of the Archbishop of Managua as mediator, the government negotiated the release of all hostages, **Dec. 30**, in exchange for free passage to Cuba for the guerrillas, a $1-million ransom, release of 14 political prisoners to Cuba, and the publication and broadcast of an anti-government statement. In the statement, the front announced that it was gaining strength in its battle against "the most despicable dictatorship in Latin America."

General

Maheu Wins Damages — A Los Angeles, Cal., grand jury, **Dec. 4**, awarded $2,823,333.30 in damages to Robert A. Maheu in his defamation suit against billionaire Howard R. Hughes' holding company, the Summa Corp. The Summa Corp. was awarded $47,-

743 of its original $4.4 million countersuit against Maheu.

Boston Board Defies Federal Busing Order — Denouncing court-ordered busing as causing "bloodshed" and "racial hatred," the Boston School Committee, **Dec. 16**, in a 2-to-3 vote, rejected a plan drawn by its staff for city-wide school busing. The action contravened an order by Federal District Court Judge W. Arthur Garrity to draw up such a plan due that day. On **Dec. 11**, violence ignited by the slaying of a white student in a south Boston high school by a black had forced the closing of 4 south Boston schools. Judge Garrity, **Dec. 27**, held the 3 school committeemen who had rejected the busing plan in civil contempt of court and, **Dec. 30**, fined and barred them from participation in desegregation matters.

Bordeaux Vintners Guilty — Two cousins, Lionel and Ivan Cruse, heads of a 160-year-old Bordeaux wine house, were found guilty **Dec. 18**, in Bordeaux, France, of illegally doctoring wines and of falsifying pedigrees for the wines. The cousins received suspended sentences, were put on strict parole for 3 years, and fined $5,400, the maximum penalty for criminal charges. They were also ordered to pay $12 million in back taxes to the Finance Ministry's fraud squad and in damages to the wine industry. Pierre Bert, a wine broker and the only one to admit his guilt in the fraud, was sentenced to a year in prison and also assesed the maximum fine.

Cyclone Devastates Darwin — With winds up to 160 miles per hour, cyclone "Tracy," **Dec. 25**, struck the city of Darwin, situated on Australia's north coast in the remote Northern Territory. The storm killed 50 people and destroyed 90% of the city. An evacuation airlift was started **Dec. 26**. By **Dec. 31**, half the city's 45,000 residents had been evacuated and the emergency ended. Prime Minister Gough Whitlam, **Dec. 31**, announced the formation of a committee to oversee rebuilding of Darwin over the next 5 years and barring of building of homes that could not withstand cyclone-force winds.

Disasters — All 92 persons aboard died, **Dec. 1**, when a TWA 727 jetliner crashed in a driving rainstorm near a secret government installation in Upperville, Va., some 20 miles away from Washington, D.C. . . . A Dutch DC-8 chartered airliner carrying Indonesian Moslems to Mecca hit a rainstorm and crashed, **Dec. 4**, southeast of Colombo, Sri Lanka, killing all 191 persons aboard . . . Shortly after take-off from Maturin airport, a Venezuelan airliner bound for Caracas crashed, **Dec. 22**, leaving all 77 persons aboard dead . . . An explosion and fire tore through a 2,100-feet deep coal mine shaft, **Dec. 27**, in Lievin, in northern France, killing 41 men and badly injuring 6 in France's worst mine disaster since World War II . . . An earthquake, measured at 6.2 on the Richter scale, **Dec. 28**, flattened at least 9 towns in northern Pakistan and caused an estimated 5,200 deaths.

JANUARY 1975
National

Unemployment Up As Recession Deepens—More discouraging economic news came, **Jan. 4**, when the Labor Department reported that unemployment had continued to grow in December, reaching a 13-year high of 7.1% of the labor force or 6.5 million workers. The Federal Reserve Board, **Jan. 15**, further confirmed fears of deepening recession in a report that industrial production had dropped 2.8% in December and at an annual rate of 12.1% for the 4th quarter of

1974, the steepest slide since World War II. In a bit of encouraging news on inflation, the Labor Department reported the wholesale price index, after adjustment for normal seasonal changes, had declined in December for the first time since Oct. 1973. Bad news continued, however, **Jan. 16**, when the Commerce Department reported that the nation's total output or "real" gross national product for the last quarter of 1974 had dropped by an annual rate of 9.1%, the worst drop in 16 years. The department further said that the 2.2% drop in GNP for 1974 as a whole was the steepest since 1946 when the nation's enormous productive capacity was shifted from wartime to peacetime use. In 2 moves to strengthen economic activity, the Federal Reserve Board, **Jan. 4**, reduced its discount rate from 7¾% to 7½% and, **Jan. 20**, reduced "reserve requirements," or the amount of money banks must keep on hand to back up deposits. Both were clearly anti-recession moves signalling an easier monetary policy to stimulate economic activity.

"Blue Ribbon" Panel, Senate to Investigate CIA— Pres. Gerald R. Ford, **Jan. 4**, established a "blue ribbon" panel to look into allegations that the Central Intelligence Agency had undertaken illegal domestic spying. Ford added that the Justice Department would also investigate "aspects of the matter within its jurisdiction." Ford, **Jan. 5**, appointed Vice Pres. Nelson A. Rockefeller to head the 8-member "blue ribbon" commission and set Apr. 4 as the target date for the group's report. The 8 men, all described as respected citizens with no CIA connections, were: former Treasury Secretary C. Douglas Dillon; former Chief of the Joint Chiefs of Staff, now NATO Commander Gen. Lyman L. Lemnitzer; former Commerce Secretary John T. Connor; former California Gov. Ronald Reagan; former Solicitor Gen. Edwin N. Griswold; former University of Virginia Pres. Edgar F. Shannon Jr.; and AFL-CIO Secretary-Treasurer Lane Kirkland. Critics immediately attacked the commission's membership as too conservative politically and lacking in experience in intelligence matters. The Senate, in an 82-to-4 vote, **Jan. 27**, set up a bi-partisan select committee similar to the Watergate Committee to launch a full-scale study of all aspects of the CIA's foreign and domestic operations as well as the FBI and all other government intelligence units. Frank Church (D-Ida.) was named chairman and John Tower (R-Tex.) was named vice chairman. In other CIA-related matters, the Senate Appropriations Intelligence subcommittee heard CIA Director William E. Colby, **Jan. 15**, testify that the agency did infiltrate agents into antiwar and dissident political groups in the U.S. But Colby denied the CIA had been involved in a "massive, illegal domestic intelligence operation." The Senate Foreign Relations Committee, **Jan. 6**, released a letter by Chairman John Sparkman (D-Ala.) to the CIA informing the agency it must abide by new legislation curbing all foreign operations not aimed solely at gathering intelligence. The restriction had been voted last year by Congress as an amendment to the 1974 Foreign Assistance Act.

Major Car Makers Introduce Rebates—The Chrysler Corporation, **Jan. 7**, announced it would offer a system of rebates on purchases of certain cars effective Jan. 12 to Feb. 16. The rebates, ranging from $200 to $400, Chrysler indicated, were aimed at stimulating lagging car sales. The Ford Motor Company followed suit, **Jan. 13**, announcing rebates of $200 to $500 on sales of its compact models. The last of the big 3 automakers, General Motors Corporation, **Jan. 20**, also announced rebates of $200 to $500 to purchasers of its compact and subcompact cars.

Dean, Magruder, Kalmbach, and Colson Released— U.S. District Judge John J. Sirica, **Jan. 8,** released John W. Dean 3d, Herbert W. Kalmbach, and Jeb Stuart Magruder from prison and commuted their sentences to the time they had already served. Although the brief order gave no specific reason for the move, it was widely believed that the cooperation of the 3 in the Watergate cover-up trial had motivated Sirica. Former presidential counsel Dean, who had pleaded guilty to conspiracy to obstruct justice and defraud the U.S., had served 4 months in prison. Former deputy director of the Committee to Re-elect the President (CRP) Magruder had served 7 months after pleading guilty to the same charges. Kalmbach, formerly personal attorney to Richard M. Nixon and chief fund raiser for CRP, had served 6 months for violating the Federal Corrupt Practices Act by raising funds for a secret congressional campaign committee in 1970 and selling an ambassadorship. On **Jan. 31,** U.S. District Judge Gerhard A. Gesell released Charles W. Colson because of "serious family difficulties." A former presidential counsel, Colson had served 7 months after pleading guilty to obstruction of justice for his role in spreading damaging information about Dr. Daniel J. Ellsberg.

Harris Joins Democratic Contenders—Former Oklahoma Sen. Fred R. Harris, **Jan. 11,** in Concord, N.H., became the 3d Democrat to enter the 1976 New Hampshire presidential primary. Labeling himself a "new populist," Harris said: "We will go to the people. The beliefs are these: People are smart enough to govern themselves; and a widespread diffusion of economic and political power ought to be the expressed goal of the government."

Levi, Coleman Named to Cabinet—Pres. Gerald R. Ford, **Jan. 14,** named University of Chicago Pres. Edward H. Levi attorney general to succeed William B. Saxbe. Ford also named William T. Coleman, a Philadelphia attorney, to replace Claude S. Brinegar as secretary of transportation. Confirmed by the Senate **Mar. 3,** Coleman became the 2d black man ever to serve in the cabinet. The Senate, **Feb. 5,** approved the Levi nomination by voice vote without debate.

House Reform Continues—In a major setback to the Congressional seniority system, the House of Representatives, **Jan. 22,** voted to remove Wright Patman (D-Tex.), F. Edward Hebert (D-La.), and W. R. Poage (D-Tex.) as chairmen, respectively, of the House Banking and Currency Committee, the Armed Service Committee, and the Agriculture Committee. Despite considerable opposition, Administration Committee Chairman Wayne L. Hays (D-Oh.) retained his chairmanship. Henry S. Reuss (D-Wis.) replaced Patman; Melvin Price (D-Ill.) replaced Hebert; and Thomas S. Foley (D-Ill.) replaced Poage.

Congress Resists High Oil Import Fees—Despite Congressional opposition, Pres. Gerald R. Ford, as he had promised in his State of the Union message, signed an executive order, **Jan. 23,** raising crude oil import tariffs $1 per barrel per month for 3 months. Ford asserted that the tariff was essential to reduce dependence on oil imports. The Democratic opposition in Congress immediately charged Ford's move constituted abuse of presidential power. Particularly vehement opposition was voiced by 10 governors of northeastern states heavily dependent on imported petroleum products. Pennsylvania Gov. Milton J. Shapp charged the plan was a "blueprint for economic disaster" and would create "a shock wave of inflation" throughout the country.

Ford Extends Amnesty Deadline—Pres. Gerald R. Ford, **Jan. 30,** extended to Mar. 1 the Jan. 31 deadline

---

Ford Proposes $16 Billion Income Tax Cut; Tells Congress State of Union Is Not Good

In a dramatic economic policy turnabout, Pres. Gerald R. Ford, **Jan. 13,** in a nationally televised address from the White House Library, proposed a $16-billion income tax cut including rebates of up to $1,000 to individual taxpayers on 1974 taxes. Two days later, Ford presented his program for economic recovery to Congress in the gloomiest State of the Union message since the Depression: "The state of the union is not good," Ford told Congress.

In the television address, Ford told the nation, "We are in trouble," but "not on the brink of another great depression." Ford asserted that the nation must wage a 3-pronged attack against inflation, recession, and energy dependence.

In addition to the tax cut, Ford called for higher taxes on oil and natural gas, demanding an austere energy conservation program that would require "personal sacrifice." The oil taxes, an estimated $30 billion, Ford said, would be returned to the economy as additional tax cuts and credits and payments to the poor.

Ford acknowledged that his new proposals differed drastically from those he had put forth in Oct. 1974, but explained that worsening economic stagnation demanded that Americans have more spending money in their pockets than in the Treasury in Washington.

Earlier in the day, the Democratic leadership in Congress, **Jan. 13,** presented their own "emergency" economic plan to restore the slumping economy. Although the plan lacked specifics, House Speaker Carl Albert said the Ways and Means Committee would act within 60 days to cut federal taxes for low-and middle-income families by $10 to $20 billion.

In the State of the Union message, **Jan. 15,** Ford urged Congress to approve swiftly his new economic plan to combat recession. He also asked Congress to pass his sweeping plan to achieve energy independence. The plan called for a reduction in oil imports to "end vulnerability to economic disruption by foreign suppliers by 1985" and development of new energy resources and energy technology. To limit oil imports, Ford said he would use his presidential power to raise fees on all imported crude oil $1 per barrel on Feb. 1, by $2 per barrel on Mar. 1, and $3 per barrel on Apr. 1.

In further gloomy news, Ford predicted the federal deficit in fiscal year 1975 would be $30 billion and as much as $45 billion in 1976 and that the national debt would rise to over $500 billion.

Ford also asked Congress not to tie his hands in the conduct of foreign policy through restrictive legislation.

The immediate reaction, **Jan. 15,** from Congressional leadership was sharply critical of many of the president's proposals. Congressional liberals criticized Ford for not limiting the tax cut to low-income earners. Conservatives vowed to resist the major budget deficits Ford had predicted.

for Vietnam-era draft evaders and military deserters to apply for clemency under his amnesty program established in Sept. 1974. Although only 8,516 of the 136,900 eligible had signed up to date, Ford cited his belief that many who could benefit from the program were just becoming aware of its application to their cases. A stepped-up publicity campaign by the Presidential Clemency Board, which handles ⅓ of the program, had significantly increased applications and inquiries over the previous week.

Dispute on Nixon Papers Continues—U.S. District Court Judge Charles R. Richey, **Jan. 31**, ruled that the government owns almost all of some 42 million documents, tapes, and other items assembled during former Pres. Richard M. Nixon's 5 years in the White House. Richey's ruling responded to 4 suits filed the previous fall after Nixon's resignation and his subsequent agreement with the General Service Administration giving the ex-president ownership and control of the materials. Richey decided that presidents are stripped of executive privilege when they leave office, reversing common practice extending back to George Washington. A few hours later, the U.S. Court of Appeals temporarily suspended the decision pending a special hearing on the matter. On **Feb. 14**, the appeals court stayed the suspension and ruled that a panel of 3 federal judges should decide the legal and constitutional issues without being bound by Richey's original ruling.

International

Kissinger Threatens Arab Oil Producers—In an interview with Business Week magazine made public **Jan. 2**, U.S. Secretary of State Henry A. Kissinger hinted that the U.S. might use military force in the Middle East "to prevent the strangulation of the industrialized world" by Arab oil producers. He stressed, however, that use of military force was most unlikely and would be "considered only in the gravest emergency." The Egyptian newspaper Al Ahram, **Jan. 4**, declared that such military intervention would cause "a catastrophe" and Algerian Pres. Houari Boumedienne, **Jan. 6**, said that "occupation of one Arab state would be regarded as an occupation of the entire Arab world."

Phuoc Binh Falls to Communists—Culminating a week-long drive marked by fierce fighting, mortar barrages, and a tank assault, North Vietnamese forces, **Jan. 7**, overran and captured Phuoc Binh, the capital of Phuoc Long province. The remote, montagnard city, 75 miles north of Saigon, was the first provincial capital taken since the fall of Quangtri on May 1, 1972, 9 months before the signing of the Paris peace accords. The Vietcong's Provisional Revolutionary Government said the stepped-up military campaign was intended to "force" the U.S. and South Vietnam to carry out the Paris peace agreements. The U.S. charged, **Jan. 13**, in a State Department note to the 7 guarantor-nations of the 1973 accords, that North Vietnam had flagrantly violated the truce accords. The note stated that North Vietnam "must accept the full consequences of its actions" in "turning from the path of negotiation to that of war." The State Department, **Jan. 14**, stated further that the U.S. was now free to break the peace agreements, a reference to a **Jan. 12** Defense Department disclosure that reconnaissance flights over North Vietnam had been resumed.

U.S.-USSR Trade Agreement Nullified—The Soviet Union, **Jan. 10**, informed the U.S. that "it does not intend to accept a trade status that is discriminatory and subject to political conditions," a reference to a Congressionally-imposed requirement in the trade reform act signed by Pres. Ford, **Jan. 3**, that Moscow agree to freer emigration for Jews. Subsequently, U.S. Secretary of State Henry A. Kissinger, **Jan. 14**, announced that the U.S. and USSR had decided to cancel the trade agreement negotiated in 1972. Kissinger indicated that the Soviet Union considered the demand for freer emigration "as contravening both the 1972 agreement, which called for unconditional elimination of discriminatory trade restrictions, and the principle of noninterference in domestic affairs." Kissinger asserted, however, "Our policy of detente remains in force." Pres. Ford, **Jan. 15**, put the blame for the cancellation of the treaty on Congress, charging it with excessive meddling in foreign policy. On **Jan. 16**, Tass, the official Soviet news agency, stated the Soviet Union was not responsible for the collapse of the treaty and that it would continue to seek trade with the U.S. when it was "mutually beneficial." Tass further asserted, "No changes have or could have taken place in the Soviet policy of detente."

Angola Granted Independence—Disbanding virtually the world's last empire, the Portuguese government, **Jan. 10**, granted independence, effective Nov. 11, to the African territory of Angola. The independence agreement, signed in Alvor, Portugal, by representatives of Portugal and Angola's 3 rival liberation movements, provided for a 10-month transitional government to be balanced between the 3 groups. After 14 years of guerrilla warfare, the 3 liberation groups, **Jan. 5**, in Mombasa, Kenya, had signed a joint political agreement which had opened up the way for the accord.

Chinese Hold National Congress—For the first time in a decade, the National People's Congress, China's highest legislative body, met secretly in Peking's Great Hall of People, **Jan. 13-17**, and solidly endorsed the political leadership of Premier Chou En-lai. Although convalescing since Apr. 1974, Chou was present to deliver the basic report in which he predicted the complete modernization of a stable, orderly China by the end of the century and offered a vision of inevitable world war. Communist party Chairman Mao Tse-tung did not appear at the congress nor did Chou offer an explanation for his absence. The congress approved a new state constitution and a slate of ministers top heavy with senior and elderly officials long associated with Chou. The post of defense minister, not filled since the death of Lin Piao, went to Yeh Chien-ying, a veteran of the Long March and one-time marshal of the People's Liberation Army. According to reports **Jan. 29**, Deputy Premier Teng Hsiao-ping was named army chief-of-staff, a move asserting the transcendance of the party over the military to a degree unprecedented in 25 years of Communist rule in China.

Greek Cypriots Protest Turkish Airlift—As Greek and Turkish Cypriots opened political talks in Nicosia on the future of Cyprus, Greek Cypriots numbering in the hundreds, **Jan. 17**, marched on the British base at Episkopi to protest a **Jan. 15** British decision to allow some 10,000 Turkish Cypriot refugees, who fled to the base during the war, to return to Turkey. According to the agreement, the refugees would later be allowed to return to the Turkish-held part of Cyprus. An 18-year-old Greek Cypriot marcher was killed as the protesters attacked a small UN convoy that was approaching the base. The Greek Cypriots charged the British decision promoted Turkey's aim to divide Cyprus. The British government asserted humanitarian reasons prompted the decision. Unrest continued **Jan. 18**, when some 5,000 Greek Cypriots ransacked British offices in Nicosia and burned a wing of the U.S. embassy.

Bangladesh Gives All Power to President—Without dissent, the Bangladesh parliament, **Jan. 25**, amended the nation's 1972 constitution to make Prime Minister Sheik Mujibur Rahman president with all executive powers. According to the new amendment, all executive authority would be exercised by the president "either directly or through officers subordinate to him." The parliament also authorized the president to declare Bangladesh a one-party state and removed a constitutional provision for "effective participation by the people through their elected representatives." Sheik Mujib announced that the constitutional changes were necessary because of a "chaotic situation" in the nation caused by "anti-national elements who sided with Pakistan during the repression preceding independence." Terming the move Bangladesh's 2d revolution, Sheik Mujib called for "all-out efforts" to make Bangladesh self-sufficient in goods.

General

Boston School Desegregation Plan Authorized—On the deadline set by federal court Judge W. Arthur Garrity Jr. to create a school desegregation plan, the Boston School Committee, **Jan. 7**, agreed to "authorize" the preparation of a plan "without forced busing." On **Jan. 8**, Judge Garrity agreed to give the committee another chance and dropped contempt of court charges against 3 of the 5 school committeemen who had defied his order to approve a citywide desegregation plan based on mandatory busing which had been drawn up by the committee's staff.

Textbook Protestors Indicted—A Charleston, W. Va., federal grand jury, **Jan. 17**, returned a 6-count indictment against the Rev. Marvin Horan, pastor of the Fundamentalist Freewill Baptist Church and leader of Concerned Citizens, and 5 others. They were charged with conspiring to "damage and destroy" 2 Kanawha county schools. According to the indictment, the alleged conspiracy took place from Oct. 1 to Nov. 15, 1974, during a controversy over school textbooks which the Concerned Citizens contended were irreligious and un-American.

Disasters—Heavy floods in southern Thailand, reported **Jan. 11**, destroyed many rubber plantations and mining facilities and left 131 persons dead. . . Some 50 persons were dead, **Jan. 14**, after blizzards with winds up to 90 miles per hour swept over the U.S. midwest and northern central plains. . . A fire raged through a 5-story commercial building in suburban Manila, Philippines, **Jan. 22**, leaving 51 persons dead and, at least 79 injured. . . At least 100 persons were feared dead, **Jan. 25**, when a ferry boat sank after a collision with a steamer in the Buriganga River, 7 miles from Dacca, Bangladesh.

FEBRUARY

National

Budget Shows Largest Peace-time Deficit—Pres. Gerald R. Ford, **Feb. 3**, presented to Congress a $349.4 billion budget for fiscal year 1976. The budget projected a deficit of $51.9 billion, the largest peacetime deficit in the nation's history. The major reason for the large deficit was the recession. Ford pointed out that the deficit might become larger if Congress failed to pass much of his $17-billion tax-cut package. The budget also disclosed the administration's forecast that unemployment would remain near 8% for the remainder of 1975 and 1976. The budget included

the first real increase in 5 years, at least $8 billion, in military spending. It also included expenditures of $18.6 billion for programs to help the unemployed, chiefly through expanded unemployment benefits. With the exception of $1.7 billion allocated for energy research and development and a proposal to allow state governments to share about $1 billion in receipts from the federal gas tax, the budget contained essentially no new programs. Reflecting the sweeping budget reforms passed by Congress in 1974, the 1976 budget included detailed agency-by-agency forecasts of spending over the next 5 years and more detailed long-term forecasts of economic trends than ever before offered by a president. The budget also incorporated changes toward a new fiscal year structure to begin Oct. 1, 1976. The Democratic leaders in Congress assailed the president's projection on unemployment. Hubert H. Humphrey, chairman of the Congressional Joint Economic Committee, said it was "unbelievable" Ford could predict record deficits and "not put America back to work."

Economic Reports Give Gloomy Outlook—Pres. Ford and his Council of Economic Advisers warned, **Feb. 4**, in their annual reports to Congress, that the economy was "in a severe recession." They warned that more government spending and larger tax cuts would increase the already record deficit in the 1976 budget. Economic adviser Alan Greenspan summed up the administration's recommendations: "If we stimulate beyond what the President is suggesting, we would be trading off some small reduction in unemployment for inflation later and an average level of unemployment higher than we want."

Congress Freezes Food Stamp Price—The Congress, **Feb. 4** and **5**, soundly rejected an administration proposal to increase the purchase price of food stamps as of Mar. 1. Seeking to stem the rapid growth of social welfare programs, the administration had proposed raising the average cost of a month's supply of food stamps from 23¢ to 30¢ of a family's net income. The House of Representatives passed, **Feb. 4**, by a 374-38 margin, legislation to freeze the cost of food stamps until the end of 1975. The Senate followed suit, **Feb. 5**, in a 76-8 vote.

Ford, Congress Battle Over Oil Imports—Despite full-scale administration lobbying in opposition, the House, **Feb. 5**, by a vote of 309-114, passed a bill suspending for 90 days the president's power to increase fees on oil imports. Pres. Ford, along with Secretary of State Kissinger, Energy Administrator Frank G. Zarb, and chief presidential economic adviser Alan Greenspan, had gone to Capitol Hill to argue that the import fees were crucial to push up petroleum prices and thereby force conservation of energy sources. Ford, speaking in Houston, Tex., in support of his anti-recession energy program, **Feb. 10**, charged that those opposed to his plan were taking a "reckless gamble" with the American economy. However, despite presidential pressure and the threat of a veto, the Senate, **Feb. 19**, also voted, 66-28, to suspend the president's power to increase fees for 90 days.

Jackson, Bentsen Join Presidential Race—Sen. Henry M. Jackson (D. Wash.), **Feb. 6**, in a 5-minute taped commercial broadcast, announced his candidacy for the Democratic presidential nomination. Jackson, who believes his traditional liberalism will appeal to those hardest hit in the current economic downturn, said, "I would use the office of the Presidency to help the people in this country who are getting hurt . . . The little people — little business, the elderly, the young, across the board — have been the ones who have taken the beating." On **Feb. 17**, Sen.

Lloyd M. Bentsen (D. Tex.), a 54-year-old insurance millionaire, became the 5th Democratic presidential candidate. Calling "economic recovery" the "paramount issue," Bentsen pledged to "restore the meaning of America's two great promises: opportunity at home and moral leadership."

Unemployment Reaches 33-Year High—The Labor Department reported, **Feb. 7**, that national unemployment had reached 8.2% in January. The rate was the highest since 1941 when 9.9% of the nation's labor force was out of work. The Federal Reserve Board indicated, **Feb. 13**, that industrial production had fallen 3.6%, the sharpest decline since December 1937. The decrease was laid to a steep drop in consumer buying, a deep slump in housing construction, and efforts by businesses to reduce inventories. Inflation, according to a **Feb. 14** Labor Dept. report, continued to abate for the 2nd month in a row. The Wholesale Price Index, after adjustment for seasonal changes, fell 0.3%. The Consumer Price Index, reported Feb. 21, rose by 0.6%, the lowest increase since April 1974.

Dunlop Named Labor Secretary—Pres. Ford, **Feb. 8**, named Harvard economist and former Cost of Living Council Director John T. Dunlop to succeed Peter J. Brennan as Secretary of Labor. Brennan resigned **Feb. 6**. The Senate confirmed the nomination **Mar. 6**.

Ford Appoints Woman to Head HUD—The White House announced, **Feb. 13**, that Pres. Ford would nominate Carla Anderson Hills as Secretary of Housing and Urban Development to succeed James T. Lynn. Immediate opposition to the nomination was voiced by Sen. William Proxmire (D. Wis.), chairman of the Senate Banking, Housing and Urban Affairs Committee. Proxmire asserted that Hills, an assistant attorney general in charge of the Justice Department's civil division, had no known qualifications for the job beyond her intelligence. Presidential Press Secretary Ron Nessen said "sex was not a factor" in the president's choice, but rather Hills' competency as a lawyer and administrator. The Senate confirmed the nomination **Mar. 5**.

Nixon Tax Attorneys Indicted—A Washington, D.C., federal grand jury, **Feb. 19**, indicted 2 attorneys for conspiracy to commit fraud and other crimes in connection with the preparation of former Pres. Richard M. Nixon's tax returns. Frank DeMarco Jr., a Los Angeles attorney who prepared Nixon's 1969 tax return, was indicted on 3 counts, each of which carried a maximum 5-year penalty and $10,000 fine. The other attorney, Ralph G. Newman, a Chicago appraiser responsible for evaluating Nixon's pre-presidential papers as a tax deduction, was charged on 2 counts, one carrying a 5-year maximum sentence and the other a 3-year possible jail term, as well as a maximum $10,000 fine on both counts. The grand jury indictment charged that both men "well knew" the gift of Nixon's papers was not made before a change in tax laws barring such a deduction and prepared documents to the contrary. The indictment, however, said nothing about Nixon's part in the alleged conspiracy.

Watergate Cover-up Sentences Imposed—U.S. District Court Judge John J. Sirica, **Feb. 21**, sentenced former Nixon associates John N. Mitchell, H.R. Haldeman, and John D. Ehrlichman to 2½ to 8 years in prison for their roles in the Watergate cover-up and conspiracy. Former Assistant Attorney General Robert C. Mardian was sentenced to 10 months to 3 years in prison. All 4 had been convicted of conspiracy to obstruct justice and various charges of lying under oath. Sirica ruled that the 4 could remain free on "personal recognizance" pending the outcome of appeals. Federal Parole Board Chairman Maurice H. Sigler said the 4 convicted men would be eligible for parole after serving the minimum sentence.

International

Ethiopian War Erupts in Eritrea—The 12-year war for Eritrean independence intensified suddenly when insurgents launched mortar and bazooka attacks, **Jan. 31**, on 3 military installations in Asmara, the capital of the beleaguered Ethiopian province. By **Feb. 6**, casualties were reported at 1,200 persons dead. Fighting continued month-long in sporadic bursts. Heaviest fighting was reported, **Feb. 27**, around Keren, 60 miles from Asmara. By month's end, casualties for both rebel and government forces were estimated at well over 2,000 persons dead. On **Feb. 2**, the Ethiopian military government ordered jet bombers, armored units, and their elite troops into Eritrea to combat the rebels. It was reported, **Feb. 10**, that government forces in Eritrea stood at 10,000, about one-half of the nation's army. By **Feb. 19**, government troop strength was reported at 22,000. Evacuation of U.S. and European citizens had begun **Feb. 4**, when Asmara was cut off from the rest of the country. The Ethiopian government, **Feb. 15**, imposed a state of emergency. A news blackout, imposed by the military government near the end of the month, seriously impaired reporting of the situation. However, the Chicago Tribune, in a **Mar. 1** report, asserted that the Eritrean insurgents held vast areas of the province.

Thieu Cracks Down on Opposition Press—South Vietnamese Pres. Nguyen Van Thieu, **Feb. 3**, shut down 5 opposition newspapers. The previous day, the government had seized editions of the 5 papers and 4 others because they had printed a new "indictment" of the Thieu regime. The indictment, issued by the Roman Catholic-led People's Anticorruption Movement, demanded that Thieu be "charged with high treason" for his many political crimes. The government also continued a wave of arrests of journalists labeled "Communist agents." The arrests, which had begun quietly over the weekend, numbered 24 by **Feb. 4**.

IRA Begins New Ceasefire—The Irish Republican Army, **Feb. 9**, announced a new, open-ended ceasefire in Northern Ireland and Britain, to begin **Feb. 10**. The IRA stated the decision had stemmed from discussions with British officials which had produced "an effective agreement to insure there would be no breakdown of a new truce." Merlyn Rees, British Secretary for Northern Ireland, **Feb. 11**, told the House of Commons that to monitor and safeguard the truce Britain would set up an elaborate network of centers to stay in 24-hour contact with IRA units in Northern Ireland. Rees also stated that, if the truce held, British Army presence in Northern Ireland would become "progressively less obtrusive."

Woman Elected to Lead British Party—In a decisive victory in Great Britain, Margaret Thatcher, **Feb. 4**, defeated incumbent Edward Heath in the first round of elections for Conservative Party leadership. On **Feb. 11**, Thatcher, formerly Secretary of State for Education in the Conservative government, defeated 4 other candidates to become the first woman to lead a British political party.

Turkish Cypriots Declare Separate State—Turkish Cypriot leader Rauf Denktash announced, **Feb. 13**, that Turkish Cypriots had proclaimed the Turkish-occupied northern section of Cyprus a separate state.

The Turkish Cypriots simultaneously offered to join in a bi-regional federal state with the Greek Cypriot community. Denktash, who would head the autonomous Turkish state, declared that the move was not "a unilateral declaration of independence," but "necessary for the existence of our community." Greek Premier Constantine Caramanlis called the Turkish Cypriot move "an insolent continuation of the policy of 'fait accompli' and armed violence." Cypriot Pres. Archbishop Makarios, addressing 2,000 Greek Cypriot demonstrators outside the presidential palace in Nicosia, **Feb. 14**, said Greek Cypriots were ready to resist and sacrifice themselves to prevent partition.

Park Frees Political Prisoners—South Korean Pres. Park Chung Hee announced, **Feb. 15**, that he would free almost all of the 203 political prisoners jailed the previous year for anti-government activities. (Prisoners believed to be Communists, chiefly members of the Peoples' Revolutionary Party, would not be released.) The conciliatory move followed a **Feb. 12** national referendum which had given wide support to Park's government and the 1972 constitution, which gives the president unlimited powers. Government critics, however, in a series of public meetings and statements, **Feb. 20**, rejected Park's attempt at reconciliation. They renewed demands that the constitution be amended to curb presidential powers, asked for an investigation of charges of torture of prisoners by government agents, and demanded amnesty for the released prisoners. Critics also charged that the recent pro-Park referendum had been rigged.

UN Commission Censures Israel—The 32-member United Nations Commission on Human Rights, **Feb. 21**, passed 2 resolutions censuring Israel for actions in occupied Arab territories. The first accused Israel of abusing the "basic norms of international law" in the territories by violating the 1949 Geneva convention on the protection of civilian war victims and by causing the "deliberate destruction and devastation" of El Quneitra in the Golan Heights. In the 2nd resolution, the commission claimed Israel had desecrated Moslem and Christian shrines. The commission also demanded the immediate release of the Greek Catholic Archbishop of East Jerusalem. Israel had convicted the archbishop of smuggling arms to the Arabs and had sentenced the cleric to 12 years in prison. Israeli Representative Eyatan Ronn, sitting as an observer to the commission, called the actions "fantastic allegations and accusations."

Administration Deems Cambodia Aid Crucial—Both U.S. Pres. Gerald R. Ford and Secretary of State Henry A. Kissinger, **Feb. 25**, asserted that the fall of the Cambodian government was imminent unless Congress provided $222 million requested by the administration for supplemental aid to Cambodia. Kissinger, at a news conference, argued in moral terms: "Is the United States, which so far has consistently stood by its friends through the most difficult times, now to condemn, in effect, a small Asian nation totally dependent on us?" The campaign for more military aid had begun **Feb. 23**, when Defense Secretary James R. Schlesinger had warned Cambodia would "absolutely" fall under Communist control without U.S. aid.

German Candidate Kidnaped—Leftist kidnapers, **Feb. 27**, seized Peter Lorenz, the Christian Democratic candidate for Mayor of West Berlin, 3 days before the election. Lorenz had based his campaign on the issue of unsafe streets and the West Berlin government's tolerance of leftist radicals. On **Feb. 28**, the kidnapers, who identified themselves as members of the June 2 Movement, demanded the release of 6 jailed German radical leftists. West German and West Berlin authorities yielded, **Mar. 3**, and flew 5 of the prisoners and one hostage, former West Berlin Mayor Heinrich Albertz, to Aden, in South Yemen. West Berlin police, in further compliance with the kidnapers' demands, also released 2 persons jailed after violent demonstrations in November 1974. Following the safe return of Albertz, Lorenz was freed **Mar. 4**. During the period of captivity, Lorenz lost the election although the Christian Democrats made substantial gains, receiving 43.9% of the vote. West Berlin police, **Sept. 10**, arrested Ralf Reinders, identified as the leader of the June 2 Movement, and a woman. Both were identified by Lorenz as members of the group that had kidnaped him.

General

Menominee Indians End Occupation—An armed band of Menominee Indians, **Feb. 4**, evacuated an unused Gresham, Wis., Roman Catholic novitiate which they had seized and held since **Jan. 1**. The occupiers had said they wanted the novitiate for use as a hospital or education facility for the Menominee people. The same day, 28 of the evacuees, members of the Menominee Warriors Society, were arraigned in Shawano, Wis., on charges of criminal trespass and disorderly conduct. Their leader, Michael Sturdevant, and 4 others were charged with armed robbery, armed burglary, and false imprisonment. The group had agreed to leave the novitiate after its owners, the Alexian Brothers of Chicago, had agreed to deed the 84-room complex to a Menominee tribal government to be elected shortly. In exchange, the Indians agreed to leave peacefully in the custody of the National Guard.

Boston Doctor Guilty in Abortion Case—Following a 6-week trial, a Boston, Mass., jury, **Feb. 15**, found Dr. Kenneth C. Edelin guilty of manslaughter in the death of a male fetus. The death had followed a legal abortion performed by Dr. Edelin at Boston City Hospital on Oct. 3, 1973. The verdict was widely considered a victory for "right-to-life" anti-abortion groups. Judge James P. McGuire sentenced Edelin to one year's probation, but immediately stayed the sentence pending the outcome of an appeal. The prosecution had contended that Edelin had suffocated the fetus while it was still in the womb. The defense had argued that the doctor could not have killed the fetus because it was not yet a person and the law does not give rights to the unborn. After the decision, Edelin, a black, **Feb. 16**, claimed that racial and religious prejudice in the Boston area had made a fair trial impossible. Ten of the 12 jury members were Roman Catholics with a stated opposition to abortion.

Ray Denied New Trial—U.S. District Court Judge Robert M. McRae, **Feb. 27**, in Memphis, Tenn., rejected a request for a new trial for James Earl Ray, the convicted murderer of the Rev. Martin Luther King Jr. Ray contended that his attorneys had enticed him to plead guilty for their own personal gain. McRae, however, ruled that the testimony had convinced him Ray "had clearly and deliberately" pleaded guilty to murder. Ray is currently serving a 99-year sentence for the 1968 assassination.

London Subway Train Crashes—At the peak of rush hour, a London subway train, **Feb. 28**, raced past its final stop and crashed into the end of a tunnel, killing 41 persons and injuring scores of others. The accident was the worst in the history of the relatively safe and trouble-free London subway system. Officials conjectured that the cause may have been a mechanical failure or a deliberate attempt to drive the train into the wall.

MARCH

National

Ford Offers Energy Compromise—Pres. Gerald R. Ford. **Mar. 4**, vetoed a bill suspending for 90 days his authority to increase fees on oil imports. but offered Congress a compromise. Ford said he would postpone for 60 days the final 2 stages of increases in the oil import tax. due Mar. 1 and Apr. 1. He encouraged Congress to develop a compromise energy plan during that time.

Senate Reforms Filibuster Rule—Following a 2-week filibuster in opposition to the vote. the Senate. **Mar. 7**, voted to reform its filibuster rule. Under the new rule. 3/5 of the Senate's membership. rather than the previous 2/3. would be sufficient to invoke cloture — the end of debate on a question. The breakthrough leading to the vote came Mar. 5, when the Senate voted. 73-21. to invoke cloture to end Sen. James D. Allen's (D. Ala.) 2-week filibuster against a motion to consider the reform proposal.

Unemployment Rate Stable at 8.2%—The nation's unemployment rate stayed at 8.2% during the month of February. it was reported **Mar. 7**. However. the total number of persons employed shrank by more than a half million. indicating continuing economic deterioration. In an attempt to alleviate the unemployment situation. Pres. Ford. **Mar. 5**, had asked for $2 billion in additional funds. above the amount projected in the budget. to create more public service jobs.

Stans Guilty of Campaign Violations—Former Commerce Secretary Maurice H. Stans. **Mar. 12**, pleaded guilty in a Washington. D.C.. federal court. to 5 misdemeanor charges of violating campaign laws. Stans. who had served as finance director of the Nixon re-election campaign. said the misdemeanors "were not willful. and at the time they occurred were not believed to be violations." Stans explained that the guilty plea. made in an arrangement with the Watergate special prosecutor. ended his liability for almost all other possible violations and established "once and for all" that he had "no guilty involvement" in the Watergate scandals. The plea subjected Stans to a possible 2 to 5 years in prison. depending on interpretation of statutes. and a $5,000-fine.

Supreme Court Rules on Offshore Waters—The Supreme Court. **Mar. 17**, decided unanimously that the federal government had exclusive title to oil and gas resources on the Atlantic Outer Continental Shelf beyond the 3-mile limit. Thirteen Atlantic states had petitioned that their original charters had given them title to resources out to 100 miles offshore. The states argued that they had not surrendered the titles when they joined the union. The states also said the 1947 and 1950 Supreme Court decisions deeding the titles to the federal government should be overturned. The court decision immediately opened the way for the Interior Department to lease tracts in the undersea Baltimore Canyon for exploration and production by oil companies.

CIA Salvage Project Disclosed—It was widely reported. **Mar. 18**, that the CIA had financed and operated. during the summer of 1974, a $250-million deepsea salvage project to recover a Soviet submarine. The sub had exploded and sunk in mysterious circumstances in 1968 in the Pacific Ocean off the coast of Hawaii. The operation, called Project Jennifer, successfully raised 1/3 of the sunken vessel, but failed to recover the portion containing hydrogen missile warheads and the code room. The salvage vessel. Glomar Explorer. had been built by millionaire Howard R. Hughes' Summa Corporation. Although thousands of employees had received security clearances to work on the project. the operation had been one of the closest secrets of both the Nixon and Ford administrations. White House. CIA. and Pentagon officials. **Mar. 19**. refused to discuss the operation. It was learned. however. that CIA Director William E. Colby had exerted considerable effort to convince newspaper. magazine. and broadcast executives that disclosure of the project would endanger national security. Several Congressional committees. including Sen. Frank Church's (D. Ida.) Select Committee on Intelligence. said they would investigate the project.

Morton Goes to Commerce Department—White House Press Secretary Ron Nessen announced. **Mar. 27**. that Pres. Ford would move his secretary of interior. Rogers C.B. Morton. to the top spot in the Commerce Department. According to Nessen. Morton's expertise with the development of exotic coal-based fuels would be valuable in the Commerce Dept. to spur private industry to manufacture such products as a substitute for oil. Morton was confirmed by the Senate **Apr. 25**. President Ford nominated former Wyoming Gov. Stanley K. Hathaway to the Interior post. Despite considerable feeling in the Senate that Hathaway's support for the strip mining bill represented a conflict of interest. his nomination was confirmed, **June 11**, by a 60-36 vote.

Congress Passes Tax Cut, Ford Signs—The Congress. **Mar. 26**, passed a compromise $22.8-billion tax cut bill which would give each individual taxpayer a minimum rebate of $100 on 1974 taxes. The bill also ended the oil and gas depletion allowance for all large oil companies. The allowance had exempted from taxation the first 22% of all income earned from oil and gas. Pres. Ford. **Mar. 29**, reluctantly signed the bill. Although Ford felt the tax cut was a "reasonable compromise" with his original $16-billion proposal, he pointed out that "this also distributes the cuts differently and. in my opinion. fails to give adequate relief to millions of middle income taxpayers who already contribute the biggest share of Federal taxes." Ford also emphasized that he would draw the line on government spending and not accept any new expenditures passed by Congress except those necessary for national security and energy developments. In addition to the individual rebate. which could go as high as $200. the bill increased the standard deduction on 1975 taxes from 15% to 16% with a maximum of $2.300 for individuals and $2.600 for married couples. Previously. the maximum amounts had been $2.000. The bill also provided a one-time $50 bonus payment to recipients of Social Security retirement. railroad retirement. and supplemental security income benefits. The bill also extended unemployment benefits 13 weeks beyond the normal 52 in 9 states with high unemployment.

International

Iran-Iraq Accord Ends Kurdish Rebellion—Iran and Iraq, in a joint communique issued in Algiers. **Mar. 6**, said they had agreed to end their long-standing border dispute. Although the rebellion was not mentioned specifically, a promise to halt subversive infiltration from both sides was interpreted as an Irani promise to end support of the Kurdish insurgency. In the major point of the agreement, the 2 nations agreed that their border would run through the middle of Shatt al-Arab, the waterway that empties into the Persian Gulf. The 2 nations agreed that the Persian Gulf area should be kept "free of all foreign influence." On **Mar. 7**, the Iraqi government launched a major offensive against the Kurdish insurgents, who had occupied border areas with Iranian support in 1974. By **Mar. 11**, Iraqi forces had driven deep into Kurdish-held territory. A rebel spokesman confirmed, **Mar. 11**, that Iran had ceased supplying military aid to the Kurds. Iraq announced a 2-week ceasefire, **Mar. 13**, to allow Kurdish rebels and civilians to cross over to Iran. Upon expiration of the ceasefire **Mar. 31**, Iraqi forces were ordered to "advance toward" control of Kurdish-held areas. Reports **Apr. 2**, stated that Iraqi armored columns, having met very little resistance, had reoccupied the border areas held by the Kurdish rebels.

OPEC Members Offer to Negotiate Oil Prices—The major oil-exporting nations, **Mar. 6**, offered to meet with industrial countries to negotiate on the "stabilization" of oil prices. The offer, coming at the conclusion of the first meeting, in Algiers, of the sovereigns and chiefs of state of the 13-member Organization of Petroleum Exporting Countries, stipulated, however, that issues of raw materials, monetary relations, and the development of the poorer nations must also be discussed. The OPEC members stated that future oil prices would be based on factors of conservation, "availability and cost of alternative sources of energy," and uses of oil for nonenergy purposes, such as chemical products. The 13 nations indicated willingness to assure the industrial nations adequate supplies of oil to meet "essential requirements." But, the OPEC members warned, any grouping of consumer countries that would have the "aim of confrontation" would endanger future availability of oil.

Lisbon Tightens Reign After Coup Attempt—After crushing an attempted coup by conservative elements, Portugal's left-wing military government, **Mar. 12**, solidified its rule through the formation of a military revolutionary council. The new council, composed chiefly of leftist officers, would hold both legislative and executive power until elections for a president and legislative assembly in April. The attempted military revolt, reportedly led by followers of former provisional president Gen. Antonio de Spinola, began, **Mar. 11**, with an air attack on military barracks in Lisbon. Spinola, his wife, and 18 other officers fled across the Spanish border. On **Mar. 13**, the government arrested more than 60 persons, including leading industrialists and bankers and 2 Spinola aides. Following a warning from Pres. Francisco da Costa Gomez that a "hard core of opposition forces" still existed, the new military revolutionary council, **Mar. 14**, nationalized almost all banks. Premier Vasco dos Santos Goncalves called the nationalization the "first firm, irreversible step" to place the economy at the service of the people. On **Mar. 15**, the government nationalized all insurance companies, thereby placing the bulk of the nation's financial power under its control. A new leftist cabinet, the 4th since the provisional government was established in April 1974, was installed **Mar. 26**.

South Korean Press Fights Curbs—Over 100 employees, **Mar. 13**, took over Dong-A Ilbo, South Korea's largest daily newspaper, to protest curbs on press reporting. The employees demanded that Kim San Man, the newspaper's publisher, take a stronger stand against the government. The government, the protesters claimed, had been stifling freedom of the press by influencing publishers to dismiss troublesome reporters and editors under the guise of economic and disciplinary measures. Dong-A Ilbo's publisher had dismissed 20 employees, **Mar. 8**, for just those reasons. The publisher countered the sit-in by dismissing 17 more newspaper employees, bringing the total fired by South Korean newspaper management over the past few months to 97. After efforts to mediate a settlement with the protesters failed, the newspaper hired some 150 youths, **Mar. 17** to forcibly evict the strikers.

Thais Seek American Withdrawal—Newly-installed Thai Premier Kukrit Pramoj, **Mar. 17**, announced his government would seek total withdrawal of the 25,000 American troops and 350 aircraft within a year, but only if "the political and military situation in this region permits." In the policy statement, issued shortly after his 7-party coalition cabinet was confirmed by King Phumiphol Aduldet, Kukrit also said he would try to establish diplomatic relations with China and open talks with North Vietnam. He indicated, however, that the demand for withdrawal was not an anti-American move. "Our good relations must continue," Kukrit emphasized. The demand for American withdrawal within one year was seen as an attempt to gain left-wing party support for Kukrit's coalition government which was 11 seats short of a majority in the lower house of parliament. Kukrit's policy won a vote of confidence, **Mar. 19**. The previous government, headed by Kukrit's brother Seni Pramoj, had been forced to resign, **Mar. 6**, after losing a vote of confidence over a proposal for American withdrawal within 18 months.

King Faisal Assassinated—At a palace reception marking the birthday of Mohammed, the prophet of Islam, Saudi Arabian King Faisal, 70, was shot dead, **Mar. 25**, in Riyadh, by a young nephew. Crown Prince Khalid, 62, succeeded the slain leader. However, because Khalid had not been very active in government it was expected that the new crown prince, Fahd, would wield the real power. The U.S. said it expected no immediate change in Saudi Arabia's pro-U.S. policies, but expressed regret at the loss of such a strong proponent of political moderation in the Middle East. As more than 100,000 people, including numerous chiefs of state, gathered, Faisal was buried, **Mar. 26** with Bedouin simplicity. On **Mar. 29**, King Khalid installed a new collective leadership, representing the 2 principle factions in the royal family. Khalid, who retained the titular position of premier, appointed crown prince Fahd as first deputy premier and interior minister. Prince Abdallah, the commander of the national guard, was named 2nd deputy premier. Sheik Ahmed Zaki Yamani remained in the influential position of minister of petroleum and mineral resources. Fahd made it clear immediately that Saudi Arabia's oil policy and close relations with the U.S. would remain unchanged. The young assassin, Faisal ibn Musad Abdel Aziz, who had a reported history of mental instability, was examined and found sane, according to reports **Mar. 30**. Faisal was tried and found guilty, **June 18**, according to Islamic law, and beheaded in the public square in Riyadh.

Kissinger Peace Mission Fails—Following 2 weeks of shuttle diplomacy, U.S. Secretary Henry A. Kissinger, **Mar. 22**, announced, in Jerusalem, that "irreconcilable differences" between Israel and Egypt had forced him to suspend his current efforts to forge a new Middle East agreement. Israel and Egypt blamed each other for the breakdown. The impasse arose because Israel refused to cede the strategically important Sinai passes and Abu Rudeis oil field unless Egypt reciprocated with a declaration of non-belligerence, which Egypt refused to do. Alternate Egyptian and Israeli proposals which softened their demands were rejected by each side as insufficient. The failure of his step-by-step approach, Kissinger said, called for "a period of reassessment . . . so that all concerned can consider how best to proceed toward a just and lasting peace." On **Mar. 24** U.S. Pres. Gerald R. Ford ordered a re-examination of U.S. policy in the Middle East. Israeli response was bitter, reflecting Israel's belief Washington was placing major blame for the breakdown on Israel. Ford, in an interview published **Mar. 27**, chided Israel for refusing to give up the Sinai passes and said chances for Middle East peace would have been enhanced had Israel been more flexible.

Cambodian Situation Worsens —Persistent and intensive shelling by communist-led insurgents of Phnom Penh's Pochentong airport forced numerous suspensions of the U.S. airlift of military supplies, fuel and food to Cambodia during March. The airlift of arms and ammunition, which had been operated from Thailand by Bird Air since the phase-out of the U.S. Air Force supply lift in October 1974, had been doubled in February as rebels intensified their blockade of the Mekong River. The U.S., **Feb. 27** had also begun an emergency 30-day airlift of rice and kerosene from Saigon. South of Phnom Penh, insurgents continued to move up the Mekong River, forcing the government to withdraw to Neak Luong. On **Mar. 17,** as the insurgents were beginning to put a stranglehold on Neak Luong, the U.S. Embassy in Phnom Penh began to evacuate international relief aides. On **Mar. 20** the British Embassy closed its doors, leaving the U.S. Embassy alone as the last important western mission in Cambodia. Rumors persisted that Cambodian Pres. Lon Nol would bow to pressure and resign. On **Mar. 11**, Lon Nol reshuffled his cabinet, ousting armed forces commander Gen. Sosthene Fernandez. The move was interpreted as a gesture toward demands of the rebels and U.S. Congressional leaders that Lon Nol and his entire cabinet resign.

General

Arson Alleged in Rubber Factory Explosion—Firebombs, **Mar. 1**, destroyed a $10-million rubber factory in Shelton, Conn. The bombs were exploded by 3 armed men after they seized 3 watchmen at the Sponge Rubber Products Co. The explosion, the biggest arson case in FBI annals, threw 900 employees out of work and disrupted the economy of the 29,000-population town on the banks of the Housatonic River. Federal and state indictments, issued **Apr. 24**, charged the plant's owner, Charles D. Moeller, his allegedly clairvoyant spiritual adviser, and 8 others with arson and conspiracy in connection with the explosion. The indictments alleged the conspirators had concocted a strange plot to get millions of dollars in fire insurance claims. The alleged scheme, according to the indictments, involved a $50,000 payoff to an arson team, interstate shipment of dynamite and gasoline, and dropping of heavy-handed false clues. On **Apr. 25**, the Sponge Rubber Products Co. filed a $62.6-million insurance claim for losses incurred in the fire-bombing. An expert close to the proceeding said the claim would almost certainly lead to a court fight and open Moeller or other officers of the company to charges of insurance fraud.

Italian Jeweler Kidnaped—Three gunmen, **Mar. 13**, in Rome, Italy, kidnaped Giovanni Bulgari, co-owner of the internationally-known jewelry company. The 40-year-old bachelor was on his way home in rush-hour traffic when the gunmen hijacked his limousine. Bulgari was freed, **Apr. 14**, for a ransom which, Bulgari said later, totaled $2.06 million.

Former Governor Guilty of Bribery—Former Oklahoma Gov. David Hall, **Mar. 14**, was convicted in Oklahoma City, Okla., on 4 counts of bribery and extortion. Also convicted was Dallas mortgage broker W.W. Taylor. The indictment had charged

that the 2 men had bribed Oklahoma Secretary of State John Rogers Jr. to vote to invest state retirement funds of $10 million in a company owned by Taylor.

Mass Slaying in Ohio—Hamilton, Oh., police, **Mar. 31**, arrested James Ruppert an unemployed draftsman, in the **Mar. 30** slaying of 11 members of his family (his mother, brother, sister-in-law and 8 nephews and nieces). Ruppert had called the police on Easter Sunday evening, the night of the murders, to report finding the bodies. The police found 10 persons shot in the head and one in the chest. There was no sign of struggle and police were unable to determine a motive. On **Apr. 8**, Ruppert pleaded not guilty by reason of insanity. Ruppert was convicted, **July 3**, and sentenced, **July 14**, to 11 consecutive life-terms in prison.

APRIL

National

Unemployment Reaches New High — Unemployment in March reached 8.7% of the labor force, unsurpassed since 1941, according to an **Apr. 4** Labor Dept. report. The total number of unemployed stood at 8 million persons, the largest amount since 1940 at the end of the Depression, when 8.1 million Americans were without jobs. The number of "discouraged workers," who dropped out of the job market entirely, reached a record 1.1 million. Pres. Gerald R. Ford, in an immediate reaction to the bad news, said he would recommend an extension of emergency benefits for the unemployed until the end of 1976. In further discouraging economic news, the Commerce Dept. reported, **Apr. 17**, that the nation's gross national product had dropped at a record annual rate of 10.4% during the first quarter of 1975. Inflation, however, had abated during the first quarter, dropping to 7.2% as compared to 11.7% during the last quarter of 1974.

United Brands Charged with Bribery — The Securities and Exchange Commission, **Apr. 9**, charged that United Brands, the multinational food concern, had bribed Honduran government officials with $1.25 million to get favorable treatment on banana shipments from Honduras. As a result of the allegations, long-time Honduran president Gen. Oswaldo Lopez Arellano was ousted from power in a bloodless coup d'etat, **Apr. 22**, in Tegucigalpa, by the Armed Forces Supreme Council. Lopez had refused to cooperate with a Honduran commission investigating the bribery charges. Armed forces commander Col. Juan Alberto Melgar Castro succeeded Lopez as president.

Connally Acquitted on Bribery Charges — A U.S. District Court jury, in Washington, D.C., **Apr. 17**, acquitted John B. Connally on 2 counts of bribery. A beaming Connally said immediately that he might resume his political career. The indictment had alleged that in 1971 Connally had accepted a total of $10,000 in 2 separate payments from the American Milk Producers, Inc. (AMPI), in return for a recommendation that the Nixon administration raise federal milk price supports. The jury deliberated for 5½ hours before bringing in the verdict. The prosecution had based its case on the testimony of Jake Jacobsen, a former AMPI attorney, and a large amount of documentary evidence, presented by 35 witnesses. Jacobsen testified, **Apr. 3**, that he had handed the money over to Connally. The defense, conducted by Edward Bennett Williams, had sought to prove Jacobsen was a known perjurer who had fabricated his account of the payoff to barter his way out of fraud charges in

Texas. Jacobsen had agreed to testify in an arrangement with the prosecution under which he pleaded guilty to bribery charges and the Justice Department. in return, dropped the Texas charges. After the defense had presented a parade of character witnesses. including Lady Bird Johnson, Billy Graham, and Texas Rep. Barbara Jordan. Connally, **Apr. 14,** had taken the stand and denied all charges.

Concord, Lexington Battles Marked — Pres. Ford, along with more than 160,000 Americans, including some 20,000 protestors, **Apr. 19,** gathered at Concord and Lexington, Mass., to mark the 200th anniversary of the 2 battles that started the Revolutionary War. The protestors, who in effect were holding a counterbicentennial celebration, jeered and booed Ford. The previous night, in ceremonies at Boston's Old North

Church marking the 200th anniversary of Paul Revere's famous ride, Pres. Ford had called on Americans to remind themselves of "the eternal truth by which we live." He also said the nation's people must "rededicate this nation to the principles of two centuries ago."

International

Military Takes Over in Chad — Chadian Pres. Ngarta Tombalbaye was killed, **Apr. 13,** in N'Djamena, in a coup d'etat by military officers. Acting army chief of staff Gen. Noel Odingar announced the coup. A military communique charged that Tombalbaye's fundamental principle had been "to divide in order to rule," thereby creating circumstances under which the nation's political and economic situation

Vietnam War Ends

Just hours after the emergency helicopter evacuation of all Americans remaining in Saigon and thousands of South Vietnamese who feared for their lives, South Vietnamese Pres. Duong Van Minh, **Apr. 30,** announced an unconditional surrender to the communists. Van Minh, in a radio broadcast to the Vietcong's Provisional Revolutionary Government, offered to meet with PRG representatives to "discuss the orderly transfer of power so as to avoid any unnecessary bloodshed." He ordered the Saigon army to cease fire and remain in place.

Shortly thereafter, North Vietnamese and Vietcong troops, in tanks and armored vehicles, poured into Saigon. The entering forces raised the National Liberation Front flag over the presidential palace, symbolizing the transfer of power. Then Saigon radio fell silent and all normal telephone and telegraph communication with the outside world was cut off.

In Paris, Dinh Ba Thi, the representative of the PRG, hailed the victory: "Henceforth South Vietnam is free and independent. The sacred testament of our beloved President Ho Chi Minh is realized." The PRG announced that it would follow a foreign policy of "peace and nonalignment" and said the lives and property of all foreigners in the country would be protected.

The final chapter in the long Vietnam war had begun, **Jan. 9,** with the fall of Phuoc Binh, the first major communist gain since the January 1973 Paris peace agreement. The fall of Ban Me Thuot, **Mar. 13,** prompted the Saigon government to withdraw forces from most of the Central Highlands; the towns of Kontum and Pleiku were overrun by communist forces **Mar. 18.** Refugees began to stream to safety in coastal areas. On **Mar. 20,** government forces began to withdraw from the northern part of the country. What was to have been an orderly retreat to defensible lines became a debacle as soldiers raced civilians south. By **Mar. 25,** Hue, the cultural capital of South Vietnam, was abandoned and Danang, the 2nd largest city, was in danger. On **Mar. 27,** the U.S. began an airlift of refugees from Danang. On **Mar. 29,** Danang was in chaos as thousands of panicked soldiers fought off civilians to get on planes trying to evacuate refugees. On **Mar. 29,** U.S. Pres. Gerald R. Ford ordered U.S. Navy ships to evacuate "helpless refugees" from the coastal cities to safety in the south. Communist forces entered Danang **Mar. 30.** Fears of a communist attack on Saigon mounted **Apr. 1,** when communist forces moved into former government enclaves on the central coast, thwarting the American evacuation of refugees. The U.S. began a symbolic airlift of military and medical supplies to Saigon, as the country's 3rd largest city, Qui Nhon, was abandoned. All evidence indicated the coastline area was falling to the

communists without much opposition. On **Apr. 2,** more coastal towns, including Cam Ranh, Tuy Hoa, and Nha Trang, the last major port on the South China Sea, were abandoned to communist forces. The communists, **Apr. 5-10,** intensified attacks in the Mekong Delta, one of the last areas outside of the capital still in government hands. On **Apr. 11,** communist forces launched an attack on Xuan Loc, 35 miles northeast of Saigon. Although government forces continued to hold Xuan Loc, communist forces began to push southward around the city. On **Apr. 15,** communist gunners reached the air base at Bien Hoa, 15 miles from Saigon, and had rendered it virtually useless by **Apr. 20.**

Pres. Nyugen Van Thieu resigned, **Apr. 21.** Communist forces held more than two-thirds of South Vietnam and were threatening to seal off Saigon from all approaches. On **Apr. 20,** senior Vietcong officials had hinted they might delay a military onslaught on Saigon to allow for a peaceful conclusion if Thieu resigned and all American "military advisers disguised as civilians" left the country. In his national farewell address, Thieu defended the accomplishments of his 10 years in office and bitterly accused the U.S. of violating its promises to support the anticommunist government in South Vietnam. He named his vice president, Tran Van Huong, as his successor who, he said, would press the enemy to cease all acts of war and begin peace negotiations.

The communists, however, rejected the resignation, indicating the U.S. must cease all involvement in South Vietnam, ending support for the Thieu clique, not just for Thieu himself. On **Apr. 24,** the Vietcong indicated that only Gen. Duong Van Minh, known as "Big Minh," and a longtime proponent of neutrality and cooperation with the communists, was acceptable to them as head of the Saigon government. With communist forces within one mile of Saigon city limits, "Big Minh," **Apr. 28,** was installed as president. The Vietcong rejected Minh's first declaration even though it included their 2 basic demands: end of U.S. intervention and dismantling of Saigon's "war machine."

U.S. Pres. Ford ordered total evacuation, **Apr. 29,** saying the move "closes a chapter in the American experience." Ford's decision had been triggered by a communist assault on Saigon's Tan Son Nhut airport, which claimed the lives of 2 U.S. Marine guards and destroyed a U.S. Air Force cargo plane. The evacuation, **Apr. 30,** conducted with 81 helicopters, carried the last 395 Americans in Saigon and 4,475 Vietnamese to U.S. ships waiting offshore. On **Apr. 30,** after the U.S. completed its withdrawal, the Vietcong accepted Minh's unconditional surrender.

ad "never ceased to deteriorate." The military also charged that social discrimination by the regime had caused animosity between tribes and spilled useless blood. Violence, chiefly disputes between Sudanic Moslems and the Bantu, had been almost continuous since 1962 when Tombalbaye imposed a constitution barring all political parties except his own Progressive party. Former armed forces commander Gen. Felix Malloum was named, **Apr. 16**, chief of state to head a 9-member Supreme Military Council.

Sikkim Merges With India — The people of Sikkim, **Apr. 15**, overwhelmingly endorsed an **Apr. 10** national legislature vote to abolish the nation's 300-year-old monarchy and to seek full statehood in India. Sikkim's ruler, Chogyal Palden Thondup Namgyal claimed, **Apr. 15**, that he had been under house arrest since **Apr. 9**, when the Indian army had surrounded the palace and disarmed his 400-man army. The Chinese government accused India of annexing the tiny Himalayan nation by force. The Indian parliament, **Apr. 23** and **26**, approved legislation granting statehood.

Moslems and Christians Fight in Beirut — A ceasefire arranged through Arab mediation, **Apr. 16**, ended 3 days of fighting in Beirut, Lebanon, between Palestinian guerrillas and the right-wing Christian Phalangist party militia. The warfare, which left 120 persons dead and 200 wounded, erupted, **Apr. 13**, when Phalangist militia commander Josef Abi Assi was killed in a dispute. In retaliation, residents of a Christian enclave in the Moslem sector ambushed a bus carrying Palestinian guerrillas from a rally, killing 27 persons and wounding 19. Under the truce agreement, arranged by Arab League Secretary General Mahmoud Riad, the Palestinians agreed to give up Assi's killer and the Phalangists agreed to surrender those responsible for the bus attack.

Shelepin Dropped From Politburo — Soviet Trade Union Chief Alexander Shelepin, **Apr. 16**, was removed from the politburo, the USSR's ruling body, by the central committee of the Communist party. A long-standing rival of Communist Party Chief Leonid Brezhnev, Shelepin had attracted attention in the West a few weeks previously when he had been hounded by demonstrators on an official visit to Great Britain. The ouster was generally seen as a power play by Brezhnev in anticipation of the 25th Communist party congress, scheduled for February 1976. One month later, Shelepin was released from all duties as chairman of the All-Union Central Council of Trade Unions, according to a **May 22** Tass report. A further report, **May 24**, stated Shelepin had been demoted to junior minister in charge of vocational training on the state committee for professional and trade education.

Cambodia Falls to Insurgents — Under heavy insurgent military pressure from all sides, the Cambodian government, **Apr. 16**, surrendered to the Khmer Rouge, ending the 5-year Cambodian war. The rebels poured into Phnom Penh and, **Apr. 17**, set up headquarters at the Interior Ministry. The Khmer Rouge immediately invited all ministers and generals of the former government "who have not run away" to help formulate measures to restore order. The beginning of the end for the Cambodian government came **Apr. 1**, when Pres. Lon Nol left the country. On the same day, the government's naval base at Neak Long was overrun by rebel forces, signalling the beginning of an intensive rebel offensive. On **Apr. 3**, the U.S. Embassy began slowly evacuating diplomatic and other personnel from Phnom Penh. U.S. military helicopters, under the protection of U.S. Marine security forces and fighter planes, **Apr. 12**, evacuated the several hundred remaining Americans and some

Cambodians, including acting president Lt. Gen. Saukham Khoy and other military and government officials, from landing zones near the American embassy. Exiled leader Prince Norodom Sihanouk announced from Peking that the U.S. had informed him that "everyone in Phnom Penh" wanted him to, return to head a new government and help work out a ceasefire. Sihanouk declined to return. The insurgents, beginning **Apr. 12**, reintensified their push on Phnom Penh from all directions and had reached the southern end of the city by nightfall **Apr. 15**. The roads to Phnom Penh were jammed with villagers and refugees fleeing from the insurgent drive. The government surrendered **Apr. 16**. Shortly afterwards, all official contact between Phnom Penh and the outside world ceased. Cambodian Communists, in Paris, **Apr. 17**, held a triumphant news conference, saying the new government would follow a policy of nonalignment and neutrality. Internally, they said, Cambodia would have "a new society, certainly different from the one that preceded the fascist coup d'etat of March 1970," when Prince Sihanouk was ousted. Sihanouk would remain chief of state and return when conditions permitted. It was reported **Apr. 18**, that thousands of Cambodians were leaving Phnom Penh under communist orders. On **Apr. 22**, in his first broadcast from Phnom Penh, Khieu Samphan, the commander of the Khmer Rouge forces, hailed the victory and said Cambodia would pursue a policy of neutrality and nonalignment.

Terrorists Seize W. German Embassy — West German terrorists, **Apr. 24**, seized the West German Embassy in Stockholm, Sweden, taking 12 hostages. Three persons, including the West German military attache and one terrorist, died during the siege. The 6 terrorists, who identified themselves as the "Holger Meins Commando," named after the Baader-Meinhof anarchist gang member who died in November 1974 following a hunger strike in prison, held the building for 12 hours and, after their demands were refused, blew up part of the embassy. The terrorists then surrendered to the police. They had demanded the release of 26 anarchists, members of the Baader-Meinhof gang, from West German prisons; $520,000; and transportation of the released prisoners from Frankfurt to an undisclosed destination.

Moderates Win Portuguese Elections — Moderate political forces, **Apr. 25**, won the majority of votes in Portugal's first free elections in more than 50 years. The Socialists, who captured 38% of the votes, and the centrist Popular Democrats, who won 26% of the votes, had campaigned for civil rights and in opposition to both communism and military dictatorship. The Communist party ran a poor 3rd, taking only 12.5% of the vote. The election results, however, meant little in light of recent political developments. Two weeks previously, on **Apr. 4**, the military forces had presented a 14-page document outlining a constitution which gave all essential power to the 28-member High Council of the Revolution. Under the constitution, the military council would run Portugal for a provisional period of 3 to 5 years and place it "irreversibly on the road that will lead it to Portuguese socialism." Pres. Francisco da Costa Gomez said years of tight military rule were needed to defend the revolution against reactionary and extreme left-wing elements and the nation's political inexpertise. Portugal's 6 major political parties, **Apr. 11**, had signed the document ceding almost all power to the military. On **Apr. 28**, after the elections, Socialist leader Mario Soares confirmed that his party would respect the pact with the military forces. The Popular Democrats promised likewise.

General

Daley Wins in Chicago — Chicago Mayor Richard J. Daley, **Apr. 1**, handily won a 6th term as mayor, defeating his Republican opponent John J. Hoellen. Earlier, in his first primary fight since he took office, Daley, **Feb. 25**, had taken 58% of the vote in a 4-man field.

Refugee Airlift Jet Crashes — On the first day of the U.S. airlift of South Vietnamese orphans, an Air Force Galaxy-C-5A cargo jet, **Apr. 4**, crashed shortly after take-off from Saigon. Of the some 300 persons aboard, at least 200 persons, including over 100 children, died, making the crash the worst disaster in U.S. aviation history. The pilot, who survived, said he lost control of his steering mechanism when the huge rear loading doors of the plane blew off.

First Attica Trial Ends — Following 25 hours of deliberation, a Buffalo, N.Y., jury, **Apr. 5**, found John Hill and Charles J. Pernasilice guilty of murder and assault in connection with the death of Attica State Prison correction officer William E. Quinn. Quinn died as a result of injuries received during the September 1971 uprising at Attica. Pernasilice and Hill, both Indian-Americans, were inmates at the prison. Hill was found guilty of murder, the highest charge he faced. Pernasilice was convicted of assault in the 2nd degree. The convictions were the first to arise from the New York state investigation into the prison rebellion. The defense, led by William E. Kunstler and former Attorney General Ramsey Clark, had contended guards and inmates who testified for the state prosecution had garnered paroles and favored treatment in return for perjured testimony. Hill was sentenced, **May 8**, to 20 years to life in prison. Pernasilice was sentenced to up to 2 years in prison.

Textbook Protestors Convicted — A West Virginia federal jury, **Apr. 18**, convicted the Rev. Marvin Horan and Larry Elmer Stevens in connection with bombings of Kanawha County public schools. The bombings, in October and November 1974, came at the height of a protest lead by Horan over textbooks used in the schools. Horan, a self-ordained fundamentalist minister and former truck driver, was found guilty on one count of conspiracy to bomb the schools. He was acquitted on 3 counts alleging overt acts to obtain dynamite illegally, to manufacture bombs, and to commit the bombings. Stevens, a young coal miner described as Horan's right-hand man, was found guilty on 6 counts, including conspiracy to bomb, possession of dynamite, manufacture of bombs, and committing the actual bombings. Horan was sentenced, **May 19**, to 3 years in prison and freed on a $50,000 bond pending appeal of the conviction. Stevens was also given a 3-year term, but with a special provision that allowed for parole at any time.

MAY

National

Stans Fined for Campaign Violations — U.S. District Court Judge John Lewis Smith Jr., **May 14**, fined former Commerce Secretary Maurice H. Stans $5,000 for 5 violations of federal campaign law. Stans, who faced up to 5 years in prison, had served as chief fund raiser for the Nixon reelection campaign. Smith said various factors, including Stans's "long public and private career," made a "monetary penalty" sufficient punishment.

Congress Votes Funds for Refugees — The House and Senate, **May 16**, approved final legislation authorizing the transportation, temporary maintenance, and resettlement of South Vietnamese and Cambodian refugees in the U.S. The legislation appropriated $405 million to fund the refugee aid program. Although the evacuation of refugees ha begun in mid-April, legislation providing authoriza tion and funds had stalled in Congress. On **May 1**, th House, in a 246-162 vote, had killed a $327 millic refugee aid bill which had stipulated use of U.: troops in the final evacuation of Saigon. By that dat an estimated 84,000 persons, including some 5,00 Americans, had been evacuated from South Vietnam Pres. Gerald R. Ford, **May 5**, asked Congress to appr priate $507 million to pay for the resettlement some 150,000 refugees over the next 28 months. Th administration had already provided $98 millio from other programs and expected to run out money by the week's end. Ford's request for refuge aid, however, encountered widespread oppositio both in Congress and from people across the countr Republican Congressional leaders who met wit Ford, **May 6**, reported the president was "damne mad" about the opposition. Ford, in a national telev sion appeal that evening, said he was upset becaus the U.S. "has had a long tradition of opening its door to immigrants of all countries." The final legislatio however, was passed with little opposition. The ir teragency task force on refugees reported, **June** that 130,000 refugees were "in the system." 30,300 c which had been processed and released for resettle ment in the U.S. Some 56,000 were at camps in th Pacific, 43,000 in Thailand, and 1,000 refugees wer on the way to the U.S. Some 3,400 had gone to othe countries, chiefly Canada.

Gulf Oil Admits Illegal Payment Abroad — Gulf O Corporation Chairman Bob R. Dorsey, **May 16**, admit ted to the Senate Foreign Relations Committee's sub committee on multinational corporations that hi company had made illegal political contribution abroad totalling $5 million over the past decade. Th Congressional inquiry had been prompted by disclo sure of Gulf's illegal payments, reported in The Wal Street Journal **May 2**. The Journal asserted Gulf offi cials had told the Securities and Exchang Commission their company had been forced to pa $4.2 million to foreign politicians to protect its o assets. Exxon Corp. Chairman James K. Jamieson **May 15**, told Exxon's annual stockholders' meetin that his company had made political contributions i Italy and Canada. Jamieson, however, asserted th contributions had been made openly and throug legal channels. Ashland Oil Co. and 3 of its to officials, **May 16**, in a Washington D. C. federal court said they would stop using corporate funds for illega political contributions. In further disclosures, Mobi Oil Corp. and Indiana and California Standard Oil **May 19**, told The Wall Street Journal they had als made legal contributions in Canada and Italy.

Moynihan Goes to UN — Pres. Gerald R. Ford, **May** **21**, named Daniel P. Moynihan, a Harvard University professor and former ambassador to India, to suc ceed John A. Scali as the U.S. Ambassador to the United Nations. The Senate confirmed the nomina tion **June 9**. The nomination had come as a surprise because it had been reported in February that Ford and Secretary of State Henry A. Kissinger had told Scali they wanted him to remain.

Ford Imposes 2nd Fee Increase on Imported Oil — Accusing Congress of wasting time on unproductive debate on energy conservation, Pres. Ford, **May 27** imposed a $1 per barrel increase in fees on imported oil effective June 1. Ford, in a nationally televised ad dress, said he was taking the action, which he had delayed twice, because "the Congress cannot drift dawdle and debate forever with America's future." Ford also announced that he would start phasing out controls on domestic oil supplies later in June. Al though Ford acknowledged the actions would inrease consumer costs of energy, he contended the American economy would eventually benefit from his efforts to stop the flow of oil money to foreign producers. The running battle between Ford and Congress over energy conservation legislation had intensified May 20, when the House Democratic leadership indefinitely postponed legislation that would have raised the federal gasoline tax and taken other steps to conserve energy.

Sanford Joins Presidential Contenders — Duke University President and former North Carolina Governor Terry Sanford, May 29, became the 6th entry in the race for the Democratic presidential nomination. He announced that a Sanford administration would guarantee a job to every American who wanted one and that moral leadership would be the cornerstone of his foreign policy. Sanford, a southerner, made it clear that a confrontation with Alabama Gov. George C. Wallace would be the central test of his candidacy.

International

New Cambodian Government Wages Peasant Revolution — The Cambodian Communist government which had come to power Apr. 17 was waging a peasant revolution that had thrown the entire country into upheaval, New York Times correspondent Sydney H. Schanberg reported May 8. Schanberg had remained in Cambodia after the take-over and had reached Thailand, May 3, by truck convoy along with several hundred other foreigners. Schanberg confirmed a May 5 U.S. State Dept. report that Cambodian communists were forcibly evacuating almost the entire population of Phnom Penh and at least 2 other cities. Schanberg said that at least 3 to 4 million people had been sent on a mammoth exodus into the countryside. The State Dept. also had reported "on the basis of reliable information" that a Khmer Rouge order to kill top political and military leaders who had served in the previous government had resulted in the deaths of 80 to 90 officers and their wives.

Fragile Laotian Coalition Imperiled — The resignation, May 9, of 5 right-wing, pro-American cabinet ministers threatened the fragile Laotian coalition government. The resignations had been preceded by widespread unrest marked by renewed military conflict between rightist forces and the communist-led Pathet Lao. The unrest was further heightened by widespread anti-American demonstrations and the seizure, May 14, by Laotian students of 14 Americans, including officials of the U.S. Agency for International Development (AID), in Savannakhet. The protestors demanded that AID in Laos be dissolved. Beginning May 16, with the seizure of Pakse, the Pathet Lao moved into the previously rightist-controlled Laotian panhandle area. They met no resistance from the rightist faction whose representatives had fled the previous week. On May 19, Pathet Lao forces took Savannakhet where the 14 Americans had remained under house arrest. Anti-Ameri-

Cambodia Seizes U. S. Merchant Vessel Mayaguez; U. S. Battles Cambodians to Regain Vessel, Crew

At the order of U. S. Pres. Gerald R. Ford, U. S. air, sea, and ground forces, May 14, engaged Cambodian forces to free the U. S. container ship Mayaguez and its 39-man crew, which had been seized by Cambodia in the Gulf of Siam 2 days previously. The rescue operation, announced by Pres. Ford, May 15, 11 hours after it began, involved the sinking of 3 Cambodian gunboats, a sharp skirmish between U. S. Marines and Khmer Rouge forces, and an air attack on the air base at Ream, near the port of Sihanoukville.

The White House announced, May 12, that a Cambodian vessel had fired on the unarmed Mayaguez, boarded it, and forced the ship into the port of Sihanoukville. Ford termed the seizure "an act of piracy" by the new Cambodian government. He instructed the State Department to "demand immediate release of the ship" because "failure to do so would have the most serious consequences." The U.S. appealed to China, through the Washington, D. C., liaison office, to help obtain release of the ship.

When diplomatic initiatives produced no results, Ford, after consulting with Congress in accordance with the war powers act, ordered the rescue operation. Despite Thai government protest, 1,100 marines were flown to U Taphao air base in Thailand for possible use in the rescue. The mission began in the early hours of May 14, when American planes sank 3 Cambodian gunboats which, according to Defense Dept. officials, were attempting to transport Mayaguez crew to the Cambodian mainland. The major confrontation occurred late in the afternoon on Tang Island in the Gulf of Siam where 200 marines battled the Khmer Rouge for more than 12 hours. The marines were landed on the island by helicopter in the mistaken belief that the Mayaguez crew was being held there. After the assault forces hit Tang Island, Phnom Penh radio broadcast an announcement stating it was freeing the ship and crew. Shortly thereafter, U. S. marines reached and boarded the Mayaguez and found no one there. Almost 2 hours later, the U.S. destroyer Wilson retrieved the crew which had approached in a small boat flying a white flag. At almost the same time, U. S. carrier planes began air strikes on Ream, ostensibly to prevent possible air interference by Cambodian planes. The operation was concluded, May 15, when 200 marines were airlifted from Tang Island. On May 17, the Defense Dept. revealed that a 2d air attack, on an oil depot close to Sihanoukville, had been made one hour after the attack on Ream.

First reports stated that the casualties had been light. However, May 20, the Defense Dept. reported 15 American servicemen were killed, 50 wounded, and 3 missing. On May 21, it was reported 23 more servicemen died in a helicopter crash related to the rescue mission.

Cambodian Information Minister Hu Him, in a May 5 broadcast from Phnom Penh, said his country had decided to release the ship because "our weak country cannot have a confrontation with the U. S." He accused the U. S. of systematic spying against Cambodia since the communist takeover.

Approval of Ford's use of force to rescue the ship and crew was widespread among the public and in Congress, although some Congressmen complained that Ford had informed rather than consulted Congress on his intentions.

Secretary of State Henry A. Kissinger, May 16, said the rescue showed "there are limits" beyond which the United States cannot be pushed." He also apologized to Thailand for embarrassment the U. S. may have caused in using U Taphao air base in the rescue. Thailand had accused the U.S., May 15, of a "breach of faith" in using the base and, May 16, had summoned her ambassador to the U. S. home for consultations. On May 19, the Thai government accepted a formal apology from the U. S.

can actions increased **May 21**, when pro-Pathet Lao students seized the AID compound in Vientiane, trapping 3 Americans inside. The U.S., **May 22**, agreed to halt all AID activities, except those in Vientiane, and to begin negotiations for total withdrawal of personnel. The 14 Americans under house arrest were released. On **May 23**, the U.S. began a major evacuation of AID personnel and dependents from Laos. On **May 28**, in exchange for the release of 3 Americans held in the AID compound, the U.S. signed an agreement terminating all AID activities in Laos and transferring all the agency's equipment to the Laotian government.

New South Vietnam Government Celebrates Victory — Marking their victory and the birthday of Ho Chi Minh, South Vietnam's Provisional Revolutionary Government, **May 13**, opened a 3-day celebration. Nguyen Huu Tho, the chairman of the PRG advisory council, called for "diplomatic, economic, cultural and friendship relations with all countries of the world provided those countries respect the sovereignty of our country and will not interfere in our internal affairs." This, Tho said, also included the U.S. if America agreed to "carry out its responsibilities as provided by the Paris agreement of 1973." On **May 1**, the PRG had broadcast a series of decrees forbidding the publication of all newspapers, books, and other printed materials by private citizens. Prostitution, dance halls, and "acting like Americans" were also banned. On **May 3**, Saigon radio announced that North Vietnam had undertaken a vast reconstruction program in South Vietnam to provide jobs and begin reversing the devastation of 30 years of war. Reports, **May 12**, on the first news conference given by the Military Management Committee administering Saigon, indicated the new rulers of South Vietnam intended to hold nation-wide elections and eventually unify North and South Vietnam. Reports, **May 19**, stated that Pham Hung, the 4th ranking member of North Vietnam's politburo, had emerged as the apparent political leader in South Vietnam. He had secretly coordinated activities against the Saigon government over the previous 8 years.

U.S. Colonels Slain in Iran — Three Iranian terrorists armed with submachine guns, **May 21**, seized and killed 2 U.S. Air Force colonels in Teheran. The 2 men, Col. Paul R. Shaffer Jr. and Lt. Col. John H. Turner, were enroute to their offices in the Iranian armed forces headquarters, where they worked for the Military Assistance Advisory Group. The Iranian People's Fighters Organization, via several anonymous phone calls, said it had committed the killings in retaliation for atrocities the Iranian government had perpetrated against political prisoners.

Portuguese Socialists Boycott Cabinet — Portuguese Socialist party leader Mario Soares, at a **May 22** press conference in Lisbon, accused the country's military leaders of discrimination in favor of the Communist party and announced his party would boycott cabinet meetings. Soares demanded union elections to test Communist power, local elections to replace Communists who had seized power illegally, and an end to Communist take-overs in the communications field. He set no deadline for these demands. A major event leading to the boycott decision was the seizure, **May 19**, of the Socialist-leaning newspaper *Republica* by Communists. Disturbances over the seizure had forced the Information Minister to close down *Republica*, May 20. On **May 25**, 10,000 Socialist supporters gathered for a 5-hour rally in Lisbon to demonstrate their determination to resist the Communists.

Karami Named Lebanese Premier — Following weeks of renewed violence and changes of government, the powerful Moslem political leader Rash Karami, **May 28**, was named premier of Lebano Premier Rashid al-Solh had resigned, **May 15**, citi as the reason criticism of the government's inabili to halt fighting the previous month between Palesti ian guerrillas and the right-wing Phalangist par militia. A renewal of fighting, **May 19**, had force Lebanese Pres. Suleiman Franjieh, **May 23**, to a point a military cabinet, the first since the natio independence in 1943. The cabinet was headed b Nureddin Rifai, a Sunni Moslem, who had been con mander of internal security forces. The new gover ment, however, came under immediate criticis from Moslem political and religious leaders, th Palestinians, and other Arab nations. Strong oppo tion by a majority of the parliament and renewed vi lence forced the military cabinet's resignation Ma 26. Rifai said he was stepping down to save Lebanc "from further bloodshed." The appointment of Kar mi 2 days later brought immediate relief to the tens capital. Karami announced that Pres. Franjieh an Phalangist leader Pierre Gemayel had agreed th armed men of both factions would withdraw from th streets and dismantle barricades.

Ford assures NATO Allies — In Brussels, Belgiun for the NATO summit meeting, U.S. Pres. Gerald Ford, **May 28**, told NATO allies that the U.S. "con mitment to this alliance will not falter." His remark reflected the growing concern of America's We European allies over U.S. commitments in wake the collapse in Indochina. In the opening address the summit, Ford, **May 29**, asserted that, despite th events in Indochina, America's "military power re mains and will continue to remain, second to non . . . Our actions will continue to confirm the durab ity of our commitments." While in Brussels, For held bilateral meetings with several NATO leader among them Portuguese Premier Vasco dos Santo The Portuguese premier rebutted statements that h country's leftist government posed a threat to th NATO alliance, telling Ford that Portugal was " loyal European state and intends to remain a loy NATO member."

Greek, Turkish Leaders Meet — For the first tim since 1967, Greek and Turkish leaders, **May 31**, me face to face for talks. Turkish Pres. Suleiman Dem rel and Greek Premier Constantine Caramanlis cor ferred for 3 hours in Brussels during the NAT summit meeting and agreed that the conflicts be tween their countries "must be resolved peacefull and through negotiations." Although no actual me tion was made of Cyprus, the source of deepest di pute between the 2 countries, the final communiqu stated both leaders "agreed to support intercommu nal negotiations in Vienna" between Greek and Turl ish Cypriots.

General

New Boston Busing Plan Released — U.S. Distric Court Judge W. Arthur Garrity Jr., **May 10**, mad public his final desegregation plan for Boston racially-troubled schools. The new plan, effectiv September 1975, called for the busing of 21,000 stu dents, 3,000 more than under the current interin plan. Under the new plan, schools in South Bostor the center of anti-busing sentiment and the gene o racial violence the previous fall, would continue t share schools with neighboring black areas. Long time busing opponent Louise Day Hicks, **May 11**, call ed Garrity's plan "the death knell of the city." O **May 12**, the U.S. Supreme Court gave support t Garrity, refusing to review his original decision find ing Boston public schools unconstitutionall segregated.

Milan Museum Hit By Second Theft — For the 2

time in 3 months, armed thieves, **May 15**, broke into Milan's Gallery of Modern Art, seizing 38 paintings valued at $8 million. Included in the theft were 28 famous impressionist paintings which had been stolen from the museum on **Feb. 11**. The paintings had been recovered, **Apr.**, in an empty Milan apartment. On **May 16**, museum staffs all over Italy called a one-week strike in protest over poor security in the country's museums.

RFK Assassin Granted Parole Date — The California Adult Authority, **May 20**, granted a Feb. 23,1986, parole date to Sirhan Sirhan, the convicted assassin of Robert F. Kennedy. Originally sentenced to death, Sirhan could now be released from prison after serving 16 years and 9 months. Philip D. Guthrie, the assistant director of the California State Department of Corrections said of Sirhan: "He was extremely well behaved all the time he has been in prison — absolutely no problem."

Landmark Marijuana Decision in Alaska — The Alaska Supreme Court, **May 27**, handed down a unanimous decision which, in effect, legalized the use of marijuana in the privacy of one's home in Alaska. Chief Justice Jay A. Rabinowitz, in the 54-page decision, wrote that "the use of marijuana, as it is presently used in the United States today, does not constitute a public health problem of any significant dimension." The judge added that its effects were less dangerous than alcohol, barbiturates, and amphetamines. The challenge to the existing marijuana law had been brought by the American Civil Liberties Union on behalf of Irwin Ravin, who had been arrested for possession of marijuana after being stopped for a traffic violation.

Disasters — A cyclone with winds up to 90 miles per hour hit Burma's Irrawaddy delta region, according to reports **May 11**, leaving 187 persons dead . . . A train, **May 19**, rammed into a truck packed with guests heading for a wedding in the Indian state of Marashtra, killing 66 of the guests and injuring 18 others . . . A Moroccan train enroute to Tangiers derailed, it was reported **May 23**, 35 miles northeast of Rabat, killing 35 persons and injuring 200.

JUNE
National
Unemployment Up Again — Unemployment continued to rise in May, reaching 9.2% of the labor force, the Labor Dept. reported **June 6**. However, for the 2d month in a row, the total number of persons employed increased. On **June 22**, top presidential economic adviser Alan Greenspan predicted that, although the recession had bottomed out, unemployment would not decline until the fall and then would decline very slowly. He said, however, that the May rate of 9.2% would be the highest of the recession and that the rate would fall to 7.5% of the labor force by the end of 1976.

Rockefeller Commission Report on CIA Released — The 8-man "blue-ribbon" Rockefeller Commission concluded, in its final report made public **June 10**, that the Central Intelligence Agency had conducted a vast network of domestic operations that "were plainly unlawful and constituted improper invasions upon the rights of Americans." However, the report stated that the "great majority" of CIA activities during its 28-year existence had complied with the law and the agency's charter. The commission, headed by Vice President Nelson A. Rockefeller, had turned over its 299-page study to Pres. Gerald R. Ford **June 6**. Ford, **June 9**, had forwarded the report, including information on alleged assassination plots against foreign leaders, to the Justice Department for possi-

ble prosecution. Ford also said he would make the report public, except for the section on alleged assassinations which was "incomplete and extremely sensitive." The commission's report described CHAOS, a 7-year espionage operation against dissident American political groups. As part of the project, the CIA created dossiers on 13,000 persons and index records on 300,000 individuals and organizations, and infiltrated agents into anti-war and black movements. The report also documented a 10-year drug-testing program which culminated in the death of a government employee who had been administered LSD without his knowledge. Also publicly documented for the first time were programs to monitor overseas telephone calls to Europe and Latin America and a 20-year program surveying mail between the U.S. and USSR. The Commission also charged that the Justice Department had "abdicated its statutory duties" for more than 20 years in a secret agreement with the CIA. The agreement, the report alleged, gave the CIA the power to decide whether or not the Justice Department would prosecute criminal charges involving CIA employees. This agreement "involved the agency directly in forbidden law enforcement activities" and in direct violation of its charter. The commission, however, found no evidence that the CIA had abused this prosecutorial power. The commission also reported it had found "no credible evidence" the CIA had been involved in the assassination of Pres. John F. Kennedy. In conclusion, the Rockefeller Commission recommended that Pres. Ford introduce a bill to set up a joint Congressional committee to oversee all intelligence agencies. The report also recommended that the president tighten executive control over the CIA by making the Foreign Intelligence Advisory Board an effective watchdog agency, by opening the CIA directorship to people outside of the government, and by limiting the director's term to 10 years.

Nedzi Quits House CIA Panel Post — Rep. Lucien D. Nedzi (D. Mich.), **June 12**, resigned as chairman of the House Select Committee on Intelligence Activities, charging Democrats on the panel had stripped him of all but "a gavel and a title." Following a **June 5** disclosure by The New York Times that Nedzi had been secretly briefed on illegal CIA activities and had failed to call for an investigation, the committee Democrats had moved to oust Nedzi. The full House, however, **June 16**, rejected Nedzi's resignation. Despite the vote, Nedzi said, "I frankly don't see how I could make a valuable contribution."

Marianas Vote to Join U.S. — In a national plebiscite, the northern Mariana Islands voted, **June 17**, by a 3-to-1 margin, to join the United States. The Marianas, comprising 14 islands, stretch for 500 miles in a north-south direction in the Pacific Ocean over 3,500 miles west of Hawaii. Currently administered as part of the United States Trust Territory of the Pacific Islands, under the proposed covenant, the islands would be a commonwealth of the U.S.

Callaway to Head Ford Election Campaign — Pres. Ford announced, **June 18**, that Secretary of the Army Howard H. Callaway would resign shortly in order to direct the president's 1976 election campaign. The announcement was the first formal indication that Ford would enter the election. Callaway, who had only limited ties with the Nixon reelection campaign, pledged "an open, candid and straightforward campaign.

Ray Quits, Scores Kissinger — Dixy Lee Ray, formerly chairman of the defunct Atomic Energy Commission, **June 20**, resigned as the top science official at the State Department, blaming Secretary of State

Henry A. Kissinger and other top officials. Ray said Kissinger and others had purposely not consulted her on key policy issues, particularly dealing with research and development of new energy sources. Ray had served for 5 months as first assistant secretary of state for oceans and international and scientific affairs. Congress had created the bureau specifically to give prestige and importance to these matters in the State Department. Kissinger, through a spokesman, said he was "sorry" about the resignation.

Mathews to Head HEW — Pres. Ford, **June 26**, nominated University of Alabama Pres. Dr. F. David Mathews, 39, to succeed Caspar W. Weinberger, who resigned the same day, as secretary of health, education and welfare. Mathews said he was honored to accept the post, but hoped "everybody fully realizes what a hard and often thankless task this post has become." Upon confirmation by the Senate, **July 22** Mathews became the youngest member of Ford's cabinet.

International

Suez Canal Reopened — Egypt, **June 5**, reopened the Suez Canal to all international shipping, except Israeli ships, exactly 8 years after its closing during the 1967 Arab-Israeli war. The first commercial ships passed through 2 hours later. Calling the event "the happiest day in my life," Egyptian Pres. Anwar el Sadat said that, although the opening was meant as a contribution to peace and international cooperation, Egypt was still determined to "liberate" Israeli-occupied Arab territories in the Sinai, the Golan Heights, and Palestine. Sadat, however, did praise Israel's announcement, **June 2**, that Israeli forces along the canal would be reduced in response to the opening. The partial withdrawal had been completed **June 4**.

Belgium to Purchase U.S. F-16's — Following a year of bitter debate, the Belgian government announced, **June 7**, that it would buy 102 U.S.-designed F-16 jet fighters to replace its obsolete force. In doing so, Belgium joined 3 other NATO allies — Norway, Denmark, the Netherlands — in opting for the F-16 over the French Mirage F-1. Altogether, the 4 countries would purchase 306 planes worth more than $2 billion, in one of the greatest arms sales of the century. In order to clinch the deal, the U.S. had offered several economic incentives, including a promise to purchase $30 million-worth of Belgian-made machine guns. French Premier Jacques Chirac deplored the decision, calling it "regrettable for the future" of the European aviation industry. The Belgian parliament, **June 13**, in a 112-91 vote, endorsed the decision.

China, Philippines Establish Relations — Philippine Pres. Ferdinand E. Marcos and Chinese Premier Chou En-lai, **June 9**, signed an agreement in Peking establishing diplomatic relations between their countries. The Chinese and Philippine trade ministers signed a trade agreement shortly thereafter. Following the announcement, the Philippine and the Nationalist Chinese government broke off all relations. Upon his return to Manila, Marcos, **June 11**, said the newly established relations with China would not prejudice his government's relations with old friends and allies.

British Cabinet Shuffled After Common Market Vote — Following an overwhelmingly pro-Common Market referendum **June 5**, British Prime Minister Harold Wilson, **June 10**, demoted outspoken market opponent and Industry Secretary Anthony Wedgewood Benn to the post of energy secretary. The industry post went to Energy Secretary Eric Varley, a less outspoken opponent of British membership in the European Community. Benn's vociferous campaign

against EC membership had made him a hero of the leftwing of the Labor party, but had alienated business and industry leaders.

Communists Gain in Italian Elections — Italy's Communist party made substantial gains nationwide, **June 15-16**, in local, provincial, and regional elections. The Communists emerged as the strongest party in the biggest cities, including Rome, Milan, Naples, Turin, Genoa, Florence, and Bologna. In final results, announced **June 17**, the Christian Democrats remained the strongest party with 35.5% of the national vote, down from 38.4% in the 1972 parliamentary elections. The Communists won 33.4%, up from 28.3% in 1972. Communist party leader Enrico Berlinguer told a victory rally that the gains made it "unthinkable" to presume Italy's problems could be solved without his party and that Communists would take "new initiatives" on the national level. On **June 22**, in a 2,000-word statement published on the first page of *L'Unita*, the Communist party outlined proposals for "necessary economic, social and political changes" in Italy. They called for the creation of "capable, efficient, honest and stable local administrations" and offered to negotiate with all democratic and anti-Fascist forces, especially the Socialist party.

Rival Rebel Groups Sign Accord in Angola — The 3 rival Angolan black liberation movements, **June 21**, signed an accord in Nakuru, Kenya, ending violence and pledging cooperation to lead the Portuguese territory to independence later in the year. Fighting among the rebel groups, **June 4-8**, had claimed some 200 lives and brought the African territory to the brink of civil war. Weeks of violence in May, which had claimed as many as 1,000 lives, had led to the imposition of martial law, **May 15**. The 3 groups — the Popular Movement for the Liberation of Angola (MPLA), the National Front for the Liberation of Angola (FNLA), and the National Union for the Total Independence of Angola (Unita) — reached agreement following 6 days of meetings called by Kenyan Pres. Jomo Kenyatta. The groups agreed to hold free elections if feasible to select the future government, but recognized that Angola's recent turmoil might necessitate another conference "to adopt another form of transfer of powers" to the black majority. They also agreed to integrate their private armed forces into a national army and to disarm the civilian population.

Israel Offers Compromise Sinai Plan — Israeli officials, **June 24**, disclosed a new plan for Israeli-Egyptian disengagement in the Sinai. The plan had been transmitted to Egyptian Pres. Anwar el-Sadat, **June 23**, by U.S. Ambassador Hermann F. Eilts. Under the proposed plan which would last from 3 to 4 years, Israel would withdraw from the western end of the Mitla and Gidi passes, but would retain control of the eastern ends and of access to electronic surveillance stations Israel maintains in the Gidi pass. Israel would also return the Abu Rudeis oil fields and establish an access corridor to the fields. Egypt, in return, would give a commitment not to use force for the duration of the interim agreement. Earlier in the month, U.S. Pres. Gerald R. Ford had met with both Sadat and Israeli Premier Itzak Rabin. Both Middle East leaders had agreed on the advantages of seeking another limited accord in the Middle East.

Mozambique Gains Independence — After 470 years of colonial rule, Mozambique, **June 25**, gained its independence from Portugal. The most militant and Marxist black government in Africa, led by Pres. Samora M. Machel, took over the leadership of the new nation. Machel, who led the Mozambique Liberation Front (FRELIMO), said he would create a militantly radical new society. However, despite some

xpectations, he did not threaten to apply United Na-
ons sanctions against the white minority
vernment in neighboring Rhodesia. Some 80% of
hodesia's trade with the outside world passes by rail
rough Mozambique to the coastal ports of Beira and
ourenco Marques.

India Declares Emergency, Gandhi Foes Arrested
In a massive crackdown on government critics, the
dian government, **June 26**, declared a state of
nergency and arrested 676 persons, including "all
e leaders" of the opposition parties. Prime Minister
dira Gandhi, in a national broadcast, announced
e government had acted against "a deep and wide-
read conspiracy" against the "very functioning of
emocracy." Press censorship was also imposed.
hose arrested included Jaya Prakash Narayan, the
idely respected leader of an anti-corruption drive
med against Gandhi, and former Deputy Prime
inister Morarji K. Desai, who had broken with the
ling Congress party in 1969. Government spokes-
an A. R. Baji reported widespread disorders and
emonstrations to protest the detention of political
aders. Scattered protest continued, **June 27** as the
overnment arrested 200 more persons. The violence
as centered chiefly in Bihar, Gujarat, and Uttar
radesh where 450 persons were arrested. By **June
8**, 1,128 persons had been detained, Baji announced.
n **June 29** the government warned foreign journal-
ts they would be treated like "criminals" and jailed
they did not present their articles for censorship. A
ine 12 high court decision that Gandhi must relin-
uish her seat in parliament because she had won it
legally had sparked the crisis. The suit had been
rought by Raj Narain, the man she had defeated in a
971 landslide victory in Uttar Pradesh. Narain was
lso arrested June 26. The court barred Gandhi from
olding any elective office for 6 years, but granted
er 20 days to file an appeal. Gandhi took her case to
e people June 13-16, holding mass rallies to seek
ipport. The ruling Congress party caucused, **June
8**, and adopted a resolution affirming their "fullest
aith" in Gandhi's "indispensable" leadership. The
overnment opposition, however, called for Gandhi
o step down and vowed, **June 24**, to conduct a nation-
ride campaign of passive resistance if she did not. On
une 24 the Supreme Court ruled that Gandhi could
emain as prime minister pending review of the ap-
eal but said she could not vote in parliament.

General

SLA Members Convicted in Foster Murder — A
acramento, Cal., Jury, **June 9**, found Joseph M.
emiro and Russell J. Little, both members of the
ymbionese Liberation Army, guilty of the Novem-
er 1973 murder of Oakland schools superintendent
r. Marcus A. Foster. The jury, which deliberated for
5 hours over 11 days, also found the 2 men guilty of
he attempted murder of Foster's assistant, Robert
Blackburn. Blackburn, who had been seriously in-
ured, took the stand but was not able to identify posi-
vely either of the defendants. Remiro and Little
vere sentenced, **June 27**, to life imprisonment for the
oster murder and to 6 months to 20 years for at-
empted murder to be served concurrently with the
fe sentences. Both men filed statements of inno-
ence, contending they had been convicted on the
asis of their association with the SLA.

Saxe Pleads Guilty — Militant antiwar radical and
eminist Susan Saxe, **June 9**, in a sudden reversal,
leaded guilty, in a Philadelphia, Pa., federal court,
o 2 crimes committed in 1970. She was charged with
he robbery of a Philadelphia savings and loan associ-

ation and with theft from a federal arsenal at Newburyport, Mass. Saxe said she did not regret the
crimes because "armed struggle against the American state was a valid and necessary escalation of the
politics of the sixties." A fugitive for 4½ years, Saxe
had been apprehended **Mar. 27**, when she had pleaded guilty to the charges. Her change of plea came as
part of a deal with the government under which she
was granted immunity from testifying in any proceedings on events that happened from 1969 to the
present.

"Big MAC" Delays NYC Default — The creation of
a new state agency, the Municipal Assistance Corporation, **June 10**, spared New York City from default
on $729 million in notes due June 11. Climaxing many
weeks of often bitter partisan political negotiations,
the New York State Legislature enacted the legislation in Albany at dawn. Dubbed "Big MAC," the agency was designed to refinance the city's immediate
short-term indebtedness, totalling $3 billion and due
for repayment September 1. "Big MAC" was empowered to sell bonds for up to 15 years to raise money to
retire the short-term loans. The long-term bonds
would be secured by a reserve fund made up of the
city's sales and stock transfer taxes. It was hoped
"Big MAC's" management of the city's debt would restore investor confidence in New York's ability to pay
its debts. In exchange for management of the debt,
New York City agreed to turn over partial control of
finances to the state agency and to tighten its budget.
Although the city always had been loath to accept
external control over its inner workings, an extremely tight money market and constant criticism of New
York City's bookkeeping methods made "Big MAC"
acceptable. New York City Mayor Abe Beame had
found all efforts to raise cash, both in Washington and
Albany, fruitless.

FBI Agents Slain on Sioux Reservation — FBI
agents Jack R. Coler and Ronald A. Williams were
shot dead, **June 26**, in disputed circumstances at
Oglala on the Pine Ridge Indian Reservation in South
Dakota. One Indian died in the shootout that followed. The FBI contended the agents were approaching a house inhabited by members of the militant
American Indian Movement to serve arrest warrants
on 4 unidentified persons when the agents were hit
by rifle fire. However, on **June 29**, the FBI released a
statement saying the agents were not carrying the
warrants at the time of their deaths. AIM members
claimed, **June 27**, that the FBI agents had killed the
Indian and then been shot by other law enforcement
officers. By **June 29**, the FBI had sent in some 300 FBI
agents to search for 16 Indian suspects in the killings.
Local residents, it was reported, were signing a petition in protest of heavy-handed tactics used by the
agents.

Disasters — An Eastern Airlines Boeing 727 enroute from New Orleans, La., crashed, **June 24** while
attempting to land at New York's Kennedy International Airport during a thunderstorm, killing 113
persons and seriously injuring 11. The crash was the
worst single-aircraft disaster in the continental U.S. .
. . Of 100 persons aboard, 80 drowned, **June 28**, when
a passenger boat capsized in the monsoon-swollen
Ganges near Patna, India.

JULY

National

Unemployment Down, Industrial Production Up —
Economic news was brighter in July, beginning with
a July 3 Labor Department report that the unemployment rate in June had fallen to 8.6% of the working

force, in contrast to 9.2% in May. Government statisticians, however, pointed out that an unusual statistical aberration had caused the 0.6% drop. Nevertheless, they maintained that unemployment had not deteriorated, pointing out that the rate had remained stable at 8.8% to 8.9% during the past few months. In further optimistic news, the Federal Reserve Board reported, July 15, that an 8-month decline in industrial production had been reversed by a 0.4% increase in June. Increased production of consumer goods, including some rebound in automobile production, had led the way.

Ford Announced Candidacy — Pres. Gerald R. Ford, **July 8**, formally announced that he would seek the Republican nomination for president in 1976 "in order to finish the job I have begun." In the brief announcement, Ford pledged "an open and above-board campaign and asked for the support of "all who believe in the fundamental values of duty, decency and constructive debate on the great issues we face together as a free people." Ford also introduced 4 campaign officials — Chairman Howard H. Callaway, Finance Chairman David Packard, Treasurer Robert C. Moot, and advisory panel head Dean Burch — as "outstanding Americans on whose integrity both my supporters and all others can depend." Callaway, **July 9**, said Ford's election campaign organization would make no effort to win support for Vice President Nelson A. Rockefeller for the 2nd spot on the ballot.

New Orleans Grain Company Indicted — A New Orleans federal grand jury, **July 21**, indicted the Bunge Corporation, one of the world's largest grain companies, and 13 present and former employees for conspiracy to steal grain by short-weighting shipments, and for conspiracy to cover up the thefts through a falsified system of interoffice accounting. The indictments raised to the highest level a spreading government investigation into alleged nationwide corrupt handling, weighing, and grading of grain for export. Previous indictments, numbering 20 in Los Angeles and Houston, had largely involved grain inspectors licensed by the Department of Agriculture but employed by private concerns and others allegedly involved with them in bribery schemes. On **Oct. 8**, the Bunge Corp., in a New Orleans federal court, pleaded nolo contendere to federal counts of conspiracy to steal grain and conspiracy to cover up the thefts. The corporation was then judged guilty and required to spend more than $2 million over the next 3 years to establish procedures to guard against corruption. Bunge was also fined $10,000 in New Orleans on the theft count and $10,000 in Houston for the coverup charge.

Ford Apologizes to LSD Suicide's Family — Pres. Ford, **July 21**, held a White House meeting with the family of Frank R. Olson to apologize "for the wrong that's been done to you." Olson, a research scientist for the CIA, had committed suicide in a New York City hotel in 1953 after taking LSD in a job-related experiment. The family had first learned of the circumstances of Olson's death while reading the Rockefeller Commission's report on CIA activities. Ford told the Olson family he would have the CIA make available to them information on the case. Ford also asked the U. S. attorney general to meet with the family's legal representatives "to discuss the claims they wish to assert against the CIA by reason of Dr. Olson's death." The New York Times had revealed, **July 18**, that Sidney Gottlieb, a biochemist who had headed the CIA's LSD program, had destroyed all the program's records in 1973, allegedly to hide details of possible illegal actions. On **July 23**, a senior U. S. Army medical official reported that none of some 600

participants in Army LSD experiments were told either before or after that they had received LSD, for fear of prejudicing the experiment. Follow-ups were done on only 10% of the cases, he said.

House Rejects Arms to Turkey — In a strong rebuff to Pres. Ford's supplications, the House, **July 24**, in a 223-206 vote, rejected an administration appeal to lift partially the 6-month-old arms embargo against Turkey. In immediate response, Turkey, **July 25**, announced it would halt, effective **July 26**, all military activities at American installations in Turkey, except at the air base at Incirlik, which houses a squadron of F-4 fighters, the only American combat unit in Turkey. Defense activities on the behalf of NATO would be allowed to continue at Incirlik. All other installations, some 20 American bases, would be placed under "the full control and supervision of the Turkish armed forces" at an unspecified date. The Turkish announcement, which stated that existing joint defense agreements had "lost their validity," came despite a personal plea from Pres. Ford to Turkish Premier Suleiman Demirel. On **July 28**, senior Turkish officials warned that some of the bases would remain closed even if Congress raised the embargo. One top official explained: "The damage has been done. No government would dare move against the pressure of public opinion." At the European Security Conference in Helsinki, Demirel, **July 31**, refused Pres. Ford's offer of $50-million in U. S. weapons in return for the reopening of the bases.

Interior Secretary Resigns — Pres. Ford, **July 2**, accepted the resignation of his recently confirmed interior secretary, Stanley K. Hathaway, for "reasons of personal health." Hathaway, who had voluntarily entered Bethesda Naval Hospital on **July 15**, had announced, **July 22**, that he was suffering from "moderate depression" caused by overwork. Interior department officials said Hathaway had been "shocked and dismayed" by White House policies "affecting his turf at Interior." The White House confirmed, **July 23**, that Ford had rejected Hathaway's original offer to resign when he entered Bethesda and had urged him to remain in office while recovering.

Congress Overrides Health Bill Veto — For the first time in the year-long struggle over government spending, the Democratic Congress, **July 26** and **29**, overrode a veto by Pres. Ford. Ford, **July 26**, vetoed $2-billion health bill because it would both "authorize excessive appropriations levels" and be "unsound from a program standpoint." The bill provided for grants to states to fund public health service programs and family planning programs, as well as programs for rape prevention and control and programs for the treatment of alcoholics and drug addicts. The House voted, **July 29**, by a 348-to-43 margin, to override the veto. The override broke the momentum of Ford's numerous veto victories on crucial bills, including a farm bill, funds for public service jobs, strip mining curbs, and a housing bill.

International

Peron Yields to Widespread Demands — Argentinian Pres. Maria Estela Martinez de Peron, **July 8**, acceded to labor union demands for industrial wage increases ranging from 100% to 135%. In response labor leaders called off a nationwide general strike which had paralyzed industry, transportation, commerce, and most public services in Buenos Aires and other cities for 38 hours. On **July 11**, Peron, yielding to pressure from labor, military, and opposition forces, named a new 8-man cabinet without Jose Lopez Rega, her private secretary and former social welfare minister. The cabinet had resigned, **July 6**, in an unsuccessful attempt to stave off the general strike. However, since most of the members of the new cabinet were considered supporters of Lopez Rega, who had emerged as the right-wing strongman of the government, opposition continued to mount against Peron from labor, opposition politicians, the army, and her own party. As Argentina came perilously close to economic chaos, reports that Peron was seeking to leave the country flooded Buenos Aires **July 18.** Lopez Rega fled the country, **July 19,** adding fuel to speculation Peron would soon resign.

Amin Releases Doomed Briton — Ugandan Pres. Idi Amin, **July 10,** freed Denis Cecil Hills, a 61-year-old British lecturer, ending month-long dickering between Great Britain and Uganda. Amin had twice threatened to execute Hills for treason. In a manuscript for a book about Uganda, Hills had compared Amin's behavior to that of "a village tyrant." On June 20 Amin had postponed the original execution, but had insisted only a personal visit by British Foreign Secretary James Callaghan to discuss British-Ugandan relations could save Hills. Although Callaghan had refused to come to Uganda under duress, Amin, **July 1,** after conferring with Zaire Pres. Mobuto Sese Seko, said he had decided to pardon Hills. Hills was released, however, only when Callaghan finally went to Uganda to discuss future relations between Kampala and London.

U. S. Colonel Released in Lebanon — Leftist kidnapers, **July 12,** released U. S. Army Col. Ernest R. Morgan unharmed to Lebanese Premier Rashid Karami. The kidnapers, described, **July 10,** by the Palestine Liberation Organization as members of a "rejection front" of the PLO who are opposed to Yasir Arafat, had, **June 29,** seized Morgan, a black, in Beirut. The kidnapers had said they would execute Morgan as a spy unless the U. S. Embassy in Beirut distributed hundreds of tons of food, clothing, and building materials to a predominantly Moslem section of Beirut which had been severely damaged in Christian-Moslem hostilities. Anonymous donors, **July 11,** acceded to the kidnapers' demands and distributed about 12 tons of foods in the Al Mashlak section of Beirut. The U. S. said it had no knowledge of the food give-away program. The kidnapers stated, in a July 12 communique, that they had released Morgan partially because he was black and blacks rarely attained high levels in the American army. By releasing him, the kidnapers said, they would safeguard black American relations with the Arab cause.

India Parliament Approves Emergency Powers — Despite vociferous opposition protest, both houses of the Indian parliament, **July 22** and **23,** gave overwhelming approval to the government's state of emergency imposed **June 26,** thereby extending it indefinitely. In debate on the question, the government opposition, **July 21,** rose one by one to protest the emergency decrees and jailing of colleagues. Following the vote in both houses, members of the main opposition parties walked out in boycott of the sessions. Prime Minister Indira Gandhi had campaigned extensively for public support of the state of emergency, arguing, **July 1,** that it "provides us with a new opportunity to go ahead with our economic tasks . . ." She announced broad economic reforms, including steps to bring down prices, reduce peasants' debts, and achieve a fairer distribution of land. On **July 2,** countering critics who had charged that the emergency decrees had "killed democracy" in India, Gandhi declared India was still "more democratic than any developing country in the world." She maintained democracy had given "too much license to people whether it were newspapers or opposition," and they had been "trying to misuse it and weakening the nation's confidence." The government, **July 21,**

tightened press curbs, further restricting the activities of foreign correspondents. Journalists were required, on pain of expulsion, to sign a pledge to abide voluntarily by a strict set of "censorship guidelines," barring reporting of arrests, anti-government demonstrations, or opposition speeches. Gandhi, in parliamentary debate **July 21,** lauded press censorship: "When there are no papers, there is no agitation."

Egypt Renews UN Mandate — At the last minute, Egypt, **July 23,** renewed for 3 months the mandate for the United Nations peace-keeping force in the Sinai. Egypt, **July 15,** had threatened to refuse to renew the mandate, which expired July 24, unless the Security Council acted to assure a quick Israeli withdrawal from occupied Arab territories. Egyptian Foreign Minister Ismail Fahmy accused Israel of using the UN presence and relative calm in the Sinai to perpetuate occupation of Arab territory. However, an appeal from the Security Council, convinced Egypt to renew the mandate. The Security Council, **July 24,** in a 12-0 vote, approved the 3-month extension.

Three-Man Junta Takes Control in Portugal — Portugal's ruling Armed Forces Movement (MFA), **July 25,** turned over political and military power to 3 key generals — Pres. General Francisco da Costa Gomes, a moderate; the communist-oriented premier, Gen. Vasco Goncalves; and the extreme leftist internal security forces chief, Gen. Otelo de Carvalho. The MFA's executive body, the Supreme Revolutionary Council, approved the 3-man junta in an all-night session, **July 31.** The creation of the junta, coming in the wake of an unsuccessful attempt by moderate MFA officials to unseat Goncalves whom they considered incompetent and too closely associated with the communists, was considered a victory for Portugal's left. The political crisis had been precipitated **July 11,** when the Socialist party resigned from the government to protest the military take-over of the Socialist newspaper Republica and the **July 9** MFA announcement of a system of rule by "direct democracy" which would bypass political parties. Under the system of neighborhood and worker committees, leaders would be chosen and decisions made by a show of hands. The ultimate authority would rest indefinitely with the Supreme Military Council. On **July 17** the Popular Democrats, Portugal's major centrist party, also resigned from the government. Military forces were placed on alert **July 18,** as Communists and their rivals took their conflict to the streets, igniting rumors of a possible coup. Socialists held a series of mass rallies culminating, **July 19** in a gathering at which Socialist leader Mario Soares called for a government headed by a military man "who gives better guarantees of neutrality" than Goncalves. Attacks on Communist party offices occurred all over Portugal, with a total of 14 reported destroyed by **July 22.** As violence continued, Gen. Carvalho, **July 30,** warned that the MFA was prepared to use repressive measures against the junta's opponents. "It is becoming impossible," Carvalho said, "to have a socialist revolution by completely peaceful means."

OAS Suspends Cuban Embargo — The Organization of American States, meeting in San Jose, Costa Rica, **July 29,** voted to lift political and economic sanctions against Cuba. The resolution, approved by 16 of 21 OAS voting members, including the U. S., allowed each country to determine its own relationship with Cuba. The embargo had been imposed 11 years previously to penalize Cuba for fostering communist guerrilla activities in the hemisphere. U. S. delegate William S. Maillard said the vote "places the issue in its proper perspective and permits us to concentrate our multilateral energies on the more fundamental problems of this hemisphere."

Coup Topples Nigerian Leader — Nigerian head of state Gen. Yakubu Gowon was overthrown, **July 29,** in a bloodless military coup, while he was attending a meeting of the Organization of African Unity in Kampala, Uganda. Brig. Muritala Rufai Mohammed, the man who had orchestrated the 1966 coup which brought Gowon's military government to power, was named to replace Gowon as both head of state and commander of the armed forces. Mohammed, **July 30,** said, in a radio broadcast, that "Nigeria had been left to drift," a situation which would have resulted in chaos and bloodshed. Gowon's retraction, last October, of a pledge to return Nigeria to civilian rule in 1976 had spurred violent student demonstrations and the army's reevaluation of the nation's future course. Mohammed, **July 30** dismissed all government members, state governors, and senior military officials and named a new 22-member Supreme Military Council to govern Nigeria. Gowon, **July 30** in Kampala, cheerfully gave his full support to the new government: "I wish to state that I on my part have accepted the change and pledge my full loyalty to my nation, my country and the new government."

General

U.S., USSR Link in Space—In a symbolic gesture of East-West detente and in the desire to cooperate in space exploration, U.S. and USSR spacecraft, **July 17** linked together in space and astronauts from both nations shook hands. The linking was the climax of the Apollo-Soyuz Test Project, a joint space effort between the 2 rivals in space exploration. The mission began, **July 15** when the Soviet Soyuz, manned by commander Col. Aleksei A. Leonov and Valery N. Kubasov, was launched from the Baikonour Cosmodrome in central Asia. The launch was televised throughout the Soviet Union for the first time in the history of Soviet space exploration. The U.S. Apollo manned by Brig. Gen. Thomas P. Stafford, Vance D. Brand, and Donald K. Slayton, lifted off from Cape Canaveral, Fla., 7½ hours later. On **July 16,** both Apollo and Soyuz crews carried out maneuvers to put their crafts in orbit for the docking. The first physical contact came **July 17** at 12:09 p.m. EDT, about 140 miles above the Atlantic Ocean and 620 miles west of Portugal. About 3 hours later, over Amsterdam, the 2 crews met face to face for the first time. Stafford and Leonov shook hands through the hatches and greeted each other in each other's language. On **July 18,** the 2 crews again exchanged visits and shared meals. At the final visit, Stafford said, "I'm sure we have opened a new era in the history of man." Leonov said, in a televised orbit-to-ground news conference, "This work became possible in the climate of detente." The 2-day joint flight ended, **July 19,** with the undocking at 11:28 a.m. EDT. The Soyuz landed safely, **July 21** on the steppes of central Kazakhstan. Leonov described the historic flight as "hard, very hard." The Apollo returned safely, **July 24,** landing almost directly on target in the Pacific Ocean. The 3 astronauts, who had seemed in excellent condition on landing, entered Tripler Army Hospital in Honolulu, **July 25** suffering from respiratory irritations apparently caused by yellowish noxious gas which filled the spacecraft during their return flight. The astronauts were reported improved **July 26.**

Congress Restores Lee Citizenship—The Senate, **July 22,** gave final Congressional approval to a resolution restoring citizenship to Gen. Robert E. Lee. The House had passed the bill in April. Robert E. Lee 4th, the great grandson of the former commander of

the Confederate Army of Virginia during the Civil War, was present to applaud the victory. Lee had originally appealed for restoration of citizenship 110 years previously, but the required oath of allegiance, signed by Lee, had been mislaid. The signed oath was found in 1970 buried among other Civil War records in the National Archives.

New York City Mayor Unveils Austerity Plan—Following 4 days of negotiations with city officials, the Municipal Assistance Corp. (MAC), and union officials, New York City Mayor Abraham Beame, **July 31,** unveiled a broad austerity package, including a wage freeze for all city union workers. Commenting on the plan designed "to overcome a crisis of confidence in our fiscal integrity," Beame said, "There is nothing I have done in public life that has been more bitter than recommending these slashing economies that affect each and every one of us." In addition to the wage freeze, Beame's plan called for a freeze in salaries of managerial employes to July 1, 1973 levels, a $32-million cut in the city university budget, a $375-million cut in the city's $1.9 billion capital budget, the consolidation and elimination of several city departments, a 15-cent increase in transit fares, increases in most bridge and tunnel tolls, a 25% increase in commuter railroad fares, and elimination of "giveaways and frills" in future collective bargaining. The mayor's announcement came shortly after union leaders representing 50% of the city's workers agreed to accept the wage freeze. Representatives of police, teachers, and firemen threatened a court test of the mayor's right to impose a wage freeze. Also on **July 31,** MAC, with its rescue effort to bail New York City out of its cash flow crisis impaired by lack of investor confidence, issued new demands to the city. MAC asked Beame to set a 3-year spending limit on the budget, to limit tax increases over the same period, and to institute a thorough reform of the city's budget practices.

AUGUST
National

Unemployment Falls, But Prices Rise—The Labor Department announced, **Aug. 1,** that the unemployment rate in July had dropped to 8.4% of the nation's work force, with an increase of 630,000 in the number of persons employed. However, while unemployment was decreasing, prices were rising again. The Labor Department revealed, **Aug. 21,** that consumer prices had risen 1.2% during July, a record increase for 1975. Higher food, fuel, and used car prices had led the way, the Labor Department noted.

FBI Enters Search for Hoffa—The FBI, **Aug. 3,** entered the search for missing former Teamsters president, James R. Hoffa. Hoffa had last been seen **July 30,** outside a restaurant in Bloomfield Township, Mich., where reportedly he was planning to meet with several persons. The investigation during the following weeks failed to produce any solid evidence on Hoffa's whereabouts. A federal grand jury investigation, thought to be the best means to get to the bottom of the disappearance, was unexpectedly postponed **Aug. 19,** and no explanation was given.

Gurney Acquitted—A Tampa, Fla., federal district court jury, **Aug. 6,** found former Florida Sen. Edward J. Gurney not guilty of 5 felony charges in connection with election campaign fund-raising. Gurney had been charged with 3 counts of lying under oath to a grand jury, bribery, and unlawful compensation involving an alleged agreement to receive a free $55,000 condominium apartment in Vero Beach, Fla., in 1971. In return for the condominium, Gurney was alleged to have promised to secure favors from federal housing authorities for a local builder. Two other counts, including a key count of conspiracy to raise secret campaign funds from Florida builders through influence peddling, were declared mistried because the jury could not reach a verdict after 10 days of deliberations.

Grain Company Affiliate—In the continuing investigation of corruption in the grain industry, a New Orleans, La., federal grand jury, **Aug. 7**, indicted ADNAC, Inc., a corporate affiliate of 2 leading grain companies, and 22 individuals on multiple charges, including conspiracy to steal grain from foreign shipments. The theft conspiracy allegedly involved large volumes of grain of an unspecified value from mid-1971 to mid-1975. The indictment also alleged that some of the defendants used an ingenious electronic device to get around inspection and enhance profits by loading low quality grain onto ships.

Appeals Court Rules Against Oil Import Fee—The U.S. Court of Appeals in Washington, D.C., **Aug. 11**, ruled that Pres. Gerald R. Ford, earlier in the year, had overstepped his authority in levying fees of $2 a barrel on imported oil. The 3-judge panel decided, 2 to 1, that the only authority granted by Congress to limit imports was through "direct" methods, i.e. import quotas. The panel, however, recognized that it was "overturning an honest attempt by the President to find a solution to a difficult crisis." The suit had been brought by the governors of 8 northeastern states, 10 utilities, and Rep. Robert F. Drinan (D. Mass.). Massachusetts Gov. Michael S. Dukakis called the decision a "great victory for consumers, home-owners, and factory owners throughout New England and the nation." Over the year, the fee had increased the price of gasoline and other oil products by an estimated 3 cents per gallon.

Unions Boycott USSR Grain Shipments—The 6 maritime unions of the AFL-CIO, **Aug. 18**, announced a boycott against U.S. grain shipments to the Soviet Union pending government action to protect against rising food prices resulting from grain sales abroad and to offer more protection for U.S. shipping interests. The boycott affected all grain shipments contracted for after July and all East Coast, Gulf, and Great Lakes ports under the jurisdiction of the International Longshoremen's Union. The USSR had contracted to purchase 9.8 million tons of grain since July 1. AFL-CIO Pres. George Meany explained the boycott: "Very simply, we are not going to load any grain to the Soviet Union unless and until a policy is set forth and agreed to that will protect the American consumer and also American shipping interests." Pres. Ford, **Aug. 20**, calling on both sides to "cool it a bit," pledged to resolve the dispute. However, a 90-minute Ford-Meany meeting, **Aug. 26** ended in a deadlock. On **Aug. 27**, District Court Judge Owen Cox, in Corpus Christi, ordered a temporary injunction against longshoremen from Lake Charles, La., to Brownsville, Tex., barring them from refusing to load USSR-bound grain. In another White House meeting **Sept. 9**, including Pres. Ford, Meany, and Labor Secretary John T. Dunlop, union leaders agreed to voluntarily resume loading for a one-month period. Ford, in return, pledged to arrange new long-term purchasing and shipping agreements with the Soviet Union and to extend the current moratorium on new grain sales to the USSR. Agriculture Secretary Earl Butz had, **Aug. 11**, called on grain companies to withhold temporarily sales to the USSR pending further crop estimates. Both Ford and Meany said they hoped a long-term agreement would serve to reduce instability of domestic food prices by stabilizing wheat and feed grain sales to the Soviet Union.

U.S. Partially Lifts Cuban Trade Ban—The United States, **Aug. 21**, ended the 12-year ban on exports to Cuba by foreign subsidiaries of American companies. However, the State Department asserted, the embargo on direct U.S.-Cuba trade would remain in effect. The move was described as a logical extension of the July decision by the Organization of American States to leave the question of trade matters to the discretion of each nation.

International

Helsinki Hosts European Security Conference — The leaders of 33 European states, the U.S., and Canada, **Aug. 1**, in Helsinki, Finland, signed the 30,000-word "final act" of the Conference on Security and Cooperation in Europe. The signing, highlight of the largest summit meeting in European history, was the culmination of 3 years of negotiations. The nonbinding document declared the basic goals of "peace, security, justice and cooperation." Divided into 4 sections, it dealt broadly with aspects of European security, economic and other forms of cooperation, humanitarian issues and increased East-West contacts, and provisions for a follow-up conference. The document also ratified Europe's post-war borders.

New Legislation "Clears" Gandhi—Both houses of India's parliament, **Aug. 5** and **6**, approved new electoral legislation which invalidated Prime Minister Indira Gandhi's June conviction for violating election laws. The Supreme Court was scheduled to consider arguments on Gandhi's appeal one week later. In further action exonerating Gandhi, the upper house, **Aug. 7**, and lower house, **Aug. 8**, approved a constitutional amendment prohibiting lawsuits, civil or criminal, against an individual serving as prime minister. The amendment voided all outstanding challenges to Gandhi's rule and also barred judicial consideration of the Maintenance of Internal Security Act under which hundreds of political opponents had been arrested. A majority of India's 22 state assemblies ratified the amendment Aug. 9, and it was signed into law **Aug. 10**.

U.S. Vetoes UN Entry of Vietnams — The United States, **Aug. 11**, in the United Nations Security Council, vetoed UN membership for North and South Vietnam. Chief U.S. Delegate Daniel P. Moynihan explained that the U.S. would not have exercised its veto if the Security Council had not. **Aug. 6** refused to consider South Korea's application for membership. By the earlier action, Moynihan asserted, the Security Council had in effect proclaimed "selective universality, a principle which in practice admits only new members acceptable to the totalitarian states."

Philippines and Moslem Rebels Sign Truce — The Philippine government announced, **Aug. 14**, that the Moro Liberation Front, the leading insurgent group in Moslem Mindanao, had accepted a government cease-fire. The group had challenged government troops in the southern Philippines for the previous 5 years. Earlier, about 20 other rebel groups had accepted government concessions and ended the warfare which had claimed many lives.

Portugal Resumes Control in Angola — Following 3 weeks of warfare between Angola's 3 chief liberation movements, Portugal. **Aug. 14** in the absence of "any functioning government," resumed administrative control of Angola. The action effectively dissolved Angola's interim government which had been placed in control until Angola gained independence in November. Two liberation movements, the National Front for the Liberation of Angola (FNLA), **Aug. 7** and the National Union for the Total Independence of

Angola (Unita), **Aug. 9**, had withdrawn from the transitional government. The Popular Movement for the Liberation of Angola (MPLA), the only liberation group with representatives and troops in Luanda, the capital, refused to abdicate its government role. The 3 liberation groups were reported to be waging heavy warfare in a battle for the southern port of Lobito. Refugees had begun fleeing fighting throughout Angola late in July. On **Aug. 2**, Portugal had announced plans for an emergency airlift to evacuate all 250,000 to 300,000 Portuguese refugees before the territory acceded to independence Nov. 11.

Mujibur Killed in Bangladesh Coup — Bangladesh Pres. Sheik Mujibur Rahman was killed, **Aug. 15**, in Dacca, in a pre-dawn army coup led by his commerce minister, Khondar Kar Mushtaque Ahmed. Mujibur had led Bangladesh to independence 4 years previously. Sporadic fighting between forces loyal to Mujibur and followers of the new government was reported in the capital and surrounding country, but no large scale resistance occurred. Mujibur's wife, son, and 2 politically active nephews were also reported killed. Mushtaque was sworn in as president.

Pathet Lao Completes Final Takeover—Some 300,000 Laotian people rallied in Vientiane, **Aug. 23** to celebrate the completion of the Pathet Lao take-over of their nation and welcome the "people's revolutionary administration." Vientiane was the last province to come under Pathet Lao control in a process of military take-over which had begun last May. Phao Phimphachan, the chairman of Vientiane's people's revolutionary administration, announced a 10-point program which included a promise to "respect and uphold the throne" and to support the coalition government of the Pathet Lao and right-wing Vientiane faction. Premier Souvanna Phouma asserted, **Aug. 24**, that Pathet Lao proclamations referred to only municipal and provincial administration and that the national coalition was still "whole and intact." The new Vientiane administration, **Aug. 26**, repeated that it would respect the position of King Savang Vatthana, the premier, and the coalition's National Political Council, headed by Pathet Lao leader Prince Souphanouvong.

Greece Commutes Death Sentences — The Greek cabinet voted unanimously, **Aug. 25**, to commute death sentences imposed on former Pres. George Papadopoulos and 2 officers, Stylianos Patakos and Nikolaos Makarezos, who had helped him engineer the 1967 military coup. The 3 men had been stripped of all military rank and condemned to death for insurrection and high treason, **Aug. 23**, by a special 5-judge criminal court. Eight other men, including former strongman Brig. Gen. **Demetrios Ioannides**, were sentenced to life imprisonment and 7 others received 5-to-20-year prison terms. The government's decision spurred widespread criticism in Greece, especially from the opposition parties.

Peruvian Leader Deposed in Coup — Pres. Juan Velasco Alvarado, who had headed Peru's leftist military government for 7 years, was deposed, **Aug. 29**, in a bloodless coup in Lima. His premier, Gen. Francisco Morales Bermudez, regarded as more conservative and pragmatic, replaced Velasco. Morales was also minister of defense and commander-in-chief of the army. A Lima radio broadcast said the military-led coup, which had been backed by the other armed forces and police would continue Velasco's "revolutionary process." The broadcast obliquely accused the deposed leader of having established a personality cult which had sidetracked the revolutionary process that had begun with his accession in 1968. Morales, **Sept. 2** relaxed government repression issuing a decree allowing political exiles to return to Peru and magazines banned under Velasco's rule to resume publication.

Goncalves Dismissed in Portugal — Portuguese Pres. Gen. Francisco da Costa Gomes, **Aug. 29**, under intense pressure from anti-Communist and military forces, dismissed his premier, Gen. Vasco Goncalves. Pres. Costa Gomes, however, immediately appointed Goncalves chief of staff of the armed forces, a move also overwhelmingly opposed by the military. Vice Adm. Jose Batista Pinheiro Azevedo, who had remained aloof from the governmental power struggle, was named premier. Pressure on the Communist-oriented Goncalves to resign had intensified during the month. Pro- and anti-Communist demonstrations and violence had wrought havoc throughout Portugal. Nine dissident military officers, **Aug. 8**, were suspended for circulating a document in which they accused Goncalves of attempting to transform Portugal into an East European Communist state. The same officers, **Aug. 12** claiming support of 90% of the armed forces, petitioned Costa Gomes to end efforts to turn Portugal into a Communist state and demanded dismissal of Goncalves. Anti-Communist violence further accelerated, forcing the Communists to cancel a major rally in Oporto **Aug. 19**. Goncalves, **Aug. 25**, resisted a deadline set by Costa Gomes to leave office, and he was ousted only after 4 days of intense bargaining.

General

Massachusetts Bar Readmits Hiss — The Massachusetts Supreme Court, in a unanimous decision **Aug. 5**, ruled that Alger Hiss should be readmitted to the state's bar. The court felt that Hiss, who had been disbarred in 1952, had shown "moral and intellectual fitness" to recommend reinstatement. The disbarment had followed by 2 years Hiss' conviction of perjury for denying that he had ever given State Department documents to self-confessed Communist spy-courier Whittaker Chambers. The court did not take into consideration whether Hiss was guilty or innocent. Hiss, now 70 years old and a printing salesman in New York City, took the oath in Boston **Aug. 7**.

Seagram Heir Kidnapped — Samuel Bronfman, the 21-year-old heir to the Seagram liquor fortune, was abducted, **Aug. 9**, from the driveway of his mother's home in Purchase, N. Y. After his father, Edgar Bronfman, **Aug. 16**, had turned over a $2.3-million ransom to his son's abductors. FBI agents and New York City police rescued Bronfman, **Aug. 17**, from an apartment in the Flatbush section of Brooklyn. Police recovered the ransom later the same day in a neighboring apartment. Mel Patrick Lynch, in whose apartment Bronfman was found, and Dominic Byrne were arrested in connection with the kidnaping and charged by federal authorities with extortion by use of the mails. At the **Aug. 18** federal arraignment, Lynch, a 37-year-old New York City fireman, was held on a $500,000 bond, and Byrne, a 53-year-old limousine service operator, was held on a $200,000 bond. Police had located Bronfman after Byrne, who had reportedly panicked when he spotted a FBI stakeout, called the police to say his life was endangered because he knew about the kidnaping.

Franklin National Aides Indicted — A New York City federal grand jury, **Aug. 11**, indicted 8 former officials and employees of Franklin National Bank and its parent company, the Franklin New York Corporation, on 76 counts involving the loss of more than $30 million through unauthorized speculation in foreign currencies. Franklin National Bank was declared insolvent in October 1974 in the largest bank failure in U.S. history.

Joanne Little Acquitted — A Raleigh, N. C., jury, **Aug. 15**, found Joanne Little not guilty of 2d degree murder charges in the 1974 stabbing death of her jailer Clarence T. Alligood. It took the jury, which was evenly divided along racial lines, just 78 minutes return the verdict in favor of Little, a black woman. The case had drawn a great deal of national attention and spurred demonstrations in support of the defendant by feminist and minority groups. The defense had contended that Little, who had been serving a breaking and entering sentence in the Beaufort County jail in Washington, N.C., had stabbed Alligood in self-defense against rape. The prosecution had contended Little had killed the jailer in an attempt to escape from the jail.

Kent State Defendants Acquitted — Ohio Gov. James A. Rhodes, former Kent State University Pres. Robert I. White, and 27 Ohio National Guardsmen were acquitted, **Aug. 27** by a Cleveland, Oh., federal court jury, of all responsibility in the 1970 Kent State shootings. The students wounded in the shooting and parents of the 4 students killed had sued the defendants for a total of $46 million in 13 separate cases. The plaintiffs were astounded at the outcome and applauded their chief counsel Joseph Kelner's assessment: "This is a sad day in American justice."

Disasters — A chartered Boeing 707 carrying Moroccan workers from France home for summer vacations, **Aug. 3**, crashed into a mountainside and burned 30 miles from Agadir, Morocco, killing all 188 persons aboard . . . Of 128 persons aboard, 126 died, **Aug. 20**, when a Czechoslovak airliner, a Soviet-built Ilyushin-62, crashed and exploded while trying to land at the Damascus, Syria, airport . . . Two Chinese river boats collided in a heavy rainstorm near Canton, it was reported **Aug. 9** leaving as many as 500 persons dead.

SEPTEMBER
National

Labor and Production Up — The unemployment picture continued to improve in August, the Labor Department reported **Sept. 5**. Although the jobless rate remained stable at 8.4% of the labor force, the total number of persons employed increased. On **Sept. 15**, the Federal Reserve Board reported a 1.3% increase in industrial production in August, the largest of 4 consecutive monthly increases. However, while the economy seemed to be recovering from the recession, inflationary pressures were worsening. The Labor Department, **Sept. 5**, reported a 0.8% August increase in the Wholesale Price Index, due primarily to higher prices for gasoline and other fuels, electric power, metals, textiles, and chemicals.

Kleppe Named to Interior Post — Pres. Gerald R. Ford, **Sept. 9**, named Small Business Administration head Thomas S. Kleppe as Secretary of the Interior. The post had been vacant since late July when former Wyoming Gov. Stanley K. Hathaway resigned following hospitalization for depression. Kleppe was formerly the representative from North Dakota.

Congress Overrides Education Bill Veto — For only the 2d time in 6 attempts since January, the Democratic-controlled Congress, **Sept. 9** and **10**, gathered the necessary two-thirds majorities to override a veto by Pres. Ford. The House, **Sept. 9**, voted, 379-41, in support of a $7.9-billion education appropriation bill. The Senate, **Sept. 20**, voted to override by an 88-12 vote. Ford had vetoed the bill because it exceeded his request by $1.5 billion.

Calley Conviction Reinstated — The U.S. Fifth Circuit Court of Appeals, in New Orleans, La., **Sept. 10**, in an 8-5 decision, reinstated the 1971 court-martial conviction of William L. Calley for the murder of 22 Vietnamese civilians at Mylai. The lower courts had overturned the conviction on the defense contention that publicity had made Calley immune to trial. Calley remained free on bail. The Army had stated previously that it would grant Calley parole regardless of the appeal decision.

Durkin Wins New Hampshire Senate Seat — Democrat John A. Durkin, **Sept. 16**, won a decisive victory over 5-term Republican Representative Louis C. Wyman in a special Senate election in New Hampshire. The seat had been disputed since the inconclusive results of the November 1974 Senate election in that state.

FBI Seizes Hearst, Harrises in San Francisco — The FBI, **Sept. 18**, captured Patricia Hearst in an apartment in the lower-middle-class Mission district of San Francisco, climaxing a 19-month search which began with her abduction by the Symbionese Liberation Army in February 1974. Three months later, Patty had announced that she had joined the SLA to fight for "the freedom of the oppressed people." Patty offered no resistance saying, "Don't shoot. I'll go with you." Seized along with her was Wendy Yoshimura, who had been missing for 3 years since being indicted in connection with a bombing conspiracy charge. An hour before the FBI seized Patty, they also captured SLA members William and Emily Harris. Patty was charged before a U.S. magistrate with armed robbery and bail was set at $500,000. She told the court that her occupation was "urban guerrilla." On **Sept. 19**, U.S. District Court Judge Oliver J. Carter, an old Hearst family friend, ordered that Patty be held without bail because of fears that she might abscond. The Harrises were charged with possession of illegal firearms and bail for each was set at $500,000. Yoshimura was turned over to Alameda County authorities where, **Sept 19**, in Oakland, she was indicted for possession of explosives, destructive devices, and a machine gun. On **Sept. 23**, in an attempt to have bail set for Patty, defense attorneys presented an affidavit by Patty which depicted her as a terrorized prisoner who had been physically mistreated, confined, and threatened to the point of hallucination and insensibility. Judge Carter delayed the bail decision pending a psychiatric report on Patty's mental condition. A tape recording of a jail conversation between Patty and an old school chum 2 days before submission of the affidavit was disclosed **Sept. 25**. On the tape, Patty said she was afraid of becoming "a prisoner in my parents' home." *Rolling Stone*, in its **Sept. 29** issue, stated that Jack Scott, a radical sports figure, who had driven Patty across the country in June 1974, had offered to take her wherever she wished. Patty had not wanted to go home, but chose to hide out with the Harrises.

Air Force to Discharge Matlovich — Following a week of hearings, a 3-member panel of U.S. Air Force officers ruled, **Sept. 19**, in Hampton, Va., that T. Sgt. Leonard P. Matlovich, a homosexual, was unfit for military service. The panel recommended that Matlovich, who holds a Bronze Star and Purple Heart, be given a general discharge. The panel said that although Matlovich "had no physical or mental defects" that would disqualify him for service, he had "engaged in one or more homosexual acts with at least two Air Force personnel and an unspecified number of civilians." The panel also ejected Matlovich as a "candidate for rehabilitation," thereby disallowing the possibility of probation. The hearing process was set off last March when Matlovich, who was serving as a human relations counselor at Langley Air Force Base, disclosed his homosexuality to a superior officer. During the hearings, Matlovich and his attorneys presented extensive testimony by psychiatrists, military students, and associates who argued that homosexuality alone should not disqualify Matlovich for military service.

Shriver, Shapp Join Democratic Race — Surrounded by many Kennedy family members, Sargent Shriver, **Sept. 20**, in Washington, D.C., formally entered the race for the Democratic nomination for president. He vehemently denied that he had entered the race as "a stalking horse" for Sen. Edward M. Kennedy. The 7th candidate to announce, Shriver was the first to state he had obtained enough campaign contributions to qualify for matching federal funds. On Sept. 25, Pennsylvania Gov. Milton J. Shapp announced, in Washington, D.C., that he was entering the race on a platform of "common sense" governmental management. Shapp, who had made a fortune as a businessman before entering politics, said "the time has come when the federal government must be run on a businesslike basis, with executive leadership and managerial skill."

Ford Announces New Energy Plan — Pres. Ford, **Sept. 22,** at a meeting of the AFL-CIO Building and Construction Trades Department in San Francisco, Calif., announced that he would ask Congress to approve a $100-billion "dramatic crash" program to give the U.S. "energy independence in 10 years or less." Ford said he would create a new agency, the Energy Independence Authority, which would cooperate with private industry to provide the massive financing necessary to develop energy sources. The plan came under immediate criticism. **Sept. 23,** at the Western Governors Conference at Sun Valley, Idaho. Washington's Republican Governor, Daniel J. Evans, said the plan was not complete and "not even worth embarking on if energy conservation aspects are being left out."

Oil Price Control Restored in Compromise — The Congress and Pres. Ford, **Sept. 25,** agreed to restore price controls on domestic oil until Nov. 15. Earlier in the month, the Senate, **Sept. 10,** had failed to override a presidential veto of extension of controls for 6 months. The controls had expired **Aug. 31.** Ford had argued that the controls had caused a massive flow of American dollars and jobs abroad. The Congress, **Sept. 26,** quickly passed legislation embodying the agreement. The stated purpose of the accord was to give the administration and Congress time to agree on a long-range energy policy.

Ford, House Committee Agree on Intelligence Data — CIA Director William E. Colby, **Sept. 30,** ended a month-long struggle between the executive and legislative branches by handing over to the House Select Committee on Intelligence classified reports dealing with the 1968 Tet offensive in Vietnam with the condition that the committee would not unilaterally make such documents public. The House committee, which had subpoened the documents, voted, **Oct. 1** to accept the conditions which also allowed the intelligence community "final appeal" to the president over continued secrecy. The stalemate between Pres. Ford and committee had begun **Sept. 12** when Ford had cut the committee off from all classified documents. Administration officials were also forbidden to appear before the committee to testify on classi-

---

Ford Escapes 2 Assassination Attempts

Two assassination attempts, both by women and both in California, on the life of Pres. Gerald R. Ford during the span of one month caused serious concern for the president's safety. The attempts also spurred criticism that intensive media coverage of the president's activities and glamorization of the would-be assassins exacerbated the possibility of further assassination attempts.

In the first attempt, **Sept. 5,** Lynette Alice "Squeaky" Fromme, 26 years old, pointed a .45-caliber pistol at Ford as he was entering the California Capitol in Sacramento, Calif. Secret Service agent Larry M. Buendorf saw the gun and grabbed it. A White House spokesman stated that although there was not a bullet in the chamber, the gun was loaded with a magazine filled with bullets.

Fromme, who was immediately identified as one of the earliest and most devoted followers of Charles M. Manson, was charged with attempted assassination of a president under the provisions of a 1965 law. A $1-million bond was set. Fromme was the first person to be charged under the law, which carries a potential life sentence.

Chief Secret Service spokesman John W. Warren refused to comment on how Fromme, clad in a long bright red dress, could have gotten so close to Ford. It was disclosed, however, that Fromme had not been on the Secret Service's list of persons who posed a potential threat to the president.

Fromme's roommate, Sandra Good, said they were both members of an organization whose objective was "killing polluters of air and water." She denied any knowledge that Fromme had been planning to kill Ford.

Fromme was indicted in Sacramento **Sept. 10.** At her arraignment in Sacramento, **Sept. 11,** Fromme was thrown out of the court room after she told Judge Thomas J. MacBride, "The gun is pointed, your honor, the gun is pointed — whether it goes off is up to you." Fromme pleaded not guilty **Sept. 19.** MacBride, **Sept. 23,** ruled Fromme was mentally compe-

tent to stand trial and could conduct her own defense.

The 2nd attempt came in San Francisco, **Sept. 22** when Sara Jane Moore, a 45-year-old political activist, shot a .38-caliber revolver at Ford as he stepped out of the St. Francis Hotel. A civilian bystander Oliver Sipple, a 30-year-old former Marine, saw the gun and deflected Moore's aim as it went off. Ford was rushed into a waiting car and onto a plane headed for Washington, D.C. Moore was charged with attempted assassination of a president. Upon arrest, Moore maintained that she was an FBI informer.

The night before, the Secret Service had questioned Moore and confiscated a .44-caliber weapon, but had not held her in custody.

Under growing pressure that he curtail his public appearances, Ford, **Sept. 23,** maintained he would no "capitulate" to would-be attackers and alter his personal, hand-shaking style or become a hostage in the White House. He said that if a president could not walk safely among the American people "something has gone wrong in our society." A special Congressional committee recommended that Secret Service protection be extended to the major presidential candidates.

On **Sept. 23,** U.S. Magistrate Owen Woodruff Jr. ordered Moore to undergo psychiatric examination to determine her competency to stand trial. She was held on $500,000-bond. Investigators reported that the twice-divorced Moore, through extensive misstatements, false names, and false documents, had tried for years to obscure her identity and background.

It was disclosed, **Sept. 26,** that Moore had not been detained prior to the assassination attempt because the San Francisco police department had told the Secret Service she was not a threat because she had, in fact, operated as an informer for the department and 2 federal agencies.

Bowing to widespread concern, Ford, **Sept. 30,** asked Congress for $13.5 million in 1975 in additional Secret Service protection. He insisted that he would continue to travel the country "not in any foolhardy spirit, but by every prudent and practical means."

ed matters. On **Sept. 11**, despite intelligence community protests, the committee had made public a '73 intelligence agency summary, of which 4 words were deemed highly sensitive. Ford, **Sept. 16**, had rejected a committee subpoena for classified documents on Vietnam unless the committee adopted procedures to safeguard the secret documents. Committee Chairman Otis G. Pike (D. N.Y.) had refused to accept any compromise.

International

Moslem-Christian Violence Flares in Lebanon — Fighting between Moslems and Christians erupted again, **Sept. 2-10**, this time in Northern Lebanon. More than 100 persons were reported to have been killed. In an attempt to halt the fighting, Premier Rashid Karami, **Sept. 10**, ordered troops to intervene between the Moslems in Tripoli and Christians in the village of Zgharta. An uneasy calm reigned **Sept. 11**, as the armed forces took up their positions. The fighting spread to Beirut **Sept. 14**, when 4 people were killed. Violence flared again in the Tripoli region **Sept. 15**, when armed Moslems clashed with army troops in a demand for removal of the buffer zone. Ceasefires, negotiated **Sept. 20 and 24**, through the mediation of Syrian Foreign Minister Abdel Halim Khaddam, brought a temporary halt to fighting. Syrian mediation also resulted in the creation of a 20-member committee of Lebanese religious and political leaders of all sides. The committee, whose goal was resolution of the crisis, held its first meeting **Sept. 25**.

Second-Stage Sinai Accord Signed — Egypt and Israel, **Sept. 4**, in Geneva, signed a second-stage interim agreement on the Sinai which provided for further Israeli troop withdrawals and the stationing of U.S. civilians in the Sinai to monitor the accord. U.S. Secretary of State Henry A. Kissinger, **Sept. 1**, had announced the accord, which culminated a round of shuttle diplomacy between Jerusalem and Alexandria which had begun **Aug. 21**. The accord consisted of 4 parts: the Israeli-Egyptian political and military agreement, a document of guidelines for the Israeli and Egyptian teams that would meet in Geneva to work out the details of implementation, a document detailing the presence of U.S. civilians in the Sinai, and an unpublished memorandum of understanding between the U.S. and Israel. In the agreement, Israel agreed to withdraw from the lengths of the Mitla and Gidi passes and to return the Abu Rudeis oil field to Egypt. The vacated areas would become an expanded UN Emergency Force buffer zone. Egyptian and Israeli strips on either side of the UN zone would be limited to 8,000 men, 75 tanks, and 60 artillery pieces. Egypt publicly pledged to allow shipment of nonmilitary cargoes to and from Israel through the Suez Canal. Both nations pledged that the Middle East conflict would be resolved by peaceful means. The agreement also included establishment of a joint Israeli-Egyptian commission to work with the United Nations in dealing with problems that might arise from the provisions of the accord. In the key provision of the agreement, a U.S. force of 200 civilians would operate an early warning system to monitor the passes in the UN buffer zone. This segment of the agreement was subject to approval of the U.S. Congress. U.S. Pres. Gerald R. Ford, **Sept. 1**, praised the agreement as "one of the most historic" peace ventures of the century and urged Congress to endorse the use of U.S. civilians. Speaking against anti-Egyptian rallies in Damascus, Syria, Egyptian Pres. Anwar al-Sadat, **Sept. 4**, maintained Egypt was standing up for the Arab cause: "We were offered the return of the whole of Sinai at the price of ending the state of war with Israel, but we said 'no' because we were negotiating for the Syrian and Palestinian cause as well as ours."

Goncalves Loses All Power in Portugal — Under intense military and political pressure, Gen. Vasco Goncalves, **Sept. 5**, rejected his appointment as chief of staff of Portugal's armed forces. Pres. Francisco da Costa Gomes signed a communique removing Goncalves from the High Council of the Revolution, the policy arm of Portugal's ruling Armed Forces Movement (MFA), effectively stripping Goncalves of all power. The crisis had begun **Aug. 29**, when Costa Gomes had dismissed the Communist-oriented Goncalves as premier and named him to the top armed forces position. Immediate opposition was voiced **Sept. 1**, by air force head Gen. Jose Morais da Silva who, referring to Goncalves' Communist connection, said he would not accept the dictatorship of any minority party. On **Sept. 3**, the general assembly of the army, in an overwhelming vote, demanded that Costa Gomes dismiss Goncalves. Goncalves' decision to bow to pressure opened the way for formation of a new broadly-based 15-member coalition cabinet, sworn in **Sept. 19**. On **Sept. 13**, premier-designate Vice Adm. Pinheiro de Azevedo had announced a 3-party accord, among the Socialists, Communists, and centrist Popular Democrats, that Portugal would pursue a more moderate revolutionary course in which all major political parties would be represented. The new government, the 6th since the military coup in April 1974, was composed of 5 military officers, 4 Socialists, 2 Popular Democrats, a Communist, and independents, 2 of whom were closely allied to the Socialists.

Plan for Poor Nations Adopted — The United Nations General Assembly met in a 2-week special session, **Sept. 1-16**, to consider problems of development and economic cooperation between the world's rich and poor nations. Despite intensive argument throughout the session, the Assembly, **Sept. 16**, unanimously agreed on a long set of principles and recommendations for "redressing the economic imbalances" between the rich and poor nations. The session agreed on the necessity of steps to guarantee the purchasing power of the developing nations by stabilizing their earnings through the aid of a new development security facility. Also needed, the assembly stated, is better access for poor nations to capital markets and to the science and technology of the developed nations. A third major point called for a redistribution of global wealth through mechanisms for automatic transfer of money to poor nations.

Peron Takes Leave of Absence — Argentinian Pres. Isabel Martinez de Peron announced, **Sept. 12**, that she was taking a leave of absence from her governmental duties effective the next day. The announcement followed weeks of speculation that Peron, suffering from exhaustion and facing a volatile political situation and persistent terrorism in Argentina, would leave office. She returned 5 weeks later and, **Oct. 17**, in her first public appearance, said she would carry on as head of state.

OPEC Raises Oil Price — The 13-member Organization of Petroleum Exporting Countries (OPEC), meeting in Vienna, Austria, **Sept. 25**, agreed to increase the price of oil 10% beginning Oct. 1. However, as a gesture of good will to the consuming nations, OPEC said it would freeze the new price level for at least 9 months. The agreement followed 4 days of bitter argument, chiefly between Iran and Saudi Arabia. While Iran argued for a 28% increase, Saudi Arabia Oil Minister Sheik Ahmed Zaki Yamani tried to convince the other member nations to keep the increase under 5%. Oil specialists predicted that the 10% increase would raise the annual oil bill by $10 billion — $2 billion for the U.S. and $5 billion for Europe. Although the Ford administration publicly criticized the increase, relief was expressed at the State Department and White House that it had been held to 10%.

Spain Executes 5 Terrorists — Despite wide international protest, including an appeal from Pope Paul VI, Spanish head of state Generalissimo Francisco Franco, **Sept. 26**, refused to commute the death sentences for 5 terrorists who had been convicted of killing policemen. However, Franco spared the lives of 6 others, including 2 women. Two of the condemned men were members of the ETA, the Basque separatist organization. The death sentences had been imposed during the previous month after a wave of terrorism during which 12 policemen had been killed. Franco's refusal spurred many European leftist groups hostile to the Spanish government to violent demonstrations and attacks on Spanish offices and properties throughout Europe. The execution of the 5 condemned men, **Sept. 27**, re-ignited anti-Spanish rioting across Europe. In a last-minute concession, the government allowed the men to be executed by firing squad rather than the more barbaric garroting. On **Sept. 28**, thousands of people in the northern Basque region protested the executions and, **Sept. 29**, some 10,000 Basques held a general strike in protest. In his first public appearance since the executions, Premier Carlos Arias Navarro, **Sept. 30**, called on Spain to unite behind Franco and condemned the protest abroad as "an intolerable aggression against Spanish sovereignty." As some 100,000 Spaniards rallied in Madrid, **Oct. 1**, to cheer Franco, gunmen shot 3 policemen apparently in revenge for the executions. Franco told his supporters the protest from European nations, which he called "aggressions," were brought about by a "leftist Masonic conspiracy" within the leadership class and by "Communist terrorist subversion."

General

Busing Spurs Violence in Louisville — Rioting and vandalism broke out, **Sept. 5**, in Louisville, Ky., following 2 relatively peaceful days of school busing. Louisville and surrounding Jefferson County, **Sept. 4**, had become the first major metropolitan area to carry out court-ordered busing between the central city and suburbs to achieve racial balance. Some 50 persons were injured and 500 arrested, and extensive property damage was sustained during the violence. The Kentucky National Guard was called in **Sept. 6**. Federal Judge James F. Gordon, **Sept. 7**, ordered armed guards to ride on all buses and prohibited protest demonstrations at schools and along bus routes. However, **Sept. 8**, after the violent weekend, busing resumed uneventfully. Public schools in Boston, the scene of extensive anti-busing violence the previous September, opened, **Sept. 8**, under heavy police guard. Despite numerous protest demonstrations, the opening day passed with no serious disturbances.

NYC Aid Plan Passed — New York State Gov. Hugh Carey, **Sept. 9**, signed into law a $2.3-billion emergency aid program for New York City to stave off default for the next 3 months. "We have begun a major effort to save a city and secure a state," Carey said. The plan, designed by Carey, also provided for state-mandated restructuring of New York City's fiscal management. Although most of those involved considered the measure risky, there was general agreement that it was the only immediate hope for containing the city's fiscal crisis and reviving confidence in the city

in order to enable it to borrow money on its own. The legislation created a 7-member Emergency Financial Control Board which would enforce austerity and control the city's flow of revenue. It brought together the $2.3 billion in cash from state loans, both state and city public employee pension funds, and other private and public sources. Carey's plan also set up a legal procedure to handle default should it occur.

Boyle Sentenced to Life — The once powerful head of the United Mine Workers, W. A. Boyle, **Sept. 11**, Media, Pa., was sentenced to 3 consecutive terms of life imprisonment for ordering the 1969 murders of union rival Joseph A. Yablonski, and Yablonski's wife and daughter. Boyle told the court he was innocent.

American-born Saint Canonized — Pope Paul VI, **Sept. 14**, in Rome, canonized the Catholic church's first U.S.-born saint, Mother Elizabeth Bayley Seton. The 2-hour canonization mass was held outdoors in St. Peter's Square to accommodate the 100,000 persons, including 16,000 Americans, who gathered for the ceremony. Mother Seton, called the "mother of Catholic education," died in 1921. Originally an Episcopalian, she converted to Roman Catholicism at the age of 30 following the death of her wealthy husband. Then, for the last 16 years of her life, she worked in the Catholic Church. She established a school for girls in Baltimore, Md., and later, in Emmitsburg, Md., Mother Seton established the Sisters of Charity of St. Joseph's, the first native American Catholic order.

Disasters — A severe earthquake registering 6.8 on the Richter scale, **Sept. 6**, shook a large area along the Anatolian fault in eastern Turkey, leveling the town of Lice. The final death toll, reported **Sept. 15**, stood at 2,312 persons, 1,000 of them in Lice; 3,372 persons were injured . . . All 60 persons aboard died **Sept. 3** when a Hungarian airliner, on approach to the Beirut, Lebanon, airport, crashed into the Mediterranean Sea.

OCTOBER
National

Employment and Production Continue to Grow — Unemployment in September slipped to 8.3% of the labor force, the Labor Department reported **Oct. 3**. The economy continued to grow during September the Federal Reserve Board reported, **Oct. 16**, with industrial production increasing 1.9%. The gain, the largest in 5 consecutive monthly increases, was also the largest since 1964 when the economy rebounded following settlement of an automobile strike. The Commerce Department, **Oct. 20**, disclosed the nation's total output of goods and services had grown at an annual rate of 11.2% during the July-September quarter, a much faster pace than most experts had expected. James L. Pate, the Commerce Department's assistant secretary for economic affairs, said the figures showed the recession was "definitely over."

Congress Reverses Itself on Turkey Arms — In a significant victory for Pres. Gerald R. Ford, the Congress, **Oct. 2** and **3**, approved legislation partly lifting the 8-month-old arms embargo against Turkey. The president, who had lobbied extensively in favor of the legislation, praised Congress and called the action "an essential first step in the process of rebuilding a relationship of trust and friendship with valued friends and allies in the eastern Mediterranean." In July, after the House had rejected similar legislation, the Turkish government had suspended operation of American military and intelligence gathering facilities in Turkey.

Ford Ties Tax Slash to Spending Cuts — Pres. Gerald R. Ford, **Oct. 6**, in a nationally televised speech ed Congress for an additional tax cut of $11-billion in 1976 and to make permanent, with some changes, the $17-billion of anti-recession tax cuts enacted last March. However, Ford asserted, he would support the tax cuts only if Congress made a commitment to reduce federal spending by $28-billion in the next fiscal year ending Oct. 1, 1977. Ford said, "I want these actions to be a first step — and they are a crucial first step — toward balancing the federal budget within three years." Rep. Al Ullman (D, Ore.) said Ford's goal of a tax reduction tied to a spending ceiling was a "mirage."

Congress Overrides Pupil-Lunch Veto—In only the second successful attempt in 8 tries, the Democratic-controlled Congress, **Oct. 7**, easily overrode Pres. Ford's veto of a $2.7-billion extension of the federal school lunch and child nutrition programs. The House voted, 397-18, and the Senate, 79-13, to override. Ford, **Oct. 3**, exercised the veto, his 39th since taking office, because the bill broadened the lunch subsidy program to "nonneedy" pupils and added $1.2 billion to the amount he had requested.

Congress Approves U.S. Civilians in Sinai—Congress, **Oct. 8** and **9**, overwhelmingly approved the administration's request to station up to 200 U.S. civilians in the Sinai to monitor the recent Israeli-Egyptian accord. The House voted, 341-69, **Oct. 8**, to place American volunteers at early warning facilities at the Mitla and Gidi passes. The Senate followed suit, **Oct. 9**, in a 70-to-18 vote.

U. S., USSR Negotiate 5-Year Grain Accord—The United States and the Soviet Union, the White House announced **Oct. 20**, concluded a 5-year agreement on grain sales, effective Oct. 1, 1976. Under the agreement, the USSR would purchase 6 to 8 million tons of American grain per year. Pres. Ford simultaneously lifted the 2-month moratorium on further grain sales to the USSR in 1975. Ford said, "The long-term agreement signed in Moscow today promotes American economic stability. It represents a positive step in our relations with the Soviet Union." The accord was negotiated by Charles W. Robinson, undersecretary of state for economic affairs, after repeated trips to the Soviet Union. The White House also disclosed that a letter of intent had been signed in Moscow to conclude an agreement for the U. S. to purchase up to 10,000 barrels of Russian oil and petroleum products per day. However, it was apparent that disagreement over the price of Russian oil was delaying a final accord.

Bayh Joins Democratic Race — Indiana Sen. Birch Bayh, **Oct. 21**, at his family farm near Shirkieville, Ind., announced his candidacy for the Democratic nomination for president. Bayh, the 9th candidate to announce officially, maintained that he could more successfully bridge the gap between the left and right of the Democratic party than any of the other contenders. Bayh promised to provide "moral leadership" that would create more jobs, close tax loopholes, break up the "monopolistic oil companies," reform the Federal Reserve System, and provide aid for the old and needy.

Moore Indicted, Arraigned—Sara Jane Moore was secretly indicted, **Oct. 22**, by a San Francisco, Calif., federal grand jury on charges of attempting to assassinate Pres. Ford. The indictment, disclosed **Oct. 24**, was kept secret at the request of F. Steele Langford, chief of the U. S. Attorney General's Criminal Division, because he "didn't see the need for more publicity since she is still undergoing psychiatric examination." At Moore's arraignment, **Oct. 28**, U. S. District Judge Samuel Conti entered a not guilty plea for the defendant. Public Defender James Hewitt had refused to enter a plea on grounds that Moore's mental

competence had not been determined. Conti ordered the trial for Dec. 15, providing Moore is found mentally competent at a hearing set for Nov. 17.

Ford Refuses to Support Federal Help for NYC—Addressing the National Press Club in Washington, D. C., Pres. Ford, **Oct. 29**, said he would veto any legislation that would rescue New York City from default by giving the city federal government loan guarantees. "I can tell you," Ford said, "and tell you now — that I am prepared to veto any bill that has as its purpose a federal bailout of New York City to prevent default." Instead, Ford proposed legislation which would enable New York to file for bankruptcy and maintain essential services after default. New York City Mayor Abraham Beame attacked Ford's proposal as a "default of presidential leadership." The New York *Daily News*, **Oct. 30**, ran a front-page banner headline: "Ford to City: Drop Dead." However, despite the threat of presidential veto and considerable anti-New York sentiment in the Congress, the Senate Banking Committee, **Oct. 30**, voted, 8 to 5, to send legislation to the full Senate to provide federal guarantees for loans of up to $4 billion if New York State would increase taxes, if unions would renegotiate pensions, and if the city's debtors would settle for longer terms at reduced interest rates. New York City had already narrowly escaped default **Oct. 17**. Only a last-minute decision by the United Federation of Teachers to use their retirement fund to purchase $150-million worth of Municipal Assistance Corporation bonds saved the city from a $95-million shortfall on obligations due that day. Mayor Beame said, **Oct. 30**, that New York City could meet its financial obligations until Dec. 1, but then would face default unless aid were forthcoming from some quarter.

International

Sakharov Wins Peace Prize — The Nobel Committee of the Norwegian parliament, **Oct. 9**, awarded the 1975 Nobel Peace Prize to Soviet dissident Andrei D. Sakharov. Sakharov, the father of the Soviet hydrogen bomb, was the first Soviet citizen to win the prize. In the prize citation, the committee said Sakharov "has addressed his message of peace and justice to all peoples of the world . . . For him it is a fundamental principle that world peace can have no lasting value unless it is founded on respect for the individual human being in society." Sakharov, who said he would travel to Norway to accept the prize if permitted, responded with a plea for release of political prisoners in the USSR. The Soviet press agency Tass, **Oct. 10**, assailed Sakharov as "a man who has taken a stand against his own country and its peaceable policy." *Literaturnaya Gazeta*, **Oct. 14**, accused Sakharov of supporting Nazi and fascist causes and claimed he "did everything he could to inflame hostility and mistrust between nations and states." The press campaign against the Nobel Prize-laureate continued **Oct. 29**, when *Trud*, the trade union weekly, called the prize "political pornography" and a traitorous award, "30 pieces of silver" for a Soviet Judas.

Beirut Fighting Widens, Foreigners Flee—Factional fighting between leftist Moslems and right-wing Christian Phalangists in Beirut, Lebanon, spread, **Oct. 20**, to the Ras Beirut district, the area where many foreigners live and work. The spread of violence to the neighborhood which houses the American Embassy, the Holiday Inn complex, and the exclusive St. Georges Hotel, was seen as a grave turn of events. As the fighting in the foreign quarter continued and the death toll mounted, the American Embassy, **Oct. 25**, following one of the city's most violent nights, began to encourage officials to evacuate their families. Gun battles intensified again, Oct. 26, when at least 52 persons were killed and the warring factions contested the Holiday Inn complex, trapping over 150 persons inside. By Oct. 27, 128 persons were dead and 300 wounded in 48 hours of fighting. As the fighting escalated to near-civil war, Premier Rashid Karami negotiated one cease-fire after another, none of which lasted. By Oct. 31, guests trapped in the Holiday Inn and St. Georges Hotel had been evacuated and shooting was continuing on a reduced scale.

Kissinger Finds Atmosphere Cool in China—Assessing his 4-day trip to China, U. S. Secretary of State Henry A. Kissinger, Oct. 23, said Chinese leaders considered the United States to be less impressive in world affairs today than it had been a few years ago. On Oct. 19, Chinese Foreign Minister Chiao Kuan-hua welcomed Kissinger with a warning about the dangers of U. S. detente with the USSR: "To base oneself on illusions is to mistake hopes or wishes for reality, and to act accordingly will only abet the ambitions of expansionism and lead to grave consequences." He urged a "tit-for-tat struggle" against Soviet "hegemonism." Kissinger responded that U. S. relations with the Soviet Union "would threaten no one." He asserted that the U. S. would stand up to the Soviet Union if the security of third countries were involved. Although Kissinger met with Chinese Communist party Chairman Mao Tsetung, Oct 21, to dramatize the soundness of Chinese-American relations, the visit ended on a chilly note Oct. 22, as both Kissinger and Chiao Kuan-hua toasted each other with words ranking near the bottom of the Chinese diplomatic vocabulary.

Explosions Shake London—A bomb exploded, Oct. 23, outside the London home of parliament member Hugh Fraser. Caroline Kennedy, the 17-year-old daughter of the late U. S. president, was staying at the Fraser home. Prof. Gordon Hamilton Fairley, a widely-regarded cancer specialist, died in the explosion. Fraser and Caroline were unhurt. At least 18 persons were wounded, Oct. 29, when another bomb exploded, this time outside an Italian restaurant near the American embassy in London's fashionable Mayfair district. The 2 incidents brought the toll to 5 deaths and almost 100 injuries since August in a spate of bomb attacks generally laid to the IRA. Two persons had been killed and 63 wounded, Sept. 5, in an explosion at the London Hilton. By Oct. 30, Scotland Yard had arrested 9 persons, including 4 women, under Britain's antiterrorism law which allows authorities to hold suspects for 72 hours without making a charge.

Egyptian President Makes First U.S. Visit—The first Egyptian president to make an official visit to the U. S., Anwar el-Sadat, Oct. 26, arrived in Newport News, Va., to begin a 10-day trip during which he would seek arms and economic aid and explain his policies to the American people. U. S. Pres. Gerald R. Ford, Oct. 27, welcomed Sadat to the White House and pledged that the U. S. was determined "not to tolerate stagnation or stalemate" in the quest for peace in the Middle East. Sadat responded that Egypt had come "with open hearts and open arms" and gave thanks for U. S. mediation efforts in the recent Sinai accord. Sadat told the National Press Club that, although Egypt wanted to buy American arms, he had come without a shopping list because his trip was chiefly a good will mission. At the United Nations General Assembly in New York City, Sadat, Oct. 29, formally asked the body's help to reconvene the Middle East peace talks in Geneva. He stressed, however, that consultations leading to the resumption of talks should include all interested parties, "including the Palestine Liberation Organization."

Juan Carlos Takes Power Temporarily—The Spanish government, Oct. 30, temporarily delegated t[...] ailing Generalissimo Francisco Franco's powers [...] chief of state to his designated successor Prince Ju[...] Carlos de Borbon. The 82-year-old Franco, who h[...] been stricken with a serious heart ailment Oct. 21, [...] mained in "extraordinarily grave" condition. T[...] transfer of power ended a political and governmen[...] vacuum which had virtually left Spain without [...] ruler since Franco had fallen ill. Juan Carlos h[...] been acting chief of state for 6 weeks in July and A[...] gust 1974 while Franco recovered from a near-fa[...] phlebitis attack.

General

Venera 9 and 10 Relay Venus Photos—The Sov[...] spacecraft Venera 9 made a soft landing on Ven[...] Oct. 22, according to a Tass report, and relayed ba[...] to earth the first photograph taken from the surf[...] of another planet. The landing climaxed a 4½-mo[...] journey over 186 million miles to Venus, one of t[...] most hostile environments which man has y[...] probed. The photograph showed rocks and smo[...] boulders in the area of the landing site. The spa[...] craft also reported that the surface temperature [...] Venus was 905 degrees F., or more than twice t[...] melting point of tin. The atmospheric pressure w[...] gauged at 90 times that of earth at sea level. The So[...] et reaction to the photograph was ecstatic. Scient[...] Boris V. Nepoklonov said, "Even the moon does n[...] have such rocks. We thought there couldn't be roc[...] on Venus, they would all be annihilated by erosi[...] but here they are, with edges absolutely not blunt[...] This picture makes us reconsider all our concepts [...] Venus." Dr. Aleksandr Badilevsky, a leading Sov[...] geologist, said the sharp, angular edges testified '[...] recent catastrophic processes like volcanic erupti[...] or earthquakes — we should say Venus-quakes [...] which took place recently. Venus, apparently, [...] internally active." A 2nd spacecraft, the Venera [...] soft-landed Oct. 25 and transmitted photos of a t[...] rain quite different from the first. The Venera [...] photographs showed an old mountain formation w[...] smooth, rounded rocks that looked like huge pa[...] cakes. Between the rocks were sections of cooled la[...] or debris of weathered rocks.

$200-Million Land Swindle Alleged—A New Yo[...] City federal grand jury, Oct. 28, brought an 80-cou[...] indictment against a real-estate group for an alleg[...] $200-million swindle in the public sale of "und[...] veloped semi-arid desert lots" in a New Mexico ar[...] called Rio Rancho Estates. The indictment charge[...] companies and 7 officers with defrauding more th[...] 45,000 people from 37 states in what could be one [...] the most massive land swindles in history. Th[...] companies charged were Amrep, a New York Ci[...] corporation, and 2 of its subsidiaries, ATC Rea[...] Corporation and Rio Rancho Estates, Inc. A spoke[...] man for Amrep stated the charges were "who[...] unwarranted and legally and morally unjust." [...] further asserted that some 6,000 residents "enj[...] Amrep-built quality homes, apartments, and recre[...] tional facilities." According to the indictment, the d[...] fendants misled buyers into believing the lots we[...] suitable for home and commercial development, se[...] ing them primarily as financial investments th[...] could be resold at substantial profits.

Disasters—All 55 persons aboard died, Oct. 2[...] when a Bolivian Air Force transport plane crashed [...] the Andes, just 10 minutes after take-off from t[...] officers' resort of Tomomoco . . . A Yugoslav-charte[...] ed jetliner carrying Czech trade union members a[...] their families home from holidays in Dalmatia cra[...] ed, Oct. 30, on approach to Prague, Czechoslovaki[...] airport, killing 72 persons aboard.

Deaths, Nov. 1, 1974 — Nov. 1, 1975

A

ons, Edward S., 58; author of 40 Assignment" spy paperback books aturing Sam Durell; New Milford, onn., June 16.

, Jane, 74; radio personality of the 0s, "Easy Aces"; New York, Nov. 11.

lerley, Julian "Cannonball", 46; zz musician; Gary, Ind., Aug. 9.

xanderson, Ernst F.W., 97; engieer, inventor of the high-frequency lternator; Schenectady, N.Y., May 14.

n, Larry, 66; AP correspondent won ulitzer prize in 1942 for his war reorting; Mexico City, May 12.

derson, Leroy, 66; pop music omposer, "Sleigh Ride", "The Syncoated Clock"; Woodbury, Conn., May 8.

dric, Ivo, 82; Yugoslav novelist won obel prize in 1961; Belgrade, Mar. 3.

le, Paul M. 74; historian and author-y on Lincoln; Chicago, May 11.

B

ley, John M., 70; Democratic nation-l chairman in the '60s; Hartford, onn., Apr. 10.

ker, George, 59; creator of the "Sad ack" cartoon character; San Gabriel, al., May 9.

ker, Josephine, 68; American-born nger and dancer gained stardom in rance; Paris, Apr. 10.

rger, Floyd, 66; former editor of the lew York Daily News; Mineola, N.Y., ug. 29.

rnes, Florence, 73; woman aviator eld many speed records; Baron, Cal., nnounced Mar. 30.

xter, James P., 82; historian won Pu-tzer prize in 1947; former president of Villiams College; Williamstown, Mass., June 17.

atty, Morgan, 72; prominent broad-aster, newsman; St. John's, Antigua, uly 4.

ch, Joseph, 88; former Premier and oreign Minister of Luxembourg; uxembourg, Mar. 8.

ll, Jack, 71; newspaper columnist for Gannett News Service; former chief olitical writer for AP; Washington, .C., Sept. 15.

nny, Jack, 80; comedian starred for 0 years on radio, television, and in lms; Beverly Hills, Cal., Dec. 20.

nton, Thomas Hart, 85; American artist emphasized regional realism; Kansas City, Mo., Jan. 19.

ckel, Alexander M., 49; a leading ex-pe.t on the U.S. Constitution; New Haven, Nov. 7.

sh James, 54; science fiction writer; Oxfordshire, Eng., July 30.

ue, Ben, 73; sad-faced comedian and pantomimist; Hollywood, Cal., Mar. 7.

yden, Larry, 49; actor appeared in the heater and on TV; TV game show nost; Agadir, Morocco, June 6.

addock, James J., 68; world heavy-weight champion of the '30s; North Bergen, N.J., Nov. 28.

anzell, Karin, 83; a leading contralto at the Metropolitan Opera for 21 sea-sons; Altadena, Cal., Dec. 15.

ent, Evelyn, 75; silent movie star of he '20s; Los Angeles, June 4.

ill, Joseph E., 71; criminal lawyer; New York, May 18.

ook, Clive, 87; British actor of stage and screen; London, Nov. 17.

own, Johnny Mack, 70; college foot-ball star appeared in over 300 western movies; Woodland Hills, Cal., Nov. 14.

Brown, Pamela, 58; British actress of stage, film, and television; London, Sept. 18.

Brundage, Avery, 87; former president of the International Olympic Commit-tee who fought for amateurism in world athletic competition; W. Germany, May 8.

Buckley, Tim, 28; rock composer and singer; Santa Monica, Cal., June 29.

Bulganin, Nikolai A., 79; former Soviet Premier; USSR, Feb. 24.

Bundy, May Sutton, 88; first woman named to the Tennis Hall of Fame; Santa Monica, Cal., Oct. 4.

Burns, John A., 66; former governor of Hawaii; Apr. 5, Kaiwi, Hi.

Bushnell, Asa, 75; leading figure in amateur sports in U.S.; Princeton, N.J., Mar. 22.

C

Cannon, Poppy, 69; syndicated food columnist and cookbook author; New York, Apr. 1.

Carpentier, Georges, 81; French boxer fought Jack Dempsey in boxing's first $1-million gate in 1921; Paris, Oct. 27.

Charles, Ezzard, 53; world heavyweight boxing champion, 1949-51; Chicago, May 27.

Chiang Kai-shek, 87; president of Na-tionalist China; last survivor of the Big Four allied leaders of WW2; Taipei, Taiwan, Apr. 5.

Childers, Erskine H., 68; president of the Irish Republic; Dublin, Nov. 16.

Coleman, Robert, 74; former drama critic for the N.Y. Mirror; New York, Nov. 27.

Connolly, Cyril, 71; British literary critic and author; London, Nov. 26.

Considine, Bob, 68; journalist and syndicated columnist, "On the Line"; radio and TV commentator; New York, Sept. 25.

Conte, Richard, 59; actor played gang-ster and hero roles in over 50 films; Los Angeles, Apr. 15.

Coolidge, William D., 101; developer of the modern X-ray tube and the ductile tungsten filament used in electric light bulbs; Schenectady, N.Y., Feb. 3.

Courtney, Clint, 48; former major league catcher; managed Richmond of the International League; Rochester, N.Y., June 16.

Craig, May, 86; former Washington correspondent famed for her penetrat-ing and persistent questions at presi-dential news conferences; Silver Springs, Md., July 15.

Cross, Milton, 77; narrator of the Metro-politan Opera Saturday afternoon broadcasts for 43 years; New York, Jan. 3.

Cruickshank, Bobby, 80; a leading money-winning golfer in the early days of the PGA tour; Delray Beach, Fla., Aug. 27.

D

Daley, Cass, 59; buck-toothed come-dienne of the 40s; Hollywood, Cal., Mar. 22.

Dallapiccola, Luigi, 71; Italian compos-er and musical theorist; Florence, Italy, Feb. 19.

Davison, F. Trubee, 78; aviation pio-neer, former president of American Museum of Natural History; Locust Valley, N.Y., Nov. 14.

De Sica, Vittorio, 73; Italian film director, "The Bicycle Thief", "Shoeshine"; Paris, Nov. 13.

DeSpirito, Tony, 39; jockey rode 390 victories in 1952 as a 17-year-old; E. Providence, R.I., announced May 26.

de Valera, Eamon, 92; Irish statesman led fight for independence; former president and prime minister; Dublin, Aug. 29.

Donohue, Mark, 38; auto racing driver won Indianapolis 500 in 1972; Graz, Austria, Aug. 19.

Dorn, Philip, 75; Dutch born film actor; Los Angeles, May 9.

Doxiadis, Constantinos, 62; Greek architect and city planner; Athens, June 28.

Dragstedt, Dr. Lester R., 81; performed first successful surgical separation of Siamese twins in 1955; Gainesville, Fla., July 16.

Driscoll, Alfred E., 72; former governor of New Jersey, 1946-54; Haddonfield, N.J., Mar. 9.

Dunning, Dr. John R., 67; scientist helped develop the method of isolating uranium 235 used in nuclear weapons; Key Biscayne, Fla., Aug. 25.

Dunninger, Joseph, 82; magician, mind reader; Cliffside Park, N.J., Mar. 9.

Durfee, Minty, 85; veteran actress was Charlie Chaplin's first film leading lady; former wife of Fatty Arbuckle; Wood-land Hills, Cal., Sept. 16.

E

Egtvedt, Claire, 83; developer of the B-17 Flying Fortress of WW2; Seattle, Oct. 19.

Ely, Gen. Paul, 77; former French army chief of staff; Val de Grace, France, Jan. 16.

Evans, Walker, 71; photographer noted for his bleak pictures of American life; New Haven, Conn., Apr. 10.

F

Faisal, King, 70; Saudi Arabian mon-arch; assassinated by his nephew; Riyadh, Saudi Arabia, Mar. 25.

Farrar, John C., 78; publisher, editor, and writer; New York, Nov. 5.

Felsenstein, Walter, 74; opera director; E. Berlin, Oct. 8.

Fine, Larry, 73; frizzy-haired member of the Three Stooges comedy team; Woodland Hills, Cal., Jan. 24.

Flanders, Michael, 53; British humorist and lyricist teamed with Donald Swann in stage hit, "At the Drop of a Hat"; Wales, Apr. 14.

Flynn, F. M., 71; former president and publisher of the N.Y. Daily News; Pel-ham, N.Y., Nov. 22.

Fresnay, Pierre, 77; French stage and film actor whose career spanned 55 years; Neuilly-sur-Seine, France, Jan. 9.

Frizzell, Lefty, 47; country music singing star; Nashville, July 19.

Fuller, Ida, 100; recipient of the nation's first social security check in 1940; Brattleboro, Vt., Jan. 27.

Furler, Hans, 71; W. German statesman helped found the European Common Market; Oberkirsch, W. Germany, June 29.

G

Gallagher, William, 52; photographer won Pulitzer prize for his picture of Adlai Stevenson with a hole in his shoe; Flint, Mich., Sept. 28.

Germi, Pietro, 60; Italian film director, "Divorce Italian Style"; Rome, Dec. 5.

Gleason, Ralph J., 58; jazz critic; editor and founder of Rolling Stone magazine; Berkeley, Cal., June 3.

Green, Martyn, 75; British actor famed for Gilbert and Sullivan interpretations; Hollywood, Cal., Feb. 8.

Griffies, Ethel, 97; British actress appeared in over 100 films and scores of plays; London, Sept. 9.

Grove, Robert Moses (Lefty), 75; baseball hall of fame pitcher; won 300 major league games; Norwalk, Ohio, May 23.

H

Hansen, Alvin, 87; principal advocate for Keynesian economics in the U.S.; Alexandria, Va., June 6.

Hayward, Susan, 55; film actress won an Oscar, in 1958, "I Want to Live"; Beverly Hills, Cal., Mar. 14.

Helfer, Al, 63; baseball broadcaster; Sacramento, Cal., May 16.

Hennessy, Helen, 51; women's editor for Newspaper Enterprise Assn.; New York, July 17.

Hepworth, Barbara, 73; British sculptress; St. Ives, Eng., May 20.

Hershfield, Harry, 89; cartoonist, toastmaster, and raconteur; New York, Dec. 15.

Hibbs, Ben, 73; former editor of the Saturday Evening Post; Penn Valley, Pa., Mar. 29.

Hogg, Ima, 93; philanthropist founded the Houston Symphony; London, Aug. 19.

Hooper, Harry, 87; baseball hall of famer; Santa Cruz, Cal., Dec. 17.

Howard, Moe, 78; member of the Three Stooges comedy team; his trademark was a "chamber-pot" haircut; Hollywood, Cal., May 4.

Howe, Helen, 70; novelist and satiric monologist; New York, Feb. 1.

Hunt, H. L., 85; billionaire oilman and political conservative; Dallas, Nov. 29.

Hunter, Ivory Joe, 63; composer-pianist of country and popular songs; Washington, D.C., Nov. 8.

Huxley, Sir Julian, British scientist and author; London, Feb. 14.

I

Ismail, Ahmed, 57; commander-in-chief of Egypt's armed forces in Oct., 1973 war; London, Dec. 25.

Ittleson, Blanche, 99; mental health pioneer; New York, Aug. 16.

J

Jenckes, Rep. Virginia E., 97; former Indiana congresswoman noted for anti-communist activities; Terre Haute, Jan. 9.

Johnson, Crocker, 68; creator of the comic strip, "Barnaby"; Norwalk, Conn., July 11.

Jordan, Louis, 66; popular bandleader of the 40s; Los Angeles, Feb. 4.

Judson, Arthur, 93; American concert manager; Rye, N.Y., Jan. 28.

Julian, Dr. Percy L., 76; research chemist held over 130 chemical patents; Waukeegan, Ill., Apr. 19.

Justice, James Robertson, 70; Scottish actor appeared in many films in England and Hollywood; King's Somborne, Eng., July 2.

K

Kalthoum, Um, 77; Egypt's most popular singer for 50 years; Cairo, Feb. 3.

Kaplan, Kivie, 71; president of the NAACP since 1966; New York, May 5.

Katz, Label, 56; former president of B'nai B'rith; activist in Jewish affairs; New Orleans, Apr. 3.

Keating, Kenneth, 74; ambassador to Israel; former U.S. Senator from New York; New York, May 5.

Kellems, Vivien, 78; industrialist gained fame for her battles against the federal tax system; Los Angeles, Jan. 25.

Kennedy, Edward R., 52; publisher of The World Almanac; Berea, Ohio, June 16.

Kenny, John V., 82; former mayor of Jersey City; one of New Jersey's most powerful political leaders; Paramus, N.J., June 2.

Keres, Paul, 59; Estonian grandmaster ranked among the world's leading chess players for 40 years; Helsinki, June 5.

Kluczynski, John C., 78; Democratic congressman from Illinois since 1951; Chicago, Jan. 27.

Kober, Arthur, 74; humorist and playwright; New York, June 12.

Kriza, John, 56; former principal dancer of the American Ballet Theater; drowned near Naples, Fla., Aug.

Kuts, Vladimir, 48; Soviet long distance runner won 2 gold medals in the 1956 Olympics; USSR, Aug. 16.

Kuznetzov, Adm. Nikolai, 72; commander of Soviet naval forces during WW2; USSR, Dec.

L

Ladejinsky, Wolf, 76; American agricultural technician played major role in postwar land reform programs in Japan; Washington, D.C., July 3.

Ladner, Wendell, 26; N.Y. Nets basketball player; in plane crash; New York, June 17.

Pham Dang Lam, 57; former South Vietnamese foreign minister led delegation at Paris peace talks of 1968; Paris June 2.

Landis, Cullen, 79; actor starred in the first all-talking movie, "Lights of New York"; Bloomfield Hills, Mich., Aug. 26.

Lane, Rosemary, 61; one of the 4 singing Lane sisters; Hollywood, Nov. 25.

Laniel, Joseph, 85; former French premier; resistance leader during WW2; Paris, Apr. 9.

Levi, Carlo, 72; Italian painter and writer, "Christ Stopped at Eboli"; Rome, Jan. 4.

Lincoln, Gen. George A., 67; military strategist in WW2; drew the 38th parallel in Korea; Colorado Springs, Col., May 24.

Lippmann, Walter, 85; columnist and author was the dean of American political journalism; New York, Dec. 14.

Litvak, Anatole, 72; film director, "The Snake Pit"; Neuilly, France, Dec. 15.

Lochner, Louis P., 87; AP correspondent won Pulitzer prize in 1939; Wiesbaden, W. Germany, Jan. 8.

Londos, Jim, 80; former professional wrestling champion; Escondido, Cal., Aug. 19.

Long, Richard, 57; film and television actor; Los Angeles, Dec. 21.

Lopez, Vincent, 80; pianist and bandleader whose popularity spanned 50 years; No. Miami, Fla., Sept. 20.

Lord, Phillips H., 73; created "Gangbusters", "Mr. District Attorney", and the Seth Parker series on radio; Ellsworth, Me., Oct. 19.

Lund, DeWayne (Tiny), 43; leading stock car racing driver; in crash during Talladega 500; Talladega, Ala., Aug. 17.

M

Mabley, Jackie (Moms), 75; veteran television, radio, and nightclub comedienne; White Plains, N.Y., May 23.

MacPhail, Larry, 85; baseball owner and executive brought night games to the major leagues; Miami, Oct. 1.

Main, Marjorie, 85; character actress in over 100 films; played "Ma Kettle"; Los

Angeles, Apr. 10.

March, Fredric, 77; star of stage a films for 50 years; twice won Oscar best actor; Los Angeles, Apr. 14.

Marshall, George, 84; directed over films during a 62-year career; Los geles, Feb. 17.

Maxwell, W. Donald, 74; former edito the Chicago Tribune, 1955-66; Chi go, May 22.

McAuliffe, Gen. Anthony C., 77; s famous reply "Nuts" to a German matum that he surrender Bastog 1944; Washington, D.C., Aug. 11.

McCann, Dora, 60; radio personality hosted "The McCanns at Home"; York, Aug. 13.

McCarthy, Babe, 51; basketball co. twice named coach-of-the-year in ABA; Baldwyn, Miss., Mar. 18.

McCormack, Gen. James, 64; form head of Comsat; Hilton Head, N Jan. 3.

McGiver, John, 62; character actor stage, television, and films; W. Full N.Y., Sept. 11.

Medwick, Joe (Ducky), 63; baseball of fame slugger; St. Petersburg, F Mar. 21.

Mesta, Perle, 85; Washington hoste and party-giver; Oklahoma City, M 16.

Mindszenty, Jozsef Cardinal, Roman Catholic primate of Hung who became a symbol of anti-comm nism following a mock treason tria Budapest in 1949; Vienna, May 6.

Moley, Raymond, 88; leader of the or nal "Brain Trust"; coined the ter "New Deal"; Phoenix, Feb. 18.

Mollet, Guy, 69; French political lea who led France during Suez cri 1956; Paris, Oct. 3.

Montana, Bob, 54; creator of "Archie" comic strip; Meredith, N Jan. 4.

Monte, Toti Dal, 81; leading sopran the '20s and '30s; Treviso, Italy, Jan. 2

Morgan, Kay Summersby, 66; c dential secretary and confidante Gen. Eisenhower during WW2; Sor ampton, N.Y., Jan. 20.

Morton, Clive, 71; British chara actor in films and television for years; London, Sept. 24.

Moscona, Nicola, 68; bass sang lead roles at Metropolitan Opera for years; Philadelphia, Sept. 17.

Muhammad, Elijah, 77; spiritual lea of the Black Muslims; Chicago, F 25.

Murphy, Sara, 91; a symbol fo the "L Generation"; model for Nicole Dive Fitzgerald's "Tender Is the Night"; lington, Va., Oct. 10.

N

Nelson, Ozzie, 68; former bandlea and singer starred in, "The Adventu of Ozzie and Harriet" for 36 years radio and TV; San Fernando Vall Cal., June 3.

Niessen, Gertrude, 62; popular sin of '30s and '40s; Glendale, Cal., M 20.

Novotny, Antonin, 70; Czech dictat 1953-68; Czechoslovakia, Jan. 28.

Nugent, Arthur, 84; wrote and drew syndicated "Funland" puzzle pag Orange, N.J., Mar. 25.

O

O'Connor, Richard, 59; writer of so 60 books, mostly biography and pop lar history; Ellsworth, Me., Feb. 15.

Onassis, Aristotle, 68; Greek shipp magnate; Neuilly-sur-Seine, Fran Mar. 15.

P

arks, Larry, 60; portrayed Al Jolson in films; career declined in 1951 after admission of past membership in the Communist party; Studio City, Cal., Apr. 13.

ayson, Joan Whitney, 72; sportswoman headed Greentree Stables; principal owner of the N. Y. Mets baseball team; New York, Oct. 4.

erse, St.-John, 88; French romantic poet won Nobel prize in 1960; Giens, France, Sept. 20.

etiot, Fernand, 74; bartender credited with inventing the Bloody Mary; Canton, Ohio, Jan. 6.

ettis, Rep. Jerry, 58; Cal. congressman since 1966; plane crash, in Cal.; Feb. 14.

ollitzer, Anita, 80; pioneer in fight for women's rights; led National Woman's party; New York, July 4.

orter, Fairfield, 68; artist whose realist style influenced many younger painters; Southampton, N.Y., Sept. 18.

refontaine, Steve, 24; leading American distance runner; Eugene, Ore., May 30.

riest, Ivy Baker, 69; treasurer of the United States during the Eisenhower administration; Santa Monica, Cal., June 23.

ulliam, Eugene C., 86; newspaper publisher; major voice in Republican conservatism; Phoenix, June 23.

R

adhakrishnan, Sarvepalli, 86; Indian philosopher and statesman; Madras, India, Apr. 17.

evson, Charles, 68; pioneer in the cosmetics industry; president of Revlon, Inc.; New York, Aug. 24.

ichards, Paul, 50; actor appeared on television and the stage; Los Angeles, Dec. 10.

obinson, Sir Robert, 88; British chemist won Nobel prize in 1947; Great Missenden, England, Feb. 8.

ojas Pinilla, Gustavo, 74; president of Colombia, 1953-57; Colombia, Jan. 17.

ooney, John J., 71; Brooklyn congressman for 30 years; Washington, D.C., Oct. 26.

ose, Rufus C., 70; puppeteer created "Howdy Doody"; New London, Conn., May 29.

oss, T. J., 81; public relations pioneer; Rye, N.Y., May 27.

yan, Cornelius, 54; wrote best sellers, "The Longest Day", "The Last Battle"; New York, Nov. 23.

S

anders, Felicia, 53; nightclub singer gained fame in the '50s with hit record, "The Song From Moulin Rouge"; New York, Feb. 7.

anderson, Julia, 87; former musical-comedy headliner and radio singing star; Springfield, Mass., Jan. 27.

astroamidjojo, Dr. Ali, 72; Indonesian political leader; Jakarta, Mar. 13.

ato, Eisaku, 74; premier of Japan, 1964-72; shared Nobel peace prize in 1974; Tokyo, June 2.

auer, Dr. Carl O., 85; geographer influenced teachers and leaders in his field for 40 years; Berkeley, Cal., July 18.

edita, Frank A., 67; former mayor of Buffalo; Buffalo, May 2.

elassie, Haile, 83; emperor of Ethiopia for 50 years; Addis Ababa, Aug. 27.

erling, Rod, 50; TV writer won 5 Emmy awards; hosted TV's "Twilight Zone", and "Night Gallery"; Rochester, N.Y., June 28.

Sheean, Vincent, 75; American journalist and author; Arolo, Italy, Mar. 15.

Shields, Frank X., 66; tennis star of the '30s; New York, Aug. 26.

Shipstad, Roy, 64; co-founder of the Shipstad & Johnson Ice Follies; Stanford, Cal., Jan. 20.

Short, Luke, 67; author wrote more than 50 Western adventure books; Aspen, Col., Aug. 18.

Shostakovich, Dmitri, 68; Soviet composer; Kuntsevo, USSR, Aug. 9.

Simon, Michel, 80; French actor appeared in 40 plays, 145 films, "The Two of Us"; Paris, May 30.

Singleton, Zutty, 77; jazz drummer; New York, July 14.

Sjoqvist, Erik, 72; archeologist discovered the ancient Greek city of Morgantina in 1954; Drottningholm, Sweden, July 16.

Slobodkin, Louis, 72; sculptor, illustrator, and author of children's books; Miami Beach, May 8.

Slocum, Bill, 62; Hearst columnist and radio reporter; Somerville, Mass., Nov. 26.

Soglow, Otto, 74; cartoonist created "The Little King"; New York, Apr. 3.

Spear, Sammy, 65; bandleader long associated with Jackie Gleason; Miami, Mar. 11.

Spottswood, Bishop Stephen, 77; board chairman of the NAACP; Washington, D.C., Dec. 1.

Sproul, Robert G., 84; educator headed the Univ. of California for 28 years; Berkeley, Cal., Sept. 10.

Stagg, Dr. James, 74; meteorologist whose weather forecast for June 6, 1944, was decisive in the allied invasion of Normandy; Seaford, Eng., June 23.

Steavenson, W. H., 81; British astronomer; Swindon, Eng., Sept. 23.

Steen, Marguerite, 81; British novelist; London, Aug. 4.

Stengel, Casey, 85; colorful baseball manager led the N.Y. Yankees to 10 pennants; managed the N.Y. Mets during their infancy; Glendale, Cal., Sept. 30.

Stevens, George, 70; film director, "Giant", "A Place in the Sun" "Shane"; Lancaster, Cal., Mar. 8.

Stevenson, Coke, 87; governor of Texas, 1941-47; lost 1948 senate race to Lyndon Johnson by less than 200 votes; San Angelo, Tex., June 28.

Stillman, Dr. Irwin M., 79; author of popular diet books; No. Miami, Fla., Aug. 26.

Stolz, Robert, 94; Austrian composer wrote 2,000 songs, 50 operettas, scores for over 100 films; won 2 Academy awards; West Berlin, June 27.

Stout, Rex, 88; mystery novelist created Nero Wolfe; Danbury, Conn., Oct. 27.

Strauss, Robert, 61; character actor and comedian; New York, Feb. 20.

Sylvester, Bob, 68; entertainment columnist for the N.Y. Daily News since 1951; Montauk, N.Y., Feb. 9.

T

Tertis, Lionel, 98; British violist; London, Feb. 22.

Thant, U, 74; third secretary general of the United Nations; New York, Nov. 25.

Thomas, Rene, 89; French auto-racing pioneer; won Indianapolis 500 in 1914; Paris, Sept. 23.

Thomson, Sir George, 83; British physicist won Nobel prize in 1937; Cambridge, Eng., Sept. 10.

Tolson, Clyde, 74; former FBI official; closest friend and associate of J. Edgar Hoover; Washington, D.C., Apr. 14.

Toynbee, Arnold, 86; British historian charted the rise and fall of civilizations in 12-volume work, "A Study of History"; York, Eng., Oct. 22.

Tucker, Richard, 60; leading tenor at the Metropolitan Opera for 30 years; Kalamazoo, Mich., Jan. 8.

Tung Pi-wu, 89; former Chinese chief-of-state; a founder of Chinese communist party; Peking, Apr. 2.

Tunnell, Emlen, 50; star defensive back; first black named to the Pro Football Hall of Fame; Pleasantville, N.Y., July 23.

U

Ure, Mary, 42; British stage and film actress; London, Apr. 3.

V

Vanderbilt, Amy, 66; author and columnist on etiquette; New York, Dec. 27.

W

Waddington, Dr. C. H., 69; British geneticist; Edinburgh, Scotland, Sept. 27.

Wahloo, Per, 48; Swedish novelist wrote the Martin Beck detective series with his wife, Maj Sjowall; Malmo, Sweden, June 24.

Weidman, Charles, 73; dancer and choreographer broadened the Participation of men in dance; New York, July 15.

Weingarten, Lawrence, 77; produced 75 films for M-G-M; Hollywood, Cal., Feb. 6.

Wheeler, Burton K., 92; Montana senator, 1922-1946; prosecutor in the Teapot Dome scandals; led opposition that halted Roosevelt's plan to enlarge the Supreme Court; Washington, D.C., Jan. 6.

Whitney, Richard, 86; former president of the N.Y. stock exchange; credited with halting the Wall Street panic of '29; Far Hills, N.J., Dec. 5.

Wightman, Hazel Hotchkiss, 87; winner of 45 national tennis titles; donor of the Wightman Cup; Chestnut Hill, Mass., Dec. 5.

Williams, David M., 74; designer of the M-1 carbine rifle; Raleigh, N.C., Jan. 8.

Wills, Bob, 70; western bandleader and composer, "San Antonio Rose"; Ft. Worth, Tex., May 13.

Wilson, Don, 29; righthander pitcher for the Houston Astros; Houston, Jan. 5.

Wodehouse, P. G., 93; author of nearly 100 novels and 16 plays; creator of Jeeves and Bertie Wooster; Southampton, N.Y., Feb. 14.

Wylie, Max, 71; novelist and playwright; Fredericksburg, Va., Sept. 21.

Y

Young, Stanley, 69; poet, playwright, and literary reviewer; Huntington, N.Y., Mar. 22.

Z

Zacchini, Hugo, 77; circus performer originated the human cannonball act; San Bernardino, Cal., Oct. 20.

Laws Passed, Bills Vetoed During 94th Congress, 1st Session (1975)

The 94th Congress convened its first session Jan. 14, 1975. During the session, Pres. Ford and Congress continued their "battle of the vetoes"; by Oct. 7, Ford had vetoed 11 bills, Congress had overridden 3 of them. Major bills passed by Congress and signed into law by Ford, as well as other actions, included:

Price of Food Stamps. Congress blocked the president's plan to raise the purchase price of food stamps by freezing the price through 1975. Ford allowed the freeze bill to become law without his signature (Feb. 13).

Emergency Funds for Railroads. This authorized $197 million in cash grants and $150 million in government-guaranteed loans to 8 northeast railroads in financial trouble (signed by Ford Mar. 1).

$22.8 Billion Tax Cut. Included $7 billion more than Ford had proposed as an anti-recession measure. It provided for $8.1 billion in rebates to individuals (maximum $400); $10 billion in cuts in current income taxes and other items including "negative income tax" payments to poor families; $4.8 billion in cuts for businesses. It also provided gradual phasing out of the 22% oil and gas depletion allowance except for small producing companies (signed Mar. 29).

Reduced Foreign Aid. Appropriated $3.7 billion for foreign developmental aid, military grants and credits, and UN programs, $2.2 billion less than Ford had requested. Postwar Indochina funds totaled $440 million, less than half what Ford had requested (signed Mar. 26).

Funds for Indochina Refugees. Authorized $455 million and appropriated $405 million of that for the Indochinese refugee relocation program (signed May 24).

Unemployment Compensation

Unemployment Pay Extended. The program guaranteeing jobless workers an extra 13 weeks unemployment compensation, in addition to the regular 52 weeks, was extended to the end of 1975; the extra 13 weeks program had been due to expire July 1 (signed June 30).

Compromise Housing Aid. After the House, June 25, failed to override a Ford veto of an earlier housing bill, Congress passed a 2d bill, authorizing the government to lend $10 billion on housing mortgages at a subsidized interest rate of 7.5%; it also provided for loans or guarantees to unemployed homeowners facing foreclosure (signed July 2).

Veto Overridden

Health Bill Veto Overridden. Authorizing $2 billion over 2 years, the bill had been vetoed by Ford July 26 as "excessive and unsound." The votes to override were 67-12 in the Senate, July 26, and 384-43 in the House, July 29. The law granted states funds for health centers and programs.

Voting Rights. Extended for 7 more years the 1965 law ensuring blacks' voting rights in southern states. It also permanently banned literacy tests and extended coverage to Spanish-speaking and Asian Americans, American Indians, and Alaskan natives (signed Aug. 6).

Office Funds. Appropriated $7.6 billion for the Executive Office, Treasury and various agencies for "old fiscal" 1976 plus the 3-month period to the new fiscal year starting date, Oct. 1, 1976. It included $210,000 in pension and office funds for ex-Pres. Nixon, $53,000 less than Ford had asked (signed Aug. 9).

Ban on Plutonium Flights. A bill authorizing funds for the Nuclear Regulatory Commission included a ban on air transport of plutonium (signed Aug. 9).

Federal Pay Increases. Approved pay boosts for members of Congress, top government executives (excepting the president), and federal judges, to match, percentagewise, cost-of-living raises due 3.5 million lower echelon federal employes and militar personnel (signed Aug. 11). The Senate, Sept. 18, an the House, Oct. 1, fixed the percentage rise at 5%, a urged by Ford.

School Aid Veto Overridden. A $7.9 billion educa tion appropriations bill, vetoed by Ford July 25, be came law as the House voted 379-41 to override, Sep 9, and the Senate, 88-12, Sept. 10. It provided federa aid for schools until the new beginning of the fisca year, Oct. 1, 1976.

Oil Price Compromise. Congress approved, in bi form, an agreement with Pres. Ford for restoratio of price controls on "old" oil (from wells in produc tion before 1973) and their extension to Nov. 15; th president was to propose after Nov. 1 a plan to rais oil prices, which Congress could accept or rejec (signed Sept. 29).

School Lunch Veto Overridden. A $2.7 billio extension and broadening of the federal school lunc program, vetoed Oct. 3 by Ford as "too costly," be came law Oct. 7 as the House voted 397-18 to overrid and the Senate, 79-13.

Turkish Arms Embargo Eased. The ban on ship ments of U.S. arms to Turkey, earlier imposed b Congress because of Turkey's use of American-sup plied arms in its invasion of Cyprus, was partiall lifted (signed Oct. 7).

U.S. Civilians in Sinai OK'd. Authorized stationin of American civilian technicians in the Sinai to hel monitor the Israel-Egypt disengagement agreemen negotiated by Sec. of State Kissinger (signed Oct. 13).

Vetoes Sustained

While Congress overrode vetoes on several majo bills (see above), it failed to override vetoes of othe important bills, including:

Oil Tariff Bill. This would have suspended th president's power to raise the tariff on imported oi Rather than seek to override the Mar. 4 veto, Con gressional leaders sought an agreement with Ford he delayed until June 1 a second $1-a-barrel boost.

Farm Bill. Authorizing increased price support and income guarantees for farmers, it was vetoed b Ford May 1 as too costly; the House tried, May 13, t override, but failed.

Jobs Bill. A $5.3 billion jobs-producing bill wa vetoed May 29, Ford saying it would produce budge and economic pressures. The House failed, June 4, b 5 votes, to override.

Strip Mining Curbs. Requiring strip mine operator to restore the landscape, this was vetoed May 20 b Ford who said it would reduce coal production. Th House failed to override, June 10, by 3 votes.

Emergency Housing. Ford, June 24, vetoed a $1. billion housing bill on grounds of "cost and ineffec tiveness." The House failed the next day to override Ford signed a compromise bill July 2 (see above).

Oil Price Controls. Ford vetoed Sept. 9 a 6-mos extension of the price freeze on "old" oil; the Senate failed to override, Sept. 10, by 6 votes. Earlier, July 21, Ford vetoed a bill to roll back the price of uncon trolled oil. A compromise oil bill was signed Sept. 29 (see above).

Tobacco Price Supports. On Sept. 30, Ford vetoed a bill to increase supports, citing costs and damage to American tobacco prices on the world market.

Change in Filibusters

Senate Filibuster Reform. The Senate, Mar. 7 ended a one-man, 2-week filibuster by Sen. James D Allen (D-Ala.) by changing its filibuster rule to per mit invoking of cloture (putting an end to debate) by only three-fifths of the Senate's membership instead of the previous two-thirds of those senators present.

Major Decisions of the U.S. Supreme Court, 1975

Notable decisions of the U.S. Supreme Court in
1975 included:

Let stand a lower court decision killing a Missouri
law which authorized the loan of textbooks to pupils
in church-related schools (Jan. 13).

Unanimously barred Louisiana from suspending a
physician who performed an abortion before the Jan.
'73 Supreme Court decision making most abortions
legal (Jan. 13).

Upheld, by 6-3 vote, an Iowa law requiring a year's
residence in the state to qualify for a divorce (Jan.
14).

Unanimously ruled a lawyer may not be held in
contempt of court for advising a client not to produce
subpoenaed material the lawyer believes would be in-
criminating. (Jan. 15).

Let stand a $650,000 award against Los Angeles
County to property owners for loss of property values
because of jet noise near its airport (Jan. 20).

Invalidated, 8-1, a criminal conviction by a jury not
representative of the community in terms of female
membership (Jan. 21).

Student Rights

Ruled, 5-4, that public school pupils cannot be suspended without being given the nature of the charges
against them, an explanation of the evidence, and a
chance to tell their side. (Jan. 22).

Let stand, in effect, the Florida system which
grants automatic jury exemption to pregnant women
and mothers of children under 18, if they request it
(Jan. 27).

Let stand a decision requiring payment of welfare
benefits to workers on strike (Jan. 27).

Let stand a decision barring a Massachusetts hospital from prohibiting elective abortions (Jan. 27).

Ordered the federal government to release $9 bil-
lion for state and local water pollution control
programs, unanimously holding that Richard Nixon,
while president, had not had the power to freeze
funds authorized by Congress (Feb. 18).

Let stand an award of support payments to a separated wife, overriding protests by the husband that
the award was discriminatory since a husband could
not obtain such payments from a wife (Feb. 18).

Ruled, 7-2, the Internal Revenue Service can issue
"John Doe" subpoenas for certain types of bank
records (Feb. 19).

Let stand the attempted burglary conviction of a
man who turned the handle of a garage door, found it
was locked, and left (Feb. 24).

Forced Retirement

Affirmed a decision upholding the federal government's right to retire employees at age 70, overriding
objectives that this constituted age discrimination
(Feb. 24).

Let stand a decision that prisoners awaiting trial
and held in jail for lack of bail cannot demand speedy
trials as a group but only as individuals (Feb. 24).

Held, 5-4, that school officials may be sued by a
pupil whose civil rights they violated by expelling
him without due process (Feb. 25).

Let stand, by a 4-4 vote, a lower court decision that
permitted a federal agency to photocopy and distrib-
ute scientific journals without payment of fees to the
author or the original publisher (Feb. 25).

Upheld the right of a trial jury to conclude that, in
a 1970 incident at Jackson (Miss.) State College, police had fired 150 shots into a group of students,
killing 2, in self-defense; the ruling meant the police
could not be sued for damages (Mar. 3).

Held that power plants could be built without
federal licenses when they would use water from
navigable streams only for cooling, not for hydroelectric power (Mar. 4).

Declared unconstitutional, 8-1, a Georgia law
which made it a misdemeanor to print or broadcast
the name of a rape victim; the court also denied the
victim or her family the right to sue for invasion of
privacy (Mar. 3).

Unanimously held that the federal government, not
coastal states, has title to oil and gas resources in the
Atlantic Continental Shelf beyond the 3-mi. limit
(Mar. 17).

Held, 5-4, Chattanooga could not bar presentation
of a musical show as obscene before the show had
been performed, extending the court's bans on "prior
restraint." (Mar. 18).

Let stand, in a Chicago case, a ruling that states and
municipalities may not impose "burdensome" regulations affecting a woman's right to an abortion during early months of pregnancy (Mar. 24).

Upheld, in effect, the right of the Federal Energy
Office to prohibit gasoline dealers from giving
preferential treatment to regular customers during a
fuel shortage (Mar. 25).

Ruled, 6-3, that federal courts should not intervene
in military courts-martial until they have been concluded (Mar. 25).

School Integration

Upheld a plan to integrate Louisville, Ky., schools
with those of surrounding Jefferson Co., noting that
both school systems were discriminatory (Apr. 1).

Let stand a decision ordering cities in Massachusetts to give preference to black and Hispanic
applicants for fire department jobs to remedy earlier
discrimination (Apr. 14).

Upheld a South Carolina law requiring awarding of
attorneys fees in a divorce action to the wife, overriding the claim that this constituted sex discrimination
against the husband (Apr. 14).

Ruled unconstitutional a Utah law declaring girls
adults at age 18 but boys at 21 (Apr. 15).

Congressional Subpoenas

Held, 8-1, a federal court could not block a Congressional subpoena issued in connection with an authorized committee investigation (May 27).

Unanimously banned fixed fees charged by
lawyers for real estate transfers (June 16).

Declared unconstitutional, 7-2, a Virginia law
which prohibited publication in Virginia of advertise-
ments for abortion services in other states (June 16).

Denied an appeal from a robbery conviction of
Jack (Murph the Surf) Murphy, saying no defendant
has a right to a jury which never heard of his previous record (June 16).

Let stand a decision holding a Georgia official liable for damages for refusing to accept a job
application from a white man because the applicant
was married to a black woman (June 16).

Declared unconstitutional, 6-3, a Jacksonville, Fla.,
ordinance which banned nudity films in drive-in
theaters that are visible from public places, calling it
interference with free speech (June 23).

Upheld the validity of a Santa Barbara, Cal., ordinance prohibiting nudity in public parks, beaches,
and streets (June 23).

Right to Remain Silent

Held that a defendant who exercised his right to remain silent on arrest could not be questioned by a
prosecutor during trial about his earlier failure to assert an alibi (June 23).

Approved invalidation of a city ordinance prohibiting multiple-family apartment houses; it was held
that the law, in effect, discriminated against blacks
(June 23).

Unanimously ruled that non-criminal, non-danger-
ous patients involuntarily confined to institutions
must either be given medical treatment or freed
(June 26).

Ruled, 6-3, that a defendant in a criminal case has a
right to conduct his own defense and to refuse to accept a court-appointed attorney (June 30).

Affirmed a decision that a teacher may paddle an
unruly pupil, but only if lesser punishments are tried
first, the student is told why he is being punished, and
other teachers witness the paddling (Oct. 20).

Off-beat News in 1975

As the United States prepared to huzzah out its second and welcome in its third century, and elsewhere the world nonchalantly greeted its four-billionth inhabitant, on or about April Fool's Day according to one calculation, the march of humanity had its share of those out of step in their own parade of off-beat news for 1975.

Leading the parade are Overreachers of the Year, the former Robert C. Weiszman family of Spokane, Washington. Seeking a name "less alien sounding," the seven-member family legally changed their names, becoming the Robert C. America family.

No less patriotic are the proud owners of Caspar the Cat, a gentleman feline from Virginia, who dressed the prize-winning puss as George Washington. So attired, Caspar became National Glamour Kitty Contest winner for 1975.

Future historians may also note that 1975 was the year when U.S. senators fought aggressively with obfuscation as they voted on the following early in the year: A motion to table a motion to reconsider a vote to table an appeal of a ruling that a point of order was not in order against a motion to table another point of order against a motion to bring to a vote the motion to call up the resolution that would institute a rules change.

Communication was no better served at the local level in Biloxi, Miss., when a local contractor finished paving a block-long street two days before another local contractor ripped up the pavement to install a new sewer line.

The sewer scene along the Seine focused on the Parisians' revolutionary step forward in man's continuing battle for cleaner streets: plans for construction of the world's first public flush toilets for dogs. The canine commodes, complete with flower and perfume, were to be placed throughout the French capital.

Perhaps nonplussed by the present state of Paris sidewalks, two men were arrested while climbing the 58-story Montparnasse Tower, the city's tallest building, using ropes and mountain picks. Their heartening and obvious explanation for climbing the building: "Because it was there."

Because it wasn't there — a 50-by-100 ft. parcel of land in New York City, that is — the deposit a Queens man paid the city for the property was returned to him. It was discovered that the parcel of land sat entirely in the roadbed of Meeker Street and all parties seemed agreed the street was no place for a house.

Reuben Webber of Mount Vernon, Me., discovered an undesirable in his water supply this year — a 900-pound bull moose. The animal fell through a log and sheet metal covering over the spring from which Webber gets his water. Webber and friends pulled the surprised moose from the water and it quickly returned to the more sedate woods.

Quite sedate were several bears near Wallace, Idaho, after gorging themselves on grain and corn which had spilled over an embankment after some freight cars overturned. Rain had fermented the grain and officials reported the bears were walking around in a daze. The area of the spillage is known as Loop Creek.

Perhaps what the bear needed was a whiff of the air some Genoans have been breathing. Some 300 Italians living near a coffee-processing plant complained that they have been forced to inhale caffeine equal to drinking 150 cups of coffee daily. A magistrate, who felt the citizens had grounds for complaint, opened an investigation.

Another individual finding coffee grounds for com-

plaint was a Long Island coffee vendor who fo[und] himself handcuffed and reprimanded by a N.Y. [Dis]trict Court judge. The judge, against whom the v[en]dor has filed a $5-million suit for damages, orde[red] the man brought to him in cuffs after purchas[ing] what he described as "terrible" coffee.

A Municipal Court judge in San Rafael, Calif., g[ain]ed notoriety this year with a familiar punitive te[ch]nique. Judge Gary S. Thomas has sentenced p[etty] offenders to writing "I will not steal" and "I will [ap]pear in court" as many as 2,000 and 3,000 times. [The] judge explains, "It's as good a deterrent as any."

Some handwriting practice might have been [in] order for a Philadelphia bank robber. "I am a b[ank] robber," he declared when the bank teller coul[dn't] read his note. "I am a policeman," said an off-duty [pa]trolman standing next in line to the would-be rob[ber] before he took the man into custody.

Thieves in Belgrade, Yugoslavia, were in for [an] even bigger shock after stealing a large wooden c[ase] containing 45 deadly Congolese snakes.

Elsewhere in the world of crime, four Sici[lian] prisoners who "diligently practiced long jump[ing] during exercise periods" used their skills to l[eap] from roof to roof in their escape, hurdling gaps [of] more than 12 feet.

Of quite a different mind was Roman Olejnicza[k of] Bay City, Mich., who reported his inability to adj[ust] to the outside world and asked to return "home[" to] Southern Michigan Prison where he had lived [for] years. He had been paroled in April.

Another fellow who might call jail home is a [66-] year-old multiple offender from New Orleans. Pol[ice] there are claiming the world arrest record for [the] man, arrested 820 times and convicted 421 tim[es] mostly for drunkenness. His name is Alfred L. Vice[.]

Depending upon one's view of classroom life[, a] Phoenix area high school senior received a very li[ght] or a very heavy sentence. Found guilty of an $85 [liq]uor store robbery, the youth was sentenced to c[om]plete two years of college as part of the terms of [his] five year probation.

Students also attended college to protect the[m]selves from crime in 1975. Mug-a-Thug 101, [an] elective at Towson State College, was one of the m[ost] popular courses offered by the school this ye[ar.] Taught by a former Green Beret, the course p[re]pared one 108-pound female to ward off an accost[ing] masher who was taken to the hospital with fractu[red] pelvis and kneecap.

Perhaps the most laborious caper of 1975 came [to] light when NYC firemen on a routine check discov[er]ed more than 15,000 New York Public Library bo[oks] in a Greenwich Village apartment. The huge coll[ec]tion was purloined over the past decade. Twenty m[en] working three days removed the books. Asked h[ow] he got the books out of the library, the law-break[ing] book lover replied: "In large quantities."

The year 1975 saw the mortality rate fall nearly [6] percent over previous weeks during a doctors' str[ike] in New York, and it was the year women in Goteb[org,] Sweden, turned to tossing sour herrings into the c[ars] of male "cruisers" who bother them.

It was a year in which 16-year-old Linda Salced[o, a] contestant in the California Teen Pageant, file[d a] half-million-dollar lawsuit against pageant offici[als] who wouldn't let her chop concrete blocks to musi[c as] part of her performance because it was too "unla[dy]like." It was, finally, the year a man in Califor[nia] claimed the world's record for lap-sitting, having h[ad] 1,539 women from 42 states and 14 foreign countr[ies] sit on his lap.

VITAL STATISTICS

Source: Division of Vital Statistics, National Center for Health Statistics, Public Health Service

First Half-Year, January-June 1975

Births

During the first half of 1975 there were 1,531,000 live births, about one percent fewer than for the first half of 1974. The birth rate for this period was 14.5 per 1,000 population compared with 14.4 for the corresponding period in 1974, and the fertility rate was 65.8 births per 1,000 women 15-44 years of age, compared with 66.2 for the earlier period.

Marriages

Provisional data for the first half of 1975 indicate a continuation of the decline in the marriage rate that started in 1973.

In the first half of 1975, 980,000 marriages were reported. This was 42,000, or 4%, fewer than in the first half of 1974. The marriage rate for the period was 9.3 per 1,000 population, a decline of 5% from the rate for the first half of 1974.

Divorces

The number of divorces granted during the 6 months ending with June was 498,000, compared with 476,000 from the corresponding period in 1974. The rate was 4.7 per 1,000 population, up from 4.5 for the first half of 1974.

Deaths

The death rate for the first half of 1975 was 9.4, unchanged from the same period in 1974.

During January-May 1975 the rates for the following causes of death were lower when compared with the same period a year earlier: cardiovascular decreased 3.4% and cirrhosis of the liver decreased 10.4%. Increases in the death rate for the same period occurred for malignant neoplasms and for influenza and pneumonia. The latter cumulative increase reflected the high rate for influenza and pneumonia during the epidemic in January and February 1975.

Provisional Statistics
12 months ending with June 1975

	Number		Rate*	
	1975	1974	1975	1974
Live births	3,187,000	3,112,000	15.0	14.8
Deaths.	1,936,000	1,950,000	9.1	9.3
Natural increase	1,251,000	1,162,000	5.9	5.5
Marriages	2,182,000	2,241,000	10.3	10.6
Divorces	993,000	940,000	4.7	4.5
Infant deaths. . .	52,500	53,100	16.5	17.1
Population base (in millions).			212.3	210.7

*Per 1,000 population

Annual Report for the Year 1974 (Provisional Statistics)

Births

During 1974 the number of live births in the United States totaled an estimated 3,166,000, resulting in a provisional birth rate of 15.0 births per 1,000 population. These data were about 1 percent higher than the final levels observed for 1973. The fertility rate, however, continued to decline to an estimated 68.4 births per 1,000 women 15-44 years of age. Still, the decline in this rate has slowed down. The rate for 1974 was 1 percent lower than the final rate recorded for 1973 (69.2); declines in the years between 1970 and 1973 averaged 7 percent.

Both the number of births and the birth rate increased slightly over 1973 levels because the 2 percent increase in the number of women in the childbearing ages (assumed to be 15-44 years) more than offset the decline in the fertility rate.

During 1974 the growth of the population due to natural increase (the excess of births over deaths) amounted to 1,233,000 persons. The provisional rate of natural increase was 5.9 persons per 1,000 population compared with the final rate of 5.5 for 1973. The increase in this rate can be attributed primarily to the decline in the death rate.

Deaths

An estimated 1,933,000 deaths occurred in the United States during 1974. The provisional death rate was 9.1 per 1,000 population, a reduction of 3 percent from the final rate of 9.4 for 1973.

In 1974 there were approximately 52,400 infant deaths resulting in an estimated infant mortality rate of 16.5 per 1,000 live births. This was the lowest annual rate ever recorded in the United States and represents a decrease of 7 percent from the final rate of 17.7 for 1973. Both the neonatal (under 28 days) and the postneonatal (28 days to 11 months) mortality rates declined in 1974 with the postneonatal rate showing a proportionately greater decline than the neonatal rate. Certain gastrointestinal diseases were the only cause of infant deaths to show an increase during 1974.

Marriages and Divorces

In 1974 marriages declined both in the number and the rate from the levels of 1973. The 1974 national total was 2,223,000, about 54,000, or 2 percent, fewer than in 1973. The decline in the number of marriages was the first annual decline since 1958. Between 1958 and 1973 the number of marriages increased every year. The marriage rate dropped to 10.5 per 1,000 population in 1974, lower than in any of the previous 5 years.

Both the number and the rate of divorces and annulments granted in the United States continued to increase during 1974. According to provisional reports 970,000 divorces were granted, an increase of 57,000 over the number granted in 1973 and more than double the number 10 years earlier. The provisional divorce rate for 1974 was 4.6 per 1,000 population, the highest national divorce rate on record and almost twice the rate for 1964. The average annual rate of increase was 8 percent for the decade 1965-74. In the previous decade, from 1955 to 1964, the rate had changed relatively little.

Births and Deaths in the United States

Refers only to events occurring within the United States, including Alaska beginning in 1959 and Hawaii in 1960. Excludes fetal deaths. Rates per 1,000 population enumerated as of April 1 for 1955 and 1960; estimated as of July 1 for all other years. (P) Provisional.

	Births				Deaths			
Year	Males	Females	Totals Number	Rate	Males	Females	Totals Number	Rate
1955	2,073,719	1,973,576	4,047,295	24.6	872,638	656,079	1,528,717	9.3
1960	2,179,708	2,078,142	4,257,850	23.7	975,648	736,334	1,711,982	9.5
1965	1,927,054	1,833,304	3,760,358	19.4	1,035,200	792,936	1,828,136	9.4
1970	1,915,378	1,816,008	3,731,386	18.4	1,078,478	842,553	1,921,031	9.5
1971	1,822,910	1,733,060	3,555,970	17.2	1,077,332	850,210	1,927,542	9.3
1972	1,669,927	1,588,484	3,258,411	25.6	1,096,198	867,746	1,963,944	9.4
1973	1,608,326	1,528,639	3,136,965	14.9	1,096,795	876,208	1,973,003	9.4
1974(P)	NA	NA	3,166,000	15.0	NA	NA	1,933,000	9.1

Births and Deaths by States

Source: Division of Vital Statistics, National Center for Health Statistics.

States	Births 1974	Births 1973	Deaths 1974	Deaths 1973	States	Births 1974	Births 1973	Deaths 1974	Deaths 1973
Alabama	58,587	59,760	34,403	35,604	Montana	12,159	11,189	6,499	6,76
Alaska	6,998	6,640	1,484	1,457	Nebraska	23,774	22,899	15,134	15,15
Arizona	39,926	37,980	17,405	17,238	Nevada	8,656	8,800	4,731	4,52
Arkansas	33,835	32,687	21,876	21,881	New Hampshire	11,310	11,077	7,604	7,70
California	303,500	300,637	166,458	174,297	New Jersey	91,136	93,478	65,507	67,82
Colorado	39,698	39,345	18,471	19,060	New Mexico	21,115	20,643	8,067	8,12
Connecticut	36,340	36,642	26,259	26,778	New York	240,085	241,349	175,991	179,44
Delaware	8,334	8,222	5,200	5,137	North Carolina	84,529	85,772	46,495	48,02
Dist. of Col.	20,349	19,919	10,347	9,769	North Dakota	10,708	10,376	5,887	6,00
Florida	108,062	107,879	89,394	90,251	Ohio	157,819	160,996	97,657	101,08
Georgia	87,371	90,048	50,124	40,402	Oklahoma	40,756	39,770	26,427	26,72
Hawaii	15,617	15,334	4,602	4,594	Oregon	33,499	31,731	20,321	20,91
Idaho	15,131	13,996	6,238	6,290	Pennsylvania	147,924	154,560	122,332	126,89
Illinois	165,850	166,844	105,594	107,871	Rhode Island	11,688	12,659	9,155	9,49
Indiana	83,523	84,388	47,919	49,761	South Carolina	47,252	47,787	23,925	24,58
Iowa	40,627	39,303	28,540	29,193	South Dakota	10,766	10,545	6,566	6,58
Kansas	31,294	30,610	21,651	22,106	Tennessee	67,376	68,484	41,340	42,38
Kentucky	54,283	55,663	33,024	34,447	Texas	221,324	218,200	100,478	103,22
Louisiana	65,867	65,887	33,786	35,272	Utah	30,575	27,958	7,745	7,68
Maine	14,533	15,314	10,787	10,906	Vermont	6,814	6,305	4,458	4,44
Maryland	46,719	47,349	32,129	32,191	Virginia	66,339	68,980	39,781	40,54
Massachusetts	71,347	74,777	55,237	62,214	Washington	47,785	45,447	29,569	30,53
Michigan	136,066	140,731	75,472	77,427	West Virginia	27,737	28,146	19,543	20,24
Minnesota	55,313	54,273	34,009	34,571	Wisconsin	65,507	62,584	41,108	41,49
Mississippi	45,242	44,399	22,649	23,766	Wyoming	6,250	5,912	3,075	3,02
Missouri	71,991	71,496	50,250	53,433	**Total**	**3,151,286**	**3,155,770**	**1,932,703**	**1,979,33**

Marriages, Divorces, and Rates in the United States

Source: Division of Vital Statistics, National Center for Health Statistics.

Data refer only to events occurring within the United States, including Alaska beginning with 1959 and Hawaii with 196_. Rates per 1,000 population.

Year	Marriages[1] No.	Rate	Divorces[2] No.	Rate[3]	Year	Marriages[1] No.	Rate	Divorces[2] No.	Rate
1890	570,000	9.0	33,461	0.5	1940	1,595,879	12.1	264,000	2.0
1895	620,000	8.9	40,387	0.6	1945	1,612,992	12.2	485,000	3.5
1900	709,000	9.3	55,751	0.7	1950	1,667,231	11.1	385,144	2.6
1905	842,000	10.0	67,976	0.8	1955	1,531,000	9.3	377,000	2.3
1910	948,166	10.3	83,045	0.9	1960	1,523,000	8.5	393,000	2.2
1915	1,007,595	10.0	104,298	1.0	1965	1,800,000	9.3	479,000	2.5
1920	1,274,476	12.0	170,505	1.6	1970	2,158,802	10.6	708,000	3.5
1925	1,188,334	10.3	175,449	1.5	1972	2,282,154	11.0	845,000	4.1
1930	1,126,856	9.2	195,961	1.6	1973	2,277,000	10.9	915,000	4.4
1935	1,327,000	10.4	218,000	1.7	1974(p)	2,223,000	10.5	970,000	4.6

(1) Includes estimates and marriage licenses for some states for all years. (2) Includes reported annulments. (3) Divorce rates fo_ 1945, based on population including armed forces overseas. (p) Provisional.

Marriages and Divorces by States 1974[1]

Source: Division of Vital Statistics National Center for Health Statistics
(Divorces include reported annulments) [1] Provisional.

State	Marriages	Divorces	State	Marriages	Divorces	State	Marriages	Divorces
Alabama	47,581	23,519	Louisiana	39,314	NA	Oklahoma	41,260	22,60
Alaska	4,342	2,423	Maine	11,756	4,924	Oregon	20,469	13,64
Arizona	27,647	NA	Maryland	47,162	14,868	Pennsylvania	92,482	31,42
Arkansas	22,202	14,604	Massachusetts	43,316	16,093	Rhode Island	7,252	2,52
California	159,386	121,944	Michigan	89,644	28,795	South Carolina	52,199	8,62
Colorado	25,592	15,120	Minnesota	33,556	12,067	South Dakota	11,930	2,02
Connecticut	24,441	10,756	Mississippi	27,887	11,864	Tennessee	54,567	24,47
Delaware	4,171	2,355	Missouri	51,752	21,567	Texas	155,916	69,52
Dist. of Col.	5,324	3,032	Montana	7,832	3,942	Utah	14,923	5,66
Florida	90,916	59,602	Nebraska	13,779	5,244	Vermont	4,726	1,50
Georgia	69,799	27,608	Nevada	99,724	9,830	Virginia	56,813	16,71
Hawaii	9,708	4,111	New Hampshire	9,289	3,523	Washington	40,309	23,20
Idaho	12,315	4,793	New Jersey	56,509	21,170	West Virginia	17,485	7,33
Illinois	117,056	48,146	New Mexico	14,158	7,246	Wisconsin	38,292	10,43
Indiana	60,366	NA	New York	155,144	54,484	Wyoming	5,933	2,55
Iowa	27,207	9,407	North Carolina	45,861	19,591			
Kansas	24,649	11,383	North Dakota	5,884	1,514	**Total**	**2,239,535**	**970,00**
Kentucky	35,121	13,720	Ohio	104,589	48,274			

Wedding Anniversaries

The traditional names for wedding anniversaries go back many years in social usage. As such names as wooden, crystal silver and golden were applied it was considered proper to present the married pair with gifts made of these products or o_ something related. While the list of permissible gifts is extensive, gifts are most appropriate when retaining a suggestion o_ the originals. Thus the wooden anniversary may call for anything of wood, including furniture, but as the years mount the gifts become more valuable until the 60th or diamond anniversary, calls for diamonds. The traditional list follows, with _ few allowable revisions in parentheses.

1st—Paper	6th—Iron	11th—Steel	20th—China	45th—Sapphire
2d—Cotton	7th—Wool, copper	12th—Silk	25th—Silver	50th—Gold
3d—Leather	8th—Bronze	13th—Lace	30th—Pearl	55th—Emerald
4th—Linen, (silk)	9th—Pottery, (china)	14th—Ivory	35th—Coral	60th—Diamond
5th—Wood	10th—Tin, (aluminum)	15th—Crystal	40th—Ruby	

Leading Causes of Death
United States: 1973 Estimates

Source: National Center for Health Statistics, U.S. Public Health Service, HEW & The American Heart Association

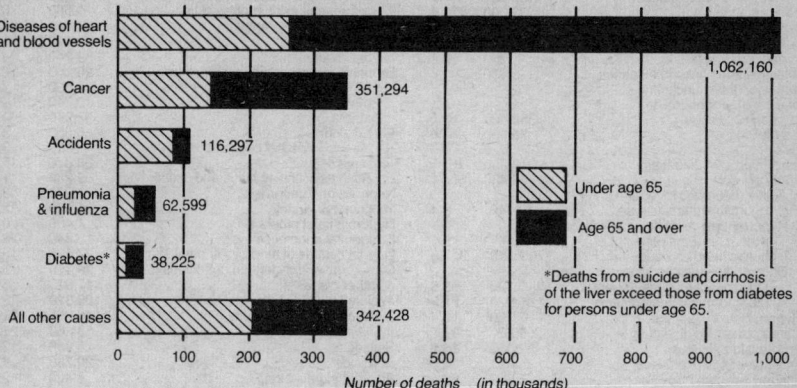

Diseases of heart and blood vessels	1,062,160
Cancer	351,294
Accidents	116,297
Pneumonia & influenza	62,599
Diabetes*	38,225
All other causes	342,428

Under age 65
Age 65 and over

*Deaths from suicide and cirrhosis of the liver exceed those from diabetes for persons under age 65.

0 100 200 300 400 500 600 700 800 900 1,000

Number of deaths (in thousands)

Warning Signs
Source: American Heart Association.

Of Heart Attack

—Prolonged, oppressive pain or unusual discomfort in the *center* of the chest
—Pain may radiate to the shoulder, arm, neck or jaw
—Sweating may accompany pain or discomfort
—Nausea and vomiting may also occur
—Shortness of breath may accompany other signs

The American Heart Association advises immediate action at the onset of these symptoms. The association points out that over half of heart attack victims die before they reach the hospital and that the average victim waits 3 hours before seeking help.

Of Stroke

—Sudden temporary weakness or numbness of face or limbs
—Temporary loss of speech, or trouble speaking or understanding speech
—Temporary dimness or loss of vision, particularly in one eye
—An episode of double vision
—Unexplained dizziness or unsteadiness
—Change in personality, mental ability
—New or unusual pattern of headaches

Major Risk Factors

Blood pressure—systolic pressure under 120 is normal; systolic pressure over 150
 = 2 times the risk of heart attack
 = 4 times the risk of stroke
Cholesterol—level under 194 is normal;
 level of 250 or over
 = 3 times the risk of heart attack or stroke
Cigarettes—with non-smoking considered normal; smoking one pack a day
 = 2 times the risk of heart attack
 = 5 times the risk of stroke

Cardiovascular Disease Statistical Summary
Source: American Heart Association

CVD Cost — $22.7 billion (AHA est.) annually.

Prevalence — 28,830,000 Americans have some form of heart and blood vessel disease.
 — Hypertension — 23,290,000 (one in six adults)
 — Coronary heart disease — 3,990,000.
 — Rheumatic heart disease — 1,750,000.
 — Stroke — 1,700,000.

CVD Mortality — 1,062,160 in 1973 (54% of all deaths); 1976 (AHA est.): 1,060,900 (52%).
 — 25% of all persons killed by CVD are under age 65.

Atherosclerosis — contributed to many of the 898,379 heart attack and stroke deaths in 1973.

Congenital or Inborn Heart Defects — 35 recognizable types of defects.
 — More than 25,000 babies are born every year with heart defects.
 — Post-natal mortality from heart defects had been reduced to 6,964 in 1973.

Heart Attack — caused 684,066 deaths in 1973.
 — 3,990,000 alive today have history of heart attack and/or angina pectoris.
 — 350,000 a year die of heart attack before they reach the hospital — average victim waits 3 hours before decision to seek help.

Stroke — killed 214,313 in 1973, afflicts 1,700,000.

CCU — two-thirds of the 7,000 general hospitals in U.S. have Coronary Care Capability.
 — 1,800 have separate CCUs; 3,000 have combined intensive care and coronary care facilities.

Hypertension (high blood pressure) — 23,290,000 adults have it but only 50% of them know it.
 — Of those who do know they have it, 50% are untreated.
 — Only 10-20% who have it are under adequate control.
 — For 90% of those with high blood pressure science doesn't know the cause; but it is easily detected and usually controllable.

Rheumatic Heart Disease — afflicts 100,000 children, 1,650,000 adults.
 — Killed 13,556 in 1973. Modern antibiotic therapy has sharply reduced mortality in 5-24 age group.

Deaths and Death Rates for Selected Causes*

Source: Division of Vital Statistics, National Center for Health Statistics
Rates per 100,000 population

1974* Cause of death	Number	Rate	1974* Cause of death	Number	Rate
All causes......................	1,933,000	914.4	Acute bronchitis and bronchiolitis........	680	0.3
Enteritis and other diarrheal diseases.....	2,370	1.1	Influenza and pneumonia..............	54,310	25.7
Tuberculosis, all forms...............	3,770	1.8	Influenza........................	2,070	1.0
Syphilis and its sequelae............	250	0.1	Pneumonia......................	52,240	24.7
Other infective and parasitic diseases....	3,330	1.6	Bronchitis, emphysema, and asthma.....	26,260	12.4
Malignant neoplasms, including			Chronic and unqualified bronchitis.....	4,580	2.2
neoplasms of lymphatic and			Emphysema......................	19,740	9.3
hematopoietic tissues...............	358,400	169.5	Asthma.........................	1,940	0.9
Diabetes mellitus....................	36,850	17.4	Peptic ulcer......................	6,950	3.3
Meningitis..........................	1,430	0.7	Hernia and intestinal obstruction........	6,300	3.0
Major cardiovascular diseases.........	1,017,350	481.3	Cirrhosis of liver...................	33,870	16.0
Diseases of heart..................	746,480	353.1	Cholelithiasis, cholecystitis and cholangitis	3,270	1.5
Active rheumatic fever and chronic			Nephritis and nephrosis..............	7,970	3.8
rheumatic heart disease.........	13,440	6.4	Infections of kidney.................	5,580	2.6
Hypertensive heart disease with or			Hyperplasia of prostate..............	1,400	0.7
without renal disease...........	11,690	5.5	Congenital anomalies................	13,840	6.5
Ischemic heart disease...........	671,140	317.5	Certain causes of mortality in early infancy.	27,960	13.2
Chronic disease of endocardium and			Symptoms and ill-defined conditions.....	29,470	13.9
other myocardial insufficiency.....	5,190	2.5	All other diseases...................	117,970	55.8
All other forms of heart disease.....	45,020	21.3	Accidents........................	103,320	48.9
Hypertension.....................	7,150	3.4	Motor vehicle accidents.............	45,060	21.3
Cerebrovascular diseases...........	205,380	97.2	All other accidents.................	58,260	27.6
Arteriosclerosis...................	32,050	15.2	Suicide..........................	26,430	12.5
Other diseases of arteries			Homicide........................	20,780	9.8
arterioles, and capillaries..........	26,290	12.4	All other external causes.............	4,420	2.1

Due to rounding estimates of death, figures may not add to total. *Provisional.
Data based on a 10% sampling of all death certificates for a 12-month (Jan.-Dec.) period.

Principal Types of Accidental Deaths

Source: Division of Vital Statistics, National Center for Health Statistics
Data for 1971 are National Safety Council estimates.

Year	All types	Motor vehicle	Falls	Burns	Drowning	Firearms	Machinery	Poison gases	Other poisons
1960......	93,806	38,137	19,023	7,645	6,529	2,334	1,951	1,253	1,679
1965......	108,004	49,163	19,984	7,347	6,799	2,344	2,054	1,526	2,110
1970......	115,000	54,600	16,900	6,700	6,400	2,400	....	1,600	3,700
1971......	113,000	54,400	16,800	6,800	6,000	2,400	....	1,600	3,800
1972......	115,000	56,300	16,700	6,700	6,200	2,400	....	1,700	3,700
1973......	117,000	55,800	16,900	6,400	8,700	2,700	....	1,500	3,700
1974(P)....	103,320	45,060	NA	NA	NA	NA	....	NA	NA

Death Rates per 100,000 Population

1960......	52.1	21.2	10.6	4.2	3.6	1.3	1.1	0.7	0.9
1965......	55.7	25.4	10.3	3.8	3.5	1.2	1.1	0.8	0.1
1970......	56.4	26.9	8.3	3.3	3.1	1.2	....	0.8	1.8
1971......	55.0	26.4	8.3	3.3	2.9	1.1	....	0.8	1.8
1972......	55.4	27.0	8.0	3.2	3.0	1.2	....	0.8	1.8
1973......	55.8	26.6	8.1	3.0	4.1	1.3	....	0.7	1.8
1974(P)....	48.9	21.3	NA	NA	NA	NA	....	NA	NA

Accidental Injuries by Severity of Injury
Source: National Safety Council

1974* Severity of Injury	Total*	Motor-Vehicle	Work	Home	Public Non-Motor-Vehicle
All Injuries*.................	22,085,000	3,646,200	4,613,400	8,025,500	5,994,000
Deaths.......................	105,000	46,200	13,400	25,500	24,000
Nonfatal injuries.................	11,000,000	1,800,000	2,300,000	4,000,000	3,000,000
Permanent impairments*........	380,000	150,000	80,000	100,000	70,000
Temporary total disabilities........	10,600,000	1,650,000	2,220,000	3,900,000	2,900,000

Certain Costs of Accidental Injuries, 1974 ($ billions)

Total*......................	$43.3	$19.3	$15.3	$5.1	$4.4
Wage loss....................	13.2	6.0	3.0	2.3	2.6
Medical expense...............	5.7	1.7	1.7	1.4	1.0
Insurance admin. costs...........	7.4	5.1	21.1	0.1	0.1

*Duplication between motor-vehicle, work and home are eliminated in total.
P-Provisions.

Birthstones

Source: Retail Jewelers of America, Inc.

Month	Ancient	Modern	Month	Ancient	Modern	Month	Ancient	Modern
January...	Garnet....	Garnet	May...	Agate...	Emerald	September	.Chrysolite .	Sapphire
February.	Amethyst.	Amethyst	June...	Emerald	Pearl, Moonstone	October....	Aquama-..	Opal or
March.....	Jasper.....	Bloodstone			or		rine	Tourmaline
		or			Alexandrite	November.	Topaz.....	Topaz
		Aquamarine	July...	Onyx...	Ruby	December.	.Ruby......	Turquoise
April......	Sapphire ..	Diamond	August	.Carne-..				or Zircon
				lian.....	Sardonyx or Peridot			

The term precious stones actually applies only to diamonds, rubies, sapphires and emeralds. All others are semiprecious. Precious gems are minerals brought to perfection by the lapidary's art. The pearl, often a gem of great value, is not a precious stone.

Average Future Lifetime in United States

Source: Division of Vital Statistics, National Center for
Health Statistics, 1974 Data

Age Interval	Number Living[1]	Avg. Life Expect.	White Male	White Female	All Others Male	All Others Female
0-1	100,000	72.0	68.9	76.7	62.9	71.3
1-5	98,340	72.2	69.1	76.6	63.7	71.9
5-10	98,044	68.4	65.3	72.8	60.0	68.2
10-15	97,863	63.5	60.4	67.9	55.1	63.3
15-20	97,672	58.6	55.6	63.0	50.3	58.4
20-25	97,170	53.9	51.0	58.1	45.6	53.6
25-30	96,496	49.3	46.4	53.3	41.5	48.9
30-35	95,818	44.6	41.8	48.5	37.4	44.3
35-40	95,069	39.9	37.1	43.7	33.3	39.7
40-45	94,023	35.4	32.6	39.0	29.4	35.3
45-50	92,443	30.9	28.1	34.3	25.6	31.2
50-55	89,985	26.7	23.9	29.9	22.0	27.2
55-60	86,431	22.7	20.0	25.6	18.8	23.4
60-65	81,200	19.0	16.5	21.5	16.1	19.9
65-70	73,949	15.6	13.4	17.6	13.5	16.7
70-75	64,568	12.4	10.6	14.0	11.2	13.6
75-80	52,191	9.8	8.3	10.8	9.8	11.8
80-85	37,655	7.6	6.4	8.1	8.6	9.8
85 and up	23,301	5.7	4.9	6.1	6.9	7.7

(1) Of 100,000 born alive, number living at beginning of age interval. (2) Average number of years of life remaining at beginning of age interval.

Years of Life Expected at Birth

Year	Total	Male	Female	Year	Total	Male	Female
1974[1]	72.0	68.1	75.9	1960	69.7	66.6	73.1
1973	71.3	67.6	75.3	1950	68.2	65.6	71.1
1972	71.1	67.4	75.1	1940	62.9	60.8	65.2
1971	71.1	67.4	75.0	1930	59.7	58.1	61.6
1970	70.8	67.1	74.6	1920	54.1	53.6	54.6
1965	70.2	66.8	73.7	1910	47.3	46.3	48.3

Based on Death-Registration States 1900-1925, and United States 1930-1974. (1) Provisional.

Purchases and Ownership of Life Insurance in U.S. and Assets of U.S. Life Companies

Legal Reserve Life Insurance Companies
Source: Statistical Services, Institute of Life Insurance

In millions of dollars.

Year	Purchases of Life Insurance Ordinary	Group	Industrial	Total	Insurance in Force Ordinary	Group	Industrial	Credit	Total	Assets
1940	7,022	747	3,318	1,087	79,346	14,938	20,866	380	115,530	30,802
1950	18,260	6,237	5,492	29,989	149,116	47,793	33,415	3,844	234,168	64,020
1960	56,183	15,328	6,906	78,417	341,881	175,903	39,563	29,101	586,448	119,576
1965	89,643	52,867*	7,302	149,812*	499,638	308,078	39,818	53,020	900,554	158,884
1970	138,356	68,939*	6,612	213,907*	734,730	551,357	38,644	77,392	1,402,123	207,254
1971	143,480	55,313	7,651	206,444	792,318	589,883	39,202	81,931	1,503,334	222,102
1972	156,859	59,953	7,394	224,206	853,911	640,689	39,975	93,410	1,627,985	239,730
1973	173,049	67,100*	7,224	247,373*	928,192	708,322	40,632	101,154	1,778,300	252,436
1974	199,239	114,665	6,657	320,561	1,009,038	827,550	39,441	109,623	1,985,652	263,349

*Includes Servicemen's Group Life Insurance $27.4 billion in 1965 and $16.8 billion in 1970, and $28.8 billion in 1974.

Home Accident Deaths

Source: National Safety Council

Year	Total Home	Falls	Fires, Burns[B]	Suffo.-Ingested Object	Suffo.-Mechanical	Poison (solid, liquid)	Poison by Gas	Firearms	Other
1950	29,000	14,800	5,000	A	1,600	1,300	1,250	950	4,100
1955	28,500	14,100	5,400	A	1,250	1,150	900	1,100	4,600
1960	28,000	12,300	6,350	1,850	1,500	1,350	900	1,200	2,550
1962	28,500	12,600	6,200	1,400*	1,400	1,400	1,000	1,000	3,500
1964	28,000	11,400	6,200	1,400	1,300	1,700	900	1,200	3,900
1965	28,500	11,700	6,100	1,300	1,200	1,700	1,100	1,300	4,100
1966	29,500	11,900	6,800	1,300	1,100	1,800	1,200	1,400	4,000
1967	29,000	12,000	6,200	1,300	900	2,000	1,100	1,600	3,900
1968	28,000	10,800	6,100	2,000*	1,200*	2,100	1,100	1,300*	3,400*
1969	27,500	10,300	6,000	2,400	1,100	2,400	1,100	1,300	2,900
1970	27,000	9,700	5,600	1,800	1,100	3,000	1,100	1,400	3,300
1971	26,500	9,300	5,600	1,900	1,000	3,000	1,000	1,300	3,400
1972	26,500	9,300	5,500	1,800	900	3,000	1,000	1,400	3,600
1973	26,500	9,200	5,300	1,900	1,100	3,000	1,000	1,500	3,500
1974	25,500	8,900	5,200	1,800	1,000	3,100	1,000	1,300	3,200

*Data for this year and subsequent years not comparable with previous years due to classification changes. (A) Included in Other. (B) Includes deaths resulting from conflagration, regardless of nature of injury.

Physical Growth Range for Children from 1 to 18 Years*

Source: U.S. Public Health Service, H.E.W.

Age	Shortest 5%	Median Height	Tallest 5%	Lightest 5%	Median Weight	Heaviest 5%
Boys						
1	28.4	30.2	32.0	18.7	23.3	27.8
2	32.1	34.6	37.1	23.3	28.3	33.3
3	35.3	37.8	40.3	27.1	32.5	37.9
4	38.3	40.8	43.3	30.0	36.1	42.2
5	40.3	43.4	46.4	33.0	40.3	47.6
6	42.8	45.9	49.0	36.0	44.7	53.4
7	44.8	48.1	51.4	40.3	50.9	61.5
8	46.9	50.5	54.1	44.4	57.4	70.4
9	48.8	52.8	56.8	48.0	64.4	80.4
10	50.6	54.3	59.2	51.4	71.4	91.4
11	51.9	56.4	60.9	53.3	78.9	102.5
12	53.5	58.6	63.7	60.0	86.0	113.5
13	55.2	61.3	67.4	65.3	98.6	131.9
14	57.5	64.1	70.7	75.5	111.8	148.1
15	61.0	66.9	72.8	88.0	124.3	160.6
16	63.8	68.9	74.0	97.8	133.8	169.8
17	65.2	69.8	74.4	106.5	139.8	174.0
18	65.9	70.2	74.5	110.3	144.8	179.3
Girls						
1	27.6	29.4	31.2	17.4	21.7	26.0
2	31.6	33.8	36.0	22.3	27.1	31.9
3	35.3	37.5	39.7	26.3	32.3	38.3
4	38.1	40.7	43.3	28.8	36.1	43.4
5	40.6	43.4	46.2	32.2	40.9	49.6
6	42.8	45.9	49.0	35.5	45.7	55.9
7	44.5	47.8	51.1	38.3	51.0	63.7
8	46.4	50.0	53.6	42.0	57.2	72.4
9	48.2	52.2	56.2	45.1	63.6	82.1
10	49.9	54.5	59.1	48.2	71.0	95.0
11	51.9	57.0	62.1	55.4	82.0	108.6
12	54.1	59.5	64.9	63.9	94.4	124.9
13	57.1	62.2	66.8	72.8	105.5	138.2
14	58.5	63.1	67.7	83.0	113.0	144.0
15	59.5	63.8	68.1	89.5	120.0	150.5
16	59.8	64.1	68.4	95.1	123.0	150.1
17	60.1	64.2	68.3	97.9	125.8	153.7
18	60.1	64.4	68.7	96.0	126.2	156.4

*This table simply gives a general picture for American children. When used as a standard, the individual variation in children's growth should not be overlooked. In most cases the height-weight relationship is probably a more valid index of weight status than a weight-for-age assessment.

Average Weight of Americans by Height and Age

Source: Society of Actuaries; based on a 4-year study of 5,000,000 persons
The figures represent weights in ordinary indoor clothing and shoes, and heights with shoes.

	MEN						**WOMEN**				
Height	20-24	25-29	30-39	40-49	50-59	Height	20-24	25-29	30-39	40-49	50-59
5'0''	122	128	131	134	136	4'10''	102	107	115	122	125
5'1''	125	131	134	137	139	4'11''	105	110	117	124	127
5'2''	128	134	137	140	142	5'0''	108	113	120	127	130
5'3''	132	138	141	144	145	5'1''	112	116	123	130	133
5'4''	136	141	145	148	149	5'2''	115	119	126	133	136
5'5''	139	144	149	152	153	5'3''	118	122	129	136	140
5'6''	142	148	153	156	157	5'4''	121	125	132	140	141
5'7''	145	151	157	161	162	5'5''	125	129	135	143	148
5'8''	149	155	161	165	166	5'6''	129	133	139	147	152
5'9''	153	159	165	169	170	5'7''	132	136	142	151	156
5'10''	157	163	170	174	175	5'8''	136	140	146	155	160
5'11''	161	167	174	178	180	5'9''	140	144	150	159	164
6'0''	166	172	179	183	185	5'10''	144	148	154	164	169
6'1''	170	177	183	187	189	5'11''	149	153	159	169	174
6'2''	174	182	188	192	194	6'0''	154	158	164	174	180
6'3''	178	186	193	197	199						
6'4''	181	190	199	203	205						

Pedalcycle Accidents

Since 1935, the number of pedalcycle-motor-vehicle deaths has more than doubled. The number of pedalcycles in use is 26 times the number in 1935; so the death rate in 1974 was about one-twelfth the rate in 1935. The proportion of deaths occuring to young adults and adults has steadily increased since 1960. Persons 15 years of age and older accounted for more than one-half the deaths in 1974 compared to one-fifth in 1960.

The Nation's Hospitals

Source: American Hospital Association

In 1974, there were 7,174 hospitals in the United States registered by the American Hospital Association. These institutions had about 1.51 million beds and reported admitting some 35.5 million in-patients. About $41.4 billion was spent to provide services for both in-patients and outpatients, or a cost of $196 per resident of the nation.

	Hospitals		Beds		Average Daily Census		Admissions		Expenses ($1,000)	
	Fed.	Non-Fed.	Fed.	Non-Fed.	Fed.	Non-Fed.	Fed.	Non-Fed.	Fed.	Non-Fed.
Ala.	8	142	2,928	23,606	2,314	17,464	36,869	625,085	$ 69,435	$ 505,194
Alask.	10	16	701	900	454	552	20,377	32,628	29,929	32,331
Ariz.	18	62	1,670	9,231	1,232	6,789	47,224	303,931	63,736	343,527
Ark.	4	92	2,049	9,528	1,754	6,901	24,056	365,499	47,333	223,202
Calif.	34	616	12,230	111,721	9,325	77,968	203,296	3,094,709	469,403	4,041,281
Colo.	7	91	2,331	12,481	1,709	9,011	39,006	413,632	77,527	389,780
Conn.	5	63	1,062	19,201	767	15,540	16,026	434,286	41,920	614,720
Dela.	2	12	404	4,306	277	3,822	6,201	70,695	11,690	103,777
D.C.	4	16	5,486	6,026	4,688	4,758	36,108	183,669	149,064	268,788
Fla.	14	214	4,275	49,229	3,554	36,844	91,109	1,303,145	162,610	1,306,077
Ga.	10	173	3,263	30,122	2,563	23,193	48,903	819,031	91,089	701,402
Ha.	1	29	750	4,239	451	3,044	19,864	88,014	29,891	106,771
Ida.	2	50	211	3,535	169	2,418	3,845	122,891	7,283	84,141
Ill.	10	283	6,876	74,286	5,823	58,080	73,941	1,909,705	180,712	2,338,688
Ind.	6	133	2,214	33,981	1,880	26,386	19,506	832,525	46,830	783,473
Ia.	3	144	1,661	20,028	1,252	13,798	15,406	530,632	46,229	419,751
Kan.	7	157	2,190	16,838	1,702	11,906	24,360	415,862	56,715	357,418
Ky.	5	122	2,382	17,560	1,691	13,537	34,065	566,817	75,297	412,772
La.	8	149	2,560	24,260	1,940	17,963	43,843	660,068	72,809	529,267
Me.	2	54	859	6,967	682	5,219	6,884	172,367	16,036	165,511
Md.	11	70	3,604	26,062	2,791	21,534	48,941	465,413	126,596	711,349
Mass.	8	190	4,018	48,205	3,388	38,334	27,815	932,196	92,025	1,607,424
Mich.	9	246	2,982	52,335	2,374	41,979	29,814	1,385,593	77,472	1,767,706
Minn.	5	187	1,943	31,236	1,633	22,300	20,073	696,517	53,407	698,540
Miss.	5	108	1,753	15,441	1,488	11,935	26,170	408,315	48,541	261,207
Mo.	8	160	3,507	33,230	2,666	25,484	51,475	865,180	121,349	852,648
Mont.	6	60	394	4,012	301	2,477	8,915	132,329	12,624	83,535
Neb.	5	100	968	10,241	755	6,990	19,363	277,068	32,617	239,347
Nev.	4	20	291	2,827	217	1,961	6,311	92,200	12,068	97,316
N.H.	2	33	288	5,987	256	4,495	6,146	125,226	10,538	112,711
N.J.	4	141	3,232	46,676	2,678	37,399	31,139	1,004,441	70,103	1,244,729
N.M.	11	44	1,045	5,383	758	3,680	30,528	146,244	35,557	116,331
N.Y.	16	399	10,419	158,052	8,710	130,564	89,369	2,686,443	276,949	4,991,913
N.C.	9	151	3,342	31,033	2,790	24,388	52,941	813,562	94,470	694,390
N.D.	5	56	421	5,487	303	3,679	11,330	124,564	13,813	94,690
Oh.	6	238	4,833	69,526	4,131	55,297	40,517	1,738,819	121,066	1,851,225
Okla.	12	135	1,392	16,044	934	11,778	38,089	456,661	50,856	354,865
Ore.	2	86	921	11,038	787	7,746	13,922	344,421	27,978	311,908
Pa.	12	309	6,982	94,632	5,986	75,265	46,783	1,845,886	153,221	2,326,908
R.I.	2	19	553	7,277	436	6,448	10,238	134,947	21,818	206,636
S.C.	7	82	1,942	17,470	1,583	13,328	45,494	402,041	64,622	313,742
S.D.	10	53	1,291	4,763	1,009	3,206	18,667	119,562	27,251	78,362
Tenn.	5	152	3,004	29,372	2,617	23,798	36,974	782,322	75,338	641,999
Tex.	25	552	8,697	70,585	7,225	51,137	147,991	2,089,591	249,605	1,646,143
Ut.	3	37	580	4,264	411	3,200	11,017	176,964	18,783	135,527
Vt.	1	20	201	3,849	157	2,824	3,243	74,678	7,135	81,538
Va.	11	117	4,143	31,581	3,393	26,710	67,621	684,505	133,853	646,513
Wash.	11	116	2,761	13,989	2,115	9,389	46,470	522,696	83,390	435,245
W.Va.	6	81	1,328	14,886	1,089	11,449	16,290	366,027	35,264	281,231
Wis.	3	179	2,096	31,390	1,741	22,687	20,674	764,452	65,212	784,005
Wyo.	3	28	601	2,132	474	1,276	5,406	61,521	12,097	37,399
Total	**387**	**6,787**	**135,634**	**1,377,050**	**109,423**	**1,057,930**	**1,840,615**	**33,665,575**	**3,971,156**	**37,434,953**

Canadian General and Allied Special Hospitals

1973	Hospitals			Beds			Admissions			Expenses ($1,000)*
	Pub.	Priv.	Fed.	Pub.	Priv.	Fed.	Pub.	Priv.	Fed.	Pub.
Canada	1,049	103	100	142,069	4,085	7,570	3,659,978	27,594	59,477	3,131,868
Nfld.	47	—	—	3,138	—	—	85,119	—	—	65,794
P.E.I.	9	—	—	751	—	—	22,996	—	—	10,874
N.S.	47	—	—	4,839	—	522	131,693	—	4,167	102,288
N.B.	38	—	—	4,398	—	—	123,053	—	—	86,741
Que.	187	44	10	37,456	2,629	1,620	804,622	12,948	4,407	921,675
Ont.	232	56	13	48,711	1,400	1,814	1,351,409	14,185	13,503	1,170,182
Man.	82	1	16	6,354	40	667	181,110	305	6,117	133,507
Sask.	139	—	3	7,605	—	114	206,759	—	2,332	116,306
Alta.	147	—	8	14,309	—	908	350,025	—	11,961	235,860
B.C.	116	2	3	14,313	16	1,501	398,390	156	8,880	285,769
Yukon	—	—	6	—	—	160	—	—	4,259	—
N.W.T.	5	—	39	195	—	264	4,802	—	3,851	2,872

*Private and Federal Hospitals do not submit Financial Returns.

How to Obtain Birth, Marriage, Death Records

The United States Government has published a series of inexpensive booklets entitled Where to Write for Birth & Death Records; Where to Write for Marriage Records; Where to Write for Divorce Records; Where to Write for Birth and Death Records of U. S. Citizens who were born or died outside of the U. S. and birth certifications for alien children adopted by U. S. citizens; You May Save Time Proving Your Age and Other Birth Facts. They tell where to write to get a certified copy of or original vital record. Supt. of Documents. Government Printing Office, Washington, D. C. 20402.

Nursing Care Homes in United States

Source: Division of Health Resources Statistics, National Center for Health Statistics

State	Nursing care homes				Personal care homes	
	Homes	Beds	Residents	Full-time Personnel	Homes	Beds
Total................	14,873	1,107,358	1,011,092	559,684	6,961	220,346
Alabama..............	188	13,997	13,350	8,320	9	847
Alaska...............	8	606	477	238	—	—
Arizona..............	75	5,969	5,332	3,189	13	461
Arkansas.............	199	17,070	15,404	7,933	12	882
California............	1,618	115,560	100,742	56,159	2,527	35,396
Colorado.............	179	15,126	13,783	7,425	35	1,544
Connecticut..........	261	19,438	18,553	9,320	104	3,856
Delaware.............	34	2,199	2,071	1,472	2	14
District of Columbia....	43	2,825	2,434	1,546	29	322
Florida...............	297	29,304	25,069	16,251	63	5,652
Georgia..............	285	24,340	23,174	12,759	21	1,596
Hawaii...............	41	2,105	1,967	1,313	101	621
Idaho................	58	4,047	3,693	2,031	6	143
Illinois...............	786	67,229	60,998	30,030	253	12,922
Indiana..............	417	29,801	26,798	14,892	78	4,446
Iowa.................	464	26,734	24,591	10,978	214	8,418
Kansas..............	305	17,821	16,460	7,856	163	5,068
Kentucky............	187	13,118	11,865	6,292	125	5,059
Louisiana............	202	16,550	15,666	7,919	10	454
Maine...............	168	7,667	7,315	4,487	173	1,560
Maryland.............	175	16,199	15,187	9,315	29	1,556
Massachusetts........	754	46,070	43,271	21,548	191	7,788
Michigan.............	444	38,735	36,860	24,117	133	9,832
Minnesota............	441	37,703	34,786	13,775	148	6,958
Mississippi...........	126	7,494	7,086	4,180	17	392
Missouri.............	415	29,191	26,827	15,001	87	4,453
Montana.............	79	3,977	3,765	2,000	26	782
Nebraska............	195	14,710	13,325	5,763	56	2,686
Nevada..............	23	1,201	1,031	763	18	281
New Hampshire.......	106	5,214	4,925	2,709	24	659
New Jersey...........	356	28,174	25,857	16,634	193	6,256
New Mexico...........	43	2,649	2,268	1,509	23	696
New York.............	691	68,024	63,439	45,461	392	24,864
North Carolina........	231	13,890	12,693	6,983	607	8,255
North Dakota.........	63	4,563	4,338	1,802	44	2,068
Ohio.................	1,015	58,189	53,305	29,446	148	6,945
Oklahoma............	386	28,213	25,270	12,953	31	1,299
Oregon..............	218	14,157	13,135	6,776	94	4,149
Pennsylvania.........	666	58,230	53,724	34,471	102	7,733
Rhode Island.........	113	5,569	5,326	2,357	46	924
South Carolina........	110	7,510	7,062	4,468	13	621
South Dakota.........	114	6,634	6,212	2,633	46	1,161
Tennessee...........	213	12,473	11,997	7,162	31	2,084
Texas...............	873	74,430	65,882	35,138	94	6,080
Utah................	92	3,941	3,674	1,698	28	615
Vermont.............	71	3,369	2,974	1,923	30	533
Virginia..............	198	13,936	12,479	7,755	150	2,796
Washington...........	327	27,954	25,475	12,151	55	3,193
West Virginia.........	75	3,510	3,290	2,153	62	1,243
Wisconsin............	421	38,104	34,484	15,949	95	13,856
Wyoming.............	24	1,569	1,403	681	10	327

Active Federal and Non-Federal Doctors by States

(as of Dec. 31, 1973)

Source: Division of Health Resources Statistics, National Center for Health Statistics

	Total	Non-fed.	Fed.		Total	Non-fed.	Fed.		Total	Non-fed.	Fed.
All areas.....	338,111	[1]311,342	26,679	Kansas.....	2,881	2,621	260	N.D........	658	581	77
United States	333,158	308,543	24,615	Kentucky....	3,781	3,511	270	Ohio........	14,725	14,173	552
Alabama.....	3,457	3,194	263	Louisiana....	4,833	4,466	367	Oklahoma....	2,929	2,647	282
Alaska......	399	281	118	Maine......	1,244	1,144	100	Oregon.....	3,428	3,266	162
Arizona.....	3,380	2,994	386	Maryland....	9,965	7,748	2,217	Pa.........	18,675	17,889	786
Arkansas....	1,973	1,794	179	Mass.......	12,931	12,183	748	R.I.........	1,686	1,549	137
California....	42,333	38,749	3,584	Michigan....	11,928	11,543	385	S.C........	2,931	2,589	342
Colorado....	4,583	4,068	515	Minnesota...	6,301	5,934	367	S.D........	595	508	87
Connecticut..	6,244	6,005	239	Mississippi..	2,143	1,889	254	Tennessee...	5,361	5,001	360
Delaware....	813	762	51	Missouri....	6,633	6,274	359	Texas......	15,829	13,885	1,944
D of C......	3,980	3,046	934	Montana....	801	730	71	Utah.......	1,745	1,631	114
Florida......	11,828	10,809	1,019	Nebraska....	1,915	1,773	142	Vermont....	861	825	36
Georgia.....	6,000	5,368	632	Nevada......	642	591	51	Virginia.....	7,067	6,072	995
Hawaii.....	1,317	1,236	81	N.H........	1,131	1,068	63	Washington..	5,641	5,110	531
Idaho......	762	710	52	New Jersey...	11,469	10,930	539	W. Va......	1,977	1,868	109
Illinois......	16,950	15,993	957	New Mexico..	1,436	1,228	208	Wisconsin...	5,815	5,548	267
Indiana.....	5,597	5,422	175	New York....	43,763	42,156	1,607	Wyoming....	372	332	40
Iowa.......	2,995	2,865	130	N.C........	6,455	5,984	471	Puerto Rico..	2,819	2,645	174
								Outlying areas	2,134	154	1,980

(1) Excludes 5,644 physicians with addresses unknown.

Transportation Accident Death Rates

Source: National Safety Council

Kind of Transportation Passenger Deaths in 1974	Passenger Miles	Passenger Deaths	Rate Per 100,000,000 Pass. Miles	1972-1974 Aver. Death Rate
Automobiles and taxis'.......................	1,790,000,000,000	22,800	1.30	1.60
Automobiles on turnpikes.....................	44,000,000,000	310	0.70	0.95
Buses..................................	73,000,000,000	150	0.21	0.21
Railroad passenger trains....................	10,300,000,000	7	0.07	0.21
Scheduled air transport planes (domestic)........	131,100,000,000	158	0.12	0.11

(1) Drivers of passenger automobiles are considered passengers.

Selected Statistics on State and County Mental Hospitals

Source: National Institute of Mental Health

Year	Total Admitted[1]	Net Releases[2]	Deaths in Hospital	Residents End of Year	Expense Per Patient[3]
1955	178,003	NA	44,384	558,922	$1,116.59
1960	234,791	NA	49,748	535,540	1,702.41
1969	379,838	373,287	35,962	373,984	4,593.61
1970	393,174	394,627	30,804	338,592	5,435.38
1973	377,020*	386,962	19,899	248,562	9,207.92
1974	374,554*	389,094	16,597	215,573	11,277.23

*Includes estimates. NA Not Available. (1) Excludes transfers.
(2) Net releases alive from hospital is computed by subtracting returns from long-term leave from the total discontinuations.
(3) Per average daily resident patient population.

Patients in State and County Mental Hospitals

Source: National Institute of Mental Health. Average Daily Census 1974

State	Number	State	Number	State	Number	State	Number
United States Total	219,102	Idaho	223	Missouri	3,840	Pennsylvania	17,618
Alabama	3,278	Illinois	8,194	Montana	1,099	Rhode Island	1,602
Alaska	142	Indiana	4,871	Nebraska	712	South Carolina	4,848
Arizona	656	Iowa	1,144	Nevada	360	South Dakota	811
Arkansas	471	Kansas	1,446	New Hampshire	1,286	Tennessee	4,429
California	8,234	Kentucky	992	New Jersey	10,810	Texas	8,872
Colorado	1,142	Louisiana	3,094	New Mexico	395	Utah	293
Connecticut	3,189	Maine	949	New York	40,752	Vermont	532
Delaware	1,042	Maryland	5,632	North Carolina	4,913	Virginia	7,304
District of Columbia	2,880	Massachusetts	7,081	North Dakota	607	Washington	1,368
Florida	6,622	Michigan	6,750	Ohio	11,399	West Virginia	3,150
Georgia	7,695	Minnesota	4,112	Oklahoma	2,748	Wisconsin	3,677
Hawaii	189	Mississippi	4,057	Oregon	1,195	Wyoming	297

The above data was based on reports of the 323 State and county hospitals. The full-time personnel was estimated at 215,604 and the expenditures $2,470,864. The average daily expenditures per patient based on the resident patient population of hospitals reporting expenditures was $30.86.

Estimated Patient Care Episodes in Mental Health Facilities

Source: National Institute of Mental Health

Year	All Facilities	Inpatient Services					Community Mental Health Centers	Other
		State & County Mental Hosp.	Priv. Mental Hospitals*	Gen. Hosp. Psych. Service	VA Hospitals	CMHC		
1973**	4,749,362	651,857	151,941	475,448	208,416	191,946	982,552	2,087,202
1971	4,038,143	745,259	126,600	542,642	176,800	130,088	622,906	1,693,848
1969	3,572,822	767,115	123,850	535,493	186,913	65,000	291,148	1,603,303
1965	2,636,525	804,926	125,428	519,328	115,843	—	—	1,071,000
1955	1,675,352	818,832	123,231	265,934	88,355	—	—	379,000

*Includes estimates of episodes of care in residential treatment centers for emotionally disturbed children. **Provisional.

Patients in Canadian Mental Hospitals

Average Patients Per Day, 1973

	Public Hospitals					Total Private	Total Mental Hospital
	Mental	Psychiatric	Retardates	Emotionally Disturbed Children	Other		
Canada	27,848	1,289	15,799	127	1,833	963	46,692
Nfld.	577	—	—	—	—	—	577
P.E.I.	270	—	22	—	—	—	291
N.S.	770	518	—	—	—	—	1,288
N.B.	1,087	—	146	—	—	—	1,234
Que.	12,404	301	3,216	—	279	—	16,199
Ont.	7,720	323	6,110	127	123	886	14,405
Man.	998	21	1,113	—	—	—	2,132
Sask.	363	66	1,217	—	—	—	1,646
Alta.	1,657	—	2,193	—	385	—	4,235
B.C.	2,002	60	1,782	—	1,046	77	4,685

Annual Fire Losses in the United States

Source: National Insurance Actuarial and Statistical Assn.

Year	Loss	Year	Loss	Year	Loss	Year	Loss
1940	$285,878,697	1960	1,107,824,000	1970	2,264,000,000	1973	2,639,000,000
1945	484,274,000	1965	1,455,631,000	1971	2,316,000,000	1974	3,190,000,000
1955	885,218,000	1968	1,829,922,000	1972	2,304,000,000	1975	1,847,000,000

Marriage Information—Canada

Source: Compiled from information provided by the various Provincial
Government departments and agencies concerned. (As of June, 1975)

Marriageable age, by provinces, for both males and females with and without consent of parents or guardians. In some provinces, the court has authority, given special circumstances, to marry young couples below the minimum age. Most provinces waive the blood test requirement and the waiting period varies across the provinces.

Province	With consent		Without consent		Blood Test Other Province Required	Blood Test Other Province Accepted	Wait for License	Wait after License
	Men	Women	Men	Women				
Newfoundland.....	—	—	19	19	—	—	—	—
Prince Edward Island	16	16	18	18	Yes	Yes	5 days	None
Nova Scotia......	(1)	(1)	19	19	None	None	5 days	None
New Brunswick.....	14-18	14-18	18+	18+	None	None	5 days	None
Quebec..........	14	12	18	18	None	—	—	None
Ontario...........	14	14²	18	18	None	—	None³	3 days
Manitoba.........	16	16	18	18	Yes	Yes	None	24 hours
Saskatchewan.....	15	15	18	18	Yes	Yes	5 days	None
Alberta...........	18−	18−	18+	18+	Yes⁴	Yes⁵	None⁶	None
British Columbia....	16⁷	16⁷	19	19	None	None	2 days⁸	None
Yukon Territory.....	15	15	19	19	None	None	None	24 hours
Northwest Territories	15	15	19	19	None	Yes	None	None

(1) There is no statutory minimum age in the Province. Anyone under the age of 19 years must have consent for marriage, and no person under the age of 16 years may be married without authorization of a Family Court Judge and in addition must have the necessary consent of the parent or guardian.

(2) Women under 14 years also require a medical certificate as to necessity of marriage to prevent illegitimacy of offspring.

(3) Special requirements applicable to non-residents.

(4) Applies only to applicants under 60 years of age.

(5) This is upon filing of negative lab report indicating blood test was taken within 14 days preceding date of application for license.

(6) Exception where consent is required by mail; depending receipt of divorce documents, etc.

(7) Persons under 16 years of age (no minimum age specified) may also be married if they have obtained, in addition to the usual consent from parents or guardian, an Order from a Judge of the Supreme or County Court in this Province.

(8) Including day of application, e.g., a license applied for on a Monday cannot be issued until Wednesday.

Grounds for Divorce in Canada

Source: Government of Canada Divorce Act

The grounds for divorce in Canada are the same for all the provinces and its territories. There are two categories of offence.

A. Marital Offence:
    Adultery
    Sodomy
    Bestiality
    Rape
    Homosexual act
    Subsequent marriage
    Physical cruelty
    Mental cruelty
B. Marriage Breakdown by Reason of:

Imprisonment for aggregate period of not less than 3 years
Imprisonment for not less than 2 years on sentence of death or sentence of 10 years or more
    Addiction to alcohol
    Addiction to narcotics
    Whereabouts of spouse unknown
    Non-consummation
    Separation for not less than 3 years
    Desertion by Petitioner for not less than 5 years
Residence time: Domicile in Canada
Time between interlocutory and final decree:
    normally 3 months before final can be applied for.

Number of Active Civilian Physicians, and Population per Physician, Canada

Source: Health Programs Branch, Health and Welfare Canada, December 31, 1974

Province	Number	Population per Physician	Province	Number	Population per Physician
Newfoundland.....................	675	809	Manitoba........................	1,629	622
Prince Edward Island..............	114	1,035	Saskatchewan....................	1,251	729
Nova Scotia.....................	1,320	620	Alberta.........................	2,621	667
New Brunswick...................	732	915	British Columbia.................	4,346	562
Quebec.........................	10,456	590	Yukon..........................	23	870
Ontario.........................	14,125	578	Northwest Territories.............	33	1,121
			Canada.........................	37,325	607

Canadian Motor Vehicle Traffic Deaths

Source: Statistics Canada

Province	Number 1973	Number 1972	Province	1973	1972
Total.................	**6,429**	**6,237**	Ontario........................	1,906	1,891
Newfoundland..................	100	118	Manitoba.......................	231	186
Prince Edward Island............	39	51	Saskatchewan...................	258	251
Nova Scotia...................	267	244	Alberta........................	536	450
New Brunswick.................	262	223	British Columbia.................	773	680
Quebec.......................	2,023	2,129	Yukon.........................	17	8
			Northwest Terr.................	17	6

Marriage Information

Source: Compiled by William E. Mariano: Council on Marriage Relations, Inc.,
110 East 42 St., New York, N. Y. 10017 (as of Nov. 1, 1975)

Marriageable age, by states, for both males and females with and without consent of parents or guardians. But in most states, the court has authority, in an emergency, to marry young couples below the ordinary age of consent, where due regard for their morals and welfare so requires. In many states, under special circumstances, blood test and waiting period may be waived.

State	With consent		Without consent		Blood test		Wait for license	Wait after license
	Men	Women	Men	Women	Required	Other state accepted*		
Alabama (b)	17	14	21	18	Yes	Yes	None	None
Alaska	18	16	19	18	Yes	No	3 days	None
Arizona	16²	16	18	18	Yes	Yes	None	None
Arkansas	17	16⁴	18	18	Yes	No	3 days	None
California	—²	—²	18	18	Yes	Yes	None	None
Colorado	16	16	18	18	Yes	. . . . .	None	None
Connecticut	16	16(q)	18	18	Yes	Yes	4 days	None
Delaware	—(q)	16⁴	18	18	Yes	Yes	None	24 hrs. (c)
District of Columbia	18	16	21	18	Yes	Yes	3 days	None
Florida	18	16	21	21	Yes	Yes	3 days	None
Georgia	18	16	18	18	Yes	Yes	None (b)	None (o)
Hawaii	17 (e)	16	18	18	Yes	Yes	None	None
Idaho	16	16	18	18	Yes	Yes	None (p)	None
Illinois (a)	—(e)	15(e)	18	18	Yes	Yes	None	None
Indiana	17	17	18	18	Yes	No	3 days	None
Iowa	16(e)	16(e)	18	18	Yes	Yes	3 days	None
Kansas	—(e)²	—(e)²	18	18	Yes	Yes	3 days	None
Kentucky	18	16	18	18	Yes	No	3 days	None
Louisiana (a)	18	16	18	18	Yes	No	None	72 hours
Maine	16	16	18	18	No	No	5 days	None
Maryland	18	16	21	18	None	None	48 hours	None
Massachusetts	—²	—²	18	18	Yes	Yes	3 days	None
Michigan (a)	—	16	18	18	Yes	No	3 days	None
Minnesota	—	16(e)	18	18	None	. . . . .	5 days	None
Mississippi (b)	17	15	21	21	Yes	. . . . .	3 days	None
Missouri	15	15	18	18	Yes	Yes	3 days	None
Montana	—²	—²	18	18	Yes	Yes	5 days	None
Nebraska	18	16	18	18	Yes	Yes	5 days	None
Nevada	—	16	18	18	None	None	None	None
New Hampshire (a)	14(e)	13(e)	18	18	Yes	Yes	5 days	None
New Jersey (a)	—	16	18	18	Yes	Yes	72 hours	None
New Mexico	16	16	21	21	Yes	Yes	None	None
New York	16	14	18	18	Yes	No	None	24 hrs.(h)
North Carolina (a)	16	16	18	18	Yes	Yes	None	None
North Dakota (a)	—²	15	18	18	Yes	. . . . .	None	None
Ohio (a)	18	16	18	18	Yes	Yes	5 days	None
Oklahoma	16	16	18	18	Yes	No	None (f)	. . . . .
Oregon	18 (e)	15 (e)	18	18	Yes	No	7 days	None
Pennsylvania	16	16	18	18	Yes	Yes	3 days	None
Rhode Island (a) (b)	18	16	18	18	Yes	No	None	None
South Carolina	16	14	18	18	None	None	24 hrs.	None
South Dakota	18	16	18	18	Yes	Yes	None	None
Tennessee (b)	16	16	18	21	Yes	Yes	3 days	None
Texas	16	16	18	18	Yes	Yes	None	None
Utah (a)	16	14	21	18	Yes	Yes	None	None
Vermont (a)	18	16	18	18	Yes	. . . . .	None	5 days
Virginia (a)	16	16	18	18	Yes	Yes (r)	None	None
Washington	17	17	18	18	(d)	. . . . .	3 days	None
West Virginia	18²	18	18	18	Yes	No	3 days	None
Wisconsin	18	16	18	18	Yes	Yes	5 days	None
Wyoming	18	16	21	21	Yes	Yes	None	None
Puerto Rico	16	16	21	21	(f)	None	None	None
Virgin Islands	16	14	21	18	None	None	8 days	None

*Many states have additional special requirements; contact individual state.

(a) Special laws applicable to non-residents. (b) Special laws applicable to those under 21 years; Alabama: bond required if male is under 21, female under 18. (c) 24 hours if one or both parties resident of state; 96 hours if both parties are non-residents. (d) None, but male must file affidavit. (e) Parental consent plus Court's consent required. (f) None, but a medical certificate is required. (g) Wait for license from time blood test is taken; Arizona, 48 hours. (h) Marriage may not be solemnized within 10 days from date of blood test. (j) If either under 21; Idaho, 3 days; Oklahoma, 72 hrs. (x) May be waived. (l)3 days if both applicants are under 18 or female is pregnant. (2) Statute provides for obtaining license with parental or court consent with no state minimum age. (3) If either party is under 18, 3 days. (4) Under 16, with parental and court consent. Delaware: Female under 18. (o) All those between 19-21 cannot waive 3 day waiting period. (p) If either under 18—wait full 3 days. (q) If under stated age court consent required. (r) Virginia blood test form must be used.

Grounds for Divorce

Source: Compiled by William E. Mariano, Council on Marriage Relations, Inc., 110 East 42nd Street, New York, N.Y. 10017. Persons contemplating divorce should study latest decisions or secure legal advice before initiating proceedings since different interpretations or exceptions in each case can change the conclusion reached.

*Exceptions are to be noted.

State	Cruelty	Desertion	Non-support	Alcohol	Felony	Impotency	Pregnancy at marriage	Drug addiction	Fraudulent contract	Other causes	Residence time	Time between interlocut'y and final decrees
Alabama	X	X	X	X	X	X				Q-K-W-F-MM	1 year*	None-R
Alaska	X	X		X	X	X		X		F-K-B	1 year	None
Arizona										QQ	90 days	None
Arkansas	X	X	X	X	X	X				B-Y-K-DD	3 months*	None
California										K-KK	6 months	6 months
Colorado										QQ	90 days	None
Connecticut	X	X		X	X				X	K-F-QQ	1 year*	None
Delaware	X	X	X		X					QQ	2 years	3 months
Dist. of Columbia		X			X					Y-Z	1 year	None
Florida										QQ-K	6 months	None
Georgia	X	X		X	X	X	X	X	X	K-M-AA-QQ	6 months	'
Hawaii										QQ	1 year	'
Idaho	X	X	X	X	X					X-K	6 weeks	None
Illinois	X	X		X	X	X		X		DD	6 months*	None
Indiana				X	X					K-QQ	6 months	None
Iowa										MM	1 year*	None-S
Kansas	X	X		X	X	X			X	K-CC-DD	6 months	None-T
Kentucky										QQ	180 days	None
Louisiana					X					X-Z	1 year*	None
Maine	X	X	X	X	X					X-K	6 months	None
Maryland		X			X					Y-K	1 year	None
Massachusetts	X	X	X	X	X	X				LL	2 years*	6 mos.
Michigan										MM	1 year*	None
Minnesota	X	X		X				X		K-W-OO-QQ	1 year*	None-T
Mississippi	X	X		X	X	X	X		X	K-M-DD	1 year*	None-U
Missouri	X	X	X	X	X	X				B-J	1 year	None
Montana	X	X	X	X						K-KK	1 year	None*
Nebraska										QQ	1 year	6 months
Nevada	X					X				K-Y-F	6 weeks	None
New Hampshire	X	X	X	X	X					D-GG-HH-II-KK	1 year*	None
New Jersey	X	X		X	X			X		NN-K-Y	1 year*	None
New Mexico	X	X		X						F	6 months	None
New York	X	X			X					X-Z*	1 year	
North Carolina					X	X		X		Q-K-X	6 months	None
North Dakota	X	X	X	X	X	X				K-KK	1 year	None
Ohio	X	X	X	X	X	X			X	BB-CC-DD	6 months	None
Oklahoma	X	X	X	X	X	X			X	F-K-BB-CC	6 months	None
Oregon										KK	6 months*	60 days
Pennsylvania	X	X		X	X					B-M-DD-K-Y	1 year*	None
Rhode Island	X	X	X	X	X			X		H-X	2 years*	6 months
South Carolina	X	X	X	X				X		Y	1 year	None
South Dakota	X	X	X	X							1 year*	None
Tennessee	X	X	X	X	X	X	X			A-DD-EE	6 months*	None
Texas	X	X	X	X	X	X				K-X-F-PP	1 year	None-T
Utah	X	X	X	X	X	X				W-K	3 months	3 mos.*
Vermont	X	X	X	X	X					Y-K	6 months	3 mos.-O*
Virginia					X				X	I-B-X	1 year	None-U*
Washington										QQ	6 months	None
West Virginia	X	X		X	X			X		X-K	2 years*[2]	None
Wisconsin	X	X	X	X	X					Y-Z-K	6 months	None-T
Wyoming	X	X	X	X	X	X	X			B-J-K	60 days	None

(1.) Determined by court order. (2.) No minimum residence required in adultery cases. (A) Violence. (B) Indignities. (D) Joining religious order disbelieving in marriage. (E) Unchaste behavior after marriage. (F) Incompatibility. (H) Any gross misbehavior or wickedness. (I) Wife being a prostitute. (J) Husband being a vagrant. (K) 5-yrs. insanity; permanent insanity in Utah; incurable insanity in Calif. Exceptions 1 yr. Wis.; 18 mos. Alaska; 2 yrs. Ga., Ha., Ind., N.J., Nev., Ore., Wash., and Wyo.; 3 yrs. Ark., N.C., Fla., Tex., Minn., Colo., Kan., Hawaii, Md., Miss., W. Va.; 6 yrs. Idaho. (M) Consanguinity. (N) In cruelty cases, one yr. to remarry. (O) Plaintiff, 6 mos.; defendant 2 yrs. to remarry. (P) If guilty spouse is sentenced to infamous punishment. (Q) Crime against nature. (R) Sixty days to remarry. (S) One year to remarry; Hawaii one year with minor child. Except Iowa, 90 days. (T) Six months to remarry; in Kan. 60 days. (U) Adultery cases, remarriage in discretion of court. (W) Separation for 2 yrs. after decree for same in Ala. and Minn.; 3 yrs. in Utah; 4 yrs. in N.J.; 18 mos. in N.H.; 5 yrs. in Md. (X) Separation, no cohabitation—5 yrs. Exceptions La., Va., Wyo., W.Va. 2 yrs.; Tex. and Maine 3 yrs.; Nev. and N.C. 1 yr. and R.I. 10 yrs. (Y) Separation, no cohabitation——3 years. Exceptions: Vt., Wash., 2 yrs.; Del., Md., N.J. and N. Y. 18 mos.; D.C. and Wis. 1 yr.; (Z) Separation for 2 yrs. after decree for Dist. of Col.; 1 yr. for N.Y., Wis. and La., per decree in Ha. (AA) Mental incapacity at time of marriage. (BB) Procurement of out-of-state divorce. (CC) Gross neglect of duty. (DD) Bigamy. (EE) Attempted homicide. (FF) Plaintiff under age at time of marriage. (GG) Treatment which injures health or endangers reason. (HH) Wife without state for 10 yrs. (II) Wife in state 2 yrs.; husband never in state and has intent to become citizen of foreign country. (JJ) Seven years absence. (KK) Irreconcilable differences. (LL) Life sentence dissolves marriage. (MM) Breakdown of marriage with no reasonable likelihood of preservation. (NN) Deviate sexual conduct. (OO) Course of conduct detrimental to the marriage relationship of party seeking divorce. (PP) Incompatibility without regard to fault. (QQ) Marriage irretrievably broken.

Adultery is either grounds for divorce or evidence of irreconcilable differences and a breakdown of the marriage, in all states. The plaintiff can invariably remarry in the same state where he or she procured a decree of divorce or annulment. Not so the defendant, who is barred in certain states for some offenses. After a period of time has elapsed even the offender can apply for special permission. The U.S. Supreme Court in a 5 to 4 opinion ruled April 18, 1949, that one-sided quick divorces could be challenged as illegal if notice of the action was not served on the divorced partner within the divorcing states, excepting where the partner was represented at the proceedings. **Enoch Arden Laws.** Disappearance and unknown to be alive—Conn. 7 years absence; N. H., 2 years; N. Y., 5 years (called dissolution); Vt., 7 years.

Motor Vehicle Traffic Deaths by States

Source: State traffic authorities

Place of accidents	Number 1974	Number 1973	Mil. death rate* 1974	Mil. death rate* 1973	Place of accidents	Number 1974	Number 1973	Mil. death rate* 1974	Mil. death rate* 1973
Total U.S.*	46,200	55,800	3.6	4.3	Montana	299	323	5.1	5.8
Alabama	976	1,235	4.1	6.2	Nebraska	388	433	3.5	3.9
Alaska	85	65	4.1	4.0	Nevada	216	267	5.2	6.4
Arizona	730	966	4.7	6.0	New Hampshire	166	145	3.4	2.8
Arkansas	527	671	3.9	5.0	New Jersey	1,112	1,355	2.4	2.8
California	4,019	4,905	3.1	3.8	New Mexico	540	638	5.7	6.7
Colorado	614	676	3.8	4.2	New York	2,620	3,082	4.0	4.6
Connecticut	398	517	2.2	2.8	North Carolina	1,580	1,892	4.5	5.3
Delaware	113	130	3.3	3.7	North Dakota	160	208	3.7	4.8
District of Columbia	78	76	2.6	2.5	Ohio	1,900	2,385	3.0	3.7
Florida	2,270	2,662	3.7	4.5	Oklahoma	750	797	3.5	3.7
Georgia	1,545	1,927	4.4	5.3	Oregon	670	636	4.4	4.0
Hawaii	129	136	3.3	3.4	Pennsylvania	2,155	2,444	3.2	3.7
Idaho	327	349	5.9	6.5	Rhode Island	98	131	1.8	2.4
Illinois	2,007	2,369	3.4	3.9	South Carolina	873	967	4.4	4.7
Indiana	1,231	1,615	3.3	4.2	South Dakota	229	286	4.5	5.6
Iowa	685	813	3.6	4.1	Tennessee	1,285	1,444	4.1	4.9
Kansas	519	623	3.4	4.1	Texas	3,046	3,692	3.9	4.6
Kentucky	795	1,117	3.3	4.6	Utah	228	361	3.1	5.0
Louisiana	844	1,165	4.4	6.0	Vermont	127	155	4.2	4.7
Maine	217	247	3.3	3.6	Virginia	1,050	1,220	3.1	3.5
Maryland	737	822	3.1	3.2	Washington	759	776	3.4	3.3
Massachusetts	961	1,010	3.4	3.4	West Virginia	448	477	4.3	4.7
Michigan	1,875	2,213	3.4	3.8	Wisconsin	911	1,157	3.3	4.0
Minnesota	852	1,024	3.5	4.1	Wyoming	195	192	5.6	5.6
Mississippi	643	883	4.7	6.4	Puerto Rico	565	568	7.7	7.5
Missouri	1,042	1,452	3.5	4.7					

*The mileage death rate is the number of deaths per 100 million vehicle-miles.

Deaths in Civil Aviation Accidents

Source: National Safety Council

Year	Total Deaths*	Scheduled flights (passengers) Domestic No.	Rate**	International No.	Rate**	General aviation No.	Rate**
1960	1,286	297	0.93	10	0.12	787	24
1965	1,279	205	0.38	21	0.12	1,029	21
1970	1,454	0	0.00	2	0.01	1,310	20
1971	1,608	174	0.16	0	0.00	1,405	21
1972	1,581	160	0.13	0	0.00	1426	21
1973	1,627	128	0.10	69	0.19	1,411	19
1974	1,757	158	0.12	262	0.80	1,290	17

*Includes some deaths not shown separately—crew members in scheduled operations and persons not in planes killed in airplane accidents. Excludes deaths in military plane accidents.
**Rates are the number of deaths per 100,000,000 passenger miles. (1) (NSC estimate) Pilots and other crew members are considered passengers for general aviation only.

Accidental Deaths by Age, Sex, and Type

Source: National Safety Council (1973)

Age and Sex	All Types	Motor-Vehicle	Falls	Drowning	Fires, Burns	Ingest. of Food, Object	Fire-arms	Poison (solid, liquid)	Poison by Gas	% Male All Types
All Ages	115,821	55,511	16,506	8,725	6,503	3,013	2,618	3,683	1,652	69%
Under 5	6,037	1,998	275	94	846	699	78	149	41	59%
5 to 14	8,102	4,124	165	1,580	526	124	463	46	71	69%
15 to 24	26,550	18,032	498	2,610	514	211	845	988	471	80%
25 to 34	14,420	8,620	429	1,090	491	196	404	736	271	80%
35 to 44	10,330	5,393	622	730	532	218	284	479	193	76%
45 to 54	11,618	5,444	1,076	680	763	362	234	449	211	73%
55 to 64	11,441	4,772	1,498	540	959	429	172	416	182	70%
65 to 74	10,243	3,892	2,331	340	856	339	94	241	112	61%
75 & over	17,080	3,236	9,612	215	1,016	435	44	179	100	46%
Sex										
Male	80,469	39,941	8,307	7,426	3,895	1,780	2,269	2,354	1,217	
Female	35,352	15,570	8,199	1,299	2,608	1,233	349	1,329	435	
Per Cent male	69%	72%	50%	85%	60%	59%	87%	64%	74%	

Accidental Deaths by Month and Type, 1973 and 1974

Month	1974 Totals	1973 Details by Type All Types	Motor-Vehicle	Falls	Drowning	Fires, Burns‡	Ingest. of Food, Object	Fire-arms	Poison (solid, liquid)	Poison by Gas
All Months	105,000	115,821	55,511	16,506	8,725	6,503	3,013	2,618	3,683	1,652
January	7,800	9,007	3,932	1,586	270	903	294	202	269	249
February	7,000	8,106	3,559	1,258	265	829	257	161	273	194
March	7,900	8,928	4,429	1,328	430	583	239	182	298	177
April	8,500	9,137	4,492	1,282	620	576	223	173	298	137
May	8,950	10,017	4,963	1,354	950	444	235	166	284	97
June	9,600	10,826	5,150	1,334	1,670	357	244	199	291	67
July	10,400	11,317	5,228	1,414	1,710	309	227	195	347	64
August	9,750	10,744	5,260	1,392	1,160	335	255	207	359	75
September	8,800	9,713	4,960	1,306	690	294	242	206	322	93
October	8,900	9,938	5,167	1,420	420	489	256	270	299	109
November	8,300	9,161	4,453	1,358	260	539	279	362	316	177
December	9,100	8,927	3,918	1,474	280	845	262	295	327	213
Average	8,750	9,652	4,626	1,376	727	542	251	218	307	138

Source: NCHS and NSC. *Includes deaths resulting from conflagration regardless of nature of injury. †Includes drowning in water transport accidents. Some totals partly estimated.

U.S. Building Fire Losses By Causes

Source: National Fire Protection Assn. Copyright 1975

These estimated figures are intended to show the relative order of magnitude of fire losses by cause, and to indicate year-to-year trends. While they are reasonable approximations based on experience in typical states, they should not be taken as exact records for each class. The figures by themselves do not show the relative safety in use of various types of materials, devices, fuels, or services, and they should not be used for that purpose.

Cause	No. of Fires	Estimated Loss
Heating and Cooking Equipment	160,000	$ 199,300,000
Defective or misused equipment.	93,300	$137,300,000
Chimneys and flues	14,000	19,300,000
Hot ashes and coals.	12,600	2,000,000
Combustibles near heaters and stoves.	40,100	40,700,000
Smoking-Related.	121,600	136,300,000
Electrical.	165,000	363,500,000
Wiring distribution equipment.	112,200	253,300,000
Motors and appliances[1].	52,800	110,200,000
Trash Burning.	177,000	5,000,000
Flammable Liquids[1].	56,100	53,200,000
Open Flames and Sparks[1].	77,500	147,600,000
Sparks and embers.	13,300	7,900,000
Welding and cutting	11,600	48,900,000
Friction, sparks from machinery.	11,900	19,100,000
Thawing pipes.	5,800	15,300,000
Other open flames.	34,900	56,400,000
Lightning.	16,600	39,100,000
Children and Fire	59,600	100,100,000
Exposure	44,200	26,200,000
Incendiary and Suspicious.	114,400	563,000,000
Spontaneous Ignition	11,000	41,200,000
Gas Fires and Explosions[1].	11,900	41,900,000
Fireworks and Explosives	4,200	38,100,000
Miscellaneous Known Causes.	91,700	268,500,000
Unknown Causes.	159,200	1,237,000,000
TOTAL BUILDING FIRES.	1,270,000	$3,260,000,000

[1]Does not include fires originating in heating and cooking equipment.

INTERPOL (International Criminal Police Organization)

The United States is one of 120 countries that are members of INTERPOL, the International Criminal Police Organization. United States participation in INTERPOL was authorized by Congress in 1938. Because of the Treasury Dept.'s activities in the suppression of counterfeiting, smuggling and the narcotics traffic, all of which have international ramifications, that department was designated as U. S. representative to INTERPOL in 1958.

Each member nation has one vote at a general assembly of INTERPOL held annually at a site chosen by the delegates at the previous year's assembly. The chairman of the U. S. delegation attending such meetings is the Assistant Secretary of the Treasury (Enforcement and Operations).

INTERPOL dates from 1914, but World War I brought suspension of all its activities until 1923. The organization's first constitution was drawn up in that year. Files on international criminals were built up gradually to a point where their value to the police of member nations became apparent. During World War II the files disappeared from Vienna, where the General Secretariat of INTERPOL was located.

The organization was reconstituted at the end of World War II. The General Secretariat was moved to Paris and is now located in the Parisian suburb of Saint-Cloud. The Secretariat functions as a central depository for fingerprints, photographs and other records of international criminals. It also operates an international radio network to 54 of the member countries.

Interpol does not employ any investigators as such. Foreign requirements for investigation are referred to the National Central Bureaus, the offices established in each country to handle INTERPOL coordination. Scotland Yard is the National Central Bureau for the United Kingdom; the Surete in France; the Italiano Di Polizia in Italy; the Canberra Commonwealth police in Australia serve as the National Central Bureaus for those countries.

In the United States the U.S. National Central Bureau is staffed by U.S. Federal Law Enforcement Agents on loan from the Secret Service, Customs Service, Bureau of Alcohol, Tobacco, and Firearms, and the Drug Enforcement Administration. All inquiries, both domestic and foreign, are channeled through the National Central Bureau at the Treasury Dept. in Washington. Unless foreign requirements for investigation in the United States involve federal jurisdiction or interest, they are referred to local and state police agencies for investigation. All U.S. enforcement agencies may call upon Interpol Washington for investigation in other member countries.

Locations of Federal Detention Areas

Source: U.S. Bureau of Prisons

Penitentiaries; Atlanta, Ga.; Leavenworth, Kan.; Lewisburg, Pa.; McNeil Island, Wash.; Marion, Ill.; Terre Haute, Ind. **Reformatories**: El Reno, Okla.; Petersburg, Va.; Women, Alderson, W. Va. **Medical center**: Springfield, Mo., Hospital, Maintenance unit. **Prison camps**: Eglin Air Force Base, Florida; Montgomery, Ala.; Safford, Ariz.; Allenwood, Pa. **Correctional Institutions**: Danbury, Conn.; La Tuna, Tex.; Lompoc, Cal.; Texarkana, Tex.; Milan, Mich.; Tallahassee, Fla.; Seagoville, Tex.; Terminal Island, Cal.; Sandstone, Minn.; Ft. Worth, Tex. **Detention headquarters center**: Florence, Ariz. **Institutions for juvenile and youth offenders**: Ashland, Ky.; Englewood, Col.; Morgantown, W. Va.; Pleasonton, Cal. **Community Treatment Centers**: Detroit, Mich.; Chicago, Ill.; Los Angeles, Cal.; Kansas City, Mo.; Atlanta, Ga.; Houston, Tex.; Oakland, Cal.; New York City; Dallas, Tex.; Phoenix, Ariz.

Total Arrest Trends by Sex — 1972-73

Source: Federal Bureau of Investigation, Uniform Crime Reports — 1973

	Males				Females			
	Total		Under 18		Total		Under 18	
Offense charged	1973	Per-cent change 1972-73	1973	Per-cent change 1972-73	1973	Per-cent change 1972-73	1973	Per-cent change 1972-73
Total[1]	5,212,599	+3.3	1,274,978	+6.1	945,915	+4.5	355,744	+.5
Murder and nonneglig. manslaughter	11,760	+9.4	1,315	+4.8	2,077	+1.5	127	—
Neglig. manslaughter	2,470	+1.0	306	+53.0	323	+2.9	21	−58.0
Forcible rape	18,387	+12.0	3,632	+13.4	—		—	
Robbery	92,190	+4.3	31,372	+12.9	6,679	+5.2	2,340	−4.3
Aggravated assault	126,717	+11.1	21,286	+7.4	19,306	+10.0	3,626	+1.9
Burglary — breaking or entering	284,679	+10.4	154,885	+16.6	16,244	+14.3	8,330	+21.3
Larceny — theft	420,049	+1.7	211,032	−1.8	193,885	+7.7	85,891	+3.0
Auto theft	106,622	+5.2	60,554	+10.1	6,747	+9.0	3,995	+13.8
Other assaults	229,227	+1.8	41,347	+4.8	36,248	+.8	10,420	−6.5
Arson	9,408	+11.1	5,645	+12.7	1,179	+28.7	539	+13.5
Forgery and counterfeiting	29,090	−1.2	3,239	+16.4	10,688	+8.2	1,224	+11.0
Fraud	54,805	+5.2	2,266	+12.8	24,808	+10.8	768	+8.6
Embezzlement	4,037	+19.2	333	+21.5	1,269	+37.5	82	+28.1
Stolen property offenses	60,020	+4.5	20,921	+15.7	6,725	+9.2	1,856	+26.2
Vandalism	106,039	+4.3	74,070	+1.8	8,906	+2.0	5,440	−1.7
Weapons; carrying, possessing, etc.	102,605	+7.7	17,040	+12.3	8,912	+15.8	962	+17.3
Prostitution and commercialized vice	10,761	+9.2	444	+23.7	31,953	+7.7	1,293	+40.4
Other sex offenses (except forcible rape)	43,364	+5.2	8,287	+2.5	3,648	−7.0	1,198	−13.1
Narcotic drug laws	394,327	+20.6	98,753	+39.8	66,604	+11.6	21,864	+25.9
Gambling	49,116	−13.2	1,373	−.5	4,706	−12.2	102	+61.9
Offenses against family, children	35,698	−2.2	622	+28.8	3,729	−4.4	257	+11.3
Driving under the influence	576,252	+18.6	7,976	+29.8	45,124	+22.5	610	+41.5
Liquor laws	146,021	−3.0	55,893	+5.3	25,761	−.2	13,904	+5.1
Drunkenness	1,053,579	−4.6	28,526	−6.0	82,282	−4.7	4,706	−13.2
Disorderly conduct	363,186	+1.0	81,786	−3.6	79,716	+15.9	17,943	−8.9
Vagrancy	31,487	−2.1	4,739	−7.5	16,897	−11.6	1,090	−10.4
All other offenses (except traffic)	682,900	−3.1	169,553	−.9	125,607	−2.6	51,268	−6.8

[1] Totals will not add due to deletion of several minor arrest categories.

Canada: Criminal Offenses and Crime Rate

Source: Statistics Canada

	1973		1974		Percent change in rate
	Actual Offenses	Rate	Actual Offenses	Rate	
Murder	475	2.2	539	2.4	11.8
Attempted Murder	483	2.2	524	2.3	6.9
Manslaughter	66	0.3	50	0.2	−25.3
Rape	1,594	7.3	1,827	8.2	13.0
Other Sexual Offenses	10,402	47.3	9,296	41.7	−11.9
Wounding	1,882	8.6	2,114	9.5	10.7
Assaults (Not indecent)	89,696	408.0	95,050	426.1	4.4
Robbery	13,166	59.9	16,953	76.0	26.9
Total-Crimes of Violence	**117,764**	**535.7**	**126,353**	**566.4**	**5.7**
Breaking and Entering	198,043	900.9	233,939	1048.7	16.4
Theft, Motor Vehicle	71,593	325.7	83,431	374.0	14.8
Theft Over $200	63,383	288.3	79,814	357.8	24.1
Theft $200 and Under	414,591	1885.9	459,845	2061.4	9.3
Have Stolen Goods	13,945	63.4	15,315	68.7	8.2
Frauds	71,774	326.5	75,705	339.4	3.9
Total Property Crimes	**833,329**	**3790.6**	**948,049**	**4250.0**	**12.1**
Prostitution	3,573	16.3	3,258	14.6	−10.1
Gaming and Betting	3,011	13.7	3,264	14.6	6.8
Offensive Weapon	8,949	40.7	10,838	48.6	19.4
Other Criminal Code	332,158	1510.9	361,444	1620.3	7.2
Arson and Attempted Arson	4,154	18.9	6,639	29.8	57.5
Total-Other Crimes	**351,845**	**1600.5**	**385,443**	**1727.9**	**8.0**
Total Criminal Code	**1,302,938**	**5926.8**	**1,459,845**	**6544.3**	**10.4**
Federal Statutes	42,786	194.6	44,409	199.1	2.3
Provincial Statutes	339,120	1542.6	369,329	1655.7	7.3
Municipal By-Laws	76,282	347.0	81,460	365.2	5.2
Addicting Opiate-Like Drugs	3,800	17.3	3,357	15.0	−12.9
Cannabis (Marijuana)	42,651	194.0	49,760	223.1	15.0
Controlled Drugs	2,129	9.7	1,576	7.1	−27.0
Restricted Drugs	4,212	19.2	3,989	17.9	−6.7

Federal Bureau of Investigation

The Federal Bureau of Investigation (FBI) is an activity of the Department of Justice, and is located at 9th St. and Pennsylvania Ave., Washington, D. C., 20535. It investigates all violations of Federal laws except those specifically assigned to some other agency by legislative action, such violations including counterfeiting, and internal revenue, postal and customs violations. It also investigates espionage, sabotage, treason and other matters affecting internal security, as well as kidnaping, transportation of stolen goods across state lines, interstate traffic in prostitution and violations of the Federal bank and atomic energy laws.

The FBI collects and classifies police and crime reports for the nation. While this division is of great usefulness in detecting criminals, it serves a wider purpose in recording the fingerprints of many other citizens who voluntarily make this record.

The FBI has 59 field divisions in the principal cities of the country. *Consult telephone directories for location and phone numbers.*

An applicant for the position of Special Agent of the FBI must be at least 23 and under 36 years old and graduate of a state-accredited resident law school or from a resident four-year college with a major in accounting with at least one year of practical accounting and/or auditing experience. In addition, applicants with a four-year resident college degree with a major in certain areas or 3 year specialized experience of a professional, executive, or complex investigative nature are presently being considered on a limited basis. An agent gets 14 weeks of training, during which he learns techniques of investigation and arrest and recognition of evidence.

Clarence M. Kelley, former FBI agent and professional law enforcement officer, became Director on July 9, 1973.

U. S. Govt. Crime Reports
Source: Federal Bureau of Investigation

Offense	1973 est.	Percent over[1] 1972	1968
Murder	19,510	+4.5	+34.8
Forcible rape	51,000	+9.0	+54.8
Robbery	382,680	+1.3	+39.2
Assault	416,270	+6.2	+39.7
Burglary	2,540,000	+7.2	+31.4
Larceny	4,304,400	+3.9	+18.9
Auto theft	923,600	+3.9	+12.9
Total	8,638,400	+4.9	+23.5

[1]Percent by which the rate of crime per 100,000 population increased in 1973 over 1972 and 1968.

Crime in the U.S. Increases 5.7% in 1973

Crime in the U.S., as measured by the Crime Index offenses, increased by 5.7% in 1973 over 1972. Violent crimes were up 4.9%, with forcible rape reports up 9.2% (partly, perhaps, because of a greater willingness of victims to report the crime), while aggravated assault (assault with a dangerous weapon including the fists) was up 7%. Murders increased 5.2% and robberies were up 2.1%. Property crimes went up 5.8%, with burglaries increasing by 8% and larceny and auto theft up 4.7% each. Serious crime in cities of 250,000 or more people was up only 1%, while crime in suburban areas grew by 9%.

Crime Index Trends by Geographic Regions
1973 over 1972
(rates per 100,000 population)

Region[1]	Total	Violent	Property	Murder	Forcible Rape	Robbery	Assault	Burglary	Larceny	Auto Theft
Northeast	+4.6	+0.9	+5.1	+ 4.1	+11.7	−3.7	+ 7.1	+4.6	+4.6	+7.5
North Central	+6.3	+5.6	+6.4	+11.8	+10.4	+1.0	+10.1	+9.0	+5.7	+3.5
South	+7.2	+4.9	+7.5	+ 1.6	+ 9.7	+8.7	+ 2.5	+9.8	+6.4	+6.4
West	+1.0	+5.3	+0.6	+ 1.3	+ 3.8	+3.3	+ 7.3	+4.7	−1.0	−2.4

[1]Northeast includes New England, New Jersey, New York and Pennsylvania; North Central extends west through Nebraska and includes Missouri; South extends from Delaware, Maryland and West Virginia to Oklahoma and Texas.

Crime Rates by States
Source: Federal Bureau of Investigation, Uniform Crime Reports—1973
(Rates per 100,000 population)

	Total	Violent	Property	Murder	Rape	Robbery	Assault	Burglary	Larceny	Auto Theft
Alabama	2,512.3	350.1	2,162.2	13.2	21.2	79.4	236.3	882.0	1,053.1	227.2
Alaska	4,943.3	384.5	4,558.8	10.0	44.5	67.0	263.0	1,167.3	2,865.5	526.1
Arizona	6,703.9	479.9	6,224.0	8.1	31.0	147.3	293.6	1,958.3	3,720.1	545.6
Arkansas	2,538.9	289.9	2,249.0	8.8	19.5	71.5	190.0	801.0	1,315.7	132.3
California	6,304.9	565.8	5,739.1	9.0	40.6	240.4	275.8	1,979.6	3,123.6	635.9
Colorado	5,495.8	414.0	5,081.9	7.9	38.7	162.9	204.4	1,598.8	2,910.6	572.5
Connecticut	3,664.4	208.7	3,455.7	3.3	11.1	84.2	110.1	1,029.3	1,909.7	516.7
Delaware	4,582.6	350.8	4,232.6	5.9	15.8	90.3	238.0	1,219.4	2,526.4	486.8
Florida	5,960.3	604.6	5,355.7	15.4	31.9	223.2	335.0	1,857.2	3,048.6	499.9
Georgia	3,430.3	412.4	3,017.9	17.4	25.8	158.1	211.1	1,268.8	1,390.7	358.4
Hawaii	4,958.8	155.6	4,803.1	5.3	20.2	83.7	46.5	1,535.5	2,830.8	436.9
Idaho	3,457.8	164.3	3,293.6	2.6	14.2	26.9	120.5	848.8	2,237.8	207.0
Illinois	4,324.9	555.9	3,769.1	10.4	24.0	272.8	248.7	1,025.1	2,236.2	507.7
Indiana	3,533.6	247.5	3,286.1	7.2	21.0	106.1	113.2	962.2	1,952.6	371.4
Iowa	2,831.6	102.3	2,729.3	2.2	11.3	32.9	55.9	634.0	1,904.6	190.7
Kansas	3,513.8	217.5	3,296.3	6.0	18.0	78.1	115.3	1,030.5	2,055.3	210.5
Kentucky	2,265.32	220.1	2,045.2	9.7	16.3	85.1	109.1	679.7	1,139.2	226.2
Louisiana	3,402.9	425.6	2,977.3	15.4	22.2	138.6	249.3	962.1	1,690.4	324.9
Maine	2,544.4	113.7	2,430.6	2.1	7.8	20.7	83.1	857.3	1,401.2	172.7
Maryland	4,791.4	641.1	4,150.3	11.3	27.8	301.6	300.4	1,144.6	2,457.9	547.8
Massachusetts	4,521.0	351.9	4,169.1	4.4	16.3	182.0	149.3	1,330.3	1,729.2	1,109.6
Michigan	5,489.4	585.2	4,904.2	12.1	35.1	282.7	255.2	1,584.6	2,771.3	548.3
Minnesota	3,535.6	177.7	3,357.8	2.7	14.9	88.7	71.5	1,016.4	2,004.7	336.7
Mississippi	1,926.3	339.1	1,587.2	16.1	17.1	46.8	259.1	593.8	879.7	113.8
Missouri	4,141.4	408.7	3,732.8	9.0	28.2	193.4	178.1	1,234.8	2,052.6	445.4

continued

	Total	Violent	Property	Murder	Rape	Robbery	Assault	Burglary	Larceny	Auto Theft
Montana	3,395.3	167.4	3,227.9	6.0	16.4	36.3	108.7	755.6	2,241.7	230.5
Nebraska	2,811.2	185.4	2,625.8	4.3	16.5	62.5	102.1	637.4	1,685.7	302.7
Nevada	6,632.1	572.1	6,060.0	12.2	46.0	262.0	251.8	2,149.8	3,299.1	611.1
New Hampshire	2,329.3	82.0	2,247.3	2.1	9.5	13.3	57.1	685.0	1,373.3	189.0
New Jersey	4,082.5	391.9	3,690.6	7.4	18.8	206.2	159.4	1,244.5	1,873.4	572.7
New Mexico	4,707.9	454.3	4,253.5	11.4	32.1	125.9	284.9	1,432.1	2,485.7	335.7
New York	4,306.7	731.2	3,575.5	11.1	26.1	439.6	254.4	1,296.7	1,671.5	607.2
North Carolina	2,811.9	437.8	2,374.0	13.0	16.1	71.4	337.4	892.0	1,308.2	173.8
North Dakota	2,078.4	60.8	2,017.7	0.8	7.3	7.3	45.3	383.4	1,502.8	131.4
Ohio	3,495.9	291.7	3,204.1	7.3	21.4	143.5	119.5	943.0	1,884.3	376.9
Oklahoma	3,466.4	246.2	3,220.2	6.6	20.0	68.2	151.4	1,163.9	1,745.2	311.1
Oregon	5,297.1	292.7	5,004.4	4.9	29.3	99.4	159.0	1,607.7	2,988.5	408.2
Pennsylvania	2,458.8	262.5	2,196.3	6.3	14.9	135.3	106.0	766.6	1,069.9	359.8
Rhode Island	4,678.3	282.5	4,395.8	3.4	8.3	97.0	173.8	1,189.1	2,312.3	894.3
South Carolina	3,327.0	394.6	2,932.4	14.4	22.5	79.2	278.6	1,194.3	1,492.1	246.0
South Dakota	2,175.8	126.9	2,048.9	3.8	12.8	24.7	85.5	498.7	1,406.0	144.2
Tennessee	3,060.1	358.0	2,702.1	13.2	26.9	130.5	187.5	1,009.8	1,362.2	330.1
Texas	4,046.2	381.5	3,664.7	12.7	25.5	142.1	201.1	1,266.4	2,051.1	347.2
Utah	4,247.1	208.5	4,038.6	3.2	22.9	62.6	119.8	989.3	2,748.1	301.2
Vermont	2,498.1	70.5	2,427.6	2.2	11.2	8.8	48.3	801.5	1,489.9	136.2
Virginia	3,238.7	285.7	2,953.0	8.5	20.7	101.0	155.5	825.8	1,859.1	268.1
Washington	5,089.9	271.5	4,818.5	4.0	26.2	96.3	145.0	1,540.4	2,902.4	375.7
West Viginia	1,471.5	123.7	1,347.8	5.7	9.3	27.9	80.8	415.8	824.9	107.1
Wisconsin	3,176.9	115.4	3,061.5	2.6	10.8	48.7	53.3	710.6	2,122.0	228.9
Wyoming	3,413.0	216.1	3,196.9	6.8	15.6	32.9	160.9	699.7	2,282.7	214.4

Reported Crime in Metropolitan Areas, 1973

Source: Federal Bureau of Investigation. Uniform Crime Reports—1973

The 27 Standard Metropolitan Statistical Areas listed below are those which appear most frequently among the top 30 cities in per capita reported crime rate for each of 7 kinds of major crime: the 5 listed below plus forcible rape and aggravated assault.

The rates are for reported crimes only; they are not an accurate index of crimes actually committed. In many metropolitan areas an unknown number of crimes go unreported by victims. This is especially true of the crimes of rape, burglary and larceny. Additionally, figures are often distorted for political reasons.

The number in parentheses following the city name indicates the number of categories (including forcible rape and aggravated assault) in which the city appears among the top 30.

The numbers in parentheses following crime rate figures give that city's rank in that category of crime. If no number appears, the city is not among the top 30 in that category. The cities are listed in order of their violent crime rate.

Rate per 100,000 population

Metropolitan Areas	Total[1]	Violent[2]	Property[3]	Murder[4]	Robbery	Burglary	Larceny	Auto Theft
New York City, N.Y. (5)	5,457.5	1,204.9 (1)	4,252.6	17.5(16)	747.0 (1)	1,691.3	1,656.5	904.8 (6)
Miami, Fla.(4)	6,726.8(12)	947.8 (2)	5,779.0(25)	15.7	382.0 (6)	1,919.9(28)	3,181.0	678.1(26)
Baltimore, Md.(3)	5,545.6	916.2 (3)	4,629.4	15.4	458.7 (3)	1,351.1	2,636.3	642.1(29)
Los Angeles-Long Beach, Cal.(5)	6,628.5(13)	837.9 (4)	5,790.6(24)	12.4	370.6 (7)	2,187(11)	2,723.9	879.1 (8)
Detroit, Mich.(4)	6,098.3	821.5 (5)	5,276.8	19.3(10)	470.3 (2)	1,661.4	2,731.9	883.4 (7)
Albuquerque, N.M.(5)	6,966.4(10)	726.2 (9)	6,240.2(12)	12.6	271.3(21)	2,231.0 (8)	3,468.7(23)	540.5
Las Vegas, Nev.(5)	7,526.3(4)	709.9(10)	6,816.5 (5)	15.0	352.8(10)	2,639.1 (1)	3,413.4(26)	763.9(15)
Orlando, Fla.(3)	6,404.3(23)	696.0(11)	5,708.4(29)	12.7	199.1	2,051.4(15)	3,158.8	498.2
Saginaw, Mich.(5)	6,617.1(14)	688.1(12)	5,929.0(20)	16.9(19)	307.1(16)	1,936.1(23)	3,778.8(11)	214.1
Baton Rouge, La.(3)	6,362.7(25)	686.6(13)	5,676.1	15.9(28)	163.1	2,018.7(20)	3,157.3	500.1
San Francisco-Oakland, Cal.(5)	7,277.8 (6)	683.6(14)	6,594.2 (7)	10.9	353.3 (9)	2,205.6 (9)	3,643.0(17)	75.6(16)
Daytona Beach, Fla.(4)	7,861.4 (2)	668.2(15)	7,193.1 (2)	10.6	283.3(19)	2,634.1 (2)	4,130.6 (3)	428.5
Jacksonville, Fla.(5)	5,861.8	668.0(17)	5,193.9	19.8(7)	260.9(24)	1,888.6	2,897.0	408.3
Gainesville, Fla.(5)	6,575.8(17)	657.6(20)	5,918.3(21)	17.4(17)	170.9	2,050.4(16)	3,477.2(21)	390.7
New Orleans, La.(4)	4,778.2	657.2(21)	4,121.0	21.6 (2)	324.7(11)	1,337.0	2,063.9	720.2(18)
Fayettville, N.C.(3)	3,884.5	646.4(22)	3,238.1	16.1(25)	180.6	1,517.7	1,478.5	241.9
W.Palm Beach-Boca Raton, Fla.(3)	7,125.2 (8)	634.8(25)	6,490.4 (9)	17.8(14)	171.5	2,243.2 (7)	3,838.8 (8)	408.3
Memphis, Tenn.(4)	5,597.1	619.8(29)	4,977.3	18.7(12)	307.9(15)	1,901.4(29)	2,633.7	442.2
Atlanta, Ga.(4)	5,273.4	616.3(30)	4,657.2	21.8 (1)	315.2(12)	2,003.8(21)	2,077.4	575.9
Ann Arbor, Mich.(4)	7,746.9 (3)	601.0	7,146.0 (3)	4.6	186.5	2,417.2 (4)	4,264.3 (2)	464.5
Phoenix, Ariz.(4)	8,165.2 (1)	569.0	7,596.2 (1)	8.3	187.1	2,509.6 (3)	4,394.2 (1)	692.4(23)
Ft. Lauderdale-Hollywood, Fla.(5)	7,519.8 (5)	542.4	6,977.4 (4)	16.7(21)	271.2(22)	2,144.2(12)	4,120.3 (4)	712.8(21)
Denver-Boulder, Colo.(5)	6,584.6(15)	519.9	6,064.8(14)	10.0	233.2(29)	1,996.4(22)	3,272.1(30)	796.3(13)
Stockton, Cal.(4)	6,819.4(11)	455.6	6,363.8(10)	16.3(24)	198.4	2,031.4(17)	3,703.2(14)	629.2(30)
Fresno, Cal.(3)	7,214.5 (7)	450.8	6,763.7 (6)	9.6	206.7	2,383.8 (6)	3,553.3(19)	826.6(12)
Santa Cruz, Cal.(3)	6,489.1(19)	436.2	6,052.9(15)	20.3 (5)	67.4	2,123.2(13)	3,495.7(20)	434.1
Santa Rosa, Cal.(3)	6,464.3(20)	331.4	6,132.9(13)	6.8	72.3	2,022.2(19)	3,649.2(16)	461.6

Other metro areas among the top 30 in total reported crime (preponderantly property crime) are Reno, Nev.(9); Sarasota, Fla. (16); Bakersfield, Cal. (18); Modesto, Cal. (21); Kalamazoo, Mich. (22); Tucson, Ariz. (24); Riverside-San Benardino-Ontario, Cal. (26); Eugene-Springfield, Ore.(27); Portland, Ore. (28); San Jose, Cal. (29); and Sacramento, Cal. (30).

[2] Violent crime includes murder and non-negligent manslaughter, forcible rape, robbery and aggravated assault. Other metro areas in the top 30 in reported violent crime are Paterson-Clifton-Passaic, N.J. (6); Chicago (7); Columbia, S.C. (8); Lttle Rock, Ark. (15); Flint, Mich. (18); Trenton, N.J. (19); Waco, Tex. (23); Washington, D.C. (24); Tallahassee, Fla. (26; Lafayette. La. (27); Greensboro-Winston-Salem-High Point, N.C. (28).

[3] Property crime includes burglary, larceny and auto theft. Other metro areas among the top 30 in reported property crime are Reno, Nev. (8); Sarasota, Fla. (11); Bakersfield, Cal. (16); Modesto, Cal. (17); Tucson, Ariz. (18); Eugene-Springfield, Ore. (19); San Jose, Cal. (22); Kalamazoo, Mich. (23); Portland, Ore. (26); Sacramento, Cal. (27); Riverside-San Bernardino-Ontario Cal. (28); Yakima, Wash. (20).

[4] Of the top 30 cities in murder all but 7 are in the South. In fact, of the 83 southern cities included in the FBI crime report, 58 had murder rates higher than that of the country as a whole.

Reported Crime, 1972-73, by Size of Place

Source: Federal Bureau of Investigation, Uniform Crime Reports - 1973

Population group (1973 estimates)	Grand Total	Violent crime	Property crime	Murder-non-neg man-slaughter	Forcible Rape	Robbery	Aggra-vated Assault	Burglary	Auto theft
Total All Agencies: 6,615 agencies; total population 172,639,000									
1972.............	7,306,145	746,462	6,559,683	16,169	41,364	353,224	335,705	2,079,546	805,7
1973.............	7,667,612	778,804	6,888,808	17,128	45,167	358,038	358,471	2,230,714	835,9
Percent change....	+4.9	+4.3	+5.0	+5.9	+9.2	+1.4	+6.8	+7.3	+3
Total Cities: 4,804 cities; total population 122,368,000									
1972.............	6,116,375	650,563	5,465,812	13,151	32,812	329,400	275,200	1,664,903	710,6
1973.............	6,370,032	673,843	5,696,189	14,054	36,177	332,434	291,178	1,774,846	731,6
Percent change....	+4.1	+3.6	+4.2	+6.9	+10.3	+0.9	+5.8	+6.6	+2
54 cities over 250,000; population 41,649,000									
1972.............	2,689,833	419,118	2,270,715	8,503	19,463	243,484	147,668	772,860	401,1
1973.............	2,718,825	418,502	2,300,323	8,953	20,968	239,314	149,267	801,327	404,7
Percent change....	+1.1	−0.1	+1.3	+5.3	+7.7	−1.7	+1.1	+3.7	+0
97 cities, 100,000 to 250,000; population 13,952,000									
1972.............	821,725	68,023	753,702	1,555	3,878	29,587	33,003	234,435	92,7
1973.............	858,892	74,313	784,579	1,634	4,389	31,733	36,557	252,045	95,5
Percent change....	+4.5	+9.2	+4.1	+5.1	+13.2	+7.3	+10.8	+7.5	+.
259 cities, 50,000 to 100,000; population 18,088,000									
1972.............	856,717	58,475	798,242	1,106	3,506	24,257	29,606	223,208	87,0
1973.............	893,014	64,617	828,397	1,154	4,108	25,811	33,544	238,109	89,1
Percent change....	+4.2	+10.5	+3.8	+4.3	+17.2	+6.4	+13.3	+6.7	+2
490 cities, 25,000 to 50,000; population 17,265,000									
1972.............	708,688	45,181	663,507	841	2,485	17,434	24,421	178,148	63,9
1973.............	766,116	50,407	715,709	932	2,824	19,132	27,519	196,100	69,2
Percent change....	+8.1	+11.6	+7.9	+10.8	+13.6	+9.7	+12.7	+10.1	+8
1,207 cities, 10,000 to 25,000; population 19,276,000									
1972.............	675,667	37,913	637,754	755	2,260	10,452	24,446	167,377	45,3
1973.............	736,696	42,650	694,046	879	2,554	11,869	27,348	187,315	50,4
Percent change....	+9.0	+12.5	+8.8	+16.4	+13.0	+13.6	+11.9	+11.9	+11
2,697 cities under 10,000; population 12,137,000									
1972.............	363,745	21,853	341,892	391	1,220	4,186	16,056	88,875	20,4
1973.............	396,489	23,354	373,135	502	1,334	4,575	16,943	99,950	22,4
Percent change....	+9.0	+6.9	+9.1	+28.4	+9.3	+9.3	+5.5	+12.5	+9
Suburban Area: 2,817 agencies; population 58,643,000									
1972.............	1,942,987	130,427	1,812,560	2,720	9,819	41,478	76,410	565,220	167,8
1973.............	2,116,212	145,897	1,970,315	2,956	10,525	45,545	86,871	624,421	184,0
Percent change....	+8.9	+11.9	+8.7	+8.7	+7.2	+9.8	+13.7	+10.5	+9
Rural Area: 1,389 agencies; population 20,653,000									
1972.............	299,152	25,819	273,333	1,243	2,270	3,382	18,924	117,546	15,9
1973.............	327,824	27,019	300,805	1,245	2,395	3,596	19,783	127,536	18,2
Percent change....	+9.6	+4.6	+10.1	+0.2	+5.5	+6.3	+4.5	+8.5	+14

858 Law Enforcement Officers Killed 1964-1973

Souce: Uniform Crime Reports (FBI)

1. Responding to disturbance calls.................. 125
2. Burglaries in progress or pursuing suspect.......... 61
3. Robberies in progress or pursuing suspect......... 166
4. Attempting other arrests...................... 209
5. Civil disorders............................. 11
6. Handling, transporting, custody of prisoners......... 3
7. Investigating suspicious persons and circumstances.. 6
8. Ambush.............................. 8
9. Unprovoked mentally deranged................. 8
10. Traffic stops.......................... 8

Geographically for the period of 1964-1973 the 858 officers who were slain in line of duty were divided in this fashion: Northeast 13; North Central 215; South 357 and West 154.

Police Roster

Police officers and civilian employees in large cities as of Oct. 31, 1973

City	Officers	Civilian	City	Officers	Civilian	City	Officers	Civilia
Anchorage, Ala.....	105	47	Indianapolis, Ind....	1,100	200	Philadelphia, Pa....	8,026	92
Atlanta, Ga.......	1,458	199	Jacksonville, Fla....	770	397	Phoenix, Ariz......	1,307	26
Baltimore, Md......	3,571	628	Jersey City, N.J....	1,041	35	Pittsburgh, Pa......	1,551	5
Birmingham, Ala....	637	121	Kansas City, Mo....	1,310	371	Portland, Ore......	714	23
Boise, Idaho......	122	39	Little Rock, Ark.....	268	63	Rochester, N.Y.....	632	10
Boston, Mass......	2,565	278	Los Angeles, Cal...	7,134	2,541	Sacramento, Cal....	521	13
Bridgeport, Conn...	457	20	Louisville, Ky.......	757	196	St. Louis, Mo.......	2,218	65
Buffalo, N.Y.......	1,359	139	Memphis, Tenn.....	1,170	292	St. Petersburg, Fla..	410	22
Chicago, Ill.......	13,415	1,460	Miami, Fla.........	764	200	San Antonio, Tex...	1,040	19
Cincinnati, Ohio....	1,125	261	Milwaukee, Wisc....	2,128	190	San Bernardino,		
Cleveland, Ohio....	2,437	(a)	Minneapolis, Minn..	850	91	Cal............	205	5
Columbus, Ohio....	1,106	220	Nashville, Tenn.....	784	148	San Diego, Cal.....	1,014	25
Dallas, Tex........	1,929	621	Newark, N.J.......	1,501	329	San Francisco, Cal..	1,958	36
Denver, Col.......	1,297	313	New Orleans, La....	1,343	458	San Jose, Cal......	654	13
Detroit, Mich.......	5,575	702	New York, N.Y......	29,861	4,427	Santa Ana, Cal.....	225	8
Ft. Worth, Tex......	656	153	Norfolk, Va.........	510	94	Seattle, Wash......	1,138	25
Fresno, Cal........	312	81	Oakland, Cal.......	722	270	Stockton, Cal......	203	4
Gary, Ind.........	394	55	Oklahoma City,			Tampa, Fla........	598	12
Hartford, Conn.....	505	80	Okla...........	621	96	Toledo, Ohio......	764	1
Honolulu, Hawaii ...	1,403	319	Omaha, Nebr......	575	125	Tucson, Ariz.......	484	14
Houston, Tex......	2,184	334	Pasadena, Cal.....	202	70	Washington, D.C....	4,937	66

POSTAL INFORMATION
United States Postal Service

The Postal Reorganization Act, creating a [gov]ernment-owned postal service under the Exec[utiv]e branch and replacing the old Post Office Depart[me]nt, was signed into law by President Nixon on Aug. [?] 1970. The service officially came into being on [Jul]y 1, 1971.

The new U.S. Postal Service is governed by an 11-[ma]n Board of Governors. Nine members are appoint[ed] to 9-year terms by the President with Senate ap[pro]val. These 9, in turn, choose a Postmaster [Ge]neral, who is no longer a member of the Presi-dent's Cabinet. The Governors and the new Postmaster General choose the 11th member, who serves as Deputy Postmaster General. A new Postal Rate Commission of 5 members, appointed by the President, recommends postal rates to the governors for their approval.

The first Postmaster General under the new system was Winton M. Blount. He resigned Oct. 29, 1971, and was replaced by his deputy, E. T. Klassen, Dec. 7, 1971. Benjamin F. Bailar succeeded him Feb. 16, 1975.

U.S. Domestic Rates (effective Dec. 28, 1975)

First Class

Letters written, and matter sealed against inspection, 13c for each ounce or fraction. U.S. Postal cards; single 9c; double 18c; private post cards, same.

First class includes written matter, namely letters, postal cards, post cards (private mailing cards) and all [oth]er matter wholly or partly in writing, whether sealed or unsealed, except manuscripts for books, periodical [art]icles and music, manuscript copy accompanying proofsheets or corrected proofsheets of the same and the [wr]iting authorized by law on matter of other classes. Also matter sealed or closed against inspection. Bills and [sta]tements of accounts.

Greeting Cards

May be sent first class or single piece third class.

Airmail

Airmail was eliminated as a separate rate category [Oc]t. 11, 1975. First class mail moves by fastest avail[ab]le carrier.

Second Class

Single copy mailings by general public 8c for first 2 [ou]nces and 4c for each additional ounce or the 4th [cl]ass rate, whichever is lower. There are special rates [for] publications, newspapers and bulk mailing. Con[su]lt local postmasters for rates and permit.

Third Class

Third Class (limit up to but not including 16 [ou]nces): Mailable matter not in 1st and 2nd classes. Single mailing: Greeting cards (sealed or unseal[ed]), small parcels, printed matter, booklets and cata[lo]gs. 13c the first 2 ounces plus 11c for each 2 ounces [th]rough 15.9 ounces.

Bulk material: Books, catalogs of 24 pages or more, [se]eds, cuttings, bulbs, roots, scions and plants; sub[je]ct to a minimum rate; consult postmaster. Other matter: Newsletters, shoppers' guides, [ad]vertising circulars. Subject to a minimum rate for [wh]ich Post Office should be consulted. Separate rates [for] some nonprofit organizations. Bulk mailing fee, [$]0 per calendar year. Apply to postmaster for per[mi]t. One-time fee for permit, $15.

Parcel Post—Fourth Class

Fourth Class or Parcel Post (16 ounces and over): Merchandise, printed matter, etc., may be sealed, subject to inspection.

On parcels weighing less than 10 lbs. and measuring more than 84 inches, but not more than 100 inches in length and girth combined, the minimum postal charge shall be the zone charge applicable to a 10-pound parcel.

Priority Mail

First-class mail of more than 12 ounces and airmail of more than 9 ounces have been merged into a "Priority Mail (Heavy Pieces)" service. The most expeditious handling and transportation available will be used for fastest delivery.

Forwarding Addresses

The mailer, in order to obtain a forwarding address, must endorse the envelope or cover "Address Correction Requested." The destination post office then will determine whether a forwarding address has been left on file and provide it for a fee.

Special Handling

Third and Fourth class parcels will be handled and delivered as expeditiously as practicable (but not special delivery) upon payment, in addition to the regular postage: Up to 2 lbs., 50c; over 2 lbs. and up to 10 lbs., 70c; over 10 lbs.; $1.00. Such parcels must be endorsed, Special Handling.

Special Delivery

First class mail up to 2 lbs. $1.20, over 2 lbs. and up to 10 lbs., $1.45; over 10 lbs. $1.70. All other classes up to 2 lbs. $1.70, over 2 and up to 10 lbs., $1.80, over 10 lbs. $2.10.

Priority Mail

Air Parcel Post (over 9 ounces to 70 lbs.): Packages not to exceed 100 inches in length and girth combined, [in]cluding written and other matter of the first class, whether sealed or unsealed, fractions of a pound being [ch]arged as a full pound. Thirteen cents an ounce or fraction for all domestic mail up to and including 8 ounces [r]egardless of distance or zone.

Rates according to zone apply between the U.S. and Puerto Rico and Virgin Islands.

Parcels weighing less than 10 pounds, measuring over 84 inches but not exceeding 100 inches in length and [gi]rth combined are chargeable with a minimum rate equal to that for a 10 pound parcel for the zone to which [ad]dressed.

Zones	To 1 lb.	1½	2	2½	3	3½	4	4½	5
2, 3	$1.56	$1.73	$1.89	$2.05	$2.21	$2.37	$2.53	$2.68	$2.83
4	1.58	1.77	1.96	2.15	2.33	2.51	2.69	2.86	3.03
5	1.60	1.84	2.07	2.29	2.50	2.70	2.90	3.09	3.27
6	1.62	1.90	2.18	2.43	2.68	2.91	3.14	3.35	3.56
7	1.64	1.97	2.29	2.59	2.88	3.15	3.41	3.65	3.88
8	1.67	2.07	2.46	2.78	3.09	3.38	3.67	3.94	4.20

Postal Union Mail Special Services

Registration. — Available to practically all countries. Fee $1.90. The maximum indemnity payable — generally only in case of complete loss (of both contents and wrapper) — is $15.76. To Canada only the fees are $1.90 and $2.10, providing indemnity for loss up to $100 to $200, respectively.

Return receipt.— Fee is 32c.

Special delivery.— Available to most countries. Consult post office. Fees: For post cards, letter mail, and airmail "other articles," $1.20 up to 2 pounds; over 2 to 10 pounds, $1.45; over 10 pounds, $1.70. For surface "other articles," $1.70, $1.80 and $2.10, respectively.

Special handling.— Entitles AO *surface* packages to priority handling between mailing point and U.S. point of dispatch. Fees: 50c for packages to 2 pounds, 70c for packages over 2 pounds to 10 pounds, and $1.00 for packages over 10 pounds.

Airmail — There is daily air service to practically all countries.

Marking.— An article intended for special delivery service must have affixed to the cover near the name of the country of destination "EXPRESS" (Special Delivery) label, obtainable at the post office, or it may be marked on the cover boldly in red "EXPRESS" (Special Delivery).

Prepayment of replies from other countries. A mailer who wishes to prepay a reply by letter from another country may do so by sending his correspondent one or more international reply coupons, which may be purchased at United States post offices. One coupon should be accepted in any country in exchange for stamps to prepay a surface letter of the first unit of weight to the U.S.

Domestic Mail Special Services

Registry. All mailable matter prepaid with postage at the first-class or airmail rate may be registered. The mailer is required to declare the value of mail presented for registration.

Insurance is applicable to 3d and 4th class matter. Matter for sale addressed to prospective purchasers who have not ordered it or authorized its sending will not be insured.

C.O.D.: Unregistered — is applicable to 3d and 4th class matter and sealed domestic mail of any class bearing postage at the 1st class rate. Such mail must be based on bona fide orders or be in conformity with agreements between senders and addressees. Registered-For details consult postmaster.

Certified mail — service is available for any matter having no intrinsic value on which 1st class or air

mail postage is paid. Receipt is furnished at time mailing and evidence of delivery obtained. The fee 50c in addition to postage. Return receipt, restrict delivery and special delivery are available upon p ment of additional fees. No indemnity.

Individual Piece Mailings
(Fourth Class Catalogs)

Weight lbs.	Local	1&2	3	4	5	6	7	
1.5	$0.45	.54	.56	.58	.61	.64	.68	
2	.46	.57	.58	.62	.65	.69	.74	
2.5	.48	.60	.61	.66	.70	.74	.81	
3	.50	.62	.65	.69	.74	.81	.88	
3.5	.52	.65	.68	.73	.80	.86	.94	1
4	.53	.68	.70	.77	.84	.92	1.02	1
4.5	.54	.69	.73	.81	.88	.97	1.09	1
5	.56	.72	.76	.84	.93	1.02	1.15	1
6	.60	.77	.82	.92	1.02	1.14	1.29	1
7	.62	.82	.88	.98	1.10	1.25	1.42	1
8	.66	.88	.94	1.06	1.20	1.37	1.55	1
9	.69	.93	1.00	1.13	1.29	1.48	1.70	1
10	.72	.97	1.05	1.21	1.38	1.58	1.84	2

Zone Mileage

1	Up to 50	3	150-300	5	600-1,000	7	1,400- 1,8
2	50-150	4	300-600	6	1,000-1,400	8	over, 1,8

Registered Mail

Indemnity to $100	$1
100.01 to 200	2
200.01 to 400	2
400.01 to 600	2
600.01 to 800	3
800.01 to 1,000	3
1,000.01 to 2,000	3
2,000.01 to 3,000	3
3,000.01 to 4,000	4
4,000.01 to 5,000	4
5,000.01 to 6,000	4
6,000.01 to 7,000	5
7,000.01 to 8,000	5
8,000.01 to 9,000	5
9,000.01 to 10,000	6

Consult postmaster for registry rates above $10,000.

Insured Mail

$0.01 to $15	$0
15.01 to 50	
50.01 to 100	
100.01 to 150	
150.01 to 200	1

Liability for insured mail is limited to $200.

C.O.D. Mail

Consult postmaster for fees and conditions of ma ing.

Parcel Post Rate Schedule

1 lb., not exceeding	Local	1 & 2	3	4	5	6	7	
2	$0.77	$0.90	$0.93	$1.04	$1.15	$1.28	$1.40	$1
3	.82	.97	1.02	1.15	1.29	1.46	1.62	1
4	.86	1.04	1.10	1.25	1.42	1.63	1.84	2
5	.91	1.11	1.19	1.36	1.56	1.81	2.06	2
6	.95	1.18	1.27	1.46	1.69	1.98	2.28	2
7	1.00	1.25	1.36	1.57	1.83	2.16	2.50	2
8	1.04	1.32	1.44	1.67	1.96	2.33	2.72	3
9	1.09	1.39	1.53	1.78	2.10	2.51	2.94	3
10	1.13	1.46	1.61	1.88	2.23	2.68	3.16	3
11	1.18	1.53	1.70	1.99	2.37	2.86	3.38	3
12	1.22	1.60	1.78	2.09	2.50	3.03	3.60	4
13	1.27	1.67	1.87	2.20	2.64	3.21	3.82	4
14	1.31	1.74	1.95	2.30	2.77	3.38	4.04	4
15	1.36	1.81	2.04	2.41	2.91	3.56	4.26	4
16	1.40	1.88	2.12	2.51	3.04	3.73	4.48	5
17	1.45	1.95	2.21	2.62	3.18	3.91	4.70	5
18	1.49	2.02	2.29	2.72	3.31	4.08	4.92	5
19	1.54	2.09	2.38	2.83	3.45	4.26	5.14	5
20	1.58	2.16	2.46	2.93	3.58	4.43	5.36	6

(Consult postmaster for parcels over 20 pounds or measuring more than 72 inches, length and girth.)

Special Fourth-Class Rate
(limit 70 lbs.)

First pound or fraction 21c, 9c for each additional pound or fraction. Only following specific articles: books 24 pages or more, at least 22 of which are print

ed consisting wholly of reading matter or scholar bibliography containing no advertisement other tha incidental announcements of books; 16 millimete films in final form (except when mailed to or fro commercial theaters); printed music in bound sheet form; printed objective test materials; sound recordings, playscripts and manuscripts for books, periodicals and music; printed educational reference charts; loose-leaf pages and binders therefor consisting of medical information for distribution to doctors, hospitals, medical schools and medical students. Package must be marked "Special 4th-Class Rate" stating item contained.

Library Rate (limit 70 lbs.)
First pound or fraction 8c; each additional pound

or fraction 4c. Books when loaned or exchanged between schools, colleges, public libraries and certain non-profit organizations; books, printed music, bound academic theses, periodicals, sound recordings, other library materials, museum materials (specimens, collections), scientific or mathematical kits, instruments or other devices; also catalogs, guides or scripts for some of these materials. Must be marked "Library Rate".

Post Office-Authorized 2-Letter State Abbreviations

Gradually replacing the traditional abbreviations for the states of the United States are the two-letter ones approved by the Post Office Department when it introduced the ZIP Code in 1963. The official list follows, including the District of Columbia, Guam, Puerto Rico and the Virgin Islands (all capital letters are used):

Alabama	AL	Kentucky	KY	Ohio	OH
Alaska	AK	Louisiana	LA	Oklahoma	OK
Arizona	AZ	Maine	ME	Oregon	OR
Arkansas	AR	Maryland	MD	Pennsylvania	PA
California	CA	Massachusetts	MA	Puerto Rico	PR
Colorado	CO	Michigan	MI	Rhode Island	RI
Connecticut	CT	Minnesota	MN	South Carolina	SC
Delaware	DE	Mississippi	MS	South Dakota	SD
Dist. of Col.	DC	Missouri	MO	Tennessee	TN
Florida	FL	Montana	MT	Texas	TX
Georgia	GA	Nebraska	NE	Utah	UT
Guam	GU	Nevada	NV	Vermont	VT
Hawaii	HI	New Hampshire	NH	Virginia	VA
Idaho	ID	New Jersey	NJ	Virgin Islands	VI
Illinois	IL	New Mexico	NM	Washington	WA
Indiana	IN	New York	NY	West Virginia	WV
Iowa	IA	North Carolina	NC	Wisconsin	WI
Kansas	KS	North Dakota	ND	Wyoming	WY

Commemorative Stamps and Regular Postal Issues 1975

Date	Commemorative Stamp	Value	From
Feb. 10	Benjamin West	10c	Swarthmore, PA
Feb. 28	Pioneer	10c	Mountain View, CA
Mar. 13	Collective Bargaining	10c	Washington, DC
Mar. 25	Sybil Ludington	8c	Carmel, NY
Mar. 25	Salem Poor	10c	Cambridge, MA
Mar. 25	Haym Salomon	10c	Chicago, IL
Mar. 25	Peter Francisco	18c	Greensboro, NC
Apr. 4	Mariner 10	10c	Pasadena, CA
Apr. 19	Battles of Lexington and Concord	10c	Concord, MA
May 1	Paul Laurence Dunbar	10c	Dayton, OH
May 27	D. W. Griffith	10c	Beverly Hills, CA
June 17	Battle of Bunker Hill	10c	Charlestown, MA
July 4	Military Services Bicentennial (block of 4)	10c	Washington, DC
July 15	Apollo-Soyuz (2 stamps)	10c	Kennedy Space Center, FL
Aug. 26	International Women's Year	10c	Seneca Falls, NY
Sept. 3	U. S. Postal Service (4 stamps)	10c	Philadelphia, PA
Sept. 14	Charles Thomson (postal card and reply card)	7c	Bryn Mawr, PA
Sept. 29	World Peace Through Law	10c	Washington, DC
Oct. 6	Banking and Commerce (2 stamps)	10c	New York, NY
Oct. 13	Seafaring Tradition Embossed Envelope	10c	Minneapolis, MN
Oct. 14	Christmas — Ghirlandaio	10c	Washington, DC
Oct. 14	Christmas — Prang	10c	Washington, DC
Oct. 31	Liberty Bell (3 booklets — 78c, 91c, $1.04)	13c	Cleveland, OH
Nov. 4	Francis Parkman (coil)	3c	Pendleton, OR
Nov. 8	Liberty Tree Embossed Envelope	13c	Memphis, TN
Nov. 10	John Witherspoon postal card and reply card	9c	Princeton, NJ
Nov. 13	Freedom of the Press	11c	Philadelphia, PA
Nov. 14	Old North Church	24c	Boston, MA
Nov. 15	American Flag (sheet & coil)	13c	Philadelphia, PA
Nov. 24	Freedom to Assemble	9c	Washington, DC
Nov. 25	Liberty Bell (coil)	13c	Allentown, PA
Dec. 1	American Eagle	13c	Juneau, AK

Postal Receipts at Large Cities

Fiscal Year	Boston	Chicago	Detroit	L.A.	New York	Phil.	St. Louis	Wash. D.C.
1971	96,205,407	292,558,518	70,256,324	149,063,344	359,170,452	107,122,556	65,104,974	84,053,982
1972	109,178,539	332,951,729	85,997,396	172,644,940	395,523,484	120,055,844	73,246,822	99,980,611
1973	114,159,472	339,770,450	84,358,518	172,365,582	392,348,195	120,173,378	75,342,257	103,152,177
1974	123,164,661	347,561,637	87,784,811	176,847,940	409,392,651	130,655,216	79,412,843	133,458,807

Other Cities for Fiscal Year 1974: Atlanta, $103,403,751; Baltimore, $67,393,399; Cincinnati, $52,719,922; Cleveland, $76,430,399; Columbus, $54,843,072; Dallas, $102,026,314; Denver, $56,504,247; Houston, $83,227,880; Indianapolis, $55,529,011; Kansas City, $60,731,477; Minneapolis, $78,673,386; Pittsburgh, $59,469,603; San Francisco, $88,996,095; Seattle, $49,626,191.

Post Offices in the United States

As of June 30, 1975, there was a total of 30,754 post offices throughout the U.S. and Possessions. Of this number 5,477 were First Class; 7,396 Second Class; 12,191 Third Class; and 5,690 Fourth Class.

Surface Mail, Air Mail, Parcel Post International Rates

Aerogrammes — 22 cents each to all countries.
Air Mail Post Cards (single) — 21 cents to all countries except Canada and Mexico (14c).

Country	Ordinary surface mail (not over 1 oz.)	Letters and letter pkgs. (per 1/2 oz.)	Other Articles First 2 oz.	Each add'l 2 oz. or fraction	Parcel Post First 4 oz.	Each add'l 4 oz. or fraction	Surface Parcel Post First 2 lbs.	Each add'l pound or fraction	Max. wt. for parcel post (surface or air) lbs.
Afghanistan	.18	.31	.86	.42	3.14	1.20	1.90	.57	22
Albania	.18	.31	.73	.29	3.33	.79	1.90	.57	22
Algeria	.18	.31	.73	.29	2.71	.80	1.90	.57	44
Andorra	.18	.31	.73	.29	2.79	.70	1.90	.57	44
Angola	.18	.31	.86	.42	2.93	1.01	1.90	.57	22
Anguilla	.18	.25	.60	.16	1.78	.36	1.90	.57	22
Antigua	.18	.25	.60	.16	1.78	.36	1.75	.50	22
Argentina	.18	.25	.73	.29	2.46	1.07	1.90	.57	44
Aruba	.18	.25	.60	.16	2.08	.45	1.75	.50	44
Ascension Isl.	.18	.25	.73	.29	(4)	—	1.90	.57	22
Australia[3]	.18	.31	.86	.42	2.62	1.21	1.90	.57	44
Austria	.18	.31	.73	.29	2.70	.74	1.90	.57	44
Azores	.18	.31	.73	.29	1.95	.56	1.90	.57	22
Bahamas	.18	.25	.60	.16	2.19	.27	1.75	.50	22
Bahrain	.18	.31	.86	.42	2.42	1.03	1.90	.57	22
Barbados	.18	.25	.60	.16	1.90	.51	1.75	.50	22
Barbuda	.18	.25	.60	.16	1.78	.36	1.75	.50	22
Belgium	.18	.31	.73	.29	2.41	.66	1.90	.57	44
Bermuda	.18	.25	.60	.16	1.77	.35	1.75	.50	33
Bhutan	.18	.31	.86	.42	(4)	—	. . .	. . .	(5)
Bolivia[3]	.18	.25	.73	.29	2.47	.69	1.90	.57	44
Bonaire	.18	.25	.60	.16	2.08	.45	1.75	.50	44
Botswana	.18	.31	.86	.42	2.66	1.27	1.90	.57	22
Brazil	.18	.25	.73	.29	2.94	.79	1.90	.57	44
Br. Honduras	.18	.25	.60	.16	2.14	.46	1.90	.57	44
Br. Virgin Isl.	.18	.25	.60	.16	1.78	.36	1.75	.50	22
Brunei	.18	.31	.86	.42	3.01	1.47	1.90	.57	22
Bulgaria	.18	.31	.73	.29	2.15	.75	1.90	.57	22
Burma[3]	.18	.31	.86	.42	3.30	1.43	1.90	.57	22
Burundi	.18	.31	.86	.42	2.76	1.07	1.90	.57	22
Cameroon	.18	.31	.86	.42	2.79	.92	1.90	.57	22
Canada[3]	.13	.17 (oz.)	(6)	—	(6)	—	1.75	.50	35
Cape Verde Isl.	.18	.31	.86	.42	2.72	.81	1.90	.57	44
Cen. Africa Rep.	.18	.31	.86	.42	2.76	1.07	1.90	.57	44
Ceylon	.18	.31	.86	.42	3.33	1.28	1.90	.57	22
Chad	.18	.31	.86	.42	2.76	1.07	1.90	.57	44
Chile[3]	.18	.25	.73	.29	2.92	.89	1.90	.57	22
China Rep.	.18	.31	.86	.42	2.46	1.05	1.90	.57	44
China, Cont.[7]	.18	.31	.86	.42	3.08	1.37	1.90	.57	44
Colombia	.18	.25	.73	.29	2.86	.50	1.90	.57	44
Comoro Isl.	.18	.31	.86	.42	3.13	1.43	1.90	.57	44
Congo (Brazza.)	.18	.31	.86	.42	2.76	1.07	1.90	.57	44
Corsica	.18	.31	.73	.29	2.98	.66	1.90	.57	44
Costa Rica	.18	.25	.60	.16	2.06	.43	1.75	.50	44
Cuba	.18	.25	.60	.16	(4)	—	. . .	. . .	(5)
Curacao	.18	.25	.60	.16	2.08	.45	1.75	.50	44
Cyprus	.18	.31	.86	.42	2.88	.85	1.90	.57	22
Czechoslovakia	.18	.31	.73	.29	2.17	.76	1.90	.57	44
Dahomey	.18	.31	.86	.42	2.36	.85	1.90	.57	44
Denmark	.18	.31	.73	.29	2.14	.72	1.90	.57	44
Dominica	.18	.25	.60	.16	2.39	.48	1.75	.50	22
Dominican Rep.	.18	.25	.60	.16	2.24	.36	1.75	.50	44
Ecuador	.18	.25	.73	.29	2.78	.48	1.90	.57	44
El Salvador	.18	.25	.60	.16	2.21	.44	1.75	.50	44
Equatorial Guinea	.18	.31	.86	.42	2.82	1.22	1.90	.57	44
Estonia[2]	.18	.31	.86	.42	2.84	.95	1.90	.57	44
Ethiopia	.18	.31	.86	.42	2.83	1.10	1.90	.57	44
Faeroe Isl.	.18	.31	.73	.29	2.14	.72	1.90	.57	44
Falkland Isl.	.18	.25	.73	.29	2.99	.85	1.90	.57	22
Fiji Islands	.18	.31	.86	.42	2.79	.90	1.90	.57	44
Finland	.18	.31	.73	.29	2.17	.79	1.90	.57	44
France incl. Monaco	.18	.31	.73	.29	2.98	.66	1.90	.57	44
French Guiana	.18	.25	.73	.29	2.19	.56	1.90	.57	44
Fr. Polynesia	.18	.31	.86	.42	2.70	.76	1.90	.57	44
Fr. Ter. Afars, Issas	.18	.31	.86	.42	2.89	1.03	1.90	.57	44
Gabon Rep.	.18	.31	.86	.42	2.76	1.07	1.90	.57	44
Gambia	.18	.31	.86	.42	2.39	.76	1.90	.57	22
Germany, incl. Saar.	.18	.31	.73	.29	2.10	.70	1.90	.57	44
Ghana	.18	.31	.86	.42	2.92	.92	1.90	.57	22
Gibraltar	.18	.31	.73	.29	2.16	.75	1.90	.57	22
Gilbert & Ellice	.18	.31	.86	.42	2.66	1.00	1.90	.57	22
Great Britain	.18	.31	.73	.29	2.08	.66	1.90	.57	44
Greece	.18	.31	.73	.29	2.62	.84	1.90	.57	44
Greenland	.18	.31	.73	.29	2.35	.93	1.75	.50	44
Grenada	.18	.25	.60	.16	2.39	.48	1.75	.50	22
Guadeloupe	.18	.25	.60	.16	2.00	.36	1.75	.50	44

| Country | Ordinary surface mail (not over 1 oz.) | Air Service | | | | | Surface Parcel Post | | Max. wt. for parcel post (surface or air) lbs. |
| | | Letters and letter pkgs. (per ½ oz.) | Other Articles | | Parcel Post | | | | |
			First 2 oz.	Each add'l. 2 oz. or fraction	First 4 oz.	Each add'l. 4 oz. or fraction	First 2 lbs.	Each add'l. pound or fraction	
⌐atemala	.18	.25	.60	.16	2.51	.46	1.75	.50	44
⌐inea	.18	.31	.86	.42	2.46	.96	1.90	.57	44
⌐yana	.18	.25	.73	.29	2.42	.50	1.90	.57	22
⌐iti	.18	.25	.60	.16	2.25	.35	1.75	.50	44
⌐nduras	.18	.25	.60	.16	2.14	.46	1.75	.50	¹44
⌐ng Kong	.18	.31	.86	.42	2.65	1.24	1.90	.57	22
⌐ngary	.18	.31	.73	.29	2.16	.76	1.90	.57	44
⌐eland	.18	.31	.73	.29	2.66	.56	1.90	.57	44
⌐dia	.18	.31	.86	.42	2.67	1.27	1.90	.57	¹44
⌐donesia	.18	.31	.86	.42	3.48	1.52	1.90	.57	22
⌐an	.18	.31	.86	.42	2.67	.96	1.90	.57	44
⌐q	.18	.31	.86	.42	2.98	.95	1.90	.57	44
⌐land (Eire)	.18	.31	.73	.29	2.06	.66	1.90	.57	22
⌐ael	.18	.31	.86	.42	2.93	.91	1.90	.57	22
⌐ly	.18	.31	.73	.29	2.63	.79	1.90	.57	44
⌐ry Coast	.18	.31	.86	.42	2.46	.95	1.90	.57	44
⌐maica	.18	.25	.60	.16	2.36	.33	1.75	.50	22
⌐pan	.18	.31	.86	.42	2.19	.80	1.90	.57	22
⌐rdan	.18	.31	.86	.42	2.72	.90	1.90	.57	22
⌐nya	.18	.31	.86	.42	2.93	1.10	1.90	.57	22
⌐mer Republic	.18	.31	.86	.42	(4)	—	1.90	.57	(5)
⌐rea (Rep. of)	.18	.31	.86	.42	2.25	.85	1.90	.57	22
No. Korea¹	.18	.31	.86	.42	(4)	....	....	....	(5)
⌐uwait	.18	.31	.86	.42	2.39	1.00	1.90	.57	44
⌐os	.18	.31	.86	.42	3.35	1.37	1.90	.57	22
⌐tvia²	.18	.31	.86	.42	2.84	.95	1.90	.57	44
⌐banon	.18	.31	.86	.42	2.72	.90	1.90	.57	¹44
⌐eward Islands	.18	.25	.60	.16	1.78	.36	1.75	.50	22
⌐sotho	.18	.31	.86	.42	2.66	1.27	1.90	.57	22
⌐beria	.18	.31	.86	.42	2.24	.84	1.90	.57	22
⌐bya	.18	.31	.73	.29	2.70	.85	1.90	.57	44
⌐echtenstein	.18	.31	.73	.29	2.39	.67	1.90	.57	44
⌐thuania²	.18	.31	.86	.42	2.84	.95	1.90	.57	44
⌐xembourg	.18	.31	.73	.29	2.47	.65	1.90	.57	44
⌐acao	.18	.31	.86	.42	3.20	1.24	1.90	.57	22
⌐adagascar	.18	.31	.86	.42	3.09	1.22	1.90	.57	44
⌐adeira Isl	.18	.31	.73	.29	2.10	.72	1.90	.57	22
⌐alawi	.18	.31	.86	.42	2.66	1.24	1.90	.57	22
⌐alaysia	.18	.31	.86	.42	3.23	1.42	1.90	.57	22
⌐aldives, Rep. of.	.18	.31	.86	.42	3.59	1.29	1.90	.57	22
⌐ali	.18	.31	.86	.42	3.46	.82	1.90	.57	44
⌐alta	.18	.31	.73	.29	2.61	.79	1.90	.57	22
⌐artinique	.18	.25	.60	.16	2.00	.36	1.75	.50	44
⌐auritania	.18	.31	.86	.42	2.36	.79	1.90	.57	44
⌐auritius	.18	.31	.86	.42	3.01	1.29	1.90	.57	22
⌐exico	.13	(oz.).17	.60	.16	1.77	.35	1.75	.50	44
⌐ontserrat	.18	.25	.60	.16	1.78	.36	1.90	.57	22
⌐orocco	.18	.31	.73	.29	2.63	.79	1.90	.57	44
⌐ozambique	.18	.31	.86	.42	3.43	1.28	1.90	.57	22
⌐auru (Rep.)	.18	.31	.86	.42	2.62	1.21	1.90	.57	22
⌐epal	.18	.31	.86	.42	2.66	1.27	1.90	.57	22
⌐etherlands	.18	.31	.73	.29	2.36	.66	1.90	.57	44
⌐eth. Antilles	.18	.25	.60	.16	2.08	.45	1.75	.50	44
⌐evis	.18	.25	.60	.16	1.78	.36	1.75	.50	22
⌐ew Caledonia	.18	.31	.86	.42	2.81	.93	1.90	.57	44
⌐ew Guinea	.18	.31	.86	.42	2.72	1.32	1.90	.57	22
⌐ew Hebrides	.18	.31	.86	.42	2.65	.93	1.90	.57	44
⌐ew Zealand	.18	.31	.86	.42	2.98	1.07	1.90	.57	22
⌐caragua	.18	.25	.60	.16	2.08	.43	1.75	.50	44
⌐ger	.18	.31	.86	.42	3.45	.80	1.90	.57	44
⌐geria	.18	.31	.86	.42	3.14	.93	1.90	.57	22
⌐orway	.18	.31	.73	.29	2.14	.72	1.90	.57	44
⌐man, Sultanate of	.18	.31	.86	.42	2.42	1.03	1.90	.57	22
⌐uter Mongolia	.18	.31	.86	.42	(4)	....	1.90	.57	(5)
⌐akistan	.18	.31	.86	.42	3.46	1.22	1.90	.57	22
⌐anama	.18	.25	.60	.16	2.50	.45	1.75	.50	¹70
⌐apua	.18	.31	.86	.42	2.72	1.32	1.90	.57	22
⌐araguay	.18	.25	.73	.29	2.47	.67	1.90	.57	44
⌐eru	.18	.25	.73	.29	2.88	.60	1.90	.57	44
⌐ilippines	.18	.31	.86	.42	3.03	1.17	1.90	.57	¹44
⌐tcairn	.18	.31	.86	.42	2.89	1.03	1.90	.57	22
⌐oland	.18	.31	.73	.29	2.61	.75	1.90	.57	44
⌐ortugal	.18	.31	.73	.29	2.05	.64	1.90	.57	22
⌐ortuguese Timor	.18	.31	.86	.42	3.64	1.72	1.90	.57	22
" W. Africa	.18	.31	.86	.42	2.93	1.01	1.90	.57	22
⌐atar	.18	.31	.86	.42	2.42	1.03	1.90	.57	22
⌐eunion	.18	.31	.86	.42	2.89	1.27	1.90	.57	44
⌐hodesia	.18	.31	.86	.42	2.66	1.24	1.90	.57	22
⌐omania	.18	.31	.73	.29	2.42	.79	1.90	.57	22
⌐wanda	.18	.31	.86	.42	2.76	1.07	1.90	.57	22
⌐yukyu	.18	.31	.86	.42	2.19	.80	1.90	.57	22
⌐abah	.18	.25	.60	.16	2.08	.45	1.90	.57	44
⌐. Christopher	.18	.25	.60	.16	2.39	.48	1.75	.50	44
⌐. Eustatius	.18	.25	.60	.16	2.08	.45	1.75	.50	44

Country	Ordinary surface mail (not over 1 oz.)	Letters and letter pkgs. (per $^1/_2$ oz.)	Air Service Other Articles First 2 oz.	Each add'l. 2 oz. or fraction	Air Service Parcel Post First 4 oz.	Each add'l. 4 oz. or fraction	Surface Parcel Post First 2 lbs.	Each add'l. pound or fraction	Max. wt. for parcel post (surface or lbs.)
St. Helena	.18	.31	.86	.42	3.01	1.22	1.90	.57	22
St. Lucia	.18	.25	.60	.16	2.39	.48	1.75	.50	22
St. Pierre, Miquelon	.18	.25	.60	.16	1.72	.35	1.75	.50	44
St. Vincent	.18	.25	.60	.16	2.39	.48	1.75	.50	22
Santa Cruz Isl.	.18	.31	.86	.42	3.10	1.39	1.90	.57	22
Saudi Arabia	.18	.31	.86	.42	3.10	1.00	1.90	.57	22
Senegal	.18	.31	.86	.42	2.34	.75	1.90	.57	44
Seychelles	.18	.31	.86	.42	2.53	1.12	1.90	.57	22
Sierra Leone	.18	.31	.86	.42	3.09	.81	1.90	.57	22
Singapore	.18	.31	.86	.42	3.23	1.42	1.90	.57	22
Solomon Isl.	.18	.31	.86	.42	3.12	1.39	1.90	.57	22
Somali Rep.	.18	.31	.86	.42	3.23	1.13	1.90	.57	22
South Africa	.18	.31	.86	.42	2.66	1.27	1.90	.57	22
Spain	.18	.31	.73	.29	2.79	.70	1.90	.57	¹44
Sp. W. Africa	.18	.31	.86	.42	2.81	.81	1.90	.57	¹44
Sri Lanka	.18	.31	.86	.42	3.33	1.28	1.90	.57	22
Sudan	.18	.31	.86	.42	3.13	1.01	1.90	.57	22
Surinam	.18	.25	.73	.29	2.24	.53	1.90	.57	44
Sweden	.18	.31	.73	.29	2.14	.72	1.90	.57	44
Switzerland	.18	.31	.73	.29	2.39	.67	1.90	.57	¹44
Syria	.18	.31	.86	.42	2.47	.92	1.90	.57	¹44
Tanzania	.18	.31	.86	.42	2.99	1.15	1.90	.57	22
Thailand	.18	.31	.86	.42	3.28	1.17	1.90	.57	22
Togo	.18	.31	.86	.42	2.57	.95	1.90	.57	44
Tonga	.18	.31	.86	.42	2.34	.93	1.90	.57	22
Trinidad, Tobago	.18	.31	.60	.16	2.37	.45	1.75	.50	44
Tristan da Cunha	.18	.31	.86	.42	2.83	1.21	1.90	.57	22
Tunisia	.18	.31	.73	.29	2.62	.75	1.90	.57	44
Turkey	.18	.31	.73	.29	2.26	.85	1.90	.57	44
Turks Islands	.18	.25	.60	.16	2.25	.33	1.75	.50	22
Uganda	.18	.31	.86	.42	2.93	1.10	1.90	.57	22
USSR²	.18	.31	.86	.42	2.84	.95	1.90	.57	44
United Arab Emir.	.18	.31	.86	.42	2.42	1.03	1.90	.57	22
Upper Volta	.18	.31	.86	.42	2.72	.89	1.90	.57	44
Uruguay	.18	.25	.73	.29	2.93	.90	1.90	.57	44
Vatican City	.18	.31	.73	.29	2.42	.74	1.90	.57	44
Venezuela	.18	.25	.73	.29	2.71	.43	1.90	.57	44
Vietnam, Rep. of.	.18	.31	.86	.42	(4)	....	....	....	(5)
North Vietnam	.18	.31	.86	.42	(4)	....	....	....	(5)
Western Samoa	.18	.31	.86	.42	2.71	.80	1.90	.57	22
Windward Isl.	.18	.25	.60	.16	2.39	.48	1.75	.50	22
Yemen	.18	.31	.86	.42	2.81	1.10	....	....	22
Yugoslavia	.18	.31	.73	.29	2.17	.79	1.90	.57	44
Zaire	.18	.31	.86	.42	2.76	1.07	1.90	.57	44
Zambia	.18	.31	.86	.42	2.66	1.24	1.90	.57	22

(1.) Restrictions apply; consult post office. (2.) To facilitate distribution and delivery, include "Union of Soviet Socia[l] Republics" or "USSR" as part of the address. (3.) Small packets weight limit one pound. (4.) No air parcel post servi[ce] (5.) No surface parcel post service. (6.) No airmail AO or parcel post to Canada; prepare and prepay all airmail packag[e] as letter mail. (7.) The Continental China Postal authorities will not deliver articles unless addressed to show name of th[e] country as "People's Republic of China"; also, acceptable spelling of capital is "Peking."

International Mails
Weight and Dimensional Limits and Surface Rates
For air rates and parcel post see pages 980-982

Letters and letter packages: All written matter or correspondence recordings, must be sent as letter mail. Weight limit: 4 lbs. to all countries except Canada, which is 60 lbs. **Surface rates:** Canada and Mexico, 13c first ounce; 11c each additional ounce or fraction up to 13 ounces; eighth-zone priority rates for heavier weights. Countries other than Canada and Mexico, 1 ounce, 18c; over 1 to 2 ounces, 31c; over 2 to 4 ounces, 41c; over 4 to 8 ounces, 82c; over 8 ounces to 1 pound, $1.58; over 1 to 2 pounds, $2.75; and over 2 to 4 pounds, $4.46. **Air rates:** Canada and Mexico, 17c first ounce; 15c each additional ounce or fraction. Central America, Colombia, Venezuela, the Caribbean Islands, Bahamas, Bermuda and St. Pierre and Miquelon, 25c per half ounce up to and including 2 ounces; 21c each additional half ounce or fraction. All other countries, 31c per half ounce up to and including 2 ounces; 26c each additional half ounce or fraction. Aerogrammes, which can be folded into the form of an envelope and sent by air to all countries, are available at post offices for 22c each.

Post cards. Surface rates to Canada and Mexico, 9c to all other countries, 12c. By air, Canada and Mexico, 14c; to all other countries, 21c. Maximum size permitted, 6 x 4¹/₄ in.; minimum, 5¹/₂ x 3¹/₂.

Printed matter. To Canada and Mexico, 13c first 2 oz., 10.5c each additional oz. or fraction; to other countries 13c for first 2 oz. or fraction, 24c for 2 to 4 oz., 45c for 4 to 8 oz., 77c for 8oz. to 1 lb., $1.15 for 1 to 2 lbs., $1.44 for 2 to 4 lbs.

To countries admitting regular prints over 4 lbs. 93c f[or] each additional 2 lbs. or fraction. (Consult post office f[or] rates and conditions applying to certain publications ma[il]ed by the publishers or by registered news agents.) Bo[ok] weight limits for most countries is 11 lbs; for exceptio[ns] see below.

Exceptional weight limits for printed matter. Printe[d] matter may weigh up to 22 lbs. to Argentina, Boliv[ia,] Brazil, Chile, Colombia, Costa Rica, Cuba, Dominic[an] Republic, Ecuador, El Salvador, Guatemala, Haiti, Ho[n]duras, Mexico, Nicaragua, Panama, Paraguay, Peru, Spa[in] (including Balearic Islands, Canary Islands and Northe[rn] Africa), Uruguay, and Venezuela. For other countries, lim[it] for books is 11 lbs., all other prints, 4 lbs.

Matter for the blind. Surface rate free; air rates to Cana[da] 17c per oz. (For all other countries, consult postmaste[r.]) Weight limit 15 lbs.

Small packets. Postage rates for small items of merchandise and samples are lower than for letter packages or parcel post; weight limits up to 2 lbs. Surface rates: Cana[da] and Mexico, 13c first 2 oz. and 10.5c each additional 2 oz. or fraction. All other countries, for 4 oz. or less 24c; 4 to 8 45c; 8 oz. to 1 lb. 77c; 1 to 2 lbs. 1.15; Air rates, Canada, 1 per oz. For other rates, see schedule "Air Service Oth[er] Articles" under heading of International Rates for Or[di]nary Surface Mail, Air Mail and Surface Parcel Post, pag[es] 979-982.

Canadian Postal Rates

Domestic Mail

First class mail costs 8c for the first oz.; between 1 and 2 oz., 14c; between 2 and 4 oz. 20c; between 4 and oz., 32c; between 8 and 12 oz., 44c and between 12 z. and a pound, 54c. Postcards 7c. Third class mail osts 6c for first 2 ounces and 3c each additional 2 oz. r fraction. All domestic first class mail not heavier han 66 lbs. and exceeding certain sizes is carried by ir if it will speed delivery.

International

All mail up to 8 oz. travels by air. An air mail stick- or the word "air mail" must be on the envelope

Cost is 15c for first oz., between 1 and 2 oz., 30c, between 2 and 4 oz., 40c and between 4 and 8 oz., 90c. Postcards 10c. Aerogrammes 15c.

To the United States, its Territories and Possessions: Air mail 10c each oz. (maximum 25 lbs.) Postcards 10c each by air mail. Surface letter mail is 8c for first oz., between 1 and 2 oz., 14c; between 2 and 4 oz., 20c; between 4 and 8 oz. 32c and between 8 oz. and a lb., 54c. Surface postcards are 8c. Printed papers are 6c up to 2 oz., between 2 and 4 oz., 9c; between 4 and 8 oz., 15c and between 8 oz. and a lb., 27c. Small packets are delivered in a speedier and alternative surface to the Parcel Post for a charge of 9c up to 4 oz., between 4 and 8 oz., 15c and 8 oz. to a lb., 27c.

United Nations Postage Stamps Issued in 1975

UN stamps in United States denominations, valid r postage only on mail deposited at UN Headquar- rs, New York, and UN stamps in Swiss denomina- ons, valid for postage only on mail deposited at the nited Nations Office, Geneva, are available at face lue from the UN Postal Administration in New ork and Geneva and through sales agencies around e world. They may be obtained by mail or automat- ally through the Customer Deposit Account service, oth in New York and Geneva. Revenue from the sale f UN stamps for postage purposes goes to the U S. ostal Service and the Swiss PTT, respectively; from philatelic sales, revenue goes to the UN.

Date	Stamp	Value
10 Jan.	Postal card.	8c
	Airmail postal cards	11c, 18c
	Envelopes.	10c, 13c
	Airletter.	18c
14 Mar.	Peaceful Uses of Outer Space.	10c, 26c
9 May	International Women's Year	10c, 18c
26 June	UN 30th Anniversary.	10c, 26c
	Souvenir sheet	36c
22 Sept.	Namibia: UN Direct Responsibility.	10c, 18c
21 Nov.	UN Peace-keeping Operations.	13c, 26c

International Parcel Post

For rates see pages 980-982

General dimensional limits—Greatest length, 3½ eet; greatest length and girth combined, 6 feet.

Prohibited articles. Before sending goods abroad he mailer should satisfy himself that they will not be onfiscated or returned because their importation is rohibited or restricted by the country of address.

Packing. Parcels for transmission overseas should e even more carefully packed than those intended or delivery within the continental United States. ontainers should be used which will be strong nough to protect the contents from the weight of other mails, from pressure and friction, climatic changes, and repeated handlings.

Sealing. Registered or insured parcels must be sealed. To some countries the sealing of ordinary (unregistered and uninsured) parcels is optional, and to others compulsory. Consult post office.

Customs declarations, and other forms. A parcel post sticker, and at least one customs declaration giving a complete description of the contents, are required for each parcel mailed to another country.

Metric Conversion Chart—Approximations

Symbol	When You Know	Multiply By	To Find	Symbol
		Length		
mm	millimeters	0.04	inches	in
cm	centimeters	0.4	inches	in
m	meters	3.3	feet	ft
m	meters	1.1	yards	yd
km	kilometers	0.6	miles	mi
		Area		
cm²	square centimeters	0.16	square inches	in²
m²	square meters	1.2	square yards	yd²
km²	square kilometers	0.4	square miles	mi²
ha	hectares (10,000m²)	2.5	acres	
		Mass (weight)		
g	grams	0.035	ounce	oz
kg	kilograms	2.2	pounds	lb
	tonnes (1000kg)	1.1	short tons	
		Volume		
ml	milliliters	0.03	fluid ounces	fl oz
l	liters	2.1	pints	pt
l	liters	1.06	quarts	qt
l	liters	0.26	gallons (U.S.)	gal (U.S.)
l	liters	0.22	gallons (Imp.)	gal (Imp.)
m³	cubic meters	35	cubic feet	ft³
m³	cubic meters	1.3	cubic yards	yd³
		Temperature (exact)		
°C	Celsius temp.	9/5 (+ 32)	Fahrenheit temp.	°F
		Temperature (exact) to Metric		
°F	Fahrenheit temp.	(−32) 5/9 of remainder	Celsius temp.	°C

Symbol	When You Know	Multiply By	To Find	Symbol
		Length		
in	inches	*2.5	centimeters	cm
ft	feet	30	centimeters	cm
yd	yards	0.9	meters	m
mi	miles	1.6	kilometers	km
		Area		
in²	square inches	6.5	sq. centimeters	cm²
ft²	square feet	0.09	square meters	m²
yd²	square yards	0.8	square meters	m²
mi²	square miles	2.6	sq. kilometers	km²
	acres	0.4	hectares	ha
		Mass (weight)		
oz	ounces	28	grams	g
lb	pounds	0.45	kilograms	kg
	short tons (2000 lb)	0.9	tonnes	t
		Volume		
tsp	teaspoons	5	milliliters	ml
tbsp	tablespoons	15	milliliters	ml
fl oz	fluid ounces	30	milliliters	ml
c	cups	0.24	liters	l
pt	pints	0.47	liters	l
qt	quarts	0.95	liters	l
gal	gallons (U.S.)	3.8	liters	l
gal	gallons (Imp.)	4.5	liters	l
ft³	cubic feet	0.03	cubic meters	m³
yd³	cubic yards	0.76	cubic meters	m³

*1 in = 2.54 cm (exactly)

QUICK REFERENCE INDEX

SPECIAL BICENTENNIAL SECTION 264-300

First Class Postal Rates in Brief

(Effective Dec. 28, 1975)

United States Domestic

Letters—13c first ounce, 11c each additional ounce.
Postal Cards—9c each (up to 4½ x 6 in.) Double cards, 18c. Private cards, 18c.

United States International

Letters—(1) Canada and Mexico, 13c first ounce, 11c each addl. ounce to 13 ounces; over 12 ounces to 1 pound, $1.67; over 1 pound to 1½ pounds, $2.07; over 1½ to 2 pounds, $2.46; over 2 to 2½ pounds, $2.78; over 2½ to 3 pounds, $3.09; over 3 to 3½ pounds $3.38; over 3½ to 4 pounds, $3.67; over 4 to 4½ pounds, $3.94; over 4½ to 5 pounds, $4.20; over 5 pounds, 52c each additional pound or fraction.
(2) Countries other than Canada and Mexico, 1 ounce, 18c; over 1 to 2 ounces, 31c; over 2 to 4 ounces, 47; over 4 to 8 ounces, 82c; over 8 ounces to 1 pound, $1.58; over 1 to 2 pounds, $2.75; and over 2 to 4 pound $4.46.
Air Mail Letters—(1) Canada and Mexico, 17c per ounce. (2). Cen. America, S. America, the Caribbean I Bahamas, Bermuda and St. Pierre and Miquelon, 25c per half ounce. (3) All other countries, 31c per h ounce.
Aerogrammes—To all countries, 18c each.
Postal cards—To Canada and Mexico 9c each. To all other countries, 12c each.
Air mail post cards—To Canada and Mexico 14c each, to other countries 21c each.

Canada

Domestic—1 oz., 8c; 1-2 oz., 14c; 2-4 oz., 20c; 4-8 oz., 32c; 8-12 oz., 44c; 12 oz.-1 lb., 54c. **Postcards** 7c.
International—Letters to U.S.: by air, 10c each oz.; surface—same as domestic first class, except: 8 oz.-1 54c; 1-2 lb., $1.50; 2-4 lb., $3.00. **Letters other than to U.S.:** 1 oz., 15c; 1-2 oz., 30c; 2-4 oz., 40c; 4-8 oz., 90c.
Postcards 10c.
Aerogrammes 15c.